DICTIONARY
OF
THE BIBLE

John L. McKenzie, S.J.

A TOUCHSTONE BOOK
Published by Simon & Schuster
New York   London   Toronto   Sydney

TOUCHSTONE
Rockefeller Center
1230 Avenue of the Americas
New York, NY 10020

First Touchstone Edition 1995

Library of Congress Catalog Card Number: 65-26691

ISBN 978-0-684-81913-6

Manufactured in the United States of America

20 19 18 17 16

IMPRIMI POTEST:
     JOHN R. CONNERY, S.J.
     Praepos. Provin.

NIHIL OBSTAT:
     JOHN B. AMBERG, S.J.
     Archdiocesan Censor

IMPRIMATUR:
     ✠ CLETUS F. O'DONNELL, J.C.D.
     Vicar General, Archdiocese of Chicago
     February 18, 1965

To the Members of
The Society of Jesus

Preface

In a conversation in the spring of 1956 the Rev. Joseph A. Fitzmyer, S.J., noticed the need for a one-volume dictionary of the Bible for general use. He pointed out that since I had a book in press at that time and no plans for another, the task could be undertaken by me, since it appeared unlikely that anyone else would undertake it in the near future. When the suggestion was presented to Mr. William C. Bruce, he accepted it with lively interest and prepared a contract. The writing was begun in November, 1956, and the last pages of the manuscript were done in July, 1962. The book was delivered to The Bruce Publishing Company in June, 1964.

It is rare in modern times that a Bible dictionary is prepared by a single writer, since the task is regarded as too massive for one man. In this judgment I am ready to concur. The idea of a volume written by a number of scholars under my editorship was considered, but never seriously. In all probability a dictionary written in this way would not yet be offered to the public. Expeditiousness of composition, however, is not the only merit desired in a dictionary. There are inevitable weaknesses in a work covering so much territory when it is done by a single writer, who cannot possibly have equal control of all the material. In the final judgment, it seemed preferable to accept these weaknesses in the hope of achieving a kind of strength which a work of multiple authorship does not have.

A number of colleagues expressed doubts about the wisdom of the project, not only because of the weaknesses which could be expected in the work, but also because they felt that it would take me from other activities which in the long run might be more useful. I mention this only because some of them who have read over the manuscript were kind enough to say that they no longer feel these doubts. This is most encouraging, and I wish to attest my gratitude for this encouragement, regretting only that I am unable to mention their names.

Any good dictionary is a work of compilation. A reference book is not the place for the most advanced creative scholarship; it is a place where the reader hopes to find a synthesis of the common conclusions of scholarship. It has been my purpose to make this such a work. I regret that the format of a dictionary does not permit complete acknowledgment of my dependence on the work of others. The practice of adding bibliographical notes after at least major articles was considered; but it was felt that this would add too much to the bulk of the book and to its cost, and that the same purpose would be served by a list of general works where the reader could find more ample bibliographical references. The books listed are those which I used most frequently in the preparation of the articles; I gladly acknowledge the use I have made of them and of the works of other writers who, because their works were less frequently used, could sometimes be mentioned only by name.

The writing was done at West Baden College, Indiana (since transferred to Bellarmine Theological School, North Aurora, Illinois) and since 1960 at Loyola University, Chicago. At both institutions I enjoyed freedom from occupations other than the minimum teaching load. Since 1961 the Very Rev. John R. Connery, S.J., superior of the Chicago Province of the Society of Jesus, has granted funds to pay a full-time secretary to handle this and other typing. Miss Carolyn Cuccia typed out the entire manuscript in quadruplicate with care and devotion far in excess of the remuneration she received, and was largely responsible for a number of corrections. When the job was finished she was without doubt better informed about the Bible than any person of her age in Chicago. Her successor, Mrs. Mildred Kearney, typed the revised pages, which themselves make a sizable book. Facilities for the work were furnished by the Rev. John B. Amberg, S.J., director of Loyola University Press. In Chicago I enjoyed the use of the library of McCormick Theological Seminary; without this resource the work could not have been done, and I thank the staff of the library for their help. The manuscript was read by eight members of the Society of Jesus whose names are not divulged to the author. Their judgment was favorable, or the work would not appear. They found several hundred points where correction removed errors or made the text clearer and more readable, or where some bold opinions were tempered or better founded. Were censorship always conducted in the manner in which these gentlemen fulfilled their responsibility, there would never be any complaint about the process. It is a thankless task, but thanks must be rendered here even though they cannot be rendered personally. Mr. William E. May has done the editorial work for the publisher, and I thank him for his extremely competent preparation of the manuscript and for his patience. Miss Anita Weisbrod assisted in preparing the manuscript for publication.

I regret that there is no way except a general expression of gratitude in which I can pay thanks to what seems an infinite multitude of friends and associates who encouraged the work, made kindly inquiries about its progress, and voiced their hopes for its successful completion. Those who have not written a book of 800,000 words probably do not realize that such a task can occasionally create a problem of author morale. At such moments one is sensible of those who share one's conviction that a job worth beginning is worth finishing. In short, these acknowledgments — and I hope no others which I have forgotten — make one keenly aware that his book is the product of many other minds and hands than his own. I am happy to testify to this; all of these have helped me in everything except making mistakes, which I am capable of handling by myself.

The work is published with perhaps more than the usual apprehensions, but it has reached the point where there is nothing else to do but publish it. Since 1956 the need for a one-volume dictionary has become less acute. But there is always room for an abundance of such aids, and it makes the author smile wryly when he recalls that even a mediocre dictionary is likely to outlive its author by many years. In such cases survival is not a mark of quality, but simply an indication that no one has replaced the work. If this book serves those for whom it is intended, it will survive; if it does not serve them, it does not merit survival.

JOHN L. McKENZIE, S.J.

Calvert House, The University of Chicago
September 8, 1965
The Nativity of the Blessed Virgin Mary

Abbreviations for Books of the Bible

OT		Mi	Micah
		Jon	Jonah
Gn	Genesis	Na	Nahum
Ex	Exodus	Hab	Habakkuk
Lv	Leviticus	Zp	Zephaniah
Nm	Numbers	Hg	Haggai
Dt	Deuteronomy	Zc	Zechariah
Jos	Joshua	Mal	Malachi
Jgs	Judges	Bar	Baruch
1 S	1 Samuel		
2 S	2 Samuel (1–2 S)		
1 K	1 Kings	*NT*	
2 K	2 Kings (1–2 K)		
1 Ch	1 Chronicles	Mt	Matthew
2 Ch	2 Chronicles (1–2 Ch)	Mk	Mark
Ezr	Ezra	Lk	Luke
Ne	Nehemiah	Jn	John
Tb	Tobit	AA	Acts
Jdt	Judith	Rm	Romans
Est	Esther	1 Co	1 Corinthians
1 Mc	1 Maccabees	2 Co	2 Corinthians (1–2 Co)
2 Mc	2 Maccabees (1–2 Mc)	Gal	Galatians
Rt	Ruth	Eph	Ephesians
Ps (Pss)	Psalms	Phl	Philippians
Pr	Proverbs	Col	Colossians
Jb	Job	1 Th	1 Thessalonians
Lam	Lamentations	2 Th	2 Thessalonians (1–2 Th)
Ec	Ecclesiastes	1 Tm	1 Timothy
SS	Song of Solomon	2 Tm	2 Timothy (1–2 Tm)
BS	Sirach	Tt	Titus
WS	Wisdom of Solomon	Phm	Philemon
Is	Isaiah (II Is, III Is)	Heb	Hebrews
Je	Jeremiah	Js	James
Ezk	Ezekiel	1 Pt	1 Peter
Dn	Daniel	2 Pt	2 Peter (1–2 Pt)
Ho	Hosea	1 Jn	1 John
Jl	Joel	2 Jn	2 John
Am	Amos	3 Jn	3 John (1–2–3 Jn)
Ob	Obadiah	Jd	Jude
		Apc	Apocalypse

Abbreviations and Symbols

AD	after Christ	JE	Jahwist-Elohist
AJ	Josephus, *Antiquities of the Jews*	LB	Late Bronze Period
Akkad	Akkadian	lit	literally
ANEP	Pritchard, *The Ancient Near East in Pictures*	Lt	Latin
		LXX	Septuagint
ANET	Pritchard, *Ancient Near Eastern Texts*	MB	Middle Bronze Period
		mi	mile(s)
		MS, MSS	Manuscript(s)
AOT	Gressman, *Altorientalische Texte und Bilder*	Mt	Mount
		MT	Masoretic Text
ARM	Bottéro and Gossin, *Archives Royales de Mari*	N	North
		NT	New Testament
AV	Authorized Version	OT	Old Testament
BC	before Christ	P	Priestly writer
BL	Driver and Miles, *Babylonian Laws*	p, pp	page(s)
CC	Code of the Covenant	passim	in numerous passages
cf	see	pers	person
ch(s)	chapters	PC	Priestly Code
circa, c	about	pl	plural
cm	centimeter(s)	Pnt	Pentateuch
D	Deuteronomist	pop	population
DBSV	Supplément au Dictionnaire de la Bible	prol	prologue
		RD	Rheims-Douay
DC	Deuteronomic Code	RDC	Rheims-Douay-Challoner
doz	dozen	S	South
E	East	sc	namely
E	Elohist	sg	singular
EA	Knudtzon, *Die El-Amarna Tafeln*	THWB	Kittel, *Theologisches Wörterbuch Zum Neuen Testament*
EB	Early Bronze Period		
e.g.	for example	v	verse
Eng	English	var	variation
etc.	and so forth	Vg	Vulgate
F	Fahrenheit	W	West
f, ff	the following verse(s)	WHA	Wright & Filson, *Westminster Historical Atlas*
ft or '	foot (feet)		
Gk	Greek	yrs	years
Hb	Hebrew	*	See article under this title
HC	Holiness Code	+	and others
ibid	the same passage	#	numbers
i.e.	that is	x	by
in or "	inch(es)	°	degree(s)
J	Jahwist	=	parallel to

Transcription of Hebrew Letters

Aleph	ʾ	Zayin	z	Mem	m	Koph	k
Beth	b	Heth	ḥ	Nun	n	Resh	r
Ghimel	g	Teth	ṭ	Samech	s	Sin	s
Daleth	d	Yod	y	Ayin	ʿ	Shin	š
He	h	Kaph	k	Pe	p	Taw	t
Waw	w	Lamed	l	Sade	ṣ		

Bibliography

I. GENERAL

Albright, William F., *History, Archaeology and Christian Humanism*. New York: McGraw-Hill, 1964.

—— *The Archaeology of Palestine*. London: Penguin Books, 1954.

—— *From the Stone Age to Christianity*. Garden City: Doubleday Anchor, 1957.

Allmen, J.-J. von (editor), *A Companion to the Bible*. Translated from the French. New York: Oxford University Press, 1958.

Arndt, William F., and Gingrich, F. Wilbur, *A Greek-English Lexicon of the New Testament*. Chicago: University of Chicago Press, 1952.

Baly, Denis, *The Geography of the Bible*. New York: Harpers, 1957.

Bauer, Hans, and Leander, Pontus, *Historische Grammatik der hebräischen Sprache des Alten Testaments*. Hildesheim: Georg Olm, 1922.

Blass, F., and Debrunner, A., *A Greek Grammar of the New Testament*. Translated and edited by Robert W. Funk. Chicago: University of Chicago Press, 1961.

Brown, Francis, Driver, S. R., and Briggs, C. A., *A Hebrew and English Lexicon of the Old Testament*. Boston: Houghton Mifflin, 1907.

Die Religion in Geschichte und Gegenwart Tübingen: J. C. B. Mohr (Paul Siebeck), 1957.

Dodd, C. H., *The Authority of the Bible*. New York: Harper Torchbooks, 1958.

Feuillet, A., and Robert, A., *Introduction à la Bible* I-II. Tournai: Desclée, 1957-1959.

Finegan, Jack, *Light from the Ancient Past*. Princeton: Princeton University Press, 1959.

Galling, Kurt, *Biblisches Reallexikon*. Tübingen: J. C. B. Mohr (Paul Siebeck), 1937.

Gesenius's Hebrew Grammar. Translated and edited by A. E. Cowley. Oxford: The Clarendon Press, 1910.

Gesenius-Kautzsch-Bergstrasser, *Hebräische Grammatik*. Hildesheim: George Olm, 1962.

Glueck, Nelson, *The Other Side of the Jordan*. New Haven: American Schools of Oriental Research, 1945.

—— *The River Jordan*. Philadelphia: Westminster Press, 1946.

Greenslade, S. L., *The Cambridge History of the Bible*. Cambridge: The University Press, 1963.

Grollenberg, L. H., *Atlas of the Bible*. Translated by J. M. H. Reid and H. H. Rowley. London: Thomas Nelson, 1956.

Harding, G. Lankester, *The Antiquities of Jordan*. New York: Thomas Y. Crowell, 1959.

Hartman, Louis F. (editor), *Encyclopedic Dictionary of the Bible*. New York: McGraw-Hill, 1963.

Hastings, James, *Dictionary of the Bible*. Revised edition by Frederick C. Grant and H. H. Rowley. New York: Scribners, 1963.

Hatch, Edwin, and Redpath, Henry A., *A Concordance to the Septuagint*. Oxford: The Clarendon Press, 1897.

The Interpreter's Dictionary of the Bible. New York: Abingdon Press, 1962.

Kittel, Gerhard (editor), *Theologisches Wörterbuch zum Neuen Testament*. Stuttgart: W. Kohlhammer, 1933.

Kittel, Rudolf, *Biblia Hebraica*. Stuttgart: Priviligierte Württembergische Bibelanstalt, 1945.

Knudtzon, J. A., *Die El-Amarna Tafeln*. Leipzig: Hinrichs, 1907-1915.

Koehler, Ludwig, and Baumgartner, Walter, *Lexicon in Veteris Testamenti Libros*. Leiden: E. J. Brill, 1958.

La Sainte Bible de Jérusalem. Paris: Les Éditions du Cerf, 1956.

Lemaire, Paulin, and Baldi, Donato, *Atlante Biblico*. Torino: Marietti, 1955.

Leeuw, G. van der, *Religion in Essence and Manifestation*. 2 Vols. Translated by J. E. Turner. New York: Harper Torchbooks, 1963.

Léon-Dufour, Xavier (editor), *Vocabulaire de Théologie biblique*. Paris: Les Éditions du Cerf, 1962.

Levie, Jean, *The Bible: Word of God in Words of Men*. Translated by S. H. Treman. New York: P. J. Kenedy, 1961.

Mandelkern, Solomon, *Veteris Testamenti Concordantiae Hebraicae et Chaldaicae*. Graz: Akademische Druck und Verlagsanstalt, 1955.

Moulton, W. F., and Geden, A. S., *A Concordance to the Greek New Testament*. Edinburgh: T. & T. Clark, 1899.

Nestle, Eberhard, Nestle, Erwin, and Aland, Kurt, *Novum Testamentum Graece*. Stuttgart: Priviligierte Württembergische Bibelanstalt, 1956.

Otto, Rudolf, *The Idea of the Holy*. Translated by John W. Harvey. New York: Oxford University Press, 1958.

Pauly-Wissowa, *Real-Encyclopädie der Classischen Altertums Wissenschaft*.

Rahlfs, Alfred, *Septuaginta*. Stuttgart: Priviligierte Württembergische Bibelanstalt.

Schmoller, Alfred, *Handkonkordanz zum griechischen Neuen Testament*. Stuttgart: Priviligierte Württembergische Bibelanstalt, 1960.

Smart, James D., *The Interpretation of Scripture*. Philadelphia: Westminster Press, 1961.

Smith, J. M. P., and Goodspeed, Edgar, *The Complete Bible: An American Translation*. Chicago: University of Chicago Press, 1939.

Wright, G. E. (editor), *The Bible and the Ancient Near East*. New York: Doubleday, 1961.

Wright, G. E., and Filson, F. V., *The Westminster Historical Atlas to the Bible*. Philadelphia: The Westminster Press, 1956.

II. OLD TESTAMENT

Alt, Albrecht, *Kleine Schriften I-III*. Munich: C. H. Beck, 1959.

Anderson, Bernhard W. (editor), *The Old Testament and Christian Faith*. New York: Harper & Row, 1963.

Anderson, Bernhard W., *Understanding the Old Testament*. Englewood Cliffs: Prentice-Hall, 1957.

Barr, James, *The Semantics of Biblical Language*. Oxford: Oxford University Press, 1961.

Baumgartner, Walter (editor), *Festschrift für Alfred Bertholet*. Tübingen: J. C. B. Mohr (Paul Siebeck), 1950.

Boman, Thorleif, *Hebrew Thought Compared with Greek*. Translated by J. L. Moreau. London: SCM Press, 1960.

Bright, John, *A History of Israel*. Philadelphia: Westminster Press, 1959.

Burrows, Millar, *What Mean These Stones?* New York: Meridian Books, 1957.

Charles, R. H. (editor), *The Apocrypha and Pseudepigrapha of the Old Testament*. Oxford: Clarendon Press, 1913.

Eichrodt, Walther, *Theologie des Alten Testaments*. Stuttgart: Klotz Verlag, 1961.

Eissfeldt, Otto, *Einleitung in das Alte Testament*. Tübingen: J. C. B. Mohr (Paul Siebeck), 1964.

Grelot, P., *Sens chrétien de l'Ancien Testament*. Paris: Desclée, 1962.

Gressmann, Hugo, *Altorientalische Texte und Bilder zum Alten Testament*. Berlin: W. De Gruyter, 1926–1927.

Heidel, Alexander, *The Babylonian Genesis*. Chicago: The University of Chicago Press, 1951.

Jacob, Edmond, *Theology of the Old Testament*. Translated by A. J. Heathcote and P. J. Allcock. New York: Harpers, 1958.

Kaufmann, Yehezkel, *The Religion of Israel*. Translated and abridged by Moshe Greenberg. Chicago: The University of Chicago Press, 1960.

Kautzsch, E., *Die Apokryphen und Pseudepigraphen des Alten Testaments*. Tübingen: J. C. B. Mohr (Paul Siebeck), 1900.

Koehler, Ludwig, *Old Testament Theology*. Translated by A. S. Todd. Philadelphia: Westminster Press, 1957.

Lindblom, J., *Prophecy in Ancient Israel*. Philadelphia: Muhlenberg Press, 1962.

McKenzie, J., *The Two-Edged Sword*. Milwaukee: Bruce, 1956.

Mowinckel, Sigmund, *He That Cometh*. Translated by G. W. Anderson. New York: Abingdon Press, 1954.

Noth, Martin, *Die Welt des Alten Testaments*. Berlin: Töpelmann, 1957.

——— *The History of Israel*. Translated by Stanley Godman. New York: Harper & Brothers, 1958.

Oesterley, W. O. E., *An Introduction to the Books of the Apocrypha*. London: Society for Promoting Christian Knowledge, 1935.

Pedersen, John, *Israel I-IV*. London: Oxford University Press, 1959.

Pritchard, James B., *The Ancient Near East in Pictures*. Princeton: Princeton University Press, 1954.

Pritchard, James B. (editor), *Ancient Near Eastern Texts Relating to the Old Testament*. Princeton: Princeton University Press, 1955.

Rad, Gerhard Von, *Theologie des Alten Testaments*. Munich: Chr. Kaiser, 1960–1961.

Roberts, Bleddyn J., *The Old Testament Text and Versions*. Cardiff: University of Wales Press, 1951.

Robinson, H. Wheeler, *Inspiration and Revelation in the Old Testament*. Oxford: The Clarendon Press, 1946.

Rowley, H. H., *The Faith of Israel*. London: SCM Press, 1956.

——— *The Servant of the Lord and other Essays*. London: Lutterworth Press, 1952.

——— *Men of God: Studies in Old Testament History and Prophecy*. London: Thomas Nelson, 1963.

——— (editor), *The Old Testament and Modern Study*. Oxford: The Clarendon Press, 1951.

Sandmel, Samuel, *The Hebrew Scriptures*. New York: Alfred A. Knopf, 1963.

Studies in Biblical Theology. Naperville, Illinois: Alec R. Allenson.

Thomas, D. Winton (editor), *Documents from Old Testament Times*. New York: Harper Torchbooks, 1961.

Vaux, Roland De, *Ancient Israel: Its Life and Institutions*. Translated by John McHugh. New York: McGraw-Hill, 1961.

Vawter, Bruce, *The Conscience of Israel*. New York: Sheed & Ward, 1961.

Weiser, Artur, *The Old Testament: Its Formation and Development*. Translated by D. M. Barton. New York: Association Press, 1961.

Wright, G. E., *Biblical Archaeology*. Philadelphia: The Westminster Press, 1957.

III. AREAS RELATED TO OLD TESTAMENT

Archives Royales de Mari. Paris: Geuthner, 1946.

Childe, V. Gordon, *New Light on the Most Ancient East*. New York: F. A. Praeger, 1953.

Drioton, Etienne, and Vandier, Jacques, *L'Egypte*. Paris: Presses Universitaires de France, 1946.

Erman, Adolf, *Die Literatur der Aegypter*. Leipzig: J. C. Hinrichs, 1923.

Forbes, R. J., *Studies in Ancient Technology I-IX*. Leiden: Brill, 1955–1964.

Frankfort, Henri, Frankfort, H. A., Wilson, John A., Jacobsen, Thorkild, *Before Philosophy*. Baltimore: Penguin, 1949.

Frankfort, Henri, *Ancient Egyptian Religion*. New York: Columbia University Press, 1948.

——— *The Birth of Civilization in the Ancient Near East*. Bloomington: Indiana University Press, 1951.

Gelb, I. J., *A Study of Writing*. Chicago: The University of Chicago Press, 1952.

Kramer, Samuel Noah, *From the Tablets of Sumer*. Indian Hills, Colorado: Falcon's Wing Press, 1956.

Lucas, Alfred, *Ancient Egyptian Materials and Industries*. London: Arnold, 1948.

Meissner, Bruno, *Babylonien und Assyrien*. Heidelberg: Carl Winter, 1920–1925.

Moscati, Sabatino, *The Face of The Ancient Orient*. New York: Doubleday Anchor, 1962.

Saggs, H. W. F., *The Greatness that was Babylon*. New York: Hawthorn Books, 1963.

Scharff, Alexander, and Moortgat, Anton, *Aegypten und Vorderasien im Altertum*. Munich: F. Bruckmann, 1950.

Schmökel, Hartmut, *Geschichte des alten Vorderasien*. Leiden: Brill, 1957.

Wilson, John A., *The Burden of Egypt*. Chicago: The University of Chicago Press, 1951.

IV. NEW TESTAMENT

Barrett, C. K., *The Gospel According to St. John*. London: S.P.C.K., 1955.

────── *The New Testament Background: Selected Documents*. New York: Harper Torchbooks, 1961.

Benoit, Pierre, *Exégèse et Théologie*, 2 vols. Paris: Éditions du Cerf, 1961.

Bonsirven, Joseph, *Palestinian Judaism in the Time of Jesus Christ*. Translated by William Wolf. New York: Holt, Rinehart & Winston, 1964.

────── *Theology of the New Testament*, Westminster, Md.: The Newman Press, 1964.

Bornkamm, Günther, *Jesus of Nazareth*. Translated by Irene and Fraser McLuskey. New York: Harpers, 1960.

Bultmann, Rudolf, *Primitive Christianity*. Translated by R. H. Fuller. New York: Meridian Books, 1956.

────── *Theology of the New Testament*. Translated by Kendrick Grobel. New York: Scribners, 1951–1955.

Cerfaux, Lucien, *Christ in the Theology of St. Paul*. Translated by G. Webb and A. Walker. New York: Herder & Herder, 1959.

Conzelmann, Hans, *The Theology of St. Luke*. Translated by Geoffrey Buswell. New York: Harpers, 1960.

Cullman, Oscar, *The Christology of the New Testament*. Translated by S. C. Guthrie and C. A. M. Hall. Philadelphia: The Westminster Press, 1959.

────── *The Early Church*. Translated by A. J. B. Higgins. Philadelphia: Westminster Press, 1956.

────── *Peter: Disciple, Apostle, Martyr*. Translated by F. V. Filson. New York: Meridian Books, 1958.

Daube, David, *The New Testament and Rabbinic Judaism*. London: Athlone Press, 1956.

Davies, W. D., and Daube, D. (editors), *The Background of the New Testament and its Eschatology*. Cambridge: The University Press, 1956.

Davies, W. D., *Paul and Rabbinic Judaism*, London: S.P.C.K., 1955.

Dibelius, Martin, *Botschaft und Geschichte*. Tübingen: J. C. B. Mohr (Paul Siebeck), 1956.

Dodd, C. H., *The Fourth Gospel*. Cambridge: The University Press, 1958.

────── *New Testament Studies*. Manchester: The University Press, 1953.

────── *The Parables of the Kingdom*. New York: Scribners, 1961.

Durrwell, F. X., *The Resurrection*. Translated by Rosemary Sheed. New York: Sheed & Ward, 1960.

Eltester, Walther (editor), *Judentum: Urchristentum: Kirche*. Berlin: Alfred Topelmann, 1960.

Grant, Frederick C., *An Introduction to New Testament Thought*. New York: Abingdon Press, 1960.

────── *Roman Hellenism and the New Testament*. Edinburgh: Oliver & Boyd, 1962.

Grant, Robert M., *Historical Introduction to the New Testament*. New York: Harper & Row, 1963.

Hennecke, Edgar (editor), *Neutestamentliche Apocryphen*. Tübingen: J. C. B. Mohr (Paul Siebeck, 1924).

Hoskyns, Edwyn, and Davey, Noel, *The Riddle of the New Testament*. London: Faber & Faber.

Huck, Albert, and Lietzmann, Hans, *Synopse der drei ersten Evangelien*. Tübingen: J. C. B. Mohr (Paul Siebeck), 1950.

James, M. R., *The Apocryphal New Testament*. Oxford: The Clarendon Press, 1924.

Jeremias, Joachim, *The Parables of Jesus*. Translated by S. H. Hooke. New York: Scribners, 1955.

────── *The Eucharistic Words of Jesus*. Translated by A. Ehrhardt. Oxford: Basil Blackwell, 1955.

Kee, Howard C., and Young, Franklin W., *Understanding the New Testament*. Englewood Cliffs: Prentice-Hall, 1957.

Macquarrie, John, *The Scope of Demythologizing*. New York: Harpers, 1960.

Manson, T. W., *Studies in the Gospels and Epistles*. Philadelphia: Westminster Press, 1962.

────── *The Teaching of Jesus*. Cambridge: The University Press, 1935.

McKenzie, John L., *The Power and the Wisdom: An Interpretation of the New Testament*. Milwaukee. Bruce, 1965.

Metzger, Bruce M., *The Text of the New Testament*. New York: Oxford University Press, 1964.

Quesnell, Quentin. *This Good News*. Milwaukee. Bruce, 1964.

Spicq, Ceslaus, *Agape dans le Nouveau Testament*. Paris: Gabalda, 1958–1959.

Stauffer, Ethelbert, *Jesus and His Story*. Translated by Richard and Clara Winston. New York: Alfred A. Knopf, 1959.

────── *New Testament Theology*. Translated by John Marsh. New York: MacMillan, 1955.

Stendahl, Krister, *The School of St. Matthew*. Uppsala, 1954.

Strack, Hermann L., and Billerbeck, Paul, *Kommentar zu Neuen Testament Aus Talmud Und Midrasch*. Munich: C. H. Beck, 1926–1928.

Taylor, Vincent, *The Atonement in New Testament Teaching.* London: Epworth Press, 1958.

————— *The Gospel According to St. Mark.* London: Macmillan, 1952.

————— *The Life and Ministry of Jesus.* New York: Abingdon Press,. 1955.

Vaganay, L., *Le problème synoptique.* Tournai: Desclée, 1952.

Wikenhauser, Alfred, *New Testament Introduction.* Translated by Joseph Cunningham. New York: Herder & Herder, 1958.

V. AREAS RELATED TO NEW TESTAMENT

Bousset, Wilhelm, and Gressmann, Hugo, *Die Religion des Judentums Im Neutestamentlichen Zeitalter.* Tübingen: J. C. B. Mohr (Paul Siebeck), 1927.

Burrrows, Millar, *The Dead Sea Scrolls.* New York: Viking Press, 1955.

————— *More Light on the Dead Sea Scrolls.* New York: Viking Press, 1958.

Cross, Frank M., *The Ancient Library of Qumran.* Garden City: Doubleday, 1958.

Deissman, Adolf, *Light From The Ancient East.* Translated by L. R. M. Strachan. New York: Harpers, 1927.

Discoveries in the Judaean Desert. Oxford: Clarendon Press, 1955.

Dupont-Sommer, A., *The Jewish Sect of Qumran and the Essenes.* Translated by R. D. Barnett. New York: Macmillan, 1956.

Foerster, Werner, *Neutestamentliche Zeitgeschichte.* Hamburg: Furche Verlag, 1955–1956.

Gaster, Theodor H., *The Dead Sea Scriptures.* New York: Doubleday Anchor, 1956.

Moore, George F., *Judaism.* Cambridge: Harvard University Press, 1927.

Prümm, Karl, S.J., *Religionsgechichtliches Handbuch für den Raum der altchristlichen Umwelt.* Rome: Pontifical Biblical Institute, 1954.

Schuerer, Emil, *A History of the Jewish People in the Time of Christ.* Translated by J. MacPherson. New York: Scribners.

Stendahl, Krister (editor), *The Scrolls and the New Testament.* New York: Harpers, 1957.

Vermès, Géza, *Discovery in the Judean Desert.* New York: Desclée, 1956.

List of Illustrations and Charts With Credits

DICTIONARY OF THE BIBLE

A

Aaron (Hb *'āhᵃrōn*, etymology unknown), brother of Moses* and Miriam*, son of Amran* and Jochebed*. Aaron is designated as the speaker for Moses (Ex 4:14; 7:1), but this is not mentioned again in the stories of the plagues* of Egypt*; in some plague stories Aaron is represented as wielding the rod, in others he is associated with Moses. The association is continued in the exodus* narratives. Aaron with Hur* sustained the hands of Moses in prayer during the battle with Amalek*. Aaron is invited to accompany Moses to the peak of Sinai* (Ex 19:24) alone; another tradition adds his two sons and 72 elders (Ex 24:1), while another leaves him with Hur in charge of the people (Ex 24:14). Aaron and his sons are designated (Ex 28:1 ff) and installed (Lv 8:1–10:20) as priests, with Aaron as high priest (cf PRIEST). Aaron was associated with the construction of the golden calf (Ex 32:1 ff), but was not punished; the tradition represented him as yielding to popular pressure. Miriam and Aaron were involved in a quarrel with Moses concerning Moses' Cushite (cf CUSH) wife; here also he is not punished, although Miriam was. The priesthood of the family of Aaron was vindicated by Yahweh against the rebellion of Korah* and his fellow Levites* (Nm 16:1–18:24). Aaron died before the Israelites reached Canaan*; he was stripped of his priestly robes, which were transferred to his son Eleazar*, and buried on Mt Hor* (Nm 20:23 ff; 33:38 f) or at Moserah (Dt 10:6). Outside of subsequent passing allusions to the exodus traditions (1 S 12:6, 8; Ps 77:21; 105:26; 106:16; Mi 6:4), Aaron is not mentioned except as the priest, the ancestor of the "house of Aaron" or "the sons of Aaron." In the NT the imperfect priesthood of Aaron is contrasted with the perfect priesthood of Christ (Heb 5:4; 7:11; cf PRIEST).

Hebrew popular tradition has obscured and transfigured the historical character of Aaron. In the episodes of Miriam and the golden calf his guilt has been minimized. His part in the plague stories has probably been enlarged; in some stories he does not appear at all. Like Moses, he is wrapped in an element of wonder, especially in the story of the vindication of the Aaronic priesthood, which seems to reflect a sacerdotal and levitical quarrel which we cannot reconstruct exactly. But tradition has honestly preserved the account of his failings; and there is no reason, with some modern scholars, to regard him as a creation of Hebrew folklore and a retrojection of the later priesthood into early Israel, although the features of the later priesthood are certainly read back into the primitive period (cf PRIEST). But early Israel must have had a priesthood, and it is worth notice that its priest was not its great leader and prophet Moses, but his brother.

Abaddon (Hb *'ᵃbaddōn*, "destruction," "perdition"), named together with death* (Jb 28:22), and Sheol* (Pr 15:11), with the grave* (Ps 88:12, cf Jb 26:6; 31:12); a name for the region of the dead (cf DEATH, SHEOL); in rabbinical literature a part of Gehenna*. In NT it occurs only in Apc 9:11 as the name of the "angel* of the abyss*," Gk *'Apollyon*, "destroyer."

Abanah (Hb *'ᵃbānāh*), one of the rivers of Damascus* with the Pharpar* (2 K 5:12); probably the modern Barada or a branch of it.

Abarim (Hb *'ᵃbārîm*), mountains in Moab, including Pisgah* and Nebo*, from which the entire land of Canaan could be surveyed (Nm 27:12; 33:47 f; Dt 32:49; Je 22:20). These are the summits and slopes which divide the plateau of Moab from the Dead Sea.

Abba (Aramaic emphatic form of *'ab*, "father", employed as vocative), a word uttered by Jesus (Mk 14:36), employed by early Christians (Rm 8:15; Gal 4:6), with Gk translation given in each passage. In prayer formulae among Gk-speaking Christians probably both forms, *'ab* and *abba*, were used. Aramaic epistles indicate that it was a familiar address used by children; in this sense Jesus used it in invoking the Father* in the great crisis of His life, and it was taken up by the early Church.

Abdon (Hb *'abdōn*, etymology uncertain; perhaps abbreviated from theophorous name meaning "slave of [name of deity]"). **1.** Personal name borne by 4 men in OT, of whom the most notable is the "minor" judge* Abdon ben Hillel of Pirathon* (Jgs 12:13), whose 40 sons and 30 grandsons rode on 70 asses, a token of fabulous wealth. **2.** A town in Asher (Jos 21:30; 1 Ch 6:59).

1

Abednego (Hb *'abēd n^egō,* probably corrupted from *'abēd n^ebō,* "slave of Nabu"), Babylonian name given to Azariah*, one of the companions of Daniel (Dn 1:7).

Abel (Hb *hebel,* which would mean "vanity," "nothingness"; but more probably derived from Akkadian *aplu,* "son," which would indicate a Mesopotamian origin of the story). Abel was the second son of Adam* and Eve*, a shepherd*. His sacrifice* was pleasing to God, and he was murdered by his brother Cain* out of envy (Gn 4:2 ff). In Gn the story of the first murder begins the account of the moral deterioration of man which follows the Fall* and grows until it is arrested by the Deluge*. The story as adapted for this purpose exhibits traits of its origin and earlier forms. Abel is a pastoral culture hero, the first herdsman — an achievement which is credited in another tradition (Gn 4:20) to Jabal*, a descendant of Cain. The murder of Abel reflects the unending guerrilla conflict between the nomadic herdsman and the peasant, represented by Cain. The story is obviously sympathetic to the herdsman, and attributes the feud of nomad and peasant to an original act of treachery by the peasant. Abel is also the first to offer sacrifice; the story accepts animal sacrifice as better than cereal offerings. This probably reflects the attitude of the early nomadic Israelites toward the cult of the Canaanite peasants, who, however, also offered animal sacrifice. Abel is mentioned in Mt 23:35 and Lk 11:51 as an innocent victim of murder; his sacrifice is praised in Heb 11:4, and in Heb 12:24 his blood, which cried for vengeance, speaks less powerfully than the atoning blood of Jesus.

Abia. 1. Cf ABIJAH. **2.** Gk form of 1; in Lk 1:5 the 8th of the 24 divisions or courses of the temple priesthood (cf 1 Ch 24:10 and PRIEST), of which Zechariah*, the father of John the Baptist*, was a member.

Abiathar (Hb *'ebyātār,* old Babylonian Abiatar, "the father [i.e., god] excels"?), son of Ahimelech* of the line of Eli*, the sole survivor of the priestly family of Nob* after the slaughter of the priests by Saul* (1 S 22:9 ff). Abiathar fled to David* and joined David's band, taking with him the priestly oracle Urim* and Thummim, which he employed in David's service (1 S 23:6 ff; 30:7 ff). He is mentioned with Zadok* as a priest in one list of David's officers (2 S 20:25; 1 Ch 15:11) and as one of David's council (1 Ch 27:34). A son of Abiathar, Ahimelech (Abimelech 1 Ch 18:16) is mentioned as priest with Zadok in 2 S 8:17 (cf also 1 Ch 24:6). This may be due to a transposition of the names in the text; but it may also signify that Abiathar's son assumed the office of priest because of Abiathar's age, which must have been advanced by the end of David's reign. With Zadok he carried the ark from Jerusalem at the beginning of the revolt of Absalom*; but at the command of David they returned the ark to the city and themselves remained there to act as spies in concert with Hushai*, one of Absalom's council (2 S 15). The messages from the spies to David were delivered by Ahimaaz* and Jonathan*, Abiathar's son. During the last illness of David, Abiathar attached himself to the party of Adonijah*, the eldest of David's surviving sons, while Zadok joined the party of Solomon*. Not long after Solomon succeeded to the throne Adonijah and Joab* were assassinated; Solomon spared the life of Abiathar because of his priesthood, but deposed him from office and confined him to his estate at Anathoth* (1 K 1–2). The list of Solomon's officers in 1 K 4:4 must therefore antedate these events.

Abib. The name of the first month in the old Hebrew calendar, corresponding to Nisan in the later calendar, roughly our March; the month in which the exodus from Egypt occurred (Ex 13:4; 34:18; Dt 16:1). Cf CALENDAR.

Abiezer (Hb *'abī'ēzer,* "the father [i.e. god] is help"). **1.** The clan of Gideon* (Jgs 6:11, 24; 8:2, 32), probably identical with the clan of Iezer of the tribe of Manasseh* (Nm 26:30; 1 Ch 7:18). **2.** One of David's heroes (2 S 23:27; 1 Ch 11:28; 27:12).

Abigail (Hb *'abīgayil,* meaning uncertain ["the father rejoices"?]). **1.** Wife of Nabal* of Carmel* in Judah. When her husband refused to assist David* and his band, Abigail averted David from his intention to massacre the entire household by meeting him with provisions (1 S 25:1 ff). After the sudden death of Nabal, David took Abigail, described as "attractive and sensible," as a wife. She followed him to Gath* during his service with Achish* (1 S 27:3), and was among those captured and rescued in the raid of the Amalekites upon Ziklag* (1 S 30:5). She also accompanied him to his accession at Hebron* (2 S 2:2), where she bore him a son, Chileab*. **2.** A sister of David (Abigal in 2 S 17:25), wife of an Ishmaelite, Jether, and mother of Amasa*, who commanded the army of Absalom* (2 S 17:25; 1 Ch 2:16, 17).

Abihu (Hb *'abīhū',* "he [the god] is father"), son of Aaron* and Elisheba (Ex 6:23; Nm 3:2; 26:60; 1 Ch 5:29; 24:1). With his brother Nadab* he accompanied Moses*,

Aaron, and the 70 elders to the theophany on Sinai* (Ex 24:1 ff). He and Nadab were installed as priests with their father Aaron, but the two sons were killed by lightning because of some impropriety in their first offering of sacrifice* (Lv 10:1 ff). Possibly this story is a fictional explanation of the extinction of two priestly families of Abihu and Nadab. Cf PRIEST.

Abijah (Hb *'abîyah*, "Yah[weh] is father"). **1.** Son and successor of Rehoboam* in the kingdom of Judah (915–913 BC); in 1 K his name appears as Abijam. His mother was Maacah*. Nothing is related of his reign in 1 K, where he is judged unfavorably, except war with Jeroboam* of Israel; the unfavorable judgment probably signifies that he tolerated worship on the high places* (1 K 15:1–8). In 2 Ch 13:1–22 there appears an account of a battle between Abijah and Jeroboam, notable chiefly for the extended speech of Abijah in which victory is assured him because of his fidelity to the worship of Yahweh. Abijah was victorious in spite of the successful ambush laid by Jeroboam, and recovered the cities of Bethel*, Jeshanah, and Ephron*. The author of Ch does not judge Abijah unfavorably (cf CHRONICLES). **2.** A son of Samuel* (1 S 8:2) who shared his father's office but not his incorruptibility. **3.** Son of Jeroboam of Israel; he died as a child and was the occasion of the denunciation of the king by Ahijah* (1 K 14:1 ff). The name was borne by three other men, one the head of a priestly family (cf ABIA) and one woman, the wife of Hezekiah* (2 Ch 29:1; Abi in 2 K 18:2).

Abilene (Gk *abilēnē*), the tetrarchy or district ruled by Lysanias* at the beginning of the public life of Jesus (Lk 3:1). The district was centered about the city of Abila, in the valley of the Barada about 20 mi NW of Damascus*.

Abimelech (Hb *'abîmelek*, "the father [i.e., god] is king"). **1.** The name of a Canaanite king of Gerar*. He took Sarah*, the wife of Abraham*, into his harem; but after he had been warned by God in a dream he released her and dismissed Abraham with gifts. His rebuke of Abraham for posing as the brother of Sarah implies a moral judgment of the author on Abraham's conduct (Gn 20:1–18). Abraham also made a covenant with Abimelech and Phicol*, the commander of his army, at Beersheba*, by which Abraham was guaranteed sure possession of a well he had dug and rights to pasture in the Negeb*. A king of the same name at Gerar appears in the story of Isaac*, whose wife he takes into his harem; in this story the ruse is discovered when Abimelech sees Isaac making love to Rebekah*. This account is no doubt a variant of the story which is read in Gn 12:10 ff, 20:1 ff, about Abraham (cf GENESIS; PENTATEUCH).

2. The son of Gideon* and a Canaanite concubine who lived at Shechem*. Abimelech appealed to the citizens of Shechem on the basis of his relationship and persuaded them to rebel against the rule of the sons of Gideon, all of whom were murdered by Abimelech except Jotham* (Jgs 8:29–9:21). Two accounts of a rebellion of the men of Shechem against Abimelech have been carelessly compiled. In one (Jgs 9:22–25; 9:42–49) a quarrel arises because the men of Shechem rob those who pass on the road. This probably reflects a quarrel over the tolls exacted from caravans on the highway which follows the ridge of the central range of Palestine*. Abimelech ambushed the men of the city when they went out to work in the fields and razed the city to the ground. Those who escaped to Migdal-Shechem, the citadel, were also killed when the citadel was burned. The other story in Jgs 9:26–41 has been interpolated into the middle of the first account. This relates a rebellion led by a certain Gaal* which was suppressed by Zebul*, the governor appointed by Abimelech. In both accounts Abimelech does not reside at Shechem, which is not explained; Arumah, not identified, is mentioned as his residence (Jgs 9:41). The destruction of Shechem is no doubt exaggerated; this important crossroads city could not long remain uninhabited. Abimelech himself was killed during an attack on Thebez* by a millstone flung from the wall by a woman (Jgs 9:50–57); this misfortune became proverbial (2 S 11:21). The story of Abimelech illustrates the unsettled conditions of Canaan during the Israelite settlement. Shechem was itself a Canaanite city, not an Israelite city, but it was ruled by Israelites, Gideon and his sons; and Abimelech himself was the issue of a mixed union. Abimelech, like Gideon, ruled the city from elsewhere, probably an Israelite city, and his armed band was either Israelite or mixed. Like the other judges*, he was a military leader who defended or expanded the territory of Israel; but his character excluded him from the list of charismatic heroes.

Abinadab '(Hb *'abînādāb*, "the father [i.e., god] is noble"). **1.** A man of Kirjath-jearim* in whose house the ark* of the covenant* was kept after it was recovered from the Philistines* (1 S 7:1) until it was removed by David* to be installed in Jerusalem* (2 S 6:2 ff). **2.** Brother of David (1 S 16:8; 17:13;

1 Ch 2:13). **3.** Son of Saul* (1 S 31:2; 1 Ch 8:33; 9:39; 10:2).

Abiram (Hb *'ªbīrām*, "the father [i.e., god] is exalted"). **1.** Cf DATHAN. **2.** Cf HIEL. The name is probably identified with Abram-Abraham*.

Abishag (Hb *'ªbīšāg*, meaning uncertain), a young woman of Shunem* who became the companion of David* in his old age (1 K 1:1–4) and slept with him to keep him warm. Although they had no sexual relations, Abishag nevertheless was the occasion of the death of Adonijah*, who asked for her from Solomon after David's death (1 K 2:13–25). Such intimate contact with the king made her a royal possession upon which it was treason to encroach.

Abishai (Hb *'ªbīšai*, meaning uncertain), brother of Joab* and Asahel*, the three sons of Zeruiah*, David's sister (1 Ch 2:16). With Joab, he was intimately associated with David during his life and reign. Abishai accompanied David to the camp of Saul by night and urged that Saul be slain there and then; David refused (1 S 26:6 ff). With Joab he pursued Abner* after Abner had killed their brother Asahel in battle (2 S 2:24), and he is mentioned together with Joab in the killing of Abner, although Joab himself struck the blow (2 S 3:30). He commanded the army of David under Joab; at the siege of Rabbah* he took command of half the army to hold the Ammonites*, while Joab attacked the Aramaeans* who had come as allies (2 S 10:9–14). He accompanied David on his flight from Absalom and asked David's permission to kill Shimei* for cursing David, but this was refused (2 S 16:9). With Joab and Ittai he commanded the army against Absalom (2 S 18:2) and in the subsequent rebellion (2 S 20:10). When Shimei met David to ask for forgiveness, Abishai again asked permission to kill him but was again forbidden to (2 S 19:19–23). During the war against the Philistines* Abishai saved David's life by killing a Philistine hero whose name is corrupted and who resembles Goliath*; this was the occasion on which David's officers refused to let him take personal part in battle (2 S 21:16–17). Abishai appears in the list of David's heroes as chief of the Thirty (2 S 23:18–19). He led a campaign into Edom* and placed garrisons in the country after a victory in the Valley of Salt (1 Ch 18:12 f). The conquest of Edom is attributed to Joab in 1 K 11:15; it is doubtful that these two traditions refer to two different campaigns. Abishai was, like his brother Joab, closely linked to David by blood and by many services both per-

sonal and official, and like Joab put loyalty to the king above every other consideration.

Abner (Hb *'abnēr*, meaning uncertain; "the father [the god] is a lamp"?), son of Ner, commander of the army of Saul (1 S 14:50). Ner and Kish, the father of Saul, were brothers, sons of Abiel. He appears at the battle with the Philistines at Socoh* (1 S 17:55). As a ranking officer he dines with the king's sons and David (1 S 20:25). He commanded Saul's forces during the pursuit of David and was rebuked by David for permitting him to enter Saul's camp by night (1 S 26:14–16). After Saul's death at the battle of Gilboa* Abner took Ishbaal*, Saul's surviving son, across the Jordan to Mahanaim* and maintained the kingdom of Israel. After David had been acclaimed king of Judah at Hebron* (2 S 2:1 ff), war broke out between the two kingdoms, and hostilities were initiated at the pool of Gibeon* (2 S 2:12 ff). The battle was opened by a tournament of 12 chosen champions from each side; perhaps what began as a mere test of arms turned to hostile conflict. Abner's army was defeated and he was pursued by Asahel*, the brother of Joab* and Abishai*; when Asahel, warned by Abner, refused to abandon the pursuit, Abner killed him. This was taken as the beginning of a blood-feud (cf AVENGER) with the family of Asahel. The war went badly for Ishbaal, who alienated Abner's loyalty by rebuking him for taking Rizpah*, a woman of Saul's harem; and Abner opened negotiations to deliver the kingdom of Ishbaal to David. David was happy to receive the message, but insisted that Saul's daughter, Michal*, who had been given to Paltiel* after David's flight, be restored to him; his honor had been grievously injured. Abner agreed and promoted the cause of David with the Israelites, especially with Benjamin*, the tribe of Saul. When he came to David with an Israelite embassy, Joab called him aside and murdered him in fulfillment of the feud. Although the murder was profitable to David, he protested that he had no part in it; but he did not punish Joab, whose fidelity here had exceeded all bounds (2 S 3). Abner's part in establishing the united monarchy of David was considerable. His loyalty to the failing house of Saul finally broke, but up to the time he changed masters he had followed Saul's house without reserve; and he must have seen that there was no hope for Israel except in the single rule of David.

Abomination of Desolation. The common English version of Dn 9:27; 11:31, Hb *šikkus mᵉšōmēm*. The passages were probably written on the occasion of the erection of an altar to Zeus Olympios in the temple sanctuary by Antiochus* Epiphanes in 168 B.C. (1 Mc 1:54; 6:7; 2 Mc 6:2). In 1 Mc the Hb words are translated into Gk. In the prophetic* and apocalyptic* literature, however, it is common to universalize particular events; and in this event is seen the profanation of the holy by the powers of unbelief and godlessness, which is a constantly recurring motif in history. It is in this sense that Jesus alludes to the words of Dn in Mt 24:15, and not with reference to any particular event.

Abraham (Hb 'abrāhām), son of Terah* and ancestor of the Israelites*. The name is most probably a dialectal variant of the original name 'abrām, identical with 'ªbīrām, "the father (i.e., god) is exalted." The etymology implied in Gn 17:5, where the change of name is related, is popular.

1. *Life.* The clan of Terah migrated from Ur* to Haran*, where Terah died. From there Abraham migrated to Canaan* (Gn 11:27 ff). This episode may preserve two variant traditions about the place of Abraham's origin. In Canaan occurred the first divine communication granted to Abraham and the promise of a great posterity (Gn 12: 1–3). At Shechem* he received the promise that his descendants would possess Canaan (Gn 12:7). He traveled to Bethel* and to the Negeb*; driven by a famine to Egypt, he posed as the brother of Sarah*, who was taken into the harem of the Pharaoh. The Pharaoh saw in a plague of diseases a warning that he had done wrong and released Sarah (Gn 12:10–20). Because of quarrels between the herdsmen of Abraham and those of his nephew Lot* they parted from each other; Lot dwelt near Sodom*, and Abraham remained in Canaan (Gn 13: 1 ff). A variant of the promise that Canaan would belong to Abraham's descendants occurs in Gn 13:14 ff. In Gn 14:1 ff Abraham appears as a military hero, the only such episode reported of him. A raiding party sent by the Mesopotamian overlords of Canaan was pursued by Abraham, who rescued the booty and the prisoners, including Lot. On his return he was met at Salem* (Jerusalem) by its king, Melchizedek*. This story preserved the memory of the first encounter of the ancestor of the Israelites with what became the most Israelite of all cities. A son was promised Abraham (Gn 15:1 ff) and a covenant* was concluded by Abraham with the God who had revealed Himself (Gn 15:9); a variant of the promise of the land to his descendants is added (Gn 15:18 ff). The childless Sarah substituted her slave Hagar*, who bore Abraham a son, Ishmael*. This practice is found in the legal codes of Mesopotamia; the rights of the substitute and her children were guaranteed by the law, but were violated by Sarah and Abraham, who yielded to his wife's jealousy and expelled Hagar and her son (Gn 16:1–16). A variant account of the covenant is found in Gn 17:1 ff; the obligation of circumcision and another variant of the promise of a son are added (Gn 17:15 ff). Abraham entertained God with two companions (Gn 18: 1 ff), and a son is promised again. The realism of the story need not blind us to the fact that hospitality is a much prized virtue in the desert; and that the tradition of Abraham's hospitality was intended to show that this virtue is most pleasing to God. He who exhibits it entertains God in the traveler. The account of the destruction of Sodom and Gomorrah* is preceded by a debate between Abraham and God (Gn 18:20–19:28). Such natural disasters posed a question to the Hebrew mind as to the justice of such punishments; for they were conceived as an act of the wrath of God. The dialogue of Gn 18:20 ff is a primitive theodicy, explaining them as the result of the total depravity of the people involved; were there even a few innocent, God would withhold His anger for their sake. In Gn 20:1 ff there is a variant of the story of Abraham and Sarah found in Gn 12:10 ff; cf ABIMELECH. The birth of Isaac is related in Gn 21:1 ff with a variant of the story of the expulsion of Hagar*. The story of the sacrifice of Isaac in Gn 22:1 ff shows the great faith of Abraham. It is also directed against the practice of human sacrifice, and this is probably its primary purpose in its original form. It may be the expression of this truth by an imaginary narrative, a parable*, or it may preserve dimly the memory of some spiritual crisis in the life of Abraham. After the death of Sarah, Abraham purchased ground at Hebron* for a burial plot; this was the first ownership of a portion of the land which was promised to the descendants of Abraham (Gn 23:1 ff). Abraham sought a bride for Isaac from his kinsfolk in Mesopotamia (Gn 24:1 ff). Gn 25:1 ff contains a genealogy* which connects Abraham with a number of Arabian* tribes.

2. *Literary character of the traditions of Abraham.* The stories of Abraham are family traditions preserved by oral tradition for some centuries before they were written down. They exhibit a number of variant accounts of single events, from which appears the freedom with which these memories were repeated in story. An element of wonder is introduced and heightened in some forms of the tradition. The stories are not preserved or related in a consecutive biography, but are strung together in a sequence which does not necessarily follow the order of time.

It is important to distinguish this type of family tradition from historical records as we understand them and to leave room for the imagination of the storytellers (cf HISTORY). On the sources and their compilation cf PENTATEUCH.

3. *Date and historical background of Abraham.* Older scholars dated Abraham as a contemporary of Hammurabi of Babylon (c 1728–1686 BC), whom they identified with Amraphel of Shinar (Gn 14:1). This identification can no longer be retained, nor can we place the five kings in any known period of Mesopotamian history, although the same or similar names occur in the first half of the 2nd millennium BC; cf the separate articles. But it is almost certain that Abraham belongs to the period 2000–1500 BC, and later in the period rather than earlier. It is no longer possible to regard Abraham as an entirely fictitious character or as the personification of a tribe, although not all the traditions concerning him have equal historical value. For historical and cultural background cf AMORITES; PATRIARCHS.

4. *The Religion of Abraham.* The importance of Abraham lies in the fact that with him begins the biblical revelation. No reason can be found for the preservation of his memory except the Hebrew belief that God first spoke to him, and this belief can be questioned only by doubting the entire chain of Hebrew and Christian belief. The substance of this fact is not affected by questions about the historical validity of separate traditions. There can be little doubt that the God who revealed Himself to Abraham appears as a family god, "the God of Abraham (Isaac and Jacob)" (Gn 26:24; Ex 3:15 +). This form of worship, in which the deity of the family was worshiped and enshrined in the family dwelling, is known from the remains of ancient Mesopotamia. Abraham knows him not as Yahweh, who was worshiped by the later Israelites, but as El Shaddai. In character He appears as a god of cosmic domain, who can give Abraham the land of Canaan, and of justice and righteousness, who gives sanction to moral obligations. He can be approached by His worshipers and He hears their prayers. He receives sacrifice, the common rite of adoration of the ancient world. He demands unreserved faith* in His promises and in His power and will to fulfill them. The morality of Abraham was in many respects no more enlightened than that of his world; the revelation of the divine moral will did not come all at once. In no tradition of Abraham does God demand that He be worshiped exclusively, and the omission is significant, since this feature of Hebrew belief is so emphasized in later history and yet is not read

back into the story of Abraham; cf Jos 24:2. But He is a God who stands alone, without associate or consort; as a family god, He has no connection with the gods of the Mesopotamian pantheon.

5. *Abraham in later Scriptures.* The promises and the covenant of Abraham, which initiated the process of salvation and culminated in the covenant, are often alluded to in the OT (Ex 32:13; Nm 32:11; Dt 1:8; 2 K 13:23; 1 Ch 16:16; Ps 105:9, 42 +). Yahweh redeemed Abraham (Is 29:22); Abraham is the rock and the quarry from which Israel came (Is 51:1–2). Though he was only one, he possessed the whole land (Ezk 33:24). References to Abraham in the NT are numerous. He was the father of the Jews (Mt 3:9 +), they are his descendants (Jn 8:33). The entire dispute in Jn 8:33 ff hinges on the Jews' pride in their descent from Abraham; Jesus takes occasion of this to point out that mere carnal descent is not enough. The climax of the dispute is reached when Jesus claimed to be greater than Abraham. John the Baptist had already said that God could raise up children of Abraham from stones (Mt 3:9). Paul takes Abraham as a hero of faith as contrasted with the works of the Law* (Rm 4:1 ff; Gal 3:6 ff). Faith in Christ makes one a true descendant of Abraham (Gal 3:29). Abraham's two wives are types of the two covenants, the covenant of bondage of Moses and the covenant of liberty of Christ (Gal 4:22). Melchizedek, a type* of Christ, shows the supremacy of Christ; for Melchizedek received tithes from Abraham, the ancestor of the priesthood of Aaron (Heb 7:1 ff).

Abraham's Bosom. Mentioned in Lk 16:22. In 4 Mc 13:17 the just at their death are received by Abraham, Isaac, and Jacob. This probably alludes to the heavenly banquet; the place of honor was next to the host, where the guest could recline on the host's bosom (cf Jn 13:25). Cf MEAL.

Abram. Cf ABRAHAM.

Absalom (Hb *'abšālōm*, "the father [i.e., god] is peace," in 1 K 15:2, 10 *'abīšālōm*), son of David* and Maacah*, daughter of Talmai*, king of Geshur* (2 S 3:3). His full sister Tamar* was raped by their half-brother Amnon*; in revenge Absalom murdered Amnon at the feast of the sheepshearing (2 S 13:1 ff). Absalom fled to Geshur, remaining there three years. Joab*, perceiving that David really yearned for his son but could not recall him without injuring the royal dignity, persuaded him through the fictitious case presented by the wise woman of Tekoa* (2 S 14:1 ff). The point of her case is that the law of blood-revenge is not valid within a family, since it is all one and the same blood, and that the family must first preserve itself even if a murder must be condoned. Absalom was recalled but not admitted to the royal presence for two years. He then set Joab's fields on fire to remind him that he should intercede with the king. During the next four years Absalom made a habit of exhibiting friendliness to all men and of pointing out weaknesses in the government of David (2 S 15:1 ff). When he felt strong enough, he proclaimed himself king in Hebron, and David was forced to flee from Jerusalem. Ahithophel*, one of David's council, joined the revolt; he persuaded Absalom to take public possession of David's harem (2 S 16:21–22). This was a paramount act of treason, since the harem partook of the sanctity of royalty, and made an irreparable breach between the two. Ahithophel also asked that he be permitted to pursue David immediately before David could gather a force. Hushai*, also one of David's council, had remained in Jerusalem at David's request to work secretly for David. He counseled delay, lest there be an immediate defeat, and urged Absalom to gather an army and head it personally (2 S 17:1 ff). Absalom, probably moved by vanity, accepted the counsel of Hushai; and Ahithophel, perceiving that this was a fatal blunder (although not aware of Hushai's duplicity), hanged himself (2 S 17:23). The battle between the two forces was joined in the forest of Ephraim. David ordered his officers to spare the life of Absalom. In the ensuing battle Absalom was defeated and fled upon a mule; but his long hair, of which he was vain (cf 2 S 14:26), was entangled in the branches of an oak. When he hung helplessly, he was discovered by one of David's soldiers, who informed Joab; and Joab immediately killed him (2 S 18:92ff). David's grief at the news was unrestrained until Joab rebuked him for thinking more of his ungrateful son than of his faithful followers (2 S 19:1 ff).

The story of Absalom reveals some weaknesses both in David's character and in his government. The household of David exhibits the vicious quarrels and hatreds which are a consequence of polygamy; it also exhibits little or no effort of David to rule his own sons, who show incredible selfishness and no sense of duty whatever. The revolt of Absalom could hardly have been so quickly successful if there had not been discontent with David's rule; perhaps his wars had been a strain upon the people, while the booty was distributed among the king and his favorites. The complaint mentioned in 2 S 15:2 ff indicates that the king was inaccessible to the people at large, and that it was difficult to obtain legal justice. While the rebellion was put down by David's professional troops, there is no evidence that the discontent ceased.

Abyss (Gk *abyssos*), in classical Gk the abode of the dead, used in this sense in Rom 10:7; in Apc the abode of the demons (cf Lk 8:31). The angel* of the abyss is Abaddon* (Apc 9:11). The beast rises from the abyss (Apc 11: 7–8). The destructive powers of the abyss are released by an angel who has the key of the abyss (Apc 9:1–2; 20:1). Cf GEHENNA; SHEOL.

Acacia (Hb *šiṭṭîm*), a tree, *Mimosa nilotica,* which grows in Palestine only in the S part of the Jordan valley. It has white round flowers and yellowish-brown light durable wood. It is mentioned in connection with the construction of the ark* of the covenant (Ex 25–27; 30; 35–38; Dt 10:13). In the messianic restoration of the land Yahweh will make the acacia grow in the desert (Is 41:29).

Accad. Cf AKKAD.

Acco (Hb *'akkō,* etymology unknown), a seaport city on the coast of Palestine N of Mt Carmel on the Bay of Acre, the Acre of medieval times, modern Akka. The site is the modern Tell el Fukkar E of Akka. The city was named Ptolemais by Ptolemy II Philadelphus of Egypt during the period when the Ptolemies controlled Palestine; the city appears under this name in 1–2 Mc. It is far and away the best harbor on the coast of Palestine and was the most important port for Palestine until Herod built Caesarea. It is inferior to the Phoenician harbors; the rocky point on which the city lay is exposed to the SW gales. It had excellent communications with the hinterland; the road from Acco through the plain of Esdraelon* was the only lowland highway route from the sea to the Jordan*.

The city is mentioned only a few times in the Bible, but its importance and antiquity are seen in other ancient texts. It is mentioned among the Canaanite cities in the Egyptian execration texts of the 19th century BC. In the Amarna* letters it is ruled by a king Zuratta, probably an Indo-Iranian name. It probably passed into the hands of the Philistines or of the Tjekker when these peoples settled on the Palestinian coast in the 12th century BC. Luli, king of Sidon, ruled it when Sennacherib* received tribute from Luli. Ashur-bani-pal of Assyria* sacked Acco in the middle of the 7th century BC. It was the administrative center of a Persian district.

Acco lay in the territory of Asher*, but the city remained Canaanite (Jgs 1:31). It was under the control of the Seleucids during the Maccabean period (1 Mc 5:15, 22, 55) and was the base of operations of Alexander* and Tryphon* (1 Mc 10:1, 39, 56–60; 11:22, 24; 13:12; 2 Mc 13:24 f), and Jonathan* was captured and imprisoned by Tryphon at Ptolemais (1 Mc 12:45, 48). The gift of the city to the Jerusalem temple promised by Alexander (1 Mc 10:39) was never made. The city was unsuccessfully besieged by Alexander Jannaeus (103–76 BC). It was the military port for Herod and the Romans. Paul landed at Ptolemais after his 3rd missionary journey (AA 21:7), where there was already a Christian church.

Achab. Cf AHAB.

Achaea (Gk *achaia*), the old name of the region lying S of the Gulf of Corinth. After the defeat of the Achaean League in 146 BC the Romans placed the district under the provincial government of Macedonia*. In 27 BC Achaea was detached from Macedonia and made a senatorial province. It included continental Greece S of Thessaly (i.e., Boeotia, Attica, the Peloponnesus, and Epirus) and included the cities of Athens and Corinth. It is mentioned most frequently in the NT in connection with Corinth (AA 18:12, 27; 19:21; Rm 15:26; 1 Co 16:15; 2 Co 1:1; 9:2; 11:10; 1 Th 1:7 f).

Achan (Hb *'ākān*, meaning unknown); son of Carmi of the tribe of Judah (Jos 7:1). At the sack of Jericho* Achan had stolen some of the booty, which had been put under the ban*. When the Israelites failed in their first attack against Ai*, some fault was suspected and the culprit was discovered by the oracle of the lot*. The sanctity of the ban was communicated to the thief and to his entire household and possessions; the people were stoned, so that no contact was made with the banned persons, and the articles were burned so that no use of them was possible.

Achaz. Cf AHAZ.

Achimaas. Cf AHIMAAZ.

Achimelech. Cf AHIMELECH.

Achinoam. Cf AHINOAM.

Achior (Gk *achior*), commander of the Ammonites* (Jdt 5:5). When questioned by Holofernes* about the Jews, Achior related their conquest of Canaan* and its peoples and warned Holofernes that he would not suc-

ceed unless the Jews had sinned and thus lost God's protection. Holofernes in anger ordered him to be bound and sent to the Jews to be executed after the city of Bethulia* was taken. Achior was present when Judith* returned from Holofernes; impressed by her deed, he professed faith in the God of the Jews and was circumcised and received into the Jewish community.

Achish (Hb *'akīsh*, probably a foreign name, etymology and meaning unknown; a connection with Anchises has been suggested), ruler of Gath*, a Philistine city, called "king" of Gath, although the Philistine rulers were not kings. Achish, king of Gath in 1 K 2:39, must be a different person. David* fled to Gath first from Saul*; but he was recognized as the Hebrew military hero and feigned madness in order to escape (1 S 21:10 ff). This is a variant account of his service as a mercenary with Achish (1 S 27:1 ff); one form of the tradition refused to accept the information that the great Hebrew hero had served the enemies of Israel for hire. Achish gave him Ziklag* as a residence with the mission to conduct guerrilla raids against the Israelites; the tradition has denied that David was faithful to these instructions, but it is difficult to see how he could have been unfaithful without discovery (1 S 27:6–12). But when David and his men were attached to the Philistine army for battle against Saul, the other Philistine leaders questioned their fidelity, and he was not allowed to take part in the campaign, in spite of his willingness to do so (1 S 29:1–10). It was with the consent of Achish and the other Philistine rulers that David became king at Hebron (2 S 2:4), and he could not have reigned except as a vassal of the Philistines. The story of Achish and David illustrates how popular tradition could gloss over the less attractive features of its hero.

Achitophel. Cf AHITHOPHEL.

Achor (Hb *'ākōr*), the valley where Achan* was stoned (Jos 7:24–26). The play on his name has no support in etymology; *'ākōr*, "trouble," is doubtfully the meaning of the name. It was a point on the boundary of Judah (Jos 15:7), probably W or SW of Jericho*, not certainly identified. In Ho 2:15 the valley of "trouble" will become a "door of hope."

Achsah (Hb *'aksāh*, meaning unknown), daughter of Caleb*, given in marriage to Othniel* in reward for the capture of Kirjath-sepher*. As a wedding gift she asked and received the springs of Upper and

Lower Gullath (Jos 15:16–19, repeated in Jgs 1:12–15).

Achshaph (Hb 'akšāp), a Canaanite town allied with Jabin* of Hazor* and defeated by Joshua (Jos 11:1; 12:20); later in the territory of Asher* (Jos 19:25). It is probably identified with the modern Tell Keisan about ten mi SE of Acco*.

Acts of the Apostles. AA is the 2nd volume of an historical work of which Lk is the 1st volume (AA 1:1). "Acts" (Gk *praxeis*) is a Hellenistic type of literature composed about famous men (Alexander, Hannibal). The Gk title is "acts of apostles," not "acts of the apostles"; the meaning of the term is somewhat indefinite (cf APOSTLE), but it is not limited to the Twelve. The prologue, unlike the prologue of Lk, does not define the scope of the work; this is implied in the words of Jesus in 1:8, "You shall be my witnesses in Jerusalem and all Judaea and Samaria and to the end of the earth." These words summarize the plan of the book. Like Lk, it imitates the form of Hellenistic history, but it is not history in the classical sense. It is the story of the growth of the Church under the impulse of the Holy Spirit* (9:31). The prominence of the Spirit in AA is evident; the book is the gospel of the Spirit, as Lk was the gospel of the Son. The fullness of the Spirit and of the mission of the Church is seen in the expansion of the Church to the Gentile world; once the gospel has reached Rome, the center of the world, the author feels that his story is complete. In this sense AA is a work of the Hellenistic Church, and in this sense it is apologetic as well as historical; cf below.

1. *Contents:*
Introduction (1:1–26): 1:1–2, prologue; 1:3–14, apparitions and ascension; 1:15–26, election of Matthias.
I. The Jewish Christian Community, 2:1–9:31.
The Jerusalem community (2:1–8:3). 2:1–47, the foundation of the Church at Pentecost; 3:1–5:16, healing of the lame man and conflict with the Jews; 5:17–42, second conflict with the Jews; 6:1–7, appointment of the Seven; 6:8–8:1, Stephen; 8:1–3, persecution and dispersal.
The Palestinian mission (8:4–9:31). 8:4–40, Philip; 9:1–31, conversion of Saul.
II. Establishment of the Gentile mission, 9:32–15:35.
The beginnings of the Gentile mission (9:32–12:15). 9:32–11:18, baptism of Cornelius and his household; 11:19–30, foundation of the community of Antioch; 12:1–25, persecution of Herod Agrippa.

First missionary journey of Barnabas and Paul (13:1–15:35). 13:1–12, Cyprus; 13:13–14:20, southern Galatia; 14:21–28, return to Antioch; 15:1–35, decision of the council of Jerusalem to admit Gentiles.
III. Paul, the apostle of the Gentiles, 15:36–28:31.
Second missionary journey (15:36–18:22). 15:36–41, departure from Antioch; 16:1–10, Asia to Troas; 16:11–17:15, Macedonia (Philippi, Thessalonica, Beroea); 17: 16–18:17, Achaea (Athens, Corinth); 18:18–22, return to Antioch via Ephesus.
Third missionary journey (18:23–20:4). 18:24–28, Apollos; 19:1–22, Ephesus; 19:23–40, riot of the silversmiths at Ephesus; 20:1–4, Macedonia and Achaea.
Final journey of Paul to Jerusalem, 20:5–21:14.
Paul the prisoner for Christ (21:15–28:31). 21:15–26, arrival in Jerusalem and visit of the Jerusalem church; 21:27–40, Paul attacked by Jews and rescued by Romans; 22:1–21, Paul's discourse to the Jews; 22:22–29, Paul in Antonia; 22:30–23:11, Paul before the council; 23:12–23, attempt on Paul's life; 23:23–35, Paul's transfer to Caesarea; 24:1–23, trial before Felix; 24:24–27, postponement of trial; 25:1–12, Paul's appeal to Caesar; 25:13–26:32, Paul before Festus and Agrippa; 27:1–8, voyage to Crete via Myra; 27:9–44, storm, shipwreck at Malta; 28:1–10, Malta; 28:11–16, arrival in Rome; 28:17–31, two year imprisonment and Paul's encounter with the Jews of Rome.
2. *Sources.* The style and vocabulary of AA are uniform with no substantial differences which betray the presence of documentary sources. There are, however, differences between the account of the Jerusalem community and the account of the Gentile missions; but it is obvious that the author depended on testimony for his account of the Jerusalem community. There is wide agreement that the evidence is against written sources for this part of the book; several attempts to identify such sources have not been successful. The author, therefore, depended on oral tradition and anecdote for the material which precedes Paul's second journey. These sources must have been more than one; Dupont points out that different sources should be postulated for the accounts of the primitive Jerusalem community (1–5), of Peter (9:32–11:18; 12), of Philip (8:4–40), of the Antioch community (11:19–30; 13:1–3), of the conversion of Paul and his first journey and part of the second (9:1–30; 13:4–14:28; 15:36 ff). The second half of AA is dominated by the "We Sections" (16:10–17; 20:5–21:18; 27:1–28:16). In these the use of "we" indicates that the narrator was present; it can be deduced that the

narrator joined Paul at Troas on his second journey, traveled with him as far as Philippi, rejoined him at Philippi on his return from the third journey, and was with him from this point to the end of the book. Efforts to make the narrator of the "We" sections a companion of Paul distinct from the author of the entire book have never convinced many scholars; the uniformity of the style of the book is opposed to this hypothesis.

3. *Language and Style.* AA has a rich vocabulary and is written generally in very good Gk which attempts to follow classical usage. The style usually but not always flows easily, and the narrative is generally lively and moving, with a flair for the dramatic. This general tone is in striking contrast to occasional vulgar Koine idioms and Semitisms. To some extent this is due to the effort of the author to adjust the language to the persons and situations of the incidents; it is also due to the fact that they were found in his oral sources for the Jerusalem community, for it is in this part of the book that most of the differences in style occur. The "We Sections" are the most lively and graphic part of the book, with abundant and exact details, frequent mention of personal names, and statements of chronology (18:11; 19:8–10; 20:31; 24:27; 28:30). The first part of the book is less graphic and attempts no chronology at all (cf below).

4. *Historical Character.* The "Tendency Criticism" of the Tübingen School of the middle 19th century placed AA in the 2nd century and interpreted it as a theological document which was intended to compromise the differences between Paulinism and Jewish Christianity represented by Peter; little historical value was given it. Modern criticism mostly avoids such extreme historical skepticism; but an excessive skepticism is shown by some writers who believe that AA is apologetic, written to vindicate Christianity both before Judaism, of which the author wishes to show it is the legitimate development, and before the Roman government, to which the author wishes to represent Christianity as a cult harmless to public order and deserving of the legal position of *religio licita,* a lawful religion. Such an apologetic purpose does indeed seem to be present; but it does not weaken the historical character of the book unless one assumes that it is impossible to present this apologetic by simply stating the truth. More evident than the ends suggested is the desire of the author to vindicate the expansion of Christianity to the Gentiles as the legitimate fulfillment of the mission of Jesus and the work of the Holy Spirit.

Questions of the historical character of AA do not arise concerning the general character of the work but about particular passages and questions; and it is possible to solve these problems only if one grants that the historical quality of the work is not uniform throughout. The differences of style noted above between the first and the second parts also extend to the contents. The atmosphere of thaumaturgy and charismatic operations is much more prominent in the first part than it is in the second, and it is not present at all in the "We Sections." This suggests that the oral tradition concerning the primitive community had heightened these elements somewhat in the accounts which the author received; and there is room for further detailed study of the single episodes and of their sources.

AA establishes no chronology, especially for the first part; but where the narrative comes in contact with extrabiblical sources no chronological difficulty is raised, and a combination of AA with these sources permits solidly probable dates. From the first Pentecost to Stephen should have been about three years (AD 30–33?). No set time can be calculated for the dispersion of the Jerusalem community and the conversion of Paul. The community of Antioch was probably founded between AD 38–40. From external data the death of Herod Agrippa is to be placed in AD 44, the famine under Claudius AD 49–55. Gallio* was at Corinth in AD 51–52, and this gives a fixed point for Paul's presence there. Festus replaced Felix as procurator most probably in AD 59–60, although AD 55 is a possible date. The end of the book is to be set at AD 63.

The discourses of AA present a special problem. They are 18 in number and occupy about ¼ of the book: Peter (1:15 ff; 2:14 ff; 3:12 ff; 4:8 ff); Gamaliel (5:34 ff); Stephen (7:2 ff); Paul (13:16 ff; 14:15 ff); Peter and James (15); Paul (17:22 ff); the clerk of Ephesus (19:35 ff); Paul (20:18 ff; 22:1 ff); Tertullus (24:2 ff); Paul (24:10 ff; 26:2 ff; 28:17 ff). It was a standard literary pattern of classical historians to compose speeches for their characters to be delivered at critical moments. Those speeches did not pretend to be records of what was said; the historian employed them as vehicles of his own analysis and interpretation of events. Thucydides said that where he had no record of the words uttered, he wrote what he thought the speaker might have said appropriate to the occasion. Were Luke's speeches of this character, he would have violated no canon of ancient historiography; and he did, with some slight differences in detail, present the characters as speaking in his own style.

There are indications, however, that Luke constructed the speeches upon a summary report of the discourses themselves. "Their historical value lies in their faithful preservation of the themes of the primitive preaching rather than in their exact agreement with the situation" (L. Cerfaux). The primitive teaching of the gospel is reconstructed by modern critics from the discourses of AA. The Christology and eschatology of the discourses of Peter are archaic; and the discourses of Paul do not contain the more elaborate teaching of the epistles. These are not the personal reflections and analyses of the author; they are for him constitutive elements of the history which he reports, for the object of the history is precisely the spread of the gospel by its preaching. When the apostles speak, they speak that which is given them (Lk 21:15).

The conversion of Cornelius, it has been argued by M. Dibelius, has received a theological interpretation which is due entirely to the author and his desire to justify the reception of the Gentiles on terms of freedom. W. C. van Unnik has argued similarly that the significance of the episode is not presented accurately; Cornelius, as a Gentile proselyte*, was eligible for membership in the community with no dispute, but the author has made it a decisive step toward a Gentile Christianity. These hypotheses presuppose a kind of apologetic which cannot be demonstrated in AA; on the difficulties which are recorded concerning Peter's acceptance of Gentile Christianity cf PETER.

AA compared to the epistles of Paul does not render an account in all respects harmonious; and it must be remembered that the epistles are a primary source, while AA is secondary. There is no discord between the personal portrait of Paul in AA and Paul as revealed in his own writings, nor between the theology of the epistles and the discourses of AA, although Pauline theology appears in AA only in isolated features. A number of critics, however, have pointed out that Paul's Judaism is emphasized in AA (13:46; 16:3; 18:6, 18; 21:23 ff; 23:6; 24:14 ff; 28:25 ff), while Paul himself is inclined to reject his Jewish background (Rm 7; Gal 2:3 ff; Phl 3:7). These critics deduce that the harmonizing of the author consisted not only in making Peter more Gentile, but also in making Paul more Jewish. The facts seem to be that both Peter and Paul showed a flexible and at times an uncertain approach to the problem (cf Rm 9:1 ff; 11:13 ff; 1 Co 9:20; 2 Co 11:18, 22; Phl 3:4 ff). The ambiguity of the documents seems to be an accurate reflection of the ambiguity of the situation. AA also omits some interesting features: details of the controversy between Jewish and Gentile Christians, the conflicts in the churches of Galatia and Corinth.

No such easy explanation is available for the differences between the accounts of some of the episodes of Paul's life in AA and the epistles. AA mentions three journeys of Paul to Jerusalem up to and including the council of Jerusalem (9:26–30; 11:30 and 12:25: 15:1); Paul insists on two separated by 14 years (Gal 2:1). If AA 15 and Gal 2:1–10 describe the same event, there are a number of striking divergences; if they do not describe the same event, it is nearly impossible to relate the two. Luke describes a council, Paul describes a discussion with three of his equals. Luke quotes a decision of the council which Paul does not mention at all. No combination of dates permits the hypothesis that Gal was written before the council. AA 15 and Gal 2 agree that a decision was made that circumcision was not necessary for Gentile converts; it can hardly be supposed that such a solemn and far-reaching decision was made twice, or that Paul was ignorant of it. Some have suggested that Paul did not mention the decree because he did not think it was relevant to predominantly Gentile churches; others suggest that it was intended only for Antioch, Syria, and Cilicia, where there was a large number of Jewish Christians. Still others have suggested that the decree was not drawn up at the council and that Luke has antedated it. These explanations are highly hypothetical and raise as many questions as they answer. J. Dupont has proposed a more radical explanation. The famine in Palestine is to be dated under the procurator Tiberius Alexander, AD 46–48; the journey of Paul and Barnabas with the collection is to be dated AD 49, the year of the council; therefore AA has made two journeys (11:30 + 12:25 and 15:1) out of one. On the other hand, Dupont suggests that AA's "council of Jerusalem" is a conflation of two different discussions, distinguished in Gal 2:1–10 and 2:11–14, one concerning circumcision and the other concerning dietary regulations. In this hypothesis AA could scarcely have obtained the data from Paul, and it is abundantly clear that AA does not employ the epistles as a source. This is confirmed by the character of the council narrative, which represents the apostles and elders as the supreme authority before whom Paul and Barnabas appear, while Paul represents a discussion between apostles of equal rank. Critics are unquestionably right in seeing here the Jewish-Christian account which is the source of AA. An effect of this source is possibly seen in the author's conception of apostle, which always means the Twelve; he does not give the title to Paul. There also seems to be little doubt that the "decree" is the author's summary of several principles laid down by the Jerusalem community which were never published in this form.

5. *Author, Place, Date.* Tradition from Irenaeus identifies the author of AA as Luke. Modern criticism generally accepts the identification and with it the identification of Luke as the narrator of the "We Sections." It is certain that Lk-AA are the work of the same author. The place appears to be Rome. The date is more ambiguous. Irenaeus says AA was written after the death of Paul; Eusebius, followed by Jerome, says it was written during Paul's Roman imprisonment, at the point· where the book ends. The question is connected with the question why AA ends so abruptly with no further data on the death of Paul and on the church of Rome, the foundation of which AA does not relate. H. F. D. Sparks suggests three explanations: (1) because that is when AA was written; (2) because an intended 3rd volume was never written; (3) because Luke chose to end his account there. #1 is extremely improbable not in itself, but because it is impossible to combine it with the dating of the Gospels (cf MATTHEW; MARK; LUKE; SYNOPTIC QUESTION). #2 is a gratuitous assumption. #3 is most in accord with the characteristics of Luke. That he selects his material is evident from the above discussion of the work. The plan of AA, Jerusalem to Rome, corresponds with the plan of Lk, Galilee to Jerusalem. Once AA has reached Rome, the center of the world, the account of the expansion of the Church has reached a terminus; the impossible has been achieved, and the gospel has become a world gospel. The critical consensus places the date of composition in the period AD 70–90.

Adah (Hb *'ādāh*, "ornament"?), wife of Lamech* (Gn 4:19); wife of Esau* (Gn 36:2).

Adam (Hb *'ādām*, "man," etymology uncertain; "ruddy"?), the first man*. The usual translation of the word as a proper name, Adam, is an error; he is called "the man" up to Gn 4:25, where the proper name first appears.

The man was made of dust from the soil (Hb *'ᵃdāmāh*); the play on words may rest upon an etymological connection. The manufacture of man from clay is found in both Egypt and Mesopotamia; the divine component in Mesopotamia was blood (Gn 2:7). The Hb account replaces this gross element with the breath of God, the principle of life* (cf SPIRIT). On the relations of Gn 1 and 2 cf CREATION. The man is placed in a garden in Eden*; the contrast between this primitive bliss and man's historical condition is evident (Gn 2:9). No restraint is placed upon the man except the prohibition to eat of the tree of knowledge (Gn 2:16–17). The superiority of man over the beasts is shown by his naming them (Gn 2:19–20). In the ancient world to give a name was a sign of authority; it also exhibits the intelligence of the man. No animal is suitable as a companion to the man; God creates woman from the body of the man (Gn 2:20–24). The creation of woman from the man signifies her true humanity and equality with the male; God did not intend her to be a depressed class, as she was in the ancient world (cf EVE; WOMAN). The couple are unclothed; this signifies control of the sexual appetite (Gn 2:25). The two are tempted by the serpent* to eat the forbidden fruit and are expelled from Eden (cf FALL). A penalty is inflicted on each of the three. The curse of the man implies that the soil shall no longer be docile and fertile for him; he must wring his living from it by hard labor, and ultimately he must die (Gn 3:17–19). Neither toil nor death were found in the unspoiled simplicity of Eden. After the expulsion the man begets Cain* and Abel* (Gn 4:1–2) and Seth* (Gn 4:25).

This account is neither a scientific explanation of the origin of man (cf MAN) nor a history of the beginning of the race in the proper sense of the word. On the literary characteristics of the story cf FALL.

Adam is mentioned in the genealogy of 1 Ch 1:1. In him and Eve is seen the ideal of marriage (Tb 8:6). He is the first man (WS 7:1), protected in his solitude by wisdom (WS 10:1). All men, like Adam, come from the ground (BS 33:10), and he was above every living thing in his creation (BS 49:16); but a heavy yoke rests upon his sons (BS 40:1, the only OT allusion which could refer to the Fall).

In contrast with the OT, Adam is very frequently mentioned in the apocryphal* books of the Jews, in which the Paradise story is embellished with many additional features. The Life of Adam and Eve contains a fanciful account of the Fall and what followed. II Baruch rationalizes the Fall by stating that each man is his own Adam.

Adam is mentioned in the genealogy of Lk (3:38). Paul makes Adam a "type* of the one to come," i.e., Christ; as death and sin came into the world through one man, so forgiveness and life come through one man (Rm 5:12 ff; cf SIN). The same typology is employed of the resurrection of the body (1 Co 15:45); as the first Adam became a living creature, the last Adam (Christ) is a life-giving spirit.

Adam (Hb *'ādām*), a town on the Jordan

near Zarethan* where the waters were blocked when the Israelites crossed the river (Jos 3:16), probably the modern Tell ed-Damiyyeh.

Adar (Hb *'ªdār*), the 12th month of the later Jewish calendar*, roughly corresponding to our February.

Adasa (Gk *adasa*), a town between Jerusalem and Beth Horon (1 Mc 7:40, 45), probably the modern Khirbet Addaseh about 5 mi N of Jerusalem.

Admah (Hb *'admāh*, etymology uncertain), one of the five cities of the plain destroyed with Sodom* (Gn 10:19; 14:2, 8), a proverbial example of the anger of Yahweh (Dt 29:22; Ho 11:8); always mentioned with Zeboiim*.

Adonibezek (Hb *'ªdōnībezeḳ*, "lord of Bezek"?), Canaanite king of Bezek*, defeated by Judah* (Jgs 1:5–7). His thumbs and great toes were cut off; this barbarous punishment he himself had inflicted upon others. The story is probably a variant of the defeat of Adonizedek* (Jos 10:1 ff); this name is read in Jgs 1:5–7 by many critics.

Adonijah (Hb *'ªdōnīyāh*, "my lord is Yah[weh]"), son of David* and Haggith* (2 S 3:4). During David's last illness Adonijah, the eldest surviving son, expected to succeed to the throne; the Israelite monarchy had as yet no regular law of succession, which lay within the appointment of the king and had to be ratified by the tribes. In his party were Joab* and Abiathar*. He summoned his supporters to a banquet to celebrate his accession. On hearing this Nathan*, who supported Solomon*, warned Solomon's mother Bathsheba* that their lives would not be safe if Adonijah assumed the throne. Bathsheba then spoke to David, who appointed Solomon co-regent (1 K 1 ff). The premature celebration of Adonijah was abruptly ended, and he fled for sanctuary to the altar (1 K 1:50); but Solomon spared his life, confining him to his house. Adonijah, after David's death, asked Bathsheba to intercede for him that he might have Abishag*, who had cared for David during his last illness. Solomon took this as an arrogation of the privileges of royalty and sent Benaiah* to kill him (2 K 2:1 ff). The name Adonijah is borne by two other men in the OT (2 Ch 17:8; Ne 10:17).

Adoniram (Hb *'ªdōnīrām*, "the Lord [i.e., god] is exalted"), also Adoram (2 S 20:24; 1 K 12:18) and Hadoram (1 Ch 10:18);

the prefect of forced labor under David* (2 S 20:24), Solomon* (1 K 4:6; 5:28) and Rehoboam* (1 K 12:18). Rehoboam sent him to quell the revolt which broke out at his accession, but Adoniram was stoned by the mob (1 K 12:18). It is possible but unlikely that the same officer survived from David to Rehoboam, and his name may have been put into 2 S 20:24 from a list of Solomon's officers. In the ancient monarchies of Egypt, Mesopotamia, and Syria each able-bodied man could be impressed for royal labor service; this usually happened during the inactive agricultural seasons. Such labor service made possible the colossal monuments of antiquity.

Adonizedek (Hb *'ªdōnīṣedeḳ*, "my lord is righteousness"? or "my lord is Sedek [a god]"?), Canaanite king of Jerusalem, one of the five kings defeated by Joshua* (Jos 10:1 ff). The five kings were hanged (or impaled) after the battle. Adonizedek and Adonibezek* (Jgs 1:5–7) may be variants of the same name.

Adoption 1. *OT*. No provision for adoption is found in Hb law*. The only two clear instances of adoption are those of Moses by an Egyptian princess (Ex 2:10) and Esther* by her uncle Mordecai* (Est 2:7). Adoption was extremely common in Mesopotamia, however; the legal codes provided for it and numerous contracts of adoption have been preserved. It is unlikely that this common practice did not occur among the Hebrews; the reception of non-Hebrew persons and families into the Hebrew community suggests their adoption. The terms of the covenants* of Yahweh with Israel* (Ex 4:22) and David* (Ps 2:7) are those of adoption.

2. *NT*. The fatherhood of God was central in the preaching of Jesus and is found through the NT (cf GOD; FATHER). Paul is the only writer to use the Gk legal term of adoption (*hyiothesia*). The legal process of adoption was based upon the despotic rights of father over children in Roman law (*patria potestas*) and conferred upon the adopted person the full rights and obligations of a son. It was analogous to the redemption* of a slave*. Paul counts adoption among the privileges of Israel (Rm 9:4; cf Ex 4:22). Christian adoption is the regeneration of the Christian as a child of God. Christ has ransomed us from slavery into adoption; we are sons and therefore heirs and free from vain observances (Gal 4:5 ff). Christians have not the fear of slaves, but the awareness of their adoption; they are heirs of the sufferings and of the glory of Christ (Rm 8:15 ff). By redemption we

have the glorious freedom of the children of God (Rm 8:21 ff). Adoption enables us to address God by the familiar title of Abba* (Rm 8:15; Gal 4:6). Christ is the firstborn of many brothers (Rm 8:29; Col 1:18). Those who believe in Christ are born not of nature, nor of carnal impulse nor human desire, but of God (Jn 1:12–13). We are sons of God in Christ through faith, which we receive through baptism (Gal 3:26–27). This makes the Christian a new being (1 Co 5:17), created in the likeness of God, as Adam was, in true righteousness and holiness (Eph 4:24). It is from the Father's love for us that we are called His children and hence we shall be like Him, because we shall see Him as He is (1 Jn 3:1 ff). The child of God has the seed of divine life in him and hence cannot sin (1 Jn 3:9); he partakes of the divine nature (2 Pt 1:4).

Adrammelech (Hb *'adrammelek*, probably Akkadian *adad-milki*, "Adad is my king"). **1.** A god worshiped by the colonists from Sepharvaim* settled in Samaria* by Sargon* of Assyria* (2 K 17:31), probably identical with Hadad*. **2.** Son of Sennacherib* of Assyria, who with his brother Sarezer* murdered Sennacherib in 681 BC (2 K 19:37; Is 37:38). The murder is recorded in Assyrian annals, but the names of the murderers are not preserved.

Adramyttium (Gk *adramytteion*), modern Edremit in Turkey, a seaport on the NW coast of Asia Minor at the head of the Gulf of Edremit; the home port of the ship in which Paul sailed from Caesarea* to Myra* in Lycia (AA 27:2).

Adria (Gk *adrias*), the sea of Adria where Paul's ship was driven by the storm (AA 27:27). The ancient name includes not only the modern Adriatic (between Italy and the Balkan peninsula) but also the sea between Crete and Sicily, where the ship of Paul was sailing when it was wrecked.

Adullam (Hb *ʽadullām*), a town of Judah (Jos 15:35), included in the list of towns conquered by Joshua (Jos 12:15), associated with the story of Judah and Tamar* (Gn 38:1, 12, 20). It was a camp of David during his flight from Saul (1 S 22:1) and his war with the Philistines, to which his heroes brought him a drink of water from the spring of Bethlehem (2 S 23:13; 1 Ch 11:15). It was fortified by Rehoboam (2 Ch 11:7) and was one of the towns resettled after the exile (Ne 11:30). Mi 1:15 may allude to 1 S 22:1; 2 S 23:13; critics suggest a slight change to read "Forever will perish from Adullam the glory of Israel." This would give a play on words (*'ad 'ôlām* [forever] = *ʽadullām*) characteristic of this passage of Mi. David, "the glory of Israel," escaped from Saul at Adullam, but the dynasty will not escape the coming disaster there. The site is probably the modern Tell esh Sheikh Madkar in the Shephelah*, about 10 mi ENE of Beit Jibrin.

Adultery. Strictly, sexual intercourse of man and woman one or both of whom is bound by marriage to another person.

1. *OT*. The Hebrew morality of adultery rested upon the primitive conception of the wife as the property of the husband. Only the rights of the husband could be violated. Hence illicit intercourse was not adultery if the woman were unmarried. The wife and her partner could violate the rights of her husband, but the wife had no rights which her husband could violate. Adultery is prohibited both in act and in desire in the Decalogue* (Ex 20:13, 17; Dt 5:18, 21). It is also prohibited in the Holiness Code (cf LAW; Lv 20:10) and in Dt 22:22. Intercourse with a betrothed maiden is treated as adultery (Dt 22:23 ff); but intercourse with an uncommitted girl involves the obligation of payment of damages and marriage (Dt 22:28 ff). The punishment of adultery is death for both parties; stoning* is the penalty in Ezk 16:40 (cf Jn 8:3); burning was threatened for Tamar*, a betrothed widow, by Judah*, but this belongs to an earlier period (Gn 38:24). Ezk 16:37 ff (cf Ho 2:5) indicates that the adulteress was stripped naked before execution; probably her hair was cropped also.

The number of warnings against adultery in wisdom literature suggests that the crime was fairly common; the sages imply some reflection on the looseness of Israelite wives. This may be founded in fact; marriages by contract of purchase must frequently have been loveless (cf Pr 2:16 ff; 5:15 ff; the vivid description of the adulterous wife in Pr 7:1 ff; 23:27 f; 30:20). Apostasy of Israel from Yahweh is termed adultery in Je 2:20 ff; 3:8; Ezk 16:1 ff; Ho 2:4 ff; 3:1; +. Cf COVENANT.

2. *NT*. Jesus repeated the 6th commandment (Mt 5:27; 19:18; Mk 10:19; Lk 18:20), adding that the desire is as malicious as the deed (Mt 5:28). The commandment is repeated in Rm 13:9; Js 2:11. On the adulteress of Jn 8:1 ff cf JOHN, GOSPEL. Fidelity to the marriage bond is enumerated among the obligations of Christians (1 Th 4:3; Heb 13:4).

Adummin (Hb *ʽadummîm*, "redness"?), the name of a pass on the boundary between

Judah and Benjamin. It is very probably to be located in the Wadi el Kelt on the modern road from Jerusalem to Jericho at the site of Khan el Hatrur, "Inn of the Good Samaritan," where the soil is heavily reddened by patches of red ochre.

Aeneas (Gk *aineas*), a Christian of Lydda* cured of paralysis by Peter* after eight years' illness (AA 9:33–34).

Aenon (Gk *ainon*), where John baptized (Jn 3:23); "near Salim" in the Jordan* valley, but the exact location is unknown.

Agabus (Gk *agabos*), probably a Gk form of a Semitic name; a Jewish-Christian prophet* from Jerusalem who came to Antioch and predicted a famine throughout the Roman Empire (AA 11:28). The famine under Claudius occurred AD 49. It was doubtless the same Agabus who later predicted the imprisonment of Paul* at Jerusalem (AA 21:10 ff).

Agag (Hb *'agag*, etymology uncertain). The word appears in Phoenician. Possibly the word is a royal title (like Pharaoh), not a personal name. **1.** A king (Nm 24:7); the context suggests a mythological character. **2.** King of the Amalekites* (1 S 15:8 ff). Under instructions of an oracle from Samuel* Saul* put the Amalekites under the ban*. When he spared the life of Agag, he was bitterly rebuked by Samuel for his disobedience. Samuel himself then hewed Agag to pieces before the altar of Yahweh in Gilgal*. In one tradition this was the occasion of the schism of Saul and Samuel; cf SAMUEL, BOOKS OF.

Agar. Cf HAGAR.

Agora. Cf MARKET.

Agrippa. Marcus Julius Agrippa (Agrippa II), son of Herod* Agrippa (Agrippa I), called Agrippa in the NT (AA 25–26). When his father died in AD 44 Agrippa was regarded by Claudius as too young to succeed him, and the rule was entrusted to his uncle, Herod*, brother of Agrippa I and king of Chalcis, a small principality lying between the Lebanon and the Anti-Lebanon. His uncle died in AD 48, and the kingdom was granted to Agrippa II in AD 50. In AD 53 in exchange for Chalcis he was granted the territories which had formerly been governed by Philip* and Lysanias* as well as some portions of Galilee and Perea. Like his father, he was careful to win the goodwill of the Jews by deference to Jewish law and custom; at the same time he was a patron of Hellenistic culture and religion. He contributed to the erection of the temple in Jerusalem, but a dispute arose when he constructed a terrace on his palace from which he could observe the temple area. Agrippa and Bernice* were present at Caesarea* when the new procurator, Festus*, found Paul in prison, and they asked that Paul might be permitted to speak to them. The discourse moved Agrippa so much that he said that Paul almost made him a Christian; it is doubtful, however, that the remark was made seriously. The Bernice who accompanied him was his sister, the widow of Herod of Chalcis, and the relation of the two was openly incestuous. When the Jewish revolt broke out in AD 66, Agrippa and Bernice returned to Palestine and did all they could to prevent the revolt from going any further. When they were unsuccessful, they remained stoutly loyal to Rome throughout the war. After the war he received territories temporarily lost together with new grants. The date of his death is not certain, but he seems to have governed his territories peacefully until about AD 100.

Agur (Hb *'āgūr*, etymology uncertain), son of Jakeh; the sage to whom the collection of proverbs in Pr 30:1–33 is attributed.

Ahab (Hb *'aḥ 'āb*, "father's brother"? but explanation uncertain). **1.** The son of Omri* and king of Israel 869–850 BC. His queen was Jezebel*, daughter of Ethbaal*, king of Tyre*. The point of interest in the biblical account of Ahab (1 K 16:29–22:40) lies not in the king himself, but in his encounters with the prophets, especially Elijah. Four of these are related. The first is the account of the drought threatened by Elijah (1 K 17:1 ff) which ended with the ordeal on Mt Carmel (1 K 18:16–46), at which Ahab was present; cf ELIJAH. The second involved two unnamed prophets, one of whom encouraged Ahab in his resistance to Ben-hadad* of Damascus* (1 K 20:22), while the other rebuked him for sparing the life of Ben-hadad after his victory (1 K 20:35–43). The third was the episode of the vineyard of Naboth*. Naboth refused to sell Ahab his vineyard; Jezebel suborned false witnesses who charged Naboth with blasphemy, and the king took possession of the land after the execution. For this Elijah threatened the total destruction of his house, and Ahab did penance for his part in the crime (1 K 21:1 ff). The fourth occurred in the beginning of the campaign of Ahab to recover Ramoth-Gilead* from the Aramaeans (1 K 22:1 ff). A group of prophets predicted success for the king. Jehoshaphat* of Judah, his ally, distrusted these prophets and asked that others be summoned. The man summoned was Micaiah* ben Imlah, who at first also predicted success; but when pressed for an honest answer, he foretold defeat. The king had him put in custody until his return from the campaign; this never happened, for Ahab was killed by an archer in the battle.

The judgment of the compiler of 1–2 K on Ahab is extremely harsh. Ahab probably did not abandon the worship of Yahweh; but he permitted Jezebel to patronize the cult of the Baal of Tyre. He did not commit the crime of Naboth's murder, but was willing to accept its profits. He seems to have been religiously indifferent; to him Elijah was the "troubler of Israel" (1 K 18:17), because he made an issue of whether Israel should worship the Baal or Yahweh.

The account in Kings does not reveal the ability and success of Ahab as a ruler. The excavations of Samaria* have disclosed the magnificence of his buildings (1 K 22:39). The two accounts of his battles with the Aramaeans of Damascus show that his father, Omri, had been unable to shake off the Aramaean hegemony. Ahab was besieged in Samaria by Ben-hadad, but defeated him by a sortie (1 K 20:15 ff). The Aramaeans excused their defeat because they had fought the Israelites on their own ground; the gods of Israel were gods of the mountains. In the following year they drew Israel into battle in the plain near Aphek*, where their chariotry could maneuver; here also Ahab defeated them. As a result Ben-hadad conceded the Israelites the same trading rights in Damascus which the Aramaeans had hitherto enjoyed in Samaria (1 K 20:34); from this we learn at least one of the causes of the constant wars of Israel and Damascus. Ahab failed to recover Ramoth-gilead; but his conduct after he was wounded by an arrow was that of a brave man. He insisted that he be propped up in his chariot so that his troops might not fall into panic if they saw the king shot down, and as a consequence he bled to death.

The overlordship of Ahab over Judah is shown by his treatment of Jehoshaphat in the campaign of Ramoth-gilead. His daughter Athaliah* married Jehoram* of Judah and held the throne for six years after Jehoram's death. Ahab also held Moab* in subjection; after his death Mesha*, king of Moab, successfully revolted. The revolt is recorded in the inscription of Mesha. The "son" of Omri mentioned by Mesha must be Jehoram* of Israel, not Ahab. Ahab is mentioned by Shalmaneser* III of Assyria as one of the allied kings at the battle of Karkar in 853 BC. Ahab's contingent of chariots, 2000, is the largest of the allies, and

the number of soldiers, 10,000, is exceeded only by Damascus.

2. The name Ahab is also born by a false prophet, the son of Kolaiah. Jeremiah accused him of adultery and impiety and threatened him with death by fire by Nebuchadnezzar (Je 29:21 ff).

Ahasuerus (Hb *'ᵃhashwērōsh*, Persian *khshayarsha*, Gk *Xerxes*), king of Persia* 485–465 BC (Ezr 4:6); a son, Darius*, is mentioned in Dn 9:1. After the defeat of his expedition against Greece at Salamis (480 BC) and Plataea (479 BC) Xerxes was assassinated. According to the book of Esther he quarreled with his queen Vashti* and sought out the most beautiful maiden in his empire to replace her; the Jewish maiden Esther* was selected. Cf ESTHER; HAMAN; MORDECAI; PURIM.

Ahava (Hb *'aḥᵃwā'*, etymology uncertain), a local name in Babylonia, given to a place (Ezr 8:15) and to the neighboring stream (Ezr 8:21, 31). It is not mentioned elsewhere and can be located only near Babylon. At this point Ezra* assembled the party which was to return to Jerusalem.

Ahaz (Hb *'āḥāz*, probably abbreviated from Jehoahaz, "Yahweh grasps the hand"), son of Jotham* and king of Judah 735–715 BC. Almost immediately after his accession he was invited by Rezin* of Damascus* and Pekah* of Israel* to join a coalition against the advance of the Assyrians under Tiglath-pileser* III (2 K 16:1 ff; Is 7:1 ff). When Ahaz refused, the two kingdoms invaded Judah and Ahaz appealed to the Assyrians for help, offering submission and tribute (2 K 16:7 ff). The Assyrians took Samaria* in 734 BC and Damascus in 732 BC, and Ahaz was saved by becoming a vassal of Assyria. This policy was stoutly opposed by Isaiah*, who counseled political inactivity and faith in Yahweh, which he offered to strengthen by a sign (Is 7:3 ff). Ahaz refused the sign and received instead the sign of Emmanuel* (Is 7:14), with a threat that his policy would prove disastrous. The Chronicler mentions military disasters suffered in the Syro-Ephraimite invasion which are not mentioned in Kings (2 Ch 28:5 ff). The same source reports invasion by the Philistines* and loss of several cities (2 Ch 28:18 ff); both sources mention the invasion by Edom* in which Elath* was recovered (2 K 16:6; 2 Ch 28:17). Ahaz initiated a religious movement of syncretism: but his model was Assyria rather than Damascus (2 Ch 28:23). A new altar for the temple was constructed after the model of an altar of Damascus (2 K 16:10 ff).

Some of the temple furniture was removed, doubtless to make up the tribute to Assyria (2 K 16:17 ff; 2 Ch 28:21, 24 ff). The "steps" of Ahaz (sundial? 2 K 20:11; Is 38:8) and the upper chamber of Ahaz removed by Josiah* (2 K 23:12) may refer to some religious innovation. Ahaz is the Iauhazi (Jehoahaz) of Judah mentioned in a list of tributary kings of Tiglath-pileser III. The harsh judgment of the historians of Kings and Chronicles upon his religion is shared by Isaiah, who also condemned his politics.

Ahaziah (Hb *'ᵃḥazyāh, 'ᵃḥazyāhū,* "Yahweh grasps [the hand]"). **1.** Son of Ahab* and king of Israel c 850–849 BC. According to 2 Ch 20:35 ff Ahaziah was associated with Jehoshaphat* of Judah in the expedition to Ophir which was wrecked at Ezion-geber*, the port of departure; a variant tradition asserts that he asked to be associated, but Jehoshaphat refused (1 K 22:48 ff). The tradition in Ch is probably a rationalization of the failure of the expedition. Moab rebelled under Ahaziah (2 K 1:1) but no action was taken. Ahaziah fell from a window and sent to ask an oracle of Baalzebul*, the god of Ekron*. For this superstition Elijah* threatened him with death, which followed shortly (2 K 1:2–18).
2. Son of Jehoram* and Athaliah* and king of Judah c 842 BC. He was allied with Jehoram* of Israel in an unsuccessful campaign to recover Ramoth-gilead* from Hazael* of Damascus* (2 K 8:28). Jehoram was wounded in the battle and rested from his wounds in Jezreel. Ahaziah visited him there, and during the visit Jehoram was assassinated by Jehu* (2 K 9:1 ff). Ahaziah fled in his chariot, but was pursued by Jehu's archers and wounded near Ibleam*; he continued to Megiddo*, where he died (2 K 9:27 ff). In the variant tradition of 2 Ch 22:7–9 he was captured, taken to Samaria, and there killed.

Ahijah (Hb *'ᵃḥîyah,* "brother of Yah[weh]"), a prophet of Shiloh* who urged Jeroboam* to rebel against Solomon*, promising him that ten tribes would follow him (1 K 11:29 ff). As a symbolic action to emphasize his prediction he tore his new garment into 12 pieces and gave ten to Jeroboam. Ahijah was the spokesman for the prophetic groups, whose dissatisfaction with Solomon's religious laxity joined with the popular dissatisfaction at his absolutism to create the rebellion. Jeroboam had to flee the assassins of Solomon, who must have heard of the message of Ahijah, and the rebellion did not occur until after Solomon's death. Ahijah in turn found that Jeroboam was no better religiously

than Solomon. When Jeroboam's son fell ill, his mother came to seek an oracle from Ahijah, who predicted the violent extinction of the house of Jeroboam (1 K 14:1 ff). The name Ahijah is borne by eight others in the OT, including a priest of Shiloh of the house of Eli* (1 S 14:3), one of Solomon's scribes (1 K 4:3), and the father of Baasha*, who assassinated Nadab, the son of Jeroboam, and succeeded to the throne of Israel (1 K 15:27).

Ahikar. Among the Aramaic papyri discovered at Elephantine* in Egypt and first published in 1906 were included extensive fragments of the story of Ahikar, which was much diffused in the ancient E. Ahikar was chancellor of Sennacherib* and Esarhaddon* of Assyria. In his old age his son Nadin succeeded to his office; but Nadin slandered Ahikar to the king, who ordered the execution of Ahikar. Ahikar escaped by persuading the officer Nabusumiskun to substitute another in his place. With the story is included a selection of wise sayings of Ahikar. This story is unquestionably alluded to in Tb, where Achiacharus is the chancellor of Esarhaddon (Tb 1:21), who supports Tobit after his blindness (Tb 2:10) and visits him after his cure with his nephew Nasbas (Nadin? Tb 11:18). The misadventure of Ahikar is alluded to in Tb 14:10, where his adversary is called Haman. Ahikar is represented as a nephew of Tobit, and therefore Jewish (1:21). Only one of these allusions (11:18) is found in the recension of Tobit which is translated in the Vulgate.

Ahimaaz (Hb *'ᵃḥîma'as,* meaning uncertain), son of Zadok*, priest. While Zadok and Abiathar* remained in Jerusalem during the rebellion of Absalom*, Ahimaaz and Jonathan* concealed themselves at En-rogel to communicate with David. The plans of Absalom were disclosed to them by Hushai* and the priests; but they were discovered by a boy and forced to hide in a well at Bahurim* with the assistance of a family of David's sympathizers (2 S 17:17 ff). Then they hurried to tell David that Absalom's pursuit, on the counsel of Hushai, had been delayed. Ahimaaz also begged the privilege of bearing the news of Absalom's death to David, but when he arrived he lost courage and announced only the victory and waited for another messenger to tell the death of Absalom; for "a good man brings good news" (2 S 18:19 ff). The bearer of bad news might easily be slain. The name Ahimaaz is also borne by the father of Ahinoam*, Saul's wife (1 S 14:50), and by the prefect of the district of Naphtali* under Solomon, who was married to Basemath, a daughter of Solomon (1 K 4:15).

Ahimelech (Hb *'aḥīmelek,* "the brother is king," or "the brother is Milk"?), son of Ahitub of the house of Eli*, and priest* at Nob*. David fled to Nob from Saul* and quieted Ahimelech's fears by telling him that he was on a secret mission. David asked for refreshment, but Ahimelech had nothing except the shewbread*, which David took (1 S 21:1 ff; cf Mt 12:1–8; Mk 2:23–28; Lk 6:1–5). David also asked for a sword, but found nothing except the sword of Goliath*. This hospitality was disclosed to Saul by Doeg* the Edomite, and Saul accused Ahimelech of conspiracy with David. Saul's retainers would not carry out the order of execution, because the priests' persons were sacred; but no scruple troubled Doeg, who killed all the priests, eighty-five in number, except Abiathar*, and sacked the city of Nob. The name Ahimelech is also borne by a Hittite*, an early companion of David (1 S 26:6).

Ahinoam (Hb *'aḥinō'am,* "my brother is delight"). **1.** Wife of Saul (1 S 14:50). **2.** A woman of Jezreel*, wife of David* and mother of his eldest son Amnon* (1 S 25:43; 2 S 3:2 +).

Ahio (Hb *'aḥyō,* meaning uncertain), son of Abinadab* and brother of Uzzah*, with whom he carried the ark from the house of Abinadab to Jerusalem (2 S 6:3 ff). The name is borne by two other men in the OT.

Ahithophel (Hb *'aḥitōpel,* meaning uncertain), a man of Giloh (a city of Judah, site unknown) and member of David's council. Ahithophel joined the rebellion of Absalom* (2 S 15:12, 31). He advised Absalom to take public possession of David's harem, a treasonable act which would create an irreparable breach (2 S 16:20 ff). He suggested that he himself pursue David with a small force immediately after David's flight and kill him before he could gather a force. This sound plan was overruled by Absalom on the advice of Hushai*, who was secretly working for David (2 S 17:1 ff). Ahithophel realized that this meant the failure of the revolt and went home and hanged himself (2 S 17:23).

Ai (Hb always with the article, *ha'ai,* "the ruin"), a city. Abraham camped between Bethel* to the W and Ai to the E (Gn 12:8; 13:3). It was the second Canaanite city to be taken by Joshua (Jos 7:2–8:29). A first attack on the city failed, which was attributed to Achan's* theft of some of the plunder seized at Jericho*, and dedicated to Yahweh. A second attack, which employed a ruse to draw the defenders from the city, was successful, and the city was utterly destroyed as Jericho had been. The account relates that the city remained uninhabited thereafter. The place was inhabited after the exile (Ezr 2:28; Ne 7:32), and it is possibly to be identified with Ayyah of Ne 11:31. The identification of Ai with et-Tell (which also means "the ruin") about two mi E of Bethel* and ten mi N of Jerusalem is generally accepted. The site contains extensive ruins and large fortifications and occupies an eminence which rises sharply in the hill country of Ephraim. The excavation of the site by Mme. Marquet-Krause in 1933–1934 disclosed occupation between 3000–2400 BC; but the site was entirely unoccupied after 2400 until a small Israelite settlement c 1000 BC. This creates problems concerning the account of the capture of Ai by Joshua. Modern explanations fall into three classes. (1) Some scholars suppose that the account is entirely fictitious and is an etiological story of the ruin. Later Israelites, it is supposed, attributed the destruction of the city to their great conqueror. This hypothesis seems improbable and has few defenders. (2) A second hypothesis supposes that Ai was an outpost of Bethel and had to be taken by the Israelites before Bethel could be attacked. It is difficult to combine this with the explicit mention of the capture and execution of the king of Ai (Jos 8:23, 29; 12:9). (3) A theory proposed by W. F. Albright and accepted by a number of modern scholars seems the most probable explanation. In this view the ruin of Ai attracted to itself the story of the conquest of Bethel. This is supported by the fact that no conquest of Bethel is mentioned in Jos, although the progress of the Israelite movement demanded the reduction of this city. The capture of Bethel is alluded to in Jgs 1:22 ff, but it is not there attributed to Joshua. The men of Bethel are mentioned among the defenders of Ai (Jos 8:17). Jos 7–8 is therefore really an account of the conquest of Bethel. A few scholars have questioned the identification of Ai with et-Tell; but there is no basis for this doubt except the literary evidence, which admits the explanation of Albright. The archaeological evidence indicates that the site was already abandoned at the time when Abraham camped there. It is most unlikely that "the ruin" was the original name of the city, which has been lost.

Aijalon (Hb *'ayyalōn,* meaning uncertain), a town located in the Shephelah*. Its history is complex; it is the scene of Joshua's victory over the confederated kings, mentioned in the victory song of Jos 10:12. It was held by the Amorites* after the Israelite settlement of Canaan* (Jgs 1:35). It is listed as a town of Dan (Jos 19:42) and as a Levitical town of Dan (Jos 21:24); the territory was abandoned by Dan after the tribe's migration to the N. It is listed as a Levitical town of Ephraim (1 Ch 6:54) and as a Levitical town of Benjamin (1 Ch 8:13), and it is very probably to this tribe that the town belonged during most of its history. A victory of the men of Aijalon over the men of Gath* is related in 1 Ch 8:13. It was involved in the victory of Saul over the Philistines (1 S 14:31) as the W limit of the Israelite pursuit. The town was fortified by Rehoboam (2 Ch 11:10) and was taken by the Philistines during the reign of Ahaz* (2 Ch 28:18). Aijalon should be read for Elon* in Solomon's 2nd district (1 K 4:9). The valley of Aijalon, the Wadi es Selman, is one of the most important routes from the coastal plain to the central mountains (cf SHEPHELAH). The site is the modern Yalo in the Wadi es Selman W of Gibeon. Another Aijalon in Zebulun, the site of the burial of the minor judge Elon*, should probably be read Elon (Jgs 12:12).

Akeldama (Gk *akeldamach,* Aramaic *hᵃkel dᵉma',* "field of blood"), the land purchased by the council with the money for the betrayal of Jesus which Judas returned to them (AA 1:19), formerly called the potter's field (Mt 27:7). Tradition locates the field S of the valley of Hinnom (cf GEHENNA), the modern Wadi er Rababi, and W of the spring En Rogel*, the modern Bir Ayyub.

Akkad (Hb *'akkad*), mentioned only in Gn 10:10 with Babel* and Erech* as part of the kingdom of Nimrod*. The city of Akkad lay on the Euphrates* in northern Babylonia*; the exact site is not certainly known. The name Akkad was also given to the region of Mesopotamia N from Babylon to Assyria; the double name "Sumer and Akkad" designated Mesopotamia S of Assyria to the Persian Gulf. Akkad was the center of a world kingdom during the 3rd millennium BC (2360–2180 BC, Albright; 2350–2150 BC, Moortgat). The two greatest kings of the dynasty were Sargon and Naram-Sin; the empire of Akkad included all of Mesopotamia and at times Syria* and Elam*. The dynasty fell under the invasion of Gutians in the 22nd century BC. The dynasty of Akkad saw great advances in culture and the arts, and was long remembered in saga, despite its brevity; perhaps some

memory of it is reflected in the biblical allusion to Nimrod (Gn 10:8 ff). The dynasty of Akkad represents the successful irruption of Semitic peoples into Mesopotamia. Its ideal of a world kingdom was reflected for centuries in the titles of the kings of Babylon and Assyria, "king of all," "king of the four quarters," " the great king," etc.

Akkadian. The name now given to the language spoken in Mesopotamia generally from about 2000 BC until about 500 BC; classified as eastern Semitic. The language was formerly called Assyrian* because the literary monuments first discovered were in the Assyrian dialect. Akkadian appears in Mesopotamia during the 3rd millennium BC. With the domination of Semitic peoples it gradually supplanted Sumerian* and remained the common language until it was supplanted by Aramaic*. It appears in two principal dialects, Babylonian and Assyrian. It was written in the cuneiform* signs of Sumerian, which had no signs for some of the consonants characteristic of the Semitic languages, and has absorbed a number of Sumerian words. The literary remains of Akkadian, which have been discovered and interpreted since 1835, are extensive; they are not only a unique source for the world of the OT, but the language itself has furnished invaluable light for the understanding of Hebrew.

Akrabbim. Cf SCORPION.

Alabaster (Gk *alabastron,* "without handles"), probably refers to the type of vessel rather than to the material. It is mentioned in the entire Bible only in Mt 26:7; Mk 14:3; Lk 7:37, in the story of the woman who broke an alabaster vessel of perfume to anoint the head of Jesus. In Hellenistic and Roman usage the word was applied to any vessel of any material without handles in which perfume was sealed; to use the contents the neck of the vessel was broken, as in the gospel episode. Alabaster now means gypsum; the material used in ancient Egypt, however, was calcite, a compact crystalline form of calcium carbonate, white or yellowish white in color. In ancient times alabaster was quarried only in Egypt and the products which have been found are either Egyptian made or imitations of Egyptian models. The little translucent vessels of alabaster, mostly for cosmetics and perfumes, which are found in Palestine come almost entirely from pre-Israelite levels and were luxury articles. It is very likely that wealthy Israelites of the 8th-7th centuries BC were able to procure these, which makes their absence in the OT and their rarity in excavated Israelite sites surprising.

Alcimus (Gk *alkimos,* Hellenized form of Hb *Eliakim*). Alcimus was a leader of the hellenizing faction among the Jews in the Maccabean* period. He was confirmed as high priest* by Demetrius* I in 159 BC and installed under the protection of Bacchides*. Shortly after his arrival he murdered sixty Hasideans who had come to discuss peace (1 Mc 7:5 ff). Judas continued the war and defeated Nicanor*, who was sent to destroy him. Alcimus accompanied Bacchides at the battle in which Judas was killed (1 Mc 9:1 ff). While engaged in razing the wall of the inner court of the temple he fell ill of paralysis and died (1 Mc 9:55 ff, 160 BC).

Aleph. The first letter of the Hb alphabet, represented by '; the sound, a glottal stop, is not represented in the English alphabet.

Alexander (Gk *alexandros,* "defending men").
1. Alexander the Great (357–323 BC), son and successor of Philip of Macedon. He acceded to the throne in 336 BC and in the following year, after imposing unity upon Greece, he embarked on the campaigns in which he conquered the Persian* Empire and reached India. He is mentioned in the Bible only in 1 Mc 1:1–9; 6:2. It was his conquests which diffused Greek culture throughout the ancient Near East; this wrought profound changes in Jewish life and thought (cf HELLENISM). Josephus's story that he visited Jerusalem is generally thought to have no historical basis. Alexander may be alluded to in the world empires of Daniel*.
2. Alexander Balas, pretended son of Antiochus* Epiphanes; the claim was accepted by the Jews, but rejected by ancient historians. Alexander took the throne of Syria when Demetrius* I Soter fell in battle in 150 BC. Both Alexander and Demetrius sought the assistance of the Jews under Jonathan* and promised many privileges; but the Jews favored Alexander, both because he appointed Jonathan high priest and because of their resentment toward Demetrius. Ptolemy* VI of Egypt also favored Alexander and gave him his daughter Cleopatra in marriage; but he betrayed Alexander in favor of Demetrius II, son of Demetrius I, seized the cities held by the Syrians in Palestine, took Cleopatra from Alexander and gave her to Demetrius. Jonathan remained faithful to Alexander and defeated the forces of Demetrius under the command of Apollonius*. The rest of the Syrian kingdom, however, accepted Demetrius; Alexander, de-

feated, fled to Arabia, where he was beheaded by the Arab chieftain Zabdiel in 145 BC (1 Mc 10:1 — 11:19).
3. Son of Simon of Cyrene* and brother of Rufus* (Mk 15:21).
4. Priest and member of the council before which Peter was summoned to justify his preaching (AA 4:6).
5. A Jew who attempted to speak in defense of the Jews during the riot at Ephesus aroused by the silversmith Demetrius* (AA 19:33).
6. A Christian who abandoned the faith and was excommunicated by Paul (1 Tm 1:20).
7. A smith who wronged Paul in a manner not specified; perhaps identical with 6 (2 Tm 4:14).

Alexandria. A city of Egypt*, mentioned in the NT as the home of Apollos*, Paul's companion (AA 18:24), and as the home port both of the ship in which Paul was wrecked at Malta (AA 27:6) and of the ship in which he traveled from Malta to Rome (AA 28:11). The Jews of the synagogue are mentioned among those with whom Stephen disputed (AA 6:9). The city was founded by Alexander* 332/331 BC, after whom it was named. It lay on a narrow strip of land between the Mediterranean and Lake Mareotis near the Canopic mouth of the Nile*, with which Lake Mareotis was joined by a canal. The harbor was largely artificial; its outstanding work was the mole connecting the city with the Island of Pharos, where stood the lighthouse which was one of the seven wonders of the ancient world. It was the capital city both of the Ptolemies* and of the Roman administration of Egypt; ancient writers praise its beauty and its extensive parks and colonnaded avenues. With Rome and Antioch it was one of the three principal cities of the Roman world, and possibly had 500,000 inhabitants at its peak. This makes it somewhat surprising that Paul, who knew the other two cities well, seems never to have thought of going to Alexandria. One of the five districts of the city was inhabited by Jews under their own municipal officer called an alabarch; this was possibly the largest concentration of Jews in the ancient world, and one of the richest and most influential. Anti-Jewish riots occurred there more than once, and reached serious proportions in 88 BC. Alexandria became the greatest intellectual center of the Hellenistic world with its libraries and its assembly of renowned scholars. Here Jews actually came to grips with Hellenistic culture and absorbed more of its thought and its way of life than they knew. In Alexandria the OT was translated into Greek (cf SEPTUA-

GINT). Here also Jewish scholars made efforts to identify their own wisdom* and law* with Greek philosophy; the most famous of these scholars was Philo, and it is possible that the intellectual currents stirred up at Alexandria have left traces in the language of the NT, especially in Paul and Heb. Hellenistic ideas are most clearly seen in the Wisdom* of Solomon, composed at Alexandria in the 1st century BC. There are no certain records of the establishment of Christianity at Alexandria; its traditions made Mark* its apostle and founder.

Allegory. A literary composition in which each detail signifies some reality. Sustained allegories are rare in any literature, and there are none in the Bible. The allegory is distinguished from the parable* and the type*, although each of these may contain allegorical elements; the parables of the sower and the tares or cockle (Mt 13:1 ff) are largely allegorical. The allegorical interpretation of the Bible first appears in Jewish interpreters and was widely practiced by many of the Fathers of the Church. In this view the entire OT signifies by allegory the entire Christian revelation; since the presupposition is false, allegorical interpretation is usually fanciful. The word is mentioned once in the NT (Gal 4:24) of the two wives of Abraham, which are interpreted "by allegory" as the two covenants. This type of allegorizing, in which a homiletic application is drawn from details of the text, is commonplace in rabbinical interpretation, of which Paul offers a number of examples; cf INTERPRETATION; PAUL.

Alleluia. A Hb word employed in the Roman Mass and breviary, Hb halᵉlū yāh, "praise Yah[weh]" (cf HALLELUJAH).

Almond (Hb šāḳēd, "the waker"); the name comes from the early blossoming of the tree in late January or early February. The tree grows wild in Palestine and reaches a height of 16 ft; its flowers are white with a tinge of pink. Je 1:11 draws from the sight of an almond twig the word that Yahweh is awake (šōḳēd) to execute His threats. The almond is a part of the allegory of Ec 12:5. The almond twig was the means by which the priesthood of Aaron was vindicated (Nm 17:23). The almond nut was and is esteemed as a delicacy in the Near East and was included in the gifts of Jacob to Joseph (Gn 43:11).

Alms. The duty of giving to the poor is not mentioned in the earlier books of the OT. The prophets often speak of the duty of compassion to the poor, but their emphasis falls upon justice rather than upon charity. Charity to the poor is praised in Pr 3:27 f; 22:9; 28:27. Almsgiving becomes one of the principal works of charity in the Greek period: Tb 4:6–11; BS 3:30–4:10; 17:22; Dn 4:24. The Talmud often praises almsgiving. Jesus mentions it to correct ostentation in almsgiving (Mt 6:2 ff) and makes the gift of all one's goods to the poor a condition of becoming His follower (Mt 19:21; Mk 10:21; Lk 18:22; cf Mt 5:42; Lk 6:30). Tabitha* (AA 9:36) and Cornelius* (AA 10:2 ff) are praised for their almsgiving, and Paul speaks of fulfilling the duty of almsgiving in Jerusalem (AA 24:17); no doubt pilgrims to Jerusalem, presumably men of means, were expected to give to the poor of the city. The social background of the practice was the rise of a numerous and extremely poor class during the Greek period, although this division between a few wealthy and a poor populace already appears under the monarchy. But the social duty of almsgiving appears just during the period when such class divisions became fixed (cf RIGHTEOUS).

Aloes. An aromatic oil derived from a tree native to India, from which both the product and the name are probably derived. It was a perfume much esteemed in Palestine; employed for the clothing, the bed, and for burial (Pr 7:17; SS 4:14; Jn 19:39).

Alpha. The first letter of the Gk alphabet, mentioned with *omega*, the last letter (Apc 1:8; 21:6; 22:13) to signify the beginning and the end, the totality.

Alphabet. Alphabetic writing is the term of a long development which was reached only once in human history; from this single term all existing alphabets are derived and man has not advanced beyond it. The earliest stage in written communication is "picture writing": for example, picture of man — spear — bear represents "man kill bear." The limitations of such communication are at once apparent; besides, it does not represent speech and can be read in any language. The next stage is the use of the conventionalized picture (sign) to represent a single spoken word (logogram). This also has limitations; abstractions and grammatical modifications (number, mood, tense) cannot be represented. This stage was reached by the Sumerians* probably in the 4th millennium BC. But almost as soon as the method was devised it was modified by the use of the logogram to represent the sound even when it occurs elsewhere than in the word (phonogram); this is "rebus writing," as if "apply" were written by the picture of the fruit and

West Semitic											Greek		Latin
AHĪRĀM	RUEISEH	AZARBAʿAL	JEḤIMELK	ABĪBAʿAL	ELĪBAʿAL	ŠAPATABAʿAL	MEŠAʿ	ZINCIRLI	CYPRUS	SARDINIA	OLD	LATE	
K	K	⋌	K,K	⋌	⋌	⋌	⋌	⋌	⋌	⋌	⋩, A	A	A
⅃	⅃	⅃	⅃,⅃	⅃	⅃	⅃	⅃	⅃	⅃	⅃	𐌁, 𐌁	B	B
⅂			⋏	⋏	⟍	⋏	⅂	⋏	⋏	⅂	⅂, ⟍	Γ	C (& G REPLACING Z)
◿	◁		◿		◬	◁	◭	◭,◬	◬	◬	Δ	Δ	D
⅌		⅌				⅁	⅁	⅁	⅊	⅊	⅁, ⅊	E	E
Ψ	Ψ	Ψ		Ψ	Ψ	Ψ	⅄	Ч	Ч	Ч	⅁, Υ, V	(Υ AT END)	F (& U,V,Y AT END)
I		I	I		I	I	I	I	I		I	Z	(Z AT END)
⍥	⊟	⊟	⍥,⊟		⊟	⊟⌄	⍥	⍥			⊟	H	H
⊕					⊘	⊖	⊕		⊕		⊗, ⊕	⊖	
⅔	⅔	⅔	⅔		⅔	⅔	⅔	⅔	⅔	⅔	⟨, ι	I	I
Ψ	Ψ	Ψ	Ψ	Ψ	Ψ	Ψ	Ϟ	⋊	⅄	⅄	⅄, ⅄	K	K
⎣		⎣	⎣	⎣	⎣	⎣	⎣	⎣	⎣	⎣	⅃, ↲	Λ	L
⟋		⟋	⟋	⟋	⟋	⟋	ꟿ	ꟿ	⟋	⟋	ꟿ	M	M
⟋	⟋	⟋	⟋		⟋	⟋	⟋	⟋	⟋	⟋	ꓵ	N	N
ⷭ	ⷭ				ⷭ	ⷭ		ⷭ	ⷭ		ⷭ	ⷭ	(X AT END)
O	O	O	O	O	O	O	O	O	O	O	o	O	O
⌐	7:⅁	⌐		⌐	⌐	⌐	⌐	⌐	⌐	⌐	⌐, ⌐	Π	P
	h		⅄	h			⊢	⊢		h	M, M	(M)	
		φ			ϙ	φ	φ	φ			Φ, Ϙ	(Ϙ)	Q
⅄			⅄	⅄	⅄	⅄	⅄	⅄	⅄	⅄	⅄, P	P	R
w	w	w		w	w	w	w	w	w	w	⦚, ᔑ, Ɛ	Σ	S
+,x		+	x		⅂	+	X	⅂	⅂	X	T	T	T
											Υ,Φ,X,Ψ,Ω	U,V,X,Y,Z	

Comparative chart of Greek and West Semitic writings. Even the order of the letters of the two writings is the same, as can be seen from the names of the first letters. The Semitic signs *wāw*, *ṣādē*, and *qōph*, which do not exist in classical Greek, occur in the older periods as *wau* or *digamma*, *san*, and *qoppa*. Furthermore, in later times these three signs continue to be used in the Greek numerical system. in which they have almost the same values as their counterparts have in the Semitic systems.

of the organ of vision. Once the device of using the sign to represent the syllable rather than the word is employed, the signs become much more flexible and can be used to write anything that is spoken. In the Sumerian syllabary, however, and in its use for Akkadian*, the logograms survive with the phonograms. The signs are so conventionalized in the cuneiform* writing that the picture cannot be identified unless the original sign is known. But the system is cumbersome and the entire syllabary of Akkadian includes several hundred signs, although they were not all in use in any one time and place. It was probably early in the 2nd millennium BC and somewhere between Asia Minor and Egypt, although it cannot be dated or located precisely, that the next decisive step was taken of isolating the consonants from the vowels. The linear scripts which remain from this area and period, many of them still undeciphered because of the scarcity of material, indicate that there were a number of efforts to reach the alphabetic prin-

ciple: the proto-Sinaitic script (1500 BC), the scripts from Gezer*, Shechem*, and Lachish* in Canaan* (1800–1500 BC), and the hieroglyphs of Byblos*, roughly the same period or earlier. At Ugarit* the cuneiform signs were adapted to an alphabetic script by 1400 BC, but this was done on the basis of the principle already discovered. The isolation of the consonants reduces the number of signs very sharply — in the Semitic languages, between 20 and 30. The oldest writing in the alphabetic script which finally prevailed is found in the inscription of Ahiram of Byblos, about 1000 BC. This alphabet was adopted by the Greeks hardly before the 9th century; no Greek inscription is earlier than the 8th century. When first adopted by the Greeks the script was written right to left, as in the Semitic alphabet, and the earliest Greek letters exhibit their derivation. The Greeks took the final step toward the true alphabet. The letters Aleph, He, Waw, Heth, Yod, Ayin, had no corresponding phonemes in Greek, and they were used to represent the vowels isolated from the consonants: Aleph/Alpha — a, He/Epsilon — ĕ, Waw/Upsilon — u, Heth/Eta — ē, Yod/Iota — i, Ayin/Omicron — ŏ. The Greeks added a few other signs (possibly derived from the Semitic script) to signify phonemes not represented in the Semitic alphabet; it is the Greek alphabet as taken over by Latin that is the parent of all modern alphabetic scripts except those which come directly from the Semitic alphabet. The Hebrew alphabet as exhibited in ostraca and inscriptions from the 8th century was identical with the Canaanite-Phoenician. The "square" characters in which modern Hebrew is printed and which appear in the Dead Sea Scrolls (earliest from 2nd century BC, cf QUMRAN) were not developed before the 5th or 4th century BC.

Alphaeus (Gk *alphaios* from Aramaic *ḥalfay,* meaning unknown), the father of the apostle James (Mt 10:3; Mk 3:18; Lk 6:15; AA 1:13); the father of Levi (Matthew) (Mk 2:14), almost certainly to be distinguished from the first.

Altar. The altar is primarily the place of sacrifice, and this is signified by its Hb name *mizbēᵃḥ;* hence it is to be found wherever sacrifice is offered, and may be temporary. It usually stood outside rather than inside ancient temples* and was found on the high places* of Canaan*, where there were no temples. Altars are mentioned in the patriarchal stories and even in the story of Noah* (Gn 8:20; 12:8; 13:18; 22:9 etc.); this retrojection is justified, since the altar appears at the beginning of human history. The altars found in Canaanite sites are of stone, either a block table of hewn stones or a single block of stone. The altar described in Ex 20:24 ff is doubtless the oldest form of Israelite altar and more primitive in general; it is to be made of earth heaped up, or of a heap of unhewn stones. Working the stone "profaned" it, i.e., established contact with the "unholy," the creature, and changed it from the state in which it came from God; hence it was unfit for sacred use. This early scruple did not remain. The altar is not to have steps; altars with steps have been discovered at Zorah* and Megiddo*. The altar described in the priestly code (Ex 27:1 ff) is made of acacia wood covered with a bronze grating and left hollow, perhaps to be filled with earth; this is doubtless a description of the altar in the temple of Solomon (1 K 8:64). The altar described in Ezk 43:13 ff is built in three stages, each stage two cubits shorter than the side below it; this recalls the ziggurat of Mesopotamian temples, and this feature

should probably be added to the description in the priestly code. The altar had horns at the corners; these have appeared on altars discovered at Megiddo.

The altar symbolized the deity in the sacrificial ritual, and the victim was presented to the deity by contact with the altar. In earlier times it does not appear that the altar was employed for burning the victim or the portions given to the deity; the offering was made by applying the blood of the victim, which symbolized its life, to the altar (cf SACRIFICE). Nor was the altar strictly a table symbolizing the sacred banquet. The horns also symbolized the deity, but with no distinct symbolism from the altar as a whole that can be detected. The priestly code also describes the golden altar of incense (probably part of Solomon's temple, Ex 30:1 ff; 1 K 6:20). The type of construction is not described, but incense altars have been discovered at Megiddo. In 732 BC, Ahaz* had an altar made after the model of an altar which he saw at Damascus, but details of construction are not given; the bronze altar was removed to the N side of the temple to make room for it and both were used (2 K 16:10 ff). The table of "shewbread*" probably should not be called an altar, since no sacrifice was involved. The NT references to altar all concern either the altar of the temple or the altar of incense or altars in pagan cults; in the NT there was as yet no altar in Christian cult. The single reference to a Christian altar is in Heb 13:10, which most probably refers to the Eucharist*. The altar of Apc 6:9; 8:3, is the altar of the heavenly temple.

Amalekites (Hb *ᵃmālēk,* meaning unknown), a nomadic tribe first mentioned in Gn 14:7, listed among the tribes in the genealogy of Esau* (Gn 36:12); not known outside the OT. Amalek dwelt in the Negeb* (Nm 13:29) in the desert between Sinai and Canaan (1 S 15:7). "The city of Amalek" (1 S 15:5) is not otherwise known; the term city may be loosely used for a nomad encampment. Amalek always appears at war with the Israelites. The first encounter was the battle at Rephidim* during the passage from Egypt to Canaan (Ex 17:8 ff). Another encounter at Hormah* may be a variant tradition of the Rephidim battle (Nm 14:45). The Amalekites attacked the Israelites in alliance with Eglon* of Moab* (Jgs 3:13) and with the Midianites* (Jgs 6:3, 33; 7:12). Under the direction of Samuel* Saul* undertook a war of extermination against the Amalekites (1 S 15:1 ff); his failure to carry out the ban* against Agag*, the king of the Amalekites, caused a breach between Samuel and himself. Amalek was one of the tribes which David raided during his service with Achish* of Gath* (1 S 27:8). In revenge the Amalekites raided David's base at Ziklag* while David was absent at Gath; they burned the city and carried off the women and children, including David's family (1 S 30:1 ff). David overtook them and destroyed all except 400 men. This blow was effective; the Amalekites do not appear again as actively hostile (cf the curse of Balaam*, Nm 24:20, and the "remnant of Amalek" 1 Ch 4:43). The enmity of Israel and Amalek, which the tradition represents as ancient, was conducted according to the primitive ethics of the blood-feud, which demanded the total extermination of the enemy (cf AVENGER). This is even read into the accounts of the early conflicts (Ex 17:14, 16; Dt 25:17, 19), and was at the base of Samuel's demand that Saul execute vengeance (1 S 15:1 ff). Since the feud was the only protection of the life of the individual and the tribe, its execution was a sacred duty.

Amana (Hb 'ᵃmānāh, meaning unknown), a peak in the Lebanon* or an alternate name for Lebanon itself (SS 4:8).

Amarna, Tell el-. The site of the ruins of Akhetaton, the royal city of the Pharaoh Amenophis IV (Ikhnaton, 1377–1358 BC), halfway between Cairo and Luxor on the right bank of the Nile*. The ruins, discovered in 1887, contained the correspond-ence from the chancery of Amenophis III (1413–1377 BC) and Amenophis IV, his successor, over 350 letters from foreign rulers. Both the great powers (Babylon*, Assyria*, Mitanni, Hittites*), and the petty kingdoms of Syria* and Canaan* (Byblos*, Sidon*, Tyre*, Ashkelon*, Jerusalem*, Gezer*, Lachish*, Megiddo*, and many others) are represented. The importance of these documents for the history of the period of the exodus* is unique. The letters with a few exceptions are written in Akkadian* in the cuneiform* script; from this we learn the wide cultural influence of Mesopotamia in the west. The language is full of Canaanite dialectal peculiarities, which are a principal source of information for the language of Canaan. It is clear that the Hebrews adopted the language of Canaan with only slight differences. The documents also furnish the political background for the settlement of the Hebrews in Canaan. Under the earlier kings of the 18th dynasty in the 16th–15th centuries BC Egypt* had effectively conquered Syria and Canaan. The documents show that under Amenophis IV the control of Egypt was ineffective and the country was disunited and disorderly. The satellite kings of the Canaanite city-states were nominal subjects of Egypt, but many of them, openly or covertly, were in revolt or plotting revolt. The documents reveal these plots and the conflicts between loyal and rebellious vassals. Lack of a strong central authority meant

Amarna, site of the royal city of Ikhnaton.

that Canaan was open to incursions from the nomadic tribes of the desert, whom the petty states could not control. It is evident that in such conditions the Hebrews had little difficulty in establishing themselves in the country; conditions had not improved in the following century, when the settlement is probably to be dated (cf EXODUS).

Amasa (Hb *ᵃmāsā'*, meaning unknown), son of Jether and Abigail, David's* sister, appointed commander of the army by Absalom* after Joab* had fled with David (2 S 17:25). After the defeat of his army Amasa persuaded the men of Judah to restore their allegiance to David (2 S 19:14). Probably in return for his demonstration of loyalty and in punishment of Joab for his disobedience in killing Absalom, David retained Amasa in command of the army and sent him to put down the rebellion of Sheba* ben Bichri (2 S 20:4 ff). Amasa joined the forces under Abishai* at Gibeon, where Joab killed him while they were exchanging greetings (2 S 20:7 ff). This treacherous murder was not merely an act of envy; Joab doubtless thought that Amasa, a kinsman of David like himself, should die for following Absalom. The crime was mentioned among those for which David charged Solomon* to kill Joab (1 K 2:5, 32).

Amaziah (Hb *ᵃmaṣyāh, ᵃmaṣyāhū*, "Yahweh is mighty"). **1.** Son and successor of Joash* and king of Judah 800–783 BC. He executed the murderers of his father but spared their families. He conducted a successful campaign against Edom and fortified the port of Elath*. He challenged Jehoash* of Israel in an attempt to shake off the overlordship of Israel and was defeated; Jehoash wrecked part of the wall of Jerusalem and plundered the temple. Amaziah himself was assassinated (2 K 14:1 ff). He is judged favorably in Kings; the judgment is repeated in Chronicles, but the Chronicler, to explain his defeat, has added an episode of doubtful historical value in which Amaziah worshiped the gods of Edom (2 Ch 25:1 ff). **2.** The priest of the sanctuary of Bethel* who forbade Amos to speak there. Amos threatened him and his family with annihilation (Am 7:10 ff).

Amen (Hb *'āmēn;* "truly," "it is true" always expressing acceptance of what has just been said [except Is 65:16, where perhaps another word should be read]). It appears in doxologies in the Pss (41:14; 72:19; 89:53; 106:48). Its use in the NT outside the Gospels is confined to doxologies; this liturgical form was taken over from Judaism. In Apc 3:14 Jesus Himself is called "the Amen," the one who is faithful to His word. Its use by Jesus Himself in the Gospels is frequent and has no real parallel elsewhere. It is used to introduce solemn affirmations and adds a note not only of asseveration but also of authority.

Ammonites (Hb *'ammōn, bᵉnē 'ammōn*, "sons of Ammon" [cf "sons of Israel" etc]); an Aramaean* tribe which settled on the upper Jabbok*, probably not much earlier than the 12th century BC. The Aramaic origin of the Ammonites is expressed by the Hebrew* account of their descent from Lot* (Gn 19:38), in which they are also connected with the ancestors of the Hebrews. They are represented as already settled at the time of the entrance of the Israelites into Canaan (Dt 2:19, 37), but this tradition may be anachronistic; in any case, the settlement of the Ammonites must have been closely contemporaneous with that of the Israelites. The Jabbok was the border of the two peoples from early times (Dt 3:16; Jos 12:2). The Ammonites displaced the Rephaim*, the earlier inhabitants, whom they themselves called the Zamzummim* (Dt 2:20). They appear at war with the Israelites in alliance with the Moabites* and Amalekites* (Jgs 3:13), and were defeated by the tribes of Gilead* under Jephthah* (Jgs 10:6 ff). Nahash, king of the Ammonites, besieged Jabesh-gilead*; his contemptuous threats against it were the occasion on which Saul* began to exercise his leadership, and he defeated the Ammonites (1 S 11:1 ff). David enjoyed friendly relations with Nahash, perhaps because both were enemies of Saul. When he sent an embassy to Hanun, son and successor of Nahash, to console him on his father's death, Hanun, suspecting treachery, insulted the ambassadors. In the campaign which followed Ammon and its Aramaean allies were defeated and the royal city, Rabbah*, was taken; David himself put on the crown of Ammon, but seems to have left a satellite king (2 S 10:1 ff). It was during this campaign that the episode of Bathsheba* and Uriah* occurred (2 S 11:1 ff). The Ammonites paid tribute to Azariah* (2 Ch 26:8) and Jotham* (2 Ch 27:5) and were probably tributary to the kingdoms of Israel and Judah until the Assyrian conquest. They raided Judah during the revolt of Jehoiakim against Nebuchadnezzar (2 K 24:2). After the fall of Jerusalem in 587 BC Baalis*, king of Ammon, sent Ishmael* to murder Gedaliah*, appointed governor of Judah by Nebuchadnezzar, and furnished him asylum after the murder. The Ammonites were among those who opposed the rebuilding of the walls of Jerusalem by Nehemiah* (Ne 4:1). Judas the Maccabee conducted a campaign against the Ammonites (1 Mc 5:6 ff). Oracles against Ammon are found in Je 9:25; 49: 1-6; Ezk 21:33-37; 25: 1-7; Am 1:13-15; Zp 2:8-11. The Assyrian records of Shalmaneser* III mention Ba'sa, son of Ruhubi, the Ammonite, among the allies at the battle of Karkar in 853 BC. Several Ammonite kings are listed as tributary by the Assyrians: Sanibu of Beth-Ammon by Tiglath-pileser* III (745-727 BC), Pudu-ilu of Beth-Ammon by Sennacherib* (705-681 BC) and Esarhaddon* (681-669 BC), Ammi-nadbi of Beth-Ammon by Ashur-bani-pal (668-626 BC). The name of Ammon is preserved in the modern city of Amman, capital of the kingdom of Jordan, on the site of the ancient Rabbah.

Amnon (Hb *'amnōn,* "faithful"? perhaps abbreviated), eldest son of David* and Ahinoam* (2 S 3:2). Amnon fell in love with his half-sister Tamar*, daughter of David and Maacah* and sister of Absalom. On the advice of Jonadab* his friend he feigned illness and asked Tamar to attend him, and raped her when she came to his room. Absalom waited two years for revenge; then he invited all the king's sons to celebrate the sheepshearing and ordered his retainers to murder Amnon at the banquet (2 S 13:1 ff).

Amon (Hb *'āmōn,* "faithful"? perhaps an abbreviation). **1.** Son and successor of Manasseh* and king of Judah (642-640 BC). He maintained the religious perversions of his father and was assassinated, perhaps by a conservative group; but the conspirators themselves were killed by the "people of the land" and his son Josiah*, then an infant, was installed as king (2 K 21:18 ff). The name is borne by two others in the OT. **2.** An Egyptian god, mentioned only in Je 46:25. The name may mean "the hidden one." Amon first appears in Thebes* in the 11th dynasty; in the opinion of some scholars he is not native to Thebes, although he became the local god of the city. His original character is obscure; some resemblance to Min can be seen in his crown and in occasional ithyphallic images, which suggest that he was a god of fertility. With the rise of the 18th dynasty and the Egyptian empire (cf EGYPT) Amon became the chief god of the Egyptian pantheon. He was identified with Re the sun god and invoked under the title Amon-Re, taking on solar attributes. Amon, his consort Mut, and their son Khonsu formed one of the divine triads of Egyptian religion. With the 19th dynasty Amon yielded ground to other gods, but never lost his preeminence. The remains of his magnificent temple at Karnak may still be seen.

Amorites (Hb *'ᵉmōrī,* etymology uncertain), one of the pre-Israelite tribes in Canaan*. In the Table* of Nations (Gn 10:16) the Amorites are classed with the other Canaanite tribes as sons of Canaan and descendants of Ham; this classification is geographical, not ethnological. They appear near the Dead Sea at Hazazontamar* (Gn 14:7); and Mamre*, an ally of Abraham*, is an Amorite (Gn 14:13). Shechem* is called an Amorite city in Gn 48:22. They have a kingdom in eastern Palestine under Sihon* which was conquered by the Israelites (Nm 21:21 ff). In western Palestine, according to Israelite tradition, they dwelt in the mountains while the Canaanites* dwelt on the seashore and in the Jordan valley (Nm 13:29), but the picture given by tradition is not consistent. The kings of western Palestine who governed in Joshua's time were Amorites (Jos 5:1), in particular the five kings who were defeated at Gibeon (Jos 10:5 ff). The Amorites kept the tribe of Dan* from the seashore and retained their cities in the Shephelah* (Jgs 1:34-35). In these traditions the Amorites are well distributed over the entire area of Canaan. The relationship of the Amorites to the Canaanites is, consequently, somewhat obscure.

Amurru appears in Mesopotamian records both as a geographic name and as a gentilic. Geographically the name signifies the territory NW of Babylonia; and this is the region from which the Amorites invaded Babylonia. Amurru is first mentioned by Sargon of Akkad* in the 3rd millennium BC, and one of his successors, Sarkalisarri, reports a victory over Amurru. Beginning with the 21st century BC there is evidence of a large Amorite invasion of Babylonia. Mari* on the Euphrates became a capital city and the Amorites established under Sumuabum (about 1830 BC) the first dynasty of Babylon, which under Hammurabi* became an empire (c 1728-1686 BC). Besides, there were numerous unsettled nomadic groups of Amorite and Aramaean nomads moving through Mesopotamia and Syria. The archaeology of Palestine shows a progressive depopulation from the 22nd to the 20th century BC, after which reoccupation begins. This fits so well the Amorite invasion of Mesopotamia that there can hardly be no connection; and it is from this period that we should date the Amorite settlements in Palestine mentioned above. The Amorite states in Mesopotamia were swallowed up in a barbarian invasion after 1780 BC, but the Palestinian settlements escaped this invasion. It is in this period of invasion and migration that Abraham* falls. Haran* and Nahor*, cities associated with Abraham, were both Amorite in the period when Abraham is best dated. Hebrew connection with the Amorites is also seen in a number of Amorite type personal names which are found in Hebrew. Hebrew ancestry, which is mixed in any case, must derive in part from the Amorites; but this is reflected in the OT only in Ezk 16:3, 45, where it is said to Jerusalem, "Your father was an Amorite." In the Amarna* letters Amurru means Syria N of the modern Beirut; but some cities N of this line are sometimes said to lie in Canaan.

Amos (Hb '*āmōs*, meaning unknown). **1.** A prophet whose discourses are preserved in the book of Amos. These were delivered in Israel* during the reign of Jeroboam* II (786–746 BC), probably between 760–750 BC. This was a period of peace and prosperity, reflected in the book. Nothing is known of his personal life except from the book. He is called a shepherd of Tekoa* in Judah (1:1), a shepherd and a dresser (?) of figs (7:14). He was not a professional prophet (7:14) but spoke in obedience to a divine vocation. Some, perhaps all, of his discourses were delivered at the shrine of Bethel*, from which he was expelled by the priest Amaziah* (7:10 ff).

2. The Book of Amos stands third among the 12 prophets in Hb and Lt Bibles, second in Gk. The book is the oldest of the prophetic books. It begins with a title (1:1) and an exordium cited from Je 25:30 and Jl 4:16. There are three major divisions: (1) Judgment against the nations (1:3–2:16); (2) The Discourses (3:1–6:13); (3) The Visions (7:1–9:8a). The conclusion (9:8b–15) is added.

I. Judgment against the nations: Amos utters oracles against Damascus* (1:3–5), Gaza* (1:6–7), Tyre* (1:9–10), Edom* (1:11–12), Ammon* (1:13–15), Moab* (2:1–3), and Judah* (2:4–5). These are all composed in similar style and structure and serve as an introduction to the judgment against Israel (2:6–16); if these nations are to be punished for their crimes, then Israel must also expect judgment, since its crimes are more serious and its responsibility is greater.

II. The Discourses. The introductory formula "Hear this word" occurs in 3:1; 4:1; 5:1; but it does not indicate three discourses so much as three collections of fragments or short utterances. We may distinguish: the election of Israel (3:1–2), the inevitability of disaster (3:3–6), the prophetic vocation (3:7–8), the sins of Samaria (3:9–11), the remnant of Israel (3:12), the fall of Bethel* and the palaces (3:13–15), the sacrifice (4:4–5), punishment — drought women of Samaria (4:1–2), the vanity of blight, pestilence, earthquake — and obstinacy in malice, followed by final judgment (4: 6–12), doxology (4:13), dirge for Israel (5:1–2), gloss (5:3), invitation to seek Yahweh (5:4–7), doxology (5:8–9), injustice (5:10–13), repeated invitation (5: 14–15), a cry of woe (5:16), the day of Yahweh (5:18–20), repudiation of superstitious worship (5:21–27), fall of Samaria (6:1–8), death by pestilence (6:9–10), destruction in war (6:11–14).

III. The Visions: the locusts (7:1–3), the fire (drought?) (7:4–6), the plumb-line of destruction (7:7–9). The visions are interrupted by the episode which relates the expulsion of Amos from Bethel by Amaziah (7:10–17). The visions are continued with the basket (a pun on *kayiṣ*, "basket," *kēṣ*, "end"), expanded by a discourse against avarice and injustice (8:4–8) and a threat of destruction and privation of the prophetic word (8:9–14). The last vision is that of Yahweh standing upon the altar, followed by a threat of total destruction from which no one can flee (9:1–4) and a doxology (9: 5–6). A final statement leaves Israel to be treated like any other nation (9:7–8a). The conclusion predicts a restoration of Israel from exile and the rebuilding of the fallen hut of David, to be followed by the marvelous prosperity of the messianic age.

The doxologies (4:13; 5:8; 9:5–6) are probably liturgical additions not written by Amos. His authorship of the conclusion (9:8b–15) is also questioned by many critics. These lines seem to presuppose the exile of Israel and the fall of the dynasty of David as something which has already happened. These messianic commonplaces may have been added by a compiler to soften the severe impact of 9:8a, with which the original book closed. The originality of the oracle against Judah is also questioned, since it lacks the vigorous concrete character of the rest of the words of Amos. It may have been added by a compiler who felt that Judah should not be spared from threats delivered to the other peoples of Palestine and Syria.

If the conclusion is detached from the work of Amos, it must be admitted that the tone of his book is almost entirely threatening, and that the hope of a messianic* future did not fall within his prophetic vision — or, at least, was not included in his prophetic message. In his historical situation there is no need to explain this omission; he was a prophet of judgment and the message of forgiveness and hope was left for others — his younger contemporary Hosea* was one of these. The dominant note in Amos is his conviction of the moral will of Yahweh imposing itself upon man through the operations of nature and the course of history. God, who is supremely good, cannot permit Himself to be overcome by evil. From this arises the insight, distinctive in Amos but adopted by later prophets, that Israel, the chosen people, cannot be excluded from the moral will of God. In this message, which is only a part of the prophetic doctrine, there is little room for emphasis upon the saving attributes of Yahweh. The place which he gives to the moral will of Yahweh in religion leads him to treat the Israelite cult not only as less important but as without value. This attitude must be understood in the light of the fact that the Israelites attached a superstitious value to the cult as a mechanical and certain means of maintaining good relations with Yahweh. The relationship between God and His people was a union of will, not of nature, which could be ruptured by malice on the side of Israel.

Amphipolis (Gk *amphipolis,* "double city," so called because two arms of the river Strymon flowed around it.) The city lay near the sea in NE Macedonia on the Gulf of Strimon, E of Thessalonica*. It was a free city, a Roman military post on the Via Egnatia, the principal route from Italy to Asia. Paul passed through Amphipolis traveling from Philippi to Thessalonica (AA 17:1).

Ampliatus (Lt *ampliatus,* found several times in Latin inscriptions as the name of a slave), a Christian at Rome greeted by Paul as "beloved in the Lord" (Rm 16:8).

Amram (Hb 'amrām, "the kinsman [i.e., god] is exalted"?), son of Kohath* and father of Moses* and Aaron* (Ex 6:18, 20), mentioned only in genealogies*.

Amraphel (Hb 'amrāpel, meaning and etymology unknown), one of the four kings who invaded Canaan and were defeated by Abraham* (Gn 14:1, 9). Amraphel was king of Shinar*, elsewhere a name of Babylonia*. The identification of this king with Hammurabi* of Babylon* has been given up, and no king is known in the first half of the 2nd millennium BC with whom Amraphel can be identified. The maneuver described in Gn 14 was classic; it was a raid, probably on a small scale, conducted by the Mesopotamian overlords to impress their unruly vassals. It is doubtful that the king or kings would be personally active in such a raid. It may be suspected that the names of the kings involved were not correctly preserved in oral tradition, and that Amraphel of Shinar is actually a garbled form of Hammurabi; cf separate articles on other kings.

Amulet. A small religious symbol worn on the person as a protection against evil spirits. There is no Hb word which directly signifies amulet and there is no polemic in the OT against them. Most of the amulets found in Palestine are of Egyptian origin and belong to pre-Israelite levels of occupation; but a few have been discovered which are of Israelite manufacture. Most of them are found in graves. The most popular Egyptian type was the scarab; an oval stone shaped like a beetle (Gk *skarabaios*), originally a seal. The flat undersurface was engraved with divine images or scenes from mythology. In addition there were small divine images of gods or of divine emblems (such as the eye of Horus or the *ded* pillar). The amulet was usually attached to the person by a cord.

Collection of Egyptian jewelry including amulets.

Anakim (Hb *ʿanāḳīm, bᵉnē ʿanāḳ,* "sons of Anak"), one of the pre-Israelite tribes of Canaan*. They were located in the vicinity of Hebron* (Nm 13:22); the names of the three chieftains (ibid) Ahiman, Sheshai, and Talmai are Aramaic. Some forms of Hb tradition described them as giants (Nm 13: 28, 33; Dt 2:10, 21; 9:2). Joshua* is credited with conquering them in Hebron*, Debir*, and Anab; the survivors settled in Philistine* territory: Gaza*, Gath*, Ashdod* (Jos 11:21–22). Another tradition credits Caleb* with the conquest of Hebron and the three chieftains (Jos 15:13–14). Israelite heroes in the Philistine wars slew Anakim, all men of gigantic size (2 S 21:16–22). The name is possibly identical with *ly-ʿanaḳ,* mentioned in the Egyptian execration texts of the 12th–13th dynasties (1900–1700 bc; ANET 328).

Anammelech (Hb *ʿanammelek*) with Adrammelech* one of the gods worshiped by the colonists from Sepharvaim* settled in Samaria* by Sargon*. Possibly the name represents Akkadian* *Anu-milki,* "Anu is my king" (W. F. Albright). Anu, the god of the sky, was the senior member of the Mesopotamian pantheon, the king of the gods; in historical times he had generally yielded his primacy to others (Bel of Nippur, Ashur of Assyria, Marduk of Babylon). This was explained as a voluntary transfer of his "Anuship" (Akkad *anutu*) to the younger god.

Ananias (*ananias,* Gk form of Hb *Hananiah**). **1.** A Jewish Christian of Jerusalem. When the Christians pooled their goods Ananias and his wife Sapphira* withheld some of their own. When charged by Peter* with falsehood, Ananias suddenly died, and the same fate came to his wife a few hours later under the same conditions (AA 5:1 ff). It seems that the traditions of the Jerusalem community invested the deaths of these two with an element of wonder and a reference to their mendacity. **2.** A Jewish Christian of Damascus to whom Paul* was directed during the illness which followed his experience on the road to Damascus. Ananias' prayer and imposition of hands restored sight to Paul (AA 9:10 ff; 22:12). **3.** The high priest at the time of Paul's arrest in Jerusalem. At the first hearing before the council Ananias ordered Paul to be struck on the mouth, for which Paul cursed him (AA 23:1 ff). Ananias was a member of the party which attended the hearing in Caesarea before the governor Felix* (AA 24:1).

Anath. A goddess of Canaan, consort of Aleyan Baal*. W. F. Albright explains the name as meaning "indication of purpose, active will" i.e., the personified will of Baal. Anath was one of a type of goddess which was diffused throughout the ancient Near East. She was a deification of the female principle; her primary function was sex, and she combined the two most desirable features of her sex, virginity and maternity. Anath is commonly represented as nude with emphasis upon her sexual characteristics. In the mythology of Ugarit* her function is to raise her consort Aleyan Baal from the dead and to fight his adversary Mot; after his resurrection, the cycle of fertility is renewed by the union of Baal and Anath. She is also a goddess of war, represented in one myth as wading in blood up to her neck; she is sometimes represented in a military posture. The worship of Anath spread into Egypt under the title Qudshu, "the holy one," where she is represented with some features of Egyptian goddesses. The only visible trace of Anath in the OT is the name of Anath, father of the judge Shamgar* (Jgs 3:31; 5:6, possibly abbreviated) and in the place named Beth-anath, a Canaanite city (Jos 19:38), possibly also Anathoth*.

Anathoth (Hb *ʿanātôt,* connected with the name of the goddess Anath*), Levitical town of Benjamin (Jos 21:18; 1 Ch 6:45). Is 10:30 places it near Jerusalem to the N. It was the home of Abiathar*, the priest deposed by Solomon* (1 K 2:26) and of the priestly family of which Jeremiah* was a member (Je 1:1; 29:27). The property which Jeremiah had to buy from his cousin Hanamel* lay at Anathoth (Je 32:7–9). The men of Anathoth were hostile to their own prophet (Je 11:21–23). The town was also the home of two of David's heroes, Abiezer (1 Ch 11:28; 27:12) and Jehu (1 Ch 12:3). The party which returned from exile in Babylon included 128 men of Anathoth (Ezr 2:23; Ne 7:27). The town was resettled after the exile (Ne 11:32). Anathoth appears as a clan name (1 Ch 7:8) and as a personal name (Ne 10:20); the text can hardly be correct in these two instances. The site is the modern Anata, which lies about 5 or 6 mi N of Jerusalem.

Andrew (Gk *andreas,* "manly") brother of Simon Peter* and one of the 12 apostles*. Andrew came from Bethsaida* in Galilee (Jn 1:44) and was a disciple of John* the Baptist before his call (Jn 1:40 ff). There are two traditions about his call: in Mk 1: 16 ff he was called with Peter while they were fishing in the Sea of Galilee; in Jn 1:40 ff he was called with John while they were in the company of John the Baptist, who pointed out Jesus as the lamb of God. Outside of the lists of the apostles Andrew appears only in Jn 6:8, where he calls attention to the boy who had the loaves and fish which were distributed, and in Jn 12:22, where he acts as mediator between Jesus and the Greeks who asked Philip* for an interview with Jesus. According to some traditions preserved by Eusebius and the *Acts of Andrew* (cf APOCRYPHA) Andrew preached in Bithynia*, Scythia*, Macedonia*, and Achaia*, where he was crucified at Patras; the historical validity of these traditions is not confirmed.

Andronicus (Gk *andronikos,* "victorious over men"). **1.** Appointed viceroy at Antioch* by Antiochus* IV Epiphanes, bribed by Menelaus*, Andronicus had the high priest Onias* arrested and murdered. He was punished by public disgrace and execution (2 Mc 4:30 ff). **2.** A Christian at Rome, greeted with Junias by Paul as fellow-Jews, companions in prison, distinguished apostles* who were Christians before him (Rm 16:7).

Angel (From Lt *angelus,* a transcription of Gk *angelos,* used in LXX to translate Hb *mal'ak,* "messenger"), in modern Christian belief, a heavenly spirit.
    1. *OT.* I. The Angel of Yahweh. The most primitive form of OT belief in angels seems to be the "messenger of Yahweh." The messenger appears to Hagar* in the desert (Gn 16:7 ff; 21:17 ff), he prevents Abraham* from sacrificing Isaac* (Gn 22:11 ff), and protects Abraham's slave on his journey to secure a wife for Isaac (Gn 24:7, 40). He speaks to Jacob in a dream (Gn 31:11), protects him from all harm (Gn 48:16) and wrestles with him at Penuel* (Gn 32: 24 ff). He appears to Moses* at the burning bush (Ex 3:2), and leads Israel through the Red Sea* and the desert (Ex 14:19; 23:20; 33:2; Nm 20:16). He halts Balaam* on his way to Balak* (Nm 22:22 ff). He is probably the man who appeared to Joshua* near Jericho* (Jos 5:13 ff), "the captain of Yahweh's host." He speaks to the Israelites at Bochim (Jgs 2:1 ff). He calls upon them to curse Meroz (Jgs 5:23). He appears to Gideon* (Jgs 6:11 ff) and to the mother of Samson* (Jgs 13:3 ff). He appears as the destroying angel of pestilence to David at the threshing-floor of Araunah (2 S 24:16 ff; 1 Ch 21:15 ff). He appears to a prophet of Bethel* (1 K 13:18), and to Elijah* on his journey to Horeb* (1 K 19:7) and before his meeting with the messengers of Ahaziah* (2 K 1:15). He slew the Assyrians before Jerusalem (2 K 19:35; 2 Ch 32:21; Is 37:36). He does not appear elsewhere in Samuel and Kings, but is used in conver-

sation as an example of fidelity (1 S 29:9), wisdom (2 S 14:20), power (2 S 19:28). Messengers occur in the plural only in Gn 19:1 ff (the two who rescued Lot* from Sodom*), in Gn 28:12 (ascending and descending the ladder seen by Jacob in a dream), and in Gn 32:2 (who met Jacob at Mahanaim*).
    From these passages it is clear that the messenger of Yahweh (in some passages *'elōhīm,* cf GOD) belongs to the earliest parts of Hebrew tradition. That the messenger occurs less and less frequently as the story advances is explained by the fact that the earlier traditions are folklore which often heighten the wonderful and appeal to the divine to explain phenomena (cf HISTORY). It is also clear that the messenger of Yahweh is not clearly distinguished from Yahweh Himself; cf Gn 16:13; 21:18; 31:13; Ex 3:2 ff; Jgs 6:14; 13:22. Thus it appears that the messenger is an emissary sent by Yahweh to speak in His name or to work wonders in His name, either of which Yahweh accomplishes elsewhere without any intermediary. In some of the passages cited it may be suspected that the messenger of Yahweh is a theological addition to the narrative, intended to preserve the divine transcendence from too intimate a contact with creatures; other forms of the tradition do not show this scruple. We may conclude that the idea of the messenger in early belief wavers between a hypostatization of the divine attributes or operations and a distinct personal heavenly being. Even in Is 63:9 it was neither a messenger nor an angel, but His presence that delivered Israel. This being is not a god. Neither is he a spiritual being; the Hebrews did not have an idea of spiritual reality and distinguished heavenly beings from men only in that they were different. The messenger is not described, but there is nothing to suggest that he was conceived in any form other than human.
    II. The Heavenly Court. Yahweh is accompanied by a heavenly retinue. This idea appears in the earlier books only in Jos 5:14 (the captain of the host of Yahweh) and in 1 K 22:19 (Micaiah* sees Yahweh surrounded by the host of heaven). This retinue is called "the holy* ones" (Ps 89:6; Jb 5:1; Dn 8:13), and "sons of *'elōhīm*" or "sons of *'ēlīm,*" cf GOD (Pss 29:1; 89:7; Jb 1:6; 2:1; 38:7). This retinue is less frequently called messengers; but the messengers have a charge to guard man (Ps 91:11), as the messenger of Yahweh led Israel through the desert. They are called to praise Yahweh (Pss 103:20; 148:2) as the choirs of Israel praise Him in the temple. The idea of a heavenly retinue is derived easily from the conception of Yahweh as king and lord,

and it is not necessary to appeal to the religions of Mesopotamia or Persia to explain its growth in Israel, although some of the imaginative features of their representation may come from these sources.

The messenger of Yahweh continues to appear in the later books. He encamps around those who fear Yahweh like the messenger of the exodus (Ps 34:8) and pursues the wicked (Ps 35:5–6). Raphael*, one of the seven holy angels who offer up the prayers of God's people, assists Tobit and his son in their needs (Tb 12:15). But he appears principally as a mediator between Yahweh and the prophets. The visions in Zc 1:7–6:15 are each explained by the angel who accompanies the prophet. The same conception is seen in Dn 8:16 ff; 9:21 ff; here the angel receives a name, Gabriel*. In Dn 10:13, 21 appears the "prince" Michael*, the angel of the people of Israel, who strives with the "princes" of Greece and Persia on behalf of Israel. The same function of interpretation is fulfilled by the "man" of Ezk 40:3 ff, and Elihu* (Jb 33:23) asserts that God will send an "angel interpreter" to intercede for the man who is chastised by suffering. There is an evident contrast between this representation and the "word of Yahweh" which comes immediately to the prophets in the older prophetic books; the revelation of Yahweh as well as His operations are conducted through a heavenly being in order that the divine transcendence may more clearly appear. On related conceptions of the heavenly retinue cf CHERUBIM; HOST OF HEAVEN; SERAPHIM.

2. *NT*. Gospels. I. The prominence of angels in the infancy* Gospels is evident. They warn Joseph of the coming birth of the child (Mt 1:20) and of the flight to Egypt (Mt 2:13) and the return (Mt 2:19). Here the angel does not differ from the "messenger of Yahweh" in the OT. Gabriel* is the angel of the annunciation; he speaks to Zechariah* of the birth of John* the Baptist (Lk 1:11 ff) and to Mary* of the birth of Jesus (Lk 1:26 ff). Both the name and the function of Gabriel are derived from Daniel (cf above). The angel of the Lord announces the birth of Jesus to the shepherds and is accompanied by a throng of the host of heaven (cf above) singing a hymn of praise (Lk 2:9 ff); here again we are in OT conceptions. Angels minister to Jesus after His temptation (Mt 4:11; Mk 1:13), and an angel strengthens Him during His agony (Lk 22:43); this line, however, is missing in several of the most important MSS. They are present at the resurrection* of Jesus, although they were seen, it seems, by only a few (Mt 28:2; Lk 24:23; Jn 20:12); here again they are "messengers." They appear as

the heavenly court, attending the Lord (Lk 12:8 f; 15:10), to whom God may be expected to manifest His designs (Mt 24:36). They are probably to be understood as guardians of little ones in Mt 18:10, and Jesus could summon them to rescue Him from His captors (Mt 26:43). They carry Lazarus* to Abraham's bosom (Lk 16:22). The angel of the pool of Bethesda* is not found in almost all of the principal MSS and is not a part of the original Gospel (Jn 5:4). The angels are ministers of God's judgment in the Parousia*; they gather the sinners for judgment (Mt 13:41, 49), they accompany the Son of Man* at His coming (Mt 16:27; Mk 8:38; Lk 9:26), they gather the elect (Mt 24:31; Mk 13:27).

This summary shows that the conception of the angels in the Gospels does not advance beyond the OT conception, and in some ways is less imaginative. The angel is still primarily a messenger or a member of the heavenly retinue, and there is not always a sharp distinction between the angel as a personal being and as a personification of the divine word or the divine action.

II. The Apostolic Writings. The "messenger of Yahweh" continues to appear in the other books of the NT. An angel releases Peter and John from prison (AA 5:19) and Peter alone (AA 12:7 ff). He tells Cornelius* to look for Peter (AA 10:3 ff) and tells Philip* to take the road to Gaza* where he will meet the eunuch of the queen of Ethiopia (AA 8:26). An angel appears to Paul in a dream during his voyage to Rome and assures him that all on the ship will be saved (AA 27:23). An angel strikes Herod* Agrippa a fatal disease (AA 12:23). Angels are less prominent in the Epistles. They witness the sufferings of Christians (1 Co 4:9) and are present invisibly at the liturgical services (1 Co 11:10). Reverence for them demands that women cover their hair, which is their glory, so that the glory of God may appear. Satan also has angels (2 Co 12:7) and can mask himself as an angel of light (2 Co 11:14). Should an angel preach another gospel he should not be believed (Gal 1:8). The Law was delivered through the ministry of angels, in contrast to the New Law which was manifested by Christ (Gal 3:19). Worship of angels, probably due to Jewish influence, is repudiated (Col 2:18). The angels are still conceived as the heavenly court (1 Tm 5:21) and will appear at the Parousia (2 Th 1:7). Christ is greater than the angels, God's messengers in the OT (Hb 1:4 ff), who delivered the "word" i.e., the Law (Heb 2:2). The concept of angels who revolted and fell appears in the NT only in 2 Pt 2:4; Jd 6; elsewhere the existence of malicious spirits is taken for granted but not explained; cf DEMON. Jd 6 is interpreted by Dubarle of the "messengers" (Gk *angeloi*) of Nm 13. The allusions in 2 Pt and Jd reflect the form which this belief took in Jewish apocalyptic literature*. Angels are very prominent in Apc, but no difference appears in their representation. They are the messengers of God, the ministers of His judgments, and His heavenly court. The "angels" of the seven churches (Apc 2:1 ff) are probably the bishops of these churches. The word archangel occurs in the entire Bible only in 1 Th 4:16; Jd 9 (Michael). The "virtues, powers, thrones, dominations, principalities" of Eph 1:21; Col 1:16, associated since Gregory the Great with the "nine choirs," have no reference to angels; they signify human or demonic power.

The belief in heavenly beings thus runs through the entire Bible and exhibits consistency. That their nature is spiritual is never clearly asserted; but the idea of spiritual reality was not possessed in its clarity. In some instances — e.g., Apc — the influence of apocalyptic literature can be traced and mythological allusions appear in their description; but the biblical conception of these heavenly beings is in general remarkably restrained compared to Jewish literature. In the NT as in the OT the angel is sometimes no more than another word for a divine communication or a divine operation personified.

Anger. The emotion of anger is often attributed to God in both OT and NT. In the OT the anger of God is mentioned more frequently than human anger. The attribution of anger to God is an anthropopathism which to many seems difficult; it is, however, an essential part of the biblical conception of God as endowed with a vigorous personality. He is a "living God," active, with a moral will to whose execution He is not indifferent; furthermore, His anger is only one feature of His personality as described in the Bible and must be understood in the context of its motivation and of other personal traits which are attributed to Him.

1. *OT*. The most frequently mentioned object of the anger of Yahweh is the people of Israel. In the Pentateuch* the stories of the exodus and wandering are a series of crises in which Israel excites the anger of Yahweh because of its unbelief, lack of confidence in Him, and rebellion against the leadership of Moses (Ex 32; Nm 11:1; 12:9; 13:25–14:35; 18:5; 32:10–14; Dt 1:34; 9:8, 19). The other historical books contain the same theme (Jgs 2:14; 3:8; 10:7). Under the monarchy Israel provokes Yahweh to anger by its worship of false gods (I K 14:15; 2 K 22:17), an anger

which ultimately issued in the destruction of the northern kingdom (2 K 17:17). The worship of false gods is conceived as a personal rejection of Yahweh, a personal insult to which there is a personal response: anger.

The prophets also emphasize the theme of the anger of Yahweh. The motive of His anger most frequently mentioned is the worship of false gods (Je 4:4, 8, 26; 7:20; 17:4; 32:31; 36:7; Ezk 6:12; 8:18; 14:19; 16:38; 20:8; Ho 5:10; 8:5; 13:11); Yahweh's anger is also provoked by human pride (Is 9:11), by practical unbelief (Is 9:16), by inhumanity (Is 9:18, 20), by failure to observe His laws (Ezk 5:13) and by all crimes (Ezk 7:3, 8).

The anger of Yahweh is also provoked by foreign nations, not so much for their worship of their own gods, for presumably they could not know better, but for their pride and arrogance (Is 13:5 ff; 30:27; 59:18; 63:3, 6). These appear particularly when they attack Israel, the people of Yahweh, for this is an implicit denial of belief that Yahweh can defend His people (Is 10:5–15; Ezk 25:15–17). Yahweh punishes men and nations for particularly obnoxious crimes and widely diffused vices; His anger is the motive of such disasters as the deluge*, the destruction of Sodom* and Gomorrah, the confusion of languages at the tower of Babel*.

In these and similar passages the anger of God is ethically motivated, an outpouring of His moral will and His justice. In other passages His anger appears unmotivated, and some writers speak of an "irrational" element in His anger. The term is admissible as long as we use it within the context of Hb thought; for while the Hebrews conceived Yahweh in human terms, they were aware that He is not human but divine, that His ways are not the ways of man, and that His actions sometimes cannot be explained in human conceptions. His anger may break out for causes imperceptible to man. Here His anger is an outpouring of His holiness* rather than of His justice. Furthermore, the Israelites shared the common ancient conception that misfortune and disaster of any kind which came without human responsibility was an effect of the divine anger; this anger was usually ethically motivated and could be presumed to be so motivated even when men did not see the cause. Yahweh attacked Jacob at Penuel (Gn 32:23 ff) and Moses on his way from Sinai to Egypt (Ex 4:24 ff). Approaching too closely to the divinity, in particular the sight of His face, would result in death (Ex 19:9–25; 20:18–21; 33:20; Nm 1:52; Jgs 13:22; Is 6:5). A lack of reverence for the holy likewise aroused Yahweh's lethal anger (1 S 6:19; 2 S 6:7). The pride which moved David to make a census and thus incur anger (2 S 24:1 ff) is an excellent example of the unsophisticated thinking of Israelite tradition. The plague was an evident sign of Yahweh's anger. The census was a sign of pride which provoked anger. But Yahweh was not angry with David alone, or He would not have stricken all Israel; hence His anger against Israel was antecedent to any anger against David. The Chronicler (1 Ch 21:1) found this simple thinking too difficult and changed the exciting cause of the census from Yahweh to Satan*. The Psalmist can ask why he experiences Yahweh's anger (Ps 88:15–17), and the apparently unmotivated anger of God is at the base of the discussions of Job* and his friends.

The anger of Yahweh could fall upon individuals and families as well as on Israel. Israel was punished because Yahweh was angry with Achan (Jos 7:1 ff). Moses incurred the anger of Yahweh for hesitation (Ex 4:14; Dt 1:37), and Aaron incurred it for his part in the episode of the golden calf (Dt 9:20) and with Miriam* for questioning the authority of Moses (Nm 12:9). Ahab* and Manasseh* provoked the anger of Yahweh by their patronage of foreign cults (1 K 16:33; 2 K 23:26).

The anger of Yahweh manifests itself as a blazing consuming fire* (Is 65:5; 30:27; Je 17:4; Ezk 21:36) or as a raging storm (Ps 83:16; Is 30:30; Je 30:23; cf THEOPHANY). It is sometimes conceived as a liquid which can be poured out (Ps 69:25; Je 6:11; Ezk 7:8; 14:19; 20:8; Ho 5:10). It is a bitter poisonous liquid which makes men stagger (Is 51:17, 22; Je 25:15). The weapons of Yahweh's anger are the nations which He brings upon Israel or upon other nations whom He has decided to destroy (Is 13:5; 10:5), or His own arm (Is 30:30; 63:5; 9:11; Je 21:5), or war (metaphorically the sword, Ezk 21). A blow given in anger is given with greater strength and with a more deadly intent, and Israel asks Yahweh not to punish it in anger (Pss 6:2; 38:2). For the anger of Yahweh annihilates unless it is restrained (Nm 16:21 f; Dt 7:4; Is 30:28; 34:2, 5; 63:1–3; Je 4:23–26; Ezk 22:31). In the OT the greatest monument of Yahweh's anger is the exile by which He destroyed His own people of Israel as a nation. The effect of Yahweh's anger is death and destruction in some form (Nm 11:1, 10, 33), leprosy (Nm 12:9 f). The day of Yahweh is a day of wrath (Pss 7:7; 79:6–8; Zp 1:15, 18).

The anger of Yahweh can be averted by petition (frequently in Pss and prophets) and by intercession such as the intercession of Moses for Israel (Ex 32:11 ff; 31 ff; Nm 11:1 ff; 14:11 ff; Dt 9:19), of Amos for

Israel (Am 7:2, 5) and of Jeremiah for Judah (Je 14:7 ff; 18:20). But the OT conceived that the anger could reach a point where intercession was no longer effective and could even be rejected (Je 14:11 f; Ezk 14:14). Yahweh's anger is also modified by His patience; He is slow to anger (Ex 34:6; Nm 14:18; Ps 103:8; Jon 4:2; Na 1:3). His anger as a work of His justice is never unjust nor excessive, and He restrains it from its fullness (Ho 11:9). The reality of Yahweh's anger in the OT is no more and no less than the reality of His love of Israel, of which it is the counterpart. For Yahweh is a jealous* God, and it is because of His election* and love of Israel that He is angered by their infidelity in a way in which He is not angered by the nations. Ultimately Yahweh swears that He will no longer be angry with Israel (Is 54:9 f).

Human anger is a passion against which frequent warnings occur in the OT, especially in wisdom* literature. One should not incite others to anger (Pr 6:34; 15:1; 16:14) nor yield to anger oneself (Ps 37:7–9; Pr 19:19; 27:4; 24:19; 14:29; 15:18; 16:32).

2. *NT.* The common belief that the anger of God is an OT theme which gives way entirely to love in the NT is inaccurate. Jesus Himself showed anger at the heartlessness of the Pharisees (Mk 3:5), and on other occasions His words and actions seem to exhibit at least a trace of anger at the Pharisees (Mt 12:34; 23:33; 15:7) and at the unbelief of the crowd (Mt 17:17); and He puts angry words in His own mouth when He represents Himself as judge (Mt 7:23; 24:51; Lk 12:46; 13:27). John the Baptist threatened the wrath to come (Mt 3:7; Lk 3:7). The common misconception is supported to the extent that divine anger appears only once in the words of Jesus in the Gospels (Lk 21:23). But Jesus attributes anger to the king or master in the parable, particularly for obstinate unbelief or for inhumanity (Mt 18:34; 22:7; Lk 19:27). Neither should one miss the allusions to fire, which in the OT is an exhibition of the anger of God and in the NT is an instrument of punishment (Mt 3:12; 18:6 ff; 25:41; Mk 9:43–48; Lk 3:17). Anger is implied in the dreadful threats of Mt 10:28; Lk 12:5.

The concept of the divine anger appears elsewhere in the NT in the Pauline writings and in Apc and once in Jn. The anger of God which falls upon all men by their nature (Eph 2:3) is broader in scope than anything else in the OT or NT, but it is a logical consequence of the belief in the universal guilt of man (cf SIN). The anger of God abides upon those who reject the son (Jn 3:36). It is revealed from heaven (not necessarily an eschatological sense here) against those who suppress the truth (Rm 1:18). Paul is particularly emphatic in his statement that the Jews who have impeded the preaching of the gospel have been overtaken by God's anger (1 Th 2:16); the added phrase, "to the end," is obscure, and is diversely rendered by interpreters as "at last" or "forever." False teachers also provoke the anger of God (Eph 5:6). The statement that the law works anger (Rm 4:15) is obscure; in the context it seems to mean that the law by imposing an obligation creates an occasion for God's anger which would not exist if there were no law. The obstinate and impenitent man stores up a treasure of wrath (Rm 2:4 f). The difficult "vessels of wrath" of Rm 9:22 should not be taken in a sense of rigid predestination. They are objects of God's anger but they are also the means by which He demonstrates His patience. They are, like all men, "sons of wrath," but they do not utilize God's patience in order to escape the anger which He withholds from them.

The anger of God in the NT is conceived as eschatological. The "treasure of anger" stored up by the impenitent man will be released against him in the day of wrath (Rm 2:4–5). God finally "brings anger" when He judges the world (Rm 3:5). The Christian should not revenge himself but should give place to the anger (of God) which will avenge all evil (Rm 12:19). The anger of God in Apc is eschatological, displayed in a great final judgment (Apc 11:18; 6:16). The anger is poured out from vials (Apc 16:1); it is a wine-press (Apc 14:19; 19:15; cf Is 63:1 ff). It is an intoxicating drink (Apc 16:19; cf Je 25:15 ff).

The anger of God in the NT also must be conceived in a wider context. For Paul it is a corollary of His justice (Rm 2:4–5), which is displayed in the day of wrath; without anger God could not judge the world (Rm 3:5). It is hardly necessary to add that the theme of love and mercy in the OT is the background of the theme of anger, and the relationship of the themes is best and most simply stated in the affirmation that it is Jesus who saves us from the anger (Rm 5:9; 1 Th 1:10). For were there no anger, there would be no need of deliverance.

The NT warns against human anger. The words of Jesus in Mt 5:22 are severe; He affirms the malice of the inner desire, for the roots of murder lie in anger. Admonitions against anger are found in Eph 4:26, 31; Col 3:8; anger does not produce the righteousness of God (Js 1:19 f). Control of anger is one of the qualities required in a bishop (1 Tm 2:8; Tt 1:7).

Anna (*hanna, anna*, Gk form of Hb Hannah*). **1.** Wife of Tobit*, who complains at his misfortunes (Tob 2:14; 5:17; 10:4). **2.** A prophetess who recognized the infant Jesus as the Messiah (Lk 2:36 ff). **3.** The name of the mother of Mary, the mother of Jesus, found in the aprocryphal* gospels.

Annas (*annas*, shortened from *ananos*, Gk form of Hb Hananiah*) father-in-law of the high priest Caiaphas* and mentioned with him in Lk 3:2; AA 4:6. Jesus was brought to him before the session of the council which condemned Him (Jn 18:13 ff). He was appointed high priest in AD 6 by the Roman procurator Quirinius and deposed by Valerius Gratus in AD 15; the influence of Annas and his family is seen in the fact that five of his sons and Caiaphas his son-in-law held the office in subsequent years. The title given him in the NT refers to his former office. Most historians think Annas was the real leader of the priestly Sadducee party and the prime mover of the plot which brought Jesus to death.

Annunciation. This name is given to the episode in Lk 1:26–38, in which Mary* learns from the angel* Gabriel* that she is to be the mother of the Messiah. The event took place at Nazareth* before Mary's marriage to Joseph. The words of the angel are almost entirely made up of OT quotations (Gn 16:11; Jgs 5:24; 6:12; 13:3; 2 S 7:12; Is 9:6; Dn 7:14; Mi 4:7); Mary raises no objection except the fact that she is not married (1:34) and then learns that the child is the Son of God and will have no human father. The virginal conception is also related in Mt 2:18–23. Many interpreters have attributed the story of the Annunciation to Mary herself as a source; but it is more probable that it is a primitive Christian retelling of the revelation to Mary of her divine maternity, in which the pattern of the heavenly messenger as a medium of revelation is imposed upon the original account of the revelation to Mary.

Anoint. The use of oil* as a refreshing unguent was extremely common in the ancient world. The origin and precise symbolism of anointing as a sacred rite cannot be traced in Israel. It is clear that the purpose of anointing a person or thing was to make it sacred. It was done to priests*, the tent of meeting, the ark*, the furniture of the tent (Ex 31:25 ff +). Kings were anointed; it is mentioned explicitly of Saul* (1 S 10:1 ff), David* (1 S 16:13; it seems to have been repeated twice at Hebron*, once for Judah 2 S 2:4 and once for all Israel 2 S 5:3), Solomon* (1 K 1:39), Jehu*

(2 K 9:6 ff), Jehoash* (2 K 11:12), Jehoahaz* (2 K 23:30). The anointing of Saul, David, and Jehu was done by a prophet, that of Solomon by a priest; probably either sacred person could perform the ceremony, and it is most likely that a prophetic oracle (of which Ps 2 may contain an example) was delivered. The anointing of Hazael* as king of Damascus* by Elijah* is commanded in 1 K 19:15, but its accomplishment is never related. The anointing of Elisha* by Elijah is commanded (1 K 19:16) but never executed, and anointing is not mentioned for any other prophet. Perhaps "anoint" is carelessly used in 1 K 19:16 to signify "appoint as successor." The unidentified speaker in Is 61:1, however, who is described in prophetic terms, affirms that he is anointed to announce the good news to the poor. Here and in other passages (1 S 10:10 ff; 16:13) anointing brings the spirit* of Yahweh upon the person and impels him to some extraordinary deed; but even where it is not mentioned, anointing made the person a charismatic officer whose mission could be executed under the impulsion of the spirit. Anointing as a sacred rite is not mentioned in the NT unless in the anointing of the sick in Js 5:14; the Gk word here used (*aleiphō*), however, is never used either in the LXX or the NT of a sacred rite, for which the word *chriō* is used. On the title *christos*, Hb *māšīah*, cf JESUS CHRIST; MESSIAH.

Ant. The ant is mentioned in the Bible only in Pr 6:6–8; 30:25; in both passages it is an example of industry and foresight.

Anthropomorphism. The representation of God in human traits. Anthropomorphism prevails throughout the OT. The OT speaks of God's eyes, ears, mouth, lips, arms, bowels (as seat of compassion), heart. In addition to the physical traits God is endowed with human emotions: kindness, love, anger, but not the ignoble emotions. God lives, speaks, hears, thinks, plans, desires, loves, hates, commands, moves from place to place, dwells. The NT continues the anthropomorphisms of the OT.

In comparison with the anthropomorphism of ancient religions, the OT is extremely restrained. The gods of these religions were human in form and were so represented (cf IMAGE). Hebrew law prohibited any image of Yahweh, affirming that He was different from any creature and so could not be represented. This apparent paradox preserves the divine transcendence, while the use of anthropomorphisms is the primary factor in the Hebrew conception of God as a living person; He is never an impersonal or demonic force. He governs the world by an intelligent plan and His moral will imposes itself upon the will of man. Thus Hebrew religion from beginning to end was a personal relation of God and man and demanded a personal response.

It is also of importance to notice that through most of the OT the Hebrews had no idea of spiritual reality. God was indeed "spirit and not flesh," but this meant to them no more than a vast difference which they were incapable of defining. In later Judaism anthropomorphisms were avoided in favor of circumlocutions, and it is evident that this made the personal religion of Judaism less intense than that of the OT.

Antichrist (Gk *antichristos*, "the adversary of Christ"), the word occurs in the NT only in 1 Jn 2:18, 22; 4:3; 2 Jn 7, where it is used as a term well known. The figure of a great adversary of God or of the Messiah whose war against God will reach its peak just before the great final judgment can be traced in Jewish apocalyptic* literature, which has derived many features of the figure from Gog* (Ezk 38) and from the beasts of Dn 7:1 ff. The NT has drawn some allusions from this Jewish mythological conception of the last days. This figure does not appear in the eschatological discourses of the Gospels, although the false messiahs and false prophets there mentioned are somewhat similar (Mt 24:5, 23 f; Mk 13:21 f). There is little doubt that the "man of sin" (2 Th 2:3–12) is the same figure; he raises himself up even above the divine and proclaims himself a god. Now he is restrained by some power which Paul had identified in his discourses, but which we can no longer identify; when this restraining influence is removed, the man of sin will be revealed and destroyed in the final consummation. But his revelation will be accompanied by signs and powers and many will be deceived; this is the great apostasy which precedes the Parousia*. A similar figure appears in Apc 11:7 ff, the beast which comes out of the abyss, and in 13:1–10, the beast which comes from the sea, uttering blasphemies and conquering the earth. This beast is followed by another beast (13:11–18) which performs wonders and makes men worship the first beast; the number of the second beast is 666. The beasts are connected with the "Scarlet Woman" of 17:1 ff, who is a thinly disguised personification of Rome (17:9 ff). The beast and its false prophet are flung into the fiery pit in 19:20 f. The picture of the beasts is derived from Dn 7:1 ff.

The figure of Antichrist has been interpreted in many ways; but there are good reasons for doubting the long established opinion that he signifies a real historical-eschatological figure. In Apc the connection of the beast with Rome is too close for him to be anything else than the persecuting imperial power; and no better explanation of the cipher 666 has been proposed than that which finds it the sum of the numerical value of the Hb letters of the name Caesar Nero (KSR NRWN), the emperor (AD 54–68) who first put Christians to death. The "man of sin" also is now at work in Paul's conception. The allusions in 1 Jn and 2 Jn seem directed against the belief of early Christians that Antichrist was eschatological; there are many Antichrists, and anyone who denies Jesus is Antichrist. Antichrist is rather a personification of the powers of evil which occasionally focus in some individual person and can be expected to do so again. The consummate wickedness of Antichrist is depicted in traits which suggest diabolical malice; but this is a poetic emphasis upon his malice rather than an indication that Antichrist is diabolically possessed, or still less that he is a diabolical incarnation.

Anti-Lebanon. A chain of mountains running N and S parallel to the Lebanon* range, from which it is separated by the valley of the Beqaa. Its summit is a plateau with an average altitude of 7500 ft. The chain terminates at Mt Hermon* on the S. In contrast with the Lebanon it is bare and rocky, especially on the nearly unpopulated E slope. The name occurs in the Bible only in Jdt 1:7.

Antioch (Gk *antiocheia*). **1.** An ancient city of Syria on the site of the modern Antakia, which preserves the name. The city was located on the Orontes river where it passes between the Lebanon and the Taurus ranges. It lay about 17 mi from the sea and was served by its port city Seleucia. The city was founded by Seleucus in 300 BC and named after his father Antiochus. The fertile plain of Antioch no doubt supported agriculture for thousands of years, but no trace of an earlier city has appeared. It was the royal city of the Seleucid kings. The city was a Greek military colony, but it grew by immigration of the neighboring indigenous peoples to become one of the largest cities of the Hellenistic-Roman world; its population in the 2nd century BC is estimated at 500,000 and some scholars believe that "Greater Antioch" included 800,000. Antioch had a large and prosperous Jewish colony which suffered losses under Caligula (AD 37–41). The city was renowned for its many splendid buildings and was a great commercial center. It enjoyed a not entirely favorable reputation as a city of pleasure and vice. After the collapse of the Seleucid kingdom it was ruled by Tigranes of Armenia after 83 BC and by the Romans after 64 BC, who made it a free city and the capital of the province of Syria. During the Roman period Antioch became a famous intellectual center; this activity lasted into Christian times, when Antioch was one of the most important theological schools of the 4th–6th centuries. The city was excavated by Princeton University and the National Museums of France 1932–1939; the remains discovered belong to the post-biblical period.

In the OT Antioch appears only in 1–2 Mc as the royal city of the Seleucids* and the base of their operations against the Jews (1 Mc 3:37; 4:35 +). The books allude to the battle in which Lysias* gained possession of the city from Philip* (1 Mc 6:63), to the assumption of the crown of Syria at Antioch by Ptolemy VI Philometor (1 Mc 11:13), and the capture of the city by Tryphon* from Demetrius* II (1 Mc 11:56). The suburb of Daphne, which was a great sanctuary of Apollo, was the refuge of the high priest Onias* (2 Mc 4:33).

Antioch first appears in the NT in AA 11:19 ff. The Christian community of the city was founded by fugitives from the persecution of the Christians in Jerusalem which followed the death of Stephen*. The preaching of the fugitives was directed to the Jews except for some Cyprians and Cyreneans, who brought some of the Greeks to accept the gospel. The success of the evangelical preaching was so great that the Jerusalem community sent Barnabas* to the city (AA 11:22). Barnabas summoned Paul* from Tarsus (AA 11:26); this is the first recorded apostolic work of Paul. They remained there a year. It was at Antioch that the name Christian* was first applied to the followers of Jesus (AA 11:26), but we do not know from what source the name came.

It is evident from other allusions to Antioch that the Christian community of the city during the first generation of the Church was large and important, second only to Jerusalem (if second). It is evident also that it was the largest community and probably the first of Gentile Christians, and that its influence was primary in widening the view of membership and observances in the Church. In its very beginning the community was large and rich enough to collect a generous subvention for the Jerusalem community, which it sent through Barnabas and Paul (AA 11:27–30); relations at this time were more cordial than they were a few years later. It is possible that Antioch was the home of Luke. It is probably no more than a coincidence that prophets* at Antioch are mentioned twice (AA 11:27;

13:1). The power and independence of the Antioch community appears in the decision to send Barnabas and Paul on a missionary journey (AA 13:1 ff), taken with no consultation of other officers of the Church; and Barnabas and Paul reported to the authorities of Antioch on the results of the journey (AA 14:26 ff). It was no doubt the broad Gentile Christianity of Antioch which Paul and Barnabas preached in the cities of Asia Minor. After their return, however, a dissension arose between the Jewish and the Christian churches concerning the necessity of Jewish observances for Gentile Christians. The episode of Gal 2:11 ff should be placed in this period, when Cephas* on a visit to Antioch associated freely with Gentiles, but withdrew from their company when some members of the rigid party arrived from Jerusalem — an action for which he was rebuked by Paul. Paul and Barnabas represented the church of Antioch at the deliberations in Jerusalem and with Judas* and Silas* communicated to the church of Antioch the decision in which the question was resolved. Barnabas and Paul again resided at Antioch for an extended visit, and Paul returned to Antioch after his second journey (AA 18:22). Antioch was the church of Paul up to this point in his life, and he did not conduct himself as its head; but the city is not mentioned again after this visit, after which Paul was associated with the churches which he himself had founded.

2. A city in Pisidia in central Asia Minor, founded by Seleucus in 280 BC. It was declared a free city by Rome in 189 BC and passed under Roman rule by inheritance from Amyntas of Phrygia in 25 BC. The remains of the city lie near the modern Turkish village of Yalvaz. Excavations of the University of Michigan have revealed a propylaeum and city squares which were built in the 1st century BC and the 1st century AD.

Pisidian Antioch was evangelized by Paul and Barnabas on their first missionary journey. They addressed themselves to the Jews, but when the Jews rejected them they turned to the Gentiles, not without success. The bitterness of the encounter was unusual; the Jews not only got them expelled from the city, but even pursued them to Lystra*, where they incited the people to stone Paul (AA 13:14–52; 14:19). These sufferings are alluded to in 2 Tm 3:11. The church of Antioch was revisited by Paul and Barnabas shortly afterwards (AA 14:21).

Antiochus (Gk *antiochos*, "withstander"), the name of ten kings of the Seleucid* dynasty, of whom four are mentioned in the OT. Antiochus III the Great (223–187 BC) is not mentioned by name; but Dn 11:10–17

mentions his two campaigns against Egypt. His initial success was arrested by his defeat at Raphia in 217 BC; the second campaign, in which he finally defeated Ptolemy V at Panion, brought Palestine under Seleucid rule. **1.** Antiochus IV Epiphanes, son of Antiochus III the Great and successor of his brother Seleucus IV Philopator as king of Syria* (175–164 BC). Antiochus had been taken to Rome as a hostage after the defeat of Antiochus III by the Romans at Magnesia in 190 BC. He was exchanged for Demetrius*, the son of Seleucus IV, in 175 and seized the throne of Syria, with the consent of Rome, when Seleucus was assassinated by Heliodorus, his chief minister. Ancient historians describe him as eccentric and capricious, mingling with the crowds in revelry and carelessly distributing huge sums of money, capable of the barbaric cruelty which disfigured the age. In 169 BC he undertook a successful war against Egypt, invaded the country and captured Ptolemy VI; an embassy from Rome halted his second campaign at the Egyptian frontier (Dn 11:25–30). He then turned his ambitions toward Armenia and Persia and died during this expedition in the east.

There was already before the accession of Antiochus a strong movement in favor of Hellenism* among the wealthy and the priestly aristocracy of Jerusalem, and it was at the initiative of this group that Antiochus permitted them, led by Jason*, to build a gymnasium in Jerusalem (1 Mc 1:11 ff). The party wished to abandon utterly the religious and cultural traditions of Israel and assimilate the nation to Hellenistic civilization. The majority of the Jews were conservative and resisted this movement; and strained relations were aggravated when Antiochus returned from Egypt. Menelaus, the brother of Jason, had expelled him from the priesthood by force and civil strife had broken out (2 Mc 4:23 ff; 5:5 ff); and to Antiochus this seemed to be rebellion. He therefore took the excuse to plunder the temple and fill up his treasury, depleted by his Egyptian campaigns (1 Mc 1:20 ff; 2 Mc 5:15 ff), and suppressed the disorders with bloody thoroughness. But the question of the Jewish religion and Hellenism was unsolved; and the Hellenizing Jews represented the religion as the root of disloyalty and rebellion. Antiochus then determined to impose Hellenistic religion and culture by force and to pacify the nation before he departed on further campaigns. His officers were empowered to suppress Jewish worship, sacred books, and religious practices, and to institute the celebration of Greek festivals and the worship of Greek gods. An altar of Zeus Olympios, the "abomination of desolation*" was erected in the temple. Resistance, at first passive, finally became revolt under Mattathias* and his son Judas*, and the Syrian forces were not numerous enough to suppress it. Before the death of Antiochus Judas had succeeded in regaining possession of the temple and rededicating it.

2. Antiochus V Eupator, son and successor of Antiochus IV as king of Syria (164–162 BC). A minor, Antiochus ruled with Lysias* whom Antiochus IV had appointed regent. Both were murdered by Demetrius I Soter*, a son of Seleucus IV (1 Mc 6:17; 7:1–4).

3. Antiochus VI Dionysos, son of Alexander Balas*, installed as king by Tryphon*, who rebelled against Demetrius* II. A minor, he ruled under Tryphon as regent (145–142 BC); he confirmed Jonathan* as high priest and made him one of the "King's Friends" (1 Mc 11:39, 57 ff). The Jews at first supported Antiochus and Tryphon against Demetrius, but the treachery of Tryphon turned them against him. Tryphon murdered Antiochus and himself assumed the throne (1 Mc 13:31 f).

4. Antiochus VII Sidetes, son of Demetrius II and king of Syria 139–129 BC. He undertook to recover the throne for the Seleucid house from Tryphon, ostensibly on behalf of his older brother, Demetrius II, who had been captured by the Parthians. He sought and received the help of the Jews under Simon*, and defeated Tryphon. After his victory, he laid claim to Joppa* and Gezer* and the citadel of Jerusalem, which the Jews had taken during the usurpation of Tryphon; but Simon refused to cede them, and a campaign by Antiochus' general Cendebaeus* to recover them was unsuccessful (1 Mc 15:1 ff).

Antipas. Cf HEROD ANTIPAS.

Antipater (Gk *antipatros*, "like the father"). **1.** Son of Jason, sent with Numenius* as ambassador to Rome and Sparta from Jonathan* (1 Mc 12:16; 14:22). **2.** Father of Herod* the Great.

Antipatris. Cf APHEK.

Antonia. Cf GABBATHA.

Apelles (Gk *apellēs*, perhaps connected with Apollo), a Roman Christian "approved in the Lord" greeted by Paul (Rm 16:10). The name occurs in inscriptions; it is probably merely coincidental that Horace uses Apella as a Jewish name (Sat. 1, 5, 100), but it suggests that it was a common Jewish name.

Aphek (Hb *'ᵃpēk*, meaning uncertain), the name of several towns. **1.** A Canaanite town included in the list of cities taken by Joshua (Jos 12:18), twice the site of the Philistine* camp before their invasion of the highlands (1 S 4:1; 29:1). The site is very probably the modern Ras el Ain in the coastal plain near Joppa* to the NE; it has a copious spring which is the source of the river Yarkon, which flows into the Mediterranean. In the 1st century BC the town was rebuilt by Herod* and named Antipatris after his father. Paul and his escort spent the night there on their journey from Jerusalem to Caesarea (AA 23:31).

2. A town of Asher (Jos 19:30) which was held by the Canaanites after the Israelite settlement (Jgs 1:31). The site is probably Tell Kurdaneh, a short distance SSE of Acco*. **3.** The scene of the defeat of Ben-hadad* of Damascus by Ahab* of Israel (1 K 20:26, 30), not held by the Israelites. In memory of this victory Elisha* directed Jehoash* of Israel to shoot in the direction of Aphek (2 K 13:17). The site is probably Fik E of the Sea of Galilee. **4.** A town vaguely located on the border of the Canaanites and the Amorites (Jos 13:4); possibly Afqa on the slopes of Mt Lebanon E of Byblos.

Apocalypse (Gk *apokalypsis*, "revelation," from which the title Revelations in Eng Protestant Bibles).

1. Contents:

Title, 1:1–3; epistolary introduction, 1:4–8.

Introductory vision, 1:9–20.

First part, letters to the seven churches, 2:1–3:22.

2:1–7, Ephesus; 2:8–11, Smyrna; 2:12–17, Pergamon; 2:18–29, Thyatira; 3:1–6, Sardis, 3:7–13, Philadelphia; 3:14–22, Laodicea.

Second part: The end of the present age and the coming of the new age, 4:1–22:5.

4:1–11, introductory vision, the throne of God.

First act of the eschatological drama, 5:1–11:14.

5:1–8:1, the seven seals; after the 6th seal there is a pause with a vision of the victory of the servants of God, 7:1–17.

8:2–11:14, the seven trumpets; there is an interlude after the 6th trumpet, the vision of the book, the temple, the death and resurrection of the two witnesses, 10:1–11:14.

Second act of the eschatological drama, 11:15–20:15.

12:1–14:5, attacks on the church by the dragon and the beasts.

14:6–20:15, the judgment of God against His enemies:

The sickles, 14:6–20; the seven cups, 15:1–16:21; the judgment of Babylon, 17:1–19:10; the judgment on the beast, 19:11–21; the judgment on Satan (binding for 1000 years, 1000 year reign of the saints, final battle), 20:1–10; resurrection and judgment, 20:11–15.

Third act of the eschatological drama: the kingdom of God and the new Jerusalem, 21:1–22:5.

21:1–8, the new creation; 21:9–22:5, the new Jerusalem.

Conclusion, 22:6–21.

On the literary background of this type of literature cf APOCALYPTIC LITERATURE. The authors of this literature did not make the distinction we make between prophecy* and apocalyptic writing; the titles prophet and prophecy are applied to Apc in the book itself (1:3; 10:7; 11:18; 22:6, 9, 18). The symbolic-allegorical vision is characteristic of apocalyptic writing, and it is the basic material of Apc. Occasionally the symbolism is explained (1:20; 4:5; 5:6; 17:9 f; 19:8). In most instances it is left unexplained, and its meaning is reconstructed by modern scholars, if at all, only by laborious exploration of the background of the passage. The free use of such cryptic symbols seems to presuppose a conventional language of symbolism known to the author and his readers. At times it is fairly obvious; the description of the Son of Man (1:13–16) clothes him with visual attributes each of which has a manifest symbolism of his attributes. The symbolism of colors is used (6:1–8; 17:4; 19:8). The symbolism of numbers is much employed: 7 signifies totality, 6 imperfection, 12 Israel (old and new), 4 the world (the four points of the compass or the four elements: land, sea, heavens, abyss), 1000 immensity.

While explicit citations of the OT in Apc are not numerous, allusions and echoes are so frequent that many parts of the book appear to be a patchwork of OT images; difficult as the book is, it is completely unintelligible without constant reference to the OT sources which it uses. The following list is only partial: 8:1, silence (Hab 2:20; Zp 1:7; Zc 2:17); 10:3, the roaring of the lion (Je 25:30; Jl 4:16; Am 1:2); 11:19; 15:8, the appearance of the ark and the cloud (2 Mc 2:5–8); 15:2–3, the seashore (Ex 14:15); 12:1–17, the woman and the serpent (Gn 3); 1:8, the revelation of the name (Ex 3:14); 4:8, hymn before the throne (Is 6:1–3); 9 and 16, the plagues (Ex 7–10); 12:4, 14; 13:1–8, 15; 17:12; 20:4, persecution (Dn 3:5–7:15; 8:10); 14:14, the Son of Man (Dn 7:13); 20:4, 12, the judgment (Dn 7:10, 22); 4:1–11, the throne of God (Ezk 1 and 10); 5:1;

10:10, the sealed book (Ezk 2:9; 3:3); 6:1–3, 8, the scourges (Zc 1:8–10; Ezk 14:21); 7:1, angels (Ezk 7:2); 7:3, the servants of God marked (Ezk 9:4); 8:5, fire as symbol of punishment (Ezk 10:2); 8:13, the release of woes (Ezk 7:5, 26); 17, the harlot (Ezk 16, 23); 18, lamentations over the fallen city (Ezk 27–28); 19:17 ff, invitation to birds of prey (Ezk 39:17–20); 20:7–10, attack of Gog (Ezk 38–39); 21:9–22:2, the new Jerusalem (Ezk 40–47). Apc is to a large extent a rethinking and a rearrangement of OT symbolism, with particular application to the time and situation of the author.

2. *Literary Composition.* Numerous critics have suggested that the book is a compilation rather than a single literary production. In several series of visions there is no apparent progress of thought and sometimes no logical link. Furthermore, the antinomies between some visions do not suggest a single author. Several hypotheses of compilation from distinct sources have been proposed; these lack a good foundation in the text and are excessively complex, and no theory has been widely accepted.

Allo attempted to explain these uneven qualities by certain laws of composition which he thought he detected in Apc. "The law of anticipation" means that the following event is anticipated in a preceding scene: 13 is anticipated in 11:1–13; 17–19 in 14:8; 16 in 14:10; 19:17–21 in 16:12–14; 21–22 in 19:7–9. These create an overlapping series of links which tie the whole together. "The law of undulation" means that the same succession of events is recapitulated in different forms. "The laws of antithesis and periodicity" refer to a kind of interruption and even reversal of movement at the 6th element of each of the series of seven of which the book is mostly composed. There are seven series of seven; each of them is preceded by a preparatory vision: the letters (1:9–20 + 2:1–3:22); the seals (4:1–5:14 + 6:1–7:17); the trumpets (8:1–6 + 8:7–11:14); the signs in the sky (11:15–19 + 12:1–14:20); the cups of wrath (15:1–16:1 + 16:2–16); the heavenly voices (16:17–21 + 17:1–19:5); the visions of the end (19:6–10 + 19:11–22:5). This structure, if indeed it is not the result of exegetical ingenuity, is the work of a unifying mind; but there are other difficulties which may make it necessary to attribute the unity to a compiler and not to the author. There is evident disorder in 22:6–21. There are two visions of the new Jerusalem, one eschatological-celestial (21:1–8), the other messianic-terrestrial (21:9–22:5). There are doublets: the beast (13:1, 3, 8; 14:8 and 17:3, 8; 18:2) with two different symbolisms; the dragon (12:9, 12 and 20:2 f), also with two different symbolisms, "two parallel employments of the same theme and two different traditions" (Boismard). Charles and Gaechter have suggested that the author died before the work was finished and that the disciples published it in a disarranged condition. Boismard has proposed a more complex scheme. He suggests that one author prepared two parallel apocalypses at two different periods, of which perhaps one or neither was complete. These were later fused in a single document. The earlier of these (I) comes from the reign of Nero (AD 54–68), the other (II) from late in the reign of Vespasian (AD 69–79) or early in the reign of Domitian (AD 81–96). The contents of each are outlined in the accompanying box:

time of the author, or traditional-mythological. This last approach (Gunkel, Bousset, Charles) proposes that the author employs material from ancient mythological traditions, both Jewish and Gentile, to present the end of the world process in terms of its beginning. All three approaches are valid, since the book represents all three elements; but no single interpretation can be proposed.

Apc is a Christian apocalypse, not a Jewish apocalypse; Jesus Christ is a dominant figure, and this is in evident contrast with the suppression of the Messiah* in most Jewish apocalyptic literature. He appears as the redeemer, the glorified and exalted Son of Man, the victor in the eschatological combat, the judge (1:5; 2:26 ff; 3:21; 5:6, 9; 7:14, 17; 12:5, 11; 13:8; 19:11,

	I	II
Prologue		10:1–2a, 3–4, 8–11
Satan against the Church	12:1–6, 13–17	12:7–12
The beast against the Church		13
Announcement and preliminaries of the great day of wrath	4–9; 10:1–2b, 5–7; 11:14–18	14–16
The great day of wrath:		
Babylon	17:1–9, 15–18	17:10, 12–14
Fall of Babylon	18:1–3	14:8
The elect delivered		18:4–8
Lamentation for Babylon	18:9–13, 15–19, 21, 24	18:14, 22 f
Songs of triumph	19:1–10	18–20 (16:5–7)
The messianic kingdom	20:1–6	
The eschatological combat	20:7–10	19:11–21
The judgment	20:13–15	20:11–12
The new Jerusalem	21:9–22; 22:6–15	21:1–4; 22:3–5; 21:5–8
Appendix: the two witnesses		11:1–13, 19

It is difficult to affirm or deny with certainty that this or any other scheme represents the composition of the book, and the authors of these schemes intend no such affirmation of their own work or the work of others. The schemes illustrate the wide agreement that the composition of Apc is not to be attributed to a single author intending to produce a unified work, and it may be taken as the consensus of scholars that Apc was not so written. Further study is necessary before a general agreement on the composition can be expected.

3. *Theology.* The allegorism and symbolism of Apc have made the book a favorite of allegorical and symbolical interpretation, and some lines of interpretation may be excluded at once. Apc is not a prophetic history of the Church, and the unfolding of its symbolism is not to be sought in contemporary history. Neither is it a purely spiritual allegory with no reference to the history contemporary with the author. Modern interpreters follow the lines of eschatology, proposing that Apc is entirely eschatological in outlook, or of history, proposing that Apc reflects the events of the

15; 21:1, 3, 22 ff; 22:1, 3, 14).

The interpretation of Apc must take account of the fact that the letters to the seven churches are not in the same literary genre with the rest of the book. The letters contain no visions and propose moral admonitions with no eschatology; the rest of the book has no moral teachings and is a succession of visions. The motivation of the moral teaching by the eschatological teaching is indirect at best; and the connection may arise from compilation.

The direction of the book toward a contemporary situation cannot be doubted. It is characteristic of apocalyptic literature that it is written for a crisis, and the crisis here is suggested by numerous allusions to persecution and martyrs. This must be the early persecutions by Roman authorities, and Apc itself suggests this. Babylon is Rome, the city of the seven hills (17:5, 9). The number of the beast, 666 (13:18), represents the sum of the numerical value of the letters of the name Caesar Nero written in Hb characters (KSR NRWN); cf ANTICHRIST. Apc is a response to the crisis of faith caused by persecution, and it is given in the apocalyptic tradition; one must await in faith and hope the salvation and the judgment of God, convinced that the persecutor must fall before he succeeds in destroying the people of God.

The salvation and the judgment are conceived in eschatological terms. Other biblical books besides Apc merge history and eschatology and use the imagery of the end-process to describe contemporary events. "In the struggle between the Church and the Roman state the author sees the decisive struggle between God and Satan which ends with the victory of God and the final annihilation of all powers hostile to God. This struggle ushers in the end of this world period and the beginning of the everlasting kingdom of God" (Wikenhauser). The attributes by which God saves and judges in any particular historical situation are the same attributes by which He finally accomplishes His purpose of saving and judgment; and thus they are portrayed in particular events. The eschatological combat is not merely eschatological but always present in the life of the Church, which thus has an eschatological perspective. The reality of the threat of evil and the promises of God to maintain His Church are valid for all times. And this is the answer to the question of the relevance of Apc for Christians of all ages; in modern times Christian readers have less sympathy for this type of literature than for any other biblical type.

Two particular problems arise in the theology of Apc. For the problem of the 1000 years of the binding of Satan and the reign of the elect cf MILLENNIUM. The problem of the identity of the woman of ch 12 is the question of whether the woman is Mary. That this was intended by the author can be sustained on no basis in the text itself. The woman is no doubt a second Eve, but the author shows no knowledge of this title given to Mary. The woman is also the mother of the Messiah (who must be the child), but her adventures cannot be explained in any intelligible form as applied to Mary. They are understood if the woman is understood as the people of God, which bears both the Messiah and the new people of God (the two are not perfectly distinguished); and this is the interpretation of most exegetes.

4. *Authorship and Canonicity.* Apc was rejected by Caius of Rome in the early 3rd century, and with serious arguments by Dionysius of Alexandria at the close of the 3rd century. Many Gk fathers rejected it; Cyril of Jerusalem, Gregory of Nazianzus, Chrysostom, Theodoret (and probably the entire school of Antioch). These doubts did not persist. They arose from a doubt of the authorship by John the Apostle, which has nothing to do with the canonicity of the book.

The author calls himself John (1:1, 4, 9; 22:8) and says he experienced his visions on the island of Patmos. That this is John the Apostle was affirmed by Justin, Irenaeus, Clement of Alexandria, Tertullian, the Canon of Muratori, Hippolytus, and most fathers after them. The internal character of Apc does not support this attribution, and the reasons were set forth by Dionysius of Alexandria. Of all the Johannine writings only Apc claims Jn as its author by name. The keywords of Jn and 1 Jn are absent from Apc: life, light-darkness, truth-lie, grace, judgment, love, world, Holy Spirit, adoption, faith. The few contacts with Jn (living water, good shepherd, lamb, witness, word) are less impressive than the differences. The Gk of Apc is the worst of the NT, much inferior to Jn and 1 Jn. It abounds with barbarisms and solecisms. The author thinks in Hb while he writes in Gk. Grammatical and stylistic irregularity is normal with him.

It is the consensus of modern scholars that Apc cannot be attributed to the author of Jn and 1 Jn, whoever this may have been. That it comes from a school of Johannine thought may be admitted; but that one man could have written all of them is an affirmation which simply rejects literary criticism as a valid process of thought. The author then must be left unidentified.

5. *Date and Place.* While Patmos may be a literary fiction, the connection of Apc with the churches of Asia is definite; one can scarcely be more precise than this. Tradition mostly dated Apc about the end of the reign of Domitian; but the tradition was somewhat confused by the attribution of Apc to John the Apostle, and an effort to fit it into the traditional (and quite unverified) career of John is evident. The source of a variant tradition which placed Apc in the reign of Claudius (Epiphanius) or Nero (Canon of Muratori, others) cannot be traced, but it should not be dismissed. The confusion, according to some critics, comes from the author himself, who wrote in the reign of Domitian but by a literary artifice placed himself in the reign of Vespasian; this antedating is not evident from the text. In favor of the date AD 94–95 can be alleged the spread and establishment of the Church in Asia and possible allusions in Apc to the cult of the divine Caesar. This was first imposed by Domitian and, if verified, would be a convincing argument for a later date. But the hypothesis of compilation (cf above) permits different dates for different parts of the book.

Apocalyptic Literature. A type of literature

which was widely diffused in Judaism from 200 BC to AD 200. On the separate examples of this type cf APOCRYPHAL BOOKS. Apocryphal literature is pseudonymous, proposed under the name ot some celebrity of the past, such as Enoch* or Moses*. It pretends to be a revelation of the future up to the time in which the reader finds himself, granted to the ancient hero and kept secret until the present. The medium of revelation is the vision, the opening of the heavens, the communications of angels. The visions usually reveal the future in complicated symbolism which is not always interpreted in the apocalypse, but can be explained if the contemporary history is sufficiently known. The apocalyptic literature deals with the final period of world history and the world catastrophe; here the powers of evil make the supreme struggle against God and are finally routed after a dreadful and bloody combat. These powers, allegorically described, are the world powers of contemporary history, which in apocalyptic literature is the last of the world periods before the end. In this combat the Jewish nation, sometimes represented with a messianic leader, triumphs over the world, and much of the false messianism* of NT times can be traced in the apocalyptic books. There are visions of the Paradise* of the blessed and the Gehenna* of the damned.

Apocalyptic literature has its roots in the OT. Prophecy* was deeply rooted in the national life of Israel and ceased to exist in its traditional form after the fall of Jerusalem and the end of the Hebrew monarchy in 587 BC. Haggai* and Malachi* are weaker imitators of the earlier prophets; but in Zechariah* almost entirely, in Jl 2:1–11; 4: 1–21, in Daniel* almost entirely, and in other compositions which were added to the books of the preexilic prophets a new form of literature appears which is the beginning of apocalyptic literature; the seer has replaced the prophet. The elements of world catastrophe, the climactic conflict of evil against God, the allegorical description of contemporary history, can be seen in Is 13 and 24–27; Ezk 38–39; Zp 1:14–18. Prophecy could focus upon the national life in the living present; once this point of interest was removed, the seer began to look for the fulfillment of God's will and the establishment of His kingdom in the future.

The single example of this type of literature in the NT is the Apocalypse*.

Apocryphal Books (Gk *apokryphos*, "hidden") books for which divine authorship is falsely claimed. Catholics apply the term apocryphal to the books listed below, both I and II. Protestants apply the term to those books which are omitted from the Protestant canon* but are found in the Catholic canon; Catholics call these books deuterocanonical*. The books listed below in I are called pseudepigrapha by Protestants. These books are written in imitation of the canonical books of the Bible and pretend to the same authority, offering supplementary revelation which is lately revealed after being long hidden, hence their name. They are classified under each Testament. As historical sources the apocryphal books have little or no value. They are, however, extremely valuable for reconstructing the popular beliefs of Judaism in NT times and for tracing certain obscure heretical currents in the early Church.

I. Old Testament

1. *Narrative:*

1 Esdras. This book, with the exception of chs. 3:1–5:6, is compiled from the canonical books of Ch, Ezr, Ne and narrates the history of Judah from the passover of Josiah* to the fall of Jerusalem in 587 BC, the decree of Cyrus* permitting the rebuilding of the temple and the return of the first group of exiles, the rebuilding of the temple against Samaritan opposition, the return of Ezra* and the reading of the Law to the people. The added chapters tell how the Jewish hero Zerubbabel*, one of three pages of Darius*, defeated his two companions in a competition of oratory by his speech defending truth as the strongest of all things. The book is also called 3 Esdras. It is an original translation of the canonical portions into Gk and may be dated in the 3rd or 2nd century BC; it was probably composed in Egypt.

3 Maccabees. This relates the attempt of Ptolemy IV Philopator of Egypt to enter the temple of Jerusalem, from which he was miraculously repelled, his efforts to persecute the Jews in Alexandria*, also miraculously foiled, and his conversion to a patron of the Jews. The historical value of this account is not confirmed. It is written in Greek, very probably in Alexandria about 100 BC.

Book of Jubilees. The book retells the events from Gn 1:1–Ex 12:51, as ostensibly revealed to Moses* on Sinai*. It teaches the eternal validity of the Law by recasting the events of Gn so that the Law, created in the beginning, is the norm for the patriarchs. It also contains a great number of Jewish legends about the patriarchs and expansions of Gn which are historically without value. It was written by a Pharisee during the reign of John Hyrcanus (134–103 BC) and is preserved in an Ethiopic version of the lost Gk version of the Hb original, also lost.

Books of Adam and Eve. These include the life of Adam and Eve, preserved in a Lt translation of a Gk original and the apocalypse of Moses, written in Gk. They fill in the period between the expulsion from Paradise* and the death of Adam and Eve. There are two accounts of the fall, one from Adam and Eve, a story of the expulsion of Satan* from heaven by Michael*, and the story of Adam's burial in heaven by the angels, where his body is preserved until the resurrection. They were most probably written between AD 20–70.

Martyrdom of Isaiah. A collection of three works: the martyrdom, the vision, the ascension of Isaiah. The first relates how Isaiah was sawn asunder by Manasseh, and is preserved in an Ethiopic version of the Hb original, written early in the 1st century AD. The other two are Christian compositions of the latter 1st and early 2nd centuries AD, relating Isaiah's vision of Christ and his journey through the seven heavens, where he sees the birth, crucifixion and resurrection of Jesus. They were written in Gk and were glossed, especially the martyrdom, by Christians in the 3rd and 4th centuries.

Letter of Aristeas. This is a splendid example of Jewish apologetic. It purports to be a letter from Aristeas, an officer of the court of Ptolemy II Philadephus of Egypt (285–246 BC). Demetrius of Phaleron, the librarian of the great library of Alexandria, suggested to the king that the library needed a collection of the Jewish sacred books. A mission was sent to Jerusalem and Eleazar appointed 72 men, six from each of the 12 tribes, to do the translation. When they arrived at Alexandria, the king proposed a philosophical question to each of the 72 at a banquet which lasted several days. The 72 finished the translation on the island of Pharos in 72 days. The letter contains an exaggerated description of the magnificence of Jerusalem and praise of the Law. The letter is not the work of Aristeas, but of a Jewish writer (145–100 BC).The story has no historical basis, but it is the origin of the name Septuagint (Lt *septuaginta,* "seventy") for the Gk translation of the OT; cf SEPTUAGINT.

2. *Apocalypses:*

Books of Enoch. These include the Ethiopic Enoch and the Slavonic Enoch. The Ethiopic Enoch relates the story of the fall of the angels and describes the coming and the judgment of the Messiah, a heavenly being who is called the son* of man or the "elect one." Enoch travels through the earth, the underworld, and the heavens and learns how to reckon the calendar. He foretells the deluge and the history of Israel to the coming of the Messiah under the allegory of animals; the history of the world is divided into ten weeks before the judgment. The book is preserved in an Ethiopic version of the lost Gk version of an Aramaic (or possibly Hb) original, also lost. It was compiled from various writings of Pharisaic origin of the 2nd century BC and was very popular among Christians in the first three centuries AD. It is quoted in Jd 14–15.

The Slavonic Enoch (also called the Secrets of Enoch), dependent on the Ethiopic Enoch, tells of Enoch's journey through heaven and hell and his visions of the angels, and his revelation of history from the fall to the deluge. It is a Jewish book written in Gk before AD 70 and preserved in Slavonic. Its present form exhibits reworking by Christians.

Testaments of the Twelve Patriarchs. The classification of this work as apocalyptic is justified by the revelations of the future of Israel contained in the testaments, but it is somewhat misleading. The principal emphasis lies in the moral exhortations which each of the sons of Jacob delivers to his sons; in each a virtue is selected which is associated with some event of the patriarch's life either in Gn or in Jewish legend. The book is preserved in a Gk version of its Hb or Aramaic original, and comes from the late 2nd or early 1st century BC. Some scholars had already assigned its origins to a devout ascetical sect of Jews; recent studies have indicated a possible connection with the group which produced the Dead Sea Scrolls; cf QUMRAN.

Sibylline Oracles. The story of the Sibyl, a prophetess, is of Gk origin and goes back at least to the 5th century BC. Rome had a collection of Sibylline books. The ancient oracles were widely imitated in later centuries. This form of literature was imitated by the Jews, who attributed to the pagan seer praises of Israel, condemnations of idolatry, and the foretelling of their own history and the Messianic times. Christians added some oracles foretelling the life of Christ and reworked some of the Jewish oracles. A compilation of all three was made about the 6th century AD. They were written in Gk from the 2nd century BC to the end of the 2nd century AD, some perhaps later.

Assumption of Moses. The testament of Moses to Joshua*, foretelling the history of Israel from its entrance into Canaan* up to the messianic times. There are clear allusions to the Hasmoneans* and Herod.* It was written in the 1st century AD in Hb or Aramaic and is preserved in a Lt version of a lost Gk version. The author was a Pharisee who was opposed to the political activities of his sect. Recent studies have suggested a connection between this book and the Dead Sea Scrolls (cf QUMRAN). Jd 9 quotes a lost portion of this book.

Books of Baruch. 2 Baruch (the Syriac

Apocalypse) is a composite from several authors in which the history of the Jews is foretold from 591 BC to the coming of the Messiah. In answer to Baruch's wonder why the judgment of the nations and the coming of the Messiah are delayed, he learns of the 12 "woes" which precede the coming of the Messiah, the four kingdoms, the 14 "floods" in which history is allegorized, and the necessity of Israel's atonement for its sins. 2 Bar is notable for its conception of a messianic kingdom upon earth before the final consummation and its conception of the resurrection, as well as for its conception of sin expressed in the line, "Each man is the Adam of his own soul." It was written after AD 70 and is preserved in a Syriac version of the Gk version (lost except for fragments) of a lost Hb or Aramaic original.

3 Baruch (the Greek Apocalypse) is the story of Baruch's journey through the seven heavens. It is a Jewish work of the 2nd century AD reworked by Christians and is preserved in Gk.

4 Esdras. This book (also called 2 Esdras) answers the question why Israel is afflicted and the messianic age delayed. The visions of Ezra* reveal the signs of the approaching end, the "woes" which precede the messianic coming, the four kingdoms with the fourth kingdom seen under the allegory of an eagle, the Messiah as the son of man coming from the sea. The general resurrection, the final judgment, and the heavenly Jerusalem are described, as well as the state of the soul between death and the judgment. This book also exhibits the conception of a messianic kingdom on earth before the final judgment. The problem of the small number of the saved is discussed. The book concludes with the story of how Ezra for 40 days and nights dictated 94 books by divine inspiration; 24 are the canonical books of the OT, restored after their destruction in the Babylonian wars, and 70 are to be concealed (*apokrypha*) until the proper time. The book survives in several ancient versions of a lost Gk version of a lost Hb original. It was composed by Jews after AD 70 and was popular in the early Church.

3. *Wisdom:*

4 Maccabees. A discussion in the manner of the Gk philosophical schools in which it is proved by examples drawn from Hb history, especially the martyrs of 2 Mc, that reason dominates the passions. It was written in Gk by a Jew of Alexandria not earlier than 50 BC.

4. *Psalms:*

Psalms of Solomon. These 13 psalms are written in the form and style of the canonical Psalms*. They illustrate Pharisaic belief and piety and messianic expectation. Allu-

sions to Pompey and Herod and the Hasmoneans indicate their composition in 50–30 BC. They are preserved in a Gk version of the lost Hb original.

II. New Testament

1. *Gospels:*

A. Infancy Gospels.

Gospel of James, also called *Protoevangelium.* This important work, of little or no historical value, is the source of the names of Joachim* and Anna* as the parents of Mary*, the presentation of Mary in the temple*, the choice of Joseph* as Mary's husband by the blossoming of his wand. It expands the details of the suspicion of Mary's unchastity and the birth of Jesus. It is preserved in Gk and was written not later than the 2nd century AD.

Gospel of Thomas. A story of the boyhood of Jesus filled with extravagant and often repulsive miracles. Doubtless from heretical sources, this book, in the words of Renan, represents the boy Jesus as a vicious little guttersnipe. Of uncertain date, it is preserved in Gk and in a Lt version.

Arabic Gospel of the Infancy. This book depends largely on the apocryphal Gospels of James and Thomas, but adds stories of the flight into Egypt again replete with extravagant miracles, some accomplished by contact with the linen or the bath water of the infant. In this book Jesus meets the two robbers with whom He was crucified. It is a late compilation of earlier stories.

History of Joseph the Carpenter. Fanciful details of the life of Joseph are added to the meager material of the Gospels, in particular his family, the story of the marriage, the flight into Egypt, his death in the presence of Jesus and Mary, and the removal of his soul by the angels. It is of Egyptian origin, not earlier than the 4th century AD, and is preserved in an Arabic version.

B. Passion Gospels.

Gospel of Peter. This is compiled from all four Gospels but casts doubt on the reality of Jesus' sufferings and is therefore Docetist. It was written about AD 150 and is preserved only in a Gk fragment.

Gospel of Nicodemus, or *Acts of Pilate.* This book exists in several recensions, expands the details of the trial of Jesus before Pilate and contains a circumstantial account of the descent into hell and the deliverance of the souls of the just. It was composed in the 4th century AD or later and is preserved partly in Gk and partly in Lt versions.

Gospel of Bartholomew. This book tells of the descent into hell, Mary's account of the annunciation, a vision of hell and the devil's account of his deeds. There is a series of questions addressed to Jesus by Bartholomew and an account of the resurrection of

Jesus. It is preserved in fragments of the original Gk and of Lt versions and is earlier than the 4th century AD.

Book of John the Evangelist. Questions addressed to Jesus and His answers. This heretical fragment attributes the creation of matter and the Jewish law to the devil. It is preserved in a Lt version and goes back to the 6th or 7th century AD.

The Assumption of the Virgin. There are a number of apocryphal accounts of this event preserved in Gk, Lt, Syriac, Coptic, and Arabic. The most important is the Gk "discourse of St. John the Divine concerning the falling asleep of the holy mother of God" from about the 7th century AD. In this account the apostles were all brought back upon clouds to witness the death and assumption of Mary.

Other apocryphal Gospels such as the Gospel according to the Hebrews (identified by some of the fathers with the Aramaic Matthew*), the Gospel of Peter, and the birth of Mary, are known only in fragments or by allusions in ancient writers. Of interest are the *agrapha* or unwritten sayings of Jesus not found in the canonical Gospels. Some of these are quoted by ancient Christian writers, and fragments of a collection of these sayings were discovered in Egypt in 1897 and 1903; they come from the 3rd century.

The Gospel of Thomas was discovered at Nag Hammadi in Egypt in 1945 and was published in 1958. It is a Gnostic collection of sayings of Jesus, some from the canonical Gospels and others clearly exhibiting Gnostic ideas. It is preserved in a Coptic translation of the Gk original and was produced in the 2nd–3rd centuries AD.

2. *Acts:*

Acts of John. This conglomeration of miracles teaches the unreality of the body of Jesus and the heresy of the Encratites, who taught that marriage was sinful. John teaches women to abandon their husbands and betrothed. The Gk original and a Lt version are both preserved in part; it was written before AD 150. The story of John cast into the caldron of boiling oil was first mentioned by Tertullian; but no Gk writer knows the story and it is not found in the extant fragments.

Acts of Paul. Preserved only in fragments, mostly Coptic; the principal events are the rescue of Thecla from martyrdom and the martyrdom of Paul. The Encratite heresy also appears here. Tertullian says it was written by a presbyter of Asia about AD 160.

Acts of Peter. This also exhibits Encratite and Docetist (denying the reality of the body of Jesus) tendencies. The episode of Simon Magus* is much expanded. This book contains the story of Jesus meeting Peter as Peter was fleeing from Rome ("Quo vadis") and of Peter's crucifixion head downward. It was written in Gk in Asia Minor about AD 200 and is preserved in fragments of the Gk and of Lt and Coptic versions.

Acts of Andrew. Like others, a series of miracles proposing Encratite teaching. The crucifixion of Andrew and his discourse from the cross are related. It was written in Gk about AD 200.

Acts of Thomas. The most frankly Encratite of all, this book is a series of episodes in which Thomas persuades wives to leave their husbands. This book places the ministry of Thomas in India and recounts his martyrdom. With the preceding four books it was assembled into a corpus by the Manicheans to replace the canonical book of Acts.

Acts of Philip. A series of fantastic miracles; in the most sensational, Philip by a magical formula opens the earth, which swallows up 7000 people. For this he was rebuked by Jesus and his entrance into paradise postponed 40 days. It is of orthodox origin and was written in Gk before the 5th century.

The number of apocryphal acts was very large, but they are all accounts of extravagant miracles. The *Apostolic History of Abdias* relates the journeys and ministry of the apostles in the countries with which they were traditionally associated. Acts were written under the names of Andrew and Matthias, Peter and Andrew, several of John and of Peter and Paul, and Thaddaeus.

3. *Epistles:*

Epistle of Abgar. A letter from Abgar, toparch of Edessa, asking Jesus to come and heal him, and the answer of Jesus promising an apostle, who in legend was Thaddaeus. It is preserved in a Gk version of the Syriac original and was written before the 4th century.

Epistle to the Laodiceans. Composed on the basis of Col 4:16, it was compiled of phrases from the canonical Epistles before the 4th century and is preserved in Lt.

Paul and Seneca. 14 short letters between Paul and Seneca in which the Roman philosopher shows sympathy for Christianity. It is preserved in Lt and was written before the 4th century.

Epistle of the Apostles. Written in the name of the 12 apostles, the epistle contains the revelations made by Jesus during the 40 days after His resurrection, concerned largely with the resurrection and the last judgment. It derives some episodes from the apocryphal Gospels. It is generally orthodox and was composed about AD 160; it survives in three ancient versions, of which the Ethiopic is complete.

4. Apocalypses:

The best preserved of the apocalypses are those of Peter (2nd century), Paul, and Thomas (both 4th century). They are similar in character, containing exaggerated descriptions of the last judgment, the joys of heaven, and the punishments of hell.

Apollonia (Gk apollōnia, "named after Apollo"), a city of NE Macedonia on the Via Egnatia between Amphipolis* and Thessalonica*, which Paul passed through on his journey through Macedonia (AA 17:1).

Apollonius (Gk apollōnios, "belonging to [the god] Apollo"). **1.** Apollonius of Tarsus (2 Mc 3:5), son of Menestheus (2 Mc 4:4), governor of Coelesyria* and Phoenicia* under Seleucus* IV, who informed the king of the treasures of the temple of Jerusalem, which the king sent Heliodorus* to plunder (2 Mc 3:5 ff). It is probably the same officer, not mentioned by name in 1 Mc 1:29, who began the campaign to hellenize the Jews under Antiochus* IV with a raid upon Jerusalem (1 Mc 1:29 ff; cf 2 Mc 4:24 ff). He was killed in battle by Judas* in 166 BC. **2.** The son of Gennaeus, a commander of Antiochus V, who raided the Jews near Joppa* and Jamnia* (2 Mc 12:2). **3.** Governor of Coelesyria under Demetrius* II, defeated in battle by Jonathan* and Simon* (1 Mc 10:69 ff).

Apollos (Gk apollōs, probably abbreviated from Apollonius [some suggest Apollodorus or Apollonides]); a Jew of Alexandria*, learned in rhetoric and the Scriptures, possibly a student of Philo. He preached Jesus as the Messiah, although he was still a disciple of John* the Baptist; but Priscilla* and Aquila* met him at Ephesus* and gave him full instruction in "the Way." He then passed to Corinth* and taught the Jews from the Scriptures that Jesus was the Messiah (AA 18:24 ff). The disciples of John whom Paul found shortly afterwards at Ephesus may have been converts of Apollos. Apollos' preaching at Corinth was successful; Paul speaks of him as watering what he had himself planted (1 Co 3:6). Unfortunately one of the cliques at Corinth had formed itself under the name of Apollos (others under Paul and Cephas; cf CORINTHIANS), and Paul found it necessary to break these up to preserve the unity of the church (1 Co 1:10 ff; 3:3 ff; 4:6 ff). Apollos, either voluntarily or at Paul's request, had left Corinth and did not wish to return; no suspicion attaches to him about the cliques. Paul later requested Titus* at Crete* to forward Apollos on his journey.

Apollyon. Cf ABADDON.

Apostle (Gk apostolos, from apostellein, "to send forth"). Most instances of the word in classical Gk refer to a ship or a fleet, either freighters or vessels of a naval expedition. The adjective is used to designate an ambassador, delegate, or messenger, but such uses are rare; the NT uses the word in this sense twice (Jn 13:16; Phl 2:25). A similar use transferred to a religious sense seems to lie behind 2 Co 8:23, where the apostles mentioned are not apostles in the technical sense (cf below), but missionaries or messengers sent by particular churches. The apostles mentioned with the prophets (Lk 11:49; Eph 3:5; Apc 2:2; 18:20) are messengers of God, not really distinguished from the prophets, unless these passages echo the Jewish conception of Moses*, Elijah*, and Ezekiel* (cf below). Jesus Himself is called an apostle (Heb 3:1), the only use of the word in this letter, as one sent from God. In the NT the word designates a small group who hold the highest position in the Church and are charged with its most responsible functions; but a closer definition of the term discloses some problems which do not admit a peremptory answer.

No clear background of the NT concept and term appears either in Gk or in Judaism. In the Cynic-Stoic school of philosophy the philosopher sometimes conceived himself as a messenger of Zeus, but the term remains vague. In Judaism, however, men who were "sent" on missions by a central authority do appear with the Hb title šālîᵃh, šālûᵃh. 2 Ch 17:7–9 describes men who were sent by Jehoshaphat to teach the book of the law*; the Chronicler here retrojects an institution which must have existed in his own time. The title is also given to rabbis who were sent from the council of Jerusalem to the Jews of the Diaspora* to proclaim the calendar, to collect donations, to make visitations of local communities, to install teachers, and to maintain communications between the Diaspora and Palestine. Most of these are attested for the period after AD 70 and thus can have no influence on the NT conception of apostle. One who prays in the name of the synagogue congregation is also called "sent." The emissaries of the council were designated by the imposition of hands. Jewish missionaries proper, however, who are sent to make proselytes (Mt 23:15) are never called "sent." Of the spiritual leaders of the OT four in particular are given the title of "sent": Moses, Elijah, Elisha, and Ezekiel. The basis of this designation is the attribution to them of thaumaturgical powers otherwise reserved to God: the procuring of water and rain, power over birth, the resurrection of the dead. The prophets are not called "sent" in Judaism.

Hence in just those offices and functions which bear some resemblance to NT apostleship the title is not used, and it is used where no more than a slight similarity can be perceived.

The name of apostle certainly belongs to the group of disciples most frequently called the Twelve, enumerated in Mt 10: 2–4; Mk 3:16–19; Lk 6:13–16; AA 1:13. This group forms a college; it is called the Eleven during the interval between the death of Judas and the election of Matthias* (Mt 28:16: Mk 16:14; Lk 24:9, 33; AA 1:26). The number 12 is evidently a sacred number which needs completion by the election of Matthias. The number seems to echo the 12 tribes of Israel which the Twelve will judge (Mt 19:28; Lk 22:30); the apostles are the foundations of the New Israel of the Church. But no replacement is mentioned after the death of James* the son of Zebedee (AA 12:2); the Twelve was not considered a perpetual institution, since the conditions of membership (cf below) could not be met except by the first generation of Palestinian Christians. The Twelve are in the first place disciples; but they are chosen by Jesus to be His constant companions, and they are submitted to a full instruction in the truths which He proclaims. The name apostles is given them several times, either explicitly or in contexts where it is clear that they are meant (Mt 10:2; Lk 6:13; 9:10; 17:5; 22:14; AA 1:26; 5:29; 15:2, 4, 6, 22 f; 16:4; Apc 21:14 +). It is evident that the designation of apostles for the Twelve is preferred by Lk, whereas it is found only once in Mk (6:30) and in Mt (10:2); this suggests that the title was not a primitive designation in the Church. It is not found at all in the ecclesiastical sense in Jn. A number of scholars consequently doubts that the title goes back to Jesus Himself, although they do not question His election of the Twelve; they believe that it was conferred by the primitive Church. Others find this rarity in the Synoptic Gospels not convincing and believe that the title originated with Jesus. R. Rengstorff compromises by supposing that the title is used only in the Gospels when the Twelve are sent on a particular mission and that it does not become a title, still less an office, in the Gospels.

The Twelve are chosen by Jesus (AA 1:2 +). They teach and preside over the fellowship of the primitive community (AA 2:42 f). They are witnesses to the resurrection (AA 4:33). They preside over the distribution of goods in the community (AA 4:34–37; 5:2). They speak in the name of Jesus (AA 5:40) and perform signs and wonders in His name (AA 5:12). Theirs

is the ministry of the word (AA 6:2). They impose hands on the Seven (cf DEACON) to authorize them to care for the distribution of goods (AA 6:6). They become identified with Jerusalem as their residence (AA 8:1, 14, 18; 9:27; 11:1), even after the Jerusalem community was scattered by persecution. With the elders of the Jerusalem church they form the supreme legislative body of the Church (AA 15:2, 4, 6, 22 f; 16:4). The twelve foundation stones of the new Jerusalem bear the names of the Twelve apostles (Apc 21:14). He who is elected to replace Judas in the Twelve must have been a member of the company from the baptism of John to the ascension of Jesus and a witness of His resurrection (AA 1:15–26). It is evident that each of the original Twelve was chosen personally by Jesus; a condition was personal knowledge of the Incarnate Word. Their first commission empowered them to expel unclean spirits, heal diseases, and announce the kingdom (Mt 10:1; Mk 3:13–15; 6:7; Lk 9:1). They are selected from the general group of disciples to share in His work. The constitution of the college of the Twelve to carry on and continue the work of Jesus is done by the Risen Christ; they are to preach repentance (Lk 24:44–49), to make disciples and baptize (Mt 28: 16–20). While the title does not appear in Jn, the commission does; Jesus confers the Holy Spirit and power upon the Twelve (Jn 20:21). The mission of the Twelve is rendered operative by the gift of the Spirit after the ascension of Jesus in Lk 24:49; AA 1:8; 2.

The peculiar position of the Twelve in the primitive Church is thus clear; but it is not equally clear that this is synonymous with their position as apostles. The singular "apostle" appears first in the Pauline writings. It is of course applied to Peter (1 Pt 1:1; 2 Pt 1:1) and James (Gal 1:19). But it is also given to Barnabas* (AA 14: 14) and to the otherwise unknown Andronicus and Junias (Rm 16:7). The apostles are also mentioned several times in contexts where it is not clear that the Twelve are meant exclusively (1 Co 4:9–13; 9:5; 15:7; 2 Pt 3:2; Jd 17). Paul includes apostleship among the charismatic offices of the Church (1 Co 12:28 f). The prophets and apostles are the foundation of the Church (Eph 2:20). The identity of the "superapostles" at whom Paul scoffs is not clear (2 Co 12:11). They are apparently the "pseudo-apostles" of 2 Co 11:13 and therefore not entitled to the name; but if the name were limited to the Twelve, there could scarcely be any possibility of men who seem to have been in good standing claiming the title. Furthermore, Lk 10:1–20 contains an account of the mission of the Seventy which does not differ in its powers and scope from the mission of the Twelve as he reports it (9:2–5); the title apostle is not given to the Seventy, but the parallelism of the missions is striking. It appears that in at least some parts of the early Church the title of apostle was extended to others besides the Twelve; but Luke of all the NT writers most clearly limits the title to the Twelve and Paul. It is somewhat remarkable that the title is never given to Apollos* and Timothy*; this can only be, it seems, because each of them lacked the prime requisite of the apostle, personal experience of the living Jesus.

Paul is insistent upon his claim to the apostolate and explicit upon the qualifications and mission of the apostle. While his first mission was committed to him by the church of Antioch* (AA 13:2), Paul never appeals to this commission; the commission of the Church did not make one an apostle. While Paul never says it expressly, the tone of his utterances indicates that he claimed to be an apostle equal to the Twelve. The claim of itself was not enough; the account given in Gal 1–2 demonstrates that the Twelve accepted his claim. His claim is based upon the qualities of the Twelve: personal election by Jesus and personal experience of the living Jesus, even though Paul knew only the risen Jesus. His conviction of his apostolate rises from the Damascus experience (Gal 1:16), given in three forms. Each form emphasizes his election: he is a chosen instrument to carry the name of Jesus before Gentiles, kings, and Israelites (AA 9:15), he is witness for Jesus to all men (AA 22:15), he is appointed to serve and bear witness, to open men's eyes that they may turn from darkness to light and receive forgiveness of sins and holiness through faith (AA 26:16–18). Jesus has appeared to Paul as He has to the Twelve (1 Co 15:8). They were apostles "before him," but he also is an apostle (Gal 1:17). Paul, like Jeremiah, was set apart before his birth and called through grace (Gal 1:15). He is called to be an apostle, set apart for the gospel (Rm 1:1), called by the will of God to be an apostle (1 Co 1:1; 2 Co 1:1; Eph 1:1; Col 1:1; 2 Tm 1:1), an apostle not from man or through man but through Jesus Christ and God the Father (Gal 1:1), an apostle by command of God and Jesus Christ (1 Tm 1:1), appointed preacher and apostle, the teacher of the Gentiles (1 Tm 2:7). As Peter has received the apostolate to the Jews, so Paul has received the apostolate to the Gentiles (AA 9:15; 22:15; Rm 11:13; Gal 2:8), and he has received it from Jesus Christ (Rm 1:5). It is to be noted that Paul associates his call not only with Jesus but also with the Father.

Paul realizes that the apostolate is a charismatic office, the work of grace and not of man (1 Co 15:10). He preaches Jesus as Lord in virtue of the illumination from God which reveals the knowledge of the glory of Christ (2 Co 4:5 f). Paul has the power of thaumaturgy, the sign of the true apostle (AA 15:12; 2 Co 12:12). But the seal of his apostolate is the church which he has founded (1 Co 9:2). The apostles are slaves of Christ and stewards of the mysteries of God (1 Co 4:1). He preaches the word of the cross (1 Co 1:18), which is the word of reconciliation (2 Co 5:19). The apostles are ambassadors of Christ (2 Co 5:20) and fellow workers with God (1 Co 3:9; 2 Co 6:1). The apostle delivers what he has received from Jesus (1 Co 11:23; 15:1 ff).

R. Bultmann has summed up the apostolic function thus: the apostle proclaims the risen Lord; he is the bearer of tradition*; he holds an office which pertains to the whole Church; he appoints other officers (but not other apostles); he is the basic constitutive element of the Church. The texts cited above illustrate the points of this summary. The authority of the apostles is most clearly seen in the acts of the Twelve in Jerusalem and in Paul's government of the churches which he founded; these always remained his responsibility, and his power of decision was questioned only at Corinth, where it was vindicated.

The qualities of the apostolic office cited above are themselves evidence that the office could not survive the first generation of the Church. But the apostolic office as the constitutive element of the Church could not end without the Church itself ending also. Hence the Church preserved apostolic power in other officers and apostolic preaching in tradition.

Apphia (Gk *apphia*), a woman mentioned in the address of the letter to Philemon*, probably the wife of Philemon (Phm 2).

Appius, Forum of or **Market of.** A town on the Appian Way from Rome to Capua where Paul was met by Christians from Rome on his journey thither as a prisoner (AA 28:15).

Apple (Hb *tappûᵃh* is usually translated "apple" [Pr 25:11; SS 2:3, 5; 7:9; 8:5; Jl 1:12]). It is not certain that the apple was cultivated in ancient Palestine; apricot, citron, lemon, and orange have been suggested as alternate translations. The identification of the fruit of Paradise* as the apple is without foundation.

Aquila (*akylas*, Gk form of Lt *aquila*, "eagle"?). A Jew, a native of Pontus*, who with his wife Priscilla* came to Corinth* when Claudius* expelled the Jews from Rome. There Paul* met them and resided with them since he practiced their trade of tentmaking. They accompanied Paul to Ephesus* where they instructed Apollos* in Christianity (AA 18). They were still in Ephesus when Paul sent their greetings to Corinth (1 Co 16:19), and again later when Paul greeted them from Rome (2 Tm 4:19). In the meantime they had returned to Rome, where Paul sent them greetings from Corinth, thanking them for risking their lives to save his, an episode not elsewhere mentioned (Rm 16:3 f). The repeated greetings such as this show Paul's attachment to these his "fellow workers in Christ Jesus" (Rm 15:3), who were probably his first converts at Corinth.

Ar (Hb *'ār*, meaning unknown), usually Ar Moab, a city of Moab* (Nm 21:15, fragment of an ancient song; Dt 2:9, 29). Another ancient song refers to its devastation (Nm 21:28); Is 15:1 refers to another and later devastation. Dt 2:18 places it at the boundary of Moab. The site is not certain; Khirbet Rabbah, on the Moabite plateau about 3 mi S of the Arnon* and 25 mi N of Kerak, is suggested. Some scholars think the word in Dt 2:9, 18, 29 means district, not city.

Arabah (Hb *'ªrābāh*, "arid"), as a common noun denotes a desert; with the article it often becomes a geographical term designating "the desert" nearest central Palestine, the Jordan valley (Dt 1:7; 2:8; 3:17; Jos 11:2, 16, 12:8; 18:18; 2 S 2:29; 4:7; 2 K 25:4; Je 39:4; 52:7; Ezk 47:8; Zc 14:10). In Dt 2:8 it seems clear that the term includes the modern Wadi Arabah, the name of the continuation of the rift from the Dead Sea to the Gulf of Aqaba*, which is a more arid region than the Jordan valley; and the term possibly always has this fuller meaning in Hb. Cf JORDAN.

Arabia, Arab. The great peninsula of Arabia is regarded by many ethnologists as the motherland of all the Semitic peoples, which have emerged in almost regular irruptions to settle in the surrounding area of the Fertile Crescent. Whether this theory is rigorously valid, it is true that such irruptions have occurred often in the historical period, and that the Semitic peoples of biblical lands and history belong racially, culturally, and linguistically to the same group with the Arabs. The central desert of Arabia extends in a wedge northward and separates Mesopotamia* from Canaan*, and the Negeb* of Palestine* touches Arabia. It was this fringe which was known in the OT, although not under a single name. The name Arab (Hb *'ªrāb*) is used to designate a nomad (Is 13:20) and a bandit (Je 3:2) and generally signifies the tribes of the Syrian desert and south of the Negeb (2 Ch 17:11; 21:16; 22:1; 26:7; Ezr 27:21; Is 21:13; Je 25:24). These tribes are also called "Sons of the east" (Hb *bªnē Ḳedem;* Gn 29:1; Jgs 6:3; 1 K 5:10 +). Ch alludes to the raids of the Arabs on the settlements (2 Ch 21:16; 22:1; 26:7). The Assyrian records of the 8th and 7th centuries BC relate campaigns against the Arab tribes of the desert and tribute received from them, but it is doubtful that these campaigns were effective very far from the desert border. Arabia was important commercially and exported minerals and spices, its chief products, through Palestine to the ports of Phoenicia*; Solomon* had commercial relations with Arabia (1 K 10:15; 2 Ch 9:14). The OT as a rule knows Arabian tribes by their own names rather than by the general designation of Arab; the 13 sons of Joktan* (Gn 10:26 ff), the 6 sons of Keturah* (Gn 25:1 ff), and the 12 sons of Ishmael* (Gn 25:12 ff) are Arabian tribes, and the genealogy recognizes the kinship between them and the Hebrews. Arabia is mentioned in the NT only in Gal 1:17; 4:25. As the place of Paul's pilgrimage it probably signifies the Syrian desert and the territory S of the Negeb, and it is impossible to define Paul's destination more closely; the vagueness of the term appears in the second allusion, which places Mt Sinai* in Arabia. On the more important Arabian tribes connected with the Bible cf DEDAN; HAVILAH; HAZARMAVETH; KEDAR; MIDIAN; NABATEANS; OPHIR; SHEBA; TEMAN.

Arad (Hb *'ªrād*, meaning uncertain); a Canaanite* city whose king attacked the Israelites on their march to Canaan (Nm 21:1 ff). The sack of the city there mentioned occurred later and is attributed to Joshua* (Jos 12:14). The site of the city is Tell Arad, 16½ mi S of Hebron, where the ruins of a Bronze Age fortress can be discerned.

Aram, Aramaeans (Hb *'ªrām*). The Aramaeans are first mentioned in the records of the Assyrian* king Tiglath-pileser I (1112–1074 BC); they are thought by many scholars to be identical with the Ahlamu mentioned in earlier records, or to be a part of the Ahlamu. Ahlamu is very probably an appellative, "nomads." They first appear as a nomadic tribe of the Syrian desert which attacks the settled country and finally settles there. During the weakness of Assyria in the

12th–11th centuries BC the Aramaeans settled in northern Syria* and in southern Babylonia, where they merged with the Chaldeans*. The Aramaeans developed a group of strong commercial city-states in Syria which prospered until the Assyrian conquests of the 9th–8th centuries BC, when they were absorbed into the Assyrian empire. The Aramaeans were not culturally creative but they were a focus of the mixture and diffusion of cultures. The religion of the Aramaeans is not well known, since the literature from the early period is limited to a few inscriptions; the names of the gods mentioned there reveal a syncretism of Canaanite and Mesopotamian deities. We find Baal* under various titles, Hadad*, the storm god, Shamash, a Mesopotamian solar god, Tammuz*, a dying and rising god of fertility whose cult was extremely popular, and Rekub-el, Sahr (solar god), Nikkal (lunar goddess), and Nusk (fire god). Sahr and Nikkal are found in Ugarit. The god Bethel (cf ELEPHANTINE) is probably Aramaic.

Israel's relations with the Aramaeans were close and ancient. In the traditions of Israel's mixed origins Aramaeans appear among their ancestors. In the table of nations* Aram is a son of Shem (Gn 10:22). According to Am 9:7 they came from Kir*, not certainly identified. Nahor*, the brother of Abraham, lived in Aram Naharaim (Gn 24:10). The name Naharina in Egyptian (Nahrina in the Amarna tablets) designates the territory of northern Syria and the upper Euphrates centered around Carchemish and Harran which became Aramaean after the 12th century BC. To this name the Hebrews prefixed Aram as they did to the names of other Aramaean states. Balaam* was summoned from Aram Naharaim (Nm 23:7; Dt 23:5 cf PETHOR). This region is called Paddan* Aram in another tradition. Jacob is once called "an Aramaean vagabond" (Dt 26:5) and Laban* is called an Aramaean (Gn 25: 20; 28:5; 31:20, 24). Cushan-rishathaim is called king of Aram Naharaim, but cf CUSHAN-RISHATHAIM. The presence of Aramaean nomads in the region where they later settled is assured for the period of the patriarchs. During the monarchy the Israelites, in spite of almost constant wars, were commercially and culturally in close touch with the Aramaean states of Syria; cf BETH-REHOB; DAMASCUS; GESHUR; MAACAH; ZOBAH. The final collapse of the Syrian states before Assyria in the 8th century BC opened the way for the conquest of Israel.

Aramaic. The language of the Aramaeans* and possibly of the Hebrews before their settlement in Canaan*. In any case, the Aramaeans did not themselves adopt Canaanite but retained their own tongue. It is classified as a northwest Semitic language. The wide diffusion of the Aramaeans and their commercial activities carried the language through the entire area of Palestine, Syria, and Mesopotamia; but the language reached its greatest diffusion after the Aramaean states ceased to have any political importance. Its use as an international diplomatic language is seen in 2 K 18:26, where it is known by the Assyrian and Hebrew officers but not by the people. Its use had become common by the period of the Neo-Babylonian empire and after the 6th century BC it became the Semitic language most commonly used. Its alphabetical script, borrowed from the Canaanites, made it a much simpler medium of written communications than Akkadian*. It was the common language of the peoples of the Persian* empire and the official language of the imperial government. It enjoyed this general use until the spread of Hellenism*; but even after Gk became the language of literary culture, politics, and commerce, Aramaic remained the language of the common people until it was replaced by Arabic after the Mohammedan conquests of the 7th century AD and later. Except for inscriptions there is no literature earlier than the 5th century, but after this point the remains are extensive. The papyri from the Jewish colony of Elephantine* in Egypt in the 5th century are Aramaic. In the OT Ezr 4:8–6:18; 7:12–26; Je 10:11; Dn 2:4–7:28 are in Aramaic, and the Aramaic documents of the Persian foreign office quoted in Ezr are now generally thought to be authentic. During these centuries the Jews, especially those living outside Palestine, found it necessary to make Aramaic versions of the OT called Targums*. Aramaic is the language of the Talmud*. It was the common language of Palestine in NT times used by Jesus, with different dialects (Mt 26:73). It was on the title of the cross (Jn 19:20, called "Hebrew") and Jesus quoted Ps 22:2 in Aramaic from the cross. The composition of the Gospels* in Aramaic, except for Mt*, is defended by few scholars; but the oral sources of the Gospel tradition were largely, if not entirely, Aramaic. The wide diffusion of Aramaic led to the development of several dialects.

1. Eastern Aramaic:
   (a) Babylonian Aramaic (the Babylonian Talmud);
   (b) dialect of the Mandaean and Manichean literature;
   (c) Syriac, developed from the dialect of Edessa into several dialects of its own with an extensive Christian literature.

2. Western Aramaic:
  (a) Jewish Aramaic (the Targums);
  (b) Palestinian Aramaic (Jerusalem Talmud), the language used by Jesus, but no literary remains until several centuries later
  (c) Samaritan
  (d) Palmyrene (inscriptions)
  (e) Nabataean (inscriptions)

Ararat (Hb *ᵃrārat̩,* meaning uncertain), the region in which the ark of Noah* settled after the deluge* (Gn 8:4) and to which the sons of Sennacherib* fled after his murder (2 K 19:37; Is 37:38), mentioned in Je 51:27. It is identical with Urartu, mentioned often in the Assyrian records of the 9th–7th centuries BC as a persistent adversary which the Assyrians were never able to subjugate effectively. Urartu was located in the mountains of Armenia around Lake Van.

Aratus (Gk *aratos,* meaning uncertain), a poet of Soloi (310–245 BC) who resided at the courts of Antigonus in Macedonia and Seleucus in Antioch. His astronomical poem *Phaenomena* is quoted by Paul in his discourse at Athens (AA 17:28)

Araunah (Hb *ᵃrawnāh,* the name may be Hittite), a Jebusite* citizen of Jerusalem*. During the plague David* saw the angel of Yahweh at the threshing floor of Araunah and purchased the land for an altar. This was the site where Solomon* built the temple* (2 S 24:16 ff). In 1 Ch 21:15 ff the name appears as Ornan.

Archaeology. From Gk *archaios + logos,* the "science of antiquities". Archaeology is a subscience of history, but only within the last century has it become a formal science with its own objective and methods. Before the 19th century the study of antiquities, as opposed to the study of written records, which is history in the rigorous sense, was limited to the examination of those artifacts which could be found on the surface of the ground. Closer examination of the sites of ancient habitation revealed that most of the remains lay under the surface of the soil, and digging disclosed that they reached a far greater depth than had been suspected. As more of these ancient remains were found, archaeological evidence as a supplement to the monumental or written source was seen to be indispensable for the study of the past; it contributes knowledge which no written document contains. In the interpretation of archaeological remains the written document is indispensable; but modern techniques have made it possible to construct a remarkably illuminating picture of the past from archaeological remains alone.

Modern archaeology is the exploration of sites of human habitation by excavation and the interpretation of the findings. There are few areas in the world which have not been so explored; for the Bible the areas of interest are Palestine and Syria, Egypt, Mesopotamia, Asia Minor, and Greece. The technique of excavation has been developed from the very nature of the Palestinian and Mesopotamian site. The Palestinian site was chosen for the availability of ground water and some elevation which made the site more defensible; in the alluvial plain of Mesopotamia neither of these factors was decisive. In each area the ancient site now appears as an extensive mound (Arabic *tell*) formed by the deposit of debris through centuries of occupation. The archaeologist selects his site, which may be identified through the persistence of the ancient name or through geographical data in ancient sources, and first clears and surveys it. The area of excavation is rarely the entire mound, for this would be very expensive; and modern archaeologists prefer to leave some material for future work. The area selected is carefully dug, measured, and photographed, and the dirt is sifted for artifacts, which are classified according to the place of discovery. Excavation discloses the levels of occupation, more clearly defined if one level was ended by destruction or followed by a long period of nonoccupation. Recording of each level is essential, since the upper level must be destroyed to reach the lower. Distinct levels in a site long occupied may be as many as 16, but the archaeologist tries to reach virgin soil or bedrock. The levels are dated by their contents. Types of building material and construction, weapons and tools, and such objects exhibit the style of their period, which is determined by amassing material sufficient for classification. Presence of foreign objects indicates commercial and other relations. If coins or written records are discovered, they date the site themselves; this is rare in Palestinian lower levels, and the most important object for dating is pottery*, which is always found in abundance, and has long been classified into different periods according to its style and texture. The entire results of the exploration are published: account of the exploration, description and photographs of the site in the various levels of excavation and of all objects discovered. Only then are evaluation and interpretation possible.

Palestinian archaeology begins with the American Edward Robinson, who in 1838 began his explorations to identify ancient sites. The Palestinian Exploration Fund, founded in Great Britain in 1865, produced the Palestine Ordnance survey map, the first detailed and accurate map of the country, based on a thorough survey of the country, printed on the scale of one in/one mi. Early excavations up to 1900 suffered from a lack of technique and of comparative material; the Englishman Flinders Petrie and the American F. J. Bliss established the pottery index of chronology in 1894, which was a revolution in the field. After 1900 a number of important excavations were done; these are noticed in the separate articles. World War I (1914–1918) interrupted archaeology, but the period 1919–1939 was the most fruitful period of modern study, dominated by the American W. F. Albright. The most recent archaeological events, both of profound interest, have been the discovery (1947) of the Dead Sea Scrolls (cf QUMRAN) and the exploration of Jericho* by Kathleen Kenyon (1952–1957).

Exploration in Mesopotamia began with the work of the Frenchman Botta at Khorsabad in 1843 and the Englishman Layard at Nineveh in 1845 and has been pursued without interruption except for the two world wars. Mesopotamia, the seat of a much older and more highly developed civilization than that of the Hebrews, drew interest because of its artistic remains, which were very attractive to the great museums; Palestine has never yielded any such treasures. Unfortunately the explorations down to the 20th century were conducted with the objective of securing museum pieces without photography and stratigraphic description, as explained above. Few Mesopotamian sites of importance have not been explored; cf separate articles. Egyptian archaeology developed at the same time.

The results of archaeological exploration cannot be summed up, but the following examples will show its value. Mesopotamian archaeology itself furnished the written documents for the history of this area, which before 1850 was unknown except for scattered allusions in the Bible and a few Greek authors. The library of Ashur-bani-pal revealed a vast collection of religious and secular literature which not only gave unique information on Mesopotamian history and religion, but also the materials for the study of Akkadian* and the hitherto unknown language and civilization of the Sumerians*. Archaeology has discovered and interpreted the legal code of Hammurabi*, the records of the Assyrian kings who conquered Judah and Israel, the Babylonian accounts of creation and the deluge, the names and characters of Mesopotamian gods, the palaces and temples of Nineveh, Babylon and other cities, Assyrian and Babylonian art, hundreds of

hymns and prayers. Mari and Nuzu have disclosed the world of the patriarchs. In Egypt there was recovered a vast literature which showed the influence of Egypt on Canaan and the Hebrews. Of special importance were the Amarna* Letters and the fragments of Egyptian wisdom literature, on which OT wisdom* depended largely for form and content. Egyptian art, like Mesopotamian art, enables us to reconstruct the daily life and occupations of ancient times. Many biblical place names appear in Egyptian lists. The chronology* of the OT has been established from Mesopotamian and Egyptian records. In Palestine there have been no comparable discoveries of written materials; but the Mesha* stone, the Siloam* inscription and the Lachish* Letters have been of primary importance. Archaeology has brought forth the palaces of Saul* and Ahab* and the stables at Megiddo*, at first attributed to Solomon*, more recently by Yigael Yadin to Ahab*. It has given abundant evidence of the Hebrew conquest of Canaanite cities. It has found Solomon's copper mining and smelting plants. It has made known the character of the ancient Hebrew city and house, its fortifications, weapons and jewelry, seals, manufactures, even the amulets and figurines of popular superstition. Ugarit* has yielded the only extensive Canaanite literary remains, and has enabled us to reconstruct Canaanite religion, the chief adversary of the Hebrew faith during its early centuries. There is scarcely a page of the Bible which has not been illuminated by archaeology, which supplies both the broad historical background of the ancient world into which the Hebrews can be placed and the real and concrete details of life and work in that world. In addition, although it is not of strictly biblical interest, Palestine has become one of the most important areas for the study of prehistoric man.

Archaeological periods (Albright)
Prehistoric
Chalcolithic 4500–3200 B.C.
Early Bronze I 3200–2900
Early Bronze II 2900–2700
Early Bronze III 2700–2300
Early Bronze IV 2300–2100
Middle Bronze I 2100–1900
Middle Bronze II 1900–1600
Late Bronze I 1600–1400
Late Bronze II 1400–1200
Iron I 1200–900
Iron II 900–600
Iron III 600–330

Archangel (Gk *archangelos*, "chief angel"), the word occurs in the Bible only in Jd 9 (Michael*, quotation from *Assumption of Moses*) and in 1 Th 4:16; an archangel will announce the Parousia*. Cf ANGEL.

Archelaus (Gk *archelaos*, "ruler of the people"), son of Herod* the Great and Malthake, ruler of Judaea 4 BC–AD 6 (Mt 2:22). Herod's last will and testament had divided his kingdom between Archelaus, Antipas*, Philip*, and Salome*. Shortly after Herod's death the Jews in Jerusalem rioted at the Passover because Archelaus refused a petition for redress of grievances, and the riot was suppressed with the loss of many lives. When Archelaus went to Rome to have Herod's will confirmed, a delegation of Jews also went to petition that his territory be put directly under the Roman governor of Syria. Augustus did not grant the petition, but withheld the title of king from Archelaus and gave him only the title of ethnarch. Archelaus had his father's cruelty but not his competence, and riots and disorders prevailed during his government; when in addition he was suspected of disloyalty, he was deposed and banished to Vienne in Gaul. He died in AD 18. After his deposition Judea was administered by a Roman procurator under the governor of Syria.

Areopagus, Areopagite (Gk *areios pagos*, "hill of Ares [English "Mars Hill"]"), a hill NW of the Acropolis in Athens*. Before the 5th century BC this was the meeting place of the supreme council and the supreme court of Athens, and the name remained with the council even after its deliberations were transferred elsewhere. When Paul was taken to the Areopagus (AA 17:19 ff) it is not clear whether he was taken before the council or to the place by that name in order that his discourse might be better heard. In any case the Areopagus in Paul's time was little more than an academic body. The discourse given was not in Paul's usual style but was an effort to speak in the manner of Gk philosophers; it was a failure, although Dionysius*, a member of the Areopagus, accepted Christianity.

Aretas (Arabic *ḥarita*), the name of four Nabataean* kings. Two are mentioned in the Bible. **1.** Aretas I; Jason* fled to Aretas but was expelled to Egypt (2 Mc 5:8). **2.** Aretas IV (AD 9–40), whose governor administered Damascus* when Paul escaped over the walls in a basket (2 Co 11:32 f; cf AA 9:23 ff). His daughter was the first wife of Herod Antipas*, who repudiated her for Herodias*, and she fled to Petra*. Not long after her father opened war with Antipas and defeated him; Antipas was rescued only by Roman legions. Aretas came into imperial favor with the accession of Caligula (37–41), and probably received Damascus from him.

Argob (Hb *'argōb*), a region of Bashan* or possibly an alternate name for Bashan (Dt 3:4, 13 f). It was included in Solomon's 6th district (1 K 4:13). Argob in 2 K 15:25 has probably been detached from its proper place in 2 K 15:29, the list of the regions conquered and made into an Assyrian province by Tiglath-pileser* III in 734 BC.

Ariel (Hb *'ᵃrī'el*, meaning uncertain; "lion of El"?, "hearth of El [altar]"?), probably identical with *hār'ēl* (Ezk 43:15), which is certainly an altar (*'ᵃrī'ēl* 43:15–16). It is a symbolic name of Jerusalem* in Is 29:1, 2, 7, possibly signifying the place of sacrifice in Jerusalem. The word in 2 S 23:20 is obscure; some scholars understand the word as "hero" here and in Is 33:7. 2 S 23:20 may be a dittography of 2 S 23:21 (*'aryeh*, "lion"). The word occurs in the Mesha* stone, where it is most probably interpreted with Albright as a proper name.

Arioch (Hb *'aryōk*). **1.** King of Ellasar*, one of the four kings of Gn 14:1. The name has been found in the Mari* texts (*arriwuk*), but Arioch cannot be identified with any known historical ruler. Cf ABRAHAM; AMRAPHEL. **2.** Captain of the royal guard of Nebuchadnezzar* (Dn 2:14 ff).

Aristarchus (Gk *aristarchos*, "excellent ruler"), a Macedonian from Thessalonica, a companion of Paul during the disturbance at Ephesus and on his third missionary journey (AA 19:29; 20:4) and on his voyage to Rome as prisoner (AA 27:2). He also shared Paul's imprisonment (Col 4:10; Phm 24).

Arimathaea. Cf RAMAH.

Aristobulus (Gk *aristobulos*, "excellent counselor"), a Christian of Rome greeted by Paul, apparently the head of a household (Rm 16:10).

Ark. Traditional English rendering of Hb *tēbāh*, the vessel in which Noah* and his family escaped the deluge* (Gn 6:14 ff); the word designates a chest or box. As described in Gn 6:14 ff, the ark was to be made of *gōper* (?) wood caulked with pitch, 300 cubits long, 50 cubits broad, 30 cubits high (about 450 ft, 75 ft, 45 ft respectively). It was to be built in three stories or decks with "nests" (cabins or cells?), with a roof and a door in the side. The ark of Utnapishtim in the Babylonian flood (cf DELUGE) had an acre of floor space and was built in a cube ten doz cubits (180 ft) on a side. It had seven decks and nine divisions (?) in the floor plan. It was caulked with pitch and had punting poles for steering. In each of these stories there is described a house of palatial dimensions, not a ship; the Babylonian ark is called "like the Apsu," the subterranean palace of the god Ea. We cannot trace the symbolism suggested here any further, but symbolism is very probable; in Mesopotamia men knew how to build a boat for river travel, knowledge which the Israelites lacked. The shape and dimensions in the two stories are similar enough to indicate that the ark of Noah is described after that of Utnapishtim, although the dimensions have been altered and the symbolism, if it is present, forgotten. In neither case is such a fantastic vessel apt even for a house boat. The ark, as a means of salvation through water, is a type of baptism in 1 Pt 3:20 f. The word *tēbāh* occurs elsewhere only in Ex 2:3 for the basket or chest of papyrus* in which Moses* was placed in the Nile* by his sister.

Ark of the Covenant (Hb *'ᵃrōn habbᵉrīt*), also called "ark of the testimony" (P), ark of the covenant* of Yahweh, ark of Yahweh, ark of elohim, ark of the elohim of Israel (both 1 S); a small portable box or chest. The name is given to the sarcophagus of Joseph (Gn 50:26). As described in Ex 25:10 ff, it was made of acacia wood overlaid with gold inside and out, 2½ cubits by 1½ cubits by 1½ cubits (about 3 ft 9 in and 2 ft 3 in respectively). On top of the ark was a gold plate, Hb *kappōret*, English "mercy seat" or "propitiatory." The Hb word probably means the place of atonement, i.e., the place where Yahweh receives atonement. On top of the ark also were two cherubim* facing each other, so constructed that their wings overshadowed the *kappōret*. This is the place where Yahweh meets Israel and reveals His commandments (Ex 25:22). While this description of the priestly source is probably later by centuries than the building of the ark, it should be regarded as a substantially accurate reconstruction. The ark contained the two tablets of stone which were thought to go back to the Mosaic period (1 K 8:9); in Heb 9:4 the author repeats an unhistorical rabbinical tradition which added a vessel of manna* and the rod of Aaron*.

The ark was carried at the head of the column when the Hebrews traveled through the desert (Nm 10:33 ff) and before the army in battle; it was notable that they did not have the ark when they were defeated by the Canaanites* (Nm 14:44). It was carried across the Jordan* first (Jos 3:3 ff) and carried around Jericho* seven days in succession (Jos 6:11 ff). It was also a place where oracles* were asked (Jgs 20:27).

After the settlement of the Israelites in Canaan the ark was finally established at Shiloh* (1 S 3:3 f); it was taken into battle against the Philistines, who defeated Israel and captured the ark (1 S 4:10-11). The Philistines, however, found it a hostile trophy; an earthquake overturned the image of Dagon at Ashdod (1 S 5:3) and plague broke out in Ashdod, Gath*, and Ekron*, to which cities the ark was carried (1 S 5:6 ff). The Philistines then put it in a cart and gave the oxen their heads, and the oxen carried it back to the Israelites at Bethshemesh (1 S 6:1 ff). But the plague also broke out at Beth-shemesh and the ark was lodged in the house of Abinadab* at Kirjathjearim* (1 S 6:19 ff). The defeat of Israel and the plague of Beth-shemesh seem to have destroyed the confidence of the Israelites in the ark, for it is not mentioned again until David brought it from the house of Abinadab to a new sanctuary in Jerusalem; and on the journey one of the porters died (2 S 6:2 ff). David, who was trying to unite a disunited Israel, saw in the ark a symbol not only of the God of Israel but also of its ancient unity; and the ark lent sanctity to his new capital city, Jerusalem, which until recently had been Jebusite. The ark was carried into battle against Ammon (2 S 11:11). It was finally placed in the temple* of Solomon (1 K 8:6 ff) and is no more mentioned in the historical books; its use in processions, however, is suggested by such passages as Ps 24:7-10. Jeremiah hinted at its future disappearance (3:16) and must have perished in the destruction of the temple in 587 BC. An unhistorical tradition that Jeremiah saved it from destruction is preserved in 2 Mc 2:5. It is mentioned in the NT in Heb 9:4 and Apc 11:19, where it appears in the heavenly temple.

The ark was a symbol of the presence of Yahweh, but both its traditions and its symbolism have become somewhat mixed. Modern studies have disclosed the existence of portable shrines among the pre-Islamic tribes of Arabia, and the ark falls into the same pattern. It is the shrine of a nomadic people who have no houses and no settled abode and therefore no temples. Lack of a detailed description of the ark prevents a detailed explanation of its symbolism. It may have resembled the sacred ceremonial boat carried in Egyptian religious processions, which symbolized the boat in which the sun god Re makes his daily circuit of the heavens. Incense altars of Canaanite manufacture have been discovered with a structure which resembles a miniature temple; this similarity has been suggested by some scholars, but neither this nor the sacred boat seems to fit the nomadic shrine. The references to Yahweh "enthroned upon the cherubim" (1 S 4:4; 2 S 6:2; Ps 80:2) suggest that the ark was the throne upon which Yahweh stood invisibly upon the cherubim. Canaanite deities are represented as standing upon the back of animals; since there was no image of Yahweh, only the footstool was represented. The images of Assyrian gods seated upon their thrones were carried in processions. Thus the ark was the symbol of Yahweh's personal presence, the place where atonement was received, where divine communications were granted. It was carried into battle to symbolize Yahweh's kingship and leadership. It was also the symbol of the covenant* of Yahweh with Israel; He was present because He had elected them as His people and imposed upon them the commandments which the ark contained.

Armageddon (Gk *harmagedon*), the place where the kings of the earth are mustered for battle on the great day of God (Apc 16:16). The name suggests Hb *har m^{c}giddō*, mountain of Megiddo. Megiddo was probably the most famous battlefield of ancient Palestine (Jgs 5:19, the defeat of Sisera* by Barak* and Deborah*; 2 K 23:29, the defeat of Josiah* by Necho*); it is also the place of mourning for Hadadrimmon (Zc 12:11). The mountain of Megiddo, however, does not appear in biblical or extrabiblical literature. F. Hommel suggested Hb *har mō'ēd*, mountain of assembly (Is 14:13), the Mt Sapon of Canaanite* mythology where the gods assemble.

Armor. The use of metal for body protection in war in Israel is at least as old as Saul* (1 S 17:38) and Goliath* (1 S 17:5). It is also mentioned as worn by Ahab* (1 K 22:34). Uzziah* was the first to equip the entire army with armor (2 Ch 26:14). The absence of remains or of pictures does not permit a reconstruction of Israelite armor. The word *nešeḳ* is now thought to mean armor in general, *širyōn*, scale armor of bronze or iron; this is mentioned in 1 S 17:5, 38. The armor of the Assyrian soldier consisted in a coat of mail of knee or ankle length, and this may have been the Hebrew type. Before Uzziah only the king and nobles wore body armor. A metal helmet also was worn, but its shape is not described; the Assyrian helmet was a rounded cone. A gold helmet, ornamental rather than practical, found in a tomb of Ur is molded to the head, even the hair and ears. Greaves are mentioned only in 1 S 17:6 (Goliath), and the Philistines may have used them. As a substitute for metal armor the common soldier may have used leather coats or jackets, perhaps reinforced with metal strips. In the Pauline writings armor is a metaphor in which the Christian virtues are described (Eph 6:14, 17; 1 Th 5:8).

1 Th 5:8	**Eph 6:14 ff**
Coat of mail of faith and love	Coat of mail of righteousness
Helmet of hope of salvation	Helmet of salvation
	Belt of truth
	Shoes of the Gospel
	Shield of the faith
	Sword of the spirit, the word of God

Army. In early Israel the army (Hb *ṣābā'*) was no more than the collection of all the men able to bear arms. In times of danger or invasion the men of the neighborhood were assembled under the clan or tribal leaders, each furnishing his own weapons. The trumpet sounded the call to war; if larger numbers were needed, they were summoned by messenger, but there was no obligation on those summoned to render assistance. The numbers were not large; Gideon* led 300 men against the Midianites* (Jgs 7:6), and the tribe of Dan* counted 600 fighting men (Jgs 18:11). Astronomically high numbers are often found in the OT; these are due not only to their growth in oral tradition, but also to the lack of exact counting and the common inability to estimate the numbers of a crowd; cf also THOUSAND. The total number of Israelite fighting men in the 11th–10th centuries BC is once estimated at 40,000 (Jgs 5:8). The Israelite forces must have been larger than those of the Canaanites, who were superior in discipline and equipment; the governors of Palestinian cities assure the Pharaoh in the Amarna* Letters that the safety of the city will be assured if he sends a garrison of 50. An organized army does not appear in Israel before Saul; its nucleus was a select group of Israelite professional soldiers (1 S 14:52). This royal guard was organized and expanded by David* from the men who had followed him as a bandit chieftain and also by hired foreign mercenaries such as the Kerethi and Pelethi (cf CHERETHITES and PELETHITES). A number of non-Israelite names occur among David's heroes. The army or "host" under Joab was also more strictly organized, although we have few details; one of the purposes of the census of 2 S 24:1 ff was to ascertain Israel's military potential. The division of the host into 12 army corps (1 Ch 27:1 ff) doubtless reflects the original organization, although it is unlikely that each corps had a month's tour of duty during the year; but since the entire host was rarely if ever called out, there must

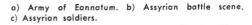
a) Army of Eannatum. b) Assyrian battle scene.
c) Assyrian soldiers.

have been some system of apportioning military service. Excuses from service are enumerated in Dt 20:5–8; 24:5, but this may describe an ideal rather than actual practice. The army was divided into thousands, hundreds, fifties, and tens, each under its own officer; these numbers are technical terms and not enumerations, and could include more or less than the number indicated; cf THOUSAND. Like all ancient armies, Israel divided its forces into light-armed (bowmen and slingers) and heavy-armed troops. The light-armed troops handled missiles and were the mobile units, having only a small shield and no body armor. The heavy-armed troops were infantry lancers with some body armor* and a large shield* and sword*. Chariots* were first introduced under Solomon. The army of Israel under the monarchy compared favorably with that of other western states; according to the records of Shalmaneser III* Ahab* had 2000 chariots and 10,000 infantry at the battle of Karkar in 853 BC.

Arnon (Hb *'arnōn*), a river mentioned frequently as the boundary between Moab to the S and the Amorite kingdom of Sihon*, later Israelite territory, to the N (Nm 21:13 f, 24, 26, 28; 22:36; Dt 2:24, 36; 3:8, 12, 16; 4:48; Jos 12:1 f; 13:9, 16; Jgs 11:13, 18, 22, 26) and hence poetically the stream associated with Moab (Is 16:2; Je 48:20). The Wadi Mojib, the modern name of the Arnon, forms a natural barrier between N and S, but nowhere does the old Eng translation of *nahal* as "brook" seem more grotesque; the Wadi Mojib is a deep and precipitous canyon cut by the stream through the plateau of Moab and it is one of the most impressive natural sights of Palestine. The highway crosses it or rather descends to the bottom about 40 mi S of Amman; at this point the canyon is over two mi wide and about 1300 ft deep. Nearer the exit of the canyon into the Dead Sea the walls of the canyon become perfectly perpendicular to a height of several hundred feet, and separated by barely more than the width of the stream at the bottom.

Aroer (Hb *ᵃrōʿēr*, meaning unknown), a city mentioned several times as lying on the edge of the valley of the Arnon (Dt 2:36; 3:12; 4:48; Jos 12:2; 13:9, 16; 2 K 10:33). It is included in the territory of Reuben in Jos 13:9, 16; 1 Ch 5:8, in the territory of Gad and Reuben in Dt 3:12; on the relation of these two tribes and their territories cf GAD; REUBEN. The town was Israelite in Jephthah's time (Jgs 11:26) and was included in David's kingdom (2 S 24:5). The site is probably Tell Arair, S of Dhiban on the N bank of the gorge of the Arnon. Geographers question whether this is the Aroer intended in Jos 13:25 (attributed to Gad) and Jgs 11:33 (involved in Jephthah's battle with the Ammonites). Jgs 11:26 cannot be questioned, since the speech attributed to Jephthah actually deals with a border dispute between Israel and Moab. Aroer is mentioned in the Moabite stone (ANET 320). Another Aroer nearer Ammon in the territory of Gad is postulated for these verses; but Jos 13:25 may refer to the Aroer on the Arnon, since Gad included the territory of Reuben to some extent. Aroer of Jgs 11:33 may have come into the text from Jgs 11:26. The Aroer of 1 S 30:28 must lie in Judah. The Aroer of Is 17:2, which would lie near Damascus, is very probably the result of corruption of the text and is not found in the LXX.

Arpad (Hb *'arpad*), mentioned several times as captured by the Assyrians in the time of Sennacherib* (2 K 18:34; 19:13; Is 36:19; 37:13; 10:9), threatened in Je 49:23 (of uncertain date). It is always mentioned with Hamath*. It is probably Tell Erfad in Syria, about 19 mi N of Aleppo. Arpad was the capital of a Syro-Hittite kingdom comprising N Syria from Mt Amanus to the Euphrates. With other Syrian kingdoms it accepted Assyria as overlord. Arpad rebelled against Tiglath-pileser III and surrendered after a siege of three years.

Arphaxad (Hb *'arpakšad*), perhaps identical with Akkadian *arrapha*, located near the modern Kirkuk; this geographical or gentilic name appears as a son of Shem in the table of nations* with Elam*, Assyria*, Lud*, and Aram* (Gn 10:22) and in the genealogy of Shem (Gn 11:10 ff). The name, derived from Gn, appears in Jdt 1:1, 5 as a king of the Medes* who founded Ecbatana*; this king is a fictional character.

Arrow. Cf BOW.

Artaxerxes (Hb *'artahšasta'*, from Persian *artakhshatra*, etymology uncertain); the name of 3 Persian kings. Artaxerxes, on the advice of a letter from the Samaritans*, prohibited further work on the temple (Ezr 4:7 ff). Artaxerxes permitted Ezra* and his company to go to Jerusalem (Ezr 7:1 ff; 8:1). Nehemiah* was the butler of Artaxerxes and obtained from him authority to rebuild the walls of Jerusalem (Ne 2:1 ff; 5:14; 13:6). There can be no doubt that the king mentioned by Nehemiah is Artaxerxes I Longimanus (464–425 BC) and the older opinion of scholars put Ezra's career in his reign also; but the many difficulties in the chronology of Ezra-Nehemiah have led many modern scholars to date Ezra about 398 BC and to identify the king mentioned in Ezr with Artaxerxes II Mnemon (404–358 BC).

Artemis (Gk *artemis*, most English versions Diana, the Roman goddess of similar character), mentioned in the Bible only in AA 19:23 ff. Artemis in Gk mythology was the virgin huntress, the sister of Apollo. Originally she was a fertility goddess; this appears from her title "queen of the wild beasts," her patronage of childbirth, and her association with the forests and springs. The Artemis of Ephesus* was an Asian mother goddess. Her image represented her fruitfulness by multiple breasts. Her temple, the *Artemision*, was one of the seven wonders of the ancient world. Demetrius* and his fellow silversmiths made miniature temples and saw in the conversions effected by Paul a threat to their trade; they incited the citizens to a riot in which the lives of Gaius* and Aristarchus*, Paul's companions, were endangered (AA 19:23 ff).

Artemis of Ephesus.

Arvad (Hb *'arwad*, meaning uncertain), a city of Phoenicia; included in the Canaanite genealogy (Gn 10:18; 1 Ch 1:16), associated with Tyre (Ezk 27:8, 11). The site is Ruad, about 95 mi N of Beirut. Arvad, like Tyre, was an island city (about 2 mi off the coast). It established a number of colonies and was the center of a small confederacy. It was in opposition to the Egyptians and furnished the Hittites* a contingent of troops at the battle of Kadesh (1280 BC). From 1125–625 BC Arvad was under the hegemony of Assyria except for brief periods; it paid tribute to Tiglath-pileser I (1114–1076 BC), Ashur-nasir-pal II (888–859 BC), Tiglath-pileser III (745–727 BC), Sennacherib (705–681 BC), Esarhaddon (680–669 BC), and Ashur-bani-pal (668–630 BC). Its submission was not perfect; it furnished troops to the coalition which fought Shalmaneser III at Karkar (853 BC). Ashur-bani-pal notes a rebellion of Arvad and his own installation of a new king; the two events may be related. The city came under Babylonian influence in 604 BC, Persian in 539 BC, Gk in 333 BC, Roman in 64 BC.

Asa (Hb *'āsā'*, meaning uncertain), son and successor of Abijah* as king of Judah (913–873 BC). He removed the fertility cults which had flourished under the protection of his mother Maacah*. When he was attacked by Baasha of Israel he used the wealth of the temple treasure to bribe Ben-hadad* of Damascus* to declare war on Israel; he then destroyed Baasha's fortification of Ramah* and used the materials to fortify Geba* and Mizpeh* (1 K 15:9–24). 2 Ch 14:8 ff adds the account of an invasion of Zerah* the Ethiopian, which was repelled. The same source expands the religious reforms of Asa and attributes them to the inspiration of the prophet Azariah* (2 Ch 15:1 ff). Another prophet, Hanani*, rebuked him for seeking the aid of Ben-hadad (2 Ch 16:7 ff); this is the prophetic policy which Isaiah* later invoked against Ahaz* (Is 7:1 ff). A final criticism of the Chronicler concerns the disease of his feet in the last years of his life, when he sought not Yahweh but the physicians (2 Ch 16:12).

Asahel (Hb *'ªsāh'ēl*, "El has done"), son of David's* sister Zeruiah* and brother of Joab* and Abishai*. In the battle with Abner's forces at Gibeon Asahel pursued Abner; the arms of the hostile commander were the most distinguished of all trophies. Abner warned him not to follow but finally had to kill him (2 S 2:18 ff). Joab later murdered Abner in blood revenge (cf AVENGER). The name is borne by three others in the OT.

Asaph (Hb *'āsāp*, probably abbreviated from *'ēl 'āsāp*, "El has gathered"). The "sons of Asaph" were a Levitical guild of singers. They were among the party who returned to Jerusalem with Zerubbabel* (128 in Ezr 2:41; 148 in Ne 7:44). The guild traced its origin to an eponymous ancestor who was

David's* chief musician (1 Ch 16:5 +) and through him to Levi* through Gershom*. The name appears in the titles of Pss 50; 73–83, where it probably indicates that the Pss belonged to the collection of this guild; cf PSALMS. The name is borne by two others in the OT.

Ascension. The ascension of Jesus is the transfer of His risen, glorious body to "heaven"*, i.e., to the world of the divine; it implies His corporeal survival, His final glorification, His departure from the material universe. P. Benoit has classified the texts which bear upon the ascension under three heads: (1) Texts which affirm the exaltation of Jesus into heaven, specifically to the right hand of the Father, but do not mention the ascension (AA 7:55; Rm 8:34; Eph 1:20; 2:6; Phl 2:9 f; Col 3:1; 1 Pt 1:21; 1 Jn 2:1). Under this heading are included texts which speak of the Parousia*, the coming of Jesus from heaven (Phl 3:20 f; 1 Th 1:10; 4:16; 2 Th 1:7; Tt 2:13; Js 5:7 f; 1 Pt 1:7, 13; 4:13; 5:1; 1 Jn 2:28).

(2) Texts which mention the ascension as a purely theological fact: He ascended far above the heavens that He might fill all things (Eph 4:10); He was taken up in glory (1 Tm 3:16); He sits at the right hand of God (Heb 1:3, 13), who has put everything under His feet (Heb 2:7–9; 8:1; 10:12 f; 12:2). In Heb the ascension is conceived as the entrance of Jesus the high priest into the innermost sanctuary to perform His priestly act of intercession (Heb 4:14; 6:19 f; 7:26; 8:1; 9:24), or His entrance into that which belongs to Him as son (Heb 1:3, 13; 2:7–9). The ascension into heaven and the sitting at the right hand of God are combined in 1 Pt 3:22. The ascension is alluded to in obscure terms in Jn 3:13; 6:61.

By "theological" Benoit means that these texts which affirm the transfer of Christ to heaven as a dogmatic fact, but do not define it as an historical fact in the sense that they fix time and place or relate ocular testimony. In particular both Eph 4:10 and 1 Pt 3:22 imply an ascension which Benoit calls "an ascension of cosmic dimensions." These passages affirm the physical reality of the heavenly triumph of Christ; by the ascension He leaves the earth and the created universe, with no implication of a particular place or time.

The exaltation of Christ and the sitting at the right hand of the Father is a more frequent motif than the ascension as such. The formulation of this belief is undoubtedly affected by the text of Ps 110:1, applied to the exaltation in AA 2:32–34.

(3) Texts in which the ascension is repre-sented as an established historical fact observed by sensible experience. Such texts appear only in Lk 24:50 f; AA 1:9 f. It must be noticed that the event is described with restraint; actually only the departure is observed, and Lk 24:50 differs from AA 1:9 in economy of details; Lk says only that "He parted from them" and does not use the word "ascend" or "was taken up." On this basis some critics have suggested that AA 1:9 f is an expanded account of the event related in Lk 24:50, in which the theological fact of the ascension is added to the event of observation. But the two accounts are more complex than this. Lk 24 in its entirety is composed so as to suggest that all the events from the resurrection to the ascension occur on the same day; AA 1:3 says explicitly that 40 days intervened between resurrection and ascension. The 40 days are very probably a round number; but the interval appears to be supported by the accounts of the Christophanies of the other Gospels, which can scarcely be compressed into a single day. It is therefore likely that Lk 24 is schematic rather than chronological, and this is a feature of his style. Benoit suggests that AA 1:3–11 is a deliberate retelling with more explicit details.

The silence of other NT books on the ascension is remarkable. Outside of 1 Tm 3:16 the ascension as an event is not mentioned in the entire Pauline corpus. In the Catholic epistles it is mentioned only in 1 Pt 3:22. It is not mentioned in Mt at all. The mention in Mk 16:19 occurs in the conclusion which is not original with Mk and appears to be composed from the data given in Lk. The Johannine conception of the ascension is suggested in Jn 20:17 and implied in the entire course of Jn 20–21, and it diverges sharply from the conception of Lk–AA; for the ascension in Jn is conceived as it is in Lk as occurring on the day of the resurrection. Of this ascension there were no witnesses. The Christophanies are therefore conceived as returns of the Risen Christ. It must be noticed that this is the conception implicit in almost all the NT allusions to the exaltation of Christ, which treat the resurrection and exaltation as a single event which completes the victory and earthly career of Jesus and marks the climax of the process of salvation. Benoit points out that there are two ways in which a double tradition and double conception of the ascension appear, in both of which Lk is set in contrast with the other NT writings: (1) The conception of the event as invisible and transcendental, not an object of observation and record but of faith and dogmatic affirmation, in contrast to Lk's conception of an event which is observed; (2) The conception of resurrection-ascension as a single event, in contrast to the 40-day interval of AA. It is suggested above that AA 1:3–11 may be explained as development of Lk 24:50 f; but the Lucan conception of the Ascension as a phenomenon is an original feature which needs some explanation.

Benoit has explained it by the removal of any real contradiction between the Lucan interval of 40 days and an invisible ascension which follows the resurrection immediately. He points out that the essence of the mystery of the ascension is the invisible transcendent accession of Jesus in His physical presence to the world of the divine, which is an object of faith and dogmatic affirmation; no phenomenon could be perceived except the departure. Such an immediate ascension, which implies that the Christophanies were returns, removes the minor but real problem of locating the physical presence of Jesus during the interval. It is also suggested by Jn 14:28, "I go but I return to you," by Mt 28:18, "All power is given me in heaven and on earth," and by Paul's belief that his own vision of the risen Jesus at Damascus was a Christophany of the same kind and equally valid as a qualification for his apostleship (cf APOSTLE) as the Christophanies seen by the Twelve. In Benoit's opinion, then, the "ascension" of Lk 24:50 f; AA 1:3–11 is really the last Christophany.

The account of Lk–AA exhibits some theological features proper to Lk. The "cloud" of AA 1:10 is clearly an allusion to the coming of the Son of Man in the clouds at the Parousia, which will take up where the ascension leaves off. Furthermore, the ascension in Lk–AA is a necessary prelude to the coming of the spirit*; here the theology of the spirit in Lk is identical with the theology of the spirit (Paraclete*) in Jn. That the account is told in terms of the cosmogony of the times, with heaven as the absolute "up" beyond which God dwells, is no more relevant than the same cosmogony in the biblical conception of creation*. Here one must remember Benoit's observation that the essence of the mystery is the transcendental accession of Jesus to the realm of the divine from the sphere of His incarnate life. The ascension is primarily His exaltation and glorification, the sign and seal of His ultimate accomplishment of His mission.

Asenath (Hb 'āsᵉnat, probably Egyptian, "belonging to [the goddess] Neit"), an Egyptian, daughter of Potiphera, priest of On*, wife of Joseph*, mother of Manasseh* and Ephraim* (Gn 41:45, 50; 46:20)

Ashdod (Hb 'ašdôd, called Azotus [Gk azōtos] in the Gk period), one of the five cities of the Philistines*. It is listed with the other four cities in Jos 13:3 (an anachronism) and in the cities of Judah (Jos 15:46 f); this notice cannot be historical, as it is doubtful that the city was ever possessed by Judah. The notice that some of the Anakim* survived there after the conquests of Joshua is likewise doubtfully historical. It was the seat of a temple of Dagon, the scene of the collapse of the image in the presence of the ark* (1 S 5:1–7). It appears elsewhere in lists of the Philistine cities (1 S 6:17) and is with them the object of a number of threatening oracles of the prophets (Am 1:8; Zp 2:4; Zc 9;6). Je 25:20 calls it the remnant of Ashdod, an allusion to its ravages by Assyrians and Egyptians. It was taken and dismantled by Uzziah (2 Ch 26:6). In Am 3:9 most critics read Assyria (with the Gk text) for Ashdod. Is 20:1 ff alludes to a rebellion of Ashdod against Sargon of Assyria in AD 711; more details of the rebellion appear in the records of Sargon (ANET 284, 286–287). Ashdod sought help from Hezekiah* of Judah, but the king refrained from sharing in the rebellion. Ashdod remained loyal during the rebellion against Sennacherib* (ANET 288) and appears as an ally of Esarhaddon* (ANET 291) and Ashur-bani-pal (ANET 294). The king of Ashdod appears in a list of satellite kings of Nebuchadnezzar* of Babylon (ANET 308). Ashdod was the capital of a district in the Persian administration; with others its people opposed Nehemiah's rebuilding of the walls of Jerusalem (Ne 4:1). Ashdod was one of the foreign communities with whom the Jews intermarried in Nehemiah's time (Ne 13:23 f). "The language of Ashdod" to which Nehemiah objected (ibid) was probably Aramaic*. In the Maccabean period the city was hostile to the Jews and was sacked by Judas (1 Mc 5:68) and burned by Jonathan (1 Mc 10:84; 11:4). It was included in Herod's* kingdom. After his death it was granted to Salome as a personal gift from Augustus. It was included in the kingdom of Herod Agrippa*. The region was evangelized by Philip* (AA 8:40). The site is the modern Eshdud, about 19 mi SW of Lydda and halfway between Jaffa and Gaza. It lies near the sea at the confluence of three watercourses from the Shephelah*. In ancient times the city was served by a port which was a satellite city.

Asher (Hb 'āšēr, meaning uncertain), the etymology in Gn 30:13 is popular; son of Jacob* and Zilpah*, the slave of Leah (Gn 30:13), and the name of one of the tribes of Israel. In the blessing of Jacob

(Gn 49:20) and the blessing of Moses (Dt 33:24–25) the tribe is described as very prosperous; but its part in Israelite history was small. Both the location of its territory, near the Phoenician coast N of Carmel, and the notices of Jgs 1:31–32 suggest that the tribe was isolated from the rest of Israel and closely assimilated to the Canaanites; it "stayed by the sea-coast" when summoned by Deborah* and Barak*, although its own territory must have been touched by this war (Jgs 5:17). It is, however, mentioned among the tribes which answered the summons of Gideon (Jgs 6:35; 7:23). The name may be geographical rather than tribal; and the tribe possibly did not become Israelite until some time after the settlement. It was included in one of the administrative districts of Solomon* (1 K 4:16). The name can be probably identified in an Egyptian document from the time of Merneptah (1234–1220 BC), possibly also in the time of Ramses II (1301–1234 BC). The name in the Ugaritic* literature has been shown to be based on a misreading.

Asherah (Hb *'ašērāh*, many older English versions "grove"), this is now known to be the name of a Canaanite goddess. In Ugaritic* mythology Asherah, "the Lady of the Sea," was the consort of El, the father of the gods. In the Baal* epic she gives birth to monsters who devour Baal, and opposes the building of a palace for Baal. In the OT, however, she appears as the consort of Baal; most frequently the word signifies a cult object, probably of wood, since it could be planted or cut down. It appears with an altar of Baal in the household of the father of Gideon* (Jgs 6:25 ff), and is mentioned in the reigns of Rehoboam* (1 K 14:23), Asa* (1 K 15:13, erected by the queen mother, Maacah*), Ahab* (1 K 16:33), Jehoahaz* (2 K 13:6), and Manasseh* (2 K 21:7); they were destroyed by Josiah (2 K 23:6 ff). Jezebel* supported 400 prophets of Asherah (1 K 18:19). The object was probably a wooden stake either incised with the symbols of the goddess or fashioned into a crude image. In Israel she seems to have assumed the character and functions of Anath*, Astarte*, and Ishtar in various forms of the myth and ritual of fertility; the numerous references attest the popularity of this superstition in Israel.

Ashima (Hb *'ašîmā'*), a deity worshiped by the colonists from Hamath* whom the Assyrians* settled in Samaria (2 K 17:30). It may possibly be connected with a deity Ashim?-Bethel worshiped by the Jewish colony of Elephantine* in Egypt, and is thought by some scholars to appear in Am 8:14, "the Ashima of Samaria," English versions "the guilt of Samaria."

Ashkelon (Hb *'ašḳᶜlôn*, meaning uncertain), one of the five cities of the Philistines; the list of Jos 13:3 is an anachronism. The notice of its capture by Judah is doubtfully historical (Jgs 1:18). It was raided by Samson (Jgs 14:19). It appears in lists of the Philistine cities (1 S 6:17) and is the object of threatening oracles by the prophets (Am 1:8; Zp 2:4, 7; Zc 9:5). The statement of Je 47:5, 7 that Ashkelon has perished is illuminated by a recently discovered papyrus (cf below).

Ashkelon is mentioned in the Egyptian Execration Texts of the 19th–18th centuries BC (ANET 329), and in the list of Canaanite cities sacked by Merneptah (1230 BC; ANET 378). The king of Ashkelon is accused of disloyalty to the Pharaoh in the Amarna* Letters and writes defending himself (ANET 488, 490). It was the site of an Egyptian temple of Ptah. It was sacked by Ramses II in his Asiatic campaigns (ANET 256). Ashkelon paid tribute to Tiglath-pileser* III of Assyria (ANET 282), who also records a revolt of the city which he suppressed (ANET 283). Sennacherib deposed its king when he refused submission and replaced him by another (ANET 287). It was an ally of Esarhaddon and Ashur-bani-pal (ANET 291, 294). Men from Ashkelon appear in lists of the dependents of Nebuchadnezzar* (ANET 308). An Aramaic papyrus* discovered at Saqqarah in Egypt in 1942 and published in 1948 is a letter from a Palestinian king (the name of the city has been lost) appealing to the Pharaoh for help against the king of Babylon. Scholars attribute this letter to Ashkelon as the most probable source. It was the only coastal city not taken by Alexander Jannaeus (cf HASMONEANS) and thus remained Hellenistic; after the Roman conquest of Palestine it had the status of a free city. The site is Khirbet Askalan, on the coast about halfway between Ashdod* and Gaza*. Ruins of Herodian public buildings can be observed. A sounding was conducted at the site in 1920 under the direction of J. Garstang and W. Phythian-Adams; the debris of Roman and medieval occupation was too thick to permit penetration to the Philistine levels of occupation. Philistine levels were reached in the excavation of 1964 directed by D. N. Freedman.

Ashkenaz (Hb *'aškᵉnāz*, meaning uncertain), in the table of nations* a grandson of Japhet* through Gomer* (Gn 10:3; cf 1 Ch 1:6), mentioned in Je 51:27 with Minni and

Ararat*; a geographical name probably to be located in or near Armenia.

Ashtaroth (Hb *'aštārôt,* derived from the name of the goddess Astarte*, Ishtar), a town of Bashan*, named with Edrei* as the royal residence of Og* of Bashan (Dt 1:4; Jos 9:10; 12:4; 13:12, 31). It is located in the territory of Reuben, Gad, and Manasseh in Jos 13:12, in the territory of Manasseh in Jos 13:31; 1 Ch 6:56. It is included in the Levitical cities of Gershom* (1 Ch 6:56). Ashtaroth Carnaim (Gn 14:5) is probably identical with Ashtaroth; cf CARNAIM. The site is probably Tell Ashtar, E of the Sea of Galilee and 15 mi N of Deraa (Edrei*).

Ashur (Hb *'aššur*), a son of Shem* (Gn 10:22); cf ASSYRIA.

Asia. In 1–2 Mc the name designates the Seleucid* kingdom, which extended after the battle of Ipsos (301 BC) from the Hellespont to the Indus. After the defeat of Antiochus III by the Romans (189 BC) at Magnesia most of the modern Asia Minor was detached from the Seleucid kingdom, but the name in Mc remains (1 Mc 8:6; 11:13; 12:39; 13:32; 2 Mc 8:3; 10:24). The territory taken from Antiochus III was transferred by the Romans to the kingdom of Pergamum*, which then included our Asia Minor W of the Halys. To this kingdom the Romans applied the name of Asia. In 133 BC the kingdom was left to the Romans by the will of Attalus III, the last of the Attalid dynasty, and the Romans established the territory as the proconsular province of Asia. The word in NT designates this province (AA 2:9; 6:9; 16:6; 19:1 ff +; Rm 16:5; 1 Co 16:19; 2 Co 1:8; 1 Pt 1:1; Apc 1:4).

Asiarch (Gk *asiarchēs,* found in AA 19:31 and inscriptions, but meaning not entirely clear). They are thought to be the priests of the cult of Caesar* in the province of Asia, elected each year by the cities of the province to preside over the festival and games in honor of the emperor. They were probably wealthy and influential men, and the title was retained for life. Some of them were friendly to Paul during the riot at Ephesus* (AA 19:31).

Asmodeus. A demon who killed the seven husbands of Sarah*, the daughter of Raguel*, on their wedding night (Tb 3:8). On the advice of Raphael*, Tobias burned some of the heart and the liver of the fish he had caught to expel the demon (Tb 16:13 ff), who was then bound by Raphael in upper

Egypt (Tb 8:1 ff). The name Asmodeus is the Persian Aeshma-Daeva, one of the seven evil spirits. The entire account belongs to the popular character of the romance of Tobias; cf TOBIT.

Asnapper. Cf OSNAPPAR.

Asp. In most Eng versions asp translates Hb *peten,* a venomous serpent mentioned in Dt 32:33; Pss 58:5; 91:13; Jb 20:14, 16; Is 11:8; cf BS 39:30. The *peten* is most probably the Egyptian cobra, now rare in Palestine and only in the S. It has an elongated flattened head (represented on the uraeus serpent head of the crown of the Pharaoh); before it strikes it swells its neck, sways, and rears. The cobra has no external acoustic organ, which is probably alluded to in its designation as "deaf" (Ps 58:5).

Ass. The Bible alludes to both the wild ass or the onager and the domesticated ass. The wild ass is a proverbial example of freedom (Gn 16:12; Jb 39:5–8). It haunts the ruins of abandoned cities (Is 32:14). The political meanderings of Israel are compared to the wandering of the wild ass (Ho 8:9). Yahweh cares for the animal (Ps 104:11). Je 14:16 pathetically describes the suffering of the wild ass during a drought.

The domesticated ass in ancient as in modern times was the most common and most useful animal in the Near East. Its importance is shown by the occurrence of the ass in Israelite law (Ex 20:17; 21:33; 22:3, 8 f; 23:4 +). The ass may not be yoked with the ox (cf YOKE). The ass is generally gray and stands about 3 ft or a little more in height, just enough for a man to ride. It is extremely sure of foot and has a tractable disposition, and can move quite swiftly when it is in the mood. Its powers of carriage are remarkable, and it can move nearly anything that can be loaded on its back. It is also proverbially sluggish, and drivers move it by a constant application of a stick to the rump. The relations of the ass to its owner are depicted with the utmost fidelity in the amusing story of Balaam* (Nm 22:21–33), apart from the fact that Balaam's ass complains about the beating. The ass was ridden both by men and by women (Jos 15:18; Jgs 1:14; 1 S 25:20, 23). It was employed as a beast of burden (Gn 42:26; 45:23; 1 S 25:18 +) and is illustrated in the tomb painting of Beni Hassan (ANEP 3). As a riding animal it was good enough for a king, although Zc 9:9 probably includes the ass as a feature of the messianic king of the poor*. Such passages as Jgs 12:14 suggest that the possession of an ass for riding was a luxury, although it would be a poor peasant who did not have one for working. The ass is also a draught animal (Is 30:24; 32:20) and was used to turn the millstone (Mt 18:6); in modern Egypt it is used to turn the water wheel. The flesh of the animal was unclean and it was eaten only during a desperate famine (2 K 6:25). The ass was not sacrificed (Ex 13:13; 34:20).

Assassins (Lt *sicarii,* "dagger men," mentioned in AA 21:38), extreme nationalist wing of the party of Zealots* who arose during the troubled years AD 50–70. They carried small daggers (Lt *sica*) under their garments and assassinated selected enemies while they mingled with crowds. AA 21:38 indicates the organization of 4000 into a band of brigands. It was probably this group which twice plotted Paul's murder (AA 20:3; 23:12 ff).

Assos (Gk *assos*), a city and seaport of Mysia* in the Roman province of Asia, where Paul met his companions for the voyage to Mitylene (AA 20:13 f). The site is the modern Behram Keui on the NW coast of Asia Minor.

Assyria (Hb *'aššûr,* etymology uncertain). 1. *Name and geography.* The name Ashur belongs primarily to the oldest Assyrian city, situated on the right bank of the Tigris between the upper and the lower Zab, then to the surrounding district, then to the people of the district. The god of the city and the people was also called Ashur; the name of the city may be derived from the god. It lay N of Akkad* and E of Mitanni and close to the Zagros mountains on the E and the mountains of Armenia on the N. The decisive geographical fact is that the district had no natural frontiers and was open to attack on all sides. In its earliest history it struggled for survival against incorporation in larger empires; its later history is an epic of conquest in which its offensive against its neighbors carried it to the limits of the world known to the ancient Semitic peoples. 2. *History.*

I. *Origins and Early Period* (to 1363 BC). The origins of Ashur are obscure. The art of later Assyria presents a distinct "Semitic" type of countenance with characteristic large hooked nose, heavy upper lip, and thick curly hair and beard; it differs not only from the Sumerian countenance but also from that shown in Babylonian art. In the time of Sargon of Akkad (2350 BC) Ashur was probably ruled by Akkadian invaders from the south; it was subject to the kings of the 3rd dynasty of Ur* (2050–1950 BC) and to Isin and Larsa (1950–1830 BC). After the

collapse of Isin and Larsa before Amorite* invaders Assyria gained its independence. The "Cappadocian tablets," discovered at Kültepe in Asia Minor, the ancient Kanish, are written in Old Assyrian and show the existence of large Assyrian commercial colonies in Asia Minor and extensive trade relations between the two regions. Assyria came under the Amorite invaders under Shamshi-Adad I (1749–1717 BC), who in turn was defeated by Hammurabi* of Babylon, and Assyria became a province of the Babylonian empire. In the disintegration of the empire Assyria regained its independence, but lost it again to Mitanni in the 16th century BC; this period, when Mesopotamia was inundated by the barbarian invasion of the Kassites, is extremely obscure.

II. *Middle Period.* The kingdom of Mitanni fell before the Hittites* in the 14th century BC and Assyria regained its independence under Eriba-Adad (1490–1364 BC). His successor Ashur-uballit (1363–1328 BC) installed a vassal king of Babylon. Adad-nirari I (1305–1274 BC), who assumed the ancient title of Sargon of Akkad, "king of the four quarters," laid the foundation of empire by again defeating Babylon, conquering the western trade centers of Harran* and Carchemish, and carrying Assyrian arms into Armenia and the Iranian plateau. Shalmaneser I (1273–1244 BC) continued campaigns in the same directions, again defeating Babylon and suppressing a revolt in Urartu (Ararat*). Assyrian power reached its greatest extent in this period under Tukulti-Ninurta (1243–1207 BC), who moved westward against the now weak Hittite empire. Babylon was once again defeated, and this time it was leveled to the ground. Tukulti-Ninurta replaced its king by an Assyrian governor and took the treasures of the great temple of Esagil and the statue of Marduk* to Assyria. At the peak of his power Tukulti-Ninurta was murdered in the revolt of his son, who was unable to maintain Assyrian strength, and Assyria was shortly reduced to a vassal state of Babylon. The relations between Assyria and Babylon were much like those of Rome and Greece; Assyria felt itself spiritually and culturally inferior to Babylon, which had become the most civilized city of the ancient Near East. Even in its period of greatest growth it sensed itself growing more and more "Babylonian" in its culture. This helps to explain the persistence of Babylon under Assyrian defeats, so that it finally outlived its stronger neighbor. But both cities were submerged in the great barbarian invasions of the 13th–12th centuries BC which caused upheavals in Greece, Asia Minor, Syria, and Mesopotamia. From the middle period survive

Assyrian victory scenes.

extensive fragments of a code of Assyrian law. Compared with the code of Hammurabi the Assyrian law is barbaric in its penalties, and in general shows a much less developed jurisprudence.

III. *Recent Period.* The barbarian invasions left Assyria reduced to a small area around Ashur; but the other great powers were equally reduced or totally destroyed, and Assyria under Tiglath-pileser I (1112–1074 BC) was the first to recover. Tiglath-pileser restored the conquests of the 14th–13th centuries in Babylonia, Armenia, and in the west as far as Syria. He organized these territories more tightly than any of his predecessors and brought to realization the ancient Akkadian ideal of a world kingdom. This ideal endured even under his weaker successors and was an objective for which later and stronger kings could strive. In the W Tiglath-pileser met the Aramaean* immigration from the desert, which he was unable to stem. His successors were much weaker than he and could not prevent the establishment of the strong merchant city-states of the Aramaeans in Syria and Mesopotamia. The destruction of the Aramaean cities became the primary objective of Ashurdan II (932–

912 BC). Adad-nirari II (911–890 BC), Tukulti-Ninurta II (889–884 BC), whose steady attacks prepared the way for the more successful conquests of Ashur-nasir-pal II (883–859 BC) and Shalmaneser III (858–824 BC). Ashur-nasir-pal set himself to restore the boundaries of the earlier empire and to pass them if possible. He conquered Carchemish on the Euphrates and the Aramaean cities between the Tigris and the Euphrates so effectively that there was no revolt there. The conquered territories were organized into provinces and districts under his own officers. He transferred the royal city from Ashur to Calah, on the left bank of the Tigris N of the upper Zab; some scholars believe that this was a move from the cultural influence of Babylon. Calah, fallen into ruins after centuries of abandonment, was rebuilt in magnificence and settled with people from the conquered Aramaean cities. Shalmaneser III (858–824 BC) moved still farther westward and southward. Babylonia as far as the Persian gulf was secure under vassal kings. Some Aramaean cities W of the Euphrates were conquered and Shalmaneser invaded Syria as far S as Damascus; two battles with an Aramaean coalition, Karkar (853 BC) and Hamath (848), were indecisive, but weakened the Aramaeans. Ahab* of Israel was among the allies at Karkar, and Jehu* of Israel paid tribute in 842 BC, together with a number of Aramaean cities which tried thus to buy off further Assyrian invasions. After his successor Shamshi-Adad V (823–810 BC) Assyrian power was retarded and much of the conquered territory was not held effectively; in other parts there were revolts. The weak frontiers of Urartu in Armenia to the N and the Iranian plateau to the E, where a people called the Medes* now appears, were neither now nor later strengthened permanently. In 745 BC a palace revolution in Calah brought Tiglath-pileser* III, a man of unknown origin, to the throne (745–727 BC). He restored Assyrian power to its former limits, made himself king of Babylon in place of the satellite king, and conquered the Aramaean cities of Syria, including Damascus*. The conquered territory was organized as provinces; cities were allowed to keep their satellite rulers, and tribute was demanded from them. Half of the kingdom of Israel was incorporated into the Assyrian province in 734 BC, and tribute was received from Judah. Shalmaneser* V (727–721 BC) devoted his entire reign to suppressing rebellion in the W; he destroyed Samaria* and the remnant of the kingdom of Israel, but died before the surrender. Sargon II (721–705 BC) was not a son of the king, and it is not known how he reached the throne. He held

and consolidated the conquests of Tiglath-pileser, and had little trouble in Syria and Palestine. He finally destroyed the kingdom of Urartu, but did not himself live to see that this opened the northern frontier to barbarian invasion from beyond. In the S a new adversary grew strong; the Chaldean* Marduk-apal-iddin (the biblical Merodach-baladan*) revolted and seized the throne of Babylon. Sargon suppressed the revolt and the Chaldeans fled to the marshes of the Persian Gulf, whence Marduk-apal-iddin was to return. Sargon moved the royal residence to an entirely new city, Dur-Sharrukin, completed only two years before his death, after which it was abandoned. He died in battle and was succeeded by his son Sennacherib (705–681 BC). Sennacherib was met by a general revolt throughout the entire empire. The revolt of the Chaldeans under Marduk-apal-iddin was aided by Elam, and the revolt of Palestine was aided by Egypt. The western revolt was quickly suppressed when Egypt was defeated at Eltekeh; Jerusalem was besieged but not taken, and Hezekiah* was left as a vassal king. The Babylonian revolt required several campaigns, and Elam was defeated; Sennacherib did not, like his predecessors, unite the two kingdoms under himself, but established a satellite king. When rebellion broke out again, Sennacherib solved the Babylonian problem by leveling the famous ancient city to the ground. Sennacherib was assassinated by two of his sons in a palace intrigue (2 K 19:37), but the throne was seized by another son, Esarhaddon*, who pursued and punished the murderers. Sennacherib transferred the royal residence to the old city of Nineveh*, on the left bank of the Tigris a little above Calah, and this remained the royal city until its destruction. Esarhaddon (681–669 BC) had to fight against the Chaldeans in Babylonia, where he rebuilt Babylon. He invaded Egypt, which had long supported revolt in the W; Memphis was sacked (671) and Esarhaddon established 20 satellite kings in Egypt, all of whom were overthrown immediately after the departure of the Assyrians. Esarhaddon died during the campaign to recover Egypt. Before his death he designated his eldest son, Shamash-shum-ukin, as king of Babylon, and a younger son, Ashur-bani-pal, as king of Assyria. The threat from the barbarians of the N and the Medes on the E continued to grow during his reign, but he was unable to do anything about it. Ashur-bani-pal (668–630 BC) continued the campaigns in Egypt and restored Assyrian power; he sacked Thebes and installed a satellite Pharaoh. In several campaigns Elam was totally defeated. But the kingdom was rocked by the revolt of his brother Shamash-shum-ukin of Babylon in 652, who was aided by several disaffected vassals; the revolt was suppressed after four years of costly warfare. After the death of Ashur-bani-pal the end came quickly. Assyria had expended its manpower in a century of world-wide warfare, while the Medes had grown strong and the Chaldeans, safe in the marshes of the "Sealand," had fostered their resources. In 616 BC the two allies began an offensive, and the heartland of Assyria was lost when Nineveh was destroyed in 612 BC. All of the Assyrian cities were so thoroughly leveled that they were never resettled. An Assyrian army under Ashur-uballit established an Assyrian kingdom at Harran but was driven westward by the allies; despite the assistance of the Egyptians under Necho*, it was finally defeated in 609 BC and the Assyrians disappeared from history.

3. *Religion.* Assyrian religion was that of Babylonia, with the exception of its national god Ashur, who gave his name to the city and the people. Ashur was primarily a warrior and a conqueror, whose symbol was an archer within a winged disk. The conquests of Assyria were his victories, and some scholars have explained Assyrian militarism as religiously motivated. He exhibits no characteristics of a nature deity and no consort; he was, in fact, an embodiment and a deification of the nation itself.

4. *Significance.* In biblical studies Assyria is the controlling factor in Israelite history during almost 200 years. Besides this its indirect cultural influences on Israel were numerous and decisive. The cultural dependence of Assyria on Babylon has been noticed. Assyria diffused Babylonian culture through its empire. It created no literature except its annals (cf below), but it is from the library of Ashur-bani-pal that most Akkadian literature has been recovered; besides collecting, the scribes of Ashur-bani-pal also drew up grammatical and lexicographical material on older Akkadian and Sumerian texts, and this has been the most important means of interpreting these languages. Their *limmu* lists, dating each year of a reign by a royal officer's name, are the only consistently reliable scheme of dating all events in the ancient Near East, including Israelite history, for the 9th–7th centuries. The Assyrian royal annals are so great a refinement of the old royal records as to be a new literary form; they are concise but detailed and unfaithful to fact only by omission. They are the only monumental record of the period except for the OT, which is more limited in scope. The annals are supplemented by Assyrian art, one field in which they excelled Babylon. Relief sculpture on a large scale was brought to a point no

other artists had reached; and their eye for detail and their realism have preserved Assyrian garments, weapons, and furniture, as well as similar details for other peoples. Politically they were the first to realize the world state, an ideal which goes back to Sargon of Akkad; had they developed an administrative machinery to compare with their military machine, it would have endured longer. They did not, despite the efforts already mentioned, and had to hold the empire together by force. A part of this force was the calculated frightfulness of their conquests, which we learn from their own records. They intended to weaken resistance and discourage revolt by making horrible examples of rebels and persistent enemies. Hence whole cities were entirely destroyed, kings and their officers were flayed or impaled, whole armies were decapitated and whole populations enslaved. Tiglath-pileser III moderated this somewhat by removing populations from one part of the empire to another, as he removed the Israelites from Samaria and replaced them by colonists likewise displaced. By uprooting them from their soil he hoped that they would become citizens of the one kingdom of Ashur, and within the empire he was successful; the final blows came from outside. Assyria was, at least at first, a frankly plundering empire and exacted heavy tribute; but it also permitted a much more free exchange of goods and peoples over a larger area, and its unification outlasted itself. The Assyrian empire passed intact to the Babylonians and from them to the Persians and then to Alexander*; it came apart only under his successors, but there was a unity of culture even in political separation. The ideal of a world state, that peoples would attain maximum peace and security under a single government, was likewise passed to Alexander and from him to Rome. Thence it lived on in such ideals as the Holy Roman Empire, "Christendom," and in all subsequent efforts to achieve over a continental area what the Assyrians did. The Hebrew prophetic idea of the world kingdom of God did not take definite shape until the Hebrews had seen the world kingdom of Assyria, which threatened to destroy the kingdom of God; and the idea of this kingdom* of God, enunciated in the Gospels, is a basic Christian belief.

Astarte (Hb *'aštōret;* the word was written with the vowels of the word *bōšet,* "shame," "shameful thing," which was to be read instead of the name of the pagan deity). With Anath* and Asherah* Astarte was one of the three Canaanite goddesses of fertility; their characteristics are not usually carefully distinguished. Astarte was in all respects similar to Anath. She was identified with the evening star. Unlike Anath she is mentioned several times in the OT. She is the goddess of Sidon* (1 K 11:5, 33; 2 K 23: 13). The Philistines* had a temple of Astarte (1 S 31:10). The name occurs in the plural with Baal, also in the plural (Jgs 2:13; 10:6; 1 S 7:3, 4; 12:10), which suggests that she was the consort of Baal in the form of fertility cult adopted by the Hebrews. A number of Astarte plaques and figurines have been found in Israelite levels of occupation; Albright believes that those found by him at Tell Beit Mirsim are amulets* worn or carried by women during pregnancy and parturition.

Astrology. The art of divination* by the heavens was incredibly developed in Mesopotamia which has left extensive literature on its interpretation. It is mentioned in the OT only in a poem on the fall of Babylon (Is 47:13). Some scholars render the Aramaic* word *gazrayya* (Dn 2:27; 4:7; 5:7, 11) as astrologers.

Atargatis (Gk *atargatis*), a temple of this goddess is mentioned in Carnaim (2 Mc 12:26). The name is probably a corrupted form of Astarte*. Her cult at Hierapolis in Syria, as described by Lucian, was an extreme form of the Semitic cults of the mother-goddess Ishtar, Anath, and Astarte. Her consort was Attis (Gk Adonis) who killed himself by self-castration; her priests castrated themselves in her honor. The festival was celebrated by sacred prostitution. The goddess was represented with the body of a fish, which is thought to represent her journey through the underworld.

Ataroth (Hb ʿaṭārôt, "sheepfold"?), the name of several towns. **1.** In the territory of Gad* (Nm 32:3, 34); the Moabite Stone (cf MESHA) says that the men of Gad had always inhabited it and that it was built by the king of Israel. Mesha* took it (ANET 320). The site is probably the modern Khirbet Attarus 8 mi NW of Dibon*. **2.** On the NE boundary of Ephraim (Jos 16:7), probably the modern Tell Sheikh ed Diab in the Jordan valley N of Jericho. **3.** On the boundary of Ephraim and Benjamin* (Jos 16:2), called Ataroth Addar in Jos 16:5; 18:13. The site is unknown. **4.** Ataroth Beth Joab in the territory of Judah (1 Ch 2:54). The site is unknown.

Athaliah (Hb ʿaṭalyāh, "Yah[weh] is exalted"?), daughter of Ahab* and Jezebel* and wife of Jehoram*, king of Judah (2 K 8:18, 26). After her son Ahaziah* was killed by Jehu* she murdered all the royal family except the infant Joash who was saved by his sister Jehosheba and hidden in the temple by the priest Jehoiada*. After Athaliah had reigned six years (842–837 BC) Jehoiada won over the loyalty of the royal guard and proclaimed Joash* king in the temple, after the doors had been secured. Athaliah was unable to escape or summon help and was led out of the temple and executed (2 K 11:1 ff), and her temple of the Baal was destroyed and its priest Mattan killed.

Athens (Gk *athēnai*), a city of Greece located in Attica, the peninsula which forms the SE extremity of the mainland of Greece. The city lay in ancient times about 5 mi from its harbor, the Piraeus. The "Long Walls" which joined Athens and the Piraeus in a single fortified enclosure in the 5th century BC did not exist in NT times. The city faces the Saronic Gulf to the SW and is almost entirely ringed by mountains to the E and N. The modern city of Athens occupies the same site but is larger by far than Athens of ancient times.

The city was visited by Paul almost by accident; he awaited his companions there after their expulsion from Berea* and before their journey to Corinth*. He found a synagogue there and was moved by the many religious buildings and images of the city to dispute in the *agora* or market*. He was heard by philosophers of the Epicurean and Stoic schools and was invited to address them formally at the Areopagus*. His discourse, much more formal and erudite than his usual style, was not impressive, and only a few men and women were convinced (AA 17:10–34). There is no further record in the NT of a Christian community at Athens.

Although settlement on the site of Athens goes back to the Neolithic period, the city does not appear in history until the 7th century BC. During the Persian wars Athens emerged as the leading Gk city and reached its peak as a leader in politics and creative culture during the 2nd half of the 5th century. The Athens which Paul visited was not the great city which produced so much in literature and the arts; it had not enjoyed political liberty since Philip of Macedon defeated it (337 BC) and had been sacked by Sulla in the early 1st century BC. But it was the city which Romans regarded as the center of philosophy and the arts and the city wherein any one who wished a genuine education must study.

Many of the remains which are now visible in Athens represent structures which were in existence in the 1st century AD; in particular, the religious buildings and art which attracted Paul's attention have survived to

a) Athens, Acropolis. b) Odeum of Herodes Atticus.

a notable extent. These include the Acropolis with the Parthenon, the Erechtheum, the temple of Victory, and the great stairs and gateway on the W called the Propylaea. The hill of the Acropolis rises steeply above the city to a height of 512 ft and despite the ruined condition of the structures is one of the most impressive sights of the world. At the foot of the Acropolis were the temple of Asclepios the healer, the theatre of Dionysius and the Odeum of Pericles. The temple of Zeus Olympios, the largest temple of Greece, lay SE of the Acropolis; although it was begun in 530 BC, it was still unfinished when Paul saw it. The *agora* or marketplace lay N of the Acropolis and has been excavated by the American School of Classical Studies in a series of campaigns since 1930. The level uncovered by these excavations represents the *agora* as it was constructed in the 3rd–2nd centuries BC, the *agora* which Paul saw. It is a large level area covering several acres which was almost completely enclosed by stoas or colonnades; from one of these, the Stoa Poikile, the Stoic school of philosophy received its name. On the E side stood the great Stoa of Attalus of Pergamum*, restored by the American

School after the recent excavations. Two smaller stoas stood on the S side and another great stoa, the Stoa of Zeus Eleutherios, on the W. The Stoa Poikile (many-colored) probably stood on the N side, where excavation was impossible. To the W of the *agora* stands the Theseum, one of the best preserved Gk temples. The *agora* was extended to the E by benefactions of Julius Caesar and Augustus*; the area contained many shops and arcades and is now called the Roman *agora*. The *agora* contained buildings for public business and numerous temples dedicated to Apollo, Aphrodite, Hephaestus, the Mother of the Gods, and Ares. On the place where Paul spoke cf AREOPAGUS.

No inscription "to an unknown god" (AA 17:23) has been found at Athens. The geographer Pausanias, however, mentions similar inscriptions at Athens and at Olympia, and a fragmentary inscription which probably contains the phrase has been found at Pergamum. An inscription to an unnamed god or goddess has been found at Rome. The inscription mentioned in AA 17:23 is not therefore unparalleled in Gk and Roman cities.

Atonement (Eng *at-one-ment*, "bringing together"), theologically it includes the ideas of expiation for sin and reconciliation of man with God.

1. *OT*. The key word for atonement is Hb *kappēr* and its derivatives, which means etymologically to cover, to conceal the offending object and so to remove the obstacle to reconciliation. In the cultic ritual the word is used in a technical sense, to make an act of atonement, which is accomplished by the application of the blood of the victim (cf SACRIFICE). The priest makes an act of atonement for himself or for another or for all Israel, or he makes an act of atonement for sin or guilt. This is the first step in reconciliation and Yahweh Himself takes the second; "he makes an act of atonement — and he is forgiven" (Lv 4:20, 31; Nm 15:25 +). The gold plate of the ark of the covenant* was the "place of atonement," *kappōret*, the place where Yahweh receives atonement. Outside of the Levitical code the word used of Yahweh Himself means to receive an act of atonement (Pss 78:38; 79:9; Ezk 16:63; Je 18:23). The effect of the act of atonement is defined by the metaphorical use of the word in Is 28:18, "your covenant with death will be *voided;*" so the sin or guilt for which atonement is made is voided and annulled, it is no longer an effective obstacle to reconciliation. One may also be reconciled by the payment of a fine or damages, *kōper;* but this leads into the pattern of ransom and redemption, which is not the same as that of atonement.

2. *NT*. Of the Gk words for *kappēr* and its derivatives the following are the most important which appear in the NT.

hilaskesthai, hilasmos, hilastērion: in classical Gk to reconcile or render favorable, reconciliation, the means of reconciliation. This use of *kappēr* is illustrated in Gn 32:20, where Jacob says of Esau, "Perhaps I will render his countenance favorable." The word *hilaskesthai* in Lk 18:13; Heb 2:17, is used in the OT sense of *kappēr*. Christ Himself is *hilasmos*, reconciliation for our sins, and for this the Father has sent Him (1 Jn 2:2; 4:10). God has set Him (or displayed?) as *hilastērion*, the means of reconciliation in His blood (Rm 3:25); the language indicates that God has made him a sacrifice of atonement.

katharizein, katharismos: in classical Gk, to cleanse, used for the ritual cleansing of the mystery cults; the LXX use introduces a new metaphor into *kapper*. But *kapper* is reflected in 2 Co 7:1; Eph 5:26, and especially in Heb 9:22–23; 1 Jn 1:7, 9, where "atone for sin" has become "cleanse from sin." Heb 1:3, making *katharismos* of sins, must be translated making atonement. *aphairein:* classical Gk, to take away, but in no religious use; to take away sins, Rm 11:27; Heb 10:4.

katallasso, katallagē: classical Gk "reconcile," "reconciliation" but not in LXX. We are reconciled to God (Rm 5:10; 2 Co 5:20); God reconciles us and the world to Himself in Christ (2 Co 5:18–19). We receive reconciliation through Christ (Rm 5:11). The apostles* have the ministry and the message of reconciliation (2 Co 5:18–19). The rejection of the Jews could be the reconciliation of the world (Rm 11:15). In these words the idea of the ritual act of atonement is suppressed. It is to be noted that except for Rm 11:15 these words appear in only two contexts. God is the agent of reconciliation but not of atonement, which is the act of Christ as the representative of men. This is seen most clearly in Heb, where the priesthood and sacrifice of Christ are compared with the priesthood and sacrifice of Aaron, who performed the act of atonement for the people (cf FORGIVENESS).

Atonement, Day of (Hb *yōm hakkipŭrīm*), the 10th day of the 7th month; the ritual is described in Lv 16:1 ff; cf Lv 23:26 ff; Nm 29:7 ff. The priest, dressed in linen vestments, takes two goats as a sin-offering and a ram as a burnt-offering for the community, and a bullock as a sin-offering for himself. Lots are cast for the two goats; one is for Yahweh, one for Azazel*. Atonement is made by applying the blood of the sin-offerings to the furniture of the sanctuary and the altar. He then lays his hands on the goat for Azazel and confesses the sins of Israel, and the goat thus laden symbolically with the national guilt is expelled into the desert. The priest then changes his vestments and offers the whole-burnt sacrifices. The atoning agent is the blood of the victim, which symbolizes life. Only in this ceremony was the sacrificial blood applied to the inner Sanctuary, the Holy of Holies. The day was also celebrated by a fast and a sabbatical rest.

Attalia (Gk *attaleia*), a seaport city on the coast of Pamphylia, the modern Adalia, founded by Attalus II, king of Pergamum 159–138 BC, from which Paul sailed to Antioch to conclude his first missionary journey (AA 14:25).

Attalus (Gk *attalos*), one of the kings to whom the Romans addressed a circular letter warning against attacks on the Jews (1 Mc 15:22); king of Pergamum in Asia Minor, either Attalus II (159–138 BC) or Attalus III (138–133 BC).

Augustus. Gaius Octavius (cognomen unknown), nephew of Gaius Julius Caesar. After Caesar adopted him as his heir he took the name of Gaius Julius Caesar Octavianus. In the civil wars which followed the assassination of Caesar Octavianus was finally triumphant in 31 BC and ruled Rome until his death in AD 14. The title Augustus (venerable) was granted him by the Senate in 27 BC. He refused the title of king, but ruled through his control of the Senate and his office as tribune and proconsul of the provinces where legions were stationed. Jesus was born during his rule (Lk 2:1; cf CENSUS; JESUS CHRIST). All succeeding emperors retained the title of Augustus. He was a patron of Herod* the Great, at first a follower of Antony, and Augustus confirmed him as king of the Jews.

Avenger. In the nomadic society of the desert there were no police or courts and the individual man could not defend himself. Hence the rights of the person were under the protection of his family and clan, each of whom was obliged to defend his kinsman or to avenge him. The Hb *gō'ēl*, "avenger," covers this complex of duties. Life and bodily integrity were protected by the assurance that the nearest kinsman would seek out the killer or the assailant. The obligation arose as soon as the death or injury was known and no further legal process took place. Naturally if the group to which the

killer belonged thought the revenge was unjust they would avenge in turn; and thus arose the feud or vendetta, which could lead to the extinction of entire groups.

The unrestricted custom of vengeance does not appear in Hb law. In the earliest laws, the code of the covenant limits the vengeance to the damage inflicted (Ex 21:23–25) and does not permit life to be taken in revenge for injury. The law is still further regulated (Nm 35:10 ff; Dt 19:1 ff; Jos 20:1 ff) by a distinction between accidental homicide and murder*; the homicide may flee to designated cities of refuge where his guilt may be determined; revenge for murder is left to the avenger of blood. Excessive vengeance is threatened in the song of Lamech* (Gn 4:23–24), the descendant of the first murderer, Cain*, who demands "seventy and sevenfold," i.e., unlimited revenge. The problem of revenge within the family itself was settled by David in the fictitious case of the woman of Tekoa (2 S 14:5 ff) by the principle that blood revenge has no place in the family, since it would consume itself; it is intended to protect the family from external aggression. From this it appears that the obligation of the *gō'ēl* is directed less to the protection of the individual than to the preservation of the group. This appears also in the obligation of the *gō'ēl* to purchase landed property of his kinsman in order to keep it within the family; if a man were forced to sell his land, the next of kin had the first opportunity to buy. Custom permitted him to pass the obligation to the next of kin after him (Lv 25:25 ff). The operation of this law is seen in Rt 4:3 ff; Je 32:6 ff. The law of the levirate*, which obliged a man to marry his brother's widow if his brother died childless, is also a form of the obligation of the *gō'ēl*. Hence the law of "revenge" is really a statement of the wider duty of each man to support his nearest of kin and thus to protect the family and clan from extinction.

It is against this social background that we find Yahweh called the *gō'ēl* of Israel or the Israelite 35 times in the OT, especially in Is 40–55. The translation "redeemer" or "redemption" fails to bring out the appeal to Yahweh as the next of kin who has the duty of protecting his clan and its individual members. The kinship thus invoked does not rest upon any physical relationship, but upon the covenant by which Yahweh has made Israel His own.

Awwim (Hb *'awwîm*), a pre-Israelite tribe of Canaan living in the neighborhood of Gaza* in territory later occupied by the Philistines* (Dt 2:23; Jos 13:3). The inclusion of the name among the cities of Benjamin* (Jos 18:23) is difficult, and some suspect that the text is corrupt.

Axa. Cf ACHSAH.

Ayin (Hb *'ayin*), the 16th letter of the Hb alphabet. The sound, written ', is not heard in English; it is close to a *g* pronounced gutturally.

Azariah (Hb *'azaryāh, '''zaryāhû,* "Yahweh helps"). **1.** King of Judah better known as Uzziah*. **2.** A companion of Daniel* who received the Babylonian name of Abednego*. With Daniel he was taken into the court of Nebuchadnezzar* (Dn 1:6 ff) and passed the test of fasting. With Shadrach* and Meshach* he was cast into the fiery furnace and escaped unharmed (Dn 3:12 ff). This popular name was borne by 20 others in the OT.

Azazel (Hb *'azā'zēl,* meaning and etymology unknown). On the Day of Atonement* the high priest* confessed the sins of the people while imposing his hands upon a goat (Lv 16:21). This "scapegoat" was then expelled into the desert "to Azazel" (Lv 16:8, 10, 20, 26). The symbolism of expelling the guilt-laden goat from the community needs no explanation; but the name Azazel is not explained. In the opinion of most scholars it is the name of a demon who inhabits the desert; such allusions to popular belief in demons* are found elsewhere in the OT. The origin and antiquity of the rite are unknown, nor is it known why the guilt-laden animal should be sent to this demon. G. R. Driver, however, translates the word as "precipice," with no demonic significance.

Azekah (Hb *'azēkāh*), a town of Judah (Jos 15:35) near the site of the battle of Joshua with the five Canaanite kings (Jos 10:10 f). and the camp of the Philistines* in their invasion against Saul (1 S 17:1). Azekah was fortified by Rehoboam* (2 Ch 11:9) and was one of the towns settled after the exile* (Ne 11:30). During Nebuchadnezzar's campaign it was one of the last cities of Judah to fall (Je 34:7). Its capture is perhaps alluded to in the Lachish* Letters; the writer observes that they are watching the signals of Lachish but can no longer see the signals of Azekah (ANET 322). The site is Tell Zakariyeh in the Shephelah*; it lies in the valley of Elah 7 mi NNE of Beit Jibrin. The site was excavated by F. J. Bliss in 1898; a fortified citadel with eight towers was found at the highest point of the mound, but the structures were not dated by the excavators. Possibly the fortifications are to be attributed to Rehoboam.

B

Baal (Hb *ba'al*, "lord" in the sense of owner or master, e.g., of a wife, a slave, a piece of property.) Most commonly it is a divine appellative (not a personal name) and as such appears as a component in many personal and local names. Baal worship appeared early in Israel; the Israelites worshiped the Baal-Peor of Moab (Nm 25:1 ff). It is

A Syrian representation of Baal brandishing the thunderbolt from Ugarit.

mentioned several times in Jgs, and Gideon tore down an altar of the Baal in his father's household (Jgs 6:28). Several of the kings of Israel and Judah permitted or patronized the cult of the Baal. It is mentioned by the prophets Hosea, Zephaniah, Jeremiah. To worship the Baal is to "serve" him, to "walk after" him, or to "commit fornication after" him. The Baal had prophets (1 K 18:19 ff; Je 2:8 +). The symbol of the Baal was the *massēbāh*, an upright stone pillar of uncertain character (2 K 3:2; 10:26 +). It may have been raw unhewn stone or possibly a crude image; in any case, it was most probably a phallic symbol. The Baal was worshiped on the high* places. Frequently the OT speaks of Baals in the plural; this does not indicate that the Baal was a local god to be found in each city; like so many ancient gods, the Baal took a number of forms and was worshiped in a special way or under some special title in a number of places. That he was a dispenser of fertility

is clearly indicated in Ho 2:2–13. This passage also indicates that Yahweh was sometimes given the attributes of the Baal and worshiped with the rites of the Baal. Hence the large number of Israelite names compounded with Baal found in the ostraka* of Samaria do not necessarily indicate Baal worship.

The character of the Baal cult has been much illuminated by the discovery of the Canaanite mythological tablets of Ugarit*. The title Baal, "lord," was applied to several gods; but when used without further qualification it signified the storm-god Hadad* (Akkadian Adad or Addu). In the Ugaritic texts he has the title Aliyan, "he who prevails" (Albright). As the storm-god who rules the weather he is the giver of fertility. The myth of the death and resurrection of Baal represents the annual cycle of the cessation and return of fertility; by the ritual enactment of the myth the recurrence of the cycle is assured. The extensive fragments of Ugarit show that the character of both the gods and the myth was fluid. Baal is killed by the monsters spawned by Asherah*. His consort Anath* attacks and kills his adversary Mot (death); perhaps another form of the myth contained the killing of Baal by Mot. The death of Mot restores Baal to life, but then Baal himself enters into mortal combat with Mot. Anath and Baal then obtain from El, against the wishes of Asherah, a palace for Baal like that of the other gods; the symbolism is obscure, but it probably represents the annual return of fertility. The inconsistency is only apparent; each of the adversaries is always dying and prevailing in turn. There are also references to a combat between Baal and various draconic monsters, Yam (Sea), and the biblical Tannin and Lotan (cf LEVIATHAN). These must be forms of the dragon of chaos subdued by the creative deity (cf CREATION). The ritual enactment of the myth no doubt included the sexual union of Baal and his consort, represented by a priest and a priestess, and sexual union of the worshipers with the goddess represented by the sacred prostitutes; by this sexual union they participated in the divine power of fertility.

Baalism was a danger to Israelite belief not merely because of its obscenities but also because it was nature worship which reduced Yahweh to the level of a personified natural force and made religion no more than a means of securing the good of nature. Ultimately the cult was a denial of any moral values or of any transcendental reality.

Baal-hazor. Cf HAZOR.

Baalis (Hb *ba'alīs,* etymology unknown), king of Ammon* at the fall of Jerusalem in 587 BC, who sent Ishmael* and his band to murder Gedaliah* and furnished them asylum (Je 40:14 ff), intending thus to disrupt the Judahite community which had survived the disaster. He was successful; the survivors fled to Egypt (Je 42:1 ff).

Baalzebub. Cf BEELZEBUB.

Baanah (Hb *ba'anāh,* etymology uncertain), with his brother Rechab* a guerrilla commander of Ishbaal*, son and successor of Saul*. Observing David's growing success, Baanah and Rechab murdered Ishbaal in his house and took his head to David, expecting a reward; but David executed them (2 S 4:1 ff). Their crime, however, hastened the accession of David to the throne of all Israel (2 S 5:1 ff).

Baasha (Hb *ba'šā',* etymology uncertain), son of Ahijah of Issachar, king of Israel 900–877 BC. He came to the throne by the assassination of Nadab*, son of Jeroboam* I, and murdered the entire family of Jeroboam. He established his royal city at Tirzah*. He was at war with Asa* of Judah for his entire reign and was at first successful; but when he blockaded Jerusalem by the fortification of Ramah*, Asa subsidized Benhadad* of Damascus* to invade Israel on the N. Baasha was rebuked for his impiety by the prophet Jehu ben Hanani (I K 15:16–22; 15:33–16:7).

Babel, Tower of. In Gn 11:1–9 is related the story of a great tower erected in the land of Shinar* and left unfinished because Yahweh confounded the speech of the builders; the city was therefore called Babel or "confusion" (from Hb *bālal,* "to mix, confuse"). Hb *bābel* represents Akkadian *bab-ilu,* Babylon. As an account of the origin of the diversity of languages the story is evidently imaginative, and the etymology *bālal-bābel* is popular. The tower is now recognized as a ziggurat, the tower which customarily stood next to a Mesopotamian temple. The tower of Babylon was called Etemenanki, "house of the foundation of heaven and earth," and was attached to Esagil, "house of the raising of the head," the temple of Marduk. Only the foundation plan of the ziggurat was discovered by the modern explorers; it was a square about 230 ft on a side. Some scholars

Reconstruction of temple tower of Esagil, Babylon.

Remains of Mesopotamian temple tower.

think that the altitude equaled the side of the base. The appearance of the ziggurat must be conjectured from a few more extensive remains and from cuneiform plans and the description of Herodotus. According to this evidence the ziggurat was constructed in an odd number of stages, three, five or seven. Etemenanki, according to Herodotus, was built in seven stages, each with a different color of brick. On the summit was a small shrine. Access was gained by stairs or ramps or a combination of both, but their construction is uncertain. The symbolism of the ziggurat is also uncertain. It has been suggested that it was, like the Egyptian pyramid, the tomb of the god or of the king; this is not well supported. More probable is the interpretation of the ziggurat as the cosmic mountain, symbolic of the earth itself; Mesopotamian seals represent a god emerging from the cosmic mountain. Not entirely unrelated to this view is the interpretation of the ziggurat as the divine mountain, the seat of the gods. It has also been regarded as an artificial mountain, built by the first settlers of the plain, who had been accustomed to worship on "high places" in their native mountains. The mountain then becomes the link between heaven and earth, by which man ascends to the gods and the gods descend to manifest themselves on the peak. This view finds some support in Gn 11:4, "a tower which shall reach to the heavens," and is perhaps suggested in the dream of Jacob (Gn 28:11–19). In historic times the symbolism of the ziggurat was no doubt already too complex for analysis and probably included some or all of the features indicated.

Babylon, Babylonia (Hb *bābel,* Akkadian *bab-ilu,* probably "gate of the gods").

1. *Geography and description.* The city of Babylon lay on the left bank of the Euphrates, not far S of the modern Baghdad, where the Tigris and the Euphrates approach each other most closely. The classical name of Babylonia, derived from the city, corresponded geographically to the ancient Akkad*. It is a broad alluvial plain whose soil is enriched by the silt of the two rivers; but their floods are devastating unless they are controlled by canals and reservoirs. These were constructed in prehistoric Babylonia. The slower and more meandering Euphrates is much more easily navigable than the Tigris, a factor which early drew the cities of the region together.

Babylon the city was excavated by Koldewey under the auspices of the Deutsches Orientgesellschaft (1899–1917), and some of the grandeur of the city so much admired by the ancients was revealed. The area of the ruins was roughly 1½ sq mi; the "new city," an expansion built by Nebuchadnezzar on the right bank of the Euphrates, is on the left bank of the present course of the stream. The city was defended by a double wall; beyond this Nebuchadnezzar built another and much more extensive wall. A number of canals passed through the city. There were eight gates, each of which opened into a broad avenue; the intersecting avenues divided the city into quarters. The Euphrates was crossed by two bridges. The city contained 53 temples, of which the greatest was Esagil, the temple of Marduk*, with its temple tower or ziggurat, the tower of Babel*. In this temple stood the statue of Marduk, from

The Ishtar gate.

Victory Stele of Naram-Sin.

each, which have been accepted as the substructure of the "Hanging Gardens," one of the seven wonders of the ancient world.

2. *History*. Babylon is mentioned for the first time by Sargon of Akkad (c 2350–2294 BC). The city was unimportant until the first dynasty of Babylon was established by the Amorites under Sumu-abum (1830 BC). Under this dynasty, and especially under Hammurabi* (1728–1686 BC), Babylon reached its first period of glory. Successful wars against Larsa, Elam*, and Assyria* united Sumer and Akkad under his rule, which extended nearly to the Mediterranean on the west. Letters to his governor Siniddinam at Larsa show that Hammurabi created a closely administered bureaucratic state which provided internal peace and security and allowed commerce and the arts to flourish. His codification of law is of special interest for biblical studies (cf HAMMURABI; LAW). The empire of the Amorites fell to pieces under the invasion of the Kassites, who succeeded them as kings of Babylon. The Kassite period, about 1530–1160 BC, is a dark period culturally, politically and historically for Babylon, and of it there are few records; but the ascendancy of Babylon as a cultural center had been so firmly established under Hammurabi that it was never lost. Politically Babylon remained weak until the 7th century BC. Assyrian expansion moved first in its direction and during the centuries of Assyrian empire Babylon was a vassal kingdom; for most of the period 745–626 BC it was united with Assyria in a dual monarchy under the Assyrian king.

The Chaldean* phase of the history of Babylon begins at the time of the invasion of the Aramaeans*, with whom they were connected. They paid tribute to the Assyrian overlord but were never effectively controlled. Under the weak rulers who preceded Tiglath-pileser* III they became the real masters' of Babylonia; but Tiglath-pileser drove them to the S and himself took the throne of Babylon. The Chaldean chief, Marduk-apaliddin (biblical Merodach-baladan*), himself seized the throne of Babylon in 721 BC and in alliance with Elam defeated Sargon of Assyria; although he was later driven S and Babylon was sacked, he continued to harass the Assyrians into the reign of Sennacherib. In 626 BC another Chaldean chief, Nabopolassar (Nabu-apil-usur), governor of the "sea lands," seized the throne of Babylon and revolted against the Assyrians. Nineveh fell to the Babylonians and the Medes in 612 BC and the last Assyrian king established his royal seat at Harran*; he was supported by the Pharaoh Necho of Egypt. He was defeated at Harran and moved westward; no more is related of

whom the king received his royalty each year when he "took the hands of Marduk" at the New Year* festival. This famous statue was removed by the Kassites in the 17th century BC and later returned by them, removed again by the Assyrian Tukulti-Ninurta (1243–1207 BC) and returned after 66 years, removed again by the Elamite Kutur-Naḥḥunte about 1176 BC and brought back by the Babylonian Nebuchadnezzar I about 1130 BC. It was brought to Nineveh by Sennacherib* of Assyria in 689 BC and restored to Babylon after 21 years by Esarhaddon. These adventures show not only the political rise and fall of Babylon but also the importance of the possession of the statue by one who claimed kingship over the land of Marduk. In the temple were shrines or cells for the statues of the other gods which were carried in procession with Marduk in the New Year festival from Esagil to the *bit akitu*, "new year house," outside the walls; the Ishtar gate, decorated with genii, through which the procession passed, was discovered by the excavators. The ruins of the great palace of Nebuchadnezzar contained what appeared to be two rows of seven vaulted chambers him. The Babylonian army, now under the command of Nebuchadnezzar*, defeated the Egyptians at Carchemish in 605 BC and in successive campaigns during the ensuing years pushed through Syria and Palestine. Nebuchadnezzar succeeded his father Nabopolassar on the throne in 605 BC, the year of his victory at Carchemish. Jerusalem surrendered to the Babylonians in 597 BC; it revolted in 588 BC and was stormed and destroyed in 587 BC. In the long reign of Nebuchadnezzar (605–562 BC) Babylon, the heir of the Assyrian empire, attained the high point of its glory. His successors were unable to maintain the empire. Nabonidus (556–539 BC) spent much of his reign in Teima in Arabia, possibly attempting to secure his empire by conquests of the Arabian tribes, and left Babylon under his son Belshazzar* as regent. He alienated the priesthood of Marduk, and when Cyrus of Anshan, who had deposed the king of the Medes in 550 BC, defeated Belshazzar in battle, the city was surrendered to him by treachery without any further defense. The city remained an important administrative center under the Persians, but after the Greek conquest it sank into insignificance.

3. *Religion.* Babylonian-Assyrian religion is a syncretism of very considerable elements from Sumerian* religion and of diverse Semitic elements. It is polytheistic; there are at least 3300 divine names in Akkadian literary remains, many of which are different names of the same deity. The gods are represented in human form, larger than men and immortal; in art they are designated by the horned cap. They are divided into two great groups, the celestial gods (*Igigi*) and the terrestrial gods (*Anunnaki*). We can mention only some of the principal deities, some of them treated under special articles.

The cosmic triad is composed of Anu, the god of the heavens, Enlil (Bel*), the god of the upper air, and Ea, the god of the watery abyss. In historic times Anu (whose sign is the sign for "god" simply) already has receded in importance. The astral triad is composed of Sin, the moon god, Shamash, the sun god, and Ishtar, identified with the planet Venus. Sin was worshiped at Ur* and Harran, both mentioned in the traditions of Abraham*. Sin is a god of destiny. Shamash is a patron of law and justice. Cf HADAD; DAGON; MARDUK; NEBO.

Babylonian religion believed in the existence of both good and bad demons*, whose malicious work could be either invoked or frustrated by magic.* It also believed in the discernment of the future by divination*. The gods were present in the temples* in their images*, and there sacrifice* was offered, and hymns (cf PSALMS) and prayers* were addressed to them. The king* was representative of the divine government, and he received his power to rule from the gods. He was also the chief priest*, but the specialized function of worship was committed to the priests. The kingship was renewed annually at the feast of the New Year*, which also was a renewal of creation*.

In general, Babylonian-Assyrian religion was a worship of nature, and most of the gods are personified natural forces, especially the forces of fertility. Many of the gods, however, have no such nature character in the form in which we know them; and many of them appear as patrons of a city. In Ashur and Marduk, at least, we seem to have the worship of the national genius. But Babylonian religion never rose to the knowledge of a god who really transcends the powers of nature or of the human person. Furthermore, it was disfigured by the gross superstitions of demonology and divination. In spite of the sometimes noble moral sentiments of its hymns, its moral force was slight. In the last analysis it was a religion of this world and its goods; it promised its worshipers nothing more and demanded of them nothing except the performance of the ritual.

4. *Importance.* The contributions of Babylonia to civilization are many and fundamental. The Babylonians adapted the cuneiform* writing of the Sumerians to their own language and produced an extensive literature, although little of any merit. Their mythology and hymns depend to a large extent on Sumerian originals, which are now often available for comparison; but they were more than mere imitators. Of particular interest for biblical studies are the creation* epic, the epic of Gilgamesh*, which contains an account of a universal deluge*, the poem "I will praise the lord of wisdom," which takes up the problem of suffering (cf JOB), and the "penitential psalms," which have some resemblance to certain Hb psalms. The vast literary remains of magic and divination are a pathetic monument to ingenious superstition. The scribes compiled extensive grammatical and lexicographical tablets. Babylonia did not produce history; but the Babylonian Chronicle and the "Synchronistic History," which correlates the kings of Babylon and of Assyria, are primary historical sources.

Babylonia is the cradle of civilization, although here also the Semites were the heirs and improvers of Sumerian institutions. Here men lived in cities, with the diversified specialization of arts, crafts, and trades which freed each family from the food quest as its principal occupation. The cities of Babylonia were governed by law with courts and police and protection for the basic human rights; these institutions, of course, were imperfectly developed and subject to abuse. The family was the social, economic, and legal unit. Transactions were governed by a law of contract; private property was guaranteed, including landed property. Slavery* was accepted, but its administration in Babylonia was relatively humane. The city-state was a closely organized political unit under a monarchic king, the viceroy of the god; but the popular will was effective through its representatives. Some modern scholars have described this society as "primitive democracy." Manufacture and commercial exchange of goods were carried on in peace and security. The Mesopotamian policy failed in securing peace between its cities and in the organization of its own and conquered territories into a larger political unit. Ultimately this failure was the cause of its ruin.

Science existed only in practical applications, but these were important. The pseudoscience of astrology created a remarkably advanced observation of the heavens and a practical calendar*. Mathematics advanced to the calculation of area and volume. In building and monumental art the Babylonians were surpassed by the Assyrians; but this is largely due to the absence of stone and the use of brick. In such things as seals, jewelry, and personal ornaments the Babylonian craftsmen exhibited a very high technique. Conservatism and stylization imposed limits upon the originality of the artist.

Bacchides (Gk *bakchidēs,* "son of [the god] Bacchus"), a royal officer, "king's friend," of the Seleucid court of Syria* under Demetrius* I Soter, and governor of the territory W of the Euphrates. After Demetrius had murdered his predecessor, Antiochus V, in 162 BC, he sent Bacchides to install Alcimus* as high priest in Jerusalem. After the defeat of Nicanor* by Judas, the king again sent Bacchides to Palestine, where he defeated Judas in the battle of Elasa in 161 BC. He did not succeed in suppressing the Maccabean party, and was defeated by Jonathan in a skirmish near the Jordan. He fortified a number of border points of the territory of Judaea* and after the death of Alcimus returned to Antioch (1 Mc 7:8 ff; 9:1, 12 ff, 32 ff, 43 ff).

Bagoas (Gk *bagōas,* from Hb *bigwai,* probably a Persian name), eunuch of Holofernes (Jdt 12:11; 13:1 ff), who discovered the dead body of his master (Jdt 14:1 ff).

Bahurim (Hb *bahûrîm,* etymology uncertain), a town or village mentioned several times in the stories of David, apparently near Jerusalem (2 S 3:16; 16:5; 17:18), the home of Shimei* (2 S 19:16; 1 K 2:8) and of David's hero Azmaweth (2 S 23:31; 1 Ch 11:33). It is identified with the modern Ras et Tmim, NE of the Mt of Olives.

Balaam (Hh *bil'ām,* etymology uncertain), son of Beor, a seer of Pethor* who was summoned by Balak*, king of Moab*, to curse the Israelites (Nm 22:5). The summons and the arrival of Balaam, with his refusal and subsequent acceptance and his visions of God and the refusal of his ass to go on the journey, and his conversation with his animal, are heavily overlaid with details of folklore. Before the ritual curse Balaam built seven altars and offered fourteen sacrificial victims. Balaam then delivered four oracles, each of which is not a curse but a blessing. The first of these (Nm 23:7 ff) praises Israel for its distinction from other nations. The second (Nm 23:18 ff) praises Israel for the fact that there is no misfortune or trouble within it, by which is probably signified the absence of idolatry in Israel; for this reason no divination or enchantment is successful against Israel. The third (Nm 24:2 ff) sees the future prosperity of Israel and its victories over its enemies. The fourth (Nm 24:15 ff) again sees the victories of Israel over its neighbors Moab and Edom*. To the fourth oracle are appended some short sayings about the Kenites*, the Amalekites*, and Ashur* and Eber*. Another and much later tradition about Balaam tells how he counseled the Moabites to seduce the Israelites into the worship of the Baal* of Peor*, and for this he was executed by the Israelites (Nm 31:8, 16; Jos 13:22). The place of Balaam's origin, in Hb "the land of the children of his people," (Nm 22:5), has been corrupted beyond recognition. Albright has argued from the language and the grammatical and syntactical characteristics of the poems that they are as ancient as the 12th or the 11th century, the period to which Balaam belongs in tradition. The same writer has shown that the "Star of Jacob" (Nm 24:17) should actually be translated, "When the stars of Jacob prevail." Balaam is mentioned as a teacher of false doctrine in 2 Pt 2:16; Jd 11; Apc 2:14.

Balak (Hb *balak,* etymology uncertain), king of Moab* who hired Balaam* to curse Israel (Nm 22:2 ff). The episode is alluded to in Jgs 11:25; Mi 6:5. A variant tradition (Jos 24:9) tells of a battle between Balak and the Israelites which is not mentioned elsewhere.

Balance. The balance, in ancient as in modern times, consisted of a standard and an

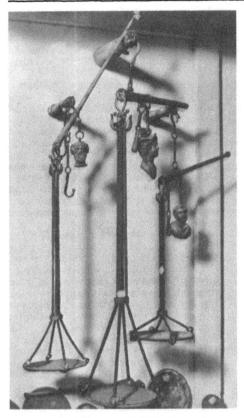

Balances and weights.

arm from which were suspended pans or baskets; some of these have been found in ancient sites and are represented in ancient art. Some Egyptian paintings show balances with standards nearly as tall as a man and an arm of proportionate size; such balances rested upon fixed bases. Merchants carried small portable balances which could be held in one hand; these are illustrated in ANEP 111, 117. Larger balances are illustrated in ANEP 133, 350, 639. Israelite law prescribed an accurate balance (Lv 19:36; Dt 25:13–16); several prophetic exhortations suggest that this was a common form of dishonesty (Pr 11:1; 16:11; Ezk 45:10; Ho 12:7; Am 8:5; Mi 6:11). The balance often appears in figures of speech (Ps 62:10; Jb 6:2; 31:6; Is 40:12, 15; Dn 5:27).

Balm, Balsam. The balm of Gilead (Je 8:22), Hb ṣ°rî, is probably the aromatic resin obtained from the mastix tree, *pistachia lentiscus,* a bushy evergreen which grew in Palestine. The identification of the tree as *balsamodendron opobalsamum* cannot be maintained; this tree is not now native to Palestine and does not appear to have been. This balm was used for healing purposes (Je 8:22; 46:11; 51:8), was handled by Midianite* merchants (Gn 37:25), was included in the gifts of Jacob to the Pharaoh (Gn 43:11), and was one of the exports of Palestine (Ezk 27:17).

Ban (Hb *ḥerem,* and the verb to make a *ḥerem*), a primitive Hb religious institution by which persons or objects were devoted to the deity. In its earliest form this practice was destruction. The ban is mentioned most frequently in the period of the conquest. It was applied to Jericho* (Jos 6:16 ff, especially 6:21) and is mentioned of other Canaanite cities (Jos 8:26; 10:28 ff). The ban was applied to the Amalekites* by Saul* at the direction of Samuel (1 S 15:1 ff). Saul's failure to execute the ban entirely was the occasion of his breach with Samuel. This policy is imposed in a number of passages of the law of Deuteronomy* (Dt 3:6; 7:2 +), and is also imposed upon the Israelites for one of their own cities if it is proved that there is idolatry in that city (Dt 13:12 ff). In later literature the word sometimes appears simply in the meaning of destroy or exterminate with no religious connotation (1 K 9:21; 2 K 19:11; Je 25:9; 50:21; 51:3). In the priestly code objects which fall under the ban go to the priests (Nm 18:14), doubtless a later modification of the earlier custom of total destruction. The word is also used in the priestly code of simple devotion of an object to Yahweh (Lv 27:28 f), with no connotation of destruction. The practice of the ban, like a number of other features of ancient Hb law and custom, is a survival from primitive and more barbarous times which finally disappeared with the growth of a more enlightened morality and a more civilized manner of life. These mass murders of hostile peoples were doubtless done in good faith by the early Hebrews, but they cannot be justified morally in any way by the fact that the Hebrews believed that the action was pleasing to God, and the growth of Hb understanding in this respect is exhibited in the historical books, where the practice does not appear after the war of Saul with the Amalekites.

Banaias. Cf BENAIAH.

Bank, Banker (Gk *trapeza,* lit "the table," "table man"). The table was the counter of the money changer. The earliest function of the banker was to change coins from one denomination to another at a discount. The banker was also a money lender; and money could be deposited with him to be invested either in money changing or in lending (Mt 25:27; Lk 19:23). Cf LOAN; MONEY. In the Hellenistic world of the 4th–1st centuries BC banking was carried on by temples*, which had great stores of deposited wealth and ample revenues, by public authorities such as city-states and in Egypt the royal bank, and by private individuals. Private banking was carried on in Babylon in the Neo-Babylonian period and in the large commercial cities of Syria and Phoenicia, and very probably also in Israel* of the monarchy; but little or nothing is known of their operations. The extensive commerce of the Hellenistic and Roman periods would have been impossible without banking.

Banner. In the camp of the Israelites as described in Nm 2:2 ff, each tribe was assembled around its own banner. The banner or standard as a military emblem was the point around which the troops assembled (Is 5:26) and which showed the direction of march or attack (Is 13:2; 18:3). The ancient military banner was a device upon a pole or a lance. There is nothing to indicate the appearance of the Hb banners. Galling thinks banners may be suggested by the animals associated with tribes in the blessing of Jacob (Gn 49); the lion of Judah, the serpent of Dan, the deer of Naphtali, the bull of Joseph, the wolf of Benjamin. Banners of ancient Egypt and Mesopotamia, as represented in ancient art or recovered by archaeology, are usually an animal device or a divine symbol; in some cases both motifs are united in one, especially in Egyptian standards. The only banner which is described in the OT is the bronze serpent of Moses (Nm 21:8; cf BRAZEN SERPENT). The standards of the Roman legions were the eagles and other symbols. Jewish prejudice against images was once responsible for a riot in Jerusalem when Pilate* attempted to introduce military standards into the temple* area.

Banquet. Cf MEALS.

Baptism (Gk *baptizein, baptisma*), in Christian belief the first of the seven sacraments. Baptism is called by the Church the sacrament of regeneration by water and is administered in modern practice by pouring water upon the forehead. In the early Church baptism was conferred by immersion; sprinkling, now in use in some Protestant churches, was never commonly practiced in the Catholic Church.

1. *Pre-Christian Baptism.* Before Jesus began His public ministry, John* the Baptist was baptizing in the Jordan*. His baptism was symbolic, expressing the repentance of the sinner, and effected of itself no interior sacramental change. This is signified by a number of NT references to the fact that John baptized with water (Mt 3:11; Mk 1:8; Lk 3:16; Jn 1:26), in contrast to the baptism of Jesus, which was effected by water and the Holy Spirit (AA 11:16). The Qumran* Scrolls now indicate that baptism was practiced by the sect of Qumran before John the Baptist; and a connection between John and this group is not excluded. In the Manual of Discipline it is stated that mere ablution cannot really cleanse a man; only by the submission of his soul to all of God's ordinances can he become clean and thus be sprinkled with the waters of ablution and sanctified by the waters of purification. God Himself will finally purge all the acts of man and refine man's substance, destroying every spirit of perversity within his flesh and cleansing him by a holy spirit and sprinkling upon him the spirit of truth like waters of purification to cleanse him — a phrase remarkably similar to Mk 1:8. The Manual, however, forbids any one to go into water in order to attain the purity of holy men, which indicates that the sect did not regard the rite in itself as effective. It had no value except as a token of the sincere inner disposition of repentance.

The baptism of John is called in the Gospels (Mk 1:4) the baptism of repentance, in contrast to the baptism of Jesus, which was the baptism of the Holy Spirit (cf AA 19:1 ff). In submitting to the baptism of John, Jesus did not confess that He was a sinner, but openly signified His real union with sinful humanity, which He had come to redeem from its sins. The theophany of the voice of the Father and of the Spirit as a dove made this the prototype of Christian baptism "in the Spirit," "in the name of the Father and of the Son and of the Holy Spirit."

2. *Baptism in the NT.* Baptism is rarely mentioned in the Gospels. Jesus is said both to have baptized (Jn 3:22) and to have committed baptism to His disciples (Jn 4:2). The necessity of baptism is stated in Jn 3:5; unless a man is born again of water and the spirit, he cannot enter the kingdom of God. The disciples are commanded to make disciples by baptizing them in the name of the Father, the Son, and the Holy Spirit (Mt 28:19). The word baptism is used metaphorically of the future passion of Jesus (Mk 10:38; Lk 12:50). The metaphor seems to be based upon baptism as the beginning of a new life or a new state, a crisis. In AA baptism is explicitly reported of almost every individual or group who accepts Christianity (AA 2:38 +). This baptism is said to be conferred in the name of Jesus (AA

8:16; 10:48; 19:5); it is extremely unlikely that this phrase indicates the formula employed in baptizing. It rather indicates that the person baptized receives the name of Jesus (Apc 14:1; 22:4), that is, he accepts the claims of Jesus and unites himself to the group which accepted Jesus as its founder and leader. Baptism is also called baptism in a holy spirit (Mk 1:8; AA 1:5; 11:16). This phrase is clearly used metaphorically in AA 1:5; 11:16; and it is probable that its use in Mk also is metaphorical, signifying the beginning of a new state, a new and critical experience. Elsewhere the spirit is received with baptism (AA 19:5 f; cf CONFIRMATION; GRACE). For Paul baptism is the Christian's experience of the passion, death, and resurrection of Jesus in himself (Rm 6:3 f; Col 1:12). Baptism symbolizes expressly not only the beginning of a new life in Christ, but also death to the old man, the old life of sin. By baptism the Christian is washed, sanctified and made righteous in the name of the Lord Jesus Christ and in the spirit of our God (1 Co 6:11). Christ sanctifies the Church, cleansing it by the washing of water in the word (Eph 5:26). By this experience the Christian is reborn, regenerated (Tt 3:5). Baptism symbolizes and effects not only the incorporation of the Christian into Christ (Gal 3:27) but also his union with his fellow Christians as members of the one body of Christ (1 Co 12:13). The Christian is redeemed through the blood of Jesus Christ and the water of baptism (1 Jn 5:6), to which the Spirit testifies. The saving power of baptism is illustrated by the ark of Noah, in which all its passengers were saved by water (1 Pt 3:20). "Baptism on behalf of the dead," alluded to in 1 Co 15:29, is mentioned nowhere else and refers to a practice which is unknown to us. It has been suggested that at Corinth it was the custom for friends of catechumens who had died before baptism to receive baptism in their place. Such a baptism could have no validity for the deceased and actually tended to endanger the concept of baptism itself. Paul simply mentions the practice without expressing either approval or disapproval.

Barabbas (Aramaic bar'abbā', "son of the father," probably a nickname). This man is mentioned in all four Gospels as the prisoner who was released instead of Jesus at the wish of the Jews (Mt 27:16 ff; Mk 15:7 ff; Lk 23:18; Jn 18:40). Mt adds the detail that it was the custom for the governor to release a prisoner of popular choice at the time of the Passover. According to the same Gospel Pilate* offered the choice to the Jews; in the other Gospels the request was first made by the Jews. Barabbas is described as a notorious prisoner (Mt), as a revolutionary and a murderer (Lk), and as a bandit (Jn). These features are not contradictory; men who combined lawlessness with a fanatic refusal to submit to the empire of Rome appear frequently in the Jewish community in the last years before the fall of Jerusalem. His name was probably Jesus; cf variant reading Mt 27:16.

Barak (Hb bārāḳ', "lightning," probably an abbreviated form of the name), son of Abinoam from Kedesh* in Naphtali, one of the judges* of Israel. Under the inspiration of Deborah* he assembled an army of 10,000 from Naphtali and Zebulun* and defeated Sisera* at Mt Tabor (Jgs 4:1 ff). He is mentioned among those who delivered Israel (1 S 12:11) and among those who by their faith conquered kingdoms, proved mighty in war, and put foreign armies to flight (Heb 11:32 ff).

Barbarian (Gk barbaros, means a non-Greek, one who does not speak Greek), the name was originally contemptuous, indicating the nonsensical sound of a foreign language; but in NT times and earlier it designated simply the non-Greek world (AA 28:2; Rm 1:14; 1 Co 14:11; Col 3:11).

Bar Jesus (Gk bar jēsous, from Aramaic bar yešûa', "son of Jesus"), also called Elymas; a Jewish magician and false prophet of Cyprus* attached to the court of the governor Sergius Paulus*. When the governor asked Barnabas* and Paul* to preach the gospel to him, Elymas opposed them. Paul then cursed him with blindness, which may have been only temporary; and this so impressed the governor that he accepted the gospel. The name Elymas seems to be not a proper name but an Arabic name meaning seer or sorcerer (AA 13:6 ff).

Bar Jonas (Gk bar iōnas, from Aramaic bar yônāh, "son of Jonah"), a patronymic applied to Simon Peter* (Mt 16:17).

Barley. Barley was cultivated in the Near East in the Stone Age; it was and still is a common crop. In Palestine it is planted in the autumn after the early rain has softened the ground but ripens a month earlier than wheat, usually in April (Ex 9:31; Rt 1:22; 2:17, 23; 3:2, 15). Barley is mentioned quite often as a Palestinian crop (2 S 14:30; Jb 31:40; Jl 1:11 +); Is 28:25 alludes to the skill of the planter. It was used as fodder (1 K 4:28). Barley bread is coarser than wheat bread, but the barley loaf was common (Jgs 7:13; 2 S 17:28; 2 K 4:42; Je 41:8; Ezk 4:9 ff; Jn 6:9, 13). Barley was offered in the ordeal of the suspected wife (Nm 5:15). Barley was included in the payment made by Solomon to Hiram for work on the temple (2 Ch 2:10, 15) and in payment of Hosea for his wife (Ho 3:2). In 2 K 7:1, 16, 18 barley is sold at half the price of wheat, in Apc 6:6 at one third the price of wheat.

Barnabas (Gk *barnabas*, from undetermined Aramaic word). In AA 4:36 the name is explained as "son of consolation"; but this popular etymology can hardly be accepted. Some scholars have suggested "son of prophecy," others *bar ncbô* "son of (the god) Nebo," the Akkadian Nabu; the surname of Joseph, a Levite of Cyprus, first mentioned in AA 4:36 as selling his property and giving the money for the disposal of the apostles. It was Barnabas who persuaded the Jerusalem community to receive Paul* as a disciple (AA 9:27). Barnabas was sent from Jerusalem to investigate the community of Antioch* in Syria (AA 11:22 ff), and brought Paul from Tarsus* to Antioch. With Paul he carried the contribution from Antioch to Jerusalem during the famine (AA 11:29 f). After their return from Jerusalem with John Mark*, Barnabas and Paul were selected by the prophets and teachers of Antioch, among whom Barnabas was numbered, to carry the gospel to cities where it had not yet been preached (AA 13:1 ff). With John Mark they traveled to Cyprus*, Perga*, Antioch in Pisidia*, and the cities of Lycaonia*, where at Lystra* they were first acclaimed as gods, Barnabas as Zeus and Paul as Hermes, and then stoned out of the city (AA 14:8 ff). After they returned to Syrian Antioch the controversy concerning the observance of Jewish rites arose, and Paul and Barnabas were sent to the council at Jerusalem (AA 15:1 ff). In his own account of this journey Paul mentions that Barnabas with Peter at first refused to eat with Gentiles (Gal 2:13); but at the council Barnabas agreed with Paul in refusing to impose Jewish observances on Gentile converts. After their return to Antioch Paul wished to revisit the cities where they had preached. Barnabas wished to take John Mark, who had abandoned them on the earlier journey (AA 13:13); Paul's refusal to accept a companion who had exhibited this weakness led to a difference so sharp that they finally separated, Paul taking Silas* as a companion and Barnabas going to Cyprus with Mark (AA 15:37 ff). No more is known of the career of Barnabas. From the mention of Mark as a companion of Paul (Col 4:10), where we learn that he was a cousin of Barnabas, and Phm 24, and from Paul's praise of Barnabas in 1 Co

9:6 and of Mark in 2 Tm 4:11, we may assume that the breach with Barnabas was ultimately healed. Tertullian proposed Barnabas as the author of Heb.

Barsabbas (Aramaic *bar sā'bā'*, a patronymic, etymology uncertain). **1.** Joseph the just, a candidate with Matthias* for the place in the Twelve left vacant by the death of Judas (AA 1:23 ff). **2.** Judas, sent with Paul, Barnabas, and Silas to Antioch with the letter of the council of Jerusalem (AA 15:22).

Bartholomew (Gk *bartholomaios*, from Aramaic *bar talmai*, "son of Tolmai," a patronymic), one of the Twelve, mentioned only in the lists of the Twelve (Mt 10:3; Mk 3:18; Lk 6:14; AA 1:13). He is identified by some with Nathanael* mentioned in Jn.

Bartimaeus (Gk *bartimaios*, from Aramaic *bar timai*, "son of Timaeus," a patronymic), a blind beggar of Jericho* whose persistent requests won healing from Jesus (Mk 10:46 ff). The man's personal name is not given; the phrase "son of Timaeus" is a doublet of his Aramaic patronymic.

Baruch (Hb *bārûk*, "blessed"), companion and amanuensis of Jeremiah*. In 605 BC Baruch at Jeremiah's dictation wrote out the discourses which Jeremiah had delivered up to that date and then read the contents of this scroll to the people in the temple. He read the scroll again before the officers of king Jehoiakim* and then on their advice fled with Jeremiah. Jehoiakim had the scroll read to him and destroyed it. Baruch then wrote another scroll at Jeremiah's dictation which contained the same material as the first with a number of additions (Je 36:1 ff). Jeremiah committed the deed of sale of the property which he had bought from his cousin Hanamel* during the siege of Jerusalem to Baruch for safekeeping (Je 32:11 ff). When Baruch complained at the sorrows of his life and the miseries of his people, Jeremiah uttered for him an oracle which contained a rebuke and a promise that he himself would survive the catastrophe (Je 45:1 ff). When the survivors of the fall of Jerusalem wished to flee to Egypt after the murder of Gedaliah*, Jeremiah uttered an oracle forbidding them to go. Baruch was blamed as inciting Jeremiah to deliver this oracle and was taken with the prophet to Egypt when the people fled there. No more is known of his life.

One canonical book and two apocryphal* books bear his name, none of which were written by him. The canonical book of Baruch is placed after the book of Lamentations in the Vulgate. This book is not found in the Hb Bible and is not contained in the Protestant canon. It is preserved in the Gk Bible and is included in the canon of the Council of Trent. The book contains the following parts:

1. Introduction (1:1–14).
2. A prayer, containing a confession of national guilt and a petition for forgiveness and the expected restoration of Israel (1:15–3:8).
3. A poem in praise of wisdom, which is not intellectual speculation but is identified with the Law given to Israel through Moses (3:9–4:4). 3:37, in which wisdom is said to appear on earth and associate with men, has been thought by many scholars to be a Christian interpolation; but the phrase simply signifies the communication of the Law.
4. A poem in which Jerusalem personified addresses her children, reminding them of their past sins and encouraging them with the hope of the messianic blessings of the future (4:4–5:9).
5. The letter of Jeremiah addressed to the exiles in Babylon, a polemic against idolatry (6:1–73).

The parts of the book are not all from one author, and many scholars believe that the three principal parts of the book were written by three different authors. It is unlikely that any part of the book is earlier than the 2nd century BC or later than the end of the 1st century BC. A Hb original is most probable for the entire book. For the apocryphal books of Baruch cf APOCRYPHAL BOOKS.

Barzillai (Hb *barzillai*, etymology uncertain; perhaps connected with *barzel*, iron), a man of Rogelim in Gilead* who with Shobi and Machir met David and his party at Mahanaim* with refreshments after their flight from Absalom* (2 S 17:27 ff). After the defeat of Absalom David invited Barzillai to accompany him and spend the rest of his life at court; but Barzillai refused because at the age of 80 he was too old for the pleasures of the court (2 S 19:31 ff). He permitted his son Chimham* to go and live at David's court. In his last words to Solomon* David recommended the sons of Barzillai and asked that they be permitted to remain perpetually at the court.

Bashan (Hb *bāšān*, "fertile plain"), a region in E Palestine* which lay N of Gilead*. Its boundaries lay generally from the foot of Mt Hermon on the N to the Yarmuk on the S, and from Maacah* and Geshur* on the W to Salhad in the Jebel ed Druz to the E. It included the lava field of the Lejja, about 350 sq mi of petrified lava, from which the Gk name Trachonitis was given

to the region. The region shows abundant traces of volcanic activity; the limestone which lies under all Palestine is here covered with a layer of black basalt, used for building stone in ancient and modern times. It gives the buildings of the area a distinctive appearance. The soil is a rich and red volcanic soil. The whole region is a plateau about 2000 ft high. In contrast with the area S of the Yarmuk it is not so well watered and has a more limited rainfall, but the region was and is a good grain producer. Its resources in ancient times included timber, which has now entirely disappeared, its fertile plains suitable for agriculture and even more for pasture, its building stone, and its position on important trade routes. Before the Israelite settlement the territory with its traditional 60 cities was ruled by Og*, who was defeated by the Israelites at Edrei*. Hb tradition is consistent in asserting that their conquest of Bashan preceded their settlement in W Palestine (Nm 21:33; Dt 3:1 ff; 29:6; Jos 12:4 f; 13:11). It is less consistent in its attribution of Bashan to the tribes. Bashan is attributed to half the tribe of Manasseh in Jos 13:30; 17:1, 5; 21:6; 22:7, but to Gad* in 1 Ch 5:11, 16. There were no doubt some tribal movements in the territory. Bashan was divided between two of Solomon's administrative districts (1 K 4:11, 19). Bashan, however, was probably never solidly Israelite. The Aramaeans began to move into the region during the period of the Judges, and they seem to have had firm control of Bashan by 900 BC. The fertility of Bashan is praised in the OT (Is 33:9; Na 1:4). More frequently its rich pasture is mentioned and its livestock is praised for its fatness (Dt 32:14; Je 50:19; Ps 22:13; Ezk 39:18; Am 4:1; Mi 7:14). In the Gk period various names appear for the whole or part of Bashan: Batanea, Trachonitis, Auranitis, Gaulanitis, Iturea. It was included in the kingdom of Herod and comprised the entire tetrarchy of Philip* (Iturea and Trachonitis, Lk 3:1), the only mention of the region in the NT.

Basin. A portable shallow vessel for holding liquids. Basins are mentioned in the Bible as holding water for washing (Jn 13:5), for receiving the blood of sacrificial victims (Ex 12:22; 24:6). They formed a part of the temple furniture and were used for many unspecified purposes, such as conveying libations.

Basket. Containers woven of fiber are represented frequently in ancient art. They were made in a great variety of sizes and shapes. They could be quite large, like the basket in which Paul was let down from the walls of

Damascus* (2 Co 11:33). A large number of Hb and Gk words are translated by "basket"; they indicate different types and sizes of the vessel which we cannot identify. They appear in two prophetic visions: Jeremiah's vision of the baskets of good and bad fruit (Je 24:2) and Am 8:2, where Amos plays on the word basket (ḳayiṣ) as signifying the end (ḳēṣ) of Israel. They are frequently mentioned as containers of food of all kinds and as used in brickmaking (Ps 81:6).

Bath. Cf WEIGHTS AND MEASURES.

Bathing. In the OT bathing is mentioned most frequently in the ceremonial laws as a means of ritual purification; it is prescribed for the priests and for any one who has incurred ceremonial uncleanness (cf CLEAN). The obligation of bathing seven times in the Jordan imposed upon Naaman* is symbolic of the cleansing from his disease (2 K 5:10 ff). The bathing of infants is alluded to in Ezk 16:4. Bathing is most frequently the washing of the feet, particularly after a journey, and it was a duty of hospitality to furnish water to guests for this purpose (Gn 24:32; 18:4; 19:2; SS 5:3). This duty was sometimes performed by slaves (1 S 25:41). Bathing was sometimes if not usually done out of doors, on the roof of a house or in its inner court (2 S 11:2) or in the garden of the house (Dn 13:15). Bathing was also done in streams; the daughter of Pharaoh bathed in the Nile (Ex 2:5). David bathed and anointed himself at the end of a period of mourning (2 S 12:20); the use of perfumes and unguents was extremely common in the ancient Orient and probably was the usual substitute for bathing or followed upon it. Herodotus in the 5th century reported that the Egyptians bathed daily or several times daily; but it is impossible to determine the frequency of the practice in ancient times. In Palestine, particularly, water for this purpose was difficult to obtain in most places. In NT times similar practices prevailed, although Pharisaic interpretation of the Law had multiplied ceremonial bathing. Water was furnished the guests at a banquet for the washing of the feet (Lk 7:44). From this incident we may deduce that the good host furnished unguents. One who had bathed needed only wash his feet to be entirely clean (Jn 13:10). The elaborate public baths of Hellenistic times were unknown in Jewish cities, but such baths were always found in the Hellenistic cities of Palestine and the adjoining regions and were known to the Jews. There were also mineral springs in the neighborhood of the Dead Sea and the Sea of Galilee which were used by Gentiles; orthodox Jews probably did not use these baths. The community of Qumran* employed numerous ablutions, most of which were ceremonial.

Bathsheba. (Hb *bat šebaʻ*, "daughter of Sheba," perhaps a divine name?), daughter of Eliam and wife of Uriah* the Hittite*, one of David's officers. David* saw her bathing from the roof of his house and invited her to his palace and seduced her. His effort to make Uriah responsible for the paternity of her child was unsuccessful, and he ordered Joab* to station Uriah in the front line of battle to be abandoned (2 S 11:1 ff). David then married Bathsheba, but the child of the adultery died (2 S 12:15 ff). The second child was Solomon*, who succeeded David as king (2 S 12:24 ff). In David's old age, Bathsheba, at the insistence of Nathan*, who had rebuked David for his adultery, persuaded David to name Solomon as his successor (1 K 1:11 ff). Her suggestion that Solomon permit Adonijah* to have Abishag*, David's companion in his old age, in his harem was less successful (1 K 2:12 ff). In 1 Ch 3:5 she is called Bathshua, the daughter of Ammiel, an inversion of Eliam; Bathshua is either a textual corruption or a variant spelling. Three other sons of Bathsheba are mentioned in this passage. She is mentioned but not by name in the genealogy of Jesus (Mt 1:6).

Battle. Cf WAR.

Bdellium (Hb *bᵉdōlah*, Gk *bdellion*), an aromatic transparent yellow gum obtained from a tree native to Southern Arabia, Babylonia, India, and Media. It is said to come from Hawilah*, a part of Arabia (Gn 2:12), and its color is compared to the color of manna* (Nm 11:7).

Bear. The bear is now practically extinct in Palestine and Syria except in remote mountain wildernesses; and it is very probable that it was nearly extinct in NT times, since it is mentioned only in Apc 13:2. In OT times the allusions to bears indicate that they were more common. They were ferocious and attacked persons as well as flocks (1 S 17:34–37; 2 K 2:24). The growling of the bear was a not unfamiliar sound (Is 59:11), and the ferocity of the bear reft of her cubs was proverbial (2 S 17:8; Pr 17:12); this image is applied to the anger of Yahweh (Ho 13:8; cf Lam 3:10). The day* of Yahweh is as dreadful as the attack of a bear (Am 5:19). The bear or its features appear in the visions of the beasts of Dn 7:5; Apc 13:2. In the peace of the messianic kingdom the bear and the cow will feed together (Is 11:7). The size and species of the ancient Palestinian bear are not known.

Beard. The ancient Semitic peoples generally wore the full beard. The Sumerians* and Egyptians* are represented in art as clean shaven; the Egyptians wore an artificial ceremonial beard, a square cut goatee. This

The type of beard worn by the Assyrians under Sargon II is illustrated in this bas-relief from Nimrud.

was so much a part of the royal costume that it was even worn by queen Hatshepsut. The beard was cultivated with great care by the Hebrews. It was anointed (Ps 133:2), and its neglect was a token of eccentricity or unsound mind (1 S 21:14) or of mourning (Je 41:5; 48:37). To have one's beard shaved or plucked was a great indignity (2 S 10:4; Is 50:6). The Holiness code prohibited the trimming of the "corners" of the beard (Lv 19:27; 21:5), probably for cultic reasons which are unknown. In NT times it was the custom of Jews to wear the full beard, although both Greeks and Romans were normally clean shaven in this period.

Beatitude. A technical term for a literary form found in both OT and NT. A beatitude is a declaration of blessedness on the ground of some virtue or good fortune. The formula begins "Blessed is . . ." It occurs 26 times in Pss, eight times in Pr, ten times in the other Hb books of the OT, and 13 times in the Gk books of the OT. It is associated with prayer* and with wisdom* utterances. One is called blessed for virtue or for enjoying the forgiveness, protection or nearness of Yahweh. The beatitude is common in the NT also, most frequently for faith

or for sharing in the kingdom of God. Best known are the beatitudes uttered by Jesus, eight in Mt 5:3 ff, four in Lk 6:20 ff. The beatitudes in Mt may be counted as nine if 5:11 is separated from 5:10. It is difficult to say which of the two formulae is nearer to the words actually spoken by Jesus. The first three of the beatitudes of Lk are very nearly identical with the 1st, 2nd and 4th of Mt, the last two inverted. These three beatitudes of Lk indicate those who suffer the misfortunes of poverty, hunger, and sorrow. These griefs will be removed. The 4th is identical with the 8th of Mt, persecution and hatred endured in the name of Jesus. The beatitudes of Mt have been expanded by the addition of meekness, compassion (almsgiving), purity of heart, and reconciliation; to each of the beatitudes has been added an explicit reward, which in each case is synonymous with the kingdom* of heaven of the 1st beatitude, described in terms which correspond to each beatitude. The beatitudes of Mt suppose a groundwork of Christian virtue. The difference between "poverty" of Lk and "poverty of spirit" of Mt is less than the translation leads one to believe; cf POOR. Both terms indicate the depressed classes of the ancient world, those who have no material possessions and enjoy no esteem or reputation. The beatitude addressed to those who hunger has been refined in Mt into an address to those who hunger for righteousness. In Mt the paradox of the beatitudes as stated in Lk has been somewhat softened. The paradox consists in this, that the beatitude is declared not because of some good fortune, but because of ill fortune — poverty, hunger, sorrow, and persecution. Jesus states that in these things men may be happy if they accept them as coming from their heavenly Father and in the spirit which Jesus teaches them. He thus declares that the opposite of these things — wealth, joy, fullness — have nothing to do with one's true happiness, which is to be found only in the kingdom of God and in His righteousness. But the paradox is still apparent in Mt, and the blessedness is now expanded by the addition of some difficult habits of virtue, which demand the suppression of self-love and ambition.

Bed. Beds as articles of furniture were used in Egypt from earliest times in the palaces of kings* and the wealthy. Most of these beds were made of wood, rather low, something like the modern daybed. In the New Kingdom there appear much more ornate beds, sometimes made of ivory plated with gold, and often so high that one approached them by steps. These were richly ornamented with animal and divine emblems;

Egyptian bed made with bronze fittings.

the foot is usually modeled after the foot of a lion. In Assyria there were in royal palaces beds made of wood plated with gold, silver, other metals, and precious stones. The temples contained a bedchamber of the gods, in which was found a highly ornamented couch for the reclining of the gods; probably also such a couch was found in the chamber where the sacred marriage was performed (cf NEW YEAR). In ancient Israel similar beds were possessed by the kings and the wealthy; Amos mentions corners of a bed (3:12) and beds of ivory (6:4). An imposing bronze bed frame from the Iron Age has been found in Tell el Fara, and ivory fragments from Arslan Tash which come from a wooden bed frame. Such beds are also indicated by the phrase "ascend" to one's bed. Ashur-bani-pal of Assyria is pictured as reclining on a bed while at dinner. Such beds were articles of luxury. The ordinary person slept on the ground wrapped in his cloak, or on a mat of straw. This mat could be rolled up and carried about with one. Such beds are indicated in the Gospels where those who are cured are told to pick up their bed and walk (Mt 9:6; Lk 5:24).

Bee. The bee is mentioned in the Bible only 4 times (Dt 1:44; Jgs 14:8; Ps 118:12; Is 7:18), although honey* is mentioned more frequently. Only Is 7:18 is possibly a reference to apiculture; the other passages clearly mean the wild bee. On the uncertainty concerning the introduction of apiculture cf HONEY. The bee cultivated in modern Palestine is smaller than the European and American species.

Beelzebub (Hb ba'al z^ebūb, Gk beel zeboub), in the OT the god of the Philistine* city of Ekron*, of whom king Ahaziah* of Israel inquired during his illness (2 K 1:2 ff). In the NT it appears as the name of the demon in whose authority the Pharisees said Jesus expelled demons (Mt 10:25; 12:24, 27; Mk 3:22; Lk 11:15 ff). The best

Gk MSS read beelzeboul instead of beelzeboub, the reading of the Vg. The meaning of the Hb name is most easily explained as "lord of flies," which is scarcely the original title of the god; it is more probably a Hb contemptuous corruption of the divine name. This name is almost certainly correctly preserved in the NT. Beelzebul was formerly explained from the Hb word z^ebūl, "habitation." It is now explained from the Ugaritic* zbl, "prince," a title frequently given to Aleyan Baal*, the fertility god of Ugarit. He is called, "prince, lord of the earth," and "prince, king."

Beer (Hb šēkār, cognate to Akkadian sikaru, is now considered to mean beer rather than distilled spirits). It is mentioned rather frequently in the OT and was apparently a common beverage (Is 24:9) which was not available in the desert (Dt 29:5). It was poured as a libation to Yahweh (Nm 28:7) and was prohibited to those under the Nazirite* vow (Nm 6:3) and to the priests before their entrance into the sanctuary (Lv 10:9). It was prohibited to the mother of Samson* before the birth of the hero (Jgs 13:4, 7, 14); in other respects she is said to lie under the Nazirite obligation. Beer was drunk at sacrificial banquets at the sanctuary (Dt 14:26). Not all the references to beer are favorable; its intoxicating qualities are mentioned (1 S 1:15; Is 29:9; 28:7) and it is with wine a beverage of drunkards (Ps 69:13; Is 5:11, 22; 56:12). It leads to quarrels (Pr 20:1) and is not the drink of rulers (Pr 31:4). "A preacher of wine and beer" is the preacher suitable to the people of Israel (Mi 2:11). Beer should be given to the perishing so that they may forget their poverty (Pr 31:6).

The technique of brewing in Israel is unknown; but it was probably not dissimilar to the techniques used in Egypt and Mesopotamia. Egyptian brewing is represented in Egyptian art (ANEP 153, 154). The beer was made from barley. The grain was made

Brewing was an art known to the Egyptians, as this scene from the Old Kingdom illustrates.

into flour and baked and the beer was produced by adding water to fermented bread.

Beeroth (Hb $b^e{}'\bar{e}r\hat{o}t$, "wells"?), one of the four Hivite (Horite*) cities which entered into a league with the Israelites (Jos 9:17); listed in the territory of Benjamin (Jos 18:25); the home of the murderers of Ishbaal, son of Saul (2 S 4:2–9) and of Naharai, one of David's heroes (2 S 23:37; 1 Ch 11:39). Men of Beeroth were included among the exiles who returned to Judah (Ezr 2:25; Ne 7:29). Beeroth is possibly identified with the modern village of El Bireh, in which the name survives, about ten mi N of Jerusalem near Ramallah; some prefer a location nearer to Gibeon in the valley of Beth-horon*.

Beersheba (Hb $b^e{}'\bar{e}r$ $\check{s}eba^c$), a town of the Negeb*. The name is literally "well of seven," possibly derived from the number of springs found there. Beersheba is associated with the patriarchs; it was a point on Hagar's flight from Sarah* (Gn 21:14). A covenant* settling a quarrel over water rights between Abraham* and Abimelech* is related in Gn 21:25–33; the meaning of the name is here doubly explained, from the seven (He $\check{s}eba^c$) lambs of the sacrifice and from the mutual oath (Hb SB^c) sworn between them. This must be regarded as a popular etymology. The story of the oath with Abimelech is also told of Isaac and the derivation of the name is also related in this episode (Gn 26:31–33). Beersheba is the home at times of both Abraham (Gn 22:19) and of Isaac (Gn 26:23; 28:10); but Abraham is not really at home at Beersheba and it is quite probable that his connection with the place is secondary. Beersheba was the scene of a theophany both to Isaac (Gn 26:23) and to Jacob (Gn 46:1–5); these were connected with Beersheba as a sanctuary. It is listed both among the towns of Judah* (Jos 15:28) and the towns of Simeon* (1 Ch 4:28). Except for the mother of Jehoash* of Judah, Zibiah, who came from Beersheba (2 K 12:2; 2 Ch 24:1), and for the court held there by Samuel's sons (1 S 8:2) Beersheba does not appear in Israelite history; but it is frequently mentioned in the phrase "from Dan to Beersheba" to designate the N-S limits of Israelite territory (Jgs 20:1; 1 S 3:20; 2 S 24:15; 17:11; 1 K 5:5; 1 Ch 21:2; 2 Ch 30:5) or as the S limit of the territory of Judah (2 S 24:7; 1 K 19:3; 2 K 23:8; 2 Ch 19:4). Beersheba was one of the towns of Judah settled after the exile (Ne 11:27, 30). Am 5:5; 8:14 attests that there was a sanctuary at Beersheba; and the allusions to Beersheba in the stories of the patriarchs indicate that the sanctuary was probably older than the settlement of the Israelites in Canaan.

The name survives in the modern Bir es Seba, about 28 mi S of Hebron*; the site of the OT settlement is probably at Tell es Seba, 2½ mi E of the modern town. Beersheba lies on the frontier of the cultivated land and the steppe of the Negeb* to the S; its altitude is only about 1000 ft above sea level, and the mountains of Judah fall to an altitude of no more than 2000 ft a little to the N of Beersheba. The antiquity of the settlement and its regional importance arose from its abundant water supply, which is the only one in the neighborhood; there are no other settlements near. This oasis was a natural point of convergence for caravan routes from the desert to the markets of the central mountains and the coastal plain.

Begging. Begging as such is scarcely mentioned in the OT; but the numerous references to the poor, the stranger, the widow, and the orphan, and the recommendations to be generous in giving to them, indicate that there were many people who had to support themselves by begging. In later Judaism and in NT times begging was very common. BS 40:28 ff says it is better to die than to beg, and describes begging as an existence which cannot be called life; only the shameless man can beg. Beggars are mentioned frequently in the NT, especially those who suffered from some bodily infirmity (Mt 9:27; 20:30; Mk 10:46; Lk 18:35; Jn 9:8; AA 3:2), who asked alms by the roadside or at the temple gates. In the economic conditions of NT times, when most of the population were extremely poor, with only a slight margin between themselves and destitution, many were reduced either to begging or to selling themselves into slavery (cf POOR).

Behemoth (Hb $b^e h\bar{e}m\bar{o}t$, pl of $b^e h\bar{e}m\bar{a}h$, "animal"). In Eng Bibles the word is a transcription of the name of the animal mentioned in Jb 40:15 ff, identified by older interpreters as the elephant*. The passage is now recognized as a description of the hippopotamus, probably written from hearsay rather than from observation. The behemoth is mentioned by the poet as an example of the creative wisdom of God.

Bel (Hb $b\bar{e}l$, Akkadian $belu$, cognate of Hb $ba'al$, "lord"), in the OT the title of Marduk*, god of Babylon* (Is 46:1; Je 50:2; 51:44). Dn 14:2 ff relates the story of the image of Bel in the temple of Babylon. In Akkadian literature the title Bel is most frequently given to Marduk, but it was actually transferred to Marduk from Enlil of Nippur, lord of the upper air and the creative deity in an older form of the creation* epic. After the title had become proper to Marduk, Enlil is often referred to as the older Bel.

Belial. The common Eng rendering of Gk *beliar*, the reading of the Gk in 2 Co 6:15. Beliar is the name of a demon found frequently in apocalyptic* literature. It is a corruption of Hb $b^e l\bar{\imath} yya'al$, a noun meaning malice or wickedness; the word is probably compounded of two words meaning, "it is of no profit." In the OT the word is often translated in Eng as a proper name, which it is not; it occurs most frequently in the combination "son of *belial*," a wicked man.

Belshazzar (Aramaic $b\bar{e}l\check{s}a'\.s\.sar$, from Akkadian *bel-šar-uṣur*, "Bel protect the king"), according to Dn 5:1 ff; 8:1, the last king of Babylon when it was captured by Cyrus*. Dn 5:1 ff relates the story of the great banquet given by Belshazzar, at which he and his guests drank from the sacred vessels of the temple of Jerusalem. A hand appeared upon the wall writing a mysterious message which no one could interpret except Daniel. Daniel revealed that it was a threat of the end of the kingdom and its transfer to the Medes and the Persians. That very night Cyrus captured the city and Belshazzar was slain. One of Daniel's visions is dated in the 3rd year of the reign of Belshazzar (Dn 8:1). The Babylonian records of this period identify Belshazzar as the son of Nabonidus, the last king of Babylon. Belshazzar was co-regent with his father and administered the capital for eight years during the absence of his father in Teima in Arabia. He was never king of Babylon; the story of his death is supported by an anecdote of Xenophon. He was the son of Nabonidus, not of Nebuchadnezzar* (Dn 5:17). The treatment of Belshazzar in Dn illustrates the legendary character of Babylon as it appears in the book. The author, who lived some centuries after the fall of Babylon, had little accurate knowledge of the history of the period, and treated it in an extremely free and imaginative style. Cf DANIEL.

Belteshazzar (Hb $b\bar{e}lt^e\check{s}a\.s\.sar$), the Akkadian name given to Daniel in the court of Nebuchadnezzar* (Dn 1:7; 2:26; 4:5 ff; 5:12). The name probably represents Akkadian *bel-balaṭsu-uṣur*, "Bel protect his life."

Benaiah (Hb $b^e n\bar{a} y\bar{a} h\bar{u}$, "Yahweh has built"), son of Jehoiada and officer of David* and Solomon*. He was commander of the Cherethi* and Pelethi, the professional soldiers who formed David's royal guard (2 S

8:18; 20:23; 1 Ch 18:17). He was one of David's thirty heroes and three of his mighty deeds are mentioned in 2 S 23:20 ff; the text of these deeds is somewhat corrupted. In the last days of David Benaiah with Nathan* and Zadok* favored the candidacy of Solomon*, the son of Bathsheba*; Benaiah and the royal guard installed Solomon as king (1 K 1:8 ff, 38 ff). At the command of Solomon he executed Adonijah*, Solomon's rival candidate for the kingship (1 K 2:25), Joab* (1 K 2:28 ff), and Shimei* (1 K 2:39 ff), the last two in fulfillment of David's last will. After the death of Joab, Benaiah was appointed commander of the army (1 K 2:35; 4:4). The name is borne by six others in the OT.

Benedictus. The first word in Lt and the usual designation of the song of Zechariah* uttered after the birth of John the Baptist* (Lk 1:68 ff). The song is divided into two parts: the first (68–75) expresses thanksgiving that the deliverance promised to the patriarchs and prophets through the house of David* has now appeared; the second part, addressed to the child (76–79), calls him a prophet who will prepare the way of the Lord. The entire song is woven of OT phrases; the first part depends mostly on Pss, the second part on Is and other prophets. The song is of value as a rare monument of genuine messianism* in the generation contemporary with the Gospels.

Ben-hadad (Hb *ben-hⁿdad*, from Aramaic *bar hⁿdad*, "son of Hadad"), the name of several kings of Damascus*, two of whom are mentioned in the Bible. **1.** Ben-hadad I, who was bribed by Asa* of Judah to rescue him by invading the territory of Israel while Baasha* was invading Judah (1 K 15:18 ff). This king is called the son of Tabrimmon and the grandson of Hezion. This invasion occurred about 878 BC. It is not certain that this Ben-hadad is the same king who was defeated by Ahab* of Israel in two successive campaigns, the first when he besieged Samaria* and the second at Aphek* (1 K 20:1 ff); as a result of this campaign, a treaty was signed in which Israel was granted the same commercial rights in Damascus which the Aramaeans* had enjoyed in Samaria*. W. F. Albright dates the reign of Ben-hadad I 880–842 BC. This war must have occurred before the appearance of both Ahab and Benhadad at the battle of Karkar in 853 BC, in which the Assyrian advance in the west was temporarily halted. The same Ben-hadad was the commander of the Aramaean army, not mentioned by name, in the unsuccessful campaign of Ahab to recover Ramothgilead*, in which Ahab was slain (1 K 22:1 ff). This battle occurred three years after the battle of Karkar. Some scholars identify the Ben-hadad of 1 K 20:1 as Ben-hadad II; recent opinion tends to eliminate this second Ben-hadad from history. The Ben-hadad who besieged Samaria (2 K 6:24 ff) cannot be identified positively, since the king of Israel in whose reign the siege occurred is not named; but it was probably Ben-hadad I. According to 2 K 8:7 ff, Ben-hadad was assassinated by Hazael*. If this were Ben-hadad I, the assassination occurred in 842 BC. The Assyrian records of Shalmaneser III* (858–824) do not mention Ben-hadad; the king of Damascus is called Adad-idri, identical with the biblical name Hadarezer*. Unless Hadarezer is supposed to follow Ben-hadad I on the throne, we must suppose that the Assyrians confused the names of two kings of Damascus, which is not entirely unprecedented in Assyrian records. Shalmaneser observes in one document that Adad-idri perished after his defeat by the Assyrians and was replaced by Hazael, "a son of nobody," on the throne; but it does not appear from the Assyrian record that he was aware of an assassination. Some scholars suggest that the name Benhadad in 2 K 8 is itself an intrusion. **2.** Ben-hadad the son of Hazael, who was defeated three times by Jehoash* of Israel (801–786) as predicted by Elisha* (2 K 13:14 ff, 24). This Ben-hadad is most probably the king meant in Am 1:4 and Je 49:27.

Benjamin (Hb *binyāmīn,* "son of the right," most probably "son of the south," southerner), son of Jacob* and Rachel* and the name of one of the 12 tribes* of Israel. Benjamin was the only of Jacob's sons born in Canaan*, at Ephrath*, and Rachel died after his birth (Gn 35:16 ff). Rachel named him Benoni, "child of my sorrow," but Jacob changed the ill omened name to Benjamin. When the brothers of Joseph* went to Egypt to purchase grain during the famine, Jacob kept Benjamin, the youngest, at home (Gn 42:3 f). But Joseph, Benjamin's only full brother, insisted that the brothers bring Benjamin as a proof of their veracity (Gn 42:15). When Benjamin arrived, Joseph was moved to tears (Gn 43:29 ff). As a test of his brothers Joseph had his silver cup put in Benjamin's sack (Gn 44:1 ff), and then accused the brothers of stealing it. Judah* responded to the test by offering himself for punishment; and this proof that the brothers had changed from what they were when they sold Joseph into Egypt finally moved Joseph to reveal himself.

A tribe of *Banu Yamina* has been found in the Mari* tablets, but this tribe has nothing in common with the Israelite tribe of Benjamin except the name. In the Blessing of Jacob Benjamin is described as a ravenous wolf, devouring prey in the morning and dividing spoil in the evening; this is an allusion to the warlike character of the tribe, verified elsewhere in the OT (Gn 49:27). In the Blessing of Moses Benjamin is the beloved of Yahweh, on whose shoulders Yahweh dwells (Dt 33:12), an allusion to the temple of Jerusalem. In the census of Nm (probably from the time of David) Benjamin is counted as 35,400 (Nm 1:37) and as 45,600 (Nm 26:41). The clans of Benjamin are listed (Nm 26:38 ff). The boundaries of Benjamin are described and its cities enumerated (Jos 18:11 ff). Its territory lay between Judah and Ephraim*, running westward from the Jordan near Jericho* up the slopes of the central highlands as far as Kirjath-jearim* and including the five Canaanite cities grouped around Gibeon*, and Jerusalem, which were not held by the Israelites. The narrative of the invasion of Jos 2–9 takes place entirely within the later territory of Benjamin, and this has led M. Noth to affirm that the story of the invasion is an account of Benjamin's invasion which was retold so as to make it the story of the invasion of all Israel. Benjamin was reckoned as the smallest tribe of Israel in numbers (1 S 9:21; Ps 68:28), but it enjoyed some renown as a fighting tribe. Ehud*, who delivered Israel by assassinating Eglon* of Moab* in his own house, was a man of Benjamin (Jgs 3:12 ff). Benjamin was among the tribes which fought with Barak* and Deborah* against Sisera* (Jgs 5:14). Benjamin was one party of an intertribal war which began because the men of Gibeah* raped the wife of a Levite and thus violated the laws of hospitality (Jgs 19:1–21:25). This is the only instance in Hb history of such a unified action in defense of Hb morality, and its historical character has been questioned by many scholars. This is due in part to the fantastic numbers of the fighting men in the story, which exceed all possibility. The story has doubtless been overlaid with a number of unhistorical elements drawn from popular tradition, and the unity of all the tribes of Israel may be such an element; but there is no serious reason to question the action of the Hb community against such a flagrant crime. According to the story the men of Benjamin routed the other Israelite tribes at the first encounter. Benjamin had 700 picked men, all left-handed slingers* who could hit a hair without missing. It is a coincidence that the Benjaminite hero Ehud was also left-handed. The men of Benjamin were defeated by a stratagem, and the tribe was very

nearly exterminated. This prospect alarmed the other tribes, but they had sworn not to give their daughters in marriage to Benjamin. They circumvented the oath by allowing the men of Benjamin to seize the maidens of Jabesh-gilead, which had not taken part in the tribal war. This number was insufficient, and they permitted the remaining men to sieze the maidens of Shiloh* while they celebrated the vintage festival. Saul*, the first king of Israel, was a man of Benjamin (1 S 9:1 ff), and his royal residence was at Gibeah of Benjamin. After the death of Saul, Benjamin adhered to Ishbaal* (2 S 2:9); but Abner*, after his quarrel with Ishbaal, persuaded Benjamin to submit to David (2 S 3:19). It is doubtful that Benjamin was ever completely loyal to David. Shimei* ben Gera cursed David as he fled from Absalom* (2 S 16:5). After the rebellion of Absalom had been subdued another rebellion broke out led by a Benjaminite, Sheba* ben Bichri (2 S 20:1 ff). In the division of the kingdom after Solomon Rehoboam* succeeded in retaining at least a part of the territory of Benjamin (1 K 12:21 ff). This territory was expanded by Asa* (1 K 15:22). Jeremiah* came from Anathoth* of Benjamin (Je 1:1). Men of Benjamin were included among those who returned to Jerusalem from Babylon (Ezr 1:5 +). Paul* also was a man of Benjamin (Rm 11:1; Phl 3:5).

Ben Sira. This book of the OT is also called the book of Sirach or Ecclesiasticus in the Vg and RD Bibles. The latter title, meaning "used in the Church," was applied in the early Church to the entire group of books now called deuterocanonical, and has been retained by this book in particular; cf CANON. The book is not found in the Hb Bible or in the Protestant canon; but it was used in the early Church and is included in the canon of the Council of Trent. The author of the book is named in 50:27 as Jesus, son of Eleazar, son of Sirach, Hb y^{e}shū$^{·a}$ ben 'el$^·$āzār ben sīra'. The prologue, written by the Gk translator whose name is not given, tells us that the translator came to Alexandria* in the 38th year of king Euergetes, which is calculated as 132 BC, in the reign of Ptolemy* VII Physcon. Since he found in Egypt that a number of Jewish books had been translated into Gk, he decided to translate the book written by his grandfather as well. The date of the translation and the mention in the book of the high priest*, Simon* (50:1 ff) indicate that the book was written in Jerusalem 190–180 BC. MSS containing about two thirds of the book in Hb were discovered in the synagogue of Cairo in 1896, and some additional fragments were discovered in 1931. More Hb fragments were discovered at Qumran*. These Hb fragments exhibit a different recension from the text of Gk, and the restoration of the original text is still an unfinished work of criticism. BS is wisdom* literature. Its author was a wise man of Jerusalem who lived in the period of the Hellenization of Palestine. To this cultural change he was opposed, and he wrote this book in order to disclose to his readers the treasures of traditional Hb wisdom, with which they could be content without seeking the novelties of Gk learning. His book resembles Pr in form and content. Like Pr, it is a compilation of detached wise sayings, which it is impossible to outline in any consecutive scheme. The wise sayings are often grouped around single topics, so that these collections somewhat resemble small essays: for example 2:1–18, admonitions of patience in tribulation; 3:1–16, admonitions of obedience and respect to parents; 4:1–10, admonitions to be generous to the needy; 6:1–17, on friendship; 9:1–13, on dealing with women; 12:30–35, on hospitality; 20:1–8, on silence; 30:33–40, on the treatment of slaves; 34:12–35:13, on conduct at banquets. Like Pr, Jb, and Ec, the book contains little poems in praise of wisdom: 1:1–20; 4:11–19; 14:20–15:8; 51:13–29. Many of the ideas of BS are the ideas of traditional wisdom. He has no theory of the origin of sin, but accepts the division of all men into the two great classes of the righteous and wicked, the wise and the foolish. His ideas of the future life do not advance beyond those of Pr. The problem of evil, which is discussed at length in Jb and also in Ec, he makes no attempt to meet. His wisdom is the traditional wisdom of skill in the management of one's life and affairs. His precepts deal with the ordinary duties and situations of ordinary life: virtues and vices such as pride and humility, the administration of wealth, self-control, the education of children, prudence and reflection, avoiding evil companions, the certain retribution of wickedness, custody of the tongue, selection and treatment of a wife. In some other respects BS is more original. Traditional wisdom, which was international in character and to some extent derived from foreign sources, did not exhibit BS's emphasis upon Israel, the covenant, and the Law. Earlier books contain no parallel to the prayer for the restoration of Israel (36:1 ff). For BS wisdom is identified with the Law. Wisdom is personified, as in Pr 8:22 ff, and represented as coming down from heaven to dwell on earth in the spot selected by the Creator. This spot is Israel, where wisdom takes up her habitation as the Law given through the covenant of Moses* (24:1 ff). BS was indeed conscious and proud of the abilities of the man learned in the Law, the scribe*. He assesses the value of the arts and crafts (38:25 ff) and finds that while each of the crafts is necessary for an ordered society, they cannot achieve wisdom. This is the privilege of the scribe (39:1 ff), whose supremacy in wisdom is described in the most enthusiastic terms. The hymn in praise of creation (42:15–43:37) also has its parallels in earlier wisdom literature. It may be compared to Jb 38:1 ff and Ps 104. He reviews the heroes of Israel's past from Enoch* to Nehemiah* (44:1–49:19). His judgment upon the kings of Israel and Judah, except for David*, Solomon*, Hezekiah*, and Josiah*, is unfavorable without reservation. The omission of Ezra* from his list is puzzling and is not easily explained with some scholars on the basis of an ideological opposition between BS and Ezra. Dn is omitted from the list of the prophets because the book had not yet been composed. But the peak of his enthusiasm is reached in the description of Simon*, the son of Onias, the high priest, who is described in all his priestly array as he appeared in the temple at the great festivals. BS represents a phase of development in which the wise man has become the scribe, the man learned in the Law of Moses. The term of this development appears in the NT. But BS is familiar not only with the Law, but also with almost the entire OT, which must have been collected by his time substantially in the canon which is still the canon of the Jews. In his attitude toward the Law and its observance he seems to belong to that group which later became the Sadducees* rather than to the Pharisees*. He exhibits no knowledge of an oral tradition of the Law, nor does he deduce from it the meticulous obligations which were characteristic of Pharisaic interpretation.

Berea (Gk *beroea*), a city of Macedonia, founded in prehistoric times. The site is the modern Verria on the left bank of the Aliakmon (ancient Astraeus), some distance from the coast; a broad plain lies to the N of Berea and Mt Olympus rises to the S. It is about 19 mi W of Thessalonica*. The Christians of Thessalonica sent Paul and Silas hastily to Berea to escape a riot in their own city; Paul and Silas preached in the synagogue of Berea and enjoyed success until Jews came from Thessalonica to incite a riot against them in Berea also. Paul was again sent off for his own safety, and Silas and Timothy remained to continue the evangelization of Berea (AA 17:10–14). Berea was the home of Sopater*, one of Paul's associates (AA 20:4).

The Berea of 1 Mc 9:4 is possibly Beeroth. The Berea of 2 Mc 13:4 is the Hellenistic name of Aleppo.

Bernice (Gk *bernikē*, abbreviation of *berenikē*, a Macedonian form of *pherenikē*, "bearing victory"). **1.** The daughter of the "king of the south" (Dn 11:6), not mentioned by name; Bernice, the daughter of Ptolemy* V Philadelphus, of Egypt (285–246 BC), who married Antiochus II Theos of Syria as a part of the peace treaty between Syria and Egypt. To marry her Antiochus divorced his wife Laodice. After the death of Antiochus Bernice and her son were murdered by Laodice. **2.** The daughter of Herod* Agrippa I, and wife of her uncle Herod* of Chalcis. After his death in 48 BC she lived in incest with her brother Herod Agrippa* II. She was present with Agrippa when Paul* was heard before the governor Festus* (AA 25:13, 23: 26:30). Later she married Polemon, king of Cilicia*, but afterwards returned to her brother. She was later the mistress of Titus, and died about AD 79 at the age of 51.

Beth. The second letter of the Hb alphabet, with the value *b*.

Bethany (Gk *bēthania*, Hb *bêt 'ᵃnîyyāh*, contraction of *bêt 'ᵃnānîyāh?* "house of Ananiyah"?). **1.** A village near Jerusalem, the modern el Azariyeh at the foot of the E slope of the Mt of Olives about two Roman mi from Jerusalem (Jn 11:18), which means the Jerusalem of Mt Zion; it is about four mi from the modern city. Mt 21:17; Mk 11:11 f indicate that Jesus spent the nights at Bethany during His last week in Jerusalem. Bethany was the home of Lazarus*, Martha*, and Mary (Jn 11:1, 18; 12:1 ff). Mt 26:6; Mk 14:3 relate the anointing of Jesus at Bethany in the house of Simon* the leper; Jn 12:1 ff places the anointing at Bethany in the house of Lazarus; on the problem created cf MARY. Mk 11:1; Lk 19:28 place the beginning of the procession of palms at Bethany. Lk 24:50 places the ascension* on the road "toward Bethany"; but it is very probable that the summit of the mountain, where the Church of the Ascension stands, is the site intended by this designation.

2. Bethany beyond the Jordan, where John the Baptist baptized (Jn 1:28). No Bethany in the Jordan valley is known; a variant reading in some MSS shows Bethabara, also not mentioned elsewhere, but preferred by some critics ("house of the crossing"?).

Bethel (Hb *bêt'ēl*, "house of El [god]"), a town. The site lies near the modern Beitin about 14 mi N of Jerusalem. Bethel is associated with the patriarchs; there are several allusions to its earlier name of Luz. Abraham built an altar at Bethel (Gn 12:8; 13:3). Since the primary associations of Bethel are with Jacob, it is possible that the introduction of Abraham into Bethel is a secondary consideration. The great cultic legend of Bethel must have been the story of the theophany of Jacob and his erection of a standing stone (Gn 28:10 ff); this was the story of the foundation of the sanctuary. The story is a combination from J and E (cf PENTATEUCH), principally from E; this sanctuary of northern Israel was an object of particular attention in the circles which produced E. The story also credits Jacob with conferring the name Bethel; this is doubtless a popular explanation rather than a certainly genuine tradition. Gn 35:1–8 (E) contains an additional account of the erection of the sanctuary by Jacob and his dedication of his clan to Yahweh there; this also is very probably a projection of later Israelite cultic practices into an earlier period. Gn 35:9–13 contains P's account of the theophany of Bethel. While these stories are from a later period, they reflect the antiquity and the importance of the sanctuary of Bethel, which must have been one of the spots earliest associated with Israelite cultic traditions.

Bethel is mentioned in the account of the conquest of Ai (Jos 7:2; 8:9, 12, 17) but only as a geographical point of reference. This account is very probably an account of the taking of Bethel itself (cf AI and below on archaeological data). Bethel is enumerated in the list of conquered kings (Jos 12:16). Jgs 1:22–25 relates the taking of Bethel by the house of Joseph*; here the change of the name from Luz is related to this conquest. In the tribal division Bethel lies on the frontier of Ephraim and Benjamin in the territory of Benjamin (Jos 16:1 f; 18:13, 22); 1 Ch 7:28, however, makes it the possession of a clan of Ephraim, and the town doubtless changed hands. In the late narrative of Jgs 20:18, 26; 21:2 Bethel appears as the place of assembly of all Israel; this also reflects its early cultic importance. The same appears in its inclusion among the places where Samuel held court (1 S 7:16). Jeroboam did not establish a new place of cult with his erection of a sanctuary at Bethel, but rather restored and maintained an old center (1 K 12:29–33). Abijah of Judah took Bethel from Israel (2 Ch 13:19); if this tradition is genuine, Judah did not hold Bethel long.

Bethel appears as a center of prophetic activity also; this may be deduced from the anecdotes of prophets which center about Bethel (1 K 13), from the presence of the sons of the prophets at Bethel (2 K 2:2 f) and the connection between Elisha* and Bethel (2 K 2:23). The sanctuary was maintained by Jehu (2 K 10:29). Bethel is the object of polemics uttered by Hosea (4:15; 5:8; 10:5) and Amos (3:14; 4:4; 5:5 f), who reprobate the calf image of Bethel. Their criticisms are otherwise not specific, but the cult of Bethel appears to have become superstitious. Hosea contemptuously calls it *bêt 'awen*, "house of wickedness" (4:15; 5:8; 10:5), and this insulting title has crept into the historical books (Jos 7:2; 18:12; 1 S 13:5; 14:23). The preaching of Amos was delivered at Bethel, "a royal sanctuary," until he was expelled by the priest Amaziah* (Am 7:10 ff). After the Assyrian conquest Bethel was the residence of an Israelite priest who was sent to teach the immigrant settlers of the land "the fear of Yahweh" (i.e., the cult of Yahweh; 2 K 17:28). The sanctuary of Bethel was destroyed in the reform of Josiah* (2 K 23:15); but Je 48:13 could still refer to the shame which Israel experienced from Bethel, their confidence.

Men from Bethel were found among the exiles who returned from Babylon (Ezr 2:28; Ne 7:32), and it was one of the towns settled after the exile (Ne 11:31; Zc 7:2).

The site was excavated in 1934 under the direction of W. F. Albright and in several seasons beginning in 1954 under the direction of J. L. Kelso. The excavations revealed the interesting fact that the urban occupation of Bethel began with the destruction of the EB level of Ai. Urban occupation continued through the MB and LB periods, apparently with no major interruption, and the city was large and prosperous with some massive structures, either temples or palaces. The fortifications* were of the massive type found in all MB levels. LB occupation was ended by a destruction and almost total conflagration in the 13th century BC; this was attributed by the excavators to the Israelite conquest. The site was rebuilt and occupied in early Iron I with a decided lowering of the cultural level; this occupation was attributed to the Israelites. The occupation of the site during Iron I and II, affirmed in the literary sources, was fully confirmed by the archaeology of the site. The city was destroyed by fire in the 6th century BC, the period of the Babylonian conquest, and reoccupied in the Persian and Hellenistic periods.

Bethesda (Gk *bethesda*, etymology uncertain), Bethesda is found in the received text and in Eng versions, but the name Bethzatha (Gk *bethzatha*, etymology uncertain) found in some MSS is the preferred critical reading. The name designates a pool in Jerusalem (Jn 5:2), but actually designated the name of the new N quarter of the city in NT times. The pool is the scene of the healing of the paralytic (Jn 5). Scholars accept the identification of Bethesda with an ancient cistern excavated adjacent to the church of St. Anne of the White Fathers in Jerusalem. The pool is a large double cistern over which a Byzantine church was built. There are remains of five colonnades (Jn 5:2). The cisterns themselves are dated in the Maccabean period, the colonnades in the Herodian period. The "troubling of the water" (Jn 5:7) was no doubt caused by the sudden inflow of water through drains.

Beth-horon (Hb *bêt-ḥōrōn*, "house of Horon [god?]"), the name of two towns, distinguished as the upper Beth-horon and the lower Beth-horon; they are identified with two modern villages likewise distinguished as the upper and the lower, Beit Ur et Tahta (lower) and Beit Ur el Foqa (upper), lying respectively 11 mi and 10 mi NW of Jerusalem. The towns lie in the valley of Aijalon*, one of the main approaches to the central highlands through the Shephelah*; they control this route and give their name to the road, called the road of the pass of Beth-horon (Jos 10:10 f). The lower Beth-horon lies about 1300 ft above sea level, the upper Beth-horon about 2000 ft above sea level. The boundary of Ephraim and Benjamin passed this point (Jos 16:3, 5; 18:13 f). 1 Ch 7:24 relates that Beth-horon was fortified by a clan of Ephraim. 1 K 9:17 relates that the lower Beth-horon was fortified by Solomon; 2 Ch 8:5 mentions both upper and lower Beth-horon. Beth-horon is included in the list of Levitical cities (Jos 21:22; 1 Ch 6:53). It appears in the list of Palestinian cities conquered by Shishak* of Egypt. It was the home of Nehemiah's enemy Sanballat* (Ne 2:10, 19; 13:28).

Bethlehem (Hb *bêt lehem*, "house of bread"? or "house of [the god] Lahm"?), the name of two towns. **1.** Bethlehem of Zebulun* (Jos 19:15), the home of the minor judge Ibzan* (Jgs 12:8–10); it is identified with the modern Beit Lahm about 7 mi WNW of Nazareth.

2. Bethlehem of Judah (but strangely not included in the list of the towns of Judah in Jos). It is identified with Ephrath, the burial place of Rachel*, in Gn 35:19; 48:7; but these allusions very probably come from a date after Bethlehem was settled by an Ephrathite clan (cf below), and the Ephrath*

Bethlehem, with shepherd's field in foreground.

of Rachel's burial is to be located farther to the N. Bethlehem appears twice as the home of a Levite (Jgs 17:7-9; 19:1 ff), which suggests that it may have been a center of Levite clans. It was the home of the family of David (1 S 16:4 ff +), of David's nephew Asahel* (2 S 2:32), of Elhanan* (2 S 21:19; 23:24; 1 Ch 11:26), of Elimelech*, Naomi*, and Boaz* (Rt). Except for the anointing of David, no episode is located there except the anecdote of David's heroes who broke through the Philistine lines to bring him a drink from the spring of Bethlehem (2 S 23:14-16; 1 Ch 11: 16-18). It was one of the cities fortified by Rehoboam* (2 Ch 11:6). Men from Bethlehem were included among the exiles who returned from Babylon (Ezr 2:21; Ne 7:26). At an uncertain date it was settled by an Ephrathite clan (1 Ch 2:51, 54; 4:4). Mi 5:1 glorifies it as the place of origin of the dynasty of David and therefore of the future scion of David who will rule all Israel.

Bethlehem was the birthplace. of Jesus (Mt 2:1 ff; Lk 2:4 ff). Jn 7:42 suggests that this was not generally known, and some scholars have suggested that the birth of Jesus at Bethlehem is a midrashic* feature of the infancy* gospels to affirm the messianic character of Jesus. Despite certain difficulties in the story of the census* which was the occasion of the journey to Bethlehem in Lk, and the absence of Bethlehem elsewhere in the NT, there is nothing in the infancy narratives themselves or elsewhere in the Gospels to indicate that Jesus was born in any other place, and the tradition should be accepted as genuine. That He was born in a cave, however, is not found in the Gospels; this is a datum of local tradition. The region of Bethlehem has a large number of caves in the limestone which

have served even in modern times as shelters both for animals and for persons; some of these lie under the present church of the Nativity, but the identification of any one of them with the scene of the birth rests on no certain foundation.

The identity of biblical Bethlehem with the modern Bethlehem about 5 mi S of Jerusalem is not questioned. The modern city is built on a double hill and the connecting saddle ridge at an altitude of 2550 ft above sea level. The ancient city lay on the S hill, where the church of the Nativity stands; archaeological exploration of the site has never been possible. The present church was erected during the Crusades; it lies on the site of the first church of the Nativity, built by Helena, the mother of Constantine (+ 327) and the successor church built by Justinian. This was also the location of the monastery built by St. Jerome. A short distance to the SE is the large artificial cone upon which Herod's fortress of the Herodium was built.

Bethphage (Gk *bēthphagē*, Aramaic *bêt paggē'*, "house of unripe figs"), a village on the Mt of Olives, the point where the procession of palms into Jerusalem began (Mt 21:1; Mk 11:1; Lk 19:29). The village lay near the summit of the mountain a short distance E of the modern Russian convent; the name survives in the modern village.

Beth-Rehob. Cf REHOB.

Bethsabee. Cf BATHSHEBA.

Bethsaida (Gk *bethsaida,* Aramaic *bêt-sayidā'*, "house of fishing"?), one of the towns of Galilee cursed by Jesus (Mt 11:21; Lk 10:13), the home of Peter, Andrew and Philip (Jn 1:44; 12:21), the scene of the healing of a blind man (Mk 8:22). The relation of Bethsaida to the "desert" nearby, the scene of multiplication of the loaves (Mk 6:45; Lk 9:10) is obscure, and Lk seems to suppose a different location of the episode from Mk.

The location of Bethsaida at the modern et Tell, 2 mi N of the Sea of Galilee and E of the Jordan, and Khirbet el Araj on the shore of the sea S of et Tell, is generally accepted. Josephus relates that Philip* the tetrarch founded his capital there and named it Julias after the daughter of Augustus. It is thought that Khirbet el Araj on the lake is the site of the original fishing village and et Tell the site of the new city built by Philip.

Beth-shan (Hb bēt-šā'n or bēt-šān, "house of [the god] šan"), an important city, located at the mound of Tell el Husn in the SE corner of the plain of Esdraelon*; the modern village of Beisan nearby preserves the ancient name. Tell el Husn was excavated under the auspices of the University Museum of Philadelphia 1921–1933. The mound was large and was built up of 79 ft of occupation debris. The earliest buildings were erected 3400–3300 BC; there were about 20 levels of occupation. The city was destroyed about 2400 BC and was rebuilt in the 15th century after a gap of 800 years in the occupation. The city became an Egyptian fortress about 1450 BC, and Egyptian control was retained until the end of Egyptian power in Palestine. The control was not absolute; the Egyptian fortress was destroyed at least twice during this period. The Egyptian city was large and wealthy and was evidently one of the most important cities of Canaan. It was a commercial center and contained a large number of imported articles. Its importance is derived from its site; it controls one of the principal roads which connect the coastal plain and the central highlands with E Palestine and Syria to the N. The Canaanite city had large temples, two of which were dedicated to Dagon* and Astarte*, which exhibited several reconstructions. In the early Israelite period it was one of the Canaanite cities which stretched across Palestine dividing Galilee* from Ephraim* and keeping the trade route in Canaanite possession. It passed under Philistine control and was destroyed in the time of David; there is no other agent to whom this destruction can be attributed, but it is not mentioned in the OT. The site lay unoccupied until the Persian period. It became a major city again with the establishment of a Gk military colony with the new name of Scythopolis, "Scythian* city"; but the origin of this name is unknown. This was the greatest of the Gk cities of the Decapolis*. It was conquered by John Hyrcanus in 108 BC and was detached from Jewish rule by Pompey in 63 BC. The excavators found the remains of a Hellenistic* temple of the 3rd century BC.

The OT twice mentions that Beth-shan was not taken from the Canaanites by the Israelites (Jos 17:16; Jgs 1:27). It is reckoned in the territory of Issachar* in Jos 17:11, in the territory of Manasseh* in Jgs 1:27; 1 Ch 7:29; actually it lay on the border of the two tribes, and Manasseh* expanded into the territory of Issachar. When it was under Philistine control the bodies of Saul and his sons were hung on its walls and their armor was hung as a trophy in the temple of Astarte (1 S 31:10, 12); the men of Jabesh-gilead* liberated the bodies. The city was included in Solomon's 5th district, but whatever settlement was there was not on the mound of Tell el Husn. The Hb name appears Grecized in 1 Mc 5:52 and 12:40 f; it was the point where Jonathan* and Trypho* met and declared a truce. Its Gk name Scythopolis appears in 2 Mc 12:39 f; the Jews of Scythopolis attested the goodwill of the Gk inhabitants toward them. Jdt 3:10 introduces Scythopolis into its fictitious narrative.

Beth-shemesh (Hb bêt-šemeš, "house of the sun" or "house of [the god] Shamash"), the name of several towns. **1.** A town in Naphtali retained by the Canaanites after the Israelite settlement; the site is unknown (Jos 19:38; Jgs 1:33). **2.** A town on the boundary of Issachar* (Jos 19:22); it is located in the Jordan valley near Beth-shan*. **3.** A town on the boundary of Judah (Jos 15:10), possibly identical with Ir Shemesh of Dan (Jos 19:41), a Levitical city (Jos 21:16; 1 Ch 6:44). It was the point to which the ark was first returned by the Philistines after its capture (1 S 6:9–20) and the scene of the defeat of Amaziah* of Judah by Jehoash* of Israel (2 K 14:11–13; 2 Ch 25:21–23). It lay in Solomon's 2nd district (1 K 4:9).

This Beth-shemesh is identified with Tell er Rumeileh near the modern Ain Shems, which preserves the name, in the Wadi Sarar (the biblical valley of Sorek*) about 15 mi W of Jerusalem. It was excavated by Duncan Mackenzie in 1911–1912 and by Elihu Grant in 1928–1933. The town was founded near the end of the EB Age, about the same time as Bethel, and flourished at its greatest 1500–918 BC. The city was destroyed by the Babylonians in 587 BC and was not reoccupied. It is mentioned in the Egyptian Execration texts of the 19th century BC. Excavation disclosed that the material culture of the Israelite period was very similar to the material culture of Philistine sites; Beth-shemesh lay on the border of Israelite and Philistine territory and the superior culture of the Philistines was influential. Some large houses* of wealthy nobles, consisting of several rooms around a court, were built in the LB Age. One large palace-citadel was identified by the excavators as the residence of Solomon's governor; it had very thick walls, long high-roofed rooms for storage of grain, and was erected on an earthen platform at first 105 ft square, later enlarged to 256 ft. The citadel, however, was built in David's reign, which suggests that David installed district governors before Solomon did. The site contained large oil presses of a size which seems to suit commercial rather than private operations, a stone lined silo 23 ft in diameter and 19 ft deep, and a small copper smelting furnace. The fortifications*, attributed to David's time, consisted of casemate walls.

Bethuel (Hb *bᵉtû'ēl*, meaning uncertain, perhaps *mᵉtû'ēl*, "man of God"?). Son of Nahor* and cousin of Abraham* (Gn 22: 22 ff) and father of Rebekah* and Laban*. Since he does not appear in the story of the wooing of Rebekah (Gn 24:1 ff), it is assumed that he was dead when this episode occurred.

Bethulia (Gk *baitoulia*), the home of Judith* and the scene of the defeat of Holofernes*. The city cannot be identified with any biblical name or any known site, and the geography of the book, like its historical background, is probably fictitious. The author represents the town as located opposite Esdraelon* facing the plain near Dothan* (Jdt 4:7).

Beth-zur (Hb *bêt-ṣûr*, etymology uncertain), a town of Judah (Jos 15:28), settled by a clan of Caleb* (1 Ch 2:45), fortified by Rehoboam (2 Ch 11:7), the center of a district of postexilic Judah (Ne 3:16), the scene of the defeat of Lysias* by Judas* (1 Mc 4:29; 2 Mc 11:5). It was apparently only after this battle that Beth-zur was fortified by Judas (1 Mc 4:61; 6:7, 26, 31), principally against Idumean* incursions. The fortress changed hands during the following years. The Jewish garrison was forced to evacuate the post because of failure of provisions (1 Mc 6:49 f) and Beth-zur was occupied by Seleucid forces, including some Jews who were members of the faction opposed to the Hasmoneans (1 Mc 10:14). Beth-zur was fortified again by Bacchides* (1 Mc 9:52) and was taken by Simon* after

a siege (1 Mc 11:65 f; 14:7); Simon again fortified it.

Beth-zur is identified with Khirbet et Tubeiqua, about 5 mi N of Hebron (the figure of 5 *schoenae* from Jerusalem, about 150 *stadia* [cf WEIGHTS AND MEASURES] is an error). The site was excavated by O. R. Sellers in 1931 and 1957. No occupation was assured before the 17th century BC; but in the Hyksos period, 17th–16th centuries, occupation was intense, although the area is not large. The city was defended by massive walls of the Hyksos type (cf FORTIFICATIONS), well enough built to be remodeled and reused in the Gk period. The site was apparently abandoned during the LB period and reoccupied about 1200 BC; the fortifications were strengthened during the Iron I period, but no trace of the fortifications ascribed to Rehoboam appeared. The site was occupied in Iron II and abandoned for an undetermined period after the 6th century. Abundant traces of fortification and occupation during the Gk period were evident. In the later part of the Gk period the territory must have been quite peaceful, as occupation spread well outside the walls. The site was abandoned about the beginning of the 1st century BC or perhaps even later in the century.

Beulah (Hb *bᵉūlāh*, lit "married woman"), a name applied to the land of Palestine to signify its restoration under the figure of marriage with Yahweh after the exile (Is 62:4).

Bezaleel (Hb *bᵉsal'ēl*, "in the shadow of El"?), the son of Uri, the son of Hur, a skillful craftsman in metal, stone, and woodwork, appointed with Oholiab to make the furniture of the tabernacle* (Ex 31:1 ff; 35:30 ff).

Bezek (Hb *bezek*, etymology uncertain), a town ruled by the Canaanite king Adoni-bezek*, defeated by Judah (Jgs 1:4 f); the point where Saul mustered the men of Israel for his campaign against the Ammonites (1 S 11:8). Bezek is identified with Khirbet Ibziq, N of Shechem and S of Mt Gilboa*; this suits Saul's rally, but not the campaign of Judah. Bezek has very probably entered the text of Jgs 1:4 ff by corruption, and its presence is responsible for the alteration of Adoni-zedek to Adoni-bezek; the story of Adoni-bezek must be a variant of the story of Adoni-zedek* of Jerusalem.

Bible (Lt *biblia*, Gk *biblia*, plural of *biblion*, "book" [diminutive], from *byblos*, papyrus*). The name, "the books" without qualification, indicates the special position which these books occupied, and also shows that the Bible is a collection or a library rather than a single literary composition. The books of the Bible are called "sacred," because they are written under divine inspiration*, and "canonical," which signifies that they are enumerated in the authentic list of sacred books called the canon*. The Bible is divided into Old Testament and New Testament; the word testament (Lt *testamentum*) here signifies Gk *diathēkē*, Hb *bᵉrît*, "covenant*," and indicates the central fact of salvation, the old covenant of Sinai* and the new covenant of Jesus Christ. The OT books are divided into historical, didactic, and prophetical; but the literary* forms of the biblical books are much more numerous than this. The NT was written in Gk and the OT in Hb, with the following exceptions: 2 Mc, WS and Dn 13 (Susanna) and 14 (Bel) were written in Gk; Jdt, Bar, BS, 1 Mc were written in Hb but are preserved in Gk (extensive fragments of Hb BS, however, have been recovered since 1896). The Qumran texts suggest that Tb may have been written in Aramaic. Je 10:11; Ezr 4:8–6:18; 7:12–26; Dn 2:4–7:28 are in Aramaic. The Hb Bible was divided into verses and into sections for synagogue reading before the Christian era. The modern division and numeration of chapters is generally attributed to Stephen Langton (+ 1228), professor at Paris and later Archbishop of Canterbury; he perhaps employed an existing division. The modern numeration of verses in the OT was made by Sanctes Pagnini, O.P., in his Lt Bible of 1528; the Paris printer Robert Etienne adopted the numeration of Pagnini and himself numbered the verses of the NT in his edition of 1555. The Bible was first printed (Lt) by Gutenberg (Mainz, 1450); over 100 editions appeared before 1500.

The Catholic Church regards the Bible as the word of God, a source of revealed doctrine and a part of the rule of faith. The Church receives her faith from the Bible and from tradition, which is the living teaching authority of the Church as it has existed from its foundation by Jesus Christ. It is the Church which defines the Bible as the word of God and determines the canon of the sacred books; hence theologians call the Bible the remote rule of faith as distinguished from tradition, the proximate rule of faith. Cf also INTERPRETATION; TEXT; VERSIONS; articles on separate books.

Biblical Commission, Pontifical. By the Apostolic Letter *Vigilantiae* of Oct 30, 1902, Leo XIII established a Commission for the promotion of biblical studies and their protection from error. The Commission was to consist of a Council of members drawn from the college of Cardinals; these were to be assisted by Consultors to be selected from reputable biblical scholars of every nation. By the Apostolic Letter *Scripturae Sanctae* of Feb 23, 1904, Pius X granted the Commission the faculty of examining candidates and conferring degrees in Sacred Scripture. By the Motu proprio *Praestantiae Sacrae Scripturae* of Nov 18, 1907, Pius X declared that the decisions of the Commission have the same authority as the decrees of the sacred Congregations: they oblige the faithful not only to external submission, but also to internal assent. From 1905 to 1915 the Commission published 14 responses, and only 5 since 1915. As a general rule the Commission speaks only in answer to questions proposed.

The Commission was established at the time when Catholic biblical studies had been deeply affected by the errors of Modernism and the responses of 1905–1915 were directed against these errors. Since that time Catholic biblical studies have taken a more definite form and the work of the Commission has been less to correct error and more to encourage scientific work. It is against this background that its responses are to be understood. The Commission has rarely decided a strictly exegetical or critical question. The Church believes in a twofold authorship of the Bible, divine and human, and consequently in a twofold interpretation, authentic, uttered by the Church alone, and scientific, reached by scientific methods. The Church speaks in order to protect her dogmas and the faithful and to restrain scientific work not only from error but also from unduly hasty and ill-founded hypotheses. Consequently, the responses more frequently deal with the certitude of various hypotheses, or indicate lines of study which the Catholic exegete cannot fruitfully pursue. Its responses are not irreformable and are subject to revision by the Commission itself.

Bildad (Hb *bildad*, etymology uncertain), the Shuhite, one of Job's three friends (Jb 2:11).

Bilhah (Hb *bilhāh*, etymology uncertain), slave given to Rachel* by Laban* when Jacob married Rachel (Gn 29:29), substituted for Rachel because of her barrenness (Gn 30:3; cf MARRIAGE), the mother of Dan* and Naphtali* (Gn 30:5 ff). Later she had incestuous relations with Reuben*, son of Jacob and Leah* (Gn 35:22), alluded to in the curse addressed to Reuben in Gn 49:4.

Birthright. Cf FIRSTBORN.

Bishop (Gk *episkopos,* "overseer"), in classical Gk used to designate an inspector, municipal officials, temple supervisors; in LXX used to translate Hb words for military officers, overseers of workmen, temple supervisors, tribal officers. The apostolate is called the office of an *episkopos* (Judas, AA 1:20) in a quotation of Ps 109:8; the office is a "good work" (1 Tm 3:1). Paul, addressing the presbyters* of Ephesus (AA 20:17), calls them "bishops," appointed by the Holy Spirit to care for the flock of which they are shepherds (AA 20:28). They are distinguished from the deacons* (Phl 1:1). Jesus Himself is called "the shepherd and bishop of souls" (1 Pt 2:25). The same officers are called "leaders" (Gk *hēgoumenoi,* Heb 13:17); they guard the souls of the flock, for which they must render an account. The "leaders" of Hb 13:7, who announced the gospel and ended their lives keeping the faith, are more probably the apostles. The qualities of a bishop are enumerated in 1 Tm 3:1–8; Tt 1:6–9; they are called presbyters in Tt 1:5. Titus is to appoint them at Crete. These texts indicate that the apostles appointed these officers to govern the churches which they founded. There is a clear distinction between bishops and deacons, but no clear distinction between bishops and presbyters. AA 20:17 and Tt 1:5 suggest that the bishop-presbyters formed a college. The institution of the monarchical episcopate, in which each church is governed by a single bishop, does not appear in the NT. Most probably the supreme government of each church rested in the apostle who founded it, and under whom the local bishops administered its affairs. Since churches appear under a single bishop before the end of the first century (e.g., Ignatius of Antioch) it is easily assumed that one of the college was elected to succeed the apostle after his death as the monarchical head of the church.

Bithynia (Gk *bithynia*), a region in the NW of Asia Minor, stretching along the coast of the Sea of Marmora and the Black Sea from Mysia to Pontus. Bithynia was a satrapy of the Persian Empire; it attained its independence after the conquest of Alexander but became a satellite kingdom of the Romans in 190 BC. Nicomedes III willed the territory to the Romans in 74 BC and with Pontus it was constituted a Roman province. Paul and Silas wished to enter Bithynia on Paul's second journey, but "the spirit of Jesus did not permit them" (AA 16:7). The Christians of Bithynia and the provinces of Pontus, Galatia*, Cappadocia*, and Asia* are addressed in 1 Pt 1:1, but the evangeliza-

tion of Bithynia is not related. Two cities of Bithynia were later seats of ecumenical councils, Nicaea (325) and Chalcedon (451).

Bitumen. Mineral pitch or asphalt, produced by the native mixture of hydrocarbons, oxygenated a thick dark substance which varies from solid to semiliquid. Species of bitumen are designated by the following Hb words: *kōper,* used for calking boats (Gn 6:14); *hēmar,* found in pits near the Dead Sea* (Gn 14:10), used for mortar (Gn 11:3) and to construct the basket in which Moses was placed (Ex 2:3); *zepet,* also used in Ex 2:3, and in figure in Is 34:9; the rivers of Edom will be turned to pitch, and the land will become flaming pitch. There are heavy deposits of bitumen near the Dead Sea and detached masses often float upon its surface; hence it was called Asphaltitis by the Greeks and Romans.

Blasphemy (Gk *blasphēmia*), abusive or contemptuous language directed toward God* or sacred things. In the Holiness code blasphemy was punished by stoning (Lv 24:16). David's adultery and murder were blasphemous (2 S 12:14); (the ancient Jewish editors inserted the word "enemies" to protect the sanctity of the divine name), making "you have utterly scorned the Lord" "you have utterly scorned the enemies of the Lord." The robber and the wicked blaspheme (Ps 10:3, 13). Disbelief in God's promises is blasphemy (Nm 14:11, 23; 16:30), as is the unbelief which thinks Him powerless or accepts other gods (Is 1:4; 5:24). The enemy of Israel blasphemes by thinking that Yahweh cannot deliver His people (Ps 74:10, 18). Infidelity to the covenant is blasphemy (Dt 31:20). The defeat of Israel causes the name of Yahweh to be blasphemed as unable to deliver (Is 52:5). The messianic claims of Jesus (Mt 26:65; Mk 14:64) and His assertion of power to forgive sins (Mt 9:3; Mk 2:7; Lk 5:21) were called blasphemy. The insults addressed to Jesus on the cross are called blasphemy in the Gospels (Mt 27:39; Mk 15:29; Lk 23:39), as well as the charges of the lying witnesses (Lk 22:65). Jesus' claim to be one with the Father was treated as blasphemy (Jn 10:33 ff). The "blasphemy against the Holy Spirit" was the attribution of Jesus's exorcisms to diabolical power (Mt 12:31; Mk 3:28 ff; Lk 12:10). This blasphemy is the one sin which is not forgiven, not because of a lack of God's mercy but because it takes away the principle which makes it possible for a man to ask forgiveness. Stephen was accused of blasphemy (AA 6:11). The refusal of the Jews to accept the gospel was blasphemy (AA 13:45; 18:6), and Paul before his conversion tried to compel Christians to curse Christ (AA 26: 11). He calls himself a former blasphemer (1 Tm 1:13). Paul elsewhere adopts the Jewish idiom and warns Christians to conduct themselves so that "the name of God may not be blasphemed" because of their faults (1 Tm 6:1; Tt 2:5). In Judaism and to some extent in Christianity also blasphemy was understood to mean not only abusive language toward or about God, but also abusive language about sacred persons or things. Warnings in the Epistles against blasphemy occur in Eph 4:31; Col 3:8; 1 Tm 6:4.

Bless, Blessing. 1. *In OT*. Blessing is conceived as a communication of life from Yahweh. With life come vigor and strength and success, which bring one peace of mind and peace with the world. Yahweh Himself is the only one who can bless; men bless by wishing and praying that Yahweh will bless. This wish is particularly effective when it is uttered by a person of authority, such as the priest, the king, or the head of a family; here the person who possesses a blessing transmits it to another. The effect of the blessing most frequently mentioned is fertility, whether in men, animals, or crops. In the first creation account God blesses birds and fish (Gn 1:22), men (Gn 1:28; 5:2); it is probable that an earlier form of the story included a blessing of animals. In each of these blessings there is a command to be fruitful and multiply. God blessed the seventh day (Gn 2:3), i.e., made it a source of blessing. After the Deluge* God blessed Noah* and his sons, again with a command to be fruitful and multiply. The patriarchs were blessed: Abraham (Gn 12:2–3), Isaac (Gn 26:3–4), and although the word is not used of Jacob in Gn 28:13 ff, the formula is otherwise the same: the result of the blessing will be an innumerable progeny. Jacob was blessed in his encounter with the heavenly being at Penuel* (Gn 32:29), and was himself a medium of blessing for Laban (Gn 30:27, 30). Joseph also was a medium of blessing for Potiphar and his house (Gn 39:5). The clan of Abraham will be a formula of blessing for all nations (Gn 12:3; 18:18; 22:18; 28:14); the phrase may possibly mean that the patriarchs and their descendants will be a medium of blessing, but it is now more commonly understood to mean that the nations of the earth will ask that God bless them as He blessed Abraham. The people Israel, with Egypt and Assyria, will be a blessing in the midst of the earth (Is 19:24). The people Israel is blessed above all people (Dt 7:14) in the fertility of its

cattle. In Dt the blessing is often represented as the recompense for the observance of the law of Yahweh (11:26 ff; 15:4, 18).

The solemn formula of blessing is uttered by a person who in some capacity represents God. Noah blesses his sons Shem and Japhet (Gn 9:26–27). The blessing of the father conferred upon his firstborn was a formula of vital importance, as may be seen in the blessing stolen from Esau by Jacob (Gn 27:28–29), which invokes fertility upon him and power to rule his family and others. By the blessing the father communicates his own life, strength and authority to his son. In this passage also appears the conception of the blessing and other solemn utterances as entities endowed with a vital reality; once the blessing is spoken, it cannot be recalled or annulled. Balaam* must bless Israel, even though he has been hired to curse them; for Yahweh has blessed Israel and the power of this blessing repels a curse (Nm 23:8, 20). Jacob blesses the sons of Joseph (Gn 48:15 f), wishing a numerous progeny and conferring the rights of the firstborn upon Ephraim*; the blessing was usually if not always accompanied by the imposition of hands, through which the blessing flowed from one person to another. The blessings of Jacob upon his sons and of Moses upon the tribes of Israel (Dt 33:1 ff) are not exact illustrations of the formula of blessing; they are artificial compositions which allude to the fates of the individuals or the tribes. In both poems Joseph is blessed with fertility, and in the blessing of Jacob Judah receives the power to rule. A solemn blessing upon Israel is uttered by Moses in Dt 28:1 ff with a corresponding curse*; again fertility is a dominant motif. David blessed his house after the enthronement of the ark* in Jerusalem (2 S 6:20), and Solomon blessed the entire people after the dedication of the temple (1 K 8:14, 55). The priestly blessing of Nm 6:22 ff is still employed in Jewish liturgy.

God blesses man, but man does not bless God; however, God is blessed frequently in Hebrew prayer, especially in the Pss. To bless God is to thank Him and to acknowledge His power and glory; the phrase, "Blessed be Yahweh" is usually a recognition of some benefit conferred by God or men. To bless in common speech comes to mean to greet; blessings were invoked not only by authorized persons, but also by one Israelite upon another at meeting; Boaz* greets his workers, "May Yahweh be with you," and they respond, "Yahweh bless you" (Rt 2:4).

2. *In NT*. Blessing is understood much as in the OT. In the Gospels it is rare. Jesus blesses the food in the miracle of the multiplication of the loaves (Mt 14:19; Mk 6:41; 8:7; Lk 9:16), the institution of the Eucharist* (Mt 26:26; Mk 14:22), and the supper of Emmaus (Lk 24:30), and blesses the apostles at the ascension (Lk 24:50). The evangelical precept to return a blessing for a curse (Lk 6:28) is repeated and expanded by Paul (Rm 12:14). Mary is called blessed among women (Lk 1:28, 42) and the Benedictus* is a hymn of blessing, i.e., thanksgiving (Lk 1:64 ff). The "cup of blessing" (1 Co 10:16, a term derived from the Jewish Passover* rite) is probably not merely the cup which is blessed, but rather the cup in which is a blessing, a gift of God. The OT formula "Blessed be God" is frequent in the Epistles, and the "blessing" most frequently means salvation through Christ.

Blindness. Blindness was and is extremely common in the Near East. The Bible recognizes only two forms of blindness: (1) opthalmia, a highly infectious disease which is aggravated by the glare of the sun, dust and sand in the air, and lack of sanitation. In its milder form it makes the eyes red and weakens the vision, as was probably the case with Leah* (Gn 29:17). (2) senile blindness, mentioned of Isaac* (Gn 27:1), Eli* (1 S 3:2) and Ahijah* (1 K 14:4). Blindness disqualified a man from the priesthood (Lv 21:18), and a blind animal was not to be offered in sacrifice (Dt 15:21). Blinding as a punishment was inflicted on Zedekiah by Nebuchadnezzar (2 K 25:7) and is mentioned twice in the code of Hammurabi; it does not appear in Hb law. The law prescribes kindness and assistance to the blind and forbids putting a "stumbling block" in their path (Lv 19:14; Dt 27:18) and among Job's works of kindness is mentioned that he was "eyes for the blind" (Jb 29:15). Jesus cured the blind three times: at Bethsaida (Mt 9:27 ff; Mk 8:22), at Jericho (Mt 20:30 ff; Mk 10:46 ff; Lk 18:35 ff), and the man born blind at Jerusalem (Jn 9:1 ff). The blind and dumb man of Mt 12:22 ff is probably a doublet of the dumb man in Lk 11:14. Jesus mentions cure of blindness as one of the signs of His messianic mission (Mk 11:5; Lk 7:22).

Blindness is a metaphor for lack of spiritual insight (Is 42:19; 29:18; 56:10; Rm 2:19; 2 Co 4:4; 2 Pt 1:9; 1 Jn 2:11; Apc 3:17), and the messianic salvation is described as light to the blind (Is 35:5; 42:16, 18; 43:8; Je 31:8, cf Ps 146:8). The Pharisees are blind leading the blind (Mt 15:14; Lk 6:39). The temporary blindness mentioned in Gn 19:11; 2 K 6:18 ff is designated by a different Hb word and is described as a psychic rather than a physical loss of vision; also cf AA 13:11. The blindness which afflicted Paul seems to have been physical and not merely psychic (AA 9:8, 18), but it cannot be identified with any known disease.

Blood. In the OT blood is the life of the living being (Gn 9:4; Dt 12:23). Man and other animals are composed of "flesh and blood." For this reason the eating of blood is prohibited (Gn 9:4; Lv 17:10 ff); life is conferred by God and is under His dominion. This prohibition was retained in the apostolic Church (AA 15:20). To take life is to shed blood, and it is avenged by the shedding of blood (Gn 9:6; cf AVENGER). The blood of the murdered man cries out from the ground (Gn 4:10) and must be atoned for, literally "covered" (Dt 21:9 +). If blood were not shed in killing (Gn 37:22) or if it were not permitted to run upon the ground (Jgs 9:5) it could be thought that blood-guilt would not follow. The conception of a family having one blood does not appear.

In the sacrificial ritual the blood represents the life and was symbolically offered to God, represented by the altar; it was dashed at the base of the altar (Lv 1:5 +) or sprinkled before the sanctuary (Lv 4:6 +) or poured at the base of the altar (Lv 4:7 +) or smeared on the horns of the altar (Lv 4:25 +). If an animal were eaten away from the sanctuary, the blood must be poured on the ground (Dt 12:24). The blood of the Passover* lamb smeared on the doorposts protected the Israelites from the angel of death in Egypt* (Ex 12:7, 13). In the covenant* ritual the blood of the victims was dashed on the altar, representing God, and on the people, signifying that the covenant partners share a common life (Ex 24:6 ff).

The blood of the Eucharist* in the NT is a departure from Hb ideas in that the blood of Jesus is proposed as drink (Mt 26:27 ff; Mk 14:23 ff; Lk 22:20; Jn 6:53 ff; 1 Co 11:25 ff). The sacramental significance, however, follows Hb patterns, since the blood is again the life which is communicated from Jesus to His disciples through the Eucharist (Jn 6:53 ff; 1 Co 10:16). The blood of the Eucharist is the blood of the new covenant in all the formulae of institution, an allusion to Ex 24:8; in Mt and Mk it is also an atoning agent, like the blood of the sin and guilt offerings; cf SACRIFICE. The blood of Jesus as a sacrificial atoning agent is much more explicit and frequent in the Epistles. He is a propitiatory offering in His blood (Rm 3:25), through which we are made righteous (Rm 5:9). We are redeemed through His blood (Eph 1:7) and through it we draw near to God (Eph 2:13), and by His blood He has made peace (between man and God; Col 1:20). The contrast and analogy between the blood of Jesus and the blood of sacrificial victims is drawn out at length in Heb. His blood excels that of animals (Heb 9:12 ff). Blood is the only effective agent of purification (Heb 9:20 ff) and of the remission of sins (9:22). But the blood of animals cannot remove sins (10:4); Christ has effected eternal redemption* by His own blood (9:12), through which we have access to the sanctuary (10:19). The blood of the new and eternal covenant (13:20) calls more loudly for forgiveness than the blood of Abel called for vengeance (12:24). His blood is sprinkled upon us (1 Pt 1:2), it is the blood of the innocent lamb (1 Pt 1:19), it purifies us (1 Jn 1:7) and delivers us from our sins (Apc 1:5). He purchases men with His blood (Apc 5:9), and by His blood the saints have conquered (Apc 12:11).

Boanerges (Gk *boanerges*, probably Hb *bᵉnê regeš*, "sons of thunder," as explained in Mk 3:17), a nickname given by Jesus to James* and John*, the sons of Zebedee*, which suggests an impetuous temper.

Boar. The wild boar is mentioned in the Bible only in Ps 80:14. It is found in the thickets of the Jordan valley in modern times and was probably much more common in ancient days. In Mesopotamia the wild boar was hunted for sport by Assyrian kings.

Boaz (Hb *bō'az*, etymology uncertain). **1.** Kinsman of Naomi*, a wealthy landowner of Bethlehem, who married Ruth* (Rt 2:1 ff); an ancestor of David. **2.** The name of one of the two columns which stood before the temple* of Solomon* (1 K 7:21).

Body. Hb has no word for body except to designate a corpse; in Israelite thought the body is not conceived as a unified totality but rather as a collection of parts and organs which are the seat of psychic activities (cf MAN; articles on separate bodily organs). In the NT the Gk word *sōma* appears in contexts which can scarcely be translated into Hb or Aramaic; this is a result of the influence of Gk thought patterns and idiom.

1. *In the Gospels.* In the Gospels the body is not a psychological or a theological conception of primary importance. It is illuminated by the eye*, which signifies the intention (Mt 6:22; Lk 11:34); if the eye has light*, it communicates light to the whole body. It is much more important than food (Mt 6:25; Lk 12:22 f); here the body is parallel with life* and is conceived almost

as the self. It is distinguished from the soul* in Mt 10:28; Lk 12:4; the death of the body is less to be feared than the destruction of soul and body by the punishment of God. The life of the body is not the totality of human life, for man survives in the resurrection of the body; but if by sin* he loses his soul, the hope and principle of resurrection is lost. (On the body of Jesus identified with bread cf EUCHARIST.)

2. *In Paul.* In the other NT writings the body becomes an important psychological and theological concept only in Paul. The first meaning of body is the concretely existing human being; in some contexts it again appears to be nearly synonymous with self (Rm 6:12 f; 8:10?; 1 Co 6:18 f), but "body" and "soul," both used for "self," have different emphases. The body is the totality rather than the conscious self, and the corporal constituent of human life never disappears from sight. Sexual sins in particular dishonor the body (Rm 1:24); by these one sins against his own body (1 Co 6:18 f). The body is "the body of death," the mortal body (Rm 7:24), from which man is delivered through Jesus Christ. The death of the body is the result of sin (Rm 8:10); but the spirit survives this death through righteousness. The body can be described as synonymous with flesh* in Rm 8:13; sins are the deeds of the body, which must be slain by the spirit in order to insure life. But flesh is normally distinguished rather as a quality of the body in its concrete existence; by union with Christ the flesh is put to death permanently, but the body will rise to a new life (cf below). Here also, however, Paul's pattern is not completely consistent; for existence in the body means that one is absent from the Lord, and one must abandon the body in order to be present with the Lord (2 Co 5:6, 8). The body therefore as existentially identified with the flesh is to be beaten and subdued (1 Co 9:27).

The body, unlike the flesh, is the object of transformation and not of death. "The body of sin," which is the flesh, is destroyed when the old man is crucified with Christ; here one notices the identification of the body with the body of Christ, a dominant theme in Paul's conception of the body. Although the body is mortal, God confers life upon it through His indwelling Spirit (Rm 8:11); and the adoption* of sons is the redemption of the body (Rm 8:23). The body therefore is to be presented to God as a living and acceptable sacrifice (Rm 12:1). It belongs to the Lord, as the Lord belongs to the body (1 Co 6:13); this remarkably strong statement of the union of the body with the Lord presupposes Paul's teaching on the identity of the Christian with Christ precisely as one body (cf below). One who suffers for Christ bears the marks of Jesus in his body (Gal 6:17). The body will be transformed from its lowly condition to the glorious condition of the risen body of Christ (Phl 3:21); for the life which it receives demands a fulfillment like the fullness of life conferred upon Jesus through His death and resurrection. The body of the Christian, which shares the experience of Christ's death and resurrection, must share the fullness of His glory. Hence Paul draws out this necessity in 1 Co 15:35-44 in speaking of the resurrection. In answer to the question what kind of body will appear in the resurrection, he points out that bodies differ in species, and that even within the same species a remarkable transformation is effected through the process of growth. This furnishes an analogy for the conferring of the life of glory upon the mortal and the corruptible body, the body of death and sin. The body become imperishable, it receives glory, it becomes a spiritual body, not after the image of the first man but after the image of the heavenly man, Christ. It must be transformed, because flesh and blood cannot inherit the kingdom of heaven. Basic to this argument is Paul's conviction that unless man rises as a body, he does not live at all; for the body is the totality of concrete human existence, and it must experience what appears impossible, a transformation which without destroying it gives it the qualities of the heavenly man. The example and the pledge of this is the transformation and the glorification of the body of the risen Jesus.

Implicit in this argument is the identification of the body of the Christian with the body of Christ; and this identification is explicit elsewhere. The Christian has died to the law through the body of Christ (Rm 7:4); he has experienced the bodily death of Jesus in his own body, otherwise Paul could not conceive the liberation of the Christian as genuine. In this union the Eucharist* is a basic principle; when the Christian eats the bread of the Eucharist he shares in the body of Christ; indeed, Christians become one body, which is the body of Christ, for there is one bread and one body (1 Co 10:16 f). He who eats and drinks the sacrament unworthily profanes the body of the Lord (1 Co 11:27), and he who eats without recognizing the body of Christ eats and drinks his own condemnation (1 Co 11:29). It is in one body, His own, that Christ has reconciled Christians to the Father by His death (Eph 2:16 f; Col 1:22). Thus He has made the Church one body, His own, in which one Spirit dwells (Eph 4:4). Christians are called in one body (Col 3:15). The physical realism of these passages is remarkable and should not be diluted to mere metaphor. The identity of Christians with the physical body of Christ is unique in Paul's presentation and is much more than the union of members of a society with the governing authority and with each other.

This physical realism lies behind those passages in which Paul speaks of the Church as the body of Christ. Scholars disagree on the precise interpretation of these passages, and some propose a development from the idea of one body "in" Christ (Rm + 1 Co) and one body "of" Christ (Eph + Col); the realistic element is more pronounced in Eph-Col, and is one of the arguments adduced for regarding these epistles as "deutero-Pauline" (cf COLOSSIANS; EPHESIANS). The argument by itself is not convincing, since the physical realism of the conception appears in all the passages cited above; but there seems to have been a development in the expression of the idea. In Rm 12:4 ff the application of the term body to the Church bears less on the unity of Christians with Christ than their union with each other; diversity of offices and of charismata does not institute a division any more than different functions of bodily members institutes a division. The members of the church belong to each other. In 1 Co 12:12-27 the same analogy of body is invoked as a motive of Christian unity with diversity of offices and functions; the church of Corinth furnished a genuine problem of unity. But Paul's language goes beyond the minimum requirements of his argument. The members are one because they are baptized by one spirit into one body (12:13). They are called not one body in Christ but one body *of* Christ (12:27). The same identity is presupposed in 1 Co 6:15 f, where Paul calls the bodies of Christians members of Christ, and adduces this identity as a motive for abstaining from fornication. The body is a member of Christ and a temple of the Holy Spirit; the Christian must glorify God in his body by preserving the holiness of Christ, for glory is manifest holiness (1 Co 6:19 f). That the temple of 6:19 does not imply physical realism is evident, and one might ask why this realism is affirmed of the body; but there is no background in Pauline language for the physical realism of the metaphor of the temple as there is for his conception of the body, and the two terms are not really parallel. It is because the Christian really is a member of the body of Christ that he can be called by metaphor a temple of the Holy Spirit.

In Eph-Col the Church as the body of

Christ is introduced somewhat abruptly with no explanation (Eph 1:23; Col 1:24); the ideas of the earlier epistles are presupposed. Development of language seems apparent; the Church is the "fullness" of the body of Christ, since the identity of the Church and her members with the circumscribed corporal extension of the body of Christ would be a manifest absurdity. But it is Paul's point that the transformation and the glorification of the body of Christ permits an identification of body (and not merely of sentiment and intention) between Christ and the Church which would have been inconceivable before the glorification of Jesus. Hence a new term is introduced; Christ is called the head of His body the Church (Eph 5:23; Col 1:8; 2:19). This term does not loosen the identity of Christ and the Church, but preserves the distinction between Christ as the principle and the Church as the term. Effectively "head and members" means nothing different from the earlier "body and members," and this is clear from Paul's explanation: it is Christ the head from whom the whole body is joined and nourished, and grows with a growth from God in love (Eph 4:16; Col 2:19). The idea of body is here enlarged to include the idea of growth, correlative with the idea of fullness. The Church and her members obviously have not reached the destiny to which their incorporation in Christ leads, and hence the body of Christ must be conceived in such a way that, while it lacks nothing which belongs to it, it is capable of expansion and perfection through growth in numbers and in the essential Christian virtue of love. Hence one can speak of "the building" of the body of Christ (Eph 4:12, 16). Finally the union of Christians with the body of Christ is compared to the union of husband and wife; the body of the wife is not her own but her husband's and so Christ cherishes the Church because we are members of His body. In this application Paul departs somewhat from the close identity of union which is implicit in other passages.

This exposition follows in general the explanation of J. A. T. Robinson in specifying the body of Christ as the risen glorified body with which the Church is one, and in emphasizing that this union involves physical realism. This is not to deny that it has a basis in sacramental union (cf EUCHARIST); but the important element is that it is distinguished from all types of merely moral and social unions. It is unique and hence all comparisons break down; because it is unique the more recent term "mystical" has come into use and appears in ecclesiastical documents. The term is not biblical and should never be explained in such a way

that the biblical elements are not included. The union of the members of Christ is the basis of their mutual union with each other; the physical realism of the union of the Church with Christ is not extended to the union of member with member, but their union with the one physical reality is a new and again unique basis for a unique type of union in society.

The antecedents of the Pauline conception of body are not obvious and a number of suggestions have been made: Stoicism, Gnosticism, the Eucharist, rabbinic speculation on the cosmic body of Adam, and the OT idea of corporate personality. It seems most probable that the idea, which in the form it has in the Pauline epistles is altogether original, has no single antecedent, but is somewhat indebted to several. The term body certainly is not derived from the OT; and the idea of a cosmic body appeared in Stoicism and in the Gnostic idea of Primeval Man. Paul could have known of these from casual conversation; he shows no profound acquaintance with either system, but the term seems to have been current enough for him to employ it. That the Eucharist is basic in the idea has been mentioned above. In principle the idea is a development of the OT conception of the corporate personality; cf SERVANT OF THE LORD for the treatment of this conception.

Book (Hb *sēper*, Gk *biblion*, Lt *liber*). The earliest form of book was the scroll of papyrus*, which was produced and marketed in rolls usually about 9 in wide and 35 ft long. These rolls could be cut into pages of desired size, but this roll uncut was the average size "book," (Hb *mᵉgillah*, Lt *volumen*) although larger books could be produced by gluing more than one roll together; one Egyptian papyrus scroll was 133 ft long and 16¾ in wide. This type of book remained in use through most of the Greek and Roman periods, although the material could be papyrus, leather (the Qumran* scrolls), or parchment*. The lines were written parallel to the length of the scroll in columns (or pages) from 2 in to 10 in in width. When not in use, the scroll was rolled up; a rod was sometimes used as an axis. In the Semitic alphabet* both writing and pages proceeded from right to left; the reader held the scroll in his left hand and unrolled it toward his right, and rolled up the portion already read. To use both sides of such a scroll was practically impossible, and a scroll written on both sides was a surprising element in a prophetic vision (Ezk 2:9 f; Apc 5:1). Scrolls could be sealed (Is 29:11; Dn 12:4). The inconvenience of the roll, especially for ready reference was at least partly responsible for the invention of the *codex*, the modern book form. Codices have now been discovered which were produced in the 2nd century AD; and since these are almost entirely biblical or Christian MSS, it is supposed by many scholars that the codex was invented by Christians. The papyrus roll was cut into pages, which were laid in a pile; the sheets could be laid singly or folded once, producing a signature of four pages. Both sides of the material could be used for writing, and the sheets were bound at the left-hand side. The form was not changed when parchment replaced papyrus, except that papyrus, which is fragile and brittle when dry, can be folded only once at most; parchment can be folded into signatures of as many as 16 pages. The codex did not exceed 14 in. in length and 10 in. in width.

Book of Life. Israelite genealogies* recorded membership and rank in Israel. When Nehemiah* came to Jerusalem those who could not prove their Israelite ancestry (Ne 7:61) or their priestly ancestry (Ne 7:64) by genealogy were not admitted to full standing. This practice probably underlies the conception of a heavenly register in which God records those who belong to Him. In Ex 32:32 to be erased from the book of life means simply to die; the same meaning is probably intended in Ps 69:29, where the wicked are erased from the book of life in which the righteous are inscribed. In Ps 87:6 God keeps a record of those who are born in Jerusalem; in Is 4:3 there is a record of those who are destined for life in the messianic Jerusalem. In Dn 12:1 the book contains the names of those who will escape the final messianic tribulation. These passages connect the book with predestination, which is also suggested in Ps 139:16; the days of the Psalmist are all written in God's book before he is born. In the NT one is inscribed in the book of life as meriting a reward for good works: the disciples (Lk 10:20), Paul's fellow-workers (Phl 4:3). Here "life" comes to mean eternal salvation. Christians are enrolled as citizens of heaven (Heb 12:23; cf Is 4:3). He who overcomes will not be erased from the book of life (Apc 3:5), and no one who is not written in the book of life will enter the heavenly Jerusalem (Apc 22:27). Elsewhere Apc explicitly suggests predestination; those who are not written in the book of life from the foundation of the world worship the beast (Apc 13:8; 17:8), and those who are not written in the book will be cast into the pool of fire (Apc 20:15). The book of life is related to the conception of a book in which the deeds of men are recorded (Mal 3:16; Dn 7:10; Apc

20:12), although the two conceptions are not identical; the book of life is a register of citizenship in the heavenly Jerusalem, while the book of accounts corresponds to a judicial or annalistic record.

Booth (Hb *sukkāh*), a temporary shelter, usually constructed of tree branches, for the use of herdsmen, harvesters, and watchmen of fields and vineyards. The Israelites constructed booths for the celebration of the feast of Tabernacles*. Jonah* built a booth in which to await the destruction of Nineveh* (Jon 4:5 ff). The booths were abandoned to collapse when they were no longer in use. Such an abandoned booth is used in a striking figure to represent the devastation of Jerusalem (Is 1:8) and the collapse of the dynasty of David (Am 9:11).

Booz. Cf BOAZ.

Bottle. Skin bottles were made of an animal's entire hide, dried slowly, and are mentioned in Gn 21:14; Jos 9:4; Jgs 4:19 +; they were the most easily obtained and the most sturdy for nomads, but were in common use in cities and villages also. When dried out they lost their flexibility and would burst by the expansion of gas, giving occasion to the figure of Jb 32:19, adopted by Jesus to express the novelty of His Gospel (Mt 9:17; Mk 2:22; Lk 5:37). Earthenware bottles of various sizes and shapes were in common use; one was employed by Jeremiah in a symbolic action to predict the destruction of Judah (Je 19:1 ff).

Bow. The use of the bow and arrow was known in Mesopotamia in the 3rd millenium BC and appears to have come in with the Akkadians* from the north. The bow was either of wood reinforced with a surface of knitted sinews on the outside or fabricated of wood with a surface of sinew and an inlay of horn. The arrow, about 32 in. long, was made of wood (sometimes polished) with a point of flint, bronze, or iron, sometimes barbed. The bowstring was of linen cord or of sinew. The "bow of bronze" (Jb 20:24) probably refers by metonymy to the point of the arrow; the technical difficulties in producing a practical metal bow seem insurmountable, and such bows as the gold-plated bow presented to Amenhotep III of Egypt by Dusratta of Mitanni must have been purely ornamental. The bow was drawn with the arm, as it always appears in art; the common Hb idiom "tread the bow" probably refers to the use of the foot to set the arrow. Wristlets to protect the left arm were

known. Some ancient bows which have been discovered are sharply angled in the center; but when set for shooting they are represented in art as forming a semicircle. The bow was used in hunting* (Gn 27:3) and in war. Until Ashur-nasir-pal II (883–859 BC) the bow seems to have been the weapon of the king and the nobles rather than the common troops; the Pharaoh is always represented in battle scenes with a bow, while the troops are armed with sword and spear. In Assyria the bowman rode in chariots with one or two companions to drive and to protect him with a shield. After Ashur-nasir-pal there also appear mounted archers; to shoot either from a chariot or from a horse presupposes no small skill. Assyrian kings are represented hunting from chariots. After the 8th century BC the Assyrians developed the technique of archery troops to a high degree. The archer was accompanied by a shield bearer; this permitted near approach to the enemy, even to fortified cities. We must suppose that the tactic of mass fire was employed; the archers are always represented in scenes of assault on fortifications. In Israel* the king (2 K 13:15 ff; Pss 18:34; 45:6), the king's son (2 S 1:22), and the commander in chief (2 K 9:24) are armed with the bow. It was no doubt under Assyrian influence that archery troops appeared among the Aramaeans (1 K 22:34) and in Judah* under Uzziah (2 Ch 26:14); we should probably suppose the same development in Israel. In poetry the bow is a figure of strength (Je 49:35; Ho 1:5 +). God Himself is armed with a bow; His arrows are the lightning (Ps 18:15).

Bozrah (Hb *bŏsrāh*, meaning unknown), an Edomite city (Gn 36:33; 1 Ch 1:44), mentioned in several prophetic threats against Edom (Is 34:6; 63:1; Je 49:13, 22; Am 1:12). The city was certainly one of the principal cities and possibly the royal residence. It is identified with modern Buseira, about 120 mi S of Amman and 25 mi E of the Dead Sea. The site lies on an isolated spur surrounded on all sides except the approach by the steep cliffs of the wadi and is naturally a very strong point. The Bozrah named among the cities of Moab (Je 48:24) can hardly be the same place; critics suggest that Bezer be read here instead.

a) Assyrian bows. b) A soldier armed with bow and short sword. c) Persian bowmen. d) Arrowhead. e) Assyrian archers behind shields.

Bracelet. Bracelets were made of gold, silver, bronze, and iron. Bracelets consisting of a closed circle were not made in Palestine; this style was Egyptian. The bracelet was a band of metal, flat or circular, bent to fit, with the ends brought next to each other or overlapped. In armbands worn on the upper arm the ends were left separated by a larger interval. There is no ornamentation on the bracelets found in ancient sites. Art shows two or three bracelets worn at once, sometimes both bracelets and armbands. They were usually worn by women

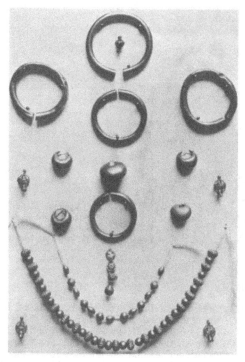

Egyptian bracelets and necklaces.

(Gn 24:22, 30, 47; Jdt 10:3; Ezk 16:11; 23:42); bracelets worn by men (e.g., by Saul in 2 S 1:10) are thought to be a sign of rank or office.

Brazen Serpent. The bronze serpent* (nᵉhuš-tān), a cult object removed from the temple* by Hezekiah (2 K 18:4 ff). According to the cult legend preserved in Nm 21:4 ff this object was constructed by Moses when the Israelites were attacked by "fiery serpents" (cf SERAPH). In both Mesopotamia and

Syria the serpent was associated with the nude goddess of fertility and the god of vegetation; it was a symbol of sex, the source of life, and its use as a symbol of healing fits this pattern. The same symbolism appears in the entwined serpent of the Greek god of healing, Asklepios, and is preserved in the caduceus of the modern physician. The worship of the serpent may be compared with the scene of the worship of a serpent god portrayed on a Mesopotamian seal. The presence of this element of foreign symbolism in Yahwism is paralleled by other elements which were only rejected with the development of Israelite belief. The bronze serpent is proposed as a symbol of salvation (WS 16:6) and as a type of the crucifixion of Jesus (Jn 3:14 f).

Bread. Bread was the staple article of diet in both OT and NT. Common bread was made of barley* flour; wheat* bread was a luxury. The meal was ground and the bread baked daily. The work was done by the wife or by slaves*, although there were professional bakers (Je 37:21). It was baked either leavened or unleavened; the latter method was used if quick baking were necessary, as to provide for guests (Gn 18:6). There were three methods of baking: (1) The tannûr (oven) was a conical cylinder in which the dough was either baked on hot stones or stuck on the inside of the oven. (2) Round metal plates were placed on three stones over a fire. (3) "Hearth-cakes" were made by placing the dough under hot ashes; Ephraim is once compared to such a cake which was not turned and is therefore half-baked (Ho 7:8). In modern times a refinement of this method is used; a hole is dug in which a fire is burned all day, and the fire is then cleared out and the bread is placed in the hole, carefully covered, and allowed to bake all night. The scarcity of wood sometimes made it necessary to use dung for fuel (Ezk 4:15). The loaf was either shaped like a stone (cf Mt 4:3; 7:9; Lk 4:3) or round and flat like our pancakes (Hb kikkar, "circle"). It was not cut with a knife, but broken with the hands. In the Bible bread often signifies food in general, as in the Our Father. The shewbread* was an offering of bread placed in the sanctuary. The price of a prostitute was a loaf of bread (Pr 6:26). Travelers carried their bread in a sack (Mk 6:8; Lk 9:3). "To eat bread in the kingdom of God" was to partake of the messianic banquet (Lk 14:15; cf MEALS). Jesus, alluding to the Eucharist*, called Himself the true bread, the living bread, the bread that comes down

a) Egyptian bread-
making: right, kneading
dough; left, tending fire.
b) Ovens at Pompeii.

from heaven (Jn 6:32 ff). Partaking of the Eucharist symbolizes the unity of Christians in one bread and one body* (1 Co 10:17).

Breastplate. Breastplate as a separate piece of armor* does not appear in the OT. It is mentioned metaphorically as a part of the Christian's armor: the breastplate of righteousness (Eph 6:14), of faith and love (1 Th 5:8). The breastplate which was a part of the vestments of the high priest* is described in Ex 28:15-30; 39:8-21. It was made of gold, violet, purple, and scarlet thread woven into linen which was folded double into a square a span (about eight in.) on a side. In it were set 12 precious stones in four rows of three, each engraved with the name of one of the 12 tribes. A pouch was attached to it by gold chains and rings which contained the oracle of the Urim and Thummim*. The breastplate symbolized the function of the high priest as the representative of all Israel.

Brethren of the Lord. The brethren of Jesus are mentioned in Mt 12:46; 13:55 f; Mk 3:31; 6:3; Lk 8:19; Jn 2:12; 7:3 ff; 20:17; AA 1:14; 1 Co 9:5; Gal 1:19. Four are mentioned by name: James*, Joses* (or Joseph*), Simon*, and Judas* (Mt 13:55; Mk 6:3). The tradition of the perpetual virginity of Mary* has always rejected the idea that these were her children and the theory proposed by a few Fathers that they were children of Joseph by a previous marriage has no foundation. The Gk word *adelphos*, brother (*adelphē*, sister) is used much as brother and sister are used in Eng. Here, however, one must recall the Hb-Aramaic background of the Gospels, which often shows that Gk words are translations of their Semitic usage. Hb words for distinction of degrees of kinship are neither as many nor as exact as our own words; and we often see reflections of the ancient nomadic usage by which all members of a tribe* or clan were called brothers, just as the tribal or clan head, the sheik, was sometimes called father. Of the four mentioned by name it is clear that James and Joses (Joseph) are sons neither of Joseph nor of Mary the mother of Jesus. A different Mary is the mother of them both; she was among the group at the foot of the cross (Mt 27:56; Mk 15:40). James is called the son of Alphaeus* in the lists of the apostles (Mt 10:3; Mk 3:18; Lk 6:15; AA 1:13). Furthermore, there is no mention of other children anywhere, and it is difficult to explain how Jesus commended Mary to the care of the disciple John* (Jn 19:26) if there were other sons. There is nothing in the Gospels or in linguistic usage which is opposed to the tradition of the perpetual virginity of Mary; and this tradition itself is difficult to explain if these allusions were ever understood as meaning uterine brothers and sisters. The exact degree of relationship between Jesus and His brethren cannot be reconstructed.

Brick. Brick was the most common building material in Palestine, Egypt, and Mesopotamia. Clay is abundant in Egypt and Mesopotamia, while stone is more abundant in Palestine; the use of brick is to be explained by the lack of adequate metal tools and skilled labor for extensive working of stone. Bricks were made by mixing the clay with the feet, the addition of a binder such as straw, and sun-drying in wooden molds; kiln-fired bricks were known in Mesopotamia (Gn 11:3), but the remains show that they were used only in areas where more durable brick was necessary. The Israelites were put to making bricks in Egypt (Ex 1:14; 5:6 ff). Clay was used in mortar; bitumen* was known in Mesopotamia. In both Egypt and Palestine stone was used only for temples and palaces; its employment was a sign of luxury (Is 9:9). The technique was not equal to that of the modern bricklayer, as can be observed in the few remains, and collapse is mentioned as a common danger (Is 30:13; Ezk 13:10 ff). Wooden beams were sometimes used as frames, but these added to the danger of fire. The bricks were easily damaged by moisture and cheaply made houses could dissolve in a heavy rain, although Nelson Glueck found at Ezion-geber* that the remains from Solomon's time resisted a torrential rain better than the brick houses of the modern inhabitants. In Hb folklore the invention of brickmaking was attributed to the builders of Babel* (Gn 11:3). Enameled bricks have been found in the remains of the buildings of Ashur-nasir-pal, Sargon, and Nebuchadnezzar (cf ASSYRIA; BABYLON), arranged in pictorial designs; but this skill does not appear in Israelite remains.

Bride, Bridegroom. Cf MARRIAGE.

Bronze. Ancient bronze was an alloy of copper* and tin*. The alloy increases the strength and hardness of copper while it lowers its melting point, and thus facilitates casting. Bronze is worked by being hammered or cast. The Bronze Age in the ancient Near East extended 3200–1200 BC (cf ARCHAEOLOGY). Neither the date nor the place of the discovery of bronze is known for certain; but it was almost certainly in Asia, and very probably in Anatolia. Probably its discovery was due to accident. It appears early in both Mesopotamia and Egypt, and was the primary metal for all purposes, not only tools and weapons, but also for ornamentation such as jewelry and statuary; cf separate articles. On the sources of the metals cf COPPER; TIN. It is not clear where the centers of the manufacture of bronze were to be found. For the bronze work of the temple Solomon hired craftsmen from Tyre* (1 K 7:13 ff), which suggests that little or no work of this kind was done by native Israelites. The casting was done in the Jordan valley between Succoth and Zarethan (1 K 7:46); the reasons for the selection of this site are not clear.

Brook. A common Eng translation of Hb *naḥal*, which, like Arabic *wadi*, signifies a seasonal stream which runs only during the

Ancient Egyptian brickmaking.

rainy months (cf *arroyo* in SW USA). The name is applied a few times to perennial streams, the Kishon* (Jgs 5:21; 1 K 18:40) and the Jabbok* (Gn 32:22).

Brother. The primary sense in both OT and NT is son of the same parents, either father and mother (e.g., Gn 27:6) or of same father and different mother (e.g., Gn 28:2). In polygamous households uterine brothers and sisters were closer to each other than half brothers and sisters. In a wider use it signifies a person of common ancestry and relationship; in particular, a member of the same clan or tribe (e.g., Nm 16:10). It is extended to members of the same race or nation (e.g., Dt 15:12) or of a kindred nation (e.g., Dt 23:7). In the NT Christians are called brothers about 160 times, and Jesus Himself said that one who does the will of the Father is His own brother (Mt 12:50; Mk 3:35; Lk 8:21). Brother is a term of polite address, especially of one monarch to another (1 K 20:32); this address is common in the Amarna* letters. In Gn 9:5; Mt 5:22; 18:35 + the word signifies a fellow human being; in these passages there is a warning against violence and anger.

Bul. The 8th month of the old Hb calendar*, corresponding to Marheswan, roughly our October-November.

Bull. On the cultivation of the bull cf ox. In the ancient Near East the bull was a very common symbol of strength and of virile fecundity and hence appears as a divine symbol. The title "the bull" is given to the moon god Sin (with reference to the horns of the crescent) and to Marduk in Mesopotamia, and to El, the head of the pantheon of Ugarit. The title *'ābîr,* given to Yahweh, usually translated "strong one," originally meant "the bull" (of Jacob, Gn 49:24; Pss 132:2, 5; of Israel, Is 1:24; 49:26; 60:16); but it is probable that the original meaning had been forgotten when this title is used in the literature. In the cult of N Israel Yahweh was represented by a bull which was the pedestal upon which He stood invisible (cf IMAGE; Ex 32; 1 K 12:26–33). This cult was reprobated with scorn by Amos (4:4; 5:5 f; 7:9) and Hosea (10:4–7; 8:4–6); although the explanation of the bull as pedestal by modern scholars is no doubt correct, it is not clear how many ignorant Israelites thought the bull was an image of Yahweh Himself in symbolic form. The value of the bull made it the most desirable sacrificial animal.

Burial. Burial was the almost universal practice in Palestine from prehistoric times; the archaeological remains of cremation occur only in pre-Israelite Gezer and Jerusalem. In the OT there is a possible allusion to cremation as an emergency measure during pestilence (Am 6:10). The burning of the bodies of Saul* and Jonathan* by the men of Jabesh-gilead probably refers to the burning of the flesh and entrails removed from the bones, which were then buried (Galling); but this practice does not appear elsewhere (1 S 31:11 ff).

1. *Archaeological Remains.* Most burials were simple inhumations which have left no traces; only the graves which were solidly constructed and presumably belonged to kings and the wealthy have survived. While burials in early times took place within the city walls and sometimes within the houses, graves are usually found outside the walls concentrated within a single area (necropolis). Prehistoric burials were done in caves or in dolmens, in which slabs of stone were set up in imitation of a house; the whole was often covered with a mound of earth (tumulus). In the Chalcolithic site of Teleilat el Ghassul were found chests and urns in which the bones of the deceased were kept in the house after the decay of the flesh. But the prevailing type of grave was the cave; and the need for more room as well as the need for using the site for more than one burial led first to the artificial enlargement of the natural cave, then to the excavation of entirely artificial caves. The simplest form of artificial cave was a chamber, natural or enlarged, entered by a shaft like a well. This appears in Middle Bronze. Technical improvements were a staircase entrance and the addition of another chamber; with variations in detail and further technical improvements this is substantially the type of grave which is found throughout the biblical period. Chambers with a vaulted masonry roof were found at Megiddo*. The entrance to the entire grave and the entrances to the separate chambers could be closed by rolling large stones before the opening, but they were not always closed; the tomb of Elisha* seems to have been open (2 K 13:21). The usual position of the body was supine, as in our burials; in early burials the bodies were sometimes interred with the knees drawn up to the chin. This has been thought to imitate the position of the fetus in the womb; it is possible also that it was no more than an economy of space. Only infants have been found buried in jars which were immured in walls or in the foundations of houses, with a few exceptions, and this type of burial is limited to the early periods. It is not clear that these were foundation sacrifices, but their position sug-

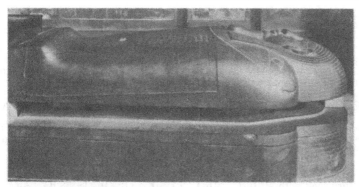

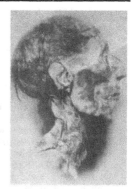

a) Sarcophagus of Eshmunazar of Sidon. b) Mummified head of Ramses II. c) Egyptian mummy. d) Tombs on the Via Appia.

gests some religious or superstitious motive. Just before the Philistine* invasion (about 1200 BC) the Canaanites had begun to bury their dead in clay coffins with human features molded upon the top; these were doubtless imitations of Egyptian sarcophagi. With the beginning of the Israelite period there appears the bench grave; the floor of the chamber was excavated to a depth of 2 ft or so, leaving a bench entirely around the wall of the chamber upon which the bodies were laid. A variation of this type is an elongated tunnel. Some have identified such a grave found on the southeastern hill of Jerusalem as the family sepulcher of the house of David, in which 13 kings of Judah were buried. Unfortunately quarrying in the area in Roman times has disturbed the

original form of the tunnel. With the beginning of the 2nd century BC there appears the catacomb type of grave, possibly introduced from Alexandria. Longitudinal niches were excavated in the wall of the chamber(s) to a depth of about 6½ ft, and 20–30 in. in width and height; the body was pushed into the niche, head or feet first, and the niche could be closed with a stone. When a new body was placed in an already used niche, the bones from the preceding burial were collected and placed in a limestone casket (ossuary), which in turn was placed either in the antechamber or in a niche in an adjoining chamber reserved for this purpose. Not until this type of grave appears was there any effort to keep the remains distinct; the ossuaries usually have a name upon them.

An ossuary of NT times was found with the name "Jesus son of Joseph"; at first it caused some excitement, but the name was one of the most common combinations of the period. The catacomb tomb, which was often entered, was closed at the entrance by a large stone rounded like a mill stone, which was usually set into a groove.

Throughout the Canaanite and Israelite periods graves appear with funerary deposits; their absence in some graves can be presumed due to disturbance or grave robbery, an extremely common crime from earliest historic times. Kings and nobles were buried with costly jewelry and with the insignia of office. The grave was furnished with all sorts of tools and utensils employed during life: weapons, personal seals, amulets, etc. A large amount of pottery shows that food and drink were left in the tombs. Pins and brooches show that the bodies were buried clothed. In later times the realism of the deposits was less pronounced, and in the Hellenistic period the most common article was the lamp.

2. *Biblical References.* The cave of Machpelah* at Hebron* purchased by Abraham* (Gn 23:1 ff) was the type of Bronze Age family tomb described above. The common biblical expression "to be buried with one's fathers" or "to sleep with one's fathers" probably refers to burial in family tombs, although the idiom becomes meaningless in this respect when it is used of burial elsewhere (e.g., David, 1 K 2:10). The Egyptian practice of mummification is mentioned only for Jacob* (Gn 50:3) and Joseph* (Gn 50:26). Jacob was buried at Machpelah, but both Rachel* (Gn 35:20) and Joseph (Jos 24:32) were buried elsewhere. The graves of men of renown were usually known, as is evident from the numerous references to grave sites, and it was worthy of note that the site of Moses's grave was not known (Dt 34:6). Barzillai* preferred to be buried in the sepulcher of his father and mother (2 S 19:38). Absalom* raised a pillar for himself (2 S 18:18); such monuments were rare, and until Hellenistic times nothing of the tomb appeared above ground. Isaiah uttered a threat against Shebna* for the vanity exhibited in hewing a new tomb in the rock (Is 22:16). The grave of the common people is mentioned in 2 K 23:6; it could scarcely have been the cave sepulcher of the type already described, and probably means an area of simple inhumation. Family tombs are mentioned for Gideon* (Jgs 8:32), Samson* (Jgs 16:31), Asahel* (2 S 2:32), Ahithophel* (2 S 17:23), the family of Kish* (2 S 21:14). The tombs of Jesus and of Lazarus* were probably the catacomb type; the tomb of Jesus was newly constructed by Joseph of Arimathea* and had not yet been used (Mt 27:60; Lk 23:53; Jn 19:41). The stone which closed it as well as the stone of the tomb of Lazarus (Jn 11:38 ff) was probably the rounded stone set in a groove. The body of Jesus was apparently not yet set in a niche, since its place could be seen from the entrance (Jn 20:5); it had been left on the bench for the completion of the burial wrapping.

Burial took place if possible on the day of death, and in OT times no preparation of the body was made, as far as we know. In NT times the body was washed (AA 9:37) and anointed with ointments and spices (Mk 16:1; Lk 16:56 ff; Jn 19:39 ff). All four Gospels mention the wrapping in linen, but only Jn mentions *othonia* (19:40; 20:7) and a handkerchief over the face (20:7). The nature of the wrapping is not clear; the word used by Jn suggests that the body was wound in linen bands. A similar word (*keiria*) is used of Lazarus (Jn 11:44), and such binding is further suggested by Jesus's command to untie him.

Burial was granted even to criminals after execution, and privation of burial was a great curse (Dt 28:26; 1 K 21:23 f; 2 K 9:36 f; Is 34:3; 66:24; Je 7:33; 14:16; 16:4; 19:7; 22:19; 25:33). Possibly the original purpose of burial was to prevent the deceased from haunting the survivors, but there is no evidence that the Israelites shared this belief. The funerary deposits likewise may have attested a belief in an afterlife in which these things would be necessary, as we know for the funerary deposits in Egypt. Without literary evidence, however, it is very difficult to deduce such beliefs. The OT exhibits no such idea (cf DEATH; SHEOL). In all cultures funeral practices exhibit many archaic features which are retained long after their original significance has been forgotten, and this is probably the explanation of the Israelite adoption of the Canaanite practice of funerary deposits. On the ritual of burial cf MOURNING.

Butter. Butter as we know it was not manufactured in biblical times. The word occurs in some Eng translations as a rendition of Hb *hem'āh,* curds of cow's or goat's milk (Gn 18:8; Dt 32:14; Jgs 5:25; 2 S 17:29; Jb 20:17; 29:6; Ps 55:22; Pr 30:33; Is 7:15, 22), esteemed as a delicacy in the Near East both in ancient and in modern times.

Byblos (Hb *g^rbal,* Gk *byblos*), a Phoenician city at the modern Jebeil, 25 mi N of Beirut on the coast of the Mediterranean. A tradition reported by Philo calls Byblos the oldest city in the world, founded and

Ruins of Byblos about
2000 B.C.

equipped with walls by the god El. It was the most important of the Phoenician cities from the beginning of recorded history down to about 1000 BC. Phoenicia was a meeting place of Mesopotamian, Egyptian, and — in the 2nd millennium BC — Mycenean influences. These mixed influences are reflected in the hybrid character of Phoenician art, most examples of which have been found at Byblos. Egyptian influence, however, was predominant. The principal commercial goods handled at Byblos were Lebanese cedars and copper from the Caucasus which was exported to Egypt. In return Byblos imported Egyptian papyrus* which it sold throughout the Mediterranean, giving its name not only to the product, but also to the Gk word *biblos,* book, from which *Bible* is derived. The Egyptian influence was strong on the religion of Byblos, but the influence was reciprocal; Baalat Gebal, "The Lady of Byblos," was identified with Hathor or Isis by the Egyptians. In the legend of Osiris the coffin of Osiris was cast into the sea by his enemies and floated ashore at Byblos, where it was recovered by Isis. The native religion of Byblos was the cult of Baal*, called by the Greeks Adonis, whom the Egyptians identified with Osiris. Byblos with the rest of the coast was conquered by the Hyksos* in the 18th century BC and regained for Egypt by Thutmose III (1502–1448). It was held by Egypt until its conquest by the Peoples of the Sea (cf PHILISTINES) in the

12th century. 64 of the Amarna* Letters come from Rib-Addi of Byblos, and these give much information on the disturbed condition of Phoenicia in the closing years of the 18th dynasty. The letters refer often to the former prosperity of Byblos, which the king refers to the protection of the Pharaoh and to the unbroken loyalty of Byblos to Egypt during the preceding centuries, which seems to be no exaggeration of the facts. Byblos is mentioned as a point on the journey of Sinuhe about 1960 BC. The story of Wen-Amon of Egypt, who was sent to Byblos to purchase cedar (about 1100 BC), shows that the city had become completely independent of Egypt, and the Egyptian envoy was treated with the utmost discourtesy. Byblos was tributary to the Assyrians. It is first mentioned by Tiglath-pileser I (1112–1074 BC) and the kings of the 9th, 8th, and 7th centuries almost without exception include Byblos among the Phoenician cities tributary to them. It is also mentioned by Nebuchadnezzar* of Babylon. The city has been extensively excavated by the French Archaeological School of Syria since 1921, and the excavations have disclosed a wealth of objects of Phoenician art. The excavators found the city walls; the earliest wall was rebuilt and remodeled and used throughout the subsequent history of the city. The temple of Baalat Gebal was identified; the oldest portion of the temple was built in the 4th millennium BC, and the temple was rebuilt after a conflagration in 2150 BC. The construction reflected Egyptian influence and the temple contained a large number of Egyptian votive offerings. Vestigial remains of two other temples equally old were discovered; one of these was dedicated to Resheph*. The excavators also found the well which provided water for the ancient city and a number of Phoenician tombs. The remains of the Roman city included the debris of a colonnade and the remains of a theater. Of importance for the history of writing were the pseudo-hieroglyphic inscriptions of the 13th century BC. These were written in a prealphabetic type of writing which has not yet been deciphered. The three passages in which Byblos is mentioned in the OT do not reflect the importance of the ancient city. It is included in the territory claimed for Israel (Jos 13:5), a claim which was never implemented, and the temple of Solomon was built with the help of carpenters and masons from Byblos (1 K 5:32). The men of Byblos were famous as skilled mariners (Ezk 27:9).

C

Cabul (Hb *kābûl,* etymology uncertain), the name of a district of 20 cities in Galilee* given by Solomon* to Hiram* of Tyre* in payment for work on the temple* (1 K 9:10 ff). Hiram's unfavorable reception of the payment gave rise to the popular etymological pun *kebal,* "good for nothing." Chronicles*, with its peculiar treatment of history, relates that Hiram gave the cities to Solomon (2 Ch 8:2).

Caesar. The *cognomen* of Gaius Julius Caesar (100–44 BC) who effectively established dictatorial rule in Rome and broke the power of the Senate, thus founding the imperial government. It was the adopted name of Octavius (cf AUGUSTUS) and after him became an official title of the emperor. Three of the Caesars are mentioned in the NT: Augustus*, Tiberius*, and Claudius*.

Caesarea (Gk *kaesareia*), a city of the Palestinian coast, the modern Kaisariyeh S of Mt Carmel. The city was built by Herod* the Great on the site of a settlement known previously as the Tower of Straton and was practically an entirely new construction. Herod created an artificial harbor by the erection of sea walls 200 ft wide standing in 20 fathoms of water. The city itself was built in the Hellenistic style with agora, theater, amphitheater, stadium, a palace, a temple of Caesar, and colossal statues of Augustus and Rome. The amphitheater was an oval enclosing an area 300 ft long and 200 ft wide, slightly larger than the area enclosed by the Colosseum of Rome. The city was 12 years in construction (25–13 BC) and was inaugurated by games in 9 BC. Excavations have been carried out at Caesarea. Underwater explorations off the shore have shown the massive character of the moles built by Herod. Caesarea became at once the principal port of Palestine, which has no natural harbor on its coast. The Roman procurator made his residence there and it became effectively the capital of the country; but it was predominantly Hellenistic. Caesarea is not mentioned in the Gospels. In AA it is the port of arrival and departure for several journeys (AA 9:30; 18:22; 21:8). It was reached by Philip* but its evangelization apparently was first conducted by Peter* at the house of Cornelius* (AA 10:1 ff), and there were disciples there who accompanied Paul on his journey to Jerusalem (AA 21:16). It was the residence of Herod Agrippa* during his short reign (AA 12:19), and as the residence of the procurator it was the place to which Paul was taken for custody from Jerusalem (AA 23:23 ff). He was detained there until his appeal to Caesar, and the hearings of his process were conducted at Caesarea (AA 24–26).

Caesarea Philippi. A town in the extreme N of Palestine, the modern Baniyas at one of the sources of the Jordan in the S foothills of Mt Hermon. The city lay near the site of the Israelite city of Dan*. During the Hellenistic* period the town received the name Panion because of the sanctuary of Pan located there. Herod* the Great built a temple to Augustus, and Philip* rebuilt it into a large Hellenistic city, naming it after the emperor and adding his own name to distinguish it from the other cities of the same name. The neighborhood (Mt 16:13) or the village (Mk 8:27) was the scene of Peter's confession; but the passage does not suggest that Jesus actually entered this largely Gentile community.

Caiaphas (Gk *kaiaphas,* meaning unknown). Surname of Joseph, high priest* at the time of the beginning of the preaching of John the Baptist* (Lk 3:2) and during the trial of Jesus. He was the son-in-law of Annas*, whose family retained the office of high priest for many years. He was appointed high priest by Valerius Gratus in AD 18 and deposed by Vitellius in AD 36. He was perhaps the first to suggest that Jesus would have to be killed to prevent trouble (Jn 11:49 ff). The plans for the arrest of Jesus were made in his house (Mt 26:3 ff), and the hearing before the Sanhedrin was held there (Mt 26:57 ff; Mk 14:53 ff; Lk 22:54 ff). Caiaphas asked Jesus the question about His messianic claims which enabled the court to vote Him guilty of blasphemy (Mt 27:62 ff; Mk 14:61 ff). Caiaphas also appears among the priests at the trial of Peter and John (AA 4:6), but Annas is called high priest. If the years of his appointment as given by Josephus are correct, this passage and others in which the title is given to Annas must be a recognition of the *de facto* control which Annas exercised over the office and its incumbents.

Cain (Hb *ḳayin,* "smith"), first son of Adam* and Eve* (Gn 4:1), eponymous ancestor of the Kenites*. There is a pun on his name, probably to be explained as *kanîtî 'iš*, "I have gotten a man-child." Several legends, probably independent of each other, are clustered about Cain. He appears as the peasant villain in the story of the feud between peasant and herdsman, which here breaks out for the first time. The motive of his murder of his brother Abel* is his envy because Yahweh has preferred the sacrifice* of Abel; this shows the excellence of animal over vegetable sacrifice. He is condemned to the life of the nomad in the land of Nod*. Since the nomads are protected from attack only by the law of the avenger*, Yahweh makes upon Cain a sign, i.e., marks corresponding to the tattooing which identifies the clan of the nomad and shows that he is protected. A different legend makes Cain the builder of the first city, which he calls Enoch*, after the name of his son; the name means or plays upon the word "foundation." The name Cain also suggests that he once was identified as the inventor of metalworking, which in the traditions of Gn has passed to his descendant Tubal-cain* (Gn 4:22). These traditions of the invention of civilization with its arts and crafts have here been collected under the one line of the first murderer, and thus Hb tradition passed an unfavorable judgment upon the civilizations of Mesopotamia and Canaan, a judgment which is reflected elsewhere in the OT. Hb 11:4 finds Cain's radical vice to be a lack of faith. 1 Jn 3:12 describes him as a child of the evil one. Heretics walk in the way of Cain (Jd 11).

Calah (Hb *kālaḥ*, Assyrian *kalḫu*, meaning uncertain), in Hb tradition one of the cities built by Nimrod* (Gn 10:11). Calah was an Assyrian city situated on the left bank of the Tigris at the mouth of the upper Zab, about 20 mi S of Nineveh*. It is first mentioned under Shalmaneser I (1273–1244 BC), but fell into ruins in subsequent years. It was rebuilt by Ashur-nasir-pal II (883–859 BC) and remained the seat of the Assyrian king until Sennacherib (704–681 BC) removed his capital to Nineveh. Esarhaddon (680–669 BC) built a new palace in Calah, but Ashur-bani-pal (668–626 BC) again transferred the royal residence to Nineveh. His successor, Ashur-etil-ilani (625–621 BC) built a new palace at Calah which is notably smaller and poorer than the earlier palaces. Excavations of the mound of Nimrud by A. H. Layard (1845–1847) disclosed the palaces of Ashur-nasir-pal, Tiglath-pileser III and Esarhaddon. It is somewhat surprising that the city is mentioned only once in the OT. At Calah was discovered the Black Obelisk of Shalmaneser III, with a picture of the tribute brought by Jehu* of Israel.

Excavations have been conducted by Mallowan since 1949.

Caleb (Hb *kālēb*, "dog?"), the name *klby* occurs in Ugarit* and in Sidon*, written the same way as variant spelling of Chelubai, *kᵉlûbāy*, 1 Ch 2:9, an early Israelite hero whose name appears later as that of a clan. In Nm 13:6; 14:6, 30; 26:65; 32:12; Dt 1:34 he is the son of Jephunneh of the tribe of Judah*, one of the 12 scouts sent to explore Canaan and the only one to bring a favorable report. For this reason he alone is spared the extinction threatened the others. He is one of the 12 appointed to apportion the land to the tribes (Nm 34:19). This is recalled in Jos 14:6 ff where Caleb receives Hebron as his portion; he evicted the three sons of Anak* (Jos 15:13 ff), and his nephew Othniel*, the son of Kenaz*, captured Kirjath-sepher* (Jos 15:16 ff; Jgs 1:12 ff). In Jgs 1:10–11, however, the capture is attributed to the tribe of Judah with no mention of Caleb; on the other hand, Jephunneh is called a Kenizzite* in Jos 14:6, 14. The allotment of Hebron to Caleb in Jos 14:14; 15:13 explains how the Kenizzites come to have a portion in the tribe of Judah. In the genealogies of Ch Caleb is called the son of Hezron* of the tribe of Judah (1 Ch 2:9, 18) and there can scarcely be question of a different person; the territory described in 1 Ch 2:42–50, in which towns of southern Judah are reckoned as children of Caleb, is the territory of Caleb and the Kenizzites. But Caleb appears again as the son of Jephunneh in 1 Ch 4:15. There is no certain explanation of these confusing data; nor is it necessary to remove Caleb as an individual figure of tradition to explain them. The genealogy of Ch is obviously artificial, in which names of cities are arranged under a clan name as "children" of the clan. The clan of Caleb in the genealogy is reckoned under the clan of Hezron, and it appears identical with the clan of the Kenizzites; on the origin of this clan cf KENIZZITES. The genealogical relationship is easily understood as representing the adoption of the clan of Caleb or the Kenizzites by the clan of Hezron, which made them members of the tribe of Judah.

Calendar. The biblical calendar is based upon a solar year of 365¼ days and a lunar month of 29½ days. A satisfactory solution of the problem of the fractions was never reached in Israel or in Judaism. Twelve lunar months give a year of 354 days; the difference as well as the fraction of a day in a solar year were made up by intercalating a second month of Adar at the end of the year. There is no reference to the means by which this was computed. The month, *yārē"ḥ*, lit "moon," or *ḥōdeš*, lit "new moon" began with the new moon and ended with the following new moon. The phases of the moon were not calculated exactly, but the length of 29½ days was known and the new moon could be expected. According to the Talmud the observation was made in Jerusalem and transmitted through the country by signal fires; but the antiquity of this practice is not attested. In early Israel the months were distinguished by number until the Canaanite names of the months were adopted, of which four appear in the OT. With the names the early Israelites probably adopted the Canaanite calendar in substance. After the exile in Babylon (587 BC) the Babylonian names of the months were adopted:

Israelite	Canaanite	Babylonian	Modern
1.	Abib	Nisan	March-April
2.	Ziw	Iyyar	April-May
3.		Siwan	May-June
4.		Tammuz	June-July
5.		Ab	July-August
6.		Elul	August-September
7.	Ethanim	Tishri	September-October
8.	Bul	Marheshwan	October-November
9.		Kisleu	November-December
10.		Tebet	December-January
11.		Shebat	January-February
12.		Adar	February-March

The OT exhibits two points for the beginning of the year. The Babylonian calendar and the Hb numeration of the months both begin in the spring with the 1st of Nisan. The feast of the new year*, however, was celebrated on the 1st of Tishri, the 7th month, in the autumn. Evidence is lacking to show the origin and the relationship of these two calculations. The Nisan new year is attributed to Moses (Ex 12:20), but it could easily have been traditional before the time of Moses, especially since the patriarchs were of Mesopotamian origin, and Canaan was under Mesopotamian cultural influence during much of the early 2nd millennium BC. Hence it appears likely that the autumn new year was of Israelite origin.

Calneh, Calno. 1. Hb *kalneh*, one of the cities built by Nimrod* in the land of Shinar* (Gn 10:10). No such name is known in Mesopotamia, and W. F. Albright has shown that the name should be read *kullaneh*, "all of them." **2.** A city mentioned with Hamath* and Gath* in Am 6:2, and probably the same as Calno (Hb *kalnō*) mentioned with Carchemish*, Hamath*, and

Arpad* among cities conquered by the Assyrians; hence a location in northern Syria is indicated. A city of Kullani in Syria is mentioned by Tiglath-pileser* III (745–727) BC).

Calvary. Cf GOLGOTHA.

Camel. The camel is mentioned frequently in the OT as a beast of riding and of burden and as a form of wealth. W. F. Albright and others have presented very serious arguments to show that the camel was not domesticated before the Late Bronze Age and that the earliest historical mention of the camel in the OT is its appearance in the story of raids of the Midianites* on Israel (Jgs 6:5; 7:12; 8:21, 26). Consequently the camels included in the patriarchal stories must be regarded as anachronisms; they are found among the wealth of Abraham (Gn 12:16) and Jacob (Gn 30:43; 32:8, 15) and of the Egyptians (Ex 9:3). They appear as riding animals and gifts (Gn 24; 31:17, 34) and in a caravan of traders (Gn 37:25). The camel was ritually unclean (Lv 11:4; Dt 14:7). The absence of the camel in documents and art from periods earlier than the Late Bronze Age is very telling against its use in the patriarchal period. After the Late Bronze Age the camel is possessed by nomadic tribes (1 S 15:3; 30:17) and by the men of Judah (1 S 27:9), and was part of the wealth of the queen of Sheba* (1 K 10:2). A caravan of 40 camels appears in the stories of Elisha (2 K 8:9). The superstitions of Jerusalem are compared to the lust of the she-camel (Je 2:23 f).

The camel mentioned in the OT is most probably the dromedary with one hump; this species was most easily acquired in Palestine and was the most common type elsewhere in the ancient Near East. The Bactrian camel with two humps was known; it appears in the tribute offered to Ashurnasir-pal II of Assyria (ANEP 351, 353). Camels are employed in battle by Arabian tribesmen in sculptures of Tiglath-pileser III (ANEP 375) and Ashur-bani-pal (ANEP 63) and are stabled in the Assyrian camp (ANEP 170). They are part of the booty of war (ANEP 187). A sculpture of the 9th century from Tell Halaf represents a camel rider (ANEP 188).

The camel represented a minor revolution in nomadic life and commerce in the ancient Near East. It gave nomadic tribes much more mobility and permitted them to claim larger areas for their pastures. "The ship of the desert" made possible a much more rapid and wide exchange of goods between areas separated by the Syrian and Arabian deserts. Its skin served for the manufacture

A desert scene. A modern camel caravan.

of tent fabric and for human clothing (Elijah, John the Baptist). Its milk is esteemed by nomads. It does not seem to have had a profound effect on the technique of ancient war.

In the NT the camel is mentioned only in figures of speech: the camel which cannot pass through the eye of the needle (Mt 19:24; Mk 10:25; Lk 18:25), and the camel which the Pharisees swallow while they strain out the gnat (Mt 23:24). The violence of both figures led a number of critics to suspect that the original reading was Gk *kamilos*, cable (pronounced like *kamēlos*, "camel," in later Gk). The MS evidence, however, supports *kamēlos* fully; and the violence of the metaphor is less in ancient Near Eastern speech than it would be in modern speech. Hyperbole is common in oriental languages. The figure of the camel passing through the eye of the needle expresses not difficulty but impossibility; and the figure of the camel which is swallowed is intended to affirm that no crime is too great for the Pharisees to tolerate if it can be in some way "legalized."

Camp. The encampment of modern nomadic tribes is set up at random in a cluster, and nothing indicates that the nomadic camps of OT times followed a more precise pattern. If there is danger of attack the tents are grouped more closely in a circle. The Israelite camp described by the P source of the Pnt in Nm 2 is set up in a square around the tent of meeting with three tribes on each side; this schematic arrangement is an ideal created by the imagination of the priestly writer, but it is not without resemblance to the formal arrangement of the fortified camp of the Roman legion, built in a square with two intersecting avenues. The Assyrian improvements in military technique probably included the arrangement and fortification of the camp, but it is not represented in their art.

Cana (Gk *kana*, meaning uncertain), a town of Galilee; the scene of the wedding where Jesus changed water into wine (Jn 2:1–11), revisited by Jesus (Jn 4:46), the home of Nathanael* (Jn 21:2). The site is uncertain; tradition places Cana at Kefr Kenna, five mi NE of Nazareth, but many scholars believe that Khirbet Qanah, nine mi N of Nazareth, is more probable.

Canaan, Canaanite (Hb *kᵉnáʿan*), the name of the land lying between Syria and Egypt in which the Israelites settled. The name occurs both in Egyptian and in cuneiform records during the 2nd millennium BC. The origin and meaning of the name are uncertain. Recently a connection with *kinahhu*

Cana.

of the Nuzu* tablets has been suggested; there the word means purple wool, one of the most famous products of Canaan (cf Gk Phoenicia* *phoinix,* "purple"), and *mat kinaḥḥi* is taken to mean "land of purple wool." The etymology, however, could run in the opposite direction; purple wool would be a "product of Canaan," a phenomenon often observed in linguistic borrowings (Eng wiener, champagne, damask, calico). The boundaries of Canaan fluctuate in the different sources. Cuneiform sources give no clear idea of what they meant by the term, preferring the designation Amurru (cf AMORITES) for the entire west, or mentioning particular regions or cities by name. In the Amarna* letters Amurru sometimes means Syria N of Beirut; elsewhere in the letters, cities N of this line are called Canaanite, and the term appears to signify the entire coast of Syria and Palestine and the hinterland as far as the Jordan. The name Amurru, consequently, is correspondingly restricted to the Lebanon* and Anti-Lebanon. The Egyptians used the name Canaanites exceptionally, preferring other names (Haru, Retenu). The population of Palestine and southern Phoenicia was Canaanite in the second half of the second millennium BC, and it is impossible at present to state when this people entered the country. The progressive depopulation of Palestine from 2300–2100 BC has no certain explanation; it is clear that the Canaanites were forced S after 2000 BC by a barbarian invasion of non-Semitic hordes; cf HURRIANS, HYKSOS. After the Egyptian conquest of Palestine in the 15th

century BC there was a further depopulation and lowering of the cultural level, which is attributed at least in part to the oppression and plundering of the Egyptian rulers. The Canaanites, thus weakened, were invaded not only by the Hebrews, but also by the Philistines* and Aramaeans*, and Canaanite civilization thereafter flourished in Phoenicia. The Canaanites in Israelite territory were either conquered or survived by treaty as distinct cities; in either case, the Canaanite population was absorbed by Israel in the course of time.

In Hb folklore Canaan was the son of Ham* and the brother of Cush*, Egypt*, and Put* (Gn 9:18 ff; 10:6); this is an artificial arrangement, since the Canaanites were as much "Semites" as were the Hebrews. Both this notice and the curse of Noah on Ham (for whose name Canaan is substituted in Gn 9:25–27) reflect the Hebrew revulsion from Canaanite civilization and religion, just as the allusion to the slavery of Canaan reflects the position of the Canaanites as a subject people. Canaan begot Sidon* as his firstborn — a reference to the antiquity of Sidon, although it was not the oldest of the Phoenician cities (Gn 10:15); he was also the "father" of the other tribes mentioned as present in Canaan at the time of the Hebrew invasion. The Canaanites were scattered from Sidon to Gaza* and Sodom* (Gn 10:19); this does not correspond precisely to the boundaries of Canaan described above. The land of the Canaanites is called the seashore (Dt 1:7; Jos 5:1), as distinguished from the mountains of the Amorites, the valley of the Jordan, the hill-country, the Shephelah*, and the Lebanon. In Dt 11:30 (probably a gloss) the Canaanites live in the Jordan valley. In Nm 13:29 the Canaanites inhabit the seashore and the Jordan valley, while the Amorites, Hittites*, and Jebusites* inhabit the mountains; this division is not always followed. Canaanite enclaves in Israelite territory are mentioned expressly in Manasseh* (Jos 17:11 ff; Jgs 1:27), Ephraim*, Zebulun*, Asher*, Naphtali* (Jgs 1:28–33), and the assimilation of the two peoples is mentioned in Jgs 3:5. The Canaanite town of Gezer* did not pass into Israelite hands until the time of Solomon* (1 K 9:16). The use of "Canaanite" to mean "merchant" or "trader" (Jb 40:30; Pr 31:24; Is 23:8; probably also Ho 12:8; Zp 1:11) in later Hb literature indicates that merchandising was largely in the hands of the Canaanites during the Hb monarchy.

The influence of the Canaanites upon the Hebrews in religion, culture, and other human activities was incalculable and is noticed under separate articles.

Candace (Gk *kandakē*, from Ethiopic *kenteky*), dynastic title of the queens of Ethiopia*, probably Meroe in Nubia. A eunuch of the queen of Ethiopia was converted to Christianity by the deacon Philip* (AA 8:27).

Candle, Candlestick. A common Eng mistranslation of "lamp"*, "lampstand." Candles i.e., tapers of wax, tallow, etc., dipped or molded around a wick of thread, while known to the Etruscans and Romans, are not mentioned in the Bible.

Canon (Gk *kanōn*, Hb *ḳāneh*, "reed," used as an instrument of measure; hence measure or rule.) In its four appearances in the NT it means either a field of apostolic labor, an apportionment (2 Co 10:13–16) or a general statement of a point of doctrine (Gal 6:16). In ecclesiastical usage the word came early to mean the rule of faith, i.e., the statement of Christian dogma, either entire or in some detail; thus the statements of councils were called canons. Disciplinary regulations of ecclesiastical authorities were also called canons, "rules" of life. The fixed part of the Mass, in contrast to the changeable parts which follow seasons and feasts, was called the canon. Canon also signifies a list or enumeration: and in this sense the canon of the Bible means the authoritative list of the books contained in the Bible. A book is canonical because it is inspired (cf INSPIRATION); but the two words do not mean the same thing. An inspired book is a book written by God through the instrumentality of a human author; a canonical

book is a book recognized by the Church as inspired and proposed to the faithful as the word of God and a source of revealed doctrine. In Catholic belief the canonicity of the Bible is determined entirely by the tradition of the Church, which alone is empowered, as the custodian of divine revelation, to determine the sacred books. Catholic belief differs here from Protestant belief, which determines canonicity by the capacity of the book to communicate religious experience, or by Jewish tradition and apostolic authorship. It is not possible to trace the earliest stages in the formation of the Catholic tradition of the canon; in general, it contains the OT as accepted by the apostles and the NT as a collection of apostolic writings, at least indirectly (Mark, Luke). The canonicity of the NT books, however, is independent of the question of their apostolic authorship.

1. The Canon of the Old Testament. It is probably not correct to speak of a Jewish canon of the Bible before the Christian era, when controversy with the Christians made it necessary to determine a canon. That the Jews had a collection of sacred books before the Christian era is evident. In the OT itself there are allusions to the writing and preservation of books or parts of books (Ex 17:14; 24:4; Nm 33:2; Dt 31:24 ff; Jos 24:25 f; 1 S 10:25; Pr 25:1; Is 30:8; Je 36:2 ff). These passages, however, do not indicate the sacred character of the books. This is seen in Dn 9:2; 1 Mc 12:9; probably also in Ne 8:1 ff; 2 Mc 2:13–15. The extent of the collection is not entirely certain. Modern Jews accept the canon as it is found in the Masoretic Hebrew text counting 24 books: (1) The Law: Gn, Ex, Lv, Nm, Dt. (2) The Prophets, divided into the former prophets: Jos, Jgs, 1–2 S, 1–2 K; and the latter prophets: Is, Je, Ezk, the 12 prophets counted as one book (Ho, Jl, Am, Ob, Mi, Jon, Na, Hab, Zp, Hg, Zc, Mal). (3) The Writings: 1–2 Ch, Ezr-Ne, Est, Rt, Pss, Pr, Jb, Lam, Ec, SS, Dn. The Alexandrian Gk translation made by Jews in the 3rd–2nd centuries BC (LXX; cf SEPTUAGINT) contains in addition 1–2 Mc, Tb, Jdt, BS, WS, Bar, and some additional parts in Dn and Est (cf DANIEL; ESTHER). These books are called deuterocanonical. Both these collections are of Jewish origin and their relations are difficult to trace. BS 44–50, "the praise of the fathers," written about 180 BC in Palestine, alludes to all the books of the Hb canon except Dn, Ezr, and Est; hence it may be suspected that these books were not included in the collection at this date. The Jewish historian Flavius Josephus, writing in AD 93, testifies to 22 sacred and divinely inspired books, which are easily identified with the Hb canon; the books were sometimes numbered as 22 instead of 24 by counting Jgs-Rt and Je-Lam as single books, thus reaching a number identical with the number of letters in the Hb alphabet. Josephus also alludes to a rabbinical tradition that Ezra closed the canon of the Bible; this tradition, which is unfounded in fact, is probably an implicit attack on the Alexandrian collection. Another rabbinical tradition attributes the definition of the canon to a synod at Jamnia in Palestine about 100 AD; but here also there is little reliable information on the activities of this synod.

Both the Palestinian collection represented by the Hb text and the Alexandrian collection represented by the Gk version almost certainly came from a gradual and unplanned development. The three divisions of Law, Prophets, and Writings may be taken to represent three stages in which the collection grew in that order; in the time of BS, for instance, the collection of the Writings was not yet complete. Neither the arrangement nor the order of the books in the Alexandrian collection follows the Hb collection; this suggests that the collection was still fluid both in arrangement and in content. Had there been a Palestinian "canon," it is difficult to see how the Alexandrian Jews, who followed the spiritual leadership of the Jerusalem rabbis, could have formed a different canon. The Samaritans, who seceded from the Jews some time after 400 BC, never accepted any book as sacred except the Law. In the NT we find Jesus and the apostles accepting, in common with the Jews, a collection of sacred books, and the titles used fit the threefold division of the Hb books; but the content of the collection cannot be determined from the NT. All the books of the Hb canon are quoted expressly except Ezr, Ne, Est, Rt, Ec, SS, Ob, Na. Of 350 quotations of the OT in the NT it is estimated that about 300 are the same as the LXX, and that the LXX was the principal source of these quotations. No deuterocanonical book is quoted, although echoes and allusions are found to Mc, BS, WS. From the time of Paul onwards there can be little doubt that the LXX, with the deuterocanonical books, was the OT of the apostolic church; it was probably adopted because Gk was the common language of the Mediterranean lands. This acceptance of the sacred books as found in the LXX perseveres in all the ecclesiastical writers of the first three centuries AD except Melito of Sardis (+ about 193), who cites the Hb canon; the fact of a difference is mentioned by Origen (+ 254), who affirms the right of Christians to employ the deuterocanonical books, even though they are not accepted by the Jews. The same canon is found in all the official canons: the Cheltenham Canon, about 350; the canons of Hippo (393), Carthage (397), and Innocent I (405), except the canon of Laodicea (360).

Hence it is difficult to explain how some fathers in the 4th century returned to the Hb canon, explicitly rejecting the deuterocanonical books: Athanasius (+ 373), Cyril of Jerusalem (+ 386), Hilary of Poitiers (+ 366), Jerome (+ 420), Rufinus (+ 410), Gregory of Nazianzen (+ 390). The root of this opinion is to be found in Jerome in his studies with Jews, and probably the same influence is to be sought in the others; it is also to be noted that the opinion appears in the east and in Lt fathers who lived for long periods in the east. The authority of these fathers was so great that their opinion survived in learned circles until the 16th century, although the council of Florence (1441) set forth the Alexandrian canon. In the sessions of the Council of Trent some of the fathers wished the opinion of Jerome to be defined, or at least to qualify acceptance of the deuterocanonical books in some way. The Reformers, in their campaign to return to the primitive faith, rejected the Alexandrian canon as a later addition and accepted only those books which are contained in the Hb text. Hence the Council of Trent made its first business the definition of the sources of revealed doctrine, and after some remarkably vigorous disputes proposed in its session of April 8, 1546, the books of the following canon of the OT, which it accepted "with equal devotion and reverence":

Five books of Moses, namely, Gn, Ex, Lv, Nm, Dt, followed by Jos, Jgs, 1–2 S, 1–2 K, 1–2 Ch, Ezr-Ne, Tb, Jdt, Est, 1–2 Mc, Rt, Pss, Pr, Jb, Lam, Ec, SS, BS, WS, Is, Je, Ezk, Bar, Dn, Ho, Jl, Am, Ob, Mi, Jon, Na, Hab, Zp, Hg, Zc, Mal.

The rejection of these books was condemned as heretical, and thus the question was closed among Catholics. The reformed churches have adhered to the Jewish canon, although many modern Protestants admit the spiritual value of some of the deuterocanonical books.

2. *The Canon of the New Testament.* The collection of the books of the NT as sacred probably began with the preservation of the writings from apostolic circles; the apostles, as eyewitnesses of the life and teaching of Jesus and as those upon whom the Holy Spirit had descended in tongues of flame, were the legitimate successors of the prophets. It is remarkable that the beginnings of such a collection appear even in the 1st century. Quotations from NT books (usually implicit) are found in the writings of Clement of Rome (+ 100), Ignatius of Antioch (+ 107), Polycarp of Smyrna (+ 156), the

Shepherd of Hermas, written at Rome about 140–155, and the anonymous *Didache Apostolorum (Teaching of the Apostles),* written 80–100 in Syria or Palestine. After 150 the NT is quoted as Scripture, a sacred book of equal standing with the OT. But the earliest canon of the NT proceeds from a heretic, not from orthodox Christians. Marcion (about 150) rejected the entire OT and of the NT accepted only an abbreviated Lk, Rm, 1–2 Co, Gal, Eph, Col, 1–2 Th, Phl, Phm. This no doubt hastened the definition of an orthodox canon, which first appeared in the Muratorian Fragment, written about 200. This fragment omits Heb, Js, 1–2 Pt.

While there was never such a doubt about the NT canon as was expressed about the OT, local and personal doubts persisted about certain books, especially in the east, down to the 5th or 6th century; the books in question were Heb, Js, 2 Pt, 2–3 Jn, Jd, Apc. Reasons for the doubts can be assigned in each case: Heb and 2 Pt because of differences in style between these works and the works of Paul and 1 Pt (cf HEBREWS, EPISTLE TO THE; PETER, EPISTLES OF); Js and Jd

because some doctrinal difficulties were suspected; 2–3 Jn because the matter was thought to be trivial; Apc because of its style and obscurity. The traditional canon was accepted with no other difficulty up to the 16th century. Erasmus and Cajetan, misled by spurious erudition, revived some of the ancient doubts. Luther and some other German reformers rejected Jd, Heb, Js, and Apc; Luther's objection to Js for teaching that faith without works is dead is well known. The other reformed churches, however, did not dispute the canon, and the Lutherans returned to the traditional canon in the 17th century. The Council of Trent in the session of April 8, 1546, defined the following canon of the NT:

Four Gospels: Mt, Mk, Lk, Jn; AA written by Lk; 14 epistles of St. Paul, i.e., Rm, 1–2 Co, Gal, Eph, Phl, Col, 1–2 Th, 1–2 Tm, Tt, Phm, Heb; 1–2 Pt, 1–2–3 Jn, Js, Jd, Apc of John the Apostle.

Capernaum (Gk *kapharnaüm,* Aramaic *kᵉpar naḥûm,* meaning uncertain), a town of Galilee, identified with the modern Tell Hum

a) Ruins of synagogue at Capernaum.
b) Roman columns at Capernaum.

on the N shore of the Sea of Galilee W of the Jordan. The site lies 23 mi from Nazareth. In the Synoptic Gospels Capernaum is the center of the activity of Jesus in Galilee; Mt 4:13 states that He established His own residence there, and in Mt 9:1 Capernaum is called "his own city." Jesus began His public ministry by teaching in the synagogue of Capernaum on the Sabbath (Mk 1:21; Lk 4:31). Capernaum was the scene of the healing of the centurion's servant (Mt 8:5–13; Lk 7:1–10), the healing of the man with the palsy (Mk 2:1–12), of the payment of the temple tax (Mt 17: 24–27) and the discussion of the disciples and the accompanying saying of Jesus about who is the greatest (Mk 9:33–37). Most of the incidents and discourses of the first part of the Synoptic Gospels occurred in or near Capernaum, although the name of the city often is not mentioned. The wonders Jesus worked at Capernaum were referred to by the men of Nazareth (Lk 4:23). Capernaum was among the Galilean towns which Jesus cursed for their unbelief (Mt 11:23; Lk 10:15).

As the Galilean ministry is less prominent in Jn, Capernaum is mentioned less frequently. In Jn's account Jesus went to Capernaum from Cana* (Jn 2:12) for a sojourn of a few days. On His return from Jerusalem He healed the ruler's son of Capernaum without entering the city (Jn 4:46–54). Jn alludes to the teaching of Jesus in the synagogue of Capernaum (Jn 6:59) and locates the miracle of the multiplication across the lake from Capernaum (Jn 6:17, 24).

The site has not been thoroughly excavated and it is not known how far back the occupation goes. The remains of a synagogue at Tell Hum were excavated by the Franciscans after the first World War; but the synagogue was built no earlier than 200 AD. It is possible that it was constructed on the foundations of the synagogue which existed there in the 1st century.

Caph. The 11th letter of the Hb alphabet, with the value of *k*.

Caphtor (Hb *kaptōr*, meaning uncertain), the original home of the Philistines* (Am 9:7); the Philistines are the "remnant of Caphtor" in later times (Je 47:4). The Caphtorim were a "son" of Egypt (Gn 10:14; 1 Ch 1:12), and from them came the Philistines. The Caphtorim occupied the territory of the Awwim (Dt 2:23); they must be identical with the Philistines. The LXX rendered Caphtor as Cappadocia*; in modern times Crete* and the coast of Cilicia* have been suggested, but there are serious difficulties against both. It may be regarded as certain that Caphtor is to be found in the Aegean basin.

Cappadocia (Gk *kappadokia*), in LXX erroneously renders Caphtor*; a region of Asia Minor N of the Taurus and east of the Halys. It was a part of the kingdom of Pontus until it was established as a Roman province in AD 17. Jews from Cappadocia were present in Jerusalem at Pentecost (AA 2:9), and Christians of Cappadocia are addressed in 1 Pt 1:1.

Captain. In Eng versions used to translate several Hb or Gk words representing army* officers in all degrees from commander in chief to leader of a small company. Cf CENTURION; LEGION.

Captivity. Cf EXILE.

Carchemish (Hb *kark^emiš*, Akkadian Gargamish), modern Jerablus; a city on the right bank of the Euphrates about 65 mi NE of Aleppo. It was an extremely important military and commercial center; the trade routes from Assyria passed through Carchemish to Asia Minor in the north and to Phoenicia on the south. It was one of the strong points of the Hittite* empire; excavations conducted by the British Museum 1912–1914 disclosed that its culture remained distinctly Hittite from the 11th to the 9th centuries, after which it yielded to Aramaean* influence. The Hittite hieroglyphs of the site are being deciphered. It is mentioned often in both Egyptian and Mesopotamian historical records. It was conquered by Sargon* of Assyria in 717 BC and reduced from a vassal state to an Assyrian province (alluded to in Is 10:9). It was the scene of a decisive battle in 605 BC between the Babylonians under Nebuchadnezzar* and the Egyptians under Necho* (alluded to in 2 Ch 35:20) for the control of the Assyrian empire. Necho, who had marched to aid the Assyrians in their last stand, was defeated and the way was opened for Nebuchadnezzar to conquer all of Syria and Palestine, including the kingdom of Judah.

Carmel (Hb *karmel*, "orchard"). **1.** A town of Judah (Jos 15:55), identified with the modern el Kirmil about 8 mi S of Hebron. It appears as the home of Nabal* and Abigail* (1 S 25:2 ff; 27:3; 30:5; 2 S 2:2; 3:3; 1 Ch 3:1) and of David's hero Hezro (2 S 23:35; 1 Ch 11:37), and was one of the points passed by Saul in his campaign against the Amalekites* (1 S 15:12).

2. A mountain on the border of Asher (Jos 19:26); the town of Jokneam lay at

a) Mount Carmel.
b) Summit of Mount Carmel.

its foot on the SW (Jos 12:22). Mt Carmel is a promontory which terminates the central range of Palestine, from which it is interrupted by the pass of Megiddo*. From the pass Carmel extends NNW to within 200 yards of the Mediterranean, making it possible for the road along the sea to be closed by a very small force; for this reason the principal route in ancient times traversed the pass of Megiddo. To the N of Carmel lies the Bay of Acre; the modern city of Haifa is built at the foot of Carmel on the bay. Carmel rises to a height of less than 2000 ft, but it ascends steeply from the sea and the surrounding country and thus is prominent in appearance and difficult of access. In ancient times it was not intensively occupied; the several levels of prehistoric occupation found there would indicate a larger population in the Stone Age than in historic times. At present Carmel is covered with heavy thickets; the OT alludes several times to its covering of forests (Is 33:9; 35:2; Am 1:2; Na 1:4) as well as to its height and prominence (Je 46:18; Am 9:3); the head of the beloved is compared to Carmel (SS 7:6). It is called a rich land in Je 50:19. Carmel was the scene of the ordeal of Elijah and the priests of the Baal (1 K 18:19 f, 42); the election of this spot suggests the presence of a sanctuary of the Baal on the mountain. Carmel seems to have been at least an occasional residence of Elisha* (2 K 2:25; 4:25), and was possibly a center of the associations of the prophets*.

Carnaim (Hh *ḳarnayim*, "horns"), a town in Bashan*, the scene of the defeat of Timotheus* by Judas* (1 Mc 5:26, 43 f; 2 Mc 12:21; Carnion in 2 Mc). The site is probably Sheikh Saad, E of the Sea of Galilee and a few miles from Ashtaroth*. The name is combined with Ashtaroth in Ashtaroth-Carnaim (Gn 14:5).

Carpenter. Simple wood* work was done before the invention of metal tools. In Egypt metal tools appeared in the late predynastic period and are easily recognized in tomb painting: adze, axe, chisel, saw, drills, mallets. In Mesopotamia the crafts were usually hereditary and were formed into guilds; the trade was learned in groups which served their apprenticeship under a master. In both Egypt and Mesopotamia wood carving and joining reached a high degree of skill. Among

Adze.

the Israelites before the monarchy the craft was not so highly developed; David* obtained carpenters for his building projects from Hiram* of Tyre* (2 S 5:11). They appear in the time of Jehoash* of Judah (837–800) and of Jehoiakin* (598), probably organized in guilds. The carpenter's tools have been found in excavations: axe, saw, chisel, hammer, drills, nails; Is 44:13

mentions measuring-line, plane, and compass. Metal saws were rare even as late as the Iron Age; flint saws were found belonging to this period. Egypt, Mesopotamia, and Palestine are all poor in wood apt for construction; on its use cf wood. Joseph, the husband of Mary, was a carpenter (Mt 13:55) and Jesus pursued the trade before He began to preach (Mk 6:3).

Carpus (Gk *karpos*), a Christian of Troas*, with whom Paul left his cloak (2 Tm 4:13).

Cart. Two-wheeled and four-wheeled carts were in use in Mesopotamia as early as the Sumerian* period. The early carts appear with solid disk wooden wheels; the Assyrian carts had wheels with spokes. They were drawn by oxen, asses, or mules. The chariot* was a more common wheeled vehicle; carts were used for the transportation of people or of goods too bulky for beasts of burden. On ancient roads beasts of burden or porters could transport goods more conveniently and quickly. Carts are sometimes represented with covered bodies. Galling believes the Israelites learned their use from the Philistines, who employed a cart to transport the ark (1 S 6:7 ff) as David did to bring it to Jerusalem (2 S 6:3 ff; 1 Ch 13:7). Otherwise the cart is mentioned rarely in the OT (Gn 45:19 ff; 46:5; Nm 7:3 ff; Is 28:27 f; 5:18; 66:20; Am 2:13).

Castor and Pollux. Two heroes of Gk mythology, the *dioskouroi* or "twins" on the figurehead of the ship which took Paul from Malta* to Puteoli* (AA 28:11). They were both sons of Leda: Castor by her husband Tyndareus, king of Sparta, and Pollux by Zeus. When Castor was killed, Pollux was offered immortality by Zeus, but he would not accept it unless he could share it on alternate days with his brother.

Catholic Epistles. Cf JAMES; JOHN, EPISTLES; JUDE; PETER, EPISTLES.

Cave. The limestone hills of Palestine are full of caves, sometimes quite large, and the Bible has numerous reference to their use as temporary or even permanent shelters (Gn 19:30; Jos 10:16; Jgs 6:2; 1 S 13:6; 22:1; 24:3; 2 Mc 6:11 +). They were a refuge for fugitives from war or from the law. They were also used as shelters for cattle, and tradition has long placed the birth of Jesus in such a cave near Bethlehem*. The Qumran* Scrolls were discovered in a cave; later exploration revealed the Qumran sectaries used an entire series of caves in the region. Caves either natural or artificially enlarged were used for burial*. Explorations of caves have disclosed their use by prehistoric man possibly as much as 100,000 years ago.

Cedar. The 400 or so cedars which are carefully preserved on the slopes of Lebanon* are a pitiful remnant of the forests which covered those slopes in pre-Christian times and furnished essential material for the temples and palaces of the ancient world. The *cedrus libani,* the cedar of Lebanon, is now found at an altitude of 6,000 ft. It grows to a height of 60–70 ft, and specimens in the Taurus range attain a height of 100 ft; in ancient times this height, mentioned in an Egyptian record, was perhaps exceeded. Its trunk reaches 40 ft in circumference, and the horizontal width of its branches approaches the height of the tree. Its cones are 3–5 in. in length. Its aromatic wood is adapted to all kinds of working, and it was the only tree in the ancient world which could furnish beams and joists for large buildings. Its use for masts (Ezk 27:5) is questioned by some scholars. Cedar imported from Lebanon was used in Egypt in the predynastic period. It was felled and seasoned in the mountains; the logs were lashed into rafts and floated down the coast from the Phoenician cities to the Nile. Allusions to the acquisition of cedar are frequent in the records of the conquering Pharaohs of the 18th dynasty. The "cedar mountain," as Lebanon was called by Baby-lonians and Assyrians, was reached by Sargon (about 2350 BC) and cedar was imported at least as early as Ur-nammu (about 2050 BC). The transportation, which was at least partly overland, must have been extremely difficult. It is mentioned often in Assyrian records as gained by tribute or conquest. The Israelite poet makes the cedars rejoice at the fall of the Mesopotamian conqueror (Is 14:8; 37:24). David was the first Israelite ruler to import it from Hiram* of Tyre* (2 S 5:11), although it was known before that time. Solomon imported it for his palace and temple; it was floated down the coast in rafts (1 K 5:6 ff). There was no one in Israel who knew how to cut timber like the Sidonians (1 K 5:6 ff). The temple was built with cedar beams and cedar paneling (1 K 5:24; 6:9 f, 15 f). It was an exaggeration of popular tradition that cedar in Solomon's times was as common as the native sycamore (1 K 10:27). It was a sign of luxury in Jehoiakim* which Jeremiah reproved that he wished to outdo others in building with cedar (Je 22:14 f), and of the vanity of the men of Samaria* that they thought they could replace sycamore with cedar after the catastrophe of the Assyrian conquest of 734 (Is 9:9). The cedar is a biblical symbol of pride (Is 2:13; Ezk 31:3; Zc 11:2), of strength (2 K 14:9; Ps 29:5; Am 2:9), of security and prosperity (Nm 24:6; Je 22:23). Ezekiel in a protracted figure describes the royal house of Judah as a mighty cedar (Ezk 17:3 ff), of which Jehoiachin* is a

A cedar grove on Mt. Lebanon.

twig transplanted. The righteous will flourish like the cedar of Lebanon (Ps 92:13).

Cenchreae (Gk *kegchreai*), the port city of Corinth* on the Saronic Gulf, about 7 mi from Corinth. Paul took a ship from there to Ephesus* and had his hair cut because of a Nazirite* vow (AA 18:18). It was the home of the deaconess Phoebe* (Rm 16:1).

Cendebaeus (Gk *kendebaios*), appointed commander of the Phoenician and Palestinian coast by Antiochus* VII Sidetes (138–129 BC). He raided Jewish towns and villages until he was routed by an army under Judas and John Hyrcanus (1 Mc 15:38 ff). Cf HASMONEAN.

Censer (Hb *maḥtāh*), a fire pan or fire holder in which hot coals were contained on which incense* was sprinkled (Lv 10:1; 16:12). Their form and appearance cannot be reconstructed; it must have been a pan or bowl with a handle. They were made of bronze* (Ex 27:3); the censers of Solomon's temple were made of gold* (1 K 7:50) and are mentioned among the plunder taken by the Babylonians in 587 BC (2 K 25:15).

Census. The enumeration of citizens and surveys of land are an ancient function of government. Land surveys were made in Egypt in the Old Kingdom. The records of Mari*, Ugarit*, and Alalakh all contain census lists, and it is easily assumed that the practice was general in the organized societies of the ancient Near East. The purpose of the census in ancient as in modern times was to establish a basis for the levying of taxes and for military service; it was a counting of the national resources.

The only census mentioned in Israel is the census undertaken by David (2 S 24; 1 Ch 21). This is generally thought to have been the first; whether it was the first or not, the narrative of the census certainly shows the popular idea of the census as a challenge of the deity, an expression of pride which is punished. The purpose of the census was no doubt the same as for other censuses; in addition, one of the purposes in Israel was very probably to determine the basis for assignment of forced labor for the king. W. F. Albright proposed that the census lists in Nm 1 and 26 represent the census lists of David. G. E. Mendenhall more recently has suggested that they belong to the early period of the tribal confederation of Israel*. Cf THOUSAND.

The census of Lk 2:1 is described as a census of the whole world (i.e., of the Roman

dominions) made at the command of Augustus. This universal census is otherwise unknown to history and there are serious reasons for doubting that Lk here reports a historical fact. The *Monumentum Ancyranum,* an inscription of Augustus, mentions three censuses of Roman citizens: 28 BC, 8 BC, and AD 14. The second of these would suit the date, but it cannot have been taken in Palestine; for it was a census of Roman citizens, and Palestine at that time was the kingdom of Herod the Great and not under Roman administration. Any census taken at this date would have been a census of Herod. The census is associated by Lk 2:1 with Quirinius, legate of Syria; in addition to the fact that Palestine was not in the province of Syria at this time, the census taken under Quirinius is dated by Josephus in AD 6–7. Outside of the difficulty of supposing a Roman census in a technically non-Roman territory, it is not unlikely that a provincial census like that of AD 6–7 may have occurred which is not mentioned elsewhere. Egyptian papyri suggest that a census was taken in Egypt every 14 years from 6–5 BC; but Egypt was a Roman province after 30 BC. Tertullian in the 2nd century mentions a census taken in Syria under the administration of Sentius Saturninus, 8–6 BC; this was the general census mentioned on the *Monumentum Ancyranum.* Tertullian, however, may from apologetic motives be extending this census to an area which was not included in it. It is furthermore striking that the Roman method of enumeration is not described in Lk; the Roman census enumerated the head of the family at his place of residence and did not enumerate his wife. The enumeration of a man and his wife in his birthplace is attested for Egypt under Augustus, and it is not impossible that it was used in Palestine also.

It is therefore difficult to accept many of the postulates demanded by the census as Lk describes it; it is not impossible, but a solution which is based on the type of literature found in the Infancy* Gospels should not be neglected. These passages contain more midrash* than the other portions of the Gospels. Here Lk or his sources can be understood as a construction based on the compilation of some elements known but not accurately recorded and other elements which are midrashic reflections on these known but not verified facts. The sources knew of the universal census of Augustus and the Syrian census of Quirinius, but from incomplete recollection the two were conflated into one. This one becomes the order of the king of all the world which brings it about that the messianic king of all the world, the son of David, is born in Bethlehem, the city of David.

Centurion (Lt *centurio*, Gk *kenturiōn* or *hekatontarchēs*), literally officer over 100 (*centum*) men; cf LEGION. Small local posts were usually commanded by a centurion. It is interesting to note that each of these Roman professional soldiers who is mentioned in the NT appears as an honest and kindly man. The centurion who commanded the squad which executed Jesus confessed that He was the Son of God (Mt 27:54) and innocent of the charges (Lk 23:47). The unusual humanity of the centurion of Capernaum (Mt 8:5 ff; Lk 7:2 ff) is evident from his care for his sick slave, whom he asked Jesus to cure, as well as by his friendly relations with the Jews, for whom he had built a synagogue. Of him Jesus said that He had not found such faith in Israel, because he knew that Jesus could effect the cure by a word alone without a personal visit; and the Church employs his profession of humility daily when the Eucharist is received. Cornelius*, the centurion stationed at Joppa*, was converted by Peter (AA 10:1 ff). One centurion helped to save Paul from a scourging (AA 22:25 ff), and another to save him from a Jewish plot to murder him (AA 23:17 ff), and Paul was taken to Rome in the custody of the centurion Julius* (AA 27:1 ff).

Cephas (Aramaic *kēpā'*, "the rock"), the nickname given to Simon* by Jesus, but found in the Gospels only in Jn 1:2; elsewhere it appears in its Gk equivalent *petros*, Peter*. It is somewhat remarkable that Paul uses the Aramaic name eight out of ten times (all in 1 Co and Gal) and the Gk twice. This doubtless represents the most primitive usage; by the time the Gospels were written the Gk had displaced the Aramaic name.

Chaff. Husks and straw; in Palestinian threshing* the chaff was thrown into the air to be blown away by the wind. Chaff or straw thus blown away or consumed by flame is a common biblical metaphor for the sudden destruction of the wicked (Ex 15:7; Pss 1:4; 35:5; Jb 13:25; 21:18; Is 5:24; 17:13; 29:5; 33:11; 40:24; 41:2; Ho 13:3; Zp 2:2).

Chain. Chains as neck ornament were worn by both men and women, especially as a badge of rank or office (Gn 41:42; Dn 5:7). They were strung with precious stones, especially pearls (SS 1:10), metal spheres (Ex 35:22), and sometimes carried amulets* (Pr 1:9). Ornate neck chains were very popular in Egypt.

Chaldeans (Hb *kasdîm*, Akkadian *kaldu*, meaning uncertain), a Semitic tribe connected with the Aramaeans. Their invasion of southern Babylonia from the 10th-8th centuries BC was contemporary with the Aramaean invasion of Syria. In Babylonia they established a number of states which resisted extinction and assimilation during the Assyrian conquests of the 8th-7th centuries, and under the dynasty of Nabopolassar and Nebuchadnezzar* destroyed the Assyrian empire (625-609 BC) and succeeded to its rule over Mesopotamia and Syria. The Chaldean empire in turn fell to Cyrus* of Persia* in 539 BC. Cf ASSYRIA; BABYLONIA. The advances of Babylonia in astronomical observation and astrology led to the use of the word Chaldean to designate astrologer in classical Gk and Lt writers; this usage is reflected in Dn 2:2 ff; 5:11. On Ur of the Chaldees cf UR.

Chariot. The chariot drawn by the horse* was introduced into Mesopotamia, Egypt, and Syria by the Hyksos* 1700-1500 BC. It immediately became popular as an instrument of war*. The possession of a chariot was limited to the king and the wealthy, and the chariot corps of the armies was formed by the aristocracy. The chariot was also used as a vehicle; Ashur-bani-pal of Assyria is represented in a chariot shaded by a parasol. Assyrian kings hunted from chariots (cf HUNTING). The railing of the carriage was rounded in both Egypt and Assyria, and the rear corners were rounded off in Egypt. The width of the axle was about 44-45 in. The rear edge of the carriage rested upon the axle. The wheels were, after an earlier four-spoke model in Egypt, built with six spokes in both Egypt and Assyria; after 800 BC the Assyrians used eight-spoke wheels. Both wheels and carriages in Egyptian chariots are represented as of lighter construction and were presumably more rapid. They were made of wood, and very little has survived. The chariot was usually drawn by two horses; one, three or four were exceptional, although it is not always possible to determine how many horses the artist intended to represent. In Egypt the chariot carried two men, the charioteer and the combat soldier, who is usually represented in both Egypt and Assyria as an archer. The crew rode standing. One man is sometimes represented with the reins tied around his waist. The Pharaoh always appears alone in the chariot, probably from artistic convention which would not show him receiving assistance; but the title "king's charioteer" designated a high ranking office in Egypt. The Hittites and after them the Assyrians had a complement of three men, adding a shield bearer. "King's

a) Assyrian war chariots with four men: a driver, an archer, and two shield bearers. b) Royal chariot of Ashur-bani-pal with canopy.

charioteer" and "king's *šālîš*," (lit "third man") designated high offices in Assyria. The chariots moved in ranks and units according to tactics; the single combat of Homer's heroes does not appear. The chariots of the Homeric period did not differ from those used in Egypt and Assyria. The Greeks shunned chariot warfare in the 6th–4th centuries, either because infantry tactics and the rise of cavalry had made them obsolete, or because, in the opinion of some scholars, the decline of the aristocracy removed the class which supported the chariot corps. They took up chariots in the 4th century, probably under Persian influence. The Persians also equipped the chariot wheels with scythes; these clumsy vehicles were more alarming in appearance than effective in battle. Chariots were used by the Seleucid* armies in the Maccabean* wars. The Romans used chariots for transportation and racing, but not in war.

The Hebrews adopted the chariot under Solomon; the word *šālîš* shows that they used a complement of three men (2 K 7:2, 17, 19; 10:25; 15:25). Its adoption aroused no small opposition from circles which regarded it as a form of luxury and vanity. Possibly it was resented because of its connection with a wealthy aristocracy. The "iron chariots" of the Canaanites inspired fear in the early Hebrews (Jos 17:16–18; Jgs 4:3 ff); but the Hebrews learned the tactics to defeat them, and Sisera* lost the battle of Tabor* because his chariots were mired

down by a heavy rain (Jgs 5:20 f). Their success against the Canaanites may have contributed to the Hebrew reluctance to employ this weapon; at least once it is reported that they hamstrung the horses they captured (Jos 11:9). The Philistines*, however, used them against the Hebrews successfully (1 S 13:5). Nevertheless, David* hamstrung the horses which he captured from the Philistines, except 100 (2 S 8:4). The first item mentioned in Samuel's indictment of kingship is that the king will have chariots (1 S 8:11). It was a sign of vanity and royal ambition in both Absalom* (2 S 15:1) and Adonijah* (1 K 1:5) when they began to ride in a chariot. Nevertheless, Solomon had 1400 chariots stationed in chariot cities (1 K 10:26); one of these cities was Megiddo*, where stables for 450 horses have been discovered. Large chariot forces were maintained by the kings of Israel; Ahab's contingent of 2000 chariots was the largest among those listed in the records of Shalmaneser III at the battle of Karkar in 853 BC. Deuteronomy warns the king not to acquire many horses (17:16). In Judah in the time of Isaiah there were chariots without end (2:7). He rebukes confidence in chariots rather than in Yahweh (30:16; 31:1), a rebuke almost identical with the mockery of the Assyrian ambassador (36:8–9). It was not unworthy of Yahweh, however, to ride in a chariot (cf THEOPHANY). It was not common in Palestine in NT times and is not mentioned except in AA 8:28 ff, where its owner is not a Jew but an Ethiopian.

Charisma. Cf GRACE; SPIRIT.

Charity. Cf LOVE.

Chebar. The "river" by which Ezekiel* had his visions (1:3; 3:15; 10:15; 43:3) was a canal, called "river" in Akkadian. A canal *naru kabari* which paralleled the Euphrates* from Babylon* to Erech* is mentioned in contract tablets from 443–424 BC.

Chedorlaomer (Hb *kᵉdōrlā'ōmer*), king of Elam*, one of the four kings who invaded Canaan in the time of Abraham* (Gn 14:1 ff). While the component *-lagamar* is the name of an Elamite deity, no Kudur-lagamar is mentioned among the 40 kings of Elam 2100–1100 BC whose names are known. W. F. Albright proposes that the Hb form be explained as arising from Elamite Kutur-Naḥḥunte (about 1625–1610 BC). This king sacked the temples and land of Akkad and carried off the statue of the goddess Nana to Elam. The expedition of Gn 14 represents Chedorlaomer as the chief of the allied kings and thus reflects the situation of the 2nd half of the 17th century BC when Amorite* power in Babylon was declining, and the name of the Elamite king may be preserved in incorrect transcription. The obscurities of the situation, in particular of the names of the other kings (cf separate articles), do not permit a precise identification.

Chemosh (Hb *kᵉmôš*, meaning unknown), god of the Moabites. Moab* is called the people of Chemosh (Nm 21:29; Je 48:46; cf also Je 48:7, 13). He was one of the gods worshiped by Solomon* (1 K 11:7, 33); his high place* was destroyed by Josiah* (2 K 23:13). In the speech of Jephthah* Chemosh has given Moab its land, as Yahweh has given its land to Israel (Jgs 11:24). In the Moabite stone of Mesha* Moab was defeated by Israel because Chemosh was angry with his land. Mesha attacked Israel at the behest of Chemosh, who expelled the king of Israel. In his honor Mesha slew the entire population of a city (cf BAN). He built the high place of Qarhoh in honor of Chemosh. Nothing is known of his character; Akkadian *kamūsh*, a title of Nergal, suggests a possible relationship. Ashtar-Chemosh, mentioned in the Moabite stone, is probably a female consort; but it may also be a title of Chemosh.

Cherethites and Pelethites (Hb *kᵉrētî, pᵉlētî*), mentioned together seven times, Cherethites alone three times. The identity of these two groups with the Philistines* or groups of the Philistines is clear — *pᵉlētî* is easily assumed to be a variant form of the name more commonly called *pᵉlistî* in Hb; *kᵉrētî* is less easily identified with Crete*, Caphtor* in Hb. Caria has been suggested. The hero Keret of the Ugaritic* myth complicates the question. The Cherethites inhabited a part of the Negeb* adjacent to the Negeb of Judah* (1 S 30:14). In Ezk 25:16 and Zp 2:5 the context shows that they are regarded as identical with the Philistines. Elsewhere the two names occur together (2 S 8:18; 15:18; 20:7; 1 K 1:38, 44; 1 Ch 18:17); in all these passages they appear as the royal guard of David under the command of Benaiah*. They accompany David on his flight from Absalom, take part in the action against the revolt of Sheba*, and at the command of David are present at the installation of Solomon as king. It is evident that they are foreign soldiers, presumably professional, immediately attached to the person of the king, and their duty is as much to protect him against his own subjects as to fight his battles against external foes.

Cherith (Hb *kᵉrît*, meaning uncertain), a seasonal stream (Arabic *wadi*) E of the Jordan, where Elijah lived during the three years' drought and was fed by ravens (1 K 17:3, 5). Abel suggests the *Wadi Yabis*.

Cherub (Hb *kᵉrûb*, pl *kᵉrûbîm*, etymology uncertain). Cherubs, armed with a "flaming whirling sword," were stationed at the entrance to the garden of Eden* to keep man from returning there (Gn 3:24). Two cherubs of gold were built upon the ark* of the covenant, facing each other with their wings spread out over the mercy-seat; "between the cherubs" was the place where Yahweh spoke to Israel (Ex 25:10–22; 37:7–9; cf Nm 7:89). The cherubs of the temple of Solomon were 10 cubits (about 15 ft) in height with a wingspread of 10 cubits, so that the wings of the two cherubs spread from wall to wall of the Holy of Holies (1 K 6:23 ff); they were made of olive wood overlaid with gold. Cherubs were also carved in the paneling of the walls (1 K 6:29, 32, 35; 7:36). Yahweh is enthroned upon the cherubs (1 S 4:4; 2 S 6:2; 2 K 19:15; 1 Ch 13:6; Pss 80:2; 99:1; Is 37:16). This refers primarily to the cherubs of the ark, which was conceived as the throne upon which Yahweh stood invisibly; the latent symbolism is more explicit in Ps 18 and Ezk. In Ps 18 (2 S 22) there is described the theophany* of Yahweh in a storm; He rides upon the cherub and flies, and speeds on the wings of the wind. Here the cherub must be the storm cloud; the same imagery is suggested by the appellation "Rider of the clouds," applied to Aleyan Baal* in Ugaritic* mythology and to Yahweh in Ps 68:5. The "living creatures" of the chariot of Ezk 1:4 ff are elsewhere in the book called cherubs (9:3; 10:1 ff). Here also Yahweh appears in a storm theophany and the cherubim as in Ps 18 are His living chariot. This may be compared to the common Canaanite representation of a deity standing upon the back of an animal. The cherubs of Ezk 1 are human in form with four faces — human, lion, ox, eagle — and four wings with human hands. This hybrid form suggests the winged sphinx of the ancient Near East with which the imagery of the cherub must be connected.

In Egypt and Canaan and in Hittite remains there are many representations of a demon* as a winged lion with a human countenance; in Mesopotamia there are winged bulls with a human countenance. The functions of these beings are parallel to those described above. The cherubs as a throne appear in Byblos and Megiddo, where the throne of the king is decorated with cherubs. In Assyria colossal winged bulls or lions with human features are found at the gates of temples and palaces; they are obviously guardian genii. A similar function is found in the cherubs which decorate sarcophagi. The sphinx of the pyramids of Gizeh in Egypt protects the tombs of the deceased Pharaohs. It is evident that the Renaissance artists who decorated their paintings with cherubs in the form of winged boys could scarcely have departed farther from the original form. The cherubs were the only images mentioned in orthodox Yahwism (cf IMAGE) and create some problems. While it is true that no cult was paid to them, the prohibition of images was taken very strictly in early Israel. In the tradition the image of the cherub was given the sanction of Moses himself; but ultimately we do not know why Israel selected this solitary plastic representation among the many external features of its cult which it had in common with ancient Near Eastern peoples.

Child. The first blessing uttered upon man in the first creation account was to be fruitful, to multiply, and to fill the earth (Gn 1:28). A numerous progeny was promised to the patriarchs* (Gn 12:2; 17:26; 26:24 +), and a large family was a blessing from God (Pss 127:3-5; 128:2-4 +). Childlessness was a curse and a great sorrow (Gn 30:1; 1 S 1:6, 11 ff; Is 4:1; Lk 1:25), although the wise man does not desire a multitude of unprofitable children (BS 16:

1-3). Sons were more desirable than daughters (cf FAMILY; WOMAN). The firstborn* son succeeded to the authority of the father*. The birth of a child, or at least of a son, was a joyous occasion, although we have no mention of any festivity as we have for circumcision (Lk 1:59 ff) or for weaning (Gn 21:8). The news was announced to the father, who presumably was not present (Jb 3:3; Je 20:15). The newborn infant was bathed, rubbed with salt, and wrapped in bands (Ezk 16:4; Lk 2:7). Circumcision was done on the 8th day after birth (Lv 12:3; Lk 1:59; 2:21), in ancient times by the father himself (Gn 17:23; 21:4). The newborn child was received upon the knees of the father, who thus acknowledged the child (Jb 3:12), perhaps by a formula such as that of Ps 2:7. When a slave substituted for the wife, the child was delivered upon the knees of the wife (Gn 30:3). The name was conferred either by the father (Gn 4:26; 5:3, 29; Ex 2:22 +) or by the mother (Gn 4:1, 25; 29:23 +), but neighbors (Rt 4:17) and relatives (Lk 1:59) could influence the choice of name. In the older accounts the name was given at birth; in the NT it is given at the time of circumcision (Lk 1:59 ff; 2:21). The mother nursed the child as a rule for a period of 2-3 years (Gn 21:7; 1 S 1:21-23); nurses were the exception (Gn 24:59; 35:8; 2 K 11:2). References to the play of children are rare (Mt 11:16; Lk 7:32) as compared to the scenes of play in Egyptian art. They helped their elders in domestic and field work (1 S 16:11; Je 7:18) and even girls herded and watered sheep (Gn 29:6; Ex 2:16). For girls the period of childhood was short, since they were marriageable at the age of puberty. Until marriage they were rather closely restrained, (2 Mc 3:19) and a real fear of sexual misadventure is expressed (BS 42:9-14); but these passages are both late, and maidens in early Israel had more liberty. The boy in Talmudic practice became a *bar mitzvah,* subject to the obligations of the law at the age of 13, and this is suggested also in Lk 2:42. The age of military service is reckoned at 20 in Nm 1:3. The education and rearing of the children was entirely in the hands of the parents; it was the duty of both father and mother to teach the children wisdom*. There was no formal instruction before the days of the synagogue*. In the earliest period the authority of the father was absolute; Abraham could sacrifice his son (Gn 22:1 ff), Jephthah* his daughter (Jgs 11:34 ff), and Judah could execute his daughter-in-law Tamar* for infidelity (Gn 38:24); but such absolute power does not appear under the monarchy. The obligation of children to honor their parents, which includes respect and obedience, is stated in the law (Ex 20:12; Lv 19:3; Dt 5:16) and is rewarded by a long life. Striking or cursing one's parents was a capital offense (Lv 20:9). Of Jesus it was written that He obeyed His parents (Lk 2:51) and Paul recommends obedience and honor to children (Eph 6:1–3). Jesus settled the dispute among His disciples about priority by placing a child before them and insisting that they must become like children (Mt 18:1 ff; 9:33 ff; Lk 9:46 ff), i.e., they must become, like the child, the least important of all. Yahweh will spare the city of Nineveh because of 120,000 infants in the city — perhaps meaning the adult inhabitants who are excused because of their ignorance (Jon 4:11). Yahweh has carried Israel as a man carries his son (Dt 1:31) and has taught Israel to walk (Ho 11:3).

Chileab (Hb *kil'āb,* etymology uncertain), David's second son, born of Abigail* at Hebron (2 S 3:3), apparently identical with Daniel of 1 Ch 3:1.

Chilion (Hb *kilyōn,* "frailty"?), son of Elimelech* and Naomi* and husband of Orpah* of Moab (Rt 1:2, 5; 4:9).

Chimham (Hb *kimhām,* meaning uncertain), son of Barzillai* of Gilead. Barzillai refused David's offer of residence at court in reward for his support of David during the rebellion of Absalom, but permitted his son to go instead (2 S 19:37 ff). There is a possible connection with the caravansary of Chimham near Bethlehem (Je 41:17), but the two names have a slightly different spelling in Hb.

Chinnereth, Chinneroth (Hb *kinneret, kin[e]-rôt,* etymology uncertain). Chinnereth was a fortified city at the NW corner of the Sea of Galilee* (Jos 19:35) which gives its name to the lake. The city is mentioned in Egyptian lists of the 18th dynasty. Chinneroth, if the difference in spelling is correct, seems to signify a region around the Sea of Galilee (1 K 15:20). The Sea of Galilee is called the Sea of Chinnereth in Nm 34:11; Jos 13:27, and the Sea of Chinneroth in Jos 12:3. The name is the origin of Gk Gennesar and Gennesareth*, used in 1 Mc and NT.

Chios (Gk *chios*), a large island of the Aegean archipelago off the coast of Asia Minor W˙ of Smyrna, one of the seven cities which claimed the birthplace of Homer. It was passed by Paul on his last voyage to Jerusalem (AA 20:15).

Chisleu (Hb *kislew*), the 9th month of the Hb calendar*, November-December.

Chittim. Cf KITTIM.

Chloe (Gk *chloe*). The members of Chloe's household, probably her slaves, informed Paul of the factions at Corinth* (1 Co 1:11). It is not clear from this whether Chloe lived at Corinth, or whether she was a Christian.

Chorazin (Gk *chorazin*), one of the towns of Galilee cursed by Jesus for their unbelief (Mt 11:21; Lk 10:13). The site is identified with Khirbet Kerazeh, about 2 mi NW of Capernaum* (Tell Hum). It contains the ruins of a black basalt synagogue built in the 3rd or 4th century AD.

Christ. Cf JESUS CHRIST; MESSIAH.

Christian (Gk *christianos,* an adjective formed in the usual way to indicate those who follow a leader). The term was coined at Antioch* (AA 11:26) and is used in 1 Pt 4:16. It gained wide usage early; it was used by Herod Agrippa* in his dialogue with Paul (AA 26:28) and appears in the writings of Pliny, Tacitus, Suetonius, and the letters of Ignatius of Antioch. In its origin it was probably a contemptuous nickname.

Chronicles, Books of. The Hb name is lit "books of the words (i.e., events) of the days." The title of Ch comes from Jerome who called them "Chronicon totius divinae historiae," "chronicle of the entire divine history." In the LXX the books were called *paraleipomenon,* Gk "things omitted" (i.e., in S and K); the title passed into Vg and RDC OT as Paralipomenon, but it is misleading. The division of Ch into two books appears first in the LXX. It is the last book of the Hb canon, most probably because it was the last to be accepted as sacred; in Vg and Eng Bibles it follows immediately after 1–2 K.

Ch + Ezr-Ne is the last of the three great collections of Hb historical traditions with the Pentateuch* and the Deuteronomistic history. It ends with the words with which Ezr begins; the inversion in Hb is due to its later acceptance. Like K, it ends not with the fall of Jerusalem but with a note of future hope: in 2 K the elevation of Jehoiachin, in Ch the decree of Cyrus permitting the rebuilding of Jerusalem. Its contents are: (1) Adam to David, 1 Ch 1–9, in the form of genealogies (2) David, 1 Ch 10–29. (3) Solomon, 2 Ch 1–9. (4) Judah from the division of the kingdom to the fall of Jerusalem, 2 Ch 11–36.

Ch and Ezr-Ne are the work of the same author, who is dated by most modern scholars not earlier than 300 BC. Recent research, however, places him nearer 400, and the identification of the Chronicler with Ezra himself, which was the Jewish tradition, has gained probability. The book was known to Ben Sira* (about 180 BC).

The Chronicler used sources. It is certain that he had either our books of S and K or, as some scholars believe, the text from which both he and the editor of our present S and K worked; but this source is never acknowledged explicitly, although extensive passages are transcribed from it word for word. He also had the books Gn–Jgs, at least in an earlier form. The following titles of sources appear: "book of the kings of Israel and Judah" (1 Ch 9:1; 2 Ch 27:7; 35:27; 36:8); "book of the kings of Judah and Israel" (2 Ch 16:11; 25:26; 32:32); "book of the kings of Israel" (2 Ch 20:34); "words of the kings of Israel" (2 Ch 33:18); "midrash* of the book of the kings" (2 Ch 24:27); "words" or "prophecy" or "vision" or "midrash" of the prophets Samuel*, Nathan*, and Gad* for the history of David; (1 Ch 29:29) of Nathan, Ahijah* and Jeddi for the history of Solomon (2 Ch 9:29); Shemaiah* and Iddo* for Rehoboam (2 Ch 12:15); Iddo for Abijah (2 Ch 13:22); Jehu* for Jehoshaphat (2 Ch 20:34); Isaiah* for Uzziah (2 Ch 26:22) and for Hezekiah (2 Ch 32:32); Hozai for Manasseh (2 Ch 33:19). Modern scholars reduce all these either to two works, one a history of the kings and the other a collection of writings by or concerning the prophets, or to one; the existence of both documents is also suggested by the compilation of K (cf KINGS, BOOKS OF). The royal document cannot be our book of K, since it is cited for events not mentioned in K.

The question of the historical value of the material peculiar to Ch has been considerably discussed (cf his conception of history below) and modern criticism is less inclined to reject it out of hand, preferring to evaluate each item in itself. The genealogies, compiled in the early sections from Gn — Jgs, show little evidence of artificial construction, although some of this may be present. The genealogy was an important document in ancient Israel. The genealogies of David and of Levi and Aaron contain many names not attested elsewhere; in some instances we can trace a corruption. The genealogies are arranged according to tribes and clans; this aspect of Hb social organization is less often mentioned in the historical books, but was the principal framework within which the Hebrews lived even after the establishment of the monarchy. It is rarely possible to date the genealogies of Ch precisely. Eissfeldt notes the following instances in which Ch has preserved certain historical information not found in S and K: David's heroes (1 Ch 11:10–47), the buildings and fortifications of Rehoboam (2 Ch 11:5–12) and his family (2 Ch 11:18–23), Uzziah's defeat of the Philistines (2 Ch 26:6) and his buildings (2 Ch 26:9–10). Other instances could be added in which a genuine tradition has been retold in the Chronicler's characteristic manner.

It is important to grasp that the Chronicler did not intend to write "history." The books of S and K existed, and he did not intend to suppress or replace them. Yet there are obvious differences both in general conception and in numerous details between the Chronicler's presentation and the course of events as his readers could find them in S and K. It may be summed up by saying that the Chronicler intended to write not what happened, but what ought to have happened; it is the story of the ideal Israel living under its law in the historical circumstances which led to its fall. Hence he omits the feud of David and Saul, the adultery of David and Bathsheba, the rebellion of Absalom, and the entire history of the northern kingdom after the division. This ideal is specified by three theological principles which he represents as governing events: a somewhat rigid scheme of retribution, direct divine intrusion into history, and the primacy of the temple and the cult. The first principle is illustrated in such episodes as the misfortunes or good fortunes of Rehoboam (2 Ch 12:1 ff), Asa (2 Ch 16:7–12), Jehoshaphat (2 Ch 20:35–37), Uzziah (2 Ch 26:16–23), which are explained as retribution for good or bad deeds not mentioned in K and sometimes certainly unhistorical. In particular the long life of Manasseh is explained as due to a conversion which is entirely unattested (2 Ch 33:10 ff) after his imprisonment in Assyria; but his journey to Assyria, perhaps to give account of a rumor of rebellion, is most probable. The second principle appears in the victories of Abijah (2 Ch 13:13 ff), of Asa (2 Ch 14:8 ff), and of Jehoshaphat (2 Ch 20:1 ff), which are accomplished entirely by prayer with no combat. The fantastic numbers of the armies in Ch are characteristic and cannot be explained as incorrect transmissions; they attest the power of God over the mightiest human forces. The third principle appears in the space and importance which the Chronicler gives to the temple and its cult and personnel, which will preserve the union of Yahweh and Israel. Here David appears as the founder of temple music; his dispositions in this regard are second only to those of Moses. While the Chronicler has probably read the institutions of his own time into the time of David, and idealized their description besides, there is a well attested tradition that David was himself a musician and the author of musical compositions (cf PSALMS). His role in the establishment of this part of the cult should not be questioned. The interest and the knowledge of the Chronicler concerning the Levites, particularly the choirs, suggest that he himself was a member of this class. David, in many respects idealized into a messianic figure, appears as a second Moses.

This presentation of the past is unsympathetic to modern readers. It is necessary to see the Chronicler's purpose: to present an ideal of a holy people living in community under a messianic ruler, governed by divine law and faithful in the observances of public worship. His affirmation of the primacy of the religious in human life, of the divine government of human affairs, and of the law of retribution, while put for his contemporaries in a form which we find somewhat strained, is in full harmony with the beliefs of the OT.

Chronology. The reckoning of fixed dates in an era determined by a fixed point of departure does not appear until late in OT times. Earlier dates must be determined by calculations from a mass of complicated and not always consistent data which is surveyed below.

1. *Egyptian*. Up to the 12th Dynasty years were identified by some event; thereafter by the king's regnal year. There are several ancient lists of kings and their regnal years (the Palermo Stone, the lists of Abydos and Saqqarah, the Turin papyrus, and fragments of the lists of Manetho). Manetho (3rd century BC) arranged the kings in 31 dynasties which are grouped under Old Kingdom, Middle Kingdom, and New Kingdom; these designations are still commonly employed.

2. *Babylonian*. From earliest times to the Kassite dynasty (17th century BC) the years were designated by some event. Lists of the kings and of the years of their reign so designated are preserved from the first dynasty of Akkad* down to the Kassite period. Neither the earlier lists nor the later regnal lists have been preserved entirely; since new material is constantly turning up, modern scholarship is engaged in putting the fragmentary lists together into a consecutive scheme. This is based primarily upon synchronisms with Assyrian history and upon backward calculations thence. Of particular importance are the "Babylonian Chronicle" for the last years of Assyria and of the kingdom of Judah and the "Synchronistic

History" (of Assyrian origin) for the relations of the Babylonian and Assyrian king lists.

3. *Assyrian*. The Assyrians as early as the 18th century BC named each year after a royal official (*limmu*). Up to Tiglath-pileser* III (745–727 BC) the first year of each king's reign was named after the king himself. These *limmu*-lists are preserved entirely for the period 911–648 BC. An eclipse in the year 763 BC enables us to formulate dates for the entire lists. For earlier periods there are two important king lists with their regnal years, one in Constantinople and the other at the Oriental Institute in Chicago. For the period of the *limmu* lists correlation with Assyrian chronology furnishes the only certain dating for the period.

4. *Biblical*. Since 1701 to recent times biblical chronology was governed by the chronology of Ussher, Anglican Archbishop of Armagh, published 1650–1654 and introduced into the margin of AV in 1701. This was based entirely upon Ussher's calculation of the biblical data, which is not entirely uniform. The creation of the world was placed in 4004 BC.

I. *Creation to Deluge:* Hb 1656 years, LXX 2242 years, Samaritan Pentateuch 1307 years. The LXX and Sam variations are both due to deliberate editorial revision. The number is reached by adding the totals of Gn 5 (cf PATRIARCH).

II. *Deluge to Abraham:* the totals of Gn 11:10–26 give 290 years from the Deluge to the birth of Terah, Abraham's father; his age at the birth of Abraham is not given. Terah's birth thus falls in 2058 BC, and Abraham's birth was put by Ussher in 1996 BC; this is too early (cf ABRAHAM).

III. *Abraham to Exodus:* from Abraham's birth to Jacob's descent into Egypt is 290 years (from Gn 21:5; 25:26; 47:9). The sojourn in Egypt is placed at 430 years in Ex 12:40, an artificial calculation reached by doubling the 215 years from Abraham's entrance into Canaan to Jacob's departure. This would place the exodus in 1276 BC (cf EXODUS). During this period there is no certain fixed point of correlation with either Egyptian or Mesopotamian chronology.

IV. *Exodus to the foundation of the temple of Solomon:* In 1 K 6:1 the foundation date of the temple is said to be 480 years after the exodus. This, no doubt, reckons 12 generations of 40 years each and may repose upon genealogical lists not preserved in the OT. The total reached by adding the 40 years in the desert, the periods assigned to each of the judges, 40 years of David and 3 years of Solomon, and without reckoning the years of Joshua, Samuel, and Saul, which are not given (Saul is given 40 years in AA 13:21) is 533 years. If 40 years each are added for Joshua, Samuel, and Saul, the total would reach 653 years. But since the temple was founded about 959 BC, this would place the exodus in 1612 BC or 1439 BC, both of which are too early. Many of the judges were contemporaneous, but they are not so represented in the book of Jgs. Actually the date of the end of the reign of Solomon* can be reached very nearly exactly (cf SHISHAK).

V. *The monarchies of Israel and Judah to the fall of Jerusalem:* for this period the OT gives for each king of Israel and Judah after Rehoboam* the year of his accession in terms of the reigning king of the other kingdom and the length of his reign. This apparently simple scheme is complicated by several factors. The first is the accession year. In Egypt the accession year of a new king was antedated, i.e., the last year of his predecessor was the first year of the new king and was counted in the total regnal years of the new king. In Mesopotamia the accession was postdated i.e., the year of the death of the predecessor was the "accession year" of the new king, and his first year began with the following calendar new year, from which point his regnal years were counted. It is certain that both systems were used in both Hb kingdoms, and postdating is very probable in Judah after Hezekiah. In 1–2 K the total regnal years for Judah from the division of the kingdom to the fall of Samaria are 258, for Israel 241; this suggests different computations of the accession year. Another complicating factor is the problem of the beginning of the calendar new year (cf CALENDAR) in Nisan or Tishri. Still another factor is the existence of co-regencies which may have been counted in the regnal totals of two kings; another is the possibility of interregna. Finally there are some textual errors, in particular a strange error consistently uncorrected for the kings of the 8th century in Judah. Against these factors are the fairly abundant data and several fixed points which can be set by correlation with Assyrian and Babylonian chronology:

853: Ahab* at the battle of Karkar (Shalmaneser III of Assyria)
842: Jehu* paid tribute to Shalmaneser III
738: Menahem* paid tribute to Tiglath-pileser III
721: Sargon* took Samaria in his accession year
609: 17th year of Nabopolassar of Babylon, Egypt marched to the Euphrates to aid Ashur-uballit of Assyria, the death of Josiah* (2 K 23:28 ff)
597: 7th year of Nebuchadnezzar*, surrender of Jerusalem and deportation of Jehoiachin* (2 K 24:10 ff)

587: 18th year of Nebuchadnezzar, destruction of Jerusalem (2 K 25:1 ff).

VI. *The fall of Jerusalem to the birth of Christ:* Ezr-Ne date events according to the regnal years of the Persian kings. Since several different Persian kings bore identical names, this sometimes leaves doubt e.g., concerning the dating of Ezra* himself under Artaxerxes* I or II. The dates of Ezk begin from an uncertain point of departure. The events in 1–2 Mc are dated by the Seleucid era, which began with the victory of Seleucus* over Demetrius at Gaza in October, 312 BC, from which the founding of the Seleucid kingdom was reckoned in Antioch. In Mesopotamia it was reckoned from Nisan 311 BC. This era was widely used in the Near East until the Mohammedan conquests of the 7th century AD. The Gk reckoning of Olympiads (four-year periods beginning with 776 BC) and the Roman era reckoned from the foundation of the city (754 BC) do not appear in the Bible.

VII. *New Testament:* chronological data in the NT are sparse. The birth of Jesus occurred at an uncertain date; 753 of the Roman era is in error by four to seven years (cf JESUS CHRIST). The 15th year of Tiberius* Caesar (Lk 3:1) may be reckoned either from his succession to Augustus (AD 14) or from his association with Augustus in the *imperium* (AD 12).

It is from this point that NT chronology must be calculated.

The chronological table (cf ENDSHEETS) contains synchronistic dates for Israel, Assyria and Babylonia, Egypt, Persia, the Seleucid and Ptolemaic dynasties, and Rome. It is based upon the chronologies of Scharff, Moortgat, Albright, Valjavec, and Freedman-Campbell. There is a large measure of approximation for the early dates, which decreases as one comes down. Assyrian and Babylonian dates from the 10th century are exact for practical purposes, as are Gk and Roman dates. The dates of the Hb kings are exact within 5 to 10 years.

Church. The Anglo-Saxon group of words (Eng *church*, Scots *kirk*, German *Kirche*, Dutch *kerk*) are derived from the late Gk word *kyriakon*, "the Lord's (house)." The Gk word *ekklēsia* signified in classical Gk the assembly of the citizens of a city for legislative or deliberative purposes. This assembly included only the citizens who enjoyed full rights, and thus the word implies both the dignity of the members and the legality of the assembly. The Gk word *ekklēsia* had no religious usage. It was adopted by the LXX to render the Hb word *ḳāhāl*, which with the Hb word *'ēdāh* signifies in later Hb the religious assembly of the Israelites. These two words were adopted for the local religious assembly of the Jews who lived outside Jerusalem, and 'ēdāh is more commonly rendered in Gk by synagōgē, the word from which Eng synagogue is derived. The earliest uses of the word in the NT reflect the idea both of ḳᶜhal yahweh, the religious assembly of God, and the local assembly. The word is first applied to the ekklēsia of Jerusalem, which was itself a local community. It was at the same time the assembly of all those who believed in Jesus Christ, and thus was the legitimate successor of the Israelite assembly of Yahweh. In its initial phases the Church of Jerusalem was not clearly aware of its distinction from Judaism. Its members were accustomed to meet and to pray in the temple and regarded themselves as in every way faithful to the Law and obligations of Judaism. The question of the relations between the Church and Judaism did not become acute until Gentiles were admitted in considerable numbers and finally formed separate local churches in other cities, of which the earliest and the largest was the church of Antioch*. It then became necessary for the Church to identify itself as a community distinct from Judaism, into which Gentiles could be admitted to full standing without becoming Jews and undertaking the full obligations of the Jewish law. This question is discussed in AA 15, Gal, and Rm; cf also Eph 2:11–22. On the council of Jerusalem (AA 15) cf ACTS OF APOSTLES.

1. *The Synoptic Gospels.* The word ekklēsia appears only twice in the Synoptic Gospels (Mt 16:18; 18:18). The teaching of Jesus Himself was stated in the framework of the kingdom* of God; but the foundations of the idea of ekklēsia are clear in the Synoptic Gospels. Jesus formed a group of disciples and followers. Of these disciples He demanded personal attachment to Himself, even at the cost of separation from friends and family; indeed, this following might cause a separation between them and the world at large which could issue in their death (Mt 4:18 ff; 10:34 ff; Mk 1:16 ff; 8:34 ff; Lk 5:1 ff; 12:51 ff). This group of followers received from Him the mission to gain other followers who would grant Him the same personal allegiance (Mt 28:19; Mk 16:15 ff). Against this background the use of the word ekklēsia in Mt 16:18 is clearly identified with this group which Jesus Himself formed and which He commanded to be continued by His disciples after His departure. In Mt 16:18 the Church is compared to a building which is erected upon the apostle Simon Peter as a rock of foundation. This passage not only indicates

the peculiar position of Peter in the assembly of Jesus' disciples, but also the unity and the permanence of the group which Jesus Himself established. In this passage Jesus assures His disciples that this single group, which is founded upon Simon Peter, will endure the attacks even of Satan. It is possible that this passage, like others in Mt, is stated in the form which had been imposed upon it in the development of Christian oral tradition. The unique instance of the word ekklēsia in this sense in the Synoptic Gospels suggests this view. But this does not alter the fact that the idea of such a group is found clearly in these three Gospels. The peculiar position of Peter is not unique in this passage. The other instance of ekklēsia (Mt 18:17) does not so clearly signify the group of Jesus's disciples. In this context, where the disciples are urged to report the recalcitrant member to the assembly, the Jewish synagogue may be signified. The difference between the group of Jesus' disciples and Judaism is not as clear at this stage of the tradition as it later became. Members are to seek redress for personal injuries from the synagogue rather than by their own acts of revenge.

2. *Acts.* The word ekklēsia occurs in AA 23 times. In no passage does it certainly mean anything except the local church, usually the church of Jerusalem, but also the local church of Antioch and other cities. The church of Jerusalem was the parent and the prototype of other churches, and possibly the first foundations were considered as expansions of the Jerusalem community. This idea did not long persist, if it was ever present at all; for each local church was called ekklēsia in the same sense in which the title was given to the community of Jerusalem, which in AA does possess the primacy of the parent church (cf AA 15:1 ff). The church of Jerusalem sends men to investigate conditions in other churches (AA 15:3) and itself in assembly decides questions which are referred to it by other churches (AA 15:22). The other churches, however, are organized with their own bishops*, presbyters*, and deacons*, and they are founded by apostles*. This early hierarchy appears in AA in the Jerusalem church itself. In AA it is clear that membership in the Church involves acceptance of the claims of Jesus and belief in the saving power of His redeeming death. Membership is gained not by Jewish birth, but by the rite of baptism*. This becomes clear when the proposal is first made to admit Gentiles who had not become proselytes* of Judaism (AA 10:1 ff). The further question of whether Gentiles admitted on these terms should then be obliged to the full observance

of the Jewish law was resolved by a lenient interpretation of Jewish obligations (AA 15:28 ff).

3. *Paul.* The word *ekklēsia* occurs 65 times in the writings of Paul, more frequently than in the rest of the NT altogether. This more likely represents a common usage which had developed when Paul wrote than any peculiar Pauline diction. In most of these instances the word signifies a local church. Paul is the first NT writer to employ the word in the plural, which signifies the equality of the separate local churches. In Eph and Col the word is used of the entire worldwide assembly of the followers of Jesus, which is here conceived as one great assembly. In these epistles the theology of the Church is worked out for the first time. Christ is the head of the Church which is His body and His fullness, a fullness which is dispensed from Him through the Church to all its members (Eph 1:22–23). As the one through whom all creation comes into being He is the head of His body the Church, a principle through which the fullness of the Church comes into being (Col 1:18 ff). It is through the Church that the mystery of God's saving will and the manifold divine wisdom are revealed (Eph 3:10). Christ is head of the Church as the husband is head of the wife, and Christ likewise is the savior of the Church. The Church is submitted to Christ as wives are submitted to their husbands, and Christ loves the Church as the husband loves his wife; He has given His own life on behalf of the Church. Through this He has hallowed the Church, cleansing it in the washing of His blood and the word of baptism, and thus He has established the Church for Himself in its glory, without spot or wrinkle. This love, Paul goes on to say, is a model of the love which husbands ought to exhibit toward their wives, and of the care which they ought to take of them; and this relationship of Christ and the Church is called a great mystery (Eph 5:22–32). This beautiful image is already suggested in the Gospels, where Jesus calls Himself the bridegroom (Mt 9:15; Mk 2:19; Lk 5:34), and in turn it is a resumption of the older image of Yahweh as the spouse of Israel (Ho 2:2 ff, 14–23; Je 2:2; cf COVENANT; MARRIAGE). The figure of the Church as the body of Christ is the basis of Paul's appeal for Christian unity and cooperation (1 Co 12:12 ff; Rm 12:4 ff). The unity of one body is symbolized by the one bread of the Eucharist* (1 Co 10:17). In the Church God has established certain offices in a set order — apostles, prophets, teachers, thaumaturges — and to assist the Church He confers charismata of healing, helpfulness, govern-

ment, of tongues. Each Christian should fulfill the function assigned him without attempting to enter into the office of others (1 Co 12:28 ff). The Church is also compared by Paul to a city (Eph 2:19) and to a building erected upon the foundation of apostles and prophets with Christ Jesus Himself the cornerstone upon which the entire building reposes. This building is the holy temple of the Lord, and the members of the Church are incorporated into its structure (Eph 2:20 ff). This suggests the figure of Mt 16:18. The Church of the living God is the house of God, the column and foundation of the edifice of truth (1 Tm 3:15). To the members of the Church Paul gives the titles of saints, those who love God, those who are called (Rm 8:27–28), the Church of God, those who are hallowed in Christ Jesus, those who are called to be holy (1 Co 1:2), the chosen holy ones of God (Col 3:12; cf 2 Tm 2:10; Tt 1:1). These titles, which are drawn from the OT, indicate that the Church is the true Israel and the legitimate heir of the covenant promises. It has now become clear that Israel itself has decided to refuse its Messiah* and with Him it has rejected the covenant which gave it its right to the titles now claimed by the Christians (Rm 9–11).

4. *John.* The word *ekklēsia* appears in the Joannine writings in 3 Jn 6, 9, 10, and 20 times in Apc, referring to particular churches. The group of the followers of Jesus is described in Jn as a flock which is gathered into a sheepfold (Jn 10:1 ff). Jesus Himself is the door of the sheepfold and the good shepherd who gives His life for His sheep. There are sheep which do not belong to His fold and He must lead them in so that they too will obey His voice and all men will become one flock under one shepherd. Jesus is the true vine which His Father cultivates. His disciples are the branches and by their union with Him they become fruitful. Unless they remain united to Him they shall be rejected (Jn 15:1 ff). Jesus commits His flock to Peter* as its shepherd (Jn 21:15 ff). He prays that His followers may be one as He and His father are one, and that His followers may be united with Him and His Father (Jn 17:20 f).

In the other NT writings the word occurs once in Js (5:14), where it most probably signifies a particular church. In these writings also there appears a clearly defined body of followers of Jesus, called once (Js 2:2) a synagogue.

From these passages it is evident that the local churches are united in a single organization, which is called the Church in the epistles of Paul. The reality is present in the other writings, even though the word is not used. This Church enjoys a union with its founder which in modern theology is called mystical (cf BODY); it derives its life and its virtue from His enduring presence within it. It is the means by which the life of Christ is communicated. It has the mission to bring into itself all men. It admits new members by baptism, and the fullness of the divine life which it possesses is communicated by the other sacraments*. It is an organized body with officials of distinct rank (cf APOSTLE; BISHOP; DEACON; ELDER; PRESBYTER). This assembly is the heir of the covenant and promises of Israel, which reach their fulfillment in Jesus and His Church.

Chuza (Gk *chouzas,* from Aramaic *kūzā',* etymology uncertain), the name appears in Nabatean and Syriac inscriptions; the steward of Herod* (Lk 8:3), whose wife Joanna* was one of the women who ministered to the needs of Jesus. Some writers identify him with the royal official whose son was cured of illness by Jesus at Capharnaum* (Jn 4:43 ff).

Cilicia (Gk *kilikia*), the coastal strip of the SE corner of Asia Minor, bounded by the Taurus Mountains to the N and Mt Amanus to the E. In OT times the region belonged to the kingdom of the Hittites. It was a part of the Seleucid* kingdom of Syria (1 Mc 11:14; 2 Mc 4:36) and under Roman rule was a part of the province of Syria until it became a distinct province in AD 57. The land route from Syria to the interior of Asia Minor traversed the rugged pass of the Taurus Mountains called the Cilician Gates. The principal city of Cilicia was Tarsus*, the birthplace of Paul. The area had Jewish inhabitants in NT times (AA 6:9) and Christian communities as early as the council of Jerusalem (AA 15:23).

Cinnamon (Hb *ḳinnāmôn,* Gk *kinnamōmon*), the well known spice. It is the product of the tree *Cinnamomum Zeylanicum,* native to Ceylon and other East Indian islands. The product is obtained from the inner bark of the tree and the oil of cinnamon is secured by boiling the ripe fruit. It is mentioned in the OT as one of the components of the oil of anointing* (Ex 30:23) and is enumerated with other perfumes in SS 4:14, and is used to perfume a bed in Pr 7:17. It is mentioned among the merchandise of Babylon (i.e., Rome, Apc 18:13).

Circumcision. 1. *OT.* The practice of cutting off the foreskin of the male organ is ancient and fairly widespread among primitive peoples even to the present time; it is estimated that 200,000,000 employ it. In the ancient Near East the practice is certainly attested for the Egyptians, but few details are known. Herodotus asserted in the 5th century BC that the practice was general, but this is not supported by evidence from Egypt itself. There is little or no doubt that it was practiced upon all priests, but it is not certain that others besides the priestly class were circumcised. A tomb painting from the 6th dynasty represents the circumcision of two boys (ANEP 629). The meaning of the practice is not altogether clear either among the Egyptians or among primitive peoples. Hygienic motives, asserted by Herodotus for the Egyptians, are not supported by the evidence. It is much more probable that it was an initiatory rite with religious or magical significance. It seems almost universally to have been conferred at the age of puberty and to be a "rite of passage" from boyhood to manhood or a preparation for marriage; possibly it was thought that circumcision facilitated sexual intercourse. This, however, does not explain its restriction to the priestly class in Egypt. The Hebrews alone practiced circumcision on the 8th day after birth. The operation in earliest times was performed by the father. The use of a flint knife indicates the antiquity of the rite. The law of circumcision appears in Gn 17:10 ff. Here it is a part of the covenant of God with Abraham. All born in the household of Abraham, whether free or slave, are to be circumcised 8 days after birth. The adult males were to be circumcised immediately. The circumcision of Isaac is mentioned in Gn 21:4. The obligation is serious, and failure to fulfill it means separation from the covenant (Gn 17:14). This anecdote contains Israelite law in the form of a story, and some scholars think that a practice of later origin has been read back into patriarchal times. The law of circumcision is stated in Ex 12:3. Circumcision is a necessary qualification for partaking in the Passover* sacrifice (Ex 12:44–48). An obscure fragment of popular tradition tells how Moses was in some way threatened with death, from which he was rescued when his wife Zipporah* circumcised their son (Ex 4:24–26). The story explains the origin of the phrase "bridegroom of blood," which is not found elsewhere. Some scholars believe that Moses son has been substituted in the story for Moses himself, and that the original story related that Moses' seizure was due to the fact that he himself was not circumcised, and that Zipporah saved his life by performing the operation upon him at the time of the consummation of their wedding. In the story of Dinah* and Shechem* (Gn 34:1 ff) the sons of Israel impose circumcision of all males as a condition of their accepting the covenant of common life and intermarriage with the people of Shechem. The sons of Israel thus trapped the men of Shechem and murdered them during the illness which followed the operation. A popular tradition related that the men of Israel were not circumcised in the desert before their entrance into Canaan, and that the operation was performed upon all Israelite males at Gibeath-araloth after the crossing of the Jordan (Jos 5:2 ff). Thus the "reproach of Egypt" was removed from Israel. The phrase "reproach of Egypt" seems to show that the account was ignorant of the practice of circumcision in Egypt. The roots of the story are difficult to trace. It is, of course, practically impossible to suppose that the entire fighting force of Israel could have submitted to this operation at the time of their entrance into hostile territory; but the tradition must preserve some account of the failure of Israel to practice circumcision for an extended time. It is unlikely that the story is actually an account of the first adoption of the practice in Israel. Neither the origin of circumcision in Israel nor its meaning is entirely clear. Jeremiah mentions as circumcised peoples of Egypt, Edom, Ammon, and Moab, and certain nomad tribes of the desert (Je 9:25 f). The name "uncircumcised" is a title of contempt applied to other peoples, especially to the Philistines* (Jgs 14:3; 15:18; 1 S 14:6; 31:4; 2 S 1:20). In Ezekiel's dirge over Egypt (32:19 ff) the curse of lying in the grave with the uncircumcised is repeated 10 times. This, however, does not signify that the Philistines alone of the neighbors of the Hebrews were uncircumcised. There is little if any evidence that it was practiced by the Canaanites. An ivory carving from Megiddo* (ANEP 332) represents two circumcised male prisoners, of uncertain origin but certainly Semitic in features, being led before an unidentified king. The practice is not mentioned in Mesopotamian literature, nor is there any trace of it in archaeological remains. Hence the hypothesis that the Hebrews adopted the rite from some desert tribes is not altogether without probability. The rite when performed 8 days after birth no longer has the meaning of initiation into adult manhood or matrimony. It is a sign of the covenant of Israel and Yahweh. The precise form of the symbolism, however, cannot be traced, and it is possible that the Hebrews first adopted the rite as an initiation. The metaphorical use of the words "circumcision" and "foreskin" as stated below indicates that the foreskin was regarded as a point where uncleanness was focused, and that this uncleanness was removed by circumcision (cf CLEAN). This, however, is doubtfully the

original significance of the rite. As a consecration of the power of generation to the deity the rite would have significance; but the symbolism is of itself less well adapted to this meaning. One may detect from such passages as Abraham's oath (Gn 24:2) that the male organ was regarded as sacred and perhaps in some sense as a symbol of the deity, the ultimate source of life. In any case circumcision appears throughout the entire OT and NT as a token of membership in Israel and of association with the covenant.

To be circumcised of heart is to be submissive to Yahweh (Lv 26:41; Dt 10:16; Je 4:4). To be uncircumcised of ears is to be disobedient to Yahweh (Je 6:10). Foreigners uncircumcised of heart and flesh should not have been admitted to the Israelite sanctuary (Ez 44:7). Israel, though circumcised of flesh, is uncircumcised of heart (Je 9:25 f). Moses is uncircumcised of lips (Ex 6:12, 30) by which is signified his inability to speak. In the opinion of some scholars this indicated a real speech impediment, but in any case it was a denial of eloquence. New fruit trees are uncircumcised (Lv 19:23) for three years, i.e., they have not yet been consecrated to Yahweh by the offering of the firstfruits*. The rite of circumcision was prohibited by Antiochus Epiphanes under the penalty of death (1 Mc 1:15).

2. NT. Jesus Himself was circumcised on the 8th day after His birth (Lk 2:21). Paul mentions his own circumcision to show that he is fully an Israelite (Phl 3:5), and Paul had Timothy* circumcised after he had reached adult years because he was the son of a Jewish mother (AA 16:3), although Titus*, whose parents were Gentiles, did not have to undergo circumcision (Gal 2:3). The Jewish members of the primitive Christian community are several times in the NT called simply "the circumcision" or "those of the circumcision" (AA 10:45; 11:2). The necessity of circumcision was proposed by Jewish Christians (AA 15:1 ff) and as a consequence a serious dispute arose. The council of Jerusalem finally decided against the necessity of circumcision for Gentile converts (AA 15:28 f). The Jewish party evidently was not entirely satisfied with this decision, for it is further discussed by Paul in both Gal and Rm, and it becomes an occasion for Paul to proclaim the efficacy of Christ's redeeming death and the freedom of the Christian from the observances of the Jewish Law. Paul insists that circumcision destroys the efficacy of the redemption; to be circumcised makes one liable to the observance of the entire Law. In Christ Jesus neither circumcision nor its absence has any

meaning (Gal 5:6). He takes up again a figure of Jeremiah to show that mere physical circumcision is without value; the true Israelite is inwardly circumcised of heart (Rm 2:25 ff). Both circumcised and uncircumcised are accepted by God because of their faith (Rm 3:30). Abraham himself was justified by his faith, not by his circumcision (Rm 4:1–12), and the descendants of Abraham are those who share his faith, not those who share only the physical sign of his circumcision (Rm 4:13 ff). Since circumcision is of no importance in the Christian dispensation, Paul prefers that those who are called, whether Jew or Gentile, remain in the state in which they are called (1 Co 7:18 ff). Christ has become a "minister of circumcision" (Rm 15:8) i.e., He has carried out the promises made to the fathers by bringing righteousness and salvation, which are promised by the covenant of circumcision. Circumcision is the work of human hands (Eph 2:11), but the initiation of Christians into Christ is effected by Christ Himself through baptism (Col 2:11 f).

Cistern. Artificial reservoirs to collect and retain rain water were extremely common in the cities of ancient Palestine. The springs which supplied fresh water were as a rule no more than adequate for the needs of the population, and in almost every city had to be supplemented by cisterns, some of which were public, others were attached to private residences. By preference a cistern was excavated in the natural rock; they were also made by digging holes in the ground and walling them with masonry. Large cisterns were sometimes reached by a flight of steps. Jeremiah compares foreign gods to broken cisterns, as contrasted with Yahweh, the spring of fresh water (Je 2:13).

City. The whole complex which we understand by civilization is the product of the city. The earliest city known is Jericho* (6800 BC). Urban centers appear in Mesopotamia in 3500 BC. Up to this time the men of Mesopotamia lived in primitive agricultural villages. Some impulse led the Sumerians* to group themselves in more closely built fortified communities. The change from agricultural and pastoral life to city life brought about specialization of labor, which permitted some men to support themselves by the crafts and released them from the necessity of procuring their own food. The city was a market, in which goods could be exchanged, not only among the citizens themselves, but also between one city and another. Manufacturing was possible, and man's use of natural resources was

much increased by specialization and exchange. The city also brought a closer political unity; the human resources of the community could be mobilized for a common purpose. Both in Mesopotamia and in Egypt, where cities appear not much later than in Mesopotamia, community effort was no doubt demanded for the common work of irrigation. In both these alluvial valleys cultivation of the soil to the best results is not possible unless each of the cultivators does his share to maintain the dikes and canals which channel the water to the fields and help control destructive floods. The military potential of the city also was more easily mobilized, and the government of the city, which was concentrated in the person of the king*, could muster men for tasks which no individual or family could or would undertake, such as the construction of temples, walls and fortifications, palaces, roads, docks, and other such works. It is clear that from earliest times the Mesopotamian city was centered about the temple, and that each city worshiped its own god. The temples were of great importance in the development of literature and the arts, both of which were employed for religious purposes from the earliest times. Mesopotamia differed from Egypt in its political structure. In Mesopotamia each city was a state, and the inhabitants of Mesopotamia never succeeded in erecting a stable political structure which would extend over a wider area than the city and the lands in the immediate neighborhood which it cultivated. Larger units took the form of empire of one city-state over others. In Egypt, on the other hand, the kingdom appears as unified from earliest historical times. This may in part be explained by the dependence of Egypt upon the Nile*, which must be treated as a single unit in order that its possibilities may be realized to the full. Canaan before the Israelites was, like Mesopotamia, a country of city-states. A list of the cities of Canaan conquered by Thutmose III contains 118 local names, most of which no doubt represent independent cities. The Papyrus Anastasi I from the times of Ramses II mentions 56 fortified cities in Syria. Many of these can be identified with biblical names. The politics of the city-states of Canaan before the Israelite conquest are described in the Amarna* Letters. In this period the city-states were ruled by kings who were vassals of the Pharaoh; the Egyptian sovereignty during the Amarna period was not very effective. But each city-state is a sovereign independent unit. When the Israelites conquered the country the city-states of Canaan were the last places to fall to them. In some instances it is clear that the cities remained

a) and b) Pompeii,
Remains of streets,
houses, and shops.
c) Pompeii. Remains
of amphitheater.

Canaanite while the surrounding countryside was Israelite. When the Hebrews did take the cities, they did not take with them the political system of the sovereign city-state. Tribal unity and Israelite unity as a whole remained even after the occupation of the cities. The political instability of the Hebrew tribal system was not healed until the establishment of the monarchy. In the OT as in Mesopotamia a city is by definition a walled and fortified enclosure. Exceptions to this use of the Hb word 'îr are rare in the OT. The Canaanite and Hebrew cities were extremely small by modern standards, running from 6 to 7 acres to 15, and in a few instances as many as 20 acres. Within these cities the population was densely packed. For some ancient cities a density of 50 to the acre is estimated by modern scholars (cf the density of about 132 to the acre for Manhattan). Within the walled enclosure there were no streets as we think of them but only narrow passages between the houses or groups of houses. The only open spaces within the city were found near the gate or gates, called "squares" in Eng versions. This space had to be left clear for defense, since the gates were the weakest points of the walls. In long periods of peace these squares were sometimes built up and the houses had to be demolished if war broke out (Is 22:10). We read also of houses built upon the wall itself (Jos 2:15). Many of the city's population, if not most, lived in villages outside the walls and cultivated the city's lands; these villages are often called the "daughters" of the city. In time of war the villagers were packed within the walled enclosure. The choice of a site was determined by the presence of water and the defensibility of the site. In the course of time the city built its own mound, called a *tell* (cf ARCHAEOLOGY). The spring was included within the walls, if possible; but frequently this was not possible. In some ancient cities we find complicated systems for securing water in times of siege (cf GIBEON; GIHON). There is no indication of any paving of the streets in early Israelite cities, and references to the dirt of the streets are not infrequent (Is 10:6; Mi 7:10). Rubbish and garbage were thrown from the houses directly into the streets. We meet references to scavenging dogs which roamed the streets and lived off the garbage (Ex 22:30; Is 5:25). The squares near the gate served as marketplaces (2 K 7:1) and courts. The elders took their seat at the gates and there adjudicated disputes (Dt 21:19; 2 S 15:2; cf GATE). Men who practiced the same trade or craft often if not usually lived in the same street; and we read that in Damascus and Samaria streets were set aside for bazaars for merchants from other cities (1 K 20:34).

In the NT the distinction between city and village is preserved. Bethany*, Bethphage*, Bethlehem*, and Emmaus* are called villages, while Nazareth*, Nain*, and Capernaum* are called cities. The Hellenistic cities in the neighborhood of Palestine, particularly the cities of the Decapolis*, were built on the model of the Greek *polis,* around the agora or marketplace, and included baths, a theater, and a stadium. They were built with one or two broad colonnaded avenues which extended across the city. The government of the Gk *polis* was conducted by a senate (*boulē*) and an assembly (*ekklēsia*) of the people (*dēmos*). But this Gk *polis* was never accepted by the Jews.

The city acquires a theological significance in the imagery of the NT. This arises from the OT conception of Jerusalem* as the city of God, the place in which Yahweh dwells in His temple. The messianism* of the OT in most of the prophetic books includes the restoration of Jerusalem from its ruins. But the earthly Jerusalem in the NT becomes a type of the heavenly Jerusalem, which is free and our mother (Gal 4:26). The Christians are citizens of the heavenly city (Phl 3:20). The Epistle to the Hebrews places a contrast between the theophany of Sinai* and the approach of the Christians to Mt Zion, the city of the living God, the heavenly Jerusalem (Heb 12:22). They are not citizens of an earthly city, but move toward a city which is to come (Heb 13:14). The city of God is the new Jerusalem which is to come down out of heaven from God (Apc 3:12); the last vision of the seer of Patmos is of Jerusalem, the holy city, coming down out of heaven from God in all the glory of God (Apc 21–22). It shines with the radiance of precious stones, and has 12 gates, each made of precious stones. It has no temple, for the Lord God and the Lamb are its temple. It needs neither sun nor moon, for the glory of God illuminates it, and the Lamb is its lamp. All the kings of the earth will bring their splendor to it, and its gates shall never be shut by night or by day. No one unclean shall enter this city. The imagery of the heavenly city is a testimonial of the conviction that it is in the life of the city that man reaches the highest fulfillment of his desires and powers, and that the life of the city offers opportunities which can never be found in the primitive pastoral or agricultural society.

Clan. Cf TRIBE.

Claudius. Tiberius Claudius Nero Germanicus, emperor of Rome 41–54, son of Drusus and nephew of Tiberius*. He was proclaimed emperor by the praetorian guard after the assassination of Caligula; but he was a weak and ineffective ruler who left most of the government to his freedmen. It was during the reign of Claudius that the famine predicted by Agabus* occurred (AA 11:22). He was a patron of Herod Agrippa* and established him as king of Judaea. At some undetermined date in his reign he expelled the Jews from Rome (AA 18:2). This expulsion brought Aquila* and Priscilla* to Corinth, where they met Paul.

Claudius Lysias. The chiliarch or tribune in command of the garrison of Jerusalem at the time of Paul's last visit to the city (AA 21:15–23:35). He rescued Paul from the riot caused by Paul's association with the Gentile Trophimus* the Ephesian and has him confined in the barracks. He permitted Paul to address the Jews from the steps of the barracks, but Paul's speech excited a new riot, and the tribune directed that Paul be examined under the lash. Paul escaped scourging by claiming Roman citizenship. The tribune, wishing to find a reason for the riot, brought Paul to a hearing before the high priest* and the council.* When the dispute became violent, the tribune broke off the hearing and returned Paul to the barracks. A centurion discovered that 40 Jews had sworn to fast until they had murdered Paul, and the centurion, to avoid further trouble, sent Paul with an escort of 200 men to the governor Felix* at Caesarea*.

Clean, Unclean. The concepts of clean and unclean appear in four categories.
1. *Food*. The clean animals are defined as those with a cloven hoof which chew the cud (Lv 11:2 ff; Dt 14:4 ff). Animals which have only one of these characteristics (or which appear to have only one) are expressly mentioned: the camel, the rock-badger, the hare, and the pig (Lv 11:4 ff; Dt 14:7). Fish may be eaten if they have fins and scales (Lv 11:9; Dt 14:10). Birds of prey and carrion birds are unclean (Lv 11:14 ff; Dt 14:11 ff). Insects are unclean unless they have jointed legs, such as the locust and the grasshopper (Lv 11:21 ff). Reptiles are unclean (Lv 11:29 ff). Animals which have died a natural death or have been killed by other animals are unclean (Lv 17:15). The code of Deuteronomy relaxes these prohibitions somewhat by permitting animals which are not killed for sacrifice to be eaten, whether they are clean or unclean (Dt 12:15, 22; 15:22).
2. *Leprosy*. Lv 13:1–14:57 contains detailed descriptions of leprosy*, which here

includes a number of skin diseases, as well as descriptions of "leprosy" of houses and garments. The leper is unclean; he must wear torn garments and hair unkempt and cover his beard. He must live outside the community and cry "Unclean" to all who approach him (Lv 13:45 f). His cure must be attested by the priest.
3. *Death*. Contact with a dead body renders a person unclean for 7 days (Nm 19:12, 14, 16). This uncleanness does not prohibit an Israelite from taking part in the Passover* rites (Nm 9:10).
4. *Sexual functions*. Uncleanness is incurred by almost any sexual function, lawful or unlawful, normal or abnormal. A man or a woman who has a discharge from the sexual organs is unclean (Lv 15:2 ff, 16 ff). A woman is unclean during her menstruation (Lv 15:19 ff) as well as during any abnormal issue of blood (Lv 15:25 ff). A woman is unclean after childbirth for seven days if the child is a boy (Lv 12:2), 14 days if the child is a girl (Lv 12:5), and she is to abstain from sexual intercourse for another 33 days after the birth of a boy and another 66 days after the birth of a girl. At the end of the 40 or 80 days there is a rite of purification. A man incurs uncleanness by adultery (Lv 18:20) or by bestiality (Lv 18:23). Normal sexual intercourse rendered one unclean for the remainder of the day (Lv 15:18; 1 S 21:4); most of the instances, however, in which the word unclean is applied to a woman refer to unlawful intercourse (Gn 34:5, 13; Nm 5:13, 27; Ezk 18:6, 11, 15; 22:11; 33:17). A woman who has married a second time after a divorce is unclean for her first husband (Dt 24:4), although she would be free to marry anyone else after the death of her second husband or divorce from him.

Priests, because of their contact with sacred articles, had particular obligations of cleanliness. They are not permitted to incur uncleanness by contact with the dead except the next of kin (Lv 21:1 ff), and the high priest may not incur this uncleanness even for father and mother (Lv 21:11). Should a priest incur uncleanness, he is unclean for the remainder of the day and may not partake of sacrificial foods (Lv 22:4 ff). Uncleanness is incurred by mere contact with the unclean person or object: unclean animals (Lv 5:2), the dead body (Nm 6:7; 19:11, 13, 14, 16). One becomes unclean not only by contact with the man or woman who has an issue from the sexual organs, but also by contact with any furniture or other objects which the person has touched (Lv 15:4–11), and any earthen vessel which he had touched should be broken (Lv 15:12, 20–23, 25–27). Uncleanness is also communicated to all those who touch the scapegoat (Lv 16:24–28) and by contact with the red heifer*, which is burned (Nm 19:1 ff) in order to obtain ashes for the water of purification.

Uncleanness endures until purification, which in some instances may not be done until a set time has elapsed. The water of purification mingled with the ashes of the red heifer are sprinkled upon the house, the furniture, and the persons in a house where a death has occurred (Nm 19:17 ff). The purification of a woman after childbirth is accomplished by the sacrifice of a lamb and a pigeon or dove (Lv 12:6), commuted to two pigeons or doves for the poor (Lv 12:8). The man or woman who has an issue from the sexual organs must take seven days for purification (Lv 15:13 ff, 28 ff) and they offer a sacrifice of two doves or pigeons. Anyone who touches them is unclean for the remainder of the day, and this uncleanness is removed by bathing (Lv 15:6 ff, 21 ff, 26 ff). The clothing also must be washed after this contact. The same bathing and washing of clothing is required after contact with the scapegoat (Lv 16:24 ff). Bathing is required to remove the uncleanness of normal sexual intercourse (Lv 15:18). After contact with a dead body uncleanness remains for seven days; the water of purification and the ashes of the red heifer are to be employed on the third and seventh days (Nm 19:12, 19). The waters of purification themselves render the person who sprinkles unclean; he must bathe and wash his clothing (Nm 19:21). For the cleansing of the leper cf LEPROSY.

Cleanness is also used in a transferred sense. Both the land (Lv 18:24 +) and the sanctuary (Je 7:30; 32:24) may be rendered unclean (cf Nm 35:34; Dt 21:23). The land or the sanctuary is rendered unclean by magicians* (Lv 19:31) or by idols (Ps 106:39; Ezk 22:3; Ho 5:3; 6:10 +) and by the offering of the firstborn child as a sacrifice (Lv 20:3). Foreign lands are unclean (Am 7:17). Isaiah speaks of himself and his people as having unclean lips (Is 6:5).

The origin of the concepts of clean and unclean and their meaning do not admit exact definition. The concepts of holy* and unclean resemble each other only in the fact that neither is to be touched and that holiness and uncleanness are both incurred by contact. But the two sets of concepts are formally unrelated. That is holy which in some way belongs to the sphere of deity. The roots of the concepts of clean and unclean are more obscure. Neither can clean and unclean be simply compared with the *tabu* of the primitives of Polynesia, except in the prohibition of touching. Similar practices are found in many primitive tribes throughout the world; in most of these instances the basis is obscure, as it is among the Hebrews. Uncleanness may be rooted in physical repulsion in leprosy and other skin diseases, but it does not appear in other diseases which are also repulsive. The same inconsistency is found in foods, which cannot be divided easily on the basis of attraction and repulsion. Sexual functions are unclean whether they are natural or unnatural. It is clear that cleanness means fitness for participation in the cult, and that uncleanness disqualifies one from cultic functions. It is not possible to determine a common basis in those things which render one unfit for the cult. Morality is not a factor. Unlawful sexual relations render one no more unclean than do lawful sexual relations or the eating of unclean food. Sin is termed unclean only when the word is used in a transferred sense (cf passages cited above). Furthermore, most uncleanness is removed simply by bathing. Uncleanness is therefore conceived as a physical entity, not a moral state. It seems that in the concept of unclean we have a number of primitive practices which may have been originally related; their basis was possibly no longer understood by the Hebrews themselves. In examining the areas of uncleanness no common element appears except that, excluding leprosy, all the unclean factors are related in some way to the beginning and end of life. The functions of sex are the human acts from which life originates; these and the body of the dead both render one unclean. Food is the means by which life is sustained, although there is no distinction in drink, nor does this tell us why some foods are unclean. It is possible, if the hypothesis is not too fanciful, to conceive that leprosy was imagined as a kind of living death, and was therefore an unclean disease. This would permit us to approach a common element in uncleanness. In ancient Hebrew and other Semitic religions life and death were the area of the divine, where the power of the deity was most obviously manifested. Man's share in the initiation of life by the functions of sex was itself considered a participation in the functions of the deity, and one whose life was just ended had been touched, as it were, by the hand of the deity. Understood in this way the concept of unclean is not entirely dissimilar to the concept of holy; possibly the ideas of unclean and clean arose in a culture which did not possess the idea of the holy, and they were not adopted without some violence and overlapping of the two sets of concepts. There remains, however, the fundamental difference that one removes uncleanness in order to participate in cultic functions, and one removes holiness in order to return to the profane world. Uncleanness, even if it is analyzed as intimate contact with the mysteries of life and death, does not tell us why this contact should render one unfit for public worship.

In NT times the laws of clean and unclean were interpreted by the Pharisees* with fanatic rigidity, which elicited some of the most severe words uttered by Jesus. He declared that all foods are equally clean (Mt 15:11 ff; Mk 7:14 ff) and accused the Pharisees of cleaning only the outside of the dish (Mt 23:36). He permitted His disciples to ignore the laws of legal cleanliness (Mt 15:1 ff; Mk 7:5 ff). Uncleanness was incurred even by contact with Gentiles (AA 10:28), and this Jewish inhibition was not entirely removed until late in the 1st century.

Clement (Gk *klēmēs*, Lt *clemens*, "mild"), one of Paul's fellow workers (Phl 4:3). The identification of this Clement with the early Christian writer and bishop of Rome is uncertain.

Cleopatra (Gk *kleopatra*, "illustrious father"), a name borne by a number of princesses of the Ptolemaic* dynasty of Egypt*. Cleopatra, daughter of Ptolemy VI Philometor, was the wife first of Alexander* Balas (1 Mc 10:57 f). Her father divorced her from Alexander and married her to Demetrius II Nicator* (1 Mc 11:12). During the captivity of Demetrius in Parthia she became the wife of his brother, Antiochus* VII Sidetes. She bore two sons to Demetrius; she murdered the elder and intrigued for the succession of the younger, Antiochus VIII Grypus, to the throne. She finally attempted to poison him, but was discovered and forced to drink the poison herself (120 BC).

Cleophas (Gk *kleopas*, abbreviated form of Gk *kleopatras* "illustrious father"). **1.** One of the disciples who met Jesus on the road to Emmaus after His resurrection* (Lk 24:18). **2.** Gk *klōpas*, the father or the husband of one of the women named Mary* who stood at the foot of the cross (Jn 19:25). If *klōpas* here is the husband of Mary, he is possibly to be identified with Alphaeus* (cf BRETHREN OF THE LORD).

Clothing. In the biblical conception clothing originates from the feeling of shame and sexual desire which was aroused by the first sin (Gn 3:7, 21) and is therefore worn primarily for modesty. The Hebrews regarded nudity as extremely shameful and it is often mentioned as a disgrace suffered by captives in war (Is 20:4; Am 2:16 +). Assyrian

and Egyptian reliefs show that captives were sometimes stripped of their clothing, which became the booty of their conquerors

Egyptian man wearing kilt and woman wearing a linen robe.

(ANEP 8, 10, 358). The word naked is sometimes used to designate a person who is clad only in the undergarment. The Bible itself tells us little of the shape and texture of clothing, and the names of the various garments cannot always be identified. This information must be supplemented by representations of clothing in ancient art. In Hb popular tradition the earliest clothing was made of the skins of animals (Gn 3:21).

1. *Men.* It is not certain that the short kiltlike skirt is mentioned in the OT, unless the word *'ēzôr* signifies this garment. The *'ēzôr* of linen is mentioned in a parable of Je 13:1 ff. It is also mentioned as worn by Assyrian warriors (Is 5:27) and by the Chaldeans (Ezk 23:15) and by Elijah (2 K 1:8). The messianic king wears fidelity as an *'ēzôr* (Is 11:5). The *'ēzôr* may, however, be the girdle. The short skirt reaching just above the knees was worn by Egyptian men of all classes in the Old Kingdom, and was the ceremonial garment of the Pharaoh during all of Egyptian history, when the short skirt had been replaced by the longer tunic for all except slaves, soldiers, and men engaged in manual labor. The short skirt is worn by Canaanites in Egyptian art up to the Late Bronze period, when it is replaced by the tunic (Hb *kuttōnet*, Gk

chitōn). This garment, made of wool* or linen*, reached almost to the ankles, and was made with or without sleeves. It was worn over the naked body. During work or travel this garment could be tucked up under the girdle (Ex 12:11; 2 K 4:29; 9:1). The tunic worn by Joseph (Gn 37:3) which aroused the jealousy of his brothers was probably not a "garment of many colors," as in Eng versions, but a tunic with sleeves. Egyptian art, however, does represent the clothing of Syrian and Canaanites as multi-colored in contrast to the clothing of the Egyptians, which was almost always white linen. In some Egyptian pictures Syrians are dressed in garments which appear to be made of strips wrapped around the body spirally; it is not clear that this garment was worn over the tunic. Such a garment doubtless represents festive attire. This garment may be meant by the *sadīn* (Jgs 14:12 ff) which Samson wagered with his Philistine grooms-men. Over the tunic was worn the cloak or mantle, which is designated by a number of Hb words. These different words probably represent different styles of the garment which we cannot distinguish. The most common word is *simlāh*. The modern mantle worn in the Near East is usually square, about 40–44 in on a side. This may be worn over both shoulders or over only one, to leave the arm free for movement. A few biblical indications (Zp 1:8) suggest that foreign styles of the cloak were easily

adopted by the wealthy and the nobles. The ambassadors of Jehu represented on the black obelisk of Shalmaneser III are clothed in a mantle which appears to be circular with a hole for the head and a fringed edge, something like a Gothic chasuble (ANEP 352–355). The cloak was used as covering at night, and the Hb legal codes prohibited the moneylender from accepting the cloak of the poor as security (Ex 22:25 ff; Dt 24:13). The cloak was not worn at work (Mt 24:18). It could be used for carrying various objects (Ex 12:34; 2 K 4:39; Hg 2:12). The girdle, a strap of leather or of fabric as much as five in wide, served not only to bind the garments and to tuck them up for work or movement, but was also slitted so as to provide small pockets for coins, knives, etc. The *mᵉˁîl* was a type of outer garment worn by kings (1 S 18:4; 24:5, 11), by the high priest (Ex 28:31 ff; Lv 8:7), by Samuel (1 S 2:19; 15:27; 28:14) and by Ezra (Ezr 9:3, 5). These passages indicate that this garment was worn as a sign of royal or sacred office. The *'adderet* is mentioned as a costly garment found in the booty of Jericho (Jos 7:21–24). It was the garment of Elijah (1 K 19:19; 2 K 2:13 ff) which was passed on to Elisha with its wonder-working properties. This garment, made of camel's hair, seems to have indicated the professional prophet* (cf Zc 13:4). The same two garments (tunic: *chitōn* and cloak: *himation*) are indicated in the NT. Jesus bids one who

a) Assyrian genius wearing a fringed kilt and robe. b) Assyrian scene showing prisoners of war, men dressed in long tunics.

is asked for his cloak to yield also his tunic (Mt 5:40; Lk 6:29). It is a sign of wealth to have a change of tunic, and Jesus forbids this to His disciples (Mt 10:10; Mk 6:9; Lk 9:3). The tunic and cloak of Jesus were taken by the soldiers at the crucifixion. The tunic was of unusual texture, being woven without seam (Jn 19:23), which indicates a garment of extremely simple construction. The garment (Gk *ependytēs*) which Peter wrapped around himself in order to meet Jesus (Jn 21:7) is mentioned only here in the NT; it probably signifies the tunic. Fishermen are often represented in Egyptian art as working in the nude, and the fishermen of the Sea of Galilee probably did the same thing. Festive garments for great occasions are mentioned frequently in OT and NT (Gn 27:15; Jgs 14:12; Mt 22:11 ff; Lk 15:22 +). These were made of more costly material and were probably more brilliantly colored.

2. *Women.* The clothing of women also consisted of the tunic and the cloak; the prohibition of exchanging the garments of the two sexes (Dt 22:5) indicates some difference in cut and style. The clothing of women in Egypt was longer and made of finer material than the clothing of men. In later Egyptian art women are represented as clothed in almost totally diaphanous linen robes. Women also wore a veil*. In an Assyrian relief Israelite women are represented as wearing a veil wrapped around the head which trails behind them as far as the ankles.

Cloud. In the OT clouds are an almost universal element of the theophany*. The rainbow in the clouds is a sign of God's covenant not to destroy mankind again by a deluge* (Gn 9:13 ff). Yahweh appears in the midst of the clouds (Jgs 5:4; Ezk 1:4) and the clouds are His chariot (Ps 18:10) or His tent (Ps 18:12; cf also Ps 104:3). Yahweh is the rider of the clouds (Ps 68:5). In popular belief the clouds could conceal men's actions upon the earth from Yahweh's vision (Jb 22:13). In the NT the cloud motif is less prominent. It appears in the narrative of the transfiguration* (Mt 17:5; Mk 9:9; Lk 9:34), in which the voice of the Father issues from the cloud which surrounds the disciples. A cloud removes Jesus from the sight of the disciples in the ascension* (AA 1:9). Jesus predicts that He Himself will come upon the clouds of heaven (Mt 26:64; Mk 14:62). This motif is drawn from the Son of Man* of Dn 7:13. The living at the time of the parousia* will be taken up upon the clouds to meet the Lord (1 Th 4:17).

The pillar of cloud by day and the pillar of fire by night which guided and protected the Israelites during the exodus* are symbolic representations of the presence of Yahweh to guide and protect them (Ex 13:21 f; 14:19 f; 16:10 +). The cloud of Sinai (Ex 19:16 ff) is no doubt one of the original elements of the association of the cloud with the theophany in the OT.

Cnidus (Gk *knidos*), a city on the SW coast of Asia Minor opposite the island of Cos. In antiquity it was renowned as a center of the study of medicine and the possessor of an Aphrodite of Praxiteles. It was one of the cities to which the Romans addressed the document warning against attacking the Jews (1 Mc 15:23), and it was touched by the ship which carried Paul to Rome (AA 27:7).

Code. Cf LAW.

Codex. Cf BOOK.

Coelesyria (Gk *hē koilē syria,* "hollow Syria"), in 1 Mc 10:69; 2 Mc 3:5, 8; 4:4; 8:8; 10:11, a part of the Seleucid kingdom ruled by the governor of Coelesyria and Phoenicia. Properly the name designates the Beqaa, the valley between the Lebanon* and the Anti-Lebanon; but the territory of the governor included Judaea, and the name therefore covered all the territory inland from the coastal plain from N Syria to the boundary of Egypt.

Colossae (Gk *kolossai*), a city of Phrygia* in Asia Minor. Colossae lay in the upper Lycus valley about 80 mi E of Ephesus. The Lycus flows into the Meander (modern Menderes) about 100 mi above its mouth. The valley of the Lycus is about 24 mi long and six mi wide at its greatest width; its altitude above sea level is 500–820 ft. At Colossae the valley is only about two mi wide and is hemmed in by steep cliffs on both sides. In this region lay Colossae, Laodicea*, and Hierapolis. Colossae was situated on a double hill on the S bank of the river. Little is known of the history of Colossae; Herodotus says it was a great city in the time of Xerxes, but in NT times it appears to have declined in importance in favor of Laodicea and Hierapolis. Like these cities it was a center of the wool and dyeing industries. The origins of the church of Colossae are also obscure; it was not founded by Paul, and its foundation is with great probability attributed to Epaphras* (Col 1:7), himself a native of Colossae (Col 4:12).

Colossians, Epistle to the. 1. *Contents.* 1:1–2, greeting.

I. Introduction, 1:3–2:5:
  1:3–8, thanksgiving.

1:9–12, prayer for further progress.
1:13–23, the primacy of Christ as redeemer and reconciler.
1:23–2:5, Paul's mission to the Gentiles and the share of the Gentiles in the salvation of Christ.

II. Doctrinal, 2:6–23:
2:6–8, perseverance in faith against misleading teachers.
2:9–15, life and freedom through Christ.
2:16–23, polemic against vain ritual practices and enslavement to the "Powers."

III. Exhortation, 3:1–4:6:
3:1–17, baptism creates a new man and imposes holiness of life.
3:18–4:1, instruction for particular classes.
4:2–6, exhortation to prayer and instructions on dealing with non-Christian neighbors.

IV. Conclusion, 4:7–18:
4:7–9, Paul's emissaries.
4:10–17, salutations.
4:18, autograph greeting.

2. *Authorship.* Several modern critics question the attribution of Col to Paul. They point out some notable differences in vocabulary; Col contains 86 words not found in the uncontested Pauline writings, of which 34 are not found elsewhere in the NT. The style likewise differs from the style of "the great epistles" (Rm, 1–2 Co, Gal); it becomes hieratic and liturgical, indeed it is often obscure and overloaded. The theology is remarkably developed over the uncontested letters; Col exhibits a more elaborate theology of the Church*, particularly the Church as the body* and Christ as the head; Col uses the term mystery* for the plan of salvation; the idea of knowledge* becomes prominent; and the cosmological-Christological synthesis, while not unparalleled in earlier writings, is here much more complex. These differences are real and should not be denied; but not all scholars believe they demand a different author. The differences in vocabulary can be attributed to the errors which the letter combats; the writer uses the terms familiar to those who had been attracted by these doctrines (cf below) and incorporates them into his own exposition of Christian belief. It must be conceded that the Christological synthesis of Col is new; it seems also that one must with Percy and Cerfaux admit that the synthesis is Pauline. To attribute it to another writer demands that one postulate another man in the primitive community with the genius and the insight of Paul. The question of the authorship and the theology of Col is complicated by its relations with Eph*.

3. *Date and Place of Composition.* Col is one the "epistles of the captivity" with Phl, Eph, and Phm. Its relations with Eph and Phm are close, and this group should be attributed to the same captivity, while Phl* may come from another imprisonment. Ephesus is an unlikely place for these letters. The traditional opinion places them at Rome in 62–63. Some scholars have placed them earlier during Paul's imprisonment at Caesarea; this also appears unlikely, as the developed theology of Col is not in favor of an earlier date.

4. *Occasion and Purpose.* Col was elicited by a doctrinal difficulty; the Church at Colossae was influenced by certain errors. Paul had not founded the Church (cf COLOSSAE); but it had been founded by his companion Epaphras* and he treats it as a Church of his own. The nature of the errors is not clear in detail; it is evident that they arose from some kind of Gnostic syncretism (cf KNOWLEDGE). Cerfaux proposes that it was a mixture of pagan and Jewish elements, perhaps arising among the Jews and accepted by some Christians. The heart of the error was belief in the "elements" or the "Powers" (2:15), intermediate beings between God and man who were thought to have power over men. A cult was paid to these cosmic powers which had features derived from the mystery* cults. L. Cerfaux adds the suggestion that these elements came from vulgar paganism and replaced the gods of paganism. In addition the new belief imposed certain prescriptions on cleanliness, the observance of holy days, and dietary practices; these have connections with the Jewish law, but the error is not simply Judaism. The error was an implicit denial of the position of Christ as sole redeemer and mediator; consequently Paul responds not only by rejecting the errors but by a positive statement of the central and unique position of Christ, both as savior and as a creative and cosmic principle. The theme is taken up again in Eph. Whether the epistle is from Paul or from one of his disciples or companions writing at his commission, it appears that the exposition of the central place of Christ is presented in terms of the Gnostic errors of Colossae, and that Christ is given the titles of honor and power which were given to the Powers.

Confirmation. In Catholic doctrine the second of the seven sacraments*, in which the Holy Spirit* is received by the anointing of the bishop for strength to profess, to defend, and to practice the faith. The sacrament reposes upon the promises of Jesus to send another comforter (Jn 14:16) who will teach the disciples everything (Jn 14:26), who will bear witness of Jesus and enable them to bear witness (Jn 15:26). He will empower the disciples to speak, for he will tell them what to say (Jn 16:13). The prototype of Christian confirmation is the descent of the Holy Spirit upon the apostles at the feast of Pentecost (AA 2:2 ff). In AA the reception of the Holy Spirit accompanied the baptism* of converts; this gift of the Spirit was usually signified externally by the charismata (cf GRACE). Only in AA 8:15 ff, however, is there any indication of a rite distinct from baptism by which the Holy Spirit is conferred; in this passage Peter and John impose hands upon some Samaritans who had been baptized previously. The Spirit fell upon Cornelius* the centurion and his companions before baptism (AA 10:44), and Peter declared that the reception of the Holy Spirit was a sufficient reason for baptism (AA 10:47). The disciples of Ephesus* who had been baptized with the baptism of John had not received the Holy Spirit, but the Spirit came upon them with the gift of tongues when they were baptized (AA 19:1 ff). There seems little doubt that the sacramental rite conferring the Holy Spirit was considered in the primitive Church to be a part of the rite of baptism, which could be separated from the baptismal rite if necessary but was normally conferred at the same time.

Conscience. There is no single Hb word which expresses the idea of conscience, and the Gk word occurs in the OT only in WS 17:11. This book, composed in the 1st century BC, is influenced by the terminology of Gk philosophy. The reality of conscience as a judgment of the morality of an act to be performed or the recognition that an act already performed is morally bad is found in the OT. The "pangs of conscience" are described with artistic skill in the account of Gn 3. The Hb word which most nearly expresses the idea of conscience is the word heart*.

In the NT the word *synīdēsīs* occurs 25 times in the Pauline writings (including Heb), 3 times in 1 Pt and twice in AA, both times uttered by Paul. The word in the meaning of conscience is derived from Stoic philosophy. In Stoicism conscience, which is the ultimate and autonomous judge of one's own acts, is the root of the independence of the sage. Paul adopted the word, as he adopted some other words from Gk philosophy which were current in popular speech, and with it adopted something of the Stoic notion of independence rooted in a good conscience. Substantially, however, his idea of one's personal judgment of moral good and evil reposes upon OT and Gospel

conceptions of sin. Paul himself has a good and clear conscience, that is, he is unaware of any charge which can be laid against him concerning his fulfillment of his apostolic mission (2 Co 1:12; AA 23:1; 24:16). Conscience, i.e., the awareness of the difference between moral good and evil, bears witness against the Gentiles, who show by this awareness that they have the law written in their hearts (Rm 2:15). Paul's conscience also bears witness in his favor that he has done nothing against his Jewish brethren (Rm 9:1). Christians should submit to civil power not only because they fear its wrath but also because of the obligations of conscience (Rm 13:5). Some Christians have a "weak" conscience, i.e., they think it is sinful to eat meat offered to idols when it is not; and those whose conscience is "strong," i.e., better informed, have the duty of not leading these weaker consciences into sin. They should abstain from their use of their liberty in order to avoid scandal (1 Co 8:7, 10, 12). Conscience is indeed a principle of liberty (1 Co 10:29), but this liberty is restrained by the necessity of building up the spiritual strength of one's neighbor (1 Co 10:23). One should eat meat freely without inquiring about its source; but if one learns that it has been offered to idols, one should abstain from eating it not because of one's own conscience, but because of the conscience of another. Paul submits himself to the judgment of the conscience of all men (2 Co 4:2; 5:11). Love proceeds from a pure heart and a good conscience and genuine faith (1 Tm 1:5); by rejecting a good conscience, i.e., Christian standards of moral good and evil, some have made shipwreck of the faith (1 Tm 1:19 ff). False apostles have seared, i.e., insensitive consciences (1 Tm 4:2). To the pure all things are pure, but to men whose intelligence and conscience are stained all things are taken in the worst sense (Tt 1:15). The sacrificial ritual of the Law was unable to purify the conscience, i.e., to remove the sense of guilt (Heb 9:9; 10:2), but Christ purifies the conscience (Heb 10:22). To purify the conscience from dead works (Heb 9:14) perhaps signifies to remove the obligation of performing the works of the Law. Where the word *synīdēsīs* is used in the NT, it is most frequently accompanied by "good," "pure," "clear." Paul is aware of the possibility of a good conscience which is in sincere error; Christian charity demands that we tolerate this weakness until the conscience can be better instructed.

Copper. Copper made its first appearance in Palestine about 4500 BC and remained the most common metal until the introduction of iron* (cf BRONZE). The mountains of Canaan are described as hills from which copper can be extracted (Dt 8:9); this is not true of the strictly Israelite territory, but extensive copper deposits existed in the immediate neighborhood. The richest deposits mined by the Egyptians were in the Sinai* peninsula; these were mined through the 19th and 20th dynasties. Nearer to Israelite territory were copper deposits in the Arabah, the gorge which extends from the Dead Sea to the head of the Gulf of Aqabah. These mines were worked from the Early Bronze Age into Middle Bronze, but were abandoned until they were again worked by the Israelites. Edom* was conquered by David, and Solomon set up mining and refining operations at Ezion-geber*. The remains of these refineries were discovered by Nelson Glueck. They were equipped with furnaces and flues which communicated with an air channel. The site was chosen in order to use the strong winds which blow south from the Arabah as a draft. With the use of proper fuel intense heat could thus be generated, and the condition of the mud brick surface of the remaining walls shows that this end was achieved. There were also copper deposits in northern Syria, and the cities of the Phoenician coast were important centers of copper refining and the manufacture of bronze articles, which are found in great numbers in the remains of these cities. For the execution of the metal vessels of the temple* Solomon brought Hiram*, a skilled metalworker, from Tyre* (1 K 7:13 ff).

Corban (Gk korban, from Hb korbān, etymology uncertain), in the priestly code (39 times in Lv, 38 times in Nm, Ezk 20:28; 40:43) signifies a gift or a consecration of an article to the deity. In Judaism the word came to mean the temple treasury (Mt 27:6). The word as used in Mk 7:11, where it is interpreted as "gift," suggests that it was employed as a formula of consecration of articles given to the temple. Pharisaic interpretation of the law permitted one to consecrate his property to the temple while continuing to enjoy its revenues. Jesus rebukes the hypocrisy which employs this device to avoid the obligation of supporting one's parents from one's property; for property consecrated to the temple could not be employed for profane uses.

Corinth (Gk korinthos), a city in the NE Peloponnesus near the E end of the Gulf of Corinth. The city lay near the shore (nearer in ancient times than now). To the S of the city rise the mountains of the Peloponnesus, most prominent of which is Acrocorinth, a steep rocky slope about 1850 ft high, the citadel of the ancient Gk city and in later times the seat of numerous temples. The importance of Corinth lay in its position on the Isthmus of Corinth, the shortest route from the Adriatic to the Aegean, and thus from Europe to Asia. The ancient Gk city was destroyed by the Romans in 146 BC. The Corinth of the NT was founded by Julius Caesar in 44 BC under the name of Colonia Laus Julia Corinthos as the capital of the senatorial province of Achaea. The first foundation was composed mostly of Italian freedmen; the position of the city, however, attracted a large and mixed population from the east; most of the citizens, it seems, were not Gk. The commercial importance of Corinth in NT times was greater than it had been in the Greek period; commerce between E and W in the Hellenistic-Roman world was more active than it had ever been before. The city of Corinth was situated between its two ports, Lechaeon on the Gulf of Corinth and Cenchreae* on the Saronic Gulf. Goods in transit were transshipped from one port to the other, and smaller vessels could be hauled, cargo and all, on the diolkos, a slipway. The distance of the transit was only about 4 mi (the length of the modern canal). Corinth depended essentially on this transfer of traffic, and we read of no major products of the city. But the traffic was enough; ancient writers testify to the splendor of its buildings, and this testimony is confirmed by the remains which have been uncovered. The old Gk city was not entirely destroyed in 146; the most imposing remains are the seven columns of the ancient temple of Apollo. The excavations have been carried on at intervals since 1896 by the American School of Athens. Not all the public buildings have been uncovered, and the residential quarters have not been touched. Both literature and archaeology testify to the large number of temples at Corinth (cf 1 Co 8:5). Besides the large temple of Apollo mentioned above, there were several other temples devoted to this god. There were temples dedicated to Athena, Poseidon, and a notable sanctuary of Asklepios, the god of healing, consisting of a temple and a hospital; the temple contained a large number of votive offerings which have been preserved. The greatest of the sanctuaries was the temple of Aphrodite on Acrocorinth, where 1000 slave girls served as hierodules. There was a Jewish synagogue and Jewish colony by AD 50. The city center was built around a large agora 600 by 300 ft surrounded by colonnades and shops. On the S side of the agora were the council chamber and the rostrum for speakers; it is most probable that Paul's case was heard by Gallio* at this rostrum (AA 18:16 f). On the same side was a basilica, a large public building of unknown purpose. The entire agora was surrounded by temples. The city had public baths, an odeum, two theaters (one seating 18,000), and an amphitheater; Corinth was the seat of the Isthmian games, and Paul's reference to the games in 1 Co 9:24–27 was altogether topical. The paved road to Lechaeon is preserved, but nothing remains of the port installations. Corinth had a reputation as a center of pleasure and of vice both in Gk and Roman times; the Gk proverb said that not everyone should go to Corinth. The city found its way into the Gk lexicon with *korinthia korē* ("Corinthian girl"), prostitute; *korinthiastēs* ("Corinthian business man"), whoremonger; *korinthiazesthai* ("to play the Corinthian"), to visit a house of prostitution. It was as unpromising a community as Paul ever chose for evangelization, and his letters perhaps reflect the character of his congregation there with allusions which are not found in other epistles (1 Co 5:1, 9 f; 6:9 f, 15–20).

Only one visit of Paul to Corinth, his first, is related in AA (18:1–18). He reached the city from Athens on his second journey, about the year 50 (cf PAUL; GALLIO). There he lived with Aquila* and Priscilla*, practicing his trade as tentmaker and preaching in the synagogue on the Sabbath; he converted Crispus*, the president of the synagogue. The Jews, however, rejected him, and he began to teach in the house of Titus Justus*. After 18 months the Jews brought him before Gallio as a teacher of unlawful religion, but Gallio would not even hear the charge. Paul left Corinth "some time" after this and went to Ephesus (AA 18:18); on other visits to the city cf PAUL: CORINTHIANS, EPISTLES TO. Apollos* also taught in Corinth after Paul's visit (AA 19:1).

Corinthians, Epistles to the. 1. *Contents,* 1 Corinthians.

I. Introduction: 1:1–3, salutation; 1:4–9, thanksgiving.

II. Abuses at Corinth, 1:10–6:20.

1:10–4:21, factions:

1:10–17, the four factions; 1:18–2:16, the wisdom of God and worldly wisdom; 3:1–23, the work of the preachers of the gospel; 4:1–13, application to Paul and Apollos; 4:14–21, the mission of Timothy and the intended coming of Paul.

5:1–6:20, scandals at Corinth:

5:1–8, a case of incest; 5:9–13, prohibition of contact with the profligate; 6:1–6, prohibition of litigation before pagan courts; 6:7–11, Christians should suffer injustice rather than do it; 6:12–20, unchastity is unworthy of the Christian.

III. Answers to Questions, 7:1–15:18.

7:1–40, marriage and virginity:

7:1–7, marriage is lawful; 7:8–11, divorce; 7:12–26, the Pauline privilege; 7:17–24, let each remain in his state; 7:25–35, recommendation of celibacy; 7:36–38, the marriage of virgins; 7:39–40, widows.

8:1–11:1, the eating of meat offered to idols:

8:1–13, freedom to eat such meat combined with duty of renouncing freedom to avoid the scandal of the weak; 9:1–27, Paul's example of renouncing his right to be maintained by the community; 10:1–22, warning against partaking in pagan sacrificial banquets; 10:23–11:1, instructions concerning eating meat offered to idols.

11:2–34, abuses in liturgical cult:

11:2–16, the veiling of women at cultic assemblies; 11:17–34, abuses at the *agapē* and instruction for the celebration of the Eucharist.

12:1–14:40, instructions about charismata:

12:1–31, variety, origin, and purpose of charismata; 13:1–13, excellence of love; 14:1–25, prophecy superior to the gift of tongues; 14:26–40, regulations governing the manifestation and display of charismata.

15:1–58, the resurrection:

15:1–11, the reality of the resurrection of Jesus; 15:12–28, faith in the resurrection (and the Parousia) based on the resurrection of Jesus; 15:29–34, folly of Christian life on any other basis; 15:35–58, the qualities of the risen body and the destiny of those who are living at the Parousia.

16, Conclusion:

16:1–4, the collection of Jerusalem; 16:5–12, Paul's plans, commendation of Timothy and Apollos; 16:13–23, final exhortations, commendations, and salutations.

2. *Contents,* 2 Corinthians

I. Introduction: 1:1–2, salutation; 1:3–11, thanksgiving.

II. Paul's defense of himself, 1:12–7:16.

1:12–2:17, the charge of instability and other matters:

1:12–2:4, omission of promised visit due to his love and consideration; 2:5–11, he commends the rebuke of the guilty party and urges that forgiveness be granted him; 2:12–17, Paul's journey to Troas and Macedonia.

3:1–6:10, the apostolic office:

3:1–3, the Corinthian community is proof of Paul's apostolic office; 3:4–18, the apostle is superior to Moses; 4:1–6, fearlessness and candor of the apostle; 4:7–18, the suffering of the apostle; 5:1–10, hope as a power in suffering; 5:11–6:10, Paul's sincerity, the greatness of his message, his testing by suffering.

6:11–7:16, Paul's reconciliation with the Corinthians:

6:11–13 + 7:2–4, request for restoration of communion; 6:14–7:1, exhortation for a complete conversion from paganism; 7:5–16, Paul's pleasure at the news brought by Titus that the community has repented.

III. The Collection for the Church of Jerusalem, 8–9.

8:1–15, exhortation to be generous, the example of the communities of Macedonia; 8:16–9:5, recommendation of his emissaries and his reasons for sending them; 9:6–15, the blessings which God grants the generous giver.

IV. The Adversaries of Paul, 10–13.

10:1–18, rejection of the charges brought by his adversaries and ridicule of their arrogance; 11:1–4 + 16–21, Paul asks them to bear with the boasting which is necessary for the defense of his apostolic mission; 11:5–15, Paul's equality with the "super-apostles," the reasons why he renounced his right to be supported; 11:21–12:13, Paul's sufferings and revelations; 12:14–13:10, his forthcoming visit, apprehensions, appeals, and threats.

V. Conclusion, 13:11–13: appeals, final salutation and blessing.

3. *Occasion*. The occasion of 1–2 Co is a complex series of events which must be reconstructed from the letters themselves. A commonly accepted reconstruction is as follows. Paul's first mission at Corinth lasted 18 months of his second journey, probably beginning in the fall of AD 51 (AA 18). From there Paul went to Ephesus, Caesarea, and Antioch. Apollos came to Corinth shortly after Paul's departure. Paul began his 3rd journey in the spring of AD 54; when he reached Ephesus he became aware of troubles in the Corinthian community. It is not clear how the news reached him; possibly it was the occasion of his dispatch of Timothy and Erastus to Corinth (AA 19:22; 1 Co 4:17; 16:10). Possibly also they bore a letter to Corinth which is not preserved (1 Co 5:9). A delegation then arrived from Corinth (1 Co 16:15–18) bearing a letter with various questions (1 Co 7:1, 25; 8:1; 12:1; 15:1); it may be assumed that they also gave Paul information by word of mouth concerning conditions at Corinth (1 Co 1:11). Paul wrote a letter in answer which they took to Corinth; this letter is 1 Co. When this letter did not have the desired effect, Paul sent Timothy as his representative; but Timothy had no more success. Paul himself then made a brief personal visit which likewise failed (2 Co 2:1); on this visit his apostolic authority was outraged by an unidentified of-

fender (2 Co 2:5–7:12). Paul then returned to Ephesus and wrote "the sorrowful letter" (2 Co 2:4), which is not preserved. This letter was sent with Titus. Paul intended to meet Titus at Troas; when his arrival was delayed, Paul in worry and impatience went to Macedonia, where Titus met him with favorable news (2 Co 2:12–14; 7:5–7). Paul then wrote 2 Co from Macedonia. Both 1–2 Co were probably written in AD 57, 1 Co in the spring and 2 Co in the fall. It is thus likely that 1–2 Co are two of four letters written to the Corinthians, arranged thus: A, the letter of 1 Co 5:9; B, 1 Co; C, the sorrowful letter (2 Co 2:4); D, 2 Co. A number of modern critics suspect that A and C are not lost but have been incorporated into 1–2 Co; cf below.

The occasion of 1–2 Co can be put simply as the encounter of the gospel with Hellenism. All we know about Corinth leads us to believe that there was scarcely a more unlikely place in the entire Roman world for the gospel to find a favorable reception. It must have been well received, however; the affection of Paul for this wayward congregation is transparent, as is his conviction that they, in spite of their faults, have accepted the gospel without reservation. The faults seem to have been something novel in Paul's experience. The factions of Cephas, Apollos, Paul, and Christ have never been identified to satisfaction. They were not factions of heresy or schism; there is no indication that the divisions split the community or bore on points of belief or doctrine. It has been suggested that the factions may have represented Judaizers (Cephas), Hellenists (Paul), exaggerated Hellenists (Apollos), extreme Judaizers (Christ), Gnostics (Apollos), extreme Gnostics who claimed special revelation and deliverance from all moral obligation (Christ). None of these identifications has any secure basis in the text, and several of them imply genuine dogmatic and doctrinal divisions which are not reflected in the words of Paul. We may conclude from other epistles (Rm, Gal, Col) that such deep divisions would not be passed over so lightly. It appears more probable that these were cases of hero worship, of various cliques boasting their favorites and creating the danger of personal jealousy and rivalry among the apostles. "The sect of Christ" no doubt pretended to be above all this and did not acknowledge even proper authority.

The moral difficulties and problems of the Corinthians can be reduced to their recent conversion from Gentile paganism; they have to do with the attitude of Christians toward sex, which is easily conceived as being an urgent problem in Corinth, with the liberty of eating meat offered to idols (the flesh of victims, after the god's portion was taken, was sold in the open market) and with the proper celebration of the Eucharist, which they seem to have not as yet distinguished from the pagan banquet, religious or secular. In addition they did not know how to deal with the charismata (cf GRACE), which they seem to have confused with ecstatic and rhapsodic manifestations in pagan cults. Finally, they had the typical Gk difficulty of accepting the resurrection of the body. The problem which still had to be dealt with in 2 Co was the reality and the nature of the apostolic mission. The adversaries against whom 2 Co is directed cannot be certainly identified. They must have included Palestinian Jews (2 Co 11:22); but the terms of Paul's controversy with them are not the same as his language when he engages with the Judaizers of Gal and Rm. Hence a number of scholars suppose that they taught some form of gnosis (cf KNOWLEDGE); this would explain why Paul appeals to his own personal revelations (2 Co 12). Kümmel has proposed that two groups united, Palestinian Jews and Gentiles who had accepted a gnostic teaching. What they had in common was opposition to the apostleship of Paul and to his person. These also seem to have claimed apostolic dignity, indeed a dignity greater than the apostles (2 Co 11:5, 12). Paul makes no specific doctrinal complaint against these adversaries, although he hints at one (2 Co 11:3 f); the words seem to show a lack of confidence in these men rather than any definite charge.

4. *Doctrinal Elements.* It is remarkable, in the words of Cambier, how the essential aspects of Christian thought and life are brought out by Paul to meet concrete situations and practical problems. This is the greatness of 1–2 Co, that belief and doctrine are so closely integrated with the urgent problems of life in the immediate present. For the major themes of the epistles cf separate topical articles: APOSTLE; BODY; EUCHARIST; FREEDOM; LOVE; RESURRECTION; WISDOM.

5. *Authorship and Integrity.* The Pauline authorship of 1–2 Co is not questioned seriously by modern scholars. These epistles have the intensely personal style which is so evident in the unquestioned Pauline epistles, with deep and changing emotions. The unity and integrity of 1 Co are likewise not questioned by modern critics; but 2 Co presents a number of problems concerning its composition which are seriously discussed.

The signs of imperfect unity are fairly evident. Chapter 9 has all the appearances of a doublet of chapter 8. There is a marked change in tone from 1–9 to 10–13; the atmosphere of joy and reconciliation of 1–9

turns without warning to one of the most severe passages of all the Pauline corpus, which employs ridicule, admonition, threat, and sarcasm; one might suspect that a reconciliation so recently and so hardly achieved would be imperiled by this passage. There is evident continuity between 6:13 and 7:2 which is broken by the insertion of 6:14–7:1. A number of critics have suggested that both chapter 9 and 6:14–7:1 are epistles or part of epistles directed to different churches; and some believe that in them or part of them we have all or what is left of Letter A to the Corinthians (cf above). Many have suggested that 10–13 contain "the sorrowful letter" (2 Co 2:4, Letter C to the Corinthians above).

The problem of unity and integrity should not be solved by denying the reality of the lack of unity between these passages and the rest of 2 Co; other critics, admitting the problem, have attempted to solve it without recurring to the hypotheses of distinct letters. Some have suggested that the brief visit of Paul to Corinth intervened between the composition of 1–9 and the composition of 10–13; this cannot be made to agree with the reconstruction of events proposed above, which seems best to suit the evidence. Others have suggested a lapse of time between the composition of the two parts; 1–9 were written after the favorable report of Titus, and 10–13 were added when new information was gained which showed that the adversaries still had a following. Still others have pointed out that the dictation of a letter as long as 2 Co consumed considerable time, more than enough for the author to experience a change of mood. Cambier has called the change of tone in 10–13 a psychological rather than a literary problem; this designation of the question seems to presuppose the unity of composition of the letter, which is precisely the problem. Cambier also adduces certain characteristics of ancient composition not only of letters but of prose works in general: the relative independence of the different parts of the composition and the absence of transitions. These characteristics should not be pressed; 1 Co, for instance, treats of a variety of topics, and the transitions are almost always clearly indicated. It seems that no hypothesis of a single composition has been proposed which genuinely fits the unusual phenomena, and a hypothesis that 2 Co has been compiled from more than one letter of Paul enjoys genuine probability. It is quite true that the situation at Corinth is not well enough known for one to be certain, and hence one must make reservations on any theory; but the obscurity of the situation also lends itself to the hypothesis of compilation. It is therefore improbable that 2 Co in its present form was dispatched to Corinth by Paul.

Cornelius. The centurion in command of the Italian cohort stationed at Caesarea* (AA 10:1). He was a proselyte* of the type called "those who fear God" (AA 10:2), who accepted the Jewish Law but did not become full members of the Jewish community by circumcision. Cornelius was visited by an angel while he was at prayer and directed to summon Peter from Joppa*. When Peter arrived and heard of the vision of Cornelius he instructed him in the story of the life, death, and messiahship of Jesus. At the end of the instruction the Holy Spirit* fell upon Cornelius and all his household and conferred upon them the gift of tongues. Peter found this sufficient justification to baptize them, although they were Gentiles. At the time when Cornelius was visited by an angel, Peter himself saw a vision of a great vessel let down from heaven containing all kinds of animals and birds. When ordered by a voice to kill and eat, Peter refused, because he had never eaten anything unclean; but the voice instructed him that nothing is unclean which God has cleansed (AA 10:9–18). When Peter met Cornelius, he understood from the vision that there was no prohibition against associating with Gentiles, as the Pharisees understood the law of cleanliness (cf CLEAN; AA 10:28 f).

The story of the conversion of Cornelius is told in such a way as to inculcate two distinct lessons. The first of these is that Gentiles may be received into the Church without circumcision or undertaking the full obligation of the Jewish law. This question was agitated in the primitive Church and was determined by the council of Jerusalem (AA 15:1 ff), but it was still active when Paul wrote Rm and Gal. Connected with the same question was the Pharisaic prohibition of associating with Gentiles and, in particular, of eating with them. Peter himself observed this Pharisaic interpretation on one occasion and was rebuked by Paul (Gal 2:12 ff). The story of the conversion of Cornelius justifies both these elements of Christian liberty by a heavenly vision: one granted to Cornelius, by which he asks for instruction in the gospel, and the other granted to Peter, by which he learns that the Jewish laws of cleanliness do not bind Christians, and that there is no distinction between Jewish and Gentile members of the Christian community. Some scholars think the narrative has been compiled from two different sources or two variant accounts of the conversion of Cornelius, one containing the account of the vision of Cornelius and his conversion, the other containing the account of the vision of Peter and his admission of Cornelius to social equality.

Cornerstone. The cornerstone, in particular the stone at the base, binds two walls and is chosen for its size. The leaders of tribes and peoples are called cornerstones in the OT (Jgs 20:2; 1 S 14:38; Is 19:13; Zc 10:4). The precious tested stone which Yahweh places at the corner (Is 28:16) is interpreted as the Messiah*, although it is doubtful that the passage means this in the context. The stone rejected by the builders which became the cornerstone (Ps 118:22) is doubtless a metaphor for the deliverance of the psalmist. The passage is applied to Jesus by Jesus Himself (Mt 21:42; Mk 12:10; Lk 20:17). The application is echoed by Peter (AA 4:11; 1 Pt 2:7). In Eph 2:20 and 1 Pt 2:4 ff the Church is represented as a building of which Christ Himself is the cornerstone. The apostles and prophets are the foundation, and the faithful themselves are the living stones of the edifice. Some interpreters believe that the metaphor here refers not to the cornerstone but to the keystone.

Corozain. Cf CHORAZIN.

Cos. An island and its city off the SW coast of Asia Minor. The city received a copy of a decree of the Roman Senate warning against attacking the Jews (1 Mc 15:23) and was the point to which Paul sailed from Miletus* on his last journey to Jerusalem (AA 21:1).

Council (Gk *synedrion*, rendered in some Eng versions as Sanhedrin). The supreme council of the Jews is first mentioned by Jewish historian Josephus as existing in the reign of Antiochus* the Great (223–187 BC). It is first mentioned in the Bible in the Maccabean period (1 Mc 11:23; 12:6; 14:28; 2 Mc 1:10; 4:44; 11:27). In NT times the council was composed of three classes: the elders, i.e., the elders of the chief families and clans; the high priests, i.e., the former high priests and elders of the four high priestly families; and the scribes*, who were mostly members of the sect of the Pharisees*. It seems that the scribes, the professional lawyers, were first admitted to the council during the reign of queen Alexandra (76–67 BC). The council was composed of 71 members including the presiding officer, the high priest then in office. It is not known how members were elected; they were probably co-opted, and probably also for life. In the time of Jesus the jurisdiction of the council was limited to Judaea* proper, which did not include Galilee*. As the supreme religious body it had some authority, which we cannot define closely, over Jewish communities of the Diaspora; it sent messengers to Damascus* to apprehend Christians (AA 9:2; 22:5; 26:12). It is possible that in this instance the council exceeded its authority; in any case, it is not certain that synagogues in foreign countries had any obligation to submit to its decisions. In general, the council was the supreme native court of the Jewish nation; this was in harmony with Roman practice in the provinces, which left native law in force and permitted its enforcement by native officers. The competence of the council was both religious and secular, and the Jewish law was the norm of its decisions. According to Jn 18:31 the council could not pass a capital sentence; capital cases in its own law had to be referred to the Roman governor for confirmation of the sentence — in the trial of Jesus, to the procurator*. It had the power of arrest and its own police (Mt 26:47; Mk 14:43; AA 4:3; 5:17 f). The stoning of Stephen (AA 7:57 ff) seems to have been an excess of the jurisdiction of the council, if it was not an incident of mob violence. The event is probably to be dated at a period when the administration of Judaea was not in strong hands. The place of meeting of the council was somewhere in the complex of the temple buildings or in its neighborhood near the SW corner. The meeting at the house of the high priest by night (Mt 26:57 ff; Mk 14:53 ff) was doubtless due to the fact that the gates of the temple area were shut at night. The Talmud describes the council as sitting in a semicircle with two clerks in front of it, one to record the votes of acquittal and the other to record the votes of conviction. When a capital sentence was involved special precautions were taken. The arguments for acquittal should be heard first, and no one who had spoken in favor of the accused was permitted to give unfavorable testimony. Sentence could not be passed except on the testimony of two witnesses. A sentence of acquittal could be pronounced on the same day, but a conviction could not be pronounced until the following day. Each member voted by rising in the sight of all, beginning with the youngest. A simple majority was sufficient for acquittal, but a conviction required a majority of two. Jesus, speaking metaphorically, says that any one who uses abusive language of another will be summoned before the council (Mt 5:22) and predicts that His disciples will be called before the council for preaching His gospel (Mt 10:17; Mk 13:9). It appears from the Gospels that the case of Jesus was heard before two sessions of the council, one at night at the house of the high priest

Caiaphas*, and the other in the regular court at the following dawn. The hearing at night is mentioned by Mt 26:59 ff; Mk 14:55 ff. Jn refers to an interrogation at the house of Annas* before Jesus was taken to the house of Caiaphas (18:12 ff). Lk mentions that Jesus was taken to the house of Caiaphas (22:54) but speaks of the morning hearing only (22:66). Neither Mt (27:1) nor Mk (15:1) use the word *synedrion* of the morning session, but it is quite probable that this was a full legal session. The council interrogated Peter and John about their preaching and prohibited them from preaching any more (AA 4:5 ff). Peter and John refused to obey, but the council released them (AA 4:18 ff). The success of the preaching of the apostles brought about a second arrest and imprisonment (AA 5:17 ff), from which they were mysteriously released. They were again arrested and the prohibition was repeated (AA 5:26 ff), and many of the council, angered by their obstinacy, wished to condemn them to death (AA 5:33). The council was persuaded by Gamaliel to let the matter rest, since the movement, if it were from God, could not be halted by human efforts (AA 5:35 ff). The case of Paul was brought before the council by the tribune Claudius Lysias* (AA 22:30 ff), but when the meeting broke up in violence, the tribune had the case transferred to Felix* the governor at Caesarea*.

Covenant (Hb *bᵉrît*, Gk *diathēkē*). **1.** OT. In early Hb society written documents were employed little or not at all. In their place the spoken word was invested with ritual solemnity which gave it a kind of concrete reality. The spoken word thus uttered could not be annulled or retracted. If it were a blessing* or a curse*, it followed inexorably after the person to whom it was directed. The covenant was such a solemn ritual agreement which served the function of a written contract. The covenanting parties bound themselves by a ritual agreement which included terrible imprecations upon the party which should violate the covenant. These agreements between men appear throughout much of the OT. The parties to the covenant were not necessarily equal; the stronger could impose his will upon the weaker, or the victor upon the vanquished; or inversely the vanquished or the weaker party could seek a covenant relationship with the stronger. Abraham had a covenant alliance with the Canaanites Eshcol and Aner (Gn 14:13). He made a covenant with Abimelech* at Beersheba which settled the dispute between the two groups about the wells of Beersheba (Gn 21:22 ff). Isaac* also made a covenant with Abimelech concerning water rights (Gn 26:26 ff); this covenant is probably a doublet of the covenant of Abraham and Abimelech. Jacob, after his flight from Laban*, made a covenant with him (Gn 31:44 ff); Jacob promised to protect the daughters of Laban and to marry no other wives, and Laban agreed not to pass the boundary marked by the stones which were set up at the point of the covenant. This covenant probably was a part of the Hb tradition concerning their boundaries with the Aramaeans. The Gibeonites* made a covenant of alliance with Joshua* by deception (Jos 9:3 ff). The covenant was valid even though the deception was discovered. The men of Jabesh-gilead* asked Nahash*, king of Ammon*, for a covenant of alliance (1 S 11:1 ff); but the terms offered were so cruel as to make acceptance impossible. Jonathan and David made a covenant of friendship (1 S 18:3; 23:18); this covenant had a tragic issue, for it forced Jonathan to choose between the obligations of blood kinship with his father and the covenant relationship with David, both of which admitted no exception. David made a covenant with Abner* on the terms that Abner should win him the allegiance of the tribes subject to Ishbaal* and restore Michal*, the daughter of Saul*, as his wife (2 S 3:11 ff). The tribes accepted David as their king by a covenant at Hebron (2 S 5:3). Solomon had a covenant alliance with Hiram* of Tyre*, according to the terms of which Hiram supplied Solomon with the materials for building the temple* (1 K 5:2 ff). Asa* appealed to the covenant between himself and Ben-hadad* of Damascus* and their fathers, and bribed him to break the covenant between himself and Baasha* of Israel (1 K 15:19). When Ahab* defeated Ben-hadad of Damascus, Ben-hadad asked for a covenant on the terms that he should restore the cities taken from Israel and that the Israelites should have trading rights in Damascus, as the Aramaeans had them in Samaria (1 K 20:34). The high priest Jehoiada* made a covenant with the royal guard to install the infant Jehoash* as king (2 K 11:4). Isaiah spoke of the alliance of Judah with Egypt as a covenant with death and a compact with Sheol* (28:15, 18). During the siege of Jerusalem Zedekiah* and the people made a covenant to liberate their Hebrew slaves; but when the Babylonian army withdrew to meet the Egyptians the people repossessed their slaves (Je 34:8 ff). The kingdom of Judah was under a covenant with the Babylonians, and their rebellion was a breach of the covenant which would be punished by Yahweh (Ezk 17:14 ff). The Israelites make a covenant with Assyria* (Ho 12:2). Tyre is threatened because it has not observed the covenant of brotherhood (Am 1:9), probably by taking part in the slave trade.

This relationship is transferred in Hb belief to be the formula of the relationship of Yahweh and the people Israel. It is not understood here as a bilateral contract between equals, but as a covenant between the greater and the lesser; the greater imposes his will upon the lesser, but it is also an act of grace and liberality. G. E. Mendenhall has shown that the external form of the covenant (historical prologue, terms, oath of fidelity, imprecations) resembles the suzerainty treaty imposed upon a vassal king as illustrated by Hittite treaties (ANET 203). In the covenant Yahweh imposes certain duties upon Israel and in return promises to be their God, to assist them and to deliver them. The Israelites accept the obligations, the most important of which is to worship no other god but Yahweh, and to observe the standards of cult and conduct which He establishes. If they are unfaithful, Yahweh will withdraw His favor. The covenant is more than a mere contract. It establishes an artificial blood kinship between the parties and is second only to the bond of blood. The word used to signify covenant affection and loyalty (Hb ḥesed) is also used to signify the affection and loyalty of kinsmen (cf LOVE). In virtue of the covenant the Hebrews appeal to Yahweh's affection and loyalty; by the covenant He has become their avenger*, obliged to protect and assist them. The prophets, speaking in the name of Yahweh, demand a corresponding affection and loyalty from Israel.

The covenant relationship between God and man is placed early in human history in Hb traditions. To some extent this is a retrojection of later theological belief into the traditions. Thus Yahweh makes a covenant with Noah* (Gn 6:18); the obligations of the covenant are the prohibition of eating blood and of homicide (Gn 9:4 ff). God promises in this covenant not to destroy mankind again by a deluge (Gn 9:11) and as a sign of the covenant places the rainbow in the clouds (Gn 9:12). The covenant ritual described in Gn 15:10 ff is probably the ritual often employed in covenants, although it is mentioned only here. Abraham killed sacrificial victims and divided them into two parts. In a vision Yahweh passed between the parts; in the covenant ritual no doubt both parties passed between the parts, imprecating upon themselves a fate like that of the slaughtered animals if they violated the covenant. Circumcision* is a sign of the covenant (Gn 17:10). The covenant with Abraham was in Hb tradition the original basis of their relationship with Yahweh;

but the covenant of Israel itself as a people was the covenant of Sinai* (Ex 19:1 ff). After ritual preparation of the people Yahweh appears in the storm and the earthquake, reveals Himself as the God of Israel, and imposes upon Israel the obligations of the covenant. The laws which are placed in Ex after this event are called the covenant code (cf LAW). Two covenant rituals are mentioned in Ex 24, perhaps from two different traditions. In the ritual of blood the blood of sacrificial animals is sprinkled on the altar*, representing Yahweh, and on the people. The contracting parties thus symbolically become one blood, one family (Ex 24:3-8). The other ritual procedure is the ritual banquet, in which Moses, Aaron and his sons, and 70 of the elders of Israel representing the entire people share a common meal with Yahweh; this also symbolizes covenant union (Ex 24:1-2, 9-11). The covenant statement of Ex 34:1 ff, which in the present text is a renewal of the covenant violated by the golden calf, is probably another tradition of the Sinai covenant. By the terms of the covenant of Sinai the Israelites become Yahweh's peculiar possession out of all the peoples of the earth, a kingdom of priests, a holy nation (Ex 19:5 f). This probably indicates that the covenant confers upon Israel the peculiar sanctity compared to other peoples which the priestly class has compared to the laity of Israel. In an obscure way it may possibly also suggest the position of Israel as a mediator to other peoples; this idea becomes explicit in later OT writings. The covenant arises from the initiative and election of Yahweh and not from the merits of Israel. The covenant of Sinai is elsewhere summed up in the formula "You shall be my people and I will be your God" (Je 7:23; 11:4; 24:7; Ezk 11:20; 14:11; Ho 2:25 +). This formula is possibly the form of the matrimonial contract, since the formula of the marriage contracts of the Elephantine* papyri is practically identical: "She is my wife and I am her husband this day and forever." The salt of the sacrificial victims is a sign of the covenant (Lv 2:13); in Arabic to eat salt with another is to seal a bond of friendship. Particular covenant obligations are sometimes called a covenant (Lv 24:8). The visible symbol of Yahweh's presence in Israel was the ark* of the covenant. The two stone tablets of the law are the tablets of the covenant (Dt 9:9, 11, 15). Renewals of the covenant are recorded in the OT; in the opinion of some scholars a covenant renewal was included in the annual cycle of feasts, although this is not expressly mentioned in the OT. Dt represents a renewal of covenant in Moab* (28:69).

This is probably a retrojection of the covenant renewal ceremony to early times. The ceremony is described in Dt 27:11 ff; there are ritual blessings for the observance of the covenant and imprecations for its violation. The people, assembled between the slopes of Ebal* and Gerizim*, accept these blessings and curses. In the covenant ceremony of Shechem* (Jos 24:1 ff) Joshua recites the great deeds of Yahweh by which He delivered Israel and in response the people accept the obligation of serving Yahweh alone. This covenant is recorded in writing (Jos 24:26). The ceremony is described as a covenant renewal; but M. Noth and a number of modern scholars believe it was the imposition of the covenant upon all the tribal groups which comprised Israel at the formation of the tribal amphictyony (cf ISRAEL). The dedication of Solomon's temple included a covenant renewal ceremony, with a recitation by Solomon of the history of the election of Israel and of the house of David, a restatement of covenant obligations, and a petition that Yahweh will, as He has promised, hear the prayers of the people in this sanctuary. There is no explicit mention of the solemn acceptance of the people, but this is easily presumed. The covenant was renewed by the high priest Jehoiada* after the assassination of Athaliah*, and the people destroyed the images of the Baal* and slew the priests (2 K 11:17 ff). Josiah renewed the covenant (2 K 23:2 ff) on the basis of the book which had been found in the temple (2 K 22:8 ff); this book is identified by modern scholars with the code of Deuteronomy. As a result of the renewal Josiah cleansed not only the temple but also Jerusalem and his entire territory of all traces of Canaanite worship. An elaborate ceremony of covenant renewal was conducted by Ezra*. This took place at the feast of Tabernacles*. The feast was observed by the building of booths and the law was read aloud to the assembly, which confessed its sins and the sins of its fathers. There was a ritual recitation by Ezra of the history of Yahweh's deliverance of Israel and of the previous sins of the people. The covenant is renewed and the written document of renewal is signed by the priests, the Levites, and the nobles (Ne 8:12 ff). Yahweh also established a covenant with David and with his house. This covenant is stated in the oracle of Nathan* (2 S 7:5 ff), although the word covenant is not employed, and is restated in Ps 89:20-38; cf also Ps 132. By the terms of the covenant Yahweh elects David and his house for an eternal dynasty. The eternity of the dynasty is absolute. David and his descendants, however, are under covenant obligations to observe the law of Yahweh; if they fail they will be punished, although the eternity of the dynasty stands (cf KING; MESSIAH). The covenant with the house of David and with the house of Levi*, by which an eternal priesthood is promised to Levi, is stated in Je 33:17 ff; while this passage is not certainly to be attributed to Jeremiah himself, it exhibits the transfer of the covenant idea from Israel itself to its charismatic officers. The covenant with the house of David tends to absorb the covenant with Israel, of which the king becomes the bearer (Is 55:3 f). It is somewhat remarkable that the word covenant is not common in the writings of the prophets of the 8th and 7th centuries. This cannot be explained by the assumption that the idea of covenant is entirely the creation of later writers; it is impossible to explain its diffusion through so much of the older material of the OT. The reality of the covenant idea that Israel has been chosen by Yahweh, that Yahweh is its God, and that it has peculiar obligations not shared by other peoples to observe the standards of worship and conduct which Yahweh has given it, is basic in the prophets. The word covenant is used by Hosea (6:7; 8:1) in a sense identical with its religious use elsewhere. The word is more common in Je than in any other prophetic book, and its use shows the influence of Dt. Jeremiah is not indebted to Dt for his original idea of the new covenant (31:27 ff). The old covenant, which was written on stone tablets, is contrasted with a new covenant which Jeremiah foresees in the future. This will not be written on stone but on the heart. Instead of external instruction this covenant will contain an interior principle of personal regeneration; hence charismatic leaders such as prophets and priests, who instruct the people in the obligations of the law of Yahweh, will not be necessary in the new covenant. Yahweh will teach each individual Israelite as He taught the prophets and the priests. It is against the traditional background of the covenant that Isaiah calls the servant* of Yahweh "a covenant of a people" (42:6; 49:8). This obscure phrase is to be explained by the parallel "light of nations" (42:8) and by the function assigned to the servant in both these passages. He is to deliver prisoners, to bring light in darkness, to restore the land. His mission, therefore, is compared to the covenant promises of Yahweh; through the servant Yahweh makes Himself known to the peoples and communicates both His promises and His obligations. The covenant is a basic and recurring motif in the OT. It is a motive urged on the Israelites for the observance

of the law (Dt 4:23). It is a motive of Yahweh's anger by which He punishes (Lv 26:15, 25; Dt 31:16 f; 2 K 17:15; Ps 78: 10, 37; Is 33:8; Je 11:3 ff; 22:9; Ezk 16: 59). The covenant is appealed to as a motive why He should assist the Israelites in distress (Lv 26:9; Dt 7:9, 12; 8:18; Pss 25:10; 74:20; 105:8; 106:45; 111:5; Je 14:21), and why He should show mercy and forgiveness (Lv 26:42; Dt 4:31; Ezk 16:60). It is the ultimate motive why His mercy is enduring, why Israel always remains His people (Lv 26:45; Ps 111:9; Is 54:10; 59:21; 61:8; Je 32:40; Ezk 34:25; 37:26).

2. NT. The Gk word diathēkē occurs 26 times in the NT. Seven are quotations from the OT, and 16 others allude to the OT. In the formula of consecration Jesus calls His blood the "blood of the covenant" (Mt 26: 28; Mk 14:24), "the new covenant in my blood" (Lk 22:20; 1 Co 11:25). This passage refers to the blood of the covenant ceremony (Ex 24). As the blood of the old covenant united the partners in one relationship, so the blood of Jesus is now the bond of union between the covenant parties, God the Father and the Christian. Paul mentions the "covenants" among the privileges of Israel (Rm 9:4); the use of the plural is obscure, but it probably refers to the renewals of the covenant in the Pnt mentioned above. The apostles are ministers of the new covenant which is not of the letter but of the spirit (2 Co 3:6 ff); this passage alludes not only to Je 31:31, but also to Is 59:21, in which the spirit is given in the covenant of the future. The old covenant is not annulled; the new covenant is a continuation of the original covenant made to Abraham (Gal 3:15 ff). The two covenants are typified by the two sons of Abraham, one the son of a slave and the other the son of a free woman (Gal 4:21 ff). The new covenant of the priesthood of Christ is superior to the old because it is confirmed by the oath of God (Heb 7:22); this is a free treatment of the idea, since God swears more than once in the OT to keep His covenant (Dt 4:31 and frequently in Dt), but not of the priesthood. The author of Heb treats the old covenant as obsolete and antiquated (Heb 8:13); this is a slightly different view from that expressed by Paul in Gal and Rm, where the old covenant is not annulled by the succession of the new, but rather fulfilled. Both authors, however, are in agreement that the obligations of the old law disappear with the coming of the new, and that the redeeming death of Jesus exceeds in virtue any means of redemption in the old covenant. Of the new covenant Jesus is the mediator (Heb 9:15). In Heb 9:16 ff the

author plays upon the meaning of *diathēkē* as last will and testament, which it has in classical and Koine Gk; and thus the new covenant is a testament in the sense that it is not valid until the testator, Jesus Himself, has died.

Creation. 1. *Mesopotamian and Canaanite myths of creation.* To understand the OT idea of creation it is necessary to have some knowledge of the mythology of creation in Mesopotamia and Canaan, since the OT incorporated some motifs from this mythology against which as a whole it took a stand in direct contradiction. The classic Mesopotamian account is found in the epic *Enuma Elish*. The form in which we possess this is a later edition of an older composition. The creative deity in the present edition is Marduk*, the god of Babylon. It is certain that in older accounts other gods had this position and these changes represent the rise and fall in importance of various Mesopotamian deities. The Mesopotamian account of creation begins with a chaos. It is easy to recognize in this chaos the sea, a formless monster which is hostile to the land and perpetually attacks it. In the beginning of the myth there is no land. The chaos is personified as two deities, the male deity Apsu and the female deity Tiamat. These two are the source by generation of all beings. They first beget the gods; but hostility arises between parents and children, and finally Apsu is slain by Ea, who was probably the creative deity in an older form of the poem. Tiamat is now revealed as the dragon of chaos, a monster. From her womb she spawns a whole horde of demons to assist her in her attack upon her offspring. The gods in terror seek a champion, but several gods refuse the challenge; it is finally accepted by Marduk, the son of Ea. In combat Marduk slays Tiamat; he catches her in his net, inflates her with the wind, and pierces her with an arrow. The gigantic carcass of the monster is the material from which Marduk creates the visible universe. Extensive portions of this part of the myth have been lost; but it is evident that Marduk creates a world in which the disk of the earth rests upon the abyss of the ocean. Over this structure arches the sky, in which move the stars, and above it are the chambers of rain and wind. The heavenly bodies become the seats of the deities of Mesopotamia; and Marduk builds himself his heavenly palace, whose earthly counterpart is Esagil, the temple of Babylon*. Man is made of clay mixed with the blood of a slain god, Kingu, an ally of Tiamat, in order to carry on the cult of the gods.

The myth clearly exhibits the belief in the

Marduk in combat with the dragon of chaos.

production of the universe from a preexisting chaos. This chaos is the ultimate principle of the origin of all things, and itself arises from nothing. It is divine in character, for it is the parent not only of men but also of gods. Creation is the victory of the creative deity over this monster. The myth had an important place in Mesopotamian cult. The cycle of nature, in which life is born anew each year to perish at the end of the year, was conceived as a recurring cycle of creation and chaos. In the spring life must be born anew; hence the New Year was celebrated by the recitation of the myth of creation and by its ritual reenactment. Extensive fragments of the Babylonian ritual have been preserved. The two principles of creation and chaos in Mesopotamian myth are equally balanced, and the victory of the creative deity is never final, since in his turn he must yield to chaos. The same pattern appears in Canaan. In the Ugaritic* tablets there is the myth of a combat between Aleyan Baal* and at least two other adversaries, Mot (whose name suggests the Canaanite word for death) and a monstrous dragon which is called Sea-River. These two adversaries perhaps represent two earlier forms of the myth. The dragon of chaos is easily recognized in Sea-River, and death is the adversary of life. Aleyan Baal is a god who annually dies but is brought to life by his female consort and again engages in victorious combat with his adversary.

2. *OT.* The Bible contains two accounts of creation at the beginning of Gn, although the word is less properly applied to the second. The first in the book, although it is now generally regarded as more recent in origin, is found in Gn 1:1–2:4a. This account is built up according to a scheme of enumeration.

Day	Work	Works of Division
1	I	Light and Darkness
2	II	Upper and Lower Waters
3 {	III	Land and Sea
{	IV	Vegetation

Day	Work	Works of Ornamentation
4	V	Sun, Moon, and Stars
5	VI	Birds and Fish
6 {	VII	Animals
{	VIII	Man

Eight works are distributed within six days. The first four are called works of division, and the second four works of ornamentation (Thomas Aquinas). The enumeration presupposes the same picture of the visible world which is seen in the *Enuma Elish.* The earth is a flat disk which rests upon the waters of the lower abyss, the ocean, which completely surrounds it. This picture has been obtained by the division of the primeval abyss into the waters of the lower abyss, the ocean, and the waters of the upper abyss, the celestial waters, which descend in the form of rain and dew. They are divided by the inverted bowl of the sky, "firmament" in Eng versions. That which first appears is light, although celestial bodies do not appear until the 4th day. The division of light and darkness, however, does not refer to the light given by sun and moon. This is the cosmic light*, the proper element of deity in both OT and ancient Semitic mythology; the first of God's creative works is to expel darkness, the element of chaos and evil, by the intrusion of the light of His own glory. The land is obtained by the division of the waters of the ocean. The works of ornamentation follow the order of the works of division: the celestial bodies of the firmament, the birds which fly beneath the sky and the fish of the lower abyss, and the land animals and man. The order of enumeration is obviously schematic and has no reference to the chronological development of the earth, of which the author had no knowledge.

A comparison of this account with the *Enuma Elish* reveals that it is an explicit polemic against the Mesopotamian and Canaanite myth of creation. Chaos appears in Gn, and the Hb word *t'hôm* is etymologically connected with the Akkadian *tiamat;* but it is no longer personfied as a deity, nor does it exhibit the primeval principle of sex. Nor is it the source and origin of all things; the sole creator in Gn is God. In enumerating the works of creation the author mentions some which were in Mesopotamian mythology identified with deity, either by personification or as the seats of deity. Light itself is a divine element, but here it appears merely as the first of creatures. The sky is in the OT also the residence of God (cf HEAVEN), but here it becomes merely an inverted bowl dividing the waters. The heavenly bodies, which were the seats of deity in Mesopotamia as well as the means by which the will of the gods was ascertained (cf DIVINATION) are here reduced to means of telling time. Man is the last of the creatures in both accounts, but his position is more significant in Gn than it is in *Enuma Elish* (cf MAN). Here man is made in the divine image, and in virtue of this image receives dominion over the rest of creation. The arrangement of the works of creation in six days followed by a Sabbath* of divine repose is not intended to indicate the time elapsed during the formation of the universe. No doubt it does suggest, as many writers propose, that the week with its Sabbath, the sacred unit of time among the Hebrews, is represented as one of the original works of creation, and that the life of man is to be modeled after the creative process which is here set forth. It is possible also that the writer, by presenting God as following the same schedule of work as man, wishes to emphasize the fact that creation is work and not a combat which issues in God's victory over the monster. This creation account is marked by a serenity and undisturbed dominion of God over the things which He makes. Creation is accomplished by the spoken word, and not by work of any kind. God is the king who needs only speak to have His will accomplished; the creator, however, has no assistant in the execution of His creative work. In wisdom literature the divine wisdom* appears with Him in the work of creation (Pr 8:22-31); but this personified attribute is not a distinct being. He is the sole operative cause. Hence there is no question of His entire supremacy; the author has represented it as best he knew how.

Whether the author represented God as creating from nothing is not easily answered. Creation from nothing is not denied by the author of Gn; but it is extremely improbable that he affirms it. Creation from nothing as it is taught in modern theology presupposes a philosophy of nature which the Hebrews did not have. They did not answer the question because they were unable to raise it; but the metaphysical affirmation of creation from nothing rests upon an idea of the divine supremacy which is identical with the biblical idea. The word which is used for creation in Gn 1 is *bārā'*. This word is used in the OT only with the deity as the subject; hence it indicates a work which is distinctively divine, which no agent less than God can accomplish. In Gn 1 it is used in the first verse, which summarizes the entire process and does not, as it is sometimes interpreted, signify the initial step in the creative work. The first step is the command that there be light. The word is used elsewhere in the chapter of the creation of animals (1:21) and of man (1:27). Since each of these works is a new stage, the production of animal life and of human life, the word is aptly used. It does not of itself, however, indicate creation from nothing, but the divine productive action. The Hb author was not able to go beyond the formless chaos which he has in common with Mesopotamian mythology. His imagination was unable to grasp a pure production from nothing. He did, however, reduce this chaos to mere shapeless matter with which God works, and in this way denied its divinity and that it was the primeval principle of creation. The account concludes with an affirmation of the goodness of all

which God has made (Gn 1:31). The author thus denies any dualism, which is implicit in Mesopotamian and Canaanite mythology. In this hypothesis evil is as primary as good; the universe contains together with the creative deity a hostile or an "evil" principle which the deity never effectively vanquishes. This the Hb author wished to reject. Again he asserts God's supremacy over His creation by this affirmation, as well as the possibility that a universe which was created totally good can in the future by the same divine power be restored to total goodness.

The second "creation account" (Gn 2:4b-25) is not properly concerned with creation itself. The origin of the world is not even described. It is conceived not as the primeval abyss but as a desert; and creation here seems to be effected by the irrigation of the desert through the streams which God sends out over the earth. The first piece of God's effective creation is the garden of Eden* (cf PARADISE), and there God places man. Man is made of clay into which God breathes His own breath (Gn 2:7). This is in contrast to the account of the *Enuma Elish* in which man is made of clay mingled with the blood of a slain god; Hb belief, of course, could not tolerate this concept, but the Hb author affirms the divine element in man, the breath of God by which he lives. Man, placed in the garden, then sees all the animals created, to which he gives names, thus exhibiting his own wisdom. The creation of the animals is merely preliminary to the next step, and is intended to show that there is among the animals no helper suitable for man (Gn 2:20). Hence woman is created, of the same species and nature as man (Gn 2:23), and intended to be the full partner of his life (Gn 2:24). Creation in this account is more anthropomorphic than in Gn 1. God is here represented as creating man as the potter molds an earthen vessel (*yāṣar;* Gn 2:7). This is creation by work rather than creation by word. At the same time the supremacy of God over His creation is no less than in Gn 1.

Elsewhere in the OT there are not infrequent and obvious echoes of the myth of creation. In these allusions Yahweh is represented as the creative deity victorious in combat. Yahweh slays the monster serpent Leviathan* (Is 27:1 ff); He hews Rahab* in pieces and pierces the sea monster (Is 51:9 f); the helpers of Rahab bow down under Him (Jb 9:13); He smites Rahab and pierces the fleeing serpent (Jb 26:12 f); He crushes the heads of dragons and Leviathan (Ps 74:13-15). Elsewhere the sea is represented not as slain but as put under restraint. It is enclosed by bar and doors

(Jb 38:8 ff); Yahweh commands its pride and suppresses its billows (Ps 89:10 f; cf also Ps 104:6 ff). If Yahweh were to relax the bonds which keep the monster under restraint, the world would relapse into primeval chaos. Some of the passages in which Yahweh is described as a warrior hero (Ex 15:3; Ps 89:14; Is 51:9), are possibly derived from His victory over chaos in creation, although elsewhere the title reflects His mighty deeds in defense of Israel.

The Sabbath rest of Yahweh after creation (Gn 2:2) is a theological conception peculiar to the author of the first creation account. Elsewhere in the OT creation is generally represented as a continuous activity which is renewed day to day. Each manifestation of Yahweh's dominion over nature may be conceived as a reenactment of the drama of creation. The Hebrews had no conception of the course or laws of nature, and looked at it as constantly regulated and governed by the will of Yahweh. Thus He brings forth the host of heaven by number and calls them by name (Is 40:26). Not only in their first creation but in their daily appearance He marshals the host of heaven (Is 45:12) and they arise when He calls them (Is 48:13). He makes dawn and darkness, turns darkness into dawn and darkens day into night (Am 4:13; 5:8). He measures the water in the hollow of His hand (Is 40:12). He sustains the life which He has given; He gives life to men upon the earth, and spirit to those who walk in it (Is 42:5). He brings forth springs in the valleys for the wild beasts and makes grass and herbage grow for the cattle. The animals wait upon Him to receive their food in due season. When He takes away His breath they die; but when He sends forth His breath they are created, and thus He constantly renews the face of the earth (Ps 104:10, 14 f, 28 ff). Yahweh is frequently praised in the OT as creator (Pss 8; 19:1 ff; 24:1 ff; 33:6 ff; 95:5; 104; Pr 8:22 ff; Jb 38:4 ff; BS 42:22–43:33; Is 40:12 ff, 26, 28; 45:18; 48:13). In Jb 38 and Pr 8:22 ff the universe is imagined in more detail as a vast edifice, with pillars which rest upon foundations laid in the abyss, chambers or storehouses for light and darkness, wind, snow, and hail. In these allusions to creation the point of admiration is often not power, as we would expect, but wisdom (Ps 104:23, 28 ff; Pr 3:19 f; 8:22 ff; Jb 38:4 ff). The creative wisdom* of Yahweh is a directive intelligence which maintains order and harmony among so many conflicting and divergent agents; the paradox of a universe which moves toward the end ordained for it by God in spite of these divergences was an object of constant admiration to the Hebrews.

Two passages in late Gk books (1st century BC) are probably affected by Gk language and thought. WS 11:17 says that God made the world "from formless matter"; the words are those of Gk philosophy, but the idea does not advance beyond Gn 1:2, which the writer desired to express in a Gk formulation. In 2 Mc 7:28 it is said that God made the heavens and the earth and all that is in them "not from existing things," which in the Gk of the writer is equivalent to "non-existing things," nothing. The idea can be paralleled from extrabiblical Jewish writings of the same period. It is very probable that the phrase is a paraphrase in Gk of *tôhû wābôhû*, the desolate waste of Gn 1:2.

3. *NT.* Creation is not emphasized in the NT. In the Synoptic Gospels even scattered allusions are few (Mt 19:4; Mk 10:6; 13:19). It is more frequent in the Pauline writings. The creative works of God manifest His invisible power and divinity, so that no one has any excuse for failing to distinguish the creator from the creature (Rm 1:20 ff). It is God from whom and through whom all things come into being, and to whom all things tend (Rm 11:36). Paul makes Christ the principle of creation, the firstborn of every creature, in whom everything in heaven and earth is created, both visible and invisible. All things are created through Him and tend to Him. Everything comes into being through Him (Col 1:15 ff). God has made the world through His Son, who bears all things through His powerful word (Heb 1:2 ff). In Jn all things were made through the Word* and without Him was made nothing that comes into being. In Him is life, and the world was made through Him (Jn 1:3 f, 9). Christ is also the principle of a new creation. If one is in Christ, one is a new creature (2 Co 5:17). Christians are God's work, created in Christ Jesus (Eph 2:10). Christ has made of Jew and Gentile one new man (Eph 2:15). There is neither circumcision nor uncircumcision but a new creature (Gal 6:15).

Crescens (Gk *krēskēs,* from Lt *crescens,* "growing"), a companion of Paul mentioned in 2 Tm 4:10 as having gone to Galatia* from Rome.

Crete. A large island of the Mediterranean, lying south of Greece in the Aegean Sea. Its western tip is about 60 mi S of the Peloponnesus. Its length E to W is about 150 mi, and its width varies from 7 to 30 mi. The history of Crete has been recovered by British excavations under Sir Arthur Evans and J. Pendlebury since 1900. These disclose that Crete in the 3rd and 2nd millennia BC was the most important center of Aegean culture. Its history is divided into three periods (called Minoan after Minos, the king of Crete in Gk mythology): Early Minoan, 3400–2000 BC; Middle Minoan, 2000–1580 BC; Late Minoan, 1580–1250 BC. The excavations disclosed a highly developed culture. The palace of Minos at Knossos was an elaborate complex of well constructed buildings which may be the original of the tale of the labyrinth. Cretan art reached a high state of technical development. The commercial relations of Crete with the Aegean islands, with Asia Minor, and with Egypt were extensive; and Cretan articles reached Syria and Palestine directly or indirectly. The Minoan culture perished in a barbarian invasion from the N which scattered the Aegean peoples as far as Palestine and Egypt. On the possible relation of Crete with the "Sea Peoples" and Philistines cf CAPHTOR; CHERETHITES AND PELETHITES; PHILISTINES. The Linear B script of Crete was deciphered after 1950 by Michael Ventris and others. This discovery proved that the language of Minoan Crete was early Greek. Crete had no political importance after 1200 BC. The Cretans were famous as archers and appear as auxiliary troops in ancient wars. The island had Jewish residents at the time of Christ (AA 2:11). Paul was shipwrecked on his voyage to Rome after the ship had left the port of Fair Havens* on Crete and was attempting to make the harbor of Phoenix* on the same island (AA 27:7, 12). Paul himself had urged the officers to winter in Crete (AA 27:21). A visit of Paul to Crete on a missionary journey is implied in his remark that he left Titus* at Crete to correct abuses and appoint presbyters (Tt 1:5). Paul also testifies to the bad reputation of Cretans in antiquity, quoting a line of Epimenides which describes them as liars, savage brutes, and lazy gluttons (Tt 1:12).

Crispus (Gk *krispos,* from Lt *crispus,* "curly-haired"), the presiding officer of the synagogue of Corinth (*archisynagōgos*), one of the first of the Jews of Corinth to accept Paul's preaching of the Gospel (AA 18:8) and one of the few Corinthians who was baptized by Paul himself (1 Co 1:14).

Crocodile. The crocodile has been extinct in Palestine since the latter part of the 19th century AD. Previous to this period it was found only in the marshes at the mouth of the Nahr ez Zerka in the coastal plain N of Caesarea*, now drained. The crocodile is described as the mythological monster

Leviathan* (Jb 41) and is possibly the "monster" identified with the Pharaoh of Egypt in Ezk 29:3; 32:2.

Cross. Crucifixion was an oriental mode of punishment introduced into the west from the Persians*. It was little used by the Greeks but was employed extensively both by the Carthaginians and the Romans. In Roman literature it is described as a cruel and feared punishment which was not inflicted on Roman citizens; it was reserved for slaves or for non-Romans who had committed heinous crimes such as murder, robbery and piracy, treason, and rebellion. It is not mentioned in the OT. Josephus reports that Antiochus Epiphanes crucified

Caricature of crucified figure with ass's head.

Jews who refused to obey his decrees of Hellenization, and that Alexander Janneus crucified his adversaries among the Pharisees. The X-shaped St. Andrew's cross was not used in antiquity. The cross on which Jesus was crucified was either the T-shaped *crux commissa* or the dagger-shaped *crux immissa* or *capitata*. The latter form is suggested by the fact that the title was affixed above His head (Mt 27:37). Since the execution of Jesus was committed to Roman soldiers, it is altogether probable that the Roman manner of execution was followed. The cross carried by Jesus to the place of execution, according to customary procedure, was not the entire cross, but only the crossbeam. As a rule, the upright beam was left permanently at the place of execution and the crossbeam was attached at each particular execution. The arms of the criminal were first attached to the crossbeam while he was stretched flat on the ground; he was then elevated together with the crossbeam to the upright beam, and his feet were then fastened to the upright beam. The fastening was done either by ropes or by nails; if nails were used, four were employed. The criminal was always attached by ropes bound around arms, legs, and belly; the nails would not support the weight of the body and the ropes prevented the victim from wriggling loose. Most of the weight of the body was supported by a peg (Lt *sedile*, "seat") projecting from the upright beam on which the victim sat astride. This is not mentioned in the NT but is described by a number of ancient Roman writers. The support for the feet (Lt *suppedaneum*), so common in Christian art, was unknown in antiquity. The victim was elevated scarcely more than a foot or two above the ground, low enough for a bystander to reach his mouth by putting a sponge upon a reed (Mt 27:48; Mk 15:36). The Romans crucified criminals stripped entirely naked, and there is no reason to think an exception was made in the case of Jesus. The clothing of the criminal went to the soldiers as a gratuity (Mt 27:35). A title with the criminal's name and his crime was written on a placard to be worn around the neck to the place of execution; this was affixed above the head of Jesus on the cross. The placard by Pilate's irony contained not a criminal charge but the title "King of the Jews" (Mt 27:37; Mk 15:26; Lk 23:38; Jn 19:19–22). This title was written in three languages: Aramaic, the vernacular of the country; Greek, the language of the Roman world; and Latin, the official language of the Roman administration. In crucifixion the victim was left to die of hunger and thirst. Death was hastened if necessary by breaking the legs with clubs, as was done to the criminals crucified with Jesus (Jn 19:32 ff). It was a surprise to the soldiers that Jesus expired so quickly, since death by crucifixion did not ensue until a few days had passed. It was a Jewish, not a Roman custom to give condemned criminals a narcotic drink before execution in order that their senses might be numbed (Mt 27:34; Mk 15:23). This was offered to Jesus, but He refused it. In Roman practice scourging* often preceded crucifixion, as it did in the case of Jesus. Under Roman law the offense for which the penalty of crucifixion was imposed on Jesus was that of treason and rebellion, as charged against Him by the Jews (Lk 23:2–5; Jn 19:12). Crucifixion as a legal punishment was abolished by the first Christian emperor, Constantine (306–337).

The theological symbolism of the cross appears in the NT only in a saying of Jesus Himself and in the writings of Paul. Jesus said that those who follow Him must take up their cross; by this they would lose their life in order to gain it (Mt 10:38; 16:24; Mk 8:34; Lk 9:23; 14:27). This is not only an allusion to His own death, but also a statement that the following of Him demands a "denial of self" (Mk 8:34), an entire disregard of one's own life, personal welfare, and personal values, which must be renounced if one is to follow Jesus. Paul preached Christ and Him crucified, although it was revolting to the Jews and folly to the Gentiles (1 Co 1:23; 2:2). He did not wish to preach the gospel of the cross in polished language lest he should deprive the cross of its value (1 Co 1:17). Although the story of the cross is nonsense to those who perish for lack of its redemption, it is the power of God to those who are saved (1 Co 1:18). If Paul must preach circumcision then the scandal of the cross has been removed (Gal 5:11), by which Paul signifies that the cross, which is a scandal to the Jews, loses its redemptive value if circumcision is necessary. Paul's only boast is the cross of Jesus Christ (Gal 6:14). By the cross Jesus has united Jews and Gentiles (Eph 2:16). Some false apostles are enemies of the cross of Christ (Phl 3:18); this probably signifies those Jewish Christians who insisted on the efficacy of circumcision. The charge of crimes which God has against mankind Christ has annulled by nailing it to the cross, i.e., by Himself becoming the victim of these crimes (Col 2:14). Those who belong to Christ have "crucified the flesh*" i.e., they have successfully mastered the sensual desires of their nature and accepted Christian renunciation. Through the cross of Jesus Christ Paul is crucified to the world and the world to him (Gal 6:14). This metaphor signifies a complete renunciation; the world is the cross upon which Paul's life is sacrificed. It is not clear what Paul means when he tells the Galatians that Christ crucified has been set forth before their very eyes, unless he refers to the vivid presentation of the crucifixion in his own catechesis (Gal 3:1); possibly this is an allusion to the representation of the redeeming death in the Eucharistic* sacrifice.

Crown. A headdress, part of the insignia of office of kings and other dignitaries; in Hb there are several words which distinguish this distinctive headdress. These words no

a) Egyptian nemes headdress. b) and c) Egyptian royal crown. d) Sumerian royal cap. e) Assyrian peaked royal cap. f) Double crown of Egypt.

doubt indicate different styles of crown which we cannot reconstruct. The *nēzer* (diadem) was worn both by the high priest (Ex 29:6; Lv 8:9) and by kings (2 K 1:12; 2 Ch 23:11; Pss 89:40; 132:18). The relation of the *nēzer* to the *ṣīṣ* worn by the high priest (Ex 28:36; Lv 8:9) and by kings (Is 28:1, 4) is obscure. The *ṣīṣ* was made of gold (Ex 28:36). The *nēzer* was ornamented with precious stones (2 S 12:30; Zc 9:16). This suggests that the *nēzer* and

the *ṣīṣ* included a metal band worn around the head; the *nēzer* of the high priest was worn over the turban (Hb *miṣnepet*). The *ʿaṭārāh* is mentioned with the *ṣīṣ* (Is 28:1, 3, 5). The *ʿaṭārāh* was worn by kings (Is 28:1 ff; Ezk 21:31; Zc 6:14) and by the image of Milcom*, god of the Ammonites (2 S 12:30). It was worn by the queen of Persia (Est 8:15) and also by bride and bridegroom in wedding festivities (SS 3:11; Ezk 16:12; 23:42).

The OT gives no evidence of the size and shape of crowns. Egyptian monarchs wore several types of ceremonial headdress. In all these crowns the distinctive sign of royalty seems to have been the uraeus, a small serpent's head which projected just above the forehead. The *nemes* headdress was a soft cloth cap which fitted closely over the hair and ended in two broad strips which hung over the shoulders on the breast. The double crown consisted of the white crown of Upper Egypt and the red crown of Lower Egypt, signifying the union of the two kingdoms which occurred in predynastic times. The white crown was a high cylindrical cap which tapered up to a knob. The red crown curved back from above the forehead to a point in the rear; a curled piece rose diagonally toward the front from the hollow of the cap. The blue crown, which seems to have been a part of the king's military insignia, was a high round helmet. The earliest representations of Sumerian kings show them with no headdress. From Gudea of Lagash to Hammurabi there appears a rounded low cap with a broad band which encircles the head. Assyrian kings wore a rounded high conical cap, truncated near the peak, at which rose a point; two strips hung down the back. This cap was sometimes adorned with precious stones and other materials. The gods in Mesopotamian art are distinguished by the horned crown. Merodach-baladan of Babylon is represented in a helmet-like cap with a streamer hanging down the back from the point of the helmet. Some Phoenician and Aramaean kings are represented wearing a rounded cap, not as high as the Assyrian crown, which tapers to a knob, resembling a helmet. The crown (Gk *stephanos*) mentioned in the NT is the laurel crown awarded to winners of athletic contests and in Gk cities to citizens for distinguished service; hence it appears almost always as a reward. Paul compares the imperishable crown of the Christian's reward to the perishable crown of the athlete (1 Co 9:25). The crown is mentioned as a reward (2 Tm 4:8; Js 1:12; 1 Pt 5:4; Apc 2:10; 3:11). The crown is worn by a number of persons in the visions of the Apc (Apc 4:4, 10; 6:2; 9:17; 12:1; 14:14).

Cubit. Cf WEIGHTS AND MEASURES.

Cummin (Hb *kammōn*, Gk *kyminon*), a plant cultivated for its seeds, which were used as spice or relish. The seeds were obtained by beating the plant with a rod (Is 28:25, 27). In Pharaisaic interpretation of the law even this small plant was subject to tithe*, and Jesus cited it as an instance of Pharisaic pettifogging (Mt 23:23).

Cuneiform. Cuneiform was the most important and the most widely used system of writing in the ancient Near East to about 500 BC. The name cuneiform (Lt *cuneus*, "wedge"), given to this type of writing in 1712, is derived from the impression of the reed stylus, narrow at one end and broader at the other, on a moist clay tablet. These impressions are combined into figures. The shape and pointing of the stylus and the manner in which its impression was made are still not entirely clear. The clay tablet after writing was dried in the sun or baked artificially, and is one of the most durable records which man has invented. This system of writing was invented by the Sumerians* before 3000 BC. The oldest texts, which come from Uruk, are almost strictly pictographic; their meaning can be grasped, but the language in which they are written cannot be ascertained. The writing was developed by the Sumerians into ideographic writing in which each sign represents a single word. The number of signs required was large; the Uruk texts exhibit almost 900 such signs. Progress in the use of cuneiform came with successive simplifications. The Sumerians employed the word sign (e.g., KI, "earth") for the syllable also (e.g., KI). When the Akkadians* adopted the Sumerian script for their own language, they developed existing Sumerian signs and employed them to signify not words, but syllables, from which new words could be formed in Akkadian. This development led to the invention of other syllabic signs. This system also was complex, and included several hundred signs; but it was much more flexible than the ideographic writing. The Akkadians retained a number of ideographic signs from Sumerian; these signs, however, are read with the Akkadian word. Since Sumerian had no way of exhibiting endings for case and number, the Akkadians, in order to assist the reader, added a system of determinants for both nouns and verbs. The syllable which indicates the inflectional ending of a noun or verb was added as a phonetic complement. The determinative added (or prefixed) to an ideogram indicates the nature or the material of the noun: for instance, male, female, god, city, country, mountain, tree (wood), stone, bronze, +. The oldest Akkadian texts come from the period of Sargon of Akkad (about 2350 BC) and the 3rd dynasty of Ur (about 2000 BC). Akkadian writing was developed in two directions: the Babylonian script, which terminated with the neo-Babylonian script of the empire of Nebuchadnezzar*, retained the archaic and more complex signs. The Assyrians moved toward greater regularity in the shape of the signs. Even in older Babylonian writing the

Cuneiform writing, Code
of Hammurabi.

picture indicated by the sign is no longer visible. Cuneiform writing was adopted by the Hittites*. The tablets found in Boghaz-koi, the site of the ancient Hittite capital in Asia Minor, were written not only in Hittite, but also in Akkadian, which was the diplomatic language of the day, in proto-Hattic for liturgical texts, in Luwian, the language of a people within the Hittite kingdom of Asia Minor, and some Hurrian* tablets were also found. Cuneiform was also adopted by the Elamites*, but their language is as yet not well known. Akkadian written in cuneiform was employed in the Amarna* letters written by satellite kings of Canaan* to the Pharaoh of Egypt. This fact of itself illustrates the wide use both of Akkadian and of cuneiform writing, since the language was native to neither party of this correspondence. Cuneiform was also employed in Ugarit*. The Akkadian texts found there are far exceeded in number by the texts written in the Ugaritic cuneiform alphabetic script. The principle of the alphabet* was already known when the Ugaritic scribe invented 31 consonantal signs. The Persians adapted the cuneiform system into an alphabetic script of 36 signs. The trilingual inscriptions of Behistun of Darius* I and of the palace of Persepolis furnished the key to the deciphering of cuneiform script about 1850. The efforts of a number of scholars, especially Sir Henry Rawlinson, Edward Hincks, and Jules Oppert, revealed that a number of royal personal names recurred in the three languages of the inscriptions, Old Persian, Elamite, and Babylonian. The decipherment was proved to the satisfaction of scholars when four men, working independently, produced in 1857 translations of a Babylonian inscription which were substantially identical.

Cup. This vessel often appears in figurative speech in the Bible. "The cup of comfort" is offered to the mourner (Je 16:7), and the cup of thanksgiving is drunk to celebrate the reception of a favor (Ps 116:13). The head of the household filled the cups of the family and guests at table; hence the cup becomes a figure of one's lot or portion (Mt 20:22; 26:39). The cup of the wrath of Yahweh is an intoxicating drink which makes men reel and stagger (Ps 75:9; Lam 4:21; Is 51:17 ff; Je 25:15, 17, 28; 49:12; Ezk 23:31; Hab 2:16). Jeremiah's prophetic mission of predicting the downfall of the nations is described as the presentation of the cup of wrath for them to drink (Je 25:15 ff). The cup was also used for divination* (Gn 44:2, 5).

Curse. Orientals both ancient and modern employ curses with a freedom which is shocking to western ears. The curse, like the blessing* and the covenant*, is a solemn utterance which cannot be retracted or annulled. The spoken word is endowed with a certain reality which enables it to pursue its object inexorably. The curse can be returned by Yahweh upon the head of him who utters it (Gn 12:3; 27:29); or it may be to some extent neutralized if the person who has uttered it follows it with a blessing upon the person who has been cursed (Jgs 17:2). The blessing of Yahweh renders the curse ineffective (Nm 23:8). In Mesopotamia solemn curses were uttered according to a ritual formula by sorcerers (cf MAGIC); such ritual curses were, of course, most effective, and it was for such a purpose that Balak*, king of Moab*, brought the seer Balaam* to curse Israel (Nm 22:5 ff). Curses are placed in the mouth of Yahweh Himself; He curses the serpent* of Eden* (Gn 3:14), the soil on man's account (Gn 3:17; 5:29), the enemies of Abraham (Gn 12:3), and promises not to curse the soil again because of man (Gn 8:21). A curse was uttered as a punishment for a crime. Noah* cursed Ham* (Gn 9:25); Jacob cursed Simeon* and Levi* (Gn 49:7). A prophet curses the Jews for dishonesty in sacrifice (Mal 1:14; 3:9), and the priests for faithlessness in their duty (Mal 2:2). David curses those who drive him into exile where he must worship foreign gods (1 S 26:19). Meroz* is cursed for failing to assist Barak* and Deborah* against the Canaanites (Jgs 5:23). Nehemiah* cursed those Jews who had married foreign wives (Ne 13:25). A curse was uttered to prevent something being done, as Joshua* cursed the man who should rebuild Jericho* (Jos 6:26). Hb popular tradition saw this curse fulfilled in the experience of Hiel* (1 K 16:34). Joshua cursed the Gibeonites for entering a covenant by deception and condemned them to forced labor (Jos 9:23). Saul cursed the man who should interrupt the battle against the Philistines* in order to take food (1 S 14:24 ff); and this curse had to be fulfilled, even though his son Jonathan* had violated it unwittingly. Only a popular tumult saved Jonathan's life. The solemn ritual curse is part of the covenant formula described in Dt 27:11 ff. To the curses uttered by the Levites* for violations of the covenant the people respond Amen. A similar solemn ritual curse is uttered in Dt 28:16 ff for breaches of the covenant (cf Je 11:3). To this may be compared the ritual imprecations of Hammurabi on those who violate or change his laws (ANET 178–180) and the imprecations in Egyptian and Hittite treaties (ANET 201, 205–206). Hb law prohibited the cursing of the deity (Ex 22:27; Lv 24:10 ff) and the cursing of one's father and mother (Ex 21:17; Lv 20:9). The penalty for these offenses was death. One should not curse a deaf person (Lv 19:14), for he could not hear the curse and take measures to prevent it. It was forbidden to curse a "prince of the people" (Ex 22:27); this prohibition was also extended to the king, the anointed of Yahweh. When Shimei* cursed David as the cause of the fall of the house of Saul, David would not permit him to be punished. Perhaps Yahweh had commanded Shimei to curse him and would be gracious to David for accepting it (2 S 16:5 ff). Ultimately Shimei was executed for his crime (1 K 2:8, 44). Both Job (3:1 ff) and Jeremiah (20:14 ff) cursed the day of their birth, and Jeremiah in addition cursed the messenger who brought the news. The curse of a prophet was especially effective (2 K 2:24). No doubt champions in single combat often exchanged curses before the actual fighting (1 S 17:43 ff). The primitive ceremony of "the waters of cursing" (Nm 5:12 ff) must have arisen from magical rites. A woman who is accused of adultery* is tested by a ritual which included the drinking of water into which a written curse has been washed. If she is guilty, the curse will take effect and all her pregnancies will end in miscarriage.

Cursing is rarely mentioned in the NT. Jesus told His disciples to return a blessing for a curse (Lk 6:28), echoed in Rm 12:14. Paul, however, curses those who preach another gospel (Gal 1:8) and any one who does not love the Lord (1 Co 16:22), as well as the high priest who ordered him to be struck while his case was being heard (AA 23:3). By an unusually vigorous figure of speech Paul says that Christ has removed the curse from man by becoming himself a curse (Gal 3:13).

It is against this pattern that such imprecatory passages as Ps 109 and Jeremiah's cursing of his adversaries (11:21; 18:19 ff) should be understood. Such utterances are not the casual explosion of a short temper, but a serious and almost ritual invocation that divine justice will be vindicated in the world through the prevention and suppression of malice. The curse thus uttered is also a means of protection for the individual himself against the malice of his enemies.

Cush. Cf ETHIOPIA .

Cushan-Rishathaim (Hb *kûšan-riš'ātayim*, etymology uncertain), according to Jgs 3:8 ff, a king of Aram Naharaim* who oppressed Israel until they were delivered by Othniel*. Most modern critics believe that Edom should be read here for Aram; the letters *d* and *r* are sometimes interchanged in the Hb text. The word Naharaim is taken as a gloss. Other scholars believe that the word Aram should be retained, but that the word Naharaim is a gloss.

Cuth, Cuthah (Hb *kûtah* [2 K 17:24], *kût* [2 K 17:30], Akkadian *kutu*, Eng often Kutha), a city of ancient Mesopotamia at the modern Tell Ibrahim, 19 mi NE of Babylon. Immigrants from Cuth were brought to Samaria to repopulate the cities of Israel conquered by Tiglath-pileser* III; they introduced the worship of the god Nergal.

Cypress (*Cupressus sempervirens*), is probably meant by Hb *tᵉʾaššûr*, mentioned with the cedar* as a tree of Lebanon* (Is 41:19; 60:13). The Italian cypress grows on Mt Lebanon; it has a tapering shape and grows to a maximum height of 90 ft. The timber is hard and close grained and of excellent quality for building. Some scholars believe that the cypress is designated by Hb *bᵉrôš*, more commonly thought to be the juniper*.

Cyprus. An island of the eastern Mediterranean lying between the coasts of Cilicia* and Syria. Its greatest width is 60 mi and its greatest length 145 mi. Cyprus is probably to be identified with Elishah* and Kittim* of the OT. Cyprus was one of the communities to which the Romans addressed a letter warning against attacking the Jews (1 Mc 15:23). It belonged to the kingdom of the Ptolemies* 294–58 BC when it passed into the hands of the Romans. In antiquity it was famous for the cult of Aphrodite, who was often called the Cyprian. It was an early source of the production of copper*, which derives its name from the island. The gospel was carried to Cyprus by fugitive Jewish Christians who left Jerusalem in the persecution which followed the stoning of Stephen* (AA 11:19 f). Paul and Barnabas preached in Salamis and Paphos in Cyprus (AA 13:4 ff). It was visited again by Barnabas and Mark* after the separation of Paul and Barnabas (AA 15:39).

Cyrene (Gk *kyrēnē*), the chief city of Cyrenaica in northern Africa (modern Libya). It was settled from Greece in the Mycenean period and was the seat of a colony from the Gk city of Thera in 630 BC. In NT times it had a large Jewish population (AA 2:10; 6:9). It was the home of Simon*, who carried the cross of Jesus to Calvary (Mt 27:32; Mk 15:21; Lk 23:26), and of Lucius*, one of the prophets and teachers of Antioch (AA 13:1).

Cyrus (Hb *kōreš*, Gk *kyros*, Persian *kurash*, "shepherd"), was the throne name of the kings of Elam*. Cyrus II the Great, the founder of the Persian Empire, the son of Cambyses, became king of Anshan, a vassal kingdom of the Medes*, in 559 BC. In alliance with Nabonidus, king of Babylon, Cyrus rebelled against Astyages, king of the Medes in 556 and by the capture of Ecbatana* made Media a satrapy of the kingdom of Persia. His conquest of Croesus of Lydia in 547 made him master of Asia Minor, including the Gk cities of the Ionian coast. In 546 he began a campaign against Babylonia which ended with the surrender of Babylon in 539. Cyrus himself was killed in battle against the Massagetae in 529. In the OT Cyrus appears, probably about 545, as the hope of restoration of Judah and of Jerusalem. Second Is calls him the shepherd of Yahweh who will accomplish Yahweh's will (Is 44:28) and gives him the grandiose title of "the anointed of Yahweh," who grasps his right hand; this title was earlier reserved to kings and priests. It is Yahweh who grants Cyrus his conquests; He does this in order that Cyrus may restore His people Israel (Is 45:1 ff). This hope was fulfilled in 538 BC when Cyrus permitted the Jews residing in Babylon to return to Jerusalem and rebuild the city and its temple (2 Ch 36:22 f; Ezr 1:1–4). The text of the decree of Cyrus is quoted in Ezr 6:3–5. This text was doubted by many older scholars, but modern scholars are inclined to accept it as an authentic copy. Cyrus' treatment of the Jews is in harmony with the policy which he followed in Mesopotamia of restoring the images of captured gods to their original temples, which he often rebuilt. The Jews, who had no divine image, received instead the sacred vessels of the temple which had been looted by Nebuchadnezzar (Ezr 1:7).

D

Dagon (Hb *dāgôn*), a god worshiped by the Philistines* (Jgs 16:23; 1 S 5:2 ff). When the ark of the covenant, captured by the Philistines, was placed in the temple of Dagon, the image of Dagon was found thrown to the ground the following morning; it was set back in its place but was found the following morning broken in pieces. Hb popular tradition thus exhibited the power of the God of Israel even in captivity. The name appears also in two Hb cities named Beth-Dagon (Jos 15:41; 19:27). Dagon was not natively a god of the Philistines but a Semitic deity adopted by them after their invasion of Canaan. The cult of the Mesopotamian Dagan (= Dagon) is traced back to the 3rd dynasty of Ur in the 25th century BC. Hence it is unlikely that Dagan was an Amorite deity, although his cult was extremely popular among the Amorites, among whom Dagan is often a component of personal names. It was also popular among the Assyrians. His character is not clearly known; he is often described as a storm god in terms which imitate the titles of Enlil. The Hb word *dāgān*, "grain," is probably derived from the name of the god. In the opinion of many scholars Dagan was originally a vegetation deity, but this character is not clear in the texts which allude to him. His cult spread to the W and is found not only among the Philistines but also at Ugarit*. Here he is mentioned in a list of gods and in a list of offerings, in which he receives a head of small cattle. A stele also was erected to Dagan by a grateful citizen of Ugarit. There was a temple of Dagan at Ugarit. Aleyan Baal* is called the son of Dagan in a few passages of the Baal epic. The temple of Dagon at Ashdod* was destroyed in Maccabean times by Jonathan (1 Mc 10:84).

Daleth. The 4th letter of the Hb alphabet, with the value of *d*.

Dalmanutha (Gk *dalmanūtha*, etymology uncertain), a city or region near the Sea of Galilee to which Jesus withdrew after the feeding of the four thousand (Mk 8:10). The place is otherwise unknown. The parallel passage in Mt 15:39 reads Magadan, which is also read in some MSS of Mk. Many modern critics believe that the name is a corruption from Magdala*.

Dalmatia. In AD 10 the ancient territory of Illyria, on the east coast of the Adriatic Sea, was established as two Roman provinces, Dalmatia in the N and Pannonia in the S. It is mentioned in the NT as a place to which Titus* had gone from Rome (2 Tim 4:10).

Damaris. A woman of Athens converted by the preaching of Paul (AA 17:34). The name occurs nowhere else in Gk literature.

Damascus (Hb *dammaseḳ* or *darmeseḳ*, meaning uncertain). The modern Syrian city of Damascus (pop 350,000) occupies the site of the royal capital of the opulent and powerful Aramaean* kingdom of the 8th–6th centuries BC. A large city is made possible on the site of Damascus by the river Barada (biblical Abanah*) which rises in the snows of the Anti-Lebanon range and gives the city an abundant water supply before it exhausts itself in the marshes of the Syrian desert. Damascus is thus a very large oasis, a gateway to the desert and a natural point of exchange between the desert and the area N and S of Damascus, as well as Lebanon, ancient Phoenicia*, over the mountains to the west. It is an ancient city, but the date of its foundation is unknown and its early history is obscure: continuous occupation of the site has destroyed or covered all archaeological evidence of pre-Christian times. Damascus under the name of Apum is mentioned in the Egyptian Execration Texts (19th century BC), and in the Mari* texts. Damascus was listed by Thutmose III (1502–1448) among the Asiatic cities subject to Egypt. The city is mentioned twice in the Amarna* tablets as located in the land of Ube and entirely submissive to the Pharaoh Amenhotep III. Later Rib-addi of Byblos* reports that Damascus has fallen into the hands of Aziru, son of Abdi-Ashirta. The history of the Aramaean kingdom of Damascus is known only from biblical and Assyrian records. Beginning with Shalmaneser III (858–824) Damascus appears frequently in Assyrian records. In the earlier records the name Aram is more frequently used, Damascus in the later. Shalmaneser III mentions victories over Damascus in four different campaigns, two against Ben-hadad* and two against Hazael*. The first of these was the battle of Karkar (853), in which Ben-hadad and Ahab* of Israel* were allied with the Aramaean states of Syria. None of these victories can have been as complete as Shalmaneser claimed. Adad-nirari III

Damascus with the Anti-Lebanon in the background.

(809–783) claimed a victory over Mari (otherwise unknown) of Damascus and tribute paid by him. Tiglath-pileser* III (745–727) received tribute from Rasunnu, the biblical Rezin*, of Aram and claims a victory over the country of Aram which is probably well in accord with the facts; but details are lacking. Except for a revolt of Damascus at the beginning of the reign of Sargon* (721–705) Damascus appears no more in Assyrian records except in the reign of Ashur-bani-pal (668–626) as an Assyrian base. The name of its governor in the Assyrian eponym list by which the years were identified shows that it was governed directly by a Assyrian officer and not by a satellite king.

The occurrence of Damascus in Gn 15:2 is probably due to a textual corruption (cf ELIEZER). The Aramaean kingdom was established by the revolt of Rezon* against Israelite rule (1 K 11:23–25). Damascus with other Aramaean territory had been subject to Israel since the conquests of David* (cf ZOBAH). On the relations of Damascus and Israel cf AHAB; AHAZ; BEN-HADAD; HAZAEL; JEHOASH; PEKAH; REZIN. Only the OT records the fall of Damascus to Tiglath-pileser III in 732 (2 K 16:9). Amos uttered an oracle threatening Damascus with destruction because of the merciless campaign conducted against Gilead* (1:3–5). The destruction of the Aramaean kingdom is mentioned in Is 17:1 ff. The oracle against Damascus in Je 49:23–27 with an allusion to Am 1:3–5 is very probably an earlier fragment inserted in Je, since in the time of Jeremiah Damascus was politically inactive. The city is mentioned in Ezk 27:18 as a producer of wine of Helbon and wool. The land of Damascus was to be the N frontier of the ideal Israel described in Ezk 47:15–17. In Zc 9:1 Damascus and its territory are reckoned as belonging to Yahweh; on the date of this allusion cf ZECHARIAH. Damascus remained politically inactive after 732 BC. When the Assyrian empire collapsed in 612 BC, Damascus passed under the neo-Babylonian empire and then under the Persians. It fell to Alexander* in 333 and became a part of the Seleucid* kingdom. When the Seleucid kingdom disintegrated, Damascus became subject to the Nabatean* kingdom in 85 BC. Pompey allowed the Nabateans to retain control of Damascus when he organized the Roman province of Syria in 64 BC. It was one of the cities of the Decapolis*. It passed under direct Roman rule in the last half of the 1st century AD, probably in the reign of Nero (AD 54–68).

The city was a thriving center of commerce and manufacture and had a large Jewish colony. Christianity appeared in Damascus only a few years after the death of Jesus; the Christians were numerous enough for Paul* to obtain authorization from the high priest to arrest any Christians he might find there. The "street called straight," on which the house of Judas* was situated (AA 9:11), followed the course of the modern Suk Midhat Pasha, running E and W. It was a colonnaded avenue of the Roman city. At the eastern end of the street at Bab Sharqi is a gate of Roman construction.

On the "Damascus Document" cf QUMRAN.

Dan (Hb *dān*, meaning uncertain). **1.** The son of Jacob* and Bilhah*, the slave of Rachel* (Gn 30:6). Here the name is explained by a play on the word *dîn*, "to judge," i.e., to give a favorable verdict. The same popular etymology is found in the blessing of Jacob (Gn 49:16).

2. One of the 12 tribes of Israel. In the blessing of Jacob (Gn 49:16 f) Dan is praised for his fighting qualities; he is a serpent by the road, a viper by the path, which bites the horse's hoof and unseats its rider. The fighting qualities of the tribe are also praised in the blessing of Moses (Dt 33:22); Dan is a lion's whelp that leaps from Bashan*. The territory of Dan, described in Jos 19:40 ff, included the cities in the neighborhood of Zorah* and Eshtaol* in the Shephelah*. This list with slight variations appears among the cities of Judah (Jos 15:33–36); the Judah list comes from the monarchy after the Philistines had been subdued, and scholars attribute it to the administrative documents of Hezekiah* or Josiah*. The Amorites* who inhabited the coastal strip would not permit the Danites to expand toward the coast (Jgs 1:34). After the Philistine conquest the pressure became even greater and the tribe of Dan was forced to migrate. Their scouts discovered a Sidonian city at the northern extremity of Hb territory, Laish (Leshem in Jgs 19:47), which the Danites sacked and settled (Jgs 18:7, 27 ff). The number of the fighting men of the tribe in this expedition is given as 600. The name Mahaneh-Dan, "camp of Dan," for Kirjath-jearim* in Judah, was derived in popular tradition from this march (Jgs 18:12). The tribe of Dan is mentioned among those which failed to give aid to Barak* and Deborah* (Jgs 5:17); the reference to ships here is extremely obscure.

In their migration from their original settlement the Danites took with them a Levite* who was in the service of a man of Ephraim* named Micah*, who had installed a small shrine and a divine image in his house (Jgs 17:4 ff; 18:15 ff). This Levite was the first to serve at the sanctuary of Dan, which afterward with Bethel* became one of the two national sanctuaries of Israel* instituted by Jeroboam I after the schism of the kingdom (1 K 12:29 ff). This sanctuary of Dan is mentioned with contempt by Amos (8:14). In spite of the debased cult the god worshiped at Dan was Yahweh. The name of the city appears frequently as the northern limit of Israel, especially in the phrase "from Dan to Beersheba." It is used anachronistically in Gn 14:14. The tribe produced the Israelite hero Samson*.

Dance. The dance is a part not only of profane celebrations but also of sacred functions with most peoples. In the OT the dance appeared in both. It was a part of the celebration of Yahweh's victory over Egypt (Ex 15:20), the procession in which David brought the ark* into Jerusalem (2 S 6:5 ff), the celebration of the golden calf (Ex 32:19; also Pss 150:4; 149:3). The dance also celebrated a victory in battle or the return of a hero (Jgs 11:34; 1 S 18:6). The dance was a part of the vintage festival (Jgs 21: 21; Je 31:4), and Jeremiah sees maidens dancing in the joy of the messianic Israel (Je 31:31). The dances mentioned in the OT seem to be performed by groups, sometimes mixed but more frequently women alone, rather than by individuals. The dance was accompanied by music* and the dancers often

Egyptian dancers.

carried tambourines (Ex 15:20). The dance which David performed before the ark is described by a word which does not occur elsewhere; it must have been unusually vigorous, to judge by the criticism of Michal* (2 S 6:14, 16, 20). The conduct of Saul with the prophets (1 S 10:10 ff; 19:20 ff) suggests that the companies called sons of the prophets conducted a cultic worship of

song and dance. Egyptian tomb paintings show that Egyptians were lovers of the dance and usually had professional dancers perform at festivals (ANEP 208, 209, 210, 211, 216). Jesus speaks of children singing and dancing in the streets (Mt 11:17 ff; Lk 7:32). The dance of the daughter of Herodias* before the guests at the dinner in honor of Herod Antipas' birthday (Mt 14:6; Mk 6:22) followed Gk, not Hb custom, and would have been regarded as in extremely bad taste by the Jews. This dance was the occasion of the execution of John the Baptist*.

Daniel (Hb *dānīyy'ēl*, "El judges"). 1. Daniel is represented in Dn 1:3 ff as a young Judahite of noble family who is taken into the household of Nebuchadnezzar* and instructed in the wisdom of the Chaldeans*. He remained in Babylon until the third year of Cyrus (537 BC). The name is borne by two others in the OT. The Daniel alluded to as a sage and a righteous man of early times (Ezk 14:14, 20; 28:3), associated with Noah* and Job*, also legendary figures of antiquity, is not to be identified with the Daniel of the book. The reference to antiquity and the slightly different spelling of the name in Ezk (*dān'ēl* instead of *dānīyy'ēl*) suggest that the Daniel mentioned by Ezk is the Danel of the Ugaritic* literature, the father of Aqhat, a wise and righteous man.

2. The Book of Daniel. I. *Authorship and Date.* The origin of the book in the neo-Babylonian period (626–539 BC), suggested to some extent by the book itself and maintained through most of the history of exegesis, is open to a number of serious objections drawn from the book and from elsewhere in the OT. The author was not familiar with the history of the neo-Babylonian period, but he is very familiar with the history of the Seleucid* and Ptolemaic* kingdoms just before the outbreak of the Maccabean wars. This is most easily explained on the assumption that he depended for his knowledge of the neo-Babylonian period on vague memories which had been handed down by oral tradition. Thus he makes Belshazzar* the son of Nebuchadnezzar, although Belshazzar was the son of Nabonidus and was never king of Babylon. The author shows no knowledge of any other Babylonian rulers. The successor of Belshazzar and the first Persian king is called Darius* the Mede, a figure otherwise unknown to history; Babylonian records begin the reign of Cyrus with the end of the reign of Nabonidus. An examination of the vision of Dn 11 shows that the information of the author is exact up to a point between 167, the year in which Antiochus Epiphanes departed on an expedition of Egypt, and 164, the year of his death, which had not yet occurred when the passage was written. Modern critics generally agree that the composition of the book in its present form is to be placed within these few years. The book is quoted in 1 Mc 2:59-60; the composition of 1 Mc is to be placed near 100 BC. Daniel is not mentioned in the praise of the fathers of Ben Sira (BS 44:1 ff), written about 180 BC, and this is most easily explained by the assumption that the book had not yet been written. In the Hb Bible Dn appears not with the prophetic books but in the third division of the Bible, the Writings; since this division of the Hb Bible most probably represents three different stages of acceptance of the sacred book (cf CANON), it is again a legitimate assumption that Dn did not exist when the prophetic books were accepted into the canon.

II. *Language.* The language of Dn creates a peculiar difficulty. 1:1–2:3 + 8:1–12:13 are written in Hb; 2:4–7:28 are written in Aramaic; 13–14 are preserved in Gk, and ch 13 at least was probably written in that language. There is no generally accepted explanation of both Hb and Aramaic in the book. Many scholars see in this a merely mechanical difference; it is supposed that the Hb original of the Aramaic portion was lost and replaced by an Aramaic translation. A more complicated theory proposed by H. H. Rowley sees in the Aramaic section a collection of preexisting stories of Daniel which the author of the book in its present form incorporated with his own compositions, chs 8–12. The introduction, originally in Aramaic, was translated into Hb by this author, who lived in Maccabean times, in order to unify the book more closely. The Aramaic section includes some Gk words for musical instruments (cf MUSIC), which would place this part of the book in the Gk period and not in the neo-Babylonian period.

III. *Purpose and Literary Form.* An examination of the material of the book (cf below) indicates that the purpose of its composition was to furnish consolation and encouragement for the Jews during the persecution of Antiochus Epiphanes. It is extremely probable that the author of the book did not invent the character of Daniel entirely but took a figure existing in popular tradition; and some of the book, especially the first part, may contain folklore tales of Daniel. For the author of the book and for his readers it was of little importance whether Daniel was a historical figure or not, since any historical character he may have had has been lost both in oral tradition and in the composition of the book. The character of Daniel as he is presented in Dn is truly fictional. The book is the first

OT specimen of apocalyptic* literature, which is foreshadowed in some parts of Is and Ezk.

IV. *Outline of the book.* The book falls into three major divisions: 1–6, the adventures of Daniel; 7–12, the visions of Daniel; 13–14 additional adventures of Daniel. The last two chapters are deuterocanonical, i.e., they are not preserved in Hb and are not found in the Bible of Jews and Protestants.

First part, the adventures of Daniel.

1:1–21: the election of Daniel and his companions, Hananiah*, Mishael*, and Azariah* (Shadrach*, Meshach*, and Abednego*) for service in the king's household. Their refusal to eat unclean foods results in their looking fatter and fairer than their associates who eat the foods prepared by the king's kitchen. This encouraged the Jews of Maccabean times, who were forbidden by the decrees of Antiochus to observe the laws of cleanliness (cf CLEAN).

2:1–49: the dream of Nebuchadnezzar. Nebuchadnezzar in a dream saw a statue with a head of gold, breast and arms of silver, belly and thighs of bronze, legs of iron, and feet of iron mixed with clay. A stone hewn from a mountain by no human hands struck this statue and broke it into pieces. The wise men of Babylon could not interpret the dream; Daniel, however, interpreted it as the dream of four kingdoms, symbolized by the various parts of the statue. Of these the kingdom of Nebuchadnezzar was the first, symbolized by the golden head. The stone was the messianic kingdom of God, erected without human power, which would destroy the kingdoms of the world. The other kingdoms are not explained by Daniel, but interpreters commonly see in the silver the kingdom of the Medes, in the bronze the Persian empire, in the iron the kingdom of Alexander*, and in the iron and clay the successor kingdoms of the Seleucid* and Ptolemaic* dynasties.

3:1–30 (Hb), 1–100 (Gk): Nebuchadnezzar made a great statue of gold and ordered all his subjects to adore it when musical instruments were played as a signal. The three companions of Daniel, who does not appear in this story, refused to obey and were cast into a furnace. They were untouched by the flame; and the king, convinced by this miracle, ordered those who had charged them with the crime to be cast into the furnace. The episode encourages the Jews of Maccabean times not to worship the gods of the Greeks, and assures them that God will preserve them. "The Song of the Three Children in the Fiery Furnace" (3:24–90) is preserved only in Gk and is not found in Hb and Protestant Bibles.

4:1–34: the madness of Nebuchadnezzar.

Nebuchadnezzar dreamed of a tree which was cut down. Its stump was bound with iron, but after seven years it grew once more. Daniel interpreted this dream as a revelation that Nebuchadnezzar would suffer for seven years from the form of insanity in which he would be like a wild beast (known today as boanthropy). After Nebuchadnezzar lived like an ox for seven years, he was restored to sanity and confessed that the God of Daniel was the true God. This madness of Nebuchadnezzar is not attested by profane historians, but scholars believe it is not impossible. The narrative shows that God can humble even the greatest power of the earth, which cannot recover from its fall unless it confesses His divinity. A fragment of a prayer of Nabonidus discovered at Qumran* tells of a very similar episode and suggests that Dn drew on this source, altering the name from the unknown Nabonidus to the famous Nebuchadnezzar.

5:1–30: the feast of Belshazzar. Belshazzar, the last king of Babylon in Dn, had a great dinner at which he and his guests profaned the sacred vessels of the temple. A hand appeared and wrote three words on the wall, which Daniel interpreted as "Mene, Tekel, Peres" (Aramaic m^{c}nē t^{c}ḵēl uparsīn, "measured, weighed, and divided") and applied to the kingdom of Belshazzar. That night the kingdom was taken by the Persians and Belshazzar was killed. The story shows that God predicts the downfall of powers hostile to His people.

6:1–29: Daniel in the lions' den. Under Darius the Mede Daniel violated a law of the Medes and Persians prohibiting prayer to any one except the king for 30 days, and was thrown into a den of lions. They did not harm him, and Darius, recognizing the miracle, had his accusers thrown into the lions' den. This story also shows that God protects His faithful in times of persecution like those of Antiochus Epiphanes, when prayer to Yahweh was forbidden.

Second part, the visions of Daniel.

7:1–28: the four beasts and the son of man. Daniel saw four beasts coming from the sea. These beasts signify the Babylonian empire, the kingdom of the Medes, the Persian empire, and the empire of Alexander. The ten horns of the fourth beast signify ten kings of the Seleucid dynasty and the little horn is Antiochus Epiphanes. The son of man* in Dn probably does not signify the Messiah* as an individual person but rather the saints of God, the people of Israel as a whole, which shall descend from heaven (a symbol of its election) and take the dominion from the kingdoms of the world.

8:1–27: the vision of the ram and the goat. This vision is explained by the angel Gabriel*. The ram with the two horns signifies the kingdom of the Medes and the Persians. The goat is the kingdom of the Greeks and the great horn is Alexander. The four others are the four successor kingdoms of Alexander, and the last horn is the Seleucid dynasty, most probably Antiochus Epiphanes himself. In this vision the time during which the sanctuary will be profaned is set at 2300 days. This may be compared with the period of a year, two years, and a half a year in 7:25. Probably these differences have no mystical significance, but are revisions to accord with the progress of the Maccabean revolt.

9:1–27: the prophecy of the 70 weeks. This vision arises from Daniel's wonder about the 70 years of Babylonian dominion predicted by Jeremiah* (25:12). In answer Daniel learns from the angel Gabriel that the 70 years signify 70 weeks of years (490 years) and that Daniel himself is now in the last and most crucial of the weeks; the time of the end is near. The prophecy of Jeremiah signified 70 years in the sense of an indefinite time, the life of a single person; no one then living would survive to see the end of the Babylonian dominion. Implicit is the difficulty real to the writer, but not in the time of Daniel, that the Babylonian empire was succeeded by others. Seventy weeks of 7 years signify an even longer indefinite time and not an exact period; by no calculation can the term 490 years from the beginning of the Babylonian dominion (605 BC) be brought into agreement either with the Maccabean or with the NT period. In 7:25, however, the beginning of the 70 weeks is reckoned from the decree permitting the rebuilding of Jerusalem (537 BC), which ignores the 70 years indicated in Je. This would place the end of the period at 47 BC, a date of no significance. The author of the book had no information on the number of years which had elapsed between the fall of Jerusalem and his own time.

10:1–11:45: the conflict of kingdoms. After a long introduction which includes a debate between the angels who preside over the destinies of nations, the history of the period from Alexander's conquest of Persia (331 BC) to the reign of Antiochus Epiphanes prior to his death (163 BC) is summed up in some detail (11:2–45). With a knowledge of the history of the period it is easy to identify the characters and events of the passage, which are not named by the author. This is a prophecy *ex eventu* and is a type which appears nowhere else in the OT; it is a technique of apocalyptic literature to relate contemporary events in the form of a revelation made to some hero of remote antiquity.

12:1-13: the vision of the end. At the end, after a period of great troubles, the dead will rise, some to life and some to everlasting reproach. This is the earliest expression of belief in the resurrection of both the righteous and the wicked. The time of the end appears to be near, but when Daniel asks when the end shall be he hears that the book is sealed; this cannot be told him. The time of the desecration of the holy place is once more set at 1290 days. The man is blessed who awaits the end after 1335 days; what the author expected at the end of this period cannot be determined.

Third part, additional adventures of Daniel.

13:1-64: the story of Susanna*. A Jewish woman of Babylon, named Susanna, accused of adultery by two lecherous elders, was delivered by Daniel, who trapped the elders in contradictory evidence. The dialogue with the elders contains puns of the Gk names of two trees (13:54-55, 58-59). The story is an example of the wisdom of Daniel.

14:1-42: Bel and the dragon. Under Cyrus Daniel proves that the food and drink set before the image of Bel is eaten secretly by his priests. A serpent worshiped at Babylon was killed by Daniel. Daniel was cast into the lions' den (a doublet of 6) where he was fed by the prophet Habakkuk, who was carried from Palestine by an angel. Daniel's escape from the lions led Cyrus to confess that the God of Israel is the true God.

Modern readers of the Bible find the type of comfort and encouragement offered by such apocalyptic writings unsympathetic. It is difficult for them to understand that the author intends to affirm the attributes of God which are exhibited in his stories and visions. Neither to him nor to his readers did it make much difference whether the events related were historical or not; for God truly possesses these attributes and does exhibit them. If they are faithful to His law and confident in His power, they can be assured that He will exhibit His power to deliver them from danger or from falling into sin under the threat of this danger. This is the sentiment uttered in the magnificent response of the three companions of Daniel to Nebuchadnezzar (3:16-18).

Daniel in the NT. Dn is quoted only once in the NT; the abomination of desolation* is mentioned in the apocalyptic discourse of Jesus (Mt 24:15; Mk 13:14). The resurrection of the dead is described in Mt 25:46 in terms taken from Dn 12:2. Most important is the phrase son of man* (Dn 7:13).

Daphne (Gk *daphnē*), a suburb of Antioch* which contained a grove and temples of Apollo and Artemis with rights of sanctuary. The suburb was named after the nymph of mythology loved by Apollo. Here the high priest Onias* took refuge after he had rebuked Menelaus* for bribing Andronicus* with the sacred vessels of the temple. He was treacherously persuaded to leave the sanctuary by Menelaus and was then executed by Andronicus (2 Mc 4:33).

Daric. Cf MONEY.

Darius (Hb *dārᵉyāweš*, from Persian *darjawaush,* meaning uncertain), the name of three Persian kings: Darius I Hystaspis (522-485 BC); Darius II Nothos (424-404 BC); Darius III Codomannus (336-330 BC). Darius I at his accession had to suppress a widespread revolt led by the usurper Gautama, who pretended to be Smerdis, the son of Cambyses. Darius organized the Persian empire into 20 satrapies and was the first monarch to put his image on gold coins (daric). The latter part of his reign was devoted to the campaigns to subdue Greece. He succeeded in suppressing the revolt of the Ionian cities but failed in his campaign against Athens. His fleet was wrecked by a storm off Mount Athos in 492 and his armies, after conquering Thessaly and winning the victory of Thermopylae, were defeated by the Athenians and their allies at Marathon (490).

The discourses of Haggai are dated in the 2nd year of Darius I (Hg 1:1, 15; 2:10), and the discourses of Zechariah are dated in the 2nd and 4th years of Darius (Zc 1:1, 7; 7:1). The building of the temple, which had been permitted by Cyrus*, was interrupted by the machinations of the neighbors of the Jews until the 2nd year of Darius I (Ezr 4:24). A letter from Tattenai*, governor of the province "beyond the river," laid the complaint before the king that the Jews were rebuilding the city and the temple and asked that the permission they claimed be verified. The obstruction was probably connected with the troubles at the beginning of the reign of Darius. A copy of the decree of Cyrus permitting the rebuilding of the temple was found in the records at Ecbatana*; consequently, Darius ordered that the temple be completed without any further hindrance (Ezr 5:1 ff). The temple was completed in the 6th year of Darius I (Ezr 6:15). Darius I is the king mentioned in Ne 12:22.

According to Dn Darius the Mede was the first Persian king of Babylon, the successor of Belshazzar* (Dn 6:1 ff). He cast Daniel into the lions' den (Dn 6:6 ff).

The vision of Dn 9:1 ff is dated in the first year of Darius, the son of Ahasuerus* (Xerxes), the Mede; obviously the same person is intended. The first year of Darius in Dn 11:1 is regarded by modern critics as a gloss. To this Darius is attributed the organization of the empire in satrapies (Dn 6:2 ff), and Daniel was one of the three presidents of the satraps; this organization was the work of Darius I Hystaspis, the successor of Cambyses. Some scholars have attempted to identify Darius the Mede with known historical characters such as Cambyses, the son of Cyrus, or Cyaxares II, but none of these hypotheses have any probability. The author had very little information about the neo-Babylonian period (cf DANIEL), and it is most probable that the name Darius was known to him and that he incorporated Darius into his writing; but he had no idea of the date at which Darius reigned, nor even of the order in which the Persian kings followed each other.

Darkness. The metaphorical use of darkness is common in both OT and NT.

1. *OT.* Darkness was the element of chaos; the primeval abyss lay under darkness, and God's first creative act was to dispel darkness by the intrusion of light (Gn 1:2 ff; cf CREATION). In Gn 1:2 the mythological character of darkness is somewhat suppressed, for God calls the darkness night and ordains the regular succession of day and night. So also God stores darkness in a chamber that He may bring it out in due time (Jb 38:19; cf also Ps 104:20). But since darkness is the element of chaos, it is also the element of evil and disorder, and it retains in its metaphorical usage some of its mythological symbolism. Darkness is disaster (Is 5:30). In the world catastrophe the sun itself is darkened in its rising (Is 13:10). Darkness is one of the plagues with which Yahweh smites Egypt (Ex 10:22). The supreme disaster is darkness at noon (Am 8:9). The day of Yahweh, which in popular belief was the day of the great deliverance of Israel, would be darkness and not light (Am 5:18 ff; Zp 1:15 ff). Darkness is ready at hand for the wicked (Jb 15:23). The kingdom of Judah is like a traveler who is overtaken by darkness in the mountains; he stumbles and perishes (Je 13:16). Darkness is defeat, captivity, oppression (Is 9:1; 42:7; 47:5). Darkness is the element of evil, in which the wicked does his work (Jb 24:16; Ezk 8:12). Darkness is the element of death, the grave, and the underworld (Jb 10:21 f; 17:13). Light* is the element of deity, and it is an exception when Yahweh is said to set His dwelling in darkness (2 S 22:12; 1 K 8:12;

Ps 18:12). Here we have an allusion to the clouds* of the storm theophany*; Yahweh must veil His light when He appears, for no man can look upon it and live. The OT imagery of darkness is also found in the Qumran document called "The War of the Sons of Light and the Sons of Darkness."

2. *NT.* The same metaphors of darkness are used in the NT. The eye which is not simple in its intentions darkens the whole soul within (Mt 6:23). Sinners shall be cast out into the darkness (Mt 8:12; 22:13; 25:30). The catastrophic darkness of the eschatological judgment is mentioned in Mt 24:29; Mk 13:24. The antithesis of light and darkness is especially prominent in Jn. Darkness is the sinful world into which the light of the Incarnate Word shines, but the darkness does not receive the light (Jn 1:5). He who follows Jesus does not walk in darkness (Jn 8:12; also Jn 12:46). God is light and there is no darkness in Him (1 Jn 1:5). Men love darkness more than the light (Jn 3:19). In Paul darkness is wickedness (Rm 13:12; 2 Co 6:14). Christians who were once darkness are now light in the Lord (Eph 5:8), and should have no share in the works of darkness (Eph 5:11). The world is darkness (Eph 6:12). Christ has saved us from the power of darkness (Col 1:13). Darkness is reserved for the wicked (2 Pt 2:17).

Date, date palm. The date palm, Hb *tāmār*, does not grow in the highlands of Palestine and is found only in the subtropical regions S of Gaza and in the Jordan valley. The tree grows to a height of 50–60 ft and is crowned by a plume of branches at the summit. The trees are mentioned as growing at the oasis of Elim (Ex 15:27; Nm 33:9) and are enumerated among the trees of the country (Jl 1:12). Palm branches were carried in procession at the feast of Tabernacles* (Lv 23:40; Ne 8:15) and in triumphal processions (1 Mc 13:51; Apc 7:9). It is as signs of triumph that they were carried in the procession which accompanied Jesus into Jerusalem (Jn 12:13). Figures of palm trees appeared in the decorations of the temple (1 K 6:29, 32, 35; 7:36; 2 Ch 3:5; Ezk 40:16–41:26). Palm branches with a gold crown were a token of peace and friendship between peoples (1 Mc 13:37; 2 Mc 14:4). The righteous in his prosperity is compared to a palm tree (Ps 92:13), and the beloved is compared to a palm tree in an erotic image (SS 7:8 f).

Dathan (Hb *dātān*, meaning unknown), the son of Eliab of the tribe of Reuben, who with his brother Abiram and Korah the Levite rebelled against the leadership of

Moses (Nm 16:1 ff). The dialogue of Moses and Korah (Nm 16:3-11) and the dialogue of Moses with Dathan and Abiram (Nm 16:12-16) are independent of each other; so also are the accounts of the punishments of the party of Dathan and Abiram (Nm 16:27b-32) and of the party of Korah (Nm 16:35), except for the introduction of Korah in Nm 16:24, 27, 32. Hence many scholars believe that the chapter has fused two accounts of two distinct rebellions. The rebellion of Korah and his party was a rebellion of the Levites against the exclusive priesthood* of the family of Aaron* (Nm 16:3); the rebellion of Dathan and Abiram was a rebellion against the leadership of Moses and a refusal to follow him into the land of Canaan (Nm 16:13-14). The punishment of the two parties differs; the party of Dathan and Abiram was swallowed up in an earthquake (Nm 16:31-32), the party of Korah was struck by lightning (Nm 16:35). Dathan and Abiram are mentioned in a genealogy of Nm 26:9. The rebellion of Dathan and Abiram (without any mention of Korah) is alluded to in Dt 11:6; Ps 106:17. All three names occur in the allusion of BS 45:18.

David (Hb *dāwīd*, formerly explained as *dôd* or *dôdô*, "beloved," possibly a divine title; a connection with Hurrian* *dawidum*, "commander-in-chief," found in the Mari* correspondence is improbable). Some suggest that *dāwīd* was the title of this Israelite ruler and that his personal name was Elhanan* (2 S 21:20). David was the son of Jesse* of Bethlehem* and the successor of Saul* as king of Israel*. The genealogy in Rt 4:18 ff connects Jesse with Perez* of Judah* through Ram, Amminadab, Nahshon, Salmon, Boaz, and Obed. Some have suggested that this genealogy is artificial, formed by adoption of the clan into the tribe of Judah, and that the family of David was of non-Israelite origin. David first appears in 1 S 16:1-13; although the youngest of eight sons of Jesse he is anointed king by Samuel as the choice of Yahweh Himself. This story authenticated the charismatic title of David to rule; like Saul and the judges* he was divinely elected. In the following episodes David is introduced to Saul as a musician (1 S 16:14 ff) and as the youthful hero who slays Goliath with a sling and a stone (1 S 17:1 ff). These two anecdotes are independent of each other, since each supposes that David is introduced to Saul for the first time. The inconcinnity of chs 16 and 17 has been removed in Codex B (Vaticanus) of the LXX, which omits 17:12-31. As a result of his musical skill David becomes Saul's squire; as the slayer of Goliath

he becomes a popular military hero who arouses Saul's envy. In 1 S 18-20 are related the stories of David at the court of Saul. Saul's envy is apparent in his sudden attempt to murder David (1 S 18:10 ff and 19:9 ff, variant accounts of the same episode). David was given Michal, the daughter of Saul, in marriage. Merab, the elder daughter, had been promised, but the promise was not honored by Saul. Michal was granted as the prize of a feat of valor against the Philistines which, Saul expected, would cost David his life (1 S 18:25 ff); but David appears throughout the story as the man of destiny. David was the close friend of Jonathan*, Saul's son and presumed successor, who saved David from his father's anger (1 S 19:1 ff); but another outburst of Saul's hostility forced David to flee, this time with the aid of Michal (1 S 19:11 ff). Even the members of Saul's own family assist the man whose destiny it is to establish his dynasty in place of their own, as Saul says to Jonathan (1 S 20:30 f). Jonathan's intercession did not restore David to favor, and David had to become a fugitive.

The course of events by which David came into royal favor, achieved fame, and then incurred Saul's hostility and became a fugitive, is fairly clear in spite of the fact that the stories are independent of each other and in some instances duplicate each other. For example, at 1 S 20:35 ff the signal of the arrows is employed according to the previous agreement because a personal meeting would be so dangerous as to be practically impossible. In the present text, the pathetic personal meeting, which must have been independent of the story of the arrows, follows immediately. After David fled from Saul he became a bandit (1 S 21-31); the ancient stories state this frankly without glossing it, something which a number of modern writers, anxious lest David's sanctity be tarnished, cannot bring themselves to do. David first fled to the sanctuary of Nob*, where he was refreshed and armed by Ahimelech* the priest. David then attempted to take service with the Philistines*, the enemies of Israel; but they would not trust the great Israelite hero and he had to flee into the desert of Judah. At the cave of Adullam* he gathered a band of about 400 men, discontented, debtors, rebels against Saul. These were the nucleus of what became a band of professional soldiers who supported David for the rest of his career. He secured the safety of his parents by sending them to Moab* (1 S 22:3 ff); this episode is one of the factors which lead some modern scholars to think that the family of David was not Israelite in origin. In asking hospitality from Ahimelech David had not disclosed the enmity of Saul. When Ahimelech's kindness was reported to Saul by Doeg*, Saul, whose madness was now apparent, had all the priests of Nob slain. Abiathar* alone escaped to David with the ephod*. Saul pursued David through the desert* of Judah. The men of Keilah* and of Ziph* were willing to betray David to Saul (1 S 23:10 ff, 19 ff); the betrayal by the men of Ziph is duplicated in 1 S 26:1 ff. On two occasions David trapped Saul in a cave (1 S 24:4 ff; 26:2 ff) and spared his life; these two stories again are probably variant accounts of one incident. In each story Saul admits he is wrong and seeks reconciliation; but no reconciliation is made, and the subsequent stories show no evidence of any acquaintance with these stories of David's magnanimity. During David's bandit career he fell in with a rich man of Carmel* named Nabal*, the husband of Abigail*. This incident illustrates the life of the bandit. David's offer of protection to Nabal, an offer no doubt made to many rich men, was nothing but a veiled form of extortion. When the offer was refused, David was ready to wipe out Nabal and his entire house. This murderous design was averted by the sagacity of Abigail, who married David shortly after the sudden death of Nabal, attributed to the shock of hearing of his narrow escape; but historians have long been suspicious of Abigail, who brought the rich estates of Nabal to David.

David finally took service with Achish* of Gath* as a mercenary of the Philistines (1 S 27:1 ff) and received for his service Ziklag* in the south of Judah; the story explains why Ziklag was the personal property of the king even to the time of the narrator. David's raids on the nomads of the desert were explained by him to his Philistine overlord as raids upon the territory of Judah; Hebrew tradition rejected the idea that the great Israelite hero had ever preyed upon his own people, which he was willing to do in the affair of Nabal, and which he could scarcely have avoided in the service of the Philistines. An even greater crisis awaited David in the mobilization of the Philistine forces against Saul. Achish wished to include David and his men with his own contingent, but the other Philistine commanders still did not trust him and insisted that he return. David found that the Amalekites* had raided his city of Ziklag; he pursued them and recovered the captives and the booty. The story attributes the Israelite policy of dividing the booty equally between those who fight in combat and those who guard the base to an ordinance of David in this campaign (1 S 30:24 f). The same ordinance is attributed to Moses in Nm

31:27, a composition of probably much later origin. Thus through no device of his own David was relieved of the necessity of taking part in the battle in which Saul and his sons were killed and Israel badly defeated. Had he been engaged in this battle, unless he turned against the Philistines, he could scarcely have presented himself to his people as the savior of Israel.

In the confusion which followed this defeat David let events guide him. He refused to accept the death of Saul as good news (2 S 1:13 ff). He accepted the kingship of Judah when elected by the men of Judah and took residence at Hebron (2 S 2:4 ff); he could not have taken this office except as a vassal of the Philistines. Probably this Philistine connection had its part in the war which dragged out between David and the remnant of the Israelite kingdom under Ishbaal*, the son of Saul (2 S 2:8 ff). David gradually prevailed over Ishbaal, and the fall of the house of Saul was certain when Abner*, insulted by Ishbaal, determined to transfer the allegiance of Israel from Ishbaal to David. Although Abner was murdered by Joab*, who feared that his own influence with David would be lessened, David accepted the betrayal of Abner. Again, however, he refused to accept the murder of Ishbaal by two bandit chieftains (2 S 4:5 ff); he punished them, but he was now the only candidate for the monarchy of Israel. He was elected to this office by all the tribes (2 S 5:1 ff).

The two most important steps in the consolidation of David's monarchy were the capture of Jerusalem and the defeat of the Philistines. The remaining records of both these events are incomplete and it is impossible to establish a chronological relation between them. As a royal residence Jerusalem had the advantage not only of a strong natural site but also of a location in neutral territory; it was not Israelite, associated with neither David's tribe of Judah nor Saul's kingdom, lying between Judah and Benjamin. The war with the Philistines is related only in a few fragments (2 S 5: 17 ff; 21:15 ff). It is evident from the subsequent course of Israelite history that the Philistines were never again a serious military threat. We cannot trace David's victory; but the Israelites probably outnumbered the Philistines and needed only strong unified leadership and equality in armament and tactics. David made Jerusalem not only his royal residence where he built his palace (2 S 5:11 ff) with the help of Hiram* of Tyre but also the religious center of Israel. The ark* of the covenant had been neglected since its failure to assist the Israelites in their war against the Philistines before the accession of Saul. David now took this ancient symbol of Israelite unity and brought it to his new capital. The untimely death of Uzzah* in the procession of the ark halted the festivities briefly and caused a postponement of the entrance of the ark; but a three months' experiment relieved his fear. The introduction of the ark into Jerusalem was the occasion of an estrangement between David and Michal; she found the vigor of David's dancing too undignified for a king. In return David excluded her from his bed for the rest of her life (2 S 6:20 ff).

There is no reason to question with some modern scholars the desire of David to build a fitting temple for the ark (2 S 7:1 ff). We know of no Israelite temple before this date; but it is unlikely that David while building himself a palace would continue to house the symbol of Yahweh's presence in a tent. Nathan* agreed when he was first consulted, but subsequently asserted that it was not the will of Yahweh that David himself should build the temple. He promised David in the name of Yahweh an eternal dynasty (2 S 7:8–16). This oracle, preserved at greater length in Ps 89:20 ff, is the root of the messianic character of David and his house (cf MESSIAH), which later took shape in the belief that a deliverer from David's house would effect the final and lasting deliverance of Israel; this belief in turn is at the base of the Christian belief in the redeeming work of Jesus Christ; cf Rm 1:3, part of an early credal formula. Other wars of David are mentioned briefly in 2 S 8:1 ff; 10:1–19; 12:26–31. It is evident from these brief notices that David established a little Israelite empire. This was possible only because of the power vacuum caused by the weakness of Egypt and Mesopotamia. David conquered the Moabites (2 S 8:2 ff), with whom he had been on friendly terms earlier, and treated the captives barbarously, killing two out of three. One may suppose that a dynastic change in Moab was responsible for the change of attitude between David and the Moabite ruler. He also defeated Hadadezer*, king of the Aramaean kingdom of Zobah*, NE of Israelite territory, Damascus*, which David garrisoned, and Edom* (2 S 8:13–14). David exacted tribute from the Moabites and the Aramaean kingdoms; the Edomites and the Ammonites were reduced to forced labor. He formed an alliance with Toi*, king of Hamath* in Syria*, who saw the wisdom of alliance rather than conquest.

The most complete record of David's life is the "family history" in 2 S 9–20. Most modern scholars believe this account was written by a contemporary eyewitness. The war with the Ammonites was the occasion of David's adultery with Bathsheba*. According to 2 S 21:15–17 David's officers were unwilling that he should expose himself in war, and thus he found himself in Jerusalem while Uriah* his neighbor, the husband of Bathsheba, was campaigning. The murder of Uriah was necessary to protect Bathsheba from the penalty of adultery for the pregnancy which followed the adultery. The son died, but the second son of Bathsheba was Solomon*. The family history of David makes this the turning point of David's life. It takes David at the point where his success is greatest both in external and internal affairs. He sins and is rebuked by Nathan; but the death of the child is only the beginning of his punishment. From this point his life is one unbroken series of misfortunes: Amnon's* rape of Tamar* and incest with her (2 S 13:1 ff), the murder of Amnon by Absalom* in revenge for the rape (2 S 13:21 ff), the exile of Absalom ended by the intercession of Joab. Absalom, who now expected to succeed, planned to usurp power before his father died (2 S 15:1 ff) and succeeded by political maneuvering in winning a sufficient number of the people and the royal officers so that David had to flee from Jerusalem when the rebellion was proclaimed in Hebron. The sudden and wide success of the rebellion suggests not only that Absalom and his associates were mendacious, but also that there were some less agreeable features of David's rule which have not been preserved in our traditions — perhaps something like the "heavy galling yoke" of Solomon (2 S 12:4). David fled E of the Jordan where he was able to organize his forces. It seems likely that the people of Hebron, possibly of all Judah, and of Jerusalem — probably non-Israelite — favored the rebellion; but it is difficult to say that the entire kingdom did. The professional soldiers were loyal to David; as soon as David could mobilize them, Absalom's forces were defeated. David's order to preserve the life of Absalom was not obeyed by Joab. To the story of the rebellion of Absalom is attached the story of a rebellion of some of the northern tribes under Sheba* ben Bichri, of Benjamin (2 S 20:1 ff). We need not suppose that this rebellion followed immediately upon the rebellion of Absalom, as it does in the narrative. Both rebellions show us that David's monarchy and empire did not rest upon the true internal unity of the people. This is borne out by the events which followed the death of his son Solomon.

Some of the misfortunes of David's reign which Hebrew tradition has preserved have been brought together in 2 S 24 in connection with the census. We cannot tell at what point in David's reign he took the census; some scholars think it is the census preserved in Nm. The census was unpopular because it was taken to determine sources of tax revenue, military service, and forced labor; and many Israelites thought it was challenging God to count one's blessings so explicitly. Hence Gad* offered David a choice of three years of famine, three months of flight from his enemies, or three days of pestilence. All three of these actually occurred; the pestilence in the story of the census, the three years of famine in 2 S 21, and the flight before Absalom. Here the history of David has been reconstructed theologically. The three years' famine was popularly attributed to the failure of the Israelite rulers to expiate the blood* guilt incurred by the house of Saul for Saul's violation of the ancient treaty with Gibeon*. An oracular response demanded that David, according to the principle of blood guilt, deliver the surviving men of the house of Saul to the Gibeonites, which he did with one exception. The famine ended with the execution of the men of the house of Saul.

In 1 K 1:1 ff David is represented as prematurely aged, while his associates and contemporaries like Nathan and Joab were still vigorous. Adonijah, the eldest surviving son of David, expected to succeed his father and began to conduct himself as king. We observe that Nathan, who had rebuked David for his adultery with Bathsheba, had now joined the party of Bathsheba and Solomon; they were supported also by Benaiah*, the commander of the royal guard, and the priest Zadok*. With Adonijah were Joab and Abiathar the priest. Bathsheba, urged by Nathan, reminded David of his oath that Solomon should succeed him; actually there is no evidence outside of Bathsheba's testimony that David had ever taken such an oath. David honored the commitment and had Solomon installed as coregent. This interrupted the coronation festivities of Adonijah and put Adonijah and all his supporters at the mercy of Solomon. The "last will" of David (1 K 2:1 ff) in which he commits to Solomon the execution of blood vengeance on Joab and Shimei* is questioned by some modern scholars as an effort to throw the guilt of this violence from Solomon to David. But Hebrew tradition moves in the opposite direction; we can trace in it efforts to remove from David some more obvious blemishes. It is far more likely that the attribution of these acts of vengeance to David's wish represents an authentic tradition; nor would they be regarded as blameworthy in the society of the blood feud (cf AVENGER).

The books of Chronicles* base their account of David on the stories of Samuel and Kings and seem to have no other source. The story of David has been edited by the omission of some disagreeable features; his bandit life, his adultery with Bathsheba, the murder of Uriah, and his family troubles are not included. The Chronicler adds some information about the preparation and plans for the building of the temple and for its worship (1 Ch 22:1 — 28:21). In particular David is credited with the organization of the Levitical* choirs and some other Levitical offices. This seems to be a claim of antiquity for the Levitical choirs; they did not claim, like the priesthood, to be of Mosaic institution. The Chronicler explains David's failure to build the temple as due to Yahweh's unwillingness to have the temple built by a man who had shed so much blood (1 Ch 22:8 f). This rationalization is not found in 2 S 7. To what extent David made plans and gathered material for the temple cannot be exactly determined; there is no reason to doubt the tradition that he did, but the details come from the free reconstruction of the past in the style of the books of Chronicles.

The fragmentary nature of our sources about David makes it difficult to evaluate his character with accuracy and fairness. We must not attribute to him the piety of the Psalms*, of which 73 bear his name in the title. David can be the author of no more than a very few of these compositions. While in many instances the type of piety expressed in the Pss is suitable for David, in many others the expressions of devotion are surprising in the mouth of the lusty turbulent warrior and bandit chieftain. David's predominant feature is violence — perhaps no more than was characteristic in his age and culture, but scarcely less. He shows no more respect for human life than his contemporaries of Canaan or Mesopotamia. From his childhood he is accustomed to violence, to a life of defense and aggression. The stories of David exhibit not only physical violence but the violence of passion, the blazing anger which would destroy Nabal and his house and the flame of desire which took the willing Bathsheba after a single glance. Like all Oriental potentates David kept a numerous harem. There is no more than poetic justice in the violence which cursed him and his sons and took all happiness from the latter half of his life. David could command loyalty; most of his followers stayed with him from his early years to his latest. Self-interest may have been involved, but very few of his old associates abandoned him for Absalom.

It has been questioned whether David returned the loyalty which he received. Many historians have refused to believe that he was as innocent of the murders which advanced his career as Hebrew tradition has made him. But the stories have a consistent pattern; and while one must marvel at the consistency with which obstacles were removed, one may not manufacture evidence to verify a suspicion. David did not remain loyal to his own people when he passed into the service of the Philistines as a mercenary. On the other hand, one must remember that the concept of a "people" to whom loyalty was owed was not clear at that time; and the king, who was identical with the people in ancient monarchies, had rejected David. Many modern writers credit David with an extraordinary degree of political skill and astuteness. David was successful; he rose from shepherd boy to king, and while it is true that events favored his advancement, one must admit that he was able to recognize opportunity and, if he could not foster it positively, he knew how to avoid any steps which would spoil it. But there were certain limitations on his political skill. The rebellion of Absalom seems to have taken David entirely unaware; and this rebellion revealed weaknesses in his control of some of his close associates, and an even more glaring loss of contact with the people at large. One must credit him with the creation of a united Israel; neither he nor any other found a principle of lasting unity.

The religion of David is of a piece with his morality. Both are the religion and the morality of a simple, ambitious and violent man, who is easily convinced that Yahweh is on his side and he on the side of Yahweh, that the cause of Yahweh and of His people are one with his own cause, and who is scarcely aware of any great demands which God makes of him. He is substantially faithful to those few demands of which he is aware.

It is necessary to have an accurate historical estimate of David because of the position which he occupies in Hebrew belief. Almost with the accession of Solomon David begins to appear as the ideal ruler of Israel. Certainly we cannot say that Hebrew tradition whitewashes him; 1–2 S, which are frank, and 1 Ch, which polishes him almost beyond recognition, are different types of literature. Hence we must realize that the concept of ideal king is to be understood in Hebrew terms. He is neither a moral ideal nor a religious ideal, nor even an ideal of success, since tradition preserved the memory of the rebellion of Absalom. He was the ideal king because he did better than any one else in Hebrew tradition what a king was expected to do. He created a united Israel, his military successes removed external danger and enriched his people and made it possible for the Israelite to sit under his vine and fig tree with none to terrify. None of his successors equaled him. The throne of Judah remained in Hebrew literature the throne of David. The authors and compilers measure succeeding kings of Judah against David and find them wanting.

David was promised an eternal dynasty in the oracle of Nathan because he best realized the ideal of kingship. His house would endure even if his successors were unworthy. The covenant of Yahweh with David would stand until it was fulfilled in another ruler who would be another and a greater David and who would establish the ideal kingdom of Yahweh. This future deliverer does not appear in the original oracle; the idea grew with the progress of time and the deterioration of the dynasty of David. If the dynasty were eternal, a greater than David would have to restore it. The ideal kingship of David is fundamental in the messianic belief of the OT (cf KING).

David is mentioned in the NT most frequently in the phrases "son of David" or "seed of David" spoken to Jesus or about Him. It is evident from Paul's references to the descent of Jesus from David (Rm 1:3; 2 Tm 2:8) that the royal descent was a key element in the messianic character of Jesus as seen in the primitive Church. The title appears in the gospel as given to Jesus by various individuals, in particular by those who sought a cure. The title must have messianic overtones, since the Gospels elsewhere express the Jewish conviction that the Messiah must be the son of David (Mt 22:45; Mk 12:35; Lk 20:41; Jn 7:42). The honorific title which could be given to any descendant of David grants that the person so addressed is eligible for the messianic claim; this must be its meaning in the context of the cures, as also in the reception of Jesus with palms on the Sunday before His death (Mt 21:9–15).

David, city of. Defined in 2 S 5:7, 9 (gloss) as "the citadel of Zion." This indicates the most ancient settlement of Jerusalem* or a part thereof. In 2 S 5:6 ff the "city of David" or "the citadel of Zion" is what David took from the Jebusites — presumably the whole city. The title is employed elsewhere to indicate the place where David brought the ark (2 S 6:10, 12, 16). It is mentioned most frequently as the place of the burial of the kings of Judah (1 K 2:10; 11:43; 15:8, 24; 22:50; 2 K 8:24; 9:28; 12:22; 14:20; 16:20 and parallels in 1–2 Ch). The breaches in the city of David were repaired in the time of Hezekiah (Is 22:9). On the extent of the city of David and of Zion cf JERUSALEM.

Solomon brought the daughter of the Pharaoh into the city of David until his palace should be finished (1 K 3:1). The ark was brought up to the temple from the city of David (1 K 8:1), and the daughter of Pharaoh went up to her own palace from the city of David (1 K 9:24).

Day. Day as signifying a period of 24 hours is found both in the OT and NT. The days of creation (Gn 1:5 ff) are reckoned "evening and morning, day x" (Gn 1:5, 8, 13, 19, 23). The Hebrews after the Exile* and in NT times, like the Babylonians, reckoned the day as beginning with sunset and extending to the following sunset (Sabbath rest, Ne 13:19; Passover and Mazzoth festival, Ex 12:6–10, 18). In earlier times the night was reckoned with the preceding day (Gn 19:34; Lv 7:15; 22:30; Jgs 19:4–9; 1 S 19:11). In popular speech day more commonly signifies the hours of daylight from sunrise to sunset. Day and night are contrasted as distinct realities in the creation account of Gn 1:4, where light* is separated from the darkness* of chaos and called day (cf Jb 38:12–20). The Mesopotamian division of daylight into 12 double hours and the night into three watches does not appear in the OT. In the NT the Jews had adopted the Greek division of the day into 12 hours from sunrise to sunset; the length of the hours varied according to the season of the year (Mt 20:3, 5, 6; Jn 11:9). Commonly also day is used to signify an appointed time, a season, or a period of time.

Day of the Lord, Day of Yahweh. The idea of the day of the Lord was a popular belief in preexilic Israelite religion. Neither its roots nor its form can be traced precisely. It first appears in Am 5:18–20 as a known popular belief which Amos takes for granted without explaining. From his brief description the day of the Lord which people desire will be in their own minds light and brightness; Amos assures them that it will be darkness and not light, blackness with no brightness in it. Amos thus incorporates this popular belief in his own prediction of the fall of Israel. If one argues from the inversion of the idea in prophetic literature one may assume that the day of the Lord was a day on which Yahweh would manifest Himself in His power and glory; in cosmic convulsions He would overturn all the enemies of Israel and establish His own people supreme. In its earliest form the Day of the Lord was probably the day of victory in the holy war* (G. von Rad). The prophets* adopt the popular imagery and apply it either to the judgment of Israel or the judgment of all mankind. The day of

Yahweh is probably the "evil day" of Am 6:3 and the "day" when the sun will set at noon and the earth will grow dark in broad daylight (Am 8:9). Yahweh has a day when He will be exalted and He will bring down all that is proud and high, all that is lofty and tall (Is 2:11 ff). The day of Yahweh is pitiless, a day of wrath and fierce anger; it makes the earth a desolation and destroys sinners from its face. There are cosmic convulsions; the stars disappear, the sun is darkened, and the moon does not shine (Is 13:9–10, a composition later than the 7th century). Zp describes the day of the Lord as a day of sacrifice, when crimes will be punished and cries of disaster will be heard all over Jerusalem. It is a day of wrath, of trouble and distress, of desolation and waste, darkness and gloom, cloud and blackness, trumpet and battle cry — language adopted by Jacopone da Todi in the *Dies Irae*. Some of the phrases of Zp are borrowed in Jl 2:2, and the cosmic catastrophes of the day of Yahweh are described in heightened colors in Jl 2:30–31. In Jl, however, the day of Yahweh is the beginning of deliverance for Zion and Jerusalem, but a day of judgment on the nations (Jl 4:14). This shift away from the emphasis of Amos back toward the early popular belief is seen also in Zc 14:1 ff; the day of Yahweh is a day when the nations shall be gathered to do battle against Jerusalem and shall be defeated and destroyed (cf Ezk 38–39; GOG). Thus even in the primitive popular belief in the day of Yahweh His cosmic dominion and His power and will to save and to judge were affirmed. In the prophetic writings the belief in these attributes is raised above a merely secular and national level to a point where Israel as well as the nations must face the salvation and the judgment of God according to a universal moral and religious standard. In the later prophetic writings Israel is expected to survive this judgment and to be vindicated as the people of God, not merely because they are the chosen people of Yahweh but because they have been morally and religiously tested.

In the NT the "day of the Son of Man" (Lk 17:24), the day when the Son of Man is manifested (Lk 17:30) as judge, is described in terms drawn from the OT day of Yahweh. It is doubtful that "my day" mentioned by Jesus in Jn 8:56 signifies the day of His manifestation as judge. In the context it is more easily understood as referring to the Incarnation. "The day of God" (2 Pt 3:12) on which the heavens shall be destroyed and elements melted in flames to be replaced by a new heaven and a new earth is likewise cast in OT language. On "the great day of God Almighty" a battle will take place between the demonic spirits and the heavenly hosts (Apc 16:14). The "Day of Jesus Christ" for which Christians must be prepared and for which God strengthens them (1 Co 1:8; Phl 1:6, 10) and on which Paul himself will boast of his Christian congregations (2 Co 1:14; Phl 2:16) can only be the day on which Jesus is manifested in His glory, the day when all shall be judged (cf PAROUSIA; JUDGMENT). This is "the day" which comes like a thief (1 Th 5:2, 4), the day which will manifest the works of each one, to be tried by fire (1 Co 3:13).

Deacon, Deaconess. (Gk *diakonos* and its cognates mean primarily one who serves at table). In some of the Gk papyri *diakonein trapezais* (AA 6:2) means to keep accounts. Both the noun and the verb are found in the NT (Lk 10:40; Jn 2:5, 9; AA 6:1 +). In a metaphorical sense the word may be translated minister or servant and is applied to the apostles* as ministers of the new covenant (2 Co 3:6), ministers of God (2 Co 6:4), ministers of justice (2 Co 11:15), of Christ (2 Co 11:23). Whether "the diversity of services" (1 Co 12:5) and the "service" mentioned with prophecy and teaching (Rm 12:7) indicate a distinct hierarchical office in the Church is open to question. These contexts do not suggest such an office. "Deacon" appears as a distinct office (Phl 1:1), where Paul addresses his letter to all the saints at Philippi with the bishops* and deacons. The qualities demanded in a deacon are listed in 1 Tm 3:8-13, immediately after the list of qualifications for the office of bishop. There is no evidence in the NT concerning the functions of the deacon in the Church. One may adduce the institution of the "Seven" in AA 6:1-6. Here a dispute arose because the Greek-speaking Christians thought their widows should receive equal treatment with the widows of the Palestinian Jewish Christian community. The Twelve refused to be involved in the dispute; it was beneath their office to serve tables. Hence they asked the community to institute other officers to take care of this duty and enable the Twelve to give themselves to "prayer and the ministry of the word." The men to be chosen should be "full of the spirit and wisdom" (AA 6:3), "faith and the holy spirit" (AA 6:5). These were instituted in their office by the imposition* of hands (AA 6:6). The accounts of Stephen* and Philip* in AA show them preaching and baptizing, much as the apostles did; and it is possible that these functions were included in the office of deacon. But the Seven are not called deacons, and one may look else-

where for the earliest form of the office. Possibly we should think of the deacon not as an officer of the community, but as an assistant to the bishop (Beyer ThWB). Here also perhaps, since deacon means primarily one who serves at table, we should think of the deacon as assisting the bishop in performing the rite of the Eucharist*. The office of minister or servant of the synagogue*, immediately under the "ruler of the synagogue" (*archisynagogus*), may also be invoked as a parallel to the office of deacon. *Diakonos* appears in Gk inscriptions referring to the personnel of pagan cults; but we have no clear information about the function of the officer so named, except that the name itself suggests that the officer would be concerned with the sacrificial banquet. In Rm 16:1 Phoebe* is called "our sister, deaconess of the church in Cenchreae*." The title here does not of itself indicate a hierarchical office; it can refer to services rendered by Phoebe to the community of Cenchreae. In 1 Tm 3:11 there seems to be a clear reference to women who either render services to the Church or assist the deacons in the performance of their duties; it seems unlikely that the qualities mentioned refer to the wives of deacons except in so far as the wives might assist the husbands in their duties.

Dead Sea (Hb *yām hammelaḥ*, "Salt Sea"; *yam ha ʿarābāh*, "Sea of the Arabah"; *hayyām hakkadmônî*, "the Eastern Sea"). The Dead Sea is formed by the inflow of the Jordan and other streams, most of them on the E side of the sea; the water has no outlet, and the evaporation is extremely heavy. The Dead Sea is covered by a haze most of the time; its entire width is easily visible, but its length can be seen only rarely. The saline content of the Dead Sea is about 25 percent, six times the saline content of the ocean, and the density of the water permits persons to float with no effort; in fact, it is impossible to sink. There are no fish in the Dead Sea, and fresh water fish which are carried in by the Jordan current die instantly. Salt cliffs at the SW corner of the sea were a source of salt in ancient times. The sea is 53 mi long and 10 mi wide at its greatest; a number of scholars believe that the S end of the sea, a bay formed by the peninsula el Lisan ("the tongue"), which extends from the E side, was formed by an earthquake about 2000 BC, which would explain the story of Sodom* and Gomorrah. The Dead Sea is the lowest point N of the Red Sea in the great rift or fault which extends from N Syria and continues as the Red Sea basin to the straits of Aden. The surface of the

Dead Sea with the
Mountains of Moab in
the background.

sea is 1290 ft below sea level, and the sea is 1300 ft deep at its deepest.

The Dead Sea, hemmed in closely by the cliffs of Moab to the E and of Judah to the W, often has a rugged beauty in its blue waters and the reddish cliffs; but the beauty is deceptive. The sea lies in the rain shadow of the highlands of Judah and its immediate neighborhood is an entirely dead wilderness of sand and bare rock. In historic times it has not been a center of population except for a few oases on its shores and the community of Qumran*.

The Dead Sea is identified with the valley of Siddim* (Gn 14:3). It is most frequently mentioned as a border point: of the kingdom of the Amorites* (Dt 4:49; Jos 12:3), of Benjamin (Jos 18:19), of Reuben and Gad (Dt 3:17), of Judah (Jos 15:2, 5), of Israel (Nm 34:3, 12; 2 K 14:25; Ezk 47:18). In the messianic land of Ezk the Dead Sea will be freshened by the stream which rises from the temple, but deposits of salt will be left (Ezk 47:8–12; cf Zc 14:8).

Dead Sea Scrolls. Cf QUMRAN.

Death. 1. *OT*. The OT exhibits a certain development in the Israelite ideas of death. This development is not progressive; one may find in BS a concept of death which scarcely differs from the concept found in the Pnt. The prevailing view in the OT is that death is terminal. One's concept of death is ultimately determined by one's concept of life*; hence the Hb concept of the human person as an animated body rather than an incarnated spirit made the end of animation appear to be the cessation of all vital activity. When a person died, the "spirit" departed; the deceased continued to exist as a "self" (*nepeš*) in Sheol*, but was incapable of any vital activity or passivity. The dead take no part in divine worship (Pss 6:6; 30:10; 88:11; 115:17; cf also Is

184

38:11, 18). It is against this background of OT belief that Jesus said that God is not the God of the dead but of the living (Mt 22:32; Mk 12:27; Lk 20:38). Death is accepted as the natural end of man (2 S 14:14). The ideal death was attained in the fullness of old age with undiminished powers (Gn 25:8; Jb 21:23 f; 29:18–20 +). One who dies such an ideal death dies easily and quickly; he goes down to Sheol "in a moment" (Jb 21:13) and is not the victim either of a premature death or of a lingering wasting disease. Such a death "embitters" one (Jb 21:15). The sense of the story of Paradise* (Gn 2–3) is that death is the consequence of the primeval fall* and that man was not created by God to be mortal. In the imagery of the Paradise story immortality is attained by eating the fruit of the tree of life, from which man is now excluded. This story has some resemblance to the Mesopotamian account of the search of Gilgamesh* for the plant of life, which Gilgamesh found only to lose it by theft at once, as well as to the story of Adapa. Adapa was admitted to the presence of the gods but warned against accepting the food of death and the water of death, which would be offered him. Actually he was offered the food of life and the water of life. The belief that death came as the consequence of a primeval fall is not reflected elsewhere in the OT before BS 25:24. There are occasional expressions in the OT of a strain of hope that death is not as terminal as it seems. Thus in Ps 16:9 the poet rejoices that Yahweh will not abandon him to Sheol nor permit him to see the pit. In Ps 49:16 the poet is assured that God will redeem him from Sheol. Similar expressions are not uncommon in the Pss and usually signify no more than preservation from sudden or premature death. The context of these Pss seems to go beyond this, since the whole problem of life and death generally is involved, particularly in Ps 49. Even clearer is the assurance of the poet in Ps 73:23 ff that he has no portion except Yahweh in heaven or in earth. If Yahweh's promises and His loving kindness are everlasting, then there must be some way in which the loyal Israelite will experience them. How he shall do it is not formulated in this early phase of Israelite belief. The Israelite conception of death was affected by the underlying cosmic myth of creation* in which so much Israelite thought was cast. The struggle between order and chaos, light and darkness, was also a struggle between life and death. In the ancient Semitic myths of creation life and death were alternately victorious. As Hb belief in Yahweh did not permit them to accept the idea that His power and will

for good were not sufficient to overcome the forces of evil, so also they could not believe that He was not victorious over death; at least death could not touch Him. Obviously, however, as they developed a belief in a final victory of Yahweh over the forces of darkness, evil and chaos, so likewise the logic of their faith demanded that He overcome death also. This development appears rather late in OT belief; we find no certain trace of a clear belief in the resurrection* of the dead before the 2nd century BC in Dn. The immortality of the soul* as proposed in WS, a product of Alexandrian Judaism, was really an element foreign to Hb belief and Hb psychology which was never assimilated into the OT or NT.

2. *NT.* The NT adds the explicit and clear belief that death is a consequence and a punishment of sin. This is stated most clearly in Rm 5:12 ff. Here the parallel is drawn out at length between death to many through the sin of one and life to many through the righteousness of one. Likewise in 1 Co 15:22 we all die in Adam, but we are all brought to life in Christ. A second element in the NT conception of death is that Jesus has overcome death by His own death. Death is the last adversary which He overcomes (1 Co 15:25 f). He has deprived death of its power (2 Tm 1:10). He has rendered powerless the devil, the lord of death (Heb 2:14). The law of the spirit of life in Christ Jesus frees us from the law of sin and death (Rm 8:2). Christ has died and come to life to rule over the living and the dead (Rm 14:9). Once Christ has risen from the dead He does not die again; death has no more power over Him (Rm 6:9). When all had died, one died on behalf of all that they might live not for themselves but for him who had died on their behalf (2 Co 5:14 f). Because Jesus humiliated Himself to death, the Father has conferred on Him glory and honor (Phl 2:5 ff). The Christian experiences Jesus's victory over death by himself sharing in the death of Jesus. This is elaborated at length in Rm 6:2 ff. The Christian is baptized into the death of Jesus, for only thus can he rise with Him to a new life. Sharing in the death of Christ is a "planting" with Him (Rm 6:5). The old man is crucified. If we die with Christ, we shall live with Him (Rm 6:8). We are dead to sin, living to God in Christ Jesus (Rm 6:11). If we live according to the flesh we shall die; but if by the spirit we kill the deeds of the body we shall live (Rm 8:13). Paul is crucified with Christ, so that he no longer lives, but Christ lives in him (Gal 2:20). He is crucified to the world and the world is crucified to him (Gal 6:14). Faith in Jesus does not protect one from death; but

it gives assurance that one shall not die forever (Jn 11:26). To partake of the Eucharist means that one shall not die but shall have eternal life (Jn 6:50 f). Parallel to the concept of eternal life is the concept of the "second death" (Apc 2:11; 20:6, 14; 21:8), by which one is deprived of eternal life. Christians who die are dead in Christ (1 Th 4:16).

Debir (Hb *d⁻bîr,* etymology uncertain), also called Kirjath-sepher, *kiryat-sēper,* an older name (Jos 15:15 f; Jgs 1:11 f); a town of Judah, located at modern Tell Beit Mirsim 12 mi WSW of Hebron in the Shephelah*. The conquest of Debir by Joshua* is mentioned twice (Jos 10:38; 11:21); it is called a city of the Anakim*. These are schematic attributions (cf JOSHUA); the city was taken by Othniel* (Jos 15:15 f; Jgs 1:11 f; cf CALEB; KENIZZITE). Debir was on the frontier of Judah (Jos 15:7) and is listed among the cities of Judah (Jos 15:49) and among the Levitical cities of Judah (Jos 21:15; 1 Ch 6:43).

The site is important not because of its historical interest but because of the thoroughness with which it was excavated by W. F. Albright 1926–1932; this excavation is a landmark in the development of the techniques of modern Palestinian archaeology. The area enclosed within the walls was about 7.5 acres. Debir was first settled in Early Bronze IV (2300–2100 BC). A 19th-century wall about 11 ft thick was uncovered. The disturbed conditions of Palestine in the 2nd millennium BC were illustrated by four general destructions and four partial destructions of the city which occurred between 1800–1500. A large number of Astarte* plaques from Late Bronze and Iron I (late

Canaanite and early Israelite) illustrate the fertility cults of Canaan and the OT. Of particular interest was a stele of a goddess and a serpent*. The city was violently destroyed by fire about 1200 BC and resettled almost immediately; this destruction and resettlement must be attributed to the Israelites. Casemated city walls of Iron I were attributed to the early reign of David, when the city was fortified against the Philistines*. Debir was destroyed by the Babylonians 598–587 BC and abandoned.

Deborah (Hb *d⁻bōrāh,* "bee"). **1.** Nurse of Rebekah, buried near Bethel* (Gn 35:8). **2.** A prophetess, the wife of Lappidoth (Jgs 4:4; 5:31). Deborah lived in Tomer-Deborah in the hill country of Ephraim* between Ramah* and Bethel*. When the Israelites were oppressed by the Canaanites* under Jabin* and Sisera*, they appealed to Deborah. She summoned Barak and in the name of Yahweh ordered him to assemble 10,000 men from Zebulun* and Naphtali* near Mount Tabor*. Barak refused to go unless Deborah accompanied him, which she did. When the army of Sisera approached Deborah gave the order to join the battle. The poem in Jgs 5 which describes the victory is attributed to Deborah and is usually called the Song of Deborah. Modern critics are unanimous in affirming the antiquity of this poem; many believe it is the oldest extant Hebrew literary composition, going back to the period of the Judges. But the traditional attribution is not enough of itself to establish the authorship of Deborah.

Decalogue. The ten commandments appear in the OT in two somewhat different formulae.

Exodus 20	Deuteronomy 5
2 I the Lord am your God who brought you out of the land of Egypt, the place of slavery.	6 I the Lord am your God who brought you out of the land of Egypt, that place of slavery.
3 You shall not have other Gods besides me.	7 You shall not have other gods besides me.
4 You shall not carve idols for yourselves	8 You shall not carve idols for yourselves
in the shape of anything in the sky above or in the earth below or in the waters beneath the earth; 5 you shall not bow down before them or worship them. For I the Lord your God am a jealous God, inflicting punishment for their fathers' wickedness on the children of those who hate me down to the third and fourth generation, 6 but bestowing mercy down to the thousandth generation on the children of those who love me and keep my commandments.	in the shape of anything in the sky above or on the earth below or in the waters beneath the earth; 9 you shall not bow down before them or worship them. For I the Lord your God am a jealous God, inflicting punishment for their father's wickedness on the children of those who hate me, unto the fourth generation, 10 but bestowing mercy down to the thousandth generation on the children of those who love me and keep my commandments.
7 You shall not take the name of the Lord your God in vain;	11 You shall not take the name of the Lord your God in vain;
for the Lord will not leave unpunished him who takes his name in vain.	for the Lord will not leave unpunished him who takes his name in vain.
8 Remember to keep holy the Sabbath day;	12 Take care to keep holy the Sabbath day as the Lord your God commanded you.

9 Six days you may labor and do all your work; 10 but the seventh day is the Sabbath of the Lord your God. No work may be done then either by you or by your son or daughter, or your male or female slave or your beast or the alien who lives with you. 11 In six days the Lord made the heavens and the earth, the sea and all that is in them; but on the seventh day He rested. That is why the Lord has blessed the Sabbath day and made it holy.

12 Honor your father and your mother

that you may have a long life in the land which the Lord your God is giving you.

13 You shall not kill.

14 You shall not commit adultery.

15 You shall not steal.

16 You shall not bear false witness against your neighbor.

17 You shall not covet

your neighbor's house; you shall not covet your neighbor's wife, nor his male and female slave, nor his ox or ass, nor anything else that belong to him.

13 Six days you may labor and do all your work; 14 but the seventh day is the Sabbath of the Lord your God. No work may be done then, whether by you, or your son or daughter, or your ox or your ass, or any of your beasts, or the alien who lives with you. Your male and female slaves rest as you do; 15 for remember that you too were once slaves in Egypt, and the Lord your God brought you from there with a strong hand and an outstretched arm. That is why the Lord your God has commanded you to observe the Sabbath day.

16 Honor your father and your mother

as the Lord your God has commanded you, that you may have a long life and prosperity in the land which the Lord your God is giving you.

17 You shall not kill.

18 You shall not commit adultery.

19 You shall not steal.

20 You shall not bear dishonest witness against your neighbor.

21 You shall not covet

your neighbor's wife. You shall not desire your neighbor's house, nor his male or female slave, nor his ox or ass, nor anything that belongs to him.

That ten words or commandments were given by God to Moses on Mt Sinai is incorporated into ancient Hebrew tradition (Ex 34:28; Dt 4:13; 10:4). The numeration of the ten commandments, however, is taken in different ways in modern times.

I. Philo, Josephus, Greek fathers modern Greek and Reformed Churches: (1) Prohibition of false or foreign gods. (2) Prohibition of images. (3) Vain use of the divine name. (4) Sabbath. (5) Parents. (6) Murder. (7) Adultery. (8) Theft. (9) False witness. (10) Covetousness.

II. This division first appears in Origen, used by Clement of Alexandria, Augustine, modern Latin church and Lutheran church: (1) Prohibition of false gods. The prohibition of images is either included in this commandment or suppressed in the enumeration. (2) Vain use of the divine name. (3) Sabbath. (4) Parents. (5) Murder. (6) Adultery. (7) Theft. (8) False witness. (9) Coveting of wife. (10) Coveting of goods.

III. Modern Jews: (1) Introduction, "I am the Lord your God" etc. (2) Prohibition of false gods and images. (3) Vain use of the divine name. (4) Sabbath. (5) Parents. (6) Murder. (7) Adultery. (8) Theft. (9) False Witness. (10) Covetousness.

The first of these three divisions is best according to sense, and is probably the most original. The first four commandments state duties toward God, the final six list duties toward human beings; parents, the source of life, are representative of God. The introduction, "I am the Lord your God," etc, often enumerated as one of the commandments, is outside the commandments proper.

The differences between the recensions of Ex and Dt are shown in the above table. It is altogether probable that neither of these recensions presents the Decalogue in its original form. Most interpreters believe that all the commandments were originally as brief as the commandments of murder, adultery, theft, and false witness. The others have been expanded by the addition of homiletic motives for their observance; the table shows the probable content of the original commandment as distinguished from the additions. There is some slight difference between the two recensions in the motivation. In Ex the Sabbath commandment is supported by an appeal to creation* in six days followed by rest on the seventh, as related in Gn 1:1–2:3. In Dt the precept of rest is extended to others besides the Hebrew family proper, for the humanitarian motive that the Hebrews were once slaves in Egypt. The original form of the prohibition of covetousness, probably the simple precept of Ex (cf TABLE), has been expanded in two ways. In Ex the first expansion was the mention of the house, which covered all the neighbor's property, and the precept was further expanded by the enumeration of the wife, slaves, and domestic animals. In Dt the first expansion was the explicit and separate mention of the wife; the precept was then extended to house, slaves, and animals. This represents a more advanced view of family life.

The formula of the direct commandment or prohibition is the type of law called "apodictic" in opposition to "casuistic" (cf LAW). Modern critics generally agree that the Decalogue in its present position in Ex is not in its original literary context; the Decalogue here is given in a priestly recension, while the surrounding context belongs to a complex tradition (cf EXODUS; PENTATEUCH). The position of the Decalogue in Dt, however, shows that the writers and editors of this book had a tradition which associated the Decalogue with the Sinai covenant*, precisely the position which the Decalogue occupies in Ex. The position of the Decalogue in Dt together with other allusions to the "ten words" (cf above), indicates the priestly recension has replaced the original older and simpler formulation.

Many older biblical critics denied that the Decalogue went back to Mosaic times. They regarded it as a summary of the ethical teaching of the prophets* of the 8th–7th centuries. This opinion was based principally on some features of the Decalogue which they thought reflected the period of Israel's settlement in Canaan rather than the seminomadic conditions of the Mosaic period: for instance, the allusions to house and field, ox and ass. Likewise the prohibition of images was thought to date only from the 8th or 7th century, and the Sabbath likewise was not a nomadic observance. Modern discoveries have removed most of the weight of these objections (cf IMAGES; SABBATH). The recension of Dt no doubt belongs to the period of the monarchy; but the Decalogue itself can be centuries earlier than this recension. It is true that there is no explicit citation of the Decalogue in later biblical literature; but this is not really convincing. The attribution of the Decalogue to the Mosaic period does not imply its attribution to Moses himself, although he is the most likely candidate. Nor does this attribution imply that the story of the stone tablets written by the finger of God (Ex 34:12; Dt 5:22) and then rewritten by Moses (Ex 34:28) is any more than a highly imaginative way of stating the divine origin and authority of the Decalogue. The prohibitions of false gods and of images are highly distinctive features of Israelite religion, and tradition constantly attributes these features to Moses (cf GOD; IMAGES).

The prohibition of the vain use of the divine name is probably directed against the use of the name in magic*. On the understanding of the other commandments in ancient Israel cf FAMILY; MARRIAGE; MURDER; SABBATH; THEFT. The prohibition of false witness as it stands refers to juridical processes. The prohibition of covetousness, which is concerned with the interior act, has often been thought to be both morally and psychologically too subtle for primitive Israelite belief. This is not convincing; no great subtlety was required to see that the inner desire was the root of wrongdoing. But the prohibition of such malicious desire is distinctive of Israelite morality at any period in which one supposes the Decalogue to have arisen.

Some modern critics believe they have discovered a cultic decalogue in Ex 34:14–26, which may be divided as follows: I. 14. II. 17. III. 18. IV. 19–20. V. 21. VI. 22. VII. 23–24. VIII. 25. IX–X. 26. Actually there are more than ten commandments in this passage, and the number ten can be reached only by some manipulation. Many critics, realizing this, have reconstructed a primitive cultic decalogue from this and other related passages, and they propose that this cultic decalogue is indicated by the "ten words" of Ex 34:28. It has in common with the Decalogue of Ex-Dt the prohibition of worshiping other gods (34:14), images (34:17), the Sabbath (34:21). Cf also Lv 19:3 f, 11 f; Je 7:9; Ho 4:2.

The separate commandments are mentioned in the NT but never as ten. The prohibitions of murder (Mt 5:21) and adultery (Mt 5:27) in the Sermon on the Mount are cited parallel with Dt 24:1 (Mt 5:31), a conflation of Ex 20:7, Nm 30:3, and Dt 23:22 (Mt 5:33), Ex 21:24 (Mt 5:38), and Lv 19:18 (Mt 5:43) in the same manner. This is the Law which Jesus came not to destroy but to fulfill, and all the citations come from the Torah, the supreme authority of Judaism (cf LAW). Ex 20:12 is cited in Mt 15:4; Eph 6:2–3. Dt 5:17–21 is cited in Rm 13:9; Ex 20:13 f (Dt 5:17 f) in Js 2:11. The young man who asked Jesus how to be perfect was told to keep the commandments. When he asked which commandments, Jesus cited some of the ten, not in the usual order nor completely. In Mt 19:18–19 are found murder, adultery, theft, false witness, honor of parents, and there is added the precept of loving the neighbor as oneself (Lv 19:18). In Mk 10:19 the same precepts are mentioned with the omission of the love of one's neighbor and the addition of the precept not to defraud, based on Dt 24:14. In Lk 18:20 the precepts of adultery, murder, theft, false witness, and honor of parents are cited. These passages suggest that even in gospel times the Decalogue had not acquired the set form and importance as a charter of fundamental morality it acquired in later Christianity.

Decapolis (Gk *dekapolis*, "ten cities"), the name given to the territory extending in eastern Palestine from Damascus* in the N to Philadelphia* in the S. The name designates a league of ten cities formed after the Roman conquest of Palestine in 63 BC. The ten cities were Hellenistic and probably formed the league not only because of their frontier position on the desert but also to protect themselves against Jewish immigration and aggression. Some of the cities had been conquered by Alexander Jannaeus (103–76 BC). The territory of the Decapolis spread over several other jurisdictions of the period; it probably did not constitute a single contiguous territory. The league was a federation of free cities, each with its surrounding territory, under the general administration of the Roman legate of Syria. The earliest literary mention of the Decapolis is found in the Gospels. The cities are also mentioned by Josephus and Pliny the Elder. Pliny lists the ten as Damascus, Philadelphia, Raphana, Scythopolis*, Gadara*, Hippos, Dion, Pella, Gerasa*, and Canatha. All the Palestinian cities except Scythopolis lay on the eastern side of the Jordan. In the 2nd century AD Ptolemy names 18 cities, omitting Raphana but including Abila and 8 others. The number was not constant. Modern scholars believe Abila was one of the original 10. People came from the Decapolis to hear Jesus (Mt 4:25), and Jesus performed a miracle of healing in the territory of the Decapolis (Mk 7:31). The demoniac who was cured on the eastern shore of the Sea of Galilee* announced Jesus in the territory of the Decapolis (Mk 5:20).

Dedan (Hb *dedān,* meaning uncertain), an Arabian tribe. Its origin is attributed to Ham through Cush* and Raamah* (Gn 10:7; 1 Ch 1:9); also to Abraham* and Keturah* through Jokshan* (Gn 25:3; 1 Ch 1:32). It is mentioned together with Sheba* (Gn 25:3; 1 Ch 1:32; Ezk 38:13), with Tema* (Is 21:13–14; Je 25:23), with the peoples who must drink the cup of wrath, here included among those who wear their hair clipped at the temples, and with Buz (Je 25:23). Its territory lay in northern Arabia bordering on Edom* (Je 49:8; Ezk 25:13). They were caravan merchants (Is 21:13) who traded with Tyre* (Ezk 27:20). The sons of Dedan who traded with Tyre (Ezk 27:5) are confused with the sons of Rodan (Rhodes*) by a textual error.

Dedication, feast of (Hb *ḥanukkāh*), the feast instituted to celebrate the recovery and purification of the temple* from the Syrians by Judas* in 165 BC. At the time of the recovery the feast was instituted to be celebrated for eight days each year, beginning with the 25th of Kislew* (1 Mc 4:52–59; 2 Mc 10:6–8). The month of Kislew falls roughly within December of the Julian calendar and brings the feast near Christmas; and in modern Judaism it is celebrated in a joyous atmosphere with an exchange of gifts. It is frequently called the Feast of Lights from the practice of illuminating homes and streets; this title appears in the writings of Josephus*.

Delilah (Hb *delīlāh*), the mistress of Samson* who betrayed him to the Philistines* by cutting off his hair while he slept (Jgs 16:4–20). A. Vincent suggests that the name is derived from the Arabic and contains a pun derived from two words from the same root: *dalla,* "to behave in an amorous manner," and *dalila,* "a guide," here betrayer. Her residence in the valley of Sorek* would permit her to be either Hebrew or Philistine, but the narrative suggests that she was a Hebrew.

Deluge. The story of the deluge is found in Gn 6:5–9:17. This story is compiled from the Yahwist (J) and priestly traditions (P) interwoven into the present single account (cf GENESIS; PENTATEUCH). Some variations in details in the two traditions are easily discerned in the present narrative. In J seven pairs of clean animals and of birds and one pair of unclean animals are taken into the ark* (Gn 7:2–3), in P a single pair of all species (Gn 7:8–9). In J the flood endures for 40 days of rain (Gn 7:12); the 40 days of Gn 7:17 is thought by most modern critics to be a gloss to provide for the abatement of the flood. In P the entire flood endures for one year and 11 days (Gn 7:11; 8:14). The waters rise for 150 days (Gn 7:24) and recede for another 150 days (Gn 8:3), and the earth is not dry enough for Noah* to leave the ark until the end of the whole period. P also exhibits other mathematical precisions besides the duration of the flood: the dimensions of the ark, 300 cubits long, 50 cubits wide, 30 cubits high (Gn 6:15), and the height of the water above the mountains, 15 cubits (Gn 7:20, calculated on the height of the ark). The two traditions differ also in their conception of the catastrophe. In J the deluge is the result of an excessive rain of 40 days and 40 nights. In P the deluge is a result of the collapse of the entire cosmos. The waters of the primitive abyss, which are divided in creation* into the waters of the lower abyss beneath the earth and the waters of the upper abyss above the earth (Gn 1:7), now return to cover the entire creation and bring back the chaos of Gn 1:2. The waters of the upper abyss enter through the broken windows or sluices of heaven and the waters of the lower abyss through the burst fountains, from which they normally issue at a moderate rate (Gn 7:11). This conception of a collapse of cosmic order is paralleled in the Mesopotamian deluge stories (cf below). Other passages in which the double tradition appears without notable variation are the decree of the flood (Gn 6:5–7, J; 6:11–13, P) and the story of the covenant* of God with Noah after the deluge (Gn 8:21–22, J; 9:1–17, P). Of these two traditions critics regard J as the older, perhaps from the 9th or 10th century BC, and P as more recent, from the 6th or 5th. P, however, in some features is more archaic and closer to the original form of the story. In both traditions the deluge was a universal catastrophe covering the entire earth as it was conceived by the ancients (cf CREATION) and destroying all life, human and animal, except that which was preserved in the ark.

Accounts of a universal deluge have been found in Mesopotamian literature. Several varieties of the Mesopotamian story are known; the longest and the best preserved appears in the XI tablet of the Gilgamesh* epic (ANET 93–95). The hero of the deluge is called Ut-napishtim, a resident of Shurippak on the Euphrates. When the gods decree the deluge, the god Ea reveals the decree to Ut-napishtim, protecting his obligation of secrecy by speaking not directly to Ut-napishtim but to a reed wall through which Ut-napishtim hears him. He is admonished to build a boat, described as a cube 10 dozen cubits on a side. The ark of Gn is rectangular, and is neither a ship nor a boat, but a large box. Ut-napishtim is warned to take ample provisions as well as "the beasts of the field, the wild creatures of the field," and this is similar to the preservation of animal species in Gn. In addition Ut-napishtim is to take craftsmen aboard lest their crafts perish entirely, and a boatman to navigate the vessel. The deluge lasts for six days and six nights, and the ark of Ut-napishtim comes to rest on Mount Nisir. Like Noah, Ut-napishtim sends forth birds — a dove, a swallow, and a raven — and leaves the ark when the raven fails to return. Like Noah, Ut-napishtim offers a sacrifice; and the gods cluster about it like flies. Instead of a covenant there follows a dispute among the gods. Enlil, angry that any one has escaped, inquires who has disclosed the secret. Ea confesses, but questions the wisdom of Enlil in sending a deluge.

On the sinner, he says, should be imposed his sin, and on the transgressor his transgression. Instead of such a universal disaster Enlil should have sent a wolf or a lion or a famine or pestilence, which would not have wiped out the entire race. Because Ut-napishtim and his wife have escaped the deluge they must now be given immortality and removed to a distant land at the mouth of the rivers where they will not mingle with common mortal men. The dispute of the gods is a piece of primitive Mesopotamian theology which attempts to explain such catastrophes which wipe out large numbers of people. They are attributed to the irrational anger of the gods, who do not show wisdom by discriminating between good and bad. The instrument chosen goes far beyond the demands of divine anger. Implicitly the story questions the wisdom and goodness of the providence of the gods. In addition to this account in the poem of Gilgamesh, which comes from the library of Ashurbani-pal, part of the Sumerian flood story has now been discovered (ANET 43–44). It is incomplete, but agrees with the poem of Gilgamesh in the residence of the hero, Shurippak. His name, however, is Ziusudra. He also receives immortality and resides in Dilmun, the land where the sun rises. The duration of the flood here is seven days and seven nights. A fragment of an old Babylonian flood story is preserved; the name of the hero is Atrahasis (ANET 104–106). Here the motive which moves Enlil to send the deluge is the clamor of mankind, which prevents the gods from enjoying their sleep. Finally, the Babylonian priest Berossus, about 275 BC, wrote in Gk some of the mythology of his people. In his summary account of the flood the hero is named Xisuthros, which is probably a Gk form of Ziusudra (AOT 200–201). His account contains no distinctive element.

The resemblance between these Mesopotamian accounts and the story of Gn are too numerous and too close to permit one to affirm the independence of the stories. It must be admitted, as almost all modern critics do, that the biblical story exhibits the same tradition which we find in Mesopotamian literature, although not necessarily the tradition in any particular form which has been discovered. The differences between the Mesopotamian and the biblical stories show how the Hebrews took a piece of ancient tradition and retold it in order to make it a vehicle of their own distinctive religious beliefs, in particular their conception of divine justice and providence. It is impossible to attach any historical value either to the Mesopotamian or to the biblical story. Excavations of Mesopotamian sites have shown more than one extensive deposit of silt which testify to disastrous floods in the early periods. But floods are frequent in the vast alluvial plain of Mesopotamia, and no deposit is such as to suggest the kind of catastrophe described in the flood story, even within a limited area. Hence the flood of the Mesopotamian and biblical stories cannot be identified with any flood of which historical or archaeological evidence has been found. Even in the most ancient forms of the story the flood was described as something which happened "long ago," long before historical records. There can be little doubt that the story preserves the memory of some unusually disastrous flood of prehistoric times, which has grown out of all proportions in successive forms of the narrative — for instance, a week of rain in the earliest story to 150 days in the priestly narrative.

The connection between the Mesopotamian and the biblical stories is easily explained by the Hb tradition that their ancestors came from Mesopotamia. Thus such traditions as that of the creation and the deluge could have been preserved orally. The retelling of the tradition has been done on the basis of religious beliefs which are attributed to Mosaic and post-Mosaic times. The Hb story faces the theological problem which, as we have seen, is involved in the Mesopotamian story; but the Hebrews did not attribute the catastrophe to irrational anger. Such a disaster postulates that "all flesh was corrupt" (Gn 6:12) except Noah and his family; there can be no question of the justice of the punishment. Nor is there any difference of purpose between various gods, one decreeing the deluge, the other revealing the decree to his favorite. In Hebrew tradition the one God decrees the deluge and reveals His plan to Noah. The Mesopotamian story of the sacrifice and the quarrel of the gods which followed is replaced by the Hb story of the covenant of God with Noah. Explicitly the deluge is a destruction of creation in P; Noah is therefore a second founder of the race and creation is restored after the deluge. The commandments which are given Noah have a resemblance both in form and content to the commandments of Gn 1:28–30 (Gn 9:1–3). In addition, after the deluge man is permitted to eat not only vegetables but also flesh; but the flesh must not be eaten with the blood (Gn 9:4–5). For no reason connected with the context except the mention of blood the prohibition of murder is inserted (Gn 9:6). The covenant of God with Noah is a guarantee that the course of nature will remain stable. Thus no similar catastrophe will again occur; that is, the whole race will not be destroyed indiscriminately. This covenant is probably an implicit reflection on the Canaanite myth of fertility, in which the victorious combat of the creative deity with the monster of chaos is annually renewed (cf CREATION). The Hb faith in the stability of nature rests on a more secure basis: the good will of the creative deity explicitly pledged by covenant. It is assured that the seasons will recur (Gn 8:22) without the necessity of any cultic myth and ritual. A sign of this stability is the rainbow (Gn 9:13–16), which is in popular belief a sign of the end of the storm. Whenever the storm occurs, fair weather will return and nature will remain within its normal cycles; and man will not again perish because of the anger of God. This covenant reflects the Hb conception of God's mercy; He is now resigned to the fact that "The inclination of man's heart is evil from his youth."

The deluge story is an extremely clear example of how the Hebrews could take popular traditions of other people, often almost entirely devoid of historical value, and retell them in such a way as to present important theological conceptions through them: here, divine justice and providence, the security and stability of nature resting on the assured good will of God to mankind in spite of the evil inclinations of man's heart (Gn 8:21).

Allusions to the deluge in the rest of the Bible are few. The covenant of God with Noah illustrates the good will of Yahweh toward Jerusalem (Is 54:9). Wisdom is praised because it saved the righteous man from the deluge (WS 10:4). Among the praises of wood, from which idols are made, is included the wood of the raft by which the hope of the world was saved (WS 14:6). Ben Sira refers to the destruction of the giants (Gn 6:1–4), although this story is not a part of the deluge narrative (BS 16:7), and enumerates Noah among the heroes of 44:1 ff (BS 44:17–18). In the Gospels the suddenness of the deluge is compared to the sudden coming of the Son of Man (Mt 24:37–39; Lk 17:26–27). Noah was saved by his faith (Heb 11:7). The deluge is an example of God's patience (1 Pt 3:20), and the waters from which Noah was saved are compared to the waters of baptism* (1 Pt 3:20). Noah was a preacher of righteousness (2 Pt 2:5).

Demas (Gk *dēmas*, possibly an abbreviation of Demetrius), a companion and fellow worker of Paul, mentioned with Luke* (Col 4:14), with Mark*, Aristarchus*, and Luke (Phm 24), charged with abandoning Paul during his imprisonment (2 Tm 4:10) because of his love of the world.

Demetrius (Gk *dēmētrios,* "belonging to Demeter"). **1.** Demetrius I Soter, king of Syria 162–150 BC. A nephew of Antiochus* IV, he had been held as a hostage in Rome*. He escaped in 162 and attained the throne of Syria by the murder of his predecessor Antiochus* V Eupator and his guardian Lysias*. He installed Alcimus* as high priest of the Jews and sent his general Bacchides* to subdue Judaea. The military operations of his general Nicanor were unsuccessful and Nicanor was defeated and killed in battle (1 Mc 7:1–50; cf 2 Mc 14–15). Demetrius then sent Bacchides with a much larger army, and Judas* was killed in the defeat of the Jews (1 Mc 9:1–21). When Demetrius was threatened by the rise of a rival king Alexander* Balas, he attempted to secure the alliance of the Jews by promising to meet all their demands. The Jews, now led by Jonathan*, the younger brother of Judas, chose to support Alexander rather than accept the terms of Demetrius; and in the ensuing battle between the two rivals Demetrius was defeated and killed (1 Mc 10:1–50).

2. Demetrius II Nicator, son of Demetrius I, king of Syria 145–138 and 129–125 BC. Demetrius came from Crete to claim the throne of his father from Alexander Balas. The operations of his general Apollonius* against Jonathan* and the Jews were unsuccessful (1 Mc 10:67–89). With the aid of Ptolemy VI of Egypt* Demetrius defeated Alexander and secured the throne of Syria (1 Mc 11:1–13). Jonathan very quickly showed his allegiance to Demetrius, who in return granted some favors to the Jews (1 Mc 11:20–37); the Jews assisted him in suppressing a rebellion at Antioch (1 Mc 11:42–52). These peaceful relations were followed by an estrangement (1 Mc 11:53). Tryphon* set up the child Antiochus* as a rival to Demetrius, and Jonathan changed his allegiance to Antiochus when the young king confirmed him as high priest (1 Mc 11:57 ff). Tryphon, however, proved to be such an impossible tyrant that Simon*, the successor of Jonathan, returned to the allegiance of Demetrius, who finally promised the Jews freedom, and "the yoke of the heathen was lifted from Israel" in the 170th year of the Seleucid* era (141 BC; 1 Mc 13:1–42). The Syrian garrison of the citadel of Jerusalem was expelled in the next year (1 Mc 13:49–51). The conflict between Demetrius and Tryphon continued, and in an expedition into Parthia Demetrius was defeated and captured by Arsaces (1 Mc 14:1–3). Demetrius regained his liberty and returned to his throne in 129; but Ptolemy VII of Egypt supported an Egyptian pretender against him, and Demetrius was defeated in battle and murdered during his subsequent flight.

3. A silversmith of Ephesus, who with other members of his guild manufactured miniature shrines of Artemis* of Ephesus. The number of converts to Christianity in Ephesus was so great that the silversmiths feared the loss of their trade. Demetrius by his harangue against the Christians incited a riot against them (AA 19:23–41).

Demon, Demonology. 1. *Mesopotamia.* The demonology of Mesopotamia, which appears in Sumerian and Akkadian literature, was extremely ancient. It influenced the Hebrews of OT times, and through the Chaldeans* entered the Hellenistic world and reached Europe; some forms of it survived into medieval and modern times. In Mesopotamia the evils of life which were less than great natural catastrophes were attributed to the evil influence of demons. Their number was almost without limit. To counteract their malice effectively the sorcerer had to know the name of the demon, and hence Mesopotamian literature contains a large number of demonic names. From literature and art it is possible to learn the imagined character and appearance of the demons. The evil demon was an *utukku.* The group of seven evil demons appears frequently in incantations. When they attacked a man, the *ashakku* attacked the head, the *namtaru* the throat, the evil *utukku* the neck, the *alu* the chest, the *etimmu,* the evil *ilu* (god), the hand, and the *gallu* the foot. Other titles are known, such as *rabiṣu,* the croucher, *aḫḫazu,* the seizer, the three night demons *lilu* (male), *lilitu* (female), *ardat lili* (maidservant of *lilu*). These three demons belonged to the incubus-succuba type. *Pazuzu* was probably the SW wind which brought the infection of malaria. *Ashakku* is death. *Namtaru,* associated with Nergal*, the god of the underworld, was the messenger of death. *Gallu* was a hideous monster without form or feature. The *etimmu* was a ghost. The *lamashtu* was an ugly and much feared monster, especially dangerous to pregnant and nursing women. Like most of the demons, its form was a mixture of human and animal features: a lion's head, a woman's body, dog's teeth, and eagle's claws on hands and feet. It held a serpent in each hand. It had an appetite for human flesh and blood, and is represented as nursing a dog and a pig at the breasts. The demons are sometimes called children of Anu, the god of the sky. In the creation* epic they are spawned by Tiamat to assist her in her combat with Marduk. They haunt graves and lonely and desert places, especially at night. Not all the demons were malevolent; the good demons, the *shedu* and

a) Demon Guardian of Gate, Babylon. b) and c) Demon Guardian of Gate of Persia. d) Demon guarding tree of life, Assyria. e) Benevolent demon, Mesopotamia.

lamassu, are invoked to repel the evil demons. These benevolent demons are represented as guardian genii at the gates of temples and palaces (cf CHERUB). The representation of demons in medieval Christian art comes from Mesopotamian art and literature.

2. *OT*. The severe prohibitions against magic* in Hebrew law seem to have excluded the practice and with it the belief in demonology from Israel. The belief is not reflected in the OT except in allusions to popular language and a few references to superstition among the Hebrews. Thus, although Saul* had expelled all witches from Israel, he himself sought one who evoked the ghost of Samuel* (1 S 28:13), here called *elohim*, a superhuman being. A difficult verse of Is (8:19) probably refers to necromancy. The *šēdîm* (Akkadian *shedu*) are mentioned in Dt 32:17 as those to whom

the Hebrews sacrificed. Here there is an identification of the gods of the nations with demons which became explicit in later Hebrew literature. Ps 106:37 mentions the sacrifice of children to the *šēdîm*. Abandoned ruins are haunted by wild beasts and by dancing *se'îrîm* (Is 13:21; 34:14) and by *lilit* (Akkadian *lilitu*), the Lilith of Jewish apocryphal literature (Is 34:14). The *se'îrîm*, "hairy ones" (?), are probably demons with goats' features. There is some similarity to demonic influence in the evil spirit from Yahweh which afflicts Saul with madness (1 S 16:14). This spirit, however, is evil only in its effects and not in its character. The language of demonology may also be reflected in Ps 91:5–6: the terror of night, the arrow that flies by day, the pestilence that walks in darkness, and the plague that lays waste at noon. Against these it is Yahweh who gives protection. Cf also ASMODEUS.

3. *Judaism.* Judaism of the intertestamental and NT periods exhibits a very active belief in demons, which is in many respects derived both from Mesopotamian demonology and Greek belief in *daimones*, beings intermediate between gods and men. But in this period Hellenism itself had been affected by Mesopotamian superstitions. Beliefs about the evil influence of demons, especially in causing ills and misfortunes, were borrowed by the Jews wholesale and almost without alteration from Mesopotamia. The origin of the demons was explained by the exegesis of biblical passages; in the apocryphal books the demons are described as fallen angels. They were identified also with the sons of God who married the daughters of men (Gn 6:1–4), from which unions were sprung the giants of mythology and folklore. This exegesis was probably correct, since this passage of Gn seems to preserve a fragment of mythology of unknown origin. Satan* was identified with the serpent* of Gn 3; this belief of Judaism is reflected in WS 2:24, "By the envy of the devil sin entered the world." Thus temptation, in addition to illness and misfortune, was now attributed to demonic influence. Furthermore, the demons were believed to be organized in a kingdom under a head who is called Mastema, Beliar, or Satan.

4. *NT.* The demonology of the NT is derived both from the OT and from Judaism; but the occurrence of demons in the NT is much rarer than in the literature of Judaism, outside of the instances of demoniac possession*. The victims of heathen sacrifices are offered to demons (1 Co 10:20–21). Deceiving spirits are responsible for false teaching (1 Tm 4:1). The demons believe and tremble (Js 2:19). The spirits of demons perform wonders (Apc 16:14). The ruins of Babylon are haunted by demons — an echo of the OT (Apc 18:2). The demons are often called spirits, especially with the adjective "unclean." A girl of Philippi had a divining spirit which was ejected by Paul (AA 16:16). The Sadducees* denied the existence of angels or spirits (AA 23:8); the distinction here possibly lies between the angels of God and the evil spirits. Christians should not believe every spirit, but test the spirits to see whether they are of God (1 Jn 4:1). Demons are also called the angels of Satan, for whom eternal fire is prepared (Mt 25:41). The conception of the demonic kingdom here is parallel to the conception of Judaism. The "principalities" mentioned with angels (Rm 8:38) as separating Christians from the love of God are probably the leaders or hierarchical powers of the demonic world. The same demonic hierarchies seem to be indicated in the "principality" (*archē*), "authority" (*exūsia*), and "power" (*dynamis*) which Christ subdues to His Father (1 Co 15:24); cf the same group of words in Eph 1:21; 3:10; 6:12, where they are clearly identified as the rulers of this darkness, the wicked spiritual beings on high, with whom the Christian must wrestle. Possibly the same beings are meant in Col 1:16 among the beings created in heaven and on earth. Here the words "thrones" and "lordships" are added. It is scarcely possible, however, that the "principality" and "authority" of which Christ is the head (Col 2:10) could be the demonic powers. But it is "principalities" and "authorities" whom Christ disarms by His crucifixion (Col 2:15). Likewise, angels, authorities, and powers are subdued to Christ (1 Pt 3:22). The angels whom Christians will judge are probably demons (1 Co 6:3). Paul attributes some physical infirmity to an angel of Satan (2 Co 12:7). Jd 6 refers to angels who did not keep their principality, but fell and are now bound and preserved for the great judgment; this echoes Jewish apocryphal literature.

The question arises to what extent the NT employs the language and imagery of mythology to personify evil. The question is more or less the same question which arises from the biblical use of popular language to describe natural phenomena (cf CREATION). Such popular language implies no dogmatic or philosophical affirmation of cosmic personal forces of evil. Such language, the origins of which can be traced in Jewish writings, seems to lie behind AA 16:16; 1 Co 10:20; Apc 16:4; 18:2; the demonic kingdom of Mt 25:41; Rm 8:38; 1 Co 15:24; Eph 1:21; 3:10; 6:12; Col 2:15; 1 Pt 3:22;

the attribution of infirmity to an evil spirit (2 Co 12:7); the great judgment of the demons (Jd 6), and probably 1 Co 6:3. But while the use of popular imagery should be understood to lie behind many details of the NT concept of demons, the Church has always taught the existence of personal evil spirits, insisting that they are malicious through their own will and not through their creation. Cf also POSSESSION; SATAN.

Derbe (Gk *derbē*), a city of Lycaonia* on the road to Iconium* from Tarsus*. It is not mentioned before the records of the Roman period. It was held by the kingdom of Galatia* until it passed under Roman suzerainty in 25 BC and was incorporated into the Roman province of Galatia under Claudius*. Paul and Barnabas made a number of disciples there (AA 14:20 f), but no incident is recorded either of Paul's first or second visit (AA 16:1).

Descent into hell. The articles of the Christian creed include the statement that Jesus died and was buried, descended into hell, and rose from the dead on the third day. The phrase "descended into hell" rests upon the language of the OT. "Hell" here represents the Hb Sheol*, the abode of the dead. The concept of Sheol in the OT implies no reward or punishment and no distinction between the state of the good and the wicked. In the OT "to die" is "to descend into Sheol" and one who rises from the dead rises from Sheol. A different concept is presupposed in Lk 23:43, where Jesus tells the penitent thief, "Today you will be with me in Paradise*." Peter applies to Jesus the text of Ps 16:10, "You do not abandon me to Sheol, nor permit your beloved one to see the pit." So God has dissolved the "pangs" of death* because death cannot have power over Jesus. "Pangs" here quotes the LXX mistranslation of the Hb "bonds" (AA 2:24–31). This text asserts no more than the reality of the death of Jesus, and consequently of the resurrection. In 1 Pt 3:19 f, however, it is stated that Jesus went to those who were kept in prison and there "announced" or "declared" to them; the verb has no object. Some MSS insert Enoch* here as the preacher. These were unbelievers in the days of Noah. It is difficult to erect on this verse a theory that Jesus descended into hell or the limbo of the fathers and there announced deliverance, since there is no indication that those who were unbelievers in the days of Noah have changed from unbelief to faith; hence they have no prospect of sharing in the salvation of Jesus. The declaration here seems to be an announcement of the triumph of Jesus over sin and

death. In 1 Pt 4:6 the good news is brought to those who have died, in order that they who were judged in the flesh according to men may live in the spirit according to God. There is no suggestion that this announcement is made by Jesus Himself. The dead here are not the unbelievers. Paul (Rm 10:6 f) combines quotations from Dt 30:12 and Ps 107:26 and asks who has ascended to bring Christ down, or who has descended into the abyss to raise Christ from the dead. Here also there is a reference to the reality of the death of Christ. In Eph 4:8 f, Ps 68:19 is applied to Christ. Here the ascent mentioned in the Ps is contrasted with the descent of Christ "into the lower parts of the earth." It is uncertain here whether the descent into the lower parts of the earth refers simply to the incarnation or to the death and burial of Jesus. "First-born of the dead" (Col 1:18) certainly refers to the resurrection of Jesus, but implies nothing of a descent. Jesus gave the Pharisees the sign of Jonah (Mt 12:40): as Jonah was three days and three nights in the belly of the whale, so the Son of Man will be in the heart of the earth three days and three nights. This is a reference to His burial. In most of these passages there is a simple employment of the language of Judaism, which conceived the heavens as the abode of God, and Sheol, the abode of the dead, as beneath the surface of the earth. This childlike view of the structure of the universe is not involved in the belief in the death, resurrection* and ascension* of Jesus. The passages quoted all affirm the reality of the death of Jesus in terms of a descent into Sheol. Christian traditions about the "harrowing of hell," the liberating visit of Jesus to the limbo of the fathers and their accompanying Him in His resurrection, have no basis in the NT.

Desert. The desert surrounds Palestine on the E and the S, and within the country itself there are some semiarid uninhabited areas to which the name of desert is given in the Bible. Very little of the desert in the immediate neighborhood of Palestine is the waste of sand and stone which the name usually suggests. Most of it has a covering of grass after the rains which permits the pasture of flocks. It is the desert to the S which is described in Dt 8:15 as "great and terrible, with venomous serpents and scorpions and thirsty arid ground." The three Hb words for desert describe different types. *Midbar*, frequently translated "steppe" in modern Bibles, is the semiarid plain with a grassy covering; *ʿarābāh* and *yeshîmôn* both describe an arid waste of sand and rock. The Syrian desert to the E is infrequently mentioned in the OT. The deserts to the S are distinguished

a) Desert of Judah between Jerusalem and Jericho.
b) Desert of Judah at sea level.

by geographical names; cf ETHAM; KADESH; PARAN; SHUR; ZIN. Within the country itself the desert of Judah is frequently mentioned. This is the area of the declivity from the central range down to the Dead Sea and the valley of the Jordan. Within the desert of Judah are mentioned the deserts of Netophah* and Tekoa*. The desert of Judah in its lower reaches is a wild and utterly barren region. In the NT "desert" sometimes means a region with few or no inhabitants (Mt 14:13; 15:33; Mk 1:45; 6:31; Lk 4:42).

The cultural influence of the desert on the Bible cannot be overestimated. Like the sea, the desert is both a barrier and a means of communication. The Israelites themselves were always aware of their desert background, and certain features of the semi-nomadic life of the desert leave their traces through the entire OT. The sharp contrast between the "Desert" and the "Sown" and the two manners of life of the two regions (cf NOMAD) leads to constant friction and often to open feuds. The desert is a perpetual reminder of the reality of danger, hardship, and death, and it is often alluded to in Hb imagery. The desert was a refuge of fugitives and bandits like David* and his men. To lose one's way in the desert was almost certain death (Jb 6:18 ff). The wrath of Yahweh turns the garden land into a desert (Je 4:26). It is a land unsown (Je 2:2), a parched land without water (Ho 2:3), a haunt of demons and dangerous wild animals (Is 13:20; 30:6).

The desert is important in the religious conceptions and imagery of Israel. Israel first met Yahweh in the desert, and the story of the desert wandering remains the type of the encounter of man with God. Subsequently in OT and NT the desert is the place where man meets God, particularly in a crisis. Israel felt that it could not have survived the passage through the desert were it not for the protection of Yahweh (Dt 8:14 ff; Je 2:6). It was in the desert that Israel was tested and failed, and Yahweh will lead Israel back into the desert in order to speak to her directly and recover her love (Ho 2:16). When Yahweh comes to redeem His people, the desert will rejoice and blossom (Is 35:1 f), an allusion to the abundant flowers which carpet the desert floor after the spring rain. The NT allusions to the desert experience of Israel are frequent. It is mentioned as a time of testing and failure (AA 7:41 ff; 1 Co 10:5; Heb 3:8 ff). It is a type of the Christian experience (1 Co 10:11). But the desert experience was also a time when Israel found favor with Yahweh (AA 7:36; 13:18). Elijah* also met God in the desert (1 K 19:8 ff). This desert motif reappears in the NT. John the Baptist began his preaching in the desert (Mt 3:1; Lk 3:2), and Jesus passed forty days of prayer and fasting in the desert before He began His public ministry. This was for Him also a time of temptation* (Mt 4:1 ff; Mk 1:12 ff; Lk 4:1 ff). The period which Paul* spent in Arabia after his conversion (Gal 1:17) was probably a sojourn in the desert. In Apc 12:6 + 14 the woman flees from the serpent to a place prepared by God in the desert.

Deuterocanonical. The name given by Sixtus of Siena (1528–1569) to those books of the Bible whose place in the canon* was at some time denied or doubted in the Church. Cf CANON.

Deuteronomy. The fifth of the five books of Moses. The word is derived from the LXX translation of the words "copy of this law," *deuteronomion* (Dt 17:18).

1. *Contents.* I. After some historical data, which place the scene in the steppes of Moab* just before the Israelites* cross the Jordan* into Canaan* (1:1–5) there follows the first introductory discourse (1:5–4:40). This discourse contains a review of the events from Sinai*-Horeb* through the wandering in the desert to the scene of the discourse (1:5–3:29). This / is followed by an exhortation to keep the law which Moses is about to promulgate (4:1–40).

II. After two detached historical notices describing the establishment of cities of refuge E of the Jordan (4:41–43) and another introduction going over much the same ground as the first (4:41–49) there follows the second introductory discourse, which is another exhortation to keep the law (5:1–11:32). This discourse contains the decalogue* (5:6–21), a description of the covenant scene of Sinai-Horeb (5:22–33), an exhortation to the love of Yahweh (6:4–9) and to keep the law, to avoid contact with the Canaanites (7:1–11), to have confidence in the power of Yahweh to give them the land of Canaan (7:17–26) based on their experience of His providence during the wandering in the desert (8:1–9:6). There is a review of the infidelity of Israel in the desert (9:7–29) and an account of the making of the ark (10:1–11), and various exhortations (10:12–11:32).

III. The code of laws of Deuteronomy (12–26); cf LAW.

IV. Conclusion of the code. Various injunctions (27:1–7), formulae of curses (27:9–26) and of blessings (28:1–14), another formula of curses (28:15–68), concluding discourse (29:2–30:20), closing words of Moses to Israel and commission to Joshua* (31:1–8), commission of the law to the Levite* priests with a prescription for its reading every seven years (31:9–13), second commission to Joshua (31:14–23), command to write the song which follows and its commission to the Levites (31:16–30), the song of Moses (32:1–43), another injunction of Moses to Israel (32:45–47), words of Yahweh to Moses (32:48–52), blessing of the 12 tribes by Moses (33), death and burial of Moses (34:1–12).

The book has a distinctive style which is easily recognized. It is full and oratorical, exhibiting a number of favorite set phrases which recur constantly. The homiletic tone even runs through the code of laws, in contrast to the style of the other Hb legal codes. Certain dominant theological ideas are emphasized by repetition: the election of Israel by Yahweh to be His people, the importance of observing the laws and statutes which Moses promulgates in the name of Yahweh, the utter repudiation not only of foreign gods, in particular the gods of the Canaanites, but also of all contact with foreign peoples (this ferocity toward the Canaanites is in contrast with the broad humanitarian tone exhibited throughout the code toward fellow Israelites and foreigners resident in Israel); the worship of Yahweh by sacrifice at one designated place of cult, by which Jerusalem is meant, although it is not named, and the joy of observing the laws of Yahweh and of celebrating His festivals; confidence in the power of Yahweh, whose own activity rather than Israelite strength or force of arms has carried Israel through the wilderness and establishes it in the promised land; the power in nature of Yahweh, the giver of fertility, who disposes of such natural means of sustaining life as rain, an implicit polemic against the worship of the fertility gods of Canaan.

2. *Origin and Composition of the Book.* Modern critics agree that the Mosaic background of the discourses and of the code is fictitious, and that the origin of the book lies in a later period. It is almost universally agreed that at least the code of laws was the book found in the temple* during the reign of Josiah* by the priest Hilkiah* (2 K 22:8–30). The religious reforms of Josiah have a number of points of relation with the code of Dt (2 K 23:1–24). Most modern critics are inclined to believe that this code contained the legal traditions of the northern kingdom (cf ISRAEL), and a number of scholars think that Shechem* was the principal legal center of the N. With the fall of Israel in 721 BC this collection was taken to Jerusalem. The origin of the laws and their collection and preservation is thought to be principally the work of the Levite priests who are mentioned so frequently in Dt. The code which was found in the temple by Hilkiah was probably not entirely the work of the Levite priests, but of the priests of Jerusalem, since it is scarcely possible to suppose that the law of one sanctuary and other changes in cultic procedure from earlier codes such as the code of the covenant (cf LAW) could have originated in any place other than Jerusalem. It seems quite unlikely that such a code would have lacked an introductory discourse, and this must be one of the two discourses which are found in the present book. Cazelles is of the opinion that the second introductory discourse is the earlier and accompanied the original code. Against this view is the fact that the second discourse contains no historical material except an account of the events at Sinai-Horeb (cf above). The first discourse, on the contrary, contains no historical material earlier than the departure from Sinai-Horeb; and Eissfeldt's suggestion that the first discourse is preserved incompletely has much in its favor. It seems unlikely also that the historical introduction would not have contained an account of the events of the exodus from Egypt more extensive than the allusion in 11:3–4, however summary it may have been. But in spite of the difficulty of distinguishing the two introductory discourses clearly, Cazelles's hypothesis that they represent two different editions of the book, one prepared before the reform of Josiah, possibly under Hezekiah, and the second during the Exile*, is probable.

The conclusion of the book (27–34) exhibits a confusing series of additions whose relations with each other are not easy to discern. The concluding discourses of Moses (29:2–30:20) with the introductory verse (29:1) is a counterpiece to the introductory discourses. Rather obvious references to the Exile suggest that this discourse belongs to the second edition of the book. In Cazelles's theory it is a companion to the first introductory discourse. In 27:1 ff it is quite probable, as Nielsen suggests, that the words of the code have replaced in the tradition the original instruction of the covenant formula, since the writing of the code on whitewashed stones is, as Nielsen indicates, extremely impractical. The formulae of curses and blessings also exhibit repetition and duplication. The first formula of cursing (27:11–26) has no counterpart in the blessings. 28 contains two corresponding formulae of blessing and curses; the curses are almost twice as long as the blessings. This is probably due to expansion beginning at 28:46, which seems to be a conclusion of the curse formula, and the following verses are again obvious allusions to the Exile. The first formula of cursing, in which the 12 tribes stand in groups of 6, is referred to also in 11:26–32 and in Jos 8:33, the execution of the commission. The two allusions in Dt must be independent of each other, and the story of the execution most probably depends on the presence of the commission in Dt.

It is unlikely that any of the material after 31:14 belongs to the original book, and it serves as a conclusion to the Pnt* as a whole. The other traditions of the Pnt are found in these passages. Certainly neither the song of Moses (32) nor the blessing of the 12 tribes (33) was a part of the original compilation of Dt. On the relations of Dt to the other Pnt traditions cf PENTATEUCH.

The work of edition and compilation which produced Dt also had effects on the other historical books of the OT from Dt onwards. Practically no effects of this work appear in the first four books of the Pnt. But the language, style, and theological ideas of Dt, in particular the rather strict ideas of temporal reward and punishment for keeping the law, are reflected in the subsequent historical books down to the end of 2 K. Hence Martin Noth, followed by a number of modern scholars, has proposed that the books from Jos to the end of 2 K form a "Deuteronomic history," a companion to the first four books of the Pnt. The history was compiled during and after the Exile by the same group of editors who compiled the final edition of Dt. This opinion does not mean that the Deuteronomic editors composed the history; they employed existing literary material which for the most part exhibits no trace of Deuteronomic thought or language. The arrangement of the material, however, particularly in Jos* and 1–2 K*, often brings out the theological ideas of Dt, which are made explicit in the editorial passages. The actual traditions of the books come from older sources. This history dealt with the events from the conquest and settlement to the fall of the monarchy.

Devil. Cf DEMON; SATAN.

Dew. Moisture brought in from the sea by the W winds condenses at night and falls in abundance as dew in Palestine during the dry months of the year. The dew falls suddenly; the attack of an army is compared to it (2 S 17:12). It is sufficiently abundant to saturate a fleece (Jgs 6:38). The dew is the only source of moisture in the atmosphere during the rainy season, and its failure during a drought is disastrous (1 K 17:1). The curse of David upon Mount Gilboa* asks that neither rain nor dew may fall upon it (2 S 1:21). Abundant dew is a blessing (Gn 27:28) which comes from heaven (Dt 33:28) or from Yahweh (Mi 5:6). The dew disappears quickly after sunrise, so that the covenant loyalty of Ephraim* is compared to the morning dew (Ho 6:4).

Diaspora (Gk *diaspora*, "dispersion"). This word became a technical term for Jewish communities settled outside Palestine during the last century BC and the 1st century AD. The settlement of Hebrews outside Palestine began with the deportation of Israelites by the Assyrian and Babylonian kings in the 8th, 7th, and 6th centuries BC. All of these Hebrew communities lost their identity and were absorbed by the surrounding population, except the community established in Babylonia by Nebuchadnezzar*, which was the source of the resettlement of Jerusalem under Cyrus* in the late 6th century. The Jewish community at Babylon became large and prosperous and retained its identity into the Middle Ages. Jewish communities were settled in Egypt as early as the 6th century BC. The precise date of the settlement is uncertain, but the Jewish colony of Elephantine* was certainly there before the Persian conquest in 525 BC. Under the rule of the Ptolemies* conditions were favorable for Jewish immigration into Egypt, and Egypt became the largest, richest, and most influential center of Judaism outside Palestine. By the 1st century AD Jews were numerous and well established at Alexandria*, where one quarter of the city was entirely Jewish and a separate self-governing municipality.

The beginnings of Jewish communities elsewhere cannot be traced. It seems unlikely that there were any Jews in Antioch* before the middle of the 2nd century BC.

The list of cities and islands in 1 Mc 13:23 where Jews resided is thought by many scholars to refer not to the period of the book but to the time of the reedition of the book in the second half of the 1st century BC. By the beginning of the Christian era it is certain that Jews were settled in Syria, Asia Minor, Persia, Greece, and Italy, and during the first half of the 1st century AD Jewish settlements are known in about 150 places within and outside the Roman empire. The number of Jews in the Diaspora is estimated in the millions; some scholars believe they numbered between 8 percent and 10 percent of the total population of the Roman empire. Parthians, Medes, Elamites, residents of Mesopotamia, Cappadocia, Pontus, Asia, Phrygia, Pamphylia, Egypt, Cyrene, Rome, Crete, and Arabia are mentioned as pilgrims to Jerusalem (AA 2:9–10). Many cities with Jewish synagogues* are mentioned in AA and the epistles (cf PAUL and separate articles). Paul's intention to visit Spain suggests the existence of a Jewish colony there, otherwise unattested for this period.

Judaism of the Diaspora was almost entirely urban and was heavily concentrated in the larger centers such as Alexandria, Antioch, and Rome. Most of the Jews of the Diaspora were merchants and craftsmen and consequently in the upper economic levels. Their position in the Hellenistic monarchies and in the Roman empire was quite favorable. It was the policy of these governments to grant freedom to private religious associations. The Jews did not always possess full rights of citizenship, but they usually enjoyed privileges granted because of their commercial importance, also because of their customary orderly behavior, which made them equal to the average citizens, if indeed they were not better off. Because of their religious beliefs they were exempted from compulsory military service, and were permitted to pay a tax to support the temple* of Jerusalem. Under Julius Caesar (+ 44 BC) the policy of conferring Roman citizenship throughout the empire was initiated. Many Jews, among them, Paul, possessed this right.

The Jews of the Diaspora regarded Jerusalem as their spiritual capital and looked to it for religious leadership. Likewise they probably had little acquaintance with Hb except for the recitation of a few daily prayers. The need of a translation resulted in the Aramaic targums* and the Gk LXX*. As many Jews as were able made the pilgrimage to Jerusalem to celebrate one of the three great annual feasts.

Relations between the Jews of the Diaspora and their neighbors were not always good;

the causes of this were varied. Sometimes the poorer masses of the cities were envious of Jewish success and prosperity. Sometimes hostility was aroused by the peculiar practices of Judaism, Jewish exclusivism, and the unconcealed contempt of the Jews for pagan superstition and immorality. This hostility was expressed in literature (Posidonius of Apamea, Apollonius Molo, Cicero, Seneca, Persius, Quintilian, Statius, Juvenal, Tacitus). The favor of the Roman emperors ended with the accession of Caligula in AD 37. He permitted severe persecution of the Jews of Alexandria, and ordered his own divine image to be erected in the temple of Jerusalem; the execution of the decree was prevented by his assassination in AD 41. Riots between Jews and the citizens of Alexandria were frequent and mutual hostility was a chronic condition. Riots also occurred at Antioch, and the Jews were expelled from Rome by Claudius*. The Jewish communities were used by Paul as points of departure on his missionary expeditions, and in all probability other apostles* followed the same policy. In the NT the word appears in the technical sense ("diaspora of the Greeks," Jn 7:35). The expression "Greeks" is applied in Jn 12:20 to non-Palestinian Jews. The meaning of the word in the superscriptions of Js 1:1 and 1 Pt 1:1 is not entirely clear, and interpreters give different explanations. The address of James to the 12 tribes of the diaspora seems most probably directed to Jewish Christians outside Palestine; the Jewish expression is adapted to those members of the community who do not reside in what was still the central city of primitive Christianity. The address of 1 Pt is less obviously directed to Jewish Christians. Here the elect who sojourn in the diaspora of Pontus, Galatia, Cappadocia, Asia, and Bithynia are probably Christians, Jewish or not, who live outside Palestine and are thus designated by the Jewish term for the world outside Palestine.

Dibon (Hb *dîbôn*, Arabic *dhiban*), 40 mi S of Amman on the highway to Kerak. The name and the site are accepted as identical with the biblical Dibon. Dibon was included in the territory N of the Arnon* which was taken from Moab* by Sihon*, king of the Amorites* (Nm 21:26–30). It was included in the territory claimed by the tribes of Reuben* and Gad* and was fortified by the men of Gad (Nm 32:3, 34); it is once called Dibon-Gad (Nm 33:45–46; cf also Jos 13:9, 17). By the time of the composition of Is 15:2 and Je 48:18, 22 Dibon was once again Moabite. The discovery of the Moabite Stone of Mesha*, king of Moab, on this site has led modern scholars to conclude that the site is identical with the city of QRHH mentioned in the Moabite Stone as the capital city of Mesha which he took from the Israelites and rebuilt and fortified. The name Dibon is absent from the stone, probably because Mesha gave the city a new name when he captured it to signify his victory; but the old name persisted. The site was excavated by the American Schools of Oriental Research 1950–1952. The excavators discovered a series of five city walls, but it was impossible to assign an absolute date to any of them. Remains of a Nabatean* building which became in turn the foundation of a Roman building not earlier than the 2nd century AD and of a Byzantine church which incorporated some of the structure of the Roman building were discovered. No certain traces of Moabite buildings or occupation were found except some tombs with pottery which could be dated to the 9th century BC, the period of Mesha. The excavators concluded that the walled cities and the main occupation remains of the Iron Age and earlier lie to the N of the site excavated. Cf BASOR 125, p 7 ff; 133, p 6 ff.

Dinah (Hb *dînāh*, perhaps "suit at law"), daughter of Jacob and Leah*, whose rape by Shechem* was bloodily avenged by her brothers Simeon* and Levi* (Gn 30:21; 34:1 ff).

Dionysius (Gk *dionysios*, "belonging to [the god] Dionysus"), an Athenian, a member of the council of the Areopagus*, one of the few who accepted Christianity when Paul preached at Athens (AA 17:34). A tradition of doubtful historical value makes him the first bishop of Athens. A number of theological writings were attributed to him by the Fathers and the medieval theologians, none of which are earlier than the 4th or 5th century AD.

Diotrephes (Gk *diotrephēs*, "nourished by Zeus"), a member of the church of which the author of 3 Jn speaks in his letter to Gaius, a member of the same church. Diotrephes appears to be in authority in the church, since he refuses to receive the brothers, and expels those who wish to receive them. He is described as loving the first place (3 Jn 9–10).

Disciple. The term disciple, Gk *mathētēs*, occurs about 250 times in the NT. Most of these occurrences refer to the disciples of Jesus. The relation of Jesus and His disciples was in many respects similar to the relation of the Jewish rabbi* and his disciples. The rabbis or teachers of the law gathered about themselves disciples to whom they transmitted their doctrine. These in turn could hope to become rabbis under his instruction, and add to the tradition which they received. The Jewish teachers and disciples are referred to in the phrase "disciples of the Pharisees" (Mt 22:16; Mk 2:18; Lk 5:33), although the phrase is used loosely here, since the Pharisees* as such were not rabbis and had no disciples. However, most of the scribes* or rabbis were members of the sect of the Pharisees. The Pharisees called themselves disciples of Moses (Jn 9:28), attaching themselves thereby to the man who was conceived as the first in the chain of the teachers of the law. The Jews themselves looked upon Jesus as a rabbi with His disciples, and the title rabbi was often given Him both by the disciples and by others. The followers of John* the Baptist, who made no pretense of being a rabbi, were also called disciples, and it was from this group that Jesus called His own first disciples (Jn 1:35). John himself directed them to Jesus. The group of John's disciples persisted after John's death. Apollos*, a companion of Paul, was a disciple of John (AA 18:24–25) and the disciples at Ephesus* whom Paul baptized knew only the baptism* of John (AA 19:1 ff). The members of this group obviously regarded themselves as followers of Jesus, but their relations to other followers of Jesus remain obscure. Quite often the invitation is issued by Jesus Himself to follow Him or become His disciple, and this invitation was extended to more than the apostles*, so that some scholars believe that vocation by Jesus Himself was one of the qualifications for discipleship. This deduction is not altogether clear from the NT. The "large crowd" of disciples (Lk 6:17; 19:37; Jn 6:60) suggests a number larger than would be gathered by personal invitation. Other interpreters suggest that the followers of Jesus were gathered in concentric circles, of which the Twelve were the innermost group, the disciples next, and then followers or "believers." The relationship between Jesus and His disciples was not entirely the same as that of the rabbi and his disciples. Jesus demanded a more complete personal surrender to Himself than did the rabbis. His disciple must be willing to abandon father and mother, son and daughter, and to take up his cross and lose his life in the following of Jesus (Mt 10:37 ff; Lk 14:26 ff). Like their master, the disciples had to leave home and had no place to lay their head. They must not remain even to take care of an aging father nor to dispose of their domestic affairs (Mt 8:19 ff; Lk 9:57 ff). The disciples of Jesus differed from the disciples of the rabbis also

because they could not hope to attain His dignity; their entire life was to be spent in His discipleship. Both in Mt and Lk the disciples share in the teaching of Jesus (Mt 10:5 ff; Lk 10:1 ff). The discourse which in Mt is addressed only to the Twelve is in Lk addressed to the 72 disciples. Quite possibly the account of Lk is so framed as to show that the commission of teaching the gospel is not limited to the Twelve. The attitude of the disciples of Jesus toward tradition was not that of the Jewish disciples. The disciple of the rabbi strove to preserve the exact teaching of the rabbi word for word to the best of his ability, and the most successful disciple was the one who could best repeat by memory what he had heard. The NT itself is the best witness of how little the disciples of Jesus were concerned with the exact word for word report of what He said. The gospel consisted not in a verbal repetition of what He had said, but in the account of His life, passion, death, and resurrection. Here the disciples were witnesses* rather than mere channels of verbal tradition. In AA the word disciple is used to describe Christians; this use is limited to the part of the book between 6:1 and 21:16. Here the word means Christian simply, and not those who had known and followed Jesus personally. This use did not endure, and was probably never common. Disciples of Paul are mentioned in AA 9:25. Here the term must be extended to cover those who assisted Paul in his ministry or were his own personal converts. There is no other instance of this use of the word in the NT.

Divination. The pseudo-science of predicting future events by occult means. This skill was widely practiced in ancient Mesopotamia, and the influence of Mesopotamian divination was extremely widespread, enduring in Europe into medieval and modern times. A vast collection of Mesopotamian literature deals with the interpretation of various divinatory signs. The Mesopotamian diviners interpreted the future by means of oracles delivered by some authorized representative of the gods or by the interpretation of omens and signs, or by various inductive practices. These are distinguished as divination by lots or by the cast of arrows (belomancy); the manipulation of rods (rhabdomancy); observations of human behavior and facial expression (physiognomy); the study of the palm of the hand (cheiromancy); the phenomena of birth, especially unusual or monstrous parturitions; the behavior of animals. The largest part of animal divination was concerned with the study of the entrails of sacrificial victims, especially of the liver (hepatoscopy); flight of birds (ornithomancy) and movements of reptiles (ophiomancy); conformations of trees (dendromancy); configurations of flames (empyromancy) and smoke (kapnomancy); the behavior of drops of oil on the surface of water (lecanomancy); the observation of the heavenly bodies and meteorological phenomena (astrology).

There are several Hb words which seem to indicate forms of divination, but their precise meaning is difficult to determine. Divination was strictly prohibited in Hebrew law under penalty of death (Lv 19:31; 20:6; Dt 18:10–11). It is a sin as grievous as idolatry* (1 S 15:23). Saul had extirpated divination from the land (1 S 28:3), but he himself consulted a necromancer (1 S 28:7 ff). The land, however, was full of diviners in the days of Isaiah (2:6; 8:19). Divination is enumerated among the sins for which Yahweh destroyed the kingdom of Israel (2 K 17:17), and among the sins of Manasseh* (2 K 21:6), and among the practices rooted out by the reform of Josiah* (2 K 23:24). The false prophets* of Judah were contemptuously called diviners by Jeremiah (14:14; 27:9) and Ezekiel 13:6, 23). Nebuchadnezzar's divination by belomancy and hepatoscopy is mentioned in Ezk 21:26; here Yahweh himself determined the signs which decided the attack on Jerusalem. Divination by lecanomancy is ascribed to Joseph* (Gn 44:4, 15).

Divorce. 1. *OT.* The Hb legal codes, unlike the codes of Mesopotamia, contain no explicit regulation of divorce. The code of Dt provides that the man who divorces his wife must certify it in writing (Dt 24:1). It is assumed, both from the analogy of Mesopotamia and the general context of the OT, that only the husband had the right of divorce. This right did not exist if the husband falsely accused his wife of premarital intercourse (Dt 22:13–19) or if he had violated her before the marriage (Dt 22:28–29). The divorced woman was free to marry again, but she could not return to her first husband if the second marriage was ended by death or divorce (Dt 24:1–4), nor could she marry a priest (Lv 21:7). The formula of divorce as given in Ho 2:4 was "She is not my wife and I am not her husband," which is probably the negative of the marriage formula. We have no indication of the frequency of divorce in Israel. In the postexilic period Malachi rebukes those who leave the wives of their youth (2:14–15) as does Ben Sira (7:26). But Ben Sira advises divorce from a wicked woman (25:26). There is no indication of the legal causes for divorce. Dt 24:1 gives only the obscure phrase 'erwat dābār, literally "naked-

ness of a thing," which suggests some immoral behavior. The phrase probably does not signify adultery, which was a capital offense, but may signify in a summary way legal causes well known by custom or contained in legal prescriptions which are not preserved.

2. *NT.* With the exception of two Gospel passages, the teaching of Jesus on divorce is clear and succinct: he who divorces his wife and marries another commits adultery, and she who is divorced and marries another man commits adultery (Mk 10:1–12; Lk 16:18). Mk 10:12 is an expansion made in view of Roman law, which permitted a woman to institute divorce; in Hb and Near Eastern law only the man could divorce. Two passages in Mt are not equally clear and have been much discussed by interpreters. In Mt 5:32 the formula of Mk and Lk is qualified by the phrase, "Whoever divorces his wife except in the case of unlawful sexual intercourse." The parallel to Mk 10:1 ff in Mt 19:1 ff contains the qualification, "Whoever divorces his wife, not for unlawful sexual intercourse." The question put by the Pharisees as found in Mt, "May a man divorce his wife for any cause?" presupposes the dispute between the rabbinical schools of Hillel, who permitted divorce for any fault which the husband might find in his wife, and Shammai, who permitted divorce for adultery only. As the biblical basis of His teaching Jesus appeals to Gn 1:27; 2:24. Many interpreters have supposed that the version of Mt represents a variant tradition in the primitive Christian community, and this tradition has been preserved in the Greek church from very early times. Few interpreters doubt that the formula of Mk and Lk is more original than the formula of Mt. J. Bonsirven, however, adverted to the fact that Mt, the most Jewish of the Gospels, alludes here to the Jewish background. The word *porneia,* translated above as "unlawful sexual intercourse," is not the ordinary Gk word for adultery (*moicheia*). Bonsirven believes that *porneia* translates the Aramaic *zᵉnût,* which means an illicit union of concubinage. This case Jesus removes from the discussion; it is a marriage only in appearance and not in reality. The form of the saying as it appears in Mk and Lk runs counter to any known Jewish interpretation and is one of the most revolutionary features of the moral teaching of Jesus. This moral teaching was repeated by Paul (1 Co 7:10–11) as a saying not of his own, but of the Lord. Paul, however, did permit divorce in the case of a believer whose unbelieving spouse departs when the partner adopts Christianity (1 Co 7:12–16).

Doeg (Hb *dō'eg* or *dōyeg,* meaning unknown), an Edomite, the head of Saul's* shepherds, who was present when David* obtained bread from Ahimelek*, the priest at Nob* (1 S 21:7), and disclosed this to Saul (1 S 22:9–10). When Saul's followers refused to commit the sacrilege of killing the priests in revenge, Doeg executed Saul's command (1 S 22:18–19).

Assyrian hunting dogs.

Dog. In ancient Hb law the dog was an unclean animal, to which unclean flesh might be thrown (Ex 22:30). "Dog," "dead dog," "dog's head" were terms of insult (1 S 17:43; 2 S 3:8; 16:9;) or of self-humiliation (1 S 24:15; 2 S 9:8; 2 K 8:13). Scavenging dogs would even devour human flesh (2 K 9:10) and would attack persons (Pss 22:17; 59:7, 15). Male prostitutes are called dogs (Dt 23:19). The warning of Jesus not to give what is holy to dogs nor to cast pearls before swine is partly based on Ex 22:30, and the two unclean animals mentioned here probably have no figurative meaning (Mt 7:6). Paul, however, uses the insulting term in warning the Philippians* to beware of dogs, evildoers, those of the "amputation," (*catatomē,* a harsh pun on *peritomē,* circumcision; Phl 3:2). Dogs, sorcerers, harlots, murderers, idol-worshipers, and those who love lies are

excluded from the heavenly Jerusalem (Apc 22:15). The word may signify those who practice unnatural vice, or it may be simply an abusive term. The comparison which Jesus apparently makes of the Gentiles to dogs (Mt 15:26) seems extremely harsh to modern readers. This saying and the sharply witty retort of the Gentile woman (Mt 15:27) was the kind of exchange which was esteemed as wisdom in the ancient Near East. Jesus was obviously pleased with her wit.

Door. The door in buildings of biblical times was made of strips or planks of wood bound by metal strips, usually bronze or iron*. The doors of houses* were generally small and low, and it is doubtful whether the houses of the poor had doors at all, and scarcely more than one outside door. The doors of temples and places often had double leaves as in the temple* of Solomon (1 K 6:34). The door was hung on two hinges; the lower hinge rested in a hollowed stone of a type which has been frequently discovered in Palestinian excavations. The upper hinge rested in a metal frame or in a hollow made in the lintel. The threshold, usually of stone, was preferably a monolith, or of large stones carefully smoothed and joined. The door was closed with a bar or with a lock*. Among ancient peoples the door was commonly decorated with amulets* to protect it against the entrance of evil spirits, and guardian genii stood at the doors of Mesopotamian palaces and temples (cf CHERUB). This practice may be reflected in the Hb practice of hanging the *mezuzah* at the door (Dt 6:9). The doorpost was smeared with the blood of the Passover* lamb to ward off the angel of death (Ex 12:7).

Dor (Hb *dôr, dō'r*), a town of the Palestinian coast identical with the modern el Burj near Tanturah, about 8 mi N of Caesarea. The name appears in the compound *nᵉpōt dor,* "the heights of Dor," which designates either the low sand hills which line the coast N of Joppa* or the slopes of Mt Carmel*, which rise to the E of Dor. Naphoth-dor is included in the confederation of N kings defeated by Joshua (Jos 11:2; 12:23). The city is assigned to Manasseh (Jos 17:11) and to Ephraim (1 Ch 7:29), but Jos 17:11 indicates that it lay in the territory of Asher. It was effectively retained by non-Israelite peoples, the Canaanites (Jgs 1:27), and after the invasion of the "Sea Peoples" by the Tjekker, who held the city when it was visited by Wenamon of Egypt about 1100 BC (ANET 26). Israelite possession of Dor was scarcely earlier than the monarchy; the city is included in Solomon's 4th district (1 K 4:11). After the Assyrian conquest Dor was the headquarters of an Assyrian province which included the coast from Akko* to Joppa. The city was a port, although it had no natural harbor; and difficult communications with the hinterland prevented it from becoming an important city. Antiochus* VII besieged Tryphon* at Dor in 139 BC (1 Mc 15:10–14).

Dorcas (Gk *dorkas,* "gazelle"), the Gk name of Tabitha*, a woman of Joppa* who was raised from the dead by Peter (AA 9:36).

Dothan (Hb *dōtan,* meaning unknown), a town of central Palestine, not mentioned in the tribal lists of Jos; the sons of Jacob pastured there (Gn 37:17) and it was the scene of Elisha's escape from the Aramaean troops sent to capture him (2 K 6:13–19). It appears in Jdt 3:9; 4:6; 7:3 as near Esdraelon. It is identified with the modern Tell Dotha 60 mi N of Jerusalem and not far S of the plain of Esdraelon. Dothan is mentioned in the list of Canaanite cities captured by Thutmose III of Egypt (ANEP 242). Tell Dotha has been excavated by J. P. Free in several seasons since 1953. The excavation disclosed a city larger and more important than the few biblical notices would indicate. There were 11 levels of continuous occupation from Early Bronze (3100 BC) to Iron II, ending in 700 BC. A smaller Hellenistic town was built on the summit of the tell 300–100 BC. The occupation debris was 30 ft thick. A massive wall 13 ft thick enclosed the Early Bronze city. A jar burial of a child in Iron II was interpreted by the excavators as a child sacrifice. A massive building with large storage facilities from Iron II was taken to be the administrative center for the collection of taxes.

Dove. Four species of dove are found in modern Palestine: the ring dove or wood dove, the stock dove, the rock dove, and the turtledove. The domestication of the dove was known from early periods; Is 60:8 alludes to dovecotes. The story of the dove and the raven in the deluge (Gn 8:8–12) seems to praise the dove implicitly. The dove is frequently mentioned in the Pnt as a sacrificial bird, particularly as the offering of the poor and for purification from ritual uncleanness (Lv 1:14; 5:7, 11 f; 12:6, 8; 14:22, 30; 15:14, 29 f). It is part of the offering of the Nazirite* vow (Nm 6:10). The two Hb words distinguish the turtledove, *tōr,* from other species, *yônāh,* which appears to include several species.

The imagery of the dove in the Bible is rich and shows familiarity with the bird. Ps 68:14 is obscure, as is the title of Ps 56:1, "the dove of the distant terebinths." The poet desires that he had wings like a dove to escape the evil of the world (Ps 55:7). The moaning of the dove is compared to the mourning of those who suffer disaster (Is 38:14; 59:11; Na 2:8). Those who are attacked by an enemy flee to the cliffs like rock doves (Je 48:28). The restored Israelites shall come like doves in flight (Is 60:8; Ho 11:11). As in modern speech, the dove is regarded as silly (Ho 7:11). The dove with other birds knows the time of its annual migrations, unlike faithless Israel (Je 8:7). The voice of the turtledove is a sign of spring (SS 2:12). The frequency of the dove in the image of SS shows that the dove was a symbol of love as it is in modern poetry. The beloved is addressed as "my dove" (SS 2:14, an allusion to the rock dove; 5:2; 6:9). Israel is called Yahweh's dove (Ps 74:19). The eyes of the beloved are doves (SS 1:15; 4:1; 5:12); the exact force of the figure is uncertain, but it possibly alludes simply to the dove as an erotic motif and not to any particular quality either of the bird or of its eyes.

In the NT the dove is the offering of the poor for the redemption of the firstborn (Lk 2:24); it was sold in the temple courts for sacrificial purposes, a practice to which Jesus objected vigorously (Mt 21:12; Mk 11:15; Jn 2:14, 16). It is a symbol of guilelessness (Mt 10:16). The dove is the visible symbol of the spirit* in the baptism of Jesus (Mt 3:16; Mk 1:10; Lk 3:22; Jn 1:32). The figurative language of the OT suggests that the primary force of the symbol here is love, the love which the Father through His beloved Son communicates to all who believe in the Son.

Dowry. The dowry is not mentioned in the Hb legal codes, and there are very few clear allusions to the dowry elsewhere in the OT. In Mesopotamian law the dowry was given to the bride by her father and remained her possession even if it was administered by her husband; it passed to her sons after her death or returned to her family if she died without sons. The gifts of the slave Deborah* to Rebekah* before her marriage to Isaac* (Gn 24:59) and of Zilpah* and Bilhah* to Leah* and Rachel* (Gn 29:24, 29) are probably to be understood as dowries. Hagar*, the slave who was certainly the personal property of Sarah*, was probably given to her as a dowry. Such gifts as a slave girl instead of a dowry are mentioned in the Mesopotamian legal records (Driver and Miles BL 274). Achsah*, daughter of Caleb*, was urged by her husband to ask her father for a gift of land, probably as a dowry (Jos 15:17–18; Jgs 1:14–15). The Pharaoh gave his daughter the city of Gezer* when she married Solomon* as a *shilluḥîm* (1 K 9:16). This rare word, which elsewhere means the dismissal of a wife or a parting gift, may here signify a dowry. The gift in this instance, however, passed to the husband and not to the wife's sons or her father.

Dream. The belief that dreams are a means of divine communication or an occult means of discerning the future was widespread in the ancient Near East. The dream was conceived as a straightforward communication or as a symbolic phenomenon whose interpretation would disclose the future. The interpretation of dreams was a part of the science of divination* (oneiromancy). Dreambooks with extensive collections of meanings have been preserved both from Mesopotamia and from Egypt. Professional dream interpreters are mentioned in Babylon in Dn and in Egypt in the story of Joseph*. In the literature of Ugarit* Anath learns in a dream that Aleyan Baal* is alive. Keret receives in a dream from El directions for offering sacrifice, and Daniel learns in a dream that he will have a son. Such a belief in the validity of dreams is found neither in OT nor in NT, nor can a belief in the efficacy of dreams as a medium of divine communication be said to be characteristic of the Bible, since dreams as a medium are found in only a few passages; and it seems that these passages should be regarded rather as a reflection of folklore narratives than instances of genuine biblical belief.

1. *OT*. Solomon (1 K 3:5–15) is invited by Yahweh in a dream to ask what he desires, and asks for wisdom rather than for wealth and power, and is promised wealth and power with wisdom. Many scholars think the story alludes to the practice of incubation, in which the worshiper passes the night in a temple expecting a divine communication. Solomon's dream occurred in the sanctuary of Gibeon*. If it is an instance of incubation, it is the only certain instance found in the Bible. It appears to be a popular fictitious explanation of Solomon's wisdom as well as a wise saying which shows that wealth and power are the fruit of wisdom. The dream vision of Jacob (Gn 28:10 ff) at Bethel* does not occur in a sanctuary; but Bethel is represented in the story as "the house of God and the gate of heaven" (28:17), and was therefore a holy place where one could seek God. The vision does not differ from others reported in the patriarchal stories except that it occurs in a dream. At Beersheba* Jacob* is assured in "a vision by night" that he would safely journey to Egypt (Gn 46:2 ff). A dream

vision is also mentioned of Abraham (Gn 15:12 ff); here, however, the sleep is described not by the ordinary word, but by a rare word (*tardēmāh*) which indicates a trance or hypnotic slumber. The call of Samuel* (1 S 3:3 ff) occurs after Samuel has retired for the night in the sanctuary, but it is not clearly a dream. It is an interesting fact that most of the dream revelations of the OT are granted to non-Israelites; Israelites believed that Yahweh spoke directly to His own people.

Dreams which contain a direct communication:

Gn 20. Abimelech*, after he has taken Sarah* into his harem, is warned in a dream that she is the wife of another and thus escapes punishment. In the parallel accounts of this episode (Gn 12 and 26) no dream is involved.

Gn 31:24. Laban* is warned in a dream not to do any harm to Jacob.

Gn 31:10–13. The stratagem by which Jacob multiplied his flocks (Gn 30:31 ff) is here explained as due to a dream vision. Cf also Gn 21:17 ff; 22:1 ff; 26:24 ff; Nm 22:9 ff, 20 ff, in which divine communications are granted at night; the text of these passages, however, does not mention dreams.

Symbolic dreams:

The largest concentration of symbolic dreams is found in the Joseph story.

Gn 37:5. Two symbolic dreams which need little interpretation signify Joseph's future preeminence over his brothers. These dreams go beyond the story of Joseph and his brothers and reflect the preeminence of the Joseph tribes in Canaan.

Gn 40:1 ff. Joseph interprets the dreams of the chief butler and the chief baker of the Pharaoh. Although the two dreams were similar, Joseph shows his skill by interpreting them differently; the interpretation involves a play on the Hb phrase "lift" or "remove" the head. His success here leads to his appearance before the Pharaoh.

Gn 41. Joseph interprets the Pharaoh's dream of the seven fat and the seven lean cows and the seven fat and the seven blasted ears as signifying seven years of plenty followed by seven years of famine. The professional dream interpreters of the Pharaoh could not interpret these dreams, and Joseph states the Hb belief that the interpretation of dreams is from God (Gn 41:16, 25).

Jgs 7:13–14. A Midianite* dreams that a barley cake rolls into the camp and overturns a tent. His companion interprets this as signifying the destruction of the camp by Gideon*. Gideon overhears the conversation and takes it as a sign of victory.

Another collection of symbolic dreams occurs in Dn.

Dn 2. This chapter is a polemic against professional dream interpretation. Nebuchadnezzar* demands that the interpreters tell him the dream itself as well as the interpretation. When they are unable to do so, Daniel, whose interpretation comes from God, interprets the king's dream of the statue which signifies the four empires. Here, as in the dreams of the Pharaoh, is reflected the ancient Near Eastern belief that the dreams of the king had political and not merely personal significance.

Dn 3:31–4:34. Daniel interprets Nebuchadnezzar's dream which foretells the king's madness.

A few passages of the OT suggest that in some circles and at some periods dreams were regarded as a regular means of divine communication. Dreams and visions of the prophet are distinguished from the personal communication of God with Moses (Nm 12:6–8). Saul could find the word of Yahweh neither by dreams nor by Urim* nor by prophets (1 S 28:6). In the eschatological future the young men will see visions and the old men will dream dreams (Jl 3:1). Eliphaz* receives an answer to Job's* problem in a dream (Jb 4:12 ff). Job is troubled by nightmares sent by God (Jb 7:13–14). Elihu* includes dreams among the means by which God speaks to men (Jb 33:14 ff). Judas* sees the high priest Onias* and the prophet Jeremiah* in a dream before his victory over Nicanor* (2 Mc 15:12 ff). The Egyptians were warned in dreams of the disasters which were about to befall them (WS 18:17–19).

A few passages of the OT seem to reject the dream explicitly as a medium of divine communication. Jeremiah (23:25 ff) distinguishes between the word of Yahweh and the dream of the lying prophets. The dream may be related, but only as a dream. Cf also Je 27:9–10; 29:9, in which the lying prophets are called dreamers. The precept of Dt 13:2–6, forbidding the Israelites to listen to any prophet or dreamer who attempts to seduce them from the worship of Yahweh, seems to be neutral toward the dreamer, and suggests that such dreamers may have been a recognized professional caste; but there is no other indication of such a caste. Lying dreams are included among the means by which false prophets deceive the people (Zc 10:2). Ec 5:2 explains dreams as due to the pressure of care.

Hb literature uses the dream as a term of comparison of the shadowy and insubstantial (Pss 73:20; 126:1; Jb 20:8; Is 29:7–8). In general the OT offers little support for the assertion that the dream was a recognized medium of divine communication. The dreams enumerated above, especially since they occur in clusters in certain books and passages and in certain literary types, must be regarded as eccentric rather than characteristic; they reflect popular belief and anecdote.

2. NT. Dreams as media of revelation occur only in Mt (1–2 and once elsewhere) and in AA. In the infancy* narrative of Mt Joseph* learns in a dream that Mary's son is of divine origin (1:20), and he is warned in a dream to flee to Egypt (2:13) and to return from Egypt (2:19–20). The Magi* are warned in a dream to avoid Herod* after they visit the child (2:12). These dreams are all direct communication. The dream of Pilate's* wife because of which she warns Pilate to abandon the case against Jesus is mentioned without any details (Mt 27:19). The word "dream" is not used in AA; Paul receives communication four times in "a vision at night." The man from Macedonia asks him to come and help them; this was the occasion of Paul's first missionary journey to Europe (AA 16:9). Paul is encouraged by a vision of the Lord to remain in Corinth (AA 18:9); a vision of the Lord assures him that he will go to Rome (AA 23:11); and an angel of God assures him that he and all the passengers of the ship will escape death (AA 27:23 ff). Both Mt 1–2 and the second half of AA exhibit a theologico-literary conception which does not occur elsewhere in the NT. It consists in setting forth the divine intervention in the story by submitting the actions of the principal characters more directly to the divine guidance as manifested in dreams.

Drunkenness. 1. OT. Alcoholic intoxication seems to have been fairly common among the Israelites. The culture hero Noah* who discovered wine* is represented as discovering its intoxicating power also (Gn 9:21). Intoxication was the normal result of festive dinners (Gn 43:34; 1 S 25:36; 2 S 11:13; 1 K 16:9; 20:16). The dinner of Joseph and his brothers (Gn 43:34) is paralleled by Egyptian art and literary allusions which show that drunkenness was normal at feasts.

David had a purpose in intoxicating Uriah* (2 S 11:13). Elah* was drunk when he was assassinated (1 K 16:9) and Benhadad* was drunk when he was attacked by the Israelites (1 K 20:16). The words of Eli* (1 S 1:13 ff) suggest that drunkenness was not unexpected at Israelite religious festivities. Isaiah speaks of the drunkards of Ephraim (28:1, 3) and describes vividly the drunkenness of a festive dinner (28:7). He also utters threats against those who drink to late hours (5:11) and the heroes at drinking (5:22). Pr 26:9 refers to the danger of a drunken man armed with a weapon. Warnings against drunkenness are uttered in Tb 4:15 and Pr 23:31. The Nazirite* vow* included abstinence from intoxicating beverages (Nm 6:3). In the story of Samson* the prohibition is extended to his mother before his birth (Jgs 13:3). The priests were forbidden to drink intoxicating beverages before entering the sanctuary (Lv 10:9). Ben Sira also warns against drunkenness (19:1). The abstinence of the Rechabites* was not due to motives of temperance (Je 35:1 ff).

Drunkenness is also used in a metaphorical sense. In particular, those who suffer disaster, especially from the punishing anger of Yahweh, are compared to those who stagger from drunkenness. The nations must drink the intoxicating cup of the anger of Yahweh (cf Ps 107:27; Lam 4:21; Is 19:14; 29:9; 51:21; Je 13:13; 23:9; 25:27; 48:26; 51:7, 39, 57; Ezk 23:33; Na 3:11). The earth totters like a drunkard in the eschatological earthquake (Is 24:20). The arrows of Yahweh are drunk with blood (Dt 32:42) and His sword drinks the blood of His enemies (Is 34:5; Je 46:10). The Israelites drink the blood of their defeated enemies (Ezk 39:19) to intoxication.

2. NT. The words of the steward at the wedding feast of Cana* suggest that intoxication was not uncommon at such festivities (Jn 2:10). The man who does not watch for the coming of Jesus is compared to a drunken servant (Mt 24:49; Lk 12:45). The gift of speaking in tongues manifested at Pentecost is explained by the listeners as due to the intoxication of the speakers (AA 2:13 ff), and Peter explains that, while drunkenness might be expected, it was not to be expected at the third hour, about 9:00 AM. Drunkenness is included in the catalogues of vices in Rm 13:13; 1 Co 5:11; 6:10; Gal 5:21. An explicit warning against drunkenness is given in Eph 5:18, perhaps with an allusion to the drunkenness of pagan rites. Christians should be filled with the spirit* and not with intoxicating liquor. Paul mentions drunkenness as one of the defects of the Corinthian celebration of the Lord's supper (cf EUCHARIST: 1 Co 11:21).

The metaphorical use of the term is found only in Apc 17:2, in which the great harlot of Babylon makes the earth drunk with her idolatry, and 17:6, where she is herself drunk with the blood of the saints.

Drusilla. A Roman name, feminine form of Drusus; the Jewish wife of the Roman procurator Felix* (AA 24:24 ff). She was the youngest daughter of Herod* Agrippa I, born in AD 38. She was betrothed by her father to Epiphanes, son of the king of Com-

magene, but the marriage did not take place because he refused to be circumcised. She was then given by her brother Agrippa* II to Azizus, king of Emesa. Felix, who had himself been married twice previously, persuaded her to desert her husband and marry him in AD 54, when she was 15 or 16 years old. Their son Agrippa died in the eruption of Vesuvius in AD 79. This couple was an apt audience for Paul's discourse on "righteousness, self-control, and the coming judgment" (AA 24:25).

Dumah (Hb *dûmāh*), an Arabian tribe mentioned among the sons of Ishmael* (Gn 25:14; 1 Ch 1:30). The oracle against Dumah (Is 21:11) is probably not directed to this Arabian tribe, but to Edom*, whose territory is elsewhere called Seir*, mentioned here. There is probably a play on the two names, but the significance of the name here is unknown.

Dura (Aramaic *dûrā'*), a plain in Babylonia where Nebuchadnezzar set up his golden statue (Dn 3:1). The name is otherwise unknown. It is thought by some scholars to be connected with Akkadian *duru,* wall or castle.

Dye. The dyer's craft was known both in Egypt and Mesopotamia from very early times. In Mesopotamia animal, vegetable, and mineral dyes were known and used. In particular, the red dye (*tulatu*), the red-purple dye (*argamannu*), and the violet-purple dye (*takiltu*) were known in the OT by the same names. The Egyptians had blue, black, brown, green, red, purple, and yellow dyes, probably all vegetable dyes applied by the use of a mordant. Egyptian paintings show that the peoples of Canaan wore brightly colored garments. Joseph's "coat of many colors" of the older English versions probably was brightly colored, but the Hb word means a tunic with sleeves. Dyed fabrics were a desirable piece of booty in war (Jgs 5:30). The similes of Is 1:18 suggest that the Hebrews knew how to manufacture fast dyes. The most desirable dyes mentioned in the OT are red and purple dyes. The red dye called *tôla'at šānî* was made by pulverizing the eggs and bodies of the kermes insect, *coccus illicis.* Albright finds a red dye in *ḥašmannîm* (Ps 68:32, from Egyptian *ḥsmn,* natron). The purple dyes were red purple (Hb *'argāmān,* Akkadian *argamannu*) and violet purple (Hb *tᵉkēlet,* Akkadian *takiltu*). Both of these were imported from the great dye manufacturing centers of the coast of Phoenicia. The dye was obtained from a mollusc (*murex*). The amount of shells found on the coast near Sidon* shows

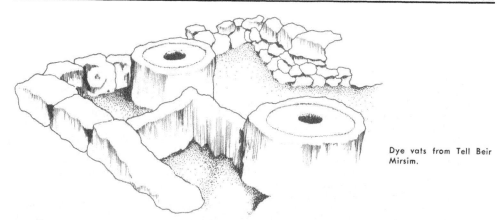

Dye vats from Tell Beir Mirsim.

that this city was at one time a great center of dye production. Dye manufacture is also mentioned at Ugarit*. The difference in the shades of the dye was the result of variations in the process. Most ancient dyes were impure and it is doubtful that the ancient dyer was ever able to produce a uniform color. The amount of dye which could be obtained from such a source was very small, and Tyrian purple is mentioned throughout the ancient world down to Greek and Roman times as a rare and costly article, within the reach only of kings and the wealthy; it was "the royal purple." Little is known of the methods of ancient dyers. W. F. Albright discovered at Tell Beit Mirsim, the biblical Debir*, what is accepted by most Palestinian archaeologists as the remains of ancient dye plants. In rectangular basins of stone and mortar stood circular vats from 28 to 32 in in height and diameter. The flat top was grooved around the edge with a drain into the vat. Albright explains this as intended to permit the excess dye to flow back into the vat; it was too precious to be allowed to run off. The openings at the top are too small to receive fabric; Albright notes that it was the ancient practice to dye the thread before the fabric was woven. The use of lime as a mordant is suggested by several jars containing slaked lime in the neighborhood of the vats. No facilities for heating the vats were found, and Albright leaves open the question of whether a hot bath or a cold bath process was employed. In NT times Asia Minor was a great dye manufacturing center; a seller of purple named Lydia* of Thyatira* was one of Paul's converts at Philippi (AA 16:14).

E

Eagle. The Hb words *nešer* and *'ayit* do not distinguish clearly between the eagle and the vulture. In Palestine there are four species of vulture and several species of eagle; the tawny eagle and the imperial eagle are common. The imagery of *nešer* seems to designate the eagle most frequently; but the vulture seems to be meant in Pr 30:17. The eagle soars and nests high in the rocks (Jb 39:27–30). Those who shave themselves in mourning make themselves bald as the eagle (Mi 1:16). Yahweh bears the Israelites on eagle's wings (Ex 19:4; Dt 32:11). The flight of the eagle is a common figure of swiftness, in particular the swiftness of an attacking enemy (Dt 28:49; Pr 23:5; Jb 9:26; Lam 4:19; Je 4:13; 48:40; 49:22; Ob 4; Hab 1:8). Saul and Jonathan are likened to eagles (2 S 1:23), as are Nebuchadnezzar and the Pharaoh (Ezk 17:3, 7). The way of the eagle in the sky is one of the four things the wise man does not understand; they leave no trace (Pr 30:19). The fable of the eagle renewing itself (the phoenix) was known to the Israelites (Ps 103:5; Is 40:31). Cyrus is compared to the *'ayit* (Is 46:11); it is unlikely that the unflattering comparison of the vulture is intended. The meaning of the word in Jb 28:7 is ambiguous. Elsewhere the *'ayit* is a carrion bird, a vulture (Gn 15:11; Is 18:6; Ezk 39:4), and probably the "speckled vulture" (?) of Je 12:9. Gk *aetos* has the same ambiguity, but the vulture is meant in Mt 24:28; Lk 17:37. The cherubim of Ezk 1:10; 10:14 have the countenance of an eagle, echoed in Apc 4:7. An eagle in flight announces doom (Apc 8:13), and the woman in flight is borne to safety on the wings of an eagle (Apc 12:14).

Earth. Earth in the Bible designates either a particular part of the earth ("land") in a geographical sense, or the earth as the place of human habitation (Is 45:18). The earth in the cosmic sense was conceived as a disk which rested either upon the waters of the abyss (Ps 24:2) or upon pillars (Ps 104:5; Jb 38:4); cf CREATION. Heaven* and earth are the comprehensive biblical designations of the biblical universe (Gn 1:1; 2:4 +). The earth belongs to Yahweh (Ps 24:1). The heavens are God's throne, and the earth is His footstool (Is 66:1; Mt 5:35). In the eschatological future God will create a new heaven and a new earth (Is 65:17; 66:22; 2 Pt 3:13; Apc 21:1). The dualistic conception of earth and earthly as opposed to heaven and heavenly appears in the NT (Jn 3:31; 1 Co 15:45–47; Col 3:2–5). In these passages the earthly is opposed to Christ, the heavenly man. The Christian regeneration consists in putting off the earthly to put on the form of the heavenly man. The only basis for this dualism in the OT is the curse put on the earth because of the sin of the first man (Gn 3:17).

Earthquake. Earthquakes in Palestine have been frequent and violent throughout recorded history. The earthquakes are due to a fault which appears on the surface as the rift of the Jordan* valley. This rift is a continuation of the rift between the Lebanon* and the Anti-Lebanon in Syria* and is prolonged southward through the Red Sea into central Africa. Disastrous earthquakes are reported in 140 BC between Tyre and Ptolemais; in 31 BC and in AD 130 at Nicopolis and Caesarea; in AD 362 at Nicopolis, Neapolis, Eleutheropolis, and Gaza; in the 4th century in Moab; in AD 530 at Antioch (ancient chroniclers note that this is the fifth time the city was destroyed by earthquake); in AD 542 in Phoenicia; in AD 551 an earthquake which was felt in Palestine, Syria, Arabia, and Mesopotamia; in AD 746 and in AD 808 at Jerusalem; in AD 1016 at Jerusalem; in 1033–1034 an earthquake which was felt for 40 days and destroyed Ramleh, Jericho, and Nablus; in 1159 in Syria; in 1170 in Palestine; in 1545 at Jerusalem; in 1759 in the Bekaa and the Lebanon; in 1733 at Aleppo; in 1837 in Galilee; in 1896 in Galilee; in 1927 at Jaffa, Gaza, Jerusalem, Nablus, and Nazareth. This latest earthquake killed over 500 people, 147 in the market of Nablus alone. It was also felt severely in Jerusalem and at other points in Palestine and Transjordan, and the Jordan was blocked by a landslide for over 24 hours. Allusions to particular earthquakes are rare in the Bible; but the number of literary and figurative allusions to them suggests that they were as frequent in biblical times as in later periods. An earthquake in the reign of Uzziah* is alluded to in Am 1:1; Zc 14:5. No details are given, but the impression is left that it was unusually severe. An earthquake is thought to lie behind the story of the "overturning" of Sodom* and Gomorrah (Gn 19:23 ff). Korah*, Dathan* and Abiron* and their followers were destroyed by an earthquake (Nm 16:31). An earthquake is mentioned at the death of Jesus (Mt 27:51 ff). The earthquakes are caused by the footstep or the voice of Yahweh, and they are a feature of the theophany* (Jgs 5:4; 2 S 22:8; Ps 18:8; 68:9; Jl 4:16; Na 1:5); the earth trembled when Yahweh revealed Himself to Elijah* on Mt Horeb* (1 K 19:11). It is a weapon of Yahweh's punishment (Ps 60:4; Je 4:24; 51:29) and a feature of the apocalyptic day* of Yahweh (Is 13:13; 24:18–19; Mt 24:7; Mk 13:8; Apc 6:12; 8:5; 11:13; 16:18).

Ebal (Hb *'ēbāl*). Mt Ebal, Jebel es Sitt es Slamiyeh, 2950 ft high, lies 40 mi N of Jerusalem on the highway near Nablus, on the N side of the road opposite Mt Gerizim* on the S side. Ebal is the scene of the ritual of blessing and cursing described in Dt 11:29 ff; 27:11 ff. The execution of the ritual is mentioned in Jos 8:30 ff. Joshua erected an altar on Ebal and the stones on which the covenant formula was written (not the entire code of law; cf DEUTERONOMY). No reason is apparent why one mountain should be chosen for the blessing and another for the curse. The topography raises some question about the reality of the ritual as described, since the bases of the two mountains do not lie sufficiently near each other. The ritual in some form, however, represents without much doubt a historical practice, and it was more probably an annual or regular ceremony than a single episode; cf COVENANT.

Ebed-Melek (Hb *'ebed melek,* "servant of the king"), an Ethiopian* eunuch in the court of Zedekiah* who interceded for Jeremiah* when the prophet was cast into a cistern and with the king's permission brought him out of the cistern (Je 38:7 ff).

Ebenezer (Hb *'eben ha 'ēzer*), according to 1 S 7:12 so named because of a memorial stone which Samuel* set up between Mizpeh* and Yeshana to commemorate a victory over the Philistines* (1 S 7:10–11). The same name is used to identify the place where the Hebrews encamped before their defeat by the Philistines encamped at Aphek* (1 S 4:1; 5:1). The two places can scarcely be the same. If they are meant to be the same, the use of the name in 4:1 must be proleptic; but it is more probable that 7:12 contains a popular anecdote explaining the origin of the name, which could have been older than either of the battles mentioned. WHA doubtfully locates Ebenezer a short distance SSE of Aphek, the later Antipatris.

Eber (Hb *'eber,* meaning uncertain), in the Table of Nations* the son of Shelah and the father of Peleg and Joktan (Gn 10:21, 24; 11:14 ff; 1 Ch 1:18, 25). In the obscure oracle of Balaam* (Nm 24:24) Eber with Ashur represents Mesopotamia. W. F. Albright, however, has reconstructed the text so that Eber does not appear. Eber (in NT Heber) is mentioned in the genealogy of Lk 3:35. On Eber as the eponymous ancestor of the Hebrews cf HEBREW.

Ecbatana. The Gk form of the Persian* city Ha(n)gmatana, Aramaic *'ahmᵉtā',* the capital city of the Medes* near the modern Hamadan, located on the slopes of Mt Orontes at an altitude of 6280 ft. Ecbatana was the capital city of the Medes and became the summer residence of the Persian kings. The decree of Cyrus permitting the rebuilding of the temple* of Jerusalem was found in the archives of Ecbatana (Ezr 6:2). The author of the romance of Tobit made it the residence of Raguel* (Tb 3:7; 7:1) and of Tobias after the death of his father (Tb 14:12). It was the capital city of Arphaxad*, king of the Medes in the story of Judith (Jdt 1:1 ff).

Ecclesiastes. The Gk title of the book, *ekklēsiastēs,* "one who calls the assembly (*ekklēsia*)" or "a member of the assembly," is a translation of the Hb *ḳōhelet* (1:1, 2, 12; 7:27; 12:9, 10). "Kohelet, son of David" (1:1, cf 1:12) signifies Solomon*, the great wise man of Israel. This is a literary attribution; but the character of Solomon is not maintained after 2:26. Modern critics, with remarkable unanimity and arguing from different reasons, propose 250 BC as the date of the book. This is suggested by its language, which is late Hb, and its position in wisdom* literature between Pr and Jb and before BS. Ec is not cited in the NT.

Ec has been described as the notebook of a sage. The contents are loosely organized about definite topics, some of which recur. The theme of the book is the vanity of human desires and achievements. This is seen in the iron cycle of nature which circumscribes man's efforts (1:2–11), the futility even of wisdom (1:12–18) and of all human efforts, even those in which men think they may find satisfaction (2:1–22), so that life offers nothing sure but the simple pleasures (2:24–26). The iron cycle is again referred to (3:1–8), and human ignorance and failure remove all security except the simple pleasures (3:9–15). There is no comfort in virtue, for righteous and wicked die alike (3:16–22). Human toil does not reward the toiler (4:1–16). Man must pay his vows to God (5:1–9). Wealth gives no satisfaction beyond the simple pleasures (5:10–6:12). Assorted maxims of traditional wisdom are collected (7:1–14), but wisdom itself gives no security (7:15–29). There is no correlation between men's righteousness and wickedness and their success and happiness (8:1–9:6). One must enjoy what pleasure life affords, for nothing else is certain (9:7–16). There is a remarkable parallelism between 9:7–9 and a passage of the Akkadian Gilgamesh* epic (ANET 90). After another collection of assorted maxims (9:17–10:20) the uncertainty of human effort is again asserted (11:1–8) and the young man is urged to enjoy his youth and vigor before old age comes and the impossibility of realizing any joy and desire (11:9–12:8). An epilogue is added by the editor (12:9–13); some critics believe 12:13 is from a second editor.

There is an evident lack of harmony between the maxims of the traditional wisdom found in the book and the pessimism of the other passages. A number of critics have attributed this to diversity of authorship; in particular, they believe that the traditional wisdom has been interpolated in order to counterbalance the harsh pessimism of the original work. In other instances (2:14; 4:5–6; 6:10; 7:5–6; 7:26; 8:1–2; 11:4, 6), the author has taken traditional maxims and used them as a text for discussion or as illustrations, in some cases contradicting them. Recent critics are inclined to minimize the work of the editor, reducing it to title and epilogue, and perhaps such lines as 3:17; 7:18; 8:5; 12:7. Once one admits, however, the "notebook" type of composition, there is no line which need be detached from the original author. The book resembles Jb, not only in the problem which it discusses, but also in the exchange of various views of the problem. Ec, however, does not employ the dialogue with different speakers to state different points of view; in a more rambling way he discourses in a soliloquy — one might almost call it a dialogue with himself, now uttering the traditional maxims of wisdom, now adding his own reflections on how the traditional wisdom fails to answer the questions he asks. In this feature the loose construction of the book gives it a resemblance to Pr and to other collections of ancient wisdom found in extrabiblical sources of Egypt and Mesopotamia.

According to rabbinical tradition the pessimism of the book caused some difficulties concerning its acceptance as a sacred book; and this pessimism is still a difficulty. In reality the difficulty arises from the profundity of Ec. Traditional wisdom often exhibited a shallow optimism and a too facile belief that virtue is always rewarded and wickedness always punished. This wisdom is criticized both in Jb and in Ec. It is contradicted by experience, by the mystery of evil, by the fact that wickedness often succeeds and virtue fails. Neither author takes this as a reason for losing faith in God, but neither finds a satisfying answer to the question; and Ec is more negative than Jb. The profundity of Ec lies in his perception of the total inability of man to work out enduring happiness by his own resources. Even man's wisdom and his virtue cannot resolve all his problems or overcome the evil which mysteriously pervades the world. The apparently negative response to the question is superficially disconcerting; the merit of Ec, as of Jb, is in putting the question rather than in answering it, in emphasizing that one cannot perceive the reality of the good unless one is aware of the reality of evil. Shallow optimism, whether of the Hb sages or of the Christian, sometimes tends to deny or to minimize the reality of evil and to draw a veil over the demands which the struggle against evil makes. Ec asserts that the struggle is beyond human power; the message has lost neither its truth nor its relevance.

The question is raised whether Ec is not at times a hedonist (2:24 ff; 3:12 f; 8:15; 9:7 ff; 11:9 f). The question misses the many obvious allusions both in OT and NT to the pleasures of life, which are always regarded as a gift of God. It also misses the unqualified polemic against hedonism of 2:1 ff, which reflects the traditions of Solomon as a lover of pleasure. It is a relieving feature of the pessimism of Ec that he believes that God grants man a certain portion of pleasure in a normal life; and he is sure that toil spent to acquire more than this portion is "vanity and the pursuit of wind."

Ultimately, of course, the pessimism of Ec rests upon the absence of a conception of a future life. In a certain sense the book postulates the future life as an answer to its problems and is an indirect vindication of the belief. Subtle as the author is, it is doubtful that his indirection is deliberate; but it was a defect of the traditional wisdom that it did not affirm this belief, and his criticisms are valid. In this respect the book must be taken in the context of Hb wisdom and the development of biblical belief. It is a great step forward to realize that human life contains no resources to achieve ultimate and enduring happiness; indeed, unless this step is taken, the need for a future life is hardly felt as real.

The wisdom of Ec is entirely in the Hb tradition. No certain traces of the influence of Gk thought appear in the book, and no indebtedness to Mesopotamian or Egyptian wisdom except those commonplaces which appeared in all ancient eastern wisdom. The place of the composition cannot be determined from the content; but the absence of any evidence of foreign residence leads most scholars to believe that Ec was a Palestinian sage.

Ecclesiasticus. Cf BEN SIRA.

Eden (Hb '*ēden*). **1.** The scene of the garden in which the first man was placed, located "in the east" (Gn 2:8), amply provided with trees (2:9), the source of the four great rivers of the known world, the Pishon*, Gihon*, Tigris*, and Euphrates*. It has been suggested that the word is the Akkadian *edinu*, "plain," the alluvial plain of Mesopotamia. Eden was also "the garden of God," proverbial for beauty (Is 51:3; Ezk 31:8–9; Jl 2:3). In it was placed the being who was perfect in all his ways and dwelt with the cherubim until he was expelled on the day that guilt was found in him (Ezk 28:13 ff). This account seems to be independent of the story of the first couple in Gn 2–3 and to be the story of the fall of a man unaccompanied by a woman. The garden was full of many beautiful trees (Ezk 31:9, 16, 18). The land before the locust plague was like the garden of Eden (Jl 2:3). The land of Israel in the messianic restoration will be like the garden of Eden (Is 51:3; Ezk 36:35). The first couple was expelled from Eden to the E (Gn 3:23 f), and Cain* also dwelt E of Eden after the murder of Abel (Gn 4:16). Eden had no definite location in Hb folklore and efforts to give it a geographical definition have not been accepted by scholars. No parallel to the conception has been found in ancient near Eastern literature. The Ugaritic god El dwelt "at the source of the two rivers," possibly a cosmic paradise similar to Eden but not a human abode. Utnapishtim and his wife were translated after the deluge* to enjoy immortality "at the mouth of the rivers," Dilmun, "the land of the living," in the Sumerian flood story. The Hb Eden seems to have borrowed some of these external features.
2. Eden (Beth-Eden, Am 1:5), threatened with captivity by Amos, mentioned with Gozan, Haran, and Rezeph among the places conquered by the Assyrians (2 K 19:12; Is 37:12), with Haran, Canneh, Assyria, and the Medes as trading in fabrics with Tyre* (Ezk 27:23); probably to be identified with Bit-Adini of the Assyrian records, first mentioned by Ashurnasir-pal in 884 BC and frequently thereafter as tributary and often at war with Assyria, incorporated into the Assyrian kingdom by Shalmaneser III in 855 BC. Bit-Adini was an Aramaean* kingdom which lay on both banks of the Euphrates in northern Syria with its capital city at Til-Barsip.

Edom (Hb '*edôm*, perhaps connected with the root '*dm*, "red," referring to reddish soil), the name of a people and a land in the OT. The land extended S of the Dead Sea to the Gulf of Aqaba. The kinship of the Israelites with Edom was explained in folklore by the descent of Edom from Jacob's* elder son Esau* (Gn 25:30; 32:4; 36:1 ff; 1 Ch 1:35 ff). Nelson Glueck has shown that there was no settled population in the territory of Edom and Moab between the end of the Bronze Age civilization about 1900 BC and the 13th century. The entrance of the Edomites into the territory which came to bear their name was a part of the ethnic movements which also brought the Hebrews into Palestine, and the Edomites were settled earlier than the Hebrews. According to Dt 2:12, 22 the sons of Esau dispossessed the Horites* from the land; but there are no archaeological remains of the Horites, and the name is either applied to nomadic tribes improperly or popular tradition has assimilated the story of Edom to the story of Israel. According to the genealogy of Gn 36:20 ff the Edomites included Horite elements. Some scholars believe that Edom originally exhibited a 12-tribe structure like Israel (Gn 36:9 ff); the tribal names of Israel also are in excess of the number 12. The Edomites were first ruled by chieftains, but Hb tradition told that they had a monarchy before Israel (Gn 36:31 ff). They appear, probably as nomads, in the Egyptian records of Merneptah (c 1225 BC) and Ramses III (1187 BC). The Israelites asked permission to pass through their kingdom on the journey from Egypt to Canaan and were refused (Nm 20:44 ff), so they traveled around Edom, probably on the western frontier, according to the opinion of many scholars (Nm 21:4). In the Deuteronomic tradition, however, the Israelites were permitted to pass through Edom (Dt 2:4 ff), but were forbidden to attack because Yahweh had given the Edomites their land. This variant tradition may have arisen from a rationalization of the older tradition of Nm which refused to admit that the Israelites could have been forced to make the difficult detour. It also exhibits a friendly attitude toward the Edomites which is rare in the OT (cf also Dt 23:8) and cannot have arisen in the time when Edom was subject to Judah, unless it is an implicit disapproval of the conquest of Edom. Edom and Israel (later the kingdom of Judah) had a contiguous frontier on the south (Nm 34:3; Jos 15:1). Edom was conquered by David (2 S 8:14; 1 K 11:14–15). Hadad, an Edomite prince, escaped to Egypt and when he grew to manhood revolted against Solomon (1 K 11:17 ff). No details are given; but Edom was again subject to Judah in the reign of Jehoshaphat*, who controlled Ezion-geber* (1 K 22:48) and was able to march through the territory with Jehoram* of Israel (2 K 3:8 ff); "there was no king in Edom" (1 K 22:47). Edom rebelled against Jehoram* of Judah (2 K 8:20 ff); Amaziah* restored the rule of Judah over Edom (2 K 14:7 ff). Azariah (Uzziah*) retained control of Ezion-geber (2 K 14:22). Edom recovered Ezion-geber in the reign of Ahaz* (2 K 16:6).

Amos uttered a threatening oracle against Edom for a merciless attack upon his brother, probably the kingdom of Judah (Am 1:11 f); and Edom itself must have been the object of an attack by Moab* otherwise unrecorded (Am 2:1). They were also engaged in the slave trade with the Philistines (Am 1:6) and Tyre (Am 1:9). In the messianic future David's rule over Edom will be reestablished (Is 11:14). Edom is mentioned among the uncircumcised by Je 9:25, and is included among those who must drink the cup of wrath (Je 25:21), and those who must bear the yoke of Nebuchadnezzar (Je 27:3). It is the subject of threatening oracles (Is 63:1 ff; Je 49:7 ff; Ezk 25:12 ff; 35:1 ff; 36:5; Ob) because of its encroachment of the land of Judah and plundering after the Babylonian conquest of 587 BC. Edom plays no active historical role after this period. For references in later centuries cf IDUMEA; NABATEANS.

Edom (Udumu) is among the countries which paid tribute to Adad-nirari III of Assyria (805–782 BC), and to Tiglath-pileser III* (745–727), to Sargon* (724–705). Malik-rammu, king of Edom, paid tribute to Sennacherib* (705–681), and Kaush-gabri to Esarhaddon (680–669) and to Ashur-banipal (668–626).

The wealth of Edom and its importance to Israel and to other peoples were due to its control of the "king's highway (Nm 20:17), the great caravan trade route between Arabia and the Syrian and Palestinian coasts, to its mineral resources (cf EZION-GEBER), and to its access to the Red Sea. Nelson Glueck found that the frontiers of Edom were defended by numerous strongly fortified positions which made it possible for them to refuse passage. Surface remains of Edomite cities attest a high degree of civilization and prosperity during the period of the Hebrew monarchy.

Edom was regarded as a seat of wisdom* in Hb tradition (Je 49:7; Ob 8).

Little is known about the religion of the Edomites. Images of a female goddess indicate that the common fertility cult was practiced as in Canaan. The name of the god Qos appears in the royal name Kaush-gabri mentioned by Esarhaddon and in the name Qosanal found on an Edomite stamped jar handle.

Eglon (Hb 'eglôn, meaning uncertain). **1.** King of Moab, who occupied the "city of palms" (cf JERICHO) and was assassinated by Ehud* (Jgs 3:12 ff). **2.** A Canaanite city, allied with Jerusalem*, Hebron*, Jarmuth*, and Lachish* against Joshua*, defeated by him (Jos 10:3 ff; 12:12) and included among the cities of Judah (Jos 15:39). Eglon is identified with Tell-el-Hesy by Albright, about 10 mi W of Beit Jibrin in the Shephelah* of Judah; the name survives in the nearby ruin Khirbet Ajlan. Elliger proposes Tell Beit Mirsim (cf DEBIR); Noth suggests Tell Eitun near Tell Beit Mirsim.

Egypt. 1. *Name.* Our word Egypt is derived from the Gk *aigyptos*, probably derived from the Egyptian *htk,'pth*, "palace of the *ka* of Ptah," a name of Memphis*. The Egyptians themselves called the country *Kemet*, "the black land," or commonly *Tawi*, "the two lands," upper and lower Egypt, the valley and the delta. In the OT Egypt is called *miṣraim* (Akkadian *muṣru*). In the Table of Nations* Egypt is included among the sons of Ham* with Cush*, Put*, and Canaan* (Gn 10:6) and is the father of Ludim* Anamim, Lehabim*, Naphtuhim, Pathrusim*, Casluhim, and Caphtorim*.

2. *Geography.* The political geography of Egypt both in ancient and in modern times included the valley of the Nile and the arid wastes of the Libyan desert to the W and the Arabian desert on the E between the Nile and the Red Sea. Egypt proper, however, consists of the valley of the Nile and the delta from the First Cataract at Aswan to the mouths of the river, latitude 24° 5′ 2″ to 31° 30′ N. The distance between northern and southern extremities in a direct line is about 490 mi; the length of the river between the same extremities is about 750 mi. The width of the valley is determined by the cultivated area, the area which can be reached by the irrigation waters of the Nile. At a few points the valley is no wider than the river itself. At Aswan its width is about 2 mi, and it generally continues to widen as the river flows N. At the delta its width is about 375 mi. The isthmus of Suez forms the natural eastern boundary of lower Egypt. The climate of Egypt is extremely regular. Outside of the delta rain is rare, about 6 days of the year at Cairo, half as much as one goes up the river, and only once or twice a year above Assiut. During the spring the strong hot wind called the *khamsin* blows frequently and often causes sandstorms. From about May to November temperatures are extremely high, dry in upper Egypt, humid in lower Egypt.

3. *Ethnography*. The origins of the people of ancient Egypt are shrouded in the obscurity of prehistory, and scholars are not in agreement on its racial origins. It is proposed that the earliest population belonged to a Hamitic African people, the same racial stock from which the African peoples of the Gallas, the Somalis, and the Berbers have arisen. During the prehistoric period Egypt was probably invaded by some Semitic* peoples from western Asia. Before the historic period the two groups had merged into a single type which most scholars, arguing from ancient Egyptian art and skeletal remains, believe has preserved itself in the *fellahin* population of modern Egypt.

4. *History*. The principal sources of ancient Egyptian history are the inscriptions of Egyptian temples. These rarely give satisfactory chronological data, since events are dated by the regnal years of the kings. A list of the kings of ancient Egypt was compiled by the Egyptian priest Manetho in the 3rd century BC. His history of Egypt is preserved only in fragments cited by ancient writers, but his king list fits the archaeological data discovered in Egypt. Manetho arranged his kings in 30 dynasties; the end of the 30th dynasty coincides with the end of the Persian domination in Egypt in 333 BC. The date of the beginning of the dynasties is uncertain. The long chronology followed by most older historians placed the beginning of the 1st dynasty in 4241 BC. Recent research has shown this to be most unlikely and a date around 3000 BC (Scharff, 2850 BC) is now generally accepted.

I. Prehistory. An absolute date for the first traces of human habitation in Egypt cannot be given, but a date about 10,000 BC for the end of the Palaeolithic period is quite probable. Traces of human habitation have been found in the Neolithic and Chalcolithic cultures, both in upper and in lower Egypt. It is certain that before the beginning of the historic period Egypt was divided into two kingdoms, the northern kingdom with its capital at Buto and the southern kingdom with its capital at Hierakonpolis. The necessity for social and political unity to carry on the irrigation and cultivation of the valley brought about political union in Egypt earlier than in other civilizations (cf NILE). The symbols of the two kingdoms such as the red crown and the papyrus flower of lower Egypt and the white crown and the lotus or lily of upper Egypt which first appeared in the prehistoric period continue as emblems of royalty through Egyptian history.

II. Archaic Period (3300–2850 BC). The unification of Egypt was accomplished, according to Egyptian tradition, by "King Scorpion" of the south who conquered the northern kingdom. His successor was probably the king called Menes by Manetho, identified by modern historians as Narmer, whose palette can be seen in the Cairo Museum (ANEP 296–297). The archaic period includes the first two dynasties of Manetho. The royal residence was fixed at Thinis near Abydos. Memphis at the head of the delta was a fortress through which the kings controlled lower Egypt. Little is known of the history of these early dynasties; the tombs of some of the kings have been discovered at Saqqarah.

III. The Old Kingdom (2850–2052 BC). The period of the Old Kingdom comprises Manetho's dynasties 3–5. At the beginning of the period the royal residence was transferred to Memphis. The great pyramid of Joser at Saqqarah was built by the first king of the 3rd dynasty, and the great pyramids of Gizeh were built by Khufu (Cheops),

Pyramids of Saqqarah.

Khafre (Chephren), and Menkaure (Mycerinus) of the 4th dynasty. Many magnificent tombs of the Old Kingdom have been excavated at Saqqarah. The rulers of the Old Kingdom conquered territory outside their frontier. In the 4th dynasty the Egyptians began to work the mines of Sinai* and made expeditions into Nubia. Pepi I of the 6th dynasty sent an expedition into Canaan*. The classical characteristic form of Egyptian art was fixed in the Old Kingdom and was retained through subsequent periods even into Greek and Roman times. During the 5th dynasty, which arose from On (Heliopolis), the worship of the sun god Re was identified with the royal house and remained of primary importance in subsequent periods.

IV. The First Intermediate Period (2190–2052 BC). The First Intermediate Period comprises the interval from the 6th dynasty to Mentuhotep II of the 11th dynasty. In the 6th dynasty the unified monarchy collapsed. This was caused by the increased power of the feudal nobility, without whom it was impossible for the king to administer a kingdom which extended from the delta to the First Cataract. The nobles of Heracleopolis declared themselves independent of the Memphite kings, and the kings of Heracleopolis are enumerated through dynasties 7–10. The princes of Thebes* were entirely independent of both northern rulers. The Memphis dynasty governed only the delta.

V. The Middle Kingdom (2052–1778 BC). The Middle Kingdom comprises dynasties 11–12 (after Mentuhotep II). Mentuhotep established a single monarchical rule over all Egypt and vindicated the royal power over the nobles. The confusion of the First Intermediate Period made Egypt ready to accept once more a single rule. The seat of dynasties 11–12 was at Thebes, which had played no part in Egyptian history up to this point. The Middle Kingdom was one of the most peaceful, orderly and prosperous periods of ancient Egypt. The power of Egypt was again asserted in Nubia and the mines of Sinai were again exploited. Conquering expeditions reached southern Canaan. A number of the classics of Egyptian literature were produced during this period. The cult of Osiris, the patron of the dead, became

Preparation of sacrificial offerings showing baking, winemaking, manufacturing of pottery, and slaughtering.

universally popular during the troubles of the First Intermediate Period and it was solidly established under the Middle Kingdom. The advent of the Theban dynasties brought with it the Theban deities Mentu (Mont) and Amon, who ultimately surpassed all other gods. Toward the end of the 12th dynasty the power of the monarchy became weak and Egypt fell once more into a period of anarchy.

VI. Second Intermediate Period (1778–1610 BC). This period saw great political and social disturbances and its records are fragmentary. The period comprises dynasties 13–17. The 13th, 14th, and 17th dynasties continue the Theban line. The 15th and 16th dynasties, roughly contemporary with the Theban dynasties, were Hyksos*. The records of this people were largely obliterated by the Egyptians of the New Kingdom, since the invasion of the Hyksos was felt to be a national disgrace. Modern historians place the beginning of the Hyksos migration into Egypt about 1730 BC. During most of the succeeding years war between the Hyksos and the princes of Thebes seems to have been fairly constant, and ultimately the Hyksos were expelled in the reign of Ahmose I, the founder of the 18th dynasty, about 1580 BC. The success of the Hyksos was largely

due to their use of chariots* and horses*, which they introduced into Egypt. Before this the animal was unknown in Egypt.

VII. The New Kingdom (1610–1085 BC). This period comprises dynasties 18–20. The royal residence remained at Thebes. This was the greatest period of ancient Egypt. The Hyksos invasion made the Egyptians aware of the danger which threatened them from Asia and they undertook conquering expeditions to secure their eastern frontier. The greatest of these conquerors was Thutmose III (1502–1448 BC), who led his armies through Palestine and Syria as far as the Euphrates and established an Egyptian empire in Asia. This empire was maintained by his successors; but Egyptian control, never well administered, began to crumble in the reign of Amenhotep III (1413–1377 BC) and collapsed under his successors. The Amarna* Letters contain contemporary records of the breakdown of Egyptian power in Canaan. Seti I (1317–1301 BC) and Ramses II (1301–1234 BC) of the 19th dynasty attempted to reassert Egyptian control over western Asia. But Ramses II met the Hittites* in a great battle at Kadesh on the Orontes about 1290; the battle was indecisive and the two powers signed a treaty guaranteeing the frontiers

Relief sculptures of Ramses II.

as they then stood. Egyptian control over its own claimed territory in Syria and Palestine was not maintained long after Ramses II. Egyptian power was also extended under the 18th dynasty up the Nile into Nubia and west into Libya. Under Merneptah (1234–1220 BC) a new danger appeared, a coalition of the Libyans and the "sea peoples," who were peoples driven from Greece and the Aegean islands. Their attack was repelled by Merneptah, but they returned under Ramses III (1196–1165 BC) and were driven off in a great land and sea battle which is commemorated in the reliefs of the temple of Medinet Habu near Luxor. Ramses III was compelled, however, to permit the Philistines to settle in S Canaan. This was the last effort of Egypt to protect its imperial possessions in Palestine, and under the 20th dynasty Egypt became an entirely ineffective political force. The 20th dynasty was also a period of internal collapse. The founder of the 18th dynasty had succeeded in asserting the authority of the monarchy against the feudal nobles. The necessity of union against the Hyksos had made central control much more desirable. As long as this strong central command endured, the power of the 18th and 19th dynasties remained. But the nobles once again recovered their power and in the 20th dynasty the king had no effective control over the country. To the 18th and 19th dynasties belong the great temple constructions of Karnak and Luxor and the most imposing tombs of the Valley of the Kings across the Nile from Luxor, as well as the mortuary temple of Hatshepsut at Deir-el-Bahari and the temple complex of Medinet Habu. Many of the most famous examples of Egyptian art also come from this period.

The queen of Punt from the tomb of Hatshepsut at Deir-el-Bahari.

The Hb traditions of the exodus* from Egypt and the settlement in Canaan fall in the period of the New Kingdom. In the decline of the New Kingdom, instead of the feudal nobility which was responsible for the breakdown of the monarchy in earlier periods, there appeared two new powers: that of the professional administrative aristocracy, created by the kings of the 19th dynasty and personally attached to the king, and the priesthood, in particular the priesthood of Amon, the god of Thebes. The power and wealth of these two groups grew to such an extent that ultimately members of these groups were able to seize the royal dignity in the 19th and 20th dynasties. Harmheb, the founder of the 19th dynasty, was an officer of the army, and Herihor, the founder of the 21st dynasty, was a priest.

VIII. Late Period (1085–332 BC). This period comprises dynasties 21–30. In the 21st dynasty power was divided between the kings of the delta, whose residence was at Tanis, the former site of the Hyksos capital, and the priestly rulers of Thebes. The kingdom was once more united by Sheshonq I, the biblical Shishak* (935–914 BC), who invaded Israel and Judah and sacked Jerusalem in the reign of Rehoboam*. Sheshonq transferred the capital to Bubastis. The royal residence was again established at Tanis during the 21st dynasty and was transferred to Sais in the 24th dynasty (730–715 BC). This dynasty, which included only two kings, was defeated by the Ethiopians* under Piankhi of Napata on the Nile just below the Fourth Cataract. Piankhi established himself as the ruler of lower Egypt just in time to be defeated by Sargon* of Assyria at Raphia, and the Saite rulers, attaching themselves to the Assyrians, succeeded in reestablishing their power over lower Egypt. The Ethiopians under Shabaka defeated Bocchoris, the last king of the 24th dynasty, and continued to resist Assyria. Shabaka was defeated at Elteqeh by Sennacherib* in the campaign in which Hezekiah* was besieged in Jerusalem. His successor, Taharka (690–663) continued the war against Assyria, but he was defeated by Esarhaddon* and his throne was given to Necho I. The Ethiopians continued their resistance to Assyria, and Ashur-bani-pal drove the Ethiopians up the Nile beyond Thebes, which he took twice, destroying it the second time. With the assistance of the Assyrians Psammetichus I (663–609) founded the 26th dynasty at Sais. Assyrian power, however, was now on the wane, and Psammetichus sustained his throne by hiring Greek mercenaries; large numbers of Greeks were permitted to establish themselves in the delta. Necho* II

Valley of the Kings opposite Luxor.

(609–594), his successor, supported the Assyrians in the struggle in which the Assyrians were finally defeated and the Assyrian state was annihilated by the Babylonians and the Medes. Necho was defeated by Nebuchadnezzar at Carchemish* in Syria in 605, and Egypt ceased to be an effective factor in Asia. Jehoahaz*, who succeeded his father Josiah after he had fallen in the battle of Megiddo, was deposed by Necho after a reign of three months. Necho installed Jehoiachim in his place. Apries, the biblical Hophra* (588–568), urged Zedekiah* to rebel against Nebuchadnezzar, and Judah and Jerusalem were destroyed by the Babylonians in the war which followed. Amasis (568–525 BC) allied himself with the Babylonians against the Persians, but Egypt was conquered by Cambyses in 525 BC, and the kings of the 27th dynasty (525–404 BC) were Persian. Egypt became a satrapy of Persia. In the troubles which followed the death of Darius II in 404 BC Egypt regained its independence, but it was again conquered by the Persians in 341 BC and the country remained a Persian satrapy until Alexander* defeated the Persians in 332 BC.

IX. Greek Period (332–30 BC). Alexander entered Egypt in 332 BC and was received as a deliverer. He showed himself favorable to the Egyptian cult. He founded the city of Alexandria. In the division of his empire after his death in 323 BC Egypt fell to one of his generals named Ptolemy*, the son of Lagus. In 306 BC Ptolemy took the title of king instead of the title of satrap. During this reign (306–285 BC) and those of his successors, Ptolemy II Philadelphus (285–246 BC) and Ptolemy III Euergetes (246–221 BC), the Egypt of the Ptolemies achieved a brilliant civilization. During this period the

Pharos, the great lighthouse of Alexandria which was one of the seven wonders of the ancient world, was built, and the great collection of the Alexandrian library was begun. Jewish tradition placed the translation of the LXX during this period. During the reign of Ptolemy IV Philopator (221–203 BC) war broke out between Egypt and the Seleucid* kingdom of Syria which endured intermittently for over the next hundred years. The first attempt of Antiochus* III to take Syria and Palestine from Egypt was successful, but the Egyptians defeated Antiochus and regained the territory. The family quarrels of the Ptolemies during the reigns of Ptolemy V Epiphanes (203–181 BC) and Ptolemy VI Philometor (181–146 BC) weakened Egypt and permitted Antiochus once again to conquer Syria and Palestine. The attempt of Antiochus IV Epiphanes to lead his armies into Egypt itself in 168 BC was halted by the intervention of Roman legates. The period of the later Ptolemies was marked by social unrest and a number of peasant uprisings. Ultimately the weakness of the kingdom led to the intervention of Rome. The assistance of Rome was invoked by Ptolemy XI Auletes (80–51 BC) who had been expelled, and he was restored to his throne by troops under the command of Gabinius. The Ptolemies took active part in the Roman civil wars. Cleopatra VII allied herself with Pompey in his war with Caesar, and after the defeat of Pompey won the favor of Caesar. After the battle of Philippi*, in which Brutus and Cassius were defeated, Cleopatra ingratiated herself with Antony, who gave her Syria, Phoenicia, and part of Cilicia as a token of his friendship. Antony was defeated by Octavius at the battle of Actium, and after the capture

Preparation of food; smiths and carpenters; glassmaking; punishment of workers; harvest; scribes.

of Alexandria by Octavius, Antony and Cleopatra committed suicide. Egypt became a Roman province.

X. Roman Period (30 BC–AD 323). During the Roman period up to the end of the 1st century AD the importance of Egypt lay in its fertility; it was called the granary. For this reason and because of its position as a frontier province at the junction of Asia and Africa it was governed directly by the emperor. The reigns of Caligula (AD 37–41), Claudius (AD 41–54), and Vespasian (AD 69–79) witnessed numerous quarrels and riots between the Jews and the Egyptians, particularly in Alexandria. Claudius granted the Jews of Alexandria the privilege of government by their own ethnarch in the Jewish quarter of the city. Christianity was established early in Egypt; tradition made Mark* the evangelist the first bishop of Alexandria.

5. *Religion.* The importance of religion in ancient Egypt is evidenced by art and architecture, which are almost entirely motivated by religion. The character of Egyptian religion is extremely complex, and some scholars prefer to speak of "Egyptian religions." The complexity arises from the absolute conservatism of ancient Egyptian religion, in which no attempt was made to synthesize data from different sources; all elements were retained, even those which were in contradiction with each other. This gave Egyptians a faculty of thinking along parallel lines; a problem could be solved in one way or in another, depending on the approach which one chose to adopt. The original character of the Egyptian gods reflects this complexity. As they appear in historic times, it is often difficult to determine whether they were nature deities or gods of nation, tribe, or clan. An extraordinary feature of Egyptian religion is the large number of theriomorphic deities; no satisfactory explanation of this phenomenon has been found. In historic times Egyptian religion has no evident traces of totemism, and totemism is absent from the most important gods. The great deities of ancient Egypt were solar gods. The number of solar deities is notably large; probably they were originally distinguished by locality, but after the unification of Egypt they were distinguished by different phases of the passage of the sun through the heavens — the rising sun, the midday sun, the setting sun, and other phases. The most important of the solar

Egyptian divine triad.

deities was Re, whose cult center was at On (Heliopolis); he combined in himself most of the attributes of the other solar deities. Of particular importance also was another solar deity Horus, called the son of Re, pictured as a falcon or as a falcon-headed man.

Osiris, the god of the dead, was almost as important as Re and perhaps more popular. Originally Osiris was a god of vegetation, but this character was submerged in his position as king of the underworld. Osiris was accompanied by his consort Isis, and Horus the son of Re was also the son of Osiris. Osiris was the central figure of a myth in which he was king of a worldwide Egyptian empire. He was murdered treacherously by his brother Seth and his body was cast into the sea. Isis, the sister and spouse of Osiris, went in search of the body and with the assistance of her sister Nephthys found it, embalmed it, and buried it. Osiris then became king of the dead. Isis was compelled to protect her son Horus against the attacks of Seth. In some variations of the myth the body of Osiris was dismembered by Seth, but was put back together by Isis. In another form the mythological combat between Horus and Seth is perpetual; Horus loses an eye, and Seth loses his testicles. The myth of Osiris, Isis and Horus is not only extremely important in Egyptian ideas of

life after death and burial practices, but also in the mysteries* of Isis which were so popular in Rome.

Several systems of cosmogony appear in ancient Egypt. Most of them synthesize different elements in which each of the deities appears in his proper place in the cosmological scheme. In the cosmogony of Heliopolis the primeval element is a watery chaos called Nu. The solar deity Atum creates himself and then by masturbation creates the first couple Shu and Tefnut, who in turn produce Geb, the earth god, and Nut, the goddess of the heavens. When Geb and Nut are locked in close embrace, Shu, who here represents the atmosphere, steps between them and separates them. He is represented in Egyptian art standing upon the body of Geb and holding the body of Nut by his hands over his head. The four gods of the Osiris cycle — Osiris, Isis, Seth, and Nephthys — were then born of Nut; these gods form the ennead of Heliopolis. Of interest also is the theology of Memphis, in which Ptah, the god of Memphis, is represented as creating the other gods and the world by his creative word.

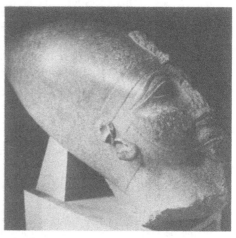

Head of Amenhotep III, wearing the white crown of Upper Egypt.

Under the Theban dynasties of the Middle Kingdom and the New Kingdom the local god of Thebes, Amon, rose to the stature of a national deity. Amon with his consort Mut and their son Khonsu is honored in the great temples of Karnak and Luxor. Amon, probably originally a god of fertility, was identified with the sun god Re, whose supremacy could not be contested, and was invoked under the title of Amon-Re and represented with solar attributes. The priesthood of his temples was numerous and the kings endowed his temples with great wealth. Under Amenhotep IV (1377–1358 BC) there occurred a unique and somewhat mysterious revolution. For reasons which we cannot trace the king broke with the priesthood of Amon and proposed the worship of the solar disk Aton. Aton was not represented in human form; apparently no figure was permitted except that of the solar disk from which emanated rays terminating in hands holding the *ankh,* the sign of life. The king forbade the worship not only of Amon but, it seems, of all other gods, including Osiris, the popular king of the dead. The name Amon was erased on Egyptian monuments, even when it occurred as a component of personal names of his own ancestors of the 18th dynasty. He changed his own name Amenhotep, which contained the component Amon, to Ikhnaton, "servant of Aton." He established a new royal city which he called Akhetaton, "horizon of Aton," at the modern El Amarna*, about half way between Cairo and Luxor. The reform of Ikhnaton outlasted his own reign barely a few years. Under his successor Tutankhamon (whose name had been changed by Ikhnaton to Tutankhaton), only a boy at his accession, the priesthood of Amon reasserted itself. The name of Ikhnaton was erased from most of the monuments which he had constructed; his new city was abandoned, and very few records of his reign have survived. On the divinity of the king and the Egyptian temple cf KING; TEMPLE.

No ancient people which we know had such an elaborate belief in the afterlife as the Egyptians. The surviving element was conceived in two forms: the *ba,* represented as a human-headed bird, and the *ka,* a concept difficult to define. It was represented in the monuments as a duplicate of the living human person, created with him, and the cult of the dead was paid to the *ka* of the deceased. The popular belief was an amalgamation of the earlier solar belief and the Osiris belief. In the solar belief the *ka* of the deceased joined the sun god and rode with him in his boat which daily circled the world. In the Osiris belief the deceased was identified with Osiris and shared his royalty. In both the deceased survived in the "field of reeds," where the afterlife, as it is represented in tomb paintings, was a continuation of the present life. Originally this type of survival was granted only to the king; but since a king needed courtiers and servants, survival was extended to these and ultimately to all. The royal tombs of Gizeh and Saqqarah are surrounded by the numerous tombs of the king's subjects. The deceased had to pass certain dangers from demons and other threats, and was judged by Osiris

and 42 gods who acted as assessors. In order that the deceased might pass these dangers, charms, magical formulae, and the vindication of innocence called the negative confession were inserted in the coffin (ANET 32–36). The vast collection of these formulae is called "The Book of the Dead." It was not conceived that anyone would fail to pass this judgment.

Survival in the afterworld depended upon the preservation of the body; this was accomplished by mummification, the ingenious process which has preserved so many Egyptian corpses into modern times. Before the process was perfected the substitute for the body was the tomb statue of the deceased, which was retained when mummification was employed. The tomb had a false door through which the deceased could make his exit at night and join in the life of the underworld by union with the body or the statue. Substitutes were provided for all the needs of life. The tomb paintings themselves were scenes into which the deceased might enter; and these paintings are an important source of our knowledge of the daily life of ancient Egypt, since almost all human activities are represented there. It was necessary also that the deceased be protected against certain demonic dangers which would prevent him from opening his eyes and his mouth after burial; and the ceremonies of "opening the eyes" and "opening the mouth" were accomplished before the tomb was sealed. Offerings of food, drink, garments, weapons, and all kinds of personal equipment were placed in the tomb. In the tombs of kings and nobles these offerings were of great value and included treasures of precious metals, most of which have been looted by grave robbers, even in ancient Egypt. The type of tomb differed at different periods. The pyramids of Gizeh and Saqqarah were employed only for kings and only during the Old Kingdom; such structures were too vast to become the normal tomb, even for the king. At the center of the pyramid was the burial chamber proper. People of lesser dignity were buried in the type of tomb called by the modern Arabs *mastabas,* which were more or less miniature houses. In upper Egypt the cliffs along the Nile made it possible to excavate hypogea in the rock. These tombs, even the royal tombs, were not as imposing as the pyramids; but the basic features of the corridor, the chapel, and the niche for the sarcophagus were retained. The tombs of the Valley of the Kings and the Valley of the Queens near Luxor were built with concealed entrances to protect them from looting; the effort was unsuccessful. The tombs of people of the lower classes as well as the tombs of kings

Games, musicians, and dancers.

and nobles were equipped with small statues, *ushebtis*, "answerers," which stood ready to answer any command for work which might be laid upon the deceased. All tombs of all periods and types were found on the west bank of the Nile, the direction of the setting sun; the dead were sometimes called "westerners."

6. *Importance.* Here it is impossible to do more than enumerate some of the contributions made to human progress by ancient Egypt. The isolated position of ancient Egypt gave almost all Egyptian institutions and inventions a peculiar and original form; at the same time, it meant that other peoples received comparatively little from Egypt.

I. Social and Political. Egypt was the first community to become a national state, with a single central political government over a widely extended geographical area. Discipline and organization were necessary in order to control and utilize the resources of the Nile. At the great periods of Egypt the monarchy was strong; when the central government was weak, disturbances multiplied and prosperity and security were imperiled. The organization of the Egyptian monarchy was complex. The country was divided into districts or nomes along the river; each nome was governed by a single administrator responsible to the king. In the 18th dynasty a refinement was added; two viziers were appointed, one for upper Egypt and one for lower Egypt, each responsible to the king. Under these chief administrators was an army of subordinates, clerks, scribes, and other officers. At its best the government, while strongly centralized and by modern standards somewhat totalitarian, was honest and efficient. In particular we notice the numerous testimonials to careful provision for irrigation and the storage of grain against future shortages; the government made efforts to keep the price of grain reasonable even in times of crop failure. We have little information about the administration of Egyptian law; but the very absence of complaint seems to show that it was well administered. Egypt was never a truly urban civilization, and the larger cities whose remains have been preserved seem to have been little more than palaces and temples with the residences of the officers and servants of the king and the priests and employees of the temples. The society was integrated in the sense that peasants, craftsmen, royal and temple functionaries each did their work and, except in the rare periods of unrest, seem to have been satisfied with it. The unstable element was the feudal nobility, which never reached a state of entire harmony with the monarchy. The stability of the Egyptian monarchy, which maintained itself through periods of disturbance, shows that the Egyptian society had a basic solidity which no other society in history has matched. While social and economic classes appear to be stratified, it was possible for an ambitious young man, even if he were a peasant's son, to rise to high position if he were educated as a scribe and exhibited sufficient talent and industry. Many of the royal officers whose names and careers appear on Egyptian monuments testify that they came from humble origins.

II. Writing and Literature. The Egyptians invented a system of writing called hieroglyphics before the beginning of the historical period. The system, in spite of its complexity, was retained throughout the subsequent history of Egypt. The signs were phonetic and ideographic, and in the hieroglyphic script the pictorial character of the signs is clearly evident. The sign represents both the object pictured and the syllable pronounced, as if a picture of a man were to represent both the English word "man" and the first syllable in the word "manner." A development followed in which the sign acquired a more nearly consonantal value. Hieroglyphic, like the early alphabet, had no means of indicating the vowels. A simplified form of the hieroglyphic signs is called hieratic; and a still more simplified form called demotic, in which the pictorial character of the signs is indiscernible, appeared in the late period.

The remains of Egyptian literature are extensive and of great interest. The Egyptians created a number of literary forms independently of external influence. The romance or tale seems to have been very popular. The account of a shipwrecked sailor of the 19th dynasty contains marvels hardly less wonderful than those of the story of Sinbad the sailor; and the story of Sinuhe, who fled from Egypt, joined the nomads and became a sheik, and returned to Egypt wealthy and powerful, is romantic enough to have furnished the subject of a modern novel and a modern moving picture (ANET 18–22). Wisdom literature appeared early in ancient literature. The wisdom books are collections of maxims and instructions, usually given by a father to his son, and often attributed to a king (ANET 412–425). This sententious type of wisdom appears in the wisdom* literature of the OT, and in some instances direct connection can be traced. Connected with this literature are some compositions from disturbed periods such as the Song of the Harper, which counsels that a man enjoy himself and place no trust in the promises of survival after death (ANET 467), or the dialogue of a man with his soul, in which a man intent upon suicide argues the desirability of death rather than life (ANET 405–407). Popular songs have been preserved: songs sung by workers at their employment and love lyrics of an extremely romantic type (ANET 467–470). A large number of religious hymns have been preserved; they are long, solemn, and formal (ANET 365–379). Historical narrative is represented by the temple inscriptions (ANET 227–264); especially admired is the account of the battle of Ramses II with the Hittites at Kadesh. The king and his corps were surrounded by the Hittites and escaped only by the personal valor of the king, who led his troops in cutting their way out of the trap.

III. Art and Architecture. Egyptian architecture appears almost fully developed at the beginning of the historic period. The Egyp-

Architect and workers.

tians were the first to build massive stone structures so stoutly constructed that they have resisted decay for thousands of years. The Nile Valley offers abundant resources of excellent granite, limestone, and sandstone, which the Egyptians used according to their suitability for the structure and according to certain canons of construction. The ordinary domestic dwelling or industrial or public building was constructed not of stone but of brick. Some of the remains of these ancient dwellings, such as the residence quarter of the tomb workers of the Valley of the Kings, show excellent construction, often superior to the huts of the modern *fellahin*. The enormous Egyptian temples have certain characteristic features: the great pylon at the entrance, the hypostyle hall (the hypostyle hall of Karnak has 128 columns built to a height of 70 ft), and the colonnaded court. The surfaces of walls and columns were covered with pictures and hieroglyphics in relief. The Egyptians were masters of the use of monoliths; they had no other way to bridge the gaps in the pylons and wide gateways. But the necessity of supporting a large roof by a large number of columns made the interior of temples almost totally dark; light was furnished only through the doorway and by clerestory windows. Several types of columns were employed. Most striking is the column with the papyriform capital, which imitates the papyrus flower either bound together or spread open. The obelisks, some of which have traveled to Europe and America, are massive monoliths carved smoothly and in perfect proportions. The same skill in carving appears in the hypogea of Luxor, which generally imitate the style of construction used in the temples. In the great temples, as in the pyramids, the stones were laid by close measurement and accurate cutting, and were not bound by mortar. The Egyptians excelled other ancient peoples in their painting, employing rich colors, many of which have survived exposure to the air for centuries. Egyptian painting was not purely representational and did not employ perspective. The perspective might be altered in a single painting by changing the point of view. The picture was less a representation than a description of what the

a) Egyptian jewelry.
b) Egyptian toilet articles in wood.

painting contained. The reasons for some features of Egyptian style are not known. The human figure is represented with the face in profile, but with the eye *en face.* The shoulders are represented *en face,* but the torso and legs in profile. The inside of both feet are shown, never the outside. A table upon which objects are laid is represented from the side, but the objects are represented as viewed from above. The same perspective is used in representing a pool or stream of water. In spite of these restraints, scenes of life are represented with vigor and vitality. Differences in station are represented by different size of figures; the king is always portrayed in colossal stature. Differences in feature between men and women and racial characteristics of foreign peoples are clearly portrayed by Egyptian painters. Buildings, garments, and objects are painted with great detail. Egyptian sculpture was not subject to the same canons of style as painting. The Egyptian masterpieces are colossal statues, many of which are preserved in the great museums of the world. The art of the sculptor was religious, and the statues were intended to convey an atmosphere of dignity and serenity. Most of the colossi are statues of kings who are identified with the gods, but even the statues of nobles and their families achieve the same serenity and dignity. The statues are very carefully worked and details are executed with precision. Ikhnaton was responsible for a revolution in art as well as religion. In breaking away from the cult he also departed from the canons of traditional art. The art of Amarna is strikingly realistic; the king himself is portrayed with a long and delicate face, a skull of such dolichocephalic character that it is almost deformed, and a protuberant paunch. The head of Nofretete, wife of Ikhnaton, preserved in the Berlin Museum, is generally regarded as the masterpiece of ancient Egyptian art (ANEP 404). The domestic scenes in which Ikhnaton and his wife and daughters and Tutankhamon and his wife are pictured enjoying themselves in their homes and gardens are an intimate representation of royalty unparalleled elsewhere in Egyptian art, although such familiar scenes are common in the tombs of the nobles (ANEP 407, 409–411). Ancient Egypt also had no lack of skilled workers in smaller objects. The tools, weapons, household and toilet articles, and jewelry found in the tombs, are executed with skill and delicacy in wood, ivory, gold, and silver.

Ehud (Hb *'ehûd,* perhaps abbreviated from *'ahihûd,* "the brother [i.e., the god] is glory"), a judge* of Israel, son of Gera, of the tribe of Benjamin*, who assassinated

Eglon*, king of Moab, who had seized the "city of palms" (cf JERICHO) and led the Israelite forces which expelled the Moabite invaders (Jgs 3:15 ff).

Ekron (Hb *'ekrôn*), the northernmost of the five cities of the Philistines, counted among the cities of Judah in Jos 15:45, of Dan in Jos 19:43. The city is not mentioned before the period of the Israelite judges* and seems to have been a new foundation of the Philistines. Jgs 1:18 and 1 S 7:14, which relate its capture by the Israelites, refer not to the period of the judges but to the conquests of David, which are here anticipated. The ark* of the covenant was taken to Ekron when it was captured by the Philistines; but a plague afflicted the city and it was sent back to Beth Shemesh (1 S 5:10–6:16). After the slaying of Goliath* the Israelites pursued the Philistines as far as Ekron (1 S 17:52). It was the seat of the worship of Baal-zebul (cf BEELZEBUB; 2 K 1:2 ff). It is threatened by Amos (1:8), Zephaniah (2:4), Jeremiah (25:20), and Zechariah (9:5). It was given to Jonathan* by Alexander Balas* as a reward for his victory over Apollonius* (1 Mc 10:89). Ekron first appears in foreign sources in the list of cities conquered by Shishak* (935–914). Sennacherib* (705–681) tells that Padi, king of Amqarruna (Ekron), refused to join the rebellion against Assyria in 701 and was dethroned by the officials, nobles and people of the city, who delivered him to Hezekiah* to be imprisoned in Jerusalem. Sennacherib took Ekron and executed the rebels and restored Padi to his throne. Esarhaddon (680–669) and Ashur-bani-pal (668–626) exacted tribute from Ikausu of Ekron. The site is to be located on the course of the Wadi-es-sarar, in the northern portion of Philistine territory. Albright has placed it at Qatra, but most scholars prefer Aqir, where the name survives.

El. Cf GOD.

Elah (Hb *'ēlāh*), son of Baasha* and king of Israel 877–876 BC. He was assassinated by his officer Zimri* at a banquet in his palace at Tirzah* (1 K 16:8 ff). The name is borne by four others in the OT.

Elam. The ancient territory of Elam lay to the E and NE of the valley of the Tigris and the Euphrates in the Zagros mountains. The ancient inhabitants of Elam are thought by modern scholars to belong to the Armenoid race. The region of Elam was also called Anshan. The Elamites are mentioned among the people conquered by Eannatum of Lagash about 2700 BC. Elam seems to have been governed by feudal lords, some of whom occasionally obtained preeminence, rather than by a monarchy in the true sense. The Elamites are mentioned also by Sargon of Akkad* and Naram-Sin (about 2300 BC), sometimes as enemies, sometimes as allies. The kings of the 3rd dynasty of Ur (2050–1950 BC) exercised sovereignty over Elam, but in the collapse of this dynasty Kutur-Naḥḥunte of Elam invaded Babylonia and ravaged the country. Ashur-bani-pal in 645 BC reported that he brought back from Susa* a statue of the goddess Nana carried off by Kutur-Naḥḥunte 1635 or 1535 years earlier, therefore 2180 or 2280 BC. The computation of Ashur-bani-pal is not accurate. The Elamite domination of Babylonia continued under Kutur-Mabug, whose sons, Arad-Sin and Rim-Sin, were kings of Larsa. Hammurabi* of the 1st dynasty of Babylon freed his country from Elam overlords. Little more is heard of Elam until the 13th century BC, when Shutruk-Naḥḥunte and his son Kutur-Naḥḥunte again invaded Mesopotamia and destroyed the Kassite dynasty. Shutruk-Naḥḥunte carried to Susa as trophies the stele of Naram-Sin and the code of Hammurabi, two of the most famous monuments of ancient Mesopotamia. They were recovered at Susa by archaeologists early in the 20th century. The Elamite power was broken by Nebuchadnezzar I of Babylon in the second half of the 12th century. Elam appears again as a rival of Assyria in its rise to world power during the 9th-7th centuries. Sargon (721–705) and Sennacherib (705–681) did not conquer Elam. Ashur-bani-pal in 649 began a series of campaigns in which the Elamite armies were annihilated and the royal city Susa destroyed. Elam no longer appeared as an independent power. Elam is mentioned among the satellite peoples of the neo-Babylonian empire, and Cyrus the Great, the founder of the Persian empire, was a prince of Anshan. Susa became an imperial center under the Persian empire. Elam is mentioned in the Table* of Nations with Ashur, Arpachshad, Lud, and Aram as sons of Shem (Gn 10:21; cf 1 Ch 1:17). For Elam in Gn 14 cf CHEDORLAOMER. Elam was among the places in which the Israelites were exiled (Is 11:11), was one of the nations which attacked Babylon with the Medes (Is 21:2) and among the attackers of Jerusalem, probably with the Assyrians (Is 22:6). Je 49:34–39 contains a threatening oracle against Elam, and Elam is included among the dead nations lying in the pit (Ez 32:24 ff). Elam is called a land of archers in Is 22:6 and in Je 49:35.

Elath. Cf EZION-GEBER.

Elder. 1. *OT*. The elders (Hb *zāḵēn*) appear as a distinct social grade or collegiate body with distinct political or religious functions. The term appears in all the books of the Pnt and in all the historical books of the Hb OT except Ne, in Is, Je, Ezk, and Jl among the prophets, and in Lam, Pss, Jb and Pr. Most frequently they are called elders simply; the most common qualification is "elders of Israel." They are also called elders of the city, of the land, of the people, of the house of Israel, of the congregation, of the tribes (or of a particular tribe mentioned by name), of Judah and Jerusalem, of the daughter of Zion, of the captivity, of the Jews, of the house of David, of the priests; and they are also mentioned in Egypt, Moab, and Midian. Their functions are as follows: (1) They represent the entire people in political or religious activity. Thus Moses gathers the elders and speaks to the people (Ex 3:16; 4:29), and the elders appear as speaking or acting for the people elsewhere in the Pnt (Ex 17:5 ff; 18:12). The elders of Israel ask Samuel to appoint a king (1 S 8:4), and David deals with the elders of Judah in order to win the favor of the tribe (1 S 30:26), as Abner* conferred with the elders of Israel about changing the allegiance of Israel to David (2 S 3:17). These elders make a covenant with David at Hebron (2 S 5:3). The elders listen to the reading of the book of the law discovered during the reign of Josiah* (2 K 23:1), and Jeremiah calls the elders to witness the symbolic breaking of the flask (Je 19:1). The 70 elders ascend the mountain with Moses, Aaron, Nadab, and Abihu to ratify the covenant in the name of Israel (Ex 24:1 ff). (2) The elders appear as associated with the leader or as his companions when he exercises his authority (Ex 3:18; Dt 27:1; Jos 8:10). (3) The elders sometimes appear as a governing body; the elders of Gibeon* (Jos 9:11), of Succoth* (Jgs 8:5 ff), of Gilead*, who conferred authority upon Jephthah* (Jgs 11:5 ff) of Jabesh*, who negotiate with Nahash* of Ammon (1 S 11:3). The elders are included among those in authority who oppress the people (Is 3:14). They are members of the royal council (2 S 17:4, 15) and they appear to have a deliberative vote on war and peace (1 K 20:7 ff). (4) Most frequently the elders appear as a judicial body (cf Dt 19:12; 21:3, 19; 22: 15; 25:8; Jos 20:4). They are not mentioned, however, in the code of the covenant (cf LAW). Judicial power of the elders is implied in the episodes of Naboth* (1 K 21:8 ff) and of the sons of Ahab* (2 K 10:1 ff). (5) The elders are mentioned with other officers: the princes (*sārîm*) (Jgs 8:8 ff; 2 K 10:1 ff; Is 3:14), the heads of tribes (Dt 5:23; 29:9). Councils of elders governed the towns and communities of the Hittites*; their powers and functions as described in the Hittite code are similar to those of the elders of Israel. A similar institution of elders appears several times in the Mari* tablets, and the elders had judicial powers in Babylon in the period of Hammurabi* as well as in the neo-Babylonian periods, sometimes under the royal governor of the city. The origin of the institution and the election of its members cannot be clearly perceived. That it was spread over the ancient Near East is evident from its presence among the Hittites and in Mesopotamia. It is probable that it was an extension of tribal, clan, and family organization of pastoral society into urban-agricultural civilization. The modern desert tribe is organized on the tent, family, clan, and tribe basis, and each group is headed by a paternal elder (Arabic *sheikh*).

Israel was organized in this fashion before its settlement in Canaan; but in the course of the settlement, particularly under the monarchy, the family-clan-tribe organization lost its solidarity when the groups were diffused among villages and cities. Where the term elder appears in the OT it seems to signify the head of a family or a clan. Once this dissolution of the family-clan organization had developed, it is conceivable that the body of elders in each community maintained itself by co-option. Possibly the ownership of land was a decisive factor in acquiring and maintaining membership among the elders. In Dt and the later historical books the elders have no function other than the judicial. This suits the general pattern which historians trace in the history of the Hb monarchy, that local and tribal self-government was weakened by the growing absolutism of the monarchy. In the early monarchy the elders were the heads of tribes, clans, and families; they formed the king's council, and as representatives of the people they exercised a limitation on the absolute power of the monarchy which cannot be paralleled exactly in other civilized states of the ancient Near East. Their power and functions were fixed not by law but by custom, and their influence was greater or less, depending on circumstances and the personal character both of king and of elders.

2. *NT*. A council of the elders (Gk *presbyteros*) is attested for Palestinian Judaism at least as early as the Seleucid* period of the early 2nd century BC. This council of elders appears as a part of the council* of the Gospels. The elders mentioned in the Gospels all represent this class; usually they are mentioned with scribes or priests or both. Mt 15:2 and Mk 7:3, 5, which refer to the tradition of the elders, employ an expression which is common in the rabbinical traditions which are collected in the Talmud. The elders here are not the members of the council but the rabbis of earlier generations, whose opinions on the Law were regarded by the Pharisees as of equal authority with the Law itself. Jesus refused to be bound by these traditions. The elders of the Jews appear also in AA 4 and 6 as taking action against the followers of Jesus. AA 11:30 is the first instance of the use of the term elders of the Christian community; the contributions of the Greek churches to the Jerusalem church were sent to the elders through Barnabas and Paul. The elders of the Jerusalem community are mentioned with the apostles* and associated with them in authority in the deliberations of the council of Jerusalem throughout AA 15; cf also AA 1:4. The elders of the church of Jerusalem with James* heard the report of Paul on his missionary work among the Gentiles (AA 21:18). Paul's farewell address to the church of Ephesus* was given to the elders of the church (AA 20:17). The position of the elders in the Jerusalem church is not unlike that of the elders in Judaism and in early Israel, and it is quite probable that the primitive church of Jerusalem adopted existing Jewish organization and institutions. The elders are not mentioned in the Pauline epistles; their functions appear more clearly in the Pastoral* epistles. Timothy receives the gift of prophecy through the imposition of hands of the *presbyterion*, which here signifies the college of elders (1 Tm 4:14). The elders govern and labor in teaching and preaching (1 Tm 5:17), for which they deserve sustenance (1 Tm 5:15), and they are not to be charged with any crime except on the evidence of two or three witnesses (1 Tm 5:19). Titus is directed to appoint elders in every town (Tt 1:5); here, however, the elders seem to be identified exclusively with the bishops, whose qualifications and functions are described in Tt 1:6–9. The elders of the Church pray for the sick and their prayer has the power to heal him (Js 5:14–15). The author of 1 Pt identifies himself as an elder and exhorts his fellow elders as shepherds to feed the flock which is in their charge. Young men are to be subject to the elders (1 Pt 5:1–5). The opposition between younger and older in 1 Tm 5:1 probably refers to a distinction of age and not of office. The author of 2–3 Jn identifies himself as the elder. Here, possibly, the title signifies not an office in the Church but the dignity of a respected teacher; the author claims no authority against Diotrephes*, although Diotrephes refuses to acknowledge the authority of the elder. The 24 elders of Apc (4:4, 10; 5:5 ff; 7:11, 13;

11:16; 14:3; 19:4) do not resemble the elders of the primitive Church. They are a heavenly divine council formed on the analogy of the OT council of elders and the representation of the heavenly council in such passages as I K 22:19; Ps 89:8; Jb 1:6; 2:1; Dn 7:9. The number 24 may be derived from the 24 classes of priests and Levites (1 Ch 24:5 ff; 25:1 ff).

Eleazar (Hb *'el'azar*, "God has helped," Gk *eleazar*), a proper name borne by seven men in the OT.

1. The most important of these is Eleazar the son of Aaron (Ex 6:23) who succeeded Aaron in the priesthood (Nm 20:24–28; Dt 10:6). Jos associates him with Joshua* in the division of the land, much as tradition associated Aaron with Moses (Jos 14:1; 17:4; 19:51; 21:1). He was buried at Gibeah* in the hill country of Ephraim (Jos 24:33). The priestly line of Zadok* traced itself to Eleazar (1 Ch 6:4 ff). The name appears in the Gk form and is borne by four men in the Gk portions of the OT.

2. Eleazar, surnamed Avaran, was one of the seven sons of Mattathias*. He commanded a division of troops in the victory of Judas* over Nicanor* (2 Mc 8:22) and was killed himself in the battle of Bethzechariah in which Judas defeated the forces of Antiochus V. Eleazar, thinking that a magnificently caparisoned elephant carried the king, cut his way through the enemy and stabbed the beast, which fell on him and killed him (1 Mc 6:43 ff).

3. Eleazar the scribe, 90 years of age, refused to eat pork during the campaign of Antiochus Epiphanes to hellenize the Jews and rejected the advice of his friends to pretend to eat the forbidden meat because the example of surrender by a man his age would weaken the courage of younger people (2 Mc 6:18–31).

4. The Eleazar who appears in the genealogy of Jesus (Mt 1:15) is not mentioned in the OT.

Electa. Cf JOHN, EPISTLES.

Election. 1. *OT.* Connected with the Hb word choose (*bāḥar*) are a number of related words which express the same or similar ideas, such as take (Ex 6:7) or know (Am 3:2; Je 1:5). This article deals with election as an act of God. Man is said to choose God's law or way or other things belonging to God, but the deity as the object of man's election occurs only in Jos 24:15, 22. This rare occurrence of the word is due to the peculiar character of the covenant tradition related in this chapter; the word signifies the response of Israel to Yah-

weh's election rather than an original election of Yahweh by Israel. The word elect or election is not used of the acts of God toward Israel in the Pnt outside of Dt. This had led many scholars to conclude that the theology of election was a development of the 8th or 7th century. Substantially the idea of Israel as determined to be the people of Yahweh by the choice of Yahweh appears in earlier passages without the word (Ex 19:5 and the certainly early song of Deborah*, Jgs 5:11). The traditions of the Pnt reduce the choice of Israel to the call of Abraham* and the promise that Yahweh would make a great people of his issue (Gn 12:3). Dt conceives the election of Israel as due to the love of Yahweh for the forefathers of Israel and to His oath to the fathers (Dt 7:6 ff; 4:37 ff) and not because of the merits of Israel (Dt 9:4 ff) or its numbers (Dt 7:7). Israel because of its election becomes a people holy to Yahweh (Dt 14:2) with the obligation of recognizing Yahweh alone as God (Dt 4:39) and of keeping His commandments (Dt 4:40; 7:9 ff; 10:16 ff). Election places a responsibility on Israel shared by no other nation. Failure to meet this responsibility brings a more severe punishment upon Israel (Am 3:2). Some passages of the prophets attest that the consciousness of election could be distorted in popular belief into national pride and unfounded assurance in Yahweh's protection (Je 7:3–10; Mi 3:11). This popular belief was in direct opposition to the deuteronomic presentation of election as implying obligation to observe the statutes of Yahweh and to recognize His unique divinity. The wider scope of the election of Israel is not explicit in Dt or in the earlier books of the OT. Israel as the servant chosen by Yahweh appears in Is 43:10. While the concept of election in the OT is theologically somewhat primitive, it should be noticed that election has as its counterpart not reprobation, but simply nonelection for the purpose for which Israel was chosen. That Yahweh is concerned with other peoples is stated explicitly by Am 9:7, and the failure of Israel to meet its responsibilities will reduce it to the level of other peoples (Am 9:8). The election of Israel is an act of divine sovereignty which is above question by any human being. It was enough for Israel to know that it was chosen that there might be a people who would recognize the divinity of Yahweh and submit themselves to His divine imperative.

Election falls also upon particular places and persons. Jerusalem is the place which Yahweh has chosen for the dwelling of His name* (Dt 12 passim; 14:23; 15:20; 16 passim and elsewhere). After the division of the kingdom Yahweh chooses the tribe of

Judah and Mt Zion which He loves, and does not choose the tent of Joseph* and the tribe of Ephraim (Ps 78:67 f). The king was chosen by Yahweh. This is said explicitly of Saul (1 S 10:24), of David (1 S 16:8; 2 S 6:21 and elsewhere). The law of the king distinguishes between the installation of the king, which is the act of the people, and the choice of the king, which is the act of Yahweh (Dt 17:15). The election of David, although the word *bāḥar* is not used, is extended to his entire dynasty (2 S 7; Ps 89:20–38). The election of Yahweh was signified in the election of Saul and David by Samuel, and it is altogether possible that the divine election of the king was signified in the ceremonial of accession by a prophetic oracle such as that which appears to be preserved in Ps 2. The name of David's son Yibhar (2 S 5:15) signifies most probably the concept of election, but it is not clear whether this name refers to the election of Israel or to the election of the king. The title of "elect" for the entire people is rare and is concentrated in 1 Ch 16:13; Ps 105:6, 43; Is 65:9, 15, 22. The word *bāḥar* is not used by the prophets of themselves, although the words of Je 1:5 and of Am 7:15 contain the substance of the idea of election. The word is applied to Abraham in Ne 9:7 and to the priesthood of the house of Eli (1 S 2:28) and to the tribe of Levi (Dt 18:5; 21:6; 1 Ch 15:2; 2 Ch 29:11). Election for a mission appears clearly in the servant of Yahweh (Is 42:1; 49:7). The servant is chosen to have the spirit of Yahweh (Is 42:1), to establish justice in the earth (Is 42:4), to be a covenant of people and a light of nations, to enlighten the blind and release prisoners (Is 42:6 f; 49:6) and ultimately to bring deliverance by suffering (Is 53: 1 ff). Apart from any discussion of the identity of the servant, it is more than coincidental that the application of election to Israel appears more frequently in Is 40–55 than elsewhere in the OT (43:10, 20; 44:1, 2; 45:4).

2. *NT.* The Gk *eklegesthai* ("choose") is used in Mk, Lk, Jn, and AA only of the choice of the apostles* by Jesus (by God, AA 15:7) as a divine act. Paul* is called a chosen vessel (AA 9:15). Election of the foolish, weak, and ignoble things of the world (1 Co 1:27 f) shows the supremacy of God over human devices. The same thought is expressed in Js 2:5. Christians were chosen before the foundation of the world to be holy and blameless in the sight of God; here the rare idea of antecedent election is combined with the responsibility of the elect. Paul repeats the idea of the election of Jacob rather than Esau (Rm 9:11; cf Mal 1:3) and

of the remnant of Israel (Rm 11:5). He alludes to the election of Christians in 1 Th 1:4. The author of 2 Pt urges Christians to make their vocation and election certain (1:10), for they may fail to live up to the demands of their election. The elect in the Synoptic Gospels (Mt 22:14; 24:22, 24, 31; Mk 13:20, 22, 27; Lk 18:7) are always mentioned in connection with the final catastrophe and the judgment*, and thus the term seems here to designate precisely those who survive the eschatological tribulations and remain faithful. A similar background appears in the use of the term in Rm 8:33. The context (8:28–38) treats of the assurance of salvation for those who are foreknown, predestined, and called. No adversary can overcome God or separate them from the love of Christ. This assures the elect of God against any charge which may be brought against them. 1 Pt 1:1 f also links the elect with the foreknowledge of God the Father and sanctification through the Spirit. In Col 3:12; 2 Tm 2:10; Tt 1:1; Apc 17:14 the term appears to have become a conventional title for Christians. The elect race (1 Pt 2:9) is an echo of Is 43:2. Jesus Himself is called the elect one (Lk 23:35). The "elect lady" and her "elect sister" (2 Jn 1, 13) are most easily taken as personifications of Christian communities. The designation of Christians as elect may reflect not only the OT but also the language of the Qumran sect, which is described in its documents as the elect of God, the elect of grace (cf the election of grace in Rm 11:5) or simply the elect; the sons of Zadok, the priests, are called the elect of the name.

Election in the NT is a continuation and enlargement of the election of Israel. The emphasis falls upon the divine initiative in the process of salvation and not upon the antithesis between election and reprobation. Theological difficulties which arise from the concept of election are generally ignored in the NT; cf however Rm 9:14–33, where Paul solves the difficulties by asserting the freedom of God to show mercy to whom He wishes. God is not bound to show it to anyone. The anger of God toward the objects of His anger is not unmotivated (Rm 9:22) and Israel failed to attain uprightness because it did not seek uprightness through faith (Rm 9:32). Election in the NT as in the OT imposes responsibility upon the elect; and the consciousness of mission which appears in the servant of Yahweh is fully explicit in the NT.

Elephant. The elephant is mentioned only in 1–2 Mc as an animal employed in war. Indian elephants were used by the Persians; Alexander was the first European ruler to

Elephantine.

use them in war, and they were used also by the Seleucids* and the Ptolemies*. The Seleucids used them against the Jews in Palestine (1 Mc 1:17; 3:34; 6:30 ff; 8:6; 2 Mc 11:4; 13:2, 15). The management of the elephant is described in 1 Mc 6:34 ff. They were excited to battle by showing them the juice of grapes and berries. They were distributed among the troops; each elephant was accompanied by 1000 infantry and 500 cavalry. The animals carried a wooden tower. The MSS give the number of men carried in the tower as 30 (1 Mc 6:37), an impossible number which is corrected to 4 by modern critics. Some ancient sources, however, say that the tower could carry 10–15 men. The animal was handled by an Indian driver. The tower was kept in place by an armored saddle and belt, not mentioned in 1 Mc.

Elephantine. The Gk name of an island in the Nile opposite the modern Aswan, called in Aramaic Yeb or Yeb the fortress. Here a large collection of Aramaic papyri was discovered 1893–1908. The papyri came from a Jewish colony settled on the island in the 5th century BC. Elephantine, immediately N of the First Cataract, where navigation was interrupted, was important as a frontier military post and as a market between Egypt* and Nubia. The papyri came from the Persian period of Egypt and contain much information on the administration of Persian satrapies. The colony is clearly identified as Jewish by its personal names, which are either identical with OT names or formed on the same type. The colony owned houses, had families and slaves, and a temple. There is little doubt that the community was a military colony of mercenaries hired to hold the frontier post. It could hardly have

been established earlier than the 7th century or later than the middle of the 6th century. Je 42–43 describes a Jewish group which fled to Egypt after the fall of Jerusalem in 587 BC, and there were probably other such groups which fled the country. The colony of Elephantine testifies that it was established on the island before the Persian conquest in 525, and thus it must have been installed under the dynasties of Sais.

The majority of the Elephantine documents are legal, and their formulation is governed by the principles of Mesopotamian law. Of particular interest are the marriage contracts; these grant the woman the right of divorce, which is unknown for women in the OT. In general women appear in the documents as quite active and possessing a degree of independence greater than that granted women in Israel. Members of the community owned slaves and transactions concerning slaves are numerous. There are also documents of transfer of property, loans, documents of suits at law, which were numerous, and some personal correspondence. The excavations conducted under Maspero in 1902, under a German expedition 1906–1908 and a French expedition 1907–1909 under Clermont-Ganneau wrecked the site rather than explored it. The excavators were searching for papyri and made little effort to record their finds and in some instances even to plot the area excavated.

The religion of the Jews of Elephantine shows some deviations from biblical religion. Their God was Yahweh of the OT, written, however, in the forms Yeho or Yahu; these forms appear in many Israelite proper names (Yehoshaphat, Yesha 'yahu, sc Jehoshaphat, Isaiah). References to Egyptian and Babylonian gods in the documents show a freedom in speaking of these gods foreign to the OT. With Yahu are grouped two names, Eshem-Bethel and Anath-Bethel (Anath-Yahu); in addition a Herem-Bethel appears. These names are most frequently taken by scholars as names of other deities associated with Yahweh; the religion of the community is thus identified with the syncretism found in Israel against which the OT prophets so often speak. The religion of the colony would thus afford a unique illustration of a phenomenon of the religion of Israel otherwise known obscurely. Anath* is a Canaanite goddess known from Ugarit*. Bethel* is with some probability identified as a divine name in the OT as well as in extrabiblical sources. Bethel, literally house of El (god), is to be identified in the opinion of many scholars with Yahweh as a hypostatization of His temple. W. F. Albright does not see in these names any deities of polytheism, but identifies all of the names as hypostatized aspects of Yahweh. There is a possible allusion to the observance of the Sabbath* and a certain allusion to the observance of the feast of Mazzoth*. It is of interest that the observance of the feast was regulated through the Persian officer Arsham. It is now known that the Persian government was quite active in regulating the diverse religions of its subjects. The evidence of the papyri together with evidence from other sources has now made it very difficult to question the authenticity of the official documents quoted in Ezr*. There is, however, no clear reference to Passover* in connection with Mazzoth; but the documents are missing large fragments and it cannot be affirmed that Passover was unknown at Elephantine. No trace of OT books has been found; but extensive fragments of the book of Ahikar* were discovered. The temple built by the Jews of Elephantine was destroyed by the native population in 410 BC. The officers of the colony appealed to Bagohi, the Jewish governer of Palestine, as well as to Sanballat*, the governor of Samaria, and to Johanan, the high priest of Jerusalem. This suggests that the schism between the Jews and the Samaritans* had not yet occurred. This harmonizes with the opinion of many scholars that Ezra*, whose severe measures would have alienated the Samaritans, came to Jerusalem in 398. The documents give no information on the issue of this correspondence, but it appears that the Jews were permitted to rebuild their temple. The troubles of 410 are probably to be connected with a rebellion of the Egyptians against Persian rule. The Persian empire was extremely unpopular in Egypt, and the Jews as foreign mercenaries must have shared the odium. Nothing is known of the end of

the Jewish colony. It appears that the colony changed its allegiance to Amytaeus, who successfully rebelled against Amyrtaeus, and that it was removed from the island under Nepherites, the king who overthrew Amyrtaeus in 399. It is possible that the colony is referred to obliquely in Is 19:16 ff.

Elhanan (Hb *'elḥānān*, meaning uncertain), one of David's heroes, the son of Dodo of Bethlehem in 2 S 23:24 and 1 Ch 11:26 (the lists of David's heroes), the son of Jaare-oregim in 2 S 21:19; this latter text appears to be corrupt and is corrected by modern critics to Jair (1 Ch 20:5). The slaying of Goliath* is attributed to Elhanan in 2 S 21:19; this tradition is probably more original than that of 1 S 17. Elhanan's adversary in 1 Ch 20:5 is Lahmi, the brother of Goliath and described in the same terms as Goliath; this is probably an editorial change to harmonize with the data of 1 S 17. The attribution of the slaying of Goliath to David seems to represent a later phase in the glorification of David. De Vaux has suggested that 1 S 17 originally mentioned the Philistine with no personal name.

Eli (Hb *'elî*, meaning uncertain; cf Nabatean *'eliel*; perhaps abbreviated from *yô'ēlî*, "Yahweh is exalted"), priest of the sanctuary of Shiloh* who received Samuel* for the service of the sanctuary (1 S 1). A prophet threatened Eli with the destruction of his house because of the transgressions of his sons Hophni* and Phinehas* (2 S 2). This lengthy passage is a doublet of the oracle attributed to Samuel in 1 S 3:1–18. Eli died when he was told of the death of his sons in battle against the Philistines, and his line survived according to this passage only in a grandson, Ichabod* (1 S 4). Other descendants, however, are mentioned: Ahijah*, Ahimelech*, and Abiathar*, who was deposed from the priesthood by Solomon (1 K 2:27). The prophetic utterances of both Samuel and the unknown prophet of 1 S 2 are no doubt written in the light of the subsequent disasters of the house of Eli. In particular, the discourse of 1 S 2 is thought to reflect the period of Josiah*. An Eli not mentioned in the OT, the son of Mathat and the father of Joseph*, appears in the genealogy of Jesus (Lk 3:23).

Eliakim (Hb *'elyāqîm*, "El will set up"), personal name. **1.** Son of Hilkiah, master of the palace under Hezekiah*, highly praised by Isaiah (22:20 ff), appointed in place of Shebna*. He was one of the ministers who negotiated with the officer of Sennacherib* about the surrender of Jerusalem and who were sent to Isaiah to ask him to pray for the escape of the city (2 K 18–19; Is 36–37).

2. Son of Josiah* and Zebidah, who succeeded his brother Jehoahaz* as king of Judah. His name was changed to Jehoiakim* at his accession, and it is by this name that he is mentioned elsewhere. The name appears in the genealogies of Jesus: the son of Abiud and the father of Asor (Mt 1:13), and the son of Melea and the father of Jonam (Lk 3:30); these are not mentioned in the OT.

Elias. Cf ELIJAH.

Eliezer (Hb *'ĕlî‛ēzer,* "my god is help"), personal name borne by nine men in the OT. Eliezer, the son of Moses* and Zipporah* (Ex 18:4) and the ancestor of a levitical family (1 Ch 23:15–17) is possibly identical with Eleazar* the son of Aaron. Eliezer the son of Dodaviah of Mareshah prophesied against Jehoshaphat* of Judah when he attempted to resume commercial fleet operations from Ezion-geber* (2 Ch 20:37). Eliezer as the name of Abraham's slave appears only in Gn 15:2; but this text is regarded as corrupt by modern critics. The Eliezer in the genealogy of Jesus, son of Jorim and father of Jesus, is not mentioned in the OT (Lk 3:29).

Elihu (Hb *'ĕlîhû',* "he is god"), personal name borne by five men in the OT. On Elihu in Job cf JOB.

Elijah (Hb *'ēlîyyah* or *'ēlîyyāhū,* "my god is Yahweh"), a prophet during the reigns of Ahab* and Ahaziah* of Israel. The name is borne by three others in the OT. The story of Elijah is contained in 1 K 17–19; 21; 2 K 1:1–2:18. Many modern critics suppose that the Elijah cycle has been taken from a biography of Elijah; this is supported by the extremely abrupt introduction of Elijah in 1 K 17:1 with no identification beyond "the Tishbite of Tishbe in Gilead." Nelson Glueck has conjectured with some probability that Tishbite and Tishbe are corruptions of Jabeshite and Jabesh*. But it may be asked why the compiler omitted the information about Elijah's origins and previous life if he possessed it, since it is usually given for other prophets. It is possible also that the stories of the Elijah cycle circulated as independent pieces and were collected by the compiler of K or one of his sources. The story shows great skill in vivid and graphic narration. The anecdotes are arranged in five groups.

1. 1 K 17:1–18:46. Elijah appears and predicts to Ahab three years of drought (17:1). He hides near the brook Cherith, where he is fed by ravens (17:2–8); from there he goes to Zarephath* in Phoenicia, where he multiplies the food and oil of a widow and raises her son from the dead (17:9–24). After three years Elijah confronts Ahab through Ahab's servant Obadiah (18:1–17) and challenges Ahab to an ordeal with the prophets of Baal to see whether Baal or Yahweh will bring rain. The ordeal takes place on Mt Carmel; the prophets of Baal appeal by ritual dance and ecstasy. Elijah's appeal to Yahweh is answered when his sacrifice is consumed by a bolt of lightning, and rain then comes from the sea (18:18–46).

2. 1 K 19:1–21. Elijah is forced to flee from the kingdom by the hostility of Jezebel*. He goes to Mt Horeb*, where Yahweh appears to him not in the earthquake or the wind or the lightning, but in a gentle whisper, and tells him to anoint Hazael* king of Damascus, Jehu* king of Israel, and Elisha* his successor (19:1–18). On his return Elijah calls Elisha from behind the plow to follow him (19:19–21).

3. 1 K 21:1–29. Elijah predicts the destruction of the house of Ahab because of the judicial murder of Naboth* by Jezebel to obtain his vineyard for Ahab.

4. 2 K 1. Elijah threatens Ahaziah with death because he sought help from Baalzebub* of Ekron* and not from Yahweh during his illness. In the course of the story Elijah invokes the lightning to consume two companies of 50 who are sent to arrest him (2 K 1).

5. 2 K 2:1–18. Elijah takes Elisha with him and is carried to heaven in a chariot of fire, leaving Elisha his mantle and a double portion of his spirit of prophecy. The legacy of Elijah is proved genuine when Elisha divides the waters of the Jordan by striking them with the mantle of Elijah (2 K 2:1–18).

It is generally agreed by critics that this cycle has collected legends about Elijah which circulated among the prophetic groups, "the sons of the prophets." The emphasis falls heavily upon the marvelous, and the cycle is exceeded in this respect only by the cycle of Elisha. It is the story of the resistance of Elijah, almost alone (cf 1 K 19:18), to the cult of Melkart, the Baal of Tyre, introduced into the kingdom by Jezebel, a princess of Tyre and queen of the tolerant Ahab. The extirpation of the cult of Baal was not accomplished by the display of wonders attributed both to Elijah and to Elisha in prophetic legend, but by the extermination of the dynasty through conspiracy and assassination; cf ELISHA; JEHU. Prophetic tradition justified the use of these unworthy tactics by attributing them to the theophany of Horeb, where Elijah learns that Yahweh is not in the earthquake, the wind, and the lightning, that is, in violence, but in the soft whisper of the breeze, which signified in the concrete the stealthy means of encouraging Hazael and Jehu to seize the thrones of their respective kingdoms and thus bring about the downfall of the dynasty which patronized the foreign cult. Possibly prophetic tradition attributed to Elijah a policy which was not his own, but was instituted by Elisha.

Elijah appears as a prophet who insists on the unique divinity of Yahweh and the repudiation of the cult of any other god. He affirms the supremacy of Yahweh over nature, which was the peculiar area of the Canaanite gods in the ritual cycle of fertility. He is also the defender of traditional Hebrew morality against the tyranny of absolutism. His greatness is attested by the numerous allusions to him in the OT and the NT. The original prophetic legend constructed his experience of God with features drawn from the traditions of Moses: the place is the same, Horeb, the features of the theophany — earthquake, wind, fire — are the same, but the antithesis between the two is also explicit; for Elijah Yahweh was not in these violent elements. 2 Ch 21:12 ff contains a letter of admonition written by Elijah to Jehoram* of Judah. The translation of Elijah in the legend was the basis of the later belief that Elijah would return. This belief already existed when Mal 3:23 was written; here Elijah returns before the Day of Yahweh. The belief is mentioned in BS 48:10 and several times in the Gospels (Mt 11:14; 17:10 f; Mk 9:11 f). Jesus Himself was thought to be Elijah by some (Mt 16:14; Mk 6:15; 8:28; Lk 9:8, 19). John the Baptist was asked whether he was Elijah (Jn 1:21, 25). Jesus Himself dismissed the belief with the remark that John the Baptist was the Elijah who was to come (Mt 11:14; 17:11 f; Mk 9:12 f). John is said to go before the Lord in the spirit and power of Elijah (Lk 1:17). Elijah, representing prophecy, with Moses, representing the law, witnessed the glorification of Jesus (Mt 17:3 ff; Mk 9:4 ff; Lk 9:30 ff). At Nazareth Jesus alluded to the episode of Elijah and the widow to illustrate the rejection of a prophet in his own country (Lk 4:25 f). The name Elijah is used once by Paul as a title of a portion of the Bible (Rm 11:2), and Elijah, "a man like us," is proposed as a model of prayer (Js 5:17).

Elim. A camp of the Israelites in the passage from Egypt to Canaan with 12 springs and 70 palm trees (Ex 15:27; Nm 33:9). Because of its position in the itinerary and the description it has been traditionally identified with the oasis of the Wadi Gharandel, near the Red Sea in the western shore of the Sinai peninsula. This oasis has palms*, tamarisks, and acacias, and a spring with a perennial flow of about 80 liters a second (Abel). Cf EXODUS.

Elimelech (Hb *'elîmelek,* "my god is king"), a man of Bethlehem, husband of Naomi*, father of Mahlon* and Chilion* and stepfather of Ruth*, who migrated to Moab* during a famine and died there (Rt 1:1 ff).

Eliphaz (Hb *'elîpāz,* meaning uncertain), personal name. **1.** Son of Esau* and Adah and father of several Edomite clans, Teman*, Omar, Zepho, Gatam, and Kenaz* (Gn 36:9 ff; 1 Ch 35 f). On the relation of Esau and Edom cf EDOM; ESAU. **2.** Eliphaz of Teman, one of Job's three friends (Jn 2:11); on his part in the dialogue cf JOB. The name and place of origin may have been taken by the author of Jb from the Edomite genealogy.

Eliseus. Cf ELISHA.

Elisha (Hb *'elîšā',* perhaps to be pronounced *'elyāšā',* "El has saved"), a prophet of Israel in the reigns of Ahaziah, Joram, Jehu, Joahaz, and Joash. Elisha, the son of Shaphat of Abel-meholah, was called by Elijah* from behind the plow, accompanied Elijah at his translation, and received from him his mantle and a double portion of his prophetic spirit, the portion of the eldest son (2 K 2:1–18). The cycle of Elisha is found in 2 K 2:19–8:15. Elisha appears in the story of the revolt of Jehu (2 K 9:1–3) and the cycle is concluded with the story of his last days and death (2 K 13:14–21). It contains the story of the purification of the water (2 K 19–22), the unsavory story of the cursing of the small boys (2 K 2:23–25), Elisha in the campaign of Jehoram and Jehoshaphat against Moab (2 K 3:11–20), the wonders accomplished by Elisha: the multiplication of the oil (2 K 4:1–7), the raising of the son of the Shunamite woman (2 K 4:8–37), the poisonous stew (2 K 4:37–41), the multiplication of the loaves and vegetables (2 K 4:42–44), the cure of the leprosy of Naaman* of Damascus (2 K 5:1–20), the clairvoyance of the theft of Gehazi* and the infliction of Naaman's leprosy upon him (2 K 5:21–27), the rescue of the ax from the Jordan (2 K 6:1–7), the deception of the Aramaeans (2 K 6:8–23), the prediction of the end of the siege of Samaria (2 K 6:24–7:26), the prediction that Hazael would become king of Damascus (2 K 8:1–15), the commission to anoint Jehu king (2 K 9:1–10), the prediction of the victories of Jehoash over Damascus (2

K 13:14–19), and the resurrection of the dead man who was placed in Elisha's grave (2 K 13:20 f). The Elisha cycle gives less of an impression of unity than the Elijah cycle and is not so easily considered a biography or selections from a biography; it is rather a collection of anecdotes. The lack of unity is evident in such passages as 2 K 6:23–24, where v 24 contradicts v 23. The cycle comes from the prophetic groups and exhibits a childish love of the marvelous which is not always edifying; indeed there seems to be an effort to make Elisha a greater thaumaturge than Elijah. The anecdotes of the multiplication of the oil and the raising of the son of the Shunamite are composed in obvious imitation of similar stories in the Elijah cycle. While Elisha is active in the story of the campaign of Israel and Judah against Moab (2 K 3:1 ff) and in the revolt of Jehu (2 K 9:1 ff), both of these accounts are probably not from the prophetic sources, since the interest lies primarily in the action of others than the prophet. Elisha employed some devices which do not appear in the stories of Elijah, such as the use of music to produce a prophetic trance (2 K 3:14 f) and the use of the symbolic action in a manner which approaches the magical rite (2 K 13:14 ff). Elisha executed the commission to anoint rival kings for the thrones of Damascus and Israel which prophetic tradition attributed to Elijah; cf ELIJAH. The encouragement of Hazael to assassinate his lord (2 K 8:9 ff) and of Jehu to assassinate not only the king but also his entire family is ethically and theologically indefensible. The use of such violent means to forward the cause of Yahweh was not in harmony with true Israelite belief; the cause of Yahweh did not need conspiracy and assassination, and this was the view of the episode taken by Hosea a century later (Ho 1:4). Behind the legends of Elijah one can discern one of· the great religious figures of Israel, a man who stood with great simplicity and integrity for the worship of Yahweh. Elisha exhibits no similar religious greatness; he was admired more as a wonderworker and a man of political dexterity and influence. He is mentioned in the NT in Lk 4:27.

Elizabeth (Gk form of Hb *'elîšeba'*, "El is fullness"), wife of Zechariah* the priest and mother of John the Baptist, relative (degree unspecified) of Mary* (Lk 1). The Hb name was borne by the wife of Aaron, mother of Abihu, Nadab, Eleazar, and Ithamar (Ex 6:23).

Elkanah (Hb *'elkānāh*, "El has produced"), a man of Zuph* of the tribe of Ephraim*,

husband of Hannah* and father of Samuel* (1 S 1–2; 1 Ch 6:12, 19). The name is borne by four others in the OT.

Ellasar (Hb *'ellāsār*, meaning uncertain), the city of Arioch* (Gn 14:1). The earlier identification with Larsa in Babylonia is now thought to be improbable, since there is nothing to correspond to the first syllable of Ellasar. An identification with the city of *Ilanṣura* mentioned in the Mari* tablets and located by Albright between Carchemish* and Harran is accepted by many modern scholars, in spite of the difference of the sibilants in the two names.

Eltekeh (Hb *'eltekēh,* meaning uncertain), listed among the cities of Dan between Ekron* and Gibbethon* (Jos 19:44) and as a Levitical city of the Kohathites (Jos 21:23). It is usually identified with Khirbet Mukanna, located in the Shephelah* about 10 mi SSE of Ekron and halfway between Ekron and Timnah*. It is listed among the cities subject to Egypt by Harmhab, Seti I, Ramses II, and Ramses III. Sennacherib records that he defeated the Egyptians and their allies at Altaku in his campaign in Judah in 701, and that he sacked Altaku and Tamna (Timnah).

Elul (Hb *'elûl,* meaning uncertain), the 6th month of the Hb calendar, roughly September (1 Mc 14:27; Ne 6:15).

Elymas. Cf BARJESUS.

Embalm. Embalming is mentioned only in connection with the burials of Jacob (Gn 50:2 ff) and Joseph (Gn 50:26.) In both of these the Egyptian process of mummification is no doubt intended. The technique of mummification varied at different periods in ancient Egypt. In general the essential feature of the process was the total desiccation of the body, probably accomplished by the use of natron. Scholars do not agree on whether the natron was used in solution or in the dry solid state. The brain and the viscera, except the heart and the kidneys, were removed. The body was washed and anointed with fragrant spices. The visceral and cranial cavities were sometimes filled with linen packing. The viscera were placed in four canopic vases which stood at the four corners of the coffin. The limbs separately and the entire body were tightly wrapped in strips of linen. The mummified bodies have survived for thousands of years. The body was buried in a sarcophagus constructed in the form of the human being; sometimes a number of sarcophagi of graduated sizes were used. The sarcophagus was enclosed in a coffin or in a series of coffins. The process was extremely expensive and it was probably not within reach of the majority of the population. The process consumed some time; the 40 days of Gn 50:3 do not correspond exactly to the 70 days mentioned in Egyptian sources. The period of mourning for Jacob, however, is put at 70 days (*ibid*).

Emim (Hb *'ēmîm,* meaning unknown), according to Dt 2:10 f the name given by the Moabites to the prehistoric inhabitants of Moab called Rephaim elsewhere. They are said to be tall like the Anakim*. Their appearance in Gn 14:5 with the Rephaim, Zuzim, and the Horites* suggests that the names in this passage are drawn at random from the names of the pre-Israelite inhabitants of Canaan.

Emmanuel (Hb *'immānû'ēl,* "God is with us," or: "may God be with us"), the name given by Isaiah to the infant whose birth is announced in Is 7:10–17. The background of the passage is the crisis of 735 BC, when Judah was threatened with attack by Pekah* of Israel and Rezin* of Damascus in order to force Judah into an alliance against Assyria. It was the intention of Ahaz* to invoke the aid of Assyria, which he actually did. Against this intention Isaiah offered the king a sign (cf MIRACLE) of assurance that the campaign of the allies would be unsuccessful. Ahaz, more from unbelief than from piety, refused the sign; he placed more confidence in Assyrian arms. Isaiah then gave the sign of Yahweh Himself: the imminent birth of a child who would feed on milk and honey, the food of the gods, during his infancy. Before the child reached the age of reason the attack of the allies would be abandoned, but there would follow troubles such as the kingdom had never known. It is most probable that Is 7:18–25 is a collection of detached sayings from Isaiah or from his editors which have been attached to this passage because of some similarity of content or catchwords; they contribute nothing to the problem of the identification of the child. In 8:8 the phrase is not certainly a proper name; it may be an ejaculation in which the phrase is used as a religious slogan.

Interpreters have proposed widely divergent views, none of which is without difficulty. Some older interpreters understood the mother and child as a collective designation referring to all children who were born at the time, all of whom would serve as a timetable of the prophet's predictions. Others have understood that the woman and child are the wife and son of Isaiah himself. A more probable view is that the child is the son of Ahaz who succeeded him on the throne, Hezekiah*. This view suffers from some chronological difficulties, but the chronology of the period is not well enough known to make these difficulties a peremptory objection.

Hezekiah seems best to fulfill the character of the sign which the prophet offers. The sign is both a threat and a promise: a promise of immediate deliverance from imminent danger, and a threat of later disaster. In the context this threat can be uttered only as a punishment for the unbelief and secular policy of Ahaz. The basis of the promise must be understood in the light of the messianic conception of the dynasty of David* (cf MESSIAH). The eternity of the dynasty of David is fundamental in messianism. The birth of an heir to the dynasty is a sign of the continuation of the dynasty and of the promises which are conferred upon it. The child is further a sign because the validity of the promises can be observed in the years of his infancy, which will follow shortly. From the promise can be concluded the validity of the threat, which will follow after a longer interval of time. The birth of the child thus assures the permanence of the dynasty in spite of the unbelief of its present representative, which will bring upon the kingdom the punishment of foreign invasion. Since the sign is so closely connected with the dynastic idea, it seems that an heir to the throne is implied in the sign rather than the children born at the time or the child of Isaiah himself.

The traditional view of the passage understands it as a direct prediction of the virgin birth of Jesus; many modern interpreters revise this in such a way as to make it a direct prediction of the birth of Jesus or of the Messiah without any determination of his personal identity. The traditional view has some serious considerations against it. It rests on the Hb word *'almāh,* translated "virgin" in the LXX (Gk *parthenos*) and the Vg (Lt *virgo*). These translations cannot be supported. *'almāh* signifies a young woman of marriageable age, and it appears that its use generally implies that the girl is not married. It does not signify virgin; for this Hb uses *beṯûlāh.* Since *parthenos* is sometimes used in Gk of women who are clearly not virgins, it is not certain that the LXX intended to express virginity by its use of the word.

The use of the text in Mt 1:22 f seems to understand it as a prediction of the virgin birth of Jesus. Here it is necessary to refer to the NT use of the OT in similar contexts (cf PROPHET). Such passages are often employed on a very broad similarity or on the principle of the catch word. Here Mt uses a catchword, *parthenos,* which has no correspondence in the Hb text. But it is not entirely clear from the context that Mt is using the text of the virgin birth. He is possibly referring to it much in the sense in which it is used in Is, as a prediction of the birth of an heir to the Davidic dynasty. Here the series of the Davidic dynasty reaches its completion, and the salvation through the dynasty which was reaffirmed in the appearance of each successive heir to the dynasty now is attained in Him who terminates the line.

Emmaus. A city in the Shephelah*, site of the victory of Judas* over Gorgias* in 166 BC (1 Mc 3:40–57; 4:3), fortified by Lysias* in 160 BC (1 Mc 9:50), and of the appearance of Jesus to two disciples after His resurrection (Lk 24:13 ff). The place cannot be certainly identified. The ancient name survives in the modern Amwas, about 19 mi WNW of Jerusalem. The original text of Lk reads 60 stadia, about 7 mi; and the distance of 19 mi makes the round trip impossible in a single day, as the incident is related in Lk. Hence other sites have been preferred, in particular the village of el Qubeibeh, about 11 mi from Jerusalem via the present roads in the same direction.

Enacim. Cf ANAKIM.

Endor (Hb *'ên dōr,* "fountain of habitation"?), a city of Manasseh* (Jos 17:11), the residence of the necromancer consulted by Saul* (1 S 28:7), associated in Ps 83:11 with the victory of Barak* over Sisera*. The name is preserved in the modern village of Endur on the N side of the plain of Esdraelon* near the foot of Mt Tabor*. This site suits the battle of Barak with the Canaanites and the visit of Saul to the necromancer.

Engedi (Hb *'ên gᵉdî,* "spring of the kid"?), a city of Judah (Jos 15:62), one of the points to which David fled when he was pursued by Saul (1 S 24:1 ff), incorrectly identified with Hazazon-Tamar* (2 Ch 20:2). It was located in the desert of Judah (Jos 15:62) by the shore of the Dead Sea (Ezk 47:10). The ancient name is preserved in the Arabic *ain jidi,* an oasis on the W shore of the Dead Sea. The site of the city is usually identified with *tell el jurn,* a mound of ruins near the oasis. The beloved in SS is compared with a cluster of henna from the gardens of Engedi (1:14), and wisdom compares herself with a palm of Engedi (BS 24:14). The oasis lies about 35 mi from Jerusalem.

English versions of the Bible. 1. Anglo-Saxon versions. A paraphrase in Anglo-Saxon verse of Gn, Ex, and parts of Dn is attributed to Caedmon (c 670). This was not a true translation. Aldhelm (✝ 709) translated the Pss, the first genuine translation. The MS of his work is preserved, but some scholars believe it is a later revision. Bede the Venerable (673–735) is said by his biographer to have translated Jn; neither this translation nor other translations attributed to him have been preserved. A translation of a few books of the Bible is attributed by early sources to Alfred the Great (849–901), but this attribution is doubtful. The liturgical importance of the Gospels and the Pss was responsible for efforts to render these books into the vernacular. Some Anglo-Saxon Gospels of unknown origin in the 10th century are preserved in MS. The earliest form of this version appears in the Lindisfarne Gospels (c 700), in which the Anglo-Saxon version is glossed between the lines of the Lt text. The most extensive Anglo-Saxon version was made by the abbot Aelfric (c 990): the Pnt, Jos, Jgs, K, Est, Jdt, Jb, Mc. All the Anglo-Saxon versions were made from the Lt. **2.** Middle English Versions. No complete version of the Bible was made in this period. The Pss were popular, and versions attributed to William of Shoreham and Richard Rolle of Hampole are preserved from the 13th and 14th centuries. **3.** Wycliffite Versions. John Wycliffe (1330?–1384) became the center of a social and religious controversy from 1370 to 1384. He was condemned as a heretic by the English hierarchy. A part of his movement was an effort to make the Bible available to everyone in the vernacular, in order that each might read and study it for himself. The Wycliffite versions, of which there are two, are doubtfully the work of Wycliffe himself. The earlier version is attributed to Nicholas of Hereford. Its stiff and pedantic style was responsible for a revision which was completed about 1400; this revision, the second Wycliffite version, is commonly attributed to John Purvey. These versions are important not only because they were the first complete versions, but also because their language left its mark on all subsequent versions. Like the earlier versions, they were translated from the Lt. **4.** 16th-century versions. The Protestant Reformation gave the impulse to a great number of translations which appeared between 1525 and 1611. The first printed English version was the NT of William Tyndale (1484–1536). Tyndale became sympathetic toward Lutheranism and most probably was moved to his work by the example of Luther's German version. He began the translation in England, but since he was suspect of heresy he left England for Germany in 1524. His NT was printed at Cologne and Worms in 1525. Several printings followed. Tyndale produced a corrected edition in 1534 (Antwerp) and another in 1536. He was executed for heresy at Brussels in 1536. He began the translation of the OT, but only the Pnt and Jos were published (1530–1531). At his death he left a MS of the translation of the OT from Jos to 2 Ch. Tyndale's version was made from Gk and Hb. His knowledge of Gk was adequate for his times, but his knowledge of Hb is uncertain. In both OT and NT he used the Vg and Luther's German version as a base. The felicity of his vernacular version is universally admired. Less admired at the time was his abandonment of such ecclesiastical words as church, bishop, and priest, for congregation, overseer, and elder or senior. These were taken as a "lutheranizing" of the Bible. Unacceptable also were the bitterly controversial notes which he inserted. This practice initiated by him was retained in all later 16th-century versions. Tyndale's NT was the basic text employed by all later versions. One writer has said that the Authorized Version of the NT was 90 percent Tyndale. His version was condemned in England and a great many copies were destroyed.

Miles Coverdale produced the first complete printed English version of the Bible (1535). Coverdale was encouraged in his work by Cromwell. The version was not original. The NT was Tyndale revised according to Luther and the Zurich Bible of the Swiss reformers. (1529). The basic text of the OT was the Zurich Bible with extensive use of the portions of the OT translated by Tyndale. Coverdale himself acknowledged the use of other aids which he did not name. They can now be recognized as the Vg and·the Lt version of Santes Pagnini produced in Italy in 1528. In spite of the secondary character of the version, it was probably more important than any other version in determining the final form which the Bible took in English. Coverdale was the first to segregate the deuterocanonical books as of less authority than the books of the Hb Bible; this feature was retained in later Protestant versions. Coverdale's first edition was published in Germany; a subsequent edition of 1537 (Southwark) was the first English Bible to be printed in England. This 1537 edition was published with the royal license.

Mathew's Bible (1537), printed in England, was the work of John Rogers. The Thomas Mathew whose name appeared in the dedication is unknown and is perhaps fictitious. This is a revision in which Tyndale was employed for Gn–2 Ch and Coverdale for the rest of the OT. Tyndale's 1535 NT was employed. Since Tyndale's edition had been condemned, no credit was given to him.

The Great Bible (1539) was a revision of Mathew's Bible made by Coverdale with the use of the Lt Bible of Sebastian Münster (1534–1535) for the OT and the Lt version of Erasmus (1516) for the NT. The name of the Bible comes from its size; it was a large and sumptuously printed version for use in the churches. Henry VIII, persuaded by Cromwell, ordered that a copy be placed in every church. Three subsequent editions appeared in 1539 and three more in 1540. The Pss of the Great Bible were used in the Book of Common Prayer published under Edward VI and have remained the Pss of Protestant worship into modern times. Taverner's Bible (1539) was an independent revision of Mathew's Bible. The revisions were few and in the OT were taken principally from the Vg. The work was superseded by the Great Bible.

With the accession of Mary Tudor in 1553 severe measures were taken against those who refused to submit to Rome. The more radical (Puritan) wing would not, as many did, accommodate itself to the new policy, and a large number of Puritans went to the continent. Many of them settled in Geneva. Here in 1557 William Whittingham produced an English NT, and with a group of colleagues the entire Bible in 1560. The Geneva NT was a revision of the Great Bible with the use of the commentaries and Lt version of Theodore Beza. The OT was the Great Bible revised according to the Hb as interpreted in the Lt version of Pagnini. The Geneva Bible was the first English Bible to divide the chapters into numbered verses. It was attractively printed and became immediately popular; it did not finally yield to the Authorized Version until the middle of the 17th century. In the bitterness of its controversial notes it exceeded any Bible which had appeared. As a model of vernacular English it surpassed all its predecessors.

The sectarian origin and tendencies of the Geneva Bible made it unacceptable to the English hierarchy of Elizabeth I for public use, but its excellence doomed the Great Bible. Under the leadership of Matthew Parker, Archbishop of Canterbury, a revision of the Great Bible for use in the churches was prepared (1568), called the Bishops' Bible. The revision was entrusted to a committee and it was uneven in quality. The Bishops' Bible was a retrogression; it was important only because it provided the basic text for the translators of the Authorized Version.

The Rheims-Douay version was the response of English Catholics to the Protestant versions. It was produced by scholars of the English college of Douay; the most active members of the group were William Cardinal Allen, Gregory Martin, Richard Bristow, and William Reynolds. The NT was published in 1582 at Rheims; the college had moved there from Douay to escape political disturbances. The OT because of lack of funds was not published until 1609–1610 at Douay. The Vg was deliberately chosen as the text in response to the Protestant emphasis on the original texts; this was a somewhat unfortunate interpretation of the authenticity of the Vg as declared by the Council of Trent. The translators, however, made use of the original texts, especially in the NT. The English of the version lacks the easy and popular style of the Geneva Bible. The desire of the translators for accuracy led them frequently to anglicize Lt words; a great many Lt derivatives now in common use entered English through the RD version. The style, however, was so dependent upon the Lt that the meaning was frequently obscure and sometimes, especially where the Lt represented a corrupt Hb text, unintelligible. The NT, however, was extensively used by the translators of the Authorized Version. The NT was reprinted in 1600, 1621, 1633, and 1749. The OT was reprinted only once (1635). The circulation of the RD Bible was limited compared to the circulation of the Geneva and Authorized versions. The early editions of the RD version contained controversial notes of a character similar to those found in Protestant Bibles; these were softened somewhat in later revisions.

The question of the English Bible was still unsettled in 1600. The Bishops' Bible was unsatisfactory, and the Geneva Bible, the work of nonconformist groups, could not be accepted by the English hierarchy. James I called a conference of the different religious groups at Hampton Court in 1604 to work for religious unity. At this conference Dr. John Reynolds, a Puritan, suggested a new translation of the Bible which would be acceptable to all. The king was pleased with the suggestion and instituted proceedings for its execution. A board of 54 translators was assembled, including almost all the prominent scholars of the country. The board was divided into three companies (Oxford, Cambridge, Westminster); the Bible was divided among the three companies, but the work of each company was to be revised by the other two. The work was begun in 1607 and finished in 1610. While this is a short time, the organization assured more careful work than had been given to any earlier

version. The directions for the translators laid down the Bishops' Bible as the basic text. They were permitted to use the versions of Tyndale, Mathew, Coverdale, Geneva, and the Great Bible wherever these seemed superior. The Rheims NT was not mentioned but it was used. Since the translation was the work of different religious groups, no notes were inserted except references to variant readings; and the ecclesiastical words (church, bishop, priest, sacrament, etc) were retained. The version was published in 1611 with royal authorization and appointed to be read in the churches. The success of the translators in meeting the public taste was immediate; the Geneva Bible had passed out of general use by 1660. The success of the AV was due principally to its choice of language. It was made when classical Elizabethan prose had taken form; the language of the AV was so entirely contemporary and intelligible that it was at once accepted. It has become a monument of classical English literature; quotations and allusions from the AV run through the whole body of subsequent literature. It was the first English version to contain a genuine new translation of the original Hb of the OT. Throughout both OT and NT the translators made use of all earlier versions.

5. 18th- and 19th-century revisions. The unsatisfactory features of the RD led Catholics to attempt to make it more attractive. It acquired the form which it retained into the 20th century from the revisions of Richard Challoner, vicar apostolic of London. He revised the OT twice (1750, 1763) and the NT five times (1749, 1750, 1752, 1763, 1772). Challoner, no scholar, was not qualified to revise the version according to the original texts; his revision consisted principally in adopting readings from the AV. This raised the quality of the English of the RD, but contributed nothing to its accuracy.

The classical beauty of the AV did not conceal its defects, some of which were due to its 16th-century scholarship, others to simple misunderstanding of the original texts. The need of a revision was rendered acute by the recognition in 19th-century scholarship that the Gk text* of the NT at the base of the AV was more remote from the original than the text of other MSS. The subject was first raised in 1865 and the Convocation of Canterbury in 1870 determined that the AV should be revised. The revision was undertaken by two companies, one for the OT and one for the NT, representing all English denominations. The NT was published in 1881, the OT in 1885. The NT incorporated changes demanded by NT textual criticism. The OT revision was less extensive and was made according to the more profound understanding of the Hb text which modern scholarship affords. Other changes were made to modernize the language. The RV, in spite of its merits, was never widely accepted by the public because of its departures from the traditional text of the AV. American scholars also were invited to take part in the production of the RV; but the changes they suggested were so extensive that no agreement could be reached on their incorporation into the RV. By a previous agreement the American revision was published 20 years after the appearance of the RV NT as the American Standard Bible (1901). A later revision of this version appeared as the Revised Standard Version (NT, 1946; entire Bible, 1953), which is regarded by many as the best English version.

An American revision of the Rheims-Challoner NT made by a committee of scholars was published by the Confraternity of Christian Doctrine in 1941. This revision depended upon the Vg, although the revisers made extensive use of the Gk text. The work was largely nullified by the encyclical *Divino Afflante Spiritu* (1943), which recommended vernacular versions made from the original texts. The Confraternity of Christian Doctrine has not yet produced a NT made from the Greek. The Confraternity NT was the most radical modification of the Rheims NT yet produced, but it left many of the archaic features of the version untouched.

The Confraternity version of the OT, undertaken after the encyclical *Divino Afflante Spiritu*, is incomplete: Gn (1948), Pss (1950), OT Gn–Rt (1952), OT Jb–BS (1955), OT Is–Mal (1961). The version combines critical use of the Hb text with a style of modern speech which entirely abandons the biblicisms of older versions.

6. Independent Versions. A large number of independent versions have been made in the 18th–20th centuries. Those listed here include only the more recent and widely read versions. Most recent versions attempt to render the Bible in modern speech.

Non-Catholic versions: James Moffatt; NT 1913, entire Bible 1926, revised edition 1935. This version has been well received for its scholarly accuracy and its successful employment of modern speech.

The Holy Scriptures according to the Masoretic Text: A New Translation (1917), a version of the Hb OT published by American Jewish scholars. Its language retains the flavor of the Authorized Version.

E. J. Goodspeed, The NT: An American Translation (1923), and J. M. P. Smith, general editor, the OT: An American Translation (1927), published together as The Bible: An American Translation (1931).

This work, in particular the NT, was the most radically modern speech version of its time. The OT was less radical. The translation also incorporates the opinions of modern scholarship, in some instances without sufficient criticism.

The NT volume of *The New English Bible* was published in 1961, to be followed by the OT and the Apocrypha*. This work was the result of a 1946 resolution of the General Assembly of the Church of Scotland. The translation was done by scholars of British universities under the supervision of a Joint Committee; the group represented all the British Protestant churches. The translation is done in modern English; it is an entirely new version and not a revision of previous versions.

Catholic versions: Francis A. Spencer, O.P., the Gospels (1898), entire NT 1935 (posthumously), a version of the original Gk respected for its accuracy, not a genuine modern speech version.

The Westminster NT, general editor, Cuthbert Lattey, S.J., 1913–1935. This version makes less attempt to use modern speech, but it is done with great care and accuracy and includes extensive exegetical and critical notes. The Westminster OT has appeared only in a few volumes.

Ronald Knox, NT (1945), OT (1949). This version was commissioned by the English hierarchy. In both NT and OT it was made from the Vg with reference to the original texts. The version is universally admired for its English style, although it retained many archaisms which modern speech versions exclude. The use of the original text is much more evident in the NT than in the OT, which shows scarcely any departure from the Vg.

James Kleist and Joseph Lilly, the NT (1954). Made from the Gk, it is possibly the most modern of modern speech versions.

Enoch (Hb *ḥᵃnôk,* meaning unknown), an antediluvian patriarch mentioned in the Cainite genealogy as the son of Cain* and the father of Irad*, after whom was named the first city (Gn 4:17 f), and in the Sethite genealogy as the son of Jared* and the father of Methuselah* (Gn 5:18–24). Enoch differs from the other members of the Sethite list in his age (365 years, notably less than the others) and in the notice that he walked with God and was taken by God; "he died," explicitly said of the others, is omitted of Enoch. On the question of the use of Mesopotamian material in these chapters cf PATRIARCHS. J. Chaine has pointed out some interesting points of resemblance between Enoch and En-men-dur-Anna of the antediluvian kings of Mesopotamia. En-men-dur-Anna was the seventh of the kings, as Enoch is the seventh from Adam. En-men-dur-Anna was king of Sippar, the city of Shamash, the sun god; and the age of Enoch, 365 years, the number of days in the year, is very probably a solar reference the background of which is not preserved in the text. En-men-dur-Anna is described as the lord of oracles, the guardian of divine mysteries, and skilled in divination. This feature is not mentioned in Gn (unless implicitly in the statement that he walked with God) but it is found in the Hb text of BS 44:16. Here Enoch pleased God and was taken up from the earth. The Gk, which calls him "a pattern of repentance for all generations," is clearly a mistranslation of the Hb, "a wonder of knowledge for all generations." BS 49:14 alludes again to Enoch and asserts that no one was ever created on earth like him, for he was taken up from the earth. Chaine also suggests that the assumption of Enoch was transferred to Enoch from the Mesopotamian hero of the deluge, Ut-napishtim (cf DELUGE; NOAH). Because he had escaped the destruction intended for all mankind, Ut-napishtim and his wife were separated from the rest of mankind and granted immortality in Dilmun. On the books attributed to Enoch cf APOCRYPHAL BOOKS. These books suggest that Enoch was a much larger figure in popular tradition than one would conclude from the brief notices of the OT, and thus Chaine's suggestion that these traditions are reflected in the OT has great probability. Enoch is mentioned in the genealogy of Jesus (Lk 3:37). Hb 11:5 is drawn from Gn 5:24 and BS. While these points are much more explicit in the Ethiopic book of Enoch, the author of Hb says nothing which he could not have drawn from the OT. The Ethiopic book of Enoch (60, 8) is cited verbally in Jd 14. The citation of this book gives the book no more authority than it possesses in itself; it may be compared to Paul's citation of Gk literature (AA 17:28; Tt 1:12), where the author quoted is also called a prophet.

Enosh (Hb *'enôš*, "man"), son of Seth* and father of Kenan* (Gn 4:26; 5:6–11). Of this patriarch* it is noticed that in his time men began to call upon the name of Yahweh. This seems to imply a form of tradition in which the name of Yahweh first became known to Enosh. On the variant traditions about the first appearance of this name cf GOD. In the context it is probably to be understood as the invocation of the name in public cultic worship; Enosh is a founder like the men mentioned in Gn 4:17–24. The name possibly signifies that this

figure existed as the first man in another form of the traditions of primitive man.

En-rogel (Hb *'ên-rōgēl*, "spy's spring"?), a source of water near Jerusalem identified with the modern *bir ayyub* (Job's well). It lies S of the point where the Kidron joins the valley of Ge-hinnom. It was a boundary point between Judah and Benjamin (Jos 15:7; 18:16) and the point where Jonathan* and Ahimaaz* waited to deliver the message from Hushai* to David (2 S 17:17), and the place where Adonijah* celebrated his premature coronation feast (1 K 1:9); it lies within earshot of ancient Zion*. The well has never been scientifically explored. It is extremely likely that it was capped during the numerous sieges which Jerusalem has experienced, since it would furnish water to the besiegers but not to the defenders. It is possible that some of the masonry of the well goes back to Israelite times. Vincent concluded that the water did not arise from a subterranean spring but was collected by seepage of rainwater to the well, which lies at the bottom of the geological basin of Jerusalem.

Epaphras, Epaphroditus (Gk *epaphras* is a shortened form of Gk *epaphroditos,* "highly desirable"). The two names probably belong to the same individual. Epaphras was a Christian of Colossae (Col 4:12), founder of the church of Colossae (Col 1:7), and a companion of Paul's imprisonment in Rome (Phm 23). Epaphroditus brought Paul gifts from Philippi (Phl 4:18) and was sent by Paul to Philippi after Epaphroditus had been ill in Rome (Phl 2:25).

Ephah. Cf WEIGHTS AND MEASURES.

Ephesians, Epistle to the. 1. *Contents.*
  1:1–2, greeting.
  I. Doctrinal, 1:3–3:21:
  1:3–14, blessing and thanksgiving for the call and redemption of Christians.
  1:15–2:10, thanksgiving for faith of Christians and prayer that they may perceive more profoundly the reality of salvation.
  2:11–22, the salvation of the Gentiles equally with the Jews and the unity of both in Christ Jesus.
  3:1–21, the revelation of the mystery to Paul and his proclamation of the mystery to the Gentiles.
  II. Moral, 4:1–6:20:
  4:1–16, the unity of the Spirit and the diversity of the gifts of grace.
  4:17–24, the old man of sin and the new man of righteousness and holiness.
  4:25–5:2, charity.

5:3–14, pagan impurity and the Christian light.

5:15–20, intoxication of the flesh and of the Spirit.

5:21–6:9, counsels of family life.

6:10–22, the Christian's armor in the spiritual combat.

Conclusion, 6:21–24.

2. *Authorship, Date, Place of Composition.* Eph is one of the "epistles of the captivity" with Phl, Col, and Phm; but there are many obscurities in its origins. It is by no means certain that the title is original, and most modern scholars believe that it is not; "in Ephesus" (1:1) is missing in the earliest MSS, and some early Christian writers show that it was not in their text. The absence of personal references and greetings to a Church in a city where Paul lived for three years is astonishing; such personal allusions are characteristic of Paul's letters. Since Marcion it has been suggested that Eph is "the letter to the Laodiceans" mentioned in Col 4:16; but the absence of personal allusions is as serious an objection against this hypothesis. The destination of the letter must be determined in terms of its origin; but this question is much more complex for Eph than for the other letters of the Pauline corpus.

Most modern scholars question the Pauline origin of Eph. Eph contains 39 words not found elsewhere in the NT, 83 words not found in the uncontested Pauline letters, and 36 words found elsewhere in the NT but not in the Pauline letters. These statistics must not be exaggerated; some similar phenomena can be observed in as certainly a Pauline letter as Gal. But in conjunction with other phenomena they become more meaningful. No one denies that the style of Eph is obviously ponderous, involved, and overloaded in comparison with the style of Paul, and any hypothesis must explain this feature. There is an evident theological development in Eph; it cannot be called non-Pauline or anti-Pauline, but critics judge it to be a remarkable development to postulate within a very few years. The question is further complicated by the entirely singular relationship between Eph and Col. This extends not only to thought but also to terminology; a number of phrases of Col are repeated in Eph. There can be no doubt that Col is the original; the phrases are sometimes used in Eph in a servile or even in an unskillful manner. At the same time Eph exhibits a more careful or at least a more labored composition than Col; it is more solemn, and doctrinal developments which are sketched in Col are elaborated in Eph, and the OT is used more extensively. The writer of Eph used Col in a way

in which no Pauline epistle is used in another.

The work is therefore frequently attributed to a disciple, whom many place near the end of the 1st century, but earlier than AD 90. M. Goguel believes the disciple heavily glossed and interpolated an original Pauline letter; but this view has found few adherents. Several, including P. Benoit, suppose that the disciple worked with Paul or at his commission, and employed Col in his composition. C. L. Mitton and others attribute it to a disciple (perhaps Tychicus*), about 87–92 in the neighborhood of Ephesus, who made a collection of the Pauline letters and composed Eph as a doctrinal summary to be attached to the collection. Those who maintain Pauline authorship assert that the disciple would need an incredible degree of penetration to write such variations and enlargements of Pauline themes without distorting them; for it is undeniable that Eph exhibits numerous close contacts with Pauline literature and thought. But the problem of style is not solved in this attribution. There are difficulties both in attributing Eph to Paul and in removing it from him. It appears that the singular character of Eph is not explained by attributing it to Paul in the same way in which Rm, 1–2 Co, and Gal are attributed to him. Actually Paul "wrote" no letters, but dictated them in general terms (cf EPISTLE; SCRIBE). The Pauline characteristics seem to demand that he have a part in the composition; the suggestions of other minds and hands are perhaps best explained by supposing, as Benoit does, that the writer was commissioned by Paul but employed more liberty in phrasing and conception than was usual in the amanuenses of Paul. The writer very probably had no part in the composition of any other Pauline letter, and it is all but certain that he used Col as an outline and as a source of phrasing.

In this hypothesis the destination of the letter is more probably no particular church. Many scholars believe Eph is an encyclical letter sent to several churches of Asia — indeed, one can say with Cerfaux that it is addressed to all Gentiles. One may ask in this hypothesis why Eph was not addressed to "the saints" or "the churches" of Asia, and the question admits no convincing answer; but it has been suggested by several that "in Ephesus" in 1:1 fills a blank which was left in the original copy, to be filled with the name of each church to which a copy was sent. It is also suggested that the letter was copied at Ephesus.

3. *Occasion and Purpose.* Eph is the most doctrinal of all the letters of the Pauline corpus; and the letter itself contains no indication of the occasion which elicited this

doctrinal summary. The relations of Eph with Col suggest that the occasion was the rise of Gnostic syncretism, the occasion of Col; and it is altogether probable that this new problem needed not only a refutation but a synthetic positive exposition precisely to meet the new errors. Contrasted with earlier letters, there is little emphasis upon the problem of Judaizing, and little attention to eschatology. In view of the Gnostic syncretism the themes elaborated in Eph are found not at all or only vestigially in the earlier letters. The term mystery* is used rather than "gospel" of the earlier letters; the mystery is revealed and is the object of true knowledge*. The mystery is the divine plan of vocation and predestination, redemption, and the recapitulation of all things in Christ. The first to whom the mystery is revealed are the apostles*, and the apostolic mission and office are emphasized. The Church is one and universal, in which Jew and Gentile become one in Christ. The Church is mysteriously one with the exalted Christ; it is His body*. That this summary is the "gospel" of Paul is not certain; but it is certainly substantially faithful to his statement of the nature of salvation and of the universality of salvation for the Gentiles.

Ephesus. A city at the mouth of the river Cayster in W Asia Minor. The Ionians occupied the site about 1100 BC; probably a city existed on the site before this period, but its foundation cannot be dated. The city passed from the hands of the king of Pergamum* into the Roman empire in 133 BC. It was the capital city of the province of Asia*. Ephesus was a wealthy city, the chief port and market center of Asia; its population is estimated at 250,000 at least in the NT period. The large amount of silt carried by the Cayster and the receding shoreline caused a displacement of Ephesus westward from its original site about 2 mi in the 3rd century BC, when the city was largely rebuilt by the Thracian king Lysimachus (287 BC). Even in the NT period, however, the port of Ephesus had again moved W. In modern times the distance from the site of Ephesus to the sea exceeds a mi. The foundations of the Artemision, the famous temple of Artemis*, were discovered in 1869. The temple was further studied by an expedition of the British Museum (1904–1905), and the entire site was explored by the Austrian Archaeological Institute in a series of campaigns beginning in 1896. Many of the principal public buildings of the Roman period were uncovered. The platform on which the Artemision stood was about 240 ft wide and 420 ft long. The temple was about 160 ft wide and 240 ft long; its 100 columns were over 55 ft high. It was one of the seven wonders of the ancient world. Other buildings included the gymnasium; the stadium or racecourse; the great theater (the site of the assembly mentioned in AA 19), seating 24,000, one of the largest Roman theaters yet discovered; the marketplace (Gk *agora*, Lt *forum*); the temple of Serapis; the library of Celsus; a smaller theater, the Odeon. The port and theater were connected by the Arcadian street, a magnificent colonnaded avenue 1735 ft long. Ephesus was renowned in antiquity not only for its temple and cult of Artemis, but also for its magicians (cf AA 19:19). Paul first preached at Ephesus on his 2nd journey on his way from Corinth to Jerusalem. He taught in the synagogue but remained in the city only a short time (AA 18:18 ff). After his departure Apollos* taught Christianity in Ephesus, although he had not yet been fully instructed. After he had been instructed by Aquila* and Priscilla* he went to Corinth (AA 18:24 ff). Paul again reached Ephesus on his 3rd journey and remained there two years (56–58). He began teaching in the synagogue; but his reception was so hostile that he moved to the lecture hall of Tyrannus, where he taught daily (AA 19:1 ff). He found at Ephesus some of the disciples of John* the Baptist. At Ephesus a riot occurred instigated by the silversmiths who made miniature shrines of Artemis (cf DEMETRIUS). No further visit of Paul to Ephesus is mentioned. At the end of his 3rd journey he summoned the elders* of Ephesus to see him at Miletus*, where he delivered his touching farewell address (AA 20:17 ff). Paul's allusion to his combat with the beasts at Ephesus is more probably to be taken metaphorically of his adversaries than of the games of the stadium (1 Co 15:32). 1 Co was written at Ephesus (15:32; 16:8); it is probable that Gal was written there also. On the question of the destination of Eph cf EPHESIANS, EPISTLE. Ephesus is one of the seven churches of Asia addressed in the beginning of Apc (2:1 ff). The Church is praised for its orthodoxy and its perseverance in the faith, but warned that its charity has fallen from its first fervor. On the relations of John with Ephesus cf JOHN.

Ephod (Hb *'ēpōd*, meaning uncertain). The nature of the object identified by this term is not altogether certain. The ephod described in Ex 28:6–14; 39:2–7 is a garment something like an apron worn over the breast of the high priest, suspended from the shoulders by two straps, made of gold, purple, violet, scarlet, and linen, and ornamented with 12 precious stones. Two stones have the name of the 12 tribes of Israel engraved upon them. The ephod had a pouch or pocket containing the oracle of the Urim* and Thummin (Ex 28:15–30; 39:8–21). The *'ēpōd bad,* the ephod of linen, worn by Samuel while serving in the sanctuary (1 S 2:18) and by David when he danced before the ark* (2 S 6:14) is likewise a garment, but it does not fit the ephod of the high priest. One may gather from the allusions in 2 S 6:14 ff that it was a short skirt or loin cloth, perhaps similar to the ceremonial skirt worn by Egyptian kings and priests. The Akkadian word *epattu* (*epadatu*) found in the Cappadocian tablets designates a garment worn by both men and women. In other passages a garment does not suit the context. Gideon* made an ephod of gold and placed it in his city Ophrah*, and all Israel commited fornication with it (Jgs 8:26 f). This is a technical term in the OT for worship of other gods and suggests that the ephod of Gideon was an image. The ephod of Micah, however, is distinguished from the carved image, the molten image, and the teraphim* (Jgs 17:5; 18:14, 18, 20). The lines, however, seem overloaded, and the distinction may not be original. The ephod is "borne" by the priests (1 S 14:3; 22:18); the word "bear" is not used in Hb of the wearing of a garment. The ephod is connected with the giving of oracles (1 S 23:9; 30:7). David orders the priest to bring the ephod, which suggests neither a garment worn by the priest nor an image. Hence some scholars have proposed that the ephod was a garment placed upon the divine image, and that this garment had a pouch for the oracle. The ephod of the high priest would be described on the model of the earlier ephod. The sword of Goliath* was wrapped in a garment behind the ephod in the sanctuary of Nob* (1 S 21:10). This also seems to suggest an image. The ephod is enumerated with sacrifice, sacred pillar, and teraphim as cult objects of which the Israelites shall be deprived (Ho 3:4).

Ephpheta (Gk transcription of the Aramaic *'etpᵉtaḥ,* "open"), the word of healing used by Jesus in the cure of a deaf and dumb man (Mk 7:34).

Ephraim (Hb *'eprayyim,* meaning uncertain), 2nd son of Joseph* (Gn 41:52; 46:20). Jacob* gave Ephraim the blessing of the firstborn and thus placed him before his brother Manasseh* (Gn 48:17–20). The name also designates one of the tribes of Israel. The tribe is not mentioned in the blessing of Jacob (Gn 49) but it is mentioned with Manasseh under the blessing of Joseph in the blessing of Moses (Dt 33:17).

Ephraim and Manasseh comprise the house of Joseph. It is quite probable that Ephraim was originally a geographical name which was taken by the Israelites who settled in the territory of that name. The story of Jacob (Gn 48:17 ff) is then most probably an imaginative explanation of the geographical division of the tribe of Joseph as well as of the preeminence of Ephraim in Israel. In the censuses of Nm Ephraim counts 40,500 (1:33) and 32,500 (26:37). The clans of Ephraim are listed in Nm 26:35–37 and in 1 Ch 7:20–27. The towns of Ephraim (1 Ch 7:28) include Bethel, Naaran, Gezer, Shechem, and Azzah, and on the border of Manasseh Beth-shan, Taanach, Megiddo, and Dor. The boundaries of Ephraim assigned in Jos 16:4–10 enclose a smaller territory than that indicated by the list of 1 Ch 7:28. Ephraim expanded its territory northward at the expense of Manasseh. In the early historical books Ephraim appears as a large and powerful tribe, perhaps the largest of the tribes of Israel. Both Ephraim and Manasseh are covertly charged with an aggressive desire for expansion in the strange anecdote of Jos 17:14–18, which suggests that they should expand by taking Canaanite and unoccupied territory and not the land of their brother Israelites. Twice in the period of the judges disputes between Ephraim and other tribes are mentioned: with Manasseh, led by Gideon* (Jgs 7:24–8:3) and with Gilead, led by Jephthah* (Jgs 12:1–6). The latter dispute ended in a bloody encounter in which Ephraim was defeated. Jeroboam I of Israel belonged to Ephraim, and the schism of the kingdom was accomplished at Shechem, the largest city of Ephraim (1 K 12:1 ff). The position of Ephraim is also indicated by the common use of the name as a poetic designation of the northern kingdom by the prophets, especially Is, Je, Ezk, and Ho (almost exclusively). The story of Shibboleth* (Jgs 12:6) suggests that the language of Ephraim had some peculiar dialectical features. The "hill-country of Ephraim" mentioned so frequently in Jos, Jgs, S, and K designates the central mountain range from Shechem in the N to Bethel in the S. The Ephraim gate of Jerusalem was a gate of the N wall leading to Ephraim (2 K 14:13; 2 Ch 25:23; Ne 8:16; 12:39). The town of Ephraim to which Jesus withdrew (Jn 11:54) is commonly identified with the modern et-Taiyibeh, 6–7 mi E of Bethel.

Ephrath, Ephrathah (Hb *'eprāt, 'ᵉprātāh,* "fruitful"). This name appears both as a clan name and as a place name. As a clan name Ephrath is the wife of Caleb*, the mother of Hur (1 Ch 2:19) and of Ashbur, the father of Tekoa* (1 Ch 2:24). The sons of Hur were Shobal, father of Kirjath-jearim*, and Salma, father of Bethlehem*, and Hareph, the father of Bethgader (1 Ch 2:50–51; 4:4). As a place name it is the place where Rachel* died and was buried and where Benjamin* was born (Gn 35:16, 19; 48:7). Ephrath is connected with Bethlehem in Rt 4:11, and Bethlehem is called Bethlehem Ephrathah in Mi 5:1. Jesse* the father of David is called an Ephrathite of Bethlehem (1 S 17:12) as are Elimelech* and his sons (Rt 1:2). Ephrath is mentioned together with the fields of Jaar (Ps 132:6), which is most probably Kirjath-jearim*; this city is mentioned also in the genealogy of Caleb (cf above). The identifications of Ephrath with Bethlehem in Gn 35:16, 19; 48:7 are almost certainly glosses which represent a later tradition placing Rachel's tomb at Bethlehem. The earlier tradition of 1 S 10:2 (cf Je 31:15) fixes the tomb of Rachel at Ephrath N of Jerusalem in the vicinity of Ramah*. The identification of Ephrah or Ephrath with Bethlehem must come from the presence of the clan of Ephrah in Bethlehem. This was a Judahite clan, at least by adoption, according to 1 Ch 2. Whether the clan name actually came from the place name cannot be determined.

Ephron (Hb '*eprôn*), a Hittite* of Hebron* from whom Abraham* purchased the cave of Machpelah* for a burying ground for himself and his family. The meaning of the name is uncertain; it bears no resemblance to known Hittite names. It is the name of a mountain (Jos 15:9) and of a town (2 Ch 13:19).

Epistle (Gk *epistolē* designates a written communication of any character). In the NT there are 21 "epistles." These can be compared with ancient letters (the following data are given according to A. Wikenhauser). There are about 14,000 letters preserved from Gk and Roman antiquity. The private letters average 87 words each, ranging in length from 18 to 209 words. The literary letters (written by men of literature with a view to publication) are longer; the letters of Cicero average 295 words, ranging from 22 words to 2530 words. The letters of Seneca (which are really epistles; cf below) average 995 words, ranging from 149 words to 4134 words. The usual material of letters was papyrus*.

By these standards the NT epistles are long; the 13 Pauline epistles average 1300 words, ranging from 7101 (Rm) to 658 (Tt) and 335 (Phm).

The letter was almost always dictated to a scribe. It appears that word for word dictation was extremely rare; the scribe was given instructions and perhaps an outline. The part of the scribe in the composition of the NT epistles was thus considerable, since the literary formulation was principally his work (cf SCRIBE).

The introduction and conclusion of letters followed a set form. The introduction, a single phrase, contained the names of the sender and destinatary with a greeting ("X to Y, health"). The final greeting was a single word (Gk *errōsō*, Lt *vale*), "good health"; but the single word was important, since it was normally the only word written by the sender himself and thus authenticated the letter; the signature of the writer was not used as it is in modern letters. The beginning and the conclusion are often expanded by a formal preamble containing longer wishes of good health.

The usual form of introduction is found in the NT only in Js and in AA 15:23; 23:26. Elsewhere the introduction follows a fairly set form of two sentences. The first contains the names of the sender and the destinatary, usually with the addition of titles, and sometimes with a doctrinal statement. The second sentence is a blessing. Gal has a doxology. Paul mentions other senders with himself 8 times; this practice is quite unusual. Paul also begins the body of the letter with an expression of thanksgiving most of the time, and concludes with a statement of his present situation and his plans for the future. Heb and 1 Jn have no greeting.

Since A. Deissmann the distinction between the literary forms of letter and epistle is accepted by almost all scholars. The letter is a communication from person to person (or a definite group of persons) in response to a defined concrete situation. It is therefore personal and intimate and presupposes mutual knowledge (omitting for the moment the peculiar classification of the business letter, which is not found in the NT). Normally no readers are envisaged beyond the destinatary, even if the possibility of other readers is recognized. The epistle is a treatise or an essay addressed to the general public; the use of the greeting is merely a literary device or a form of dedication. It deals therefore with general topics directed to a general audience with no concrete reference, and is neither personal nor confidential. A large number of epistles are preserved from antiquity (Horace, Seneca, +; many of Cicero's letters are really epistles).

Deissmann has defined the 13 Pauline letters and 2–3 Jn as letters; the others he calls epistles. The importance of the distinction lies in the fact that the interpretation of the letter requires some knowledge of the personal character of both sender and destinatary and of the concrete situation which has elicited the letter. The importance of this knowledge is obvious in 2–3 Jn, where we lack it. Scholars are no doubt right, however, in pointing out that the distinction must not be imposed mechanically. In many parts of the Pauline letters Paul produces little doctrinal treatises which are not tied to the concrete situation. But the general principle is still valid that one must study closely the churches to which the letters are addressed and the situation of the letters. The fact that the destinataries are a a church and not a person does not alter the principle. In most of the later letters Paul must have been aware that his letters would receive a wider circulation than the church to which they were addressed, and the epistolary tone of these letters becomes more pronounced in contrast to the highly personal tone of the early letters.

Erastus (Gk erastos, "lovable"), a companion of Paul sent with Timothy* from Ephesus* to Macedonia* (AA 19:22); not certainly the same as the Erastus who was city treasurer of Corinth (Rm 16:23), who is probably the Erastus mentioned in 2 Tm 4:20.

Erech (Hb 'erek, meaning unknown), a city of Mesopotamia mentioned with Babylon and Akkad as a part of the kingdom of Nimrod* (Gn 10:10). The site of Erech is the modern Warka, about 160 mi SSE of Baghdad. Archaeology has disclosed that Erech was one of the oldest cities of Mesopotamia, founded before 3000 BC. Its earliest culture was Neolithic; the use of metal was known before 3000 BC. It was also the earliest of the known Mesopotamian sites to employ monumental architecture. The site has revealed substantial remains of the ziggurat, the step tower of the temple* complex (cf BABEL, TOWER OF). Erech was not an important political factor in Mesopotamia after 2200 BC and its mention in Gn probably reflects quite old traditions. The building of its wall was attributed to the epic hero Gilgamesh*, one of its kings in Mesopotamian legend.

Esarhaddon (Assyrian ashur-ah-iddin, "Ashur has given a brother"), son and successor of Sennacherib*, king of Assyria* 681–668 BC, whose succession after the assassination of Sennacherib is mentioned in 2 K 19:37; Is 37:38. He transferred some settlers into the territory of the former kingdom of Israel (Ezr 4:2). His records relate that he was appointed successor to Sennacherib, although he was not the eldest son, and that he made good his succession by suppressing a widespread rebellion led by his brothers. He also relates his victory over Taharka (cf TIRHAKAH) of Egypt, which first opened Egypt to conquest by the Assyrians, and mentions Manasseh* of Judah as a vassal king.

Esau (Hb 'ēsāw, meaning unknown), eldest son of Isaac* and Rebekah* and twin brother of Jacob* (Gn 25:22–26). The two boys pushed each other in Rebekah's womb striving for the rights of the firstborn, and Esau was the first to emerge. He was a hunter, while Jacob was a herdsman (Gn 25:27). Esau sold Jacob his rights of primogeniture in exchange for a dish of stew when he returned fatigued from a hunting expedition (Gn 25:29–34). He displeased Jacob by marrying two Hittite women (Gn 26:34). Jacob disguised himself as Esau and obtained the blessing of the firstborn (Gn 27). The blessing granted Esau after the deception was discovered (Gn 27:39–40) describes Esau as a desert bandit; he will serve his brother but shall finally free himself. Esau's hatred of Jacob was so bitter that their parents feared it might issue in murder, and Jacob was sent away to seek a wife among their kinsmen (Gn 27:42 ff). While Jacob was working for Laban*, Esau also prospered in a manner not related; and when Jacob returned, Esau met him with 400 men (Gn 32:3 ff). Jacob sent gifts in advance to placate Esau, and Esau met him in a friendly manner; but Jacob refused Esau's invitation to dwell with him in Seir*. Esau was also present with Jacob at the burial of Isaac (Gn 35:29). Esau, a wealthy man, made his home in the highlands of Seir (Gn 36:6–8). In other occurrences of the name Esau is clearly identified with Edom*, and the name is used as a pathetic title of Edom in poetry. The list of Edomite clans, kings, and chieftains (Gn 36:9 ff) lists them as descendants of Esau. The Edomites are called sons of Esau (Dt 2:4, 5, 8, 12, 29). Yahweh gave them the land of Seir as He gave the land of Canaan to Israel (Dt 2:8; Jos 24:4). Esau appears as a title of Edom in postexilic prophetic passages which pronounce doom against Edom for its plundering of Judah and Jerusalem in the fall of the kingdom to the Babylonians in 587 BC (Je 49:8–10; Ob passim). Mal employs the story of the birth of Esau and Jacob and the transfer of the rights of primogeniture to show Yahweh's love of election* for Israel (1:2–4). But the identification of Esau and Edom runs through the stories of the two brothers in Gn 25–33 as well. Thus the story of the twins in the womb is composed in terms of the struggles of Israel and Edom under the monarchy; although Edom was the older people in Hb tradition — that is, settled in their land earlier than Israel — ultimately they bowed to the younger people. In the explanation of the name of Esau (Gn 25:25) he is called *ᵃdmōnî*, "red," which contains a word-play on Edom, and "like a hairy garment" (*'adderet sē 'ār*), which probably contains a play on Seir (*sē'îr*), the name of the mountain range of Edom; one might think that the story was originally a story of the birth of Israel and Edom (Seir) rather than a story of the birth of Jacob and Esau. The two sons follow different manners of life; Hb traditions do not describe the Edomites as hunters, and they were settled people before Israel. The sale of the rights of primogeniture for food and the deception by which Jacob obtained the blessing of the firstborn appear to be doublets, each of them presenting a claim for the sovereignty of Israel over Edom in spite of the greater antiquity of Edom. These claims seem to be rejected in Dt 2:8; Jos 24:4. Both anecdotes reflect the popular belief that the Edomites were people of slower wit than the Israelites who told the stories; cf, however, the traditional wisdom* of Edom. The story of the meeting of the brothers (Gn 32–33) is more sympathetic to Edom; he is a wealthy man who can afford to be magnanimous to his brother, who fears him. In spite of these traits, the Esau of Gn 25–33, like the Jacob of the same chapters, is not simply the personification of a people with no reference to an individual person. The Israelites thought of the Edomites as their kinsmen and the kinship is explained by a connection of blood relationship in the remote past (cf AMMON; MOAB). How Esau came to be connected with Edom cannot be determined from the literature of the OT without the folk traditions of Edom; it is possible that the position of Esau in Edomite tradition was something like the position of Jacob in the traditions of Israel.

The story of the birth of Esau and Jacob as interpreted by Mal 1:13 is used by Paul to illustrate the freedom of God's election before any merit or demerit (Rm 9:11 ff). The rejection of Esau is explained in Hb 12:16 in harmony with Jewish interpretation as based upon his "wickedness" in selling his rights of primogeniture, and the author draws the moral that this transaction could not be reversed, even by repentance and tears. The point of view adopted differs from the antecedent election of Mal 1:3 and Rm 9:11 ff.

Esdraelon (Gk *esdraēlon*, a corruption of Hb

The Plain of Esdraelon with Mount Tabor in left center.

Jezreel [*yizre'e'l*], "God sows"), the name most commonly given to a plain lying between Galilee* on the N and Samaria* on the S, also called the valley of Jezreel. The plain is roughly triangular in shape. Its western corner lies near the point where the river Kishon*, which drains it, flows between Mt Carmel* and the southern extremity of the Lebanon* range into the Mediterranean. Its northern edge runs almost due E to the Jordan; its southern edge runs in a southeasterly direction to the Jordan valley. It is divided in its eastern half by the hill of Moreh into two valleys. The plain is very fertile. A number of well known biblical cities were built around it: Megiddo*, Taanach*, Jezreel, and Beth-shan*. The plain was an important route of commerce. For travel N and S along the coast the best road came through the pass of Megiddo into the plain, since the shore at the foot of Mt Carmel is extremely narrow. From Megiddo roads went eastward toward Galilee, Beth-shan and the valley of the Jordan, and the regions E of the Sea of Galilee and Damascus. Passage of the plain can be difficult during the winter rains, since the plain is not well drained; for the same reason it is marshy and somewhat insalubrious. The importance of the plain in communications has made it the most famous battleground of Palestine: Thutmose III of Egypt and the Canaanites, Saul* and the Philistines*, Gideon* and the Midianites*, Barak* and the Canaanites, Josiah* and Necho* of Egypt, Saladin and the Crusaders, the Napoleonic wars, and the British and the Turks in 1917. The Gk name Esdraelon occurs only in Jdt 3:9 in the Bible; it is used by Josephus. The valley of Jezreel (Jos 17:16; Jgs 6:33; Ho 1:5) is not clearly the entire plain, and some geographers restrict the valley of Jezreel to the SW arm of the valley lying between Mt Gilboa* and the Hill of Moreh. The plain is called sometimes simply "the valley" (Jos 17:16; Jgs 1:19; 5:15; 7:1, 8, 12; cf "the great plain" in 1 Mc 12:49).

The valley of Jezreel derived its name from the city of Jezreel, mentioned among the cities of Issachar* (Jos 19:18), located at a point on the S side of the plain opposite the foot of the W extremity of the Hill of Moreh on the slopes of Mt Gilboa. The Philistines pitched camp at Jezreel before the engagement in which Saul lost his life (1 S 29:11). Ahab had a palace in Jezreel. Naboth* had his vineyard in Jezreel, and the elders of Jezreel brought about his death by false evidence (1 K 21:1 ff). It was in the palace of Jezreel that Jehu killed Joram of Israel, Jezebel, and all the members of the family of Ahab (2 K 9–10). About 100 years later Hosea said that Yahweh would demand the blood of Jezreel from the house of Jehu (1:4).

Esdras. Cf APOCRYPHAL BOOKS; EZRA.

Essenes. Cf QUMRAN.

Esther (Hb *'ester*, of uncertain origin and meaning; suggested Persian *stareh*, star, more commonly now Akkadian *ishtar*), the Persian name of the heroine of the book of Est, whose Hb name was Hadassah*.

The book of Est begins with the decision of Ahasuerus*, king of Persia, to put away his queen Vashti* because of disobedience (ch 1). Another queen is sought among the beautiful maidens of all the provinces of his empire, and the Hb maiden Hadassah, niece of Mordecai*, is chosen. She receives the Persian name of Esther. Her uncle Mordecai discovers a conspiracy against the king's life and reveals it to the king through Esther (ch 2). Mordecai, however, won the enmity of Haman*, the grand vizier; he refused to bow to Haman out of Jewish religious scruples, and Haman obtained from the king a decree that all the Jews of the kingdom should be slain (ch 3). Mordecai asked Esther to appeal to the king on behalf of her people (ch 4), and Esther presented the appeal at a banquet which she gave for the king and Haman. Before he went to the banquet Haman prepared a gibbet 50 cubits high for Mordecai. When the king granted Esther's petition, she revealed that Haman was the adversary of the Jews. Haman threw himself at Esther's feet; the king, interpreting this as an indecent motion, ordered Haman to be hung on the gibbet he had prepared for Mordecai (chs 5–7). The king then granted another decree permitting the Jews to defend themselves against their enemies (ch 8). The permission for self-defense was executed by giving the Jews freedom to kill all those whom they regarded as their enemies; since one day was insufficient, Esther obtained permission from the king for another day (ch 9). This victory of the Jews was celebrated in the feast of Purim*, and Mordecai became grand vizier (ch 10).

The form of the book differs in the Hb and Gk texts. The Gk text contains additional material; these passages were translated into Lt by Jerome and placed in an appendix at the end of the book, since Jerome did not accept them as part of the canonical* book. The Catholic Church, however, accepts the books of the OT as they appear in the Gk version, including the deuterocanonical* portions. With their relationship to the Hb text they are as follows:

Before 1:1: (1) The dream of Mordecai. (2) The plot against the king's life.

After 3:12: (3) The royal decree of extermination of the Jews.

After 4:8: (4) Mordecai's appeal to Esther.

After 4:17: (5) The prayer of Mordecai. (6) The prayer of Esther. (7) Esther's appeal to Ahasuerus.

After 8:12: (8) The royal decree permitting the Jews to defend themselves.

After 10:3: (9) The interpretation of Mordecai's dream. (10) The account of the reception of the Gk version of the book in Egypt. The Gk portions add one notable feature to the book. The Hb text does not contain the divine name, nor indeed any reference to God or His activities except the implicit allusion of 4:14. This omission is so singular in the Hb OT that it demands some explanation; but scholars are unable to assign a cause. The prayers and other allusions to God in the Gk additions most probably are intended to render the book more acceptable as sacred. The Gk additions, however, are not properly additions to the Hb text but fragments of a variant recension. There are two accounts of the conspiracy against the life of the king, and the Gk texts of the royal decrees are not entirely in harmony with the summaries given in the Hb text. Cf also the variations in the hatred of Haman for Mordecai (Gk 12:6; Hb 3:1-5); the position of Mordecai in the palace (Gk 11:3; Hb 2:19); the reward of Mordecai for his service to the king (Gk 12:5; Hb 6:3). The question of whether the Gk text represents a Hb or Aramaic original is answered, according to Eissfeldt, affirmatively for some of the additions; others were composed in Gk.

The date of the work cannot be determined with certainty. The story is set in the reign of Xerxes (485-465). The Gk translation, attributed to a certain Lysimachus of Jerusalem, son of Ptolemy, was brought to Egypt by Dositheus in the 4th year of the reign of Ptolemy and Cleopatra. Five of the Ptolemies had queens named Cleopatra: Ptolemy V Epiphanes (203-181), Ptolemy VI Philometor (181-146), Ptolemy VII Euergetes II (146-116), Ptolemy VIII Soter II (116-107), and Ptolemy XI Auletes (80-51). Modern scholars generally identify the Ptolemy mentioned in Est as Ptolemy VIII or Ptolemy XI. Some indications point not only to a late composition of the book, but also to its late reception as a sacred book. It is not quoted in the NT, and it is the only book of the Hb OT whose text has not been found at Qumran*. Both Esther and Mordecai are missing from the praise of the fathers in BS 44-49, written about 180 BC. The "day of Mordecai" (2 Mc 15:36) almost certainly means the feast of Purim; but this allusion does not necessarily imply knowledge of the book of Est. The historical character of the book and its literary form also suggest a later rather than an earlier date. While Ahasuerus (Xerxes) is a historical character, and the writer exhibits some knowledge of the city and palace of Susa and Persian life and customs, there are a number of improbabilities in the book which lead most modern scholars to consider it a historical romance. It may reflect actual events, but with our sketchy knowledge of the history of Judaism for the period of the book it is impossible to identify these events with any certainty. The queen of Xerxes was Amestris, and nothing like the story of Vashti can be traced in Persian records. Furthermore, a decree which permitted the Jews to kill all their enemies is most improbable, and it should have left some trace in extrabiblical records. Mordecai, transported from Jerusalem in 597 BC, is still living in the reign of Xerxes (485-465 BC). The opinion that the book was composed for the feast of Purim, which had another origin, is not without probability. The tone of the book is suitable to the 2nd century BC, when Antiochus* Epiphanes attempted to hellenize the Jews of Palestine at the expense of their religion.

The religious significance and value of the book have always been difficult for readers to appreciate. This is especially true of the Hb text, which omits any mention of God. Modern Christian ethical standards are offended by the attitude toward their enemies shown by the Jews of the book, no matter how odious the enemies may be; and the bloody revenge which Esther obtains for the Jews is not edifying. The religious value of the book, however, does not lie in the models of conduct furnished by Esther or Mordecai. Rather the whole story exhibits the providence of God which preserves His people from annihilation. The means by which His providence operates in this book are human plans and actions; the divine action is hidden, and no marvels are related. Yet the Jews escape. The figure of Esther is modeled in some respects after that of other OT heroes who reached high place in foreign governments and were thus in a position to assist their people in times of crisis, such as Joseph*, Nehemiah*, and Daniel*. This view of providence, implicit in the Hb text, becomes explicit in the prayers of the Gk additions.

Eternity. The philosophical concept of eternity is not clearly expressed in either OT or NT. The Hb 'ôlam and the Gk aiōn both signify primarily an indefinitely extended period of time, beyond the lifetime of a single person. This duration extends either into the past or into the future. Thus the prophets are said to be "from old" (Lk 1:70) as is the house of David (Am 9:11). The indefinite period is lengthened by the addition of the adjective "all" or by the use of the superlative, "age of age," or "ages of ages." A similar idea is expressed by the word "generation," again heightened by the superlative, "generation and (of) generation," or "age" and "generation" may be combined. When these words are applied to God, they acquire the meaning of an indefinite duration with no beginning or end. The title *'ēl 'ôlām* (Gn 21:33) is an early title of God in the OT. God exists before creation, and He exists from age to age (Ps 90:2). In contrast to man, whose days are a shadow, God endures unto age, and His memory from generation to generation (Ps 102:12 f). God created the heavens and the earth. Though they wear out, He remains what He is, and His years are never finished (Ps 102:26–28). To Him a thousand years are but as a day (Ps 90:4; 2 Pt 3:8). Yahweh is a God "of age"; He does not fail (Is 40:28). He is the first and the last (Is 41:4). The adjective *aiōnios* applied to God in Rm 16:26 may signify the kind of existence which transcends time. This adjective, however, is applied to other things besides God: glory (2 Co 4:17; 2 Tm 2:10), honor (1 Tm 6:16), the gospel (Apc 14:6), salvation (Heb 5:9), redemption (Heb 9:12). *Aiōnios* is applied to the kingdom (2 Pt 1:11), life and inheritance (Heb 9:15), tabernacles (Lk 16:9), dwellings, meaning the risen body (2 Co 5:1), fire (Mt 18:8; 25:41), destruction (2 Th 1:9), sin (Mk 3:29), judgment (Heb 6:2). God is the Alpha and Omega, the first and last letters of the alphabet (Apc 1:8), the beginning and the end (Apc 21:6). He lives through all ages (Apc 4:9). Jesus Christ is sometimes given the same terms of duration in the NT which are given to Yahweh in the OT (Heb 1:10; 13:8; Apc 2:8). The duration expressed by these phrases seems to differ from the philosophical concept of eternity in that it is an indefinite duration of time without beginning or end and does not, except for an occasional suggestion, reach the idea that eternity involves not only endless duration but also changeless duration.

Ethan (Hb *'êtān,* meaning uncertain), a famous wise man mentioned with Heman*, Chalcol, and Darda (1 K 5:11). To him is attributed Ps 89 in the title. Ethan is included among the sons of Zerah* in 1 Ch

2:6–8 and among the Levites in 1 Ch 6:27–29; 15:17–19. The primary mention of the name is most probably found in 1 K 5, and from this mention the attribution of the Ps is derived. On the basis of this attribution Ethan was included in the genealogies, first of Judah, because of the assonance Zerah-Ezrahite, and then among the Levites with Heman and Asaph. The legendary wise men have become cantors and composers of David's choir of 1 Ch.

Ethanim (Hb *'ētānîm,* meaning uncertain), the older Canaanite name of the 7th month (Sept-Oct; 1 K 8:2).

Ethbaal (Hb *'etba'al*), king of the Sidonians and father of Jezebel*, queen of Ahab* of Israel (2 K 16:31). The name is possibly the Phoenician equivalent of the Hb Ishbaal, "man of Baal." The name appears in Phoenician inscriptions, and Sennacherib mentions a Tubalu installed by him as satellite king of Sidon. In all probability, however, king of the Sidonians in 2 K 16:31 means king of Tyre; cf SIDON; TYRE.

Ethiopia (Gk *aithiōpia,* long explained by a popular etymology as "burnt-facedom," is derived by modern scholars from Egyptian *htk,'pth,* the same Egyptian phrase from which *aigyptos,* "Egypt," is derived.) The ancient Ethiopia was not the same region as the modern kingdom of Ethiopia; the name designated the ancient Nubia, the modern Sudan: the valley of the Nile* from the 2nd Cataract to the 6th Cataract. The length of the river from the 1st Cataract at Aswan to the junction of the Blue and the White Nile at Khartum, a little above the 6th Cataract, is about 1080 mi. Relations between Egypt and Nubia are reported as early as the 3rd dynasty and no doubt go back even earlier. The Egyptians made a sustained effort throughout their history to extend their dominion S into Nubia and thus control the profitable trade between the two regions. Effectively Egypt generally sustained its rule as far as the 2nd Cataract; its deepest penetration reached the city of Napata at the 4th Cataract under the 18th dynasty. The people of ancient Ethiopia were negroid, as appears from Egyptian art; but the Negro component of the population appears to have been less than it is in modern Sudan. The Egyptianization of Ethiopia was so thorough that Egyptian culture endured longer in Ethiopia than it did in Egypt. About the year 1000 BC the Nubians made themselves independent of Egypt and established a kingdom with its royal city at Napata at the 4th Cataract. This kingdom in the following centuries extended its rule over the region of Thebes. When Tefnakht of the 24th dynasty of Sais threatened Thebes from the N, the Ethiopians under Piankhi in a single campaign brought all Egypt under their power except for a small portion in the N (about 725). The campaign is related in detail in a stele of Piankhi preserved in the Museum of Cairo. The 25th dynasty (715–663) was an Ethiopian dynasty. The names of Shabaka, Shabataka, Taharka, and Tanutamon are preserved (cf SO; TIRHAKAH). The Ethiopian dynasty came just in time to feel the weight of the Assyrian attacks upon Egypt. Esarhaddon conquered the whole country in 670 and established an Assyrian province. Tanutamon continued his resistance in upper Egypt and was driven into Ethiopia by Ashur-bani-pal, who destroyed Thebes in his second campaign (666 BC); the destruction is mentioned in Na 3:8. This campaign ended Ethiopian influence N of the 2nd Cataract. About 300 BC the royal city was transferred for unknown reasons from Napata to Meroe at the 5th Cataract. This kingdom endured until about 355 AD. During this period the population became predominantly Negro. The isolation of Meroe permitted it to retain many features of ancient Egyptian culture, but prevented any development.

The Hb Cush represents the Egyptian *k,'s*. Cush in the Table* of Nations is a son of Ham*, the brother of Egypt, Put*, and Canaan*, and the father of Seba*, Havilah*, Sabtah, Raamah, and Sabteca (Gn 10:6–7). Cush the father of Nimrod* (Gn 10:8) is probably not derived from the Egyptian *k,'s* but from the Akkadian *kashshu*, the Kassite invaders of Mesopotamia in the middle of the 2nd millennium BC. Am 9:7 mentions the Cushites as a people over whom Yahweh has no special providence. The oracle of Is delivered to the people beyond the rivers of Cush (18:1 ff) is directed to the Ethiopians, very probably at the time of the rise of the Ethiopian dynasty. The symbolic action of Is in 20:1 ff, dated 711 BC by the allusion to Ashdod*, is directed to Egypt and Ethiopia, and falls within the period of the 25th dynasty. A campaign of Tirhakah* of Ethiopia against Sennacherib* is mentioned in Is 37:9; 2 K 19:9; on the chronological difficulties of this allusion cf ISAIAH; SENNACHERIB; TIRHAKAH. Cush is a land of merchants (Is 45:14). With Egypt and Seba Yahweh will give Cush in ransom for Israel (Is 43:3). A threat of doom is pronounced against Cush in Zp 2:12; on the date of this allusion cf ZEPHANIAH. It is included among the peoples allied to Egypt in Je 46:9. Cush is called the frontier of Egypt at Syene* (Ezk 29:10), and a threat is directed against them as allies of the Egyptians

(Ezk 30:5, 9). It is one of the enemy peoples of the apocalyptic war under the command of Gog* (Ezk 38:5). Cush is called the strength of Thebes (Na 3:9), an accurate reflection of the Ethiopian control of Thebes. Cush is invited to stretch forth her hands in prayer to the God of Israel (Ps 68:32). It is one of the countries of which a man may boast of his birth (Ps 87:4). It is a source of topaz (Jb 28:19). Je 13:23 alludes to the negroid complexion of the people of Cush. Pathros* (upper Egypt) and Cush are among the lands from which Yahweh will recover His people (Is 11:11). Two Cushite slaves appear in Israel (2 S 18: 21 ff; Je 38:7; 39:16). The Ethiopian eunuch* of the queen of Ethiopia (AA 8: 27 ff) who believed in Jesus when Philip* instructed him and was immediately baptized came from the kingdom of Meroe.

Eubulus (Gk *eubūlos*, "well advised," "prudent"), a Roman Christian who sent greetings to Timothy* (2 Tm 4:21).

Eucharist. The name Eucharist (Gk *eucharistia*, "thanksgiving") to designate the sacramental rite of the offering and consumption of bread and wine does not appear in the NT; it is first employed in the *Didache* (late 1st century) and is used by Ignatius of Antioch and Justin. In the NT it is called "the Lord's Supper" (1 Co 11:20), the *agapē* (Jd 12; cf LOVE), and possibly "the breaking of bread" (AA 2:42, 46; 20: 7, 11). Some modern scholars question whether the sacrament is intended in AA 2:46; 20:7, 11, and it is not as clear in these passages as it seems to be in AA 2:42.

1. *The Institution of the Eucharist.* The institution is related in Mt 26:26–29; Mk 14:22–25; Lk 22:15–20; 1 Co 11:23–25. In spite of variations in detail, these four sources are in remarkable accord on the substance of the words used and on the significance of the rite. The accord is due to a large extent to the fact that the four sources are really two; Mt-Lk depend on Mk. The formula of Lk presents special problems which are discussed below. In the opinion of many modern critics, both Mk and Paul give liturgical formulae, Mk the formula of the Palestinian communities and Paul the formula of the Hellenistic communities.

The problem of Lk's account is superficially the problem of "the two cups" (22: 17–18, 20); but the problem is deeper than this. Some critics have supposed that Lk has simply conflated two formulae of institution; but this would seem to imply that Lk scarcely knew the meaning of the rite which he describes. H. Schürmann has suggested that Lk does indeed conflate two traditions, one of them a "Passover Supper tradition" (22:15–18) and the other an "Institution Tradition" (22:19–20). Schürmann does not believe that Lk depends on Mk or Paul for either of these; both are derived from special sources peculiar to Lk. P. Benoit, on the other hand, believes that the language does not suggest independent sources, and that 22:15–18 is derived from Mk 14:23–25; and 22:19–20, from 1 Co 11: 23–25. This immediately raises the question why Lk should have conflated in this manner; Benoit suggests that it is done to place the institution explicitly against the background of the Passover* (cf below), which does not appear in the institution formulae of Mk and Paul. This is done by anticipating the mention of the bread and wine as the elements of the supper; the cup is mentioned in 22:17 f, and the bread is implicitly anticipated in the word "Passover" in 22:15. But the Passover meal is not bread but the Passover lamb; the Passover lamb of the new Christian Passover is the bread which becomes the body of Christ. Hence the cup of 22:17 is not yet the cup of the Eucharist; it is the Passover cup which becomes the Eucharist. Lk thus achieves the theme by the artificial construction of two panels, as Benoit calls them, from existing traditions.

The sacramental symbolic themes of the institution narrative are seen more clearly if the variations of the several accounts are noticed. Only Paul adds the words "for you" to "body"; Paul does not have the phrase "poured out for you" which Mt and Lk add to "blood" (Mk "poured out for many"; Mt adds "for the remission of sins"). "Many" is an Aramaism meaning "all" which is retained in Mt-Mk; the "you" of Lk is a liturgical formula which makes the Eucharist immediate to those participating. Mt's addition makes the atoning character of the sacrament explicit; cf below. The cup is associated with the covenant in all formulae: Mt-Mk, "my blood of the covenant" (thought by many critics to be an overloaded expansion); Paul-Lk, "this cup is the new covenant in my blood." It is suggested that the alteration in the Hellenistic formula of Paul-Lk is intended to remove the realism of the Aramaic formula, which may have been somewhat offensive; but surely Mt-Mk also had Hellenistic groups in mind, and the variation probably is not significant. Each of the four sources contains an eschatological allusion. In Mt-Mk this is the final cup which Jesus drinks with His disciples until He drinks new wine in the kingdom; Lk alludes simply to the coming of the kingdom and omits the allusion

to the new cup. Paul calls the sacrament a proclamation of the death of the Lord "until he comes" (1 Co 11:26). Lk and Paul contain the precept to repeat the rite.

2. *Symbolism of the Eucharist.* The Eucharist is remarkably rich in symbolic significance; it presents almost all the major themes of the primitive Christian preaching and teaching. There can be no doubt that the rite existed from the very beginning of the Church (AA 2:42; the witness of 1 Co is the earliest witness to the rite, cf CORINTHIANS, EPISTLES TO). Nor can there be any doubt that the Eucharist was the cult of the primitive community; the Christians of Jerusalem participated in the temple cult (cf SACRIFICE), but there was no such participation in communities outside Jerusalem, and by no means for Gentile communities. No other ritual cult is attested. It was celebrated on the day after Sabbath, very probably because this was the day of the resurrection, the day which initiated the new week and the new age of salvation. The choice of the day of the resurrection was not without its symbolism also; the Eucharist, while it commemorates the death of Jesus, commemorates not the death simply but the death as a phase in the saving process which is fulfilled in the glorification of Jesus. The Eucharist was celebrated as a supper, and very probably at the usual Roman hour of dinner, the late afternoon.

In the wealth of Eucharistic symbolism it is not easy to disengage the primary theme; but it appears to be the Eucharist as the Christian Passover. While the Passover allusion is explicit only in the formula of Lk (cf above), all the sources unite in affirming that the supper itself was the Passover dinner of Jesus and His disciples. Jn creates some difficulty here, since he alone presents the supper as occurring not on the eve of Passover (and in Jewish reckoning the beginning of the day) but a day earlier; and Jn's chronology seems to suit the probabilities better, since Passover itself is an unlikely day for a long legal process and an execution; cf PASSION. However this problem is to be explained, the Passover supper in the Synoptic Gospels is beyond question. The Passover commemorated the great saving event, the deliverance of Israel from slavery and its constitution as the people of Yahweh; and the P source of the Pnt places the first Passover supper in Egypt as an anticipation of the saving event which occurred that night. The new Passover is likewise anticipated by a dinner; and at this dinner the new Passover lamb, whose blood on the doors was a sign of deliverance, is consumed by the disciples, the little core of the New Israel. The Lamb is consumed sacramentally.

The Passover lamb is not clearly a sacrificial animal, and the sacrificial motif is implicit rather than explicit in the formulae of institution. But the motif of atonement is explicit; the body and blood are "for many," "for you," and the atoning character of the death is stated as clearly in these formulae as anywhere in the NT. P. Benoit points out that these phrases seem to echo the description of the Servant* of Yahweh (Is 53). The Eucharist is a "proclamation" of the atoning death (1 Co 11:26). It is a "memorial" (Lk 22:19; 1 Co 11:24 f) in the sense of cultic recital and reenactment of the saving event, by which each participant experiences the event and is personally integrated into the death and the resurrection of Jesus, in terms of which Paul often describes the new life of the Christian. Modern theologians have perhaps less felicitously coined the term "mystical mactation" to designate the reenactment; the Eucharist is nowhere in the NT even hinted as a ritual killing of Jesus, which is what the theological term implies. The term is based upon a more rigid conception of the sacrificial character of the death and the Eucharist than the NT exhibits; the sacrifice of Jesus, like other elements in His life and teaching, breaks through the framework of Jewish institutions.

The sacrificial character appears explicitly in the allusions to the covenant and the covenant sacrifice (cf Ex 24). The covenant is sealed by sacrifice which symbolizes the bond; Jesus, as the bond of the new covenant through His death, is the victim of the covenant sacrifice. The sacrificial motif is likewise explicit in the conception of the Eucharist as a sacrificial banquet; this is clearly stated by Paul (1 Co 10:14–22), where the consumption of the Eucharist is a decisive motif for the prohibition of any participation in pagan sacrifices by Christians.

The sacrificial element prominent in this passage of 1 Co and implicit in the formulae of institution is communion with the deity in the sacrificial banquet. Through the Eucharist the deity is rendered present in a striking and unique fashion. Communion is achieved only through Jesus Christ, who is man, and as man is body. The body is therefore rendered really present; the language of the four sources (and of Jn; cf below) leaves no room for mere symbolism in this respect. The manner in which the bread and wine are the body is a mystery of faith, the term which the Church herself has consecrated; theological speculation, necessary and useful as it is to protect the belief against misunderstanding, has not achieved and will not achieve an understanding of the reality of the sacramental presence of Jesus. The body which is present is the glorified body; we seem justified in believing that the NT implies that it is through His resurrection and exaltation that the body of Jesus becomes the Church (cf BODY). But this is the body "which was delivered for you," one and the same Lord Jesus who died, rose, and sits at the right hand of the Father. Communion is achieved through the participation of the body and the blood of the victim. The salvation of the NT is not directed to the soul*, but to the man, and man in Hebrew thought is body; if salvation is to reach man, his communion with the Savior must be a communication of body.

The body of Christ is the Church, and this makes the Eucharist an effective sign of Christian unity. The instructions of 1 Co 11:17–33 disclose that the Eucharist was united with a meal taken in common by all the members of the Church, the *agapē* or feast of love. Such a common meal is implied in AA 2:46, whether the Eucharist was a part of this common meal or not. Paul notes certain abuses and lack of decorum in this communal banquet, and it appears that it was divorced rather early from the Eucharist in the early Church; discipline was preserved at the cost of some symbolism. But the Eucharist is a participation in the body of Christ, in which Christians are all one; the many are one body, for they partake of the one loaf (1 Co 10:17).

The Eucharist is associated with the messianic banquet, if it is not explicitly identified with it; on this theme cf MEALS. Efforts to find a parallel with the Eucharist in the Qumran* writings have failed; but it is clear that the Qumran community did celebrate an anticipation of the messianic banquet, and this feature it has in common with the Eucharist. Lk alters the eschatological allusion of Mt-Mk from the end of the passage to follow his anticipation of the Eucharist in the Passover (cf above) and by this change of position seems to identify the Eucharist with the messianic banquet. Certainly the Eucharist stands, in the words of Benoit, in "the eschatological present," the present which is a memorial of the past and a hope of the future, because in the Eucharist the Christian apprehends the enduring reality of the atoning death and the glorified body of Jesus. The Eucharist is therefore celebrated "until He come," and affirms the assured hope of the eschatological fulfillment of the salvation into which it integrates the Christian.

3. *Jn.* John does not relate the institution of the Eucharist, but he clearly knows it, and in Jn 6 presents it in an original manner

which makes more explicit the theme of communion. The Eucharist is primarily the food which nourishes man to eternal life. The point of departure of the dialogue and discourse of Jn 6:25–59 is the miraculous feeding of the five thousand. The discourse begins with the bread which perishes (6:27), contrasts the manna*, the bread from heaven (6:32), with the bread from heaven which gives life to the world (6:33). Jesus Himself is the bread of life which comes down from heaven (6:35). The Jews object not to the idea of bread but to the heavenly descent of Jesus (6:42). Jesus reaffirms that He is the bread of life, the living bread, and makes the eating of this bread a condition of eternal life (6:51); and identifies the bread which He gives for the life of the world as His flesh. The Jews now object to the eating of His flesh (6:52); Jesus reaffirms that one must eat His flesh and drink His blood to have eternal life; He dwells in the person who eats and drinks, and raises him up. This is the genuine heavenly bread (6:53–58).

The Eucharistic intent of the latter portion of the discourse is clear; but the first part of the discourse is not interpreted the same way by all. Hence some suggest that Jn has combined two discourses, one in which Jesus is the bread of life by His preaching, or in which the bread of life is His word, and combined it with a Eucharistic discourse. It is not to be doubted that the discourse is a Johannine construction; but the theme of the bread of life is so central and so consistently developed that no point of conjunction appears. "I am the bread of life" is repeated in 6:48 from 6:35, forming an *inclusio*, and the discourse between these lines turns on Jesus as the bread which is accepted by faith in His teaching (6:40, 44–47). The phrase which ends this part of the discourse also begins the second, in which the bread is accepted not only by faith, but also by sacramental consumption; faith without sacramental union with Jesus will not secure eternal life. The realism of the language of Jn is greater than the realism of the Synoptic Gospels and Paul, but it is thoroughly consistent with them. The salvation motif and the eschatological motif are joined in Jn's insistence on the sacrament as a principle of life, a theme which Jn develops in his own distinctive way. The atoning motif is less prominent, but it is present in "the bread which I give for the life of the world is my flesh" (6:51).

Eunice (Gk *eunikē*, "victorious"), a Jewish Christian, mother of Timothy* (AA 16:1), praised for her genuine faith (2 Tm 1:5).

Eunuch (Gk *eunouchos*, "keeper of the bed"). The castration of the human male was not practiced in Egypt, as far as is known, nor in Greece and Rome except under Oriental influence. Eunuchs are mentioned in the Code of Hammurabi*. In Mesopotamia they were members of cult personnel, particularly in the cult of Ishtar, and frequently royal officers. The Hb word *sārîs* is derived by some scholars from Akkadian *ša reši* or *šut reši*, "head" or "chief." It is not entirely clear that this word in

Eunuch, Assyrian sculpture.

Akkadian always signifies eunuch. The reason for the choice of eunuchs as servants and managers of the palace, particularly of the harem, is evident. It is also rather obvious that eunuchs succeeded in winning the confidence of the king and securing important and influential positions. Attendants of the king with evident physical characteristics of eunuchs are often represented on Assyrian monuments. The word *sārîs* in some OT passages seems to signify clearly a eunuch; thus Est and Dn 1 *passim*, which deal with Oriental courts, the eunuchs of the women's apartments of the palace of Jezreel (2 K

9:32), the prediction that Israelites will be eunuchs in the royal palace of Babylon (2 K 20:18; Is 39:7). Eunuchs are probably also intended when they are grouped with other servants and attendants of the royal palace of Judah or Israel (1 S 8:15; 2 K 24:12, 15; Je 29:2; 34:19; 41:16). Since the Egyptians did not practice castration, it is improbable that the Egyptian royal servants and officers (Gn 37:36, 39; 40:2, 7) were eunuchs. But the word may have entered these passages when the stories were retold in a time when royal servants were usually castrated. In such passages as 1 K 22:9; 2 K 8:6; 23:11; 25:19; Je 29:2; 52:25; it is not clear that the officer mentioned is designated as a eunuch. The code of Deuteronomy (Dt 23:2) prohibited the eunuch from becoming a member of the Israelite community. A later prophet (Is 56:3 ff) permits both foreigners and eunuchs to become members of the redeemed community of Israel; cf also WS 3:14. In the NT eunuchs are mentioned only in AA 8:27 ff (the eunuch of the queen of Ethiopia) and Mt 19:12, where Jesus distinguishes between those who are naturally impotent, those who have been castrated, and those who "make themselves eunuchs for the kingdom of heaven." In spite of a few instances of crass literal interpretation in the early centuries of Christianity, Christian tradition has always understood the words metaphorically as the proposal of the ideal of the voluntary renunciation of sexual intercourse as exemplified in the life of Jesus Himself.

Euphrates (Akkadian *purattu,* Hb *perat,* Gk *euphratēs*), the largest river of W Asia, about 1700 mi in length from its source in the Armenian highlands to its mouth in the Persian Gulf. It is formed by the union of two streams, the modern Murad-su and Kara-su; Kara-su, the principal source, rises near the modern Erzerum. The river follows a somewhat wild course through the mountains of Armenia, reversing itself twice. When it reaches the lower ranges near the frontier of Turkey and Syria it takes a SW direction toward the Mediterranean, coming within less than 100 mi of the sea near ancient Carchemish. The range of Amanus blocks it to the E and it flows due S and then due E for a short distance, finally taking the southeasterly course which it follows to its mouth through the alluvial plain of Mesopotamia. The mountains through which it flows become progressively smaller, and from the modern city of Hit its course lies in the broad flat desert plain. The course of its lower reaches is erratic and slow, and it carries very little water in the dry season. Its principal tributaries, the Balik and the Habur, both enter it from the left bank. Before it reaches the Persian Gulf it joins the Tigris* in a single stream, the Shatt el Arab. In ancient times each of the two rivers flowed into the Gulf separately. The lower course of the river above and below its junction with the Tigris is extremely marshy; the country had this character in the ancient world also. The Euphrates was vital in the civilization of ancient Mesopotamia, as the Nile* was vital to Egypt*, since it permitted the irrigation of what would otherwise be arid desert. It is doubtful whether even in modern times

The Euphrates near ancient Babylon.

the waters are as fully exploited as they were in the ancient world. The modern course of the Euphrates reaches nearest the Tigris opposite Baghdad. In ancient times the two rivers lay nearer each other and were joined by a number of canals; the Borsippa canal, the Pallukatu canal, and the Kabaru canal (cf CHEBAR) are mentioned frequently in ancient records. Many of the most famous cities of Mesopotamia lay on the banks of the Euphrates; Babylon*, Sippar, Nippur, Shuruppak (the city of the deluge*), Erech*, Larsa, Ur*, and Eridu. The river has altered its course since ancient times. The ruins of Babylon, Sippar, Nippur, Shuruppak, Erech, and Larsa now lie E of the Euphrates; the ruins of Ur and Eridu lie to its W. The Euphrates was one of the four rivers which rose in Eden*.

Eutychus (Gk *eutychos*, "fortunate"), a young man of Troas* who fell asleep during a long discourse of Paul and plunged from a third story window. He was revived by Paul (AA 20:9–12).

Evangelist (Gk *euangelistēs*, "one who announces good news"; cf GOSPEL). In Eph 4:11 the evangelist stands in the third place in the list of officers of the Church after apostles and prophets, and the term must here designate a regular office. Elsewhere it is applied to Timothy* (2 Tm 4:5), and to Philip*, one of the seven (AA 21:8); in these two places an office is not so clearly indicated. The word by its etymology should signify one who proclaims the gospel (cf also PREACH), and may therefore be applied to apostles also. As an office, however, it most probably designates those men who were associated with the apostles in the proclamation of the gospel.

Eve (Hb *ḥawwāh*), the name of the first woman (Gn 3:20; 4:1), the mother of Cain*, Abel*, and Seth*. The explanation of the name given in Gn 3:20, which connects it with *ḥayāh*, "to live," is obviously popular; but none of the etymologies suggested by several modern scholars has been generally accepted. She was created from the rib of the first man and brought to him to be his wife. The symbolism of the rib signifies the equality and community of woman and man, explicitly stated in Gn 2:23, and establishes her as a fitting partner for the man, not an inferior being. On her seduction by the serpent and the following sin cf FALL. The name occurs elsewhere in the OT only in Tb 8:6, an explicit allusion to Gn 2:18–24. The deception of Eve by the serpent is mentioned in 2 Co 11:3; in 1 Tm 2:13 the creation of man followed by woman is presented as an argument for the authority of man over woman; cf 1 Co 11:12.

Evil Merodach (Hb *'ewīl merōdak*, Akkadian *amel marduk*, "man of Marduk"), son and successor of Nebuchadnezzar* as king of Babylon (562–559 BC), assassinated by his brother-in-law Neriglissor (Nergal-sar-usur) who succeeded him. In the year of his accession he showed favor to Jehoiachin*, former king of Judah, releasing him from confinement, elevating him above other captive kings, and admitting him to dine at the royal table (2 K 25:27; Je 52:31).

Exile. The exile in exegetical literature designates the period from the destruction of Jerusalem* by the Babylonians in 587 BC to the rebuilding of Jerusalem under the Persians beginning in 537 BC. The practice of removing conquered peoples on a large scale was ancient in the Near East. It appears that Tiglath-pileser* III of Assyria (745–727 BC) was the first to refine this simple enslavement by resettling peoples in different parts of the empire. The policy was devised to detach people from their land and thus to destroy the spirit of resistance by suppressing their sense of national identity. Deportation did not as a rule include the entire population; those selected for removal included the royal and noble families, the wealthy, the landowners, and the skilled artisans — people who were most influential in shaping the popular will and in whom the spirit of resistance was most likely to endure. The peasant population generally lived the same way no matter who governed the country, and it appears that the peasants were mostly left on the soil.

Tiglath-pileser III removed the inhabitants of Gilead*, Galilee*, and Naphtali* to Assyria (2 K 15:29) and Sargon* carried Israel to Assyria and settled its people in Calah, along the Habor* and the river Gozan and in the cities of the Medes (2 K 17:6). The land was resettled by people from Babylon*, Cutha, Avva, Hamath*, and Sepharvaim. Another resettlement of foreign peoples in the land of Israel is suggested in Ezr 4:2; the inhabitants say they have worshiped Yahweh since they were settled there by Esarhaddon* (681–668). These people were not accepted by Zerubbabel* and Jeshua* as genuine Israelites. The Israelites deported from the northern kingdom disappeared as a group from history; but individual members of the northern tribes occur in later passages of the OT. Sennacherib* claims to have captured 200,150 people during the rebellion of Hezekiah* in 701 BC. This figure may be exaggerated or a scribal error; and no resettlement of other peoples in Judah is mentioned. Nebuchadnezzar* of Babylon in 597 deported from Judah the king and the royal family, the nobles, the warriors, and the artisans (2 K 24:14 f). The number is given as 10,000 in 24:14, 7,000 in 24:16. When the city was destroyed in 587 by the Babylonians, the rest of the population was deported (2 K 25:11) except for some of "the poorest of the land," who were left as vinedressers and ploughmen (2 K 25:12). The totals given in Je 52:28 ff are 3,023 in the 7th year of Nebuchadnezzar (597), 832 from Jerusalem in his 18th year (587), and 745 in his 23rd year (582), in all 4600. The third deportation (Je 52:30) is not mentioned elsewhere. The numbers given here are small and can scarcely represent the entire population which was removed. Several places in Mesopotamia are mentioned where the Judahites were settled: Tel-Abib* by the river (canal) Chebar* (Ezk 3:15) and the cities or villages otherwise unknown mentioned in Ezr 2:59. Modern scholars do not agree entirely on the number of people removed to Mesopotamia nor on the percentage of the population included; but the opinion of some older scholars that the "exile" was not a historical reality but an invention of Hb tradition is no longer seriously defended. Some scholars, however, believe that the percentage of the population deported was extremely small; the more common view is that Judah was extensively depopulated by the Babylonian wars and that few people remained in the country after 587.

The importance of the exile lies in the fact that the center of gravity of Israelite life and national and religious consciousness was moved to Babylon during the years 587–537 BC. It is clear that the exiles and not the peasants left in the land by the Babylonians thought of themselves as Israel. Jeremiah had encouraged them to build houses, plant vineyards, and marry the people among whom they settled (29:4 ff). He urged them to accept the exile because it was the will of Yahweh that they should be punished, and to await His good pleasure for the redemption of Israel. That the Jews did this, whether on the advice of Jeremiah or not, is clear from Babylonian records. The Jews were allowed to live freely in Mesopotamia. They appear in some Babylonian tablets as landowners and money-lenders, and OT allusions suggest that they gathered in their own communities. Some of them prospered so well that the Jewish colony begun by the deportations of Nebuchadnezzar still existed in the medieval period. The religious importance of the exile appears not only in the survival of national and religious consciousness but also, as most scholars are convinced, in extensive work on the sacred books and traditions of Israel. It seems quite likely that most of the historical books of the OT were collected and edited during the exile. The same is true in much of prophetic literature, and two major prophetic works, Ezk and Is 40–55, were written during the exile. It is suggested also that the codification of Hb law in the form in which it appears in the Pnt was at least begun during the exile. It is possible that the synagogue*, of such vital importance in the subsequent history of Judaism, first made its appearance in the exile as a substitute for the worship of the temple.

Exodus (Gk *exodus*, "departure"). The name designates the events of Ex 1–15, in particular the events of Ex 12:29–15:21. Ex 1–15 narrates the oppression of the Israelites in Egypt, the vocation of Moses*, the 10 plagues* of Egypt, the departure of the Hebrews, and the passage of the sea. From these events the Gk name *exodus* was given to the 2nd book of the Pnt (cf EXODUS, BOOK OF).

1. *Geography*. Modern scholars are generally agreed that the Hb *yam sûp*, "Red Sea" in most Bible translations, cannot be the Red Sea of modern geography. The Hb phrase means "sea of reeds," which does not describe the Red Sea. The occurrence of an Egyptian phrase meaning "Papyrus (Reed) Marsh" in a document of the 13th century to designate a body of water near the city of Ramses suggests that *yam sûp* should be sought in this area, or at least a body of water in the Isthmus of Suez. There are three modern theories of the route of the exodus. In each theory the departure route crossed the Isthmus, which extends about 72 mi in width from the Mediterranean to the head of the Gulf of Suez, an arm of the Red Sea. It was formerly supposed that the modern level of the Red Sea is lower than it was during the period of the exodus, and that in consequence the marshes and the Bitter Lakes of the southern Isthmus were more extensive than they are at present. Explorations in the areas of the N end of the Red Sea have shown that this supposition is false; the fall of the water level, if any, was inconsiderable. There are, however, a number of lakes and marshy areas in the Isthmus: from S to N, the Bitter Lakes, Lake Timsah, and Lake Balah. Lake Menzaleh, E of the Damietta mouth of the Nile, and Lake Bardawil, the Sirbonis of the Greeks, are separated from the Mediterranean only by sandy spits and islands. The land at the mouth of the Nile has been built up by deposits of silt over the cen-

Suez Canal.

turies, and it is almost certain that the shoreline of the Mediterranean and of these lakes lay farther S in the period of the exodus than it does now. This is well verified for Lake Menzaleh. The geographical data of Ex are as follows: The Hebrews worked at the cities of Pithom and Ramses (1:11) and they traveled from Ramses to Succoth* (12:37 f). They did not take "the road of the Philistines" or "travel in the direction of the land of the Philistines" but took the road of the desert and of the "Reed Sea" (13:17 f). From Succoth they encamped at Etham on the edge of the desert (13:20). They camped then "before" Pihahiroth, between Migdol and the sea, "before" Baal Zephon by the sea (14:2). Here they could be described as "shut in by the desert" (14:3). From the Reed Sea they traveled through the desert of Shur* for three days (15:22). The route of the exodus is affected to some extent by the geography of Sinai*; but the theory of the route neither demands nor excludes the traditional identification of Sinai in the modern peninsula of Sinai. Modern archaeological exploration has identified a number of the places mentioned. The road of the Philistines (mentioned anachronistically here) was the main highway between Egypt and Canaan which ran along the coast of the Mediterranean. This route and the entire frontier of Egypt and Canaan were protected by a line of strong Egyptian fortresses across the Isthmus. The Hebrews had to bypass these fortresses to get out of the country without opposition. Ramses, the point of departure, was the "house of Ramses," the royal city of Egypt in the delta in the 19th dynasty, at the site of Tanis, the Hyksos* capital Avaris, the OT Zoan*. Pithom is located at Tell el Ertabeh ESE of Ramses, toward Lake Tim-

sah in the Wadi Tumilat. Succoth is identified by many scholars with the Egyptian Theku or Thel at the modern Tell el Mashkhuta, 8 mi E of Pithom. Etham and Pihahiroth have not been identified, and their location depends on the theory which one accepts of the further course of the route. The theory of a southern crossing proposes that the Hebrews moved from Ramses toward the head of the Gulf of Suez and that they crossed the Bitter Lakes, the "Reed Sea" of Ex. In the theory of a central crossing they proceeded E of Succoth toward Lake Timsah, which would be the Reed Sea. Neither of these sites seems to fit the data concerning the wind and change of level of the waters (Ex 14:21 ff). Hence a number of modern scholars suppose that the crossing took place in the extreme N of the Isthmus. This is equally in harmony with the location of Pithom, Ramses, and Succoth. It supposes that the Israelites met at Succoth an Egyptian fortress or series of fortresses which they could not safely pass, and turned NE toward Lake Sirbonis, which is the "Reed Sea" of the passage. Here they avoided the road of the Philistines by traversing the sandy spit which divides Lake Sirbonis from the Mediterranean. It is of interest that Titus and his army followed this route in their passage from Egypt to Jerusalem in AD 68. Migdol, named as the northernmost point of Egypt in Je 44:1; 46:14; Ezk 29:10; 30:6, is now identified with Tell el Her, which lies near this route. Baal Zephon, the name of a Canaanite deity (cf BAAL), is mentioned in a Phoenician letter discovered in recent years which groups him with the gods of Tahpanhes. This is the Gk Daphne, the modern Tell Defneh, which again brings the route of the Hebrews to the N. This identification supports the view that the Hebrews escaped by the sandy spit. Other scholars identify the sea with a southern extension of Lake Menzaleh which does not exist in modern times. In both of these sites the gales affect the water level. But anyone who attempted a crossing during a gale would place himself in great danger. While we propose the northern crossing as the route which best suits the evidence available at the present time, the Ex account appears to incorporate more than one geographical tradition; and it is possible that the tradition as it appears in Ex is a reconstruction of the route from several accounts without any certain knowledge of the places mentioned and therefore of the route followed.

2. *Date*. The settlement of the Israelites in Canaan described in Jos and Jgs could scarcely have happened except in a period when Egyptian control of Canaan was ineffective or nonexistent. According to 1 K 6:1 the exodus occurred 480 years before Solomon built the temple of Jerusalem. This would place it in the 18th dynasty of Egypt, or about 1440 BC during the reign of the great conqueror Thutmose III. This seems extremely improbable. The figure 480 was in all likelihood reached by computing 12 generations of 40 years each. In the genealogy of the high priests (1 Ch 6:1 ff; 6:50 ff) the high priests from Aaron to Azariah are 12. Azariah follows Zadok* and Ahimaaz*, who are mentioned as priests in David's time. The Israelites cannot be identified with the Habiru of the Amarna* letters, who invaded Canaan in the reign of Amenhotep IV, Ikhnaton (1377–1358), except in the theory of H. H. Rowley that the Israelites entered Canaan in two separate waves of invasion (cf JOSHUA; JUDAH). A term of the settlement is set by the stele of Merneptah (about 1220 BC) which enumerates peoples defeated by him: Libya, Hatti (the Hittites), Canaan, Ashkelon, Gezer, Yenoam, and Israel. Israel is written with the determinative for "foreign people," not "foreign land." The mention of Pithom and Ramses in Ex indicates that the Hebrews were in Egypt when Ramses was rebuilt by Ramses II (1301–1234). Hence many modern scholars find a date 1290–1260 for the exodus and the wilderness period of Israel most acceptable, and the period 1250–1200 for the settlement.

3. *Theology*. The allusions to the exodus throughout the OT are far too numerous to list. It became, early in Hebrew tradition, the great saving act of Yahweh by which He redeemed Israel and established it as a people. Here rather than in the history of the patriarchs Israel saw the roots of its nationality and its religion and its great historical motive for belief in the power and will of Yahweh to save. In the early forms of the tradition the event was explained as due to the movements of wind and waters (Ex 14:21); in the P traditions, which are later, the event was expanded into a separation of the waters and the production of a path on dry land (Ex 14:22). The wonder of the event is heightened elsewhere in P (Ex 14:27–29) and in poetic accounts in the song of Miriam (Ex 15:8) and in the Pss. The exodus was commemorated in the Passover* festival, part of which was the liturgical recitation of the story of the event (Dt 6:20 ff; cf also 26:6 ff). Among the allusions in the historical books cf Jos 2:10; 24:6 (possibly this also is a liturgical passage); Jgs 6:8, 13; 1 S 4:8; 2 S 7:23. The prophets frequently allude to the exodus as a motive of faith or as a point of contrast between the saving works of Yahweh for Israel and the infidelity of Israel toward Yahweh: Is 10:26; 43:16 f; 51:10; 63:11 ff; Je 2:6; 31:32; Ezk 20:5 ff; Ho 11:1; Mi 6:4. The exodus is prominent in the Pss in the recitals of the saving acts of Yahweh: 78:12 ff; 105:23 ff; 106:8 ff; 114:1 ff; 135:8 ff; 136:10 ff. In the second part of Is images drawn from the exodus and the passage through the desert are often employed to describe the future salvation and the establishment of the kingdom of Yahweh (41:18; 42:16; 43:19; 48:21; 49:10). The passage through the sea is a figure of Christian baptism* (1 Co 10:1 f).

Exodus, Book of (Gk *exodos*, "departure"), the 2nd of the five books of the Pnt*.

1. *Contents:* 1:1–22, the oppression of the Hebrews in Egypt; 2, the birth and early career of Moses; 3–4, the vocation of Moses; 5:1–6:1, Moses before the Pharaoh; 6:2–7:7, a second account of the vocation and his appearance before the Pharaoh; 7:8–12:28, the plagues of Egypt; 12:29–15:21, the departure from Egypt and the passage of the sea; 15:22–18:27, from the sea to Sinai; 19:1–40:48, at Sinai: 19, the theophany of Sinai 20, the Decalogue; 21–23, the code of the covenant (cf LAW); 24, covenant of Moses and the elders; 25–31, directions for the construction of the ark and the sanctuary; 32–33, the golden calf; 34:1–28, another account of the covenant and the cultic decalogue; 34:29–35, the glory of Moses; 35–40, construction of the ark and the sanctuary.

2. *Sources*. The three narrative traditions of the Pnt appear to Ex; but most critics believe they can be analyzed only with difficulty in this book. The substance of the book outside of 25–31 + 35–40 is J. Among passages in which one tradition appears relatively free of admixture may be mentioned

the revelation of the name of Yahweh (3:13–15), attributed to E, since J employs the divine name from the beginning; the P account of the vocation of Moses and his appearance before Pharaoh (6:2–7:7); the liturgical prescriptions of P (12:43–13:2) and the historical summary of P (12:40–42). On the analysis of the account of the plagues cf PLAGUES. The analysis of the Sinai episodes is especially difficult. 19 and 24 appear to be parallel to 34, but it is not clear that 24 is the continuation of 19, as it appears to be. The covenant code has been inserted between the two chapters, and it is unlikely that this is its original position. The elders who ratify the covenant on Sinai in 24 seem to be expressly excluded from doing this in 19:24. The parallelism between 19 + 24 and 34 has been editorially removed in 34:1, which makes 34 a renewal of the covenant after the episode of the golden calf (32–33). The marks of the J tradition are clearest in 34, hence 19 and 24 are assigned in substance to E, as is the story of the golden calf. The instructions concerning the sanctuary and the account of their fulfillment, which is a word for word repetition of the instructions except for textual variations and the change of the verbs from imperative to narrative, are both from P, and the narrative from the latest phase of that tradition. For the religious and doctrinal importance of Ex cf EXODUS; PENTATEUCH.

Eye. The eye in biblical usage appears not only as the organ of vision, but also by a very common figure of synecdoche in the OT for the entire person as the subject of psychic functions. The fixing of the eyes signifies both attention and intention, whether favorable or unfavorable. The eye is also the organ of judgment and decision. A bribe blinds the eye of judges (Ex 23:8). The eyes exhibit pride (Pr 6:17), covetousness (BS 14:9; Je 22:17) and the intention of bloodshed and violence (Je 22:17) as well as lust (Jb 31:1, 7). To have one's eyes always directed toward God is to regard His will (Ps 25:15) or to seek some sign of His favor in prayer (Ps 123:2). To ask God to enlighten the eyes is to ask for a sign of His good will, which will remove the dimness of grief and tears and return the brightness of a cheerful gaze (Ps 13:4). The eyes of God are mentioned in the OT in similar terms. His eye judges as it judged the sin of David (2 S 11:27). It is a sign of attention whether for good or for evil (Dt 11:12; Pss 33:18; 34:16; Am 9:8). More than the eyes of man the eyes of God observe all things (Pr 15:3). The figurative use of the eye is much less common in the NT. The eye which is the light of the body is the intention (Mt 6:22; Lk 11:34), which illuminates the entire body. The evil eye (Mt 20:15; Mk 7:22) is envy. The eye is the seat of concupiscence together with the flesh (1 Jn 2:16), here probably avarice. The eye in the sense of desire can be a source of scandal (Mt 5:29; 18:9; Mk 9:47).

Ezekiel (Hb $y^ehezke'l$, "may El strengthen"), a prophet to whom is attributed the third of the books of the major prophets. Very little personal information about Ezk is contained in the book. He was a priest, the son of Buzi, and he lived by the river (canal) Chebar* in Babylonia (Ezk 1:3) near Telabib* (3:15). He was married, and the death of his wife is related in 24:16 ff. This passage is the only one in which Ezk expresses any personal feeling. The earliest date mentioned in the book is 593 BC (1:3) and the latest is 571 BC (29:1). He was one of those deported by Nebuchadnezzar* to Babylon in 597 BC (1:1).

1. *Contents of the book.* The book falls into four major parts: 1–24, threatening discourses before the fall of Jerusalem; 25–32, oracles against the nations; 33–39; discourses of promise after the fall of Jerusalem; 40–48, description of the future restoration of the temple, Jerusalem, and Israel.

I. 1, the vision of the chariot; 2:1–3:15, the eating of the scroll; 3:16–21, the prophet as watchman; 3:22–27, mutism; 4:1–5:17, symbolic actions predicting the fall of Jerusalem; 6, against the mountains of Jerusalem; 7, the day of doom; 8–11, vision in Jerusalem; 8:1–18, idolatry in Jerusalem; 9, the idol worshipers marked for destruction; 10 + 11:22–25, the departure of the glory of Yahweh from Jerusalem; 11:1–12, the false counselors of Israel; 11:13–21, a promise of restoration; 12:1–20, symbols of the fall of Jerusalem; 12:21–28, fulfillment of prophecy; 13, false prophets; 14:1–11, against idol worshipers; 14:12–23, the inevitable fall of Jerusalem; 15, allegory of the vine; 16, allegory of the unfaithful wife; 17, allegory of the eagles and the vine; 18, personal responsibility; 19, lamentation for the royal princes and the queen mother; 20, review of the history of the sins of Israel; 21, the threat of fire and sword against Jerusalem; 22, the guilt of Jerusalem; 23, the allegory of the two sisters; 24:1–14, the allegory of the rusty pot; 24:15–27, the death of the prophet's wife.

II. 25:1–7, against Ammon; 8–11, against Moab; 12–14, against Edom; 15–17, against the Philistines; 26:1–28:19, against

Tyre; 28:20–26, against Sidon; 29–32, against Egypt.

III. 33:1–20, the prophet as watchman; 33:21–33, the fall of Jerusalem is announced; 34, bad shepherds and good shepherds; 35, victory over Edom; 36:1–15, restoration of the land of Israel; 36:16–38, the interior regeneration of Israel; 37:1–14, the vision of the dry bones; 37:15–28, the allegory of the two sticks; 38–39, the overthrow of Gog and his hosts.

IV. 40:1–43:4, the new temple; 43:5–46:24, prescriptions for the cults; 47:1–12, the river issuing from the temple; 47:13–48:35, the division of the land among the tribes.

The book exhibits a number of features which distinguish Ezekiel sharply in his personality from the other prophets. The outstanding trait which sets him off is the number of visions and raptures which the book contains (1:4 ff; 3:14 f; 8:1 ff; 11:1 ff; 37:1 ff). Another peculiarity is the mutism which the prophet experienced for some time (3:26; 24:27; 33:22). The problem of the mutism is to some extent solved by modern critics by a rearrangement of these sections of the book; cf below. The reference to confinement within his house (3:25) may indicate that the mutism meant only silence in public. Connected with the mutism are the symbolic actions of Ezk, again more numerous than in other prophetic books (4:1–3, the siege of Jerusalem in miniature; 4:4–8, lying upon his side; 4:9–12, preparing the food of starvation; 5:1–4, the shaving of the hair and beard; 12:7, the symbolic escape from his house). The symbolic action probably means that the prophet uttered no discourse while he performed them; the explanation which accompanies them in the text does not belong to the context of the action itself and was added later by the prophet himself or by another. The audience was left to divine the meaning of the actions. Ezk experienced ecstasy of a type which we rarely find in other prophets, if at all. This has led some modern scholars to question his mental balance. Such a question presupposes that any extraordinary religious experience can come only to a person who is mentally unbalanced. This view is indefensible; it is refuted by the large number of mystics who have proved themselves active and efficient in practical enterprises. The degree, however, to which the passages in Ezk actually reflect the details of his experience is uncertain. A great amount of the details must be taken as literary imagery — for instance, the description of the chariot of Yahweh (1). It is possible that here and in one or two similar passages we have the description of a vivid dream recalled — or rather reconstructed —

after awakening. The general tone of the passages, however, leaves little room for doubt that Ezk experienced rapture and unconsciousness. Another personal trait of Ezk is his powerful visual imagination, exhibited in 1; 8–11 (the vision of Jerusalem); 37:1 ff (the vision of the dry bones). Related to this is his gift for allegory: cf the allegory of the unfaithful wife (16), of the two sisters Ohollah and Oholibah (23), the ship of Tyre (27:4–11, 25–36), Pharaoh as the crocodile (29:3–7), the descent into Sheol* (32:19 ff). Paradoxically this verdant imagination and elaborate allegory are expressed in a style which is generally stiff and dry.

2. *Authorship*. The book gives a greater impression of organized unity than do the other larger prophetic books. Criticism for the last generation, however, has come to a more and more general agreement that this unity is superficial and deceptive and that the book exhibits signs of compilation and of the work of different hands. For instance, critics point out doublets: 3:17–21 = 33:7–9; 18:25–29 = 33:17–20; 13:11 = 13:12; 13:13 ff = 14:4 ff; 14:6 ff = 18:21–24; 18:26–28 = 18:32. Furthermore, 11:22 should follow immediately after 10:22, but the description of the false counselors has been inserted. Likewise 33:21 should follow 24:26 ff. The oracles against the nations interrupt this sequence; these, as in Is* and Je*, are placed in the middle of the book. A number of modern critics have proposed theories which would remove the book entirely or almost entirely from Ezk of Babylon. Hölscher in 1924 found a mutually exclusive opposition between the luxuriant imagination and colorful language of the poet and the dry thinking and style of the priest. To Ezk himself he attributed only 170 verses of the 1273 in the book and attributed the rest to priestly expansion and commentary. The criterion of originality was metrical form. C. C. Torrey in 1930 took an even more radical stand. The entire book consists of a pseudepigraphical nucleus composed in 230 BC and attributed to the time of Manasseh, king of Judah (693–642). Not long after 230 this was reworked and expanded and attributed to Ezk of Babylon. W. A. Irwin in 1943 accepted Hölscher's criterion of metrical form as valid and by a somewhat different application accepted 250 verses of the book as original. The rest of the book was expansion and commentary from priestly literary circles. For Irwin Ezekiel was not the father of Judaism, as he is frequently called, but the product of Judaism. Nils Messel in 1945 proposed the opinion that 1–24 and 40–48 were composed about 500 BC and that they were reworked, expanded and given an exilic setting about

450 BC. A number of other theories have been proposed which are omitted here because few scholars have accepted them. The most recent criticism has reverted to an acceptance in general of the unity of authorship, but it does not understand it as the organized unity formerly attributed to the book. In spite of the presence of many hands, the book as a whole leaves a decided impression of a single personality with his own manner of thought and expression; the more radical criticism has failed to take this impression into account. The contemporary view of this unity takes the book as substantially the work of Ezekiel, who lived in the time attributed to him and spoke under the conditions described in the book; but it is admitted that the book exhibits reworking and expansion, in some passages to an extensive degree. There is a consensus among modern critics that the book is a collection and not a single composition, and that the origins of the collection are similar to the origins of the other large prophetic collections of the OT: Isaiah, Jeremiah, and the 12 prophets. Some critics describe the writings of Ezekiel as entries of his journal. From this comes the dating of the oracles, more common in Ezk than in other prophetic books: 1:2 (the 5th day of the 4th month of the 30th year of 1:1 is a riddle as yet unexplained); 8:1; 20:1; 24:1; 26:1; 29:1, 17; 30:20; 31:1; 32:1, 17; 33:21; 40:1. These dates do not appear in entirely consecutive order, nor does each date apply to any more than the passage which follows. This material passed through several phases into the book as we have it. It was the opinion of Herrmann that Ezekiel himself collected and organized the material; few modern scholars follow this opinion. Herrmann's view that Ezekiel's journal contained two series, a series of discourses against Jerusalem and Israel and another series of discourses against the nations, is accepted by Eissfeldt and others. Some disorder in the early chapters is generally admitted, and the following scheme is widely accepted as the correct sequence: 3:22–27; 4:4–8; 24:25–27; 33:21–22. This arrangement brings the passages describing Ezekiel's mutism together and compresses it into a brief space of time. The remaining undated discourses between 5 and 24 were collected by other hands than those of Ezekiel, and they exhibit considerable expansion. For instance, the allegory of the unfaithful wife has been expanded by the addition of. 16:44–63, and the allegory of the two sisters by the addition of 23:36–49. Much expansion is found in 1–3; 8–11; 38–39; and 40–48. In particular, 38–39 in their present form are attributed by some scholars to the period of

Alexander the Great. The oracles against the nations are rejected by some critics, but their arguments do not appear convincing except for 25. Georg Fohrer has distinguished three stages in the origin of the book. The first stage was that of detached pieces or loose leaves. Ezk was not, as some older critics thought, a "writing prophet," but a man who spoke in public. He did however, record his ecstatic experiences, of which Fohrer counts 8, his symbolic actions, of which he counts 12, and the words of Yahweh which are found in the discourses. Some of these pieces, he believes, were written before they were spoken, others long after the discourse had been given. In each case they were retouched later. The phase of detached pieces was followed by separate collections, gathered according to their material — thus ecstatic experiences or symbolic actions — or around catchwords such as "idol" and "sword." Fohrer distinguishes the following separate collections: 1:1–3:15, the vocation of Ezk; 3:16–5:17 (except 3:16b–21), symbolic actions; 6, idols; 7, judgment; 8–11 and 21, ecstatic visit to Jerusalem (the words of promise in 11:14–21 are secondary); 12:1–20, symbolic actions; 12:21–13:21, on prophets and prophecy, to which 14:1–11 and 14:12–23 have been added; 15:1–16:43; 20:1–31, the sins of Israel, to which the expansions of 16:44–63 and 20:32–44 have been added; 17 and 19, sins and punishment of the kings (the messianic promise in 17:22–24 is not original, and 18 has been inserted out of place, since Fohrer thinks it was thought to treat of Zedekiah); 21, the sword collection; 22, various sins, in particular blood guilt; 23, the two sisters; 24:1–27, symbolic actions (with which the symbolic actions of 3–4 and 33:21–22 originally belonged); 25, the neighboring peoples of Judah; 26–28, Tyre; 29–32, Egypt; 33:1–20, the prophet's pastoral duty, with which 3:16b–21 was originally connected (33:23–29; 30–33 have been added); 34, the shepherds and the flock; 35, Edom; 36–39 restoration of Israel, into which the oracle against Gog, 38:1–39:20, has been violently introduced; 40–48. The final phase, the book itself, is the arrangement of the collections in a chronological and topical order, neither of which is without dislocation. Fohrer believes that the oracles against the nations were the last to be inserted in the book, and that the collection was finished before the resettlement of Jerusalem in 538, since the temple of Ezekiel does not correspond to the temple of Zerubbabel.

A number of critics, although they differ in their views of the origin of the book, agree on a solution of some of its literary problems which supposes that the book in its present form does not narrate the career of Ezekiel as it happened. Herntrich suggested that Ezekiel's entire ministry was in Jerusalem and that he never went to Babylon. Bertholet, followed by Irwin, van den Born, Steinmann, and Auvray, believed that Ezekiel was in Jerusalem until 587, and that he was then taken to Babylon. They see a double account of his vocation: the symbolic eating of the scroll (2:1–3:9) relates his vocation in Jerusalem, and 1:4–28, with which belongs 3:10–15, relates his vocation in Babylon. The evidence for this hypothesis, however, is not regarded as convincing by a number of modern scholars.

3. *Theology.* The term "father of Judaism," so long applied to Ezekiel, is somewhat exaggerated; the characteristic features of later Judaism do not appear in the book. He is, however, a link between preexilic Israel and the Judaism of the restoration. He looks both ways; with the former prophets he insists upon the vitality and the interior nature of religion, on the reality of sin, and the certainty of God's judgment, upon the demands made upon Israel and its failure to fulfill them. But with Judaism he lays emphasis upon the temple and upon cultic observances as the earlier prophets do not. His conception of God is transcendent and does not exhibit the familiarity so characteristic of Je; nor is his attitude comparable to that of Is, although both emphasize the holiness* of God, His transcendent divinity and His "wholly other" nature. The conception of God in Ezk is perhaps most explicitly seen in the vision of the chariot of the glory of God (1). The chariot is a carriage constructed of a platform of crystal sustained at the corners by four cherubim*, self-propelled by the power of the cherubim and the spirit* which was in the wheels, and flashing fire, the element of divinity, symbolizing the holiness of God, which consumes all that is unholy. The chariot symbolizes the divine attributes; the four faces of the cherub — man, lion, ox, and eagle — signify intelligence, aggressive courage, strength, and swiftness. The chariot moves in any direction instantly; the work of Yahweh is not limited by place. But the form of Yahweh is not perceived; it is "something like a man." Ancient tradition believed that no man could look upon Yahweh and live, and it refused to give Yahweh the likeness of any creature, even of man. Ezk here brings forth his own conception of the traditional theophany* in which Yahweh appears to judge His people. In the earlier theophanies the judgment was the vindication of Israel against its enemies; here Yahweh vindicates His holiness against His own people. For

Ezk is conscious of the guilt of Israel to an extreme degree; it seems to be almost a preoccupation with guilt. In reviewing the past history of Israel (16, 20, and 23) he presents it as an unbroken course of infidelity. Each of God's saving acts of mercy is met with new rebellion, until finally the guilt of Jerusalem has become ingrained (24:1 ff). It is beyond repair and the evil can be cured only by destruction. This destruction the prophet presents not only as inevitable but as entirely just. The holiness of Yahweh in punishing, even by such punishments as those which Ezekiel predicts for his people, is entirely in accord with the demands of justice, and Israel cannot complain that it is treated unfairly. Ezk, like Je, represents a complete break with the past, a new beginning after destruction of the past with all its evil. It is evident that the question of Yahweh's justice was raised by some of the contemporaries of Ezk (18:2; 33:10). The complaint took the form of a protest that the present generation was punished for the sins of earlier generations. To this Ezk responds that each man is responsible for his own life and will be punished for his own guilt, not the guilt of another. This statement is sometimes taken as a distortion of the truth and a denial of the suffering of the innocent; but it must be understood in the concrete situation in which it was uttered. Traditional Hb religion was institutional, and the security of the individual in his union with God rested on his membership in an institution which united him with God. When the institution perished, one could attain God only by one's personal endeavor. This is the point which Ezekiel makes and perhaps overemphasizes; but it was a point of great importance. He did not, however, invent the principle of personal responsibility, which was known in the earliest traditions and laws of Israel; but he restated it in a form and with an emphasis which his own time demanded (18 + 33). With this principle goes a declaration of the vital interior character of the future restoration of Israel. It is not merely a restoration of Hb institutions, but an interior regeneration, a new heart and a new spirit within each individual man (36:26 ff). The heart* is the principle of thought and decision, the spirit is the impulse to act; by these each person will submit himself to the will of Yahweh. This inner regeneration must be borne in mind when one reads the schematic, artificial, and almost entirely external program of restoration in 40–48. The New Israel and Jerusalem will be inhabited by the type of person described in 36:26 ff. The messianism of Ezk, in the ordinary sense of the word, is minimal; the scion of David occupies an insignificant place in his scheme of the future (34:23 ff). But messianism in the broader sense of man living in a society fully submitted to the will of God is found in Ezk.

The conception of the office of the prophet receives a new development in Ezk (3:16–21; 33:1–9). Like the older prophets he must proclaim the judgment to come; but he incurs the guilt of the wicked if he fails to warn him. Here too is a refined insight of personal responsibility. Je had spoken of the prophets who told the people only what the people wanted to hear (4:11–13; 23:16–18). The people whom the prophets thus satisfy with delusions that all is well will perish; but Yahweh requires their blood from the prophets who failed to warn them. There is not yet what many interpreters call the birth of the pastoral office of the prophet; but there is a more urgent sense of the responsibility of the prophet to those whom he addresses.

Ezion-geber (Hb 'eṣyôn-geber, meaning uncertain), an ancient city lying at the head of the Gulf of Aqaba a few miles W of the modern village of Aqaba, precisely at the point where the Wadi Arabah opens into the Gulf. It is mentioned as one of the camps of the Israelites on the journey from Egypt to Canaan (Nm 33:35), but it is almost certain that no settled community existed here at this period (cf also Dt 2:8). It was a seaport "near Eloth on the shore of the Red Sea in the land of Edom" from which Solomon sent a fleet manned by seamen furnished by Hiram* of Tyre* on voyages to Ophir* (1 K 9:26–28; 2 Ch 8:17). Jehoshaphat* also attempted to send a fleet from Ezion-geber to Ophir, but the fleet was wrecked by storms in the port (1 K 22:48; cf 2 Ch 30:35 ff, where the failure is explained by the partnership of Ahaziah* of Israel with Jehoshaphat, which is denied in 1 K 22). The site, the modern Tell el Kheleifeh, was excavated by Nelson Glueck in three campaigns 1938–1940. The excavation disclosed that this was the only Early Iron Age site in the entire area. The mound lay about 1500 ft from the shoreline; this distance represents the recession of the shoreline in 3000 years. The recession is caused by the deposit of sand laid down by strong and almost constant north winds which blow through the Wadi Arabah. It is these winds, which render the climate of the spot extremely disagreeable and sometimes raise sandstorms which last for hours, that determined the choice of the site. The modern village of Aqaba lying a short distance to the E escaped the fury of these winds. Occasionally the wind reverses itself and blows violently from the S; this prob-

ably explains the wreck of Jehoshaphat's fleet, whose seamen were not familiar with the local winds. The excavation revealed dwellings of mud brick, the native material of the area. The bricks of Period I were very well constructed and better in quality than the bricks used in modern times. Some of the buildings were too large for dwellings and were identified as industrial complexes for the smelting and refining of the copper* mined in the Wadi Arabah. These buildings were equipped with flues and vents built into the walls; the wind from the Wadi Arabah furnished the draft for the fires. Traces of intense heat and copper were left upon the brick walls. The first occupation was built upon virgin soil, and the excavators concluded that it was designed and built entirely for industrial purposes. The extremely disagreeable conditions of the site indicate that the labor was forced labor or slave labor. Water is available from wells. The excavators found no fuel in the vicinity and concluded that the fuel was probably charcoal brought from some distance. The buildings of Period I were attributed to Solomon and represent one of his greatest achievements. This level was destroyed by fire in the 10th century, and the destruction was attributed to the invasion of Judah by the Pharaoh Shishak* in the reign of Rehoboam (922–915). It was impossible for Judah to control Ezion-geber unless it also controlled Edom, and Glueck supposes that the frequent wars of Judah and Edom during the monarchy revolved principally around control of this important site. Period II showed an extensive rebuilding of the site, including the industrial facilities, and it was attributed by Glueck to Jehoshaphat (873–849). This level also was destroyed by a conflagration. Period III was attributed to a rebuilding by Uzziah of Judah (783–742). This level also was destroyed by a conflagration, and the industrial village of Period IV was Edomite. From Period III came a seal inscribed with the name YTM, which is with great probability identified with the king of Judah, Jotham* (742–735). Period IV disclosed a royal seal stamp inscribed with the name of "Qausanal, the servant of the king." This is an Edomite name containing the name of the Edomite god Qaus or Qos. The excavations have shown that Elath or Eloth is to be identified with Ezion-geber. Elath is mentioned with Ezion-geber in Dt 2:8, and Ezion-geber is said to be near Eloth in 1 K 9:26; cf 2 Ch 8:17. Uzziah (Azariah) built Elath and restored it to Judah (2 K 14:22; cf 2 Ch 26:2). The Edomites recovered Elath from Judah in the reign of Ahaz* (735–715; 2 K 16:6). Glueck mentions four main activities at Ezion-geber:

the smelting and refining of copper iron, the manufacture of copper and iron implements, sea trade including shipbuilding and fishing, and caravan trade with Egypt, Edom, Judah, and Arabia.

Ezra (Hb *'ezrā'*, "help"?, perhaps an abbreviated name), a priest (Ezr 7:11), a scribe skilled in the law of Moses (Ezr 7:6), a member of the Jewish community of Babylon who went to Jerusalem in the 7th year of the Persian king Artaxerxes (Ezr 7:7) with a large party and a letter of Artaxerxes which authorized him "to make investigation of Judah and Jerusalem according to the law of your God which is in your hand, and to carry silver and gold which the king and his counselors have freely offered to the God of Israel" (7:14 f). The episodes of Ne 8–9 probably followed immediately upon the arrival of Ezra in Jerusalem, narrated in Ezr 8. Ezra assembled the community and proclaimed the "law," which was written in a book, while the scribes who accompanied him explained the law to the people (Ne 8:1–9). The reading of the law took at least two days (Ne 8:3, 13), and the reading of the law was followed by a celebration of the feast of tabernacles* (Ne 8:14 ff), and by a fast and a confession of sins (Ne 9:1 ff). After the proclamation of the law, Ezra learned that a number of Palestinian Jews had married foreign women (Ezr 9:1 ff). Ezra's distress at this so moved the people that they took an oath that they would no longer marry foreign women (Ezr 10:5 ff). Investigation was then made of all who married foreign wives, and they divorced the wives and abandoned the children (Ezr 10:44).

The older opinion, still defended by a large number of modern scholars, took the Artaxerxes mentioned in Ezr 7:7 as Artaxerxes I (465–425 BC). This would put Ezra's mission in 458 BC before Nehemiah* went to Jerusalem. A. van Hoonacker in 1890 suggested that some features of Ezr–Ne cast some doubt on this date (cf EZRA-NEHEMIAH, BOOK OF) and proposed that the king meant was Artaxerxes II (404–359) and that Ezra went to Jerusalem in 398, over 30 years after Nehemiah's second journey. In this hypothesis the two men lived a generation apart and their activities were completely unrelated. Among the reasons alleged for this hypothesis are: There is no contact between the two men in the book except Ne 8:9 and 12:36, which are easily explained as the work of the compiler. The dispute concerning foreign wives, in which both men were involved with no relation with each other, has the appearance of two separate events. Jehohanan, the son of Eliashib (Ezr

9:6), although he is not called the high priest, is very probably to be identified with the high priest Jehohanan, grandson of Eliashib, mentioned in the Elephantine* papyri about 408 BC. It is scarcely possible that Ezra could have lived in the same generation with Nehemiah, in whose time Eliashib was high priest. This opinion of the date of Ezra seems more probable, although the arguments are not peremptory.

The purpose of Ezra's mission was not the same as the purpose of Nehemiah's mission. Ezra is described (Ezr 7:6) as a scribe skilled in the law of Moses. It is most unlikely that the term scribe had in Ezra's time the meaning which it acquired in later Judaism. It is rather (de Vaux, Noth) to be explained as an official administrative title, "secretary for Jewish affairs." Ezra was an officer of the Persian court sent to impose the "law" upon the Jewish community of Jerusalem. It is doubtful that the initiative for this step came from the Persian court; but the interest of the Persian court in religious affairs within the empire has been demonstrated beyond doubt by the modern discovery of Persian documents which exhibit this interest. Such a mission as that of Ezra, which would bring the Jewish community under what was described to the Persian king as its own manner of life, would suit the Persian policy of permitting its subject peoples to preserve their own religion and customs. Noth has suggested that the proximity of Judah to Egypt, which was one of the most troublesome provinces of the empire, moved the king to consent to a measure which was calculated to preserve peace and order in that territory.

The question of the contents of the book of the law cannot be determined, and modern scholars present a wide variety of opinion. Some believe that the law was substantially the Pnt* as it appears in our Bibles. Others think that it was a part of the collections of law* in the Pnt, and more probably one of the later collections, the Holiness Code or the Priestly Code. Whether the book of the law contained any narrative portions is uncertain. The whole conception of law or Torah as it appears in Judaism included a recital of the saving acts of Yahweh on behalf of Israel, and the historical background against which He revealed Himself. Hence it seems probable that the book of Ezra contained at least that abstract of history in the Pnt called P. The narrative suggests that Ezra's law was not previously very well known to his audience (Ne 8:9–12). It is significant that the law which Ezra imposed had to be brought from Babylon and was not possessed in Jerusalem. It was in Babylon that the laws and traditions of

Israel were preserved, edited, and codified. Ezra, it seems, came at the term of this movement, when the law had been assembled to the point where it could be imposed on the community as the will of God revealed to their fathers. The effect of Ezra's mission was permanent. It is remarkable that Ezra is not mentioned in the praise of the fathers (BS 44-49). This can no longer be explained, as older scholars did, by the hypothesis that Ezra was an entirely fictitious character. Nor is the omission due to the refusal of BS to accept the law of Ezra, since BS himself identified wisdom* with the knowledge of the law (BS 24:1 ff; 39:1 ff).

Ezra-Nehemiah, Book of. The book of Ezr-Ne was originally a single book. The division into two books first appears in Origen († AD 254) and found its way into the Lt Vg and into the Hb Bible in 1448. Ezr 1:1–3a is identical with 2 Ch 36:22–23. Most modern critics include Ezr-Ne with 1–2 Ch as a single historical work (cf CHRONICLES; HISTORY).

1. *Contents*. 1:1–11, the return of some of the Jews from Babylon to Jerusalem in the 1st year of Cyrus (539/538 BC), including the decree of Cyrus permitting the return (1:2–4); 2, list of those who returned with Zerubbabel* and Jeshua*; 3:1–6, the renewal of sacrifice at Jerusalem; 3:7–13, the foundation of the second temple 4:1–6, opposition to the building of the temple from the neighbors of Judah; 4:7–24, correspondence concerning the rebuilding of the wall, including a letter from the Persian officers of Samaria (4:12–16) and the response of the king (4:18–22) prohibiting any further work on the walls; 5:1–5, opposition to the building of the temple; 5:6–6:12, correspondence concerning the building of the temple, including a letter of Tattenai*, governor of the territory beyond the Euphrates (5:8–17) and the response of the king quoting a decree of Cyrus (6:3–5, parallel to 1:2–4) and granting the permission to build the temple (6:6–12); 6:13–22, completion of the temple; 7:1–28, departure of Ezra for Jerusalem, including a letter of Artaxerxes permitting Ezra to proclaim the law of his God and granting a subsidy for the worship of the temple (7:11–26; 8:1–14, list of those who accompanied Ezra; 8:15–36, journey of Ezra and his company to Jerusalem; 9:1–10:17, dispute with the Jews who had married foreign women; 10:18–44, list of those who had married foreign women; Ne 1:1–11, Nehemiah learns of the destruction of the walls of Jerusalem; 2:1–9, Nehemiah, butler of Artaxerxes, obtains permission to go to Jerusalem and

build the walls; 2:11–20, Nehemiah's examinations of the walls; his determination to rebuild them; opposition in Samaria; 3:1–32, list of those who worked on the wall; 4:1–9, plot of Sanballat and others to prevent the building of the walls; 4:10–23, measures of protection while the walls were built; 5:1–19, complaints of Jews who were in debt to other Jews; 6:1–19, attempt of Nehemiah's enemies to get him out of the city, and completion of the wall in 52 days; 7:1–5, directions concerning the gates and notice that the population of the city was insufficient; 7:6–72, list identical with Ezr 2; 8:1–9:38, Ezra proclaims the law in Jerusalem; 10:1–27, list of those who signed the "sealed document" with Nehemiah; 10:28–39, compact of the people led by Nehemiah not to marry foreign wives, to observe the Sabbath and the sabbatical year, and to sustain the expenses of the temple and the sacrifices; 11:1–2, arrangements for the repopulation of Jerusalem; 11:3–12:26, lists of those who dwelt in Jerusalem (11:3–21), heads of the Levites (11:22–24), the districts of Judah (11:25–36), the priests and Levites who came with Zerubbabel (12:1–9), the high priests (12:10–11), the heads of the priestly families (12:12–21), the Levites (12:22–36); 12:27–47, dedication of the city wall; 13:1–3, correction of the abuse of foreign marriages; 13:4–31, correction of abuses on Nehemiah's second visit to Jerusalem: the expulsion of Tobiah* from his chamber in the temple (7–9), the refusal to give portions to the Levites and singers (10–14), the observance of the Sabbath (15–22), foreign marriages (23–31).

The book employs several documentary sources, most of which are quoted without any modification. Ezr 7:12–9:15 comes from the memoirs of Ezra. Most modern critics believe that Ne 8–9 also comes from the memoirs of Ezra. Ne 1:1–7:5; 12:27–47; 13:4–31 comes from the memoirs of Nehemiah. It is possible that both these collections include the entire memoirs of these two men. In addition there are the lists of Ezr 8:1–14; 10:18–44; Ne 3:1–32; 10:1–27; Ezr 2, duplicated in Ne 7:6–72; Ne 11:3–19; 20–36. Some modern scholars regard the lists of Ne 11 as later additions, since they do not seem to belong to the time of Nehemiah. Most of the other lists are accepted as authentic documents. Ezr 4:8–7:28 is in Aramaic, while the rest of the book is in Hb. This Aramaic section is made up almost entirely of documents from the Persian archives. The authenticity of these documents, often questioned by scholars of earlier generations, has been placed beyond doubt by the modern discovery of Persian documents which are written in the style of these documents and treat similar business; in particular, the letter of the Persian court ordering a celebration of the Passover, found among the Elephantine* papyri, exhibits the interest of the Persian administration in religious questions, which was the chief reason why older scholars rejected the documents of Ezra. In addition the author almost certainly had a Hb documentary source for Ezr 1 + 3 + 4:1–6. The other material in the books is the work of the author and compiler. To him Eissfeldt assigns most of Ezr 3; 6:19–22; 7:1–11; Ne 12:27–43, and with some probability Ezr 9:6–15 and Ne 9:6–37 (prayers of Ezra). To these Ne 13:1–3, not from the memoirs, should be added. There is a wide but not universal agreement that the compilation of these documents was done at a time when the chronology neither of the Persian kings nor of Ezra and Nehemiah was accurately known, and that the present arrangement gives rise to a misconception of the order of events and the relations between the two men. On the chronology of Ezra and Nehemiah cf EZRA; NEHEMIAH. Apart, however, from the question of the dates of Ezra and Nehemiah, the following dislocations are observed. The Aramaic documents concerning the building of the wall are out of place (Ezr 4:6–23). The question of the walls was not raised when the party of Zerubbabel came to Jerusalem. This correspondence is, with all probability, to be placed shortly before the coming of Nehemiah and is to be connected with the event alluded to in Ne 1:3. It is remarkable that the two men never meet or cooperate; they are mentioned only in Ne 8:9; 12:36. It is extremely probable that the author has here introduced Nehemiah into the proclamation of the law and Ezra into the dedication of the walls in an effort to bring the two more closely together. Ne 8–9 belongs with the memoirs of Ezra; Eissfeldt restores them to follow Ezr 8:36. The autobiographical style was changed from the 1st person to the 3rd when these chapters were detached from the memoirs and placed in their present position. There is a lack of consequence between Ne 9 and 10. The "sealed compact" of Ne 9:38–10:1 does not follow the reading of the law by Ezra. It is the opinion of Eissfeldt that the compiler has replaced the compact imposed by Ezra after the reading of the law with the compact imposed by Nehemiah on another occasion, again in an effort to bring the two together. Hence the sealed document of Ne 9:38 is a document of Nehemiah and not of Ezra. Although the activity in Ne 9:38–10:39 is that of Nehemiah, modern critics do not think this chapter was taken from the memoirs of Nehemiah, and Noth proposes that the compact really belongs after the disputes mentioned in Ne 13.

2. *Authorship and Date*. Modern critics generally believe that Ezr-Ne is the work of the Chronicler*, and that this work was not composed earlier than 300 BC. Some propose a date 400–300, and Albright identifies the Chronicler as Ezra himself. The later date seems more probable in view of the manipulation of the documents described above and of the apparent uncertainty concerning the relations of Ezra and Nehemiah and of the identity of the Persian kings. Critical analysis, however, shows that by far the greater part of the material of the book consists of contemporary documents. For this reason the historical value of the books is more highly esteemed now than it was in earlier generations. Ezr 1–6 is almost the only source of information for the first return of Jewish exiles and the resettlement of Jerusalem.

3. *Religious Significance*. The religious significance of the book lies more in its history than in its message. Ezr-Ne relates the practical steps which were taken to restore a Jewish community in Jerusalem and Palestine. These steps were taken in faith in the continued life of Israel, based on the conviction that Israel was the people of Yahweh and the promises that this people would survive that He might be known to all nations. This community was the beginning of Judaism. Judaism preserved the literature of Israel and composed its own contributions, and created a religio-political society based on Israelite traditions. It was in this society that the NT and Christianity arose.

F

Fable. A short story embodying a moral and introducing persons, animals, or inanimate things as persons or actors. Examples of this literary species appear in the OT in the fable of Jotham* (Jgs 9:7–15) and the fable of Jehoash* of Israel (2 K 14:9; 2 Ch 25:18). In the fable of Jotham the thorn tree, representing Abimelech*, is chosen king rather than any of the more useful trees. In the fable of Jehoash the thistle, representing Amaziah* of Judah, challenged the cedar of Lebanon and was destroyed by a wild beast. Paul also uses the language of fable in 1 Co 12:14–21 in describing the unity of the members of the Church in one body* of Christ. He perhaps alludes to a popular fable of a dispute between different members of the body.

Face (Hb *pānîm;* the word always appears in the plural, probably because the face is a combination of a number of features). The face identifies the person and reflects the sentiments and attitudes of the person. Hence it is frequently used as a substitute for the self and the feelings and desires of the self. The hard face expresses stubbornness or impudence or ruthlessness (Dt 28:50; Pr 7:13; 21:29; Is 50:7; Je 5:3; Ezk 3:8). The face that shines expresses joy or cheerfulness (Jb 29:24). The shamed face (2 S 19:6; 2 Ch 32:21; Ezr 9:7; Pss 34:6; 44:16; 69:8; 83:17; Is 29:22; Je 7:19; Ezk 7:18) may express defeat, frustration, humiliation, or fear. The flaming face (Is 13:8) manifests terror, which may even cause the face to turn green (Je 30:6). The "evil" face (Gn 40:7; Ne 2:2), rather the evil looking face, is a sign of distress and worry. The innocent man is able to hold up his face (2 S 2:22). The fallen face, however, is an expression of anger (Gn 4:5). To sweeten or soften the face of another is to win his favor (Ps 45:13; Pr 19:6; Jb 11:19). The idiom may signify literally to soften the face by gently stroking the face. To hide the face is to show aversion or disgust (Is 53:3). Similarly, to turn away the face of another is to reject him or to refuse his request (2 K 2:16 ff). To raise the face of another is to grant his request or to show him favor or regard (Gn 19:21; 32:21; Dt 28:50; 1 S 25:35; 2 K 3:14; Jb 42:8). But when a judge or person in office is said to raise the face of another, it means to show partiality (Lv 19:15; Ps 82:2; Pr 18:5; Jb 13:8, 10; 32:21; Mal 2:9). To see the face of another is most frequently simply to see the person. But to see the face of a king or other dignitary is to be admitted to his presence, with the implication that the reception would be favorable (Gn 43:3, 5; 44:23, 26; Ex 10:28; 2 S 3:13; 14:24, 28, 32). "Those who see the face of the king" (2 K 25:19; Je 52:25) are the personal retinue of Nebuchadnezzar* of Babylon.

These idioms are applied to God. When the face of Yahweh shines, it manifests His favor and good will (Nm 6:5; Pss 4:7; 31:17; 44:4; 67:2; 80:4, 8, 20). Yahweh is frequently asked to let His face shine upon the petitioner. When the face of Yahweh falls, He is angry (Je 3:12). To sweeten or soften the face of Yahweh (Ex 32:11; 1 K 13:6; 2 K 13:4; 2 Ch 33:12; Je 26:19) is not merely to win His good favor, but appease Him when He is angry. This connotation, however, does not appear in 1 S 13:12 and Ps 119:58, where the phrase means simply to seek His good will by ritual cult. Yahweh, like men, shows His anger by hiding His face (Dt 31:17 ff; Pss 13:2; 27:9; Jb 13:24; Is 54:8; Je 33:5 +). Yahweh also shows His favor to man by raising the man's face (Dt 10:17; Jb 34:19). To see the face of Yahweh (Gn 33:10; Jb 33:26) is to be received favorably by Him. But in Ex 23:15; 34:20; Ps 42:3; Is 1:12 the phrase appears to have the technical sense of visiting the sanctuary for cultic worship. In the last four passages cited the Hb text has been pointed in such a way as to mean "be seen before the face of Yahweh." This later Jewish interpretation removes from the text the idea that man could see the countenance of Yahweh. The face of Yahweh is also used as a substitute for self or person; but in such passages as Ex 33:14 ff; Dt 4:37; Is 63:9, an allusion to the exodus* traditions, the use of "face" is emphatic. Yahweh in person accompanies the Israelites to guide and protect them. The "shewbread" or "bread of the presence" of English Bibles (Ex 25:30; 1 S 21:7 +) is literally the bread of the face, the bread which is placed in the presence of Yahweh. The bread of the presence, like the phrase "sweeten" or "soften" the face, possibly uses cultic language from worship in which images were placed in the temple. Both Jacob* (Gn 32:31) and Moses* (Ex 33:11) encountered God face to face. This extremely rare experience is extended to all Israel (Dt 5:4); but Dt 34:10 expresses the general belief that the experience was unique for Moses. In early Hb belief the sight of the face of God was regarded as fatal (Jgs 6:22; cf also Jgs 13:22). The phrase signifies a more intimate personal communion than was known to normal experience; Moses was the mediator of the words of Yahweh to the people of Israel. Later prophets received or heard the word, of Yahweh. A late popular tradition told how the face of Moses became resplendent after a conversation with Yahweh, so that he had to wear a veil when he spoke to the Israelites (Ex 34:29–35). Paul, alluding to this tradition, compares the veil of Moses to the veil which prevented the Jews from understanding the books of Moses when they were read and so kept them from seeing Christ. Christians now see the splendor of the Lord with unveiled faces, and through this vision are changed into likeness with Him (2 Co 3:12–18). The NT usage of face often reflects the Hb usage.

Fair Havens (Gk *kaloi limenes*), a small bay on the S coast of Crete* E of Cape Matala. Here, near the town of Lasea, the ship bearing Paul put in on its voyage from Cnidus (AA 27:8). It was after leaving Fair Havens that the ship was wrecked.

Faith. Modern Catholic theology defines faith with St. Thomas Aquinas as "the act of the intellect when it assents to divine truth under the influence of the will moved by God through grace" (II. II. q. 2 a. 9). This somewhat strictly intellectual concept of faith was developed in the intellectualistic theology of the medieval period, and the controversies aroused by the Reformation teaching on faith as an act of confidence led Catholic theology to emphasize still more the intellectual quality of faith. The biblical understanding of faith, which is antecedent to these movements, is not so severely intellectual; it has some intellectual content, but biblical faith viewed as a whole is a more comprehensive psychic act than the faith defined by St. Thomas.

1. *OT.* The Hb word which lies at the base of the NT *pistis* and *pisteuein* is *'āman.* Basically this word means to be firm or solid, and hence to be true. The Niphal of the verb means to be trustworthy, and hence of a person to be sure or reliable, of a thing to be true or genuine. The Hiphil or causative stem of the verb does not signify to make firm or sure, but to accept something as *ne'emān* — firm, sure or true, trustworthy or dependable. Thus one accepts a word or report as true (Gn 45:26). The Hebrews accepted Moses' account of his experience as true and accepted him as the leader designated by God to bring them out of Egypt

(Ex 4:5, 8, 31; 19:9; cf also 1 K 10:7; Je 40:14; Is 53:1; Hab 1:5). One believes in an inferior (1 S 27:12), in a friend (Je 12:6; Mi 7:5); in a servant (Jb 4:18); by this belief one professes that they are true and genuine and can be depended on to act according to their orders or their friendship. The nouns derived from this verb are *'emûnāh,* solidity or firmness (Ex 17:12) and *'emet.* That which is firm gives *security* (Is 33:6). God offers firm security because of His *fidelity* (Ps 36:6). Hab 2:4 almost certainly means "a righteous man shall live by his fidelity" i.e., his fidelity to Yahweh; the term nowhere signifies the subjective act of belief or confidence. *'emet* is firmness or solidity, in particular of words or personal conduct, hence *truth* or *truthfulness* or *fidelity.* The word is commonly included among the attributes of God (Ps 30:10; 40:11; 71:22; 91:4). This fidelity is often coupled with the attribute of *ḥesed,* covenant love*, and the two words together indicate His fidelity to His promises and to His covenant. Weiser notes that the Hiphil of *'āman* always indicates a personal relation; when one places faith in a thing, it is because of the credit one gives to the person who stands behind the thing or the word.

The word used of God declares that God is *ne'emān,* sure or faithful (Weiser). One then believes the word of God or accepts His command (Dt 9:23; Ps 119:66 +). In particular one declares that God is sure and faithful by accepting His promises; cf Abraham, Gn 15:1 ff. Abraham, although he and his wife were childless, was promised numerous descendants. Abraham's belief in the promise was reckoned to him as righteousness; he did what he ought to do. To believe here is to accept the promise with confidence in its fulfillment, and with it to accept the power and will of God to fulfill His promise. In some instances the word can be said to summarize the entire attitude of man to God (Weiser); thus Ex 14:31; 19:9; Nm 14:11; Dt 1:32; Ps 78:22. Used in such an absolute sense, the word indicates that one believes God and trusts Him; one commits oneself to Him as sure and dependable. The use of the word in Is has some features peculiar to this prophet. The fundamental demand which Isaiah made upon Ahaz* in the Assyrian crisis of 735 BC was faith; and it is this faith, by a word play, in which Judah will find its *security* (Is 7:9). The word play cannot be reproduced in English; roughly, one can only be firm by accepting God as firm. The content of the faith demanded by Isaiah is an acceptance of the power and will of God to deliver Judah from this political crisis; the acceptance will be demonstrated by abstinence from all political and military action. To take these means is to refuse to believe in God, to trust Him. Similarly in another passage, probably to be placed in the crisis of Sennacherib* in 701, Isaiah says that he who believes shall have no worry (Is 28:16). The scope of the faith demanded by Isaiah shows that faith was a total commitment to Yahweh, a renunciation of secular and material resources, a seeking of security in the saving will of God alone. This is indeed to accept Him as faithful and genuine.

The intellectual quality of faith is more prominent in Second Is. Thus the Israelites are witnesses that the nations may know Yahweh and believe Him and understand that He is Yahweh (Is 43:10). They are to accept Yahweh as Himself on the declaration of the Israelites, and through this to know and understand that He and He alone is God. Normally, however, the intellectual quality of faith as it is set forth in modern theology is expressed in the OT by other words, such as "knowing" God, which is not speculative knowledge, but experience of Him through His revealed word and His saving deeds. The common word to describe the response of man is not "believe" but "hear" in the sense of "hearken" — to hear so as to accept or to obey. Unbelief in the OT often consists in not listening to the words of Yahweh. The use of believe in an apparently intellectual sense in Ps 27:13 is unusual in the OT and especially in the Pss, where the word he'emin is rare. Elsewhere the word is commonly used in synonymous parallelism with other words which mean "trust" or "have confidence." The above analysis, however, shows that he'emin is not accurately rendered by these synonyms; it is rather the word which contains the basis of the trust and confidence, the profession that the person trusted is sure, truthful, and faithful. This basic sense of the Hb word lies at the root of the NT vocabulary and ideology.

2. NT. "Believe" and "faith" in our English Bibles translate the Gk pisteuein and pistis. The verb pisteuein in classical Gk means to trust, to show confidence, and to accept as true. The noun pistis expresses assurance, confidence, and belief, as pistis theōn, belief in the gods, i.e., belief that the gods exist. The common meanings appear often in the NT; but the specifically Christian meaning of the word is a development of the classical usage and of the OT concept of faith.

I. The Synoptic Gospels. Jesus Himself demands faith (Mt 9:28; Mk 4:36; Lk 8:25), praises faith (Mt 8:10; Lk 7:9) and declares that faith has saved (Mt 9:22; Mk 5:34; Lk 8:48) — in the context, saved from an illness which is miraculously cured; cf also Mt 15:28. To one who believes all things are possible (Mk 9:23), and even a small amount of faith can move mountains and do other wonders (Mt 17:20; 21:21). The content of this faith is not stated in the Synoptic Gospels. In its most simple and general terms, it is an acceptance of Jesus Himself as being what He claims to be. Implicit in this acceptance is a conjunction with the power which He exhibits in His own person; this is the faith which moves mountains. The faith of the Gospels, like the OT faith, is not simply trust and confidence; it is trust and confidence which arise from faith, which in turn is an acceptance of a person and his claims.

II. AA. The importance of faith in primitive Christianity is evident from the use of the word in AA. Here "believers" is a common designation of those who accept the preaching of the apostles and join the Christian community. To become a Christian is "to believe" (AA 4:4; 13:12; 14:1; 15:7 +). In most of these passages the object of belief is the preaching of the apostles. This belief is faith in the Lord (AA 5:14; 9:42), in the Lord Jesus Christ (11:17), belief that one is saved through the grace of the Lord Jesus (15:11). The specific Christian sense of faith is supposed in the usage of AA, and this sense is explicit in the Pauline writings.

III. Paul. Faith joined with baptism is that which renders a man righteous (Rm 1:17; 3:22, 26, 28, 30; 4:5; 9:30; Gal 2:16; 3:8, 24). The life which Paul lives since his conversion is a life by faith in the Son of God (Gal 2:20). This is a life of crucifixion with Christ so that Christ lives in him; cf also Rm 6:8. It is through faith that Christians become sons of God in Christ Jesus (Gal 3:26). Hence through faith the Christian is saved by grace (Eph 2:8). Paul adapts Hab 2:4, "a righteous man will live by his fidelity," to his own meaning (Rm 1:17; Gal 3:11), making faith the principle of the life of the righteous. This use of the text is based on the LXX, in which the Hb 'emûnāh is rendered by pistis; pistis is not fidelity, but the act of belief or confidence. Faith, for Paul, is not only faith in Christ Jesus (Gal 2:16; Eph 1:15; Col 1:4), but in the specifically Christian sense it is faith in the preaching, "the word of faith" (Rm 10:8). No one can be saved unless he invokes the name of the Lord, but no one can invoke His name unless he believes in Him; and how is one to believe in Him unless one has heard of Him through the preaching (Rm 10:13-15)? Hence faith comes through the preaching of those who are witnesses of the life, death, and resurrection of Jesus

Christ. The content of the Christian faith is summed up briefly in Rm 10:9: Jesus is Lord and God has raised Him from the dead. It is faith in Him who raised the Lord Jesus from the dead, who was delivered to death for our sins and raised for our righteousness (Rm 4:24 f). It is summed up best in what is more probably an early Christian hymn and profession of faith; He was revealed in flesh, proved righteous in spirit, seen by angels, preached among nations, believed in the world, and assumed in glory (1 Tm 3:16). The content of Christian faith for Paul was that Jesus is the Christ (Messiah), Lord, Son of God, that He died and through His death delivered us from our sins and was raised from the dead and through His resurrection communicates new life to those who believe in Him and are baptized.

In Rm, particularly Rm 4, and in Gal Paul draws an antithesis between faith and the law*. Faith as described in the profession cited above brings man things which the law could not bring and was not instituted to bring; hence faith is superior to circumcision and to the law. No one, by observing the law without faith in the Lord Jesus, can attain the righteousness promised to those who believe. The Pauline antithesis between faith and works is really an antithesis between faith and the law. Those who think they can be saved by the works of the law without faith are no better than the unbelieving Gentiles. In the early part of Paul's apostolic career it was not yet clear to any one that faith entirely relieved the Jews from the obligations of the law; but it was clear to Paul from the very beginning that those who had never been under the law had no need to undertake its observance, since faith in the Lord Jesus saved them effectively. But faith carried with it obligations and "works" of its own. Paul never professed faith which was a mere inoperative sentiment. He who believes in the heart must also confess with the mouth (Rm 10:9); faith must be externalized at least by public profession. Paul twice sums up all the obligations of the law in the single commandment to love one's neighbor (Rm 13:8–10; Gal 5:6, 14).

Faith looks not only to the past, but also to the future; it is a belief that the work begun by the redeeming death and justifying resurrection of Jesus will be consummated in eternal life (1 Th 4:14). Faith retains a degree of obscurity; it grants complete assurance and confidence, but it does not grant the fullness of knowledge. The Christian walks by faith and not by vision (2 Co 5:7). The Christian does not see the consummation of which he is certain.

For Paul, faith is also an obedience (Rm 1:5; 16:26). The acceptance of Christ, as in the Synoptic Gospels, is not merely an intellectual acceptance of a body of truth, but a surrender and a total commitment to a person. This commitment is not made by a single act; even Christians may show defects of faith (1 Th 3:10) or a weakness in faith (Rm 14:1), and they ought to grow in faith (2 Co 10:15). The single act of belief finds its fulfillment in a progressively fuller commitment to Jesus Christ, until it reaches the point where the believer lives with Christ, crucified with Him (Gal 2:20).

Heb 11 contains a lengthy discussion of faith which follows its own lines. Faith is defined somewhat obscurely in Hb 11:1 as "the assurance of things hoped, the proof of things unseen"; the translation is not entirely certain. The word *hypostasis* (assurance) means confidence in 2 Co 9:4; 11:17, and possibly in Heb 3:14 — here possibly conviction. The word confidence, however, is a transferred meaning of the Gk word. *Hypostasis* is that which stands underneath, hence that which gives support to a building, its foundation, or to a conviction, its arguments or evidence. Hence one could translate here "the foundation of the things hoped," or "the reality of things hoped"; faith is that which gives a conviction of their reality and furnishes the motive of hope. In the examples of faith in Heb 11, drawn from the OT, this conviction of the reality of the things hoped and the proof of things unseen is the virtue which is praised. Finally, the Christian, with this cloud of witness, should fix his eyes upon Jesus, who initiates and consummates faith (Heb 12:1 f). The content of this faith is in part indicated as the faith by which we perceive that the universe was created at God's command (Heb 11:3). Without this faith it is impossible to please God; for one who approaches God must believe that He is and that He rewards those who seek Him (Heb 11:6).

IV. John. The Johannine usage of faith, while substantially identical with the usage described above, has a few peculiarities of its own. Faith is here also faith in the Son of Man (Jn 9:36, 38), in Jesus (Jn 11:45, 48); but in Jn the object of faith is frequently more explicit. It is faith that Jesus came from God (Jn 16:30), that He is the holy one of God (Jn 6:69), that He is the Messiah (Jn 11:27). Unique in Jn is faith in the words of Jesus (Jn 2:22; 5:47; 8:45). Those who hear the apostles will believe on the word of the apostles (Jn 17:20); the Johannine faith also is faith in the preaching. Faith in the Son brings life (Jn 3:36). He who does not believe is already condemned (Jn 3:18 f). The Jews do not believe because

a) Assyrian kings accompanied by demons bearing offerings to the Tree of Life. b) Tree of Life and guardian demon. c) Mesopotamian seal showing divine figures seated at a tree with serpent in background.

they are not of God (Jn 8:47). These texts do not imply a crass doctrine of predestination. The Jews are not of God, that is, they are of the world and the devil; faith does not come from the world; it comes only from God, and in order to believe one must renounce the world. When the preaching is uttered, and in particular when Jesus presents Himself, one refuses to believe only because one refuses to renounce the world. As Paul says that the Christian walks by faith and not by vision, so also in Jn faith is praised when it is faith without sight (Jn 20:29). In Jn also the work of faith is the love of one's neighbor (1 Jn 3:23).

The other NT books speak of faith in the same or similar terms. Faith is a precious gift of God (2 Pt 1:1). Js 2:14–20 discusses faith and works; it is idle to assert that here Js is saying the same thing that Paul says of faith and the law. It seems obvious that Js thought that Paul's views on freedom from the law needed further explanation, especially among the Jewish Christians to whom the epistle is addressed. Paul's teaching was open to misunderstanding; and some probably thought that liberation from the obligation of the law was deliverance from all obligations. The texts of Paul quoted above show that this was not Paul's teaching; and Js also insists that faith without works is dead and no better than the faith of the demons. The works proposed by Js, however, are not the works of the law. They are charity to the needy (2:15 f), assistance to those in danger (2:25), and the supreme obedience of Abraham in offering Isaac for sacrifice (2:21). The works of the law mentioned in 2:8–11 are the love of one's neighbor and the prohibition of adultery and murder, fundamental commandments which are also cited by Paul; neither writer imposes the strict Pharisaic observance of the law.

Falcon. Several species of falcon are known in Palestine. A number of scholars identify Hb *nēṣ* as *Falco peregrinus;* it is an unclean bird (Lv 11:16; Dt 14:15), and its soaring flight is mentioned in Jb 39:26.

Fall, the. The fall of man is related in Gn 2:4b–3:24.

1. *Literary Character:* The story of the fall of man, attributed to the J tradition of the Pnt*, cannot be traced in its present form to any known earlier literary material. Analysis, however, leads scholars to suspect that the episodes of the chapters existed originally in an independent form in oral or written tradition. They were combined in their present form by J. Comparison with ancient Near Eastern literary material shows

that the author or his sources drew heavily, in composing the account, on ancient Near Eastern myths for most of the external features of the narrative, and that the symbolism of these external features is in almost every instance quite obvious, especially where the source of the material can be traced. These external features are as follows: man created from clay by the hand of a divine being and infused with life is found both in Mesopotamia and in Egypt. The Hb account alone describes the infusion of life as the inspiration of the divine breath. The concept of a single pair living in isolated bliss bears a resemblance to the description of Ut-napishtim and his wife, the survivors of the deluge*, in the Gilgamesh* epic; they live in "A paradise of delight at the mouth of the two rivers," which in Mesopotamian myth are the Tigris* and the Euphrates*. The external features of Eden*, including the rivers, resemble this picture. The same Gilgamesh epic contains a description of Enkidu, the companion of Gilgamesh. He is not the first man, but he is created of clay by the goddess Aruru to do battle with Gilgamesh. He is half man and half beast and lives with the wild beasts in the open field. Gilgamesh instigated a harlot to seduce him, and after his experience with the harlot Enkidu abandoned his wild manner of life and became a city dweller. This episode also bears some external resemblance to the progress of man as described in Gn 2–3 ff. The tree of life appears both in Mesopotamian literature and in Mesopotamian art. Life is communicated, however, not by eating the fruit of the tree, but by contact with its branches. There is no parallel to the tree of knowledge of good and evil, but it is not difficult to suppose that the Hb narrator created the tree of knowledge as a counterpiece to the tree of life. The symbolism of the serpent* in the ancient Near East is broad. The serpent also appears to be a symbol of life. More precisely, however, the serpent is often represented in connection with a nude goddess in a manner which scarcely permits one to deny that the serpent is a symbol of life as it is originated by sexual intercourse, and hence the serpent may be taken as a sexual symbol, although not precisely as a phallic symbol (ANEP 470–474). On the cherubim (Gn 3:24) cf CHERUB. The flaming, whirling sword is probably the lightning represented elsewhere as a weapon of Yahweh (Dt 32:22; Ps 104:4) and as the weapon of Baal and Hadad in Mesopotamian and Syrian art (ANEP 490, 500, 501, 531, 532). Critics have not reached an agreement on the number or the character of the separate stories which are woven into the present account, although there is very general agreement that the stories existed separately. To the present writer it seems that one can distinguish an account of the origin of woman and of sex in ch 2, the story of the sin of a man alone, and the story of the sin of a woman. The detachment of ch 2 from ch 3 is suggested because the narrative of ch 2 almost demands as its conclusion the statement that man and woman fulfilled the union of sex for which they are destined. This statement does not appear; ch 3 replaces it. The distinction between the story of the sin of man alone and the story of the sin of woman is suggested by the parallel to the story of the fall of man which is found in Ezk 28:12–15. Here also external features can be traced which appear in Near Eastern mythology, but there is no woman in the story. On the other hand, in the story of Gn 3 the man is strangely inactive; the dialogue takes place between the serpent and the woman, who plays the leading role in tempting the man.

It may be concluded from this that the story of the fall of man existed in several variant forms in Hb tradition, of which only two have been preserved in the text of the OT. It is furthermore easily assumed that these stories circulated in oral tradition before they were fixed in writing. The presence of these external descriptive and symbolic features makes it difficult to accept the hypothesis that the Hebrews enjoyed a divine revelation of the fall of man, since it is unlikely that these somewhat common mythological traits would be contained in a direct divine revelation. It is also difficult to retain the older view that the story was preserved by tradition from the first generation of mankind, since the age of man is now known to be much greater than the time during which traditions could be preserved, even substantially. Hence modern scholars prefer to treat the account as a story through which the Hebrews enunciated their belief that man fell from his primitive harmonious relationship with God. The story was constructed by the use of elements drawn from the beliefs and traditions of the ancient Near Eastern world, but it was governed by the unique Hebrew conception of God which made it impossible for them to accept the beliefs concerning the origin of man found in ancient Near Eastern myths. The condition of man and his relations with God could not be explained by the assumption that man was created evil, or that man as he actually existed could be in harmonious relations with a God who imposed His moral will on the world. The present condition of man can be due only to his own failure to meet the standards which God has set for him. The question of the reality of the fall of man, which is theologically connected with the reality of the redemption*, is distinct from the question of the historical character of Gn 2–3. If man had not fallen, man needed no redemption nor was he really redeemed by the death of Jesus Christ. This theological certainty, however, does not repose on a "history" of the fall of man understood in the sense in which we employ the word, but on the biblical awareness of the reality and universality of the hostility which man exhibits to God, which is responsible for his estrangement from God. From this estrangement only God can deliver him.

2. *Theology.* The theology of the account is Hebrew in character, and is based on the importance of the woman in Gn 2–3. The account of Gn 2 is not really an account of creation, but rather an account of the origin of the distinction of the sexes. The distinction of the sexes in ancient Near Eastern belief was found in the divine world. The Hebrews rejected this belief; sex was instituted in the animal world and in man by God's creative act. Furthermore the distinction of sex implied a relation between man and woman which did not correspond to the historical position of woman known to the Hebrews. In the ancient world woman was depressed, less fully human than the male. Her rights in law, marriage and the family, and civil society were inferior to the rights of the man. The double standard of morality existed, and restraint was imposed only upon the woman. Woman was regarded as the creature of man's pleasure and as the drudge who performed lowly domestic duties while she bore man's children. At the same time woman, who could give man his supreme animal pleasure, was worshiped as a goddess precisely in her sexual character, as the goddess Ishtar, Astarte, or other such deities found in almost all ancient Near Eastern religions. To the Hebrew this view of woman was a perversion of the position assigned woman by God in creation, depressing her on the one hand from her place as a helper fit for man (Gn 2:20) and elevating her on the other hand to a deity. This perversion of the position of the female sex found expression in the cult of the goddess of fertility. She was recognized as the source of life; and her union with the male deity, celebrated in the annual myth-ritual cycle of fertility, was the sign and symbol of the renewal of life. The worshipers entered into communion with the deities of fertility by themselves participating in the rites through intercourse with priestesses who represented the goddess of fertility. Thus the worshipers became "like gods" (Gn 3:5, 22). Hence it appears that

the Yahwist account describes the fall of man in the terms of his own time and his own civilization as identical with the cult of fertility, which he represents as the radical rebellion which alienates man from God and takes away the dominion over nature which God conferred upon man in creation. This does not mean that the writer intended to affirm that the original fall was historically the adoption of the fertility cult, but rather that in the fertility cult there appeared the rebellion which originally sundered man from God and made the achievement of happiness impossible for him. It is a result of man's rebellion against God that he is doomed to death. It may be noticed that the absence of any personal name of the man (the common designation, Adam*, represents the Hebrew ha'adam, which means "the man" or "Man") shows that the writer emphasizes the representative character of his hero rather than his individual personality. Similar representative traits appear elsewhere in the OT in the stories of individuals who head or represent a group; cf ABRAHAM; ISAAC; JACOB; PATRIARCHS.

There is no certain allusion to the story of the fall in the Hb text of the rest of the OT. Allusions appear only in the late books: BS 25:24; WS 2:22–25. These passages make the connection between sin and death. On the NT references (Rm 5:12 ff; 1 Co 15: 20–22) cf SIN. The story is also alluded to in 1 Tm 2:13 f.

Family. The Hb word for family is bêt'āb, "father's house," and the name indicates the patriarchal character of the Hb family. The family is the smallest social unit beneath the clan and the tribe*. The family of the OT included all those of the same blood or who lived in a common dwelling. Thus it included the husband and father, the head of the family, his wife or wives and concubines, his children, slaves or retainers, clients or resident aliens (cf STRANGER), widowed or expelled daughters, and unmarried adult sons or daughters. Such a large household appears in the patriarchal accounts of Gn. The family was a religious unit. The Passover* was celebrated within the family (Ex 12:3 f). Elkanah* and his family, who made an annual pilgrimage to Shiloh* (1 S 1:3 ff), probably exhibited the usual devotion of the period. The family was also in some sense a moral unit, although this unity was relaxed with the development of civilization. Yahweh Himself punished sin even to the third and fourth generation of the family (Ex 20:5 f; Dt 5:9 f). In the story of Achan* his whole family is punished with him for his theft (Jos 7:24). This punishment, however, is

unique in the OT and was forbidden in Dt 24:16; cf 2 K 14:6. The Hb sense of family solidarity was extremely close, since the individual depended entirely on his family for support and protection, and life was not conceived as possible outside the family. For the protection which the family furnished its members cf AVENGER. The family shared the guilt of the offender in the sense that it owed him protection. Passages such as 1 Ch 4:14, 21, 23 suggest that in Israel after its settlement in Canaan trades and crafts were hereditary in families. The priesthood* is the outstanding example of a hereditary profession. The archaeology of Palestinian sites shows that the large patriarchal family described in Gn appeared in Israel under the monarchy only in the royal palace and in the homes of the few wealthy nobles. The houses of the period of the monarchy are altogether too small for such huge family groups, even granted that one family perhaps had no more than one room in the house. The family as an institution experienced developments during the settlement and the monarchy which were not entirely wholesome. It was no longer a self-sufficient independent unit. Its size was limited by the economic conditions of life in cities and villages. While the Hebrews always retained a strong sense of blood kinship, a sense of kinship could not exert itself when families rapidly split into separate units. Cf also CHILD; FATHER; INHERITANCE; MARRIAGE; MOTHER.

Famine (Hb rā'āb) is mentioned frequently in the OT. Abraham* (Gn 12:10), Isaac* (Gn 26:1) and Jacob* (Gn 47:1) migrated to Egypt during famines in Canaan. Similar migrations of nomadic peoples are mentioned in ancient Egyptian records. Egypt also frequently experienced famine in ancient times, and famine is represented in Egyptian art (ANEP 101, 102). Famine could be caused in Canaan by lack of sufficient rain or in particular areas by plagues of locusts, blight, or mildew. Famine in Egypt could easily happen if the annual inundation of the Nile* were excessive or defective, or if the irrigation system was disturbed because of external or civil war. A famine is mentioned during the reign of David (2 S 21:1) and the description of the drought and famine in Je 14 probably reflects an actual event. Acute famine leading to cannibalism could happen in a city under siege (2 K 6:25 ff; 25:3). A famine caused by drought occurred during the reign of Ahab* (2 K 18:2). Migrations like that of Elimelech and his family to Moab (Rt 1:1) were probably frequent. Famine is mentioned frequently in Je as a weapon with which God punishes the sins of Israel, and only less frequently in Ezk. The other prophetic writings, however, contain few allusions to famine as a punishing weapon (Am 4:6). The famine during the reign of Claudius* (AD 41–54) is mentioned in AA 11:28. The famine occurred in the second year of the reign of Claudius and is mentioned by Tacitus, Suetonius, and Dio Cassius. The latter writer adds that the metropolitan center of Rome was in chronic danger of famine because all of its grain was imported from abroad, and shipping by sea was impossible during the winter months.

Farthing. Cf MONEY.

Fast. Abstention from food is found in many ancient and modern religions.

1. *OT.* In the Bible fasting does not appear as an ascetic practice but as a token of sorrow. Thus fasting is mentioned with sackcloth, ashes, and wailing among the ceremonies of mourning (1 S 31:13; 2 S 1:12; 3:35). Fasting is also a sign of repentance (1 S 7:6; Ne 9:1 ff; Je 14:12; Jl 1:14; 2:15 ff; Jon 3:8). Fasting also accompanies prayer in crisis or great need. David fasted when the son of Bathsheba* fell ill, but stopped his fasting when the child died (2 S 12:16 ff). His servants were astonished at this, since fasting was expected as a sign of mourning; but David explained that his fasting was part of his petition that the child might live. Cf also Pss 35:13; 69:11. Public fasts were sometimes proclaimed as part of public petitions; such was probably the fast mentioned in Jgs 20:26; 1 S 14:24; 1 K 21:9; Ezr 8:21–23; Je 14:12; 36:6, 9; Jon 3:5 ff. Moses and Daniel both fasted in preparation for the reception of divine revelation (Ex 34:28; Dt 9:9; Dn 9:3; 10:2 ff). No fast is prescribed in Israelite cultic law except the fast of the Day of Atonement (Lv 16:29 ff; 23:17 ff; Nm 29:7). After the fall of Jerusalem in 587 BC the disaster was commemorated by four fast days in the course of the year (Zc 7:3 ff; 8:19). The prophets sometimes speak unfavorably of fasting as a mere external observance without any interior sentiment (Is 58:1 ff; Je 14:12; Zc 7:5 ff). In Pharisaic Judaism fasting was very common and highly esteemed as an act of devotion. Fasting in the OT generally meant one day from sunrise to sunset. A fast of 72 hours is mentioned in Est 4:16. The fast during the daylight hours was total.

2. *NT.* Fasting is mentioned rarely in the NT. The attitude of Jesus toward fasting was casual and certainly different from the attitude of the Pharisees. When Jesus was asked why His own disciples did not fast (presumably because He did not impose it upon them) while the disciples of the Pharisees and of John the Baptist did, Jesus pointed out that fasting is not appropriate to times of joy, and He compared Himself to the bridegroom and His disciples to the companions of the groom. They were joyful because He was with them; and they would fast after His departure. In this passage fasting is a sign of mourning with no ascetical significance implied (Mt 9:14 ff; Mk 2:18 ff; Lk 5:33 ff). Jesus supposes that His disciples will fast; when they do so He wishes them to conceal it and to make no public display of their devotion (Mt 6:16). Jesus Himself fasted for 40 days before beginning His ministry; Christian tradition saw in this a resemblance to the fasting of Moses (Ex 34:28). The reference in the received text of the Gospels (Mk 9:29) to fasting with prayer as a means of exorcising evil spirits is not found in the critical text. Fasting is not mentioned as a cultic practice in the apostolic writings. It occurs only as accompanying a petition for divine assistance in making an important decision, such as the election of Paul and Barnabas at Antioch (AA 13:2 f) and the appointment of elders in the newly established churches of Asia (AA 14:23).

Fat. The fat and the blood* are the portions of the sacrificial animal which belong to the deity, the blood because it was the seat of life, the fat because it was considered the most desirable portion of the animal; it was offered as food. The fatty portions are enumerated in Lv 3–7 as the fat of the entrails, of the kidneys, and of the liver; in a few passages the fat of the tail is added. The fat is to be removed and burned on the altar. Fat is often mentioned in the OT as signifying the entire sacrificial victim (1 S 15:22; Is 1:11; 43:24 etc).

Father. 1. *OT.* I. Social. The father was the head of the Hb family in the OT with extensive rights. Quite probably in the early period the father possessed the power of life and death over his children; cf Judah's treatment of his daughter-in-law Tamar* (Gn 38:24). Normally the father had the right to arrange the marriages of his sons and daughters, although it appears that in Israel the wishes of the contracting parties were not disregarded; cf Isaac and Rebekah (Gn 24), Caleb and Achsah (Jgs 1:12 f), Samson (Jgs 14:2 f), Amnon and Tamar (2 S 13:13). Jacob's marriage with the daughters of Laban was accomplished without any consultation of his father (Gn 30: 15 ff). The right which was exercised by Jacob in conferring the rights of primogeniture upon Ephraim* instead of Manasseh*

(Gn 48:13 ff) and by David in preferring Solomon* to Adonijah* (1 K 1:30) is prohibited in Dt 21:15 ff. The law of Ex 21:7 supposes the right of a father to sell his daughter into slavery. Respect for father and mother is commanded in the decalogue: (Ex 20:12; Dt 5:16). Striking or insulting one's father or mother is a capital offense (Ex 21:15, 17; Lv 20:9). These punishments may be compared with the Code of Hammurabi, 195, where the son who strikes his father is punished by the cutting off of his hand. The Code strangely prescribes no punishment for the natural child who curses or insults his parents, but commands the removal of the tongue of the adopted child who denies his adoptive parents and the removal of the eye of the adopted child who abandons his adoptive parents for his natural parents (192, 193). According to Dt 21:18–21 death is the punishment for pertinacious rebellion against parental authority. The religious position of the father appears in the patriarchal stories, where he prays and offers sacrifice (Gn 12:7; 26:25; 33:20; 35:14). This early practice survived only in the Passover*, which was a domestic feast (Ex 12:1–14, 21–28).

II. Theological. A large number of Hb personal names* apply the title of father to the deity such as Joab, "Yahweh is father," Abiel or Eliab, "El is father," Absalom, "the father i.e., the god is peace." These Israelite names do not differ in number or type from similar names in Mesopotamia and Canaan. Yahweh is called the father of Israel. There is no trace in the OT of the term father applied to Yahweh as the begetter of the people; this idea seems to be applied in the allusion to Canaanite religion in Je 2:27. The title of father of Israel is a theological metaphor which expresses the love of father for his son (Ho 11:1). This love exhibits itself in His paternal care of Israel (Ex 4:22 f; Dt 1:31; 8:5; Is 43:6 f), in His compassion and forgiveness (Ps 103:13 f; Je 3:19; 31:9, 20; Ho 2:1). This paternal affection stands in contrast to the ungrateful rebellion of Israel (Is 1:2; 30:1). The paternity of Yahweh also signifies His creation of Israel as a people (Ex 4:22; Dt 32:6, 18 f; Is 63:16; 64:7). The paternity of Yahweh is a motive for observing His law (Dt 14:1). Only in Mal 1:6 is authority the primary motif of the title. The title also signifies the unity of Israel (Mal 2:10). The employment of the title in prayer (BS 23:1, 4; 51:10) has become rather colorless, but it reflects a more frequent use of the title in the last two pre-Christian centuries which can be traced in extrabiblical literature. Cf also WS 2:13, 16, 18; 5:5, where the title carries

no particular force. Yahweh adopted David and his descendants as His sons (2 S 7:14; 1 Ch 22:10; Pss 2:7; 89:27 f).

2. NT. I. Social. The family morality of the OT is presumed in the Gospels. Jesus adds an admonition against evading the duty of supporting one's parents through a form of casuistry permitted by the scribes (Mt 15:4–7; Mk 7:10–13; cf CORBAN). Children must leave their father, however, in order to follow the gospel (Mt 10:37; Lk 12:53; cf Mt 8:21; Lk 9:59; 14:26). Traditional morality is repeated and expanded in Eph 5:22–6:9. The head of the family must love his wife; children must obey their parents; and fathers must give their children a Christian education. Slaves must obey their masters, and masters must treat their slaves with compassion. Cf Col 3:18–4:1.

II. Theological. (a) Synoptic Gospels. It is evident from the texts cited above that Jesus did not introduce the concept of the fatherhood of God as something entirely new. It is, however, broadened and deepened. The concept of God as father includes the notion of paternal love and care (Mt 6:5–8, 26 ff; 7:11; 10:29–31; 18:14; Lk 11:13). The love of the Father in heaven is a model of the love with which the disciples should love even their enemies (Mt 5:43–45). The Father is the model of the perfection which the disciples should seek to attain (Mt 5:48). The Father likewise is an example of forgiveness (Mt 6:14 f; 18:35; Mk 11:25 f). Perhaps the supreme statement of God's paternal forgiveness appears in the parable of the prodigal son (Lk 15:11–32). The Father's love is accompanied by His authoritative will which imposes an obligation upon the disciples (Mt 7:21–23). Jesus often speaks of the Father with relation to Himself in a different tone from that which He uses in speaking of the Father in relation to the disciples. It is not without significance that most of these passages in which the distinction between "my Father" and "your Father" is explicit or implicit are concerned with the mission and authority of Jesus. One such passage occurs even in the infancy narratives (Lk 2:49; cf also Lk 22:29). The phrase "my Father" is most frequent in Mt (15:13; 16:17; 18:10, 19, 35; 20:23). The union of Jesus with the will of His Father is emphasized in the Passion account (Mt 26:39–43; Mk 14:35–39; Lk 22:41 f; 23:34, 46). The difference is clearest in Mt 11:25–27; Lk 10:21 f. Here Jesus thanks the Father for what He has revealed to the little ones and concealed from the wise and knowing. He then affirms that the Father has revealed Himself to the Son, i.e., Jesus, and that the Father and the Son know each other in a way which is not revealed and by implication cannot be revealed to any one else.

(b) John. In Jn the Father appears almost entirely as the Father of Jesus in contrast to the Father of the disciples. Jesus has a unique relationship with the Father, who communicates Himself to men through Jesus His Son and confers upon Him power and authority to execute His mission. Jesus is the only-begotten of the Father (1:14, 18); He is the object of the peculiar love of the Father (3:35; 5:20; 10:17). Jesus alone knows the Father (1:18; 6:46; 10:15), and Jesus and the Father are one (10:30). To know and to see Jesus is to know and to see the Father (14:7–9), because Jesus is in the Father and the Father in Jesus (10:38; 14:10). Jesus teaches what He has learned from the Father (8:28–38) and does the works of the Father (10:32; 14:10). No one can come to the Father except through Jesus (14:6). The Father is greater than Jesus (14:28), as the father is always superior to his son, and the sender to the one sent; but Jesus has received all power and authority from the Father (16:15), so that He can grant any request which the disciples may make (16:23). Jesus is sent by the Father and lives through the Father (6:57) and thus is able to communicate life to those who believe in Him; and He can send His disciples with the fullness of ·power, as He Himself was sent by the Father (20:21).

(c) Paul. God the Father is invoked in the exordium of each of the 13 epistles attributed to Paul and He is invoked as God our Father in the body of each of them except Gal, 1–2 Tm, Tt. The distinctive relationship of Jesus with the Father is asserted, especially when Jesus and the Father are joined in invocation (2 Co 1:3; Gal 1:1; Eph 1:3; Col 1:3). The Father is the Father of our Lord Jesus Christ (2 Co 1:3; Eph 1:3; Col 1:3). The characteristics of the divine paternity noted in the Gospels are usually implicit in Paul, but the use of the title shows that the understanding of the divine paternity was common to him and to the members of his churches.

Felix. Marcus Antonius Felix, freedman of Claudius* and brother of the notorious Pallas, freedman and favorite of Claudius, Roman procurator* of Palestine AD 52–59. Felix was married three times, twice to women of royal blood. His first wife was a granddaughter of Mark Anthony and Cleopatra, his second was the Jewish princess Drusilla*. The harshness and misgovernment of Felix was, in the opinion of historians, principally responsible for the permanent rebellion of the Jews against Rome which

issued in the war of AD 66–70. A number of insurrections occurred during his term of office; one of these, led by an Egyptian who claimed to be a prophet, is mentioned in AA 21:38. Felix was procurator at the time of Paul's arrest and imprisonment in AA 21–24, and with Drusilla granted Paul a personal interview. He would not release Paul without a bribe (AA 24:26), and Paul was still in prison when Felix was succeeded by Porcius Festus*. Felix was acquitted of charges laid against him by the Jews after his recall to Rome.

Festus. Porcius Festus, appointed by Nero, Roman procurator* of Judaea AD 60–61 (AA 24:27). Festus seems to have been an honorable man who made genuine efforts to resolve the growing conflict between the Jews and Rome; but his death in office after only two years frustrated all his efforts. Immediately after his arrival he granted Paul a hearing, and when Paul appealed to Caesar, Festus had him removed to Rome. He invited Agrippa* and Bernice* to hear a discourse of Paul (AA 25–26).

Fig. (Hb $t^e\bar{e}n\bar{a}h$, Gk $syk\bar{e}$ [tree], $sykon$ [fruit]). The fig is one of the most common trees of Palestine and its fruit is liked and plentiful. The tree grows to a height of 35–40 ft; it has spreading branches and broad, thick leaves which afford shade in the summer (Jn 1:48). They are often planted in vineyards, since they flourish in stony soil; "to sit under one's vine and one's fig with none to terrify" is a proverbial description of the peace and serenity of the peasant's life (1 K 5:5; Mi 4:4; Zc 3:10). The fruit is eaten fresh or dried; dried figs are made up into cakes (1 S 25:18; 30:12; 1 Ch 12:41), which were applied for soothing medicinal effects (2 K 20:7; Is 38:21). With the vine*, the olive*, and the pomegranate* it is one of the most common fruit trees mentioned in the Bible (Nm 13:23; 20:5; Dt 8:8; 2 K 18:31; Is 34:4; 36:16; Je 5:17; Ho 2:14; Jl 1:7; Hg 2:19; Am 4:9). In Jotham's parable of the trees the fig is one of the trees which serves mankind too well to leave off its services and become king (Jgs 9:10 f). The blossoms of the fig are a sign of spring (SS 2:13; Mt 24:32 f; Mk 13:28 f; Lk 21:29–31).

The fig tree appears in the parables of the overripe, rotten figs (Je 24:1 ff) and the barren fig tree (Lk 13:6–9); Jesus asks whether figs are gathered from thistles (Mt 7:16). The cursing of the fig tree by Jesus (Mt 21:18–22; Mk 11:12–14, 15–25) has long been a difficult passage, particularly because of Mk's note that it was not the season for figs. Many commentators observe that the fig tree carries fruit about 10 months of the year: (1) the green figs which appear with the first blossoms, many of which fall from the tree before ripening; these are the "first ripe figs," esteemed as most delicious (Mi 7:1), which fall easily from the trees (Na 3:12); (2) the late figs, which grow from August to winter. Other commentators with, it seems, greater probability, interpret the action of Jesus as entirely symbolic, with no reference to the quality of the tree itself; the fig tree which is bearing no fruit is a symbol of unbelieving Israel, which is cursed for its unbelief and remains barren.

Fire. 1. *OT*. Fire had its place in the cult. The fire on the altar of whole-burnt offerings was to burn perpetually (Lv 6:12 f), probably as a symbol of the presence of the deity (cf below and ALTAR). It is a means of purification of booty taken in battle (Nm 31:23). The symbolic cleansing of the lips of Isaiah is accomplished by fire (Is 6:6). Articles which have been consecrated but not used are to be burned to keep their holiness from being profaned, such as the remains of the Passover* lamb (Ex 12:10), the ram of priestly installation (Ex 29:34), the portions of the sin-offering (cf SACRIFICE) which in peace-offerings are given to the worshipers or the priests (Lv 4:11 f). The liturgical use of fire and its symbolism raises the question whether the punishment of certain offenses by burning (fornication by a betrothed widow, Gn 38:24; sexual intercourse by one man with a woman and her daughter, Lv 20:14; fornication by the daughter of a priest, Lv 21:9; theft of consecrated booty, Jos 7:15) is not also a ritual purification of the community from a particularly heinous moral stain. The same idea of purification may lie in the burning of cult utensils and images of foreign gods (Dt 7:5, 25; 2 K 23:4, 6, 11).

The "fire of God" (Jb 1:16), "fire from heaven" (2 K 1:10-14), and "fire of Yahweh" (Nm 11:1; 1 K 18:38) is the lightning*. Fire is often used metaphorically to signify anger, which always "burns" or "blazes." This is frequently said of the anger of Yahweh (Pss 79:5; 89:47; Je 4:4; 21:12; Ezk 21:36; 22:21, 31; Na 1:6; Zp 1:18 +). The fire of the smelting furnace is a common metaphor for tribulation, such as the sojourn in Egypt (Dt 4:20; 1 K 8:51; Je 11:4), especially tribulation which tests and separates the righteous from the wicked (Is 1:22, 25; Je 6:27 ff; Ezk 22:17-22; Mal 3:2).

Fire is an element in the theophanies*. The original place of this conception is probably the theophany of Sinai* (Ex 19:18 +), and it appears in Ex 3:2 (the burning bush); Ex 24:17; Jgs 6:21 (where it is the glory* of Yahweh; cf Ps 18:9, 13; Ezk 1:4, 13 f, 27). Fire is a sign of the presence of Yahweh, for fire is the element proper to deity. The pillar of fire of the exodus* traditions (Ex 13:21; 14:24; Nm 14:14) was a symbol of the divine presence in Israel. Yahweh is a consuming fire (Dt 4:24; 9:3; Is 33:14); this signifies His holiness* which makes it impossible for man to approach Him. Fire, however, may be a sign of His good pleasure and His acceptance of sacrifice (Gn 15:7; Lv 9:24; Jgs 6:21; 1 K 18:38). In view of these passages the statement in the theophany of Elijah* that Yahweh is not in the fire (1 K 19:12) seems to be a departure from the usual pattern. It is probably to be understood as a more reflective view of the theophanies, an explicit denial that Yahweh is to be identified with fire or any other natural phenomenon. In the context it also expresses the belief that Yahweh acts by other means more hidden than natural convulsions; even events whose course cannot be so easily traced are His work.

Fire is the element of judgment* by which Yahweh destroys the wicked: Sodom and Gomorrah (Gn 19:24), Nadab and Abihu (Lv 10:2), the messengers of Ahaziah (1 K 1:10 ff), the Israelites (Nm 11:1), the enemies of Israel (Am 1:4 ff), Egypt (Je 43:12), Judah (Am 2:5), Israel (Je 5:14; 11:16; 17:27; 21:14; Ezk 15:7; 24:9 f; Ho 8:14). It also appears in the eschatological judgment (Is 66:15; Ezk 38:22; 39:6; Jl 3:3; Mal 3:19).

The Qumran* texts repeat the OT ideas of the fire of purification and judgment.

2. *NT*. The NT continues the theological use of fire as in the OT. On the fires of punishment cf GEHENNA. Fire is the agent of God's judgment announced by John the Baptist (Mt 3:10; Lk 3:9; 3:17). Similar expressions are used by Jesus (Mt 7:19; 13:40; Lk 17:29; Jn 15:6, echoing Gn 19:24) and by the disciples (Lk 9:54, echoing 2 K 1:10).

The fire of eschatological signs and judgments is most frequent in Apc; cf 8:7 (echoing Ex 9:24); 8:8 (the blazing mountain); 9:17 (fire proceeds from the mouth of the four angels); 11:5 (fire from the olive trees and the lampstands). Mk 9:49, "Everyone must be salted with fire" is obscure. Many interpreters understand it of the eschatological fire of judgment. Since salt is a preservative, it can also be understood of the fire of testing. Lk 12:49, "I have come to bring fire on the earth and desire that it be kindled" is also understood by many of the eschatological fire of judgment; but it is, like Mk 9:49, a deliberate riddle. Here also the fire of testing seems more probable but also inadequate. The saying is perhaps too obscure to be an allusion to the fire of the theophanies and the symbol of the divine presence in the OT, but this allusion is possibly at the base of the saying. The fire of the eschatological judgment also appears in Heb 10:27. Heb 12:29 repeats the sentence that God is a consuming fire (cf above). 2 Pt 3:7 is the only NT writer to describe the eschatological fire as a universal end-conflagration; it is evident that 2 Pt and Apc refine the OT image of eschatological fire in the manner of midrash*. Fire is also a manifestation of glory (Apc 1:14; 2:18; 19:21). This is of some importance; in these texts, as in 2 Th 1:8, the fire of the OT theophany is transferred to Jesus Christ. Unless we understand Mk 9:49 and Lk 12:49 of the fire of testing, Paul is the only NT writer to refer to it (1 Co 3:13–15); this fire is clearly eschatological.

Firmament. The word is derived from the Lt *firmamentum,* which in turn represents the Gk *stereoma,* "a hard object." The word is used in most Eng Bibles to translate the Hb *rāki‘a,* which signifies a thin beaten metal plate. The Hb word signifies the sky and implies the ancient conception of the sky as a thin bowl-shaped surface which covers the earth. In its creation (Gn 1:6 f) the sky divides the waters of the lower abyss from the waters of the upper abyss (cf CREATION). Outside of Gn 1 the Hb word occurs only in Gn 17:20; Pss 19:2; 150:1; Dn 12:3; and in the description of the chariot in Ezk 1:22, 23, 25; 10:1.

Firstborn. In a polygamous family* firstborn can signify either the firstborn of the father or the firstborn of any particular wife. The position of the firstborn of the father was assured by the law of Dt 21:15–17, which forbade the father to prefer the firstborn of his favorite wife. The firstborn succeeded the father as head of the household and possessed patriarchal authority over his brothers and sisters (Gn 27:29, 37). He was also entitled to a special blessing* of his father (Gn 27:33–36). The patriarchal narratives, however, exhibit some instances in which the rights of primogeniture were conferred upon a younger son. Jacob acquired the rights of primogeniture by deception, but they were not taken from him. Jacob also reversed the positions of Ephraim and Manasseh (Gn 48:17–20). In the blessing of Jacob (Gn 49) the position of firstborn is ascribed to Judah, actually the fourth (49:8). Reuben was cursed because of his incest (49:3 f; cf Gn 35:22) and Simeon and Levi because of their crime

against the men of Shechem (Gn 34). The firstborn was conceived as "the first fruits of the manhood" of the father (Gn 49:3) and thus presumably he was more generously endowed with physical and mental qualities than the younger sons. The male firstborn of the mother, whether human or animal, belonged to Yahweh (Ex 13:2; 22:28 f; Dt 15:19). The animal was to be sacrificed if it were a sacrificial animal; otherwise it was to be redeemed or destroyed. The firstborn son was redeemed (Ex 34:19–20); the price was set in a later law at five shekels of silver (Nm 18:15–17). In another and still later and artificial conception the tribe of Levi was the ransom for the firstborn of all Israel (Nm 3:40–51). There is no evidence that the sacrifice of the firstborn son was ever practiced in Israel except as an aberration (cf SACRIFICE). The motivation of the offering of the firstborn (Ex 13:14–16) is the slaying of the firstborn in Egypt during the exodus. This is probably a later interpretation of the practice. The early view of the firstborn was more probably that the firstborn was sacred to Yahweh as opening the channel through which life flowed. The designation of firstborn does not imply subsequent children (cf Lk 2:7). Christ is called the firstborn of many brothers (Rm 8:29) as the founder of the Church, the community of the adopted children of God, and the firstborn of the dead, first to experience the glorious resurrection (Col 1:18; Apc 1:5). The title "firstborn of all creation" (Col 1:15) was an occasion of difficulty in the Arian controversies. The context, however, is evidently a denial that Christ is the same in dignity, character, and origin as created beings (Col 1:16–17), since it is in Him and for Him that all things were created. But the Son is here placed in a position between the Father and the created world (Col 1:13); a more precise definition of this position awaited the Christological controversies of the 4th century.

First fruits. The first fruits were sacred to Yahweh. The directions in the various Hb codes reflect differences in practice and a growing precision in the requirements for the offering. In Ex 23:19; 34:26 the first fruits of the soil are required. Dt 18:4 mentions first fruits of grain, wine, oil, and fleece. In Dt 26:1 f only a portion of the first fruits, enough to fill a basket, is required. In Lv 19:24 the first fruits of trees are required, but the trees must not be harvested for three years after the Israelites enter the land. Lv 23:9–11, 15–17 specifies sheaves of grain and loaves of bread. Nm 18:12 f mentions oil, wine, and grain, but it is to be eaten by the members of the family who are clean. Ezk 44:30 treats the first fruits as destined for the priests. The motivation of offering the first fruits is not expressed; and while it may be a thanks offering for the annual harvest, this does not appear in the text. It was perhaps conceived as sacred in the same sense in which the firstborn* was sacred. The only explicit motivation which accompanies their offering is the Credo of Dt 26:3–10, in which the offerer professes his thanks for the deliverance from Egypt and settlement in Canaan. By metaphor Israel is called the first fruits of Yahweh (Je 2:3). As the first to rise to a new life Christ is the first fruits of the dead (1 Co 15:20). Christians even in this life possess the first fruits of the spirit (Rm 8:23). The first generation of the Church is the first fruits of God (Js 1:18; Apc 14:4). Other Christians are called first fruits because they were the first to be converted (Rm 16:5; 1 Co 16:15).

Fish. Fish are found in the Mediterranean and in the Sea of Galilee and in the Jordan; the Sea of Galilee is particularly well stocked, and 26 species have been recorded there. Neither in OT nor in NT are species of fish distinguished. Clean* fish are those which have fins and scales (Lv 11:9 f); aquatic animals of any other kind are unclean. The skill of fishing and the use of fish as food was known in both Egypt and Mesopotamia from earliest times (cf NET; an Egyptian fishing boat, ANEP 109; an Assyrian representation of line fishing, ANEP 114). Fish were preserved either by salting or drying, and Nm 11:5 suggests that this

was an esteemed part of the diet. Fish were included among the topics of Solomon's wisdom (1 K 5:11). Line fishing was known to the Israelites (Jb 40:25; Is 19:8; Am 4:2; Hab 1:15). It is probably merely an accident that the consumption of fish is mentioned so rarely in the OT (Nm 11:5, 22). There was a Fish Gate at Jerusalem before and after the exile (2 Ch 33:14; Ne 3:3; 12:39; Zp 1:10) and a fish market in the time of Nehemiah (Ne 13:16). Historians think, however, that the importance of fish in the diet was less in pre-exilic Israel than it was in the postexilic, Hellenistic, and NT periods. Fish as food is mentioned more frequently in the NT (Mt 7:10; 14:17; 15:36; Mk 6:38; Lk 9:13; 11:11; 24:42; Jn 21:9–13). Many of the first disciples of Jesus were fishermen on the Sea of Galilee, where there was a flourishing fish industry in NT times. Two miraculous catches of fish are related in the Gospels (Lk 5:1–11; Jn 21:1–8). The story of the fish with the *statēr* in its mouth (Mt 17:27) probably alludes to the bream of the Sea of Galilee, which carries its young in its mouth.

Fish are mentioned among the divine images prohibited to the Israelites (Dt 4:18); but no cult of ichthyoid deities appears in ancient Egypt, Mesopotamia, or Canaan. The Babylonian priest Berossus of the 3rd century BC, who compiled Mesopotamian mythology in Gk, tells of the fish god Oannes who came out of the sea and taught men the arts and crafts of civilization. Oannes must be the Sumerian Enki (Akkadian Ea) to whom wisdom and the teaching of the arts are credited; but in Mesopotamian sources Enki-Ea, while a subaqueous deity,

Fishing with nets in Sea of Galilee.

is not represented or described as a fish. Two fish men appear in an Assyrian seal impression of a cultic scene standing near the sacred tree (ANEP 706); but the literature affords no identification of their character.

Flax. Cf LINEN.

Flesh. 1. *OT*. Hb has no word which literally designates the living body, and "flesh" in many contexts comes nearer to this meaning than any other word. Flesh and *nepeš* (cf SOUL) designate the whole living man* (Jb 14:22; Is 10:18), sometimes as the seat of emotion (Ps 63:2). The totality is also expressed by flesh and heart*; in this phrase the emotional totality is emphasized (Ps 16:9; 84:3). The flesh, like *nepeš*, sometimes means the conscious self (Pr 14:30; 4:22; Ps 16:9 f; Ec 5:5).

Flesh designates kindred in a very concrete sense; all the members of a single kinship group have one flesh, which is conceived as a collective reality possessed by all (Gn 29:14; Jgs 9:2; 2 S 5:1; 19:13 f; Ne 5:5; Is 58:7). The community of flesh is a motive why kinsmen should not harm one another, for they harm their own flesh (Gn 37:37). Man recognizes that woman is flesh of his flesh (Gn 2:23); this does not express kinship, but community of species. Woman is unique, appearing nowhere else in nature, a help "corresponding to man" (Gn 2:18, 20). When a woman marries she becomes one flesh with her husband (Gn 2:24); she is now a member of his kinship group.

It is rare that flesh is used to express delicacy and sensitivity, as it is when Ezk contrasts Israel's heart of stone with the heart of flesh which Yahweh will give it (Ezk 11:19; 36:26). When flesh is mentioned in contrast to spirit or to the divine, it connotes the weakness and the mortality of man (Gn 6:3). When one is assured of the help of God, flesh can do one no harm (Ps 56:5). Because man is flesh and mortal, Yahweh has compassion on him (Ps 78:39). God does not have eyes of flesh, like man, and His vision is not limited (Jb 10:4). Israel's enemies oppose an arm of flesh to the power of Yahweh (2 Ch 32:8). The man who makes flesh his arm is cursed (Je 17:5). The Egyptians are men, not gods, and their horses are flesh, not spirit (Is 31:3).

"All flesh" designates all living beings (Gn 6:17, 19; 7:21; 9:11, 15–17; Lv 17:14; Nm 18:15; Ps 136:25; Jb 34:15) or all animals (Gn 7:15 f; 8:17). When it designates all mankind, it is almost never a neutral expression, but it contrasts the weakness and mortality of man to God. When the total depravity of mankind is mentioned, man is called "all flesh" (Gn 6:12 f). Mankind, "all flesh," has never before heard the voice of God (Dt 5:23). All flesh must come to God because of sins (Ps 65:3). An unusual title of Yahweh, "God of the spirits of all flesh" (Nm 16:22; 27:16) salutes Him as the master of life and death. When mankind sees the glory of God, it is called "all flesh" (Is 40:5); for all flesh is grass which withers, but the word of Yahweh endures forever (Is 40:6–8). Similarly all flesh shall know that Yahweh is the savior of Israel (Is 49:26); this revelation discloses not only the power and majesty of Yahweh but the powerlessness of man. It is as all flesh that man meets the judgment of Yahweh (Is 66:16; Je 25:31). Because man is sinful, no flesh shall have peace (Je 12:12). When Yahweh asserts His unlimited power, He calls Himself the God of all flesh, which cannot resist Him (Je 32:27). He brings evil upon all flesh (Je 45:5), bares His sword against all flesh (Ezk 21:9 f), and all flesh shall see that Yahweh has kindled the fire of judgment (Ezk 21:4). In His hand is the spirit of all flesh of man (Jb 12:10). Jl 3:1 departs somewhat from the usual associations of the word when he affirms that Yahweh will pour out His spirit upon all flesh; for the flesh is generally an object of threat and judgment rather than of promise. When "all flesh" is invited to bless the name of Yahweh (Ps 145:21), to worship Him (Is 66:23), to be silent before Him (Zc 2:17), the term is not neutral; it is the awareness of his flesh that impels man to blessing, adoration, and silence before Him who is not flesh and therefore is neither weak nor mortal.

Flesh is not conceived in philosophical terms as the material component opposed to the formal or the spiritual; it designates properties of man's nature which can be summed up radically as man's corruptibility. Corruptibility may be either physical or moral; the OT does not distinguish sharply between one and the other, for the one leads to the other.

2. *NT*. The flesh is the subject of illness (2 Co 12:7; Gal 4:13), of suffering (1 Pt 4:1), of circumcision (Rm 2:28; Gal 6:13; Eph 2:11; Col 2:13). None of these expressions is entirely neutral; the suffering of the flesh is, like the flesh itself, transitory; and a religious sign which exists only in the flesh has no lasting reality. Paul insists on the essentially carnal and impermanent nature of Judaism; cf below. The flesh is also the subject of the sexual urge (Jn 1:13); in this passage the urge is viewed neutrally in its morality, but it is contrasted with the

birth to a new life created by the will of God.

It is remarkable that Jn 6:51–56 uses flesh in speaking of the Eucharist* rather than body*. The flesh is not identical with the body, as the texts cited below illustrate; and the connotations of flesh are such as to set the language of Jn rather clearly against the language of the Synoptic Gospels and Paul. W. Bauer points out that Ignatius of Antioch speaks of flesh in the Eucharistic context because of his desire to eliminate Docetism, the heresy which denied the physical reality of the body of Christ. It seems probable that the same emphasis lies behind Jn's choice of flesh rather than body to emphasize the realism of the sacrament. I Jn 4:2 makes the confession that Jesus has come in the flesh a test of genuine faith; and this suggests an implicit controversy with Docetism. The flesh as designating the physical reality of the body is also seen in Col 2:1, where the flesh means the physical presence of the person. When Jn says somewhat paradoxically in the same context that the spirit gives life, while the flesh avails nothing (Jn 6:63), he adds a necessary element to his exposition of the Eucharist*. The incarnation is the first step in a process of salvation which is completed by the coming of the Spirit*, without whom there could be no Eucharist.

The same emphasis on the physical reality of the incarnation is expressed elsewhere by the use of flesh. Jesus is manifested in the flesh (1 Tm 3:16). He has come in the flesh (1 Jn 4:2), and in the classic formula of Jn 1:14 the word became flesh. It is particularly apt to speak of the flesh when the atoning suffering and death of Jesus are mentioned, for the flesh is the subject of suffering. Jesus abolished the law in His own flesh to create a new man (Eph 2:15). He has opened the way for us through His flesh (Heb 10:20). He suffered and was put to death in the flesh (1 Pt 3:18; 4:1).

Flesh and blood designate the totality of human nature; but here, as in the OT, the designation is not neutral. Peter did not receive his revelation from flesh and blood but from the Father (Mt 16:17). Paul did not confer with flesh and blood about his gospel (Gal 1:16); he received it by revelation. The warfare of the Christian is not against flesh and blood but against spiritual enemies (Eph 6:12).

Flesh designates human nature as a principle of generation. Abraham is the ancestor of the Jews in the flesh (Rm 4:1; cf Heb 12:9), and the Jews are Paul's kinsmen according to the flesh (Rm 9:3; 11:14). The carnal descent of Jesus from the Jews is also emphasized (Rm 8:3; 1:3; 9:5); but here Paul is less concerned with affirming

the reality of the incarnation against Docetism than he is with denying that mere association according to the flesh has anything to do with salvation in Christ. The Jews are children of Abraham according to the flesh, but the Christians are children of the promise (Rm 9:8; Gal 4:23).

To be in the flesh or to live in the flesh is to live in the present life, subject to weakness and mortality (2 Co 10:3; Gal 2:20; Phl 1:22, 24; 1 Pt 4:2). In the flesh one experiences tribulations (1 Co 7:28), and in the flesh Paul fills up what is lacking in the sufferings of Christ (Col 1:24). But even in this mortal flesh the life of Jesus is manifested in us through our sufferings (2 Co 4:11).

When human nature is called flesh, it is signified in the state of unregenerate nature, in its earthly and secular condition. The world has those who are wise, powerful, and noble according to the flesh (1 Co 1:26). The master is superior to his slave only in the flesh (Eph 6:5; Col 3:22). Confidence in any human or worldly qualities, or boasting of such qualities, is confidence in the flesh (2 Co 11:18; Phl 3:3 f). The worldly man desires to make a display in the flesh (Gal 6:12). Hence Paul by a somewhat daring statement affirms that he regards no one according to the flesh, not even Christ (2 Co 5:16); this thought is obscure, but Paul at least alludes to the carnal descent of Jesus from the Jews. More probably he implies also that Christ means simply nothing to "the flesh," i.e., to secular and unregenerate human nature. To judge according to the flesh is to judge by external features (Jn 8:15). Paul recommends Onesimus* to Philemon* as "dear both in the flesh and in the Lord," as a member of the household of Philemon and as a member of the same Christian fellowship (Phm 16).

Against this background, which emphasizes certain OT uses of the word, the NT goes beyond the OT in making the flesh the subject of sin, and identifying "the flesh" with man as sinner; and this is the most common use of the word in the NT. Even Jesus was sent in the likeness of sinful flesh (Rm 8:3). The flesh is weak (which means morally weak, Rm 6:19); in the flesh nothing good dwells (Rm 7:18), with the flesh one serves the law of sin (Rm 7:25). Walking in the flesh is sin, opposed to walking in the spirit (Rm 8:4); life in the flesh is thinking in the flesh, opposed to life and thought in the spirit (Rm 8:5). To set the mind on the flesh is death, it is enmity to God; the flesh cannot please God (Rm 8:6 f). He who lives according to the flesh will die (Rm 8:13). Christian liberty must not become an opportunity for the flesh (Gal

5:13); those who belong to Christ crucify the flesh with its passions and desires (Gal 5:24). The indulgences of the flesh must be checked (Col 2:23). The Galatians have begun in the spirit, but they are ending in the flesh (Gal 3:3); it is clear from the context of Gal that "the flesh" here does not signify what are now called "carnal vices," i.e., sins "of the flesh," but errors in faith. So the desires of the flesh which are opposed to the desires of the spirit are not merely sexual concupiscence (Gal 5: 16 f). He who sows for his flesh reaps corruption, but he who sows for the spirit reaps eternal life (Gal 6:8). Flesh and spirit are contrasted as this life and life eternal (Jn 3:6). The lust of the flesh with the lust of the eyes and pride is one of the capital vices (1 Jn 2:16). The works of the flesh are sins (Gal 5:19), and the passions of the flesh are sinful desires (Eph 2:3; 2 Pt 2:18); to walk according to the flesh is to sin (2 Co 10:2). "The will of the flesh" is a vacillating and indecisive will (2 Co 1:17). By a paradox Paul can speak of "the mind of flesh" (Col 2:18), which is a proud mind. The body of flesh in this sense is put off in Christian baptism, the circumcision of the Christian (Col 2:11). In the same sense flesh and blood cannot inherit the kingdom of God (1 Co 15:50); this line is certainly not a denial of the resurrection of the body, which Paul is at pains to assert, but an affirmation that the risen body cannot be a body of flesh, understanding flesh as the subject of sin. It must become a "spiritual" body (cf SPIRIT).

The adjective "carnal" is used in the same senses. The carnal is synonymous with the worldly (1 Co 3:3). Carnal wisdom is opposed to the grace of God (2 Co 1:12). Carnal passions war against the soul (1 Pt 2:11). Where there is jealousy and strife, Christians act like carnal men (1 Co 3:3). Though Christians live in the flesh, they are not carrying on a war in the flesh; for their weapons are not carnal but have divine power (2 Co 10:3 f). Christians have resources which the flesh does not confer, in order that they may achieve a victory which is beyond the power of the flesh.

In the NT as in the OT the flesh must not be conceived as synonymous with the body, nor in any philosophical sense as the material component. The flesh is the psychophysical complex of man not in abstraction but in its concrete existent totality, historical man with his past and with his concupiscence and sin. To think of the flesh as merely the material component can lead and has led Christians to a false ascetical and mystical ideal which conceives that man is to be spiritualized by being dematerialized. A study of the ideas of flesh and spirit shows that this fragment of Platonism has no place in the NT scheme of salvation; and by the same study it becomes clear that there is an impassable chasm between the salvation of the NT and the salvation of the Gnostic cults (cf KNOWLEDGE).

Flood. Cf DELUGE.

Flower. After the winter rains in Palestine and in the desert areas on its fringes the usually bare and stony ground is literally covered with large masses of an enormous variety of flowers. The beauty of this display is one of the rare features of the Palestinian landscape; it is literally rare, for these flowers are withered within two weeks. Hence the biblical allusions to flowers, which appear in the spring (SS 2:12), almost entirely use them as figures of the transitory and impermanent (Ps 103:15; Jb 14:2; Is 5:24; 18:5; 40:6–8; Na 1:4; Js 1:10 f). The figure of the city of Samaria, "the fading flower of glorious beauty" (Is 28:1), is particularly striking. Floral decorations on the lampstand (Ex 25:31; 37:17) and on the paneling and doors of the temple (1 K 6:18, 29, 32, 35) were the work of Phoenician craftsmen and are paralleled in other ancient Near Eastern decorations. Few flowers are mentioned by specific names, cf separate articles.

Flute. Cf MUSIC.

Fly. It is surprising that the fly is mentioned so rarely in the Bible. Dead flies cause perfume to stink (Ec 10:1); Yahweh hisses to bring the fly from Egypt against Judah (Is 7:18); fly here means the Egyptian troops. The deity Beelzebub* (lit "lord of the flies") is in all probability a corruption of another name. The word "fly" is not used to designate the 4th of the plagues of Egypt (Ex 8:21, 24, 29; Pss 78:45; 105:31), but a word which designates a swarm of insects.

Fool. 1. *OT.* The word fool renders a group of Hb words ('ᵉwîl; kᵉsîl; nābāl) but the Eng translation is not entirely accurate. The fool in the OT is one who is witless, but the words imply much more than a lack of intelligence. Folly in the OT is malicious, and the malice comes from the fact that the fool rejects wisdom. According to the teaching of the sages of Israel, which here no doubt represents the ordinary Israelite view, all young men are fools, and they can acquire wisdom only by listening to the instruction of their elders, in particular of their parents. Through this instruction they will become wise; if they reject it they will become confirmed in their folly. Thus for the sages all mankind is divided into two classes, the wise and the fools, and they do not envisage a passage from one class to the other. Since wisdom is a gift of Yahweh and consists in the fear of Yahweh, the fool Ḣas no fear of Yahweh. The malice of the fool appears in the description of the fool in wisdom literature. The mouth of the fool by its unrestrained speech causes ruin (Pr 10:14). The fool is stingy to his household and so reaps the wind (Pr 11:29). The fool is wise in his own eyes (Pr 12:15) and self-assured (Pr 14:6). He is quick to show his anger (Pr 12:16). He scorns his father's instruction (Pr 15:5). He is quarrelsome (Pr 20:3). There is no hope of his reform (Pr 27:22), and he cannot attain wisdom (Pr 24:7). He squanders wealth (Pr 21:20) and thinks it is sport to do wrong (Pr 10:23). He is obdurate in evildoing (Pr 13:19) and denies that there is a God who watches and judges (Pss 14:1; 53:2). Israel in its rebellion against Yahweh is foolish (Je 4:22; Dt 32:6). Certain heinous crimes are called folly "in Israel:" the rape of Dinah (Gn 34:7), the fornication of an unmarried girl (Dt 22:21), the theft of devoted objects by Achan (Jos 7:15), the rape of the Levite's wife by the men of Gibeah (Jgs 19:23 ff; 20:10), and the rape of Tamar by Amnon (2 S 13:12). Nabal* is called a fool according to his name (1 S 25:25) for his churlish refusal to grant hospitality to David and his men. Thus the fool is regarded as morally corrupt, unprincipled, and irreligious.

2. *NT.* The OT conception of folly is to some extent reflected in the Gk terms of the NT (*mōros; aphrōn; asynetos; anoētos*), although the word has been weakened in its force. The severe penalty which Jesus lays upon the use of the word as invective (Mt 5:22) creates an exegetical problem. The severity of His words may be explained if one understands fool here as it is understood in the OT. But it seems doubtful that any climax is intended in the triple denunciation of anger, the use of the word *raca**, and the use of the word fool, all three of which are roughly equivalent. The climax is rather in the punishment which is threatened; and the point of the saying is that Jesus is not, like the Pharisees, satisfied with the minimum observance of the prohibition of murder. Other lesser crimes against the human person such as anger and insult, which arise from the same hatred as murder, are also worthy of severe punishment. Jesus Himself spoke of the foolish man who built his house upon sand (Mt 7:26) and of the foolish virgins who forgot to provide oil for their lamps (Mt 25:2 ff); folly here

is improvidence. When Jesus called the Pharisees blind fools (Mt 23:17, 19), the word here seems to reflect the OT conception. A similar connotation seems to be reflected in the rebuke to the Pharisees who are fools because they clean the outside of the dish but not the inside (Lk 11:40) and in the designation of fool for the man in the parable who fills his barns and makes no provision for his impending death (Lk 12:20). The rebuke seems gentler, and a different word is used, when the disciples are called "without understanding," "witless," for failing to understand the parable of the leaven of the Pharisees (Mt 15:16; Mk 7:18), and when the two disciples on the road to Emmaus are called "foolish and slow of wit" (Lk 24:25) for not understanding that the Messiah had to suffer. Paul called the Galatians "senseless" (Gal 3:1, 3) for accepting a teaching about the law which detracted from the redeeming value of the death of Jesus. The play on the words wise-fool and wisdom-folly which runs through 1 Co 1:18–27 presupposes the Gk conception of wise-wisdom which signifies philosophy rather than OT wisdom. To the educated Gk the gospel was the folly of the cross. Paul in irony accepts these designations and affirms that the folly of God is the wisdom of men and the wisdom of God is the folly of men, and he makes no effort to reconcile the gospel and the cross with Gk philosophy. Cf also 1 Co 3:18; 4:10. The man is foolish (*aphrōn*) who because of philosophical difficulties refuses to accept the doctrine of the resurrection (1 Co 15:36). *Anoētoi* in Rm 1:14 seems to signify simply the uneducated. In Rm 1:21 the "witless mind" of the heathens is shown by their refusal to recognize the reality of God. Paul himself apparently was charged with being foolish (*aphrōn*; 2 Co 11:16–19; 12:6, 11). Here again Paul in irony accepts the charge and admits that he was foolish in submitting to such toils and persecutions and in giving such devotion to his apostolic duties. This is the folly of the cross. In general the NT conception agrees with the OT conception that folly is malice rather than lack of wit and that the fool is foolish because he chooses to be so and refuses the wisdom of God communicated by Jesus Christ.

Foot. Like other parts of the body, the foot often represents by synecdoche the person or the character of the person. The foot is a symbol of power and to place one's enemies at one's foot or under one's foot is a token of victory (Jos 10:24; 2 S 22:39; 1 K 5:17; Pss 8:7; 18:39; 47:4; 110:1; Mal 3:21). To place the foot upon land was a sign of possession (Dt 11:24; Jos 1:3; 14:9).

The slipping or stumbling of the foot signifies calamity (Dt 32:35; Pss 38:17; 66:9; 121:3; Jb 12:5; Je 13:16). The slipping of the foot in Ps 73:2 signifies weakening in faith. The direction of the foot indicates the character of the person as turned toward evil (Pr 1:16; 6:18; Jb 31:5; Is 59:7) or in the direction of the law of Yahweh (Pss 119:59, 101; Pr 4:27; Is 58:13). God also is described as having feet. The 24 elders saw the footstool under His feet (Ex 24:10) and His feet are said to stand upon storm clouds (2 S 22:10; Ps 18:10). The ark* was called His footstool (1 Ch 28:2; Pss 99:5; 132:7). The royal footstool in Egypt was decorated with the symbols of the enemies of Egypt. In the OT the feet are occasionally a euphemism for the sexual organs (Ex 4:25; Is 6:2; 7:20). "To cover the feet" (Jgs 3:24; 1 S 24:4) is a polite expression for providing for the needs of nature, and probably describes the posture. In the NT also the foot is used as synonymous with the person (Lk 1:79; Heb 12:13 +). The foot is also a symbol of power, but the symbol is used almost entirely of Christ in His eschatological victory, illustrated by the use of OT texts (AA 2:35; 1 Co 15:25–27; Eph 1:22; Heb 1:13; 2:8; 10:13). The posture of sitting at the feet of another, which is the position of the disciple before his master, is mentioned in AA 22:3. To shake the dust of a place from one's feet signifies repudiation (Mt 10:14; Mk 6:11; Lk 9:5; AA 13:15). In the Gospels people frequently cast themselves at the feet of Jesus. This is more than a gesture of ordinary politeness; it is a recognition of His extraordinary dignity and power. It is the position of the petitioner and of the subject before his sovereign. It is not, however, clearly a profession of faith in His divinity; cf Mt 15:30; Mk 5:22; 7:25; Lk 8:41; 17:16; Jn 11:32. Baring the feet to enter a holy place is mentioned in Ex 3:5; Jos 5:13–15. The inference is legitimate that this was the common practice for entering a sanctuary, although it is not mentioned elsewhere. Priests were to wash their feet before entering the sanctuary (Ex 30:19–21). The washing of the feet when one entered a house was necessary, since people walked barefoot or in sandals, and it was the duty of the host to offer this courtesy to his guests (Lk 7:44). The service of washing the feet was performed by the sinful woman for Jesus (Lk 7:36–50) and by Jesus for His disciples (Jn 13:1–16). The symbolism was explained by Jesus Himself in the latter episode as a lesson that none of His disciples should be too proud to perform mean services for each other, since this duty was usually performed by slaves, and that no dignity excused anyone from devotion to the service of others.

Forgiveness. 1. *OT.* That Yahweh is forgiving is a commonplace in the OT (Ex 34:7; Nm 14:18; Pss 99:8; 103:3; Dn 9:19; Mi 7:18–20). The forgiving character of Yahweh is conceived in anthropomorphic terms (cf Gn 50:17; 1 S 15:25; 25:28). It is noteworthy that Samuel is once asked to forgive a fault against Yahweh (1 S 15:25). Prayers for forgiveness are common (Ex 10:17; 32:32; 34:9; Ps 25:11 +). Often the prayer for forgiveness contains no explicit motive which is adduced for forgiveness; the forgiving character of Yahweh is enough to justify such a prayer. He is asked to forgive according to His great covenant love (Nm 14:19) and once rather pathetically to forgive Jacob because Jacob is so small (Am 7:2). The conditions for forgiveness explicitly mentioned in Ho 14:3 are confession of sin, conversion from sin, and prayer for forgiveness; cf these elements in Ps 32:1–5; Is 55:7; Je 14:20; 36:3; cf also the formal prayer for forgiveness in Pss 6 + 51. It is possible also that Yahweh will forgive a guilty group because of the righteousness of some members of the group. Thus Abraham asks the forgiveness of Yahweh for Sodom and Gomorrah if as few as ten righteous men can be found in these cities (Gn 18:26–32), and Yahweh asks Jeremiah whether even one righteous man can be found in Jerusalem for whose sake He might pardon the city (Je 5:1). Sometimes Yahweh is said not to forgive. In such passages a lack of the conditions mentioned is implied or expressly stated (Ho 1:6). Yahweh will not forgive Judah because of its pride (Is 2:9), or Israel because of its rebellion (Ex 23:21) or because it has renounced Yahweh for other gods (Dt 29:19; Je 5:7) or because of its obduracy in evil (2 K 24:4). Forgiveness meant restoration to former favor (Ex 33:15). The sin was forgotten or not reckoned against the sinner. The punishment, however, might not be entirely dismissed; David's sin was forgiven and his own life was spared, but the sin is punished by the death of the child of Bathsheba (2 S 12:13). Forgiveness of sin is one of the features of the messianic future (Is 33:8, 24; Je 31:34). The OT knows no forgiveness which is obtained by cultic propitiation for sins of formal guilt, and forgiveness is obtained through cultic rites only for ritual and inadvertent faults (Lv 4:22–6:7). The same term "forgive" which is used of sin is also used of Yahweh's forgiving vows made by a wife but annulled by her husband (Nm 30:6, 9, 13).

2. *NT.* John the Baptist preached the baptism of repentance for the remission of

sins (Mk 1:4; cf BAPTISM). Jesus Himself claimed and exercised the power to forgive sins; when this power was challenged He vindicated it by an appeal to His power to heal. It was clearly understood to be a divine power which He claimed (Mt 9:2 ff; Mk 2:5 ff; Lk 5:20 ff). In this episode Jesus forgave sins because of the faith of the petitioner. Faith is also a disposition of forgiveness in AA 10:43; 26:18. The sinful woman was forgiven many sins because of the greatness of her love (Lk 7:47). Repentance is implicit in these passages and is explicit in the apostolic preaching (Lk 24:47; AA 2:38; 5:31; 8:22). The forgiveness of sins is prominent in the primitive preaching of the apostles (AA 2:38; 5:31; 10:43; 13:38; 26:18). The Christian knows salvation through the forgiveness of sins (Lk 1:77). The forgiveness of sins is a work of God's patience (Rm 3:25). The essential difference between the OT and the NT conceptions lies in the fact that in the NT forgiveness of sins comes through Christ (AA 13:38; Eph 1:7; Col 1:14; 1 Jn 2:12). The forgiveness comes through Christ not only by His own personal forgiveness as in Mt 9:2; Mk 2:5; Lk 5:20 but is also gained through His redeeming death. This appears in the eucharistic formula of Mt 26:28; but it is not found in the eucharistic formulae of Mk and Lk. The redeeming death of Jesus stands in contrast to the sacrifices of the OT (cf above). The forgiveness which is obtained through the redeeming death of Christ annuls the sacrifices of the Law (Heb 9:22; 10:18). Confession of sins as a step toward forgiveness is mentioned explicitly in AA 19:18; Js 5:16; 1 Jn 1:9. Forgiveness is also gained through the prayers of the Church (Js 5:15 f). Throughout the NT it is presupposed that forgiveness is a free gift of God, not due to the merit or the repentance of the sinner, and not to be obtained by the sinner except through Christ. An exception to forgiveness is the sin against the holy spirit (Mt 12:32; Mk 3:28 f; Lk 12:10). The sin is not identified; in the context it can scarcely be anything but the sin of the Pharisees for which they are not forgiven (Mk 4:12). No other reason for the omission of this latter passage in Mt and Lk appears except its apparent harshness. These evangelists, however, retain the passage concerning the sin against the holy spirit. This was the sin by which the Pharisees not only rejected the revelation of God through Jesus, but attributed His power to the evil spirit; this is to reject the very motive of credibility. As a corollary of God's forgiveness Jesus deduces the duty of Christians to forgive one another (Mt 6:14; Mk 11:25; Lk 17:3 f). This virtue is made a

condition of obtaining forgiveness of one's own sins from God, and the duty is emphasized in the parable of the unjust servant (Mt 18:21–35).

Jesus conferred upon the Twelve the power to forgive sins (Jn 20:21–23). This can only be understood in the light of the personal power exercised by Jesus (cf above). This power is communicated through their reception of "a holy spirit," symbolized by the breath of Jesus upon them. They are therefore empowered to perform the kind of forgiving act described in Mk 2:5 ff etc, although this power does not appear in Jn. The antithesis "forgive-retain" contains a play on the word *aphienai,* which means not only to forgive, but also to release from one's grasp; retain, *kratein,* also means to retain within one's grasp, hence to deny forgiveness.

Fortifications. Throughout most OT history fortifications were erected to defend a small site against a small attacking force. Before the Assyrian campaigns of the 9th and 8th centuries the attacking force had no offensive tactics except undermining the walls and direct assault; cf SIEGE. The Assyrians introduced the ram. The most important element in fortifications, especially in early periods, was the choice of the site. The desirable site lay on an eminence, preferably with steep slopes, and had a perennial spring. The early city walls followed the contours of the slope; often the area thus enclosed was quite limited, as little as 5–10 acres. The walled city proper, however, was the center of an extended cluster of villages in which dwelt the peasants who cultivated the soil; and a large number of houses were built immediately outside the wall. In time of war this scattered population was crowded within the walls.

A precise date for fortifications is usually difficult to determine, since it is impossible to date masonry by itself. Furthermore, most fortifications exhibit several phases of remodeling, and the fortifications are never preserved to any great extent. It seems that the earliest form of city wall was a simple vertical stone structure. The glacis of earth outside the wall was in use in the early period; this made it more difficult for the attackers to mine the wall. For the same reason the walls were built upon bedrock. The excavations of Jericho directed by Kathleen Kenyon 1951–1958 have disclosed a massive system of fortifications earlier than 5000 BC, much older than any remains of fortifications discovered elsewhere. The fortifications consisted of a wall of large undressed stones which had a vertical outside face but a terraced inside face. Miss

Assyrian representations of city walls and towers.

Kenyon estimates that the wall originally stood 15–20 ft high. Before the outside face was a fosse cut in the rock about 30 ft wide and 10 ft deep. A massive defensive tower was included in the defense system. The tower was round and about 30 ft in diameter and is a remarkably skillful work in the masonry of large stones. As yet there is nothing in Palestinian archaeology to compare with the fortifications of prepottery Neolithic Jericho. The fortifications of the Middle Bronze period — a period known for other reasons to be the most prosperous period of ancient Palestine — were the most massive and elaborate of ancient Palestinian history. In the Middle Bronze period the erection of towers and bastions at gates and corners became common, and the modification of the walls by recesses and salients in order to permit the defenders to set up a crossfire of missiles on an assaulting force came into use. This type of construction became more common in the Iron Age. Everyone participated in the defense; the death of Abimelech* from a millstone thrown by a woman was proverbial (Jgs 9:53 ff; 2 S 11:20–21). Many of the Middle Bronze walls were extremely thick, as much sometimes as 16–24 ft. Such walls were usually not single walls, but double walls filled with rubble. The stones of the Middle Bronze period were rough and unfitted, and the gaps left in the courses were chinked with smaller stones. The late Middle Bronze period saw the introduction of a new, more complex and more effective fortification. This was basically an earthwork of extreme thickness with a sloping outer face. The earthwork was covered with stones and the sloping outer face with a pavement of stones called a revetment. This made it necessary for the attacking force to advance at a slow pace over a smooth and slippery surface without any effective cover. The summit of the revetment was equipped with another rampart, of which very few vestiges remain in any site; in at least some sites this upper rampart was made more difficult still by an outer bulge. The revetment was faced with a fosse and a counterscarp with a perpendicular wall. The *migdol* (tower; cf Jgs 9:46 ff) was an inner citadel, itself again fortified with extremely massive walls and towers, into which the defending force could retire if the outer walls were breached. Some think that the Millo* of Jerusalem was such a citadel.

The fortifications which can be assigned with any certainty to premonarchic Israel are of poor quality, much inferior to the massive Middle Bronze fortifications. This is attributed by scholars with great probability to the different social structure of the Israelites of the period. The Israelites at the time of their entrance into Canaan were a pastoral people organized in clans and tribes. The Canaanites with a city culture some centuries old had forced labor and slave labor with which massive fortifications could be erected. The premonarchic Israelites did not draft their own members for such tasks. The fortifications of Israelite cities before the monarchy consisted of the Canaanite fortifications, generally deteriorated, rebuilt and remodeled. Strong large scale fortifications were not erected in Israel before David, perhaps not before Solomon, who is credited in Israelite tradition with the introduction of

forced labor (1 K 9:21 f; 12:4, 10 f). The first fortifications built of fitted and bonded stones are attributed to Solomon; this type of construction appears at Megiddo* and Gezer*. The introduction of this improved technique of masonry made the thick walls of the Middle Bronze period unnecessary. The use of the double or even the triple wall also appears in the fortifications of the monarchy. Such multiple walls were not always planned; they were often the result of an expansion or contraction of the site within a new wall. The older wall was left standing or remodeled. The casemated wall is attributed to the Hittites. In this type of construction the double wall filled with stones and rubble is divided into compartments by transverse walls. Should the assaulting force breach the outer wall, their maneuvers are then confined within the cramped space of the compartment, where they were an easy target for missiles. The use of bricks* in fortifications, in spite of their weakness compared to stone, appears not only in early levels of settlement but also in the period of the monarchy. The brick wall, insufficient in itself, was erected upon a foundation of stones and was often if not generally built into a double wall, sometimes casemated. With the beginning of the Greek and Roman periods the types of fortifications used in Palestine were those imported by the Greeks and Romans. No basic new feature was found in these types; the difference lay in the superior techniques of masonry and design. This may be seen in the fortifications of Herod the Great, which have resisted time better than any other ancient Palestinian structure. The defensive walls of Herod were built of massive hewn and dressed stones, laid very closely and to a great height and thickness. Herodian walls may still be observed in the structure of the Haram esh Sharif and the lower courses of "the Tower of David" near the Jaffa gate in Jerusalem and in the remains of Herod's desert fortresses of Machaerus and the Herodium.

Fortunatus (Lt *fortunatus,* "blessed, well off"), a Christian of Corinth who with Stephanas* and Achaicus visited Paul in Ephesus (1 Co 16:17) and probably brought the letter from the Corinthians to which 1 Co is the answer.

Forum. Cf MARKET.

Fowl. It was long believed that the barnyard fowl was not known in Mesopotamia, Syria, Palestine, and Egypt until it was introduced during the Persian period. There is now sufficient evidence to show that the domesticated fowl was known in the 2nd millennium BC in these regions. An Israelite seal from Tell-en-Nasbeh, dated about 600 BC, shows a game cock (ANEP 277). The fowl, however, is not mentioned in the OT. Its cultivation in Palestine was very common in the Hellenistic and Roman periods, and it is mentioned in the Gospels (Mt 23:37; Lk 11:12). The crowing of the cock was the sign by which Jesus affirmed His prediction of the denial of Peter (Mt 26:34, 74 f; Mk 14:30, 72; Lk 22:34, 60 f; Jn 13:38; 18:27).

Fox. Two species of fox are found in modern Palestine. The fox is probably designated by Hb *šûʿal*, which infests vineyards (SS 2:15) and ruins (Ezk 13:4; Lam 5:18). Samson* sent foxes into the Philistine fields (Jgs 15:4) and Tobiah* scoffed at Nehemiah's* wall as something which a fox could break down (Ne 3:35). Jesus called Herod* Antipas a fox (Lk 13:32), and contrasted His own homelessness with the holes of the fox (Mt 8:20; Lk 9:58). Many scholars believe that the word *šûʿal* designates the jackal, or does not distinguish between the fox and the jackal.

Frankincense. Cf INCENSE.

Free, Freedom. The words free and freedom are used in the NT with a few exceptions only in a theological sense. This theological conception is not based upon the OT, in which freedom as a social or a theological concept is not found. In OT times to be free was to be not a slave*. Freedom was also understood to be independence of foreign domination. The pastoral life with its patriarchal organization (cf FAMILY; FATHER) permitted the individual man a great deal of freedom, in spite of the theoretically absolute power of the patriarch. This freedom is contrasted unfavorably with life under the monarchy in 1 S 8:11–18. In the beginning of the monarchy as throughout its history there seem to have been circles in Israel which regarded the monarchy as an infringement upon traditional freedom.

The conception of the political freedom of the individual and the independence of the city is a Gk conception, and the NT use of the word freedom seems to reflect the Gk idea rather than the Hb idea. The theological conception of freedom appears almost exclusively in the Pauline and Johannine writings. The Christian obtains freedom from sin (Rm 6:18–23; Jn 8:31–36), freedom from the obligation of observing the Jewish Law (Rm 7:3 ff; 8:2; 1 Co 10:29; Gal 2:4; 4:21–31; 5:1–13), and freedom from death (Rm 6:21 ff; 8:21). Indeed freedom

from bondage to decay is conferred upon the entire creation through the Christian dispensation (Rm 8:21). Freedom is brought to the Christian by Christ (Gal 5:1), and the Son frees from sin (Jn 8:36). It is also knowledge of the truth revealed by the Son which frees from sin (Jn 8:31 ff). The freedom of the Christian is a freedom under discipline; freedom is obtained through obedience (Rm 6:17 f). Freedom from sin is not only freedom from guilt and punishment for past sins, but freedom also from the bondage to concupiscence which impels men to sin; through Christ man is delivered from slavery to his own desires (Rm 7:3–25). Christian freedom is freedom under a new law, the law of love (Gal 5:13), and the old law is replaced by the law of the gospel which frees (Js 1:25; 2:12). Christian freedom replaces slavery to the law or to sin with slavery to God (1 Pt 2:16). Christian freedom is not a social revolutionary element; the Christian who is freed from sin is urged to be content with the social status which is his, and to submit to established authority (1 Co 7:17–25; 1 Pt 2:16). The principle of Christian freedom, however, as enunciated in the NT, contains the principle of social and political freedom; for within the Christian community all have secured equal freedom through baptism, whatever their social status (1 Co 12:13). All are equally free in Christ, so that within the Christian community national, social, or racial distinctions are of no validity (Gal 3:28; Col 3:11). The NT not only contains no plan for realizing this new conception of freedom, but does not even urge its members to realize it. The force of the principle, however, had tremendous consequences in both the theory and the practice of politics within the history of Christendom. The principle of Christian freedom is the spirit; for where the spirit of the Lord is, there is freedom (2 Co 3:17). It is through the infusion of the spirit, in contrast to the letter of the law and Jewish tradition, that the life of the Christian is governed. Freedom which implies license and absence of restraint is a spurious freedom and slavery to destruction (2 Pt 2:19).

Fringes. Israelite law prescribed that the Israelite should wear four tassels, one at each corner of his mantle, as a memorial of the commandments of Yahweh (Nm 15:38 f; Dt 22:12). Such tassels appear on representations of other ancient peoples (ANEP 351–355; 441); it is possible that the tassels had a magical value which was transformed in Israelite law to a religious value. Jesus wore the tassels on His cloak, and people thought they were endowed with healing powers (Mt 9:20; 14:36; Mk 6:56; Lk 8:44). Among the forms of external display with which Jesus charged the Pharisees was the wearing of large elongated tassels as a testimony of their fidelity to the law (Mt 23:5).

Frog. Although several species of frog are known in Palestine; they are not mentioned in the OT except in allusions to the plagues* of Egypt (Ex 8:1–15; Pss 78:45; 105:30). In Apc 16:13 three foul spirits appear in the likeness of frogs.

G

Gaal. Cf ABIMELECH.

Gabbatha (Aramaic *gabbᵉta'*, the name of the place called in Gk *lithostrōtos*), the scene of the judgment of Jesus by Pilate (Jn 19:13). This event took place in the praetorium* (Mt 27:27; Mk 15:16). There are two generally accepted sites which can be identified with the palace which Pilate occupied while he was in Jerusalem; one is the site of the modern Citadel near the Jaffa Gate, the other is the site of the fortress of Antonia adjacent to the NW corner of the temple area. The meaning of the Aramaic *gabbᵉta'* is uncertain, but it appears to mean "height," perhaps something like Eng "knob." The Gk *lithostrōtos* means a flagstone pavement. Under the convent of Notre Dame de Sion in Jerusalem there has been discovered an extensive flagstone pavement. The stones are of limestone, about 3 ft square. The remains indicate the existence of a flagstone court about 165 ft on its NS side and about 150 ft on its EW side. These flagstones have been worn smooth by traffic and they are striated for the movement of horses. These are traces of the W entrance to the court, which was a double arched gate; it is altogether probable that a matching double arched gate lay on the E side of the court. Near the W entrance there are traces of a chamber which is identified as the guardroom. At the NW corner of the court there was a stairway which led to a terrace. There were also stairways on the E side of the court and in the SE corner. The remains at the NW corner suggest the foundations of a tower. Under the court is a vast double vaulted cistern, 170 ft long by 46 ft wide. On the flagstone pavement near the guardroom was a peculiar complex of markings which can be identified as the board of a game something like our parchesi, in which the players advanced from one position to the next, probably by the throw of the dice. One line terminated in a crown and another in what appears to be a saber. The Gk letter Beta, which appears a few times in the diagram, suggests that this was the board of the game called *basilikos* (royal), in which the winning course ended in a crown, the losing course in the symbol of death. The game is thought to reflect the practice of the substitute king which goes back to ancient Mesopotamia. For the week of the festival of the New Year in Mesopotamia and of the

The paved court of the fortress Antonia.

Sacaea in Persia and the Saturnalia of Rome a slave or a condemned criminal was allowed to live as king; at the end of the festival he was executed. No archaeologist questions that the pavement represents the site of the fortress of Antonia built by Herod at the NW corner of the temple area on the site of an earlier Hasmonean fortress. The fortress stood upon the eminence of Bezetha, which can now scarcely be distinguished. The stairs in the E and SE give direct access to the temple court, permitting the Roman cohort to move immediately to the court if action was necessary. Some archaeologists, however, have questioned whether the pavement belongs to the period before the destruction of Jerusalem in AD 70 or to Aelia Capitolina, the city built by Hadrian after the suppression of the rebellion of AD 132–135. The evidence supports the opinion of most achaeologists that the pavement is the actual pavement of the court of the fortress of Antonia. It is another question whether Pilate resided at this fortress or at the palace at the site of modern Citadel. Strict archaeological demonstration is impossible, and the literary sources do not decide the question. The game board offers an explanation of the crowning with thorns; if the soldiers were playing the game during the hearings of Jesus, the game might have suggested their rude sport. In fact, they may have made Jesus Himself the pawn of the game. The fortress of Antonia was destroyed in the fall of Jerusalem in AD 70. In the excavation of the area there was found a rounded stone weighing about 770 lbs which was a ballistic missile of the Roman artillery.

Gabelus (Vg form of Hb *gᵉbāh'ēl*, "El is lofty"), a man of Rages* with whom Tobit* deposited 10 talents of silver (Tb 1:14) which his son Tobias was sent to repossess (Tb 4:1, 20; 9:6).

Gabriel (Hb *gabri'el*, "El is strong"), the name of an angel*. Gabriel is not called an archangel in the Bible; he is one of the seven archangels in the book of Enoch (cf APOCRYPHAL BOOKS), probably one of the seven who stand before God (Tb 12:15; Lk 1:19). In Dn Gabriel is an interpreting angel who explains the vision of the ram and the he-goat (8:16–26) and the meaning of the 70 years of captivity of Je 25:11; 29:10 (Dn 9:21–27). Gabriel appears in the infancy* Gospel of Lk as the angel who announces the birth of John the Baptist* to Zachary* (Lk 1:11–20) and the conception, birth, and mission of Jesus to Mary (Lk 1:26–38). Gabriel is probably chosen here because it is the only angelic name of the OT which is connected with the messianic fulfill-

ment. Gabriel appears several times in the books of Enoch, but not as a messenger. His appearance in Lk is modeled after his mission in Dn and is conceived as the completion of his mission in Dn.

Gad (Hb *gad*, "good fortune (?)"). **1.** Son of Jacob* and Zilpah*, slave* of Leah* (Gn 30:11), and one of the 12 tribes of Israel. The etymology and meaning of the name are uncertain. A deity Gad is mentioned with Meni (Is 65:11, a late passage), and the two are thought to be deities of fortune. Albright believes that the name Gad is an abbreviation. The territory of Gad (Jos 13:24–28) lay on the eastern side of the Jordan*, W of the territory of Ammon* and extended generally from the southern end of the Sea of Galilee to the Arnon*. The territory N of the Arnon was often in dispute between Israel and Moab*, and the Moabite Stone of Mesha* reports the conquest of part of this territory from the men of Gad, who had dwelt in Ataroth* "for ages." This suggests a settlement before Moabite occupation, i.e., before the exodus* of Israel from Egypt. The territory of Gad is frequently called Gilead*, a name also applied to the tribe. The territory of Gad as usually described in the OT leaves no room for the territory of Reuben*, which also lay N of the Arnon; Reuben and its territory must have been assimilated early into the tribe of Gad. The tribe was never settled in western Palestine; this early tradition, reported in Nm 32, a late composition, is supported by all the other literary evidence, and the apportionment of the territory to Gad is attributed in tradition to Moses himself. A quarrel between the tribes of eastern and western territory over the construction of an altar in eastern Palestine is reported in Jos 22. This narrative is of late origin and is probably only a dim reflection of the quarrel which it reports. The narrative as it stands has become the basis of a double theological affirmation: of the religious unity of the tribes in the worship of Yahweh, and of the worship of Yahweh at a single sanctuary. The census of Nm, which is thought to belong to the period of David, gives the tribe 45,650 members (Nm 1:24–2:14) or 40,500 members (Nm 26:18). It is not surprising that Gad, as a frontier tribe, should be praised for its warlike qualities in both the blessing of Jacob, where by a play upon its name it is called a raider (Gn 49:19), and in the blessing of Moses, where it is called a lion, a leader of the people (Dt 33:20 f). Besides its border wars with Moab it was ravaged by the Aramaeans* under Hazael* 850–800 (2 K 10:33) and after the fall of Jerusalem in 587 its territory was possessed by Milcom, the god of the Ammonites* (Je 49:1).

2. A prophet of David, who accompanied David as an outlaw and once gave him a warning oracle (1 S 22:5). Gad rebuked David for taking the census of Israel (2 S 24:11 ff; 1 Ch 21:9 ff) and signified the end of the plague by designating the threshing-floor of Araunah* as the place of sacrifice (2 S 24:18; 1 Ch 21:18). The Chronicler includes the writings of Gad among his sources for the reign of David (1 Ch 29:29; cf CHRONICLES).

Gadara. A Hellenistic city of eastern Palestine, one of the cities of the Decapolis*. A demoniac was healed by Jesus in its territory according to Mt 8:28. The variant reading of Gerasenes for Gadarenes (Mk 5:1; Lk 8:26) refer to the city of Gerasa*. Another variant, Gergesenes*, has no critical support. The city was situated at the modern Umm Qeis, about 3-4 mi NW of Irbid. There are remains of a theater, tombs, and an aqueduct.

Gaius. A Lt *praenomen* borne by four men in the NT. **1.** A Macedonian, a traveling companion of Paul, who with Aristarchus* was seized by the mob in the disturbance at Ephesus (AA 19:29). **2.** Gaius of Derbe, a companion of Paul on his journey to Macedonia (AA 20:4). **3.** Gaius of Corinth, baptized by Paul himself (1 Co 1:14) and the host of Paul and the whole Church (Rm 16:23). **4.** "The Beloved" to whom 3 Jn is addressed.

Galaad. Cf GILEAD.

Galatia. The geographical and political name Galatia is used in two senses. In its first meaning it designates the plateau of central Anatolia between Pontus, Bithynia, and Lycaonia*. The name is derived from the Gauls who invaded Macedonia, Greece, and Asia Minor in 279 BC and the following years; they finally settled in Anatolia, where they established a kingdom. In 64 BC Galatia became a client state of Rome, and in the following years the territory of the kingdom was extended into adjoining regions. In its second meaning Galatia designates the Roman province of Galatia, established in 24 BC after the death of the last king, Amyntas; it included the region of Galatia and the regions of Pisidia*, Pamphylia*, and part of Lycaonia. After this date the name Galatia was used to designate the province.

Galatia in 1 Mc 8:2 means European (Cisalpine) Gaul. 2 Mc 8:20 alludes to the presence of Jewish mercenaries in the service of the Seleucid kingdom against the Gala-

tians. Galatia was reached by Paul on his 2nd journey (AA 16:6) and again on his 3rd journey (AA 18:23), and the churches of Galatia contributed to the collection taken up by Paul for the Jerusalem community (1 Co 16:1). Crescens* was active in Galatia (2 Tm 4:10), and Galatia is included among the destinataries of 1 Pt (1:1).

The two senses of the term have led to a division of opinion on the destination of Gal. "The N Galatian theory" maintains that Gal is addressed to communities of Galatia proper i.e., the original Galatian kingdom of central Anatolia. "The S Galatian theory" maintains that Gal is addressed to the communities mentioned in AA — Antioch* of Pisidia, Derbe*, Lystra*, and Iconium*. These cities lay in the province of Galatia, although they were not in the original territory; AA designates them according to the districts, Pisidia and Lycaonia, which were the older and probably the usual names of the regions. The question cannot be regarded as settled. A number of recent commentators incline to the N Galatian theory because of the territorial names (above), because of Paul's illness (Gal 4:13) not mentioned in AA, and because the Galatians were former pagans. Hence Galatia in AA 16:6; 18:23 is taken to signify Galatia proper, even though the foundation of churches there is not mentioned by AA.

Galatians, Epistle to the. 1. *Contents:*

1:1-5, salutation; 1:5-10, reprimand.

I. Apologetic and Argumentative, 1:11-4:11.

1:11-2:21, apostolic authority of Paul: 1:11-17, his call; 1:18-24, his early preaching; 2:1-10, his approval by Jerusalem; 2:11-21, his defense of his gospel before Peter.

3:1-4:11, the solidity of his teaching: 3:1-5, his teaching proved by the working of the Spirit; 3:6-14, argument from Scripture; 3:15-18, the blessing promised to Abraham; 3:19-29, the place of the law; 4:1-11, liberation by Christ.

II. Exhortation, 4:12-6:10.

4:12-20, personal appeal; 4:21-31, the allegory of Sarah and Hagar; 5:1-12, the uselessness of circumcision; 5:13-24, the contrast of Christian virtue with the vices of the flesh; 5:25-6:1, counsels.

Conclusion, 6:11-18.

2. *Occasion.* The letter was written against certain individuals who had disturbed the faith of the Galatians. They were obviously Judaizers whose teaching is summed up from the letter thus by A. Wikenhauser: They argued that Paul's gospel was a dangerous heresy; the law was not repealed by Christ;

salvation is available to the Gentiles only if they first become Jews and submit to circumcision and the law. Paul was not a real apostle; he had not seen Jesus nor been with him; only the 12 were real apostles, and they had said nothing about the repeal of the law; Paul had received no mission from Jesus, he was only an agent of the original apostles from whom he had learned and on whom he was dependent. Probably they represented themselves as preachers of the only genuine Christianity, the gospel which was proclaimed in the Jerusalem community, the mother Church which was nearest to the traditions of Jesus.

Scholars have asked further whether these men taught this as an unconditionally necessary part of the gospel or as necessary for those only who sought Christian perfection. The opinion of commentators is in favor of the first of these. It was suggested by Lütgert that Gal looks two ways, against the legalists who sought to impose the law and against "spirituals" who claimed that the gospel liberated men from all moral obligations. Munck has proposed that the disturbers were not Jews but Gentile converts whose zeal led them to think that Judaism was a necessary part of the gospel. Most commentators believe that one cannot be so precise about the disturbers. It seems altogether probable that they are connected with the Judaizing movement mentioned in AA 15. Paul seems anxious to show that they have no authorization from James and the community of Jerusalem, and that Peter recognized that he had acted imprudently in yielding to them at Antioch.

The occasion gave Paul an opportunity to work out for the first time his gospel on the freedom* of Christianity from Judaism and the total efficacy of the salvation obtained through Christ. This leads him in turn to see the unity of Christianity, which makes no distinction between Jew and Gentile. Cf CIRCUMCISION; JUDAISM; LAW. It also gives Paul an opportunity to state his position as apostle and thus to clarify the nature of this office; cf APOSTLE.

3. *Date and Destination.* On the destination cf GALATIA; it seems more probable that it is addressed to N Galatia rather than S Galatia, although each theory has difficulties. The destination determines the date. Those who defend the S Galatian theory must date the letter about 50, from Corinth*; those who defend the N Galatian theory date it about 54, from Ephesus*. The early date seems improbable; Gal is the first of the four "great epistles" (with 1-2 Co and Rm), but the early date would make it the earliest of all the epistles. The question of the relation of the Antioch affair with the Council of Jerusalem also affects the date; cf AA.

4. *Authorship.* No one questions the Pauline authorship of Gal. The letter does not have rigorous literary unity; it is bound by a unity of sentiment and psychological context. It is more deeply permeated with anger and emotion than any other letter, and it is the only letter which lacks the thanksgiving at the beginning and the final salutations (Wikenhauser). The conclusion (6:11–18) was written in Paul's own hand; the depth of feeling and lack of schematic approach is shown by the way in which he repeats once more the urgings of the letter, feeling that his point will never be sufficiently clear.

The content is related to Rm on the question of the law and the gospel, and to 2 Co on the vindication of Paul's title as apostle.

Galilee (Gk *galilaia,* Hb *gālîl, haggālîl,* probably "circle," "district"), the region of northern Palestine* bounded by Nahr el Qasimiyeh on the N, the Mediterranean on the W, the plain of Esdraelon on the S, and the Jordan and the Sea of Galilee on the W. This area is about 50 mi N to S and 25–35 mi E to W. Upper or Northern Galilee has different physical characteristics from those of Lower or Southern Galilee. Northern Galilee is rugged and mountainous and is a continuation of the Lebanon* range; its peaks rise to an altitude of 4000 ft. Southern Galilee is gentle rolling hill country; the hills rise to about 1500 ft, and they are frequently interrupted by plains. The soil is generally fertile, especially in the plains. Northern Galilee is called simply "the mountain" (Jos 11:2) or "the mountains of Naphthali" (Jos 20:7). The geographical character of Galilee turns it southward, and thus throughout biblical history it has been connected with Samaria and Judah, to which it opened easily through the plain of Esdraelon and the valley of the Jordan. The situation of Galilee made it a crossroads of important routes radiating in all directions and gave it a mixed population, which appears in most periods of recorded history and is reflected in *gᵉlîl haggoyim,* "The region of the nations" (Is 8:23). It was mixed to a very high degree in NT times, when the Hellenistic civilization and people of the region were centered about Sepphoris, the administrative capital of the territory, and Tiberias* on the Sea of Galilee. The conquest of Galilee attributed to Joshua (Jos 11) probably telescopes a much longer process of infiltration. Important Canaanite cities such as Kedesh and Yanoam remained Canaanite after the settlement. The territory of Galilee was the territory of the tribes of Zebulun, Naphtali, Asher, and Issachar. These tribes were led by Barak* and Deborah* in the battle against Sisera* (Jgs 4–5). Galilee is unimportant in OT history from Solomon to NT times. It was one of the districts of the northern kingdom which were detached by Tiglath-pileser III in 734 BC and incorporated into an Assyrian province. Galilee was the scene of the campaign of Simon* (1 Mc 5:14–23). The passage is somewhat revealing, because at the end of the campaign Simon transferred the Jews of Galilee to Judaea*. The Jews soon returned to Galilee, and a Jewish population in Galilee appears throughout 100 BC–AD 100. Galilee formed a part of the kingdom of Herod* the Great and was a part of the tetrarchy of Herod* Antipas during the public ministry of Jesus. Most of the events of the Synoptic Gospels occurred in Galilee, and there Jesus spent most of His life and most of His ministry. He was generally regarded as a native of Galilee. The somewhat supercilious attitude of the Jews of Jerusalem and Judaea toward Galilee is reflected in Jn 1:46; 7:52. Galilee is not important in the history of the primitive Church; outside the Gospels it is mentioned in the NT only in AA 9:31. After the Jewish war of AD 66–70 it became a center of Jewish settlement and Jewish learning.

Galilee, Sea of. The Sea of Galilee is formed by the Jordan where it flows between the hills of Galilee to the W and the plateau of Hauran to the E. The surface of the lake lies 696 ft below sea level and it is 165 to 230 ft deep. It is about 13 mi long and about 8 mi wide at its widest. The lake is shut in by surrounding hills for almost its entire

a) Sea of Galilee near Capernaum.
b) Storm on the Sea of Galilee with the wall at Tiberias.

circumference. The hills on the E lie closer to the water than the hills on the W and the slope is steeper, rising shortly to about 2700 ft above the surface of the lake. Hence communication with the eastern plateau is more difficult, and in ancient times the larger centers lay on the W side of the lake. The ruins, however, indicate that in NT times the lake shore was built up for almost its entire circumference. Nine fairly important cities on the shore of the lake are mentioned during NT times. A modern estimate would give these cities a population of about 15,000 each, and the lake area was one of the greater centers of population in NT Palestine. The climate is tropical, since the depth of the depression cuts off the W winds, and the heat can be extremely uncomfortable. The natural resources of the area in ancient times supported a large population and a number of industries. Josephus describes the area as a fertile fruit-growing center. This seems to have been concentrated at the plain of Gennesareth* on the NW corner of the lake. Agriculture also was possible in the fertile soil of the plain on the western side of the lake, and the cities were the seats of tanning and dyeing industries. Fishing and fish packing were important activities, and fishing is mentioned frequently in the NT. The city of Tarichaeae, not mentioned in the Gospels, seems to have been the principal industrial center of the lake cities. The lake is mentioned rarely in the OT under the name of Chinereth or Chinneroth, and only as a boundary point (Nm 34:11; Jos 12:3; 13:27); it is mentioned in the account of the campaign of Jonathan* in Galilee (1 Mc 11:67), where it is called the sea of Gennesar. The name Gennesareth*, apparently a variation of the name Gennesar, is the name of the lake in Mt 14:34; Mk 6:53; Lk 5:1. It is most frequently designated in the NT as the Sea of Galilee (Mt 4:18; 15:29; Mk 1:16; 7:31; Jn 6:1). It is also called the Sea of Tiberias* (Jn 6:1; 21:1) after the city built by Herod the Great. The ministry of Jesus in Galilee was centered about the Sea of Galilee and in particular about the city of Capernaum*, "his own city." Gospel events which occur on the Sea of Galilee include the miraculous draught of fishes and the vocation of four apostles (Lk 5:1–11), the walking upon the waters (Mt 14:21–33; Mk 6:45–52), the stilling of the storm on the sea (Mt 5:23–27; Mk 4:35–41; Lk 8:22–25) and the apparition of the risen Jesus by the sea (Jn 21:1 ff). In modern times the population on the shore of the sea is much smaller than it was in the 1st century, and the agriculture, fruit growing and fishing mentioned in ancient sources have all but vanished.

Gall. The Hb word $m^e r\bar{e}r\bar{a}h$ (once only), $m^e r\hat{o}r\bar{a}h$ signifies either the gall bladder (Jb 20:25) which is there located in the back, or the gall itself, which is poured out on the ground through a wound (Jb 16:13). The poison of a venomous serpent is its gall (Jb 20:14). Metaphorically gall signifies something bitter to the taste, as bitter grapes (Dt 32:32). The metaphorical use of the word, probably to signify poison, occurs once in the NT (AA 8:23). Wine mixed with gall, given to Jesus on the cross (Mt 27:34) probably comes from a mistranslation of the Aramaic source of Mt and should be understood as wine mixed with myrrh (Aramaic *môr;* Mk 15:23).

Gallio. Marcus Annaeus Novatus took the name of Lucius Junius Annaeus Gallio after his adoption by the orator Lucius Junius Gallio. He was born about 3 BC in Spain and was a member of a distinguished family. He was a brother of Seneca, the philosopher and tutor of Nero, and of Marcus Annaeus Mela, a geographer and the father of the epic poet Lucan. All the members of this family were compelled to commit suicide by Nero near the end of his reign. Gallio was proconsul in Corinth* when the Jews brought Paul* before him on a charge of teaching a worship of God contrary to the law* (AA 18:12–17). Gallio refused to hear the case because it had no standing in civil law and he would not decide a religious controversy. He expelled the Jews from the court and permitted them to beat Sosthenes, the president of the synagogue, in the court itself. Gallio here reflects the typical attitude of the haughty educated Roman toward the contemptible sect of the Jews. This attitude had no doubt been rendered more hostile by the recent expulsion of the Jews from Rome by Claudius (AA 18:2), which probably happened no more than a year before Gallio came to Corinth as proconsul. An inscription discovered at Delphi during the excavations conducted by the French School at Athens 1892–1903 mentions Gallio as proconsul of Achaea. The inscription is dated in the 12th year as tribune of Tiberius Claudius Caesar Augustus Germanicus and the 26th occasion on which he was saluted as imperator. This dates the inscription between January and August of AD 52. Normally the proconsul held office for only a year. Not infrequently, however, especially in provinces where disturbed conditions demanded a more delicate administration, the emperor permitted an officer to remain for a longer time. The event related in AA 18 must therefore be dated in 51 or 52. It seems probable that Gallio held office only from the opening of navigation in April of 52 to late summer or early fall of the same year. Consequently, the process before his tribunal fell within these months. Since Paul stayed in Corinth a year and a half, his arrival in Corinth falls in 50.

Gamaliel (Hb *gamli'ēl,* "El has repaid me"), a teacher of the law, called Gamaliel the Elder or Gamaliel I to distinguish him from his grandson Gamaliel II, who lived about AD 100. In the rabbinical sources he is given the honorific title of Rabban and is regarded as one of the great teachers of the law*. In spirit he belonged to the gentler school of interpretation of Hillel, and a not entirely reliable tradition makes him the son or grandson of Hillel. He was the teacher of Paul* (AA 22:3), who probably studied under him for the usual three or four years. He was a member of the council which passed judgment on Peter* and the apostles for teaching the gospel, and advised the council to take no positive action, on the ground that the movement would collapse of itself if it were from men, and if it were from God they would be wrong in opposing it (AA 5:34–39). Early Christian legend made Gamaliel a Christian.

Garden. The gardens of Egypt, usually attached to palaces of kings or the wealthy, were enclosures in which trees were cultivated by irrigation. The Egyptian garden was also equipped with pavilions and the irrigation water was diverted to form pools and artificial streams. The garden was a welcome resort from the heat of the sun. Flowers were also cultivated, and Egyptian art represents the family entertaining itself and its guests in the garden, or children at play. The Mesopotamian garden was an enclosure of cultivated trees which were principally fruit trees, as in the Egyptian garden. The Mesopotamian garden was also irrigated and enhanced as a pleasure resort by shaded pavilions; but it seems that flowers were not cultivated. The Mesopotamian garden was also at times a park or preserve in which game was hunted. Such preserves belonged only to royalty. The skill of constructing gardens for the cultivation of fruit and vegetables and as an annex for rest and recreation was more highly developed by the Greeks and Romans. The garden of the OT (Hb *gan*) was not as highly cultivated as the Egyptian or Mesopotamian garden and corresponded rather to our orchard. The garden in which man was placed in creation (Gn 2–3) resembles a Mesopotamian rather than a Palestinian garden. The garden of the king in Jerusalem was no doubt attached to the royal palace (2 K 25:4; Je 39:4; 52:7). It is uncertain whether this garden is identical with the garden of Uzzah in which Manasseh (2 K 21:18) and Amon (2 K 21:26) were buried. The vegetable garden which Ahab wished to make of Naboth's vineyard (1 K 21:2) appears to have been a rare type of garden in Palestine. To be like an irrigated garden was to be prosperous and peaceful (Is 58:11; Je 31:11). To plant gardens and eat their fruit was likewise a sign of peace and prosperity (Je 29:5, 28; Am 9:14). The gardens of the Israelites were also places of rest and repose, as we see in SS, where the beloved is called a garden (SS 4:16; 5:1; 6:2, 11; 8:13). On Eden and the garden of God cf EDEN. The enclosed garden of Joachim, the husband of Susanna*, was used to entertain his guests as well as for strolling and bathing. Gethsemani*, a grove of olive trees, is called a garden (Jn 18:1,

Garden of Ashur-bani-pal. The king and his queen are feasting, the king on a couch and the queen seated in a chair. Musicians are performing, and the head of the king of Elam is hung from the tree on the left.

Restoration of the
Ishtar Gate of Babylon.

26) and Jn also observes that the tomb of Jesus was in a garden (19:21).

Gate. In the Bronze Age the city walls were pierced by one or two gates, seldom more. In the Iron Age city gates were more numerous, and seven gates are mentioned by name for Jerusalem of the monarchy. The gates were at least as deep as the thickness of the city walls, and usually the depth of the gate was lengthened by additional fortifications. The gate, as the weakest point of the defenses, was the most strongly fortified; from the Bronze Age the gates were strengthened by towers and bastions. The principal gate of the city was often if not usually a multiple entrance with several pairs of doors. The multiple entrance was created by flanking piers, two to four in number. These piers enclosed bays or chambers which could be used as guardrooms and converted to defensive positions if the gate were forced. The gate was covered by a roof or an upper story. The arch was not used in OT times, and the roof was supported by heavy wooden beams. The width of the principal gate was 13–14 ft. Other gates were too low and narrow for vehicular traffic and permitted the passage of pedestrians or a single ass. There was usually a drain at the gate to permit rain water to flow out without damaging the substructure of the defenses. A number of gates from the Bronze Age and the Iron Age have been preserved. In MB appears the indirect access gate which appears at Megiddo* and at Gezer*. In this type of gate one is forced to turn left sharply on the approach ramp to reach the gate and thus to expose the right side, not protected by the shield, to the city wall. The gateway proper is at right angles to the line of fortifications. In LB fortifications the walls overlap at the point of entrance and are strengthened by one or two towers at the outer entrance to the gateway. The Iron II gateway of Tell en Nasbeh is a more complex example of this type of gateway with overlapping walls, double gate with a right angle turn to the left, guard chambers, and twin towers. The "gate between the two walls" at Jerusalem (2 K 25:4) may be such a gate. The outer approach to the gateway was an exposed ramp. The Iron II gate at Megiddo exhibits a ramp with a double outer gate, within which the entry turns leftward, then reaches the main gate, behind which are three smaller entries. The corridor of the gateway is lined by guardrooms. The gate was a place of assembly. It was necessary for defense to keep the area inside the gate clear of buildings in order that defensive forces could be massed. These areas were the only squares or plazas of the ancient city, which was otherwise built very closely. Public assemblies at the gate are mentioned frequently. This square was also a public market (2 K 7:1 +). The hospitality of the ancient city was extended to the stranger* by meeting him at the gate (Gn 19:1); here Lot* seats himself at the gate to offer hospitality to any stranger who might come in. The area of the gate was also the place where the elders sat (Dt 21:19; 25:7; Pr 31:23) as a court (Ps 69:13; 127:5; Jb 31:21; Am 5:10) and to witness transactions which needed legal authentication (Gn 23:10; Rt 3:11; 4:1). In the Iron Age gate at Tell en Nasbeh long stone benches were found in the gate area which were probably intended for the elders and judges. "Those who enter the gate" (Gn 23:10, 18) probably designates the citizens, those who have the vote in the city assembly. The metaphorical use of the term is extremely common. The gate stands for the entire house or the entire country (Ex 20:10; Zc 8:16 +). It is a point of weakness, and thus to possess the gates (Gn 24:60) is to conquer; and when the enemy is at the gate (Gn 4:7) the danger of defeat is imminent. The gate also signifies power, as in the gates of death (Ps 107:16, 18; Is 38:10), the gates of Sheol* (Mt 16:18). The house of God and the gate of heaven (Gn 27:17) is a holy place where man may meet God. The narrow gate in contrast to the wide gate (Mt 7:13) is the subsidiary gate which was wide enough only for pedestrians in contrast to the main gate, which could accommodate vehicular traffic and was the most frequented passage.

Gath. (Hb *gat,* "wine press"), one of the five Philistine cities, on the frontier of Philistine and Judahite territory in the Shephelah*. Gath (*gimti*) is mentioned in the Amarna* letters in connection with Gezer* and Keilah* in the same region (EA 290), and was conquered by Sargon* of Assyria* in his campaign against Ashdod* in 711 BC. The site of Gath is not certainly identified. Most modern scholars place it at Araq el Menshiyeh, about 7–8 mi W of Beit Jibrin. In the OT Gath is one of the cities of the Anakim* (Jos 11:22) and is mentioned several times in connection with an ancient belief that it was the place of origin of the giants* (2 S 21:22; 1 Ch 20:8). The most famous of the giants of Gath was Goliath*, slain by David* (1 S 17:4 ff). Gath was one of the cities to which the ark* was taken after its capture by the Philistines* (1 S 5:8 ff). David took service as a mercenary with Achish* of Gath (1 S 21:11 ff; 27:2 ff). The city was taken by David in his campaigns against the Philistines (2 S 21:20; 1 Ch 18:1). Possibly it was David's service at Gath which was responsible for the presence of two men of Gath among his own professional soldiers, Obededom* (2 S 6:10 ff) and Ittai* (2 S 15:18 ff). It is listed among the cities fortified by Rehoboam (2 Ch 11: 8), but its possession by Judah* seems to have been uncertain. A tradition that Uzziah took it from the Philistines is preserved in 2 Ch 26:6, and it is called a Philistine city as late as Amos 6:2. This designation may not however, indicate actual Philistine possession at the time. It was taken from Judah by Hazael* of Damascus (2 K 12:18). The tradition of the feud between Ephraim* and Gath cannot be dated (1 Ch 7:21; 8:13). It is not clear that Gath is in these passages regarded as a Philistine city. The proverb "Tell it not in Gath" is original in 2 S 1:20, where it refers to the defeat of Israel and death of Saul* and Jonathan* in battle; it is repeated in Mi 1:10.

Gaza (Hb *'azzah,* meaning uncertain), one of the five cities of the Philistines. The position of Gaza on the main route of travel between Egypt and Asia, 45 mi S of Jaffa and 3 mi from the sea, made it a point of importance from earliest recorded history. The city was conquered by Thutmose III of Egypt (1502–1448) and was still held under Merneptah (1234–1220). It is mentioned in the Amarna* letters, which show that it was an Egyptian residence and a military base. It was conquered by Tiglathpileser II of Assyria in 734 and an effort to regain its independence was defeated by Sargon. In the rebellion against Sennacherib* in which Hezekiah* of Judah was active Gaza remained loyal to Assyria and as a reward received some of the territory of Judah. Gaza is mentioned as an ally by Esarhaddon and Ashur-bani-pal. It is listed among the cities subject to Nebuchadnezzar. Cambyses of Persia conquered it in 529, and it was a Persian headquarters and military base during the Persian rule of Palestine. Gaza was conquered by Alexander in 332. After the death of Alexander it passed back and forth in the wars of the Ptolemies and Seleucids until it was finally secured for the Seleucids in 198. Rebuilt by Antiochus III, Gaza became an important and populous Hellenistic city and as such it was besieged by Jonathan in 144 BC (1 Mc 11:61 f). The inhabitants capitulated on Jonathan's terms. It was attacked and destroyed by Alexander Jannaeus in 95. Pompey in his conquest of Palestine freed Gaza from Jewish control and made it a free city attached to the province of Syria. Augustus as a favor to Herod the Great attached it to Herod's kingdom; after the death of Herod it was again made a free city. Gaza was an agricultural and commercial center and the principal market of Palestine, the terminus of caravans from Arabia. Gaza is counted as a Canaanite city in the Table of Nations* (Gn 10:19). Another tradition identifies these Canaanites as the Awwim*, who were exterminated by the Caphtorim*, here identical with the Philistines (Dt 2:23). With Gath and Ashdod it is also a city of the Anakim* (Jos 11:22). The city was taken by Judah (Jgs

1:18) and is included among the list of
Judahite cities (Jos 15:47). This list, however, belongs to the monarchical period. Gaza
was lost to the Philistines before the foundation of the monarchy. At Gaza Samson
performed the feat of carrying off the doors
of the city gates (Jgs 16:1 ff). Gaza was a
point on the boundary of Solomon's kingdom
(1 K 5:4). It was, however, reckoned as a
non-Israelite city in the time of Amos
(1:6 ff). It was conquered by Hezekiah
in the revolt of Sennacherib, but was immediately lost (2 K 18:8). The site of the
ancient city is covered by the modern city,
which before the civil war of 1948 had a
population of about 21,000 and was still
the chief agricultural and commercial center
of the area. Gaza is mentioned in the NT
only in AA 8:26.

Gazelle. There are several species of gazelle
or antelope in Palestine and related areas:
the Eng word gazelle is derived from the
Arabic *ghazzal*. It is the largest of the game
animals of Palestine and is the most abundant.
In Israelite law the gazelle was a clean
animal (Dt 12:15, 22; 14:5; 15:22). It was
included in the daily provisions of food for
Solomon's household (1 K 5:3). It is praised
for its swiftness (2 S 2:18; Pr 6:5) and its
grace; the lover is compared to the gazelle
(SS 2:9, 17; 8:14), and the breasts of the
beloved are compared to two fawns of the
gazelle (SS 4:5; 7:4). People under the
judgment of Yahweh are pathetically compared to the hunted gazelle (Is 13:14).

Geba (Hb *geba'*, meaning uncertain), a city
of Benjamin (Jos 18:24; 1 Ch 8:6). The
name is preserved in the modern Jeba which
occupies the site between Tell el Ful and
Muhmas on the S side of the Wadi es Su-
weinit. It is enumerated between Michmash
to the N and Ramah and Gibeah to the
S (Is 10:29). It is one of the priestly cities
(Jos 21:17; 1 Ch 6:45) and is a boundary
point of the kingdom of Josiah* (2 K 23:8)
and of Judah (Zc 14:10). It is mentioned
in the tribal war of Jgs 19–21; but Gibeah
should probably be read in Jgs 20:10, 33.
Geba and Michmash were the site of the
action between Saul* and the Philistines*
(1 S 13–14); the names Geba and Gibeah
are confused in the Gk and Hb texts, Geba
certainly lay across the ravine from Michmash (1 S 14:5), and the location of Saul's
camp at a point from which the Philistine
camp at Michmash could be seen and heard
(1 S 14:16 ff) suggests that Geba should be
read for Gibeah as the site of Saul's camp
(1 S 13:2, 15; 14:2, 16). The Hb reads
Gibeah in 13:16. It is not equally certain
that Geba was the site of the Philistine

nasib (1 S 13:3); some critics read Gibeah
here, as in 1 S 10:5. Gibeon should be read
for Geba in 2 S 5:25. Geba was fortified
by Asa against Israel (1 K 15:22; 2 Ch
16:6). It was included in the territory of
Jerusalem in the Persian period (Ezr 2:26;
Ne 7:30; 11:31; 12:29).

Gebal. Cf BYBLOS.

Gedaliah (Hb *gedalyāh*, "Yahweh is great"),
son of Ahikam*, son of Shaphan*, appointed
by Nebuchadnezzar* governor of Judah after
the fall of Jerusalem in 587 BC (2 K 25:
22 ff; Je 39:14; 40:5 ff). Gedaliah set up his
residence at Mizpeh* and attempted to restore some order in the country ravaged by
war. He was, however, murdered by some
discontented fugitives from the army led by
Ishmael*, son of Nethaniah (Je 41). This
outburst of lawlessness led the rest of the
community to flee in fear to Egypt (Je
42–44). The members of this family appear
in Je as friendly to the prophet. A seal
impression reading, "Belonging to Gedaliah,
who is over the house," was found in the
excavation of Lachish*. In the opinion of
most scholars this is the individual mentioned
in Je and 2 K. The name is borne by three
others in the OT.

Gehazi (Hb *gehazî*, meaning uncertain), servant of Elisha* who is mentioned only in
the stories of the miracles of Elisha (2 K
4:12–31; 5:20–25; 8:4 ff). Gehazi was sent
to cure the son of the Shunemite woman by
stretching the prophet's rod over him, but
the cure failed. Because of his greed in attempting to secure a gift from Naaman*
of Syria* for the cure of his leprosy*, the
leprosy of Naaman came upon him. The
motif of the story shows that the prophetic
gift and power were not to be diverted to
personal gain.

Gehenna (Gk *geenna* represents Aramaic
ge-hinnam, which in turn represents Hb
ge-hinnōm, an abbreviation of the full title,
"valley of the son of Hinnom"). The name
probably is that of the original Jebusite owner
of the property. In the OT this is a geographical term which divides ancient Jerusalem (Zion) from the hills to the S and
W. It is the modern Wadi er Rababi, which
joins the Wadi en Nar (the Kidron) at the
southern extremity of the hill of Zion. The
valley was a point on the boundary between
Judah and Benjamin (Jos 15:8; 18:16).
This usage is reflected in Ne 11:30. The
valley had an unholy reputation in later OT
books because it was the site of Tophet*,
a cultic shrine where human sacrifice was
offered (2 K 23:10; 2 Ch 28:3; 33:6; Je

7:31; 19:2 ff; 32:35). It is called simply "the valley" (Je 2:23). Because of this cult Jeremiah cursed the place and predicted that it would be a place of death and corruption (7:32; 19:6 ff). This valley is referred to, not by name in Is 66:24, as a place where the dead bodies of the rebels against Yahweh shall lie. Their worm shall not die nor shall their fire be quenched — an allusion to the passages of Je cited above. This passage is of importance in tracing the origin of the concept of Gehenna as a place of punishment after death in extrabiblical Jewish writings. It appears in the Assumption of Moses 10:19 and in the Syriac Apocalypse of Baruch 59:10; Jn 4; in Esdras 7:36 it is a furnace, a place of fire and torments which lies in sight of Paradise. 1 Enoch often mentions this place of torment, although the name Gehenna is not always used. It is for the accursed (27:2); it is a fiery abyss (90:26 f) where the impious will burn like straw (48:9). It is a place of darkness, chains, and burning flames (103:8), a valley of burning fire (54:1). Gehenna is also mentioned frequently in the rabbinical literature where it also appears as a pit of fire, a place of punishment for the wicked. In rabbinical literature, however, the eternal fire is not surely eternal punishment. The rabbis at times see the possibility of annihilation of the wicked or even of their release after a period of punishment. Gehenna in the NT is mentioned seven times in Mt, three times in Mk, once in Lk, once in Js. It is a place of fire (Mt 5:22; 18:9; Js 3:6). The fire is unquenchable (Mk 9:43). It is a pit into which people are cast (Mt 5:29 f; 18:9; Mk 9:45, 47; Lk 12:5). It is a place where the wicked are destroyed body and soul, which perhaps echoes the idea of annihilation (Mt 10:28). The Pharisees are sons of Gehenna — in Semitic idiom destined to Gehenna (Mt 23:15), and they will incur the judgment of Gehenna (Mt 23:33). The punishment of fire is mentioned in other passages where the name of Gehenna is not used (Mt 3:10, 12; 7:19; Lk 3:9, 17). Sinners are punished in fire which is eternal (Mt 18:8), prepared for the devil and his angels (Mt 25:41). The worshipers of the beast shall be tortured with fire and brimstone (Apc 14:10), and the scarlet woman will be burned with fire (Apc 17:16; 18:8). The final destination of all the wicked is the pool of fire, which is the second death (Apc 19: 20; 20:9–15; 21:8; cf 2 Pt 2:4; Jd 6 f). Gehenna is also supposed in passages which do not mention fire, but which describe the place of punishment as a prison and a torture chamber (Mt 5:25–26), a place of misery, "weeping and gnashing of teeth" (Mt 8:12; 13:42, 50; 22:13; 24:51; 25:30),

or as the grave where the process of corruption is never ended, "where the worm does not die" (Mk 9:48, quoted from Is 66:24), or as a place of darkness* (Mt 8:12; 22:13; 25:30). Comparison of these NT passages with the passages of the apocryphal books cited above show that the Synoptic Gospels, Jd, Js, 2 Pt, and Apc employ the language and the imagery of contemporary Judaism. It is remarkable that this language and imagery does not appear in other NT writings; Chaine has suggested that it does not appear precisely because the other NT writers found the imagery of popular Jewish apocalyptic eschatology unsuitable for Gentile Christians. Hence they chose other imagery through which to portray the grim truth of the anger* of God and the punishment of sin; these images must be included in a complete synthesis of NT thought on the subject. In Jn the punishment of sin is accomplished through judgment* (3:8; 5:24ff; 12:31, 48; 16:11); and through death i.e., exclusion from the eternal life communicated by the Son (5:29; 8:24; 10:28; 11:25 f; 12:25), and darkness (8:12; 12:44–46). Paul's language is even less concrete. The wicked stores up wrath for the day of wrath when the justice of God will burst forth (Rm 2:5). Death is the wages of sin (Rm 6:23). Sinners have no share in the kingdom of God (1 Co 6:10; Gal 5:19–21; cf Mt 5:20). The enemies of the cross of Christ are doomed to destruction (Phl 3:19). The impious will be punished with eternal destruction (2 Th 1:9). For obdurate sinners there is no prospect except judgment and the blazing consuming anger of God; it is fearful to fall into the hands of the living God (Hb 10:26–31). These passages suggest that the apocalyptic imagery of other NT passages is to be taken for what it is, imagery, and not as strictly literal theological affirmation. The great truths of judgment and punishment are firmly retained throughout the NT, and no theological hypothesis can be biblical which reduces the ultimate destiny of righteousness and wickedness to the same thing; the details of the afterlife, however, are not disclosed except in imagery.

Genealogy. The importance of genealogies in Israelite culture arose from the clan and tribal organization of Israelite society; cf FAMILY; TRIBE. Most of the personal rights and privileges of the individual flowed from his membership in the clan and tribe; the genealogy was a written record of his membership. Furthermore, it furnished a numeration of those whom the clan or tribe could summon. The importance of the genealogy for proof of descent appears in the ex-

clusion from the priesthood after the exile*
of those who could not prove their priestly
descent from the genealogies (Ezr 2:59–63;
Ne 7:61–65). A large number of Israelite
genealogies are preserved in Gn, Nm, 1 Ch,
Ezr, Ne, and Rt. These genealogies often contain historical notes which are not elsewhere
preserved. In the priestly tradition the patriarchs and their immediate family are the
objects of the stories; the other members
of the family who are of no further interest
in the transmission of the promises are listed
in genealogies. The system of genealogies
is used to fill the interval between Adam
and Abraham. These early genealogies contain the names of nations, tribes, and geographical areas as well as the names of
individuals. This artificial arrangement is intended to show a historical or a geographical
connection; cf TABLE OF NATIONS. The artificial character of the genealogies appears
also in the number of ten generations from
Adam to Noah and of another ten from
Shem to Abraham.

The Gospels contain two genealogies of
Jesus (Mt 1:17; Lk 3:23–38). The genealogy of Mt runs from Abraham to Jesus in
a descending order; the genealogy of Lk runs
from Jesus to Adam in an ascending order.
The genealogy of Mt has 42 names divided
into 3 groups of 14 names (Mt 1:17). The
numbers are obtained by the omission of some
members of the royal line of David between
Joram and Uzziah. Furthermore, Jechoniah is counted twice (11–12). The genealogy of Lk has 56 names for the same
period and a total of 76 names. From David
to Joseph the two genealogies have only
two names in common, Zerubbabel and
Shealtiel. The difference has never been
satisfactorily explained, and it is perhaps
attributed with most probability to the fact
that one genealogy gives the natural descent
of Joseph, the other his legal or adopted
descent. Joseph himself was the legal father
of Jesus, and in Jewish law legal paternity
conferred all the rights of natural paternity.
The genealogy does not state that Mary
also was descended from David. It is probable that the longer genealogy of Lk is in-
tentionally more universal, implying that Jesus
is the savior not only of the Jews but of
all mankind.

Generation. In general the word generation in
the Bible refers to any contemporary group.
The Hb phrases "generation and generation"
or "from generation to generation" mean
"generation after generation," an indefinite
period extending usually into the future, but
also into the past. Besides designating a
contemporary group, the word is used to
designate a group which exhibits common

moral traits, implicitly or explicitly mentioned
(Dt 32:5, 20; Pss 14:5; 95:10), and more
frequently in the NT (Mt 11:16; 12:41 f;
12:39, 45; 17:17; Mk 8:12, 38; 9:21; Lk
7:31; 11:29 f; 16:8; AA 2:40).

Genesis (Gk *genesis*, "origin," "beginning"),
the first book of the Bible and the first of
the five books of the Pnt*. The narrative
traditions of which the Pnt is compiled are
more evident and easily analyzed in Gn and
are exhibited (following R. de Vaux) in the
following summary of contents:
I. Primitive History (1:1–11:26)
  1:1–2:4a: creation (P)
  2:4b–3:24: Paradise and the Fall (J)
  4: Cain and Abel and the Cainites (J)
  5: the antediluvian patriarchs (P)
  6:1–4: the giants (J?)
  6:5–9:17: The deluge, 6:5–8; 7:1–5,
7–10, 12, 16b, 17, 22–23; 8:2b–3a, 6–12,
13b, 20–22 (J); 6:9–22; 7:6, 11; 8:1–2a,
3b–5, 13a, 14–19; 9:1–17; 13:16a, 18–21,
24 (P)
  9:18–27; Noah and his sons (J)
  10: the table of nations, 1–7, 20–23, 31–
32 (P); 8–19, 24–30 (J)
  11:1–9: tower of Babel (J)
  11:10–26: Semite genealogy (P)
II. Patriarchal history
  12: Call of Abraham and arrival in Canaan
(J)
  13: Abraham and Lot (J)
  14: Abraham and the kings (?)
  15: Promises and covenant of Abraham
(J + E?)
  16: Birth of Ishmael (J + P, 3, 15–16)
  17: Promise and covenant of Abraham
(P)
  18:1–15: promise of a son (J)
  18:16–19:38: Sodom and Gomorrah (J)
  20: Abraham at Gerar (E)
  21:1–7: birth of Isaac (J + P)
  21:8–21: expulsion of Hagar and Ishmael (E)
  21:22–34: Abraham and Abimelek (J
+ E)
  22: sacrifice of Isaac (E + J)
  23: death of Sarah and purchase of Machpelah (P)
  24: wooing of Rebekah (J)
  25:1–10: Abraham's descendants and death
(J + P)
  25:7–18: death of Abraham and Ishmaelite
genealogy (P)
  26: Isaac (J + P, 34–35)
  27:1–45: Isaac, Esau, and Jacob (J)
  27:45–28:9: Jacob's journey to Mesopotamia (P)
  28:10–22: Jacob's dream (JE)
  29–30: Jacob and Laban (J + E)
  31:1–32:3: Jacob and Laban (E + J)

32:4–33:20: Jacob and Esau, 32:4–14, 23–33; 33 (J); 32:14–22 (E)

34: Dinah at Shechem (JE)

35: Jacob at Bethel, 21–22a (J); 1–19 (E + P in 6, 9, 15); 22b–39 (P)

36:1–5: genealogy of Esau (J or E?)

36:9–39: Edomite lists (?)

36:40–37:1: Edomite chieftains (P)

37: Joseph sold into slavery (JE, Reuben intercedes in E, Judah in J)

38: Judah and his family (J)

39: Joseph in Egypt (J)

40: Joseph in Egypt (E)

41–43: Joseph in Egypt (E + J)

44: Joseph and his brothers (J)

45:1–46:7: Joseph and his brothers (JE)

46:8–27: family of Jacob (P)

46:28–47:31: Jacob and Joseph in Egypt (J + P in 47:6–11)

48: adoption of Ephraim and Manasseh (48:1–2, 7–22, JE; 3–6, P)

49: blessing of Jacob (?)

50: death of Joseph, 1–11, 14 (J); 15–26, (E); 12–13 (P)

It is evident that the Yahwist tradition (J) is dominant in the book. It will be observed that the Elohist tradition (E) preserves nothing of the primitive history, and it seems probable that it never contained any of this material, but began with Abraham. J therefore is more universal in its outlook. J is the only tradition which preserves the story of the fall*; it also preserves the somewhat parallel story of the tower of Babel*. In P the deluge* probably served the purpose which the fall* serves in J. A number of incidents occur in more than one tradition, such as the covenant of Abraham, the expulsion of Hagar, and the patriarch's wife in the harem of a foreign king.

The compilation makes of these traditions the introduction to the history of Israel. Beginning with the creation of the world and the estrangement of man from God followed by his progressive degeneration, the book introduces with Abraham its dominant theme of promise. The promise in Gn scarcely looks beyond a numerous progeny in possession of its own land, but it is the root from which the OT conception of messianism springs. The relations of God with the patriarchs are conceived in the form of a covenant*, which is the relation of God with Israel.

On the literary origins of the book, its historical character, and its theological content cf CREATION; DELUGE; FALL; HISTORY; PATRIARCHS; PENTATEUCH and articles under personal and geographical names.

Gennesareth. In ancient times the name given to the plain lying at the NW corner of the Sea of Galilee. This region is highly praised by Josephus for the fertility of its soil, the verdance of its gardens and orchards, and the salubrity of its air. Capernaum* probably lay very near the plain. It is mentioned in the Gospels as the point where Jesus and the apostles reached land after the multiplication of the loaves (Mt 14:34; Mk 6:53), and once the Sea of Galilee is called the lake of Gennesareth (Lk 5:1).

Gentile (Lt *gentilis,* member of [foreign] people). Two Hb words, *'am* and *goy,* both

The Plain of Gennesareth between Magdala and Capernaum.

signify "people." In later OT books a usage appears in which the two terms are distinguished, '*am* for Israel and *goyim* for peoples other than Israel. The LXX reflects the same usage by rendering '*am* as *laos* and *goyim* as *ethnē*. This usage is also reflected in the NT, although neither in the LXX nor in the NT is the distinction always observed. The distinction which Jews made between themselves and the Gentiles arose after the exile and seems to have risen from a combination of several factors. One was the union of people and religion in Judaism. The national character of Israelite religion was not remarkable before the exile, since all peoples of the ancient Near East had their own religion. The subjection of the Jews to imperial foreign powers, which were often oppressive, bred hatred and resentment. The religious difference was sharpened when the Jews came into contact with the supranational religions of Hellenism; and the conflict was acute between Judaism, people and religion, and the Seleucid* kingdom in the period of the Maccabees*. The attitude of the Jews becomes supercilious, and the judgment of the Gentiles in extrabiblical Jewish literature is extremely harsh. This unfavorable judgment is reflected in some of the later books of the OT, such as Est and WS 10–19, a polemic against the Gentiles and idolatry. The Gentiles were called idolaters, although this is an oversimplification of Greek religion. Sometimes the Gentiles were called, not idolaters, but demon worshipers, since the demons were identified with the gods of the Gentiles. They were denied credit for any sound moral instincts and no vice was beneath them. In this they stood in contrast with the people of the revealed Law. Bousset points out that there were two judgments of the Gentiles by the Jews. One, which was derived from Second Is, asserted that the gods of the Gentiles were nothing and that Israel had a mission to bring the worship of the one true God to the Gentiles. The other fastened upon the consciousness of Israel as an elect nation and treated the Gentiles as reprobated by God and condemned to the worship of false gods. With this second judgment no missionary zeal was possible.

The Jewish use of the term Gentile (*ethnē*) is often reflected in the NT. Thus the Gentiles illustrate the minimum of morality which deserves no praise (Mt 5:47). The Gentiles make long prayers of empty phrases (Mt 6:7). The first mission of the apostles excluded the Gentiles from its scope (Mt 10:5). The Christian who will not accept fraternal rebuke is to be expelled like the Gentile and the publican (Mt 18:17). It is the Gentiles who will be the agents of the death of Jesus (Mt 20:19; Mk 10:33; Lk 18:32).

The Gentiles seek the things of this world (Mt 6:32; Lk 12:30). This use of the word does not appear in Jn. In past ages God permitted the Gentiles to follow their own ways (AA 14:16). Christians, when they were Gentiles, were separated from Christ, alienated from the community of Israel, strangers to the covenant of promise, without hope and without God (Eph 2:11 f). The Gentiles have a frivolous mind and darkened understanding (Eph 4:17). There is no depth of sexual immorality which is not found among the Gentiles (1 Co 5:1). They worship dumb idols (1 Co 12:2). They are slaves of their passions and know not God (1 Th 4:5). Thus, although the Christians themselves are Gentiles (Eph 3:1), frequently the same line is drawn between Christians and Gentiles which was drawn between Jews and Gentiles by Jews. This is not only an unreflecting adoption of Jewish idiom, but an implication that Christians are now the true Israel. Nevertheless, the attitude of the NT toward the Gentiles stands in total opposition to the attitude of the Jews. Paul calls himself an apostle of the Gentiles (Rm 11:13), and the number of passages in which it is expressly stated that Jesus and His apostles have a mission to the Gentiles are too numerous to need quotation.

Gerar (Hb *gᵉrār,* meaning uncertain), a city of the Negeb*. It was a point on the southern boundary of the Canaanites (Gn 10:19) and is called a Philistine city in the time of Isaac by an anachronism (Gn 26:1). Its king, Abimelech*, is related to have taken Sarah, the wife of Abraham (Gn 20:2 ff) and Rebekah, the wife of Isaac (Gn 26: 6 ff), into his harem. No doubt the same king is meant, but the story of a patriarch's wife has been duplicated. Abraham was a *gēr* in Gerar (cf STRANGER), but Isaac entered into a covenant with Abimelech (Gn 26:6 ff). Gerar was the site of a battle between Asa* and the Kushites, and the territory of the city was conquered by Asa (2 Ch 14:12 f). The OT gives no certain identification of the site. The most probable site according to modern archaeologists is Tell Jemmeh, a point about 8 mi S of Gaza. The site was sounded by Phythian-Adams in 1922 and partly excavated by Flinders Petrie in 1926–1927. The excavators report that they discovered six levels of occupation from the 14th to the 5th century BC. The site showed evidences of strong Egyptian and Mediterranean influence.

Gerasa. A Hellenistic city whose foundation was attributed to Alexander; more probably it was founded by his general Perdiccas or even later by Antiochus* Epiphanes. The city

Remains of Gerasa.

was located at the modern Jerash, about 37 mi N of Amman. According to the best readings Jesus and His apostles landed in the territory of Gerasa after the calming of the tempest (Mk 5:1; Lk 8:26); cf GADARA; GIRGASHITES. The inhabitants of the place have the unhappy distinction of asking Jesus to leave their territory because they feared Him after the exorcism of the demoniac (Lk 8:37). The ruins of Jerash, which are among the most impressive Roman ruins of the world, include a theater, the forum, and several temples; these were all built in the postbiblical period after the visit of Hadrian in the 2nd century AD and in the 3rd century when Gerasa became more important as a market after the Roman war against Palmyra.

Gergesenes. Cf GIRGASHITES.

Gerizim (Hb gᵉrizzîm, meaning unknown), the mountain which lies opposite Ebal* on the S side of the pass E of Nablus, the modern Jebel et Tur. Its altitude is about 2900 ft. In the OT it is the scene of a ceremonial blessing and curse which was a part of the ritual of the renewal of the covenant; half the representatives stood on Mt Gerizim to utter the blessing, and half stood on Mt Ebal to utter the curse (Dt 11:29 f; 27:12; Jos 8:33). Jotham* stood on the slopes of the mountain to utter his

fable against Abimelech* (Jgs 9:7 ff). At an uncertain date after the exile* and after their secession from the Jews of Jerusalem, the Samaritans built a temple on Mt Gerizim. This temple was destroyed by John Hyrcanus in 128 BC. The site, however, was still a place of Samaritan worship in NT times (Jn 4:20). It was the scene of a massacre of Samaritans by Pilate in AD 36, which was responsible for his recall to Rome. In the Jewish war the Samaritans made a stand on the mountain, but were reduced by thirst until the Romans under the command of Cerealis stormed the mountain and killed the entire force, which refused to surrender. Exploration of the mountain disclosed nothing earlier than the remains of a church and fortifications of the Byzantine period.

Gershom (Hb gēršôm, etymology and meaning uncertain). **1.** Son of Moses* and Zipporah* (Ex 2:22; 18:3, where the name is explained by a popular etymology); traditional ancestor of the priesthood of Dan (Jgs 18:30), by another tradition the ancestor of a Levitical family (1 Ch 23:15; 26:24). **2.** The head of the family of Phinehas* in the time of Ezra (Ezr 2:2). **3.** Appears in 1 Ch 6:1 ff instead of Gershon*.

Gershon (Hb gēršôn, etymology and meaning uncertain), eldest son of Levi* (Gn 46:11;

Ex 6:16), eponymous ancestor of the Levitical clan of Gershon (Nm 3:17 ff; 4:22 ff; 7:7; 10:17; 26:57). The cities and territories of the clan are described in Jos 21:27 ff; I Ch 6:56–61.

Geshem (Hb *gešem,* probably *gašmu,* etymology and meaning unknown), called the Arabian, and with Tobiah* and Sanballat* an adversary of Nehemiah* (Ne 2:19; 6:1 ff). Nothing else is known of him, and it is conjectured that he was an Arabian chieftain whose tribe had perhaps occupied former Judahite territory. The name appears in Lihyanite inscriptions. A silver bowl found in the Delta of Egypt inscribed as a votive offering to the goddess Han-'ilat offered by Qaynu, son of Gashmu, identifies Gashmu as king of Kedar*. This Gashmu is very probably the biblical Geshem.

Geshur. A kingdom E of the Jordan and N of Bashan, mentioned as a frontier of the occupation of early Israel (Dt 3:14; Jos 12:5), probably extending as far N as Mt Hermon. It was claimed as Israelite territory but never possessed (Jos 13:11, 13); one tradition related that Geshur took territory from the Israelites (1 Ch 2:23). David entered into friendly relations with Geshur, and his son Absalom* was the son of Maacah*, the daughter of Talmai*, king of Geshur (2 S 3:3; 1 Ch 3:2). Absalom fled to the king of Geshur after his murder of Amnon and stayed there three years until he was brought back by Joab (2 S 13:37; 14:23).

The Geshurites of Jos 13:2, from their position in the enumeration, belong to the S of Palestine. Their territory also was claimed by the Israelites: in 1 S 27:8, however, where they are raided by David, they are clearly non-Israelite.

Gethsemani (Gk *gethsēmanei,* probably Aramaic *gat šᵉmānê,* "oil press"), the place where Jesus went to pray after the last supper and where He was arrested (Mt 26:36 ff; Mk 14:32 ff). Lk says that He went to the Mt of Olives (22:39), as He was accustomed to do; Jn says that He went to a garden* on the Mt of Olives, where He often went with His disciples (18:1 f). The modern Gethsemani is an enclosed grove of 8 olive trees which were old in the 16th century, but they are not certainly 2000 years old. This grove lies at the foot of the Mt of Olives at the point where the modern highway to Jericho* diverges from the path over the mountain to Bethany*. A short distance to the N, adjacent to the crypt of the Church of the Tomb of the Virgin, which is all that remains of a medieval church, is a grotto which was called the grotto of the agony in the 14th century. While none of these precise identifications can be accepted as certain, Gethsemani must have been situated at or very near the spot.

Gezer (Hb *gezer,* meaning uncertain), a city which joined in the war of the 5 kings against Joshua but was not taken by the Israelites (Jos 10:33; 12:12; Jgs 1:29). It was located on the frontier of Joseph (Jos 16:3) and was claimed as a city of Ephraim (1 Ch 7:28) and as a Levitical city (1 Ch 6:52). It was the scene of a battle between David and the Philistines (2 S 5:25; 1 Ch 14:16, 20:4). It was taken from the Canaanites by the Pharaoh and given to Solomon as a dowry to his daughter when Solomon married her (1 K 9:15 ff). Solomon fortified it; this was the first time that the city passed into Israelite possession. It was taken from the Seleucid forces by Judas (2 Mc 10:32 ff) and fortified by Jonathan (1 Mc 9:52) and maintained as an important Jewish stronghold (1 Mc 13:53; 14:7, 34). Antiochus* VII laid claim to Gezer, Joppa, and the

Olive tree in Gethsemani.

citadel of Jerusalem but was unable to take them. Gezer, commanded by John Hyrcanus, was the center of resistance (1 Mc 15:28; 16:1, 19, 21).

Gezer is included among the Canaanite cities conquered by Thutmose III of Egypt (1502–1448 BC). It appears in the Amarna* Letters and seems to have fallen early to the invading Apiru. Merneptah (1234–1220) claims to have recovered it for Egypt.

The site of the city is the modern Tell Jezer, 18 mi NW of Jerusalem. The area of the city, about 22 acres, was fairly extensive for ancient Palestinian cities. The tell was excavated by R. A. S. Macalister in 1902–1909. A sounding was conducted by Alan Rowe in 1934. The excavations of Macalister, while extensive, lacked the technique and methods which have been developed since 1910 and many of his conclusions are doubtful; correction on the basis of other explorations is sometimes possible. The site was occupied in the Chalcolithic period (4500–3200 BC). Three major walls were identified. The first was built before 3000 BC during the Chalcolithic, the second about 3000 BC, and the third and principal wall about 1500 BC. This wall was remodeled in later periods and was used even in the Hellenistic period. A remarkably well-constructed tunnel built about 3000 BC connected the city with its well and secured the water supply in time of war. An area identified by the excavators and most archaeologists as the Canaanite high place* had several standing stones which suggest the pillars (*maṣṣēbôt*) of the OT. Some scholars, however, regard these as memorial stelae for funerary rites, and a few are not entirely convinced that the area, a large level artificial stone platform, was a cultic area. Gezer yielded not only some cuneiform contract tablets of the 15th-14th centuries BC — thus attesting Mesopotamian influence at this period — but also the Gezer calendar of about the 10th century BC, the earliest important Hb inscription. It is thought to be a school exercise. The months are not named but identified by the work of the agricultural seasons. The excavation did not correspond entirely to the biblical data. There is a gap in the history of the occupation from about the 9th to the 5th centuries BC, beginning at the time when the city was given to Solomon by the Pharaoh. No evidence of destruction in the 9th century was found; but the statement that the Pharaoh "burned" the city need not be taken crassly.

Giant. Cf ANAKIM; NEPHILIM; REPHAIM.

Gibbethon (Hb *gibbᵉtôn*, "little hill (?)"), included among the cities of Dan (Jos 19:44) and the Levitical cities (Jos 21:23). It belonged, however, to the Philistines at least into the 9th century; it was unsuccessfully besieged by the Israelites under Nadab* (1 K 15:27) and Omri* (1 K 16:15–17). Scholars identify it with Tell et Melat between Ekron* and Gezer*. It was very probably included in the territory of Ekron and was an outpost against the Israelite frontier.

Gibeah (Hb *gibᵉʿāh*, "hill"), the city of this name enumerated with the cities of Judah (Jos 15:57) can scarcely be identical with the city of Benjamin (Jos 18:28), but a Gibeah of Judah is not mentioned elsewhere. Gibeah of Benjamin was the scene of the crime against the Levite's wife which was the occasion of the intertribal war of Jgs 19–21. Saul met the prophets at Gibeah and joined them in ecstasy (1 S 10:5, 10). Since the name "Gibeah of Elohim" which appears here is most unusual, some interpreters prefer to render the word here "the hill of Elohim" as a designation of a sanctuary. Gibeah was the home of Saul both before (1 S 10:26) and after (1 S 10:26) his accession to the throne and it appears as his royal residence throughout his reign (1 S 22:6; 23:19; 26:1). As the royal residence the city was called Gibeah of Saul (1 S 15:34; Is 10:29). Hosea's allusions to the crime of Gibeah are too indefinite to be referred certainly to the episode of Jgs 19 (9:9; 10:9). As a frontier point of Benjamin it is a place where the alarm of an approaching enemy is raised (Ho 5:8). It is one of the points near Jerusalem on the road from the N (Is 10:29). On the confusion of Gibeah and Geba in 1 S 13–14 cf GEBA. Gibeon should be read for Gibeah in Jgs 20:31, and "Gibeon, on the mountain of Yahweh" should be read for "Gibeon of Saul, the chosen of Yahweh" in 2 S 21:6 as the scene of the execution of the descendants of Saul.

Since the excavations of W. F. Albright at Tell el Ful in 1922 and 1933 the identification of this site with Gibeah is not questioned. The tell lies about 4 mi N of the Damascus Gate, just outside the suburban areas of modern Jerusalem. Three phases of occupation were distinguished. The first, about the 12th century, left few remains and was ended by a conflagration; Albright suggests that this may be connected with the war against Gibeah of Jgs 19–21. The second phase was marked by a strong citadel with double casemated walls and bastions. Only one bastion was preserved, but parallel constructions elsewhere show that the fortress had these bastions at each of its four corners. This citadel belongs to the 11th century and must be the citadel of Saul. It also was destroyed by fire, no doubt by the Philistines. Albright believes that this occurred during Saul's life, perhaps early in his reign, since the reconstruction of the citadel in another phase of the same period followed very closely the lines of the original construction. In the period of the divided monarchy (9th-8th centuries) a tower was built over the remains of the citadel. The village was probably destroyed during the Babylonian invasions of 598–587 and was most intensively occupied during the Hellenistic and Roman periods. It was probably destroyed by Titus in his attack on Jerusalem in AD 70.

Gibeon (Hb *gibᶜʿôn*, meaning uncertain), a town of Benjamin (Jos 18:25) and a levitical city (Jos 21:17). With Chephirah, Beeroth*, and Kiriath-jearim* Gibeon was one of the cities of the Horites*. A story doubtless considerably transformed in transmission explains the connection of the Horite league of towns with Israel by a covenant obtained by the Gibeonites through craft (Jos 9:3 ff). The importance of the story is not in the details, but in the clear attestation that the Israelites obtained the Horite territory by compact. In virtue of the covenant Gibeon was able to summon aid from the Israelites, and the battle of Joshua with the five Canaanite kings took place near Gibeon (Jos 10:1–27). The great pool of Gibeon (cf below) was the scene of the tournament between the men of Joab and the men of Abner which was followed by a battle (2 S 2:12 ff), and "the great stone in Gibeon" was the scene of the assassination of Amasa* by Joab* (2 S 20:8). The men of Gibeon were able to appeal to David for revenge on the house of Saul in virtue of an oracle (2 S 21:1–14). Precisely what the complaint against Saul was is not clear; very probably it was based upon the covenant by which Gibeon had been accepted into Israel. Gibeon had a notable high place where Solomon worshiped (1 K 3:4 f); the Chronicler* explains this by placing at Gibeon the tabernacle* (1 Ch 21:29; 2 Ch 1:3, 13). Gibeon was a point on the Assyrian march from the N described in Is 28:21. Gibeon was the home of Hananiah*, the prophet who opposed Jeremiah (Je 28:1) and of Ishmaiah, one of David's heroes (1 Ch 12:4). The Chronicler mentions a victory of David over the Philistines near Gibeon (1 Ch 14:16), and gives the name of the Benjaminite clan which settled at Gibeon (1 Ch 8:29; 9:35). The pool of Gibeon recurs in Je 41:12, 16 as the scene of the defeat of the brigand Ishmael*, the murderer of Gedaliah*. Gibeon was settled after the exile (Ne 3:7; 7:25). It is mentioned in the list of Palestinian towns taken by Shishak* (ANET 242).

Gibeon is identified with the modern El Jib, 8 mi N of Jerusalem. It lies near the head of the valley of Aijalon* (cf SHEP-HELAH) which connects the highlands with the coastal plain. The ancient town lay upon a hill somewhat larger and higher than the adjacent hill on which the modern village is built. Gibeon was excavated by J. B. Pritchard through four seasons beginning in 1956. The excavation confirmed in a surprising way the description of Gibeon as "a great city, like a royal city" (Jos 10:2); while the outer walls were uncovered in several places, the perimeter of the city is still undetermined, but it was spacious — larger than the area which is usually attributed to the fortified area of Jerusalem when David took the city. Occupation levels have been definitely identified for Middle Bronze I and II and Iron II; the Middle Bronze II level shows destruction by fire. A necropolis of 14 tombs contained abundant pottery from Middle Bronze I–II and Late Bronze. Part of a large building which was very probably erected in Iron I has been uncovered. The gaps in the occupation in the excavated sites are here irrelevant, as by far most of the area enclosed by the wall has not been excavated, and occupation through Middle Bronze to Iron II is easily assumed. Little of any traces of occupation during the Hellenistic period have been discovered, but occupation is sure for the Roman period. From the Roman period came a large rectangular reservoir, stepped and plastered. The ancient spring was reached by a stepped tunnel cut into the rock which gave access from within the walls and permitted the outside of the spring to be concealed; similar installations were found at Jerusalem (cf GIHON), Megiddo*, and Gezer*. This tunnel was dated with probability in Iron II. The most remarkable hydraulic installation was a cylindrical rock cut pool 35 ft in diameter, descending 33 ft to a floor below which was a water chamber 42 ft deep, a total of 75 ft in depth; a spiral stairway of 79 steps was cut to the bottom. The excavators dated the excavation of the pool tentatively in Iron I. The identification of this pool with "the great pool of Gibeon" (Je 41:12; cf 2 S 2:12) is tempting, if only because one wonders what other pool of Gibeon would receive this name; it is the largest hydraulic excavation from such an early period.

The excavators believe that the size and prosperity of Gibeon was based during the Israelite monarchy upon its wine industry; there are good reasons for supposing that Gibeon was the largest center of the manufacture of wine in ancient Israel. In what the excavators called "industrial areas," which included several acres, there were 63 vats, 5–6 ft in depth and 4–5 ft in diameter, cut in the rock, far too numerous and too closely spaced to serve as cisterns for dwellings. The fact that most of them were not plastered made it impossible to suppose that they were cisterns; the porous limestone will not hold water. Some had been later connected to form caves. Since the temperature of the vats is a fairly steady 65° F, it was easily supposed that wine was stored in them in large jars. This theory was confirmed by the presence of channels cut in the rock connecting smaller basins, of a convenient size for treading the grapes and for settling. The site also disclosed a large number of stamped jar handles with the royal stamp, names of towns, and apparently names of private owners (Azariah, Hananiah). Some of the handles bore the name of the town, Gibeon. During the Roman period one of the plastered vats was used for the storage of olive oil.

Gideon (Hb *gid^{e‘}ôn*, "hewer," "warrior" [?]), son of Joash of the clan of Abiezri of the tribe of Manasseh, one of the judges of Israel. When the Israelites were afflicted by the incursions of Midianite* raiders from the desert (Jgs 6:1–7), they were rebuked by a prophet (6:7–10), and Gideon was called by the angel of Yahweh to save Israel (6:11–16). He asked a sign of assurance; as a sign his sacrifice was consumed by fire, and he built an altar to Yahweh-shalom to commemorate the event (6:17–24). He overturned an altar to the Baal which belonged to his father and received from his father the name of Jerubbaal, "Let Baal contend" (6:25–32). It is possible that Gideon is here conflated with another figure, Jerubbaal, the head of the clan which ruled Shechem (Jgs 9:1 ff). Gideon called warriors from his own clan, from the rest of Manasseh, and from Asher, Zebulun, and Naphtali and received another sign, the sign of the fleece (6:33–40). He took his army to En Harod but sharply reduced its numbers by the ordeal of the drinking water (7:1–8). In a nocturnal vision both Gideon and two of the Midianites were warned in a dream of the victory of the Israelites; the victory was accomplished when Gideon's small force by noise excited the Midianites to panic and flight. They were cut off by warriors from other tribes at the fords of the Jordan (7:9–25). The tribe of Ephraim, which claimed a preeminence, was angered at Gideon's independent action, but he soothed their anger by his humble words (8:1–3). Gideon pursued the Midianites across the Jordan. He was refused hospital-

ity at Succoth* and Penuel* and threatened reprisals (8:4–9). He overtook the Midianites, defeated them and captured their two kings, and took revenge on the two inhospitable cities (8:10–16). He then executed the two kings in blood vengeance (cf AVENGER) for the killing of his brothers on Mt Tabor (8:18–21). His attempt to get his youngest son Jether to perform the action was unsuccessful, because the boy was too young; such an introduction of the younger generation to the blood feud is a recognized practice. The Israelites then offered Gideon the crown, but he refused it because Yahweh is Israel's only king; he did, however, make an ephod* of the leader's portion of the booty which came to him (8:22–28).

The allusions to Gideon's victory elsewhere in the OT (Ps 83:10; Is 9:3; 10:26) suggest that it was one of the more popular pieces of Israelite tradition. Most modern critics find clear indications of several versions of the story in Jgs 6–8. There is quite general agreement that the story of 8:4–21 is independent of the story in 7:1–8:3. In the first story there is a tribal war against a general invasion; in the second Gideon and his clan pursue a single group in execution of a blood feud not mentioned earlier. This story has lost its introduction. The names of the chieftains differ: Oreb and Zeeb in 7:1–8:3, Zebah and Zalmunna in 8:4–21. The first story has been embellished by a number of details (the vocation of Gideon, the multiple signs assuring his victory, and the ordeal which reduces the number of his forces) which emphasize that deliverance is the work of Yahweh and not of human strength. With A. Vincent we may distinguish two accounts of the vocation of Gideon in 6:11–24 and 25–35, and very probably the remnant of a third account in 6:36–40. The appearance of the angel* of Yahweh is composed in a pattern which can also be traced in the apparition of the angel to Manoah and his wife (Jgs 13:3–23). The introduction (Jgs 6:1–10) is placed in the Deuteronomic framework of the book; cf JUDGES.

The story shows Israel as a settled agricultural people, not strong enough to resist the incursions of the nomad raiders even in western Palestine; cf OPHRAH. The camels of the Midianites here are the first certain mention of domesticated camels in the OT; cf CAMEL. The swiftness and capacity for long distance travel of these animals made it difficult for the peasants to defend themselves against raids.

The conclusion (8:22–28), while it may preserve genuine tradition, is couched in its present form as a polemic against monarchy;

cf KING. On the problem of the ephod of Gideon cf EPHOD.

Gihon (Hb *gîḥôn*, meaning uncertain; perhaps from *gîᵃḥ*, "burst forth"). **1.** One of the four rivers of Paradise* which flows around the land of Cush* (Gn 2:13). This river cannot be identified with any known geographical reality and probably, as a creation of early folklore, is not intended to be so identified.

2. A spring on the eastern slope of the hill of Zion*, the modern Ain Umm ed Daraj or Ain Sitti Maryam; one of the two springs of ancient Jerusalem*. This was the principal source of water for Jebusite and Israelite Jerusalem. Explorations of the spring and excavations in the hill of Zion reveal that the Jebusites made a passage from the city to the spring, which lay too low on the slope to be included within the fortifications; it was necessary both to protect the water supply for the city and to make the spring unavailable as far as possible to invading enemies. It seems that this was done by diverting the natural flow of the water down the slope into a pool cut in the rock of the hill which was reached from the city by a shaft. This is very probably the *ṣinnôr* mentioned in 2 S 5:8 through which David's men succeeded in capturing Jerusalem. The text is too corrupt to permit us to reconstruct the operation. In addition, L. H. Vincent distinguished four artificial transformations of the spring, all belonging to the period of the Israelite monarchy. The latest

of these is attributed to Hezekiah* and is identified with the tunnel mentioned in 2 K 20:20; 2 Ch 32:30; BS 48:17. This work was done in anticipation of the siege of Jerusalem by Sennacherib*. The tunnel passed completely under the hill of Zion from the eastern slope to the western slope in the valley of the Tyropoeon. It was cut in a circuitous S-shaped route, and it is thought that at least one reason for this devious route was the necessity of avoiding the royal necropolis. The length of the tunnel, including the works necessary to connect the new tunnel with the spring through the older tunnels, is about 1760 ft. The level of the tunnel falls 7 ft from the spring to the western outlet. The traces of the work in the tunnel shows that it was executed by two companies beginning at opposite ends and meeting near the middle. The completion of the tunnel was marked by an inscription on the wall of the tunnel near the spring. The inscription was discovered in 1880 and has since been removed from the wall to the museum of Istanbul. The inscription is one of the few examples of 8th-century script. It is thus translated by W. F. Albright (ANET 321): "[. . . when] (the tunnel) was driven through. And this was the way in which it was cut through: — While [. . .] (were) still [. . .] axe(s), each man towards his fellow, and while there were still three cubits to be cut through, [there was heard] the voice of a man calling to his fellow, for there was *an overlap* in the rock on the right [and on the left]. And when

The inscription of Hezekiah in the tunnel of Siloam.

the tunnel was driven through, the quarrymen hewed (the rock), each man towards his fellow, axe against axe: and the water flowed from the spring towards the reservoir for 1,200 cubits, and the height of the rock above the head(s) of the quarrymen was 100 cubits." On other biblical references to the reservoir of Hezekiah cf SILOAM. Gihon was the scene of the coronation of Solomon* (1 K 1:33 ff). Its connection with wall of Manasseh is obscure (2 Ch 33:14).

Gilboa (Hb *gilbô'a*, meaning uncertain), a mountain at the northern extremity of the chain of hills of Samaria which rises from the S side of the plain of Esdraelon* W of Beth-shan*. It rises to a height of about 1650 ft and is now called Jebel Fuqu'a. It was the scene of the camp of Saul in his last campaign against the Philistines (1 S 28:4) and of the battle in which Saul and his sons were killed (1 S 31:1, 8; 2 S 1:6, 21; 21:12; 1 Ch 10:1, 8).

Gilead (Hb *gil'e'ād*, etymology uncertain; the connection of the name with *gal'e'ēd*, "heap of testimony" [Gn 31:47 ff] is fanciful), a geographical designation of the territory E of the Jordan and W of Ammon bounded roughly by Heshbon* on the S and the Yarmuk on the N. The territory included in the name fluctuates in various instances of its usage. The land is a rolling plateau watered by many streams and enjoying a good annual rainfall which gives it fertile soil. It is called a desirable land (Je 22:6). Its fertility is counterbalanced by the fact that its E frontier offers no natural barrier to the invasion of desert tribes. From ancient times it was regarded as excellent pasture land (Nm 32:1) and this feature of the land is emphasized in the messianic restoration of Israel (Je 50:19; Mi 7:14; cf also Zc 10:10). A woman's hair is compared to

flocks streaming down the hills of Gilead (SS 4:1; 6:5). The geographical name becomes a personal name in some of the clan lists. Gilead is the son of Machir*, a Manassite clan which settled in N Gilead (Nm 26:29; 1 Ch 2:21, 23). The clans of Gilead are listed under Gilead as their father (Nm 26:30–33; ·cf Nm 27:1; 36:1; Jos 17:3; 1 Ch 7:14 ff). Jephthah* is called the illegitimate son of Gilead (Jgs 11:1 ff). Here the name of Jephthah's father must have been lost in an early stage of the tradition. It was in Gilead that Laban* overtook Jacob* when the latter returned from Mesopotamia (Gn 31:21 ff); the story of the covenant made by the two is no doubt written in such a way as to reflect the claims of Israel to Gilead against the Aramaean* kingdom of Damascus* in the 9th and 8th centuries by basing the claim upon a covenant made by the ancestors of the two peoples granting Jacob the possession of Gilead. The assignment of Gilead to the tribes of Reuben*, Gad*, and half of the tribe of Manasseh* was attributed in the traditions to Moses himself. The southern portion of Gilead S of the Jabbok was assigned to Reuben and Gad (Nm 32:1 ff). Reuben, which vanished early as a tribe, is not elsewhere mentioned in connection with Gilead. N Gilead is assigned to half the tribe of Manasseh (Dt 3:13); the term is used here includes Bashan*, N of Gilead proper (cf also Jos 13:25 ff, 29 ff; 17:1 ff). The territory of Gilead was formerly a part of the kingdom of Og* of Bashan to the N and of Sihon* of Heshbon* to the S (Dt 3:1 ff; Jos 12:1, 6). Gilead is mentioned among the Israelite tribes which took no part in the campaign of Barak* and Deborah* against the Canaanites (Jgs 5:17). Thus this early song exhibits a sense of the unity of Gilead with the tribes of W Palestine. Gilead was the home of two of the judges, Jair* (Jgs 10:3 ff)

Mount Gilboa and the Plain of Esdraelon.

and Jephthah* (Jgs 11–12). Gilead is mentioned among the tribes which took part in the war against Benjamin* (Jgs 20:1). In the reigns of Saul and David Gilead was a point where resistance to the Philistines and loyalty to the monarchy survived disturbances in W Palestine. Thus Gilead was the seat of the kingdom of Ishbaal*, the son of Saul, after the Israelites were defeated in the battle of Mt Gilboa (2 S 2:9). David also saved himself in the rebellion of Absalom by flight to Gilead, where he was able to organize the resistance which defeated the rebellion (2 S 17:22). The territory of Gilead was divided among three of the administrative districts of Solomon (1 K 4:13 f, 19). Gilead was the place of origin of Elijah* (1 K 17:1). In the division of the kingdom under Rehoboam* Gilead remained with N Israel. The N border of Gilead was an object of dispute between Israel and Damascus during most of the 9th and 8th centuries, and the territory was taken from Israel by Hazael* during the reign of Jehu* (2 K 10:32 f). This campaign is probably alluded to in Am 1:3. We may assume that it was recovered by Israel under Jeroboam* II; but it was taken from Israel by Tiglath-pileser* III in 734 and incorporated into an Assyrian province (2 K 15:29). A raid or a campaign of the Ammonites against Gilead alluded to in Am 1:13 is not mentioned elsewhere. Two allusions of Ho to Gilead as a city of evildoers (6:8) and as wicked (12:12) are unexplained. Obscure also are the allusions of Je to the balm of Gilead (8:22; 46:11), which suggest that the country was a producer of balm. Gilead was not included in the ideal restored Israel of Ezk (47:18). In the Maccabean period a campaign in Gilead was carried on by Judas to rescue the Jews in E Palestine from their Gentile neighbors. After military victories Judas finally decided to evacuate the Jews of E Palestine to W Palestine (1 Mc 5:9–54).

Gilgal (Hb gilgal, "circle" [of stones]), the name of a place the geography of which is not entirely certain; the name appears to be given to more than one place. Gilgal was the base of operations of Joshua*, where the circle of 12 commemorative stones was set up (Jos 4:19 f) and where the Israelites were circumcised (Jos 5:9; here another popular etymology of the name is given (Jos 10:6 ff; 14:6; Jgs 2:1). Gilgal appears as the end of the journey of the Israelites from Moab to Canaan (Mi 6:5). Not only the geographical context suggests proximity to Jericho, but this is explicitly stated in Jos 4:19. Gilgal also appears as a holy place in the days of Samuel* (1 S

7:16) and the place where Saul was installed as king (1 S 10:8; 11:14 ff), hence very probably a sanctuary. It was also a base of operations for Saul against the Philistines and the Amalekites (1 S 13:4 ff; 15:12 ff), but it was also a holy place where Yahweh was symbolically present (1 S 15:33). Gilgal in the valley of the Jordan* was the place where the men of Judah went to meet David when he returned from Gilead (2 S 19:16, 41). The Gilgal of Elijah and Elisha appears to be also in the valley of the Jordan (2 K 2:1; 4:38). A Gilgal is one of the great sanctuaries of N Israel, mentioned by Am (4:4; 5:5) and by Ho (9:15; 12:12). There is no reason to suppose that more than one place is meant in these passages. It is to be located in the Jordan valley near Jericho. Opinions of modern scholars are divided between Khirbet en Nitleh, about 3 mi SE of Tell es Sultan, and Khirbet Mefjer, about 1¼ mi N of Tell es Sultan. No certain traces of Iron Age occupation have been discovered at Khirbet en Nitleh. Traces of Iron Age settlement at Khirbet Mefjer were found by Muilenburg in 1954. Three other occurrences of the name cannot be applied to Gilgal of the Jordan valley. The Gilgal near the terebinth of Moreh (Dt 11:30) must be located near Shechem*. Since this place is not mentioned elsewhere, some scholars suspect that the text is not correctly preserved. A Gilgal opposite Adummin was located on the S boundary of Judah (Jos 15:7). For Gilgal in Jos 12:23 most scholars prefer to read Galilee*.

Gilgamesh, Epic of. A Mesopotamian poem named after its hero Gilgamesh, "two-thirds god and one-third man." It is divided into 12 tablets or cantos and may be outlined as follows:

Tablet I: Gilgamesh, king of Uruk (Erech*), disturbs the citizens by his violence and his lust. They petition the gods for aid. Aruru creates Enkidu, who lives in a state of nature with the wild beasts. Gilgamesh hears of him and sends a prostitute to seduce him. After this experience Enkidu loses his wildness and becomes a dweller of Uruk and a bosom comrade of Gilgamesh.

Tablet II: For some reason (the text is broken at this point) Gilgamesh and Enkidu engage in furious combat, but Gilgamesh suddenly repents of his fury and the friendship of the two is strengthened.

Tablet III: Gilgamesh determines to slay the monster Huwawa who resides on the cedar mountain.

Tablet IV: Gilgamesh and Enkidu reach the cedar forest.

Tablet V: Gilgamesh has a favorable dream, but Enkidu has a dream which seems ominous; the text is badly mutilated. Only a fragment of the account of the slaying of Huwawa is preserved.

Tablet VI: Ishtar offers herself to Gilgamesh, but he refuses her with contempt, recounting the names of those who have perished because of her love. Ishtar petitions her father Anu to send the bull of heaven against Enkidu. The bull kills hundreds, but is itself slain by Enkidu and Gilgamesh.

Tablet VII: The gods decree that one of the two must die; it is Enkidu. He curses those who brought him from the wilderness to the city, but is persuaded to change the curses to blessings. Enkidu dreams of the nether world, which is described in customary terms.

Tablet VIII: The mourning of Gilgamesh for Enkidu.

Tablet IX: Gilgamesh, frightened by death, determines to seek life by journeying to Utnapishtim, the survivor of the deluge, the only man who has escaped death. He reaches a mountain and a "scorpion-man," who tries to discourage him from continuing the dangerous journey.

Tablet X: He reaches the ale-wife Siduri, who also tries to discourage him, affirming the inevitability of death; but he pushes on to the waters of death, where he meets the boatman Urshanabi, who tells him how to cross the waters. There he finds Utnapishtim.

Tablet XI: Utnapishtim relates the story of the deluge and his escape. He reveals to Gilgamesh the place of the plant of life. Gilgamesh finds the plant, but while he is bathing a serpent steals it.

Tablet XII: An appendix. Here Enkidu has perished because he went to the underworld to recover the *pukku* and *mikku* dropped by Gilgamesh. Finally the shade of Enkidu is permitted to rise to tell Gilgamesh of the underworld, which he does with the deepest pessimism: "If I tell thee the order of the nether world which I have seen, sit thou down and weep."

The epic is preserved in numerous fragments. The principal tablets come from the library of Ashur-bani-pal of Assyria (668–626) and the First Dynasty of Babylon (1830–1580). The above outline is based on a text reconstructed from these Akkadian sources (ANET 72–99). A Hittite translation is known. Much of it has now been found in Sumerian* (partly presented in ANET 42–52). S. N. Kramer lists the following episodes: (1) Gilgamesh and the Land of the Living (Tablets III–V); (2) Gilgamesh and the Bull of Heaven (Tablet VI); (3) The Deluge (Tablet XI); (4) The Death of Gilgamesh (no correspondence);

(5) Gilgamesh and Agga of Kish (no correspondence); (6) Gilgamesh, Enkidu, and the Nether World (the Akkadian text is a translation of the Sumerian original).

The stories must go back into the 3rd millennium BC. It appears that they were a part of a cycle of heroic tales. The Deluge story, in particular, appears to have had no original connection with the Gilgamesh cycle. The Babylonians of the First Dynasty, however, wove the stories together into an epic which revolves around the theme of the paradox of the joy of life and the inevitability of death, and of man's unsearching and hopeless quest for life.

There are a number of points of possible and probable contacts with the OT. Wherever these contacts appear the Hebrew poets and storytellers have transformed the material into a vehicle of their own beliefs. On Enkidu as man in the state of nature changing through sexual experience into historic man, and on the serpent which steals the plant of life cf FALL. On the deluge cf DELUGE.

Gimel. The 3rd letter of the Hb alphabet, with the value of *g*.

Girgashites (Hb *girgāšî*, etymology uncertain), one of the pre-Israelite peoples of Canaan; a descendant of Canaan in the Table* of Nations (Gn 10:16; 1 Ch 1:14), mentioned only in enumerations (Gn 15:21; Dt 7:1; Jos 3:10; 24:11; Ne 9:8). The name does not occur elsewhere and nothing is known of this people. The Gergesenes of the NT appear in some MSS as a variant reading for Gadarene (cf GADARA) or Gerasene (cf GERASA; Mt 8:28; Mk 5:1; Lk 8:26, 37); the reading has no critical support, and is probably formed from the OT name.

Glass. The manufacture of glass was known in the Old Kingdom in Egypt. Its discovery was probably connected with the manufacture of glaze, and was to some extent due to the fact that much of the sand of Egypt has a high content of calcium carbonate. The manufacture of glass in ancient Egypt reached its highest technique during the 18th–19th dynasties. Glass was cast, and hence its use was limited to the manufacture of beads, amulets, and small vessels. The technique of glassblowing was not discovered until the 1st century BC, probably in Phoenicia. The sand near Sidon also has the proper chemical content for the manufacture of glass. Glass vessels were quite common during NT times in the Roman empire. Transparent glass was not produced in the ancient world, and in the early Egyptian period even translucent glass was generally beyond the capacity of the manufacturers.

Colored glass was preferred to plain glass; the color was obtained by the addition of metal oxides. Egypt was the principal center of the production of glass until the Persian and Hellenistic periods, when Syria and Phoenicia became active and proficient in glass manufacture. The glass objects found in Palestinian sites in Bronze and Iron Age levels are entirely Egyptian imports. Glass beads and amulets are much more common than vessels. Glass is mentioned only once in the OT (Jb 28:17), with gold, which indicates its comparatively high price in ancient times; it was used in the manufacture of imitation jewelry for personal ornamentation and for luxury vessels. In the NT it is mentioned only in Apc 4:6; 15:2; 21:18. The sea of glass of Apc suggests a large glass mass, the kind which was prepared by glass manufacturers for the production of cut glass.

Glean. Hb law prohibited the farmer from reaping his field to the extreme limit and in the corners (Lv 19:9 f; 23:22; Dt 24:19–22), nor was he to glean after the reapers. The leavings of the reapers were to be left in the field for the poor, the resident alien (cf STRANGER), the orphan, and the widow. The same generosity was to be exhibited in the harvest of the olives and the grapes. Such gleaning by the poor is described in Rt 2.

Glory 1. *OT.* Hb *kābôd* signifies weight or heaviness. Glory is importance, that which exhibits a man's inner worth and demands the respect of others. References to the glory of man are common in wisdom* literature, which deals so frequently with the attainment of success in one's life and business. Glory sometimes appears to be identified with riches and possessions, which win the esteem of others (Ec 6:2; Gn 31:1; 1 K 3:13 +). The glory of God is a complex theological concept which exhibits several aspects. The most primitive form of the conception appears to be found in the Pnt. Here the glory of Yahweh is described in terms suggesting the pillar of cloud and the pillar of fire; in the exodus* traditions these were the visible manifestation of Yahweh's presence and protection. Glory is expressly said to be a cloud or in a cloud (Ex 16:10; 24:16 ff; Lv 9:6, 23; Nm 14:22; 16:19; 17:7; 20:6). This is the glory which the Israelites can see (Ex 16:7). The glory is described as smoke and fire (Dt 5:21); here also the glory of Yahweh is visible to the Israelites. The glory of Yahweh as a cloud dwells in the tabernacle (Ex 40:34; Nm 14:10). The glory as a cloud also dwells in the temple of Solomon (1 K 8:11 +), and in this manner was manifested to Isaiah*

(Is 6:3 f). The imagery of the exodus appears elsewhere in the OT to describe the glory of Yahweh. The glory is a cloud canopy over Israel (Is 4:5; cf also Is 58:8; Mi 1:15). Elsewhere, however, the glory of Yahweh appears rather as a brilliant light, and it is visible to men only when it is veiled by a cloud which is rendered luminous by that which it contains. The luminous character of the glory of Yahweh is clear in Is 24:23; 60:1. In the imagination of Ezekiel the luminous cloud becomes the object of a detailed description. The prophet at first sees only the luminous cloud which, as it approaches nearer, is seen to contain the brilliance of Yahweh Himself riding upon His chariot. The term glory is applied to the cloud, to the chariot, or to Yahweh Himself, who is rendered invisible by the brilliance (Ezk 1:28; 3:12; 3:23; 8:4; 10:18 f; 11:22 f; 43:2, 5; 44:4).

The conception of glory as light is very probably at the base of passages which say that the earth is full of the glory of Yahweh, i.e., light (Nm 14:21), or that the earth is bright with the glory of Yahweh (Ezk 43:2), or that the glory of Yahweh is above the heavens (Ps 113:4). The same conception of glory as light too brilliant to be seen is reflected in the story of Moses' request, which was refused, to see the glory of Yahweh (Ex 33:18). He must cover his face while the glory of Yahweh passes and he may view it only as it departs (Ex 33:22). That which was refused Moses in this episode was granted to all Israel in the passages cited above.

In later books the concept of glory loses some of its primitive concrete reality, and to see the glory of Yahweh means to witness His saving acts (cf Is 35:2; 40:5; 59:19; 66:18 f; Ps 63:3). The glory of Yahweh is then a visible manifestation of His divinity, and glory has been defined as holiness* manifest. To give glory to Yahweh is to recognize His divinity. One gives glory by confessing sin (Jos 7:19; Je 13:16). This can be done by non-Israelites (1 S 6:5). One gives glory to Yahweh by confessing His divinity in hymns of praise (1 Ch 16:28; Pss 29:1, 9; 96:7; 30:13; 66:2; 115:1; Is 42:12). The priests give glory to Yahweh by performing the functions of cult (Mal 2:2). The glory as a recognition of the divinity of Yahweh is also intended in the knowledge of the glory of Yahweh which will fill the earth (Hab 2:14), and in the same sense the heavens declare the glory of Yahweh (Ps 19:2; cf Ps 96:3). The glory of Yahweh, the recognition of His divinity, is cited as a motive why He should assist Israel (Ps 79:9), and the recognition of His divinity is to endure forever (Ps 104:31).

In the same sense the glory of Yahweh is great (Ps 138:5), and this is the glory which Yahweh will not grant to another (Is 42:8; 48:11). Likewise the Israelites are created for the glory of Yahweh, i.e., the recognition of His divinity (Is 43:7), and in this sense the Psalmist prays that the nations will see the glory of Yahweh (Ps 97:6). Once at least in the mouth of Yahweh "my glory" is a simple substitute for the personal pronoun "me" (Je 2:11, altered by Jewish scribes out of reverence to read "its glory").

Glory is also used in an adjectival sense: thus throne of glory (1 S 2:8; Is 22:23; Je 14:21; 17:12), the king of glory (Ps 24:7 ff), the God of glory (Ps 29:3), the dwelling of glory (Ps 26:8), the dwelling of the messianic king (Is 11:10). In these adjectival uses, however, the original primitive conception can be seen. The throne of glory is the throne on which Yahweh sits in luminous brilliance, and the glorious king and the glorious God is the God-king of cloud and fire.

2. *NT.* I. The Synoptic Gospels. The Gospels reflect the OT use of the word glory, especially in the phrase "to glorify God," to give Him glory by confessing His divinity. The glory of God which illuminated the shepherds at Bethlehem was a brilliant light (Lk 2:9). Jesus shares the glory, i.e., the luminous brilliance of His Father, and this will be manifest in His Second Coming as judge (Mt 16:27; 24:30; 25:31; Mk 8:38; 13:26; Lk 21:27). Once in the Synoptics Jesus is said to arrive at His glory through His passion and death (Lk 24:26). The throne of glory which belongs to Yahweh in the OT is attributed to Jesus in the Synoptics (Mt 19:28) and the disciples ask that they too may sit on thrones of glory (Mk 10:37). The brilliance of the glory of Jesus is manifested by anticipation in His transfiguration* (Lk 9:31 f).

II. The Apostolic Writings. AA continues the OT usage. Stephen*, just before his death, saw the glory of God in the opened heavens, the only visible manifestation of divinity which man can perceive (AA 7:55). The glory is also the luminous brilliance of Paul's vision on the road to Damascus which prevented his companions from seeing the vision (AA 22:11). The glory of the incorruptible God which the Gentiles exchanged for the likeness of creatures (Rm 1:23) is an echo of Je 2:11. Sinners are deprived of the glory of God, here no doubt His presence as in the tabernacle and temple (Rm 3:23). Paul explains elaborately that just as the ministry of the Old Law was granted in an atmosphere of glory, so there is an element of glory in the manifestation of the New Law (2 Co 3:7 ff). The glory

of God, the recognition of His divinity, is alleged as a motive for His plan of salvation in Christ (Eph 1:12; Phl 1:11). In the NT God is glorified through Jesus (1 Pt 4:11). The glory of Christ is more prominent in the apostolic writings outside the Pauline corpus. Christ through His sufferings is in the glory of the Father (Phl 2:11), and He is taken into heaven in glory (1 Tm 3:16). He is the reflection of the glory of the Father (Heb 1:3). The glory which is proper to Jesus Christ as redeemer is obtained through sufferings (Heb 2:9; 1 Pt 1:11). God is glorified through His raising of Jesus from the dead (1 Pt 1:21), and Christians await the future revelation of His glory, no doubt an allusion to His Second Coming (1 Pt 4:13; 5:1). Twice Jesus is given the title of lord of glory, glorious lord (1 Co 2:8; Js 2:1).

In the Pauline writings the concept of glory as referred to the Christian receives a new and original elaboration. Christians have the hope of sharing in the glory of God (Rm 5:2). They shall be glorified with Christ through their sharing of His passion (Rm 8:17), and through this sharing of His passion the glory of God will be revealed in them (Rm 8:18). This glory confers perfect freedom upon the Christian (Rm 8:21), and the translation of the Christian into glory terminates the process of foreknowledge, predestination, and justification (Rm 8:30). The Christian, like Christ, will rise to glory (1 Co 15:40). He will be conformed to the glorious body of Jesus Christ (Phl 3:21). He will appear glorified with Christ (Col 3:4) and will share in the glory of the Lord (2 Th 2:14). The Christian reflects the glory of the Father by being changed into His likeness (2 Co 3:18), and this is the glory proper to the revelation of the new covenant. Paul tells Christians to do whatever they do for the glory of God, that His divinity may be recognized (1 Co 10:31), and to glorify God in their bodies by observing the ideal of Christian chastity (1 Co 6:20). In a sense, then, the manifest holiness of the NT is the Church itself, which puts on the likeness of Christ, shares in His sufferings, and so enters into His glory. The NT also employs the term glory of God's saving acts: Christ is raised through the glory of the Father (Rm 6:4). Glory also signifies manifestation in the sense of image: man is the image and glory of God, and woman is the glory i.e., image of man (1 Co 11:7).

III. John. In the Johannine writings the glory of Jesus is prominent, but it is the mutual glory of Jesus and the Father. The Father gives glory to Jesus, demonstrating that Jesus is what He claims to be (Jn 8:54), and the Father Himself receives glory from the Son (Jn 14:13), as He receives glory from the disciples of Jesus (Jn 15:8). Jn speaks of the glorification of Jesus as a critical point before which the Spirit has not come and the disciples do not fully understand His words (Jn 7:39; 12:16). The time when Jesus is to be glorified comes just before the passion of Jesus (Jn 12:23; cf 13:31), and the solemn prayer that the Father will give Him glory concludes the last discourse of Jesus recorded by Jn before the passion (Jn 17:1–5). Jesus Himself promises that the disciples will see His glory (Jn 17:24). The glory which the Father gives Him He will communicate to the disciples (Jn 17:22). Jn asserts that the disciples saw His glory (Jn 1:14). This must mean more than the display of thaumaturgic power, which is called His glory in the miracle of Cana (Jn 2:11). Rather it seems that in Jn the glorification of Jesus is His passion, death, and resurrection. This is the supreme manifestation of the holiness of the Father and His greatest saving act. The Spirit also shares in the glorification of Jesus by giving the disciples understanding of His words and works (Jn 16:14). In Apc glory appears in the conventional senses. The cloud of glory of Israelite tradition reappears (Apc 15:8), and the glory of God is a brilliant light which illuminates the whole earth (Apc 18:1) and the new Jerusalem (Apc 21:11, 23).

Gnosticism. Cf KNOWLEDGE.

Goad (Hb *dārᶜbôn, malmad*), the oxgoad was a wooden stick 6–7 ft long with which the plowman could prod the ox. It could therefore be employed as a weapon (Jgs 3:31). The Philistines held a monopoly on iron working and forced the Hebrews to buy oxgoads and other tools from them (1 S 13:21). Metaphorically the words of the wise are like oxgoads (Ec 12:11). "Goad" (Gk *kentron*) is used metaphorically in the NT. Paul relates that in the vision on the road to Damascus Jesus told him that it is hard to kick against the goad (AA 26:14). This is a common Gk proverbial expression which is not found in Semitic literature. It does not occur in the other accounts of the vision. Hence it is thought that the phrase is put in the mouth of Jesus here by Paul or by Luke. The word also means the sting of a serpent or insect and is used in this sense metaphorically in 1 Co 15:55 in a quotation from Ho 13:14. There is nothing in the Hb which corresponds to the Gk word. The sting of death here is probably sin, that which gives death its power. With the victory of Christ over sin death has lost its power to do harm.

Goat. The goat is common in modern Palestine and is frequently mentioned in the Bible. In modern times there are two species; one is distinguished by its large curved horn and long pendulous ears. The goat was ritually clean (Dt 14:4) and a sacrificial animal (Lv 1:10 +); it was in particular the victim of sin and guilt offerings (cf SACRIFICE; Lv 4:23; 9:3, 15; Nm 28:15; 29:38; Ezr 6:17; Ezk 43:22; 45:23 +). Large flocks of goats were kept by wealthy owners; Jacob* had 220 (Gn 32:15), and Nabal* had 1000 (1 S 25:2). Goat's milk* was and is esteemed (Pr 27:27). The meat of the goat is eaten, and its skin can be used for water bottles (Gn 21:15) and for the manufacture of fabric (Nm 31:20; 1 S 19:13), which is used for tent* cloth (Ex 35:6, 23, 26; 36:14) and for garments (Heb 11:37). Most Palestinian goats are black; the black hair of the beloved, bound in two tresses, is compared to two flocks of goats descending the hill (SS 4:1; 6:5). Speckled goats are rare, and this is the point of the bargain between Jacob and Laban* (Gn 30:32). Goats lead the flock (Je 50:8), and therefore political leaders and powerful kings are called goats (Ezk 34:17; 39:18; Dn 8:5; Zc 10:3). The army of Israel, however, is compared to two little flocks of goats in comparison with the Aramaean forces (1 K 20:27). The "hairy ones" (Lv 17:7; 2 Ch 11:15; Is 13:21; 34:14) are demonic beings, probably of goat form, satyrs. In the parable of the judgment (Mt 25:31–46) Jesus employs a scene which can still be commonly observed in Palestine; the sheep and the goats share the same pasture, but when it is time to take them to market the two are separated into different enclosures. The parable alludes merely to the division and implies no symbolism of the goat as an emblem of wickedness.

God. In this article treatment centers mainly upon the names of God in the Bible; for more complete discussion cf ANGER; ANTHROPOMORPHISM; AVENGER; BAAL; CREATION; COVENANT; ELECTION; FAITH; FATHER; GRACE; HOLY; JUDGMENT; KING; LAW; LORD; LOVE; REVELATION; RIGHTEOUS; SALVATION; SPIRIT and related articles.

1. OT. The existence of a divine being is never a problem in the OT, and no discussion or demonstration is required. This conviction Israel shared with other peoples of the ancient Near East; the difference between Israel and these peoples turned on the identity of the divine being, not upon his reality

and existence. It is more accurate to speak of "identity" than of nature; at the same time, a concept of the "nature" of the divine being is implicit in the biblical language and thought patterns which is explicit in assertions of the difference between the God of Israel and the gods of the nations on the one hand and the difference between God and man on the other.

The Hb words for divine being are 'ēl, 'elōhîm, and 'elōāh. The third of these is relatively rare and appears most frequently in poetry; there is no difference in meaning between Eloah and the first two words. El represents the common word for deity in the Semitic languages (Akkadian ilu, Arabic 'ilah, etc). El is originally a specific name; an El is a member of the divine species as a man is a member of the human species. But El appears as a personal name of the head of the pantheon of Ugarit*; and it is possible that the name reflects an original conception in which El was the truly supreme god and the other deities were sons and daughters of El, a phrase which occurs in the OT. Elohim, on the contrary, has no known cognate in other Semitic languages. The noun is plural in form and is often plural in sense; but it is also used of a single divine being, both of the God of Israel and of other gods. It is important to notice that the usage of these titles reflects the pantheistic beliefs of the ancient Semitic world; the linguistic resources of Hb were not sufficient to express the singular Israelite conception of the divine being, and certain circumlocutions became necessary to express it.

Etymology furnishes no clue to the radical meaning of El and Elohim; most commentators and lexicographers believe that the words designate power, but this conclusion is drawn from the concept of deity rather than from etymology. Power is certainly a basic component in the conception of deity. Their meaning in usage, if not in etymology, can be to some extent perceived in a biblical use of these terms as adjectives or appellatives; a person or thing is said to be identical with El-Elohim or to belong to El-Elohim because of some quality which raises it above the ordinary (Gn 3:5; 23:6; 30:2, 8; 33:10; 35:5; Ex 4:20; 1 S 14:15; 28:13; 2 S 9:3; 1 K 3:28; 2 K 5:7; Ps 8:6; 36:7; 45:7; 68:18; 80:11; Is 9:5; 14:13; Jon 3:3; Zc 12:8). This use is not adequately rendered by such paraphrases as "great." The world of El-Elohim was the superhuman world of being and power superior to man. We have no instance which shows that the ancient Semitic peoples conceived this as an impersonal world; but these uses seem to suggest that the superhuman world was more extensive than the divine world. Actually, no

rigorous line was drawn between the superhuman and the divine. The gods were like man, but larger and immortal. Words which designated such beings could not properly be applied to the God of Israel without modification.

Israel was aware that its ancestors had worshiped other gods (Jos 24:2), presumably the gods of some part of the ancient Semitic world. The distinctive worship of the God of Israel begins with Abraham and is continued to Moses. It is the view of the E and P sources of the Pnt that the God of the fathers was known by another name than Yahweh before Moses. This name is Shaddai (in P, Gn 17:1; 28:3; 35:11; 43:14; 48:3; Ex 6:3); the name is also attested in older poems (Gn 49:25; Nm 24:4, 16). It is common in Jb; here and in Pss 68:15; 91:1; Ezk 1:24; 10:5 it appears to have become an archaizing poetic name. Shaddai was rendered in the LXX by pantokratōr, "almighty," and as such has passed into Eng versions. W. F. Albright, followed by many, has interpreted it as "The One of the Mountain"; the cosmic mountain in ancient Semitic mythology was the home of the gods (cf NORTH). The title is not attested elsewhere.

The title Elyon (LXX "Most High") is very probably not Israelite. Gn 14 identifies El Elyon with the god worshiped by Melchizedek* at Jerusalem, and identifies this deity with the God of the fathers worshiped by Abraham. The name appears as Yahweh Elyon in combination with the proper name of the God of Israel (Pss 7:18; 47:3). It is found in an early poem (Nm 24:16); elsewhere, like Shaddai, it seems to be an archaic poetic title (Dt 32:8; 2 S 22:14; Is 14:14; Ps 18:14; + Pss, Lam).

When the name El is applied to the God of Israel, it usually has a defining genitive: El Bethel (Gn 35:7), El of your fathers (Gn 49:25), El of Israel (Ps 68:36), El of Jacob (Ps 146:5), El of eternity (Gn 21:33), El the Elohim of Israel (Gn 33:20). Elohim likewise most commonly has a defining genitive when applied to the God of Israel. These genitives seem to express a desire to distinguish the God of Israel sharply from other beings to whom these names were applied.

The God of Israel is called by His personal name more frequently than by all other titles combined; the name* not only identified the person, it revealed his character. This name is now pronounced Yahweh by scholars; the true pronunciation of the name was lost during Judaism when a superstitious fear of the name prevented its enunciation. In its place was read Adonai, "Lord"; the combination in writing of the consonants YHWH and the vowels of Adonai, a-o-a, created the hybrid Jehovah of the Eng Bibles. The meaning of the name etymologically is much disputed. The LXX rendered it by "He who is," and the Vg "I am who am." There is general agreement that the name is derived from the archaic form of the verb *to be, hāwāh;* but other etymologies proposed are too numerous for listing. W. F. Albright has interpreted the name as derived from the causative form and proposes that it is only the first word of the entire name *yahweh-'ᵃšer-yihweh,* "He brings into being whatever comes into being." The name therefore designates Him as creator, and this etymology is regarded as most probable by many scholars.

In E and P this name was first revealed to Moses on Mt Horeb (Ex 3); the J source seems unaware of this tradition and uses the divine name Yahweh from the beginning of history. This name needs no defining genitive; Yahweh is the God of Israel without further definition. The name implies that a divine personal being has revealed Himself as the God of Israel through the covenant* and the exodus*; it designates the divine personal reality as proclaimed and experienced. It affirms the unique Yahweh-Israel relationship; and it affirms the unique character of Yahweh.

The unique character of Yahweh is the answer to the question about the monotheism of early Israel. Monotheism as a speculative affirmation is simply not found in the earlier books of the Bible; the affirmation presupposes a pattern of philosophical thinking which was foreign to the Israelite mind. Nor is there a clear and unambiguous denial of the reality of other Elohim before Second Isaiah in the 6th century. This does not mean that early Israel was polytheistic or uncertain about the exclusive character of Yahweh. They perhaps would have said that there are many Elohim but only one Yahweh, and would have denied to any Elohim the unique character which they affirmed of Yahweh. Or they may have granted that the Elohim were real, but not that they were real Elohim; we noted above that the vocabulary was not sufficient to express the Israelite faith in Yahweh. The Israelites did affirm that Yahweh alone creates, that Yahweh alone reveals Himself, that Yahweh alone imposes His will upon man and upon history, that Yahweh alone saves and judges, that to Yahweh belongs the kingdom which is as wide as creation. Against Him the other Elohim were ineffectual competitors who did not deserve worship; and it was a logical if not an immediate development to the conviction that such Elohim can be no reality at all. The personal reality of Yahweh is clearly distinguished from any reality alleged for other Elohim. In fact, His char-

acter became more clearly known by the encounter between the faith of Israel and other religions. The OT shows that Israel was under steady pressure to assimilate Yahweh to the fertility deities represented by the Canaanite Baal*. The OT likewise shows that the faith of Israel survived this temptation to assimilate Yahweh to the vague world of superhuman power perceived particularly in the forces of nature.

The same resistance to assimilation is seen in the cult of Yahweh without images*. Yahweh is like nothing in the visible world; the anthropomorphism* of the biblical language about Yahweh expresses the vigorous reality of His personality, but Yahweh is not man. The spirituality of Yahweh could not be affirmed in Hb; but Yahweh was not flesh*. For fuller statements of His transcendence cf the articles cited above. Perhaps no word better sums up the biblical conception of Yahweh than the word "living" (cf LIFE); for the life of Yahweh includes His personal reality, His activity and His will, His nearness joined with His utter transcendence over man, over creation, over all beings, whether they are real or not, to whom the title El or Elohim is falsely given.

2. NT. The word *theos* is used to designate the gods of paganism. Normally the word with or without the article designates the God of the Old Testament and of Judaism, the God of Israel: Yahweh. But the character of God is revealed in an original way in the NT; the originality is perhaps best summed up by saying that God reveals Himself in and through Jesus Christ. The revelation of God in Jesus Christ does not consist merely in the prophetic word* as in the OT, but in an identity between God and Jesus Christ. Jn 1:1–18 expresses this by contrasting the word spoken by the prophets with the word incarnate in Jesus. In Jesus the personal reality of God is manifested in visible and tangible form.

In the words of Jesus and in much of the rest of the NT the God of Israel (Gk *ho theos*) is the Father* of Jesus Christ. It is for this reason that the title *ho theos,* which now designates the Father as a personal reality, is not applied in the NT to Jesus Himself; Jesus is the Son of God (of *ho theos*). This is a matter of usage and not of rule, and the noun is applied to Jesus a few times. Jn 1:1 should rigorously be translated "the word was with the God [= the Father], and the word was a divine being." Thomas invokes Jesus with the titles which belong to the Father, "My Lord and my God" (Jn 20:28). "The glory of our great God and Savior" which is to appear can be the glory of no other than Jesus (Tt 2:13). And the identity of Jesus and the Father is expressed clearly without the title in Jn 10:30, "I and the Father are one." The application of the noun is less certain in Rm 9:5; Paul's normal usage is to restrict the noun to designate the Father (cf 1 Co 8:6), and in Rm 9:5 it is very probable that the concluding words are a doxology, "Blessed is the God who is above all." 2 Pt 1:1 is slightly more ambiguous than Tt 2:13, to which it is not strictly parallel; it may be rendered "our God and Jesus Christ savior." The pronoun "this" in 1 Jn 5:20 is easily referred to God, who is implicit in Jn 5:19, although "Jesus Christ" is the nearest noun. It should be understood that this usage of *ho theos* touches the personal distinction of the Father and the Son and not the divinity i.e., the divine sonship of Jesus Christ.

The identity of *ho theos* (*theos*) with the Father appears in the large number of texts in which the word is joined with father: Rm 1:7; 15:6; 1 Co 1:3; 15:24; 2 Co 1:2 f; Gal 1:3; Eph 1:2; 5:20; 6:23; Phl 1:2; 2:11; Col 1:2 f; 2 Th 1:2; 2 Tm 1:2; Tt 1:4; Phm 3; Js 1:27; 1 Pt 1:2 f; 2 Jn 3.

The revelation of God in and through Jesus Christ is often expressed in the complete union of Jesus with God and of the entire integration of the mission of Jesus with the will of God. God sends Jesus (Jn 3:34; AA 7:35), constitutes Him (AA 10:42), demonstrates Him (AA 2:22), seals Him (Jn 6:27), exalts Him (AA 5:31; Phl 2:9); Jesus comes from God (Jn 8:42; 3:2; 9:16, 33; 13:3; 16:27 f). God pardons in Jesus (Eph 4:32), empowers Him (Mt 28:18; Jn 3:35; 5:22; 13:3; Eph 1:21), reconciles in Him (2 Co 5:19). The Christian belongs to Christ, and Christ belongs to God (1 Co 3:23). In Christ the fullness of deity dwells bodily (Col 2:9). In His preexistent state Christ existed in the form of God (Phl 2:6).

In Jesus Christ therefore not only the word of God is made flesh, but all of the saving attributes of Yahweh in the OT. In Him God is known (cf KNOWLEDGE) in a new and more intimately personal manner, and through Him God is attained more nearly; for He speaks of "my Father and your Father, my God and your God" (Jn 20:17).

Gog (Hb *gōg*, etymology uncertain), king of Magog*, Meshech*, and Tubal*, who in the remote future will lead his hosts against Israel. He and his armies will be annihilated by Yahweh without the intervention of man (Ezk 38–39). Meshech and Tubal are to be found in Asia Minor, and Gog is possibly Gyges, king of Lydia about 650 BC. It seems, however, that Ezk has no historical figure in mind. He is a typical figure whose features are drawn from the conquering kings of Israel's historical experience, and he comes from the N, the traditional route of invaders (cf Je 4:5 ff). Gog does not seem to be an apocalyptic figure in the proper sense of the word. Ezk seems to believe that even the restored Israel will not be entirely removed from the operations of historical forces. But should a conquering power invade Israel in the future as so many had done in the past, the restored Israel, because of its perfect union with Yahweh, will be protected by His power from all harm. In Apc 20:8 Gog is permitted to attack the kingdom of God after the 1000 years during which Satan* is bound. Apc borrows the figure from Ezk without change.

Golan (Hb *gôlān*, etymology uncertain), a city of refuge and a Levitical city in Bashan* (Dt 4:43; Jos 20:8; 21:27; 1 Ch 6:56). The site of the city has not been identified.

Gold. Gold was known in the ancient Near East in prehistoric times. Egypt controlled sources of gold of such abundance that silver* was a more precious metal in Egypt; the wealth of Egypt in gold was regarded as fabulous in Mesopotamia and Canaan. Gold had a value in proportion to silver of 6:1 in Babylon under Hammurabi, and of 4:1 at Nuzu*. In the Persian period the value of gold had advanced to 13½:1. The principal gold deposits in the Near East were found in Nubia and in Egypt between the Nile and the Red Sea; in southern and western Arabia, probably the biblical Ophir*; in Armenia; in Asia Minor on the banks of the Pactolus and in Troas. Both alluvial deposits and gold veins in quartz were worked by methods which differed little from those still in use in the 19th century AD. In the ancient Near East gold was used exclusively for jewelry and ornamentation. It was worked by hammering and casting, and excellent work of the goldsmiths of Egypt, Mesopotamia, and Canaan has been preserved. Gold was generally used in plating; solid gold objects were too expensive to be common. The technique of the manufacture of gold thread was known. Ancient refining processes have not been thoroughly studied. It is all but certain that the process of refining was not known before 1000 BC, and the process was discovered gradually 1000–500 BC. The gold was employed in its natural state. Hb and other ancient languages have a number of words for gold (Hb *zahab, haruṣ, beṣer, sagur, ketem, paz*). Some of these are loan words from other languages; but some also seem to designate gold of different colors, which are the result of natural alloys. Weighed gold was used as a medium of exchange before the invention of minted money*. According to Hb tradition gold was not common in Israel before the reign of Solomon*, who in cooperation with Hiram* of Tyre imported gold from Ophir* (1 K 9:27 f; 10:11). The amount of gold implements and vessels in Solomon's palace may be somewhat exaggerated in popular tradition (1 K 10:16–21). The interior of the temple was richly ornamented with gold (1 K 6:15 ff). The vestments of the high priest contained a generous amount of gold (Ex 28:5 ff). The most imposing article of the temple furniture was probably the altar of incense, entirely overlaid with gold (Ex 30:1 ff; 1 K 6:20). It is noteworthy that the guild of the goldsmiths was represented even in impoverished postexilic Jerusalem (Ne 3:8, 31).

Golgotha (probably Aramaic *gulgultā'*, "skull"), the place of the execution of Jesus (Mt 27:33; Mk 15:22; Jn 19:17). The three Gospels which mention Golgotha also identify it by the Gk translation *kranion*, skull. Lk gives the name of the place as Kranion, but does not use the Aramaic word (23:33). Calvary comes into our language in the Rheims NT translation of the Vg *calvariae locus,* the Lt translation of Gk *kraniou topos,* place of the skull. Golgotha is explicitly said to lie outside the city (Mt 27:32; Mk 15:21). Jn says it was near the city (19:20), and a location outside the city is implicit in the account of Lk. The city is here defined by the Second Wall; cf JERU-SALEM. Golgotha was near the tomb of Jesus, explicitly in Jn 19:41 and implicitly in the other Gospels. The traditional site of both is occupied by the present Church of the Holy Sepulcher. While the events of two thousand years of occupation have altered the topography of the site beyond all recognition, it is important to remember that there is no literary or archaeological evidence to support the popular belief that the place of execution was a hill or even a small knoll. Nor is this implied by the name "Skull." The first literary record of the traditional identification appears in the 4th century AD. According to Eusebius, the site of Golgotha and the tomb was occupied by a temple of Aphrodite in the Roman city of Aelia Capitolina, built by Hadrian on the ruins of Jerusalem after the Jewish rebellion of AD 132–135. We have no way of tracing this identification, since it is in no way certain that Hadrian wished deliberately to erect the temple on the spot of the execution and burial of Jesus, or even that the spot was known as such to the Roman builders. This temple lay within the walls of Aelia Capitolina, but these walls did not follow the course of the older walls. Even at this early date the identification of the site after the damages and reconstruction in the wars of AD 70 and AD 135 would have been extremely difficult. Constantine wrecked the temple of Aphrodite, which was pointed out to him as the place of Golgotha and the tomb, and erected a basilica on the spot. The basilica was destroyed by the Persians in 614 and rebuilt shortly after. This structure was destroyed by the Moslems in the 11th century. The Crusaders began to build on the spot after the conquest of 1099, and their church, the present edifice, was consecrated in 1149. Certain archaeological identification of the site is impossible. The dispute concerning the site which has endured for over 100 years revolves around the question whether the Second Wall included or excluded the site of the Church of the Holy Sepulcher. If the Second Wall included the present church, the traditional identification of the site cannot be maintained. Neither proposition can be affirmed with certainty. The probabilities, however, have led most modern scholars to trace the course of the wall E and S of the church, and thus to maintain the possibility of the traditional identifications. If the church does not occupy the spot, it is as close as one can possibly come to the place.

Goliath (Hb *gŏlyāt,* etymology uncertain; a connection with the Gk name Alyattes has been suggested), a hero of the Philistines whose height was 6 cubits and a span (1 S 17:4) = 8–9 ft. The armor of Goliath as described in 1 S 17:5–7 bears a close resemblance to the armor of the Homeric heroes. A circumstantial account of the slaying of Goliath by David is given in 1 S 17. The challenge of Goliath to single combat — a feature again reminiscent of Homeric heroes — was not accepted until David appeared and killed him with a slung stone. Another tradition preserved in 2 S 21:19 attributes the slaying of Goliath to Elhanan of Bethlehem, otherwise unknown. 1 Ch 20:5, which credits Elhanan with the slaying of Lahmi the brother of Goliath, is an obvious attempt to harmonize the divergent traditions. On the problem cf DAVID; ELHANAN.

Gomer (Hb *gōmer,* etymology uncertain). **1.** Son of Japheth* and father of Ashkenaz*, Riphath, and Togarmah* (Gn 10:2 f; 1 Ch 5 f), the Gimirrai of the Assyrian records and the Cimmerians of the Greeks; a Thracian people who were driven from their home N of the Black Sea in the 8th century BC and invaded Asia and Asia Minor through the Caucasus. **2.** Daughter of Diblaim and wife of Hosea, who bore him three children (Ho 1:2–9). On the prophetic significance of the marriage cf HOSEA.

Gomorrah. Cf SODOM.

Gorgias (Gk *gorgias*), a general of Antiochus* Epiphanes in the campaign of that king against the Maccabees (1 Mc 3:38; 2 Mc 8:9). His forces were defeated by Judas near Emmaus (1 Mc 4:1–22). Gorgias repelled a raid led by Joseph and Azarias (1 Mc 5:58 ff). As governor of Idumea he conducted harassing operations against the Jews (2 Mc 10:14) and was defeated by Judas (2 Mc 12:32–37).

Goshen (Hb *gōšēn*), the part of Egypt in which the Israelites were settled by Joseph. The land was granted them because they were shepherds and it was apt for pasture, indeed it is called "the best of the land"; they pastured the flocks of the Pharaoh together with their own (Gn 45:10; 46:28 f, 34; 47:1, 4, 6, 27; 50:8; Ex 8:18; 9:26). The territory is doubtless to be located NE of the Delta. It is also called the land of Ramses (Gn 47:11), a proleptic designation, and the field of Zoan* (Ps 78:12). These indications also suggest the region NE of the Delta, and modern scholars generally believe that Goshen is the region of the Wadi Tumilat. The name does not appear in Egyptian records, and it is thought by Albright and others to be Canaanite; it appears also as the name of a town in Canaan (Jos 10:41; 11:16; 15:51). This city was located in the hill country of Judah. A text from the tomb of Horemheb, general of the Pharaoh Ikhnaton about 1350 BC, relates that Asian peoples wished permission to escape disaster in their own country by admission to Egypt "after the manner of their fathers' fathers from the first times" (ANET 251). Another text of a frontier official about 1230 BC relates that he has granted permission to nomadic peoples to pass the frontier (ANET 259). The permission granted the Israelites to reside in Goshen was not extraordinary.

Gospel (Eng *gospel*, from Anglo-Saxon gōd-spell, "good tidings," translates Gk *euangelion*, good tidings, and *euangelizesthai*, to announce good tidings). The NT use of these words is no doubt influenced by Hb *BSR* and derivatives as used in Is 40:9; 41:27; 52:7, to designate the good news of the salvation of Zion, and 61:1, which describes the same salvation as the comforting of the afflicted and the release of captives. The use of the word in classical and Hellenistic Gk to designate good news, particularly the news of a victory, is not clearly reflected in the NT; but it is altogether probable that the NT reflects the use of the word *euangelion* in Roman times for the news of the birth of an heir of the Caesar or the accession of a Caesar to the throne. Against this good news the NT places its own good news of the birth of the one true savior and the coming of the greatest reign of all. In the NT the verb does not appear in Mk, Jn, Js, 2 Pt, 1–3 Jn, Jd. The noun does not appear in Lk (who prefers the verb), Jn, Heb, Js, 2 Pt, 1–3 Jn, Jd. The noun is found far more frequently in Paul than in the rest of the NT together; Lk-Paul contain the verb more than twice as much as the rest of the NT together.

1. *The Oral Gospel as a part of the Preaching.*

The NT nowhere uses gospel to designate a writing; this meaning occurs later (cf below). One may deduce that the use of the word in a technical sense, while it did not begin in Pauline usage, became more common and acquired a more definite meaning in Paul.

In the Synoptics the "good news" by anticipation includes the announcement of the birth of the precursor, John the Baptist* (Lk 1:19) and the birth of Jesus, which is a great joy to all the people (Lk 2:10). By anticipation also John the Baptist is said to announce the good news (Lk 3:18). Jesus brings the good news; this is the gospel of the coming of the kingdom* (Mt 4:23; Lk 4:43; 8:1; 16:16) or the gospel of God (Mk 1:15). Jesus unites the gospel with himself as a motive of renunciation of one's family (Mk 10:29) and life (Mk 8:35); Mt-Lk do not use the word in these contexts. The good news of the kingdom includes a call to repentance (Mt 4:17; Mk 1:15). Jesus applies to Himself the role of bringer of good news of Is 61:1 (Lk 4:18) and declares that the bringing of good news to the poor is a messianic sign (Mt 11:5). The gospel of the coming of the kingdom is announced by the disciples sent by Jesus (Lk 9:1–6).

In the title of Mk (1:1) the meaning of the gospel changes from the coming of the kingdom to the meaning which it has elsewhere in the NT, the coming of Jesus Himself and the account of His life, death, and resurrection. This is the activity in which the apostles and disciples engage after Pentecost (AA 5:42, combined with teaching; 8:4, 12). It is announcing the good news of the Lord Jesus (AA 11:20). It is probably in this later sense that the word is used in the gospel passages which speak of the preaching of the gospel to the whole world (Mt 24:14; 26:13; Mk 13:10; Mk 14:9; Mk 16:15). It is a frequently used and obviously intelligible word to describe the missionary work of Paul (AA 14:7, 15, 21; 16:10; 17:18; Rm 15:20; 1 Co 15:1 f; 2 Co 10:16; 11:7; Gal 1:8, 11, 16; 4:13). The office of announcing the gospel is a grace committed to the apostle (Eph 3:8), and a necessity lies upon him to preach it (1 Co 9:16). Paul can often refer to "the gospel" simply as something which is known to his readers (Rm 1:1; 1 Co 9:14, 18; 2 Co 2:12; 8:18; Phl 4:3; 4:15).

That the gospel had a definite content is indicated by the use of such words as announce, declare, preach, speak, know, teach, hear, receive (1 Co 15:1; 9:14; 2 Co 11:7; Gal 1:11; 1:12; 2:2; Col 1:23; Eph 6:19; 1 Th 2:2, 9 +). This content is summarized briefly as "concerning the Son, descended from David according to the flesh, designated Son of God in power according to the spirit of holiness by his resurrection from the dead" (Rm 1:3 f), that Christ died for our sins, was buried, and that He appeared to the disciples (1 Co 15:3–5). It is the mystery of God concealed through long ages, disclosed through the prophets and revealed to the nations (Rm 16:25). The object of the gospel is Jesus (AA 5:42; 8:12, 35; 11:20; 17:18; Gal 1:16), the riches of Jesus (Eph 3:8), the passion and glory of Jesus (1 Pt 1:1 ff), the resurrection of Jesus (AA 17:18), the kingdom of God and the name of Jesus (AA 8:12), the word (AA 8:4; 15:35; 1 Pt 1:23), faith (Gal 1:23). It is the gospel of Christ (Rm 15:19; 1 Co 9:12; 2 Co 2:12; 9:13; 10:14; Gal 1:7; Phl 1:27; 1 Th 3:2 +) or the gospel of God (Rm 1:9; 1 Th 2:2, 9). Christ is not only the object of the gospel, but also the subject, for He is its author. Evidently it is not a mere recital of the events of the life of Jesus, although it certainly includes such a recital; it presents Jesus as the Messiah and Savior through His word, His life, death and resurrection, and as the fulfillment of the Old Testament (cf TEACHING). The cross is central to the gospel (1 Co 1:17–25; 2:2). It is the good news of God's grace (AA 20:24), the good news of salvation (Eph 1:13), the wisdom of God (1 Co 2:6).

The gospel is salvation history and is conceived as a power-laden entity which effects that which it declares. It comes not only in word but in power and a holy spirit and a full conviction (1 Th 1:5). It grows and bears fruit everywhere (Col 1:5). It is the bond of union between Jews and Gentiles (Eph 3:6). It works salvation (Rm 1:16; 1 Co 15:2; Eph 1:13). It brings hope (Col 1:5, 23). Participation in the gospel is shar-

ing in salvation (Phl 1:5). The gospel of the glory of Christ sheds light (2 Co 4:4). Through the gospel Christ has brought life and immortality (2 Tm 1:10).

Paul often speaks of "our gospel" or "my gospel" (Rm 2:16; 1 Co 15:1; 2 Co 4:3; Gal 1:11; 2:2; 1 Th 1:5; 2 Th 2:14; 2 Tm 2:8). This cannot mean that Paul had a different gospel from others, for he is at pains to affirm that there is only one gospel, and this he preaches (Gal 1:11; 1 Co 15:1). The pronoun may signify, as Friedrich suggests, the identification of the apostle with the gospel, which is committed to him as a charge; he is a herald, an apostle, a teacher of the gospel (2 Tm 1:10), and to this he is called (Rm 1:1; 1 Co 1:17; 9:16). On the other hand, the tone of Paul's letters suggests that he regarded the gospel to the Gentiles as his charge in a peculiar way, with its message of the universality of salvation and the equality of Jew and Gentile in the Church (Gal 2:8), and this is possibly what he means by his own gospel.

The gospel is not merely a recitation or an announcement; it commits the hearer to standards by which he must live (Phl 1:27), and this includes moral teaching such as is illustrated in the discourses of our written gospels.

2. *From Oral Gospel to Written Gospel.* Since 1920 NT critics have questioned whether the origin of the Gospels can be explained purely by literary criticism (cf SYNOPTIC QUESTION). The method of analysis which attempts to show how the oral traditions arose and were fixed in writing is called in German *Formgeschichte,* in Eng somewhat inexactly Form Criticism or Form History (cf LITERARY FORMS). This method, whose most prominent exponents were M. Dibelius and R. Bultmann, postulates that our Gospels are compilations of material which already existed in set forms. These pieces arose in popular circles and exhibit the traits of popular narrative. The framework in which they are cast in the present Gospels (here only the three Synoptic Gospels are in question) is artificial, created by the authors; tradition gave them no chronology and very little topography. The Gospels are testimonials of faith, not biographies. The term "form" indicates the postulate that stories of the same type dealing with similar material tend to be cast in a certain form and structure. Dibelius distinguished in the narratives paradigms (short stories which lead to an exemplary saying or action), *Novelle* (miracle stories), legends (edifying narratives), myths (baptism, temptation, transfiguration). Dibelius grouped the sayings under "exhortation" with various subforms: wisdom sayings, similes, parables,

prophetic utterances, short commandments, long commandments, revelatory sayings (disclosing the character of Jesus). Bultmann's classification is simpler and more widely accepted. He divides the material into two large classes, sayings, and narratives. The narratives are divided into miracle stories and biographical legends. The sayings are more complex: (1) apophthegmata, sayings encased in a narrative, which are controversies and instructions or biographical apophthegmata; (2) proverbs; (3) prophetic and apocalyptic sayings; (4) community rules; (5) personal proclamations ("I" sayings) of Jesus about Himself and His mission; (6) parables.

The difference between the two are more apparent than real; under variant names and different classifications almost the same division of material appears in each. Where the division seems overrefined scholars have been slow to follow it. No scholar claims that the forms appear in our Gospels very frequently in their purity; most of the Gospel material presents mixed forms, and this to Form Criticism is evidence of a modification of the primitive form. Not all scholars accept the postulate that only the pure form is the primitive form.

An early form of the oral gospel is found in the sermons of AA 2:14–40; 3:12–26; 10:28–43. The primitive character of these discourses is supported by the fact that they appear in a work of Luke, who wrote at a time when written Gospels, including his own, already existed, and the teaching of Paul had been developed; nevertheless, these sermons do not exhibit ideas characteristic of these later developments. The content of these discourses is thus summed up by H. F. D. Sparks: the election and rebellion of Israel, the mission of Jesus, His life, works, death, and resurrection, Jesus as the fulfillment of the promises, and a call to repentance. Our written Gospels are a filling in of this outline with details.

In both the composition and the transmission of the material attention must be paid to the oral style, of which L. Cerfaux enumerates these features: balance of rhythm, techniques to aid the memory, repetitions, alliterations, rhymes, grouping in numbers, and connection by catchwords. These give oral tradition a peculiar tenacity, and it is by no means to be assumed that oral tradition is incapable of preserving genuine memories. But it is incapable of preserving them without some transformation; the analysis of forms is not satisfied with merely noting the principle, but seeks to ascertain the motives of the transformations and to recover if possible the primitive form of the story detached from its context in the present framework.

In Form Criticism the principle by which this is solved is the *Sitz im Leben*, "the situation in life" of the separate narratives. Form Criticism presupposes that the community, the primitive Church, is the true author of the Gospel materials. The community forms the stories according to its spiritual needs and transforms them as new needs arise in order to find a response to new questions. This analysis is rendered possible by the existence of three Gospels; the parallel accounts of incidents often permit the critic to assign the cause of variations in the "situation in life" of the separate accounts. A very obvious and frequent application of this principle appears in the Jewish or Gentile direction of the different Gospels.

Form Criticism has reached a dominant position in Gospel studies; as a method of literary analysis it is accepted and practiced by almost all NT scholars. Their acceptance is made with reservations, the most important of which touch Form Criticism as involved in historical criticism and sociological theories; cf below. The refinement and application of the method is described here, following in general the treatment of X. Léon-Dufour.

There is little doubt that the Church rather than individuals should be regarded as the true author of gospel tradition and the written Gospels; but it must be remembered that the primitive Church was not a mob. It was what Léon-Dufour calls "a structured community." It was hierarchically organized about the apostles, even though the organization was much simpler than it later became. Primary in the formation of the gospel tradition was the witness* of "the eyewitnesses and ministers of the word" (Lk 1:2). The traditions were formed to express a single faith believed in the churches diffused within 30 years after the death of Jesus through much of the Hellenistic-Roman world. In this context the gospel tradition was not the work of free invention.

At the same time, the formation was influenced by the gospel as lived in the Church as well as by the gospel proclaimed to Jews and Gentiles. Léon-Dufour points out three "situations in life" which affected the formation: the liturgical situation (as in the cultic recital of the narratives of the Last Supper [cf EUCHARIST] and the Passion*); the catechetical situation, i.e., the need for instruction in the teachings, life, and person of Jesus; and the missionary situation, i.e., the need for apologetic reference to the OT for the Jews and a certain broadening of the gospel for the Gentiles. The OT is a factor in the gospel both in the catechetical situation, which includes references to the law, and the missionary situation. Because of these situations the critic must, contrary to Dibelius and Bultmann, allow for more than one answer to the question, "Why was this story told?" Léon-Dufour notes three such motivations (1) the evocation of memories of the words and life of Jesus to resolve new problems (the Sabbath, fasting, the attitude of the Church toward Gentiles and sinners, the law, the coming of the kingdom, the attitude of the convert toward his family and kin); (2) the apologetic motivation in the recounting of miracles and in developing the material for controversies with Jews; (3) the historical motivation: this refers not to history in the technical sense, but to the conviction that the saving acts of God, the life, death, and resurrection of Jesus were real and actual events which could be observed and reported.

Most critics believe that the written Gospels were preceded by earlier written collections; but there is much less agreement on their nature and contents. Albertz proposed a collection of controversy stories. Some form of separate collection of miracle stories on the one hand and of discourses or sayings grouped in discourses on the other is widely accepted (cf MATTHEW; MARK; LUKE; SYNOPTIC QUESTION). The Gospels themselves exhibit summaries and transitions which sometimes appear to be earlier than themselves. Fragments of a collection of sayings of Jesus were found in the papyri of Oxyrhynchus in Egypt, containing both canonical and noncanonical sayings. The collection is dated about AD 200 and thus is later than the Gospels; but it illustrates the existence of such collections. Many scholars believe that much of the OT quoted in the Gospels comes from a *florilegium* of messianic texts. This is suggested by the known *Testimonia* of Cyprian, which was such a collection, by the groupings of certain texts which recur in different early Christian writers, and by the OT texts peculiar to Mt, which are not used elsewhere and follow neither the Hb text nor the LXX. The structure of the three Synoptics, in spite of individual variations, does not depart from the plan: Galilee, journey to Jerusalem, Passion, death and resurrection. Most critics believe that the Passion narratives took form before any other part of the Gospels. The structure is probably earlier than Mk and was traditional when Mark wrote.

3. *Historical Character of the Gospel Tradition.* Many exponents of Form Criticism expressed the utmost skepticism about the historical character of the Gospels and doubted that even the primitive traditions presented "the historical Jesus." It has now become evident that Form Criticism is a method of literary criticism, not of historical criticism, and that such skepticism is not warranted by the method itself. But the problem is not solved by an antiquated apologetic which leans heavily upon the Gospels as the documents of eyewitnesses and stands or falls with the personal connection of the authors with the events. The Gospels are not eyewitness documents. They are "catechetical booklets reporting history" (Léon-Dufour). The historical value of the gospel tradition is seen rather in the fact that it is a single tradition, in spite of the triple source; there emerges a single commanding personality thoroughly consistent in His person and His mission. The single gospel reposes on a single fact, which is the fact of Jesus; it does not repose on a doctrine. By comparison with other historical sources the scene of the Gospels is in language, history, politics, geography, and religion the Palestine before AD 70. The institutions and teachings of the primitive Church, which had taken definite form by AD 50, do not appear in the Gospels. Taken together, this is an impressive body of evidence. It becomes less significant if it is pushed to mean that each detail is equally historical; one must allow for transformation and for the use of narrative as a vehicle of an idea (cf MIDRASH). The central fact, however, resists deformation; and the critic is wise if he remembers that this unique historical event will always remain somewhat obscured by an atmosphere. The analysis of the gospel traditions solves a celebrated question by affirming that the Jesus of history is the Christ of faith.

Gourd (Hb *ḳîḳāyôn*), the word occurs only in Jon 4:6–10 to designate the plant which shaded the prophet and was suddenly destroyed. The meaning of the word is unknown; commentators most frequently suggest the castor bean because of its large palmate leaves.

Gozan (Hb *gôzān*, etymology uncertain), a region of Mesopotamia to which Tiglath-pileser* III transferred some of the inhabitants of N Israel in 734 BC (2 K 17:6; 18:11), and enumerated by the Assyrian officer before Jerusalem among the places conquered by the Assyrians (2 K 19:12; Is 37:12). The place is called strangely the river Gozan in 2 K 17:6; 18:11; 1 Ch 5:26. Gozan is the Guzanu of the Assyrian records, conquered by Adad-nirari II (909–889) and tributary to Shalmaneser III (854–824). The site of Gozan is identified with Tell Halaf on the river Habur in Syria, excavated by Max von Oppenheim 1911–1913 and 1927–1929.

Grace. The modern theological concept of grace is a complex of themes which appear separately in the Bible; cf BAPTISM; BODY; EUCHARIST; LIFE; LOVE; RIGHTEOUSNESS; SALVATION; SPIRIT and related articles. In this article are considered the Hb words *ḥānan,* to show favor; *ḥēn,* favor; and the Gk words *charis, charisma* and their cognates.

1. OT. The noun *ḥēn* designates a quality which arouses favor; it may lie in external appearance (Pr 11:16; 31:30) or in speech (Ps 45:3; Pr 22:11). The noun appears most frequently in the phrase "to find favor in the eyes of" God or man. One who intercedes for another "gives favor" in the eyes of the person to whom the intercession is made. The "favor" is shown in the favorable reception of the petition, in manifesting kindness and compassion, in rendering aid. One who seeks favor throws himself entirely on the good will of the person from whom favor is sought; by definition any claim upon the person whose favor is sought is excluded.

The verb *ḥānan,* to show favor, is used of men; it is an attitude which is proper toward the needy, the poor, the orphan, and any who are in distress. One shows favor by sparing from punishment, by rendering assistance, by gifts. When the word is used of Yahweh, the same benevolence is seen in Him. The petition or acknowledgment of favor from Yahweh is sometimes conventional and general in sense (Gn 43:29; Nm 6:25; Ps 67:2 +). Usually the context shows what the exhibition of favor means in the concrete. Yahweh shows favor by giving prosperity (Gn 33:11), by giving children (Gn 33:5), by accepting sacrifice (Mal 1:9). Most frequently He shows favor by deliverance from distress (Pss 4:2; 6:3; 9:14; 25:16; 26:11; 27:7; 30:11; 31:10; 56:2; 57:2; 77:10; 86:3, 16; 102:14). His favor is shown particularly by delivering Israel from its enemies (2 K 13:23; Is 30:18 f; 33:2). When deliverance is granted from distress which is punishment merited by sin, favor is also forgiveness* (Pss 41:5, 11; 51:3; Is 27:11; Am 5:15). Yahweh could show favor to David by sparing the life of the child of Bathsheba; He did not do so (2 S 12:22). He shows favor to the wicked when He spares them from the punishment they deserve (Ps 59:6).

The favor of Yahweh is distinguished from His righteousness*, by which He is in a way committed to help Israel, the people of His covenant*; and it is thus a counterweight against a too rigorous conception of the relation of Yahweh to Israel. His favor is under no compulsion; He shows it to whomsoever He pleases; this means that He is absolutely free to give or withhold it (Ex 33:19).

2. NT. The frequency of the word *charis* and its cognates in the NT stands in contrast to the simple and undeveloped idea of favor in the OT. It is closely and fundamentally identified with the entire gospel* and ultimately becomes a technical term, a key word. It does not acquire all the connotations which it has acquired in the development of Christian theology; but it is, even in the NT, a characteristic description of the NT message.

The verb *charizesthai* is comparatively weak in theological content. It means to grant freely as a favor. With God as the agent, the object of the granting is all things in Christ (Rm 8:32), the inheritance to Abraham (Gal 3:18), unspecified gifts of God (1 Co 2:12), the gift of faith and of suffering with Christ (Ph 1:29). As effects of the saving will of God these are more clearly seen in the use of the noun *charis;* cf below. Jesus granted sight to the blind (Lk 7:21). He Himself is the indirect object of the divine good will when He is granted the name which is above all names (Phl 2:9).

Charis occurs frequently in the introductory and final greetings of the epistles; here it has clearly become a key theme word, almost a slogan, of the early Christian communities (Rm 1:7; 16:20; 1 Co 1:3; 16:23; 2 Co 1:2; 13:13; Gal 1:3; 6:18; Eph 1:2; 6:24; Phl 1:2; 4:23; Col 1:2; 4:18; 1 Th 1:1; 5:28; 2 Th 1:2; 3:18; Phm 3; 25; 1 Tm 1:2; 6:21; 2 Tm 1:2; 4:22; Tt 1:4; 3:15; Heb 13:25; 1 Pt 1:2; 2 Pt 1:2; 2 Jn 3; Apc 1:4; Apc 22:21). It is usually joined with peace* in these greetings; it is the atmosphere of the early Church and the condition which one Christian wished for another.

Charis is used in the profane sense of attractiveness, charm (derived from *charis*), the quality which wins favor. Its characteristic theological use in the NT designates the good will of God, sometimes in the general sense: The good will of God was upon Jesus, i.e., God was pleased with Him (Lk 2:40); Paul and Barnabas are recommended by the brethren to God's good will (AA 14:26; 15:40). In particular and most frequently it means the saving will of God executed in Jesus Christ and communicated to men through Him. It is not easy to draw a precise distinction in the NT between this saving will conceived as the act immanent to God and the effects of the saving will as they appear in the life of Jesus and in the Church; hence the term "grace" is better as a translation than "favor" or "good will," since, like *charis,* it designates the reality of God's saving will both in its principle and in its effects.

This grace of God is the totality by which men are made righteous* (Rm 3:24; Tt 3:7). By grace Paul was called (Gal 1:15). God bestows His glorious grace on us in His Son (Eph 1:6). The grace of God has appeared (in the incarnation of Jesus Christ) for the salvation of all men (Tt 2:11). By the grace of God Jesus suffered death for all (Heb 2:9). The throne of grace is the point from which Christians should seek help (Heb 4:16). The grace of God is not distinguished from the grace of Jesus Christ, for only through Jesus does grace reach men. Paul speaks of the grace of Jesus Christ who became poor to enrich us (2 Co 8:9). The grace of our Lord has overflowed with the faith and love which are in Christ Jesus (1 Tm 1:14); the speech here is somewhat obscure, but it is clear that faith and love, communicated through Christ, are the fruits of grace.

Elsewhere the emphasis falls rather on that which is given through grace than on the saving will which gives it. God is the God of all grace (1 Pt 5:10), of every deed of grace. Grace is something which is given (Js 4:6; 1 Pt 5:5). The Word is full of grace, i.e., of saving deeds, which we receive (Jn 1:14, 16). Grace is a store to which we have access through Christ (Rm 5:2). It is a state or condition in which we stand (Rm 5:2). It is received in abundance (Rm 5:17). The grace of God has abounded more than sin (Rm 5:15, 20; 6:1). It is given us in Christ (1 Co 1:4). Paul has not received it in vain (2 Co 6:1). The surpassing grace of God is within the Christian (2 Co 9:14). It extends to more and more people (2 Co 4:15). Christians are called in the grace of Christ (Gal 1:6). It can and should be obtained by the Christian (Heb 12:15). The prophets foretold it (1 Pt 1:10). By a rather singular turn of phrase it is described as coming in the revelation (i.e., the Parousia*) of Jesus Christ (1 Pt 1:13). The Christians are heirs to the grace of life (1 Pt 3:7). They should grow in the grace and knowledge of Jesus Christ (2 Pt 3:18). Some have perverted the grace of God to licentiousness (Jd 4). The spirit* is called the spirit of grace (Heb 10:29); grace is received with the spirit.

Wide as may seem to be the range of these passages, they have in common the conception of grace as something given, received, a reality in the Christian and in the world in which the Christian lives. Grace cannot be conceived in these passages as exclusively the saving will of God.

Grace stands in opposition to works, which lack the power to save; if they had the power, the reality of grace would be annulled (Rm 11:5 f; Eph 2:5, 7 f; 2 Tm 1:9). Grace stands in opposition to the law. Both Jews and Gentiles are saved through the grace of the Lord Jesus (AA 15:11). To hold to the law is to nullify grace (Gal 2:21); and when the Galatians accept the law, they have fallen from grace (Gal 5:4). The Christian is not under the law but under grace (Rm 6:14 f). Grace is opposed to what is owed (Rm 4:4).

The gospel* itself, which is the good news of grace, can be called grace. It is the true grace in which the Christian should stand (1 Pt 5:12), in which he should continue (AA 13:43). It is the grace and knowledge of Jesus Christ (2 Pt 3:18) in which the Christian should grow. The gospel is the gospel of the grace of God (AA 20:24) or the word of His grace (AA 14:3; 20:32).

Grace is a principle of Christian life and action. This appears first of all in the concept of mission; Stephen was full of grace and power by which he spoke (AA 6:8). Paul speaks several times of his apostleship as a grace which he has received (Rm 1:5; 12:3; 15:15; 1 Co 3:10; 15:10; Gal 2:9; Eph 3:7 f). In this grace his hearers are partakers (Phl 1:7). He has the stewardship of God's grace for those to whom he preaches (Eph 3:2). The grace of the apostleship is something which the apostle must communicate and share. But it is not merely a static quality; it is dynamic, the grace by which the apostle performs his apostolic functions (Rm 12:3; 1 Co 3:10; 15:10; Eph 3:7 f). Grace is also a principle of Christian life and action even when the apostleship or other particular offices are not in question. Grace fructifies in good works in the churches of Macedonia (2 Co 8:1). The grace of God is sufficient to enable Paul to resist temptations; it is the power of God in contrast with the weakness of men (2 Co 12:9). The grace of God and not earthly wisdom is the principle which guides Paul's conduct (2 Co 1:12). The law and its works are replaced by an entirely new principle of activity. The Christian, while he is absolutely a recipient of grace, is not an inert recipient; the saving good will of God enables him to hear the Gospel, to believe it, to become one with Jesus Christ and to live in union with Christ according to the ideals proposed by Christ.

The verb *charitūn,* to bestow *charis,* is rare. It occurs with *charis* as its object in Eph 1:6. The participle *kecharitomenē* is addressed to Mary (Lk 1:28). The common version "full of grace" is correct as long as the word is not made to bear the entire weight of a theology of grace which is subsequent to the

NT. Literally the word means "highly favored"; but in the NT context of God's favor as "grace," described above, it signifies the saving will of God and all its effects, here in particular the first step in the process of salvation, the incarnation of Jesus Christ.

Strictly speaking, the Gk word *charisma* as the favor granted should be distinguished from *charis,* the good will by which the favor is granted. Actually the NT uses this word rather rarely in a general sense. Paul wishes by his letter to impart some spiritual charisma to the Romans (Rm 1:11), and he observes that the Corinthians lack no spiritual charisma (1 Co 1:7). In Rm 6:23 the charisma of God is life everlasting in Jesus Christ. The charismata of the OT are all the gifts of God to Israel (Rm 11:29); such gifts are irrevocable. But rather early the term charisma is used to designate a particular type of spiritual gift which enables its receiver to perform some office or function in the Church. These are the gifts which each has received and which are to be employed for speech and service (1 Pt 4:10). The charisma is conferred upon Timothy by the imposition of hands, the rite by which he is ordained to his office (1 Tm 4:14; 2 Tm 1:6). Celibacy or marriage is each the fruit of a charisma (1 Co 7:7).

There are several enumerations of these offices or functions. Rm 12:6 mentions prophecy, service, teaching, exhorting, contributing, helping, works of mercy. Eph 4:11 mentions apostles, prophets, evangelists, pastors, teachers. Historians of the Church no longer distinguish between the primitive "charismatic" age, in which such offices were presumably filled only by some charismatic manifestation, and the later "hierarchical" age, in which they were filled by organizational methods. The Church has never forgotten that her offices, which are not secular, cannot be filled without the saving will of God, which she believes is still directed toward her.

A particular problem is presented in 1 Co 12–14, where Paul speaks at length of charismatic manifestations in the church of Corinth which are not paralleled elsewhere. These are enumerated in 1 Co 12:8–11 as wisdom, knowledge, faith, healing, thaumaturgy, prophecy, the distinction of spirits, tongues, and the interpretation of tongues. The gift of tongues (glossolaly) is mentioned also as an effect of the spirit in AA 10:46; 19:6; the account of Pentecost, AA 2. To Paul all of these are inferior to love (1 Co 13); prophecy is superior to the rest, and Paul frankly seems to regard tongues as a less desirable gift.

Of the charismata in general, most of which can be easily identified, it must be said that the effusion of the spirit in the primitive Church should not be measured according to western European standards; and this is said with no concession to the excesses of some Christian sects. The spirit, as Paul says, has different gifts but is the same spirit; and the atmosphere of religious exaltation which was normal in the Hellenistic world could scarcely have been irrelevant in the primitive development of Christianity. Such external manifestations were a visible sign that a new force, a new spirit was at work. It is evident from the NT and from the literature of the postapostolic age that these phenomena were elements of the birth of the Church which did not endure once it was securely established in communities.

What is meant by the gift of tongues is somewhat perplexing. It may help to recall that to the Gk-speaking world all foreign languages were "barbarian," literally "babbling." One who spoke a foreign tongue spoke unintelligibly, and one who spoke unintelligibly spoke a foreign tongue. The speaker of tongues needed an interpreter; it is probable that the tongues spoken at Corinth were the utterances of ecstatic speakers who expressed their exaltation in unintelligible cries. The glossolaly of Pentecost (AA 2) is described more precisely as speech understood by a number of foreign visitors mentioned by name. Here the tradition has no doubt employed symbolism. The diversity of mankind is signified in the OT by the story of the tower of Babel* (Gn 11:1 ff), where diversity of speech separated peoples from each other. The Church is a principle of the unity of mankind; it will break down the walls of separation between peoples and bring them together in one body in Christ. The gospel which the apostles preach is equally intelligible to all men.

Grape. Cf VINE; WINE.

Grave. Cf BURIAL.

Greek. The term Greek (Gk *hellēn*) was used after 700 BC by the Greeks themselves to designate the group of peoples, cities, and states which possessed a common language, religion, civilization, literature, and art. The rest of the world were barbarians (*barbaroi*). There is an interesting comparison between the self-consciousness of the Greeks as the most civilized of people and the self-consciousness of the Jews as the chosen people. The pride of the Greeks was not based on any awareness of divine election or revelation nor upon any religious element whatever, but upon their own cultural achievements, principally philosophy, literature, and art. The essence of Greek civilization lay in the Greek conception of the *polis*, the city*, the manner of life in community in which man was capable of his highest achievements. After the conquests of Alexander the term Greek was extended to all those who spoke Gk and adopted Gk civilization. On this expansion of Gk civilization into the E and its effect upon the Jews cf HELLENISM. It is in this wider sense that the term Greek is used in the Bible. The most common use of the term in the NT is found in AA, Rm, 1 Co, Gal, once in Col. In the missionary journeys of Paul it is usually stated that he spoke in each city to Jews and to Greeks, and in that order. Greek here signifies the non-Jewish population, including those who had adopted Jewish beliefs; cf PROSELYTE (AA 11:20; 14:1; 18:4; 19:10, 17; 20:21; Rm 2:9 f; 1 Co 1:24; 10:32). Paul singles out as the characteristic of the Greeks their pursuit of wisdom (*sophia*); the term here, as commonly in Gk, signifies philosophical thought and literature (1 Co 1:18–2:16). To the Gk philosopher the gospel of the cross is folly. As a Jew, even Paul, the apostle of the Greeks, was aware of the Jewish exclusivism in which he had been reared. While it was his duty to bring the gospel to the Greeks (which in his writings signifies the inhabitants of the Gk-speaking cities of Syria, Asia Minor, and the Gk mainland), it seems that he came only gradually to realize that the gospel was a unifying and equalizing force. Thus, in spite of the privileges of the Jews, who had received the old covenant (Rm 9:4 ff) he recognized that there is no difference between Jew and Greek as far as the need of salvation in Jesus Christ is concerned (Rm 10:12). Furthermore, in the Christian community the differences between the two groups were ultimately to be annihilated (Gal 3:28; Col 3:11), since Jew and Greek by baptism* form one body* (1 Co 12:13). The term Hellenist (AA 6:1; 9:29) designates Gk-speaking Jews residing or visiting in Jerusalem and Damascus, and in AA 6:1 members of this group who had joined the Christian community.

Guest. Cf HOSPITALITY.

Guilt. Cf SIN.

Guilt Offering. Cf SACRIFICE.

Gymnasium (from Gk *gymnos*, "naked"). The gymnasium was regarded by ancient Gk writers as an essential feature of the city, without which the community was not a true *polis*. The gymnasium was erected and supported by public funds. It was a place of

Ancient boxer.

exercise and of instruction. The youth were trained and exercised in military skills. Athletes practiced for competition in games. The Gk idea of the care of the body included a great love of sports; the gymnasium served both for athletic competition and for exercises calculated to build a strong and beautiful body. The gymnasium was also used for public lectures, and it was the most important center of the instruction of youth in literature and the humanities. It was also a place for the celebration of festivals. The gymnasium often if not usually had a library attached. At least from the 6th century BC, if not earlier, the Greeks carried on athletic activities in the nude. The chief competitive sports were originally skills of the warrior which were cultivated for their own sake: racing, jumping, boxing, wrestling and the cast of the discus and the javelin. As a part of the Hellenization of the Jews a gymnasium was erected in Jerusalem at the request of the high priest Jason* (1 Mc 1:14; 2 Mc 4:12). The gymnasium was a solid monumental building which included colonnaded porticoes, a racecourse, the palaestra or arena for boxing and wrestling, other open courts, and halls for lectures and instruction. A public bath was usually a part of the gymnasium complex. Paul alludes to the exercises of the gymnasium several times: boxing (1 Co 9:26), wrestling (Eph 6:12), racing (1 Co 4:24; Gal 5:7; Phl 3:12–14), which he likens to the contest of the Christian against evil. The practice of virtue is the Christian gymnastic (1 Tm 4:7 f).

H

Habakkuk (Hb *ḥᵃbakkuḳ*), one of the 12 minor prophets. The meaning and etymology of the name are uncertain; perhaps Akkadian, *habbaququ*, "plant" or "fruit tree." Nothing is known of his life and person; the story of his mission to Daniel in the lion's den (Dn 14:33 ff) has no historical value.

Analysis of the book: 1:1–4, complaint of the prophet against violence and oppression. 1:5–11, Yahweh predicts the coming of the Chaldean* conquerers. 1:12–17, complaint of the prophet against an oppressor. 2:1–5, the prophet as watchman is commissioned to write his vision and asserts that the righteous* shall live by his fidelity while the wicked shall perish. 2:6–20, a collection of five woes against oppressors. 3:1–19, a psalm describing the coming of Yahweh in a theophany* to save His people.

The obscurity of the book affords occasion for a wide variety of interpretation. Some (Rothstein, Humbert, Nielsen) have identified the oppressor with Jehoiachim* and his followers; most commentators, however, identify the oppressor with some external foe, either the Assyrians* (Budde, Eissfeldt, Weiser) or the Babylonians* (Chaldeans, mentioned by name 1:6; the majority of commentators). Wellhausen and Giesebrecht, however, thought that 1:5–11, which does not speak unfavorably of the Chaldeans, was a later addition. Duhm and others read *kittîm* (Macedonians) for *kasdîm* (Chaldeans) in 1:6 and interpret the book as referring to the Greeks in the period of Alexander. Some writers who believe that the oppressors of 1–2 are the Assyrians think that the prediction of the coming of the Chaldeans (1:5–11) should follow 2:4 as the answer to the complaint of the prophet about the oppressor. Several authors agree in thinking that the book is either a cultic-prophetic liturgy or composed in the style of such a liturgy. This view has much to recommend it, since the book is not explained to entire satisfaction on the hypothesis either of the Assyrians or of the Babylonians as the oppressor. On the hypothesis that the Assyrians are the oppressor the book is to be dated between 625, when the Chaldeans appeared as a threat to Assyria, and 612, the date of the fall of Nineveh. If the Chaldeans are meant throughout the book, then it is more probably dated 605–600, the period following the battle of Carchemish

when it became clear that no power would oppose Babylon's supremacy in the Near East. Among the Qumran Scrolls was found a commentary on Habakkuk which interpreted the Chaldeans (Kasdim) as the Macedonians (Kittim); on the meaning of this word in the scrolls cf QUMRAN. It is clear, however, that the textual tradition of Qumran has rendered the opinion of Duhm untenable. The book deals with the problem of evil, and the question of the prophet may be compared with the question of Je 12: 1–6. The problem, however, is not merely personal, but extends to the wider problem of how God permits His ends to be accomplished by wicked and unbelieving oppressors. The answer of the book to this question is twofold, or, if one distinguishes between the Chaldeans and the Assyrians, threefold. The first step in the answer is that Yahweh brings down one oppressing nation by another. The second step is that in the rise and fall of nations the righteous man shall survive by his fidelity to Yahweh, and the third step that Yahweh Himself is the ultimate deliverer (ch 3). Contemporary critics are generally agreed on a date near the end of the 7th century for the book and on the unity of authorship and of composition; they believe it is not a collection of detached utterances (except perhaps for ch 3) but one or at the most two single compositions. On the use of Hab 2:4 in the NT cf FAITH.

Habiru. Cf HEBREW.

Habor (Hb *ḥābôr*, etymology uncertain), the modern Khabur, a river which flows into the Euphrates from the E between the modern Deir ez Zor and the site of ancient Dura Europos; the ancient Circesium stood at the confluence. The Israelites were transferred to the region of the Habor by Tiglath-pileser III in 734 (2 K 17:6; 18:11; 1 Ch 5:26).

Haceldama. Cf AKELDAMA.

Hadad (Hb *hᵃdad*, etymology uncertain). **1.** A Mesopotamian and Syrian storm god. As a storm god, Hadad's character was destructive, and in hymns and prayers he is asked to restrain his destroying hand. The storm, which brings rain, however, is also a principle of life and fertility, and thus Hadad as a god of fertility exhibits a con-

329

tradictory character. He is the Baal* of the fertility cults of Ugarit* and Canaan*. He is also a warrior god, and as such he was especially cultivated by the Assyrians. Because of meteorological omens Hadad is a god of oracles and divination, often mentioned in connection with Shamash. His symbol is the bull, upon which he is frequently represented standing, and he usually brandishes the thunderbolt (ANEP 501). The thunder is the voice of Hadad, a figure which is transferred to Yahweh in the OT (cf THEOPHANY). The name Hadad appears as a divine component of personal names of non-Hebrews in the OT.

2. A personal name borne by two kings of Edom before the Hebrew monarchy (Gn 36:35 f, 39; 1 Ch 46 f, 50). Gn 36:39 reads Hadar, a corruption. The name is borne by an Edomite prince who escaped to Egypt after the conquest of Edom by David. There he was supported by the Pharaoh, who gave him one of his daughters in marriage. After the death of David Hadad was permitted to return to his own country, where he rebelled against Solomon (1 K 11:14–22).

Hadadezer (Hb *hᵃdadʿēzer,* "Hadad is help"). The Aramaean king of Zobah* twice defeated by David* (2 S 8:3 ff; 10:16 ff; 1 Ch 18:3 ff; 19:16 ff). The name is corrupted in Ch to Hadarezer.

Hadad-Rimmon (Hb *hᵃdad rimmōn*). Mentioned in connection with mourning in the plain of Megiddo* (Zc 12:11). Some scholars interpret the name as a place name, others with more probability as the names of two gods of similar character (cf HADAD; RIMMON) syncretized into a single deity who in the fertility rites was ritually mourned as the dying (and rising) god of vegetation.

Hadassah (Hb *hᵃdassāh,* "myrtle"), the Hb name of Esther*.

Hades. Cf SHEOL.

Hadrach (Hb *ḥadrāk,* etymology uncertain), called the land or district of Hadrach in Zc 9:1. Hatarikka, however, is always called a city in the Assyrian records. Both the city and the district lay in N Syria between Hamath* and Arpad*.

Hagar (Hb *hāgār,* etymology uncertain), an Egyptian slave of Sarah*, the wife of Abraham. Since Sarah was childless, she gave Hagar to her husband as a substitute, and Hagar bore Ishmael* to Abraham (Gn 16: 1–4). Hagar, proud of her son, began to despise her mistress, who treated her so cruelly that Hagar fled into the desert. There she had a vision of the angel of Yahweh, who bade her return to Abraham (Gn 16:4–14). The spring where she had the vision is given the name of Beer-lahai-roi. The name actually is of uncertain meaning, and is no doubt mentioned because of the similarity in sound between the name and El-roi (Gn 16:13), the title which Hagar gave to the deity who appeared to her. The title probably means a god who is seen. After the birth of Isaac, Sarah saw Ishmael playing with her son Isaac and insisted that Hagar and her son be expelled from the household. Abraham sent the two of them into the desert. When Hagar and her son were in danger of death from thirst, Hagar found water in a spot revealed to her by the angel of God (Gn 21:9–21). On the relations of Abraham, Sarah, and Hagar cf MARRIAGE. The provision of a slave as a substitute by a childless wife is permitted in the code of Hammurabi*, and is imposed as an obligation upon the wife in some of the marriage contracts of Nuzu*. The expulsion of such a slave is expressly forbidden in the code of Hammurabi; but the slave girl who is disrespectful to her mistress may be reduced to the status of slave, and this is probably implied in Gn 16:6. Modern critics regard the accounts of Gn 16 and 21 as duplicates. They have in common the departure of Hagar and the preservation of her life through a vision. They differ in the following: in Gn 16 Hagar flees before the birth of Ishmael, in Gn 21 she is expelled with Ishmael. The return of Hagar after her flight in Gn 16 and the allusions to the greater age of Ishmael in relation to Isaac in Gn 21 are probably due to the harmonizing of the compilers. In some verses of Gn 21 Ishmael appears as a child small enough to be carried (21:14 f). The visions of Hagar show that tradition extended Abraham's familiarity with God to all the members of his household; Hagar, who had borne his son, is rescued from death through a divine intervention. Gn 16 is referred to J, Gn 21 to E (cf PENTATEUCH).

St. Paul, basing his argument upon an "allegory" (Gal 4:24), argues from the relations of Abraham, Sarah, and Hagar to the freedom of Christians from the obligations of the law* (Gal 4:21–31). Carnal descent from Abraham is not enough for salvation; salvation was transmitted not through Ishmael, who was the carnal son of Abraham, but through Isaac, who was the son in virtue of the promise. The carnal descent of Ishmael is associated with the slavery of his mother; but Isaac, the son of the promise, was the son of a free mother. Thus Hagar represents Sinai* in Arabia (whither Hagar fled), and this in turn represents the present Jerusalem, which is enslaved to the law. The new Jerusalem on high, the mother of Christians, is free; for Christians, like Isaac, are the children of the promise. The Jews, by rejecting the promises of which Jesus Christ is the fulfillment, have chosen slavery. The Christian, by accepting the fulfillment of the promise, becomes the true descendant of Abraham; as the son of a free mother, he is liberated from the law. The argument involves a clever rebuttal of Jewish pride in descent from Abraham, which in Hagar and Ishmael is shown to be slavery.

Haggai (Hh *haggai,* meaning uncertain, probably derived from *hāg,* "feast"), one of the 12 minor prophets. Nothing is known of the life and person of the prophet; his prophetic work is mentioned in Ezr 5:1; 6:14.

Analysis of the book:

1:1–13, an exhortation to Zerubbabel* and Shealtiel* to complete the building of the temple*, begun shortly after the reestablishment of the Jewish community in 537 BC, but permitted to lapse. The prophet attributes the failure of agriculture and the poverty of the community to its neglect. 1:14 f relates that the leaders of the community heeded the prophet and completed the building of the temple.

2:1–9, although the external features of the second temple lacked the storied grandeur of Solomon's temple, the prophet assures his listeners that the glory of the second temple will be greater than the glory of the first because Yahweh will overturn the nations and bring the treasures of the world to this temple — an allusion to the riches of the messianic period.

2:10–14, a priestly *torah* enunciating the principle that uncleanness is more contagious than cleanliness; "this people" is unclean (cf CLEAN). The oracle is obscure; most commentators understand it as a rejection of the offer of the Samaritans* to participate in the construction of the temple.

2:15–19, a promise that agricultural blessings will follow the completion of the temple instead of the present distress.

2:20–23, addressed to Zerubbabel; a prediction that Yahweh will shake the heavens and the earth and overturn the nations, but Yahweh will keep Zerubbabel as a signet ring. The promise of the messianic dynasty survives in Zerubbabel, and the dynasty will endure through the cosmic disturbances which will precede the establishment of the messianic kingdom.

The five utterances of the prophet are all dated from August to December of 520 BC. Outside of the discourses the book is written in the third person; this, however, means nothing in determining the authorship of the book. Most modern critics suppose that 2:15–23 have been misplaced and should follow 1:13, before the completion of the temple.

Haggith (Hb *haggit,* meaning uncertain, perhaps derived from *hāg,* "feast"), wife of David and mother of Adonijah* (2 S 3:4; 1 K 1:5, 11; 2:13; 1 Ch 3:2).

Hagiographa. The name given to the third part of the OT in the Jewish collection, which comprises the books outside the Pnt and the former prophets (historical books) and the latter prophets (prophetical books); cf CANON.

Hagrites. A nomadic tribe of eastern Palestine which engaged in war with the tribe of Reuben* (1 Ch 5:10) and the tribes of Gad* and Manasseh* (1 Ch 5:19 f). They are mentioned with Edom*, Moab*, and the Ishmaelites* among the enemies of Israel* (Ps 83:7). Jaziz the Hagrite was the chief herdsman of David* (1 Ch 27:31). There is no certain connection between the name of the tribe and Hagar*, the mother of Ishmael.

Hai. Cf AI.

Hail. Hail accompanied by thunder and lightning is common in Palestine during the rainy season. In the OT it is one of the features which accompany Yahweh in His appearance in the storm to punish His enemies (Is 28:2, 17; 30:30; Pss 18:13 f; 148:8). Hail can be destructive to crops (Hg 2:17). In Hebrew tradition hail was a weapon which Yahweh employed against the Canaanites Jos (10:11), and Ezk sees it as destroying the hosts of Gog* (38:22). Yahweh stores hail in storehouses (Jn 38:22). The hail storm of Egypt (Ex 9:18–34) is described in Palestinian rather than Egyptian terms.

Hair. For our information about ancient styles of hairdress we depend on Egyptian and Mesopotamian art and on casual allusions in the literature, neither of which is an entirely satisfactory source. Close study of the abundant representations of Egyptian art has led modern scholars to conclude that the Egyptian artists were often quite arbitrary in details. Egyptians always represent the people of Canaan and western Asia as wearing long hair and beards, in contrast to the Egyptians themselves (ANEP 1–8). The Egyptians from the Old Kingdom generally cut the hair short, both men and

a) Woman's headdress. Phoenician. b) Woman's headdress. Assyrian sculpture. c) Man's headdress. Assyrian sculpture.

women, and wore wigs of various styles. Long hair and beards appear only on peasants and slaves. Egyptian men are represented as clean-shaven, and priests, at least under the New Kingdom, shaved not only the beard but the entire head. OT allusions show that men wore the hair long (2 S 14:26; 18:9; Ezk 8:3 +). The hair, however, was occasionally cut. The Nazirite* was distinguished by the fact that his hair was not cut during the term of his vow (Jgs 13:5; Nm 6:5). The moustache, however, was trimmed (2 S 19:25). To cut the hair and beard short was a dishonor (2 S

10:4). The hair and beard were cut short as a sign of mourning (Is 15:2; Je 41:5; 7:29; Mi 1:16). This practice was followed by both men and women. The hair was cut with a knife. While combs are not mentioned in the Bible, they are comparatively numerous in Palestinian sites, considering the perishable material of which they were usually made, and there is no doubt about their use (ANEP 67). Women, it seems, generally wore the hair loose, hanging down the back below the shoulders. It was sometimes bound by a band around the temples and was worn long in tresses or sometimes in braids. Curls are mentioned once (Is 3:24); these may have been the mode of a particular period. The dressing of the hair by women is alluded to several times (SS 4:1; 2 K 9:30; Jdt 10:3). It was a practice to pour olive oil on the hair, sometimes in such abundance that it ran down off the beard (Ps 133:2). Egyptian representations of banquet scenes show the diners sitting with a cone of oil on the head which dripped down in the course of the banquet; its cooling and refreshing effect was most appreciated (ANEP 209).

In NT times the styles of hairdressing were much the same among Palestinian Jews as in OT times. Men and women wore the hair long, and men wore the full beard. The long hair of Palestinian women is illustrated in Lk 7:38, 44; Jn 11:1; 12:3. The Roman styles of hairdressing of the 1st century bore a rather close resemblance to modern styles. Roman men were clean shaven and cropped the hair closely as do modern Europeans and Americans. Roman women had many elaborate styles of hairdress. Matrons preferred a mass of hair built high on the crown of the head. Younger and more sophisticated women preferred a more complicated coiffure of curls and ringlets. Paul in speaking to the Corinthians accepts the Roman rather than the Palestinian style and says it is degrading for a man to wear his hair long (1 Co 11:14). He admits also that it is becoming for a woman to cultivate and dress her hair, which is her glory (ibid). For a woman to have her hair cut short or her head shaved is a disgrace (1 Co 11:5 f); possibly the short haircut was a token of the prostitute. Elsewhere the NT writers warn Christian women against excess in attention to the dressing of the hair (1 Tm 2:9; 1 Pt 3:3).

Halah (Hb *ḥᵃlaḥ*, meaning uncertain), a region in Mesopotamia to which Tiglathpileser* III transferred some of the Israelites in 734 (2 K 17:6; 18:11; 1 Ch 5:26). The exact location of the area is not known, but it is probably to be located in the neighborhood of the river Habur, NW of Nineveh. Sennacherib* mentions a gate of Nineveh named "the gate of the land of Halahhi."

Hallelujah (Hb *hallᵉlû-yāh*, "praise Yah[weh]"), an ancient liturgical invitation glossed in a number of the Pss (beginning of 111 and 112; end of 104, 105, 115–117; beginning and end of 106, 113, 135, 146–150). As a liturgical direction it was probably uttered at the beginning as an invitatory by the precentors, and as a response at the end by the entire choir. The textual tradition of the LXX differs from the Hb text in its insertion of Hallelujah. Cf ALLELUIA.

Ham (Hb *ḥām*, etymology and meaning uncertain), one of the three sons of Noah* (Gn 5:32; 6:10; 7:13). After the deluge* Noah cultivated the vine and, unaware of the strength of fermented grape juice, became intoxicated and lay naked in his tent. Ham discovered him and called his brothers to look at their father; but they, walking backwards so that they would not see their father's nakedness, covered him with a garment (Gn 9:22–24). The curse which Noah uttered against Ham has been edited so as to apply to Canaan* (Gn 9:25–27). Some commentators suspect that the fault of Ham consisted not only in looking at his father's genital organs but also in the commission of some unnatural act; "to look upon a person's nakedness" sometimes means to have sexual relations with the person (Lv 20:17; Ezk 16:37). The ancient story of Ham has become in its present form an ancestral example of the proverbial licentiousness of the Canaanites. In the Table* of Nations Ham is the father of Cush*, Egypt*, Put*, and Canaan* (Gn 10:6; 1 Ch 1:8), and through Cush the ancestor of a number of Arabian tribes. On the descent of Nimrod from Ham cf NIMROD. The grouping of the descendants of Ham is not ethnographic but a combination of geographic and historical factors. With the exception of Nimrod the peoples lie generally to the S of Palestine. Canaan is perhaps attached to Ham in memory of the Egyptian domination of Canaan before the settlement of the Hebrews, and the Caphtorim* perhaps because of the commercial relations of this people with Egypt.

Haman (Hb *hāmān*, etymology uncertain), son of Hammedatha the Agagite, promoted by Xerxes of Persia to grand vizier. The prostration which was given him by the subjects of the king was refused by Mordecai*. In his anger Haman planned a revenge which would involve the extermination of all the Jews in the Persian Empire, and he obtained a decree to this effect from Xerxes. Mordecai urged Esther* to intercede for her people with the king. She invited the king and Haman to a banquet, where she disclosed Mordecai's services to the king and obtained for Mordecai the right to royal honors. At a second banquet she revealed the purpose of Haman against the Jews. The king left the room in anger, and when he returned he found Haman pleading for his life and prostrate on the couch where Esther sat. Taking this as a sign of Haman's lustful intentions toward the queen, Xerxes ordered Haman to be hung on a gallows 50 cubits high which he had prepared for Mordecai (Est 3:1–7:10). The name Haman is possibly a Persian name, although it has not been found in Persian records. On the historical character of Haman and his anti-Jewish plot cf ESTHER.

Hamath (Hb h^amāt, etymology uncertain), a city of Syria. The modern city of Hama, about 130 mi N of Damascus and 30 mi N of Homs, built on both banks of the River Orontes, occupies the site. The city has a population of about 65,000. It encircles the tell of the ancient city. The area is fertile, but the climate of the city, built in a depression between the surrounding hills, is disagreeably warm and humid. The tell was excavated by Harald Ingholt 1931–1938. Occupation goes back to the Neolithic period. The Bronze Age occupation was ended by a destruction about 1750 BC, probably by the Hyksos*. The city was rebuilt and enjoyed prosperity 1550–1450, the years of Egyptian control of Syria. It is included in the list of Asiatic cities conquered by Thutmose III (1502–1448). There is then a gap in the history of the tell until its occupation by the Aramaeans* about 1100 BC. Sometime before 900 BC it became Hittite* and from 900 to 720 it was the capital of a small kingdom which seems to have been powerful and prosperous. The city is first mentioned in the Assyrian records by Shalmaneser III; Irhuleni of Hamath was one of the allies of Ahab* of Israel and Hadadezer* of Damascus in the coalition which fought Shalmaneser III in the battle of Qarqar 854–853 BC. Hamath was conquered by Tiglath-pileser* III (745–727 BC), who imposed tribute upon it. It warred against Sargon* and was conquered and destroyed by him in 720 BC. Sargon recorded that he settled Mannaeans and a reliable group of Assyrians in the region. The "entrance of Hamath" is the northern boundary of Canaan and Israel in the OT. Israelite possession of the territory up to this point was actually effective only under David, Solomon, and Jeroboam II of Israel (Nm 13:21; 34:8; Jos 13:5; Jgs 3:3; 1 K 8:65; 2 K 14:25; 1 Ch 13:5; 2 Ch 7:8; Am 6:14). It is the boundary also in the ideally restored Israel of Ezk (47:16 f, 20, probably to be read also in 47:15). Toi*, king of Hamath, made a treaty with David (2 S 8:9 f; 1 Ch 18:9 f). The territory of N Israel, conquered by Tiglath-pileser III in 734, included people of Hamath among the colonists settled there by the Assyrians (2 K 17:24). There are a number of allusions to the Assyrian conquest of Hamath (2 K 18:34; 19:13; Is 10:9; 36:19; 37:13; Am 6:2). The city is called Hamath the great in Am 6:2. The

threats uttered against Hamath in Je 49:23 and Zc 9:2 are of uncertain date and background. Hamath-Zobah, conquered by Solomon according to 2 Ch 8:4, is unexplained; Hamath was distinct from the territory of Zobah*. Modern scholars suspect the integrity of the text.

Hammurabi. Son of Sin-muballit and sixth king of the First (Amorite*) dynasty of Babylon (1728–1686 BC, according to the chronology of W. F. Albright). At his accession Hammurabi was a vassal king of the Elamite dynasty of Larsa. By a series of wars which endured for the first 30 years of his reign he conquered Isin, Larsa, Eshnunna, and Mari and created an empire which extended from the Persian Gulf to the Mediterranean. This empire endured 1700–1550. These conquests gave the city of Babylon a political and cultural importance which it had never had before and which it never entirely lost for more than a thousand years. Hammurabi was a great builder of canals and temples. He promoted religion, in particular the cult of Marduk, the local god of the city of Babylon, as the head of the pantheon. He strove to unify his empire politically and culturally; the Babylonian culture which arose during his reign was an enduring fusion of Sumerian* and Akkadian* elements. He was a patron of learning; large collections of tablets were made and Sumerian writings were translated into Akkadian, including works on philology, lexicography, astronomy and astrology, mathematics, magic and divination, religious texts, and the epics of creation* and of Gilgamesh*. His interest in the organization of society is shown in his great collection of laws. The identification of Hammurabi with Amraphel* of Gn 14 is generally rejected by modern scholars.

The Laws of Hammurabi. The laws of Hammurabi are engraved on a diorite stele which was found at Susa in Elam* in 1902. The stele was probably carried there as a trophy by the Elamite king Shutruk-naḫḫunte (1207–1171 BC). The text of the laws has been partly effaced; some of the missing portions are supplied from fragments of other copies of the laws. The text of the code suggests that a similar stele stood in Esagila, the temple of Marduk in Babylon. The stele is now in the Louvre in Paris. It stands about 6 ft high. At the top is a bas-relief which shows Hammurabi standing before Shamash, the god of justice, seated on a throne, who hands him the royal insignia of the ring and the staff. The laws of Hammurabi are not the earliest collection of Mesopotamian law now known. The laws of Ur-nammu, Lipit-Ishtar and of Bilalama

The law code of
Hammurabi with detail
of Shamash conferring
on Hammurabi the
power to rule.

of Eshnunna are 100–200 years earlier. Both collections are much smaller than the laws of Hammurabi. The laws contain 282 articles, arranged under the following heads (Driver and Miles): offenses against the administration of justice; offenses against property; land and houses; trade and commerce; marriage, family, and property; assault; various professions; agriculture; wages and hire; slaves. The formulation employed in the laws is the type called casuistic (cf LAW); the situation is described in a conditional clause, and the governing law is stated in the apodosis. This formulation is thought to reflect judicial decision of cases. Although the laws are usually called the code of Hammurabi, this designation is not entirely correct, since the collection is not a complete codification of existing law, nor was it intended as such. A number of topics which must have been treated in law are not found in the collection. A comparison of the laws of Hammurabi with other ancient legal materials shows that a common customary law existed in the Fertile Crescent in the 3rd millennium BC. This common customary law can be traced in the legal collections of the OT and in the patriarchal stories of Gn. These passages have numerous illuminating parallels in the laws of Hammurabi. The laws are the single most important source of information about the life, manners, economy, and structure of Meso-

potamian society in the 2nd millennium BC. The laws are enclosed between a prologue and an epilogue. In the prologue Hammurabi proclaims himself the king appointed by the gods, who has brought peace, justice, and good order to the land, both by his conquests, which pacified the area, and by his promulgation of the laws. He attests his devotion to the gods by enumerating the temples which he has built or repaired throughout his domain. The epilogue again proclaims a panegyric of the justice of the rule of Hammurabi, especially as it is shown in his protection of the poor, weak, and oppressed, who are now defended by his laws, and closes with a long formal imprecation upon any one who changes his laws.

Hamor (Hb *ḥᵃmôr*), the father of Shechem*. He sold a piece of ground in Shechem to Jacob* (Gn 33:19; Jos 24:32) and when his son Shechem raped Dinah*, the daughter of Jacob, he arranged the marriage of Shechem and Dinah. With the rest of the men of the city he was murdered by Simeon* and Levi* in revenge for the rape (Gn 34). The Hb meaning of the name *ḥᵃmôr* is "ass"; and while this meaning is not impossible, some scholars suspect that the name is not Semitic. Hamor is called a Hiwwite (Gn 34:2), which is probably to be understood as Horite* or Hurrian*. While the patriarchal narratives generally deal with persons rather than with clan or tribal groups personified, in this instance it appears that the names Hamor and Shechem (the name of the city) are tribal and geographical names. It appears likely that the Hurrian population of Shechem at this time called itself *bᵉnê ḥᵃmôr*, "the sons of Hamor," and so Shechem, the city, was regarded as the son or descendant of the eponymous ancestor of the tribe. The men of Shechem are called the men of Hamor, the father of Shechem, in Jgs 9:28. The narrative combines the story of the rape of an Israelite woman by a man of Shechem with memories of a feud between the Israelites and the men of Shechem during the patriarchal period, neither of them very well remembered.

Hamutal (Hb *ḥᵃmûṭal* or *ḥᵃmîṭal*, etymology uncertain), daughter of Jeremiah of Libnah, queen of Josiah* and mother of the kings Jehoahaz* and Zedekiah* (2 K 23:31; 24:18; Je 52:1).

Hanamel (Hb *ḥᵃnam'ēl*, perhaps *ḥᵃnan'ēl*, "El is gracious"), cousin of Jeremiah, who obliged Jeremiah to purchase his property at Anathoth* while the Babylonians were besieging Jerusalem in the campaign of 588–587 BC; cf AVENGER (Je 32:6 ff).

Hananel (Hb *ḥᵃnan'ēl*, "El is gracious"), a fortified tower in the wall of Jerusalem which existed in the time of Jeremiah (Je 31:37). The date of its construction is not known. It was also included in the wall built by Nehemiah (Ne 3:1; 12:39), and is alluded to in Zc 14:10 as the northernmost point of the city. Modern archaeologists believe that the tower stood at the NW corner of the ramparts near the head of the valley of Tyropoeon, a naturally weak point in the defenses of Jerusalem. It stood on the spot which was later occupied by the Hasmonean citadel mentioned by Josephus* and the fortress of Antonia of Herod at the NW corner of the temple area; cf GABBATHA; JERUSALEM.

Hananiah (Hb *ḥᵃnanyāh*, "Yah[weh] is gracious"), son of Azzur of Gibeon and a prophet contemporary with Jeremiah. Jeremiah predicted to Zedekiah and other kings gathered in Jerusalem to form an allegiance against Nebuchadnezzar* that the alliance would be defeated, and symbolized his oracle by wearing a yoke made of thongs and bars (Je 27). Hananiah denied the prediction and foretold that the plunder and captives already taken by Nebuchadnezzar would be restored in two years, and broke the yoke of Jeremiah. Jeremiah had no immediate answer, but returned later to re-

affirm his threat, adding that Hananiah himself would soon die. Hananiah died the same year (Je 28). Hananiah illustrates the type of false prophet described in Je 23, those who say that all is well when it is not (Je 6:14; 8:11). Such men spoke without the true inner conviction that they had received the word of Yahweh. In the mind of Jeremiah they should have known that their predictions of peace and prosperity were false, because the infidelity of the people to Yahweh was a firm obstacle to such blessings. The name is borne by seven others in the OT.

Hand. The hand is mentioned in a large variety of literal and figurative uses in the Bible, most of which exhibit no subtlety; many of these idiomatic uses have passed into common modern speech. To fill the hand is to consecrate priests to their office (Lv 8:25 ff; Jgs 17:5, 12 +); the phrase denotes the placing in the hand of the priest pieces of meat from the victim offered in his consecration. To "send" or put the hand to something is to undertake action. The work of the hands of Yahweh is His creatures (Jb 14:15 +). The hand is lifted in the taking of the oath*. To strike hands is to pledge an agreement. The hand is brandished in threat or in judgment (of Yahweh, Is 11:15). The hand should be strong; to assist one is to strengthen his hands. The hands droop and become weak when one fails. The "hand of Yahweh" occurs frequently; most frequently it smites or "is heavy," but it also delivers. Is 9:7–10:4 describes a pageant of Yahweh's punishments with the refrain, "His hand is still stretched out." The hand of Yahweh is not shortened (Nm 11:23; Is 59:1 +); nothing is beyond His power. It is somewhat unusual when prophetic inspiration is described as the hand of Yahweh upon the prophet (2 K 3:15; Ezk 1:3; 3:14, 22; 37:1; 40:1).

Metaphorically the hand is power and strength. What a man can do is that which is in his hand or to which his hand reaches. To give into the hand of someone is to deliver into his power or possession; and to take out of the hand is to deliver. To demand from the hand is to take from the possession; and since the hand is the agent of action, to demand from the hand is to call to account, to judge. "By the hand of" signifies by the agency; the phrase is so conventional that it is used even when the agent is an animal or an inanimate object. There is little reflection of the common superstition concerning the good and evil omen of right hand and left hand respectively.

Impalement. Assyrian
sculpture.

On the liturgical rite cf IMPOSITION OF
HANDS.

Hanging. This method of execution is signified by Hb *tālāh,* which otherwise means
to hang or suspend an object. It is mentioned
as used in Egypt (Gn 40:19, 22; 41:13)
and in Persia (Est 2:23; 5:14; 6:4; 7:9 f;
8:7; 9:13 f, 25). In Jos 10:26 death · is inflicted before hanging, and it is possible
that this was a usual practice. In Jos 8:29
it is inflicted upon the king of a captured
city. The Hb word *hôkîaʻ* is more obscure
in meaning; some suggest on the basis of
etymology that it means to expose or suspend after the breaking of arms and legs.
It is probable that the word signifies impalement, practiced widely in the ancient Near
East and illustrated in Assyrian sculptures
(ANET 362, 386, 372–373). It is mentioned only as a punishment for the worship
of foreign gods (Nm 25:4) and as the revenge taken upon the house of Saul by the
Gibeonites (2 S 21:6, 9, 13). The bodies
of Saul and Jonathan were hung or impaled
after their death in battle (1 S 31:10).
Neither hanging nor impalement is mentioned as a punishment in Israelite law for
any particular crime; but Dt 21:22 f prescribes that the body of one hung must be
removed the same day.

Hannah (Hb *hannāh,* possibly an abbreviation of Hananiah*), one of the two wives
of Elkanah* of Ephraim. Although she
was the preferred wife, she was childless.
Finally, in answer to her prayer and her

vow to devote the child to Yahweh, she
gave birth to Samuel*. She bore Elkanah
three other sons and two daughters (1 S
1–2). The song of Hannah (2 S 2:1–10)
is not written by Hannah but has been
placed here by the compiler because of 1 S
2:5. The song is a psalm, and like most
of Pss contains no evidence for an exact
date. The poet exults in the security which
he feels in the power of Yahweh, who defeats the powerful, impoverishes the rich, and
raises up the poor and needy. His wicked
adversaries will be destroyed. The content is
paralleled in Jb 12:7–25. The allusion to
the anointed king in 2:10 suggests that the
psalm was composed during the monarchy.
It is a source and prototype of the Magnificat* of Lk.

Hanun (Hb *hānûn,* etymology uncertain),
son and successor of Nahash* as king of
the Ammonites, a contemporary of David
(2 S 10:1–4; 1 Ch 19:2–6). David sent an
embassy to manifest the continuation of the
friendship which he had exhibited toward
Nahash. Hanun, badly advised by his counselors, treated the ambassadors as spies and
sent them back disgraced. This was the occasion of the war between David and the
Ammonites which in turn was the occasion
of the episode of Uriah* and Bathsheba*.

Haran. 1. Hb *hārān,* a city on the river
Balikh; the modern Eski Harran a short
distance SSE of Urfa (Edessa) in Turkey
on the Turkish-Syrian frontier. Haran
appears as a flourishing trade center in the

19th–18th centuries BC; it was an Amorite* community with a mixture of Hurrian* population. It retained its importance as a market and caravan town down into the Hellenistic period, when it was overshadowed by Edessa. It lay on the main route between Nineveh and the commercial cities of N Syria. It was an important center of the cult of the moon god Sin, who was also venerated at Ur*, the city from which Terah* migrated to Haran. Haran was conquered by the Assyrians under Shalmaneser I in the 13th century BC. It is doubtful that they retained control of the city during subsequent centuries; but it seems to have been an Assyrian city at least from the time of Shalmaneser III (858–824 BC). It was the last center of Assyrian resistance to annihilation; the last king of Assyria, Ashur-uballit, established his capital at Haran in 612 BC after the destruction of Nineveh. He was forced to abandon the city in 610, and an attempt to retake it by assault in 609 failed. In Greek and Roman times the city was called Carrhae. It was the scene of the annihilation of the army of Crassus by the Parthians in 53 BC and of the assassination of Caracalla during a campaign against the Parthians in AD 217. Terah and his family migrated to Haran from Ur (Gn 11:31 f). It was from Haran that Abraham was called to go to Canaan (Gn 12:4 f). Laban, the kinsman of Isaac and Jacob, lived at Haran, and it was here that Jacob stayed during his sojourn in Mesopotamia (Gn 28:10; 29:4). The capture of the city by the Assyrians is alluded to in 2 K 19:12; Is 37:12. This, however, can scarcely have been a recent event during the campaign of Sennacherib*. Haran is mentioned among the cities which traded with Tyre* (Ezk 27:23). Sultan Tepe, the site of ancient Haran, was excavated by a British-Turkish expedition in 1951–1952. The exploration did not go beneath the levels of 9th–8th century occupation. They found the remains of a large substantial Assyrian structure identified as a palace or temple, more probably the latter. The site was rather rich in literary remains; 150 tablets and several hundred fragments were discovered, practically all of which came from the period 700–612. They included copies of religious texts and some fragments of the annals of a king, probably Shalmaneser III, which speak of a victory over the Hittites.

2. Hb *hārān*, son of Terah and brother of Abraham and father of Lot*, who died in Ur before the family migrated to Haran (Gn 11:27–32). The personal name Haran is not the same as the name of the city.

Hare. The hare is meant by Hb *'arnebet*, mentioned only in Lv 11:6; Dt 14:7 as an unclean animal, because it chews the cud but does not divide the hoof. The hare is not, of course, a ruminant, and is probably so described because of the movement of its throat and lips. There are several species of hare in modern Palestine and Syria.

Harlot. Cf PROSTITUTION.

Harmagedon. Cf ARMAGEDDON.

Harosheth (Hb *hᵃrōšet haggōyim*, "Harosheth of the nations"), the home of Sisera* and the scene of his defeat by the Israelites led by Deborah* and Barak* (Jgs 4:2, 13, 16). The place is not certainly identified; some modern scholars locate it at Tell 'Amr at the foot of Mt Carmel near el Haritiyeh, which preserves the ancient name.

Harp. Cf MUSIC.

Hart. In Eng versions *hart* is the usual translation of Hb *'ayyāl*, fem *'ayyālāh*. The hart is extinct in Palestine now; and many scholars believe that the *'ayyāl* is not the hart or the red deer but the fallow deer, pale yellow in color and smaller, standing only about 3 ft high at the shoulders. The *'ayyāl* is clean and may be eaten (Dt 12:15, 22; 14:5; 15:22). It was part of the provisions of Solomon's household (1 K 5:3). Both the buck and the doe appear in figurative speech; the animal is admired for its leaping (SS 2:9, 17; 8:14; Is 35:6;) and its sureness of foot and its grace (Gn 49:21; 2 S 22:34; Ps 18:34; Hab 3:19). Jb 39:1 alludes to its shyness. Lam 1:6 and Je 14:5 allude to its pathetic suffering in time of drought. The beloved wife is called a doe (Pr 5:19); and SS 2:7; 3:5 suggests that the doe is an erotic emblem.

Harvest. The harvests of Palestine are enumerated on a limestone tablet from Gezer* of the 10th century BC; two months are designated for the olive* harvest, followed by five months of planting and cultivation, then two months of grain harvest (cf BARLEY; WHEAT) "and feasting," two months of vine cultivation, and a month of fruit harvest (ANET 320). This 12-month period runs roughly from September through August. Ancient harvesting was done with primitive tools. The tool of the grain harvest was the curved sickle of stone or metal. The cutter was followed by the gatherers (who could be men or women) who bound the ears into sheaves. The sheaves were carried by hand to the threshing* floor. The harvest was a time of fulfillment of promise, of the renewal of hope, of security in food supply;

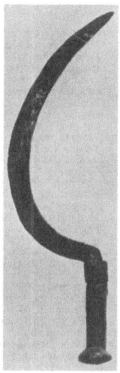

Egyptian harvest scenes, and a serrated sickle.

if the harvest fails, there is no hope (Je 8:20). Therefore the harvest is a time of feasting and rejoicing, and it is celebrated in three major festivals of Israel (Ex 34:22; cf MAZZOTH; PENTECOST; TABERNACLES). The shout of victory is like the shout of joy at harvest (Is 9:2). The restoration of Israel is the joy of harvest after the sowers have sown in tears (Ps 126:5 f).

The sequence of harvest after sowing is a figure of the moral necessity by which actions have their due consequences. Who sows injustice reaps calamity (Pr 22:8). In a famous phrase Hosea says that Israel sows the wind and reaps the whirlwind (Ho 8:7); but if Israel sows righteousness it

will reap love* (Ho 10:12). The apostle* who sows the spiritual good of the gospel* should reap material good, his own support (1 Co 9:11).

The harvest is a figure of the growth of the kingdom; but apostles are necessary to reap the abundant harvest which is there (Mt 9:37 f). The harvest, however, is not sown by the apostles, but by Jesus Himself; the apostles reap what He has sown (Jn 4:35–38).

The harvest is a figure of the eschatological consummation; in the end of days all men are gathered for judgment as the harvest is gathered (Mt 13:39). The figure is made more vivid by the angel with the sickle who reaps the earth (Apc 14:15 f).

Hasideans (Gk *asidaioi*, probably from Hb *ḥᵃsîd*, "devout" or "pious"), a group of Jews in the Maccabean period called the synagogue of the Hasideans, described as devoted to the law (1 Mc 2:42). They attached themselves to the Maccabean cause. While they were blamed by Alcimus* for keeping the rebellion alive (2 Mc 14:6), they were the first to ask for peace when Alcimus came with Bacchides. Alcimus, abusing their confidence in him, had 60 of them killed in a single day (1 Mc 6:12 ff). The group is not mentioned by Josephus. The name occurs frequently in the rabbinical writings, but it is not certain that here it means a definite group or "synagogue." Modern scholars believe that this group, distinguished by its devotion to the law, was the group from which the Pharisees* developed. On a possible connection between the Hasideans and the Qumran sect cf QUMRAN.

Hasmonean. The name of the dynasty which ruled Judaea from the Maccabean wars to the conquest of the Romans under Pompey in 63 BC. The name Maccabees and Maccabean is generally given to Mattathias* and his sons, and the name Hasmonean to their descendants from 135 to 63 BC. Hasmonean is derived from Asamonaeus (Hb *hašmōn*), named as the father of Mattathias by Josephus. The dynasty after 135 included the following rulers:

(1) John Hyrcanus, son of Simon* (135–105); after the death of Antiochus* VII Sidetes in 128 Judaea was practically independent. John ruled with the titles of ethnarch and high priest. He extended Jewish rule over E Palestine* and Edom. where he forced the Idumeans to submit to circumcision. He attacked Samaria and destroyed the temple of the Samaritans on Mt Gerizim*. The Pharisees, alarmed at his political ambitions and the secular character of his rule, broke with the Hasmoneans during his reign.

(2) Aristobulus I, son of John Hyrcanus (105–104); he imprisoned his mother, to whom the sovereignty had been bequeathed by the will of John, and imprisoned his brothers except Antigonus, whom he associated with himself in government but later assassinated. Aristobulus assumed the title of king.

(3) Alexander Jannaeus (Jonathan), brother of Aristobulus I (104–76); Salome Alexandra, widow of Aristobulus, released her brothers-in-law from prison and set Jonathan, who preferred to go by his Gk name, upon the throne. Alexander extended the Jewish kingdom, in spite of a number of setbacks, almost to the limits of the ancient kingdom of David. An attempt to take some of the territory of the coast from Ptolemy Lathyrus of Egypt at first failed, and Alexander was soundly defeated by Ptolemy. Internal disturbances in Egypt, however, forced Ptolemy to abandon the conflict, and Alexander extended his rule over Philistia and those parts of E Palestine which were still free of Jewish rule, including some of the Hellenistic cities. In his expansion northward in Palestine he confronted the Nabatean king Obodath, who held Damascus and halted his advance in that direction. This defeat aroused his adversaries among his own people, who summoned help from the Seleucid king Demetrius III Eukairos. Demetrius invaded Judea and defeated Alexander. The defeat, however, turned the patriotism of the Jews to sympathy with Alexander; Demetrius, thus deprived of support, was forced to withdraw. Alexander then revenged himself by having 800 of his Jewish captives and their wives and children executed before their eyes; he himself dined with his concubines, watching the spectacle. Antiochus XII Dionysus, the successor of Demetrius III, invaded Palestine, and Alexander was unable to resist him; but after Antiochus was defeated and killed by the Nabateans, Alexander continued his conquests in E Palestine. The enmity between Alexander and the Pharisees was deep and irreconcilable, and Josephus reports that he counseled Salome Alexandra, his wife, to whom he bequeathed the kingdom, to seek a reconciliation with the Pharisees after his death.

(4) Salome (75–67), widow of Alexander Jannaeus; she appointed Hyrcanus II, the elder son of Alexander, high priest and, recognizing the unchecked ambition of Aristobulus II, the younger son, kept him in private life. After her death the civil war between Hyrcanus and Aristobulus led each brother to seek the assistance of Pompey, then engaged in his eastern conquests. Aristobulus, however, finally refused Roman arbitration; and Pompey attacked and took Jerusalem in 63 BC. He ended the Hasmonean monarchy, detached the territories conquered by earlier Hasmonean rulers, and made Judaea part of the province of Syria. Aristobulus II was taken to Rome as prisoner, and Hyrcanus II was made high priest with the title of ethnarch.

Hate. 1. *OT.* The ancient Oriental had more sensitive and profound feelings than the modern western man, and expressed them more easily and fully; hence hatred is a rather common word; and the sentiment seems to have arisen easily. Hatred of men for men occurs often; Isaac is hated because of disputes about water rights (Gn 26:27), Jephthah is hated by his brothers because of his illegitimate birth (Jgs 11:7), Absalom* hated Amnon* because of the rape of Tamar* (2 S 13:22). Ahab* hated Micaiah* because he did not prophesy according to the king's wishes (1 K 22:8), and it seems normal that one would hate another in the Israelite community (Ex 23:5). Even in a family hatred could arise between brothers, especially if they were sons of different mothers, as between Joseph* and his brothers (Gn 37); but such hatred was prohibited in Hb law (Lv 19:17). Such hatred was normally murderous, and Hb law prescribed that in cases of homicide it should be ascertained whether the manslayer was known to hate the victim; if he did not hate him, the homicide is presumed to be accidental, but if he did malice is presumed (Dt 4:42; 19:4, 6, 11; Jos 20:5). The Hb language lacks the refined and precise vocabulary of modern languages, and the OT often uses "hate" where we would say "not love" or "love less." Thus Yahweh "hates" Esau, i.e., He prefers Jacob (Mal 1:3). A wife is hated when her husband ceases to love her (Dt 21:15; 22:13; 24:3; Mal 2:16), or when in a polygamous household she is loved less than another wife (Gn 29:31, 33). Israel is called the unloved or rejected wife of Yahweh (Is 54:6; 60:15). When Amnon is said to hate Tamar after he has raped her, however, the author, with fine psychological insight, means that the brutal lust which impelled Amnon to the crime turns to hatred of self which is directed toward the innocent victim. The righteous hate evil (Ps 97:10; Pr 8:13; BS 17:26; Is 33:15; Am 5:15). With simple directness they hate the sinner (Ps 139:21 f); the Bible is ignorant of the modern distinction between loving the sinner and hating the sin. The wicked hate God (Ex 20:3; Dt 5:9; 7:10; Pss 68:2; 74:4; 83:3; 139:21), for to oppose the will of another is to show hatred. They hate the righteous and seek to destroy them (Pss 34:22; 35:19; Pr 29:10 +). By anthropomorphism hatred is attributed to God. Yahweh hates the worship of false gods (Dt 12:31; 16:22; Je 44:4 +). Perhaps even more He hates the superstitious worship paid by the Israelites with no interior devotion and submission to His will (Is 1:14; Am 5:21). He hates injustice (Jdt 5:17; Is 61:8), pride (BS 10:7). Yahweh also hates sinners (BS 12:6; 27:24; Ps 5:6; Ho 9:15) and various vices (Pr 6:16–19).

2. *NT.* The NT departs from the casual OT acceptance of hatred among men as a part of normal life. Jesus commands His disciples to do good to those who hate them

(Lk 6:27; cf LOVE). One who hates his brother is still in darkness (1 Jn 2:9, 11), indeed, he is a murderer (1 Jn 3:15); the normal issue of hatred is still murder. It is a lie to say one loves God when he hates his brother (1 Jn 4:20). Hatred is characteristic of the Gentiles*, not of Christians (Tt 3:3)'. The NT also uses the word "hate" in the sense of "love less"; it is interesting that the most Gk of the gospels, Lk, preserves the Hebraism by demanding that the follower of Jesus hate father and mother (14:26), while the more Semitic Mt softens the phrase to "He who loves father and mother more than me is not worthy of me" (10:37). He who would follow Jesus must hate even himself (Jn 12:25), in the sense that he brings his own life into danger. It is almost a commonplace in the Gospels that the disciples will be hated by the world (Mt 10:22; 24:9; Mk 13:13; Lk 6:22, 27; 21:17) as the world hates Jesus (Jn 7:7; 15:18). The sinner hates the light (Jn 3:20). The NT avoids the anthropomorphism which attributes hatred to God; in Apc 2:6, however, Jesus is said to hate the works of the Nicolaites* at Ephesus.

Hauran (Hb *ḥaurān*, etymology uncertain), the later (and modern) name of the region called Bashan* in the OT. The name occurs only in Ezk 47:16, 18. The Haurina of the Assyrian records is called a mountain, once written with the determinative for city.

Havilah (Hb *ḥᵃwîlāh*, etymology uncertain), a geographical name. The name is otherwise unknown except for biblical allusions. In the Table* of Nations Havilah appears both as a descendant of Ham* through Cush* with Seba, Sabtah, Raamah, and Sabteca (Gn 10:7), and as a descendant of Shem* through Joktan with Almodad, Sheleph, Hazarmaweth, Jerah, Hadoram, Uzal, Diklah, Obal, Abimael, Sheba, Ophir, and Jobab (Gn 10:29; cf 1 Ch 1:9, 23). It was a region rich in gold, encircled by the river Pishon* (Gn 2:11). It was the territory in which Ishmael* lived which extended to Shur* on the frontier of Egypt (Gn 25:18); the same territory was inhabited by the Amalekites (1 S 15:7). These indications are too vague for definition; but Havilah is grouped with Arabian tribes, and the references of Ishmael and the Amalekites also suggest Arabia.

Havoth-Jair. Cf JAIR.

Hawk. Cf FALCON.

Hazael (Hb *ḥᵃza'ēl*, "El sees" [var *ḥᵃzahēl*]), a king of Damascus*. His exact dates are uncertain, but he was a contemporary of Jehoram (849–842), Jehu (842–815), and Jehoahaz of Israel. His name occurs as a future king of Damascus and enemy of Israel in the vision of Elijah (1 K 19:15–17). He was encouraged by Elisha to assassinate his master, Ben-hadad I and to seize the throne of Damascus. Shalmaneser refers to him at his accession as "son of nobody," i.e., usurper. He immediately began to war against Jehoram of Israel for the territory of E Palestine (2 K 8:28 f; 9:14 f; 2 Ch 22:5 f). His conquests of Israelite territory were interrupted by the western campaigns of Shalmaneser III (858–824) of Assyria, who records that he defeated Hazael in 841 and again in 838. Shalmaneser did not, however, claim to have taken Damascus, and he campaigned no more in the W after 838. Hazael then continued his campaigns against Israel under Jehu and Jehoahaz with great fury and success; apparently his anger was heightened because Jehu had paid tribute to Shalmaneser III without offering any resistance. He conquered all of E Palestine from Israel (2 K 10:32) and ravaged the territory during the reign of Jehoahaz (2 K 13:3, 22), forcing Israel to disband almost its entire armed forces (2 K 13:7). He carried his campaigns to the S, taking Gath, but was bribed by Jehoash of Judah to abstain from attacking Jerusalem (2 K 12:18 f). The date of his death is unknown; he was succeeded by his son Ben-hadad (2 K 13:24 f). The "deliverer" who liberated Israel from the Aramaeans did not arise until after the death of Hazael (2 K 13:5, 23). He is not named; some modern scholars suggest Jeroboam II of Israel, others Zakar of Hamath, whose victory over Ben-hadad is reported in an inscription; others Adad-nirari III of Assyria (809–782), who claims a victory over a king of Damascus whose name has been lost. It is uncertain whether Hazael or Ben-hadad is meant. Amos alludes to the dynasty of Hazael and probably to the cruelty of the wars of Hazael (1:3–5).

Hazarmaweth (Hb $h^a \bar{s}ar$-$m\bar{a}wet$, etymology uncertain), a region of Arabia, the modern Hadramaut, in the Table* of Nations grouped with other Arabian tribes as a son of Joktan* (Gn 10:36; 1:20).

Hazazon-tamar (Hb $ha\bar{s}\bar{s}\bar{o}n$ $t\bar{a}m\bar{a}r$, etymology uncertain), an Amorite* settlement (Gn 14:7), probably to be located in the S of Palestine. The identification of the site with Engedi* in a gloss of 2 Ch 20:2 is doubtful.

Hazeroth (Hb $h^a\bar{s}\bar{e}r\hat{o}t$, perhaps the plural of $h\bar{a}\bar{s}\bar{e}r$, "court" or "enclosure" [corral]), a stopping place on the exodus* from Egypt, the scene of the quarrel of Miriam and Aaron with Moses in which Moses was vindicated (Nm 11:35–12:16; 23:17 f; Dt 1:1). The place has not been identified.

Hazor (Hb $h\bar{a}\bar{s}\hat{o}r$, etymology uncertain), a city of Galilee; the site of the city is located at the modern Tell el Qedah, 9 mi N of the Sea of Galilee and S of Kadesh in Naphtali, 5 mi SW of Lake Huleh. Hazor was the capital of Jabin*, overlord of the kings of Galilee, whom he summoned to an alliance against the Israelite invaders, Joshua attacked them by surprise near the waters of Merom, defeated them, and destroyed Hazor with all its inhabitants (Jos 11:1–11; 12:19). Jabin is probably an interpolation in Jgs 4:2, 17. Hazor belonged to the territory of Naphtali (Jos 19:36). Solomon rebuilt Hazor (1 K 9:15). The city was taken by Tiglath-pileser* III of Assyria (2 K 15:29). The plain of Hazor was the scene of a battle between Jonathan* and Demetrius* I Soter of Syria (1 Mc 11:67–74). The allusions to Hazor in extrabiblical records and the recent excavations show the importance of the city in the 2nd millennium BC. Hazor is mentioned among the Asiatic cities in the Egyptian execration texts of the 12th–13th dynasties (19th–18th centuries) and in the lists of Asiatic cities captured by Thutmose III and Seti I. It is also one of the cities mentioned in the satirical papyrus Anastasi I. It appears in the Mari tablets in the correspondence of Bahdi-lim to Hammurabi (ARM VI, 24, 78) and in the Amarna* Letters, where Abdi-milki of Tyre says that Hazor has abandoned its allegiance to the Pharaoh to go over to the Habiru. The Amarna collection also contains two letters from the king of Hazor (EA 227, 228). A sounding of Tell el Qedah was conducted in 1926 by John Garstang. The exploration was only superficial, and the techniques used at the time did not permit the much more precise conclusions derived from the thorough exploration of Yigael Yadin in four seasons, 1955–1958. The area contains two outstanding features: the tell or mound, and a large enclosure, identified by Garstang as a camp. The area of the tell covers about 25 acres. The recent excavations uncovered 21 strata over 2500 years of occupation. The earliest settlement was limited to the tell, and goes back to the 2nd quarter of the 3rd millennium BC. Hazor reached its peak in the 2nd millennium. Garstang's camp turned out to be a lower city covering approximately 180 acres, easily the most extensive city of this period hitherto discovered. The city was enclosed by a gigantic earthwork rampart which was uncovered on the western side of the enclosure. This earthwork was about 110 ft thick at its base and still stood to a height of about 45 ft. The entire area was occupied by buildings, including a Canaanite temple in four levels or phases, belonging respectively to the 18th, 15th, 14th, and 13th centuries. The temple was dedicated to Hadad*. Its dimensions, 80 ft x 50 ft, were close to those of the temple of Solomon, and like the temple of Solomon it had three divisions, a porch, a main hall, and an inner chamber. An unexampled five ton monolithic altar was found in the Canaanite levels. The large enclosed area was occupied about 1700–1300 BC, and was destroyed in the 13th century. Later occupation did not use the enclosure and was limited to the area of the tell. The destruction of the 13th century city can be attributed to no one but the Israelites. Two pre-Solomonic Israelite settlements left traces on the tell. These, however, were unfortified; but they were of interest, since the remains of an Israelite sanctuary dedicated to some deity other than Yahweh were found. This illustrates the high places* of the OT. The rebuilding of Solomon (1 K 9:15) left distinct traces, which the excavators identified with certainty. The Solomonic city was surrounded by a casemated city wall, and a gate of this period was identical with a type of gate found at Megiddo* in the Solomonic level. The Israelite occupation exhibited several phases, one of which was due to an extensive reconstruction of the 9th century, probably under Ahab. To this period was attributed a strong and imposing Israelite citadel with walls 6–7 ft thick. The citadel had been totally destroyed by fire, most probably in the invasion of Tiglath-pileser III in 732 (2 K 15:29). There were traces of an unfortified occupation after 732. No extensive occupation of the site appeared later than the 8th century. The citadel, however, was used during the Assyrian, Persian, and Hellenistic periods. Baal-hazor (Hb ba‘al ḥāṣôr), where Absalom had his sheep sheared (2 S 13:23) is identified with the modern Asur, about 15 mi N of Jerusalem.

He. The fifth letter of the Hb alphabet, with the value of *h*.

Head. In Hb thought the head is not the seat of thought, consciousness, and decision. Its metaphorical use is limited to persons or things which are first in order, rank, or quality; thus the beginning of a series, the best of a collection, the top (of mountains), the chief or ruler of a community. The headship of Christ in the NT is an original conception which is only in part from the OT usage of head, and not from profane Gk, which did not use head to designate the ruler of a community. In 1 Co 11:2–4 the word head signifies the first in rank and order. Thus the head of Christ is God the Father, and Christ is the head of man, and man the head of woman. In a more profound sense Christ is the head of the Church which is His body* (Eph 1:22; 5:23; Col 1:18). This signifies that Christ is the beginning of the Church, the first to rise to glorious life (Col 1:18), but it also signifies a community of life which is communicated from the head to the body (Col 2:19). Christ as the head of the Church is not only the principle of life but also the governing and unifying principle (Eph 4:16; Col 2:19). The Church is the fullness of the body of Christ (Eph 1:22), for Christ as the head does not reach the destiny which is assigned Him by the Father until He has formed for Himself the body of the Church. The body of the Church is cosmic in scope, for in the fullness of time everything in heaven and earth is to be brought under one head, Christ (Eph 1:10).

Heart. Psychic activity is usually associated in the Bible with various organs of the body. The chief of these and the organ most frequently mentioned is the heart. The ancients were unaware of the circulation of the blood and the physiological functions of the heart; but its emotional reaction is easily recognized, and the heart is the chief bodily focus of emotional activity. The heart is glad or cheerful (Jgs 18:20; Pr 15:13; Jn 16:22; AA 2:26); it experiences religious exultation (1 S 2:1; Pss 13:6; 28:7; 84:3). The heart is made merry by wine (Rt 3:7; Ps 104:15). The heart feels grief and sadness (1 S 1:8; Ps 13:3; Pr 14:10, 13; 15:13; Je 8:18; Jn 14:1; 16:6; AA 2:37; Rm 9:2; 2 Co 2:4), disappointment (Pr 13:12), impatience and vexation (Ps 73:21), worry and anguish (Pss 25:17; 55:5; Je 4:19; 23:9), anger (Dt 19:6; 2 K 6:11), hatred (Lv 19:17), fear (Dt 28:67; Ps 27:3; 1 S 4:13), love (2 Co 7:3; 6:11). A firm or strong heart is a sign of courage (Pss 27:14; 31:25; Am 2:16). Biblical idiom differs from modern idiom in considering the heart as the seat of intelligence (Mt 12:34; Mk 7:21; 11:23; Jn 12:40; AA 7:23; 28:27) and decision (AA 11:23; 2 Co 9:7), and heart is used in the Bible where in English we should use mind or will. Great searchings of heart (Jgs 5:15 f) signify thought and planning without decision. To set the heart is to give attention (Lk 21:14). The heart is the source of thoughts, desires, and deeds (Dt 15:9; Mk 7:21–23; Lk 6:45). One's plan or purpose lies in the heart (Is 10:7). What one has never thought of has never entered one's heart (Je 7:31; 19:5). The extremely common idiom, "To say in the heart," means simply to think (Rm 10:6). To reckon in the heart is to plan (Gn 6:5; Pr 6:18; 16:9). Wisdom, discernment, and knowledge are seated in the heart (Ex 28:3; Dt 8:5; 1 K 3:12). When Yahweh gives Solomon breadth of heart (1 K 5:9), this signifies not magnanimity but intelligence; so also one who is lacking in heart is not cowardly but short of wit (Pr 6:32; 7:7; 9:4). To steal one's heart is not to win his affections but to deceive him (Gn 31:20, 26; 2 S 15:16). To be stubborn is to be heavy or hard of heart (Ex 7:14; 8:11; 9:7; Je 3:17; 7:24; 9:13), and stubbornness is overcome by the exchange of a heart of stone for a heart of flesh (Ezk 18:31; 36:26). Moral qualities are attributed to the heart as the seat of decision. It may be pure (Pss 24:4; 73:1), "whole" i.e., sincere (Gn 20:5), or upright (Dt 9:5; 1 K 3:6). Thus a man is what his heart is, and heart is used to designate the character (Mk 7:21; 2 Co 5:12). Yahweh examines the heart (Ps 17:3; Je 12:3; Lk 16:15; Rm 8:27); indeed, only Yahweh can know the heart, which is deceitful above all things (Je 17:9 f). The regeneration of Israel includes an interior regeneration, a change of heart which is a transformation of character (Ezk 18:31; 36:26). Jeremiah sees the terms of the new covenant written not on tablets of stone i.e., promulgated externally, but written upon the heart i.e., understood by the mind and accepted by the personal decision of each member of the restored Israel (31:32 f). The man who confesses his sins acknowledges that his heart is crushed and broken i.e., that he has experienced the suffering which Yahweh inflicts upon those who sin (Ps 51:19), and asks that he may be morally regenerated, that Yahweh will create a clean heart within him. Thus in the NT the heart is the seat of the divine operations which transform the Christian. The Spirit is sent into the heart (Gal 4:6), and the love of God is poured into the heart through the holy spirit (Rm 5:5; 2 Co 1:22). Christ dwells in the heart (Eph 3:17). Je 31:31 ff is echoed in Rm 2:15 and 2 Co 3:3. The spirit of wisdom and revelation and the knowledge of Christ Jesus enlighten the eyes of the heart (Eph 1:17 f). Hardness of heart, on the other hand, is slowness to believe the words of Jesus (Mk 3:5; 6:52; 8:17).

Heathen. Cf GENTILE.

Heave Offering. Cf SACRIFICE.

Heaven. In the Bible the heavens are both a natural phenomenon and a theological conception. The common ancient Semitic conception of the visible universe divided it into several levels or stages, which vary from one people to another and from one period to another. The threefold division of the Hebrews is reflected in Ex 20:4 — the heavens, the earth, and the abyss of water under the earth — or the heavens, the earth, and Sheol* (Ps 115:16 f). The phrase "heavens and earth" signifies as a rule simply the visible universe (Gn 1:1; Mt 5:18; 6:10; AA 4:24; 17:24 +). The heavens are conceived as a vast hemispherical vault which covers the earth; cf CREATION. This vault is sometimes described as stretched out like a tent (Is 40:22; 45:12; Ps 104:2). Another conception (Gn 1:6 f) treats it as a firmament, a thin beaten metallic plate. Heaven is also implied to be a building which is sustained by columns (Jb 26:11) and which rests upon foundation (2 S 22:8). Neither of these features appears in the account of creation of Gn 1. The heavens also have windows through which rain falls (Gn 7:11; 2 K 7:2, 19). In the heavens are storehouses for snow and hail (Jb 38:22), for the winds (Jb 37:9), and for water (Jb 38:37 +), whence Yahweh brings out these phenomena when needed. The heavenly bodies are demythologized in Gn 1:14. Divination* by astrology was extremely widespread in the ancient world; the creation account of Gn 1 denies that the heavenly bodies serve any purpose except the measurement of time. The heavens are the dwelling of God (Gn 11:5; 19:24; Dt 10:14; 1 K 22:19; Pss 11:4; 148:4; Jb 22:13 ff; Is 63:19; Mt 5:16, 45; 6:1 +). In some passages the dwelling of God is said to be "the heaven of heavens," the height of heaven (Dt 10:14; 1 K 8:27; Ps 148:4). Yahweh is also present in earthly sanctuaries; on the reconciliation of His heavenly presence with His presence in the sanctuaries cf ARK; TEMPLE. When Elijah is taken up from among the living he is assumed into the heavens; in the Hb conception there was no other place to which he could be assumed, and it was impossible for one who escaped death to remain upon earth, however remote his dwelling might be. This privilege of Elijah is unique in the OT (cf ENOCH), and there is no other reference to the passage of a man to heaven. Cf, however, WISDOM OF SOLOMON. The end catastrophe includes a collapse of the heavens (Is 13:13; 34:4; 51:6; Je 4:23; Am 8:9; Mk 13:31 +), and the eschatological renewal includes the creation of a new heaven and a new earth, i.e., a new universe (Is 65:17; 66:22; 2 Pt 3:13; Apc 21:1). This eschatological renewal concerns the heavens as a natural phenomenon and not as the dwelling of the deity. Jewish literature, influenced in part by the fact that the Hb word šamāyim, "heaven," is a grammatical plural, distinguished a number of heavens or stages. The numbers vary between three, five, seven, and ten. This conception lies at the base of Paul's statement that he was taken up to the third heaven (2 Co 12:2). This third heaven is identified with Paradise*. In Jewish literature the scruple against the use of the divine name in speech and writing led to substitutes, one of which was heaven. This Jewish practice is reflected at times in the NT; cf Mk 11:30; Lk 15:18, 21. The kingdom of God, which is always used in Mk and Lk, always appears in Mt as the kingdom of heaven except in 19:24; 21:31, 43. The connection between Jesus Christ and heaven in the NT has no antecedents in the OT. In Mk 16:19 (cf MARK) and AA 1:9, 11; 2:33 Jesus is taken up into heaven after His resurrection (cf ASCENSION). At His second coming Jesus will return from heaven or on the clouds of heaven (Mt 24:30; 26:64; Mk 14:62; 1 Th 1:10 +). In Jn Jesus comes from heaven even in the incarnation (3:13, 31; 6:38 ff); but the same idea is to some extent implied in the narrative of the baptism* of Jesus, which in all four Gospels includes the opening of the heavens and the manifestation of the Father by the voice and of the Spirit by the dove (Mt 3:16 f; Mk 1:10 f; Lk 3:21 f; Jn 1:32). The opening of the heavens in the OT signifies the coming and the activity of Yahweh (Gn 28:12, which is probably reflected in the Gospels; Is 63:19; Ezk 1:1). After His ascension Jesus sits in heaven at the right hand of the Father (Mt 26:64; Mk 14:62; Lk 22:69; AA 7:55 f; Rm 8:34; Eph 1:20; Col 3:1; 1 Pt 3:22). St. Paul calls Jesus the second man, heavenly and spiritual, in opposition to Adam the first man, who was of the earth, earthy. The second man, like the first man, is the founder of a new race; He is the image of the risen glorious race (1 Co 15:45–49). The heavens which in the OT are invisible and unattainable by man (with the exception of the Elijah episode) become in the NT the place of dwelling and reward for the Christian. The Christian is a citizen of heaven (Phl 3:20). He looks forward to a home which God will build for him in heaven (2 Co 5:1–5). The Christian's inheritance (1 Pt 1:4), reward (Mt 5:12 +), and treasure (Mt 6:20 +; Col 1:5) are all in heaven. The Father and Jesus prepare mansions in heaven for the disciples (Jn 14:1–3). The names of the disciples are written in the records of heaven (Lk 10:20), and those who rise with Christ are with Him taken into heaven (1 Th 4:16 f). The

risen, like Christ who is their prototype, are endowed with the qualities of the heavenly body, which differs from the earthly body: incorruptible, glorious, powerful, and spiritual (1 Co 15:42–49). The quality of glory* most probably signifies luminosity. The qualities of the glorious body are the negation of the "carnal" defects of the present life. The present body of man is unfit to enter heaven, but must experience the transformation which gives it the qualities proper to heaven. Paul does not pretend to understand or to explain what his transformation is in detail; but he is certain that flesh and blood, the present body, cannot share in the kingdom of God (1 Co 15:50). On the angels in heaven cf ANGEL.

Heber (Hb heber, "companion"? perhaps abbreviated from a theophorous name), a Kenite* who lived apart from his clan in Galilee*, where he entered into friendship with the Canaanite Sisera*. His wife Jael* killed Sisera in the tent of Heber when Sisera fled there after his defeat by Barak* (Jgs 4:11, 17–23).

Hebrew (Hb 'ibrî, a name of the Hebrew or Israelite people). The name appears most frequently as applied to Israelites by foreigners (Gn 39:14, 17; 41:12; Ex 1:16–19; 2:6, 9; 1 S 13:19; 14:11; 29:3) or by Israelites when speaking to foreigners (Gn 40:15; Ex 2:7; 3:18; 5:3; 7:16; 9:1, 13; Jon 1:9). It is also used by the Hb narrator, but it is almost always found in a context which is concerned with the relations of Israelites with foreigners (Gn 14:13; Ex 1:15; 2:11, 13; 1 S 13:3, 7; 14:21; the text of 1 S 13:7 is uncertain). The Hb slave who is to be freed after six years of servitude (Ex 21:2 ff; Dt 15:12 ff) is a slave of the same ethnic community as the owner, and this is emphasized by the designation Hebrew. The term is used in the NT (AA 6:1; 2 Co 11:22; Phl 3:5) to designate an Aramaic-speaking Jew, not necessarily a Palestinian Jew, since Paul, a native of Tarsus, boasts that he is a Hebrew (2 Co 11:22). For many years the question of the identity of the Hebrews of the OT with a people who are mentioned in a number of ancient records as the Ḫabiru, Ḫapiru, or 'Apiru has been raised. The question still cannot be answered definitely; but the information concerning this people is much more abundant in recent times, and permits one to reject certain older views and to draw some limited conclusions. This people, designated in Sumerian as SA.GAZ., appears in documents from Ur and Larsa of the 20th century BC and in the documents of the Assyrian trading colony of Cappadocia in

Asia Minor (2000–1800 BC) and in the Mari* texts of the 18th century. A fairly consistent picture emerges from these texts. The Habiru appear as fighting men, since most of the texts refer to their military services for a certain king or to their raids upon communities. It is of interest that they are always associated with towns, and from this M. Greenberg concludes that it is unlikely that they were a nomadic people. Other scholars (G. E. Wright, G. E. Mendenhall) believe that the Habiru were members of nomadic tribes who settled in the neighborhood of cities; cf below. It is also of interest to notice that in the first half of the 2nd millennium the Habiru were widely distributed from Ur in the far S of Mesopotamia to N Syria. The documents from Alalakh in N Syria of the 15th century give the same description of the Habiru as fighting men, mercenaries or lawless raiders. Here also they are associated with cities, and it is clear in these documents, although it is indicated in the other documents, that the Habiru are a social group of lower status in the community rather than an ethnic group. The documents from Nuzu* in Assyria, which come from the period of Hurrian control of the city in the 15th century, exhibit the Habiru in contracts in which they enter the service of a patron. The status is above that of a slave and corresponds to the terms of a contract of indenture. The Habiru in the Nuzu documents all have Akkadian names. In the Amarna* texts of the 14th century the Habiru are prominent but only obscurely identified. They are associated with Abdi-Ashirta, a Canaanite king, and his son Aziru, who do not appear themselves to be Habiru. They are rebels against Egyptian authority and are associated with rebellious Canaanite kings either in taking the cities of Egyptian satellites by assault or in persuading the peoples of cities to abandon their allegiance to the representatives of Egypt. Here also they appear as mercenary troops, more frequently as lawless raiders. The degree of their lawlessness, greater in the Amarna texts than in earlier records, probably reflects the more generally lawless condition of the country at the time. Likewise they do not appear as an ethnic group but rather as a distinct social group. The Apiru are mentioned in Egyptian records from the 15th to the 12th centuries; here they are foreigners with the status of slaves or unskilled laborers. Apparently they were captives in war; cf EXODUS. The occurrences of Habiru in these records show a wide variety of nomenclature, from which modern scholars deduce that the Habiru had a heterogeneous ethnic composition. Scholars are more inclined to believe that they were

a distinct social group within the various communities. This social group was found through the Fertile Crescent from Canaan to S Mesopotamia. M. Greenberg has suggested that the core of this group was formed by "uprooted propertyless persons who found a means of subsistence for themselves and their families by entering a state of dependence in various forms. A contributory factor in their helplessness appears to have been their lack of rights as foreigners in places where they lived. In large numbers they were organized in military bodies to serve the needs of their localities" (*The Hab/piru,* 88). In times of unsettled political conditions it was possible for these bands of warriors to turn to banditry to support themselves. Greenberg also suggests that since the first mention of the Habiru is contemporary with the infiltration of the Amorites* into Mesopotamia, it is possible that the original Habiru were Amorites. In any case, in subsequent centuries they attracted to themselves members of other peoples who were in a similar social condition. G. E. Mendenhall has summed up the details of the various texts as applying to the members of a group existing outside the bounds of a given legal community and not completely controlled by its laws and mores. Although they are usually connected with cities, it is not necessary that they should be regarded as an urban population, and scholars are not agreed on whether the propertyless persons who formed the Habiru were drawn from the cities or from the drift of nomadic tribes toward the cities. In the OT Hebrew clearly seems to be a gentilic name and not the designation of a social status. It is therefore difficult to identify the biblical Hebrews with the Habiru. On the other hand, it is difficult to separate them entirely. According to the biblical genealogies, the descendants of Eber* include Aramaeans as well as Israelites; but in biblical usage the term Hebrew is applied only to Israelites, and this is emphatically shown in Ex 3:18; 5:3; 7:16; 9:1, 13, where Yahweh is called the God of the Hebrews. It is most unlikely that the Hebrew narrator would have applied this designation to Yahweh if he had meant to include Aramaeans under the term Hebrews. In the OT Eber is probably a fictitious eponymous ancestor invented to explain the existence of a group under a name which had become a gentilic instead of a social designation. A hypothetical connection between the two uses of the name may be found in the suggestion that the clan of Abraham originally had the status of Habiru, and that the descendants remembered the name but forgot that it was a social term. It is impossible to identify the Hebrews with the Habiru of the Amarna texts; the modern calculation of the date of the exodus* places the invasion and settlement of the Hebrews at least 100 years later than the troubled period from which the Amarna texts come. The inclusion of the Hebrews among the Apiru who performed forced labor in Egypt is possible, but as members of a larger group. A. Alt has suggested biblical parallels to the social type indicated by the records of the Habiru. The hired brigands who joined Abimelech* to establish his usurpation at Shechem (Jgs 9:4), the bandit troops of Jephthah* (Jgs 11:3) and of David* (1 S 22:2 ff), who finally hired out himself and his troops as mercenaries to the Philistines (1 S 27:1 ff), correspond rather closely to the propertyless class suggested in Mesopotamia which was forced to support itself by the profession of arms, by banditry, by hiring itself out, or finally by enslavement. This class is explicitly described in David's band, which was composed of those who were in distress and in debt and embittered (1 S 22:2).

Hebrew language. Hb, the language of the OT, belongs to the NW Semitic* language group, which comprises Aramaic* and Canaanite*. The dialects of Canaanite known from existing literary remains are Ugaritic, Hamathite, Phoenician (with several dialects), Hebrew, and Moabite. Canaanite was spoken throughout Syria and Palestine during the last two millennia BC. In the 2nd half of the 1st millennium BC Hb yielded to Aramaic as the common spoken language of Palestine. Hb exhibits in common with other Semitic languages certain characteristics; these include the existence of guttural consonants (ḥ and ʻ), emphatic consonants (ṭ, ṣ, ḳ), and the almost universal appearance of triliteral roots. The triliteral root conveys the basic meaning of the words; modifications and inflections are signified by prefixes, affixes, and changes in the vocalization of the inflected forms of the root. The script of Hb is consonantal (cf ALPHABET), and it was relatively late in the history of Hb writing that methods of signifying the vowels appeared in the written language. The Hb text of the OT is equipped with a system of points to indicate the vowels. This system of vowel pointing was the creation of rabbinical scholars of the 1st millennium AD (cf TEXT). These scholars were no longer in possession of the living tradition of Hb speech, and the grammar of Hb based upon their pointing of the text is, to an undetermined point, artificial. Early Hb is found in a number of Palestinian inscriptions. Most of these are very brief, written on potsherds, containing little more

than a single personal name. The most important inscriptions are found in the Gezer* calendar, the ostraca* of Samaria*, the Siloam* inscription, and the Lachish* letters. These inscriptions show that the consonantal script of the period of the Hb monarchy differs only slightly, apart from the formation of the letters, from the script of the OT. The pronunciation of early Hb can also be reconstructed to some extent from the transcription of Hb local and personal names in the records of Assyria; the cuneiform* script designated the vocalization of words. These transcriptions and some differences in the writing of the Hb inscriptions show that the ancient pronunciation differed from the pronunciation of the Massoretic tradition. Scholars have long thought that Hb as a means of communication had disappeared before the NT period. This opinion is now rendered doubtful by the texts of Qumran* which are written in Hb. The Hb is not that of the early literature of the OT; but it does not appear to be an artificial scholastic language like rabbinical Hb or medieval Lt. In general it resembles the Hb of the later books of the OT. The language is not called Hb in the OT; it is called either Canaanite (Is 19:18) or Judahite (2 K 18:26; Ne 13:24; Is 36:11). In the opinion of some scholars the text of the OT represents the dialect of Jerusalem, which is meant by the term Judahite in 2 K 18:26; Is 36:11, and probably in Ne 13:24. Dialectal differences among the Israelites are suggested in Jgs 12:6, which indicates that the Ephraimites were unable to pronounce the sibilant Shin (Shibboleth; Sibboleth). The isolation of the villages in modern Palestine permits local dialectal differences within a remarkably small area. Neo-Hebrew, which was employed in the Talmud, was a scholastic language. Modern Hb, the written and spoken language of Israel, is a modern construction which differs widely from biblical Hb.

Hebrews, Epistle to the. 1. *Contents* (here the outline of J. Cambier is followed).

I. Christ the high priest brings a new covenant to be accepted in faith and fidelity, 1:1–10:18.

1. The new and last spokesman of God, 1:1–5:10:

a) Christ is superior to the angels.

This is affirmed in the OT, 1:1–14.

Exhortation to fidelity to Him, 2:1–4.

His humiliation in human nature was necessary to secure His solidarity with us, 2:5–18.

b) Christ is superior to Moses.

Jesus is superior as the son is superior to the slave, 3:1–6.

Exhortation to fidelity to His preaching, 3:7–19.

c) The message of Christ is addressed to us.

The announcement of the "rest" promised to Israel, 4:1–11.

The living and effective word of God, 4:12–13.

Through Him we approach the throne, 4:15–16.

d) Christ the high priest and the Son has received the priesthood of Melchizedek; He has taken human nature and merited salvation by His suffering, 5:1–10.

2. Preparatory Exhortation, 5:11–6:20:

a) Reproach that the readers are like children rather than adults, 5:11–6:3.

b) Warning of the hopelessness of the apostate, 6:4–8.

c) Encouragement based on their charity, 6:9–12.

d) The promise to Abraham and the merits of Jesus are a motive of hope, 6:13–20.

3. The religious institutions of Old and New Covenant, 7:1–10:18:

a) Jesus the eternal high priest.

The priesthood of Jesus is superior to the levitical priesthood, 7:1–10.

The new priesthood and sacrifice replace the old and achieve what was impossible to the old, 7:11–28.

b) Superiority of the heavenly· cult, the heavenly sanctuary, and the perfect sacrifice of the new covenant.

The heavenly sanctuary, 8:1–13.

The earthly sanctuary, 9:1–10.

The unique sacrifice of Christ in the heavenly sanctuary, 9:11–14.

The new covenant established by the blood of Christ, 9:15–22.

Superiority of the new cult; Christ enters the heavenly sanctuary, 9:23–28.

The sacrifice of Christ brings true remission, 10:1–18.

II. Necessity of fidelity to the new covenant and of advancing toward the everlasting city, 10:19–13:25.

1. Counsels of perseverance in faith in Christ, 10:19–39.

a) Necessity of retaining faith and hope received in baptism and of fraternal love, 10:19–25.

b) The hopeless condition of the apostate, 10:26–31.

c) Encouragement based on the faith and love already shown by the community, 10:32–39.

2. The example of the faith of heroes of the past, 11:1–12:13.

a) Examples of faith in the OT, 11:1–40.

b) Encouragement to sustain patience in present trials, 12:1–13.

3. Counsels of perseverance in Christian virtue, 12:14–17.

4. Exhortation of fidelity to the new covenant.

a) Comparison of the old earthly covenant and the new heavenly covenant, 12:18–24.

b) It is a greater sin to refuse the new covenant than to refuse the old covenant, 12:25–29.

5. Various counsels:

a) Love, purity, detachment, gratitude, 13:1–7.

b) Exhortation to detachment from the world and to be faithful to Christ in suffering until arrival at the heavenly city, 13:8–14.

c) Counsels of praise, fraternal love, obedience, mutual aid in prayer, confidence, 13:15–21.

6. Final recommendations and greetings, 13:22–25.

2. *Authorship.* Very few modern scholars still maintain that Heb is the work of Paul. The thought and language (cf below) are too different from the Pauline epistles to permit this attribution. Tradition is not uniform on this question. Heb was not accepted as canonical in the W before 350, although it was known to Clement of Rome, the Shepherd of Hermas, Hippolytus, and Tertullian (who attributed Heb to Barnabas and did not consider it canonical). It was accepted in the E at least from Pantaenus of Alexandria, who attributed it to Paul. Clement of Alexandria recognized the striking differences of style and explained them by the hypothesis that Paul wrote Heb in Hb, which was translated into Gk. Origen went further; he believed that the ideas were those of Paul, but that Heb was written by an unknown who wrote what he remembered of what Paul had said. Modern critics do not believe that the dependence on Paul was any more than indirect; the writer knew Paul's thought, but the epistle was neither written nor commissioned by Paul (Spicq). Heb is a personal work of the writer.

The writer has not identified himself in any way, and both ancients and moderns have made various suggestions: Clement of Rome, Barnabas, Jude, Apollos, and even Priscilla the wife of Aquila. These are no more than guesses. Modern critics are agreed that Heb shows that its author had an Alexandrian background; C. Spicq has suggested that he was a disciple of Philo who became a Christian. He uses a number of terms drawn from Hellenistic literature and philosophy which are rare or absent in the rest of the NT. In contrast to the antithesis of present-future world which is found in Judaism and the NT, Heb presents an antithesis of the visible-earthly-OT reality against the invisible-heavenly-NT reality. It is this invisible reality which gives reality to the prophetic words of the OT.

The divergences from Paul in vocabulary, style, sentence structure, and patterns of thought are more numerous and more notable than the resemblances. The style of Heb is the most polished of all the NT writings. The author knows and uses the rhetorical figures and periods of style.

The exegesis of the OT in Heb stands apart from the other NT books. Heb usually quotes the LXX, but sometimes exhibits a text with variations which are found neither in the LXX nor the MT. All citations are treated and quoted as the words of the Holy Spirit, of Christ, of God; this method of citation is characteristic of Philo but not of the other NT books. The author employs rabbinical methods of interpretation and the allegorical commentary used by Philo (cf INTERPRETATION). All these taken together suggest a Hellenistic Jew with an Alexandrian intellectual background; of the Christians known to us from the NT Apollos* fits this description better than any other, but there is no reason to say that only Apollos comes under it.

3. *Date, Place of Composition, Destination.* Heb and 1 Jn are the only epistles which have no introductory greeting; but Heb has a concluding greeting. The absence of the introduction cannot be due to damage; in all the MS letters of ancient times there is no instance in which only the salutation was lost by damage. Since Heb is otherwise more like a treatise than an epistle, some have asked whether it is an epistle at all, i.e., whether it was addressed to any particular church or group. Unlike the Pauline letters, Heb does not fall into a clear doctrinal and moral division; the exhortations are interspersed among the doctrinal expositions (cf outline above). The closest parallel to its form is found in the Hellenistic synagogue discourse as found in the apocryphal 4 Mc — another suggestion of Alexandrian influence. Most scholars now believe that it was addressed to a particular group or community; but there is no agreement on the identification of the group.

The title was known in the 2nd century but is probably not much earlier; it appears that the title was deduced from the emphasis upon OT institutions. Most modern scholars doubt that Heb was addressed to Jewish Christians; they believe its terms are equally suitable for a Gentile community without any reference to the division between Jews and Gentiles, or to a Gentile community which was strongly influenced by Judaism, such as Colossae (cf COLOSSIANS, EPISTLE).

There seems no doubt that the group, whoever it was, was under stress because of persecution and disappointment, and was weakened in its faith. The writer believed that the primitive gospel needed development and application to their needs. C. Spicq has proposed the interesting view that this group consisted of priests of Jerusalem who had become Christians and who fled, perhaps to Caesarea, after the fall of the temple* in 70; the message would comfort them with its announcement of the eternal heavenly priesthood, temple, and sacrifice. Others do not believe that the central theme of the epistle — which is somewhat difficult to define — is so exclusively the priesthood of Christ; J. Cambier puts it as "fidelity to Christ, the heavenly high priest, rendered perfect by His obedience in suffering, the last spokesman of God; Christ invites us, in spite of persecutions, to remain faithful to the new definitive heavenly covenant, merited by his perfect priestly sacrifice."

The place is unknown, although Italy is suggested in 13:24. The date is likewise unknown; the use of Heb by Clement of Rome indicates a date earlier than 90, and modern scholars place it between 60 and 90, most 80–90.

4. *Theological Elements.* While the central position of Christ is in the line of Pauline theology, the centrality of Christ precisely as priest is not a characteristic Pauline idea. Christ is the eternal preexistent Son and high priest (1; 7:1–10:18; 13:8–14). The writer affirms His humanity, for it is through His humanity that He achieves the solidarity which makes Him the one mediator (2:11–18; 3:15; 5:1–5). The redeeming death has the efficacy of sacrifice* (6:4; 9:26, 28; 10:2; 12:26 f). The emphasis of Heb on covenant is peculiar to Heb in the NT. Heb, like Paul, considers the law* as voided; but strangely he considers the law as merely the ceremonial law and does not advert to its moral content. Unlike Paul, he conceives the saving efficacy of the death of Jesus as assured not by the resurrection but by the entrance of Jesus into heaven and His glorification (cf ASCENSION). Käsemann has drawn attention to the theme of the people of God on the march to salvation; the advance of the Christians is illustrated by allusions from the exodus and the wandering, in which the Pnt places the construction of the sanctuary and the institution of the levitical sacrifice and priesthood.

Hebron (Hb *ḥebrôn,* etymology and meaning uncertain), a city in the hill country of Judah. The modern Hebron lies about 20 mi S of Jerusalem. Its Arabic name is El Khalil, "the friend" (Abraham). There

Hebron.

is no doubt that the modern Hebron lies at or near the site of the ancient city. The ancient site has never been positively identified, and most scholars think that its remains lie under the modern city. Hebron lies in a depression in the mountains of Judah; the hills which surround it rise to an altitude of 3300 ft. According to Nm 13:22 Hebron was founded 7 years before Zoan* (Tanis) in Egypt. This probably refers to the Hyksos* foundation of Tanis about 1700 BC; therefore Hebron did not exist as a city in the time of Abraham, who is usually associated with Mamre*, which is identified in the Hb narrative with Hebron. The city is also called Kirjath-arba (Gn 23:2; 35:27; Jos 14:15; 15:13, 54; 20:7; 21:11; Jgs 1:10; Ne 11:25). This name, which means "city of four," is obscure. Traditions concerning the pre-Israelite inhabitants of Hebron vary in different sources. The city is said to belong to the Amorites* in Gn 14:13, a document of uncertain date, to the Hittites* in Gn 23, a later tradition, to the Anakim* in Nm 13:22; Jos 11:21; 14:15 (earlier sources) and to the Canaanites in Jgs 1:10 (a later tradition). Jacob also is associated with Hebron (Gn 35:27; 37:14). The city was scouted by the Israelites before their entrance into Canaan (Nm 13:22) and was described by the scouts as strongly fortified. The king of Hebron was one of the confederated kings defeated by Joshua (Jos 10:3, 5, 23; 12:10). The Israelite possession of Hebron also reflects varying traditions

from different periods. The earliest tradition is no doubt that contained in Jos 14:13 ff and Jgs 1:20, in which the city belongs to Caleb* the Kenizzite*. That the city belonged to Caleb is retained in the later traditions which list Hebron among the cities of refuge (Jos 20:7) and the Levitical cities (Jos 21:11, 13; 1 Ch 6:40, 42). In Jgs 1:10, however, it is stated simply that the city was taken by Judah. This is a later tradition which arose at a time when the Kenizzites had been merged with the tribe of Judah. The tradition of Caleb, however, is preserved in Jgs 1:20. Mareshah*, a city name, is called the son of Caleb and the father of Hebron (1 Ch 2:42), an obscure reference which no doubt reflects the movements of clans in the early period of Israelite settlement. Hebron is included in the list of Judahite cities (Jos 15:54). Samson carried the city gates of Gaza* to the hill which overlooks Hebron (Jgs 16:3), an exaggeration of popular tradition. Hebron, where he reigned for seven years, is prominent in the history of David*. It was the first seat of his kingdom, which was extended over Judah alone (2 S 2:1 ff). It was the scene of his treaty with Abner*, which delivered to him the sovereignty of the tribes ruled by Ishbaal* (2 S 3:20 ff) as well as the murder of Abner (2 S 3:27) and his burial (2 S 3:32). The news of the murder of Ishbaal was brought to David at Hebron (2 S 4:1 ff) and the assembly of Israel which conferred the kingship of all Israel upon David was held at

Hebron (2 S 5:1 ff; 1 Ch 11:1 ff). According to the Chronicler it was also the point of assembly of David's army (1 Ch 12:23 ff). In the time of David Hebron appears as the principal city of Judah, and this is scarcely insignificant in the story of the revolt of Absalom, which was first proclaimed at Hebron (2 S 15:9); Jerusalem had overshadowed Hebron. Absalom's excuse for going to Hebron was the necessity of paying a vow he had made during his exile in Geshur* (1 S 15:7 f). This suggests that Hebron was also the principal cultic center of Judah at this period. Shechem* was the scene of the assembly which ratified the accession of Rehoboam* (1 K 12:1); the monarchy had become Israelite, not Judahite, and had to look to the N, where the majority of the Israelite population resided. After the reign of David Hebron scarcely appears in the OT except for the mention of its resettlement after the exile (Ne 11:25). The name of Hebron and of three other cities of Judah appears on jar handles of the 8th century BC. These handles are stamped with the name of the city and the inscription "to the king." They appear to be official royal measures, and scholars believe that the cities mentioned, including Hebron, were places of the manufacture of pottery vessels of royally determined measures. The city was sacked by Judas* during the Maccabean wars (1 Mc 5:65); it is evident that at this time the city had become Idumean*. It was burned by the Romans during the Jewish wars in AD 68. The absence of any reference to Hebron as a city during the Byzantine period suggests that it was abandoned for centuries after the Roman destruction. The city is not mentioned in the NT. It was, however, a place of Christian pilgrimage as the burying ground of the patriarchs. A Crusader church was built upon the site of an earlier Byzantine church in the 12th century and Hebron became the seat of a bishop. It was repossessed by the Moslems toward the close of the 12th century.

The modern city of Hebron has a population of about 35,000. It has been locally famous for the manufacture of glass since the Middle Ages. Its great monument is the mosque Haram el Khalil, which is built over a cave which non-Moslems are not permitted to enter. Only a few Christians since the Middle Ages have seen it, and these unfortunately included no qualified observers. It is a possibility accepted by scholars that the cave is the cave of Machpelah*. The mosque includes the massive masonry of the type which is usually identified as Herodian. There is no literary evidence, however, of any building activities of Herod at Hebron.

Heifer. Cf OX; RED HEIFER.

Heir. Cf INHERITANCE.

Helam (Hb ḥêlām, etymology uncertain), the place on the E side of the Jordan where the Aramaeans assembled in alliance with the Ammonites and were defeated by David (2 S 10:16 f). The place is mentioned only here in the Hb OT. The fact that it was a point of assembly for the Aramaeans suggests some connection with Alema (1 Mc 5:26), described as a large fortified town, mentioned with other towns in the region of Hauran (cf BASHAN).

Heli. Cf ELI.

Heliodorus (Gk hēliodōros, "gift of Helios" [the sun]), the central character of the midrash* of 2 Mc 3:1–40. Simon, governor of the temple of Jerusalem, because of a quarrel with the high priest Onias*, reported the existence of the temple treasures to Apollonius* of Tarsus, governor of Coelesyria and Phoenicia. This in turn was reported to Seleucus IV Philopator (187–175 BC), who sent his chief minister, Heliodorus, to confiscate the treasury. Heliodorus was prevented from executing his mission by the appearance of a horseman who knocked him down and of two strong young men who flogged him within an inch of his life. He was cured of his wounds by the prayers of Onias and testified to the presence of a deity who protected the temple of Jerusalem. Historians identify Heliodorus with the Heliodorus mentioned in an inscription of the citizens of Laodicea in Phoenicia discovered in the temple of Apollo at Delos. He was the son of Aeschylus of Antioch, reared with the king Selecus IV, and chief minister of Seleucus; the Gk phrase which is translated "chief minister" is the same as that which appears in 2 Mc 3:7. This Heliodorus later murdered Seleucus IV.

Heliopolis. Cf ON.

Hell. Cf GEHENNA.

Hellenism. Hellenism designates the diffusion of Gk civilization throughout the E Mediterranean basin and W Asia following the conquests of Alexander. The centers of this diffusion were the military colonies founded by the Macedonians and the Gk cities built in great numbers in W Asia, each following the standard Gk city plan with its marketplace* (agora), colonnaded avenues, temples, theater, and gymnasium*. Intellectually Hellenism brought the study of Gk literature and philosophy and the cultivation of Gk forms of the plastic arts. In the process Gk civilization lost its most distinctive Gk features and took on a more general and universal form. At the same time there was an exchange; Gk civilization assimilated something from the various areas in which it was diffused. The Gk language became the *Koine* spoken throughout the area, differentiated into various local dialects and borrowing a number of foreign words. Hellenism also assimilated with some enthusiasm features of Oriental religion and cult, and Gk art took on native features which can be clearly discerned in the art of Hellenistic Egypt and Syria. Hellenism penetrated most deeply into the cities; the peasant population and the hinterlands were more lightly touched. Judaism also was influenced by this development. The Jewish communities of the Diaspora*, which supported themselves by commercial activities in large Hellenistic cities, were scarcely able to resist the impact of Hellenism, retaining only the law and the worship of the synagogue. The external features of Hellenistic civilization overwhelmed them. The common articles of daily use — food, clothing, furniture, etc — were Gk in name and in style. A large number of Gk personal names appear among Jews both in the Diaspora and in Palestine during the Hellenistic period (e.g., Andrew, Philip, Alexander), and often Jewish personal names were altered to Gk names of similar sound (e.g., Joshua to Jason). Gk architecture affected even the construction of synagogues, and in the government of Jewish communities the organization and titles of Gk government were adopted. The first impact of this civilization on Palestinian Judaism was equally strong, and it reached its peak in the first half of the 2nd century BC, when Hellenism was adopted and fostered by members of the sacerdotal aristocracy. Antiochus* Epiphanes attempted to unify his scattered empire by imposing Hellenism on all his subjects to the point of the abolition of local differences, including religions (1 Mc 1:41 ff). A gymnasium, which was an educational as well as an athletic establishment, was built in Jerusalem (1 Mc 1:11–15; 2 Mc 4:9–16). Gk learning was studied and Gk costume was adopted. But the prohibition of Jewish religion aroused resistance which ultimately issued in the wars of the Maccabees*. These wars did not establish a lasting independent Jewish state, but they left as their heritage Pharisaism, the focus of zeal for the preservation of Jewish religion and the Jewish way of life (cf PHARISEE). The intellectual influence of Hellenism on Palestinian Judaism has left no profound trace in Jewish literature, and it was probably never more than superficial. This is in contrast to the Judaism of Alexandria, the principal intellectual center of the Diaspora. The writings of Philo and WS both exhibit an acquaintance with Gk thought (cf WISDOM OF SOLOMON). Philo was a student of Gk philosophy and it is evident that he regarded it with favor. It was his purpose to show that the law*, which was the sum of all wisdom for the Jew, was a philosophy like Platonism or Stoicism and capable of producing the same intellectual growth. If Philo is typical of Alexandrian Judaism, then the assimilation of Gk thought by the Jews had gone quite far. The Hellenistic world offered favorable conditions for the diffusion of Christianity; a universal civilization which had brought together peoples of widely differing regions and cultures into a common way of life was sympathetic to a universal religion which imposed no particular national or racial conditions upon its members and taught the unity and equality of all men under one divine father. In addition the community of language and the easy communications of the Hellenistic world made it easy for the apostles of Christianity to spread the gospel rapidly over a surprisingly wide area.

Hellenist. Cf GREEK.

Helmet. Cf ARMOR.

Heman (Hb *hêmān*, etymology and meaning uncertain), a famous wise man mentioned with Ethan*, Chalcol, and Darda (1 K 5:11). Heman also appears in the genealogy of Judah as the son of Zerah* with Zimri, Ethan, Chalcol, and Darda (1 Ch 2:6) and in the genealogical lists of Levi as the son of Joel of the Levite clan of Kohath* (1 Ch 6:18). Heman was one of the heads of David's choir with Asaph* and Ethan* (1 Ch 15:17 ff), with Jeduthun* (1 Ch 16:41 f), and with Asaph and Jeduthun as the head of a family of singers (1 Ch 25:1 ff; 2 Ch 29:13 f; 35:15), and with Asaph and Jeduthun at the dedication of Solomon's temple (2 Ch 5:12). As with Ethan, the mention of the famous wise man is primary, and from this comes the attribution of Ps 88. On the basis of this attribution, Heman was included in the genealogies of Judah and then of the Levites. The legendary wise men become cantors and composers in David's choir.

Hen. Cf FOWL.

Henoch. Cf ENOCH.

Heracles (Gk *heraclēs*, Lt *hercules*), a hero of Gk mythology who was apotheosized in a number of Hellenistic cities. At Tyre* he was identified with Baal Melkart, and the high priest Jason* of Jerusalem sent 300 silver drachmas in the name of the Jews of Jerusalem for a sacrifice to Heracles (2 Mc 4:18 ff).

Heresy (Gk *haeresis*, primarily a "taking" or a "choice"), in later Gk literature the word designates a philosophical system or school, and it is no doubt from this usage that the word appears in the NT to designate a religious party or sect. The term is applied to the Sadducees* (AA 5:17) and to the Pharisees* (AA 15:5), which is called by Paul the strictest sect of our (Jewish) religion (AA 26:5). The term is also applied to the Christians, who were called the sect of the Nazarenes (AA 24:5), a term which Paul rejects (AA 24:14; cf AA 28:22). The concept of Christian unity did not favor the admission of sects, parties, or other divisive influences within the early Church; Paul admits their inevitability, but he does not praise them (1 Co 11:19), and they are mentioned together with dissension and envy in a list of the most serious vices (Gal 5:20). They are called destructive parties or divisions (2 Pt 2:1). The word is not used in the NT in the technical theological sense of denial of dogma.

Hermas (Gk *hermas*), a Christian of Rome to whom Paul sends greetings (Rm 16:14). The name is probably an abbreviation of a name compounded with the name of the god Hermes*.

Hermes (Gk *hermes*). **1.** A Greek god, Lt Mercury, the messenger of the gods. Hence the people of Lystra* took Barnabas for Zeus* and Paul, the spokesman of the two, for Hermes (AA 14:12). **2.** A Christian of Rome to whom Paul sent greetings (Rm 16:14). The name, like Hermas*, is probably an abbreviation of a name of which Hermes is a component.

Hermogenes (Gk *hermogenēs*), a Christian who deserted Paul (2 Tm 1:15).

Hermon (Hb *ḥermôn*, etymology and meaning uncertain), the mountain which terminates the Anti-Lebanon* range in the S. Hermon rises to a height of 9232 ft and has three peaks. Its summit carries perpetual snow, and this is one of the sources of the Jordan*. Hermon rises well above the other mountains of the Anti-Lebanon and is a landmark which can be seen for many miles; it is usually visible from the Sea of Galilee.

According to Dt 3:9 its Phoenician name was Sirion and its Amorite name Senir. It was the N boundary of the Amorite kingdom (Dt 3:8; 4:48) and thus it is said to lie in the territory of Og* (Jos 12:5; 13:11). The Hittites* dwelt at the foot of Hermon in the land of Mizpeh* (Jos 11:3). In tradition it was the N limit of the conquests of Joshua (Jos 11:17; 12:1; 13:5) and the N limit of the territory of Manasseh* (1 Ch 5:23). There are a number of poetic allusions to Hermon: its waterfalls (Ps 42:7), its dew (Ps 133:3); it is one of the scenes in SS 4:8, and with Tabor* it celebrates the name of Yahweh (Ps 89:13), and it is one of the scenes of storm (Ps 29:6). The name Senir occurs outside of Dt 3:9 in SS 4:8; 1 Ch 5:23; Ezk 27:5 (cedars). The name Sirion occurs outside of Dt 3:9 only in Ps 29:6. Both of these names are found in extrabiblical literature. Mt Sariyana is included in the list of deities who witness the treaty of the Hittite king Mursilis and Duppi-Teshub of Amurru (ANET 205). Mt Saniru was the site of a stronghold of Hazael* of Damascus which was attacked by Shalmaneser III (858–824 BC).

Herod (Gk *hērōdēs*), the name is common in profane Gk literature, history, and inscriptions; satellite king of Judaea under the Romans 37–4 BC, and founder of the Herodian family, several members of which appear in the NT. Herod was the son of the Idumean* Antipater, associated with Hyrcanus II (cf HASMONEAN), and appointed procurator of Judaea by the Romans while Hyrcanus II held the title of ethnarch. Hyrcanus was restricted to religious activity, and political power was held by Antipater. The mother of Herod was Cypris, an Arabian princess; hence Herod was at best half-Jewish, since the Idumeans, forcibly brought into Judaism by John Hyrcanus, were not accepted as genuine Jews. Antipater strove to win the favor of Julius Caesar and succeeded; and as a result of Caesar's friendship he won concessions for the Jews not only in Judaea but also in the Diaspora*. Herod himself was first active in public affairs when he was appointed *strategos* of Galilee by his father in 47 BC at the age of 25 (according to the generally accepted correction of the text of Josephus, which gives 15 years of age). Herod was a man of unusual powers: physical vigor, extremely astute, and a master of political maneuver, and endowed with boundless energy and ambition. At the same time his passions were wild and ungoverned, and especially in his later years degenerated into tyranny and brutality. Herod's political astuteness was early tested in the crises of the Roman civil war which followed the assassination of Julius Caesar in 44 BC. At first he attached himself to Cassius, one of the assassins; after the death of Cassius in the battle of Philippi he transferred his allegiance to Mark Antony, who received the eastern portion of the Roman dominions. In 40 BC Herod had to flee the country. The entire Roman E was menaced by an invasion of the Parthians; Antigonus, brother of Hyrcanus II (cf HASMONEAN), took the occasion to invite them to assist him to regain his throne. The inaction of Antony, then enmeshed in his affair with Cleopatra, permitted the Parthians initial successes, and Antigonus was established king of the Jews. Herod first fled to Arabia; but his reception there was hostile, and he went to Rome, where beyond his expectations he received the title of king of the Jews. It was necessary for him to win his kingdom. The Roman legions defeated the Parthians and expelled them in 39–38 BC, and Herod after three years of war defeated Antigonus and installed himself as king in 37 BC. Politically the reign of Herod was generally peaceful and externally prosperous. He was, however, universally unpopular among the Jews, not only because of his foreign origin but also because he was dependent upon Rome, which was already hated by the Jews as a foreign tyranny. Furthermore, he was religiously indifferent, externally faithful to Jewish observances in public but a patron of Hellenistic cults in non-Jewish parts of his kingdom. He did not hesitate to employ violence immediately and indiscriminately to suppress any sign of trouble. In 31 BC with the defeat of Antony at Actium Herod's political skill was again tested. He went to Rome and appealed directly to Augustus, promising him the same fidelity which he had shown to Antony. Augustus accepted his appeal, and with the exception of a single episode Herod retained the friendship of Augustus for the rest of his reign. Through successive grants of Antony and Augustus the kingdom of Herod was expanded from its original limits of Judaea proper to include Idumea*, Samaria*, Galilee, Perea*, and the ancient territory of Bashan*. A disastrous earthquake in 31 BC killed 30,000 people, and Herod showed himself generous in assisting the survivors. Herod's building program was the most grandiose which the country had ever witnessed. He rebuilt, in some instances entirely from the foundations, Samaria* (which he renamed Sebaste), Caesarea*, which was an entirely new foundation, Jerusalem*, Jericho*, and Antipatris*, named after his father. To keep the country in submission he fortified a number of strong points which served him

also as palatial residences: Herodium S of Bethlehem, Masada on the W shore of the Dead Sea, Machaerus on the E shore of the Dead Sea (the scene of the death of John the Baptist), Alexandrium (Qarn Sartabeh) N of Jericho, and Hyrcania S of Jericho. The massive remains of Herodian masonry can be seen in many places in modern Israel and Jordan.

The family history of Herod is a story of violence and terror. His career was governed by two desires which ultimately proved irreconcilable; one was to win the acceptance of the members of the aristocratic Hasmonean family, the other was to protect himself against any danger of conspiracy on the part of the Hasmoneans. His first measure to raise his social position was to repudiate his Idumean wife Doris and to marry Mariamme, the granddaughter of Hyrcanus II. At the same time, in order to keep the Hasmoneans in their place, he refused to install Aristobulus, the brother of Mariamme, as high priest, and instead selected an unknown Ananel. At the insistence of Mariamme Aristobulus was finally installed, but Herod had him murdered a few months after his installation on suspicion of conspiracy. Herod's household was riven by envy and factions which centered around his sister Salome on the one hand and the members of the Hasmonean family on the other. Mariamme, although she seems to have been innocent of any designs against Herod, was a tool employed by both factions. The tragic result of these family quarrels, almost all instigated by Salome, was a series of deaths by assassination or execution in the family of Herod. The envious slanders of Salome moved Herod to execute his brother Joseph, Hycanus II, the grandfather of Mariamme, and finally Mariamme herself on charges of plotting against his life. Alexandra, the mother of Mariamme, more insistent than her daughter on family prerogatives and a match for Salome in intrigue, also fell to Herod's anger. The envy of Salome did not spare her own spouses; both her first husband, Joseph, and her second husband, Costobar, were executed by Herod on her testimony. The sons of Mariamme, Alexander and Aristobulus, were sent to Rome by Herod to be educated. On their return, in addition to the grudge they held against Herod for the killing of their mother, they were further incited by the whispers against Herod which filled their household. As in most of the other cases, the exact degree of their guilt cannot be ascertained; but Herod, against the advice of his friend Augustus, had them both tried and executed. Antipater, the son of his first wife Doris, became his favorite instead of Alexander and

Aristobulus; but Antipater unwisely attempted to consolidate his own position against his father's wishes, and was himself executed on the charge of conspiracy. These family tragedies were responsible for many changes in Herod's will and testament. His first will designated Antipater as his successor, but it was modified so as to include Alexander and Aristobulus. After the execution of the sons of Mariamme Antipater again became sole heir. After his fall the succession passed to another son, Herod* Antipas. The last will of Herod, made shortly before his death, conferred upon another son, Archelaus*, the title of king, and gave two other sons, Antipas and Philip*, shares of his territory as tetrarchs. This will was ratified by Augustus and was executed. The NT gives the reign of Herod as the time of the birth of Jesus (Mt 2:1; Lk 1:5). Elsewhere Herod is mentioned only in connection with the murder of the infants of Bethlehem (Mt 2:1 ff). Such a crime is in harmony with the violence of his reign, especially in his closing years, and where his own security on the throne was concerned. On the historical problems created by this account cf MAGI. On the problem of chronology cf JESUS CHRIST.

Herod Agrippa. Son of Aristobulus and Bernice, grandson of Herod* the Great and Mariamme, daughter of Hyrcanus. In the NT he is called Herod (AA 12) but he himself used the name of Agrippa (I, to distinguish him from his son Agrippa* II) after a Roman patron of Herod the Great. He was born in 10 BC and was educated in Rome. There as a young man his career was that of a wastrel. Finally he had to leave Rome on account of the debts he had contracted. He had formed, however, a number of friendships with members of the imperial family, in particular with Gaius Caesar (Caligula), emperor AD 37–41. He was imprisoned by Tiberius six months before the death of Tiberius because of a chance remark that he hoped Caligula would succeed Tiberius. Caligula immediately released him from prison and gave him a gold chain equal in weight to the iron chain which he had worn as a prisoner. He also granted Agrippa the territories of Philip*, who had died in AD 34, and the title of king. To this was added in AD 40 the territory of Herod Antipas* after the latter's disgrace. After the assassination of Caligula in 41 Agrippa rendered some services to Claudius* in securing the succession, and in return Claudius not only confirmed him in his dignity but also granted him the territory of the province of Samaria and Judaea. He

THE FAMILY OF HEROD

Dates given are dates of death. Persons marked with an asterisk* are mentioned in the NT. *m* — married. *d* — daughter. *k* — king.

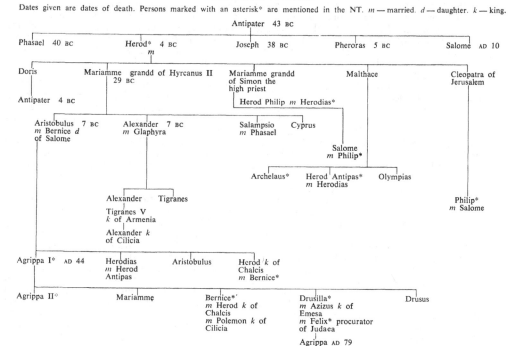

was very careful to observe all the prescriptions of the Jewish law and thus won the favor of his subjects. This, however, was only a superficial pose; outside Jewish territory he lived in the Hellenistic manner. It was probably because of his zeal for the Law that he attempted to suppress the Christian sect; he executed James* the son of Zebedee, and imprisoned Peter, who escaped (AA 12:1 ff). His most important work of building was the so-called Third Wall, the northernmost of the walls of Jerusalem. The exact course of this wall is uncertain; cf JERUSALEM. The wall was not completed, either because the imperial government prohibited it or because Agrippa, fearing to arouse suspicion, abandoned it spontaneously. He ruled his territories only from 41 to 44, and died suddenly during a public function; the description of his death in Josephus suggests a ruptured appendix.

Herod Antipas. Son of Herod the Great and Malthace, tetrarch of Galilee under the terms of Herod's will. He is designated by his father's name Herod not only in the Gospels but also on his coins. His territory included Galilee* and Perea*, which were separated from each other by the Greek cities of the Decapolis*. Herod rebuilt and fortified the city of Sepphoris N of Nazareth and founded the city of Tiberias*, named after the emperor Tiberius*, on the W shore of the Sea of Galilee. Herod acted as a spy for Tiberius upon Roman officers and satellite kings in the E. This probably accounts for the enmity of Pontius Pilate* (Lk 23:12) and of Vitellius, the legate of Syria. Like Archelaus* and Philip* he had been educated in Rome. His first wife was the daughter of the Nabatean* king Aretas*. While on a visit to Rome about AD 28 he met Herodias, the daughter of Aristobulus, son of Herod the Great and Mariamme the granddaughter of Hyrcanus II, who was then the wife of Herod Philip, son of Herod the Great and Mariamme the granddaughter of Simon. They had one daughter, Salome*. The two fell in love and planned to divorce their respective spouses. The husband of Herodias made no objection, but the wife of Antipas fled to her father Aretas. Herod and Herodias were then married. The marriage not only caused great scandal among the Jews but also incurred the vindictive anger of Aretas. John the Baptist publicly reproached Herod and the Gospels tell the story of Herod's imprisonment of John. Herod was unwilling to execute him, but the dance of the daughter of Herodias at his birthday dinner so enchanted the intoxicated ruler that he promised her anything she desired. Salome at her mother's prompting asked the head of John the Baptist on a platter; the execution was accomplished immediately, and the head of the Baptist was brought to the dining hall (Mt 14:3 ff; Mk 6:17 ff). Herod played a part in the passion of Jesus. Pilate* in an attempt to rid himself of the troublesome case had Jesus sent to Herod because he was a resident of Galilee. Herod, although he had been desirous of seeing Jesus, had never had the opportunity of doing so. The silence with which Jesus met his questions is perhaps the most severe rebuke administered by Him in the entire Gospels, and Herod in anger labeled him a fool and returned him to Pilate (Lk 23:7-12). The episode mentioned in Lk 13:31 in which the Pharisees warn Jesus that Herod wished to have Him murdered may have reflected an actual plan of the tetrarch; his remark that this was John the Baptist risen from the dead (Mt 14:1 f; Mk 6:14 ff) may have expressed his fear that another popular preacher had arisen to make him more odious to the people. It is more probable, however, that the Pharisees had been sent by Herod himself to get Jesus to leave his territory; this may be implied in the epithet "fox" which Jesus applied to Herod in the conversation. In AD 36 the Nabatean king Aretas, still angry over Herod's dismissal of his daughter, declared war over a border dispute and defeated Herod. Herod appealed to Tiberius, who sent Vitellius, the legate of Syria, against Aretas. Before any action was taken, news of Tiberius's death arrived, and Vitellius, no friend of Herod, broke off the campaign. Agrippa*, the brother of Herodias*, was a favorite of the new emperor Caligula, who granted him the territories of Philip* with the title of king. Herodias, envious of the honors paid to her brother while her husband did not have the royal dignity, persuaded her husband to go to Rome and ask the title of king. Agrippa sent a representative to present charges against Herod. The charges were credited and Herod was exiled to Lyons in Gaul; Herodias accompanied him of her own choice. No further record of them appears.

Herodians. Mentioned in Mk 3:6 as plotting the death of Jesus with the Pharisees; in Mt 22:16-22; Mk 12:13-17 as proposing with the Pharisees the question whether the Jews should pay tribute to Caesar. The identity of this group has been considerably disputed both among the ancients and among modern scholars. It has been proposed that they were a sect which believed that Herod the Great was the Messiah; a religious sect founded by Herod; the Sadducees; anti-Roman Jews who wished to see Palestine independent under the house of Herod. None of these views has any probability; it is almost impossible that they were a religious sect, and most unlikely that an anti-Roman group could have been associated in any way with the house of Herod, whose one consistent principle was loyalty to Rome. More recent scholars have proposed that they were soldiers of Herod, his courtiers, or members of his household staff. The adjective, however, is of the type which is never used to designate such a group. It is more probable that they were those who favored the house of Herod i.e., they supported the Herodian rule and the Roman rule upon which it rested (H. H. Rowley), the same group which is called in Josephus "those who think with Herod."

Herodias (Gk *hērodias,* feminine of Herod), daughter of Aristobulus, son of Herod the Great and Mariamme. She was first married to Herod Philip, son of Herod the Great and Mariamme, granddaughter of Simon the high priest. They had one daughter, Salome*. This Herod was a man without ambition who took no part in public life. Herodias met Herod Antipas* in Rome about AD 28 and the two formed a passionate attachment for each other, and each obtained a divorce. The scandalous union was detested by the Jews of Galilee and was publicly rebuked by John the Baptist. Herod imprisoned John but was unwilling to execute him. Herodias, however, cherished her vengeance, and through the dance of her daughter Salome shamed Herod into ordering the execution of John during his birthday dinner (Mt 14: 3 ff; Mk 6:17 ff). The ambition of Herodias was responsible for the downfall of her husband. Envious at the royal dignity granted to her brother Agrippa* I by Caligula in AD 37, she persuaded Herod to go to Rome and ask the title of king. Agrippa sent a member of his staff to lay charges of disloyalty against Herod. Herod could not refute the charges and was exiled to Lyons in Gaul. Herodias, as the sister of Caligula's favorite, was excused from accompanying her husband into exile; but she, in the only noble gesture recorded of her, freely chose to accompany him. They are not further mentioned in history.

Herodion (Gk *herōdiōn*), a Jewish Christian of Rome greeted by Paul (Rm 16:11).

Heshbon (Hb *ḥešbôn,* etymology uncertain), a city of Moab; the site is that of the modern Hesban, approximately 16 mi E of the Jordan and 9 mi N of Madaba*. The site has not been explored. Heshbon was the capital city of Sihon*, king of the Amorites; it was taken from him by the Hebrews in the earliest phases of the invasion of Canaan (Nm 21:25 f; Dt 1:4; 2:26 ff; Jgs 11:19 +). It is mentioned frequently as a proverbial great victory. It is mentioned in the list of the cities of Reuben* (Jos 13:17) and as a boundary point between Reuben and Gad* (Jos 13:26), as a city of refuge (Jos 21:37) and a Levitical city (1 Ch 6:66). It lay in a country suitable for pasture (Nm 32:2). There are a number of poetical allusions to the city: the pools of Heshbon (SS 7:5) and its fall mentioned in an ancient poem, possibly Moabite, of uncertain date which is preserved in variant forms in two prophetic books (Is 15:4; 16:8 f; Je 48:2, 34; 49:3).

Heth. The 8th letter of the Hb alphabet, with the value of ḥ.

Heth, Hethite. Cf HITTITE.

Hexateuch (Gk *hexateuchos,* "six books"), in modern literary criticism, a term to designate the books of Gn, Ex, Lv, Nm, Dt, Jos, which are taken as a single compilation. Most recent criticism tends to separate Jos from the Pnt and group it with other books; cf JOSHUA; PENTATEUCH.

Hezekiah (Hb *ḥizkîyāhû,* "Yahweh is my strength," var *yᵉḥizkîyāhû,* "may Yahweh strengthen me"), son of Ahaz* and Abi (2 K 18:2), shortened from Abijah (2 Ch 29:1), king of Judah 715–687 BC. He instituted a religious reform, destroying the places of Baal worship and the bronze Nehushtan* (2 K 18:4). Many more details of uncertain historical validity (cf CHRONICLES) are related in 2 Ch, including the cleansing of the temple (29:5–24), the celebration of the Passover* (30:1–27) and other reforms in the temple cult. According to 30:1–6, 10 f; 31:1 Hezekiah attempted to make Jerusalem the cult center of the former kingdom of Israel. Conquest of Philistine territory is credited to him (2 K 18:8); this was probably in the course of the rebellion against Sennacherib* (cf below), in which some of the Philistines remained loyal to the Assyrians. When Sennacherib succeeded Sargon on the throne of Assyria in 705 BC he was greeted by a widespread revolt throughout the Assyrian empire, extending from Babylonia in the S to Armenia in the N and the states of Syria, Phoenicia, and Palestine. Hezekiah first surrendered and paid tribute (2 K 18:13–16; omitted in Is 36 and 2 Ch). Sennacherib, however, moved against the city anyway; the negotiations with his officer before the city wall, the prayer of Hezekiah, the oracle of Is promising deliverance, and the extermination of 185,000 Assyrians by the angel of Yahweh are related in 2 K 18:17–19:37 (2 Mc 15:22). This text is duplicated in Is 36:1–37:38 and an abbreviated version of the episode is found in 2 Ch 32:1–23. The records of Sennacherib add many details to the biblical passage (ANET 287–288). The people of Ekron* had dethroned their loyal king Padi and committed him to confinement in Jerusalem. The states of Syria and Phoenicia summoned an Egyptian army to their assistance, but the Egyptians were defeated at Eltekeh near the frontier of Egypt. Sennacherib took 46 fortified cities in Judah (2 K 18:13; Is 36:1), took 200,150 captives, and besieged Jerusalem. Hezekiah surrendered and paid heavy tribute, including 30 talents of gold and 800 talents of silver (30 talents of gold and 300 talents of silver in 2 K 18:14). Sennacherib detached some of his territory and gave it to the Philistines. This disaster is implicitly mentioned in 2 Ch 32:25. The omission of any defeat or disaster in the Assyrian records need not be due to suppression of unfavorable reports. Modern scholars have noticed certain features in the accounts: Sennacherib is at Lachish in 2 K 18:14, 17 (Is 36:1), at Libnah in 2 K 19:8 (Is 37:8), and it is quite possible that 2 K 14:17; 19:8 (Is 36:1; 37:8) contain harmonizing glosses. The omission of 2 K 18:13–16 in Is can scarcely be due to anything but a desire to remove an episode which seemed to reflect discredit on the power of Yahweh to protect His chosen city and king. Tirhakah*, king of Ethiopia, is mentioned as approaching with an army in 2 K 19:8 (Is 37:8), but Tirhakah (Taharko) of the Ethiopian dynasty of Egypt did not accede to the throne until 690–689. The narrative closes with an allusion to the assassination of Sennacherib (2 K 19:37; Is 37:38), which occurred in 681, 20 years later. There are no records of Sennacherib later than 689. Hence, W. F. Albright and others suppose another campaign of Sennacherib, against the rebellious states of the W, which was connected with the accession of the anti-Assyrian Taharko; and this campaign is related in 2 K 18:7–19:37; Is 36:1–37:38. One must therefore suppose that an interval of 10–12 years lies between 2 K 18:16 and 2 K 18:17. The number 185,000 is an impossible exaggeration of popular tradition for the Assyrian army. "The angel of the Lord" was most probably a pestilential disease. Other episodes of Hezekiah's life are connected with the Assyrian invasion. He was cured of a boil by the prayer of Isaiah and the application of a fig poultice (2 K 20:1–11; Is 38:1–8). The sign of the regression of the shadow upon the "steps of Ahaz" is obscure; the usual English trans-

lation of sundial has no basis in the language. In any case the marvel is probably a part of the general character of the passage, which is a theological interpretation of events rather than an account of events. The theological problem was created by Hezekiah himself, who exhibited contradictory qualities. On the one hand tradition made him a reformer of religion and an opponent of foreign cults; on the other hand, it is impossible that his rebellion against Sennacherib should have won prophetic approval; Isaiah was totally opposed to foreign alliances and military defense against Assyria. In the view of later compilers this should not have won him a long life, which was a sign of the blessing of Yahweh; furthermore, the disaster of 701 must have been a sign of Yahweh's anger. But because of his other merits the threat of death was postponed and 15 additional years of life were granted — the interval from 701–687. This theologumenon was introduced into a story of his sickness and healing. In Is the psalm of Hezekiah is interpolated at this point (Is 38:9–20). It is a song of thanksgiving for deliverance from serious illness, but belongs to no definite event. The threat of Isaiah that the treasures of the palace and temple would be plundered by the Babylonians is, it seems, another theological construction as it stands, since it postpones the threat from the time of the devout Hezekiah; but it probably reflects the prophet's disapproval of the negotiations with Merodach-baladan* of Babylon for rebellion. The story of Hezekiah's repentance and the postponement of the threat of Mi 3:12 is related in Je 26:18 f. The oracle and the strange symbolic action of Isaiah at the time of the revolt of Ashdod* in 711 BC (Is 20:1–6) were also directed against Hezekiah; here the revolt never matured. In connection with the siege Hezekiah's fortification of Jerusalem is mentioned in 2 Ch 32:1–5, and his construction of the tunnel of Siloam from the spring of Gihon* is mentioned in 2 Ch 32:30; 2 K 20:20. The praise of Hezekiah in BS 48:17–22 is based upon biblical material; the implicit qualifications in 2 K (cf above) and in 2 Ch 32:24 f, where his illness and cure were followed by pride, disaster, and repentance (an implicit allusion to 2 K 18:13–16) are forgotten in BS. The dates of Hezekiah in 2 K create a problem in chronology. With the exception of 2 K 18:1, 9 f, the data all point to a reign of 29 years 715–687 (by ancient reckoning). But 2 K 18:1, 9 f date his accession in the 3rd year of Hoshea* of Israel, the investment of Samaria by Shalmaneser V in his 4th year, and the fall of Samaria in his 6th year. Since the siege and fall of Samaria must lie in 724/723–722/721 BC these data agree neither with the accepted dates of Hoshea* nor with those of Hezekiah. They represent an erroneous calculation by ancient compilers, to be corrected on the basis of other data.

Hiddekel (Hb *ḥiddekel* [Akkadian *idiklat*]), the Tigris* (Gn 2:14; Dn 10:4).

Hiel (Hb *ḥi'ēl*, shortened from *'aḥi'ēl*, "my brother is El"), a man of Bethel* who rebuilt Jericho* during the reign of Ahab* (1 K 16:34). He founded the city "upon" his eldest son Abiram and set up its gates "upon" his youngest son Segub; the phrase is that of the curse attributed to Joshua in the destruction of the city (Jos 6:26), to which the passage of 1 K alludes. The formula of the curse may come from the story of Hiel. It is possible, and many modern scholars accept it, that the phrase signifies that the two sons were offered as foundation sacrifices.

Hierapolis (Gk *hierapolis*, "sacred city"), a city in Asia Minor in the valley of the Lycus, the seat of an early Christian community (Col 4:13). The city was under Seleucid, Pergamene, and then Roman rule after 133 BC. It was famous for its medicinal hot springs. The site has remains of two Roman theaters and the baths, and was the place of origin of the philosopher Epictetus and the early Christian writer Papias (c AD 130).

High place (Hb *bāmāh*). The word is most frequently used to designate a cultic place, but instances of its use in a noncultic sense indicate that originally it was a simple topographical designation: a deserted hill (Mi 3:12), high places of the earth i.e., mountain tops (Dt 32:13; Is 58:14; Am 4:13; Mi 1:3), of the clouds (Is 14:14), of the sea i.e., the waves (Jb 9:8), heights as security against attack (2 S 22:34; Ps 18:34; Hab 3:19). The cultic high place is first mentioned in 1 S 9–10; Samuel is conducting worship at the high place, probably of Ramah*. Solomon worshiped at the high place of Gibeon* and there had his vision (1 K 3:1 ff). Elsewhere the high places are mentioned frequently in 1–2 K and in Am, Ho, Mi, Je, Ezk, and they are always repudiated as a place of illegitimate and immoral cult, either of Yahweh or of Canaanite gods. The biblical allusions give little information about the high places and their equipment; but other allusions to objects and instruments of worship suggest what they contained: the *asherah**, the tree or stake which was the symbol of the goddess of fertility; the sacred pillar (*maṣṣēbāh*), the

symbol of the god of fertility; altars for sacrifice and for incense. The high places of Petra*, while they come from a much later period, are the most complete and the best preserved. The largest, built on the highest point inside the walled city, consists of a rectangular court 47 ft × 21 ft, hewn into the rock to a depth of 16–21 in; to the W of the court a 6 ft square altar, 5 ft high, hewn from the rock, with a flight of steps to the top; a round altar 3 ft 9 in. in diameter; a small pool cut in the rock; a larger pool cut in the rock (9 ft × 8 ft, 3–4 ft deep) to the S of the court. Another high place was a circular processional way around a sacred rock. The high place was essentially a rural open air sanctuary in contrast to the urban temples, and represented a more primitive cult. W. F. Albright has proposed that the standing stones (*maṣṣēbôt*) which were sometimes numerous at the high places were not symbols of the male deity but funerary stelae, and suggests a cult of the ancestors similar to the Greek hero cults. The Mesha* inscription mentions the Moabite high place of Qarhoh.

High priest. Cf PRIEST.

Hilkiah (Hb *ḥilkīyyāh* or *ḥīlkiyyāhû*, "my portion is Yah[weh]"), the high priest who discovered a book of the law in the temple during the repairs commissioned by Josiah* (2 K 22:4 ff; 2 Ch 34:8 ff; cf DEUTERONOMY). The name is born by five others in the OT, including the father of Jeremiah* (Je 1:1), who was also a member of a priestly family.

Hinnom. Cf GEHENNA.

Hiram (Hb *ḥîrām*, shortened from *'aḥirām*, "the brother [god] is exalted"), king of Tyre*, who enjoyed friendly relations with both David* and Solomon*. David traded with him for materials and craftsmen to build his royal palace in Jerusalem (2 S 5:11; 1 Ch 14:1 ff). Solomon traded with him also for materials and craftsmen for his own much grander building projects (1 K 5:15 ff; 2 Ch 2:3 ff); Solomon paid him in foodstuffs. This apparently did not meet the expenses, and Solomon ceded some villages of Galilee after the work was finished (1 K 9:10 ff). In 2 Ch 8:2, in accordance with the principles of composition of Ch*, this is converted into a cession of territory from Hiram to Solomon. Hiram joined Solomon in the Red Sea trade with Ophir* in Arabia, furnishing the ships and seamen (1 K 9:26 ff; 10:11, 22; 2 Ch 8:17 f; 9:10 f). This Hiram was Hiram I of Tyre (969–935), whose reign also saw the beginning of the great Phoenician colonial movement which ultimately established Phoenician cities and markets in Sardinia, Africa, and the Iberian peninsula. The name was also borne by the Tyrian bronzesmith sent by Hiram to do the bronze work for the temple (1 K 7:13 ff; 2 Ch 2:12 ff).

History, historical writing. The historical books of the OT include the group from Gn to 2 K, and in addition 1–2 Ch, Ez-Ne, Est, Tb, Jdt, 1–2 Mc; in the NT the four Gospels and AA. The term "historical" is here used in such a broad sense to cover such a mixed group of writings that it is easily misleading. In the Bible the narrative passages come from a period and a civilization in which history in the modern sense of the word was entirely unknown. By this no definition of history in the modern sense is implied; modern historians are not agreed on the theory and the definition of their science, but none of the concepts of history proposed by modern scholars can be read back into the ancient Semitic world. The type of historical writing which the Greeks began was likewise unknown, and some general understanding of the literary forms which we include under historical writing is necessary to prevent misunderstanding.

In the ancient world history may be generally designated as "the remembered past" (Cicero); it was the past as it was remembered, as it was told, and it was not supposed that it could be further recovered by critical investigation of documents and other remains of human activity. The modern concept of "historical fact," a historical event certainly established as occurring in a definite place and time, was therefore not within the scope of the ancient historian; neither therefore is the correlative concept of "historical error," an event of which historical reality is falsely affirmed. The past was what was told (German *Sage*), and was not distinguished from "what actually happened" (German *Geschichte*), as the German historian von Ranke defined history. The past could be told either in oral tradition or in written records, but in the ancient world the medium of communication did not change the species of the literature. The material, whether oral or written, in which the ancient world remembered its past is the source from which we construct a "history" of this past in our sense, and the historical books of the Bible are included in this material. No single book or passage presents that narrative of the past which we call "historical"; the memory of the past is imperfect and incomplete.

Ancient historical memory, however, was not mere brute memory. The past becomes meaningful only to a group which has a sense of unity and continuity, a true political society; such a society is civilized. Tribes which never advance beyond primitive civilization, such as the tribes of the Americas, of the Asian and African deserts, of the East Indies, preserve little or no memory of their past. Like animals, they have no progress to record. A civilized society is aware of its past as that on which its unity and identity rest, and the principal function of history is to affirm the unity and identity of the society in the present. Cazelles has said that every literary work is a dialogue between the author and his contemporary society, and this is particularly true of history. As for other forms of literature, the society furnishes the material and dictates the form in which it shall be uttered. This is of particular importance in the ancient world in which literature is anonymous; the speaker or the writer is the voice of his society, which authenticates him by its acceptance.

Without a concept of historical fact, the critical means of ascertaining historical fact and an interest in the knowledge of the past for its own sake, what was the ancient society intending to do when it retold its past, besides affirm its own distinct identity? Apart from deliberate falsification, which is an ineradicable feature of human discourse, the society usually intended to present a true portrait of itself as well as such a portrait could be drawn from its remembered past. It is important for survival that a society, like an individual person, should know itself for what it is and not cherish delusions about itself. The society was not interested in the detailed accuracy of historical knowledge, but in seeing itself as it was. As in the portrait of a person, what was most important was not accuracy but whether the portrait captured and rendered visible the genuine personality of the subject. In ancient history, as in painting, this could not be done without distortion, exaggeration, and omission; but this is the "historical truth" which was the object of ancient history. This historical truth was within the reach of ancient history.

Comparative literary studies show that in all cultures poetry is prior to prose as a medium of narrative, and oral tradition is prior to written tradition; here, however, we may begin with what comes last, since it is this which has been preserved more extensively. The written records of Mesopotamia and Egypt show that ancient Israel shared with them many of the literary forms of narrative. From Mesopotamia are preserved economic and administrative documents, legal collections and legal documents, letters, myths, tales and romances, and lists. Royal inscriptions record the deeds of the king (usually including building and military operations); these are developed into annals, statistical annual reports, which in turn are woven into chronicles, summary reports of reigns or longer periods. As is explained in more detail below, the Israelites employed almost all these same forms. From Egypt are preserved likewise royal inscriptions and annals, myths, tales and romances, and biographical inscriptions of private citizens, usually men who held some political or sacerdotal office. Scholars, however, doubt that a concept of history is to be found either in Mesopotamia or Egypt, although each exhibited an awareness of the past and of the continuity between the past and the present. But there is no awareness that history is a process, no perception of development and retrogression, no perception of cause and effect. The static character of Egyptian civilization made its historical record an affirmation of the unchanging identity of Egypt through its 2500 years, even when this affirmation became a historical falsehood; but antecedent to this refusal to accept history it was Egypt's proud knowledge of its past which, as much as anything else, kept life in Egyptian society. In Mesopotamia the consciousness of unity and continuity with the past was rather the consciousness of a civilization than of a political society; Mesopotamia was never a true political society, but each of its members felt itself the heir of common traditions. It may be thought, as some scholars think, that the view of history taken in each region reflects their view of nature and of the gods: a static reality in Egypt, an unceasing conflict of independent wills in Mesopotamia. In historical consciousness neither of these great civilizations equalled Israel.

Behind the documents lies oral tradition, and under this heading we consider the forms of historical narrative used in Israel. As a preliminary we should note that the original form, when it is incorporated into a larger composition, does not have precisely the same meaning which it had when it existed independently. The forms, however, are often easily discernible in the existing literary complexes. Modern scholars are largely agreed that the forms which occur in writing were shaped in oral tradition long before they were committed to writing. Oral tradition itself exhibits general characteristics which must be noticed. It is popular (hence the designations "popular tradition" or "folklore"), not erudite; it is the possession of a whole people, not of a particular class. It is the dialogue between the author and his society, as mentioned above; through the dialogue the society expresses its own identity. It has most frequently been preserved by professional raconteurs, who probably appeared in Israel also. It is the professionals who are responsible for set artistic forms.

The attitude of the storyteller toward his material, the remembered past of his society, is so different from that of the modern historian that it must be emphasized. The storyteller is master of his material and is not constrained by it. He is uncritical and unaware of the existence of "historical fact," which he had no means to ascertain. He speaks the living tradition of his group and must make it pertinent to the contemporaries he addresses, that they may see the identity of the present with the past. It surprises us that he should seem indifferent to the preservation of the exact memory of the past, that he feels free to add, to omit, to alter, to interpret; but he is a creative artist. Each generation must retell for itself the story of the past from which it comes, and he is the instrument through which this is accomplished. And so he does not merely recount the story of the past, he recreates it, and in so doing he loses many of the details of the past. This is not the only factor at work to dim the memory of historical facts; there is also the inevitable variation in reporting and transmitting the reports which can be observed in modern times as well. These considerations show us with what reserve we must apply the modern concept of "historical truth" to such ancient traditions.

Recent studies have established the priority and importance of oral tradition in Israel and have left no doubt that most premonarchic Israelite history was preserved orally for some centuries before it was written. Scholars of the Scandinavian school take an extreme position and deny that any of the traditions were written before the exile. Other scholars cannot accept this; there are sound indications that the earliest writings in the historical books were written about the 12th century BC. The use of writing in Canaanite and neighboring cultures was so common that it seems highly improbable that the Israelites also would not have employed it. The collection and writing of traditions on a large scale, from which the biblical books arise, is very probably placed in the early monarchy. In both Mesopotamia and Egypt the palace and the temple were centers of schools of writing and the preservation of records and other literature. We should assume the same not only for the palaces and temples of the Israelite monarchies, but also for the sanctuaries of premonarchic Israel. The OT itself indicates that at least three groups were active in writing: the scribes* (of the royal court); the priests*; and the prophets*. We may assume that each group had its own traditions, its own form and style.

With Otto Eissfeldt and many others we may distinguish certain forms or types of popular tradition. Myth* is a category which demands a treatment by itself. The "tale" is a story which lacks definition of time and place, like our "Once upon a time in a country far away" tales; such tales may be given a local and temporal connection, however, when they are incorporated into a larger collection. One may instance much of Gn 4–11, some of the patriarchal stories, and possibly some other pieces which have been given geographical and temporal definition. The saga is defined in place and time, at least broadly, and deals with the tribe, in particular with its chieftains and heroes. In the OT one may instance the sagas of Moses, Joshua, the Judges, David, and certain patriarchal stories; indeed, most of the OT narratives fall into this category. The legend has a primarily religious interest and usually centers about sacred places, rites, or persons, often dealing with the origin of these things; thus the accounts of the origin of circumcision, the Passover, various sanctuaries, and the stories of prophets. The legend often becomes a liturgical recital, of which some appear in the OT (Passover in Ex 12; Pss 78; 105; 106). The story or romance is a more extended narrative, often a means of entertainment, and often involving love and women; one may illustrate by the stories of Joseph, Ruth, Samson, Tb, Est, Jdt. According to the principles of form criticism these types are distinguished purely by form; but in practice the distinction reposes on content as well, and in the existing text the pure form is not always preserved. One must not, however, distinguish the forms on the basis of greater or less credibility; this is a modern distinction which would be meaningless to the ancient. It was all the past remembered and retold, no doubt with some degree of elementary criticism, but all worth preserving because it was the past on which the present society was founded. From the modern point of view, the story or romance in some instances was written with a degree of skill and objectivity which was not equalled by any document from Mesopotamia or Egypt and not surpassed even by the Greeks. Such is the story of David in 2 S 9–20; some passages of 1–2 K; the story of Abimelech* in Jgs 9 (now defaced by conflation of two documents). 1 Mc should be added, since it is written in the style of Hb narrative prose; but it comes long after the Jews had been affected by Hellenistic culture.

The original piece of folklore was essentially brief, expanded according to the ingenuity of the individual storyteller, who supplied dialogue, scenery, and descriptive details of the action. In oral tradition the anecdotes are collected in complexes or cycles centered about a person, a place, or a series of events. Thus, we may suppose, there were cycles of the patriarchs, of the exodus*, of Moses, of Sinai, of the wandering, of the conquest, of the judges, of David, of Elijah and Elisha. Some of these complexes must have been collected in writing before the composition of larger historical works; Jgs, for instance, is a complex which has no parallel elsewhere. But the work which distinguished Israelite historiography from all others of the ancient Near East was the composition of larger historical works which took a unified view of long periods of time and presented the history of Israel as a series of crises. The number of these larger works is now generally put at four, of which only three can be easily identified. J and E (cf PENTATEUCH) were histories of early Israel i.e., premonarchic Israel. J began with creation; E has left no trace of anything earlier than Abraham. Both agreed in seeing in Abraham's life an event initiating a series which culminated in the settlement of Israel in Palestine. According to most older and many modern critics, J was carried at least up to the end of the conquest. Martin Noth, however, has contended that it carried the narrative only up to the end of Nm. D (cf DEUTERONOMY) carried the history to the fall of the kingdom of Judah, either including the conquest (Noth) or beginning with the monarchy. There is general agreement that J should be placed in the 10th or 9th century, E in the 9th or 8th century, and D in the 6th or 5th century. The fourth large composition is the Chronicler's history of the postexilic community prefaced by a summary of preexilic history (Chr; Ez-Ne). Each of these works exhibits its own style and conceptions; but they all have an idea of history as a continuous process. These works have been further compiled into the present books of the OT.

Israel, then, had a concept of history; when we examine the concept, it turns out to be the fruit of what we would call a theology of history. The unity and continuity of the historical process comes from Israel's recognition of itself not only as a people, but as the people of Yahweh. Its history is the history of its encounter with Yahweh and of its response to the encounter. Its interest is cosmic because there is only one God and one historical process. And history is a process, a development through crisis, a development in which Yahweh is more clearly recognized in His true reality.

History tends to a term; it is not the mere chronicle of the Mesopotamians nor the recurring cycles of the Greeks. The purpose of Israel, which spoke through its storytellers, was to present a true picture of the reality of God operating in history and of man's response to God's operations; this to them was "historical truth," and they must be judged on this basis and not on their success or failure in recounting "historical fact." On the NT cf GOSPEL and separate articles; ACTS OF THE APOSTLES.

Hittites. A people of Asia Minor and N Syria, known from Egyptian records as Kheta, from Assyrian records as Hatti, and from the OT as Hethites or sons of Heth. The Hittites are known from their own records and remains only since the excavations begun at Boghazköy in Turkey in 1906. Boghazköy alone yielded extensive ruins of the royal city of the Hittites and over 10,000 cuneiform records. These, with records discovered at other sites, added a new chapter to the history of the ancient Near East. The Hittites are first identified about 1900 BC, although the Hittite sites were occupied during the 3rd millennium BC; but it is doubtful that these occupants were Hittites. The Hittites themselves were an Indo-European people who settled in Asia Minor before 2000 BC. Their great royal city of Hattusas, the modern Boghazköy, did not pass into their hands until after 1900 BC. They are mentioned in the records of the Assyrian trading colonies of Cappadocia about 1900 BC. Modern historians divide their history into three periods.

1. *The Old Kingdom.* From about 1900 BC to some time in the 16th century the Hittite kingdom, centered in Anatolia, conquered N Syria and even invaded Mesopotamia as far as Babylon. The territory was lost due to dynastic instability which permitted the invading Hurrians* to establish independent kingdoms in N Syria. The foundation of the Old Kingdom was attributed to Labarnas; this name, in the form Tabarna, became the title of later Hittite kings, as the Roman emperors took the title of Caesar.

2. *The Hittite Empire.* The Hittite kingdom under Tudhaliyas II in the 15th century was able to resist external attacks and expand to even greater limits. The empire reached its peak under Suppiluliuma (about 1380 BC) and ruled N Syria and much of N Mesopotamia. Egypt under Ramses II attempted to move northward into Hittite territory and was defeated by Muwatallis at Kadesh on the Orontes. The battle is described in detail in Egyptian records, where it is made into a victory; but the terms of

the treaty concluded a few years later, which is preserved both in Egyptian and in Hittite, show that the Hittite Empire lost nothing to the Egyptians. The treaty was sealed by the marriage of a Hittite princess to the Pharaoh. The records of the fall of the empire are obscure and fragmentary; there can be little doubt that it gave way after 1200 BC before the invasion of the "Peoples of the Sea," which created unsettled conditions as far S as Egypt and Palestine (cf PHILISTINES).

3. *The Neo-Hittite kingdoms.* These kingdoms emerged in the Taurus and in N Syria, where they shared the land with Aramaean* kingdoms, during the 12th century. They were centered about Carchemish*, the most powerful of the group; the southernmost kingdom had its capital at Hamath*. The Assyrian records from the 12th to the 8th century designate N Syria as the land of Hatti. These kingdoms were conquered by the Assyrians in the 9th-8th centuries and were incorporated into Assyrian provinces.

The political organization of the Hittites was monarchical. In the early period the power of the king was less absolute than it appears in the empire; it was limited not only by the nobles, but also by an assembly of the whole people, the *pankus*, which disappears after the troubles which ended the old kingdom. The economy of the Hittites was principally agricultural; they did, however exploit the rich mineral resources of Asia Minor, from which the use of iron* spread into Mesopotamia, Syria, and Canaan. Two fragmentary collections of Hittite laws have been preserved; they are less important than the code of Hammurabi* for biblical studies, but show some parallel to the OT. The Hittites contributed the development of the light horse-drawn chariot*, which was a dominant offensive weapon for a thousand years, to ancient Near Eastern warfare.

The Hittite kingdom was multilingual. Hittite itself is an Indo-European language. Proto-Hittite (Hattian), an older language which is used only in archaic cultic formulae, is known from few remains and has not been related to any known group of languages. Luwian is another Indo-European language which is close to Hittite; Palaic also is Indo-European, but it is imperfectly known from few remains. The Hittite records also employed foreign languages: Sumerian, Akkadian, and Hurrian. The type of Hittite script called hieroglyphic Hittite is still undeciphered.

The religion of the Hittites included more deities than can be counted, but otherwise exhibits no remarkable features. They adopted the Hurrian* deities: the weather-god Teshup, depicted with the thunderbolt in his hand;

his consort Hepa; and their son Sharruma. In the official public cult, however, the sun-goddess of the shrine of Arinna was the patron of Hatti.

The abundant Hittite literature shows no distinctive originality except in one feature; the Hittites created an original conception and style of historical narrative which offers the only ancient Near Eastern parallel to Hb historical writing (cf HISTORY). The narrative is not only annals or chronicle, but conceives a period as a unified development centered about a theme.

Hittite art and architectural remains are preserved in abundance. The buildings and fortifications were substantial and well suited to topography and climate, but lacked origi-nality except in one feature, the *bit hilani* (cf HOUSE). Most of the products of Hittite art come from the Neo-Hittite period and are strongly influenced by Assyrian and Canaanite-Phoenician models; the art has, however, a distinctive style in relief sculp-ture, which is its most frequent and most characteristic medium of expression.

4. *Hittites in the OT*. Heth, the eponymous ancestor of the Hittites, is with Sidon* the

Hittite god
Teshup.

son of Canaan* (Gn 10:15; 1 Ch 1:13); the Hittites are thus clearly grouped with the Canaanites and Phoenicians of Syria and Palestine. According to Gn 23 the Hittites inhabited Hebron* in the time of Abraham*. Esau married Hittite wives (Gn 26:34; 27:46; 36:2). They are frequently mentioned

in the enumeration of the pre-Israelite in-habitants of Canaan. In Jos 1:4 the land of promise is defined as "from the desert and the Lebanon to the great river, the Euphrates, all the land of the Hittites, and to the great sea of the west." The phrase "land of the Hittites" is missing in the LXX and is regarded as a gloss by many modern editors; the phrase is borrowed from the Assyrian "land of the Hatti." The boundaries described, however, correspond to no other description of the boundaries of Canaan; the terms are obscure and doubtfully original, and it is possible that the phrase originally described the boundaries of the land of the Hittites, which is suggested in the received text. O. R. Gurney has proposed that the definition is a guess from an editor who understood the Hittites not as Palestinian, but as the Neo-Hittites of Syria. The Hittites, Jebusites, and Amorites* inhabited the hill country at the time of the Israelite invasion (Nm 13:29). The land of the Hittites in Jgs 1:26 is the Assyrian Hatti land, N of Syria. David's men included the Hittites, Ahimelech (1 S 26:6) and Uriah* (2 S 11:3 ff). There were still Hittites in the land under Solomon (1 K 9:20), and Solomon's foreign wives included Hittites (1 K 11:1). The Neo-Hittites are mentioned as partners in Solomon's trade in horses and chariots (1 K 10:29) and as a possible military threat to the kingdom of Israel (2 K 7:6). The tradition of the Hittites still lived when Ezekiel wrote of Jerusalem that its father was an Amorite and its mother a Hittite (Ezk 16:3, 45). There is nothing in the Hittite records which would put Hittite groups in Canaan in the pre-Israelite period, and some scholars believe this is an anach-ronism in a late source. M. Lehmann, how-ever, has pointed out that some features of the contract of Abraham and Ephron at Hebron seem to reflect Hittite law: the in-sistence of Ephron that Abraham purchase the whole field, thus engaging himself to the feudal duties of proprietorship, and the ex-plicit mention of trees on the property (Gn 23:11, 17). It is possible that the movement southward which was responsible for the Neo-Hittite kingdoms of N Syria reached farther than extrabiblical records show. It is also possible that the term Hittite was joined with Canaanite after the foundation of the kingdoms anachronistically at the time the OT documents were written. There is no difficulty in supposing scattered Hittite fami-lies and clans from which Ahimelech and Uriah could have come. O. R. Gurney sug-gests that the Palestinian Hittites were rem-nants of the Hattians, the pre-Hittite in-habitants of Anatolia, whose language was spoken over a much wider area.

Hivites. Cf HURRIANS.

Hobab (Hb *ḥōbāb,* etymology and meaning uncertain), a Midianite*, the son of Reuel* and the father-in-law of Moses (Nm 10:29), the ancestor of the Kenites* (Jgs 4:11); modern scholars on the basis of some MSS read his name also in Jgs 1:16. Another tradition gives Jethro* as the name of the father-in-law of Moses. It is possible that the non-Israelite clan of the Kenites attached themselves to the great leader of Israel through this connection.

Holofernes (Gk *holophernēs,* etymology uncertain), in Jdt' the general of the armies of Nebuchadnezzar* king of Assyria*, who invaded Judah and besieged Bethulia*, where he was received and killed by Judith*. This Holophernes is not a historical character (cf JUDITH), but like other characters in the book he bears a name which is probably taken from a historical person. The name is very probably a variant or corruption of the Persian name Orophernes in its Gk form; the name Orophernes is twice spelled Holophernes by the Gk historians Diodorus Siculus, and Appian. Orophernes, the son of the Persian satrap Ariamnes, ruled the province of Cappadocia in the 1st half of the 4th century BC. Another Orophernes seized the throne of Cappadocia from Ariarathes IV in 160 BC with the help of Demetrius* I Soter of Syria. He was forced by Rome, however, to divide the kingdom with Ariarathes and later suffered other troubles. He last appears in Antioch as a client of Demetrius shortly before the latter's defeat and death. The proximity of his date to the date of the composition of Jdt and his relations with an enemy of the Jews suggests that he is the source of the name in Jdt; this does not imply, however, that Holofernes is drawn in imitation of him or that Orophernes had any part in the Palestinian campaigns of Demetrius.

Holy. 1. *OT.* In the opinion of most scholars the Hb root *ḳdš* has the basic meaning of separate. In usage, however, the word signifies properly divinity, the essence of deity itself. In creatures the quality is derived from the divine by some peculiar contact. The holiness of God as His proper nature is seen in such passages as Am 4:2, where Yahweh swears by His holiness (i.e., by Himself) and Ho 11:9, where Yahweh affirms that He is God and not man, the holy one. It is therefore a quality unique to Yahweh (1 S 2:2 +). Rudolf Otto's analysis of the nature of holiness is widely accepted and casts light on the biblical concept. Otto identifies the holy with the "numinous," the mysterious quality of the divine, which he describes as "wholly other"; that which strikes man in the presence of the divine is the difference between the divine and the created. The effect of the numinous is twofold and paradoxical: it is "tremendous," fearful, and so repels, but at the same time it is "fascinating" and attracts man. In the OT holiness is primarily neither a physical nor a moral quality but an attribute which combines both; it affects man now in one order and now in the other. Physically the near presence of deity in speech or action is dangerous to man and the vision of deity is normally fatal (cf FACE); the "wholly other" character of the divine reality suffers no lesser reality to approach it. What men see or perceive is not the "holiness" of God but His "glory*," the manifestation of His holiness. When Yahweh shows Himself to be holy, He demonstrates His divinity. This is always a demonstration of power, but it is power directed to some purpose worthy of the divinity, and Yahweh shows Himself holy also by demonstrating His moral will. Thus He shows Himself holy through righteousness (Is 5:16). He shows His abhorrence of moral evil, which is a quality of holiness, by His judgment upon sin (Nm 20:13; Ezk 28:22; 38:16). He also shows His holiness in His deliverance, which is the great work of His righteousness and His fidelity. Thus His holiness is often mentioned in contexts where the restoration of Israel occurs; for this restoration is the establishment of an order in which His moral will is supreme and His power over the forces of evil is asserted (Is 29:23; 41:14; 43:3; Ezk 20:41; 36:23; 39:27 +). Isaiah created the title "The Holy One of Israel," which is frequent in Is and rare elsewhere in the OT. The force of this title is seen in the inaugural vision of Is 6. The triple invocation of "Holy" is the formula of adoration employed by the heavenly retinue of Yahweh. The initial response of Is to the manifest holiness of Yahweh is a sense of his own personal danger, but also a sense of his moral unworthiness to stand so near to the holy. This has nothing to do with the number and degree of the sins of which he may have been conscious; morally the gulf between the divine and the human is so great that no man can approach the holy without the danger of being consumed by it. It is the duty of man to declare the holiness of Yahweh, to confess that He is "wholly other" in His physical reality and in His moral character and not to reduce Him to the level of creatures (Lv 10:3; Nm 20:12; Is 8:13; 29:23 + especially in liturgical formulae). The name* of Yahweh (which stands for the person) is holy, and men "profane the holy name" when they act in a manner unworthy of the holy one, fail to confess His holiness, or prevent others from confessing it (Lv 20:3; 22:2; Ezk 20:39; 36:20).

Holiness is derived in creatures by some peculiar association or contact with the divine. Most occurrences of the word are found in liturgical contexts. The personnel and the furniture of the cult belong to Yahweh in a peculiar way, and very probably this more primitive meaning of holiness is the primary meaning from which holiness as a moral quality in men is derived. The heavens, of course, are the holy place or the holy dwelling of Yahweh (Dt 26:15 +). Holy also are the places where He manifests Himself to men: the burning bush (Ex 3:5), the apparition to Joshua near Jericho (Jos 5:15), Canaan, the land of the earthly dwelling of Yahweh (Ps 78:54; Zc 2:16), Jerusalem (Ps 46:5; Is 48:2; 52:1 +), Zion, the temple hill (Is 27:13; Je 31:22 +), the tent of meeting (Ex 28:43 +), the temple (Ps 5:8 +). The sacred seasons are times holy to Yahweh (Lv 25:12, the jubilee; Gn 2:3; Ex 20:8; Je 17:22, the Sabbath). The holiness of persons and furniture in liturgical cult is signified by a ritual consecration: the priests (Ex 28:41 +), the altar (Ex 29:37). Sacrificial victims and all gifts to Yahweh become holy by the offering. The vestments of the priest are holy (Lv 16:4). Cultic holiness is opposed to the profane, which here is a morally neutral quality. The profane may be used for any purpose, but the holy is to be used only in worship, and persons or objects which have not been hallowed have no place in liturgical cult. Cultic holiness is a physical quality which passes from one object or person to another by physical contact (Ex 29:37; 30:29; Lv 6:11 +; Is 65:5; Hg 2:12). It should be noticed that holiness is the dominant quality in this conception; the contact sanctifies the profane, but the profane does not destroy holiness. The concepts of holy and profane bear a resemblance to the parallel and originally unrelated concepts of clean* and unclean; the unclean, however, contaminates the clean. That the distinction was not always observed appears in 2 S 11:4, where Bathsheba* sanctifies herself from her uncleanness (of menstruation) where we would expect the word "cleanse" to be used.

The concept of Israel as a people holy to Yahweh is broader than the concept of cultic holiness, which is, however, included; Israel is a holy people in the sense that it is in a condition for the liturgical worship of Yahweh. Israel is holy because it belongs to Yahweh and thus has been admitted to the sphere of divinity; it belongs to Him by His election* and His covenant* (Ex 19:6; Lv 20:8 +; Dt 7:6; Je 2:3; Ezk 37:28). Holiness is maintained not only by cultic ritual but also by meeting the demands of the moral will of Yahweh; Israel is to be holy because Yahweh is holy (Lv 19:2). This principle introduces a series of moral precepts in Lv 19 ff. Even though the people is holy, it must sanctify itself to prepare for a demonstration of the presence and power of Yahweh (Ex 19:10; Jos 3:5; 7:13). This sanctification can scarcely be anything but ritual, and this motif is probably a later modification of the traditions. By extension men are sanctified for a mission on behalf of Yahweh. War* was a sacred activity not only in Israel but also in other ancient peoples, and warriors are consecrated (Mi 3:5; Je 6:4). By a prophetic turn of the idea the foreign armies sent to destroy Judah are consecrated for the mission (Je 22:7). Once a prophet also is consecrated for his mission (Je 1:5). The road by which the redeemed Israel returns to Jerusalem is protected by Yahweh's presence and power and is the scene of His redemptive righteousness; hence it is called "the holy way" (Is 35:8) on which only the redeemed may travel. The spirit* of Yahweh is rarely called holy (Ps 51:13; Is 63:10) this concept becomes much richer in the NT.

Occasionally the angelic retinue of Yahweh is called the holy ones; they also belong to the sphere of the divine (Ps 89:6, 8; Jb 5:1). A few instances occur of the non-Israelite use of the term "holy one" to designate not only temple personnel, but the male and female prostitutes of the temples of the fertility deities (male: Dt 23:18; 1 K 14:24; 15:12; 22:47; 2 K 23:7; female: Gn 38:21; Ho 4:14).

2. NT. The holiness of God is rarely mentioned in the NT. The petition of the Lord's Prayer (Mt 6:9; Lk 11:2) that the divine name be sanctified is couched in OT terms; the name is to be sanctified by the acknowledgement of the divinity of God. The title "holy father" is employed in Jn 17:11, and God is called the holy one in 1 Jn 2:20; holy lord in Apc 6:10; and the threefold holy of Is 6:3 is quoted in Apc 4:8.

Some other passages reflect OT usage. The temple and the altar sanctify the gifts (Mt 23:17–19). The sanctification of a person for a mission (cf Je 1:5) is applied both to Jesus (Jn 10:36; 17:19) and to the apostles (Jn 17:17, 19). The blood of the sacrificial victim sanctifies by bringing the worshiper into contact with God (Heb 9:13). Christians must sanctify the Lord Jesus (1 Pt 3:15); the verb, employed in the OT of God, is applied to Jesus with no hesitation or qualification. Jerusalem is the holy city (Mt 4:5; 27:53; Apc 11:2; 21:2, 10; 22:19), and the temple the holy place (Mt 24:15; AA 21:28; Heb 8:2) and its furniture holy (Heb 9:1 ff). The "holy ones" of 1 Th 3:13; 2 Th 1:10; Jd 14; Apc 18:20 are somewhat ambiguous; they may signify the angels or the heavenly company of the blessed. The angels are called holy in Mk 8:38; Lk 9:26; AA 10:22; Apc 14:10.

The term is not often applied to Jesus Christ, and its meaning is not derived from the OT usage. He is called the holy one or the holy one of God (Mk 1:24; Lk 1:35; 4:34; Jn 6:69; AA 3:14; Apc 3:7), the holy servant of God (AA 4:27, 30). The title holy one suggests the designation of Yahweh in the OT and is a tacit profession of the divinity of Christ. The holy one of God or the holy servant of God (an application of the "Servant of the Lord*" to Jesus) is less a profession of His divinity than of His unique origin and relationship to the Father. He is holy in a unique degree and communicates holiness to the Church. On the frequent use of the term holy spirit in the NT cf SPIRIT.

It is to the Church and its members that the term is more frequently applied. The basic meaning of the NT term is derived from the idea of Israel as a people holy to Yahweh (Ex 19:6, quoted in 1 Pt 2:9), which explicitly refers both to the union of the Church and its members with the Father through Jesus, and to the moral quality of the Church. Christians are those who have been sanctified (AA 20:32; 26:18). The common designation of the members of the Church in AA and the epistles is "the saints"; this appears in the earliest documents of the NT. The primary agent of the sanctification of the Christian is God (1 Th 5:23), through whose will the sanctification is accomplished (1 Th 4:5). God sanctifies through Jesus, who is Himself called the sanctification of the Christian (1 Co 1:30) in the spirit (2 Th 2:13; 1 Pt 1:2). The media of sanctification are faith (Rm 15:16) and baptism (1 Co 6:11) and union with Christ, which is instituted by faith and baptism (1 Co 1:2). The Christian is sanctified through righteousness (Rm 6:19), here the righteousness of the Christian, which consists in entire submission, "slavery" to God, and not the righteousness of God (Rm 6:19, 22). The indwelling of the spirit in the Christian makes him a holy temple (1 Co 3:17); the holiness is to be maintained by avoiding sin (1 Co 6:19). The Church as a whole is likewise a temple holy to the Lord (Eph 2:21), and the Church and her members are to be holy and unstained (Eph 1:4; 5:27; Col 1:22). It is evident that the primary effect of Christian holiness is the obligation of meeting Christian moral standards (holy behavior, 2 Pt 3:11). In 1 Pt 1:15, however, where holiness is to be achieved, it becomes almost identical with morality rather than a principle which demands morality. The concept of holiness in Heb is somewhat peculiar to this epistle, combining OT cultic holiness with the redeeming sacrifice of Jesus. Here, where Jesus sanctifies Christians (Heb 2:11), who are sanctified from sin through His sacrifice (Heb 10:10) and through His blood of the covenant (Heb 10:29), to sanctify means very nearly to achieve ritual reconciliation; cf ATONEMENT.

In other miscellaneous uses the term indicates the sacred character of persons or objects as belonging to God: the Scriptures (Rm 1:2), the law* (Rm 7:12), the commandment (2 Pt 2:21), the apostles (Eph 3:5), the Christian vocation (2 Tm 1:9), the prophets (Lk 1:70; 2 Pt 3:2; Apc 11:18), faith (Jd 20). Indeed, all things can be sanctified through prayer and the Scriptures (1 Tm 4:5), probably a protest against the remnants of levitical holiness in the Church. The mutual greeting of Christians is itself holy with their holiness and not a mere casual, polite good wish (Rm 16:16; 1 Co 16:20; 2 Co 13:12; 1 Th 5:26).

Honey. Honey appears in lists of produce which describe Palestinian abundance (Dt 8:8; 2 Ch 31:5; Ezk 16:13, 19) and it was also one of the boasts of the Mesopotamian officer in his speech before Jerusalem (2 K 18:32); it is missing, however, in the version of this speech in Is 36. It was regarded as a delicacy (Gn 43:11; 2 S 17:29; Ps 24:13; SS 4:11). It was essential in the diet of the nomadic tribes who did not cultivate cereals, and was not esteemed by settled peoples as a steady diet (Is 7:22 and probably also in the obscure Is 7:15, where honey is eaten in defect of cereals). It was not acceptable for sacrifice (Lv 2:11). It is not clear when apiculture was introduced into Palestine, and not much more is known about it in Egypt and Mesopotamia. The Akkadian* word which is a cognate of the Hb $d^ebaš$, honey, means usually date syrup. Apiculture was introduced in the Hellenistic period; but there is no certain sign of it earlier. Wild honey is mentioned in Dt 32:13; Jgs 14:8; 1 S 14:25 ff. Many scholars doubt, however, that stores of honey (Je 41:8) could be produced from wild honey alone, or that wild honey could be an export (Ezk 27:17). This last passage, however, is very probably later than the period of Ezk. On the honey taste of manna cf MANNA.

Hope. 1. *OT*. It seems no exaggeration to say that the OT breathes an atmosphere of hope throughout; but it is true that Hb seems to have no word which corresponds exactly to "hope," and no precise concept of hope in the sense of "desire accompanied by expectation." The words which most frequently express hope are *kawah*, "to expect," and *batah*, "to trust or have confidence." As a religious concept hope rests entirely upon Yahweh, "the hope of Israel" (Je 14:8; 17:13). He is also the hope of the individual Israelite (Ps 71:5). He who hopes in man is cursed (Je 17:5), but he who hopes in Yahweh is blessed (Je 17:7). One must hope in Yahweh even when He "hides His face" (Is 8:17), i.e., seems to withdraw His favor, or when hope is deferred (Is 26:8). The motive of hope is the past deeds of Yahweh (Gn 15:7), which recurs throughout the OT, which gives confidence in His power to fulfill His promises (Gn 17:8; Ex 3:8, 17; 6:4; Dt 1:8). His fidelity to His word is guaranteed by His covenant love*, which is granted according to the degree in which Israel hopes in Him (Pss 13:6; 33:18, 22). Israel hopes in the power of Yahweh, His "arm" (Is 51:5), or in His protection ("shield and strength," Ps 28:7). Hope which reposes on such security can never perish (Ps 9:19). This atmosphere of hope, as we have observed, runs through the OT. In the Pnt it is the hope of a great people promised to the patriarchs and in the possession of the land which was promised to them. But with the collapse of the kingdom of Israel before the Assyrians in 721 BC and of the kingdom of Judah before the Babylonians in 587 BC hope was put to a new test. The test was not given without warning. Amos assured the Israelites that hope for the Day* of Yahweh was foolish, since it would be judgment and not the deliverance which they expected (Am 5:18). Nor could they hope in security through foreign alliances rather than through Yahweh (Is 31:1 ff). In the disaster of Israel no one could open "a door of hope" (Ho 2:17) except Yahweh, and He would do it because of His unfailing love; but the objects of hope would have to be something different. The motive of hope remains the same; only Yahweh can give Israel a future and a hope (Je 29:11; 31:17). Here the prophets differ from one another. Jeremiah presents the hope of a new covenant* which is an interior regeneration and is written in the heart of each individual person (Je 31:31; 32:38 ff). Ezekiel rests hope on the promise of Yahweh to remember His covenant with Israel (Ezk 16:59 ff), but he also presents the hope of an interior regeneration, the exchange of the heart of stone for the heart of flesh (Ezk 36:25 ff). Second Isaiah also presents the hope of a future restoration based on Yahweh's remembering of His covenant (Is 55:3).

The hope of the Israelite falls short at the grave, since the OT has no idea of survival until its very latest parts (cf LIFE; RESURRECTION). It is almost a commonplace that the living have hope (Ec 9:4); when death becomes certain and imminent, hope ceases. Job* has no prospect of escaping from his fatal illness and has lost all hope (Jb 6:11; 7:6; 17:15). There is hope for a tree, since there may be life in the stump even after the tree is felled; but there is no hope for man (Jb 14:7). The dead have no hope (Is 38:18), and some of the vast despair of exiled Israel appears in Ezk 37:11; the nation of Israel was like the scattered bones of the dead for which there is no hope. The OT shows flashes of a hope that the power and covenant love of Yahweh will find a way to exhibit themselves even beyond the grave (Pss 16:16; 73:25), but this hope takes no definite form.

2. *NT*. The Gk words *elpis* and *elpizein*, meaning "expectation," "expect," are neutral in profane Gk and may refer either to expected good or to expected evil. The words appear in this sense in the NT; but hope as a religious concept is a much enriched development of the OT hope.

The theological concept of hope is not found in the Gospels except for an allusion to the false messianic hope of the disciples (Lk 24:21) nor in the Johannine writings except in 1 Jn 3:3, where the object of hope is to become like God by seeing Him as He is. The hope of the Pharisees in Moses (Jn 5:45) means rather confidence and assurance. The word occurs in AA in reference to the Jewish hope of the resurrection (AA 23:6; 24:15) and in the promises (AA 26:6). Paul was imprisoned for the hope of Israel (AA 28:20, a reference to Je 14:8; 17:13); the phrase is not defined, but it seems that the OT title of Yahweh is transferred to Jesus.

The concept of hope is most fully developed in the Pauline writings, especially in Rm. Abraham himself is the model of hope; we should translate the paradox of Rm 4:18 as "hoped against expectation." God can accomplish the impossible. Hope is of the unseen both as to its object and its motive (Rm 8:24; Heb 3:6). It is the hope of the glory of God (probably here considered as communicated to the Christian, Rm 5:2), which is the boast of the Christian, which must ultimately issue in the liberation of all creation from sin (Rm 8:20). Thus the Christian is saved through hope (Rm 8:24), which is his joy (Rm 12:12). Paul does not think that hope is easily attained; it is the fruit of proved virtue, which in turn is produced through patient suffering (Rm 5:4), and it is sustained through patience and the encouragement afforded by the Sacred Scriptures (Rm 15:4). God can be called simply the God of hope (Rm 15:13). With faith and love, hope forms the great triad of the most precious charismata* of the Christian (1 Co 13:13). Hope bears on other eschatological goods, since Paul hopes that God will deliver him from danger (2 Co 1:10); but if one had hope in Christ in this life only, he would be the most miserable of men (1 Co 15:19). Hope may be directed either to God, as most frequently (above and 1 Tm 4:10; 5:5; 6:17; 1 Pt 1:21) or to Christ (1 Co 15:19; Col 1:27). The object of hope is most frequently eschatological: the glory (above; Col 1:27), the resurrection (above), the hope stored up in the heavens (Col 1:5), the grace which will be granted in the (eschatological) revelation of Jesus Christ (1 Pt 1:13). Hope bears not only on the term of the Christian life, however, but also on righteousness produced by the spirit through faith (Gal 5:5); as the Christian hopes to receive the term from God, so also he hopes to receive from God the means by which he can attain the term. Christians have one and the same hope, as they are one body in one spirit (Eph 4:4). This hope distinguishes them from the Jews, for it is a better hope than the law (Heb 7:19), and from the Gentiles, who are without God and without hope (Eph 2:12), especially for anything beyond death (1 Th 4:13). Hope is therefore a safe and secure anchor (Heb 6:18 f); it is not only the fruit of patience (above) but also a motive of patience (Heb 6:11). The object of hope, presented in the gospel (Col 1:23), is made real through faith (Heb 11:1), with a reality which should enable the Christian to give an account of his hope to any inquirer (1 Pt 3:15).

Hophni (Hb *hŏpnî,* from Egyptian *hfnr,* "tadpole"), son of the priest Eli* (1 S 1:3), who with his brother Pinehas* stole from the sacrifices (1 S 2:12–17) and sinned with women who served at the door of the tent (1 S 2:22; some scholars regard this as a gloss based on Ex 38:8). The two carried the ark into battle against the Philistines (1 S 4:4) and were killed (1 S 4:11, 17); their death was viewed as a divine chastisement.

Hophra (Hb *hŏprac,* etymology uncertain), the Egyptian Pharaoh Apries (588–568). His name occurs in the OT only in Je 44:30, where the prophet threatens him

because he has permitted Jews to settle in Egypt after the fall of Jerusalem in 587. It was probably during his reign that the Jewish colonies in Egypt (cf ELEPHANTINE) began to arise. Although his name does not occur, he is the Pharaoh who made an abortive movement against the Babylonians during the siege of Jerusalem (Jer 37:5–11) which caused them to raise the siege temporarily. Herodotus mentions a war of Apries against Tyre. Both Herodotus and an Egyptian monument tell of his fall. An Army sent to assist the Libyans against the Gk colony of Cyrene was defeated and the general of the armies, Amasis, rebelled against Apries, defeated him and imprisoned him; shortly afterwards he was killed.

Hor (Hb *hōr,* perhaps identical with Hb *hār,* "mountain," therefore "the mountain"), a mountain, scene of the death of Aaron* (Nm 20:23 ff; 33:38 f; Dt 32:50) and a point of encampment in the journey of the Israelites from Kadesh* to the frontier of Edom (Nm 21:4; 33:37); the Mt Hor on the northern frontier of Israel cannot be the same and is otherwise unmentioned (Nm 34:7). Modern critics attribute the mention of Mt Hor to P, the latest of the patriarchal sources. In the opinion of some scholars Mt Hor is Jebel Nebi Harun, "mount of the prophet Aaron," SW of Petra; but this identification is not certain.

Horeb (Hb *hōrēb,* perhaps "dry"?). It was "the mountain of God," the scene of the apparition of the burning bush (Ex 3:1) and of the worship of the golden calf (Ex 33:6; Ps 106:19), the point from which the Israelites journeyed to Kadesh-barnea* (Dt 1:2, 6, 19), the scene of the promulgation of the covenant (Dt 4:10, 15; 5:2; 9:8; 18:16; 28:69; 2 Ch 5:10; 1 K 8:9) and of the vision of Elijah* (1 K 19:8). Thus it is obviously the same as Sinai*; but the location of Sinai-Horeb is not altogether certain. Modern critics find that Horeb occurs in the E and D sources of the Pnt, while Sinai occurs in the sources J and P. But while the two names are the scene of the same events, it is not certain that the different sources localized the event in the same place. No geographical data for Horeb are given except that it was 11 days' march from Kadesh-barnea (Dt 1:2); this is true of Sinai, but it is not of itself convincing. It is possible that the same mountain or range had more than one name (cf e.g., Hermon*). At the time the traditions of Elijah took form the location of Horeb had been entirely forgotten, since no conceivable point for the Sinai episodes could be located 40 days and 40 nights of travel from the land of

Israel (1 K 19:8). The addition of the phrase "in Horeb" in Ex 17:6 to identify the scene of the striking of the rock is regarded by modern critics as a gloss.

Horites. Cf HURRIANS.

Hormah (Hb *hormah,* from *herem?* [cf BAN], but perhaps a popular etymology [Nm 21:3]), a city in the Negeb* taken by the Israelites early in the settlement; but the conquest appears in variant forms in tradition. Modern scholars think the original tradition is best preserved in Jgs 1:17; the conquest is attributed to Judah and Simeon*. The city is included in the lists both of Simeonite cities (Jos 19:4; 1 Ch 4:30) and of Judahite cities (Jos 15:30). On the relations of these tribes cf JUDAH; SIMEON. The city was Canaanite and was previously called Zephath. It is mentioned as a point in the campaign in which Israel attempted to enter Canaan from the S and was defeated; here also there is a variation in the names of the opposing peoples, who are Amalekites* and Canaanites* in Nm 14:45 and Amorites* in Dt 1:44. In Dt 1:44, however, the limits of the campaign are not in the Negeb, but "from Seir* [in Edom] to Hormah." The king of Hormah is mentioned in the list of kings conquered by Joshua (Jos 12:14); this list, however, is a schematic tabulation of conquests which were extended over a longer period. The attribution of the conquest to all Israel before the entrance into Canaan (Nm 21:3) comes from a late source in which the earlier defeat was counterbalanced by victory. The city was Judahite in the time of David (1 S 30:30). The site is uncertain; scholars have suggested Tell es Seba near Beersheba* to the E, or Tell el Mushash ESE of Beersheba, or Tell el Milh farther to the E of Beersheba.

Horn. The horn (of ram, goat, or ox) is a common OT figure for strength and dignity. When one's horn is raised one has achieved success, victory, or vindication (1 S 2:1, 10; Pss 75:5 f; 89:25; 92:11; 112:9; 148:14). To have one's horn lowered in the dust (Jb 16:15) or cut off (Ps 75:11; Lam 2:3; Je 48:25) is to be defeated or to suffer loss of dignity and esteem. To gain strength is to acquire horns (Am 6:13) or to have a horn sprout (Ezk 29:21; Ps 132:17). Great strength is signified by a horn of iron (Mi 4:13) or the horn of the wild ox (Dt 33:17). Hence God can be called "my horn," my strength (2 S 22:3; Ps 18:3). The OT imagery appears in Lk 1:69. The oil used in the ritual of anointing the king was poured from a horn (1 S 16:13; 1 K 1:39). Since this use of the horn as a vessel

is not mentioned elsewhere, it is possible that its use in this ritual was symbolic. Cf also ALTAR; MUSIC.

In Dn 7:7 f, 20 f the ten horns of the beast symbolize not only strength but also the kings of the Seleucid* dynasty; the last "little horn" (7:8) with "eyes and a mouth speaking great things" is Antiochus* Epiphanes. The vision of 8:3–13 is explained in 8:14–22; the ram with two horns is the kingdom of the Medes and the Persians, the goat with the great horn is Alexander, the four horns are the kingdoms of the Diadochi, and the little horn is Antiochus Epiphanes. Similar imagery is used in Apc, to some extent borrowed. The lamb has seven horns, which symbolize prodigious strength. The draconic serpent has ten horns (12:3), as does the monster from the sea (13:1) and the monster on which the scarlet woman is seated (17:3); the second monster from the sea has two horns (13:11). The ten horns are interpreted as ten kings of the future (17:12); here the writer borrows from Dn. These probably signify satellite kings of Rome who will destroy Rome (17:16).

Horse. The horse was known in Mesopotamia during the 3rd millennium BC, as one may observe in the art of Ur; but it was rare until after 1800 BC. It was introduced in large numbers by the Indo-European peoples who entered the Fertile Crescent at this period (cf HITTITES; HURRIANS), and who had developed the horse-drawn chariot* as a weapon of war. A treatise on the care and training of the horse from Mitanni was found in the Hittite literature at Boghazköy and a treatise on veterinary medicine was found at Ugarit*. The horse was employed only to draw the chariot, which was used almost exclusively in war. It is uncertain when horsemanship was developed as a common skill in the ancient Near East. It does not appear in Assyrian records or art before Ashur-nasir-pal II (883–859 BC). The Assyrians after this date employed cavalry in war; but cavalry was not used on a large scale until the Persian and Greek periods. It became less important with the Romans, who developed the infantry tactics of the legion to a point where cavalry enjoyed little success against the legion.

The OT mentions horse-drawn chariots during the New Kingdom in Egypt (Ex 14:9, 23; 15:1, 19, 21); it was under the New Kingdom that the Egyptians first employed the chariot, introduced into Egypt by the Hyksos*. From early Israel through the monarchy the OT exhibits a prejudice against the use of the horse and chariot in

a) Horses in Assyrian
sculpture. b) and c)
Assyrian cavalry.

war, the base of which is not entirely apparent. The law of the king of Dt 17:16, which reflects conditions under the monarchy, prescribes that the king shall not acquire large numbers of horses from Egypt (Dt 17:16); here the prejudice possibly implies a dependence upon Egypt to obtain the horses. Some warnings are uttered against confidence in horses as means of deliverance from the enemy (Ho 1:7; Pss 20:8; 31:1–3;

33:17); here, however, the speakers probably do not object to the horse in itself, but to military means as such, of which the horse was the most impressive weapon. Joshua hamstrung the horses he captured from the Canaanites (Jos 11:4 ff) and David hamstrung all but 100 teams of those he captured from the Aramaeans (2 S 8:4). In the first instance this may have been motivated by ignorance of the use of the horse in war, and in the second by the inability of David to feed such a large number of horses. In any case this attitude was sharply changed under Solomon. Wealth in horses was both a sign of a strong military posture and a display of the magnificence of the monarch, and Solomon cultivated horses. Even under David, Absalom began to travel in a horse-drawn chariot (2 S 15:1). Solomon is credited with having 40,000 stalls of horses (1 K 5:6); the number may seem exaggerated, but the stables at Megiddo*, one of his "chariot cities" (1 K 10:26), could accommodate 500 chariots. Horses are mentioned frequently in 1–2 K as weapons of war; how far the kingdom fell from Solomon to Hezekiah is seen in the contemptuous offer of the Assyrian officer to give the Judahites 2000 horses if they can find men to ride them (2 K 18:23; Is 36:8). On the numbers of horses employed in war during this period cf CHARIOT. There was a horse gate of the royal palace in Jerusalem (2 K 11:16) and of Jerusalem (Je 31:40), more accurately a chariot gate; there was probably only one gate of sufficient width for chariots in the entire defenses. Here also there is some uncertainty when the Israelites learned horsemanship, since Hb lacks a lexicographical distinction between "riding" in a chariot and "riding" a horse. A rider as messenger seems certain in 2 K 9:17 ff; this occurs in the 2nd half of the 9th century, which is not too early, particularly since the horseman was used as a messenger before he became a cavalryman. Other instances where riding is probably signified are not early. Under Solomon the kingdom of Israel played an important part in the horse trade of the ancient Near East. An easy correction of the text of 1 K 10:28 f, accepted by modern scholars, shows that Solomon bought horses from Kue in Cilicia and chariots of Egyptian manufacture and sold them to the Hittites and the Aramaeans of Syria. The Hb poets did not fail to observe the behavior of the horse: its sure footed speed (Is 63:13), its inability to travel in rocky country (Am 6:12), and the lust of the stallion (Je 5:8). The description of the war horse in Jb 39:19–25 is one of the finest classic tributes which poetry has paid to the horse. The sound of the horses coursing is the sound of war (Je 8:16; Ezk 26:10).

Hosanna (Hb *hošîyāh nā'*, "save, we ask"), an invocation of Yahweh (Ps 118:25). The word was employed in later Jewish liturgy, especially at the feast of Pentecost*, and was uttered as an acclamation by the crowds who met Jesus at His solemn entrance into Jerusalem (Mt 21:9, 15; Mk 11:9 f; Jn 12:13). It was probably used to signify the recognition of His royal messianic dignity; cf MESSIAH.

Hosea (Hb *hošeʻa*, probably an abbreviation, "Yahweh saves"), a prophet whose book is the 1st of the 12 (minor) prophets.

1. *Date and Person*. Ho 1:1 dates the oracles of Hosea in the reigns of Uzziah, Jotham, Ahaz, and Hezekiah of Judah and Jeroboam II of Israel. These two series of kings are not coincidental. It is probable that the editor should have added the kings of Israel contemporaneous with the kings of Judah enumerated. The oracles of Ho probably begin during the last years of Jeroboam II (786–746 BC). It is uncertain when the latest should be dated. The tribute of Menahem* of Israel to Assyria in 738 and other relations with Assyria are probably reflected in 5:13; 7:11 f; 8:9; 10:5 f; 12:2. Some scholars would bring the date down to 725, just before the final siege of Samaria by the Assyrians, others to the fall of the city in 721; there is no certain trace in the book, however, of Hosea's knowledge of this catastrophic event. Hosea was a subject of the N kingdom, and his words are directed to that kingdom. Of his life and person nothing is known except the name of his father Beeri and the story of his marriage (Ho 1–3; cf below).

2. *The Book*. The book falls into two major parts, 1–3 and 4–14:

1–3: Title, 1:1; biographical account of Hosea's marriage to Gomer, 1:1–2:9; oracle of restoration, 2:1–2; Yahweh the spouse of Israel, 2:3–25; autobiographical account of Hosea's marriage, 3:1–5.

4–14. This is a collection of oracles arranged with no visible order or plan. The text of this section is much more poorly preserved than in 1–3. The oracles are grouped by Eissfeldt as follows:

4:1–10, rebukes and threats against the corrupt priesthood. 4:11–19, rebukes and threats against the people for obscene superstitions. 5:1–7, rebukes and threats against the priesthood, the royal house and the people for worship of false gods; 5:8–6:6, rebuke and threat against Israel and Judah for the folly of the Syro-Ephraimite war (cf ISAIAH). 6:7–11, rebuke of Israel for worship of false gods and other vices not specified. 6:11–7:7, rebuke of Israel for civil strife. 7:8–16, rebuke of Israel for seeking foreign alliances. 8:1–14, rebuke and threat against Israel for false cult and for political machinations. 9:1–9, rebuke and threat against Israel for superstitious and immoral cult. 9:10–14 begins a series of oracles which refer to the past wickedness of Israel; the cult of Baal-Peor. 9:15–17, the sin of Gilgal. 10:1–8, rebuke and threat for superstitious cult and faithlessness. 10:9–15, rebuke and threat for the sin of Gibeah. 11:1–11, rebuke of Israel for its ingratitude; promise of divine compassion. 12:1–15, rebuke and threat to Israel for its faithlessness to Yahweh. 13:1–11, rebuke and threat to Israel for superstitious cult and ingratitude. 13:12–14:1, threat of utter destruction for impenitent Israel. 14:2–9, invitation to repentance and forgiveness. 14:10, editorial conclusion.

Modern criticism accepts the book as the product of Hosea or his immediate disciples and admits no major interpolation by later hands. Older critics questioned both the oracles of forgiveness and the mention of Judah, but these are rarely doubted now. The mention of Judah in 1:7; 4:15; 5:5 may be due to the work of Judahite scribes.

1–3, which contain the account of the marriage of Hosea and Gomer, raises a number of celebrated exegetical questions, and opinions are almost as numerous as the scholars who have discussed them. Recent exegesis tends to agreement on some questions, as follows: Few now doubt that the account of the marriage relates facts and is not an allegorical fiction of the relations of Yahweh and Israel. There is wide, although less general agreement, that 1 and 3 speak of the same woman; there is less agreement on whether the two passages speak of the same marriage, some scholars preferring to interpret the passages of a marriage, a divorce, and a remarriage. If the two accounts refer to the same marriage, then it seems best to accept what the text suggests, that the autobiographical account of 3:1–5 is the original account and that the biographical account of 1:2–9 is an expanded story of the event by a disciple of Hosea, possibly the collector of his oracles. There is disagreement on whether Gomer was a temple prostitute or a woman whose infidelity was discovered only after the marriage. Connected with this is the disputed question, at what point in the events Hosea became aware of the prophetic significance of his own marriage and of his own prophetic vocation. If Gomer was a temple prostitute, then the marriage was explicitly symbolic from the beginning. This opinion seems less preferable, since the discourses of the prophet apply to God all the passionate grief of a man who has discovered that he has been betrayed; but an apodictic answer to the question of this symbolic feature of the experience seems impossible. The divine command of 1:2 does not solve the question, since either Hosea or his collector could easily read the explicit divine will into the government of affairs after their course became known fully to the participants. The names of Hosea's children complicate the

question further, because they have prophetic significance. It seems possible that here, on the basis of the treatment of the names in 2:25, they may be a strictly allegorical feature of the narrative, admitting that this is perhaps a violent solution of the problem.

Despite these difficulties in detail, the symbolism of Hosea's experience with Gomer is quite clear and forms the basis of the magnificent discourse of 2:1–23. As we reconstruct the events, Hosea married a woman who was unfaithful. We cannot now be certain when the infidelity was discovered; perhaps it was known before the birth of the second child. Hosea ultimately divorced her, but found that his love for her was too great to admit a final separation, and he strove to win her fidelity. His prophetic vocation came with the realization that the love of Yahweh for Israel was like that of his love for an unfaithful wife, great enough to forgive her infidelity if she will return to him, and ready to return to the beginning of their love — the desert — that they may start anew. This becomes the dominating note in the fragments of oracles which follow.

The book receives its distinctive character from the manner in which Hosea transfers to Yahweh his own emotional conflict and represents Yahweh as moved by conflicting emotions: the sentiment of justice, which moves Him to punish the sins of Israel by irreparable destruction, and His love of Israel, as passionate as the love of a man for a woman. The book often refers to the period of "first love," the desert period of Israel's history; some interpreters see in this an implicit repudiation not only of Canaanite cults, but also of Canaanite civilization, and a belief that Israel can find Yahweh only by returning to a simpler manner of life. The emphasis, however, falls upon Canaanite cults. It is not always easy to discern whether Hosea is speaking of the worship of the Baal* or of the worship of Yahweh with the rites of the Baal cult. No doubt both perversions occurred, and it is not unimportant that Hosea does not distinguish them carefully; the worship of Yahweh as a fertility deity is scarcely better than the explicit cult of the Baal.

While love is, as it is often called, the dominant motif of the book, it does not seem to be the final resolution. It is difficult to affirm anything about the final resolution, since we have only fragments rather than discourses. As they are collected, however, it seems that Hosea represents Yahweh as finally permitting His justice to overcome His affection and decreeing the total destruction of Israel. Is there then any room for the repentance and forgiveness to which he invites? In a sense there is not; the historical Israel must perish, and there is no future for Israel except in a return to the desert, a new beginning. This must come from Yahweh, just as the first election of Israel came from Yahweh. The prophet has no eschatology in the proper sense of the term; but neither does he see any salvation for Israel in the historical process. Whatever future it may have must be initiated, as its history was in the beginning, by the intervention of Yahweh.

Hoshea (Hb *hošē'a*, the same as the name of the prophet Hosea*; the double spelling of the name in English was an effort to avoid confusing the two). Hoshea ben Elah was the last king of Israel (732–724). His predecessor Pekah* was defeated by Tiglath-pileser* III of Assyria* in 732 and was assassinated by Hoshea. Hoshea certainly represented the pro-Assyrian faction in the kingdom, as Pekah had represented the anti-Assyrian faction, and he was installed by the Assyrians (2 K 15:30). He remained a faithful vassal king until about 724; then he conspired with Sewe (cf So) of Egypt and refused tribute. Shalmaneser V of Assyria immediately invaded Israel and in some way — the details are not related — seized Hoshea in person without delay. The subjection of Samaria took another three years. The records of Tiglath-pileser III do not mention the assassination of Pekah; the king says that he deposed Pakaha (Pekah) and installed Ausi (Hoshea) as king.

Hospitality. In the desert hospitality is a necessity for survival; and since this necessity falls upon all alike, any guest is entitled to hospitality from any host. Should host and guest be at enmity, the acceptance of hospitality involves a reconciliation. The guest, once the host has accepted him, is sacred, and must be protected from any danger even at the cost of the life of members of the family. To be generous in hospitality is a primary virtue among the modern Bedawi. The guest is expected to remain one to three days, depending on local custom; no charge is made and no return gift is accepted. The guest is also entitled to protection as long as he remains within the territory of the clan or tribe which has received him. In return the guest is bound to commit no offense against any one which would bring odium upon his host, who is bound to protect him. One anecdote about Abraham shows him as the model of a generous host (Gn 18:1 ff). The good host makes a feast for his guest, such a feast as is never prepared for the family. The duty of the host to protect the guest is illustrated by the stories of Lot at Sodom (Gn 19:1, 8) and the man of Gibeah (Jgs 19:16–24), both of whom are willing to sacrifice the women of their family in order to protect the guest against the lust of their attackers. The stories of both Lot and Gibeah exhibit the practice in cities. The traveler sat in the marketplace until one of the citizens invited him to his house. The churlishness of the men of Sodom and of the men of Gibeah, who do not extend this invitation, is evidence of their depravity. Cf other typical instances of hospitality in Gn 24:23 ff; 1 S 9:22 ff. Job boasts of his hospitality (Jb 31:32). The virtue of hospitality is praised in the NT also (Rm 12:13; 1 Tm 3:2; Tt 1:18; Heb 13:2; 1 Pt 4:9). Hospitality is enumerated among the works of charity by which men will be judged (Mt 25:35 ff). It is also of interest that the work of Jesus Himself and the spread of the early Church was facilitated by the common practice of hospitality. Jesus had no home and was frequently a guest (Lk 7:36 ff; 9:51 ff; 10:38 ff; 14:1 ff; 19:5 ff; cf also Mk 1:29 ff; 2:15 ff; 14:3 ff). It was the practice of Paul on his journeys first to visit the Jews and to stay with them, and to stay with the Gentiles only if the Jews refused him (AA 14:28; 15:33; 16:15, 34; 17:1 ff; 18:3, 27; 21:16). God is the generous host (Pss 15:1; 23:5).

Hosts, Lord of; Host of heaven. Hb *ṣābā'*, pl *ṣebā'ôt*, means an army ready for war, and more precisely in Israelite military terminology the army drawn from the general population in contrast to the professional soldiers. Yahweh of hosts then means Yahweh of armies rather than Yahweh of battles, although the second idea is no doubt connoted. The original phrase, which is rarer than "Yahweh of hosts," is "Yahweh God of hosts"; Hb does not form genitives upon proper names and the common noun must be supposed, although it is more frequently omitted and the shorter form employed. In postbiblical Judaism Sebaoth became a substitute for the divine name. The title in variant forms occurs 284 times in the OT but its distribution is uneven. It is most frequent in some of the prophets (Is 1–55; Je; Ho; Am; Mi; Na; Hab; Zp; Hg; Zc; Mal), less frequently in some other books (1–2 S, 11 times 1–2 K, 8 times; 1 Ch, 3 times; Pss, 13 times). The contexts offer no certain clue to the identification of the armies, and scholars have proposed the armies of Israel or the hosts of heaven, either the angels* or the heavenly bodies (cf below), or the "hosts" of all the cosmic forces, heavenly and earthly. Others suggest a semantic and theological development by which the title, which originally designated Yahweh as the God of the armies of Israel, in the prophets comes to mean Yahweh the God of all cosmic forces. This view has some probability, but there are considerations against it, as there are against any view.

The host of heaven appears only in texts of the 8th century and later, and means the heavenly bodies, frequently as astral deities which the Israelites worshiped. It never signifies angelic hosts, which is a factor against this interpretation of the title Yahweh of hosts. Furthermore, the noun in "host of heaven" always appears in the singular (ṣᵉba' haššāmayim, not ṣᵉba'ot), which does not recommend this identification of the hosts in the title Yahweh of hosts. Cosmic hosts and heaven and earth appear only at the conclusion of the creative narrative in Gn 2:1. This passage in its present form comes from one of the later sources of the Pnt and is a doubtful witness to the early appearance of this conception. The hosts of Yahweh are led by the man who appears to Joshua (Jos 5:14 f); angelic hosts come to mind, but one thinks also that "The stars in their courses fought against Sisera" (Jgs 5:20). This midrash of Jos is again of uncertain date and doubtfully an early witness to the meaning of the term; but it is not impossible that the hosts of Yahweh whom the man comes to lead are the armies of Israel itself, in particular since the following victory is described as occurring without any human effort. The armies of Israel are called the hosts of Yahweh in Ex 7:4; 12:41. Ex 12:41 comes from a late source, but Ex 7:4 comes from the early sources of the Pnt and is perhaps the best and earliest witness to the identification of the hosts in the title Yahweh of hosts. It seems therefore more probable that the original title designated Yahweh, God of the hosts of Israel; the title never appears in this form but it is suggested by the form "Yahweh of hosts, God of Israel" (36 times) in which the two terms may be taken as parallel.

Hour. Biblical Hb has no word for hour, and it appears that the Israelites did not employ this mode of calculating time. In NT times, however, Jews employed the Gk and Roman division of the daylight period into 12 hours, which were calculated roughly and varied in length with the varying length of the daylight. This calculation goes back to the 12 double hours of the Mesopotamian day*. In the NT an hour also signifies a brief period of time, or the point of time at which an event occurs.

The hour is also the proper or appointed or expected time of an event; cf TIME. Thus the hour of temptation (Apc 3:10), the hour of the fulfillment of the predictions of Jesus (Jn 16:4), the hour for the Christian to rise from sleep (Rm 13:11). The present age is the last hour of the world (1 Jn 2:18).

"The hour of Jesus" is a conception prominent in Jn but mentioned also in the Synoptic Gospels. This is the hour which is said several times not yet to have arrived (Jn 7:30; 8:20). When it comes, it is the hour in which the Son of Man is glorified (Jn 12:23; 17:1). It is the hour which Jesus asks might pass (Mk 14:35) and from which He may be saved (Jn 12:27). The hour is explicitly the hour when Jesus departs from this world to the Father (Jn 13:1), the hour when the Son of Man is delivered to the hands of sinners (Mt 26:45; Mk 14:41). The hour of Jesus is also the hour of His enemies and of the power of darkness (Lk 22:53). The hour of Jesus is the time of His passion and death; the use of the term shows that it is an appointed event, not merely the casual issue of conflicting forces. It is the event toward which His life is pointed as to a fulfillment, the hour which He controls because it is His hour.

The same phrase, "my hour has not yet come," is used in Jn 2:4 with a more obscure reference; the context does not suggest a reference to the passion. It does, however, suggest a reference to the glorification of Jesus. This illustrates another aspect of His "hour," which is larger even than the passion; His hour is the time of His messianic manifestation, or His glorification, as it is called in Jn 12:23; 17:1.

House. The Palestinian dwelling never stood alone and isolated. Security and certain essential services such as water could be obtained only by dwelling in clusters of houses in towns and villages. In detail not much is known about the type of construction of houses in ancient Palestine. Archaeological excavation never recovers more than fragments of walls a few feet high at most, and usually scarcely more than the floor plan. The material of construction was rarely wood, except for joints and planks; the structure was stone or mud brick, depending on which material was more easily available. The remains indicate that the ordinary dwelling was a very shabby construction. Constant deterioration, repair, and remodeling of houses adds to the difficulty of recovering a clear idea of their structure. The houses which survived to any degree were larger and more substantially built, and thus presumably belonged to wealthy families. Some literary allusions cast light upon the structure of the house.

The house was a shelter within which

a) Inner court of house at Pompeii. b) and c) Egyptian house furniture.

the family ate and slept. Basically it consisted of a single all-purpose room; the number of additional rooms (what are now called "utility rooms") varied according to the means of the family. The large room could not be more than 15 ft long, the usual length of the joist, without pillars, which were frequently employed; the roof was heavy. The craftsman's shop was a part of his house. Small chambers for storage of grain and water jars often appear in the remains of houses. Sleeping rooms were found only in the large houses of the wealthy. The houses of the poor, which have been scarcely preserved, were no better than shacks. The Israelite family*, however was larger than the modern family, and the ordinary house was usually a multiple-family dwelling by our standards. There was no privacy. Throughout the entire archaeological history the common type of house was built adjacent to a court, enclosed sometimes on one side only, more frequently on two or three. There was only one small outside door, which opened into the court. No windows have been preserved, and they had no covering except a lattice; but it is most unlikely that they were numerous or large. Perhaps, as in the house of the modern Palestinian peasant, the windows were stuffed closed during the winter. The house consequently was dark, but the absence of many windows and doors was the best protection against both heat and cold. It also was the best protection against housebreaking, which is not infrequently mentioned in the Bible (Jb 24:16; Mt 6:19). The walls could be "dug" (Ezk 12:5 ff), whether they were mud, brick, or stone; the rubble masonry employed offered little difficulty to a diligent and patient effort to remove the stones. The floor was of clay, partly covered with rush mats. The mats were the principal furniture of the house of the poor; they served for sleeping and for sitting and for eating. The wealthy had chairs, tables, and bedsteads. The kitchen, if possible, was outside the large room where the family ate and rested. The roof afforded supplementary living space to the dark, crowded, dirty, and noisy interior. The ordinary roof consisted of a thick layer of marl and straw supported by wooden beams and planks and a network of branches. The roof was leaky at best (Pr 19:13; 27:15) and had to be rolled after each rain. It could easily be removed (Mk 2:4). It was accessible by a ladder or outside stairs. A parapet offered protection against falls (Dt 22:4; 2 K 1:2). A booth protected it against the sun. The family could sleep on the roof during the warmer months (1 S 9:25). The upper chamber mentioned often in the Bible may have been no more

than such a booth; in larger houses the upper chamber was another story. The chamber was, however, open to the breeze on all sides and could be refreshing in the cool evening (2 S 11:2). The thickness of some house foundations has suggested to some archaeologists the construction of houses of two or even three stories; but there is no demonstration that houses were built so high.

In the Hellenistic cities of Palestine of NT times, houses were built in Gk or Roman style. The large Hellenistic house was built around two courts: the large outer court (*atrium*), open to the public and often let out for shops, and the inner court (*peristyle*) around which were built family chambers. In Hellenistic and Roman cities the poorer classes lived in large multiple-family blocks which were not unlike the modern tenement. In towns and villages the basic one room shack was still the normal housing of most of the population.

The word "house" often designates not the material structure but in particular a dynastic family (house of David); in a transferred sense it designates a larger group such as a tribe (house of Levi, of Judah) or an entire people (house of Israel). To the house moral traits may be applied (rebellious house). The house can also signify a condition of existence (Egypt, the house of slaves). The temple was called the house of Yahweh.

Huldah (Hb *ḥuldāh,* meaning and etymology uncertain), the wife of Shallum, the keeper of the royal wardrobe (2 K 22:14–20; 2 Ch 34:22–28). She was consulted by the officers of Josiah* after the discovery of the book of the law in the temple and responded with a prediction of disaster for the kingdom because of its failure to observe the law, from which Josiah is excepted for his piety. Her words are obviously reported in the light of subsequent events.

Hunting. Hunting is not mentioned often in the Bible. Nimrod* was a mighty hunter before Yahweh (Gn 10:9) and was presumably the folklore inventor of the skill. No circumstantial account of hunting is found except the story of Esau (Gn 25:27; 27:1 ff). Esau here hunts with the bow. The story in its characterization of Esau expresses contempt for the man who lives by hunting in contrast to the herdsman, who has meat readily available. The casual allusions elsewhere in the OT presuppose that the Israelite supplemented his food supply with game (Je 16:16; Lv 17:13). A catalogue of game which may be eaten is found in Dt 14:5. Predatory animals also were hunted (1 S 17:35; 2 S 23:20; Jb

Assyrian hunting scenes.
Shown are archers,
mounted lancers,
fowlers, and hunting
the wild ox from a
chariot.

10:16). It is doubtful that the list of weapons in Jb 41:18–20 is meant to be a list of hunting weapons. Trapping rather than hunting is presupposed in the allusions to snares, nets, traps, and pits. The antelope is netted (Is 51:20). The lion is taken in a net or pit and caged (Ezk 19:8 f); the caged lion is represented in Assyrian art. There is no indication that the Israelites ever hunted for sport; Josephus says that Herod was a sportsman. The Israelite countryside was not suitable for the hunting of the lion and the wild ox from the chariot, which so often appears in Assyrian sculpture. For this royal pleasure the animals were enclosed in a royal park. A bowl from Ugarit* represents a Canaanite king hunting from his chariot.

Hur (Hb *ḥûr,* meaning and etymology uncertain, but probably an Egyptian name [the god Horus]), a contemporary of Moses*. He is mentioned as an equal with Aaron in Ex 17:10 ff, where with Aaron he supports the arms of Moses at prayer, and in Ex 24:14, where with Aaron he governs the Israelites while Moses was absent.

The Hur of the genealogical lists of 1 Ch was a Judahite of the clan of Caleb, connected with Bethlehem (1 Ch 2:19 f, 50; 4:1, 4). It is not clear that this is the Hur of Ex. It is strange that a man so prominent in the early traditions of the exodus* should disappear so suddenly without trace. The name is born by three others in the OT.

Hurrians. A people of western Asia of the 2nd millennium BC. Recent studies have clarified the use of certain names in ancient records; Hurrian is an ethnic name, Mitanni a political name, and Subartu a geographical name designating Mesopotamia N of Akkad. About 1500–1400 BC the three names are concretely identical, Mitanni designating the kingdom of the Hurrians located in Subartu. The evidence suggests that the Hurrians were neither Semitic nor Indo-European, but Armenoid. They entered Mesopotamia in the 22nd century BC and Syria and Palestine in the 17th century. They first appear in ancient records about 2400 BC. In the 2nd half of the 1st millennium they appear widely diffused through Mesopotamia, Syria, and Canaan. Their historical and cultural influence was greater than their short-lived political independence might suggest; the appearance of large numbers of Hurrian proper names in Mesopotamia, in the Hittite* kingdom, at Ugarit*, and in the Amarna* letters, particularly as names of chieftains, shows that they were a large and influential portion of the population. They founded independent kingdoms in N Mesopotamia and N Syria with the weakening of the old Hittite kingdom about 1500 BC and ruled Assyria as a vassal kingdom; the largest and most frequently mentioned of these kingdoms were Mitanni and Hanigalbat. Mitanni extended from the Zagros region to the Mediterranean and from Lake Van in Armenia to Assyria. The kingdoms endured scarcely more than a hundred years. They were weakened by wars with the Pharaohs of the 18th dynasty of Egypt in the 15th century, and reduced to vassal states by the Hittite Suppiluliuma in the 14th century. They appear as petty kings in Canaan during the Amarna period and in the OT at the time of the Hebrew settlement. The Hurrian language is unrelated to other languages of the area and is not yet completely understood. The structure of Hurrian society was distinctive in the ancient Near East. The mass of the Hurrian population was ruled by an alien aristocracy of Indo-Iranian (Aryan) extraction which in the course of time was absorbed by the lower grades. This aristocracy was chariot* warriors (*maryannu*). Their religion was syncretized with the cults of Mesopotamia; but the Hurrian weather-god Teshup with his consort Hepat and their son Sharruma was adopted by the Hittites. While their political importance was less than that of other peoples, modern historians now see in them the mediators of Mesopotamian culture to the peoples of Syria, Phoenicia, and Canaan. Their laws and customs are known through the tablets of Nuzu*, which they ruled in the 15th century; these tablets show a number of remarkable contacts with early Hebrew history.

The OT. The Hurrians (Hb *hôrî*) are placed in the hill country of Seir* in Edom* in the time of Abraham (Gn 14:6). They were dispossessed by the Edomites (Dt 2:12, 22). The names of some Horite chieftains are given in the genealogy of Esau (Gn 36:20–22, 29–30; 1 Ch 1:39) and the geographical name Seir becomes the name of a Horite chieftain (Gn 36:20). It is altogether probable, following the opinion of most scholars, that the name Hivite is a corruption of Horite. The Hivites are mentioned in Gn 10:17 and frequently in the lists of the pre-Israelite inhabitants of Canaan, and one of Esau's wives was a Hivite (Gn 36:2). More specifically, the Horites (Hivites) are said to dwell in Shechem* in the time of Jacob (Gn 34:2), in the confederated cities of Gibeon*, Chephirah, Beeroth*, and Kirjath-jearim* in the time of Joshua (Jos 9:7; 11:19), at the foot of Mt Hermon* (Jos 11:3) and in the Lebanon* (Jgs 3:3). Some were left in the reigns of David (1 S 24:7) and Solomon* (1 K 9:20). Some modern scholars read "Hittite" for "Horite" in these last four passages; but the emendation does not impose itself. In view of the wide diffusion of the Hurrians, especially their presence in Canaan during the Amarna period, no question arises concerning their presence at the time of the Israelite settlement. Nothing in ancient records, however, suggests their presence in Edom before the Edomites; the name here may be an anachronism.

Hushai (Hb *ḥûšai*, meaning and etymology uncertain, possibly an abbreviation), "king's friend" of David. The title "king's friend" was an official title of the royal cabinet and probably designated the supreme royal adviser. Hushai was an Arkite; the name of the town or clan does not appear except in this appellative form. David did not permit Hushai to accompany him on his flight from Absalom but urged that he could best serve the king by retaining his office under Absalom (2 S 15:32–37). Hushai was accepted by Absalom (2 S 16:16–19), and did indeed serve David well by advising Absalom against an immediate pursuit of David (2 S 17:7–14). The import of this advice was clearly perceived by Ahithophel (2 S 17:23), for it afforded the delay which David needed to gather an army.

Hyksos. The Gk form of the Egyptian name of Asiatic invaders of Egypt in the Second Intermediate Period between the Middle Kingdom and the New Kingdom (cf EGYPT). The Egyptian historian Manetho as quoted by Josephus interpreted the name as "shepherd kings" (nomad chieftains); modern Egyptologists identify the word as the Egyptian "rulers of foreign lands." It is an appellative, not a gentilic name; the gentilic name of this people is unknown. The Hyksos have left no records of their own, and Egyptian records are meager; the Egyptians preferred to delete them from their records as far as possible. It appears that Asiatic groups began to invade Egypt about 1720 BC and continued to come in several waves for some years. In the anarchy which followed the 12th dynasty Egypt could offer no effective resistance. The causes which lay behind this irruption can be conjectured; the movement of the Hyksos is contemporaneous with the invasion of Hurrians* and other non-Semitic peoples into NW Mesopotamia, and it appears that the Semitic inhabitants of the area were driven southward. That the Hyksos were Semitic is indicated by the appearance of some NW Semitic types of personal names (Jacob-har, Anat-har). The Hyksos constitute the 15th–16th dynasties of ancient Egypt. They reached their peak of power about 1650–1590 under Apophis I and Khayana, ruling an empire which extended from Nubia to Syria. They located their capital first at Memphis and then at Avaris in NE Egypt (cf TANIS). They worshiped the Egyptian god Set, probably identifying him with the Semitic storm god (cf HADAD). They were ultimately expelled from Egypt after 1580 by the kings of the 18th Theban Dynasty, who pursued them into Canaan and successfully besieged them at Sharuhen for three years. The Hyksos have left no evidence of creative culture; they were important, however, as the first who formed a medium between Egyptian and Asiatic culture; the contact was not broken thereafter. They were also the first, as Noth points out, to bring Syria and Palestine into the theater of international history; after the Hyksos this area played its natural part as bridge between Egypt and Asia. Their empire was taken by the kings of the 18th dynasty. Their chief contributions were in warfare; they introduced the horse* and the chariot* into Egypt, and a massive earthwork type of fortification* is regarded by some scholars as a Hyksos invention.

Most scholars agree that the Hyksos period is the most likely background for the story of Joseph* and the settlement of the Israelites in Egypt. It is not improbable that there was some kinship between the two groups. During no other period is it conceivable that the Israelites could have enjoyed the royal favor which is described in their traditions.

Hymenaeus (Gk *hymenaios*, "pertaining to Hymen," the god of marriages), a Christian who with Alexander has lost the faith and has been delivered to Satan (by excommunication; 1 Tm 1:20), probably the same who with Philetus taught that the resurrection had already occurred (2 Tm 2:17).

Hymn. The literary form of the hymn is common in the Pss* and in other books of the Bible. The hymn is a song of praise; the scheme is not rigid, but the form most frequently begins with an invitation to praise God (which may be repeated in the course of the hymn), followed by an enumeration of titles to praise: the divine attributes and virtues and the divine deeds, in particular His deeds in creation and His deeds of salvation* for Israel either in the past or in the messianic future. Some hymns consist entirely of invitations to praise. The titles to praise are sometimes mere enumerations, like a litany; the grammatical form employed is the declarative sentence, the attributive adjective, the participle, the relative clause. The hymn is a cultic composition. Examples of hymns outside the Pss are found in Ex

15:1 ff (which develops into a narrative poem); Jgs 5:3–5 (exordium to the song of Deborah*); Jb 5:9–16; 12:13–25; Is 42:10–12; 44:23; 52:9–10; BS 39:14–35; 42:15–43:33. The Israelite hymn may be compared with many examples of Egyptian and Mesopotamian hymns (ANET 365–368, 370–375, 383, 385–386, 387–389); there are certain similarities in form, which are due largely to the identity of subject matter. The Israelite hymn is distinctive in its use of its own history in hymns which recite the saving deeds of Yahweh. Hymns were sung in the cultic assemblies of the early Christian communities (AA 16:25; Eph 5:19), and the NT contains examples of hymns (Lk 1:46–55, the Magnificat*; 1:68–79, the Benedictus*; 2:29–32; Phl 2:5–11; Col 1:13–20 suggests the hymn style; 1 Tm 3:16 is thought to be an early Christian hymn; Apc 11:17 f; 15:3 f; 19:1 f, 5, 6–8).

Hyssop (Hb *'ēzôb,* Gk *hyssopos*), a marjoram of the mint family, native to Egypt. It has a strong wiry stem with bunches of flowers and leaves. Its absorptive qualities rendered it apt as an aspergill in Hb liturgical practices; to sprinkle the blood of the Passover on the doorposts (Ex 12:22), to sprinkle the blood of the covenant on the people (Hb 9:19), to sprinkle blood in the rite of the purification of the leper (Lv 14:4–6) or of the "leprous" house (Lv 14:49–52), to sprinkle water on the unclean man (Nm 19:18). Metaphorically God's forgiveness is called sprinkling with hyssop (Ps 51:9). Solomon* discoursed of plants from the largest (cedar) to the smallest (hyssop, 1 K 5:13). According to Jn 19:29 the wine was given to Jesus on the cross in a sponge set on hyssop (on a reed, *kalamos,* in Mt 27:48; Mk 15:36).

I

Ibleam (Hb *yible'am,* a city [called Bilam, Hb *bile'am* in 1 Ch 6:55], etymology uncertain). The site is identified with the modern Khirbet Belame about 5 mi S of En-Gannim*. The site has not been explored. Ibleam is listed among the Canaanite cities conquered by Thutmose III (1502–1448). The list of Jos 17:11 includes Ibleam among the cities of Manasseh; it passed to this tribe from Asher and Issachar. In Jgs 1:27 it is included among the Canaanite cities which the Israelites did not take. It is listed as a Levitical city of the Kohathites in Manasseh (1 Ch 6:55). It is probably the Belmain mentioned in Jdt 4:4.

Ibzan (Hb *'ibṣān,* etymology and meaning uncertain), one of the minor judges (Jgs 12:8–10), of Bethlehem. He was remarkable for his success in marrying outside his clan; his 30 sons and 30 daughters (a fabulous figure) all married outside his own clan.

Ichabod (Hb *'ikābôd*), son of Phinehas*, son of Eli*. He was born at the time of the defeat of the Israelites by the Philistines, and his name is explained as Hb *'i-kabod,* "no glory" (dishonor) (1 S 4:21). This etymology is popular; Eissfeldt suggests that the name is shortened from *'aḥikābôd,* "the brother is glory." Others connect it with the *i*-prefix in such names as Jezebel* (Izebel) and Ithamar*, which is unexplained. Ichabod does not appear again, but he is mentioned in the lineage of Ahijah*, who wore the ephod* in the time of Saul (1 S 14:3), although Ahijah was not a direct descendant of Ichabod.

Iconium (Gk *ikonion,* "little image"), a city of Asia Minor. The site is occupied by the modern city of Konya in Turkey (population, 65,000). It lies on the southern edge of the plain of the Anatolian plateau at an altitude of about 3500 ft. In NT times it lay in the region of Lycaonia*. The city was probably first settled by the Phrygians some time before the 7th century BC. It was ruled by the Lydians, the Persians, the Seleucids, the kingdom of Pergamum, and was a part of the legacy of Attalus III to Rome in 133 BC.
Iconium was reached by Paul and Barnabas on their first missionary journey after they had left Antioch* in Pisidia (AA 13:51–14:6). As in Antioch, the Jews stirred up popular hostility against them so that they were forced to flee. They revisited Iconium on their return (AA 14:21), and probably Paul returned once more on his second journey, when he visited the neighboring towns of Derbe and Lystra (AA 16:1).

Iddo (Hb *'iddô,* etymology and meaning uncertain). The author of Chronicles* cites the visions of Iddo the prophet as a source for Rehoboam* (2 Ch 12:15) and the midrash of Iddo as a source for Abijah* (2 Ch 13:22). Most modern critics read Iddo for Jeddi in 2 Ch 9:29.

Idol, Idolatry. Cf IMAGE.

Idumaea (Gk *idumaia* from Hb *'edôm,* Edom*), the word used in the LXX for Edom. The Edomite occupation of southern Judah after the fall of Jerusalem in 586 BC is attested in several biblical allusions (Ps 137:7; Ezk 25:12; 35:12–15; Ob). This movement was due not only to the land hunger of the Edomites, but also to the pressure upon them by invading Arabian tribes, who seem to have occupied ancient Edom after the 4th century BC; by NT times ancient Edom was a Nabatean kingdom. The frontier of Idumaea and Judaea ran along a line near Beth-Zur* just N of Hebron*, and Idumaea included the territory S of the line into the Negeb*. Idumaea is called an eparchy of the Seleucid kingdom by the Gk historian Diodorus; Josephus uses the less apt Persian term of satrapy. Idumaea was conquered by the Hasmonean* ruler John Hyrcanus (135–105 BC), who forced the Idumaeans to accept Judaism*. The family of Herod* the Great was Idumaean. After the conquest of John Hyrcanus Idumaea was treated as a unit with Judaea by the Hasmonaeans, Herod, and the Romans.

Illyricum (Gk *illyrikon*), the ancient name of the territory on the E coast of the Adriatic N of Macedonia. It is mentioned by Paul as a limit of his journeys (Rm 15:19); there is no other allusion to his reaching the country. Illyricum was not finally conquered by the Romans until AD 9, when it was erected into the provinces of Dalmatia, Pannonia, and Moesia.

Image. 1. *The divine image (idol).* A large

a) The Egyptian god Bes. b) and c) Egyptian representations of the fertility goddess Kadesh with Min on the left and Resheph on the right. The goddess stands on a lion and holds the lotus and serpents. d) Mesopotamian seal showing divine figures standing on lions making offerings to Tree of Life.

number of divine images have been preserved from Egypt*, Syria*, and Mesopotamia*; but outside of Egypt not many of the principal temple images of the gods have been preserved, and Palestine has revealed no image that can be certainly identified as such. Smaller images, reliefs, and plaques have been discovered in abundance. These were employed in the domestic cult or in accessory shrines in the temples. Some of the smallest images and plaques may be amulets* rather than cult images; they could be worn on the person and sometimes are pierced with small holes through which they could be attached by a cord.

The images are cast in bronze, hewn in stone, or modeled in clay. Casting was employed only in small images; larger metal images were made by plating metal over a hewn wooden core. All these types of images are mentioned in the OT.

A few of the more common types of images may be described. By far the most common is the small plaque of the nude goddess of fertility, usually modeled with the sexual organs exaggerated (ANEP 469). Of interest is the contamination of Kadesh, the Canaanite goddess, with Egyptian artistic motifs, reflecting the Egyptian influence on Canaan 1500–1300 BC (ANEP 470–474). Here the goddess appears nude, standing on a lion, and holding the Egyptian lotus symbol or a serpent. She has the hairdress of the Egyptian goddess Hathor, and is sometimes accompanied by the Egyptian god Min and the Syrian god Resheph. An interesting variant was found at Ugarit representing a goddess dressed in a skirt, bare above the waist, flanked by animals; this is thought to be a Canaanite adaptation of the Aegean *potnia thērōn,* "queen of the wild beasts," a title applied to Artemis* (ANEP 464). Images of a god brandishing or holding an axe or a thunderbolt are common both in Syria and Mesopotamia (ANEP 476, 486, 490, 500, 501, 531). The god sometimes stands upon a bull (ANEP 500, 501, 531). This image represents the god of the storm, who is at once a god of war and of fertility (cf BAAL; HADAD). In Mesopotamian art the deity is identified as such by the horned cap (ANEP 513–516); the symbolism of this motif is unknown. In stylized Egyptian art each deity was identified by a distinctive headdress or crown (ANEP 573). The history of Egyptian religion offers no certain explanation of the large number of Egyptian gods represented in human form with animal heads; there is nothing in Syrian and Mesopotamian images to correspond to this peculiarly Egyptian practice.

The conception of the meaning and value

of the image in Egypt, Syria, and Mesopotamia, is difficult to analyze; and it is not possible to arrive at a coherent rationalization of the image. This is of some importance for the interpretation of the OT polemic against idolatry (cf below). The image was more than a simple representation; at the same time, the image was not absolutely identified with the god. The god's dwelling and sphere of operation were not limited to the temple in which the image was placed. The temple and the image were the earthly counterparts of the celestial reality, and they were the only means by which cult could reach the gods. On this basis the image was treated as the god himself would be treated; and the treatment was that which courtiers gave their monarch. In both Egypt and Mesopotamia the god was awakened in the morning, washed and purified or anointed, clothed, and served his meals. Yet there was awareness of the image as such; both in Egypt and in Mesopotamia the morning cult included a rite called "the opening of the mouth," by which the image was animated to receive the cult and the petitions of the worshipers of the god. In Egypt and in Babylon the image was carried about on feast days; in Babylon it was carried as a guest to the temples of other gods whose festivals were being celebrated. Yet all this was not idolatry in the gross sense of the term; nevertheless, without the divine image no cult of the god was possible.

2. *The Israelite prohibition of images.* The 2nd commandment of the decalogue* (Ex 20:4–6; Dt 5:8–10; cf Lv 26:1; Dt 4:15–23) prohibits the manufacture of images of anything "in the heavens above, or the earth below, or the waters beneath the earth." The enumeration is comprehensive and includes every visible object which can be represented. It is unlikely that it is a total prohibition of representational art, as it was understood by some rabbis of strict views. In early Israel the cherubim* were images, and in Judaism of the 1st century AD and later artistic decorations of tombs and synagogues were permitted, as can be seen in the Roman catacombs and the synagogue paintings of Dura-Europos, and the synagogue of Beth Shearim. But even if the precept was not understood in the rigorous sense in the early monarchy, very little representational art has survived except the plaques of the nude goddess (cf above). Nothing has been discovered in Israelite levels of occupation in Palestine which can be called an image of Yahweh. The bull calves erected by Jeroboam of Israel (1 K 12:26–30; cf Ex 33:2–4) are regarded by many modern scholars not as images of Yahweh, but as pedestals upon which Yahweh stood invisible,

not represented by any image. This is in harmony with the animal pedestal found in Canaanite art (cf above; ANET 470–474; 500, 501, 531) and with the absence of theriomorphic images of the divine in Syria and Mesopotamia. Some instances of divine images are found in the OT, but their character is obscure. The image of Micah (Jgs 17:1 ff; 18:30 f) is never called an image of Yahweh. The teraphim of Laban (Gn 31:19–21, 31–35) were small household gods (cf above) so small that a woman could conceal them by sitting upon them. The teraphim in the house of David (1 S 19:13–16) was larger, apparently nearly human size; but this teraphim is not called an image of Yahweh.

There is nothing in the civilizations of the ancient Near East nor in Israel's cultural origins from which this prohibition can be derived. Parallels adduced from uncivilized peoples who have no representational images of the deity are not accompanied by such an explicit prohibition. We are justified in interpreting this precept as an expression of an article of the faith of Israel in the cult. Yahweh was not to be represented by an image because no image could represent him. He was totally different from any object in nature; to represent him by an image would be to reduce him to the level of nature and thus to bring him down to the level of the gods who were worshiped through images. Through this precept Israel was taught that Yahweh was entirely outside and above nature.

3. *The OT polemic against idolatry.* In several OT passages (cf Is 40:18–20; 44:9–20; Je 10:1–9 +) there is an explicit polemic against the worship of idols. The idols are not gods, they are the work of human hands, and their worshipers are ridiculed. Since the cult of the image in the ancient Near East was not gross idolatry (cf above), and it seems unlikely that the Israelites were unaware of this, a question arises concerning the meaning of such passages. Are they a rhetorical oversimplification of the position to be attacked, the erection of a "straw man" to be demolished? Y. Kaufmann has asserted that the Israelites were entirely unaware of the ideological basis of the cult of images. This appears altogether unlikely. H. H. Rowley has, it seems, better interpreted these passages as a denial of the reality of the gods. The heathens worshiped the god of whom the image was the earthly counterpart, and not the image itself. But since the Hebrews denied any reality behind the image, then the cult fell upon the image itself because there was nothing else to receive it. The heathens were therefore effec-

tively idol-worshipers, even if they intended to be something else.

4. *Man in the image of God.* The creation* account (Gn 1:26 f) states that God made man in His own image and likeness. Precisely in what the likeness consists is not expressed, and modern interpreters have proposed several explanations. In spite of the anthropomorphism* of the OT, there are few who believe that the likeness lies in man's physiological structure; such a view is too sharply in conflict with the transcendental nature of God as expressed in the prohibition of images (cf above) and elsewhere in the OT. Köhler has modified this view by proposing that the likeness consists in the erect stature of man, which symbolizes his elevation over the animals and his power to rule them. Th. C. Vriezen thinks that the likeness means a direct and positive relation of community between God and man which does not place the two terms of the relation on the same level. W. Eichrodt places the likeness in the spiritual qualities of man, his capacity of self-consciousness and self-determination — in a word, his personality. It seems most probable that the likeness lies in this area. In the OT Yahweh is distinguished from the other gods by the designation "living;" He is an extremely vigorous and sharply defined personality who plans, desires, achieves, and responds personally to the words and deeds of men. In this "living" quality man resembles Him.

5. *Image in the NT.* The idea of man as the image of God is developed theologically in the Pauline writings. The image of God is first and most properly Christ, the new Adam* and the head of a new race of men (2 Co 4:4; Col 1:15). Men realize the fullness of the image of God in them by "sharing the form of the image of the Son," to which they are predestined (Rm 8:29). Through sharing in the image of the Son the Christian is changed in form to the image of the Lord (2 Co 3:18); the new man which he puts on, the image of Christ, renders him in the image of his creator, an allusion to Gn 1:26 f (Col 3:15). This "image of the glory" (2 Co 3:18) is not to be found only in the attributes of grace and virtue, but ultimately in the resurrection, which alters the physical form of man also into the image of the glory* of Christ; as man first bears the image of the earthly man, Adam, so finally he wears the image of the heavenly man, Christ (1 Co 15:49). In 1 Co 11:7 Paul limits the image of God to the male; the female shares in the glory of the image only by reflection. From this he adduces an argument for the authority of man over woman.

Immanuel. Cf EMMANUEL.

Imposition of Hands. The rite of the imposition of hands is ancient in Israel and exhibits multiple symbolism. The offerer lays his hands upon the victim (cf SACRIFICE) probably to symbolize that the victim is his; the gesture affirms identity rather than substitution. This is probably the symbolism of the imposition of hands upon the Levites by the entire people of Israel (Nm 8:10 f); while the Levites do take the place of the firstborn of Israel in the service of Yahweh in the cult, the imposition of hands affirms the solidarity of the Levites and the rest of Israel in cultic worship. The imposition of hands in stoning seems to symbolize the acceptance by each person of the judgment and sentence executed upon the guilty one (Lv 24:14). The imposition of hands in blessing* (Gn 48:9, 13 f; Mt 19:15; Mk 10:16) symbolizes communication; blessing is conceived as a substantial reality which flows from the one conferring the blessing to the one receiving. Similarly the imposition of hands in healing symbolizes the transmission of blessing. Jesus sometimes is narrated to have imposed His hands in healing (Mk 6:5; Lk 4:40; 13:11–13), but more frequently it is not mentioned or it is clear that it was not done. The apostles also imposed hands in healing (Mk 16:18; AA 9:12, 17; 28:8).

The imposition of hands in ordination to an office appears in the OT only in the appointment of Joshua by Moses (Nm 27:18–23; Dt 34:9); the imposition of hands upon the Levites, as noted above, has another symbolism. The two passages concerning Joshua differ in conception; in Nm Joshua, "in whom is the spirit*," receives the imposition of hands, but in Dt Joshua receives the spirit by the imposition. The symbolism is the communication of power and authority, more specifically the spirit; for the spirit must be possessed by one who exercises leadership in the Israelite community. In the NT the apostles impose hands upon the Seven (AA 6:6) and the elders* impose hands upon Paul and Barnabas (AA 13:3). Elders (AA 14:23) and Titus (2 Co 8:19) are appointed by the imposition of hands. In these passages there is no mention of the communication of the spirit; the symbolism is the communication of power and authority, and the solidarity of those who impose hands and those who receive the imposition is affirmed. The imposition of hands which Timothy received conferred upon him a grace* (1 Tm 4:14; 2 Tm 5:22). By the time 1 Tm was written the imposition of hands seems to have become the normal rite of ordination to office in the Church (1 Tm 5:22).

The imposition of hands is in the NT a

symbolic rite by which the spirit is conferred, but it is not restricted to officers in the Church. The imposition of hands which accompanied baptism* conferred the spirit upon those baptized (AA 8:17–19; 19:6; cf CONFIRMATION). Ananias, however, imposed hands upon Paul, who received the spirit and recovered his vision before he was baptized (AA 9:17 f).

Incense (Hb *l^ebonah*, Gk *libanos*). The use of burning incense as a perfume both in cultic practice and in profane life was widespread in the ancient Near East. It was

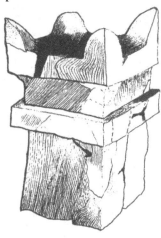

A horned incense altar from Megiddo.

possibly included in the pharmacopoeia of Mesopotamia*. Its cultic use is pictured in Egyptian temples and tombs. The profane use is mentioned in Pr 27:9. The genuine incense is frankincense, described by A. Lucas as a fragrant gum-resin occurring in the form of large tears light yellowish-brown in color. Its quality was judged by its approach to whiteness. The gum is yielded by Boswellia trees native to Somaliland and S Arabia; Je 6:20 mentions incense from Sheba* in S Arabia. Other aromatic substances were burned as perfume; Lucas lists myrrh*, galbanum (a gum-resin), ladanum (a resin), storax (a balsam), and a few other less important varieties. The prescription for the manufacture of incense in Ex 30:34 ff is a compound of frankincense and several other aromatic substances.

The *hammanim* of Lv 26:30; 2 Ch 14:4; 34:4, 7; Is 17:8; 27:9; Ezk 6:4, 6, translated in older Bibles as idols, are now recognized as incense altars. The incense altar described in Ex 30:1 ff bears a resemblance to a Canaanite incense altar found at Megiddo (ANEP 575), a small limestone cube with horns. Similar cubes without horns, but with supporting legs, are found in S Arabia

(ANEP 579, 581). Portable hand censers are represented in Egypt (ANEP 334) and Syria (ANEP 493). An incense spoon in the form of a lion's paw was found at Tell Beit Mirsim in Palestine (cf DEBIR). An Assyrian incense stand consists of a narrow broad-based column on which the burner rested (ANEP 625–628).

The offering of incense on the incense altar was a priestly office in Israel (1 S 2:28; cf Nm 16:5 ff). "Strange fire" was a possible ritual defect (Lv 10:1 ff) but we are not told in what the defect consisted. Incense accompanied sacrificial offerings (Lv 2:1, 15; 6:8; Is 43:23; Je 17:26; 41:5), but was excluded from at least some types of sin-offering (Lv 5:11; Nm 5:15). A cloud of incense obscured the "mercy-seat" (cf ARK) when the high priest entered the sanctuary, concealing the priest from the sight of the deity and protecting his life. Ezk refers to the use of incense in foreign image cults practiced by Israelites (Ezk 8:11; 16:18; 23:41); this should be offered to Yahweh alone.

Incense is one of the gifts offered to the infant Jesus in Mt 2:11, which is probably an echo of Is 60:6.

Incest. The Hb prohibitions of incestuous unions are listed in Lv 18:6–18. The penalty of death is imposed on incest together with some other sexual perversions in Lv 20:10–21. The prohibitions are based both on consanguinity and on affinity. According to Lv 18:27 incest was practiced by the Canaanites*. Such unions are to be avoided either because of nearness of kin ("she is your flesh") or because she belongs to a male kinsman ("it is the nakedness of X"). The prohibitions are addressed only to the male, since it was conceived that only the male was the active party in sexual intercourse. The prohibitions are directed not only against marriage, but against extramarital intercourse. The forbidden degrees are thus summed up by E. Neufeld:

A man is not allowed to have intercourse with his:

Mother	
Stepmother	Granddaughter
Sister	Stepsister
Half sister	
Paternal aunt	Paternal aunt by marriage
Maternal aunt	
Daughter-in-law	Stepdaughter
Sister-in-law	Stepgranddaughter
(brother's wife)	
Mother-in-law	Sister-in-law (wife's sister, during life)

It is remarkable that there is no prohibition of union of father and daughter. It seems altogether likely that it was prohibited, but that the prohibition has fallen out of the list. The prohibition against marriage with a father's wife was violated by Reuben* with Bilhah* (Gn 35:22); no punishment is reported, but the offense was cursed in Gn 48:4. When Absalom wished to assert his possession of David's throne he took possession of his father's harem "before all Israel" (2 S 16:22); this was the action which made the breach between the two irreparable. The prohibition of marriage of brother and sister seems to be unknown in the patriarchal stories, since Abraham and Sarah were half brother and half sister (Gn 20:12). But even under the monarchy Tamar* thought that David would permit her half brother Amnon* to marry her (2 S 13:13); Amnon's crime seems to have consisted rather in rape than in incestuous union. It is difficult to see whether the story of Lot* and his daughters (Gn 19:30–38) reflects disgrace on the daughters or praise for their boldness and ingenuity in finding their feminine fulfillment. There is no doubt that the device by which Tamar deceived her father-in-law Judah into having extramarital intercourse with her is accepted as "righteous" (Gn 38:12 ff; 38:26); she recovered a right of which Judah had defrauded her. Hence, while he was ready to have her burned for extramarital intercourse, no punishment was inflicted for the incest. The marriage of a man with his stepmother was treated by Paul as an exceptionally base form of sexual perversion for which the offender was not only excommunicated but placed under a solemn curse (1 Co 5:1–5).

India (Hb *hōddû,* of Old Persian *indu-u, hi-in-du-is*), mentioned as the eastern limit of the empire of Ahasuerus* (Est 1:1; 8:9).

Infancy Gospels. Accounts of the infancy and childhood of Jesus appear in Mt 1:18–2:23; Lk 1:5–2:52. There is no account of the infancy in Mk and Jn, nor is it alluded to elsewhere in the NT. The infancy, however, was perhaps the most popular topic of the apocryphal* gospels.

Mt and Lk have in common only the basic elements of the birth of Jesus in Bethlehem and the virginal conception of Mary. Catholic tradition has from earliest times understood the virginity of Mary as perpetual. In other respects the differences at times raise a difficulty in combining them. Lk not only knows nothing of the episode of Herod* and the Magi* and the flight to Egypt*, but it is nearly impossible to combine these events with his account. Lk also has nothing of the problem of Joseph. Mt has none of the temple incidents which Lk relates, and

again it is difficult to combine them with his narrative. Mt seems to know of no residence at Nazareth before the return from Egypt. Certain problems are raised by external history; cf CENSUS; MAGI. In addition the infancy accounts in Mt-Lk are generously endowed with quotations from the OT which show Jesus as Messiah and king.

It is hardly possible that Mt and Lk have drawn from a common source. In addition to the differences noted above, the infancy narrative of Mt is colored by tragedy and sorrow, while the account of Lk has a spirit of joy. The language in both Mt and Lk demands a Semitic original for each; this is particularly evident in Lk, where the style differs sharply from the rest of the Gospel. There is nothing in the text to suggest that the material comes from a firsthand witness of the events. In Mt Joseph is the prominent figure, in Lk Mary and the other women predominate; but an attribution of the material to these is not warranted.

These features of the Infancy Gospels, together with the absence of the infancy elsewhere in the NT, have led modern scholars to suppose that the primitive Church possessed little or no living memory of the infancy and childhood of Jesus. This implies that no messianic features were obvious in His infancy and childhood, a supposition which is easily made, since such features leave no echo in the accounts of His public life. The Infancy Gospels, which apparently arose only in certain areas of the primitive Church, were intended to be theological expansions of the bare data contained in the memory of the early life of Jesus by the use of the OT and of the developed belief in His divine sonship and His Messiahship. Thus the infancy narratives are proclamations of His supernatural origin and character and anticipations of the revelation of Him as Messiah and Lord to both Jews and Gentiles. In Mt the revelation meets with profound hostility; Lk does not exhibit this element. In both Mt and Lk the infancy anticipates the passion and death of Jesus.

Such freedom in handling the material is in harmony with the purpose of the Gospels as a proclamation of faith, and with the characteristic literary feature of the Gospels by which they adapt the traditions to the belief of the Church which they set forth. Where material concerning the public life of Jesus was more abundant and the living memory of His person and words was more vivid, the Gospels do not employ a midrashic type of composition. But the composition of the Infancy Gospels does not differ in principle from the composition of the rest of the Gospels; they are intended to present the real Jesus as He was known by the Church, and differ from the rest of the Gospels only in that the material which was available was more scanty. Complete historical skepticism concerning the infancy and childhood of Jesus is unjustified; the difference between Mt-Lk and the apocryphal gospels is sufficient evidence of the restraint which was exercised in the composition of these narratives. The nature of the material likewise does not permit an uncritical acceptance of all features of these narratives as equally historical; as theological expansions they are intelligible, and in Christian tradition and cult have been of primary importance in forming the popular idea of the person, character, and mission of Jesus. This is precisely the purpose for which the Church composed them; and historical criticism, practiced with due reservations, does not alter this conception of Jesus nor remove any of the value of the Infancy Gospels as witnesses of the Christian faith.

Inheritance. 1. *Law*. The Hb codes contain no general laws of inheritance, and most of the law must be deduced from practices related in the narratives. It is not always certain that these practices prevailed during the entire course of Israelite history. All sons shared in the inheritance; this included even sons of slaves (Ishmael, Gn 21:10) or illegitimate sons (Jephthah, Jgs 11:1). Ishmael, however, was the son of a substitute wife and thus the real firstborn of his father, and it is by no means certain that this represents the usual position of sons of slaves. The eldest was granted a double portion of the inheritance, twice that of each other brother; the father was forbidden to transfer this to another son (Dt 21:15–17; the "two-thirds" of the text is to be understood as a proportion of 2:1 between the eldest and each of his brothers, and not of ⅔ of the estate absolutely). The eldest also succeeded to the headship of the family. Neither Jacob, in his treatment of Joseph nor David in his treatment of Solomon observed the law of the firstborn. The wife did not inherit; if she returned to her father's house as a widow, the man's property would go outside the family. Daughters likewise did not inherit because the property would pass outside the family to their husbands. A law which most critics regard as late includes daughters in the succession of inheritance if a man dies with no sons: daughters, brother, paternal uncle, nearest male relative (Nm 27:8–11). A supplementary law prescribes that daughters who inherit must marry within the tribe of their father to keep the inheritance within the tribe (Nm 36:6–9).

Mesopotamian general laws of inheritance are not preserved, and the practice is deduced from some laws governing special cases and from contracts and legal tablets. The Babylonian laws may be summed up thus, following Driver and Miles: The heirs divided the whole estate, movable and immovable goods. The sons divided equal shares; the eldest or favorite could receive a larger share if the father had so disposed. Sons of slaves probably could not inherit unless they were legitimated. Whether the widow and daughters had claims is disputed by historians; from the documents it appears that daughters sometimes inherited, but these may have been exceptional cases. Brothers inherited if a man died with no sons. A son could be disinherited for unworthy conduct, but only after a judicial process granted the father the right to disinherit. All these practices were subject to both local and temporal variations.

The Assyrian laws may be summed up thus, following the same scholars: All sons inherit, even the sons of concubines. The Assyrians were more rigorous than either Hebrews or Babylonians in excluding women from inheritance. The eldest son is granted a double portion, as in Israel. The harem was included in the goods which were divided among the sons.

The Nuzu* tablets afford a parallel to the possibility that the slave Eliezer* might inherit the estate of Abraham in defect of sons (Gn 15:3). Numerous contracts of adoption show that slaves were commonly adopted at Nuzu and designated as heirs. But if the adoptor begot a son after the adoption, the adopted son must yield the inheritance to the son of the body. The Nuzu tablets also expressly prohibit the expulsion of a substitute wife and her son as Sarah* expelled Hagar* and Ishmael (Gn 21:10). They likewise afford a certain imperfect parallel to the sale of the rights of the firstborn by Esau to Jacob; but the parallel is sufficient to show that such a transfer was possible.

2. *Theological*. Inheritance becomes a theological concept of some importance both in OT and in NT. Inheritance is a correlative to promise*, which is the source and the title of inheritance; the inheritance cannot be due to community of blood, as it was in law. The NT, however, adds a new modification to the title of inheritance. The analysis of the theological concept is somewhat obscured by the poverty of the Hb vocabulary, which is reflected in the Gk of the NT. The group of Hb words in question all exhibit too large a meaning for any single English word. In Hb law inheritance was the most secure title of possession, and the Hb words do not distinguish the two ideas; thus a man may "possess" something which he did not inherit.

A development in the content of the promise-inheritance relation should be noticed; it begins with the land and ends with the eschatological kingdom.

A. OT. The inheritance, as noted above, rests on the title of the promise made to the patriarchs. The content of the promise is the land of Canaan; the nomadic tribes of Israel are to receive a land where they may live in the stability and the distinct identity of a settled people. The land is called an "inheritance" or a "secure possession" (Ex 32:13; Nm 16:14; 34:2; Dt 4:21, 38; 12:10; 15:4; 19:10; 20:16; 21:23; 24:4; 25:19; 26:1; 1 K 8:36; Je 3:19; Ezk 35:15; 36:12). As the whole land is the inheritance of Israel, so the portion of each tribe is its inheritance (Gn 48:6; Nm 26:52–56; 32:18; 33:54; 34:14; 36:2; Jos 13:7; 14:2; 19:49, of Joshua*; 24:30, of Joshua). Since inheritance means secure possession, the land is called the inheritance of Yahweh (1 S 26: 19; 2 S 21:3). By a further extension Israel is called the inheritance of Yahweh (Dt 9:26, 29; 1 S 10:1; 2 S 14:16; 20:19; 1 K 8:51, 53; Is 63:17; Je 12:7–10; Pss 33:12; 74:2 and frequently in Pss).

The concept of inheritance means that the land is given to Israel; it is not won, acquired, or conquered. By its conquest Israel simply enters into the possession of its inheritance, which it receives as a gift from Yahweh; it is not a trophy of Israel's armed might (Dt 8:17 f). This gift comes from the initiative of Yahweh, who promised the land to them in their fathers, who did not possess the land, and consequently could not bequeath it. The analogy, however, is imperfect; there is no suggestion that the land comes to Israel by right, as an inheritance came to sons under the law. The concept of inheritance emphasizes the idea that the land is given, not acquired or merited.

B. NT. In the NT the object of inheritance is usually the kingdom* (1 Co 6:9 f; Gal 5:21); it is also salvation* (Heb 1:14), eternal life* (Tt 3:7), glory* (Rm 8:17), an incorruptible inheritance (1 Pt 1:4). The NT modifies the concept by introducing the idea of sonship, which is the normal correlative of inheritance. Christians inherit in virtue of their adoption* as sons and their union with Christ the true son and heir. Christ is the heir (Mt 21:38; Mk 12:7; Lk 20:14; Heb 1:2); the idea is not frequently expressed, but it is implicit in the development of the concept of inheritance. Inheritance follows the adoption of the Christian, and he becomes co-heir with Christ (Rm 8:17; Gal 3:29; 4:7). The inheritance is not limited to the Jews, the carnal descendants of the patriarchs, but is extended to the Gentiles through the Gospel (Eph 3:6; cf Heb 6:17).

The problem of the title of inheritance is discussed at length in Gal 3–4. The claims of the Jews, based on carnal descent, are negated by the basic title of Abraham to righteousness, which was his faith; there must have been something antecedent to carnal descent to establish the title. All those who share Abraham's faith share his righteousness and his promises. If the inheritance rests on the law* (as of right, Gal 3:18), then it does not rest on a promise. Faith, however, makes all men, not merely Jews, sons of God through their union with Christ in baptism (Gal 3:26–29). Now the heir, as long as he is a minor, is little better off than a slave, and so were the Jews under the law. The coming of the true son, Christ, is the hour of their majority and their liberation, which they realize only by union with the true son (Gal 4:1–7). Finally, Paul* emphasizes his point by the allegory of Sarah and Hagar; the natural son was the son of the slave, the son of the freewoman was the son of the promise. It was the son of the free woman who became the heir. The Christian receives his inheritance by rejecting the slavery of the law and accepting the liberty which Christ confers (Gal 4:21–5:1).

Ink (Hb $d^e y\bar{o}$, Gk *melan* [black]), mentioned in the Bible only in Je 36:18; 2 Co 3:3; 2 Jn 12; 3 Jn 13. Ancient ink was manufactured from carbon, probably obtained from soot, suspended in a solution of gum or glue. Ink was used in Egypt* before the 1st dynasty (2850 BC). Metallic ink does not appear before 400 BC; it was in common use in classical times. At the ruins of Qumran* inkpots with dried ink were found; the ink was a carbon product.

Inn. Inns or hotels for travelers in the modern sense did not exist in the ancient world. In the OT the inn is mentioned only in Je 41:17 (*gērût*); the text, however, is not certain. In the NT (Gk *kataluma*) it is mentioned at Bethlehem (Lk 2:7), as the place of the last supper of Jesus, and as the place where the Samaritan lodged the wounded traveler (Lk 10:35, Gk *pandocheion*). In these passages is no doubt signified a place similar to the more recent caravansary or *khan*. This is a large walled enclosure, open to the sky except around the inner walls, where a roof furnishes shelter from sun and rain. Cf MANGER.

Inspiration. In Catholic doctrine the Bible and tradition are the sources, written and oral, of revealed doctrine. Inspiration in general signifies the divine origin of the

Bible. We treat it under these heads: the belief in inspiration; the extent of inspiration; the theological theory of inspiration; inerrancy.

1. *The belief in inspiration.* The roots of the belief, which affect the form it later developed, lie in the Israelite belief in the inspiration of Moses*, of the prophets*, the authors of wisdom* literature, the priests* in giving priestly instruction. These differ in kind. Moses was the unique mediator who communicated the will of God to Israel. The prophet was one who spoke the word of the Lord. Wisdom was a gift of Yahweh. The priests continued in a derived manner the instructional office of Moses. Je 18:18 speaks of a triple charisma: the instruction of the priest, the counsel of the wise, and the word of the prophet.

Between 400 BC and AD 100 there appears in Judaism a firm belief in the divine origin of the sacred books. The rabbis attributed the highest grade of inspiration to the Pentateuch*, a lower grade to the Prophets, and a still lower grade to the Writings (cf CANON). Inspiration was understood as dictation by which God communicated the words of the text to the inspired writer. Hence in rabbinical discussions each verse is treated as a divine oracle which contained revelation, a peremptory argument to settle any dispute. One should distinguish between the belief of Judaism in the divine origin of their sacred books and the theory of verbal dictation.

The OT is cited or quoted in the NT about 350 times in such a way as to show that Jesus and the NT writers share the belief of Judaism in the divine origin and authority of the sacred books. The NT idea of inspiration is explicitly contained in 2 Tm 3:14–17 and 2 Pt 1:19–21. The text of 2 Tm is the source of the word *inspiration* in Christian theology; the word, however, is not explained, nor does it suggest the idea of verbal dictation. The text of 2 Pt deals explicitly with prophecy; the prophets are borne or carried by the Holy Spirit. This metaphor suggests the divine impulse and movement, but not the idea of verbal dictation.

The NT itself does not claim inspiration, nor can the development of this belief be traced. The early Church, however, believed that it had the charisma of prophecy which Israel had possessed (AA 2:16–20; 11:27; 13:1; 1 Co 12:28 f; 14:37; Eph 4:11).

The Fathers of the Church from the beginning accept the belief in the divine origin and authority of the Bible. Many use the word "dictate" to explain inspiration; the word is borrowed from Judaism, and many of the Fathers accepted the idea also. Other patristic formulae do not contain this implication: God is the author of the Bible; the human author is God's instrument; the Bible is the word of God. Patristic literature of the 2nd century begins to quote the NT as equal to the OT in authority; the belief cannot be traced, but its roots can be seen in the conception of apostolate (cf APOSTLE) and prophecy in the early Church.

The question of inspiration did not become an urgent theological problem in the Church until the 19th century, and no declaration of the Church touches the question of set purpose before the declaration of the Council of the Vatican in 1870. The Council declared that the Church accepts the sacred books not because they are approved by her authority, although of human origin, nor because they contain revelation free from error, but because God is their author through the inspiration of the Holy Spirit; the rejection of the divine inspiration of the Bible is condemned as formal heresy. The Council's declaration initiated vigorous theological discussions of the nature of inspiration (cf below); Leo XIII intervened in these in 1893 with the encyclical *Providentissimus Deus*, declaring that "God so moved the inspired writers by His supernatural operation that he incited them to write, and assisted them in their writing so that they correctly conceived, accurately wrote down and truthfully expressed all that He intended and only what He intended; and only thus can God be the author of the Bible." This affirmation that God is active as a principal cause in all the essential operations of the composition of a book laid down the lines upon which theological speculation since 1893 has operated.

2. *The extent of biblical inspiration.* Here we treat two questions: (a) How is it determined what books are inspired? (b) Are there any portions of the single books which are not affected by inspiration?

(a) Inspiration is not a fact of experience and cannot be attested from the form and character of the books themselves. The question became urgent with the Reformation. The Reformers, rejecting dogmatic tradition, could find no criterion except the inner testimony of the Spirit speaking to the reader. Search for a more objective criterion led many Protestant theologians to formulate a criterion based upon prophecy and apostleship. In modern scholarship the view of the literary origins of the books makes this theory difficult to defend. The Catholic Church has always maintained that no other criterion is possible except her own traditions, for there is no other medium through which revelation comes to man; and inspiration can be known only by divine revelation.

(b) Certain exegetical difficulties led some theologians to suggest that inspiration was not extended equally to all parts of the text. These theories generally took the form of affirming inspiration only of those parts of the text which contained revealed doctrine (Holden, 1662; Rohling, 1872; Newman, 1884), or which were revealed (Grotius), or of excluding things which seemed less important such as the quotations of the OT (Erasmus, 1536) or *obiter dicta* (Newman). These theories rightly emphasize the primacy of religion in the Bible, but they contain a false overidentification of religion with doctrine and ignore the principle of literary forms*. All such theories were expressly rejected by Leo XIII in *Providentissimus Deus*.

3. *The theological theory of inspiration.* The data of traditional belief in inspiration may be summed up in the elements of *inspiration, divine authorship,* and *the word of God*. These elements are not formally the same, and the difference may be seen in the proposition: Through *inspiration* God is the *author* of the Bible in such a way that the Bible is His *word*. Traditional belief did not explain the meaning of these elements, and it is the task of theology to explain them in an intelligible and doctrinally sound manner.

The rabbinical theory of verbal dictation was accepted by many of the Fathers and dominated both Catholic and Protestant theology down to the 19th century. This is a gross and mechanical conception which takes no account whatever of the differences in form and style in the sacred books. Some premature efforts of theologians to escape from verbal dictation were not well conceived. Leonard Lessius (1587) suggested that a book composed by human effort could become inspired by subsequent divine acceptance and approbation, and Sixtus of Siena (1575) affirmed that mere ecclesiastical approbation is sufficient; this theory was revived by Haneberg (1850) shortly before the Vatican Council. Jahn (early 19th century) suggested that inspiration consisted in the charisma of inerrancy. The opinions of Sixtus and Jahn were expressly rejected by the Vatican Council.

Recent theological opinion proceeded from the datum that inspiration consists in a positive divine influence upon the composition of the sacred books which is more than subsequent divine or ecclesiastical approbation or negative assistance against error. It also is aware of the bankruptcy of the theory of verbal dictation. From these discussions emerged the distinction between inspiration, which produces the sacred books, and revelation, which is the attestation of a truth by God. What is written by the inspired writer is revelation to the readers, but not necessarily revelation to the writer, who may acquire his knowledge in the normal human manner.

In 1870 Franzelin proposed a theory of revelation which distinguished the ideas of the Bible and their verbal formulation. Inspiration affects only the ideas, which are communicated to the writer through revelation or "suggestion" of ideas which he already possesses. The verbal formulation is left to the writer with no divine influence except negative assistance against error. Theologians have criticized the system for its introduction of a distinction between articulate and inarticulate thought which cannot be justified by modern psychology. Furthermore, the recent study of literary forms makes it difficult to divorce form and content in this way. The theory also takes no account of the fact that much of the content of the Bible cannot be reduced to doctrinal ideas; it expresses hopes, fears, desires, anger and other similar psychological processes which are not dialectical. Finally, the theory seems to be reduced to verbal dictation applied to the ideas instead of the words and the addition of negative assistance for the words.

M.-J. Lagrange in 1895–1896 proposed a theory which has been widely accepted. Instead of the idea of *author*, which Franzelin took as his basic principle, Lagrange built upon the idea of *inspiration*. The cooperation of God and the human writer is to be understood as a cooperation of principal and instrumental causality. In the Thomistic understanding of instrumental causality this is the only cooperation of causes in which each cause is a cause of the total effect. The instrumental cause possesses its own proper virtue, but it attains the effect through its application and elevation by the virtue of the principal cause. God therefore assumes the entire man as a concrete reality with his date and situation in history, his personality, his habits of thought and speech. Assumption by the principal cause changes none of these, but simply applies them to the end intended. The instrumental virtue of the man is his capacity to write a book. Since the whole man is assumed as he is, the book which he produces is his and not another's. Lagrange and others have added St. Thomas's concept of "prophetic illumination," which aids the prophet to understand the truth which he expresses, whether this truth be revealed or learned by experience. This illumination is conceived as a distinct movement upon the powers of understanding which makes possible an insight above the natural conditions of these powers. The assumption, which is total, also moves the appetitive and executive powers; thus in the theory of Lagrange the verbal expression is no less inspired than the conception of ideas. This understanding of "verbal inspiration" is not to be confused with the antiquated theory of "verbal dictation."

More recent writers have refined the theory further. P. Benoit observed that the problem of the writer is not a problem of understanding but a problem of communication. Hence precisely the "prophetic illumination" as it touches the inspired writer is not a speculative but a practical movement enabling the writer to choose the form and style best suited to his purpose. The charisma of inspiration he places in the illumination of the practical judgment of what is to be written. Benoit is the first to examine the problem in the light of what is now known about the complex literary processes by which the books of the Bible were produced. The illumination of the practical judgment affects all who contributed to the production of the inspired text in proportion to their part in its production. "Author" and "book" are modern conceptions which cannot be transferred to the ancient world.

Karl Rahner has further suggested that the charisma of inspiration was one of the unique elements of the primitive Church which did not pass on to subsequent generations. It is the Church which wrote the NT rather than individual writers. B. Brinkmann has further suggested that this charisma was a part of the apostolic office, understanding here apostles and their intimate associates.

Theologians generally agree that the theory of inspiration is incomplete in many respects. The bookish character of the theory, which understands "author" and "book" in the modern sense, has not been sufficiently eliminated even after Benoit's work. Few biblical books have a single author, and most of them are anonymous; they are the term of a long process of development. Many, if not most of the biblical books were composed and transmitted orally; it seems unrealistic to speak of a charisma of inspiration which affects only the *writing* of such books. Future studies will no doubt emphasize the social character of inspiration, which will be conceived in accordance with the social character of ancient literary composition. The early writer or speaker did not consider himself an individual artist but a spokesman of the society for which and in which he spoke. In some sense Israel and the Church must be conceived as the real authors of the Bible. Each executed its work through those who were regarded in some sense as its represen-

tatives: priests, prophets, scribes, wise men in the OT, and apostles in the NT.

4. *Inerrancy.* Inerrancy has never been the object of an ecclesiastical definition, but it has been so long and so clearly believed in the Church that theologians regard it as an article of faith. The conception of inerrancy, which is a corollary of inspiration, depends on the conception of inspiration, which is somewhat complex. A fundamentalist understanding of inerrancy is indefensible. Certain exegetical difficulties led modern theologians to attempt to formulate a more accurate conception of inerrancy; many of these theories were premature and not well conceived. Lenormant (1880) proposed that Gn expresses truths through myths which are false. Di Bartolo (1889) and Didiot (1891) limited the inerrancy of the Bible to matters of faith and morals, like the infallibility of the Church. D'Hulst (1893) distinguishes between revelation, which is infallible and deals with faith and morals, and inspiration, which is not infallible. Loisy (1892) proposed a theory of "relative truth;" there is no absolute truth, but propositions which are true only within their historical and cultural context. Zanecchia (1903) employed the words "relative truth" in a different sense: the concepts of one culture are not those of another culture.

These theories were attempts to refine the concept of inerrancy according to modern historical and natural science, which makes it impossible to defend a homogeneous oracular infallibility of the Bible. Modern exegesis does not seek such a simple and comprehensive formula but thinks that each problem must be solved in its own context. Certain general principles, however, have emerged from exegetical studies which govern the treatment of these problems.

(a) The words of the Bible are always true in the sense which the human author conveys by them, and only in this sense. One must master the patterns and speech of the biblical writers before one can be sure of what this sense is.

(b) One must distinguish the fallible man from the infallible writer. The man may have erroneous beliefs which will certainly betray themselves at times. Inerrancy means that these are not affirmed, not that they are imperceptible.

(c) Inerrancy must be understood in terms of customary human linguistic usage. The Bible uses popular nontechnical language, figures of speech, paradox, approximation, telescoped narrative, nonchronological narrative, inexact quotations, folklore, legend, myth.

(d) Inerrancy must take account of the Oriental mind and of the character of the

Semitic languages. The Oriental mind is not metaphysical or dialectic; Hebrew cannot express sustained abstract thought and subtle distinctions; its propositions have all the same grammatical weight and are not nuanced.

(e) Inerrancy must be conceived in terms of literary forms.

(f) Inerrancy must be conceived in terms of the personal style of the writers.

(g) The writer does not always intend to speak of things as they are in themselves. Thus things are described according to their external appearance, common inaccurate designations are used, advice is given which is valid only in a particular context, the *argumentum ad hominem* is employed — in a word, all the realities of common discourse appear.

The difficulties raised against inerrancy from the natural sciences show that the language of the Bible is unscientific and that its conceptions of physical realities are those of its times. We now see that "scientific truth" and "scientific error" are modern conceptions; neither appears in the Bible, which makes no "scientific" assertion of any kind, true or false.

The difficulties raised against inerrancy are met in terms of literary forms and the ancient conception of history* and historical writing.

Interpretation. The science of biblical interpretation is usually known technically as *exegesis* (Gk *exēgēsis*, explanation). Exegesis is the investigation of the meaning of the biblical text. Its practice is governed by a set of general principles called *hermeneutics* (Gk *hermēneutikē*, interpretation). This article is a summary of hermeneutics and includes an explanation of what is understood by the *meaning* of the Bible and the methods which are employed to ascertain its meaning.

The meaning of the text must be studied with respect to the twofold authorship of the Bible, divine and human (cf INSPIRATION). The two authors of the book cooperate to produce a single text with a single meaning; the twofold authorship does not and cannot imply a twofold meaning. Hence what God means in the Bible can be investigated only by discovering what the human author means, since God does not make His meaning known except through the human writer. The twofold authorship, however, has in the course of biblical study been responsible for a large number of meanings attributed to the Bible. It is now apparent that these must be reduced to a single meaning unless one wishes to incur the danger of breaking down communications. This single meaning is called *literal*.

The *literal* meaning is simply the meaning which in all human speech is communicated by words arranged in sentences and larger units of discourse according to usage. The name *literal*, which was coined in the patristic age, is not altogether felicitous, since it implies in modern usage an opposition to metaphorical. As we point out below, *literal* here is not opposed to metaphorical or figurative, but to *typical* or *spiritual*. Since common usage permits one to express his meaning by the use of figures of speech, the *literal* meaning of the Bible is communicated by such figures. The figurative diction of the Bible is that of the ancient Near East and not the diction of modern speech; hence it is sometimes obscure to modern readers. No figured expression is of itself alien to the literal meaning of the Bible.

The *consequent* meaning of the Bible is a conclusion derived from the literal meaning of the Bible, by the combination of biblical propositions with propositions drawn from nonbiblical senses. Such a meaning is only virtually present in the Bible, not formally; that is, the writer does not intend to communicate it by the language which he employs. The fact that God knows all the implications of speech does not alter the laws of human speech which He employs as a means of communication.

Many modern Catholic writers have introduced what is called a *fuller* meaning of the Bible. Those who propose this meaning are not in perfect agreement on its explanation. In general they base their hypothesis upon the twofold authorship of the Bible, admitting that it is sometimes possible that God intends to communicate more than the text, taken according to usage, could be understood to communicate. This meaning cannot be grasped from the text in question but only from some other text or from a declaration of the Church that the text does contain a meaning fuller than the literal meaning. Other scholars believe that this hypothesis either imperils communication or that it is an unnecessarily complicated statement of the truth that the meaning of the whole Bible is greater than the meaning of any single passage.

The terms *spiritual* meaning and *typical* meaning are used in modern writing with some ambiguity. Pius XII (*Divino Afflante Spiritu*) used the term *spiritual* of a sense which has generally been called *typical* (cf TYPE). In the writings of the Fathers the term spiritual (*pneumatic*) is used in opposition to literal (*somatic*) and *psychic* (difficult to explain, but perhaps best paraphrased by *inner*). The distinction is based on the Pauline trichotomy of the Christian: body, soul, and spirit. One's power to understand the meaning of the Bible is determined by one's degree of advancement in Christian perfection. The somatic meaning is superficial and can be grasped even by the unbeliever. The psychic meaning can be grasped by the less advanced Christian. The spiritual meaning can be grasped by the perfect Christian. In modern literature the term spiritual meaning is used generally of an insight into the meaning of the Bible which gives a more profound understanding of Christian doctrine and of its application to Christian life. Often it is used of meanings which are not expressed by the text of the Bible in any sense. As a term to designate the understanding of the *fullness* of the meaning of the Bible as a whole the term is less apt. It is frequently difficult to distinguish the spiritual meaning of the Bible, as proposed in modern literature, from the *accommodated* meaning of the Bible; this is the application of the text of the Bible to persons or events which have some resemblance with the persons and events of the biblical text. Accommodation is found in the NT, frequently in ecclesiastical documents and in the liturgy, and very often in some writings of the Fathers, where it is clearly called the *spiritual* meaning of the Bible. Such accommodation, however, is not an interpretation of the Bible, but an allusive use of the Bible in the exposition of Christian doctrine.

The Investigation of the Literal Meaning. Catholic exegetes admit a twofold interpretation of the literal meaning based on the twofold authorship of the Bible. The Bible is a part of the public revelation committed to the Church, and as such it is subject to the *authentic* interpretation of the Church as the ultimate authority. As a document of human authorship it is subject to *scientific* interpretation, which applies to the text the laws of human discourse. No true conflict can arise between the two interpretations, since the Bible has a single meaning; but conflicts can arise because of the imperfect understanding of the text. The technique of scientific interpretation is called *grammatico-historical* interpretation.

Grammatico-historical interpretation proceeds first from a study of the language in which the text is written and employs lexica and grammars which contain the material collected on the usage of the language to be studied. The individual interpreter must control this information by personal familiarity with the language. The study of the Bible is supplemented by the study of the ancient versions* which are early witnesses of the understanding of the text as well as of its form. In modern times the knowledge of languages of the Bible is enlarged by extensive literature in the cognate languages, such as Akkadian* and Ugaritic*, which add lexicographical and grammatical information.

Meaning is conveyed not by single words, as a general rule, but by larger units of discourse. The minimal unit is the sentence, which again is rarely a complete utterance (cf WISDOM) but is a part of a larger complete unit. This complete unit is the vehicle of meaning. One of the most important and valuable contributions of modern exegesis to the study of the Bible is the identification and definition of various forms of discourse (cf LITERARY FORMS) and the style proper to each. These units of discourse cannot be understood in the abstract nor in the context of modern western literary forms; the forms of the Bible belong to ancient Near Eastern culture, and must therefore be studied in themselves and in comparison with the forms of other Near Eastern literature, with which they have numerous points of contact. This study was explicitly encouraged by Pius XII (*Divino Afflante Spiritu*), who affirmed that an understanding of the Bible is impossible without such comparative studies.

Each literary unit arises in a definite historical and geographical and cultural milieu, and the understanding of its meaning is attained only by knowledge of the usages which prevail in the milieu. Since most biblical books are anonymous, knowledge of the person of the writer is usually not available; but modern scholars can identify passages which come from certain individuals or groups and can reconstruct to a large extent the characteristic patterns of thought and speech of the individual or group.

The unity of any given context is a unity of subject and of the development of discourse. In the Bible, which is literature of the ancient East, this unity is not the same as the unity of literary discourse with which western readers are familiar. The ancient Semitic peoples did not express themselves in the logical discourse with which we are familiar. Their concepts and their expression are much more simple and much less precise than the concepts and expressions of modern speech. In poetry and in high impassioned prose the unity of the context is often rather a unity of mood than a unity of subject. The development of the discourse may proceed by mere association — verbal, temporal, local.

Authentic interpretation can be given only by the teaching authority of the Church. The actual definition of the meaning of a passage is extremely rare in ecclesiastical teaching; no more than four or five such texts can be adduced, and it may be doubted that in these there is more than a negative definition, i.e., the denial that the passage can be understood in a heretical sense. The effect of authentic interpretation is much more extensive in certain general rules derived from the teaching of the Church which govern Catholic interpretation.

(1) The inspired writer teaches nothing erroneous. This is not limited to religious and doctrinal passages. Where difficulties arise they are to be solved by investigating more exactly the meaning of the text.

(2) The unity of the Bible must be maintained so that no contradiction between its various parts may be admitted. Here also difficulties may arise; they are to be solved by a more profound understanding of the development of biblical belief, or by more complete information concerning the course of biblical history.

(3) No contradiction may be admitted between the Bible and the certain conclusions of the profane sciences. It is now realized that the Bible is not a "scientific" document and that its popular language has no reference to modern scientific formulations.

(4) The Bible is to be understood according to the analogy of faith. This principle seems vague but is of wide practical importance. It does not mean that one is to find propositions of the articles of faith where they do not exist. It is rather an understanding of the Bible which arises from an understanding of the whole of the Christian fact in its development and its completion, in virtue of which the interpreter recognizes by a habitual insight how the meaning of the Bible in a particular context is in harmony with the stages of the total revelation.

Irad (Hb *irad,* etymology and meaning unknown), in the genealogy of Cain* the son of Enoch* and the father of Mehujael (Gn 4:18). On the parallelism between Irad and Jared* in the genealogy of Seth* cf PATRIARCHS.

Iron. Although iron is the most common metal in nature, the Iron Age in the ancient Near East begins only in the 2nd half of the 2nd millennium BC. Archaeological remains show that the metal was known and worked before this date; but the technical difficulties of working it were not solved well enough before this date to make the metal practical for common use. The Hb word for iron, *barzel* (Akkadian *parzillu*) suggests by its character that it is, like the metal itself, of foreign origin; but the etymology of the word is not known. Small iron objects appear in predynastic times in Egypt and in the 3rd millennium BC in Mesopotamia and Asia Minor. The rarity and the size of these objects suggest that the iron of which they were made was acciden-

tally discovered or produced. In Egypt the percentage of nickel in the iron objects indicates that they were made of meteoric iron; the Egyptian name for iron means "metal from heaven." Iron was a rare metal in Hammurabi's* time (1728–1686) and was exchanged for silver at the proportion of 1:8. Iron becomes much more plentiful after 1400 BC. Although there is no apodictic proof, the evidence indicates that the technique of working iron was originated in Asia Minor in the Hittite* Empire. The Hittites exercised a monopoly of the making and merchandising of iron for a short period, very probably in order to maintain an advantage in the quality of military weapons. When the Hittite Empire crumbled under the irruptions of the Sea Peoples after 1200 BC, the use of the metal became widely diffused throughout the ancient Near East. In Assyria* iron was common after the beginning of the 9th century. Egypt was the last of the regions of the Fertile Crescent to enter the Iron Age; the technique of working iron did not reach Egypt until the 7th century, after which the use of iron became common.

Technical difficulties retarded the development of iron. Copper can be hammered cold, but iron had to await the accidental discovery that it is malleable only when it is red-hot. The variety of impurities in iron ore made it impossible to develop a universally valid technique; apparently each ironsmith had to learn the tricks of his trade by trial and error. The production, of which little is known, seems to have followed the lines of primitive production as known elsewhere. The ore was preroasted to remove some impurities and then smelted and fused in a furnace. This produced a spongy lump of metal called a bloom which was then worked in the forge and cut and hammered into the desired shapes. Only wrought iron was known in the ancient world; the furnace could not produce a sufficiently high temperature for the manufacture of cast iron. "The early wrought iron, on account of the way it was made, would contain little or no carbon (less than 0.2 percent) and such iron is not hardened but softened if heated and suddenly cooled; but with an increase in the proportion of carbon present, this property of being hardened is acquired, and it is this higher proportion of carbon (from 0.2 percent to not more than 2.0 percent), with the resultant virtue it imparts, that constitutes the difference between wrought iron and steel, steel being iron containing small proportions of added carbon (the carbon content of the ordinary modern product ranging from about 0.7 percent to 1.7 percent) that imparts to it the property mentioned, and iron only became a thoroughly serviceable metal for weapons and tools after the discovery of the method (for a long time purely empirical and without any understanding of the underlying principle) of adding a little carbon (carburizing, it is termed) so that when heated and suddenly cooled (quenched) it became hardened. This result may have been brought about by allowing the iron to remain in contact with carbon at a high temperature for some time, when a certain small proportion of the carbon is absorbed by the iron, the amount depending upon the length of time the two are kept in contact, being greatest at the surface and gradually lessening toward the center. At one time a process (called the cementation process) employed for making steel, which is still used to some extent, was to pack the iron in charcoal and heat it strongly for several days. Such a considered method, however, is a comparatively late invention, but a similar result can be brought about by the frequent heating and reheating of iron in a charcoal fire, and this must have been the method practiced anciently, probably an outcome of the hammering and reheating necessary to free the lumps of iron at first produced" (A. Lucas, *Ancient Egyptian Materials and Industries*, pp. 274–275).

The principal ore deposits of the ancient world lay in Egypt (these were never worked), between the Lebanon* and the Anti-Lebanon (some scholars doubt that these were worked), Syria, Cyprus, the Aegean islands, and in abundance in Asia Minor, Armenia, Caucasia, and Persia. There are some deposits in eastern Palestine; but Dt 8:9 can refer only to the ore deposits of Edom*. On the Israelite mining and smelting operations in Edom cf EZION-GEBER. Iron in all probability was introduced into Canaan by the Philistines; in the time of Samuel the Philistines permitted no ironsmith in Israel and compelled the Israelites to bring their tools to Philistine smiths for sharpening (1 S 13:19 ff). This effectively prevented the Israelites from producing iron weapons. The Canaanites had at least iron chariots (Jos 17:16; Jgs 1:19; 4:3). Iron became common in Israel after the Philistine power was broken by David. The texts and the archaeological remains show that iron was used for arms, tools, griddles, gate-bars, plow-points, threshing-sledges, and armor*. The smelting furnace is a common metaphor for foreign oppression (Dt 4:20; 1 K 8:51; Je 11:4). The iron from the N (Je 15:12) may be iron from Asia Minor; the text suggests that this was metal of superior quality. The altar stones were not to be hewn with iron (Jos 8:31). This prohibition was not directed against iron as such, but against the working of the native stone (cf ALTAR).

Irrigation. Cf WATER.

Isaac (Hb *yiṣḥāḳ*, "he laughs," to which a divine name was probably originally attached), the son of Abraham* and Sarah* and father of Esau* and Jacob*. In the present text the name is explained by more than one popular etymology; it is connected with the laughter of Abraham (Gn 17:17 f) and Sarah (Gn 18:11–15) at the promise of a son in their old age, and with the "laughing-stock" which Sarah becomes at the birth of the son (Gn 21:6). It is probable that the word *ṣāḥaḳ*, used of the behavior of Ishmael* toward the infant Isaac, is also an allusion to the name; the word means not only laugh but play, and possibly in this context suggests obscene play. Isaac was a son of promise* and the bearer of the covenant* (Gn 17:19–21; 18:14). On the sacrifice of Isaac cf ABRAHAM. Abraham sent his slave to procure a wife for his son from his kinsmen, and the slave brought Rebekah* the daughter of Bathuel and the sister of Laban* (Gn 24). Rebekah bore Isaac twin sons, Esau and Jacob (Gn 25:19–26).

The only stories of Isaac which are not really stories either about his father or about his sons occur in Gn 26; and these on examination are evidently imitations of the stories of Abraham. Thus the story of Isaac, Rebekah, and Abimelech (Gn 26:1–11) is an imitation of Gn 12:10–20 and 20:1–18, even to the name of Abimelech. The story of the covenant with Abimelech at Beer-sheba is likewise an imitation of Gn 21:22–34 (where there are two accounts of Abraham's covenant with Abimelech at Beersheba). This leaves only the quarrels about the wells (Gn 26:12–22); but cf Gn 21:25 ff. The blessing of Jacob is a story which has Jacob as its protagonist. The death and burial of Isaac are related in Gn 35:27–29. Isaac thus appears to be a shadowy figure, and it seems quite probable that the original information contained about him in tradition was purely genealogical; this gap was filled by the composition of anecdotes about Isaac which attached to him adventures similar to those related of Abraham. Isaac remains a shadowy figure in the OT, mentioned most frequently with Abraham and Jacob; the use of his name as a title of Israel (Am 7:9, 16) is extremely rare. In the poem of the praise of the fathers (BS 44:22) he is merely mentioned by name. Paul makes of Isaac a type of the Gentile Christian community (Rm 9:7; Gal 4:28–31) in that Isaac was a son not merely by carnal descent but by promise. All who by faith like Abraham's accept the promises are true sons of Abraham and heirs of the promises; those who are carnally descended but refuse the promises are expelled like Ishmael.

Isaiah (Hb *yᵉšaʻyāhû*, "Yahweh" is salvation").

1. The prophet to whom the canonical book of Isaiah is attributed. The name in the same form or in the alternate form *yᵉšaʻyāh* is borne by several others in the OT. Nothing is known of the life of Isaiah except what is found in the book. He lived in Jerusalem and his prophetic activity extended at least from 742 to 701 BC. He was the son of Amoz and was married; two sons, Shear-jashub* and Maher-shalal-hashbaz*, are mentioned in the book. Most commentators think that his easy contacts with the court indicate that he was a member of an aristocratic family. A legend in the apocryphal* *Martyrdom of Isaiah* that he was sawn asunder in the reign of Manasseh* is historically worthless. The stirring events which occurred during his career give his discourses a political and supranational scope. He was a contemporary of the Assyrian conquest of western Asia under Tiglath-pileser* III, Shalmaneser* V, Sargon*, and Sennacherib*. Cf also AHAZ; DAMASCUS; HEZEKIAH; SAMARIA.

2. *Book of Isaiah.* Most of the book of Isaiah does not come from the prophet Isaiah, and even those discourses which are his come in the reports of those who wrote them down from audition or from memory (cf PROPHECY, PROPHET). The book is a compendium of many types of prophecy from diverse periods; this is shown in detail in the analysis which follows. It is a "collection of collections." The book existed in its present form by the time of Ben Sira* (180 BC, BS 48:24 f), and the Qumran* scroll of Isaiah, probably from the 2nd century BC, has the contents of the present book. The book is easily divided into two major parts, 1–39 and 40–66. The analysis given below further divides these parts.

3. *Analysis of Contents.*

I. 1–39.

(1) 1–12: oracles concerning Judah and Jerusalem. 1:1 is intended as a title of the whole collection, which probably included no more than chs 1–35 when the title was appended. The two doxologies in ch 12 appended by an editor mark the end of the first collection. 1:1 now serves as a preface to the collection; it is composed of detached sayings: 1:2–3, ingratitude of Israel; 1:4–9, national disaster (probably the Assyrian invasion of 701); 1:10–17, superstitious cult; 1:18–20, Judah's profound guilt and Yahweh's forgiveness; 1:21–26, lamentation for Jerusalem; 27–31, fragmentary sayings on salvation and judgment (possibly not original).

2–4: the title in 2:1 indicates a smaller collection. 2:2–4, the messianic peace (duplicated in Mi 4:1–4, probably an anonymous piece included in both books); 2:5, liturgical invocation added to verses 2–4; 2:6–21, the day of Yahweh against the proud; 2:22, added wisdom saying; 3:1–15, the failure of leadership in Jerusalem; 3:16–4:1, the frivolous women of Zion; 4:2–6, Yahweh's protection of Zion, probably added by the editor. This probably concludes the collection of 2–4.

5:1–7, song of the vineyard; 5:8–24, the six woes, belongs with 10:1–4, the seventh woe (the passage has been disturbed by the insertion of the collection 6:1–9:6); 5:25–30 follows 9:7–20 (cf below).

6:1–9:6, "the book of Emmanuel." 6:1–13, the inaugural vision (this must have stood at the beginning of the first collection; it is dated 742); 7:1–9, the necessity of faith* (the Syro-Ephraimite war, 735); 7:10–17, the sign of Emmanuel*; 7:18–25 (placed here in association with the gloss "the king of Assyria" at the end of 17), detached threats of Assyrian invasion; 8:1–4, the sign of Maher-shalal-hash-baz*; 8:5–15, against Ahaz's policy of seeking the help of Assyria; 8:16–23, resolution to preserve his teaching among the disciples (contaminated in 21–23 by the addition of a fragment of another saying which is almost unintelligible); 9:1–6, the heir of David (cf MESSIAH). The collection belongs to the period of 735.

9:7–20, the plagues (notice the refrain); 10:1–4, concludes 5:8–24; 5:25–30, concludes 9:7–20 (the refrain of 10:4b belongs with this passage); 10:5–19 and 10:24–34, various sayings against Assyria (probably to be dated in 701); 10:20–23, predictions of deliverance and of judgment, probably placed here because of their similarity with the context, but doubtfully from Isaiah; 11:1–9, the scion of Jesse (cf MESSIAH; the authorship of Isaiah is doubted by many critics, and since its point of view, e.g., "stump of Jesse," is different from that of 9:1–6, it should be placed late in the Prophet's life); 11:10–16, joined by the gloss of 10 to the preceding, the return of the exiled Israelites (therefore exilic).

The material of these early collections is to be placed, with the exceptions noted, in the early years of Isaiah.

(2) 13–23, a collection of "oracles against the nations," each preceded by Hb *massā'* (Eng versions "burden," literally "utterance"). Their position in the middle of Is 1–33 is similar to the position of parallel oracles in

Jeremiah* and Ezekiel*. 13, an oracle against Babylon from the 6th century; 14:1–2, the restoration of Israel, a later composition; 14:3–21, taunt-song against the king of Babylon from the 6th century; 22–23, prose addition, the destruction of Babylon; 14:24–27, threat against Assyria (probably 701); 14:28–32, threat against Philistia* (dated 715); 15–16, Moab* (probably not from Isaiah, but can be given no definite date; partly reproduced in Je 48:29 ff); 17:1–11, Damascus* and Israel (the period of the Syro-Ephraimite war, 735); 12–14, "many peoples" (probably Assyria, 701); 18, Ethiopia* (713 or 705, when an embassy from Ethiopia was in Jerusalem to negotiate an alliance against Assyria); 19:1–15 (poem) and 19:16–25 (prose), Egypt (almost all critics believe 19:16–25 is later than Isaiah, many think the poem is also later; the universalism of 19:18–25 is remarkable); 20, the only symbolic action of Isaiah, dated 711; 21:1–10, "the desert of the sea," probably Babylon (later than Isaiah); 21:11–12, "Dumah," to be read Edom* (later than Isaiah); 22:1–14, "the valley of vision," i.e., Jerusalem (its presence in this collection is due to a careless collector who noticed only the title; probably 701, damning the frivolous irreligious joy of the people at escaping destruction by the Assyrians); 22:15–25, Shebna* and Eliakim*, officers of Hezekiah* (probably collected with 22:1–14 and therefore included here); 23, Tyre* (later than Isaiah, of uncertain date, possibly combines two utterances, one against Tyre and one against Sidon*, cf 2 and 12; glossed in 13 by an editor who attributed it to Isaiah).

(3) 24–27, the apocalypse of Isaiah. The collection is not a single composition; modern critics distinguish eschatological prophecies and songs interspersed among the prophecies. Prophecies: 24:1–3, 13, 17–23 (the destruction of the world); 25:6–8, the eschatological banquet; 27:1, destruction of the world powers; 27:6, 12–13, restoration of the exiled Israelites. Songs: 24:4–6, the corruption of the earth; 24:7–9, the failure of wine; 24:10–11, fall of the city of chaos (probably no definite city is meant); 24:14–16, hymn of the redeemed; 25:1–5, hymn to Yahweh; 25:9–12, hymn to Yahweh who protects Zion and destroys Moab; 26:1–6, hymn to Yahweh, who destroys the city of the world and builds the city of righteousness; 26:7–19, lamentation of the righteous for deliverance from their tribulations; 26:20–21, response of Yahweh, promising them deliverance from the impending end-catastrophe; 27:2–5, hymn in which Yahweh calls Judah his true vineyard; 27:7–11, reflections: Yahweh spares Israel if they forsake idolatry.

It is generally accepted by critics that this collection is not the work of Isaiah. Apocalyptic* literature is a later appearance in biblical and extrabiblical literature; neither the contents (cf below, theology) nor the style bears a resemblance to the thought and expression of Isaiah. There is no agreement on the date which should be assigned the collection except that it belongs to the postexilic period.

(4) 28–33. A second collection (after 1–12) of Isaiah's sayings. 28–31 are called the Assyrian cycle and come from the period 705–701, when Isaiah exerted all his influence in an unsuccessful attempt to divert Hezekiah from taking part in the rebellion against Assyria. These sayings are interspersed with brief messianic sayings which are generally not the work of Isaiah. 28:1–4, against Israel (probably 735); 28:5–6, Yahweh the crown of His people (not from Isaiah, placed here by the catchword); 28:7–22, against priests, prophets, and politicians; 23–29, wisdom reflections (Yahweh acts like the wise farmer); 29:1–8 threat against Jerusalem (Ariel) with promise of ultimate escape (the two passages may have been originally separate); 29:10–12, spiritual blindness; 29:13–14, hypocritical worship; 29:15–16, the all-powerful plan of Yahweh; 29:17–24, restoration of the land (later than Isaiah); 30:1–8, against Egypt (which promised assistance in the rebellion); 30:8–14, the unbelief of Judah; 30:15–17, false security of Judah; 30:18–26, riches of the messianic period (later than Isaiah); 30:27–33, threat against Assyria; 31:1–3, against Egypt; 31:4–5, 8–9, defeat of Assyria (interrupted by 6–7, against idolatry, later than Isaiah); 32:1–8, the righteous king and noble rulers (by most critics regarded as not from Isaiah, because of general terms and conception different from 9:1 ff; not clearly a reference to the messianic king); 32:9–14, the women of Jerusalem (regarded by some critics as not from Isaiah); 32:15–20, the messianic peace (later than Isaiah); 33, probably a prophetic liturgy in which prophetic utterances are interspersed among liturgical songs; 1, woe; 2, lamentation; 3–6, prophetic utterance; 7–9, lamentation; 10–13, oracle; 14a, prophetic utterance; 14b–16, torah-liturgy; 17–24, prophetic utterance (probably postexilic).

(5) 34–35. 34:1–4, destruction of the nations; 34:5–17, destruction of Edom*; 35:1–10, the regeneration of the desert as a highway for the redeemed. These poems are written in the spirit and the style of Is 40–66, which they probably imitate; cf below.

(6) 36–39, historical appendix; taken from 2 K 18:13–20:19, with the addition of the psalm of Hezekiah (38:9–20) and the important omission of 2 K 18:14–16 (cf

HEZEKIAH). 36:1–37:38, Sennacherib* before Jerusalem; 38:1–9, the illness and recovery of Hezekiah; 38:9–20, psalm of Hezekiah; 39:1–8, embassy of Merodach-baladan*. On the historical background and problems of these chapters cf HEZEKIAH. The oracle of Hezekiah (37:21–35) is widely accepted as genuine by modern critics, at least as in harmony with other pronouncements against Assyria, although its present form may represent the work of disciples of Isaiah.

The addition of these excerpts from 2 K matches the excerpts from the same book at the end of Je and comes from a desire to have all the material about the prophet in a single collection. This addition was earlier than the addition of 40–66.

The compilation of the various collections of 1–39 is a complex process which can be recovered only by conjecture. A. Weiser suggests: 6:1–9:6 and 28–31 from Isaiah himself or his time; 2–4 + 5 + 9:7–11:9 (in some way interrupted by 6:1–9:6), the original pieces in 13–23, collected by Isaiah's disciples; assembling of 1–12 and 13–23 by addition of other pieces thought similar in style and content; interspersing of prophetic promises into 28–31 and addition of 34–35; addition of 24–27; addition of 36–39. The collection by the disciples of Isaiah and their successors was intended to represent not so much a single prophet as a school of prophecy which was derived from Isaiah (cf PROPHECY). Hence despite the diversity of origin it is possible with only a few reservations to speak of the theology of Is 1–39.

Theology. If any idea can be called basic in the theology of Isaiah, it is his conception of the holiness* of Yahweh, which is the theme of the inaugural vision (6:1 ff): the physical and moral transcendence which makes Yahweh "wholly other" than man. This is reflected in Yahweh's abomination of sin and superstition (1:15 ff), the fear which He inspires (8:13), His anger (9:7 ff), His supreme power (31:1–3). It is at the basis of the plan of God, which is so different from the plans of men that they cannot understand it (28:21, 23–29; 29:14). For this is a second basic idea in Isaiah, that God has a plan by which He governs the course of events and brings them to a term set by Himself. This plan can be frustrated by no human effort (8:10; 10:6–7; 30:1; 31:1). The plan is achieved by the activity of Yahweh in events (9:10 f; 7:18–20; 10:5 f); He and not human agents is responsible for the course which events take. The only proper response of man to the plan and activity of God is faith (7:9; 28:16; 30:15), by which Isaiah means an acceptance of the plan of Yahweh and of His power and will to execute it. The

genuinity of faith is shown by a refusal to place reliance upon human means, and it is unbelief to think that these means can deliver (7:10–13; 8:6; 28:15; 30:1–3; 31:1–3). This faith is a complete surrender to the plan and to the wisdom of Yahweh. It involves a rejection of political means, and Isaiah tried unsuccessfully to bring the kingdom of Judah to manage its foreign affairs by faith and not by policy. The refusal of faith becomes in Isaiah the basic sin: the nonrecognition of the reality and activity of Yahweh (5:18 f; 7:10–13; 8:6, 14; 10:15; 29:9–12; 30:8–11). From such practical unbelief flow all other vices, individual and social, which Isaiah saw in the society of his time.

The plan of Yahweh has a twofold term, distinguished according to the response of men to it: it is judgment or salvation. Judgment appears in such events as the vindication of Yahweh against human pride in the Day* of Yahweh (2:6 ff) and His visitation upon sin (3:8 f; 5:8–24; 10:16 f). The salvation described by Isaiah is distinguished by the important place assigned to the scion of David (9:1 ff; 11:1 ff; cf MESSIAH). Many passages added by the disciples present salvation as a reign of peace, enlarging upon the effects of the attributes of the Davidic ruler (2:1–4; 4:2–6; 28:5 f; 29:17–24; 30:18–26; 32:15–20).

The idea of a "remnant" of Israel is characteristic of Isaiah and his school (4:3; 7:3; 10:20 ff; 11:11, 16; 28:5; cf SHEAR-JASHUB). Outside of the name of Isaiah's son, Shear-jashub, most of the passages come from the school of Isaiah, and here they appear as a promise of certain survival of at least a few from the crisis of Israel's history. The maxim "a remnant will return" (the meaning of Shear-jashub) seems to be studiously ambiguous. That a remnant will survive is a threat as well as a promise; cf e.g., 6:13; Am 3:12. But the maxim does express Isaiah's assurance that Israel would not entirely perish. This assurance is probably the key to what some have called a change in his attitude toward the threat of Assyria. In the early passages of the book Assyria is a threat, an instrument through which Yahweh punishes the sins of Israel (10:5 ff). In the crisis of 701, however, Isaiah assures the men of Judah, still unregenerate as far as we know, that the danger will not strike them. It must be admitted that Isaiah did not, like Jeremiah*, envisage the total destruction of Israel as a nation; this was a later development of prophetic insight. But while his attitude did change, it was not a reversal of his prophetic affirmation of the necessity of repentance. He did not utter threat and promise in the same oracle. It is quite possible that the discourses come from two different campaigns in 701 and 691 (cf HEZEKIAH). Nor could Judah be said to have experienced a deliverance which left it unpunished when we recall Sennacherib's report that he sacked 46 cities and looted the country for heavy tribute; while he did not take Jerusalem, he reduced Judah to a state of vassalage which endured 75 years. The "rod of God's anger" had done its work. But the nation did not perish. That Isaiah did not see it perish in this instance is not a sufficient reason to affirm that he believed in its indestructibility, although it is probable that its destruction never entered his mind.

The theology of 34–35 is of the same type as the theology of 40–66; cf below. The theology of 24–27 is apocalyptic. It describes not the judgment of Yahweh in history (cf above) but the judgment of Yahweh in a cosmic end-catastrophe. From this catastrophe only the redeemed escape. This vast conception of a world final judgment reaches a fuller development in apocalyptic* literature and in the NT (cf JUDGMENT). Whether Is 26:19 expresses a hope of the resurrection* of the dead is not certain. It is possible that the resurrection may be a metaphor to express the hope of the restoration of Israel, as in Ezk 37:1–14.

II. 40–66.

Döderlein in 1775 and Eichhorn in 1782 were the first to suggest that these chapters of Is were not from the author of the first part. Modern critics accept this view as established and raise the further question whether 40–55 and 56–66 are not from distinct authors. We discuss 56–66 below.

(1) 40–55. The reasons for assigning 40–55 to a different author are historical, doctrinal, and literary. The background of 40–55 is evidently the period near the end of the exile*. Cyrus*, mentioned by name (44:28; 45:1) has arisen as a threat to Babylon and a liberator of Israel. The course of the conquests of Cyrus permits one to date this allusion about 545 BC; the whole composition most probably falls 550–540 BC. Doctrinally the explicit formulation of monotheism and the conception of the messianic deliverance are developments beyond the doctrine of 1–39; and the cast of mind which these chapters reflect is in general that of another man and another period. The literary style of the chapters is distinctive and powerful and cannot be confused with the style of Isaiah. Hence, since the chapters are anonymous, the author is usually called Deutero-Isaiah or Second Isaiah. In 1908 the Pontifical Biblical Commission declared that the arguments in favor of this opinion were not compelling; criticism, however, has made great progress since 1908, and the arguments have gained much more weight. Some modern critics suggest that 40–55 are the work of several authors; to others their arguments are not convincing, and we accept the unity of authorship as probable, except for one passage. The "Servant Songs" (42:1–9; 49:1–7; 50:4–9; 52:13–53:12) are discussed under SERVANT OF THE LORD.

The chapters fall into two sections: 40–48, "hymns of Yahweh and Israel," and 49–55, "hymns of Jerusalem and Zion." Critics count about 50 different utterances in the chapters; unlike the detached sayings of earlier prophetic books (e.g., in 1–12 and 23–33) they are here arranged into a pattern of longer poems so that the distinction is lost. A great variety of poetic and prophetic forms is used by the author: the vision, the oracle, the reproach, the message, the debate, the taunt-song, interspersed with hymns and doxologies.

a) 40–48.

40:1–8, three sayings from Yahweh and heavenly voices; 9–11, message to Judah; 12–31, poem on the power of the creator as an assurance of His power to redeem Israel (41:6–7 should follow 40:19); 41:1–4, address of Yahweh to the nations affirming that He has called Cyrus; 41:5, 8–20, promises of Yahweh to Israel His chosen servant; 41:21–29, debate of Yahweh with the nations, appealing to prophecy and to His call of Cyrus; 42:10–13, hymn to Yahweh; 42:14–17, declaration of Yahweh of His intention to redeem; 42:18–25, apostrophe of Yahweh explaining His treatment of Israel; 43:1–8, declaration of Yahweh that Israel is His people; 43:8–9, prophecy; 43:10–13, oracles affirming the truth of prophecy; 43:14–15, 16–21, oracles of deliverance; 43:22–44:5, apostrophe of Yahweh contrasting Israel's infidelity with His saving grace; 44:6–8, oracle affirming the truth of prophecy; 44:9–20, prose polemic against idolatry (cf IMAGE), probably inserted by a later editor; 44:21–22, declaration of Yahweh's forgiveness; 44:23, doxology; 44:24–28; 45:1–7, two apostrophes of Yahweh to Cyrus; 45:8, Yahweh's righteousness and salvation; 45:9, certainty of Yahweh's purpose to save; 45:11–13, oracle that Yahweh will save in His own way; 45:14–17, Israel the people of Yahweh; 45:18–25, Yahweh's appeal to all nations; 46:1–13, fall of the gods of Babylon; 47:1–15, taunt-song addressed to Babylon; 48:1–16, apostrophe of Yahweh confirming His power by prophecy; 48:17–19, Yahweh explains His punishment of Israel; 48:20–22, summons to the Israelites to depart from Babylon.

b) 49–55.

49:8–13, oracle assuring Yahweh's saving purpose (8b probably added to connect this passage with the preceding Servant Song); 49:14–21, 22–23, 24–26, 50:1–3, apostrophes of Yahweh promising the restoration of Zion; 50:10–11, commentary on the preceding Servant Song; 51:1–3, apostrophe of Yahweh to Israel; 4–6, apostrophe of Yahweh to the nations; 7–8 apostrophe to Israel; 9:11, invocation of Yahweh; 12–16, response of Yahweh; 17–23, address to Jerusalem and oracle explaining the punishment of Jerusalem and promising restoration; 52:1–3, apostrophe of Jerusalem and oracle of restoration; 4–5, oracle of deliverance; 7–10, hymn; 11–12, summons to depart from Babylon; 54:1–18, poem in which the words of the prophet and the words of Yahweh are mingled to declare the acceptance of Jerusalem by Yahweh; 55:1–13, apostrophe of Yahweh (interrupted by the prophetic saying in 6–7), affirming that in Him alone is salvation, that He has an eternal covenant with David, that His saving purpose will surely come to pass.

Theology. In a truly magnificent and elevated poetic style Second Isaiah succeeds in creating a synthesis of prophetic belief up to his time. The synthesis is accomplished by uniting into one great conception the Israelite beliefs in creation, in the divine government of history, and in the divine will to save. Because Yahweh is creator even the greatest world powers are insignificant before Him (40:14 ff, 21 ff). As creator He disposes of the powers of nature as His instruments to accomplish His will. And His will is to deliver Israel. Yet this must not be understood in a narrow national sense. The deliverance of Israel is the first step in the establishment of His reign. In this reign Israel is His servant (41:9; 42:18 ff; 44:2, 21), His witness (43:10 ff; 44:8), His mediator to the nations (45:14). For the salvation of Yahweh is to be made known to all the nations, that they may share in it (42:10 ff; 45:6 f; 45:14, 18–24). To this end He governs history. His government may be seen in the prophecies to which so many allusions are made. These can be referred to no definite passages in earlier books; they are based rather upon the prophetic world view of history as formulated in earlier prophets (cf e.g., above on 1–39), that Yahweh governs the course of events and leads it to a term which He has established. This world view was shared by no other people. It is visible in the prophet's time in the appearance of Cyrus, the unexpected means who will perform the impossible: restore life to a people effaced from the pages of history by their conquerors. Thus Israel will survive Baby-

lon; with it will survive faith in Yahweh and a testimonial of Yahweh's power and will to save. It is a notable feature of Second Isaiah that salvation is the coming of Yahweh, not merely His deeds or His message. That Israel is the people of Yahweh is an ancient and basic belief; what Second Isaiah has added to the belief is the expression of a tender love and compassion, of a forgiveness now magnificently manifested in His restoration to life of a people who deserve to remain dead.

The synthesis of creation, history, and saving will has resulted in an explicit and polemic profession of monotheism which has no parallel in earlier writings. There can be no doubt that the world view of Israel broadened from the 8th century, when it first was touched by world powers, to the 6th century, when Israel was absorbed into a world empire and transferred from its own soil to another. Reflection on this course of events, as we see from Second Isaiah, destroyed the faith of some Israelites; for the prophet himself his concept of God grew with his view of the world as He perceived that the moral will and world government of Yahweh were as broad as His creative acts. Therefore the gods of the nations were not His competitors; they were nothing and should be designated as such.

The redemption and restoration of Israel is described as a new exodus* and its imagery is taken from the exodus traditions, but much enlarged (41:17 ff; 42:16; 43:2, 16 ff; 48:21; 49:10; 51:10). The desert through which they pass will blossom, the land of Judah will be regenerated, and restored Jerusalem will exhibit the grandeur which befits the city where Yahweh dwells (49:18–23; 52:1 f; 54:1 f, 11–14). The question has been raised concerning the relation of these magnificent descriptions to the shabby reality of the postexilic Palestinian community. One must misunderstand such prophetic passages if one thinks of them as mere predictions; as such, they are unfulfilled and therefore false. But they are more than mere predictions. They are attempts to present the saving acts of God which will reach their fullness only in the end of history. The end of history, unseen and beyond experience, is imagined by the prophet as well as he can in exaggerations of present experience, which are applied to present events. The application is valid, in his mind, because it is the same saving will which is exhibited in all history, and it is too magnificent for description even in its less spectacular manifestations. For the Israelites in conceiving history as a process described the past in terms of the present and the present in terms of the future; thus they expressed its unity and continuity.

(2) 56–66.

Duhm in 1892 first suggested that these chapters are from a different author whom he dated about 450. Since the chapters are anonymous the author is called Trito-Isaiah or Third Isaiah. Criticism has generally accepted the diversity of authorship but regards the chapters as a collection of the works of diverse authors. The dating is less firm; some place most or all of the chapters in the 6th century, others place some passages in the 4th or even 3rd century. Such a late date seems improbable. The chapters are certainly influenced by Second Isaiah, whose writings are echoed (56:1, 8; 57:14–19; 58:8–12; 60–62; 65:15–25; 66:6–16), and the collection as a whole is regarded by many critics as the work of the "school of Second Isaiah." O. Eissfeldt thinks that some parts (63:7–64:11; 66:1–4) may come from the early 6th century, and 57:1–13 even before 587. These passages are placed by others between 538 and 510, when the restored Jerusalem was a miserable village inhabited by a mixed population with many superstitions. The difficulty of dating the chapters comes from the total absence of any concrete allusions to history. Some of the chapters (e.g., 60–62) may have been preexisting collections.

56:1–8, foreigners may enter the Israelite community; 56:9–12, the unworthy rulers of the community; 57:1–2, indifference of men to the death of the righteous; 57:3–13, against superstitious rites in Jerusalem; 57:14–21, Yahweh, who has punished, will now restore; 58:1–12, the true fast demands charity; 12–14, the observance of the Sabbath; 59:1–15a, a psalm of lamentation (the enemies of 5–8 are not identified, as in such Pss); 15b–20, the theophany of Yahweh the warrior (in apocalyptic terms); 21, the covenant of Yahweh; 60, poem of the glory of the new Jerusalem; 61–62, the consolation of Zion, the bride of Yahweh; 63:1–6, the day of Yahweh's vengeance; 63:7–64:11, psalm of lamentation; recalls the past saving acts of Yahweh (63:7–14), describes present tribulations (15–18), combines confession of sin with petitions for deliverance (64:1–11); 65:1–25, response of Yahweh, who destroys idol-worshipers (1–12) but establishes those who worship Him in the messianic kingdom (13–25); 66:1–2, oracle against superstitious veneration of the temple; 3–4, against superstitious sacrifice; 5–16, apocalyptic poem: the restoration of Zion and the destruction of Yahweh's enemies; 17, fragment against superstitious worship in the gardens (the allusion is obscure); 18–25, eschatological poem: return of the Israelites of the Diaspora*, the new heavens and the new earth, judgment of rebels.

Theology. The theology of Third Isaiah shows some resemblances to the theology of Second Isaiah and a degree of dependence; but the differences are manifest. The consciousness of national guilt in Third Isaiah, particularly of guilt as an obstacle which retards the accomplishment of salvation, is a distinctive note (58:8–10; 59:1–2; 54:5–7; 65:1). This consciousness of sin and frequent confession is characteristic of postexilic piety and can be paralleled frequently in the Pss and Ch. Although the sins of Israel delay salvation, it is nevertheless with Second Isaiah regarded as still imminent (60–62, which may come from another author; 64:1). 58 exhibits the influence of the legalism which was characteristic of the postexilic period; Third Isaiah, himself no legalist, insists that the merit of external observances such as fasting and the Sabbath comes only from adherence to more substantial obligations.

The new Jerusalem of 60–62 has the closest relations to the conceptions of Second Isaiah. At first glance it appears to be more exaggerated and grandiose and more national — and therefore less broad. The imagery and the exaggeration are explained as above (cf theology of Second Isaiah). The nationalism seems to be present, but it is present to some extent in all messianic passages (cf MESSIAH). The Israelites always conceived the reign of Yahweh concretely in terms of Israelite institutions, since there was no other way to conceive them; the awareness that the reality was too great for these terms is sometimes more explicit, sometimes less, but never entirely absent. The universalism of 56:1–8 is as broad as anything in the OT.

Salvation is explicitly in Third Isaiah a new creation, modeled after the creation of Gn 1:1 but enlarged and altered (65:17–25; 66:22). The traits of the new creation are derived from Paradise and from Second Isaiah. The judgment is described in terms more grisly than those employed in Second Isaiah (63:1–6; 66:24), and these have scandalized some readers. One can say no more than that the reality of judgment is indeed grim, and it is dishonest to pretend that it is anything else, although we might use less concrete terms to say so.

Is in the NT. In the NT the use of Is is exceeded only by the use of the Pnt and of the Pss; but next to the Pss Is is the most frequently quoted single book. 41 different passages of Is are quoted explicitly or implicitly in 66 passages of the NT. The influence of Is on the thought of the NT is vast, but cannot be traced here; some references will be found in separate articles on the theology of the books of the NT.

Iscariot (Gk *iskariōtēs* or *iskariōth*), an appellative often added to the name of Judas*, one of the Twelve, who betrayed Jesus to His enemies. The meaning and etymology of the word are uncertain. It is derived by some from the Judean village Kerioth, which is assumed to be the home of Judas, by others from Gk *sikarios* (borrowed from Lt *sicarius*, "daggerman," "assassin"), a name given in NT times to outlaws who united patriotism and banditry. Judas may have come from this group or the title may be an opprobrious designation alluding to his treachery.

Ishbaal. Cf ISH-BOSHETH.

Ish-bosheth (Hb *'îš-bōšet*, literally "man of the shameful thing"). The name has been deliberately altered from *'îš-ba'al*, "man of Baal," from an unwillingness to write the name of the Canaanite deity Baal*, although the title was undoubtedly applied to Yahweh in this name. This scruple was not always followed by the OT scribes. Ishbaal was the son of Saul who was installed as Saul's successor by Abner after the defeat of Saul and his death at Mt Gilboa (2 S 2:8–11). His kingdom included "Gilead, the Ashurites, Jezreel (cf ESDRAELON), Ephraim*, Benjamin, and all Israel." The last member is probably a gloss which extends Ishbaal's kingdom beyond its bounds. Judah was ruled by David, and the power of Ishbaal in western Palestine was probably reduced to nothing or nearly nothing by the. Philistines. The war between David and Ishbaal which opened with the tournament of Gibeon* (2 S 2:12 ff) continued to Ishbaal's disadvantage (2 S 3:1). Ishbaal committed the indiscretion of insulting his most faithful officer, Abner, because of his union with Rizpah* (2 S 3:6 ff), and Abner dealt with David to deliver the kingdom of Ishbaal to him. David insisted that Ishbaal return to him Michal*, the daughter of Saul (2 S 3:12 ff). The murder of Abner by Joab broke off the negotiations, but it also ended any hope that Ishbaal could resist David (2 S 4:1). He was murdered by two of his officers who were bandits, Baanah and Rechab. They brought his head to David, thinking to win his favor; but David refused to accept such devices and had them executed (2 S 4). The inevitable transfer of the allegiance of the kingdom of Ishbaal to David followed (2 S 5:1 ff).

Ishmael (Hb *yišmā'ēl*, "let El hear"), a personal name. **1.** Son of Abraham* and Hagar* (Gn 16:15). A late tradition recorded his circumcision* at the time when Abraham and his household were circumcised (Gn 17:25). After the birth of Isaac* he was expelled from the household with his mother (Gn 21:8–21). He survived the expulsion and lived to be a desert nomad and a skillful archer. It is noteworthy that this entire anecdote does not contain the name Ishmael; this form of the tradition probably had no knowledge of the name of the son of Hagar. Another late tradition made him present at the burial of Abraham (Gn 25:9). He is the ancestor of a number of Arabian tribes (Gn 25:12–18); here his territory (that is, the territory of these tribes) extended from Havilah* to Shur*. Esau married a wife from the tribes of Ishmael (Gn 28:9; 36:3). Ishmaelite nomadic traders purchased Joseph and sold him into slavery in Egypt (Gn 37:25–28, 39:1; called Midianite* in Gn 37:28). The nomads captured by Gideon are called Midianites everywhere in the passage except in Jgs 8:24, where they are called Ishmaelites; it is noticed that they had gold earrings, since they were Ishmaelites.

The absence of the name Ishmael in Gn 21 suggests that the name has been introduced into Gn 16–17 from the gentilic nam "Ishmaelites," a desert tribe. The desert raider is described in the prophecy of Ishmael's career (Gn 16:12). This established an artificial connection between Israel and these tribes, with whom Israel had some real kinship. That they were associated with Midian is indicated in the passages cited above.

2. The son of Nethaniah, a bandit chieftain in Judah* after the conquest of Nebuchadnezzar*, who operated under the protection of the king of the Ammonites*. Ishmael probably was one of many who had not surrendered to the Babylonians and regarded the regime established under Gedaliah* at Mizpeh* as a form of collaboration with the enemy. He assassinated Gedaliah and a number of his companions and carried off the women and children of the settlement as captives. The captives were recovered by Johanan*, but Ishmael himself escaped to the Ammonites (2 K 25:25; Je 40:13–41:18).

Israel (Hb *yisrā'ēl*, etymology and meaning uncertain). The popular etymology of Gn 32:28 suggests, "he contends against El," but the form would signify "let El contend." Modern scholars have proposed more probable etymologies in "let El rule," or "let El shine"; but none of these are demonstrated. The name is given to the patriarch Jacob* in the account of his wrestling at Penuel*. Another brief account of this event without the wrestling is reported from a later tradition (Gn 35:10). The name Israel is not consistently used in later passages of Gn, however, as Abraham* replaces Abram in earlier chapters; Jacob is used with about as much frequency.

The name Israel is much more common in the Bible as a gentilic. It is used alone or in phrases such as "sons of Israel," "house of Israel," "kingdom of Israel." The gentilic designates that ethnic group which was united in the worship of Yahweh and which occupied, first in a loose tribal organization and later in a single monarchy, then in two, the territory of Canaan or Palestine. Modern historical research shows that the origin and nature of this group cannot be explained simply by descent from Jacob through his 12 sons; hence the question of when Israel began to exist as Israel and what it included territorially and ethnically is complex and admits no easy answer. The earliest occurrence of the name in nonbiblical sources is found in the stele of Merneptah of Egypt dated about 1230 BC. The stele reports victories of Merneptah over peoples of Canaan and includes Israel among them: "Israel is desolate, his seed is not." Otherwise the name appears in the Assyrian records only under Shalmaneser III (858–824) who mentions Ahab* of the land of Israel as present at the battle of Karkar; the Assyrians elsewhere called Israel "the land" or "the house" of Omri*. The name here clearly designates the northern kingdom; cf below. It is also used by Mesha* in the Moabite Stone in the same sense.

The family of Jacob is called both "sons of Israel" and "sons of Jacob" in Gn. The designation "sons of X" is commonly used to identify nomadic tribes of the Syrian and Arabian deserts. It always includes more than the direct descendants of the person named. Hb tradition therefore places the name before the sojourn in Egypt and attaches it to the group which left Egypt under Moses. Whether the 12 sons of Jacob, or the 12 tribes of the tribal system of Israel, are all included in this group is another question. History permits no certain answer; the reasons for asking the question may be found in the articles on the separate tribes. The stele of Merneptah is a difficulty against the theory of Martin Noth that "Israel" began to exist as a tribal confederacy with the covenant* of Shechem described in Jos 24. Noth conceives the confederacy thus formed after the manner of the Gk amphictyony, a group of tribes which are united about a common shrine and the worship of the same god. The narrative does suggest that some of the tribes here accepted Yahweh as their god, and one may accept Noth's view to this extent;

but it seems more probable that the Israel which worshiped Yahweh existed before the Shechem covenant and was enlarged, not formed, by this covenant. Otherwise Noth's conception of an amphictyony suits well the tribal organization reflected in Jgs and 1 S 1–8. The 12-tribe system is at least as old as the Shechem covenant. The 12-tribe system is itself, however, not free of difficulties. Ephraim* and Manasseh* are always counted as separate tribes, which raises the number to 13; where 12 are counted, Levi* as a landless tribe is not counted. This suggests that the linking of the tribes with the traditional 12 sons of Jacob is an artificial conception, including some geographical names and some names of tribes which were not a part of the earliest Israel.

Saul was king of Israel, but the extent of his kingdom and the tribes included are not given. His son Ishbaal (cf ISH-BOSHETH) ruled Gilead, the Ashurites, Jezreel, Ephraim, and Benjamin "and all Israel"; the last phrase is probably not a part of the original tradition. Large sections of the later Israel are not mentioned. David* ruled over Judah. The diminution of the kingdom of Ishbaal, however, is easily ascribed to the Philistine aggression which cut off the northern tribes from the monarchy. There is no doubt that the kingdoms of David and Solomon included all Israel.

A difference between Israel and Judah appears even in David's reign (2 S 19:42; 20:1 ff). Since this part of 2 S is almost universally assigned by critics to a contemporary author, it is not a reflection of the later schism; cf JUDAH. The name Israel is used after the schism of Jeroboam* of the northern kingdom. This, despite the fact that the historical books must have been finally edited by Judahite editors, shows that both northern and southern Israelites accepted the northern kingdom, which included the majority of the Israelites, as the true Israel and Judah as the seceding party. This usage is also found in the writings of Hosea* and Amos* and in those parts of Is which precede the fall of Samaria in 722. After the collapse of the northern kingdom in 722 the name Israel passes to Judah. This remarkable transmission of the name shows that it was not a purely political designation even in the early monarchy, but that it was, as it is clearly seen to be in later prophets, a political and religious designation. Israel is the people of Yahweh; as such, it survives even the political collapse of the larger of its political divisions. The basic unity of Israel was religious. Thus the name survives even the political collapse of Judah. The messianic hopes of Israel (cf MESSIAH) included a restoration of Israel to its full dignity as a people, i.e., a political society. This restoration always included the full restoration of the 12 tribes; but the messianic importance of the dynasty of David meant that they were conceived as ruled by the heir of David (Is 49:5–6; 56:8; 66:20; Je 30–31; Ezk 36:1–15; 37:15–28 +). This is also the view of the Chronicler, whose ideal Israel contains 12 tribes; but he passes over the history of the northern kingdom in silence, since the secession of the 10 tribes from the house of David was conceived in his time as a secession from Israel. This is an interesting development from the view of the contemporaries of the two monarchies (cf above).

In extrabiblical literature of late centuries BC and early centuries AD Israel is used only as a designation of Jews among themselves; they are called Jews by foreigners (cf JEW). K. G. Kuhn has pointed out a difference between Palestinian Judaism and Hellenistic Judaism in 1–2 Mc. In 1 Mc, a product of Palestinian Judaism, "Jews" is the official title of the community used by Jews in dealing with foreigners; Israel is used only among Jews themselves. In 2 Mc Israel is used much more sparingly; it appears only in prayer.

In the Synoptic Gospels Israel is used of the people and the religion, Israel as the people of God; occasionally, however, the religious element is not apparent. The name is rare in Jn, who generally uses the term Jews; where Israel is used it has the same meaning as in the synoptics. It is possible that Jn's preference for "Jews" reflects the growing conviction at the time Jn was written that the Jews had forfeited the title which designated the people of God. There is a strange difference between the first and second parts of AA; in the first part Israel is used in the same sense mentioned above, but in the second part the term "Jews" is employed. This may reflect the same idea as suggested above for Jn. Paul also uses Israel in the sense of the people of God, but the roots of a new usage are evident. He distinguishes the Israelite who is an Israelite merely by blood (Rm 9:6) or merely according to the flesh (1 Co 10:18). It is remarkable that neither he nor any other NT writer goes on to the concept of the Christian community as the new Israel; "the true Israel of God" (Gal 6:16) certainly approaches such a concept. The ideal restored Israel of the OT appears in Apc. Those sealed with the sign of servants of God include 12,000 from each of the 12 tribes of Israel (Apc 7:4–8), and the heavenly city, the new Jerusalem has 12 gates named after the 12 tribes (21:12). The eschatological Israel may appear also in Mt 19:28; Lk 22:30, in which the apostles sit on 12 thrones judging the 12 tribes of Israel. "Judge" here is used in the sense of rule (cf JUDGE). Some interpreters here see the Church conceived as the new Israel, as it probably is so conceived in Apc; but in both passages it is more probably the eschatological Church and the eschatological Israel.

Issachar (Hb *yissākār,* popularly explained in Gn 30:18 as "there is a reward," possibly "He [the god] gives a reward"), son of Jacob* and Leah* and one of the 12 tribes of Israel. The sons or clans of Issachar were Tola, Puwwah, Job, and Shimron (Gn 46:13; Nm 26:23; 1 Ch 7:1 ff); the minor judge Tola, son of Puah, a man of Issachar, seems to represent these clan names (Jgs 10:1). Issachar counts 54,400 fighting men in the census of Nm 1:29; 2:5, and 87,000 fighting men in 1 Ch 7:2. The boundaries of the tribe are not given in Jos; but the names of its cities and other allusions locate it in the plain of Esdraelon* from Mt Tabor* on the N to Mt Gilboa* on the S and from about the middle of the plain on the W to the Jordan on the E. The towns of Issachar are listed in Jos 19:17–23. The Levitical cities in Issachar (Jos 21:28; 1 Ch 6:57) fall within this area. An encroachment of Manasseh* upon Issachar is mentioned in Jos 17:11–13; the cities mentioned here were actually Canaanite, however. The territory of Issachar was strongly Canaanite, and the submission of the tribe to Canaanites is probably reflected in the unflattering allusion in the blessing of Jacob (Gn 49:14–15). This passage also alludes to the prosperity of the tribe, reflected again in the blessing of Moses (Dt 33:18 f). Issachar was not entirely submissive to the Canaanites; it was one of the tribes who participated in the conflict with Sisera* led by Deborah* and Barak* (Jgs 5:15), and the Israelites assembled on Mt Tabor, in its territory. Issachar was one of the 12 administrative districts of Solomon (1 K 4:17). Baasha* of Israel was a man of Issachar (1 K 15:27), and some historians believe that Omri*, who had a residence in Jezreel, may also have been a man of Issachar.

Italy. Mentioned in NT only in AA 18:2 and 27:1, 6 in the sense of the mainland of the Italian peninsula. Cornelius* was centurion of the Italian cohort (AA 10:1); in Roman usage Italian designated non-Roman inhabitants of the peninsula.

Ithamar (Hb *'îtāmār,* etymology and meaning uncertain), youngest son of Aaron* (Ex 6:23) and head of a priestly clan. The priestly tradition related how he and his brother Eleazar* survived the plague which destroyed Nadab* and Abihu* (Lv 10:1 ff; Nm 3:2 ff). To Ithamar was committed the supervision of the construction (Ex 38:21) and the transportation (Nm 4:28, 33; 7:8) of the tabernacle*. One member of the clan of Ithamar returned to Jerusalem with Ezra* (Ezr 8:2). The clan was smaller than the clan of Eleazar and received 8 of the 24 courses of priestly service (1 Ch 24:4 ff).

Ittai (Hb *'ittai,* probably an abbreviation of a Hb name such as *'ittî'ēl,* "El is with me"), a Philistine of Gath, captain of a mercenary troop under David*, who refused to abandon David even at the king's orders when David fled before Absalom* (2 S 15: 19–22) and commanded his troops in the battle with Absalom (2 S 18:2, 5, 12). The name is also borne by one of David's heroes, a man of Benjamin (2 S 23:29, spelled *'itai* 1 Ch 11:31).

Ituraea. Cf BASHAN.

Ivory. Ivory, called in Hb *šen,* "tooth," was widely used for ornamentation in the ancient Near East, and ivory carvings are among the finest remains of ancient Near Eastern art. The ivory was obtained from Africa or from NW Mesopotamia, where the elephant* was hunted by Egyptian and Assyrian kings in the 15th and 12th centuries BC. The Syrian elephant was extinct after the 8th century BC. Ivory was always a luxury article. It was used in panels inlaid in boxes, chairs, tables, and beds, as handles for combs, knives, and other instruments, particularly toilet articles. Often it was encrusted with semiprecious stones or faïence. Ivory carvings from predynastic Egypt have been found; the importance of Egypt as a source and the traditions of its craftsmen were responsible for a wide diffusion of Egyptian style and motifs in ivory carvings.

The influence was especially strong in Canaan and Phoenicia. The Phoenician craftsmen developed a peculiarly distinctive modification of Egyptian style which in turn reached farther than the Egyptian influence. The largest collections of ivory carvings from Palestine were found in the Canaanite levels of Megiddo* (14th century) and from Samaria; the Palestinian ivories were probably largely imported from Phoenicia. Cf from Megiddo a comb (ANEP 67), a handle of a cosmetic container (ANEP 70), female figurines (ANEP 125, 126), a small box (ANEP 128), and inlaid panel (ANEP 332), and from Samaria* inlaid panels (ANEP 129, 130, 649). These may be compared with inlaid panels from Nimrod in Mesopotamia (ANEP 131, 132, 133) and from Ugarit* (ANEP 464). Of particular interest not only for craftsmanship but for light on a hidden corner of cultural history are the ivory game boards from Thebes in Egypt (ANEP 213), from Tell Beit Mirsim (ANEP 214; cf DEBIR), and from Megiddo (ANEP 215). Of interest for its antiquity is the predynastic knife handle from Egypt which already shows advanced technique (ANEP 290). The Egyptian influence through Phoenicia is clearly seen in the sphinx from Samaria (ANEP 649). Solomon's throne of ivory (1 K 10:18; 2 Ch 9:17), and the ivory beds of Am 6:4 were made with inlaid panels of ivory similar to those illustrated above. The "house of ivory" of Ahab* (1 K 22:39), perhaps the source of the allusion to houses of ivory in Ps 45:9; Am 3:15, was not a palace constructed of ivory. but a house with furniture paneled in inlaid ivory. Even the decks of Tyrian ships were inlaid with ivory according to Ezk 27:6. A fair complexion is likened to ivory in SS 5:14; 7:5. Ezk 27:15 mentions Tyre* as a Phoenician ivory market; the ivory of Solomon, however, is said to come from Ophir* (1 K 10:22), an African source.

J

Jaazaniah (Hb *ya'azanyāh* or *ya'azanyāhû*, "let Yahweh hear"), a name borne by several men in the OT. **1.** A chieftain of the Rechabites* (Je 35:3). **2–3.** Two men of this name are mentioned in Ezk 8:11 and 11:1 as taking part in idolatrous worship in the temple; they have different patronymics. **4.** An associate of Gedaliah* at Mizpeh* (2 K 25:23; Je 40:8). The name appears on two Palestinian seals. One, belonging to Hanun ben Jaazaniah, is of unknown provenance. The other, belonging to Jaazaniah, servant of the king, was found at Tell-en Nasbeh (cf MIZPEH) and was attributed by W. F. Badé, its discoverer, to the Jaazaniah # 4 above. The name is also found on a Lachish* ostrakon.

Jabal (Hb *yābāl*), one of the sons of Lamech* and Adah* (Gn 4:20); the inventor of the life of the nomadic herdsman. There is a possible play on this occupation in the name; L. Koehler connects it with Obil, a camel-driver mentioned in 1 Ch 27:30. Possibly he is a doublet of Abel*, to whom also the invention of nomadic life is attributed.

Jabbok (Hb *yabbōk*), etymology uncertain), a river of E Palestine, the modern Nahr ez Zerqa, "the blue river." It rises near the modern Amman, the ancient Rabbath Ammon and Philadelphia, and flows in a loop before it turns westward to enter the Jordan near the ford of ed-Damieh, the biblical Adam. The river flows through deep cut canyons in order to reach the Jordan; the country through which it passes is heavily wooded even today. The wrestling of Jacob* occurred at the ford of the Jabbok near Penuel*. Elsewhere the stream is mentioned as a boundary: between the kingdom of Sihon* and Ammon* (Nm 21:24; Jos 12:2), of Ammon (Dt 2:37; 3:16), between Israel and Ammon (Jgs 11:13, 22). The Jabbok descends from its source at about an altitude of 1900 ft to a level of about 1155 ft below sea level where it joins the Jordan. Its length is about 230 mi.

Jabesh-gilead (Hb *yābēš gil'ād*, etymology uncertain), a town in Gilead*. According to the tradition of the intertribal war of Jgs 19–21 Jabesh-gilead did not take part in the war against Benjamin*. Hence wives were sought for the surviving Benjamites from Jabesh-gilead, which the Israelites took, slaughtering all the men and married women and sparing 400 virgins (Jgs 21:8–12). The historical character of this late tradition is doubtful, but a close relationship between Jabesh-gilead and Benjamin is also indicated in its relations with Saul*. When the city was threatened by Nahash*, king of Ammon*, they asked help from Saul, who mustered the Israelites and delivered the city (1 S 11:1 ff). In gratitude the men of Jabesh-gilead rescued the body of Saul after it had been hung on the wall of Beth-shan* (1 S 31: 11 ff) and gave it decent burial. David sent a message of gratitude for this act (2 S 2:4 ff). The bodies of Saul and his sons were later translated to a grave in Benjamin by David (2 S 21:12 ff). The night march from Jabesh-gilead to Beth-shan gives some clue to its location, and Nelson Glueck has identified it with two tells in the Jordan valley, Tell Abu Haraz and Tell el-Meqbereh, a few hours' walk SSE of Beth-shan, which is within sight, lying on the Wadi Yabis, which preserves the ancient name. Glueck also suggests that the text which describes Elijah* as a Tishbite is corrupt and should be read Jabeshite, a man of Jabesh-gilead (1 K 17:1 +).

Jabin (Hb *jābîn*, meaning unknown), king of Hazor* and head of a coalition of kings defeated by Joshua; Jabin himself was executed by Joshua (Jos 11:1 ff). Jabin of Hazor also appears as the king whose army under Sisera* was defeated by the Israelites led by Deborah* and Barak* (Jgs 4:2 ff). Jabin himself was killed later (4:24). Jabin is not mentioned in the poem (Jgs 5) and must be regarded as an intrusion in the prose narrative. On the Israelite conquest cf HAZOR. It is not altogether certain that the conquest should be attributed to Joshua.

Jabneel (Hb *yabne'ēl*, "El will build"), Jabneh (Hb *yabneh* in 2 Ch 26:6), Gk *iamnîa*, Jamnia; a city of the border of Judah (Jos 15:11) about 12 mi S of Joppa, the modern Yebna; in 2 Ch 26:6 it is a Philistine city captured by Uzziah*. It was a base of operations for the Syrian armies in the Maccabean wars (1 Mc 4:15; 5:58; 10:69; 15:40) and according to 2 Mc 12:8 f was burned with its port city by Judas. The population of the town in Hellenistic and Roman times was mixed at best and probably mostly Greek. After the fall of Jerusalem in AD 70 Jews settled in Jamnia; in Talmudic tradition it was the seat of Jewish learning where a notable council was held in AD 100 which among other things determined the canon* of the OT.

A town of the same name appears in Naphtali* (Jos 19:33).

Jachin and Boaz. Cf TEMPLE.

Jackal. The jackal is common in Palestine; it prefers uninhabited areas. Most of the biblical allusions to the jackal describe it as haunting ruins (Is 13:22; 34:13; 35:7; Je 9:10; 10:22; 49:33; 51:37; Ps 44:20) or the desert (Jb 30:29). The cry of the mourner is compared to its howling (Mi 1:8). Its suckling of its young is contrasted with the cruelty of Israel (Lam 4:3). When the prophet says that even the jackals will honor Yahweh, he means that the glory of Yahweh will be manifested even in places where no man dwells (Is 43:20).

Jacob (Hb *ya'aḳōb;* the etymology of Gn 25:26, "he will trip by the heel," from *'aḳēb,* heel, is popular; the name is more probably shortened from a name similar to Jacob-el or Jacob-har, "let [the deity] protect"); son of Isaac*, twin brother of Esau*, and eponymous ancestor of the 12 tribes of Israel*. The place name *ya'qubel* appears in the list of Canaanite places conquered by Thutmose III of Egypt, and the name *Ya-ah-qu-ub-il* is found in Mesopotamian tablets of the 18th century BC. The name *Ya 'qob-har,* "let Har (the mountain god) protect" was the name of a Hyksos* chieftain. No connection can be established between these names and the biblical Jacob, but they show that the name was neither rare nor distinctively Hebrew. Some scholars suspect a connection between Jacob and the Jacob-el of the list of Thutmose III, which occurs in a place where Jacob could easily have been; the list is too late, however, for Jacob to be a contemporary.

1. *Life.* Jacob was the son of Isaac and Rebekah* and the younger twin of Esau* (Gn 25:19–26). He purchased the rights of the firstborn* from Esau for the price of a luncheon (Gn 25:27–34) and secured by stealth the blessing* of the firstborn from Isaac (Gn 27:1–42). Two motives are given for his journey to Paddan-Aram*: fear of his brother's vengeance and the desire of Isaac that Jacob should marry one of his kinswomen and not a Canaanite (Gn 27:42–28:5). On his way to Paddan-Aram Jacob had a dream vision of Yahweh at Bethel* in which he was promised a numerous posterity which should possess the land (Gn 28:10–22). Jacob erected a sacred pillar; a place where God has revealed Himself was a sanctuary. In Paddan-Aram he met Rachel*, the daughter of Laban*, at the well where the shepherds watered the sheep, and Laban invited him to stay with him and enter his employ. In return for seven years' service Jacob asked to marry Rachel; but Laban deceived him by substituting his daughter Leah*, who was unattractive because of her dull eyes. The substitution was possible because the bride was veiled not only at the wedding ceremony but also during the consummation of the marriage (Gn 29:1–25). Jacob then performed another seven years' service for Rachel. Leah was fortunate in bearing children, but Rachel was barren and substituted her slave Bilhah*. Leah also substituted her slave, Zilpah*; and Rachel finally bore a son (Gn 29:26–30:24). Jacob then desired to return to his own country and arranged a contract with Laban which through his cleverness resulted in the increase of his own flocks and the impoverishment of Laban. The ensuing quarrel led Jacob to flee with his wives and flocks. Laban pursued him but was warned in a vision not to harm him; he was indignant because Rachel had stolen his household gods, the symbol of his authority as head of the house. Rachel concealed them so that he could not discover them. Jacob and Laban concluded a covenant, agreeing that Jacob should not maltreat Laban's daughters or marry other wives and that neither party should pass the heap of stones which was erected to commemorate the covenant (Gn 30:25–31:55). Jacob sent gifts to meet Esau; and at Penuel* he wrestled all night with a mysterious being who lamed him and changed his name to Israel* (Gn 32). The meeting with Esau was amicable and Jacob settled at Shechem* (Gn 33). There, because of the rape of his daughter Dinah* by Shechem, his sons Simeon* and Levi* by deception rendered the Shechemites incapable of fighting and then sacked the city (Gn 34). Jacob then moved to Bethel; near there Rachel died giving birth to her second son Benjamin* (Gn 35). Jacob's partiality to Joseph led his brothers to plot his murder, but instead they sold him into slavery in Egypt (Gn 37). After Joseph had been made vizier of Egypt a famine afflicted Canaan and Jacob sent his sons to secure grain. Through these meetings Joseph came to recognize his brothers; finally he revealed his identity and invited his father and family to live in Egypt (Gn 42:1–45:28). Jacob moved to Egypt and was settled in Goshen* (Gn 46:1–47:12). In his last illness Jacob blessed Joseph and his sons Ephraim* and Manasseh* and made Ephraim the firstborn (Gn 48). The blessing of Jacob (Gn 49) is partly individual and partly tribal; cf JACOB, BLESSING OF and articles on the various tribes. Jacob died in Egypt, but Joseph and his brothers removed the

body to Machpelah* for burial (Gn 49:29–50:13).

2. *Date and Historical Background.* W. F. Albright suggests a date of about 1750 BC for Jacob; this date is indicated by all the evidence. Several episodes in the Jacob traditions have parallels in the Nuzu* tablets, which belong to this period and come from N Mesopotamia, the region in which the origins of the patriarchs are placed in the traditions. Among these parallels G. E. Wright notices the sale of the birthright for a low price (perhaps — indeed, very probably — other factors were involved which tradition did not preserve); the oral blessing and testament; the relations of Jacob and Laban, which presuppose that Laban, having no sons of his own, adopted Jacob as his son (cf Gn 31:43, in which Laban claims patriarchal rights over the family of Jacob). The family gods which Rachel stole were at Nuzu the symbol of headship of the family and of the rights of inheritance.

The racial background of Jacob is said to be Aramaean* in Dt 26:5; this is in harmony with his recognized kinship with Laban the Aramaean. Later Israel was not Aramaean but recognized their relationship with the Aramaeans. The story of the covenant of Jacob and Laban is no doubt a historicizing of an ancient boundary tradition of Gilead*. The kinship of Israel and Edom* also is recognized in the stories of Jacob and Esau; in some of these the individual hero takes on the character of the tribe of which he is the ancestor. Both the story of the birthright and that of the blessing express Israel's claim to superiority over Edom even though Edom is the elder; these may reflect the conditions of the time of the conquest of Edom by David. The story of the birth of the twins seems to fall in the same category; indeed that the story of the birth came from an explanation of the name Jacob is more probable than the reverse process.

The relation of Jacob with the Israelite tribes, which are named after his 12 sons, is quite complex; cf ISRAEL; TRIBES. Whether Jacob actually had 12 sons by these names or not, there are very weighty reasons for considering the 12-tribe system an artificial grouping of tribes not connected as sons of a single ancestor, Jacob. Jacob himself is associated with E and central Palestine, Gilead* and the region around Shechem and Bethel. These are the territories associated with Ephraim and Manasseh, the two tribes which represent the tribe of Joseph, the favorite son of Jacob. This is in contrast with Abraham, who is associated with Hebron* and the Negeb, the territory associated with Judah. That Jacob was the grandson or even the direct descendant of Abraham

cannot be regarded as certain; they may represent two different movements into the land of Canaan. These movements are to be distinguished from the invasion associated with Joshua and the tribe of Ephraim after the exodus*. The traditions of the conquest contain no account of the conquest of Shechem and the region of central Palestine, which nevertheless were Israelite. The story of Jacob, however, contains allusions to the sack of Shechem by his sons (Gn 34) and to his own conquest of Shechem by arms (Gn 48:22). These suggest that the Israelite possession of Shechem was reckoned as earlier than Joshua, and that the Israelites who dwelt in these regions did not join the migration of the sons of Israel to Egypt.

3. *Religion of Jacob.* The religion of Jacob is less prominent in the traditions concerning him than is the religion of Abraham in the Abraham traditions. Jacob inherits the promises of Abraham (Gn 28:13–15; 48:3 f) in the Abraham traditions. The divine title *'abbîr ya'akōb* (or "of Israel"; Gn 49:24; Is 1:24; 49:26; 60:16; Ps 132:3, 5) is of uncertain meaning. It is usually translated "strong one" or "champion" of Jacob; but the word *'abbîr* elsewhere means "bull," a divine designation found in Ugarit but most offensive to later Israelites. The wrestling of Jacob with a divine being at Penuel (Gn 32) is a story whose original theme is difficult to detect. The significance of the story very probably lies in the fact that it occurs at the boundary point; Jacob as an intruder had to overcome divine resistance in order to enter the land of Canaan. Like the story of the birthright and the blessing of Isaac, it authenticates the rights of the Jacob group to enter the country. Jacob is associated with the sanctuaries of Bethel (Gn 28) and Shechem (Gn 33:20). At Bethel he erected a sacred pillar* as a symbol of the deity, a *maṣṣēbāh*. Such pillars of stone were a part of the Canaanite cultic furniture and were stoutly repudiated in the later sanctuaries of Yahweh; the candor of Hebrew tradition in retaining this story of Jacob is admirable, and it must have been adduced in favor of the *maṣṣēbāh* in later Israelite sanctuaries. The fusion of the religion of Jacob with the religion of Abraham probably did not occur before the settlement of the Israelite tribes in Canaan.

4. *Jacob in other Scriptures.* Elsewhere in the OT the name of Jacob is a common designation for Israel: as equivalent to Israel (Dt 32:9; 33:28; Pss 44:5; 59:14; 79:7; 87:2; 99:4; 147:19; Is 27:9; 48:20; 59:20; Je 10:25; 30:7, 18; 31:6, 10; 46:27 f; Ob 10; Mi 2:12; 5:6 f), parallel with the name Israel (Gn 49:7; Nm 23:2, 7, 10, 21, 23; 24:5, 17, 19; Dt 33:10; Pss 14:7; 53:7;

105:10; 135:4; Is 9:7; 27:6; 40:27; 41:8, 14; 42:24; 43:1, ·22, 28; 44:1, 5, 21, 23; 45:4; 48:12; 49:5, 6; Je 30:10; 46:2; Mi 3:8; Na 2:3), in the phrases "house of Jacob" (Ex 19:3; Is 2:5; 8:17; 10:20 f; 14:1; 29:22; 46:3; 48:1; 58:1; Je 2:4; 5:20; Ezk 20:5; Am 3:13 and 9:8 [referring to the northern kingdom]; Ps 114:1; Ob 17 f; Mi 2:7; 3:1, 9), congregation of Jacob (Dt 33:4), seed of Jacob (Ps 22:24; Is 45:19; Je 33:26), sons of Jacob (1 K 18:31; 2 K 17:34; Pss 77:16; 105:6; Mal 3:6). Jacob designates the northern kingdom in Ho 10:11; Am 6:8; 7:2, 5; Mi 1:5. Yahweh is called the God of Jacob (Pss 20:2; 46:8, 12; 75:10; 76:7; 81:2, 5; 84:9; 94:7; 114:7; 146:5; Is 2:3; Mi 4:2), the pride of Jacob (Am 8:7), the holy one of Jacob (Is 29:23), and the king of Jacob (Is 41:21; 44:6). This usage shows that the name Jacob was almost equivalent to the name Israel as a designation of the people and it is not paralleled for Isaac and Abraham. Ho (12:2–4, 12) identifies Jacob with the people Israel and sees in Jacob's deceit of Esau, his struggle with an angel, and his flight to Aram signs of Yahweh's displeasure. But Israel can find mercy and forgiveness as Jacob did. This unfavorable judgment of Jacob is implicit at best in the traditions of Gn.

The NT references to Jacob most frequently associate him with Abraham and Isaac. There are some allusions to episodes of his life, particularly in the speech of Stephen* (AA 7:8 ff). Jesus compares Himself to the ladder of Jacob's vision at Bethel, a mediator between heaven and earth (Jn 1:51). Paul uses the transfer of the birthright from Esau to Jacob as an example of free divine election*, basing his exposition on the same thought as that expressed in Mal 1:2.

Jacob is the name of the father of Joseph* in Mt's genealogy* of Jesus (Mt 1:15 f).

Jacob, blessing of. The name of Jacob appears in the introduction and conclusion (referring the blessing to the tribes of Israel) in Gn 49. On the significance of the formulae of blessings cf articles on separate tribes. Modern critics do not believe that the blessing of Jacob is a unified composition; it is rather a collection of detached sayings of varied provenance. It cannot be attributed to Jacob himself nor to his time. Ancient conceptions regarded the dying man as granted a peculiar insight into the future; the words of a dying man, especially a blessing* or curse*, were regarded as having even greater power than the ordinary blessing or curse. The formulae are not "blessings" nor are they predictions. The date of the various sayings can scarcely be determined; the blessing of Judah seems to come

from the reign of David*. The earliest of the sayings may be 300 years earlier than David. The reign of David, when the national and historical consciousness of Israel as a whole first awakened and engaged in literary self-expression and collection of traditions, is the most probable time for the compilation of the blessing of Jacob.

Jacob's well. The scene of the conversation of Jesus with the Samaritan woman (Jn 4:5 ff). The traditional identification of the well, which is most probably accurate, places it at the well which lies about 2 mi E of Nablus, almost due E of Balata, the site of Shechem*, about 40 mi N of Jerusalem. Here the road forks to the W to Galilee through Nablus and to the N to Beisan (Bethshan*) and the plain of Esdraelon*. A Byzantine church was built over the well in the 6th century AD; a modern restoration of the Gk church has never been finished. The well is about 100 ft deep (Jn 4:11). This is the traditional site of the property which Jacob purchased "before" Shechem (Gn 33:19), inherited by the tribe of Joseph, where the bones of Joseph were interred (Jos 24:32). Cf SYCHAR.

Jael (Hb yā'ēl, perhaps "mountain-goat"?), wife of Heber* the Kenite* who admitted the fleeing Canaanite general Sisera* to her tent but killed him with a mallet and tentpeg (Jgs 4:17 ff; 5:6; 24 ff), praised for her valor in the song of Deborah*; actually she seems to have violated the customs of hospitality*.

Jair (Hb yā'îr, "may he [the god] enlighten"), a personal clan and geographical name in the OT. Hawwōt-yā'îr, "the villages of Jair," lay in Gilead* (Nm 32:41), in Argob* (Dt 3:14); they consisted of 60 towns in Bashan* (Jos 13:30), of 23 towns in Gilead which were taken by Geshur* and Aram* (1 Ch 2:22 f). These different geographical data must represent an expansion of the territory of Jair from its original holding in Gilead into Argob and Bashan and a subsequent loss of territory to Geshur. The loss of territory must be later than Solomon. The villages of Jair are included in one of Solomon's 12 administrative districts, attached to Ramoth-gilead (1 K 4:13). While Jair appears as a personal name in the above passages, it must be a clan name. The clan of Jair is called a son of Manasseh* (Nm 32:41; Dt 3:14); but the territory is assigned to Manasseh in Jos 13:30 with no reference to a conquest. This leads to the possibility that the clan of Jair associated itself with Israel by covenant and that the conquest tradition is a later explanation. B. Mazar suggests that the name appears in Assyrian records as early as Adadnirari I (1305–1274), who conquered the Iauri, and that the name may appear also in Mt Iauri mentioned by Tukulti-Ninurta I (1243–1207), and "the house of Iahir" conquered by Ashur-nasir-pal II (883–859). 1 Ch 2:21 ff derives the clan of Jair from Machir* on one side and from Judah through Hezron on the other; this may be understood as a migration of Judahites to the territory in the early monarchy.

The minor judge Jair who possessed the 30 "villages of Jair" is obviously a fictitious character created to explain the title of the villages. The name is also borne by the father of Mordecai* (Est 2:5).

Jairus (Gk *iairos* from Hb Jair*), president of the synagogue* in Capharnaum*, whose daughter Jesus raised from the dead (Mk 5:21–43; Lk 8:40–56). The episode is related in Mt 9:18–26, but the name of Jairus is not given; he is called simply "a ruler."

James. Anglicized form of Hb Jacob through Spanish Jaime, the personal name of several men in the NT.

1. Son of Zebedee*, called with his brother John* by Jesus while they were in the fishing boat with their father (Mt 4:21; Mk 1:19 cf Lk 5:10), accompanied Jesus when He entered the house of Peter and Andrew (Mk 1:29). The mother of James and John asked that they might sit next to Him in His kingdom; when He asked whether they could drink His chalice, they answered that they could (Mt 20:20–28; Mk 10:35–45). John and James also asked Jesus whether they should ask that fire from heaven should strike the inhospitable Samaritans (Lk 9:54); it was probably on this account that Jesus nicknamed them Boanerges, "sons of thunder" (Mk 3:17), although Mk does not have the episode. James was admitted with Peter and John to some episodes of Jesus' life from which the rest of the Twelve were excluded: the raising of the daughter of Jairus (Mk 5:37; Lk 8:51), the transfiguration* (Mt 17:1; Mk 9:2), and the agony of Gethsemani (Mt 26:37; Mk 14:33). James appears in the lists of the Twelve (Mt 10:2; Mk 3:17; Lk 6:14; AA 1:13). He was beheaded by Herod Agrippa* in AD 42 (AA 12:2).

2. The son of Alphaeus*, another member of the Twelve, mentioned in the lists (Mt 10:3; Mk 3:18; Lk 6:15; AA 1:13). Cf below.

3. The "brother of the Lord" (Mt 13:55; Mk 6:3; Gal 1:19; cf BRETHREN OF THE LORD), brother of Joseph* or Joses, Simon*, and Judas* of Nazareth (Mt 13:55; Mk 6:3),

head of the primitive community of Jerusalem (AA 12:17). In the deliberations concerning the status of Gentile Christians and their obligations to practice Judaism James presented a defense of the liberty of the Gentiles and suggested that only four Jewish obligations be imposed upon them; this proposal was adopted (AA 15:13–23). Paul reported his success to James and the elders of Jerusalem (AA 21:18). A separate apparition of the risen Jesus to James is mentioned in 1 Co 15:7. Paul mentions a visit to James in Jerusalem and a discussion with James, Cephas, and John, "the pillars" (of the Church) in Gal 2:9; these passages show that Paul regarded the approval which James gave to his gospel to the Gentiles as very weighty. "Some who came from James" opposed his release of his converts from Judaism (Gal 2:12); but Paul's appeal to the approval of James as well as the discourse of James (AA 15:13 ff) shows that these emissaries did not represent the mind of James. James was martyred in AD 62. It is this James to whom the Catholic Epistle is attributed.

The texts of Mt 27:56; Mk 15:40 are not entirely clear; but it is unlikely that Mary* the mother of James and Joseph would be any other than the mother of "the brethren of the Lord." James is called "the little" in Mk 15:40, a title which as "James the Less" is popularly given to # 2 above. The text of Mk 16:1 reads "Mary of James," a phrase which would usually designate the husband of Mary rather than her son.

James is the name of the father of Jude* (Lk 6:16), and is read in the text of D of Mk 2:14 instead of Levi as the original name of Matthew* (cf TEXT, NT).

Even in patristic times the question of the identity or the distinction of # 2 and # 3 was raised. The conventional opinion has been that the two are identical. Perhaps a majority of modern scholars think that they are two different individuals. The "brother of the Lord" is never said clearly to be one of the Twelve (cf APOSTLE), nor even an apostle; the claim is not made in the exordium of the epistle (Js 1:1). 1 Co 15:7 actually suggests a distinction between James and the apostles. Gal 1:19 is sometimes understood to indicate that James was an apostle; but the Gk particle used here often has a simple adversative meaning, not "except" but "but only." Some scholars suggest that the unbelief of the brethren of Jesus (Mk 3:21; Jn 7:5; cf Mt 12:46 ff; Mk 3:31 ff; Lk 8:19 ff) could scarcely have been said of one of the apostles. This is, however, by no means impossible at this early date, but the argument seems irrelevant; nothing indicates that James was or was not one of the brethren present on these occasions.

James, Epistle of. Js, with 1–2 Pt, Jd, 1–3 Jn, is one of the seven "Catholic" or "General" epistles, so grouped because they are addressed to no particular church.

1. *Contents.*
1:1, greeting.
1:2–12, spiritual profit to be drawn from suffering.
1:13–18, defense of the holiness of God who sends suffering.
1:19–27, Christian duty of truthfulness.
2:1–13, impartiality toward persons.
2:14–26, vanity of faith unaccompanied by the works of love.
3:1–12, control of the tongue.
3:13–18, genuine wisdom.
4:1–12, causes of strife and quarrels.
4:13–17, divine providence.
5:1–11, divine justice.
5:12–20, various recommendations.

2. *Literary Form and Purpose.* Although Js contains an epistolary salutation (1:1), it has no final greeting nor does it have the tone of a letter. It is entirely lacking in personal allusions. It contains no doctrinal instruction so characteristic of the NT epistles; it is entirely an exhortation of morality. Its literary affinities are to be found with the wisdom literature of the OT and with the synagogue homilies illustrated in the apocryphal* books of the Testaments of the 12 Patriarchs, 1 Enoch, 4 Mc, and some of the literature of Qumran*. The author is also acquainted with the diatribe of Stoic philosophical writings, the use of question and answer and imaginary dialogue (2:4 f, 8, 14 ff, 18 f; 3:11 f; 4:4 f; 5:13 f). There are traces of the texts of the liturgy and of the baptismal catechism. The literary antecedants of Js are thus wide and varied; the prevailing form is the Jewish-Hellenistic exhortation.

3. *Authorship.* The title attributes the epistle to James; on the identity of this James and the problems connected with the attribution cf JAMES. The Jewish tone and interest of Js is so strong that F. Spitta and A. Meyer suggested that Js is a Jewish work which was christianized by an unknown redactor about 80–90. The certainly Christian character of the work does not permit this view, but the combination of Jewish and Christian features creates some problems; cf below.

The author is without doubt a Jew. Js contains many echoes of OT wisdom; it exhibits Semitisms in its language; its thought patterns are the concrete mentality of the OT, not the abstract thinking of the Greek; Js uses typical Jewish terms. There can like-

wise be no doubt that the author is a Christian; numerous relations with the Gospels and the NT epistles can easily be traced, e.g.:

Gospels: 1:2, 12 = Mt 5:11 f; 2:5 = Mt 5:3; 2:13 = Mt 5:7; 1:22 = Mt 7:24 f; 5:15 = Mt 12:32; 5:12 = Mt 5:34 f; 5:1–11 = Mt 24; 1:27 = Mt 18:7; Jn 15:19; 2:1 ff = Mt 25:31 ff; Jn 15:12 ff; 2:5 ff = 5:1 ff = Lk 6:24 ff.

Epistles: 1:2 ff = Rm 5:3 ff; 1 Pt 1:6 ff; 1:17–21 = 1 Pt 1:22–2:2; Eph 1:5; 1 Jn 2:29; 3:9; 5:1; 1:26 f = 1 Pt 2:5; 4:6–10 = 1 Pt 5:5–9; 2:5 = 1 Co 1:27; 1:12 = 2 Tm 4:7 f; 1:13 = 1 Co 10:13; 4:3 = 1 Jn 5:14; 1:22 f = Rm 2:13 ff.

These affinities do not suggest literary dependence in one way or the other with the exception of 1 Pt, which possibly uses Js. What they do indicate is the common living teaching of the early Church in which the author of Js was completely immersed.

Almost all modern critics are certain that this Jewish Christian author writes for Jewish Christians. It is altogether unlikely that a work with such a thoroughly Jewish tone would have been written for Gentile Christians without some effort to broaden it.

There is some support in the letter itself for the attribution to James the head of the church of Jerusalem (Gal 1:19; 2:9; AA 12:17; 21:18 ff; 15:13 ff). The writer speaks with a tone of authority (1:2 ff, 13 ff; 3:1, 13 ff; 4:13 ff; 5:7). This does not demonstrate that James is the author, but it shows that Js contains nothing which is inconsistent with the position of James. But other indications from the content and style have led modern scholars (Dibelius, Windisch +) to propose that the attribution to James is pseudonymous. They date the epistle at various points in the period 70–132 (between the two Jewish rebellions). The author, some suggest, possibly had himself the common name of Jesus. Others believe that he employed a document of James, or wrote as an interpreter of James.

Against the authorship of James is alleged the tradition which makes James extremely devoted to Jewish legal observance (Eusebius, the Pseudo-Clementine homilies); Js ignores the ceremonial law and deals with the law only as a moral law. The tradition of James's devotion to legalism, however, is not as well established in the NT, where he appears as moderate and tolerant of Gentile departure from the law (AA 15:1, 5, 22; 21:18 ff; Gal 2:4 f).

More serious is the objection based on the startling lack of attention given to the work and person of Jesus in Js. Jesus is named only in 1:1; 2:1 f; He is mentioned in 5:7 f and probably in 2:7; 5:14. This seems improbable in a work written either by an apostle or by one of "the brethren of the Lord." But it seems surprising in any NT book, and the difficulty is scarcely solved by proposing an author who had not known Jesus personally. The contacts of Js with Christian teaching are numerous (cf above); but it is strange that he says so little of Jesus, and no explanation is offered by scholars except the literary form of Js, the laudatory homily of Jewish-Hellenistic wisdom.

Still more serious is the difficulty based on the language of Js. The Gk of Js is the purest Gk of the NT after Heb. Critics ask how it is possible that a Galilean peasant who never, as far as we know, left Palestine, could have acquired a vocabulary and a skill in sentence structure which exceeds the qualities of the writings of Luke and Paul. Indeed it is altogether unlikely that James could have acquired such skill, and his authorship can be defended only by attributing the formulation of the epistle to a secretary who was endowed with good Gk style.

4. *Date.* If Js is the work of James, it is earlier than 62, the date of his death. Some have proposed a date as early as 35–50, basing this upon the primitive organization of the Church in Js (2:2; 3:1; 5:14), his ignorance of the Gentile mission and the problem of Judaizing, and his undeveloped Christology. Others point out that the treatment of faith and works may echo Paul's treatment of righteousness* and faith in Rm and is therefore to be dated after 57–58. Neither of these reasons compels assent. Those who believe it is pseudonymous propose a date late in the 1st century or early in the 2nd century; many modern scholars believe that the archaic quality of its doctrine does not permit a date so late.

5. *Canonicity.* Origen is the first witness to the canonicity of Js. Eusebius remarked that it was contested by some churches. It appears in the canon of the western church after 350.

6. *Doctrinal Elements.* In addition to the primitive Christology already mentioned, there is not even an insinuation of the Trinity of persons in God. Jesus is given the titles of Lord*, Messiah*, savior*, but the meaning of the titles is not elaborated; the second coming of Jesus and probably His glorification are alluded to. On the concept of faith and works cf FAITH; RIGHTEOUSNESS. The visit of the elders* to the sick (5:14 f) is treated by the Council of Trent (Session 14, Nov 25, 1551); the interpretation that this is a mere charitable visit is rejected, and it is affirmed that the elders anoint in virtue of their priestly powers and that the unction is sacramental in character. The Council thus affirms the traditional understanding of the rite in the Church without affirming that this is explicitly stated in Js. The effects of the anointing*, recovery, and forgiveness of sins, are certainly sacramental, and the position of the elders in the primitive Church, while not as well defined as in the later hierarchy of bishops-priests-deacons, was certainly a position with ecclesiastical character and functions.

Jamnia. Cf JABNEEL.

Jannes and Jambres. Mentioned in 2 Tm 3:8; in Jewish tradition the names of the Egyptian magicians who strove with Moses (Ex 7: 11 f). The existence of an apocryphal book of Jannes and Jambres is suggested by Origen and the decree of Gelasius on the canon. The Vg reads the second name as Mambres.

Japheth (Hb *yepet,* meaning and etymology uncertain; connected by popular explanation with the verb *pātah,* "to be spacious" [Gn 9:27]), third son of Noah* (Gn 5:32; 6:10; 7:13; 9:18). In the Table of Nations* Japheth is the ancestor of Gomer*, Magog*, Madai*, Javan*, Tubal*, Meshech*, and Tiras. These are non-Semitic peoples located mostly in the region of the Black Sea (Gn 10:1 f). The blessing of Japheth which is attributed to Noah (Gn 9:27) is obscure. It must refer to a movement of the non-Semitic peoples of Asia Minor into Semitic territory. Such movements occurred more than once in ancient history, but there is no particular movement which can be associated with this verse. The verse presupposes peaceful relations between the two groups. The refrain, "Let Canaan be his slave," is probably not a part of the original saying.

Jared (Hb *yered,* perhaps Akkadian *wardu,* "slave" [with the theophorous component omitted]), in the Sethite genealogy son of Mahalel and father of Enoch* (Gn 5:15–18; 1 Ch 1:2). On the parallelism between Jared and Irad (Gn 4:18) cf PATRIARCHS.

Jarmuth (Hb *yarmût,* etymology uncertain), a Canaanite city, one of the five confederated cities which was defeated by Joshua (Jos 10:3, 5, 23; 12:11); enumerated among the cities of Judah (Jos 15:35; Ne 11:29). It is identified with Khirbet Yarmuk in the Shephelah* of Judah near the modern Zakariya.

Jashar, Book of (Hb *sēper hayyāšār,* "book of the upright"?; O. Eissfeldt suggests "book of the valiant"); an Israelite literary collection older than the present biblical books. Two items from this collection are contained in the OT: the words of Joshua* at the battle of Gibeon* (Jos 10:12 f) and the dirge of David for Saul and Jonathan (2 S 1:17–27). These two items suggest that the collection contained poems and ballads of wars and heroes. Eissfeldt and others suggest that the collection was secular rather than religious, although the Israelites did not regard wars as a purely secular activity. The LXX adds after the saying of Solomon* in 1 K 8:12 f, "Is it not written in the books of songs?" Since song (ŠYR) and Jashar (YŠR) differ in Hb only by the metathesis of the first two consonants, most critics believe that Jashar should be read here also. Eissfeldt, however, points out that the saying of Solomon is of a cultic-religious character and suggests that "the book of songs" containing such cultic-religious poems was a different collection from the book of Jashar. He also deduces from the phrase (2 S 1:18) "to teach the sons of Judah the bow" that such songs were a part of the inspirational training of the young Israelite in the skills of war.

Jason (Gk *iasōn*, etymology uncertain), the name of several men in 1–2 Mc.
1. Jason of Cyrene, a historian whose lost history of the Maccabean* wars in five books was condensed by the author of 2 Mc (2 Mc 2:19–23).
2. Son of Eleazar, sent by Judas* as ambassador to Rome (1 Mc 8:17; 12:16) and to Sparta (1 Mc 12:17; 14:22).
3. Brother of the high priest Onias* who secured the high priesthood by bribing Antiochus* Epiphanes (2 Mc 4:7). He is called Jesus by Josephus (Hb Joshua); like many Jews of the period, he altered his name to a similar Gk name. He was a leader of the party which desired to Hellenize the Jews and built a gymnasium* in Jerusalem and introduced Gk clothing, games, and other practices (2 Mc 4:9–17). An even greater broadness was shown when he contributed to the sacrifice of Heracles at Tyre (2 Mc 4:18–20). Jason held the high priesthood 174–171 BC. In 171 he sent his brother Menelaus* on a mission to Antiochus and Menelaus secured the high priesthood by offering a larger bribe; Jason was expelled and fled to Ammon (2 Mc 4:23–26). He secured a band of 1000 men and attacked Jerusalem; he forced an entrance, but the attack was unsuccessful and he returned to Ammon. He was charged before Aretas*, the Nabatean king, fled to Egypt, and then to Sparta, where he died (2 Mc 5:5–10). Cf Josephus AJ XII, v. 1.

Javan (Hb *yāwān*, Gk *iōn*, meaning uncertain), in the Table* of Nations the son of Japheth* and the father of Elishah, Tarshish, Kittim, and Rodanim (Gn 10:2, 4; 1 Ch 1:5, 7). The word here designates the Ionian cities of the W coast of Asia Minor, and the word is used in the same sense in Is 66:19; Ezk 27:13 (many modern critics regard the word in Ezk 27:19 as a scribal error). The word is used to designate Greece proper only in some later writings (Dn 8:21; 10:20; 11:12; Jl 4:6; Zc 9:13).

Jealousy. The conventional translation of "jealous" and "jealousy" renders the Hb verb *ḳānā'* and cognate words, *ḳineʾāh*. The translation is unsatisfactory; the Hb words seem to render an emotional complex for which English has no single word. The Philistines feel this emotion at the prosperity of Isaac (Gn 26:14), the brothers of Joseph because their father favored Joseph (Gn 37:11), and Rachel because Leah bears children (Gn 30:1). In these passages "envy" renders the sense; this is also the feeling of the trees toward the cedar (Ezk 31:9). Envy of the authority of Moses and Aaron was also the feeling of the rebels (Ps 106:16). The *ḳineʾāh* which is hard as Sheol is coupled with the love as strong as death (SS 8:6) and is the jealousy which defends the possession of the beloved. Phineas showed his *ḳineʾāh* for Yahweh by smiting the guilty Israelite and his companion (Nm 25:11, 13). Elijah showed it for Yahweh by defending His right to be worshiped as the one God of Israel (Is 19:10, 14), and Jehu showed it by murdering the members of the house of Omri (2 K 10:16). For this feeling one suggests "zeal," the second English word (with jealous) which is derived from the Gk *zēlos*. The Psalmist experiences this feeling for the temple (Ps 69:10). Joshua expressed the feeling when the authority of Moses seemed to be challenged (Nm 11:29). The Psalmist feels something which is not envy or jealousy against fools (Ps 73:3); they are a challenge to the power and authority of God. Saul was "zealous" for Israel and Judah in slaying the Gibeonites (2 S 21:2); the motive for the slaying is not given, but the phrase suggests that in some way they had been a danger to Israel and Judah. The feeling of Ephraim against Judah (Is 11:13) is paralleled by the "enmity" of Judah for Ephraim. The complex emotional reaction designated by "jealousy" may be friendly or unfriendly, "for" or "against." It arises against another when he arrogates something to himself which he should not have, especially when it is taken from oneself; it arises for another when he is deprived of something which is rightfully his. The complaint need not be reasonable; the feeling is aroused whether it is reasonable or not.

This emotion, like many others, is transferred to God. Yahweh is "zealous" for His land (Jl 2:18) which has been attacked by enemies, for His people who have been attacked (Is 26:11), for His own name, which has been challenged because His people have not been restored to their land (Ezk 39:25), and for Jerusalem because it has not been rebuilt (Zc 1:14). The *ḳinᵉ'āh* of Yahweh is also hostile: it is directed against the nations (Ps 79:5; Ezk 36:5; 38:19; Zp 1:18; 3:8) for their pride, which is an implicit denial of His divinity, or for their aggressions against His people and His land. It is also directed against Zion (Zc 8:2); against Judah (1 K 14:22) for its cult of other gods. The "image of jealousy" which Ezekiel saw in the temple (Ezk 8:3, 5) is the image which makes Yahweh "jealous." The *ḳinᵉ'āh* of Yahweh is an active force; it is a fire* (Ezk 36:5; 38:19; Zp 1:18; 3:8). It is coupled with the anger* of Yahweh (Dt 29:19; Ezk 35:11). It is the sentiment of Yahweh when He appears as a warrior (Is 42:13) and it is coupled with His valor (Is 63:15); in the panoply of Yahweh's attributes it is the cloak in which He wraps Himself (Is 59:17). In Jl 2:18, however, it is coupled with the pity of Yahweh. That which the "zeal of Yahweh" accomplishes may be either destructive (the destruction of the Assyrians: 2 K 19:31; Is 37:32) or saving (the establishment of the messianic king: Is 9:6).

The title *'el ḳannā'*, "jealous God," appears five times; in each instance it is a warning that the prohibition against the worship of other gods must be observed (Ex 20:5; 34:14; Dt 4:24; 5:9; 6:15). It is the denial of the exclusive divinity of Yahweh which most excites His *ḳinᵉ'āh*. Almost all of the passages in which the word appears are explicitly or reductively associated with Yahweh's response to such a denial or to a desire to display His divinity by some manifestly divine work.

The *ḳinᵉ'āh* group of words signify anger rather than envy, jealousy, or zeal, but it is anger in a specific situation; it is a passion for justice, which is excited, as indicated above, at the arrogation of something which does not belong to the one who arrogates it to himself or at the privation of something from its proper possessor. It issues in a desire to attack the aggressor and to defend the person who is the victim of aggression.

Jebus, Jebusite (Hb *yᵉbûs, yᵉbûsî*, etymology uncertain). Jebus appears as a name of Jerusalem in Jgs 19:10 f; 1 Ch 11:4 f. These are later passages; the name Jebus is formed after the gentilic name Jebusite. The Jebusites appear in the enumerations of the pre-Israelite inhabitants of Canaan (Gn 15:21; Ex 3:8, 17; 13:5; 23:23; 33:2; 34:11; Nm 13:29; Dt 7:1; 20:17; Jos 3:10; 9:1; 11:3; 12:8; 24:11; Jgs 3:5; 1 K 9:20; Ezr 9:1; Ne 9:8; 2 Ch 8:7), and they are mentioned in Zc 9:7. They are said to live in "the mountain," the central range, in Jos 11:3. In the Table of Nations* the Jebusites are descendants of Canaan* (Gn 10:16; 1 Ch 1:14). The geographical designation "Jebusite shoulder" for part of the central range (Jos 15:8; 18:16) is defined as Jerusalem in Jos 15:8, but it may have included more than the spur on which Jerusalem was built. The Jebusites inhabited Jerusalem at the time of the Israelite invasion (Jos 15:63; Jgs 1:21) and held the city until it was captured by David* (2 S 5:6–8; 1 Ch 11:4–7). The presence of Araunah* the Jebusite in Jerusalem in David's reign leads some historians to think that the Jebusite population of Jerusalem was left undisturbed and that there was no Israelite settlement of the city after its capture by David, who preferred to leave his royal city neutral.

Jeconiah. Cf JEHOIACHIN.

Jedidiah (Hb *yᵉdîdyāh*, "beloved of Yah[weh]"), the name conferred upon Solomon* through an oracle of Nathan* (2 S 12:25). Jedidiah was probably the given name and Solomon the throne name taken upon his accession.

Jeduthun (Hb *yᵉdûtûn*, meaning and etymology unknown), the name of a Levitical choir. Members of the choir ("sons of Jeduthun") mentioned by name are Obadiah (1 Ch 9:16), Obed-edom* (1 Ch 16:38) and Abda (Ne 11:17). Some scholars suggest that Jeduthun was originally the same as Ethan*. In Ch, however, the choirs appear as distinct, and Jeduthun has been created as a distinct person who leads the choir with Heman* (1 Ch 16:41 f), with Asaph* and Heman (1 Ch 25:1–6; 2 Ch 5:12) during the reigns of David and Solomon, and who appears again as the king's seer in the reign of Josiah (2 Ch 35:15). If Jeduthun is not to be identified with Ethan, it is probable that he also is a legendary wise man like Asaph, Heman, and Ethan. The name appears also in three Ps titles, 39:1; 77:1; 62:1), which probably signifies that these Pss belonged to this temple choir. In a few passages the spelling of the name wavers between Jeduthun and Jedithun.

Jehoahaz (Hb *yᵉhô'āḥāz*, "Yahweh grasps"), personal name of a king of Israel* and a king of Judah. **1.** Jehoahaz of Israel (815–801 BC), son and successor of Jehu* (2 K 10:35). The brief record of his reign (2 K

13:1–9) relates that he suffered severe losses in war with Hazael* of Damascus until Yahweh sent a "deliverer." Some scholars suggest that the deliverer was Adad-nirari III of Assyria (809–782) who reports a successful campaign against Damascus in the 5th year of his reign.

2. Jehoahaz of Judah (609 BC), son and successor of Josiah*. He reigned only three months and was deposed by Necho* of Egypt, who had defeated and killed Josiah at Megiddo. Jehoahaz was first imprisoned at Riblah and then taken to Egypt, where he died (2 K 23:30–35). He is called Shallum in Je 22:11; this was probably his given name, and Jehoahaz his throne name, taken at his accession.

Jehoahaz is the full form of the name Ahaz*. It appears as a variant of the name Ahaziah*, with which it is identical in meaning, in 2 Ch 21:17.

Jehoash (Hb *yᵉhôʾāš*, "Yahweh has given"?), personal name of a king of Israel and a king of Judah and of several other men in the OT. It is frequently written *yôʾāš*, Joash.

1. Father of Gideon* (Joash), of Abiezer (Jgs 6:11). Although he had an altar and a sacred pole, he refused to take action when Gideon destroyed them (Jgs 6:9–31).

2. King of Judah (837–800), sole survivor of the sons of Ahaziah*, who were murdered by Athaliah*. He was an infant and was hidden in the temple by Jehosheba, his aunt, for six years. He was then installed as king by the priest Jehoiada* and Athaliah was assassinated (2 K 11:1–20). During his minority Jehoiada acted as regent. Jehoash was responsible for repairs on the temple (2 K 12:1–16). He was attacked by Hazael* of Damascus and bought him off by paying tribute (2 K 12:17 f). It may have been this humiliating failure which was responsible for his assassination (2 K 12:19 f).

The story of Jehoash is an interesting example of how history is rewritten and made the vehicle of theological instruction in Chronicles*. The theological problem is the combination of the devotion of Jehoash in restoring the temple with such a disaster as the payment of tribute to Hazael. The Chronicler therefore describes the first half of the reign of Jehoash, as prosperous, due to the guidance which Jehoiada gave the king. After the death of Jehoida the king turned to the worship of false gods; and when he was rebuked by the prophet Zechariah*, the son of Jehoiada, he had the prophet killed. "It was a year later" that the Aramaeans devastated the country, and Jehoash was assassinated.

3. King of Israel (801–786), son and successor of Jehoahaz (Joash). He appears in one of the prophetic legends of Elisha*, who promised him victory over the Aramaeans through the symbolic action of striking the ground with arrows; but he struck only three times, and the prophet was angered that he did not strike to annihilation (2 K 13:14–19). The story is based on the triple victory of Joash over Ben-hadad*, successor of Hazael (2 K 13:24 f). He was foolishly challenged by Amaziah* of Judah and defeated Amaziah soundly after he failed to dissuade him from the challenge. He looted the temple treasures and destroyed part of the wall of Jerusalem (2 K 14:8–16; 2 Ch 25:17–25).

Jehohanan (Hb *yᵉhôḥānān*, also written *yôḥānān*, Johanan, "Yahweh is gracious"), a personal name borne by several men in the OT, the Hb from which the Gk *iōannēs* comes. Of these men the only one who is more than mentioned by name is Johanan ben Kareah, a military officer and an associate of Gedaliah* at Mizpeh* (2 K 25:23; Je 40:8). He attempted to warn Gedaliah of the danger of attack from Ishmael* (Je 40:13–15). Johanan was absent when Gedaliah was murdered; but he pursued Ishmael and rescued the people whom Ishmael had captured and removed them from Mizpeh (Je 41:11–18). He and others asked Jeremiah to tell them whether Yahweh wished them to stay in the country or to flee to Egypt (Je 42:1–6). But when Jeremiah declared that the word of Yahweh was for them to stay, Johanan and others said that this was a lie and went to Egypt, forcing Jeremiah to accompany them (Je 43:1–7).

Jehoiachin (Hb *yᵉhôîākîn*, "may Yahweh establish"; also written Hb *yᵉkŏnyāh*, Jeconiah [meaning identical] 4 times in Je, 3 times elsewhere, once *yôyăkîn* [Ezk 1:2]), personal name of a king of Judah (598–597 BC) son and successor of Jehoiakim*. He was 18 years of age at his accession and reigned only three months. His father had revolted against Nebuchadnezzar* but died before the Babylonians came to Jerusalem. Nebuchadnezzar laid siege to the city after the accession of Jehoiachin, who offered no resistance. The king, the royal family, the nobles, and 10,000 men drawn from the warriors and craftsmen were settled in Babylon (2 K 24:6–16; 2 Ch 36:9 f). Je 22:24–30 alludes to this event and describes it as the rejection and end of the dynasty of David; Jehoiachin was childless in the sense that his sons did not succeed to the throne (Zedekiah* was his uncle). Possibly Je did not regard Zedekiah as a legitimate successor. 2 K 25:27–30 (Je 52:31–34) is an expression of the messianic hope; after the death of Nebuchadnezzar in 562 BC. Jehoiachin, still living in Babylon, was restored to some of his royal dignity. The dynasty of David still lived in him.

The name of Ia-ku-u-ki-nu, son of the king Ia-ku-du, appears in a list of those who receive rations from the royal table in the reign of Nebuchadnezzar; the identification with Jehoiachin is obvious. The name is also found on a seal of Eliakim, na'ar of Yaukin. The word na'ar, child or slave, is here interpreted as "slave," a common title of a high ranking official. W. F. Albright translates it as "steward."

Jehoiada (Hb *y^ehôiādā'*, "Yahweh knows" [i.e., recognizes as His own; cf Am 3:2]), personal name of several men in the OT. **1.** Father of Benaiah*, one of David's officers. **2.** Priest in the reigns of Athaliah* and Jehoash* of Judah. In the 7th year of the reign of Athaliah Jehoiada arranged to have the full temple guard on duty at the same time. He then introduced the boy Jehoash, who had been hidden in the priests' apartments of the temple, and proclaimed him king. Jehoiada then ordered the guard to kill Athaliah outside the temple enclosure, renewed the covenant* between Yahweh and the people, and destroyed the temple of Baal (2 K 11:1–20). Jehoash later in his reign found fault with Jehoiada for not employing the money collected to repair the temple (2 K 12:7 ff). The Chronicler repeats the text of 2 K (2 Ch 23:1–7), adding that Jehoiada reorganized the temple cult (2 Ch 23:18–21). The Chronicler also credits Jehoiada for inspiring Jehoash to uprightness (2 Ch 24:2, 17) and removes the blame for failure to repair the temple from Jehoiada to the Levites (2 Ch 24:6). The name is borne by two others (written *yôyādā'*, Joiada) in Ne.

Jehoiakim (Hb *y^ehôyāķîm*, "may Yahweh raise up"; also written *yôyāķîm*), personal name of a king of Judah (609–598 BC), son of Josiah* and successor of Jehoahaz*. He was installed as king by Necho* of Egypt in place of Jehoahaz. His original name, Eliakim, was changed by Necho to the throne name of Jehoiakim. Necho extracted heavy tribute from Jehoiakim at his accession. The course of events related in 2 K 24:1–3, 10–12, has been much clarified by the publication of the Babylonian Chronicle; cf NEBUCHADNEZZAR. The submission of Jehoiakim to Nebuchadnezzar occurred in 604 BC after the defeat of the Egyptians at the battle of Carchemish*; the rulers of all the small states of Syria and Palestine accepted the Babylonian hegemony. The submission lasted for three years. In 601 BC Nebuchadnezzar marched and fought an indecisive battle with the Egyptians, after which he returned; this was the occasion on which Jehoiakim rebelled. Nebuchadnezzar was not able to return to Syria until 599/598 BC; desert tribes loyal to him, however, harassed the rebellious kingdom, Jehoiakim died only three months before the surrender of the city in 597. There is no support in the Chronicle for the unhistorical tradition of 2 Ch 36:6–8, repeated in Dn 1:1–2, that Jehoiakim was captured and taken to Babylon and the temple looted. It is likely that this is a theological modification by the Chronicler of a genuine tradition of a visit of Jehoiakim to Nebuchadnezzar to submit his allegiance; the two need not have met in Babylon.

Between Jehoiakim and Jeremiah there was a deep mutual hatred. While Jehoiakim is not named, the scathing "woe" of Je 22:13–17 is addressed to him; he is charged with extravagant remodeling of the palace with money extorted from the poor, and with oppression and murder. Jeremiah scornfully contrasts his character with the simple life and the just rule of his father Josiah. Je 22:18 f, which promises Jehoiakim "the burial of an ass," is difficult; it suggests that the king was assassinated and his body dishonored. There is no record of this, but it is suspected by some historians that this was the fate of Jehoiakim.

The attack upon Jeremiah and his trial for the temple discourse (Je 26:1–19) occurred at the beginning of the reign of Jehoiakim; the text does not say that the king was involved, and Jeremiah was acquitted. His hostility, however, had grown by his 4th year. When Baruch read the scroll of Jeremiah in the temple, the royal officers at once warned him and Jeremiah to hide themselves. When the scroll was read to Jehoiakim, he sacrilegiously destroyed it as it was read and sent men to arrest Jeremiah; but the prophet could not be found (Je 36:1–27). Je 26:20–25 relates that Jehoiakim had the prophet Uriah*, who spoke in the same spirit as Jeremiah, murdered, even though he had to send officers to Egypt to pursue him.

Jehonadab (Hb *y^ehônādāb*, "Yahweh is noble"? or "Yahweh is liberal"?; also written *yônādāb*, Jonadab), personal name. **1.** Son of David's brother Shimeah, who advised Amnon* of the plan by which he might rape Tamar* (2 S 13:3–5; cf 13:32 f). **2.** Jonadab ben Rechab, chieftain of the Rechabites*, who accompanied Jehu* in his chariot while he exterminated the worshipers of the Baal (2 K 10:15 ff). The Rechabites of the time of Je referred the rules of their manner of life to Jehonadab (Je 35:6–10, 14).

Jehoram (Hb *yᵉhôrām*, "Yahweh is exalted"; also written *yorām*, Joram), personal name.

1. King of Israel (849–842 BC), son and successor of Ahaziah* (2 K 1:17; 3:1–3). Mesha*, king of Moab, rebelled against Israel at the death of Ahab* in 850 BC, and Jehoram undertook a campaign to subdue him in which Jehoshaphat of Judah, at the time a vassal of Israel, had to take part. They marched a week and their water was exhausted. They sought a prophet to give them an oracle and found Elisha*, who promised them water and a victory over Moab. The water came from a rain in the mountains, and they pursued the Moabites until they besieged them in Kir-hareseth*. There Mesha sacrificed his firstborn son. The "wrath" which came upon Israel can mean only that Israel was defeated. Mesha himself claims a victory over Israel and the repossession of Moabite territory from Israel (ANET 320). Jehoram also engaged in war with Hazael* of Damascus and was wounded at Ramoth-gilead*. While he was convalescing in Jezreel he was assassinated by Jehu*. His body was cast into the field of Naboth* (2 K 8:28–9:29; 2 Ch 22:5–9).

2. King of Judah (849–842 BC), son and successor of Jehoshaphat* (1 K 22:51). He was the husband of Athaliah*, daughter of Ahab* and Jezebel*. During his reign Edom* revolted against Judah, which never regained its suzerainty, and Jehoram himself was in danger of capture or death in battle against Edom. Libnah* also revolted during his reign (2 K 8:16–24). The Chronicler adds traditions that he murdered all his brothers (2 Ch 21:4) and that the kingdom was invaded by incursions of the Philistines and Arabs (2 Ch 21:16–17). He also presents a fictitious threatening letter of Elijah to Joram (2 Ch 21:12–15), and adds that he died of a lingering illness of the bowels (2 Ch 21:18 f). It is difficult to evaluate the historical worth of these traditions, since the Chronicler's theological purpose was to present a scheme of crime and punishment, and the disasters of Jehoram's reign mentioned in K were scarcely proportionate to the wickedness of a king who was married to a daughter of the accursed house of Ahab.

The name is borne by three others in the OT.

Jehoshaphat (Hb *yᵉhôšāpāṭ*, "Yahweh is judge"; also written *yôšāpāṭ*, Josaphat), personal name of a king of Judah* (873-849 BC), son and successor of Asa* (1 K 15:24).

Jehoshaphat was allied with Ahab* in the campaign against Ramoth-gilead (1 K 22) in which Ahab was fatally wounded and with Jehoram of Israel in his unsuccessful attempt to subdue Moab* (2 K 3). His long reign was peaceful and prosperous; he failed, however, in an attempt to restore the Red Sea trade of Solomon* when his ships were wrecked in the port. He refused to enter a partnership with Ahaziah* of Israel in another attempt at the venture (1 K 22:41–51). The Chronicler* disapproved of the alliance of Jehoshaphat with Ahab; but his traditional piety made it impossible for him to tell a story of punishment (2 Ch 19:1 f). The Chronicler has a very probable historical tradition of a reform of the judicial system instituted by Jehoshaphat (2 Ch 19:4–11). His tradition of an invasion of the Philistines*, Ammonites*, and Meunites*, which was repelled without a stroke by any Judahite soldier, is much less probably historical in detail, although the tradition of some incursion may rest on fact (2 Ch 20:1–30). The misfortune of the wrecking of the Red Sea fleet is explained by exactly reversing the data of 2 K; the Chronicler explains it as due to his partnership with Ahaziah* of Israel (2 Ch 20:35–37). The name is borne by three others in the OT.

Jehoshaphat, Valley of. In Jl 4:2, 12 the scene of the apocalyptic judgment of Yahweh upon the nations, the "valley of decision" of 4:14. The traditional identification of this valley with the Kidron* valley has no foundation. The name is symbolic, not geographical, signifying the place where Yahweh judges (*yᵉhôšāpāṭ*).

Jehosheba (Hb *yᵉhôšebaᶜ*, "Yahweh has sworn"), a personal name; daughter of Jehoram* of Judah* and sister of Ahaziah* of Judah, who hid the infant Jehoash* in the priests' apartments and saved him when Athaliah* murdered all the other members of the royal family (2 K 11:2; 2 Ch 22:11).

Jehovah. Cf GOD.

Jehu (Hb *yēhû'*, probably shortened from *yohu'*, "Yahweh is He," i.e., "Yahweh is God"), personal name.

1. King of Israel (842–815), son of Nimshi. The prophetic legends explain his rise to kingship from a commission to Elijah to anoint him (1 K 19:16 f); the prophetic group supported him and considered themselves as acting in the name of Yahweh. The anointing of Jehu by a prophet actually occurred after the death of Elijah and at the instigation of Elisha (2 K 9:1–10); it was done at Ramoth-gilead,

where Jehu, general of the armies, was continuing the campaign against the Aramaeans. Neither he nor his officers seemed to have much respect for prophets, and Jehu thought his officers had sent the prophet; but when all realized that there had been no collusion, his officers saluted him king. Jehu drove at once to Jezreel before the wounded Jehoram could be informed; but Jehoram, seeing his approach and recognizing him by his furious pace, went to meet him in his own chariot, accompanied by Ahaziah* of Judah, suspecting a conspiracy. Jehu at once shot him with an arrow and cast his body into the field of Naboth*. He wounded Ahaziah, who escaped. Jezebel the queen mother was in the palace of Jezreel; he ordered two eunuchs to throw her to the pavement where he drove his chariot over her body, then went in to dine while scavenger dogs consumed all but her bones (2 K 9:11–30). Jehu then sent a message to the elders of Samaria ordering them to defend themselves; in fear they asked what he desired, and he ordered the massacre of all the members of the royal house. Their heads were sent to Jehu at Jezreel and he piled them in two heaps at the city gate and the following day he killed the members of the family who were in Jezreel (2 K 10:1–11). He continued the slaughter by killing some kinsmen of Ahaziah who had come to visit Jehoram (2 K 10:12–14). In company with Jonadab (Jehonadab*) ben Rechab he convoked all the priests and worshipers of the Baal and killed them (2 K 10:15–27). An oracle from the prophets commending him for his work is preserved in 2 K 10:30; cf 2 K 15:12. This prophetic judgment is of course to be understood in terms of the primitive morality of Jehu and the prophets, who believed that the cause of Yahweh should be served by all means. Hosea later affirmed that Yahweh would demand the blood of Jezreel from the house of Jehu (Ho 1:4). The OT says nothing of Jehu's reign. Both the annals and the Black Obelisk of Shalmaneser III of Assyria mention Ia-u-a son of Hu-um-ri as paying tribute (ANET 280–281), and he is pictured on the Black Obelisk (ANEP 355). This occurred in the 18th year of Shalmaneser's reign, 841 BC. The designation of Jehu as son of Omri* shows that the Assyrians were not informed on the dynastic revolutions of Israel.

2. A prophet, son of Hanani, who gave a threatening oracle to Baasha* of Israel (1 K 16:1–4, 7, 12). The Chronicler introduces him into the history of Jehoshaphat* of Judah (2 Ch 19:2) and includes his writings among his sources (2 Ch 20:34). The name is borne by three others in the OT.

Jehudi (Hb $y^e h\hat{u}d\hat{i}$, "Judahite"), a personal name; a servant or retainer of Jehoiakim* who acted as messenger (Je 36:14, 21) and who read the scroll of Jeremiah to Jehoiakim (Je 36:21–23). The name is surprising and so is the genealogy through three generations of Je 36:14. The name of his great-grandfather Cushi is also a gentilic (cf CUSH) and suggests that the family was originally of foreign origin.

Jephthah (Hb $yipt\bar{a}h$, "may he [the god] open [the womb?]"), personal name; a judge of Israel. Gilead* was attacked by the Ammonites* and could find no leader except Jephthah, a bastard son who had been expelled from his family and had become a bandit chieftain. The name of his father had been replaced by Gilead, a geographical name. Jephthah accepted leadership only on condition that he receive the chieftainship of Gilead (Jgs 10:8–11:11). Jephthah first attempted to negotiate an agreement on the boundary with the Ammonites; when the negotiations failed, he went to war, vowing that he would sacrifice "whatever" came out of his house to meet him (Jgs 11:12–31). He was victorious and was met by his only child, a daughter; he allowed her two months to mourn because she had not married and then executed his vow (Jgs 11:32–40). A feud broke out between Gilead and Ephraim, and Jephthah led the Gileadites to victory, cutting off the Ephraimites at the fords of the Jordan. The password "Shibboleth" indicates a dialectical difference between eastern and western Palestine (Jgs 12:6).

The vow of Jephthah can be understood as nothing but a vow to offer a whole burnt sacrifice; and it is unlikely that an animal was more likely to come from the door of his house than a human being. Many exegetes have attempted to deliver Jephthah from his vow by supposing that his daughter was consecrated to Yahweh. There was no such consecration in Israelite religion. The vow and its fulfillment are indicative of the primitive character of the religion of Jephthah, and of many of his contemporaries, who retained this story as an example of genuine devotion.

The story of Jephthah has been conflated from two accounts or from an account of an entirely different event, since the speech of Jephthah (Jgs 11:15–27) is, except 27, entirely addressed to the Moabites.

Jeremiah (Hb $yirm^e y\bar{a}h\hat{u}$ or $yirm^e y\bar{a}h$, meaning uncertain), personal name of a prophet. 1. *The person.* Jeremiah's prophetic vocation came to him in the 13th year of Josiah* (1:2; 626 BC). While his description of himself as *na'ar*, a boy, at the time of his vocation (1:6) may be slightly exaggerated, it suggests a date for his birth no earlier than 650 BC, 645 according to some exegetes. He was born at Anathoth* near Jerusalem of a priestly family and was possibly a descendant of Abiathar*. At the time of his call Judah* lived in peace as a vassal of Assyria*; but the prophet's career spanned the troubled years which ended in the destruction of Jerusalem. In 621 BC a book of the law (cf DEUTERONOMY) was discovered in the temple and became the basis of a religious reform under Josiah. The revolt of the Babylonians* under Nabopolassar and the war of the Babylonians and the Medes* against Assyria ended in the fall of Nineveh* in 612 and the defeat of the last Assyrian king at Harran in 609. The end of effective Assyrian rule led Josiah to attempt to incorporate the former "land of Israel" into a single kingdom; but this led to conflict with Egypt, which supported the Assyrians against Babylon, and Josiah was killed in battle at Megiddo in 609. Necho* of Egypt deposed his son and successor Jehoahaz* and installed another son of Josiah, Eliakim, whose name he changed to Jehoiakim*. Both Egypt and Babylon desired to inherit the empire of Assyria; the issue was settled at the battle of Carchemish in 605 BC, in which the Babylonians under Nebuchadnezzar* defeated the Egyptians. The states of Syria and Palestine, including Judah under Jehoiakim, submitted to Nebuchadnezzar with little or no resistance. Jehoiakim, however, revolted after a few years; but he died before Nebuchadnezzar reached Jerusalem, and his son and successor Jehoiachin* surrendered. The royal family, the nobles, and 10,000 craftsmen and warriors were transported to Mesopotamia; the remnant of the kingdom was ruled by Zedekiah*, installed by Nebuchadnezzar. The anti-Babylonian party of Judah was stronger than any other group, and they forced Zedekiah to revolt. Nebuchadnezzar laid siege to the city and took it in 587. He leveled the city to the ground, destroyed Judah as an independent state, and transported another large group of Judahites to Babylon.

We are better informed of the personal life and adventures of Jeremiah than for any other prophet. His manner of life was governed by his vocation; he did not marry as a sign that children would not survive (16:1–4), nor did he take part in mourning or festivities as a sign that none would be left to mourn and that there would be no occasion for festivities in the disastrous future (16:5–8). His prophetic teaching aroused deadly hostility. There were conspiracies against his life in his own town (11:18–23; 18:18). He was confined in the stocks for one night in the temple for announcing the destruction of the city (19:14–20:6). For announcing the destruction of the temple he was tried for blasphemy; he escaped condemnation because of his prophetic commission, and also because he was supported by Ahikam* ben Shaphan, one of the royal officers; another prophet, Uriah*, was not as fortunate (26:1–34).

The relations of Jeremiah with Jehoiakim were extremely hostile on both sides. Jeremiah delivered a scathing charge against the king (22:13–19), and it was probably during the reign of Jehoiakim that he was flogged and put in the stocks in the temple (19:14 ff). In the year 605 Jeremiah compiled all his discourses up to that point in a scroll which Baruch was to read in public in the temple; Jeremiah realized that the supremacy which Babylon had achieved in the battle of Carchemish would enable Babylon to fulfill the will of Yahweh to punish His people. When the scroll was read the royal officers at once realized its inflammatory character and asked to have it read to them. When they heard it they told Jeremiah and Baruch to conceal themselves before they had it read to the king. Jehoiakim destroyed the scroll column by column as it was read; but the guilty parties had already escaped. Jeremiah then dictated another scroll which contained additional material (36:1–32).

Zedekiah consulted with Jeremiah more than once (21:1 ff; 37:17 ff; 38:14 ff) but was unable to resist the pressure of his officers, who believed that Jeremiah's prophecies of disaster destroyed the will to resist the Babylonians. During a brief interruption of the siege of 588–587 Jeremiah left the city briefly and was arrested and imprisoned for desertion (37:11–16); he was released from the dungeon but not from confinement by Zedekiah (37:17–21). He continued to announce defeat and was placed in a cistern with the intention that he should starve there; but Zedekiah authorized his release (38:1–13). After the capture of Jerusalem, Jeremiah, because of his predictions of the fall of the city, was well treated as a Babylonian sympathizer and offered his choice of residence in Babylonia or in Judah. Jeremiah chose Judah and urged those who were left in the country to live in peace (39:1–40:12). After the murder of Gedaliah* the community, fearing Babylonian vengeance, appealed to Jeremiah for a divine oracle on whether they should stay or flee to Egypt. Jeremiah after 10 days told them to stay; but the people, led by Johanan (Jehohanan*), called this a lie and forced him and Baruch to accompany them to Egypt (40:13–43:7).

There Jeremiah predicted the downfall of Egypt before the Babylonians (43:8–13). When the Israelites in Egypt took up the worship of "the queen of heaven*", Jeremiah rebuked them; but his protest was rejected (44). A later Jewish legend of doubtful historical value told that he was stoned to death by the Jews in Egypt.

2. *The Book*. Je is the longest book of the Bible. There are interesting variations between Hb and the LXX; LXX is shorter by about ⅛, 2700 words, and places the oracles against the nations (46–51) after 25:13. These oracles are also arranged in a different order. Hb: Egypt, Philistines, Moab, Ammon, Edom, Damascus, Kedar and Hazor, Elam, Babylon; LXX: Elam, Egypt, Babylon, Philistines, Edom, Ammon, Kedar and Hazor, Damascus, Moab.

A. Outline:

I. 1–6, mostly from the reign of Josiah.

1:1–3, introduction; 1:4–10, vocation; 1:11–13, the almond tree and the boiling pot (not necessarily connected with the inaugural experience); 1:14–25, commission to speak; 2:1–3:5, apostasy of Israel (a poem probably composed of separate utterances); 3:6–13, invitation of apostate Israel; 3:14–18, future restoration of Judah and Jerusalem; 3:19–4:2, dialogue between Yahweh and Israel; 4:3–4, oracle to Judah; 4:5–6:26, poem on "the foe from the north," composed from separate utterances which are arranged antiphonally between different speakers: Yahweh, the prophet, and the people; 6:27–30, the prophet as assayer.

II. 7–20, mostly from the reign of Jehoiakim.

7:1–8:3: the cult, including the temple discourse (7:1–15; cf 26), the worship of the queen of heaven (7:16–20), the vanity of superstitious sacrifice (7:21–27), fragment of a poem (7:28–29), human sacrifice (7:30–8:3); 8:4–9:26, assorted sayings and fragments: hopeless condition of Judah (8:4–7), the lying scribes and sages (8:8–9), a fragment duplicated in 6:12–15 (8:10–12), Judah a barren vine (8:13), the coming doom (8:14–17, similar in style and tone to the poem of the foe from the N), the grief of the prophet (8:18–9:1), sayings against dishonesty and violence (9:2–9), the coming disaster and its causes (9:10–16), the dirge of death (9:17–22), vanity of human means (9:23–24), uncircumcision of flesh and of heart (9:25–26); folly of idolatry (10:1–10, 11–16); 10:17–22, invasion from the N (three speakers, as in the poem 4:5 ff); 10:23–25 (three fragments of prayers; cf Ps 79:6 f); 11:1–5, 6–8, 9–14, three discourses on the covenant*; 11:15–16, vanity of hypocritical worship; 11:17, worship of the Baal; 11:18–20, 21–

23, plot against Jeremiah; 12:1–6, riddle of the prosperity of the wicked; 12:7–13, desolation of Judah; 12:14–17, restoration of Judah and others; 13:1–11, parable of the girdle; 13:12–14; parable of the jars; 13:15–17, warning of disaster; 13:18–19, lament for the king and queen mother; 13:20–27, the guilt and punishment of Jerusalem; 14:1–15:9, poems and sayings collected on the drought: a dialogue (14:1–10), impossibility of intercession (14:11–12), false prophets (14:13–17), disasters of war and famine (14:17–18), prayer for rain (14:19–22), denial of intercession (15:1–2), four fates (15:2–4), destruction of Jerusalem in war (15:5–9); 15:10–21, from the "confessions" (cf below); 16:1–4, celibacy of Jeremiah; 16:5–9, mournful life of Jeremiah; 16:10–13, explanation of the punishment of Judah; 16:14–15, fragment found also in 23:7–8; 16:16–18, 21, hunters and fishers of Judah; 16:19–20, vanity of false gods; 17:1–4, the ineradicable guilt of Judah; 17:5–11, wisdom sayings; 17:12–13, sanctity of the temple; 17:14–18, from the "confessions"; 17:19–27, the Sabbath; 18:1–12, parable of the potter; 18:13–17, infidelity of Israel; 18:18–23, from the "confessions"; 19:1–13, parable of the broken flask; 19:14–20:6; Jeremiah in the stocks; 20:7–18, from the "confessions."

III. 21–25, various dates.

21:1–23:8, the kings: Zedekiah (21:1–10), the royal house (21:11–12), Jerusalem (21:13–14), the royal house (22:1–5, 6–7), the reason for disaster (22:8–9), Shallum (Jehoahaz*; 22:10–12), Jehoiakim (22:15–19), rebellious Judah (22:20–23), Coniah (Jehoiachin*, 22:24–30), the messianic king (23:1–8); 23:9–40, a collection of sayings on the prophets; 24:1–10, parable of the figs; 25:1–14, summary of Jeremiah's preaching from 626 to 605; 25:15–29, the cup of wrath; 15:30–38, poems against nations (30–32) and kings (34–38) with prose threat (33).

IV. 26–45, mostly biographical.

26, the temple discourse (cf 7:1–15) and the trial of Jeremiah; 27:1–22, the symbolic yoke; 28:1–17, dispute of Jeremiah and Hananiah*; 29:1–23, letter to the exiles; 29:24–32, message of Jeremiah defending himself against Shemaiah; 30–31, "the book of consolation": introduction (30:1–4); poems of restoration (30:1–11, 12–17, 18–22); the storm of Yahweh's vengeance, (30:23–24); poems of the restoration of Israel and Judah: introduction (31:1); 31:2–6, 7–14, 15, 16–22, 23–26; the new covenant (31:27–30, 31–34), assurance of Yahweh's fidelity (31:35–37), rebuilding of Jerusalem (31:38–40); 32, Jeremiah's purchase of family property during the siege; 33, collected promises of restoration; 34:1–7, warning to Zedekiah, 34:8–22, the broken pledge of the slave owners; 35:1–19, fidelity of the Rechabites; 36:1–22, the writing of Jeremiah's discourses (605 BC); 37:1–10, warning to Zedekiah; 37:11–21, imprisonment of Jeremiah; 38:1–13, Jeremiah placed in a cistern and rescued; 39:1–10, capture of Jerusalem; 40:1–12, Jeremiah urges the survivors to settle in peace; 40:13–41:18, murder of Gedaliah*; 42:1–43:13, migration to Egypt against Jeremiah's oracular decision; 44, rebuke of the worship of the queen of heaven; 45, oracle promising deliverance to Baruch.

V. Oracles against the nations.

46, Egypt (605 BC, the battle of Carchemish); 47:1–7, the Philistines; 48, Moab; 49:1–6, Ammon; 49:7–22, Edom; 49:23–27, Damascus; 49:28–33, Kedar and Hazor; 49:34–39, Elam; 50:1–51:58, Babylon; 51:59–64, symbolic prediction of the fall of Babylon.

VI. 52, historical appendix, taken from 2 K 24:18–25:34, with the omission of the murder of Gedaliah (related in Je 40:13 ff) and the addition of 52:28–30.

The above outline shows that Je exhibits a more complex process of compilation and recension than any other book of the OT. The divisions and groupings of the above outline are homogeneous neither in topics, literary form, nor chronology. Some passages are found duplicated. Modern criticism, however, believes that the great mass of the material comes from Jeremiah or from his associates, although often not in the form in which it is preserved here. The disorderly character of the book is in part probably to be explained by the circulation of the words of Jeremiah in detached collections or even pages. Some critics have held that Hb and LXX represent two different editions of the book which may perhaps be reduced to the time of Jeremiah himself; but this opinion is not well supported.

Critics often begin with an effort to determine what elements may have been contained in the scroll of 36, described as containing "oracles against Israel and Judah and the other nations" (36:2). When this scroll was destroyed by Jehoiakim, Jeremiah dictated the same material again "with many additions" (36:32); this most probably refers to an expansion in the second copy and not to expansions added later by others, although doubtless there were such. O. Eissfeldt proposes with great probability that all the material of the scroll is to be sought in 1–25, which ends with a summary of Jeremiah's words. The battle of Carchemish in that year made it clear which power would dominate the Near East and be the agent of Yahweh's chastisement of His people. Eiss-

feldt includes in the scroll the words of Jeremiah framed in an autobiographical account, and omits the "confessions" and wisdom sayings. There are other minor additions also.

The book exhibits three different forms of material: (a) the oracular poem in several forms (including dialogue); (b) autobiographical prose, each of which is a setting for an oracle or a prophetic saying; (c) biographical accounts, some of which are settings for prophetic sayings or oracles, others, especially 39–42, an account of events in the prophet's life. The autobiographical portions all occur in 1–25, the biographical portions (except 21:1–11) all in 26–45. The biographical portions are with great probability attributed to Baruch. The autobiographical portions should be attributed to him to some extent also, it seems; these are narratives which lead to a prose summary of the prophet's word, quite different in style from the oracular poems. In some instances the prose narrative or summary is concluded by a poetic saying or fragment. These three forms of material are not grouped, although a. is found mostly in 1–17, b. in 7, 18–25, c. in 26–45. Nor can they be reassembled into anything that looks like an earlier compilation, so it is doubtful that this principle was employed in earlier compilations. Some earlier compilations are discernible; they all center upon topics: 7:1–8:3, the cult; 11:1–17, the covenant (3 discourses in which the word covenant occurs); 14:1–15:9, the drought (14:10–18 and 15:1–9 from other occasions); 17:5–11, wise sayings (not from Jeremiah); 21:1–23:8, the kings (21:1–10 and 23:1–8 displaced because of catchword "king"); 23:9–40, the prophets; 30–31 and 32–33, the book of consolation; 46–51, oracles against the nations. It seems likely that all these compilations are later than Baruch. 45 has been displaced in the collection, Eissfeldt thinks, in order that it may be clear that Baruch, who lived in Egypt, is excepted from the threats of 44. 51:59–64 has been placed after 50–51, which are certainly not from Jeremiah. 36 has been displaced probably because the compiler took the scroll to include 1–35.

The confessions, on the other hand, probably existed as an independent collection. These prayers and meditations, often very impassioned in tone, are unique in prophetic literature and shed much light not only on the person of Jeremiah but also on the character of the prophetic vocation. It is doubtful that they were ever intended for public reading or delivery. Jeremiah, who is the first prophet of whom we read that he compiled his own discourses, also kept some record of his inner conflicts.

The autobiography and the biography probably constituted a single compilation, and this should be attributed to Baruch. It seems doubtful that the entire compilation is preserved in the present book. This compilation formed a unit with the "words" of the prophet.

The position of the oracles of the nations in LXX, in the middle of the book between oracles of threat and oracles of promise, corresponds to the position of the oracles against the nations in Is 1–39 and Ezk; the scheme is too rigid, however, for Is 1–39 and even more rigid in Je. The LXX therefore most probably represents an earlier compilation of the book than Hb. But the position of this material after 25:13 is not the original position of the oracles. Eissfeldt explains their position in Hb as due to the attachment of 46, against Egypt, to 44, and this drew the other oracles with it.

Je has been expanded by some passages, among which most critics include: 10:1–16; 17:19–27; 25:12–13 (in part), 14; 30:10–11, 23–24; 31:10–11, 26, 38–40; 32:17–23; 50:1–51:58. There are a few other smaller glosses. A special problem is created by the autobiographical prose summaries. These are written in the "Deuteronomic" style (cf DEUTERONOMY), and some critics believe that they are entirely from the Deuteronomic redactors of the book. More recent critics, while admitting the Deuteronomic edition, are inclined to attribute them to Jeremiah or Baruch in their original form. Some suggest that the Deuteronomic style is simply the common Hb prose style of the late 7th and early 6th century. There is also a peculiar difficulty in discerning what is original in the oracles against the nations. 50–51 cannot be from Jeremiah. It is most improbable that the Moab oracle (48) is original; its affinities with Is 15–16 suggest that a common source was employed in the two compilations. The Edom oracle (49:7–22) is closely related to Ob and can hardly be original. The Philistine oracle (47:1–7) may be in part original. The Egypt oracle (46) very probably contains original material in 3–12 and 14–24 (Eissfeldt), expanded by the addition of other lines.

B. Theology. Je exhibits a life and a spirit rather than a "theology"; there are, nevertheless, some lines of thought which it cultivates in a distinctive manner. Perhaps more than any other prophet except Amos the idea of national guilt as deep and ineradicable dominates his words. This gives his discourses a tone of despair, but it is only despair of any change in the present generation; as we point out below, he does not lose faith in the power and will of Yahweh to save. But the hopelessness of any change

in Judah leads him to insights which are not found in earlier prophets. He is the first to see clearly that the guilt of Judah demands that Judah, the only survivor of historic Israel, must be destroyed as a nation and a people. He faces the problem of what is to survive this collapse (cf below). But the institutions of Israel, through which Israel was united to Yahweh, will all disappear: the kingship* (22:29–30), the temple* (7:14 f), and the ark* (3:16). Nor will there be any priestly instruction (31:34).

How then will the worship of Yahweh survive? The prophetic insight of Jeremiah does not inform him, but he has a sure faith that it will survive in a restored form. This restoration will be a restoration of the old united Israel (3:18 ff; 31:2–9, 18–22). Critics suggest with great probability that Jeremiah conceived this restoration in its first form when Josiah* attempted after the collapse of the Assyrian empire to repossess the land of Israel. This attempt was very quickly defeated, but the idea of a new and whole Israel did not die with Josiah's failure. The theme of the messianic scion of David is not prominent in Je, but a messianic passage is repeated in 23:5 f and 33:15 f. This passage is thought by many critics to be a later expansion, and there is some probability in the view, since the theme has practically no echo elsewhere in the book.

The most distinctive element in the messianic ideal of Je is the new covenant (31:31–34). Many critics have doubted the originality of this passage; but this view is no longer widely held. A new covenant* replaces the old. The institutions which Je saw destroyed (cf above) will not be necessary. The old institutions were media through which the knowledge* of Yahweh came to the Israelites. In the new covenant Yahweh will make Himself known to each person as He once made Himself known to Moses and the prophets. The "law" (instruction) which came from Moses and the priestly tradition will now be written on the heart of each Israelite and not on tablets of stone. This bold conception proposes a degree of intimate union with God which is scarcely paralleled elsewhere in the OT. Yahweh can reach His people without the traditional media of the covenant. It is for this reason that Je has sometimes been called the beginning of "personal" as opposed to "institutional" religion. The collapse of the state and worship of Israel left a spiritual vacuum which the individual Israelite was unable to fill. Je taught that Yahweh would fill it.

Jeremiah is the most revealing of the prophets concerning the prophetic vocation. Only in the confessions (cf outline above) do we find evidence of an inner conflict between the prophet's commission on the one side and his personal desires and sympathies on the other. Jeremiah deeply loved his people and his land — no other prophet has so many homely descriptive touches which illustrate town and village life — and he suffered because his threatening oracles erected a barrier between himself and his people. He confesses that he more than once wished to abandon the message, but the compulsion was too much for him. Hence he is the only prophet to explore the difference between "true" and "false" prophecy* (23:9 ff; 28:1 ff). The prophet who feels no similar compulsion speaks his own word and not the word of Yahweh. The confessions exhibit a very human attitude toward those who persecute him in which Jeremiah rose little above the usual ideas of his time; but these expressions are not entirely dissimilar to the words which Jesus addressed to the Pharisees*.

C. Jeremiah elsewhere in the Bible. The "70 years" of Je 25:12, long past in the time of the composition of Dn, are the basis of the "70 weeks of years" of Dn 9:2 ff. Passages on the fall of Babylon and the restoration of Judah are alluded to in 2 Ch 36:21 and Ezr 1:1. To Jeremiah was attributed the authorship of Lam*. To him also was attributed a dirge at the death of Josiah* (2 Ch 35:25) and the letter of Bar 6. The praise of Jeremiah in BS 49:7 is no more than a quotation of Je 1:5, 10. 2 Mc contains an apocryphal story of how Jeremiah concealed the sacred fire from the temple (2:1–8). The conception of Jeremiah as intercessor for his people based on the confessions (Je 18:20) appears in the vision of Judas in 2 Mc 15:12–16. Je is quoted seven times in the NT, not including the quotation of Zc 11:13 attributed to Jeremiah in Mt 27:9. P. Benoit suggests that this attribution arises from association with the purchase of a field (Je 32:6–15) which lay near the pottery region of Jerusalem, also mentioned by Je (18:2 ff).

Jericho (Hb $y^e r\hat{\imath}h\hat{o}$, perhaps $y\bar{a}r\hat{\imath}h$, "the moon [god]"?), a city. Joshua* sent two men to spy out the city before he crossed the Jordan; they were concealed by the prostitute Rahab* and reported to Joshua that the city feared the Israelites and would be easily taken by them (Jos 2). Joshua crossed the river and camped in "the steppes of Jericho," the broad plain of the Jordan valley on

Jericho: the trench dug by the expedition of 1952–1958 with the Mountain of Temptation in the background.

the W bank just before the river enters the Dead Sea (Jos 4:13). The Israelites marched around the city once each day for six days; on the 7th day they marched around the city seven times; on the seventh march they sounded the horns, the walls of the city collapsed, and the Israelites killed all the inhabitants except Rahab and her family. Joshua cursed the city and the man who should attempt to rebuild it (Jos 6).

Jericho was a point on the frontier of Benjamin and Joseph* (Jos 6:1, 7; 18:12) and was included in the cities of Benjamin (Jos 18:21). 2 S 10:5 suggests that there was a town at Jericho in the time of David. The "building" of Jericho by Hiel* of Bethel must refer to a remodeling of the fortifications (1 K 16:34). A town at Jericho is also indicated in 2 K 2:4 f, 15, 18. Jericho was fortified by Bacchides* (1 Mc 9:50). It was the scene of the murder of Simon* by Ptolemy (1 Mc 16:11 ff).

Jericho was the scene of the healing of the blind man Bartimaeus* (Mt 20:29 ff; Mk 10:46 ff; Lk 18:35 ff). Lk alone tells the story of Zachaeus* the publican who was Jesus' host at Jericho (Lk 19:1 ff). The road from Jerusalem to Jericho was the scene of the parable of the good Samaritan* (Lk 10:29 ff). This road was a favorite haunt of highway robbers even into modern times.

Modern Jericho lies about 23 mi from Jerusalem via a winding mountain road which descends from 2250 ft above sea level to 900 ft below sea level. It lies S of the abundant spring, called the Fountain of Elisha, whose waters make the oasis of Jericho one of the richest agricultural areas of the entire Near East. The site of OT Jericho is an elongated tell called Tell-es-Sultan which lies just W of the spring. The site of NT Jericho lies under the modern city. Herod* built a palace in the neighborhood; its site has not yet been certainly identified.

The excavations of Tell-es-Sultan by the British School of Archaeology 1951–1957 have raised problems concerning the Israelite conquest. Earlier hypotheses about the site were proved false; there was no trace whatever of any settlement which could be dated about 1250 BC (cf EXODUS). Dr. Kenyon explains this by the erosion of the site, which showed frequent traces of upper levels which had been washed to a lower point on the slope or completely down to the base of the tell. This could not have happened to Late Bronze Jericho unless it were a very small settlement, a conclusion which Dr. Kenyon suggests. It is most improbable that a site so rich as Jericho should ever have been entirely abandoned for long. Exegetes had long seen that the account of the conquest of

Jericho belongs to a late priestly source and is a theoretical reconstruction of the capture of Jericho rather than a living memory of the event. No trace likewise was found of the Jericho of the period of the monarchy, which also must have been a small settlement whose remains were washed away.

The chief interest of the Jericho exploration lay in pre-Israelite levels which showed the existence of walled towns long before the Israelites, the earliest to be dated at least 6800 BC. This has important effects in the prehistory of Palestine as well as on the dating of the earliest city cultures, all of which previously known are later than Jericho.

Jeroboam (Hb yārŏbʻām, meaning and etymology uncertain; perhaps a distortion of yarbeh ʻām, "may he [the god] increase the people"), personal name of two kings of Israel*. **1.** Jeroboam I ben Nebat (922–901 BC), first king of Israel after the secession of the N tribes from Rehoboam*. A lacuna in 1 K 11:27 appears where the reason for the breach between Jeroboam and Solomon occurred. He was prefect of forced labor under Solomon (1 K 11:28). A prophetic legend tells how he was commissioned king of the seceding tribes by Ahijah* of Shiloh (1 K 11:29–39). This legend of the N Israel prophets was written to authenticate the monarchy of N Israel; the actual causes of the schism are not of interest to the prophetic authors. Whatever the reason, whether attempted rebellion or something else, Jeroboam had to flee to Egypt until the death of Solomon (1 K 11:40), when he returned to take part in the tribal assembly which convened for the accession of Rehoboam (1 K 12:2–3). Jeroboam would scarcely have been proclaimed king unless he had been a leader in the rebellion (1 K 12:20). The causes of the rebellion indicated in 1 K 12:4, 10–14 were the heavy taxes and forced labor imposed by Solomon. The prophetic legend of Shemaiah* (1 K 12:21–24) is also of N origin; it disapproves of any attempt by Judah to submit the tribes of the N again to the throne of David. The other prophetic legends which fill out the account of Jeroboam place him in a most unfavorable light and are probably of Judahite origin: the establishment of sanctuaries at Bethel* and Dan* (1 K 12:25–33) and the rebuke of the prophet (13:1–10); the illness of his son and the discourse of Ahijah delivered to his wife (1 K 14:1–18). "The sin of Jeroboam with which he made Israel sin" is alluded to in the account of the accession of nearly every king of Israel after Jeroboam. This sin of Jeroboam was worship at sanctuaries other than Jerusalem; the formula is due to the Deuteronomic compiler of K, who viewed the history of Israel in the light of the law of Dt 12:1 ff that Yahweh should be worshiped at only one sanctuary, Jerusalem. The sin was not viewed so severely by the men of the period of the Israelite monarchy.

2. Jeroboam II, king of Israel (786–746 BC), son and successor of Jehoash* (2 K 13:13). The prosperity and peace of Jeroboam's long reign is briefly passed over in 2 K 14:23–29; it is indicated by his restoration of the frontiers of Israel to their farthest limit since the division of the kingdom (14:25) and his victories over the Aramaean kingdom of Damascus*, which had been a constant menace to his predecessors (14:28). He was a contemporary of Hosea* (Ho 1:1) and of Amos*, whose book contains an oracle threatening the house of Jeroboam with destruction; this oracle was reported to the king by the priest Amaziah* (Am 7:9–11).

A seal discovered at Megiddo* bears the name of Shema, slave (officer) of Jeroboam; epigraphers identify this as Jeroboam II.

Jerubbaal. Cf GIDEON.

Jerusalem (Hb *y^erûšālayim,* but probably pronounced *y^erûšālēm,* "foundation of [the god] Salem"?). In the Execration Texts of the 12th–13th dynasties of Egypt the name appears as *,'w,'š mm,* in the Amarna* Letters as Urusalim, in Assyrian* texts as Urusalimmu; cf SALEM.

1. *Location.* Jerusalem lies on the crest of the central range of the mountains of W Palestine; it is reached by the main road which traverses the watershed of the range and by comparatively easy wadi routes which connect it with the coast and the Jordan valley. The altitude of modern Jerusalem varies from 2400 ft to 2255 ft above sea level; most of ancient Jerusalem lay slightly lower. The modern city has moved N and W from the ancient site, and the city area of the time of David lies entirely S of the walls erected by Suleiman the Magnificent in the 16th century. Jerusalem was built upon two hills (hereafter E hill and W hill) which extend S from their connection with the central range. The hills are bounded by the biblical Kidron* on the E, which has several names in modern times, and the Wadi er Rababy, the biblical Ge-Hinnom (cf GEHENNA) on the W. The E and W hills are divided from each other by a central valley called by Josephus* the valley of the Tyropoeon (Gk *tyropoei,* cheese-makers). The central valley has been filled with 40 to 70 ft of debris over the centuries and is now a perceptible depression which begins

Jerusalem. The wailing wall, the retaining wall of the temple esplanade of Herod.

just N of the modern Damascus Gate and broadens and deepens until it reaches the S extremity of the E and W hills. The Wadi er Rababy and the Kidron are both steeply sloped, in spite of the fact that the banks have been smoothed by erosion and the beds have become more shallow with the deposit of debris; indeed it seems that the bed of the Kidron has moved somewhat to the E since ancient times. The hills which surround the two hills of Jerusalem are all higher than the hills of the city itself. The steep slopes, however, made the city an excellent defensive position which could be stormed only on the N; and the ancient city had a sure water supply in the spring of Gihon*. The two stream beds of the Kidron and the Wadi er Rababy join to form the extremity of the S hill and the single bed which flows to the Dead Sea is now called the Wadi en Nar.

Even in pre-Christian times, as Josephus shows, the name of Zion was given to the W hill, which is larger and higher than the E hill, and down to the 20th century it was commonly believed that the site of the early city lay on this more imposing eminence. Archaeological exploration (cf below) and the fact that the only spring which was available to ancient Jerusalem is found on the E hill show conclusively that the early city was built on the E hill S of the site of the temple*, the present Haram esh-Sharif. Connected with this question is the meaning of the terms Zion and "the city of David," which are said to be synonymous in 1 K 8:1 = 2 Ch 5:2. Zion is called "the citadel of Zion" in 2 S 5:7 = 1 Ch 11:5. H. Vincent has identified Zion and the city of David with the citadel of the E hill as opposed to the entire walled area of the city. J. Simons has suggested that Zion means the walled city of the E hill and Jerusalem the unwalled extension of the inhabited area on the W hill; this unwalled extension was found in all ancient cities, and the name Jerusalem, Simons believes, was given when the unwalled area was incorporated into the enclosure by Solomon.

2. *Archaeology.* The Bible and extrabiblical literary sources give very little information on the extent and the buildings of Jerusalem at any period of its history, and archaeology has been singularly unsuccessful in the neighborhood of Jerusalem. The failure of archaeology is largely due to the fact that exploration was carried on before the development of modern methods; the discoveries were poorly recorded and interpreted, and they permit scarcely more than the affirmation that the E hill is the site of the earliest settlement. Charles Warren explored the four sides of the Haram 1867–1870 and discovered "the Ophel Wall," a structure of early but uncertain date. Hermann Guthe explored the E hill in 1881 with lamentable methods and no results. F. J. Bliss explored the W hill 1894–1897 and found some ancient walls, and on the E hill began to perceive the complex waterworks of the spring of Gihon. These channels were more thoroughly examined by Montague Parker in 1911. Raymond Weill in 1913–1914 and 1923–1924 identified some pre-Israelite remains on the E hill. R. A. S. Macalister and J. G. Duncan in 1923–1925 uncovered large sections of the defensive E wall. J. W. Crowfoot and G. M. FitzGerald in 1927 found a city gate on the W side of the E hill. The excavations on the E slope of the E hill conducted in 1961–1962 by the British School of Archaeology and the Ecole Biblique uncovered buildings and walls from 1800 BC and buildings from the period of the Judahite monarchy. These remains lay well down the slope, showing that the extent of Canaanite and early city was larger than had been previously estimated. The excavations suggested that the W hill was not included in the walled enclosure in the period of the monarchy. The archaeologists concluded that the enclosure of Nehemiah* was much smaller than the enclosure of the city of the monarchy.

3. *Extent.* The extent and growth of the

Jerusalem, the southeast corner of the Haram-esh-sharif with the Dome of the Rock to the right.

Jerusalem, the east wall of the Haram-esh-sharif with the Valley of the Kidron in the foreground.

city from the walled enclosure on the E hill to the enclosure of both E and W hills in the 1st century AD is uncertain. Josephus described three walls which stood in his time, distinguished by modern scholars as First, Second, and Third Walls. He attributes his First Wall to David and Solomon, but this conception is vitiated by his belief that Zion is the W hill. Modern historians agree that the walled enclosure of the pre-Israelite settlement and of David lay on the E hill exclusively and entirely S of the modern Haram. This area was extended to the N by Solomon when he built the temple and palace. Whether Solomon also extended the wall to the W hill is less certain; it is highly probable and accepted by several recent writers. The Second Wall of Josephus lay farther to the N, about the line of the modern David Street and Street of the Chain. Wherever this lay more precisely, the extent of the Second Wall is thought by scholars to define the area of the city in the later monarchy of Judah, the area enclosed by the walls of Nehemiah, and the walled Jerusalem of the NT. The uncertainty here again touches the time at which the W hill was brought into the enclosure. J. Simons believes that the N line of the Second Wall was built by Hezekiah* and Manasseh*. The efforts to bring the water of Gihon* into a reservoir in the central valley, which were made before Hezekiah, presuppose that the W hill was at least partly enclosed with the E hill on the S. On the connection of the Second Wall with the site of the crucifixion of Jesus cf GOLGOTHA. A quarter of the city

called the Mishneh ("The Second") is mentioned in 2 K 22:14; 2 Ch 34:22; Zp 1:10; most scholars believe that this name designates the extension of the city to the N incorporated in the Second Wall. The name *maktēš* ("the Mortar") given to a quarter of the city (Zp 1:11) is more obscure; the name suggests a depression or hollow, and therefore more probably an area in the central valley rather than in the N extension.

The Third Wall was begun by Herod Agrippa* (41–44 BC) but was not finished by him for fear it might be construed as a rebellious act. It was completed by the Jews during the insurrection 66–70. There is wide agreement that this wall followed the line of the existing Turkish wall on the N, which forms a natural line of defense. Sukenik and Mayer in 1925–1927 found the remains of a wall much farther N (near the École Biblique), which was also traced in the property of the American School; the majority of scholars believe that this was never a city wall, but a temporary outwork erected during the insurrection of Bar Cochba 132–135.

Nehemiah's description of the walls and the gates (Ne 2:11–15; 3:1–32; 12:27–43), while the fullest literary source, is too vague to be satisfactory. A list of the gates of Jerusalem can be prepared, chiefly from Ne 3:1–32; 12:27–43, the narratives of the building and the dedication of the walls: the Sheep Gate (Ne 3:1; 12:39), the Fish Gate (2 Ch 33:14; Ne 3:3, 12:39; Zp 1:10), the Old Gate (Ne 3:6; 12:39), the Valley Gate (2 Ch 26:9; Ne 2:11; 3:13), the Dung Gate (Ne 2:13; 3:14; 12:31), the Fountain Gate (Ne 2:14; 3:15; 12:37), the Water Gate (Ne 3:26; 8:1; 16; 12:37), the Horse Gate (Ne 3:28; Je 31:40, not certainly identified with "the horses' entrance" of 2 K 11:16; 2 Ch 23:15), the Muster Gate (Ne 3:31), the Ephraim Gate (2 K 14:13; 2 Ch 25:23; Ne 8:16; 12:39), the Gate of the Guard (Ne 12:39), the gate between the two walls (2 K 25:4; Je 39:4; 52:7), the Benjamin Gate (Je 37:13; 38:7; Zc 14:10), the Corner Gate (2 K 14:13; 2 Ch 25:23; Je 31:38; Zc 14:10), "the former gate" (Zc 14:10), the Middle Gate (Je 39:3), the Potsherd Gate (Je 19:2); Josephus mentions of Gate of the Essenes. It is possible that some gates had several names. The location of them is uncertain. The Valley Gate, the Dung Gate, and the Potsherd Gate are commonly thought to be in the S wall. "The gate between the two walls" (possibly identical with one of these three, by which Zedekiah* fled toward the Jordan valley, is almost certainly in the S wall. The Ephraim Gate and the Benjamin Gate, if they looked to the territory for which they are named,

A street; the steps show the slope which was originally the valley of the Tyropoeon.

should have been in the N wall. The Fountain Gate is most probably named for the spring of Gihon and would be in the E wall. The Water Gate may probably be located in the S wall near the reservoir fed by a tunnel from the spring of Gihon. The Corner Gate is thought to be named after the NW corner of the walls. The W wall must have had its gates and some of the others are probably to be located there. Little is known in detail of the fortifications of OT Jerusalem; cf HANANEL.

4. *Buildings*. A citadel for the Syrian garrison of Jerusalem called the Acra, mentioned frequently in 1 Mc, was established by Antiochus* IV in 168 BC and taken by the Jews under Simon* in 141 BC. The site of this fortress is not certain. H. Vincent locates it on the NE corner of the W hill, the site of the Hasmonean* palace which replaced it. J. Simons accepts the same site for the Hasmonean palace, but believes that the Acra designates the entire S hill, the original area of Jerusalem (Zion), enclosed by the Syrians with a new set of defensive walls which set it off from the rest of the city.

Herod* the Great added considerably to the structures of Jerusalem. Besides the temple*, he built the fortress of Antonia* at the NW corner of the temple area and his own palace on the W side of the city; the site of this palace is identified with the modern Citadel, and Herodian masonry appears in the lower courses of this building. Josephus adds that he built a theater and an amphitheater, but does not say whether these were within or without the walls. Herod and later Pontius Pilate*, procurator of Judaea AD 26–36, both improved the water supply of Jerusalem by building pools and aqueducts which brought water from distant springs.

5. *History*. Jerusalem was settled in prehistoric times. It appears among the cities of Canaan in the Execration Texts of the 12th-13th Dynasties of Egypt in the early 2nd millennium BC (ANET 329). In the Amarna* Letters it is ruled by a satellite king named Abdu-Heba (a Hittite name?). After the Israelite settlement the city lay in neutral territory on the boundary of Judah and Benjamin; it was occupied by the Jebusites*. The account of its conquest in Jgs 1:8 must be an anticipation of the conquest of the city by David; if an earlier conquest occurred, it gave the Judahites no permanent possession of the city. The capture of the city by David (2 S 5:6–9) is probably not to be placed immediately after his accession. Several motives besides the mere desire for territory seem to have been at work. David was king of all Israel in a sense in which Saul* had not been; and his identification with Judah would not recommend him to the other tribes. He preferred for his royal city a community which had no tribal associations whatever. In addition Jerusalem was a stronger defensive site than any of the older Israelite cities which he might have chosen. The name "city of David" may indicate the character of the royal city (cf DAVID, CITY OF); some historians have suggested that the population of the city in David's time was composed entirely of David's court, palace personnel, and personal military force.

Jerusalem looking toward the Mount of Olives to the East with the Dome of the Rock in the center and grove of Gethsemani just behind it.
Jerusalem from the Mount of Olives with the Valley of the Kidron in the center.

The city suffered a number of invasions and total or partial destructions during its history. In the reign of Rehoboam* it was taken by Shishak* of Egypt (1 K 14:25 ff; 2 Ch 12:1 ff). An invasion by Arabs and Philistines in the reign of Jehoram* is mentioned in 2 Ch 21:1 f. It was taken by Jehoash* of Israel in the reign of Amaziah* and part of its fortifications were dismantled (2 K 14:11–14; 2 Ch 25:21–24). The city was invested by the Assyrians under Sennacherib in the reign of Hezekiah* (2 K 18:13–19; 2 Ch 32:1–22; Is 36–37); it is not clear that the Assyrians actually took the city. On the possibility of two separate campaigns cf HEZEKIAH; SENNACHERIB. The city was taken, apparently without fighting, by Necho* of Egypt after the death of Josiah* (2 K 23:33 ff; 2 Ch 36:3). The city surrendered to the Babylonians under Nebuchadnezzar* in 598 BC, apparently without fighting or substantial damage; but when Nebuchadnezzar took it by storm in 587 BC, after a siege of 18 months, the entire city was destroyed and left depopulated. It was resettled after 537 BC (Ezr 1–7; Ne 1–4). No events are recorded during the Persian and early Gk periods; but the city was the scene of strife during the Maccabean period. The city was besieged and stormed by the Romans under Pompey in 63 BC. It was again besieged and stormed by the Romans under Vespasian and Titus in AD 70 and suffered substantial destruction. This was effectively the end of Jerusalem as a Jewish center, although the city was not left uninhabited. In the insurrection of Bar Cochba (AD 132–135) Jerusalem was again a center of resistance and was again stormed. After its fall Hadrian forbade Jews to dwell there and founded a Roman colony on the site with the name of Aelia Capitolina.

6. *Jerusalem as a Theological Symbol.* The theological symbolism of Jerusalem rests not upon its identification with the dynasty of David but upon the temple. Jerusalem is "the place which Yahweh chose for His name to dwell there" (1 K 11:13; 2 K 21:4; 23:27 +). Zion is His holy mountain upon which He has set His king (Ps 2:6). Thus Jerusalem is a holy city, the dwelling and throne of Yahweh (Je 3:16 f; Jl 4:17). The sentiments with which the Israelite venerated Jerusalem are expressed in Pss 87; 122; 125; 128; 137. This devotion to the place of Yahweh's presence among His people gives a peculiar poignancy to the prophetic threats that the city will be destroyed by the righteous anger of Yahweh (Je 9:11; 13:9, 27; Ezk 4–5; 8–10; Mi 3:12). But Jerusalem becomes a vital messianic conception. Its restoration is a work of the fidelity of Yahweh and it is the focus of the messianic kingdom. It is

the center of worship of Yahweh to which all nations will resort (Is 2:2 f; 60:1 ff; 66: 18–20; Mi 4:1–3; Hg 2:7 ff; Zc 8:20–22; 14:16–19). It is again the dwelling of Yahweh (Is 60:1 ff). It is the source of revelation to the world, of law* and word* (Is 2:2 f; Mi 4:1–3). The restored Jerusalem, the work of Yahweh, is a city of joy (Is 35:10; 65:19) and of moral perfection (Is 52:1 ff; 54:11 ff; 60:1 ff). In it appear the symbols of Yahweh's saving power as seen in the exodus*, the pillar of fire and of cloud, and it will be covered with the canopy of His glory* (Is 4:5 f). The restored Jerusalem is eternal (Jl 4:20). It is the source of the river of life which flows from the temple (Ezk 47:2–12; Zc 14:8). One is clearly beyond the Jerusalem of history and geography in this conception; Jerusalem has become the symbol of the contact between God and men, and the point from which salvation radiates.

This conception is retained in the NT. The Gospels echo the poignancy of the prophetic threats against Jerusalem in the predictions of Jesus. He expresses His desire to save this city, the murderess of the prophets, from the judgments which it has deserved (Mt 23:37; Lk 13:34). In Lk and AA Jerusalem is given a central position; it is the point toward which Jesus moves throughout the Gospel, and it becomes the focus from which the preaching of the Gospel goes out to the entire world (Lk 24:47; AA 1:8). Paul also makes Jerusalem the point of origin of his personal ministry (Rm 15:19). But the general refusal of Judaism to accept Christianity and the judgment which in the NT either threatens it or has overtaken it causes a transformation of Jerusalem into the messianic symbol which it already is in the OT. It is the Jerusalem above that is free and the mother of Christians (Gal 4:26), the heavenly Jerusalem which is the end of the pilgrimage of the Christian (Heb 12:22) and the throne of the Lamb (Apc 14:1). The vision of Apc culminates in the descent of the heavenly Jerusalem, which is now synonymous with the kingdom of God and the point of meeting of heaven and earth (Apc 3:12; 21:9–22:6).

Jeshua. Cf JOSHUA.

Jeshurun (Hb *yᵉšurûn*), a name applied to Israel (Dt 32:15; 33:5, 26; Is 44:2). The meaning of the name is obscure. M. Noth suggests that it is artificially formed from *yāšār*, "upright," in opposition to Jacob*, understood as "deceiver" in Gn 27:36.

Jesse (Hb *yišai*, possibly shortened from Abishai*); father of David*. He was a man of Bethlehem* (1 S 16:1 ff). His sons are enumerated in 1 S 16:6 ff; 17:13, as seven in number, but only four are named. After David had fled from Saul to the life of a bandit he transferred his father and mother to Moab that they might escape Saul's vengeance (1 S 22:3 f). This is not only in harmony with the tradition of Rt 4:21 f that David's family was descended from Ruth* the Moabite, but suggests an even closer kinship. The messianic king is called "the sprout of Jesse" (Is 11:1, 10) to signify his descent from David.

Jesus Christ. 1. *Name.* Gk *iēsūs* represents Hb and Aramaic *yēšûʻa,* a late form of Hb *yᵉhôšûʻa* (cf JOSHUA). The name Yeshua was very common in NT times. The meaning of the name ("Yahweh is salvation") is alluded to in Mt 1:21; Lk 2:21; the title of savior (cf SALVATION) was one of the Christian appellatives of Jesus. Gk *christos* translates Hb *māšîaḥ,* "anointed one"; by this name Christians confessed their belief that Jesus was the Messiah*.

2. *Sources.* Jesus is mentioned by three Roman historians. Suetonius (*Life of Claudius,* 25, 4) says that Claudius* expelled the Jews from Rome because of riots instigated by Chrestos. Obviously Suetonius was ignorant of the date and the place of residence of Jesus and thought he was a Jew of Rome in the reign of Claudius. He confused the title Christus with the common Gk name of Chrestos. It is possible, however, that Suetonius has misunderstood the true occasion of the riots, which probably arose because of the enmity of Jews and Christians. Tacitus, writing of the persecution of the Christians under Nero on the charge that they had set fire to Rome, explains the name as referring to Christ, who was executed by the procurator Pontius Pilate in the reign of Tiberius (*Annals,* 15, 14). This information is exact; but Tacitus writes *chrestiani.* Pliny the Younger in his letter to Trajan asking for instructions on how to deal with the Christian sect in Bithynia writes that the Christians assemble on certain days before sunrise and sing hymns in honor of Christ as a god (*Epistles,* 10, 96). Pliny betrays no knowledge of the life or even of the historical identity of Jesus.

Josephus* mentions Jesus twice. In relating the execution of James* he identifies James as the brother of that Jesus who was called Christ (AJ 20, 9, 1). This allusion is brief and unquestioned. In AJ 18, 3, 3 there is a much longer allusion: "Jesus, a wise man — if he can be called a man — accomplished incredible deeds and taught all men who receive the truth with joy. He drew to himself many Jews and many others who came from Hellenism*. Although Pilate condemned him to death on the cross at the instigation of the leaders of our people, his early followers remained faithful. For he appeared to them on the third day restored to life, as the prophets sent by God had foretold this and a thousand other wonders of him. The Christian sect, which is named after him, survives to this day." It is patent that this passage as it stands is the work of a Christian interpolator who has glossed the original text of Josephus beyond recovery. There is no reason to think, however, that Josephus did not mention Jesus in this context at all.

The only sources of the life and teaching of Jesus are the four Gospels (cf separate articles). The contents of the apocryphal* gospels are historically worthless. The other NT writings place Jesus Christ in the central position but add no details of His life to the data of the Gospels.

3. *Life.* The writing of the life of Jesus has been the major problem of NT scholarship for more than a hundred years; after numerous shifts of opinion, the consensus of scholars is that the life of Jesus cannot be written. The reason is that the data for a historical biography do not exist. Refinements on this statement diverge all the way from the historical skepticism which asserts that the historical Jesus cannot be known to the conservative position which believes that we lack only an exact chronological scheme. Better is the statement of M. J. Lagrange that the life of Jesus cannot be written because it has already been written in the Gospels. In these sources (cf separate articles) the purpose of the authors was not to write a life but to present the object of the Christian faith and preaching. The object which they presented was the real historical person Jesus Christ, but they did not and were unable to present His historical biography. Even the personality of Jesus, it seems, was not the primary object of interest. The compelling personality which emerges from the Gospels is one and vividly real, but little effort is made to delineate Him fully. We can believe that the atmosphere of mystery in which He appears reflects the atmosphere of His historic presence; those who knew Him and related the anecdotes from which the Gospels were written knew that there were depths in Him which they never comprehended. The modern historian will do well to respect their reserve.

A chronology of the life of Jesus can be given only within broad lines; cf CENSUS; HEROD; PASSION; PONTIUS PILATE. Mt 2 places the birth of Jesus before the death of Herod in 4 BC. Lk 3:1–2 places the beginning of His public life in the 15th year of the reign of Tiberius*, which may mean either AD 26 or 28. Jn 2:20 reckons the cleansing of the temple in the 46th year of its construction, which was begun in the 18th year of Herod; according to the chronology of Josephus this must be reckoned in 20 BC. The exact dates of the birth and death of Jesus cannot be ascertained, but His life must fall almost entirely between the death of Herod (4 BC) and AD 30, which is near the year of His death.

The three Synoptic Gospels agree on a scheme of His public life; the baptism of John, the temptation, the preaching in Galilee, the journey to Jerusalem, a brief ministry in Jerusalem, His passion and death. It is somewhat surprising that the events of the Synoptic Gospels could be compressed into one year; only one Passover is mentioned, and a number of scholars have attempted to fit the events into a year. This is generally rejected. Jn mentions three Passovers, and the public life is calculated by most scholars as including two to three years. Jn, however, nearly ignores the ministry in Galilee and locates most of the discourses and miracles in Jerusalem. It is difficult to compress these into the week or so suggested by the Synoptic Gospels, nor is it necessary to do so; neither the Synoptics nor Jn intended to compose a historical biography, and the divergence of Jn from the Synoptic Gospels here raises no serious historical problem.

Many particular questions in the life of Jesus are treated in separate articles. Cf ANNUNCIATION; GOSPEL; INFANCY GOSPELS and separate articles; APOSTLE; ASCENSION; BEATITUDES; BRETHREN OF THE LORD; DISCIPLE; GENEALOGY; JOHN THE BAPTIST; MIRACLES; PASSION; PHARISEES; RESURRECTION; SADDUCEES; TEMPTATION; TRANSFIGURATION; WITNESS.

4. *Teaching.* As with the life of Jesus, so it is impossible to write a synopsis of His teaching. There is an implicit fallacy in any attempt to synthesize "the teaching of Jesus" as distinct from the teaching of the primitive Church. The primitive Church made no attempt in its earliest phases to isolate the teaching of Jesus; this can be seen in Mk*, which contains little formal teaching. The apostles conceived themselves as empowered by Jesus to carry on His teaching, and the principal element in His teaching and theirs was Jesus Himself. The only object of investigation is the teaching of the primitive Church itself, which was derived from its memory of the life, person, and teaching of Jesus and the expansion and application of its teaching to the growth of the Church and to new questions which arose. Cf CHURCH; KINGDOM; PARABLE and separate articles on theological topics.

5. *The Jesus of history and the Christ of faith.* A celebrated question of the late 19th and early 20th centuries was the distinction between the historical Jesus and the Christ presented in the NT. In the opinion of many scholars the historical Jesus was so overlaid and transfigured by the faith of the early Church that His genuine figure could no longer be recognized. They proposed that it was necessary by historical and literary criticism to prune off the elements added by the primitive Church to recover both the person and the message of Jesus of Nazareth; the results of such criticism were almost always a sharp reduction of all transcendental elements and a presentation of Jesus as a simple Galilean villager with no message other than, in Harnack's famous phrase, the fatherhood of God and the brotherhood of man. In recent writers, such as Bultmann, Jesus becomes the most insignificant figure of the early Christian Church; all the creative work of Christianity is done by anonymous disciples who made of Him what He never was and never intended to be, the founder of a world religion.

There is an obvious difficulty in this theory in any form in which it has been proposed. There is no genuine reason why we should attribute to Jesus Himself any less importance than the primitive Church attached to Him as its founder. If He was as unimportant as radical criticism makes Him, we should have to discover some other individual or group which was responsible for Christianity. The anonymous mass of the early Church is simply not an adequate cause of the effect which was produced. The personal influence of Jesus dominates every page of the NT; no historical parallel can be adduced by which the reality behind this influence can be doubted. More recent scholarship therefore accepts the identity of the Jesus of history and the Christ of faith.

The identity does not solve all historical and critical problems. It is or ought to be obvious that the faith of the disciples of the living Jesus lacked the depth, the strength, and the understanding of His person and mission which it acquired with the growth of the Church. When the anecdotes of His life and words were retold, He was seen without reflection in the fullness with which He was proclaimed. A degree of transformation and glorification of Him in the traditions and the Gospels must be admitted if on no other basis than normal psychological experience. The questions arise only in determining the degree, and it is doubtful that all the problems of detail in this area will ever be solved. The basic question is whether the preaching of the primitive Church distorted His person and His mission to the point where a substantial identity no longer existed, where the Christ of faith whom it proclaimed was not the historical Jesus of Nazareth. The amount of investigation which has been done in this area for over a hundred years has failed to show any such distortion; rather, it has vindicated the extraordinary fidelity with which the primitive Church preserved the memory of the Jesus of history. For discussion of some problems in detail cf articles cited in the following section.

6. *Jesus the Christ.* Even in the NT Christ becomes a personal surname, as it is in modern usage. Originally it was a title, the Gk form of "Jesus the Messiah." The title identifies Jesus as the Messiah of the OT and of Judaism. This should not be understood as a simple identification. In many ways the title of Messiah is too narrow as a description of Jesus and His mission. Hence in the NT it is supplemented by a number of titles which are "messianic" only in the sense that they describe some aspect of the person and mission of Jesus, and define the sense in which Messiah-Christ was understood in the primitive Church. Here the observations concerning the identity of the proclamation of Jesus by Himself and by the Church are particularly relevant. Cf BODY; KING; LORD; MEDIATOR; PRIEST; PROPHET; SAVIOR; SERVANT OF THE LORD; SON OF GOD; SON OF MAN; WORD. A literal application of the term Messiah as it was understood in contemporary Judaism was impossible; the popular understanding of the title would have been altogether misleading. Hence there are certain reservations in the use of the title in the Gospels; cf below.

(*a*) The Gospels. There are several allusions to popular messianism in the Gospels. The Christ is the Son of David (Mt 22:42; Mk 12:35; Lk 20:41). He is expected in the eschatological catastrophe (Mt 24:5, 23; Mk 13:21). He has the power of clairvoyance (Mt 26:68). He is the king of Israel and a wonderworker (Mk 15:32; Lk 23:35, 39). He will appear from a place known to no one (Jn 7:26 f) and will work many wonders (Jn 7:31). He is a scion of David from Bethlehem (Jn 7:41). He remains forever (Jn 12:34). Some of these features are innocent enough; it was the messianic complex of OT texts and popular misinterpretation which could not be applied to Jesus without modification. The title had to be transformed before it could be used in a Christian sense, and the agent of transformation was the life of Jesus. The question has arisen whether Jesus ever applied the title of Messiah to Himself (denied by a number of scholars) or whether He used

it in public beyond the circle of His disciples (denied by a large number of scholars). In either hypothesis we should have an instance of use of a title by the Church which Jesus did not employ of Himself. The theory of the "messianic secret" (cf MARK) proposed that Jesus simply had no idea that He was the Messiah and that Mk created the explanation that Jesus prohibited its use (Mt 16:20 f; Mk 1:34; 8:30; Lk 4:41; 9:21). Most modern scholars, in the words of Cullmann, are convinced that the messianic secret goes back to Jesus Himself, who actually used the title with great reserve.

There are several passages in which an affirmation that He is the Messiah appears to be made by Jesus. In Mt 26:63 ff; Mk 14:61 ff; Lk 22:67 ff Jesus is asked directly by the high priest if He is the Messiah. The answer is given with interesting variations. In Mk the answer is affirmative, but the expansion of the answer affirms not the title of Messiah but the title of Son of Man. O. Cullmann points out that in Mt the Aramaic phrase "You have said it," contrary to popular opinion, does not mean an affirmative but evades a direct answer. In Mt also the expansion affirms the title of Son of Man. In Lk the answer of Jesus in clearly evasive, and the expansion deals with the title Son of God, again with the phrase "You have said it." It is not therefore clear that at this solemn moment Jesus affirmed that He was the Messiah.

In Mt 27:11; Mk 15:2; Lk 23:3; Jn 18:33 Jesus is asked by Pilate if He is king of the Jews, a messianic title. The answer in all three Synoptic Gospels is "You have said it." O. Cullmann interprets this phrase here in the same way, and supports the interpretation from Jn 18:33, where Jesus never affirms that He is king of the Jews but that He is a king in a nonpolitical sense. Hence it is not clear that Jesus accepted this ambiguous messianic title.

In Mt 16:33 ff; Mk 8:27 ff; Lk 9:18 ff Peter, in answering Jesus when He asked the disciples who they thought He was, answers that He is the Messiah. While the praise of Peter's faith appears only in Mt, there is scarcely any doubt that Jesus accepts the confession. But it is important to notice that the confession is followed immediately by a prediction of the passion which explains the character of the messianic mission of Jesus. The theme of suffering is not drawn from any OT messianic passage in the strict sense, but from the theme of the Servant* of Yahweh and from the theme of Son of Man. Hence the acceptance of Jesus is qualified by an interpretation which removes the title from its popular interpretation.

Jn is more explicit than the Synoptic Gospels in the use of the title of Messiah, and there can be little doubt that Jn is more explicit than Jesus Himself was. Thus in Jn 10:24 Jesus answers a question whether He is the Messiah in the affirmative, and in 4:25 declares that he is the Messiah without being asked. In Jn 9:22 expulsion from the synagogue is threatened to any who should confess that Jesus is the Messiah. Where Jesus identifies Himself with the Messiah to His disciples (Jn 17:3) or where a close follower confesses that He is the Messiah, the Son of God, who comes into the world (11:27) there is less of a problem. A similar explicit note occurs in Mk 9:41, where the followers of Jesus are called those who belong to the Messiah, a Pauline phrase (cf below). In the infancy narratives of Lk Jesus is announced as Christ Lord (Lk 2:11), the Christ Lord (2:26).

In their narratives the evangelists use the title more freely; it was in current use in the Church when the Gospels were written. Jesus is the one called the Messiah (Mt 1:16). Mk opens the Gospel with the title "the beginning of the Gospel of Jesus Christ" (to which many MSS add the title son of God, Mk 1:1). Jn opposes Jesus Christ, the source of grace and truth, to Moses, the source of the law (1:17), and writes the Gospel that its readers may believe that Jesus is the Christ, the son of God (20:31); this statement of purpose does not differentiate Jn from the Synoptic Gospels.

The Gospels identify the messianic mission of Jesus with His suffering, more frequently by the use of other titles but also explicitly. In the groups of passages discussed above (Mt 16:13 ff; 26:6 ff; 27:11; Mk 8:27 ff; 14:61 ff; 15:2; Lk 9:18 ff; 22:67 ff; 23:3;) the messianic mission, however obscurely it appears, is seen in the context of the passion in the first two groups, and in the confession of Peter the affirmation of the messianic mission is followed by a prediction of the passion. In the postresurrection narrative of Lk it is said that the Christ must suffer and enter His glory (24:26) and that it is written that He must suffer and rise on the third day (24:46). This appeal to the OT is seen frequently in the early apostolic preaching; cf below.

(b) The Apostolic Preaching. The material for the apostolic preaching is derived from AA*. The burden of the apostolic preaching to the Jews is often described simply as the proclamation that Jesus is the Messiah (AA 3:20; 5:42; 8:5; 9:22; 18:5, 28) or the proclamation of the gospel of the kingdom and the name of Jesus Messiah (8:12). The messianic mission of Jesus is based upon the OT, particularly His passion and death and resurrection (AA 2:31, 36; 3:18; 17:3;

26:23). The messianic character of Jesus is fulfilled in His glorification and exaltation: God has made Him Lord and Messiah (AA 2:36), He is Lord of all (AA 10:36). The expansion of these themes is seen in the epistles; cf below.

(c) The Epistles. Almost all of the material here is derived from the Pauline and deuteropauline writings (cf PAUL and separate articles on epistles), where the title Christ is more frequently used than in the rest of the entire NT.

The great Christological text of St. Paul is found in Phl 2:5-11. Here the preexistent Christ is in the form of God and equal with God; the incarnation is an emptying of Himself and the assumption of the form of a slave — a very probable allusion to the Servant of the Lord — humiliation and obedience to death by crucifixion. As a result of His mission God has glorified Him and given Him the name of Jesus, a title of adoration, and a confession that Jesus is Lord. This one passage sums up the principal themes of Pauline and even of NT Christology. The transcendence of Jesus, so clear in this passage, is more apparent in the Pauline writings than it is in the Gospels; but A. Feuillet has drawn attention to a number of passages of the Synoptic Gospels which imply preexistence and transcendence, particularly the use of the phrases "I am sent" (Mt 15:24; Lk 4:43) and "I have come" (Mt 5:17; 9:13; 10:45; 20:28; Mk 2:17; Lk 5:32). He who receives the disciples of Jesus receives Jesus Himself, and he who receives Jesus receives the one who sent Jesus (Mt 10:40). Jesus compares Himself to the beloved son sent by his father (Mk 12:6), and presents Himself as eschatological king and judge (Mt 25:34-40). The greater reserve in the use of these themes in the Synoptic Gospels certainly reflects the reserve of Jesus Himself; but they are not pure creations of the apostolic Church.

In the epistles Jesus is the Messiah of the Jews (Rm 9:5; 10:4); in the Johannine epistles, as in Jn, the confession that Jesus is the Messiah is the primary article of faith (1 Jn 2:21; 4:2; 5:1). The Messiah accomplishes His mission through His suffering and death on behalf of sinners (Rm 5:6, 8; 14:9; 1 Co 15:3). Paul knows nothing but Christ crucified (1 Co 1:23; 2:2), and Paul is crucified with Him (Gal 2:20) as all Christians must suffer with Him (Rm 8: 17). God has reconciled man with Himself through Christ, indeed God is in Christ reconciling the world to Himself (2 Co 5: 18 f).

The effect of the saving work of Jesus Christ is union and incorporation of the faithful into Him. Baptism* incorporates the

Christian into the death and resurrection of Christ and confers upon him a new life (Rm 6:3 f); those who die with Christ live with Him (Rm 6:8). Those who are baptized in Christ put on Christ (Gal 3:27); Christ is formed in them (Gal 4:19). Christ and the spirit of Christ dwell in the Christian (Rm 8:9-11). The Christian is an heir with Christ (Rm 8:17). When Paul is crucified with Christ, it is no longer Paul who lives but Christ who lives in him (Gal 2:20). To live is Christ (Phl 1:21). Cf BODY. In these passages Christ takes on a dimension which is larger than that of the historical Jesus, but Paul is not thinking of two distinct realities. Jesus through His passion, resurrection, and glorification becomes the Christ who is the Church and in whose life* His members live.

The glorification of Christ is a prominent theme in the epistles. Through His passion He acquires the name which is adored (Phl 2:5-11). He dies and lives again to be Lord of the dead and of the living (Rm 14:9). He is the power of God and the wisdom of God (1 Co 1:24). The Christians await the appearing of the glory of our God and savior Jesus Christ (Tt 2:13). This theme is more fully developed under the title of Lord*. With the title of Christ are associated other titles which exalt Him: son of God (2 Co 1:19), mediator (1 Tm 2:5), God and savior (Tt 2:13; 2 Pt 1:1), Lord and savior (2 Pt 1:11).

(d) "In Christ." This characteristic phrase of Paul expresses more than any other phrase the dominant place of the Christ in the faith and the thought of Paul. The phrase falls into none of the usual grammatical classifications of the Gk language, but it is not so broad as to lose all meaning; the survey which follows shows that a profound insight into the mystery of Christ is revealed by Paul's usage.

One group of uses of the phrase can be broadly classified as instrumental. In this group the phrase is associated with the redemptive work of Christ, which the Father accomplishes in Him. Redemption and salvation occur in Christ Jesus (Rm 3:24; 2 Tm 2:10). Christians are sanctified in Christ Jesus (1 Co 1:2). God leads us to triumph in Christ (2 Co 2:14), He has blessed us in Christ (Eph 1:3 f). In Christ we have redemption (Eph 1:7; Col 1:14). The Christian is created for Christ Jesus for new works (Eph 2:10). The saving will of God is in Christ Jesus (1 Th 5:18). This use of the phrase emphasizes a prominent element in Paul's conception of redemption* and salvation*, the cooperation of the Father as the initiator and prime cause with the Son as agent-instrument.

The effect of the saving work of Christ is a new life, and this new life is lived not only from Christ but in Christ. In Christ the Christian is alive to God (Rm 6:11); he receives eternal life in Christ Jesus our Lord (Rm 6:23; 8:2). In the resurrection the dead shall be made alive in Christ (1 Co 15:22). Cf 1 Co 1:30; Col 2:6; 2 Tm 1:9. Christ is not only the agent-instrument by which new life is conferred; He is also the sustaining cause, the principle by which the new life endures.

The new life of the Christian is achieved by his membership in the Church, which is an incorporation into Christ. Hence Paul uses the phrase almost as a dative of place to indicate that to be in the Church is to be in Christ; and Christians are said simply to be in Christ (Rm 8:1; 1 Co 15:19; 16:7). Paul's collaborators are his collaborators in Christ (Rm 16:3). Probably this is the meaning of the phrase "many guides in Christ" (1 Co 4:15). Those who die in the Church die in Christ (1 Co 15:18; 1 Th 4:16). To be in Christ is to be a new creature (2 Co 5:17). The phrase is peculiarly apt when it is used of the Church with respect to its unity in one body (Rm 12:5), in one structure (Eph 2:21 f; Col 2:7), a unity which suppresses all differences of race and nation (Gal 3:28). Indeed, the final unity in Christ to which God's saving acts tend is the unity of all things in Christ (Eph 1:10).

Christ is a principle of grace and virtue, and these things are fulfilled in Christ: the love of God (Rm 8:39), the grace of God (1 Co 1:4), spiritual enrichment (1 Co 1:5), the righteousness of God which the Christians become (2 Co 5:21), freedom (Gal 2:4), strength (Gal 2:17), faith and love (1 Tm 1:14). Christ is not an exterior principle of law or doctrine, but a life and a state in which and only in which the fullness of Christian grace and virtue is possible. These are the necessary effects of genuine incorporation in Christ.

Hence in some instances the phrase "in Christ" appears to designate the element or the atmosphere in which the Christian lives and acts: 1 Co 16:24; 2 Co 2:17; Eph 2:6 (a reference to eschatological union with Christ); Phl 1:1; 4:21; 1 Th 1:1; 2 Th 1:1. In these phrases one sees the cosmic dimensions of Christ in the thinking of Paul. In Col 1:16 f "in Christ" designates Christ as the instrument of the Father in creation and the preservation of the entire universe.

Jethro (Hb *yitrô*, meaning and etymology uncertain, but probably a foreign word), a Midianite*, father-in-law of Moses* (Ex 3:1; 4:18), called Reuel* in Ex 2:18; cf also HOBAB. He was a priest. Moses' wife Zipporah* and his sons Gershom* and Eliezer* had stayed with Jethro while Moses returned to Egypt and led the Israelites out of Egypt. He met Moses in the desert and offered sacrifice to Yahweh (Ex 18:1–12). He is credited also with suggesting the institution of subordinate judges (Ex 18:13–27). The story relates the separation of sacral functions from the judgment of civil cases and reduces this division to the authority of Moses (M. Noth). It is curious that the institution should be credited to the suggestion of Jethro; this must reflect a tradition of some dependence of early Israelite judicial practice upon the practice of the Midianites or Kenites. The division of thousands, hundreds, fifties, and tens is military, not civil.

It is impossible to harmonize the different names given to the father-in-law of Moses; Jethro is the name found in the E traditions.

Jew (Hb *yᵉhûdî*, Gk *ioudaios*). The term *yᵉhûdî* in the preexilic books of the OT designates a Judahite, a member of the tribe of Judah*. After the fall of the kingdom of Israel* in 721 BC the title Israel survived only in Judah. In postexilic books the term designates an inhabitant of the Persian province of Judah, which consisted of Jerusalem and its environs. From this time forward the term Jew is used in a varied but distinctive manner in Palestinian and in Hellenistic Judaism. In Palestine the term is a political-ethnological term which designates the Jew as a member of a people; for the religious community the term Israel is employed. The usage is best illustrated in 1 Mc, in which the term Jew is used only by Gentiles and by Jews when speaking to Gentiles (e.g., 1 Mc 8:20) or in official documents of a secular character (e.g., 1 Mc 14:27–46). In the Hellenistic Judaism of the Diaspora* the term Israel was rare, and the term Jew was commonly used by Jews to designate themselves even within the community and in religious contexts. Thus in 2 Mc the term Israel is used only in prayers and in the title "God of Israel"; these are echoes of OT usage. Similar use of the term is found in the papyri of Elephantine*, Philo, Josephus, and the inscriptions on Jewish tombs in the Roman catacombs.

In the Synoptic Gospels the term is rare; this reflects the Palestinian character of their sources. It is used only in the phrase "king of the Jews" uttered by Gentiles and in Mt 28:15; Mk 7:3; Lk 7:3; 23:51. The latter four passages no doubt reflect the address of the Gospels to Gentile readers or listeners.

Jn exhibits the Palestinian usage (18:33, 39; 19:3, 19, 21), and also a use similar to that of Mt 28:15 + cited above (Jn 2:6; 5:1; 6:4). The most distinctive usage of Jn is the employment of the term to designate the adversaries of Jesus in contexts where the Synoptic Gospels would use Pharisees* or Scribes* (e.g., 2:18; 7:1; 8:48, 52, 57; 9:18; 10:24, 31, 33; 11:8; 19:38; 20:19). The technical sense of "adversary" is particularly clear in such passages as 7:13; 9:22; 19:38; 20:19, where believers in Jesus, themselves Jews, are said to act "out of fear of the Jews." Gutbrod suggests aptly that this usage shows that the Gospel was written at a time when the division between Jews and Christians had become deep enough to be recognized as what it was, and that "Jews" used in this sense designates exactly those who refuse to accept Jesus because He seems to demand abandonment or modification of Jewish beliefs and practices which ultimately must issue in the loss of identity of the Jewish community as such.

The use of the term in AA is sometimes parallel to the Johannine usage (e.g., 9:23; 12:11; 13:50; 17:5, 13 +). The term is also used to designate Jewish members of the Christian community (14:1; 18:2; 21:39; 22:3).

The term Jew in Paul is also used to designate members of the Christian community (Gal 2:13 f); these are Jews by birth (Gal 2:15). Most frequently the term is used to designate a type rather than individuals (Gutbrod). The type is described in Rm 2:17–29; he is a man of the law*, conscious of his obligations under the law and placing all his hope in the law; cf 1 Co 9:20. The heritage of the law makes the Jew different from the Greek (Rm 3:1; 9:4). When the Jew becomes a Christian, he creates the problem of the reconciliation of the law and faith. Because of his membership in the people of God he is slow to accept the Christian message that in Christ there is no longer any difference between Jew and Greek (Rm 3:9) either in the necessity of deliverance from sin (Rm 3:9) or in the union achieved in Christ (Gal 3:8, 28; Col 3:11).

The relations of Jew and Christian in the first generation of the Church were complex and not worked out without a process of development which ultimately gave the Church a deeper insight into her nature and mission. The apostles and their first disciples were Jews who naturally continued the cult and the observances of Judaism; they prayed in the temple (Lk 24:53; AA 2:46; 3:1), observed the Jewish practice of vows (AA 18:18), observed Jewish festivals (AA 20:16). The apostles at first selected the temple as the place where they taught and proclaimed Jesus (AA 5:42). They could not believe the report that Paul taught Jewish

Christians that they did not have to observe the law* — a report which Paul himself denied — and counseled him to make a display of Judaism while he was in Jerusalem (AA 21:20–24). The early expansion of Christianity to Damascus* is thought to be the work of Jewish Christians (AA 9:2); Paul was careful to point out that Ananias*, who had received him into the Church, was an exact observer of the law (AA 22:12).

But a certain lack of harmony appeared early. The Jerusalem community included some Hellenists*, Gk speaking Jews; it is probable that the dissension mentioned in AA 6:1 was deeper than the issue mentioned, since Jews of the Diaspora were not as rigid in their view of Jewish obligations as were the Jews of Jerusalem. The question was settled amicably. A more urgent question was the admission of Gentiles to the Church. This was solved by Peter* when he admitted Cornelius (AA 10:1 ff). But Cornelius was a proselyte (AA 10:2) and it is likely that his admission to the community included the obligation to practice Judaism. When Paul and Barnabas admitted Gentiles to the Church they laid no Jewish obligations upon them at all. Some members of the Jerusalem community rejected this policy entirely (AA 15:1, 5), thus putting the issue clearly: one could not become a Christian unless one first became a Jew, and circumcision and the law were necessary means of salvation. This was the question discussed at the meeting of Jerusalem (AA 15) which decided it by a compromise, imposing only three dietary laws and the observance of Jewish matrimonial impediments (AA 15:29). It did not settle the question of the obligation of Jewish Christians to observe the law, and in fact it seems the question was not even raised.

The incident at Antioch*, which was the center of Gentile Christianity as Jerusalem was of Jewish Christianity, shows that the influence of rigorous Judaism was strong even there (Gal 2:11–14). It is uncertain whether this occurred before or after the meeting at Jerusalem; it is probable that it was later, and this shows the persistence of the Jewish party. Even when Gal was written the influence of the Jewish party had spread into Galatia*, and the purpose of the letter is to controvert this party. Apparently they were active at Corinth also (2 Co 11:22). These rigorists should not be taken as representative of the entire Jerusalem community and its leaders. In the NT Js, Heb, and to some extent Mt are products of Jewish Christianity.

The Jerusalem community fled to Pella when the Romans came to suppress the Jewish rebellion; after AD 70 its numbers and influence were diminished to very little. The Fathers mention some obscure sects such as the Nazareans and the Ebionites which were later degenerations of Jewish Christianity.

Jezebel (Hb 'îzebel, meaning and etymology uncertain; the component -zebel represents the divine title "prince" cf BEELZEBUL), personal name; daughter of Ethbaal* of Sidon* and queen of Ahab* of Israel (1 K 16:31). She fostered the worship of the Canaanite Baal in Israel and supported 450 prophets of the Baal (1 K 18:19); this was not mere syncretism, for in her hostility to Yahweh worship she attempted to exterminate all the prophets of Yahweh (1 K 18:4,13). When Elijah stirred up a popular movement which resulted in the killing of the prophets of the Baal, Jezebel decreed death for him (1 K 19:1–2). It was Jezebel who persuaded Ahab to permit her to secure the vineyard of Naboth* for him and who accomplished this end by the judicial murder of Naboth (1 K 21:5–15). For this she was cursed by Elijah in terms which were written in view of the story of her death at the hands of Jehu* (2 K 9:29–37). That Jezebel was a strong-willed woman who had a powerful influence on Ahab, himself not a man of weak will, is evident not only in these stories of her life but also in the boldness with which she met death. It seems likely that Ahab had little interest in religion and permitted her to have her way. The name is used in a cryptic way in Apc 2:20 with an obvious allusion to the Jezebel of 1–2 K; it is probably applied to a prophetess of Thyatira*.

Jezreel. Cf ESDRAELON.

Joab (Hb yô'āb, "Yahweh is father"), personal name; son of Zeruiah* the sister of David, and brother of Asahel and Abishai (1 Ch 2:16). It is curious that the name of Joab's father is never mentioned. Joab was the commander of David's forces after David's accession as king of Judah at Hebron, and he led them to victory over Ishbaal's men, commanded by Abner (2 S 2:12–32). He was no doubt a companion of David with his brothers during David's outlaw career, but his name does not occur except as the brother of Abishai* in the narrative of this period (1 S 26:6). Joab murdered Abner in revenge for Abner's killing of his brother Asahel* in combat (2 S 2:18–23; 3:24–27). Joab alleged as an excuse his belief in Abner's duplicity (2 S 3:24–25), but the narrator makes it an act of revenge (2 S 3:27). Such revenge of a slaying in combat does not seem in accord with the ethics of the feud even in the primitive form in which they were practiced, and it was disapproved by David, who cursed Joab for the murder (2 S 3:28 f) and gave Abner an honorable burial (2 S 3:31–37). It was certainly David's purpose to dissociate himself publicly from the murder (2 S 3:37), which actually was unprofitable to him. But the mysterious hold which Joab retained over him most of his life is seen in his confession of his inability to punish the crime (2 S 3:38 f). 1 Ch 11:6 preserves a tradition that Joab was the first to enter Jerusalem (cf GIHON) which was not preserved in 2 S; but it is a later interpretation which makes this deed the cause of his promotion to chief command. Joab is listed as commander in both lists of David's cabinet officers (2 S 8:16; 20:23; cf 1 Ch 18:15; 27:33). Joab was the commander in the victories over Ammon* and the Aramaeans* (2 S 10:7 ff; 12:26 ff); David took no active part in the campaign until Joab summoned him to take possession of the city. During this campaign Joab executed David's plan to abandon Uriah* at an exposed point of the battle; David was then able to marry the widowed Bathsheba* (2 S 11:14–25). Joab's influence secured David's permission for Absalom to return from exile after the murder of Amnon (2 S 14); it was no doubt Joab's involvement in this act of clemency which drove him to take such savage vengeance on Absalom after the rebellion was defeated, a rebellion to which he had been an unwitting contributing cause, even though David had expressly ordered that Absalom be spared (2 S 18). Joab rebuked David in frank terms for valuing his rebellious son above his loyal followers, assuring him that the men who had fought for him were ready to desert him at this ingratitude (2 S 19:1–7). David accepted his counsel but made Amasa* commander in his place (2 S 19:13). Joab, in a subordinate command, followed Amasa to subdue the rebellion of Sheba*; disgusted at Amasa's dilatory tactics, he murdered Amasa treacherously, assumed command, and suppressed the rebellion (2 S 20). Joab was opposed to the census which David took, expressing a no doubt general superstitious fear that to count your blessings is to challenge God (2 S 24:3) but Joab and the officers of the army presided over the census (2 S 24:4–9). Joab was a member of the party of Adonijah* (1 K 1:7) and fell into disfavor when Solomon was installed as co-regent by David. David before his death left a charge with Joab for Solomon to execute vengeance upon Joab for the murders of Abner and Amasa (2 S 2:5 f). Some critics doubt the historical value of this tradition and believe it is created to give Solomon the authority of David for the execution of Joab (1 K 2:28–34). The command and the execution, however, are quite in accord with the Israelite view of the danger of unavenged blood.

The importance of Joab in the career of David and the foundation of the monarchy of David can scarcely be overestimated. It is unnecessary, with some modern historians, to see in him the military genius who was responsible for David's victories, but he must have been a skillful warrior. It was this combined with his unswerving and dedicated loyalty to David, it seems, which gave him such a hold upon David that David could not punish him for acts of which he disapproved. These dark and violent deeds were done from no other apparent motive than to protect David in his rise to the throne and in his retention of it. David could not reject them, nor was he unwilling to profit by them; but it is far more probable that he wished Solomon to execute the justice which he felt himself unable to execute.

Joanna (Gk *ioana*, from Hb *yᵉhôhānān* [Jehohanan*]), a personal name; wife of Chuza*, steward of Herod* Antipas. She was one of the women whose contributions helped to support Jesus (Lk 8:3) and was among the party who discovered the empty tomb of Jesus (Lk 24:10).

Joash. Cf JEHOASH.

Job (Hb *'iyyôb*, meaning and etymology uncertain, but probably the same as the name Ai-ia-ab-bu which occurs in the Amarna* Letters), the hero of the book of that name.

1. *Analysis*. The prologue (1:1–3:1), in prose except for the speeches, relates how Job, a wealthy and pious man, was stripped of all his goods and afflicted with a fatal disease (probably leprosy) in order that a dispute between Yahweh and Satan* about the disinterestedness of Job's virtue might be settled. Job refuses to blame God for his misfortunes.

3–31. A dialogue between Job and his friends, Eliphaz*, Bildad*, and Zophar*. After the introductory speech of Job (3), the dialogue is arranged in three cycles (4–14; 15–21; 22–27). Each cycle contains six speeches: a speech by each of Job's friends and a reply of Job to each. This is followed by a poem in praise of wisdom (28) and Job's final speech (29–31). The third cycle has apparently been disturbed. The speech of Bildad (25) is very brief, and the speech of Zophar is missing. There is general agreement among critics that 26:5–14 and 27:7–23, whose contents are altogether in accordance with the ideas of Job's friends throughout the dialogue, contain part or all of the disarranged speeches of Bildad and Zophar.

32–37, four speeches of Elihu*.

38–39, two speeches of Yahweh, followed by submission of Job (40:1–5).

40:6–41:34, two additional speeches of Yahweh, followed by a second submission of Job (42:1–6).

Epilogue (42:7–16), again in prose, in which Yahweh renders the verdict in the debate to Job and restores all his possessions double.

2. *Criticism.* The inquiry into the literary origins of the book has concerned itself chiefly with these questions:

(1) Prologue and epilogue and their relation to dialogue. The opinion that the two parts were originally independent and unrelated has been abandoned. Most critics, however, believe that the prologue and epilogue come from a much older tradition of Job which the author used as the setting for the dialogue which he composed. Some older critics proposed that the present prologue and epilogue were adopted from preexisting literature as they are; the more widely accepted opinion is that the author has modified the tradition. The existence of Job as a figure in early folklore is suggested by Ezk 14:14, 20, who mentions Noah*, Daniel* (not the Dn of the OT), and Job as three righteous men. Job and his friends are not represented as Israelites, which suggests a foreign origin of the popular story. R. H. Pfeiffer proposed that not only the original story but also much of the book itself was of Edomite* origin, adapted by an Israelite poet; this solution has not recommended itself to critics, although the Edomite character of the Job story is not improbable.

There is no reason to affirm or to deny the historical existence of Job. The allusion to his patience in Js 5:11 implies his historicity no more than the parable of the Good Samaritan demands a historical background.

(2) Praise of wisdom (28). This poem does not fit easily into the speeches of Job or his friends. Most critics regard it as a fugitive piece of wisdom literature, possibly from the author of the book, which has wandered into its present context.

(3) The speeches of Elihu* (32–38). Almost all recent critics believe these were added by a later hand. Elihu does not appear outside his own speeches. In style and depth of thought his speeches do not reach the level exhibited throughout the dialogue. They are an example of the process of expansion of Hb literature by the reflections of later readers who desired to contribute their own ideas on the subject discussed in the text. Some older critics believed that Elihu's doctrine of the educative value of suffering was actually the solution to the problem proposed by the author of the book. This opinion is generally rejected. The author of the dialogue could scarcely have constructed his work so as to reach such an inadequate solution as a climax; and this opinion makes it difficult to incorporate the speeches of Yahweh into the book.

(4) The speeches of Yahweh (38–41). The first two speeches of Yahweh (38–39), formerly questioned by several critics, are now more generally accepted, not only because they reach the quality of style and content which is characteristic of the dialogue, but also because they seem necessary to complete the book. C. Kuhl, however, believes that the completion is achieved by the theophany alone without the speeches (cf below). The second two speeches describing Behemoth* (the hippopotamus) and Leviathan* (the crocodile) are more seriously questioned as original. Whether they add anything to the first two speeches is not altogether clear, and they seem to fall somewhat in style and conception. These are not convincing arguments, and some modern critics believe they do not demonstrate the secondary character of these passages.

Jb has some relations to ancient wisdom literature, but they are relations of subject matter only; Jb is perhaps the most profound and original literary work of the entire OT. Its problem was explicitly proposed in a Mesopotamian poem called after its first line *Ludlul bel nemeqi,* "I will praise the lord of wisdom" (ANET 434–437). The designation of this poem as "the Babylonian Job" is overenthusiastic. Its author is afflicted, but he knows no reason, since he has been faithful in all his duties to the gods; why is the god angry? His real mind is expressed in the thought that perhaps man does not know: what man thinks is good is evil to the gods, and what man thinks is evil is good to the gods. This thought he does not allow himself to retain; he is delivered from his sufferings by a deliverance as mechanical and unreal as the epilogue of Job.

The literary form of the dialogue has no parallel in the OT. It is found, however, in extrabiblical literature such as the Egyptian dialogue of a man with his soul (ANET 405–407). No ancient Near Eastern writer, however, used it with the perfection with which it appears in Jb. Within the dialogue there are many reminiscences of the hymns and lamentations of the Pss*. Some other more extreme critical theories which are generally abandoned are mentioned only to show that the book is more complex than it appears. In general these theories, accepting the principle that much of the OT grows by successive additions of meditation and reflection — a principle which must be accepted — explain the entire dialogue as due to successive deposits of thought on the problem of the book. E. Sellin believed that these were the successive deposits of a single author, whose mind grew and changed with his reflections. The obstacle to such theories is the rather obvious presence of a literary genius of the highest order, a unity of spirit and conception which can scarcely be the result of coincidental additions.

3. *Authorship and Date*. There is nothing whatever to identify the author of the book; all critics except R. H. Pfeiffer and a few who have accepted his view believe the author was an Israelite. The book offers no concrete evidence of its date. It seems very probable that the discussion of the problem of the book did not occur in Israel until the time of the exile and afterwards; on this basis most critics believe it was composed between the 5th and 3rd centuries, with the probability inclined toward the earlier part of this period.

4. *Theology*. The term "theology" is apt to be misleading here. Jb is not a philosophical dialogue; as A. Lefèvre has remarked, it is a lived experience. It presents a problem, but it never proposes the problem as such nor does it formulate a solution. The meaning of the book has been extensively discussed; it is extremely difficult to formulate the author's thought in a scheme which does it full justice. The problem is the living reality of Job himself, and the solution, if it may be called a solution, is the spiritual progress of Job from the beginning to his submission to Yahweh. The problem in the large sense is the problem of evil; more precisely, it is the problem of unmerited evil, the suffering of the innocent and its corollary, the prosperity of the wicked. The problem is raised in Je 12:1–6, which is possibly reflected in Jb 21.

The doctrine of Job's friends is consistent throughout. It is wisdom teaching which has its roots in passages like Ps 37; Pr 2:21 f +, and ultimately in the theology of Dt*. They affirm that God grants prosperity to the righteous* and punishes the wicked with adversity; therefore Job is a sinner. This carries the doctrine of the wise men to the point of absurdity by applying it to each individual case. The teaching of the wise was collective rather than individual and ascribed all evil and suffering to human malice; this is true, but it cannot be applied in proportion to individuals.

The speeches of Job exhibit no such consistency; they wander from one point to another, sometimes replying to the friends and sometimes ignoring them. Job touches on such questions as whether he is an enemy of God by nature, whether God is more pleased to destroy than to make, whether God is sheer irrational power and nothing more, whether justice is only what God wills it to be. These and all such ideas are rejected, and Job arrives at one clear conclusion: the justice of God cannot be defended by affirming that it is realized in the existing world. God must be just, or there is no such thing as justice; and if He is just He must know that the world does not display perfect justice. It appears that the author in these speeches wishes to present the problem in all its urgency and to look at it from all possible angles. Job's friends exhibit the kind of smug prosperity which leads men to deny the reality of the problem; all is well with them, and if all is not well with another it must be his fault.

The Vg translation of 19:25–27, which introduces the idea of the resurrection into Job, is an unfaithful translation of a corrupted Hb text. The idea can be traced nowhere else in the speeches of Job; and it is so relevant to the problem that it is most unlikely that it should be mentioned only once and then dismissed. Nevertheless, Job wonders whether there may not be some possibility of a future vindication which ordinary experience does not offer. It is possible that the author leads the discussion toward this point but does not carry it further; Hb belief of the period presented nothing to which he could carry it. But it is in a sense demanded once the problem of evil is attacked as he attacks it.

The progress of Job's realization that both he and his friends find no answer to the problem ends in the bankruptcy of wisdom, of human reason, before evil. The term of Job's spiritual progress is the theophany. God, to whom he has desired to plead his innocence, appears, but God does not listen to Job's plea. Nor does God take the trouble to defend Himself. The speeches of Yahweh are an affirmation of Yahweh's wisdom and it is necessary to understand what wisdom means in the OT to perceive their relevance. As the wisdom of man is demonstrated in his management of his life, so the wisdom of God is manifested in His management of the universe. The world is full of the mystery of Yahweh's wisdom; in spite of its paradoxes, it does not fall apart, it does not return to chaos (cf CREATION). Of this world men, and one man in particular, are but a small part. Job must accept the world as it is and from this accept God as He is.

This is not, as we have remarked, a speculative solution; the author does not offer Job's experience as a way to understand evil, but as a way to live with it. The experience of Job is that one can support evil only when one experiences a theophany, an insight into the reality of God. Without this insight the problem ultimately drives one to the solution of the Mesopotamian poet; there is really no difference between good and evil. Before evil human wisdom and human reason are bankrupt; the book of Job ends with the conviction that only faith* makes evil tolerable, faith which brings insight through the experience of God which is within the reach of one who desires it.

Jochebed (Hb *yôkebed*, meaning and etymology uncertain), a personal name; daughter of Levi*, aunt and husband of Amram*, mother of Moses* and Aaron* (Ex 6:20) and of Miriam* (Nm 26:59). The names of Moses's parents are not mentioned in J's account of his birth (Ex 2:1 ff) and it is most probable that the two genealogical lists of P where the name Jochebed occurs are late artificially constructed genealogies. It is quite unlikely that names compounded with Je — (Yahweh) should occur before Moses.

Joel (Hb *yô'ēl*, "Yahweh is El" [god]), a personal name; the title of one of the twelve prophets. No data are given on his life. The book stands second in the collection of the twelve prophets.

1. *Analysis.* The book falls into two parts: 1–2, the plague of the locusts; 3–4, the day of Yahweh. LXX and Vg combine 2–3 of Hb into one chapter 2.

1–2. This is a prophetic liturgy of lamentation; descriptions of the plague of locusts (1:4–7, 10–12, 17; 2:2b–10) are interspersed with lamentations (1:8, 19) and calls to fasting and repentance (1:13–16; 2:12–17). The liturgy of lamentation is answered by an oracle of deliverance delivered by the prophet (2:18–27).

3–4. An apocalyptic poem compiled from several short sayings: the outpouring of the spirit* upon Israel (3:1–2), portents of the day of Yahweh (3:3–5), the judgment of the nations in the valley of Jehoshaphat* (4:1–8, 9–14), the deliverance of Israel (4:10–21).

2. *Criticism.* A number of critics have proposed that the liturgy of lamentation and the apocalyptic poem are from different authors; they point out differences in style and spirit and the somewhat violent union of the two themes in a single book. They explain the allusions to the day of Yahweh in 2:2, 11 as due to the redactor who fused the two. Many other modern critics believe that these are not convincing and maintain the unity of the composition.

3. *Date.* The conception of the day of Yahweh exhibited in the book and the tone of the lamentation suggest a date in the postexilic period after Nehemiah*. A. Kapelrud among modern critics is almost alone in proposing a date about 600 BC. The position of the book after Ho in the collection of the 12 prophets shows that the collectors of the prophetic writings regarded the book as early.

4. *Theology.* The interpretation of the book depends on whether the locusts are to be taken as a historical event, as a metaphorical description of an invasion of a foreign army, or as an apocalyptic prophecy of the future. Almost all modern critics think that the locusts are a historical event. The language may seem somewhat exaggerated, in spite of the severity of such locust plagues in the Near East. Joel applies to this plague of nature in terms which in preexilic prophets are used to describe the armies of Assyria and Babylonia. In the postexilic period, however, there were no longer any such threats as these invaders.

In the assumption of single authorship, the prophet represents the locust plague as a type and a portent of the day of Yahweh. As Israel can escape the plague by fasting and repentance, so by the same means it can escape the judgment which will fall on all nations. This conception of the day of Yahweh is a later development of the idea from the form it has in earlier prophets; cf DAY OF THE LORD.

Jl 3:1–5 is quoted in AA 2:16–21 with reference to the charisma of Pentecost, and Jl 3:5 is quoted in Rm 10:13.

Johanan. Cf JEHOHANAN.

John (Hb *yᵉhôhanān*, "Yahweh is gracious," Gk *iôannēs*), the name is borne by several in the NT.

1. The son of Zechariah* and Elizabeth* called "the baptizer" (Gk *baptistēs*). Lk 1 relates the story of his birth: the announcement to Zechariah by the angel Gabriel*, the old age of his parents, the dumbness of Zechariah, the divinely chosen name, the recognition by the unborn John of the presence of the unborn Jesus. The motifs of the child of aged parents, the announcement of the birth by an angel, and the divinely chosen name echo the narratives of Abraham*, Isaac*, Samson*, and Samuel*; and the account of the conception and birth of John seems to contain an admixture of midrash* in which the story expresses through symbolism the anticipation of the saving event of the gospel. But the symbolism does not mean entire creation; and the kinship of Jesus and John is very probably a piece of genuine tradition. John next

appears (Mt 3:1–10; Mk 1:4–6; Lk 3:1–9) in the desert of Judah announcing the kingdom (Mt), the coming of the judgment (Mt-Lk), inviting to baptism and repentance (Mt-Mk). John was dressed in a manner reminiscent of Elijah (Mt), and his appearance in the desert also echoed the way of life of Elijah. Lk adds details of his moral teaching (3:10–14): generosity to the poor and renunciation of cheating and oppression. John announced the coming of the Messiah as judge (Mt 3:11 f; Mk 1:7 f; Lk 3:15–18). The Messiah will baptize in a holy spirit and fire, for which John's baptism, which was a symbol of the repentance to which he invited, was merely a preparation. When Jesus joined those who wished to be baptized by John, John recognized Him as the Messiah (Mt 3:13–17; Mk 1:9–11; Lk 3:21 f). The Synoptics attest the large numbers who heard him and went out to see him (Mt 3:5, 7; Mk 1:5).

Jn's representation of the Baptist does not differ. He was sent from God to bear witness to the light (1:6, 15); and Jn 1:19–36 relates that John denied that he was the Messiah (Lk 3:15 f) and designated Jesus as "the lamb* of God." It was because of this designation that Jesus made His first disciples. The witness of John to Jesus is reiterated in Jn 3:25–30.

John was imprisoned by Herod* Antipas because of his public rebuke of the tetrarch for his adulterous and incestuous marriage with Herodias* (Mt 4:12; Mk 1:14; Lk 3:19 f); in the account of the Synoptics Jesus did not begin His own ministry until John had been imprisoned. John recurs in the public life of Jesus. A question was raised why the disciples of Jesus did not fast like those of John (Mt 9:14 ff; Mk 2:18 ff; Lk 5:33 ff), and Jesus elsewhere calls attention to the contrast between the austere life of John and His own ordinary manner of life (Mt 11:18; Lk 7:33). John sent his own disciples from his prison to ask Jesus the question about His Messiahship directly (Mt 11:2–6; Lk 7:18–23). The answer of Jesus, couched in terms of the Servant* passages of Is, was equally direct to those who knew the OT. There is no reason to think that this was a theatrical manifestation by John in order to convince not himself, but his disciples; it is not at all improbable that he lost some of the assurance with which he had first borne witness and wished to be reassured. The answer of Jesus not only reassures him but also defines the character of His Messiahship. The testimony of Jesus to John makes John the greatest of all the Israelite heroes (Mt 11:7–19; Lk 7:24–35). In John the Jewish belief that Elijah would return before the Messiah

has been fulfilled (Mt 17:13; Mk 9:13). Some thought that Jesus Himself was John returned from the dead (Mt 16:14; Mk 8:28; Lk 9:19). Jesus was able to silence the Pharisees by asking them to say whether the baptism of John was from heaven or from men (Mt 21:25–27; Mk 11:30–33; Lk 20:4–8); the popular esteem of John as a prophet was so great that the Pharisees dared not question his authentic mission. The NT presents him as the last of the prophets of the OT, the precursor of the Messiah.

John was finally executed as a result of a foolish pledge made by Herod during a drunken orgy (Mt 14:1–12; Mk 6:14–28; Lk 9:7–9). The murder of John is also attested by Josephus*, who witnesses the popularity and influence of John among the people. Jn 5:33–36 adds a testimony of Jesus to John as a witness to the truth, a burning and shining lamp, and notes his popular influence (Jn 10:41).

The baptism of John is from the beginning the point at which the ministry of Jesus is thought to begin (AA 1:22; 10:37). John's own antithesis between his baptism and the baptism with the holy spirit and fire is repeated in AA 1:5; 11:16, and the witness of John to Jesus in the gospel appears in Paul's discourse at Antioch of Pisidia (AA 13:24 f). The disciples of John survived as a distinct group some years after his death in places as remote as Ephesus (AA 19:3); and Apollos*, a native of Alexandria, who became a Christian at Ephesus, knew only the baptism of John (AA 18:25).

The Qumran* texts have cast some light on John and raised some questions. If John baptized in the Jordan valley near the Dead Sea — and this is what all topographical indications suggest — he could scarcely have failed to have some contact with the Qumran group; the buildings were literally within sight. The place of baptism in John's call to repentance is paralleled not in orthodox Judaism but in the Qumran rites; and the hostility of John to the priestly and scribal circles also has its parallels in Qumran; cf BAPTISM; QUMRAN. But there is nothing in the simple proclamation of John as related in the Gospels which would suggest that he was at the time a member of the group, and nothing in the literature of Qumran which would prepare one of its members to recognize Jesus as the Messiah. But we should not think that the lines of such groups were drawn so hard and fast as to exclude all association. One need not go so far as to assume with some scholars that John was a member of the Qumran community who became dissatisfied with it and turned to the solitary life; but it is easy to assume that some of John's disciples had shared the Qumran experience before they joined themselves to him.

2. The son of Zebedee* and brother of James*, one of the Twelve (Mt 10:2; Mk 3:17; Lk 6:14; AA 1:13). Mk 3:17 adds that they received from Jesus the nickname Boanerges*, "sons of thunder"; whatever the name may mean, it scarcely suggests a retiring and contemplative disposition. James and John were called from their father's fishing boat to follow Jesus (Mt 4:21 f; Mk 1:19 f). Peter, James, and John occur together as chosen by Jesus to accompany Him where the rest of the Twelve were left behind: the transfiguration (Mt 17:1; Mk 9:2; Lk 9:28); the healing of Peter's mother-in-law (Mk 1:29) and of the daughter of Jairus* (Mk 5:37; Lk 8:51); asking about the time of the Parousia* (Mk 13:3); Gethsemani* (Mt 26:37; Mk 14:33). These incidents suggest that the three were more intimately associated with Jesus than the rest of the Twelve. John and Peter are sent to prepare the Passover (Lk 22:8). James and John ask that they may be seated beside Jesus on two thrones; they receive a mild rebuke and the promise that they shall drink of His cup (Mt 20:20–28; Mk 10:35–45). Of John alone it is related that he complained about an unauthorized exorcist (Mk 9:38; Lk 9:49) and that he asked that the inhospitable Samaritans be struck by lightning. He appears together with Peter in the cure of the lame man (AA 3:1, 3, 4, 11) and in the hearing before the council (AA 4:13, 19) and as conferring the spirit upon the disciples baptized at Samaria (AA 8:14). Paul names him with Peter and James among the three pillars of the Jerusalem church (Gal 2:9). No character sketch can be drawn from these details which permits one to say that this John must be or could not be the author of the 4th Gospel.

John is not named in Jn. Those who maintain that he is its author identify him with the beloved disciple (13:23; 19:26; 20:2 f; 21:7, 20–24) and the unnamed disciple of 1:40; 18:15 ff; cf JOHN, GOSPEL OF. While there is no difficulty in identifying him with the beloved disciple, there are difficulties against identifying him with the unnamed disciple. The call of the two is not the same (cf above); John was a working fisherman at the Sea of Galilee, not a follower of John the Baptist in the desert of Judah; and it is not as easy to combine the two as one would think. How John the son of Zebedee could not only enter the palace of the high priest but introduce a friend is scarcely conceivable; and the hypothesis that he was known

there because he delivered the fish does not deserve serious mention.

John, Epistles of. 1. 1 Jn: I. *Content and Plan.* Many commentators renounce any effort to find a logical arrangement and progression of thought; the sentences are strung together with no order except that of a loose community of topics and occasional catchwords. With H. Braun, A. Feuillet, and A. Wikenhauser, the epistle can be divided into three groups of remarks, preceded by a prologue and concluded by an appendix:

Prologue, 1:1–4: the life manifested on earth as a principle of communion with the Father and the Son.

I. Communion with God (or walking in the light), 1:5–2:27 (or 2:29): the antitheses of light-darkness and truth-lie, the necessity of confessing sin and keeping the commandments, of abstaining from the world and rejecting false teachers.

II. Living as children of God, 2:28–4:6 (or 3:1): likeness to God, the transforming vision, the urgency of the commandments, particularly the primary commandment of love, the need of faith, the dangers of false teaching.

III. Love and faith, 4:7–5:12: God is love, union with God through love and faith that Jesus is the Son of God, love of God and one's fellow man, faith in Jesus the principle of the new birth from God, the witness given by God that Jesus gives eternal life.

Conclusion of the epistle, 5:13.

Appendix, 5:14–21: prayer for a sinful brother, summary of three truths.

Some more subtle plans have been proposed by scholars. Haring and Brooke suggest a triple development: 1:5–2:27; 2:28–4:6; 4:7–5:17. In each of the first two they find a moral thesis followed by a Christological thesis; in the third the two theses are merged. Bonsirven suggests two developments: the conditions of divine communion and of ecclesiastical communion (1:5–2:29) and the love of God and of God's children (3:1–5:4). Chaine also presents a double development: communion with God (1:5–2:28), divine sonship (2:29–5:13). Schnackenburg presents a triple arrangement: communion with God (1:5–2:17), the present situation of the community (2:18–3:24), the true children of God (4:1–5:12). These and other plans attest the ingenuity of their writers rather than the art of the author of 1 Jn; the epistle simply rambles on a set of topics which are generally agreed upon by commentators.

II. *Main Themes.* These main themes can be summarized as follows: Christian life is "a vital ontological relation" (Feuillet) of communion with God arising from rebirth, knowledge of God, the indwelling of God. The communion is mysterious, realized at present only by faith but creating a likeness to God fulfilled in the present by the observance of commandments. The commandments are summed up in the commandment of love; there is only one Christian love, which attains God in the love of one's fellow man. This moral realism is united with a mystical awareness of God possessed. The reality of the union depends on the reality of the Incarnation of Jesus the Son of God, who is the medium by which the Christian life is communicated.

III. *Literary Unity*. A number of critics have questioned the literary unity of 1 Jn. There are some antinomies in the present text (1:8–10; 2:1; 3:3; 5:16 f vs 3:6–8; 5:18). The lack of plan indicated above leads to a suspicion of a process of compilation. Dobschütz suggested that 1 Jn is a compilation of a didactic composition and a homiletic composition. R. Bultmann has proposed a much more elaborate theory; he believes the author used an existing collection of pagan-gnostic revelations to which he adds homiletic glosses and commentaries to make them vehicles of Christian faith. The revelation document included 32 verses: 1:5–10; 2:4 f, 9–11, 29; 3:4, 6–10, 14 f, 24; 4:7 f, 12, 16; 5:1, 4; 4:5 f; 2:23; 5:10, 12. Bultmann claims to recognize the document by parallel clauses arranged in pairs and its sententious style. This compilation Bultmann thinks was then rewritten to adapt it to traditional eschatology and sacramental theology. Preisker modifies this theory to a compilation of the revelation document and an eschatological text found in 3:13 f, 19:21; 5:18b–20; 2:18 ff; 4:1 ff. It must be conceded that the style of 1 Jn does shift between the didactic and the homiletic, and some degree of compilation is probable; whether the materials can be recovered is another question. It is certain that the appendix 5:14–21 is added after 5:13, the conclusion of the epistle.

IV. *Authorship*. Tradition attributes 1 Jn to John the apostle. 1 Jn is used by Polycarp and by Papias (as quoted by Eusebius). The explicit tradition begins with Irenaeus and is affirmed by Clement of Alexandria, Tertullian, and Origen. Internal evidence supports the identity of the author of Jn and 1 Jn. There are a number of close contacts in vocabulary and style, and in particular there are a number of phrases common to Jn and 1 Jn which are rare or absent in the rest of the NT. There are several characteristic ideas in common such as word*, the only-begotten, savior, the coming in the flesh, new birth of the Christian, the primacy of faith and love, the antitheses of light-darkness and truth-lie, the children of God, the world, the spirit. But there are also differences. Several key words of Jn are missing in 1 Jn: glory*, holy spirit*, mission, judgment* and others. Likewise there are some keywords of 1 Jn absent from the Gospel: anointing*, the seed of God, communion, parousia*, propitiation, antichrist*, and others. The style of 1 Jn is less Semitic than Jn. It is remarkable that the OT is not cited in 1 Jn. Christ is called the paraclete* (2:1). The eschatology of 1 Jn is less spiritualized and realized than the eschatology of Jn. The differences seem to be less weighty than the verbal and doctrinal similarities; and the difference may have an explanation in the literary form and purpose of 1 Jn.

V. *Literary Form and Purpose*. 1 Jn lacks some of the marks of the epistle*; it has no name of sender or receiver, no formulae of greeting or of conclusion. Hence some suggest that it is not a letter but a didactic composition. Most scholars, however, believe that it was written for a determined audience, more probably as an encyclical to a group of churches in Asia. Certainly the author seems to have definite adversaries in mind. They deny that Jesus is the Messiah or the Son (2:22 f); they reject the coming in the flesh (4:2 f, 5–6). They seem to claim extraordinary revelations. These adversaries have been variously identified as Judaizing Christians, Gnostics, or Docetists. Meager information about these sects does not permit certain definition; but it is altogether probable that the polemic intention of the author is sufficient to account for the differences between Jn and 1 Jn mentioned above.

The Comma Joanneum, 5:7–8 of the Vg, is missing in all Gk MSS except four later MSS and in the Oriental versions. It is quoted by no Church father before Priscillian (380). There is no doubt that it is a gloss on the preceding lines, probably added in Africa or the Iberian peninsula.

2. *2–3 Jn*. These differ from 1 Jn in form and content; they are letters, and indeed occasional letters. 2 Jn is addressed to *Eklektē Kyria*, "The Elect Lady," which in all probability designates a church of Asia. The church is troubled by false teachers, who appear to be the same as the false teachers of 1 Jn. The church is exhorted to faith, love, and rejection of the false teachers. 3 Jn is addressed to Gaius. It arises from a conflict with Diotrephes, who has an undefined headship in the church. Gaius is praised for his faith and loyalty; some think Demetrius, the bearer of the letter, is sent to depose Diotrephes and install Gaius. It is a tantalizing peep into an early jurisdic-

tional dispute which is otherwise obscure.

Authorship and Canonicity of 2–3 Jn. Not only the authorship of John the apostle but the canonicity of 2–3 Jn was questioned in the early Church. Their use in the E is not attested before Dionysius of Alexandria; they are cited by Athanasius, Cyril of Jerusalem, and Gregory of Nazianzan. Origen, Eusebius, and Jerome all relate that they were not received in some eastern churches; these probably included the church of Antioch, since writers of this school do not use 2–3 Jn. The two letters exhibit close verbal affinities with Jn and 1 Jn. There is no difficulty about the joint authorship of all the Jn documents; a difficulty is raised by the title of John the Elder in 2–3 Jn. This title is unique in the NT; many think it is the John the Elder mentioned by Papias (cf JOHN, GOSPEL OF). Not enough is known about the titles and functions of officers in the early Church to speak with complete assurance; but it does seem that one would expect the title of apostle if the author possessed it. The title appears in the other NT writings which are alleged to be the work of apostles. The absence of the title in these letters casts some doubt on the authorship of John the apostle and by implication on his authorship of Jn and 1 Jn.

John, Gospel of. 1. *Contents:*

Prologue, 1:1–18.

I. The ministry of Jesus, 1:19–12:50.

Preparation, 2:1–4:54: testimony of John the Baptist, 1:19–34; call of first disciples, 1:35–51.

Beginnings, 2:1–4:54: miracle at Cana, 2:1–12; cleansing of temple and discourse with Nicodemus, 2:13–3:21; testimony of John the Baptist, 3:32–36; Jesus in Samaria, 4:1–42; healing of ruler's son at Capernaum, 4:43–54.

The ministry of Jesus, 5:1–10:39.

Cure of paralytic followed by discourse and debate, 5:1–47; miracle of the loaves and discourse on the eucharist, 6:1–71; discourse and debate at Jerusalem, 7:1–52; discourse and debate on the light, 8:12–59; cure of the man born blind, 9:1–41; discourse on the good shepherd, 10:1–21; discourse and debate at the feast of the Dedication, 10:22–39.

Conclusion of the ministry, 10:40–12:50.

Resurrection of Lazarus and decision of the council to have Jesus put to death, 10:40–11:54; journey to Jerusalem, anointing at Bethany, triumphal entry into Jerusalem, discourse, 11:55–12:50.

II. Passion and Resurrection, 13–21.

The last supper, 13:1–31; farewell discourses, 14:1–16:33; final prayer, 17:1–26.

The Passion, 18:1–19:42.

Apparitions, 20:1–29; conclusion, 20:30–31; apparition at the Sea of Galilee, 21:1–23; second conclusion, 21:24–25.

2. *Plan and Structure.* The above outline attempts to describe no plan of the book. Scholars agree that the book is carefully, even artfully planned; but the plan must be quite subtle, for there is no general agreement on it. Thus E. Allo finds that Jn is composed of the prologue, five major divisions, and the resurrection accounts; the five major divisions are: first manifestations, 1:19–4:42; Galilean ministry, 4:43–7:9; public proclamations of the person and mission of Jesus, 7:10–11:57; "the great week," 12:1–17:26; the Passion, 18–19. D. Mollat believes that Jn after the prologue is arranged in nine parts grouped around the major liturgical feasts of the Jews which appear in Jn (cf below): the first week of the messianic ministry, 1:19–2:11; the first Passover, 2:12–4:54; the Sabbath, 5:1–47; the second Passover, 6:1–71; the feast of Tabernacles, 7:1–10:21; the feast of the Dedication, 10:22–11:54; the third Passover, 11:55–19:42; the resurrection and the week of apparitions, 20:1–29; appendix, 21. Mollat adds that the idea which emerges from this plan is that Jesus brings the institutions of Judaism to an end by accomplishing them. A. Feuillet borrows from C. H. Dodd the name of "The Book of Signs" for 1–12, which is balanced by "The Book of the Passion," 13–20(21). Feuillet finds that the climactic point is "the hour" mentioned in Jn, the hour of the fulfillment of Jesus in His redeeming death. The dramatic progression of Jn, as Feuillet describes it, is exhibited in a double movement; the progressive revelation of the person and mission of Jesus set against the growth of faith in His disciples and the growth of unbelief in the Jews to its climax in their decision to put Him to death. Jesus first reveals Himself as the founder of a new economy of salvation: the Messiah who institutes a new covenant with the baptism of regeneration and the coming of the spirit (1:19–4:42). Jesus then reveals Himself as being with the Father the source of life (4:43–5:47), as the bread of life (6:1–71), as the life and light of the world (7–12). The second part is the supreme manifestation of Jesus: first His intimate revelation of Himself to the disciples, centering on the themes of love, consolation, and union (13–17), the Passion, oriented toward the foundation of the Church (18–19), and the resurrection, dominated by the coming of the spirit and the atmosphere of peace and joy and the foundation of faith and the Church. There is a common element in these various plans: an agreement of commentators that the Gospel is schematic and symbolic,

and that schematism and symbolism are basic in the theology of Jn (cf below).

It is also widely agreed that the structure is not rigid and that a number of anomalies suggest either disarrangement of the original form or a complex and not entirely unified process of compilation. The passage of the adulterous woman (7:53–8:11) is almost universally regarded as secondary by critics. It is missing in most MSS; it is cited by no Gk writer earlier than the 11th century; the style is not that of Jn; and Papyrus Bodmer, dated about 200, does not contain it. Some MSS place it after Lk 21:38. The angel of the pool of Bethesda (5:3b–4) is likewise missing in the most important MSS and in the Papyrus Bodmer and is generally regarded as secondary. There are two conclusions (20:30 f; 21:24 f), which suggests that 21 is not a part of the original Gospel. 15–16 seem to be a retreatment of the themes of 14. In addition a considerable number of transpositions have been suggested by critics: 3:31–36 should follow 3:21; chapters 5 and 6 should be inverted; 10:1–18 should follow 10:29; 10:19–21 should follow chapter 9; 12:44–50 should follow 12:36; chapters 15–16 are either secondary or displaced from their original position (14:31 seems to conclude the supper discourse); 18:14–23 should follow 18:24. Of these transpositions the inversion of chapters 5 and 6 is the most popular among critics. The others are not generally accepted. The evidence of the MSS does not support any of them; and it is notable that the Papyrus Bodmer contains none of them. The theories do, however, attest a general consensus of critics that the present arrangement of the text does not come from a single plan and process; to some extent it is the result of casual compilation (cf below).

3. *Language and Style.* The vocabulary of Jn is limited. The syntax is stiff and the style is somewhat monotonous. In spite of this, Jn achieves a sublimity which is universally admired; it is achieved not by literary polish but by the depth and simplicity of conception. Jn also has a vividness of concrete detail which is excelled only by Mk. The style is Semitic, it employs parallelism and parataxis, and is particularly abundant in inclusions, the device by which a passage is set off by the repetition of the same phrase at the beginning and the end. Some (Wellhausen, Burney, Torrey) have suggested that Jn is a translation of an Aramaic original; the majority of scholars have not accepted this proposal, since the Gk is not evidently a translation. There are some Hb and Aramaic words which are interpreted (1:38, 41 f; 4:25; 5:2; 9:7; 19:17; 20:16, 24). Boismard cautiously concludes that while it

is too much to say that the entire Gospel had an Aramaic original, it is possible that parts of it may have been composed in Aramaic.

Jn alone among the Gospels contains personal reflections of the author (1:15–17; 3:16–21 or 13–21; 3:31–35; 12:37–43, 44–50). These are sometimes difficult to distinguish from the words of Jesus; A. Feuillet has said that it is significant that one passes easily from the words of Jesus to the commentary of the author. The style and tone of the words of Jesus in Jn differ notably from the style and tone of the words of Jesus in the Synoptics; Feuillet has called the language abstract, monotonous, learned, almost metaphysical. Some have suggested that the difference in language comes from the fact that Jn contains a higher doctrinal catechesis addressed to a restricted circle of disciples. This is not suggested by Jn, which represents Jesus as addressing crowds. The difference admits no explanation except that Jn has given Jesus his own manner of expression, while the Synoptics have preserved a more primitive form of His words.

The words of Jesus occur in discourses; these differ from the discourses of the Synoptics, which are really collections of sayings. In Jn the discourses are developments of single themes. The development is neither that of Gk dialectic, nor rabbinical discussion, but a peculiar intuitive-mystical presentation; the theme is seen in successive visions, slightly modified at each advance. The discourses arise from some incident. Jesus is often interrupted by questions or objections; this never occurs in the Synoptics. The responses of the listeners are always noted; this is a part of the dramatic progression of faith and unbelief. E. Schweizer has noticed a number of formulae which are rare or absent in the rest of the NT; many of these will be found under articles on separate theological topics.

4. *Jn and the Synoptic Gospels.* The relations of Jn with the Synoptics are peculiar and raise questions concerning the literary form of Jn. Most of the matter of Jn is peculiar to Jn. He has in common with the Synoptics only these episodes: the baptism of Jesus (1:32–34), the cleansing of the temple (2:13–16), the miracle of the loaves (6:1–13), the walking on the water (6:16–21), the anointing at Bethany (12:1–8), the triumphal entry into Jerusalem (12:12–19), the announcement of the betrayal (13:21–30). He has of course the Passion and the Resurrection, but Jn has his own presentation of these. The differences are wider than the material itself. The cleansing of the temple occurs at the beginning of the public life in Jn, at the end in the Synoptics. Little

of the Gospel is set in Galilee, most of it in Jerusalem. There are only seven miracles, of which five or six are peculiar to Jn (4:43–54 is probably parallel to Mt 8:1–13; Lk 7:1–10). The chronology is more detailed and in the opinion of scholars it is reliable; Jn mentions three Passovers and four journeys to Jerusalem whereas the Synoptics mention only one. It is possible and the attempt has been made to reduce the public life of Jesus to no more than a year on the basis of the vague chronology of the Synoptics; Jn demands at least more than two years. Jn lacks the temptation, the choice of the Twelve, moral teachings, the transfiguration, the eschatological discourse, the institution of the Eucharist. It has therefore been asked whether Jn knew the Synoptics, and if he did, what his intention in writing a Gospel so different may have been.

Many modern scholars believe that John certainly knew Mk, probably knew Lk, and probably did not know Mt. The literary affinities with Lk are closer than they are with Mk; cf 13:2, 27 = Lk 22:3; 16:4, 21 = Lk 22:43. The following "Johannisms" are listed in Lk: 2:34 f, 49; 4:22, 29; 7:35; 9:51; 10:21 f; 12:4; 16:31; 24:42. In addition the spirit* is more prominent in Lk and Jn than in Mt-Mk. On the assumption that Jn is the latest of the four he could have known the Synoptics; on the assumption that he is not the latest (cf below), he could not have known all of them. What he did know was the oral gospel*. There are differences in theological perspective also (cf below).

The differences between Jn and the Synoptics are great enough to permit the question whether Jn is to be classified in the same literary form of gospel. Many modern scholars say cautiously that they are not to be purely and simply all grouped together. Jn is preaching* and gospel in the sense that he announces Jesus as Messiah-Son of God (20:31, which may, however, be editorial). But if the Synoptics represent the common gospel tradition, then Jn does not represent it; like them, he does not present a biography of Jesus, but unlike them he presents a comparatively small selection of episodes and many discourses which are cast in his own language (cf above). Numerous explanations have been proposed by scholars. Some suggest that the differences arise from a polemic intention; Jn is directed against incredulous Judaism or against an exaggerated cult of John the Baptist. The second is an unlikely explanation of the whole Gospel; and it is not obvious that the polemic of Jn against Judaism is any more intense than the polemic included in Mt-Mk-Lk. Others have suggested that it is directed against

early heresies, the Docetists (1 Jn 4:2 f) or the Gnostics. We do not know these heresies well enough to discern clearly a polemic against them. Others have suggested that Jn was written either to complete the Synoptics or to correct them or even to supplant them. The last two of these are completely unfounded; the first is an easy explanation which many have accepted. But it is by no means evident that John intended to complete the Synoptics, nor that he does in fact complete them. E. Allo says Jn cannot be understood as an original presentation; it must presuppose and complete the Synoptics. Other modern critics are ready to affirm precisely the opposite: that Jn is an autonomous composition written with no relation, affirmative or negative, to the Synoptics. It is not a complete sketch of the life and mission of Jesus but rather a collection of essays, a presentation of the personal conception of Jesus in a series of sketches.

5. *Authorship, Date, Place of Composition.* Early tradition attributes the Gospel to John* the son of Zebedee* and brother of James*. A. Feuillet notes that authorship here may be taken loosely; the work may have come from John in substance and have been reworked and completed and published by his disciples. The question does not turn on these details. The influence of Jn can be traced in Justin and the Shepherd of Hermas (140–150). The earliest affirmation is found in Irenaeus (180), who traces the line of tradition from himself to his master Polycarp who, he says, knew John personally. The same tradition is found in Clement of Alexandria and in the Canon of Muratori (cf CANON). While it does not touch the question of authorship directly, a date late in the 2nd century proposed by some 19th century critics is rendered nearly impossible by Papyrus Egerton 2 and Papyrus Rylands 457; these fragments of Jn from Egypt in the middle of the 2nd century show that Jn was known there at this early date. Papyrus Bodmer shows that it existed in its present form in 200. The same traditions locate the composition of Jn at Ephesus near the end of the 1st century. Early tradition, however, was not unanimous. Irenaeus says that some whom he does not identify denied the authorship of Jn; these were probably an anti-Montanist sect. Eusebius and Hippolytus report that it was denied by Caius, a priest of Rome (about 200). Epiphanius mentions the *Alogoi,* "opposed to the *Logos,*" so called because they denied that Jn wrote the Gospel.

In support of the tradition some internal features are adduced. "The beloved disciple" (21:24; 21:20) was present at the supper (13:23), at the cross (19:26), where he received the care of Mary, which surely indicates some intimacy, at the tomb with Peter (20:2 f), and at the Sea of Galilee (21:7), where he was the object of a saying of Jesus (21:20–23). The identity of John with the unnamed disciple of 1:40; 18:15 ff is alleged; but cf above, under JOHN. Thus it seems likely that this beloved disciple is Peter, James, or John, one of the three privileged disciples; he cannot be Peter, and James was martyred in 44, too early to be the author of the Gospel. In addition there are some curious statistics: John is mentioned twice in Mt, 9 times in Mk, 6 times in Lk, never in Jn. James the brother of John is mentioned twice in Mt, 9 times in Mk, 4 times in Lk, never in Jn. Of the Twelve Mt is the only other not mentioned in Jn. The silence about James and John suits well the authorship of Jn. It is generally agreed that the author was an eyewitness; his occasional vivid details, his exact knowledge of Palestinian geography and topography and of Jewish customs, and his chronology do not suit one who had never been there. The claims of ocular witness in 1:14; 15:27; 19:35 are to be taken seriously.

Critics who deny or doubt the authorship of John the apostle raise some difficulties. The internal arguments which are drawn from the advanced Christology and alleged disagreements with the Synoptics are less weighty; one cannot set standards of Christology in advance, and the differences, while real, are not such as to prove that John is not the author. More serious is the contention that Irenaeus was wrong in thinking that Polycarp knew John; the letter of Polycarp does not mention his personal acquaintance with John. Irenaeus also says that Papias knew John, but according to Eusebius this was not John the apostle, but John the Elder. The residence of John at Ephesus, attested by Irenaeus, is also doubted because it is not mentioned in the letter of Ignatius of Antioch to the Ephesians; the argument from silence is subject to caution, but it is not without weight. In addition there is a tradition of uncertain value that John suffered martyrdom under Agrippa* with his brother James in 44 and thus could not have lived to the traditional date of the composition of the Gospel. This is attested by Philip of Side (430), by the Byzantine monk George Hamartolos (9th century), and in a Syriac martyrology of 411. These sources are not of impressive reliability, and the silence of tradition elsewhere on the martyrdom of John at this date is also a factor. But all these elements must be taken into account in evaluating the tradition of authorship.

Many modern critics believe that the tradition of the name and the composition at Ephesus around 100 are best preserved by attributing the Gospel not to the apostle but to John the Elder, mentioned by Papias. An extremely hypothetical reconstruction of this person identifies him with the beloved disciple, scarcely more than a boy at the time, the son of a priestly family of Jerusalem (thus explaining 18:15 f, long a difficulty against the authorship of Jn), the eyewitness of some of the events, all at Jerusalem, who lived to old age at Ephesus. A response of the Pontifical Biblical Commission of May 29, 1907, denied that the arguments against the authorship of John are convincing and affirmed the historical character of the Gospel.

The question is now affected by the relations of Jn with the Qumran* documents; these have more affinities with Jn than any other NT book, and this seriously concerns the question of the origin of the thought of Jn. Many critics have questioned the authorship of Jn because they thought the Gospel was the product of Hellenistic rather than Jewish thought; specifically, elements of Hellenistic-Oriental mysticism or mystery* religion, or Syrian or Iranian Gnosticism were proposed. Even before the discovery of the Qumran documents many studies had shown that the roots of the thought of Jn are satisfactorily shown in the OT; cf separate articles on theological topics. The affinities of Jn with Qumran go far to exclude anything but a Palestinian origin for the Gospel. If this be accepted, the question of the date becomes urgent once more. If Jn is the most Jewish rather than the least Jewish of the Gospels, it becomes doubtful that it is the latest. If it is to be dated at the latest before 70, it is probably earlier than both Lk and the Gk Mt, and possibly as early as Mk. In this hypothesis it is a primitive conception of the Gospel, not a mature meditation, a form in which, unlike Mt-Mk-Lk, the themes and the presentation are entirely Jewish, unaffected by the expansion of the Church to the Gentiles. The original form of the Gospel, however, need not be the present form, which exhibits certain anomalies (cf above). Mollat has attributed these anomalies to the method of composition and redaction; it is a slow elaboration including elements from different periods with retouches and additions and different redactions of the same teaching. The whole was finally published not by John in all probability but posthumously by his disciples, who inserted fragments they did not wish to lose but did not know where to place.

6. *Theology.* Jn has long been called the most theological of the Gospels; the term "spiritual Gospel" was coined by Clement

of Alexandria. The dominant themes of Jn are treated under separate articles: BAPTISM, EUCHARIST, FAITH, LIFE, LIGHT, LOVE, SIN, SPIRIT, WORD, and the distinctive treatment of these themes in Jn is seen. The sacramental interest of Jn (baptism, Eucharist) is more emphatic than it is in the Synoptics. The unique feature of Jn's presentation lies in his use of symbolism. Each of the discourses arises from an episode, and the episode is so constructed as to symbolize the theme of the discourse. E. Allo and A. Feuillet have summarized this symbolism as follows: 1:1 echoes Gn 1:1 and indicates that the incarnation of the word initiates a new creation. There are seven days from the confession of the Baptist to Cana. There are seven miracles. Water is a symbol of faith, of baptism, and of purification; wine is a symbol of blood, of sacrifice, of love, of the Eucharist. The episodes and discourses are arranged in eight pieces. (1) The miracle of Cana presents water and wine, baptism growing into union with the death of Jesus in the Eucharist. (2–3) In the cleansing of the temple Jesus is revealed as the new temple. The episodes of Nicodemus and the Samaritan present Jesus as the giver of the water of regeneration in baptism, offered to Jew and non-Jew, to man and woman. (4) Jesus gives life to the ruler's son. (5) The word of Christ to the paralytic has the power of healing water; He gives life to men and raises them from the dead. (6) Jesus is the bread of life, the new manna, in the Eucharist. (7) Jesus is the life and light of the world; He gives light to the blind man, in contrast to the spiritual blindness of the Jews, through the purification of water. (8) The climax of the presentation of Jesus as the resurrection and the life is the resurrection of Lazarus, who emerges from the darkness of the tomb to the light of life.

In contrast with the Synoptics Jn has some striking omissions. It is not the gospel of the kingdom but the gospel of the person of Jesus Himself. Jn speaks of (eternal) life rather than of the kingdom, but eternal life in Jn is not clearly eschatological; in fact the eschatology of Jn seems to be more of a realized eschatology in the present than the eschatology of the Synoptics, and there is no reason to say that the presentation of the Synoptics is more primitive. The resurrection is emphasized in Jn; but the judgment* is usually conceived as present. The Christology is certainly different from the Christology of the Synoptics; this does not necessarily mean that it is "more advanced." Jesus is clearly the preexistent Son and Word in whom the Father is revealed. There is no moral doctrine in Jn as in the Synoptics,

except for general recommendations to keep the commandments.

7. Historical Value. Many critics of the 19th and 20th centuries, impressed by the differences between Jn and the Synoptics and by the deliberate use of symbolism, have denied that Jn is or is intended to be a historical presentation. It is necessary to define "historical." Many meant that Jn does not present "the historical Jesus," that the Jesus of Jn never existed. To this one must point out that the Jesus of Jn and of the Synoptics are not two different persons presenting two different missions and two different teachings. The basic themes are identical; the differences do not change the character of Jesus or of the gospel. In the sense that Jn presents the real Jesus in whom faith is demanded, Jn is as historical as the Synoptics.

The use of symbolism and schematism, however, seems to make it evident that Jn is not historical in the same sense as the Synoptics, and that both the words of Jesus and the incidents have received a transformation beyond that which they receive in the Synoptics — and they are transformed there also. The symbolism, it must be understood, arises from the person of Jesus and from the events of His life; but events represented symbolically are not represented in their pure historical character. One must concede, it seems, that Jn permits himself a freedom in constructing the episodes which is considerably greater than the freedom exercised by the Synoptics; to what extent this freedom has transformed the event from its past actuality cannot be settled by any general principle, but only by an examination of each passage.

Joktan (Hb *yŏḳtān,* meaning and etymology uncertain), in the Table* of Nations the son of Eber* and the father of a number of S Arabian tribes (Gn 10:25–30; 1 Ch 1:19–23) with whom the Israelites were ethnologically connected.

Jonadab. Cf JEHONADAB.

Jonah (Hb *yônāh,* "dove"?), a personal name; a prophet, Jonah ben Amittai of Geth-hepher of the reign of Jeroboam* II; the hero of the book of Jonah.

1. Analysis. 1:1–16. Jonah receives a commission from Yahweh to preach to the Assyrians of Nineveh. To evade the commission he sails to Tarshish*; but the ship is threatened by a great storm. By lot the blame falls upon Jonah; and the ship is saved when Jonah is thrown overboard.

1:17–2:10. Jonah is swallowed by a great fish, in which he remains three days and nights, and where he sings a psalm (2:2–9); then the fish vomits him upon the shore.

3: Jonah preaches in Nineveh. The king and the entire people proclaim a fast of repentance and the threat of destruction is averted.

4: Jonah, angry that his threat has been nullified, sits in a booth under the shade of a gourd. When the gourd is attacked by a worm it withers and Jonah is exposed to the sun. His grief at the destruction of the gourd becomes a lesson from Yahweh Himself; Yahweh is even more unwilling that a large city with all its people and cattle should be destroyed.

2. Authorship and Date. The book is anonymous. A date in the postexilic period is accepted by most critics not only on the basis of the doctrine of the book (cf below) but also because of numerous Aramaisms and features of later Hb prose style and grammar.

3. Criticism. There is no reason for assigning the book to more than one author except for the psalm 2:2–9. This song has no relation to the situation of Jonah; indeed, it is a psalm of thanksgiving rather than a petition. It has been added, more probably by an editor than by the author.

4. Literary Form and Doctrine. The meaning of the book can be understood only in the light of its literary form. Jon is unique in the prophetic canon; it is entirely a narrative and not a collection of sayings. Exegetical tradition down to the 19th century regarded the book as historical and even attempted in recent times to date it according to the known kings of Assyria. There are convincing reasons why the book cannot be historical. There is little doubt that the author has adopted Jonah of 2 K 14:25 as his hero; but the name was chosen apparently almost at random. The book knows nothing of Nineveh, which is only a vague memory at best. It is altogether impossible that Nineveh, the ruins of which have been explored, could have been a city of "three days' journey," by which the author clearly means a city which it takes three days to walk through (3:4). A city of 120,000 infants implies a total population of over a million, far too large for Nineveh. Our knowledge of Assyria both from Assyrian and from biblical records leaves no room whatever for a conversion of Nineveh to the worship of Yahweh; to say, as some apologists do, that the conversion was only temporary, destroys all the point of the story. The title "king of Nineveh" (3:6) never appears in Assyrian nor in biblical records; it is always "king of Ashur." The author understands a "ship of Tarshish" as a ship bound for Tarshish, which is not what the term means. It is not merely the fish which is wonderful in the story, but the entire story is motivated by wonders from beginning to end: the storm, the fish, the gourd, and the greatest wonder of all, the instantaneous conversion of Nineveh. A search therefore after the species of fish which swallowed and regurgitated Jonah or for parallels to this wonder is idle; the fish is the creation of the author. The literary type of the book is didactic fiction or parable.

Thus understood the teaching of the parable is clear; it is the opposition between the attitude of Jonah toward the Assyrians and the attitude of Yahweh. One must recall here the place of Assyria in Israelite and in ancient history; it was the first great imperial power, a bloody, aggressive, and plundering nation. The attitude of contemporary Israelites toward Assyria is exhibited in the book of Na*. This is the city which the author represents as the object of a prophetic mission from Yahweh; and Yahweh receives the repentance of Assyria. Clearly His compassion and forgiveness can go no farther.

In contrast to this is the attitude of Jonah, the typical Israelite: narrow, unwilling to bring the message of Yahweh to the enemies of his people, and angry when they accept it. Jon, like Rt, is a protest against the narrowness and exclusivism which often appeared in postexilic Judaism. This narrowness frequently expressed itself in a hate of foreign nations, a desire for their destruction rather than their recognition of the divinity of Yahweh. Hence Jon marks one of the greatest steps forward in the spiritual advancement of biblical religion. It is unfortunate that so much discussion of its historical character has obscured the meaning of the book for many readers.

5. Jon in the NT. "The sign of Jonah" (Mt 12:39–41; Lk 11:29–30, 32) is slightly modified in Lk, who does not present the three days and three nights as a sign explicitly. It is not certain that Lk deliberately omitted this feature to alter the meaning from the sojourn in the fish's belly to the success of Jonah's preaching; rather Lk's sign of Jonah consists in the authentication of God's messenger by his deliverance from death (J. Jeremias). The success of Jonah's preaching is part of the sign, however, both in Mt and Lk, whose words in this part of the passage are identical.

Defenders of the historical character of Jon have always appealed to the sign of Jon, urging that the deliverance of Jon and the resurrection are placed parallel and that one must be as historical as the other. Modern studies of the way in which the OT is cited in the NT make it clear that the OT is always taken as a single work and cited with no distinction between its various literary forms. There is no more reason for the historicity of Jon in this passage than there is for the historicity of the rock of 1 Co 10:4 or of Jannes* and Jambres in 2 Tm 3:8. A fictitious narrative, such as the parable of the Good Samaritan, is just as effective a sign as a historical allusion.

Jonathan (Hb *yônātān* or *yᵉhônātān,* "Yahweh has given [a son]"), a common personal name in the OT. **1.** Eldest son of Saul*. He distinguished himself as a warrior by his feat of capturing single-handed a Philistine outpost at Michmash*; his boldness incited the Israelites to attack and defeat the Philistines. Saul, however, uttered a foolish curse on anyone who should touch food before evening. Jonathan, unaware of the curse, ate some wild honey. On the following day the failure of the oracle (cf URIM AND THUMMIN) to deliver an answer led Saul to inquire who had violated the curse; the oracle revealed that it was Jonathan, and Saul would certainly have had him executed were it not for a popular outcry against this judgment (1 S 14:1–45). Jonathan and David became close friends when David entered the service of Saul (1 S 18:1–4). In the conflated account of David's troubles with Saul (cf SAMUEL, BOOKS OF) there are accounts of Jonathan's successful intercession for David with Saul (1 S 19:1–7) and of an unsuccessful attempt to reconcile the two (1 S 20). The farewell of David and Jonathan (20:41 f) can scarcely belong to the preceding narrative, which presupposes that the two were unable to meet personally. There is another account of the last meeting of the two in 1 S 23:16–18. Saul and his sons were killed in battle with the Philistines at Mt Gilboa* (1 S 31) and their bodies hung on the city wall of Bethshan*, whence they were rescued by the men of Jabesh-gilead*. Saul and Jonathan were the subjects of a poem of lamentation by David (2 S 1:17–27).
2. One of the Maccabees*, a son of Mattathias*, surnamed Apphus (1 Mc 2:5). He accompanied Judas* in the campaign in Gilead which ended in the removal of all Jews from E Palestine (1 Mc 5:17, 24 54). After the death of Judas (160 BC) Jonathan was elected leader of the Jewish forces (1 Mc 9:28–31). The approach of Bacchides* forced him to flee to the desert near Tekoa*, whence he went on an expedition against the Nabateans who had killed his brother John. In an indecisive battle with Bacchides on the banks of the Jordan Jonathan and his men escaped by swimming the Jordan (1 Mc 9:32–49). After a short

interval of peace (1 Mc 9:57) due to the death of Alcimus* (159 BC) the Hellenizing party of the Jews secretly conspired for the sudden return of Bacchides and the seizure of Jonathan while he suspected nothing. Jonathan learned of the plan and withdrew again to the desert, whence he moved against some of his opponents while Simon defeated Bacchides. The defeat angered Bacchides against the Hellenistic party and he withdrew, leaving Jonathan undisputed ruler of the Jews (1 Mc 9:58–73; 157 BC). He was approached by Demetrius* I when his throne was threatened by Alexander* Balas and obtained generous terms for his alliance with Demetrius (1 Mc 10:1–14). Alexander capped this offer by making Jonathan high priest, an offer which Jonathan accepted (1 Mc 10:15–21; 152 BC). Demetrius made in turn such a generous offer, amounting to practical independence, that Jonathan did not believe it and remained an ally of Alexander (1 Mc 10:22–47). After Alexander's victory he entertained Jonathan as a king (1 Mc 10:59–66). When Demetrius* II claimed the throne he sent a force under Apollonius* against Jonathan, which Jonathan defeated (1 Mc 10:67–89). Demetrius II was successful in obtaining the throne (145 BC); in spite of early hostility, Jonathan, too powerful to be easily dislodged, was accepted as an ally (1 Mc 11:20–41). Jewish troops were sent by Jonathan to help Demetrius suppress a rebellion in Antioch (1 Mc 11:42–52); an estrangement followed of which 1 Mc does not give the cause. When Tryphon* claimed the throne in the name of the child Antiochus VI Jonathan shifted his allegiance to Antiochus (1 Mc 11:54–62) and defeated a detachment of the forces of Demetrius (1 Mc 11:63–74). He renewed the alliances with Rome and Sparta (1 Mc 12:1–23). Tryphon moved against him with an army, but saw that Jonathan was too powerful for him. Tryphon invited him into the city of Ptolemais, where he killed the small force which accompanied Jonathan and held him as hostage (1 Mc 12:39–53). Tryphon offered to release him for payment of an alleged debt to the royal treasury; Simon, successor of Jonathan, made the payment, but Tryphon murdered Jonathan (1 Mc 13:12–23).

Joppa (Hb *yāpô* or *yāpô',* Gk *ioppē,* modern Jaffa), a city on the seashore of Palestine WNW of Jerusalem. From ancient times it was the nearest port to Jerusalem; but it has no true harbor and cannot be used in rough weather. It is listed among the Canaanite cities captured by Thutmose III of Egypt. The Papyrus Anastasi I of the 19th dynasty of Egypt (13th century BC) praises the beauty of its gardens, "where you find the meadow blossoming in its season." In the Amarna* Letters it appears as an Egyptian administrative center. It is included among the cities of Dan* (Jos 19:46) but it was never Israelite; it was possessed by the Canaanites or the Philistines and was Phoenician in the Persian period. Sennacherib* of Assyria took it in 701 BC from Sidqia of Ashkelon*. It is the port to which cedar timber was floated both for the temple of Solomon (2 Ch 2:15) and the temple of Zerubbabel (Ezr 3:7). Otherwise it is mentioned in the Hb OT only as Jonah's port of embarkation (Jon 1:3). Possession of the city shifted from the Jews to the Syrians and back in the wars of the Maccabees; it surrendered to Jonathan* (1 Mc 10:75 f) but was subsequently twice recaptured by Simon* (1 Mc 12:33; 13:11). In 142 BC Simon acquired it permanently (1 Mc 14:5) and fortified it (1 Mc 14:34; 15:28, 35). After the conquest of Pompey Caesar returned the city to the Jews in 47 BC and they held it until AD 67, when the Romans retook it at the beginning of the rebellion.

A Christian community was established early at Joppa which included the devout Tabitha*, raised from the dead by Peter (AA 9:36–42), and Simon* the tanner, at whose house Peter was staying when he had the vision which moved him to receive Cornelius* of Caesarea, the first Gentile to be accepted into the Church (AA 10:7–22).

Joram. Cf JEHORAM.

Jordan (Hb [always with the article] *hayyardēn;* the popular etymology, "the descender," is improbable; the word may be non-Semitic), the largest river of Palestine. The valley of the Jordan is a part of a rift formed by a large geological fault which extends from the valley between the Lebanon* and the Anti-Lebanon to the Red Sea. The river is formed by the junction of four sources near Banias (ancient Paneas) near the Israelite city of Dan. The sources are fed by melting snows from Mt Hermon*. After flowing through the marshy region of Lake Huleh at an altitude of 6–8 ft above sea level, the river plunges through a gorge to the Sea of Galilee* at an altitude of 696 ft below sea level in a course of 10 mi. At the S end of the Sea of Galilee the valley of the Jordan is about 4 mi wide. From the Sea of Galilee to the Dead Sea is 65 mi airline, but the river has a course of 200 mi in this distance. The river descends from 696 ft below sea level at the Sea of Galilee to 1286 ft below sea level at the Dead Sea. Its average width over this course is 90–100 ft and its depth 3–10 ft.

The deep valley of the Jordan between the mountains of W Palestine and the plateaus of Gilead and Moab dominates the Palestinian landscape and is visible from most points on the mountains. An unprejudiced observer must agree with Naaman* that the rivers of Damascus are fairer than the rivers of Israel (2 K 5:12); for the valley is impressive more because of its austere nakedness than for any real attraction of natural beauty. The bed of the river itself is frankly one of the ugliest streams in all nature. The valley has two levels which the Arabs distinguish as ez-Zor, the lower level, and el-Ghor, the upper level, which sometimes lies 150 ft above the river. The tortuous river winds through a dense thicket of small trees and underbrush. This is called "the pride of the Jordan" in Je 12:5; 49:19; 50:44; Zc 11:3; in the last three passages cited the jungle of the Jordan is a haunt of lions*. The thicket varies in width from 200 yards to 1 mi. The Zor is separated from the Ghor above it by a range of bare and eroded marl hills. The valley is arid; the annual mean rainfall at Jericho is 15–16 in. The width of the valley varies from 4–8 mi until the river reaches Jericho, where it is about 14 mi wide. The river is flooded in the spring. Its waters are not clear; it carries a large amount of silt which is deposited where it enters the Dead Sea. It has numerous tributaries, more on the E than on the W; but these are almost entirely seasonal streams except the Yarmuk (not mentioned in the Bible) and the Jabbok*, both of which enter the Jordan from the E.

The river is almost entirely useless; its low bed makes it impractical for irrigation. Historically it has been a barrier between E and W Palestine rather than a means of communication. The climate is disagreeable to Europeans; the winters are mild, but the summers are extremely hot and humid. In modern times the valley supports only a small population. The explorations of Nelson Glueck have shown that this was not always the case: in prehistoric times the valley, it seems, was more densely populated than the mountains, and certainly more densely populated than it is now.

Fords, impassable during the flood season, are mentioned in the Bible at Beth-shan, Jericho, Adamah (Jgs 12:5), Beth-barah (Jgs 7:24), and Bethany (Jn 1:28). The crossing of the Jordan by the Israelites (Jgs 3:10–17) is preserved in a late tradition which has transfigured a simple crossing beyond all recognition. The event on which the story is probably constructed has recurred several times in recorded history, as recently as 1927. The earthquakes* to which

The Jordan near Jericho
with the marl hills in
the background.

The Jordan valley north
of the Dead Sea with
the marl hills in the
foreground and the
mountains of Moab in
the background.

The Jordan at high
water near Jericho.

The Jordan Valley
looking toward the
mountains and desert
of Judah.

the rift is subject have dislodged large land-slips into the river which have blocked its flow for more than 24 hours.

Joseph (Hb *yôsēp,* "let him [the god] add"; some scholars suggest the original form was *y'ôsēp,* "let him gather"), a personal and tribal name. **1.** Son of Jacob* and Rachel* (Gn 30:24; 35:24; 1 Ch 2:2). His brothers, envious of their father's favoritism toward Joseph, sold him to some slave traders who took him to Egypt (Gn 37). Both Reuben* (37:21 f, 30) and Judah* (37:26 f) are credited with efforts to save his life; these two elements probably come from earlier variants of the story. Joseph in Egypt was sold to Potiphar*, who imprisoned him be-cause his wife, failing to seduce Joseph, falsely accused him of rape (Gn 39). In prison Joseph interpreted the dreams of two of the Pharaoh's household who were in prison (Gn 40). One of the officers called Joseph to Pharaoh's attention when the Pharaoh had a disturbing dream; Joseph's interpretation of the dream as portending seven years of plenty followed by seven years of famine so impressed the Pharaoh that he appointed Joseph vizier of the kingdom (Gn 42). When the famine touched Canaan, Jacob sent his sons to Egypt to purchase grain; they did not recognize Joseph. He tested them by accusing them of spying, by holding Simeon as a pledge, and by return-ing their money, and learned that they were sorry for their treatment of him; but he demanded they bring his own uterine brother, Benjamin*, on their next trip (Gn 43). When they brought Benjamin, he tested them again by accusing Benjamin of steal-ing his cup; and when Judah offered to sub-stitute himself for Benjamin's punishment, Joseph revealed his identity and told them to bring their father and his family to Egypt (Gn 44–45). Jacob accepted the invi-tation and was settled in Goshen* (Gn 46:1–47:12). By his monopoly of grain storage Joseph forced the Egyptians to part with their land (except the priests) so that the Pharaoh became the sole landowner in Egypt (Gn 47:13–26). Joseph presented his two sons, Ephraim* and Manasseh*, to Jacob, who blessed them and transferred the rights of primogeniture from Manasseh to Ephraim (Gn 48). Joseph took Jacob's body to Canaan for burial at Machpelah* (Gn 50). After his death the oppression of the Is-raelites occurred under another king who knew not Joseph (Ex 1:8; cf EXODUS). The bones of Joseph were taken out of Egypt by the Israelites (Ex 13:19) and buried at Shechem* (Jos 24:32).

The historical character of the Joseph story is complex. The Egyptian coloring and background is mostly authentic but shows signs of editing in oral or written tradition. The Egyptian names in the story are types found in the 10th century BC rather than the 17th or 16th (cf ASENATH; POTIPHAR; ZAPHENATH-PANEAH). The land monopoly of the Pharaohs and the temples appears in Egypt at the beginning of the 18th dynasty (1580 BC) but its origins are obscure; the tradition credited the great Hb hero with a condition which almost certainly arose after his time. The relations of Joseph with the other tribes of Israel make it probable that the story of Joseph and his brothers is mostly a creation of edifying fiction (cf below); it presents Joseph as an ideal, a man who by his generosity and readiness to for-give upholds the family unity and prevents the family from destroying itself by such quarrels. The story of Joseph and Potiphar's wife has affinities with the Egyptian story of the two brothers (ANET 23–25) and it is quite probable that this story of moral heroism was added to the legends of Joseph.

The sojourn of Israel in Egypt, however, is too solidly imbedded in Israelite tradition to be explained as entirely created. Tradi-tion explained the presence of Israelites in Egypt as due to the promotion of one of their members to a high office in Egypt who admitted them during a famine; they fell from favor in a dynastic change after his death. This suits very well the period of the Hyksos* and their expulsion under the 18th dynasty, and most modern historians place the background of the story here. An Egyptian tomb painting of the 19th cen-tury BC at Beni Hassan shows such a group of nomads seeking admission to Egypt (ANEP 3).

2. Joseph also appears as an eponym; but it is not clear that the name should be in-cluded among the 12 tribes* of Israel*. He is one of the 12 in the blessing of Jacob (Gn 49:22–26); but in the blessing of Moses, which here imitates rather closely the blessing of Jacob, an added line identi-fies Joseph as Ephraim and Manasseh (Dt 33:13–17); the number 12 is preserved by the exclusion of Simeon*. Joseph is also one of 12 in Dt 27:12.

Elsewhere, however, Joseph is either ex-plicitly not one of the 12 tribes or the desig-nation is too ambiguous to show whether Joseph is included in them. Joseph always represents a larger group within the twelve. The usage of the Pnt* and Jos* differs here from the usage of the other books. In the Pnt and Jos Joseph is identified with Ephraim and Manasseh singly or together. These tribes are described as "sons of Joseph" (Jos 18:11; 17:14, 16; 24:32) or the identification is made simply with both

(Nm 1:10, 32; 26:28, 37; 34:23; Jos 14:4; 16:1, 4; 17:17) or with Manasseh alone (Nm 13:11; 27:1; 32:33; 36:1, 5, 12; Jos 17:1–2). It is obvious at once that the identification is never made with Ephraim alone; and this recalls the story of Jacob's transfer of the rights of primogeniture from Manasseh to Ephraim (Gn 48). In some of these passages the identification is made by what appears to be a gloss without which Joseph would appear as a tribal name (Nm 13:11; Jos 14:4). In Jos 18:11; 24:32 the sons of Joseph stand in opposition to the sons of Judah.

In the other books the phrase "house of Joseph" is used. There can scarcely be any doubt that the house of Joseph represents Ephraim and Manasseh in Jgs 1:22 f, 35. But in David's time one passage indicates that the house of Joseph includes Benjamin (2 S 19:21). The relations of this small tribe were no doubt much closer with the larger tribes to the N than with any other. The house of Joseph most probably signifies the same tribes of Ephraim and Manasseh with perhaps Benjamin in 1 K 11:28. Ezk 47:13 in an obscure allusion to the 12 tribes gives an equal portion to all except a double portion to Joseph. Joseph, however, is not included in the list of the 12 (Ezk 48:1–8, 23–28); Ephraim and Manasseh receive the double portion, and the number 12 is retained by excluding Levi. Am uses "house of Joseph" (5:6) and "remnant of Joseph" (5:15) in what appears to be a wider sense of the entire kingdom of Israel; this usage is quite intelligible, since the house of Joseph was the largest portion of the kingdom. Cf Ho's use of Ephraim. Ob 18 likewise uses house of Jacob and house of Joseph in a sense which seems to be synonymous. In Zc 10:6 the house of Joseph is parallel to the house of Judah, again a reference to the two kingdoms. In the Pss Joseph is synonymous with the tribe of Ephraim (78:67), with Israel (80:2), and with Jacob (81:6). In Ps 77:16 the sons of Jacob and Joseph are the people of Yahweh. Thus the term is sometimes used as nearly synonymous with Israel.

The obscurities involved in this usage are discussed by scholars but no substantial agreement has been reached. The identity between Joseph and Ephraim-Manasseh is too frequently mentioned to be regarded as a late artificial creation. M. Noth is no doubt correct in defining the house of Joseph as a federation of the central tribes: at least Ephraim-Manasseh and, possibly at a later date, Benjamin. The occurrence of the name Joseph-El in the list of Thutmose III of Egypt does not indicate that this federation existed in Palestine in the 15th century.

Joseph, then, is a smaller federation just as Israel is a federation, and neither is used as a tribal name. The boundary of Joseph and Ephraim-Manasseh is consistently given as Bethel* on the S; the N boundary is not given, but every indication points to the plain of Esdraelon*. The wavering of the 12-tribe system is probably to be explained by the hypothesis that the "house of Joseph" occupied first one place and then two. The story of Gn 34 suggests that Joseph occupied central Palestine after Simeon* and Levi*.

The house of Joseph, if any Israelite group, is associated with the traditions of Egypt and the exodus*. They must also be the possessors of the traditions of Moses. Joshua was a man of Ephraim. The ark* was usually found in the territory of Joseph. The position of Joseph and Benjamin as sons of Jacob's favorite wife also suggests that the house of Joseph was the original possessor of the Jacob traditions. The original Israel is to be sought in Joseph rather than in any other tribe or group of tribes.

The origin of the other tribes and their relations with the Joseph tribes are questions which cannot be answered with the evidence now available; cf ISRAEL; TRIBE; and articles on the separate tribes. It is scarcely possible to reduce the story of Joseph and his brothers to a history of personified tribes, nor to trace the manner in which the eponyms of the tribes acquired the associations which they have in the present form of the traditions. It appears that the story of the sale of Joseph and his deliverance of his brothers now associates Joseph with the others in a form which reflects the later unity of Israel.

The Joseph tribes were the focus of the rebellion against the house of David under Rehoboam* and comprised the majority of the population and territory of the kingdom of Israel.

3. Son of Jacob (Mt 1:16) or of Eli (Lk 3:23; cf GENEALOGY), husband of Mary*, the mother of Jesus*. Joseph appears in the infancy narratives of Mt and Lk, otherwise only as the patronymic of Jesus (Lk 4:22; Jn 1:46; 6:42). He is called a "righteous man" (Mt 1:19); to him the virgin birth was revealed (Mt 1:20–25). He was also responsible for the care of Mary and Jesus in the flight to Egypt (Mt 2:13–15, 19–23). Mt mentions no residence of Joseph in Nazareth* prior to the return from Egypt. Lk 1:27, however, places the residence of Mary and presumably of Joseph also in Nazareth before the birth of Jesus. The necessity of the journey from Nazareth to Bethlehem in Lk comes from the Bethlehem origin of Joseph's family (2:4). Else-

where in the infancy narrative of Lk Joseph is an accessory figure, present at the birth of Jesus (2:16), the circumcision (2:21), the redemption of the firstborn* (2:22), and the loss of Jesus and his finding in the temple (2:41–52). Joseph was a carpenter by trade (Mt 13:55) as was Jesus also (Mk 6:3).

4. A wealthy man of Arimathea, a member of the Sanhedrin* and a disciple of Jesus, who obtained the body of Jesus after His death and buried it in his own family tomb (Mt 27:57–60; Mk 15:43–46; Lk 23:50–54; Jn 19:38–42).

5. One of the "brethren* of the Lord" (Mt 13:55; 27:56), elsewhere called Joses.

6. Surnamed Barsabbas or Justus; proposed with Matthias* to fill the place of Judas* among the Twelve (AA 1:23).

Josephus. A Jewish historian, born AD 37/38. At the beginning of the Jewish war in AD 66 he was a commander in Galilee but was captured in that year and spent the remaining years of the war with the Romans attempting to persuade the Jews to abandon the war. He took the name Flavius Josephus after the family name of his Roman patrons, the generals Vespasian and Titus, who commanded the Roman armies in Palestine; both of them became emperor. He wrote in Gk. His works: *The Jewish War* (7 books), the *Antiquities of the Jews* (20 books, from the creation to Nero), the *Life* (an autobiography), *Against Apion* (a reply to an anti-Jewish writer). As a historian Josephus is often uncritical and engages in special pleading on behalf of the Jews or on his own behalf; but he is the only source for much postexilic history, especially the period from 142 BC to AD 70.

Joshua (Hb *yᵉhôŝú'a*, "Yahweh is salvation"), personal name; changed by Moses* from Hoshea, salvation, (Nm 13:16). **1.** Lieutenant and successor of Moses and hero of the book of Jos (cf below). The picture of Joshua in the Pnt is not entirely consistent; he appears as military leader (Ex 17:9–14) and as an attendant of Moses (Ex 32:17; 24:13; Nm 11:28) who guarded the tabernacle* (Ex 33:11). He was one of the men sent to scout Canaan before the entrance of the Israelites and with Caleb* resisted the timidity of the other scouts (Nm 13:1–14:38). These differences come from variant traditions. In D (Dt 1:38; 3:21, 38; 31:3, 14 f, 23) and in P (Nm 27:18–23; 34:17) Joshua was solemnly commissioned to succeed Moses. This commission is also found in Jos 1:1–9.

2. The book of Joshua.

1. *Contents:* The book is divided into three parts: 1–12, the conquest of Canaan; 13–21, the division of Canaan; 22–24, appendices.

1, prologue; 2, the scouting of Jericho; 3, the crossing of the Jordan; 4, the erection of commemorative stones; 5, circumcision at Gilgal and apparition of an angel to Joshua; 6, conquest of Jericho; 7:8–29, conquest of Ai; 8:30–35, proclamation of the law with blessings and curses; 9, treaty with the Gibeonites; 10, defeat of the federated kings of S Canaan and conquest of the territory of Judah; 11, conquest of Hazor and Galilee; 12, list of conquered cities.

13–21, description of the boundaries and cities of the tribes.

22, dispute with the tribes of E Palestine about an altar; 23, discourse of Joshua; 24, tribal covenant assembly at Shechem.

2. *Criticism.* The classical documentary hypothesis of the Pnt* included Jos with the Pnt under the designation of Hexateuch and found in Jos the same documents which were identified in the Pnt. Many recent critics have raised reasons for doubt whether the same sources can be found in Jos. M. Noth, followed by several critics, insists that Jos was never part of a single collection with the Pnt but belongs to the "Deuteronomic history" (cf DEUTERONOMY; HISTORY). In the OT Jos replaces an account of the conquest which must have stood in the Pnt sources, since it is impossible that these documents should have ended in the steppes of Moab*. Perhaps some remnants of this other account are found in Jgs 1 (cf below). Modern critics, however, admit that the book is a compilation from diverse sources; but the identification of the separate sources is difficult and there is wide disagreement on the subject. To a large extent this analysis is closely connected with the historical character of the book discussed below.

3. *Historical Character.* There is evident a certain discrepancy between what appears in Jos to be a unified campaign of all Israel which conquers all of Canaan from N to S and a series of separate movements of individual tribes briefly narrated in Jgs 1. This, together with certain features of the account of the conquest in Jos, suggests that Jos is a telescoping of the Israelite conquest into a single movement. M. Noth suggests that the campaign of 2–9 is really an account of the entrance of the tribe of Benjamin. It may be suggested that it was the movement of the house of Joseph*; Joshua was a member of the tribe of Ephraim. But the tradition must be a later reworking of the story; cf the archaeological problems of Jericho and Ai. There are difficulties in supposing that the house of Joseph under Joshua was engaged in the conquests of the terri-

tories of Judah; (10) and Galilee (11). On the other hand, there is no record whatever of a conquest of Shechem* and central Palestine, the territory of the house of Joseph; and many historians suppose that this region was inhabited by Israelite tribes which were never in Egypt. It is seen therefore that there is some difficulty in associating Joshua with almost every conquest attributed to him. But the Israelite movement into Canaan is attested not only by Israelite tradition but also by archaeology, which exhibits a destruction and resettlement in the 13th century of almost every site excavated. This can be attributed to no one but the Israelites. The telescoping of the traditions at a date when the living memory of the conquest was dimmed has altered the form so that it is extremely difficult to recover the original course of events.

The relations of Joshua to Moses are somewhat obscure and many critics have suggested that the connection is entirely artificial, i.e., that Joshua was never connected with Moses. Others believe on the contrary that Joshua is original in the Pnt and from there has become the Israelite leader of the unified conquest created by historical theory. There is a considerable element of theoretical reconstruction in the Joshua traditions, and, as noted above, the position of Joshua in the Pnt is ambiguous; nevertheless, Joshua is too deeply imbedded in the traditions both of the exodus and of the conquest to be easily dismissed. Since he was a member of Ephraim, which with the house of Joseph was most certainly in Egypt, his presence both in the Pnt and in Jos fits the pattern which must be basic in the conquest and settlement, even if the actual conquests attributed to him come largely if not mostly from other tribal traditions.

The lists of 13–21 contain historical data, but not from the time of Joshua. The lists in their present form combine two originally separate lists: a list of tribal boundaries, and a list of the cities within the tribal territories. Neither list is complete. The list of tribal boundaries includes Judah (15:1–12), Joseph (16:1–3), subdivided into Ephraim (16:5–8) and Manasseh (17:7–10), Benjamin (18:11–20), Zebulun (19:10–16), Issachar (19:22), Asher (19:25–29), Naphtali (19:33–35). Some of these boundaries are very sketchily described. The lists of cities include Reuben (13:10–21), Gad (13:25–27), Judah (15:20–62, the most complete), Manasseh (17:11, cities lying in the territory of other tribes), Benjamin (18:21–28), Simeon (19:2–8, cities within the territory of Judah), Zebulun (19:15, a fragment), Issachar (19:18–21), Asher (19:25, 29, fragments), Naphtali (19:35–38), Dan (19:41–46). The list of cities was assigned by A. Alt to the reign of Josiah*; W. F. Albright prefers an earlier date under David or Solomon. The list of tribal boundaries are thought by many to be premonarchic and to represent an ideal rather than a real division, although the tribal territories followed closely the ideal. To these lists is appended a list of the cities of refuge* and of the cities of Levi*. 22 seems to be a late retelling of an early tradition of a dispute between the tribes of E and W Palestine. 23 is a discourse of Joshua written in the style and thought patterns of the Deuteronomic historian.

The tribal assembly at Shechem (24) is regarded by M. Noth as an event of primary importance in the history of Israel; he believes that at this assembly the Palestinian elements of Israel (the tribes which had never been in Egypt) entered into the covenant with Yahweh. This view of the assembly is now accepted by many historians. The words of Joshua, however, are written in the theory of a united Israel with no diversity in its past; they represent the form of a covenant renewal ceremony, including the recital of the deeds of Yahweh, and of the obligations of the covenant and the acceptance by the people of the covenant. There can be little doubt that the assembly was a renewal of the covenant for those tribes which had been in Egypt.

4. *Theology.* The theme of the book, which is among the less edifying books of the OT to many readers, is the possession of the land in fulfillment of the promises made to the fathers. To appreciate this theme one must realize the desire for land which often arises in a nomadic group. Without land a tribe has no roots and no place in history; from the land it acquires stability and identity as a people. Without "the land of Israel" there could be no "Israel." The Israelites realized this and regarded the land as a gift of Yahweh.

The moral tone of the book in such episodes as the entire annihilation of the population of Canaanite cities has been distressing to many readers; to others, unfortunately, it has furnished an example. The use of this example to justify similar treatment of one's religious adversaries shows how much evil can come from faulty exegesis. Knowledge of ancient history now shows us that Joshua and the Israelites were altogether people of their time in the morality of warfare. Their practice can be justified on no ground whatever, and their primitive morality is no example for anyone. The Israelite view of the charismatic leader as one under the guidance of Yahweh must be understood in Israelite terms and not pressed into a crass literal sense. Furthermore, the form of the tradition which we have contains itself the evidence that the practice of annihilation from a religious motive was not practiced generally by the Israelites and may have been actually a rare incident. Their relations with the Canaanites were generally friendly.

The wonders attributed to Joshua are clearly the creations of popular tradition. The crossing of the Jordan is an expression of the theme that Joshua is another Moses (also seen in his lawgiving, Jos 24). The fragment of poetry quoted in 10:12 has caused no small theological difficulty because it was not recognized as a war cry found in an ancient ballad.

2. Son of Jozadak, high priest of Jerusalem in the time of Zerubbabel*, Haggai*, and Zechariah*; written Joshua in Hg and Zc, yĕšûʻa (Aramaic form) in Ezr and Ne. Jeshua is listed among the exiles who returned from Babylon to Jerusalem with Zerubbabel in 537 BC (Ezr 2:2, 36; Ne 7:7, 39). With Zerubbabel he rebuilt the altar (Ezr 3:2) and the temple (Ezr 3:8 f, 5:2). The genealogy of his descendants is given in Ne 12:10 f. With Zerubbabel he was charged by Haggai to build the temple (Hg 1:1) and to serve faithfully after its completion (Hg 2:2, 4).

Jeshua occurs in two passages of Zc. In the first (Zc 3:1–10) Jeshua appears in soiled garments (a sign of mourning) before Yahweh where he is accused by the Satan. He is then clothed in his priestly garments and guaranteed access to the temple. In his presence Yahweh will introduce the Branch (cf MESSIAH; ZERUBBABEL). Jeshua in the vision represents the priesthood, often accused in preexilic writings of sins and crimes. In him the priesthood is absolved from these faults and restored to its proper dignity. The postexilic priesthood will witness the advent of the Messiah.

The second passage describes the coronation of the Branch by Zc. Since the Branch is without doubt Zerubbabel, exegetes regard the name of Jeshua in Zc 6:11 as a substitution for Zerubbabel. The Branch will enjoy harmonious relations with the priest (6:13) who sits at his right hand (Gk; Hb reads "on his throne"); this demands a distinction between the Branch and the priest, and Jeshua should be inserted before "the priest." This modification raises the priest to replace the Messiah; for the reasons behind this modification cf ZERUBBABEL.

Josiah (Hb y'ôšîyyah, y'ôšîyyahu, "may Yahweh give"), personal name; king of Judah (640–609 BC), son and successor of Amon*. Josiah was installed as king at the age of eight after the assassination of Amon (2 K 21:23 f). He was installed by "the people of the land," i.e., the people of Judah outside the royal city and the royal court; the motivation of the assassination of Amon and of the installation is not clear from the records. The narratives of 2 K 22–23 and 2 Ch 33–34 emphasize the religious reforms of Josiah. These began with the repair of the temple and culminated in a sweeping extirpation of all forms of foreign cult. The reform was based on the book of law discovered in the temple by Hilkiah* (2 K 22:8 ff); there is general agreement that this was the original form of Dt*. Josiah renewed the covenant* (2 K 23:1–3; 2 Ch 34:29–33) and celebrated the Passover* according to the terms of the book of the law (2 K 23:21 f); this is much enlarged by 2 Ch 35:1–19. 2 Ch 34:3–7 advances the reform to the 8th year of his reign (631 BC), but this can scarcely be historical.

The political developments of the reign of Josiah can be reconstructed from extrabiblical references to the events briefly alluded to in 2 K. The collapse of Assyria* between 625 and 612 BC meant that after 625, if not earlier, there was no effective Assyrian government of Palestine. M. Noth points out that the religious reform of 2 K 23:4 was an effective declaration of independence from Assyria. With no major power at the moment asserting itself in Palestine, Josiah attempted to restore the kingdom of David. Noth also points out that the activity of Josiah in Bethel* (2 K 23:15), Samaria* and the cities of Samaria (2 K 23:18 f), and Megiddo* (2 K 23:29) shows that Josiah repossessed the land of Israel as far N as the plain of Esdraelon. Political events made it impossible for this repossession to remain permanent. Ashur-uballit of Assyria was expelled from Harran* in Mesopotamia by the Babylonians and Medes in 610 BC. Necho* of Egypt, fearing that another Mesopotamian power would move into the vacuum created by the fall of Assyria, marched to the aid of Ashur-uballit. Josiah, more afraid of a restoration of Assyria or of Egyptian hegemony, met Necho at Megiddo. The text of 2 K 23:29 does not suggest that Josiah was killed in battle, and some historians think he was assassinated. The fuller tradition of 2 Ch 35:20–27 speaks clearly of a battle.

Josiah occurs in Je (1:2 f; 3:6) as a contemporary of Jeremiah and in Zp 1:1. Je 22:13–16 praised Josiah as a man who lived simply, acted justly and righteously, and defended the poor.

Jot. In Mt 5:18 the English rendition of the Gk iōta, representing the Hb Yod*, the smallest letter of the Hb alphabet; the figure thus indicates that not even the smallest piece of the law* will pass.

Jotham (Hb *yôtām*, "Yahweh is perfect"?), personal name. **1.** Youngest son of Gideon*; he alone escaped the murder of his family by Abimelech* and delivered the fable of the trees and their king (Jgs 9:5–21). **2.** King of Judah, son and successor of Uzziah*. He became regent about 750 when Uzziah was struck with leprosy, and reigned 742–735 after the death of Uzziah (2 K 15:5). 2 K relates nothing of his reign except that he built the upper gate of the temple (2 K 15:32–36) and that the campaign of Rezin* and Pekah* against Judah was begun during his reign; but he died very shortly afterwards. 2 Ch 27:1–9 adds a story of his victory over the Ammonites*. Jotham is mentioned as a contemporary in the titles of Is 1:1; Ho 1:1; Mi 1:1.

Jubal (Hb *yûbal*), son of Lamech* and Adah*, a culture hero who invented music (Gn 4:21). The name is very probably a play on the word *yôbēl*, horn.

Jubilee. The name given in English to the law of Lv 25:8–17, 29–31. The name comes through the Gk form of Hb *yôbēl*, horn; the beginning of the year was proclaimed by the blast of a horn. The law prescribes that after 49 years each man shall return to his own landed property; the soil is not to be cultivated. Property sold between jubilee years is rather leased than sold; the price is to be calculated on the number of years remaining until the jubilee. A distinction is made in 25:29–31 between property within a walled city, which may be transferred in perpetuity, and houses in villages, which must be restored in the jubilee.

It is the universal opinion of exegetes that the law represents an ideal rather than a practical law. No reference in the OT suggests that it was ever practiced. It is a later addition to the Holiness Code (cf LAW), which develops further the law of the sabbatical year (cf SABBATH). It expresses an ideal, however, which was ancient in Israel and probably goes back to premonarchic times: the idea that Yahweh was the true owner of the land and all the Israelites His tenants. His land should be shared by all the members of His people equally; should an Israelite be forced to part with his land, it should return either to him or to his family. There is a strong Israelite conviction that land monopoly in the hands of a few was contrary to the will of Yahweh; land monopoly is among the social evils denounced by the prophets (Is 5:8–10).

Ezk 46:17 shows some knowledge of this ideal; the passage is probably earlier than the law of jubilee. But Ezk refers also to an ideal future dispensation. There is some question about the reckoning of the jubilee; 49 years are mentioned in Lv 25:8; the 50th year in 25:11. R. North and several others point out that in Hb reckoning 50th and 49 may mean the same year, and suppose that the jubilee year and the seventh of seven sabbatical years fall in the same year.

Judaea (Gk *ioudaia*, adjective with *chōra*, "land," understood, from Hb *yᵉhûdāh*, Judah*), a geographical term; the S portion

The mountains of Judaea with Ain Karim in the center.

of Palestine in Gk and Roman times, distinguished from Samaria*, Galilee*, Peraea*, and Idumaea*. The extent of the territory of Judaea varied from period to period. The province of Judah in the Persian empire included no more than the neighborhood of Jerusalem; but it grew somewhat during the period between Nehemiah and the Maccabees, as may be seen from the list of Ne 11:25-36. Judaea, however, was subject to pressure from the Idumaeans* on the S, who moved N as far as Beth-Zur*. The territory was expanded in all directions by the Maccabees and the Hasmoneans* to include Joppa* and the coastal plain, Idumaea, and both sides of the Jordan valley. The Roman province of Judaea as settled by Julius Caesar included Idumaea to the S, a coastal strip including the immediate neighborhood of Joppa, N as far as a line drawn E and W on Antipatris, and E as far as the Jordan.

Judaea sits astride the central range of W Palestine. The altitude of the mountains falls somewhat from the altitude of Samaria and the country becomes more abrupt; the natural point where the change is perceptible, if gradual, occurs near modern Ramallah or the ancient Geba*. The distance from Geba to Beersheba* is 30 mi airline, notably longer by road; the distance from Kirjathjearim* on the W slope to the Dead Sea is 18 mi airline. Within this compressed area the altitude varies from −1300 ft sea level at the Dead Sea to 3370 ft at Hebron, and the variations in the type of soil and the amount of rainfall match this diversity. Judaea may be distinguished into three zones N–S and three zones E–W. N–S there is the plateau of Benjamin, somewhat below 3000 ft altitude, the depression of the Jerusalem region, 2000–2500 ft, from which the range rises gradually to its peak of 3370 ft at Hebron, whence it slopes again gradually to the plateau of the Negeb*. The area S of Hebron, which is broader and less broken than the regions N, has a lower rainfall and is pastoral rather than agricultural. E and W Judaea are distinguished into the E slope and the W slope; the range mostly approaches the "hogback," and the distance between points from which one may view the Mediterranean to the W or the Dead Sea to the E is never more than a few miles. The W slope receives the average Palestinian rainfall of 20–25 in and is cultivated; the E slope is almost entirely arid desert, descending steeply through broken clay hills to the Dead Sea; this is the biblical wilderness or desert of Judah. The slopes of the hills are usually not gentle and extensive terracing is required for cultivation; the land produces fruit and grain and vegetables of satisfactory quality and quantity. The visitor is impressed by the almost incredible number of stones which litter the ground and the outcroppings of rock on every hillside. These are evidences of almost 2000 years of neglect, deforestation, and erosion. Historians generally believe that the land was more heavily forested in ancient times; the annual rainfall is sufficient and there are numerous allusions to trees and "forests" in the OT. The deforestation, almost entirely done by man, has stripped the soil of its protection and the violent winter rains have washed much of it away.

The W slope is protected by a range of foothills called the Shephelah* which do not extend N of Jerusalem. The central range proper is divided from these hills by a steep transverse valley which throughout history has rendered Judaea difficult to attack directly from the W.

Judah (Hb *yᵉhûdāh*, meaning and etymology uncertain), personal, tribal, and national name. **1.** Son of Jacob* and Leah* (Gn 29:35; the name is explained by a popular etymology based on assonance with the word *yādāh*, praise). In the story of Joseph* Judah proposes that Joseph be sold into slavery rather than murdered (Gn 37:26 f). He pledged himself to Jacob as security for the return of Benjamin* from Egypt (Gn 43:8 f), and when Joseph threatened to execute Benjamin for the theft of his cup, Judah offered himself as substitute (Gn 44:18–34). Judah thus is assigned an honorable role in the story of Joseph. There are serious arguments, however, against the original presence of Judah as a son of Jacob in the story; and the anecdote is probably so formed as to express the unity of the tribes of Israel.

In Gn 38 Judah marries his son Er to Tamar*, a Canaanite; but Er died as did Onan*, his younger brother, to whom according to the levirate* law Judah assigned Tamar. Doubtless in superstitious fear, he postponed her marriage to his son Shelah. Tamar then disguised herself as a prostitute and seduced Judah himself, to whom she bore two sons. In this story Judah appears entirely unconnected with Jacob and his sons, and this is more probably the original form in which he appears in Hb tradition. He dwells near Adullam* in the later territory of the tribe of Judah.

2. One of the 12 tribes of Israel. In the blessing of Jacob (Gn 49:8–12) Judah is the ruler of his brothers. The difficult 49:10 is best rendered with W. L. Moran as "The scepter shall never depart from Judah, nor the staff from between his feet, until he comes to whom tribute is due." The passage is written during the united monarchy and most probably during the reign of David, who is the one "to whom tribute is due." The blessing of Moses (Dt 33:7) is more obscure. Judah is separated from "his people" and in straits of some kind. It is more probably dated during the divided monarchy and is of N Israelite origin.

The clans of Judah are enumerated in Gn 46:12; Nm 26:19–22; 1 Ch 2:3–8. The tribe is numbered at 74,600 in the census of Nm 1:27, and at 76,500 in the census of Nm 26:22. The boundaries of Judah are given in Jos 15:1–12 and the cities of Judah are listed in Jos 15:20–62.

Judah was the principal tribe of the S group. It included Simeon* and a number of clans of uncertain or mixed origins such as the Kenites* and the Kenizzites* (cf CALEB). Very little is heard of Judah as a tribe before the monarchy; in Jgs 15:10–13 they are unable to offer any resistance to the Philistines. The conquest of its territory by Judah in Jgs 1:1–15, 17–20, presents some difficulties which are the result of the fusion of detached pieces of tradition. The conquest of Jerusalem (1:5–8) and of Gaza, Askelon, and Ekron (1:18) cannot be historical. Judah has been introduced into the conquest of Hebron and Debir (1:10 f), which were cities of Caleb. Some historians suggest that the entrance of Judah into Canaan was from the S; M. Noth believes that entrance was possible only from the E. Of all the tribes Judah was most probably not a part of the Israel which entered with Joshua and not a part of the Egyptian sojourn and the covenant of Sinai. Judah and Simeon are not mentioned among the tribes in the song of Deborah* (Jgs 5).

That relations between Judah and Israel were never close is evident in the history of the monarchy; and this supports the view that the two groups had distinct origins. David, a Judahite who took service with Saul, did not hesitate to take service with the Philistines, the enemies of Saul, when he was expelled from court. One should not think David guilty of treason to "Israel" when an "Israel" against which treason could be committed did not exist. David was a professional soldier, not a subject of Saul, who was not king of Judah. David was elected king of Judah, but he was elected king of Israel only after the death of Ishbaal*; both he and Solomon ruled a dual monarchy. After the death of Solomon the two parts of the kingdom returned to their ancient and habitual division; and the name Israel* belonged to the tribes other than Judah.

M. Noth has suggested that the name of Judah is not an eponym but a tribal title derived from a geographical designation, "mountains of Judah," the name of the central range S of Jerusalem. The clans of Judah took the name to signify their unity. The name is not a Hb type and it is uncertain whether it is a personal or a geographical name. While the relations of Judah with Jacob are apparently artificial, its relations with Abraham* and Isaac* are more deeply rooted in history. The regions with which Abraham and Isaac are associated lie almost entirely in the territory of Judah. It is most probable that the clans of Judah had these traditions of their ancestors as the N tribes had their traditions of Jacob.

3. The name Judah is given to the S kingdom ruled by the dynasty of David which endured until its destruction by Nebuchadnezzar* in 587 BC. Its territory included the territory of the tribe of Judah (including Simeon) and at least part of the territory of Benjamin. The name continued as a designation of a province of the Babylonian and Persian empires and passed into Gk in the Grecized Judaea*.

Judas (Gk *ioudas*, from Hb *yᵉhûdāh*, Judah*), personal name of several men in the OT and NT. **1.** Judas surnamed Maccabee*, son of Mattathias* and leader of the military resistance of the Jews to the Seleucid kingdom of Antiochus* Epiphanes 165–161. Mattathias appointed him to command the rebel band which he had raised (1 Mc 2:66), and Judas enjoyed a series of successes against small forces sent to suppress the rebellion; he defeated and killed Apollonius* (1 Mc 3:10–12), Seron* (1 Mc 3:13–26), Gorgias* (1 Mc 3:38–4:25), and Lysias* (1 Mc 4:28–35). As a result of these successes he was able to purify and dedicate the temple* of Jerusalem in 165 BC (1 Mc 4:36–60). The failure of the Seleucid rulers to renew the campaign permitted him to send a punitive expedition against the Idumaeans (1 Mc 5:1–8, 65) and against Timotheus* in Gilead (1 Mc 5:24–44). The position of the Jews in Gilead was untenable and Judas transported all of them into Judaea (1 Mc 5:45–54). He also attacked the cities of Philistia (1 Mc 5:66–68). Lysias*, regent of Antiochus* V, sent a larger force against Judas and defeated him at Beth-Zur* (1 Mc 6:28–47); the rebellion of Demetrius* prevented him from following up his victory. Demetrius I, who acceded to the throne in 162, sent Nicanor*, who was defeated and killed by Judas (1 Mc 7:32, 39–50). Judas made a treaty with the Romans (1 Mc 8) which had no effect on the course of events. Demetrius then sent a much larger force under Bacchides*; Judas, deserted by most of his forces, was defeated and killed (1 Mc 9:1–21). 2 Mc 8:15 covers the series of events up to the defeat of Nicanor; for the differences between the two accounts cf MACCABEES.

2. Judas the Galilean, mentioned by Gamaliel* as an example of a false Messiah* and by Josephus as the leader of an insurrection against Rome under the procurator Quirinius* about the beginning of the Christian era.

3. Judas Iscariot*, one of the twelve. To his name in each of the lists of the 12 is added the note that he was a traitor (Mt 10:4; Mk 3:19; Lk 6:16). Jn adds that he was a *diabolos*, possibly here "adversary" or "informer" (Goodspeed; Jn 6:71, but cf Jn 13:27) and a thief, and credits him with the ungracious and hypocritical remark about the anointing of Jesus at Bethany (Jn 12:4–6); Mt 26:8 and Mk 14:4 attribute the complaint to "the disciples" (Mt) and "some" (Mk). The Synoptic Gospels all relate the previous visit of Judas to the priests and the agreement on the betrayal and the price (Mt 26:14–16; Mk 14:10 f; Lk 22:3–6). The price, 30 pieces of silver, is mentioned here only by Mt and probably comes from Zc 11:12. The need for betrayal arose from the fact that the popularity of Jesus would not permit a public arrest; and the Jewish leaders apparently did not know where He retired for the night. The Synoptics also relate the incident at the supper in which Jesus mentions the betrayal without the name of the traitor except to say that it was one who eats with Him, i.e., shares the most effective token of fellowship (Mt 26:20–25; Mk 14:17–21; Lk 22:21–23). In Jn the meaning of this phrase differs; here it is a sign known only to the disciple who asks the question, as Judas dips bread with Jesus (Jn 13:21–26). The account of the betrayal in Gethsemani in Mt 27:47–56 and Mk 14:43–52 presupposes the necessity of some identification of Jesus by the traitor in the darkness; Lk retains the kiss but not the purpose of the kiss (22:47–53). Jn again modifies the story, here to the point where the treachery of Judas is rendered superfluous, since Jesus identifies Himself (18:2–8). Mt 27:3–10 alone among the Gospels relates the rejection of the bribe by Judas and his suicide. The suicide probably echoes the death of Ahithophel* (2 S 17:23). AA 1:18 has another tradition concerning the end of Judas; the purchase of the field which in Mt 27:7 was made by the priests is attributed in AA to Judas himself, and his death is attributed to a fall with no hint that it was a suicide. This passage probably echoes the fate of the wicked in WS 4:19.

4. A Christian of Damascus, to whose house Paul was taken after the vision on the road and where he was baptized by Ananias* (AA 9:11).

Jude, Epistle of. 1. *Contents.*

1–2, greeting.

3–4, occasion: the appearance of false teachers.

5–16, certainty of the punishment of the false teachers.

17–23, how the faithful should meet false doctrine.

24–25, conclusion.

2. *Literary Form and Purpose.* The epistolary form appears artificial; the form is Jewish Hellenistic homily; cf HEBREWS, EPISTLE; JAMES, EPISTLE. The letter is written to combat false teachers who abuse the freedom of the gospel and equivalently deny Christ. The author quotes the OT (5, 7, 11); remarkably, he quotes apocryphal books extensively in a short space: Enoch (14 f), the Assumption of Moses, and the Testament of the 12 Patriarchs (6 f). This use of apocrypha gives them no authority; they are used as illustrations and their content is not affirmed as historically or theologically valid.

3. *Author, Date, Destination.* The author calls himself Jude the brother of James. Jude appears in the list of the Twelve only in Lk 6:16; AA 1:13. In the lists of Mt-Mk the name Thaddaeus* appears in the place of Jude, and there is little doubt that the two names designate the same individual. Jude is also mentioned among the brethren of the Lord (Mt 13:55; Mk 6:3). Most modern scholars believe that Jude of the Twelve and Jude the kinsman of the Lord are two distinct individuals, and it is to Jude the kinsman of the Lord that the epistle is traditionally attributed. Several reasons are adduced by critics against this attribution. In 17 it seems that the apostles are dead. If this is a general statement Jd must certainly be put in the postapostolic age; but it is possible that "the apostles" meant here are the apostles of the group to whom the letter is addressed. The mention of tradition in 3 is also alleged for a later date; but tradition* is mentioned in some of the apostolic writings, and is a concept which appears before the end of the apostolic age. The errors which the writer combats are said to be the errors of Gnosticism of the 2nd century; but the errors are very obscurely identified, and this affirmation is not well grounded. In fact the "false teachers" are not explicitly called heretics; they seem to be immoral rather than heretical, and their denial of Christ is practical rather than theoretical. Their error consists in interpreting Christian freedom as license. It is also pointed out that the Gk of Jd is very good for a Palestinian

Jew, and it is; here as elsewhere the traditional origin can be maintained only by supposing that an amanuensis had a very large part in the composition of the epistle.

The letter does not appear to be addressed to Jewish Christians; there is no specifically Jewish interest. Indeed it is addressed to no particular group; this does not strengthen the traditional attribution. It is directed to Gentile Christians or to Christians in general with no reference to the difference between Jews and Gentiles.

No date can be assigned with any certainty; critics place it late in the 1st century on general probabilities.

3. *Canonicity.* The earliest witness is the Canon of Muratori. With 2 Pt it was rejected by a number of eastern churches; its quotation of apocryphal books was one of the reasons why its canonicity was doubted. It was accepted in the western church in the 4th century.

Judges. The book of Jgs follows Jos and covers the period of Israelite history which falls between the settlement of Israel in Canaan and the establishment of the monarchy.

1. *Contents.*

1:1–36, introduction: some scattered traditions of tribal conquests.

2:1–5, fragment of a discourse.

2:6–3:6, second introduction: summarizes the theology of the book.

3:7–16:31, the Judges, 3:7–11, Othniel; 3:11–30, Ehud; 3:31, Shamgar; 4 (prose) and 5 (poem), Deborah and Barak; 6–8, Gideon; 9, Abimelech; 10:1–2, Tola; 10:3–4, Jair; 10:6–11:7, Jephthah; 12:8–10, Ibzan; 12:11–12, Elon; 12:13–15, Abdon; 13:1–16:31, Samson.

17–21, appendices. I. 17–18, Micah and the tribe of Dan; II. 19–21, the holy war against Benjamin.

2. *Criticism.* The literary origins of the book are complex and no generally accepted theory exists among critics. There is an evident difference between the stories of the "major" judges (Othniel, Ehud, Deborah-Barak, Gideon, Abimelech, Jephthah, Samson) and the brief notices of the "minor" judges (Shamgar, Tola, Jair, Ibzan, Elon, Abdon). Abimelech is doubtfully a "judge" (cf below); without him, and counting Deborah-Barak as one, the number of judges is 12. They do not, however, match the 12 tribes of Israel; Reuben*, Simeon*, and Levi* have no judges attached to them.

There are two introductions plus the fragment 2:1–5. The first introduction does not deal with judges. 1:1 presupposes the existence of Jos with which it connects Jgs. But 1:1 is an editorial gloss, and the intro-

duction contains fragments of tribal traditions which must have existed in greater number; cf JOSHUA. The second introduction exhibits the Deuteronomic style and thought, which are not reflected in the stories of the judges themselves. The appendices (17–18, 19–21) also are not stories of judges. Within the separate stories there are signs of compilation from different sources; cf separate articles.

In general critics agree on the broad outline of the process of composition. At the base of the book are oral traditions, local and tribal in scope, which contain heroic tales. For some of these we must suppose a wide circulation and a notable variation in form before their written composition. The writing of them can scarcely be earlier than the early monarchy. The collection of the stories into a single compilation is often put after the fall of Israel in 721; the stories from Israel (Ehud, Deborah-Barak, Gideon) were joined to Jephthah, Othniel, and Samson. This first edition was subject to a Deuteronomic revision in the 7th–6th century which added the introduction 2:6–3:6 and the framework in which the stories are set; cf below. The story of Abimelech probably was not included before this edition. A third edition of an uncertain and later date added material which made the book a complete record of the period between the settlement and the monarchy. This edition was expanded by certainly old material in 1:1–36 and 17–18, and by the later account of the tribal war against Benjamin (19–21). The notices of the minor judges, also older material, were inserted into the book. The chronology comes from this edition.

3. *Chronology and Background.* The sum of the various periods mentioned in the course of the book is 410 years. Since the exodus* must be placed 1290–1260 and the accession of Saul* 1050–1040, this period is far too long; it was reached by artificial calculation with a generous use of 40, the length of a generation. In the Deuteronomic edition of the book the judges were made judges of all Israel; in the original story they were local and tribal heroes. There is no way to relate the stories to each other chronologically. No set date is proposed for any of the events except Barak's victory at Taanach, which is to be placed about 1125 BC.

The Israelites appear simply as a group of tribes leading a sedentary village agricultural life without any political unity. There is no unity except that of common tribal feeling and the worship of Yahweh. It is known that other peoples were passing through a similar period of settlement, such as the Philistines* in Canaan and the Aramaeans* in Syria. The great powers of Egypt and Mesopotamia were inactive.

4. *Theology*. Two motifs are exhibited, one of the separate stories and the other of the Deuteronomic edition. The motif of the separate stories is deliverance by Yahweh through a "judge." The function of the judge in Hb thought is not precisely to determine justice according to law, but rather to restore righteousness; therefore — from the point of view of the injured party — to defend one's rights, to vindicate. The judge is therefore a deliverer. He is conceived as a "charismatic leader" (Max Weber). The charisma is explicit in 6:34; 11:29; 14:6, 19; 15:14; here it is the spirit* of Yahweh, conceived as a supernatural impulse which leads one to do or say things which are beyond one's ordinary capacities. In the stories of Gideon (6:11–23) and of Samson (13:2–23) the motif has been emphasized by the story of a vocation; these are very doubtfully parts of the original heroic tale. In the chronological additions of the last edition of the book and in the notices of the minor judges the term judge is used in the sense of a ruler. The word is used of Moab* in this sense in Am 2:3 and appears also in the title *suffetes* (Hb *šôpēṭ*) of the rulers of Carthage, a Phoenician colony. This late conception of the function of the judges does not appear in the original form of the stories, and the title is not used in this sense elsewhere in the OT. The minor judges were more probably tribal chieftains to whom the name is given by the compiler.

The Deuteronomic motif arranges the stories in a cycle of sin, punishment, repentance, and deliverance. Foreign invasions are sent by Yahweh in punishment for sin, in particular the worship of Canaanite gods; when the Israelites repent of their sin, the punishing agent is removed by the deliverer. This appears in the introduction (2:6–3:6) and in the Deuteronomic formulae in which the stories are set (3:7 f, 11 f, 4:1; 6:1; 10:6–16; 13:1). This exhibits the scheme of retribution which is characteristic of the school of Dt* and expresses through rearrangement of the narratives the profound Israelite conviction that evil doing was followed by evil and doing good was followed by good.

Some portions of the book, such as the Gideon-Abimelech stories, exhibit an antimonarchic tendency; cf SAMUEL. The belief in the charismatic leader as a sufficient guarantee of Israel's security under the promises of Yahweh was no doubt a part of the belief of those Israelites who believed that human kingship infringed upon Yahweh's kingship. But no such tendency appears as a purpose of any of the editions of the book.

The judges are included in the praise of the fathers (BS 46:11).

Judgment. There is no single Hb word to express our concept of justice; what we mean by justice is included in the concepts of judgment and righteousness*: Judgment, *mišpāṭ*, is that which is pronounced by a judge, *šōpeṭ*. The judgment does not lie merely in the declaration; one who has a *mišpāṭ*, a case or plea (Jb 13:18), presents it to the judge. One who has a *mišpāṭ* is *ṣaddîḳ*, righteous. But one is not fully righteous nor is *mišpāṭ* realized until it is declared by the judge; it must then be recognized. *Mišpāṭ* may be stolen or "bent," and the judge may deprive one of his *mišpāṭ*. If he does, he fails in the essential function of a judge, which is to render *mišpāṭ*. *Mišpāṭ* comes nearest in a single word to our "justice"; but it is conceived concretely, not abstractly. *Mišpāṭ* also then is a right, a juridical claim (Je 32:8) antecedent to the "judgment," fully established after the judgment. Hence the judge is a defender of one's rights, a vindicator (cf JUDGES). As a judicial declaration *mišpāṭ* establishes a precedent, and comes to mean a law. In a weaker sense it means a procedure; the *mišpāṭ* of a god (2 K 17:26 f) is the proper way of worshiping him by ritual cult. The *mišpāṭ* of the king (1 S 8:9–11) set forth by Samuel is the rights of the king, the claims of the king, and simply the way the king will act. The judgment looks two ways, to the vindication or liberation of the righteous, the one who receives his *mišpāṭ*, and the punishment of the wrongdoer (1 K 8:32); hence the word is polarized to mean "punishment," but this usage is less frequent.

Judgment was exercised by the king (1 S 8:5; 2 S 8:15); he was the supreme court, but theoretically he heard the case of any one who brought his plea (2 S 12:1–6; 14:4–11; 1 K 3:9, 16–28; 2 K 8:3). Absalom justified his rebellion by the claim that David no longer fulfilled his office as judge of the people (2 S 15:4). One of the public rooms of the palace of Solomon was the hall of Judgment (1 K 7:7), where the king appeared to hear cases. Judgment was one of the attributes of the ideal king (Is 9:6; Ps 72:1–2). Before the institution of the monarchy judgment was exercised by judges whose institution was attributed to Moses (Ex 18:13–26). In the concrete these judges were usually the elders* of the clan, tribe, or city. Judges as distinct officers are mentioned in Dt 16:18–20; the royal officers in cities and towns no doubt also exercised judicial functions. The judicial reform attributed to Jehoshaphat* in 2 Ch 19:4–11 was accomplished by the institution of royally appointed judges. To some extent the priests* also exercised judicial functions; their power is difficult to determine exactly. Certainly they had the decision in cases of cultic law; but de Vaux has noted that it is not impertinent that in early Israel judgment was often exercised at the sanctuaries (1 S 7:16; 8:2). The religious character of Israelite law* must have given them more power than we suspect, and more than we see in other ancient Near Eastern peoples; it was probably least during the monarchy, when all Israelite institutions were somewhat secularized.

Several instances of legal process are described in the OT: Abraham's purchase of land at Hebron (Gn 23); the transfer of the rights of the levirate to Boaz* (Rt 4); David's judgment of the fictitious case of Nathan* (2 S 12:1–6) and of the fictitious case of the woman of Tekoa (2 S 14:4–11); Solomon's judgment of the two women (1 K 3:16–27); the process of Naboth (1 K 21:13–14), and, the most circumstantially described, the acquittal of Jeremiah (Je 26:7–19). In some of these cases the description is summary, but the process of justice also appears summary to us. Two or three witnesses were required for conviction in the law of Dt (17:6; 19:15), and false witness was severely punished (Dt 19:18–19) by the infliction of the penalty of the charge which was falsely laid. The judges could also act as witnesses. While the case of the woman of Tekoa illustrates the right of appeal, the sentence in most instances was carried out immediately. There is no evidence of legal counsel; plaintiff and defendant each managed his own case. The process was usually heard in the city gates*; the judges sat, the litigants stood.

Palestine in the NT was administered under Roman law; the Roman administration, however, generally left local law in force as far as possible. Little information is available on the local administration of law in NT Palestine; cases were heard by local judges (elders) and by Roman officers. The supreme court of Judaism and Judaea was the council*; capital sentence, however, was pronounced only by the Roman governor or procurator. This was a key element in the trial of Jesus before the council. Outside of the trial of Jesus the NT describes only the hearings of Peter* and John* (AA 4:1–21; 5:26–40) and of Stephen* before the council (AA 7:12–56); the last case obviously occurred at a time when the Roman authorities for some reason were not enforcing their monopoly of the capital

sentence. Paul and Silas were summarily condemned on a charge of inciting a riot at Philippi (AA 16:20–22); this summary treatment could not be given a Roman citizen, who was entitled to a trial, and when Paul mentioned his citizenship the magistrates were alarmed (AA 16:36–39). Gallio* refused to hear a charge against Paul at Corinth (AA 18:12–17). Paul again appealed to his Roman citizenship in Jerusalem to escape a summary flogging (AA 22:24–29). This removed him from the jurisdiction of the council and his case was brought before the governor of Syria (AA 23:26–30). The Jews employed a professional advocate to deliver their case, but Paul conducted his own defense (AA 24:1–22). When the case was heard again under Festus*, Paul ended the proceedings by appealing to Caesar, which as a Roman citizen was his right (AA 25:1–12).

The Judgment of God.

1. *OT* — Yahweh had a covenant* relation with Israel, and the covenant partner or kinsman who defends one's rights acts as an avenger* rather than as a judge. Israel appeals less frequently to Yahweh's judgment than to His *ḥesed* (cf MERCY), *ṣedāḳāh* (cf RIGHTEOUSNESS), and *'emûnāh* (cf FAITH). Yahweh is the judge of the whole earth, and it is inconceivable that He should render anything but *mišpāṭ* (Gn 18:25). He does *mišpāṭ* (Je 9:23 +) and loves *mišpāṭ* (Ps 37:28; Is 61:8 +). He is a spirit of *mišpāṭ* (Is 28:6) and gives a righteous judgment (Je 11:20). In a dispute men appeal to the judgment of Yahweh: Sarah* against Abraham* (Gn 16:5), Jephthah* against Ammon* (Jgs 11:27), David against Saul (1 S 24:12). Yahweh "judged" (delivered) David from his enemies (2 S 18:31). Yahweh is the defender of the *mišpāṭ* of the poor, the orphan, and the widow (Dt 10:18; Ps 76:10; 82:3; 103:6; 140:13; Jb 36:6). The Pss petition Yahweh for judgment, i.e., for defense and vindication (7:7; 9:5 +). The judgment of Israel is a defense of Israel against foreign nations or a restoration to its former state; thus Zion will be redeemed in judgment (Is 1:27). This development of the term leads to a somewhat paradoxical combination of attributes; Israel may be assured of Yahweh's favor and pity because He is a God of *mišpāṭ* (Is 30:18). Because of the sins of Israel *mišpāṭ* (deliverance) is remote (Is 59:9). 1 K 8:49 appeals to the *mišpāṭ* of Yahweh to forgive the sins of Israel; here the term has lost almost all suggestion of judgment.

Yahweh's *mišpāṭ* of Israel may also be His punishment, although it is more frequently

His anger* than His *mišpāṭ* which is operative in His punishment of Israel. Ezk is preeminently the book of Yahweh's punishing judgment (Ezk 5:7 ff; 7:3 ff; 16:38; 11:10; 24:14 +; cf also Je 1:16; 4:12; Zp 3:5). The imagery of the judicial process between Yahweh and Israel is used (Is 1:2, 18 ff; Ho 2:4 ff; 5:3; Mi 1:2–4), but Yahweh appears as plaintiff or witness rather than as judge.

Yahweh has no covenant relations with other peoples, and so He is the judge of the world, of nations, and of peoples (Pss 7:7; 9:8 f; 96:13; 110:6; 1 S 2:10; Gn 18:25). In the messianic era He judges between nations and ends their wars (Is 2:4; Mi 4:3). He judges the nations which unjustly attack Israel (Ezk 25:11). The idea of a great judgment of all nations is characteristic of apocalyptic* literature rather than of the OT. The idea appears in Jl 4:9 ff, where the nations are assembled in the valley of Jehoshaphat*, "Yahweh judges," and in Dn 7:9–11. In these passages the idea is suggested without any of the florid descriptions which appear in apocalyptic writings.

2. *NT*. I. The Synoptic Gospels. The idea of judgment appears far more frequently in Mt and Lk than it does in Mk. "Judgment" often means condemnation; the Pharisees are threatened with this judgment (Mt 23:33; Mk 12:40; Lk 20:47). It is called the "judgment," i.e., punishment of Gehenna* (Mt 23:33). Condemnation is also threatened to the man who is angry (Mt 5:22) and who refuses to be reconciled (Mt 5:25; Lk 12:58). Jesus here plays on the word judgment; the process to which murder is submitted (Mt 5:21) is obviously not the same process to which anger is submitted; this is the judgment of God.

The "day of judgment" is mentioned in Mt 10:15; 12:36; Lk 11:22, 24. Not too much stress should be laid on the word "day," since the parallel passages have simply judgment (Mt 12:41, 42; Lk 10:14; 11:31 f). The judgment of condemnation in Mt 12:41 f; Lk 11:31 f is given not by God but by the Gentiles whose belief is compared with the unbelief of the Jews; here it is evident that we are dealing with metaphor. A similar metaphor assigns the function of judgment to the twelve (Mt 19:28; Lk 22:30), unless "judge" in these passages is used in the Hb sense of "rule," which seems more probable. Jesus warns men against arrogating to themselves the function of judgment, and He makes our judgment of others the measure of the judgment which we shall receive (Mt 7:1 f; Lk 6:37). The scene described in Mt 25:31–46, usually called the last judgment, has little or no resemblance to a judgment scene; actually no words suggesting judgment appear in the passage. It may seem to be carping on words, but legal terminology was available to the NT writers when they wished to use it, and the scene described here is more properly described under PAROUSIA. On the nature of the judgment suggested in the Gospels cf below.

II. Paul. Paul is quoted in AA 24:25 as speaking of "the coming judgment"; and this does indeed appear in the epistles. Repeating the warning not to judge another, Paul asks how the one who does this is to escape the judgment of God (Rm 2:1–3). The judgment of God will be accomplished on "the day of wrath" (Rm 3:5; cf ANGER; DAY OF THE LORD). This is the day when God will judge (Rm 2:16), when He will judge the world (Rm 3:6) and when Jesus Christ will come to judge the living and the dead (2 Tm 4:1). What Paul means by the judgment of the world and angels by the saints is not clear (1 Co 6:2 f); the verse is perhaps an echo of Mt 19:28; Lk 22:30. It is clear from the context that judge here means "render a judicial decision," not "rule."

There is also a past judgment in Paul, the judgment which issued from one (Adam) to the condemnation of all men (Rm 5:16, 18). From this universal condemnation those who are in Christ Jesus escape (Rm 8:1) because the condemnation of sin in the flesh has been destroyed by the death of Christ in the flesh (Rm 8:3). The Jews are a special case; they are judged according to the law* (Rm 2:12).

There seems also to be a sense in which the judgment is present. Despite Rm 8:1, Paul in 1 Co 11:32 foresees the possibility that Christians may be condemned with the world; they escape this condemnation because they are chastised by the Lord. One who eats and drinks the Eucharist unworthily eats and drinks his own condemnation (1 Co 11:29). On the nature and the relation of these views of the judgment cf below.

As objects of judgment are mentioned slander (Rm 3:8), violation of the vow of virginity (1 Tm 5:12), the Judaizers who disturb the Galatians (Gal 5:12), those who do not believe the truth (2 Th 2:12), and those who disobey public authority (Rm 13:2); the judgment in the last passage is probably the judgment of the public authority. Finally, Paul was aware that the judgment of God is unsearchable (Rm 11:33).

III. John. Jn's theology of the judgment appears at first to be nothing but a series of paradoxes. God did not send His son to judge the world but to save the world (Jn 3:17), and Jesus Himself says the same thing (Jn 12:47). Yet Jesus says also that He has come into the world for judgment (Jn 9:39). Another paradox appears in the identity of the judge. The Father judges no one (Jn 5:22); yet the one who seeks the glory of Jesus and judges can scarcely be any other than the Father (Jn 8:50). Jesus says that the Father judges no one because He has given judgment to the son (5:22, 27), and Jesus affirms that He judges justly (5:30) and truthfully (8:16). Yet He also affirms that He does not judge (8:12; 12:47).

Yet there is a unity of thought in these paradoxes, and it lies in the nature of the judgment, which is peculiar to Jn. In Jn the judgment is always present and is, so to speak, the act of man himself. The believer is not judged, but the unbeliever is already judged by his very unbelief (3:18; 5:24). The unbeliever has his judge on the last day, and the judge is the word which Jesus has spoken (12:48). The spirit will not judge the world but will demonstrate that there is judgment by showing that the prince of the world, the spirit of evil, is already judged (Jn 16:11). And Jesus affirms that the judgment of the world is *now*, when the critical hour of His rejection by His own people is near (Jn 12:31). It seems clear, then, that in Jn the judgment is the rejection of faith in Jesus Christ. Those who refuse faith will rise to the resurrection of judgment, which is opposed to the resurrection of life (Jn 5:29). Jesus is judge in the sense that He presents Himself as the object of decision, and it is thus that the Father judges no one but has committed judgment to the Son. He comes not for the judgment of unbelief but to save those who believe.

IV. Hebrews and Catholic Epistles. Heb looks to the resurrection of the dead and eternal judgment (Heb 6:2). This is probably the judgment which is appointed to men after death (Heb 9:27) and of which the expectation is fearful (Heb 10:27). Adulterers and fornicators are singled out as objects of judgment (Heb 13:4). The word is also used in a transferred sense; Noah by his faith and obedience condemned the world (Heb 11:7). Js 2:12 points out that those who expect to be judged by the law of freedom must live according to that law; if they are merciless, they will be judged mercilessly (Js 2:13). Christian teachers will be judged with special severity (Js 3:1). Js 4:12 echoes the warning of Mt 7:1; Lk 6:37 not to judge others. God will judge the living and the dead (1 Pt 4:5); this suggests that the dead have not yet been judged. The judgment begins with God's house, the Church (1 Pt 4:17). In 2 Pt and Jd the judgment takes on apocalyptic coloring. The judgment is compared to the judgment of

Sodom and Gomorrah (2 Pt 2:6); the wicked are stored up for the day of judgment (2 Pt 2:9), and the heavens and earth are stored up for fire on the day of judgment (2 Pt 3:7).

V. Apocalypse. Apc is the book of the apocalyptic judgment. The climactic act of judgment is the judgment of the great harlot, Babylon (Rome). Judgment here is the downfall of a world power (17:1–19:2). There is an hour of judgment (14:7). Judgment is committed to others not named, but they must be the saints (20:4); and the rider on the white horse is an agent of judgment (19:11). The final act of judgment is an assizes at which the dead are judged (11:18; 20:12 f).

VI. Summary. The meaning of the judgment and its place in Christian belief have been discussed at length and widely variant views have been maintained. The question revolves around the eschatological character of the judgment. The principle that the Bible employs eschatological imagery drawn from apocalyptic* literature and even from mythological sources (cf MYTH) is well established; and very few modern interpreters would understand the judgment of 2 Pt and Apc as anything but eschatological image.y; by this they do not intend to deny the reality of the judgment. Others believe that the eschatological-apocalyptic judgment is entirely imagery. They interpret the judgment exclusively in Joannine terms (cf above) as the confrontation of man with Jesus Christ and His acceptance or rejection. The judgment is always present, and occurs only in history. The judgment of nations is also exclusively historical.

No synthesis seems to be faithful to the biblical passages unless it combines both the historical and the eschatological character of the judgment. The confrontation of man with Jesus Christ is indeed a *crisis* (Gk *krisis,* judgment), and one is effectively judged when he accepts or rejects. For each man the "day of judgment" is the day on which he makes a permanent decision to accept Jesus Christ or to reject Him. The biblical view of judgment is that the attributes and operations of God's judgment are exhibited in the course of the individual life and in the course of history.

On the other hand, the eschatological element is too deeply imbedded in biblical thought to be understood as entirely imagery, even though one may understand this of the apocalyptic imagery. Biblical belief is that the judgment of God is in some way finally decisive, that this judgment is outside of history and ends history. Without some such final judgment there is no effective victory of God over evil; if He does not once finally overcome it, then evil becomes as eternal as God Himself. This at least is expressed in the imagery of the judgment, and there is no sense in which the images refer to reality unless some such final and extrahistorical judgment be maintained. The scenery of the judgment is another question, and it is false exegesis to insist upon apocalyptic details to the extent that the reality of the judgment itself becomes impossible to grasp.

Judith (Gk *ioudith*, "Jewess"?), the heroine of the book of that name.

1. *Contents.* 1, Nebuchadnezzar, king of Assyria, decides to invade the countries of western Asia because of their refusal to aid him in his war against the Medes; 2, he sends Holofernes with an army of 132,000 men; 3, Holofernes encamps near Bethulia; 4, the Israelites refuse to surrender to Holofernes; 5, Achior the Ammonite explains to Holofernes that he cannot defeat the Israelites unless they have sinned against their God; 6, Holofernes sends Achior to Bethulia to perish with the Israelites in the fall of the city; 7, Holofernes besieges Bethulia and cuts off the water; Judith, young widow of Bethulia, argues against surrender, urges trust in God, and promises to deliver the city; 9, the prayer of Judith; 10–11, Judith enters the camp of Holofernes and flatters him by promising him victory; 12–13, Holofernes invites Judith to a banquet with him alone in his tent, after which she cuts off the head of the intoxicated general and takes it into Bethulia; 14–15, Achior is converted to Judaism; the Israelites attack and rout the leaderless Assyrians; 16, the canticle of Judith; her death, still a widow, at the age of 105.

2. *Literary Form and Historical Character.* The unreal background of the story makes it highly improbable that the author intends to relate historical events. Nebuchadnezzar*, who was king of Babylon 605–562 BC, is here made king of Assyria*, resident in Nineveh*; the Assyrian empire and the city of Nineveh were both destroyed, Nineveh in 612 BC, by the campaigns of Nabopolassar, the father of Nebuchadnezzar. Nebuchadnezzar is made a contemporary of the postexilic period after the rebuilding of the temple in 515 BC (4:3). The names Holofernes* and Bagoas* are not Babylonian but Persian. The strategically important Bethulia is unknown and cannot be identified with any Palestinian site; it is a creation of fiction. The name Judith occurs elsewhere only as the name of a Hittite wife of Esau* (Gn 26:34) and is an unlikely name for a Jewish woman. It is chosen either because of its meaning, *yᵉhûdît*, Jewess, or because of its assonance with Judas*, a

possible allusion to the Maccabean* leader. Some scholars seek a recollection of a historical event by associating the story with the campaigns of Artaxerxes III Ochus of Persia against Egypt in 351–350, against Sidon in 345, and against Egypt in 344–343. There is no historical record that these campaigns touched Palestine at all; and there seems to be no reason for associating Jdt with them except an implicit principle that some historical association must be found. The book in background as well as in its contrived plot has all the marks of an entirely fictitious historical romance.

3. *Theology.* The deed of Judith has often been judged harshly. Her deed was assassination; furthermore, she achieved her end by an implicit seduction. She did not actually seduce Holofernes, but the narrator leaves the impression that this was due to the mercy of God (13:16), and that Judith was willing to do whatever was necessary to accomplish her purpose.

This criticism of Judith, valid as it may be, fails to grasp the lesson conveyed by the writer, which is that the Jews should trust in God to protect them. In a historical tradition which included such heroes as Joshua*, Jephthah*, Samson*, and David* the character of the heroes or their methods of war were not the object of a rigorous moral examination. God saves His people by the deeds of men acting as men. Furthermore, the deliverance of the Jews rests on their fidelity to the law. This is the burden of the discourse of Achior (5:5–21), of the words of Judith (8:17–20), and of the example of Judith as a woman who lives according to the law strictly interpreted (8:6; 10:5; 12:2, 19). For God is "the God of the depressed, the helper of the lowly, the avenger of the helpless, the protector of the contemptible, the savior of the desperate" (9:11). Jdt is a profession of this faith.

4. *Date.* The theological content of the book, its emphasis on the hope of deliverance from foreign enemies and its emphasis on the law, suggest that it belongs to the literature of the Maccabean period, written to encourage the Jews in their political and religious resistance to the Seleucids. The book was written in Hb or Aramaic but is preserved in the Gk version, of which there are several recensions.

Julius (Gk *ioulios*, Lt Julius), the name of the great Roman family, the *gens Julia*, of which Caesar was a member, and probably adopted by the centurion* to whom Paul was committed on his voyage from Caesarea* to Rome, praised for his kindness to Paul (AA 27:1, 3). He was responsible for insisting that the voyage continue even during the dangerous winter months (AA 27:11), and thus risked the shipwreck which actually occurred. He prevented the sailors from abandoning the ship (AA 27:31 f) and his own men from killing Paul lest he escape in the shipwreck (AA 27:42 f).

Juniper. It is probable that the Phoenician juniper, an evergreen cone bearing tree, is meant by Hb $b^e r \hat{o} \check{s}$. The timber of this tree was used in the construction of the temple of Solomon (1 K 6:15, 34) and for planking on ships (Ezk 27:5). It was cut on Mt Lebanon* (2 K 19:23; Is 14:8; 37:24; 60: 13) and shipped to Israel from Phoenicia (1 K 5:22, 24: 9:11). In the messianic restoration the juniper flourishes in the desert (Is 41:19; 55:13). The identification is not certain, and many scholars identify the $b^e r \hat{o} \check{s}$ with the cypress*.

Just, Justice, Justification. Cf RIGHTEOUS, RIGHTEOUSNESS.

Justus (Gk *ioustos* from Lt *iustus*), surname of Joseph Barsabbas (AA 1:23; Col 4:11), and of a proselyte* of Corinth, Titius Justus, whose house stood next to the synagogue. Paul preached in the house of Justus when he was rejected by the synagogue (AA 18:7).

K

Kadesh (Hb *ḳādēš,* also called Kadesh-barnea, *ḳādēš-barnēaʿ,* etymology uncertain), a point in the desert in the journey of Israel from Egypt to Canaan. It is by general agreement located at a spring in the Negeb* now called Ain Qudeirat, near which there are two smaller springs. The identification is almost compelled, since the arid Negeb contains very few springs of sufficient flow to support a tribe which must have numbered a few thousand. Ain Qudeirat lies in the SW corner of the Negeb near the Sinai* region. Kadesh appears in the stories of Abraham (Gn 14:7; 16:14; 20:1); a gloss in Gn 14:7 identifies it with *ʿēn mišpāṭ,* "the spring of judgment," no doubt an allusion to the experience of Israel at Kadesh. Several widely variant forms of the tradition of the stay at Kadesh appear in the Pnt. In Nm 20 Kadesh is the scene of a dispute between Moses* and the Israelites, the striking of the rock, and the message to Edom* asking passage, which is refused; the Israelites then proceed to Mt Hor*. This passage identifies Kadesh with the waters of Meribah*. In Nm 13:26, however, Kadesh is the point from which the scouts are sent into Canaan (cf also Jos 14:7), and the unsuccessful attack on Canaan was launched. In Dt 1:2 the Israelites reach Kadesh after 11 days travel from Horeb*; in Dt 1:46 they remained there "a long time," more explicitly 38 years (Dt 2:14), setting out from Kadesh to the stream Zered*. Kadesh is mentioned in the list of "stations" (Nm 33:26), and the Kadesh sojourn is alluded to in the speech of Jephthah* (Jgs 11:16). It is said to lie in the desert of Zin* (Nm 20:1; 33:36) and in the desert of Paran* (Nm 13:26). The history of the exodus* as reconstructed by modern scholars follows the tradition of Dt in making Kadesh the center of the nomadic life of Israel for an indefinite number of years before the entrance into Canaan. Kadesh is included in the territory of Judah* near the S border in Jos 15:3. The desert of Kadesh is mentioned in Ps 29:8.

Kedar (Hb *ḳēdār,* etymology uncertain), an Arabian tribe. The Hebrews reckoned them as remote kinsmen through Ishmael*, the son of Abraham* (Gn 25:13; 1 Ch 1:29). They enjoyed some renown as archers (Is 21:16 f) They were a nomadic tribe of herdsmen (SS 1:5; Is 60:7; Je 49:28) who engaged in trade with Tyre* (Ezk 27:21). Is 42:11 describes them as villagers. They were defeated by Ashur-bani-pal of Assyria (668–626 BC); he describes them as ruled by a king. He mentions their deity Atarsamain, ʿAttar of the heavens. The deity ʿAttar is known from later Arabic inscriptions. The name is Aramaic rather than Arabic, and the deity may have been borrowed. It is not certain at this period whether ʿAttar was a male or female deity.

Kedesh (Hb *ḳedeš;* the word suggests the Canaanite goddess Kadesh), a town of Naphtali* (Jos 19:37) in N Galilee*, NW of Lake Huleh, about 11 mi N of Safed and 22 mi W of Tyre. The site is identified with the modern Qades; one of two tells is the site of the Canaanite city, the other the site of the Israelite city. Its inclusion in the list of cities conquered by Joshua* is doubtfully historical (Jos 12:22). Kedesh was a city of refuge* (Jos 20:7) and a Levitical* city of Gershom* (Jos 21:32; 1 Ch 6:61). It was the city of the judge Barak* (Jgs 4: 6–11). Kedesh was taken by Tiglath-pileser* III in 734 BC. It is not certain that the Kedesh taken by Thutmose III of Egypt was the Kedesh of Galilee. Kedesh was the scene of a victory of Jonathan* over the forces of Demetrius* II (1 Mc 11:63–73).

Keilah (Hb *ḳeʿîlāh,* etymology uncertain), a town of Judah (Jos 15:44). David repelled a Philistine attack on the town, but had to leave when the oracle predicted that the men of Keilah would hand him over to Saul (1 S 23). Keilah was included in Jewish territory in the time of Nehemiah (Ne 3:17 f). Keilah is mentioned several times in the Amarna* Letters. The site is identified with the modern Khirbet Qila, an isolated hill in the Shephelah* about 8 mi E of Beit Jibrin. The site contains ruins of houses and a city wall and some rock cut tombs.

Kenaz. Cf KENIZZITES.

Kenites. A non-Israelite clan closely associated with Judah*. Kain, mentioned as a town of Judah (Jos 15:57), doubtlessly refers to the clan of the Kenites and the situation of the Kenites found in other passages. According to Jgs 1:16 they accompanied

Judah from the city of palms (usually identified as Jericho*) and settled in the steppes of Arad* in the Negeb* with the Amalekites*. They dwelt with the Amalekites in the time of Saul*; their relationship with Judah was the reason why Saul warned them to move when he made his raid on the Amalekites (1 S 15:6). The Negeb of the Kenites lay in the S of Judah, the region of Arad (1 S 27:10). Some of the Kenites dwelt in towns and were among the clans of Judah to whom David sent gifts (1 S 30:29); it seems probable therefore that they were included among "the men of Judah" who installed David as king at Hebron (2 S 2:4). The Kenites claimed a connection with Moses* through Hobab* (Jgs 4:11; some MSS read his name also in Jgs 1:16). The connection of the Kenites with the Rechabites* in 1 Ch 2:55 is obscure. The presence of Heber the Kenite in Galilee is explained by his separation from his clan (Jgs 4:11); friendship existed between him and Sisera* (Jgs 4:17). The oracles of Balaam* contain a threatening oracle against the Kenites (Nm 24:21 f); the background is obscure and the text is corrupted. W. F. Albright believes that the oracles as a whole should be dated AD 1250–1100, more or less the period of the Israelite settlement.

The story of Cain*, the eponymous ancestor of the Kenites, as the first murderer (Gn 4:2–15) can scarcely have come from the Kenites, particularly since Cain appears as a peasant, while the Kenites were nomads. But Gn 4:15–17 contains independent legends of Cain* which originally were unconnected; why the story of murder should have been attached to him is not evident. The name means "smith," and many scholars believe the Kenites were nomad smiths.

Kenizzites (Hb *kᵉnizzî*, etymology unknown), a clan closely associated with Judah*. An Edomite* origin of the clan is attested by the genealogy of Gn 36:11 which makes Kenaz, the eponymous ancestor of the clan, a grandson of Esau*. The name reappears among the clans of Edom (Gn 36:15); 1 Ch 1:53 makes it the name of a chieftain. In 1 Ch 4:13 Kenaz appears among the clans of Judah. The relations of the Kenizzites with Caleb* and the clan of Caleb were somewhat complex, and the divergent relationships mentioned in the Bible probably come from attempts to systematize these relationships after they had been forgotten. Caleb is called simply a Kenizzite (Nm 32:12; Jos 14:6, 14). Kenaz the father of Othniel*, however, is the brother of Caleb in Jos 15:17; Jgs 1:13; 3:9, 11. Kenaz is a son of Caleb in 1 Ch 4:15. Hebron* belonged to Caleb and the Kenizzites (Jos

14:14), as did Kirjathsepher*, which was taken by Othniel* the Kenizzite (Jos 14:16; Jgs 1:13). The Kenizzites in Gn 15:19 are an anachronism; and the verse must have come from a time when it was not known that the Kenizzites were one of the clans of Judah.

Keturah (Hb *kᵉṭûrāh*, probably connected with *kᵉṭōret*, "incense"), wife of Abraham of lower rank. It was through Keturah that the Hebrews established their connection with the Arabian tribes (Gn 25:1–4; 1 Ch 1:32 f).

Key. The ancient type of lock and key is still in use in some parts of the Near East. It consists of two pieces of wood at right angles to each other. The upright piece, nailed to the door, has four or five holes bored into its upper part in which pins are set. The crosspiece or bolt fits into a slot cut into the bar and has a corresponding number of holes bored in its top. When the bolt is pushed into the bar the metal pieces fall into the holes in the bolt and lock the door. The bolt is hollowed to receive the key, which is a piece of wood about 9 in long with pins at one end placed to correspond to the pins in the bolt and bar. When the key is pushed upward the pins in the lock are pushed upward through the holes and can be pulled out. Such a key is cumbersome and can conveniently be carried over the shoulder (Is 22:22). The key in the same passage is a symbol of authority of the master of the palace. Otherwise keys are mentioned in the OT only in Jgs 3:25; 1 Ch 9:27.

The key appears in the NT only in a transferred sense as a symbol of power. Jesus holds the keys to death and Hades (Apc 1:18); it is probable that death and Hades are here personified as monsters which are under restraint and not as spatial entities (J. Jeremias). He has the key of David, an allusion to Is 22:22; but the house of David here has become the kingdom of God which He rules. The fallen star of Apc 9:1 is given a key to the abyss and power to release its evil operations upon the earth. The angel who has the key to the abyss (Apc 20:1) binds the dragon and locks him in the abyss. The key of the abyss is also found in 2 Enoch 42:1. These are all symbols of power; Jesus Christ, in particular, is not conceived as the porter of the kingdom of heaven but as its ruler.

In Lk 11:52 the lawyers have the key of knowledge; they have not themselves entered and they prevent others from entering. The meaning of the metaphor becomes clear from the parallel in Mt 23:13; the Pharisees* and scribes* close the kingdom of heaven; they neither enter themselves nor permit others to enter. While the "key of knowledge" is found in the rabbinical writings, it is most probable that Lk here has altered the typical phrase of Mt to knowledge. The power of the key is possessed by the scribes in their function of teaching, by which they should instruct men in such a way that they are brought to the kingdom which Jesus announces.

These passages are the background of Mt 16:19, in which Jesus gives Peter* the keys of the kingdom of heaven. The phrase is found only once in extrabiblical Jewish writings; the archangel Michael* holds the keys of the kingdom of heaven (2 Baruch 11:2). Michael likewise is an archangel, not merely the porter of heaven. The key is here a symbol of the power to rule, as it is elsewhere. The kingdom of heaven here cannot be "heaven*"; it has its usual meaning in Mt of the kingdom which is announced and instituted by Jesus, beginning in His preaching and His community of disciples, looking to an eschatological term. The power to rule conferred upon Peter can have reference only to the temporal phase of the kingdom. The meaning of the metaphor is also clarified by the power to bind and loose. It is extremely doubtful that the phrase here reflects the technical term of the rabbinical writings in which bind signifies a prohibitive interpretation and loose a permissive interpretation. Behind the rabbinical phrase is the original significance of the judicial power to bind or to release; this also signifies the power to rule. Further specification of the nature and exercise of the power, and of the relation of Peter* to the other apostles*, are treated in these articles.

Kibroth-hattaavah (Hb *ḳibrôt-hatta'ᵃwāh*, "the graves of desire"), a point in the wilderness sojourn of the Israelites where a number of them died from eating quail (Nm 11:34 f; 33:16 f; Dt 9:22). The name originally meant in all probability the graves of Ta'awat, a desert tribe; a popular etymology has associated it with the tradition of the quail.

Kid (Hb *gᵉdî*), the young of the goat. The flesh of the animal was esteemed as a delicacy (Gn 27:9; Jgs 13:15). It was offered in sacrifice (Jgs 6:19; 13:19), but it does not appear in the priestly rules of sacrifice. A kid was the price of a prostitute (Gn 38:17); by what may not be sheer coincidence, it was also the gift which Samson took to visit his wife, who remained in her father's house (Jgs 15:1). It was also a gift

to a king (1 S 16:20). The boiling of a kid in the milk of its dam was prohibited (Ex 23:19; 34:26; Dt 14:21); the origins of this ritual prohibition are obscure, but it may be an expression of the natural repugnance that the liquid which is the life of the young animal should be employed in its destruction. Possibly it was a Canaanite* rite. The kid which lies down with the leopard is a symbol of the peace of the messianic age (Is 11:6).

Kidneys. The kidneys and kidney fat were a choice portion of the sacrificial animal which were to be offered to Yahweh in sacrifice (Lv 3–4; 8–9). Metaphorically the kidneys, often mentioned with the heart*, are the seat of thought and desire in a vague and unspecified manner. The frequently mentioned "testing" of the kidneys by Yahweh suggests that they are the seat of desire and intention (Pss 7:10; 26:2; Je 11:20; 17:10; 20:12). They are also the seat of excitement (Ps 73:21), and probably of desire in Jb 19:27, where they are "consumed." They are also thoughts which instruct (Ps 16:7). In general Hb does not draw a sharp distinction between these various psychic processes.

Kidron (Hb *qidrôn*, "turbid?"), the ravine or seasonal stream bed which lies E of Jerusalem between the city and Mt Scopus and the Mt of Olives to the E. The hill of the city rises steeply above the bottom of the ravine to a height varying from 90 ft to 180 ft at present; it is estimated that the level of the bottom has been raised by accumulated debris 50 ft to 100 ft since ancient times, so that the difference was even greater. The spring of Gihon* lies on the E side of the city not far above the bottom of the ravine. Kidron was crossed by David* on his flight from Jerusalem (2 S 23:15) and it was set as a limit by Solomon* which Shimei* was not to cross (1 K 2:37). It was the place where Asa* burned the idol of Maacah* (1 K 15:13; 2 Ch 15:16) and Josiah* burned the cult furniture of the Baal shrines (2 K 23:4, 6, 12; 2 Ch 30:14); 2 Ch 29:16 adds that a similar destruction was performed there by Hezekiah. The point mentioned in Je 31:40 is the junction of the Kidron with the valley of Hinnom which meets it from the W; the junction terminates the hill of Ophel on which ancient Jerusalem was built. The Kidron is mentioned in the NT only in Jn 18:1 as crossed by Jesus on His way to the garden, identified as Gethsemani* by the other Gospels; it lay across the ravine from Jerusalem.

The Valley of the Kidron with the village of Silwan.

King. 1. *Ancient Near East:* I. General. G. E. Mendenhall has said that in the ancient Near East the functions of kingship were two, war and law. To these a third may be added, the cultic function of the king. But the cultic position of the king should scarcely be included on the same level as war and law; it is the basis and the source of the power by which the king governs. The cultic position of the king expresses

Assyrian king receiving submission of defeated enemy.

ritually his position between gods and men; for the power of kingship is a divine power. Royal power is the basis of ordered society; indeed, it is identical with ordered society, for no other form of ordered political society was conceived except the monarchical form. The king was the state, and his acts were the acts of the state. Order in society is achieved by war, which protects the state from the attack of external enemies, and law, which maintains internal stability. The king is the source of law both as lawmaker and as judge.

II. Egypt. The history of Egypt as an independent state, which extends from about 2800 BC to 525 BC, exhibits a remarkable dynastic stability. This is part of the pattern of Egyptian thought and life, which was generally stable and conservative; cf EGYPT. The theoretical basis of the stability of the Egyptian monarchy was the divinity of the king; the king was a god, Horus the son of Re and Horus the son of Osiris. The divine power of kingship reached the Egyptian state directly through the person of the monarch. Hence the king was not a cultic officer but an object of cult. In Egyptian art the king is represented as gigantic in stature. In military scenes he appears as routing the enemy almost single handed, accompanied by a number of diminutive figures who do little more than mop up after him. Not until the Amarna* period is there any attempt at portrait representation of the king; all the Pharaohs have the same serene divine appearance.

The rule of the god was in theory absolute. All the acts of the administration were acts of the king, for he alone possessed the divine power of rule. In practice the Egyptian state was administered by a highly centralized bureaucracy in which the chain of authority reached from the king down to the lowest administrative level. Only in times of stress (cf EGYPT) was the control of the palace over administration relaxed; and the return of a strong stable government meant the restoration of close bureaucratic control.

There is no real parallel elsewhere in the Near East to the divinity of the king and the absolute centralized administration of Egypt; and historians point out that the peculiar conditions of life in Egypt suit this conception of government. The climate of Egypt is stable, and its food supply depended upon the regular inundation of the Nile. To secure these benefits a close social organization which could maintain the irrigation system was necessary. Nor is it merely accessory that in the Nile the Egyptian monarchy had an easy and rapid means of communication with the entire country; without this geographical base it is difficult to see how the Egyptian bureaucracy could have been maintained.

III. Mesopotamia. Kingship was a divine power in Mesopotamia also, but it was conceived in a manner different from the manner of Egypt. Kingship came down from heaven; it was a divine institution. The model of human kingship was the kingship of the gods; and here Mesopotamian myth has revealed the early conception of kingship, which left traces in later periods when early institutions no longer survived. The monarchy of the gods, possessed by different deities in different periods and different places, was not absolute like the Egyptian monarchy. It appears in a system which modern scholars have called primitive democracy. The king governs with a council of elders and with the general assembly of the whole people. To an extent which cannot be precisely determined the acts of the king must be ratified by the general assembly; the annual decree of the destinies is validated by the assembly of the gods. In historical times the popular assembly has generally disappeared; but it survived in a conception of the monarchy as limited.

The theoretical basis of monarchical power was the position of the king as representative of the gods. The king is the elect of the gods; what ritual practice lies behind this designation is not known, as the manner of election and succession is not well known. In the early Sumerian cities the city was a temple community, the estate of the god of the city, ruled by the god through his viceroy, the *ensi*. This conception also did not endure, but it determined the place of the king in relation to the gods. The king was the head not only of the city but also of the cult; he was the high priest and the chief cultic officer, without whom men could not communicate with the gods. Habitually the king was not himself a divine figure; the few exceptions to this habitual practice are obscure.

The king as ruler of a city-state did not appear in Egypt, but this was the earliest form of kingship in Mesopotamia. Mesopotamia developed the nation-state through conquest of one city-state by another. The true nation-state does not appear in Mesopotamia; the larger states were empires, and the king remained ruler of his own city, adding the kingship of other cities. The gods of the other cities were not conquered nor could their identity be destroyed. But in the expansion of the rule of strong city-states there was no room for the popular assembly.

Mesopotamian dynasties were unstable compared to Egyptian dynasties; Thorkild Jacobsen has related this to the Mesopotamian view of the cosmos. Mesopotamian climate is unstable compared to the climate of Egypt; Jacobsen calls the Mesopotamian conception of the cosmos an integration of many wills. What stability it has is maintained by the agreement of these wills under an elected ruler. This is the conception of the divine assembly which is transferred to the political community; it limits absolutism at the same time that it fails to furnish a principle of stability.

The principal cultic function of the king was to represent the god in the New Year* festival. The integration of society with nature was assured through the king, who here more than elsewhere was identified with the state. This role also was a vital part of the theoretical basis of the power of the king, who here sustained life. The rare texts in which a king is called a god are thought by scholars to be connected with his role in the New Year festival.

The Mesopotamian king was a savior; the emphasis upon this title reflects the threat of chaos lurking under the unstable integration of wills. Both as victor in war and as lawmaker and judge the king delivers the kingdom from present threatening evil. He is the principle of peace and of justice, the defender of the weak and the vindicator of rights.

IV. Other States. Little is known of the ideology of kingship of the city-states of Canaan and the neighboring nation-states of Edom, Ammon and Moab. It is unlikely that the kingship of Israel was not influenced by these peoples, but no certain points of contact can be traced. That the Canaanite gods were called kings is clear from many personal names compounded with the title "king" given to the deity.

2. *The Kingship of Yahweh.* That Yahweh is king is clear in numerous passages of the OT from various dates; but the conception is strangely lacking in unity, and it can be asked whether the kingship of Yahweh was a basic element of Israelite belief. Yahweh is king of Israel (Nm 23:21; Dt 33:5; Jgs 8:23; 1 S 8:7; 12:12). He is king of all nations (Ps 22:29; Zc 14:16 f). He is king in virtue of creation* (Ps 74:12). The title is given Him without any specification (Ex 15:8; 1 K 22:19; Ps 146:10; Is 6:5). He is the king savior who vindicates His kingship by His saving deeds on behalf of Israel (Ps 145:11–13; Is 33:22; 43:14 f; 52:7). The saving deeds of Yahweh are sometimes eschatological rather than historical, the final establishment of His reign and of Israel as the center of His reign (Is 24:32; Ob 21; Zp 3:15; Zc 14:16). These aspects are all combined in the royal Pss 47; 93; 95–99. Here Yahweh is king and con-

queror of nations (Ps 47), king of creation (Ps 93; 97), creator and king of Israel (Ps 95), creator and king and judge of nations (Ps 96), king of Israel and of all nations (Ps 99). It is extremely difficult to identify one of these aspects as primary. Connected with this difficulty is the problem of the period in which the concept of Yahweh as king arose. The traditions of the origin of the monarchy include the argument that human kingship is an infringement on the monarchy of Yahweh (Jgs 8:23; 1 S 8:7; 12:12). This argument was certainly overcome in Israel; many critics believe that it was not urged at an early date but was a theological construction by later writers who were opposed to the monarchy. In addition there can be urged for a later date the argument that the kingship of Yahweh was not likely to be formed until Israel had instituted a monarchy. These arguments are not convincing. A. Alt has associated the idea of the kingship of Yahweh with the ark* of the covenant, the throne of Yahweh, and places the origin of the idea between the settlement of Israel in Palestine* and the institution of the monarchy. W. Eichrodt, on the other hand, connects the title of king with the eschatological saving deeds of Yahweh, which would place the origin of the title in a later period. A. R. Johnson connects it with the covenant festival which he proposes in the monarchy (cf below), and thus would make it nearly contemporary with the rise of the monarchy. It seems probable that Yahweh was first conceived as king of Israel before the institution of the monarchy, that the kingship of Yahweh over all nations was a result of the consideration of His saving deeds, and that His cosmic kingship was a third development. The title must have been to some extent an attribution to Yahweh of titles and powers which were claimed for other gods and could not be withheld from Him. In the framework of mythological thinking Israel found ways in which the power and sovereignty of Yahweh could be described.

3. *Israelite Kingship.* The origin of Israelite kingship is related in 1 S 1–12. On the complex character of these traditions cf SAMUEL, BOOKS OF. They impose the conclusion that the institution of the kingship was a response to the crisis created by the Philistines*. This conclusion is supported also by the description of the kingship of Saul in 1 S 13–31; he appears primarily, indeed almost entirely, as a military chieftain, exercising only one of the two functions of war and law. He gathered a small force of professional soldiers attached personally to his service (1 S 13:2, 15; 14:2, 52; 18:5);

David was one of this corps. While Saul is more than once conventionally said to rule Israel or all Israel, it is impossible to determine how many of the tribes accepted his sovereignty; it is very probable that Judah* was not among them. In Saul, consequently, one does not see the full character of Israelite kingship; he is more like a permanent judge*. The absence of any lawmaking or judicial activity is not, however, due merely to the crisis in which his kingship arose. Even at this early date there was already a long tradition of Israelite law* which had another source than civil power; this legal tradition was prior to the monarchy and neither in Saul's reign nor later was the king free to flout it. The lawmaking function of the king is never emphasized in tradition, but the judicial function of the king is; cf JUDGE.

The theoretical basis of royal power in Israel differed notably and sharply from the theoretical basis of kingship in other peoples; cf above. The king was a charismatic leader like the judges; this meant that he was endowed with the spirit* of Yahweh to perform his functions. A difficulty in the kingship was the conception of the spirit as a permanent possession; in the judges the spirit came in a period of crisis and remained only for the duration. The conferring of the spirit was ritually symbolized by the rite of anointing*, which made the king a sacred person. But he is not the representative of Yahweh as the Mesopotamian king was the representative of the gods. As the charismatic leader who possesses the spirit he is king by divine election proclaimed through a prophetic oracle. This election is transferred to the dynasty of David as a whole (2 S 7; Ps 89:20–38), and it is quite likely that this conception contributed to the stability of the dynasty of David, which endured from David to 587 BC, in contrast with the dynastic instability of N Israel. The charismatic quality of the king disappears after Solomon except in liturgical songs (cf below on the royal Pss) and is sought in the messianic king; cf MESSIAH.

The premonarchic society asserts itself in the ratification of the elders* and of the people which follows the accession of a king. This is mentioned for Saul, David, Solomon, Rehoboam, and Jehoash, and it is easily assumed that it occurred at the accession of each king. It seems clear that the traditions of premonarchic Israel were never perfectly combined with the monarchy. The "antimonarchic" account of the rise of Saul (1 S 8 + 10:17 ff + 12) regards the kingship as a rejection of the kingship of Yahweh; and there is no reason for believing that this tradition is entirely the creation of

later experience with the monarchy. Dissatisfaction is expressed in the "law of the king" (Dt 17:14–20; 1 S 8:11–17), both of which are later compositions. The same antimonarchic attitude seems to be reflected in Ho 8:4; 10:3 f; 13:11; these passages go beyond such criticisms of the monarchy as Je 22:1–5, 15 ff; Ezk 22; 34, which accept the institution and reject its abuses.

The accession of the king is described in 1 K 1:32–48; 2 K 11:12–20. Both of these incidents were exceptional and describe a ceremony performed in urgency. The essential ritual was the anointing and the tradition of the symbols of royalty: throne*, crown*, and scepter*. The "testimonies" mentioned in the coronation of Jehoash (2 K 11:12) are thought by several scholars to be a document containing either the titulary of the king or the oracle of his accession; Ps 2 is alleged as a possible example of such an oracle. Other parts of the liturgy are deduced with more or less probability from the royal Pss. Whether the Israelite king took a throne name at his accession as the Pharaohs of Egypt did and as a few Mesopotamian kings are known to have done is not certain. A throne name was conferred upon Jehoiachim* and Zedekiah* by the foreign conqueror who installed them. A double name is indicated for Shallum-Jehoahaz*, Azariah-Uzziah*, Jedidiah-Solomon*, and possibly Elhanan-David*.

The administration of the Israelite monarchy shows the influence of the Egyptian court. No administration existed when David became king and it is not improbable that he should borrow the administrative structure of an old neighboring state. R. de Vaux collects the following list of royal officers and attendants. Those who see the face of the king (2 K 25:19; Je 52:25) are those who are regularly admitted to his presence. De Vaux suggests that they are his personal attendants, the same persons mentioned in 1 S 16:21; 2 S 14:24; 1 K 12:6; Je 52:12. The counsellor (2 S 15:12, 31 16:23; 2 Ch 25:16) was a professional sage; cf WISDOM. On the "eunuchs" cf EUNUCH. The squire bore the arms of the king in war and attended him personally (1 S 16:21; 31:4–6; 1 K 9:22; 2 K 7:2 ff, Naaman; 9:25; 10:25; 15:25). "The King's Friend" (2 S 15:37; 16:16; 1 K 4:5) was probably also a counsellor; the meaning of the word is not entirely certain. David organized the personal royal guard much more extensively than Saul had done; cf CHERETHI AND PELETHI. The runners (1 S 22:17; 2 S 15:1; 1 K 1:5; 14:27 f; 2 K 11:4 ff) were the escort of the king when he traveled abroad and the palace guard when he was in residence. The lists of officers of David and Solomon (2 S

8:16–18; 20:23–26; 1 K 4:1–6) include the commander of the host (cf ARMY; WAR), the commander of the royal guard, the herald, the scribe*, the priests, the chief of forced labor (except in David's first list), the king's friend (Solomon), the master of the palace (Solomon), and the chief of district governors (Solomon). The master of the palace (1 K 16:9; 18:3; 2 K 15:3; Is 22:15 ff) was probably the chief executive officer of the king corresponding to the vizier in Egypt. A seal of Gedaliah* with the name of this office has been found. The functions of the herald (Hb *mazkîr,* "reminder") are reconstructed from the office as it is known in Egypt; he was in charge of audiences, presented the business of the day to the king, and proclaimed the king's decisions to the people. Whether the "princes" (*sarîm*) represent an office distinct from all these royal officers and their subordinates is doubtful. This group formed a court aristocracy called the princes or "the king's slaves" (cf SLAVE). They were rewarded by gifts from the king's estates and by shares in the revenue of the royal enterprises.

Solomon organized the entire kingdom except for Judah into 12 districts. This organization did not survive him, but it may have been retained by the kings of Israel. Some believe that 12 districts of Judah can be found in Jos 15:21–62, and suggest that these were instituted by David or Solomon. They are also attributed to Jehoshaphat* or Josiah*.

The administration was totalitarian, modified by some degree of local government. The king paid all expenses and received all revenues, and it is difficult to distinguish between crown property and state property. The revenues came from war, tribute, gifts from foreign sovereigns, and regular taxes; taxes are very probably indicated by numerous jar handles with the royal stamp, although these may be produce of crown lands. Forced labor was a form of taxation. The estates of the crown consisted in lands and flocks; the mines of Ezion-geber* were a crown enterprise. It is not unlikely that foreign trade was a crown monopoly. The acquisition of vast estates by the crown was not in harmony with Israelite legal tradition; cf INHERITANCE; NABOTH. A. Alt has suggested that crown land was acquired at first by purchase or seizure of the land of Canaanite enclaves within Israel and by reversion to the crown of the land of Israelites who died without heirs or who abandoned their land

A coregency is attested for Solomon during the life of David and for Jotham* during the life of Uzziah*. It is highly probable that Jehoshaphat*, Uzziah, and Manasseh* of Judah and Jeroboam* II of Israel were coregents with their predecessors. It is unlikely that the eldest son did not hold high office if he was old enough, and perhaps something like a coregency was normal. The principle of primogeniture, however, was not obvious in Israel, as it seems it was not in Mesopotamia. There is no indication that Saul's eldest son was designated as his successor, and the successor of David was unknown until David designated him. Both Absalom and Adonijah seemed to expect that they as the oldest surviving brothers would inherit as the firstborn*; but in the early monarchy it was not self-evident that the kingship was part of the goods of inheritance.

In theory the king as judge was available to any of his subjects; this is illustrated in 2 S 14; 1 K 3. These were not only cases of appeal from lower courts. It is suggested in 2 S 15 that David's failure to hear the cases brought to him was partly responsible for popular discontent.

The cultic position of the king has been extensively discussed. A number of members of the Scandinavian school believe that the cultic position of the Israelite king belonged to a myth and ritual pattern which they attempt to trace throughout the ancient Near East. In this pattern it is alleged that the king is divine in the sense that he is identified with the dying and rising god of the fertility festival; cf NEW YEAR. The majority of scholars do not find this pattern in the ancient Near East as a whole, and do not admit that it can be harmonized with the peculiar Israelite conceptions of Yahweh and of the king. They believe, however, that the cultic position of the king was more important than one would gather from the narrative passages of the OT.

R. de Vaux has assembled these passages. The king erects an altar (2 S 24:25). He plans to build a temple (2 S 7:2) and executes the plan (1 K 5–8). He builds a sanctuary, designates priests, and regulates the festal calendar (1 K 12:26–33). He designates priests (2 S 8:17; 20:25; 1 K 2:26 f; 4:2). He regulates the temple revenues (2 K 12:5–9). He institutes cultic reforms (2 K 22:3–7; 23). He offers sacrifice (1 S 13:9 f; 2 S 6:13, 17 f; 24:25; 1 K 3:4, 15; 8:5, 62–64; 9:25; 12:33; 2 K 16:12–15). He blesses the people (2 S 6:18; 1 K 8:14). These passages are mostly from the early monarchy; they suggest that the king in this period was the head of the priesthood as he was in Mesopotamia.

The cultic position of the king can be deduced also from the royal Pss. Most of these Pss see the king under messianic aspects; cf MESSIAH. Ps 110 is a song assuring the king of divine election and victory. It is probably connected with the accession and coronation ceremonies. On the priesthood of the king cf MELCHIZEDEK. Ps 2 is widely recognized as an accession song containing the divine oracle of election. Ps 89:20–38 celebrates the oracle of Nathan* and the covenant* of election of the dynasty of David. Ps 72 celebrates the universal dominion of the king and in numerous allusions to fertility suggests that the king was a medium of the prosperity asked from Yahweh. The king in this Ps is the king savior, the deliverer of the needy and the vindicator of righteousness; cf also 2 S 19: 10; 2 K 6:26. Ps 72 also appears to be connected with the accession of the king. Ps 20 is a prayer for the king with a favorable oracle in response; it is possibly a prayer in war. Ps 21 is both a petition and thanksgiving for victory for the king. Ps 18 is aptly conceived as spoken by the king or in his behalf; it is also a thanksgiving for victory. Ps 132 celebrates the transfer of the ark to Zion and the covenant of Yahweh with the house of David. Ps 101 is a profession of justice and righteousness, suitable for the king.

A number of scholars believe that these Pss were not merely occasional. H. J. Kraus suggests that Pss 132; 2; 24:7–10; 72; 78:65–72; 89:4–5, 20–38 belong to a royal Zion festival on the first day of Tabernacles* celebrating the election of the dynasty of David and of Jerusalem. A. R. Johnson connects these and several other Pss with a covenant festival celebrating the covenant of Yahweh with Israel and with David and presenting Yahweh as king in creation, in His saving deeds of Israel, and in His future eschatological triumph. The objection that these festivals are not mentioned in the OT is not convincing; we are not well informed on the preexilic liturgy of Israel and Judah. It seems highly probable that there was a festival celebrating the anniversary of the king's accession, and the elements mentioned by Kraus and Johnson would be most suitably included in such a festival.

4. *Kingship in the NT*. The kingship of Jesus is not emphasized in the NT. This is a part of the transformation of OT messianism in the NT; cf JESUS CHRIST. The royal messianism of the OT (cf MESSIAH) presents an incomplete picture of the reality of Jesus. The title is given Jesus in Mt 2:2; indeed His royal character is the key to this entire narrative, which has as its principal purpose to present the true kingship of Jesus as devoid of external pomp and recognized only by a few Gentiles. Jesus accepts rather than claims the title in His dialogue with Pilate* (Mt 27:11; Mk 15:2; Lk 23:3). The

longer version of this dialogue in Jn 18: 33–39 is written to make clear the unworldly character of the kingship of Jesus. Other allusions in the passion narratives show the popular belief, accepted also by the soldiers who executed Jesus, that He wished to restore the monarchy of Israel (Mt 27:29, 37, 42; Mk 15:9, 18, 26, 32; Lk 23:37 f; Jn 19:3, 14 f, 19, 21). The title king of Israel coupled with Son of God (Jn 1:49) professes belief in the messianic character of Jesus. The title king appears in the procession of palms in Jn 12:13, but not in the account of this episode in the Synoptic Gospels; the difference is not important, since the incident explicitly reflects the coming of the king in Zc 9:9. The king here is lowly, and Jesus therefore accepts the identification; it is doubtful that those who greeted Him understood the full force of His meaning. Otherwise the kingship of Jesus is mentioned only in 1 Co 15:24 f; here it is clearly eschatological, achieved after the conquest of all His enemies.

Kingdom of God. In the Synoptic Gospels the term kingdom of God is frequently used to designate the central theme of the mission of Jesus. The term is comparatively rare in other NT books and there can be little doubt that it goes back to Jesus Himself. The abandonment of the term in the apostolic writings is probably due to the heavily Jewish coloring of the term, which was not easily intelligible to Gk speaking Christians; cf SON OF MAN.

The idea of the kingdom of God reflects the OT conception of the kingship of Yahweh; cf KING. The term "kingdom," however, is not frequently used of Yahweh in the OT, and mostly in later books. In Dn 7:14, 18, 22, 27 the kingdom is given to the Son of Man and to the saints. In Dn 4:3 the everlasting kingdom of God is mentioned. The throne of the reign of God appears in Dn 3:54 (Gk). The kingdom of Yahweh is universal and everlasting, a kingdom of glory*, power*, and splendor (Pss 103:19; 145:11–13). Cf also Ws 6:4; 10: 10; in the latter passage the "kingdom" is synonymous with display of power. The kingdom of David* is called the kingdom of Yahweh (1 Ch 28:5). The term as used in the NT goes beyond these OT allusions and incorporates themes from judgment* and the Day* of Yahweh. The idea of kingdom is more frequent in Jewish apocalyptic* literature. The kingdom here is not only the catastrophic display of power and judgment but also the establishment of the reign of God identified with the reign of Israel over the nations. These allusions show how Jesus could employ the term with no introductory explanation; but the NT idea of the kingdom of God is not dependent upon the apocalyptic literature except in some details of imagery. Mt by preference uses the phrase "kingdom of heaven," reflecting the substitution of "heaven" or some other word for the divine name characteristic of Jewish speech of the 1st century AD.

Interpreters point out that the word kingdom (Gk *basileia*, Hb *malkut*) means "reign," not "realm" or "domain." This is generally true; but there are a number of passages where the translation "reign" is awkward. The basic meaning of the phrase is reign of God, but the idea of reign grows into the idea of realm or kingdom. The kingdom is sometimes called the reign of Christ; this phrase almost always is used with one aspect of the kingdom (cf below). Where "kingdom" is used without any defining modifier it is clear that the kingdom of God is meant.

The kingdom of God is preached or announced by Jesus; it is the object of His "good news," His gospel*, and it was announced before Him by John the Baptist (Mt 4:23; 9:35; 13:19; 24:14; Lk 4:43; 8:1; 16:16; 9:2, 60). The announcement is that the kingdom of God is near or has arrived (Mt 3:2; 4:17; 10:7; 12:28; Mk 1:15; 11:10; Lk 10:9, 11; 11:20; 17:20; 19:11; 21:31). At the same time the arrival of the kingdom is something for which Jesus tells His disciples to pray (Mt 6:10; Lk 11:2). The kingdom is a mystery* which men do not perceive and which Jesus reveals to His disciples (Mt 13:11; Mk 4:11; Lk 8:10).

What is meant by the kingdom which is announced and which is near or has even arrived cannot be deduced from the OT passages in which the phrase occurs nor from apocalyptic literature. The numerous occurrences of the phrase disclose an apparent duality of sense. A number of passages clearly suggest an eschatological event which lies outside history and closes history. This meaning is particularly clear in the phrase "the kingdom of Christ," explicitly or implicitly so designated. The Parousia* is called in Mt 16:28 the coming of the Son in His kingdom; Mk 9:1 speaks of the coming of the kingdom, Lk 9:27 of the kingdom simply, but the eschatological event is clear. The kingdom of the Messiah is everlasting (Lk 1:33); it is the kingdom to which the thief asks admission at death (Lk 23:42). The eschatological kingdom is obvious in the epistles; the kingdom of Christ is eternal (2 Pt 1:11), heavenly (2 Tm 4:18), it is the kingdom in which the Son is manifested (2 Tm 4:1; cf Mt 16:28). The kingdom is the scene of the messianic banquet (cf MEALS; Mt 8:11 f; 22:1–10; 26:29; Mk 14:25; Lk 13:28 f; 14:

16–24; 22:30). The righteous will shine like the sun in the kingdom (Mt 13:43). The disciples will sit on thrones (Mt 19:28; 20:21; Mk 10:37; Lk 22:30). The kingdom is a reward given to the disciples (Lk 12:32; Js 2:5) which they inherit (Mt 25:34; AA 14:22; 1 Co 6:9 f; Gal 5:21; Eph 5:5). To enter the kingdom is synonymous with entrance into eternal life* (Mk 9:47; 2 Pt 1:11). In such passages the word "reign" is not an apt translation. Nor do these phrases simply echo the rabbinical phrase "take the yoke of the kingdom," which means to accept the sovereignty of God.

In an even larger number of passages the eschatological character of the kingdom is not apparent. The kingdom is rare in Jn. The kingdom of Jesus is not of this world (Jn 18:36), which in the context does not affirm an extratemporal or celestial reality, but simply a denial that the reign which Jesus claims is secular. Baptism* is a necessary condition for seeing or entering the kingdom (Jn 3:3, 5). In the theology of Jn, which places "eschatological" events in the present (cf JUDGMENT; LIFE), it is unlikely that the kingdom here means the eschatological state. It is identical with life and consists in personal union with Jesus. The kingdom here is practically identical with the Church* (cf below). Similarly the kingdom of the Son to which God transfers the faithful (Col 1:13) and the kingdom which Christ delivers to the Father (1 Co 15:24) are not purely eschatological. This is the kingdom formed by the saving act accomplished by the Father through Jesus.

Jesus tells His disciples to seek the kingdom of God and His righteousness (Mt 6:33; Lk 12:31); the text is somewhat parallel to the definition of the kingdom as righteousness, peace and joy in the Holy Spirit (Rm 14:17), a state which is achieved by present submission to the rule of God. When Jesus is asked the time of the coming of the kingdom, He answers in an obscure phrase that it is "in your midst" (Lk 17:20 f). This phrase is best understood as signifying that the kingdom is a present but unrecognized reality, and most probably identifies the kingdom with Jesus Himself (cf below), in whom the establishment of the reign of God is being accomplished. Admission to the kingdom demands that one become as a child (Mt 18:3; Mk 10:15; Lk 18:17), that one exhibit righteousness (Mt 5:20), do the will of the Father (Mt 7:21), abandon one's wealth (Mt 19:23; Mk 10:23; Lk 18:24). For the sake of the kingdom men accept celibacy (Mt 19:12). The kingdom belongs to the poor and the lowly and those who suffer for righteousness (Mt 5:3, 10; 19:14; Mk 10:14; Lk 6:20;

18:16). These texts do not define the kingdom purely as a moral ideal but show that the reign of God is in complete opposition to merely human values and to sinful desires. The accomplishment of the reign of God demands a moral revolution in those who submit themselves to the reign and is itself the means by which the moral revolution is achieved.

The double aspect of the kingdom as present reality and future reality is apparent in the parables* of the kingdom (Mt 13; 18:23–35; 20:1–16; 25:1–13; Mk 4; Lk 8:4–18; 13:18–21). The kingdom is the preaching of the word; it contains both good and bad; it grows to greatness from imperceptible beginnings; it is a treasure for which a man should trade all his possessions. It imposes obligations of love and forgiveness. It admits all comers. It demands an alert readiness. The emerging conception is of a single reality which is present and operative but which inevitably must reach a fulfillment of cosmic scope. It presents a challenge to each man which cannot be evaded: the challenge whether he accepts the sovereignty of God or not. If he accepts it, he must submit to the revolution in his life which it imposes. The coming of the kingdom is synonymous with the execution of the will of God (Mt 6:10; Lk 11:2). The kingdom is the object of violence (Mt 11:12; Lk 16:16). This is one of the most obscure passages of the Gospels. Some interpret the violence as the attitude of those who must do violence to themselves in order to secure the kingdom; probably a more common interpretation understands the verse as an allusion to the violence of the Zealots* who attempted to restore the kingdom of Jews by violence against Rome. The use of such secular means is repudiated by Jesus.

In some passages the kingdom seems to be identified with the person of Jesus Himself, in whom the kingdom comes. In certain passages Jesus appears where the parallel passages speak of the kingdom (Mt 16:28; 19:29; 21:9; Mk 9:1; 10:29; 11:10; Lk 9:27; 18:29; 19:38; AA 8:12; 28:31; Apc 12:10). Where Jesus Himself proclaimed the kingdom, the apostolic Church proclaimed Jesus. This identification is most probably to be attributed to the Church itself rather than to the words of Jesus.

The identification of the kingdom with Jesus and the imposition of faith and moral regeneration by the inbreak of the reign of God in the mission of Jesus lead naturally to an identification of the kingdom with the group formed by Jesus Himself, the Church. This identification is particularly clear in Mt*, but it is not limited to this Gospel. The kingdom which contains both good and bad is most easily understood as the Church. "The sons of the kingdom," those to whom the kingdom belongs, are the good seed (Mt 13:38). The same phrase is used elsewhere of the Jews, who are destined to belong to the kingdom; but they are expelled (Mt 8: 11 f; Lk 13:28 f) and the kingdom of God is taken from them and given to others (Mt 21:43). The Church is most probably meant by the kingdom which cannot be shaken (Heb 12:28). The scribes and Pharisees close the kingdom to others (Mt 23:13); the parallel (Lk 11:52) speaks of the key of knowledge, and it is difficult to say which form is more original, but the kingdom in Mt seems to refer to the revelation which Jesus brings. There is scarcely any doubt that the Church is meant by the kingdom of which Peter holds the keys (Mt 16:19). The scribe learned in the kingdom (Mt 13: 52) and the doer and teacher in the kingdom (Mt 5:19) are officers of the Church. John the Baptist is lesser than the least in the kingdom (Mt 11:11; Lk 7:28), which is best understood as a contrast between John as a precursor of the Church and apostles as its proclaimers. Tax collectors and prostitutes enter the kingdom of the Church before the Jews (Mt 21:31). The wise scribe is not far from the kingdom (Mk 12:34); Mk rarely if ever identifies the kingdom with the Church as Mt does, but this text makes the kingdom nearly identical with faith in Jesus. The demands made by the kingdom (Lk 9:62) are the demands made on those who take up the mission of preaching the gospel. Paul's fellow workers for the kingdom (Col 4:11) are his fellow workers in the Church.

In neither the present nor the future aspect of the kingdom should a complete division of one from the other be made. A large number of interpreters have insisted that it is impossible to suppose that both aspects can be attributed to Jesus Himself; believing that one must choose between contradictories, some have asserted that His own view of the kingdom was purely an imminent eschatological event and others that His kingdom was simply a program of submission to the moral will of God. The contradiction is by no means explicit and irreducible. Oscar Cullmann has pointed out that there is an implicit fallacy in imposing rigid categories of time* upon biblical conceptions. Neither Jew nor Christian would regard the reign of God as an event which could be placed in space and time like the reign of Caesar Augustus. Yet the coming of Jesus and the proclamation of the reign by Him are such historical events. The kingdom of God is not entirely identical with its proclamation. One and the same metahistorical and heavenly reality is manifested in different points of time and reveals itself as moving toward a complete and total manifestation. It comes not as an imperial conquest but as a challenge to the individual person; unlike the reign of Caesar, the reign of God is established by the free surrender of men to His sovereignty. When the proclamation calling for surrender is made by Jesus, the reign of God enters upon a new and a final phase. No further inbreak of the divine sovereignty is promised beyond the mission of Jesus and its living continuation in His Church. Hence He Himself and the Church which is one with Him become the kingdom of God, at once its fulfillment and the means by which it moves toward fulfillment.

Kings, Books of. 1–2 K follow 1–2 S in the Hb text and in Jewish and Protestant English versions. The LXX, followed by the Vg and the Douay OT, designate 1–2 S as 1–2 Kings and 1–2 K as 3–4 Kings (the LXX title is actually "kingdoms," not "kings"). There is some reason for thinking that the four books originally formed a single work; 1 K 1–2, the story of the accession of Solomon, belongs to the court history of David which extends through 2 S 9–20, from which it has been detached. But it seems unlikely that the four books represent a single work or compilation; the detachment of 1 K 1–2 from 2 S 9–20, however, more probably was the final step in the compilation of S and K. 1–2 K were originally a single book; the division into 1–2 K was made by LXX in its four books of kingdoms. It was followed by Vg and came into the Hb Bible in the Middle Ages.

1. *Contents:* 1 K 1–11, history of Solomon; 1 K 12–2 K 17, history of the divided monarchy to the fall of Israel; 2 K 18–25, history of Judah to the fall of Jerusalem.

K has through most of the book a unity imposed upon it by a framework into which the stories of the kings are set. This framework employs formulae which introduce and conclude the account of each reign. The introductory formula for the kings of Judah gives the king's paternity, the year of the reign of the contemporary king of Israel in which he acceded to the throne, the name of the royal city (always Jerusalem), the number of years of his reign, his maternity, and a moral evaluation. For the kings of Israel the introductory formula contains the year of the reign of the contemporary king of Judah in which the monarch acceded to the throne, the paternity only when a son succeeded his father, the name of the royal city (Tirzah or Samaria), and a moral evaluation. The concluding formula for the

kings of Judah contains a reference to the sources of further information, the statement of death, the place of burial, and the name of his successor if he was his son. For the kings of Israel the formula contains a reference to the source of further information, the statement of death, and the name of his successor if he was his son. These formulae are varied only when the course of events demand it: in particular, the numerous dynastic changes in Israel, the accession and death of Athaliah* of Judah, the deaths of Ahaziah* and Josiah* of Judah, the dynastic uncertainties after the death of Josiah. This unity is attributed to the Deuteronomic* editor (by M. Noth, to the author of the Deuteronomic history, of which he takes 1–2 K to be the concluding portion). The work of the Deuteronomic editor is also visible in several passages which contain characteristic theological reflections (cf below): the prayer of Solomon (1 K 8), the last days of Solomon (1 K 11), the fall of the kingdom of Israel (2 K 17).

The framework is imposed upon a collection of various literary types and forms drawn from a number of sources. K itself names only three sources explicitly: the acts of Solomon (1 K 11:41), the chronicles of the kings of Judah and the chronicles of of the kings of Israel (in the concluding formulae). The nature of these documents is not entirely clear. The title suggests the royal archives; but some of the material drawn from these sources does not seem to be the type which would be found in the royal archives, if one is to judge their content by the annals of Mesopotamian kings. Scholars further question whether these were so available to the public that the compiler could refer to them for further information; but we simply do not know how available the works of the royal scribes were to the public. Many scholars therefore suppose that these sources are not official records but historical works composed on the basis of official records, with other information added. The official records, however, were available to the authors of the stories of the kings. How long these records may have survived the fall of the kingdoms of Israel and Judah, or whether they survived these disasters at all, is a question to which no answer can be given except on analogy. The conduct of the Medes and Babylonians at the sack of Nineveh (612 BC), who deliberately broke the thousands of tablets of the library of Ashur-bani-pal, suggests that the annals of Israel and Judah had little chance of survival.

There were other and more important sources which are not mentioned explicitly. The temple* certainly had its scribes and archives, and some have postulated that these were the source of the stories in which the temple is involved; this seems improbable except for the description of the building of the temple in 1 K 6–7. But the most important source was "prophetic legends." This is apparent from an enumeration of those episodes (after the reign of Solomon) which are treated in more than a summary and statistical form: the schism of the kingdom (1 K 12–14); Elijah* and Elisha* (1 K 17–2 K 10); Athaliah* and Jehoash* (2 K 11); cultic changes of Ahaz* (2 K 16); Hezekiah* (2 K 18–20); Josiah* (2 K 22–23); fall of Jerusalem (2 K 24–25). In these episodes prophets are the principal actors and objects of interest in all except 2 K 11; 16; 22–25. The type of story contained in the prophetic legend is distinctive and quite unlike the report of events from other sources; cf AHIJAH; ELIJAH; ELISHA; SHEMAIAH. These prophetic legends, however, are not all from the same source, although most of them are of northern origin; the story of the schism, for instance, places all the blame on Rehoboam. The prophets of 1 K 20 cannot belong to the same group as Elijah, nor even Elisha, who was willing to encourage Hazael* to attack Israel as long as Israel was ruled by the hated house of Omri. The story of the prophet of Bethel (1 K 13: 1–6) is a Judahite reprobation of the cult of Jeroboam*; it has been prefixed to another prophetic legend unrelated to the king which has as its object to teach the obligation of the prophet to follow the word of Yahweh without qualification.

The character of the material suggests to a number of scholars that the book experienced two redactions, one under Josiah and the other after 562 BC, the year in which Jehoiachin was released from confinement (2 K 25:27). This opinion rests very heavily on 2 K 22:20, in which Huldah* predicts a peaceful death for Josiah; this verse could hardly have been written after the king's death at the hands of Necno* in 609 BC. The opinion has some probability; the reign of Josiah was a period of national optimism, when the worship of Yahweh was restored by his reforms and it seemed that he was about to restore the ancient "land of Israel" under the sovereignty of David. It is altogether probable that the history of the kingdom would be recapitulated at this point, which seemed to mark the end of a period of troubles and the opening of an era of almost messianic peace and prosperity. This work was completed by the redactor who added 2 K 23:26–25:30; these could have been composed largely from his own experience and the reports of contemporaries. Both of the redactors deserve the title "Deuterono-

mic," since they share the same conception of history. The later redactor is credited with some notes which modify the optimism of the early redactor by alluding to the future disaster (e.g., possibly 2 K 17:19 f; 20:12–19; 21:11–15; the oracle of Huldah, 2 K 22:15–20 in its present form).

2. *Theology*. The moral evaluation of each king is based on the Deuteronomic principle that sacrifice should be offered only in Jerusalem in the temple. Hence every Israelite king is condemned because of "the sin of Jeroboam," which was the establishment of royal sanctuaries at Bethel* and Dan*. Of the kings of Judah only Hezekiah and Josiah, who are credited with religious reforms, are praised without reservation. Asa, Jehoshaphat, Jehoash, Amaziah, Uzziah, and Jotham are praised with the qualification that the high places* were not removed. The evaluation is unhistorical in the sense that the Deuteronomic theory of one sanctuary was unknown before Josiah.

1–2 K is the finest enunciation of the Deuteronomic theology of retribution. The explanation of the fall of Israel and Judah does not lie, to this historian, in the political events of the period. His account of the political history of the Hebrew monarchy is sketchy at best. What brought the kingdoms down was the corruption of their religious belief and cult. Except for the reflection in 1 K 11 and 2 K 17 he lets the history speak for itself; and it cannot be denied that this synthetic view of history is impressive. It arises from the words of the prophets contemporaneous with the monarchy, but it adds the impact of actual rather than predicted disaster. Such a historical analysis of the fall of a nation by its own members is without parallel in the ancient Near East and is a striking demonstration of the unique character of the faith of Israel. The Deuteronomic conception was also of vital importance in assuring the survival of the faith of Israel. Yahweh did not perish with His people, as the gods of other ancient peoples perished, because the history of Israel demonstrated His moral will which raised Him above the level of political and national interests. In such a god, faith was possible even after the nation perished, because He was the agent of its destruction. The fall of Israel was His success, not His failure.

The note of messianism which was present in the redaction of Josiah remains in another form in the closing words of the book, which remind the Hebrews that the dynasty of David still lives in a contemporary descendant. The hope of the historian rests in the continuance of the house to which was given the promise of an eternal destiny (2 S 7; Ps 89:20–38).

Kir (Hb *k̠îr*, etymology uncertain), a geographical name; the land to which the Aramaeans of Damascus* were deported by Tiglath-pileser* III in 732 BC (2 K 16:9; Am 1:5); associated with Elam* among the invaders of Jerusalem (Is 22:6); the place of origin of the Aramaeans (Am 9:7). The name is not attested outside the Bible; its associations suggest only that it lay in the E in or near Mesopotamia.

Kir-heres (Hb *k̠îr-ḥeres*, also Kir-hareseth, *k̠ir ḥᵃreset*, once Kir Moab [Is 15:1]; probably corrupted from original *k̠ir-ḥādăš*, "new town"), a city of Moab. Jehoram* of Israel and Jehoshaphat of Judah besieged Mesha* of Moab in the city, but were repelled (2 K 3:25). Otherwise it is mentioned only in the poems of Is (15:1; 16:7, 11) and Je (48:31, 36). These allusions suggest that it was the royal city of Moab. In the inscription of Mesha* the royal city is called Qarhoh. Kir-heres was located on the site of the modern el Kerak, about 80 mi S of Amman.

Kirjath-Arba. Cf HEBRON.

Kirjathaim (Hb *k̠iryātayim*, dual of *kiryah*, "city"?), a city E of the Dead Sea; inhabited by the Emim* in the archaizing notice of Gn 14:5; in the kingdom of Sihon* (Jos 13:19); a city of Reuben* (Nm 32:37), but historically a Moabite city (Je 48:1, 23; Ezk 25:9); mentioned by Mesha* as a city which he rebuilt. The site lies at modern Khirbet el Qureiyat, about 13 mi SW of Madaba.

Kirjath-jearim (Hb *k̠iryat-yᵉʿārîm*, "forest city"), one of the Gibeonite* federated cities which formed a covenant with Joshua (Jos 9:17); located on the frontier of Judah and Benjamin (Jos 15:9; 18:14 f), listed among the cities of Judah (Jos 15:60). It was the site of the camp of the tribe of Dan* on their journey to seek new territory in the N (Jgs 18:12), from which it received the name of Mahaneh-Dan, "camp of Dan," otherwise unattested. In 1 Ch 2:50–53 it is treated as a personal name in the genealogical scheme of the clans and towns of Judah. It was the site where the ark* was kept for 20 years after its return by the Philistines (1 S 6:21; 7:1 f; 1 Ch 13:5 f; 2 Ch 1:4). It was the home of Uriah*, the prophet murdered by Jehoiakim* (Je 26:20). Men from Kirjath-jearim are included in the list of Ezr 2:25; Ne 7:29. Kirjath-jearim is given

the alternate names of Kirjath-baal (Jos 15:60; 18:14) and Baalah (Jos 15:9). The city was located at the modern Tell al Azhar, a few mi W of Jerusalem.

Kirjath-Sepher. Cf DEBIR.

Kish (Hb *k̠iš*, meaning and etymology uncertain; a connection with Akkadian *qasu*, gift, is suggested), the father of Saul*. He was the son of Abiel (1 S 9:1) or of Jeuel (1 Ch 8:29 f) or Jeiel (1 Ch 9:35 f), of the clan of Matri of the tribe of Benjamin* (1 S 10:21). The name is borne by several Levites in 1–2 Ch.

Kishon (Hb *k̠îšôn*, meaning and etymology uncertain), a stream which drains the plain of Esdraelon* and the mountains N and S of the plain and flows into the Mediterranean at the N base of Mt Carmel. The stream is perennial only in its lower course and normally is no more than a brook. When fed by the winter rains it floods and the entire plain becomes a marsh difficult to traverse. This is the flood alluded to in the story of the victory of Barak* over the Canaanites (Jgs 5:21; it is not clear that "the waters of Megiddo," Jgs 5:19, signify the Kishon). The poem is slightly exaggerated in describing the stream as "sweeping away" the Canaanites; its swollen waters made chariot maneuvers impossible. The flood is not referred to in the later prose account (Jgs 4:7, 13; cf also Ps 83:10). The stream was the scene of the killing of the prophets of the Baal by Elijah (1 K 18:40); for what reason it was chosen is not clear.

Kiss. The kiss, exchanged between persons of the same sex or persons of opposite sexes, was a common token of affection at greetings and farewells between persons of the same family or kin, proximate or remote, by blood or by marriage (Gn 27:26 f; 29:11; 29:13; 31:28; 32:1; 33:4; 45:15; 48:10; 50:1; Ex 4:27; 18:7; 2 S 14:33; 1 K 19:20; Rt 1:9, 14) and between friends (1 S 20:41; 2 S 19:40; Pr 24:26). The kiss of an enemy is treacherous (Pr 27:6); such was the kiss with which Joab* greeted Amasa* when he stabbed him (2 S 20:9). The kiss was exchanged between lovers (SS 1:2; 8:1). Absalom's kiss of petitioners was noted as something which won the hearts of the men of Israel; presumably such a greeting from a superior to inferior was an unusual sign of condescension (2 S 15:5). The ceremonial kiss appears in the anointing of Saul by Samuel (1 S 10:1). In worship one kissed the divine image (1 K 19:18; Jb 31:27; Ho 13:2). The harlot kisses the man whom she solicits (Pr 7:13). The kiss of Judas, by which he identified Jesus in the darkness to the temple police, was the usual kiss of greeting (Mt 26:48; Mk 14:44; Lk 22:47). It was an expected courtesy for the host to greet the guest with a kiss (Lk 7:45). Members of the Christian communities greeted each other with a kiss (Rm 16:16; 1 Co 16:20; 2 Co 13:12; 1 Th 5:26; 1 Pt 5:14); this ancient greeting survives in the ritual *Pax* of the solemn Mass of the Roman rite.

Kittim (Hb *kittîm*, etymology uncertain), a people descended from Japhet* through Javan* (Gn 10:4; 1 Ch 1:7). They enjoyed friendly commercial relations with Tyre* (Is 23:1, 12; Ezk 27:6). In Dn 11:30 the name is used to signify the Romans. In 1 Mc 1:1; 8:5 Kittim means Macedonia; this is an instance of its late use to designate the countries N of the Mediterranean. Most scholars believe that the name originally designated the Phoenician colony of Kition in Cyprus; but in the passages cited above Cyprus simply is meant. On the identification of the Kittim of the Qumran scrolls cf QUMRAN. W. F. Albright by rearrangement of the consonants removes the Kittim from the text of Nm 24:24.

Knee. The knee is bent to Yahweh as a token of adoration (Is 45:23) or in the posture of prayer (1 K 8:54; Ezr 9:5). It is bent to the Baal (1 K 19:18). The same token is given to a human being Elijah, (2 K 1:13), perhaps not usually to any except "the man of God." The child was apparently received on the father's knees at birth as a sign of acknowledgment (Jb 3:12; Gn 50:23). When the mother substituted a slave for herself the child was received on the mother's knees (Gn 30:3). Weak, trembling, or "watery" knees are a sign of fear and terror (Ps 109:24; Jb 4:4; Is 35:3; Ezk 7:17; Dn 10:10; Na 2:11).

In the Gospels petitioners sometimes kneel to make their requests of Jesus (Mt 8:2; 17:14; Mk 1:40; the parallel in Lk 5:12 has the prostration with the face to the ground; Mk 10:17). This was a proper gesture in approaching a person of rank and power and indicates no profession of belief in the divinity of Jesus. Subjects knelt before kings, as the soldiers did in the mock crowning of Jesus (Mt 27:29; Mk 15:19). Kneeling was also a posture in prayer (AA 7:60; 9:40; 20:36; 21:5). Lk 22:41 describes Jesus as kneeling in prayer in Gethsemani; Mt 26:39 and Mk 14:35 describe Him as prostrate with face on the ground. Bending the knee is a gesture of adoration to the Father (Eph 3:14) and to Jesus as Lord* (Phl 2:10).

Knife. Palestinian sites exhibit knives of flint, bronze, and iron. The most common shape shows a blade which is broadened with a convex cutting edge toward a point. Others curve toward the point, others have two cutting edges which broaden and then converge to a point, others straight with a

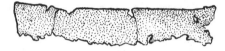

Knife.

single cutting edge which ends in a point. The flint knife (*ṣōr*) was used ritually in circumcision* (Ex 4:25; Jos 5:2). The butcher's knife (*ma'ᵃkelet*, "eater") is mentioned in Gn 22:6; Jgs 19:29; Pr 30:14. The type meant by *sakkîn*, mentioned only in Pr 23:2, is unknown. The *ta'ar* was a very sharp knife, used as a razor (Nm 6:5; 8:7; Ps 52:4; Is 7:20; Ezk 5:1) or as a penknife to sharpen pens and cut the writing material (Je 36:23).

Know, knowledge. Knowledge in western philosophy, which is ultimately derived from Greece, is an intellectual apprehension of reality, distinguished from the sensible and the intellectual appetites. The term of knowledge in western philosophy is the judgment, an affirmation of the truth perceived. In biblical patterns of thought the words which we translate "know" and "knowledge" express a more complex group of psychic activities.

1. *OT.* The Israelite knew with the heart*, and Hb has no word which corresponds exactly to our "mind" or "intellect." The distinction between intellect and appetite therefore is imprecise. In general it may be said that in Hb to know is to experience; experience develops into acceptance or possession. The meaning of "experience" is clear in such passages as 1 S 14:12 (the experience of battle), Is 47:8 (the experience of bereavement), Is 53:3 (the experience of pain), Je 16:21 (the experience of the hand and strength of Yahweh), Ezk 25:14 (the experience of Yahweh's vengeance). In such contexts "know" is equivalent to our "feel." The experience of possession is clear in the use of the word "know" to designate sexual intercourse (Gn 4:1, 17, 25; Nm 31:18, 35; Jgs 21:12 +). Similarly to make known means to make felt, to make another person experience (Pss 77:15; 98:2; 106:8). One who has experience of another person knows him, is acquainted with him (Ex 1:8; Dt 9:2, 24; 1 S 10:11). Even the knowledge which Yahweh has of men is in some contexts a knowledge which is based upon

experience of their behavior (Pss 94:11; 139:1). One who knows an art or a craft is experienced with it, skilled in it (Gn 25:27; 1 S 16:16; 1 K 9:27; Is 29:12). Hence "knowledge" absolutely is a skill of the wise man; he is experienced in the art of living (Dn 1:4; Pss 73:22; 82:5; Pr 1:4; 2:6; Ecc 1:18; cf WISDOM).

Knowledge as acceptance is dynamic, issuing in action; it is appetitive as well as perceptive. To "know" someone or something is to take care, to provide (Gn 39:6, 8; Pss 50:11; 73:11; 144:3). This arises from a basic understanding that to know is to acknowledge (Pr 29:7; Jb 9:21). To know no evil is to refuse it (Ps 101:4). To know the decrees of Yahweh is to accept them by obedience (Ps 119:79). To know what to do is to decide what to do, to make an effective choice (Jgs 18:14; 1 S 25:17). It is usually implied that one cannot know unless one wishes to know, unless one has a desire of the object known. Knowledge is at least the initiation of the satisfaction of desire.

This conception of knowledge is supposed in certain theological uses of "know" and "knowledge." One "knows" the saving deeds of Yahweh by experiencing them and recognizing that He is the doer (Dt 11:2; Is 41:20; Ho 11:3; Mi 6:5). One knows that Yahweh is God by experiencing His divinity in His words and deeds and by acknowledging it (Dt 4:39; 8:5; 29:5; 1 Mc 4:11; Ps 46:11; BS 36:4; Is 43:10). Not to know that Yahweh is God is more than a failure of intellect, an error in judgment; it is a refusal to know, a rejection of Yahweh who is experienced (1 S 2:12; Jb 18:21; Is 1:3; Je 2:8; 9:2-5). The appetitive quality of such knowledge is apparent in most of these contexts, where it is clear that the speculative judgment that Yahweh is God, as we would call it, is not denied by the people who are said not to "know" that Yahweh is God.

To "know" sin in some contexts is more than the experience of sin; it is the acknowledgment of sin, the confession of guilt (Ps 51:5; Je 3:13).

To "know" Yahweh and "knowledge" of Yahweh is a basic religious virtue in the OT; the breadth of the concept of knowledge makes it difficult to define. It seems probable that we should distinguish between knowledge of God ('elohîm) and knowledge of Yahweh (cf GOD); these two terms are not synonymous. Knowledge of 'elohîm is not a common phrase; where it appears it seems to be a technical term, nearly synonymous with the content of the priestly instruction (cf LAW), which deals with the manner in which one should conduct oneself: hence

cultic and moral principles of conduct (Ho 4:1, 6; 6:6). But just as the name Yahweh is a personal name in contrast to the general 'elohîm, which can be applied to any being which is or is thought to be superhuman, so the knowledge of Yahweh is a personal experience. It includes the elements we have seen: experience of the reality of Yahweh and of His divinity, acceptance of Him, acknowledgment that He is God, acquaintance with what He is and the way in which He acts and in particular of His will. The knowledge of Yahweh may be summed up in experience and response. The land will be filled with the knowledge of Yahweh in the peace of the messianic reign (Is 11:9). Similarly Jeremiah affirms that each individual will know Yahweh in the revelation of the new covenant (Je 31:33). Wisdom literature states that the essence of the knowledge of the wise man (cf above) is the fear of Yahweh (Pr 1:7), and knowledge of the holy is discernment (Pr 9:10). The response of the knowledge of Yahweh is stated in Je 22:16: to know Yahweh is to do justice and righteousness and to defend the poor and the needy.

The dynamic quality of the subjective knowledge of Yahweh corresponds to the surpassing dynamism of His person. Hence when Yahweh knows one He accepts him as His own, He chooses him, as He knows Abraham* (Gn 18:19), Moses* (Ex 33:12), Israel* (Ho 13:5; Am 3:2), Jeremiah* (Je 1:5).

2. *NT.* — Synoptic Gospels, Pauline and Catholic Epistles. In the NT we find many of the same qualities of knowledge which appear in the OT; but since much of the NT was composed for Gentile readers and under the influence of Hellenistic civilization, the intellectual quality of knowledge makes an appearance. To know is to experience (sin, Rm 7:7; 2 Co 5:21). To know, especially when the verb appears in the imperative, is to be willing to recognize, to accept (Mt 24:43; Lk 12:39; 10:11; Eph 5:5; 1 Co 14:37; 2 Tm 3:1; Js 1:3; 5:20; 2 Pt 1:20; 3:3). To know is to accept commands by obedience (Lk 19:42, 44; Rm 10:19), to accept the will of God and obey (Rm 2:18; AA 22:14; Col 1:9). To know the grace of God or Jesus Christ is to have experienced it and to accept it (2 Co 8:9; Col 1:6) and to acknowledge it (Gal 2:9). The enemies of Christians will know that Jesus loves the faithful when they experience His vengeance (Apc 3:9). The knowledge of God is something which can be refused (Rm 1:28). One knows the truth i.e., one recognizes and accepts the truth (1 Tm 2:4; 2 Tm 2:25; 3:7; Tt 1:1; Heb 2 Pt 2:20).

To know God is mentioned in the NT 10:26). Likewise one recognizes and accepts God who calls (2 Pt 1:3, 8) or Jesus Christ much in the same sense as in the OT (2 Co 2:14; 10:5); in the same way one knows His glory (2 Co 4:6). The law through which God revealed Himself to Israel is the knowledge of God (Rm 2:20). The key of knowledge which the Pharisees withhold from others (Lk 11:52) is probably the understanding of the law. The knowledge of salvation is the experience of salvation (Lk 1:77).

When knowledge is mentioned absolutely (Rm 15:14; 1 Co 1:5; 2 Co 8:7; Phl 1:9) or explicitly as a charisma (1 Co 12:8; 14:6) it is conceived as a habitual gift possessed by the Christian not acquired by investigation. It is an insight which is the fruit of the process of revelation, faith, and experience. It thus replaces the knowledge of the wise man in the OT but is knowledge of a far higher type and of a higher object. In virtue of this gift one knows particular revealed truths (Mt 13:11; Lk 8:10; Rm 6:6; Col 2:2; Gal 3:7; Eph 1:17; 3:19; 4:13; Js 2:20). This is more than speculative or theoretical knowledge, especially when the object of this knowledge is the mystery* of God's saving will revealed in Jesus Christ.

The knowledge of God is conceived mostly in OT terms. The knowledge which no one perceives (Rm 11:33) is the dynamic knowledge by which He has chosen the Gentiles and rejected Israel. In the NT also God knows in the sense that He recognizes as His own, chooses (Gal 4:9; 1 Co 8:3; 13:12; 2 Tm 2:19). This gives additional fullness to the mutual knowledge of God and the believer in 1 Co 13:12. To know as one is known is to accept God with the same totality with which God accepts the believer. The perfection of knowledge and the perfection of love merge into one; to know fully one must choose without reservation.

The influence of the Greek conception of knowledge appears in Rm 1:18–23 and in 1 Co 1:21: these verses deal with the knowledge of God possessed by the heathens and derived from their experience of Him in creation. The allusions to philosophy in these passages suggest that Paul was referring to philosophical conclusions about the deity. To the Jew such conclusions were unworthy of the name of "knowledge," but Paul goes on to castigate the arrogance of those who believe that they know when actually they do not. The Christian after his conversion really knows God where he did not know Him before conversion (Gal 4:8). The intellectual conception of knowledge probably appears also in the knowledge that there is one God (1 Co 8:4–6) and in the statement that no one can know the mind of God (Rm 11:34; 1 Co 2:16); but even here the "mind" of God is more His intention and will than His knowledge in the intellectual sense. The dynamic conception of knowledge is nowhere more explicit than in Phl 3:8–10, where to know Christ is to gain Him, to be united with Him, to share in His holiness, and through sharing in His suffering to attain to His resurrection.

The Johannine writings. The dynamic and experiential character of knowledge is so apparent in John that his writings must be separately classified; his conception of knowledge exhibits a number of original elements. In John knowledge and love grow together, so that it is difficult to say whether love is the fruit of knowledge or knowledge is the fruit of love. Actually this is a false antithesis in John, since the two mutually enrich each other (1 Jn 4:7–8, 16, 20). One who knows God keeps His commandments, and one who sins cannot know God (1 Jn 2:3–5; 3:6). To know God and Jesus Christ is eternal life (Jn 17:3). Love is joined with knowledge when the relation between Jesus and His Father is described as a mutual knowledge (Jn 7:29; 8:55; 10:15). The same mutual knowledge is the bond between Jesus and His disciples (Jn 10:14 ff, 27). The unity of Jesus and the Father in mutual knowledge is also stated in Mt 11:27; Lk 10:22. This passage, which is altogether singular in the Synoptic Gospels, has been regarded by many exegetes as a piece of Johannine theology which has wandered from its original context. Yet the Johannine conception of knowledge, while original, is foreign neither to the OT nor to the rest of the NT; it simply explicitates what is elsewhere implicit, and it is by no means impossible that this dynamic and experiential knowledge should have found expression outside of Jn.

The knowledge which is the full acceptance of experienced love is implicit in the antithesis between the Jews, who do not know Jesus nor the Father (Jn 8:19; 16:3) and the disciples, who know Jesus and in knowing Him know the Father (Jn 6:69; 10:38; 14:20). The Jews do know Jesus in the vulgar sense (Jn 7:28), since they know His identity and origin; but they do not know Him with the Christian and Johannine knowledge (Jn 8:19). The disciples know Him because to know another puts one "in" another (Jn 10:38; 14:20); it is thus that they know the Father by knowing Jesus (Jn 14:7) and know the love of Jesus for the Father (Jn 14:31). Hence John associates knowledge with vision (Jn 14:7–9, 17, 19 f), emphasizing its experiential quality.

This knowledge the world*, which knows neither the Father (Jn 16:3; 1 Jn 3:1) nor Jesus (Jn 16:3) nor the Spirit (Jn 14:17) nor the Church (1 Jn 3:1), does not have. The Jews and the world do not know because they reject love.

John associates knowledge with faith as well as with love. The two words occur together (Jn 6:69; 8:31 f; 10:38; 16:30; 1 Jn 4:16), and other passages suggest the same connection; one does God's will and knows (Jn 7:17), hears and knows (Jn 8:43), hears, believes, and knows (Jn 17:7 f). Knowledge is then the fruit of faith as well as of love; it comes from the experience and acceptance of God in faith and love and not from human investigation. Hence in John as in the other NT writings it is a gift which is communicated to all Christians (1 Jn 2:13 f, 21; 5:20).

There is a false knowledge against which Christians are warned in several NT writings (1 Co 1:17 ff; 2:6 ff; 8:1, 7, 10 f; 13:8; 1 Tm 6:20; Apc 2:24). The nature and origin of this knowledge are not specified in a way which permits us to identify it with any known system of thought. Modern scholars have suggested a connection with the movement called Gnosticism. This was not a unified speculative system; the groups which are lumped under the name had in common the conviction that salvation was to be achieved through revealed esoteric knowledge. The knowledge, in most groups, was the esoteric revelation that evil was to be explained by dualism; that being was lowered in quality by successive emanations from the source; and that man was saved from evil by retracing the emanations until he arrived at the supreme principle of good. The forms of *gnōsis* (knowledge) of which there are literary expressions are all later than the NT and are therefore more influenced by it than influencing, in particular those forms of *gnōsis* which pretended to be Christian. Many scholars, however, believed these could be traced to earlier pre-Christian forms of *gnōsis* both Jewish and Hellenistic which arose from the mingling of Oriental cults and mythology with Greek philosophy and mythology in the eastern Mediterranean. More recent discoveries of Gnostic literature have rendered these hypotheses untenable, or at best precarious. It seems that there was in the air, particularly in the E, some movements at least akin to Gnosticism and that Christian communities in and near this region were affected by it. The use of some terms in the NT which are known to be Gnostic does not prove that these terms were explicitly used as Gnostic, since they are common Gk words. But when these words appear in such documents as Col and Apc, which were written in Asia Minor or addressed to it, and in 1–2 Co, which were addressed to a port where E and W met and mingled, it is not impossible that the terms should come into use, and that the false knowledge against which the NT warns is an early form of Gnosticism.

Kohath (Hb *kᵉhat*, meaning and etymology unknown), son of Levi (Gn 46:11; Ex 6:16) and eponymous ancestor of the Levite clan of Kohath (Nm 3:17 ff; 4:34 ff; 7:9; 10:21; 26:58). The cities and territories of the clan are described in Jos 21:4 f, 20–26, its territories and clans in 1 Ch 5:27 ff; 6:42 ff. Moses* and Aaron* belonged to the clan of Kohath (Ex 6:20).

Koheleth. Cf ECCLESIASTES.

Koph. The 19th letter of the Hb alphabet, with the value of *ḳ*.

Korah (Hb *ḳōraḥ*, "bald"?). 1. An Edomite clan (Gn 36:5, 14, 16, 18). 2. A Judahite clan of Hebron (1 Ch 2:43). 3. A Levite family of the clan of Kohath* (Ex 6:21, 24; 1 Ch 6:7). Some members of this family were included among the exiles who returned to Jerusalem (1 Ch 9:19, 31). The family of Korah were one of the Levite choirs and the name of the family appears in the titles of Pss 42; 44–49; 84; 85; 87; 88. In Nm 16 the eponymous ancestor of the clan perished by a bolt of lightning when he attempted with others to arrogate the priestly office of offering incense. This rebellion has been conflated with the lay rebellion of Dathan and Abiram; on the analysis of Nm 16 cf DATHAN. A gloss in Nm 26:11 notes that "the sons of Korah," the well known Levite choir, did not perish with Korah. While the origin of this account in the priestly tradition (cf PENTATEUCH) makes it probable that its literary form is much later than the time of Moses*, it is very difficult to suppose that an anecdote which reflected so much discredit on the eponymous ancestor of a well known Levite family could have been composed in the later period. Modern critics with some probability give the anecdote little if any historical value, taking it as an explanation of the subordinate position of the family of Korah. They are very likely right in questioning the details of the story; but there is nothing to show that the position of the family of Korah differed so much in its subordination from the position of other Levite families that it required such an elaborate etiology as this. It is better therefore to accept the unlikely and to take the story as retaining in a much altered and largely invented form the genuine old tradition of a rebellion of the family of Korah and its failure to raise itself to a higher station in the priestly clans. Whether the family of Korah was originally identical with the Edomite and Judahite clans (1 and 2 above) can only be conjectured; if it were, the story of the rebellion may have been concerned with their admission to the priestly clans.

L

Laban (Hb *lābān,* "white"? perhaps a title of the moon-god), son of Bethuel* and brother of Rebekah* (Gn 24:29, 50). Bethuel (Gn 25:20; 28:5) and Laban (Gn 31:20, 24) are both called Aramaeans*. The home of Laban was in Paddan-Aram* or Aram-naharaim* near Haran*. The story of Jacob's employment with Laban for 14 years in order to win as wives his daughters Leah* and Rachel* has been illuminated by the Hurrian* tablets of Nuzu*; according to the customs reflected in these tablets Laban, who had no male heirs, adopted Jacob as his son. This included the legacy of the family gods, the signs of ownership and headship, to the son-in-law through the daughters, unless the adopter subsequently begot a son of his own. This happened to Laban, and hence Rachel's theft of the family gods was theft in law. The story of Jacob and Laban (Gn 29–31) cannot be regarded as a personification of clan and tribal groups, since it is too realistic for this, and reflects Nuzu customs too accurately to be a later fiction. It is, however, a complex literary collection into which a number of motifs have been woven, such as the 12-tribe scheme of Israel and the relations between Israel and the Aramaeans E of the Jordan. There can be little doubt that the covenant which established a boundary between Jacob and Laban E of the Jordan (Gn 31:44–55, especially 31:52) was appealed to in the boundary disputes of Israel and the Aramaeans under the monarchy, and that it justified an ancient Israelite claim. The story also exhibits a popular view of the ability of the Israelite to outwit the Aramaean; the adversary succeeds initially, but in the end he is totally defeated. Upon this popular account is superimposed the religious view which attributes the success of Jacob to the protection of His God (31:24, 42).

Lachish (Hb *lākîš,* etymology uncertain), a city of Judah; its site is identified with the modern Tell ed Duweir 25 mi SW of Jerusalem in the Shephelah*. The city is mentioned in the Amarna* Letters (ANET 321–322) as supporting the Habiru and killing their king, loyal to Egypt. A famous relief sculpture of Sennacherib* represents the capture of Lachish and the reception of captives and tribute by the king (ANEP 371–373).

Lachish was one of the cities in the league which was defeated by Joshua* (Jos 10). It is listed in the cities of Judah (Jos 15:39). It was the base of Sennacherib's* movement against Jerusalem (2 K 18:14, not in Is; Is 36:2; 37:8; 2 K 18:17; 19:8; 2 Ch 32:9). It was the scene of the assassination of Amaziah* (2 K 14:19; 2 Ch 25:27). It is listed among the cities fortified by Rehoboam* (2 Ch 11:9). In the campaign of Nebuchadnezzar* against Zedekiah* Lachish and Azekah* were the two last cities to fall before Jerusalem itself (Je 34:7).

The excavation of Lachish was skillfully directed by J. L. Starkey 1932–1938; the murder of Mr. Starkey by bandits in 1938 left a number of questions unanswered. The city enclosed 18 acres within walls, which made it larger than Jerusalem of the early monarchy. The Bronze Age city was destroyed 1250–1200 BC, almost certainly by the Israelites. No evidence of occupation 1200–900 was found; but the occupation may have covered a smaller area not reached by the excavators. Evidence of the destruction by the Assyrians in 701 BC was clear; the city was occupied and fortified almost immediately afterwards. The destruction by the Babylonians in 588–587 was total, and the site was deserted 586–400. It was the site of a Persian residency after 400, and was finally deserted after the 2nd century BC. The Iron Age fortifications are probably to be attributed to Rehoboam. These included a palace-citadel built on an elevated platform and a double wall; the upper wall was of brick and the lower wall was a stone revetment. Towers were spaced at intervals in the wall. The remains of a small temple which stood 1600–1200, with two rebuildings during the period, contained images and traces of cult, in particular the offering of incense*. The most important discoveries of Lachish were epigraphic. These included seals, stamped jar handles, and inscriptions in an archaic alphabetic script 1800–1500. Of sensational interest were the Lachish letters, written to the commander of the garrison during the last years of Zedekiah, shortly before the fall of the kingdom to the Babylonians. They probably came from Mareshah* or Debir*. They refer to a prophet, who has not been identified with any known biblical figure. Some of the princes are accused of "weakening the hands" (lowering the morale), an accusation which was leveled at Jeremiah (Je 38:4). The writer of the letters is in a position to see the fire-signals of both Lachish and Azekah

Assyrian relief sculpture of siege of Lachish showing infantry and archers advancing up siege ramps, city tower with defenders, mobile covered battering ram, lines of prisoners, and impalement.

(Je 34:7); the letters must be earlier than the date of this verse.

Ladder of Jacob. The ladder (Hb *sŭllām*, Gn 28:12) is probably not to be imagined as a ladder or a flight of stairs, but rather as a connection between heaven and earth like the temple tower (cf BABEL, TOWER OF) of Mesopotamia. The temple tower of Marduk at Babylon was called Etemenanki, "the house of the bond of heaven and earth." The angels ascending and descending are on missions to execute the divine will (von Rad).

Laish. Cf DAN.

Lamb. The lamb is most frequently mentioned in the OT as a sacrificial victim in the ritual passages of Ex-Nm-Lv; cf SACRIFICE; PASSOVER. The flesh of the lamb was regarded as a delicacy (Dt 32:14; Am 6:4). The lamb is a figure of innocence (Is 53:7; Je 11:19) and of helplessness (Ps 119:176; Ho 4:16). The parable of Nathan* (2 S 12:3 ff) represents the affection of the family for its one ewe-lamb.

The title "Lamb of God" (who takes away the sin of the world) is applied by John the Baptist to Jesus in Jn 1:29, 36. This singular title probably arises from a combination of the application to Jesus of the Servant of Yahweh* (Is 53:7), which is also applied in AA 8:32, and of the Passover lamb, which is also applied in Jn 19:36. Many critics question whether this combination of themes is original with John the Baptist or is the result of the reflection of the early Christian community. J. Jeremias has suggested that the title arises from a mistranslation of the original Aramaic *talyā'*, which means both lamb and slave, and that the original saying was "Here is the Servant of God," an allusion to Is 53:1 ff. Jesus is also compared to a lamb, either as sacrificial victim or Passover lamb, in 1 Pt 1:19.

The title of lamb is applied to Jesus 28 times in Apc in a way which has no parallel elsewhere in the NT. He is the sacrificial victim (slain, 5:6, 12; 13:8; His saving blood 7:14; 12:11); but primarily He is represented as enthroned and glorified (5:8, 12–13; 7:9 f; 15:3; 22:1, 3), wrathful (6:16), victorious in war (17:14), the judge who has the book of life (13:8; 21:27). The themes of the sacrificial death and the eschatological triumph of Jesus are joined in such a way that the basis of His glorification is clearly perceived to be His redemptive death.

The believers of Jesus are called lambs (Jn 21:15) of whom Peter* is to be the shepherd; the figure of shepherd* as ruler is common in the OT.

Lamech (Hb *lemek*, meaning and etymology

unknown). **1.** In the Sethite genealogy the son of Methuselah* and father of Noah* (Gn 5:25, 28, 30); he lived 777 years (which would bring him to the year of the deluge in the chronology of P). **2.** In the Cainite genealogy the son of Methushael* and the father of Jabal*, Jubal*, and Tubal-cain* (Gn 4:18–22). To him is attributed the song of the sword (Gn 4:23–24). Lamech is a culture hero in the inverse sense, since he is presented as the author of moral deterioration; he is the first polygamist and the author of the blood feud in its most barbarous and unrestricted form. On the relation of 1 and 2 cf PATRIARCHS.

Lamed. The 12th letter of Hb alphabet, with the value of *l*.

Lamentation. The lamentation as a literary form* exhibits several species. The dirge, (*ķînāh*) the lamentation for the dead, is found in the lamentations of David for Saul and Jonathan (2 S 1:17–27) and for Abner (2 S 3:33 f). The dirge usually begins with the word '*êkāh*, "How . . ." These songs were sung by relatives and friends (2 S 1:17 ff; 3:33 f) or by professional mourners (Je 9:16). This literary form is imitated in the prophets, who apply it to the downfall of nations or individuals: Israel (Am 5:2), Shallum (Je· 22:10), Judah (Je 9:21 f), the princes of Judah (Ezk 19:13), Tyre (Ezk 26:17 f; 27:32–36), the king of Tyre (Ezk 28:12–19), Egypt (Ezk 32:19 f), and perhaps the greatest poem of this species, the lamentation for the king of Babylon* in Is 14:4–21. Most of these pieces exhibit the characteristic *ķînāh* rhythm of an unbalanced 3:2 distich (three stresses in the first stich, two in the second), which is rather easily imitated in translation: "How quiet the tyrant/ quiet the troubler!/Yahweh has broken the staff of the wicked/the scepter of rulers" (Is 14:4 f). The dirge, when addressed to foreign peoples and rulers, becomes a mocking "taunt-song."

The more common species of lamentation is a form of prayer in which the speaker laments his need or misfortune and petitions Yahweh for assistance and deliverance. About ⅓ of the Psalms* fall into this class of prayer. These lamentations are both personal (Je 11:18–23; 12:1–4; 14–18; 15:10–12, 15–18; 17:14–18; 18:18–23; 20:7–13, much of the "confessions," cf JEREMIAH), and collective, uttered in the name of the community (Ezr 9:6–15; Ne 1:5–11; Je 63:7–64:12; Je 14:7–9, 17–22; Ho 6:1–3; Jl 1–2 +). Several of these lamentations are followed by a divine utterance which was spoken by a prophet in the liturgy; cf

PSALMS. In the prophets this oracle is often threatening instead of favorable.

There is some similarity in form and content between the lamentations of the OT and the lamentations used in the cult in Mesopotamia. The dirge was employed in the festival of the New Year for the liturgical death of the god of fertility. The relations between the two groups may be seen in the lamentation to Ishtar (ANET 383–385) and the prayer to "any god" (ANET 391–392). Like many biblical lamentations, these include a hymnal prologue and a confession of guilt.

Lamentations. Lam appears in the Hb Bible in the third part among the writings (cf CANON), in the Gk and Lt Bibles attached to Je.

1. *Contents.* 1, the desolation of Jerusalem conquered by the Babylonians; 2, the angry judgment of Yahweh against Jerusalem; 3, the lamentation of one smitten by God's anger, the hope of mercy, petition for relief; 4, the present misery of Jerusalem contrasted with the glorious past; 5, the sufferings of the vanquished, petition for release.

2. *Form and Style.* The five poems of the book are written in the form of the lamentation*. In 1, 2, and 4 the form of the dirge is retained; 3 is a personal lamentation, and 5 is a collective lamentation. While 3 is personal in form, the speaker can scarcely be an individual Judahite; most of the poem is better applied to the city or the people than to an individual. 1–4 are alphabetical acrostics; in 1–2 and 4 each couplet begins with the successive letters of the Hb alphabet, in 3 there are three lines under each letter. 5 is not acrostic, but has 22 verses, the number of letters of the Hb alphabet. The poems may be compared with a Sumerian lamentation for the fall of Ur shortly after 2000 BC (ANET 455–463). The two compositions have nothing in common except the topic and the spirit of lamentation.

3. *Author, Date, Place of Composition.* The attribution of Lam to Jeremiah is as old as the LXX arrangement of the books; the Hb arrangement, however, does not support this tradition. The tradition probably rests on 2 Ch 35:25. Modern critics are almost unanimous in agreeing that the language and the conceptions are too different from those of Jeremiah to permit the traditional attribution; the author is unknown. Indeed, it is most improbable that the five poems should be attributed to a single author; but criticism cannot demonstrate any more than this diversity. Critics also generally agree that the poems are not much later than the date of the event which they lament, the fall of

Jerusalem to the Babylonians in 587 BC. 2 and 4 appear to be the poems nearest the event, 3 the most recent poem. Rudolph, followed by some critics, proposes that 1 was written after the submission of Jerusalem to Nebuchadnezzar* in 597 BC. While one can hardly speak of literary affinity and still less of dependence, the style and tone echo the literature of the period, Je, Ezk, and Is 40–55. Several critics suggest a liturgical origin for the poems. An annual commemoration of the disaster of 587 is suggested by Je 41:5 and Zc 7:3; these poems may have been written for the commemoration.

4. *Religious Significance.* While the poems are not strictly prophecies, they inherit the prophetic teaching and apply it to the crisis of 587, which was a crisis of faith. The destruction of Judah did not show that Yahweh was too weak to save it or that He had abandoned His people. Rather the disaster was His own work (1:15; 2:1–8, 17, 20; 3:1–18, 43–45; 4:11), which He did to His people because of their sins (1:5, 8, 14, 18; 3:40–42; 4:6; 13; 5:7, 16). Only by confession of guilt and hope in Yahweh's mercy and forgiveness can Israel survive (1:18; 3:21–36, 40, 58; 4:22; 5:20–22). The acceptance of these beliefs enabled Israel to survive as a people and as a faith after it had lost its independent national existence, and the themes of Lam recur frequently in later postexilic literature.

Lamp. Ancient lamps have been discovered in large numbers and the development is easy to trace. Lamps were made of clay until the 5th century BC when metal lamps appear; they did not displace the clay lamp. The Middle Bronze lamp was a shallow bowl or saucer to contain the oil with the edge pinched at one point to contain the wick. In LB period this was modified only by making the pinch somewhat longer and narrower. In Iron II the edge of the bowl is bent outward and the base is flattened. After the 5th century the pinch is brought together so that there are two apertures, one to receive the oil and one to receive the wick. The Hellenistic lamp then becomes a round vessel with a long neck for the wick and a circular opening in the cover to receive the oil. The Roman lamp is a covered saucer, usually decorated, with a small opening in the cover to receive the oil and a slight projection for the opening to receive the wick. The lamp was always kept burning, not only because the house* had very little daylight illumination, but also because it was not easy to light it. The lamp stood upon a lampstand (Mt 5:15; Mk 4:21; Lk 8:16; 11:33). Some lamps are built in a single piece with the stand. Lamps with multiple holders for the wicks, as many as seven, appear; the famous seven-branched lampstand is illustrated on the arch of Titus, and similar elaborate lampstands were found in other ancient sanctuaries and in the homes of the wealthy. The burning lamp was maintained even in the poorest home. Its presence was a sign that the establishment was, so to speak, still in business; the extinction of the lamp was total disaster.

Roman lamp.

Roman lampstands.

The metaphorical use of lamp is common in OT and NT. David is the lamp of Israel (2 S 21:17), and the survival of his dynasty is a lamp for David (1 K 11:36; 15:14). The extinction of the lamp signifies the destruction of Judah (Je 25:10), the downfall of the wicked (Jb 21:17), and the destruction of the sanctuary of Shiloh* (1 S 3:3). Yahweh is a lamp for the psalmist (2 S 22:29; Ps 18:29), and the word of Yahweh is a lamp for his feet (Ps 119:105); Yahweh is a lamp for the king of Israel (Ps 132:17).

The bridal party was met with lamps (Mt 25:1 ff), and the master of the house was met by his servants with lamps (Lk 12:35); both of these are applied to the coming of Jesus. The eye is the lamp of the body (Mt 6:22; Lk 11:34). John the Baptist was a lamp (Jn 5:35); many authors think the distinction between John as the lamp and Jesus as the light* is explicit. The Lamb* is the lamp of the heavenly Jerusalem (Apc 21:23). The lamp of the apostles is explained in Mt 5:15 as their good works, which are to lead men to glorify God. This explanation of Mt does not appear in Mk 4:21; Lk 8:16; 11:33, and the earlier form of the saying may have had another significance, the lamp possibly signifying the preaching of the Gospel.

Laodicea (Gk *laodikeia*), a city of Phrygia in Asia Minor, an early seat of Christianity; associated with Colossae* (Col 2:1; 4:15) and Hierapolis* (Col 4:13); Paul wrote a letter to Laodicea which is not preserved (Col 4:16). Laodicea was one of the seven churches of Apc (Apc 1:11); it is severely rebuked for being neither hot nor cold, but lukewarm (Apc 3:14–22).

Laodicea was founded by Antiochus* II (261–246 BC) and named after his queen, Laodice. It passed under the rule of Pergamum* after the defeat of Antiochus III at Magnesia in 190 BC and with the rest of the kingdom of Pergamum was willed to Rome in 133 BC. It was besieged and captured by Mithridates of Pontus in 88 BC and was repossessed by Rome in 84 BC. After a severe earthquake in the 1st century AD Laodicea began to decline in importance. The ruins are situated at the modern Eski Hisar in the valley of the Lycus, near the ruins of Colossae and Hierapolis, about 160 mi ESE of Izmir. There are remains of a stadium built by Titus in AD 79, a building which was either a gymnasium* or a bath, and two theaters.

Lasea (Gk *lasaia*), a town on the S coast of Crete* near the harbor of Fair Havens* (AA 27:8).

Last Supper. Cf EUCHARIST.

Latin. An Italian dialect which, as the language of Rome, was widely spoken in the western portion of the Roman Empire in the later centuries of the empire and became the parent of the "Latin" languages: French, Italian, Spanish, Portuguese, and affected most other modern European languages. In Hellenistic and NT times, however, Gk was the language of the empire and was more common than Lt even in Italy and Rome itself. It is mentioned only once in the NT; John alone (19:20) remarks that the title of the cross was trilingual: Hb (i.e., Aramaic), Gk and Lt. There are several Latinisms (Lt words written in Gk) in the NT; some of these are loan words in common use, others may be due to the Lt background of the readers for whom the Gospels, particularly Mk (who has more Latinisms than any other writer), were written: *denarion* (Lt *denarius*, cf MONEY); *kenturion* (Lt *centurio*, cf CENTURION); *kensos* (Lt *census*, cf CENSUS); *kodrantēs* (Lt *quadrans*, cf MONEY); *legion* (Lt *legio*, cf LEGION); *xestēs* (Lt *sextarius*, cf WEIGHTS AND MEASURES); *spēkulator*, (Lt *speculator*), scout, then messenger, then executioner (Mk 6:27). On Lt versions of the Bible cf VERSIONS.

Laugh, laughter. Laughter is presented rather unfavorably in the Bible. The word sometimes means to be merry or to make merry or to play: Ishmael with Isaac (Gn 21:9), Isaac with Rebekah (Gn 26:8; these two passages may suggest sexual play), the proper time for merriment (Ecc 3:4), the wise woman "laughs at the future," looks at the future with gladness in her security (Pr 31:25); cf the house of laughter (Je 15:17), the sound of laughter (Je 30:19), the dance (Je 31:4) of merrymakers, boys and girls making merry in the streets (Zc 8:5), wisdom playing or making merry in the presence of Yahweh (Pr 8:30 f); women meet David with song and merriment (1 S 18:7); the frolicking of the crocodile (104:26); or of beasts (Jb 40:20); playing with a bird (Jb 40:29). The word also refers to cultic merriment: the Israelites before the calf-image (Ex 32:6), David and Israel before the ark (2 S 6:5, 21; 1 Ch 13:8; 15:29). But laughter is more frequently unkind or cruel. It is a sign of disbelief: Abraham (Gn 17:17) and Sarah (Gn 18:12–15) both laugh at Yahweh's promise of a son (the name Isaac plays on the meaning of laughter to express disbelief and to express gladness), Lot's father-in-law laughs at the threat of the destruction of Sodom* (Gn 19:14), the people of Judah at Hezekiah's warning messengers (2 Ch 30:10). Most frequently laughter expresses one's gladness at the downfall of an enemy or indeed of anyone who is cast down from eminence or success: the Philistines want the blinded Samson* to be brought out to give them something to laugh at (Jgs 16:25), men laugh at the afflictions of Job (Jb 30:1), the enemies of Jerusalem laugh at its fall (Lam 1:7), wisdom laughs at the doom of fools (Pr 1:26), the righteous at the downfall of the wicked (Ps 52:8); in the spirit of haughtiness Nicanor laughs at the priests and elders (1 Mc 7:34). Laughter expresses scorn or contempt: Daniel laughs at Bel (Dn 14:19 7, 19), the wicked laugh at the righteous (WS 5:4), Tobit's neighbors laugh at his good works (Tb 2:8), Job will laugh at the threat of destruction and famine (Jb 5:22), the Chaldeans laugh at fortifications (Hab 1:10), the wild ass laughs at the city (Jb 39:7), the war horse laughs at terror (Jb 39:22), the ostrich laughs at the horse (Jb 39:18), the crocodile laughs at the lance (Jb 41:21). Perhaps only in Jb 29:24 does Job's laughter at those who have lost faith exhibit a kindly encouraging quality. To be made ridiculous is extremely painful: Potiphar's wife accused Joseph* of making her and the household ridiculous (Gn 39:14, 17), the adulterous wife is exhibited to ridicule (Ezk 23:32). The wise man believes that one who deceives his neighbor in play ("to get a laugh") is no better than a madman (Pr 26:19). By a nearly intolerable euphemism the tournament at arms of Gibeon* is described by the commanding officers as play by the young men: "Let them give us something to laugh at" (2 S 2:14). Ben Sira is perhaps above all others unsympathetic to laughter: twice he points out that laughter, in particular loud laughter, is the sign of a fool (BS 21:20; 27:13), and his remark that laughter tells what a man is has a disparaging tone (BS 19:30). When people laugh at a fool he gets only what he deserves (BS 20:17), and only a fool would laugh at one who is sad (BS 7:11). With this background it is somewhat surprising that laughter is three times attributed to Yahweh; it is the laughter of scorn and contempt at the plots and threats of the enemies of the king (Ps 2:4) or the enemies of the righteous (Ps 37:13; 59:9).

It has sometimes been remarked that Jesus never laughs in the NT. Neither does anyone else; the only people in the entire NT who laugh are the mourners in the house of Jairus* who laugh in disbelief at Jesus' promise to revive the girl (Mt 9:24; Mk 5:40; Lk 8:53). One of the beatitudes of Lk (6:21) promises the laughter of gladness

to those who mourn, and one of the woes promises mourning to those who now laugh, where laughter is a sign of frivolity.

Law. 1. *Outside the OT.* The first extrabiblical parallel to biblical law from the ancient Near East to be discovered was the Code of Hammurabi*, found at Susa in 1902. Since that date the Sumerian* collection of Lipit-Ishtar, the Akkadian laws of Eshnunna, the Assyrian* laws, the Hittite* laws, and some neo-Babylonian* laws have been discovered; these texts are all translated ANET 159–198. With the exception of the laws last mentioned, all of these collections are older than the Israelite laws. The laws of Lipit-Ishtar go back to 1900–1850 BC, the laws of Eshnunna to about the same period, the laws of Hammurabi (1728–1686) slightly later, the Assyrian laws in their inscribed form to the 12th century, the laws themselves perhaps to the 15th, the Hittite laws in their inscribed form to the 13th century, in their origin to the 17th century; the Neo-Babylonian laws probably come from the 7th century. These collections, when compared with the Israelite collections and with each other, lead scholars to conclude to the existence of a widespread customary law of the ancient Near East, which varied in detail but not in principle from one collection to another. It is evident from the comparison that the Israelite civil and criminal law is a product of this customary law. Comparison is not possible in all details; none of the collections (they are not true "codes") is complete, and all except the damaged stele of Hammurabi are preserved only in fragments. Hammurabi introduces the laws with a historical prologue and concludes them with an epilogue, including imprecations on those who alter the laws. Lipit-Ishtar has a fragment of a historical prologue. It may be concluded that prologue and epilogue appeared in all collections. It is evident from the prologue of Hammurabi (ANET 164–165) and the epilogue (ANET 177–180) that the laws are not received by divine revelation; Hammurabi receives from the gods the commission and the authority to write the laws and wisdom to write them well, but the laws are his own composition. This last is in fact exaggerated; the king speaks as if there had been no law before his collection. Lipit-Ishtar (ANET 159) also speaks of his commission as king. Besides some principles and practices in common, these laws all exhibit the same formulation, called "casuistic" by Albrecht Alt: the case is described in a conditional clause, and the decision, penalty, or compromise is stated in the apodosis: "If a seignior's wife was accused by her husband, but she was not caught while lying with another man, she shall make affirmation by god and return to her house" (Hammurabi 131). This formulation is retained even when the description of the case and a complex settlement make the sentence unwieldy; one must suppose that it was traditional even in the early 2nd millennium.

Scholars do not think that the connection of Israelite law with the common consuetudinary law of the Near East was direct with the codes of Mesopotamia, but mediated through Canaanite law; but there are no literary remains of Canaanite law. Recently, however, a number of documents containing contracts and other legally valid formulae have been discovered at the Canaanite sites of Ugarit* and Alalakh; these are the type of documents found in ANET 217–223, and the laws governing the cases can often be deduced from such documents. Both these collections indicate that the juridical activity of the king in daily administration was extremely great, even in the hypothesis that "the king" sometimes means a bureau and not the person of the monarch. They also indicate that these Canaanite cities at least lived under the common consuetudinary law in the areas which are touched in the documents. There are no sources of ancient Egyptian law, neither collections of laws nor even such juridical documents as those mentioned above.

2. *Law in the OT.*

The Israelite laws are contained mostly in collections (improperly called "codes") in the Pnt:

(1) The Decalogue*;

(2) The "Code of the Covenant" (CC), Ex 20:22–23:33. 20:22–26, the altar; 21:1–11, slaves; 21:12–27, personal damages with intent; 21:28–32, personal damages without intent; 21:33–36, damages to animals; 21:37–22:3 theft; 22:4–16, property damages (including unmarried daughter!); 22:17–23:9, religious and humanitarian laws; 23:10–19, festivals and offerings; 23:20–33, epilogue.

The name "code of the covenant" is derived from the "book of the covenant" (Ex 24:7); critics, however, are generally agreed that this collection has been inserted here out of its proper context, and that the book of the covenant of Ex 24:7 is the decalogue. The insertion, however, was meant to include the CC as a part of the terms of the covenant of Sinai; these were the laws which Israel was to observe as its covenant obligations. The CC is consequently attributed to Moses and given the supreme authority which Israel attributed to all its laws (cf below).

Critics are also agreed that the CC is the earliest of the codes after the decalogue; some place it before the decalogue. Its date can be determined only relatively and it is deduced from the social and economic background of the laws. This is not the nomadic life, since the code presupposes the ownership of oxen, cisterns, fields of grain, and vineyards. On the other hand, its few references to real property and no references to mercantile transactions presuppose a period earlier than the monarchy. It is therefore most probably dated late in the premonarchic period. The civil and criminal laws (21:1–22:17) which show several contacts with the code of Hammurabi, are the Israelite adaptation of Canaanite customary law to themselves. The laws of 20:22–26, 22:18–23:19 are humanitarian and religious and have a different formulation from the civil and criminal laws (cf below); these are more probably distinctively Israelite. The epilogue of the CC may be compared with the epilogue of Hammurabi and the other Israelite collections; its insertion in its present context has made the entire Sinai revelation its historical prologue. Since the CC is associated with the E source of the Pnt*, critics generally believe that it originated in N Israel.

(3) The "Jahwist ritual decalogue" (Ex 34:17–27). This collection is entirely religious, dealing with the prohibition of images, festivals, and offerings. Most of its prescriptions are paralleled elsewhere in the Pnt. It is regarded as an early collection, as old as the CC, and containing some of the earliest cultic practice of Israel.

(4) The Deuteronomic Code (DC), Dt 12–26. 12, prohibition of the worship of other gods and the law of worship at a single sanctuary; 13:1–5, prophet; 13:6–18, punishment of those who tempt to Canaanite worship; 14:1–2, funeral observances; 14:3–21, clean* and unclean foods; 14:22–29, offerings; 15:1–18, the sabbath* year; 15:19–23, offering of firstborn animals; 16:1–17, festivals; 16:18–20, judges; 16:21, superstitious divine symbols; 17:1, sacrificial animals; 17:2–7, punishment of superstitious worship; 17:8–13, the priests as a court of appeal; 17:14–20, the king; 18:1–8, the Levites*; 18:9–14, sorcery; 18:15–22, prophets; 19:1–13, homicide and cities of refuge; 19:14, landmark; 19:15–21, witnesses; 20, war; 21:1–9, unidentified homicide; 21:10–17, marriage; 21:18–21, rebellious sons; 21:22–23, execution; 22:1–8, humanitarian laws; 22:9–12, cultic laws; 22:13–30, marriage and illicit intercourse; 23:1–7, admission into the community of Israel; 23:9–14, cleanness of the camp; 23:15–16, runaway slaves; 23:17–18, cultic prostitution; 23:19–20, loans; 23:21–23, vows; 23:24–25, liberality; 24:1–4, divorce*;

24:5–25:4, humanitarian laws; 25:5–10, the levirate*; 25:11–12, aggravated assault; 25:13–16, weights (25:17–19 is not a law); 26, epilogue.

The DC has received a historical prologue in 1–12 which includes more than one composition (cf DEUTERONOMY). In addition to the epilogue of Dt 26, which prescribes an offering, confession of the saving deeds of Yahweh, and profession of observance of the law, the DC has an additional epilogue in Dt 27–30 which contains blessings and imprecations and exhortations to observe the law. Critics are agreed that the DC in some form, not necessarily the present form, was the book of the law found in the temple under Josiah*. On its literary origins cf DEUTERONOMY. The DC exhibits a more complex urban-agricultural society than the CC; in particular, its refinements of the law of blood revenge (cf AVENGER), distinguishing between voluntary and casual homicide, are evident. The DC stands out from the other collections by its hortatory tone; the laws are preached rather than promulgated. The DC is emphatic on the rejection of Canaanite beliefs and cultic practices, which it regards as a genuine threat to Israel. Its distinctive cultic law is the law which permits sacrifice only at a single sanctuary; in the present form of the law this can only be Jerusalem, which in accordance with the fictitious attribution of the DC to Moses is not mentioned by name. The style of the DC falls easily into no class of juridical formulation found in other ancient Near Eastern and Oriental codes; where the casuistic formulation is employed, it is couched in the oratorical style of Dt. The DC as a whole represents an Israelite transformation of the customary law which it contains. This transformation affects not only the practice of the law in details but also the spirit in which law is conceived and expressed. In the DC also the law is a covenant obligation, but it is more; it is a gift of Yahweh, it is Yahweh revealing Himself as the deliverer of Israel.

(5) The Holiness Code (HC), Lv 17–26. 17, prohibition of eating blood; 18, incest and unnatural vice; 19, moral, cultic, and humanitarian laws; 20:1–6, superstitious worship and magic; 20:7–9, filial respect; 21:10–21, adultery, unnatural vice, incest; 20:22–26, clean and unclean; 20:27, sorcery; 21, the priests; 22:1–16, cleanness in priests and laymen; 22:17–33, qualities and defects of sacrificial animals; 23, festivals; 24:1–4, the sanctuary lamp; 24:5–9, the shewbread*; 24:10–23, blasphemy; 25:1–7, the sabbath* year; 25:8–55, the jubilee* year, slavery*; 26:1–2, idols and sabbath; 26:3–46, epilogue of blessings and curses.

The HC has the epilogue but no historical prologue; since the prologue is found so generally, it is probable that the prologue of the HC was detached when the HC was inserted in its present context, which in the opinion of critics is not original. It contains no civil or criminal law at all, but is entirely religious and cultic. Critics generally believe that it is an exilic compilation (about 550 BC or late monarchic) of material which is of undetermined antiquity, some of it perhaps as old as anything in the Israelite collections. It has a characteristic formulation (cf below). The nature of the material suggests that the HC is more closely connected with the priests in its origins than the CC or the DC; but cf below. On the conception of holiness in the HC cf HOLY. The HC has a remarkable series of moral precepts in Lv 19 and the most extended laws of all the collections on marriage and sexual morality.

(6) The Priestly Code (PC). Unlike the other collections, the PC is not gathered in one place but is scattered over the P source of the Pnt*. Some parts are collected; these probably represent collections earlier than the P source itself:

Lv 1–7, sacrifice; Lv 11–15, cleanness* and uncleanness; Nm 28–29, festivals.

It is characteristic of the PC to place the law in a historical context, i.e., to attach the origin of the institution to some event. It is scarcely necessary to add that these events are not always historical in the genuine sense. Cazelles offers as examples the prohibition of blood after the deluge (Gn 9:1–7), the law of circumcision following the covenant established with Abraham (Gn 17:9–14), the Passover* ritual at the departure from Egypt (Ex 12), the law of the priesthood at Sinai (Ex 28:1–29:37), the law of the Levites at the departure from Sinai (Nm 3–4; 8:5–28), other laws concerning the priests and the Levites after the rebellion of Korah* (Nm 18). Other laws have no particular context in events; they are all cultic-ritual, and their position in P is such as to attribute them to Moses. The compilation of P is postexilic, and some of these cultic-ritual laws are of more recent origin; but it is impossible to make a general judgment about their antiquity, which must be settled in each individual case.

It is altogether probable that the PC is in many cases a priestly law in the sense that its directions are not intended for laymen; indeed, some of the strictly cultic-ritual laws could have no one in view except the priests.

3. *Israelite Terms for Law.* There are several Hb words for various species of law. No doubt in their original sense they referred to definite laws of distinct form and content;

but in the present text critics have not succeeded in identifying them with any particular material or enunciation:

Tôrāh. This became the most general word for law in Judaism (cf below). The etymology of the word most frequently given, although it is disputed by some scholars, derives the word from *yārāh*, to throw or cast (lots), and thus finds that its original meaning is divine oracle (revealed by the lot). Hence it comes to mean a divine response in general; and since divine responses were communicated by the priests, it comes to mean priestly instruction. This instruction dealt with cultic and moral precepts. The *tôrāh*, probably in this sense of priestly instruction, is mentioned in Is 8:20; Je 2:8; 18:18; Am 2:4. The word emphasizes the law as the revelation of Yahweh given through the priests.

'Ēdôt, "testimonies"; A. R. Johnson suggests that this word is a technical word for the terms of the covenant of Yahweh and Israel, and may designate either the promises of Yahweh or the obligations which He imposes upon them. Thus the king wore a written formula of the *'ēdôt* at his coronation (2 K 11:12). The term emphasizes, like *tôrāh*, the revealed will of Yahweh in the laws and also the conception of law as covenant obligation.

Mišpāṭ, "judgment*"; this word designates a judicial decision. The term is applied to the civil and criminal laws of the CC (Ex 21:1). The word designates judicial precedent as a source of law (cf below). This term can with great probability be identified with the casuistic formulation of law (cf below). Unlike *tôrāh*, *'ēdôt*, and *dābār* it signifies the human origin of law.

Hôk, "statute"; literally something engraved. Some writers think they detect an antithesis between *mišpāṭ*, customary law, and *hôk*, written law. The source of *hôk* seems to be public authority rather than judicial precedent or custom.

Dābār, "word*"; this term signifies a divine utterance and is used of such solemn laws as the decalogue* (Ex 20:1; 24:3, "words and judgments"). This term also emphasizes the law as the revealed will of Yahweh and can most probably be identified with the apodictic formulation of law (cf below).

Miṣwāh, "commandment"; this term signifies the ordinance of authority, whether divine or human, and is a general term which is applied to other ordinances than law in the strict sense.

4. *Formulation of Israelite Law*. The casuistic formulation of law is found in the civil and criminal laws of CC. The same formulation is employed in the DC with the stylistic modifications of Dt. There are certain variations on this formulation found in Israelite but not in other ancient Near Eastern laws; instead of the conditional clause, the participle is employed (CC, particularly in laws which state offense and penalty) or the relative clause (HC, Lv 20). The first is illustrated by Ex 21:15: "Whoever strikes his father and his mother shall be put to death." The second is illustrated by Lv 20:10: "The man who commits adultery with a married woman, with the wife of his neighbor, shall be put to death — the adulterer and the adulteress." But in the latter portion of the CC, and in most of the other codes, a formulation appears whose classic form is seen in the decalogue: a simple imperative or prohibition couched in the 2nd pers singular imperfect. The plural 2nd pers is occasionally used. This formulation has no parallel in other ancient Near Eastern collections. Furthermore, it is employed in moral and cultic-ritual laws and not in civil and criminal laws. A. Alt proposed that this formulation, which he called "apodictic," is original with Israelite law, and that the formulation and the contents of apodictic laws are the creation of Israelite religious belief. Almost all scholars have accepted Alt's view. The speaker in the apodictic laws is Yahweh Himself; these laws, in contrast to the "judgments," are the revealed will of Yahweh and the terms of the covenant.

5. *The Sources of Israelite Law*. The conception of Yahweh as a source of law is discussed below; here we consider the law-making persons or bodies of Israel. Noth, followed by de Vaux and many others, has shown very probably that the Israelite king was a judge, not a lawmaker. The source of customary law was custom itself; many laws existed simply because it was the way in which things had always been done. Proximately, the person who determined precisely what the formulation of custom should be was the judge. When a case arose (cf the casuistic formulation), the judge decided on the basis of known and accepted custom. Where sacral laws were concerned the judge was the priest; to an undetermined extent the priest also was a judge in civil and criminal cases. Certain cases were brought to the sanctuary for decision (Ex 22:7–8; Dt 17:10; 1 K 8:31–32), in particular cases of the ordeal*; it is important to remember that the ordeal, while it is not a judicial decision in the modern sense, was understood as a judicial act by the ancients. In general, then, the source of Israelite law was tradition as determined by the judge: the king, the elder, the priest.

The collections, as the outlines above show, were not true "codes." Topics are not treated systematically, and the relation between one law and another is sometimes no more than a broad similarity or a catchword. Furthermore, the same question is treated in two or three codes in a different manner. These retreatments and expansions of the collections show the growth of Israelite law with the growth of Israelite society. From a seminomadic group which entered Canaan and began to settle on the land Israel developed into a typical monarchical state of western Asia. The growth of towns, the rise of commerce and industry, the changes in landholding, the needs of a rigid military organization, the creation of an autocratic monarchy — all these meant that the sources of law continually transformed the tradition which they interpreted. Laws which were supplanted by other laws or which fell into desuetude were not expunged from the collections; indeed, this is never done in written collections of law until the law is codified. There is one instance of a law which is attributed both to David (1 S 30:25) and to Moses (Nm 31:27).

6. *Law and Covenant.* The authority of the tradition reposed upon the conception of the covenant*. It is immediately obvious to any reader of the Pnt that the Israelite collections are all attributed to the revelation of Yahweh mediated by Moses. Our understanding of this conception must be such as to take account of the known facts of the derivation of many of the "judgments" from the common customary law of the ancient Near East and of the literary origins of the DC, the HC, and the PC centuries after Moses; and in fact it is now extremely difficult to maintain a Mosaic date for the CC. It is not a matter of defending the position that the Israelite collections are collections of divinely revealed positive law, but of ascertaining the theological significance of the attribution. This significance lies in the Israelite belief that the obligation of their law flowed from the covenant, that life under law was the duty which Yahweh's covenant promises laid upon them. All law was ultimately the will of Yahweh and was endowed to a degree with that supreme obligation which was imposed upon Israel through Moses. All law became a part of the covenant tradition; Yahweh, in revealing His moral will to Israel, had given His own sanction to law. Thus Noth, followed by de Vaux and several others, has insisted that there is no distinction in Israel between secular and religious law. All law is viewed as a religious duty and imposes a sacred obligation. No matter who enforces the law, it is Yahweh who ultimately rewards and punishes its observance and its violation. When collections of law were promulgated, as by Josiah (2 K 22:23) and Ezra (Ezr 9:5 ff),

it is promulgated as the revealed will of Yahweh. Noth, again followed by de Vaux and others, has suggested that the CC is truly a covenant law, although it has been removed from its original context; this context is said by these scholars to be the covenant ceremony of Jos 24:25–26 (combined with Jos 8:30–35; cf JOSHUA). In this ceremony the CC was adopted as the common law of the amphictyony of Israel and imposed upon the tribes as the will of Yahweh sanctioning the covenant. From this passage one notices that the sacred character of the law is also signified by the preservation of the text in the sanctuary; this is not a peculiarly Israelite practice. In addition Dt 31:10–13 provides for periodic public reading of the law as a cultic ceremony; this was doubtless an older practice than Dt.

The conception of the law as the revealed will of God is not paralleled in other ancient Near Eastern collections. Both Hammurabi and Lipit-Ishtar receive from the gods the authority to promulgate the laws and the wisdom to formulate them; but the laws are their own work. Hence the conception of law as a sacred covenant obligation is unique with Israel, as far as is known, and it is fundamental in the OT conception of society as governed by the will of God, and of history as determined by man's attitude toward the law.

7. *The Torah in Judaism.* After the exile the law was no longer the rule of an independent political society; Judaism preserved it by making it a guide of life. The word *tôrāh* is used to describe the whole law, a use which appears in preexilic texts also (Je 8:8; 9:12; Ho 4:6; 8:12), and comes to mean the Pnt (2 Mc 15:9; BS prol 1, 8, 24). The postexilic scribes identify the law with wisdom* (BS 24; 39:1–11) and find in it all knowledge, human and divine. The joy of the Jew in the law is reflected in the Torah Pss 19 and 119. The rabbis included the Torah among the beings which existed before creation. Since the observance of the law was perfection, a school of belief (cf PHARISEES) arose in Judaism which understood the obligations of the law in the strictest sense. To protect the perfect observance of the law they "built a fence" around the law; the fence consisted of legal opinions which advanced the obligations of the law beyond the sense of the words, and thus made it more difficult to violate. This was the "oral law," which was regarded as second in authority only to the Torah itself, and which was by an artificial construction projected in its origin back to Moses himself. The law was reckoned to include 613 distinct "commandments."

8. *Law in the NT.* The Gk word *nomos,*

"law," to translate *tôrāh* comes into Gk from the LXX. The word is never used in the NT of the "oral law," which is called human tradition (Mt 15:3, 6; Mk 7:8 f, 13; Col 2:8). The use of the word is flexible; *nomos* may designate the law as such, the Pnt, the entire OT, the decalogue, or a particular law of the Pnt.

I. The synoptic Gospels. Jesus Himself observed the law and never accepted the charge that He violated it; when He was so accused, He insisted that it was the oral law and not the Torah on which the charge was based (Mt 15; Mk 7). The word is not common in the synoptics (8 times in Mt, 9 in Lk, 0 in Mk) and Gutbrod has remarked that the attitude of Jesus to the law must be sought in other contexts than those in which the word *nomos* occurs. The following texts are drawn from his treatment.

The attitude of Jesus toward the law must in a sense be described as negative. Publicans and sinners are saved before the Scribes and Pharisees (Mt 21:28–32), and repentant sinners are better than the unrepentant righteous (again the Scribes and Pharisees; Lk 15:1–10). The beatitudes (Mt 5:3–10) contain no praise of observance of the law. Acknowledgment by the heavenly Father depends on confession of Jesus (Mt 10:32 f; Lk 12:8 f). He claims to be lord of the Sabbath (Mt 12:8; Mk 2:28; Lk 6:5). The repentant publican is forgiven when the righteous Pharisee is not (Lk 18:9–14). Those who obey all the master's commandments are useless slaves doing no more than their duty (Lk 17:7–10). The scribes and Pharisees have taken away the key of the kingdom, neither entering themselves nor permitting others to enter (Mt 23:13; Lk 11:52). The law in relation to the words of Jesus is like a new patch on an old garment or new wine in old bottles (Mt 9: 16–17; Mk 2:21–22; Lk 5:36–39). Jesus as a son of the kingdom is free of the obligation of the law (Mt 17:24–27). He does not hesitate to restate the law (Mt 5:21–48), and His treatment here is not in the rabbinical manner; His antithesis is, "It was said," and "I say."

On the other hand, the attitude of Jesus is not purely negative rejection. His mission is not to annul the law but to fulfill it, and the kingdom of heaven is entered by its observance (Mt 5:17–20). When He is asked how one is to obtain eternal life, His answer is "keep the commandments" (Mt 19:16–19; Mk 10:17–19; Lk 18:18–20). He reduces the whole law to the commandment of the love of God and of one's neighbor (Mt 22:34–40; Mk 12:28–34; Lk 10:25–28). The righteousness of His disciples must exceed the righteousness of the Scribes and

Pharisees (Mt 5:20). The Scribes and Pharisees strain at the minutiae of observance and omit the essential virtue; they ought to do one without losing the other (Mt 23:23 f).

One may synthesize this double attitude only against the larger conception of the mission of Jesus. He rejects the law as a sufficient means of righteousness; in addition to the law a person must accept Him as one whose words are not only equal to the law, but who comes as a new Moses revealing the Father. If one accepts Him, then one's sinfulness will not be an obstacle to the kingdom of heaven, for the Father is forgiving. But those who place their confidence in their observance of the law make an obstacle of the law. For the law is of itself an insufficient means of reaching God; it must be fulfilled, reach its fullness, in Him. The law is fundamentally what Jesus insists that it is, the revealed will of God; those who accept this revelation cannot make it an excuse for rejecting the fullness of the revelation of God to which the law is directed.

II. The Pauline writings. The attitude of Paul toward the law is universally affected by the problem of the law and Gentile converts to Christianity. The first reaction of the Christian community to the reception of Gentiles was that the Gentiles must become Jews in order to become Christians; it is obvious that they thought of themselves as a Jewish community. But the Church rejected this contention; in the Council of Jerusalem it accepted the saying of Peter that both Gentiles and Jews were saved by the grace of Jesus Christ (AA 15:11) and the saying of Paul that man becomes righteous not by the works of the law but by faith in Jesus Christ (Gal 2:16). The speculative problem of the meaning and value of the law was not solved as easily as the practical problem of its observance. For the law is for Paul the revealed will of God, and it was impossible for him to reject it.

Yet it was evident to him that life and holiness came through Jesus Christ and not from the law (Gal 2:21). If baptism* is a death* to one's former life, one is released from the law (Rm 7:1–6). Jesus Christ has effected what was impossible to the law, deliverance from sin, which is also a "law" (Rm 8:1–3). Paul appeals to the history of Israel to show that the law was not an effective barrier to sin (Rm 2:17–24); indeed, the law is no better than the "law" which Gentiles have in their hearts, which makes them do the works of the law without knowing it (Rm 2:14–16). The spirit comes through faith and not through the law (Gal 3:2). The law "works wrath" in the sense that it reveals sin, it manifests man's sinfulness and his impotence to overcome sin (Rm 4:15; 5:20; 7:9; 2 Co 3:6; Gal 3:19). For the law as revealing sin is an instrument of condemnation and not of salvation. The Christian fact is then a new creation (Gal 6:15); Christians have died to the law (Rm 7:4) with Christ (Gal 2:19); and as Christ is the new Adam (Rm 5:15–19), the old creation has been supplanted (Rm 10:4). The law by its revelation of sin brought a curse; now that Christ has taken the curse upon Himself, no one is subject to it (Gal 3:13). Hence the destiny of the law was not to save man but to lead him to Jesus, the savior; the law was the slave who leads children to school. When the child attains his majority, the slave's work is done. Here Paul's conception of the law reaches a synthesis.

Paul repeats the saying in which Jesus reduced the entire law to the commandment of love (Gal 5:14). Likewise, as a trained rabbi, he occasionally quotes the law to illustrate a point in the manner of rabbinical discussions (1 Co 9:8; 14:21, 34).

III. Hebrews. The law is mentioned frequently in Heb, but the emphasis falls upon the cultic-ritual law which explains the dignity and function of the priesthood. The priesthood of Jesus is explained as fulfilling and surpassing the priesthood of Israel. Here also the principle of the insufficiency of the law is applied (7:11, 18 f; 10:1).

IV. James. The well known antithesis of Js is an antithesis not between faith and the law, but between faith and works. The Gospel is a new law, a perfect law of liberty (Js 1:25). A conception of Christian liberty which would believe that no obligations of the law lay upon the Christian would be false; and one must obey the whole law (Js 2:8–11; 4:11 f). Js obviously does not mean the entire Torah; after Jesus and Paul, the "royal law" is reduced to the single precept of love (Js 2:8), and for the Christian it includes all those works of the law which love demands.

V. John. Jn reports two disputes about the sabbath, but the question of the law is not important to him; the disputes are the occasion of the discussions which follow (Jn 5:16 ff; 9:14). To Jn the law is revelation (Jn 1:17). It is revelation which speaks of Jesus and is His witness (Jn 1:45; 5:39 f). Jesus appeals to the law as an argument for Himself (Jn 8:17; 10:34; 15:25). Brief as is the allusion in 1:17, it is clear that Jn conceives Jesus as the new law surpassing the old; and to express this he chooses that Hb legal term which designates the most solemn promulgation of the revealed will of God, "word*."

Lawyer (Gk *nomikos*), once in Mt, 9 times in Lk 7:30; 10:25; 11:45–53; 14:3, to designate one learned in the law, identical with the group usually called scribes*.

Lazarus (Gk *lazaros* from Hb *'el'āzār*, "God has helped"), a personal name. **1.** The beggar in the parable of Lk 16:20 ff. That a character of a parable should be named is rare, but there is no evident symbolism and no obvious explanation.

2. A man of Bethany*, the brother of Martha* and Mary*, raised from the tomb by Jesus (Jn 11–12). That this, the most striking of the resurrection stories, is not found in the Synoptic Gospels is an old and unsolved problem; and many critics have solved the problem by interpreting the account as purely symbolic and nonhistorical. This explanation does not of itself deny the power of Jesus to raise from the dead; the Synoptic Gospels have episodes in which this power is exhibited, and one may not reject all of them on any antecedent principle. Nor can it be denied that the account in Jn relates the resurrection not merely as an event but as a "sign*" in the Johannine sense (cf GOSPEL; JOHN). It is a part of his presentation of Jesus as the life*, which Jesus renders even after all hope is gone. The description of the exit of Lazarus from the tomb and the lapse of time between burial and resurrection are curiously and deliberately anticipations of the resurrection of Jesus Himself. It is probable that Jn has amplified the account of the event in order to incorporate it into his major themes.

Lead. In Palestine, as in most of the ancient Semitic world, lead was rarely used. There were no deposits of the ore in Palestine. It was widely known, since silver is obtained from deposits of lead ore; but the metal is chemically inactive and was not of much use. Je 6:29 alludes to the lead obtained in the smelting of silver. It is listed among the metals to be purified by fire in Nm 31:22 f. A similar enumeration is found in Ezk 22:18–20. Lead was an object of trade from Tarshish* to Tyre (Ezk 27:12). The vessel in which the woman is contained in Zc 5:7 f is closed with a leaden weight. The allusion to lead in writing in Jb 19:24 probably refers to the filling of inscribed letters with molten lead. The Egyptians sink like lead in Ex 15:10, probably an allusion to the use of lead for sinkers of fishing nets. Lucas mentions as uses of lead in Egypt small human and animal figures; sinkers for nets; rings and beads; ornaments; dishes and trays; addition to bronze to lower the smelting point; headdresses of divine images; filling of bronze weights and cores of bronze statutettes.

Leah (Hb *lē'āh*, "cow"?), daughter of Laban*, given to Jacob in marriage by the deception of Laban (Gn 29:16–24), mother of Reuben*, Simeon*, Levi*, Judah* (Gn 29:32–35), Issachar* (Gn 30:17–18), Zebulun* (Gn 30:19–20), Dinah* (Gn 30:21). The sons of her slave Zilpah*, Gad* (Gn 30:9–11) and Asher* (Gn 30:12–13), were also reckoned as sons of Leah (Gn 35:23–26). Her death is not related; a late tradition tells of her burial in the sepulcher of Abraham at Mamre* (Gn 49:31).

The story of the sons of Leah has to some extent been contaminated by tribal history. The "Leah tribes" exhibit some distinctive features. Reuben, Simeon, and Judah belong to the S of Palestine. Two of these, Reuben and Simeon, disappear very early in Israelite history as distinct tribes; Simeon is scarcely more than a clan of Judah, and Reuben is assimilated by the Moabites*. Levi as a tribe does not appear at all. Judah, however, is a tribal group which can stand opposite Israel. The other two Leah tribes, Zebulun and Issachar, are found in Galilee*. Some historians propose that the Leah tribes were resident in Palestine when the Joseph* tribes entered from Egypt under Joshua and established themselves in the central highlands between the two groups of the Leah tribes. The tribes recognized a certain community of ancestry and of religion.

Leather. The Hb vocabulary does not distinguish leather; it has only one word, *'or*, to designate skin, pelt, hide, and leather. Tanning is not mentioned in the Bible except for Simon the tanner at whose house Peter stayed in Joppa (AA 9:43–10:6, 32). Tanning was known in ancient Egypt even in predynastic times and among the Sumerians in Mesopotamia. Oil, vegetable, and mineral tanning were employed. From archaeology and literature it is known that leather was used in Egypt for bags, braces, bracelets, cushion covers, chariot flooring and tires, sheaths, harnesses, quivers, ropes, sandals, dog collars, seats of chairs and stools, writing material and other purposes (Lucas). Its uses in Mesopotamia were similar and it is easily assumed that the Israelites also employed it. Their tanning processes are not known. The word *'or* in the OT must refer to leather when it is used to describe the girdle of Elijah (2 K 1:8) and in connection with sandals*. Shields which were anointed with oil (Is 21:5) were manufactured of leather; this was a common type of shield* in the ancient world. Body armor* also was manufactured of leather.

Leaven. Leaven was usually employed in the baking of bread; on the significance of unleavened bread in the cult cf MAZZOTH. Leaven is mentioned metaphorically in the parable of the kingdom of heaven (Mt 13:33; Lk 13:20 f); the figure indicates not only the insignificant beginnings of the kingdom of God, but also its inevitable progress. The leaven of the Pharisees (Mt 16:5–12; Mk 8:14–21; Lk 12:1) is explained as the doctrine of the Pharisees in Mt 16:12, as hypocrisy in Lk 12:1; in either case the popular view of leaven as an agent of corruption is presupposed as well as its activity on the mass in which it is placed. Similarly Paul compares the scandalous behavior of one man (1 Co 5:6) and the false doctrine of his adversaries (Gal 5:9) to leaven.

Lebanon (Hb *lᵉbānôn*, "white," probably from the snows which cover the upper slopes of Lebanon most of the year), the chain of mountains which extends N and S along the Syrian coast through the modern country of Lebanon from the Nahr el Kebir until it slopes off into the hills of N Galilee a length of about 106 mi. The average altitude of the chain is about 10,000 ft, and since it rises rather abruptly from the Mediterranean, leaving a coastal plain which is never more than a few miles wide, it is an impressive sight. The slopes both E and W are rather steep and are cut by streams and gorges, particularly on the W. The W slope is well watered and has abundant growth of trees and vegetation, and the variation in altitude permits a wide variety of cultivation of fruits and vegetables. The Lebanon is divided from the Anti-Lebanon* range by a valley, the Beqaa, which is the northern portion of the cleft which becomes the valley of the Jordan*, the Dead Sea*, and the Arabah which extends to the Red Sea. The Beqaa, about 575 ft average altitude, is from 5 to 8 mi wide and 75 mi long. It is watered by the Orontes, which flows N, and the Litany, which flows S. It is a rich agricultural area.

Most of the biblical occurrences of Lebanon refer to its cedars*, but it also occurs in poetic and figured language rather frequently. It is mentioned several times in Jos as a vague N boundary of Israelite territory. In Is 29:17 Lebanon is a wild forest which in the day of Yahweh shall become a vineyard. In Is 33:9 Lebanon withers before the coming of Yahweh. Ho 14:6–8 praises the fragrance of Lebanon; cf also SS 4:11. Lebanon skips like a wild ox in the thunderstorm (Ps 29:6). "The glory of Lebanon" (Is 35:2; 60:13) is its magnificent forests. Je 22:6 alludes to Lebanon as too beautiful for Yahweh to destroy. Ps 72:16 alludes to the richness of its fruits.

Legion (Lt *legio*), the largest division of the Roman armies, which numbered 6000 infantry and 120 cavalry in NT times besides auxiliary and special service troops. The word does not appear in the NT of a military unit, but only of the demons* by which the man of Gerasa* was possessed (Mk 5:9, 15; Lk 8:30, missing in Mt 8:28–34) and of the 12 legions of angels* which Jesus said His Father could send to liberate Him (Mt 26:53). Both occurrences reflect the popular belief of Judaism* that there were vast numbers of both angels and demons, and also the power which Jesus exercised over both parts of the world of spirits.

Lemuel (Hb *lᵉmû'ēl*, etymology and meaning uncertain; some scholars suggest it is a variation of *lā'ēl*; king of Massa [?]). The name appears in the title of the small collection of proverbs in Pr 31:1–9, which the king learned from his mother. The father is always the teacher of wisdom elsewhere; the mother's teaching and counsel, however, are mentioned in parallelism with the teaching and counsel of the father (Pr 1:8; 6:20).

Lentils. A small pea-like plant which grows freely in soil unsuitable for other plants and is cultivated intensively in Syria and Palestine. It can be mixed with flour and baked in bread (Ezk 4:9) or made into a porridge (Gn 24:34).

Leopard (Hb *nāmēr*), the *felis pardus,* a fierce carnivorous cat found in most of W Asia and Africa. It is about 6–7½ ft long including the tail. It is distinguished by the black spots upon its yellow brownish fur; black mutants occasionally appear. It does not appear W of the Jordan in modern times, but is found occasionally in the unsettled areas of Lebanon and E of the Jordan. Ancient Egyptian paintings show the leopard skin as a ceremonial garment of the king. It is mentioned in the OT only in metaphorical language. The enemy which attacks Judah is like a leopard stalking its prey (Je 5:6); the horses of the Chaldeans* are swifter than leopards (Hab 1:8). Yahweh Himself is like a leopard lurking for Israel (Ho 13:7). Judah can no more change its wicked habits than the leopard can change its spots (Je 13:23). In the peace of the messianic kingdom the leopard and the kid will lie down together (Is 11:6). The heights of the Anti-Lebanon are haunts of leopards (SS 4:8). A leopard with four wings symbolizes one of the world kingdoms (Dn 7:6).

Leprosy (Hb *ṣara'at,* Gk *lepra*). The disease now called leprosy, the scourge of medieval Europe and still common in hot, humid climates, is always fatal unless it is treated. It is a bacterial disease, distinguished according to its prevailing symptoms into nodular, anesthetic, and mixed. There is a long period of incubation, perhaps some years. In nodular leprosy the patient exhibits eruptions which develop into nodules which in turn become ulcerated. Anesthetic leprosy exhibits a degeneration of the nerves, loss of sensation and muscular movement, and progressive paralysis with loss of extremities. The mixed type exhibits both sets of symptoms.

It is not certain that the Hb and Gk words always refer to leprosy, although it is highly probable that the disease was known; but the words are applied in some cases when no more than some infectious but milder skin disease, it seems, can be intended. The only "lepers" mentioned in the OT are Moses (Ex 4:6 ff), Miriam (Nm 12:10 ff), Naaman and Gehazi (2 K 5), Uzziah (2 K 15:5), and the four lepers at the siege of Samaria (2 K 7:3 ff). The attacks of Moses and Miriam were brief and miraculously cured; it is impossible to determine what disease the folk story may have intended. The position of Naaman at court and in the administration of the kingdom makes it very unlikely that he suffered from leprosy, and the disease of Gehazi in the story is understood to be the same type. The four lepers of Samaria and Uzziah seem to have been isolated; this suggests that there was more to their case than a mild skin infection.

The priestly rules (*tôrāh*) for the diagnosis of leprosy and of its cure are given in Lv 13–14. Modern medical science can ascertain little from the symptoms here described, but they are not the symptoms of leprosy. It seems that the description sums up a number of infectious skin diseases, which are common in the Near East; the priestly *tôrāh* included a number of skills in diagnosis which are not contained in the text. Lv 13:29–37, for example, is thought to be a description of ringworm. In all cases the victim was isolated for a period until it was determined that he was healed, "clean," or that the disease was not infectious, or that it was chronic. "Leprosy" can also attack garments (Lv 13:47–59) and houses (Lv 14:33–53); this leprosy must be some kind of mold or mildew or dry rot.

The cure of a leper by Jesus is related in Mt 8:1–4; Mk 1:40–45; Lk 5:12–16, and the cure of ten lepers in Lk 17:11–19. The power to cure leprosy is included in the mission of the apostles (Mt 10:8), and the cure of leprosy is one of the messianic signs which Jesus points out to the disciples of John the Baptist (Mt 11:5;

Lk 7:22). Jesus was received as a guest by Simon "the leper" of Bethany (Mt 26:6; Mk 14:3). The word here can scarcely mean one who suffers from true leprosy, and it probably refers to an affliction from which Simon had been cured. In the NT, as in the OT, leprosy may designate a wide variety of mild skin infections.

Levi, Levite (Hb *lēwî*, meaning and etymology uncertain [cf below]), one of the 12 sons of Jacob* and one of the 12 tribes* of Israel*. The OT data concerning Levi are not consistent and present a number of problems which scholars have not yet solved. Levi was the son of Jacob and Leah* (Gn 29:34); his name is explained by a popular etymology as "joined." Levi and Simeon* treacherously attacked the men of Shechem* in revenge for the rape of Dinah* and brought the name of Israel into bad repute (Gn 34). Modern historians are inclined to see in this story some reflection of the action of tribes and clans rather than individuals and to take the story as a dim recollection of an unsuccessful attempt of Simeon and Levi to settle in the later territory of Ephraim*. The blessing of Jacob (Gn 49:5–7) alludes to this action of violence and treachery and curses the two tribes as divided and scattered in Israel. The blessing of Moses* (Dt 33:8–11) knows nothing of this curse. Levi is the priestly tribe faithful to Yahweh. Levi, however, does not always appear in the enumeration of the 12 tribes of Israel; as a landless tribe (cf below) it yields place to Ephraim and Manasseh*, who represent the double portion of Joseph*. Moses and Aaron* belonged to the tribe of Levi (Ex 2:1 ff).

In Ex and all later references Levi appears as a priestly tribe or as a tribe associated with the priesthood as inferior ministers of the sanctuary; but neither are the data here consistent. In Dt the designation "the Levite priests" is common and usual (Dt 18:1; 21:5; 24:8; 27:9; 31:9, 25). The same designation is used in Jos 3:3; 8:33 and Ezk 43:19–44:15, with the additional specification that these are Levite priests of the house of Zadok* (cf below). Je 33:18–21 speaks of a covenant of Yahweh with the Levite priests, as does Mal 2:4. The rarity of the Levites in 1–2 S and 1–2 K is surprising and significant. They appear in 2 S 15:24 with Zadok bearing the ark*. It is noticed that Jeroboam* established priests, at Bethel* and Dan*, who were not Levites (1 K 12:31). While the date of these allusions is not certain, they certainly must have come from a period when all priests were Levites.

But most of the passages in which Levites occur suppose that there is a difference between priests and Levites, or at least that the term "Levite" has a wider extension than the term "priest." In Dt the Levite frequently appears as a *gēr*, a stranger*, presumably homeless and unemployed, who is mentioned with the widow and the orphan as an object of charity (Dt 12:12; 12:18–19; 14:28; 16:11; 26:12–13). It is difficult to combine such a social status with the priestly office. It is still more puzzling to find in the same code that the Levite has a right to serve in the sanctuary and share in the priestly portions whenever he desires to do so (Dt 18:6–8). Such a Levite stranger appears in the stories of Jgs 17:7–13 and 18: 18–20; 19:1 ff. The Levite of Jgs 17–18 became priest of the sanctuary of Dan, and his line endured as priests at Dan until "the land was taken captive" (721 BC; Jgs 18:30). The distinction between the priests and the Levites establishes the Levites as inferior ministers who assist the priests and perform sacred but not sacerdotal functions in the sanctuary. These are set forth in several passages, and mentioned by allusion frequently. The Levites are "to oversee the work of the house of Yahweh," as *šôṭerîm* (an administrative office whose functions are not precisely known) and judges, as doorkeepers and instrumental musicians (1 Ch 23:4–5), according to an ordinance of David. They attend the priests, purify the holy things, prepare the bread, sing praises, and have general care of the sanctuary — also according to an ordinance of David (1 Ch 23:28–32). They collect tithes (Ne 10:37–40). They render vocal and instrumental music and act as cultic prophets (1 Ch 25:1–8). They are excused by David from carrying the utensils of the service, which they had presumably done earlier (1 Ch 23:26). They lead in prayer (Ne 9: 4–5) and instruct the people in the law* proclaimed by Ezra* (Ne 8:7–9). There are frequent allusions to the Levite choirs (1 Ch 9:14 ff, 33 f; 15:16–23; 2 Ch 5:12; 7:6; 20:19; Ne 11:22 f; 12:24, 45–47), and to the Levite gatekeepers (1 Ch 9:14 ff; 26: 12 ff; Ne 12:45–47; 13:22). In the P source of the Pnt they are assigned the care of the ark and the tabernacle* and they alone have the privilege of carrying the ark (Nm 1:49–53; 4). The privilege of carrying the ark is mentioned in other sources also (Dt 31: 9, 25, which speaks of "the Levite priests"; 10:8–9; 2 S 15:24; 1 Ch 15:2, where the concession is attributed to David rather than to Moses).

The inferior position of the Levites has historical roots; but here again several variant accounts are given or suggested. In Ex 32: 25–29 the priesthood is awarded to the tribe of Levi for its fidelity to Yahweh and to Moses in the episode of the golden calf, in Dt 33:8-11 for its fidelity at Massah* and Meribah*, not mentioned in the Pnt account of these episodes. The suggestion of many critics that this account is a theological explanation rather than a historical narrative has some probability; but the account does imply that the priesthood came to the tribe of Levi by some concession, that there was a time when it was not a priestly tribe. In Nm 16-17 some of the Levites led by Korah* claim equality with the priests; the claim is rejected and the Levites are punished. Here the inferior position of the Levites is taken for granted. The historical character of this episode also is subject to question; but it must be founded on a memory of some dispute about the exclusion of the Levites from the priestly position which in the tradition mentioned above they possessed. The priestly family which is here vindicated in its rights is the family of Aaron. Ezekiel, however, speaks of the priestly family of Zadok*, which is a Levite family, but which alone possesses priestly rights and privileges (Ezk 40:46; 43:19; 44:15). The privilege is accorded to the family of Zadok because it alone among the Levitical families did not worship false gods (Ezk 44:10). The Levites who returned with Ezra are clearly distinct from the priests and clearly also inferior to them (Ezr 2:40-42; Ne 7:43-45); in this source they are also clearly distinct from the temple servants. In Nm 3:44-51; 8:1 ff the Levites are the substitutes for the firstborn sons of Israel, who belong to Yahweh, i.e., to the sanctuary, and in Nm 8 they are offered to Yahweh after the manner of the sacrificial portions.

It is frequently stated that the Levites have no portion or possession; unlike the other tribes they receive no allotment. This is a motive in Dt for charity which the Israelites should show them (Dt 18:1-5; Jos 13:14, 33). In contrast with this statement, however, is the assignment of cities and their environs to the Levites. This assignment is attributed to Moses (Nm 35:2-8) and its execution to Joshua (Jos 21, which lists the 48 cities of the Levites; cf Ch 6). The list offers a number of difficulties, including some cities which were not Israelite or not held by them very long, and many scholars have concluded that the list is entirely unhistorical. W. F. Albright suggests that the institution of Levitical cities is to be attributed to David, but that it was never completely established and did not long endure, and may perhaps be regarded rather as an ideal piece of legislation than as an accomplished fact. But the landless Levite appears fre-

quently in Dt and must have been a historical phenomenon.

The picture of the Levites and their position in the cult and their relations to the priests is most consistent in 1-2 Ch and the P source of the Pnt. Both of these sources are late and the institution as they describe it reflects the postexilic period. It does not seem possible to assume with some scholars that the entire conception is a postexilic cultic institution retrojected into the earlier periods. It is evident from the above survey that the preexilic history of the Levites includes a complex historical process which thus far has defied analysis. The tradition that Levi had the priesthood and lost it occurs too frequently in too many varied forms to be rejected entirely, but it is impossible to reconstruct the events. It seems more probable that the Levites were the oldest of the Israelite priesthoods.

The relations of the Levites to the tribe of Levi likewise defy analysis. The hypothesis that they were scattered members of the tribe who in some way fell into the priesthood is most improbable. The most likely explanation seems to be the theory suggested by Eichrodt and others that we have here two similar names which in the course of tradition became fused into a single name. The popular etymology of Gn 29:34 is not probable, but it may represent a different name from that of the cultic tribe, which W. F. Albright suggests comes from the root *lawiya,* "pledged by debt or vow." Albright believes that the name and the "tribe" are an official and functional group rather than a family or ethnic group; it was the sacred personnel of early Israel which was maintained not only by generation but also by adoption. Thus Samuel*, a member of Ephraim, is given a Levite genealogy (1 Ch 6:18). The vicissitudes through which this group passed are reflected in the variants in their traditions, which attribute their functions to Moses, David, Solomon, Hezekiah, and Nehemiah.

Levi appears in the NT as another name of Matthew* (Mk 2:14; Lk 5:27, 29) and in the Lucan genealogy of Jesus (Lk 3: 24, 29).

Leviathan (Hb *lewiyatan,* "the fleeing serpent, the coiled serpent"). The serpent struck by the sword of Yahweh (Is 27:1); his heads are shattered by Yahweh (Ps 74:14); he is aroused by conjurers (Jb 3:8). The title was also applied to the crocodile (Jb 40:25) and to a frolicking large fish (Ps 104:26). These allusions suggest a monstrous being, to be identified with the mythological monster of chaos, Lotan, "the serpent slant, the serpent tortuous, Shalyat of the seven heads," slain by Baal in the Ugaritic* Baal epic (ANET 138). Is 27:1 is borrowed from the Ugaritic poem; cf also the "heads" of Ps 74:14. The victory of the creative deity over the monster of chaos is transferred to Yahweh; cf CREATION.

Levirate marriage (From Lt *levir*, "brother-in-law"), the law which obliged a brother to marry the widow of his deceased brother if the brother died without male issue. The nature of the obligation is obscure because the three OT passages which refer to the practice exhibit different forms of the law at different periods. In Gn 38 Judah* is clearly obliged to give Tamar*, the widow of Er to Er's brother Onan*. Onan's refusal to fulfill the duty and his subsequent death aroused a superstitious fear in Judah so that he did not give Tamar to the next son, Shelah. Then Tamar disguised herself as a prostitute and seduced Judah himself. Instead of burning her for illicit intercourse Judah was forced to admit that she was "more righteous" than he was, since she secured her rights. This is supported by the Hittite laws (# 193; ANET 196), in which the obligation falls upon the father-in-law after the brother-in-law.

The law of Dt 25:5–10 is valid when brothers live "together," i.e., on property owned by the family. The purpose of the law is stated here to be "to raise up seed for the (deceased) brother that his name be not blotted out of Israel." The first son born is to bear the patronymic of the deceased brother. It was a disaster for a family line to be extinguished. Although it is not stated in the law, the family property must have had some bearing on the practice; the marriage and the provision of an heir would have removed the possibility of dispute and litigation which could have arisen if the widow married outside the family. Without information on the laws of inheritance of the period it is difficult to answer this question. The brother could escape the obligation by submitting to a ceremonial degradation; it seems that this was a small price to pay to evade what could have been a burdensome duty.

The marriage of Boaz* and Ruth* (Rt 4) resembles the levirate marriage. Here, however, the right of marriage is involved with the right to purchase landed property; the legal background is not at all clear. Furthermore, the right or duty of marriage is extended beyond the circle of brothers to the next of kin, who happens here to be quite remote. It seems that one can hardly speak of a duty of marriage in this transaction; the duty is conditioned upon the desire to purchase the property which Naomi* wanted

to alienate. As in Je 32, it was first offered to the next of kin; cf AVENGER. The ceremony of removing the shoe (Rt 4:7) does not include the element of degradation mentioned in Dt 25:9; possibly custom had softened this practice.

The prohibition of intercourse with a brother's wife (Lv 18:16; 20:21) seems to include marriage as well as illicit intercourse and makes no distinction between a widow and a divorced wife. It is uncertain whether this law is intended to prohibit the levirate or whether it assumes the exception.

Although the levirate marriage is a widespread practice in many cultures and is still practiced among nomad Arabs, it is not attested in the Babylonian and Assyrian laws; its only parallel in the ancient Near East is the Hittite law # 193. Historians have sought for a uniform basis of the custom in such postulated institutions as group marriages or polyandry. Whatever may be said of other peoples, the Israelite law is expressly intended to raise up a son and heir of the deceased and so to continue his family. Thus it is best regarded in Israel as an instance of the duty of the avenger*. In practice, as we have seen, it was probably complicated by questions of property and inheritance.

It cannot be deduced from the question of the Sadducees* (Mt 22:23–33; Mk 12:18–27; Lk 20:27–40) that the levirate marriage was practiced in NT times. It is abundantly evident that the rabbis were accustomed to discuss scholastic questions of the interpretation of the law which had no reference to existing reality.

Levitical cities. Cf LEVI, LEVITES.

Leviticus. The third of the 5 books of the Pnt. The name comes from the LXX and designates the "Levitical" laws which the book contains. Contents. 1–7, laws governing sacrifice*; 8–10, the installation of the Aaronic priesthood*; 11–15, laws of cleanness* and uncleanness; 16, ritual of the day of atonement*; 17–26, the holiness* code (cf LAW); 27, votive offerings and dues.

The entire book is assigned to the P source of the Pnt*.

Libertines (Lt *libertini*, "freedmen"). The opposition to Stephen* is said in AA 6:9 to have come from the two groups: "the synagogue of the Libertines, the Cyreneans, and the Alexandrians," and Jews from Cilicia* and Asia*. The Libertines, unlike the others, are not a geographical name. Strathmann suggests with great probability that they represent the descendants of Jews captured and enslaved by Pompey and taken to Rome who had obtained their freedom. Philo attests that the Jewry of Rome was largely composed of the descendants of captives in war.

Libnah (Hb *libnāh,* etymology uncertain), a city in the Shephelah*, identified either with Tell es Safi, about 25 mi WSW of Jerusalem, or with Tell Bornat, about 5 mi S of Tell es Safi. Tell es Safi, explored by Bliss and Macalister in 1899, showed occupation from 1700 BC into the Seleucid* period. Libnah was a Canaanite royal city taken by Joshua* (Jos 10:29 f; 12:15). It is listed among the cities of Judah* (Jos 15:42) and among the priestly cities (Jos 21:13). It freed itself from Judah under Jehoram*, probably under Philistine* influence (2 K 8:22; 2 Ch 21:10). Sennacherib* was besieging Libnah when he sent a letter to Hezekiah demanding surrender (2 K 19:8; Is 37:8); the siege apparently had to be raised. Hamutal*, queen of Josiah, came from Libnah (2 K 23:31; 24:18; Je 52:1).

Libya (Hb *lûbîm*), mentioned only in the OT as neighbors (Dn 11:43) and auxiliary troops of Egypt* (2 Ch 12:3; 16:8; Na 3:9). They are mentioned among defeated enemies by Thutmose III (ANET 374), Amen-hotep III (ANET 376) and Merneptah (ANET 376) of Egypt. Libya's defeat is predicted in the prophecy of Nefer-rohu of the Middle Kingdom of Egypt (ANET 446). Libya is listed among the countries of the empire of Xerxes of Persia* (485–465 BC). Other allusions to war with Libya run through the entire history of Egypt from early times; the wealth of Egypt was a constant temptation to the impoverished nomads of Libya. They were among "the peoples of the sea" whose invasion was repelled by Ramses III in 1187 BC. Their attempts to penetrate Egypt succeeded after the 19th dynasty and Sheshonq, the biblical Shishak*, was a Libyan. The biblical texts which describe them as allies of Egypt come from this later period. In the NT Libya is mentioned in AA 2:10. The designation in ancient times is loose, but covers generally the N coast of Africa W of Egypt.

Life. 1. *OT.* The OT does not distinguish between "life" as a principle of vitality and life as living, the concrete experience of vitality. Its language is concrete rather than abstract, and life is viewed as the fullness of power, the pleasure which accompanies the exercise of vital functions, integration with the world and with one's society. Loss of these is a diminution of life, and the approach of death. When the Assyrian promises life to the inhabitants of Jerusalem

he also promises the good things of life: that each should eat from his own vine and fig and drink from his own cistern, and live in a land of grain and wine, of bread and vineyards, of olives and honey (2 K 18:31 f). Israel is promised that it shall live and possess the land (Dt 4:1; 16:20); for the earth or one's own land is "the land of the living" or "the land of life" (in Hb the two phrases are scarcely distinguished), the place where life belongs and can be fully experienced (Dt 12:1; 31:13; Is 38:11; 53:8; Je 11:19; Ezk 32:23; Pss 52:7; 142:6; Jb 28:13). The greeting to the king, "May the king live," or "Let the king live forever" was much more than a wish for mere survival (1 S 10:24; 1 K 1:25, 31, 34, 39; 2 K 11:12). Israel desires that it may be well with them and that Yahweh may give them life (Dt 6:24). Man desires life and length of days that he may see good (Ps 34:13). God gives life and loving-kindness to Job (10:12); He gave life and peace* to Israel's priests (Mal 2:5). A calm heart is life to the flesh (Pr 14:30). Life is made joyful by wine (Ec 10:19) and by the love of one's wife (Ec 9:9). The rewards of humility and the fear of Yahweh are wealth, honor, and life. When Yahweh gives a man life, He makes the man happy and does not deliver him to his enemies (Ps 41:3). Thus life is itself the basic good without which no other good is possible; a living dog is better than a dead lion (Ec 9:4). It is more sophisticated reflection which perceives that life can be something else than an experience and asks whether there is any value in a long life without good (Ec 6:3), or why life is given to the embittered of spirit (Jb 3:20). One may come to hate life which brings no lasting good (Ec 2:17), and to prefer death to life in the hour of disaster (Je 8:3). It was possible for Job to play on the meaning of the word *rûªḥ,* "wind" or "spirit," and to declare that his unhappy life was indeed "wind" (Jb 7:7); life is often said to come from the spirit* (cf below).

The conception of life implied above shows that the Israelites did not conceive of the living man as an incarnate spirit, as many scholars have said, but as an animated body. It is the vigor and power of the body and its functions, its capacity for pleasure, which is the fullness of life. "Living water" is running water (Gn 26:19; Lv 15:13; Nm 19:17; Je 2:13; 17:13). Death* is total and Israel knew of no vital activity which survived it. The dead do not live (Is 26:14). It is the living, not the dead, who praise Yahweh (Is 38:19). The OT knows of no life after death until its latest books (cf SHEOL); when the idea arises, it could be conceived only as a restoration of the life which the Hebrews knew, a resurrection* of the body.

The title of "living" is applied primarily to Yahweh (Jos 3:10; 1 S 17:26, 36; 2 K 19:4, 16; Pss 42:3; 84:3; Is 37:4, 17; Je 10:10; Ho 2:1). The title no doubt implies a distinction between the living reality of Yahweh and the lifeless images of foreign gods, but it also emphasizes the living reality: the possession of the power and freedom and movement which is life. As living, Yahweh is perceptive, responsive, and active. It is Yahweh alone who gives life. In the story of the origin of man life is maintained by eating of the tree of life, which could confer the power of living forever (Gn 2:9; 3:22, 24). This figure may be borrowed from foreign mythology and is accessory to the general conception in the OT of how Yahweh confers and sustains life. In Gn 2:7 man becomes a living being when Yahweh breathes into his nostrils. It is a common conception in the OT that life endures while man possesses the spirit, the breath which was inspired in him by Yahweh. This spirit is not a living personal being in man (Gn 6:17; Jb 33:4). When a man recovers from a faint, his "spirit" returns (Gn 45:27). The dry bones of Ezekiel's vision (37) live again when the wind, the "spirit," moves them. The spirit is not the same as the nepeš (cf SOUL), which is rather the "self" of the living being. When Elijah* raises the widow's son, the nepeš of the body returns and he lives (1 K 17:22); actually the phrase describes the phenomenon: "consciousness returned to him." A comparison between this line and Gn 45:27 shows that "spirit" and "soul" are used loosely. The righteous lives by his fidelity (Hab 2:4).

Yahweh is often said to give life where we should speak of His preserving it; since every nepeš is in His hand (Jb 12:10), life is in a way a constantly new gift. At His command the dying child lives (Ezk 16:6). It is Yahweh who kills and gives life (Dt 32:39; 1 S 2:6), who shows men the path of life (Ps 16:11). By His blessing life is conferred (Ps 133:3). Those will live who are written in His book of life (Is 4:3; Ps 69:29). The fountain of life is with Him, and men see light* in His light (Ps 36:10); "to see light" is not an uncommon paraphrase for "to live." The man whom God protects walks in His presence in the light of life (Ps 56:14) or in the land of the living (Ps 116:9). Light is the element of life and good, darkness* the element of death and evil. The king asks and receives of Yahweh long life (Ps 21:5); the life here given is the fullness of life worthy of a king. The Pss frequently ask Yahweh for life or thank

Him for its gift when the petitioner has been delivered not only from the danger of death but even from the danger of some loss to his vitality or his personal dignity; for honor is an important function of life (Pss 30:4; 71:20; 80:19; 143:11). The unique conception of 1 S 25:29 represents life as carried in a "bundle" by Yahweh; as long as one's life is wrapped in the bundle, he is safe.

Since Yahweh is the lord of life and death, He gives life with respect to one's character and deeds. It is the teaching of Dt that Israel must choose between life and death, good and evil, blessing and curse; Israel chooses life by loving Yahweh and by observing His commandments (Dt 30:15-20). Life here is not mere vital existence but life in its fullness of goodness and blessing; whether man receives life in this proper sense (as the Hebrews understood it) was determined not by chance but by his own free choice. It is a fairly constant theme in Dt that life is given and maintained by the love of Yahweh and fidelity to His commandments (Dt 4:1; 6:24; 16:20; 30:6; also Lv 18:5). Man does not live by bread alone, but by the utterance of Yahweh (Dt 8:3). Life, then, is not a merely physical and biological reality, nor even primarily such; it is an ethical and religious function whose health and vigor ultimately rest upon integration of the human will with the divine will.

The same idea appears in the prophets, but less frequently and schematically than in Dt. To live one must seek Yahweh (Am 5:4, 6) or seek good and not evil (Am 5:14). One may live by hearkening to the word of Yahweh (Is 55:3), by keeping His commandments (Ezk 20:11, 13, 21). In two passages parallel in thought Ezekiel (18 + 33:1-20) insists that life is obtained by abstaining from wickedness or by turning away from the wickedness one has committed. The thought here seems to mean more than mere survival, and more than the thought of Gn 3 that death is a consequence of wickedness; Ezekiel is not promising eternal life to those who turn from sin. Life here is again taken in the sense of the fullness and the joy of life, a good achieved by moral and religious perfection.

In the wisdom* literature life is the fruit of wisdom and of righteousness; this is stated frequently (Pr 3:2, 18, 22; 4:4, 10, 22 f; 6:23; 8:35; 9:6; 10:11, 16 f; 11:30; 12:28; 13:14; 14:27; 19:23; 21:21). Wisdom (3:18) or righteousness (11:30) is a tree of life; the figure is probably from Gn 2-3 and the ethical symbolism is added. This wisdom which is life includes the fear of Yahweh (14:27; 19:23). Ps 119 repeats the petition that Yahweh will give life; the source of life is the word and the commandment of Yahweh. Life here is understood in the sense of fullness of well-being; for it is a commonplace of wisdom literature that the fruit of wisdom is success, health, and good fortune. The man who pursues righteousness will find life and honor. This life God does not give to the wicked (Jb 36:6). It is with horror that Hb narrative relates of the rebellious Israelites that they went down to Sheol* alive (Nm 16:30). They did not experience the fullness of their days in the normal span of years nor pass from the prime of life through the normal disintegration of age. Such a gradual disintegration was to the Hebrews a gift of Yahweh, a token of His good pleasure and of a man's righteousness. The wicked who went down to Sheol alive were struck down in their fullness; they died, so to speak, a living death.

The Gk books of the OT echo earlier themes without modification except for the distinctive view of WS* of life after death influenced by Gk thought. Life is the fruit of wisdom (BS 4:12); the same book repeats the older belief that only the living praise God (BS 17:27 f). Almsgiving saves one from death (Tb 12:9). God kills and gives life (WS 16:13). Life is given by the commandments (Bar 3:9) and by wisdom (Bar 3:14). The life of human beings is not the gift of the parents but of the creator (2 Mc 7:22 f).

2. *NT*. I. The Synoptic Gospels. The synoptics echo the OT. Dt 8:3 is quoted in Mt 4:4; Lk 4:4. Life is obtained by keeping the commandments (Mt 19:16 f; Mk 10:17–19; Lk 10:28; 18:18–20). Life is granted to those who renounce all things for Jesus (Mt 19:29; Mk 10:30; Lk 18:30). Life is not assured by wealth (Lk 12:15). God is not the God of the dead but of the living; this OT conception is employed by Jesus in an *argumentum ad hominem* in response to an absurd question of casuistry proposed by the Sadducees* (Mt 22:32; Mk 12:27). This life which is thus obtained is specified as eternal life in the world to come, and thus it goes beyond the OT conception of life as the experience of the fullness of vitality in a morally integrated life. The synoptic teaching does not have any regard to the fulfillment of the life of the present experience; the fullness of life is obtained after death. The idea of eternal life, somewhat casually mentioned in the synoptics without explanation, is more fully developed in other NT writings. The return from sin is described as a return from death to life (Lk 15:24), and it is altogether likely that this passage shows the influence of Pauline

thought (cf below). The way to eternal life is narrow and few pass through it (Mt 7:14).

AA also echoes the OT in its quotation of Pr 16:11 in 2:28 and in Stephen's allusion to the words of life given to Moses (AA 7:38). The words of the Gospel are also the words of this life (AA 5:20). Jesus is the "leader of life," the one who leads men to life (AA 3:15). Eternal life is given only to those whom God has appointed for it (AA 13:48); this apparently rigid conception of God's will for man's life states no more than the common biblical belief that God is the lord of life and death and that life is obtained only through the word and the commandments of God. In Paul's discourse at Athens he describes life in the biblical conception as given by God to all creatures with the breath (AA 17:25); but his assertion that in God we live and move and are has no OT precedent and is probably influenced by current Gk philosophical terms. AA, like the synoptics, does not further specify what "eternal life" is understood to be.

II. The Pauline writings. Paul echoes the OT frequently, especially by quoting passages which refer to life; for him too the commandment of God gives life, but it is a part of Paul's thought on the law* that the commandment instead of life gives death (Rm 7:10). Paul also speaks of eternal life as do the synoptics. God gives eternal life to those who persevere in good deeds (Rm 2:7); eternal life is the gift of God (Rm 6:23), it is the product of holiness (Rm 6:22). Eternal life is particularly prominent in the pastoral epistles; it comes through faith (1 Tm 1:16), it is assured by hope (Tt 1:2; 3:7), the Christian should grasp it (1 Tm 6:12). It is the true life (1 Tm 6:19).

Eternal life in the Pauline writings is not merely the life of the world to come; it becomes a present reality begun by baptism (Rm 6:4). It is a new life (Rm 6:4), initiated by union with the death and resurrection of Christ which is symbolized and effected by baptism. It is death of the life according to the flesh (Rm 8:12), but a resurrection from the death of sin (Rm 6:13). It is life conferred by holiness (Rm 5:18, 21), it is active within the Christian (2 Co 4:11), it is a conferring of the life of the risen Jesus (Rm 8:11). The Christian is reconciled by the death of Jesus and saved by His life (Rm 8:11). Hence this life cannot be considered purely eschatological in Paul.

The new life of the Christian is a life of the spirit*. The spirit here is not the OT conception of breath or wind merely, but the spirit which appears in the Gospel and the

Johannine writings: the spirit which is communicated by Jesus. The Christian lives if he kills the deeds of the flesh by the spirit (Rm 8:13). He lives by the spirit (Rm 5:25), by the law of the spirit of life in Christ Jesus (Rm 8:2). The mind of the spirit is life and peace (Rm 8:6). The spirit is life through righteousness (Rm 8:10). The "letter" (the law*) kills, but the spirit gives life (2 Co 3:6). The newness of the life is consequent upon the newness of the spirit; the spirit is an operative principle first revealed and communicated by Jesus, and the vivifying effect of the spirit, while described in OT terms, is a reality not produced by the law.

The newness of the Christian life consists in the relationship established between the Christian and God through Christ in the spirit. The Christian does not live to himself (2 Co 5:15), indeed it is no longer the Christian who lives but Christ who lives in him; the life that Paul lives in the body he lives by faith in the Son of God (Gal 2:20). Thus the Christian lives to God in Christ Jesus (Rm 6:11; 1 Co 15:22; Eph 4:18; 2 Tm 1:1; Tt 2:12), he lives to Christ Jesus (Rm 14:8). His life is hidden with God in Christ (Col 3:3). For him to live is Christ (Phl 1:21); Christ is his life (Col 3:4), the life of Jesus is manifest in his body (2 Co 4:10 f). The concept of the life of Christ continued and extended in the Church to each of its individual members is one of the great Pauline themes and one of his most original insights. The new life, as we have seen, is instituted by the sacramental participation of the Christian in the redeeming death and the saving resurrection through baptism and sustained by the indwelling spirit conferred through baptism. It is a participation in the risen life of Jesus which moves to its fulfillment in the resurrection of the Christian. But even while the Christian yet "lives in the flesh," he receives the powers of the new risen life which free him from sin and make him superior to the forces of sin; he is now free from the death of sin.

III. John. Of the preexisting word* John says that life which is the light of men is in Him (Jn 1:4). Here John seems to combine the themes of creation and salvation; the same word which is a creative principle of life also confers life through the light which He brings, the light of salvation. Jesus Himself is the way, the truth and the life, through whom one comes to the Father and knows the Father (Jn 14:6). He is the living and vivifying word which manifests life, which the apostles saw and touched (1 Jn 1:1–2). This life is forgiveness of sin (1 Jn 5:16), it is living water (Jn 4:10; 7:38). Jesus has the words of eternal life

(Jn 6:68). One obtains eternal life through faith in Him (Jn 3:15, 36; 20:31) and by keeping the commandment of God (Jn 12:50). One retains eternal life by fraternal love (1 Jn 3:14 f). To preserve one's soul* for eternal life one must be ready to lose one's natural life (Jn 12:25).

The mission of Jesus in John is often conceived as the bringing of life. This is eternal life, primarily viewed as an eschatological reality and in this different from the Pauline view (cf above). This seems to be the Johannine view even though the one who believes Jesus is said to possess eternal life and to have passed from death to life (Jn 5:24); for the following verses of this discourse (Jn 5:25–29) place the conferring of eternal life in the resurrection, when life is given by the Father at the command of the Son. The same emphasis appears in the discourse of Jn 6:33–58. Jesus is the bread which comes down from heaven, the living bread, the bread of life. One must eat His flesh and drink His blood in order to have life; and one has this life because of the mutual indwelling of Jesus and himself, through which one shares the life which Jesus has from the Father (Jn 6:56 f). The assurance which this bread gives against death (6:50, 58) cannot be construed as a promise that physical death will not come in its natural course; it means that death is not final, that one receives eternal life in the resurrection (6:39, 44, 54). This is stated even more clearly in Jn 11:25 f; Jesus is the resurrection and the life, and those who believe in Him live forever even though they die. The light of life (Jn 8:12) is the salvation which Jesus confers. So also is "the more abundant life" which Jesus brings (Jn 10:10), the eternal life which is assured because no one can snatch His sheep from the hand of Jesus (Jn 10:28). God gives eternal life by sending His Son who has this life, and those who partake of the Son have eternal life (1 Jn 5:11 f). Eternal life consists in knowledge* of the one true God and Jesus whom He has sent (Jn 17:3). John's conception should not be taken as implying that there is no present transformation of the Christian through faith and sacramental participation in the life of Jesus; but he emphasizes more than Paul the difference between the inchoate life in the believing Christian and the fullness of eschatological realization.

Light. The symbolism of light is universal and occurs in the ancient Near East as a whole in a manner similar to the symbolism of light in the Bible.

1. *OT*. Light is vision, and Yahweh gives light to the eyes (Ps 13:4; Pr 29:13). Meta-

phorically the commandment of Yahweh gives vision (Ps 19:9). The light of the eyes is also hope (Ezr 9:8).

In the ancient Near East light is the element proper to deity. This is not often formally the symbolism of light in the OT; it is a feature of the theophany* (Ezk 43:2), but the term more frequently used is glory*. Yahweh is the creator of light (Gn 1:3–5; Is 45:7); this affirmation is very probably intended to raise Him above the level of the dualism of light and darkness. Light is conceived as stored in a chamber during the night (Jb 38:19). Light is more frequently the element of Yahweh when it is a symbol of His saving power. The light of Yahweh's countenance is His favor to man (Nm 6:25; Pss 4:7; 31:17; 44:4; 67:2; 80:4, 8:20; 89:16; 119:135; Dn 9:17). Light is the deliverance and salvation wrought by Yahweh (Is 9:1; 60:1; Am 5:18, 20; Pss 43:3; 118:27); this is probably the meaning of the light of Yahweh in Is 2:5. The Servant* of Yahweh is a light to the nations, an agent of salvation (Is 42:6; 49:6). Yahweh Himself is called the light when He is conceived as the savior (Ps 27:1; Is 10:17; 60:19 f; Mi 7:8). The effect of deliverance is life*, which is to see light (Jb 33:30; Pss 36:10; 56:14), prosperity (Jb 22:28; 30:26), joy (Ps 97:11; Lam 3:2). Light is the element of moral good (Is 5:20).

Light is less frequently the symbol of revelation*, which is usually conceived as the hearing of the word* rather than as vision. The light to peoples (Is 51:4) is more probably revelation.

2. *NT*. In the NT light is the element of deity. Light in Peter's prison reveals the angel of deliverance (AA 12:7); Paul recognizes the presence of God in a blinding light (AA 9:3; 22:6). The angel of God is an angel of light (2 Co 11:14). The luminous cloud* at the transfiguration* shows the presence of God (Mt 17:5), as does the light which shines on the shepherds at the birth of Jesus (Lk 2:9). God dwells in inaccessible light (1 Tm 6:16). God is light (1 Jn 1:5), and those who obey His commandments walk in the light (1 Jn 1:7). The light of God is seen in Jesus, who is the light of the world (Jn 3:19; 8:12; 9:5; 12:35 f, 46). He is the light which enlightens every man (Jn 1:9) through the life which is in Him (Jn 1:4). He is the true shining light (1 Jn 2:8–10) in whom the Christian abides, the light to the revelation of the Gentiles (Lk 2:32). Those who are sons of God are called sons of light (Lk 16:8; Jn 12:36; 1 Th 5:5; Eph 5:8). Light is identified with the life which Christ communicates (Jn 1:4; Eph 5:14; Col 1:12; 1 Pt 2:9). Because the Christian has re-ceived the divine light through Christ the Christian Himself becomes the light of the world (Mt 5:14–16; Eph 5:8). The symbolism of light makes this figure wider than good example. The Christian through his participation in the light and life of God through Jesus becomes himself a medium of light to those who are in darkness.

Light is less frequently a symbol of revelation; this appears to be meant by the light of the gospel (knowledge) of the glory of God (2 Co 4:4, 6). Revelation is probably also meant by the enlightenment of the eyes of the heart (Eph 1:18), or the charismatic gift of understanding of revealed truth. Light is the element of moral good (Jn 3:20).

The NT does not reflect the dualism of light and darkness which runs through much of Oriental and Hellenistic religion and Gnosticism; but the language of these beliefs has affected the choice of language in both OT and NT. The dualism of light-darkness can also be seen in the writings of Qumran*, where one of the names of the righteous community is sons of light.

Lightning. Conceived in the Bible as a sign of the active presence of God, and therefore a part of the theophany*. It is His weapon and the instrument of His judgment*. The conception is by no means unique in the Bible. The Syrian and Mesopotamian and Anatolian storm gods are often represented in art brandishing the thunderbolt as an arrow or a lance (ANEP 490, 500, 501, 531, 532).

Lily. Translation of Hb *šôšān*, a flower mentioned several times in SS and rarely elsewhere (only of carved lilies in the temple of Solomon, Ho 14:6 and four Ps titles). A reddish flower is indicated by SS 5:13; the *lilium chalcedonicum* or Scarlet Martagon is suggested, which has brilliant scarlet petals. In the titles of three Pss (45:1; 69:1; 80:1) the words "upon lilies" occur, and in Ps 60:1 "upon the lily of testimony," a suspect and scarcely intelligible phrase. It is possible that these designations refer to the title of the song to whose melody the Ps was sung.

The lilies of the field are an example of brightly colored (not white) clothing in Mt 6:28; Lk 12:27.

Linen. Linen was manufactured in Egypt and Mesopotamia from the earliest periods, and many samples of Egyptian linen have been found. Its texture varied from a coarse weave to a fine, almost transparent fabric. Egypt produced more and finer linen than other regions of the ancient Near East. The

The manufacture of linen, from an Egyptian tomb painting.

cultivation of flax and the manufacture of linen are often represented in Egyptian tomb paintings (ANEP 122). The fine linen robe or tunic also appears often, its fineness probably exaggerated by the artist (ANEP 208, 211, 415).

Flax was grown in Palestine only in the coastal plain and in the Jordan valley, and archaeology has yielded samples of ancient linen. Hb has three words for linen: *bad, šeš, buṣ;* the last word appears as a loan word in Gk *byssos.* The distinction between the three terms is not known; possibly they designate linen from different sources. The occurrence of the words in the Bible suggest that linen was a luxury article. *Bad* was used for priestly vestments (Ex 28:42; Lv 6:3; 16:4, 23, 32; 1 S 2:18; 22:18 +). It was probably a ritual vestment of linen that David wore when he danced before the ark* (2 S 6:14; 1 Ch 15:27). It appears in two prophetic visions worn by a heavenly "officer" (Ezk 9:2 ff) and a heavenly "prince" (Dn 10:5; 12:6 f). *Buṣ* appears in the hangings of the palace of Xerxes (Est 1:6) and of the temple of Solomon (2 Ch 3:14), and is mentioned in 1 Ch 15:27 with *bad* in the garments worn by David during his ritual dance. It is worn by Levites (2 Ch 5:12). It is an object of trade between Tyre* and Edom* (Ezk 27:16). A village of linen workers of Judah is mentioned in 1 Ch 4:21. Solomon, however, imported a skilled worker in fine linen for the temple (2 Ch 2:13). *Šeš* was the fabric of the garment given to Joseph* when he was appointed vizier of Egypt (Gn 41:42). It was employed in the hangings of the tabernacle and priestly vestments (Ex 25–26; 28). It was worn by the princess of Jerusalem in the allegory of Ezk 16:10, 13. The good wife is clothed in purple and linen (Pr 31:22). It was the fabric of sails (Ezk 27:7); sails of linen are also mentioned by classical writers. In the NT *byssos* is mentioned only as the clothing of the rich man of the parable of Lk 16:19.

Linus (Gk *linos* [a legendary singer]), a Christian of Rome (2 Tm 4:21), according to a Roman tradition reported by Irenaeus and Eusebius the successor of Peter* as bishop of Rome.

Lion. The lion has been extinct in Palestine since the 12th century AD. The frequent allusions to the lion in the OT and the seven Hb words which designate the lion indicate that lions were common in OT times. The Asiatic lion is not as large as the African lion. The Palestinian lion was of the same species represented so frequently in ancient art: Palestinian (ANEP 128, 130, 228, 276), Assyrian (ANEP 184, 355), and Sumerian (ANEP 192). The seal of Shema, steward of Jeroboam (ANEP 276) is an Israelite representation of the lion. Gods (ANEP 486) and goddesses (ANEP 470–474) appear standing on lions in Syrian art. The lion appears frequently as a decorative motif in art and furniture; the lions on the throne of Solomon (1 K 10:19 f) are paralleled in the throne shown on one of the ivories of Megiddo (ANEP 332), and the lions carved on the temple furniture (1 K 7:29, 36) have many parallels in the Near East (ANEP 128–130, 456–459, 586, 592, 762). The cherubim* of Ezk 1:10, 14 have a lion's face, and similar cherubim are described as decorations in the temple of Ezk (41:19). The roar of the lion was a familiar and terrifying sound in ancient Palestine (Ps 104:21; Ezk 22:25; Ho 11:10; Am 3:4, 8). The lion lurked in thickets or forests (Je 5:6; Am 3:4), particularly in the jungle of the Jordan (Je 49:19; 50:44), and in caves (SS 4:8; Am 3:4). It roamed the desert (Is 30:6). It crouched to spring on its prey (Gn 49:9; Ps 10:9). Lions became numerous in territory which was depopulated by war (2 K 17:25; Is 15:9; Je 25:38). A Hb poetic name of the lion, "sons of pride," suggests our "king of beasts" (Jb 28:8; 41:26). It could be caught in pits (Ezk 19:4), snares and nets (Ezk 19:8) and caged (Ezk 19:9). The hunting of lions was a favorite sport of Assyrian kings (ANEP 184); when there were no wild lions, they were released from cages to afford sport for the king. The lion usually preyed on flocks and herds, but it would attack a man (1 K 13:24 f; 20:36). A strong and dexterous man, however, could kill a lion with his bare hands (Jgs 14:5 ff; 1 S 17:34; 2 S 23:20).

The lion is prominent in the wisdom literature of Israel (Pr 19:12; 20:2; 22:13; 26:13; 28:1, 15; 30:30) and in its poetry. An enemy, whether the enemy of Israel or another nation (Is 5:29; Je 2:15; 4:7; Ezk 32:2; Na 2:12 f) or of the individual person (Pss 7:3; 10:9; 17:12; 22:14, 22), is compared to a lion; Israel itself (Nm 23:24; 24:9; Mi 5:7), its tribes (Judah, Gn 49:9; Dan, Dt 33:22; Gad, Dt 33:20), its queen and princes (Ezk 19:2 ff), are like lions in boldness and ferocity. Saul and Jonathan were stronger than lions (2 S 1:23). Yahweh Himself is compared to a lion; He roars against Israel and attacks and rends them (Lam 3:10; Ho 5:14; Am 1:2; 11:10; 13:7 f). But He is also a lion against the enemies of Israel (Is 31:4) and against nations whom He punishes (Je 49:19; 50:44). A poetic element of the peace of the messianic age is the reconciliation of the lion with the animals upon which he preys (Is 11:6 f; 65:25).

The few allusions in the NT suggest that the lion was much less common in Palestine in NT times; most of these allusions are poetic and drawn from the OT. The lion appears most frequently in Apc (4:7; 9:8, 17; 10:3; 13:2) in the monsters of the visions. The title of "the lion of the tribe of Judah" is given to Jesus in Apc 5:5, but the animal which appears to the seer is a lamb*.

Literary forms. By literary forms are meant types or species of literature distinguished from each other by distinct form and structure adapted to content. One may make an analogy between literary forms and architectural forms: the form and structure of buildings differ according to the purpose for which they are constructed, so that one may simply by the external form and structure distinguish a residence, a church, a factory, a railway station, a post office, etc. Thus in all civilized cultures distinctions of form and structure appear as early as the writing itself. The earliest distinction and the most general is that between prose and poetry. As such these two genera do not exist; they exist only in more specific forms such as epic, lyric, and dramatic poetry, and narrative, rhetorical, and expository prose. These species in turn exhibit many more precise subspecies; and the number and complexity of forms grow with the complexity of the intellectual culture of a people. As with architectural forms, however, one must

be familiar with the culture in order to recognize the purpose of the form and structure. When one is not familiar with architectural form, he does not recognize the purpose of a building; when one is not familiar with literary form, he does not perceive the meaning of the writing. Furthermore, as a building may exhibit a combination of architectural forms, due to remodeling, diversity of purpose, or length of time in construction, or simple archaizing, so a literary work may exhibit diversity of forms due to compilation or to archaizing.

The literary form is a part of the communication of meaning; neither the word nor the sentence is meaningful out of context, and the form furnishes the proximate context. Diversity of literary forms arises because of a desire to deal with different subjects in a more meaningful way and to express different conceptions of a truth which is too large for expression through a single form. A single event, for instance, may be the subject of a prose narrative, a ballad or an epic poem, a tragedy, an oration, a philosophical reflection, and a prayer of lamentation or thanksgiving. Such diversity is possible only because the event can be conceived and represented in so many different ways. The "meaning" of the event lies not in its bare reality, but in the diversity of conceptions which it originates; and the "truth" of the event lies in no single form in which the event is represented. The truth of poetry is not the same as the truth of prose, nor is the truth of narrative the same as the truth of the drama. All of these forms are different efforts to express the truth; but because the truth is larger than any single form, the truth expressed, while it is a conception of the same reality, is often quite different in one form from what it appears to be in another.

More obvious is the diversity of forms which arises from the diversity of content. Some mental conceptions are not fit subjects of poetic expression, and others are inadequately expressed in prose. The prose of the narrator is not the prose of the lawyer. Here likewise the analogy of architecture helps us to understand the process of development. The more specialized the thinking of a society becomes, the more it generates new forms to suit the specialties, just as it develops new architectural forms to suit more highly specialized activities. More primitive peoples are extremely simple both in their buildings and in their forms of expression.

The creation of literary forms is the work of a society; Cazelles has said that every literary work is a dialogue between the author and the society of his time. This does not mean that literary forms are never the creation of the individual genius; but the form does not endure unless the society accepts the form as its own. The symbolism of the form, like the symbolism of the word, must be validated by usage. In the ancient Near East literature, like other arts and crafts, was produced anonymously. The student of ancient Near Eastern forms must study the society because there are no individual artists to study.

While different literary forms have long been recognized by students of classical and modern languages, the study of biblical literary forms has been carried on seriously only since 1900. The school which is identified with this study originated in Germany; it is called *Gattungsgeschichte* or *Formgeschichte,* popularly but inaccurately rendered in English as "Form Criticism." The impulse to the study of biblical forms came from the discovery of the literature of Babylonia* and Assyria* and Egypt* and in more recent times of the Canaanite* literature of Ugarit*. Certain evident similarities in form and structure at once appeared; and since, as we have noticed above, form and structure are determined by conception and content, it was asked whether the similarities did not extend to conception and content also.

The conception of biblical forms was also seriously affected by the realization that "literary" forms in the Bible had a long history in oral tradition and that much of the OT and the NT is simply the writing down of forms which were developed in oral tradition. A study of other cultures makes it clear that oral forms are substantially different from literary forms, and the Bible exhibits the effect of oral formation. The major difference between the two is that oral tradition is not capable of the sustained book size composition; it collects smaller units, whether songs, stories, or other forms, and groups them around a person or a place. The constant repetition of the oral material by singers or reciters who recreate as often as they retell means that the material is subject to a constant revision; it is conceived and expressed anew in each generation. The meaning of a biblical passage, consequently, is not explored thoroughly unless one traces as closely as one can the development through which it reached the form which it has in the text.

The exploration of this development proceeds in a horizontal dimension by comparing the Bible with contemporary nonbiblical literature and in a vertical dimension by comparing the development of forms within Hb literature itself. The horizontal comparison observes similarities and differences in form, structure, and content, but it cannot be merely literary; it must study the separate cultures which produced the literature. The vertical comparison also must study the different phases from which the literature proceeds. This is known as the study of the *Sitz im Leben,* the "situation in life" of literature. The need to express oneself obviously differs from one culture to another and from one cultural phase to another. The meaning of forms cannot be the same when they proceed from the oral tradition of Israelite herdsmen or peasants and from the erudite priests of the Jerusalem temple or the inspired zeal of the prophets. This demands a study of cultural history and social psychology as well as of the events of external history. One tries to ascertain the need which this literary production was intended to fill; one must understand not only one term of the dialogue, the author, but also the other term, the society of his time.

Form Criticism proceeds on the now generally accepted assumption that our biblical books are, with a few exceptions, compilations. The compilation itself may be the work of a single mind and thus become a new literary form; but Form Criticism seeks to isolate and analyze the smallest independent units of the compilation, find their "situation in life," and see how they met in their original utterance the need for the society to express itself, whether to itself or to others. It must be admitted that the reconstruction of the "situation in life" of a particular passage is often based upon a hypothetical reconstruction. At times a familiarity with form and structure and their relations to content and conception and an understanding of the history and culture of Israel and of the ancient Near Eastern civilization of which it was a part permit the scholar to make his reconstruction with assurance; he sees patterns emerge which are impressive by their intrinsic probability.

Form Criticism is a method, not a theology, and many objections to the method are really objections to the theology or the philosophy of critics. The method has proved itself fruitful both in OT and NT; by determining more precisely what Israel had in common with other cultures, it is possible to see much more clearly what was original with Israel and is in no way derived from other cultures. One can observe the transformation of known literary forms by the faith of Israel seeking to express itself by developing new forms and modifying old ones. The process is less complex in the NT, which was written over a period of about 60 years; but there also a study of the forms reveals their originality, an originality which arose from the originality of content and conception of the material.

For details cf articles on the separate books; EPISTLE; GOSPEL; HISTORY; LAW; POETRY; PROPHECY; PSALMS; WISDOM and references given in these articles.

Loan. Before the invention of minted money* loans in kind were much more common than loans of hard metal; the ancient laws and records of Mesopotamia show loans of both kinds in the earliest periods. The laws of Eshnunna and of Hammurabi (cf LAW) both contain laws regulating the rate of interest; this suggests that rates had reached a point considered intolerably high. Since the rates of which we have information were quite high by modern standards, the rates before regulation may have reached 50 percent or 75 percent or even more. The interest to be paid in kind was higher than the interest to be paid on hard metal. In Babylonia the rate on payment in kind was about 33⅓ percent and on hard metal about 20 percent. The Assyrian rates were higher, about 50 percent on payment in kind and about 25–33⅓ percent on hard metal. The code of Hammurabi contains some laws which were evidently intended to restrain moneylenders and creditors and help the debtor. The debtor was released from payment of interest in crops and produce if the yield was destroyed by a year of flood or drought. A debt in grain was annulled if the creditoɪ exacted payment by forced seizure of the grain. Loans of hard metal could be repaid in grain. An investment was remitted if the debtor took an oath that the goods were taken or destroyed by "an enemy," a term which probably included both hostile troops and brigands. The debtor's pledge could be seized by the creditor if the pledge were a person — wife, child, or slave — not, apparently, if it were an animal, and the person of the debtor seems to have been immune from seizure.

In the Hellenistic period (323 BC–30 BC) banks* were the principal lending agencies. The prevailing rate of interest in the Hellenistic world was a reasonable 8 to 10 percent except in Egypt, where the scarcity of hard money was responsible for a 24 percent rate. Rome also enjoyed a reasonable 6–10 percent on investments and a much higher 50 percent on payment in kind. A senatorial decree of the 1st century BC established a 12 percent rate in the provinces of Asia which corrected some extortionate rates.

The attitude of the OT toward loans is expressed in Dt 28:12, 44: it is a blessing to be a creditor and not a debtor. A number of laws restraining creditors suggest that the reality of debt was grim. The cloak (Ex 22:25), other garments (Am 2:8), the ox and the ass (Jb 24:3), and children (Jb 24:9) were given as pledges; the pledging of animals does not appear in Mesopotamian law (cf above). The millstone, without which the family food of the day could not be prepared, was prohibited as a pledge (Dt 24:6), nor could the lender take the garment of a widow. If the cloak were pledged, it had to be returned at sunset that the borrower might sleep in it (Ex 22:24 f). Enslavement of the debtor is clearly mentioned in Lv 25:36 ff; Am 2:6; this may be the debtor himself or members of his family. The lender may not enter the house of the borrower in order to collect his pledge (Dt 24:10). There are a number of passages both in the laws and in other books which present it as an obligation or as an ideal to lend without interest (Ex 22:24 ff; Ps 15:5; Pr 28:8; Ezk 18:13, 17; 22:12); the Israelites may exact interest from foreigners, but not from each other (Dt 23:20). It appears that this was far more of an ideal than a real practice. The same is to be said of the exhortations to the creditor not to exact the pledge when the debtor is unable to pay (Ezk 18:16). Ne 5:1–13 exhibits practically all the abuses which are mentioned above. In the Jerusalem community debtors pledged their lands and their children, who were enslaved when the debt was not paid, and were being charged interest; Nehemiah persuaded the creditors to remit their demands, but he appeals to no law nor even to any tradition.

Wisdom literature contains a number of reflections on loans and debts which view them unfavorably. It is the wicked man who does not pay his debts (Ps 37:21). The borrower is the slave of the creditor (Pr 22:7). The good lender is kind and just (Ps 112:5). To lend to a powerful man is to lose one's money (BS 8:12). The fool lends today and demands payment tomorrow (BS 20:15). A series of reflections in BS 29:1–10 commends the payment of debts, patience with the poor debtor, and generosity in the lender to the point where he is willing to risk the loss of his loan.

In the NT interest is mentioned only in the parable of the talents (Mt 25:27; Lk 19:23); the investor could let out his money to banks and expect interest. The forgiveness of the bankrupt debtor is presented as an example of generosity which is not entirely unexpected (Lk 7:41 ff). The forgiveness of one's debtors is a condition of forgiveness from God (Mt 6:12; Lk 11:4); "debtor" here may be taken in a wider sense to include those against whom one has any claim. Lk makes the prayer a petition for forgiveness of sins where Mt has debts; but the metaphor in Mt means the same. The allusion to the imprisonment and torture of defaulting debtors (Mt 5:25 f; 18:28 ff; Lk 12:58 f) refers to no contemporary practice and is probably a heightened description of enslavement.

Lock. Cf KEY.

Locust. The generic Hb word for locust is *'arbeh* ("multiplier?"), which designates the migratory locust (*Schistocera gregaria*). Besides this there are eight other words which designate species of locust or similar insects; the precise meaning of the words is uncertain: *sŏl'ām*, "devourer"?; *ḥargōl*, "galloper"?; *ḥāgāb*, "concealer"?; *ṣelāṣal*, "whizzer"?; *gēb*, "swarmer"?; *gāzām*, "shearer"?; *yeleḳ*, "lopper"?; *ḥāsîl*, "finisher"? The *gāzām* may be the caterpillar and the *yeleḳ* the locust in the creeping stage. The advance of the locust swarm and its disastrous effects are vividly described in Ex 10:4–19 (the plagues of Egypt; cf Pss 78:46; 105:34 f) and Jl 1:4–19; 2:2–11. They cover the land and consume all vegetation; famine and starvation are threatened to men and flocks; they advance like an army or a raging fire. The plague of locusts is mentioned frequently; it is one of the punishments of Yahweh (Dt 28:38; 1 K 8:37; 2 Ch 6:28; 7:13). The Israelite imagination was impressed by the resemblance between the locust swarm and an advancing army (Jgs 6:5; 7:12; Pr 30:27; Je 46:23; 51:14, 27; Na 3:15, 17) both in numbers and in destructive power. The leap of the war horse is like the leap of the locust (Jb 39:20); snow falls like a swarm of locusts (BS 43:17).

The OT does not exaggerate the disastrous effects of a locust swarm in the Near East. The swarm in flight can obscure the sun and the noise of their flight sounds like a heavy rain. The destruction comes not so much from the flying swarm, which rests during the night and resumes its migration when the sun rises, but from the larvae of the eggs which are laid while the swarm is at rest. The larvae hatch in 15–20 days. They are black and literally darken the ground (Ex 10:15) and devour every piece of green vegetation, even stripping the bark from trees. Modern scientific control arrests the plague to some extent; but the area which suffers a swarm of locusts experiences a severe loss. Without control the loss of crops is total.

Locusts are included among the clean edible animals (Lv 11:22); modern nomads eat them after stripping off the head, legs, and wings. They are toasted or ground into meal. These were the food of John the Baptist (Mt 3:4; Mk 1:6). The improbability of this food has led many interpreters to believe that the pod of the carob tree was meant here; but the word *akris* can designate only the insect. The monstrous locusts of Apc 9:3–11 are a real nightmare; the locust becomes an apocalyptic horror, and "in those days men will look for death but will not find it" (Apc 9:6).

Lodebar (Hb *lo'debar*), a town E of the Jordan near Mahanaim*, exact site unknown; residence of Meribaal (2 S 9:4) and of Machir, a friend of David (2 S 17:27). It is probably to be read in Jos 13:26 instead of Lidebir or Debir*. Its presence in Am 6:13 is doubted by some scholars, since the words can be translated "nothing"; the verse may allude to the conquest of Lodebar and Karnaim by Jeroboam* II.

Lois (Gk *lōis*, meaning unknown), a personal name; grandmother of Timothy*, praised for her genuine faith (2 Tm 1:5).

Lord 1. *OT*. The Hb *'ādôn* appears also in Canaanite* (Ugaritic* and Phoenician*) as the honorific title of a king, a god, or a husband. In the OT it is used of the owner of a slave, of a husband, and of a king, especially as a polite form of address; it may also be applied to any person of superior rank. It differs from *ba'al* (cf BAAL) which signifies ownership; *'ādôn* rather signifies authority, the power to command. It is frequently applied to Yahweh and suggests His kingship*. In most of the instances where the title belongs to Yahweh it appears in the unique and grammatically anomalous form of Adonai, *'adōnāi;* this is probably a vocalization of uncertain late date and origin to distinguish the divine title from the usual *'adōnî*, "my lord," addressed to human beings. *Adonai* is used even when Yahweh is not addressed directly. The title is most common in Pss and Is; it is more frequent in these two books taken together than in the rest of the entire OT. It is a solemn hymnic title, used most frequently in invocations.

The Gk *kyrios*, "lord," is used in the LXX as a translation of the divine name Yahweh (cf GOD). At some early date the Jews began to abstain from the pronunciation of the name Yahweh in the belief that it was too sacred for utterance. Whenever the name occurred in the Hb text the title Adonai was read in its place. Since at least some of the LXX was translated in the 2nd century BC and the abandonment of the name Yahweh in speech cannot be certainly dated before the 1st century BC, some scholars doubt that the use of *kyrios* for Yahweh in the LXX comes from the use of Adonai in speech. They think that *kyrios* is a theological interpretation of the name Yahweh by the 2nd century Jews of Alexandria which emphasized the dominion of Yahweh. This view is complicated somewhat by the fact that Gk usage does not exhibit the use of *kyrios* as a divine title until the 1st century BC. It does not therefore seem possible to affirm with assurance the course of development of the use of this term.

2. *NT*. The use and meaning of *kyrios* in the NT is affected by the background of the term in Hellenistic* civilization. In the classical Gk period (500–300 BC) the word *kyrios* is more common as an adjective than as a noun; it signifies power and authority, more precisely the power to dispose of a person or object. Thus is it used of the owner of a slave, of the ruler or conqueror of subject peoples, of the head of a family or the master of a house, of the guardian of a minor, rarely of the owner of property. It does not appear as a title absolutely (without an accompanying genitive) until the 1st century BC in Egypt, when it is applied to a goddess. From this period on the title is common in Egypt, Syria, and Asia Minor as an honorific designation of gods and kings. With the beginning of the imperial rule of Rome under Augustus (30 BC) the title is applied to the Caesars. Until the end of the 1st century the Caesars in Rome refused the title of lord (Lt *dominus*) while accepting it in the E. Since the conception of "lordship" expressed in *kyrios* was foreign both to Gk and to Roman political conceptions, it is probable that the use of *kyrios* in Egypt, Phoenicia, and Asia Minor was a translation of native forms of address into Gk; cf above on the title "lord" in Hb and Canaanite.

The use of *kyrios* in the Synoptic Gospels offers no new development. It is common as a form of address of Jesus; this reflects Aramaic usage and is no more than "Sir." It is also a designation of God in quotations from the LXX or as a substitute for the name of God, and in the common profane sense of owner or master. For some exceptions in Lk and Jn cf below.

The distinctive application of *kyrios* to Jesus seems to be original with the early Christian communities; in Rm 10:9; 1 Co 12:3; Phl 2:11, the title appears to be a liturgical invocation or acclamation. Scholars are not agreed on whether this title was first employed in the Jewish or in the Hellenistic churches; but it seems more probable that it was Hellenistic in origin. The title (cf above) was a contemporary designation of gods and of kings; and at least once (1 Co 8:5 ff) Paul adverts to this usage, contrasting the one God, the Father, and the one Lord, Jesus, of the Christians with the many

gods and the many lords of the Hellenistic world.

The theological use of the title is more frequent in Paul than in the other NT epistles. The belief appears already in AA 2:36 that Jesus is established as Lord by His resurrection*. The connection is established in Rm 10:9, and most clearly in Phl 2:6–11; God has exalted Jesus because He emptied Himself and submitted to the death of the cross. Therefore He is to be universally confessed as Lord. The exaltation in the verse is identical with the resurrection. The mission of the apostles is to announce that Christ Jesus is Lord (2 Co 4:5). Christians are therefore the slaves of the Lord whom they must serve (Rm 12:11; Eph 6:7; Col 3:24). His commands are to be obeyed (1 Co 4:19; 14:37; 2 Co 10:18). He assigns to the apostles their mission (1 Co 3:5) and to the Christians their state in life (1 Co 7:17); He confers power and authority upon the apostles (2 Co 10:8; 13:10), indeed He governs the course of the apostle's life (1 Co 16:7). It is to Him that Christians give themselves (2 Co 8:5). It is for Him that Christians live and die; for the purpose of His life and death was that He might become Lord of the living and the dead (Rm 14:8–9). He is the one and the same Lord of all, Jews and Greeks (Rm 10:12). He is recognized as Lord in the Eucharist* which announces His death (1 Co 11:26 f).

Lord appears as a trinitarian title in 1 Co 12:4–6, where Paul enumerates spirit, Lord, God; cf also the triple enumeration in 2 Co 13:13. These verses are in contrast to 2 Co 3:17, where Paul affirms that the Lord is the spirit. This is to be interpreted in the context; the Christian dispensation is compared to the Sinai events, where Moses had to veil his face from the Israelites to hide the brightness, the "glory*" reflected from his communion with Yahweh. The Christian knows the risen Jesus who is not "according to the flesh," and because He is spirit the Christian contemplates Him, and by reflecting His glory is transformed into His image, the image of "the Lord spirit" (2 Co 3:18). The passage, which is difficult, exhibits the belief that the Lord is the risen Lord.

The total union of the Christian with the Lord appears in the common phrase of Paul, "in the Lord," which is applied to a great number of actions and events; the phrase reflects Rm 14:8–9. For the Christian who is united to the Lord is one spirit with Him (1 Co 6:17); and the spirit, the principle of life, is one and the same in the Lord and in those who are His members. Hence they live in Him, and all that happens to them happens in Him.

By retrospection the title Lord is sometimes applied by Paul to Jesus before the resurrection (AA 20:35; 1 Co 7:10, 25; 9:5, 14; Gal 1:19), also in AA 11:16. It is perhaps not insignificant that all of these except Gal 1:19; 1 Co 9:5 refer to the words or sayings of the Lord, which are adduced as authoritative decisions. The same usage is found 13 times in Lk and 5 times in Jn; these no doubt reflect the spread of the title in Hellenistic communities.

The title is, of course, most appropriate when the second coming is mentioned (cf PAROUSIA); cf 1 Co 4:5; 2 Th 1:9. It also appears commonly in conjunction with glory. The title is relevant to Paul's conception of the divinity of Jesus. There can be no doubt that it is intended to raise Jesus above the level of common humanity; the very fact that it is associated with the resurrection and with the second coming is sufficient for this. To Paul it means more than the title kyrios as applied in the Hellenistic world to gods, kings, and Caesars. The claims which the Lord makes upon Christians and their total union with Him (cf above) cannot be reduced to the concept of the Hellenistic kyrios. The Lord Jesus Christ has powers which are divine in any sense of the word. The concept of the divinity of Jesus in Paul cannot be determined on the basis of this word alone. Nevertheless, it is not without significance that the use of the word kyrios in the LXX is the usual divine name. Josephus records that some Jews suffered death rather than give the title kyrios to Caesar. Paul, on the contrary, not only uses the title frequently, but he uses it in such a way that we cannot always determine whether he means Jesus or the Father. Furthermore, he applies to Jesus in Phl 2:10–11 the words which in Is 45:23 are spoken by Yahweh, demanding a tribute of adoration which no Jew would pay except to God alone. Paul never identifies Jesus with ho theos, "the god," the Father; but the title kyrios is used in harmony with Phl 2:6, which we may paraphrase by saying that Jesus stole nothing in being equal to God.

Lord's day (Gk kyriakē hēmera), the day on which the seer of Apc came under the inspiration of the spirit (Apc 1:10). This is the earliest reference to the dedication of a day of the week to the Lord; scarcely any other day than the first day, the day after the Sabbath*, can be meant. It was "the Lord's Day" as the day on which He rose (Mt 28:1; Mk 16:1; Lk 24:1; Jn 20:1).

Lord's Prayer. The Lord's prayer, the only formula of prayer which is attributed to Jesus Himself, is preserved in Mt 6:9–15; Lk 11:2–4 (see parallel comparison below).

Commentators generally agree that Lk has the prayer in its original context, a question of the disciples on how to pray; Mt has incorporated it into the sermon on the mount and prefaced it with some general remarks on prayer. Mt's longer form is regarded as more original and was employed liturgically as early as the *Didache* (1st century AD). The doxology, "for thine is the kingdom and the power and the glory," in common use among Protestants in English-speaking countries, is a later expansion which is omitted from the modern critical text. In Mt the prayer is composed of an invocation and seven petitions. The style of the petitions is modeled on the Pss; the content, however, especially in the 2nd and 5th petitions, is originally Christian. The kingdom* must be understood against the Gospel preaching of the kingdom as the messianic reality. The 5th petition includes a common NT teaching on forgiveness*. The word translated "necessary" appears only once (in the papyri) outside of these passages in all Gk literature; this translation appears most probable, but many scholars and most versions prefer "for the day." "Evil" in the 7th petition is ambiguous in Gk and may also be rendered "the evil one"; which is meant cannot be determined.

Lk's variation in the 4th petition seems to be merely verbal; the other variations, which may be attributed to Lk's sources, possibly reflect the influence of the Gk communities.

Mt	Lk
Our Father in heaven,	Father,
Hallowed be your name;	Hallowed be your name;
May your kingdom come,	May your kingdom come,
May your will be done,	
As in heaven, so on earth;	
Our necessary bread give us today;	Our necessary bread give us each day;
And forgive us our debts,	And forgive us our sins,
As we forgive our debtors;	As we forgive each of our debtors;
And do not lead us into temptation,	And do not lead us into temptation.
But deliver us from evil.	

The 3rd and 7th petitions, which are instances of Hb parallelism, might appear purely tautological when the prayer was repeated in Gk. The metaphor of "debt" for sin is rendered explicit in Lk.

Lord's Supper. Cf EUCHARIST.

Lot (Hb *lôṭ,* meaning and etymology unknown), son of Haran* and nephew of Abraham* (Gn 11:27), taken with the family of Terah* in their migration to Haran (Gn 11:31), accompanied Abraham on his migration to Canaan (Gn 12:4 f). Because of quarrels between their herdsmen Lot parted from Abraham and settled near Sodom* (Gn 13:5–13). He was taken prisoner by the Mesopotamian kings and was delivered by Abraham (Gn 14:12–16). Because of his hospitality to the two heavenly messengers he was spared with his family from the destruction of Sodom (Gn 19:1–26). He then lived in a cave with his two daughters. Since there were no survivors whom they might marry, the two daughters seduced Lot while he was drunk and bore him sons, the ancestors of the Moabites* and the Ammonites* (Gn 19:30–38). The story contains a popular pun on these names: Moab and Hb *mē'āb,* "from the father," and *'ammôn* and Ben-*'Ammî,* "son of my kinsman." These two peoples are called "the sons of Lot" in Dt 2:9, 19; Ps 83:9, where the kinship of Israel with these peoples is adduced as a reason why the Israelites should not attack their land.

The stories of Lot contain a large admixture of folklore from various sources, and their heterogeneity suggests very strongly that they have been grouped artificially around a single figure. To most Bible readers Lot's wife is better known than Lot; her story is easily explained by the similarity of a standing column in the eroded country at the S end of the Dead Sea* to the figure of a standing woman. It is impossible to place the story of Sodom and Gomorrah in the period of Abraham; and it is highly probable that the story of this deliverance originally dealt with some other hero and was incorporated into Hb traditions by identifying this hero with Lot, who in tradition dwelt in the region. "The sons of Lot" is a title which suggests to some scholars that Lot was an eponymous ancestor who in the artificial genealogies of the Pnt became the nephew of Abraham. The meaning of the story of the incestuous origin of the peoples of Moab and Ammon may not be as repulsive in its origin as it is to modern taste; to a more primitive people the daughters of Lot could be heroines who against all hope found a way to fulfill their

destiny as women. Whether this is an Israelite story or not is difficult to determine; it seems probable that it was not, and that the Moabites and Ammonites both traced their descent from an earlier tribe, "the sons of Lot." This story may be independent of the story of the destruction of Sodom; the conjunction of the two stories in the present text is artificial, and the situation when "there is no man in the land" (Gn 19:31) is not that of the rest of the stories of the Abraham cycle. These factors support the hypothesis that Lot is a native Canaanite figure of folklore who has been accepted in Hb tradition because of the recognized kinship between the Israelites and the Moabites and the Ammonites.

Lot. The lot is an oracular device employed to make a selection among a number of choices. In the OT most of the words used with the noun lot suggest that the lot was thrown or cast. The lot was used in the division of land (Jos 18:6 ff +), the assignment of duties among a group such as the priests and Levites (1 Ch 24:8; 25:8; 26:13 +), the selection of those who were to settle in Jerusalem during its restoration (Ne 11:1), the assignment of military duties (Jgs 20:9), the division of slaves and other booty of war (Jl 4:3; Ps 22:19). The use of the lot for such divisions differs from its use to answer questions as a substitute for investigation (Pr 18:18), especially the determination of the guilty individual among a group (Jon 1:7, 17). While the word lot is not used, it is implied in the stories of the election of Saul* (1 S 10:17 ff) and the determination of the guilt of Achan* (Jos 7:14 ff) and of Jonathan* (1 S 14:41 ff). The lot in such instances is a form of divination* to ascertain knowledge by occult means. Presupposed, however, in the use of the lot to determine guilt in a group is a pattern of thought somewhat foreign to our thinking. The guilt falls first upon the group, and the duty of bearing it to save the group is not dissimilar to the duty of bearing any community service. In the stories which we have this primitive conception of the lot is no longer explicit, and it becomes a preternatural means of detection. Lot also means metaphorically one's portion in life or one's fortune (Pr 1:14). In the NT the use of lot is mentioned only in the division of the garments of Jesus by His executioners (Mt 27:35; Mk 15:24; Lk 23:34; Jn 19:24) and the appointment of Matthias* among the Twelve (AA 1:26). The use of the oracular device here implies two beliefs about the office: the number 12 should be maintained, and the selection of the man must come from God. The two persons available were equally qualified, and the final decision was left to the lot; cf APOSTLE.

Love. 1. *OT*. The Hb word *'āhab* and its cognates are used in a variety of contexts which are much the same as the uses of the Eng word love. Basically it signifies a voluntary attachment. It is used somewhat improperly, as the Eng word is used, of attachment to objects or to abstractions; these may be good or evil. Of attachments between persons the word is used most frequently of love between the sexes. It may signify simple sexual concupiscence (Gn 34:3; Jgs 16:4, 15; 2 S 13:4, 15; Is 57:8; Je 2:25, 33; Ezk 16:33–37; 23:5, 9, 22; Ho 2:7–15); this is probably the sense implied in Solomon's love of his many wives (1 K 11:1). The word, however, again like the Eng word, also designates the attachment of man and woman in a nobler sense than the sense of mere concupiscence (Gn 24:67; 29:20; 1 S 1:5; Ec 9:9). The emotional side of sexual love is prominent in SS 1:7; 2:4 f; 3:1; 4:10; 5:8; 7:7; 8:6 f; on the OT conception of love between the sexes cf MARRIAGE; SONG OF SOLOMON. The ardent passion which is implied in the word is apparent in such passages as Gn 29:20; SS 8:6 f, and the depth of quiet attachment in Ezk 24:16. The antithesis of the loved and the hated wife (Dt 21:15 f) is better rendered by "loved more" and "loved less." The word is used less frequently of other family attachments, such as father for son (Gn 22:2; 25:28; 37:3 f; 44:20) and mother for son (Gn 25:28). These passages, however, are an important clue to the meaning of the word; for in each context where it is used love signifies a love of preference. This undertone is not always explicit; the love of Ruth for Naomi, her mother-in-law, is signified by her devotion and fidelity to the last survivor of the family of her husband (Rt 4:15). People are also said to be loved where we would say that they enjoy popularity; David is loved by Saul (1 S 16:21), but also by the retainers of Saul (1 S 18:22) and by all Israel (1 S 18:16). Love is also exhibited by a slave toward a kindly master (Ex 21:5; Dt 15:16), and the Israelite is commanded to love the foreigner (cf STRANGER; Lv 19:34; Dt 10:19); the sentiment therefore can be mutual between superior and inferior. Love is also friendship, and one's friends in Hb are called one's lovers (1 S 18:1; 20:17; 1 K 5:15; Ps 38:12; Jb 19:19; Je 20:4, 6). The intensity of feeling which could exist between friends is reflected in 2 S 1:26; the love of one's friend surpasses the love of women. This expression is not attractive to modern

tastes, but it does not have in Hb the unpleasant connotation which it has in Eng. The love of friendship, like other emotions, was expressed in the OT without the restraints which we are accustomed to impose upon it. The Israelite is commanded to love his neighbor (Lv 19:18); the identification of the neighbor is far more explicit in the Gospel than it ever was in the OT (cf below). The word "neighbor" as commonly used does not signify any other Israelite, but rather the Israelites to whom one is "near," those with whom one lives and deals habitually. Only once is the word love used of the self (Pr 19:8); here we could paraphrase by saying that he who acquires wisdom takes good care of himself.

As a theological concept love appears as a mutual sentiment between Yahweh and Israel. The concept cannot be called early; it is not found before Hosea*, who in all probability must be regarded as the first to express it. Hosea gives it form in the analogy of the marriage of Yahweh and Israel. A not insignificant feature of this analogy is that the initiative in matrimonial love comes from the man and not from the woman; Yahweh is the first to love Israel, and Israel's love is a response. The love of Yahweh is the cord by which Yahweh draws Israel to Himself (Ho 11:4). Hosea also speaks of the paternal love of Yahweh for Israel (Ho 11:1), which also places the initiative in Yahweh. Hosea is also the first to speak of the end of the love of Yahweh for Israel (Ho 9:15); the violently passionate character of Hosea's conception of love makes room for the possibility that this love can be cooled by continued flagrant infidelity. It is a voluntary, not a natural attachment, and the direction of the will can be changed.

Dt is the first book of the OT to incorporate the idea of love in a systematic way into its thought, and it remains the OT book in which the conception has the largest place. In contrast to Hosea and other prophets who employ the idea Dt's idea of love appears cool and dispassionate. The love of Yahweh for Israel is a continuation of His love for the patriarchs (Dt 4:37; 7:8; 10:15). Usually the word love is coupled in Dt with the word choose (cf ELECTION); the love of Yahweh is a love which prefers, and which is the root of election. The idea of love and election appears also in Is 43:4; Mal 1:2 f; Ps 47:5; and in Pss 78:68; 87:2 it is transferred from Israel as a whole to Judah and Jerusalem, the seat of the dynasty of David. The love of Yahweh for Israel recurs in Dt (7:13; 23:6 +) and in books influenced by the Deuteronomic redaction (1 K 10:9), and the terms of Dt are used in 2 Ch 2:10; 9:8; Ne 13:26. In Dt 7:13 + love is coupled with blessing*, which is an outpouring of love. Je 31:3 is in the tradition of Hosea rather than of Dt; the love of Yahweh is everlasting, which may look to the past as well as to the future, and it is a love which draws Israel. The love of Yahweh rarely falls upon individuals, and then it is almost synonymous with election, as of Solomon as heir (2 S 12:24) and Cyrus, who is called to conquer nations and liberate Israel (Is 48:14). In some later Pss the love of Yahweh falls upon virtues such as righteousness and justice (Pss 11:7; 33:5; 37:28; Cf Is 61:8) and upon the righteous(Ps 146:8).

With the exception of Jgs 5:31, which is possibly a later doxology added to an early song, the love of Israel for Yahweh is certainly the creation of Dt. The word occurs in the decalogue* (Ex 20:6; Dt 5:10), but the formula of Ex may be due to the influence of Dt. The command to love Yahweh appears frequently in Dt (6:5; 10:12; 11:1, 13, 22; 13:4; 19:9; 30:6, 16, 20) and in Jos 22:5; 23:11 under the influence of the Deuteronomic redaction. The language of Dt (e.g., 6:5) is intended to represent the love given to Yahweh as a genuine sentiment and not a mere conviction; Israel is to love Yahweh with its whole heart, its whole self, and its whole strength. The chief work of the love of Yahweh is the observance of His commandments; this is indeed the summary of the message of Dt, that Israel must repay Yahweh's electing love by observing the laws which the book sets forth (Dt 5:10; 7:9 +). The conjunction of love and observance appears in later books also (Dn 9:4; Ne 1:5), and the idea of love simply (Ps 145:20). Je 2:2 is again in the tradition of Hosea; the youthful love of Israel for Yahweh was a part of her desert history, like the love of a bride for her husband. The individual person is not said to love Yahweh, except Solomon (1 K 3:3). In later literature the reverence for the divine reality leads to the use of the name of Yahweh (Pss 5:12; 69:37; Is 56:6) or the salvation of Yahweh (Pss 40:17; 70:5) as a substitute for Yahweh Himself as an object of love. In such a context of excessive reverence, it could hardly be expected that the idea of the love of Yahweh could grow.

2. *NT*. Gk uses the word *erōs, philia,* and *agapē* and their cognates to designate love. *Erōs* signifies the passion of sexual desire and does not appear in the NT. *Philein* and *philia* designate primarily the love of friendship. *Agapē* and *agapān,* less frequent in profane Gk, are possibly chosen for that reason to designate the unique and original Christian idea of love in the NT. In Eng also the word "charity" is used to show the unique character of this love, and is used in most Eng versions of the Bible to translate *agapē* and *agapān*.

I. Synoptic Gospels. The love of God and of one's neighbor is called the greatest commandment of the law by Jesus, who quotes Dt 6:5 and Lv 19:18 (Mt 22:34–40; Mk 12:28–34; Lk 10:25–28). The two commandments are placed on an equal plane; and it is in this precisely that the Christian revolution of charity consists. Only Lk, however, relates the further question, "Who is the neighbor?" Jesus answered with the parable of the good Samaritan* (Lk 10:29–37). The hostility between Jews and Samaritans was deep, and by this parable Jesus identified the neighbor with that group from which Jews felt themselves most alien. The parable is a sharply picturesque explanation of the love of one's enemies (Mt 5:43–48; Lk 6:27 f, 32–36). Here Jesus presents God's attitude toward men as the model of the Christian's attitude toward those who hate him. Love of one's neighbor is a general and regular attitude which the Christian exhibits, and it is no more dependent upon the behavior of one's neighbor than is the course of nature, which God maintains for sinners as well as for righteous. In this Christian love must show itself different from pagan morality; no one questions the duty of loving one's friends, but Jesus demands more.

In Lk 7:36–50 Jesus presents growth in the love of God as a result of gratitude for the forgiveness of sins. This implies that genuine love of God can only arise from the recognition of one's sinfulness, and that self-righteousness like that of the Pharisees is incompatible with love. 7:47 is a compressed sentence in Gk and the usual Eng translation is misleading. The sentence means, in accordance with the preceding and following context, "Many sins are forgiven her, seeing that she has shown so much love," i.e., her extraordinary display of love manifests her awareness of great forgiveness. One who has no such awareness cannot show love.

The love of God is possessive, and one cannot have two masters (Mt 6:24; Lk 16:13). In this saying the meaning of "prefer" in *agapān* appears clearly. The antithesis love-hate in Hb and Aramaic has not quite the same force as it has in Eng.

The love of Jesus and the Father appears in the Synoptic Gospels only in the designation of Jesus as the beloved son (Mt 3:17; 12:18; 17:5; Mk 1:11; 9:7; 12:6; Lk 3:22; 9:35; 20:13). The Semitic original of this phrase means "only son," but the Gk paraphrase is exact; the only son was, of course, the loved son. The relationship is developed more fully in Jn and Paul; cf below.

Jesus uses the word *philein* of the attitude of His disciples toward Himself by demanding greater love than one gives to parents or to children (Mt 10:37). The word *agapān* describes Jesus's sentiment toward the young man who asked Him how to become perfect (Mk 10:21) and the love of the centurion of Capernaum for the Jewish people (Lk 7:5).

II. The Pauline writings. *Agapē* and *agapān* in the Pauline writings refer to the love of God and Christ for man, the love of man for God and Christ, and the mutual love of men. God's love is "poured" into men's heart through the Holy Spirit*, who is a token and an effect of the love of God (Rm 5:5). Through love the Father predestines the Christian (Eph 1:4) and is moved to give life to the Christian (Eph 2:4). The proof of God's love for man is the death of Christ to deliver man from sin (Rm 5:8). No power can separate the Christian from such abiding love, which assures him of victory (Rm 8:35–39); God who loves the Christian gives him encouragement and hope (2 Th 2:16). The love of Christ for men is shown in His surrender of Himself on behalf of sinful man (Gal 2:20; Eph 5:2, 25). The love which Christ shows for His Church is the model of the love which husbands should show their wives (Eph 5:25); here there appears the OT theme of love as conceived in Hosea and Jeremiah.

When Paul speaks of the love of man for God, it is usually in order to announce the blessings which man receives as a fruit of this love. The love of God is something to which God Himself directs the heart of the Christian (2 Th 3:5). All things work together for good to those who love God (Rm 8:28), and the Christian should be rejoiced and encouraged by the thought of what God prepares for those who love Him (1 Co 2:9). Those who love God are approved by Him (1 Co 8:3). Paul's love of Christ impels him to the labors of the apostolate (2 Co 5:14).

The exhortations to mutual charity are numerous and a standard part of Paul's exhortations to Christian life and virtue. Paul restates in his own words the teaching of the Synoptic Gospels: one who loves his neighbor fulfills the entire law, for this commandment sums up the other commandments (Rm 13:8–10; Gal 5:13 f). Love should appear in an excellent form between husband and wife, who should love each other as Christ and the Church love each other (Eph 5:25–33). Love shows itself in bearing with inconvenience in order not to wound a brother by scandal (Rm 14:15), and by giving alms to those in need (2 Co 8:7 ff). Love also receives the repentant sinner (2 Co 2:8). The Pauline conception of fraternal *agapē*, it is true, seems to have no room for those who are not Christians, and in a sense it has none; the union of hearts and the exchange of the duties of love which a community makes possible cannot be communicated to those who are not members of the community. But Paul does not exclude those who are not Christians from the kindness of Christians; *agapē*, however, becomes in Paul almost a synonym for the Church (cf below), of which one must be a member in order to partake of the fullness of *agapē*. Paul frequently addresses the members of the Church as "beloved," which designates primarily the affection which Paul has for them and which they have for each other. *Agapē* as a mutual relationship can exist only between Christians.

The most remarkable and most frequent use of the word *agapē* in the Pauline writings employs the word absolutely with no object explicitly mentioned, so that it is sometimes impossible to affirm that the word refers formally to the love of God or to the mutual love of Christians. This use is especially frequent in the pastoral epistles and other epistles which are Pauline in influence and spirit rather than in their literary origins. *Agapē* thus becomes a kind of atmosphere in which God and Christians live together; communicated from God, *agapē* permeates the Christian community and the individual Christian. Love builds the Christian (1 Co 8:1). The Christian is rooted and grounded in love (Eph 3:17), and love is his guide of conduct (Eph 5:2). It is the bond which unites all the virtues (Col 3:14), and it is the activity of faith (Gal 5:6). It inspires the Christian to labor (1 Th 1:3), and he grows in love by fidelity to the truth (Eph 4:15 f). *Agapē* in this absolute sense is praised in the hymn of 1 Co 13:1–13. It is the most excellent of *charismata*, superior to languages, knowledge, thaumaturgy, and martyrdom (1–4), which are of no value without it. It exhibits all the virtues (4–7). Unlike other *charismata* and virtues, it endures; even faith and hope will yield to the final reality, but the Christian will remain eternally in *agapē* (8–13).

III. The Johannine writings. In John *agapē* is presented in three terms of a mutual relation: the Father, the Son, and the disciples. The love of the Father for the disciples moves Him to adopt* them as His children (1 Jn 3:1). Jesus loves His disciples to the extreme (Jn 13:1) and lays down His life for them (1 Jn 3:16); this is the greatest proof of love (Jn 15:13). God is *agapē* (1 Jn 4:8, 16); without *agapē* one cannot know God.

The love of God and Christ for man demands a response. The Jews are blamed because they do not love God (Jn 5:42). This love should not consist in mere profession of love, but should be demonstrated as genuine by deeds (1 Jn 3:18). The chief work of love is to keep the word of God and the commandments of Jesus (Jn 14:15, 21, 23; 15:10; 1 Jn 2:5; 5:3). One who loves the world does not love God (1 Jn 2:15 f). Nor does one love God who withholds his gifts from one in need (1 Jn 3:17). Those who love Jesus rejoice at His return to the Father, for this means the accomplishment of His mission and His glorification (Jn 14:28).

The chief of the commandments, the new commandment of Jesus, is that the disciples should love one another (Jn 13:34 f; 15:17). They should love one another with the same selfless total love with which Jesus has loved them (Jn 15:12 f). The peculiar force of John's conception of Christian mutual love lies in his presentation of love as a reality which is communicated from the Father through the Son to all the disciples, who share it with each other. Jesus loves the disciples with the love which the Father exhibits toward Him (Jn 15:9). The Father loves the Son and puts all things at His disposal (Jn 3:35); He loves the Son because the Son lays down His life (Jn 10:17). One who loves Jesus is loved by the Father; to him the Son will reveal Himself, and the Father and the Son abide in the one who loves Jesus and keeps His word (Jn 14:21, 23). The Son shows His love of the Father by His obedience (Jn 14:31). The unity of the disciples is sealed by the love which the Father bestows upon them, the same love with which He loves the Son; through this love the Father and the Son dwell in the disciples (Jn 17:23, 26). The unifying principle of love which originates from God and is diffused through the Church is the theme of the great discourse of 1 Jn 4:7–21. God is love and through love sends His Son to communicate life. The love of God consists not in loving Him but in being loved by Him; God initiates, man responds. God abides in the community through the mutual love of its members. In the same way He abides in the individual Christian through the *agapē* of that Christian. When love is perfect, there is no longer room for fear; the potential hostility which fear implies is annihilated in perfect love, which unites totally. The perfection of the Christian's love for God is tested by his love of his brother.

Unlike the other NT writings, Jn does not always distinguish between *agapān* and *philein*. *Philein* is used of the love of friendship, its normal use; Jesus loved Lazarus, Martha, and Mary (Jn 11:3, 36). But the love of Jesus for "the beloved disciple" is expressed by *agapān* (Jn 13:23; 19:26; 21:7, 20). *Philein* is used of the mutual love of Father and Son (Jn 5:20), which elsewhere is designated by *agapē* and *agapān*, and of the love of the Father for the disciples and of the disciples for Jesus (Jn 16:27). These passages suggest that it is improbable that any special significance is to be found in the variation of the two words in the triple question and answer of Peter in Jn 21:15–17. In the first two questions *agapān* is used, in the third *philein; philein* is used in each of the three answers of Peter.

IV. The other NT writings. The other NT writings exhibit no distinctive feature in their conception of *agapē*. Most of the instances of the word exhibit the Pauline conception of *agapē* as an absolute and the Johannine conception of a mutual all-embracing unifying force. Jd 12 is the single NT instance of the use of *agapē* to designate the Eucharistic* rite, a use which is more common in postapostolic Christian literature.

Lubim. Cf LIBYA.

Lucius (Gk *lūkios* from Lt Lucius), the name of two Christians: **1.** A Cyrenian, one of the prophets and teachers of Antioch* (AA 13:1). **2.** A companion and fellow-countryman of Paul* (from Tarsus? Rm 16:21).

Lud, Ludim (Hb *lûd, lûdîm*, etymology uncertain), a gentilic and geographical name. In the table of nations* the name is given to two peoples: a descendant of Ham* through Egypt (Gn 10:13; 1 Ch 1:11) and a descendant of Shem* (Gn 10:22; 1 Ch 1:17). It is associated with peoples of Asia Minor in Is 66:19 and with African peoples in Je 46:9 and Ezk 30:5; Ezk 27:10 is ambiguous. The two peoples cannot be identified and we must suppose that carelessness has conflated two names into one. The Asian Lud is most probably the same as the Gk Lydia, a kingdom of W Asia Minor. The Lydians first appear in the 7th century and are mentioned with their king Gugu (Gyges) by Ashur-bani-pal of Assyria (668–630 BC) as vassals and as rebels in 665 BC. Under the dynasty of the Mermnades (685–546 BC) Lydia dominated the W coast of Asia Minor; the most famous kings of the dynasty were Alyattes and Croesus. The kingdom of Lydia was subjugated by Cyrus* in 546 BC. Cf SARDIS.

Luke. Cf LUKE, GOSPEL OF.

Luke, Gospel of. 1. *Authorship*. The 3rd Gospel is attributed to Luke* by a tradition which goes back to Marcion and the Canon of Muratori (cf CANON) of the 2nd century, and to an anti-Marcionite prologue added to the Gospel at an uncertain date, but placed by many scholars in the 2nd century at Rome. The same tradition is found in Irenaeus, Tertullian, Clement of Alexandria, Origen, Eusebius, and Jerome. This tradition cannot be tested; but the very obscurity of Lk in the NT suggests that it rests upon a genuine memory. Luke appears as a companion and fellow worker of Paul* in Col 4:14; 2 Tm 4:11; Phm 24. Some scholars believe he should be identified with Lucius of Cyrene, one of the prophets and teachers of Antioch (AA 13:1), and the Lucius who was a companion of Paul at Corinth (Rm 16:21). The designation of him as "the beloved physician" (Col 4:14) led some scholars, notably A. Harnack, to attempt a demonstration that Lk and AA show a specialized knowledge of medical terminology; the demonstration is not regarded as successful. The internal evidence does not demonstrate the authorship of Lk but it fits very well with the traditional attribution; Lk is written for Gentile Christians (cf below) and is the work of the man who wrote AA*.

2. *Date, Place, Destination*. There is no firm tradition about either date or place of composition. Irenaeus said that Lk was written before the death of Paul; Jerome, depending on Eusebius, places it after the death of Paul. Some modern critics defend a date around 63, or 63–70; the majority prefer a date after 70, but there is very little probability in the opinion that it was written after 90. There is no dispute about the destination; the literary characteristics and the theological perspectives of Lk show beyond doubt that it is the work of a Gentile Christian written for Gentile Christians (cf below).

3. *Contents and Plan*. L. Cerfaux notes four types of composition in Lk: the material produced by Lk as redactor, the material in which Lk depends on Mk, the material common to Mt-Mk, and the matter proper to Lk alone. In the following outline the relation of Lk to Mt-Mk is noted; matter not noted is found in Lk alone.

Prologue: 1:1–4.

Infancy* Gospel: 1:5–2:52.

I. Galilean Ministry: 3:1–9:50.

(1) 3:1–4:13, preaching of John, baptism, temptation (Mt-Mk-Lk).

(2) 4:14–6:11, Nazareth, Capernaum, call of disciples, miracles (Mk-Lk).

(3) 6:12–8:3, choice of Twelve, discourse, miracles (Mt-Lk).

(4) 8:4–9:50, parables, miracles (Mk-Lk).

II. Journey to Jerusalem: 9:51–21:38 (most of the material proper to Lk is found here).

(1) 9:51–13:21, Samaria, mission of the 70, sayings, controversies, parables.

(2) 13:22–17:10, sayings, controversies, parables.

(3) 17:11–18:14, miracles, discourses, parables, sayings.

(4) 18:15–21:38, sayings, Zacchaeus, discourses (Mk mostly).

III. Passion: 22:1–23:56 (while Lk follows the common tradition, a large number of details are proper to him).

IV. Resurrection: 24.

4. *Sources*. The above outline shows that the question of the sources of Lk is somewhat different from the question of the sources of Mt-Mk (cf GOSPEL). There is wide agreement that Lk's principal source is Mk; statistics presented by A. Wikenhauser show the extent of the dependence. Out of 1149 verses 548 are peculiar to Lk. Lk has taken about 350 of the 661 verses of Mk. About 325 verses of Lk are common to Mt-Lk and not to Mk. The prologue mentions "many" who have written narratives of the life of Jesus based on the traditions of those "who from the beginning were eyewitnesses and ministers of the word" (1:1–2). The "many" (which in Gk need only mean more than one) certainly include Mk; it is not certain, and many critics doubt, that Lk knew our Gk Mt. There is a common consensus that written collections of sayings and narratives were composed before our Gospels, and Lk could have had access to these. Such a source has been suggested in several forms. Schlatter, Rengstorff, Cerfaux, and others believe that most if not all of the material proper to Lk was contained in a "gospel of the disciples," which originated in the groups of Palestinian disciples and which was distinct from "the gospel of the Twelve," best illustrated by Mk. This source, according to Schlatter, was produced shortly after 55 by a disciple who was an eyewitness. B. H. Streeter proposed an earlier form of the Gospel which he called Proto-Luke. The majority of scholars hesitate to identify such a single source and believe that Lk's material comes from distinct and scattered sources, oral and written. AA indicates that Luke was in Palestine for some time, and this would have given him an opportunity to collect Palestinian oral traditions from contemporaries of Jesus.

5. *Literary Form and Composition*. The prologue of Lk is modeled on the prologues

of Hellenistic historical writers and conveys the impression that Luke writes primarily as a historian; he has investigated the matter closely and intends to set forth the material (1:3). He relates the events to the contemporary scene by synchronisms (2:1–3; 3:1 f). He gives the age of Jesus (3:23). But the Gospel itself shows that Luke, like Matthew and Mark, is primarily an evangelist; he writes that Theophilus may know the truth of the things in which he has been instructed (1:4). In the words of X. Léon-Dufour, the expressions of the historian are the literary vesture of the original Christian reality. The gospel form, which was established when Luke wrote, broke through the forms of Gk historiography. Unlike Mt and Mk, which A. Wilkenhauser describes as impersonal community books written for liturgical purposes, Lk is a literary work written to be read.

The language of Lk is more polished Gk than Mt or Mk, but it is still the popular (*Koinē*) language. He does not, however, avoid all Aramaisms and Hebraisms; these include the periphrastic verb form, the superfluous participle, the *casus pendens,* the excessive use of pronouns, and the adjectival genitive. His vocabulary is larger than the vocabulary of Matthew-Mark. A difference can be noticed in his treatment of Mk; in the words of Jesus Luke merely polishes the Gk, but in the narratives he curtails Mk, especially by omitting graphic details, and adds explanatory notes. In the narratives Luke acquires a Semitic tone, in the opinion of many scholars, not from his sources but by deliberately imitating the Gk of the LXX.

Luke's treatment of his sources can be traced only where he is compared with Mk, but the comparison is revealing. It is evident that the threefold plan of the gospel: Galilee, journeys, Jerusalem, was fixed when Luke wrote and he did not feel free to vary it. For this reason he strangely inserts most of his own material in the long "journey account," which is evidently a literary framework; there was no other point in the existing framework where this material could be inserted. This is the so called "great insertion," which in the plan of Mk would occur between Mk 9:50 and 10:1. The "little insertion," which contains Lucan material or material common to Mt-Lk (Lk 6:20–8:3), would occur in the plan of Mk between Mk 3:19 and 3:20. On the other hand, "the great omission" of Lk is the absence in Lk of the material in Mk 6:45–8:26; this is probably due to theological motives (cf below). Luke felt free to alter episodes from their position in Mk, to conflate events which have common features, to add dramatic touches in narrative. He did not feel obliged

to retain all the topographical notices of Mk, e.g., Capernaum (5:17; 9:46), the sea of Galilee (5:27; 6:17; 8:4), Galilee (9:43), the Decapolis (8:39). In the journey narrative all topographical notices are suppressed, if indeed this material was included in Luke's sources. The narrative is rendered continuous by the use of transitions (5:33; 8:11, 16, 40; 9:22, 28 +); but at times Luke has only the vague "at that time" characteristic of Mt-Mk (6:12; 7:11; 8:1). The composition of some lines evidently shows an intention to presage an event which occurs later (1:80 = 3:1–3; 3:20 = 9:9; 9:1–6 = 10:1; 5:33 = 11:1; 20:19 = 22:2; 21:37 = 22:39; 20:25 = 23:2 +). This artistic weaving together of episodes is a part of Luke's own theological interpretation of events and is not from his sources. The narrative is centered upon Jerusalem, where the Gospel begins and ends; Mk's account of the journeys to the borders of Galilee is "the great omission."

These traits show that while Luke was faithful to his sources, he permitted himself remarkable freedom both in interpreting a Palestinian-Jewish account for Gentile readers and in casting the narrative in a theological mold (cf below). Some differences and modification are due less to deliberate recasting than to his ignorance of Palestinian houses (5:19; 6:47–49), dress (6:29; 7:14; 8:5 f), climate and topography (4:29; 9:10; 12:55; 21:29).

6. *Theology.* While none of the Synoptic Gospels can be called nontheological, Lk may be called the most theological; it should be noticed that he is candidly so. It should be noticed also that while Luke was a companion and a disciple of Paul, the characteristic Pauline ideas are not expressed in Lk; the theology which he presents is the theology of his sources i.e., the apostolic and Palestinian traditions. The theology of Lk is not sharply different from the theology of Mt-Mk, still less in opposition; Lk contains no theological element which is not found in his predecessors and differs from them in emphasis rather than in any positive doctrine. But Lk does show in his theology that he writes as a Gentile Christian when the first generation of the Church was well advanced.

In the words of X. Léon-Dufour, Luke projects on the events of the life of Jesus the light of the mystery of the Passion-Resurrection. By establishing a connection through anticipatory notice of coming events (cf above) he shows that he views the life, death, and resurrection of Jesus as a complete unit; and he alone relates the ascension* of Jesus. He retains the triple prediction of the passion which was a part of the common tradition, and he adds allusions to the passion in 2:34; 9:31; 12:50; 13:32 f;

17:24 f. Alone of the evangelists Luke uses the title Lord* in the Christological sense of the early Christian community. Luke also conceives Jesus as the savior (cf SALVATION); this is not due merely to his Hellenistic origins and background, for salvation is a biblical idea, but also to his universalism (cf below) and his desire to find the Gk words which would be both an intelligible and a faithful presentation of the gospel traditions.

The universalism of Luke is his belief and his expression of the belief that the gospel is addressed to all men. This is neither peculiarly Lucan nor Pauline but belongs to the primitive tradition (cf GENTILES); Luke, writing more for Greeks than for Jews, wished the Greeks to share the consciousness of universalism which he himself possessed. The genealogy of Jesus in Lk begins not with Abraham, but with Adam, the father of all men, "who was of God" (Lk 3:38). Certain distinctively Jewish traits and practices in Mk are removed or obscured in Lk. There are explicit allusions to the universal scope of the Church peculiar to Lk (2:14, 32; 24:47). He introduces Samaritans as models of charity (10:25–37) and of gratitude (17:11–19), and Gentiles as models of good conduct and ready faith (7:9). Cerfaux calls Luke's universalism as it stands the fruit of the union of the primitive traditions with the Hellenistic Christianity of Antioch and the preaching of Paul. Of a piece with Luke's universalism is the prominence given to women; more women appear in Lk than in the other Gospels. In the Hellenistic world the social and legal position of woman* was higher than it was in Judaism, and Luke wished to show clearly that the Gospel did not include the Jewish attitude toward woman. Perhaps the most paradoxical feature of Luke's universalism is that Luke is less hostile to Jews than Mt, Mk, or Jn.

To Luke's universalism also belongs his emphasis upon Jesus as "the friend of sinners" — again not a feature peculiar to Luke. Only Luke contains the saying that the Son of Man has come to seek and save what is lost (19:10). A number of episodes, sayings, and parables peculiar to Luke present the friendliness and compassion of Jesus to sinners: the parable of patience with the barren fig tree (13:6–9), the parables of the lost sheep, the lost drachma, the prodigal son (15), the sinful woman (7:36–50), Zacchaeus (19:1–10), the parable of the Pharisee and the publican (18:10–14), the promise to the thief on the cross (23:40–43).

In a similar mood Luke emphasizes in miracle stories the compassion of Jesus for the sufferer (7:11–17; 13:11–17; 14:1–6; 17:11–19). The expressions of strong feelings

in Jesus found in Mk are omitted in Lk, as are some harsh statements concerning the disciples. Some rather grim sayings in Mk (4:12; 9:43–48; 14:21) are omitted in Lk.

The kingdom of God, which is a peculiarly Jewish-Palestinian conception, does not receive the emphasis in Lk which it receives in Mt-Mk. Luke follows Mk rather than Mt in conceiving the kingdom primarily as the eschatological kingdom of the future. The present reality of salvation in Lk, as in AA, is not the kingdom but the spirit. It is a gift (11:13), it is active in the initiation of the Incarnation (1:5, 35, 41, 67, 80), in the early witness to Jesus (2:25–27), and in the activity of Jesus Himself (4:1, 14, 17; 10:21). The coming of salvation creates an atmosphere of joy, mentioned much more frequently in Lk than in Mt-Mk (1:4, 28, 58; 2:10; 10:17, 20 f; 13:17; 19:6, 37; 24:41, 52). There is joy even in heaven at the repentance of sinners (15:7, 10, 32). Joy breaks out in expressions of praise, again more frequent in Lk than in Mt-Mk (BENEDICTUS; MAGNIFICAT). The coming of salvation also creates an atmosphere of prayer (3:21; 5:16; 6:12; 9:18, 28 f; 10:21; 11:1; 22:32; 23:34). Peculiar to Luke are the parables of the importunate friend (11:5–8) and the unjust judge (18:1–8) which recommend perseverance in prayer.

In his attitude toward wealth* and poverty (cf POOR) Luke is the spokesman of what has come to be called the evangelical attitude. This appears in his formulation of the Beatitudes* compared with Mt (Lk 6:20–26). The emphasis is seen again in material which is peculiar to Lk: the parable of Dives and Lazarus (16:19–31), of the rich fool (12:13–21), the recommendation to invite the poor to the banquet (14:12–14). Luke likewise emphasizes the total renunciation demanded of the followers of Jesus (5:11, 28; 11:41; 12:13–33; 14:26, 33; 18:29).

Léon-Dufour is certainly right in pointing out that in Lk the gospel becomes explicitly a rule of life, and that the somewhat repulsive modern term "social gospel" can with reservations be applied to Lk. Lucan passages are explicit on the duty of giving to the poor (3:10 ff; 14:12–14), the penalty of failing to share with the poor (16:25 f), and the duties of those who are in a position to cheat and oppress (3:10–14).

7. *Historical Value.* The historical quality of Lk can be tested remarkably well in his treatment of Mk. As mentioned above, here he is faithful to his source although free in his use of it. He does not distort the reality of Jesus or the events which he draws from Mk. It would be gratuitous to assert that he handles his other sources, which cannot be compared with him, in a different manner.

The theological modification of the gospel in Lk is obvious and should not be denied; neither is it a distortion. Luke did not pretend that his Gospel should replace the others and be regarded as the only authentic account of Jesus. Apparently he thought that the gospel traditions as he knew them failed to render Jesus fully in a way easily comprehensible to Hellenistic Christians like himself. For this he used new material and rewrote the old. Since one and the same Jesus emerges in Lk who emerges in Mt-Mk, it would be captious to question Luke's fidelity.

Lute. Cf MUSIC.

Luz. Cf BETHEL.

Lycaonia. A region of central Asia Minor, a plateau of about 3000 ft altitude, bounded by Cappadocia*, Galatia*, Phrygia*, Pisidia*, and Cilicia*. It was economically poor and of no historical importance; in ancient times it was infested by bandits. Its principal cities, Derbe*, Lystra*, and Iconium*, were visited by Paul and Barnabas on their first missionary journey (AA 14:6). Jews resided in Lycaonia. According to AA 14:11 the Lycaonians spoke their own language or dialect, but it has not been identified. Lycaonia was under Roman rule after 25 BC.

Lycia. A region and Roman province on the S coast of Asia Minor. At Myra*, the principal city of Lycia, the party which bore Paul* to Rome transferred from their Adramyttian ship to an Alexandrian ship bound for Rome. It is not mentioned as a field of evangelization in the NT.

Lydda (Hb *lôd*, Gk *lydda*, etymology uncertain), modern *Ludd*, a town of Judah about 12 mi SE of Joppa* and about 25 mi from Jerusalem. It is mentioned in the list of Palestinian cities conquered by Thutmose III of Egypt (ANET 243). According to 1 Ch 8:12 it was founded by Shemed of Benjamin; this can refer only to a rebuilding. It was one of the towns of Judah inhabited in the period of Nehemiah* (Ezr 2:33; Ne 7:37). Under Jonathan* the toparchy of Lydda was transferred from Samaria to Judah (1 Mc 11:34). One of the early Christian communities was established at Lydda, and Peter* cured a paralytic of Lydda, Aeneas (AA 9:32–35). The town was an administrative center under the Seleucids, the Maccabees, and Herod.

Lydia (Gk *lydia*, meaning uncertain), a feminine name attested frequently in ancient literature; a dealer in purple (cf DYE) of Philippi* who was a native of Thyatira* in Asia. She was a Jewish proselyte* and was the first in Philippi to be baptized by Paul. She gave the apostles hospitality in her house (AA 16:14 f, 40).

Lyre. Cf MUSIC.

Lysanias (Gk *lysanias,* "freeing from sorrow"), tetrarch of Abilene* at the beginning of the public life of Jesus (Lk 3:1). The younger Lysanias, son of the better known Lysanias executed by Antony and Cleopatra in 34 BC (according to Josephus), is known from three inscriptions from Abila dated in the reign of Tiberius (AD 14–37) earlier than AD 29. Lysanias was dead by AD 37.

Lysias (Gk *lysias,* a short form of Lysanias), a personal name; an officer of Antiochus* IV Epiphanes. When Antiochus IV departed to Persia to raise money in 166 BC, he left Lysias as regent of his son Antiochus* V Eupator, who was a boy, and commissioned him to carry on the campaign against the Jews. Lysias sent a force under three commanders, Ptolemy*, Nicanor*, and Gorgias* (1 Mc 3:27–41), who were defeated by Judas*. Lysias then led an expedition personally, but he also was defeated (1 Mc 4:27–35; 2 Mc 11:1–15; 12:1). After the death of Antiochus in 164 Lysias installed Antiochus V as king and undertook another campaign in Judaea, defeated Judas at Beth-Zechariah, occupied Beth-zur*, and besieged the Jewish forces in the citadel of Jerusalem (1 Mc 6:17–54; the acts of the boy king in this passage are the acts of Lysias; 2 Mc 13:9–26). He was forced to abandon the campaign when he was threatened by the approach of Philip*, to whom Antiochus IV had committed the regency before his death, and he made an agreement with the Jews giving them freedom to follow their Law. He returned to Antioch and defeated Philip. Both Lysias and Antiochus V were murdered in 162 BC when Antioch was seized by Demetrius* I (1 Mc 7:1–4; 2 Mc 14:1–2). 2 Mc adds the account of Lysias's execution of Menelaus* (2 Mc 13:1–8), and gives Antiochus V credit for appointing him regent (2 Mc 10:11); 2 Mc or his source probably did not know that Antiochus V was a boy. Ancient historians also relate that he executed Laodice, daughter of Antiochus IV, after her father's death because she was accused of favoring the claims of Demetrius I. They also tell of a journey which he made to Rome in order to clear himself and Antiochus V of the charge of the assassination of a Roman legate.

Lystra. A city of Lycaonia*, to which Paul* and Barnabas* passed after they had been forced to leave Iconium* (AA 14:6). Here the people, astonished at Paul's cure of a lame man, saluted them as gods, Zeus and Hermes (AA 14:6–18), and Paul with difficulty prevented them from offering sacrifice. The fickle citizens were easily persuaded by Jews from Iconium that Paul and Barnabas were charlatans and they stoned Paul into unconsciousness (AA 14:19 f). This did not prevent them from returning to Lystra to encourage their converts (AA 14:21; 16:1). Lystra was the home of Timothy* (AA 16:2). Paul's persecution at Lystra is mentioned in 2 Tm 16:2. The site of Lystra is known, but nothing remains of the ancient city.

M

Maacah (Hb *ma'ᵃkāh*, meaning uncertain).
1. A geographical name; a region S of Mt
Hermon and N of Lake Huleh around
the town of Abel-Beth-Maacah. It was an
Aramaean kingdom which fought against
David in alliance with the Ammonites
(2 S 10:6–8; 1 Ch 19:6–7). In Gn 22:24
Maacah with other Aramaean tribes is a
descendant of Nahor*. They are mentioned
on the N frontier of Israel in Jos 12:5;
13:11, 13. The kingdom was incorporated
into Israelite territory, probably by David,
and several Maacathites appear among the
Israelites (2 S 23:34; 2 K 25:23; Je 40:8;
1 Ch 4:19).
2. A personal name borne by both men
and women, including a wife of David, the
mother of Absalom* (2 S 3:3); the wife of
Rehoboam* and mother of Abijah* (1 K
15:2); Maacah the daughter of Abishalom
(granddaughter, if the son of David is meant)
appears as mother both of Abijah* (1 K
15:2) and of his son Asa* (1 K 15:10).
She was deposed as queen mother by Asa
because of her cult of a fertility image (1 K
15:13). It seems unlikely that two successive
queens had identical names and patronymics.
Some scholars suppose that Maacah was
queen mother in place of the deceased mother
of Asa, others that there has been a confusion
of names. 2 Ch 11:20–22 gives a number
of additional details on Maacah, wife of
Rehoboam and mother of Abijah; but in 1
Ch 13:2 she is called Micaiah, elsewhere
a masculine name.

Maccabee (Gk *makkabaios*, from Hb *mak-
kebet,* "hammer"), a nickname of Judas* son
of Mattathias* (1 Mc 2:4), leader of the
insurrection of the Jews against Antiochus*
Epiphanes 165–161. The nickname is extended to his brothers, who succeeded him
in the leadership of the Jews, and is used
to designate the entire period of Jewish history. The period is surveyed in the articles
HASMONEAN; JONATHAN; JUDAS; MATTATHIAS;
SIMON; and articles referred to in these
articles.

Maccabees, Books of. 1–2 Mc, while grouped
under a single heading in the Bible, are actually two books unrelated except for community of subject; cf below. On 3–4 Mc cf
APOCRYPHAL BOOKS. 1–2 Mc are deuterocanonical* books not accepted in the Jewish
and Protestant canons.
1. *1 Mc.*

I. *Contents and structure:*
Prologue in two parts: 1, survey from
Alexander to the accession of Antiochus
Epiphanes, the rise of the Hellenistic party
in Judaea, the profanation of the temple,
and the attempt of Antiochus to suppress
Judaism and Hellenize the Jews; 2, the
resistance of Mattathias and his sons and
the organization of a guerrilla campaign
against the Seleucid forces.
3:1–9:22, the campaigns of Judas.
9:23–12:53, the campaigns and diplomacy
of Jonathan.
13:1–16:24, the liberation under Simon.
The structure of the book is not without
art. The entire story recounts the successful
struggle of the Jews to survive against the
cultural and military forces brought against
them. The prologue introduces the antagon-
ists: on the one hand, the Greeks and the
Hellenizing Jews, on the other the family
of Mattathias, which becomes the heart of
the resistance. Each of the three brothers
who carries on the struggle is distinguished
in some way: Judas is a hero of battles,
Jonathan* a master diplomat, and Simon*
the man who combines both gifts and achieves
the final liberation.
II. *Language and Text.* 1 Mc was written
in Hb; its style makes this evident and no
scholar doubts it. It is preserved in Gk
only; with a few exceptions the Gk reflects
the Hb original in such a way that its accuracy can be presumed. Jerome relates that
he saw a copy of the Hb original. Maccabees
cannot be the original title; Origen gave the
Hb title in Gk transcription as *sarbeth-
sabaniael*, of which no certain reconstruction
has been proposed.
III. *Author and Date.* The author is unknown. On the basis of 16:24 the book must
be dated after 104 BC, the date of the death
of John Hyrcanus. Several scholars, however, question the originality of 14–16, which
are not employed by Josephus in his history
of the period. Some of these would date
1–13 as early as 135 BC, the year of the
death of Simon, or shortly after. More recent opinion finds the absence of these chapters in Josephus an insufficient argument for
detaching them from the rest of the book,
with which they have a unity in style and
conception.
IV. *Literary Form and Historical Character.* The author evidently intended to write
in the style of classical Hb narrative prose
as in S and K and succeeded in doing so.

529

The narrative is moving and vivid. It is, however, episodic; gaps occur in the sequence of events which are only vaguely noted.

The historical importance of 1 Mc is primary; it is the only document for the entire period which it covers, from the accession of Antiochus in 175 BC to the death of Simon in 135 BC. Modern historical science and criticism show that the book is an extremely reliable historical source. Jewish defeats and Jewish treachery are not concealed nor transformed. We learn from the data of 1 Mc that Jewish liberty came from the collapse of the Seleucid kingdom. 1 Mc does not refer to sources except in 9:22 and 16:23 f, and these references are ambiguous. The source mentioned in 16:23 f is not used for the book itself, and 9:22 states that "the rest of the deeds" of Judas are not recorded. The formula imitates the well known concluding formula which ends the account of each reign in 1–2 K. It is difficult to determine whether this verse implies that the author was using a documentary source for the events of the life of Judas which he does narrate. On the hypothesis of a date after 104 it can hardly be supposed that he was himself a witness of the events 175–165. There is very great probability that documentary sources for the period 175–135 were in existence.

The author gives exact chronological and geographical details and is evidently familiar with Palestine. The dates are given according to the Seleucid era, reckoned from 312 BC. His familiarity with the geography, ethnology, institutions, and history of external peoples is not remarkable; for instance, he is poorly informed about Rome* and Sparta, and it appears that, in accordance with a local tradition, he has placed the death of Antiochus IV (6:1–17) later than it actually occurred. The numbers of men engaged in the battles are exaggerated; neither he nor his sources had any idea of what the actual number of combatants may have been.

Thirteen documents are quoted: the letter of the Israelites of Gilead, 5:10–13; the letter of the Romans to Judas, 8:23–32; the letter of Alexander Balas to Jonathan, 10:18–20; the letter of Demetrius I to Jonathan, 10:25–45; the letter of Demetrius II to Jonathan, 11:30–37; the letter of Antiochus VI to Jonathan, 11:57; the letter of Jonathan to the Spartans, 12:6–17; the reply of the Spartans to Jonathan, 12:20–23; the letter of Demetrius II to Simon, 13:36–40; the letter of the Spartans to Simon, 14:20–23; the letter of Antiochus VI to Simon, 15:2–9; the letter of Lucius to Ptolemy, 15:16–21; the inscription in honor of Simon, 14:27–45. Many modern historians regard these quotations as entirely fictitious, composed in the spirit of ancient historical narrative. They support their opinion from the speeches which the author often puts in the mouth of his characters (cf below); this technique, through which the author himself often interprets events, was common in Gk historians. It is not characteristic of preexilic Hb historiography but occurs in postexilic writings. Recent opinion, however, places more confidence in the documents as authentic. These scholars believe that the author saw the documents but composed a resume of them in the form in which they appear in the book.

V. *Religious Ideas.* In 1 Mc the ideas of religion and patriotism are very closely merged; the survival of belief in the one true God is dependent upon the survival of the Jewish community. The heroes of the book are not the martyrs of Judaism — although the author admires them — but the fighters and diplomats who make it unnecessary for anyone to submit to martyrdom. The author is a candid partisan of the Maccabees, "the family through whom it was given to save Israel" (5:62), and by implication of their successors, the Hasmoneans*. Some scholars have affirmed that he was a Pharisee, others have affirmed with equal assurance that he was a Sadducee; hence it seems most probable that he was neither, and that he wrote at a time when these divisions had not yet become significant.

The theme of the book is the opposition which exists between Israel, the people of God, and the Gentiles. Unless Israel resists Hellenism by every means, political and military as well as religious, it will succumb and lose its distinct identity and its distinct beliefs and cult. In this struggle the Hellenizing Jews play the role of villains; the Greeks, after all, are only doing what they think they ought, but the Jews are traitors to God and to Israel. Thus the Maccabees can treat and deal with the Seleucids and their officers, but not with the treacherous Jews. It is vital in the struggle that the Jews show fidelity to the law* (1:11–2:68; 3:47, 51; 13:3–6); Judaism is now identified with the observance of the law. It is also identified with a devotion to Zion and the temple (3:43, 45, 49; 4:36, 60; 7:33–38, 41–42). The author does not reject Judaism of the Diaspora*, but he is sure that Judaism both in Palestine and in the Diaspora cannot survive unless it has Zion and the temple as a focus.

The author interprets the course of events by the speeches and prayers which he puts in the mouth of his characters, and by reflections on passages of the Bible: 1:37–40; 2:7–12, 19–22, 49–68; 3:18–22, 45, 58–60;

4:9–11, 30–33; 6:11–13; 7:17, 41–42; 9:10; 13:3–6; 16:2–3. He exhibits the belief that the sufferings of Israel are due to its sins, and that it will recover by observance of the law. God in His judgments governs the course of events; in this belief, however, he differs from 2 Mc in that he relates no marvelous interposition of God. His view of God and God's action emphasizes the divine remoteness and transcendence, in which he shares the common view of the Judaism of his time. He never employs the divine names or titles, and speaks of God as "heaven" or simply as "He." There is no element of messianism* in the book; the establishment of a free state of Israel is not the establishment of the kingdom* of God, and the dynasty of David has no place in his thought. Like BS he shows no awareness of an afterlife, although this awareness appears in Dn.

2. *2 Mc.*

I. *Contents:* Two letters from the Jews in Jerusalem to the Jews in Alexandria (1:1–10a; 1:10b–2:18); 2:19–32, author's preface.

3, under the high priest Onias the temple is miraculously protected from a raid on the treasury attempted by Heliodorus.

4–7, the acquisition of the high priesthood by Jason through bribery; intrigues of Jason and Menelaus for the high priesthood; pillage of the city and profanation of the temple by Antiochus; martyrdom of Jews who refuse to abandon the law, in particular Eleazar the scribe and the seven brothers.

8:1–10:9, success of Judas against the Seleucid armies; death of Antiochus; purification of the temple.

10:10–13:26, success of Judas against Gorgias, Timotheus, Lysias, and neighboring peoples; execution of Menelaus; withdrawal of Seleucid forces.

14:1–15:37, expedition of Nicanor; heroism of Razis; defeat of Nicanor.

II. *Author and Date.* The author is unknown. The book is written in Gk and in the opinion of almost all scholars is the work of an Alexandrian Jew. The work is an epitome of an otherwise unknown lost historical work of Jason of Cyrene (2:19 ff). The author speaks as if he had epitomized the entire work of Jason (15:37–39). This would mean that Jason's five books ended before the death of Judas; this, however, seems unlikely. The death of Judas followed rather closely after these events, and it is more probable that the author of 2 Mc chose to end his epitome on a note of triumph rather than to carry it on to the tragic death of the hero. There is no solid reason for assigning a precise date to the work of Jason; most scholars believe it was earlier than 1 Mc, perhaps as early as 150. The date of

2 Mc likewise is uncertain. If the letter of 1:10 was prefaced to the book by the author, then the book is later than the 188th year of the Seleucid era, 124 BC. Some, however, believe these letters were prefixed by an editor. Estimates of the date of 2 Mc vary from 120 BC to AD 50; the probability favors an earlier date within this period.

III. *Literary Form and Historical Character.* A. Lefèvre has remarked that 2 Mc 2:19–32 is the only biblical passage in which the author explicitly identifies the literary form of his work. It is an epitome of a historical work, in which the author for details and profound investigation relies entirely upon the source which he epitomizes. He himself desires to produce a work which will be easy and agreeable to read, and compares himself to the decorator of an existing building. Evidently he has adopted a very free style of narrative and composition. The work is actually rhetorical rather than narrative and can be viewed as a series of discourses. In this it is in the style of midrash*. Modern scholars call it "pathetic history."

As a historical source 2 Mc is of primary importance for the material in 3:1–4:6, of which there is no other documentary account. The material in 4:7–7:42, which is summarized briefly in 1 Mc 1:10–64, is related at greater length and with more details. Not all of these details can be regarded as historical; cf below. The chronology of 2 Mc (and perhaps of Jason) is somewhat uncertain. In 8–15, in which he is parallel to 1 Mc, the course of events is generally the same, with the exception of a single block of material, and 2 Mc has a few events which are not found in 1 Mc; the historical value of each of these must be judged in detail. The exception in the course of events is the displacement of the death of Antiochus. In 1 Mc the events in 4:26–7:50 are arranged: the victory over Lysias, the dedication of the temple, the wars with neighboring peoples, and the death of Antiochus Epiphanes. In 2 Mc the events in 9–12 are arranged: the death of Antiochus, the dedication of the temple, the victory over Lysias, and the wars with neighboring peoples. 2 Mc agrees with the Seleucid king list, which indicates that Antiochus IV died in 164. The numbers of combatants engaged in battles are grossly exaggerated. Why 2 Mc was not employed by Josephus is difficult to explain except on the hypothesis that he was not acquainted with the book.

2 Mc contains some documents: 1:1–10a, letter and 1:10a–2:18, letter (cf above); 9:19–27, letter of Antiochus to the Jews; 11:16–21, letter of Lysias to the Jews; 11:22–26, letter of Antiochus V to Lysias; 11:27–33, letter to Antiochus IV to the Jews; 11:34–38, letter of the Roman legates to the

Jews. Many scholars believe these are fictitious compositions, but the majority of recent opinion finds nothing in their form or contents which casts suspicion upon their authenticity in substance, if not in form. It is of interest, however, that the letter of Antiochus IV in 11:27 ff is placed out of order. The documents were of importance because they contained explicit grants to the Jews of liberty to follow their own law. These grants were not faithfully observed.

IV. *Religious Ideas*. Like 1 Mc, 2 Mc views the history as a deadly struggle between Hellenism and Judaism (a word which appears for the first time in 2 Mc) conceived as civilizations and as religions. Unlike 1 Mc, and no doubt because he was a Jew of the Diaspora*, the author of 2 Mc does not identify religion and patriotism. Probably for the same reason he assigns the primacy of honor to the martyrs of Judaism and not to her military defenders. He is somewhat cool toward the Hasmoneans, with the exception of Judas. Like 1 Mc he insists on the sanctity of the temple, and much of the book revolves around the profanation and the purification of the temple. In a sense the book is an explanation of two Jewish feasts of recent institution, the feast of the Dedication* and the Day of Nicanor*. These are two events on which the survival of Judaism depended, and they are the only achievements of the Hasmoneans which the writer thinks worth commemorating.

The religious ideas of the author have affected his composition, which in some passages appears to be imaginative rather than historical. This is particularly evident in the account of the martyrdoms of Eleazar and the seven brothers (7), in which the torments of the martyrs are unquestionably heightened and the discourses of the martyrs are the vehicles of profession of faith. His entire conception of history is that it is the action of God rather than the deeds of men, and this is in striking contrast to the conception of 1 Mc (cf above). When 1 Mc relates no marvels, 2 Mc finds many of them. In particular one notices the "epiphanies" at various crises which resolve the issue in favor of the Jews (3:24–30; 10:29–30; 11:8; 15:12–16). In these the author no doubt hypostatizes the help from heaven which the Jews believed they received. The issue of battle is not decided by armed combat, but by prayer, after which the enemy is rendered helpless. The author's conception of providence also appears in his somewhat rigorous presentation of judgment, particularly in the death of Antiochus Epiphanes, the details of which are almost entirely imaginative, and the execution of Menelaus. Unlike 1 Mc, the divine names and titles are used frequently. 2 Mc exhibits a conviction of the afterlife and the resurrection of the body (7:9, 11, 14, 23, 29; 12:39–45). In general he stands nearer to the beliefs of Pharisaism than does the author of 1 Mc. He also exhibits a unique conception of creation* (7:28).

The religious ideas of the book are of great value in ascertaining the beliefs of Judaism of the period; and it is not unfair to the author to assume that his primary purpose was to present these beliefs in a rhetorical and persuasive fashion. History was a means to this end, not an end in itself, and he used it with utter freedom according to his purpose.

Macedonia (Gk *makedōn*), a region N of Greece; in classical times Macedonia was regarded by the Gks as "barbarian." It became prominent in history with the accession of Philip, who conquered Greece, and his son Alexander*, who conquered the entire Near East. Alexander and Philip were known to the writer of 1 Mc (1:1; 6:2). The allusion to the Macedonian mercenaries in 2 Mc 8:20 is obscure; it probably refers either to the war between Antiochus II Soter (281–261 BC) against the Galatians or to the defeat of the rebellious satrap Molon by Antiochus III (221/220 BC). In NT times Macedonia was a Roman province with its capital at Thessalonica*. It was visited by Paul* on his 1st journey after a dream in which he was asked to come to Macedonia (AA 16:9 ff) and revisited on his 3rd journey (AA 20:2 ff). Paul founded churches at Philippi* and Thessalonica in Macedonia. Paul alludes to his troubles in Macedonia (2 Co 7:5), but praises the churches of Macedonia for their generosity in spite of their poverty (2 Co 8:1 ff).

Machaerus (Gk *machaerus*), a fortified point E of the Dead Sea between Zerka Main and the Arnon, at an altitude of about 3600 ft above the Dead Sea. A castle was erected there by Alexander Jannaeus about 90 BC to protect the trade route against the Nabataeans*. This castle was a center of resistance against the Romans by the Hasmoneans*, who took the castle and destroyed it in 57 BC. It was rebuilt both as a fortress and a villa by Herod* the Great 25–13 BC. It was inherited by Herod Antipas*, and according to Josephus* John* the Baptist was imprisoned and beheaded at Machaerus. It was again a center of resistance in the wars of Vespasian and Titus and was taken and destroyed by the Romans in AD 71–72. The remains have been identified at the modern Khirbet el Mukawer, but they have not been system-

The site of the desert fortress palace of Herod where John the Baptist was executed.

atically explored. The name does not appear in the Bible.

Machir (Hb *mākîr*, etymology uncertain), a clan name in the OT. In the genealogies Machir is the son of Manasseh* (Gn 50:23; Nm 26:29; 27:1; 32:39 f; 36:1) and the father of Gilead* (Nm 26:29; 36:1; 1 Ch 7:14–17). The "paternity" of Machir over Gilead refers to the conquest of Gilead by Machir (Nm 32:39 f). The territory of Machir, described in Jos 13:31; 17:1 included half of Gilead (N of the Jabbok*) and Bashan*. A gloss in Jos 13:31 explains that this territory went to half of Machir; the other half of Machir included the clan of the daughters of Zelophehad* (Jos 17: 3–6). Jair* is listed among the descendants of Manasseh in 1 Ch 2:21–23. The relations of Machir with Manasseh and Israel are somewhat complex. The clans of Gilead (1 Ch 7:14–17), which is a geographical name, are no doubt the clans of Machir. In the enumeration of Jgs 5:14–18 Machir and Gilead are the only names which are not names of the 12 tribes. This suggests that Machir was originally more than a clan of Manasseh. The clue may be found in Gn 50:23; the birth of the children of Machir upon the knees of Joseph is a symbol of acceptance by the father. This adoption was very probably created to explain the presence of Machir among the sons of Joseph; hence it is possible that Machir was a non-Israelite group which entered into the Israelite tribal community through union with Manasseh. The territory of Machir is elsewhere attributed to the half-tribe of Manasseh. Machir always appears in E Palestine,

and most historians believe that the clan migrated to the E from the territory of Manasseh in the W. This is supported by Nm 32:39 f. It should be noted, however, that Machir is included among the tribes and clans whose traditional claim to their territory rested upon the apportionment of Moses and not of Joshua; this may signify that these groups were recognized as in possession of their territory before the settlement of Israel in W Palestine.

Machir also appears as a personal name of a contemporary of David* who lived in Lodebar* in E Palestine (2 S 9:4 f; 17:27).

Machpelah (Hb *hammakpēlāh* [always with the article], etymology uncertain), a name given to a cave and the field in which the cave was situated, purchased by Abraham as a family burying ground at Hebron* (Gn 23). Those buried there were: Abraham and Sarah (Gn 25:9 f); Isaac, Rebekah, and Leah (Gn 49:30); Jacob (Gn 50:13). The tradition of the purchase in Gn 23 is attributed to the priestly source (cf PENTA-TEUCH), but most modern scholars now accept it as an ancient tradition. The importance of the story in the traditions of the Pnt is that it was the first instance of the ownership of land by the ancestors of Israel in Palestine. By the purchase Abraham became a landholder and one of "the men of Hebron." The situation of Machpelah is uncertain. The mosque of Hebron is built over a cave of which little can be seen through a grating in the floor of the mosque. The tradition identifying this cave with Machpelah is attested in the 4th century AD. Access to the cave is prohibited and it has never been systematically explored. An account from the Crusades tells that coffins with bones were discovered there which were, of course, identified with those of the patriarchs. No other site in the neighborhood of Hebron has a better claim, but in the absence of exploration the claim must remain doubtful.

Magdala (Gk *magdala,* probably from Hb *migdōl,* "tower"), a town on the W shore of the Sea of Galilee* about 4 mi N of Tiberias*. It was a center of fishing and fish packing. Magdala is probably identical with the Tarichaea mentioned by Josephus. The town is not mentioned in the Bible, but occurs in the epithet "Magdalen" applied to Mary*. It is located at the modern el Mejdel.

Magdalen. Cf MARY.

Magi. In profane Gk the word *magos* is used in four meanings: (1) a member of the Persian priestly caste; (2) the possessor of occult knowledge and power; (3) magician; (4) mountebank, charlatan. In Mt 2:1–12 the Magi are the possessors of occult knowledge, which is here identified by implication as astrology. Their coming from "the East" is vague, but probably Babylonia, in the NT period the traditional home of astrology, is meant; the OT passages which are alluded to, however, suggest Arabia.

The story of the Magi is primarily theological in interest and purpose. Jesus is presented as the King-Messiah of the Gentiles, recognized by the Gentiles but not by His own people, the Jews; cf GOSPEL; MATTHEW. The presentation is compiled from a number of OT texts. The star is the star which rises from Jacob (Nm 24:17). The coming of the ruler of Judah is an echo of Gn 49:10. The birth of the Messiah in Bethlehem is based upon Mi 5:1–3. The tribute from kings of Tarshish* and the coastlands, the gifts of kings from Sheba* and Seba, the worship of kings and the service of nations, and gold from Sheba are promised the king of Judah in Ps 72:10 f, 15. In the restored messianic Jerusalem camels will come from Midian* and Epha, and gold and frankincense will be brought from Sheba; cf Is 49:23. These allusions show that the account has been transformed by theological reflection on the OT (cf MIDRASH). The theme of Jesus as the Messiah accepted by the Gentiles and rejected by the Jews is basic in the entire NT, but especially in Mt. Particular details of the narrative, consequently, scarcely can be submitted to historical analysis. The star is evidently described as wonderful and lies beyond any astronomical investigation. The absence of

the massacre of Bethlehem in Josephus should not be treated as inconsequential. Popular devotion has added to the story since early medieval times such details as the number three (based on the gifts), the transformation of astrologers into kings (from Ps 72:10; Is 60:6), and the names of the three (Caspar, Melchior, Balthasar) and their connection with certain countries. These details have no biblical basis.

Magic. Magic is "the art which claims or is believed to produce effects by the assistance of supernatural beings or by a mastery of secret forces in nature" (Webster). It is characteristic of magic that it is *occult:* its powers are concealed from all but the few who are enabled to employ them. It is *infallible,* recognizing no higher power. It is *disproportionate;* the means which it employs are not adapted to the end which is desired and there can be no question of the natural operation of these means. Few scholars would now maintain the older view that magic is the ancestor of religion. Magic is irreligious rather than religious, since its powers are not dependent upon the divine and escape divine control; it is a superstition which takes some elements of religion and erects them into a competing system. Divination* seeks to ascertain the future course of events by occult means; magic seeks to influence the course of future events by occult means. Magic is not always used logically; the peoples of Mesopotamia (cf below) combined invocations of the gods with magical formulae.

1. *Mesopotamia.* If we may judge from the amount of literature given to the subject, no people was ever more deeply convinced of the value of magic and more devoted to its practice than the peoples of ancient Mesopotamia. Magic rested on the belief that almost all human troubles were caused by demons*. Demons attacked men not only because of their own malice, but also because they were conjured up by sorcerers and sorceresses. There is, naturally, no literature from these practitioners of "black magic"; the practice of sorcery was prohibited by law in Babylon (Code of Hammurabi 2, ANET 166). It is difficult to believe that the numerous references to the work of sorcerers did not rest on their existence, and we may safely assume that this class of magicians operated very secretly for hire in behalf of those who wished to do evil to their enemies. The literature all comes from the magicians of the temple priesthood, who were called to relieve the victim of his spell. The magician-priests were a recognized class in the temple hierarchy; the magician himself was called *ašipu,* and

he was assisted by other priests designated *mašmašu* (?) and *kalu* (chanter). The extremely complex ritual of magic was practiced according to the tablets; it is not possible from these tablets to reconstruct any actual rite, but the elements of the ritual are clear. The tablets are classified according to the names of the demons against which they are directed (*utukku; lamaštu*), or according to the characteristic feature of the rite described (*šurpu*, "burning"; *maklu*, "combustion"; "lifting of the hand"). The ritual was based upon the magical value of certain material objects, colors, sounds, forms and figures. Fire and water, the elements of purification, were particularly effective. The rite of transfer was accomplished by the use of figurines which represented the object or the person, such as the sorcerer, against whom the magical operation was directed (sympathetic magic). The value of these and of magical gestures rests on the magical principle that likeness means identity; that which is done by symbolism actually reaches the thing which is symbolized. These, however, received their power from the incantation, which was the essence of the rite. The incantation usually began with a hymn* in invocation of the gods; it was here that the Mesopotamian peoples merged magic and religion. The gods most frequently invoked were Ea, the god of water, Marduk, and the gods of fire Gibil and Nusku. The magician recited his qualifications. The demons who attacked the patient must be described and addressed by name. The sorcerer must also be addressed; the sorcerer was unknown, but could be reached through the symbolic figurine. The patient must be purified of impurity which made him liable to the attack of the demons. This rite included a long list of questions which were an examination of conscience, except that deliberate and indeliberate faults were not distinguished; whether the patient actually admitted to any such fault is not certain, since the purpose of the ritual would be served by denial. Whether by denial or by repudiation, the impurity was removed. The rite sometimes included the recitation of a myth which exhibited the power of the god invoked or the defeat of the demon to be exorcised or which justified the rite employed. In addition to curative magic, preventive magic was widely practiced by the wearing of amulets*, the carrying of figurines or their erection in the house, devices engraved on cylinder seals, and inscriptions. While medicine was practiced in Mesopotamia in a primitive way, there seems no doubt that illnesses whose symptoms were not obvious and which could not be healed by the simples in use were taken to the magician. Many of the magical formulae of Mesopotamia passed into Europe and have survived even in modern times; indeed Mesopotamia seems to be the single most important source of magical practices in the western world.

2. *Egypt.* The ancient Egyptians were scarcely less devoted to magic than the Mesopotamian peoples. Evils could come from black magic, the dead, demons, or gods. The only allusion to legal coercion of black magic in Egypt occurs in the process of the conspiracy against Ramses III (about 1164 BC), in which two of the accused were charged with fabricating a scroll against the king. Egyptians expressly believed that the gods were subject to magical practices; the Mesopotamian people did not express this belief. Examples of Egyptian magical practice and formulae can be found in ANET 29–30 (the exorcism of the princess of Bekhten) and 326, 328 (incantations). Sympathetic magic was practiced in Egypt, not only by figurines but also by the use of tablets on which the name of the enemy was inscribed; the king before going to war had this magic practiced on tablets which listed his enemies. Preventive magic was employed by the use of amulets. The Egyptian magicians were not exclusively members of the priestly class, but included learned laymen. The incantation, accompanied by gestures and action, was the central rite. As in Mesopotamia, the incantation included an invocation of the gods and allusions to mythology. The magician not only accredited himself but actually identified himself with the gods in whose name he spoke. The demon or enemy was addressed by name; the Egyptians treated knowledge of the name* as the essential factor in magical control. Some invocations were no more than a hymn to the gods or the recital of a myth.

The purposes of Egyptian magic were perhaps wider than the purposes of magic in Mesopotamia. It was practiced not only for prevention and for the cure of illness and the bite of animals and reptiles, but also for more positive purposes. The number of magical formulae which were intended to arouse or restore sexual potency or to secure the affections of one's desired is very large. This was sought not only by the use of love philtres and the recitation of formulae and sympathetic magic calculated to excite the desire of the beloved, but also by magic directed against the rival for the affections of the beloved.

3. *Bible.* Prohibitions of magic appear in three of the Hb codes of law* (Ex 22:17; Lv 19:31; 20:27; Dt 18:10); the death penalty for witchcraft is explicit in Ex 22:17. That these prohibitions were not idle is evident not only from the background sketched

above, but also from numerous allusions to the practice of magic in Israel (2 K 21:6; 23, 24, abolition of magic by Josiah*; 2 K 9:22, sorceries of Jezebel*; 2 K 17:17; 2 Ch 33:6; Is 3:3; 57:3; Je 27:9; Ezk 13:18 f; Mi 5:11; Mal 3:5). The nature of these practices is not indicated except in Ezk 13:18 f, and the allusion here is obscure; it seems to refer to the use of bands and knots, which are extremely common in magical rites. Moses and Aaron surpassed the feats of the magicians of Egypt (Ex 7:10–13, 19–23; 8:1–7, 17 f; 9:8–12). Na 3:4 calls Assyria a witch. The magic of Babylon is alluded to in Is 47:12. These allusions to foreign magic are always contemptuous; magic is ineffectual. In the NT also allusions to magic are not infrequent both among Jews (AA 13:6–11, Bar Jesus or Elymas*; 19:13–17) and Gentiles (cf SIMON MAGUS). Converts at Ephesus brought magical books to be burned (AA 19:18 f). Paul had to warn converts against magic (Gal 5:20). Magic and sorcery are practiced by the great harlot (Apc 18:23) and are included in the list of heinous vices (Apc 9:21; 21:8; 22:15).

The Bible nowhere simply asserts that magic is fraudulent, and many Bible readers have thought it implicitly affirms the existence of magical powers. But the Bible makes no speculative general assertion about magic. In the patterns of its times such an assertion was scarcely possible. The Bible does not indeed expressly deny that magic is effective; it does repudiate the practice every time the subject is mentioned, and affirms that magic is helpless against the power of Yahweh. This is the point of the stories of Ex 7–9, which are extremely popular in character; the magicians are unable to frustrate the will of Yahweh and even to imitate His displays of power. The attitude of the Bible toward magic is something like its attitude in early books toward other gods; it does not take the trouble to deny their existence, but affirms that for those who believe in Yahweh other gods are meaningless.

Magnificat. The name popularly given to the song of Mary in Lk 1:46–55. The song borrows extensively in theme, tone, and phrase from the song of Hannah* (1 S 2:1–10), with which it should be compared; cf 1 S 2:1, 4, 5, 7, 8. Like the song of Hannah, it expresses the themes of the favor of God to the poor* and His judgment of the rich and of His favor to Israel, who is identified with the poor. In form and style it is an individual thanksgiving psalm*. It is scarcely possible that the Magnificat is intended to be a literal report of the words of Mary; it is a song put in her mouth as apt to the situation, despite the fact that it makes no concrete reference to this situation and does not refer to the Messiah. Its position in the present context is to be attributed to the source on which Luke* drew for the infancy narratives. One cannot be certain that it was composed for this position by the author; the hypothesis seems more probable that it was an existing hymn which the author applied to this passage. The song was possibly a Jewish psalm adopted by the early Christian community. Israel is the speaker in the song; the early Christian Church identified itself as the new Israel.

Magog (Hb *māgôg*), the land of Gog* (Ezk 38:2; 39:6) with Meshech* and Tubal*; in the table* of nations a son of Japheth* (Gn 10:2; 1 Ch 1:5). The association of Magog with Meshech and Tubal would lead one to seek Magog on the S coast of the Black Sea. Many modern critics, however, suggest that Magog is a gloss introduced into the text of Ezk because of the assonance of the names Gog and Magog. In Apc 20:8 Magog becomes with Gog a personal name.

Mahanaim (Hb *maḥᵃnayyim*, from *maḥᵃneh*, "camp"), a local name; a town in E Palestine. The name is explained by a popular etymology as derived from a vision of Jacob* at the site (Gn 32:3). It is listed among the Palestinian towns conquered by Shishak* of Egypt (935–914 BC). The city lay on the boundary of Gad and Manasseh (Jos 13:26, 30) and was a priestly city of the territory of Gad (Jos 21:36; 1 Ch 6:65). Mahanaim was the royal residence of Ishbaal* (2 S 8:12, 29). It was at Mahanaim that David paused in his flight from Absalom* to organize resistance (2 S 17:24, 27). It was the headquarters of one of Solomon's administrative districts (1 K 4:14). The location of Mahanaim is uncertain; the sites suggested all lie near the junction of the Jabbok* and the Jordan*.

Mahaneh-dan (Hb *maḥᵃnēh-dān*, "camp of Dan"), a town in the Shephelah* near Zorah* in the S territory of Dan (Jgs 13:25; 18:12). The name is explained in Jgs 18:12 on the basis of the story of the migration of Dan; more probably it reflects the early period before the tribe of Dan had settled (Abel).

Maher-shalal-hash-baz (Hb *mahēr-šālāl-ḥāš-baz*, "speeds the spoil, hurries the prey"); a symbolic name given by Isaiah to his son during the reign of Ahaz*. The name of the child is a prophetic threat that Israel* and Damascus*, which threatened to attack

Judah, would themselves quickly be despoiled by the Assyrians (Is 8:1-4).

Malachi (Hb *mal'ākî*, "my messenger"), the last of the minor prophets*.

1. *Contents:*
1:1, title; 1:2-5, the election of Israel and the rejection of Edom*; 1:6-2:9, failure of the priests to observe the ritual of sacrifice and the duty of giving instruction, with a prediction of worldwide worship of Yahweh (1:11); 2:10-16, against marriages of foreign wives and divorce; 2:17-3:5, the approach of the day* of Yahweh; purification of the priests; judgment against various crimes; 3:6-12, refusal of the Jews to pay tithes to the temple; 3:13-21, the unbelief of those who see the prosperity of sinners; the salvation of the righteous and the judgment of the wicked in the day of Yahweh; 3:22, exhortation to observe the law of Moses; 3:23-24, the coming of Elijah to reconcile families before the day of Yahweh.

2. *Author and Date.* The book is anonymous. The title has taken the name Malachi from the word "my messenger" in 3:1 and identified the messenger with the prophet, who is anonymous. The LXX converted the Hb word into a proper name *malachias* on the analogy of such names as Elijah, Isaiah, etc. The book is dated by critics after the rebuilding of the temple in 516 BC (1:10; 3:1, 8), during the Persian period (the word *pehāh*, governor, in 1:8) and before the reforms of Nehemiah and Ezra, i.e., before 432 BC. A distinctive feature of the style of the book is its employment of the dialogue (1:7, 12; 2:14, 17; 3:7-8, 13).

3. *Integrity and Structure.* Mal is composed of six addresses and an epilogue or appendix (3:22-24). Sellin followed by Weiser suggested that the redactor has not grouped the addresses according to their original arrangement and proposes the following rearrangement: (1) Preaching of repentance: 1:2-5; 3:6-12; 2:10-16. (2) Against the priests: 1:6-2:9. (3) Against doubters: 2:17-35; 3:18-21. The unity of the book is not questioned by any scholar except for a few verses. Some believe that 2:11-13 is an addition to include the marriage of foreign wives (cf EZRA; NEHEMIAH) with the speech against divorce. Most scholars believe that the appendix (3:22-24) is a later addition. Mal actually knows nothing of the law in the course of the book; and Elijah is identified with the messenger of the covenant of 3:1. On the coming of Elijah cf ELIJAH.

4. *Theology.* Mal lays the troubles of the postexilic community to its failure to observe properly the ritual of cult; in particular he blames the priests. The idea of the priestly instruction is put in 2:7 in as noble a form as it appears in the OT. His invective against divorce* runs counter to what seems to have been the common Hb practice and raises a new and better ideal of marriage. His view of the day of Yahweh is conventional and adds nothing to earlier conceptions. He sees Israel as the chosen people. Election does not relieve them of their responsibilities; nevertheless, his view of election is not the same as that which appears in Am 9:7. The antithesis between Israel and Edom and their ancestors, Jacob and Esau, probably reflects the hostility between the two peoples which arose when Edom seized the territory of S Judah after 587 BC. His utterances against other vices are conventional (3:5) and do not show the feeling which he exhibits when he speaks of the cult. Like Jeremiah and Job he deals with the doubts caused by the prosperity of the wicked; his answer is the answer of the sages, that judgment will overtake the wicked.

His vision of a worldwide sacrificial worship of Yahweh (1:11) is one of the high points of the messianism and universalism of the OT; the nations will not only recognize the divinity of Yahweh but will offer acceptable sacrifice. Christian theology has long seen in this verse a prediction of the Eucharist*, arguing in particular from the word *minhāh*, which designates an offering of meal in the priestly ritual. Much more frequently, however, the word designates a gift or an offering in general; the technical use of the term is restricted to P. The prophet speaks of a universal sacrificial worship; he does not specify the sacrifice which is to be offered.

Malchus (Gk *malchos* from *maliku*, "king" [i.e., god]), a personal name; the name of the slave of the high priest whose ear Peter* cut off (Jn 18:10). The name is common in inscriptions, most frequent in Nabataean*. It is not unlikely that the slave of the high priest was a Nabataean.

Malta. Cf MELITA.

Mammon (Gk *mamōnas*, from Aramaic *mamôna'*, the definite state of the noun *māmôn*). The word occurs in the NT only in Mt 6:24; Lk 16:9, 11, 13, and not at all in the OT. It is found frequently in the targums* and the Talmud* and once in the Damascus document (cf QUMRAN). In these documents it has the meaning of property, not only money but any possession. In the rabbinical writings, as in the NT, it is sometimes used in a pejorative sense. The saying of Mt 6:24 from the sermon on the mount is attached by Luke to the parable of the dishonest steward. In the saying *mammon* is personified almost in the manner of a god. The phrase "unjust *mammon*," "dishonest gain" (Lk 16:9, 11) is paralleled in the rabbinical writings.

Mamre (Hb *mamrē'*, meaning and etymology uncertain); a place near Hebron* connected with the patriarchs Abraham, Isaac, and Jacob. Mamre was distinguished by an oak (Gn 13:18; 18:1); it was probably a sanctuary, but the patriarchal narratives do not reflect this. It is said to be "opposite Machpelah*" (Gn 23:17, 19; 25:9; 49:30; 50:13). Isaac also resided at Mamre (Gn 35:27). An ancient oak is shown at the Russian convent near Hebron as the oak of Mamre; this cannot be correct, and the site is doubtful. Mamre is also possibly to be located at Ramet-el-Khalil about 2 mi N of Hebron; the excavations of Mader disclosed the foundations of a Herodian structure at the spot which attests the identification of this site with Mamre during NT times. Ramet-el-Khalil, however, cannot be considered "opposite" the mosque of Hebron, where the cave of Machpelah is claimed to be. The identification remains uncertain.

Mamre also appears as a personal name in Gn 14:13, 24. In all probability this person has been created by folklore out of the topographical name.

Man. 1. *OT*. The OT does not conceive man as a species in the sense of a logical abstraction, but as a concretely existing group. The word which designates man in this concrete sense is *'ādām*. The popular etymology implicit in Gn 2:7 derives this name from *'ªdāmāh*, soil or clay, and this popular etymology is important in ascertaining the biblical conception of man (cf below); the two words, however, are more probably to be connected with a single root, *'DM*, "red" or "ruddy," the color both of the Caucasian complexion and of the clay soil of much of Palestine.

It is basic to the OT conception of man that he is a creature (Gn 1:26 f; Gn 2:7 ff; cf CREATION). From creation follows "an unconditioned obligation imposed by the divine will" (Eichrodt). Man is clay which lives by the breath of God (Gn 2:7). His life* is not his own and he must yield it when God recalls the breath of life. Under God, however, man is supreme in the universe and may employ it to his purposes (Gn 1:26).

The OT does not contain a consistent psychology; it speaks of various "elements" of which the human being is compounded

without reducing these elements to any system. The basic element is the soul*; the word "soul" is not an accurate translation of the Hb *nepeš*, but it is consecrated in English versions of the Bible. The soul is a psychophysiological totality which at times signifies the entire psychic reality of man, at times a kind of psychic principle, at times "self" or consciousness; the OT does not distinguish these various concepts. The soul is rather that which lives than that by which man lives. The soul and the flesh* are not contrasted as two principles which are compounded into a single reality. Scholars point out that the Hebrews conceived man as an animated body, the Greeks conceived him as an incarnated spirit. The flesh, however, signifies man's mortality and weakness rather than his power; it is the clay which returns to its proper nature when the breath of life is withdrawn. Consciousness is diffused through the flesh rather than seated in any particular organ. Indeed all the organs of the body in Hb speech are hypostatized and endowed with psychic attributes; this does not signify that the OT regards man as an association of independent psychic principles, but that it is aware of the externalization of consciousness through the operations of the organs of the body. Man has from God a spirit*; this concept is somewhat fluid, but it is not the soul nor does it seem to be a part of the human compound. It is rather a principle of power, of activity, which is infused by God; it is conceived either as a temporary infusion or occasionally as a permanent infusion. If any single organ is to be conceived as the seat of consciousness it is the heart*, which is most frequently mentioned as the agent of thought and decision.

Man is made in the image* and likeness of God (Gn 1:26 f), which raises him above the level of the beasts. He is created bisexual (Gn 1:27; 2:20 ff; cf WOMAN). From this difference arises the fundamental form of society, marriage* and the family*. Man is a social being; without the security of family, tribal, or political society he cannot even survive, much less attain the degree of happiness and fulfillment which he ought to expect. The relations of individual and society in the OT are different from our own conception of these relations and are not easily and simply stated. The individual man is a responsible agent within society and receives individual goods from the society; yet in OT society the individual person could not reach that form of independence and self-assertion which has so long been the ideal of modern society. Man's dependence on society demanded a total integration with the social group and an acceptance of its ideals, its ambitions, and its means of achieving them.

Man is mortal, and man is sinful; in the OT these two limitations go together (Gn 3; cf SIN). These more than anything else distinguish him from the Creator. While the story of the Fall* is rarely alluded to in the OT, the belief that man is hopelessly subject to his own defective will is a commonplace, and he depends on the mercy of God not to be compelled to bear the full effects of his waywardness. But he cannot evade his mortality (cf DEATH). It is remarkable that the OT so rarely expresses the despondency which the finality of death should elicit. It was, it seems, the Hb belief in the active interest of God in human life and affairs which created some degree of optimism in the face of man's mortality and sinfulness.

2. *NT*. The NT, which does not contain literature parallel to the historical, legal, and wisdom literature of the OT, contains even less of a system of thought on man; it views man purely in his encounter with God, and its ideas on man are gathered from what is implicit. The conceptions of the creation of man, of flesh, soul, heart, and spirit appear in the NT with their own developments. Paul adds to the OT conceptions a distinctive conception of the body as the organized totality of man. The NT is even more explicit than the OT on the reign of sin* in man and on mortality as a consequence of sin. If anything, it heightens the conception of man's responsibility and the importance of the decisive choice which man must make. It is more aware of the width and depth of the corruption of mankind (e.g., Rm 1:18–32). It emphasizes the principle of concupiscence within man (cf FLESH).

But the NT adds particularly the concept of the "new man" who receives a new life* by his incorporation in Christ. The "old man" is the slave of sin (Rm 6:6); this old man must be put off (Eph 4:22; Col 3:9) so that the new man may be put on. The new man is created through the death of Christ (Eph 2:15), and it is the new man who is created in the likeness of God, as man was originally created in God's likeness (Gn 1:26 f; Eph 4:24; Col 3:10; cf IMAGE). The new man living by the new life is "the inner man," while "the outer man" is the psychophysiological totality which is subject to mortality (2 Co 4:16).

Man is also used by Paul in a pejorative sense. "According to man" is opposed to "the revelation of Jesus Christ" (Gal 1:11–12), to spiritual man (1 Co 3:3), to faith (1 Co 15:32). Man is of himself unable to think, speak, or achieve any of the things that are wrought by God in Christ; he re-

mains man and therefore hopelessly sinful and mortal.

Manaen (Gk *manaēn*, Grecized form of Hb Menahem*), a personal name; one of the leaders of the church of Antioch (AA 13:1), a *syntrophos* of Herod* (Antipas) the tetrarch. *Syntrophos* means literally "foster-brother," "nursed together," but is also used in the sense of reared or educated together, and finally comes to be an honorific title of the "companions" of a king. It is probably in this latter sense that the word is used here; it is paralleled in inscriptions.

Manasseh (Hb *mᵉnaššeh*, meaning and etymology uncertain; the etymology of Gn 41:51 is popular). 1. The name of the eldest son of Joseph*, brother of Ephraim* and eponymous ancestor of one of the 12 tribes of Israel. He was born to Joseph in Egypt (Gn 41:51; 46:20) and was adopted by Jacob* as his son with his brother Ephraim (Gn 48). In the adoption Manasseh, the firstborn, was placed after Ephraim; this must reflect the later position of the tribes and the preeminence of Ephraim. The adoption itself most probably is an explanation of tribal relations too complex for recovery from the existing sources; cf EPHRAIM; ISRAEL; JACOB; JOSEPH. Manasseh is given 32,200 fighting men in the census of Nm 1:34 f, and 52,700 fighting men in the census of Nm 26:29–34. The clans of Manasseh are listed in Nm 26:29–34; 1 Ch 7:14–29. Manasseh does not appear in the blessing of Jacob (Gn 49), but is mentioned with Ephraim in the blessing of Moses (Dt 33:17) as one of the elements of "the house of Joseph."

There is a steady tradition that Manasseh dwelt both E and W of the Jordan. Its territory in the E is the former kingdom of Bashan* and the N half of Gilead* (Dt 3:13–14; Jos 13:29–31; 17:1–6). At least N Gilead, however, is identified with Machir*, which is treated as a clan of Manasseh; the relations of Manasseh and Machir are not entirely clear. This E territory was based upon an apportionment of Moses (Nm 32:33, 39 f; 34:14; Dt 3:13–14; Jos 1:12; 12:6; 18:7). Here as for other tribes the claim to an apportionment from Moses antecedent to the traditional division of the land under Joshua suggests the occupation of these territories before the entrance of Israel into Palestine. This is difficult to accept for Manasseh, who with Ephraim, "the house of Joseph," must be included in any conception of the group which migrated as Israel from Egypt to Canaan. The claim of Manasseh was possibly extended because of the migration of part of the tribe from

W to E Palestine, possibly also because the clan of Machir, adopted into Manasseh, was in occupation of its territory before the entrance of Israel. Manasseh seems intruded in Nm 32:33, 39–40; it is not mentioned with Gad and Reuben in the preceding verses. It is included with these two tribes in the story of the dispute about the altar (Jos 22). The territory of Manasseh in W Palestine lay N of Ephraim and included the confederation city of Shechem* (Jos 17:7–13); the Canaanite cities in its territory (Jgs 1:27) are all in W Palestine. Gideon*, who summoned Manasseh to war, lived in W Palestine (Jgs 6:15, 35; 7:23). There seems to have been some uncertainty in the boundary between Ephraim and Manasseh; Ephraim resided in the territory of Manasseh (Jos 16:9; 17:7–13). The Canaanite towns in the territory of Manasseh (Jgs 1:27) have become towns of Ephraim in 1 Ch 7:29. Whether this expansion came through Ephraimite aggression or through compact is not related.

Ephraim and Manasseh designate the N kingdom in Is 9:20, and Manasseh is associated with Gilead of E Palestine in Pss 60:9; 108:9. In Ch, which does not refer to the N kingdom, Ephraim and Manasseh also designate the territory of the N kingdom (2 Ch 15:9; 30:1, 18; 31:1). 1 Ch preserves a tradition of the conquest of Manasseh by the Assyrians in 734 BC which is not found elsewhere and mentions the cities of Mesopotamia to which the tribe was transported.

2. A king of Judah (687–642 BC), son and successor of Hezekiah* (2 K 20:21; 2 Ch 32:33). The record of Manasseh (2 K 21:1–17) is the blackest of all the kings of Judah; he is credited with the worship of foreign gods, superstition of all kinds, oppression and murder, and he becomes the occasion of the decision of Yahweh to destroy Judah. 2 Ch parallels these charges in 33: 1–10, but adds data of its own in 33: 11–20. This passage relates that Manasseh was taken captive to Assyria; there he experienced a change of heart, and after his release put away the idolatry and superstition of his early years. This can scarcely be regarded as historical; allusions to the consummate wickedness of Manasseh as a motive for Yahweh's destruction of Judah are too numerous elsewhere to permit one to accept these data as historical (2 K 23:26; 24:3; Je 15:4). The Prayer of Manasses (cf APOCRYPHAL BOOKS) is a fictitious composition written on the basis of 2 Ch. This is an instance of the theologizing of tradition by Ch; Manasseh, in spite of his well known wickedness, enjoyed a long peaceful reign and died a natural death; such rewards are the fruit of repentance. The

information concerning his fortification of Jerusalem (2 Ch 33:14) is a much more authentic piece of tradition.

The religious policy of Manasseh, admitting the possibility of some exaggeration in the traditions concerning him, was doubtless based on the fact that the peace of his reign was earned by his docility as a vassal of Assyria. The campaigns of Sennacherib* had reduced Judah to a state of submission. Manasseh, it appears, wished to assimilate Judah religiously and culturally to Assyria, and suppressed violently the resistance which he met from loyal worshipers of Yahweh. He is mentioned as a vassal by the Assyrian kings Esarhaddon (680–669 BC) and Ashurbanipal (668–630 BC; ANET 291, 294). The story of 2 Ch of his captivity in Babylon possibly grew out of a journey to Mesopotamia which is suggested by the account of Esarhaddon.

Mandrake (*Mandragora officinarum*), a plant which grows abundantly in Syria and S Europe. It has a large root shaped like a human body, yellow leaves, and a bright red small fruit shaped like a tomato which is soft and pulpy. It has long been and still is esteemed in the E as an aphrodisiac, and it appears as such in Gn 30:14–16; SS 7:14. The Hb word, *dûdā'îm*, is derived from a root meaning love. It is of interest that the tomato, which resembles the fruit of the mandrake, was formerly called the love-apple in the U.S.A.

Manger. The Gk *phatnē* is used to designate the place in which Mary laid the infant Jesus after He was born (Lk 2:7, 12, 16 and once in Lk 13:15). In classical Gk the word always means manger. The LXX, however, uses it to translate three rare words which mean stall, fodder, and enclosure for cattle. It seems most probable that the LXX did not understand these words and used the more common *phatnē*, which does no violence to the context. Some scholars, however, have suggested that *phatnē* in Lk 2 means stall, not manger; in this view Mary and Joseph actually were lodged in the inn* (Gk *katalyma*), but laid the child in a stall because the inn was crowded. They believe that it is much more credible to suppose that Mary and Joseph lodged in the inn than in a cave in the hillside. The frequent use of the caves as shelter and even as dwellings throughout Palestinian history does not render this view any more credible. It is true, however, that no cave is mentioned in Lk, and there seems to be no reason for mentioning the *katalyma* except that Mary and Joseph were lodged there, but had to place the infant either in a stall or in a manger. The tradition that Jesus was born in a cave is attested in the 2nd century AD; but it is impossible to trace a continuous living tradition from the birth of Jesus.

Manna (Hb *man*), a food which the Israelites ate during their sojourn in the desert between Egypt and Canaan. It is described in Ex 16:12–35, a narrative compiled from several sources (cf PENTATEUCH), as falling on the ground like frost, white and sweet. It would keep overnight except over the Sabbath; it did not fall on the Sabbath. It melted when the heat of the morning sun reached it. According to Nm 11:7–8, it could be ground or pounded like meal, boiled and made into cakes. It continued to fall until the Israelites reached the border of Canaan (Ex 16:38), specified in Jos 5:12 as Gilgal*. A vessel of manna was to be preserved in the ark* of the covenant (Ex 16:33); but this vessel is not mentioned in 1 K 8:9, and probably never existed. The Israelites professed weariness with the manna (Nm 11:6) and it is elsewhere represented as a principal article of diet (Dt 8:3, 16). It appears in all the traditions of the Pnt, early as well as late. It seems most probable that popular tradition has amplified an original datum and enveloped it in some marvelous features. The original datum appears to be a sweet resinous substance which is exuded from a desert tree known as the *tamarix mannifera* as well as by two or three desert shrubs. The tree exudes the substance when it is punctured by the insect *Gossyparia mannipara*. It is edible, but it appears only in small quantities and has none of the other properties attributed to manna. The memory of this food, found and eaten occasionally in the desert, was expanded in tradition to become the regular diet of all Israel, treated much as grain, and not available on the Sabbath. In Ps 78:24 f the manna is called "the grain of heaven" and "the bread of the mighty."

The manna appears in the discourse of Jn 6 on the Eucharist. The Jews, alluding to manna, "the bread from heaven," ask Jesus what sign He, the new Moses, will give them comparable to the manna (6:30 f). Jesus responds that the manna was not the genuine bread of heaven, for those who ate it died. The genuine bread from heaven is the bread of life* which preserves from death. Jesus Himself is this bread, indeed His flesh is this bread (6:32–34, 49–51). The tradition of the jar of manna is referred to in Heb 9:4. This also is the manna "hidden" in the tabernacle which is promised to him who conquers (Apc 2:17).

Mantle. Cf CLOTHING.

Maon (Hb *mā'ôn,* meaning uncertain), a town in the hill country of Judah; it is identified with the modern Tell Main S of Hebron*. It is mentioned among the cities of Judah (Jos 15:55) and was the residence of Nabal*, whose widow Abigail* married David (1 S 25:2). It gives its name to "the desert of Maon" (1 S 23:24 f and to be read instead of Paran in 1 S 25:1), a not infertile plateau where David* fled from Saul*.

Marah (Hb *mārāh,* "bitter"), a place mentioned in the narratives of the desert sojourn of Israel (Ex 15:23–26). The name is explained as an allusion to the brackish water of the spring of Marah. The episode is conflated by the redactor with the story of Massah*, "temptation," in 15:25, and with Sinai* and Kadesh* in the reference to the "statute and ordinance" delivered at Marah. This statute and ordinance is contained in 15:26, which is a summary and somewhat inadequate formulation of the covenant*. The name possibly contains a play on the word *mārāh,* to be rebellious.

Maranatha. An Aramaic phrase occurring in 1 Co 16:22. It may be turned back into Aramaic either as *māran'ªtā,* "Our Lord has come," or as *māranā' tā,* "Come, our Lord." The occurrence of the phrase, "Come, Lord Jesus" in Apc 22:20, which is, except for the personal name, a translation of *māranā' tā',* makes this meaning of the phrase somewhat more probable. Paul* could not have placed an Aramaic invocation in a letter to the church at Corinth* unless it were already known to them, and they could hardly have known it unless it were a well known liturgical invocation. Its origin must lie in the Palestinian communities, whence it passed into the Hellenistic churches. It is thus an attestation to the extremely early use of the title Lord* given to Jesus. The invocation must have had its place in the celebration of the Eucharist*. The "coming" for which it prays may be either the eschatological coming (cf PAROUSIA) or the coming in the celebration of the Eucharist. More probably the two comings should not be too sharply distinguished. The Eucharist was a messianic banquet and was a perpetual symbol and assurance of the Parousia (1 Co 11:26). The use of the Aramaic phrase in the liturgy is parallel to the use of the Hb words *Amen, Alleluia,* and *Hosanna* and the Gk words *Kyrie eleison* in the modern Roman liturgy.

Marduk. The god of Babylon*. Marduk was as obscure as the city of which he was the patron until Hammurabi* established Babylon as the center of an empire and made it permanently the cultural heart of Mesopotamia. Marduk then became the head of the pantheon and was given the titles and attributes of other gods. The epic of creation* was rewritten so that Marduk, by concession of the other gods, wins the headship of the pantheon by his victory over the monster Tiamat and his work of creation. As the son of Ea of Eridu Marduk, like his father, was a patron of the arts of magic* and is frequently invoked in incantations. What the character of Marduk may have been before his glorification in the First Babylonian empire is obscure. He does not exhibit the features of a nature deity; some scholars suspect, however, that he may have been a solar deity before he became identified with the genius of Babylon. His temple was called Esagil, "the house of the uplifted head," and the great *ziggurat,* probably the original of the story of the Tower of Babel*, was called Etemenanki, "the house of the foundation of heaven and earth." Marduk is mentioned in the Bible only once by name (Je 50:2), but he is the god signified by the title Bel*. Marduk also appears in the names Merodach-baladan* and Mordecai*.

Mareshah (Hb *mārē'šāh* or *mārēšāh,* etymology uncertain), a town of Judah (Jos 15:44; 1 Ch 4:21; Mi 1:15). It was among the towns fortified by Rehoboam* (2 Ch 11:8) and was the scene of the defeat of Zerah* the Ethiopian (2 Ch 14:9 f). It was the home of the prophet Eliezer* (2 Ch 20:37). In the Maccabean wars it was held by the Seleucid forces (2 Mc 12:35). It became Idumaean after 587 BC, and is mentioned in a document of the 3rd century BC as an Idumaean slave market. It was conquered from the Idumaeans by John Hyrcanus (134–104 BC; cf HASMONEAN). It was taken by Pompey in 63 BC and was destroyed by the Parthians in 40 BC, after which it was uninhabited. The town was removed to Eleutheropolis, the modern Beit Jibrin, about 2 mi N.

The site is identified with the modern Tell Sandahannah, which was excavated by Bliss and Macalister in 1900. The excavation penetrated to the 8th century BC level of occupation. It was most successful in uncovering a large section of the street plan of the Hellenistic city, with a broad avenue and narrower streets running nearly at right angles dividing the houses into blocks. One building was a palace with a large court, adjacent to the marketplace, and at the E end of the town was a large enclosure which probably was a part of the temple complex. The city was fortified with a strong wall.

Mari. An ancient city on the middle Euphrates at the modern Tell el Hariri, near Abu Kemal. Mari is not mentioned in the Bible. The site was excavated 1933–1939 under the direction of A. Parrot. Excavations were resumed in 1951; but the first six campaigns demonstrated the importance of the site. The excavators uncovered the remains of the royal palace, one of the largest known from the ancient world, covering about 15 acres. The tell itself was an oval over ½ mi long and about ½ mi wide. There were also discovered numerous examples of ancient art of an original type. Historically the most valuable discovery consisted in the 20,000 tablets of the royal archives, containing royal correspondence and juridical, economic, and religious texts which permit an extensive reconstruction of the life and society of Mari. The tablets have made possible a more accurate chronology of the early 2nd millennium BC, illustrated the ethnological background of the period of the biblical patriarchs, and contributed a surprising number of parallels to Israelite law and custom. Mari was occupied at least at the beginning of the 3rd millennium BC. Its position between the Mediterranean and Mesopotamia made it a natural site for a commercial center, and its history exhibits the struggle between various powers for its possession. It was conquered by Hammurabi*; but when it rebelled he destroyed the city and it was abandoned.

Mark. Cf MARK, GOSPEL OF.

Mark, Gospel of. 1. *Authorship.* Early Christian tradition uniformly attributes the 2nd Gospel to Mark, and there is no reason to doubt that this is the John Mark mentioned several times in the NT. He was the son of Mary*, who resided in Jerusalem (AA 12:12) and a cousin of Barnabas* (Col 4:10). When Barnabas and Paul* left Jerusalem after the persecution of Herod Agrippa, Mark accompanied them (AA 12:25) and went with them to Cyprus on their first missionary journey (AA 13:5). For reasons not given he left them at Perga* in Pamphylia and returned to Jerusalem (AA 13:13). Evidently this destroyed Paul's confidence in him, because Paul would not take him with them on the second journey (AA 15:37). This was the occasion of the separation of Paul and Barnabas, and Mark accompanied Barnabas to Cyprus (AA 15:37). Mark must have restored himself to the good graces of Paul, who calls him a fellow worker (Phm 24), and he appears with Paul in Rome (Col 4:10). An association with Paul is testified in 2 Tm 4:11. The only association of Mark* and

Peter in the NT appears in 1 Pt 5:13. It is not certain that Mark is the young man who attempted to follow the arrest of Jesus (Mk 14:51 f). The tradition that Mark was bishop of Alexandria is not well founded.

The earliest tradition for Mark as the author is found in Eusebius, who quotes Papias, bishop of Hierapolis about AD 130. Papias in turn quotes John* the Elder (probably not John the Apostle), who said that Mark was the interpreter of Peter and wrote carefully, but not in order, all that he remembered, both words and deeds of the Lord. Papias adds that Mark had not himself heard the Lord*, but knew Him only from Peter's account. Peter had arranged his instructions according to the needs of the audience and made no attempt to set the words of the Lord in order. Papias therefore defends Mark against the charge, which some must have made, that he wrote the words of the Lord in a disorderly manner; Mark wrote only what he remembered, taking care neither to omit nor falsify.

Although it is impossible to verify the information either of Papias or of his source, John the Elder, most modern critics find his account so much in harmony with the internal evidence of the Gospel itself that they accept it, and the skepticism of earlier critics has been abandoned. "Interpreter" is taken to mean translator; Peter, it is thought, did not know Gk well enough to teach in that language. "Not in order" may refer merely to chronological order; it may also mean, as many scholars think, that Papias denies any schematism. If he does, he said too much, although the plan of Mk is not so clear that it admits no dispute; cf below. But Mark wrote "carefully," "exactly."

Mk is not cited explicitly in any writer earlier than 140; but probable allusions and implicit citations are found in Clement of Rome, Polycarp, the Epistle of Barnabas, and the Shepherd of Hermas. The Gospel is placed 2nd in the canon by all early sources (The Canon of Muratori, Origen, Irenaeus); some later writers who list him 3rd do this on the principle that the Gospels which contain genealogies should come first. It is not certain that Justin means Mk by a work which he calls the Memoirs of Peter, but it is extremely probable. The Gospel is clearly attributed to Mark, the disciple and interpreter of Peter, by Irenaeus, Tertullian, and Clement of Alexandria, and no question is ever raised.

2. *Date.* The date is not so well established. Irenaeus affirms that Mk was written after the death of Peter and Paul; Clement of Alexandria has a story that Mk was written at the request of Roman Christians while Peter was still living. Neither tradition can be tested. Modern critics are generally agreed that Mk was written in the decade 60–70; efforts to show an earlier or a later date have not been successful. The question turns principally on the "apocalypse" of Mk 13; some critics think that it reflects the destruction of Jerusalem in 70. Most contemporary scholars believe that the event would leave much more distinct and numerous traces if it had occurred before Mk 13 was written.

3. *Place and Destination.* Tradition is uniform that Mk was written in Rome for Gentile Christians. This tradition is supported, at least for the destination of the Gospel, by some characteristics. A number of Aramaic phrases are explained, obviously for those who do not know the language, and the number of such explanations is greater than in any other Gospel (2:26; 3:17; 5:41; 7:11, 34; 14:36; 15:22, 34, 42). Lt words, also more numerous than in any other NT book, do not of themselves suggest a Roman audience, for Gk was spoken at Rome more than Lt; the terms, however, refer to military and judicial processes and to money, where Lt was no doubt the language used even where Gk was spoken. A Gentile audience is also suggested by the rarity of citations from the OT and by less emphasis on the controversies of Jesus with the Scribes and Pharisees compared to the other Gospels.

4. *Sources.* The tradition that Mark was a disciple and interpreter of Peter is less questioned by contemporary critics; but it is scarcely possible, as V. Taylor has remarked, to think of Mark as simply following Peter with notebook in hand. While the teaching of Peter is a source of Mk, it is only one of the sources. In fact, it is difficult to trace Peter as a distinct source with much assurance. In a few instances Peter is mentioned by name where the parallel accounts mention simply the disciples (Mk 1:36; 11:31; 13:3). Otherwise Peter is not given greater importance in Mk than in Mt-Lk. Turner and Lagrange, however, have pointed out a strange feature of Mk's style which may reflect Peter's narratives: this is the exceptional use of an indefinite 3rd person plural (1:21; 5:1 +) which may easily represent an original 1st person plural uttered by the narrator, Peter.

Other sources appear in the analysis of the structure of Mk presented by V. Taylor, who finds 18 "complexes" or groups of material: (1) 1:1–13; (2) 1:21–39; (3) 2:1–3:6; (4) 3:19b–35; (5) 4:1–34; (6) 4:35–5:43; (7) 6:30–56; (8) 7:1–23; (9) 7:24–37; (10) 8:1–26; (11) 8:27–9:29; (12) 9:30–50; (13) 10:1–31; (14) 10:32–52; (15) 11:1–25; (16) 11:27–12:44; (17) 13:5–37; (18) 14:1–16:8. These Taylor divides into three types of groups: (A) Groups of narratives and sayings formed on the basis of existing tradition (## 1, 12–15); (B) Groups of narratives based on personal testimony, probably that of Peter (## 2, 6, 7, 9, 11, 18); (C) Groups of narratives topically arranged consisting of sayings and pronouncement-stories (## 3–5, 8, 16–17). Groups A and C evidently presuppose an existing body of oral tradition (possibly to some extent already written) of the sayings and the deeds of Jesus; Mark is responsible for their grouping, but not for their form, which he found already in existence. In addition Mark is responsible for the summaries and connections in 1:14 f; 3:7–12. Mark has less material peculiar to himself than any other Gospel: the healing of the deaf mute (7:31–37) and of the blind man of Bethsaida (8:22–26); the parable of the seed (4:26–29); the episode of Jesus and His relatives (3:20 f); the young man of Gethsemani (14:51 f). Some of these materials are attributed by Taylor to an existing source of *Logia* or sayings of Jesus (e.g., 4:21–25; 8:34–9:1; 9:42–56).

Mark's methods in his use of materials are thus summarized by Taylor: (1) When Mark takes over an isolated story from tradition, he leaves it as he finds it. (2) He leaves previously existing complexes almost intact. (3) He rarely comments upon the material. (4) He does not impose a narrative form on topical complexes already existing in the tradition. (5) When Mark finds doublets in the tradition he uses both elements and does not select or conflate.

These methods perhaps best solve the question of the two feedings of the crowd (6:30–44; 8:1–10). Mark's two versions have all the appearance of a duplicate account. On the hypothesis of Peter as a single source this is difficult to understand. If Mark uses preexisting traditions in the manner described above, it is apparent that the story of the feeding appeared more than once in his sources with a sufficient number of variations in detail for him to incorporate both forms, retaining each in the complex in which it already existed. His use of sources also appears in the absence of a context of place and time for many episodes; these must have existed as isolated stories which had not been woven into any complex.

5. *Style.* Mk's Gk lacks literary finish. It contains a large number of colloquialisms. The vocabulary is limited and the syntax is elementary; Mk's favorite grammatical structure is the stringing together of parallel independent clauses (parataxis). But he has a greater degree of realism and concrete vividness than the other Gospels; this comes from a wealth of specific detail which does not appear in Mt-Lk. Many scholars point out that these details are not from Mark but from the traditions which he employs. There are several traits of popular narration, such as vague or general affirmation followed immediately by a precision (e.g., 1:28), a parenthetic explanation (e.g., 2:5, 10), and a supplementary detail added somewhat violently (e.g., 5:42). Certain set patterns or forms in which stories are cast appear; this is illustrated in the miracle stories of 1:25–27 and 4:39–41, each of which follows the scheme: command; effect; effect on witnesses; remark of the witnesses. X. Léon-Dufour observes on these somewhat paradoxical features of Mark's style that Mark has a double origin, the witness of the event and the community; the witness furnishes the realism and the details, the community furnishes the schematic tradition. The wealth of detail is illustrated in such stories as 2:1–13; 5:1–20, 21–43; 7:31–37; a comparison of these episodes with the parallels in Mt-Lk is instructive. Mark refers to the sentiments of the actors, including Jesus Himself (1:41, 43; 3:5; 7:34; 8:12; 10:24, 32), more than the other Gospels. Vividness is found in his frequent use of the historical present. Wealth of circumstantial details sometimes leads to prolixity, although he is the shortest of the Gospels.

6. *The Conclusion of 16:9–20.* This passage is missing in the most important MSS and many of the Fathers seem to be unaware of it. In content and form and style it is unlike the rest of the Gospel; and an examination of its contents shows that it is a harmony and summary of the apparitions related in Mt-Lk-Jn. These features are sufficient to warrant the assertion that it is not from the author of Mk. Its appearance in Tatian and Irenaeus, however, shows that it existed after 150. A conclusion at 16:8 would be extremely abrupt, and it is possible that the present conclusion replaces a lost passage. It belongs to the canonical text. The response of the Biblical Commission of June 26, 1912, denies that its secondary character is demonstrated; but the negative character of this response should be noted.

7. *Plan.* Mk falls into three major divisions:

Prologue: teaching of John, baptism and temptation of Jesus (1:1–13).

I. The Galilean Ministry (1:14–6:6a):

(1) Capernaum and the surrounding district (1:14–45; the ministry in Capernaum is described as the events of a single day, an instance of Mark's schematizing).

(2) Conflict of Jesus and the Jews: 5 controversial discourses (2:1–3:6).

(3) Success of Jesus and further conflicts (3:7–35).

(4) The parables (4:1–34).

(5) Four miracles at the Sea of Galilee (4:35–5:43).

(6) Conclusion of Galilean ministry; rejection at Nazareth (6:1–6a).

 II. The Journeys of Jesus (6:6–10:52).

(1) Mission of the apostles (6:6b–29).

(2) Journey and return, feeding of 5000, controversy (7:1–23).

(3) Journey and return, miracles, controversy (7:24–8:12).

(4) Journey and return, cures, confessions of Peter, predictions of Passion, transfiguration (8:13–9:50).

(5) Journey to Jerusalem, controversy, instructions, cure of blind man (10:1–52).

 III. Ministry in Jerusalem, Passion and Death, Resurrection (11:1–16:8).

(1) Messianic activity (11:1–26).

(2) Messianic teaching (11:27–12:44).

(3) Apocalypse (13:1–37).

(4) Jesus and His disciples (14:1–42).

(5) Jesus tried by the Jews (14:43–72).

(6) Jesus tried by Pilate and crucified (15:1–47).

(7) The Risen Jesus (16:1–8).

Appendix (16:9–20).

The above outline gives the superficial impression of a topographical scheme; actually it is much more. The theme of the structure is rejection and misunderstanding. Rejection begins with the controversies with which each division of the Galilean ministry is concluded and reaches a climax at the end of the Galilean ministry. Misunderstanding appears in the circle of the disciples and mounts with the triple prediction of the Passion; but the second phase is marked by the confession of Peter, which makes future understanding possible. The true character of Jesus is progressively manifested through Galilee, the journeys, and the ministry in Jerusalem; but for Mark the whole revelation of the true Jesus comes with His death and resurrection. Without this He cannot be understood nor accepted. The plan of the Gospel itself is therefore an element in the theology of the Gospel.

8. *Theology.* The doctrinal purpose of Mark is set forth in the title (1:1): to proclaim the gospel*, the "good news" of Jesus Christ, the Son of God. This purpose is more clearly seen in some striking characteristics of Mark's style in contrast to Mt-Lk: he relates fewer of the words of Jesus than Mt-Lk, with only two discourses (4:1–34; 13:1–37), and says often that "Jesus taught" without telling the content of His teaching. His narrative is more concerned with the deeds of Jesus, which he narrates, as noted above, with more circumstantial detail than Mt-Lk. It is Jesus Himself as a person, the Son of God, whom he wishes to portray;

Jesus Himself is the primary and basic element in His own teaching. That Jesus is the Son of God is revealed less in dogmatic statements than in the exercise by Jesus of divine power: the forgiveness* of sins (2:10–12), dominion over the Sabbath (2:28; 3:1–5), the expulsion of demons (1:28, 34; 3:11+), the knowledge of secrets (2:8; 8:17; 12:15), predictions (8:31 ff; 10:39; 13:1 ff). The title "Son of God" occurs at critical points: the prologue (1:1), the transfiguration (9:7), the confession of the centurion (15:39).

But Jesus, the Son of God, is genuinely man, and Mk reveals His human traits more than the other Gospels: He is said to be out of Himself (3:21), He is a carpenter whose family is well known (6:3), He cannot work miracles because of unbelief (6:5 f), He forbids men to call Him good (10:18), He does not know the hour of the judgment (13:32), He exhibits human sentiments (3:5; 6:34; 8:2, 12; 10:14, 16, 21; 14:41), He works miracles progressively (7:31–35; 8:22–26), He asks questions (5:30; 8:5; 9:16–21). The genuine humanity of Jesus is basic both to His rejection by His own people and to His triumph in His real death and resurrection. That the death of Jesus is redemptive is clear in Mk (10:45; 14:24; cf REDEMPTION), but it is not a belief which is discussed or elaborated; in Mk the mission of Jesus is to die and to rise.

The most explicit doctrinal feature in Mk is the idea of the kingdom, and the kingdom is eschatological; this does not imply an explicit belief in an imminent Parousia*, but simply an absence of any other aspect of the kingdom than eschatological. Here Mk represents the most primitive form of the understanding of the kingdom. The kingdom is also apocalyptic, reaching its fulfillment in a world catastrophe and judgment. The elements of the church as kingdom are not excluded, but they have not yet become explicit.

That Jesus is the Messiah is clear in Mk, but since the writing of W. Wrede in 1901 the question of "the messianic secret" in Mk has been raised. Wrede presented the theory that Jesus Himself never claimed to be the Messiah, and that the title was given Him by early Jewish Christians. They created the story that Jesus forbade the proclamation of His Messiahship, and thus explained why He was not accepted as Messiah by the Jews. Of this "messianic secret" Mk is the first witness.

It must be conceded to Wrede that Mk exhibits a definite pattern of concealment of the messianic character of Jesus (1:34, 44; 3:12; 5:43; 7:36; 8:26, 30; 9:9). But there is no reason whatever to say that Mark did not find this in his sources. The Messiahship of Jesus (cf MESSIAH) is so transformed from Jewish messianism of the NT period that a simple claim of the title would certainly be misleading. Mk has therefore preserved a genuine element in the pedagogy of Jesus, which is exhibited in other passages, such as His proclamation of the kingdom and His predictions of the passion. Jesus did not openly claim the title of Messiah until His death had shown the meaning of the title clearly (X. Léon-Dufour).

Other critics have affirmed that the apparently simple and artless narratives of Mk are really a subtle proposition of Pauline Christology in narrative form. This theory has not been widely accepted; its defenders conclude that Mk's primary source is Pauline theology rather than tradition, and that therefore he is not a historical witness. The theory cannot stand with the remarkable absence from Mk of just those ideas which are most characteristic of the Pauline writings. Where he expresses theological ideas in a somewhat primitive manner, such as the redeeming death (10:45; 14:24) or the universalism of the kingdom (12:8–12; 13:10; 14:9), he does not express them with Pauline modalities; he rather attests that these ideas belong to the earliest traditions and the primitive catechesis.

9. *Historical Value.* Mk is a gospel, not a history or biography; it is "a work of faith addressed to faith" (X. Léon-Dufour). Apologetic, doctrinal, and catechetical themes are visible in Mk (cf above). These dictate his arrangement of his material; he is therefore not a historical source for the chronological order of the events, in which he is not interested. Nor is he interested merely in reporting what was observed and transmitted; he presents the events as moments in the process of salvation, as transformed by faith and understanding which comes from the passion and resurrection. He presents the events in popular style and conception because neither he nor his sources were capable of an exact and critical account. His traditional sources arise in the historical reality of Jesus Christ the Son of God, who proclaimed the kingdom, taught, worked wonders, suffered and died, and rose. This is the saving event, and this is historical. But for a "historical" perception of the events in the modern sense of the word, the historian must employ Mt-Lk-Jn and those instruments of historical criticism which he has at his disposal. Cf HISTORY.

Marketplace. In the OT $r^e\dot{h}\hat{o}b$, lit "wide place," Eng versions often "street" or "square." The congested structures of the ancient walled city* left little room for open spaces. It was essential for defense, however, that the area inside the gates be left clear of buildings in order to mass troops against an assault on the gates*. These "wide places" furnished the only open areas in the city and the allusions to the marketplaces offer a little compendium of life in the ancient city. It was a place where strangers went either to be offered lodging or to sleep (Gn 19:2; Jgs 19:15 ff). It was a place of assembly for any purpose (2 Ch 32:6; Ne 8:1, 3, 16); the allusions to mourning suggest that it was here that formal mourning for the dead was conducted (Ps 144:14; Is 15:3; Je 48:38; Am 5:16). Here were hung trophies of war, including the bodies of slain enemies (2 S 21:12). The men of the city assembled in the marketplace for war, and action frequently occurred here (Je 49:26; 50:30; Na 2:5). Here prostitutes solicited (Ezk 16:24, 31; Pr 7:12). Old people sat or strolled and children played (Zc 8:4–5). It was the place to seek a friend (SS 3:2). There is only one obscure allusion to business (Ps 55:12), but it is altogether probable that the open market so typical of the Near East today was found in the "wide place" of the ancient city. It was a place for public proclamations (Pr 1:20), and the place of judgment*.

The marketplace of NT Palestinian towns (Gk *agora*) was like the marketplace of OT towns; it was the place where children played (Mt 11:16; Lk 7:32), where one met one's friends (Mt 23:7; Mk 12:38; Lk 11:43; 20:46), where one could be sure of finding the person one desired to meet (Mk 6:56), where unemployed casual laborers awaited employment (Mt 20:3). But the Palestinian marketplace was not the true *agora*, which was an essential feature of the Gk and Hellenistic *polis*. In early Gk times the *agora* was the assembly of the people; in classical times it had become the large open space, and the assembly was held in another space designated for the purpose. The *agora* became the commercial center of the *polis*, but it was far more than a mere commercial center. It was surrounded by public buildings and porticos where one could walk protected from sun or rain, and the Gk citizen spent most of his day in or near the *agora*. It was the scene of philosophical discussions; both the Peripatetic ("strolling") and Stoic ("portico") schools drew their names from the *agora*. It was a political and intellectual center as well as a commercial center. It was natural that Paul should propose Christianity in the *agora* at Athens, the intellectual center of the Mediterranean world; but he was received so coolly by the wits of the *agora* that we read of no more preaching in this

a) Roman forum, Temple of Saturn. b) Roman forum, the Sacred Way. c) The forum of Trajan, Rome, showing the shops.

atmosphere (AA 17:17). It was also the place of public offices (AA 16:19).

Marriage. 1. *OT*. Hb has no single word which means "marriage." The law* on the subject is fragmentary, and the allusions to marriage in the text, while numerous, leave many questions unanswered. Comparative information from other ancient codes of law is more abundant; but since these exhibit some striking differences from each other, it is unsafe to draw analogies between these codes and Israelite practice.

The end of marriage as conceived in the two accounts of the origin of man is stated with some differences. In Gn 1:27 f the differentiation of sex has as its purpose that man should multiply. In Gn 2:18–25 marriage is conceived on a somewhat more elevated tone; it is a union in which the wife is to be the helper of man, for it is not good for the man to be alone. It is implicit in the account that the ideal union of the sexes is monogamous. Sex and marriage are divine institutions through which man finds fulfillment. The account is alluded to in Tb 8:5–7, with the additional note that the husband does not take the wife in lust, but in truth.

Marriage in Israel was neither a religious nor a public concern; it was a private contract, and it is this conception which leaves so little room for it in Hb law, which deals only with exceptional cases. The contracting parties were not the bride and groom but the families, i.e., the fathers of the spouses; the brothers of the bride had the disposal of the girl if the father were dead. Thus in Gn 24 the slave acts as the agent of Abraham* in selecting a wife for Isaac, and the brothers of Rebekah give her in marriage. Judah* selected Tamar as the wife of his firstborn son Er (Gn 38:6) and continues to

dispose of Tamar after Er's death. In Dt 7:3 the injunction not to marry Canaanites is expressed in terms of giving and receiving daughters in marriage. This did not mean that the bride and groom had no voice in the matter. Rebekah was asked whether she would go with the slave of Abraham (Gn 24:57 f), and Samson chose a bride against the wishes of his parents; it was, however, necessary for him to demand that his father obtain the bride of his choice for him (Jgs 14:2, 5). Esau grieved his parents by marrying women whom they had not chosen (Gn 26:34).

The contract between the families was sealed by the payment of the *mōhar* to the parents of the bride; on the gift made by the parents to the bride cf DOWRY. There is some disagreement among scholars on the meaning of the *mōhar*, and some insist that it is incorrect to translate it as "price of the bride." It seems more probable, however, that the *mōhar* is an ancient custom which goes back to a conception of marriage by purchase; this conception left other traces in Israelite marriage practice (such as the terms *ba'al*, "owner," to designate the husband, and *be'ûlāh*, "owned," to designate the bride). It is true that Israelite marriage as it appears in the OT is not properly marriage by purchase; but few institutions have the capacity to retain archaic rites which no longer have meaning as marriage does. The *mōhar* is mentioned in Ex 22:16; a man must pay the *mōhar* and marry the girl whom he has seduced, unless her father refuses to give her, in which case the offender must pay the *mōhar*. The similar law of Dt 22:28 f makes 50 shekels of silver a fair price; but the *mōhar* was no doubt negotiated in each instance. The *mōhar* could be paid in service, as Jacob paid Laban for his wives (Gn 29:18–20, 27–30). A

A Roman marriage.

father could offer his daughter as a reward for prowess in war* (Jos 15:16); the price demanded by Saul* from David* for Michal*, however, can scarcely be anything but an eccentric exception (1 S 18:25). The payment of the *mōhar* is described in Gn 24:53. A suitor who eagerly desired the bride offered to pay any price required (Gn 34:12). The dowry of the bride must often have included one or more slave girls who remained the personal property of their mistress (Gn 16:1; 24:61). It could also be a piece of property (Jos 15:18); for a king's daughter it could be a city (1 K 9:18). With the completion of the agreement between the families the couple were betrothed (Gn 24:54–56) and the woman was treated as married as far as extramarital intercourse with another man was concerned (cf Dt 22:23 ff).

The OT gives no information of the age at marriage; it is altogether probable that marriage was contracted at an early age as in most less civilized communities; for girls, it was probably not long after puberty was attained. The OT contains no information on the ceremonial of marriage, and possibly there was no formal ceremonial at all except the introduction of the wife to the home of the husband. An allusion to the spreading of the husband's garment upon the wife to indicate possession (Rt 3:9; Ezk 16:18) may refer to the marriage ceremonial. On the significance of the veil cf VEIL. The marriage was an occasion of community festivity; this lasted a week (Gn 29:27 f; Jgs 14:12). Jeremiah* refers several times to the merriment of the wedding festival (7:34; 16:9; 25:10).

A large family, in particular sons, was a joy and a blessing from Yahweh (Gn 24:60; Ps 127:3), and a barren wife was accursed (Gn 30:1 ff; 1 S 1:6 ff). The desire for progeny was no doubt largely responsible both for polygamy and for concubinage; cf below.

Historians of the Near East point out that the Babylonian marriage was basically monogamous, while the Assyrian and Hb marriage was basically polygamous. This was subtly contested by the J tradition in Gn, which presented a monogamous relationship as instituted in creation (Gn 2:18–25) and then described polygamy as a part of the deterioration of mankind which is outlined in Gn 4. Kings and very probably the noble and wealthy had a large harem* (David, 2 S 3:2–7; 5:13). The 700 wives and 300 concubines of Solomon (1 K 11:3) must, however, be an exaggeration of popular tradition. Dt 17:17 contains a mild protest against the king who "multiplies" wives, but this seems to moderate excess rather than to impose monogamy. Besides Gn 2:24 a number of sayings in the wisdom* literature propose monogamy as the ideal state (Pr 5:15 ff; 12:4; 18:22; 19:14; 31:10 ff; BS 9:1; 26:1–4). There appears to have been little or no polygamy practiced after the exile. How deeply rooted it was before the exile may be seen from the parable of Ezk 23, which represents Yahweh as the husband of two wives. The law of Dt 21:15–17, which is parallel to several Mesopotamian laws, protects the "hated" wife and her children, especially if she has borne the firstborn son ("hated" here means less loved). Almost every polygamous household of which any extended account is given exhibits the bickering and envy, sometimes breaking into hatred and murder, which are the natural consequences of polygamy; cf ABRAHAM; DAVID; JACOB.

There is some suggestion in the OT of the institution called *errebu* marriage, in which the wife does not join her husband but the husband becomes a member of the wife's family. This seems to be involved in the marriages of both Jacob and Moses (Ex 2:21; 3:1). In the light of the Nuzu* marriage contracts it now appears that Laban, who had no sons when Jacob married his daughters, adopted Jacob as his son and heir on condition that Laban had no heir. When Laban begot sons of his own, Jacob obtained a division of Laban's property. There is only one instance of marriage by capture; this is the furnishing of wives to the sons of Benjamin by war upon Jabesh-gilead* and by the rape of the girls of Shiloh (Jgs 21). The historical value of this chapter is not great, and the incident, which is echoed in the rape of the Sabines in Roman folklore, is certainly not typical.

On the dissolution of marriage cf DIVORCE.

That concubinage existed as an institution regulated by custom and to some extent by law is clear; but there is some uncertainty as to its practice. The term *pilegeš* (perhaps connected with the Gk *pallakis*) designates a woman who cohabits habitually with the same man; she does not appear to have the rank of wife and there is no indication that the union is permanent. 300 of Solomon's harem have this designation (1 K 11:3). They were possessed by Abraham (Gn 25:6), Esau's son Eliphaz (Gn 36:12), a Levite of the period of the judges (Jgs 19:1 ff), Gideon (Jgs 8:31), Saul (Rizpah*, 2 S 3:12 ff), David (2 S 5:13; 15:16; 16:21), Rehoboam (2 Ch 11:21, 18 wives and 60 concubines), Caleb (1 Ch 2:46, 48), Manasseh (1 Ch 7:14). From these data it is difficult to form an idea of the legal standing of the concubine, if indeed she had any. In some instances, her sons seem to be legitimate, in other instances it is not clear that they were. Hb custom here was perhaps the same as the law of Hammurabi which left it to the option of the father whether he would acknowledge the children of the concubine (170–171; ANET 173). There is always a distinction between "women" (wives) and concubines, and it does not seem that they should be regarded as wives of a lower or secondary rank. A few passages suggest that the *pilegeš* was always a slave. An obscure law of Ex 21:7–11 deals with the sale of the daughter (of an Israelite) into slavery. The purchaser may acquire her either for himself or for his son; if she is unsatisfactory he shall let her be redeemed and not sell her to a foreigner; if she is purchased for his son she must be treated as a daughter; and if he takes another woman (either as wife or as concubine?) the slave shall not lose her support from him (food and clothing) nor her cohabitation (the word *'ōnāh* appears only here). She is not, however, subject to the seven year period of slavery mentioned in Ex 21:3, but is sold permanently. This law, it seems, was designed to protect Israelite girls whom their father was forced by economic necessity to sell into slavery as concubines; the restrictions which are imposed upon the purchaser show clearly what the position of the concubine was ·who was not protected by law. The *pilegeš* could also be a captive in war (Nm 31:9; Dt 20:14). The law of Dt 21:10–14 deals with the man who *marries* a captive in war, and seems to be designed to protect a woman who has been married from the treatment which could be given to a captive who was taken as a *pilegeš*. In general, it appears that the harem of the Hb householder consisted of all his wives and all the female slaves who were not the personal property of his wives or of his sons. The female slave could be substituted for the childless wife; this occurred with Sarah and Hagar (Gn 16:1 f), Rachel and Bilhah (Gn 30:3 f); Leah substituted Zilpah even after Leah herself had borne sons (Gn 30:9). The substitution of a slave for a childless wife occurs as a condition imposed upon the wife in Nuzu marriage contracts. When this happens the son must be acknowledged by the father, and the wife may not expel the children of the concubine. The law of Hammurabi provides that such a slave may not be sold, but may be reduced to the condition of slavery (146; ANET 172). Bilhah is called the *pilegeš* of Jacob in Gn 35:22. Such a union is obviously more firm and has more complex legal effects than a simple union of concubinage. In the family of Jacob all the sons have equal rights.

It is not accurate to speak of matrimonial impediments in the OT in the modern sense of the term; cf INCEST. Passages such as Gn 24:3 f and 28:1 f suggest that endogamy was proposed as an ideal; but the number of marriages of foreign women mentioned in the OT show that the ideal was not sustained. Dt 7:23 is an exhortation not to marry Canaanites, not a law.

There is no reference in the OT to a written marriage contract except in the late book of Tb 7:14. In Mesopotamia, however, the written marriage contract was demanded by law, and it would be surprising if it was not written in Israel, particularly since the divorce had to be recorded in writing (Dt 24:1). A written marriage contract was found at the Jewish colony of Elephantine* (ANET 222 f). The formula, "She is my wife and I am her husband from this day forever," which was no doubt uttered by the groom before witnesses, is as close as we come to the formula of marriage in ancient Israel, if we may suppose that this remote Jewish colony preserved the rites and customs of marriage as their ancestors in Palestine had known them. Considering the tenacity of marriage customs, this is not unlikely.

The highest tribute which is paid to marriage in the OT is the adoption of the union of marriage as an image of the covenant* union and love* of Yahweh for Israel. This idea first appears in Ho 2; the theme of the passage is not the power and ownership of the husband, but the love of the husband which is more enduring than the infidelity of the wife and strives with endless patience to recapture her affections. The image is resumed in Is 54:4 f; 62:4 f; Je 2:2; 3:20, where the theme of affection is maintained. The use of the image in Ezk 16 and 23 exhibits less delicacy of sentiment and emphasizes more the power of the husband and the faithlessness of the wife. It is these passages with SS* and the passages from wisdom* literature quoted above which show more than anything in the narrative and legal portions of the OT that marriage was a union of love in ancient Israel.

2. *NT*. The NT adds little information on wedding customs. It appears that the wedding feast was celebrated at night (Mt 25:1 ff; Lk 12:36). The festive character of the occasion and the high conviviality are illustrated in the account of the wedding at Cana* which Jesus attended (Jn 2:1 ff).

The teaching of Jesus on marriage is limited to His affirmation of its indissolubility (cf DIVORCE). In this affirmation He goes back to the conception of Gn 2:18–25 and applies the divine institution of marriage not only to marriage in general but also to each particular marriage (Mt 19:4–6; Mk 10: 6–8). Yet there is in His words a subtle implication that marriage is or at least can be treated as a thing of this world, a thing which can blind a man to vital decisions. Marriage is one of the activities of the heedless generation which perished in the deluge (Lk 17:27); it is an excuse offered by the man who is not ready to accept the call of God (Lk 14:20); it will not exist in the kingdom of God (Mt 22:30; Mk 12:25; Lk 20:35 f). One should not conclude from this that Jesus expressed an opposition to marriage, but rather that He wished its value to be seen in proper perspective.

Paul appeals in 1 Co 6:16 f to the text of Gn 2:24 not in reference to marriage but in an exhortation to avoid fornication. Carnal union is union in one flesh and unworthy of the Christian who, united to the Lord, forms one spirit with Him. This introduces a lengthy discussion of marriage in 1 Co 7, the fullest treatment which the subject receives in the NT. Marriage, while less perfect than virginity, is normal and necessary to avoid fornication. It involves a mutual surrender of the rights over one's own body (7:1–11). The Christian spouse may depart from an unbeliever who refuses to consent to the conversion of the partner (7:12–16). Those who contract marriage should do it in the awareness that marriage, like the world in which we live, passes quickly (7:29–31). The married person is of necessity concerned with the things of the world and how to please the spouse, which may distract him from concern about the things of the Lord (7:32–35).

The epistles exhort husbands to love their wives and wives to be subject to their husbands (Col 3:18; 1 Pt 3:1–7). Marriage is conceived as a hierarchy; this belief rests not only upon the common conception of the social position of women*, but also upon the likeness between marriage and the relation of Christ and the Church, which is set forth at some length in Eph 5:22–33. The husband is the head of the wife, as Christ is the head of the Church. As Christ loved the Church and delivered Himself that the Church might be saved and sanctified, so the husband should love and cherish his wife as he cherishes his own body; for husband and wife are one body, as Christ and the Church are one body. This is a great "mystery*" (Eph 5:32). The verse is obscure and is interpreted in various ways. Mystery in Eph refers to the divine plan of salvation in Christ revealed in Him (3: 3–6). The word in 5:32 must refer to this mystery of salvation, and seems to signify that one aspect of the mystery is the relationship between Christ and His Church

which is established by His saving act, a relation so intimate that it is like the relation of husband and wife. This in turn illuminates the nature of the matrimonial union, which reaches its fullness in Christians only when the spouses love and cherish each other as Christ and the Church love each other. The same relationship is alluded to briefly in 2 Co 11:2.

There are several passages in the Gospels in which the messianic period is described as a wedding feast (Mt 9:15; 25:1 ff; Mk 2:19; Jn 3:29). J. Jeremias seems to be right in pointing out that Jesus is not here expressly identified with the bridegroom; the sayings are parables* rather than allegories and refer to the messianic period in general as a period of great joy. The messianic period here begins with the appearance of Jesus. Jesus is the bridegroom, however, in 2 Co 11:2. The Church as bride and Christ as bridegroom appear in Apc; the wedding of the Lamb occurs in the eschatological consummation when He accepts the Church, perfect and purified (19:7–9; 21:2; 22:17). This conception of the Church as bride echoes Eph 5:27.

Mars Hill. Cf AREOPAGUS.

Martha (Aramaic *martā',* "lady"), sister of Mary* and of Lazarus* (Lk 10:38–42; Jn 11), a resident of Bethany*. On the basis of Lk 10:38–42 Martha in Christian tradition has, somewhat unfairly, become the very type of the unrecollected activist. The saying addressed to her contains nothing that is not a summary of sayings found elsewhere in the Gospel on the uselessness of concern about material objects and worldly affairs (Mt 6:25–34; Lk 12:22–31) and the obligation of hearing the words of Jesus (Mt 7:24; Lk 6:47–49; 8:21; 11:28). It is evident from the tone of the few episodes in which Martha appears that she enjoyed the friendship and esteem of Jesus.

Martyr. Cf WITNESS.

Mary (Gk *maria* or *mariam,* from Hb Miriam*), the name of several women in the NT.

1. The mother of Jesus, the wife of Joseph*; the names of her parents are not mentioned in the NT. The account of the conception of Jesus (Mt 1:18–25) clearly affirms that Jesus was not conceived of a human father. The same belief is affirmed in the account of the annunciation* (Lk 1:26–38). The messianic character of Jesus is affirmed also in both passages and in the account of the visit of Mary to Elizabeth* (Lk 1:39–56; cf MAGNIFICAT). Mary appears in the story of the birth of Jesus (Lk 2:1–20), her purification after childbirth (Lk 2:22–39), in the story of the Magi* and the flight to Egypt (Mt 2) and the story of the finding of Jesus in the temple (Lk 2:41–52). Lk in particular emphasizes the fact that Mary thought about the things she heard concerning the infant (Lk 2:19, 51). Outside of the infancy narratives Mary appears in the Synoptic Gospels only in Mt 13:55; Mk 6:3 (cf also Jn 6:42), where she is well known to the people of Nazareth, and in Mt 12:46–50; Mk 3:31–35; Lk 8:19–21, where a visit of Mary and the kinsmen of Jesus is the occasion of the saying of Jesus that one who does the will of the Father is as close to Him as His nearest relations. In Jn 2:1–5 Mary suggests the failure of wine which is the occasion of the miracle; in Jn 2:12 she goes to Capernaum with Jesus, which suggests that she no longer resided at Nazareth. Only Jn 19:25–27 mentions her presence at the death of Jesus and the commission of her care to John. This clearly suggests that there were no relations with whom she could live. Mary was present with the disciples during the days which preceded the giving of the Spirit (AA 1:14). Neither the NT nor any other sources gives reliable information of the further course of her life and her death.

The two basic Christian beliefs concerning Mary, the divine maternity and the virginal conception of Jesus, are clearly stated in the Gospels. Other beliefs are developed from these basic beliefs or are found in the traditional belief and cult of the Church. The relatively minor role which Mary plays in the Gospels is entirely in accord with Jewish life and with biblical history in general, in which women play a minor role, most frequently limited to their feminine functions as wife and mother. The words of Mary are few, and often they contain or are the occasion of an exegetical difficulty. Thus the matrimonial status of Joseph and Mary in Mt 1:18 ff is difficult to define; it seems to be betrothal rather than marriage. The messianic texts of Lk 1–2, which are frequent, are difficult to combine with the "wonder" which Lk attributes to Mary (Lk 2:33, 48) and lack of understanding (Lk 2:50). Lk's sources apparently had two variant conceptions of Mary; in one she was aware to some extent of the messianic character of her son, and in the other she was unaware of it. The messianic texts come very probably from the expansion of the infancy narratives by early Christian teachers. While Luke in his prologue asserts that he has made diligent investigations, there is no direct evidence in the infancy narratives that Mary was the source of his information.

The words which Jesus addresses to Mary in the Gospels cause some difficulty. In general the relationship of Jesus and Mary is not presented as different from the relationship of any son to his mother. But it is undeniable that in Mt 12:49 f; Mk 3:34 f; Lk 2:49; 8:21; and Jn 2:4 the words of Jesus addressed to Mary or mentioning her imply a detachment which is greater than usual between an adult son and his mother. The title of "woman" by which Jesus addresses Mary (Jn 2:4; 19:25) is unparalleled in Gk literature as an address of a son to his mother. It is important to observe that in none of these passages is a genuine rebuke implied, since no fault is charged to Mary. One may suggest the hypothesis that these sayings are a part of the primitive teaching of the Church which removed the implication that any carnal connection with Jesus was a substitute for faith in Him. Jesus, who was a Jew of Galilee and related to the "brethren* of the Lord" mentioned in the NT, was no more of a Messiah-savior to the Jews or to His relatives than He is to any one who believes in Him. It is altogether probable that others of His kinsmen than James* were members of the early Christian community, and it is not unlikely that some of them considered that this entitled them to a peculiar position. Paul speaks of "a party of Christ" at Corinth (1 Co 1:12), and in a difficult line denies that any importance should be attached to knowing Christ "according to the flesh*" (2 Co 5:16). The positive reticence of the primitive preaching not only about Mary, but also about the entire life of Jesus and His family and village connections before the baptism, seems to suggest a movement against any such attempt to make kinship the basis of special claims. A by-product of this reticence is our almost total lack of genuine information concerning the life and person of Mary.

2. Mary Magdalen (of Magdala* in Galilee), from whom Jesus expelled seven demons (Mk 16:9; Lk 8:2), one of the women who ministered to the needs of Jesus (Lk 8:2), a witness of the crucifixion (Mt 27:56; Mk 15:40; Jn 19:25), the burial of Jesus (Mt 27:61; Mk 15:47), and of the empty tomb (Mt 28:1–10; Mk 16:1–8; Lk 24:10). An apparition of the risen Jesus to Mary Magdalen alone is related in Mk 16:9; Jn 20:1–18. The picture of Mary Magdalen as the classic example of the penitent sinner is due to the identification of her with the sinful woman of Lk 7:36–50; but this woman is not named, and there is no basis for the identification with Mary Magdalen except the anointing, which is probably Lk's variant of the anointing of Bethany*. The Mary of this anointing, however, was a different person; cf # 3.

3. The sister of Lazarus* and Martha* of Bethany. She is the occasion of the saying that it is the better part to listen to the words of Jesus (Lk 10:39–42). She appears in the account of the resurrection of Lazarus (Jn 11) and is in Jn 12:3–8 the woman who anointed Jesus at Bethany. The name of the woman is not given in Mt 26:6–13; Mk 14:3–9. She is not represented as a penitent in any of these passages; and there is no basis in Lk or Jn for identifying her with Mary Magdalen.

4. The mother of James* and Joses, a witness of the crucifixion of Jesus and of the empty tomb (Mk 15:40, 47; 16:1; Lk 24:10); perhaps identical with # 5.

5. The wife of Clopas, a witness of the crucifixion of Jesus (Jn 19:25).

6. The mother of John Mark* (AA 12:12).

7. A Christian of Rome greeted by Paul (Rm 16:6).

Masora, Masorete, Masoretic. Cf TEXT.

Massah (Hb *massāh*, "testing"), the name of a point in the desert sojourn of the exodus* where Moses* drew water from the ground by striking the ground with his staff (Ex 17:1–7). In this passage the name is explained by the Israelites' "temptation" of Yahweh by their lack of faith. The episode, however, has contaminated the account of Marah* (Ex 16:25), of which it is quite likely a variant account, and in Ex 17:7 it is related to the story of Meribah*. The "testing" receives several different explanations besides the explanation given in 17:7. In Ex 16:25 Yahweh puts the Israelites to the test; in Dt 33:8 Yahweh puts Levi* to the test and proves him. In Dt 6:16; 9:22; Ps 95:8 the explanation is the same as in Ex 17:7. In Ps 95:8 Massah is joined with Meribah. It is evident that the story of the water discovered in the desert was told in several forms and in connection with more than one place; the theme of unbelief and rebellion, however, was constant in all the accounts. The compiler of the traditions has made them so many distinct incidents according to the popular etymologies of the names mentioned in the traditions.

Mattaniah. Cf ZEDEKIAH.

Mattathias (Gk *mattathias* from Hb *mattityāh*, "gift of Yahweh"), a priest of Modin*, father of Judas* Maccabee. When the officers of Antiochus* Epiphanes came to Modin to compel the inhabitants to offer sacrifice contrary to Jewish law, Mattathias killed the royal officer and a Jew who offered sacrifice. With his sons he fled to the mountains. A number of Jews left the towns and went to the desert of the Jordan and were killed when they refused to take up arms on the Sabbath. Mattathias determined that his group would defend themselves even on the Sabbath. He was joined by a group of Hasideans and with his small force carried on guerrilla warfare against the Hellenizing Greeks. He died in 166 BC and was buried in Modin (1 Mc 2).

Matthew. Cf MATTHEW, GOSPEL OF.

Matthew, Gospel of. Matthew, Gk *maththaios* or *matthaios*, comes from Aramaic *mattāi*, a shorter form of Hb *mattanyāh*, "gift of Yahweh." The name appears in the lists of the Twelve (Mt 10:3; Mk 3:18; Lk 6:15; AA 1:13). Only in Mt 9:9–13; 10:3, however, is Matthew identified with the tax collector Levi, whose call is related in Mk 2:13–17; Lk 5:27–32.

1. Authorship. Papias, bishop of Hierapolis about 130, as quoted by Eusebius, attributes to the apostle the composition of the discourses (Gk *logia*) of Jesus in Aramaic and adds that "each one" translated these as best he could. The same attribution is made by Irenaeus, who adds that Mt was written while Peter and Paul were founding the church of Rome* (i.e., 60–65). Irenaeus, however, depends on Papias for the attribution; his source for the date is unknown. Origen and Eusebius also attest that Matthew wrote a Gospel in Aramaic, which they call "Hebrew." Other witnesses are not independent. The value of this tradition for the present Mt depends on the solution of the question of the original language of Mt.

2. Original Language. Basic to this question is the meaning of the "sayings" mentioned by Papias and the meaning of "arranged"; Papias credits Matthew with an orderly arrangement in contradistinction to Mark. By "arrangement" he probably means chronological order. Matthew is no more chronological than Mark or Luke, but Papias did not understand this. Many scholars have long asserted that Papias means a collection of sayings or discourses of Jesus, not a Gospel as we have them with narratives of miracles, controversies, and other episodes. That such a collection was first made in Aramaic seems altogether likely; but these scholars believe that the attribution of this collection to the apostle Matthew cannot be tested. Since, however, it is all but certain that the Gk Mt was known and used by 130, other scholars think that Papias must mean the Gk Mt, and that he knew (or had heard) that several translations had been made. There is no evidence that he had seen either the Aramaic Mt or more than one translation.

There are, however, serious difficulties against the hypothesis that Mt was written in Aramaic. It does not show the signs of a translation; in particular, it is difficult to retranslate Mt into an Aramaic original. There are some word plays (6:16; 21:41; 24:30) which are possible only in Gk. The citations from the OT number 41, of which 21 are common to Mt-Mk-Lk; these 21 are all given according to the LXX, which makes an Aramaic original unlikely and also weighs heavily against any common Aramaic source for all three. In the 20 citations peculiar to Mt the Hb text is followed more closely, but there are affinities to the LXX here also; the variations are not always easy to define, but it is clear that the author is not using the Hb OT, as one would expect an Aramaic writer to do. Finally, there is an evident dependence on Mk in almost all the narrative passages (cf SYNOPTIC QUESTION). It is therefore possible to maintain an Aramaic original of Mt only if one understands that the Gk Mt is a thorough and substantial revision of the Aramaic original and not a mere translation, and that no traces are left from which the Aramaic original can be reconstructed. It follows that Matthew is not the author of the Gk Mt.

3. *Date, Place of Composition, Destination.* There is no clear tradition on the date; the testimony of Irenaeus (cf above) cannot be tested. Critics conclude on internal evidence that the work cannot be earlier than 55, and believe this early date is improbable even for the Aramaic Mt. There is wide agreement that it is later than 70, although the evidence for this is not great; a date after the fall of Jerusalem is favored by Mt 22:7. The place of composition and destination are much clearer. Mt is the most Jewish and the most Palestinian of all the Gospels. Mt gives more space to the relations of Jesus with the Scribes and Pharisees than any other Gospel. He is more interested in the relation of Jesus to the law* (cf Doctrine, below). He mentions Jewish customs which are not mentioned in Mk-Lk (5:19, 32; 6:1-6, 16-18; 12:5; 23:5, 15, 23, 27). He emphasizes the personal mission of Jesus to Israel (10:5; 15:24). He cites the OT more frequently than Mk-Lk, and in his own name; cf below. There is no doubt that Mt was written by a Jewish Christian for Jewish Christians, and that both the author and his intended readers were of Palestinian origin; but if the work was written after 70, it could have been produced in Syria. Some scholars suggest Antioch.

4. *Contents and Plan.* The plan of Mt is itself a factor in his doctrinal perspective; cf below.

Prologue: 1:1-4:11.

1:1-2:23, genealogy and infancy* narratives.

3:1-4:11, preaching of John, baptism, temptation.

I. Galilean ministry: 4:12-13:58.

(1) 4:12-25, Capernaum, call of disciples, summary.

(2) 5-7, Sermon on the Mount.

(3) 8:1-9:34, cycle of 10 miracles.

(4) 9:36-11:1, missionary discourse.

(5) 11:2-12:50, incredulity and hostility of the Jews.

(6) 13:1-52, parables.

(7) 13:53-58, rejection at Nazareth.

II. Journeys of Jesus: 14:1-20:34.

(1) 14:1-12, death of John.

(2) 14:13-15:20, Jesus in Peraea, feeding of 5000, walking on lake, cures, controversy.

(3) 15:21-16:4, Jesus in N Palestine, cures, feeding of 4000, controversy.

(4) 16:5-17:27, instruction, confession of Peter, prediction of Passion, transfiguration, cure, 2nd prediction of Passion, temple tax.

(5) 18, discourse on the Church.

(6) 19:1-20:34, journey to Jerusalem, instructions, parables, 3rd prediction of Passion.

III. Ministry in Jerusalem, Passion and Death, Resurrection: 21:28.

(1) 21:1-22, messianic activity.

(2) 21:23-22:46, messianic teaching.

(3) 23, denunciation of Scribes and Pharisees.

(4) 24-25, eschatological discourse, and parables.

(5) 26:1-46, Jesus and disciples, last supper, Garden of Gethsemani.

(6) 26:47-75, Jesus before Jewish court.

(7) 27, Jesus before Roman court, crucifixion and death.

(8) 28, the risen Jesus.

The artificial character of Mt's arrangement is more obvious than it is in Mk-Lk; he employs a number of seams, particularly connecting particles such as "at that time" far more frequently than Mk-Lk. The arrangement of the five major discourses (5-7; 10; 13; 18; 24-25) is apparent; each of these is followed by an explicit conclusion (7:28; 11:1; 13-53; 19:1; 26:1). These discourses are synthetic; a comparison with Mk-Lk shows that the materials of Mk-Lk occur in scattered sayings, which Mt has collected, grouping them in each discourse about distinct themes. The invective against the Pharisees is also a discourse (23); this is a difficulty against the scheme proposed by L. Vaganay, who proposes that Mt consists of

5 "booklets," each composed of narrative followed by discourse. Vaganay further supposes that this was the structure of the source common to Mt-Mk-Lk (cf SYNOPTIC QUESTION). The structure actually can be traced clearly only in 5–9 and appears somewhat contrived in other portions of the Gospel. In 5–9 Jesus is presented in discourse as the messianic teacher and in miracles as the messianic wonder-worker. The plan can be discerned in 11–12 + 13, where, however, the order is inverted.

The emphasis on discourses shows that Matthew intends to present Jesus as a teacher superior to the rabbis, the teachers of Judaism. It also shows that the Gospel is conceived as a presentation of the teaching of Jesus as much as a recital of His life, and in this Matthew is less primitive than Mark. K. Stendahl has described its origin as "the school of St. Matthew," a group of Christian rabbis who wished to produce a catechism of Christian conduct. Thematic grouping can be observed in the narrative portions as well, particularly in 8:1–9:34, which focus upon the revelation and the confession of Jesus as Messiah.

5. *Composition and Style.* The Gk of Mt is evidently superior to the Gk of Mk; but it is also evident that an effort to write good Gk is more obvious in the narratives than it is in the discourses, which have retained much more Aramaic flavor than the narratives, and thus exhibit the Aramaic source. The explanation of Aramaisms in Mt is rare compared to Mk, for Mt was intended for Jewish readers.

X. Léon-Dufour notes certain features of "Semitic style": the use of catchwords ("little ones," 18:4–6; light-lamp, 5:4 f +), which were aids to the memory; numerical groupings (3 × 14 ancestors in the genealogy of Jesus, Mt 1:17; 7 petitions of the Lord's Prayer, 7 parables in the parable discourse, 7 woes against the Pharisees, 3 temptations of Jesus); inclusions i.e., the use of the same sentence or phrase at the beginning and the end of a passage (6:19, 21; 7:16, 20; 16:6, 12; 18:1, 4; 12:39, 45; 15:2, 20; 18:10, 14 +), synonymous and antithetic parallelism (7:24–27; 16:25), repetition of formulae (which occurs 15 times in Mt against 3 in Mk and 2 in Lk), and strophic structure (5:3–10; 12:22–32). Some of these are no doubt due to the Aramaic original source; others seem to come from the author of Mt.

Schematism appears in details as well as in the plan of the book. The accounts of miracles often follow a set pattern: the introduction of the persons, the request, the reaction of Jesus, command and effect, the reaction of the spectators. A comparison with Mk shows that in the narratives Mt has by far fewer details, and many of those which he has are obviously artificially added coloring, such as "on the mountain," "by the seashore," etc. These are not mere abbreviations; Léon-Dufour believes that this style is deliberately adopted in order to give the miracle stories the solemnity of a recital in which the symbolic meaning of the miracle becomes more apparent. The miracles are detached from a close connection with space and time and become an earthly manifestation of the heavenly reality. In consequence Mt's miracle stories are less vivid than the stories of Mk, but the style flows more smoothly. In the sayings of Jesus the words of Jesus are reduced to their essential content with no personal details. The genius of the author appears nowhere more than in this feature; for the Gospel sayings most frequently quoted in both ancient and modern literature are quoted from Mt, whose economy of phrase gives the sayings of Jesus their greatest force and impact.

6. *Doctrinal Themes.* The Jewish Christian character of Mt is evident in his conception of Jesus as the fulfillment of the OT, a theme which is more prominent in Mt than in Mk-Lk. He has more citations of the OT than Mk-Lk; 21 are common to Mt-Mk-Lk, and 20 are peculiar to Mt. Of these 10 are found in Mt and nowhere else in the NT. 37 OT citations are introduced with a formula, frequently "that it might be fulfilled." Peculiar to Mt is the reflective citation in his own name, in which he attaches the verse cited to a saying of Jesus or an episode. These are marked by ingenious applications which have long been recognized as rabbinical in style; it is now evident that they are similar to the exegesis applied to Habakkuk in the Qumran* scrolls. The idea of fulfillment is basic in Mt and perhaps original with him; but it would be a misconception to understand fulfillment in terms merely of prediction of future events. Jesus fulfills the OT by being the reality which is initiated in the OT, which, because it is the earlier phase of a single saving act, exhibits a community of character and traits with Jesus. It is noteworthy that 6 of the reflective citations are found in the infancy and passion narratives.

Jesus is therefore presented as the Messiah, the Christ, the Son of David; the element of the "messianic secret" is present, since it belonged to the original tradition, but it does not have the prominence which it has in Mk*. The genealogy shows that Jesus is the Son of David. Mt's theme is that Jesus could be recognized as the Messiah whom the Jews expected; they recognized Him and rejected Him, and thus cut themselves off from the messianic kingdom. He is not concerned with excusing them. Jesus did not come to destroy the law*, but to fulfill it (5:17–19). Mt alludes several times to the law, which is treated with reverence (5:31 f; 7:12; 12:5–7), to legal practices (8:4; 18:16; 24:20), and to the personal mission of Jesus exclusively to Israel (10:5, 23; 15:22, 24, 26). But because the Jews have rejected Jesus the kingdom is given to the Gentiles (3:8 f; 21:43–46; 23). The story of the Magi* (2:1–12) presents Gentiles as the first worshipers of Jesus. Pilate's washing of his hands, peculiar to Mt (27:24 f), emphasizes the rejection of Jesus by the Jews.

But Jesus is the fulfillment of the law, and therefore He is superior to it; He is Lord of the Sabbath (12:8), greater than the temple (12:6). One does not put new wine in old bags nor sew new fabric upon old (9:16 f). The "six antitheses" of the Sermon on the Mount (5:21–48) show Jesus as the new Moses, pronouncing a new law of equal authority with the old. Indeed, the very location of the discourse "on a mountain" where Lk places it "in a plain" (Lk 6:17) is a deliberate evocation of the first revelation of the law upon a mountain, Sinai-Horeb. The antitheses also show the novelty of the law proposed by Jesus; they are classic expressions, perhaps quoted more than any other Gospel passage, of the new dimension of Christian morality which aims at a perfection which imitates the perfection of the Father (5:48). A new righteousness* is presented; all the forceful implications of the word in the OT are retained, but an entirely new level is reached. It seems altogether likely that Mt's righteousness, although Mt is later than the Pauline writings, preserves a more primitive expression of the teaching of Jesus.

As in Mk-Lk, Jesus proclaims the kingdom (cf KINGDOM for fuller discussion). In the idiom of Judaism Mt generally avoids the term "kingdom of God" in favor of the euphemism "kingdom of heaven." In contrast to Mk the kingdom is more clearly a present reality (3:2; 4:17, 23; 9:35; 10:7; 12:28). It is also a future reality (5:3, 10, 19 f; 7:21; 8:11 f; 13:43; 18:3; 19:23 f; 25:34) and is identified with eternal life (5:19; 7:21). Where Mt's originality lies is in his explicit identification of kingdom and Church*; only Mt has the word ekklēsia (church) in the Gospels (16:18; 18:17). The kingdom as an existing society is clearly presented in the parables (13:24–30, 36–43, 47–50); this is the kingdom of the Son of Man (13:11; 16:28). That the kingdom-church is a hierarchical society, of which the disciples are the present existing reality

and the future governing body, is clear from "the ecclesial discourse" (18).

This feature of Mt's understanding of the kingdom has been much discussed, and many scholars have denied that it represents the original tradition; it comes, they say, from the reflective self-consciousness of the Church of the late 1st century. There is no need and no possibility to deny that Mt's expression is influenced by the language of his time; neither he nor Mk-Lk-Jn present the "very words" of Jesus. That the tradition is not genuine, however, can be shown only by adducing unquestionably genuine elements of a tradition which excludes Mt's kingdom-church; this has not been done and cannot be done.

7. *Historical Value.* From the above summary of the composition and form of Mt it appears that, like Mt-Lk, Matthew had no intention of writing a history or a biography of Jesus according to modern standards. His style lacks the immediacy of the eyewitness, and he depends on Mk and other sources for his material (cf GOSPEL; SYNOPTIC QUESTION). This of itself does not invalidate him as a historical source. Nor does his intention to write a gospel rather than a history invalidate him as a source; cf remarks on the historical value of MARK. His freedom in the arrangement of material, of his choice of themes and emphases, and in his adaptation of the gospel to his intended readers, is apparent and not devious; where he can be compared with Mk-Lk, no deformation either of the person of Jesus or of the events related appears. It remains popular history with its limitations, but faithful to its material.

Matthias (Gk *Mathias,* shortened from Mattathias*), chosen by lot to take the place of Judas* Iscariot as one of the Twelve (AA 1:23–26). He is not mentioned elsewhere in the NT, and the traditions about him found in the apocryphal* books and in the Fathers are historically worthless.

Mazzoth, Feast of (Hb *maṣṣōt,* lit "unleavened cakes"; Gk *azyma,* whence Eng Azymes). In Ex 12 Mazzoth is combined with Passover* as a historical feast commemorating the deliverance of Israel from Egypt. Only unleavened bread was to be eaten for a week beginning with the day of Passover (Ex 12:15–20; 13:3–7). The three feasts of Ex 23:15 ff include Mazzoth, to be celebrated in the first month of the year (in the spring); it is here associated with the exodus, but Passover is not mentioned. Mazzoth is described in the same terms in Ex 34:18, again with no mention of Passover. These two sources are regarded

A couple reclining at dinner, a painting from Herculaneum.

Egyptian banquet scene, showing men and women guests, a servant, musicians and dancers, and decorated wine jars.

Egyptian banquet scene at which all the guests are women. The guests wore cones of fat on their heads which cooled them.

as extremely early by critics, and it is consequently deduced that the historicization of Mazzoth occurred before its combination with Passover. Mazzoth and Passover are combined in the holiness code (Lv 23:6) and in the priestly code (Ex 12; Nm 28:17; cf LAW). Dt 16 exhibits a somewhat inconsistent pattern, drawing no doubt from different sources; Mazzoth and Passover are combined (16:1–8), but in the list of three major feasts of the year Mazzoth is mentioned without Passover (Dt 16:16). It is combined with Passover in the calendar of Ezk (45:21). The celebration of the feast without Passover is mentioned in 2 Ch 8:13; 30:13, 21; Ezr 6:22, and with Passover in 2 Ch 35:17.

It seems altogether probable that the historicization of Mazzoth is a later element introduced into the feast to connect it with the liturgical celebration of the saving deeds of Yahweh. The character of the feast indicates that it was an agricultural festival of thanksgiving for the beginning of the harvest. That which comes forth from nature is holy as coming immediately from the deity and must be offered to the deity before man can use it. The ritual of offering consisted in part in abstaining from the use of leaven for a week; to put leaven, a foreign matter, into the dough profanes its holiness. Scholars further ask whether it was a Canaanite agricultural feast adopted by the Israelites. That the Canaanites had such a harvest festival may be assumed, since all peoples have them; but there is nothing in Mazzoth which can be identified as specifically Canaanite.

The feast is mentioned in the NT in connection with the Passion narratives. The supper was eaten "on the first day of Mazzoth" (Mt 26:17; Mk 14:12), on "the day of Mazzoth" (Lk 22:1, 7); on the chronological problem involved cf PASSION. It is also mentioned in AA 12:3; 20:6. Paul's allusion to the feast in 1 Co 5:7, 8 (cf LEAVEN) suggests that the practice of eating unleavened bread at the time of the Passover was retained even by Gentile Christian communities. Mazzoth still survives in the Roman liturgy in the use of unleavened bread for the Eucharistic species.

Meals. In OT and NT times meals were taken twice a day, morning and evening. Pharisaic Judaism demanded that one wash before eating, a practice which was often omitted by the poor and less observant (Mt 15:1 f; Mk 7:1–5). When one came in from out of doors the feet were washed. Jesus observes that Simon* did not show Him the ordinary signs of courtesy to a guest; the water to wash the feet, the kiss of greeting, and the anointing of the head (Lk 7:44–

46). Egyptian art represents guests at formal dinners with cones of oil upon their heads, which melted and cooled them during the repast. For a formal dinner a guest was expected to wear a festive garment, usually white (Ec 9:8; Mt 22:11). It was a mark of courtesy for the host to extend a tasty morsel to a guest (Jn 13:26). In the ordinary house of OT and NT times meals were served on a mat laid upon the floor and the diners squatted about the mat. The remains of pottery show that there was no lack of number and variety of dishes; but all food was reached by the hands, since the knife, fork, and spoon had not yet been invented. Chairs and tables were known both in Egypt and Mesopotamia; ANEP 451 shows Ashurbanipal and his queen at dinner, the king reclining upon a couch before a table and the queen seated in a chair. Such furniture was available only to the wealthy in Israel*, but it is probable that the wealthy did imitate these foreign manners. It appears that Palestinian Jews of NT times to some extent adopted the Hellenistic and Roman style of eating, at least for more formal meals. The table was semicircular or horseshoe in shape and was built at a low level so that it could be reached from the couches on which the diners reclined. These were placed perpendicular to the table; the diner leaned on one elbow and helped himself with the other hand. That Jews ate in this way appears from the Gk words *anakeisthai, anaklinein, anapiptein,* and *kataklinein* to designate the posture taken while eating. The words are sometimes used improperly, as we might say "sit at table," when there was neither table nor couch, as in the multiplication of the loaves (Mt 14:19; 15:35; Mk 6:39 f; 8:6; Lk 9:14 f). Only in the Roman style of eating is it possible to represent the posture of the disciple seated next to Jesus at the last supper (Jn 13:23; 21:20). It is not known whether Jews followed the rather heavy Roman diet of four meals a day. The principal and formal meal was the fourth, the *cena,* which was taken about the 9th hour (3–4 PM). It included a large number of courses, and was often, especially if it was a festive dinner, protracted long after nightfall. The last supper was such a protracted meal. On the contents of the diet cf separate articles.

The messianic banquet is a figure of the joys of the messianic kingdom. The theme appears in the OT: Yahweh prepares a banquet for those who are redeemed on Mt Zion* (Is 25:6). It was found in the ritual banquet of the sect of Qumran*. Jesus uses it to describe the beatitude of heaven (Mt 8:11). It is implicit in the parable of the banquet (Lk 14:15–24). The last supper is presented as the messianic banquet in anticipation; the cup which Jesus shares with the disciples is a symbol and a pledge of the cup which He will share with them at their next banquet in the kingdom of the Father (Mt 26:29; Lk 22:16, 18) and Lk adds a promise that they will be seated at the messianic banquet in the kingdom (22:29 f). It is also a theme of beatitude in Apc 3:20; 19:9. In the Christian liturgy the Mass and the Eucharist retain the theme of the messianic banquet by anticipation.

Measure. Cf WEIGHTS AND MEASURES.

Medeba (Hb *mêdᵉba'*, etymology uncertain), according to Hb tradition a Moabite city taken from Moab by Sihon* king of the Amorites (Nm 21:30); included in the territory of Reuben* (Jos 13:9, 16); it is not clear to whom it is considered to belong in 1 Ch 19:7, but it is Moabite in Is 15:2. It is included in Moabite territory in the Moabite stone of Mesha* (ANET 321). With the rest of the territory of Moab it became Nabataean* after the exile. It was captured by the Jews in 128 BC but returned to the Nabataeans by Hyrcanus II (cf HASMONEAN). After the 4th century AD it became an important Christian center. The site, which lies about 25 mi S of Amman, contains two churches. Medeba is most famous for the mosaic floor of one of these churches, which preserves fragments of a map of Palestine in mosaic. This map is dated by R. T. O'Callaghan AD 578–608 and for the parts preserved is an important source for the topography of Palestine and the identification of biblical sites at this period.

Medes (Hb *mādai*, etymology uncertain), a people of the Iranian plateau. They are first mentioned by Shalmaneser III of Assyria (858–824 BC) who received tribute from them. Raids on their territory and tribute received are mentioned by Shamshi-Adad V (823–810) and by Sargon (721–705), who claims to have detached several districts of Median territory and incorporated them into the Assyrian kingdom. Up to the reign of Sargon the Medes appear as an extremely loose confederation of petty principalities. Herodotus relates that they were united into a single kingdom by Deioces (Daiukku, about 715 BC), who established the royal residence at Ecbatana*. That the claims of earlier Assyrian kings of sovereignty over the Medes were somewhat exaggerated may be deduced from Sennacherib's* (704–681) declaration that he received tribute from the Medes, a people whose name the kings his fathers had never heard. Esarhaddon (680–669) also invaded Median territory —

whose territory the kings his fathers had never invaded! The earlier claims probably arise from an indefinite idea of what the territory of the Medes was, particularly before the kingdom was united. Ashurbanipal (668–630) claims to have taken 75 cities of the Medes. The Medes were, nevertheless, a vigorous kingdom when under Cyaxares they formed an alliance with Nabopolassar of Babylon in 625 and waged the campaign which issued in the total destruction of Assyria. In 553 Cyrus*, prince of Anshan, rebelled against the Median king Astyages and united the Medes and Persians* into a single kingdom.

In the table of nations* the Medes are the sons of Japheth* (Gn 10:2; 1 Ch 1:5). According to 2 K 17:6; 18:11 the N Israelites were transported by the Assyrians to the cities of the Medes; this is probably a vague and loose designation of territory to the E. Other biblical allusions illustrate the duality of the Medo-Persian kingdom. The Medes are among those who attack Babylon, which was taken by Cyrus (Is 21:2; cf also Je 51:11, 18, where Cyrus is "the king of the Medes"). The Medes are included in the enumeration of foreign peoples in Je 25:25. In Ezr 6:2 Ecbatana is correctly located in the "province" (satrapy) of Madai. Medes and Persians are mentioned together in Est 1:3, 14, 19; Dn 5:28; 6:9, 13; 8:20, and Xerxes is said to be of "the race of the Medes" (Dn 9:1). The Medes remained a distinct people honored equally with the Persians in the Persian kingdom; and the biblical use of Mede alone to designate the Persian kingdom has extrabiblical parallels.

Mediation, Mediator. The concept of mediation is fundamental in most forms of historical religion. Commerce between the divine and the human is conceived as possible only through some recognized person who transmits communications from one to the other. From the divine point of view the mediator has some quality which makes him acceptable; from the human point of view the mediator is endowed with a charismatic power which places him in nearer contact with the divine, and with a representative quality in virtue of which he is enabled to speak and act on behalf of the human community. The idea of mediation appears in the religions of Mesopotamia, with both gods and men as mediators. The individual person was conceived as living under the patronage of a particular god or goddess who presented his petitions to the great gods and communicated to him the blessings which the great gods chose to bestow. This conception appears not only in the formulae of prayer but also in the large number of seals which represent the individual as introduced into the presence of the great god by another god who leads him by the hand or stands by while he prays and worships (ANEP 692, 697, 700, 701). The principal human mediator in Mesopotamian religions was the king*, who in the older Sumerian religion was an *ensi,* a viceroy of the god, who was the true king of the city. The king represented the people in cult and was the medium through whom the will of the gods was communicated and blessings were conferred. He was by office the head of the priesthood, which was a mediating office; the priesthood by divination made known the revealed will of the gods and by offering sacrifice was the mediator of prayer and worship. Egyptian religion likewise knew the mediation of king and priest, but its conception of mediation was distinguished by the unique position of the Pharaoh. The Pharaoh was himself a god, and as the incorporation of the people in his own person he brought the two worlds of god and man together.

Hb has no word to express mediator and mediation, but the concept is fundamental in Hb belief. Israel knows Yahweh because Yahweh has spoken, but Yahweh speaks to individual men who communicate the revelation. Of all Hb mediators Moses is the chief and the mediator after whom others are conceived. He was the mediator of the covenant*, the agent who in the name of Yahweh presented the covenant to Israel and in the name of Israel accepts the covenant. He is the revealer of the law*, the manifest will of Yahweh. He stands on a higher level of mediation than the priests, who also mediate through the communication of *tôrāh* (cf LAW), through the worship of the cult, which the priests alone could perform in the name of Israel, and through their power to bless*. In the monarchy the king also becomes a mediator; the Israelite king, however, should be distinguished as a mediator from the king in Mesopotamia and in Egypt. He is, at least in the earliest conception, a charismatic figure; he receives the spirit* of Yahweh and thus becomes the agent of deliverance. Like all ancient kings he is the incorporation of his people and a medium through whom blessing* comes. The covenant of David* absorbs the covenant of Israel because the king is Israel. But the Israelite king exhibits none of the divinity of the Pharaoh, nor even that superhuman quality which at times appears in the Mesopotamian monarch.

The Hb prophet* is the true successor of Moses as mediator, for he mediates the revealed will of Yahweh. The Servant* of Yahweh seems to be a prophet, but he adds an element of mediation unique in the OT and basic to the NT conception of mediation; for he mediates not only by communicating the word of Yahweh and by acting on behalf of Israel, but by bringing a blessing on Israel which is obtained through his own death. By taking upon himself the sins of Israel he removes from Israel its guilt and brings it the good will of Yahweh (Is 53).

Meditation in the OT rests on the election* of Yahweh, who alone designates and accepts the mediator and imparts to him the necessary charisma. Mediation is also an aspect of religion as a social reality; in a sense Israel itself as a community is the mediator for the individual Israelite, who cannot approach Yahweh except as a member of the Israelite community.

Angels* in the OT can be conceived as mediators only in a rather wide sense, and should be called intermediaries rather than mediators; they are not representatives of Israel. Their intermediation also is not a simple conception, and is not prominent in the early books of the OT; cf ANGEL.

The NT uses the Gk word for mediator (*mesitēs*), but the word is rare and found in only a few books. In Gal 3:19–20 the law is compared to the promises, and is considered inferior to the promises because it came through a mediator; only Moses can be meant by the mediator. The promises came to Abraham immediately from Yahweh, and the Christians, heirs of the promises, thus have a nearer approach to God than Israel. Gal 3:20 is entirely obscure and seems to presuppose a discussion which is not reported in the NT; one may suggest that Paul means that God, being one, does not need a mediator, and employs one only because He does not choose to act as immediately as He does in the promises, and still more immediately in His revelation in Jesus Christ. In any case the verse is an argument in a particular context and contains an overemphasis. 1 Tm 2:5 affirms that because there is only one God there is also only one mediator, Jesus Christ, a man. The emphasis on unity here is opposed to the multiplicity of mediators in Israel, all of whose functions are now summed up in the saving acts of Jesus Christ; but it is also in opposition, very probably, to the large number of intermediaries which were presented in the Gnostic beliefs of the time. The unity of the mediation of Jesus Christ also is a correlative of its universality; there is no other through whom man can approach God. The humanity of Jesus is emphasized; unlike the Gnostic mediators, He is a truly human being, and it is His human solidarity with the race which enables Him to act as its representative.

The term is used elsewhere in Hb 8:6; 9:15; 12:24. These verses assert the superiority of the mediation of Jesus Christ to the mediation of the old covenant. The mediation is conceived here chiefly as a priestly mediation, and the superiority lies in the excellence of that which is offered, which is the blood of the mediator Himself. The superiority lies also in the excellence of the new covenant over the old; a more efficacious offering secures a full redemption and establishes a far more intimate communion between God and man.

The theology of mediation in the NT goes far beyond the use of the term mediator. The mediation of Jesus rests upon His identity as Son of God and as man. He alone knows the Father and can reveal Him to others (Mt 11:27 f). He therefore surpasses Moses and the prophets as a mediator of revelation. He is the agent of reconciliation and through His redeeming death He communicates to men the new life which He possesses. Men reach God through their incorporation into Him (cf BODY). He is the way, the truth, and the life, through whom alone one comes to the Father (Jn 14:6).

Medicine. Professional physicians appear as far back as the Old Kingdom in Egypt (3rd millennium BC). There are several medical papyri from the Middle kingdom and the Hyksos period (2nd millennium BC). Ancient medicine was closely connected with magic* and it is sometimes difficult to dissociate the two. Thoth, the patron of the scribes, was also the patron of the physician. The papyri suggest by implication that there were medical schools. The skill of the physician lay in his diagnostic ability and his mastery of the pharmacopoeia, which is contained in the medical papyri. Both the diagnosis and the remedies depend almost entirely on tradition uncritically accepted and do not rise above the level of the · old fashioned home remedies. The pharmacopoeia contains some useful vegetable substances; the prescriptions, however, usually contain a fantastic mixture of repulsive elements which are fully as revolting as the witches' brew of *Macbeth*. In Egypt as elsewhere magic, which was largely responsible for this sort of concoction, was an obstacle to the progress of medicine. The Papyrus Edwin Smith is an exception among the medical papyri; it shows some anatomical observations, is sane and rational, and depends for the efficacy of its remedies on cooperation with nature.

Mesopotamia, it seems, was even less advanced medically than Egypt. The relation of magic and medicine was the same; the medical documents exhibit the same superficial diagnosis of symptoms and the pharmacopoeia contains the same type of simples. The Egyptians because of the practice of embalming* had at least an opportunity to learn some anatomy; but the Mesopotamians show practically no knowledge of anatomy. The practice of medicine was under the patronage of Ea, who was also the patron of magic. Primitive surgery was practiced; the code of Hammurabi* mentions operations on the eye, the setting of bones and the treatment of sprained muscles or tendons. The fee for such operations is set by the law. If the surgeon is responsible for the loss of life or sight, his hand is cut off (ANET 175).

The OT does not exhibit any certain trace of belief in the demonic character of disease, which was presupposed in the magic and medicine of Mesopotamia. Disease is an affliction sent from Yahweh, usually a punishment, and it is Yahweh who can heal (Ex 12:12; 1 S 5:6; 2 S 24:15; 2 K 19:35; Ps 39:11 f; Is 53:4). Sometimes the angel* appears as an agent of punishment instead of Yahweh Himself; this is probably the "destroyer" of Ex 12:23; cf also 2 S 24:16 f. The *deber* and the *keteb* of Ps 91:6 are personified agents of death; some scholars believe these may be demonic names. The medical knowledge exhibited in the OT is primitive, and it is scarcely possible to determine with certainty what diseases are meant by most names of diseases or to adduce the disease from the symptoms as described. It is also probable that some diseases are meant which are no longer known. The principal and only reliable treatment of disease was prayer and repentance; many of the Pss are petitions for healing (Pss 32, 38, 88, 91; Is 38, the prayer of Hezekiah). Physicians are mentioned more than once in the OT (Ex 21:19; Is 1:6 describes the treatment of wounds; Je 8:22; 46:11; Tb 2:10). The Chronicler finds fault with Asa* because he sought help not from Yahweh but from physicians (2 Ch 16:12). BS 38:1–15, written after the influence of Gk medicine had probably made itself felt in Palestine, praises the physician and the use of medicines; 38:15 is not, as it seems, a harsh judgment on the medical profession, but a devout wish that the traditional punishment of illness may be inflicted on the sinner. The OT, however, makes no reference to the details of the practice of medicine; Isaiah prescribed a fig poultice for the boil from which Hezekiah suffered (Is 38:21).

The NT exhibits the OT belief in the connection between sin and illness, which Jesus Himself at times expresses (Mt 9:2; Mk 2:5; Lk 5:20). He rejects this belief in its gross and exaggerated form; illness is one of the evils which afflicts mankind, and God in His providence permits it for other reasons than the personal guilt of the afflicted person (Jn 9:3). According to an early tradition Luke* was a physician; it is suspected that this may account for his omission (8:40–43) of the hostile remark of Mark* concerning physicians (Mk 5:26). On the healing miracles of Jesus cf MIRACLE.

Megiddo (Hb *m^egiddô*, etymology uncertain), a town located at the pass through the Carmel range connecting the coastal plain with the plain of Esdraelon. The strategic situation of the town where it commanded this highway made it important from early history. It is listed among the Palestinian cities conquered by Thutmose III, Seti I, and Shishak (ANET 242–243). It was the focus of Canaanite resistance to the invasion of Thutmose III, and this Pharaoh has left a lengthy account of his defeat of the Canaanite forces and his capture of Megiddo (ANET 234–238). The Amarna* Letters contain several communications from the prince of Megiddo, a satellite of the Egyptians, which show the importance of the city at this period (ANET 485).

Megiddo is listed among the cities conquered by Joshua (Jos 12:21); this list, however, is schematic and includes cities taken long after Joshua. Jos 17:11 f notes that Megiddo was one of the cities which Manasseh* was unable to take from the Canaanites; cf also Jgs 1:27. Jgs 5:19 mentions "the waters of Megiddo" but not the city; W. F. Albright and others conclude that the site was unoccupied at the time, and this fact, along with the archaeology of the site, affords a date for the battle of Barak* and Deborah* (cf below). Solomon rebuilt Megiddo (1 K 9:15; 1 Ch 7:29) and made it the administrative capital of one of his districts (1 K 4:12). Ahaziah*, king of Judah, died at Megiddo in flight from Jehu* (2 K 9:27). Megiddo was the scene of the death of Josiah at the hands of Necho* (2 K 23:29 f; 2 Ch 35:22 ff; on the ambiguity of these two accounts cf JOSIAH). The allusion to the mourning of Hadad-Rimmon in the plain of Megiddo (Zc 12:11) is obscure.

The site of Megiddo is a large tell, Tell el Mutesellim. The site was excavated by Schumacher 1903–1905 and by the Oriental Institute of the University of Chicago 1925–1934 and 1935–1939. This extensive exploration of the site was justified by the wealth of the material which it disclosed. The excavators distinguished 20 levels of occupation; the earliest was dated in the Chalcolithic period,

the 4th millennium BC. The first fortified wall of the town appeared in the EB period (3rd millennium BC). The city was totally destroyed about 2500 BC; this destruction appears in all EB Palestinian sites but no historical cause is known. The MB city (2100–1500) was the largest and most prosperous phase of the ancient city. From MB I (2100–1850) came the remains of three Canaanite temples and a large altar and a high place*. The exact extent of the MB city was not determined, but it was larger than the Israelite city, which covered about 13 acres inside the walls. The discovery of the base of an Egyptian statue in the MB I period showed that Egyptian influence was active in Palestine earlier than had previously been thought. The MB city was destroyed and rebuilt by Thutmose III about 1479 BC, and it became the headquarters of Egyptian administration in N Palestine. At the close of the 18th dynasty the city broke from Egyptian suzerainty; it was taken and destroyed by Seti I about 1300 BC, but rebuilt immediately. This phase of the city, LB II (1300–1150 BC), disclosed the Megiddo ivories* (ANEP 125, 126, 128). The LB II city experienced a violent destruction about 1150 and there is a hiatus in the occupation until about 1050. Albright places the battle of Barak and Deborah during this hiatus. Historical records disclose no agent of this destruction; it was not the Israelites. The city was reoccupied 1050–950, perhaps by the Philistines, who enjoyed their greatest successes during this period. The city was Israelite after 950; it was, however, probably taken by David before this date, since it is difficult to see how he could have achieved his conquests in the N without reducing Megiddo. The Israelite city of Solomon was unusually well built; the wall was carefully constructed of hewn and fitted stones and contained a complex gate* with several towers, the most elaborate fortification disclosed by Palestinian archaeology. The administrative importance of the city was reflected in the large palace, which must have been the residence of the governor, and in the enormous stables which housed a squadron of chariots; the stables would accommodate 480 horses. While there is little archaeological evidence, the city was probably destroyed and rebuilt by Tiglath-pileser* III in his conquest of Israel; it remained the administrative capital of the district. About 350 BC the tell was abandoned and the occupation moved to its foot; but Megiddo had lost its importance some centuries before. Recent exploration by Yigael Yadin has cast some doubt on the Solomonic origin of many of the large structures of the Israelite city, which Yadin thinks should be attributed to Ahab*.

Melchizedek (Hb *malkî-ṣedek,* "my king is righteousness," or more probably, "my king is Sedek" [a divine name]), king of Salem (Jerusalem; Gn 14:18–20). In this tradition Melchizedek met Abraham after Abraham's expedition against the four kings, gave him bread and wine, blessed him, and received a tenth of the booty of Abraham. Melchizedek as king was also priest* of the god of the city, El Elyon (cf GOD). In Ps 110:4 an oracle of Yahweh announces that the person addressed will be a priest forever "according to the manner of Melchizedek," as it is generally translated; but the Hb must be corrected according to the Gk in order to obtain this translation. The Hb reads, "on my account, Melchizedek," a certainly obscure and doubtful reading which makes the correction of the Gk probable; but what "the manner of Melchizedek" may be is left unidentified. On this and the identity of the person addressed cf below.

Melchizedek occurs only twice in the OT and it is improbable that the two passages are unconnected. Many critics point out that Gn 14:18–20 are not related either to what precedes or to what follows, and in fact disturb the dialogue between Abraham and the king of Sodom; they suggest that this tradition has been interpolated in its present context, perhaps because of the "king's valley" mentioned in 14:17. The tradition appears to preserve the first contact between the Israelite patriarch and the city which was later to become the heart of Israelite polity and faith. The identification of Salem and Jerusalem is not to be doubted. That Abraham should give portions (literally "tithes") to a priest who had blessed him was no more than correct ritual procedure and implies no superiority of Melchizedek to Abraham. The divine name Elyon, applied elsewhere in the OT to Yahweh but not yet verified as a Canaanite divine name, would have attracted the attention of the compilers of Israelite traditions. The text gives no indication that the bread and wine brought out by Melchizedek were a sacrifice; bread and wine alone were not the material of sacrifice. The priestly function performed by Melchizedek was not the offering of bread and wine but the blessing of Abraham. The connection between the bread and wine and the Eucharistic sacrifice was first made by Clement of Alexandria and Cyprian, and from this patristic interpretation Melchizedek has entered the Canon of the Roman rite of the Mass.

H. H. Rowley has suggested with great probability that Gn 14 in its present form is not merely an account of a contact of Abraham with Jerusalem and a blessing conferred on him by the priest-king of Jerusalem, but that its background lies in the period when David took Jerusalem. The priest Zadok*, who appears in the story of David only after Jerusalem became the royal city, is thought by many scholars to be the priest of Jerusalem who became priest of Yahweh under David. This story may be understood as a development of the tradition by the Jerusalem priests by which they established an ancient connection between themselves and Abraham. They affirmed that in worshiping El Elyon they had really worshiped Yahweh; and when they blessed Abraham in the name of El Elyon, Yahweh fulfilled the blessing by giving Jerusalem to David.

Rowley also suggests that this conception explains the allusion to Melchizedek in Ps 110:4. The "manner of Melchizedek" can only be understood to signify the priest-kingship of Canaanite city-states; but this conception of kingship was, if not rejected in Israel, certainly not accepted in its Canaanite form. If, with Rowley, the Ps is understood as a liturgical dialogue (a form paralleled often elsewhere in the Pss), this difficulty disappears. Zadok is the speaker in 110:1–3, 5–7; he addresses David and confirms his kingship in the name of Yahweh. David is the speaker in Ps 110:4, responding to Zadok by confirming his priesthood.

The allusions to Melchizedek in Heb 5–7 must be understood not as exegesis as we understand the word, but as a free use of biblical allusion to illustrate theological doctrine. Thus Heb mentions "the manner of Melchizedek" (5:6, 10; 6:20) in a way which suggests that Christ, who unites in His person all the messianic themes of the OT, here unites the functions of priest and king, as Melchizedek did. The explanation of the Melchizedek-Christ relationship in Heb 7 is somewhat involved. Christ is like Melchizedek in having no human father, for no genealogy is given of Melchizedek (Heb certainly did not intend to imply that Melchizedek was unbegotten, but seizes upon this external similarity as a point of illustration). Therefore Christ, unlike priests of the line of Aaron, is priest by divine appointment and not by descent. But Abraham, the carnal ancestor of Aaron, recognized the priesthood of Melchizedek by giving him tithes and receiving his blessing; therefore the priesthood descended from Abraham had to await the greater priesthood which its ancestor had recognized. This priesthood is that of Christ.

Melita (Gk *melitē,* etymology uncertain), the island upon which Paul was shipwrecked

(AA 28:1 ff). There can be little doubt that Melita is to be identified with Malta, although this form of the name is comparatively late in appearance; a few scholars have proposed an island in the Adriatic. Malta lies 60 mi S of the SE tip of Sicily and 200 mi from Cape Bon, the nearest point in Africa. It is 17 mi long and 9 mi wide at its greatest extent, 60 mi in circumference, and 95 sq mi in area. Little is known of its early history; it passed under Carthaginian rule at an unknown date and was permanently acquired by Rome in 218 BC during the Second Punic War. Its people acquired Roman citizenship at an unknown date, but before Paul's visit to the island; Luke calls them *barbaroi* (AA 28:1) in the technical sense of people who did not speak Gk. Their language was probably Punic. The title *prōtos* (first) given to Publius (AA 28:7) appears also in an inscription from Malta. "St Paul's Bay" on the N side of the island suits the narrative of AA well, even to the direction of the prevailing winds.

Mem. The 13th letter of the Hb alphabet, with the value of *m*.

Memphis (Gk *memphis*, Hb *mōp* in Ho 9:6, *nōp* elsewhere, represent the Egyptian Mennofer), one of the greatest and most ancient cities of Egypt. The site lies about 20 mi S of Cairo on the W bank of the Nile. Memphis was the royal residence during most of the 3rd–4th dynasties, its greatest period, and occasionally up to the 6th. Even after it was no longer the royal residence it was an important city, and its necropolis is large and imposing, containing most of the pyramids erected by the Pharaohs for their tombs. It was rebuilt by the pharaohs of the 18th and 19th dynasties. Because of its position Memphis was often exposed to the attacks of invading enemies; it was taken by the Ethiopians, the Assyrians, and the Persians. The city declined in importance after the foundation of Alexandria. Today nothing remains of Memphis except a few scattered stones. It is mentioned in Is 19:13; Je 2:16; Ho 9:6. The threat of Babylonian invasion in Je 46:14 was never verified. The destruction of Memphis is predicted in Je 46:19; Ezk 30:13, 16 not in particular, but as an Egyptian city. Je 44:1 mentions Jews living in Memphis, one of the places in Egypt to which they migrated after the fall of Judah in 587 BC.

Menahem (Hb *menaḥēm*, "consoler"), a personal name; king of Israel 745–738 BC. He seized the throne of Israel 745 by the assassination of his predecessor Shallum, himself a usurper; he put down resistance to his reign with extraordinary barbarity. He submitted to Tiglath-pileser* III of Assyria and paid tribute. This tribute is also mentioned in the annals of Tiglath-pileser III, which unfortunately do not give the date; the event is variously dated from 742 to 738 BC. The tribute no doubt secured Menahem on his somewhat unstable throne, and both he and his successor Pekahiah* represented the pro-Assyrian faction in Israel.

Mene, mene, tekel upharsin. The Eng transcription of the Aramaic words written on the wall during the banquet of Belshazzar* (Dn 5:25). That no one in the Babylonian court could read Aramaic is part of the element of the marvelous in the story. As the words are vocalized (*menē' menē' tekēl uparsīn*) they designate three measures (cf WEIGHTS AND MEASURES): a mina, a shekel, and two (?) half-minas. Dn's interpretation proceeds by a play on the words, which suggest *menāh*, "he has measured," *tekiltā*, "you are weighed," *perīsat*, "it (your kingdom) is divided"; the last word contains an additional play on *paras*, Persians. Such discoveries of meaning in assonant words appear in earlier prophets (Je 1:11 f; Am 8:1 f) and are also a demonstration of wisdom*.

Menelaus (Gk *menelaos*, "withstanding men"), In 172 BC Menelaus supplanted Jason* as high priest in Jerusalem by offering a bribe to Antiochus* IV. When he failed to make the expected payment he was called to account at Antioch and left his brother Lysimachus in charge of affairs at Jerusalem (2 Mc 4:23–29). At Antioch he bribed Andronicus, the king's representative; and when he was rebuked for this by the retired high priest Onias* he urged Andronicus to have Onias executed. Andronicus was executed by Antiochus for his share in the crime; but Menelaus, charged with this as well as with responsibility for disturbances, bought his way out by bribing Ptolemy, an officer of the king (2 Mc 4:30–50). In 169, when a false rumor arose that Antiochus had perished during his campaign in Egypt, Jason revolted and took the city; Menelaus and his followers were besieged in the citadel. Antiochus returned and crushed the revolt and Menelaus was restored as high priest (2 Mc 5:1–23). Menelaus is mentioned in the letter of Antiochus to the Jews dated 164 BC (2 Mc 11:29, 32). In 163 BC Antiochus, convinced by Lysias* that Menelaus was at the root of his troubles with the Jews, had Menelaus executed in a cruel and unusual manner (2 Mc 13:1–8). Josephus adds that Menelaus was the Gk name and that the Jewish name was Onias, and that he was the brother of the high priest Onias and

Jason. This must be due to a confusion of names, since it is most unlikely that each of two brothers would have been named Onias.

Meni (Hb *meni*), the name of a god mentioned with Gad* as worshiped by the Israelites (Is 65:11) with offerings of food and drink. The word possibly means "portion" and is thought to signify a god of destiny or fortune; but the name is not attested elsewhere.

Mephibosheth (Hb *mepibōšet*, altered from *meriba'al*, the form of the name which appears in 1 Ch 8:34; 9:40 in order to remove the divine name Baal), a personal name borne by two men, both of the house of Saul. **1.** Son of Saul and Rizpah*, executed by the Gibeonites* in atonement of the wrong done them by Saul (2 S 21:7 ff). **2.** A son of Jonathan*, crippled when his nurse dropped him while she fled after the death of Saul and Jonathan in battle. David* brought him, as the only survivor of the house of Saul, to the palace and supported him from the royal table (2 S 9:1–13). In the insurrection of Absalom Mephibosheth took the part of Absalom, or at least was so charged by his servant Ziba* (2 S 16: 1–4). When David returned after his victory Mephibosheth pleaded that he had been slandered by Ziba and that he had remained in Jerusalem because of his lameness; David, apparently not believing either one entirely, made Mephibosheth divide his estate with Ziba (2 S 19:25–31).

Merab (Hb *mērab,* meaning and etymology uncertain), elder daughter of Saul* (1 S 14:49); promised to David in marriage but given to Adriel (1 S 18:17–19). This was a slur upon David, since the eldest daughter, like the eldest son, was regarded as the most desirable (cf FIRSTBORN).

Merari (Hb *merārî*, meaning and etymology uncertain), son of Levi* and eponymous ancestor of the Levite clan of Merari (Gn 46:11; Ex 6:16, 19; Nm 3:33 ff; 4:29 ff; 7:8; 10:17). The cities and territories of the clan are described in Jos 21:7, 34–40, its clans and territories in 1 Ch 6:14, 29, 62 ff.

Mercury. Cf HERMES.

Mercy. The Hb word *hesed,* translated in the LXX by *eleos* and in the Vg by *misericordia,* is rendered by *mercy* in all but the most modern Eng Bibles. The translation *mercy* is unfortunate; but scholars are not agreed on the proper translation of *hesed.*

They are agreed, however, that there is no single Eng word which is an adequate translation. They agree also that the divine and human attitude designated by *hesed* is basic in Hb religion and Hb morality. This article presents a summary description of the usage of the word and does not attempt to employ any single Eng word as its equivalent.

The meaning of *hesed* is seen most clearly by studying the words with which it is associated. Perfect consistency should not be sought, since there is a development of the term over the centuries of its usage; a basic meaning does appear, however, which is modified but not substantially changed. The most common word used with *hesed* is *'emet* (cf FAITH), which signifies solidity, steadfastness, loyalty; and thus *hesed* is associated with the quality which makes another person dependable and worthy of faith. When the two words are joined they signify dependable *hesed. Hesed* is something which one can "do" for another, either God (Gn 24:12) or man (Gn 40:14); in each of these instances the person who does *hesed* is in a superior position, and in the story of Joseph it is the return of a kindness which is expected. But when Abner does *hesed* to the house of Saul (2 S 3:8) he is doing what is expected of a faithful retainer. The word in these and similar instances seems to suggest that a person does something which he is not obliged to do; but the object of the deed depends on him to do it from generosity and not from obligation. The warning which Lot receives from his guests to leave Sodom is a great *hesed* (Gn 19:19); while the guest and the host become members of the same family during the period of hospitality*, Lot seems to imply that the guests are going beyond the duty of a guest when they deliver him. Elsewhere *hesed* is expected as a normal part of good human relations. When the Psalmist curses his enemy he wishes that no one will show him *hesed* (Ps 109:12) because the enemy himself has not shown it (Ps 109:16). The wisdom literature praises *hesed* as the thing which wins *hesed* for oneself and assures success (Pr 11:17; 14:22; 19:22; 21:21).

Hesed is associated with *mišpat,* judgment*, which here signifies justice; the two virtues are a part of the conversion demanded by Yahweh (Ho 12:7), and are two of the three demands in which Micah makes the will of Yahweh consist (Mi 6:8). They are with righteousness* the attributes of Yahweh's dealing with men (Je 9:23). Zc 7:9 imposes them as a duty, and they are the first attributes mentioned in the list of the virtues of a ruler (Ps 101:1). *Hesed* in the judgment is a part of the conception of the judge* not as an arbiter but as a deliverer;

and here it may be described as the will to save; cf Gn 19:19; 40:14).

Hesed is associated with ṣᵉdāḳāh, righteousness. These are attributes which Yahweh manifests to the righteous and those who know Him (Pss 36:11; 40:11; 143:11 f). The last of these three passages again signifies the will to save. They are also the attributes of the human ruler, the Davidic king, by which his throne is established (Is 16:5; the same thought occurs in Pr 20:28); the hesed of the king is exhibited in his execution of judgment.

Hesed as the will to save is more clearly perceived in its association with yᵉšûʻa, salvation* and cognate words. The psalmist who trusts in the hesed of Yahweh rejoices in the deliverance of Yahweh (Ps 13:6), and asks that Yahweh will show His hesed and grant His salvation (Ps 85:8). The same element appears in the association of hesed with šālôm (cf PEACE; Ps 85:11). Where Yahweh withdraws His hesed there is no longer any šālôm (Je 16:5).

Other associations unite hesed with states of feeling; hesed is not merely a quality or an attribute, but a sentiment. As a youthful bride of Yahweh Israel exhibited hesed and love* (Je 2:2); and in the restoration of Israel Yahweh shows His own hesed and love of Israel (Je 31:3). It is also frequently joined with raḥᵃmîm, another word difficult to translate; but its relationship with reḥem, womb or belly, shows that it indicates a genuine emotional state and is often best rendered by mercy or pity. The sentiment of raḥᵃmîm is exhibited toward those who have suffered misfortune or those who, like children, are helpless; thus it is seen in parents, to whose raḥᵃmîm the raḥᵃmîm of Yahweh is compared (Ps 103:13). The saving deeds of Yahweh demonstrate His hesed and his raḥᵃmîm for Israel (Is 63:7). Yahweh withdraws them together (Je 16:5). Yahweh exhibits them, together with His righteousness and judgment, when He betroths Israel to Himself (Ho 2:21). They are to be exhibited by the Israelites to each other (Zc 7:9), and the psalmist appeals to these attributes for forgiveness (Pss 25:6; 40:12; 51:3).

The hesed of Yahweh is most frequently associated with the covenant*. In the covenant narratives of Ex (20:6; 34:6) the continuation of the hesed of Yahweh to Israel is conditioned upon the fidelity of Israel to His commandments. Yahweh preserves His covenant and His hesed to those who walk before Him (1 K 8:23). The covenant itself is called a hesed (Is 55:3). This conjunction of covenant and hesed is noticed especially in the covenant by which David is promised an eternal dynasty; the covenant is a hesed,

a preservation of hesed, a demonstration of hesed (2 S 7:15; 1 K 3:6; Ps 89:29, 34, 50). While the preservation of hesed is said to depend on the fidelity of Israel to the covenant (cf above), this is only a partial view of the hesed of the covenant; for it is the covenant hesed to which Israel and its representatives appeal as a motive why Yahweh should forgive their infidelity to the covenant. Hesed in Yahweh is more enduring than hesed in man and is a forgiving attribute which maintains good relations even when men attempt to destroy them (Ex 34:6; Nm 14:19; Je 3:12 f). As a consequence of covenant Yahweh expects hesed in Israel (Ho 4:1; 6:4, 6). The context in these passages suggests that the hesed which is desired is directed to Yahweh rather than to men; hesed toward Yahweh could be only that dependable good will which is reflected in most of the uses of the word sketched above.

It has been indicated above that the hesed of Yahweh sometimes indicates or implies His will to save. There are some passages in which hesed appears as the movement of the will of Yahweh which initiates and sustains the history of Israel (Is 54:10; 63:7; Je 31:3; Mi 7:20). The entire history of the dealing of Yahweh with Israel can be summed up as hesed; it is the dominating motive which appears in His deeds and the motive which gives unity and intelligibility to all His dealings with men, including such things as anger* and judgment*. This is emphasized in the numerous passages which affirm that the hesed of Yahweh endures forever (Is 54:8; 55:3; Je 33:11; Mi 7:20; Pss 85:8; 90:14; 100:5; 106:1; 107:1 +). It sustains the history of Israel's salvation into the indefinite future. The endurance of hesed tends to identify it with Yahweh Himself as other attributes are not so clearly identified, and to make the hesed of Yahweh the key to the understanding of His character.

This survey of some of the uses of the word illustrate why a single word cannot translate its richness of meaning. We have more than once adverted to "the will to save," but this would be too narrow a translation. N. Glueck proposed that it should be related to covenant and that it indicates the affection and fidelity which should unite members of a covenant. Other writers (Jacob, Stoebe) point out — correctly, it seems — that while this relationship is indicated in many contexts, there are other contexts in which hesed appears not only as covenant love, but as the movement of the will which initiates the covenant. The word indicates a broad and embracing benevolence, a will to do good to another rather than evil. It is not precisely love or kindness but the goodness of the heart from which love and kindness arise.

The NT use of *eleos,* also translated "mercy" in most Eng versions, is broader than the word "mercy" suggests. *Eleos* appears frequently in contexts where it renders *ḥesed* or is used in a way reminiscent of *ḥesed.* This is true, for instance, of the Benedictus* and the Magnificat* of Lk 1. The Gospels present *eleos* as the duty of one man to another; Jesus applies Ho 6:6 to this duty and makes His own attitude toward sinners the model of *eleos;* His attitude is one of readiness to associate with them, unlike the exclusivism of the Scribes, and He calls to them to enter the kingdom of God (Mt 9:13). The same verse is applied by Jesus in Mt 12:7 to the harsh judgment of the Pharisees* on those who do not observe the Pharisaic traditions and interpretations of the law*. With righteousness and fidelity, *eleos* is one of the more important features of the law (Mt 23:23); the reference here is once again to the rigid interpretation of the law. In these passages *eleos* signifies breadth and tolerance. Jesus makes the *eleos* which one shows another the condition of the *eleos* which one may expect from God (Mt 5:7; 18:33). The proof of the love of one's neighbor is the demonstration of *eleos* (Lk 10:37), and in this parable *eleos* is the rendering of assistance to one in need. In Mt 18:33 *eleos* is a readiness to forgive, and Mt 5:7 is very probably to be understood in the same way. Js 2:13 echoes this saying; here judgment without *eleos* may easily be rendered judgment without mercy. *Eleos* is a component of the wisdom from above; in contrast to worldly wisdom it shows itself in good deeds (Js 3:17).

The *eleos* of God appears most frequently as the will to save, echoing the OT use of *ḥesed.* With His love it is the *eleos* of God which moves Him to confer life in Jesus Christ (Eph 2:4; 1 Pt 1:3). The *eleos* of God is the motive of His saving will, not the merits of man (Tt 3:5). In Rm 9:22 f *eleos* and anger* are contrasted as motives of God's dealing with men; the passage is difficult, but *eleos* is clearly the antecedent will to save. *Eleos* is the motive which moves God to confer the apostolic office on Paul* (1 Co 7:25; 2 Co 4:1). It is also the divine attribute which heals illness (Phl 2:27).

The NT *eleos* can, when it is the *eleos* of God, much more easily be understood as His saving will which is antecedent to any deed of man. It initiates and consummates the process of salvation in Christ. In men it comes very near *agapē* (cf LOVE). It is chiefly manifested in the readiness to do good and to forgive, and "mercy" appears

to be too narrow a rendition. The NT *eleos* between men is transformed by the NT conception of love, which is a revolutionary development in the NT and places a deeper motivation behind *eleos* than we find in the OT.

Mercy seat. Cf ARK OF THE COVENANT.

Meribah (Hb *mᵉrîbāh,* "quarrel"?), the scene of a dispute between the Israelites and Moses* in the desert of Zin* (Nm 20: 1–13). Moses produced water from the rock. It was here that Moses committed the mysterious fault which has not been preserved in the traditions (Nm 20:12). In this context Meribah is identified with Kadesh*; the same identification appears in the name Meribath-kadesh (Nm 27:14; Dt 32:51; Ezk 47:19; 48:28). The story is difficult to distinguish from the story of Massah* of which it is a variant; Ps 81:8 speaks of a "testing" at Meribah, and Massah and Meribah are parallel in Ps 95:8. Other allusions (cf above and Ps 106:32) add no information. In Dt 33:8, however, Meribah is connected with the conferring of the priesthood on Levi; this is not amplified in the traditions. Meribah means a legal contention as well as a quarrel, and so it is somewhat synonymous with the alternate name of Kadesh, 'en mišpāṭ, spring of judgment. In Ezk 47:19; 48:28 it is simply a boundary point in the S.

Merodach-baladan (Hb *mᵉrodak-bal'adan* = Akkadian *Marduk-Apal-Iddina,* "Marduk has given a son"), a king of Babylon who sent an embassy to Hezekiah. Hezekiah showed them the treasures of the palace, and this was the occasion of a prediction of Isaiah that the treasures would be taken to Babylon (2 K 20:12–19; Is 39:1–8). This king was the Marduk-apal-iddina of the Assyrian records, an Aramaic prince of Bit-Jakin in the S of Mesopotamia who first appears as submitting to Tiglath-pileser* III (745–728). Under later Assyrian kings Merodach-baladan appeared as a persistent rebel whom Assyria found it difficult to suppress. He established himself as king of Babylon under Sargon in 721, but was expelled from Babylon after a year or so of rule and fled to Elam. He reappeared as a rebel against Sennacherib and once more took the throne of Babylon in 701. He was defeated by Sennacherib and continued the struggle until Babylon was destroyed by Sennacherib in 689. His ultimate fate is not recorded. This background of the narrative of 2 K and Is indicates that the embassy of Merodach-baladan must be dated in the neighborhood of 701, that the display of treasures was actually a calculation of resources for war, and that the purpose of the embassy was to secure the alliance of Hezekiah in a general revolt against Assyria, in which Hezekiah against the advice of Isaiah did engage.

Merom (Hb *mērôm*, etymology uncertain), "the waters of Merom," the scene of the battle between Joshua* and Jabin* of Hazor* (Jos 11:5, 7). The waters of Merom have traditionally been identified with Lake Huleh (cf JORDAN); modern geographers reject this identification. The name Merom is probably to be identified with the modern village *Meron* and the stream *Wadi Meron* in upper Galilee WNW of the modern town of Safed.

Meroz (Hb *mērôz*, etymology uncertain), a town cursed because it took no part in the battle of Barak* and Deborah* against the Canaanites (Jgs 5:23). The site has not been identified; Khirbet Maruz, SW of Lake Huleh, has been suggested.

Mesha (Hb *mêša'*, etymology uncertain), king of Moab*. He was subject to Ahab*

The inscription of Mesha of Moab.

but rebelled against Jehoram* after the death of Ahab. Jehoram and Jehoshaphat undertook a campaign against him and besieged him in Kir-hareseth, but the campaign was unsuccessful after Mesha sacrificed his eldest son (2 K 3:4–27). Mesha is also known from his own inscription, the Moabite Stone discovered in 1868 and brought to the Louvre in 1873 (ANET 320 f). Unfortunately the Arabs who discovered it broke it into several pieces in the hope of obtaining a higher price for the separate fragments. The expedition of Jehoram should be dated about 849 BC; W. F. Albright suggests that the contents of the inscription fit a date later in the reign of Mesha, between 840 and 820. The inscription relates the reconquest of Moabite territory from Israel, in particular from the men of Gad*, and the rebuilding of several cities. Mesha's own city was Dibon*. The subjugation of Moab is attributed by Mesha to Omri*. Mesha himself asserts that he freed Moab from the son of Omri, but this must be used loosely to refer to the grandson. The inscription is written in 8th century Hb characters in a language which does not differ from Hb of the period. Several idioms and phrases parallel biblical language and show the linguistic and ideological community of Israel and Moab.

Meshach (Hb *mêšak*, meaning and etymology uncertain), Babylonian name given to Mishael, one of the companions of Daniel (Dn 1:7).

Meshech (Hb *mešek*, etymology uncertain), a geographical or gentilic name; a son of Japhet* (Gn 10:2; 1 Ch 1:5, 17 also lists Meshech among the sons of Shem*); one of the conquered peoples enumerated by Ezk (32:26); one of the lands ruled by Gog* (Ezk 38:2 f; 39:1); mentioned with Kedar* in Ps 120:5, which suggests either ignorance of the location of Meshech or another name entirely. Meshech is probably to be identified with the Mushki of the Assyrian inscriptions. The Mushki were conquered by Tiglath-pileser I (1112–1074 BC), who describes them as a powerful people. They appear again under a king Mita in the reign of Sargon (721–705 BC). The Mushki appear to be identical with the Phrygians of Gk records and Mita is very probably the same name as Midas. Meshech except in Ps 120:5 is always mentioned with Tubal*.

Mesopotamia (Gk *mesopotamia*, "the land between the rivers," i.e., the Tigris* and the Euphrates*). Cf ASSYRIA; BABYLONIA; SUMER.

Messiah, Messianism. Messiah, Hb *mašîaḥ*,

"anointed," is used in the OT as a designation of the king of Israel* and of the priest (cf ANOINTING). There are a few passages in which the application of the term is doubtful; some scholars suggest that the nation is meant in Hab 3:13 and the patriarchs in Ps 105:15; 1 Ch 16:22. The word is rendered in Gk by *christos,* whence Eng Christ. The word messianism designates a complex of biblical ideas which it is difficult to define, and the opinions of scholars on the constituents of messianism differ widely. In general messianism includes those ideas which represent the Israel of the future as identical with the universal kingdom of Yahweh. It is not quite the same as eschatology, which deals with the end of history as accomplished by an intervention of Yahweh, although messianism is at least partly eschatological; nor is it quite the same as apocalyptic* thought, which represents the end of history as a world catastrophe, although some forms of messianism contain apocalyptic elements. In spite of the derivation of the word, messianism does not always include the idea of a future king or deliverer; some scholars insist that the term should be so restricted in order to distinguish messianism from eschatology. In this article are included with brief comments those texts which are usually treated as messianic in the broad sense of the term; references are given to treatment of some texts in other articles. The material is arranged according to the treatment of A. Gelin, DBS V 1165–1212.

A number of theories have been proposed which place the origins of Hebrew messianism in non-Israelite cultures and religions; none of these theories have been generally accepted and they are all open to serious objections. They may be grouped under theories which associate messianism with the place of the king in Mesopotamian cult and with the dualism of Persian religion. Mesopotamian and Canaanite religions contain the myth of the annual dying and rising god whose death and resurrection is the heavenly event which assures the renewal of the cycle of fertility. The king to some extent not clearly known played the part of the god in the cultic representation of the myth. Persian dualism exhibits a struggle between the god of light, Ahura Mazda, and the god of darkness, Ahriman or Angra Mainyu, which issues in the victory of light. Israelite messianism exhibits neither the cyclic conception of history, which imitates the conception of nature, upon which the Mesopotamian-Canaanite myth rests, nor the dualism of Persian religion. The unique character of Hebrew messianism arises from the biblical conception of history as a process which moves toward a final term. This term

is the kingdom* of Yahweh. Israel, and in particular the king of Israel, is the medium through which the kingdom of Yahweh is to be established. This conception obviously exhibits several stages of development which reflect the evolution of Israelite cultural and political institutions and the catastrophes of Israelite history, as well as Israel's growing awareness of the character of Yahweh; this development appears in the texts listed below.

The treatment of messianism is usually begun with Gn 3:15; on the context cf FALL, THE. This text is often misunderstood because of the erroneous Vg translation, "she will crush your head" where the Hb has "it (the seed) will crush your head." The translation "crush" is not certain; the same word designates both the attack of the serpent on the man and the defensive movement of the man against the serpent; some word like "strike" is more accurate. The seed of the woman most probably designates man; the nature of the struggle must be understood according to the identification of the serpent*; cf FALL, THE. In the most general messianic sense the verse speaks of a struggle between man and evil, however the serpent be interpreted, in which man will not be defeated. In the scheme of messianism the passage takes a broad view of the conflict between man and evil, looking at humanity at large and not merely at Israel. The passage is not certainly the earliest in which messianism can be found; in its present form it is probably no earlier than the 10th century BC (cf FALL, THE; PENTATEUCH).

The Patriarchs. Gn contains a series of promises and blessings (Abraham, 12:1–3; 13:15–17; 17:1–8; 22:15–18; Isaac, 26: 2–5, 24; Jacob, 28:1–4, 13–15; 35:9–12; 48:3–4). On the literary character of the patriarchal narratives cf ABRAHAM; ISAAC; JACOB; PATRIARCHS. These blessings and promises are constructions formed on oral tradition; but the tradition exhibits a consciousness of destiny arising from the personal relations between the patriarchs and the God who revealed Himself to them. The promises and blessings are messianic in the broadest sense; they refer explicitly to the possession of the land and the growth of Israel as a people, and to some extent are formed in the light of the history of Israel.

The Covenant*. The covenant is the basic conception upon which the religion and the polity of Israel are built. The covenant not only establishes the union between Yahweh and Israel but also constitutes Israel a people. In the covenant is communicated the code which is to regulate the life of Israel as the people of Yahweh, and by its election* Israel is directed in its historical progress by the government of Yahweh according to the moral will which is revealed in the covenant. By the covenant the reign of Yahweh is established in Israel; this is the core from which messianism becomes universal.

The Oracles of Balaam* (Nm 23–24). These oracles, which probably come from the premonarchic period, are likewise messianic only in the broadest sense; they identify Israel as a distinct people not like other nations, successful in war and prosperous. They are therefore expressions of the national consciousness of Israel and of its destiny, but they do not extend to properly messianic ideas. The usual translation of "the star of Jacob" (Nm 24:17), which is taken as an allusion to royal messianism (cf below), is questioned by W. F. Albright (cf BALAAM).

Royal Messianism. With the establishment of the monarchy (cf KING) the messianic idea takes on the political form of the Israelite monarchy, and the king himself, David and his dynasty, become the dominant element in messianism. The prominence of the king rises from the conception of king and kingship in the ancient world; the king was the visible incorporation of his people, a "representative personality" through whom and in whom the people act as a political unit. Hence the messianism of the king is not really distinct from the messianism of Israel as a people.

The blessing of Judah* (Gn 49:8–12) is very probably written under the monarchy, and in the earlier period, perhaps in the reign of David himself. David is the one "to whom tribute is due" (cf JUDAH). The tribe of Judah is promised an eternal rule; this is an important conception which perseveres in later developments of messianism. The king also appears as the agent of prosperity; this is one of his functions as "savior."

The Oracle of Nathan. This oracle appears in three forms: 2 S 7:5–16; 1 Ch 17:4–14; Ps 89:20–38. Which of these three best represents the original form of the oracle has been vigorously debated; an apodictic statement is impossible, but the weight of the probability seems to lie with Ps 89. The oracle promises an eternal dynasty to David; this is the object of a covenant which in a way supplants the covenant with Israel. The monarchy is the agency through which Yahweh will fulfill the destiny of Israel; and the eternity of the dynasty includes the eternity of Israel. The messianic idea takes the form of a kingdom ruled by the king established by Yahweh. The oracle is echoed in 2 S 23:1–7; Ps 132:11–18.

The Royal Psalms*. The group of royal Pss (2; 20; 21; 45; 72; 89; 101; 110) are now generally dated under the monarchy; Ps 110 may very probably be attributed to the reign of David and Ps 2 to the accession of Solomon. In some passages it is evident that it is the historical king who is addressed or spoken of; in other passages terms are used which can be applied to no historical king, and these are understood by many interpreters to refer to the eschatological messianic ruler, the ideal king who will terminate the line of David and realize the reign of Yahweh upon earth. There are difficulties against assuming such a change of person in the individual Pss; and many interpreters suggest that the king meant in the Pss is always the historical contemporary ruler who is addressed in messianic terms. The basis for this address is the conception of the dynasty as a continuing living reality; each king is theoretically a new David who carries on the covenant of David and is the charismatic leader of Israel, the man through whom Yahweh saves Israel. The accession of the king is a pledge of the covenant and a step toward the realization of Israel's destiny; and the king is addressed in terms which anticipate the realization of the destiny. Therefore they speak of complete victory over the enemies of the king and of the marvelous prosperity which his reign will bring.

The preexilic Prophets. The messianism of the preexilic prophets was profoundly affected by the world kingdom established by Assyria* during the 8th and 7th centuries. The empire was a threat to the survival of the Israelite monarchy, and did in fact extinguish the kingdom of N Israel; but it also presented the political framework of a world kingdom which was easily transferred to the reign of Yahweh. This does not imply that the idea of the universal reign of Yahweh arose only as a response to the Assyrian empire; but the form of the conception was no doubt drawn from the Assyrian achievement.

Isaiah. In Is 6–9 the Davidic monarch appears as a savior in even more grandiose terms than in the royal Pss. The birth of an heir to the throne (Is 7:10 ff; cf EMMANUEL) is a pledge that Yahweh is with the kingdom; and the king is saluted in Is 9:1–6 as the agent of Yahweh's victories who will inaugurate a kingdom of justice and righteousness. His superhuman qualities are seen in the four titles "wonderful counselor, divine hero, father forever (?), prince of peace" (Is 9:5). A similar passage in Is 11:1–9 is attributed to a later writer by many scholars; this conclusion is not imperative, but it seems that the passage must at least be placed in the later years of Isaiah, after Assyria had reduced Judah to a vassal kingdom and Isaiah could look only to a resurgence of the dynasty in the future, "a shoot from the stump of Jesse." Here the king receives the spirit* which fills him with the six virtues of the ruler. A new theme is introduced which appears often in later literature, the conception of the messianic age as a restoration of paradise*. In these passages of Isaiah the political structure of the messianic kingdom is more clearly defined; but the moral regeneration of the kingdom is also more clearly stated, and the messianism of Isaiah can by no means be called a political messianism. The agency of the messianic king is obscure. Yahweh is the true creator of the messianic kingdom.

Mi 5:1–5. The text and meaning of this passage are obscure; it is clear, however, that it refers to a king of the Davidic line (cf BETHLEHEM), an ancient house, who will save his people. The assurances against Assyria which follow these lines may be an addition to the original utterance.

Exilic and postexilic Prophets. With Je 23:5 f; Ezk 34:23; 37:24 f there appears the conception of the Messiah as a *David redivivus*, a returning David. This does not signify a return of David in person but the restoration of the fallen dynasty and kingdom through a king who will exhibit the traits of the ideal king, which David was thought to have been. In Ezk 21:32 the blessing of Judah (Gn 49:10) is applied to the ideal ruler of the future. Such passages as Je 30:9; Am 9:11 ff are probably exilic additions to the text of these prophets.

In Hg 2:20 ff; Zc 6:9 ff the messianic hope is attached to Zerubbabel*, the surviving head of the house of David. On the somewhat obscure and complex political background of these passages cf ZERUBBABEL; ZECHARIAH. Here it is sufficient to note that the hope of the future is still centered upon the royal house of David, and that the existence of an heir to the throne of David is an assurance that the saving will of Yahweh will be accomplished.

In Zc 9:9 f, a passage of still later and uncertain date, the king is represented as a bringer of peace, but not precisely as a conqueror. The grandiose external character of royalty is explicitly taken away from him, and he is one of the "poor," the great lower class with which postexilic Judaism identified itself (cf POOR). Here also the political realities of the time affect prophetic conceptions; the terms of the preexilic royal psalms could scarcely be employed in the Judah of the Persian period.

The Reign of Yahweh. A number of passages are understood in a broad sense as messianic, although they do not refer to a personal agent of deliverance. They are derived from the idea of Israel as the people of Yahweh by covenant and from faith in the promises and saving will of Yahweh,

which is not frustrated even by the sins of Israel. The destiny of Israel is to attain perfect union with Yahweh through unqualified submission to His will; only then will it attain peace* and salvation*, and the reign of Yahweh thus established in Israel will be extended to all men. The salvation of Israel is conceived by Hosea (2) as a return to the desert and a reestablishment of the covenant under conditions similar to the conditions of Sinai. The psalms of the kingship of Yahweh (Pss 47; 93; 96–100) present the universal reign of Yahweh. In Is 2:1 ff; Mi 4:1 ff Zion is the center from which the word of Yahweh will reach all men and inaugurate universal peace. The second part of Is describes the restoration of Israel (40–48) and of Zion (49–52; 54–55; 60–62) as a center to which the nations shall come in submission to Yahweh. In Je 30–31 the restoration of Israel and of Jerusalem is dominated by the idea of a moral regeneration of the people and by the new covenant which is written on the heart and not on tablets. Ezk 34–37 likewise represents the restoration and the regeneration of Israel, even to the resurrection of the nation from apparent death (Ezk 37:1–14). The temple and Jerusalem are to be the symbols of Yahweh's presence among His people (Ezk 40–48) which was withdrawn when He punished them (Ezk 10). The establishment of the reign of Yahweh is sometimes combined with the theme of judgment*.

On the Servant* of Yahweh and the Son* of Man cf these articles. Both of these ideas are somewhat abrupt departures from the common messianic themes.

Messianism thus outlined appears as a consistent development of certain themes and beliefs which have their origins in early Israelite religion. It is faith in the power and will of Yahweh to save and takes form as Israel learns more clearly what that power is and how it is exercised, how it is the moving force of history, and what it means to be "saved." There is a certain desecularization of an idea which in its earliest form is rather social and political than moral and religious. Through its history Israel learns that salvation is not achieved through cultural and political institutions; salvation is achieved only through the intervention of Yahweh, and since the obstacle to salvation is man's refusal to accept it, the intervention frequently takes the form of judgment. Messianism precisely understood, i.e., with reference to a personal human agent of deliverance, brings out the human factor in deliverance; while it is the work of Yahweh, it is a work in which man must share.

While the messianism of extrabiblical Judaism lies somewhat outside our scope, it is necessary to allude to it because it is presupposed in many NT allusions. As messianism is reconstructed from the apocryphal* books, it appears to have been rather thoroughly secularized into a hope of a Jewish empire established by the intervention of God. This made it necessary for Jesus to use great reserve in the employment of messianic terms, in particular those which refer to royal messianism. The messianic future looked to the restoration of the kingdom of Israel and to the consummation of the world. There is no consistent conception; sometimes the restoration of Israel is followed immediately by the consummation, at other times there is no earthly kingdom of Israel at all, but the entire messianic consummation is extraterrestrial. Not infrequently the earthly kingdom is said to endure 1000 years before the consummation; this idea passed into early Christian thought. The nations are judged or destroyed and Palestine is renewed and turned into an earthly paradise. The Messiah himself is likewise not consistently understood; but often he is a preexistent superhuman being who comes from heaven. He is the conqueror of the nations and the ruler of the earthly kingdom. The importance of the priesthood in later Judaism, particularly under Hasmonean* rule, led to the conception of two Messiahs, a Davidic royal Messiah and a priestly Messiah of Levi or Aaron. This idea, formerly known in only one apocryphal book, has now appeared also at Qumran*.

On messianism in the NT cf CHURCH; ISRAEL; JESUS CHRIST; KINGDOM.

Methuselah (Hb *mᵉtûšelaḥ*, "man of Shelah [god?]"), in the Sethite genealogy son of Enoch* and father of Lamech* (Gn 5:21–27; 1 Ch 1:3; Lk 3:37); died at the age of 969 years. Methuselah is possibly a variant of Methushael* in the Cainite genealogy; cf PATRIARCHS.

Methushael (Hb *mᵉtûšā'ēl*, "man of El" [god?]), in the Cainite genealogy son of Mehujael and father of Lamech* (Gn 4:18); possibly a variant of Methuselah*; cf PATRIARCHS.

Meunim (Hb *mᵉûnîm*, etymology uncertain), a nomadic tribe of S Palestine; exterminated by the tribe of Simeon* in the reign of Hezekiah* (1 Ch 4:41); attacked by Uzziah* (2 Ch 26:7); they are probably to be read instead of Ammonites* in 2 Ch 26:8. They are probably to be read in 2 Ch 20:1 as attacking Judah with the Moabites and the Ammonites. Some of the tribe appear among the temple servants in the postexilic community (Ezr 2:50; Ne 7:52). The tribe

is not mentioned elsewhere and is connected by most scholars with the modern place name Maan SE of Petra.

Micah (Hb *mîkāh*, abbreviation of *mîkāyāhū*, "who is like Yahweh"), a prophet to whom is attributed the 6th of the books of the 12 minor prophets.

1. *Contents*. The book is apparently divided into two collections (1–5; 6–7), each of which is divided into a collection of threats (1–3; 6) and promises (4–5; 7).

1:1, title; 1:2–4, invocation and theophany; 1:5–9, sins of Israel and Judah and threat of the destruction of Samaria: 1:10–16, dirge for the cities of Judah invaded by an enemy; 2:1–11, woe against rich oppressors; 2:12–13, ingathering of the remnant of Israel; 3:1–4, against oppressive rulers; 3:5–8, against false prophets; 3:9–12, against oppressive rulers, threat of the destruction of Jerusalem; 4:1–5, Zion the center of the messianic salvation; 4:6–10, ingathering of the exiles from Babylon; 4:11–14, fall of the enemies of Zion; 5:1–3, the messianic king; 5:4–5, promise of protection against Assyria; 5:6–8, the power of the remnant of Jacob; 5:9–14, Yahweh removes superstition from Israel; 6:1–5, the charge of Yahweh against Israel; recital of His saving deeds; 6:6–8, virtue preferred to sacrifice; 6:9–16, threat against the city; 7:1–6, breakdown of morality among the people; 7:7–20, a prophetic liturgy: the conquest of enemies; the restoration of the exiles; the renewal of the favor of Yahweh.

2. *The Prophet*. Micah came from Moresheth-Gath* in SW Judah. The work is dated in the title in the reigns of Jotham*, Ahaz*, and Hezekiah* (750–687 BC). Many critics feel that this is too long a period and find no trace of any utterances in the reign of Jotham. 1:6 refers to Samaria* as still in existence and is therefore to be dated before 721. The unnamed city of 6:9–16 is thought to be Jerusalem by some critics, Samaria by others (6:16). The military disaster of 1:10–16 is in all probability the invasion of Sennacherib in 701. Nothing else is known of the life or person of the prophet; the evidences of his village or peasant origin found in the book itself are for the most part fanciful. Micah is a contemporary of Isaiah and exhibits similarity of thought, although he is quite independent.

3. *Criticism*. There is quite general agreement that 1–3 are original with the exception of 2:12–13 which presupposes the exile* and the diaspora*. 6:1–7:6 likewise are generally accepted as original. Some earlier critics refused in principle any oracles of promise in preexilic prophecy and therefore treated 4–5; 7:7 ff as secondary. Modern criticism does

not accept this principle and deals with each passage by itself. Passages which presuppose the exile (2:12 f; 4:6–10; 5:6–8) must be regarded as postexilic commentaries on the text, 4:1–5, which is duplicated in Is 2:1–4, is generally regarded as a postexilic addition to both Is and Mi. The passage on the messianic king (5:1–3) is more difficult to judge; many critics regard it as postexilic, but there is nothing which demands a later dating. It is in harmony with the messianic passages of Is 7:10; 9:1 ff; 11:1 ff, and it is likely that these outbursts of royal messianism at this particular period have a common origin in the feelings of the time. The lines on Assyria (5:4–5) are probably a later commentary. 5:9–14 is a threat in the collection of promises and contains nothing which casts doubt on its originality. The prophetic liturgy of 7:7–20 is questioned by most critics, but several recent writers (Eissfeldt) observe that there is nothing except 7:11–13 which indicates a later origin.

4. *Theology*. The thought of Micah is simple; he proclaims that the political disasters which threaten Israel and Judah come from the anger of Yahweh which the people have excited by their sins. The themes in which this is expressed are common in the preexilic prophets: the sins of oppression and dishonesty; the practice of superstitious worship; the primary importance of genuine morality. Like Jeremiah, Micah describes a breakdown of morality and mutual confidence. Accepting as original the passages mentioned above, Micah views this punishment as something through which Israel must pass in order to survive. Yahweh will not destroy His people completely, but He will impose upon them the standards of traditional morality. Ultimately the hope of Israel rests upon the forgiving mercy of Yahweh; Yahweh will restore the nation through a new David (5:1–3).

Unlike Isaiah, Micah envisages the destruction of Jerusalem (3:12). If the passages mentioned above are secondary, he does not attend to the destiny of the nations which attack Israel as Isaiah does; and these passages (e.g., 4:11–14) bear a strong resemblance to some parts of Is 40–66. Micah is also aware of the nature of the true prophetic vocation in contrast to the professional prophets, to whom, like Jeremiah, he contrasts himself; the charisma of the prophet is power and the spirit of Yahweh, judgment and strength to declare iniquity and sin (3:8).

Micah's prediction of the fall of Jerusalem was alleged in favor of Jeremiah when Jeremiah was tried on a charge of blasphemy for a similar threat (Je 26:18). The mes-

sianic passage (5:1–3) is quoted in Mt 2:6 and is referred to in Jn 7:42.

Micaiah (Hb *mikāyāhû*, "who is like Yahweh"), a prophet of N Israel, son of Imlah (1 K 22:8–28; 2 Ch 18:7–27). Micaiah predicted the defeat and death of Ahab* in battle with the Aramaeans at Ramoth-gilead. He was known as a prophet who "always prophesied evil"; in Je 28:6–9 this is proposed as a mark of the genuine prophet. It may be supposed that Micaiah spoke in the same terms as the later prophets Amos and Hosea and was in the same prophetic spirit as Elijah, although no contact between the two is mentioned. Micaiah attributes the hopeful utterances of the court prophets to a lying spirit sent from Yahweh to deceive them; this is a more primitive view of the false prophets than we read in Je 23:16–32. It is not impossible that the words of Micaiah express profound irony. Micaiah was imprisoned by Ahab to await the victorious return of the king, which never happened; nothing further is related of him.

Michael (Hb *mīcā'ēl*, "who is like El"), a personal name. In Dn 10:13 Michael is the name of one of the "chief princes" who assists Gabriel* on behalf of the Jews against the "prince" of the kingdom of Persia. In Dn 10:21 Michael is "your prince" who strengthens Gabriel, and in 12:1 he is the "great prince who stands over your people." Michael is conceived as the heavenly spirit who watches over the Jews; and the "prince of the Persians" implies the conception of a guardian angel for each nation. Michael is prominent in the apocryphal* books in the role of protector of the Jews. Jd 9, where Michael is called an archangel, refers to a dispute between Michael and the devil concerning the body of Moses; this allusion probably comes from a lost portion of the *Assumption of Moses* (cf APOCRYPHAL BOOKS). In Apc 12:7 Michael is the leader of the angelic hosts in the battle between the dragon and his angels. In the Christian liturgy Michael is the protector of the Church and the angel who escorts the souls of the departed into heaven, a *psychopompus*.

Michal (Hb *mīkāl*, meaning and etymology uncertain, possibly an abbreviation), a personal name; younger daughter of Saul (1 S 14:49), given to David as wife at the price of a hundred foreskins of the Philistines, although Saul had promised his elder daughter Merab* (1 S 18:20–28). Michal loved David (1 S 18:20) and proved her loyalty when Saul attempted to murder David. She revealed her father's plot to David and deceived Saul's emissaries by placing a dummy in David's bed while David escaped (1 S 19:11–17). After David's flight Saul gave Michal to Paltai (Paltiel) as wife (1 S 25:43); and one of the conditions David imposed in his treaty with Abner was the return of Michal (2 S 3:13–16). Michal's pride and sense of dignity were offended by the dance of David before the ark, and David in fury refused to cohabit with her (2 S 6:20–23). Merab is to be read for Michal in 2 S 21:8.

Michmash (Hb *mikmāš*, etymology uncertain), a place name; town near the scene of Jonathan's exploit against the Philistines and the battle which followed (1 S 13–14). Is 10:28 locates it N of Jerusalem near the city. In the period of Nehemiah it was settled by the tribe of Benjamin (Ne 11:31). It is mentioned in the list of Ezr 2:27; Ne 7:31. In the Maccabean period is was the residence of Jonathan* (1 Mc 9:73). The modern village of Muhmas a short distance N of Jerusalem occupies the site.

Midian (Hb *midyān*, etymology uncertain), a nomadic tribe. Israelite kinship with Midian was recognized in the genealogy of Abraham, which included Midian among the descendants of Abraham through Keturah* (Gn 25:2–4; 1 Ch 1:32 ff). They appear as traders both in an early story (Gn 37:28, 38, where the group is also called Ishmaelites*), and in a late prophetic passage (Is 60:6). Moses fled to Midian from Egypt and married a Midianite wife (Ex 2:15 ff) and the vision of the burning bush occurred in Midian (Ex 3:1). The father-in-law of Moses, Jethro* or Reuel*, was a Midianite priest (Ex 18:1), and Hobab*, the son of Reuel, acted as guide of the Israelites through the desert from Sinai. These early friendly relations with Midian were not maintained. They appear with the Moabites in the story of Balaam* (Nm 22:4–7); it is possible that the name is intruded here, but the Midianites appear elsewhere connected with the land of Moab. In Nm 25, where the Israelites practiced the orgiastic worship of the Moabite Baal* of Peor, one of the worshipers was a Midianite woman who was killed with her Israelite partner by Phinehas*. The war of vengeance in Nm 31 can scarcely be historical; but the story attaches the anecdote of Baal Peor to the Midianites. In Jos 13:21 Midianite chieftains are mentioned as vassals of Sihon* king of Moab. Midianite raids on Israelite territory were a scourge in the period of the judges (Jgs 6–8); here the domesticated camel* appears for the first time in the OT. Gideon's victory is alluded to as a saving deed of Yahweh in Is 9:3; 10:26; Ps 83:10. The Midian-

ites appear as neighbors of Edom* in 1 K 11:18. A tradition of uncertain date relates the conquest of Midian by Edom (Gn 36:35; 1 Ch 1:46).

Midian appears as a nomadic tribe every time it is mentioned and hence "occupied" no territory; but nomadic tribes exercised a vague claim to certain pasture lands. The biblical data suggest a place not far from Sinai, between Edom and Paran on the road to Egypt (Abel). Other scholars suggest that this should be regarded as an extension of Midianite habitation, and prefer the identification of Midian with the Madian of ancient Gk and Arab geographers which is located in N Arabia, SE of Edom and E and SE of the Gulf of Aqabah. This raises complications concerning the location of Sinai but has much in its favor. Midian is not mentioned in extrabiblical records. Abel suggests that the Arabian desert tribe Haiappu is identical with the Midian clan Ephah (Gn 25:4; 1 Ch 1:33). Tiglath-pileser* III (745–727 BC) received tribute from the Haiappu, and Sargon* (721–705 BC) conquered them and settled them, by an ironical coincidence of history, in the territory of Bit-Humri or Samaria, the Israelite territory conquered in 721 BC.

Midrash (Hb *midrāš*), the word occurs only twice in the OT to designate the source used by the Chronicler (2 Ch 13:22; 24:27), and it is impossible to determine what kind of writing is referred to here. In modern exegesis *midrāš* designates a type of writing based on a distinctive Jewish use of the OT; here *use* is a better word than interpretation. This type of writing can be seen clearly in the literature of Judaism and can be recognized in both OT and NT. The earliest forms of midrash occur in the OT. The Hb word *dāraš* means to seek. It is used of the seeking of an answer from Yahweh through the oracle, and it is probable that this meaning of the word is at the base of its use to designate the study of the sacred text. BS 51:23 speaks of the *bêt midrāš*, the "house of midrash," which must designate a school where the sacred text is studied. In rabbinical literature midrash means the study of the sacred text in general, but more particularly a commentary or an explanation of a homiletic character. Two types of midrash are distinguished, the *halakhah* ("walking," i.e., conduct) and the *haggadah* (narrative). The *halakhah* is an explanation of the law, deriving principles of conduct; the *haggadah* is an explanation of the narrative passages of the Pnt with an extremely wide scope of edifying lessons. Midrash is not an attempt to investigate the literal sense of the sacred text (cf INTERPRETATION);

indeed the literal sense as we understand it is a concept not found either in the rabbinical writings or in the biblical writers. Midrash looked for the maximum of edifying lessons; it is a meditation on the sacred text or an imaginative reconstruction of the scene and episode narrated. Its goal is always the practical application to the present; thus a precept may be restated or an episode retold not in the terms of its own historical context, but in such a way that it gives light and direction to the generation which writes the midrash. There is no parallel to midrash in Gk and Lt literature because there is nothing in these literatures which corresponds to the Torah, the law*. In postexilic Judaism the law was revelation; it fulfilled the function which had earlier been fulfilled by the prophets*, and it was the work of the scribe to propose lessons from the law which would have the same impact for life which the word of the prophets had had. The scribe was Moses in his own generation, but he elicited all that he uttered from the words of Moses; Moses spoke to the present generation as well as to the fathers, and it was simply a mätter of seeing how his meaning was extended to fit the contemporary scene. The practice of midrash often appears arbitrary to us, who think first of all of "meaning" i.e., the literal sense; where no such limitation in concept is present, midrash was not regarded as arbitrary but as necessary.

The OT exhibits numerous examples of midrash which is an edifying meditation on an earlier biblical utterance, an imaginative reconstruction of an episode, or the construction of a fictitious episode on the principles deduced from biblical material. The priestly source of the Pnt* has its own account of the creation*, the deluge*, the episodes of the patriarchs*, and of the exodus* and covenant*; a comparison of this material with the material of the older sources shows that the priestly source has no intention to relate the history of the past but to draw lessons from tradition by a homiletic retelling. The same principles explain the treatment which is given in Ch* to the stories of S and K. Midrashic retellings of the past are found also in Pss 78; 105; 106; BS 44–50; WS 16–19. The early history of Israel is told by Ezekiel in the form of an allegory (Ezk 16). Is 60–62 takes the discourses of Is 40–55 and transforms them into a new application to Jerusalem. BS 24, employing Pr 8:22 ff, explains that wisdom* is the law. The narratives of Dn; Jon, Tb, Jdt, Est take some principle of the law or Jewish belief and present it in a fictitious narrative. The popular explanation of proper names, which is often not the

philological explanation, finds meaning in the names based on assonance. The LXX is frequently a paraphrase rather than a translation; this comes not from ignorance of Hb nor from deliberate infidelity, but from a desire to reinterpret and explain the text so that it would be more meaningful for Hellenistic Jews of the 2nd century BC.

The NT also exhibits no small amount of midrash. In the Gospels Mt is especially fond of midrash. Mt 2:1–12 is written around the re-use of Nm 24:17, Mt 2:13–15 around Ho 11:1, and Mt 2:16–18 around Je 31:15. Mt 2:23 connects Nazareth with Jgs 13:5 on the assonance with *nāzir* (cf NAZARITE) and with Is 11:1 on the assonance with *neṣer*, "shoot." Mt 27:3–10 conflates Zc 11:12 f and Je 32:6–15 and applies them to the episode related. The infancy narrative of Lk 1–2 is a splendid example of midrash; where little genuine recollection of the events was preserved, the narrative is filled out by an anthology of citations from the OT appropriate to the birth of the Messiah. Mt 5:32, 19:9 on divorce are examples of the *halakhah*, the derivation of a rule of conduct from the Law; the *halakhah* is rare in the NT. Paul often employs midrash to apply the OT to the Christian fact; cf his use of the Abraham-Sarah-Hagar theme in Gal 3–4; the faith of Abraham in Rm 4; the use of several passages in his discussion of the mystery of the unbelief of the Jews in Rm 9–11; the use of the exodus traditions in 1 Co 10:1–13. Heb employs midrash throughout; cf especially the recital of the heroes of faith, Heb 11. The NT cites several midrashic traditions which do not appear in the OT and have no historical value: AA 7:22–32; the rock which followed the Israelites in the desert, 1 Co 10:4; the angels as promulgators of the covenant, Gal 3:19; the Egyptian magicians, 2 Tm 3:8; the dispute of Michael and the devil, Jd 9.

It is quite impossible to accept midrash as literal exegesis, and it is unjust to reject it as the simple play of fancy. A sympathetic understanding of something so important in the Bible requires that we attempt to place ourselves in the intellectual and religious atmosphere in which midrash was almost the only possible way in which the Bible could be kept relevant to the life of the Jewish and then of the Christian communities. Midrash was serious, and it was extremely important in the development of the mind of Judaism and of the early Church. We should not, on the other hand, think that midrash is a terminal explanation of the Bible. It arose in a particular historical situation in which it was at home; but it can no more be transferred to another culture as such than other intellectual patterns.

Migdol (Hb *migdōl,* "tower"), the name of one or several places in Egypt. The Egyptian Canaanite frontier was defended by a string of fortresses across the Isthmus of Suez, and Migdol very probably is the name of one of them. Migdol lay on the route of the exodus (Ex 14:2). It is not clear that this is the same Migdol where Jews lived after the fall of Jerusalem (Je 44:1), addressed in the poem of Je 46:14. Migdol is mentioned in an Egyptian papyrus of the 19th dynasty (ANET 259) and in the Amarna* Letters (ANET 485); but these texts do not inform us of its location. Magdolum of the Roman period lay in the NW corner of the Sinai peninsula.

Milcom (Hb *milkōm,* formed from *melek,* "king," with mimation [addition of m]), the god of the Ammonites*. The cult of Milkom is not mentioned outside the OT. Solomon* built a high place for Milcom in Jerusalem (1 K 11:5, 33). It was still in existence in the reign of Josiah*, who demolished it (2 K 23:13). Milcom is to be read for "their king" (Hb *malkam*) in 2 S 12:30; 1 Ch 20:2; Je 49:1, 3; Zp 1:5. The Massoretic vocalization removes from the text the offensive name of a false god (cf BAAL). No information about the cult is contained in these passages except that the image was crowned (2 S 12:30; 1 Ch 20:2); for David* to wear this crown himself was a supreme insult.

Miletus (Gk *milētos,* etymology uncertain), a city of Asia Minor situated on a bay at the ancient mouth of the Meander (Menderes). There is no record of the foundation of a church at Miletus, but it is altogether probable that one was established there in the apostolic period. Paul met the elders of Ephesus at Miletus (AA 20:15, 17), and Tychicus sojourned there during an illness (2 Tm 4:20). Miletus was a large port and commercial center. Excavations at the site, the modern Balat, disclosed remains from the Hellenistic and Roman period which included the theater, the senate house, the marketplaces, the baths, and the foundations of some temples. The port has been useless since the Middle Ages because of the silt deposited at the mouth of the river.

Milk. Canaan is often described as a land "dripping milk and honey" (Ex 3:8, 17; 13:5; 33:3 +), and abundance of milk is one of the signs of prosperity and peace (Dt 32:14; Jb 21:24; Is 7:22), particularly of the prosperity of messianic times (Gn 49:12; Jl 4:18). Metaphorically milk signifies wealth (Is 60:16). The milk used in OT times was sheep or goat's milk kept in skin bottles; in the arid and semiarid neighborhood of Palestine and even within the country itself in some regions water is scarce or unsafe, and milk was often used to quench the thirst. The milk could not be kept fresh, but sour curdled milk was and still is a delicacy in the country. It was offered to a guest (Gn 18:8; Jgs 4:19; 5:25). Hb law prohibits the boiling of a kid in the milk of its dam (Ex 23:19; 34:26; Dt 14:21); a reference to this practice in the Ugarit* tablets shows that it was a Canaanite cultic rite.

Milk is mentioned only four times in the NT, and three of these are metaphorical (with the exception of 1 Co 9:7). In 1 Co 3:1 f Paul* compares his instruction to the Corinthians to milk given to infants who are not ready for solid food. It is not obvious what he means by the solid food; the milk must be the most elementary instruction, but what might be the content of the "wisdom spoken to the perfect" (1 Co 2:6) is not clear; but Paul distinguishes between this wisdom and the instruction given to the Corinthians. The same metaphor of milk for elementary instruction is used in Heb 5:12–6:1; here the writer finds fault with his readers for not advancing from the milk, the elements, to the solid food of the perfect; these elements of instruction seem to be enumerated in 6:1–2. The "unadulterated spiritual milk" of 1 Pt 2:2, however, is not opposed to mature doctrine. "Spiritual" (Gk *logikos*) is an ambiguous term; it is used in Gk to signify metaphorical as opposed to literal, and many take it so here; but it could be a genitival adjective, the milk of the word (*logos*).

Mill. The mill of the biblical world, whether larger or smaller, with or without mechanical devices for motion, consisted of an upper stone (the "rider") and a lower stone. The earliest type of hand mill consisted of a slightly concave nether stone and an oval upper stone which was rubbed back and forth. Examples of this mill found at Megiddo have a lower stone 15 in to 30 in long, 12 in to 15 in wide, and 2 to 3 in thick; the upper stone is 12 in to 15 in long, 4 in to 6 in wide, and 2 to 3 in thick in the middle. The usual material was basalt. The upper stone of this type was the stone with which Abimelech was killed (Jgs 9:53). This type of hand mill was in use until Hellenistic times when it yielded to the rotary stone. The nether stone is convex, at times nearly pointed, and the upper stone is correspondingly concave both above and below, something like an hour glass in shape. The grain was poured in through

Mill stones from Pompeii.

the upper concavity. The upper stone had two handles through which wooden bars could be placed and two could work the mill (Mt 24:41; Lk 17:35). In Roman times mills powered by water or by animals or human beings were known; a mill stone drawn by an ass is mentioned in Mt 18:6; Mk 9:42; Lk calls it simply a millstone. Such mills were used only by professional millers; the hand mill was universally used by the poor. Milling was obviously extremely hard work and was done only by women and slaves (Ex 11:5; Ec 12:3; Mt 24:41). Samson was humiliated by the Philistines when he was put to the hand mill (Jgs 16:21). The women's working day began with the grinding of the meal for the day's baking (Pr 31:15), and the sound of the mills with which the day began is alluded to in the OT (Je 25:10; Ec 12:4). Since the mill was essential to the preparation of the daily food the lender was forbidden to take it as a pledge (Dt 24:6).

Millennium (Lt *millennium, mille anni,* a period of 1000 years). In Apc 20:1–10 the devil is bound for a period of 1000 years; the righteous rise and reign with Christ during this period. At the end of the period the devil is released and musters his forces against the holy city but is consumed by fire from heaven. There follows the resurrection of all the dead and the judgment and condemnation of the wicked. This conception seems to be based on a passage of the book of the Secrets of Enoch (cf APOCRYPHA) in which the world period is said to be 7000 years, 1000 for each day of creation. The 1000 years of Apc is the period of Sabbath rest. The idea of the reign of the Messiah on earth also appears in 4 Ezra (cf APO-CRYPHA), but in this book it endures 400

years. No doubt there were other forms of the conception.

This extremely imaginative conception of Apc is not in harmony with the universal teaching of the NT concerning the resurrection and can be combined with them only by taking it at its obviously symbolic value. Nevertheless, the opinion called chiliasm (Gk *chilioi,* 1000) not only was sustained by a number of heretical sects in the early Church but also by not a few of the fathers of the Church. It was thought that the period after the birth of Christ was the 6th millennium, and that the earthly kingdom would be initiated by the Second Coming in the year AD 1000.

Millo (Hb *millô',* lit "filling"), a topographical name of uncertain location and meaning. It was a point in the fortifications of Jerusalem*, more precisely of the original city called "the city of David" fortified by Solomon through the use of forced labor (1 K 9:15, 24) and rebuilt by Hezekiah* at the time of the invasion of Sennacherib* (2 Ch 32:5). The allusions to Millo in the reign of David (2 S 5:9; 1 Ch 11:8) are attributed to a writer who names the point as it stood in his own time; David is not said to build the Millo. Many theories have been advanced and discarded concerning the nature and location of the Millo. Vincent takes the name literally, i.e., an earth fill of the Tyropoeon valley which lay on the W of the city of David; this natural depression was a weakness in the N wall of Jerusalem, the weakest wall in any case, and Solomon thus raised the level of the wall and "closed the breach" of the city (1 K 11:27). Breach here is taken to signify not a gap in the fortifications but a natural weakness. J. Simons objects that this theory presupposes that the fortifications extended to the W hill, which is not demonstrated, and makes no effort to define the term other than that it signified some particular piece of fortification in the N wall.

Minister. Cf DEACON.

Miracle. Modern theology defines miracle as a phenomenon in nature which transcends the capacity of natural causes to such a degree that it must be attributed to the direct intervention of God. This definition presupposes a conception of "nature" as a unity and a philosophy of nature and of natural "laws." The law of nature is a constant mode of action rooted in a fixed principle of the natural body; a miracle can be discerned because the constancy of the action and the consistency of the principle permit the observer to see beyond doubt that nature itself is incapable of producing the effect in question. The philosophy and science upon which this common conception of miracle is based are the products of the 18th and 19th century and have been seriously revised in the 20th century; scientists are now much more hesitant in affirming the constancy of action and the fixity of natural principles. There is still no question, however, that nature exhibits a certain constancy; questions arise only concerning individual events whose transcendence of the capacity of nature is uncertain.

OT. In considering the OT conception of miracle it is essential to realize that a concept of nature such as is described above did not exist in ancient Near Eastern thinking. Nature was not conceived as a unified system; these languages have no single word which is equivalent to "nature." Natural phenomena were the perceptible effects of the operations of divine personal beings, often in conflict with each other. Israelite belief did not arrive at a conception of nature; it regarded natural phenomena as the operations of a single divine personal being. The apparent conflicts in nature were seen as the effects of man's conflict with the supreme will of Yahweh, who punishes rebellious man· through the instrumentality of nature. The OT conception of nature is that it exhibits the constant activity of Yahweh directed by His providence toward men. The whole of nature is personalized, and there is no idea of natural causes acting according to constant laws and fixed principles. The course of nature exhibits the unpredictability which we attribute to personal beings.

The ideas of nature and miracle in the OT are further complicated by the character of the popular tradition in which events are related (cf HISTORY). Where the analysis of the event depends upon its exact recon-struction, it is usually impossible to determine "exactly what happened." The narrative reflects not only the impressions of unskilled and excited observers, but it also shows the effects of the heightening of the unusual which is always and everywhere characteristic of popular tradition. Critical and historical elements are therefore of primary importance and impose caution in the study of the miraculous in Hb tradition.

As Hb has no word for nature, so it has no word which corresponds to "miracle." Three words are used to signify the marvelous: *'ôt*, sign, something which attracts attention; *mōpēt*, a wonder or portent, often a sign of a future event; *pālā'*, to surpass the ordinary or the expected. *'ôt* is used of such things as Gideon's fleece (Jgs 6:17), the regression of the shadow on the sundial (Is 38:3–9), the proofs of Moses' commission (Ex 4:9, 28, 30), the plagues of Egypt and the events of the exodus (25 times). But *'ôt* also designates the rainbow as a sign of the covenant (Gn 9:13), the names of Isaiah and his sons (Is 8:18, *'ôt* and *mōpēt*), the strange conduct of Isaiah when he went about naked and barefoot (Is 20:3, *'ôt* and *mōpēt*). *Mōpēt* is used of the feats of a false prophet (Dt 13:2 f), of the afflictions of the psalmist (Ps 71:7), of Ezekiel's grief for his wife (Ezk 24:24, 27), of the plagues of Egypt (19 times). *Pālā'*, especially in the participle *niplā'ôt* ("wonders") is used of the crossing of the Jordan (Jos 3:5), frequently of the plagues of Egypt, of things which surpass understanding (Pr 30:8; Ps 131:1; Jb 42:3; Is 29:14). The word is frequently used of Yahweh's works of judgment and redemption (Pss 9:2; 26:7; 40:6; 71:17; 75:2; 98:1; 105:2, 5; 106:22; 107:8, 15, 21, 31; 111:4; 145:5; Je 21:2), of His works of creation (Pss 107:24; 136:4; Jb 5:9; 9:10; 37:14), or of His works without specification (Pss 72:18; 86:10; 96:3; 119:18, 27). This survey shows that none of these words have the specialized sense of "miracle." In the OT no work of Yahweh is more "wonderful" than His work of creation* (Jb 4:8–10; 9:5–10; 26:5–14; 36:26–37:28; 38:1–41:26). This wonder is exhibited daily in the course of nature; every work of Yahweh is wonderful and exhibits the mysterious supremacy of Yahweh. This conception is more than ignorance of physical laws and physical causes; it is an insight into the reality of God in nature.

It is rare in the OT that the power of thaumaturgy is communicated to men. The cluster of wonders associated with Elijah* and Elisha* is complicated by the literary character of these narratives. Wonders are associated with Moses*; but these narratives also exhibit the peculiar conception of the wonderful found in early Israel. The feats of Moses are matched up to a point by the magicians of Egypt (Ex 7:20–8:19). The narrative is therefore cast somewhat artificially in the form of a contest between Yahweh and the magicians of Egypt in which Yahweh is finally victorious. The existence of magic* was taken for granted; it was also taken for granted that the power of Yahweh is superior to all magic.

The greatest wonder of the history of Israel was the exodus, and attempts to reconstruct these events have been numerous (cf EXODUS; PLAGUES). It seems methodologically superior to renounce any effort at exact analysis of the events and of their miraculous character in the strict sense of the term; the traditions do not afford the evidence. The emphasis in the traditions falls not upon the "miraculous" character of the events, but upon the "wonder" of the power and will of Yahweh to save. With no conception of nature upon which to reason the Hebrews did not distinguish degrees in this wonder; it was the key to their history, in whatever way this power and will to save was exhibited. The modern reader falls into the trap either of thinking that the historical character of the events can be affirmed only by denying any miraculous character of the events or of affirming that the Hb idea of miracle was the same as the idea of modern man. The traditions exhibit not so much a faith in "miracle," an unknown concept, but a faith in Yahweh as the lord of history and the lord of nature, who bends nature to His purposes in history. The marvelous is His interposition in history.

NT. The NT likewise, although it was written after the birth of Gk philosophical and scientific speculation, shows little or no conception of nature as a systematic unity governed by fixed principles and laws of causality. The NT conception of God and nature is much more a reflection of the OT conception than it is of the Gk idea. A study of the words which are employed in the NT bears out this view. The wonders worked by Jesus and the apostles are called *dynameis,* "powers," works of power (Mt 7:22; 11:20–23; 13:54, 58; 14:2; Mk 6:2, 5, 14; 9:39; Lk 10:13; 19:37); the words *dynamis, sēmeion* ("sign" Hb *'ôt*), and *teras* ("portent," Hb *mōpēt*) are sometimes grouped as designations of wonders (Mt 24:24; Mk 13:22; Jn 4:48; AA 2:22; 2:43; 5:12; 6:8; 8:13; 14:3; 15:12; 19:11; Rm 15:19; 1 Co 12:28; 2 Co 12:12; Gal 3:5; 2 Th 2:9; Heb 2:4). The word *sēmeion,* sign, does not mean "miracle" as such, but rather a manifest evidence of the intervention of God. The "sign of Jonah" is the resurrection of Jesus (Mt 12:39; 16:4; Lk 11:29; omitted by Mk 8:11–13). The signs of the Parousia* are certain events not miraculous in character (Mt 24:3 ff; Mk 13:4 ff; Lk 21:7 ff). The sign of the birth of the Messiah is the manger* (Lk 2:12). John, however, has a distinctive use of the word and a distinctive conception of the wonders worked by Jesus. More than the other evangelists he employs the word to designate wonders, and in the narrative of the miracles he chooses those episodes and constructs his narrative in a way which makes them "significant." They are signs which confute the Jews' rejection of Jesus and demonstrate His claims to be the way (restoring the power to walk, Jn 5), the light* (restoration of sight, Jn 9), the life (food, Jn 6; drink, Jn 2; resurrection, Jn 11). They are signs of the reality of Jesus as the Son of God and savior of mankind, of the manifest intervention of God in the world in Jesus.

The most common designation of miracle is *dynamis,* "power"; and the use of this word in other contexts contributes to the understanding of the NT conception of miracles. This concept may be summed up in general in these terms: the Incarnation is the entrance of the power of God into the world in the person of Jesus Christ. Jesus was constituted the Son of God in power (Rm 1:4); indeed He is the power of God (1 Co 1:24). His conception occurs when the power of God overshadows Mary (Lk 1:35). This is not simply a power of working wonders; as the power of God, mysterious, supreme, and subject to no restraint, it breaks out in all directions. The entire Christian fact is thus enveloped in an atmosphere of power and wonder. Primarily it is the power of God to salvation (Rm 1:16). The Gospel itself, the words of Christ uttered by Jesus Himself and preached by the apostles, are the power of God (Rm 1:16; 1 Co 1:18). This outbreak of power first resides in Jesus Himself; in at least one episode it is conceived as a palpable substance which flows out at contact with Him (Mk 5:30; Lk 8:46). It is a power to save not only from the evil of sin but also from ills of the body, a power to heal (Lk 5:17). The power which resides in Jesus is communicated by Him to His apostles (Lk 9:1); and after the ascension the power of the kingdom of God (Mk 9:1) resides in the Church in which He continues to live. The fullness of the power is communicated to the apostles by the reception of the Spirit* at Pentecost; they receive it, they are clothed with it (Lk 24:29; AA 1:8). The apostles feel themselves full of the power of Jesus, which enables them to preach, to bear witness to Him, to heal

(AA 6:8; 2 Co 12:9; Eph 3:20; Col 1:29). The power exhibits itself also in the charismata which appeared in the primitive Church (1 Co 12:10; cf GRACE). It is therefore a part of the lasting presence of Jesus in His Church and an enduring "sign" of the present operation of God.

The conception of miracle as a function of power is vital in the NT conception of Jesus and the Church. This idea is derived neither from the OT nor from Judaism nor Gk thought; it is a creation of the early Christian community. It may be granted, as many have urged, that there are stories of healing and other wonders from the contemporary NT scene; it may be granted also, as we observed above for the OT, that almost any NT miracle account must be submitted to literary and historical criticism. These do not alter the original and unique conception of the power of Jesus which appears in the NT. The wonders which He works are classified under nature miracles and healing miracles (including under healing the resurrections). One difference which is immediately apparent between the OT and the NT is the small proportion of nature miracles in comparison to the healing miracles. In the healing miracles Jesus appears as savior*; the power and will of God to save is not restricted to the preaching of the word and the forgiveness of sins, although these are great and fundamental, but it also operates to remove the consequences of sin, human infirmity and suffering. There is an absence of miracles in the Gospels which affect any one adversely; and while the Christian community told such stories of the apostles as those of Ananias* and Sapphira* (AA 5:1–11) and Elymas* (AA 13:8–11), it did not tell them of Jesus. It is for this reason that one may suspect that the stories mentioned in AA have more symbolism than history in them. One may compare the Gospels in this respect with the apocryphal* gospels, which abound in offensively cruel miracles, in order to grasp the difference. The primitive preaching of the Church presented Jesus as one "who went about doing good" (AA 10:38). The nature miracles also are not mere demonstrations of power; the calming of the storm, the provision of food and drink, are also exhibitions of the power and will to save. The conception of power shows that Jesus is effectively able to give that which He offers men. The power is a perfect example of the complete gift and of unmixed benevolence; it works entirely outward and draws nothing to itself. There is no instance in which the power is exercised for Jesus Himself. The conception of Jesus and of the Church would scarcely be the same without this unique idea of the power to save. It is strange that the word does not occur in John, although his conception does not differ; but his emphasis, as we have seen, falls upon the power as a sign.

Miriam (Hb *miryam,* meaning and etymology uncertain, perh Egyptian *mrjt,* "beloved"), a personal name; sister of Moses* and Aaron*, daughter of Amram and Jochebed (Nm 26:59; 1 Ch 5:29). The sister of Moses in Ex 2:4–9 is not named; but the early history of Moses is complex. Miriam led the women of Israel in song and dance after the passage of the sea (Ex 15:20 f). With Aaron she was involved in a dispute with Moses and was afflicted with leprosy (Nm 12:1–15). The text is compiled; the occasion of the dispute is said to be Moses's wife (12:1), but the rest of the passage is concerned with the vindication of the unique position of Moses as a messenger of Yahweh. Aaron and Miriam claimed equal authority with him. The leprosy of Miriam is alluded to in Dt 24:9. Miriam died at Kadesh* (Nm 20:1). Mi 6:4 seems to rest on the tradition which is controverted in Nm 12:1 ff; the prophet mentions Moses, Aaron, and Miriam as leaders of Israel out of Egypt. These allusions, together with the designation of Miriam as a "prophetess" in Ex 15:20, have led some scholars to suspect that the position of Miriam in the earlier preliterary forms of the tradition was considerably larger than it is in the written text, and that her importance has been suppressed to some degree in favor of Moses.

Mirror. The ancient mirror was a circular

A hand mirror from Praeneste, showing the judgment of Paris.

plate of metal, smooth and highly polished on one side, to which a handle was attached; examples of mirrors of Egyptian manufacture have been found in Syria and Palestine (ANEP 71, 76, 78). Mirrors of glass did not come into use until Roman times, and they are not mentioned in the NT. Women's mirrors, obviously metallic, were used as the material of the lavers of the tabernacle (Ex 38:8). The skies are compared to the beaten metal mirror (Jb 37:18). Such mirrors needed careful cleaning and protection from rust (BS 12:11). They gave an imperfect reflection, which Paul uses as a metaphor for man's obscure vision of God (1 Co 13:12) and James for mere hearing of the Gospel without obedience (Js 1:23).

Mishna. Cf TALMUD.

Mitanni. A powerful state on the upper Euphrates* between 1500 and 1370 BC known from the Amarna* Letters and the Hittite* records. Mitanni was a feudal kingdom which was formed of a symbiosis between a Hurrian* population and a ruling class of Indo-Aryan extraction. It was conquered and absorbed by the Hittite* kingdom early in the 14th century. Some historians believe there is a connection between the kingdom of Mitanni and the Hyksos* who established themselves in Egypt at the close of the Middle Kingdom.

Mitylene (Gk *mitylēnē*), the principal city of the island of Lesbos, touched by Paul on his journey from Macedonia to Jerusalem (AA 20:14). No Christian community of Mitylene is mentioned.

Mizpah, Mizpeh (Hb *miṣpāh, miṣpeh*, from *ṣāpāh*, "to scout or spy"), the name of several towns. The land of Mizpeh at the foot of Mt Hermon occupied by the Horites* cannot be located any more clearly (Jos 11:3, 8). Ramath-mizpeh in Gilead* (Jos 13:28) is probably the same as the Mizpah attacked by the Ammonites (Jgs 10:17), the residence of Jephthah* (Jgs 11:11, 29, 34). David fled to the king of Moab at Mizpeh in Moab (1 S 22:3). The location of the Mizpeh in S Judah is uncertain, but it lay near Lachish* (Jos 15:38). Mizpah of Benjamin (Jos 18:26) is now located by most scholars at Tell en Nasbeh 8 mi N of Jerusalem; the remains of a fortified town occupy the summit of a hill. The site was excavated in 1932–1935 and disclosed massive Iron Age fortifications*, burial vaults, and a Canaanite high place. Mizpah appears as an important cultic and political center in premonarchic Israel. It was a

place of assembly of the tribes (Jgs 20:1–3; 21:1–8; 1 S 7:5–12; 10:17), and Hosea mentions it as a place of cult (Ho 5:1). It was fortified by Asa against Israel (1 K 15:22); the border of Judah and Israel must have run very near Tell en Nasbeh. After the destruction of Jerusalem Gedaliah resided at Mizpah as governor (2 K 25:23–25; Je 40:10, 15), and Mizpah was the scene of the mass murder of Gedaliah and his companions by Ishmael* (Je 41). In the time of Nehemiah* Mizpah was occupied (Ne 3:7); it gives its name to a district (Ne 3:15), and the "ruler of Mizpah" (Ne 3:19) was probably head of the district. It appears in the Maccabean period as a place of assembly, and the author notes that it was formerly a place of cult (1 Mc 3:46).

Mnason (Gk *mnasōn*), a personal name; a Christian from Cyprus, one of the first to accept Christianity, who gave Paul and his companions hospitality on Paul's journey to Jerusalem (AA 21:16). The text is somewhat uncertain, and it cannot be determined whether Mnason lived in Jerusalem or on the road between Caesarea* and Jerusalem. The latter is more probable, and is explicitly stated in the text of D, which here may be exegetical rather than original.

Moab (Hb *mō'āb*, meaning uncertain), a geographic and gentilic name designating the territory E of the Dead Sea and S of the river Arnon*, the modern Wadi el Mojib, and the people who inhabited this territory. The OT is our chief and almost our only source of information concerning Moab. The explorations of Nelson Glueck revealed the existence of a flourishing urban civilization in Transjordan between the 23rd and the 20th centuries BC which was suddenly ended about 1900 BC, probably by a catastrophe which is not as yet identified. Between the 20th and the 13th centuries there was no sedentary occupation of the territory. In the f3th century, not long before the Israelite entry into Canaan, an urban-agricultural civilization appeared in Moab which endured as long as the Israelite monarchies. Moab was itself a monarchy before Israel adopted monarchial government. The Moabite stone (cf MESHA) shows that the language of Moab was practically identical with Hb, and excavation of Moabite sites shows that the two peoples possessed substantially the same material culture. Glueck's exploration shows that the boundaries of Moab were fortified in the 13th century, thus illustrating the refusal of the Moabites to let Israel pass through their territory. Little is known of the religion of Moab; the chief deity was Chemosh*. The name of

Moab appears in several geographic designations: the field of Moab, which designates the plateau N and S of the Arnon; the steppes of Moab, which designates the plain of the Jordan E of the river and N of the Dead Sea.

J. A. Wilson suggests that Moab is meant by Shutu in the execration texts of the 12th dynasty of Egypt (19th-18th centuries BC); cf the sons of Shet in Nm 24:17. It is listed among the Asiatic countries conquered by Ramses II (1301–1234 BC). Tiglath-pileser* III of Assyria (745–727 BC) includes Salamanu of Moab among kings who pay tribute. Sargon* (721–705 BC) received tribute from Moab. Sennacherib* (705–681 BC) mentions Kammusunadabi (Chemosh-nadab) of Moab as a tributary contemporary with the rebellion of Hezekiah* of Judah. Musuri of Moab was a vassal of Esarhaddon* (681–668 BC). Ashurbani-pal (668–630 BC) campaigned against nomadic tribes in Moab and received tribute from Moab.

Israelite folklore reckoned Moab as the descendants of Lot* and his daughter (Gn 19:37). This anecdote recognizes the kinship of Moab and Israel. The Edomite king-list refers to a defeat of the Midianites* in Moab (Gn 36:35); cf MIDIAN. Nm 21:13–29 contains some allusions to the history of Moab before the Israelite settlement. Moab claimed the territory N of the Arnon, but was expelled S of the river by the Amorite kingdom of Sihon*; the poem quoted in these verses refers to the defeat of the Moabites in this war. When Israel conquered the Amorite kingdom it claimed the territory N of the Arnon; the dispute about this territory remained constant between Israel and Moab. The boundary fluctuated with the successes of the contending parties; but Israel was more successful in maintaining its territory. Moab seems to have been a smaller kingdom than Israel and it prevailed only when Israel was unable to bring its united forces against Moab. Nm 22–24 reports the attempt of Balak* of Moab to obtain a curse upon Israel from Balaam*. Nm 25:1 ff relates how the Israelites adopted the cult of the Moabite Baal of Peor, not otherwise identified. This is made the occasion of the fictitious war of vengeance against Moab in Nm 31, composed by P as the model of an avenging war. This is at variance with the friendly attitude exhibited in Dt 2:9, which recognizes the Moabite claim to its territory as confirmed by Yahweh and the kinship between Israel and Moab. This claim was probably not understood to extend N of the Arnon. Dt 2:10 mentions the Emim* as early inhabitants of Moab. A less friendly attitude appears in the law of Dt 23:4, which permits no Moabite to marry into Israel nor to become a member of the Israelite community until after ten generations; this law recalls the hostility of Balak. The death and burial of Moses occurred in Moab (Dt 34). Jgs 3:11–30 relates the conquest of Benjamin* by Eglon* of Moab and the deliverance of the tribe by Ehud*; this conquest occurred against a disunited Israel. The speech of Jephthah* (Jgs 11:15–27) curiously states the Israelite claim to the territory N of the Arnon, basing it upon Israel's conquest of the Amorite kingdom of Sihon, and has lost its original context. Saul was victorious over Moab, but no details are given and no territory, it seems, was acquired (1 S 14:47). The friendly relations of David with the king of Moab are somewhat puzzling (1 S 22:3 f); the story of Ruth*, however, shows that the family of David was partly of Moabite extraction, and the degree of relationship may have been closer than the story of Ruth suggests. For reasons which are unknown this friendship of David with Moab did not endure after his accession as king, for he conquered Moab in a particularly brutal fashion and made it a vassal kingdom of Israel (2 S 8:2). Israel's rule of Moab endured through the reign of Ahab*; at least there is no record of successful rebellion either in the OT or in the Moabite stone of Mesha. The rebellion of Mesha is mentioned both in the OT (2 K 1:1; 3:4 ff) and in the Moabite stone; they agree that the rebellion was successful, but vary in some details. It is obvious from these accounts that it was the northern kingdom and not the kingdom of Judah which retained the rule over Moab. There are allusions to raiding bands from Moab which plundered Israel in the reign of Jehoash* (2 K 13:20) and against Judah in the reign of Jehoiakim* (2 K 24:2), probably as allies of Nebuchadnezzar*. The story of an invasion of Judah by Moab and other peoples during the reign of Jehoshaphat* (2 Ch 20), while composed in the peculiar style of Chronicles*, probably represents an actual event.

The oracles against Moab in Is 15–16 and Je 48, which to a large extent are variant editions of the same poem, are among the most obscure passages in the OT. They are probably original with neither prophet and contain no information which permits a date and occasion to be assigned. The disaster of Moab is described, probably in exaggerated terms, as extremely severe; but the conqueror is not named, and does not appear to be Israel. Am 2:1 f refers to an act of barbarism committed by the Moabites in a war with Edom. Jeremiah predicts the fall of Moab (9:25; 25:21) and includes Moab among the peoples to whom he sends warning against rebellion (27:3); these kings had ambassadors in Jerusalem during the reign of Zedekiah*, but there is no record that Moab joined Judah in rebelling against Nebuchadnezzar. Zp 2:8 f, which is probably later than the fall of Jerusalem, threatens Moab for its taunts against defeated Judah, which rather suggests that Moab did not join the rebellion. Ezk 25:8 f indicates that Moab joined the other neighbors of Judah in plundering the defeated nation and seizing its territory. Moab does not appear after the fall of Judah and was probably, like Edom, submerged by the Nabatean* migration from Arabia.

Modin (Gk *modein*), not mentioned in Hb OT; a town NW of Jerusalem, located near the modern El Arba'in, the home of Mattathias*, patriarch of the family of the Maccabees*, and the family place of burial (1 Mc 2:1, 15, 23, 70; 9:19; 13:25, 30); encampment of Judas* (2 Mc 13:14) and of Simon* (1 Mc 16:4).

Molech (Hb *mōlek,* the consonants of *melek,* "king," with the vowels of the word *bōšet,* "shame"), a divine name or title, probably *malik.* The title of king* was given to the deity by the Israelites as well as by other ancient Semitic peoples; the evidence for the divine name MLK, however, is rather slender. A god Muluk is mentioned in the Mari* texts; Milcom*, the god of the Ammonites*, is the same name with mimation (addition of *m*), and the divine name MLKM is mentioned in the Ugarit* tablets. The Israelites were forbidden to offer their children to Molech and to "commit fornication" after Molech (Lv 20:2–5); the last phrase usually means to worship false gods. The offering of sons and daughters to Molech by "passing them through the fire" is mentioned in 2 K 23:10; Je 32:35; cf GEHENNA; TOPHET. The immigrants settled in Israel by Tiglath-pileser* III sacrificed their children in the fire to Adrammelech and Anammelech, divine names compounded with the title *melek* (2 K 17:31). O. Eissfeldt, arguing on the basis of Carthaginian inscriptions, has maintained that the word is *molk,* a technical term for a votive offering, and that human sacrifice, rare at any time, was not practiced by the Semitic peoples at this period. His arguments have great probability, but most scholars believe that the terms used in biblical passages indicate a personal deity and that the references to fire can mean only human sacrifice.

Money. It is not certain when and where minted coins were first employed; the earliest known coins come from Asia Minor, probably from the 7th century BC. Before the invention of minted coins, metals and semiprecious metals were used as media of exchange by weight. Minted money issued by public authority guarantees the weight and value of each piece; without this guarantee metal in exchange had to be weighed in each transaction. Most of the Hb and Gk names for coins are originally names of weights*. Minted coins were introduced into Palestine during the Persian period; the Persian daric (Gk *dareikos,* Hb *'ªdarkōn,* named after Darius*) is mentioned in 1 Ch 29:7; Ezr 8:27. The Gk drachma (Hb *darkᵉmôn*) is mentioned in Ezr 2:69; Ne 7:70–72; here, however, the two names have probably been confused and the daric is meant. During and after the Persian period several systems of coinage were in use concurrently, and it is impossible as a rule to determine their relative values. Exchange was handled by the bankers*. The Persian imperial government retained the exclusive right to mint gold and silver coins and permitted the provinces to issue coins of baser metals. Syro-Phoenician coins were, of course, common in Palestine; Gk coins became common after the conquests of Alexander. The relations of these currencies are further complicated by the debasing of coins at different periods. Gk, Ptolemaic, and Seleucid coinage reckoned the silver drachma as the unit; coins were issued to the value of four drachmas (tetradrachma), two drachmas (didrachma), and one-half drachma. The gold stater had the value of four drachmas. The Hasmonean kingdom issued its own coins; John Hyrcanus (135–104) was probably the first ruler to issue them. Under Roman rule Roman coins, the only valid money for tax payments, were introduced. The imperial government reserved gold and silver coinage to itself. The free cities within the empire were permitted to issue their own coinage. Coins were struck by Herod, the tetrarchs, and the Roman procurators of Judaea. The Roman units were the gold aureus and one-half aureus, and the silver denarius (not a penny, as in the older English versions). The denarius was the basic daily wage of an unskilled worker. It is impossible to translate the value of these coins into modern terms either of coinage or of purchasing power. With relation to each other, the various systems of coinage in NT times can be reckoned roughly as follows: 240 aurei were equal to a talent of silver (a weight, not a coin), and the talent was equal to 6000 drachmas. The mina was equal to 100 drachmas. The silver stater was equal to the silver shekel, and the silver didrachma to the silver half-shekel. The gold aureus was officially exchanged for 25 denarii. Both the denarius and the drachma were divided into fractions, represented by copper coins. The drachma was worth 6 obols, and the obol was worth 8 coppers. The denarius was worth 10 to 16 *as* (Gk *assarion*), and the as was worth 4 *quadrantes* (Gk *kodrantēs*). The *kodrantēs* was worth 1–2 *lepta;* the *lepton* was the smallest coin in circulation. The issue of coinage was a declaration of political independence, and coins were issued by the Jews during the first (AD 66–70) and the second revolt (AD 132–135) against the Romans.

Monotheism. Monotheism means the belief in the existence of one only God and exclusive worship of this one God. Monotheism in the Bible and in Israelite-Jewish-Christian religion is questioned by no one for the period after the 6th century BC. The monotheism of Israel before this date has been questioned by many historians. To answer the question one must distinguish between the popular religion of early Israel and the religion of the OT itself. The OT is our chief source for the polytheism of the popular religion of Israel; the religious leaders of Israel whose utterances are preserved in the OT engage in almost uninterrupted polemic against the adoption of polytheistic cults. The polytheism of early and monarchic Israel has been confirmed by archaeological exploration, which has disclosed numerous divine images in Israelite levels of occupation. The question is raised about the religion of the OT and of the religious leaders of Israel; admitting that their conception of the deity differed from that of popular and Canaanite religion, does it deserve the name of monotheism as defined above? Here again a distinction must be made. A speculative philosophical affirmation of monotheism appears nowhere in the Bible. Nor can we find in the OT the monotheism which is evident in the NT. Modern historians have invented the terms "henotheism" and "monolatry" to describe the religion of early Israel as they reconstruct it. The terms, while used loosely as equivalent, are not exactly the same; they designate the exclusive cult of one deity, with the admission of the existence of other deities, or at least without any explicit denial of the existence of other deities. This reconstruction of early Israelite belief, it must be said, has no parallel in the history of religion anywhere in the world; but since the Israelite religious experience is unique in any hypothesis, this lack of parallel does not settle the question by itself.

Historians of religion also draw our attention to tendencies toward unification of the gods of polytheistic peoples. Historically polytheistic religions seem to follow a pattern: gods are multiplied for various reasons, such as diversity of place, diversity of natural powers and phenomena, etc. The multiplication of deities seems to reach a point of saturation at which the worshipers begin to merge the gods into fewer individual deities. It must be said also that historically no religion is known which followed this process down to a conclusion in which all gods were reduced to a single deity. Of interest for the biblical historian is the cult introduced into Egypt by Ikhnaton (1377–1358 BC), who probably lived a century before Moses. The successors of Ikhnaton made a serious effort to efface his name and memory from Egyptian records, and hence his religion is not completely known. It appears that at least in the royal court and city no deity was worshiped except the sun-disk Aton. Aton, unlike other Egyptian deities, was not represented by a human or theriomorphic image, but by the symbolic image of the disk emitting rays which terminated in hands holding the *ankh,* the sign which symbolized life. Ikhnaton certainly attempted to eradicate the cult of Amon-Re of Thebes, the patronal deity of Thebes and of his own 18th dynasty. Beyond this not enough is known to permit the affirmation that Ikhnaton was an explicit monotheist, an affirmation which needs solid evidence.

In determining the nature of the monotheism of early Israel the cosmic character of Yahweh's power is not peremptory. There is no period of Israelite belief in which Yahweh is not represented as possessing supreme power over nature. But supreme cosmic power is attributed in almost the same terms to deities in religions which are certainly polytheistic; in particular, Hb hymns* often have parallels in Mesopotamian hymns. The contradiction implicit in these hymns did not seem to trouble Mesopotamian worshipers. Of more importance is the conception of Yahweh's dominion over history, which is a conception not derived from other religions; they simply do not exhibit this conception. Here, however, one must admit that this conception does not become fully explicit until the 8th century, a period when almost any scholar is willing to admit that monotheism appeared in Israel.

The religion of the patriarchs (cf ABRAHAM; ISAAC; JACOB) appears to have been the exclusive worship of a God who was conceived as the god of family or clan. This worship is represented in Gn as given to Him exclusively; but we here meet the problem of the gap in time between the patriarchs and the form in which these traditions appear in Gn. Preserved and retold for many generations, including peoples who in all probability were not members of the original group of Israel*, the patriarchal stories exhibit some retrojection of later religious ideas. This means that they are often represented as devout Israelites of a later period. This element should not be exaggerated, because in many respects the patriarchs are not represented as devout Israelites of a later period; but it does mean that caution is necessary in affirming that they were monotheists. In Gn 14 Abraham is represented as present at the worship of a Canaanite deity; his active participation is not explicitly mentioned, but it is highly improbable that he would be present and inactive. It would be impossible for a devout Israelite of a later period even to be present at such a sacrifice. The Israelites obviously identified the deity of Melchizedek* with the deity of Abraham. Rachel* stole the household gods of her father Laban*, which gives a clue to his religion; yet Jacob was a member of his family for some years. Joseph* was completely Egyptianized; the story of Joseph says nothing of his attitude toward Egyptian religion, but it hardly needs to be said. These elements in the patriarchal traditions suggest, although they do not demonstrate, that monotheism is scarcely the word to describe the religion of the ancestors of Israel.

Recent discussion of the question has centered about the monotheism of Moses. W. F. Albright has maintained from a study of biblical and comparative material that Moses must be called a monotheist, but not a speculative monotheist. A basic question is the first commandment of the decalogue*. Some scholars maintain that this prohibition of worship is merely practical, with no affirmation implied; but this is difficult to maintain. The attitude of Israel toward other gods, as expressed in this commandment, is so singular that some affirmation must be implied. It is difficult to see how they could depart so far from the common belief and practice of the ancient Semitic world. It is true, as scholars point out, that the OT often refers to other gods as existing beings; but most of these references come from a period of Hb literature when monotheism was certainly explicit. These references are best explained as allusions to the only existing reality which foreign gods possessed, and this is the reality of the divine image. Behind the image, however, there was nothing. Yahweh, in contrast, could be represented by no image, because He is like nothing else. The prohibition of images is most easily explained as an expression of the Israelite belief in the unique character of the reality of Yahweh; He was like nothing in the heavens or the earth, but He was also like no other god. Relevant here

also is His solitary character. Alone of ancient Semitic deities He has no feminine consort and no divine family; even angels* and the host* of heaven are rare in early literature and possibly come from later narrators and not from the original story. It seems that to some degree to ask whether Moses and early Israel were monotheists is to answer it; for other ancient Semitic religions the question cannot even be asked. Therefore, scholars who do not believe that Israel reached this conception of God before the monarchy attribute the first commandment not to the period of Moses but to a later period. The attribution seems to be based on a theory of the development of Israelite religion rather than on critical analysis of the text. There is nothing in the history of early Israel to indicate that the first commandment goes beyond the belief and practice of early Israel. It must be granted that this monotheism is practical rather than speculative; but the first commandment can scarcely be interpreted as a selection of one god out of many. Other gods are totally rejected as simply irrelevant for Israel; they are not recognized as possessing any power or as active in any way, and Yahweh is not engaged in a combat with them.

Monotheism becomes more explicit in the 9th century. The combat of Elijah* on behalf of Yahweh (1 K 18) is a more explicit rejection of the divinity of the Baal*. In the 8th century Amos, Hosea, and Isaiah leave no doubt of their monotheism. But the most explicit and formal profession first appears in Is 40–55. Here the gods of the nations are said to be nothing, nonexistent. This is not a departure from earlier belief, which never affirmed the reality of the gods beyond the images, but never formally denied it. The monotheism of Second Isaiah appears also in his presentation of Yahweh as lord of nature and lord of history — ideas which appear in earlier prophets also, but not explicitly connected with the unity of Yahweh.

Judaism distinguished itself from the Hellenistic world by its profession of belief in only one God. Philosophical monotheism was taught by many Gk philosophers, but the religions of the Hellenistic world were still polytheistic.

Month. Cf CALENDAR.

Moon. The month in the OT was reckoned from new moon to new moon. The moon is a symbol of permanence (Pss 72:7; 89:38). Ps 121:6 alludes to the popular belief that the moon, like the sun, emits harmful rays (cf Lt *lunaticus,* Eng "moon-struck"). The worship of the moon is mentioned in Dt

4:19; 2 K 23:5; Jb 31:26; Je 8:2; cf below. The moon is made by Yahweh to illuminate the night as the sun illuminates the day (Gn 1:16; Je 31:35). The eclipse of the moon is frequently mentioned as one of the phenomena of the day* of Yahweh (Is 13:10; Ezk 32:7; Jl 3:15; Mt 24:29; Mk 13:24), or the moon will turn the color of blood (Jl 2:31; AA 2:20; Apc 6:12). In the messianic restoration of Jerusalem the light of the moon will be as bright as the light of the sun (Is 30:26); in another conception the moon will not shine in the perpetual daylight of the heavenly Jerusalem (Apc 21:23).

A number of Semitic peoples worshiped a moon god, called Wadd in S Arabia, Shahar by the Aramaeans, and Warah or Yarah by the Amorites. The Akkadian moon god was called Sin. Ur* in S Babylonia was the ancient seat of his worship. A number of hymns to Sin have been preserved, but they are rather general in character and do not give the god a very sharply defined character. He was a patron of divination*. His consort was called Nin-gal. He was venerated at Harran* in NW Mesopotamia; it is remarkable that the family of Abraham* was connected with both these cities. The Sumerian moon god was called Nannar; the seat of his worship was Shuruppak. Many scholars believe that Sin was a Semitic adaptation of the Sumerian Nannar; but J. Bottéro has proposed the hypothesis that, in view of the fact that moon worship was so widespread among Semitic peoples, Nannar acquired a lunar character from assimilation to Sin.

Mordecai (Hb *mordᵉkai*, formed from the Akkadian divine name Marduk*), uncle of Esther* who reared her (Est 2:5–8). Mordecai revealed to Esther a plot to assassinate the king (Est 2:10–22). He refused on religious grounds to make obeisance to Haman*, and this was the occasion of Haman's plot to exterminate the Jews (Est 3). Mordecai appealed to Esther to intercede for her people (Est 4). It happened by accident that the king was reminded of Mordecai's service to him, and Mordecai was rewarded with royal honors (Est 6). After Haman's fall Mordecai was given the office of vizier and he obtained a decree permitting the Jews to exterminate their enemies (Est 8). Mordecai instituted the feast of Purim*, which is called in 2 Mc 15:36 the day of Mordecai (Est 9). The Gk edition of Est contains the dream and the prayer of Mordecai at Est 10:4. Mordecai is the real hero of Est; he represents the Jew who is entirely devoted to the welfare of his people in foreign lands, who maintains his duties even at great risk, is a faithful citizen of his adopted country, and is wise and skillful enough to succeed in the foreign environment.

Moresheth-gath (Hb *morešet-gat*, meaning uncertain), the home city of the prophet Micah* (Mi 1:1, 14; Je 26:18). It is identified with Tell el Judeideh E of Gath. The site was excavated by Bliss and Macalister 1899–1900; the excavation showed that the site was occupied during the Bronze Age, abandoned, and reoccupied during the latter centuries of the monarchy of Judah.

Moriah (Hb *mōrīyyāh*, meaning and etymology uncertain), a topographical name; the site of the sacrifice of Isaac (Gn 22:2). The ancient versions did not take Moriah as a proper name: Gk, "high land," Vg, "land of vision," Syriac, "land of the Amorites." The site lay three days' journey from Abraham's home (22:4), which is Beersheba* in 22:19; but this connection with Beersheba may be redactional. The hill on which Solomon's temple was built is called Moriah (2 Ch 3:1), the only other incidence of the name; but this is in all probability due to theological invention, which identified the temple, the place of Yahweh's dwelling and of Israel's worship, with the site of the sacrifice of Isaac. This identification appears also in Josephus*. There is no way to identify Moriah, and it is possible that no real geographical site is intended.

Moses (Hb *mōšeh*, explained by a popular etymology in Ex 2:10 from Hb MŠH, "to draw," but now generally identified with Egyptian *mešu*, ". . . is born," a common type of Egyptian name with a divine name as subject: Ramses, "Re is born"; Thutmose, "Thoth is born," and thus the name is probably only a fragment of the original Egyptian name). The parents of Moses are not named in the early legend of Ex 2:1 ff, and the genealogy of Ex 6:14 ff, which gives their names as Amram* and Jochebed* (Ex 6:20) is a late document which may contain an artificial genealogy of Moses.

1. *Sources.* There is no extrabiblical information concerning Moses. The biblical information is not homogeneous in quality. Of primary importance are those narratives to which literary criticism assigns an earlier date (cf PENTATEUCH). Later narratives of the Pnt and other allusions to Moses in the OT depend upon the earlier narratives for historical information, and often exhibit the features of midrash*. Even for the earlier narratives it is important that their reduction to writing can scarcely be dated before the 10th century BC in their earliest form, and

the composition of the forms which are at the basis of the present Pnt must be put a century or more later. The redaction of the Pnt itself cannot be earlier than 400 BC. Consequently, even the literary history of the traditions of Moses is complex and does not issue in a simple and unified narrative. Even more important is the gap of perhaps two to three hundred years which lies between the date of Moses and the first reduction of the traditions to writing. Criticism finds that the oral traditions which preserved the memory took two, perhaps three or four forms in different Israelite circles, and that the traditions were submitted to a process of selection, expansion, and interpretation which was considerable before they were written. Consequently, Moses is not a historical figure in the sense that David or Solomon is a historical figure; this implies no question of his existence nor of his importance as the founder of Israel and of many Israelite institutions, which no modern historian denies. But it does show that the traditions of Moses are to a large extent the work of imaginative reconstruction by Israelite narrators, and that many questions of the details of his life admit no certain answer on the basis of historical information; there is room for a theoretical construction of the history of Moses by modern scholars, and here notable differences of opinion appear.

I. Birth and Early Years (Ex 2). Moses was saved from infanticide by his mother and sister and was adopted by an Egyptian princess who had him reared as a scribe. Aware of his Israelite origin, he attempted to defend his countrymen and to reconcile their disputes, but was forced to flee to Midian*, where he joined a nomad tribe and married a Midianite woman.

Historians find several features in this narrative which raise questions concerning its historical character and suggest that folklore here has supplied from invention some things which tradition did not give it. A policy of infanticide is altogether alien to all that is known of Egypt. The story of Moses in the basket is so similar in detail to the Mesopotamian legend of Sargon of Agade (ANET 119) that it is legitimate to ask whether the story of Moses was not composed in imitation, especially since the story of Sargon has now been found in Canaan. It is possible that no historical details of the birth and early years of Moses were known at all. The question has been raised whether he was of Israelite extraction, and it has been suggested that he was an Egyptian who identified himself with the Hebrews. Moses' flight to Midian has some resemblance to the adventure of Sinuhe, an Egyptian noble of the Middle Kingdom who

went into exile and lived with a nomad tribe; the resemblance does not suggest borrowing, but illustrates the story of Moses with a similar episode.

II. The Vision of the Burning Bush and the Return to Egypt (Ex 3:1–7:7). Moses sees a burning bush in which a god who identifies himself with the god of the patriarchs reveals His name as Yahweh (cf GOD) and commissions Moses to lead Israel out of Egypt into Canaan. Moses, accompanied by his brother Aaron, presents his petition to the Pharaoh, who rejects it.

This section exhibits the compilation of several traditions (cf PENTATEUCH) which it is difficult to disentangle, except for the late priestly tradition in Ex 6:2–7:7. The traditions agree in attributing the revelation of the divine name Yahweh to Moses. In following the leadership of Moses the Hebrews accepted the same deity who was worshiped by their fathers, and to whom still older traditions attributed the coming of their ancestors to Canaan. The anecdote of Ex 4:22–25, the circumcision of the son of Moses, is similar to the anecdote of Jacob* at Penuel* (Gn 32:24–32) and is difficult to explain. Some interpreters think it is simply a piece of demonic legend of foreign origin which was attached to the story of Moses. Others suggest that it was originally a story of the circumcision of Moses, and that it was altered to his son because it was inconceivable that the great leader could have been uncircumcised. Since the practice was extremely common in Egypt, it is unlikely that Moses was uncircumcised; but this explanation of the story seems unlikely. It is most probably to be taken as a cult legend expressing the importance of circumcision and the danger of omitting it.

III. The Plagues* of Egypt and the Passover* (Ex 7:8–12:36).

The Exodus (Ex 12:37–15:21).

From the Sea to Sinai* (Ex 15:22–18:27). This section bears a number of resemblances to Nm 10:11–14:45; 20–21 (cf below); and it appears that divergent traditions of identical events were arranged by the compilers of the traditions so that one version appears before Sinai and the other version after Sinai. The Israelites passed Marah*, were nourished with manna* and quail, were given water from the rock, fought the Amalekites, met Jethro*, Moses' father-in-law, who worshiped Yahweh and advised Moses to institute judges; cf ELDER; JUDGE.

IV. The Sojourn at Sinai (Ex 19:1; Nm 10:10). Cf ARK; COVENANT; DECALOGUE; HOREB; LAW; PRIEST; SACRIFICE; TABERNACLE.

V. From Sinai to Paran (Nm 10:11–19:22). The Israelites, guided by Hobab*, continued their journey, were fed with manna and quail, and the elders* were given the spirit* of Yahweh. A quarrel arose between Moses and his brother and sister, Aaron and Miriam*. A scouting party was sent to Canaan; their reports were so much at variance that a serious rebellion against the leadership of Moses sprang up. An attempt to invade Canaan from the S was defeated and the Israelites were condemned to continue their desert sojourn for 40 years. Two other rebellions are related, one led by Korah* and the other by Dathan* and Abiram.

This section contains variant accounts of episodes related in Ex 15–18 (cf above). The stories of rebellions against Moses have been grouped in this section. The story of the scouts probably conflates two rebellions into one: one in which the Hebrews refuse to follow Moses into Canaan, and the other in which they attempt unsuccessfully to invade the country. Two different groups were probably involved. The rebellions of Korah, Dathan and Abiram have been even more closely fused into one.

VI. From Kadesh* to Moab* (Nm 20–36). Here also are contained variant versions of some episodes. The Hebrews were forced to march around Edom. The conquest of Sihon* is placed here, although it probably belongs elsewhere. Cf BALAAM; MIDIAN; MOAB.

VII. The Steppes of Moab and the Death of Moses (Dt). Cf DEUTERONOMY. The death of Moses occurred before the Hebrews crossed the Jordan; it is highly significant that his burial place was not known and that there is no indication that any site was ever claimed for it; the OT makes frequent references to the graves of notable persons, and such graves are still shown in Palestine, usually with little justification for the claim.

2. *The Person of Moses.* The traditions do not attempt to recreate the personality of Moses, and he is not one of the more vividly portrayed characters of the OT. But in spite of the complex character of the oral and written traditions concerning him, a consistent personal character emerges who remains discernible as the same individual through the developing course of events. A certain diffidence which approaches timidity is noted in the story of the burning bush, and this characteristic recurs in later episodes. It may appear that this is not in harmony with the impulsive boldness exhibited in the slaying of the Egyptian and the violent temper which breaks out in the episode of the golden calf and elsewhere; but flashes of violent passion are not out of harmony with habitual diffidence. The dominant trait of the Moses of the Pnt is perseverance. The various traditions represent him as the one man who sustains the purpose of the journey

from Egypt to Canaan against the opposition at one time or another of almost the entire group which he leads. Moses is not presented as a plaster saint; the tradition is constant on the story of a fault which excluded him from entrance to Canaan. To some extent this is a theological conclusion; that Moses did not live to see the final success of his leadership must, in Israelite thinking, have been a punishment for some fault, and this is alluded to more than once. But in the context where the fault seems to be related (Nm 20:12), no fault is mentioned, and one must conclude that the tradition rejected it in the course of transmission. Some historians have concluded that it was found not in the context of Nm 20 but in the story of the scouts and the rebellion in Nm 13–14.

Some uncertainties concerning Moses's extraction are mentioned above. To these should be added the mention of a Cushite* wife in Nm 12:1. This can scarcely be reconciled with the story of his sojourn in Midian except by the hypothesis of polygamy, which is not impossible; but it is possible that the anecdote of Nm 12 knew nothing of the sojourn in Midian. The relations of Moses with the priesthood* are likewise somewhat vague. Although he was a member of the tribe of Levi* (perhaps by an artificial genealogy), he is not connected with priestly functions, and one must conclude that this exclusion preserves a genuine tradition. A further question then arises whether Moses and Aaron are not reckoned as "brothers" by an artificial connection.

3. *The Work of Moses.* In Israelite tradition Moses was simply the founder of Israel, and no lesser designation does justice to the place he occupies. Modern historians are less inclined to question the historical validity of this tradition, despite the fact that the tradition has to some extent magnified his work. He is not, for instance, the lawgiver in the sense that all Israelite law* is to be attributed to him, nor the founder of the cult in the sense that the priesthood and the ritual of sacrifice* are to be attributed to him. Nor is he in any sense the founder of political institutions; Israel* before the monarchy was a tribal confederation, as loose a political unity as can be imagined. The authorship of the Pnt by Moses cannot be sustained, and there is scarcely a line of the Pnt which can be attributed to him with certainty. He does not appear as a military leader; he orders men to battle and inspires them, but does not command them.

The traditions are consistent on certain achievements, and this consistency is such that, to borrow a phrase, if Moses did not exist we would have to invent him. He is the founder of Yahwism, the worship of Yahweh as the God of Israel. The ancestors of Israel did not worship Yahweh by this name nor was He conceived by them as He was revealed by Moses. Moses presented Yahweh to Israel as a deity with an irresistible moral will who imposes His standards of conduct on the people. He presents Yahweh also as the lord of history, who moves events so as to bring His people to their destiny, and the lord of nature, who employs the forces of nature to realize His purpose; He uses human activity, but He is not dependent upon it. The basic Israelite knowledge of Yahweh is found in the traditions of the Pnt; it is clarified and expanded in later books, but it suffers no essential alteration. The Yahweh of the Pnt is the Yahweh of the entire OT.

Moses is the mediator* of the covenant*. The covenant relation of Yahweh and Israel is a unique phenomenon in the religions of the ancient Near East. The establishment of this relationship is attributed to Moses and to no other. The terms of the covenant in the traditions of the Pnt have no doubt been expanded by later religious thought, but the essence of the relationship again remains unchanged.

Moses, however, is not precisely conceived as a prophet. The final verses of Dt, one of the later passages of the Pnt, remark that no prophet like Moses ever appeared. The unique quality of Moses is placed by this note in a feature which recurs in the traditions of the Pnt: the immediacy and intimacy of Moses's knowledge of Yahweh. Israelite tradition affirmed that this was not granted to any other; Moses is more than the first of the prophets. The religious ideal of knowledge* of Yahweh, which is so frequently mentioned in the OT, is reduced to Moses as its originator.

Moses is thus the creator of Israel. That which unified Israel not only before the political unification of David but also under the monarchy, and which survived the division of the monarchy into two kingdoms, was Israel's consciousness of itself as the people of Yahweh. This consciousness rested upon the covenant of Israel with Yahweh. The ethnic unity of early Israel is obscure; but its unity as a people of Yahweh appears in all its traditions, and in this unity the various groups which made up Israel were incorporated. Tradition attributes to Moses the inspiration which brought Israel out of Egypt and thus prevented it from absorption into Egypt; it does not attribute to him the ideal of the possession of Canaan, which is expressed in the stories of the patriarchs. The realization of this ideal, however, Israel frankly attributed to the energy and

persistence of Moses, and it did not blush to represent him as maintaining the ideal against the opposition of the entire people.

On the date of Moses cf EXODUS.

4. *Moses in the OT*. Moses is not mentioned frequently in the Hb books of the OT outside the Pnt: twice in 1 S, 10 times in 1–2 K, 5 times in the prophets, twice in Dn, 8 times in Pss, but 31 times in Ezr-Ne-Ch. Many writers have noticed this, and have deduced that Moses was an unimportant figure in preexilic Israel, or even unknown to many Israelites. Modern criticism has rendered this position untenable. The traditions of Moses are early and many allusions testify that they were known; it is impossible that they should have been known without Moses. But it is to be conceded that Moses does not appear to have been regarded in preexilic Israel as the lawgiver, and not as the author of a book of law before Dt, which has influenced several of the allusions. Most of the allusions outside of Ezr-Ne-Ch refer to the deliverance from Egypt (1 S 12:6, 8; Pss 77:21; 105:26; Is 63:11 f; Mi 6:4). He is the giver of *torah* (1 K 2:3; 2 K 23:25; Mal 3:22), of commandments (2 K 18:6, 12; 21:8). He is the mediator of the covenant (1 K 8:9, 53, 56; Ps 99:6) and the intercessor for Israel (Ps 106:23; Je 15:1). In Ezr-Ne-Ch, which are contemporary to the redaction of the Pnt or later, he appears chiefly as the author of the book of the law. Except for the latter allusions, these allusions are obviously dependent on a form of the traditions quite substantially identical with those in the present Pnt. 2 K 18:4 recalls the story of the brazen serpent in Nm 21:6–9.

The Gk books of the OT, which are of late origin, show the influence of the compilation of the Pnt; Moses appears principally as the lawgiver (Bar 2:2, 28; Tb 7:11–13). The panegyric in BS 45:1–5 praises Moses as wonderworker (a character not mentioned often in other allusions), revealer, and lawgiver; but from the fact that the panegyric of Moses is much briefer than the panegyric of Aaron, which follows, it is evident that BS is not in the dominant strain of Jewish thought about Moses (cf below). 2 Mc not only knows Moses as the lawgiver and the author of the book of law but quotes the Pnt several times (Ex 15:17; Dt 30:5 quoted in 1:29; Lv 9:24 quoted in 2:10; Lv 10:16 ff quoted in 2:11; Dt 32:36 quoted in 7:6). 2 Mc also alludes to the cloud of glory* (2:8) and the law of Moses (7:30).

5. *Moses in Judaism*. The primacy of the law in Judaism was naturally accompanied by an enormous increase of the prestige of Moses. This can be seen both in the Judaism of the apocryphal books and in the Judaism

of the rabbinical schools. The apocryphal*
book of Jubilees was attributed to Moses.
His powers as wonderworker were enhanced
in legend; in particular the wonders of his
death and burial were elaborated, as in the
apocryphal *Assumption of Moses*. In the
rabbinical schools Moses was the lawgiver
and the author of the Torah, the supreme
authority in the decision of any question. He
was regarded not only as the author of the
book of the law, but also as the founder
of the oral tradition interpreting the law,
of which the scribes* were the continuators.
There are also indications, not entirely clear,
of his function in messianic eschatology. In
some forms of this belief, Moses was expected
to return before the end; in other forms, he
would not himself return, but would have as a
successor "the prophet like Moses" (Dt 18:
15), who would be the precursor of the
Messiah. Other forms of the belief presented
a form of typology in which the Messiah
would incorporate in himself many of the
qualities and functions of Moses, would repeat in his career some of the experiences
of Moses, and would be for the new Israel
the founder which Moses was for the old
Israel. Much of this conception of Moses is
reflected in the NT.

6. *Moses in the NT*. Moses is mentioned
80 times in the NT, more frequently than
any other personage. Many of these instances
exhibit the use of the name of Moses as a
designation of the Pnt, or of the Law, and
he appears most frequently as the lawgiver
(Mt 8:4; 19:7 f; 22:24; 23:2; Mk 1:44;
7:10; 10:3 f; 12:19, 26; Lk 2:22; 5:14;
20:28; Jn 1:17; 7:19, 22 f). In Mt 23:2 the
seat of Moses is the authority of interpreting
the law, which Jesus concedes is possessed
by the Scribes and Pharisees*. The Jews
boast that they are disciples of Moses, to
whom God spoke (Jn 9:28 f). The discourse
of Stephen (AA 7:20–45) exhibits several
traits from legend (cf above, Moses in Judaism): he was a beautiful child (20), educated in Egyptian wisdom and skilled in
speech (22, but cf Ex 4:10), heard the
revelation at Sinai from an angel (38). But
the position of the early Church has already
begun to take form in Stephen's discourse;
Moses is the medium of revelation and the
deliverer, but Stephen does not mention his
function as lawgiver.

In Jn and the apostolic writings Moses
becomes a typological figure. He stands as
the type of Jesus, who is a second but also
a greater Moses, and is in the new Israel of
the Church what Moses was in the old Israel,
the founder, the mediator, the revealer. Moses
is the prophet who points to the reality of
the Messiah (Lk 24:27, 44; Jn 1:45; 5:
45 f; AA 3:22; 26:22). Moses wrote that

life came through the righteousness of the
law; but the righteousness of Christ is perfect and communicated to all men (Rm
10:5 ff). The passage of Israel through the
sea was a baptism "in Moses" (1 Co 10:2).
In the transfiguration* Moses, representing
the law, and Elijah*, representing prophecy,
stand with Jesus, who as the Son who is
the word of God is the fulfillment of them
both (Mt 17:1–8; Mk 9:2–8; Lk 9:28–36).
The glory of the religion of the law was
such that Moses had to veil his face, because the Israelites could not look upon its
brightness; the glory of the revelation of
Christ is far greater, but it is revealed in
its fullness with nothing to hide it (2 Co
3:7–18). Moses gave the law, but Jesus
gave grace and truth (Jn 1:17). Moses
gave manna*, but Jesus gives the bread of
life (Jn 6:32). Moses lifted up the serpent
that Israel might live, but Jesus is Himself
lifted up that believers may have eternal life
(Jn 3:14). Moses was in charge of the house,
but Jesus is its builder (Heb 3:2 ff). The
priesthood and the covenant of Jesus surpass
the priesthood and the covenant of Moses;
the new covenant was promised by Jeremiah
(Heb 8:5 ff). Moses ratified the covenant
with the blood of victims, but Jesus ratifies
the new covenant with His own blood (Heb
9:11–22). Violations of the law of Moses
are punished by death; violations of the law
of the Son of God deserve a more severe
punishment (Heb 10:28 f). It is evident
that the controversies with the Jews and
Judaizing Christians, which forced the Christians to assert the excellence of Jesus and
His revelation, involved a certain deprecia-
tion of the law and of Moses. The emphasis
in such passages as those cited here is somewhat misleading simply because they are
selected. It is not that Moses is depreciated
but that Jesus is the one who finishes,
"fulfills" the work of Moses by establishing
the new Israel. It was necessary to point out
to those who admitted no fulfillment that
they adhered to something which was necessarily imperfect, unfulfilled.

Moth. The moth appears in the Bible only
in metaphor. The moth-eaten garment is a
figure of the corruptibility and mortality of
man (Is 50:9; 51:8; Jb 13:28), and man
is compared to the moth which quickly
perishes (Jb 4:19). The moth-eaten garment
is also a figure of the corruptibility of riches
(Mt 6:19; Lk 6:29).

Mourning. Funeral rites in the OT are known
only from casual allusions. Hb law prohibits
some practices, such as shaving the head and
incisions of the body (Dt 14:1) and food-
offerings for the dead (Dt 26:14). Contact

Mourning women represented on Egyptian sarcophagus.

with the dead rendered a person unclean (cf CLEAN AND UNCLEAN) and was not permitted to the priests (Lv 21:1 ff). The dead were mourned by ritual lamentation*. The climate of the Near East and the absence of any practice of preservation such as Egyptian mummification made early burial imperative, and it was usually done on the same day. A number of tokens of mourning are mentioned in the OT: the rending of garments (2 S 1:2; 3:31; 15:32), the wearing of sackcloth (2 S 3:31) or other mourning garments (Ezk 26:16; 2 S 14:2), the smearing of dust on the head (2 S 1:2), the covering of the head (2 S 15:30), walking barefoot (2 S 15:30), wearing the hair loose (Lv 10:6), the omission of the customary employment of unguents (2 S 14:2), wild gestures such as slapping the thigh (Je 31:19), fasting (1 S 31:13; 2 S 1:12), the burning of spices (2 Ch 16:14; 21:19). The Gospel account of the burial of Jesus relates that the body was washed, anointed, and bound tightly in linen. The period of mourning is mentioned as 30 days for Moses* (Dt 34:8) and 7 days' fast for Saul* and Jonathan* (1 S 31:13). Funeral practices among other peoples are illustrated in art, in particular the ceremonial funeral banquet (ANEP 630, 632, 633, 635, 637). The Egyptian scenes of mourning in ANEP 634, 638 are of great interest. These show the wild gestures of dismay and the

tearing of the hair, which is worn loose, and garments; women bared themselves to the waist, and were expected to mourn more ardently than men. The tokens of mourning mentioned above have as a common element the effort to disfigure the appearance, and some scholars have suggested that this was a kind of ritual disguise to conceal oneself from the spirits of the dead. This may have been their origin, but in practice mourning customs are always archaic and usually have no meaning beyond that of conventional expressions of grief. It was the Israelite practice to express festive joy by washing, anointing, and the wearing of a clean festal garment; the expression of grief was the abandonment of the tokens of joy and the adoption of their opposite: the soiling of the person, the wearing of old garments, and loud stylized cries of grief.

Mouth. The mouth is the organ of eating and drinking; and the metaphor of the mouth is used in a few striking instances of the earth, which swallows the blood of the murdered man (Gn 4:11) or the enemies of Yahweh (Nm 16:30, 32; 26:10 +), and of Sheol*, which devours the frivolous (Is 5:14). The mouth is the external manifestation of the character and the disposition. The mouth is opened in the laughter of scorn (Ps 35:24; Jb 16:10; Is 57:4) or of exultation and triumph (1 S 2:1). The mouth is most frequently the organ of speech; to guard the mouth is to preserve one's life (Pr 13:3), to keep oneself from trouble (Pr 13:3); the prudent man guards his mouth (Mi 7:5) or muzzles it (Ps 39:2). Solemnity of utterance is expressed by the introductory phrase, "he opened his mouth and spoke" (Nm 22:28; Mt 5:2). Restoration of speech to the dumb is the opening of the mouth (Lk 1:64). The speech which is an expression of pride against God is arrested by the closing of the mouth (Is 52:15; Jb 5:16; Rm 3:19), and the wise man will put his own hand over his mouth (Jgs 18:19; Jb 21:5; Mi 7:16). Those who live in harmony are of one mouth (Jos 9:2; 1 K 22:13). To speak to another directly is to speak mouth to mouth (Je 32:4). Yahweh reveals His word to man by putting His words into the mouth (Ex 4:12; Nm 22:38; 23:12, 16), as one person puts words into the mouth of another (2 S 14:3, 19). The words which Yahweh puts into the mouth of Moses are in turn put by Moses into the mouth of Aaron, who becomes the mouth of Moses (Ex 4:12–16). Jesus gives His disciples a mouth and wisdom when they must respond to their adversaries (Lk 21:15).

As the organ of speech the mouth is endowed with moral traits; it is crooked (Pr 4:24; 6:12; 8:13) or flattering (Pr 26:28). God fills the mouth with laughter when He delivers one (Ps 126:2; Jb 8:21). It is the source of evil words (Eph 4:29). The mouth reveals the character, for it speaks from the fullness of the heart (Mt 12:34). The speech which comes from the mouth defiles man, not the food which enters it (Mt 15:11, 17 f).

By anthropomorphism* Yahweh has a mouth; when it speaks, it speaks with finality (Is 1:20; 40:5). The mouth of Yahweh is His revelation (Je 9:11) or His command (Nm 14:41; 1 S 12:14 f ;15:24). The idols have mouths but they cannot speak (Pss 115:5; 135:16 f). The word which proceeds from the mouth of Yahweh is an agent of power (Dt 8:3; Is 45:23). Yahweh creates by the breath of His mouth (Ps 33:6). The intimacy of His revelation to Moses is speech "mouth to mouth" (Nm 12:8). The fire of judgment proceeds from the mouth of Yahweh (2 S 22:9; Ps 18:9). The messianic king smites the wicked with the rod of his mouth (Is 11:4); a sword proceeds from the mouth of the lamb with which He combats His enemies (Apc 1:16; 2:16).

Mulberry. Mentioned only in 1 Mc 6:34 and Lk 17:6; older Eng versions sometimes translated mulberry where balsam or sycamore is the tree signified in Hb. The black mul-

berry, *morus nigra* or sycamine (Lk 17:6), is a large tree with green heart-shaped leaves and clusters of berries. In 1 Mc 6:34 the juice of grapes and mulberries is shown to elephants* before they are led into battle.

Mule (Hb *pered*, fem *pirdāh*, designates the mule [the offspring of a male ass and a mare] and the hinny [the offspring of a stallion and a she ass]. The law of Lv 19:19, which is probably ancient, would prohibit the breeding of mules, and they must have been secured by importation. The properties of the mule were highly appreciated, since many of the incidences of the word mention the mule as the beast upon which members of the royal family ride (2 S 13:29; 18:9; 1 K 1:33 ff). A sign of Solomon's accession as David's successor was permission to ride upon the king's mule (1 K 1:33 ff). They are mentioned among the gifts received by Solomon from foreign rulers (1 K 10:25; 2 Ch 9:24). The census of the Jerusalem community of the Persian period includes the number of mules and other animals owned by the community (Ezr 2:66). Most of the incidences refer to riding, but the mule was also employed as a beast of burden (2 K 5:17; 1 Ch 12:40). Horses and mules were imported at Tyre from Togarmah* (Ezk 27:14).

Murder. Murder is prohibited in the decalogue* (Ex 20:15; Dt 5:18); but the crime was not precisely defined in early Israel. The taking of human life by any means and for any cause was the shedding of blood*, and some degree of blood guilt was incurred. The primitive form of the law of blood revenge (cf AVENGER) prescribed the punishment of the killer with no distinction between malicious and casual homicide. The statement of the law by the priestly source in the story of Noah (Gn 9:4–6) speaks simply of the shedding of blood. The law of the code of the covenant (Ex 21:12–14) distinguishes between killing "by hunting," with malice, and killing "when God delivers into one's hands"; the second member must refer to casual homicide if one compares it with other laws, but the words as they stand may reflect a primitive stage of custom in which killing by plan or in ambush was prohibited, but not in combat. The refinements in Dt 19:1–13; Nm 35:10–34 distinguish only between willful and casual killing; willful killing is murder, whatever be the occasion or the means, and is punished by revenge. The guilt is to be determined on the basis of known enmity between the killer and the slain man; known enmity establishes a presumption of guilt. The casual homicide may escape the avenger by flight to a city of refuge; but the concept of blood guilt persists here, for he is safe from the avenger only as long as he remains within the city of refuge. Israelite law is distinguished from other ancient Near Eastern laws by its extension of murder to slaves (Ex 21:20); the phrase is obscure, and the process followed is not clear.

Murder is regarded with abhorrence in the OT. The story of Cain* and Abel* (Gn 4) makes murder the first crime in the moral deterioration of man which is sketched in Gn 4–11. The prophets mention it among the crimes of Israel several times (Is 1:21; Je 7:9; Ho 4:2; +). At the same time, a number of killings which would be murders in modern law and morality were not regarded as murders in ancient Israel. Murder was the killing of an "innocent" man, one who had done nothing worthy of death; the judgment of what was worthy of death and the conception of the moral power to inflict death differed sharply from modern ideas. Jesus expanded the 5th commandment by treating anger and insults as crimes which, like murder, strike at the dignity of the person (Mt 5:21 f). Parallel to this teaching is the statement that one who hates his brother is a murderer (1 Jn 3:15). The 5th commandment appears among enumerations of the commandments (Mt 19:18; Mk 10:19; Lk 18:20; Rm 13:9; Js 2:11). It is one of the crimes of the Gentiles (Rm 1:29), and it proceeds from the malice of the heart (Mt 15:19; Mk 7:21).

Music. No information is available on the music of the ancient Near East; a number of obscure terms which are apparently musical appear in the titles of the Pss*, but their interpretation is unknown. Music is one of early arts of civilization which is attributed to Jubal*, the son of Lamech* (Gn 4:21). There are numerous references to music, vocal and instrumental, on festive occasions and as a part of the cult (Ex 15; Jgs 5), and even to the psychic influence of music; Saul's* disturbed mind was soothed by music (1 S 16:23), and Elisha* summoned a musician to assist him in eliciting prophetic inspiration (2 K 3:15). Sennacherib's account of the booty he took from Jerusalem includes male and female singers. Barzillai includes music and song among the joys which the aged are no longer able to appreciate (2 S 19:35). These allusions are matched in the literature and monuments of other ancient Near Eastern peoples, and it is evident that music played a large part in daily life and religious activity. Ch, a late book, credits David* with the invention of the entire musical system of the temple, which after the exile was complex and re-

quired a large staff of vocalists and instrumentalists. While Ch here no doubt projects a contemporary institution into an early period, the tradition that David was a skilled musician appears in the oldest portions of the accounts of David. David himself played before the ark (2 S 6), and the tradition that he was the major factor in the earliest organization of cultic music seems to rest on a solid historical memory.

A number of musical instruments are mentioned in the OT. Some of these terms are obscure; but with the aid of the cognate languages and the representations of musical instruments in the art of Israel's neighbors, it is possible to arrive at a definition of most of the terms. The following classifications and definitions are taken from O. R. Sellers. The *tōp* was probably a hand drum like the tom-tom. The *kinnôr* was the lyre; the strings, made of the intestines of sheep, were stretched across a sounding board with an aperture and attached to a cross bar. The player struck the strings with a plectrum and with the other hand deadened the strings which he did not wish to sound. The *nēbel* was the harp. The *'āsôr*, lit "ten," is thought to be a zither, a rectangular instrument with ten strings. The Israelites almost certainly had the flute, which is represented in Old Kingdom art in Egypt, but it is uncertain precisely what musical term designates it; the *'ugāb* is very probably a flute. It is represented as a hollow reed pipe with finger holes near one end. The *ḥālîl* is now thought to be the oboe; the double pipe is common in art. Sellers believes that the term may be a more general term for woodwind and may include the double clarinet, a type of instrument found in Egypt. The general word for horn is *keren;* the *šôpār* is the ram's horn, which is still used in modern synagogues. The *šôpār* produces two tones, but a skilled player can introduce variations on these tones. The horn, like the bugle, was used for signals rather than for musical notes, and the blast of the horn seems to have been a regular accompaniment to the charge in battle. The *ḥaṣōṣerāh* was a metal trumpet. The *ṣelṣelîm* and the *meṣiltayim* were cymbals. Sellers believes that the *mena'anîm* was the same as the Egyptian sistrum, a handled metal loop with a hole through which wires were inserted; it gave a jingling sound when shaken.

For illustrations of ancient musical instruments cf ANEP 191–209, 604, 626, 637, 679.

a) Mesopotamian musicians playing the lyre.

c) Egyptian musicians with lute and harp.

b) A lyre from Mesopotamia.

d) Egyptian musicians and dancers with harp, lute (almost entirely disfigured), pipes, and lyre.

Mustard. A tree, *brassica nigra,* which grows both wild and cultivated in Palestine. Its flowers are yellow and its leaves dark green; it grows to a large size (Mt 13:31). The spice is made from the seeds ground to powder.

Myra. A seaport of Lycia on the S coast of Asia Minor, touched by Paul* on his journey to Rome (AA 27:5). The city was of great antiquity. Its ruins lie near the modern village of Dembre.

Myrrh (Hb *mōr*), a spice produced from the gum resin of a large bush or small tree, *commiphora myrrha.* The aromatic gum appears when the thin bark is pierced; it hardens and turns red when exposed to the air. The myrrh of some Eng versions in Gn 37:26; 53:11 is not myrrh but Hb *lōṭ,* the aromatic gum of the rockrose, a small shrub with rose-like pink flowers which grows abundantly in Palestine.

Myrtle (Hb *hᵃdas*), a large evergreen shrub, common in Mediterranean countries. It grows to a height of 18 in or more, and bears white flowers with a pleasing perfume and smooth shiny oval-shaped leaves. The name appears only in late biblical books. Hadassah was the Hb name of Esther*.

Mysia. A region in the NW of Asia Minor, the major portion of the kingdom of Pergamum* from 280 to 133 BC and containing the cities of Pergamum, Troas, and Assos. It was reached by Paul* in his 2nd missionary journey (AA 16:7 f).

Mystery (Gk *mystērion*). *1. Gk usage.* In profane Gk the word appears most frequently in the plural designating religious rites (cf below), and it is uncertain whether this is the primary usage from which the more general meaning of secret or mystery is derived. The mystery cults became extremely popular in the Hellenistic and Roman worlds; they responded to the religious hunger which was created by the bankruptcy of classical religion, and the exotic foreign elements which most of them exhibited fascinated the curiosity of many. All the mystery cults were esoteric; the participants were bound by an oath not to reveal the rites. Because of this there is no explicit description of the mysteries, which must be reconstructed from scattered allusions.

I. The Eleusinian mysteries. This cult originated at Eleusis near Athens and was incorporated into the state religion of Athens in classical times. It was based on the myth of the rape of Proserpine, daughter of Demeter, the earth goddess, by Pluto, the god of the underworld, and Demeter's recovery of Proserpine for one half of the year. The myth represents the cycle of vegetation and the annual renewal of life; the participants were integrated into the cycle and assured of life and fecundity.

II. The mysteries of Dionysus. These rites were probably of Thracian origin. Several forms of the myth of Dionysus appear, but the basic element is the return of the god to life after death; it also is a vegetation myth. The Dionysiac rites were much more licentious and orgiastic than the Eleusinian rites, and were likewise a means by which the participants were integrated with the natural forces of life and fecundity.

III. The Orphic mysteries. The myth of Orpheus relates how he rescued his deceased wife, Eurydice, from the underworld by his music, but lost her again because he looked back at her before they had fully emerged. The origins of these rites are obscure but are probably prehistoric. The myth includes a cosmogony and a theogony which explains the origin of man. Orphism professed belief in the immortality and the transmigration of the soul.

IV. The mysteries of the Great Mother and Attis. These extraordinarily repulsive rites, which included the self-castration of many of the initiates, seem to have come from Asia Minor. The myth related how Attis castrated himself in grief for his infidelity to Cybele, the Great Mother. The rites were a cult of the material force in nature.

V. The mysteries of Adonis. Adonis (cf LORD) was a dying and rising god of vegetation identical with the Baal* of Canaan. The rites originated at Byblos* in Phoenicia.

VI. The mysteries of Isis and Osiris. On the myth cf EGYPT. These mysteries also integrated the participants in the cycle of life.

VII. The mysteries of Mithra. These rites were of Iranian origin and were extremely popular among the soldiers of the Roman legions of the imperial period. Mithra is a solar deity who restores fertility by slaying the bull and releasing the vital force.

The mystery cults exhibit certain common elements; these are not mutual borrowings and imitations, but expressions of certain basic patterns of religious thought and behavior. In all of them the essential rite is the ritual enactment of the myth, which by the reenactment is eternally present. They are all nature cults which are intended in some way to integrate the participants into the cycle of the renewal of life. They do not rest on a historical event but on the recurring events of the cycle. They are an effort to gain life, to strengthen its forces,

Initiation rites of the mysteries of Dionysus, wall paintings from Pompeii.

to prolong it, and in some instances to prolong it beyond death. Survival in those cults which profess belief in it comes through initiation into the mysteries; it is not a natural consequence of human existence nor a gift of the deity. The fact that the mystery cults are entirely enclosed by the concept of nature and its cycle justifies K. Prümm in denying that they contain any genuine idea of salvation*, which, however it is conceived, must include some escape from the confines of nature to be genuine. The mystery cults offered only a "naturist rebirth." The mystery cults all include a rite of initiation

and a progress through various grades of purification to "perfection;" the summit of perfection was reached with the *epopteia* or vision of the essential act in the ritual enactment of the myth. In most of the mystery cults the perfection and the vision were actually a pretended insight into the mystery of sex and a participation in sexual rites.

Several scholars, led by Bousset and Reitzenstein, proposed in the first half of the 20th century that Christianity exhibited a number of resemblances to the mystery cults which suggested some dependence. This theory did not of necessity involve a denial

The mysteries of Isis, a wall painting from Pompeii.

A priestess
of Isis holding
the sistrüm.

of the originality of Christianity, but suggested that Christianity employed many of the rites and the terms of the mystery cults which were so popular in the 1st century AD. In principle, of course, Christianity has taken terms and rites which were older and invested them with a new significance. Scholars pointed out in particular the rites of initiation (cf BAPTISM), the sacred banquet, the concept of purification, the reenactment of a saving event, and the concept of a new life*. More mature consideration of these factors has led scholars in general to abandon the theory of dependence on the mysteries and to regard Christianity as more of a formal and explicit movement against the mystery cults. It is historical, not mythical, in its conception of the saving event, and in fact, as noted above, the mystery cults really include no "saving" event. The conception of God, of redemption*, of the new and eternal life, and the moral elevation of Christianity, which is in obvious contrast to the moral relaxation in which "perfection" consisted in the mysteries, permit no dependence. It must be conceded, however, that the NT use of the word mystery is to be understood against what appears to have been the common understanding of the term in the NT world; but the NT has invested the term with a new meaning (cf below).

2. *In the LXX*. The word is used in the LXX twice of the mystery cults (WS 14: 15, 23) and several times in the meaning of secret (BS 22:22; 27:16, 17, 21; 2 Mc 13:21). "The secret of the king" (Tb 12:7; Jdt 2:2) is the plan or decision of the king; this meaning is certainly reflected in the Pauline use of the word (cf below). "The mysteries of God" (WS 2:22) are the saving designs of God; this use also is reflected in the NT.

This rather infrequent use of the word in the LXX does not match the use of the Aramaic and Hebrew *raz* in the texts of Qumran*, where it occurs more than 40 times (E. Vogt). The word occurs in Dn 2:18 f, 27–30; 4:6 to designate the secret meaning of a dream which God reveals to Dn. In the Qumran texts the word designates the plans or decisions of God concerning the eschatological period; these refer both to salvation and to judgment. This use of the word furnishes a background for the NT use of the word which could not be perceived in profane Gk or in the OT. The word occurs also in the apocryphal* book of Enoch of the messianic-eschatological mystery (Prümm).

3. *In the NT*. The word occurs in the Synoptic Gospels only in Mt 13:11; Mk 4:11; Lk 8:10 of the mystery of the kingdom* which is revealed only to the disciples; to others it is revealed in parables*. The mystery of the kingdom is not defined here and can be defined only from the general context of the Gospels; most interpreters believe that it is the present reality of the kingdom in the person of Jesus, which is recognized only by revelation. This passage exhibits the basic sense of mystery in the NT: an object of divine revelation.

Paul rejects oratorical skill and human wisdom in order to propose the wisdom of God, which is a mystery (1 Co 2:7), unknown to the world's rulers, (2:8), revealed to the apostles through the spirit* (2:10), intelligible only to the spiritual man (2:13 f). These truths are the mysteries of which the apostles are stewards (4:1). The content of the mystery is stated briefly in 2:2; Paul says he preached only Christ and His crucifixion, which is a compendium of his entire teaching on redemption and salvation. The mystery is the divine plan and decision to save men through the death of Jesus.

The concept of mystery is much more explicit in Eph* and Col* (cf these articles on the authorship of these epistles). God has revealed to the apostles the mystery of His will, which is to bring all things under one head in Christ (Eph 1:9 f). This is the mystery unknown to former ages, revealed by the Spirit to the apostles and prophets; and it is the divine decision not only to save through the death of Jesus, but to make all nations equally joint heirs, members of the same body, and partakers of the promise in Christ (3:3–6); it is a "wonderful plan" (3:9), hidden from eternity in God; cf Rm 16:25 f. Eph 5:32 uses the word with reference to the comparison of marriage to the union of Christ and the Church; in the light of other uses, the word here must refer to the union of Christ and His Church, which is the effect of the divine plan of salvation. To make known this mystery is the mission of the apostle (6:19). Col, here as elsewhere, shows affinities with Eph. The mystery, hidden for ages but now revealed to the saints, is "Christ in you" (1:26 f). Christ, in whom are hidden all the treasures of wisdom and knowledge, is the divine mystery (2:2 f). Mystery in the prologue of the hymn of 1 Tm 3:16 refers also to Christ Himself; and the hymn recites the saving career of Jesus. Belief in Christ is no doubt the "mystery of faith" of 1 Tm 3:9. Rm 11:25 identifies the mystery with God's will to save the Gentiles while permitting the Jews to reject salvation.

Other Pauline uses of the word are less precise. 1 Co 13:2; 14:2 seem to speak of mysteries (NB plural) as knowledge of secrets, probably by divine revelation, particularly 14:2, "in the spirit he speaks mysteries." 1 Co 15:51 is an explicit statement of a truth known to Paul by revelation, and the context suggests that he has not uttered this truth to the Corinthians before; it is the revelation of the change of the body in the resurrection. "The mystery of iniquity" of 2 Th 2:7 has no parallel in the NT, and could be understood as an inversion of the "mystery" of salvation applied to the cosmic power of evil, which has a plan of perversion; the phrase is now paralleled in the Qumran documents in precisely this way.

The word does not occur in Jn or 1–3 Jn. In Apc 1:20; 17:5–7 the word is used as in Dn (cf above) of a symbol which needs interpretation. In Apc 10:7, however, the word seems to be used in the Pauline sense.

In general, then, mystery in the NT signifies, as already noted, an object of revelation. In by far most of its incidences the truth known only by revelation is the plan and decision of God to save all men, including the Gentiles equally with the Jews, through the death of Jesus Christ. In the concrete Christ Himself can be called the mystery, and in Eph 5:32 the Church also is identified with the mystery.

Myth (Gk *mythos*, "story"), defined in the Oxford Dictionary as "a purely fictitious narrative usually involving supernatural persons, actions, or events, and embodying some popular idea concerning natural or historical phenomena." Myth in some form appears in almost every culture known to history and anthropology; it deals with questions of cosmic and human origins, the origins of human institutions, man's quest for happiness and his success or failure in finding it, and the end of the world. Its particular interest lies in the relations of nature with gods and with man. It has long been accepted among scholars that myth is by its nature polytheistic and that a monotheistic religion rejects myth. Recent studies have led some scholars to the view that myth is neither polytheistic nor religious by definition, but a pattern of thought and expression. Most of these studies come from the work of Ernst Cassirer. The view may be briefly and inadequately summarized by describing myth so understood as a symbolic expression; myth, art, language, and science are "forces each of which produces and posits a world of its own" (Cassirer). The reality which myth presents in symbolic form is the unknown transcendental reality which lies beyond observation and simple deduction, but which is recognized as existing and operative; myth may represent it as personal beings divine or demonic, a "Thou" rather than an "It." The mythic form is always symbolic of the reality which it apprehends obscurely and only through an intuition. This reality is perceived and represented in events and not in abstraction, and the event is portrayed in the form of a story. The mythical event occurs on a cosmic scale; it is the action and interaction of personal beings on the cosmic scale which is the pattern and the foundation of events in the phenomenal world. This is not causality as it is understood in modern philosophy and science.

This approach to reality is contrasted with the logical discourse of philosophy and science. It claims to represent reality, and recent scholars point out that it should be examined to see to what extent it is successful and how far its claim is valid. Myth to some extent in the view of these scholars is an essential part of the patterns of human thought and discourse which can never be entirely replaced by logical discourse, particularly in those questions for which logical discourse fails to render an answer which satisfies the mind. The newer view of myth is summed up by Millar Burrows as "a symbolic, approximate expression of truth which the human mind cannot perceive sharply and completely but only glimpse vaguely, and therefore cannot adequately or accurately express. . . Myth implies, not falsehood, but truth; not primitive, naïve misunderstanding but an insight more profound than scientific description and logical analysis can ever achieve. The language of myth in this sense is consciously inadequate, being simply the nearest we can come to a formulation of what we see very darkly." And G. Henton Davies: "Mythology is a way of thinking and imagining about the divine rather than a thinking or imagining about a number of gods."

1. *Myth in the OT*. The question of myth in the OT is concerned with the relation of similarity or dependence between the OT and the myths of Mesopotamia and Canaan. The mythological literature of these two civilizations has been extensively recovered and comparison is possible; cf CREATION; DELUGE; FALL, THE. It is evident that the OT often employs language and imagery which is either drawn from this mythology or which very closely resembles it; cf Gn 1 and allusions to the victory of the creative deity (CREATION); Gn 2–3 (FALL, THE); the eschatological catastrophe as a return to chaos (Is 17:12 ff; 24:19); the golden age as a new creation (Is 11:6 ff); imagery of the theophany*. Whether such passages as the creation accounts, the deluge, the condition and fall of primitive man should be called theological reconstructions or interpretations is doubtful, if theology is to be understood as logical discourse. Of these things the OT actually tells stories; the representation of the unknown reality and its relations to the phenomenal world in a single event is a trait of mythopoeic thinking. These passages are equally well designated approximate expressions through symbolic forms of truths vaguely perceived through intuition. The unknown reality is personal will and the world of phenomena is determined by a personal will. What distinguishes these passages of the OT from ancient myths is not the patterns of thought and language, which seem in every respect to be the same, but the Hebrew idea of God as known through His revelation of Himself. This knowledge they themselves attributed to a personal encounter with God, and in this respect the unknown reality is not entirely unknown. When we compare the thought processes of the OT with the processes of Semitic myth, we observe that the OT rejects all elements which are out of character with the God whom they knew. But what they knew of God could be expressed only through symbolic form and concrete cosmic event, and the relations of God with the world and with man were perceived and expressed through the same patterns and processes which elsewhere we call mythical. This is the quality of OT thought and language, by whatever term it may be designated.

2. *Myth in the NT*. In 1835 D. F. Strauss proposed the "mythological" interpretation of the life of Christ, by which mythological signified "fictitious," not in the sense that Jesus was not a historical figure but that the Gospels were fictitious accounts of His life. This conception of the mythical dominated NT studies until 1941. R. Bultmann then initiated a vigorous discussion on the "demythologization" of the NT. Bultmann found the NT "mythological" in its conception of a three storied world with heaven and hell, angelic and demonic beings, the preexisting Son of God, the redeeming death, the resurrection, ascension, and enthronement at the right hand of the Father, the eschatological catastrophe and the world judgment. These Bultmann found entirely unacceptable to the modern mind and demanded a restatement of the NT gospel of salvation in the terms of philosophical and scientific logical discourse. Bultmann's demand was criticized from many quarters as a demand to reduce the NT to a philosophy. In particular, his definition of myth was carelessly constructed with no reference to the recent studies mentioned above. But the question he raised demanded an answer. In the light of the newer concept of myth, here summarized by J. Henninger as "the complex expression of man's global experience of himself and of certain mysterious realities with which he finds himself in relation," there is no difficulty in designating some NT patterns as mythical. This implies no denial or doubt of the historical reality of Jesus and the apostolic Church, for myth is not concerned with events of the phenomenal world which can be observed, nor with the truth and reality of the process of salvation; for a symbolic form is an expression of truth, not a denial of truth. But the sym-

bolic form must be recognized as an inadequate and approximate expression of the mysterious (cf MYSTERY). The patterns of myth which one may find in the NT are not drawn from the myth and mystery religions of the Hellenistic world but from the mythopoeic thought and language of the OT.

N

Naaman (Hb *na'amān*, "[the god is (?)] love"), general of the king of Damascus, cured of his leprosy* by bathing in the Jordan seven times at the command of Elisha* (2 K 5). The story is extremely popular in character, but it illustrates several features of life in Israel at the period: the raids of slave traders; the hegemony of Damascus over Israel; the easy communications between the two kingdoms. Several theological motifs are implied also: the superiority of the waters of Israel over the waters of Damascus, and by implication of the God of Israel over the gods of Damascus; the power of the prophet not only as healer but as savior and vindicator of Israel; the gratuity of the works of the prophet. The request of Naaman for two loads of the soil of Israel shows how the popular mind conceived the deity as identified with the land where he is worshiped; and the prophet's approval of his entry into the temple of Rimmon* with the king draws a fine distinction between material and formal communication in worship. At the same time, it shows that one who becomes a worshiper of Yahweh may not worship other gods.

Nabal (Hb *nābāl*, "fool"; but this etymology seems doubtful; the play on the name [1 S 25:25] has perhaps made the assonance of the name and the noun nearer than it was originally), a wealthy herdsman of Maon* in Judah (1 S 25). When Nabal refused gifts to David* and his band, David was insulted and swore to exterminate the entire household of Nabal. He was diverted from his intention by Abigail*, Nabal's wife. Nabal died suddenly when Abigail told him how near he had been to destruction, and David married the widow. Some have, perhaps unjustly, suspected that Abigail was not entirely innocent of Nabal's sudden death. The demand of David for gifts, although couched in polite and courteous terms, is a veiled form of extortion, the modern "protection money" for not doing violence.

Nabataeans. An Arabian tribe; mentioned in 1 Mc 5:25; 9:35 as friends and allies of the Maccabean party. Originally a nomadic desert tribe, they emerge into history with the beginning of the Seleucid era (312 BC) as settled in the former territory of Edom* and Moab* and the regions to the S of these territories. Their importance was due to the fact that the caravan routes between Arabia and Syria passed through their territory and were controlled by them. They erected numerous caravan cities and fortified posts along the routes; their capital and most famous city, Petra, the "rose red city half as old as time," was a great emporium. The explorations of Nelson Glueck have shown that the Nabataean civilization was of a high quality. The nomadic tribe developed urban life and agriculture to a high degree; the area maintained a larger population in the Nabataean period than it ever maintained before or since. The Nabataeans created this civilization by large and carefully constructed systems of water conservation and distribution. The area contains few springs and has a small annual rainfall; the Nabataean cisterns, dams, and canals were built to conserve almost every drop. The rock-cut tombs and houses of Petra and other Nabataean centers are famous; but their art and architecture was largely derived and eclectic, exhibiting Egyptian, Parthian, and Hellenistic influences. The Nabataean community became a monarchy under Aretas I (110–96 BC); four kings named Aretas* are known. The Nabataeans engaged in successful campaigns against Alexander Jannaeus and against Herod* Antipas, who divorced the daughter of Aretas IV to marry Herodias and incurred the wrath of his father-in-law. Aretas IV also secured the rule of the region of Damascus from Caligula. The Nabataeans, situated between the great powers of Rome and Parthia, could maintain themselves only by skillful diplomacy, and they were finally incorporated into the Roman province of Arabia in AD 106. They have left numerous inscriptions, but no literature. Exploration of temples at Petra and Khirbet Tannur and a few smaller places show that their religion was a syncretism of Semitic and Hellenistic deities. Their own deities were principally fertility deities: Dushara and the feminine Allat. Images show Zeus (with the characteristics of Hadad*) and Atargatis, a Semitized Artemis*. The Nabataean temples were equipped with the broad open high place*, the cult area mentioned so frequently in the OT.

Naboth (Hb *nābôt*, meaning and etymology uncertain; possibly "sprout"), a man of Jezreel, victim of a judicial murder engineered by Jezebel* in order that Ahab* might acquire his land, which he had refused to sell (1 K 21). This cynical crime was the occasion of Elijah's* oracle against the house of Ahab, and Jehu* deliberately had the body of the dying Jehoram* flung into the field which had been owned by Naboth (2 K 9:25 f). The refusal of Naboth was motivated by the ancient Israelite belief that land should be retained in the family and should not be allowed to pass into large estates; and the crime was particularly repugnant not only as a perversion of justice but as a sin against the ideal of land ownership.

Nadab (Hb *nādāb*, shortened form of such names as Nedabiah, Jehonadab, Amminadab). **1.** Son of Aaron* and brother of Abihu*, heirs of the priestly office; the succession passed to Eleazar* and Ithamar* after the violent and sudden death of Nadab and Abihu (Lv 10:1 ff; cf PRIEST). **2.** King of Israel 909–908, son and successor of Jeroboam* I, assassinated with his family by Baasha* (1 K 14:20; 15:25–31). The name is borne by two others in the OT.

Nahash (Hb *nāhāš*, "serpent"?), king of Ammon*. He besieged Jabesh-gilead* and promised peace on harsh and insolent terms, and was defeated when Saul rallied Israel to rescue the city (1 S 11). David was indebted to him for a kindness which is not related, probably exhibited while David was in flight from Saul (2 S 10:2; 1 Ch 19:1 f).

Nahor (Hb *nāhôr*, meaning and etymology uncertain). Nahor appears as the grandfather of Abraham (Gn 11:22–25) and as the brother of Abraham (Gn 11:26–29; 24; Jos 24:2), the father of Bethuel* and the grandfather of Rebekah* (Gn 24), and the father of Laban*, brother of Rebekah (Gn 29:5); the name in the last instance may be used loosely, but there is possibly some uncertainty in the genealogy also. That grandfather and grandson should have the same name is not impossible, but there are other complexities. Nahor is the name of a city in Gn 24:10. The city Nahur in NW Mesopotamia near Haran* has been known for many years from the Assyrian inscriptions; the Mari* tablets now reveal that it was one of a group of cities whose names appear in the patriarchal narratives (cf PELEG; SERUG). Furthermore, Nahor appears as the ancestor of a number of Aramaean* tribes (Gn 22:20–24). It is possible that the clan gave its name to the city; but in any case it seems that either the clan or the city or both have been hypostatized in the genealogy of Abraham and his family.

Nahum (Hb *nahûm*, probably a shortened

form of Nahumiah, "Yahweh comforts"), the 7th of the minor prophets.

1. *Contents of the Book*
1:1, superscription; 1:2–10, an incomplete acrostic psalm describing the theophany and the judgment of Yahweh; 1:10–2:2; probably disarranged pieces containing threats against Assyria (1:11, 13–14) and promises to Judah (1:12, 15, 2:2); 2:1 is probably to be joined to the following poem; 2:1, 3–13, the attack upon Nineveh*; 3:1–19, the sack of Nineveh, the despair of its citizens, allusion to the Assyrian conquest of Thebes in Egypt, the futile defensive efforts, the joy of those who see the fall of the city.

2. *Occasion.* The book clearly refers to the capture and destruction of Nineveh by the Babylonians and Medes in 612 BC (cf ASSYRIA; NINEVEH). This event marked the climax of the campaign which had begun in 625 to overthrow the Assyrian empire. The significance of this historic event was clearly perceived by the Israelite prophet.

3. *Author and Date.* Of Nahum nothing is known except his name. He is called the Elkoshite; the town of Elkosh is not mentioned elsewhere, and there is no clue to its location. The book must be later than 663 BC, the date of the sack of Thebes by the Assyrians (3:8 ff); very few critics regard it as later than the fall of Nineveh in 612 BC, and it can scarcely be later in any case than 609 BC, when the defeat and death of Josiah* showed that Judah's hope of independence after the fall of Assyria was fallacious. The tone of the book suggests that the prophet describes an impending event, and it was most probably written after the siege of Nineveh had begun.

4. *Criticism.* Few if any critics doubt that the poems of 2–3 come from the period and from a single author; they exhibit homogeneity in style and conception. Some doubts are raised about 1; the introductory poem is general, not historical, and the section 1:11–2:2 seems to be disarranged. These considerations are serious but not convincing. The acrostic poem is not complete, and it is a question whether the compiler of the book possessed it in its complete form.

5. *Theology.* Many modern writers deny that Nahum deserves the title of prophet. They assert that he voices nationalism rather than faith, and that the poem is a cry of cruel exultation over the fall of Nineveh; this tone is not excused by the character of the Assyrian empire. Nahum does not, like the other prophets, attack the sins of his own people nor threaten them in any way. The name of Yahweh occurs in the poems only in 2:13 and 3:5. These considerations are exaggerated; on the other hand, there is no reason to affirm that Nahum represents

the highest level of prophetic thought. It seems altogether possible that the compiler, struck by the nearly secular character of the poems, introduced the acrostic as a general reflection on the judgments of Yahweh, of which the fall of Nineveh was the greatest example in the history of Israel. Yahweh, however, is the agent of the destruction of Nineveh in the poems themselves; the two passages where the divine name occurs introduce oracles in which this is stated clearly. Judah is not the avenging agent; nor is there in 2–3 any allusion to the benefits which Judah might expect from the collapse of Assyria. The fall of Assyria was indeed a tremendous demonstration of a principle of Israelite belief, that Yahweh does not permit the wicked and the godless oppressor to survive; it was a theme worthy of an Israelite prophet, although we may concede that he did not reach what we consider a high theological level.

He did, however, reach a high poetic level; Na is one of the most powerfully written compositions of the OT. It is rapid and vivid and creates a picture of the terror and confusion of the doomed city and the rush of the attackers. The description speaks for itself and needs no explicit moralizing by the prophet; it is a great poem to match a great critical event of history which is its theme.

Nain (Gk *nain* in the critical text, Lt and some MSS *naim;* probably from Hb *nāʿîm,* "lovely"?), a village of Galilee mentioned in Lk 7:11, where Jesus raised the son of a widow. It is very probably to be identified with the modern village of Nein near Nazareth.

Naioth (Hb *nāyôt* or *nᵉwāyôt*), mentioned as being "in Ramah*" (1 S 19:18–23; 20:1); the place where David fled to Samuel and a company of prophets, and where Saul himself was seized by the spirit. Both the meaning and the spelling of the word are uncertain; some modern scholars suggest that it is not a proper name, as it is usually translated, but a designation of the place where the prophets dwelt or assembled.

Name. It is a widespread cultural phenomenon that the name is considered to be more than an artificial tag which distinguishes one person from another. The name has a mysterious identity with its bearer; it can be considered as a substitute for the person, as acting or receiving in his place. The name is often meaningful; it not only distinguishes the person, but it is thought to tell something of the kind of person he is. In magic* rites the name is extremely important: Knowledge of the name gives control, and utterance of the name is effective either upon its bearer or as containing the power of the person whose name is uttered. Vestiges of such beliefs survive even in civilized societies when they retain ancient customs which surround the conferring of the name with solemnity. Many of these beliefs occur in the Bible, and where the name of the deity is concerned the conception of the name becomes a theological idea.

1. *OT*. Hb personal names were significant, and most of them express a religious belief or a prayer of petition. Occasionally we see that a name was given to a child in connection with an event which was contemporaneous with his birth (Ichabod*, 1 S 4:21 f). The name of the son of Isaiah, Shear-jashub*, was a statement of the prophet's teaching, and the name of the child Emmanuel* was likewise a statement of the teaching of Is. The name of Nabal* is explained by Abigail as describing the character of the man (1 S 25:25). Frequently in the OT names are explained by etymologies which are no more than assonance; but to treat them as mere puns is to miss the Hb conception of the power of the name. For the name not only suggested its proper meaning, but also words of similar sound; it was a part of the mysterious fullness of the power of the name that it should signify more than the word itself, and when such assonances could be observed they were taken as instances of the power of the word*.

The name was not merely an identification mark; the name must be known, and in this sense it is fame or reputation; we also use "name" in this sense. A person's name survives in his descendants; but the name here is also something of the person. It is a disaster when one's name is destroyed or blotted out (1 S 24:21; 2 K 14:27). The supreme threat to the wicked is that he will have no name (Jb 18:17), that his name will rot (Pr 10:7). The men who built the Tower of Babel hoped to establish a name for themselves (Gn 11:4); something of themselves would survive in their work.

A change of personal name indicated a change in the person; the change of Abram to Abraham (Gn 17:5) and of Jacob to Israel (Gn 35:10) showed a new development in the relation of the patriarchs to Yahweh. The change of Mattaniah to Zedekiah showed that the king was a vassal of Nebuchadnezzar (2 K 24:17). Yahweh shows His redeeming love for Zion by conferring a new name (Is 62:2); this proves that its sinful and troubled past is blotted out and that it begins to live anew. Man shows his intelligence and his superiority to the brutes by giving them names (Gn 2:20).

The divine name has all the significance

and power of the human name raised to a fitting degree. In solemn hymns of praise which sing either the creative works of Yahweh (Am 4:13) or His redeeming deeds (Ex 15:3) the solemn affirmation that Yahweh (or Yahweh of hosts*) is His name says all that need be said; for Yahweh has proved that He is what His name signifies. In postexilic literature the "name" is frequently used as a substitute for Yahweh Himself; this is the step toward the hypostatization of the name which appears in later Judaism. In earlier literature the name is the person; Yahweh is present and active where His name is invoked, where He is known and recognized. To call upon His name is to summon Him. His name is in Zion (Is 18:7) or in Shiloh* (Je 7:12), the places where He is worshiped and invoked. Modern scholars point out a theology of Dt in which the name of Yahweh is conceived as dwelling in the temple, while Yahweh Himself dwells in heaven (Dt 12:11; 14:23; 16:11; 1 K 3:2).

One may speak in the name of a king or of a powerful man (I S 25:9; 1 K 21:8); and so the prophet speaks in the name of Yahweh (Ex 5:23; Dt 18:22; Je 26:20; 14:15 +). The ancient messenger identified himself with the person whose message he bore; the formula, "Thus speaks Yahweh," followed by an utterance in the first person, was the usual message formula. The messenger spoke with the power of the one who sent him; and the power was communicated by the utterance of the name, itself a bearer of power, at the beginning of his message. The power is also communicated to those who bear Yahweh's name, for He thus recognizes them as His own (2 Ch 1:14; Je 25:29). Likewise a name conferred by Yahweh Himself, which is an act of ownership, gives to the person named the protection of the one who confers the name; and thus Yahweh recognizes Israel by giving it the name (Is 43:1; 48:1). In the same way He recognizes Moses (Ex 33:12, 17). Yahweh's power over creation is demonstrated when He calls the stars by name (Is 40:26).

Yahweh guides Israel through the desert by an angel in whom is His name (Ex 23:20 f). Possibly two ideas have been conflated in this passage (cf ANGEL); in any case, the work of Yahweh is attributed to His name. So His name is glorious (Ps 72:19); great (1 K 8:42), awful (Dt 28:58), exalted (Ps 148:13). Through His name one is delivered (Ps 54:3), exalted (Pss 20:2; 89:25;). One trusts in His name (Ps 33:21; Is 50:10), finds help in His name (Ps 124:8). Goliath approaches David with spear and javelin but David meets him with the name of Yahweh (1 S 17:45). The

name in such passages is the invocation of the name; it is an utterance of power which renders present Him who is invoked.

To know the name of Yahweh is to experience the reality which the name signifies, the reality of assured confidence and deliverance (Ps 9:16; Is 52:6) or of avenging judgment (Is 64:2); to know Yahweh's name is to learn what He is. So it was vital to the mission of Moses that he should be able to tell the Israelites the name of the God who sent him (Ex 3). The name is therefore to be uttered respectfully; it must not be profaned (Lv 24:11) or used "vainly" i.e., probably in magical formulae (Ex 20:7; Dt 5:11). The prohibition of mentioning the name in Am 6:10 is obscure and probably reflects popular belief; where Yahweh has just struck disaster, He is obviously angry, and it is unwise to irritate Him again by mentioning His name.

The name of Yahweh is also His reputation and His glory, His recognition by men (Ex· 9:16; Jos 9:9; Ps 48:11; Is 55:12). Where His deeds are recited His name is recalled and He is recognized as what He is.

2. *NT*. The divine name in the NT is used in OT idioms. The work of Jesus is to make known the name of the Father (Jn 17:6, 26), to reveal His true character. He glorifies the name of the Father by bringing recognition of His divinity (Jn 12:28). He prays that the Father will keep the disciples in His name (Jn 17:11), that He will preserve them as His own. He works in the name of the Father (Jn 10:25), which here means what He says elsewhere, that He is in the Father and the Father is in Him (Jn 14:10). The first petition of the Lord's Prayer is that the name of the Father may be sanctified, that His divinity may be manifested (Mt 6:9; Lk 11:2; cf HOLY).

The most remarkable development of the concept of name in the NT is the way in which the theology of the name is applied to Jesus; this is a testimonial of the divinity of Jesus Himself. J. Dupont collects the use of the name of Jesus under the following seven themes; the texts are too numerous to permit more than a sampling:

(1) The supernatural power of the name of Jesus. The invocation of the name of Jesus empowers the disciples to work wonders (Mk 16:17), in particular to heal (AA 3:6; 4:12) and to expel demons (Lk 10:17). This power of the name is seen even when the one who invokes it is not a member of the company of the disciples (Mk 9:38). Jesus, however, tolerated this use of His name; it is evident that it was used in genuine faith. That any magic power was thought to reside in the name is explicitly repudiated in the episode of AA 19:13–16,

when the attempt of unbelieving Jews to use the name of Jesus in exorcisms brought disaster upon themselves. But the power of the name of Jesus appears most eminently in its quality as an instrument of salvation. Men receive forgiveness of sins in His name (AA 10:43; 1 Jn 2:12), they are washed and sanctified in His name (1 Co 6:11), and there is no other name in which salvation can be attained (AA 4:12). The name here means Jesus in His character as savior, in which He is accepted by faith and invoked in the rite of baptism*.

(2) The name of Jesus is above every name. This is stated in the Christological confession of Phl 2:9–11 and Eph 1:21. It expresses His total transcendence over every creature; the name here is the reality of the person, and it is expressed formally in the confessional formula of Phl 2:11: "Jesus is Lord*."

(3) The invocation of the name of Jesus. Christians are defined as those who invoke the name of Jesus. They invoke it in the confession of their faith and in ritual invocation, of which the most important is baptism "in the name of Jesus." This does not identify the formula of baptism as such, which is the Trinitarian formula of Mt 28:19; but it is a common designation of the sacrament (AA 2:38; Rm 6:3 +). To be baptized "by" or "in" or "into" the name of Jesus is to be called by His name, according to the OT usage (cf above); by baptism Jesus accepts and recognizes the Christian as His own, and the Christian submits himself to incorporation in the community of which Jesus is the head. Anointing in the name of Jesus helps the sick and brings forgiveness of sins (Js 5:14).

(4) The preaching of the name of Jesus. The preaching of the gospel is compendiously defined as the preaching of the name of Jesus (AA 5:40; 8:12; 9:15, 28), which is further defined (AA 9:20) as "preaching Jesus as the son of God." To preach Jesus is to declare who and what He is, and this is the content of the gospel, the good news, which is the object of faith.

(5) Faith in the name of Jesus. In the same way, the belief of the Christian is compendiously defined as faith in the name of Jesus (Jn 3:18; 1 Jn 5:13); through faith in the name of Jesus the Christian obtains eternal life.

(6) Jesus asks renunciation of the goods of this world for His name (Mt 19:29) and His disciples must suffer for His name (1 Pt 4:14–16; AA 5:42; 9:15; Jn 15:21). This does not mean suffering for the person of Jesus, but for the confession that Jesus is son of God and Lord.

(7) The name of Jesus in the life of the Church. Other passages which do not fall under the six themes previously mentioned illustrate the use of the name of Jesus in the Church and the conception of the name. The invocation of the name in prayer or in confession was not a casual matter; to utter the words "Jesus is Lord" demanded an impulse of the spirit* (1 Co 12:3). The name of Jesus is the power in which the apostle commands (2 Th 3:6); as in the OT (cf above), the one who pronounces the name speaks with the power of the one who sends him. The prayers of the Church and of the individual Christian are uttered in the name of Jesus (Jn 14:13; 16:26); this is also an instance of the supernatural power of the name. The Church approaches the Father invoking the name of Jesus, which it bears and with whom it is identified; and it is assured of a hearing. The Christian acts in the name of Jesus and performs good deeds in His name (Mt 18:5; Col 3:17), i.e., he acts in the character which he has received by his incorporation into Jesus and according to the teaching and example of Jesus, so that the name of Jesus works in him. Finally, the name of Jesus is the principle of the unity of the Church, for He is present where two or three are assembled in His name (Mt 18:20). This recalls the OT use of the name of Yahweh to signify His presence, particularly in cultic assemblies.

J. Dupont makes the important point that the NT lacks formulae such as person and nature to speak of the relations of the divine persons. It does not identify Jesus with "God" (Gk ho theos), which is a personal name identical with the Father (cf GOD); but here and elsewhere it applies to Jesus formulae of the OT which belong to Yahweh. Within the limits of its vocabulary it could say no more to elevate Jesus to a level which is properly and formally the level of a divine person.

Naomi (Hb nŏ'ŏmî, "my delight"), a personal name; wife of Elimelech* of Bethlehem, mother of Mahlon* and Chilion*, mother-in-law of Orpah* and Ruth*.

Naphtali (Hb naptālî, meaning and etymology uncertain), explained by popular etymology in Gn 30:8 as "wrestlings"; son of Jacob* and Bilhah* (Gn 30:8) and one of the 12 tribes of Israel* (Gn 35:25; 1 Ch 2:2). The clans of Naphtali are listed in Gn 46:24; Nm 26:48–50; 1 Ch 7:13. The numbers of its fighting men are given as 53,400 in Nm 1:42 f, as 45,400 in Nm 26:48–50. It is mentioned in the processional enumeration of tribes in Ps 68:28. Its frontiers are described in Jos 19:32–34; its cities are listed in Jos 19:35–39. The Levitical* cities of

Naphtali are listed in Jos 20:32. The principal city of Naphtali was Kedesh*, which is a city of refuge (Jos 20:7). The territory of Naphtali lay in Galilee between the Sea of Galilee and the mountains of central Galilee. Non-Israelite enclaves in the territory are mentioned in Jgs 1:33.

Barak* was a member of the tribe, and Naphtali was prominent in the campaign against Sisera* (Jgs 4:6, 10; 5:18). It was one of the tribes which marched with Gideon* against the Midianites* (Jgs 6:35; 7:23). Naphtali formed the 8th administrative district of Solomon* (1 K 4:15). The position of the territory in the N exposed it to invasion; it was conquered by Ben-hadad of Damascus (1 K 15:20; 2 Ch 16:4) and was one of the Israelite territories which first fell to the Assyrians under Tiglath-pileser* III in 734 BC (2 K 15:29; Is 8:23). The expressions in the blessing of Jacob (Gn 49:21) and the blessing of Moses (Dt 33:23) describe the tribe as prosperous; and the country of Naphtali is one of the fairest pieces of the land of promise.

Naphtali is a geographical rather than a tribal name in Dt 34:2, and the phrase "the mountain of Naphtali" (Jos 20:7) also seems to have a geographical meaning; this has led some scholars to ask whether the name may not have been attached to the tribe from the territory rather than the reverse. The complexity of early tribal history is shown in this feature of the name, as well as in the relations of Naphtali with Dan*. The two tribes, reckoned as sons of Bilhah*, obviously had some connection; but their territories were adjacent only after the move of Dan* to the N, which is well attested in the traditions.

Narcissus (Gk narkissos, meaning uncertain), a personal name; the mythological hero Narcissus drowned when he fell into a pool while admiring his own reflection. The name was extremely common in imperial Roman times. "Those of the household of Narcissus" in Rome, probably slaves of Narcissus, were Christians (Rm 16:11); it is not clear that Narcissus himself was a Christian.

Nard (Hb nerd, Gk nardos), a loan word from Indo-Germanic; a perfume derived from the oil of Nardostachys Jatamansi, a plant native to India. Eng "spikenard" is derived from Lt spica nardi, which designates the spikes characteristic of the plant. The perfume is mentioned in SS 1:12; 4:13; Mk 14:3; Jn 12:3. The NT passages indicate that it was an extremely costly unguent. It is called nardos pistikos in the NT, usually translated "genuine nard"; but it is more probable that the adjective pistikos is a Gk

corruption of a name which indicates the origin of the perfume. R. Köbert suggests that it is a mistranslation of the Aramaic kšṭ', which represents Costum, an Indian perfume, as "truth."

Nathan (Hb nātān, "[the god] gave," an abbreviation), a personal name borne by a number of men in the OT, of whom the most important is the prophet of David's court. Nathan first appears in 2 S 7:1–17 (1 Ch 17:1–15); he encourages David in the project of building a temple to Yahweh, but after a nocturnal communication from Yahweh he reverses himself and declares that Yahweh does not desire that David should build Him a house, and promises David an eternal dynasty. The oracle is built around a play on the word bayit, "house," which means both a temple and a family. The text of 2 S 7:8–16 shows many signs of editorial reworking, and the original oracle is probably much better preserved, with some expansions, in Ps 89:20–38. This oracle, which is now generally regarded as originating in the Davidic period, is the earliest statement of the belief in the eternity of the dynasty of David, and is the root of the messianic expectation of the rule of David; cf DAVID; KING; MESSIAH.

Nathan next appears in 2 S 12:1–25; he rebukes David severely for his adultery and murder and threatens him with death. Because of the repentance of David the threat of death passes from him to the child who is born of Bathsheba*. With other passages (cf ELIJAH; ELISHA; ISAIAH; JEREMIAH) this story illustrates the freedom which the prophet exercised in speaking to the king. Nathan here exhibits the prophetic duty of defending the traditional morality of Israel as imposed by Yahweh.

Nathan's final appearance in 1 K 1:8 ff relates that he, with Bathsheba, Zadok*, and Benaiah*, favored the accession of Solomon after David against Adonijah*. Nathan's share in the proceedings consisted in persuading Bathsheba to ask for the succession of Solomon and in himself presenting the case of Solomon. It is strange to find Bathsheba and Nathan so thoroughly reconciled; one imagines that the episode of 2 S 12 would not have furnished a basis for their friendship. Nathan does not here act as a prophet and presents no oracle concerning the succession; he appeals to a promise made to Bathsheba. It is not surprising to find two of his sons among Solomon's officers (1 K 4:5).

No information is given of Nathan's origin. The absence of any Israelite genealogy and the fact that he does not appear in David's life until David established his residence in Jerusalem has led some scholars to ask whether Nathan may not have been a Jebusite of Jerusalem; cf ZADOK. He is the earliest example of the "court prophet," and indeed approaches the prophetic ideal much more nearly than most other court prophets; it seems that the king's cabinet normally included one or more men who possessed the charisma of prophecy. Like other prophets, Nathan was capable of purely political intrigue (1 K 1).

Nathanael (Hb $n^e tan'\bar{e}l$, "El has given"), personal name; a man of Cana*; he was summoned by Philip to Jesus, and his initial unbelief was overcome by a demonstration of the superhuman knowledge of Jesus, so that he confessed that Jesus was the Messiah (Jn 1:45–51). He was one of the party which saw the apparition of Jesus at the Sea of Galilee (Jn 21:1). The absence of the name of Nathanael in the lists of the Twelve (cf APOSTLE) creates an exegetical problem; he is most easily identified with Bartholomew*, but some scholars suggest that he is the same as Matthias*.

Nazareth (Gk *nazareth*, Hb *naṣret*, meaning uncertain), the name of the town or village of Galilee where Jesus spent most of His

Two views of Nazareth.

life. Nazareth is not mentioned in the OT. In Lk Nazareth is the home of Mary and Joseph, the scene of the annunciation (Lk 1:26) and the place from which Mary and Joseph went to Bethlehem (Lk 2:4), whither they returned after the purification rites (Lk 2:39), and where Jesus grew to maturity (Lk 2:51). Mt apparently knows of no residence at Nazareth before the return of the family from Egypt (Mt 2:23). The quotation from the prophets in this verse, "he shall be called a Nazarene," is not found in the OT; most interpreters believe that it is a play on the word *neṣer*, "shoot" (of Jesse) in Is 11:1. This illustrates the biblical conception of the significance of the word* by assonance. Mk 1:9 makes Nazareth the point from which Jesus departs to be baptized; Mt 4:13 makes it the point of return from the baptism and of departure on the mission of preaching. All three synoptic Gospels relate the rejection of His preaching at Nazareth (Mt 13:54–58; Mk 6:1–6; Lk 4:16–30). This passage clearly attests that Nazareth was the home of Jesus, where His parents and His relatives were known, and where both Joseph and He were carpenters. Only Lk relates the violent ejection from the city and the attempt upon the life of Jesus. This episode is in keeping with the remark of Nathanael (Jn 1:45 f), which indicates that Nazareth enjoyed a very poor reputation. Jesus is often called a "Nazarene" in the Gospels and AA; two Gk forms, *nazarēnos* and *nazōraios* are used to indicate His origin. Once (AA 24:5) the followers of Jesus are called "Nazarenes."

The identification of Nazareth with the modern en-Nasira cannot be seriously questioned. The population, about 10,000, must be much larger than the population of the place in NT times; this growth is due purely to the interest of pilgrims and tourists in Nazareth's only famous son. Occupation has covered practically all remains of early Nazareth; soundings show occupation in Iron II (cf ARCHAEOLOGY). The "brow of the hill" mentioned in Lk 4:29 has long caused difficulty, since there is no topographical feature which corresponds to this description; but recent explorations have disclosed a rock formation below the surface, long covered by later occupation, which could fit the passage of Lk. The precipice must not be imagined as of very great height.

Nazirite (Hb *nᵉzîr,* "one set apart or of high rank"), in cultic usage, one who has pronounced a certain type of vow. Samson is described as Nazirite (Jgs 13:5, 7; 16:17); the feature which is emphasized is the prohibition of the use of the razor on the hair and the beard. Samson's mother is to drink no alcoholic beverage nor eat unclean food during her pregnancy; these were obligations of the Nazirite. Am 2:11 accuses the Israelites of making the Nazirites drink wine. Nazirites are mentioned in 1 Mc 3:49. It was almost certainly a Nazirite vow which Paul pronounced, after which he had his hair cut (AA 18:18); and the four men at Jerusalem also had their hair cut and submitted to rites of purification. All of these instances except Samson suggest that the vow was a temporary vow. The late priestly law of Nm 6 permits the law to be taken by either a man or a woman. It includes abstinence from intoxicating beverages, the use of the razor, and contact with the dead. When the period of the vow is finished the Nazirite offers sacrifice and has his hair cut and burned in the fire of the sanctuary. No motive is given for the making of the vow, and it appears to have been a voluntary act of devotion.

Neapolis (Gk *neapolis,* "new city"), the port city of Philippi*, touched by Paul on his 2nd journey (AA 16:11).

Nebaioth (Hb *nᵉbayôt,* meaning uncertain), a tribe descended from Ishmael* (Gn 25:13; 1 Ch 1:29). It brings tribute to the new Jerusalem (Is 60:7). The Ishmaelite tribes are tribes of the Arabian desert. The Nebaioth may possibly be identified with the country of Nabaiate, mentioned by Ashurbani-pal of Assyria (668–630 BC) in accounts of his campaign in Arabia (Cf NABATAEANS).

Nebo (Hb *nᵉbo*). **1.** A geographical and local name; probably derived from the Babylonian god Nabu (cf below). (a) A mountain in Moab, identified with Jebel en Neba, which rises to a height of 2600 ft. Nm 33:47 places it W of the mountains of Abarim. It is the traditional site of Moses' view of Canaan and his death (Dt 32:49; 34:1); the latter passage identifies it with the headland of Pisgah*. (b) A town of Moab near the mountain of the same name. It lay in the territory of Reuben and Gad (Nm 32:3; 1 Ch 5:8) and was built by Reuben (Nm 32:38). The inscription of Mesha* relates that Mesha took Nebo from Israel. In Is 15:2; Je 48:1, 22 the town is Moabite. 2 Mc 2:1–8 relates the legend that Jeremiah concealed some of the sacred fire of the temple, the ark*, and the tabernacle* in a cave on Mt Nebo where they were not to be discovered until the ingathering of Israel in the messianic age.

2. In Is 46:1 Nebo mentioned with Marduk* is a Babylonian god, the son of Marduk. The seat of his worship was the temple of Ezida in Borsippa, which lay across the Euphrates from Babylon. Nabu was the scribe god, the patron of scribes and the god of wisdom. He was closely associated with Marduk in the New Year* festival and the ceremony of the determination of the fates. Names compounded with Nabu were extremely popular in the neo-Babylonian period.

Nebuchadnezzar (Hb *n^ebukadne'ṣṣar*, incorrectly transcribed from Akkadian *nabu-kudurri-uṣur*, "Nabu protect the boundary"; the incorrect spelling is much more common in the OT; the correct *n^ebukadre'ṣṣar* appears in most of the incidences of the word in Je and 4 times in Ezk), a personal name; Nebuchadnezzar II, king of Babylon 605–562 BC. The records from the reign of Nebuchadnezzar (ANET 307–308), despite his great historical importance, are fragmentary; they have been much clarified by the publication of a large portion of the Babylonian Chronicle from the British Museum by D. J. Wiseman in 1956. Together with the portion of this Chronicle published by C. J. Gadd in 1923 (cf BABYLONIA; ASSYRIA) they permit a better reconstruction of the period (625–587, the final years of the kingdom of Judah).

Nebuchadnezzar was the son of Nabopolassar (Akkadian *nabu-apil-uṣur*, "Nabu protect the son"), a Chaldean* chieftain appointed by the Assyrians governor of "the Sea lands," the extreme S of Mesopotamia. The weakness of Assyria, then in its decline, made it possible for Nabopolassar to revolt and proclaim himself king of Babylon in 626 BC. The Assyrians resisted; but in addition to their enfeebled condition a new factor, the Medes*, entered against them, and their empire was destroyed by the Medes and Babylonians in a series of campaigns 625–609 BC. Nabopolassar moved to keep under his control the old Assyrian provinces of the W, Syria and Phoenicia; Egypt stood in opposition to this movement. Nebuchadnezzar appears as general of his father's armies in the W 607–605, and he defeated the Egyptians at Carchemish on the Euphrates in 605, thus assuring Babylonian control of the Syrian and Phoenician coast. After this victory, however, he was recalled to Babylon by the death of his father; with the succession assured, he returned to pursue the Egyptians, who retired slowly S, and to secure the submission of the territory. These campaigns continued through 603–602 and culminated in an unsuccessful attempt to invade Egypt in 601. During this period Nebuchadnezzar received the submission of Jehoiakim* of Judah. In 600–599 Nebuchadnezzar campaigned in the

Syrian desert. Jehoiakim, encouraged by Nebuchadnezzar's failure to conquer Egypt, withheld tribute; but the Babylonians moved against Jerusalem in 598–597 and Jehoiachin*, successor of Jehoiakim, submitted after a brief resistance. Nebuchadnezzar deported a large number of the population, especially from the upper classes, to Babylonia, and appointed Mattaniah, whose name he changed to Zedekiah*, king in place of Jehoiachin. Zedekiah revolted in 590 and the city was taken and destroyed after a bitter siege in 589–587.

The OT adds valuable details to our information concerning Nebuchadnezzar. 2 K 24 relates that the submission of Jehoiakim to Nebuchadnezzar endured three years. The campaigns of the Babylonians against Judah in 600–599 were conducted not by regular Babylonian troops, but by mercenary bands of marauders recruited from neighboring peoples. All of Syria and Phoenicia N of Egypt was securely held by the Babylonians. Nebuchadnezzar himself was present at the capitulation of Jehoiachin. The temple was looted; 10,000 captives, nobles and skilled craftsmen, were deported (2 K 24:14), and the royal household (24:15). 24:16, however, gives the number as 7000 landowners and 1000 craftsmen; this is regarded as a variant tradition (but cf below). Nebuchadnezzar was not present at the siege in the reign of Zedekiah, but directed events from Riblah* in Phoenicia, where he executed a barbarous revenge on Zedekiah and his family.

Jeremiah (25; 27–29) affirms that the success of Nebuchadnezzar is granted him by Yahweh and that resistance cannot succeed; cf also 32:1–5, 28 ff; 34:2 ff, 21; 37:1–11; 38:14–23. This fixed theme of Jeremiah's preaching infuriated the defenders of the city, who attempted to have him executed for sedition. The Babylonian officers, however, regarded him as favorable to their side, and treated him with consideration after the city was taken (39:11–14). Jeremiah predicted that Nebuchadnezzar would conquer Egypt (43:10–14; 46:13–26); there is no record that this ever happened. A fragment records an attack on Egypt in the 37th year of his reign (568 BC), but the success of the attack is not known. Je 52:28–30, not found in 2 K 25, from which the rest of the chapter is drawn, mentions three deportations of the Judahites by Nebuchadnezzar: in 598, 3023; in 587, 832; in 582 (not mentioned elsewhere and unexplained), 745, totaling 4600 persons. These figures are notably smaller than those given in 2 K 24 (cf above); the discrepancy may arise from the fact that the smaller counting includes only adult males, but it is also possible that we have simply different traditions.

Ezekiel also predicts the conquest of Egypt by Nebuchadnezzar (30:10 ff). Ezekiel describes Nebuchadnezzar as casting lots at Riblah whether to attack Jerusalem or Ammon (21:24 ff); Yahweh directs the lot to Jerusalem. Ezekiel predicts for Nebuchadnezzar the conquest of Egypt (30:10 ff) and of Tyre (26:7). The prediction of the conquest of Tyre is corrected in 29:18 ff, where we learn that Nebuchadnezzar unsuccessfully besieged Tyre for 13 years. Ezekiel promises him Egypt instead; but there is no correction of this prediction.

Nebuchadnezzar is the adversary of Yahweh and Daniel in Dn 1–4, and the scene is laid at his court; but Dn has no reference to the historical Nebuchadnezzar. Nebuchadnezzar in Dn is simply a fictitious character representing the Seleucid* monarchy, in particular Antiochus* IV Epiphanes.

The remains of Babylon, which were best preserved from the time of Nebuchadnezzar, show that he was a great builder who made his city one of the wonders of the world of his time.

Nebushazban (Hb *nᵉbûšaz-ban,* Akkadian *nabu-sezib-anni,* "Nabu save me"), a personal name; one of the Babylonian officers present at the capture of Jerusalem in 587 BC. The usual translation of his office is "chief eunuch*," and it is known that eunuchs often held high office in Mesopotamia; but some scholars believe the term had come to mean simply an officer of high rank.

Nebuzaradan (Hb *nᵉbûzar'ᵃdān,* Akkadian *nabu-zer-iddin,* "Nabu has given off-spring"), a personal name; one of the Babylonian officers present at the capture of Jerusalem in 587 BC. He was commander of the (royal) guard, in charge of the destruction of the city and the gathering of prisoners for deportation (2 K 25:8–20; Je 52:12–30), who at the command of Nebuchadnezzar set Jeremiah at liberty (Je 39:9–14; 40:1–5). He appointed Gedaliah* governor of the settlement at Mizpeh* (Je 41:10; 43:6).

Necho (Hb *nᵉkōh,* representing Egyptian *nk',w,* always "Pharaoh-necho" in the OT, etymology uncertain); a king of Egypt of the 26th dynasty, Necho II (609–594 BC). Biblical data relate that he defeated and killed Josiah* at Megiddo* (2 K 23:29; 2 Ch 35:20–24, a more circumstantial account), replaced Jehoahaz* by Jehoiakim* (2 K 23:33–35), and was defeated by Nebuchadnezzar at the battle of Carchemish (Je 46:2). Almost all information concerning Necho comes from non-Egyptian records; but recently-discovered Babylonian chronicles have clarified the events of his reign (cf NEBUCHADNEZZAR). It is now certain that he marched to Syria to support the falling kingdom of Assyria, really to secure for Egypt the Assyrian provinces of the W; Josiah, desirous of independence both from Assyria and Egypt, attempted to prevent him from taking part in the war. It is not certain that Necho was present at the final defeat of the Assyrians at Haran in 609 BC, although Egyptian troops were present; some historians believe that the battle of Megiddo and the battle of Haran occurred in the same campaign. Necho was decisively defeated by Nebuchadnezzar at Carchemish in 605 BC and lost any power over the Syrian coast; he repelled, however, a Babylonian attempt to invade Egypt in 601 BC. He encouraged Jehoiakim to revolt against Nebuchadnezzar but furnished no help to Judah. The events of his reign after 601 are not known.

Necromancy. Cf DEMON; DIVINATION; MAGIC.

Negeb (Hb *negeb,* usually translated "south," since from the point of view of Palestine it designates that point of the compass; lit "dry," desert), the designation of the territory which begins in the area of Beersheba* and extends to the Gulf of Aqaba; in a narrower sense, it runs from Beersheba on the N to Kadesh* on the S. Only in this narrower sense does the OT designate it by regions: the Negeb of the Kerethi (1 S 30:1) the S portion of Philistia; the Negeb of Judah, roughly equivalent to the territory of Simeon* (Jos 18:19 +); the Negeb of Caleb, the region of Ziph*, Maon*, and Carmel*; the Negeb of the Kenites*, in the vicinity of Arad* (1 S 27:10); the Negeb of Jerahmeel, S of the Kenites (1 S 27:10). The Negeb was associated with the patriarchs Abraham and Isaac, who dwelt in it or traveled in it (Gn 12:9; 20:1; 24:62 +; cf BEERSHEBA). Kadesh to the S was the center of Israelite life in the period of the wandering. Relations, both friendly and hostile, were close between Israel and the Negeb tribes of the Kenites and the Amalekites*.

The Negeb is broken country which averages 8 in rain annually in its most favored parts down to 1 in or even less in its most arid parts. The summers are hot and the winters cold, and the wind blows hard in both seasons. The country is partly flat plain, partly hilly, but everywhere broken, cut by numerous wadis and often showing nothing but fields of broken rock. Despite these apparently unattractive features, the modern efforts of Israel to colonize the region are based on sound archaeology, to which the explorations of Nelson Glueck have contributed immensely. Glueck found that the underground water table of the Negeb is comparatively generous, and that wells can often be dug without going to a great depth. There are a fair number of small springs; these have long been known to the Bedawi who pasture their flocks in the Negeb. Glueck found remains of numerous villages of the 21st-19th centuries BC, after which occupation ended. There were a number of fortresses from the period of the Israelite monarchy, obviously intended to protect caravan routes; the Negeb was a center of mining, metallurgy, and caravan traffic initiated by Solomon* (cf COPPER; EZION-GEBER). The region was intensively settled and laid under cultivation by the Nabataeans*; but the Roman frontier was withdrawn to the N under the empire. It was again intensively settled and cultivated during the Byzantine period (4th–7th centuries AD), and since then has been allowed to relapse into desert. Glueck found that in all periods of cultivation serious efforts were made to conserve and distribute water by the digging of wells, cisterns, and canals, and the erection of dams in the wadis. This, he believes, proves that nothing but water conservation is needed to make cultivation possible in the Negeb, since the climate has not changed.

Nehemiah (Hb *nᵉḥemyāh*, "Yahweh comforts"), son of Hacaliah, butler of Artaxerxes, king of Persia (Ne 2:1), appointed by Artaxerxes governor of Judah (Ne 5:14). Ne begins with the news brought to Nehemiah of the troubles in the territory of Judah and of the destruction of the walls and gates of Jerusalem (Ne 1:3). In his position as butler Nehemiah was in intimate contact with the king; and while he was serving the king's dinner he found occasion to tell the king that he was unhappy because of the condition of Jerusalem. The king granted his request to go and rebuild it and gave him letters of recommendation to the Persian governors of the territory beyond the Euphrates (2:1–8). Nehemiah's mission was opposed by a group centered around Samaria: Sanballat*, Tobiah*, Geshem* and others (2:9–10). Nehemiah first rounded the walls and examined their condition, and convinced the leaders of the Jerusalem community of the necessity of fortifications (2:11–20). The building of the wall was begun (3:1 ff), but the work was opposed by Sanballat and his company, who threatened war (4:1–9). Against this Nehemiah armed the builders of the wall and in addition set up armed posts and instituted

an alarm system (4:10–23). Objections were raised because a number of the people of Jerusalem had incurred debt by borrowing from their fellow Jews at exorbitant rates of interest; Nehemiah rebuked the landlords and persuaded them to lend money without interest (5). He himself gave a notable example of generosity. Sanballat and his associates continued their opposition. Since their threat of violence was ineffective, they invited Nehemiah to a conference outside the city. Nehemiah refused to fall into the trap, and the walls were finished in 52 days (6). Nehemiah formed a covenant, signed by the leaders of the Jerusalem community, to abstain from foreign marriages, to observe the Sabbath, and to support the worship of the temple (9:38–10:39). The occasion of this covenant is not found in the present book; cf EZRA-NEHEMIAH, BOOK OF. The population of the walled city of Jerusalem was not sufficient to support it; hence Nehemiah took a step which is related also of the foundation of new cities in the Hellenistic period called *synoekismos*. He obliged the rural population to draw lots to choose 10 percent of their number who would reside in the city (11:1 ff). The new city wall was dedicated (12:27–47). Nehemiah returned to Persia in 432, the 32nd year of Artaxerxes (Ne 13:6). He came back to Jerusalem not long after at an unspecified date and found a number of abuses. The high priest Eliashib had admitted his old enemy Tobiah* to a chamber in the temple courts; Nehemiah expelled him (13:7–9). The Levites had not received portions for their support, and Nehemiah imposed contributions for this purpose (13:10–13). The Sabbath observance was violated by men who marketed produce and in particular by Tyrian merchants. Nehemiah ordered the city gates to be closed at dusk on the eve of the Sabbath and threatened to arrest any who continued to trade on the Sabbath (13:15–22). Nehemiah attacked publicly the Jews who had married foreign wives, cursing them and beating them and plucking out their hair; he extracted an oath that they would give up their foreign wives. One of these men came from the family of the high priest (13:23–31).

The date of Nehemiah is determined as the 20th year of Artaxerxes I (465–425), therefore 445 BC. This date is confirmed by a reference to the sons of Sanballat in the Elephantine* papyri about 408 BC, a generation after Nehemiah. The occasion of his petition of the king was the destruction of the walls of Jerusalem by fire (Ne 1:3). This can scarcely be referred to the destruction of Jerusalem in 587 BC. The allusion rather suggests that there was an unsuccessful attempt to rebuild the walls of Jerusalem, and this is the episode mentioned in Ezr 4:12–22. This attempt occurred in the days of Artaxerxes (Ezr 4:7). The work was halted by the letter of the king; the allusion of Ne 1:3 suggests that the enemies of the Jerusalem community, probably the same group mentioned in Ne, destroyed the unfinished walls in an affair otherwise not mentioned.

It is now known from the customs of the Persian court that the office of butler was always held by a eunuch*. While Nehemiah says nothing of this himself, it is a legitimate inference; he makes no reference to a wife or family. His position in Judah is that of governor (pehāh, Ne 5:14) and the appointment endured at least from the 20th year of Artaxerxes to the 32nd. This appointment is not mentioned in 2, which speaks only of letters of recommendation and a military escort (2:9). It is clear that Nehemiah's power is greater than merely personal influence. In comparison with the governor the high priest has none of the political power and influence attached to the office in later periods. Alt and Noth have suggested that Nehemiah's appointment as governor included the erection of a new separate province of Judah, which had previously been a part of the province governed from Samaria. This would certainly arouse the opposition of the authorities in Samaria. Alt and Noth also see in 11:25–36 a list of the districts into which the province was divided by Nehemiah. On the date of Ezra cf EZRA; EZRA-NEHEMIAH, BOOK OF. There is no reference to the law as governing the Jews of Palestine in connection with Nehemiah except in Ne 13:1, a passage which comes not from the memoirs of Nehemiah but from the Chronicler.

Nehushtan. Cf BRAZEN SERPENT.

Nephilim (Hb nᵉpilîm, lit "abortions," but this seems impossible; perhaps a corruption of a foreign word), the "ancient heroes, men of renown" born of the union of the sons of Elohim and the daughters of men (Gn 6:1–4). It is most probable that this is a fragment of an ancient myth* incorporated by the author as a prelude to the story of the deluge; it is similar to the Gk myth of the Titans. The pre-Israelite inhabitants of Canaan are elsewhere identified with the Nephilim (Nm 13:33) and other gigantic beings (cf ANAKIM; REPHAIM). BS 16:7 alludes to the rebellion of the giants, probably with reference to this passage.

Nereus (Gk nereus), a personal name, the name of a water god; a Christian of Rome, greeted with his sister by Paul (Rm 16:15).

Nergal (Hb and Akkadian nērgal, a divine name), the god of Arallu, the underworld and the realm of the dead. The seat of his cult was at Kutu, the biblical Cuth*. Nergal was originally a solar deity, representing the sun in its menacing aspects of heat and burning; and his menacing character obscured his solar origin. He was a god of pestilence. Consequently he was much feared and was invoked as a god of vengeance. His cult was introduced into the territory of Israel by settlers introduced from Kutu by Tiglath-pileser* III (2 K 17:30). The personal name Nergal read in many translations of Je 39:3, 13 should be read as Nergal-sharezer*.

Nergal-sharezer (Hb nērgal šarᵉēzer, Akkadian nergal-sarri-uṣur, "Nergal protect the king"), a personal name; a Babylonian officer present at the capture of Jerusalem in 587 BC (Je 39:3, 13). He is called rab-mag, which indicates a high ranking officer whose functions are not entirely known. From 39:3, which is somewhat corrupt, modern critics restore his title of "prince of Sin-Magir."

Net. The net was used in hunting, fishing, and fowling. The Hb word pah designates a spring net used in hunting and fowling; rešet is a large draw net for trapping birds or game. The ḥērem is a large dragnet for fish. ANEP 112 shows the use of the seine and the hand casting net for fish; the large seine is pulled by several men with the aid of cords and shoulder straps. ANEP 189 shows a large cage net for fowling which is drawn by three men. ANEP 298 shows a Sumerian king catching his enemies in a bag net; a similar scene is shown in ANEP 307. In the NT nets are mentioned frequently in connection with the Sea of Galilee* (cf FISH). The general word for net is diktyon. The large dragnet for fish, sagēnē, is mentioned only in Mt 13:47. The amphiblēstron, the casting net, is mentioned only in Mk 4:18. Today in the Sea of Galilee large seines 300 ft long, requiring 16–20 men, are in use. These are spread from the bank and from boats.

Nethinim (Hb nᵉtînîm, "given"? usually translated "temple slaves" or "temple servants"). They appear only in postexilic books. They were in the first group to return to Judah from Babylon (1 Ch 9:2), and others returned with Ezra* (Ezr 7:7; 8:17–20). A list of their clans is given in Ezr 2:43–54; Ne 7:46 ff. In the time of Nehemiah they dwelt in Ophel (cf JERUSALEM).

They could scarcely have been included in the covenant of Nehemiah (Ne 10:29) unless they had been regarded as Israelites. There is no account of their origin; it is generally believed that they were originally prisoners of war who were given to the temple* as slaves; such temple slaves appear in Mesopotamia*. In the course of time their descendants acquired either Israelite status or full freedom. An early tradition relates that the Gibeonites* were made temple slaves by Joshua* (Jos 9:23); but no connection is established between the Gibeonites and the Nethinim.

New Moon. Cf MOON.

New Year. The celebration of the New Year in some form is an extremely widespread cultural and religious phenomenon. It is a matter of some wonder that it is so unimportant in the text of the Bible (cf below), especially since the New Year is one of the more important feasts of postbiblical Judaism. Recent discoveries of Mesopotamian literature have shown that it was the most important religious feast of the year. These considerations have led scholars to a theoretical reconstruction of the New Year feast of preexilic Israel. The discussion of this question, which touches upon a large number of elements in Israelite religion, is one of the most interesting and significant events of recent biblical scholarship.

1. *Mesopotamia.* The Mesopotamian New Year, most frequently called the feast of *akitu* or the feast of *zagmuku*, is best known as it was celebrated in the neo-Babylonian period in Babylon. Indications of its celebration at other places and times show that it did not fall at the same date nor was it celebrated by the same ritual at all times. The meaning and motifs of the feast, however, are basically the same; this uniformity has permitted scholars to suggest a common pattern of myth and ritual in the ancient Near East which, they believe, must have affected Israel. Other scholars do not find the uniformity so great that it exhibits a "pattern"; it arises from the common conception of deity and nature in the naturistic religions of the ancient Near East.

At Babylon the New Year feast began with the 1st of Nisan* (March-April), the 1st month of the Mesopotamian year, and endured for 11 days. A large portion of the ritual of this festival is now known (ANET 331–334). This can be supplemented by myths and hymns which can be surely attached to the New Year festival. Of these the most important is the myth of creation* (ANET 60–72) which was recited in the festival. The myth of the descent of Ishtar

or Inanna into the underworld (Sumerian, ANET 52–57; Akkadian, ANET 106–109) is also a part of the mythical cycle of the New Year, as is the Sumerian myth of Enki and Ninhursag (ANET 37–41). The hymn to Marduk found in ANET 389–390 is a sample of the type of hymn connected with the feast. The feast was a ritual enactment or rather reenactment of the myth, but the details of this reenactment are obscurely known.

The *ziggurat* (cf BABEL, TOWER OF) was properly the scene of the New Year feast. It was the tomb of the dying god; in Mesopotamian art the god is often shown emerging from the mountain. It was the temple of the hierogamy or sacred marriage (cf below); and it was the temple of the determination of the destinies. In addition the texts speak of a "rural temple" of the god which was one of the terms of the New Year procession; the meaning of this temple is obscure.

The ceremonies, in which the myths were recited at appropriate points, included the following elements, not set forth here in order, as pointed out by R. Largement: (a) processions; the images of the gods were carried from temple to temple. They were all ultimately brought to the temple of the host god, Marduk, for solemn assembly and the determination of the fates. The sacred processional way of Babylon has partly been recovered by archaeology. (b) sacrifices. (c) the ritual of the death of the god; this included lamentations, a number of which have been preserved, and royal humiliations, in which the king was stripped of his royal insignia and struck in the face by the priest. It is possible that in early times the ritual was accomplished upon a human victim, but this was never common in historic times. These ceremonies included the purification of the temple and the sacred furniture by aspersion with water, the burning of perfumes, and incantations. (d) the exaltation of the god; the symbols of royalty were restored to the king. (e) the hierogamy; the sexual union of king or priest with a priestess, representing the union of the god and his consort. A special temple or cell seems to have been provided for this ceremony. (f) the proclamation of destinies, prepared by diviners. (g) The libation of the tree* of life; this or similar libations are shown in ANEP 619, 706.

Significance of the feast. The ritual reenactment of the myths was based upon the conception that the cycles of nature were the earthly counterpart of heavenly events. These heavenly events were the death of the god who represented life, his restoration through his female consort who brought him from the underworld, his combat over the monster of chaos and his victory, the creation of the universe, and the determination of the destinies. The seasonal and cosmic cycle of life and death was itself a reenactment of the myth, and the continuance of the cycle could be assured only by man's incorporation of himself through ritual into the heavenly cycle. Each new year was a new creation and a new victory over chaos, a new birth of the god from whom life came. The place of sex in this myth and ritual was primary; for it is evident that life comes from the union of the male and female principles. The existence of sacred prostitutes shows that the individual worshipers received in this way communion with the divine principle of life and renewal of their vital forces.

2. *Judaism.* Although this is a postbiblical feast, it is mentioned first because scholars seek in it some vestiges of an earlier New Year feast which is not mentioned in the OT. The Jewish New Year falls on the 1st of Tishri (September-October), not the 1st of Nisan; cf CALENDAR. It is the first of three feasts (with the Day of Atonement* and Pentecost*) which fall in the first half of Tishri; this fact may be significant; cf below. The New Year observance is characterized by the use of the blast of the horn and the recitation of texts which allude to the judgment and the kingship of Yahweh. The motif of creation is less clearly seen. The origin and significance of these themes are variously assessed by scholars; cf below.

3. *Israel under the monarchy.* The New Year observance is mentioned in the OT only in Lv 23:24 f; Nm 29:1-6; these laws prescribe the blast of the horn, sabbath* observance, and sacrifices. The theory that the older New Year festival included much more was first proposed by Sigmund Mowinckel in 1922. Mowinckel suggested that the New Year feast of monarchic Israel was a feast of the enthronement of Yahweh as king. This theory was based on a large number of passages of the OT which Mowinckel asserted could have their "situation in life" only in some cultic observance which is not enumerated among the biblical feasts. The chief piece of evidence is the Pss in which Yahweh is hailed as king (Pss 47; 93; 95-99). There are also numerous references to a procession and to the carrying of the ark* (Pss 15; 24; 84; 118; 132; cf 2 S 6 and the dedication of Solomon's temple, 1 K 8). Mowinckel placed in this context the numerous allusions to the victory of Yahweh over chaos in creation. But the kingship of Yahweh in Israel was not only His power in nature, but also His power in history, His saving deeds on behalf of Israel; therefore the enthronement feast included a renewal of the covenant*, the terms under which Israel

served Yahweh as king. The enthronement feast was substantially the liturgical "day* of Yahweh," the day of His manifestation as king, savior, and judge.

This theory initiated a vigorous discussion which is still active. Critics were quick to point out that the OT contains no trace of such a festival. Other scholars, impressed by Mowinckel's hypothesis, admitted that it was difficult to demonstrate by solid historical arguments, but that it was not impossible that the absence of the festival from the OT was simply casual; the OT does not contain a complete description of Israel's cultic observances. Furthermore, they suggested that the festival lapsed into desuetude during the exile, and that the postexilic compilers did not include it for this reason. Recent modifications of the hypotheses have strengthened it.

H. J. Kraus sees in the passages employed by Mowinckel not an enthronement of Yahweh but an ancient covenant and amphictyonic feast (cf ISRAEL). This, Kraus believes, was transformed under David into a royal Zion festival; the monarchy tended to absorb into itself the covenant of Israel. This festival included the recital of the Sinai traditions, the reading of the law, of the blessings and curses attached to the law, and of the royal covenant of the house of David. With the end of the monarchy the royal features lost their meaning and the feast became the New Year of Judaism.

A. R. Johnson describes the same festival in substance as Mowinckel, but adds the highly important element of eschatology; the feast looks forward as well as backward to the ultimate realization of Yahweh's universal kingship.

G. Widengren more than other scholars has asserted the similarity between the Israelite New Year and the Mesopotamian New Year. He puts in the festival the combat against chaos, the death and resurrection of the god, the sacred marriage, and the enthronement of the god.

H. Gross, admitting that the kingship of Yahweh is a dominant motif, believes that the passages in question can be assembled under the celebration of the exodus described in terms of creation and a cosmic achievement. This celebration need not have been a regularly recurring festival.

H. Cazelles has observed that the concentration of three major festivals in the first half of Tishri raises a question, and he suggests that they arise from a fractioning of an early New Year festival. The festival instituted by Jeroboam* (1 K 12:26 f, 32 f), he thinks, was a royal festival which contained these elements: Yahweh as warrior (the blast of the horn), ritual illumination

(Am 5:18), creation (Ps 104, which Cazelles thinks may have been one of the sources on which the recital of Gn 1 was composed).

In summary: recent scholars have been in very general agreement that such theories as those of Widengren, which find that the Israelite New Year is derived from the Mesopotamian New Year, cannot be sustained. If there is such a festival, it had its own peculiar Israelite character and rejected such elements as the death of the god and the hierogamy. Beyond this, the fact that the OT does not mention such a festival even by allusion remains a difficulty, although it is not decisive. A growing number of scholars are inclined to believe that the texts which have been connected with this hypothetical festival demand some explanation; with the growth of form criticism and the explanation of literary forms by a "situation in life" in the cult the feeling has grown that such passages must be connected with some festival which is not mentioned. The elements of the festival, however, are not clearly determined by any consensus. It must be admitted that it is highly probable that the New Year was celebrated by the Israelites with more solemnity than we find in Lv 23 and Nm 29. There is high probability that Israel celebrated creation and the renewal of the covenant. It is altogether likely that the monarchy also had a celebration of the accession of the king and that this included the recital of the covenant with David. It seems very probable also that the creation of the world was linked liturgically with the creation of Israel by the exodus and the conferring of the land. It is doubtful that the ark simply reposed in the temple of Solomon without ever being brought forth and carried in procession as it had been in earlier times. To what extent these and other related elements may have been combined into a single feast different from the great feasts mentioned in the OT cannot now be affirmed with certainty; but the discussion of the question has shed great light upon the meaning and practice of early Israelite cult, through which so much of the faith of Israel was expressed, and has furnished an extremely probable theory of the composition of much of the OT.

Nicanor (Gk *nikanōr*, "conqueror of men"), a personal name; "king's friend" and officer of the Syrian armies in the Maccabean wars. He was defeated by Judas at Emmaus* in the campaign led by Gorgias* in 165 BC in the reign of Antiochus* IV (1 Mc 3:38–4:25; 2 Mc 8:9–34). He was again defeated by Judas in 160 BC at Beth-horon* in the reign of Demetrius* I; in this battle he was killed and his head and right hand were

hung as trophies in Jerusalem. The day of his defeat, the 13th of Adar, was celebrated as the Day of Nicanor (1 Mc 7:26–50; 2 Mc 14:11–15:36). Because of his duplicity and his contempt for Jewish piety he was the object of particular hatred from the Jews.

Nicodemus (Gk *nikodēmos*, "conqueror for the people"), a personal name; a Pharisee, a "ruler of the Jews" (Jn 3:1), which probably means a member of the Sanhedrin*, who visited Jesus secretly at night and admitted His divine mission; this visit is the occasion of the discourse on baptism* of Jn 3:1 ff. He spoke in the council on behalf of Jesus, observing that the law demanded that the accused be given a hearing (Jn 7:50). He took part in the burial of Jesus, bringing a large and costly quantity of spices (Jn 19:39). It appears altogether likely that he became a disciple, although this is nowhere expressly stated.

Nicolaitans (Gk *nikolaitēs* (sing), "follower of Nicolaus"), a sect found in the early church at Ephesus* (Apc 2:6) and Pergamum* (Apc 2:15). The allusions tell nothing about the origin of the sect or its teaching and practices, which the author of Apc repudiates. Efforts to connect it with Nicolas*, one of the seven appointed to assist the apostles (AA 6:5), have no foundation.

Nicolas (Gk *nikolaos*, "conqueror for the people"), a personal name; one of the seven appointed to assist the apostles in the Jerusalem Church (AA 6:5; cf DEACON). He was a Gk proselyte* to Judaism from Antioch*.

Nicopolis (Gk *nikopolis*, "city of victory"), mentioned as a place of Paul's sojourn (Tt 3:12). Of the numerous cities so named Nicopolis in Epirus is very probably meant here. The city lay on the site of the modern Prevesa on the peninsula which encloses the Ambracian Gulf on the W, facing the Adriatic. It was founded as a Roman colony by Augustus to commemorate his victory over Antony at the battle of Actium, the promontory which lies opposite Nicopolis.

Niger (Lt *niger*, "black"), appellative of Simon or Simeon, one of the prophets and teachers of Antioch* (AA 13:1). The name Simon-Simeon was extremely common and appellatives to distinguish its bearers were probably common also. The name does not indicate African extraction; it was a Roman family name which, like the Eng "black," had long lost any connotation which it may have had when it was first imposed.

Night. In Jewish usage the night was divided into three watches; in Gk and Roman usage it was divided into four watches. The Gk-Roman usage is employed in Mt 6:48; 14:24.

In most of the ancient world the night was the time when demons* were abroad; cf DARKNESS. Paradoxically it is also the time of dreams and visions (Gn 15:12; 26:34; 28:12; 31:24; 46:2; AA 16:9; 18:9; 23:11; 27:23). Night is used in a figurative sense of the time when man can no longer work (Jn 9:4) and the time when a man is in danger of stumbling when he travels (Jn 11:10). The day here probably does not mean simply the time of the present life, but rather the period which precedes the eschatological night of judgment. Paul also uses night figuratively, but it is the night which precedes the day (Rm 13:12; 1 Th 5:5–7). The day here seems to be the eschatological day, the day of the Lord*, the beginning of realized salvation, and the night is the period of the present world. Christians do not belong to the night, but to the day, and should live in the light of this day which they expect.

Nile. The largest river of Africa and the second longest river of the world. The distance from the source of the White Nile, the main stream, at Lake Victoria Nyanza to the Mediterranean is 3473 mi. The length of the river in Egypt proper from the 1st cataract at Aswan to the beginning of the delta 12 mi below Cairo is 600 mi. The Nile is carried through the delta by two streams, the Rosetta and the Damietta. The Damietta to the E has a length of 75 mi; the Rosetta to the W has a length of 50 mi. The width of the Nile varies from 1500 ft to over 1 mi in upper Egypt, from 600 ft to 2800 ft in the delta. The Nile is fed in its upper courses by streams which carry the melted snow from the mountains of central Africa; the principal tributary is the Blue Nile, which joins the White Nile at Khartoum. Below Khartoum the Nile has no other tributary. Between Khartoum and Wadi Halfa, at the modern frontier of Egypt and the Sudan, the Nile flows in a great S-shaped curve through the Nubian desert. Six cataracts, numbered 1–6 counting upstream, lie in this portion of the river; the 1st cataract is at Aswan. The cataracts are formed where the limestone shelf which lies beneath the desert crops out to the surface and the river falls steeply.

The regular annual inundation of the Nile makes it possible to cultivate the rich soil of its valley, which is bordered immediately by the desert where the irrigation ceases. Records of the rise of the Nile have been kept since the 4th millennium BC, and an ancient Nilometer can still be seen at Aswan. The crest takes a month and a half to two months to move from Khartoum to Cairo. At Khartoum the river reaches its low point (average 18 ft), in April-May, and its crest in August-September (25 ft). At Aswan the river is at its lowest at the end of May, at its crest at the beginning of August. At Cairo the river is at its lowest in the middle of June, at its crest at the beginning of October. The average rise at Aswan is 26 ft, at Cairo 21 ft. From prehistoric times the Egyptian peasants had devices which lifted the water to pools from which it could be channeled into the fields; the *shaduf* is a waterwheel which may be seen both in the tomb paintings of the Old Kingdom and in the fields of modern Egypt.

In ancient times the delta had seven mouths of the Nile (W to E): the Canopic, the Bolbitine, the Sebennytic, the Phatnitic, the Mendesian, the Tanitic, and the Pelusiac; these courses were named after neighboring cities. The modern delta has only two streams, the Rosetta (ancient Bolbitine) and the Damietta (ancient Phatnitic). The other courses have been converted to canals or have silted up entirely.

In the OT the Nile is called *haye'ōr* (always with the article), an Egyptian loan word which means stream; it is the stream *par excellence*. The Israelites were acquainted with this great river and knew its vital importance to Egypt. Not without some exaggeration Egypt, "watered by hand," is compared unfavorably to Canaan, a land watered by rain (Dt 11:10 f). The story of the infancy of Moses begins in the papyrus marshes on the banks of the Nile where the royal princess bathed in the stream (Ex 2:1 ff). The Nile appears in the first two of the ten plagues* of Egypt (Ex 7:14–8:15). The arrogance of Egypt is like the rising of its Nile (Je 46:7 f), and an earthquake is compared to the rising and falling of the Nile (Am 8:8; 9:5). Egypt is compared to a crocodile lying in the Nile (Ezk 29:3). Thebes* was a city which sat by the great Nile with its waters as a rampart (Na 3:8). The Assyrian conqueror boasted that he dried up the Nile (2 K 19:24; Is 37:25), and the ultimate threat of the prophet to Egypt is that Yahweh will dry up the Nile, destroying crops, fish, and life itself in Egypt (Ezk 30:12; Is 19:5–8).

a) The Nile at Luxor looking west; the valley of the kings is on the opposite bank.

b) The Nilometer on the island of Elephantine at the first cataract, built during the Old Kingdom.

c) The Nile at the first cataract, below the Aswan dam.

d) The Nile at the first cataract; the red granite of the region appears in the upper right.

e) and f) Ancient Egyptian boats.

Nimrod (Hb *nimrōd*), in the table* of nations (Gn 10:8–10) son of Cush*, the first *gibbôr* (probably warrior) and a mighty hunter, ruler of Babel (cf BABYLON, Erech*, and Akkad* in the land of Shinear*. Nimrod is probably a figure of foreign myth or legend who has not yet been identified with certainty. Some have suggested the Mesopotamian god Ninurta, patron of war and the chase; others see faint reflections of the hero Gilgamesh*. His father Cush* should probably be read Kash, a reference to the Kassites of Mesopotamia; cf BABYLON.

Nineveh (Hb *nîneweh*, Akkadian *ninua*), a city of Assyria*; its site, the tells of Neby Yunus and Kuyunjik, lies on the left bank of the Tigris* across the stream from the modern city of Mosul. The destruction of the city (cf below) and the total collapse of the Assyrian kingdom brought the site into almost complete oblivion and it was not identified until the first half of the 19th century.

Occupation probably goes back to the 4th millennium BC, and the city is first mentioned in cuneiform literature at the end of the 2nd millennium BC. Nineveh was the royal residence of Assyria from the time of Tiglath-pileser I in the 11th century to the reign of Sargon* (722–705 BC), who built a new city in the neighborhood at Dur Sharrukin, modern Khorsabad. The royal residence was restored to Nineveh by Sennacherib* (705–681 BC), who built a new palace and other massive constructions and fortified the city with a wall of a perimeter of about 7½ mi. The city covered more than twice the area of modern Mosul. Palaces were built by his successors Esarhaddon* (681–668 BC) and Ashur-bani-pal (668–630 BC). The city was besieged by the Babylonians and the Medes in 614 BC and was taken by storm in 612 BC. The victors destroyed the great city entirely; this event is celebrated in the prophecy of Nahum*.

Archaeological exploration was undertaken briefly and with few results by E. Botta in 1842, and much more thoroughly by Rawlinson, Layard, and Rassam in 1845–1851. These primitive explorations were principally directed to the acquisition of museum pieces, and most of the Assyrian collection of the British Museum came from these years. But the site was not studied historically at all and these early explorers actually damaged the site for further and more scientific study. The site was explored again in 1904 by L. W. King and in 1927–1932 by H. Mallowan, the first truly scientific exploration of the site.

Nineveh has been an extremely rich source of materials for the study of ancient Mesopotamia. The relief sculptures from the palaces of Sennacherib, Esarhaddon, and Ashur-bani-pal are the finest examples of Assyrian art. The library of Ashur-bani-pal contained 25,000 cuneiform texts, including most of the important religious and mythological texts known. The scribes of Ashur-bani-pal collected the remains of Sumerian* literature and translated it into Akkadian*, preparing bilingual texts, dictionaries, and grammatical material in the course of their task; this collection has been the chief aid to modern scholars in the recovery of the Sumerian language.

Gn 10:11 f relates that Nineveh was founded by Ashur, the eponymous ancestor of the Assyrians. It is the theme of the prophecy of Nahum and the scene of the ministry of Jonah*. Zephaniah*, a contemporary of the fall of Nineveh, also alludes to the event (2:13). Sennacherib was murdered by his sons at Nineveh (2 K 19:36; Is 37:37).

Nisan. The month which fell roughly during our March and April; the month of the feasts of Passover* and Mazzoth*. It was the first month of the year in the Babylonian calendar*, followed by Israelites and Jews in some periods and for some reckonings, the 7th month of the year reckoned as beginning with Tishri*.

Nisroch (Hb *nisrōk*, meaning uncertain), the name of the Assyrian god in whose temple at Nineveh* the Assyrian king Sennacherib* was murdered by his sons (2 K 19:37; Is 37:38). The name represents no known Assyrian god; Marduk*, Ninurta, and Nusku have been suggested.

No. Cf THEBES.

Noah (Hb *nōªḥ*, "rest"?), personal name; the hero of the deluge*; son of Lamech* in the Sethite genealogy (Gn 5:29 f). Noah is combined from two and perhaps three figures of tradition. As the hero of the deluge he is substantially the same as the Mesopotamian Ut-napishtim; as the inventor of viniculture (Gn 9:20 f) he is a culture hero belonging to the same group as the men of Gn 4:20–22, with which group he was perhaps first associated in tradition; as the father of Shem, Ham, and Japheth he is perhaps a third genealogical figure. It appears that the figure of Noah, the culture hero, has attracted to himself the account of the deluge. Noah in the deluge story bears the blessing (Gn 8:21 f) and the covenant (Gn 9:9–16) by which the stability of the course of nature against catastrophe is assured. He is also the first to receive the permission to eat flesh (Gn 9:3) and the fundamental precepts of eating meat without the blood and the prohibition of homicide (Gn 9:4–6). The character of Noah in the story of the vine is much less edifying than his character in the deluge story and exhibits the diversity of the sources; the conception of wine* in this account is less favorable than it usually is in the OT and may reflect a nomadic* culture which does not drink wine. The connection of Noah with the table* of nations is still more obscure; the curse of Canaan* has almost without any doubt been transferred from its original context to its present position (Gn 9:25–27), and it is doubtful that Canaan was the villain of the original story concerning Noah's drunkenness.

Allusions to the deluge (Is 54:9) and to Noah as a hero of righteousness (Ezk 14: 14, 20) do not go beyond the material of Gn. The praise of Noah in BS 44:17 f likewise reflects the stories of Gn. Mt 24:37 f and Lk 17:26 f refer to "the days of Noah" and not to Noah himself. Noah is saved by faith and righteousness (Heb 11:7) and is called a herald of righteousness (2 Pt 2:5).

Nob (Hb *nōb*, meaning uncertain), a town of Benjamin. It was the residence of Ahimelech and the priests and presumably a sanctuary; David fled to Ahimelech at Nob from Saul, obtained refreshments and the sword of Goliath, and Ahimelech and the priests were killed at Saul's command for this friendly gesture (1 S 21–22). Modern critics read Gob for Nob in 2 S 21:16, as in 2 S 21:18 f. Is 10:32 suggests that Nob was the nearest town to Jerusalem on the N and lay within sight of the city. Ne 11:32 mentions Nob between Anathoth and Ananiah. Abel locates Nob on Mt Scopus on the site of the modern Augusta Victoria hospital; traces of ancient construction were found when the building was erected.

Nod (Hb *nôd*), the land E of Eden* to which Cain* went after the murder of Abel* (Gn 4:16). Nod represents no known geographical name, and may be formed from the word "wanderer" which Cain applies to himself in Gn 4:14, "the land of wandering."

Nomad. Nomadism is a form of life and culture which has its beginnings much earlier than recorded history and has persevered in many parts of the world into modern times. Its modification during the last few centuries, particularly where it has come into close contact with western civilization, shows the peculiar capacity of the nomad to modify his institutions and adapt them to new features of civilization without losing his essential nomadic character. Nomadism of SW Asia is simply a mode of life which is formed for the single purpose of survival in the desert. The techniques of nomadism which have been proved by survival are in consequence changed very slowly and reluctantly. The importance of nomadism in the early history of Israel demands that the reader of the Bible have some grasp of this strange and unfamiliar cultural institution.

Scholars warn against hasty comparisons between the nomadism of the OT and life of the modern Bedawi. The basic difference lies not in the associations of the Bedawi with contemporary civilization but in his domestication of the camel*; recent studies indicate very strongly that the camel was not domesticated in SW Asia before the 13th or 12th century BC. Without the camel the mobility of the nomad is much restricted, and the area which he covers is much smaller. Other nomadic institutions, however, bear a close resemblance to institutions mentioned, rarely described, in the OT, and permit analogies to be drawn which illustrate the life of the patriarchs and of early Israel.

Nomads of the Syrian desert are mentioned in Mesopotamian and Egyptian texts of the 2nd millennium BC. These texts show that the nomad could not and did not range far into the interior of the desert; he lived on the fringe of the area of cultivation. In fact, they are more accurately described as seminomads than as nomads. Egyptian records relate that occasionally in times of food shortage nomads asked and were granted permission to enter Egypt and seek pasture there; such a permission was granted to Jacob* and his clan. A group of such nomads appears in a tomb painting of Egypt of about 1890 BC (ANEP 3). This painting, nearly contemporary with Abraham, gives us an excellent idea of the appearance of Abraham and his family. The close contact of the nomads with civilization meant a constant interchange between the two cultures. The nomad, it appears, generally practiced some cultivation of the soil; he differed from the peasant in that his cultivation was occasional, limited to crops which could be rather quickly harvested, and did not occur in the same soil year after year.

The chief support of the nomad was herds of sheep and goats, which furnished him with food, clothing, and tent fabrics. Meat was rarely eaten — only to serve a guest and to celebrate a few great religious festivals. A vivid picture of nomad life of the 20th century BC is contained in the Egyptian story of Sinuhe (ANET 18–22). The nomad group exercises a loose claim over the territory in which it pastures its flocks and herds. The land is held in common, not individually, and boundaries between neighboring groups are loosely drawn. The claims to wells and springs are much more closely defined and are more likely to become the object of bitter quarrels (Gn 26:15–22). In addition to the herds the nomad cultivates the ass as a beast of burden. Movements over a great distance are possible but rare, and would usually be a desperate move for survival. The nomad does not build houses; he is identified as a "tent-dweller." The tents* are made of goatskin with the hair to the outside.

The nomad group is organized in families* ("tents"), clans, and tribes. Survival is obtained only by close cohesion of the group; the strongest feeling of the nomad is the feeling of blood-kinship, which exhibits itself in the law of blood vengeance (cf AVENGER). The individual has no protection except from his group, which is the only judiciary and enforcing agency of the customary law of the desert. The clans and tribes are ruled by sheikhs in a rather loose familial government; the solidarity of the group is matched by a remarkable degree of individual freedom within the group. The nomad regards the peasant as a slave in comparison to himself. Several tribes may form a confederation; the amphictyony of Israel* was such a union. Growth may force tribes to divide into smaller groups to find pasture (Abraham and Lot*, Gn 13:5–13); tribes which are weakened by shrinking numbers may be absorbed into other tribes or disappear entirely (cf LEVI; REUBEN; SIMEON). Where such fusion and division of groups occur the connection is established by artificial genealogies, of which a number occur in the OT.

The history of the Near East has been a rather constant story of the defeat of some nomad groups in the struggle for survival. The margin between sufficiency and starvation is so slender that there has been a perpetual immigration of nomad groups into the settled areas. Many great movements which have determined the course of Near Eastern history appear to have their origin in the mass movement of nomad groups to escape the desert (cf AMORITES; ARAMAEANS), and the movement of Israel into Canaan was such a nomadic immigration. Nomads living near the cities, moving into them, or raiding settled areas are mentioned frequently in the records of Mesopotamia and Egypt. Israel itself after the settlement experienced the raids of such nomads as the Midianites* and the Amalekites*.

The OT has far more phrases and figures of speech drawn from the nomadic life than it is possible to list here; one may compare this to much vigorous American slang which is drawn from life and work on the farm and is constantly used by urban dwellers who scarcely know what it means. We may notice that the OT, which contains both nomadic and agricultural traditions, exhibits as a collection a certain ambivalence toward the nomad. Abel* the nomad was murdered by Cain* the peasant (Gn 4:2 ff); but Cain himself after his curse becomes a nomad (Gn 4:11–16). Ishmael* the nomad is the enemy of every man (Gn 16:12), although his father Abraham is a nomad. The "nomadic ideal," as some scholars call it, may be traced in certain prophetic passages (Je 2:2; Ho 2:16 f; 13:5; Am 2:10). These prophets conceive the nomadic period of early history as an ideal period when Israel had not yet been corrupted by Canaanite religion and civilization; and they see no hope for the salvation of Israel except through a religious and cultural reversion to the desert life. The Rechabites* seem to have made the preservation of the nomad life a religious profession.

Noph. Cf MEMPHIS.

North. This point of the compass has a peculiar significance in the OT. In Canaanite mythology it was the seat of divinity, "the mountain of the north," "the mountain of assembly." This conception is reflected in Is 14:13, where Helal desires to establish his throne in "the recesses of the N," and in Ps 48:3, where Zion is identified with "the recesses of the N," Zion is truly the mountain of divinity. The N is also the source of disaster; foreign invasion comes from the N, since invading armies had to follow the roads through Syria (Is 14:31; Je 1:14; 4:6; 6:22; 10:22; 16:15; 25:9; Ezk 26:7 +). It is also the land of exile from which Yahweh will gather Israel (Is 43:6; Je 3:18; 31:8). It is the direction from which the theophany of Ezk 1:4 appears; Ezekiel finds himself in Babylonia, and the chariot of Yahweh follows the usual route of travel from Palestine to Babylonia.

Nose. The organ of breath and of smell is a sensitive sign of emotion. In the OT it is the organ in which breath, i.e., life, is situated (Gn 2:7; Jb 27:3 +). The dilation of the nostrils is characteristic of anger, the usual Hb word for anger is lit "nostrils." The earthy metaphor of "stink" for persons or objects which elicit dislike is common in Hb (e.g., Gn 34:30).

Number. The symbolism of number and numerology is extremely common in religion and in magic. No apparent numerical symbolism can be traced in the Bible in the sense that any particular number indicates any particular person, object, phenomenon, or idea. Numbers are used, however, in other senses than a strictly arithmetical sense, and here they convey a meaning apart from their numerical value. This meaning, it seems, was simply a part of common usage and not part of any numerological speculation; similar use of number occurs in our own speech. The following numbers deserve notice.

3 — while the number 3 occurs in blessings, invocations, and apostrophes, it appears to have no particular significance. There are 3 sons of Noah*, the ancestor of all nations (Gn 10).

4 — the original significance of 4 probably comes from the 4 points of the compass, from which come the 4 winds. The 4 rivers of Paradise irrigate the whole earth (Gn 2:10 ff). Thus the number 4 is associated with the conception of the visible universe. The chariot of Yahweh is borne by 4 creatures in the theophany* of Ezk 1. Mesopotamian kings include among their titles "king of the 4 quarters" i.e., of the world.

7 — the number 7 is regarded almost universally as endowed with special significance. The Hb word for swear and oath* is formed from the root ŠB', 7, and may refer to a ceremony of swearing not mentioned. Mary Magdalene was possessed by 7 demons (Lk 8:2). In the hypothetical case of the Sadducees they presented a man who had married 7 wives (Mt 22:25 ff; Mk 12:18 ff; Lk 20:27 ff). Disaster strikes the mother of 7 sons (Je 15:9), and Ruth is declared to be better than 7 sons (Rt 4:15). There are 7 days of the week (Gn 2:2). The Seven are appointed to assist the apostles (AA 6:3 ff). The case of forgiveness shows a particular use of the number. Peter asks whether he shall forgive his brother 7 times (Mt 18:21 f; Lk 17:4), and Jesus answers that he should forgive 70 × 7 times. These uses indicate that the number 7 signifies a certain fullness. Peter probably does not mean 7 numerically, but a certain required number, beyond which the obligation is fulfilled and ceases to exist; by giving 7 the multiple of 7 × 10 Jesus removes any limit. The rites of Balaam revolved around the number 7 (Nm 23:1). The Israelites marched 7 days around Jericho with 7 priests blowing horns (Jos 6:1 ff). The 7th year is the year of the Sabbath. The number 7 appears all through Apc: there are 7 churches (1:4), 7 spirits (1:4), 7 lamps (4:5), 7 seals (5:1), 7 angels (8:2), 7 trumpets (8:2), 7 heads of the dragon (12:3), 7 horns of the beast (13:1), 7 plagues (15:1), 7 vials (15:6). These all exhibit the idea of fullness and completeness.

10 — a round number quite frequently. 10 is composed of 2 pentads, the sum of the fingers, the root of the decimal numeral system. The decalogue exhibits 10 as a number of fullness.

12 — the significance of 12 comes from the Sumerian sexagesimal system, which survives in our dozen. There are 12 tribes of Israel, even though more than 12 tribal names appear; this is the fullness of Israel. In a similar manner and probably in deliberate imitation Jesus selects the 12, although there are more than 12 apostles* in the NT. The 12 found it necessary to fill out their number after the death of Judas* by electing Matthias*. There are 12 months, the fullness of the year. Hence 12 is in the sexagesimal system much what 10 is in the decimal system.

40 — is a round number. There are 40 days of the deluge (Gn 7:4), 40 years of Israel in the desert (Ex 16:35; Nm 14:33; Dt 29:5), 40 years of the reign of David (2 S 5:4). The 40 days of the journey of Elijah (2 K 19:8) and the 40 days of Jesus in the desert (Mt 4:2; Mk 1:13; Lk 4:2) are deliberate imitations of the 40 years of Israel in the desert. The earthly sojourn of Jesus after the resurrection was 40 days (AA 1:3). 40 years is roughly a generation.

70 — a multiple of 10 × 7, again a round number with a suggestion of unknown dimensions. The sons of Israel numbered 70 at their entrance into Egypt (Gn 46:27; Ex 1:5). The years of the exile number 70 (Je 25:11). There are 70 elders* of Israel (Nm 11), but the number is no doubt really 72, 6 × 12, as there were 72 disciples (Lk 10). 70 years is the ideal life of a man (Ps 90:10), consequently a period of time beyond the memory of a single individual.

In addition one may notice the number of 144,000 sealed in Apc 7:4 ff; 14:1 ff. This is 12, the number of the tribes of Israel, multiplied by itself and then multiplied by 1000, the number of a military unit in the ancient Israelite army*. The number indicates the fullness of Israel; the Church in the NT is conceived as the fullness of Israel, and this is the heavenly Church in its final completion.

Numbers. The 4th book of the Pnt*. The name is given from the census with which the book begins.

Contents.

1:1–4:49, census of Israel.

5:1–6:27, laws, in particular the law of ordeal of the suspected wife (5:11–31) and of the Nazirite* (6:1–21); the formula of the priestly blessing* (6:22–27).

7, offerings of the tribal chieftains.

8, laws governing the Levites*.

9, laws governing the Passover*.

10:1–10, the silver trumpets.

10:11–28, the order of march.

10:29–12:16, Sinai to Paran; 13–14, the story of the scouts.

15, laws.

16–17, rebellion of Korah, Dathan and Abiram.

18, laws governing priests and Levites; 19, various laws.

20–21, Kadesh to Moab; 22–24, Balaam; 25, episode at Baal Peor.

26, a second census.

27:1–11, law of the inheritance of daughters.

27:12–22, appointment of Joshua.

28–29, laws of sacrifice for festivals, 30, laws of vows.

31, sacred war against Midian; 32, dispute of tribes of E and W Palestine; 33, list of Israelite encampments; 34, instructions for the division of the land.

35, laws of Levite cities and cities of refuge; 36, law of the inheritance of daughters.

Nm exhibits the interweaving of narrative and law which is characteristic of the Pnt. It comes from the sources of the Pnt, but the narrative sources are not easily isolated. A number of the episodes present law in the form of a story which illustrates the law or creates the occasion of its promulgation.

The census lists can hardly represent Israel in the period of the desert sojourn. W. F. Albright has proposed that they come from the period of David, who was probably the first to make a census of Israel (2 S 24); the numbers, he believes, suit Israel of this period very well.

The list of encampments (Nm 33) raises a number of questions. It is composed in the manner of P (cf Pnt). Where it was compiled from names given in earlier sources it is easy to trace, as in 33:1–11, 14–17, 36–40, 47–49. The other names are impossible to trace. It seems unlikely that the list was to such a large extent a simple invention of P; and most scholars suppose that he had access to another source, or that the names were contained in oral traditions which were not incorporated into the written form of the sources of the Pnt. The historical value of the names cannot be rated very highly, and the geographical location of most of them is impossible in the present state of our knowledge.

Nun. The 14th letter of the Hb alphabet, with the value of *n*.

Nunc Dimittis. The canticle of Simeon* (Lk 2:29–32). The song is a thanksgiving psalm for the coming of the messianic salvation; in spite of its brevity, it draws on Is (cf Is 40:5; 42:6; 49:6; 52:10). Luke has very probably put in Simeon's mouth a liturgical song of the primitive community.

Nuzu. The ancient city of Nuzu lay at the modern Yorgan Tepe, about 14 mi SE of Kirkuk in Iraq. The site was excavated 1925–1931 through the cooperation of a number of American institutions. The material discovered was rich and important both for the history of NW Asia in the 2nd millennium BC and for the patriarchal period of biblical history. Several thousand tablets in Akkadian* from the 15th century BC, mostly contracts, furnished much information on the society, law and commerce of the period. Nuzu, originally a Semitic settlement, was a Hurrian* city in the period of the tablets. A number of parallels to customs and laws mentioned by allusion in Gn showed that the customary law of these narratives was closer to the customary law of Nuzu that to any other legal system, closer even than it is to later Israelite law. This fact confirms the traditions of the origins of the patriarchs from NW Mesopotamia. These parallels include the adoption of a slave by a childless couple; marriage customs, in particular the substitution of a slave for a childless wife; the contract of Jacob* and Laban*; the teraphim* of Laban stolen by Rachel*; the presence of Habiru (cf HEBREW) in Nuzu; the importance of blessings* uttered when death is near.

O

Oak. Eng translations render by "oak" 5 Hb words: *'ayil, 'ēlāh, 'ēlôn, 'allāh,* and *'allôn.* Possibly these words do not all signify "oak"; cf TEREBINTH. G. E. Post notes 9 species of oak in Palestine and Syria. We may note *Quercus coccifera,* the holly oak or holm oak, which grows to a height of 25–30 ft and a diameter of 40–50 ft in its crown. The holm oak near Hebron* called "Abraham's oak" is shown to tourists, but it can scarcely be more than 400 years old. This tree, which usually grows in isolation, is often seen near Moslem holy places, and is possibly the tree which is associated with sanctuaries in the OT (Ho 4:13). The oaks of Bashan* were proverbial in the OT (Is 2:13; Ezk 27:6; Zc 11:2), and many oaks are still found in the region of the Hauran, especially the holm oak and *Quercus Aegilops,* the Valonia oak.

Oath. By an oath one invokes the deity in attestation of the truth of one's word; by what is probably an exaggerated reverence, some sacred object is often substituted for the name of the deity. The oath is assertory, attesting the truth of a declaration, or promissory, attesting that one will abide by a promise.

The laws and records of ancient Mesopotamia show that the oath was frequently administered both in public and private transactions, and the biblical conception of the oath largely reflects the same ideas. An oath of loyalty to the king was exacted from royal officers. Parties to treaties and to private contracts confirmed the agreement by an oath to observe it. In legal processes oaths were exacted not only from witnesses but also from the parties to the suit. The oath was sometimes combined with the ordeal*; a suspected wife must swear to her innocence, but had to submit to the ordeal in addition. In charges of loss or damage, however, the responsible party could clear himself by an exculpatory oath that he was not responsible for the loss or damage, and no further testimony was required. The oath was a sacral act and was usually pronounced before the divine image. Perjury was treated as the extreme of sacrilege and blasphemy and was severely punished.

Hb uses two words, *šaba'* and *ālāh,* to designate the oath. The first of these comes from the root which means "seven" (cf NUMBER) and probably alludes to a rite of swearing which does not appear in the OT.

The second means "curse"; the oath was often accompanied by imprecations. In the OT the imprecation is often omitted, leaving the fragment, ". . . If I do (or do not do) such a thing." The imprecation is sometimes elliptically stated, "May Yahweh do so and so to me, and add to it." The full formula would contain an explicit curse: "May Yahweh do . . . to me, if I do not fulfil my oath (or if what I say is not true)."

The Israelite was to swear by Yahweh alone (Dt 6:13; 10:20; Is 19:18; 45:23; 48:1; Je 12). The oath was a profession of faith in the divinity of the deity who was invoked, and to swear by other gods was a denial of the exclusive divinity of Yahweh (Je 5:7; 12:16; Am 8:14; Zp 1:5). The formulae included "as Yahweh lives" (Jgs 8:19; 1 S 14:39, 45; 19:6; Je 4:2), the life of the person addressed (1 S 1:26; 20:3; 2 S 15:21), "Yahweh (God) is witness" (Gn 31:50, 53; 1 S 20:12; Je 42:5), "Yahweh is between us" (1 S 20:23) and other similar formulae. In Mt 23:16–22 Jesus rejects any evasion of the oath on the plea that the sacred object sworn by is not really sacred. He mentions oaths by the sanctuary, the gold of the sanctuary, the altar, the victim, and heaven. These are all substitutes for the divine name, the pronunciation of which was avoided in Judaism, but Jesus points out that they are no less an invocation of the deity.

By an anthropomorphism Yahweh also takes oaths, but He can swear only by Himself, as men swear by Him (Gn 22:16; Ex 32:13; Is 45:23; Am 6:8; 8:7), or by His holiness* (Ps 89:36).

The hand was raised in swearing (Gn 14:22; Ex 6:8; Dt 32:40). To bring one "before Elohim" for an oath (Ex 21:6) is a phrase which is probably taken from common Semitic law to indicate that the oath is taken before the divine image; in Israelite law it indicates that the oath was in some occasions pronounced "in the presence of Elohim" i.e., at the sanctuary; cf 1 K 8:31. A peculiarly solemn oath was the oath pronounced with the hand of the person swearing upon the genital organ of the person to whom he made a promissory oath (Gn 24:2; 47:29); the source of life was a sacred object.

The oath is not mentioned frequently in Hb law: the exculpatory oath for loss or damage (Ex 22:10 f), for homicide by an unknown agent (Dt 21:1–9). Perjury is prohibited in the decalogue* (Ex 20:7; Dt 5:11) and in the holiness code (Lv 19:12). As in Mesopotamia, the promissory oath was a part of the contract (Gn 21:22 ff; 31:43 ff; the covenant of David and Jonathan, 1 S 20:12 ff). Ezk 17:13–21 treats Zedekiah's violation of his vassal oath to Nebuchadnezzar as perjury against Yahweh.

The warning against excessive swearing in BS 23:9–12 indicates that the use of the oath was frequent in ordinary speech, as it is in the earlier books of the OT; but in the 2nd century BC reverence for the divine name* had developed to the point where such speech was regarded as almost certainly involving some wrongdoing. The free use of the oath, although with rare use of the divine name, is probably behind Mt 5:33–37. Here Jesus simply forbids His disciples to swear at all. It does not seem to do justice to His words to regard this, with other peculiarly "evangelical counsels" (Mt 5:23 f; 39–42; 44–47; 6:25–32), as unreal and impractically high moral ideals. In a regenerated society there is no room for oaths, for the word of a truthful man is sufficient (5:36); the necessity of the oath comes from "the evil one" (5:37), from the fact that men are mendacious. Js 5:12 probably preserves this saying of Jesus in a form closer to the original. It is not without interest that only in the passion narrative of Mt 26:63 is the exaction of an oath from Jesus by the high priest preserved; in Mk 14:61 the adjuration is simply a question, and in Lk 22:67 the high priest is no longer the questioner. It is also not without interest that Paul uses oaths to attest his veracity (Rm 1:9; 2 Co 1:23; 11:31; Gal 1:20).

Obadiah (Hb *'ōbadyāh* or *'ōbadyāhū,* "slave of Yahweh"), a personal name; the 4th of the 12 prophets.

Contents: 1, title and introduction; 2–14, 15b, curse and threat of Edom*; 15a, 16–21, the restoration.

Although Ob is the shortest of the prophetic books, it has been the occasion of a wide variety of critical opinion. Some scholars believe that 2–14 is composed of two different oracles, one written on occasion of the disaster of Edom at some date in the 5th or 4th century (2–9), the other (11–14) referring to the predatory attacks of Edom on the territory of Judah after the disaster of 587 BC. Such imprecations are common in exilic and postexilic literature (Is 34:5 ff; Lam 4:21 ff; Mal 1:2 ff; Ezk 35:4 ff). Others see in this passage a single poem, which must be dated not too long after the fall of Jerusalem. 2–9 are employed in Je 49:7–22; but most critics do not attribute this passage to Jeremiah.

and it seems more probable that the smaller Ob was incorporated into Je than that these verses were transcribed from Je. Most modern scholars do not believe that 16–21 come from the same author; they are postexilic, but nothing indicates a more precise date. A few have dated the poem on Edom in the time of the wars of Edom and Judah in the 9th century. The *terminus ad quem* for the book as a whole must be 312 BC, when the territory of Edom was entirely overrun by the Nabataeans*.

Some interpreters have found the book narrow, vengeful, and nationalistic — that is, unworthy of divine inspiration and of a place in the canon of sacred books. These criticisms take Ob very narrowly and without consideration of the wider context of prophecy; for Ob says nothing which is not found in other prophetic works. The downfall of Edom is seen as a morally motivated act of providence. The restoration of Judah does not explicitly speak of the regeneration of Israel, as Isaiah and Jeremiah and Ezekiel and Hosea do; but this prophetic idea is easily presupposed. If Ob is, as a few critics believe, a collection of prophetic fragments, such theological criticisms have no relevance.

The name is borne by 9 others in the OT; the most prominent of these is the officer of Ahab (1 K 18:3 ff).

Oblation. Cf SACRIFICE.

Ochozias. Cf AHAZIAH.

Odollam. Cf ADULLAM.

Offering. Cf SACRIFICE.

Og (Hb *'ôg,* meaning unknown), a personal name; king of Bashan*, defeated at Edrei* by the Israelites before they crossed the Jordan (Nm 21:33–35; Dt 1:4; 3:1–13). His defeat became a proverbial example of the victories which Yahweh gave Israel (Dt 4:47; 31:4; Jos 2:10; 9:10) and is included in recitals of the saving deeds of Yahweh (Ne 9:22; Pss 135:11; 136:20). Israelite popular tradition associated him with an enormous "iron bed," a tomb at Rabbath Ammon (Dt 3:11); this is generally thought to be a dolmen, and the iron is probably basalt. It was probably this tradition which made Og the last of the Rephaim*, a race of giants. The territory of Og was given to the tribes of Reuben*, Gad*, and Manasseh* (Nm 32:33; Dt 29:6; Jos 13, 12, 30 f).

While the scheme of traditions places the defeat of Og before the entrance of Israel into Canaan, there are good reasons for thinking that this arrangement is artificial and that Israel's expansion into Bashan occurred in a late phase of the settlement; such a conquest seems to suppose a more organized and stronger military society than Israel had in this early period. The story of Og is associated with the claim of Reuben, Gad, and Manasseh to territory on the E side of the Jordan, which is consistently attributed to Moses and was thus affirmed to be a more ancient claim than the claim of the other tribes. It is possibly the antiquity of this claim which drew the story of the conquest of Og into an earlier period.

Oholah, Oholibah (Hb *'ŏholāh,* "her tent" ?, *'ŏholībāh,* "my tent is in her" ?), names signifying Samaria and Jerusalem respectively in the allegory of Ezk 23. If the usual explanation of the names is correct, the names refer to the sanctuaries of the two cities. The two cities are represented as wives of Yahweh (who here is described as bigamous) who turn to harlotry with other nations. The allegory is an extension of the parable of marriage employed by Hosea and Jeremiah, but is couched in much more explicit terms which by modern standards are sometimes gross.

Oil. Olive* oil was the oil of ancient Palestine, as it was in most of the ancient world. The OT and other ancient sources contemporary with the OT tell nothing of the methods used for extracting the oil; the olive press and the olive mill did not come into use until Hellenistic times. It is probable that primitive methods were used before the press and the mill were introduced; the Hb word for the process is "tread," the word which also designates the pressing of the grape*, which was done with the foot; the word probably designates simply the crushing of the oil. This was possibly done by pressing a large stone upon the mass of olives by the hands and its own weight. Cup-shaped depressions in the rock, natural or artificially enlarged, appear frequently near Palestinian towns, and these may have been the area in which the oil was collected; a channel cut from these depressions permitted the oil to flow into containers. The olive presses and mills used in Hellenistic times brought large stones upon the mass of olives by the use of weights and levers. The mill is a rotary stone which rolled in a circular depression; the power was supplied by man or beast. The oil was kept in large jars for commercial distribution. The usual domestic container was a small bottle or flask (1 S 10:1; 1 K 17:12 f; 2 K 4:2; 9:1; Mt 25:4).

The uses of oil were many and it was a valued product of the land, often mentioned in enumerations of the products of Palestine (Dt 7:13; 11:14; 33:24; 2 K 18:32; Je 31:11). A man's words are said to be "smoother than oil" (Ps 55:22), and the name of the beloved is compared to precious oil (SS 1:3). Oil as a condiment was an important part of the diet (Dt 32:13; Jgs 9:9; Ezk 16:13; Ho 2:7), and it made the face shine (Ps 104:15). It was medicinal and was used in the anointing of wounds (Is 1:6; Lk 10:34). It was used as a refreshing unguent (Dt 28:40; 2 Ch 28:15; Mi 6:15), especially after a bath (2 S 12:20; Rt 3:3). The use of the unguent was a sign of joy and of festive attire and was omitted during fasts and mourning (Mt 6:17). It was the base of the mixture of perfumes such as myrrh* and nard*. It was also a ceremonial unguent (cf ANOINTING). Olive oil was the usual fuel for the lamp*; it is surprising that its use for domestic illumination is mentioned only in connection with the lamp of the sanctuary (Ex 27:20; Lv 24:2). Oil was an important item in the export trade of Palestine (1 K 5:25; 2 Ch 2:14; Ezr 3:7; Ezk 27:17; Ho 12:2).

Ointment. Cf ANOINT; OIL.

Olive. The olive tree is an evergreen which is common in the entire Mediterranean basin and is the most common tree in Palestine. The base of the olive tree is a thick knotted trunk; at the height of 6 ft to 9 ft it divides into 3 to 6 branches which expand into a crown which ranges from 15 ft to 35 ft in height. The tree reaches a great age which is sometimes exaggerated; the trees of Gethsemani* are not 2000 years old, as tourists are told, but they are 500 years old. The olive grows wild and demands cultivation if its full fertility is to be realized. The leaves are grayish green, long and slender, and do not as a rule afford much shade. Its pale yellow flowers blossom in May. A fully grown tree will yield ½ ton of oil a year.

The olive was highly esteemed (cf OIL; Dt 8:8; 2 K 18:32; Hg 2:19). In the parable of Jotham* it is the most honored of the trees (Jgs 9:8 f). The restored Israel will be like the olive in beauty (Ho 14:6; cf Ps 52:10; Je 11:16). The olive survives the deluge (Gn 8:11); Hb folklore did not imagine the earth at a time when the olive was not cultivated. This feature of the story does not appear in the Mesopotamian myth; the olive does not grow in Mesopotamia. Asher* is blessed for its wealth of oil (Dt 33:24): the olive grows more abundantly in Galilee* than in other parts of Palestine.

The cultivation of the olive included grafting the branch of the cultivated tree into the trunk of a wild olive tree; this was

Olive trees near Tiberias on the Sea of Galilee.

probably practiced in OT times also, but the OT does not distinguish between the wild and the cultivated olive. The analogy of Paul in Rm 11:17 f reverses the normal practice by speaking of the grafting of the wild olive into the cultivated olive; the inversion is no doubt deliberate and is intended to show the paradoxical character of the will of God to save the Gentiles while permitting the Jews to reject His salvation.

In Palestine the olive is harvested in October; the fruit is beaten off the trees with hands or clubs and gathered off the ground (Dt 24:20). There is no mention of the eating of olives in the Bible and it appears that the olive was cultivated solely for its oil*.

Olives, Mount of. The principal eminence to the E of Jerusalem, from which it is separated by the Kidron*. The summit rises about 250 ft above the terrace of the Dome of the Rock (cf JERUSALEM). The mountain extends its shoulder northward; this elevation is called Mt Scopus. The name indicates the number of olive trees which grew on its slopes in ancient times; there are few olives on the hill in modern times.

The mountain is mentioned in the OT only in 2 S 15:30; Zc 14:4, and without any name in Ezk 11:23. It is mentioned much more frequently in the NT. On the E slope, the side opposite from Jerusalem, lay the villages of Bethphage* and Bethany*. Gethsemani* lies on the lower W slope of the mountain only a short distance from Jerusalem. The triumphal entry of Jesus into Jerusalem began on the Mt of Olives (Mt 21:1 ff; Mk 11:1 ff; Lk 19:28 ff). In Mt 24:3; Mk 13:3 it is the scene of the eschatological discourse. It was the scene of the agony and arrest of Jesus (Mt 26:30 ff; Mk 14:26 ff; Lk 22:39 ff) and of His ascension* (AA 1:12).

The Mount of Olives, with Gethsemani in the foreground.

Olympas or **Olympias** (Gk *olympas*, "belonging to Olympus"), a personal name; a Christian of Rome greeted by Paul (Rm 16:15).

Omega. Cf ALPHA.

Omer. Cf WEIGHTS AND MEASURES.

Omri. (Hb *ŏmrî*, meaning uncertain, perhaps not a Hb name; some suggest Arabic), the name of a king of Israel and of three others in the OT. Omri (876–869 BC) is treated briefly in the OT, but historians generally regard him as one of the strongest rulers of the kingdom and the true founder of the strength which permitted the kingdom of Israel to endure as long as it did. Omri was general of the armies under Elah*. When Zimri*, another royal officer, assassinated Elah and made himself king, Omri was proclaimed king by his army. He defeated and killed Zimri, but the resistance continued under Tibni* for four years (1 K 15:15–23). The OT records in addition only Omri's transfer of the royal capital from Tirzah* to Samaria*, a new foundation of his own. He secured alliance with Tyre by marrying his son Ahab to Jezebel* and with Judah by marrying his daughter Athaliah* to Jehoram* (2 Ch 22:2). His conquest of Moab*, not mentioned in the OT, is attested in the inscription of Mesha* (ANET 320). His influence is attested by the use of his name by the Assyrians (bit Humri) to designate Israel long after his death; even Jehu*, who destroyed the dynasty of Omri, is called "the son of Omri" by the Assyrians. His religious policy followed the policy of Jeroboam, and he is one of the few Israelite kings to have the disapproval not only of the compiler of 1–2 K but also of a canonical prophet (Mi 6:16).

On (Hb *'ôn*, Egyptian *'iwnw*, Gk *heliopolis*, "city of the sun"), a city of ancient Egypt, situated at the modern Matariyeh, 5 mi NE of Cairo. Nothing is left of the ancient city but two obelisks of Sesostris I. The city is one of the oldest foundations of ancient Egypt and is frequently mentioned in Egyptian lists and records. It was never politically important; its importance was religious. It was probably the oldest and certainly the chief seat of the worship of the solar deity Re (cf EGYPT) and of the solar deity Atum, who was the sun as the creator. Joseph* was married to Asenath*, daughter of Potiphera*, a priest of On (Gn 41:45, 50; 46:20).

Onan (Hb *'ônān*, "the strong"?), a personal name; son of Judah* and the Canaanite Shua*. Judah commanded Onan to take Tamar*, the widow of Er*, in a levirate marriage. Onan withdrew during intercourse with Tamar and Yahweh killed him because of the evil which he had done (Gn 38:4–10). The vice of onanism, frustration of conception by withdrawal, has received its name from him.

The anecdote creates the situation for the story of Judah and Tamar, which is the real point of the whole story. There can be little doubt that in the intention of the narrators of the story the vice which Onan exhibits is not what is meant by the modern conception of "onanism," but his refusal to fulfill the duty of the levirate and to beget sons who should bear his brother's name. This flagrant contempt of the duties of kinship struck at the very conception of solidarity which was the chief protection of the family, clan, and tribe in nomadic* life.

No doubt the ancedote preserves only obscurely some clan or tribal episode. Judah* elsewhere appears as a tribe with a large admixture of Canaanite blood which distinguishes it from "Israel" of the N. The stories of Gn 38 are constructed around traditions of the intermarriage between some of the clans of Judah and the Canaanites. The tradition bears the memory of a disaster which overtook the clans of Er and Onan in connection with this connubium, and one can scarcely go beyond this in reconstructing the story. In many respects the literary character of the story is similar to the character of the story of Dinah*, Simeon*, Levi* and Shechem* (Gn 34).

Onesimus (Gk *onēsimos*, "useful"), a common personal name; a slave of Philemon* of Colossae* who ran away, met Paul at Rome and was converted to Christianity. Paul sent him back to Philemon with a letter of recommendation, our epistle Phm, to receive him. Onesimus appears in Col 4:9 as Paul's "dear faithful brother" sent with Tychicus*, the bearer of the letter.

Onesiphorus (Gk *onēsiphoros*, "bringer of profit"), a personal name; a householder of Ephesus* who sustained Paul in his troubles (2 Tm 1:16–18; 4:19).

Onias (Gk *onīas*, a Grecized abbreviation of Jechoniah*, or Honnai from Johanan), a personal name borne by several members of the high priestly family during the period 300–150 BC.

1. Onias I (about 300 BC), who concluded a treaty with Arius, king of Sparta (1 Mc 12:7 f, 19–23).

2. Onias II (about 227 BC), father of Simon, the high priest praised in BS 50:1 ff.

3. Onias III, son of Simon, high priest about 195 BC. He enjoyed excellent relations with the Seleucid kings; but according to the midrash* of 2 Mc 3 the cupidity of the king was excited by a certain Simon, and the king sent Heliodorus* to seize the temple treasures. He was prevented by an apparition which struck him down and was healed by the prayers of Onias. Onias had to go to Antioch to clear himself of charges; during his absence Menelaus* by plotting secured the favor of the court and persuaded a royal officer named Andronicus to murder Onias (2 Mc 4:1–6, 30–38). His death occurred about 170 BC.

4. Onias IV, son of Onias III, never held the high priesthood and is not mentioned in the OT. He fled to Egypt during the troubles of the Maccabean period and secured permission from Ptolemy Philometor about 154 BC to build a temple to Yahweh at Leontopolis.

Ophel. Cf JERUSALEM.

Ophir (Hb *'ôpîr*, meaning uncertain), a geographical name; listed with Arabian tribal and geographical names in the table* of nations (Gn 10:29; 1 Ch 1:23). Its position can be deduced from the information that it was reached by sea from Ezion-geber* and that it was a gold producing region (1 K 9:28; 10:10; 22:49; 2 Ch 8:18; 9:10). This practically demands a location on the SW coast of Arabia on the Red Sea. The gold* of Ophir (1 Ch 29:4; Ps 45:10; Jb 22:24; 28:16; Is 13:12) was highly esteemed.

Ophni (Hb *ḥŏpnī*, probably Egyptian *ḥfn(r)*, "tadpole"), a personal name; a priest of Shiloh*, son of Eli* (1 S 1:3). With his brother Phinehas* he abused the privilege of the priesthood by extorting unjust tariffs from the offerers of sacrifice and was threatened by a prophet with destruction (1 S 2). The two brothers perished in battle with the Philistines* while escorting the ark* (1 S 4).

Ophrah (Hb *'oprāh*, meaning uncertain), a local name. **1.** A town of Judah (Jos 18:23; 1 S 13:17; the reading of Mi 1:10 is doubtful). It is to be identified with the Ephron of 2 Ch 13:19 and the Ephraim* or Ephrem of 2 S 13:23 and Jn 11:54. The site is identical with the modern et-Taiyibeh, a village NE of Jerusalem and E of Beitin (Bethel*) on the crest of the Jordan valley with a magnificent view of the valley. **2.** A town of the clan of Abiezer of the tribe of Manasseh*, the home of Gideon (Jgs 6:11). It probably had a sanctuary from pre-Israelite times. Gideon built there an altar

to Yahweh (Jgs 6:24) and an ephod* (Jgs 8:27), repudiated by the compiler of Jgs but no doubt intended to honor Yahweh. Gideon was buried at Ophrah (Jgs 8:32) and his sons were murdered there by Abimelech* (Jgs 9:5). It is identified with another et-Taiyibeh about 8 mi N of Beisan (Beth-shan*).

Oracle Cf DIVINATION; PROPHET; REVELATION; URIM AND THUMMIM.

Ordeal. Ordeal is a primitive method of deciding cases at law which cannot be decided by evidence through the submission of the accused to pain or risk of life on the assumption that the deity will protect the innocent. This primitive and cruelly unjust method had little place in the collections of Near Eastern law. In the Code of Hammurabi* #2 (ANET 166) one charged with sorcery without proof must submit to the ordeal of the river i.e., the guilty person will drown; it is probable that the charge of sorcery was not only difficult to prove but also that people were afraid to lay such a charge. A woman against whom an unproved charge of adultery is laid must also submit to the ordeal of the river (#132, ANET 171); here, it seems, the assumption was that the charge was probably true. In the Middle Assyrian laws of the 15th–12th centuries BC the ordeal of the river is also employed in a charge of adultery (#17, ANET 181); but the text does not define the ordeal, and it is not clear whether the wife or the accuser or both were submitted to the ordeal. #22 also imposes the ordeal in a charge of adultery, but the text is even more obscure; apparently a man who is charged with adultery with another's wife but denies either the fact or the knowledge that she was married must, if the woman accuses him, be submitted to the ordeal. #24 (ANET 182) imposes the ordeal upon a man whose wife receives the runaway wife of another; if he pleads ignorance, he must submit to the ordeal. Here the husband of the runaway, it seems, must also submit to the ordeal if he has charged the householder with knowledge.

The ordeal in Hb law survives only in the case of a wife suspected of infidelity (Nm 5:11–31); this case also is found in the Mesopotamian laws. But the ordeal is reduced in Hb law to a merely symbolic ritual; the woman, if guilty, must consume water into which has been washed the writing of the imprecations laid upon her. The exculpatory oath* is also a mild form of the ordeal.

Oreb (Hb *'ōrēb*, "raven"), a personal name;

a Midianite* chieftain defeated and slain by the Israelites led by Gideon* (Jgs 7:25; 8:3; Ps 83:12).

Original Sin. Cf FALL; SIN.

Ornan. Cf ARAUNAH.

Orpah (Hb 'ŏrpāh, meaning and etymology uncertain), a personal name; a Moabite woman who married one of the sons of Elimelech* and Naomi* (Rt 1:4) and, unlike Ruth*, returned to her father's house after the death of her husband (Rt 1:14).

Osnappar (Aramaic 'ŏsnappar, a corruption of Assyrian Ashur-bani-pal, "Ashur has given a son"), personal name, a king of Assyria who is said in Ezr 4:10 to have settled a number of peoples of Mesopotamia in the province of Samaria*. Osnappar is Ashur-bani-pal (663–630 BC), and the deportations probably followed the civil war between Ashur-bani-pal and his brother Shamash-shum-ukin, viceroy of Babylon.

Ostraka (Gk ostrakon, plural ostraka). An ostrakon is a potsherd. In the ancient world, where writing material was comparatively rare and expensive, potsherds were much in use for occasional writing: brief letters, both official and private, lists, accounts, and similar ephemeral notes. Because of the durability of the material most Palestinian literary remains have been preserved on ostraka. For the most important collections cf BETH-SHEMESH; GEZER; LACHISH; SAMARIA.

Ostrich. The ostrich, a bird of the deserts of Asia and Africa, is found in the Syrian desert. In Hb law it is unclean (cf CLEAN; Lv 11:16; Dt 14:15). The OT refers to it as a dweller of the desert (Is 13:21; 43:20; Je 50:39), and its presence is a sign of abandonment of human habitation. The wailing of the mourner is compared to the cry of the ostrich (Jb 30:29; Mi 1:8). It is praised for its plumage and its swiftness (Jb 39:13–18). Its cruelty to its young (Lam 4:3) and its thoughtless lack of care for them (Jb 39:14–17) refer to a popular belief concerning the ostrich which is based on the fact that it does not nest like other birds.

Its eggs are laid in the sand and covered to a depth of about a foot; they are warmed by the sun during the day and incubated at night. The ostrich is unable to defend its eggs and abandons them when it is pursued.

Othniel (Hb 'ŏtnî'ēl, meaning and etymology uncertain), a son of Kenaz (i.e., a Kenizzite*, 1 Ch 4:13), who appears as a clan name in 1 Ch 27:15. In the traditions of the conquest Othniel captured Kirjath-sepher* and in reward was given Achsah*, daughter of Caleb*, as his wife (Jos 15:16 ff; Jgs 1:12 ff). A compiler placed Othniel in the list of the judges as first, although he had no information concerning the deliverance which Othniel effected (cf CUSHAN-RISHATHAIM).

Oven. Cf BREAD

Ox. The unit of the bovine species without respect to age or sex; commonly used, however, of the castrated male. Allusions to oxen in the Bible are too numerous for citation. They were used for plowing and for draught and for beasts of burden. They were also used to thresh grain by treading it; in this operation the owner was forbidden to muzzle them (Dt 25:4). This law is cited by Paul (1 Co 9:9 ff) in order to show that the minister of the Gospel is entitled to support from those whom he evangelizes. Oxen were the most precious animal for sacrifice and the most esteemed animal flesh for food; the practice of fattening them is mentioned. It is unlikely that they were eaten except by the extremely wealthy and on great festivals. Possession of herds of oxen meant great wealth. The abundance of grass and water which the cultivation of oxen demands is not found frequently in modern Palestine and it is doubtful that it was much more available in biblical times, although most historians think that the land has lost much of its grass cover due to deforestation and erosion. Oxen can be cultivated, however, in areas which have no greater annual rainfall than Palestine, and the allusions to oxen in the Bible certainly indicate that they were not rare.

P

Paddan-Aram (Hb *paddan-'ᵃrām,* a geographical name; the element *paddan* is uncertain, *'ᵃrām* designates Aram* or Aramaean). The name is given in the priestly tradition to NW Mesopotamia, the home of Bethuel* and Laban*, where Jacob* served Laban and married his daughters; it is the same region called in the other traditions of the Pnt Aram-naharaim (cf ARAM; Gn 25:20; 28:2–7; 31:18; 33:18; 35:9, 26; 48:7, Paddan).

Palace. The palace in the ancient city was the residence of the king. It was also with the temple a focus of civic life. It employed a large domestic and administrative staff and owned a large number of slaves. The palace was a self-contained community with its garrison, craftsmen, storehouses; it was the center of administration of the palace lands, flocks, and herds. As the center of administration it had a large staff of scribes* and extensive collections of records and archives. It was the center of reception of payments of taxes and other imposts and its treasury exercised control over the circulation of gold and silver and sometimes over other metals. It was a court of law where cases were heard by the king himself or by royal judges. In the reign of Solomon* the Jerusalem palace was the principal economic and marketing center not only of Jerusalem but of the entire kingdom.

Archaeology tells us nothing of the construction of the palace of Solomon. The brief description of the palace in 1 K 7:1 ff gives no information about the arrangement of the various rooms mentioned. These are: (a) the house of the forest of Lebanon, so named because of its columns and paneling of cedar. The purpose of the hall is uncertain. (b) The purpose of the hall of columns is also uncertain. (c) The throne hall was the seat of judgment and doubtless also the audience chamber. These were large public rooms; there may have been other such rooms. They were distinct from the royal apartments. (d) Separate apartments were built for the daughter of the Pharaoh, the most distinguished of Solomon's wives. The description says nothing about the offices, shops, and storehouses which must also have been included in the palace complex. On the analogy of other ancient palaces these buildings were arranged around a series of courts; most palaces which have been explored had one large central court on which the main gate opened. Access to the state chambers and still more to the royal apartments was not open to the public. The entire complex of temple and palace was surrounded by a single enclosure.

The palace of Omri at Samaria* has been only partially identified and no ground

Restoration of the Palace of Sargon at Khorsabad.

plan can be reconstructed. The excavators propose that the palace was begun by Omri, finished by Ahab*, and remodeled by Jeroboam* II.

The palace of Herod* at Jerusalem was the scene of the encounter of Herod Antipas* and Jesus during the passion (Lk 23:6–16). The magnificence of this palace is extravagantly described by Josephus. It is to be located on the site of the modern "Citadel" of Jerusalem just inside the Jaffa Gate in the W wall. One of the towers of the Citadel, popularly called "the tower of David," contains remains of the Herodian masonry and represents one of the three towers mentioned by Josephus as part of its fortifications. The measurements of the tower of David fit none of the three towers described by Josephus and its identification with any of them is uncertain. The towers were named after Hippicus, a friend of Herod, his brother Phasael, and Mariamne, the wife whom he murdered. Most archaeologists think the tower of David is the tower Phasael.

Palestine. 1. *Name.* The designation of the region which lies between the Taurus mountains to the N and the deserts of Sinai and Arabia to the S, the Mediterranean to the W and the desert to the E as Syria* goes back to the Gk sailors and merchants of the 5th century BC. This land mass was subdivided into Upper Syria, the plain which extends from the Mediterranean to the Zagros mountains; Coelesyria, "hollow Syria," the region of the Lebanon and the Anti-Lebanon; and Syria Palestina, the region S of the Lebanon and Mt Hermon. From the 2nd century AD the official title of the Roman province of this region was Syria Palestina. The name "Palestina" alone (the adjective used as a noun) appears in Herodotus, Philo, and Josephus. Palestine is the Grecized form of the Hb word which is anglicized as Philistine*.

2. *Position.* The historical importance of Palestine is largely determined by its relation to the surrounding land masses of Asia and Africa. J. H. Breasted gave the name "Fertile Crescent" to a strip of land of varying breadth which begins at the mouth of the Tigris and Euphrates, follows the valleys of these two rivers NE, turns W to the Mediterranean from ancient Assyria to N Syria, turns S along the coast to the Wadi el Arish, the traditional boundary of Egypt and Palestine. If one adds to this the valley of the Nile*, the crescent extends to the First Cataract. This strip is characterized by the presence of enough water, either from rainfall or from irrigation, to assure the annual cultivation of the soil. Palestine

on E and S is surrounded by desert, which was an effective barrier to travel in ancient times. Communication between Mesopotamia and Egypt and between Arabia and N Syria and Phoenicia must pass through Palestine because there is no detour or short cut. Control of the area was therefore vital to each of the power centers between which Palestine lay, and its history has been decisively determined by the actions of these two political centers. The Mediterranean is a barrier, not a gateway. Unlike Phoenicia, Palestine has no natural harbor. During the ancient period it never looked seaward and was reached late by the Greeks. The Bible shows little interest in the sea and sea travel, and some fear of them.

3. *Boundaries.* The political boundaries of Palestine have fluctuated remarkably during its recorded history; yet there is a certain fundamental unity to the country determined by its natural frontiers. The traditional biblical formula is from Dan to Beersheba. This line, however, does not correspond to the line on the sea coast, which more properly runs from the Ladder of Tyre or even farther S at Accho (Acre) to the Wadi el Arish. The Negeb* S of Beersheba was during most Israelite history related politically and culturally to the history of Israel. The boundary to the E is determined by the line where the desert begins. From Dan to Beersheba is about 150 mi. From Accho to the Sea of Galilee is 28 mi, and from Gaza to the Dead Sea is 54 mi. The area of Palestine W of the Jordan is about 6000 sq mi, and the area of Palestine E and W of the Jordan is about 10,000 sq mi (cf Vermont, 9609 sq mi). The country is therefore small in area, and this must be borne in mind if one is to appreciate the variations of topography and climate which the country exhibits (cf below). One may note also that these variations are such as to render the country apt for internal political divisions.

4. *Physical Geography.* Here we touch only the main general characteristics of the entire country; cf separate articles for more details upon the various regions.

The determining factor in the physical geography of Palestine is its position astride a rift which is the largest geological fault on the land surface of the globe. This position gives the country an interesting history of earthquakes*. This rift appears as a cleft between two mountain ranges which extend N-S from N Syria to the Gulf of Aqabah. The W range includes the range of Amanus in N Syria, the Lebanon in Syria, and the mountains of Galilee*. It is interrupted by the plain of Esdraelon*, and resumes as the mountains of Samaria and Judaea* (with a spur thrown to the sea at Mt Carmel). S of Hebron the mountains gradually diminish into the plateau of the Negeb. The E range appears in the N as a range running NE from a point between Damascus and Homs into the desert toward Deir ez Zor, proceeding S as the Anti-Lebanon*, terminating at Mt Hermon*. It then proceeds southward as the high plateau of the Hauran, Gilead, and Moab, through Edom to the Gulf of Aqabah. The cleft between the two ranges narrows in Lebanon into the Beqaa, and at the foot of Mt Hermon, where the Jordan rises, it becomes the valley of the Jordan with its lakes of Huleh, the Sea of Galilee, and the Dead Sea. S of the Dead Sea it is the arid cleft of the Wadi el Arabah, which sinks into the Red Sea, which is itself a continuation of the continental rift. In Palestine proper the altitude of the W range varies from 4000 ft in N Galilee to 2000–3000 ft in Samaria and Judaea, rising to 3300 ft at Hebron. In E Palestine the altitude rises slightly higher but the country is less broken. The Jordan valley drops from sea level N of the Sea of Galilee to 1290 ft below sea level at the Dead Sea.

This feature divides the country naturally into five zones running N and S: the coastal plain, the central range, the Jordan valley, the E plateau, the steppe. The steppe is a thin belt which divides the country from the desert on S and E. It averages 8–16 in of rain a year and therefore is marginal for cultivation; but it has a grass cover which affords pasture. The desert extends an arm into the country in the Jordan valley itself, which is arid, except for a few oases, up to half the distance between the Dead Sea and the Sea of Galilee. Each of these zones has its own peculiarities of climate (cf below).

Further lateral divisions are created by other features. Mt Carmel effectively splits the coastal plain in two. The plain of Esdraelon and its extension through the valley of Beth-shan divides Galilee from Samaria. The character of the central range changes perceptibly but not abruptly between Samaria and Judaea, and the change begins about the neighborhood of the modern city of Ramallah, 10 mi N of Jerusalem. In Samaria the valleys are wider and the slopes of the mountains gentler; hence conditions for cultivation are more favorable. From a point a little S of Jerusalem the central range is divided from the coastal plain by a range of foothills called the Shephelah*. The transverse cleft between these hills and the central range was an effective frontier of Judah in ancient times. The eastern slope of the range of Judah is the wilderness or desert

of Judah. The Jordan receives no important tributaries from the W; from the E it is fed by the Yarmuk and the Jabbok*. These two with the Arnon*, which flows into the Dead Sea, by their drainage systems create the divisions of E Palestine into the ancient Bashan, Gilead, and Moab. These physical divisions are reflected in the tribal and political divisions of ancient Palestine.

5. *Climate.* The five N-S zones mentioned above are five climatic zones. The entire country has only two real seasons; the rainy season, extending from October to June at its greatest, and the dry season, during which no rain falls at all, from June to October. There are only brief transitional seasons between these two seasons. The summer is hot, but the heat varies in the different zones. The highest temperatures are recorded in the Jordan valley, followed by the E Jordan plateau, the steppe, the central range, and the coastal plain with not much difference in average summer temperatures. The averages, however, are meaningless; the Jordan valley is nearly intolerable for foreigners. The coastal plain has a smaller temperature variation but greater humidity and nights are not cool. In the other four zones the temperature drops, sometimes sharply, at night. The afternoon breeze from the sea moderates the heat in the coastal plain and is most appreciated on the heights of the central range; but it is not felt at all in the Jordan valley and reaches E Jordan quite late in the afternoon.

The coastal plain receives over 20 in of rain annually; the figure drops as one moves E, but the mountains of the central range receive nearly as much as the coast. The Jordan valley receives practically none in its S portion. The sharp rise of the E Jordan plateau, however, means that the moisture remaining from the clouds is again condensed, and the rainfall nearly approaches the rainfall of the central range. The coastal plain has warmer winter temperatures than any other zone; in the Jordan valley the days are warmer, but the temperature falls at night. The central range, the E Jordan plateau, and the steppe are all exposed to the cold land winds. It is rare, however, for the temperature to drop to frost; snow is also rare, and a heavy snowfall which lies on the ground is a newsworthy event.

A heavy fall of dew is characteristic of the summer climate; this moderates the heat and deposits a small but extremely useful amount of moisture in the soil. The dew also is a result of the prevailing W winds, and it falls most heavily where the temperature variation between day and night is greatest. It does not fall in the Jordan valley.

The winds, as observed, are prevailing W

winds from the sea, and they bring moisture as rain or dew. At the beginning of the rainy season, when temperature and pressure vary sharply, thunderstorms occur; they are less frequent as the rainy season advances. Rain falls in heavy showers, and the foggy all-day drizzle of Europe and N America is almost unknown. The land wind is rarer but usually more violent than the W wind. In winter it is a cold wind. The sirocco (Arabic *sharqiyyeh*, Hb *ḳadīm*, both meaning E wind) is the most unpleasant feature of the climate. It comes not in the summer but in the two brief transitional seasons. It is a violent and extremely hot and dry wind. It dehydrates not only human beings and animals, causing extreme discomfort and in human beings unpleasant psychological repercussions and great fatigue, but also vegetation, which it kills if it blows long enough. It fills the air with fine gritty dust which pervades clothing and habitation. It is frequently mentioned in the Bible.

6. *Hydrography*. Palestine has only one true river system, the Jordan and its tributaries. The wadi is a seasonal stream bed (cf BROOK). These are both barriers and means of communication; they break the country up into smaller parts, but also afford the easiest ascent of the mountains. In the central range they run E-W, as noted above, are broader and more numerous on the W slope of Samaria than in Judaea. The base of the soil in Palestine is mostly limestone, which is porous and easily traps water; hence the country, except in the S portion of Judaea, is generously supplied with wells and springs (cf WATER).

7. *Political Geography*. For details on this aspect of geography cf separate articles. In general it may be noticed that the political and historical geography of Palestine exhibits two dominant traits: the country has rarely been politically unified; and the country has rarely been politically independent. Independence and unity together in the historical period have been achieved only in the monarchy of David and Solomon and briefly in the Hasmonean* period; and it is questionable whether the Hasmonean period showed true political independence. The unity of the country, as we noticed, is broken by several geographical features. Its independence is compromised by its proximity to the power centers of Egypt and Mesopotamia, to each of which the country is important. Normally each of these two centers supports a far larger population than Palestine, and each of them has a far closer natural geographical unity. It has therefore been normal that the country should be wholly or partly controlled by one of the two.

8. *Prehistory*. Palestinian prehistory has developed almost entirely since 1920 and the field has been dominated by the work of Dorothy Garrod and her associates. No other country except France has yielded so much evidence of prehistoric man. The oldest cultures found correspond to the Tayacian and Acheulian of the 2nd interglacial period, 230,000–180,000 years ago (Albright). From the Middle Palaeolithic period (150,000–120,000 years ago) comes the culture called Levallo-Mousterian, since it exhibits traits of these two cultures found in France. The "Carmel Man" of this period was identified as a mixed race intermediate between Neanderthal man of the palaeolithic period and *homo sapiens*. Palestine also exhibits a brief period of Aurignacian culture; but its most distinctive prehistoric culture, which has left the most abundant remains, is the Mesolithic Natufian culture of 8000 BC. These were cave dwellers and cultivators of grain; racially they were a Mediterranean type. The following prehistoric phase is the pre-pottery Neolithic culture of Jericho* discovered by Kathleen Kenyon.

Palm. The date palm, *phoenix dactylifera*, grows in a single trunk without branches and sometimes reaches a height of 100 ft. At the top it flowers into a coronet of fronds 6 ft long, beneath which the dates hang in clusters. The date palm was a basic staple in Mesopotamia, where the tree grows in abundance, and it is common in Egypt also; in Palestine it grows only in the coastal plain and in the Jordan valley, and cannot survive the winters of the mountains. It grows in oases in the desert; Elim, mentioned in Ex 15:27; Nm 33:9, had 12 springs and 70 palms. Jericho is called the city of Palms in Dt 34:3; 2 Ch 28:15, and it is altogether probable that Jericho is meant by the designation in Jgs 1:16; 3:13. According to Jn 12:13 the disciples bore palm fronds at the entry of Jesus into Jerusalem. On the basis of Apc 7:9 the palm in Christian liturgy and art has become the symbol of the martyr. The righteous flourishes like the palm (Ps 92:13), and the maiden of SS is compared to a palm (7:8 f). Palms as a decorative motif in the temple were probably the work of the Phoenician artists of Hiram; the palm grows abundantly in Phoenicia and appears on Phoenician coins, while it is not seen in the region of Jerusalem.

Pamphylia (Gk *pamphylia*, "all tribes"), a region on the S coast of Asia Minor between Pisidia* to the N, Lycia* to the W, and Cilicia* to the E; its principal cities were Perge* and Attalia, its port. It was the seat of a Jewish community (1 Mc 15:23; AA

2:10). Paul preached there on his first missionary journey (AA 13:13; 14:24 f).

Paphos (Gk *paphos,* meaning uncertain), a city on the W coast of Cyprus, visited by Paul on his first missionary journey (AA 13:6–13). It was the residence of the proconsul Sergius Paulus*, and the scene of the dispute between Paul and the magician Elymas* or Barjesus.

Papyrus (Gk *papyros,* Hb *gōme',* loan word from Egyptian *km,'; Cyperus papyrus*), a reed which in ancient times grew abundantly in the marshes of the delta in Egypt and less abundantly along the banks of the Nile above the delta. It was the symbol of Lower Egypt in art. The reed is now found N of the Sudan. In Palestine it grows in the marshes of Lake Huleh. The reed consists of a stalk composed of rind and pith which grows 4–15 ft above the surface of the water and bears an umbrella shaped crown of leaves at the top; for representations of the reed in ancient art cf ANEP 296. The reed was extremely useful in ancient Egypt, which was poor in wood; it was used for the manufacture of boats (ANEP 124), baskets, ropes, cords, and other articles where it could be used as a fabric. Egypt was the only producer of papyrus in antiquity and

shipped it to the Near East and later to the Gk countries and Italy. Its most important use was as a material for writing. It was used for this purpose in Egypt at least ·in the 3rd millennium BC, if not earlier, and it was universally used in the Gk countries by 450 BC. The Gk word *papyrus* is the word from which Eng *paper* and cognate words in modern languages are derived, although paper is quite a different substance.

The papyrus sheet or scroll (cf BOOK) was manufactured by stripping the rind off the reed and cutting the pith into strips. The strips were laid in vertical rows, slightly overlapping each other, and another layer of strips were spread across the first layer in horizontal rows. The sheet was beaten and pressed; after drying the sheet was finished. The *recto,* the side on which the strips lie horizontally i.e., in the parallel plane with the script, was normally the only side used for writing in the ancient world; use of the *verso* also, the vertical side, was a sign of the poverty of the writer. As a writing material papyrus is nearly as good as paper and it has proved itself more durable. But it cannot survive storage in damp places and if dried out becomes brittle, much like a dried leaf. In spite of this, ancient Egypt has yielded over 30,000 papyri in Gk alone. A sheet of papyrus rolled up,

A fowler with his family in the Papyrus marshes of the Nile.

tied, and sealed is shown in ANEP 265; sample pages of ancient Egyptian papyri are shown in ANEP 266, 542. These illustrate the clarity with which writing on papyrus can be preserved when conditions are suitable.

Although papyrus must have been commonly used in Palestine, its use as a writing material is not mentioned in the Bible. It was the material of the vessel in which Moses was exposed in the Nile (Ex 2:3), and boats of papyrus are mentioned in Is 18:2. Jb 8:11; Is 35:7 allude to papyrus as growing in water.

On papyrus biblical MSS cf TEXT.

Parable. The Gk word *parabolē* in the LXX represents the Hb *māšāl*, which designates a wise saying, a maxim (cf WISDOM) or a taunt song (cf POETRY). In the NT *parabolē* is not used of the taunt song; it designates the wise saying or the fictitious short story used by Jesus to set forth His teaching. The parables of the Gospel are a unique development of a literary form which has its roots in the OT and in rabbinic literature. T. W. Manson lists nine such parables in the OT: the ewe lamb (2 S 12:1–14), the two brothers and the avenger (2 S 14:1–11), the escaped captive (2 K 20:35–40), the vineyard (Is 5:1–7), the eagle and the vine (Ezk 17:3–10), the lion whelps (Ezk 19:2–9), the vine (Ezk 19:10–14), the forest fire (Ezk 21:1–5), the boiling pot (Ezk 24:3–5). Two other anecdotes are classified by Manson as fables rather than parables: the trees (Jgs 9:7–15) and the thistle and the cedar (2 K 14:9). The purpose of these anecdotes is to bring the listener to concede a point which he does not perceive as applicable to himself. In addition the anecdote whets the curiosity and attracts attention; the listener is trapped because of his desire to hear how the story comes out. The rabbinic parables, of which it is estimated that there are about 2000 in the rabbinic literature, have not the same practical purpose. They are told in answer to the question of a disciple, and the anecdote shows that the scope of the answer is broader than the disciple perceived. These last two purposes also appear in the parables of Jesus.

The number of parables in the Gospels is estimated as low as 35 and as high as 72; the variation arises from the difficulty of classifying the parables. A larger number is attained by including sayings which most scholars would call not parables but similes or metaphors; and this more limited definition seems preferable. That the parables come from Jesus Himself is doubted by no one; they are present in all the Synoptic Gospels. In Jn only the good shepherd (Jn 10:1 ff) and the vine and the branches (Jn 15:1–7) can be called parables; but these should be called allegories rather than parables. The parables of the Synoptic Gospels show a number of interesting variations among the three Gospels; these have led all modern scholars to conclude that the primitive Church did not hesitate to adapt the parables to its own homiletic needs. There is a wide area of agreement on the nature and the extent of this adaptation.

For most of the parables a double situation in life should be sought: a situation in the life and teaching of Jesus Himself and a situation in the life and teaching of the primitive community. In 1899 A. Jülicher enunciated a principle which became a commonplace in interpretation until quite recent times: there is no allegory in the original parables of Jesus Himself, and any allegorical elements in the parables have been added by the primitive Church. Modern interpreters do not accept this principle rigidly; the analysis of the elements which the Church added to the parables is too complex to be done by the use of this or any other single rule. As a general guide Jülicher's principle is still valid in the sense that most allegorical elements appear to be the work of the primitive Church. J. Jeremias lists the following passages as examples of the allegorization by the Church: Mt 12:1–11; 13:36–43, 49–50; 21:34–36; 22:1–14; Mk 4:13–20 = Mt 13:18–23 = Lk 8:11–15. In particular Jeremias denies that any allegorization in Lk is original with Jesus Himself.

The parables at times appear to have experienced a change in meaning when they were translated from Aramaic into Gk. Jeremias and other modern scholars believe this element has been insufficiently explored. The alterations go beyond mere vocabulary; they include implicit changes in the cultural background of the parables such as differences in houses, furniture, agricultural methods, the names of officials, the types of implements used in domestic, industrial, and agricultural work, and similar items. These changes are minor and do not affect the meaning of the parable substantially.

The parables are sometimes abbreviated from one Gospel to another with no apparent purpose except to omit details which are obscure or less meaningful to the audience of the Gospels. Lk 8:6–8 abbreviates Mt 13:6–9; Mt 18:12–14 abbreviates Lk 15:4–7; Mt 22:4 f abbreviates Lk 14:18–20. The expansions of the parables from one Gospel to another are almost always a reinterpretation of the parable. The only two commentaries on the parables (Mt 13:36–43; Mk 4:13–20 = Mt 13:18–23 = Lk 8:11–15) are almost universally regarded as additions made by the primitive Church with reference to its own missionary activities. Lk 14:23 is an expansion peculiar to Lk with a missionary outlook. Mt 22:11–13 is another and an independent parable added by Mt to the parable of the marriage feast, again with a missionary outlook. Lk 20:10–12 seems to be the more original form of the parable of the wicked farmers; Mt 21:34–36 = Mk 12:3–5 expand by adding details which refer more explicitly to the persecution of prophets and apostles by the Jews. The delay of the Parousia* was responsible for some added applications to the Parousia in parables where this theme was not original: Lk 12:39 f (= Mt 24:43 f in a different context); Mt 25:5; Mt 24:48 = Lk 12:45.

The primitive Church also adapted the parables by creating a new setting in the narrative for the utterance of the parable. The variation in the settings is best explained by supposing that collections of parables existed before the composition of the Gospels; the collections either had no setting for the separate parables or a setting which was already artficially constructed. Expansions also and more frequently occur in the conclusions of the parables, especially by the addition of a saying of Jesus; in some instances the parable becomes an occasion for a saying which in all probability was originally in some other context or in no context at all: the quotation of Ps 117:22 f in Mk 12:10 f = Mt 21:42 = Lk 20:17; Mt 18:14; 20:16 = 19:30; Lk 11:9–13 added to the parable of 11:5–8; Lk 16:8–13; Lk 18:8b; 18:14b.

J. Jeremias enumerates eight major themes which occur in the parables: the assurance of the approach of the reign of God (cf KINGDOM); the present arrival of the new age; the mercy of God for sinners; the imminence of judgment; the necessity of an immediate personal response; the conditions of discipleship (cf DISCIPLE); the passion; the consummation. These themes are original in the teaching of Jesus Himself; and it should be noticed that the primitive Church in its adaptation of the parables to the Gentile mission and to exhortation and universal application has not distorted or concealed these themes; rather it perceives a meaning for them in its own life and the life of the individual Christian which was not explicit in the original parables. Hence a search for the original parable as Jesus uttered it can be deceptive; one does not recover Christian teaching in a purer and finer form by removing it from its context in the life of the Church.

The purpose of the parables is set forth in the difficult saying of Mt 13:10–15; Mk 4:10–12; Lk 8:9–10. The passage distinguishes between the disciples and others, "those outside." T. W. Manson observes that it is the listener who places himself in one category or the other by his response to the parables. If he refuses to believe, they become unintelligible. The saying is regarded by most interpreters as original with Jesus Himself; they agree also that it is not in its original context in any of the three Gospels. In all of the three, it seems, the saying is phrased in terms of the rejection of Jesus by the Jews. This mysterious event is seen as a fulfillment — or a reenactment — of the words of Is 6:9 f. The harshness comes ultimately not only from the thought, but from the inadequacy of Semitic idiom, which does not distinguish grammatically from purpose and foreseen result. The idiom is rooted in Israelite and Jewish belief, which could not conceive of a result foreseen by God but not intended by Him; in Israelite and Jewish thought such a conception would imply that God's sovereignty was less than complete. The Aramaic particle which probably underlies the Gk *hina,* "in order that," is ambiguous; some suggest that it may indicate here the relative pronoun rather than purpose. The text is quoted in Mk according to the Palestinian Targum* and not according to the Hebrew; T. W. Manson has suggested that the Aramaic particle has been mistranslated in Gk. Probable as such explanations are, the question ultimately is a theological and not an exegetical or grammatical problem; it is the problem of the rejection of Jesus by the Jews.

Paraclete (Gk *paraklētos*), the word is not used in the LXX and only 5 times in the NT. In profane Gk the word means the person *called to the side* of one in need of assistance, particularly in legal processes; but it does not signify a professional advocate (which Lt *advocatus* does mean). Hence the general meaning of *paraclete* is helper. Profane Gk also employs the word as an active verbal adjective, i.e., one who speaks on behalf of another, an intercessor. The roots of the NT usage are difficult to trace, and they have not been found in comparative religious phenomena of the Hellenistic world. It is probable that the phrase is closely connected with the function of the spirit of truth as "helper" in the Qumran* documents, and this meaning best suits the biblical occurrences of the word.

Jesus Himself is called paraclete before the Father (1 Jn 2:1); since it is He to whom the sinner turns, the word in this passage must mean intercessor. It is not clear, however, that this meaning of the word is at the base of the use of the word in Jn 14:16, 26; 15:26; 16:7. Jn 14:26 implies that Jesus

Himself is primarily the paraclete, for the spirit who is sent is "another" paraclete. The meaning of paraclete as applied to the spirit* can be deduced only from what is said of the mission of the spirit. He is the spirit of truth (Jn 14:16); He will teach the disciples all truth and bring to their minds what Jesus has told them (14:26; 16:13); He will bear witness to Jesus (15:26); He will demonstrate the error of the world concerning sin, righteousness, and judgment (16:6–11); He will give glory to Jesus (16:14). These items, it must be admitted, do not give an entirely coherent picture. They are almost entirely fulfilled by speech, either formally or equivalently, but the speech is not the speech of intercession. In a broad sense the paraclete, then, is conceived as a helper. Scholars are quite generally agreed that the word as applied to the spirit should not be translated "comforter" or "consoler," as an active verbal adjective derived from the verb *parakalein,* and the context justifies this exclusion.

Paradise (Hb *pardēs* [only SS 4:13; Ec 2:5; Ne 2:8, in the proper sense defined below], Gk *paradeisos,* loan word from Old Persian *pairi-daeza*). In Persian the word designated an extensive park enclosed by a wall, attached to the royal palace. The park was planted with trees and grass, watered by natural streams or channels which were diverted into pools, and sometimes stocked with game.

The religious significance of the word as a proper name, "Paradise," goes back to the use of *paradeisos* in the LXX to translate the Hb word, *gan,* garden, of the garden of Eden in Gn 2–3. This primeval park deserved a special name (although *paradeisos* is used elsewhere in the LXX with no special connotation). It was a normal development of biblical and Jewish messianic and eschatological thinking that the end of history should be conceived as a return to the beginning. This is alluded to in such passages as Is 11:6–9; 51:3; Ezk 36:35. But the explicit conception of the end as a restoration of Paradise by this name becomes explicit in the apocryphal* literature of pre-Christian Judaism. Paradise was created before the earth (4 Ez 3:6). After the fall of Adam it is preserved in heaven (2 Bar 4:6; 59:8), more specifically the third heaven (Secr Enoch 8). It is a paradise of delight for the righteous (4 Ezr 4:7; 7:36, 123; 8:52; Secr Enoch 42:3; 65:10). The paradise of the righteous is in some conceptions represented as an intermediate state between the death of the righteous and the final judgment.

The highly imaginative, not to say fantastic, nature of these conceptions must be borne in mind when we see that the NT adopts the language of apocalyptic Judaism in the three passages where Paradise is mentioned. Paul locates his ecstatic vision in the Paradise of the third heaven (2 Co 12:4; cf Secr Enoch above). Lk 23:43 makes Paradise the place where both Jesus and the repentant thief go after their death; this is the Paradise of the righteous, possibly conceived as an intermediate state. Apc 2:7 represents the Paradise of God with the tree of life as the place where the victorious are destined to go. This is a clear instance of the Paradise preserved in heaven as a reward for the righteous. Paradise is only one aspect of the NT conception of life after death; cf HEAVEN; JERUSALEM; KINGDOM; LIFE.

Paran (Hb *pā'rān,* most frequently the name of a desert region). The place name Elparan (Gn 14:6) no doubt is associated with the desert; this place is thought to be identical with Elath* by some scholars. The desert of Paran was the home of the Ishmaelites (Gn 21:21). It was, in the itinerary according to P (cf PENTATEUCH), reached by the Israelites after the desert of Sinai (Nm 10:12), and they camped in this desert for some time (Nm 10:12; 13:3, 26, mission and return of the scouts). In Dt 1:1 Paran is vaguely defined as a place in the desert. Hadad of Edom passed through the desert of Paran on his journey from Midian* to Egypt (1 K 11:18). The mountains of Paran are the place from which the theophany* appears (Dt 33:2; Hab 3:3); like most other names mentioned in the theophanies, Paran reflects the region S of Judah. The desert of Paran is probably that region of the desert of the Negeb* which lies S of Kadesh-barnea*.

Parchment. Eng parchment and cognate words in modern languages are derived from Lt *pergamena* (charta), Gk *pergamenē,* adjective formed from the name of the city of Pergamum*. Pliny the Elder reports that parchment was invented by Eumenes II (197–159 BC) of Pergamum when an embargo was laid on the export of papyrus from Egypt by Ptolemy V Epiphanes (205–185 BC). This story is without historical value; the name, however, indicates that Pergamum was certainly an important center of the manufacture and distribution of parchment. Strictly speaking parchment designates sheepskin, and vellum calfskin, a material of finer quality; in popular use this distinction is not always made, and both materials are included in this article.

Parchment is not tanned. The animal skin is washed, depilated, soaked in lime, stretched tight in a frame, and scraped entirely clean; it is then moistened, rubbed with pulverized chalk, and polished with a pumice stone. After drying it is ready for use. In many ways it is the finest of all writing materials. It is nearly white, has a smooth surface which does not easily wrinkle or scratch, retains ink well, can be used on both sides, is extremely durable, and the ink can be rubbed off and the parchment used again — the palimpsest.

Parchments have been found at Dura Europos on the Euphrates from the early 2nd century BC, the very period of Eumenes II; it is concluded that it must have been in fairly wide use in the 3rd century BC, but no date can be assigned to its invention. In fact, "invention" is probably not the word; parchment was a development and improvement of animal skin and leather, which had been used for writing in earlier periods. Considering the superior qualities of parchment, it is surprising that for several centuries it did not displace papyrus; one factor was its cost, but this seems irrelevant when even emperors and wealthy men preferred papyrus. Parchment is heavier than papyrus and does not make a good scroll, the usual book* form until the codex displaced it, and the page is shiny. The codex is almost its natural form. With the 4th century AD, which coincides with the liberation of Christianity, parchment displaced papyrus in common use. Its cost was no doubt less with more abundant use, but the desire of Christians to copy their sacred books and other religious works on a finer and more durable material may have contributed to its popularity. It remained the usual material of books until the invention of printing.

Parchment is mentioned in the Bible only in 2 Tm 4:13 (*membrana*), together with *biblia,* probably papyrus scrolls.

On parchment biblical MSS cf TEXT.

Parents. Cf FAMILY; FATHER; MOTHER.

Parmenas (Gk *parmenas,* hypocoristicon of Parmenides or a similar name), one of the Seven appointed to assist the apostles in the Jerusalem Church (AA 6:5; cf DEACON).

Parousia (Gk *parousia,* "presence" or "arrival"), used in a technical sense of the ceremonial visit of a ruler to a city or country, or of the apparition of a god to help. In the NT the word is sometimes used to designate the eschatological coming of Jesus; here we treat the NT passages which deal with the Second Coming.

The coming of Yahweh is a conception which appears in the OT (cf THEOPHANY); but the OT conception which lies at the root of the NT Parousia is the coming of the Son* of Man (Dn 7:13).

In the Synoptic Gospels the Parousia is described as the coming of the Son of Man in glory (the glory of the Father) with the angels (Mt 16:27; 25:31; Mk 8:38; Lk 9:26), as a coming on the clouds with power and glory (Mt 24:30; 26:64; Mk 13:26; 14:62; Lk 21:27, omitted in Lk 22:69). The Parousia will be preceded by signs in the heavens, the departure of the heavenly bodies from their courses (Mt 24:29; Mk 13:24; Lk 21:25–27). The coming will be like a flash of lightning (Mt 24:27; Lk 17:24); this image no doubt refers primarily to the sudden and unannounced appearance of the Son of Man, but it also suggests the brilliance of His appearance. He will come in the manner in which He ascended into heaven (AA 1:11). He takes His throne in the heavens (Mt 25:31). The time of the Parousia is indefinite; the disciples will not finish their preaching to all the cities of Israel before the Son of Man comes (Mt 10:23), and the present generation will not pass before all these things happen (Mt 24:34; Mk 13:30; Lk 21:32). On the other hand, the hour is known to no one, not even to the Son of Man Himself; it is a secret which the Father has reserved to Himself (Mt 24:36; Mk 13:32). Therefore Jesus warns His disciples to be ready for His coming at all times, for, like a thief in the night, He will come without previous announcement; this is the point of the parables of the wise and foolish virgins (Mt 25:1–13), the talents (Mt 25:14–30), and the pounds (Lk 19:12–27). This insistence is not entirely concordant with the signs of the coming of the Son of Man mentioned obscurely in Mt 24:32 f; Mk 13:28 f; Lk 21:29 ff, and it seems most likely that the traditions concerning the sayings of Jesus about the Parousia began to take divergent forms extremely early; cf below. "The sign of the Son of Man" in heaven, mentioned only in Mt 24:30, is a different sign from the celestial convulsions described in the same context; the popular belief that it means a cross is without foundation.

The external traits of the Parousia in the Synoptic Gospels are clearly derived from the coming of the Son of Man in Dn 7:13 f with very little elaboration. In Dn the coming of the Son of Man is the last act of world history, the erection of the reign of God and the subjection of all hostile powers. Early Christian tradition, no doubt basing itself upon the words of Jesus Himself, applied this image to Jesus as Savior and Judge.

The Parousia appears in the Pauline writings as a fully developed concept which is substantially identical with the concept in the Synoptic Gospels. It is the day of our Lord Jesus Christ (cf DAY OF THE LORD; 1 Co 1:8). Jesus comes with His saints (1 Th 3:13); His coming is preceded by an archangel and a blast of a trumpet, and He comes in the clouds (1 Th 4:13 ff). He comes from heaven (Phl 3:20) with the angels in a blaze of fire with glory (2 Th 2:7 ff). His coming is preceded by signs through which its nearness can be discerned (2 Th 2:1–12; cf ANTICHRIST). He comes at the appointed time*, the *kairos* (1 Co 4:5). His Parousia is the hour of the resurrection* of the dead, and the righteous will join Him in glory in the clouds, and the living also will be snatched up in glory (1 Co 15:23; 1 Th 4:13 ff; Col 3:4). The Eucharist* is a proclamation both of His death and of faith in His Parousia (1 Co 11:26), and the Christian community uttered invocations that His coming might occur (cf MARANATHA; 1 Co 16:22). Paul's constant teaching is that the Christians should await His coming, expect it, hope for it.

The same conception appears in the Catholic epistles, although less frequently (Js 5: 7–9; 1 Pt 4:7). At the Parousia heaven and earth will be consumed in flame (2 Pt 3:10–12). The Parousia is called the revelation of Jesus Christ (Gk *apokalypsis*) in 1 Co 1:7; 2 Th 1:7; 1 Pt 1:7, 13; 4:13), and the appearance or manifestation (Gk *epiphaneia*) in the pastoral epistles (1 Tm 6:14; 2 Tm 4:1, 8; Tt 2:13; the same word is applied to the Incarnation in 2 Tm 1:10). It is a time of judgment (1 Pt 1:7, 13), a revelation of the glory of Jesus (1 Pt 4:13), an appearance in power (2 Tm 4:1). Christians love His epiphany (2 Tm 4:8); it is the realization of their hope (Tt 2:13).

The almost entire absence of the Parousia from the Johannine writings is a problem. It is called the *epiphaneia* (1 Jn 2:28) which Christians await, and the glorified Jesus is represented as saying that He comes quickly (Apc 3:11; 22:20). R. Bultmann has explained this by suggesting that in Jn the resurrection of Jesus and the Parousia have merged into a single event. This can be connected with the development of the belief in the Parousia in the first generation of the Church, particularly with the question of its time (cf below); on the hypothesis that Jn is a later composition, he did not speak of the Parousia because at his time it was no longer regarded as proximately imminent. But even if this possible connection is unfounded, it is important that the Johannine conceptions of judgment*, life*, and resurrection* lack the vivid eschatological-apocalyptic imagery of the Synoptic Gospels and

Paul. This feature of the Johannine writings permits us to locate the imagery of the Parousia in the wider scheme of early Christian and NT belief; cf below.

The attitude of the NT and the early Church toward the time of Parousia creates one of the more vexing problems of NT exegesis and theology. A number of texts seems to suggest with all desired clarity that the Parousia is an imminent event (Mt 10:23; 24:34; Mk 13:30; Lk 21:32; 1 Th 4:13 ff; 1 Pt 4:7; Apc 3:11; 22:20). It has been suggested that the texts from the synoptic apocalypse (Mt 24:34; Mk 13:30; Lk 21:32) have reference not to the Parousia but to the fall of Jerusalem, which is equally prominent with the Parousia in this discourse. This is possibly evasive of the real problem, which is the conjunction of the fall of Jerusalem and the Parousia in ʼthe discourse. Modern form criticism now shows that the eschatological discourse may be a compilation of sayings of Jesus like the sermon on the mount of Mt 5–7 and thus need never have been delivered in the form in which it stands. The impression of the proximity of the Parousia, however, does not arise from any single text, but from a number of texts found in different books, and it is not altogether honest to attempt to rationalize it out of existence. That the impression was common in the early Church seems to admit no doubt.

One may ask whether this impression should be reduced to the words of Jesus Himself, and there is serious doubt that it should. The current of tradition which contains warnings that the time is entirely unknown is as solidly embedded in early tradition as the impression of the proximity of the Parousia, and one is no more justified in rationalizing this qualification out of existence, or in explaining it as a development which occurred in the literary tradition after the belief in the proximity of the Parousia had been abandoned. On critical grounds these qualifications are as primitive as the passages which suggest that the Parousia is near.

One may combine these themes, it seems, only by preserving both of them. The Parousia was never described by Jesus as an event which was in the remote future; and to be altogether accurate the attitude of the early Church should be described as a hope and an expectation that the Parousia was near rather than a firm conviction that it was near. To this generation the Parousia, which was the consummation of the work of Jesus and of history and the providence of God, was not an event to be feared but to be desired. In a world of such limited geographical and historical horizons the "end of all things" did not appear to be necessarily remote.

The theme of the indefinite time of the Parousia was stronger in the early Church than many students have realized. Many critics have defined the early Church as an "eschatological community" which did nothing except live in common awaiting the Parousia. The Church had no awareness of its mission, these critics say, until it was necessary to renounce the hope that the end was near. This conception can scarcely be combined with the evangelistic work of the apostles, particularly of Paul and his associates; the community which extended itself through so much of the Roman world was not an eschatological group withdrawn from the world. And this movement occurred while the hope that the Parousia was near was still strong, as one can see in the Synoptic Gospels and the epistles of Paul. To describe this uniquely vital and energetic movement as a tight little eschatological group which was content to let the world go to perdition while it awaited the coming of its savior in the clouds seems to be as great a perversion of Jesus and the Church as anyone has ever proposed.

Finally the question of the imagery of the Parousia, which has stimulated so much Christian art and poetry, should be faced. The imagery, as we have observed, is derived mainly from Dn 7:13 f with additions from other OT apocalyptic passages. This imagery the NT did not invent; it found it and applied it to its own conceptions, transforming it in the application. It seems exegetically more secure to treat it as what it appears to be, imagery, and to draw no unwarranted conclusions in detail about the external features of the Parousia. A belief that history tends to a term in which judgment* will be final, God vindicated, and evil definitively overcome, is basic to biblical and Christian faith and cannot be renounced or "demythologized" without reducing that faith to zero. This faith includes no detailed apocalyptic images. A world catastrophe, which the Parousia and the judgment are, must indeed elicit images, but they should be understood as such. One may affirm that Jesus not only asserted that the time of the Parousia is unknown, but also that He uttered no concrete and detailed description of its external features.

Parthians. An Iranian people who appeared in history after the Medes and Persians were absorbed into the Hellenistic empire of Alexander. Under Arsaces I the Parthians won their independence from the Seleucid kings; the dynasty which reigned from this date until AD 225 is called the Arsacid dynasty. In AD 225 the Arsacids were succeeded by the Sassanids. The Parthian kingdom had its heartland SE of the Caspian Sea. In 92 BC they came into contact with Rome; Rome's efforts to extend its frontiers eastward led to a perpetual conflict which was never ended during the entire period of the Roman empire. The Romans were unable to defeat the Parthians and their eastern frontier, the *limes,* was finally erected in order to secure their territory against Parthian incursions; Rome conceded to them the territory of the Euphrates and eastward. 1 Mc 14:2 alludes to the defeat and capture of Demetrius II by the Parthians in 140 BC. The Parthians mentioned in AA 2:9 were Jews resident in the Parthian kingdom.

Pashhur (Hb *pašḥûr*), a personal name; the etymology appears to be Egyptian, *ps ḥor;* there are a number of Egyptian names in priestly families. Pashhur son of Immer was the priest and officer in charge of the temple (Hb *pāḳîd nāgîd*) who had Jeremiah flogged and set in the stocks for predicting the downfall of the temple. On his release Jeremiah predicted disaster and exile for Pashhur and his family (Je 20:1–6). The play on the name of Pashhur, "Terror on all sides" (Hb *māgôr missābîb,* 20:3) cannot be explained by any etymology of the name Pashhur nor by simple assonance; such use of the personal name often involves a paronomasia which cannot be discerned here. The name is borne by two others in the OT, one also a priest contemporary with Jeremiah (Je 21:1).

Passion. The passion narrrative appears in all four Gospels. Scholars believe that it was the first portion of the Gospel to acquire a set form and unity; while it is, like the rest of the Gospels, composed of detached anecdotes (cf GOSPEL), these were woven into a consecutive account almost with the first preaching. It is very probable that the first proclamation of the Gospel consisted in the recital of the passion with no further material concerning the words and deeds of Jesus; and several allusions of Paul to his gospel suggest that he never expanded his preaching by allusions to the life and sayings of Jesus. The passion is proclaimed, not simply narrated; it is the central saving event of the history of salvation, the climax and fulfillment of the saving and judging acts of God. Hence there are numerous allusions to the fulfillment of the OT in the passion; it is the event which gives intelligibility to the law and the prophets. The same kind of interpretation is seen in the triple predictions of the passion (Mt 16:13–23; 17:22–23; 20:17–19; Mk 8:27–33; 9:30–32; 10:32–34; Lk 9:18–22; 9:43–45;

18:31–34). Jesus Himself presents the passion as the goal and the fulfillment of His life and teaching; and in the passion narrative itself the elements of His perfect foreknowledge and freedom in submission to the passion are emphasized.

The passion narrative comprises Mt 26–27; Mk 14–15; Lk 22–23; Jn 18–19. These accounts show a substantial uniformity in the course of events with a large number of small variations. The variations are not merely the result of the flexibility of popular memory and tradition; they also show features of midrash*, interpretation and expansion of the events based on OT texts. Each account proclaims the saving event in its own way. The number or significance of the variations can be seen in the comparative table which follows.

The conspiracy of the Jews, Mt 26:1–3; Mk 14:1–2; Lk 22:1–2 (placed by Jn outside the passion narrative, Jn 11:47–53).

The anointing at Bethany, Mt 26:6–13; Mk 14:3–9 (placed by Lk 7:36–50; Jn 12:1–8 outside the passion narrative). The change in arrangement in Lk–Jn does not alter the interpretation of the passage as an allusion to the burial of Jesus.

The betrayal by Judas, Mt 26:14–16; Mk 14:10–11; Lk 22:3–6 (omitted by Jn, who retains the incident in the garden). Mt introduces in 26:15 a fulfillment of Zc 11:12.

The preparation of the Passover, Mt 36:17–19; Mk 14:12–16; Lk 22:7–13 (omitted by Jn). Mt omits the incident of the man carrying the water pitcher and compresses the rest of the passage.

The designation of Judas as the traitor, Mt 26:20–25; Mk 14:17–25; Lk 22:14 (resumed in 22:21–23). Lk compresses the account and emphasizes the freedom of Jesus in accepting the passion. Omitted in Jn.

The Eucharist*, Mt 26:26–29; Mk 14:22–25; Lk 22:15–20.

Greatness in the kingdom of God, Lk 22:24–30 (placed by Mt 20:25–28 + 19:28; Mk 10:42–45 outside the passion narrative, probably the more original context). Lk emphasizes the connection of the saying with the passion, which is present in Mt–Mk. The washing of the feet (Jn 13:3–16) is parallel.

The two swords, Lk 22:35–38, peculiar to Lk, but expressing the theme of renunciation of defense; cf below. Is 53:12 is quoted in 22:37.

The way to Gethsemani and the prediction of Peter's denial, Mt 26:30–35; Mk 14:26–31; Lk 22:39; Jn 18:1. Zc 13:7 is quoted in Mt 26:31 = Mk 14:27. Lk 22:31–34 and Jn 13:36–38 place the denial slightly earlier.

Gethsemani, Mt 26:36–46; Mk 14:32–42; Lk 22:40–46 (omitted by Jn). Mk is clearly harsher in his description of the mental anguish of Jesus. Lk alone introduces the comforting angel (22:43); the bloody sweat (Lk 22:44) is missing in several important MSS. Lk compresses the event so that the indolence of the disciples is less evident, and omits the saying concerning the spirit and the flesh (Mt 26:41; Mk 14:38). Ps 42:6 is quoted in Mt 26:38 = Mk 14:34.

The arrest of Jesus, Mt 26:47–50; Mk 14:48–52; Lk 22:47–53; Jn 18:2–11. Mt expands the refusal of Jesus to permit defense by the saying of the sword and the angels (Mt 26:52–54). Lk compresses to make the kiss of Judas less offensive. Jn omits the kiss and by the expansion of 18:4–9 shows the freedom and independence of Jesus in submitting to the passion. Lk omits the flight of the disciples. Mk adds the incident of the young man who followed the arresting party.

Jesus before the council and denial of Peter, Mt 26:57–75; Mk 14:53–72; Lk 22:54–71. Lk differs from Mt–Lk in his arrangement of the denials of Peter and in his omission of any reference to a nocturnal session of the council; probably he wished to simplify a complicated course of events. The double title of Messiah-Son of God in Mt–Mk becomes the object of two questions in Lk; the divine sonship is thus more explicitly professed. All three quote Dn 7:13 in the answer of Jesus; cf SON OF MAN. Jn 18:13–27 goes his own way; he alone places Jesus in the house of Annas* and omits the profession of Messiahship and sonship. In Jn the blow is given to Jesus for His bold answer and not in mockery of His power of prophecy.

The delivery of Jesus to Pilate, Mt 27:1–2; Mk 15:1; Lk 23:1; Jn 18:28.

The death of Judas, only in Mt 27:3–10; Zc 11:12 f is quoted in 27:9 f.

The trial before Pilate, Mt 27:11–14; Mk 15:2–5; Lk 23:2–5; Jn 18:29–38. Only Lk and Jn mention the charges laid against Jesus. The question of the kingship of Jesus, found in Mt–Mk–Lk, is expanded by Jn into a dialogue on the nature of Jesus's kingship. Both Lk and Jn mention Pilate's affirmation of the innocence of Jesus in this context.

Jesus before Herod, only in Lk 23:6–16. Here also Lk emphasizes the innocence of Jesus.

The sentence of death, Mt 27:15–26; Mk 15:6–15; Lk 23:17–25; Jn 18:39–19:16. Variations are numerous here. Mt alone has the episode of the wife of Pilate and the washing of hands by Pilate. Lk omits the scourging. The conditions under which Barabbas* is released are obscure. Jn elaborates the passage notably; he places the scourging and the mocking before the sentence and makes them an effort by Pilate to satisfy the Jews, adding the scene of the display of Jesus. He expands the dialogue between Pilate and the Jews and Pilate and Jesus, introducing here the motif of the sonship of Jesus and making explicit the pressure which the Jews put upon Pilate.

The mocking of the soldiers, Mt 27:27–31; Mk 15:16–20; Jn (above). Lk omits, most probably from delicacy. The incident brings out the kingship of Jesus.

The journey to Calvary, Mt 27:32; Mk 15:21; Lk 23:26–32; Jn 19:17. Jn omits the assistance given to Jesus by Simon. Lk expands by the incident of the meeting of Jesus with the women of Jerusalem and introduces the theme of judgment, quoting Ho 10:8.

The crucifixion, Mt 27:33–44; Mk 15:22–32; Lk 23:33–43; Jn 19:18–27. There is some variation in the order of the incidents between Lk and Mt–Mk. Only Lk introduces the title of king in the mockery of the Jews. Only Lk has the prayer of Jesus for His executioners and the dialogue between Jesus and the repentant thief; these bring out the theme of mercy. Lk–Jn omit the offer of a narcotic drink. Jn alone has the controversy between Pilate and the Jews concerning the title affixed to the cross; this emphasizes the kingship of Jesus. Ps 22:19 is quoted in Mt 27:35; Mk 15:24; Lk 23:34; Jn 19:24. Ps 22:8 is quoted in Mt 27:39; Mk 15:29; Lk 23:35. Ps 22:9 is quoted in Mt 27:43. The use of this Ps in the narrative is probably expanded from its use in the following section. Only Jn has the words commending Mary to the care of the beloved disciple.

The death of Jesus, Mt 27:45–56; Mk 15:33–41; Lk 23:44–49; Jn 19:28–30. The darkness which covers the earth (missing in Jn) makes the death of Jesus a cosmic event. The words of Ps 22:2, put in the mouth of Jesus in Mt–Mk, are missing in Lk–Jn; Lk has a quotation of Ps 31:6, and Jn the words "I thirst" and "It is finished." Ps 69:22 is alluded to in Mt 27:48; Mk 15:36. The rending of the veil in Mk, a symbol of the evacuation of the law and of Jewish cult, is expanded in Mt by earthquake and appearance of the dead, making the death of Jesus again a cosmic event; Lk–Jn omit these. The profession of the centurion in Lk is altered from son of God to a righteous man; it is missing in Jn. Lk alone mentions the compunction of the bystanders.

The burial of Jesus, Mt 27:56–61; Mk 15:42–47; Lk 50–56; Jn 19:31–38. The expansion of Jn (19:31–37) is intended to affirm the reality of the death of Jesus. Ex 12:46 (the Passover lamb) and Zc 12:10 are quoted. Mk 15:44–45 (missing in Mt–

Lk) is also intended to affirm the reality of the death.

The watch at the tomb, only in Mt 27:62–66, affirms the reality of the burial and looks forward to the resurrection; the guard makes the Jewish explanation of the empty tomb impossible.

From this synopsis it is evident that most of the themes in the proclamation of the passion are common and must belong to the earliest traditions. The most significant theme is that Jesus fulfills His Messiahship and His kingship in the passion. The numerous OT allusions show that the event is achieved by God and not by men, who in their own evil purpose accomplish His saving will.

Date of the Passion. A number of data drawn from early Christian traditions and extrabiblical information have led the majority of scholars to retain the established opinion that AD 30 was the year of the death of Jesus. A considerable number of modern scholars, however, maintain the date AD 33, a smaller number the date AD 29. Dates proposed by individuals as far divergent as 21, 24, or 36 must be disregarded as merely eccentric. The problem of the date is complicated by a clear divergence between Mt–Mk–Lk and Jn on the Passover. Jn, who does not present the last supper as a Passover meal, clearly makes the Friday of the death of Jesus the eve of the Passover, the 14th Nisan. Mt–Mk–Lk with equal clarity present the supper as the Passover meal and by implication make Thursday the 14th of Nisan. There is no generally accepted solution of this problem; here its elements are presented.

It has been suggested that Jn altered the date in order to connect the death of Jesus with the killing of the Passover lambs. The use of this theme in Jn is undeniable (cf LAMB), but the alteration is not immediately evident. It could be argued with some probability that Mt–Mk–Lk altered the date in order to show the Eucharist* as the Christian Passover. At the present state of knowledge it seems wiser not to appeal to theological considerations as the reason for the variation.

The argument adduced by some that Passover was an improbable day for a trial and execution is not convincing, at least for the execution; parallels are known.

Jn appears to be supported by two passages of the Talmud. One places the death of Jesus on the 14th Nisan; the other places the Passover amnesty (cf BARABBAS) on the eve of the Passover, the 14th Nisan.

Astronomical calculations unfortunately are not sufficiently established to be decisive. According to a calculation widely accepted the 14th Nisan fell on Friday in 30 and 33 in the years under consideration, the 15th Nisan on Friday only in 34. This would be decisive for Jn if it were certain. But in addition to some difficulties, the calculation itself assumes that the Jewish calendar was regulated with astronomical precision. It appears certain that it was not. The observation of the new moon in Jerusalem was the point from which the beginning of the month was calculated, and it is obvious that this could not be rigorous.

Many scholars believe that one must choose between one date and the other; and since the year 30 on other factors seems most probable, this means that they accept the date of Jn. Others believe that it is possible to reconcile the two dates by discovering different calendars employed. The theory of Mlle A. Jaubert has been accepted by a large number of distinguished scholars, although they form as yet a minority. Jaubert has pointed out that the Qumran* documents, the book of Jubilees, the book of Enoch and the Damascus Document (cf APOCRYPHAL BOOKS) exhibit a solar calendar in which Passover always falls on Wednesday. How much this calendar was used is not known; Jaubert points out that in this calendar the Passover supper would be celebrated on Tuesday. It was by this calendar that Jesus and the disciples celebrated the Passover supper; and she draws the surprising conclusion that Jesus was arrested on Tuesday night and executed on Friday. Jn, who follows the official calendar, places the death on the 14th of Nisan (in the year 30). The three day interval is not an impossible objection to the theory; such telescoping is not foreign to the Gospels or to biblical narrative in general. What must be preserved is the agreement of the four Gospels that Jesus died on a Friday.

M. H. Shepherd has proposed a divergence of calendars without invoking an unattested three day interval. He believes that Palestinian Jews reckoned the beginning of the month from the observation of the new moon and the Jews of the Diaspora* by a fixed calendar, since observation would allow far too much variation. Jn, the most Palestinian of the Gospels, follows the Palestinian calendar; Mk, written for Gentiles and followed by Mt–Lk, employs the Diaspora calendar. The date, he believes, was reached by calculation from the Diaspora calendar to the year of Jesus's death, 30, which was recent enough to be remembered exactly. This calendar variation is as yet unattested by documents.

Passover (Hb *pesaḥ*, meaning and etymology uncertain), an Israelite festival. In usage the word seems to designate both the feast and the animal eaten at the festival banquet. The Passover ritual is set forth in Ex 12:1–28, where it is combined with the festival of Mazzoth*. The rite consists of a banquet in which a yearling lamb is eaten. The lamb is to be roasted entire, and what is not eaten at the banquet must be burned before the next day. The diners eat it standing and dressed for a journey. Blood is smeared on the doorpost to ward off the destroying angel who slew the firstborn of the Egyptians. Ex 12:43–49 adds that no one is to eat of the Passover who is not circumcised. The feast is mentioned in the festival lists of Lv 23:5; Nm 28:16; Ezk 45:21. Dt 16:1–5 modifies the observance; the killing of the lamb becomes a quasi-sacrificial act which is to be performed only at the sanctuary, and the banquet also is to be eaten at the sanctuary. Nm 9:2–14 lays down requirements of ritual cleanness* for the Passover. Passover is not mentioned in the festival list of the covenant code (cf LAW), where the feast of Mazzoth appears. Jos 5:10 f relates the observance of the Passover at the entrance of the Israelites into Canaan; the historical value of this notice is slight, and it appears to state the ideal of observance and to make the entrance into Canaan coincide with the anniversary of the exodus. The festival is not mentioned in the historical books thereafter until 2 K 23:21–23, which relates the observance in the reform of Josiah*. The notice that no such Passover had been observed since the time of the judges has led many scholars to conclude that the Passover celebration fell into abeyance under the monarchy, and some to believe that the Passover did not exist until it was instituted by Josiah. This view is now generally regarded as unfounded. 2 Ch 35:1–20 describes the Passover of Josiah in a much expanded form; there is little doubt that this represents some of the liturgy of the postexilic period. The Passover attributed by 2 Ch 30 to Hezekiah* is doubtfully historical; it is more probably an instance of the manner in which Ch attributes various virtues and devotions to pious kings (cf CHRONICLES).

The descriptions of the festival show a number of variations which indicate a complex origin and development. It is a very common opinion of scholars that the Passover was originally a pastoral festival which celebrated the spring yeaning; many modern scholars believe that it is older than the period of the exodus, and that it was the festival which is mentioned in Ex 5:1. The festival has been historicized; it becomes a celebration of the exodus which is symbolized in the Passover dinner by the posture and garb of the diners. It has also acquired the motif of the substitution of the animal for the firstborn of Israel who belong to Yahweh (Ex 13:11–16). The firstborn are not only redeemed by the substitution of the animal; they are spared from the death inflicted on the firstborn of Egypt by the destroying angel. The smearing of the blood upon the doorpost is an apotropaic rite of rather wide use, and it is very probable that the rite was in use before its connection with the story of the firstborn. Indeed, a number of scholars suggest that the story of the firstborn has been created from the ritual practice. By historicization Passover became the great national feast of Israel which celebrated its establishment as the people of Yahweh. The festival is a reliving of the exodus. It is very likely that the exodus accounts of Ex 4–15 are taken from the recitals which were a part of the Passover festival; such a recital is prescribed in Ex 12:27. There is no satisfactory explanation of the absence of Passover in the code of the covenant; one may hazard the guess that this code came from those Israelite tribes which had not shared in the exodus experience and had not yet begun to celebrate Passover.

According to the Synoptic Gospels the supper (cf EUCHARIST) which Jesus celebrated with His disciples the night before His death was the Passover supper (Mt 26:2, 17–19; Mk 14:12–17; Lk 22:7–14). Jn does not explicitly affirm or deny that this was a Passover supper; but Jn 18:28; 19:14 says clearly that the Jews had not yet eaten the Passover supper when Jesus died. This celebrated difficulty has received no generally accepted solution; cf PASSION; CALENDAR.

The title of lamb is applied to Jesus in Jn 1:29, 36, possibly with an allusion to the Passover lamb; but cf LAMB. Jn 19:36 certainly applies the typology of the Passover lamb to Jesus, as does Paul in 1 Co 5:7. The application is somewhat loose, since the Passover lamb is not clearly a sacrifice in the OT. The Passover typology is by no means clear in 1 Pt 1:19. A typological connection between the Passover supper and the Eucharist is suggested only in Lk 22:16 among the Eucharistic passages. Since the death of Jesus occurred at Passover, many Passover themes have been introduced into the Christian liturgy of the Holy Week and Easter cycle.

Pastoral Epistles. Since 1750 1–2 Tm and Tt have been grouped under the title "Pastoral Epistles." The three have common subject matter, theological direction, and vocabulary and style, and are best treated together.

1. *Contents.*
A. 1 Tm.

1:1–2, greeting.
I. False Teachers, 1:3–20:
1:3–7, description of false teachers of the Law.
1:8–11, the meaning and value of the Law.
1:12–17, the call of the apostle to preach the gospel.
1:18–20, combat against the false teachers.
II. Problems of Discipline, 2:1–3:16:
2:1–15, public worship, prayer for all men, position of men and women.
3:1–13, qualities of bishops and deacons.
3:14–16, the divine mystery entrusted to the Church.
III. Practices of False Teachers, 4:1–11:
4:1–5, certain false prohibitions and false attitude toward creatures.
4:6–11, method of combating these practices.
IV. Counsels to Timothy, 4:12–6:2:
4:12–16, exemplary life and diligence in his work.
5:1–6:2, how to deal with different ages, widows, elders, slaves.
Conclusion, 6:3–19:
6:3–10, vices of false teachers.
6:11–16, exhortation to Timothy.
6:17–19, right use of wealth.
Final recommendation and warning, 6:20–21.
B. Tt is very similar in form and content to 1 Tm:
1:1–4, greeting.
I. Duties of Titus, 1:5–16:
1:5–9, qualities of bishops.
1:10–16, combat against false teachers.
II. Problems of Discipline, 2:1–2:11:
2:11–15, the grace of God which imposes Christian ideals.
3:1–3, duties toward superiors and fellow men.
3:3–8, the regeneration which imposes the duties of a new life.
3:9–11, counsels against errors and false teachers.
Final Instruction and Greetings, 3:12–15.
C. 2 Tm.
1:1–2, greeting.
I. Exhortations to Timothy, 1:3–2:13:
1:3–5, thanksgiving for Timothy's fidelity.
1:6–14, fearless profession of the faith and patience in suffering.
1:15–18, Paul's sufferings in Ephesus.
2:1–13, fidelity to apostolic tradition and patience in suffering.
II. Instructions concerning False Teachers, 2:14–4:8:
2:14–21, warning against useless disputes.
2:22–26, charitable instruction the best means of conversion.
3:1–9, the confusion created by false teachers.

3:10–17, fidelity to traditional teaching and the Scriptures.

4:1–8, duty of preaching with zeal and strength.

Conclusion: requests, counsels, greetings, 4:9–22.

2. *Authorship.* Most modern critics seriously question the Pauline origin of the Pastoral Epistles; the discussion involves all the problems of their language, style, theology, and occasion. Critics point out these features of the Pastoral Epistles:

They are addressed not to the congregation, as are the other letters of the Pauline corpus, but to the head of the Church. They are less concerned with exposition of doctrine than with questions of church organization and government. A hierarchy of bishops, elders, and deacons is evident. The mission of the bishop is to govern the church and to teach. The teaching rests not on a gospel* or a preaching* but on apostolic tradition*; with the Scripture this forms a deposit of faith, and the office of the bishop is to preserve this deposit against false doctrines. An idea of apostolic succession both in doctrine and in government of the Church has appeared.

Compared with the earlier epistles the Church is now seen as a reality existing in the present world; there is almost no eschatological tension. Dibelius said that the Pastoral Epistles present "a Christianity of orthodoxy and good works"; the statement is exaggerated, but there is certainly a shift of emphasis. There are no charismata* in the churches of the Pastoral Epistles. Orthodoxy and good works are not foreign to the earlier epistles, but they occupy a more subordinate position to the exposition of the gospel. The definition of the Church in 1 Tm 3:15 is new in Pauline thought. The hymn of the mystery of salvation in 1 Tm 3:16 is, in the words of L. Cerfaux, "quite independent of Pauline ideas." Heretical teachers have appeared of a character not known in the earlier epistles; they are apparently connected with Judaism and Gnosticism (1 Tm 1:4; 4:3; 2 Tm 2:18; Tt 1:14; 3:9).

The language and style exhibit obvious differences from the earlier letters. Of a vocabulary of 848 words 306 do not appear in the other 10 letters. J. Jeremias writes: "When compared to Paul's general usage, the vocabulary of the Pastoral Epistles as a whole shows closer contacts with the educated everyday language of the Hellenistic world, and with the language of Hellenistic-Jewish wisdom teaching, of popular philosophy, and of court style." The style is smooth and dull compared to the earlier letters; it is never impassioned, usually assertive and instructive. Many critics call it

an imitation; theological ideas are elaborated in dependence on the earlier epistles, and psychological and rhetorical traits foreign to Paul are introduced. AA, according to some critics, is used to create situations (cf 2 Tm 3:11 in relation to AA 13:44–14:22). But it is impossible to fit the allusions of the Pastorals into the situations of Paul's life as narrated in AA. They must therefore be placed after his imprisonment in Rome, which ended in 63. Tradition, however, places his death in 67, but this is not certainly established; his death may have followed the imprisonment with which AA concludes.

These considerations led many scholars of the 19th century to place the Pastoral Epistles as late as AD 150. This view is now abandoned; they are quoted by Polycarp (155), are very probably alluded to by Ignatius of Antioch (107), and are to be placed before 1 Clement (95), which shows a more highly developed hierarchical structure than the Pastoral Epistles. Those who maintain the Pauline authorship point out that the principal Pauline themes are retained in the Pastoral Epistles and that the hierarchy of the epistles is archaic and primitive. They point out that the letters of the captivity (Phl, Eph, Col) form a link between the early letters and the Pastoral Epistles; in these there appear the themes of the mystery*, of knowledge*, of moral instruction and of the combat against false doctrines. They postulate a development of the thought and language of Paul, observing that his creative period ends with the letters of the captivity; after these his attention is drawn to formalizing his teaching, to preserving it against distortion, to organizing his churches on a stable basis which can survive his departure. These are valid points; but the time allowed for this development is very brief, 63–67 at most.

Recent and prevailing modern theory attempts to combine the Pauline features with the marks of other hands. Scholars propose that an unknown author collected what remained of the correspondence of Paul with Timothy and Titus and incorporated it into his own work, conceived and written in terms of the needs of his own times. This author need not be put as late as the early 2nd century with most critics; indeed, there is no reason to deny that he was a disciple and companion of Paul who intended to relate the teaching of Paul to new situations. In any case, it seems impossible to attribute the Pastoral Epistles to Paul in the same way in which the great epistles are attributed to him. Those who maintain the Pauline origin of the letters concede that they must be proximately the work of an amanuensis who composed from very general instructions and wrote like himself rather than like Paul. This explanation is not entirely satisfactory, since all of Paul's letters were written by an amanuensis, and it is hard to find a reason why this liberty should have occurred here (and in Eph) and nowhere else.

A response of the Pontifical Biblical Commission of June 12, 1913, affirmed that the Pauline origin of the Pastoral Epistles is to be maintained. This statement stands; but the developments of criticism have added no strength to their Pauline origin. They should therefore be used with caution and reserve as sources of Pauline theology or as sources for the organization of the Church during the life of Paul.

Patara (Gk *patara*, meaning uncertain), a port of Lycia* at the mouth of the Xanthus on the S coast of Asia Minor, touched by Paul on his journey from Ephesus to Tyre (AA 21:1). The ancient harbor has been silted up. Remains of a theater and a triumphal arch can be seen at the site, which has not been explored.

Patmos (Gk *patmos*, meaning uncertain), a small island of the Sporades in the Aegean Sea off the W coast of Asia Minor, W of Samos and WSW of Ephesus, where the author of Apc had his visions (Apc 1:9).

Patrobas (Gk *patrobās*, shortened form of Patrobius, "life of the father"), a Roman Christian greeted by Paul* (Rm 16:14).

Pathros, Pathrusim (Hb *patrôs, patrūsîm*, Egyptian *p,'-t,'-rsy*, "south country"), a geographical name designating upper Egypt, i.e., Egypt S of the delta. It was one of the places to which the Israelites were scattered after the fall of Jerusalem (Is 11:11; Je 44:1, 15) and is threatened by Ezk (30:14). These passages suggest a distinction between Egypt proper (the delta) and Pathros. In the table* of nations (Gn 10:14; cf 1 Ch 1:12) the Pathrusim are the descendants of Egypt.

Patriarch. In exegesis the name "patriarch" has long been given to those biblical personages who appear in Gn from Adam to Joseph. For further details of separate articles.

Gn 5 (the P tradition) lists 10 generations between Adam and Noah whereas Gn 4 (the J tradition) lists 8:

J			P
1 Adam			1 Adam
2 Cain	Abel	Seth	2 Seth
		Enos	
3 Enoch			3 Enosh
4 Irad			4 Kenan
5 Mehujael			5 Mahalalel
6 Methushael			6 Jared
7 Lamech			7 Enoch
8 Jabal, Jubal, Tubal-cain,			8 Methushelah
Noah?			9 Lamech
			10 Noah

A comparison of the names in the two lists suggests that they come from the same source: Cain-Kenan, Enoch-Enoch, Irad-Jared, Methushael-Methushelah, Lamech-Lamech. Furthermore Enosh (Hb *'enôš*, "man") is quite possibly a duplicate of Adam; and Mehujael-Mahalalel are not so remote from each other that a single name as their common source is impossible. A source has been suggested in Mesopotamian literature in the list of kings who reigned before the deluge. This list is preserved in Gk fragments of the work of Berossus, a Babylonian priest of the 2nd century BC, and in a Sumerian king list. The years of reign attributed to each king are added for comparison with the ages attributed to the patriarchs in Gn 5.

These two lists are not identical but, like the lists of Gn, must be related in origin. The first four names in each list exhibit possible connections, as do Daos-Dumuzi, En-men-dur-Anna-Evedorachos. Ubaradudu-Xisuthros is the hero of the deluge*. As in Gn, one list has 10 generations, the other has 8. Pautibibla is probably Badtibira, and Laracha in Larak. Babylon, the home of Berossus and the great city of later Mesopotamia, has been substituted for the Sumerian Eridu as the city to which "kingship

Sumerian (ANET 265)		Berossus	
1 Alulim of Eridu	28800	1 Aloros of Babylon	36000
2 Alalgar of Eridu	36000	2 Alaparos of Babylon	10800
3 Enmenluanna of Badtibira	43200	3 Amelon of Pautibibla	46800
4 Enmengalanna of Badtibira . . .	28800	4 Amenon of Pautibibla	43200
5 Dumuzi of Badtibira	36000	5 Megalaros of Pautibibla	64800
6 Ensipazianna of Larak	28800	6 Daos of Pautibibla	36000
7 En-men-dur-Anna of Shurippak . .	21000	7 Evedorachos of Pautibibla	64800
8 Ubaradudu of Shurippak	18600	8 Amempsinos of Laracha	36000
		9 Otiastes of Laracha	28000
		10 Xisuthros	64800

came down from heaven." A connection between these names and the biblical lists is difficult to establish on the basis of the names. But the conception of 10 or 8 generations who lived to great ages before the deluge is certainly common to Gn and to the Mesopotamian lists. The idea of king has disappeared from Gn; the Gn traditions were formed at a period when the Israelites thought of their ancestors as nomads*. Despite the difficulty of connecting the names of the Mesopotamian lists with the lists of Gn, the basic conception is too similar to be explained as merely coincidental, and the biblical lists must be at least in a wide sense derived from the same source.

The lists, while the names may preserve memories of persons who existed, are without historical value. In both Mesopotamia and Israel they are a substitute for history and tradition; they are used as "fillers" for the long period of unknown length which lay between the beginning of man and the beginning of historical recollection. Both sets of lists exhibit the popular belief that prehistoric man lived to a great age; this has been supported by no research in prehistory and must be regarded as a popular belief and no more. The Mesopotamian figures are notably higher than the biblical figures, but no certain conclusions can be drawn from this difference. The ages of the patriarchs have notable variations in Hb, the LXX and the Samaritan Pentateuch, although the variations remain in the same general range and do not approach the Mesopotamian figures. All three systems appear to be the result of artificial calculations which probably have some symbolic meaning; but efforts to uncover the symbolism have not been successful. There is little doubt that the ages and the synchronisms are intended to convey an impression of the family unity of primitive man. Thus Adam survives to the time of Lamech, the father of Noah. Noah himself outlives Nahor* and lives into the life of Abraham, and Shem, the eponymous ancestor of the Semites, outlives Abraham. Seth sees the "taking" of Enoch and dies only a few years before the birth of Noah. This is the family which is wiped out except for one group in the deluge. The genealogy of P appears to know nothing of the Eden story of J (Gn 2–3) and of Cain and Abel. The progressive deterioration of man sketched by J is replaced by the single catastrophe of the deluge.

The patriarchal narratives of Abraham*, Isaac*, Jacob* and his sons form the prologue to the history of Israel. They are not properly a history of tribal origins; the historian seeks in them faint memories of earlier tribal history, but fails to reconstruct a picture which even approaches completeness. Even at the time when the patriarchal traditions were compiled in the literary sources of Gn they had lost much of the detailed memory of the events. The patriarchal traditions are primarily a prologue to the history of salvation, not to political and economic history.

The "history of salvation" theme, however, has been imposed upon the traditions by the authors of the sources of the Pnt, and was not primary in many of the anecdotes of the traditions. Upon examination the stories of the patriarchs appear as detached anecdotes clustering about the person of the patriarch with no particular chronological arrangement. Some of them were probably in their original form centered not upon the patriarch but upon some place or some other person. How much of a selection was made by the authors of the Pnt it is difficult to say. The compilations of J and E reduced the anecdotes to unity around the person of the patriarch and certain leading themes: the revelation of God to the patriarchs, the promise of a numerous posterity which should become a great people, and the promise of the land of Canaan in which the patriarchs lived as nomadic herdsmen. The fidelity of the compilers to their material appears in the fact that the patriarchs are not represented as Israelite (understanding here Israelite after Moses) in their beliefs and their cult; the few retrojections of later belief and practice belong to P. It appears also in their rather pedestrian description of the patriarchs; the patriarchs are not heroes of arms nor wonderworkers nor paragons of virtue, but rather humble nomad sheikhs who are not able to meet the kings and chieftains with whom they come in contact on any better than even terms. The fidelity to their material, however, does not imply that the material is more historical than they found it. The character of the traditions permitted the writers to impose upon them a dominant theological interpretation of revelation and providence. The God of Israel was the God of the fathers, and the providence of Yahweh which Israel admired in the exodus and settlement was the same providence which had carried their nomadic fathers through the lands of their wandering until their descendants became numerous enough to take possession of the land. The fathers were not indeed paragons of virtue, but they were presented as ideal figures of men who lived in worshipful submission to the God who had revealed Himself to them and expected from His hand whatever blessings they were to receive. In a word, Yahweh had always been the God of Israel, even if His manifestation of Himself to the ancestors of Israel was less brilliant and overpowering than His manifestation in the exodus. There was a continuity between the will of Yahweh as known to the Fathers and as known to Israel; His election in both cases imposed responsibilities which must be met if harmonious relations are to be maintained. He is a God who can do what He promises, but He demands fidelity.

Paul (Lt *Paul(l)us*), a Roman patrician name taken by Saul of Tarsus and the name by which he is known; the use of a Gk or Lt name in addition to or in place of a Jewish name was common among Jews of the Diaspora*.

1. *Sources.* The sources for the life of Paul are found almost entirely in the Bible: AA 7:58, 9:1–30; 11:25–30; 13–28; autobiographical allusions in the epistles: Rm 11:1; 1 Co 15:8 f; 2 Co 11:22–12:12; Gal 1:11–2:14; Phl 3:4–6; 2 Tm 1:5; 3:10–11: For the period of Paul's life later than the biblical allusions there are a few traditions preserved by Clement of Rome; cf below.

2. *Chronology.* Paul's life can be related to three dates fixed by external history: the death of Herod Agrippa* (AD 44); the administration of Gallio* at Corinth* (AD 50/51 or 51/52); the administration of Felix* at Caesarea* (AD 58–60). Paul himself puts 14 years between his conversion and his visit to Jerusalem after his first journey; cf below.

Birth	AD	5–15
Arrival in Jerusalem		30
Conversion		34–36
Sojourn in Damascus and Arabia (3 years)		
Visit to Jerusalem		37–39
Sojourn at Tarsus		
Arrival at Antioch		43–44
1st missionary journey		45–49
Visit to Jerusalem		49
2nd missionary journey		49–52
At Corinth		50–52
1–2 Th		51–52
3rd journey		53–58
Ephesus		54–57
Gal		54
1 Co		54
Macedonia		57
2 Co		57
Corinth		57–58
Rm		57–58
Jerusalem		58
Caesarea		58–60
Voyage to Rome		60–61
Rome		61–63
Col, Phl, Eph, Phm		61–63
Voyage to Spain? and to E?		63–67
Roman captivity		
Death		67–68?

3. *Life.* Paul was born at Tarsus (AA 22:3) of Jewish parents who traced their ancestry to the tribe of Benjamin (Rm 11:1; Phl 3:5). The date of his birth is calculated from the statement that he was a young man at the time of the death of Stephen* (AA 7:58), an event itself of uncertain date but not much later than the death of Jesus. Paul spoke both Gr and Aramaic (AA 21:40; 26:14). The extent of his education in Gk learning is uncertain; many scholars postulate it, but his writings show no definite traces of Gk learning which Paul's alert mind could not have picked up by his associations. That Paul had a married sister residing in Jerusalem (AA 23:16) has led some to conclude that his entire family moved to Jerusalem when Paul reached the city as a young man. Paul possessed the citizenship of Tarsus and of Rome (AA 16:37 ff; 21:39; 22:25 ff; 25:10 ff); this privilege was of service to him in his missionary journeys. He was a tentmaker by trade (AA 18:3); the rabbis refused to accept fees for instruction and learned a trade by which they could support themselves independently. Paul did not extend this rabbinical principle to the apostolate, but himself never renounced the independence which self-support gave him (1 Co 9:1–18). It is all but certain that Paul came to Jerusalem after the death of Jesus and that he never saw Jesus during His earthly life; it is scarcely less certain that he came no more than a few years after the death of Jesus. In Jerusalem he was a student of Gamaliel* (AA 22:3); from his rabbinical studies or from his home training or from both he became what in his own terms can only be understood as a rigid Pharisee* (AA 23:6; 1 Co 15:9; Gal 1:13; Phl 3:6). His part in the stoning of Stephen seems to have been more than that of a simple participant (AA 7:58); and he became an agent of the council of Jerusalem in its attack upon the Christians (AA 9:1 ff).

The conversion of Paul occurred as a result of his experience on the road to Damascus; Jesus appeared to him and Paul was ill and blinded for a few days until he was cured and baptized by Ananias* (AA 9). The experience is narrated in two other passages (AA 22:6–16; 26:12–18); the variations in these accounts are slight. All the accounts make clear the decisive importance of the Damascus experience not only in the conversion of Paul, but also in determining the personal qualities of his faith and his gospel: its focus on Jesus as the glorified Lord who has risen from His saving death and lives in His Church; Paul's own commission to preach Christ to the Gentiles, with implications for the universal scope of the gospel which even Paul did not see immediately; the concept of election*; the total salvation which Jesus brings; the importance of the resurrection*.

The experience is difficult to analyze; there is scarcely any parallel instance in recorded history of such a sudden and complete personal reversal. For this reason many historians have postulated some degree of preparation in Paul's previous experience. Of such preparation there is no trace; and the candor and keenness of Paul's insight makes it most unlikely that he should have been ignorant of such a gradual transformation or that he should have concealed it. Paul himself based his entire career on his conviction that he had seen the real Jesus in the flesh — the risen and glorified Jesus; and this experience was the base of his claim that he was an apostle* of the same rank and rights as the Twelve (1 Co 9:1).

After his conversion Paul was uncertain of his future. Combining the data of AA 9 and Gal 1, it appears that he first went to Arabia for three years; Arabia here most probably means the Nabataean* kingdom. Paul himself gives no reason for this interval; it must be understood as a retirement to the desert* like the retirements of Moses*, Elijah* and Jesus Himself. When he returned he began to preach Jesus in Damascus, apparently to the Jews; his mission to the Gentiles was not yet clear, or the manner in which he should execute it had not yet become practical. In his first preaching he encountered the hatred of the Jews which pursued him the rest of his life; he was then what he has been since, the great renegade. It was probably after his flight from Damascus that he returned to Jerusalem for the first time since his departure as a persecutor and there met the apostles (Gal 1:18 f). Paul's brief allusion to this visit is intended to affirm that he was accepted by the Jerusalem group, but that he did not derive his gospel from their instruction; he received his gospel from Jesus Himself. From Jerusalem — where several allusions make it clear that he was welcome neither to Jews nor Christians — he went back to his home city of Tarsus for a few years. There is no record of any activity there; and it is possible that Paul was idled and discouraged by his failure to win the acceptance even of his fellow believers. The first Gentile church, the church of Antioch*, can scarcely be attributed to Paul; it seems rather that it was this Gentile church which made him the apostle of the Gentiles.

Saul was rescued from oblivion by Barnabas*, who brought him to Antioch and secured him a position as teacher in the church there; he was sent to Jerusalem as a companion of Barnabas with a donation. Paul himself does not mention this journey, which seems to have included no further conferences with the Jerusalem church. After their return to Antioch Barnabas and Paul were commissioned by the church of Antioch to preach the gospel where it had not yet been proclaimed. The first journey, 45–49, took them to Cyprus, Perga, Antioch of Pisidia, and the cities of Lycaonia (AA 13–14). Their practice was to preach first in the synagogue of the city to the Jews. This was continued in later missions; the statement attributed to Paul and Barnabas at Antioch (AA 13:46 f) is probably a summary of the principle that the apostles turned to the Gentiles only when the Jews refused the message. The hostility shown by the Jews of Lycaonia was violent.

At the end of the first journey the controversy concerning the obligation of the Gentiles to observe the law* came to a head. On the variations between AA and Paul's account in Gal cf ACTS OF THE APOSTLES. The accounts agree that Paul's principle that Christianity imposed no obligations of Judaism on Gentiles was accepted by the Jerusalem church; from Paul's letters we learn that it was not accepted by many Jewish Christians. The incident of Antioch involving Peter and Gentile Christians is placed by Paul (Gal 2) after the agreement of Jerusalem was reached.

The 2nd journey was begun shortly after the return of Paul and Barnabas to Antioch (AA 15:36–18:21). The beginning of the trip was marred by the dissension of Paul and Barnabas over Mark, and Paul's companion on the 2nd journey was Silas*. This was the most significant of the three journeys; after passing through Cilicia, Lycaonia, Phrygia, and Galatia, Paul in consequence of a dream (which probably confirmed him in a decision already formed) first preached the gospel on the continent of Europe. He founded churches in the Macedonian cities of Philippi, Thessalonica, and Beroea, and experienced again the hostility of the Jews, who had both Paul and Silas imprisoned in Philippi. His forced retirement from Beroea was responsible for his presence in Athens, where his discourse on the Areopagus* made a very slight impression. From Athens he went to Corinth; there he met Priscilla* and Aquila*. Jewish hostility was neutralized by the indifference of Gallio*, and Paul during a residence of about two years founded the most famous of his churches. 1–2 Th were most probably written from Corinth.

The 3rd journey was begun after a short rest at Antioch (AA 18:23–21:14). Paul again visited Phrygia and Galatia, but most of the journey was spent establishing the church of the large and important city of Ephesus. The visit to Asia brought Paul into contact with Apollos* and some others who had received the baptism of John the Baptist. The riot of the silversmiths at Ephesus is the first recorded instance of hostility to the Christians exhibited by Gentiles, and the hostility is explained as not genuinely religious in origin. Whether the riot is intended by Paul's reference to his "conflict with beasts" at Ephesus (1 Co 15:32) is uncertain. The troubles of the church of Corinth complicated his travel plans on this journey and his course is not altogether certain; cf CORINTHIANS, EPISTLES TO. 1 Co was written from Ephesus; Paul then reached Macedonia, where he wrote 2 Co. Rm was written from Corinth. Paul did not return to Antioch after this journey but reached Jerusalem via Tyre. The account of his meetings with the elders of Ephesus at Miletus and with the disciples at Caesarea contains premonitions of suffering which awaited him at Jerusalem. Paul's intention, suggested by the choice of his companions, seems to have been to go to Jerusalem for a decisive demonstration that Gentiles were full Christians. The advice of the Jerusalem officers that he perform rites of purification in the temple was the occasion of the riots of the Jews which led to Paul's arrest and his appearance before the council. The incidents show how deep was the hatred of Paul felt by the Jews of Jerusalem. To protect him from assassination the Romans transferred him to Caesarea. The venal Felix*, governor at the time, heard the charges of the Jews, but allowed the case to pend until he received a bribe, which Paul did not give him. Festus*, who succeeded Felix, reopened the case; but Paul, apparently not certain of Festus, employed his privilege as a Roman citizen to appeal to the tribunal of Caesar in Rome. Before he was sent to Rome Festus invited him to address Agrippa* and Bernice*. The ship on which Paul sailed from Myra was wrecked off the coast of Malta, and Paul landed at Puteoli in the following spring. AA describes him as confined under an easy house arrest in Rome for two years, but says nothing of the final disposal of his case. "The captivity epistles" (Phl, Phm, Col, Eph) are to be attributed to this period.

Clement of Rome attests a voyage of Paul to the W (Spain?) after his imprisonment in Rome. The pastoral* epistles, however, suppose another journey to the E. Neither of them could have been long, since Paul's imprisonment and execution in Rome must be put before the death of Nero, therefore 67–68. The place of the martyrdom in local Roman tradition is the site of the basilica of St. Paul "outside the walls." Since he was a Roman citizen, the mode of execution according to the same tradition was decapitation.

4. *Personality*. The reader of the epistles is probably first impressed by the depth of feeling which they exhibit, and he concludes correctly that Paul was a man of strong passions. Less obvious is the keen mind which composed the letters and which is always disciplined; Paul's fiery personality does not obscure his thought. His qualities of leadership and organization are evident in the account of his missionary journeys. The epistles show a capacity for attention to detail which at times may have been a little annoying to his associates.

Paul often speaks warmly of his friends and companions, and there is no doubt of his friendly personality. One who spent most of his life meeting strangers and establishing close relations with them must have been warm and outgoing. Gal, 1–2 Co and Phl exhibit what is almost overidentification with his congregations. Paul seems to have been equally at home with Jews and Gentiles everywhere; he is the most cosmopolitan figure of the entire Bible. He is familiar with the Old Testament, but also with the life of the cities of the Mediterranean. There is a sharp contrast between the country and village atmosphere of the Gospels and the urban atmosphere of Paul's epistles; Paul was a man of the city, and nowhere in his writings shows any awareness of the countryside and the villages, or interest in them.

That Paul was a sturdy and determined individual both in mind and in body is evident from his career. His spiritual determination was steeled by his complete identification with Jesus Christ whom he preached. He speaks of himself as under compulsion (1 Co 9:16 f). It is not merely his zeal which is impressive; it is also his calm assurance that he can preach the gospel with success anywhere, an assurance which he founds on faith and hope (2 Co 12:9 +). Christians almost from the day of his death have called him simply "the apostle."

Nothing is known of his personal appearance. He quotes his adversaries as calling him "weak in presence and unimpressive in speech" (2 Co 10:10). This suggests at least that he was short of stature and that his discourses, like his letters, were without the form and polish esteemed in Hellenistic rhetoric. He has only one certain reference to illness (Gal 4:13–15), which seems to have been a form of the ophthalmia so common in the Near East. "The sting of the flesh" (2 Co 12:7) is not certainly an illness; some interpret it as the persecutions of the Jews.

5. *Theology.* The theology of Paul is treated at length in separate articles on the epistles and on theological topics. No one questions his position as the most creative thinker in the history of Christianity; indeed some have gone too far, asserting that historic Christianity is more Pauline than Christian. It is not difficult to imagine Paul's response to this; his entire career was devoted to obliterating himself behind the Christ with whom he identified himself. The Damascus experience was central in determining the direction of his thinking (cf above). To this one must add an undetermined degree of mystical experience, concerning which Paul is reserved (2 Co 12:1 ff). Scarcely less important in determining his theology was the controversy concerning Judaism*. In the solution of this problem Paul arrived at almost all of the dominant ideas which we now regard as characteristic of him. Less explicit but highly important was the fact that he was a man of two worlds, Judaism and Hellenistic urban civilization. Paul never outgrew his rabbinical training nor the profound knowledge and acceptance of Judaism in which he had been reared. His handling of the OT is rabbinical; cf INTERPRETATION. The term "Christian rabbi" which some have applied to him does more than justice to his rabbinical schooling; like most epithets, it fails to capture his extraordinarily rich and complex personality. His Gk, while not classic, is easy and good; it is obscure only because of the packed density of his thought and his habit of proceeding to his conclusions by intuitive leaps rather than by measured steps. The weight of his writing comes from his ability to muster all the resources of his learning and experience for the exposition of any question and the solution of any problem. His preference for statements which are extreme and absolute rather than qualified and tempered is characteristic of Semitic speech, not of Gk; and this habit has been responsible for the unfortunate fact that most heresies have based themselves upon the writings of Paul. One should notice also that none of the great movements of Christian thought have developed without a base in Paul. In him for the first time the Church and Jesus living in the Church encountered world civilization; and the Church has never learned a better language in which to address the world than the language of Paul.

Pe. The 17th letter of the Hb alphabet, with the value of *P*.

Peace. 1. *OT.* The Hb word *šālôm,* translated in Eng Bibles by "peace," is a word so widely used and with such rich content that no single Eng word can render it. This breadth of use, however, has not made the word vague of meaning; and its use is consistent enough to permit us to summarize its contents with what we think is a high degree of accuracy.

The cognate verb of the noun signifies such things as to finish, to complete, to pay (i.e., to complete a transaction by paying a debt); thus the word may be said to signify in general completeness, perfection — perhaps most precisely, a condition in which nothing is lacking.

Sālôm was the ordinary greeting, an expression of good wishes. The Israelite conceived peace as a gift of Yahweh, and as such it becomes a theological concept. Gideon's altar had the title "Yahwehshalom" (Jgs 6:24); if the title is rendered according to the usual structure of such titles, it means "Yahweh is peace." The state of perfect well-being which the word designates is identified with the deity; when one possesses peace, one is in perfect and assured communion with Yahweh. Yahweh desires the peace of those who serve Him (Ps 35:27). The priestly blessing invokes the peace of Yahweh upon Israel (Nm 6:26), and the prayer for Jerusalem asks peace for the city (Ps 122:6-8). Yahweh "speaks peace" upon His people i.e., His words effect peace (Ps 85:9), and righteousness and peace are joined where His peace is to be found (Ps 85:11). The elements of peace are mentioned in Lv 26:3-13: rain, abundant harvests, no enemy to terrify, no wild beasts, the covenant of Yahweh and His dwelling in the midst of His people. Peace is in contrast to blood vengeance, which brings a curse (1 K 2:33).

The false prophets of Jeremiah's time prophesied peace when there was no peace (Je 6:14; 8:11; 28:9). Peace does not consist in mere prosperity and well being; an essential component of peace is righteousness, and where there is no righteousness there is no genuine peace. Should it appear to be present, it will be proved specious when disaster comes. To affirm that it is peace is to heal the breach with falsehood (Je 6:14; 8:11) or to whitewash a collapsing wall (Ezk 13:10-12). Obedience to the commandments of Yahweh would have made the peace of Israel like a flowing river (Is 48:18). Peace will govern, and righteousness will rule (Is 60:17), and prosperity will be great when Israel is established in righteousness (Is 54:13 f). But there is no peace for the wicked (Is 48:22). Yahweh creates both peace and evil (Is 45:7) and allots them as men deserve them.

Perfect peace is to be expected in the messianic salvation. The Messiah is the prince of peace (Is 9:5 f), and in His kingdom there will be peace without end.

2. *NT*. The Gk word *īrēnē*, "peace," is most frequently used to render the Hb *šālôm* rather than the classical Gk sense. There are exceptions, however, e.g., the saying of Jesus that He came to send not peace but a sword (Mt 10:34; Lk 12:51). "Peace" is the usual greeting in the NT. "Peace" in 1 Co 14:33 designates good order and harmony. The OT sense of the word appears in Lk 1:79; 2:14; 19:42. Peace, likewise in the OT sense, is the fruit of the preaching of the gospel (Eph 6:15); it is brought by Jesus and is an achievement which is not possible to the world (Jn 14:27; 16:33). The greeting of peace, when uttered by the messengers of Jesus, is a word* of power, for to their words is communicated some of the dynamism of the utterances of Jesus; when one refuses to accept this greeting, the peace which it conveys returns to the one who utters the greeting (Mt 10:13; Lk 10:5). Peace comes through union with Jesus Christ and surpasses all human thought; it cannot be effected by human ingenuity (Phl 4:7). It reigns in the hearts of Christians, who are joined in the peace of the one body of Christ (Col 3:15). Peace is the fruit of spiritual-mindedness (Rm 8:6); in this verse peace is coupled with life, of which it is the fullness. Paul's phrase, "the God of peace" (Rm 16:20; 1 Th 5:23 +) is equivalent to "saving God," as peace in the NT becomes very nearly synonymous with salvation*.

Peace is communion with God, and Jesus Himself is our peace in this sense, since He is the bond of communion (Eph 2:14–17); we live in peace with God through our Lord Jesus Christ (Rm 5:1). It is also a state of interior calm and of harmonious relations with the Christian community, both of which are implied in the Christian vocation to peace (Rm 14:17; 1 Co 7:15).

Peace Offering. Cf SACRIFICE.

Pearl (Gk *margaritēs*), the well known precious stone is not certainly mentioned in the OT, and was unknown in the Gk world before the conquests of Alexander. Archaeology does not exhibit it in OT times. The pearls so prized in the Gk and Roman world were produced in the regions of the Red Sea, the Persian Gulf, and the Indian Ocean. They are used in figured speech in the NT. One single pearl could be worth the investment of one's entire possessions (Mt 13:45). The preaching of the gospel is compared to pearls (Mt 7:6). They are

an expensive ornament which women should shun (1 Tm 2:9). They appear frequently in the imagery of Apc (17:4; 18:12, 16; 21:21).

Pekah (Hb *peḳaḥ*, shortened form of Pekahiah* [?], which would give him the same name as his predecessor), son of Remaliah, king of Israel 737–732 BC. A royal officer of Pekahiah, he reached the throne by assassination. In 734 Tiglath-pileser* III of Assyria conquered Galilee and Gilead and detached them from the kingdom of Israel. Pekah was assassinated by a conspiracy led by Hoshea*, who succeeded him (2 K 15:25–31). Is 7:1–9 adds the information that Pekah, in league with Rezin* of Damascus*, invaded Judah in an attempt to force Ahaz* to join them in a defensive alliance against the Assyrians before the conquest of 734. The records of Tiglath-pileser mention the conquest of Israel and add that the Israelites overthrew Pekah and that Tiglath-pileser installed Hoshea on the throne (ANET 284). The name Pekah appears on a seal discovered at Shechem, but there is no reason to attribute the seal to the king. In the factional strife of the last years of the kingdom of Israel, when the throne passed from the pro-Assyrian to the anti-Assyrian faction in a series of rapid changes, Pekah represented the anti-Assyrian faction which believed in resistance.

Pekahiah (Hb *peḳaḥyāh*, "Yahweh has opened [the eyes]"), a personal name; king of Israel 738–737 BC, son and successor of Menahem*. He was assassinated by Pekah*, one of his officers, after a brief reign (2 K 15:22–26). Pekahiah and his father Menahem represented the political faction in Israel which believed in collaboration with the Assyrian advance.

Pekod (Hb *peḳōd*, etymology uncertain), a geographical name mentioned with Babylon* in Je 50:21; Ezk 23:23. An Aramaean* tribe, the Puqudu, dwelling in Babylonia, was defeated by Tiglath-pileser* III of Assyria* (745–727 BC), Sargon* (721–705 BC), and Sennacherib* (705–681 BC).

Peleg (Hb *peleg*), personal name; son of Eber* and father of Reu (Gn 10:25; 11:16–19; 1 Ch 1:19, 25). The name is explained from the root PLG, "divide." Related words in Akkadian mean "canal" and a "district." The word may conceal a culture hero to whom was attributed the construction of irrigation canals.

Pelethites. Cf CHERETHITES AND PELETHITES.

Pen (Hb *ēṭ*, Gk *kalamos* [lit "reed"]), the pen is rarely mentioned in the Bible (Ps 45:1; Je 8:8; 3 Jn 13). The pen of iron (Jb 19:24; Je 17:1) was used for inscriptions in stone. The ancient pen was a reed

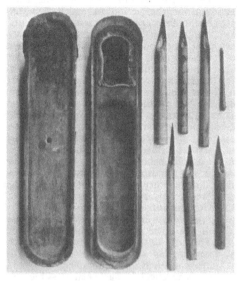

Ancient pens and inkwells.

Girl with case, tablet, and stylus, a painting from Herculaneum.

cut obliquely across the bottom to form a point. The point was slit so that it would hold and feed ink*. The scribe carried a pen knife to keep the point sharp (Je 36:23). Since the material wore out easily, the scribe included a large number of reeds among his equipment.

Penny. Cf MONEY.

Pentateuch (Gk *pentateuchos,* "[the book of] five volumes"), the first five books of the OT. The Pnt is called the *tôrāh,* the law* in Judaism in the NT (cf CANON). For contents cf GENESIS; EXODUS; LEVITICUS; NUMBERS; DEUTERONOMY.

1. *Literary Criticism.* Jewish and Christian tradition alike from the pre-Christian period to the 19th century attributed the Pnt to Moses*; a few isolated questions raised by some writers suggested that the origins of the Pnt were more complex than this, but these questions had no lasting influence and cast no serious doubt on the customary attribution. In the NT Moses, the law of Moses, or the book of Moses is the normal title of the Pnt. In accepting the common designation of the Pnt the NT does not determine the critical question and should not be employed to determine it.

Criticism begins with the observation of certain features of the Pnt which suggest more than one author. There are two accounts of creation* (Gn 1:1–2:4a; 2:4b–24). Two distinct accounts of the deluge* (Gn 6:5–9:18) can be reconstructed from the present text, which contains two mentions of most details, sometimes separated and at variance with each other (the entrance into the ark; the number of animals taken into the ark). Ex 4:19 should follow Ex 2:23a. The rebellion of Dathan* and Abiram can be entirely removed from the story of the rebellion of Korah* (Nm 16). The two genealogies of the antediluvian patriarchs* (Gn 4–5) in some instances exhibit the same names. The expulsion of Hagar* (Gn 16 and 21), the call of Moses (Ex 3 and 6), the miracle of the quail and the manna* (Ex 16; Nm 11) are related twice, and the wife of a patriarch is taken into the harem of a foreign ruler three times (Gn 12; 20; 26). The decalogue* appears twice (Ex 20; Dt 5). When these pieces of narrative are set alongside each other, it becomes evident that certain common features of vocabulary and style appear in various groups. The deity is called by different titles, the holy mountain of the exodus is called both Sinai* and Horeb*, the pre-Israelite inhabitants of Canaan are called Amorites* and Canaanites*. Reasoning from these features critics have reconstructed several sources of the Pnt; since these sources appear in all five books, it is impossible to attribute them to a time earlier than Moses.

The French physician Jean Astruc and the German scholar Eichhorn (1781) proposed independently that two documents could be discerned in Gn, one of which employed the divine name Yahweh and the other the divine name Elohim (cf GOD); they were therefore called the Jahwist document and the Elohist document, and were regarded as preexisting sources which Moses compiled into Gn. Ilgen (1798) made the second important step toward the critical theory when he suggested that the Elohist document must be two and not one. De Wette (1805–1807) isolated Dt as a distinct source; but the prevailing theory at the beginning of the 19th century (Geddes, 1792; Vater, 1802–1805; de Wette) was "the theory of fragments"; the Pnt, it was thought, was not compiled from "documents" but from fragments of written sources. This theory expresses one of the two extremes between which criticism of the Pnt moves; the one extreme is the obvious unity of its sources, and the other is the equally obvious diversity which makes the unity imperfect. The theory of fragments did not long survive; it yielded to "the complementary theory" (Ewald, 1823; de Wette, 1840), which supposed that one basic source (the Elohist) was expanded by the addition of fragments from other sources.

The modern documentary theory was first proposed in the form which it has substantially retained by Hupfeld (1853). Returning to Ilgen's theory, he distinguished three sources in Gn-Nm: the first Elohist, the oldest; the Jahwist; and the second Elohist, the most recent. The Jahwist and the second Elohist were combined before their union with the first Elohist. With Dt this includes four documents.

The decisive step was taken by Graf (1865). Accepting the documents as analyzed by Hupfeld, he observed that Hupfeld's first Elohist must be the most recent document; it is the work of the postexilic Jerusalem priesthood and exhibits sacerdotal and legalistic interests. He called this the priestly source. Thus the four document hypothesis was complete. The documents are usually symbolized by code letters: J, the Jahwist; E, the Elohist; D, the Deuteronomist; P, the priestly source. Kuenen (1869) announced that he had reached the same conclusion independently. The writings of Julius Wellhausen from 1876 to 1901 did more than anything else to recommend the theory to the public as well as to scholars. Wellhausen was endowed with the gift of brilliantly clear and persuasive exposition, and the hypothesis has become identified with his name, although he received it substantially complete from others. He did, however, strengthen it by argument and discussion; but his most important and most controversial contribution to the theory was his union of the documentary hypothesis with

a theory of the religious and cultural evolution of Israel. In accordance with the prevailing type of historical thinking of his generation, Israelite traditions were regarded with considerable skepticism as valid witnesses for the time of their composition, but not for the period to which they referred. Wellhausen reconstructed the evolution of the religion of Israel from primitive polytheism through the ethical monotheism of the prophets, whom he regarded as the great creative thinkers of Israel and the high point of Israelite religion, to the formal and legalistic religion of the priesthood and the scribes of the postexilic period.

Failure to distinguish between the literary hypothesis and the historical hypothesis led many to reject the whole theory as an attack upon revealed religion. The reaction of a few Catholic scholars at first was favorable, but in the atmosphere of Modernism of the early 20th century it was difficult to judge the theory objectively, and the Pontifical Biblical Commission in a response of June 27, 1906, rejected the literary and evolutionary theories in the form in which they were proposed. This arrested discussion by Catholic scholars, and it was not resumed until after the encyclical *Divino Afflante Spiritu* of 1943. Since the encyclical it has been possible to make the necessary distinctions between the literary problems and the problems of historical and cultural evolution.

The documentary hypothesis dominated biblical criticism after 1900, and most critical work after 1900 was devoted to further analysis of the sources and to the isolation of other special sources besides the four documents. The analysis of the sources into further strata (J^1, J^2, E^1, E^2, etc), successful within limits, soon developed to the point where a new theory of fragments appeared to be suggested. It became evident that this analysis could easily be pushed to excess, and scholars began to wonder whether literary analysis alone was sufficient. This, combined with certain weaknesses in the Wellhausen hypothesis, stimulated investigation along the lines which contemporary scholars pursue. The philosophical presuppositions of the evolutionary theory of Israel's development have become antiquated. The theory was conceived at the very beginning of the great discoveries of the literature and culture of the ancient Near East, which have much illuminated the history and culture of Israel and offered early parallels to many biblical texts. These studies have shown that the skepticism of the Wellhausen theory is indefensible, and proved that a construction of the history of Israel without reference to ancient Near Eastern material is impossible. The literary theory was conceived in too bookish a manner; the "documents" were described after the manner of documents of another and later culture.

These considerations have led scholars to think that the complexity of the literary origins of the Pnt is so great that it can never be solved entirely, and that scholarship is more sure of its results if it proceeds along broader lines; the analysis and identification of each sentence and even of each word, as practiced by earlier critics, is insecure. Recent studies have emphasized literary form* and oral tradition. The members of the "Scandinavian school" in particular have pushed the importance of oral tradition beyond the point which other scholars are willing to accept; they not only deny that the "documents" are documents in the modern historical sense, but deny that they were written at all until after the Exile. The Jahwist and the Elohist represent collections of traditions which were composed and transmitted orally. Our knowledge of ancient Near Eastern culture renders it most improbable that the traditions were not written before this late date. But the "bookish" element in the theory is now generally denied to the extent that scholars think the traditions were almost entirely composed orally and transmitted orally until the early monarchy, with some exceptions.

The investigation of literary forms seeks the "situation in life" in which the traditions were composed and attempts to deduce from this their scope and style. Study not only of ancient Near Eastern traditions but also of other traditions shows that narratives tend to fall into certain set forms which have each their own associations. In the view of many scholars, particularly von Rad and Noth, the traditions of the Pnt should not be viewed merely as tribal folk tales; they are "history of salvation," the profession of the faith of Israel. Even where their origin is secular rather than religious, they have their present form and character from their incorporation into the history of salvation. The written traditions are the result of the oral transmission of cultic recitals attached to great festivals and to sanctuaries; these recitals tell of the saving and forgiving deeds of Yahweh, His election and deliverance of Israel, the institution of the covenant, the laws, and the cult of Israel. Many scholars are inclined to give this principle of cultic recital a more narrow scope; but the principles of literary form, of situation in life, and of the cultic influence on the traditions must be regarded as established conclusions of scholarship. The conceptions of oral tradition and of literary form better than any other principles seem to explain the conflict

of unity and diversity in the traditions mentioned above.

Many modern critics do not speak of "documents," although (cf below) one must allow room for the work of some who deserve the name of authors rather than compilers. But these authors have often left traces of the complex character of the preliterary traditions in their work; furthermore, the traditions even in writing received numerous modifications after their literary composition. Some speak of "schools" rather than documents or writers; others (de Vaux) prefer to call them simply traditions, without affirming their oral or literary origin, or the unity or multiplicity of the compilers. This term seems preferable; and the reasonably assured results of modern criticism may be summed up in the description of the traditions which follow.

The Jahwist tradition. The following analysis is taken from A. Weiser. * indicates passages which have been conflated from more than one source, indicated in parentheses by their symbols.

Gn 2:4b–4:26; 5:29; 6:1–8; 7–8* (P); 9:18–27; 10:8–19, 25–30; 11:1–9, 28–30; 12; 13* (P); 15* (E); 16* (P); 18:1–19:20, 30–38; 21:1–7* (P), 32–33* (E); 22:14–24* (E); 24* (E); 25* (P); 26* (P); 27* (EP); 28:13–16; 29:2–14, 31–35; 30:9–16, 24–43* (E); 31* (EP); 32* (E); 33* (E) 34* (E); 36* (EP); 37* (EP); 38; 39* (E); 40–42* (E); 43; 44; 45* (E); 46* (EP); 47* (P); 48* (EP); 49:1–27; 50:1–11.

Ex 1* (EP); 2–5* (EP); 11:4–8; 12:21–27; 13–14* (E); 15:22–27* (E); 16* (EP); 19:20–25; 23–24* (EP); 32* (E); 33* (E); 34:1–28.

Nm 10:29–32; 11* (E); 13–14* (EP); 16* (EP); 20–21* (EP); 22–24* (E); 25:1–5* (E); 32* (EP).

Dt 34* (EDP).

The Jahwist tradition therefore contains the story of Paradise and the fall; primitive man; the sons of God; the deluge; Noah and the vine; part of the table of nations; the tower of Babel; the call of Abraham and his journey to Hebron; the promise of the land and a numerous posterity; Hagar and Ishmael; Abraham's guests; the destruction of Sodom and Gomorrah; Lot and his daughters; the birth of Isaac; the wooing of Rebekah; the story of Isaac; Esau and Jacob; the birth of the sons of Jacob; Jacob and Laban; Jacob at Shechem; the Edomite genealogy; Joseph and his brothers; Joseph in Egypt, the blessing of Jacob; the death of Jacob; the oppression of Israel in Egypt; the birth and call of Moses; probably seven of the ten plagues; the passage of the sea; the journey from the sea to

Sinai; the quail and manna; a very brief notice of the Sinai theophany; the golden calf; the departure from Sinai; the commandments of Ex 34; the departure from Sinai; the story of the scouts; the rebellion of Dathan and Abiram; the journey from Kadesh to Moab; the oracles of Balaam; the worship of Baal Peor; the dispute between eastern and western tribes; the death of Moses.

In the classical form of documentary hypothesis the composition of J was placed in the 9th century BC. Recent critics are inclined to place it in the reign of Solomon or even of David; it has been called "the Israelite national epic," and is an expression of the national consciousness of Israel which arose from the victories of David and the prosperity which his reign initiated. J is one of the most expert narrators of the OT; it is evident from the summary above that many of the best known stories of the OT belong to this document. His narrative is vivid and moves rapidly, and his characters are depicted with earthy realism; they are not plaster saints. His conception of the deity is extremely anthropomorphic, but it does not lack dignity. Yahweh is the lord of history. Beginning with the primeval fall of man and the human deterioration which followed, J shows how the divine will to save exhibits itself in the promises made to Abraham, how the chosen family and its offspring are led through various adventures and dangers to settlement in the land of promise; the reader is left to conclude that the monarchy of David is the fulfillment of the saving promise. As a Judahite author, his emphasis and interest lie chiefly in the persons and regions of later Judahite territory. But he is extremely conscious of the unity· of Israel, and he incorporates those elements from what was no doubt an existing cycle of Jacob stories (cf below) which bring the 12 tribes together in a common origin. He makes Judah the chief of the brothers in the story of Joseph — which also he probably found already in existence.

The Elohist tradition. The following analysis is taken from A. Weiser; symbols are used as above.

Gn 15* (J) 20–21* (J); 22* (J); 24* (J); 27* (JP); 28:10–12, 17–22; 29–34* (J); 35* (P); 36* (JP); 37* (JP); 39* (J); 40–42* (J); 45* (J); 46* (JP); 48* (JP); 50* (JP).

Ex 1* (JP); 2–5* (JP); 7–10* (JP); 11:1–3; 12* (JP); 13–14* (J); 15:20 f; 16* (JP); 17–18; 19* (J); 20:22–23:19; 23–24* (JP); 32* (J); 33* (J).

Nm 10* (JP); 11* (J); 12; 13–14* (JP); 16* (JP); 20–21* (JP); 22–24* (J); 25:1–6* (J): 32* (JP).

Dt 31:14 ff; 32; 33; 34* (JDP).

The Elohist traditions therefore contain the covenant of Abraham; Abraham; the birth of Isaac; the expulsion of Hagar; the sacrifice of Isaac; the wooing of Rebekah; Esau and Jacob; Jacob at Bethel; the marriages of Jacob, the birth of the sons of Jacob, Jacob and Laban; Joseph and his brothers; Joseph in Egypt; the death of Jacob; the oppression of Israel in Egypt; the birth and call of Moses; probably five of the ten plagues; the passage of the sea; the journey to Sinai; the sojourn at Sinai; the golden calf; the departure from Sinai; the quail and manna; the scouts; the rebellion of Dathan and Abiram; the journey from Kadesh to Moab; the oracles of Balaam; the worship of Baal Peor; the dispute between eastern and western tribes; the commission of Joshua to succeed Moses; the song of Moses; the blessing of Moses; the death of Moses.

The classical documentary theory placed the composition of E in northern Israel in the 8th century BC. More recent critics would advance this date; it is a statement of Israelite traditions like J, but a statement which originated in the northern kingdom. Compared to J, E appears to be a torso. This may be due to redaction; E was fused with J after the fall of Israel in 721 BC in an effort to preserve Israelite traditions, and it seems that the Judahite editors preferred their own form of the tradition where the two were parallel. E exhibits, however, no tradition earlier than Abraham, and it is doubtful that these would have been suppressed entirely. This indicates that E took a more narrow view of history than did J; it may be said of his work in general that it does not show the sweeping scope of which J is capable. His style is less vivid and his characters less realistic. In fact E is difficult to distinguish from J outside of Gn, as the above summary shows. This has led Volz and Rudolph to conclude that E is a fiction created by modern critics; but this view has found no general acceptance. Diversity and duplication do not permit one to reduce the accounts to a single source or to a main source expanded by the addition of fragments.

E is less anthropomorphic in his presentation of the deity than is J, preferring more sublimated and less direct dealings of Yahweh with men. He places the revelation of the name of Yahweh in the period of Moses (Ex 3). J, probably in line with his presentation of Israel as one people with one God, refers to Yahweh throughout. Where his story parallels J, there is evidently some effort to make the actions of the heroes morally more acceptable. A northern tradition, E shows more interest in the northern heroes, Jacob, Joseph, and Joshua. He conceives the relation of the patriarchs with the deity as covenant rather than as blessing.

The Priestly tradition. The following analysis is taken from A. Weiser, with symbols used as above.

Gn 1:1–2:4a; 5:1–28, 30–32; 6:5–9:19* (J); 9:28 f; 10* (J); 11:10–26, 27, 31–32; 13:6, 11 f; 16:1, 3, 15 f; 17; 19:29; 21:3–5; 23; 25:7–20; 26:34 f; 27:46–28:9; 31:18; 35:9–13, 15, 22–29; 36* (JE); 37:1–2; 46:6–27; 48:3–6; 49:28–33; 50:12 f.

Ex 1:1–5, 7, 13 f; 2:23–25; 6:2–30; 7:1–13, 19 f, 23; 8:1–3, 12–15; 9:8–12; 11:9–12, 20, 28; 12:40–51; 16* (JE); 24:16–18; 25–31; 34:29–35; 35–40.

Lv entirely.

Nm 1–10; 13–14* (JE); 15; 16* (JE); 17–19; 20* (JE); 25:6–31, 54; 27:12–23; 32* (JE); 33–36.

Dt 32:48–52; 34:1a, 7–9.

In the classical theory P was composed in the 5th century and incorporated with JED into the Pnt about 400 BC. Recent critics accept this late date, but are now much more willing to grant that P sometimes contains ancient materials; he is not dependent entirely on JE.

The narrative of P is rather a sketch or an outline and never seems to have been anything more. Longer pieces appear only in the creation account, the deluge, and the origins of cultic institutions, in which P takes primary interest; many of these are retrojected into an early period. He expands the theme of covenant and makes it run even through the primitive history.

The style of P is dry and statistical and is the most easily recognized of all the traditions, even in translation. Most of the material mentioned above is genealogical and statistical. P frames Gn in an artificial chronology which issues in some startling figures for the ages of the patriarchs. The theory on which this is based is not clear; but it is now known since the discovery of the Qumran* material that interest in calendars and calendrical speculation ran high in later Judaism, and it is probable that this interest existed when P was composed.

P goes into detail concerning priesthood, sacrifice, festivals, and cult. He describes the tabernacle* and its furniture in great detail; it is the prototype of the temple* and its description is based on the temple. It is the center of the life and worship of early Israel as the temple was the center of postexilic Israel. Moses is primarily the lawgiver rather than the prophet and the deliverer.

For the special problems of Dt cf DEUTERONOMY. The above summaries do not include the legal collections, which are discussed under LAW. The relation of the legal collections to the narratives is not entirely clear. P made the narrative merely a framework for his collection of law; but it cannot be determined whether the other collections originally were a part of J and E or whether they were added by redactors at some later date. For J at least it seems unlikely that his epic conception included any legal collections as such. But whether it was due to P or the final redactor, the Pnt as a whole and to some extent in its sources exhibits the peculiar fusion of law and narrative which is characteristic of the Pnt and of no other biblical or ancient Near Eastern work. Law rises out of the history of Israel; it is the revealed will of Yahweh, the God of blessing and of covenant, who elects Israel as His own people and furnishes the constitution under which Israel is to live. This is the chief theological feature of the Pnt; for its repercussions in later Judaism and Christianity cf COVENANT; LAW. The other theological features of the Pnt are of the highest importance; cf pertinent articles such as BLESSING; COVENANT; CREATION; DELUGE; ELECTION; EXODUS; FALL; PASSOVER; SIN; TABERNACLE.

The summary of the traditions given above does not include all the passages of the Pnt, such as Gn 14 and several poems or fragments of poems. On Gn 14 cf ABRAHAM; MELCHIZEDEK. The poems and fragments are discussed under separate headings of persons and places and biblical books. Many of these cannot be assigned to any one of the traditions with certainty; it is possible that they were added by redactors. Modern critics now regard most of these poetic fragments as among the oldest written portions of the Pnt.

Pentecost. (Gk *hē pentēkostē* [*hēmerā*], "the 50th [day]"), an Israelite-Jewish festival. The festival is one of the three listed in Ex 23:14–17, where it is called simply the harvest festival, the feast of the first-fruits of the grain harvest. In Ex 34:22 it is called the feast of weeks, the first-fruits of the grain harvest mentioned with Mazzoth* and the feast of Ingathering (cf TABERNACLES). In Lv 23:15–21 the feast is reckoned by counting 7 weeks from the beginning of the grain harvest; it is a day of Sabbatical observance (cf SABBATH). In Nm 28:26–31 it is called the feast of weeks, the day of first-fruits. In Dt 16:9–12 it is the feast of weeks, which occurs 7 weeks after the beginning of the grain harvest. Elsewhere the feast is mentioned only in 2 Ch 8:13, which has led some scholars to conclude that it was not an important festival.

This conclusion does not seem well founded. It is one of the three major festivals in all the older lists of feasts.

As Pentecost is described it is evidently an agricultural feast with no historical motif. It is probable that it was later in origin than Passover* and did not take form until the Israelites had become a primarily agricultural community in Canaan. The time of the festival in its original celebration must have been indefinite, since the beginning of the grain harvest cannot be put at a certain day in the calendar. The beginning of the grain harvest corresponds with the feast of Mazzoth. When Passover and Mazzoth were combined and set on the 14th of Nisan, the feast of weeks received a regular date in the calendar 7 weeks (50 days) after Passover.

In Judaism the feast received a historical motif; it became the anniversary of the giving of the law* to Moses. This motif does not certainly appear until after the beginning of the Christian era. Scholars suspect that the ancient Israelite festal calendar contained a festival which was a renewal of the covenant*, and the Jewish motif of the giving of the law may have its roots in a much earlier practice.

Pentecost is mentioned more frequently in the NT than in the OT; it receives its importance in Christian belief and liturgy from the event related in AA 2, the descent of the Spirit upon the disciples, the gift of tongues, the discourse of Peter, and the formation of the first Christian church. Lk makes Pentecost "the birthday of the universal church" (Lohse). The event as it is described in AA is placed in a somewhat complex theological interpretation, which many critics believe was already incorporated into the account when it reached Luke. On the gift of tongues cf GRACE. The antecedents of the gift of tongues at Pentecost appear in such OT passages as NM 11:25-29; 1 S 10:5 f, 10-19; 19:20-24. In these episodes the elders* and Saul* under the impulse of the spirit "prophesy," which in the context appears to signify unintelligible ecstatic discourse, "a foreign tongue." Under the impulse of the Spirit given by Jesus the same charisma appears in the Church, but in a higher form. Through the outpouring of the Spirit the Church is empowered to address herself to all nations and to be understood by them. The discourse to all nations in their own tongue seen in this event is actually fulfilled in the mission of the apostolic group to the peoples of the world. There is possibly an implicit allusion to the story of the tower of Babel*, in which mankind was divided by the diversity of languages. The lost unity is restored in the Church which speaks all languages but is a single unified society.

The outpouring of the Spirit renders the Church articulate in preaching the gospel. The discourse of Peter is the first proclamation of the Gospel. Lk deliberately sets a contrast between the inactive and somewhat helpless group which assembles before the Spirit is given and the active and eloquent speaker who appears at Pentecost. By the Spirit the Church is now empowered to fulfill the mission which was committed to her by Jesus.

The narrative concludes with a description of the Jerusalem community, the first *ekklēsia* (cf CHURCH), which is the fruit of the Pentecostal manifestation. This Church is the Jerusalem community, a Judaeo-Christian group. The Pentecost account is actually composed in the light of the subsequent awareness of the universal mission of the Church and its extension to Gentiles. The account then sums up in a single event the work of the first generation of the Church, the Spirit which inspired and moved it, and the fruits of the Spirit working in the Church.

Penuel (Hb *penû'ēl* or *penî'ēl*, "face of El"), a local name; the scene of Jacob's wrestling (Gn 32:31 f). The men of the town refused aid to Gideon* in his pursuit of the Midianites and he sacked the city (Jgs 8:8 f, 17). The city was fortified by Jeroboam* (1 K 12:25). The name appears in the list of Palestinian cities conquered by the Pharaoh Shishak*. The allusions place the city E of the Jordan near a ford of the Jabbok*, but the exact site is uncertain. Modern opinion prefers a small tell called Tululat ed-Dhabab.

Peor (Hb *peôr*, meaning uncertain), a place name, occurring only in combination: Beth-Peor (Dt 3:29; 4:46; 34:6; Jos 13:20) and Baal-Peor (Nm 25:3, 5; Dt 4:3; Ps 106:28; Ho 9:10). In Dt the valley opposite Beth-Peor was the final camping place of the Israelites in Moab. Peor or Beth-Peor was the seat of the cult of a deity, Baal-Peor (cf BAAL) whom the Israelites worshiped (Nm 25:1-9; Dt 4:3; Ps 106:28; Ho 9:10). The site is not certainly known; Khirbet esh-sheikh-Jayil, N of Mt Nebo, is suggested by many geographers.

Perazim (Hb *perāṣîm*, "divisions"? "breaches"?), local name, appearing in Baal-perazim (2 S 5:20) and Mt Perazim (Is 28:21). Baal-perazim was the scene of a victory of David over the Philistines; Is probably alludes to this victory, despite the difference in the names, as an example of the power and wonder of the works of Yahweh. Its location is uncertain, but it lay S of Jerusalem; the modern Sheikh Bedr near the city has been suggested.

Perez (Hb *pereṣ*, explained by a popular etymology in Gn 38:29 as meaning "breach"; possibly means "spreading" [of family or clan]), a personal and clan name, one of the twin sons of Judah* and Tamar* (Gn 38:29) and eponymous ancestor of one of the clans of Judah (1 Ch 4:1).

Perfect. 1. *OT.* The Hb word *tōm* and its cognates signify radically that which is complete, finished. The ethical use of the word designates a quality which can be rendered "simple" or "integral." Where the word is applied to those who do not know (Gn 20:5 f; 2 S 15:11) it denies any evil intention. The archer who shoots in the simplicity of his heart shoots without aim (1 K 22:34). The simple heart of a king (Pss 78:72; 101:2) is a heart which is not corrupted by partiality. The quality of "perfection," which belongs to the righteous (Pss 26:1, 11; 64:5; Jb 1:1, 8; 2:3; 4:6; Pr 10:9; 13:6; 19:1; 20:7; 28:6; 2:7; 29:10) is probably the denial of duplicity and deception; it is a quality of the way* in which he walks. It preserves the righteous man (Ps 25:21); it is a motive why Yahweh defends him (Pss 7:9; 41:13) and regards him favorably (Ps 37:37). It is an axiom of wisdom literature that God does not reject the perfect (Jb 8:20) and Job asserts that he is perfect (9:20–22).

2. *NT.* The Gk word *teleios* has a more complex meaning than Hb *tōm*. Radically *teleios* also means complete, finished, and when used of a person signifies adult, mature. This is the sense in which it is used in 1 Co 14:20; Heb 5:14; 6:1. In profane Gk the word sometimes signifies moral development; this is the most obvious sense of the word in Col 4:12; Js 1:4; 3:2. Elsewhere the word is somewhat obscure. In the mystery* cults the "perfect" were those who had been initiated into the cults. It is suspected that "perfect" means initiated into Christianity, baptized, in 1 Co 2:6; Phl 3:15; Col 1:28, although the meaning of adult is satisfactory in these passages. "The perfect man" which Christians must become in Eph 4:13 is understood in a peculiarly Christian sense; it is both maturity and moral completeness, but understood as the full identity of the Christian with Jesus Christ; this is probably suggested in Col 1:28 also. Love is called the bond of perfection (Col 3:14); this may be an adjectival genitive (= perfect bond) or it may signify that love is the bond which unites all the virtues. The

use of the term in Mt 19:21 supposes that perfect means more than the observance of the law; Jesus defines it as the abandonment of one's goods and becoming His disciple. The word scarcely means quite the same thing in Mt 5:48; coming as it does at the close of the discourse of the antitheses, it imposes upon the Christian the obligation of going beyond the Pharisaic interpretation of the commandments. The use of the word in this verse of the Father is quite unusual, and the relationship between the Father and the Christians in perfection is therefore somewhat obscure. More than moral completeness seems to be implied; it is a moral completeness derived from the personal and experiential knowledge of God, not from the law.

Perga (Gk *perge*, meaning uncertain), a city in Pamphylia* situated 7–8 mi above the mouth of the Kestros, near the Pamphylian port of Attalia*. The city had a well known temple of Artemis in Roman times. It was visited by Paul and Barnabas on their first missionary journey (AA 13:13 f), and it was at Perga that John Mark* abandoned them. It was perhaps because of this disagreement that they did not preach the gospel there until their return from the interior (AA 14:25).

Pergamum (Gk *pergamon*, meaning uncertain), one of the seven churches addressed by the author of Apc (1:11; 2:12). The church tolerated some obscure heretical sects. There is no record of its foundations; it is possible that it was a Pauline foundation, since Paul was active in this area of Asia Minor. Pergamum was one of the largest and most illustrious cities of Asia. It lay N of Smyrna* about 15 mi from the sea, but ships could reach its port through the river Caicus. Attalus I founded the kingdom of Pergamum (241 BC) which preserved itself through close alliance with Rome; the kingdom passed to Rome by the legacy of Attalus III in 133 BC, and it was substantially the territory of the kingdom which was erected by the Romans into the province of Asia*. It was the residence of the Roman provincial governor. Excavations at Pergamum were begun by the Berlin Museum in 1878. The city had a temple of Athene, its patron goddess, a temple of Dionysus, and a great altar of Zeus. It had the typical colonnaded marketplace, theater, stadium, and amphitheater. It was a center of the cult of Asklepios "the healer" (cf SAVIOR). Its library was second only to the library of Ahasuerus. Artaxerxes I (465–425) (*apgamentum*) is derived from the name of the city; it was an important center of the manufacture of parchment, but the legend that parchment was invented there has no foundation.

Perizzites (Hb *p^e rizzîm,* a gentilic name; meaning possibly "dwellers in the open country"), one of the pre-Israelite inhabitants of Canaan. A degree of importance may be seen in the fact that they are sometimes mentioned with the Canaanites alone (Gn 13:7; 34:30; Jgs 1:4 f). Jos 17:5 suggests that they lived in the wooded hill country. Elsewhere they are mentioned in conventional enumerations of the six or seven peoples of Canaan (Gn 15:20; Ex 3:8, 17; 23:23; 34:11; Dt 7:1; 20:17; Jgs 3:5; 1 K 9:20; 2 Ch 8:7; Ne 9:8). The gentilic name Pirizzi occurs once in the Amarna* Letters and is probably to be identified with the biblical Perizzites.

Perseus (Gk *perseus,* "Persian"), the last king of Macedonia, conquered at Pydna by L. Aemilius Paullus in 168 BC, mentioned in 1 Mc 8:5.

Persepolis (Gk *persepolis,* "Persian city"), a Persian royal residence (2 Mc 9:2; cf PERSIA).

Columns of the palace at Persepolis.

Persia (Hb *paras,* from Persian *Parsa* [cf below]; a people of the Iranian plateau; the names Iran and Aryan come from the Iranian *aryanam,* "the land").

1. *History.* The Iranian peoples include the Medes* and the Persians; the early history of both these peoples is extremely obscure, and the Persians became historically important later than the Medes. The Aryans appear to have reached the Iranian plateau from their original homeland in central Asia in the 2nd millennium BC. For centuries they continued to live as nomadic groups; the important political society of the region was the kingdom of Elam* with its capital at Susa*. The old Elamite kingdom disappeared in the disturbances of the 12th century BC (cf ASSYRIA; BABYLON), permitting the Iranians to expand into former Elamite territory. They settled in Parsua W of Lake Urmia at an undetermined date; the name is first mentioned in the 9th century BC. From here the Persians, at this period and until Cyrus* vassals of the Medes, expanded S into old Elamite territory.

Persian history proper begins with Hachmanish (Gk *Achaemenes),* the eponymous founder of the Achaemenid dynasty (700–675 BC). His son Teispes (675–640) extended Persian rule to Anshan NW of the Persian Gulf. During his reign and the reign of his successor Cyrus I (640–600) the Persians moved into the territory E of the Persian Gulf, which thereafter bore the name of Parsa and was considered the homeland of the Persians. The royal residence in Parsa was Parsa-garda, "Persian camp," called by the Greeks Pasargadae. The founder of the Persian kingdom and empire was Cyrus II the Great (559–529 BC), who rebelled against his Mede overlord Astyages and united the Medes and the Persians into a single kingdom. Ecbatana*, the Mede royal residence, was captured by Cyrus and became the capital preferred to Pasargadae. Cyrus' conquest of Croesus of Lydia (547 BC) made him lord of Asia Minor and established Persian sovereignty over the Ionian Greeks of Asia Minor. After this conquest he moved easily against the moribund monarchy of Babylon; Gubaru (Gobryas), the Babylonian commander of Susa, delivered the city and his troops to Cyrus in 546, and Babylon surrendered without a struggle in 539. Cyrus thus became heir to the Neo-Babylonian empire of Nebuchadnezzar.

In comparison with Assyrian and Babylonian conquerors the government of Cyrus was remarkably humane; this humanity was not equally evident in his successors, but the Persian Empire never exhibited the cruelty and rapacity of the Assyrians. It endured for over 200 years with a notable stability in the Asian parts of the empire; it was fought and finally defeated by the Greeks, whose culture was too foreign to permit them to adjust to an Asian empire. A. Moortgat has suggested that the difference between the Mesopotamian and the Persian empires lay in the difference between the Persian god Ahura Mazda (cf below) and the Assyrian god Ashur (cf ASSYRIA); Ashur was a military god and a national genius, while Ahura Mazda was "the lord of wisdom" and a god with a more cosmic appeal. The tolerance and humanity of Cyrus is seen in his attitude toward the gods of conquered peoples, whose worship he promoted and whom he venerated in their own regions; this tolerance is the motive of the permission which was granted the Jews to resettle Jerusalem and rebuild the temple.

The empire was expanded by Cambyses II (528–522 BC), who conquered Egypt, and by Darius I (521–486 BC), the organizer of the empire. At his accession Darius was greeted by widespread revolts and dynastic rivalries; his victory over his adversaries is told in the celebrated inscription of Behistun; this trilingual monument (Persian, Elamite, Babylonian) was an important key to the decipherment of cuneiform* writing in the 19th century. Darius founded the new royal city and palace of Persepolis (Parsawardana), enlarged by his successors, particularly by Xerxes; the palace, whose imposing remains have been excavated, is the greatest monument of Persian art and architecture. Darius stabilized the empire at its greatest extent; its territory went from central Asia in the E through all of Asia Minor, Mesopotamia, Syria, Palestine, and Egypt. The attempts of Darius and his successor Xerxes (486–465) to extend the empire to continental Greece failed; these are the episodes of Persian history best known because they were immortalized in Gk literature, but they lie outside the area of biblical studies. The relations of Persia with Greece, however, were the first occasion for the penetration of Gk civilization into the Near East, and this penetration had profound and permanent results on Palestine and related countries (cf HELLENISM). After the Persian invasions of Greece in 490–479 had failed, the relations between Greece and Persia became rather friendly; there were a large number of Greeks who admired Persian culture, and the number of Greeks who entered Persian military and diplomatic service was considerable. Persian influence on Gk politics was almost as great as it would have been if they had won the Persian wars; there were many Greeks who favored Persian

influence, but most of these who worked for Persia in Gk cities did it because they were bribed to do so. When Philip and Alexander conceived the idea of uniting the Greeks under a single ruler for a decisive victory over Persia, they moved against a genuinely powerful influence in Gk life.

The empire was organized by Darius into satrapies, each ruled by a satrap. The satraps were always Iranian nobles, often related to the Achaemenids. The number of satrapies varied; 23 are listed in the Behistun inscription, but the number sometimes went as high as 29–30. The satrap was granted almost unlimited power and freedom in administration; he was a viceroy in his territory with a court, palace, and officials like a king. He was a feudal vassal rather than a subordinate administrator. There was a danger in such power wielded at such a distance from the royal residence, and rebellions of satraps were numerous in the later periods of Persian history. The king, assisted in the central government by the "Council of Seven," exercised some control over the satraps by a vast bureaucracy and by separately appointed inspectors. Each satrap had a secretary and separate commander of military forces appointed by the king. This supervision was supplemented by espionage. The really new feature in control was the establishment of a courier system between the satrapies and the central government, described by Herodotus in the famous line inscribed on the post office of New York: "Nor rain nor cold nor heat of day nor dark of night shall stay these couriers from their appointed rounds." The erection of stations along the roads permitted messages to be carried by riders without interruption; horses and riders were changed, and refreshments were stored. This was the first rapid overland communication known in history, and centuries passed before anything like it appeared again. The chief responsibility of the satrap was to collect and send to the central government the annual tribute, paid both in precious metals and in kind. As a means to more efficient administration Aramaic* was adopted as the official language of the government. This practical step had enormous cultural effects. Aramaic remained the language of most of the area of the Persian empire for centuries.

The details of the collapse of the empire in Alexander's wars lie outside biblical studies. The Persians are mentioned in the Bible only in later books: Est, Dn, Ezr-Ne passim. Ezk 27:10 and 38:5 are most probably added to Ezk by later writers. The Persian kings were responsible for the establishment and survival of the postexilic community of Jerusalem. Cyrus granted permission which was reaffirmed by Darius (cf EZRA-NEHEMIAH). Xerxes appears in Est as Ahasuerus. Artaxerxes I (465–425) appointed Nehemiah* governor of Jerusalem, and it was probably Artaxerxes II (404–359) who authorized the mission of Ezra* to Jerusalem.

2. *Religion*. A distinction must be made between the old Iranian religion, the reform of Zoroaster (Zarathustra), the religion of the Achaemenids as exhibited in their inscriptions, and the later popular religion. In comparative religion the reform of Zoroaster alone is of importance. The old Iranian religion was a naturalistic polytheism much like the religion of Greece or Mesopotamia; Ahura Mazda, "the lord of wisdom," was the head of the pantheon, and other great deities were Mithra the god of light and Anahita the goddess of fertility.

Zoroaster, while certainly a historical figure, is obscurely known; his character has been heavily overlaid with myth and legend so that even his date is uncertain. Dates suggested by scholars range from about 1000 BC to 500 BC. He was probably a member of a Mede noble family. The Gathas, in which his teaching is preserved, date only from the 3rd century AD, although they were probably written first about the 1st century AD. This means a long period of oral transmission, and the original teaching of Zoroaster has been somewhat modified in the course of transmission. Scholars feel certain, however, that the tradition has preserved Zoroaster's teaching in substantial integrity.

Zoroaster was a monotheist, not as clearly as the OT prophets, but in evident opposition to Iranian polytheism. He reduced the gods of Iranian polytheism to *daevas* (demons) and raised Ahura Mazda to a position of unparalleled eminence. The divinity of Ahura Mazda was limited only by dualism (cf below); he had no consort and no accompanying pantheon, no mythology, no images or temples, and he is conceived in an abstract, almost spiritual manner. He is creator, lawgiver, and judge. The teaching of Zoroaster attempts to reconcile monotheism with the problem of evil. The universe is dominated by the conflict of two dualistic principles: the good spirit (Spenta Mainyu) and the evil spirit (Angra Mainyu, Ahriman). Dualism is expressed in the opposition of good and evil, spirit and matter, truth and lie, and (later) light and darkness. There is a certain inconsistency in the doctrine at this point; Ahura Mazda is sometimes identified with Spenta Mainyu, and sometimes stands above the dualistic conflict. The origin of Angra Mainyu is never clearly seen. In the doctrine of Zoroaster the ultimate resolution

of the problem (cf below) is much more important than its origin.

Both Ahura Mazda and Angra Mainyu are accompanied by other beings which they create. The character of these beings is not clear; they are not gods as Ahura Mazda is a god; they are conceived as emanations or aspects or attributes or functions, but they are also conceived as distinct spirits. The good spirits are called Amesha Spentas, "immortal saviors"; their number varies from the original five or six to the later seven. Their names are Good Thought, Best Order, Desirable Domination, Beneficent Devotion, Holiness, Immortality, Beneficent Spirit. In accordance with these rather abstract concepts Zoroaster rejected magic and sorcery and animal sacrifices and the principal cult permitted was the cult of fire, the element and the symbol of the deity.

The conflict of Ahura Mazda and Angra Mainyu is to be resolved in the triumph of Ahura Mazda and the annihilation of Angra Mainyu and the evil spirit. This resolution takes the form of a world judgment by fire and a resurrection of the dead. The eschatology of Zoroaster is both individual and social. Each man is rewarded or punished in the afterlife according to his deeds. In eschatology the later developments of the doctrine became much more concrete and were described with more vivid imagery. An interesting development was the idea of a birth of a savior (Saoshyant) from a virgin in the last world period. Here there is a possible influence of Christianity. Men are judged according to the ethical law which Ahura Mazda imposes; but the ethical standards set forth by Zoroaster are general and simple. The ethical law is social as well as individual; the life of the peasant is the good life, and the life of the nomad bandit is the evil life.

The influence of Zoroastrianism on the official religion of the Achaemenids is uncertain. Some scholars are inclined to deny it altogether; others believe that Darius and his successors down to 405 BC were followers of Zoroaster, while earlier and later kings adhered to Iranian polytheism. The popular Zoroastrian religion did not maintain the integrity of the doctrine; it descended to a rather crass dualism of two equal and opposing principles and embroidered the ideas of judgment and paradise with luxuriant imagery.

This brief sketch is enough to indicate why historians of religion have affirmed a strong influence of Zoroastrianism upon Judaism and Christianity. This opinion is now largely abandoned; closer study of the materials has shown that the resemblances are superficial and coincidental. Dualism in the sense that there is a cosmic adversary of the deity does appear in Judaism and in Zoroaster; both have an organized celestial hierarchy (cf ANGEL); both have judgment and retribution after death. The conceptions, however, differ sufficiently to permit a denial of positive influence of Zoroaster upon Judaism. The positive influence is limited to such items as the seven archangels of Judaism, whose number may come from Iranian influence, and to certain details in the imagery of the judgment and retribution. As suggested above, later Iranian religion may be influenced by Judaism and Christianity.

Peshitta. Cf VERSIONS.

Peter. The original name of Peter was the Hb name Simeon*, which appears in the Grecized form of *symeōn* only in AA 15:14; 2 Pt 1:1. Elsewhere it appears as the Gk name *simōn* in Mt 17:25; Mk 1:16, 29 f, 36; 14:37; Lk 5:3–10; 22:31; 24:34; Jn 1:41 f; 21:15–17. Usually he is called by the surname *petros,* a masculine name formed from the feminine noun *petra,* "rock"; on the conferring of this name cf below. The original name was the Aramaic *kêpā',* "rock"; this is used in the Grecized form of *kēphas* in Jn 1:42; 1 Co 1:12; 3:22; 9:5; 15:5; Gal 1:18; 2:9, 11, 14. His father was John (Jn 1:42; 21:15–17) or Jonah (Mt 16:17). His home was Bethsaida* of Galilee and he was a fisherman (Mt 4:18–22; Mk 1:16–20; Lk 5:1–11; Jn 1:40–42). In Mt 8:14, however, he has a home in Capernaum*. A mother-in-law is mentioned in Mt 8:14, and 1 Co 9:5 suggests that his wife was still living at the time the letter was written.

1. *Life.* There are two and possibly three variant accounts of the call of Peter (Mt 4:18–22; Mk 1:16–20; Lk 5:1–11; Jn 1: 40–42). These agree that he was called with his brother Andrew* and that their call was closely linked with the call of James* and John*. The call in the Synoptic Gospels occurs at the Sea of Galilee (Lk alone associates it with the marvelous catch of fish); in Jn it occurs near the Dead Sea, and in Jn they are disciples or at least listeners of John the Baptist. The accounts agree also that the call occurred early in the public life of Jesus.

Peter is mentioned much more frequently in the Gospels than any other disciple; this together with other considerations (cf below) indicates an undefined special position in the group of disciples and a special interest in him in the gospel traditions. The special position is most easily defined as close association with Jesus not shared by the others, a vague responsibility assumed or committed as the representative and spokesman of the

group and some degree of initiative. These do not of themselves add up to leadership, but they furnish a basis for the leadership which he evidently exhibits after the resurrection of Jesus. He is mentioned first in the lists of the Twelve (Mt 10:2; Mk 3:16; Lk 6:14; AA 1:13). Jesus cured his mother-in-law (Mt 8:14). Peter attempted to walk on the water (Mt 14:28–31). He asks an explanation of sayings of Jesus (Mt 15:15; Lk 12:41). He attempts to object to the prediction of the passion and is sharply rebuked by Jesus (Mt 16:22 f; Mk 9:32 f). With James and John he was a witness of the transfiguration* (Mt 17:1; Mk 9:2; Lk 9:28), the raising of the daughter of Jairus* (Mk 5:37; Lk 8:51) and the agony (Mt 26:37; Mk 14:33). With John Jesus sent him to prepare the Passover (Lk 22:8). Jesus paid the temple tax for Himself and Peter (Mt 17:24–27). He proposed the question about forgiveness (Mt 18:21). He asks what reward the disciples shall receive for their renunciation (Mt 19:27; Mk 10:28; Lk 18:28). He affirms that he will take no scandal at anything that happens to Jesus and is warned of his coming denial (Mt 26: 33–35; Mk 14:29–31; Lk 22:33 f; Jn 13: 36–38). To Peter Jesus addresses a mild rebuke when the disciples fall asleep in Gethsemani (Mt 26:40; Mk 14:37). He asks a question about the fig tree (Mk 11: 21). With James, John and Andrew he asks the signs of the second coming (Mk 13:3). He leads the disciples when they pursue Jesus into the desert (Mk 1:36). He answers the question of Jesus when Jesus was touched by the woman with a hemorrhage (Lk 8:45). He objects when Jesus washes his feet (Jn 13:6–9). He inquires about the traitor (Jn 13:24). When Jesus was arrested he assaulted Malchus* with a sword (Jn 18:10). The resurrection is announced to "the disciples and Peter" (Mk 16:7). Lk 24:34 and 1 Co 15:5 suggest that he was the first witness of the Risen Jesus; this tradition is not at the base of the narratives of Mt and Jn. With John, Peter investigated the empty tomb (Jn 20:2–10). On other Gospel texts which state more formally the special position of Peter cf below. It should be noticed that the special position of Peter is found in all four Gospels.

In the first Christian community of Jerusalem Peter appears as the leader immediately after the ascension of Jesus and retains this position through AA 1–12. He proposes the election of a successor to Judas in the Twelve (AA 1:15–26). He is the spokesman of the disciples at Pentecost (AA 2), after the cure of the lame man (AA 3), and before the council (AA 4; 5:29). He more than any other exhibits the healing power of Jesus (AA 3; 5:15; 9:32–43). In the episode of Ananias* and Sapphira* he is the spokesman of the community (AA 5:1–11) and he rejects the proposal of Simon* Magus (AA 8:20–24). His leadership is not exercised in a monarchical manner, and it is said that he and John are sent to Samaria to confer the spirit on the disciples (AA 8:14). He is the first to preach the gospel to Gentiles (AA 10) and explains this as the result of a heavenly revelation (AA 11: 1–18). The same attitude is shown in his discourse at the council of Jerusalem (AA 15:7–11). Paul likewise attests his importance in the primitive Church both in Jerusalem and elsewhere. At Corinth one party called itself the party of Cephas, although there is no evidence that Peter had been in the city except this allusion (1 Co 1:12; 3:22). Paul sets him apart as a witness of the resurrection (1 Co 15:5). On Paul's first visit to Jerusalem he conferred with Peter but saw no other apostle except James (Gal 1:18).

Except for AA 15:7–11, Peter disappears after AA 12; and information on the further course of his life is uncertain. "The other place" of AA 12:17 is often said to be Rome; but the text does not imply this. The silence of Rm about Peter makes it difficult to affirm not only that he was in Rome when Rm was written, but that he had ever been there. 1 Pt was written from "Babylon" (1 Pt 5:13); it is far more likely that this is a cryptic allusion to Rome than that it means the city of Mesopotamia. 1 Pt is not certainly the work of Peter (cf PETER, EPISTLES OF) but the line attests a belief that Peter had been in Rome, and the attestation is early.

The residence, death and burial of Peter in Rome are so strongly imbedded in tradition that few recent historians doubt it; and no other church claimed him. The literary form of the tradition, however, does not clearly appear before late in the 2nd century, and the idea of Peter as bishop of Rome does not appear in the literature before the 3rd century. Two early witnesses, Clement of Rome (1 Clement 5, about 96) and Ignatius of Antioch (shortly after 100) explicitly affirm neither the martyrdom of Peter nor Rome as the place of his death, but the texts are most easily understood as implying it; and it is altogether probable that they do not affirm it because it was so well known that it did not occur to them to affirm it. The earliest traditions concerning the place of Peter's death and burial are somewhat imprecise. The Vatican was accepted as the site of Peter's tomb in the time of Constantine. Gaius of Rome in the 3rd century claimed that Rome had the

"trophies" of Peter and Paul on the Vatican and the Via Ostiensis respectively. The recent excavations under St. Peter's basilica have disclosed a pagan cemetery in which the earliest dated burial belongs to AD 70; Christian burials occur in later centuries, but the inscriptions make no allusion to the proximity of the graves to Peter's grave. There can be no doubt that this cemetery is the site which was identified in the time of Gaius with the tomb of Peter. The Vatican as the place of execution of Christian martyrs in the reign of Nero is otherwise well attested. The possibility must be recognized that the bodies of the martyrs were thrown into a common pit or burned, and that only the site of the death could be retained. The convergence of probabilities leads most historians to accept the Roman tradition that Peter was executed in the reign of Nero between 64 and 67 on the Vatican hill, possibly as one of a large number. There is no basis for the tradition that he was crucified, either upright or reversed.

2. *The Primacy of Peter.* The position of Peter in the Church rests primarily upon a few texts of the Gospels; these texts harmonize fully with the texts cited above, which give only a somewhat vague special position to Peter. In Mt 16:16–18, after Peter in the name of the disciples has recognized Jesus as Messiah, Jesus confers upon him the name of "Rock," promises him that He will build His Church* upon this rock, and gives Peter the keys of the kingdom of heaven and the power to bind and loose. The importance of the confession of Peter, in which he is the spokesman of the disciples, is evident in the parallel accounts also (Mk 8:29; Lk 9:20). The absence of the saying addressed to Peter in Mk-Lk has led many scholars to conclude that the saying is not from Jesus, but from the primitive Church, and in particular from the Jewish Christian community. The question here is not whether the Gospels reproduce the very words of Jesus, for they frequently do not. The question is whether the Gospels reproduce the teaching of Jesus accurately in their own words as well as in His. If the community creates the formal saying, it does so through its resources of apostolic memory and tradition and expresses the mind of Jesus. The texts from other Gospels (cf below) are in agreement with the commission insofar as they too represent a special office of Peter within the Church. O. Cullmann has pointed out that the language and the ideas of Mt 16:16–18 are Semitic and Palestinian. The word "church," found in the Gospels only here and Mt 18:17, represents Hb ḵāhāl or 'ēdāh, the sacred community of Israel. The word play on "rock" is Aramaic and

is reproduced in Gk by forming a new masculine name from the feminine *petra*. Cullmann concludes that everything points to the originality of the saying; and its absence from Mk-Lk is most easily explained on the hypothesis that it did not appear in their sources.

The metaphors used clearly imply a leadership in the Church which is not shared by Peter with the other apostles. The leadership is described in metaphorical not juridical language; and the OT background of both metaphors does not specify them further (cf Is 22:22). "Rock" is a common title of God, but not of a human ruler in the OT. "Bind and loose" are not used in the OT in any sense which is pertinent to this passage; the only usage which may be relevant is the rabbinical use of "bind" and "loose" of rabbinical decisions to prohibit or to permit respectively. Actually it is the use of metaphor rather than juridical language which leaves the leadership open to development in the life and growth of the Church.

How Peter understood his leadership is best determined by the manner in which he exercised it; and this is seen most clearly in the narratives of AA (cf above). In Mt alone the conferring of the name Peter is associated with the confession. In Mk-Lk the change is noted with no context, and in Jn 1:42 it is placed in the first meeting of Jesus and Peter.

Cullmann asks whether the commission comes from Jesus before or after the resurrection; and on the basis of Jn 21 (cf below) he believes that tradition based Peter's leadership on a commission granted both before and after. He denies, however, that Mt 16 is to be identified with Jn 21; but the absence of the saying in Mk-Lk suggests, he thinks, that the scene of the confession of Peter was not the original situation of the saying, and possibly the original scene was not remembered. Cullmann proposes that Mt has transferred the saying from the Passion account, where he found it, and where Lk has a related saying; cf below.

A parallel to the confession appears in Jn 6:68, without any accompanying commission. Lk 22:31 f contains a commission which likewise confers leadership with no definition, the commission to Peter to strengthen his fellow disciples. In a context which speaks of faith the strengthening is best understood of faith, and passage suggests the rock metaphor in the name of Peter. In Jn 21 Peter is commissioned to feed the lambs and the sheep, i.e., to be the shepherd* of the flock of Jesus. Against the biblical background of this figure this is perhaps an even clearer commission to govern than Mt 16:16–18.

In Jn 21 occurs a manifest balance between the triple confession of Peter and the triple denial; and it is unlikely that the denial, which is narrated so circumstantially in all four Gospels, is not connected with the idea of the primacy. The connection suggests that the leaders of the Church are human and weak like anyone else; that the weakness exhibited by Peter does not make him unacceptable for the leadership of the community; and that human weakness in the Church is sustained only by the vitalizing presence of Jesus in the Church.

The leadership of Peter, so clear in AA 1–12, is somewhat obscured by the accounts of AA 15 and Gal 2, in which James assumes an eminence which is sudden and surprising. Peter is one of the pillars with James and John (Gal 2:9). Paul attests the importance of Peter in the Antioch incident (Gal 2:11–14); had Peter not been such a massive figure, his example would not have been so damaging. But in the same passage Paul attests that Peter was afraid of the emissaries. This does not imply that superior authority of James; neither does it imply the absolute authority of Peter. A number of exegetes, most recently Cullmann, have proposed the hypothesis that after AA 12 Peter yielded the leadership of the Jerusalem church to James and himself undertook the mission among the Jews of the Diaspora*. In favor of this can be quoted Gal 2:7 f; but in this passage Paul appears to give himself a position equal to the position of Peter in the direction of missionary work. But here there are problems also; neither Peter nor Paul clearly observed the division between the Jewish mission and the Gentile mission before the date of Gal. In AA Paul in his first two journeys opened each mission by speaking in the synagogue, and in AA also Peter is the first to preach to Gentiles (cf above).

This division of labor can scarcely mean that Peter resigned his leadership of the Church; nor does it appear possible for him to resign a leadership which rested on a commission from Jesus. The uncertainties are much more easily resolved if one remembers that the Church of the first generation found its organization and structure as it went along. It is clear that the Jerusalem church remained "the mother Church" in a sense until AD 70. But before one thinks of Jerusalem as central headquarters one should note that Antioch is not known to have sought the approval of Jerusalem for the mission of Barnabas and Paul. The head of the church of Jerusalem was not by that very fact the head of the entire Church. Peter most probably did not remain as head of the church of Jerusalem once the expansion of Christianity had begun. How he fulfilled his commission of "feeding the flock" after he left Jerusalem is not reported in the NT. One should not look in Peter or in the primitive Church for the developed conception of the primacy which appears no earlier than the 3rd century. The NT does not show Peter exercising a monarchical leadership. The development of the power possessed by the Church and by Peter into monarchical leadership lies outside of biblical theology; it is an example of the development of dogma, of the office of the Church to define the exercise and the application of the powers she has received from Jesus Christ in historical situations which were never encountered by the primitive Church.

Peter, Epistles of. 1. *1 Pt.*

A. Contents.

1:1–2, greeting.

1:3–12, thanksgiving for the regeneration of baptism.

1:13–2:10, exhortation to maintain the holiness of life imposed by the new condition of baptism.

2:11–3:12, exhortation to observe Christian standards in family relations and in dealing with others.

3:13–4:6, exhortation to sustain persecution by adhering to virtue and following the example set by Jesus in His suffering.

4:7–19, the Paròusia is a motive to Christian virtue and to patience in suffering.

5:1–11, duties of the chiefs and members of the Christian community toward each other.

5:12–14, final greetings and blessing.

B. Literary Form and Purpose. The epistolary form of 1 Pt appears only in the greetings and conclusion; there are no personal allusions about the writer or those addressed. The destination is general, and nothing is known of the churches of the regions mentioned; some scholars have suggested that it is a homily to which the epistolary form has been added. While 1 Pt is homiletic and parenetic, it contains doctrinal elements interspersed as motivation for its exhortations.

Recent scholarship has paid much attention to the allusions to baptism (1:3, 23; 2:2; 3:18 ff); and there is a consensus that the author has used the baptismal catechesis as a source. The degree to which it is used is disputed. Boismard has suggested that 1:3–2:10 reproduce the baptismal liturgy; 1:3–12 is a hymn, and 1:13–2:10 is the baptismal catechesis. Others carry the theory further. Bornemann identified 1:3–5:11, the entire epistle, as a baptismal sermon, and believes that an editor added the introductory and concluding salutations to give it epistolary

form and apostolic origin. Others find a compilation of two documents: 1:3–4:11 is a baptismal sermon, and 4:12–5:14 is an epistle written to a community which was experiencing persecution. These theories go well beyond the evidence of the text; but the relation of 1 Pt to the baptismal liturgy and catechesis is assured.

C. Authorship. Peter is identified as the author in 1:1, and he is indicated in 5:1 f, 13. The early tradition is unanimous in attributing 1 Pt to him. A number of modern scholars have raised objections against the attribution, not all of equal weight and not convincing even taken together. In the hypothesis that most or all of the letter is a baptismal liturgy it can scarcely be attributed to Peter. More serious is the objection based upon the allusions to persecutions. Critics point out that the persecution is described as official and general (2:12, 19 f; 3:9, 14–17; 4:4, 12–16, 19; 5:9 f). No such general and official persecution occurred during the life of Peter and cannot be attested before the end of the reign of Domitian (81–96), in the opinion of some not before the reign of Trajan (98–117), late in the reign. The traditional date of the death of Peter falls late in the reign of Nero; Nero's persecution of the Christians seems to have been brief and local. Those who maintain the authorship of Peter point out that these passages, examined carefully, do not indicate a general and official persecution. The strongest passage is 4:12, but this is obscure and metaphorical. The terms in which 1 Pt recommends submission to public authority (2:13 f) do not in any way suggest that the authority is persecuting the Church. The passages seem therefore to allude not to the persecution by public authority but to the annoyances and hardships to which, it is easily supposed, Christians were submitted by hostile neighbors.

A more serious objection is drawn from the language. 1 Pt has a rich vocabulary, many skillful turns of phrase, such devices as antitheses and synonyms, and a very good knowledge of the LXX. Such mastery of the language seems highly improbable in Peter, and is; one must attribute the composition of the letter to another person. There is no difficulty in this attribution; the part of Silvanus (cf SILAS) in the composition of the letter is stated in 5:12. It must be supposed that the part of Silvanus was much more than the work of amanuensis; his part in the composition of the letter was equal to the part of Peter, if indeed it was not greater.

It is very probably to Silvanus, who had also been a companion of Paul, that we may attribute the numerous affinities with the language of Paul: 1:14 = Rm 12:2; 2:4–8 = Rm 9:32 f; 2:13–17 = Rm 13:1–7; 3:9 = Rm 12:17; 3:18 = Rm 5:2; Eph 2:18; 3:12, 22 = Eph 1:20 f; 4:1 = Rm 6:7; 4:10 f = Rm 12:6. These need not be understood as literary allusions or dependences, but as memories of Paul's diction. 1 Pt also has affinities with Js: 1:1 = Js 1:1; 1:6 f = Js 1:2 f; 1:23–2:2 = Js 1:17–22; 4:8 = Js 5:20; 5:5 f = Js 4:6, 10. These are less easily explained than the affinities with Paul, and seem to demand that Js was available to Silvanus in the composition of 1 Pt — unless one supposes that there was a greater community of phrase between James and Peter themselves than one might otherwise suppose.

If 1 Pt is to be attributed to Pt, it must almost certainly fall in 64. It was written from Rome (Babylon of 5:13).

D. Doctrinal Elements. As noted above, 1 Pt is parenetic, and the doctrinal elements occur as motivation for his counsels. Nevertheless, 1 Pt contains an excellent summary of some of the chief heads of the early teaching. Jesus is preexistent; the emphasis, as in Paul, falls upon His atoning death; He is the model of Christian conduct. On the peculiar passage 3:19–4:6 cf DESCENT INTO HELL. The emphasis upon baptism is noted above; with it is emphasis upon regeneration and new life conferred upon the Christian. The Church is represented as a building (2:4–8); it has officers (5:1–3), and the beginnings of the hierarchical structure can be discerned.

2. 2 Pt.

A. Contents.

1:1–2, greeting.

1:3–11, the gifts of salvation received from God and the duties which they impose.

1:12–21, assurance that the prophecies of the Parousia are valid.

2:1–3, the appearance of false teachers.

2:4–9, certainty of judgment upon false teachers illustrated from the fall of the angels, the deluge, Sodom and Gomorrah.

2:10–22, the sins of the false teachers.

3:1–13, reasons for the delay of the Parousia; apocalyptic description of the Parousia and the judgment.

3:14–18, concluding warnings.

B. Literary Form and Purpose. It is more evident in 2 Pt than in 1 Pt that the epistolary form is merely external; no particular group is addressed, and the form is the Jewish-Hellenistic homily (cf HEBREWS, EPISTLE: JAMES, EPISTLE). The author is a Jew who has been deeply imbued with Hellenistic culture. His vocabulary is erudite and his style is impersonal. He writes to reassure Christians whose faith has been shaken because the predictions of the Parousia have not been verified.

C. Authorship and Date. The author clearly affirms that he is Peter (1:1, 16–18; 3:1, 15). In spite of this, tradition is by no means uniform in this attribution. Origen and Eusebius said that it was contested, and several eastern churches did not accept it. The objection was particularly strong in the Gk churches because of the manifest difference in style between 1 Pt and 2 Pt. Modern scholars are almost unanimously convinced that Peter (or the author of 1 Pt) cannot be the author of 2 Pt.

2 Pt seems to presuppose a collection of the letters of Paul which are regarded as Scripture (3:15 f). Whether this collection existed before the end of the 1st century or not, it certainly did not exist with this quality during the life of Peter. The delay of the Parousia is not of itself a convincing argument against a later date; but the reference to the first generation of Christians as "the fathers" (3:2) who are dead cannot come from a first generation Christian. So also the apostles are joined with the prophets as heroes of the past (3:2). The dependence of 2 Pt 2:1–3:3 on Jd 4–18 is evident, and scholars agree that Jd is prior. It is granted that 2 Pt 2:1–3:3 seems to be a digression and an interruption, but it does not show a lack of unity of authorship. 1 Pt has a vocabulary of 469 words and 2 Pt a vocabulary of 330 words, of which they have only 100 in common. These indications are now accepted as convincing arguments that 2 Pt is not from Peter.

If it is not, the author and the date remain unknown. A date later than the fall of Jerusalem in 70 is as early as one may go; a date at the end of the 1st century or early in the 2nd century is much more probable, but the dates ranging from 120 to 180 suggested by some appear altogether too late. The attribution is a literary fiction, which was not regarded in the ancient world as we regard it now; but the attribution to Peter may indicate that the author had been a disciple of Peter who attempted to answer the question of the delay of the Parousia in terms which he remembered as those of Peter.

D. Canonicity. Origen is the first witness to the canonicity of 2 Pt. In the 4th century, because of its doubtful authorship, it was denied or doubted as much as it was accepted. It was accepted in the west after 400.

E. Doctrinal Elements. The principal and indeed the only topic is the Parousia* and the judgment*. 2 Pt is remarkable in its apocalyptic coloring. The epistle has some often quoted passages: the partaking of the divine nature (1:4) and the inspiration of the prophets (1:20 f).

Pethor (Hb *p^etôr*, meaning uncertain), the place of origin of Balaam*, near the Euphrates* (Nm 22:5), in Aram*, in the mountains of the E (Nm 23:7). It is possible that Pethor is to be identified with Pitru, a city on the Euphrates in N Syria mentioned in the records of Shalmaneser III of Assyria (858–824 BC). Shalmaneser III marks that the name Pitru was used only by the inhabitants of the city; other peoples knew the place by a different name.

Phanuel. Cf PENUEL.

Pharaoh (Hb *par`ōh*, Egyptian *pr–,* "great house" [an expression similar to "The White House"]), a title (not a personal name) of the Egyptian king which appears in the 18th dynasty (16th century BC) and is used thereafter. The Hb "Pharaoh king of Egypt" corresponds exactly to *pir'u sar musri,* a title used in Assyrian records.

Pharisees (Hb *p^erûšîm*, Aramaic *p^erîššayya,'* meaning uncertain; possibly "separated," the "separate ones," or "separators," i.e., distinguishers, expositors [of the law*]). This party or sect within Judaism is mentioned frequently in the Gospels, almost entirely as extremely hostile to Jesus. The origin of the group is uncertain; scholars connect them with the Hasideans* of the Maccabean period. Josephus* first mentions them as appearing in the reign of John Hyrcanus (135–104 BC; cf HASMONEANS), but it is probable that the group appeared earlier. Their number was probably small. Josephus says there were 6000 in Herod's time. Josephus and some allusions in the Talmud* are our only source of information on the Pharisees outside the NT. They are the heirs of Ezra* rather than of the prophets; they conceived Judaism as a religion centered upon the observance of the law, and they interpreted the obligations of the law in the most severe manner. The Israel under the law which the Pharisees conceived was a theocracy, a nation-religion, and their conception was nonpolitical. They were opposed to the later Hasmonean rulers and to Herod, despite the fact that these rulers were Jewish or, in the case of Herod, not as foreign as Rome, on the ground that these rulers were in opposition to the law either in their conception of the Jewish nation-state or in their manner of life and government. They were realists and in general, it seems, nonmessianic; they had as a group little sympathy with the fanatic nationalists who attempted to rebel against Rome, and preferred submission to Rome, which was generally tolerant of the religions of subject peoples and permitted the Jewish nation-state to live under its law. Their politics were flexible; their opposition to Alexander Jannaeus finally issued in civil war and persecution of the Pharisees, but his successor Alexandra permitted the Pharisees to exercise a powerful influence on her government.

The Pharisees were a lay group and stood in opposition to the Sadducees*, the sacerdotal party. They were in close alliance with the scribes*, the teachers and interpreters of the law. In the other direction they stood in opposition to "the people of the land," the ignorant who neither knew nor cared about the niceties of Pharisaic observance. The Gospels allude several times to the proud exclusiveness of the Pharisees (Mt 9:9–13; Mk 2:13–17; Lk 5:27–32; 18:9–14; Jn 7:49). But their adhesion to the law and their conception of the nation-state was vital in Judaism, and Pharisaic Judaism alone survived the catastrophe of AD 70 when the Jewish community of Palestine was destroyed by the Romans.

The NT and Josephus allude to some distinct Pharisaic beliefs, particularly in contrast with the beliefs of the Sadducees. The Sadducees admitted only the law, the five books of Moses, as imposing valid obligations upon Jews. The Pharisees accepted also the oral traditions of the elders (Mt 15:2; Mk 7:5), which was attributed to a chain of elders which went all the way back to Moses. These traditions erected a "fence" about the law, and exact observance of the traditions was a safeguard against violations of the law itself. They believed in the existence of angels and spirits, the resurrection of the dead, and the judgment; these beliefs were denied by the Sadducees.

The mutual hostility of Jesus and the Pharisees is evident in the Gospels, and some historians have charged that the Gospels have presented a false and slanderous picture of the Pharisees. It should be noted that the Talmud itself, which is strongly Pharisaic in origin, also contains some remarks hostile to the Pharisees which find the same faults in them which appear in the NT. The picture which the Gospels present is consistent and scarcely exaggerated on the face of it. The hostility of the Pharisees toward Jesus appears at the very beginning of the Gospel accounts, and seems to have arisen from the fear of the Pharisees that Jesus threatened their position as religious leaders. Even John the Baptist called them a brood of vipers who were excessively proud and confident of their Jewish blood (Mt 3:7–10; Lk 3:7–9). The authors of the Gospels often mention them together with the chief priests (who were Sadducees), scribes and lawyers (two names for the same group), all of whom were hostile to Jesus, and make no careful distinction in attributing remarks to one group or to the other or to all together.

In the Gospels the Pharisees watch Jesus closely to find some fault in Him (Jn 4:1); they try to trap Him into a wrong answer (Mt 22:15; Mk 12:13; Lk 20:20 ff), and propose questions about the interpretation of the law (Mt 22:34; the Pharisees are not named in the parallel passages in Mk and Lk; Mt 19:3; Mk 10:2) and points of Jewish belief: the coming of the kingdom (Lk 17:20), the Messiah (Mt 22:41; the Pharisees are not named in the parallel passages of Mk and Lk). They investigate the mission of John the Baptist (Jn 1:24). They are scandalized at the conduct of Jesus: His association with publicans and sinners (Mt 9:9–13; Mk 2:13–17; Lk 5:27–32; 7:36; 15:2), at His laxness in the Sabbath observance (Mt 12:2 ff; Mk 2:24 ff; Lk 6:2 ff), at His healing on the Sabbath (Lk 14:1–3), at His neglect of ritual ablutions (Mt 15:1 ff; Mk 7:1 ff). In these examples of scandal they exhibit an excessively meticulous idea of the obligations of the law. They object to Jesus' claim of power to forgive sin (Lk 5:17 ff; they are not named in the parallel passages in Mt and Mk). They attribute Jesus' exorcisms to a league with Beelzebub (Mt 12:24; they are not named in the parallel passages in Mk-Lk). They object when Jesus is triumphantly saluted by His disciples (Lk 19:39). Jn emphasizes their hostility (8:13; 12:19, 42) and their incredulity (7:45–48; 9:13–16). They plot against the life of Jesus (Mt 12:14; Mk 3:6; not named in Lk 6:11; Jn 11:46–53, 57), but only Jn places them in the arresting party (18:3). In Mt 27:62 their hostility to Jesus extends even to the tomb. Lk calls them avaricious and says they frustrate the plan of God (16:14; 7:30).

Perhaps the mildest saying of Jesus concerning the Pharisees is that His disciples must be more righteous than they to enter the kingdom of heaven (Mt 5:20). When they ask for a sign to confirm His mission He calls them a wicked and adulterous generation (Mt 12:38 ff; 15:1 ff; Mk 7:1 ff). He condemns their exclusiveness as harsh (Mt 9:9–13; Mk 2:13–17; Lk 5:27–32; 7:36 ff), and their rigor in the law as intolerable (Mt 12:2 ff; Mk 2:24 ff; Lk 6:2 ff). They commit the unforgivable sin against the spirit (Mt 12:31 ff; Mk 3:28 f). Their rigor in the law is a device to evade its obligations (Mt 15:1 ff; Mk 7:1 ff). They are the wicked husbandmen of the parable (Mt 21:33–46; not named in Mk 12:1–12 and Lk 20:9–19). They are blind with self-

inflicted blindness (Jn 9:40). Their self-righteousness is castigated in the parable of the Pharisee and the publican (Lk 18:9–14); this parable, together with the words of Jesus about their exclusiveness, make it clear that He implies that they are not the most admirable element in the Jewish community, as they pretended to be, but the lowest. In the invective discourses of Mt 23 and Lk 11:37 ff the recurring word is "hypocrites"; the Pharisees evade the more sacred obligations of the law and insist on mere external formalities, do not themselves observe the obligations which they impose, and are "whited sepulchers," concerned with looking devout while vicious at heart.

It would no doubt be inaccurate to say that the Pharisees were the only group of Jews which were mortally opposed to Jesus. Their responsibility for His death seems to have been less than the responsibility of the priests and Sadducees. Nor does the group condemnation imply that there were no Pharisees who did not deserve the condemnation. Among the Pharisees were men like Nicodemus* (Jn 3; 7:45–48) and Gamaliel* (AA 5:34). The Christian community of Jerusalem included Pharisees (AA 15:5), and Paul was not ashamed to call himself a Pharisee (AA 23:6–9; 26:5; Phl 3:5). It is not unlikely that Jewish Christians included a large number of Pharisees; the ideal of life under the law was not foreign either to Christian messianism nor Christian morality, and where the defects of Pharisaism did not reach the peak described in the Gospels it seems that Pharisaism should have been as receptive to the teaching of Jesus as any other Jewish group. The basic fault of the Pharisees was their refusal to admit that Judaism could reach any further development beyond themselves; they called a halt to the saving activity and power of God.

Pharpar (Hb *parpar*, meaning uncertain), with the Abanah* one of the rivers of Damascus; probably a branch of the Barada (2 K 5:12).

Phicol (Hb *pîkōl*, etymology uncertain; Egyptian *p,'-rkw*, "Lycian," has been suggested, and thus the word would be a title rather than a personal name), the commander of the (mercenary?) soldiers of Abimelech* (Gn 21:22, 32; 26:26). The Lycians must be an anachronism in this period.

Philadelphia (Gk *philadelphia*, "brotherly love"), one of the seven cities addressed by the author of Apc (1:11; 3:7–13). Philadelphia was an important and prosperous city of Lydia*. It lay on the slopes of Mt

Tmolus E of Sardis* on the road between Sardis and Hierapolis*, and was included in the administrative district of Sardis. The region was fertile but subject to earthquakes; the city was wrecked by an earthquake in AD 17. Cf also RABBAH.

Philemon, Epistle to. 1. *Contents.*

1–3, greeting.

4–7, thanksgiving for Philemon's faith and fraternal love.

8–21, request that Philemon should receive Onesimus, his slave who had fled, met Paul, and been received as a Christian, not as a slave but as a brother in Christ; Paul will meet charges for any damage done by Onesimus.

22–25, request for lodgings and final conclusion.

2. *Authorship and date.* The Pauline authorship of Phm is questioned by no one. Alone among the epistles it is a private personal letter. Philemon (Gk *philēmon,* "loving") was a Christian of Colossae, converted by Paul (probably at Ephesus). In 11 Paul plays on the name Onesimus (Gk *onēsimos,* "useful") and alludes to the services which Onesimus had rendered him. Paul does not ask for the manumission of Onesimus directly; he asks that Philemon forgive Onesimus any harm he has done and receive him as a brother, not as a slave. The appeal does not attack the institution of slavery* directly, but creates an atmosphere in which it would be difficult for slavery to survive.

Phm is with Col, Eph, and Phl, one of "the epistles of the captivity" and was sent to Colossae through Tychicus* with Col, most probably from Rome; cf COLOSSIANS, EPISTLE. It is to be dated 62–63.

Philetus (Gk *philētos,* "beloved"), a personal name; with Hymenaeus* an early heretic who asserted that the resurrection had already occurred (2 Tm 2:17).

Philip (Gk *philippos,* "lover of horses"), a personal name. 1. One of the Twelve, mentioned in the lists (Mt 10:3; Mk 3:18; Lk 6:14; AA 1:13). Philip is prominent in Jn. His call is related in Jn 1:43–48; he came from Bethsaida* in Galilee, was called by Jesus Himself, and in turn brought Nathanael* to Jesus. He engages in a brief dialogue with Jesus in the multiplication of the loaves (Jn 6:5, 7). The request of the Hellenistic Jews to introduce them to Jesus suggests that he was regarded as being more closely associated with Jesus than others of the Twelve (Jn 12:21 f). He asked Jesus to show them the Father (Jn 14:8). Of his later life and career nothing is known.

2. One of the seven chosen to assist the apostles in Jerusalem (AA 6:5; cf DEACON). He was the first to announce the Gospel in Samaria* (AA 8:5–13), where he converted Simon* the magician. He converted the eunuch of the queen of Ethiopia (cf CANDACE) on a journey from Jerusalem to Gaza (AA 8:26–40), and from there he announced the Gospel in the cities of the costal plain. In AA 21:8 f he is still residing in Caesarea* with four unmarried daughters who "prophesied"; the word here is probably used in the OT sense of ecstatic song and dance.

3. Son of Herod* the Great and Cleopatra of Jerusalem, granted a part of Herod's kingdom in the will of Herod; the grant was confirmed by Augustus. The territory of Philip included the ancient Bashan*: according to Josephus, Gaulanitis, Trachonitis, Batanea, Panias, Auranitis; Lk 3:1 mentions Trachonitis and Iturea. The territory was almost entirely Gentile. Philip had been educated at Rome and remained loyal throughout his life. Little is recorded of him, and he seems to have administered his territory in peace and order. He built a new city at Panion near the ancient Dan, which he named Caesarea* Philippi in honor of the emperor; his own name was added to distinguish it from Caesarea on the sea built by Herod the Great. He rebuilt entirely the village of Bethsaida* on the Sea of Galilee and named it Julia in honor of the daughter of Augustus. His wife was Salome*, the daughter of Herodias*; there were no children to this marriage. He died in AD 33–34 after 27 years of rule. After his death his territory was incorporated into the province of Syria* in AD 37 and was shortly thereafter granted to Agrippa* I by Caligula.

4. The son of Herod the Great and Mariamme the daughter of Simon (not the granddaughter of Hyrcanus II), the husband of Herodias in Mt 14:3; Mk 6:17. This Philip is called Herod in Josephus and is otherwise unknown. Herodias abandoned him to marry the tetrarch Herod Antipas.

Philippi. A city of NE Macedonia on the Gulf of Neapolis, 8 mi from the sea. It lies in a plain surrounded by mountains. The city is named after its founder, Philip II of Macedon; it was founded on the site of an older city, Crenides. The city passed under Roman rule after the conquest of Macedonia in 167 BC. The site was the scene of the defeat of the Roman republican forces led by Brutus and Cassius in 42 BC. After this victory the city became a Roman *colonia* with a large population of Roman veterans; it was subject to Roman law. This was its position when it was visited by Paul.

Archaeological exploration disclosed the forum, temples, library, baths, necropolis, aqueducts, porticos, gates, and some residential quarters of the Roman period; the streets identified included the Via Egnatia, the principal Roman road from Italy to Byzantium. A crypt of Roman construction is traditionally identified with the dungeon of Paul. In AA 16:12 Philippi is called "the first city of the district of Macedonia," probably the first city of *its* district, an administrative division, of Macedonia.

Philippi was visited by Paul and Silas on his second missionary journey in response to a dream which Paul had in Troas (AA 16:9–12). This is the first known visit of Christian missionaries to the continent of Europe. Paul first spoke in the Jewish place of prayer, then was offered lodging by Lydia*, a woman whom he converted. Paul and Silas were charged with illegal religious practices by the owners of a girl who had a divining spirit which Paul expelled. The two apostles were flogged and imprisoned. The refusal of Paul and Silas to escape when an earthquake shattered the prison gates so impressed the warder that he was baptized. The next day Paul revealed his Roman citizenship; this should have protected him from imprisonment and flogging, and the municipal authorities in fear asked the apostles to leave the city. Paul revisited Philippi on his third journey (AA 20:6). The affection which Paul felt for his first European congregation is evident in Phl.

Philippians, Epistle to the.
1. *Contents.*
1:1–2, greeting.
1:3–11, introduction: thanksgiving and prayer.
I. Imprisonment of Paul and the preaching of the gospel: 1:12–26.
1:12–18, Paul's imprisonment promotes the gospel.
1:19–22, life or death will be a blessing.
1:23–26, Paul is torn between desire for death and desire to remain active.
II. Instructions: 1:27–2:18.
1:27–2:11, exhortation to maintain the faith and to be humble and unselfish after the example of Christ.
2:12–18, one must work out one's salvation in fear and trembling and present a good example in preparation for the day of judgment.
III. Personal Messages: 2:19–3:1.
2:19–24, plans to send Timothy and to visit Philippi.
2:25–3:1, the mission of Epaphroditus.
IV. Final Exhortation: 3:2–4:9.
3:2–3, warning against agitators.
3:4–16, worthlessness of external merits;

value of knowledge of Christ and of righteousness.
3:17–21, the wicked who strive for the things of earth.
4:1–9, recommendations to individuals and to the community.
Conclusion: thanks, greeting, blessing, 4:10–23.
2. *Authorship, Date, Place of Composition.* The authorship of Phl by Paul is not questioned by modern critics; the unity of Phl, however, is not evident. There are breaks in the continuity at 2:19; 3:2; 4:2, 10. These have led some scholars to propose that Phl is not a single epistle but a conflation of several epistles sent by Paul to Philippi. This suggestion has not won general acceptance, but the problem of unity is not solved. The Christological hymn of 2:6–11, one of the most admired passages of all the Pauline letters, exhibits some differences in vocabulary from the other Pauline passages. These are not so significant that they impose the conclusion that Paul did not write this passage; but they are sufficient to furnish a basis for the theory that Paul has incorporated into his letter a hymn which was used in early Christian liturgy; cf below.

Phl, with Col, Eph, Phm, is one of "the captivity epistles"; these allude to an imprisonment of Paul, not necessarily the same imprisonment in all four. Early tradition unanimously identified this imprisonment with the imprisonment at Rome with which AA ends, and this is supported by 1:13 (the pretorium) and 4:22 (Caesar's household). This is still the easiest view of the composition of the letter, which would thus fall in 62–63. But it is not entirely satisfactory, and scholars have suggested the imprisonment of Paul at Caesarea before his voyage to Rome or an imprisonment at Ephesus not elsewhere recorded. The hypothesis of Caesarea has won little support; the arguments for an imprisonment at Ephesus are more serious. Phl 1:26, 30; 4:15 suggest that Paul has not revisited Philippi since its foundation; this would place Phl before the events of AA 20:1 ff and those mentioned in 2 Co. Paul gives the preaching of the gospel as the reason for his arrest (1:7, 12 f, 30); the reason for his imprisonment in AA 21:28; 24:6; 25:8 was his alleged defilement of the temple. The journeys of 2:25 ff suggest that the place of Paul's imprisonment was not far from Philippi; Ephesus is nearer and communications were easier, but Rome was a journey of at least 5 to 7 weeks from Philippi. Paul intends to visit Philippi (1:26; 2:24); but Rm reveals his plans at the moment of his imprisonment as a journey to the W. Paul did revisit Philippi after his sojourn at Ephesus (AA 19:21 f; 20:1; 1 Co 4:17; 16:5, 10; 2 Co 2:12 f; 7:5). The controversy over Judaizing falls better into the period of Gal and Rm than in the period of the Roman imprisonment. These reasons are not convincing, but they lead a number of modern scholars to withhold any certain affirmation that Phl was written at Rome or at Ephesus.

3. *Doctrinal Elements*. Phl is one of the least doctrinal of the Pauline epistles; but it contains the unique Christological hymn of 2:6–11, one of the most remarkable monuments of primitive Christian faith, whether it is written by Paul himself or cited by him from the liturgy. The six verses of the hymn are six strophes enunciating the following themes: the divine preexistence of Christ; the abasement of the incarnation; the abasement of death; the heavenly glorification of Christ; the adoration of the universe; the new title won by the glorified Christ. The incarnation is conceived as an "emptying," a renunciation of the glory which is proper to the person who is "equal to God," i.e., to the Father. Literary antecedents of the hymn have been sought in several places in Jewish and Gk literature; but the clearest literary connections are found with the Servant* poem of Is 53.

The identity of the adversaries of Paul in 3:2–3, 18–19 is not entirely clear, and it is unlikely that the same adversaries are meant in both passages. It appears more probable that the adversaries of 3:2–3 are Jewish agitators who arouse hostility toward Christianity. The adversaries of 3:18–19 are enemies of the cross, but the context does not indicate that they are Jews or Judaizing Christians as it does in 3:2 ff. The suggestion of Dibelius and others that they are Christian libertines who propose that the gospel is a removal of all restraint upon desire is well founded in 3:19; but no interpretation of the passage imposes itself.

Philistia, Philistines (Hb *peléšet* [geographic], *pelištim* [gentilic], meaning uncertain), a region and a people of Palestine. The geographic name is formed from the gentilic. The name Philistia designates the coastal plain of Palestine from just N of Gaza to the Wadi Ghazza; the coastal plain between the sea and the Shephelah* is narrow, reaching its widest at the latitude of Gaza, about 15–16 mi. The Philistine territory at its greatest extent included territory to the N and E. The coastal plain is rolling rather than flat. It is swampy and has extensive sand dunes, which sometimes cover arable land. Like the rest of the Palestinian coast, it has no natural harbors.

The Philistines are first mentioned in history by Ramses III of Egypt (1196–1165 BC). The Purasati were one of the "Sea Peoples" who invaded Egypt and were repulsed by Ramses III in the great amphibious battle recorded in the inscriptions and relief of Medinet Habu (ANET 262–263). After the repulse the Philistines settled in the coastal plain of Palestine; another of the Sea Peoples, the Tjekker, settled in the plain N of the Philistines. The city of Dor was in the hands of the Tjekker about 1100 BC; they are mentioned in the story of Wen-Amon (ANET 25–29). The settlement in

Relief sculptures from the tomb of Ramses III at Medinet Habu, showing his defeat of the Sea Peoples.

Palestine may have been made by an agreement with the Egyptians.

The Philistines were of Aegean-Asian origin, although the exact place of their origin is uncertain; they may have reached the Aegean basin from the mainland of the Balkan peninsula. A connection with Pelasgi has been suggested. Their race was Indo-Germanic or Mediterranean. They are represented in Egyptian art with the panache of Gk warriors, and the armor of Goliath* described in 1 S 17 is reminiscent of the armor of Homer's heroes. Their movement from their homeland was occasioned by the barbarian invasion of Europe about 1200 BC which excited a great movement of peoples throughout the lands of the E Mediterranean. The OT mentions Caphtor* as their place of origin, but this cannot be certainly identified; cf CHERETHI AND PELETHI. They have left no documents nor trace of their language, which is unknown; some names suggest an Aegean origin. Achish* has been related with Anchises, found in Homer, and Goliath with Alyattes, a name found in Hittite records. The name of the Philistine chieftains, *seren,* is thought by many scholars to be connected with the Gk *tyrannos,* "ruler." Their pottery was a distinctive Philistine ware which emerges in the early 12th century in Palestine; it is an imitation of 13th century Mycenean ware with contacts with Cyprian and Rhodian ware, and is painted with geometric designs and birds. They adopted some Canaanite cultural features. Their religion, known only from OT allusions, shows exclusively Canaanite features; the names of their gods Dagon*, Astarte*, and Baal-zebul* are all Semitic. Is 2:6 mentions their practice of divination. Eissfeldt and others have suggested that they were a ruling military aristocracy who imposed their sovereignty upon the native Canaanite population. They were obviously superior to the Canaanites and the Israelites in arms and military organization, and perhaps in physique also. They introduced the use of iron* into Palestine, and for some time exercised a monopoly of iron weapons and tools (1 S 13:19–22). The Philistine confederacy of the Pentapolis (Ashdod*, Ashkelon*, Ekron*, Gath*, Gaza*), each ruled by a *seren,* was more closely organized than any other Palestinian group of the period, and Philistine hegemony endured from about 1150 to about 1000 BC, when the Israelite monarchy was unified by David. The Israelite awareness of the racial and cultural difference between themselves and the Philistines is reflected in the frequent designation of the Philistines as "uncircumcised" (cf CIRCUMCISION).

The geographic name occurs in Ex 15:14, where it is anachronistic, in the oracle against Philistia delivered by Is (14:29–31) about 715 BC, and in Joel 4:4, where the Philistines with Tyre and Sidon are threatened for engaging in the slave trade; cf below. It occurs as a poetic title in Pss 60:10; 83:8; 108:10, where it occurs in an enumeration of the enemies of Israel, and in Ps 87:4 as one of the countries which has borne famous men. The gentilic in the singular is used only of Goliath*. Elsewhere only the plural of the gentilic is used.

In the Table of Nations* (Gn 10:14) the Philistines are the son of Caphtorim (cf CAPHTOR) and the descendant of Egypt; in 1 Ch 1:12 the lists have been garbled so that the Philistines are the son of Casluhim. This is a purely geographical explanation of the origin of the Philistines; cf above. A number of anachronistic uses of the name (Gn 21:32, 34; 26:1, 8, 14 f, 18; Ex 13:17; 23:31; 15:14; Jos 13:2 f; Jgs 3:3) betray that these passages are later than the early 12th century. The sea of the Philistines (Ex 23:31) is the Mediterranean. The influence of Philistine religion on the Israelites is mentioned in Jgs 10:6; this is a schematic editorial passage.

The Philistine conquest of Israelite territory appears in the story of Samson* (Jgs 13–16); Judah is subject to the Philistines (Jgs 15:11 ff), and Samson's tribe of Dan, whose territory lay between Judah and Philistia, was forced to migrate N to seek another home (Jgs 18). Israel, however, resisted the Philistine invasion, but it was soundly defeated at Aphek* (1 S 4), and the Philistines captured the ark* (1 S 5–6). The victory ascribed to Israel at Ebenezer* (1 S 7) cannot be historical; the passage is a midrash*. The penetration of the Philistines into the central range, the heart of Israelite territory, is shown by the presence of a Philistine post or garrison at Gibeah* (1 S 13:3; on Gibeath Elohim of 1 S 10:5, where there was a garrison) and by the fact that they easily advanced to Michmash* before Saul dared to give them battle. The battle at Michmash was Saul's first victory over the Philistines (1 S 13–14); it was not decisive, and war with the Philistines continued during the rest of Saul's reign (1 S 14:47, 52). Saul won another victory at the valley of Elah (1 S 17). The Philistines continued to raid Israel (1 S 23:27 f). The defeat and death of Saul at Mt Gilboa* (1 S 31) was a serious setback to Israel, and the Philistine hegemony was unchallenged until David united the monarchies of Israel and Judah. David himself appears to have been a mercenary. As a man of Judah he was probably a subject of the Philistines; he took service with Saul, but turned to the Philistines when

Saul attempted to assassinate him. Although it is not explicitly mentioned in the text of 2 S, David was probably installed as king of Judah as a vassal of the Philistines. It is doubtful whether his acceptance of the crown of Israel was acceptable to the Philistines. War broke out; the occasion is not mentioned, and no details of the wars have been preserved except some anecdotes of battles which occurred at Baal-perazim and the valley of Rephaim (2 S 5:17–25) Gob (2 S 21:15–22), Pasdammim, Lehi, and Bethlehem, probably the same campaign as the valley of Rephaim (2 S 23:9–17). David's victory over the Philistines was complete (2 S 8:1); it is not clear whether they became vassals or tributaries, but it does not seem that they were incorporated into David's kingdom. Israel's suzerainty over the Philistines was continued during the reign of Solomon (1 K 5:1). After the division of the monarchy Israel's control over the Philistines was not effective; it seems likely that they rendered themselves practically independent, but they were never again the menace to the very existence of Israel which they had been before Saul and David. There are several allusions to war with the Philistines and raids of the Philistines on Israelite territory during the monarchy: they held Gibbethon* under Nadab* and Zimri* of Israel (1 K 15:27; 16:15); they raided the territory of Judah in the reigns of Jehoram* and Ahaz* (2 Ch 21:16; 28:18); they paid tribute to Jehoshaphat* (2 Ch 17:11) and were defeated by Uzziah* (2 Ch 26:6 f). They were defeated by Hezekiah (2 K 18:8; this may refer to Hezekiah's seizure of Ekron*, cf HEZEKIAH). Several prophetic oracles indicate the enmity of Israel and the Philistines as late as the time of Ezk (Is 14:28–31; 9:11; Je 25:20; 47:1–7; Ezk 16:27, 57; 25:15 f; Zp 2:5). Is 11:14 and Zc 9:5–8, as well as Ps 83:8, are later passages in which the name is used in an archaism. Am 1:8 threatens them for their part in the slave trade. Am 6:2 alludes to the fall of Gaza, and Je 47:1–7 to the sack of Gaza by the Pharaoh; neither of these events is mentioned elsewhere.

The Philistines are not mentioned frequently in the Assyrian records, where they are called Palastu. Adad-nirari III (805–782 BC) advanced into Philistia, and Tiglath-pileser III conducted an expedition into Philistia in 734 BC. Sennacherib accepted the submission of Philistia after his suppression of the rebellion of 705–701. Esarhaddon (680–669) mentions Philistia as a province in a treaty with Baalu of Tyre; this indicates that it no longer existed even as a satellite kingdom. There are, however, several allusions to the separate Philistine cities and

their kings (cf ASHDOD; EKRON; GAZA) in earlier Assyrian records; possibly the confederacy of the Pentapolis was no longer maintained. Indeed, since the names of these kings are Semitic, it seems that the original Philistine immigrants had been entirely assimilated by the 8th century. As a political factor the Philistines are insignificant after the conquests of Nebuchadnezzar; the name Philistia for the territory was retained into Roman and Christian times, and survives in the modern name Palestine. The hostility of Jews and the people of Philistia is attested in the 2nd century BC by Ben Sira, who mentions the Philistines with the Samaritans and the Shechemites as peoples whom he detests (BS 50:26).

Phinehas (Hb pînᵉḥas, etymology uncertain; possibly Egyptian p,'nhšj, "the Negro"), a personal name. **1.** Son of Eleazar* and grandson of Aaron* (Ex 6:25; 1 Ch 5:30; 6:35); he was an ancestor of Ezra* (Ezr 7:5) and of the priest Gershom, a companion of Ezra (Ezr 8:2). Phinehas was celebrated for his zeal; when an Israelite was having intercourse with a Midianite woman in the rites of Baal Peor, Phinehas killed them both with a single thrust of a spear in the genital organs (Nm 25:7–11). For this he was promised an abiding priesthood. Among the several clans who had titles to the priesthood (cf PRIEST) this story validated the claim of the house of Phinehas; cf also Ps 106:30. Phinehas appropriately appears in the midrash* of the war of vengeance against Midian (Nm 31:6). In Jos 22:13, 30–32 he is the spokesman of Israel in the dispute with the tribes of E Palestine about the altar. Gibeah* was given him as a residence (Jos 24:33). The Levites claimed him as their chief (1 Ch 9:20).

2. Son of Eli* and brother of Hophni* (1 S 1:3), who with his brother abused the priestly office (1 S 2:12–36); both of them were killed in the battle of Aphek* (1 S 4:4, 11, 17). Phinehas' wife bore Ichabod* shortly after the battle. Ahijah*, priest in the time of Saul, was the grandson of Phinehas; the line survived until Abiathar* was deposed by Solomon. The stories cited above indicate that the house of Phinehas did not renounce its claim to the priesthood.

Phlegon (Gk phlegōn, "flaming"?), a Roman Christian greeted by Paul (Rm 16:14).

Phoebe (Gk phoebē, fem of phoebus, a title of Apollo), a Christian woman of Cenchreae*, recommended by Paul to the Roman congregation when she visited Rome and praised for her assistance of the apostles (Rm 16:1). On her position in the Church* cf DEACON.

Phoenicia (Gk *phoenikē*, "crimson," "purple-red"), a geographical name; the coastal strip of modern Syria and Lebanon from Jebel Akra, the ancient Mons Casius, to Mt Carmel, a distance of about 250 mi. Ancient Phoenicia included only the coastal strip and the W slope of the mountains and did not extend inland. The region is well watered; it has only five dry months during the year, and it has a number of rivers which are fed by mountain snows. Its soil is good and produces grain and excellent fruit. The climate is mild and generally agreeable; the summers are extremely hot. The most striking differences between the Phoenician coastal strip and the Palestinian coastal strip were decisive in the histories and cultures of the two regions: Phoenicia has a number of natural harbors, while there are none in Palestine; and the mountain barrier to the E is much more rugged in Phoenicia (cf

LEBANON). Phoenicia therefore looked to the W and the Mediterranean. Between the fall of Crete c 1500 BC and the rise of Gk sea power c 700 BC the Phoenicians enjoyed a monopoly of navigation in the Mediterranean.

The Phoenicians were a Semitic people, identical with the Canaanites* and related to the Israelites. They no doubt entered Phoenicia from the S or E, but this immigration occurred in prehistoric times. They called themselves Sidonians (cf SIDON). The Gk name Phoenicia is derived from *phoenix*, "purple," and alludes to the purple dye* which was one of the most celebrated products of Phoenicia.

From earliest history (about 2800 BC) there were close relations between Egypt and Phoenicia, with Egypt usually exercising a hegemony over Phoenicia. Egypt desired cedar*, another celebrated product

a) The Nahr-el-Kelb in Lebanon, where conquering armies have inscribed their exploits at the mouth of the river. b) Assyrian inscription at the mouth of the Nahr-el-Kelb. c) and d) Phoenician gods and goddesses.

which was widely exported. Egyptian influence ended with the 19th dynasty. 1200 to 750, the beginning of the Assyrian empire, was the period of the independence of Phoenicia and its greatest activity. It was in close cultural and political relations with Israel (cf TYRE). The Phoenician cities paid tribute to Assyria after the 9th century, but their independence was not seriously affected until after 750. The Neo-Babylonian empire attempted to maintain Mesopotamian control of Phoenicia with less success than Assyria. The Phoenicians appear to have accepted the Persian empire gladly; they were the most important naval allies of the Persians in their campaigns against Greece. The conquests of Alexander rendered the Phoenician cities politically impotent. They were incorporated into the Roman empire by Pompey in 64 BC.

Phoenicia was never a political unity. It was organized in city-states, each independent and ruled by a hereditary monarch assisted by a council of elders and magistrates. The most important cities were Tyre*, Sidon*, Byblos*, Arwad, and Ugarit*. The city-states were usually jealous and hostile to each other; but they generally maintained peace. The Phoenicians were commercial minded above all else, and disliked war as a hindrance to trade; they preferred to pay tribute to conquerors, which they could well afford, since they were among the wealthiest communities of the ancient world. Their economy was based on agriculture and industry; the work of Phoenician craftsmen, as can be observed from archaeological discovery, was extremely good and was much admired abroad. They excelled in the production of "luxury goods," executed with great skill. But the chief source of their wealth was commerce and trade. We have noticed their monopoly of the Mediterranean sea trade. They were the terminus of caravans from the Asiatic mainland, and their markets were the points of exchange for the entire Mediterranean world. To them is attributed the circumnavigation of Africa in the 6th century. Their network of colonies and factories extended through the entire Mediterranean basin, with the most important centers at Cyprus, Sicily, Sardinia, and the Iberian peninsula; the most famous colony was Carthage in N Africa, Karthadasht, "Newtown," founded from Tyre.

Phoenician culture was not original, but the Phoenicians were skillful adapters of alien cultures. Situated at a point of diffusion and exchange they were subject to mixed influences from many quarters; they were the most cosmopolitan people of the ancient Semitic world. The mixed character of their culture is seen in their art, which is skillfully done but always affected by foreign models — Egyptian, Mesopotamian, Anatolian, Aegean. Their cosmopolitan attitude made them open to Gk influence, and the Phoenician cities were foci of the diffusion of Hellenism* in the Near East. Phoenician art and architecture furnished the plans and the craftsmen for the construction of the temple* of Solomon. Samples of Phoenician art appear in ANEP 283, 456–459, 477.

The religion of the Phoenicians was Semitic, identical with the Canaanite worship mentioned in the OT. Our knowledge of Canaanite religion has been vastly increased in recent times by the discoveries at Ugarit*. Each city, however, had its own gods and its own cult. At Byblos* there were Baalat, Byblos, El, and Adonis; at Sidon* there were Astarte and the Baal of Sidon; at Tyre there were Baal Shamem, Eshmun, Astarte, and Melkart; cf UGARIT. Under the difference of names there seems to have been a prevailing nature cult of myth and ritual which celebrated the annual death and resurrection of the god of fertility; cf BAAL.

Phoenicia is mentioned in the NT as the place of origin of a woman who sought a cure of Jesus and was a first refused because she was not a Jew (Mt 7:26). The gospel was announced in Phoenicia by Christians from Jerusalem after the dispersion of Jerusalem Christians which followed the stoning of Stephen; Gentiles were not included in this evangelization (AA 11:19; 15:3).

Phrygia. A region of NW Asia Minor; its boundaries fluctuated, but it was bounded on the N by Bithynia*, on the E and SE by Galatia* and Lycaonia*, on the S by Pisidia*. It is the region called Mushki by the Assyrians, Meshech* in the OT. The Phrygians entered Asia Minor about 1200 BC in the great movement of peoples of this period and established a kingdom with its capital at Gordion which endured for several centuries; its most famous king was Midas. Its principal cities were Laodicea*, Colossae*, and Hierapolis*, of which the first two were evangelized by Paul*. Paul passed through Phrygia on his 2nd (AA 16:6) and 3rd journeys (AA 18:23), but AA does not relate any preaching which he did in the country.

Phygelus (Gk phygelos, a personal name), a Christian of Asia who turned away from Paul (2 Tm 1:15).

Phylactery (Gk phylaktērion, "protection," means an amulet*, which is a misrepresentation of the Jewish understanding of the article). This article, still in use in Jewish worship, is mentioned in the NT only in Mt 23:5 as worn by the Pharisees*. The Aramaic word is *t*^e*pillîn,* etymology and meaning uncertain. Phylacteries were worn on the head and on the arm. The head phylactery consisted of a small capsule made of parchment 10–15 mm wide. It was constructed with four hollow spaces in which were inserted four miniature scrolls, containing the following four passages from the law: Ex 13:1–10 (the Mazzoth* Torah), Ex 13:11–16 (the Passover* Torah), Dt 6:4–9 (the "Shema," the profession of belief in one God), Dt 11:13–21 (commandment to love Yahweh and not to serve other gods). All these passages contain allusions to keeping the law of Yahweh before one's eyes and in one's heart. These metaphorical allusions were literally fulfilled by the wearing of phylacteries. The capsule was fastened around the head by straps so that it hung in the middle of the forehead. The arm phylactery was a similar capsule with only one hollow space; the same four passages were written on a single miniature scroll. The capsule was fastened to the upper left arm by straps so that it hung at the level of the heart. The date when the phylactery was introduced is unknown; it is first mentioned in the Letter of Aristeas, also of uncertain date, but probably of the 3rd or 1st century BC. The phylactery was worn by the adult Jewish male (over 14 years) and strict observance required that it be worn all day.

Physician. Cf MEDICINE.

Pilate. Anglicized form of the Lt name *Pontius Pilatus,* procurator* of Judaea from AD 25–27 to AD 35. Pilate is named in all Christian creeds as the officer who pronounced sentence of death on Jesus. Information concerning him comes from the NT, Josephus, and Philo; the few brief allusions in classical writers mention him only in connection with the death of Jesus. Both Josephus and Philo, who quotes a letter of Agrippa I, give an extremely unfavorable picture of him: obstinate and harsh, violent, a plunderer, cruel, guilty of executing persons without legal process. Josephus relates anecdotes which illustrate these defects. Roman procurators did not bring into Judaea the standards of the legions with the images of Caesar out of deference to the Jewish prohibition of images. When Pilate assumed office he had the images brought in secretly by night. The Jews then sent a large delegation to him at Caesarea* (the residence of the procurator) who petitioned him for five days; he then assembled them in the stadium, but turned his soldiers loose on the crowd and a large number of Jews were killed. He spent some of the temple funds on an aqueduct for Jerusalem; this misuse of sacred treasure, in spite of the utility of the project, caused a crowd to assemble in protest. Pilate sent his soldiers disguised among the crowd, and at a signal they began to kill wantonly. In AD 35 he attacked a Samaritan religious procession at Mt Gerizim, killed some, imprisoned others, and scattered the rest. The Samaritans represented to Vitellius, the legate of Syria, that they were not in insurrection, and Vitellius sent Pilate to Tiberius at Rome to give an account of himself. Nothing more is known of him; a number of Christian legends concerning his later years and death are without historical value. Modern historians ask whether Philo and Josephus have not blackened Pilate's reputation; they observe that even the NT is less unsympathetic to Pilate. There is a single allusion (Lk 13:1) to an episode similar to those which Josephus narrates, but no details are given and Pilate's bloody attack on the Galileans may have had some excuse.

Lk 3:1 dates the beginning of the ministry of Jesus by the term of Pilate's administration, which unfortunately cannot be dated exactly at its beginning. He is mentioned in AA 3:13; 4:27; 13:28; 1 Tm 6:13 in terms which resemble the later Christian credal formulae. Elsewhere he appears in the Passion narratives of Mt 27; Mk 15; Lk 23; Jn 18–19. Mt, Mk, and Lk relate that Pilate asked Jesus whether . He were the king of the Jews and that Jesus answered in a simple affirmative. Jn expands this datum of primitive tradition into a dialogue in which Jesus explains that His reign is not secular, but a kingdom of truth — an idea incomprehensible to the Roman. All four evangelists relate that Pilate did not think Jesus guilty and tried to release Him; Mt, Mk, and Lk add that he tried to substitute Barabbas* for Jesus. The Passover amnesty, not mentioned by Jn, was evidently no longer clearly understood when the Gospels were written. Mt has two details of his own: the warning given to Pilate by his wife, and Pilate's explicit profession of innocence of the death of Jesus and the symbolic washing of hands. Mt-Mk-Jn relate the flogging of Jesus and the mock salutation of Jesus as king by the soldiers of Pilate's guard. Mk adds that the flogging was done from a desire to satisfy the desires of the Jews, perhaps hinting that Pilate hoped that a flogging would be sufficient. Pilate alone was empowered to pronounce the sentence of death, and he obviously did so under pressure. Jn no doubt preserves the urgent character of the pressure employed — a threat to delate Pilate to Caesar for tolerating a claimant to royalty. Neither in the Gospels nor in Philo and Josephus does Pilate appear noble; but it is evident that the administrator who yielded to pressure in the manner described is out of character with the ruthless and violent Pilate of Philo and Josephus. Any further judgment of his motives runs the risk of being not only unhistorical, but unfair.

Pilate was less scrupulous of Jewish law after the death of Jesus. Jewish law and custom prescribed that the bodies of criminals should be thrown into a common pit. All four evangelists relate that Pilate delivered the body at the petition of Joseph* of Arimathaea, who arranged for its burial. Only Mt mentions the guard which Pilate permitted the Jews to set at the tomb of Jesus to prevent the theft of His body.

Pipe. Cf MUSIC.

Pirathon (Hb *pir'āṭôn*, meaning uncertain), a town of Ephraim*, the home of the judge Abdon* (Jgs 12:13–15) and of one of David's heroes, Benaiah* (2 S 23:30; 1 Ch 11:31; 27:14). It is probably to be identified with Farata, 5 mi NW of Nablus.

Pisgah (Hb *pisgāh*, always with the article, the Pisgah, meaning uncertain), the slope of the mountains between the Moabite plateau and the Dead Sea (Nm 23:14; Dt 3:17, 27; 4:49; 34:1; Jos 12:3; 13:20). Mt Nebo*, from which Moses saw the land of Canaan, is a point in the Pisgah.

Pishon (Hb *pîšôn*, meaning uncertain), one of the four rivers of Eden* (Gn 2:11). It can be identified with no known stream and is probably an imaginative feature of the account.

Pisidia. A region of central Asia Minor, N of Pamphylia* and Lycia*, lying between Lycaonia* to the E and Phrygia* and Caria* to the W. The region is mountainous and has many large lakes; most of Pisidia consists of a plateau 3000 ft above sea level. The chief city of Pisidia, Antioch*, was evangelized by Paul on his 1st journey (AA 13:14; 14:24). Pisidia had its own native language, which has not yet been identified.

Pit. Cf SHEOL.

Pithom (Hb *pᵉṯōm*, Egyptian *pr-itm*, "house of [the god] Atum"), one of the cities in Egypt on which the Israelites worked (Ex 1:11). The city is most probably to be located in the valley which connects the Nile with Lake Timsah in the Isthmus of Suez. It was built after the accession of Seti I (1317 BC).

Plagues of Egypt. Plagues is the traditional name given to the series of disasters inflicted upon Egypt before the Pharaoh permitted Moses and the Israelites to leave Egypt (Ex 7:14–12:30). In the present text the plagues are ten: the Nile and the water

of Egypt turned into blood (Ex 7:14–25); frogs (Ex 8:1–9); mosquitoes (or flies; Ex 8:16–19); gnats (Ex 8:20–32); cattle plague (9:1–7); boils (9:8–21); hail (9:22–35); locusts (10:1–20); darkness (10:21–29); death of the firstborn (11:1–12:30). Analysis of the passage according to the literary criticism of the Pnt* shows that the 10 plagues are compiled from the accounts of the three sources of Ex. J has 7 plagues, E and P each have 5 plagues as follows:

J	E	P
The red Nile	(Water turned into blood)	(Water turned into blood)
Frogs		Frogs
Gnats		(Dust turned into mosquitoes)
Cattle plague		(Ashes producing boils)
Hail	Hail	
Locusts	Locusts	
	Darkness	
Firstborn	Firstborn	Firstborn

Various types of compilation appear in the various plagues; in some the sources have been juxtaposed, in others they have been interwoven. Certain motifs are evidently peculiar to each of the sources and justify the analysis. In J the staff of Moses is employed to perform the wonder (not in each plague); J employs the refrain "Let my people go," etc, and uses the threat of the plague given in advance; after some of the plagues the Pharaoh yields; Israel is exempt from the plagues. In E the wonder is accomplished when Moses raises his hand; the plague is sometimes preceded by a commission given by Yahweh to Moses to execute the plague; E also exhibits the yielding of Pharaoh and the exemption of Israel. Except for the darkness, which is proper to E, less is preserved of this source than the others. In P the plagues are attributed to both Moses and Aaron; the staff of Aaron is used; the Egyptian magicians imitate the plagues; P also uses the commission given to Moses and Aaron to act. The table shows that E and P have modified some of the plagues. In J the Nile turns to blood, in E and J all the water of Egypt turns to blood. The gnats of J become in P mosquitoes produced by the scattering of dust particles. The cattle plague of J becomes in P boils afflicting men as well as beasts, and the boils are produced by the scattering of ashes. The modifications are all in the direction of heightening the wonder; this illustrates the progress of popular tradition.

The historical criticism of the passage has ranged from complete denial of any historical value to total acceptance of the 10 plagues as described. A more moderate view is suggested by modern literary and historical criticism. The 10 plagues are the result of compilation and J, the oldest source, has only 7. Of the 10 two are doublets, mosquitoes-gnats and cattle plague-boils. But even in J the popular features of the tradition (the easy access of Moses to the Pharaoh, the affliction of the entire country of Egypt in a manner which leaves no trace in nonbiblical records) suggests that the living memory of the events had been much transformed at the time of the composition of J.

It is evident that the plagues are phenomena natural to Egypt and indeed to many parts of the Near East. The Nile is red at the time of the inundation, when it carries large quantities of loam from the mountains in which it rises; it is green at its low point, when it is filled with algae, and the pools in the vicinity of the river become stagnant. It is no doubt the "green Nile" to which the tradition refers, but in its present form it shows little acquaintance with the behavior of the river. The variant forms of the plague in E and J have extended the phenomenon to all the water of Egypt. The darkness very probably means a sandstorm, which obscures the sky and the air for hours. The death of the firstborn, however, is probably a cult legend formed upon the Passover* rite and the dedication of the Israelite firstborn* to Yahweh. Many older exegetes, observing the character of the phenomena, attempted a kind of rationalization which proposed that the phenomena, natural in themselves, were heightened at the word of Moses and were preternaturally announced by him.

A more probable explanation seems to lie in literary criticism rather than in historical criticism or in an appeal to the natural sciences. The literary form of the plagues is a recital of the saving deeds of Yahweh. Each of the traditions has taken features of Egyptian geography, climate, zoology, etc and presented them as strokes by which Yahweh punishes the Pharaoh and his people for refusing to liberate the Israelites. The phenomena are not described as "heightened," but as introduced by the word of Moses and Aaron, the word which contains the power of Yahweh. Egypt therefore is cursed for its oppression of Israel by these plagues of nature. Through such works in nature Yahweh's saving power delivers His people; He renders their enemies helpless, in spite of the superior numbers and power of the enemy. The plagues are judgments* on the Pharaoh, who refuses to obey the command of Yahweh.

The materials which were available to J for the composition of this recital were some knowledge of Egypt and some traditions which it is no longer possible for us to recover; it is certainly unlikely that they can be recovered by the type of rationalism mentioned above. That the traditions contained some account of natural phenomena which accompanied the exodus of Israel is altogether likely; but the schematic character of the account indicates that they were cast in highly imaginative form when J compiled his account.

It is remarkable that the plagues do not appear explicitly in most of the allusions of the OT to saving deeds of the exodus (cf EXODUS). They are found in Pss 105:23 ff; 135:8 ff; 136:10. The material of Ex is expanded in the long midrash* of WS 16–18.

Pledge. Cf LOAN.

Plow. The ancient plow was composed

Plowing and sowing, an Egyptian temple painting.

mostly of wood, often entirely of wood without even a metal tip. Iron plowtips have been found by archaeologists; it is remarkable that no bronze tips have been found. Plowing was done with two animals, usually oxen, sometimes asses (Is 30:24). The yoking of an ox and an ass together is prohibited in Dt 22:10. The animals were driven by the goad. The modern plow used in the Near East is often not dissimilar from the ancient plow. For representations of plows and plowing cf ANEP 84–88, 91, 122, 686, 688, 697.

Poetry. The Israelites, like all peoples, exhibit a poetic type of utterance which is early, long before any of their literature was written. Since the work of Lowth in the 18th-century scholars agree that the essence of Hebrew poetic structure consists in parallelism of members. This differs somewhat from the poetry familiar to modern readers which is, of course, built upon some form of parallelism of lines. Hb poetry is logically and stylistically parallel, and this is the most obvious parallelism; whether it is also metrically parallel, with balanced schemes of rhythm through stress or quantity, is less certain (cf below). Lowth distinguished three types of parallelism which are universally accepted: synonymous, antithetic, and climactic.

The unit of Hb poetry is the *stichos* or line; except in climactic parallelism the stichos is a complete sentence. The parallel structure admits a balance of two, three, or even more stichoi. In synonymous parallelism the balanced lines each express the same proposition or sentiment through the use of synonyms. The balance may be mechanical, with each synonymous word balanced by another in the corresponding stichos: "Does God pervert justice?/Does the Almighty pervert the right?" (Jb 8:3). Usually, however, the monotony of such parallelism is relieved by making the balance slightly imperfect: "The heavens and the earth will praise Him/the sea and all that stirs therein" (Ps 69:35); "may he descend like rain upon the mown grass/like showers that water the earth" (Ps 72:5). The more complex parallelism of Ps 92:10, which older critics emended as a dittography, has an exact parallel in the poetry of Ugarit*: "For lo! your enemies, Yahweh/for lo! your enemies will perish/all evildoers will be scattered." The number of possible variations on synonymy permits Hb poetry to exhibit a pleasing suppleness, especially when it is combined with the other two forms. It is rare that any single type of parallelism is sustained for a long passage.

Antithetic parallelism balances a statement against its opposite: "A wise son makes a glad father/but a foolish son is a grief to his mother" (Pr 10:1). "The mouth of the righteous is a fountain of life/but the mouth of the wicked is full of violence" (Pr 10:11). This form also is varied slightly: "Fear of Yahweh prolongs life/but the years of the wicked will be shortened" (Pr 10:27). Antithetic parallelism prevails in Pr, but this is not in contradiction with what was said above about the variation of parallelism in Hb poetry; each wise saying of Pr is an independent poem in itself (cf PROVERBS; WISDOM) and the occasional monotony is due to their collection.

Climactic parallelism is the broadest of Lowth's forms, and includes everything which is not clearly synonymous nor antithetic. The name is, however, descriptive; the second member (more are possible) completes the thought of the first: "You love righteousness and hate iniquity/therefore God your God has anointed you/with the oil of gladness above your companions" (Ps 45:8); "though I walk in the dark valley/I fear no harm, for you are with me" (Ps 23:4). Climax especially appears in the simile which is common in wise sayings: "Like a golden ring in a swine's snout/is a woman fair and foolish" (Pr 11:22).

The complete interweaving of forms of parallelism and the variety of effects which can be obtained are seen in Is 1:2–3, analyzed as follows:

a   Hear, O heavens, and listen, O earth,
b   For Yahweh has spoken:
c   "Sons I have reared and brought up
d   But they have rebelled against me.
e   The ox knows its owner
f   And the ass its master's crib
g   But Israel does not know
h   My people does not understand."

Here a-b is a climactic distich; c-d is an antithetic distich; e-f and g-h are synonymous distichs, but e-f and g-h are antithetic to each other. Thus the skillful use of the three types of parallelism gives the passage a stately but easy movement. The parallelism of Hb poetry is a common feature of ancient Near Eastern literature; it is seen in the poetry of Mesopotamia (Sumerian and Akkadian), Egypt, Canaan, and Phoenicia. The Israelites therefore adopted an existing form; but no other people who used it succeeded so well in the composition of great poetry.

The analysis of Hb prosody is extremely uncertain. The pronunciation of Hb indicated in the Masoretic text* does not represent the pronunciation of OT times, and no living tradition has been preserved. Some idea of the pronunciation has been gained from

Akkadian, which has written signs for vowels; but Hb lacked such signs and it is impossible to construct a metrical scheme upon a purely consonantal text with any assurance. Scholars have proposed a number of systems, none of which have met with wide acceptance. There is agreement that Hb meter was accentual, like English verse, and not quantitative, like Lt and Gk. It appears all but certain that the meter was loose and permitted a number of unstressed syllables to be run together; it is this laxity which is the chief obstacle to discerning a metrical scheme. There is wide agreement that the stichos usually has 2, 3, or 4 stresses; but it is often difficult to find the corresponding number of stresses in the parallel stichos. It is, however, again all but certain that the distich or the tristich could be composed of lines unbalanced in stress; but to permit this to occur regularly would approach a total destruction of metrical structure.

Poetry occupied a large place in Hb life; the difference between verse and elevated prose is not as great as it is in English, and it seems to have been fairly easy to speak in verse when the solemnity of the occasion required it. Such a solemn poetic utterance is called a "saying," often no more than a single distich. Such sayings were uttered at the more solemn occasions of daily life, such as the birth and naming of a child, espousals and weddings (Gn 24:60; Rt 4:11), in blessings* and curses*, at the beginning of wars (Ex 17:16 and probably Nm 10:35, but not in its present context), victories (Ex 15:20; 1 S 18:7; Jgs 5; 15:16; 16:23 f [the Philistines]; Jos 10:12 f). Poetry was the proper form of cultic sayings such as the oracular response (Gn 25:23), the blessing* and the curse*, and in particular of cultic song (cf PSALMS). It was also the form of the prophetic oracle and discourse (cf PROPHECY) and of the wise saying (cf WISDOM). There are several allusions to the songs of daily Hb life and some fragments are preserved: work songs (Nm 21:17 f), the song of the night watchman (Is 21:11 f), harvest songs (Jgs 9:27; 21:21), drinking songs (Is 5:11–13; 22:13), love songs (Is 5:1 ff; cf SONG OF SOLOMON). The taunt-song, originally directed to individuals (as in Is 23:15 f) becomes in the prophetic literature a type of song applied to Israel and to other peoples (Is 37:22–29; 47; cf also Nm 21:27–30, possibly an Amorite song). Frequently songs which were probably current were attributed to some historical or legendary situation (e.g., Nm 10:35; 21:17 f). In the other direction, it seems certain that songs often preserved the oldest living tradition of events in the past of Israel. It is often possible to trace with great probability the development of a prose narrative account of an event to a reconstruction based upon a song which was composed at or at least very near the event itself; cf DEBORAH. This is an important factor in the historical criticism of OT narrative.

Polygamy. Cf MARRIAGE.

Pomegranate (Hb *rimmôn, punica granatum*). The pomegranate tree grows to a height of 10–15 ft. It has oblong deciduous leaves. The fruit resembles an apple in shape; it is yellowish or brownish with a trace of red, has a large number of seeds, and has a juicy pulp sweet or acid. It grows wild in Syria. The numerous allusions to the fruit in the OT show that it was regarded as a delicacy (SS 4:3, 13; 6:11; 7:12). It is enumerated among the fruits of Canaan (Nm 13:23; Dt 8:8; 1 S 14:2) and it was one of the Egyptian delicacies which the Israelites desired in the desert (Nm 20:5). The withering of the tree is a sign of disaster (Jl 1:12). Representations of the fruit were used as decoration in embroidery (Ex 28:33) and sculpture (1 K 7:18).

Pontus (Gk *pontos*, "sea"), a geographical name; the region of NE Asia Minor from the Black Sea to the Caucasus. It was included in the Persian* empire. After the conquests of Pompey part of Pontus was incorporated into a Roman province. It is mentioned as a residence of Jews of the Diaspora* (AA 2:9) and as one of the regions to which 1 Pt was addressed (1 Pt 1:1).

Poor, Poverty. 1. *In ancient world.* In the ancient world, both in OT and NT times, society had no middle class of the kind found in modern industrial nations. Wealth was concentrated in the hands of a few, and the mass of the population was poor to a degree which is rare in modern western countries, although it is found in countries outside of Europe and the United States. The concentration of wealth in monarchical countries was focused upon the king and his court. One does not find in the ancient world any expression of discontent with the prevailing poverty, and still less any ideal of social justice; the existence of widespread poverty was taken for granted as much as the processes of nature, for no other condition was known to be possible. What the poor could legitimately expect was that the wealthy would not take advantage of them, particularly by using their wealth to corrupt the administration of the government and the processes of justice. This ideal appears as far back as the code of Hammurabi*, who says that he was appointed king by Enlil "to cause justice to prevail in the land, to destroy the wicked and the evil, that the strong might not oppress the weak" (ANET 164). His laws are promulgated "in order that the strong might not oppress the weak . . . to give justice to the oppressed" (ANET 178). "Let any oppressed man who has a cause come into the presence of my statue" (ANET *ibid*). In Egypt also there was a consciousness of the rights of the poor. The instruction of Merikare warns that the king should not show partiality against the poor in selecting candidates for office (ANET 415). The wisdom of Amenemope knows, in terms reminiscent of OT wisdom, that "better is poverty in the hands of the god than riches in a storehouse" (ANET 422). He warns the rich not to be greedy for the property of a poor man (ANET 423) and urges him to forgive ⅔ of the debt of the poor man (ANET *ibid*). Akkadian wisdom counsels the rich to give alms to the poor (ANET 426). These quotations from Mesopotamia and Egypt antedate any OT saying about poverty by at least several centuries.

The Gk world, on the contrary, seems to have exhibited very little humanity toward the poor. The poor were not regarded as enjoying any special divine protection, as is clearly said in the OT (cf below) and is hinted in the code of Hammurabi. To give alms is the gentlemanly rather than the morally good thing to do, and Gk cities, so advanced in other institutions, exhibit no public care for the poor. The poor, if they lost all income, could always sell themselves and their families into slavery*.

2. *In the OT*. There are several Hb words to express poverty, but none of them can be translated exactly by "poor." *'ānî* is literally "afflicted"; in usage the affliction consists in membership in a lower class which is indigent and subject to oppression with no power to defend itself. The related Aramaizing form *'ānaw* is synonymous, but is more frequently used of the poor in a religious sense (cf below). The weakness implied in the word makes it possible at times to translate it as "meek," having no will to fight. *dal* is literally "languishing," again a socially weak class whose weakness comes from its indigence. *'ebyōn* means more properly poor and needy.

In the nomadism* of early Israel there was no great distinction between wealth and poverty. In nomadic groups every one is equally poor; there is a close family and clan interdependence and a degree of community of ownership, especially of the flocks and herds on which the nomads subsist,

which protects the individual and the smaller group against extreme need as long as the group has anything to share. Israel's settlement on the land with the growth of individual ownership and life in villages and cities brought with it a greater individual responsibility for subsistence. Israel's expanding economy also brought the rise of a wealthy class and a depression of the circumstances of the peasant and artisan. The code of the covenant, Israel's earliest collection of law*, contains statutes which protect the poor. The debtor who sells himself into slavery must be liberated without any compensation after six years (Ex 21:2). In the sabbatical* year the fields are to be left fallow, and the poor may eat what grows there (Ex 23:10 f). Judges must not pervert justice due to the poor (Ex 23:6). More fundamentally, Yahweh is declared to be the avenger of all needy classes (Ex 22:21–24).

It is clear from the prophetic literature that the increase in wealth and the spread of dire poverty became even more of a social problem under the monarchy, due largely to the conquests of David and the trading of Solomon and his successors. Oppression of the poor, the denial of even basic human dignity to the poor, and harsh exactions of debts are crimes rebuked by Amos (2:7; 4:1; 5:11). Isaiah utters a woe against those who expand their holdings of land (5:8), and speaks of the denial of rights and justice to the poor (10:2) and of those who crush and grind the poor by exacting the full measure of their debts (3:15). Dt 15:7–11 prescribes liberality to the poor both by loan* and by gift, and clearly alludes to the crime of defrauding the poor day laborer of his wages (Dt 24:14 f). The oppression of the poor and needy is a crime for which Yahweh will destroy the kingdom (Ezk 22:29). Ps 82:3–4 refers to the duty of judges to render justice to the poor and needy and to protect them from oppression, and the Pss frequently refer to the oppression of the poor by the wicked rich (e.g., Ps 10:2, 9, 17 f). Yahweh does not forget the cry of the poor (Ps 9:13, 19). In the Pss, however, we meet a conception of the poor which is religious and no longer merely social and economic.

This conception appears in Zp 3:12, which is a later supplement to the book; the remnant which survives the fall of Israel will be poor and needy. The purification of Israel demands the destruction of the rich, who are such wicked oppressors that they are beyond redemption; there is no place for them in the restored Israel. In a number of postexilic Pss the petitioner gives his poverty and need as a motive why Yahweh should hear his prayer; here evidently "poor" is becoming synonymous with pious and devout (Pss 25:16; 40:18; 69:30; 86:1; 109:22). Yahweh is the deliverer of the poor and needy (Pss 22:27; 35:10; 76:10). The poor rejoice when they hear the praise of Yahweh (Ps 34:3). They shall possess the land (Ps 37:11). This line is the base of Mt 5:4, translated in most Eng versions as "meek"; but the word designates the lowly class as described above. In Ps 69:33 the parallelism of the line makes the poor synonymous with those who seek God. Similar conceptions appear in later prophetic passages. The poor and lowly find joy in Yahweh (Is 29:19), hear good news from Yahweh (Is 61:1). Yahweh is the savior of the needy (Je 20:13). The terms to designate poor and needy are applied to exiled Israel (Is 49:13) and to Zion (Is 51:21; 54:11). These passages indicate that postexilic Judaism identified piety with poverty and lowliness. There is little doubt that the postexilic community of Palestine was indeed poor, at least in its earlier history. Possibly also the designations reflect the catastrophic story of the fall of the Israelite monarchies which left the Jews subjects of the powerful Babylonian and Persian empires. More basic perhaps is the fact that the titles of poverty are a denial of the pride of wealth and position, so often excoriated by the preexilic prophets. The titles certainly mean more than the identification of true religion with membership in the depressed classes and indicate an attitude of mind rather than social standing.

The attitude of the wisdom literature toward poverty is ambiguous, due to the fact that the collection comes from widely scattered periods. Poverty is often regarded as a curse, the punishment of sloth, intemperance, frivolity (Pr 6:11; 10:15; 13:18; 21:17; 23:21; 28:19; 31:7). Wisdom literature is also aware of the duty of justice and liberality to the poor (Pr 14:31; 22:22). Ben Sira shows disgust with the poor man who does not recognize his lowly potion (25:2), but shows a genuine insight into the pathos of poverty with his remark that the poor man who is wronged must beg pardon (13:3). Other sayings show a moderation which sees both wealth and poverty as evil (Pr 30:8 f; BS 11:14), and notice that poverty is not the supreme evil; poverty is better than mendacity (Pr 19:22), than dishonesty (Pr 28:6), than illness (BS 30:14), than folly (Ec 4:13). These are not said in praise of poverty. Job boasts of his compassion and liberality to the poor (Jb 29:12, 16; 30:25; 31:16), and the book contains the most genuine and touching description of abject poverty not only in the

OT, but in the entire ancient world (24:2-12). Here as elsewhere Jb exhibits an empathy with human suffering which is unique in the OT.

The writings of Qumran show even more clearly than the OT the development of the piety of poverty. The community identifies itself with the poor and needy who are devout and of whom God is the avenger. Indeed the community practiced a kind of community poverty; cf QUMRAN.

The rabbinical sources which can be dated before AD 70 show a different attitude. Here poverty is simply a curse, and there are some sayings which exhibit haughtiness and contempt toward the poor. After the fall of Jerusalem the piety of poverty prevails in the rabbinical literature.

3. *In the NT*. The dominant idea of poverty in the Gospels comes not only from the words of Jesus but from His life. He belonged Himself to the lower classes and made no attempt to escape or to disguise it. His attitude toward wealth* was simple; it is an obstacle to the kingdom of heaven. His refusal to accept any income, even by earning, is a striking feature of His public life. It must not be thought that the poverty of Jesus was excessive in comparison with the common poverty of His time; the economic conditions of the place and time were such as to emphasize the excess both of wealth and of poverty. The social and economic condition of Jesus was not preached as an ideal; it was simply taken for granted. Jesus does not exhibit the "piety of poverty" of the OT; He does indeed recommend the attitude, but the attitude arises from a real social and economic depression. The background must be understood in order that the words of Jesus as reported in the Gospels may not seem less emphatic than they are.

The story of the widow's mite (Mk 12:41-44; Lk 21:1-4) is less a praise of the poor than a condemnation of the rich. The story of the rich man who would not renounce his possessions to follow Jesus is the basis of "the evangelical counsel" of poverty and is found in all three synoptics with slight variations (Mk 10:17 ff; Mt 19:16 ff; Lk 18:18 ff): where Mk and Lk have "one thing is lacking to you," Mt has "if you wish to be perfect." Jesus here makes the total renunciation of wealth a condition of "following Him," i.e., of joining the group of disciples, who lived as He did and had given up homes and income (Mt 19:27-29; Mk 10:28-30; Lk 18:28-30). The recommendation to give all to the poor was not a part of His general preaching to all listeners. Nevertheless, He adds a remark on the difficulty which wealth creates to admission to the kingdom of heaven; this indicates that while He does not impose total renunciation universally, those who do not make it should know what they are doing; cf WEALTH.

Jesus' simple acceptance of poverty as an existing fact appears in Mk 14:5 ff; Mt 26:11; Jn 12:8, "the poor you have always with you," to which Mk adds, "you can do them good whenever you wish." The whole saying seems to imply that poverty deserves less concern than the disciples are showing for it at the moment; there are other things of greater importance.

The poor are called blessed in Mt 5:3; Lk 6:20; Mt has "poor in spirit," a much tortured phrase. It does not mean detachment, but reflects the OT words cited above, which it makes explicit; the poor in spirit are the lowly classes, whose spirit is crushed by their need and by oppression. "Poor in spirit" is not only synonymous with Lk 6:20 but also with "meek" of Mt 5:5; which also reflects the OT vocabulary; cf above. The revolutionary character of this statement should not be missed; the curse of poverty is removed by it, and the blessing consists in the kingdom of heaven, which surpasses all wealth. The saying does not mean that only the poor enter the kingdom of heaven, but *even* the poor; it is an implicit response to the haughtiness of the Pharisees. A similar response to the Pharisees lies in Jesus' employment of Is 61:1 (Mt 11:5; Lk 4:18) to announce the messianic character of His mission; the good news is brought to the poor, who are not excluded from the kingdom.

Lk has a number of passages touching poverty peculiar to himself which show a special interest in the question; possibly the teaching of Jesus on this point was discussed more intensely in Hellenistic communities; cf also WEALTH. The admission of the poor to the kingdom of heaven is found in the parables of the banquet (14:15) and of the rich man and Lazarus (16:19–31); they are admitted to the eschatological banquet (14:21). The story of Zacchaeus praises Zacchaeus for giving a generous portion of his goods to the poor (19:1 ff). Whatever be the source of the influence, the 3rd Gospel exhibits in these places a sympathy for the poor and a hostility toward the rich which is more pronounced than anything in the other Gospels.

In the other NT writings little attention is given to the poor and to poverty. Most of the Pauline passages are concerned with the aid which he asks from the Hellenistic churches for the poor in Jerusalem; in this connection he makes spirited exhortations to generous almsgiving (Gal 2:10; Rm 15:26).

The longest passage is found in 2 Co 8–9. Paul proposes that the wealthy should give so much of their superfluous goods that equality may be established between them and the poor (2 Co 8:14). He conceives of the Incarnation and death of Jesus as an impoverishment by which the wealth of Jesus is distributed to the redeemed (2 Co 8:9). His allusions to the poverty and sufferings of the apostolate are casual (2 Co 6:3 ff).

In conclusion it may be noticed that Christianity was the only movement of importance in the Roman world which had its origins and its growth in the poor and lower classes. It conquered society not from above, but from below. The example and teaching of Jesus were such that the Church of the early centuries easily thought of itself as the Church of the poor.

Possession, Diabolical. By diabolical possession is meant the seizure of a human person by an evil spirit in such a way that the spirit assumes the personality of the human being and controls all his bodily movements, including speech. Belief in diabolical possession does not appear in the OT nor in any ancient literature prior to the literature of Judaism in the last centuries BC. The antecedents of the belief in possession lie in the belief of the power of demons* to cause afflictions of which no natural cause is known. In Mesopotamia diseases were usually attributed to demons. In Judaism psychic diseases were regarded as manifestations of the seizure of the person by a demon. Jewish exorcists are mentioned in the NT (Mt 12:27; Lk 11:19), and in AA 19:13–16 the efforts of Jewish exorcists to employ the names of Jesus and Paul issue in failure.

In the Gospels and AA a number of instances of possession are mentioned (Mt 8:16; Mk 1:34; Lk 7:21; AA 5:16). Of particular interest are episodes in which the behavior of the possessed person and the expulsion are described with some detail. The "unclean" spirit confesses Jesus and "tears" the person when it is expelled (Mk 1:23–27; Lk 4:33–36). The demoniac of Gerasa lived in cemeteries, exhibited extraordinary strength, inflicted injuries on himself, and confessed Jesus. The "legion" of demons expelled from him entered a herd of swine, which they drove to death in the Sea of Galilee. The demoniac of Mt 12:22; Lk 11:14 was blind and deaf. The boy of Mt 17:14–21; Mk 9:14–29; Lk 9:37–43, from whom the disciples could not exorcise the demon, exhibits symptoms recognized by modern medicine as proper to epilepsy. In AA 16:16–18 Paul exorcises a girl whose demon was used by her employers in divination.

Many modern writers have explained the accounts of possession in the Gospels as exhibiting the simple view of antiquity that evils of an unknown cause were the work of demons; the people who are called possessed suffer from psychic disorders which can now be recognized as such. An exorcism similar to the exorcisms of the Gospels is attributed to Apollonius of Tyana in the life written by Philostratus; this work, however, comes from the 3rd century AD. These writers think that Jesus accommodated Himself to this popular belief and used language which agreed with it. In doing this, these writers say, He did no more and no less than He did in other areas where modern science has advanced far beyond the knowledge of His times. Just as His language assumes the flat earth and the geocentric universe, so it also assumes the demonic explanation of psychic disorders. The parallelism between the two is not perfect. In the Gospels the episodes of possession are a part of a larger pattern of thought. The coming of Jesus is a crisis for the kingdom of Satan, the powers of evil. They recognize the presence of supreme power and rebel at its proximity. The discourse of Jesus given when the Pharisees explain His power as due to a pact with the demons is one of the most severe in the Gospels; refusal to believe that He exhibits the power of God precisely in His power over demons is the sin against the Holy Spirit which is not forgiven. The severity of the discourse makes one slow to accept an explanation which proposes that there were no demons to expel.

This problem should not be confused with the reality of the cures related in the episodes. The demoniacs do in fact exhibit psychic disorders. The question is not whether Jesus accommodated Himself to popular language, but whether the authors of the gospel traditions had any resources of language to describe these psychic disorders and their cure other than the language of possession and exorcism. This, it seems, should be taken as a principle of the interpretation of the narratives; and it is likely that in such details as the incident of the pigs (Mt 8:31 f; Mk 5:11–13; Lk 8:32 f) the popular tradition has expanded the symbolism implicit in the unclean spirits and the pig, the unclean animal. The discourse of Jesus makes the power of exorcism a theological motif of some importance. The disorders exhibited in the demoniacs are consequences of the reign of sin in man; the powers of evil have usurped their liberty to the point where man is a helpless victim of them even in the inner sanctuary of his personality. The solid biblical belief that sin and human defects are connected is given here a new expression. When Jesus cures, in particular those mysterious disorders of the mind, He introduces the power of the kingdom of God against sin and its consequences. This should not be reduced to mere medication; it is a part of His redemptive mission and an exhibition of a power possessed by Him alone.

Potiphar, Potiphera (Hb *pôṭîpar, pôṭîpera'*, Egyptian *p,'dj p,'re*, "he whom [the god] Re gives"), a personal name. **1.** Potiphar, an officer (cf EUNUCH) of the Pharaoh, who bought Joseph as a slave from the Midianites (Gn 37:36). Potiphar made Joseph his major-domo; he was solicited by Potiphar's wife, falsely accused by her of rape, and imprisoned by Potiphar, who apparently did not believe his wife (Gn 39:1 ff). Joseph's imprisonment was the occasion of his interpretation of dreams and his introduction to the Pharaoh. **2.** Potiphera, priest of On* and father of Asenath*, the wife of Joseph (Gn 41:45, 50; 46:20). It is possible that tradition separated an original single figure into two different individuals.

Potter's Field. Cf AKELDAMA.

Pottery. Ceramic ware appears in all levels of Palestinian archaeology* from Chalcolithic onwards, as it does in excavation of all ancient sites. It is, however, far more important in Palestine than in Gk and Roman archaeology, and each fragment is collected; a choice is then made of fragments for recording according to level and context, for preservation, and for possible restoration. The importance of pottery comes from the universal absence of coins before the Persian period and the extreme paucity of epigraphic material. This material is the normal evidence for dating finds and remains; where it is lacking, a substitute must be found or the material excavated hangs in the air. The discovery that pottery can furnish a chronological index was made by Flinders Petrie at Tell el Hesy in 1890. Petrie's chronology was relative only and contained some striking errors; subsequent work, above all the excavation of W. F. Albright at Tell Beit Mirsim (1926–1932), established an absolute chronology which has not been substantially modified since. For the periods of Palestinian archaeology as determined by pottery cf ARCHAEOLOGY. The pottery index is weak for EB and earlier periods and for the period after Iron II (postexilic); this later gap is being closed by contemporary work.

The fragility of pottery means frequent

Pottery making. Ancient Egyptian models.

breakage and replacement with the newest style. Study of pottery discloses patterns of change in form, especially rims, bases, and handles, and the existence of some forms characteristic of certain periods (e.g., the chalice of Iron I and the "hole-mouth" jar of Iron II). Changes also occur in decoration, such as painting and combing, and in the ware itself (type of clay, methods of firing, finish, burnishing, glaze). Once a type can be related to a certain historical context, the induction from the presence of this type is valid for all Palestinian sites. The presence of imported ware and imitation foreign ware is a valuable indication of cultural contacts, and often it is the only indication.

Pound. Cf WEIGHTS AND MEASURES.

Power. Cf MIRACLE.

Praetor. The Roman office of praetor (Gk *stratēgos*) is not mentioned in the NT. It was the popular but inaccurate designation of the magistrates of Philippi*, whose proper technical name was *duumviri*. This designation appears not only in AA 16:20, 22, 35 f, 38 but also in several inscriptions.

Praetorium. Cf GABBATHA.

Prayer. 1. *OT*. The only Hb words which can properly be translated "pray" are the rare *'ātar* and the more common *pālal*, which more frequently means "to intercede," "to pray for another." The proper word for prayer is *tᵉpillâh*. The large group of Hb words which are used to designate prayer show the elements and sentiments of prayer as they are conceived in the OT. *šā'al*, "ask," *ḥānan*, "ask for favor or mercy," designate

the prayer of petition, including petition for forgiveness. *kārā'*, "call" or "invoke," is neutral but indicates that prayer was said aloud; *'ānaḥ*, "sigh," and a similar group of words indicate deep feeling. A large group of words designates the prayer of praise: *halal*, "praise," with the noun *tᵉhillāh*; *hodāh*, "praise," especially in thanksgiving; *higdîl*, "magnify," *harîm*, "extol," *bērēk*, "bless" (the name of Yahweh). *gîl*, "rejoice," and other similar words indicate the joy and exaltation of prayer, particularly of public liturgical cult; *hāgāh*, "meditate," and a few other words, indicate prayerful consideration: *hištaḥāwāh*, "adore" (lit "to prostrate oneself") indicates the posture of respect which is given to kings and dignitaries as well as to the deity. This group of words shows that the traditional ends of prayer: adoration (praise), thanksgiving, and petition are characteristic of Israelite prayer. The emphasis on the prayer of praise is even greater than the word list indicates; cf HYMN; PSALMS.

Prayer in the OT implies and expresses a number of theological ideas which determine its character. It is addressed to Yahweh alone; and this at once distinguishes it from Akkadian and Egyptian prayers, which are often similar in tone and phrase. The epithets and petitions of these prayers, however, can be addressed to any god, and their force is by that very fact weakened. Israelite prayer always implicitly and sometimes explicitly affirms that the titles and petitions of its prayer can be given only to Yahweh, in whom alone is salvation. Yahweh is addressed as the God of Israel; this means the God of the covenant, the God of revelation who has manifested Himself to Israel, the God of election who has chosen Israel as His people. The character of Yahweh is revealed in the history of Israel, which is the recital of His saving deeds; hence allusions to this recital are frequent in prayer. In the exodus* and the covenant traditions Yahweh is seen as a God with the power and will to save Israel, and as a God who imposes His moral will upon Israel. His moral will issues from the same power which delivered Israel. The Israelite therefore always approaches Yahweh as an Israelite, a member of a covenanted community. It is his membership in Israel which enables him to approach Yahweh with the assurance that he will be heard. J. Herrmann has remarked that Israelite prayer is not the address of man to God but of Israelite to Yahweh. It is a later development in Israelite theology and prayer, which probably begins with the exile, when Yahweh is invoked as the sole cosmic deity and the creator. Earlier prayer neither denied nor was ignorant of these attributes of Yahweh, but addressed Him within the enclosure of the covenant; for it was the covenant revelation which revealed that it was possible for Israel to invoke Yahweh.

Yahweh is invoked as a living personal being, and the conception of Him in prayer is highly anthropomorphic. The tone of Israelite prayer is often quite familiar, even importunate, and complaints are freely expressed. The object of petitions includes every desirable good; but the OT reader notices that what he calls "spiritual" goods are rarely asked. Most Israelite prayer asks the blessings of this life, social and individual. This apparent narrowness is due to Hb patterns of thought; the absence of abstract thinking and their lack of any clear idea of an afterlife made it difficult for them to conceive "spiritual" goods. Their petitions are not as narrow as they appear to the modern reader; in the OT life* is the supreme good which Yahweh gives, and prayer asks the fullness of life. The fullness of life includes joy in Yahweh, which is certainly a "spiritual" good. Modern readers are also disturbed by the prayers of imprecation of evil upon enemies; cf CURSE.

Because of the social character of Israelite piety (cf above), cultic prayer was of primary importance. The proper place of cultic prayer was the sanctuary, because it is the place of the presence of Yahweh; cf TEMPLE. At an undetermined date the practice arose of directing one's countenance toward the temple during prayer when one was elsewhere (1 K 8:38; Dn 6:11), a practice which modern Moslems imitate when they pray toward Mecca. But prayer could be uttered anywhere. The entire land of Israel is conceived as ·a sanctuary with reference to foreign lands, for it is the land where Yahweh chooses to dwell; hence the Aramaean Naaman* takes Israelite earth with him to Damascus to have a sanctuary of Yahweh in his own house (2 K 5:17). The chief cultic prayers were sacrifice* and psalms*.

Israelite prayer of petition is characterized by an assurance that the prayer is heard, and in the Pss the conclusion of the petition usually describes the petition as already granted. The assurance rests upon the history of Yahweh's saving deeds and upon His fidelity and love, also upon the need of the petitioner. By election and covenant Yahweh has made Himself the savior of Israel and of the individual Israelite.

Prayer is far too common in the OT to permit a complete citation. The Pss are the complete handbook of OT prayer; in addition the following examples may be noticed as illustrations: the prayer of Eliezer (Gn 24:12–14); Jacob (Gn 32:10–13); Moses (Ex 32:11–14; 34:8 f; Nm 14:13–19); Gideon (Jgs 6:36–40); Samson (Jgs 15:18; 16:28); Hannah (1 S 1:10 ff); David (2 K 7:18–29); Solomon (1 K 3:6–9, 8:23–53); Elijah (1 K 19:36 f). While practically none of these prayers as they stand can be attributed to the persons with whom they are associated, they do reflect Israelite forms of prayer from the monarchy and the early exilic period. Of interest are the prayers of Moses, which are intercessions on behalf of Israel; that the prayer of intercession was possible is seen also in the story of Abraham and Sodom (Gn 18:20–32). The prayers of David (2 S 7:18–29) and Solomon (1 K 8:23–53) are composed in the style and spirit of Dt*. Otherwise it is obvious that the prayers are short, dignified, and humble. The prayers found in postexilic books are considerably longer and more formal: Ezra (9:6–15); Mordecai (Gk Est 4:18 ff), Tobit (3:1–6; 13:1–18), Judith (9:2–14), Judas (2 Mc 15:22–24). The postexilic prayers exhibit a profound sense of guilt, arising from the judgment of Yahweh upon Israel and Jerusalem, and petitions for forgiveness are a normal part of these prayers; this element is much less prominent in earlier prayers.

Prayer is extremely common in the prophetic literature; the conception of prophecy* as the reception of the word of Yahweh makes prophetic books frequently a dialogue between the prophet and Yahweh. Such a dialogue is explicit in the "confessions" of Jeremiah*. The relations of the prophet with Yahweh were not normative for Israelites generally; but the prophetic addresses to Yahweh are in the spirit of Israelite prayer and are obviously of great influence upon it. The prophet, like Moses, was an intercessor for Israel (Am 7:1–6; Je 7:16; 11:14; 14:11–13). Jeremiah heightens the corruption of Israel by the prohibition of intercession which Yahweh lays upon him. The prophets are occasionally critical of cultic prayer, particularly of sacrifice*; and Isaiah affirms that the prayer of his people is insincere (29:13). Among the prophetic warnings are admonitions to prayer and promises that in prayer the Israelites will find salvation (Is 55:6; 58:9; Je 29:13–14). These utterances come from the exilic period, when the sacrificial cult was suspended because of the destruction of the temple. Public cultic prayer therefore became of primary importance, and formulae of prayer for public recitation arose. Some of these formulae have been preserved and are still in use among Jews: the Shema, the morning and evening recitation of Dt 6:4–9; 11:13–21; Nm 15:37–41; and the Shemone Esre, the 18 blessings. These were probably in use in NT times. The synagogue was primarily a "house of prayer."

2. *NT.* Jesus was highly critical of some practices of prayer of Pharisaic* piety; He warned His followers not to utter long prayers in public, but to pray briefly and in private (Mt 6:5–8); long prayers are characteristic of pagan rather than Christian piety. Pharisaic hypocrisy is never more severely pilloried than when Jesus describes them as "devouring the houses of widows while they make long prayers in public" (Mk 12:40; Lk 20:47). The brief petition for pardon uttered by the publican is the prayer which makes a man righteous (Lk 18: 10 ff). Obviously the Church has not always literally followed this injunction of Jesus, and there seems to be no point in trying to show that certain devotional practices are in accord with these Gospel texts. When Jesus was asked to teach His disciples to pray, He gave them the Lord's Prayer*.

The prayer of Jesus Himself dominates the Gospels, although there is here a relationship between Jesus and the Father* which is unique even beyond the relationship of the prophets with Yahweh. Jesus illustrated His own recommendation (Mt 6:6) by praying in solitude (Lk 6:12). One of the most precious documents on the prayer of Jesus is the Gethsemani episode, in which an internal conflict is subdued through prayer (Mt 26:36–46; Mk 14:32–42; Lk 22:40–46); here also Jesus prayed in solitude. There is no indication, however, that Jesus was opposed to cultic prayer; besides explicit notices of His presence at festivals, it is certain that any refusal to participate in Jewish cult would have been noticed by the Pharisees. Models of prayer are also Jesus' thanksgiving to His Father in an hour of failure (Mt 11:25 f; Lk 10:21). The prayers in Jn (11:41 f, the priestly prayer, 17:1 ff) are freely composed in the Joannine style.

Jesus teaches that the Christian must pray with complete assurance that his prayer will be answered; the Father deals with us as a father with his children (Mt 7:7–11; Lk 11:9–13). Christians are to pray with importunity, like a man who knows that his neighbor will assist him simply to be rid of the inconvenience of the petition (Lk 11:5–8). He even employs the parable of the dishonest judge who yields to the widow's petition because she annoys him; Christians are to persevere in their petitions and not to give up (Lk 18:1–8). The same assurance that prayer is answered is found in Jn 15:7, 17; 16:26. Early Christian prayer shows an assurance which is based on this teaching. But the "answer" may sublimate the petition; when Paul asked to be delivered of his "thorn," whatever this may have been, he received instead the strength to bear it (2 Co 12:7–9). Early Christian prayer was uttered in the name* of Jesus (Jn 15:7). Jesus is the eternal high priest who intercedes for those who approach God through Him (Hb 7:25). Christians invoke the Father in virtue of the spirit* which Jesus gives them (Rm 8:15; Gal 4:6), without which they cannot even profess their faith that Jesus is Lord (1 Co 12:3).

The early Christian communities imitated the synagogues whose model they followed in the recitation of common prayers (Mt 18:19; 1 Co 14:13). The posture was either kneeling (AA 21:5) or standing (Mk 11:25). Probably they used the posture common in the OT and also among Greeks and Romans of outstretched arms. The allusions to prayer in the epistles show a variety of objects of prayer: a safe journey (Rm 1:10), the salvation of the Jews (Rm 10:1), deliverance from enemies (Rm 15:31), spiritual strength (Eph 3:14–17), for various·spiritual goods (Eph 6:18–20; Phl 1:4, 9–12), for peace for all men (1 Tm 2:1–4), for the sick (Js 5:14 ff). It is obvious that spiritual goods are predominant in Christian prayer, as noticed above; the NT revelation has made known what the spiritual goods are for which men should pray. Paul frequently exhorts to prayer, especially to perseverance in prayer (Rm 13:4; Eph 6:18–20; Phl 4:6). In Col 3:16 the prayer of praise is encouraged. A characteristic of Paul's prayer is the thanksgiving which is found in the introduction and conclusion of most of his epistles.

Prayer of Manasses. Cf APOCRYPHAL BOOKS.

Preaching (Gk *kērussein*, "to proclaim,"

kērygma, "proclamation," is the work of the *kēryx,* "herald"). "Preach" is a slightly inadequate version of the word, since it has acquired in contemporary usage the meaning of pulpit oratory, which includes instruction and exhortation, and usually is thought to suppose personal preparation and elaboration of the theme through logical and rhetorical means. "Proclaim" is a peculiarly NT word for the presentation of the Christian message, the gospel*. It presupposes that the preachers are heralds who announce simply that which they are commissioned to announce, not in their own name but by the authority of the one who sends them. There is no background in classical Gk or the LXX or Judaism for the NT use of the word, which thus exhibits an original conception. John the Baptist is the messianic herald (Mk 1:4; Mt 3:1; Lk 3:3). The proclamation is the task and mission of Jesus Himself (Mk 1:38; Lk 4:18 f). Jesus and those who proclaim in His name announce a present reality and not the future, and thus "proclamation" is distinguished from prophetic utterance, which looks to the future. It is necessary that the gospel be proclaimed, and it cannot be proclaimed unless the preacher has a mission (Rm 10:14). Proclamation implies a public utterance; the early Church did not conceive itself as an exclusive esoteric group. What the preachers had heard was to be proclaimed from the housetops (Mt 10:27; Lk 12:3) and to the whole world (Mt 24:14; Lk 24:46 f). The preaching is addressed to all peoples (Col 1:23; Mk 13:10; 16:15, 20). It is to be preached in season and out of season (2 Tm 4:2). The preaching depends not upon the persuasive words of human wisdom but upon the demonstration of spirit and power (1 Co 2:4). The preacher is a herald of another; he preaches not himself but Christ Jesus the Lord (2 Co 4:5). The content of the preaching is the word of God which the preacher has received from Jesus (Tt 1:3). "Preaching" is sometimes joined with "teaching" (Mt 4:23; 9:35; 11:1; AA 28:31); the preaching is the proclamation of the gospel, the teaching* is the explanation of the OT which follows the proclamation. The purpose of the proclamation is faith (1 Co 2:4 f).

The object of the proclamation is simply the gospel; "proclaim" and "announce the good news" are often synonymous, as are "kerygma" and "gospel." It includes baptism (Mk 1:4; Lk 3:3; AA 10:37), repentance (Lk 24:47), forgiveness (Lk 4:18), Jesus (AA 19:13), Jesus Son of God (AA 9:20), Jesus Lord (2 Co 4:5), Jesus Messiah (AA 8:5; 2 Co 1:19; 4:5; Phl 1:15), Christ crucified (1 Co 1:23), the

kingdom of God (Lk 8:1; 9:2; AA 20:25; 28:31), the gospel (Mt 26:13; Mk 13:10; 14:9; 16:15; Gal 2:2; Col 1:23), the gospel of the kingdom (Mt 4:23; 9:35; 24:14), the word (2 Tm 4:2), the word of faith (Rm 10:8). There is no real diversity of objects in this enumeration. The theme is the coming of the kingdom, which is the coming of Jesus Himself. This is the saving act of God which is proclaimed, and in particular the supreme saving act, the redeeming death of Jesus and the resurrection by which He is manifested Son of God, empowered to communicate the salvation which He promises. It is a proclamation which imposes upon those who hear it the necessity of responding either by acceptance, which means repentance and faith, or rejection, which means judgment. The proclamation is seen in the discourses of AA 2:14–40; 3:12–26; 10:28–43 (cf GOSPEL).

Presbyter. Cf ELDER.

Priest. 1. *Mesopotamia.* Priesthood appears in all periods and regions in Mesopotamia and certain common features appear. The priesthood was generally hereditary; it was divided into a very large number of classes with specialized functions, many of which are obscure; it was headed by a chief priest or chief priests; it included diviners* and magicians*; the temple personnel included women; the priests were scribes* and teachers (cf TEMPLE). In Assyria, at least at some periods, they were exempt from taxes and military service. The influence of the priesthood was powerful because of the large holdings and land and slaves which belonged to the temples*; but there is no trace of such political influence as they acquired in Egypt. A peculiar feature of Sumerian* priesthood is the ritual nakedness required during the cult. For illustrations of Mesopotamian priests cf ANEP 20, 599, 600, 603, 658, 665, 673, 680; an exorcism is represented in 658, an offering in most of the rest, and the performance of the ritual sacred marriage in 680.

2. *Egypt.* Occasionally at least the priests were exempted from taxes and forced labor. The number of priests in Egypt was large; from a record of Ramses III, J. A. Wilson projects that 450,000 persons and 1100 sq mi belonged to the temples; this he estimates as $\frac{1}{10}$ of the population and $\frac{1}{8}$ of the arable land. As in Mesopotamia, the priests were divided into a large number of classes with specialized functions; for illustrations cf ANEP 629, 640. They also functioned occasionally as judges and magistrates. The power of the priesthood seems to have been always great; in the New Kingdom, under the 18th–

20th dynasties, the political power of the priesthood of Amon at Thebes, in particular of the high priest, became strong enough to challenge the Pharaoh. The priesthood was certainly very active under the successors of Ikhnaton, who had challenged the supremacy of Amon; and in the 20th dynasty the priests of Amon seized the kingship itself.

Little is known of the priesthood of the Canaanites; they were designated by the same word as the Hb *kōhēn,* priest.

3. *OT.* The origins of the priesthood are obscure; behind the apparently clear picture of the Pnt, in which the priesthood belongs to the clan of Aaron*, there is much complexity. Later redaction has covered the historical complexity by reckoning all claimants to the priesthood under the genealogy of Levi*. The position of Levi itself is uncertain in the traditions. There are several anecdotes which seem to have as their purpose the vindication of priestly claims; cf

Nude Sumerian priest.

AARON; ELEAZAR; ELI; LEVI; PHINEHAS; ZADOK. It is not necessary to suppose that these anecdotes arose as expressions of rivalry between Levi and Aaron or between Levi and Zadok. Hb tradition is explicit that before the construction of the temple of Solomon (and indeed after it) the Israelites worshiped at numerous sanctuaries scattered

through the land. Each of these sanctuaries was served by its own hereditary priesthood; these in all probability were of distinct origins. It is difficult to say at what period precisely the rivalry between the groups became acute; David accepted the priesthood of Abiathar* but added the priestly line of Zadok (2 S 8:17; 20:25). Solomon displaced the house of Abiathar in favor of Zadok (1 K 2:26 f). Genealogies, real or artificial, connect Zadok with Levi and with Aaron (1 Ch 5:34); no such connection is established for Eli*, whose priestly line was rejected. Jeroboam of Israel established a new priesthood in his sanctuaries of Dan* and Bethel*; but whether they came from old priestly families, as they most probably did, is not stated (1 K 12:31). The connection of Aaron with the period of Moses is clearer than for any other group; these are related to Aaron by genealogies.

The centralization of cult effected by the reform had a violent impact upon the priesthood, but information is insufficient to determine its nature. Dt often refers to landless Levites who have no share in the office of their brothers in Jerusalem. The priesthood of Jerusalem was still the possession of the house of Zadok in the time of Josiah, and one may suppose a distinction between the house of Zadok and the Levites. But the term Levite is also applied to the priests of the temple, and there is evidently some ambiguity in its use (cf LEVI). There is no mention of the house of Aaron in this proceeding.

The high priest presents a further problem. The high priest is clearly present in the post-exilic Jerusalem. The house of Zadok held the office by hereditary succession down to Onias* II (175 BC). Antiochus* Epiphanes replaced Onias with Jason* (175–172), who was the last Zadokite; appointments were made by the Seleucid kings until Jonathan* assumed the office in 153 BC. The Hasmoneans held the office until Aristobulus (37 BC). From this date under the Herods and Roman rule the office was a political office in the hands of the secular government; it was monopolized by a few great priestly families (cf ANNAS; CAIPHAS).

The high priest was the most important person in the Palestinian Jewish community in the postexilic period. He was not only the head of the cult; he was the president of the Sanhedrin* and the chief representative of the people to the ruling officers of the foreign powers who ruled Palestine during these centuries. The eminence of the high priest is clearly seen in the extravagant praise of Onias in BS 50.

This commanding figure has nothing to correspond to it in the monarchy. Except for the activity of the priest Jehoiada* in the dethroning of Athaliah* (2 K 11), priests are politically unimportant in the monarchy, as they are in the premonarchic period. Even the title of high priest is not common: he is mentioned as the great priest (Lv 21:10; Nm 35:25; Jos 20:6; 2 K 22:4, 8), the head priest (2 K 25:18; 2 Ch 19:11; Ezr 7:5), and more rarely the anointed priest (Lv 4:5). Most of the texts in which these phrases are found are regarded by critics as late, and many think that the words "great" and "head" are interpolated into earlier texts. It was formerly a widely accepted view that the high priest did not appear until the postexilic period, and that his appearance in earlier periods is a projection of the high priest into the past. Since high priests or chief priests were found in all other priesthoods of the Near East, it seems quite improbable that he did not appear in Israel also. It is true, however, that the details concerning the high priest and his functions found in the Pnt come from P and are postexilic. We know little or nothing of the functions of the preexilic high priest.

The functions of the Israelite priest were diversified, although we can be certain of no extreme specialization such as appeared in Egypt and Mesopotamia; the analogy suggests that similar specializations were found in Israel. In the postexilic period at least the number of priestly clans or families was large; 21 families or classes appear in the list of Ne 10:3–9 (cf Ne 12:1–7, 12–21). In 1 Ch 24:1–19 the number has grown to 24. One of these 24 classes is mentioned in Lk 1:5; in NT times the 24 classes served in the temple in weekly turns, and the families within the classes served in daily turns. Zechariah* who offers incense*, has a specialized office. Although the evidence is comparatively recent, these divisions no doubt represent older divisions, or are developed from older divisions.

Three priestly functions can be found in certainly older texts: the priest is the giver of oracles (Dt 33:7–11; Jgs 18:5; 1 S 14:41; 28:6); he instructs in the law* (Dt 33:10); he offers sacrifice* (Dt 33:10). Some scholars have wondered whether the oracle was not the primary function of the priest; they point out that in earliest Israel sacrifice was offered by the head of the family (Gn 22; Jgs 6:26; 13:19; 1 K 18: 30 ff, by Elijah). Instruction in the law is a development of the oracular function; the oracle is a communication of the revealed will of Yahweh as a guide of action, and instruction in the law is a more systematic communication of the same thing. Mal 2: 6–8, a late composition, treats instruction in the law as one of the priestly duties;

but in the postexilic period instruction in the law began to pass into the hands of specialists, the scribes*. Mal 1:6 ff deals with the function of sacrifice; the oracular function at this date has been sublimated in the office of instruction. Instruction in the law in the monarchy is mentioned in Ho 4:4–6; Je 2:8. W. Eichrodt sums up the position of the priests in Israel as "the indispensable mediator for entrance into the sphere of the divine." They were the custodians of the sacred traditions of cult and of the knowledge* of God; and it is altogether likely that the priests of Israel, like the priest of other ancient peoples, were also the custodians of their historical traditions and that they had a large part in the writing of these traditions. The great single monument of priestly tradition and theology is the P source of the Pnt*.

The priests occasionally fall under the criticism of the prophets, but less frequently than other leading groups in Israel; this is not necessarily a sign of their greater fidelity, but falls in with the general infrequency of mentions of the priests in the historical books. They are rebuked for their failure to give proper instruction (Je 2:8; Ezk 22:26; Ho 4:4–6; Mal 2:6 ff, after the exile), for revelry (Is 28:7). Jeremiah associates them with false prophets as deceivers of the people (5:30–31; 6:13–14; 8:10–11; 23:11) and includes them among those who attack him (18:18).

3. *NT*. Priests are not often mentioned in the Gospels. It may be noted that the title "chief priests" in the plural does not designate more than one high priest, but designates the heads of priestly families. Jesus refers to the office of the priests to decide between clean and unclean (Mt 8: 14; Mk 1:44; Lk 5:14; 17:14). He vindicates freedom of action on the Sabbath by showing that priestly privileges must yield to need (Mt 12:4; Mk 2:26; Lk 6:4), to which Mt adds that priestly service in the sanctuary is not a violation of the Sabbath (12:5 f). There is an implicit criticism of priests and Levites in Lk's parable of the good Samaritan (10:31 f). The priests are most active in the passion narratives; all four Gospels leave the impression that the priestly aristocracy was the most malevolent and the most active of all the groups which cooperated in bringing Jesus to death. That this is not a condemnation of the entire class is suggested by AA 6:7, which notes that a large number of priests were members of the Jerusalem church.

Jesus applies the title "priest" (Gk *hiereus*) neither to Himself nor to His disciples, and the idea of a Christian priesthood is implicit in the NT (cf EUCHARIST; SACRIFICE). The designation of priests is first applied to the Christian community in 1 Pt 2:5; Apc 1:6; 5:10; 20:5. These passages are all applications of the title of Israel, "a kingdom of priests" (Ex 19:6) to the Church. The Church as the new Israel fulfills also this character of the old Israel; it is probable that the application has the same meaning as the original text, that the group so designated has a priestly character because of its election and consecration. On the title *presbyteros* cf ELDER.

The missing element is supplied in Heb, which deals almost entirely with the priesthood of Jesus. Jesus was not a member of the tribe of Levi and could not be a "priest" in the mind of a Jew; His priesthood is vindicated by the application to Him of the priesthood of Melchizedek (Ps 110:4; Heb 5:6, 10; 6:20). This priesthood is superior to the priesthood of Aaron, because Abraham, the ancestor of Levi and Aaron, acknowledged the superiority of Melchizedek by giving him tithes (7:1–17) and because, as a man without father, mother, and genealogy (not mentioned in Gn 14), he is a type of the timeless Son of God. He has a superior covenant, the new covenant mentioned by Je 31:31 ff (8:6–13), the covenant which is a "testament" (a play upon the Gk word *diathēkē*) rendered effective by the death of the testator; this death is sacrificially effective, for it is a death by the shedding of blood (9:15–22). As the priest He has access to the sanctuary, and He brings others in with Him (4:15–16; 9:11 f; 7:19). His priesthood is heavenly, not earthly, which vindicates it against the exclusive claims of Aaron (8:4). The dignity of His priesthood rests ultimately upon His sonship (3:2 ff; 5:1–10), which is a far higher claim to mediation and union with God than Aaron possessed. The ancient sacrificial cult, which was imperfect, is fulfilled in the sacrifice of Jesus (9–10); its atonement is perfect because of the excellence of the victim, Himself. He has the solidarity with men which the priest as mediator must have: He has experienced human weakness (4:14 f; 5:2), He has suffered (5:7–10), He is like His brothers in every respect (2:17), although He is Himself sinless (7:26 f; 2:18; 4:15) and therefore has no need of offering atonement for Himself. He is the victim which He offers (7:27; 9:12, 14, 25; 10:5 ff), not the animal victims of the old law. And therefore His one single offering need not be repeated and cannot be repeated, because it is totally offered and totally effective (7:27; 9:24–28; 10:10, 12, 14). So the ancient sacrificial cult is abolished (10:9; 7:18; 8:13). The sacrifice of Christ effects redemption (9:12), salvation (10:18), forgiveness (9:15), purifica-

tion (10:18; 9:14), sanctification (10:10, 22), perfection (10:14). It is the foundation of a new cult (9:14; 13:15 ff).

This is perhaps the most systematic theological exposition of the entire NT, and the effects of Heb on the formation of the Christian priesthood in the early Church are incalculable.

Prisca, Priscilla (Lt *prisca*, diminutive *priscilla*, meaning uncertain), personal name, wife of Aquila*, who came to Corinth from Rome with her husband; in Corinth Paul was their guest (AA 18:1–3). Priscilla joined her husband in instructing Apollos* (AA 18:26). The two are commended by Paul as his helpers; they had a Church in their house (Rm 16:3; 1 Co 16:19).

Prison. Imprisonment was not employed as a punishment in the ancient world; it occurred when there was need of detention for trial or for the execution of a sentence (AA 12:4 f). There were no prisons as distinct institutions; chambers or dungeons habitually used for detention were found in other establishments. Joseph and his companions were detained in a "dungeon," possibly in the house of Potiphar* (Gn 40:15; 41:14). Samson* was probably imprisoned in a workhouse (Jgs 16:21, 25). Micaiah* was probably detained in the palace of Ahab (1 K 22:27), as Hoshea* in the palace of the king of Assyria (2 K 17:4) and Jehoiochin* (2 K 25:27) and Zedekiah* (Je 52:11) in the palace of the king of Babylon. Jeremiah was put under confinement in several places: the barracks of the palace (Je 32:2; 37:21; 38:28), a dungeon in the house of the secretary Jonathan (Je 37:15), and the cistern of a private home (Je 38:6–11); it was intended that he die in the cistern. John the Baptist was imprisoned in the fortress of Machaerus by Herod (Mt 11:2; 14:3; Mk 6:17); John was confined neither for trial nor for execution, but simply to remove him from the public; Herod was afraid to have him killed. The prison in which the apostles were confined was probably in the temple area (AA 5:18 f). The prison of Philippi in which Paul and Silas were confined was probably a private home (AA 16:23 ff). Paul mentions imprisonment among the perils of the apostolate (2 Co 6:5).

Prochorus (Gk *prochoros*), one of the seven ordained to help the apostles in the Jerusalem church; cf DEACON (AA 6:5).

Proconsul (Lt *proconsul*, Gk *anthypatos*), a Roman office, originally *pro consule*, possessing consular authority; in NT times the proconsul was the governor of a senatorial province. In the NT are mentioned Sergius Paulus*, proconsul of Cyprus* (AA 13:7–12), and Gallio*, proconsul of Achaea* (1 Co 18:12). The plural in AA 19:38, referring to the governor of Asia, does not indicate that there was more than one proconsul in the province; the plural is used loosely, much as we might say "there are mayors to make these decisions."

Procurator (Lt *procurator*, Gk *hēgemon*, "leader"), a Roman officer. The appointment and functions of procurators varied over the centuries of Roman imperial government, and there are a number of uncertainties about the nature of office. The procurator was an imperial provincial officer, appointed by the emperor and responsible to him. Originally the procurator had the charge of the *fiscus*, the treasury. Occasionally he governed a province with the powers of a governor. Such appointments were usually transitional pending the full organization of a province. Judaea*, however, was governed by procurators, except for the reigns of Herod* and Agrippa*, from 63 BC to the destruction of Jerusalem and the abolition of Judaea as a distinct territory in AD 70. The appointment of procurators was probably due to the peculiar character of the Jewish people and their laws; and the territory, as its history shows, was frequently a trouble spot for Roman administration. The procurator was subordinate to the nearest governor; the procurator of Judaea was subordinate to the legate of Syria*. The procurator had auxiliary troops (not legions) under his command. He administered the collection of taxes. He had exclusive jurisdiction in capital cases. He had the power to nominate and depose the high priest.

The term is used loosely in the sense of "rulers" in Mt 10:18; Mk 13:9; Lk 21:12; 1 Pt 2:14. Individual procurators of Judaea are mentioned: Pilate*, Felix*; Festus*. The procurator of Judaea regularly resided at Caesarea*, visiting Jerusalem only when close supervision seemed necessary. On the question of his residence in Jerusalem cf GABBATHA.

Procurators of Judaea AD 6–41:

6–9	Coponius
9–12	M. Ambivius
12–15	Annius Rufus
15–26	Valerius Gratus
26–36	Pontius Pilatus
36–37	Marcellus
37–41	Marullus

AD 44–66:

44–46	Cuspius Fadus
46–48	Tiberius Alexander
48–52	Ventidius Cumanus
52–60	Antonius Felix
61–62	Porcius Festus
62–64	Albinus
64–66	Gessius Florus

Profane. Cf HOLY.

Promise. 1. *OT*. While there is no Hb word which can be translated "promise," the theological theme of promise, which is first explicit in the NT, is evident in the OT also. Martin Noth has pointed out that "promise and fulfilment" is one of the great themes of the Pnt. Gn 12–50 contains a chain of promises made to the patriarchs: blessing*, numerous progeny, and possession of the land in which they dwell. The rest of the Pnt and the book of Jos is a story of the fulfillment of these promises. With the fulfillment of the promise in the OT runs the unfolding of new promises: of the reign of Yahweh, of an eternal dynasty of David*, and after the exile of the restoration of Israel. It is a basic article of OT faith that Yahweh is able and willing to keep His promises, that He is faithful; and His fidelity to promise is a motive for the fidelity of Israel to the commandments of Yahweh.

2. *NT*. Promise in the NT is a restatement of the promises of the OT, an affirmation of their fulfillment, and again an unfolding of new promises. The promises were made to the patriarchs (Heb 11:9–11; 7:6; 6:13–15; AA 7:15, 17). Paul, on trial in Caesarea, affirms his hope in the promises made to the fathers; this establishes the genuinity of his Judaism and establishes the continuity between the gospel and the OT (AA 26:6). The recital of the promises and their fulfillment is a new motive for affirming that God is faithful to His promises (Heb 10:23).

The promises therefore belong to Israel (Rm 9:4); this creates a problem, for the Israelites have rejected the fulfillment, and the Gentiles, to whom the promises were not given (Eph 2:12), are now sharers in the fulfillment through the Gospel (Eph 3:6). Paul twice discusses the relations of the law and the promises (Rm 4:13–25; Gal 3:15–29). In Gal he notes that a promise is absolute and is not nullified by the subsequent law, which was promulgated because of transgressions. The promise is a promise of life, which the law could not give. Consequently, when the fulfillment of the promise comes, the law, which was transitional, is invalidated. In Rm Paul adds to this that Abraham, who was not under the law when he received the promise, accepted the promise by faith*; so faith alone is required when the fulfillment of the promise arrives.

Now it is Christ who realizes the promises made to the fathers, and by realizing them He demonstrates the fidelity of God (Rm 15:8). He is the promised messianic salvation (Heb 12:26), He is the savior whom God brings according to promise (AA 13:23); and God fulfills His promise not only by bringing Jesus but by raising Him from the dead (AA 13:32 f). This is the promised Rest which the fathers did not receive (Heb 4:1–13).

Equally, if not more prominent, is the theme of the promises of the Gospel. The new promises and the new covenant surpass the old (Heb 8:6). The first fruits of the new promises is the Spirit* granted to the apostles (AA 1:4; 2:33) and then to all Christians (AA 2:39; Eph 1:13). To those who love Him God promises a kingdom (Js 2:5) and a crown of life (Js 1:12), eternal life (1 Jn 2:25). Christians obtain the promised reward by doing the will of God (Heb 10:36).

The theme of promise is basic to the themes of faith* and hope*; these virtues rest upon the promises of the OT which, as noticed above, establish the continuity of the process of salvation from OT to Gospel, and of the promises of the NT, which are assured not only by conviction of the saving power and will of God, but also by the experience of the fulfillment of promises.

Prophet, Prophecy. The Eng word prophet is derived from Gk *prophētēs*, "one who speaks before others"; the Gk word almost always denotes one who communicates divine revelation. In the Gk Bible *prophētēs* translates Hb *nābî'*, the usual word for prophet. The meaning of the etymology of the word is uncertain; many scholars connect it with an Akkadian root meaning "to call," "speak aloud," and interpret it as speaker; others suggest an Arabian root which means "to bubble" and interpret it of the frenetic character of prophetic utterance. W. F. Albright with great probability derives it from the Akkadian root in the sense of "one called" (by God to speak for Him). In Hb a verb is formed from the noun which appears in two senses: to conduct oneself as a prophet, to act in the manner of a prophet (Nm 11: 25, 27; 1 S 10:5 f, 10 ff; 19:18 ff; 1 K 18: 29; 22:10), and to be a prophet, to speak as a prophet (Am 3:8; 7:15 f, frequently in Je and Ezk, only Jl and Zc of the other prophetic books). On the prophetic manner of action cf below. The prophet is also called a man of God (['elōhîm] 1 S 2:27; 9:6–10; 1 K 12:22; 13:1; 17:18, 24; 20:28; 2 K 1:9–13; 4:38 ff, 42 ff; 6:1 ff). Most of these incidences indicate that this was an honorific address. The prophet is also called a

seer (*rō'eh*, 1 S 9:9, 11, 18, 19; *ḥōzeh*, 2 S 24:11; Am 7:12); on the relation of prophet and seer cf below.

Hb prophetism is generally recognized by scholars as a uniquely distinctive Hb phenomenon; parallels which can be adduced from other ancient Near Eastern sources are superficial. In the letters of Mari* there appears a priest called the *muhhu* who delivers oracles of the god Hadad to king Zimri-lim. These oracles resemble the utterances of OT prophets in their introductory formulae and in their form and style, and in their content they refer to the relation of the king and the god in terms which are not dissimilar to the dynastic oracle of David* (2 S 7). In an Egyptian narrative Wen-Amon, an emissary of the Pharaoh to Byblos*, finds a young man at the court of Byblos who delivers oracles of the god in an ecstatic manner (ANET 26). The records of Ugarit* disclose that there were ecstatic and oracular phenomena in the cult. The stele of Zakir king of Hamath* tells how he receives favorable oracles of Baal-shamim through seers and diviners. The resemblance between these phenomena and Israelite prophecy is merely in the form; the ethical and religious content of Israelite prophecy has no parallel whatever in the ancient world.

The origins and early development of Hb prophecy are somewhat obscure. Shortly before the establishment of the early monarchy there appear groups called "the sons of the prophet(s)." As they are described in 1 S 10:5–12; 19:20–24, it seems that they were groups organized for worship in cultic song and dance, and the behavior of Saul in 19:20 ff strongly suggests that their worship was frenetic. They do not appear as attached to any temple or liturgical cult; in 1 S 19:20 Samuel exercises a kind of presidency of the group. A group of the same name in 1 K 22:6–12 predicts victory for Ahab* over the Arameans; it is hinted, although not with all certainty, that their performance also was frenetic. The name occurs in 1 K 20:35; here and elsewhere the distinction between "the sons of the prophets" and the prophets is not sharp. They appear several times in 2 K (2:3–17; 4:1, 38–44; 5:22; 9:1–11) as associates of Elijah and Elisha, to some extent living in community outside of towns and cities, and acting as aids and messengers (9:1 ff). Frenetic cult is not mentioned; the officers of Jehu* call Elisha's prophetic messenger a madman (9:11), which does not necessarily indicate frenzy; it may be a sign of the low esteem of the prophetic groups among worldly men like these officers. Frenetic cult is certainly evident in the prophets of the Baal* (1 K 18·22–29); one may ask, however, whether these cult functionaries have not been given a Hb title which they did not possess. Even so, the application indicates that their behavior was regarded as "prophetic." Elisha, who never participates in such rites, once calls for music to stimulate him to deliver an oracle requested (2 K 3:16 f).

The occurrences of the "sons of the prophets" and their relations to Samuel, Elijah, and Elisha, obscure as they are, suggest that these were independent groups of worshipers, in the sense that they were not regular cult personnel, and that they were organized under a leader who was called "the prophet." The leader himself was not an ecstatic worshiper as far as he was described, but a religious leader of a different type (cf below). The sons of the prophets identified themselves with the cause which the prophet represented.

Of these prophets the first who can be discerned with any degree of clarity is Samuel, and his character has been overlaid with a heavy layer of highly imaginative details. His vocation as a prophet is related (1 S 3:1 ff). He is a judge as well as a prophet. At the word of Yahweh he installs Saul as king (1 S 7–10). He delivers an oracle deposing Saul as king (duplicate accounts in 1 S 13 and 1 S 15). The form in which Samuel delivers his oracles is the form we see in the later prophetic books, but it is unlikely that this is a retrojection of a later form; Amos, the first of the writing prophets, disposes of a form which is already well defined. Samuel is called a seer, and a gloss explains that seer was the older title of prophet (1 S 9:9, 11, 18 f). "Seer" is evidently the title employed in the original narrative, and the question arises of the relation of these two. A seer like Samuel who may be expected to find lost animals approaches the Mesopotamian diviner* in character and function, and has in common with the later prophet only the possession of superhuman knowledge. He is not an ecstatic; he is a giver of oracular responses. Similar oracular responses are given by other prophets (1 S 28:6; 1 K 14:2; 22:5, 7; 2 K 3:11; 22:13). As such, and as one who guides Israel by the revealed will of Yahweh, Samuel is more directly the ancestor of later prophecy than are the sons of the prophets.

The prophets Gad* and Nathan* were associated with David both as an outlaw and as king. Gad delivers an oracular warning to David (1 S 22:5) and a threat of punishment to him for taking the census (2 S 24: 11–13). Nathan delivers the dynastic oracle (2 S 7) and rebukes David for adultery and murder (2 S 12:1–14). Except for 1 S 22:5, these prophetic actions are in the type of address which is later identified with

prophecy: moral censures, threats of divine punishment, and statements of the saving will of Yahweh for Israel. The form is likewise that typical of prophecy.

Samuel was active in the external and internal politics of Israel, although his attempt to depose Saul failed; later prophets also are politically active, but a division of policy appears which is rooted in religious belief. Ahijah* commissioned Jeroboam to rebel against Solomon and establish the distinct kingdom of Israel (1 K 11:29–40); he is clearly in opposition to the dual monarchy of David and the policies of David and Solomon and believes that the purity of Israelite belief will be most securely preserved if the northern tribes, the heart of ancient Israel*, detach themselves from Judah* and its king. The same Ahijah, however, threatens destruction to the house of Jeroboam for its infidelity to Yahweh (1 K 14:1–19). Jehu predicted the total extinction of the house of Baasha* (1 K 16:1–4, 7, 12). Micaiah* predicts the defeat and death of Ahab at Ramoth-gilead in opposition to the predictions of victory delivered by other prophets (1 K 22). Elijah and Elisha were in mortal opposition to the house of Omri. In Israel, therefore, one sees a developing opposition between prophecy and the monarchy; the prophets were convinced that the monarchy was an irreligious institution, and the prophetic opposition culminates in conspiracy and assassination instigated by the prophets (1 K 19:16 f; 2 K 8:7–15; 9:1–10). The conversation of Elisha with Hazael* shows the extent to which the prophets would go; Elisha encouraged Hazael, whom he knew believed in total war with Israel, to assassinate Benhadad*, who made a treaty with Ahab. The prophets placed the integrity of Yahwism above any national or patriotic consideration.

But this was not true of all prophets. The prophets who threatened Ahab for his treaty with Ben-hadad (1 K 20:35–42) and who predicted victory for Ahab at Ramoth-gilead (1 K 22:6–12) were passionately attached to the nation and its political and military success, and encouraged war by their predictions of victory. No doubt they too had their religious beliefs; they were convinced of the saving power of Yahweh and His will to deliver Israel from its enemies and establish it as His kingdom. To them too is given the title of prophet, and they speak in the name of Yahweh.

The title is given to some persons in early Israel by a retrojection: Abraham (Gn 20: 7), Aaron (Ex 7:1), Miriam (Ex 15:20), Moses (Nm 12:6–8; Dt 34:10; 18:15–19), the elders (Nm 11:16, 24–26). The retrojection shows the conception of prophecy; these men are in conversation with Yahweh

(Abraham, Moses) or by inspiration speak in His name (Aaron, Miriam). Moses is indeed the head of all prophets and greater than any one; he is the supreme example of one who receives the word of Yahweh and speaks it to Israel, who leads Israel through the affirmation of basic Israelite beliefs. The conception is illustrated in Ex 4:16; Moses, who cannot speak, will be like a god to Aaron, and Aaron will be his *nābî'*, his spokesman. But in the time of Amos the title must have suggested the type of prophet seen in 1 K 20; 22, for Amos refuses the title and appeals simply to a command of Yahweh to speak. To us nothing could be more "prophetic" than such a command; this shows the necessity of care in stating the Israelite conception of prophecy. In the preexilic prophetic books the title is rarely employed outside of editorial passages; Hosea apparently applies it to himself (9:7), Jeremiah is a prophet to the nations (1:5), and he is regularly given the title in the biographical passages (cf JEREMIAH); it is more common in Ezk (2:5; 14:4), and usual in the postexilic books. It is used in a favorable sense in the plural of men who speak the word of Yahweh: Ho 6:5; 12:11; Je 5:13; 28:8 (and in the prose summaries cf Je 7:25; 25:4; 26:5; 29:19; 35:15; 44:4); in Ezk 38:17 the prophets are called the servants of Yahweh, a title also found in the prose summaries of Je.

Most occurrences of the title in preexilic prophetic books are hostile, referring to what we call "false" prophets (cf below; Is 3:1–3; 9:13 f; 28:7 ff; 29:10; Je 5:31; 6:13; 8:10; 14:13 f; 23:9–40; Ezk 13:1–23; Ho 4:5; Mi 3:5–7; Zp 3:3 f). They are named several times with king and priests as leaders of the people.

Modern scholars have raised the problem of groups which are called professional prophets, court prophets, or cultic prophets; these terms may designate the same group under different names, or they may designate different groups. Theories concerning these groups attempt to explain the character and purpose of those groups which we find in opposition to the individual prophets in the monarchical period and to the literary prophets. The groups are characterized by a strong nationalistic patriotism. The professional prophet is what the name implies; he lives by prophecy, as is suggested by Am 7:12. A prophet had to have the charisma of the word of Yahweh; how did the professional prophet obtain the charisma? Presumably he obtained it by joining a group. The groups associated with the king seem to have been court functionaries, supported by the king and available for inquiry concerning the will of Yahweh. Gad and Nathan may be court prophets, and the 400 who predict Ahab's victory (1 K 22:6). Court prophets need not be merely tools of the monarch, uttering what he wishes; they stand in opposition to him in 1 K 20:35 ff. Micaiah seems to have been a court prophet who was habitually in opposition to Ahab (1 K 22:8); Nathan rebuked David for his sins, and Gad threatened him for taking the census. Nevertheless, it appears that dependence on the monarchy could easily be a corrupting influence on prophecy.

The existence of cultic prophets who exercised a regular function in the cult is proposed by several writers, mostly of the Scandinavian school. They find a basis for this hypothesis in certain prophetic utterances in the Pss (60:8–11; 75:3–6; 82:2–4; 110:1, 4). These oracular sayings are in the form of prophetic utterances, and these scholars believe that the cult provided for such oracular responses in contexts of inquiry, petition, or royal Pss such as 110 and 2. The theory is supported also by "prophetic liturgies" which these scholars find in Je 14; Ho 6:1 ff; Hab 3; Jl 1:2 +, where the prophet speaks in a context of dialogue which resembles the petitions of the Pss. The theory has some probability, and a relation between prophecy and liturgy at least in form may be regarded as established; but the existence of prophets who were cultic personnel is still doubted, perhaps by the majority of scholars.

The question of prophetic inspiration must be answered in terms of the prophetic experience as described by the prophets themselves; and in these descriptions there is no small amount of imagery and symbolism. A simple and crass understanding of the experience as vision and hearing does justice neither to the prophets themselves nor to any possible parallels (cf below) which can be adduced to the experience. The prophets themselves exhibit a creative faculty of utterance which stamps most of them with a distinctive and highly personal style; and their own genius is largely responsible for their utterances. Nevertheless, they attribute their utterances to "the word of Yahweh"; this is the charisma proper to the prophet, as law* belongs to the priest and wisdom* to the wise man (Je 18:18). This "otherness" in their utterances is also the pivotal point of the inaugural experiences which are described in Is 6; Je 1; Ezk 2. These are full of symbolism, but the common point is the reception of what is uttered from Yahweh through purification of the lips for His word (Is), putting the word in the mouth (Je), eating a scroll (Ezk). These might be mere fanciful elaborations of the traditional phrase, "the word of Yahweh came to . . . ," were it not for other elements mentioned, particularly by Jeremiah, the only introspective prophet. This element is principally a compulsion by a personal external will, which the prophet cannot overcome in spite of his own unwillingness to speak the word of Yahweh, an unwillingness which is manifest in Jeremiah (Je 1:7; 6:11; 20:9; Am 3:8).

An obvious theory of prophetic inspiration which has been proposed by a large number of scholars is that they were profound religious thinkers. Granting the remarkable insight of the prophets, their own description of their experience, symbolism and all, does not attribute their words to their own insight; and if they actually spoke the fruits of their own reflection, it is difficult to see how they could be credited with profound insight if they could not tell their own thoughts from the experience of Yahweh. In other men who claimed divine revelation this is the result of insincerity or fanaticism. This theory is explicitly rejected in Je 23:16, 18, 21 f, 25–29; the prophets who do not speak the word of Yahweh speak their own minds, they are not sent, Yahweh has not spoken to them, they speak their dreams. Je insists upon the authenticity of his prophecy precisely because it is not the word of man.

Many scholars have followed G. Hölscher in calling the prophets ecstatics; the frenetic element in "the sons of the prophets" has been noticed above. Divine communications in Canaan and in Greece were often accompanied by an ecstatic frenzy, and Hölscher adduced a number of abnormal phenomena, almost all from Ezk (Ezk 3:15, 25; 4:1–3; 6:11; 9:8; 11:13; 21:19; 24:27; Is 20:1 ff). It is now generally admitted that ecstatic behavior is not characteristic of Israelite prophecy, rather it is distinctly nonecstatic in sharp contrast to Canaanite and Gk phenomena. The prophetic inspiration cannot be reduced to simple frenzy or ecstasy, although it must be conceded that the element of ecstasy or enthusiasm is a universal religious phenomenon. But prophecy is not a universal phenomenon, and for this reason cannot be reduced to ecstasy.

The only satisfactory parallel to the prophetic experience is the phenomena of mysticism as described by writers like Teresa of Avila, John of the Cross, and others. They affirm that the immediate experience of God is ineffable; like the prophets, they must employ imagery and symbolism to describe it, with explicit warnings that these are used. They describe it as a transforming experience which moves one to speech and action beyond one's expected capacities. It grants them a profound insight not only into divine reality but into the human scene. Thus the prophetic experience is such a mystical immediate experience of the reality and presence of God. The prophets disclose the nature and character of the God so experienced, and they state the implications of the divine nature and character for human thought and action. But the conception and formulation of their utterance is their own. For Jeremiah the false prophet is one who has no such awareness; the false prophet may be sincere, but he is nonetheless false. Because he lacks the prophetic insight into the moral will of Yahweh and the reality of sin, the false prophet sees no evil where it is and prophesies that all is well when it is not. He easily identifies Israel and its cause with Yahweh and His will and predicts victory; he has no conception of the sweeping and rigorous justice with which Yahweh governs. He speaks less than the truth and perverts sound religious belief to merely national and personal good.

The prophetic form of utterance rises from prophetic inspiration, which it affirms. It is introduced by set formulae, "Thus speaks Yahweh," etc, and often concludes with the phrase, "the oracle of Yahweh." This is the oracular utterance, in which Yahweh Himself is the speaker. It is now clear from ancient Near Eastern literature that these formulae are epistolary. The epistolary formulae of the ancient Near East are the formulae of oral messages, memorized and delivered with the introduction, "Thus speaks X: Speak to Y, and say to him: Thus speaks X." The four original species of the oracle are defined by scholars as the threat, the promise, the reproach, and the admonition. The oracle is thought by most scholars to have been brief; obviously the prophetic books exhibit longer sayings. These often arise from the collection of sayings into longer poems or discourses; the sayings are grouped around a single topic, or they pass from one to another by catchwords. In some instances the prophet takes the oracle as a kind of text and then delivers a discourse or commentary; in such discourses he passes from speech in his own person to speech in the person of Yahweh. But the prophetic literature shows an adaptation of most forms of Hb literature as vehicles for the prophetic message of threat, promise, reproach, and admonition: lamentation*, taunt-song, drinking song, love song, wise saying, priestly response, legal plea, dialogue. The use of these popular forms add much to the power and appeal of the prophetic discourse, which is far removed from what is conventionally conceived as "preaching."

The prophet occasionally performs symbolic actions (Is 20:1 ff; Je 13:1–11; 19:1–13; Ezk 4:1–5:17), and sometimes features in his manner of life or of the events of his life are invested with prophetic significance (Je 16:1 ff; Ezk 24:15 ff; Ho 1–3). The symbolic action is an extension of the prophetic word*, which is a dynamic agent. The performance of the action emphasizes the word and brings the reality it signifies and effects into incipient being. It is, of course, a rhetorical device to attract attention, but it is much more. The action has force only from the prophetic word which accompanies and interprets it.

Prophecy gradually lapsed after the exile. The postexilic prophets lack the vigor and urgency of the preexilic and exilic prophets, possibly because the Jewish community was politically inactive. Zc 13:2–6, a passage of uncertain but late date, is as severe a polemic against prophecy as any in the preexilic prophets; but it is not a total renunciation of prophecy, and seems to be directed to the "false" prophets. Josephus speaks of an uninterrupted succession of prophets from Moses to Artaxerxes I (464–424 BC). The date no doubt reflects the belief of Josephus concerning the date of Mal, but it also coincides with the beginning of the work of Nehemiah* and Ezra*. In the postexilic community the written word of the law* replaced the spoken word of the prophet as the vehicle of the revelation of Yahweh; prophecy yielded to the scribe* as the guide of the faith of Israel, and to the authors of apocalypses* as a seer. Passages such as 1 Mc 4:46; 9:27; 14:1 obviously regard prophecy as inactive in the time of the Macabees and to be expected in some indefinite future.

NT. In the NT the word *prophētēs* most frequently designates the OT prophets; it is twice applied to non-Israelites, Balaam (2 Pt 2:16, not called a prophet in the OT) and the Cretan poet Epimenides (Tt 1:12). Hannah* is called a prophetess (Lk 2:36); she spoke in the prophetic manner. The verb "prophesy" likewise is used to designate the prophetic manner of speech (Lk 1:67; Jn 11:51; AA 19:6; 21:9; Apc 10:11). The utterance of Zechariah* was a messianic pronouncement, and Caiaphas uttered a messianic pronouncement unwittingly; Apc 10:11; AA 19:6; 21 possibly mean by prophecy ecstatic speech. Prophecy is also a display of occult knowledge (Mk 14:65; Mt 26:68; Lk 22:64). It is synonymous with instruction and exhortation (1 Co 14:3, 24, 31). The noun "prophecy" means either the charisma itself (Rm 12:6; 1 Co 12:10; 13:2) or a prophetic utterance, a very common use. *Pseudoprophētēs,* false prophet, is used in Mt 7:15; 24:11, 24; Mk 13:22; AA 13:6; 2 Pt 2:1; 1 Jn 4:1; Apc 16:13; 19:20; 20: 10; except for Mt 7:15 and AA 13:6, these

appear in the future, possibly the eschatological future.

Of the OT prophets, Isaiah is named most frequently in the NT; others named are Samuel, Enoch, Elisha, Jeremiah, Daniel, Joel, Jonah. Hosea, Amos. Micah, Habakkuk, Haggai, Zechariah are cited without being named. The concept of OT prophecy is that God spoke through the prophets (Mt 1:22; 2:15 +; Lk 1:70; AA 3:18, 21; Rm 1:2) or in the prophets (Heb 1:1). The spirit* is also said to reveal in them (1 Pt 1:11); the prophets spoke moved by a holy spirit (2 Pt 1:21). It is to be noticed that God speaks through the prophets rather than to them. There are many references to written prophecy; the "prophets" sometimes signifies the historical and prophetic books of the OT; cf CANON.

The word most frequently used to describe the prophetic utterance is "foretell" (Lk 24: 27; Jn 1:45; AA 2:3; 3:18, 24; 7:52; 8:34; 28:23; Rm 1:2; 9:29; 1 Pt 1:11; 2 Pt 3:2). It is a common misconception of OT prophecy that it means prediction; cf above and articles on separate books. This misconception cannot be based upon the NT conception nor on the formula "that it might be fulfilled." Often there is obviously no prediction (e.g., Mt 2:15); there is reference to an OT character or event which illustrates the reality of the process of salvation, the reality which is "fulfilled" in Jesus Christ. He and the Church are the new Israel and their experience appears in the experience of the old Israel, much as the OT ancestor shows in his life and character the life and character of his descendants. Many of these predictions are intended to illustrate the place of the redemptive suffering in the process of salvation; the Jews were not receptive to the idea of a Messiah who saved through suffering and death, and it was necessary to show that the scandal of the cross appears in the messianism of the OT; cf SERVANT OF THE LORD. In these passages the NT writers take a specialized and apologetic view of the OT which is not intended to be a general exhaustive interpretation. "Fulfillment" is more than fulfillment of a prediction; it is the fulfillment of a hope, a destiny, a plan, a reality.

The prophets are also canonical authorities, to which one may appeal as one appeals to the law* (Mt 21:13; Mk 11:17; Lk 19: 46; Jn 6:45; AA 10:43; 15:15). We find here the Christian understanding of the OT, which does not raise the law to a higher degree of inspiration and authority.

There are several references to the persecution and martyrdom of the prophets (Mt 23:29–37; 21:35; 22:6; 5:12; Lk 13:33 f; 6:23; 11:47 f +). These are based on Jewish traditions rather than on the text of the OT, which has little information of this type. Some of these traditions can be traced in the apocryphal* literature.

There are prophetic figures in the NT, of whom the most outstanding is John* the Baptist. Was Jesus Himself a prophet? The title is applied to Him by others (Mt 16:24; 21:11, 46; Mk 6:15; 8:28; Lk 7:16, 39; 9:8, 19; 24:19; Jn 4:19; 6:14; 7:40; 9:17; AA 3:22 f; 7:37). But it is never applied to Jesus by Himself or by the evangelists, which suggests that He did not claim the title, although He did not reject it. The unique character of Jesus makes it difficult to fit Him into any of the charismatic figures and religious leaders of Israel and Judaism. He was not a scribe, although He was often addressed as rabbi*. He was not a priest. He resembles the prophet more than any other Hb religious figure; He speaks for God, He stands outside the cultic and political structure. Yet He never uses the prophetic formulae, but speaks with His own authority. There was a Jewish belief in the prophetic precursor of the Messiah, the last of the prophets, and some of the occurrences mentioned above attempt to identify Jesus with this precursor (Mt 21:11; Mk 6:14; Lk 7:16; Jn 6:14; 7:40); Jesus implicitly rejected this identification by hinting rather strongly that John the Baptist was the prophet precursor (Mt 11:7–10; Lk 7:24–27).

That there were prophets in the early Christian communities is evident from a number of passages (AA 11:27; 21:10 f; 13:1 ff; 1 Co 13:2; 14:3–5, 24 f; Eph 3:5; 1 Tm 1:18; 4:14; Apc 22:6 f). These are mentioned with other officers as leaders of the Church (Rm 12:6; 1 Co 12:10, 28 f; Eph 2:20; 3:5; 4:11). Their office and function, however, is not entirely clear. Prophecy was a charismatic office; this is to be expected, and Paul calls it the best of the charisms (1 Co 14:1). Their occurrence in the lists of officers indicates that they had a regular place and function, cultic at least, in the community, and thus they resemble the cultic prophets postulated for the OT by some scholars (cf above). They must have spoken in the name of God, and would not have the name unless they spoke inspired utterances; but except for a few passages (cf above), there is no more reason to think that they were ecstatic than there is for the OT prophets. In 1 Co 14 ecstasy is associated with the gift of tongues, the prophet edifies, exhorts, and encourages (1 Co 14:3). Prophecy does not appear after NT times; as OT prophecy yielded to the scribe, so NT prophecy was submerged in the development of the hierarchical offices. After the 1st cen-

tury prophecy was claimed almost exclusively by heretical sects.

Propitiation. Cf ATONEMENT.

Proselyte (Gk *prosēlytos,* "one who approaches"). The religion of the OT with its belief in one supreme God who must be recognized and served by all mankind has in itself universalist tendencies. These tendencies find expression in the OT in such passages as Is 42:6 ff; 45:14 ff; 56:1–8; 66: 19; Jon; Zc 13. When the Jews of the Diaspora* spread out over the Hellenistic world, they began to present their religion in a way which was attractive to their neighbors. This was due not only to religious zeal, but also to a desire to create friendly relations in the foreign cities in which they lived. There were many features in Judaism which recommended it to the Hellenistic world. The old polytheism of the Greeks had been destroyed by the criticisms of the philosophers and was regarded as superstition and ignorance by most Greeks, whether educated or not. The philosophy of the schools of Plato, Aristotle, and Stoicism had elaborated a conception of one supreme god and an advanced system of morality. Philosophy, however, did not satisfy the religious hunger; and the Hellenistic world welcomed oriental cults such as those of Mithra and the Great Mother (cf MYSTERIES). Judaism with its monotheism and its high moral code had in addition the aura of oriental mysticism which heightened its attraction. Hence a number of Greeks adopted Judaism in whole or in part. There was opposition to proselytism in Judaism itself, especially in Palestinian Judaism. In the period of the Maccabean wars exclusivism and insistence upon beliefs and rites peculiar to Judaism seemed to be the only protection of the Jews against assimilation by the vigorous leveling civilization of Hellenism. Hence Talmudic tradition quotes a number of great rabbis who had no faith in proselytes and no readiness to accept them into the Jewish community.

The name proselyte belongs strictly to the Gentile who accepted Judaism in its entirety. The rites of initiation included circumcision, a ritual bath, and the offering of a sacrificial victim. The Jews regarded proselytism as a new birth and the beginning of a new life which nullified previous relationship. It is doubtful that this extreme theory could often be carried out in practice; but it meant that the proselyte renounced his wife and his family, if married. His children could not be his heirs unless they were born after his circumcision. The proselyte abandoned his citizenship or nationality and became a member of the Jewish community. How many Gentiles were able to make such a violent change in their lives is not known. Among the hundreds of Jewish tomb inscriptions which have been discovered less than 20 can be certainly identified as those of proselytes. The Herodian family (cf HEROD) were Idumean proselytes, perhaps in the campaign in which John Hyrcanus (AD 135–104) forcibly imposed circumcision upon the Idumeans. The royal family of Izates of Adiabene in Syria passed to Judaism and the tomb of Queen Helena of this family can be seen in Jerusalem; this occurred about AD 60. The number of Gentiles who accepted Judaism in part without accepting circumcision and the full observance of the law was much larger, and such half-converts are mentioned by Greek and Roman writers. These are called "those who fear God." They accepted the Jewish teaching on God, the sacred books, the observance of the Sabbath, the laws of cleanliness (cf CLEAN), and Jewish morality. They attended the synagogue and observed the seven precepts of Noah*. Both proselytes and fearers of God are mentioned in the NT. Jesus alludes to the zeal of the Pharisees in making proselytes (Mt 23:15). Proselytes were present at the feast of Pentecost in Jerusalem at which Peter preached (AA 2:11). Nicholas of Antioch, one of the seven ordained by the Twelve at Jerusalem (cf DEACON), is singled out as a proselyte; this implies that the other six were Jews. Proselytes were included among the first converts made by Paul and Barnabas at Antioch in Pisidia (AA 13:43). These are the only passages in which proselytes appear in the NT. "The fearers of God" are mentioned more frequently. The centurion Cornelius* of Joppa with his household feared God (AA 10:2, 22). When Peter baptized him without first making him a Jew by circumcision, Jewish Christians found fault with him; but they were finally convinced by Peter's revelation (AA 11:1 ff). Many of Paul's first converts, if not most of them, came from "the fearers of God" who heard him in the synagogues (AA 13:16, 26, Antioch in Pisidia; 14:1, Iconium, here called Greeks; 16:14, Philippi; 17:4, Thessalonica; 17:12, Beroea; 17:17, Athens; 18:4, 7, Corinth). The growth of Christianity from proselytes in addition to the other factors which favored exclusivism brought the Jewish community as a whole into opposition to proselytism by AD 100, although proselytes are reported after this date. Roman law dealt an additional blow to proselytism when Hadrian prohibited circumcision about AD 132. Historians think this may have been one of the reasons for the Jewish insurrection of 132–135. The successor of Hadrian, Antoninus Pius (138–161), excepted Jews from this law, but the circumcision of proselytes remained prohibited.

Prostitution. The practice of prostitution in the ancient Near East seems to have been under no moral censure whatever and was extremely common. A peculiar feature of Mesopotamian and Canaanite culture was ritual prostitution. To the temples of the goddess of fertility (Inanna, Ishtar, Astarte) were attached bordellos served by consecrated women who represented the goddess, the female principle of fertility. Intercourse with these women was communion with the divine as the principles of fertility. Cultic prostitution was especially associated with the festival of the New Year*.

OT. The number of allusions to prostitutes and houses of prostitution in the OT show that the practice was found in Israel (Gn 38:15 f; Jos 2:1 [the scene here is, however, the Canaanite town of Jericho and not an Israelite town]; Jgs 11:1; 16:1; 1 K 3:16, two prostitutes sharing a common house). Prostitution lay under moral censure in Israel; it was prohibited in Dt 23:18 and the prophets include it in lists of sins (Je 5:7; Ho 4:14; Am 2:7). The priestly code forbade the high priest to marry a prostitute (Lv 21: 7, 14). Wisdom* literature contains warnings to the young man not to be seduced by prostitutes (Pr 6:26; 7:6–27; BS 23:16 ff).

There are allusions to cultic prostitution in the OT. The word used to describe Tamar*, whose actions were those of the commercial prostitute, is not *zōnāh* but *kᵉdēšāh*, "holy woman," which designates a temple prostitute in the cognate languages. Cultic prostitution is prohibited in the worship of Yahweh (Dt 23:18). The prohibition was not merely theoretical; male cultic prostitutes were removed from the land by Asa* (1 K 15:12) and Jehoshaphat* (1 K 22:47). Although the neutral phrase "the land" is used, it is possible that they, like Josiah*, removed them from the temple of Jerusalem (2 K 23:7).

The infidelity of Israel to Yahweh is called prostitution a number of times by the prophets (Is 1:21; 57:7–13; Je 2:20; 3:1–4, 6–10; Ezk 16 and 23; Ho 1–3). The same figure is used in the historical books also (Ex 34:16; Lv 17:7; 20:5; Nm 14:33; Dt 31:16; Jgs 2:17; 8:27). This somewhat vigorous metaphor is the reverse of the conception of the union of Yahweh and Israel as a union of love* and marriage*; the metaphor of adultery* is used in the same sense. Nineveh*, the royal city of Assyria, is called a harlot for its wantonness (Na 3:1–7). Tyre* is called a harlot by Is (23:15–18); to the prophet the mercantile and commercial activity of this great market city was harlotry.

NT. Allusions in the Gospels show that prostitution appeared in Palestine in NT times (Mt 21:31 f; Lk 15:30; 7:39). Judaism, however, in contrast with the Hellenistic world, laid a severe moral censure upon prostitution.

The word is used in AA 15:20, 29; 21:25 of the prohibition laid upon Gentile Christians; here it does not mean prostitution, but marriage within the degrees of kinship prohibited in Lv 18:6–18. The morality of the Hellenistic-Roman world concerning prostitution was, if possible, looser than the morality of the ancient Near East; sexual intercourse was regarded as a normal and necessary part of a healthy and well ordered life, and prostitutes furnished a service to the community as well respected as the services of the butcher or the baker. Hence the allusions to prostitution and the warnings against it in the Epistles are more numerous (Rm 1:24 f; 1 Co 6:9; 5:9–12; 6:15–20; 2 Co 12:21; Gal 5:19 f; Eph 5:3, 5; Col 3:5; 1 Th 4:3 ff). The allusions to Corinth* reflect the character of the city as perhaps the capital of the industry in the Roman world. It is in a warning against prostitution that Paul brings out two of his most vital conceptions of the Christian life; the Christian is a member of the body of Christ and a temple of the Holy Spirit (1 Co 6: 15–20).

The prostitution mentioned in Apc 2:14, 20 is associated with cultic practices; in the eastern Roman empire many forms of the old cultic prostitution survived. Babylon (Rome) is described in Apc 17–19 as the great harlot; the figure echoes Na 3:1–7.

Proverbs. The book of Pr belongs to the class of wisdom* literature and is the oldest biblical book of this type. It is formed by the union of a number of preexisting collections; scholars are not entirely in agreement on the number of these collections, but the following seven are pointed out by several writers:

1. 1:1–9:18, "The proverbs of Solomon ben David king of Israel" (1:1). This collection differs from the others; whereas the others are collections of single sayings arranged with scarcely any perceptible pattern, this collection groups sayings into discussions which approach the essay; cf especially 1:10– 19, 20–33; 2:1–22; 4:1–27; 5:1–23; 6:20– 35; 7:1–27; 8; 9. The theme is the invitation to acquire wisdom extended by the father to his son and by wisdom personified. The antithesis between personified Wisdom and Dame Folly (9:1–6, 13–18) is one of the most picturesque figures of the book.

Wisdom is the possession of Yahweh, His attendant in creation (8:22–31); the word which defines her position in 8:30 is unfortunately obscure and is translated by some "architect" or "master workman"; by others, "ward" or "fosterchild." The conception of wisdom in Pr 8 is paralleled in Jb 28; BS 24; WS 7; cf WISDOM. This collection is the latest part of Pr and can scarcely be earlier than the 4th or 3rd century BC. A. Weiser believes that the expansion of the single wise saying into the essay may be due to Gk influence. Weiser also traces the influence of the prophetic discourse and the hymn in Pr 1–9. It is possible that this collection was written as an introduction to Pr in its final and present form.

2. 10:1–22:16, "the proverbs of Solomon." This collection is composed of 375 single sayings arranged in no pattern. They are almost entirely practical rules of good conduct. The collection contains a number of doublets (10:1 = 15:20; 10:2b = 11:4b; 10:6b = 10:11b; 10:8b = 11:10b; 10:13b = 19:29b; 16:2 = 21:2; 19:5 = 19:9); this suggests some carelessness in compiling, but also the presence of these sayings in more than one of the collections which the compilers had available. A hint of preexisting compilations may be found in the fact that 10–15 are almost entirely antithetic parallels, while 16:1–22:16 are mainly synonymous and comparative parallels (cf POETRY). While the collection in its present form is probably not earlier than the exile, the collection in its earliest form is not only preexilic, but may very probably go back to a collection made in the reign of Solomon (961–922 BC), and this is the oldest of the collections of Pr.

3. 22:17–24:22; the title "words of the wise" has become part of the saying in 22:17 This collection has no arrangement; it emphasizes duties to the neighbor and rules of temperance. The prevailing form is the synonymous tetrastich with a few variations, some longer and some couplets. There are evident relations between this collection and the Egyptian Wisdom of Amenemope preserved in the British Museum and first published in 1923–1924 (ANET 421–424). Amenemope is also written in tetrastichs; the Egyptian poet called his collection "30 sayings," and 30 sayings are mentioned in Pr 22:20. The parallelism in content is not exact, but a number of lines in the two collections are substantially identical. The wisdom of Amenemope can only be dated within the broad limits 1000–600 BC. Pr 22:17–24:22 is very probably put in the preexilic period. Pr is not necessarily dependent on Amenemope; the two collections may have a common source.

4. 24:23–24:34: an additional collection of "words of the wise" (24:23). These sayings are mostly tetrastichs and emphasize industry as opposed to sloth. The collection is also very probably preexilic.

5. 25–29; "proverbs of Solomon which the men of Hezekiah copied" (25:1). This is a second collection of Solomon attributed in its present form to the scribes of Hezekiah; modern critics are inclined to accept this attribution and to date the collection about 700 BC. The material is diverse, as in the first collection of Solomon (10:1 ff). The prevailing form is the antithetic and comparative distich. The number of sayings is 128. The emphasis on religious and legal interests in 28–29 leads some scholars to suspect that these chapters represent a distinct earlier collection.

6. 30; "the words of Agur ben Jakeh" (30:1). The collection is characterized by the use of the rhetorical question and of zoological proverbs. The numerical sayings (30:15–31) are thought by some scholars to form a distinct collection. This type of saying is an answer to a riddle; what is the common feature in these curiously dissimilar items? The prevailing form is the synonymous and antithetic tetrastich. No definite date can be assigned to the collection.

7. 31; "the words of Lemuel king of Massa which his mother taught him" (31:1). 31: 1–9 contains advice to kings, and it is probable that the title belongs to these sayings only. 31:10–31 is an alphabetical acrostic poem in praise of the good wife, composed of synonymous distichs. No date can be assigned to this collection.

Pr is a speculum of the business and interests of Israelite daily life; it touches upon the activities of government, civic and social life in community, mercantile pursuits, courts, agriculture, the family and slaves, work and play, joy and sorrow. On the doctrine of wisdom and its principles concerning moral ideals and conduct cf WISDOM.

The book cannot be attributed to Solomon as its author nor is he responsible for the collections; on Solomon as the traditional wise man cf SOLOMON; WISDOM. But two of the collections bear his name, and it is altogether probable that these two collections represent work which was done under Solomon. Compilation or editing is explicitly attributed to the scribes of Hezekiah for one (25–29) and must be assumed for the other. To these Solomonic collections, which form the bulk of the book, 5 appendices have been added. Their present position indicates that the two collections of "words of the wise" (# 3 and # 4) were added to the first collection of Solomon before it was united with the second collection (# 5). It cannot be

determined whether # 6 and # 7 had already been added to # 5 when the fusion was made. It is altogether likely that # 1 (1–9) was not prefixed until the entire book was compiled.

The book is quoted several times in the NT.

Psalms. The book of Pss is a collection of 150 Israelite religious lyrics. In the Hb text it is the first of the writings, the third part of the canon*. In the LXX and Vg it is somewhat improperly included among the "didactic" books. The numeration of the Pss differs in the Hb text and versions derived from it (Authorized Version, Revised Version, Revised Standard Version and all Eng Protestant versions) from the numeration of the LXX and Vg and Eng versions derived from the Vg (Douay, Knox, Confraternity, most Catholic versions). The following scheme shows the difference

Hb	LXX–Vg
1–8	1–8
9–10	9
11–113	10–112
114–115	113
116	114–115
117–146	116–145
147	146–147
148–150	148–150

1: *Division of the Psalter. Sources.* The present Pss is divided into 5 books: 1–41; 42–72; 73–89; 90–106; 107–150. The last Ps in each of the first 4 books is concluded by a doxology to mark the end of the book; Ps 150 is a doxology which marks the end of the whole book. This division imitates the Pnt and is quite recent. The gloss at the end of Ps 72, "the prayers of David ben Jesse are ended," belongs to an earlier collection.

Critics agree that the present Pss is a compilation of existing collections, and the larger collections can be somewhat easily determined. The existence of several collections is indicated by the presence of doublets: 14 = 53; 40:14–18 = 70; 57:8–12 + 60:7–14 = 108; also Ps 18 = 2 S 22. There appear to be two distinct collections of Davidic Pss, 3–41 and 51–71. 120–134 are grouped under an obscure title, "songs of ascents (?)," usually translated "pilgrim songs." The collection 42–83, called "the Elohist psalter," cuts across other collections; it uses the divine name Elohim much more frequently than the name Yahweh, but in the rest of the Pss Yahweh is far more common than Elohim. 90–150 shows signs of being compiled from 4 smaller collections: 90–104, to which 105–107 have been added; 108–110 (David), to which 111–118 have been added;

120–134, the pilgrim songs, to which 135–136 have been added; 138–145 (David), to which 146–150 have been added.

The titles of the Pss are obscure, but they lead to evidence of still earlier collections. There are 34 Pss without any title, called "orphans" by rabbinical interpreters; the LXX has only 19 without title. There are 73 Davidic Pss in the Hb text, 84 in the LXX. Other personal names are the sons of Asaph*, 12 Pss (50 + 73–83); the sons of Korah*, 11 Pss (42 + 44–49 + 84–85 + 87–88); Heman*, Ps 88; Ethan*, Ps 89; Jeduthun* (identical with Ethan, Pss 39; 62; 77); Moses, Ps 90; Solomon, Ps 72; 127. Some of these are names of choir guilds in the temple; cf the relevant articles. It is possible therefore that the proper names indicate collections of Pss belonging to particular guilds of choirs, although this is unlikely for Moses and Solomon. Nor is it likely that "David" represents a choir guild; but it is extremely probable that it represents a collection, and most probably the oldest collection of Pss, which was in the course of time attributed to David and may be the development of a collection begun in the early monarchy; on David as "author" of the Pss cf below.

On the assumption that the proper names represent collections, some other obscure terms in the titles may be taken to indicate the same thing. The most common title after David is the Hb *lammᵉnaṣṣēᵃḥ*, translated in Gk and Vg "unto the end" (thereby affording an opportunity for some rather glowing comments by expositors of earlier generations). The term is not altogether certain; it is most frequently translated "the choirmaster," and thus very probably indicates another collection. It occurs in 55 Pss. The Hallelujah* Pss (113–118) form a distinct group. Some other even more obscure terms which appear to designate the type of Ps may also indicate a collection made under these types. The most common such term is Hb *mizmôr*, which occurs in 57 titles; it is usually translated "psalm," and probably indicates a song to be accompanied by stringed instruments (cf MUSIC). The title "song" is found in 30 Pss, prayer in 5, hymn in 1; but the Hb word for hymn is used in the plural (*tᵉhillîm*) to designate the book of Pss in the Hb text. Other titles of unknown meaning are *miktām*, 6 Pss; *maskîl*, 13 Pss; *šiggāyôn*, 1 Ps (and Hab 3).

Other words in the titles appear to be musical notations: Pss 4; 6; 54; 55; 61; 76 are to be accompanied by the strings, Ps 5 by the flute, and 8; 81; 84 by "the harp of Gath" (but. cf below). The mode may be indicated for Pss 6; 12 (the octave? or the 8-stringed harp?) and 46 (soprano?).

Some extremely obscure phrases are thought to indicate the melody, just as modern hymns are often set to secular tunes; a hymn book might contain such notations as "Flow gently, sweet Afton." Thus we have "Do not destroy" (Pss 57; 58; 59; 75); "the hind of the dawn" (Ps 22); "the dove of the far terebinths" (Ps 56); "the death of the son" (Ps 9); "the Gittite (woman)" (Pss 8; 81; 84); "lilies" (Pss 45; 69; 80); "The lily of the testimony (?)" (Ps 60). "To teach" (Ps 60) and "to respond" (Ps 80) are unintelligible. The word *selāh* occurs 71 times in 39 Pss; it is thought to be a musical notation, but its meaning is unknown. There are a few notations for the liturgical use of the Pss: for the dedication of the temple, Ps 30; for the Sabbath, Ps 92; for the "commemoration," Pss 38; 70. These are believed to be quite recent.

There are a number of notations in the titles which relate the Pss so entitled to events in David's life: Pss 3; 7; 18; 34; 51; 52; 56; 57; 59; 60; 63; 142. Little historical value can be given to the events mentioned in these titles, and the titles are of no value whatever in determining the literary origin of the Pss. They were composed at a date when the Pss were attributed to David and are a primitive attempt at historical exegesis.

With these collections at the base of Pss, it is evident that the compilation of the book in its present form was an extremely complex process. The process can scarcely have been completed until the exilic period. In form and style the David collections appear to be the earliest; but no hard and fast general rules can be stated. Modern critics discuss each Ps on its own merits, trying to find its literary and theological relations in other books which can be more easily dated. There is a special difficulty in handling the Pss because the book was obviously submitted to an unceasing process of development and adaptation; individual Pss become collective, private prayers become liturgical, songs of local sanctuaries are adapted to the temple of Jerusalem, royal psalms become messianic, historical psalms become eschatological. Modern interpreters speak of the "rereading" of the Pss; an earlier Ps which has in some way become antiquated (e.g., by the fall of the monarchy, the destruction of Jerusalem and the temple, the loss of political independence) is reworked to fit a contemporary situation and given a direction to the future which was not present in the original composition.

A generation or two ago it was a commonly accepted critical opinion that the Pss were all late compositions; the Pss were called "the hymnbook of the Second Temple," and few Pss were dated before the exile.

Indeed there was a strong tendency to place most of them in the Maccabean period. Contemporary critics have almost entirely abandoned the hypothesis of any Maccabean Pss; the study of the literature of the intertestamental period, and in particular of the Qumran* material, has shown that the Pss in form, style, and content do not belong to this period. A large number of the Pss are now widely regarded as preexilic, and most of the references to the king are taken to refer to the historical kings of Israel and Judah (with some "rereading"; cf below). Critics, however, are very doubtful of their ability to date any particular Ps beyond rather wide limits. The Scandinavian school of criticism is inclined to doubt whether any Ps is postexilic; this extreme view has not been widely accepted. W. F. Albright believes that Ps 29 is an Israelite adaptation of a Canaanite poem and may be the earliest Ps of the entire book, written before the monarchy.

That David is the author of all the Pss is seriously maintained by no modern critic; that the Pss, which reflect the whole spectrum of Israelite belief and piety over the entire history of Israel, should have come from this one author is inconceivable. On the other hand, it is uncritical to affirm that he had nothing to do with the composition of the Pss. In the NT "David" has become a title of the Pss, as "Moses" is a title of the Pnt*; both of these titles have led Christian interpreters into some unfortunate literary attributions. It is a solid Israelite tradition that David was a musician (1 S 16:18–23; 18:10; Am 6:5), a poet (2 S 1:19–27; 3:33 f; 22; 23:1–7), and an organizer of the liturgical cult (2 S 6:5–16; 1 Ch 15:28; Ezr 3:10; Ne 12:24, 36). These traditions do not stand or fall with the attribution to David of the poems or the liturgical organization mentioned in these passages; here again we meet the development of institutions and literary works and the attribution of the developed phenomenon to its earliest known author. These traditions are independent of the attribution of the Pss to David; indeed, they were the base of the attribution. But they suggest that just as David is with great probability the founder of Israelite historical writing (cf HISTORY; PENTATEUCH), so also he organized the music of the cult. The earliest collection of the Pss, the David collection, no doubt bears this name because its origins lay in the early monarchy. The attribution of any particular Ps to David with any certainty is beyond the powers of criticism; we have noticed that the assignment of any Ps in particular is also beyond these powers.

The most constructive step in the criticism and exegesis of the Pss in modern times was taken by Hermann Gunkel, whose first essays in the criticism of literary* forms were made in the Pss. The analysis of the Pss shows that the poems exhibit consistent structures which correspond to their subject matter. Comparative studies show that these structures appear in other passages of the OT where similar subject matter is found, and that the structures appear in other ancient Near Eastern literatures. Cf relevant articles noted below. The purpose of form criticism is not only to determine the typical structure, but also to ascertain the "situation in life" from which the structure arises; this analysis answers the question of the purpose of the narrative and the identification of the social body in which the composition is written. Recent criticism of the Pss has affirmed that the liturgical cult is the proper situation in life of almost all the Pss. As a general explanation this is not accepted by all scholars; no doubt many, perhaps most of the Pss, were written for liturgical use, but many of them can only be explained as the productions of private individuals. A more moderate view, again, avoids a general hard and fast critical rule.

Connected with this question of the situation in life is the identity of the "I" of the Pss, the speaker. A generation ago the view was widely held that the "I" of the Pss is always the community personified as an individual, that there are no Pss which express or were intended to express the sentiments and petitions of the individual Israelite. All the Pss were taken as expressions of social liturgical piety. This opinion has now been widely abandoned for the reasons indicated above; one must often do violence to the Pss to interpret them as community prayers.

2. *Typical Forms.* The following forms are generally accepted:

I. Royal Pss: 2; 18; 20; 21; 72; 101; 110; 132; 144:1–11. The situation of life of these Pss can be assigned with good probability. 2; 21; 72; 110 can easily be identified as songs for the enthronement of the king, possibly 101 and 132 as well. 20 is a battle prayer, 18 a thanksgiving for victory. The royal Pss contain some obvious examples of the oracular response (cf PROPHET) delivered to the petitioner: 2:7–9; 20:7; 21:5; 110:1–4; 132:11–12. The royal Pss also offer examples of the adaptation of the Pss to different cultic purposes; with the fall of the monarchy prayers for the king had no further meaning, and the royal Pss were "spiritualized," usually by textual modifications and additions which identify the king with the messianic king (cf KING; MESSIAH).

II. Hymns*: a large classification: 8; 19; 29; 33; 46; 48; 65; 67; 68; 76; 84; 87; 105;

111; 113; 114; 117; 122; 135; 136; 145–150 (here and below the enumeration is not intended to be complete; it mentions the most typical examples of the form). In addition there are fragments in the hymnal style in other Pss. The structure of the hymn is simple: (a) introduction with invitation to praise Yahweh; (b) description of the motives of praise; (c) conclusion, which may repeat the introduction, utter a blessing or vow, or a brief petition. The motives of praise are found in the attributes of Yahweh, His power in nature (8; 19:2–7; 29; 104) or His saving deeds in the history of Israel (114; 136). In some instances the entire hymn is an invitation to praise. The Zion songs (46; 48; 76) are included among the hymns.

A special class of hymns are the Pss of the kingship of Yahweh: 47; 93; 96–99. On the connection of these with the cult cf KING; NEW YEAR.

III. The lamentation or supplication is the form most frequently found; it is divided into two classes with different structures:

A. Collective lamentations: 44; 60; 74; 79; 80. The situation in the cult is proposed as days of fast and penance in public calamity. The structure is: (a) recollection of the past mercies of Yahweh; (b) expression of confidence; description of the need; plea of innocence; assurance of confidence. In these Pss also there sometimes occurs the favorable oracular response. The plea of innocence may be replaced by a confession of guilt.

B. Individual lamentations: 3; 5; 6; 7; 13; 22; 26; 27:7–14; 28; 31; 35; 38; 39; 42 + 43; 51; 54; 55; 57; 59; 61; 63; 64; 69; 70; 71; 80; 88; 102:1–12 + 24–29; 109; 120; 130; 140; 141; 142; 143. The structure of these Pss includes: (a) invocation of Yahweh, asking for help; (b) description of the need; (c) petition for deliverance; (d) motivation for granting the petition; (e) expression of confidence. The motivation for granting the petition exhibits variety; it may be a plea of innocence, a confession of guilt, the divine attributes, the divine promises, Yahweh's saving deeds in the past, considerations of the misery and helplessness of man, the brevity of life, and similar considerations. It is probable, if these were used in the cult, that the final expression of confidence was uttered after a favorable oracular response. Modern critics, however, believe that these are not all cultic in origin and that here as much as anywhere we have monuments of Israelite personal piety. These Pss, however, have been adapted for liturgical use; and this is no doubt the reason why the need described is sometimes ambiguous. The same poem may mention illness, danger from external enemies, slander, suits at law; these are more easily understood as an enumeration of needs for which one might petition assistance, much after the manner of our own formal liturgical prayers.

IV. Individual song of confidence: 23; 27: 1–6; 121; 131. In these Pss one element of the lamentation (cf above) becomes the entire poem.

V. Thanksgiving songs: these are collective (136; 67; 124; 129) or individual (30; 32; 34; 40:2–12; 66:13–20; 107; 116; 138). They are structured as follows: (a) introduction in the style of the hymn; (b) narrative of the need from which one has been delivered, mention of the petition made; (c) recital of the saving deed; (d) conclusion, which may be an expression of confidence, a promise to praise, an invitation to join in praise, a blessing. The situation in the cult of such Pss is easily identified as the thank offering (cf SACRIFICE).

Some other forms include fewer Pss and are less formally structured.

VI. Prophetic Pss: 50; 75; 82. These are influenced by the prophetic discourse (cf PROPHET) in form and style.

VII. Historical meditations: 78; 105; 106. These are not precisely either hymns or songs of thanksgiving, and in some instances approach the prophetic admonition. The history of Israel is recited as a motive for maintaining or restoring fidelity to Yahweh.

VIII. Wisdom Pss: 1; 14; 19:8–14; 37; 49; 53; 73; 112; 119; 127; 128. These are evident examples of wisdom discourse — not the single maxim (cf WISDOM) but the reflection on some problem with appeal to the characteristic principles of wisdom literature.

In addition mixed Pss must be noted; by this is meant not merely Pss which by accident have been composed of two originally independent compositions, but Pss in which the styles and motifs of more than one form are employed. The flexibility of the form permitted such variations.

3. The "Teaching" of the Psalms. It is difficult to speak of the "teaching" of the Pss. The book is a collection of the spontaneous popular piety and beliefs of Israel from the monarchy to the postexilic period It is not prophetic or wisdom in conception and style, but lyrical; in one sense the Pss are a summary of all the beliefs of the OT, but in another sense only the entire OT is a sufficient commentary on the Pss. The themes of the Pss are rather implicit and presupposed; one does not expound in prayer, especially when one's prayer is a song. One may note, however, that the dominant themes of the Pss flow naturally from the forms mentioned above. Yahweh is conceived in the hymns as a God of power and the savior of Israel. In the lamentations He is con-

ceived as the savior of the individual Israelite, merciful and forgiving, faithful to His promises. It is obvious that the saving power and will of Yahweh for Israel is effective for the individual Israelite. Israel in the Pss is the people of election* and covenant*. Man is viewed in the lamentations as miserable and helpless, utterly dependent on Yahweh for his deliverance from evil. The confessions of guilt which occur in some Pss, both individual and collective, are characteristic of postexilic rather than of preexilic piety. Israel, collective and individual, lies under the obligation of the moral will of Yahweh and is governed by His action in history; the sense of Israel under the law* is again characteristic of the postexilic period. On the problem of the "imprecatory" Pss (e.g., 69:23–29; 109; 137) cf CURSE.

Psalms of Solomon. Cf APOCRYPHAL BOOKS.

Psaltery. Cf MUSIC.

Pseudepigrapha. Cf APOCRYPHAL BOOKS.

Ptolemais. Cf ACCO.

Ptolemy. The name of the founder of the Hellenistic dynasty which ruled Egypt 323–30 BC, borne by each of his successors.

Ptolemy I Soter: 323–283
Ptolemy II Philadelphus: 283–246
Ptolemy III Euergetes: 246–221
Ptolemy IV Philopator: 221–203
Ptolemy V Epiphanes: 203–181
Ptolemy VI Philometor: 181–145
Ptolemy VII Euergetes II Physcon: 145–116
Ptolemy VIII Soter II Lathyrus: 116–108
Ptolemy IX Alexander: 108–88
Ptolemy X Alexander II: 80
Ptolemy XI Auletes: 80–51
Ptolemy XII & Cleopatra VII: 51–48
Ptolemy XIII & Cleopatra VII: 47–44
Ptolemy XIV Caesar & Cleopatra VII: 44–30

Ptolemy Lagi, the founder of the dynasty, was one of the generals of Alexander. After the death of Alexander he was given Egypt and Cyrenaica in the division of Alexander's empire. In 320 he added Palestine to his territory and maintained his hold in wars with Antigonus until 312; Palestine was given, however, to Seleucus of Syria (cf SELEUCID) in the peace of 311. Ptolemy took the title of king, as did the other successors of Alexander (*Diadochi*) in 305. He took no part in the battle between the Diadochi at Ipsus in Asia Minor in 301, but received Palestine in the treaty which followed the battle. Palestine was ruled by the Ptolemies 301–198.

There is no contemporary Jewish historical source for this period and very little mention of Palestine and the Jews in other sources; the very silence strengthens the impression that this was a period of tranquil prosperity. Relations between the Jews and the Ptolemies were perhaps more cordial than the relations of the Jews with any other foreign imperial power. It was during this period that the great Jewish communities in Egypt, particularly at Alexandria*, were founded, and that the translation of the OT into Gk was undertaken (cf VERSIONS). The production of Jewish literature in Gk also advanced under the favorable conditions which Jews enjoyed in Egypt.

The rule of the Ptolemies was challenged by the Seleucid king Antiochus III the Great, who invaded Palestine in 219 and was successful for three campaigns; but Sosibius, the general of Ptolemy IV Philopator, defeated him in Raphia in SW Palestine in 217 and forced him to abandon the campaigns. Antiochus returned in the reign of Ptolemy V Epiphanes and by his defeat of the Egyptians at Panias, the biblical Dan*, in 198 detached Palestine from the Ptolemies and subjected it to the Seleucid kingdom. This was a decisive turning point in the history of the Jews; cf MACCABEES.

The Ptolemies are referred to rarely by name in the Bible, but there are several cryptic allusions to the Egyptian kings. 1 Mc 10:51–58 relates that Ptolemy VI Philometor allied himself with Alexander Balas*, a claimant to the Seleucid throne, and gave Alexander his daughter Cleopatra in marriage. 1 Mc 11:1–19 tells of the attempts of the same Ptolemy to secure the Seleucid kingdom, his betrayal of Alexander for Demetrius*, and his dealings with Jonathan; his attempt was succeeding well when it was halted by his death.

Dn 11, a review of history in the form of prediction, refers to the Ptolemies under the designation "king of the south." 11:6 refers to the marriage of Antiochus II (261–247) of Syria to Berenice, the daughter of Ptolemy II, in 252. This political marriage was unsuccessful; Berenice and her son were assassinated by Laodice, the divorced wife of Antiochus II. 11:7–8 mentions the war of revenge against Laodice conducted by Ptolemy III, who invaded Syria in 246. 11:9 refers to the war which Seleucus II of Syria conducted without success in 242. 11:10 refers to the campaigns of Antiochus III in 219–217 and his defeat at Raphia. 11:13–17 refers to the second campaign of Antiochus III and his victory at Panion, and the marriage of Cleopatra, the daughter of Antiochus, to Ptolemy V. 11:25–30 refers to the invasion of Egypt by Antiochus IV Epiphanes in 169–168; his first campaign was successful, and Ptolemy VI was captured; the second campaign (168) was abruptly halted at the frontier of Egypt by three Roman legates who forbade him to advance any further.

The name Ptolemy is borne by two others in 1 Mc. Ptolemy, the general of Antiochus IV, was an officer of the force defeated by Judas at Emmaus* (1 Mc 3:38 ff). Ptolemy the son-in-law of Simon*, governor of Jericho, assassinated Simon in order to win favor with the Seleucid court (1 Mc 16:11 ff).

Puah (Hb *pûʻāh,* etymology uncertain; Ugaritic *pgt,* "girl," has been suggested), a personal name; one of the Egyptian midwives who refused to obey the Pharaoh's order to kill Hebrew male infants (Ex 1:13).

Publican (Gk *telōnēs,* Lt *publicanus*), name given in many Eng versions to an official mentioned often in the Gospels. The *publicanus* in Roman administration was a private business man, usually of the equestrian class, who was a tax farmer. The publican leased from the government for a fixed annual sum the right to collect taxes. The sum was fixed on the calculated revenues, which were determined by law, and was sufficiently lower than the expected return to offer an attractive commission to the publican. The publican retained any excess, but had to pay the fixed sum whether he collected it or not. In Palestine in NT times only the customs were farmed out, not direct taxes. The abuses which such a system is easily subject to are obvious, and Roman history contains many complaints of the dishonest extortions of publicans.

The "publicans" of the Gospels are not the *publicani,* the tax farmers, but agents and collectors of a minor grade (except Zacchaeus*, who was an *architelōnēs,* a chief collector at Jericho). The universal unpopularity of publicans which appears in the NT is not necessarily a sign of their dishonesty; even in the modern Near East the tax collector is detested by definition. But the tax collector was an agent of the foreign imperial government and thus he worked against what his fellow citizens considered their welfare. In the Gospels "publicans and sinners" form a usual pair (Mt 9:9–13; 11:19; 21: 31 f; Mk 2:13–17; Lk 5:27–32; 7:34; 15:1). Publicans are also paired with Gentiles (Mt 18:17). The morality of the publicans is presumed to be at the lowest level (Mt 5:46; the parallel in Lk 6:32 reads "sinners").

Despite this, the publicans enjoy a certain favor in the Gospels. Matthew* or Levi*, one of the twelve, was not only a publican, but was called from the tax collector's table (Mt 9:9–13; Mk 2:13–17; Lk 5:27–32). In the list of the Twelve in Mt 10:3 he is called a publican, but not in the other lists. Matthew invited Jesus to a dinner with his friends, who could not be anything but publicans and sinners, and Jesus accepted. This gave the Pharisees an occasion to charge that Jesus was a friend of publicans and sinners, a charge repeated elsewhere in the Gospels (Mt 11:19; Lk 7:34). Jesus did not disclaim the charge, but answered it with the saying that He came to call not the righteous, but sinners. Certainly His teaching and His person must have given such social outcasts reason to believe that He could accept them and they Him, for it is mentioned that they were among His listeners (Lk 15:1), as they had listened to John the Baptist and believed him (Mt 21:32; Lk 7:29). Twice the publican is proposed as an example to the Pharisees: Zacchaeus* for his candid confession and repentance (Lk 19:1 ff) and the publican of the parable for his prayer, a simple appeal for mercy to a sinner (Lk 18: 10–13). Jesus Himself warns the Jews that the publicans and sinners are advancing before them into the kingdom of heaven (Mt 21:31).

Against this background the harsh formula of excommunication, "Let him be to you as the Gentile and the publican" (Mt 18:17) seems somewhat strange. It should be noticed that the formula is preserved only in Mt*, who preserves more Jewish idioms than the other Gospels. It may be taken as a formula in use among the early Jewish Christian communities, which was never employed in Gentile churches and lapsed with the submersion of Jewish Christianity in the much larger Hellenistic church.

Pudens (Lt *pudens,* Gk *poudēs,* "shame"?), a personal name; a Christian of Rome (1 Tm 4:21). The family of Pudens belonged to the Roman aristocracy, and was probably the first family of this social level in Rome to accept Christianity; the appeal of the Gospel was directed rather to slaves and the lower classes.

Pul (Hb *pûl,* meaning uncertain), personal name; the king of Assyria who received tribute from Menahem* of Israel (2 K 15: 19). The chronology alone would identify this king with Tiglath-pileser* III; a Babylonian king list gives his name as Pulu, his throne name in Babylon. This identification was unknown to the author of 1 Ch 5:26, who distinguishes Pul and Tiglath-pileser as two men.

The geographical name Pul in Is 66:19 is probably to be read Put*.

Purification. Cf CLEAN.

Purim (Hb *pûrîm,* etymology uncertain [cf below]), a Jewish feast. The feast fell on the 14–15 Adar (February-March) and according to Est, which is read in the synagogue on the feast, it is a commemoration of the deliverance of the Jews in Persia from the plot of Haman (cf ESTHER). The celebration is ordained, according to Est 9:17–32, in letters of Mordecai* and Esther addressed to the Jews of the Diaspora*. The popular etymology of the name is derived from *pûr,* "lot" (Est 3:7; 9:24). The feast is attested by Josephus. But it is not mentioned elsewhere in the Bible, and certain difficulties about its origin have been raised to which there is no satisfactory answer. 2 Mc 15:36 alludes to "the day of Mordecai," which could be the anniversary of the deliverance, but the absence of the name Purim is puzzling, if it was the common name of the feast. Certain historical difficulties about the episodes related in Est also raise the question whether the feast commemorates events which did not occur. One may ask whether the feast of Purim comes from the book of Est or whether the book of Est comes from the feast. A number of attempts have been made by scholars to find a Mesopotamian or Persian feast from which Purim has been derived; no such feast has been successfully identified, but despite this the opinion of scholars is widely in favor of the theory that Purim is an adaptation of a Mesopotamian or Persian spring festival by the Jews. As such it is a feast primarily of the Diaspora and not of Palestine, and it seems that it was very slowly adopted in Palestine. The motif of deliverance is attached also to the principal spring festival of Israel, the Passover*; and a new deliverance in the exile is not an improbable object of a new feast. It is unnecessary to appeal to the names of Mordecai and Esther, which are related to the Mesopotamian divine names Marduk and Ishtar respectively, to find the origin of this feast; here there may be a sheer coincidence, although a rather striking one. H. Lusseau has proposed that the first step was the adaptation of a Mesopotamian spring feast to Jewish worship. This feast was subsequently "historicized" by relating it to a deliverance of the Jews in Persia, which was first designated "the day of Mordecai"; finally the Gk additions to Esther were made to accredit the feast (cf ESTHER). Lusseau's theory may be modified by introducing the composition of Est as a festive reading and an accreditation of the feast.

Traditionally Purim has been the most secular of the Jewish feasts, on which excess in food and drink were easily tolerated, and cheers for Mordecai and Esther and curses of Haman were shouted.

Purple. Cf DYE.

Put (Hb *pûṭ*), a geographical name; mentioned in the Table* of Nations as the son of Ham* and the brother of Cush*, Egypt*, and Canaan* (Gn 10:6; 1 Ch 1:8). This arrangement places it very probably in Africa; Canaan is included here for special reasons. Other incidences of the name place it in relation with other African territories; Cush, Egypt, Lud* (Na 3:9); Cush and Lud (Je 46:9). The occurrence of the name with Persia as an ally of Tyre (Ezk 27:10), with Cush, Lud, Arabians, and Cherethites (Ezk 30:5), and with Cush and Persia (Ezk 38:5) is ambiguous, and suggests that these passages come from a period when the geographical names were mere archaisms. On the ambiguity of Lud in these passages cf LUD. The name has often been connected with Punt, mentioned several times in Egyptian records as a place to which the Egyptians sent trading expeditions. It lay on the Red Sea, very probably on the Somali coast. Punt, however, is judged to be phonetically impossible. L. Koehler suggests the Egyptian *pd.t,* Elamite *pu-u-ti-ja-ap,* Babylonian *pu-u-ṭa,* Persian *putaya,* "a people of Libya"; this geographical location suits the OT allusions better.

Puteoli (Lt *puteoli,* "little wells," Gk *potioloi*), a seaport city on the Bay of Naples where Paul and his company landed after their shipwreck on the voyage to Rome (AA 28:13). The site is the modern Pozzuoli on the peninsula of Posilipo. There was already a Christian community in Puteoli when Paul arrived there.

Q

Quail (Hb *šᵉlāw*), the *coturnix vulgaris,* a migratory bird (although some remain in Palestine and Syria throughout the year). The quail migrates across Palestine, Syria, and Egypt, arriving northbound at the beginning of March and southbound in November. It flies mostly at night. The bird is extremely heavy and it sustains long flights with difficulty, sometimes falling from fatigue. It always flies with the wind and crosses the Mediterranean at the narrowest points. There are two accounts of the fall of quail, probably doublets, during the passage of the Israelites through the desert (Ex 16:13; Nm 11:31 f; cf Ps 105:40). The brief description is entirely in accord with the habits of the quail.

Queen. In the polygamous societies of the ancient Near East the position of the wife of the king did not correspond to the position of the queen in modern monarchies, as indeed the position of woman generally was quite different. The king had a harem as all men could have if they could afford it, and the harem of the king was presumably the largest of the kingdom; the harem of Solomon was legendary (1 K 11:3). Uncertainty in the rank of the wives could lead to uncertainty in the succession; cf 1 K 1. After the accession of Solomon this problem was not permitted to arise again in Judah. One of the wives was first in rank; how this primacy was determined is not clear. 2 Ch 11:21–22 suggests that it was determined purely by the choice of the monarch. In normal matrimonial law both in Israel and in Mesopotamia the first wife to be married was also first in rank; and the most important function of the first wife was to bear the heir to the throne.

In other ancient Near Eastern countries the position of the queen was perhaps higher than it was in Israel and Judah. In Egypt one wife was the royal spouse whose dignity was not rivaled by any of the harem. Some of these Egyptian queens were influential in the history of Egypt, although the influence must be deduced by modern historians. The most famous piece of Egyptian sculpture, the bust of Nefertete, queen of Ikhnaton, represents a woman who is thought to have had much to do with her husband's religious revolution. Hatshepsut, daughter of Thutmose I, sister of Thutmose II, and wife of Thutmose III, was able to seize the throne after the death of Thutmose II and maintain it until her death, successfully suppressing the ambitions of her husband, who on his accession turned out to be the most aggressive and victorious ruler in the entire history of Egypt. The clear primacy of the Egyptian "Great Royal Spouse" no doubt had much to do with the fairly consistent evidence of the influence of the queens in government.

In Assyria the first wife in rank was "the Lady of the Palace," but there are fewer traces of her influence. Shammuramat, a Babylonian, mother of Adad-nirari III, acted as regent during the minority of her ,son, and was powerful enough to become the object of the Gk legends of Semiramis. Historians think that she was responsible for the promotion of the cult of the Babylonian god Nabu during the reign of Adad-nirari III. The Aramaean Naqia, mother of Esarhaddon*, helped him to secure the throne when his brothers murdered their father Sennacherib*. She was influential in the selection of Ashur-bani-pal as successor to Esarhaddon over his older brother Shamash-shum-ukin, and her influence remained powerful after the accession of Ashur-bani-pal.

In Judah the highest rank in the harem was held by the *gᵉbîrāh,* the mother of the reigning king. This seems actually to have been a kind of official position from which a woman could be deposed, as Asa* deposed Maacah* (1 K 15:13; 2 Ch 15:16). Hamutal*, wife of Josiah*, appears to have held the position twice, once in the reign of her son Jehoahaz* and again after an interruption in the reign of Zedekiah* (2 K 23:31; 24:18). With two exceptions the name of the queen mother is given for all the kings of Judah. Of these no doubt Bathsheba* was the first, although the title is not used of her; her influence in the succession of Solomon is obvious. The queen mother sat at the right of the king (2 K 2:19) and perhaps wore a crown (Je 13:18). She was taken into exile with the king (Je 29:2). One queen mother, Athaliah*, seized the throne while her son was a minor (2 K 11). Jezebel* is called the queen mother by Judahite nobles (2 K 10:13); the same verse distinguishes between the king's sons and the sons of the queen mother, i.e., the king's full brothers. But the title is not mentioned elsewhere for the kingdom of Israel and it is not certain that it existed. The influence of the queen mother in Assyria has been mentioned above; a similar title and dignity existed among the Hittites and possibly at Ugarit.

Queen of Heaven. The title given to an unnamed foreign goddess in Je 7:18; 44:17–19, 25. She is worshipped by the usual rites of vows, sacrifices, and libations, and in addition by the making of cakes stamped with her image, a practice not attested elsewhere. The women in particular were faithful to her cult and protested that during the long time they practiced it they suffered no harm. There can be little doubt that the queen of heaven is the Mesopotamian Ishtar, mother goddess of fertility, love, and war, and that her cult became popular in Judah during the long period of Assyrian vassalage during the first three quarters of the 7th century. The images stamped on the cakes were very probably similar to the plaques and figurines of the goddess of fertility found in large numbers throughout the Near East, including Israel (ANEP 465, 467, 469; 469 shows figures found in Palestine).

Quirinius (Lt *quirinius,* Gk *kyrenios;* meaning uncertain), in Lk 2:2 the governor of Syria at the time of the census which was being taken when Jesus was born. This man is known from Tacitus and a few inscriptions; he was P. Sulpicius Quirinius, a senator, governor of Crete and of Cyrene, consul 12 BC, legate of Syria in AD 6–7 for an uncertain length of time. Josephus reports a census made in his administration at this date. This, however, is much too late for the date of the birth of Jesus as calculated by all scholars; on the problem cf CENSUS. Quirinius can be put at the time of the birth of Jesus only by postulating an earlier term of office, which is not mentioned; Josephus mentions the legates of Syria from 9–1 BC and does not include Quirinius. Others have supposed that the word "governor" is used loosely, as indeed it is in the NT, to denote any officer; but it is improbable that he would be said to "govern Syria" except as legate.

Qumran Scrolls. 1. *Discovery.* In the spring of 1947 two shepherds of the Bedawi Ta'amireh tribe discovered by accident some jars containing scrolls in a cave of the cliffs near the place where the Wadi Qumran descends into the Dead Sea. The tribesmen attempted to dispose of the scrolls through some antiquities dealers of Bethlehem, and ultimately four scrolls came into the hands of the Syrian patriarch of Jerusalem, Mar Athanasius Yeshue Samuel. Three other scrolls were purchased by Prof. E. L. Sukenik for the Hebrew University of Jerusalem. The scrolls of the patriarch were identified as ancient by scholars of the American Schools of Oriental Research of Jerusalem in February, 1948, and Prof. Sukenik reached the same conclusion independently for his scrolls. The unsettled political conditions of Jerusalem at the time seemed to Mar Athanasius to make it advisable to smuggle his four scrolls to the United States in 1948. Three of them were published by the American Schools, but the fourth could not be opened without the risk of destroying it. These four scrolls were purchased by the state of Israel in 1954 and are now displayed in the Shrine of the Book in Jerusalem. The fourth scroll was opened after its acquisition by the state of Israel. Once the value of the scrolls became known to the Bedawi, they began to explore the almost innumerable caves in the cliffs of the western shore of the Dead Sea. The appearance of fragments from these caves in the hands of antiquities dealers finally led scholars to undertake an exploration conducted by the Department of Antiquities of the Hashemite Kingdom of Jordan in cooperation with the École Biblique et Archéologique Francaise and the American Schools of Oriental Research, both of Jerusalem. The exploration of the area was begun in 1951 and continued in five campaigns through 1956. The systematic exploration of the area disclosed thousands of fragments in the caves, and also disclosed that the clandestine explorations of the Bedawi had caused incalculable damage to the scrolls which they themselves had discovered. Explorations were extended to the region of the Wadi Muraba'at, S of the Wadi Qumran and about 15 mi S of Jerusalem, where documents of the second rebellion of the Jews against the Romans (AD 132–135) were discovered, and to Khirbet Mird, the site of a ruined Byzantine monastery and of the Hasmonean fortress Hyrcanium. At Khirbet Mird documents from the first six centuries AD in Greek, Christian-Palestinian Aramaic, and Arabic were discovered. The documents of the Wadi Muraba'at and Khirbet Mird lie outside the field of biblical studies proper.

2. *The Archaeology of the Site.* At the foot of the cliffs in which the scrolls were discovered there is a large natural esplanade upon which lay the almost entirely buried ruins of some unidentified buildings, called by the Arabs Khirbet Qumran and previously regarded by explorers of Palestine as the ruins of a Roman fort. Adjacent to the ruins was a large cemetery which had always aroused questions, since the burials, which were in the N-S axis, were certainly not Moslem. The proximity of the ruin to the scroll caves suggested excavation, which was carried on under the direction of G. Lan-

kester Harding, Director of the Department of Antiquities of Jordan, and Père R. de Vaux of the École Biblique of Jerusalem. This excavation, continued through five campaigns, disclosed an extensive building complex which had been inhabited in three periods. The buildings were constructed upon the foundations of an Israelite fortress abandoned in the 6th century BC. Period I was divided into two phases. Period Ia consisted in temporary structures which were occupied before the central building complex was erected. Most of the remains of Ia were incorporated into the structures of Ib. The exact date of the building of the central complex could not be ascertained. The coins began in the reign of John Hyrcanus (134–104 BC) and continued to the end of the Hasmonean period in 37 BC. Coins were most numerous from the reign of Alexander Jannaeus (103–76 BC). Period I ends early in the reign of Herod* the Great (after 37 BC), and there were signs of destruction by earthquake. This earthquake is almost certainly to be identified with the great earthquake of 31 BC mentioned by ancient historians. The site seems to have been abandoned until the reign of Archelaus* (4 BC–AD 6). The occupation of Period II continued from the reign of Archelaus to AD 68 and was ended by a violent destruction. Evidence of undermining the fortifications and of conflagration and Roman arrowheads indicate that the site was a point of Jewish resistance during the rebellion against Rome of AD 66–70 and that it fell before a Roman attack. In Period III the site was occupied by a Roman garrison from the capture of the site to some time toward the end of the first century AD. The site was then permanently abandoned. The relation of caves to the buildings is obscure. There are signs of occupation in many of the caves. Possibly the members of the community which inhabited the building overflowed into caves and tents. Archaeologists are certain that the caves were not regularly employed for the storage of MSS and other valuables. They believe that the MSS were stored in the caves at the time of the rebellion against Rome as a temporary measure. But the group never returned. The MSS were enclosed in jars which seem to have been made precisely to contain them. This, however, does not indicate that the jars were made at the time the MSS were put in the caves. It is now known that jars were frequently used for the storage of MSS in the ancient world.

The area occupied by the ruins is roughly square, about 250 ft on a side, and the central building complex, also roughly square, is about 125 ft on a side. The buildings were enclosed by a defense wall, and a fortified tower stood in the NW corner. These defenses were not military, but were intended to protect the site against desert raiders. A large room about 40 ft × 13 ft belonging to Period II contained long plaster tables and wooden benches. The construction of these tables and the presence of two inkwells, one of which contained traces of dried ink, furnish a basis for identifying this room as the scriptorium. A great hall with plastered floor and walls and plaster pillars was probably the place for general assembly, possibly also for ritual assembly. A round stone pavement in one end of the hall was taken to be the podium of the reader or the presiding officer. In this room also the group possibly took community meals. An adjoining room called the pantry contained about 780 pieces of pottery, an almost complete table service. There were other rooms for storing food, a bakery, a pottery, and a forge. The water system was surprisingly extensive and complex. The water was secured from the Wadi Qumran, which flows only during the rainy season. This stream was dammed and the water was channeled to the buildings by aqueducts and distributed by canals. The excavators cleared seven large cisterns and at least six small pools. It is quite improbable that the cisterns were used for bathing or for ritual baptism, as some scholars have proposed. The flight of steps into the cisterns makes it possible to fetch water when the water level is low and is not intended for the entrance of bathers; this type of cistern is common in ancient Palestinian sites. Some of the smaller pools were quite probably baths. The 1100 graves in the cemetery to the E of the buildings are too numerous for the number of people who are calculated to have occupied the site, even if we suppose that a large number of people lived outside the enclosure. They were buried with the head to the S and the body extended to the N and the hands crossed over the breasts. Some of the skeletons were female. Scholars have suggested that the community had members or associates living elsewhere in the country who desired to be buried near the establishment. Contrary to Jewish practices of the times, no objects were buried with the bodies.

3. *The Scrolls of Cave I*. These scrolls (all except one written in Hb) include the seven scrolls of the first discovery:

(1) The Isaiah MS published by the American Schools of Oriental Research, containing the complete text of the book.

(2) A second Isaiah scroll, fragmentary.

(3) A commentary on Habakkuk 1–2.

(4) The rule of the community or "The Manual of Discipline": regulations for the

government of the group, admission of candidates, conduct, punishment of infractions, and some ritual prescriptions.

(5) A collection of thanksgiving hymns written in the style of the individual petitions and lamentations of the canonical books of Pss.

(6) The war of the children of light and the children of darkness: regulations for the conduct of a campaign against enemies of the Jews and of the sect, probably to be understood as an apocalyptic war.

(7) A Genesis apocryphon (Aramaic), the last of the seven scrolls to be published. The condition of the scroll when it was acquired made it seem quite doubtful that it could ever be opened. It was at first called the book of Lamech*, because a detached legible piece contained the name of Lamech. It is now recognized as the type of literature called midrash*, an imaginative expanded account of the episodes of Gn. The portions hitherto published are parallel to Gn 5:28–29; 12:10–15:2.

Other MSS besides the first seven are fragmentary. Fragments have been found of every OT book except Est. Among the deuterocanonical* books fragments of Tb and BS have been discovered. The apocryphal* books include the book of Jubilees, the book of Enoch, the Testament of the 12 Patriarchs. The Damascus Document (cf below), hitherto known only in a MS discovered in the genizah of the synagogue of Old Cairo, was found at Qumran. The "Rule of the Community" is parallel and supplementary to the Manual of Discipline and seems to represent a later phase of the community organization. There are commentaries on Is, Ho, Mi, Na, Zp, and Pss. In addition there are some sectarian works, in which particular interest is attached to formulae of blessings for the high priest, the priests, the prince of the congregation, and the congregation. Some other liturgical texts and what might be called wisdom literature also appeared. A curiosity was a copper scroll which was unrolled only by a difficult and complicated process. It turned out to be not a scroll but a copper plate rolled up containing a list of about 60 treasures concealed in the vicinity of Jerusalem. The amount of gold and silver mentioned is fantastic (about 200 tons) and can represent nothing in reality, and scholars have not yet found a reason why this catalogue should have been inscribed upon a copper plate.

4. *Date of the Documents and Identification of the Community.* When the scrolls were first examined, W. F. Albright and some other scholars identified the script as characteristic of the 1st century BC and the 1st century AD. The archaeology of the site

has confirmed this date. A few scholars, of whom the best known is Solomon Zeitlin, maintain that the scrolls are medieval forgeries. This, however, is rendered extremely unlikely, not only by the archaeological data and the pottery of the site, but also by a Carbon 14 test made on the linen wrappings of the scrolls which gave them a median date of AD 33 with a margin of roughly 100 years' error each way. G. R. Driver and a few other scholars have preferred a date in the 6th or 7th century AD, but neither can this date be harmonized with the archaeological data. Interest therefore has fastened on a Jewish sect called the Essenes, described by Philo Judaeus in the first half of the 1st century AD (*Quod omnis probus liber sit,* xii–xiii, 75–91) and the Jewish historian Flavius Josephus in the second half of the 1st century AD (*The Jewish War,* book ii, 119–161). The Essenes were also mentioned by Pliny the Elder (*Naturalis Historia,* book V, xv, 73). Pliny describes the Essenes as living on the western shore of the Dead Sea in a place which must be identical with Qumran or very near it. Josephus, accommodating himself to his Greek and Roman readers, called the Essenes one of the three philosophical sects of the Jews, of which the other two were the Pharisees* and the Sadducees*. They have a reputation for peculiar sanctity, abstain from marriage but adopt children. They practice community of goods and they demand that new members surrender their property. They occupy no single city but dwell in various towns. They offer worship at sunrise and spend the day in manual crafts. Then after bathing they partake of a common meal. Their garment, when they are not engaged in work, is white. They speak only in turn. They are completely governed by the officers of the community. A candidate is not admitted without three years of probation. When the candidates are admitted they must take solemn oaths to observe the rules of the community and to conceal its secrets. Offenses against the rules are punished by expulsion or by privation of food. Both admission and expulsion as well as punishment are determined by the vote of the community. Their Sabbath observance is more rigid even than that of the Pharisees. They are divided into four grades. They believe in the immortality of the soul. They have holy books and believe they can foretell the future. They had a kind of lay order which observed the other rules but permitted marriage. They had a profound interest in the Torah, the law of Moses, which they studied and discussed in groups. They emphasized the complete supremacy of God and believed in a kind of predestination. Philo gives substantially the same picture.

Most of these points are paralleled in the Qumran documents, but there are some differences. The period of probation differs in some details. The four divisions or classes do not appear in the Qumran documents. The emphasis upon God's supremacy and belief in predestination does appear, but there is no evidence of belief in immortality of the soul. Josephus says that the Essenes rejected the animal sacrifices of the temple, but the scrolls seem to presuppose that animal sacrifices are offered. The ancient sources say nothing about priests among the Essenes, but in the Qumran scrolls the priests are prominent. It is not clear from the scrolls that the sect of Qumran practiced celibacy. In the opinion of most scholars the differences in detail are not as decisive as the similarities. The geographical area and the general identity of spirit and practice convince them that the community of Qumran was Essene, and they explain the differences by the hypothesis that the Qumran scrolls and the ancient sources represent different phases of development; or it is possible that the ancient sources, which were written by Jews for Gentile readers, omitted some peculiar Jewish details.

The Damascus Document, also called the Zadokite Fragment, discovered in the genizah of the synagogue of Old Cairo, was published by Solomon Schechter in 1910. This curious document, which had no context by which it could be explained, is now seen to have remarkable affinities with the Qumran scrolls, and the discovery of a fragment of the Damascus Document at Qumran has made it all but certain that the document originated in the Qumran group. The Damascus Document is so called because it describes a group which migrates to Damascus and there enters into a new covenant. The covenant idea is extremely prominent in the Qumran documents. Scholars, however, are not certain that Damascus here represents the city of that name. It is thought by some that the name may signify the Qumran region, by others that it indicates simply that the group departed from orthodox Judaism. It is supposed that it indicates a movement away from Judaism during the Hasmonean period, when the office of high priest was assumed by the Hasmonean kings. Some regarded this as a usurpation. The Damascus Document contains doctrinal exposition and rules for the community which are in general harmony with the Qumran documents. It is difficult to say which represents the older phase of the group.

Other identifications suggested for the Qumran group such as a sect of the Pharisees or of the Sadducees, of the Samaritans, of the Zealots*, or even the early Christian heretics known as the Ebionites, are not generally accepted by scholars. The Qumran documents themselves contain no clear historical allusions except to a Greek king Demetrius and to the lion of wrath who crucified his enemies (a fragment of a commentary of Nahum). This allusion is most frequently referred to Alexander Jannaeus (103–76 BC). The crucifixion is taken to refer to the crucifixion of 800 Pharisees by Jannaeus after Demetrius III Eukairos had retired from his invasion of the country. Historical allusions elsewhere in the scrolls employ fictitious names, and the data do not permit a certain identification.

The most important episode is the encounter of "The Teacher of Righteousness," a leader of the sect, with "The Wicked Priest" on the Day of Atonement. The Wicked Priest later fell into the hands of his enemies. It is not clear that the Teacher of Righteousness suffered death at his hands, as some scholars have maintained. This episode cannot be defined with certainty. The Wicked Priest is identified with Simon* (142–135 BC) by F. M. Cross, with Jonathan*, Simon's predecessor (160–142 BC) by J. T. Milik. A later date is proposed by A. Dupont-Sommer, who identifies the Wicked Priest with Aristobulus II, high priest 67–63 BC, son of Alexander Jannaeus, and connects the episode with the Roman conquest of Jerusalem by Pompey in 63 BC. H. H. Rowley suggests an earlier date and places the episode in the period of Antiochus IV Epiphanes (175–164 BC); the Wicked Priest is Menelaus*, who purchased the office of high priest from Antiochus. Most scholars agree, however, that the origins of the sect go back to the period of Antiochus Epiphanes and the Maccabean wars. They suppose that the sect came originally from the Hasidim, the early Pharisees, who supported the Maccabees in their struggle for independence and that this group, together with some other Pharisees, rejected the Hasmoneans when they assumed the office of high priest, to which in the strict view of the Qumran sect and of some of the Pharisees they had no right. Connected with this question is the identification of a people called the Kittim* in the Qumran scrolls. They are described as powerful and cruel conquerors and must be identified either with the Seleucids* (H. H. Rowley) or the Romans (F. M. Cross, A. Dupont-Sommer, and perhaps the majority of scholars).

5. *Organization and Discipline of the Community.* The sect was composed of the priestly class and the laity. The priests were called the sons of Aaron* or the sons of Zadok*, probably a reference to the priestly line of Zadok, the priest appointed by David. Legislative and judicial powers were

vested in the sons of Aaron. In addition there was an assembly of "The Many," who seem to be the members who enjoyed full standing. The group was governed by a council of twelve laymen, one for each tribe of Israel, and three priests, according to the Manual of Discipline. Other officers are mentioned. The Damascus Document speaks of a priest inspector of the Many and a superintendent of the camps. The Manual of Discipline also speaks of an inspector at the head of the Many and a superintendent of the Many. The assembly of the Many voted on the admission of new members, the infliction of punishment, and the readmission, on condition of proper repentance and atonement, of members who had been expelled. Members were admitted after two years of probation (Josephus mentions three years). The oath was taken at the beginning of the probation. After one year the candidate was admitted to some of the community functions; after two years he was admitted to full membership. Property was held in common. The rules emphasize those virtues which are most necessary in close community life and punish severely those defects which are most opposed to this life. Only full members were admitted to the common meal. No ceremony is mentioned in connection with the meal except that the priest first blesses the bread and the wine. It is quite possible that this ceremonial meal represented the eschatological banquet which in Jewish belief would be celebrated in the Day of Yahweh (cf Is 25:6). In the assembly members were seated according to rank: priests, elders, and the rest of the people, and they were to speak only in turn. Wherever ten are assembled there shall be a priest among them and there shall be one who studies the law day and night. The members are to stay awake together a third of each night to read, to study the law, and to recite the blessings in common. During the day they engage in manual labor. The Qumran documents exhibit a calendar* independent of that employed by Jews of the period which would involve the celebration of Jewish feasts on different days.

6. *Doctrines of the Sect.* The group regarded itself as the true Israel which would survive the eschatological tribulations. Membership in the true Israel was obtained not only by birth but also by the free choice of the individual member. The group preserved the covenant; indeed, they thought of it in terms of the new covenant of Je 31:31–34 and Ezk 36:22–28. Their belief in the absolute supremacy of God included a somewhat rigid doctrine of predestination. Man is subject to the conflicting influence of the two spirits, the spirit of light or good and the spirit of darkness or evil, also called Belial*. The doctrines emphasize the sinfulness of man, but also the forgiving mercy of God, who will cleanse man from every spirit of error and will sprinkle him with a spirit of truth.

The messianic belief is stated in the Manual of Discipline; in fact, they believed in two Messiahs, the Messiah of Aaron and the Messiah of Israel. The Messiah of Aaron and Israel (in the singular) appears also in the Damascus Document, and some scholars think we have here either a scribal error or an editorial change. This doctrine of the two Messiahs is derived from the importance which the Qumran sect gave to the priesthood. The Messiah of Aaron takes precedence over the Messiah of Israel, who is no doubt to be identified with the Messiah of the house of David. It is not clear whether the group expected the Messiah to appear in the present age. The messianic character of the Teacher of Righteousness is obscure and doubtful. The Teacher of Righteousness appears to be the founder of the sect and in the sect enjoyed a respect second only to the respect granted to Moses. He is thought also to be the author of at least some of the Thanksgiving psalms. The documents suggest that a Teacher of Righteousness was to appear in the last days. It is not entirely certain, as some scholars believe, that the group expected the return of the Teacher of Righteousness who was their founder. Neither is it clear that the Teacher of Righteousness who was expected in the last days is to be identified with the Messiah of Aaron.

The scrolls reveal the importance of the sect in apocalyptic Judaism, the section of Judaism which produced the apocryphal* books. The group was extremely conscious of the end of days and regarded themselves as the last generation. The end of days would involve an eschatological conflict both on the heavenly plane and the earthly plane. The battle of the spirits of light and darkness on the heavenly plane would be paralleled by the battle of the sons of light and the sons of darkness on earth. This battle is described in the war scroll, and the sons of darkness are given the names of traditional enemies of Israel in the OT. There is no explicit reference either to the resurrection of the dead or to the punishment of the wicked after death. The final salvation includes not only the bliss of the righteous, the establishment of a new heaven and a new earth and a new Jerusalem, but also the moral regeneration of the redeemed. The redeemed will be cleansed from all error and sin; they will have everlasting joy in the life of eternity, and will receive a crown of glory and a raiment of light.

7. *Relations with the NT.* Before the discovery of the Qumran scrolls apocalyptic Judaism was known only from certain of the apocryphal books. It is now evident that the Qumran group was at least one of the sects which held apocalyptic beliefs. The apocalyptic strain, which was derived from the OT, did not appear in the Judaism of the Pharisees or the Sadducees. The apocalyptic books, the Qumran scrolls, and the NT have apocalyptic doctrines in common. The scrolls disclose features of the Jewish background of the NT which were not known before. The points of community which have been observed can at the present only be enumerated; their origin cannot be traced nor can their significance be precisely evaluated. But some contact between the members of the two groups seems to be established beyond doubt.

Of the separate books, the closest contacts in language and ideas appear between the Qumran scrolls and the Johannine writings (cf JOHN, GOSPEL OF and EPISTLES OF). The following phrases have been noted by F. M. Cross as appearing both in the Johannine writings and in the scrolls: "the spirits of truth and of deceit" (1 Jn 4:6), "the word of life" (Jn 8:12), "to do the truth" (Jn 3:21), "sons of light" (Jn 12:36), "life eternal" (Jn 3:15 +). The idea of knowledge as "a revealed eschatological knowledge" (Cross) appears in the scrolls and in Mt, Jn, and Paul. The antithesis of flesh* and spirit*, which is derived from the OT, is emphasized both in the scrolls and in the NT writings. Cross compares the Qumran belief in the spirit of truth and the spirit of wickedness and the conflict of the sons of light and the sons of darkness to 1 Jn 3:7–10; 4:1–6.

The Qumran "spiritual" interpretation of the OT, particularly the eschatological interpretation, has no parallel in rabbinic exegesis (cf INTERPRETATION), but does have some resemblance to NT uses of the OT. The organization of the Qumran group has some affinities with the organization of the primitive Church described in AA. Cross points out that the primitive Church exhibits no parallel to the importance of the priestly order in the Qumran group. The usual designation of the Qumran assembly, "the Many," is applied to the members of the Jerusalem council (AA 15:12), to the assembly which chose the seven (AA 6:2, 5), and to the members of the church of Antioch* to whom Paul and Barnabas reported (AA 13:30). The resemblance between the twelve laymen of the Qumran council and the twelve apostles* should not be pressed, since the number in each instance is no doubt drawn from the twelve tribes of Israel. The supreme executive officer of the Qumran community, called the Inspector (Hb *pāḳîd,* Gk *episkopos*) is in power and functions somewhat similar to the *episkopos* (bishop*) of the early Christian churches. The solemn meal of the group, as we have noted above, appears to be a liturgical anticipation of the messianic banquet. This feature appears also in the account of the Lord's supper as given in Mk 14:25 and Lk 22:14–19. The anticipation of the second coming also appears in Paul's mention of the Eucharist* in 1 Co 11:26. There is, however, no parallel in the Qumran meal to the Eucharist of the Lord's supper and the early Christian celebration of the supper.

The primitive Church, like the Qumran group, practiced community of possessions (AA 4:32 ff). This need not be attributed to Qumran influence, since Jesus Himself recommended that His followers bestow their goods on the poor (Mt 19:21; Mk 10:21; Lk 18:22). The counsel of Jesus concerning riches is not couched in terms which are reminiscent of Qumran, but the manner in which early Christians executed this counsel does bear a resemblance to Qumran practice. The question of celibacy at Qumran, as we have noticed, cannot be answered clearly. The evidence does not permit the affirmation that the members of the sect practiced perpetual celibacy. Temporary abstinence from conjugal intercourse was known in the OT (cf WAR). The counsel of Jesus Himself (Mt 19:10–12), which is repeated by Paul (1 Co 7:7–8, 25–31), shows no dependence whatever on Qumran. K. Schubert has pointed out that both the Qumran documents and the NT emphasize poverty as a virtue; the idea, however, appears in the OT (cf POOR). But the emphasis is common to both Qumran and the NT. The same writer has pointed out resemblances between Qumran and the gospel attitude toward persecution for the sake of righteousness (Mt 5:11). There is a parallel in the directions given for correcting an offending brother in the Manual of Discipline and in Mt 18:15–17 which is remarkably close, although it is not exact. In both instances the rebuke before witnesses is prescribed before the charge is brought before the church or the assembly.

E. Stauffer has pointed out eight substantial differences between the primitive Church on one side and the Qumran group on the other: (1) Clericalism, the important place occupied by the priests in Qumran; (2) Ritualism; the ceremonial prescriptions of Qumran are far more extensive than ritual prescriptions in the NT; (3) The direction given in the Manual of Discipline to love the children of light and to hate the children of darkness, to which the command of Jesus to love one's enemies is directly contradictory (Mt 5:43 ff; Lk 6:27 ff); (4) Militarism, which appears in the war of the sons of light and sons of darkness, even if this be conceived as an imaginary apocalyptic battle. Jesus expressly rejected violence as a means of advancing His own doctrine (Mt 26:52); (5) The extraordinary interest at Qumran in the calendar; (6) The esoteric character of the Qumran group and its teaching. Jesus denied expressly that He had taught anything which was not public knowledge (Jn 18:20); (7) The belief in the Messiah of the house of Aaron in addition to the Messiah of the house of David, to which no parallel appears in the NT; (8) The attitude of the Qumran group toward the Jerusalem priesthood and the temple worship. Jesus celebrated Jewish festivals and expressed no repudiation of the temple cult. The members of the primitive Jerusalem Church prayed and worshiped in the temple (Lk 24:52; AA 3:1). In addition Stauffer notes that while the Qumran group had an excessive veneration of the authority of the law of Moses, Jesus presented Himself as superior to the law of Moses and permitted His followers to depart from it. This is especially evident when one compares the attitude of the Qumran group to the Sabbath, which was more rigid than the attitude of the Pharisees, to the liberalism of Jesus, who more than once failed to observe the pharisaic regulations concerning the Sabbath (Mk 2:32 ff; Jn 5:8 ff; 9:1 ff).

8. *The Qumran Scrolls and the Text of the OT*. The extensive fragments of OT books and especially the complete Is scroll from Qumran have had a decisive effect on OT criticism; more results can be expected as the texts are published. Except for the book of Daniel* no major portion of the Hb OT was composed during or after the Maccabean period. One fragment called the prayer of Nabonidus contains an anecdote about Nabonidus which is extremely close to the story of the madness of Nebuchadnezzar* in Dn 4. Nabonidus, not mentioned in Dn, was the father of Belshazzar*, called the son of Nebuchadnezzar in Dn; and it appears that the story of the madness of Nebuchadnezzar was taken from this source with the name of the hero altered from the unknown Nabonidus to the famous Nebuchadnezzar. The Qumran texts show that the Hb text* which we possess was fixed before the beginning of the Christian era. The Hb source of the LXX has also been discovered at Qumran. Scholars have long disputed whether the differences between the LXX and the Masoretic text are to be attributed to the failure of the translators to render the original correctly or to the existence of a different Hb text. The Hb MS of S discovered at Qumran exhibits a text which is not that of the Masoretic text but of the LXX. Similar texts of Jos and K have been found at Qumran. Some other MSS exhibit a conflation of features of both the LXX and the Masoretic text. The evidence indicates that both the LXX and the Masoretic text were the products of recensions made earlier than the Qumran period, i.e., earlier than the 1st or 2nd century BC, and thus represent the termination of an editorial process. The Egyptian origin of the LXX has suggested to W. F. Albright and others that Egypt was the place where this recension arose. The presence of this recension in the Qumran MSS, however, casts some doubt on the Egyptian origin of this text, and it appears equally possible that the text behind the LXX may have a Palestinian origin. But it seems quite likely that this was the text which was taken early to Egypt and that it was in Egypt that it developed into the form in which it was used in the LXX.

R

Raamah (Hb *ra'mā', ra'māh;* meaning uncertain), in the Table* of Nations (Gn 10:7; 1 Ch 1:9) an African tribe, descendant of Ham* and a son of Cush*, otherwise unknown.

Raamses (Hb *ra'm^{e}sēs, ra'am^{e}sēs;* "Re has begotten him"), a city in Egypt. The Hebrews were forced to work on its construction (Ex 1:11) and from there set out on their journey to Canaan (Ex 12:37; Nm 33:3, 5). There is no doubt that Raamses is the Egyptian "House of Ramses" built by the celebrated Pharaoh Ramses II and named after him. Egyptian inscriptions attest the magnificence of its construction. It was not until the 19th dynasty that the Pharaohs moved the royal residence from Thebes to the delta. The site of Raamses is also the site of Tanis*, the Hyksos* capital of Egypt. On its situation and its relation to the date and route of the exodus cf EXODUS. The "land of Raamses" (Gn 47:11) is anachronistic.

Rabbah, Rabbath Ammon (Hb *rabbāh,* "great," *rabbat b^{e}nê 'ammōn,* "Rabbah of the sons of Ammon"), the royal city of Ammon*. The ancient city is completely covered by the modern Amman and no remains earlier than the Roman period are visible. It is very probable that the Ammonite city was built upon the hill of the citadel which rises steeply from the valley of the Jabbok. "The city of waters" (2 S 12:26) may designate a lower city in the valley. The city lies near the W edge of the great plateau of Trans-Jordan 65 mi E of Jerusalem by road; it is exposed to the winds and its temperatures both hot and cold are more extreme than those in Jerusalem. The city was besieged by Joab* (2 S 11:1), who summoned David to lead the army when the city was actually ready for capture (2 S 12:27 ff). This campaign was the occasion of the murder of Uriah*, husband of Bathsheba*. The city possessed a sarcophagus reputed to be the sarcophagus of Og* of Bashan (Dt 3:11). Rabbah was threatened

Modern Amman, the site of the ancient Rabbah, with the valley of the Jabbok in the foreground and the Roman theater visible in left center.

with destruction in the oracles of Je (49:2 f) and Am (1:14) against Ammon. During the Hellenistic period the city was named Philadelphia by Ptolemy II Philadelphus (285–247); it is not mentioned by this name in the Bible. It is one of the cities of the Decapolis* in NT times.

There was also a Rabbah in the territory of Judah (Jos 15:60).

Rabbi (Aramaic *rab*, "master" + first person pronominal suffix, "my master"), Aramaic *rabbônî* (*rabban*) is an emphatic form of *rabbi*. In the Talmudic period the suffix lost its force and the word became a title instead of a form of an address; this use is still found in modern times, when we speak of "a rabbi" or "the rabbi." The NT (the Gospels except Lk) use it as a form of address; the title is always given to Jesus. It is often translated by *kyrie* ("lord*") or *didaskale*, "teacher." Rabbi was the address given by a student of the scribes* to his teacher. Talmudic traditions show the absolute respect which the scribes demanded from their students, and Jesus finds fault with the pride which demands exaggerated respect (Mt 23:7–8) and forbids His disciples to accept the titles of rabbi or father, another title given to scribal teachers. The saying is not found in Mk and Lk, and it may be an instance of Mt's not infrequent rejection of some features of Judaism; in any case, the practice of Christians toward honorific titles has from early centuries treated this saying as a pious and somewhat impractical hyperbole. The use of the address to Jesus is significant; it shows that both His disciples and those outside His circle, uncertain of what precisely His character and His mission were, treated Him as one of the only class of religious leader which they knew.

Raca (Gk *raka*, Aramaic *rêķā'*), a term of abuse frequent in the Talmud; it means an "empty" one, a dolt who cannot understand the teaching of the rabbis. It is a less opprobrious term than "fool." Jesus forbids the use of such opprobrious terms under severe penalties (Mt 5:22); they destroy good relations and are a sign of the superciliousness of the man who uses them.

Rachel (Hb *rāḥēl*, "ewe"), a personal name; the younger daughter of Laban* and wife of Jacob*. Jacob worked for Laban for 7 years as the purchase price of Rachel; but Laban substituted Leah* for Rachel in the wedding ceremony and Jacob had to work another 7 years (Gn 29:6–31). Rachel was barren and substituted her slave Bilhah* (Gn 30:1–25; cf MARRIAGE), and finally herself bore Joseph*. When Jacob returned to Canaan Rachel stole Laban's *teraphim,* the household gods which were the token of the headship of the family (Gn 31:14–35); the story reflects the claims of Israel to predominance over the Aramaeans*. The episode is similar to the story of Rebekah* (Gn 27); through a woman the headship is transferred from one holder to another. Rachel bore Benjamin* after the arrival of Jacob in Canaan and died at Ephrath* shortly after (Gn 35:16–20; 48:7); the story of 1 S 10:2 places the tomb of Rachel at Zelzak in the territory of Benjamin; on the ambiguity of the location of Rachel's tomb cf EPHRAH. In Rt 4:11 Leah and Rachel are a formula of blessing upon a bride. The weeping of Rachel for her sons (Je 31:15) refers to Ephraim*; Ephraim, which to Je means the kingdom of Israel, had been destroyed as an independent state by the Assyrians in the 8th century.

In the Israelite tribal confederacy the Rachel tribes are Ephraim, Manasseh, and Benjamin. This territory was the heartland of Israel, and it is with the Joseph tribes that the exodus from Egypt is certainly associated. The story of the conquests in Jos 8–10 is mostly within the territory of Benjamin. On the position of these tribes within the Israelite confederacy cf ISRAEL and articles on the tribes. The genealogy in which these tribes are the sons of Jacob's preferred wife no doubt reflects their claim to be the most genuinely "Israelite" of all the tribes.

Ragae (Gk *rhagae*, meaning uncertain), the city to which the young Tobias journeyed to collect from Gabelus* the money which his father Tobit had deposited (Tb 1:14; 4:1, 20; 5:4; 9:2). Ragae lay in Media. The ruins of the city, which have not been excavated, lie about 5 mi SE of Teheran. Remains of walls, towers, and the acropolis in the NE corner of the area are visible.

Raguel (Gk *raguel*, Gk form of the Hb name Reuel*), father of Sarah*, who was married to the young Tobias (Tb 3:7 ff; 6:10 ff; 7–10).

Rahab. In Eng versions this one name represents two different Hb words.

1. Hb *rāḥāb*, meaning uncertain; a personal name; a prostitute of Jericho who hid the spies of Joshua in her house (Jos 2:1–21) and was spared with her household when the Israelites took the city (Jos 6:17–25). The story exhibits more breadth than is usually associated with Jos; faith in Yahweh is sufficient to save a woman who was not only a Canaanite, but also a prostitute. The scarlet cord which hung from her

window is thought by some interpreters to signify the character of the establishment.

2. Hb *rāhāb,* a mythological being; the etymology "the stormer" has been suggested. Rahab seems clearly to be associated or identified with the monster of chaos which is slain by the creative deity in ancient Semitic myths of creation*. In the OT this victory is attributed to Yahweh. Yahweh hewed Rahab in pieces, pierced the dragon, dried up the sea (Is 51:9). He rules the raging sea, stills its waves, crushes Rahab (Ps 89:10 f). He stilled the sea, smote Rahab, slew the fleeing serpent (Jb 26:12). The helpers of Rahab are bowed under His power (Jb 9:13). These allusions to the sea, the dragon, and the serpent, which can be traced in other literatures, place Rahab clearly in the context of the myth. The name Rahab, however, has not been found elsewhere, and it is possible that it is a native Hb name of the monster.

The name is scornfully applied to Egypt in Is 30:7; Egypt is a "sitting Rahab," a monster of threatening appearance which is really inactive. Possibly on the basis of this allusion Rahab appears with Babylon in Ps 87:4 as a home of famous men; the name must mean Egypt, but it is doubtful that this was a common appellative of Egypt.

Rain. The rain pattern of Palestine is determined by the position of the country as a relatively narrow strip between the Mediterranean and the desert; the pattern is complicated somewhat by the central range of mountains running N–S and by the deep rift of the Jordan valley. The pattern is remarkably regular; the forces of climate from the sea and the desert create by their opposition a regular cycle of weather throughout the year, which varies from zone to zone of the country but is regular within the zones. The rain decreases in quantity from W to E and from N to S, with one exception; the rain in the central mountain range decreases from S to N until the mountain range is close enough to the sea to fall into the general W–E pattern. The W slopes of the mountains are wetter than the E slopes and have more moderate temperatures both winter and summer.

The rainy season normally begins after October 15 and is ended by May 15. Rain in the dry season is an extraordinary event. In good years cyclonic storms come once a week when the rain is at its maximum; there are three days when rain falls followed by four fair days. All visitors to Palestine notice that the line between rain and fair weather in the winter is clearly drawn; the approach of clouds means rain, which will fall within 24 hours, and after the rain the sky clears rapidly and the air

is fresh, cool, and agreeable. The rain is always accompanied by a heavy W wind. The quantity of rain follows a haystack curve through the season. It begins in October with occasional heavy but brief local showers. In November the number of rainy days increases and the storms are longer in duration. In December there begins the alternation of periods of rainy and fair days; the alternation continues through January, when the rainfall reaches its maximum, usually 10–12 days of rain in the month. The rain diminishes gradually through February and March; April, like October, is limited to short heavy showers, and rain is rare in May.

The annual quantity of rain varies in the four principal topographical areas of the country. The coastal plain ranges from 24 in in the N to 17 in the S. The central mountains range from 26 in the S to 25 in in the N, an insignificant variation. The Jordan valley ranges from 16 in at the Sea of Galilee to 2 in in the desert of the Dead Sea region. Transjordan ranges from 30 in in the N to 11 in in the S. The belt of steppe which lies between the rain area and the desert to the E and S has a range of 16 in to 2 in.

The distribution of the rain is as important for agriculture as its quantity. It is essential that the early rains of December fall normally; a deficit here is not made up even if unusually heavy rains during the rest of the season should bring the annual rainfall up to the average. Actually the rainfall is so marginal that little can be spared from any part of the season; the late rains, while appreciated, are perhaps the most easily missed; their absence means an early and longer summer drought. The limestone soil erodes easily and hard driving rains are damaging. But the soil retains moisture; archaeologists find that the soil is moist 3–4 feet below the surface in summer even after several years of less than normal rainfall. Most rainfalls are local; the rain fronts over several hundred miles and the prolonged drizzles of Europe and N America do not occur in Palestine. C. C. McCown observed that with respect to the salubrity of climate the ancient Israelites were much better situated than the Egyptians and the Mesopotamians and scarcely worse off than the Greeks and Romans.

The Israelites had different words for the phases of the rainy season. Rain in general is *māṭār; yôreh (môreh)* designates the early rains, *gešem* the heavy showers of November–January, and *malḳôš* the later rains (Dt 11:14; Je 5:24; Jl 2:23; Ho 6:3; Ezr 10:9, 13). Rain in harvest time, the summer, is extraordinary and a sign that Yahweh has acted (1 S 12:17; Pr 26:1). There are numerous allusions to the rain and accompanying phenomena in the Bible. Ezra held a meeting in the hard driving showers of the 9th month, Kisleu, November-December (Ezr 10:9, 13). Am 4:17 alludes to the local character of the showers which fall on one city or field and not on another. Three years of drought occurred in the reign of Ahab* (1 K 17:1 ff); this is not unprecedented in the history of Palestine. During a severe drought "the sky turns to bronze, the earth to iron, and the rain into powder and dust" (Dt 28:23). The clouds and wind which do not bring rain are normal on Palestinian summer days (Pr 25:14). The rapid clearing of the sky after a winter rain is described in Jb 37:21. The rare but violent rain storms of the desert wreck both tents (Hab 3:7) and houses (Jb 1:16, 19). After the summer the air is full of dust which creates some remarkably colored sunsets and permits the experienced observers to predict that rain is near (Mt 16:3).

In the OT rain is a gift of Yahweh which He gives or withholds at His pleasure; His pleasure is determined by the moral attitude of men. Dt 11:11–13 contrasts this gift of Yahweh with the hard labor of irrigation in Egypt to the disadvantage of Egypt. This gift of Yahweh was life to the soil and to man who cultivated it, and relief from the heat of summer; the present help of Yahweh is compared to the refreshing and vitalizing winter rain (Ho 6:3).

Rainbow. The "bow" of Yahweh is mentioned in Gn 9:12–17. In the conception of creation* in the P source of the Pnt* the rainbow is a supplementary creation. The deluge* was a relapse into chaos, and the visible universe is restored at its conclusion. The rainbow is now added as a symbol of the covenant of Yahweh with Noah as the representative of all mankind. The covenant is Yahweh's promise that He will not again reduce the world to chaos, even for the sins of man; the rain will always be followed by fair weather. The J source has the same assurance of the regular cycle of the seasons without the symbol of the rainbow (Gn 8:21 f).

Ramah (Hb rāmāh, "height"), the name of several Palestinian towns.

1. Ramah in the territory of Benjamin (Jos 18:25; Ne 11:33). Its location is well defined by its enumeration with other towns of Benjamin: Gibeah* (Jgs 9:13; Is 10:29; Ho 5:8), Bethel* (Jgs 4:5; Ho 5:8), Geba* (Ezr 2:26; Ne 7:30; Is 10:29), Gibeon*, Beeroth*, Mizpeh* (Jos 18:25). It lay near Jerusalem (Jgs 19:13; Is 10:29). These data fit the site which preserves the ancient name,

er-Ram, a hilltop village about 5 mi N of Jerusalem. This distance explains why the fortification of Ramah by Baasha* of Israel was such a serious threat to Judah, and Asa* bribed the Aramaeans to draw Baasha from his plans against Jerusalem. Asa himself did not fortify Ramah, since it was useless to him, but demolished it (1 K 15:17–22). Jeremiah was kept at Ramah by the Babylonians for a short time after the fall of Jerusalem (Je 40:1). It is the place where Rachel, the mother of Benjamin and Joseph, weeps for her sons, the Joseph tribes of Ephraim and Manasseh (Je 31:15).

2. A town in the hill country of Ephraim, called Ramathaim-sophim in 1 S 1:1; the home of Elkanah* (1 S 1:1, 19; 2:11) and of Samuel (1 S 7:17; 8:4; 15:34; 16:13; 19:18; 20:1) and the place where Samuel was buried (1 S 25:1; 28:3). Saul* pursued David to Ramah; here he met the prophets and fell into a prophetic frenzy (1 S 19:18–23). In the Maccabean period it was the administrative center of a district (1 Mc 11:34). It appears in the NT under the Grecized form of Arimathaea, the home of Joseph, who buried Jesus (Mt 27:57; Mk 15:43; Lk 23:51; Jn 19:38). The site is located by scholars at the modern Rentis, a hilltop village on the W edge of the hills of Ephraim and on the road which leads through the valley from the coastal plain to Shiloh. It is about 9 mi NE of Ludd (Lydda).

The name is borne by four other towns which cannot be exactly located:

3. A town on the frontier of Asher near Tyre and Sidon (Jos 19:29).

4. A town of Naphtali (Jos 19:36).

5. Ramah of the Negeb* (Jos 19:8), probably the same as Ramoth of the Negeb (1 S 30:27).

6. Ramah in 2 K 8:29; 2 Ch 22:6 is identical with Ramoth-Gilead*.

Ramoth-Gilead (Hb ramōt-gilʿād, "heights of Gilead"), a town in eastern Palestine; its location has been long disputed, but Nelson Glueck's identification of the site with Tell Ramit, a little more than 1 mi S of Ramtha, on the modern Jordan-Syria frontier on the road from Damascus to Amman, is now generally accepted. The site is listed as a Levitical city of Merari* (Jos 20:8; 1 Ch 6:65) and a city of refuge (Jos 21:38; Dt 4:43). It was the administrative center of one of Solomon's districts (1 K 4:13). At some time between the division of the monarchy and the accession of Ahab* it passed into the hands of the Aramaean kingdom of Damascus; Ahab, with Jehoshaphat of Judah as his ally, undertook a campaign to recover the city but was defeated and killed in the battle (1 K 22; 2 Ch 18). The city was, however, recovered by Israel not long after; when Jehoram* of Israel was wounded in the defense of the city against the Aramaeans, and it was at Ramoth-Gilead that Jehu* was anointed king of Israel (2 K 8:28 f; 9:2–14). The site lies in the plateau of Gilead and no doubt lay on the main road in ancient times as it does now.

Ramses. Cf EGYPT; EXODUS; RAAMSES.

Ransom. Cf REDEMPTION.

Raphael (Hb *r^epā'ēl*, "El heals"), the name of an angel. Raphael plays a principal role in the book of Tb; he is the guardian of a journey (Tb 5–6), the healer (6; 11:1–15), the expeller of demons (6:15–17; 8:1–3). He is one of the 7 angels who offer the prayers of God's people and enter the presence of the Holy One (12:15).

The character of Raphael in the beliefs of Judaism is further disclosed in the apocryphal* book of Enoch. This book exhibits two conceptions of archangels: one of 4 angels (Michael, Gabriel, Raphael, and Uriel or Phanuel; 9:1; 40:9; 70:1 ff), the other of 7 archangels (20:3). After the fall of the angels Raphael is commissioned to bind the fallen angel Azazel hand and foot and cast him into the darkness, and to heal the earth. This commission not only echoes the name but is also very close to Tb 8:1–3. In 20:3 Raphael is in charge of the spirits of men. In 40:9 he is one of the four angels of the presence, who heals all the illnesses and injuries of men; the conception of angels of the presence is found in Tb 12:15, but the number there is 7. In 68:1 ff he questions Michael about the severity of the punishment of the fallen angels.

In Enoch, Raphael is a hypostatization of the healing power of God, and there is no reason to think that he is anything else in Tb. The healing power is not limited to illness and injury; it also protects travelers and defends men from the attacks of demons who inflict corporal injury. Cf ANGEL.

Ras Shamra. Cf UGARIT.

Raven (Hb *'ōrēb*, "dark"?). Several species of raven are known in Palestine; they are carrion birds (Pr 30:17). In many peoples the raven is a bird of evil omen, as it is in the poem of Poe; this belief is not evident in biblical usage. The raven is unclean* (Lv 11:15; Dt 14:14). In the story of the deluge* the raven, sent forth first, does not return; the compiler has probably garbled the tradition as it is found in the poem of Gilgamesh*,

where the failure of the raven to return is a sign that the waters have receded. The ravens appear in the saga of Elijah; they bring food to the prophet in the desert (1 K 17:4–6). The hair of the beloved is as black as ravens (SS 5:11). Ravens with other carrion birds and beasts haunt the ruins of Edom (Is 34:11). Three times in the Bible God's provision of food for the ravens is an example of His providence (Ps 147:9; Jb 38:41; Lk 12:24, where Mt has "birds").

Razis (Gk *razis*, Hb ?, meaning uncertain), an elder of Jerusalem in the Maccabean period (2 Mc 14:37–46). When Nicanor sent troops to arrest him, he attempted to fall upon his sword; but in his haste he missed his stroke and and plunged from the wall of his house to the pavement. Still living, he ran to a rock, pulled out his bowels and threw them at the crowd. This was done that he might not suffer treatment unworthy of his rank (2 Mc 14:42). This example of heroism is not certainly historical; cf MACCABEES, BOOKS. But this does not alter the rather casual attitude toward suicide which disturbs many modern readers. They should remember that even in early Christian times the morality of suicide was not as elaborate as it has since become; stories are told of Christian martyrs who thought that once one's death was certain one might anticipate it, and these stories were examples of heroism in the early Church.

Razor. There are two Hb words for razor: (1) *ta'ar.* Assyria* is Yahweh's hired razor with which He will shave the hair of the head, the pubic hair, and beard (Is 7:20). The razor is not to touch the head of the Nazirite* (Nm 6:5). The Levites* for ritual cleanliness are to shave the entire body (Nm 8:7). Ezekiel is to shave his hair and beard with a sharp sword used as a razor (Ezk 5:1). The sharp tongue is like a razor (Ps 52:4).

(2) *môrāh:* the razor was not used on the heads of Samson* (Jgs 13:5; 16:17) and Samuel* (1 S 1:11), who were Nazirites. No doubt the two words indicate two different types of razor, but the difference cannot be determined. There is no indication that the Israelites shaved the beard as the Egyptians and Sumerians did, and a close shave with a blade of flint or bronze or even with a primitive iron blade would have caused acute discomfort; the shaving of the Levites is an exception and is reminiscent of the clean shaven Sumerian and Egyptian priests who appear in art. Types of razors are illustrated in ANEP 81, 82, 83. 81 is only the handle of a flint or obsidian blade. The bronze blade of 82 is 16.2 cm long, 6–7 in

and has a concavo-convex blade tapering to a rounded point. The handle of a similar blade, shown in 83, is not unlike the handle of the modern safety razor. Cf BEARD; HAIR.

Reaping. Cf HARVEST.

Rebekah (Hb *ribḳāh,* a personal name, etymology uncertain), daughter of Bethuel* of Paddan-Aram* (Gn 22:23) and wife of Isaac. The story of the wooing of Rebekah (Gn 24) contains some points of information on marriage practice: the wooing was done by a slave who represented the father of the groom; the purchase price was paid; the negotiations were conducted by the family of the bride, but the bride herself was given the decision of going immediately without awaiting a prolonged farewell party. Bethuel strangely does not appear in Gn 24, and the bride, presumably on the death of her father, becomes the property of her elder brother, the heir of the estate. The slave was attracted to Rebekah because of the courtesy she showed him at the well.

The story of the birth of twin sons to Rebekah is explained by the oracle of Gn 25:23 in terms of the later conflict of Israel and Edom*; although Israel was a younger people, its preeminence was guaranteed by an ancient oracle which antedated the birth of the eponymous ancestors. In Gn 26:6–11 the story of the wife of the patriarch in the harem of a foreign prince is told of Rebekah. It is also told twice of Sarah*, and it is more probably original in the story of Sarah.

The most important role of Rebekah in the patriarchal stories appears in Gn 27. At her instigation and with her assistance Jacob steals the blessing of the firstborn from Isaac and with it all the rights of primogeniture (cf FIRSTBORN). As in the story of Rachel and the household gods, the headship is transferred by craft from one holder to another, who is the ancestor of Israel. The headship here is again taken by Israel from Edom; the motif is the same as in the story of the birth of the twins and the oracle, and both stories authenticate Israel's claims of hegemony over Edom.

Although the death of Rebekah's nurse is mentioned in Gn 35:8, the death of Rebekah herself is not explicitly noticed. She was buried at Machpelah* with Abraham, Sarah, and Isaac (Gn 49:31).

Rechab (Hb *rēkab,* "rider" ?). **1.** The eponymous ancestor of an Israelite clan, who appears only in the phrase "son(s) of Rechab." The genealogy of 1 Ch 2:55 relates the Rechabites to the Kenites* through Hammath, father of the house of Rechab. Jonadab*, a member of the clan, was invited to accom-

pany Jehu* and see his "zeal for Yahweh" in the killing of the members of the house of Ahab and of the worshipers of Baal (2 K 10:15, 23). One may deduce from this that the Rechabites represented the conservative defenders of Israelite traditions which were also represented by Elijah, Elisha, and Jehu, each in his own way. This impression of conservatism becomes clear in Je 35. The Rechabites, compelled to live in Jerusalem during the siege of the city, were invited by Jeremiah to drink wine. They answered that they have obeyed the traditions of their ancestor Jonadab: they do not drink wine, nor dwell in houses, nor sow, nor plant, nor own vineyards, but they live in tents. Nomadism* was then and is now a way of life in the steppe and the desert; but this nomadism was undertaken for religious motives, and Jeremiah praises them for their fidelity to their traditions, which he contrasts with the infidelity of Judah and Jerusalem. It seems a legitimate conclusion that the Rechabites identified fidelity to Yahweh with a cultural archaism; they clung to the nomadic way of life which is found in the traditions of Israel, and rejected the urban-agricultural society of Canaan, which Israel had adopted centuries before, as betrayal of Israelite traditions. They may be compared to a number of sects in the history of Christianity which have refused cultural changes from religious motives, like the Amish in the United States.

2. One of the assassins of Ishbaal*, executed by David (2 S 4:2–12).

Reconciliation. "Reconciliation" is the Gk legal term used of husband and wife (1 Co 7:11 and in Gk papyri). Paul applies the term to the process of salvation. In 2 Co 5:18–20 God is the agent of reconciliation, and man is reconciled. Christ is the means of reconciliation, which is extended to the world. God reconciles the world to Himself "in Christ"; the preposition "in" here has the Semitic idiomatic use which is called "the instrumental in," equivalent to the preposition *through, by means of.* The reconciliation in this context is expressed through the phrase, "not reckoning against men their sins" (5:19); in the proximate context it also consists in man's becoming a new creation (5:17), in becoming the holiness of God (5:21). The reconciliation is accomplished more precisely through the death of Christ for all (5:14). The reconciling death is more explicit in Rm 5:10, as is the enmity of man to God which needs reconciliation. In Col 1:20 God is the agent of reconciliation and Christ the means; reconciliation here is paralleled by "making peace," and the means again more precisely is the blood shed on the cross (1:20), the death of Christ in His body (1:22). Men are reconciled from a state of estrangement and hostility which comes from their evil deeds (1:22). The conception of reconciliation in Eph 2:15 f is not quite the same. Here Christ is the agent of reconciliation, who makes peace and kills hostility (2:16). The means of reconciliation, however, is not precisely the redeeming death; Christ reconciles by breaking down the wall of separation and abolishing the law* (2:14–15). He creates from the two races of Jew and Gentile one new being (2:15), and reconciles both races in one body to God by the cross — here the redeeming death. In calling Christ "our peace" (2:14), it is not clear that the author of Eph is thinking of reconciliation of man with God; the terms themselves and the preceding context suggest rather that the reconciliation here is made between Jews and Gentiles in the one body of the Church.

Red Heifer. The rite of the red heifer (Nm 19) is intended for the removal of uncleanness contracted by contact with death (cf CLEAN). An unblemished red heifer, never worked, is to be slain outside the camp and burned with cedar wood, hyssop, and scarlet string; the blood of the slain heifer is to be sprinkled toward the tabernacle seven times. The ashes are to be gathered and kept. They are put into the "water of impurity" which is sprinkled on the dwelling where a death has occurred and upon its furniture, and upon the person who touches the dead body. The ashes are a kind of focus of uncleanness; they render unclean all persons involved in the slaying and burning of the animal and the gathering of the ashes and the sprinkling of the water of impurity, but they cleanse the objects and persons upon which the water is sprinkled. The color of red is no doubt significant, but its significance is not clear and probably was not when the rite was described in writing. Although the chapter comes from the late source P, the rite is probably extremely ancient.

Red Sea. The Red Sea, lying between the continent of Africa and the peninsula of Arabia and enclosed by the Isthmus of Suez to the N and the Straits of Aden to the S, is mentioned several times in the Bible; the Hb name yam-sûp, which almost certainly means "sea of reeds," is ambiguous in some passages. The name certainly means the Red Sea in 1 K 9:26; 2 Ch 8:17, where Solomon's fleet and port at Elath* — Eziongeber* is mentioned. The name almost certainly means the Red Sea in Nm 14:25; 21:4; Dt 1:40; 2:1; here the yam-sûp is a point toward which the Israelites turn in

their sojourn in the desert, particularly to make a circuit of Edom; this latter datum makes it nearly impossible to suppose that any other body of water could be meant. It probably means the Red Sea in Jgs 11:16; here the Israelites are said to travel through the desert as far as yam-sûp and then to Kadesh*. This, however, may be a compendious statement of the route of the exodus* in which the geographical data are not altogether clear. The boundaries of Israel are stated in Ex 23:31, "from yam-sûp to the sea of the Philistines, and from the desert to the river." "The river" without qualification in the OT means the Euphrates*, which is elsewhere mentioned as an ideal boundary of Israel; the desert should therefore be the S point, but it appears that it is more intelligible as the E point; the country to the S of Israel is always the Negeb*. The yam-sûp as the Red Sea (i.e., the Gulf of Aqaba) is the most obvious S point, and the sea of the Philistines must be the Mediterranean. The boundaries therefore run S to W to E to N in the enumeration. In all these incidences not the Red Sea proper but the Gulf of Aqaba is meant. All other incidences of the name refer to the water crossed by the Israelites in the exodus, and this is most probably not the Gulf of Suez but the "sea of reeds," one of the lakes which lie near the Mediterranean on the N coast of the Isthmus of Suez; cf EXODUS (Ex 10:19; 13: 18; 15:4, 22; Nm 33:10 f; Dt 11:4; Jos 2:10; 4:23; Ne 9:9; Pss 106:7, 9, 22; 136: 13, 15). The LXX and the Gk books of the OT and NT habitually render yam-sûp by the Gk geographical term thalassa erythra, Red Sea, which had the same meaning in Gk geographically as Red Sea in Eng (1 Mc 4:9; WS 10:18; 19:7; AA 7:36; Heb 11:29).

The term yam-sûp is not particularly apt for the Gulf of Aqaba, and the application of the term to this body of water seems probably due to an ancient misunderstanding of the term yam-sûp in the traditions of the exodus. On the assumption that this meant the Gulf of Suez, the term was applied to the Gulf of Aqaba, another arm of the Red Sea.

Redemption. 1. *In the OT*. The Hb words for *redeem* and *ransom,* like the Eng words, mean primarily payment of a sum for the release of a person or object which is held in detention. This use of the word appears in passages such as Ex 34:20; 13:13, 16; Nm 18:15, where the firstborn* of men and animals, which belong to Yahweh, are released from this obligation by the payment of a price. In Nm 3:46 ff the Levites* are the ransom for the firstborn; this approaches the metaphorical use of the word, for in this conception it is the substitution of the Levites for the service of Yahweh which makes the ransom payment acceptable. The metaphorical use of the word in the sense of *liberate* appears in 1 S 14:45; the people deliver Jonathan* from the penalty of death which he has unwittingly incurred, but there is no mention of a ransom; they liberate him by the pressure of popular demand, and the word does not imply, as some scholars have thought, that the death penalty was inflicted upon some hapless substitute.

The word is used often metaphorically of the saving action of Yahweh. Even where Yahweh is said to redeem the Israelites from slavery in Egypt, He does not do it by the payment of a ransom; He does it by His power (Dt 7:8; 13:6; 15:15; 24:18; Mi 6:4). Elsewhere the word means simply to liberate from distress and trouble (2 S 4:9; 1 K 1:29; Ps 25:22) or from the hand of the strong (Je 31:11) or from one's enemy (Ps 78:42). It is used absolutely without mention of that from which one is redeemed (Dt 9:26; Ne 1:10; Ps 44:27; Ho 7:13). Redemption is a work of Yahweh's power (Dt 15:15) or of His love* (Ps 44:27). In a few passages it has almost the sense of acquire, which is implicit in the idea of redemption; Yahweh redeems Israel to be a people (2 S 7:23; 1 Ch 17:21) and His inherited tribe (Ps 74:2). In one passage which approaches the NT use Yahweh redeems Israel from its iniquities (Ps 130:8), and in Ho 13:14 Yahweh asks, implying a negative answer, whether He shall redeem Israel from death.

The idea of the redemption of Israel is transferred to the redemption of the individual person; here it is always used in the metaphorical sense of liberate, as Jeremiah from the grasp of the cruel (15:21), and David from distress (2 S 4:9; 1 K 1:29). It occurs in the Pss practically in the sense of "save one's life" either as a petition (Ps 34:23; 26:11) or in thanksgiving (Ps 55:19; 71:23; 31:6). This sense appears also in BS 51:2, where the body is redeemed from destruction. It also means to liberate from oppression (Ps 119:134).

2. *In the NT*. The NT use of the words *lytron*, "ransom," and the cognate verbs and nouns reflects this OT usage; but in addition it also reflects the LXX usage of these Gk words, which are employed somewhat loosely also to translate the words for "avenge*" and "atone*." In the LXX the root idea of redemption, release by purchase, had been submerged in the idea of liberation, as had the ideas of vengeance and atonement. In profane Gk the words signify release from detention by payment of ransom; they are used in particular of the redemption of slaves and of prisoners of war, and also in a meta-phorical sense of the release from a civic obligation by the payment of a stipulated sum. The cultic use of the word in Gk is similar to this last use; it means the payment of a fine for guilt.

The words are used only twice in the Gospels in the parallel passages of Mt 20:28; Mk 10:45; the Son of Man has not come to receive service but to render service and to give His life as a ransom for many. The saying comes at the end of a short discourse on not seeking eminence; Luke preserves the discourse but not the ransom saying. "Life" (lit *soul*) here has the usual Semitic meaning of *self*, although the Eng "give one's life" is an accurate paraphrase. Jesus Himself is the ransom and He becomes the ransom payment by His death. The idea of ransom implies the voluntary offering of Himself. It also includes the vicarious nature of His death. The ransom is paid for another who secures the good for which the payment is made; the good does not come to the redeemer. The phrase seems reminiscent of the Servant of Yahweh (Is 53:6, 12). The passage does not say from what "the many" are redeemed, but the general context of the Gospels leaves no doubt that they are redeemed from sin. Neither is it said to whom the ransom is paid. Here one may ask whether the metaphor should be pushed too far; if it is paid to anyone, it is paid to God, but this approaches allegorizing. Jesus offers Himself to the Father, and submits Himself entirely to His will, but it is doubtful that the idea of ransom should be extended so far. Some of the Fathers of the Church permitted themselves some unsound speculations on the hypothesis that the ransom was paid to Satan. Büchsel has asked why a ransom should be necessary, in view of the easy forgiveness of sins which Jesus Himself extended (Mk 2:5 +) and of the gratuity of grace, and observes that the idea of redemption is a necessary corrective; it implies the reality of man's sin and guilt, which is as real as the death of Jesus, and it shows how easy forgiveness has become possible. The ease with which it is granted may mislead one concerning the tremendous work which was done to establish it. Büchsel sums up neatly with the sentence, "The ransom exhibits the living unity of God's grace and God's judgment." These two Gospel passages are imitated in 1 Tm 2:6.

In the other NT incidences of the words there is almost no implication of ransom; in some passages redemption has become a technical term for the saving work of Jesus. Setting aside Heb 11:35, in which the word means simply release, one finds it used in passages reminiscent of the OT usage of the redemption of Israel (Lk 1:68; 2:38; 24:21);

these, however, speak of the messianic redemption of Israel and have an eschatological rather than a soteriological implication. The eschatological consummation is clearly signified by redemption in Lk 21:28; Rm 8:23, where it means the resurrection of the body; Eph 1:14, where redemption as God's possession is the ultimate purpose of God's saving acts; Eph 4:30, sealed for the day of redemption. Here the phrase seems to have a merely technical sense. In other passages it is used of the saving work of Jesus by His death and of its immediate effects in the Christian life. Jesus has redeemed us from iniquity (Tt 2:14). Christians are redeemed from their worthless manner of life by the precious blood of Christ (1 Pt 1:18 f); here the blood rather than Jesus Himself has become the ransom. Through God's grace, which is redemption in Christ, the Christian is sanctified (Rm 3:24). Christ has become for us wisdom, holiness, sanctification, and redemption (1 Co 1:30); in this heap of epithets the term "redemption" has lost its peculiar force. Redemption through the blood of Jesus is the remission of sins (Eph 1:7; Col 1:14). Christ died for the redemption of transgressions (Heb 9:15). There is scarcely any of these passages in which the metaphor has not become rather loose.

Büchsel seems at least near the truth in saying that redemption is not one of the major basic ideas of primitive Christianity to describe the saving work of Jesus. Of this saving work the word is not used at all in Lk, Jn, the Catholic epistles, and Apc. It appears only twice in Mt-Mk, and it is much less common in Paul than other ideas which are used to describe the process of salvation. By a paradox the word has become a technical term in theology and popular language to describe this saving work.

Refuge, Cities of. Six cities of refuge are enumerated in Jos 20:7-9: Kedesh* in Galilee, Shechem*, Hebron*, Bezer*, Ramoth-Gilead*, and Golan*, three on the W side of the Jordan* and three on the E. Dt 4:43 relates the institution of 3 on the E side; this notice is probably a historical fiction arising from the attribution of the cities of refuge to Moses. The law governing the cities is found in Dt 19 (D) and Nm 35 (P). The law makes a distinction between accidental homicide and willful murder and provides that the accidental homicide may flee to the city of refuge until his case is adjudicated. The customary law of blood revenge (cf AVENGER) made no distinction between casual and deliberate homicide, at least in theory. In the law of D the elders* of the city are to judge the case, in the

law of P the community, which means practically the same thing.

Most historians have regarded the law of the cities of refuge as a fiction of the priestly writer. Such fictions are indeed found in P, but it is very doubtful that this is one. In early times the man threatened with execution could flee to the shrine for sanctuary, as did Adonijah* (1 K 1:50) and Joab* (1 K 2:28); in these two cases the sanctuary was violated. W. F. Albright and others have proposed that the institution of the cities of refuge should be attributed to the reign of David. The cities were probably selected because of the presence of a shrine. In the settled urban-agricultural community of monarchic Israel the unrestrained operations of the ancient customary law of blood vengeance could not easily be tolerated. The law of the cities of refuge is an early effort to distinguish between murder and homicide and to protect the homicide from the penalty of death through a legal process; but since it was the duty of the avenger to act expeditiously, the protection was not secure unless the culprit could find sanctuary in a place which was even holier than the obligation of vengeance. Such a legal step should be placed in the early monarchy in any case, if not in the reign of David Himself.

Reed. Several species of tall grass are found in Palestine; in the borders of the streams which run into the Dead Sea, the Jordan valley, and the region of Huleh these grasses grow to a height of 15-20 ft. Particularly stout types were used as walking sticks (2 K 18:21; Is 36:6; Ezk 29:6). The reed was used as a measuring rod (Ezk 40:3, 5 +; Apc 11:1; 21:15 f). The reed is used in metaphor as a symbol of weakness, especially of deceptive weakness; it is bent by the wind (Mt 11:7; Lk 7:24) or shaken in the water (1 K 14:15). The servant of Yahweh will not crush the bent reed (Is 42:3). The reed which is used as a walking stick breaks easily and pierces the hand of its holder; such is the help of Egypt to Judah (2 K 18:21; Is 36:6; Ezk 29:6-7).

Regeneration. The concept of initiation into the Christian community as a birth into a new life is scarcely found in the NT outside of Jn and 1 Pt, and it has no antecedents in the OT. Scholars have pointed out that the initiation into certain mystery* cults was called a regeneration, and some have sought here the antecedents of the NT use. Modern scholarship is less inclined to see much positive influence of the mysteries on early Christianity. The nature of the regeneration contained in the mysteries is too obscure to draw clear parallels, and in addition it is uncertain whether these features of the mysteries are pre-Christian or post-Christian in origin. One can scarcely define the influence as consisting in more than the entrance of the term "regeneration" from the mystery cults into popular language, from which it came into these NT books. Whether Judaism exhibits a concept of regeneration is not clear; the proselyte* was regarded as a new man who begins an entirely new life; all relationships contracted before circumcision are voided. This is effectively a new birth, even if the term is not used, and it is as likely to have influenced the NT as the mystery cults.

In 1 Jn those who are born of God are those who do righteousness (2:29), who love their neighbor (4:7), who believe that Jesus is the Messiah (5:1). As a fruit of regeneration those who are born of God do not sin, indeed cannot sin because they are born of God (3:9; 5:18); regeneration from God raises them to the level of God, to whom sin is impossible. In virtue of their regeneration they overcome the world (5:4), as Jesus has overcome the world (Jn 16:33). In the Gospel of Jn those who are born of God are those who believe in His name; they are not born of blood, i.e., they are not distinguished by human racial origin such as Jew and Gentile, nor of the flesh, i.e., by human copulation, nor of the will of man, i.e., of carnal desire, but of God (Jn 1:13). They live in a new life and in a new nature of divine origin. This new birth is baptism*. It is a birth of the spirit (Jn 3:3–8).

In 1 Pt 2:2 the Christians are newborn babes nourished on unadulterated spiritual milk. The Father has begotten them anew to a living hope through the resurrection of Jesus Christ (1:3); here the regeneration to a new life looks to eschatological fulfillment. The same eschatological outlook is implied in 1:23; the Christian is born anew through an imperishable seed. Here the birth comes through the living and eternal word of God; "word" here does not mean precisely baptism, which is not called the "word," but the preaching of the Gospel. Baptism is the bath of regeneration and renewal through a holy spirit (Tt 3:5).

The regeneration of Mt 19:28 refers to the Jewish eschatological belief in the resurrection* of the body and the renovation of the material world.

Perhaps because the concept of regeneration has certain echoes in the mysteries, it has little place in the NT; but it is closely parallel to Paul's conception of baptism as death to the old life and resurrection to the new life in Christ.

Rehob (Hb $r^e\d{h}\bar{o}b$, "wide"?), the name of at least two towns: **1.** a town of Asher* (Jos 19:28, 30), a Levitical town (Jos 21:31; 1 Ch 6:60), one of the Canaanite towns not conquered by the Israelites (Jgs 1:31). The site is not certainly known; it may be the modern Tell es Sarem 3 mi S of Beth-shan.

2. An Aramaean town, near the northern limit of Canaan (Nm 13:21), which engaged in David's war with Ammon as an ally of Ammon (2 S 10:8), called Beth-rehob in 2 S 10:6, probably also in Jgs 18:28.

A town of Rehob in Canaan is mentioned in the lists of the Pharaohs Thutmose III and Shishak* (ANET 253) and in an Egyptian geographic text of the 13th century (ANET 477). It seems that this should be identified with the Aramaean Rehob.

Rehoboam (Hb $r^e\d{h}ab\cdot\bar{a}m$, "[the deity] enlarges the people"?), a personal name; son and successor of Solomon as king of Israel 922–915 BC (1 K 11:43; 1 Ch 3:10; 2 Ch 9:31). The crude attempt of Rehoboam to assert autocratic authority at the assembly of Shechem alienated most of the Israelite tribes from him and furnished the occasion for the rebellion which set up the distinct kingdom of Israel (1 K 12:1–20; 2 Ch 10:1–19). For the latent schism in the monarchy cf JUDAH. Rehoboam at this early period in the monarchy did not succeed simply by inheritance; the confirmation of the assembly of tribal elders was necessary. During his brief reign there occurred the disastrous invasion of Palestine by the Pharaoh Shishak* (1 K 14:21–31); the text notices only the plundering of the palace and the temple, but the inscription of Shishak indicates that it was a much larger operation. The parallel narrative of 2 Ch 12 adds a theological explanation, asserting that the invasion was a punishment of the guilt of Rehoboam but adding that the disaster was less than total because of the repentance of Rehoboam; cf CHRONICLES. 2 Ch 11:1–4 relates that the prophet Shemaiah* forbade Rehoboam to make war against Israel; this is midrash*, which authenticates the failure of the house of David to reconquer its territory by an explicit statement of the divine will. The list of the fortifications of Rehoboam (2 Ch 11:5–12) and the list of his wives and children (11:18–23) very probably come from genuine records.

Rehoboth (Hb $r^e\d{h}\bar{o}b\bar{o}t$, "wide places"?). **1.** The name given by Isaac* to a well which he dug in the Negeb* (Gn 26:22). It is possibly identical with Ruheibeh 7–8 mi SW of Beersheba*.

2. A town of Edom (Gn 36:37; 1 Ch 1:48) of uncertain location.

3. Rehoboth-ir, "wide places of the city," in Mesopotamia, one of the cities built by Nimrod* (Gn 10:11). No identification of this site is known; but it is similar to the Akkadian *rebit Nina,* "wide places (i.e., suburbs) of Nineveh*," upon which the phrase may be modeled.

Rehum (Aramaic *rᵉḥûm,* etymology uncertain), a personal name; the Persian officer in the district of Samaria* at the time of the return of the Jewish exiles. His Aramaic title *bᵉᶜel ṭᵉᶜēm* represents the Akkadian *bel ṭemi,* "commander," "officer." Ezr 4:8–24 contains his letter to the Persian imperial court objecting to the rebuilding of Jerusalem as a possible focus of future rebellion, and the response from the court prohibiting further building; cf ZERUBBABEL. The name Rehum is not Persian and the officer was no doubt one of the native population to whom the government of the district was entrusted, as Nehemiah* was made governor of Jerusalem. The two letters are regarded by most scholars as copies taken from the Persian archives.

Remnant (Hb *šᵉār, šᵉᵉrît,* "the remainder," and thus often "the rest [of]"), the word when used of a nation or a people means that which is left after conquest, hence the translation remnant. To destroy without leaving a remnant is to destroy totally (Is 14:22; Je 11:23; Ezk 25:16; 2 S 14:7). The term is used of other peoples: Moab (Is 16:14; 15:9), Aram (Is 17:3), Kedar (Is 21:17), Ashdod (Je 25:20), Caphtor (Je 47:4), the Philistines (Is 14:30; Am 1:8), Edom (Am 9:12) +. It is used in the same neutral sense of Israel and Judah to designate the people after the conquests of Assyria and Babylon. The term "remnant" is the normal designation of the group of Judahites which settled at Mizpeh after the fall of Jerusalem and then, when Gedaliah was murdered, moved to Egypt (Je 40:15 ff). In Ezk 9:8; 11:13 the remnant of Israel is the kingdom of Zedekiah, and in Am 5:15 the remnant of Joseph is that which survives foreign conquest as yet in the future; this remnant may experience the favor of Yahweh. Isaiah is asked to pray for "the remnant" (Is 37:4; 2 K 19:4); here it is the kingdom of Judah after the invasion of Sennacherib, which had reduced the territory held by Hezekiah to scarcely more than the city of Jerusalem.

From this use of the word there develops a sense which can only be called technical and theological; "the remnant," with or without the addition of Israel, Judah, Jerusalem, or "this people," to define it, means Israel which survives after conquest, an act of the judgment of Yahweh, and which is the bearer of the promises of Israel. This remnant is the object of threats; Yahweh will glean the remnant of Israel as a vine (Je 6:9), he will treat the remnant like bad figs (Je 24:8), death will be preferable to life for the remnant (Je 8:3). The remnant of Je 40–44 is threatened with destruction (Je 42:15, 19). Yahweh will scatter the remnant of Judah to the winds (Ezk 5:10); He will give it to the sword (Je 15:9); He will reject the remnant of His inheritance (2 K 21:14). Though the people of Israel be as numerous as the sand of the sea, only a remnant will return (Is 10:22).

But since the remnant is the only existing Israel, it is the only object of the promises made to Israel, and frequently it is the one to whom promises of messianic restoration are addressed. On general critical grounds the passages where the remnant has acquired this messianic sense are later expansions of the prophetic books. Thus Is 10:20–22 groups three sayings, one of which is a threat; the other two are promises, all probably expansions, and grouped on the catchword "remnant." The remnant is scattered in distant countries from which it will be gathered and restored to the land of Israel (Is 11:11, 16; Je 23:3; Mi 2:12; Zc 8:6 ff). The remnant shall possess not only the land of Israel, but the land of their former enemies (Zp 2:7, 9). The remnant will lean upon Yahweh (Is 10:20), Yahweh will be its crown and diadem (Is 28:5). Yahweh has saved the remnant of Israel (Je 31:7); it will triumph over the nations (Mi 5:6 f). The remnant will find refuge in the name of Yahweh (Zp 3:13). The remnant shall enjoy fabulous prosperity in Israel (Zc 8:10–12). The complete conversion of the term from an implication of defeat and conquest to a term of messianic hope is seen in Mi 4:7, where Yahweh promises that He will make the lame a remnant.

There is a certain polarization in this development. In early prophets such as Amos as well as in the more surely original utterance of Jeremiah and Ezekiel the term is either neutral or an implied threat; to say that a remnant of the nation will endure is more of a threat than a promise, although it is something of a promise as well. The actual survival of a remnant made the term a token of Yahweh's fidelity to His promise; Israel did not totally perish and therefore the remnant was a sign of His fidelity and of His saving power and will.

It is a question whether this development of the idea of the remnant into a technical messianic term is to be found in Isaiah, particularly in the name of his son, Shear-yashub, "a remnant will return" (Is 7:3). The name is of itself ambiguous: a remnant will return, and therefore the nation will suffer conquest; but it will not be destroyed totally. Perhaps it is better to attribute the ambiguity to Isaiah himself, who wished the term to look both ways, as indeed his prophetic message does; cf ISAIAH. But there is no trace in the original writings of Isaiah of that technical messianic sense which occurs in later prophetic texts; it seems that this development of the term is a result of history, which created the remnant and compelled the Jews to rethink their position in the promises of Yahweh and the process of salvation.

Repentance. Under this heading are grouped several related ideas: change of "mind" or change of "heart" i.e., change of intention, disposition, attitude; regret; conversion; sorrow for sin. Repentance in the sense of a change of intention is by an anthropomorphism attributed to God in the OT. Yahweh "repents" of His plan to destroy by plague (1 Ch 21:15), of His creation of man (Gn 6:6), of the election of Saul as king (1 S 15:11). Jeremiah's parable of the potter (18:8–10) is explained to signify that the determination of Yahweh to punish is not inflexible; if man turns from his evil ways, Yahweh will "repent" of His purpose to punish; cf 26:13. Yahweh repents of His anger and exhibits compassion (Ps 106:45). Anthropomorphism does not impose a consistent pattern, and elsewhere Yahweh is said to decide without repentance; this is said of His intention to punish (Je 4:28; Ho 13:14). The pattern is explicitly reversed when it is affirmed that Yahweh is unlike man in that He does not change His mind (Nm 23:19; 1 S 15:29). He swears that David is a priest forever and does not repent (Ps 110:4). He overthrew Sodom and Gomorrah without regret (Je 20:16). His gifts and His vocation are bestowed with no condition of recall (Rm 11:29).

The term is used both of God and of man in the sense of simple regret; Judas regrets his betrayal of Jesus (Mt 27:3), but it is clear from the context that his regret does not fulfill the biblical idea of conversion and repentance. He does indeed confess his sin, which is one of the elements of repentance and conversion; one could say that he repents but does not convert. The theological sense of the term implies a movement from one term to another.

1. *In the OT.* There are a number of OT passages which modern scholars now identify as references to cultic liturgies of repentance, or selections from such liturgies. These litur-gies may easily be connected with the Pss of lamentation (cf PSALMS). The liturgies are mentioned or quoted in Ne 9; Is 63:7–64:12; Bar 1:15–3:8; Dn 9:3–19; Ho 6:1 ff; 7:14; 14:2 ff; Jl 2:15–18; Jon 3:7 f. From these passages the following elements can be found in liturgies of repentance: fast, assembly of the people, public lamentation and petition, loud cries and wails, the cutting of oneself, the wearing of sackcloth and ashes, the public confession of sins, the recital of the sins of Israel in its history. These liturgies are submitted to criticism by the prophets as merely external symbols of repentance with no interior change of disposition. The refrain of Am 4:6–11 denies the reality of conversion. Ho 6:4–6, after quoting a liturgy of repentance, says that the devotion of Israel evaporates like the morning dew. Is 58:5–7 asserts that there is no genuine repentance in a liturgy which does not interrupt the pursuit of business and one's ordinary habits of quarreling; true repentance is shown by helping the needy; similarly Zc 7:5 ff makes the aid of the needy the test of true repentance; fasting and lamentation without it are merely works for oneself. Jl 2:13 demands that one rend one's heart and not one's garments. These criticisms are in the same line of thought as the prophetic criticisms of the ritual of sacrifice, and they show that repentance cannot be merely signs of sorrow and public confession of sin; it demands what is signified by the word *šûb,* "turn," which is quite common in the OT to denote the attitude which sinful man must take to God.

"Turn" of itself is a neutral word which may mean deviation from the right as well as from the wrong, as it does in Je 8:4; Ezk 18:24; 33:18. But the word is so common that it becomes nearly a technical term for conversion. One turns most frequently to Yahweh, sometimes to His law or to righteousness. One turns from sin, evil, the evil way, evil deeds, idols. Conversion is a personal change and not merely a participation in community ritual; it is a total change, the adoption of an entirely new attitude toward Yahweh and an abandonment of all previous attitudes and habits. Both the personal and the total quality of conversion appear most clearly in Ho 2:4–24. It is the return of a faithless wife to a loving husband, a restoration of love and an entire rejection of one's past life and of the false values to which one has been attached. Conversion is the acquisition of love and knowledge (Ho 6:6). The summary of Jeremiah's words in 26:3–5 is not as vigorous, but the totality of conversion is apparent in the demand that one follow the law of Yahweh and hearken to the words of His prophets.

The totality of conversion is also apparent in the frequent demand of confidence in Yahweh; by this confidence one admits His supremacy and repudiates false security. Repentance means a rejection of trust in foreign alliance or military means (Is 10:20; 30:15; Ho 14:4). One expects salvation from Yahweh alone (Je 3:22 f) and not from other gods (Je 25:5 f). Conversion thus means that one accepts Yahweh's total supremacy in all phases of human life and activity and expects no lasting good from any other source.

The question arises whether the prophets always speak as if repentance and conversion are possible. The generally pessimistic tone of Amos is obvious, and perhaps from Amos alone we would not know that he is describing a fact, the obduracy of Israel, and not denying the theoretical possibility of conversion. Pessimism equally profound is expressed in Is 6:10, which makes the prophet's words the means by which conversion becomes less probable, and in Jeremiah's proverbial saying about the Ethiopian's skin and the leopard's spots (13:23). Even Hosea says that the deeds of Israel do not permit conversion; they have an apostate spirit and do not know Yahweh (5:4). Such pessimism is less characteristic of Hosea, who has drawn the brightest picture of repentance and conversion in the entire OT (Ho 2). He foresees the conversion of Israel after punishment (3:5) and the book closes with an invitation to repentance (14:2).

The fruits of repentance and conversion are the messianic salvation (Je 4:1), salvation (Is 30:15), deliverance from the evil planned by Yahweh (Je 26:3; 36:3). These latter passages must be read against the general context of the prophetic utterances on the reality and the mysterious power of sin. Deliverance does not imply an immediate change in the course of history; Israel by its sins has set evil in motion, and its repentance, while it assures survival and maintenance of union with Yahweh, does not have its fruits in the merely political and economic order. Repentance does mean that transgressions are blotted out (Is 44:22). Its interior character is described as a new heart and a new spirit which are created by Yahweh (Ps 51:12; Ezk 11:19; 18:31; 36:26). The wicked who turns from his evil way will live (Ezk 33:11).

Conversion is not always directly to Yahweh. It is conversion to righteousness (Ezk 18:21, 27; 33:9, 11, 12, 14). One returns to Yahweh by heeding His commandments (Dt 30:2, 10), by putting away foreign gods (1 S 7:13; 2 K 17:13).

In the Gk books of the OT conversion and repentance generally are seen in the framework of the earlier books. Repentance is the forsaking of sin (BS 48:15). Postponement of conversion runs the risk of sudden destruction (BS 5:7). One who is converted turns to God in his heart (BS 21: 6). Enoch is a pattern of repentance (44:16); this conclusion is a midrash* on Gn 5:22, 24; since all mankind before the deluge was wicked (Gn 6:5), Enoch must have been repentant. A new element is introduced in BS 17:24; WS 11:23; 12:10, 17; it is God who gives repentance or the way of repentance, leads men to repentance, gives an opportunity of repentance by judging only a little.

2. *In the NT*. In the NT repentance and conversion are much more prominent in the Gospels and in the apostolic preaching of AA than in the other books, and this emphasis must be reduced to the preaching of Jesus Himself. The preaching of John the Baptist was a call to repentance, and his baptism* was baptism of repentance (Mt 3:2–11; Mk 1:4–6; Lk 3:1–14). He demands repentance because the kingdom of God is at hand. Repentance is shown by baptism, confession of sins, and the production of fruits worthy of repentance. He imposes good works: alms given to the poor and the faithful execution of one's duty. Jesus alludes to John's call to repentance and charges the Pharisees with refusing to heed it (Mt 21:30, 32). The beginning of the preaching of Jesus is stated in the same formula as the preaching of John: repent and believe, for the kingdom is at hand (Mt 4:17; Mk 1:15). This message is easily understood against the OT background of repentance and conversion; it must have been more than slightly odious to the Pharisees, since the prophetic call to repentance was spoken to historically sinful Israel, the old Israel with which the Pharisees would not compare themselves. Therein lies the irony of Jesus' remark that He came to call not the righteous (i.e., those who refuse to admit their sinfulness) but sinners to repentance (Lk 5:32). He contrasts the repentance of Nineveh with the unrepentance of the Jews (Mt 12:39 ff; Lk 11:29–32), and finds the towns of Galilee less disposed to repentance than Tyre and Sidon, Sodom and Gomorrah (Mt 1:20–24; Lk 10:13–15). The first words of Peter in his own conversion were a confession that he was a sinner (Lk 5:8). The danger of perdition lies upon the unrepentant, and this means every one (Lk 13:3–5). The publican becomes righteous by confessing his sins (Lk 18:13 f), and there is joy in heaven at a repentant sinner more than there is for the righteous who do not need repentance; this is another piece of irony, for these are the "righteous" who fail

to recognize the need of repentance. Repentance is a genuine and total conversion; Jesus describes it as becoming like a child: repudiation of one's past and beginning a new life (Mt 18:3). It is evident that the call to repentance is fundamental in the preaching of Jesus; it implies the reality, the power, and the universality of sin, and the genuine, entire, and interior change of belief and attitude which is necessary to escape from sin. For it is a call to repent and to believe (Mk 1:15); one turns from sin by repentance and turns to the Father through Jesus Christ by faith.

The emphasis on repentance is continued in the early apostolic preaching as it is reported in AA (2:38; 3:19; 5:31; 8:22; 11:18; 17:30; 20:21; 26:20). The greatest discovery of this period was the perception of the truth that God has given repentance to the Gentiles as well as to the Jews (AA 11:18); this is the gospel which Paul preached (AA 20:21; 26:20). In Apc failure to repent is the dire step which leads to ultimate catastrophe (2:21 f; 9:20; 16:9, 11). Repentance is the return of the lost sheep to their shepherd and guardian (1 Pt 2:25).

Heb 6:1-6 denies the possibility of a second repentance for those who have once experienced conversion to God through Christ. The passage is the occasion of a celebrated theological discussion, and the question is usually solved by saying that Heb speaks of the fact rather than the possibility. This solution may oversimplify; the passage is in the same line of thought as the sin against the Holy Spirit which will not be forgiven (cf FORGIVENESS). Both passages warn against too facile a presumption of the mercy of God which would imply a denial of the seriousness of sin. In both passages the heinousness of the sin consists in its rejection of the very principle of life and salvation; it sunders man from God more effectively than man is sundered before his conversion, and that which rendered his first conversion possible is no longer a factor.

It seems somewhat strange that repentance and conversion should occupy a comparatively small position in the Pauline writings and the pastoral epistles. He observes that men are led to repentance by the goodness of God, but that they store up wrath by their refusal to repent (Rm 2:4 f). Failure to repent causes him to mourn (2 Co 12:21). God gives repentance and knowledge of the truth (2 Tm 2:25). Paul, however, has produced the most striking play on the word repentance in the entire Bible: sorrow which is from God produces salutary and "unrepentant" repentance (2 Co 7:10) i.e., repentance which is not subject to a change of heart. Behm has observed that in Paul repentance is submerged in faith*, which is the first fruit and the converse of repentance, the attitude by which one turns to God from sin. It may be noticed also that the epistles are addressed not to unbelievers who are called to repentance, but to churches which have accepted the gospel.

Rephaim (Hb $r^e p\bar{a}'im$, "ancestors"?), a proper name used in two senses in the OT.

1. One of the pre-Israelite peoples of Canaan. The inclusion of the Rephaim among the peoples conquered by Amraphel* and the other kings of the E (Gn 14:5) is probably an archaism, one of several in this chapter. In Dt they are identified with several other pre-Israelite peoples: they are the same as the people who lived in Moab called Emim* by the Moabites* (Dt 2:11); they are the Zamzummim* who inhabited the territory of Ammon* (Dt 2:20). They were also placed in Bashan* (Dt 3:13), and Og* is called the last survivor of the Rephaim (Dt 3:11; Jos 12:4; 13:12). They are also mentioned in the territory of Ephraim*, the only passage where their presence in W Palestine* is suggested (Jos 17:15). This wide distribution of the Rephaim casts some doubt on their identity as a distinct people, and the etymology of "ancestors," suggested by some scholars, gains some probability; all the pre-Israelite peoples of Canaan are "ancestors." Israelite tradition, unaware of the etymology, identified them with several of the peoples.

2. The Rephaim are also the dead, the inhabitants of Sheol*. They greet the coming of the great king to Sheol (Is 14:9). They do not rise (Is 26:14). They do not praise Yahweh (Pr 88:11). They quake at the conquering approach of Yahweh (Jb 26:5). They are in the house of Folly (Pr 9:18). The paths of the adulteress lead to the Rephaim (Pr 2:18), and he who wanders from wisdom will rest in their assembly (Pr 21:16). They are thus inactive; the Hb conception of death* is simply a negation of life. In Is 26:19 the Rephaim which rise are probably Israel restored from exile; cf the resurrection of the dead in Ezk 37 in the same sense.

The word in the same meaning (*rpum*) is found in Ugaritic* literature. The etymology of "ancestors" is even more plausible for this conception of Rephaim, and it is not impossible that the pre-Israelite people of Canaan is actually a creation of popular tradition by which the "shades" became an early tribe.

Rephidim (Hb $r^e p\hat{\imath}dim$, "plains"), a point on the journey of the Israelites from Egypt to Canaan where Moses provided water and where an engagement between Israel and the Amalekites* occurred; Moses prayed with extended arms during the entire battle (Ex 17; 19:2; Nm 33:14 f). The place cannot be located with any probability. The present form of the text has identified it with Massah* and with Meribah*; on the uncertainty of these sites cf these articles.

Resen (Hb *resen*, etymology uncertain), "the large city lying between Nineveh and Calah" built by Nimrod* (Gn 10:12). In spite of this precise datum, there is no identification of the place; Nineveh and its neighboring cities seem to have formed a large urban complex which cannot be sorted out.

Resh. The 20th letter of the Hb alphabet*, with the value of *r*.

Resheph (Hb *rešep*). This word appears as a proper name only in more recent Eng translations, and indeed in some passages of the OT it appears to have become a common name. In such phrases as "the reshephs of the bow," clearly arrows (Ps 76:4) and "the reshephs of passion are flaming reshephs" (SS 8:6), also clearly arrows, the word has become a common noun. In Hab 3:5, however, where *rešep* is one of the attendants of Yahweh in the theophany*, there is a personification. In Dt 32:34; Ps 78:48 the usual translation is "plague"; interpreters, however, point out a metaphor. The plague is the arrow or bolt of Yahweh. The sons of *rešep* which fly (Jb 5:7) have long been obscure, and commentators vary between "birds" and "sparks." There can be little doubt that the common noun is originally the proper name of an Asian god. In the 18th and 19th dynasties of Egypt, when several Asian gods received cult in Egypt, Resheph is mentioned with Astarte, who is certainly Canaanite; in inscriptions of Thutmose III and Amenhotep II (ANET 245, 246). Other Egyptian texts call Resheph "the great god, lord of heaven, ruler of the Ennead [the nine first gods of Egypt], lord of eternity" (ANET 250). Resheph is represented in Egyptian art with the Canaanite goddess Kadesh and the Egyptian god Min; he is armed with a spear (ANET 473, 474), or holds a spear and brandishes an ax (ANET 476). His pose and character are reminiscent of Hadad*; he appears to be a god of war and storms who brandishes the thunderbolt. The OT allusions suggest in addition a fiery character. This is reminiscent of the Gk Apollo, whose fiery bolts strike men and beasts with plague and pestilence. More proximately, Resheph is similar to the Mesopotamian Nergal, both a solar and a chthonic deity, who represents the noonday sun whose fiery darts are fatal. The "sons of Resheph" appear in a list of guilds at Ugarit. It is not clearly a divine name here, but the probability is solid; the character of the god, however, does not permit an identification of the trade; smiths or armorers are not unlikely.

Resurrection. The resurrection of the dead can be conceived in two ways: the restoration of a deceased person to the conditions of the present life or the conferring upon the deceased of a new and permanent form of life. It is the resurrection in the second sense which is properly the object of biblical belief. The resurrection in the first sense is stated or implied in a few passages.

1. *In the OT*. Resurrection as restoration of life. Resurrection in this sense can be found only in the stories of Elijah (1 K 17:17–24) and Elisha (2 K 4:18–37; 13:20 f). These episodes must be understood in the light of the literary character of the passages in which they are found; cf ELIJAH; ELISHA. In none of them is a genuine restoration of life obviously implied; in each no more than an apparent death recently supervened is described. When the entire absence of a conception of the resurrection in the early books of the OT is considered (cf below), it is unlikely that such a power would be so casually attributed to these prophets.

Resurrection to immortality. The absence of the resurrection in most of the OT is a part of the silence of the OT on the afterlife in any form. The Hb conception of man made it impossible for any idea of the afterlife to arise which was not a restoration of life to the body (cf LIFE; MAN; SOUL). The novelty of the belief makes its appearance all the more startling when it appears in the Maccabean period. Dn 12:2 presents a resurrection to life and to reproach in terms which imply that it is a belief already possessed. The belief is also attested in 2 Mc 7:9, 11, 23; 14:46, where it is clearly attested only of the righteous. From Josephus* and the NT we learn that the resurrection was believed by the Pharisees* but not by the Sadducees* and the Samaritans* (Mt 22:23; Mk 12:18; Lk 20:27; AA 23:8). It is also found in apocalyptic* literature.

The roots of the belief cannot be traced either in the OT or in extrabiblical religions. Passages in which the resurrection may be implied lack clarity. Ezk 37:1–14, the earliest of the passages in question, refers to the restoration of Israel under the image of the resurrection of the dead. A resurrection is not clearly affirmed of the Servant of Yahweh in Is 53:10–12, although some form of survival or of restoration of life seems intended by the language. The meaning of the survival is complicated here by the probability that the Servant* is not a purely individual figure and the survival may therefore be referred to Israel as a whole. Is 26:19 clearly mentions the resurrection of the dead; but this passage may be nearly as late as Dn (cf ISAIAH) or it may refer, like Ezk, to the restoration of Israel.

2. *In the NT*. Resurrection as restoration of life. Three of the miracles of Jesus are usually classified as resurrections: the daughter of Jairus (Mt 9:18–26; Mk 5:21–42; Lk 8:40–56), the son of the widow of Nain (Lk 7:11–17) and Lazarus* (Jn 11:1–44). The best witness, Jesus Himself, denied that the raising of the daughter of Jairus was a resurrection (Mt 9:39; Mk 5:24; Lk 8:52). The son of the widow of Nain should also most probably be classified as a cure; in ancient Palestine as in most of the modern Near East burial occurred on the day of death. The account of the raising of Lazarus must be treated by itself. The restoration of Eutychus* at Troas by Paul* is also more obviously a cure than a resurrection (AA 20:8–12).

The Resurrection of Jesus. (*a*) The event. The resurrection itself is not narrated in the NT; what is narrated is the empty tomb and the apparitions of the risen Jesus. The earliest literary witness of the NT is 1 Co 15:3–8. Modern critics also regard as extremely early those NT passages which are probably derived from credal formulae (AA 8:37; Rm 10:9; 1 Co 12:3) and from hymns and prayers of the primitive Christian liturgy (Eph 5:14; 1 Tm 3:16) and from the apostolic preaching* and catechesis (AA 2:24–28; 3:15, 26; 4:10, 33; 5:30 f; 10:41 f; 13:31–37; 17:3, 31; 26:22 f). These passages, which represent both the Palestinian and the Pauline preaching and catechesis, make it abundantly clear that the resurrection was a primary object of the apostolic proclamation from the very beginning. The Twelve must be witnesses of the resurrection (AA 1:22).

The gospel narratives exhibit a basic consistency joined with variations and uncertainties which have been celebrated in exegesis since the patristic period. There is substantial agreement in Mt 28:1–10; Mk 16:1–8; Lk 24:1–11 that the empty tomb was discovered by women; that the resurrection was announced to the women by a messenger (Mt), a youth (Mk), men (Lk); that Jesus Himself appeared shortly thereafter to the women; that the women announced the resurrection to the disciples. The names of the women are given with variations but no substantial disagreement by all three. This section is no doubt the

original core of tradition; beyond this each Gospel has features of its own. Mt has the guard at the tomb, the bribing of the soldiers, and the apparition on a mountain in Galilee. Lk has the apparition on the road to Emmaus* and to Simon, to the disciples in Jerusalem, and the ascension*. Mk 16:9–20, not originally a part of Mk, is compiled from Mt-Lk-Jn. Mt-Mk allude to an apparition in Galilee; Lk places the entire scene in Jerusalem. Jn mentions only Mary of Magdala at the tomb and as seeing the risen Jesus and as announcing the resurrection. Peculiar to Jn are the investigation of the tomb by Peter and the beloved disciple; the two Jerusalem apparitions on the day of the resurrection and one week later, with the episode of Thomas; the apparition by the Sea of Galilee with the catch of fish and the commission to Peter. A complete reconciliation of these accounts in all details is simply impossible and should not be attempted. In some instances the variations are due not simply to the flexibility of oral tradition but to theological interpretation; cf in particular ASCENSION; JOHN; LUKE and related articles.

In the synoptic tradition Jesus foretells His death and resurrection several times (Mt 16:21; 17:9; 17:23; 20:19; Mk 8:3; 9:9; 9:31; 10:34; Lk 9:22; 18:33). These predictions are accompanied by explicit notices that they were unintelligible to the disciples. In addition the resurrection accounts themselves emphasize the doubt and uncertainty of the disciples. The predictions show that Jesus Himself gave some explanation of the meaning of His death and resurrection in obscure terms; but these explanations were not comprehended at the time nor even in the resurrection itself. Clarity of insight is given the disciples only after Pentecost. Obscurity of understanding at the time of the resurrection is seen in one rather striking way: in four passages the witnesses fail to recognize the risen Jesus (Mk 16:12; Lk 24:16; Jn 20:14; 21:4). Evidently the resurrection of Jesus was not a return to His previous condition of life. Nor is Jesus seen by any who are not His disciples (with the exception of Paul).

These and related considerations have moved W. Grossouw to write that the risen Jesus (and the apparitions of the risen Jesus) is a supernatural reality which does not belong to this world and cannot be the object of historical investigation as such; He is exclusively an object of faith. The resurrection, he points out, is a real fact, but as a mystery of faith it is not a fact which can be demonstrated with certainty by the methods of historical investigation. History can demonstrate only the faith of the disciples in the resurrection. Grossouw here formulates the position which is more commonly maintained in modern interpretation. Many apologetic writers have presented the resurrection exclusively as the convincing demonstration of the claims of Jesus or of His divinity. Whatever may be the merits of this approach, it is not the NT approach to the resurrection. In the NT the resurrection is not an argument for faith but that which faith first apprehends, the risen and glorified Jesus. The resurrection is the climactic achievement in the saving deeds of God. To recognize the event as a fact is nothing; to accept it as a saving deed is to believe in it and to receive the salvation which is achieved by it. In Jn 20:29 it is faith in the resurrection, not observation of the fact, which is blessed by Jesus. The importance of the resurrection in the preaching and catechesis of the NT rests upon its theological significance.

(b) The theological significance of the resurrection of Jesus. In much theological literature since the 11th century (St. Anselm) the emphasis has been laid upon the redeeming death of Jesus. The theological need for this emphasis arose from the necessary effort to conceive the redemption as an act at once of justice and of grace; in achieving this conception the value of the resurrection as a saving act was somewhat obscured. It was in consequence of this obscurity that the resurrection, as noted above, came in more recent times to be considered primarily as an apologetic demonstration. In the NT, particularly in Paul, redemption is achieved by death and resurrection together; this is often explicit and always implicit.

The redemption, especially in the Pauline writings, is the work of the Father; and it is the Father who raised Jesus from the dead (Rm 4:24; 8:11; 10:9; 1 Co 6:14; 2 Co 4:14; 13:4; Gal 1:1; Eph 1:20; Phl 2:9; 1 Th 1:10; 1 Pt 1:21). The attribution of the resurrection to the Father is a part of the general attribution of the redemption to the Trinity of persons in their respective roles. The resurrection of Jesus places Him in a new life, and this new life comes from the Father who is the source of all life. Closely associated with the resurrection of Jesus is His exaltation and glorification; in some passages of the Synoptic Gospels the theme of exaltation appears without explicit mention of the resurrection. Christ raised from the dead sits at the right hand of the Father as intercessor (Rm 8:34). God has raised Him and exalted Him above all creatures (Eph 1:20). He receives honor from the Father after His resurrection (1 Pt 1:21). "Justified by the spirit" (1 Tm 3:16) is very

probably referred to the resurrection. Particularly emphatic is the hymn of Phl 2:9–11; God has exalted Him to a position where every creature must adore Him and confess that He is Lord*. Several passages connect the resurrection and the exaltation with the title of Lord in such a way as to suggest that Christ fully possesses the title through His resurrection and glorification (Rm 10:9; 14:9; Eph 1:21; Phl 2:7–11; Col 1:18). Paul declares that Christ is constituted son of God by the resurrection (Rm 1:4). Unless one wishes, as certain heretics have done, to understand these passages as meaning that Jesus received a personality which He did not possess in His incarnation, one must understand them to mean that the titles which signify His redeeming work are not fully verified in Him until He is raised to the right hand of the Father. Not until He has received the fullness of the life which is properly His as son of God and son of man, not until in His own person are exhibited the full fruits of the new life which He confers by His redeeming act, is the redemptive work complete and effective. He is the firstborn of those who rise (Col 1:18).

The saving effect of the resurrection as such is clearly stated; it is through the resurrection that Jesus communicates a new life to those who believe in Him. Jesus was delivered to death for our sins and rose for our righteousness (Rm 4:24 f). Baptism is burial with Christ in death, from which the Christian is raised to a new life like His, a life of freedom from sin; the Christian, like Christ, is dead to sin and lives to God (Rm 6:4–11). Christ was raised from the dead in order that we might bear fruit to God (Rm 7:4). Christ died for all that those who live might no longer live for themselves but for Him (2 Co 5:15). The new life is no longer the life of the individual Christian; Christ lives in him (Gal 2:20); the life of Jesus is visible in his body (2 Co 4:10). One who is united to (the risen) Christ is a new being (2 Co 5:17–21). The Christian is born anew to a life of hope through the resurrection of Jesus Christ (1 Pt 1:3–4). The Spirit*, the principle of the new life of the Christian, is not given until Jesus is raised and glorified (Jn 7:39; 16:7; 20:22). The spirit of Him who raised Jesus from the dead takes possession of the Christian, and He who raised Jesus gives life to our bodies through the spirit which possesses us (Rm 8:11).

The resurrection of Jesus is the principle of the resurrection of the Christian to the eternal life of glory. The Father who raised Jesus will also raise the Christian (2 Co 4:14). Paul wishes to know Jesus in His resurrection, to share His sufferings and death in the hope of attaining the resurrection (Phl 3:10). Those who die with Christ will live with Him (2 Tm 2:11). Jesus is the resurrection and the life and He will raise on the last day those who believe in Him (Jn 11:25; 6:39–44, 54). This theme receives its greatest elaboration in 1 Co 15. Paul resumes his gospel of the resurrection and the witnesses of the resurrection. The resurrection of Jesus and the future resurrection of the Christian are a testimonial that the Christian is liberated from sin. Christ is the first of the risen; men rise in Him as they died in Adam. The resurrection of the faithful completes the victory of Christ over sin and death. The resurrection is not a return to the conditions of the present life, but to a life of the spirit, the life already possessed by the risen Jesus and communicated from Him to those who believe in Him.

D. M. Stanley has pointed out that only in Eph-Col are the preceding two themes combined in the statement that the Christian is raised with Christ in the present existence. Christ is the firstborn of the dead; as He is the principle of creation*, so likewise is He the principle of the new life initiated by His own resurrection (Col 1:18). We are dead with Him and raised to life with Him (Col 2:12 f). God has not only made us live with Christ, but has raised us and made us sit with Him in heaven (Eph 2:5 f). It is Christ risen and exalted who is the head of the Church His body* and the principle of its life and unity. All these themes are thus summarized by D. M. Stanley: Salvation, originating in God the Father of Christ and the Christian, has been completely realized by Jesus Christ in His humanity, and through that humanity, now glorified, is in the process of realization in the Christian. Against this background the heresy that the resurrection has already occurred is viewed as pernicious (2 Tm 2:18).

The general resurrection. The Jewish belief in the general resurrection (cf above) is not emphasized in the NT. All the texts cited above deal with the resurrection of the Christian; for the rise to a new life in Christ alone deserves the name, and a resurrection to anything else is almost a contradiction in terms. The reward granted in the resurrection of the righteous reflects the Jewish rather than the Christian conception (Lk 14:14). A resurrection to life and to judgment is mentioned in Jn 5:28 f in terms which scarcely differ from the language of Dn 12:2; the same conception is reflected in 2 Co 5:10. Apc 20:5 f, 11–14 exhibits a curious idea of the resurrection of the righteous for 1000 years of life on earth, followed by a resurrection of the wicked for judgment which issues in the second death*.

This conception involves certain features of imagery which must be understood in their proper sense; cf MILLENNIUM.

Reuben (Hb *re'ûbēn*, etymology uncertain; in Gn 29:32 connected by assonance with *rā'āh be'ônî* "[God] has looked on my affliction"), eldest son of Jacob* and Leah* and one of the 12 tribes of Israel*. As the eldest son Reuben appears first in the enumeration of the sons of Israel (Gn 35:22; 46:8; Ex 1:2; 1 Ch 2:1). Reuben is prominent in the traditions of E and several anecdotes are preserved about him in Gn: the story of Leah and the mandrakes (30:14), his intervention to save the life of Joseph* (37:21 f, 29 f), his warning to his brothers that their troubles are a judgment for their cruelty to Joseph (42:22), and his offer of his own sons as surety for the safety of Benjamin (42:37). These anecdotes, which correspond in the Joseph story to the place of Judah in the J traditions, show Reuben in a favorable light. This is not true of the story of his incest with Bilhah*, the slave who substituted for Rachel* (35:22).

The clans of Reuben are enumerated in Ex 6:14; 1 Ch 5:1 ff. The territory of Reuben is defined in Jos 13:15–23; here and in other passages it is said to be N of the Arnon* (Dt 3:12, 16). With Gad* and Manasseh* it is involved in the agreement to aid in the conquest of W Palestine (Nm 32; Jos 1:12) and in the dispute about the altar (Jos 22). The territory of Reuben was one of the regions conquered by Hazael* (2 K 10:33) and the tribe of Reuben is mentioned among the Israelites deported by Tiglath-pileser* III of Assyria (1 Ch 5:26). In the song of Deborah* Reuben is accused of inaction, sitting at the sheepfolds debating while the battle was going on (Jgs 5:15 f). The Chronicler adds a note that Reuben warred against the nomad Hagrites* in the time of Saul and seized their territory (1 Ch 5:1–11).

There are a number of uncertainties in the tribal data. The importance of primogeniture was such that Reuben must have had some ancient claim to antiquity and preeminence; but the tribe is anything but preeminent in the traditions. In the blessing of Jacob it is unfavorably described as turbulent and the story of the incest is recalled (Gn 49:3 f). In the blessing of Moses it is described as failing and near extinction (Dt 33:6). The story of the incest hints at an explanation of the fall of the tribe from an earlier hegemony. Even the Chronicler essays an explanation of the depressed position of Reuben; the princedom of the tribes passed to Judah and the primogeniture passed to Joseph (1 Ch 5:1-11). The territory which is assigned to Reuben in the lists never appears as Reubenite in the passages where the boundary disputes between Israel and Moab are mentioned; the territory, claimed by Israel, is always referred to Gad* or Gilead*. This silence has led most historians to conclude that Reuben either lost the territory or had ceased to exist as a distinct tribe, perhaps as early as the 11th century. The notice of Jos 13:23 describing the territory of Reuben as "the Jordan and the boundary (?)" is not in harmony with the boundaries N of Moab and possibly indicates a displacement from the territory N of the Arnon. J. Bright has suggested that it was the invasion of Eglon* of Moab (Jgs 3) which wrecked Reuben as a tribe; Israel, however, repossessed the territory under the monarchy if not before. M. Noth has proposed a more complex theory. He suggests that the association of Reuben with Simeon* and Judah* (cf LEAH) and the occurrence of the name in the song of Deborah indicate that the original seat of Reuben lay in W Palestine near Judah and Benjamin. Its position as firstborn indicates that it was one of the older tribes which did not enter Canaan from Egypt. After some unmentioned disaster the tribe disintegrated and some elements settled N of the Arnon on the fringe of Israelite territory; but Noth believes that in the written traditions Reuben has no real territory. Against the W Palestinian origin may be urged the tradition which Reuben shares with Gad and Manasseh of an early pre-Israelite claim to its territory in E Palestine. But in any hypothesis it seems that the tribe, once large and distinguished, was sharply reduced and absorbed. The disaster which weakened it may perhaps be concealed under another form in the story of the rebellion of Dathan* and Abiram* (Nm 16); the rebels were of the tribe of Reuben, and the tribe may have been a victim of intertribal strife.

Reuel (Hb $r^{e\cdot}\hat{u}'\bar{e}l$, etymology uncertain). **1.** a clan of Edom* (Gn 36:4, 10, 13, 17; 1 Ch 1:35, 37. **2.** The name of the father-in-law of Moses in the J traditions (Ex 2:18; Nm 10:29).

Revelation. By the term "revelation" in this article is understood the self-manifestation of the divine; in speaking of the biblical background of the term one must go beyond the common theological definition of revelation as a divine speech attesting to a proposition. This self-manifestation is ultimately some kind of communication, but in the Bible it is not always the communication precisely of a proposition. No particular word or group of words in Hb or Gk can be set down as expressing the idea; revelation is a broad term which involves several related ideas; cf references below to related articles.

Some kind of revelation in the sense described above is found in all religions. Man regards the divine as "hidden" from normal experience, and the manifestation of the divine must then be an extraordinary event. The perception of the hidden divine reality is usually limited to certain chosen charismatic individuals who enjoy some special relationship with the divine. There is a tendency so general that it may be called universal to establish the revelation once received as a tradition, and in the course of time to codify the tradition.

In naturalistic polytheism the divine usually manifests itself first of all in nature, particularly in the more unusual and violent aspects of natural phenomena. These are conceived as personal actions and interpreted as revealing the personal attitude of the being or beings who produce the phenomena. This experience is really more the foundation of revelation than revelation itself; the exact interpretation of the events requires the revealing speech of a charismatic interpreter.

Revelation was the peak experience of the mystery* cults of the Hellenistic world. This revelation produced a vision, a direct experience of the divine in ritual and symbolism; actually the vision and the experience were a surrender to the forces of nature and to certain inner psychological impulses. In seeking the manifestation of the divine man usually satisfies his quest within himself and the world about him, and believes that the divine is best manifested in an integration of himself with nature. These remarks on the general character of revelation in religion will help to make clear the unique nature of biblical revelation. The religions of the ancient world practiced in the cultures which ancient Israel knew best conceived revelation as obtained through divination* and through participation in the myth* and ritual of fertility.

1. *In the OT.* Early Israelite religion exhibits regular channels through which the divine will may be ascertained which have some superficial resemblance to the arts of divination. Thus the Israelites placed some store by signs and omens (Gn 24:12 ff; 25:21 ff; Jgs 6:36 ff; 1 S 15:27 ff). The ambiguous function of the seer was at least in part to answer questions by occult means (1 S 9:6 ff; 9:15 ff; 2 S 24:11; cf PROPHET). The dream* was sometimes a means of divine communication. The oracular device of Urim and Thummim* was used. It should be noticed that these devices are found in the primitive phase of Hb belief and practice, that they occur in isolated instances, and that they appear to represent an unenlightened early belief. They are not a part of the revelation which is characteristic of the OT and the NT (cf below), and they disappear with the growth of Israelite religion.

A fundamental presupposition of OT revelation is that Yahweh is a living God (Dt 5:23; Jos 3:10; Is 37:4 +). His vitality stands precisely in opposition to the confused identification of foreign gods with their images, which the Israelites scornfully point out can neither speak nor act. The vitality of Yahweh is perceived in His words and His actions, which are His self-manifestation, His revelation. All ancient gods were anthropomorphic, and of this the Israelites were aware; Yahweh is anthropomorphic* in the OT, but He is still totally unlike man and is a personal reality who is unique; the gods of the nations do not exist. Israel knows this distinct and highly personal being because He has manifested Himself as personal. This self-manifestation may be distinguished in several steps without attempting to determine which step is logically prior.

Yahweh manifests Himself as the lord of history; this does not mean that man is not a free agent, but that history moves toward a term which Yahweh intends. He directs its movements, even when man is opposed to His purpose, in such a way that His end is attained. The fundamental event of history in which Yahweh manifests Himself as lord is the exodus* of Israel from Egypt. In this event appears His power and His will to save Israel; this event occurs that even Egyptians may know "that I am Yahweh" (Ex 14:18). The manifestation of Yahweh as the savior in history is often recalled by the prophets (Je 7:22; Ho 11:1; Am 2:10); they need not present a new self-manifestation of Yahweh, but they only have to remind Israel that Yahweh has already made Himself known. His lordship is reaffirmed in the events contemporary to the prophet (Is 7:1–9; 8:1–4; 10:5 ff).

Yahweh also manifests Himself as creator and lord of nature (cf CREATION). The typical poetic form in which Yahweh's manifestation in nature is conceived is the theophany*. The presence and activity of Yahweh in nature is universal; all phenomena of nature are produced by Him. Israelite belief in the manifestation of Yahweh in nature is distinguished from naturalistic polytheism not only by the unity of Yahweh, but also by the fact that His manifestation in nature is one with His manifestation in history; in each sphere He manifests the same qualities and the same moral will. When nature is convulsed at His appearance at Sinai, it is at His coming to reveal Himself in the covenant* (Ex 10:16). The theophany reveals Him as the defender of Israel and the judge of His enemies.

Yahweh reveals Himself in judgment*; this is a particular aspect of His self-manifestation in history. He appears in the fall of nations (Is 13; Je 25:12 ff; Am 1:3–2:3). He is revealed in His judgment upon Israel even more clearly than in His judgments upon the nations, for His integrity as judge appears nowhere more clearly than in the sentence pronounced upon the people of election. Ezekiel in pronouncing judgment upon Israel repeats the refrain that Yahweh does these acts of judgment in order that the Israelites may know that He is Yahweh, that it is Yahweh who acts, that Yahweh is holy (Ezk 6:14; 7:9, 27; 11:12; 12:20; 13:23 +).

The revelation of Yahweh is ultimately destined for all peoples through Israel (Is 2:2–4 = Mi 4:1–3). Indeed all peoples experience the self-manifestation of Yahweh in history and nature, but they have not the peculiar manifestation of Himself to Israel in election* and covenant. In particular they do not have the "word" of Yahweh; and it is the word* which makes it impossible to reduce the self-manifestation of Yahweh to His deeds in history and in nature, as some interpreters seem to do. The deeds of Yahweh need an interpreter; and in Israel one may distinguish a triple stream of revelation which interprets His deeds.

Moses* stands at the head of this triple stream in an unparalleled position of face to face communication with Yahweh (Ex 33:11; Nm 12:6 ff; Dt 34:10). The first of the streams is law*, the revelation of the covenant will of Yahweh establishing standards of conduct for Israel. History and nature alone do not manifest the moral imperative which Yahweh lays upon Israel; this is explicitly stated by the founder of Israel as the community of Yahweh. Of the three this source is the best example of revelation preserved in tradition and codified in writing (cf LAW). Moses had no successor, but the priests as the interpreters of the law were spokesmen of the revealed will of Yahweh.

The second stream is prophecy*. Revelation in prophecy is normally conceived as the reception of the word. The prophet experiences the present activity of Yahweh in history and nature and interprets the deeds of Yahweh according to the word which is given him, the mystic intuition of the present divine reality. He discloses according to the word the will of Yahweh for Israel in the present and the plans of Yahweh for the destiny of Israel in the future, and gives directions how Israel must submit itself to these plans.

The third stream, and perhaps the weakest as revelation, is wisdom*. Wisdom, however, is also a charisma and it is the gift of Yahweh. It does not deal with cosmic and historical events, but with the will of Yahweh as it governs the ordinary events of the life of the individual person. This revelation is more strongly the preservation of a tradition than even the law*. Thus in all three of these sources revelation, the self-manifestation of Yahweh as lord of history, creator and lord of nature, and source of law and wise conduct, is seen to be the governing factor of Israelite life and belief to the point where there is no other factor. Human intelligence and prudence best fulfill themselves by learning what Yahweh is. Thus the result of revelation in the OT is knowledge* which is not the philosophical knowledge of understanding but the knowledge of the living and active personal reality of Yahweh, experience of Yahweh as He is and as He acts.

2. *In the NT*. I. Synoptic Gospels. The Synoptics really do not seem to consider the idea of revelation formally, and it is clear from the other NT writings as well as from the Synoptics themselves why they do not; Jesus is the self-manifestation of God, and in relating His life, death and resurrection they propose the ultimate in revelation. This is seen in the symbolic story of the baptism of Jesus (Mt 3:13–17; Mk 1:9–11; Lk 3:21–22). When Jesus first appears before the public the heavens are opened and the voice of the Father, the voice which spoke the word of Yahweh in the OT, is heard authenticating Jesus as His Son, and at the same time the Spirit becomes visible, the Spirit which Jesus communicates to those who believe in Him. When one considers the quality of the law as the fundamental revelation of the OT, one appreciates the words of Jesus when He says that He comes to fulfill the law; He thereby asserts a position of equality with the law and with Moses (Mt 5:17–20). He proposes Himself as that which the ancients desired to see and hear and did not (Mt 13:16 f; Lk 10:23 f). He not only continues the prophets, but He is the full revelation which the prophets foretold. One who accepts Him as the Christ does it in virtue of a revelation received from the Father (Mt 16:17). The most formal text concerning revelation is found in Mt 11:25–27; Lk 10:21 f: Jesus has received all things from the Father; He alone knows the Father, and no one can know the Father except through the revelation of the Son. Jesus is the revelation of the Father.

I. AA and Epp. In the preaching of the apostles the revelation of God lies in their own gospel* and their preaching*; in these God manifests Himself. The preaching is the gospel of Jesus Christ, the story of His life, death, and resurrection. In Jesus the revelation of the OT reaches its fullness; that which God spoke through the prophets He has made entirely clear in His Son (AA 3:17–26; 10:36–43; Heb 1:1; 1 Pt 1:11 f). In addressing Jews the apostles found it necessary to emphasize the continuity of the revelational process through Moses and the prophets to Jesus.

Paul finds it necessary to insist on the divine origin of the gospel which he preaches. It comes to him from the revelation of Jesus Christ (Gal 1:12, 16); it is not the word of man but the word of God (1 Th 2:13). It is the gospel which he has received from the Lord (1 Co 15:1 ff; 11:23). Revelation is the faith, that which is believed (Gal 3:23); it is the teaching of the apostles (Rm 6:17; 16:17). That which is revealed is the mystery*, the divine plan of salvation (Rm 16:25 f; Col 1:26, made known through the spirit to the apostles and prophets, Eph 3:3, 5). For Paul also Jesus is revelation; but by a kind of inversion he sees the incarnation as a concealment of the divine which is at once a revelation of the divine (Rm 8:3; Gal 4:4; Phl 2:7). This is similar to the paradox by which he makes revelation consist in the mystery, and adds a new note; the revelation of the divine is always less than the total reality.

Paul likewise speaks of "private" revelations to himself (2 Co 12:1–7; Gal 2:2) and expects that Christians also will experience revelations which will give them a deeper understanding of the gospel (Eph 1:17; Phl 3:5). These personal revelations are mystical insights which refer to the individual; they are not the type of self-manifestation of the divine which occurs in the incarnation, the prophets, the apostolic teaching and preaching. But they aid the preacher; the charismata of knowledge, prophecy, and teaching aid the Church (1 Co 14:6, 26, 30).

The Epp look to an eschatological revelation which will complete the self-manifestation of God. The coming of Jesus in the Parousia reveals Him more fully than He is revealed in the incarnation (1 Co 1:7; 2 Th 1:7; 1 Pt 1:7, 13). This is also the moment when the glory of the Christian is fully revealed (Rm 8:18–21; 1 Pt 1:5; 4:13; 5:1). By a transfer of the term to a similar manifestation Paul speaks not only of the revelation of wrath (Rm 1:18) but even of the revelation of Antichrist* (2 Th 2:3, 6, 8).

In Rm 1:19 f Paul seems to speak of what theologians call a "natural" revelation. In the OT Yahweh manifests Himself in nature, and so also He does for Paul, and in such a way that His essential divinity cannot be mistaken. The same kind of "natural" revelation is extended to the law; the Gentiles do not know the law, but they have it in their hearts and thus are informed of their obligations. A similar conception, influenced by Gk philosophy, appears in WS 13; more precisely, the author of WS states that observation of nature should show the pagans that natural forces, and still less idols, are not the divinity which is manifested in nature. In fact this passage shows how sharply Paul distinguishes between revelation and the knowledge which arises from the manifestation of God in nature and in man. Revelation is Jesus Christ, the fulfillment of prophecy and law, the wisdom and the power of God; it is the gospel of the cross, unintelligible to human wisdom; it is the mystery of the divine will and plan of salvation, the thoughts of God revealed by the spirit of God and understood only by the spiritual men; it is the mind of Christ (1 Co 1:17–2:16, which is perhaps the most formal passage dealing with revelation in the Pauline Epp).

II. Jn. In the Johannine writings the idea of revelation seems to be more consciously exhibited than in the other NT writings. Jesus is the self-manifestation of God; no NT passage states this so simply and so sublimely as the Johannine title of word (Jn 1:1 ff). Jesus is the Only-Begotten who declares God, unseen by men (Jn 1:17 f), and the apostles declare the word of life which they have heard and seen, the Word who is and imparts life, who has manifested Himself (1 Jn 1:1 f). But in Jn Jesus is not only the revelation, He is the revealer. He who has come down from heaven speaks what He knows and attests what He has seen (Jn 3:11–13, 31–33). The word of Jesus is the word of Him who sent Jesus (Jn 5:24). One who comes to Him hears the Father's voice and is taught of God (Jn 6:45 f). The teaching of Jesus is not His own, but the teaching of God who sent Him (Jn 7:16 f). He proclaims the truth which He has heard spoken by the one who sent Him (Jn 8:26); He speaks what He has seen with the Father (Jn 8:38). The Father who sent Him commands Him what to say (Jn 12:49). Who sees Jesus sees the Father, for He and the Father are in each other (Jn 14:10 f). The spirit completes the revelation of Jesus; He will teach the apostles everything (Jn 14:26); He will teach them all truth, the truth which He has heard (Jn 16:13). This emphasis in Jn no doubt arises from some peculiar need of the Christian communities of the time and place where the gospels arose, and it does not seem difficult to find this need in the rise of

pseudo-revelation and pseudo-prophecy which claimed to enlarge or to change the revelation of the Gospel and the preaching. Jn responds by reiterating the unique sonship of Jesus, who is the self-manifestation of the Father. This sonship is the origin of what the apostles teach, and to attempt to propose anything in addition is to claim a relation to God which belongs to Jesus alone. The emphasis of Jn is stated more briefly in Mt 11:27 ff; Lk 10:21 f (cf above), and is altogether in harmony with the apostolic teaching of other books of the NT.

Revenge. Cf AVENGER.

Rezin (Hb $r^e\hat{s}\hat{\imath}n$, Akkadian *rasunnu*, etymology uncertain), Aramaean king of Damascus. In 735 bc he formed an alliance with Pekah* of Israel against Judah, then ruled by Jotham*, to compel Judah to join a coalition against Assyria. Jotham died very shortly afterwards, and his successor Ahaz* offered tribute to Tiglath-pileser* III of Assyria and asked for assistance. The Assyrians defeated both Israel and Damascus and Rezin was killed (2 K 15:37; 16:5–9). Isaiah predicted the defeat of Rezin and Pekah but urged faith instead of alliance with Assyria (Is 7:1–8; 8:6). The records of Tiglath-pileser III, which are not complete, claim less of a victory than 2 K 16:9 attributes to him; he relates that he conquered and looted some of the territory of Damascus.

Rezon (Hb $r^e z\hat{o}n$ [not the same as Rezin*]), a rebel and bandit leader who established himself as king of Damascus* in the time of Solomon (1 K 11:23–25). The ascription to him of the sovereignty over Edom* is suspicious and some data have possibly been omitted in the compilation of the material which would refer this item to another person.

Rhegium (Lt *rhegium*, Gk *rhēgion*, meaning uncertain), a seaport of S Italy on the Italian side of the Straits of Messina. The ship bearing Paul touched there on the voyage after his shipwreck (AA 28:13). The name survives in the modern Reggio di Calabria.

Rhoda (Gk *rhoda*, "rose"), the slave of Mary the mother of John Mark* who answered Peter's knock when he was released from prison (AA 12:13 ff).

Riblah (Hb *riblāh*, meaning uncertain), a city in Syria. It is identified with the modern Rableh, a village on the right bank of the Orontes about 25 mi S of Homs. No traces of the ancient city have been found. In the last years of the kingdom of Judah it appears as an important military base. It was held by the Pharaoh Necho* and it was there that he imprisoned Jehoahaz* (2 K 23:33). It was the base from which Nebuchadnezzar* conducted his campaign against Judah and Jerusalem; he did not attend the siege of Jerusalem in person. Sentence was executed upon Zedekiah*, and the sons of the king and a number of officers and people of Judah were executed at Riblah in the presence of Nebuchadnezzar (2 K 25:6, 20 f; Je 39:5 f; 52:9 f, 26 f). Riblah is mentioned as a frontier point of Israel in Nm 34:11, but many critics suspect the text at this point.

Riddle (Hb *ḥîdāh*). The riddle is a favorite form of the wise saying (cf WISDOM). It was a mark of genuine wisdom to couch one's saying in an obscure form which aroused the curiosity of the listener and impressed the lesson by forcing the hearer to search out the meaning, or to admit his ignorance by asking the explanation. It was therefore a mark of wisdom to solve the riddle, and it seems that the discussion of the sages often consisted in duels of wit in which riddles were exchanged. Although the characters involved are not sages, such an exchange occurs at the wedding of Samson*, who proposes a wager to his groomsmen that they cannot solve his riddle (Jgs 14:12). When they extort its solution from his bride, their answer takes the form of another riddle (Jgs 14:18). The queen of Sheba tested Solomon by riddles (1 K 10:1; 2 Ch 9:1). The wisdom literature contains sayings which appear to be the answer to riddles such as "What is like X?" or "Why is X like Y?"; cf Pr 11:22; 27:3, 8. Pr 30:15a is a riddle as it stands. A paradoxical saying like Pr 26:4, "Answer a fool according to his folly; do not answer a fool according to his folly" implies a riddle which demands an explanation. Numerical climactic sayings such as Pr 30:15b–16, 18–19, 21–23, 24–28, 29–31 likewise imply riddles. The riddle of Ps 49:5 is doubtless the prosperity of the wicked, with which the Ps is concerned. The riddle of Ezk 17:2 is the allegory of the eagle and the vine; the listener should be able to identify the persons veiled under the allegory. In Pr 1:6; Ps 78:2 the riddle practically becomes equivalent to wise saying. The "scornful riddle" of Hab 2:6 is a veiled insult. Moses is distinguished from other prophets in that Yahweh speaks to him plainly and not in riddles (Nm 12:8). In the late passage Dn 8:23 the riddle has become a wily or devious saying, not far removed from the lie.

Righteous, Righteousness. 1. *In the OT.* There is no single Hb word to express our idea of justice; what is meant by justice is contained in the concepts of judgment* and righteousness. The concept of righteousness (Hb *ṣedek, ṣᵉdākāh* and cognate words) is somewhat complex and a summary survey of its usage will best elucidate its content. The basic meaning of the word perhaps appears best when it is applied to things such as a weight (Dt 25:15; Lv 19:36; Jb 31:6; Ezk 45:10); a "righteous" weight is one which is what it is supposed to be. A straight path goes in the right direction (Ps 23:3); correct sacrifices are those which are offered according to cultic prescriptions (Dt 33:19; Ps 4:6; 51:21). The righteous seed which Yahweh raises for David is probably a legitimate seed (Je 23:5). Here appears the common element of righteous: that which meets a standard. Yahweh gives rain in righteousness (Jl 2:23), i.e., in the right time and measure. The sanctuary is made righteous (Dn 8:14), i.e., purified for divine worship.

In common usage the word group *ṣedek* etc is applied to legal processes, and the legal meaning usually underlies its application to other situations; it is in this usage that it is often best translated by *just* or *justice*. Judges should judge not with partiality but with justice (Lv 19:15; Dt 1:16). Their verdicts should be just (Pr 31:9; Dt 16:18, 20), and the decrees of rulers should be just (Pr 8:15). Malfeasance of legal process throws justice to the ground (Am 5:7) and turns its fruit to poison (Am 6:12). Hence one who sues at law believes that he has a "righteousness," a just claim, a *right* (Pss 7:9; 17:1; 18:21, 25; Is 59:4; Je 51:10). This claim or right stands in opposition to the lie (Ps 37:6). Job clings to his just cause as his security with God (Jb 27:6), and one who asks for mercy does not urge his claim (2 S 19:29). Perversion of justice distorts just cases, rights (Is 5:23).

Hence one who has *ṣedek* or is *ṣaddîk* is in the right, whether legally (Ex 23:7 f; Dt 25:1; 2 S 15:4; 1 K 8:32; Pr 17:15, 26; 18:5, 17; 24:24; Is 5:23; 29:21; Am 2:6; 5:12) or in some other context (1 S 24:18; Jb 27:5; 32:1). "Righteousness" means innocence of a charge, in law or in some other situation, or absence of any charge (Gn 20:4; 44:16; 2 S 4:11; 1 K 2:32). The afflictions of Job are conceived in primitive wisdom thinking as evidence that he is guilty before Yahweh (cf JOB), and Job reiterates his righteousness, his innocence (Jb 9:2, 15, 20; 10:15; 13:18; 33:12; 34:5), and Elihu desires to declare Job innocent (Jb 33:32). The Servant* of Yahweh, whose afflictions likewise make it appear that Yahweh is his enemy, will be proved innocent (Is 53:11). Tamar* is "more righteous" than Judah, i.e., less guilty (Gn 38:26), and Israel has been more righteous than Judah in the same sense (Je 3:11; Ezk 16:52). Neither the nations nor Israel have a just case against Yahweh (Is 43:9, 26).

Since righteousness in these uses is measured by the standard of law, law itself can be called "righteousness," especially the law of Yahweh (Ps 119:7, 62 +), and righteousness i.e., justice is a property of law (Dt 4:8). But more frequently righteousness is viewed as a personal quality which should be found in the king, who is the source of law and the administration of justice (2 S 23:3). The throne is established by righteousness (Pr 16:12; 25:5). The good king loves righteousness (Ps 45:8); the bad king, Jehoiachim*, builds his palace in injustice (Je 22:13). To "do righteousness" (cf below) has a peculiar force when it is said of a king (Je 22:15), for it refers to his administration of justice. Righteousness was found in the greatest of Israelite kings, David (2 S 8:15; 1 K 3:6) and Solomon (1 K 10:9). But it is especially envisaged as a quality of the ideal or messianic king (Ps 72:1–3; Is 9:6; 11:4 f; 16:5; Je 23:5; 33:15; Ezk 45:9). The emphasis on this quality in the ideal king no doubt reflects its frequent and glaring absence in the ordinary royal and judicial administration of the later period of the monarchy of Judah.

Since ṣedek is a quality rooted in law and found most properly in the makers and the administrators of law, it easily develops the meaning of conduct in accordance with the law; this is the sense which is most properly rendered by the English translation "righteous, righteousness." ṣedek as right conduct is opposed to sin, wickedness, etc. Jerusalem, the city of righteousness, was formerly the place where righteousness lodged (Is 1:21, 26). To seek righteousness is parallel in poetry with "seek Yahweh," for it is through good conduct that Yahweh is to be found (Is 51:1; Zp 2:3). More specifically right conduct is honesty as opposed to deception and truthfulness as opposed to mendacity (Gn 30:33; Je 4:2). To "do righteousness" is usually righteous conduct in general and not the administration of justice (Gn 18:19; Ps 106:3; Pr 21:3; Is 56:1; 58:2). The righteous is the man who serves God (Mal 3:18). The righteous lives by his fidelity (cf FAITH). It is a perversion of cosmic order when the righteous perishes in his righteousness (Ec 7:15). Yahweh rewards a man according to his righteousness (2 S 22:25). Righteousness saves from death (Pr 10:2); life is found in its path (Pr 12:28); it wins a crown (Pr 16:31). Yah-

weh wishes that in Israel judgment* should roll like water, and righteousness like a perennial stream (Am 5:24); judgment and righteousness here are right conduct in opposition to the cult performed with mechanical exactness but no inner devotion. God does not turn His favorable gaze away from the righteous (Jb 36:7); He blesses the righteous (Ps 5:13), He makes the righteous stand firm (Ps 7:10). The use of the ṣedek wordgroup in the sense of good moral conduct is extremely common in the Pss and in the wisdom literature; but it is not limited to later books.

The use of ṣedek to mean good conduct in a few passages exhibits an idea which is more fully developed elsewhere. Thus it has been noticed that the context often shows that the word means a right or a claim; ṣedek as the means of salvation in Ezk 14:14, 20 is good conduct which establishes a claim upon Yahweh to deliver one from evil. When Abraham's faith is reckoned to him as righteousness (Gn 15:6), this implies that his faith is not only the proper attitude of response to the promises of Yahweh, but that it also establishes a title to their fulfillment. Elsewhere right conduct implies salvation (cf below); this is probably meant in the fields or dwellings of righteousness (Je 31:23; 50:7). The play on the word is clear in Ho 10:12; Israel is to sow ṣedek, right conduct, and Yahweh will rain ṣedek, salvation; cf righteousness as a means of salvation in Pr 11:4–6. When Yahweh restores to a man his ṣᵉdākāh, He restores him to the wellbeing which is the proper condition of the righteous.

Here we have the transition to the numerous passages in which ṣedek etc. can be translated simply as salvation, deliverance, vindication. When one has a just claim or a right, or when one is charged, the process by which his right is established or his innocence vindicated is not only justice under the law, it is also personal salvation. With this element we meet the more properly theological use of the ṣedek group; for this righteousness is the work of Yahweh who intervenes to establish or to bestow "righteousness," salvation. The "righteous dwelling" of Job is the dwelling which God protects (Jb 8:6). The friends of the Psalmist are happy at his vindication (Ps 35:27); he will see the countenance of Yahweh in ṣedek i.e., when he is saved (Ps 17:15). Indeed the word is often used with salvation* in synonymous parallelism. In particular ṣedek designates the messianic salvation (Is 24:16; 45:8, 25; 54:14; 58:8; 62:1). Yahweh is our salvation, ṣedek (Je 23:5). The priests are clothed with ṣedek, salvation, parallel to joy (Ps 132:9); the gates of ṣedek are the gates of salvation (Ps 118:19). The fruit of ṣedek and judgment is well-being and security (Is 32:17). The work of the Servant of Yahweh is to deliver many (Is 53:11). When the messianic king appears, he will be "righteous," victorious (Zc 9:9).

Against this background the attribute of righteousness in Yahweh is to be conceived. The legal quality of righteousness appears in Yahweh also, for He is a just judge (2 Ch 12:6; Jb 8:3; 34:17; Pss 7:10; 11:7; Is 10:22; 28:17; Je 11:20; Zp 3:5). He is just and fair also in His general administration; the "righteousness" proper to the king is found in an eminent degree in Yahweh (Dt 32:4; Ps 119:137; Jb 36:3; Is 5:16). Hence the law of Yahweh is called simply "righteousness" (Ps 119:142).

By far the larger number of applications of the ṣedek word group to Yahweh signify His "righteousness" as a saving attribute, His saving power and will. The righteousness of the salvation which He works (cf above) is transferred to Him, its agent. Yahweh shows Himself righteous in effecting deliverance, in vindicating His people. Since the deliverance is a fulfillment of His promises*, "righteousness" is often combined in these passages with fidelity; cf FAITH. These two qualities are personified as His attendants (Ps 85:11–14). They are the foundations of the throne of Yahweh, as they are the foundations of the throne of a human king; but in Yahweh they are conceived as saving attributes (Ps 97:2). He calls His Servant and Cyrus in ṣedek, in His will to save (Is 42:6; 45:13). His righteous hand is His saving hand (Is 41:10). This saving attribute is combined with love, fidelity, and judgment (Ps 36:7), with power (Ps 71:19), with blessing (Ps 24:6), with healing (Mal 3:20). It is celebrated by those who experience it (Pss 22:32; 40:11; 51:16; 71:15–16; 89:17). The "righteousnesses" of Yahweh is His saving deeds either in the historic experience of Israel or of the individual or in the messianic future (Jgs 5:11; 1 S 12:7; Ps 103:6; Is 45:24; Dn 9:16; Mi 6:5). Cf also Pss 31:2; 35:24, 28; 36:11; 40:10; 48:11; 50:6; 97:6; 103:17; Pr 8:18; Is 1:27; 42:21; 46:13; 51:5; 54:17; Mi 7:9; Zc 8:8. A number of other instances can be adduced; but these are sufficient to illustrate the use of the term, which is common in Is 40–66 and in texts which are contemporary or later. This development of the term, while it is not unknown in earlier literature, seems to have become a set epithet of Yahweh only in exilic and postexilic literature.

This summary shows that the idea which we translate somewhat inaccurately as "righteous" is complex and that it must be read in its context. It must be remembered that this complex development is the background of the still more complex NT use of the corresponding Gk word.

2. *In the NT.* The Gk words in the NT are the adjective *dikaios*, the noun *dikaiosynē*, the verb *dikaiûn*, the noun *dikaiōma*, the product of the verb, and the noun *dikaiōsis*, the process. In most instances these words are used either in the OT senses noticed above or with a transformation through some specifically Christian idea. Thus "righteous" means "innocent" (Mt 27:4, 19; Lk 23:47); the parallels to "innocent" in Lk 23:47 (Mt 27:54; 15:39) have "son of God," but it is doubtful that Lk intends "righteous" as synonymous with this title; cf, however, the messianic use of the word righteous below. The adjective appears in the meaning it has in daily use in Mt 20:4; Lk 12:57; Phl 1:7; Col 4:1; 2 Pt 1:13 i.e., right, proper etc; but even this sense receives a Christian modification in AA 4:19; Eph 6:1; 2 Th 1:6 by the addition of "before God," "with God," and by the addition that what is righteous is the divine law. The judgments of God are just (1 Pt 2:23; Apc 16:7; 19:2). The righteous is frequently the man of good moral conduct (Mk 2:17; Lk 5:32, but the word is used here with irony; Mt 5:45; 13:49; 23:28; 25:37, 46; Lk 15:7; 18:9; 20:20; the righteous are opposed to the wicked in the eschatological judgment; Heb 12:23; Js 5:16; 1 Pt 3:12; 4:18; Apc 22:11). Lk 14:14 and AA. 24:15 allude to two different conceptions of the resurrection* which appear in Judaism, one limiting the resurrection to the righteous and the other extending it to the wicked as well. The triple repetition of the adjective in Mt 10:41 may not be insignificant; "the righteous" in whose name the cup of water is given is possibly God. A specifically NT usage appears in the designation of Jesus the Messiah as "the righteous one" (AA 3:13 f; 7:52; Js 5:6; 1 Pt 3:18). These contexts, which allude to the death of Jesus, no doubt emphasize His innocence; but they also hint at His vindication and His triumph, particularly 1 Jn 2:1, where Jesus is called righteous and glorified.

The "righteousness" which Jesus must fulfill (Mt 3:15) is that which is required. The righteousness which is the object of hunger and thirst (Mt 5:6) appears in the context of the other beatitudes to be good deeds; by itself the line could indicate the saving will or the judgment of God. The salvation of the kingdom appears to be meant by its righteousness in Mt 6:33. The righteousness of which Jesus convinces the world is His own vindication by His ascent to the Father (Jn 16:8, 10). Is 32:17, "the effect of righteousness (salvation) is well being," is quoted or alluded to in Heb 12:11; Js 3:18. Righteousness is good conduct in Mt 5:10, 20; 6:1; Lk 1:75; AA 10:35; 13:10; 24:25; 2 Pt 2:5, 21. In other passages the NT transformation of the word which is so radical in Paul (cf below) appears in an initial form. Deliverance from sin to live to righteousness (1 Pt 2:24) sounds like an echo of Paul; righteousness is the peculiarly Christian state of moral goodness and deliverance from sin (= salvation) conferred by Jesus. So also the dwelling of righteousness in Christians (2 Pt 3:13) suggests the saving work of Jesus. Noah, partaker of the righteousness which comes from faith (Heb 11:7), is granted in Heb the position which Abraham has in Rm and Gal. The Christian who "does righteousness," an OT phrase, is righteous as Jesus is righteous (1 Jn 3:7); and this righteousness is specified in 1 Jn 3:10 as the love of one's brother. In Js 1:20 the righteousness of God is His justice.

The verb *dikaiûn* in Apc 22:11 means to act righteously, a singular use. Elsewhere outside the Pauline writings it means, to declare (God) righteous (Lk 7:29), to be proved right (Mt 11:19; Lk 7:35; Rm 3:4, quoting Ps 50:6) and it is used in a popular forensic sense in Lk 10:29; 16:15. It means to be acquitted (Mt 12:37). Lk 18:14, however, approaches the Pauline use, to be delivered from sin. The hymn of 1 Tm 3:16 uses the word of Jesus, elsewhere in the NT "the righteous one" (cf above); Jesus is proved righteous in the spirit, probably proved by His resurrection* to be what He claimed.

The noun *dikaiōma* means a law (Lk 1:6; Rm 1:32; 2:26; 8:4; Heb 9:1, 10), a saving deed of God (Apc 15:4), or the righteous acts of the righteous (Apc 19:8). In Rm 5:18 it designates the death of Jesus, which is both a righteous deed and a saving deed.

Paul. The concept of "righteous" is perhaps the most complex of all the Pauline ideas; the concept of "justification" was one of the key points of Luther's teaching which was controverted by the Council of Trent. Here the exposition must be limited to a summary analysis of the Pauline usage.

Paul employs the words in a neutral sense, as in "the weapons of righteousness" (2 Co 6:7); "innocent" (1 Co 4:4). He found himself with an OT vocabulary which had to be expanded to fit the fullness of his insight into the Christian mystery; he develops the OT righteousness to a point where it acquires a content which without the OT background seems entirely new. He knows that righteousness is observance of the law, morally right conduct (Rm 2:13; 10:5). A problem arises from the conversion of the Gentiles without observance of the law; plainly they do not achieve the traditional righteousness, but they must be nevertheless righteous. Hence the Christian fact opens to man a new righteousness through Christ; and since it is through Christ, it is not and cannot be achieved through the works of the law. Therefore Paul reaches the conclusion (with which he actually begins his exposition in Rm 3:10) that no one is righteous, neither Jew nor Greek; all are sinners.

In Rm and Gal, where the question is treated explicitly and polemically, Paul insists that the law and the deeds of the law do not achieve righteousness (Rm 3:11, 28; Gal 2:21; 2:16; 3:11). Paul does not mean the righteousness of the OT, but the new righteousness brought by Christ. This righteousness can be acquired only by faith in Christ, and here Paul quotes more than once Hab 2:4 (Rm 1:17; 3:28; 4:5; 5:1; 9:30 f; Gal 2:16; 3:8, 11, 24). This is represented in AA 13:38 f as a principle of Paul's early preaching. He calls the righteousness of the law "my own righteousness," in contrast to the righteousness which comes from God through faith in Christ Jesus (Phl 3:9). This righteousness of man is not the work of man by achievement or merit; it is God alone who makes man righteous (Rm 3:30). Whom God calls He makes righteous (Rm 8:30); and no one can condemn the man whom God makes righteous (Rm 8:34). Through the gift of righteousness we reign in life (Rm 5:17). God works this righteousness through the death of Jesus. Christ is righteousness (1 Co 1:30). Christians are made righteous in His name (1 Co 6:11). We are made righteous freely through God's grace by the redemption of the Lord Jesus Christ (Rm 5:1); the righteous saving deed of Christ makes many righteous and confers upon them life (Rm 5:18). The Christian becomes righteous, delivered from his sin, by death to the flesh in Christ (Rm 6:7); he is delivered from the wrath when he is made righteous through the blood of Jesus (Rm 5:9 f). This righteousness is received in the spirit (1 Co 6:11).

A few more explicit and formal treatments may be reviewed. Rm 4 proceeds from Gn 15:6, the faith of Abraham was reckoned as righteousness. This happened before his circumcision (according to the arrangement of Gn made by the compiler) and therefore did not depend on his circumcision nor on his subjection to the law. The same righteousness therefore is within the reach of all who like Abraham believe, even if they are uncircumcised and not subject to the law. In Rm 5:15–21 Paul proceeds from the one sin which made many sinners to the one righteous deed by which many were constituted righteous. This righteousness is a gift conferred through the death of Christ. Rm 10:1–6 takes up the problem of the Jews before the Christian fact. Christ has annulled the law as a means of righteousness and made righteousness available to all who believe. One is now righteous if he confesses that Jesus is lord and that God has raised him from the dead.

What, then, is this new righteousness? One may first proceed by examining Paul's conception of the righteousness of God, which is also new. The righteousness of God is revealed in the growth of faith (Rm 1:17), without the works of the law (Rm 3:21), it is established (i.e., clearly proved to be such) by our unrighteousness (Rm 3:5), it is demonstrated through His forgiveness of sin (Rm 3:25 f). Indeed we ourselves *are* the righteousness of God through Christ, who has been made sin for us (2 Co 5:21). The righteousness of God is the saving attribute which appears in the OT (cf above), but now specified by the nature of the salvation which it operates; it is the will of God to deliver men from their sin through the redeeming death of Jesus Christ. In this work God is eminently the deliverer, the vindicator.

The new righteousness of men is the righteousness conferred upon them through this saving will. It is not merely the moral rectitude which was achieved by the observance of the law. It is deliverance from sin (Rm 5:16). It is life in the spirit (Rm 8:10). The Christian, delivered from sin, is enslaved to righteousness (Rm 6:18 f). Righteousness and lawlessness are opposed as light* and darkness* (2 Co 6:14). The kingdom of God is peace, grace, righteousness, in the Holy Spirit (Rm 14:17). The Christian is filled with the fruit of righteousness through Jesus Christ to the glory and praise of God (Phl 1:11); the fruit of light is contained in all goodness, righteousness, and truth (Eph 5:9). Indeed, perfect and complete righteousness is still an object of hope to be achieved eschatologically (Gal 5:5).

These texts, taken together with others in which the key related words are used, show that Paul develops the OT idea of righteousness in a thoroughly Christian sense. The "righteous" is "right" with God, he is saved and vindicated, he has received a new life from his vindication. So the righteousness of the Christian is his state of vindication and deliverance achieved through the death of Christ. This is precisely deliverance from sin and the restoration of a state of innocence, but it is also positive in character. The "righteousness" of the Christian is a principle of right conduct which consists in his communion in the death and resurrection

of Jesus Christ, through which he begins a new life in the spirit — a life in which he lives in Christ and Christ lives in him. This is the righteousness which cannot be achieved by the observance of the law; it is a free gift, which God alone can effect, and which reaches its fullness in the eschatological life to come.

Rimmon (Hb *rimmôn*), a god worshiped at Damascus* (2 K 5:18). The name is identical with Akkadian *rammanu,* which appears in Assyrian personal names. Rimmon is an alternate name of the storm god Hadad*; this name also appears at Damascus.

Ring. The Hb word *nezem* designates *ring* in general, and the addition of "nose" or "ear" specifies where it is worn. As a female ornament the nose ring is mentioned in Gn 24:47; Is 3:21, the ear ring in Ezk 16:12 +. The ear ring was worn by men as well as by women (Gn 35:4; Ex 32:2 f). The finger ring was almost always a signet ring (*ṭabba'at*); it was worn by kings and officials (Gn 41:42; Est 3:10; 8:2) but also as a personal ornament by ordinary persons, both men and women (Ex 35:22; Is 3:21). The ear ring is illustrated in ANEP 4, 6, 8 (worn by Negroes but not by the Syrians in the same reliefs), 26, 30 (Mede and Elamite men), 49–51 (probably Hittite men) 74–75 (Palestinian from 14th–13th centuries; the ear rings here are quite broad crescents), 173 (Assyrian soldiers), 398 (an Egyptian queen), 410 (Egyptian princesses), 441, 446, 448–449 (Assyrian kings), 479 (Egyptian representation of a Palestinian goddess), 498 (a Palestinian god), 539 (Hittite gods), 614, 647 (Assyrian genii). These illustrate how general the wearing of ear rings by both sexes was. The type illustrated is mostly a narrow ring, sometimes with pendants. The lunate gold ear rings of Queen Shubad (Sumerian, ANEP 72) are an alarming 11 cm in diameter.

Rizpah (Hb *riṣpāh,* a personal name, etymology uncertain; the connection with *reṣep,* "live coals," seems unlikely). Rizpah was a concubine of Saul, her seizure by Abner* after Saul's death was the occasion of a quarrel between Abner and Ishbaal* as a result of which Abner transferred his allegiance to David (2 S 3:7–11). A woman who had been possessed by a king partook of the sanctity of royalty and sexual commerce with her by another was regarded as treason; cf ABSALOM; ADONIJAH. Rizpah appears a second time in 2 S 21:10–11 as an example of heroic maternal devotion; she would not let scavenging birds and beasts devour the bodies of the sons she had borne Saul, even though custom required that men so executed be left exposed. David rewarded her heroism by giving her sons and the five grandsons of Saul who were executed with them decent burial.

Rock (Hb *ṣûr*), used as a divine title. The title clearly suggests ancient warfare; if one could establish a position on one of the precipitous crags which are so numerous in the mountains of Palestine, one could resist almost any attack. This explains the divine title without any appeal to an earlier cult of rocks, which was suggested by some older scholars. Yahweh is the rock of Israel (2 S 23:3; Is 30:29), the rock of refuge (Dt 32:37; 2 S 22:3; Pss 18:3; 62:8; 94:22; Is 17:10), the rock of deliverance (Dt 32:15; Pss 62:3, 7; 89:27; 95:1). He is the rock who bore Israel (Dt 32:18), an everlasting rock (Is 26:4). There is no rock like the God of Israel (Dt 32:31; 1 S 2:2; 2 S 22:32; Ps 18:32). Yahweh is addressed as "Rock" (Hab 1:12), "Rock and avenger" (Ps 19:15), and the Psalmist says, "Blessed is my Rock" (Pss 18:47; 144:1; 2 S 22:47). The title twice suggests the appropriate attributes of Yahweh: He is the righteous and faithful rock (Dt 32:4), the Rock in whom there is no wrong (Ps 92:16). The title was meaningless or not sufficiently reverent to the translators of the LXX, who substituted other titles for it; these were reproduced in the Gallican Psalter used in the· Vg*. The title appears in the classic Eng hymn "Rock of Ages" (Is 26:4).

Rodanim (Hb *rôdānîm*), in 1 Ch 1:7 one of the sons of Javan*; Gn 10:4 has Dodanim, which can scarcely be correct. If the reading of 1 Ch 1:7 is correct, the name designates the people of Rhodes, one of the largest islands of the Aegean archipelago, lying off the SW coast of Turkey. A number of critics, however, believe that both Rodanim and Dodanim come from an original *dananim,* the Gk *danaoi,* "Danaans," a people of the Peloponnesus during the Mycenean period.

Romans, Epistle to the. 1. *Contents:*
1:1–7, introductory salutation with dogmatic summary; 1:8–15, thanksgiving.
I. *Dogmatic Exposition:* The righteousness of God, 1:16–11:36.
1:16–17, proposition of the theme.
1:18–3:20, man's incapacity to gain righteousness:
1:18–32, unbelief and sinfulness of pagans.
2:1–3:8, sins of the Jews, incapacity of the law and circumcision to secure righteousness.
3:9–20, summary: Jew and pagan both incapable of righteousness.

3:21–4:25, the manifestation of the righteousness of God in Christ: 3:21–26, God's plan to confer righteousness; 3:27–31, the power of faith and the powerlessness of works of the law; 4:1–12, Abraham became righteous by faith; 4:13–25, the promise to Abraham's descendants is verified in righteousness secured by faith.
5:1–21, the righteousness of God saves gratuitously through Christ: 5:1–11, the righteousness of God is a pledge of salvation; 5:12–22, the righteousness is given to all through one as sin came to all through one.
6:1–23, righteousness liberates from sin: 6:1–14, the sequence of sin-death is defeated by the sequence of death in Christ through baptism to life; 6:15–23, liberation from sin to the slavery of God and righteousness.
7:1–25, liberation from the law: 7:1–6, faith liberates from the law; 7:7–25, the relations of the law and sin.
8:1–39, righteousness is life in the Spirit and the eschatological hope: 8:1–13, the indwelling of the Spirit; 8:14–17, the adoption in the Spirit; 8:18–30, the possession of the Spirit is the hope of glory; 8:31–39, hymn of Christian hope.
9:1–11:36, the righteousness of God and the problem of the Jews: 9:1–5, Paul's grief for Israel, the chosen bearers of the promises; 9:6–24, the promise and the mystery of election; 9:25–29, the mystery of election shown in the Scriptures. 9:30–10:3, the fault of the Jews in seeking their own righteousness instead of the righteousness of God; 10:4–15, Scripture shows that righteousness is obtained by faith; 10:16–21, Israel has rejected the salvation offered it; 11:1–6, God has saved a remnant of his people; 11:7–12, through Israel's rejection salvation has come to the Gentiles; 11:13–24, the Gentiles must confess the mysterious mercy of God; 11:25–32, Paul's assurance of the salvation of Israel; 11:33–36, hymn of praise of God's wisdom.
II. *The Moral Imperatives* imposed by the righteousness of God, 12:1–15:13.
12:1–3, the living sacrifice of a Christian life.
12:4–8, the charismata and the unity of the body.
12:9–21, love of the community and of enemies.
13:1–7, obedience to civil authority.
13:8–10, love is the fulfillment of the law.
13:11–14, the Parousia imposes Christian duties.
14:1–12, the "strong" and the "weak" should tolerate each other.
14:13–23, the strong must show special consideration for the weak.

15:1–13, both should follow the example of Christ.

III. *Conclusion,* 15:14–16:27.

15:14–21, why Paul writes the letter.

15:22–23, Paul's plans.

16:1–2, recommendation of Phoebe.

16:3–16, list of greetings.

16:17–20, warning against deceivers.

16:21–23, greetings from Paul's companions.

16:24–27, final doxology.

2. *Date, Place, Occasion.* There is universal agreement that Rm was written from Corinth in early 58. It was Paul's intention after he returned to Jerusalem to resume his missionary journeys in Spain and to reach Spain via Rome, where he probably intended to establish a base. Rome was unknown to him personally; the Christian community had been in existence there for an undetermined number of years, but it does not appear to have been new; the time and circumstances of its foundation and the names of its founders are unknown. Indeed, Rm is the oldest and most reliable source of information concerning the Roman church. These plans of Paul were never carried out; when Paul went to Jerusalem he was arrested, and his adventures in the procurator's court, his appeal to Caesar, and his voyage and shipwreck brought him finally to Rome in quite other circumstances than he had planned, probably in the spring of 61.

The purpose of the letter was to announce his coming and to prepare the Roman Christians for it (1:10–15; 15:14–33). The authenticity of the letter is not questioned. The style is that of Paul as seen in Gal and 1–2 Co, although it is less impassioned, more solemn and much more expository. This difference, which is slight, is easily explained by the fact that he was writing to a church personally unknown to him; one could not expect the deep personal interest which is seen in Gal and 1–2 Co. But this does not answer the major question of the purpose of the letter. Rm is the longest of the Pauline letters; it is the most carefully written and organized, and the fullest in theological content. It is not a complete summary of the gospel* of Paul; but it appears to be intended as a fairly complete exposition of that which was most characteristic and distinctive of Paul's doctrine, the salvation of the Gentiles through faith in Jesus Christ. Certainly this seems more than is demanded by his intended appearance as a passing traveler in a strange church. Some of the fathers of the Church thought that the letter was written to heal existing divisions between Jewish and Gentile Christians; this is not reflected in the letter and is now regarded as improbable. One may

discuss as lacking in probability the view that a mission of Judaizers led by Peter had come to Rome with the teachings of Judaism; there is no basis for this in Rm or in the entire NT. Hence modern scholars deduce that it was written not to meet any particular situation in Rome but as a recommendation of Paul by himself. The importance of the Roman community is implied in the length of the letter and the care with which it is written. Paul was known only by hearsay to the Romans, but we must suppose that he was known; and not improbably he was known as a controversial figure, if not as a disturber. Paul thought that his best introduction was a full exposition of those elements in his preaching which were most controversial; this could be set against any distortion which might have arisen in oral reports.

The character of the letter must have been determined to some extent by the character of the Roman congregation. This was no doubt better known to Paul than it is to us; he could have learned about the Roman community from Aquila* and Priscilla* and others. The older view, now generally abandoned, is that the Roman community was predominantly Jewish. To support this view proponents pointed to 2:17–3:8; 3:21–31; 4:1; 6:1–7:6; 9–11; 14:1–15:3 (understanding the "weak" to be Jewish Christians, which is very probable). These verses, together with the general argument and the vindication of Paul's gospel of salvation without the works of the law, were thought to be addressed to a Jewish Christian audience. But these are generalities which would be in place in any early Christian community; the relation of Christianity to Judaism was an urgent and controversial problem which was of concern to Gentiles as well as Jews. Modern critics are inclined to think that the Roman community was predominantly Gentile. They deduce this from the fact that Paul addresses the readers as Gentiles (and not rhetorically, as he addresses the Jew in 2:1, 3–5, 17–24); this address appears in 1:5 ff, 13 ff; 6:17 ff; 11:23, 28, 31. Paul also notices with some emphasis his own mission to the Gentiles (9:3 ff; 10:1 ff; 11:13; 15:15 f). The community probably had a considerable Jewish minority (the "weak").

3. *Integrity.* Some MSS lack chs 15–16. The absence of both is probably due to Marcion's exclusion of them from his text; but modern critics raise some serious questions about 16:3–20. The autograph conclusion of the letter appears in 15:33. The list of salutations (16:3–16) contains 26 names, which seems rather large in a community which Paul had never seen. Furthermore, the list contains some names which appear

inappropriate: Epaenetus, "the first fruits of Asia," must have moved from Asia, probably Ephesus; but so must Aquila and Priscilla (16:3 f), who went to Ephesus with Paul. 16:17–20, the most direct part of the letter, seems more direct than one would expect to a strange community. The oldest MS of Rm, P⁴⁶, places the doxology of 16: 25–27 after 15:33.

These data have led a number of modern critics to conclude that 16:3–20 come from another letter and have been attached to Rm. Manson and Munck have proposed a plausible theory that Rm, because of its doctrinal content, was circulated by Paul in a number of the churches which he founded, accompanied in each case by a separate covering letter. The mention of Epaenetus, Aquila, and Priscilla, suggests that Rm 16 is the covering letter of the copy which was sent to Ephesus, and that Rm is the "Ephesian edition" of the letter; the "Roman edition" consisted only of 1–15. Nonetheless the reasons advanced for detaching 16 are not convincing; the communications of the early churches were frequent enough for Paul to have made 26 acquaintances at Rome, and one may even admit that Epaenetus, Aquila, and Priscilla had moved there. But the attachment of 16 to the body of the letter cannot be regarded as altogether assured.

4. *Literary Form.* It should be noticed that Rm contains a rich variety of literary forms of expression: liturgical fragments (1:1–7; 16:25–27), the Stoic diatribe, the procedure by question and answer (2:1–25), the rabbinical argument from the OT (3:1–20; 4:1–25; 9:6–11:10), hymns (8:31–39), exhortation (12:1 ff; 13:11–14). These show that more art went into the composition of Rm than Paul was accustomed to put in his letters.

5. *Theological Elements.* The theological wealth of Rm touches most of the theological themes of the NT. These are discussed under separate articles; cf ELECTION; FAITH; LAW; LIFE; RIGHTEOUSNESS; SALVATION; SIN; SPIRIT; related articles. Here more explicitly than in any other letter Paul sets forth the meaning of Christian salvation, the powerlessness of man and the fullness of the redeeming work of God.

Rome. The Romans are mentioned under the cryptic name of Kittim* in Dn 11:30, an allusion to their arrest of the campaign of Antiochus Epiphanes against Egypt (168 BC). They enter the history of Palestine in 1 Mc 8, which relates the treaty negotiated with the Romans by Judas. The text of the treaty is prefaced by a review of recent Roman conquests: Gaul, Spain, Macedon, the Seleucid* kingdom, and the mainland of Greece. This review represents the Romans in a very favorable light in

The Roman forum.

contrast with the Seleucid monarchy against which the Jews were contending; the Romans were known only by hearsay and they were idealized. This illustrates the readiness with which many eastern people accepted Roman intervention. The influence of the treaty with Rome (which was heavily loaded in favor of Rome) is alluded to in 1 Mc 14: 40; 15:16; in the latter instance it does not appear to have been very effective. 2 Mc 4:11 alludes to an earlier mission to Rome not reported elsewhere. 2 Mc 8:10, 36 refers to the fact that the Seleucids were a tributary kingdom of Rome after the defeat of Antiochus the Great at Magnesia in 190 BC. A letter of the Romans to the Jews is quoted in 2 Mc 11:34–38; on the authenticity of this document cf MACCABEES, BOOKS.

In the Gospels the name of Rome appears only in Jn 11:48 in the warning of Caiaphas that a messianic movement could bring the Romans to destroy both the temple and the Jewish people; the sentence no doubt reflects the events of AD 70, in which the disaster occurred which Caiaphas is here represented as ready to avoid by sacrificing the life of Jesus. The Latin language is called the "Roman" language in Jn 19:20. AA 18:2 alludes to the decree of Claudius* expelling Jews from Rome. Paul's intention and desire to visit Rome is seen in AA 19:21; 23:11; he finally arrived in Rome as a prisoner appealing his case to the imperial tribunal. The allusions to Rome in AA 16:21, 37 f; 22:25–29; 23:27; 25:16 are concerned with Roman citizenship, possessed by Paul. The extension of Roman citizenship outside the city began under the Republic and was intended for the benefit of the central government, not of the citizens; Roman citizens were subject to Roman military service. But citizenship proved more of a benefit than an obligation; Julius Caesar extended it to many communities which had supported his cause in the civil war, and Augustus extended it still further. Tarsus*, the native city of Paul, was made a free city by Augustus, and it was probably through this concession that the family of Paul acquired citizenship. The privileges of the citizen are appealed to by Paul in the passages cited above; the Roman citizen could not be sentenced for any crime without due process of Roman (not provincial) law; he could not be scourged or submitted to any other degrading punishment; he could not be put to the question under torture; and he could appeal the verdict of a lower court to "Caesar," the imperial tribunal at Rome. Under Claudius the citizenship could be purchased, and it was by the venality of this period that the tribune Claudius Lysias* obtained his citizenship.

The entire course of Jewish and Palestinian history was dominated by the imperial power of Rome after the incorporation of the territory into a Roman province; but even before this event it was the Roman conquests in the E which rendered the Seleucid kingdom unable to retain its hold on Palestine. After the conquest of Mithridates of Pontus in 65 BC Pompey decided to establish Roman order in W Asia; this involved the liquidation of the now decayed Seleucid kingdom, which still claimed Palestine and was reduced to the territory of Syria and a fringe around it. Palestine came into the decision through the quarrel of Aristobulus and Hyrcanus (cf HASMONEANS), both of whom appealed to M. Aemilius Scaurus, the legate of Pompey. Scaurus chose Aristobulus, but withheld action. In 63 Pompey himself went to Damascus, where Antipater (cf HEROD) appealed to him on behalf of Hyrcanus. The impatience of Aristobulus issued in armed resistance; the city was surrendered after a few skirmishes, but the partisans of Aristobulus in the temple area resisted Gabinius for a siege of three months. After the surrender Pompey horrified the Jews by entering the inner sanctuary of the temple. Pompey then organized the *provincia Syriae*, which included Syria and Palestine, and appointed Scaurus as governor. Judaea was detached from the territories conquered by the Hasmoneans — the Decapolis*, the coastal cities, and Samaria — and united in one administrative unit with Galilee and Peraea (a part of E Palestine). This area was intended to represent the religious community of Jerusalem, Jews who accepted the temple as the center of the cult and the high priest as its head. The priesthood was conferred upon Hyrcanus, but he was deprived of all political authority. Conditions were unsettled during the years following the organization due to the continued quarrels of the factions of Aristobulus and Hyrcanus. In 57 BC Gabinius divided Judaea proper into three administrative districts, Jerusalem, Gazara (Gezer*), and Jericho*, probably to break up the unity of the Jews; the system was not successful and endured only a few years. Gabinius was succeeded as governor of Syria by M. Licinius Crassus in 54 BC, who plundered the province magnificently; he was killed the following year in a campaign against the Parthians. He was succeeded by C. Cassius Longinus (known to readers of Shakespeare's *Julius Caesar*) in 53– 51 BC; a revolt of the Jews occurred during his administration. The Roman administration of Palestine was temporarily disrupted during the Roman civil war; Hyrcanus and Antipater took the side of Caesar and were generously rewarded after his victory. Hyr-

The Arch of Titus
in the Roman forum.

canus was given the title of Ethnarch and made a Roman *confederatus;* Antipater was granted Roman citizenship and was made procurator of Judaea. For the events which followed the assassination of Caesar in 44 BC and the rise of Herod to the throne of Judaea; the reign of Herod and the family of Herod in Palestinian political and religious affairs cf HASMONEANS; HEROD. From the deposition of Archelaus* (AD 6) to AD 66 Judaea was administered by Roman procurators (for list cf PROCURATOR), except for the brief reign of Agrippa* (AD 41–44). The quality of the men appointed to this office deteriorated sharply during the reigns of Claudius and Nero, and the last two, Albinus and Gessius Florus, were tyrannical and venal to an intolerable degree.

The disaster of AD 70 was prepared by a period of 30–35 years of disquiet in Palestine. For the troubled administration of Pilate cf PILATE. During his administration there arose the faction of the Pharisees* called the Zealots*, whom the Romans called *Sicarii,* "dagger-men"; these developed assassination, especially of their Jewish opponents, to a fine art. During the reign of Caligula (AD 37–41) the intention of the emperor to erect a statue of himself in the temple of

Jerusalem excited profound hostility; a large delegation of Jews protested to Petronius, the governor of Syria, who delayed the erection of the work, even secretly instructing the workmen not to hurry, while he wrote temporizing letters to Caligula. An open rebellion was averted only by the assassination of Caligula. Cuspius Fadus (44–46) was a fair but severe administrator; he suppressed banditry and scattered a messianic uprising led by Theudas, who had promised to divide the waters of the Jordan. Three incidents arose under Ventidius Cumanus (48–52): a riot caused when a Roman soldier made an obscene gesture in the temple; another when a soldier tore up a scroll of the Law publicly; and the third when the Jews sacked and burned some Samaritan villages in retaliation for attacks on pilgrims traveling to Jerusalem. Cumanus was removed from office, and the confidence of the Jews in their ability to bait the Roman government was increased.

The maladministration of Felix* (52–60) permitted the assassins to ravage almost without check. Riots occurred between Jews and Greeks in Caesarea. Albinus (62–64) and Florus (64–66) were both in league with bandits. A judgment rendered in favor of the Greeks at Caesarea and the barbarous repression by Florus of a riot in Jerusalem at the Passover of 66 kindled the flame; the Jews attacked the Roman troops and killed or scattered them. Rebellion then broke out over the entire country; Jews and Greeks fought each other in towns where they lived together, and the army gathered by the governor of Syria was routed at Beth-horon. The Jews declared themselves an independent state and fortified for war. The rebellion was not of major proportions, and Nero appointed Titus Flavianus Vespasianus to attack with a large army. The Romans moved slowly and methodically from Caesarea through Galilee, which they first subdued, southward until they were able to invest Jerusalem. This had been accomplished when Vespasian was declared emperor by his troops in 69, after the assassination of Nero and the proclamation of three emperors in one year. He left his son Titus in command. The attack and the resistance were one of the most bitterly fought campaigns in military history; it was even more remarkable that the siege was prolonged, for from the very beginning of the war factions of the Jews had fought and killed each other with no less vigor than they fought the Romans, and this continued until the final assault on the city. Titus, as reported by Josephus his defender, desired to negotiate a surrender with as little destruction of property and loss of life as possible. But the Jews contested every inch of the Roman advance; the walls were breached near the temple and the temple was accidentally fired. Resistance was continued until most of the defenders had been killed and the city was almost totally leveled. Bands of the Zealots escaped to maintain resistance in the deserts and mountains, and Roman mopping up operations continued for several years. The victory is commemorated on the triumphal arch of Titus at Rome. Jerusalem was not rebuilt until the reign of Hadrian; it was rebuilt as a Roman military colony with the name Aelia Capitolina, and no Jews lived there. In the political reorganization which followed the defeat the name of the country was changed from Judaea to *Palestina;* it was no longer Jewish territory. The status of Jews in the diaspora*, however, was not affected; there were a few riots here and there. The disaster made a decisive change in the nature of Judaism; the destruction of the temple and the disappearance of the priesthood made Judaism a religion without a cult, and it became the religion of the Law* and the synagogue* exclusively.

There can be no doubt that Rome is meant by Babylon in Apc 14:8; 16:19; 17:5; 18:2, 10, 21. The hostility of these passages is in contrast to the favorable or at least neutral attitude toward Rome expressed elsewhere in the NT, and it is probably a reflection of the hostility toward Christians shown by Nero and in particular by Domitian, whose reign is closer to the composition of Apc.

On the question of Peter's presence in Rome cf PETER.

Historians point out that there was no period before the 1st century AD when travel and communications over such a wide area were possible. Roman administration after the civil troubles of the 1st century BC joined the entire Mediterranean basin by a network of roads; Roman suppression of banditry and piracy removed the major hazard to travel by land or sea. The entire region was under a single government and one language, Gk, was spoken everywhere. The rapid expansion of Christianity was possible only under Roman imperial administration.

Roof. Cf HOUSE.

Rufus (Lt *rufus,* "red-haired"), a personal name; the son of Simon* of Cyrene and the brother of Alexander (Mk 15:21); a Roman Christian, "the elect in the Lord" (Rm 16:13). The name was quite common and it is not known whether these passages refer to one man or to two.

Ruth (Hb *rût,* possibly a contraction from *re'ût,* "lady friend[s]"), a personal name; the heroine of the book of Ruth.

1. *Summary.* During the period of the judges Elimelech of Bethlehem migrated to Moab during a famine with his wife Naomi and his two sons Mahlon and Chilion. He died in Moab and his sons married two Moabite women, Orpah and Ruth. The two sons died, and Naomi wished to return to Bethlehem; Ruth went with her, but Orpah returned to her family. They arrived at Bethlehem during the harvest, and Ruth went out to glean for the two destitute women. She worked in the field of a wealthy landowner named Boaz, who was attracted by her. Naomi urged her to seek marriage with Boaz, since he was her kinsman, although remote, and Ruth crept under his mantle while he slept on the harvesting floor. Boaz accepted the implied proposal of marriage, but first had to redeem Ruth from a nearer kinsman, according to the levirate* law. The kinsman renounced his claim; Boaz married Ruth, and their son was Obed, the grandfather of David.

In the Hb canon the book is placed in the 3rd part among the Writings (cf CANON), which suggests a later date of its acceptance and probably of its composition. The LXX and Vg (and Eng Bibles) place it after Jgs.

In the Jewish liturgy it is read on the feast of Pentecost*.

2. *Date and Criticism.* Most modern critics place the book after the exile. This judgment rests principally upon a large number of Aramaisms in such a small book and on its general style and tenor. There is no sign of diversity of authorship; but many critics regard the genealogy of David in 4:17b–22 as secondary. This opinion is connected with the historical character of the book; cf below.

3. *Literary Form and Historical Character.* Modern critics are nearly unanimous in thinking that the book is a fictitious composition; there are differences of opinion on the extent to which genuine traditions are used and on the theme of the book (cf below). The symbolic character of several of the names supports the fictitious nature of the narrative: Mahlon (sickness), Chilion (failing), Orpah (she who turns her back), and this may be taken as a safe hypothesis. The question turns rather on whether the genealogical information is a genuine ancient tradition, and whether the story is composed on the datum that one of David's ancestors was a Moabite. While the question must be left open, it appears that there is no reason to think that the genealogy is not original. One may therefore take the genealogical data as a reliable piece of historical information while regarding the story as a whole as a free invention; the interpretation of the story depends on what its theme is understood to be (cf below). The literary qualities of the story are much admired. It is an idyl, quite in contrast to the battles and brutality of the stories of Jgs and 1 S. The story is a simple adventure of daily life, with fine portrayal of character and realistic dialogue. Everyone in the story, even Orpah, appears in a favorable light.

4. *Theme.* There is again general agreement on the theme of Rt, or rather the themes. It exhibits the heroism of two women, which arises from their unswerving faith and trust in Yahweh. Yahweh is the protector of widows and rewarder of fidelity. The house of Elimelech is rebuilt on the virtues of Naomi and Ruth and the good fortune of any house depends on such virtues. There can be no doubt that these qualities stand out in Ruth, a foreign woman, who chooses Naomi's kin and people and God as her own; her noble profession of fidelity to her adopted family (Rt 1:16 f) has been incorporated into the marriage ceremony of some Protestant churches. Like Israel itself, Ruth chooses Yahweh as her God. It is Ruth who is the proximate agent of Naomi's deliverance; her beauty and her nobility excel those of the Israelite maidens, who had not been able to woo Boaz from single blessedness. To this foreign woman Yahweh exhibits the same gracious providence which He exhibits to the daughters of Israel. This conception is certainly in accord with other books which express generosity toward Gentiles*, such as Jon; Is 56:1–8 etc.

Some critics have gone further and found that the specific theme of the book is a protest against the rigorism of Ezra* and Nehemiah* in the repression and even the divorce of marriages between Jews and Gentiles (Ezr 10; Ne 13:23–27). The presentation of a noble Gentile woman who fulfills the Israelite wifely ideal and who was an ancestor of the great Israelite kings shows that such narrowness could exclude worthy members from the Israelite community. The polemic, if it is there, is so gentle and subtle that other scholars deny any such purpose; the book, they think, is a book of breadth and tolerance, but no more. The question does not admit a decision; it seems, however, that if it is to be dated in the period of Ezra and Nehemiah (which is not certain), the author could scarcely be unaware of the rigorism of Ezra and Nehemiah; and it certainly expresses a totally different attitude toward the marriage of Jew and Gentile.

S

Sabacthani. The Gk word *sabachthani* in Mt 27:46; Mk 15:34 represents the Aramaic *šᵉbaḳtānî* for the Hb *'azabtānî,* in the phrase *lammah šᵉbaḳtānî,* "Why hast thou forsaken me?" (Ps 22:2), quoted by Jesus on the cross.

Sabaeans. Cf SHEBA.

Sabaoth. Cf HOSTS.

Sabbath (Hb *šabbat*), the seventh day of the week in the Israelite and Jewish calendar. From early Israelite times the Sabbath was a holy day marked by religious and most probably some kind of cultic observance; but its antiquity and the nature of the earliest observances cannot be determined with full clarity. The laws of the Pnt retroject the Sabbath into the Mosaic period; this seems to be historically improbable, at least with respect to the type of observance which appears later, since it is scarcely possible for nomads to observe a day of complete cessation from labor. There are witnesses to the Sabbath which according to generally accepted criticism come from the period of the monarchy; beyond this period is it hardly possible to assert anything with certainty.

The name *šabbat* is connected with the root *ŠBT,* which means to rest or to cease; the "rest" may have different connotations in different contexts (cf below). Etymologically a connection has been sought with Akkadian *sapattu* mentioned in some ritual texts. This name designates the 15th day of the month; with other days which mark 7-day intervals, this day was regarded as a day of ill omen on which it was unsafe to undertake activities. The etymological connection is not certain, and there is not even a slight resemblance between the evil omen which inhibits new undertakings and the "rest" of the Sabbath. Even if a connection existed, one would be forced to recognize such a transformation in the Hb Sabbath that it is clearly a unique and peculiarly Hb institution.

The Sabbath during the monarchy is attested in only a few passages. It was a day on which merchandising was prohibited (Am 8:5). It was a day on which one might be expected to visit the "man of God," the prophet (2 K 4:23). It was a day of rest from work, for animals and slaves as well as for Israelites (Ex 23:12; 34:12). It appears from 2 K 11:5–9 that the number of men posted in the palace guard was reduced by one half on the Sabbath. It was a day of rest for Israelites, their animals and their slaves, because the Israelites, themselves once slaves in Egypt, should have compassion on those forced to labor (Dt 5:12–15). The addition of the humanitarian motive for the Sabbath observance is characteristic of Dt. This text is not as surely preexilic as those quoted above; but it is certainly earlier than the formula found in the Decalogue* of Ex 20, which is a P recension (cf below). Dt also adds a phrase not found in the other early texts: that the Sabbath is to be kept holy. This phrase is common in later texts. These scattered notices of the nature of the Sabbath indicate rest from work and in Dt some kind of sanctification and in 2 K 4:23 a day apt for religious activity.

The other passages are all exilic or postexilic. One observes the Sabbath by keeping it holy (Ex 20:8–10; 31:13–16; Is 56:2, 6); to violate the Sabbath is to "profane" its holiness (Ne 13:15–22; Is 56:2, 6; Ezk 20:16–26; 22:8, 26). The Sabbath is profaned by merchandising, and Nehemiah closed the gates of Jerusalem on the Sabbath to halt trading (Ne 13:15–22). The carrying of loads violates the Sabbath (Je 17:21–27, a postexilic expansion of Je). A midrash* in Nm 15:32–36 comments that the gathering of wood on the Sabbath is a capital offense; this extremely rigorous view shows the ideal of Sabbath holiness which was characteristic of postexilic Judaism. Another midrash in Ex 16:22–30 tells how Yahweh Himself observed the Sabbath by not distributing manna, and this compelled the Israelites to keep the Sabbath by not gathering manna. Certain sacrifices are prescribed on the Sabbath (Nm 28:9 f; Ezk 46:1 ff). The creation account of P makes the Sabbath the day of Yahweh's rest after creation; this cosmic event is the theological basis of man's rest at the end of the week, which also is a representation of the cosmic event of creation (Gn 2:1–3). The commandment of the Decalogue in Ex 20:8–10 (revised by P), makes the creation rest the motive for the Sabbath observance, which consists in keeping the day holy and permitting neither man nor beast to labor. The Day of Atonement* is called a Sabbath (Lv 16:31), which signifies the observance of the Sabbath rest. In the Maccabean period the Sabbath rest was understood to prohibit combat even in self-defense, and some Jews were killed because of their refusal to resist attack. The Maccabees themselves then determined that they would not maintain such a rigorous Sabbath observance (1 Mc 2:31–41; cf 2 Mc 15:2–4). There is one severe prophetic criticism of the Sabbath observance; it is mentioned with other ritual practices as vain without interior devotion (Is 1:13; the passage is not regarded as original by many critics).

The meaning of the Sabbath rest is somewhat ambiguous in these texts. "Rest" may signify either repose or simple cessation from work. Dt proposes the Sabbath rest as a humanitarian repose. The later priestly observance is not so clearly humanitarian. The Sabbath was a day holy to Yahweh; as persons and things could be consecrated and so removed from profane use (cf HOLY), so could a period of time be consecrated. Work was a secular element which profaned the holy; the fact that the cessation of work involved repose was merely incidental. This view of the Sabbath rest came to prevail in later Judaism and was criticized by Jesus (cf below).

In Judaism the Sabbath became one of the most important observances. It was developed with the religion of the synagogue*; it did not depend upon the temple and could be observed everywhere. It was a day of religious assembly (first prescribed in Lv 23:1–3) and of the Sabbath repose. The Sabbath was one of the observances which was most distinctive of Judaism; it identified Jews and marked them off from Gentiles and became a sign of genuine Judaism (much as many modern Catholics make Sunday Mass and Friday abstinence the sign of the "practicing" Catholic). The nature of the Sabbath rest was the subject of much casuistic discussion of the rabbis, who enumerated 39 types of work which were prohibited on the Sabbath; some prohibitions seem to us unreasonably petty, such as the prohibition of lighting a fire, clapping the hands, jumping, slapping the thigh, visiting the sick. One could walk only so far from one's home (unless one established a temporary domicile by depositing personal possessions at some distance from the home); the Sabbath day's journey (AA 1:12) was 2000 cubits, about 3000 ft.

That the rigorous Sabbath observance of Judaism was a point of frequent and serious dispute between Jesus and the rabbis is attested in all the Gospels. Jesus Himself observed the Sabbath according to reasonable standards, and occasionally taught in the synagogues on the Sabbath (Mk 6:2; Lk 4:16, 31). The Pharisees found fault with His disciples for rubbing grain between their hands on the Sabbath, which was a

preparation of food, one of the 39 prohibited works. Jesus appealed to the example of David, who ate holy food when he was in need, and to the priests who minister in the sanctuary on the Sabbath. He affirmed that He Himself is lord of the Sabbath, able to determine what may and may not be done on the Sabbath. He was particularly severe when the Pharisees objected to healing on the Sabbath, insisting that there is no time when it is prohibited to do good to another; the fellow man has at least as much right to assistance as the animal which strays and falls into a pit, from which its owner or anyone else will rescue it on the Sabbath (Mt 12:1–14; Mk 2:23–28; Lk 6:1–11; 13:10–16; 14:1–5; Jn 5:9–18; 7:22 f; 9:14–16). Only Mk 2:27 has preserved the saying that the Sabbath is made for man, not man for the Sabbath, which sums up the teaching of Jesus in a single sentence better than any other. Without rejecting the Sabbath observance as a whole, Jesus points out that the rabbinical practices were mere human interpretations of the precept, which basically is for human welfare (thus aligning Himself with the Deuteronomic view of the Sabbath); the Sabbath is indeed to be kept holy, but one profanes the Sabbath by making it an excuse to evade one's duty of providing one's own essential needs or doing good to another. There are many things more important than the Sabbath observance. Jesus lays down no particular precepts but leaves it to prudent and humane judgment to determine when the Sabbath observance should yield to greater matters.

The burial of Jesus on the eve of the Sabbath led to the need for hurry and was responsible for the presence of women at the tomb on the morning following the Sabbath (Mt 28:1; Mk 16:1 f; Lk 23:54 f; 24:1).

AA alludes to the reading of the prophets (13:27) and of the Pnt (15:21) in the synagogue on the Sabbath. The Sabbath synagogue meetings were used by Paul as opportunities to present the gospel to Jewish audiences (AA 13:14, 42–44; 16:13; 17:2; 18:4). In the NT the term Sabbath comes to mean simply the week (AA 20:7; 1 Co 16:2). Judaizing Christians attempted to impose the Sabbath observance upon Gentile Christians; Paul affirms that no one may be called to account for Sabbath observance (Col 2:16), thus finally and completely liberating Christians from the obligations of the Sabbath law.

Sabbatical Year. The law of the 7th or sabbatical year appears in three of the legal collections of the Pnt (cf LAW): the code of the covenant (Ex 23:10–11), the code of

Dt (Dt 15:1–3), and the holiness code (Lv 25:2–8). Ex and Lv agree on the substance of the prescriptions; the law requires that the land should not be cultivated, but is to lie fallow in the 7th year; like man and beast, it is to have a Sabbath rest, which for land can be arranged only by seasons. The threats appended to the holiness code predict that the land shall enjoy its Sabbaths if the Israelites fail to observe these laws; the land shall lie fallow not by choice, but because invasion and conquest shall have rendered it desolate and removed its cultivators (Lv 26:34 f, 43). The law of the 7th year in Dt 15:1–3, 9 is not directed to the land and does not speak of a Sabbath or rest; it is a law directing that debts should be remitted after 7 years; 15:9 implies that a regular cycle of 7 years is meant. This remission would easily coincide with the law of the fallow.

It is not altogether certain that the sabbatical year is connected with another law found in Ex 21:2; Dt 15:12–14, which prescribes that a Hebrew slave is to be given his choice of freedom or continued enslavement in the 7th year of his servitude. This law rather implies that no recurring cycle is meant, since the 7 years are measured from the acquisition of the slave. It is related to the law of the fallow only by the expression of the idea that the 7th year is a year of repose or deliverance from servitude.

Many scholars have asked whether these laws are intended to be realistic legal precepts or whether they are the statements of a religious ideal in the form of law. As such they may be compared to midrash* which expresses the obligation of the Sabbath*. There is no clear reference to the observance of these laws in other books of the OT; this is not of itself convincing, but it makes the laws stand alone. To this consideration is added the somewhat impractical character of the law; ancient agriculture was not so successful that a year's reserve could be surely expected, and it is idle to demand a 7 year cycle of miraculous crops when it is possible to explain the law as an ideal and not as a practical direction. Je 34:8–22 refers to the law of the remission of the slaves and charges the Israelites with not observing it; but the general manumission of slaves proclaimed by Zedekiah* during the siege of Jerusalem was not done in observance of the law. It went beyond the law and was an emergency measure of devotion in a desperate situation. Furthermore, the discourse assigned to Jeremiah on this occasion is composed in the style of the prose summary (cf JEREMIAH), which least of all the portions of the book reflects the words of Jeremiah; the allusion to the law of re-

mission may come from the compiler and not from the contemporary scene. The difficulties involved in supposing that the law was ever intended to be practical seem too serious to permit this opinion to be proposed as more probable. Some remission of debts to relieve general economic distress was practiced more than once in more than one region in the ancient world, and such an emergency measure may have occurred in Israel. It is difficult to suppose that the remission could be made cyclic, and it is probable that the emergency measure was erected by the Dt writers into a law which expressed the ideal of generosity for the money-lender.

Sackcloth (Hb *saḳ,* Akkadian *šaḳḳu*), the word is obviously a loan word in Gk *sakkos,* from which it has passed into Lt *saccus* and Eng *sack,* but it is not certain that the word is originally Semitic; Egyptian has been suggested. The word designates a rough fabric woven of hair, dark in color, used among other purposes for grain bags (Gn 42:25, 27, 35; Jos 9:4). It occurs most frequently in the Bible to designate garments of ritual symbolism. The OT does not distinguish sharply between the situations of mourning, penitence, and supplication, all of which elicit expressions of grief; the change from usual garments to sackcloth indicates that one is afflicted. Sackcloth was worn in mourning for family (Gn 37:34) and friends (2 S 3:31), national disaster (Is 15:3; 22:12; Je 4:8; 6:26; 48:37; 49:3; Ezk 27:31) and personal disaster (Ps 30:12). Affliction is the work of the anger of Yahweh and hence elicits penitence for the sins which have aroused His anger; sackcloth is the garb of the penitent (1 K 21:27; Ne 9:1; Is 22:12; Jon 3:5 f, 8; Mt 11:21; Lk 10:13). Sackcloth is also the humiliating garb of the suppliant who petitions for relief from affliction; it is worn by man making supplication to man (1 K 20:31) and by man making supplication to Yahweh (2 K 6:30; 19:1; Pss 35:13; 69:12; Jb 16:15; Is 37:1 f; 58:5; Ezk 7:18; 2 K 19:1 f; Est 4:1; Dn 9:3). It is often associated with other tokens of mourning: the shaving of the head and beard (Is 22:12; Je 48:37; Ezk 27:31), the scattering of dust and ashes on the head and person (Is 58:5; Je 6:26; Ezk 27:31; Dn 9:3; Mt 11:21; Lk 10:13), fasting (Ps 69:12; Is 58:5; Dn 9:3). Sackcloth is the garment of captivity (Is 3:24). In Apc 11:3 it is the garment of prophecy, no doubt because the prophets who wear it announce disaster. Metaphorically the heavens put on sackcloth, i.e., they are darkened, a portent of coming disaster (Is 50:3). Although the situation of Rizpah* in 2 S 21:10 was tragic in the extreme, it seems that the sackcloth which she spread on the rock had a practical and not a symbolic intent. Sackcloth could be worn concealed under the outer garments next to the skin (2 K 6:30), a sign visible to Yahweh alone. It is said to be girt or worn upon the loins (2 S 3:31; Is 20:2; Je 4:8) as the tunic or the loin cloth was girt (cf CLOTHING).

Sacrament. Sacramental theology in general scarcely appears in the NT at all; there is no single word which renders the idea, nor are there any passages which group those rites which the Church counts as sacraments under a common heading or common traits. The common traits must be deduced from the passages which treat of the individual rites; cf BAPTISM; CONFIRMATION; EUCHARIST; FORGIVENESS; MARRIAGE; PRIEST.

Certain common elements in the separate rites can be perceived. There is a contrast both explicit and implicit with Jewish rites, institutions, and events: cf ATONEMENT; CIRCUMCISION; FORGIVENESS; MANNA (in contrast with the Eucharist); SACRIFICE. There is a general abolition of the Jewish ritual system for Christians; the ritual system is ineffective after the saving work of Jesus Christ. Those scholars who see in this abolition simply an antiritualist position have forgotten that the primitive Church had rites of its own for which it claimed an effectiveness which was never possessed by the rites of the OT. Circumcision is vain, but baptism is absolutely necessary. The sacrificial banquet is annulled, but the Christian must partake of the body and blood of Christ. The priesthood of Levi has lost its commission, but the Church has its appointed leaders.

The effect of the rites of the Church is never summed up under one head and is most clearly stated for baptism. If one collects the effects of the rites in general, one finds that they achieve a new life in the Christian; they work a complete liberation from sin; they incorporate the Christian into Jesus Christ; they confer the spirit which Jesus promised. All the effects of the rites arise from the fact that they are in some way a reenactment of the redeeming death of Jesus, who is the sole source of grace and salvation. The Church is the minister of the rites through her leaders. Of baptism, the Eucharist and forgiveness the NT expressly states the commission of Jesus to perform these rites. The power of the priesthood is not explicit, but it is implied in the idea of succession in the ministry of the Church. There is no explicit reference of the other rites to Jesus Himself as the agent of institution.

Sacrifice. The limits of this article do not permit a sketch of the place of sacrifice in the general history of religions. It should be noticed that it is a universal phenomenon and that scarcely any religion is known which does not have a sacrificial ritual. The rituals of sacrifice exhibit a basic similarity which is not due to mutual borrowing; the nature of the symbolism of sacrifice and of the ideas from which it arises are the result of the belief in the deity and the desire to worship him. In particular areas and in details there is a communication of ritual practices and presuppositions; not much is known of the sacrificial ritual of Mesopotamia and Canaan, but what is known suggests that the sacrificial ritual of these areas was in many respects like the sacrificial ritual of the Israelites. OT sacrifice is not one of the distinctive features of OT religion, and its peculiar qualities arise from the unique character of the Israelite God and not from the ritual practices themselves.

1. *A general theory of sacrifice.* Sacrifice can be descriptively defined in general as a material oblation made to the deity by means of a consecration and consumption of the thing offered. The purpose of this oblation is to establish or maintain communion with the deity. Communion with the deity can be conceived under various aspects, and the symbolism of the various types of sacrifice expresses these differences; cf below. Historians of religion have proposed a number of theories which attempt to isolate the essential idea on which the sacrificial ritual and symbolism reposes. These theories point out the following elements in sacrifice: (1) the gift of man to the deity; (2) the homage of the subject to the lord; (3) the expiation of offenses; (4) communion with the deity in the sacrificial banquet; (5) life released from the victim, transmitted to the deity, and conferred upon the worshipers. The discussions concerning the theory of sacrifice turn upon which of these elements is the primary element from which the others can be derived. Actually the practice of sacrifice seems too complex to be reduced to a single radical element. The practice has not arisen from theoretical considerations of the nature of communion of man with the deity. Where one or more of the above elements is missing, the symbolism of the sacrificial act is altered. Not all sacrifices are expiatory; if the communion of man with the deity is conceived as established, sacrifice cements it; expiation is necessary only if it is conceived as sundered by human sin, which angers the deity. The common meal among many peoples is the supreme symbol of fellowship, and the sacrificial banquet is a symbol of existing fellowship with the deity; but this element does not appear in several types of OT sacri-

Assyrian sculpture representing the offering of an animal for sacrifice.

fice. If there is a basic element, it is the gift; in the ancient world the subject was expected to bring a gift to the sheikh or king to assure his benevolence if it was assumed to exist, or to restore it if the visitor was afraid that he was not in good standing. The element of the banquet is clear in the nature of the victims, which in the OT are food and drink, even when these are not shared by the worshipers. The victim proper is an animal; cereal offerings and libations appear only as accompaniments of animal sacrifices; they make the sacrifice a complete meal.

The common symbolic element in all OT sacrifices is the manipulation of the blood*; and since it is universal, it very probably symbolizes the essential note of the sacrificial symbolism. The blood is sprinkled on the altar*, or dashed at its base, or smeared on the horns*. The altar symbolizes the deity. In OT thought the blood is the life*; and the ritual of the blood is the precise symbolic act of oblation by which the life of the animal is transmitted to the deity. The mere slaughtering of the animal is not a ritually symbolic act. Another common ritual act is the imposition of hands upon the victim; this does not appear to support any theories of the ritual substitution of the victim

for the offerer, but rather is an act by which the offerer declares that this is his offering.

2. *Types of Israelite sacrifice*. The number of technical sacrificial terms in the OT is large. Some terms denote an offering without specifying the type: *'iššāh*, an offering by fire; *minḥāh*, in the early period a tribute, in the later period specialized to signify a cereal offering; *ḳōrban*, a gift. Of sacrifices in general it is noticed that they went to the priests (Dt 18:1; Jos 13:14; Ezk 44:29); only holy persons could eat food that had been consecrated, and the priests here represent the deity. The portions of the priests were taken only from some partly burnt offerings; cf below. The temple had chambers for storing the cereal offerings for later consumption (Ezk 42:13; Ne 13:5, 9). *Minḥāh*, meaning tribute paid to a human ruler, is used in Jgs 3:15 ff; 2 S 8:2, 6; 1 K 5:1; 2 K 17:3 f +, as a gift from man to man in Gn 32:14 ff; 33:10; 43:11 ff. This illustrates the original conception of sacrifice; the tribute was theoretically in the ancient Near East a free will offering of the vassal to the overlord. The word is used a few times to denote sacrifice in general (1 S 2:13–17; 26:19; Ps 96:8; Is 1:13), but by far the greater number of its occurrences are found in the P ritual prescriptions of the Pnt*. The spe-

cialized meaning of cereal offering is probably earlier than P; it appears in Ezk and in a few isolated passages elsewhere. The cereal offering is almost always an accompaniment of an animal offering (Jgs 13:19, 23; 1 K 8:64; 2 K 16:13–15; Is 43:23; 57:6; 66:3; Je 17:26; 33:18; Ezk 46:5, 7, 11, 14, 20; frequently in Ex, Lv, Nm). A tariff of the amount of cereal offerings to be made with various sacrifices is found in Ezk 45:13–24; 46:5–15; Lv 14:10, 21; 23: 13–17; Nm 15:4–9; 28–29; similar sacrificial tariffs have been found at the Phoenician colony located near Marseilles. The ritual of the cereal offering is set forth in Lv 2; part is burned, part goes to the priests. No leaven or honey is to be used.

Animal sacrifices were whole burnt offerings ('ôlāh, the ascender), or several types of partly burnt offerings. The ritual of these offerings is preserved only in the P portions of the Pnt, except for scattered allusions elsewhere. The P ritual is the ritual of the postexilic temple of Jerusalem, but this ritual must preserve preexilic ritual traditions; nothing is more conservative than ritual traditions. It is impossible, however, to write a history of the development of the ritual.

The whole burnt offering (Lv 1) must be unblemished; the offerer lays his hands on the victim; it is slaughtered and the blood dashed at the base of the altar; it is flayed and cut into pieces which are burned. In the P ritual it is to be offered only at the altar of whole burnt offerings (Ex 30:28 +; Lv 4:7–34; 1 Ch 6:34; 16:40 +). The symbolism of the whole burnt offering is obscure; it does not fall into the types of partly burnt offerings (cf below), and it is not an expiatory sacrifice. The totality of the offering obviously indicates greater solemnity; and it seems that the whole burnt offering is a ritual act of supreme adoration. It is offered at purification after childbearing (Lv 12:6, 8), the purification of the leper (Lv 14:19, 22), and after purification from uncleanness arising from sexual diseases (Lv 15:14–30); at the consecration of the Nazirite* (Nm 6:10–14); at the consecration of priests (Lv 9); regularly morning and evening in the temple ritual (2 K 16:15; Ezr 3:3; in the postexilic period it was supported by a tax on the general population, Ne 10:33 f) and on the major festivals (Nm 28–29). It was offered with peace offerings and a sacrificial banquet at the feast inaugurating the golden calf* (Ex 32:6) and at the covenant ritual of Sinai (Ex 24:5). Whole burnt offerings celebrated the destruction of a Canaanite high place (Jgs 6:26). It is offered at times of crisis, both of lamentation and exultation: in war (Jgs 20:26), especially before battle (1 S 7:9 f; 13:9–15), at the introduction

of the ark to Jerusalem (2 S 6:17 ff), at the theophany at the threshing floor of Araunah* which marked the halting of the plague (2 S 24:24 f), at Gibeon and Jerusalem, probably to celebrate the accession of Solomon (1 K 3 f, 15), at the consecration of the temple (1 K 8:64). Whole burnt offerings were offered in the cult of the Baal (2 K 10:24 f). These occasions seem to have no common motif except their solemnity; the whole burnt offering is made in times of supplication, atonement, and thanksgiving without expressing any one sentiment.

Partly burnt offerings. The general designation of these is zebaḥ, literally a slaughter victim; the name does not usually include whole burnt offerings. This is an extremely common designation of sacrifices in general; they are offered to other gods besides Yahweh (Ex 34:15; Nm 25:2; Dt 32:38; Jgs 16:23; 2 K 10:19–24; Ho 4:9 +). The name is used to designate sacrifices which do not come under the types mentioned below: the covenant sacrifice sealing an agreement (Gn 31:54, Jacob and Laban, Ex 24:5, Yahweh and Israel), the sacrifices at the installation of Saul as king (1 S 11:15), the family feast of David at Bethlehem (1 S 20:6, 29). It also designates the Passover* lamb, which is doubtfully a sacrifice. Sacrifices could be offered as votive offerings (Lv 23: 38; Dt 12:11, 17, 26; Ps 22:26; Is 19:21).

Peace offering. The partly burnt offerings are either peace offerings or atonement sacrifices. The peace offering (Hb šelem, usually in pl) is a symbol of good relations between man and Yahweh, which it expresses and cements. The ritual of the peace offering is given in Lv 3. The animal is to be unblemished; the imposition of hands occurs; the blood of the animal is dashed at the base of the altar; the fat of the entrails and kidneys is burned on the altar as the portion of Yahweh. The breast, which is "waved" before Yahweh, and the right thigh, which is "heaved" before Yahweh, go to the priests; the rest of the animal is consumed in the sanctuary as a sacrificial banquet. All of it must be eaten the same day; if anything is left over, it is to be burned. Ritual cleanliness* is demanded for participation in the banquet (Lv 7:11–36; 19:5). Peace offerings were offered after victory (1 S 11:15), at the inauguration of the golden calf, before battle (1 S 13:9), at the introduction of the ark to Jerusalem (2 S 6:17 f), at the halting of the plague (2 S 24:25), at the installation of Solomon (1 K 3:15), at the consecration of the Nazirite (Nm 6:14), at the consecration of the temple (1 K 8:64), with the morning whole burnt offering (Ezk 46:2), and other regular occasions (Ezk 45:17).

Particular types of the peace offering are the thank offering, the votive offering, and the free will offering. The ritual of these offerings is essentially the same (Lv 7; Nm 15:3). There are several allusions to the thank offering outside of P (Pss 27:6; 50:14, 23; 56:13; 107:22; 116:17; Am 4:5). The free will offering was offered at Pentecost* (Dt 16:10), at the restoration of the altar of Jerusalem (Ezr 3:5), at festivals (Nm 29:39) and outside of prescribed festive offerings (Lv 23:38). The animal offered as a free will offering need not be entirely perfect (Lv 22:23).

The symbolism of the peace offering is the fellowship of the sacrificial banquet. The offerers present a banquet to the deity, who in turn accepts it and invites the worshipers to dine with him. This signifies the most cordial and friendly relations. The occasion of the peace offering is almost always a joyous occasion, and the sacrificial banquet is frequently described in Dt as eating and drinking and rejoicing before your God (12: 7, 12, 18).

Atonement sacrifices. These presuppose that there has been a rupture of good relations between the deity and the worshiper, and the sacrifice is a propitiation to appease the deity and restore his good favor. The ritual of P distinguishes the guilt offering (Hb 'āšām) and the sin offering (Hb ḥaṭṭa't). The ritual of the oblation is given in Lv 4; the differences express the symbolism of atonement. As in the peace offerings, a portion goes to the priests and the fatty portion is burned on the altar for the deity. The blood is applied not by dashing it at the base of the altar but by smearing it on the horns (in some cases sprinkling it before the sanctuary also) and pouring the rest on the ground before the altar. There is no sacrificial banquet; what is not offered to Yahweh or given to the priests is burned outside the camp. A special holiness is attached to atonement sacrifices (Lv 14:13; Ezk 46:20). The distinction between the sin offering and the guilt offering is not clear and probably has its roots in ritual practices no longer understood by the P writers. The 'āšām is conceived by most scholars as damages or compensation rendered to the deity. The sin offering is offered in purification after childbirth (Lv 12:6, 8), purification from leprosy (Lv 14:19, 22, 31), purification from contact with death (Nm 6:11, 14, 16), purification from bodily uncleanness (Lv 15:15, 30). The list of faults for which the atonement sacrifices may be offered (Lv 4:1–6:7; Nm 15:22–31) shows clearly that it is offered only for faults committed unwittingly, and this shows an important feature of the Israelite sacrificial ritual: there is no

ritual atonement or expiation for sins committed "with a high hand," with full and deliberate malice. Forgiveness for such sins is obtained only by repentance. The Servant* of Yahweh makes himself a guilt offering (Is 53:10).

In the early period sacrifice could be offered by the king or the head of the family, as the patriarchs offered sacrifice and Solomon offered sacrifice at the dedication of the temple (1 K 8:5, 62–64). By the time the code of holiness (cf LAW) was prepared sacrifice had been restricted to the priests. The dispute was still active when Samuel rebuked Saul for offering sacrifice before battle without awaiting the arrival of Samuel (1 S 13:8–14). An even more important modification was the centralization of cult introduced in the law of Dt 12. This law, of uncertain origin, did not certainly exist in practice before it was implemented by Josiah*. Before this law the slaughtering of any animal for food was done only in sacrificial ritual; every meat dinner was a peace offering at the nearest sanctuary. The law of Dt permits the profane slaying of animals for food and restricts the offering of sacrifice to the temple of Jerusalem. This was the final step in making the Jerusalem temple the sole seat of sacrificial cult, a position which it maintained in Judaism until AD 70.

There are occasional references to the practice of human sacrifice both by Israelites and by other peoples. The story of Abraham and Isaac (Gn 22) is a theological statement of Yahweh's rejection of this sacrifice in the form of a story. This extreme measure was adopted by Mesha* of Moab when he was besieged by the Israelites (2 K 3:27). Most of the references to the practice in Israel can be traced to the Assyrian period, roughly 750–620 BC; but the practice is not Assyrian, and it seems to have been rare in the peoples of the ancient Near East in the entire historical period; cf FIRSTBORN.

The prophetic literature contains a number of passages which are critical not only of externalism in ritual, but which are interpreted by many scholars as a rejection of the ritual system itself (1 S 15:22; Ho 6:4–6; Ps 50; Is 1:10–17; Je 7:21 f; Am 4:4; 5:21–25; Mi 6:6–8). No such rejection is implied when the prophets demand genuine virtue and not sacrifice; this is evidently not only rhetorical, but it is Hb idiom to say "not X but Y" where we say "Y rather than X." Nor is such a rejection implied even when Yahweh is said to hate and reject sacrifices; when the offering conceals unrepented sin and unchanged malice, the symbol of holiness becomes a mask of unholiness. Ps 50 rises to an unaccustomed irony when it declares that Yahweh is not hungry. But many critics take Je 7:21 to be a denial of the early origin of the law of sacrifice, and Am 5:25 to be a denial even of the practice of sacrifice in Israel before its entrance into Canaan. Many more recent scholars, finding it very difficult to suppose that these two prophets could take a stand opposed to such a weight of literary and traditional evidence, have not accepted this radical interpretation. Je 7:21 f makes an antithesis between sacrifice and obedience (cf 1 S 15: 22); and Am 5:25 is best understood to mean that it was not *only* sacrifices that early Israel offered in the desert; the same antithesis is understood to be present, but it is implicit.

3. *NT*. Jesus repeats the prophetic criticism of sacrifice by quoting Ho 6:6 (Mt 9: 13; 12:7); His insistence on the need of genuine interior piety is entirely in accord with the prophetic teaching (cf LAW; PHARISEES). Sacrifice is metaphorically good deeds ("Spiritual sacrifices," 1 Pt 2:5) or submission to God ("present your bodies as a living sacrifice," Rm 12:1).

The sacrificial character of the death of Jesus and of the Eucharist* has been doubted as original with the Gospels and Paul by many theologians, who deny that there is any reference to sacrifice in these documents. The sacrificial character of the death of Jesus, they say, was first explained by the author of Heb. There is no doubt that sacrificial terms are rare in the Gospels and the Pauline literature; but there are good reasons for believing that Heb makes explicit what was believed and taught in the primitive apostolic instruction. In Heb 9–10 the priesthood* and sacrifice of Jesus are contrasted with the priesthood and sacrifice of Israel and Judaism. The atoning blood of the new covenant is the blood of Jesus (9:12–14). A covenant cannot be ratified without blood (9:15–21), and there is no forgiveness without the shedding of sacrificial blood (9:22). The atoning sacrifice of Jesus need be offered only once, since it is totally effective (9:25–28). The sacrifices of the law did not achieve true deliverance from sin (10:1–5); as we noticed above, there was no sacrificial remission for sins committed with a high hand. But Christ has offered a single perfect sacrifice which brings perfect forgiveness and holiness (10:5–18); and the Christian can approach the sanctuary with solid faith and hope that he is delivered from sin (10: 19–25).

This conception is expressed in Eph 5:2; Christ loved us and delivered Himself for us as a fragrant offering and sacrifice. Both Heb and Eph here emphasize the voluntary offering of Jesus; it is essential to sacrifice that it be offered with the free consent of the worshiper. The background is implicit in the formulae of institution of the Eucharist (Mt 26:26–29; Mk 14:22–25; Lk 22: 15–20; 1 Co 11:23–26). The allusions to blood and the covenant clearly reflect Ex 24:5–8, in which the covenant of Sinai was ratified by the communion of the blood of the sacrificial victim. The manipulation of the blood is the essential rite of offering in OT sacrifice (cf above) and the words of Jesus recall the sacrificial character of blood. Thus there is no reason to doubt, as some scholars do, that the communion of the body and blood of Jesus Christ (1 Co 10:16–22) alludes to the sacrificial character of the Eucharist; the context contrasts the eating of the Eucharist with the sacrificial banquets of both Jews and pagans. The Eucharist is the sacrificial banquet which is prepared by the offering of Jesus Christ (cf above); it is the sign and seal of the communion of the worshipers with the deity.

Sadducees (Gk *saddukaioi* [always in pl in NT], etymology uncertain; some suggest that Sadducee = Zadokite, a descendant of Zadok* [cf QUMRAN]; others derive it from *ṣaddîk*, "righteous"). The Sadducees were a party or group within Judaism in the NT period. They are known only from the NT and from Josephus* and not much information is available. The Sadducees were the priestly aristocracy and their dependents and supporters. It seems that they are more accurately designated as a religious rather than as a political party. Josephus and the NT ascribe to them distinct beliefs different from the beliefs of the Pharisees; they denied the resurrection of the dead and the existence of angels and spirits (AA 23:6–8); apparently they had no messianic doctrine, unless it was the belief in the priestly Messiah*; they accepted only the Torah, the written law* as authoritative and rejected the Pharisaic doctrine of the traditions of the elders. Josephus adds that they defend freedom (as contrasted with the Pharisaic belief in predestination); but this is very probably an effort to present the two groups as philosophical schools. Josephus also relates that they were more rigorous than the Pharisees in the interpretation of penal legislation; in general the Pharisees represented rigorous standards of observance.

The origin of the party probably lies in the position of the high priest* during the Persian administration. The high priest was accepted by the Persian authorities as the representative of the people; this naturally gave the priestly families a certain amount of prestige and political influence. Under the Hasmonean* kings the Sadducees were the ruling party. While they were not precisely a political party, they did represent certain ideas on how to live under the Roman administration; and it appears that the Sadducees included the conservative class of landowners and merchants. They believed in stability and therefore in peaceful collaboration with a foreign rule which could not be dislodged. This was odious to the extreme nationalist wing of Judaism (cf ZEALOT). As a group the Sadducees disappeared with the destruction of the temple and the priesthood in AD 70, and the Judaism which survived the disaster was rabbinical and Pharisaic.

In the Gospels the Sadducees are condemned with the Pharisees by John the Baptist (Mt 3:7) and by Jesus (Mt 16:1–12). Their only encounter with Jesus reported in the Gospels is the question concerning levirate marriage (Mt 22:22–33; Mk 12:18–27; Lk 20:27–40). The question was a trap, intended to make the belief in the resurrection appear ridiculous. In AA 4:1; 5:17 the Sadducees appear as extremely hostile to the apostles, whom they imprisoned to prevent their preaching. Paul made use of the doctrinal difference between Pharisees and Sadducees to divert an attack on himself (AA 23:6–8).

Salamis (Gk *salamis*), in NT times the largest city and port of Cyprus*. Its ruins lie on the bay of Famagusta N of the modern city of Famagusta. It was the first point reached by Paul and Barnabas in their first missionary journey; they preached in the synagogues of the city (AA 13:5).

Salem (Hb *šālēm*, meaning uncertain), the name of the city of Melchizedek* (Gn 14:18), identified with Jerusalem* in Ps 76:3 and in early Jewish tradition, which is accepted by modern interpreters. That this name was ever used is extremely doubtful; the city is called Urusalim in the Amarna* Letters, and this component represents a god known in Akkadian as Shulman and in Canaanite (Ugarit*) as Shalem. The abbreviation of the title may be intended to conceal the divine name.

Salim (Gk *saleim*), in Jn 3:23 the point of reference for Aenon (which cannot be located) where John was baptizing. Two identifications have been suggested, one near the Jordan about 8 mi S of Beisan, another in the hill country 3–4 mi E of Balatah (Shechem*).

Salmon (Hb *salmā'* and *sālmôn*, Gk *salmōn*), the father of Boaz* (Rt 4:20–21; 1 Ch 2:11;

Mt 1:4 f; Lk 3:32). On the originality of the genealogy in Rt cf RUTH. The name is very probably the name of a clan of Judah, called in 1 Ch 2:51, 54 "the father of Bethlehem," and was inserted as a personal name into the partly artificial genealogical lists found in Ch and Rt and transcribed in Mt and Lk; cf GENEALOGY.

Salome (Gk *salōmē*, from Hb *šālôm*, "peace"). 1. Wife of Zebedee* and mother of the apostles James* and John*. She stood by the cross of Jesus and took part in His burial (Mk 15:40; 16:1). She also, although her name does not occur in the passage, asked that her sons might sit one on the right hand of Jesus and one on the left in His kingdom. This elicited the affirmative answer to the question whether they could drink the chalice He had to drink (Mt 20:20 ff).

2. Daughter of Herod Philip and Herodias, daughter of Aristobulus. Her name is not mentioned in the Gospels, but it was her dance which trapped Herod Antipas into the promise which could be fulfilled only by the execution of John the Baptist (Mt 14:1 ff; Mk 6:17 ff). She was the wife of Philip* the tetrarch, and after his death married Aristobulus, the son of Herod of Chalcis. Her birth probably took place about AD 10, so that she was still a young girl at the time of the dance. At the time of her marriage to Philip there must have been a difference between them of about 30 years.

Salt. The chief Palestinian source of salt in the ancient period was the Dead Sea area, in particular Jebel Usdum, a cliff of rock salt about 6 mi long and 650 ft high. The erosion of the wind creates fantastic figures and the face of the mountain is constantly changing. The importance of this source of salt is attested in Ezk 47:11; the stream which rises from the temple in the New Jerusalem will flow into the Dead Sea and sweeten it, but the swamps and marshes of the Sea will remain bitter; they will be sources of salt. Lot's wife was changed into a pillar of salt (Gn 19:26); this story is no doubt created from one of the formations of Jebel Usdum (cf above); in modern times the Arabs give personal names to some of these figures which resemble human beings. A story of Elisha* relates that he sweetened a brackish spring by salting it; the story illustrates the principle of sympathetic magic. Salt was to be offered with all sacrificial victims (Lv 2:13; Ezk 43:24).

Salt is mentioned in several metaphorical senses. A covenant of salt is a covenant of friendship (Nm 18:19; 2 Ch 13:5); the eating of the salt of another is a symbol of friendship in many languages. "Salt land" is a common name for desert wasteland (Dt 29:22; Ps 107:34; Jb 39:6; Je 17:6; Zp 2:9). Salt is scattered on the ruins of a city which has been destroyed by a conqueror (Jgs 9:45) to signify that he has made it a desert; similar symbolism was practiced by Greeks and Romans. To season one's speech with salt (Col 4:6) is to speak with intelligence. The saying of Jesus about salt (Mt 5:13; Mk 9:49 f; Lk 14:34 f) differs slightly in Mt from Mk-Lk; Mt expressly identifies the disciples as the salt, which is probably an exegetical expansion. They are the salt in that they diffuse their teaching and example (parallel to "light of the world" in 5:14). Without this expansion the saying in Mk and Lk refers to the possibility of defection from the gospel. Mk on the principle of the catchword has collected three sayings about salt, each of which is obscure. The salting of the condemned (9:49) probably refers to the extreme character of the punishment. The second saying is identical with the saying in Lk. The third saying, "Have salt in you and keep the peace with each other" probably refers to salt as the charity which seasons the relations of men with each other.

Salvation. 1. *OT*. The word and the idea of salvation are basic in the faith and theology of both OT and NT. Like so many theological terms, salvation has originally a secular significance; but in OT usage this appears much less frequently than its religious significance. The Hb root *YŠ'* and its derivatives appear to signify primarily the possession of space and the freedom and security which is gained by the removal of constriction; "save" frequently stands in antithesis to the root *ṢRR* and its derivatives, which signify narrowness, straits. J. Pedersen has remarked that Ps 91 is a compendium of what salvation means. One saves by defending or assisting in war and battle (Jos 10:6; 1 S 23:2, 5; 2 S 10:19 +). Salvation is frequently deliverance from war and invasion (Jgs 2:16; 8:22; 12:3; 13:5; 1 S 9:16; Pss 44:8; 69:14; 80:4, 8, 20; 85:8, 10; Je 42:11 +). Frequently "save" and "salvation" can be translated simply by "victory" (Dt 33:29; 20:4; Jgs 15:18; 1 S 14:45; 2 S 23:10, 12; Ps 68:20; Pr 21:31). Jehoash shoots "Yahweh's arrow of victory" over Damascus (2 K 13:17). Hence to save means to render help or protection in any "straits": Yahweh preserves the life of men and beasts (Ps 36:7); a girl who is assaulted calls for salvation (Dt 22:27).

That Yahweh saves is stated hundreds of times in the OT and quotations are not necessary. When it appears that He will not save, there is none to save (Jgs 12:3; 1 S 11:3; 2 S 22:42; Ps 18:42 +). It is affirmed explicitly that Yahweh alone saves (Ho 13:4) and that the safety of Israel is in Yahweh (Je 3:23; 1 Mc 3:18; 4:11; 2 Mc 1:11; 2:17). Yahweh is frequently invoked or described by titles which employ the words "save" and "salvation," and these can be called His most characteristic appellatives in the OT. The frequently recurring phrases "God of my (your, his) salvation" (Pss 18:47; 24:5; 25:5; 27:9; 65:6; 79:9; 85:5 +; Is 17:10; Mi 7:7; Hab 3:18) and "rock of my (your, his) salvation" (Dt 32:15; Pss 62:3, 7; 89:27; 95:1) are adjectival uses of the noun; the phrases are better rendered "my saving God" and "my saving rock." Yahweh is called "my light and my salvation" (Ps 27:1) or "my salvation" (2 S 22:3; Ps 18:3). Yahweh saves by His own power, His own arm (Is 59:16; 63:5). The vanity of other gods is shown by their inability to save (Is 45:20; 46:7; Je 2:28; 11:12). It is foolish to expect salvation from men or from any human devices: the sword (Ps 44:7), the nation (Lam 4:17), Assyria (Ho 14:4), horses and chariots (Ps 33:17), man (Is 26:18).

Yahweh does save through human means, but it is clearly understood that He raises men to be saviors and empowers them to save. This is the conception of charismatic leader which is so fundamental in the theology and the sociology of Israel; cf KING; SPIRIT. The judges* of Israel are saviors (Jgs 2:16; 3:9; 6:36 f; 7:7; 8:22; 10:13; 12:3; 13:5), and the same conception is transferred to the king in the beginning of the monarchy (1 S 9:16; 11:3; 14:23, 29). The unnamed savior of 2 K 13:5 is probably the king of Assyria, whose war against Damascus drew the Aramaeans from their attacks on Israel. The association of the king with salvation is close. The idea of the king-savior is not peculiar to Israel nor original with Israel; it appears in some fashion in most of the ancient Near East (cf KING). But the Israelite king is associated with the salvation of Yahweh. He is in the first place the peculiar object of the salvation of Yahweh (2 S 8:6, 14; Pss 20:6 f, 10; 21:2). He is then the savior of his people, particularly in war (Ps 33:16). He is the savior of his people also through the law, the saving power which any of his subjects may invoke in any need (2 S 14:4; 2 K 6:26 f). He is the savior of those who because of their weakness most need a savior, the poor* (Ps 72:4, 13). In a well ordered society the king is a channel of salvation to the people; to him they may look, for Yahweh has incorporated in the king His own power to save.

The saving power of Yahweh is exercised through His dominion over nature, which is the instrument of His salvation and His judgment. His saving power is manifested in the theophany (Hab 3:8) and in His victory in creation (Ps 74:12). The most marvelous saving act of Yahweh is His deliverance of Israel in the exodus* (Ex 14:13; 15:2; Ps 78:22; Is 63:9). The power which is revealed in this work cannot be conceived as limited by any superior power.

The will of Yahweh to save Israel is rooted in the covenant* relationship of Yahweh and Israel, and therefore in His promises* and His righteousness* and His fidelity (cf FAITH). But it is also connected with the qualities of the person who seeks for salvation. Security comes from integrity (Pr 28:18). Israel's assurance against Assyria comes from "resting," a synonym here of faith* (Is 30:15). Judah will be saved from invasion through repentance* (Je 4:14). The righteous* may hope for salvation (Pss 7:11; 17:7; 34:19; 37:40; Jb 13:16), as may the innocent (Ps 37:39) and the obedient (Ps 50:23). But the favorite object of the salvation of Yahweh in the later books of the OT are the poor and the helpless (Pss 12:6; 18:28; 76:10; 109:31; Jb 5:16; 22:29 +). These can invoke Yahweh with an urgency possible to no one else, for His salvation is dispensed most readily to those who are most hopeless.

In this attitude toward the poor the personal aspect of salvation emerges; and many of the Pss of personal lamentation contain petitions for the salvation of the individual man. In these liturgical prayers the salvation which is asked is usually vague and undefined; the petition is suitable to any need. Most frequently the prayer is for salvation from enemies (Pss 3:8; 7:2; 31:17; 54:3; 55:17; 57:4; 69:2; 71:2 f +), also from the lion's mouth (Ps 22:22), from the wicked (Ps 59:3). Ps 6:5 is probably a petition for salvation from illness.

The idea of salvation is deepened and expanded after the exile; for the power and will of Yahweh to save must be exhibited in a manner which exceeds even the greatness of His saving deeds in the exodus if Israel is to survive this crisis. The simplest form on which this salvation is expected is the restoration of Israel to its own land (Pss 14:7; 69:36, exilic doxologies added to the Pss; Je 30:10). But the future salvation soon becomes messianic in character and is seen as a new creation of Israel, an event in which all the themes of victory and deliverance implied in the word are brought to their fullness. The messianic king is a savior in a way in which the historic kings never were (Je 23:6; 33:16; Zc 9:9). The mes-

sianic salvation is eternal (Is 45:7; 51:6, 8). Salvation is a garment worn by Zion (Is 61:10), a helmet donned by Yahweh (Is 59:17). It sprouts from the earth (Is 45:8). The walls of the new Jerusalem are named Salvation (Is 26:1; 60:18). Salvation is wells from which water is drawn with joy (Is 12:3). The salvation of Jerusalem glows like a burning torch (Is 62:1). The frequency of the word in Is 40–66 is remarkable; it is a refrain which dominates the entire composition of these passages. Salvation means a new Zion and a new Israel, a new revelation of the character of Yahweh, and by implication a new world. Salvation approaches the idea of liberation from all evil, collective and personal, and the acquisition of complete security. It does not explicitly reach the idea of the attainment of spiritual good as such. In Ps 51:16 the petitioner asks to be delivered from guilt, by which possibly is meant the consequences of guilt; but the entire Ps asks for an interior and moral regeneration. In Ezk 36:29; 37:23 the new Israel is saved from impurities and from apostasies. The supreme threat to the salvation of Israel in both the historical and the prophetic literature is the sins of Israel, in particular its disloyalty to Yahweh. The full and eternal salvation of the messianic Israel is inconceivable unless this threat is removed. But the OT does not see the removal of the threat precisely as a saving act of Yahweh.

The extension of the salvation of Yahweh beyond Israel is less clearly presented. It is extended in the sense that the saving acts and power of Yahweh must be proclaimed and recognized by all the world (Pss 67:3; 98:2 f; Is 43:3; 49:6; 52:10). Thus all men will confess that Yahweh alone can save; and they must then seek salvation from Him alone who can give (Is 45:22) and listen to the salvation proclaimed by the Servant* of Yahweh (Is 49:6).

2. *NT.* The background of OT usage is the principal factor in the creation of the NT use of the words save, savior, and salvation; but the use of *sōzein,* "save," *sōtēr,* "savior," and *sōtēria,* "salvation" in Gk and Hellenistic literature and inscriptions is probably not without effect on the NT. The title *sōtēr* is applied to several gods and goddesses: Zeus, Heracles, Serapis and Isis in the mystery* cults, and in particular to Asklepios the healer; and in this last instance the title means "healer." *Sōtēr* is applied in Gk inscriptions to distinguished men who have rendered public service. It is frequently assumed by the Hellenistic kings after Alexander (cf PTOLEMY; SELEUCUS) or applied to them, and from this usage it is applied to the emperors of Rome. In at least some of these instances *sōtēr* as a royal title re-

flects the deification of kings. Against the OT background it is scarcely possible to think that the NT usage of the words is derived from the Hellenistic usage; the influence shows rather in another direction. The title *sōtēr* is strangely rare in the early books of the NT — the Synoptic Gospels, the Pauline epp, and even in Jn, and is found much more frequently in the Catholic epp and the pastoral epp. Vincent Taylor thinks that the absence of the title must be deliberate; the use of the word in Gk forms of the imperial cult and the mystery cults restricted and delayed its Christian usage. No such inhibition appears in the words *sōzein* and *sōtēria*. When the title does appear in the NT, it means that the Christians now present Jesus as the one true *sōtēr*, effecting that salvation which is falsely promised in the cults. *Sōtēria* is also achieved by those who are initiated into the mysteries. After the 1st century the title *sōtēr* is very frequently given to Jesus in Christian literature.

The word "save" in the Synoptic Gospels means a healing accomplished by Jesus (Mt 9:21; Mk 3:4; 5:23, 28; 6:56; Lk 6:9; 8:36, 50; 17:19). This saving is attributed to the faith of the person cured (Mt 9:22; Mk 5:34; 10:52; Lk 8:48; 17:19; 18:42); here and in some other passages it is very probable that the word "save" is used in a pregnant sense to suggest that the healing is a visible sign of the saving power of Jesus, which confers a far great salvation than the health of the body; cf below.

That God (or the Father) saves is basic in the NT (Lk 1:47; 1 Tm 1:1; 2:3; 4:10; Tt 2:10; 3:4; Jd 25). More significant is the emphasis on the truth that salvation is the work of the divine initiative and election (1 Th 5:9; 2 Th 2:13; 2 Tm 1:9; Heb 1:4). Salvation is a work of God's mercy and not of man's activity (Tt 3:5), a work of His grace (Eph 2:5; Tt 2:11) and His patience (2 Pt 3:15). Even more frequently is it affirmed that salvation comes through Jesus Christ (Lk 2:11; Jn 10:9; AA 13:23; Rm 15:11; 16:30 f; Tt 1:3 f; 2 Pt 1:1, 11; 3:2, 18; 1 Jn 4:14). Jesus is the savior of the Church His body (Eph 5:23); the meaning of "save" here is explicit in Eph 5:26 f. Salvation is in Jesus alone (AA 4:12; 2:21; Rm 10:13). That Jesus is the one savior became clear in the controversy concerning the observance of the Law* by Gentile Christians, and was stated in opposition to the claim that circumcision was necessary for salvation (AA 15:1, 11). The salvation which comes to the house of Zacchaeus* is identical with the person of Jesus (Lk 19:9). Jesus is the "pioneer" and the source of salvation (Heb 2:10; 5:9). Simeon saw salvation when he saw the in-

fant Jesus (Lk 2:30). Salvation comes through the cross*, which is the power of God to those who are saved (1 Co 1:18).

The salvation which Jesus confers is salvation from sin. He gives repentance and forgiveness of sins (AA 5:31). Through the knowledge of salvation Christians escape from the defilements of the world (2 Pt 2:20). The coming of the Messiah brings salvation and forgiveness of sins (Lk 1:77). The name of Jesus is interpreted by the angel who speaks to Joseph as signifying that the child will deliver His people from their sins (Mt 1:21). Christ Jesus came to save sinners (1 Tm 1:15). Sinners are meant by "the lost" whom Jesus comes to seek and to save (Lk 19:10). There is very probably a play on the significance of save in such apparently neutral uses of the word as those of the disciples and Peter when they are in danger on the Sea of Galilee (Mt 8:35; 14:30); by their invocation of Jesus when they are threatened by the powers of nature they confess that He is savior. The play is even more apparent in the incidents in which the healing of the sick is called salvation (cf above). Faith is the principle of salvation by healing as it is the principle of salvation from sin (cf below), and Jesus attributes the healing in several instances to faith (Mt 9:22; Mk 5:34; 10:52; 18:42; Lk 8:48; 17:19). The same phrase, "your faith has saved you," is addressed to the penitent woman of the forgiveness of her sins (Lk 7:50). A tragic play on the word appears in the passion narratives when Jesus is said in mockery to be unable to save Himself, although He saved others (Mt 27:40, 42; Mk 15:30 f; Lk 23:35–39); the phrase is spoken in the place and the hour of the climactic saving act. Salvation is deliverance from the judgment* (Jn 3:17; 5:34; 12:47) and the anger* of God (Rm 5:9 f).

The reception of salvation by the saved is conceived as a process rather than a single act. In some instances "to be saved" means to accept the faith; this is the "salvation" which the believing husband or wife can communicate to the unbelieving spouse (1 Co 7:16), and the salvation desired by God for all men is synonymous with "coming to the knowledge of the truth" (1 Tm 2:4). This salvation comes from the Jews (Jn 4:22), who are the channels of God's revelation and His saving acts, but it is intended for all men. It is a serious theological problem for Paul that salvation reaches the Gentiles through the defection of the Jews (AA 28:28; Rm 11:11). God is the savior of all men (1 Tm 2:4; 4:10). The means of salvation are the gospel and preaching*, in which salvation is proclaimed (AA 13:26;

16:17; Rm 1:16; 1 Co 1:21; 15:2; 1 Th 2:16; Eph 1:13; 1 Tm 4:16;, Heb 2:3; Js 1:21). The believer is saved through baptism* (1 Pt 3:21). The essential act of the person is faith*, through which he accepts the gospel preached to him and the salvation which it proclaims — in the concrete, salvation is identified with Christ Jesus dead and risen (AA 16:30 f; Rm 10:10; 1 Co 1:21; Eph 2:8; 1 Pt 1:9). Faith is identical with the love of truth which saves (2 Th 2:10). The sacred books (of the OT) instruct to salvation through the faith in Christ Jesus (which they inspire, 2 Tm 3:15). The hope of salvation is a helmet in the armor of the Christian (Eph 6:17; 1 Th 5:8), and through hope* we are saved (Rm 8:24).

The reception of salvation by the Christian is not conceived as a purely passive inaction. The emphasis on the divine election and initiative, the grace of God in Jesus Christ and the vital importance of faith do not release the Christian from those actions which salvation demands. The works which Paul repudiates as saving are the works of the Law*. His own sufferings work for the salvation of the Corinthians (2 Co 1:6), and his imprisonment is salutary for himself (Phl 1:19). Repentance leads to salvation (2 Co 7:10). Christians must work out their salvation in fear and trembling (Phl 2:12); this passage indicates that salvation is a process whose term lies in the future (cf below). The firmness of the Philippians is a token of their salvation (Phl 1:28). Even childbearing is salutary for women (1 Tm 2:15). Faith without works cannot save (Js 2:14); one who reclaims a sinner from his evil ways will save himself (Js 5:20).

A large number of texts present salvation as finally achieved in the eschatological event. The achievement of our savior Jesus Christ is life and immortality (2 Tm 1:10). The glory of Christ our savior is manifested in His eschatological appearance (Tt 2:13). The salvation which is nearer than when Christians began to believe must' be the eschatological salvation of the Parousia* (Rm 13:11). Salvation in Christ Jesus accompanies eternal glory (2 Tm 2:10). Salvation grows until its final accomplishment (Heb 6:9). Christ saves in His second coming (Heb 9:28). Salvation will be revealed on the last day (1 Pt 1:5), and Christians must grow to the fullness of salvation (1 Pt 2:2). The eschatological victory of Apc is called salvation (Apc 7:10; 12:10; 19:1). Salvation is attained by him who perseveres to the end (Mt 10:22; 24:13; Mk 13:13); this saying is uttered in the context of the eschatological discourse. One must lose his life in order to save it (Mt 16:25; Mk 8:35; Lk 9:24). Salvation is entrance into the eschatological

kingdom (Mt 19:25; Mk 10:26; Lk 13:23; 18:26). The salvation of the elect comes from the shortening of the time of the eschatological tribulations (Mt 24:22; Mk 13:20). The man who is saved by the fire of testing (1 Co 3:15) is ready for the final judgment of his acts. The spirit of man is saved in the day of the Lord (1 Co 5:5).

One of the recurring heresies of the history of Christianity has been the belief that salvation could be finally and completely achieved by a single act, whether that act be conceived as the predestination of God, the saving death of Jesus Christ, or the reception of faith and baptism. There is in these texts a massive witness of the NT teaching that the salvation conferred by the death of Christ and accepted by faith and baptism and membership in the Church the body of Christ is real and genuine, but inchoative; it demands growth and can be regarded as finally achieved only in the eschatological event which marks the term of human activity. Salvation in the eschatological sense returns to the OT idiom in which salvation means victory; the salvation of man is God's final victory over evil.

Samaria (Hb *šōmᵉrôn*, meaning uncertain), a royal city of the kingdom of Israel located at the modern Sebastiyeh, 7 mi NW of Nablus. The site was purchased by Omri* from its owner Shemer* for 2 talents of silver; the city was named after the owner (1 K 16:24). The site is agreeable and defensible. It occupies the top of a hill which is steep on all sides, offering a good view of the Mediterranean and exposure to the sea breezes. To the N and E the mountains rise higher, but Jerusalem can be seen to the S. Isaiah called it the proud crown of the drunkards of Samaria, the fading flower of its glorious beauty, at the head of a rich valley (28:1-4). The city is mentioned frequently in 1 K 17–2 K 17 as the royal residence of Israel. It was besieged by Ben-hadad* of Damascus during the reign of Ahab*; the besiegers were defeated by a sortie (1 K 20:1-21). A prophetic story of Elisha* relates that he led Aramaean attackers into the city by casting temporary blindness upon them (2 K 6:19-23). Another siege by Ben-hadad is related during the reign of an unnamed Israelite king (6:19-23). The members of the royal house and the worshipers of the Baal were massacred in Samaria by Jehu* (2 K 10). When Hoshea* rebelled against Assyria the city was besieged 724–721 and finally taken; the siege was begun by Shalmaneser V and completed by Sargon*, who acceded to the throne in 721. Sargon records the capture of the city and the deportation of 27,290 in-

The Hill of Samaria.

habitants, his restoration and improvement of the city, the institution of an Assyrian province called Samerina in the territory and the installation of an Assyrian governor (ANET 284–285). The account of the fall of the kingdom in 2 K 17 adds that Sargon settled people from Babylon, Cuthah, Avva, and Sepharvaim in the cities of Samaria (2 K 17:24; the name Samaria appears here for the first time as the name of a district, not a city). These peoples added the worship of Yahweh to the worship of their own gods. 2 Ch 30:1–11 relates that Hezekiah* attempted to impose a cultic reform upon the territory of Samaria; many modern historians are inclined to see in this the trace of a genuine historical notice of a claim exercised by Hezekiah upon former Israelite territory during the rebellion of 705–701 BC. There is no doubt that Josiah* extended his religious reform to the district of Samaria and that he attempted to incorporate the territory into the kingdom of Judah (2 K 23:19).

The prophets of the 8th century mention Samaria frequently, always with hostility. Isaiah (7:9) calls it the head of Ephraim, threatens it with destruction (8:4; 28:1–4), alludes to its contemporary defeats by Assyria (9:8–12), and puts in the mouth of the Assyrian king boasts of its conquests (10:9–11; 36:19). Amos sees tumults and oppression in its midst (3:9) and threatens it with

destruction (3:12; 6:1). Its women are fat cows (4:1); its inhabitants worship the Ashimah* (8:14). Hosea speaks of its corruption and wickedness (7:1), alludes to the calf which it worshiped (8:5 f; 10:5) and threatens the city and its king with terrible destruction (10:7; 14:1). Micah (1:5–7) calls it the transgression of Israel, as Jerusalem is the sin of Judah, meaning that the wickedness of the nation reaches its peak in the capital, and threatens it with total desolation. A. Alt proposed a theory which may explain some of this hostility; he believes that Samaria, like Jerusalem, was strictly a royal city consisting of the palace and the residences of the palace personnel. It was owned by the king. In Israel, Alt suggests, Samaria was populated entirely by Canaanites; Omri, he thinks, united in the one crown a dual monarchy of Israel and Canaanites as David had united in one crown Israel and Judah. The Israelite royal city Alt places in Jezreel*.

Later settlements of foreign peoples in the district of Samaria by Esarhaddon* and Osnappar* (Ashur-bani-pal) are mentioned in Ezr 4:2, 10. The city continued as the seat of Persian administration of the district, which included Jerusalem after the disappearance of Zerubbabel* until the coming of Nehemiah*. The Jews of Elephantine* addressed a letter to the authorities at Samaria and at Jerusalem after the destruction of their temple in 408 BC. The Hellenization of Samaria began with the conquest of Alexander; Perdiccas established a Macedonian military colony in the city, and it remained predominantly Hellenistic through the rest of the biblical period. Shechem rather than Samaria was the center of the Samaritans*. The city was besieged and destroyed by John Hyrcanus in 108 BC (cf HASMONEAN). It was rebuilt by Pompey and Gabinius; but a new city in magnificent style was constructed by Herod*, who settled there 6000 Roman veterans. Herod named the city Sebaste (Gk sebastē, Lt augusta, after his patron Augustus). The district was detached from Judaea in the Roman organization of the province of Syria but was included in the kingdoms of Herod and Archelaus*. After the deposition of Archelaus it was administered by the procurator of Judaea, except during the short reign of Agrippa* I (AD 41–44).

In the Gospels the district is mentioned in Lk 17:11; Jesus traversed Samaria on His way from Galilee to Jerusalem; and Jn 4:4–7 (cf SYCHAR). In AA 1:8 Samaria is mentioned as the first point out of Judaea where the apostles will bear witness to Jesus. The line is probably composed as a reflection of the events related in AA 8–9. When the Jerusalem community was scattered in the persecution in which Stephen* was killed, the members of the community preached in the district of Samaria with good success (AA 8:1–25), and churches established there are mentioned in AA 9:31; 15:3.

The site was excavated 1908–1910 by G. A. Reisner and C. S. Fisher under the auspices of Harvard University, and in 1931–1935 by a joint British-American-Hebrew University expedition directed by J. W. Crowfoot. The archaeology of the site was difficult, since the Hellenistic and Roman builders trenched and leveled the Israelite remains to build right on top of them. The fortifications of the city walls of the Israelite city contained the best masonry recovered from the Israelite period. The royal palace* area, a rectangle of 5 acres, was identified; since Omri could have had only a few years' residence on the site, the palace is attributed principally to Ahab*. This was a citadel within the fortress. An older "inner wall" was later strengthened by a casemate wall which made the fortifications 31 ft thick. Traces of some destruction were attributed to the attacks of Hazael* of Damascus, 815–805 BC. Later phases of reconstruction were attributed to Jehu* and Jeroboam* II. The pottery of the site has convinced most archaeologists (except the excavators themselves) that Omri did not buy an empty hill; it was occupied by a village. The Roman remains come from the period of Herod and later, and there are well preserved ruins of Byzantine churches. Herod built a temple of Augustus over the Israelite palace, new fortifications enclosing an oval about ⅝ mi at its widest dimension, and a forum; some of the columns of the colonnades of the forum are still standing. From the Hellenistic period there remains a round tower of excellent masonry.

In the palace area were recovered 65 ostraka*. These are administrative documents ("chits" is a more proper word) from the Israelite monarchy dealing with the delivery of jars of wine and oil. District names, some identical with the clan lists of biblical genealogies, and personal names, several of which occur in the OT, are found in the ostraka. Scholars do not think these are records of taxes, but rather of the delivery of produce from the tenants of the crown lands. The ivories* of Samaria illustrate the luxury of which the prophets speak (ANEP 129, 130, 566).

Samaritans. In the NT Samaritans is the name given to the inhabitants of the district of Samaria*; but the name has deep religious overtones. To the Jews the Samaritans were a heretical and schismatic group of spurious worshipers of the God of Israel, who were detested even more than pagans. The origins of the schism between Jews and Samaritans lie deep in early Israelite history; indeed, it probably reflects the fact that Judah and Israel were never really one. Political and religious divisions between Judah and the other tribes appear both before the reigns of David and Solomon and after the establishment of the kingdom of Israel by Jeroboam I.

The Jews who settled in Jerusalem after the edict of Cyrus* (538 BC) did not regard the community which inhabited the district of Samaria, the ancient heartland of Israel, as true Israelites. They were the descendants of a mixed population: Israelites who had survived the Assyrian deportations (cf SAMARIA) and peoples from various Mesopotamian communities who had been settled in Israel. These peoples had introduced the worship of their own gods into the land of Israel (2 K 17). These foreign beliefs do not appear to have survived; in all the hostile remarks made of the Samaritans by Jews there is no charge of worshiping foreign gods. When the Jewish community led by Zerubbabel* and Jeshua* began the rebuilding of the temple the Samaritan community wished to join them in the construction; they were rudely rebuffed and harassed the project in various ways so that it was delayed (Ezr 4:1–6). When the construction of the walls was begun, the Samaritan authorities took stronger measures; they protested to the Persian court that this was an act of rebellion, and the work was halted until Nehemiah* came as governor (Ezr 4: 7–24). The Samaritans attempted to frighten and to discourage Nehemiah from building the walls, since his authority from the Persian court could not be shaken; they scoffed at the work, threatened armed opposition, and apparently attempted to assassinate Nehemiah (Ne 4; 6:1–13). The opposition was unsuccessful. But the breach between Jews and Samaritans had been made and it was irreparable. At some date between the time of Nehemiah and the beginning of the Maccabean period the schism became open and complete when the Samaritans built a temple to Yahweh on Mt Gerizim*. Josephus reports that this happened when Alexander* visited Palestine, but there are some inaccuracies of detail in his account which lead to the suspicion that he did not have primary sources for the date. The insistence of the Jews on genealogies to prove purity of blood probably comes from the time of the Samaritan disputes. It is clear that the schism occurred before the Jews accepted the prophets and the writings as canonical (cf CANON); the Samaritans accept only the Pnt. The MS now to be seen at Nablus is thought by scholars to belong to the 12th century AD. The text has some minor differences from the MT (cf TEXT), and has an added verse which identifies Gerizim as the temple mountain. Some readings of the Samaritan Pnt appears in the MSS of Qumran*.

During the Maccabean wars the Samaritans were allied with the Seleucid forces (1 Mc 3:10). When the Seleucid rulers found themselves unable to subdue the Jews they granted part of the district of Samaria to them (1 Mc 10:30, 38; 11:28, 34). In 108 BC John Hyrcanus (cf HASMONEANS) destroyed the Samaritan temple and ravaged the territory. Josephus reports that a band of Samaritans profaned the temple of Jerusalem in the administration of Coponius (AD 6–9) by scattering the bones of dead men in the sanctuary. Pilate* attacked a religious procession of the Samaritans led by a messianic prophet in AD 35; the protest of the Samaritans was the occasion of his recall.

The beliefs of the Samaritans are obscurely known. They now accept the rule of a theocratic high priest, and this was probably their traditional government; the priesthood traced its origin back to Aaron, and Ne 13:28 relates that Nehemiah expelled one of the family of the high priest who went to Samaria. Like the Pharisees*, they believed in the authority of oral tradition as interpreting the law. Their eschatology, derived from the Pnt exclusively, was primi-

tive, but they did not exhibit the radical denial of eschatology which is seen in the Sadducees*. Their messianism (alluded to in Jn 4:25) was also vague, centered upon a figure called Taheb, "the Restorer," a prophet from the tribe of Levi modeled on Dt 18:15. The community still survives and numbers about 350 in Nablus; they have their own ritual of celebrating the Passover.

The hostility of Jews and Samaritans is reflected several times in the Bible. BS 50: 25–26 calls the foolish people who live in Shechem no nation. A deadly insult to Jesus was to call Him a Samaritan (Jn 8:48). A Samaritan village refused hospitality to Jesus and His disciples on their way from Galilee to Jerusalem (Lk 9:52); Jesus rebuked the disciples for their anger. Josephus reports instances of attacks by Samaritans on pilgrims traveling to or from the temple of Jerusalem. Jn 4 relates the conversation of Jesus with the Samaritan woman of Sychar*, His preaching to the villagers, and their sympathetic reception; but the narrative reflects the extreme hostility of the two groups. One would not ask or receive even a drink of water from the other (4:9); and even a village woman was acquainted with the theological dispute about the mountain of the temple (4:20). But the Samaritans believed in prophecy and expected a Messiah who would be a teacher (4:19, 25). The disciples were shocked that Jesus would converse with a Samaritan woman (4:27). It is unlikely that the prohibition which Jesus lays upon the disciples against preaching to the Samaritans reflects this hostility (Mt 10:5); the Samaritans are mentioned with the Gentiles, and it is basic in the Gospels and the apostolic writings that the Gospel is first to be preached to the Jews. Breadth of view is evidenced in Jn 4 and in several passages of Lk. The Samaritan is proposed as an example of love of one's neighbor (Lk 10:33 ff), and the only one of 10 lepers whom Jesus cured who thanked Him was a Samaritan (Lk 17:16). There was no deeper breach of human relations in the contemporary world than the feud of Jews and Samaritans, and the breadth and depth of Jesus' doctrine of love could demand no greater act of a Jew than to accept a Samaritan as a brother.

Samech. The 15th letter of the Hb alphabet, with the value of s.

Samos (Gk samos, meaning uncertain), an island in the Aegean Sea lying WSW of Ephesus*, touched by Paul on his voyage from Troas* to Miletus* (AA 20:15); mentioned also in 1 Mc 15:23.

Samothrace (Gk samothrakē, "Thracian

Samos"), an island in the N Aegean Sea lying WNW of the Hellespont, touched by Paul on his second missionary journey on his voyage from Troas* to Neapolis* (AA 16:11).

Samson (Hb *šimšôn*, perhaps connected with *šemeš*, "sun," and the divine name Shamash). This etymological connection led some earlier scholars to suggest that Samson was a mythological solar figure; this view has now been generally abandoned. Samson, the son of Manoah*, was a member of the tribe of Dan*. His family lived in Zorah* in the Shephelah* in the territory which the tribe inhabited before its migration under Philistine pressure to Dan in the N. The stories of Samson are grouped loosely; each of them no doubt was originally independent.

His birth, Jgs 13; his marriage and the slaying of the lion (the story of the lion and the riddle is possibly intruded into the story of the marriage), 14; the loss of his wife and the story of the foxes (now interwoven, possibly unconnected originally), 15: 1–8; his betrayal by the Judahites and the slaying of a thousand Philistines at Lehi*, 15:9–17; the spring of En-hakkore, 15:18; the gates of Gath*, 16:1–3; Samson and Delilah*, three stories which follow an identical pattern succeeded by the story of his capture, 16:4–22; the great deed performed at his death, 16:28–31.

The hero of these stories is a peasant of the tribe of Dan, a giant, endowed with extraordinary physical strength, who carried on a private war of revenge against the Philistines. As a "judge" of Israel Samson is a surprising figure; he leads no armed bands, he is obviously an amoral giant of violent angers and lusts. But he was the sole pride of the Israelite tribes in the time and place of Philistine domination where he lived, and he became a hero of popular folktales. That these tales have been richly embroidered is evident; the feats of Samson's prowess have reached extravagant proportions. In the stories themselves there is no effort to give their hero any religious aura; this is done by the compiler of the stories, who is probably the creator of the story of Samson's birth. Such a man, who was the weapon which Yahweh gave Dan against the Philistines, should have his providential place in the history of his people presented in the form of a prenatal divine election and prediction. That his great strength was a gift of Yahweh appears in the stories themselves; some stories attribute it to the irruption of the spirit* of Yahweh (13:25; 14:6, 19; 15:14), others to his consecration as a Nazirite* and his uncut hair (16:17, 22). It is the purpose of the compiler to make clear

that this unlikely murderous bandit was the instrument through whom Yahweh helped His people. It is Samson so transfigured who is cited in Heb 11:32 as a hero of faith.

The stories illustrate better than any other OT narratives the relations between Israelites and Philistines. They live in adjoining villages on the frontier, with relations which are sometimes friendly, sometimes viciously hostile. They move freely into each others' territory. They intermarry. Because of the Philistine supremacy the Judahites are compelled to deliver Samson to the Philistines. The realism of the background of the stories shows that they come from the time and place of Samson's feats, even though popular tradition has magnified the feats. He was a witness of the saving power and will of Yahweh, who ultimately delivered His people from , the Philistine threat.

Samuel (Hb *šemû'ēl*, "name of El", or "his name is El"?; it is explained in popular etymology of 1 S 1:20 as formed from *S'L*, "ask," which has suggested to some scholars that the story of 1 S 1 was originally told of Saul*; a leader of Israel at the time when the tribal confederacy became a monarchy). The precise character of the leadership of Samuel is somewhat complex; cf below. Samuel was the son of Elkanah* of the tribe of Ephraim* and of Hannah*.

The stories of Samuel in 1–2 S are compiled from several diverse traditions (cf SAMUEL, BOOKS OF); and within these compilations materials of diverse origins are used. The earliest of these is the story of the rise of Saul (1 S 9:1–10:16 + 11). Here Samuel is a seer (cf PROPHET) in an unnamed town in the land of Zuph. To him Yahweh reveals that the young man who inquires about the lost asses of his father is the king whom Yahweh has chosen for Israel. Samuel is a cultic officer (9:12 f). He reveals the election of Yahweh to Saul and anoints Saul king. In this account Samuel is the man who designates and anoints the king, but the climax of the narrative is the election of Saul, the charismatic leader who defeats the Ammonites (1 S 11) and the Philistines (13–14); this is the promonarchic account of the institution of kingship (cf SAMUEL, BOOKS OF).

Samuel appears in the story of the rise of David, another early source. Here he is an accessory figure, who presides over "the sons of the prophets*" at Naioth* and protects David from Saul (1 S 29:18–24). His death is reported in 1 S 25:1, which is probably a redactional insertion into the story of the rise of David.

Were this all the material concerning Samuel, the picture would be simple. But the theologically reflective expansion of 1–2

S (cf SAMUEL, BOOKS OF) gives Samuel a somewhat different character and a far greater importance. In 1 S 15 Samuel announces that Yahweh has repudiated Saul for his disobedience to Samuel's command to carry out a war of extermination against Amalek*. Here Samuel represents the old barbarous tradition of the desert war of revenge, the blood feud, and Saul represents the more civilized and secular war of conquest and plunder. Another story of Saul's rejection (1 S 13:7–15) makes the motive of Samuel's repudiation the offering of sacrifice by Saul. This story gives Samuel a priestly character and the motivation of the repudiation is priestly rather than prophetic; but both stories have a tradition of the repudiation of Saul by Samuel. Somewhat parallel to these is the account of the evocation of the ghost of Samuel by the witch of Endor (1 S 28); this story resumes the motive of 1 S 15, the war with the Amalekites.

In the antimonarchic account of the election of Saul (1 S 8 + 10:17–27) the demand for a king comes from the elders* of Israel. Samuel is opposed to the demand; it infringes upon the kingship of Yahweh over Israel. The king is chosen not by divine designation by oracle, as in the promonarchic account, but by lot, and the elected king must be summoned from his hiding place in the baggage.

In 1 S 7 + 12 Samuel has become the last of the judges*; he is both a victorious leader in battle and a magistrate. The victory must be judged unhistorical, and probably the magistracy also. This conception of Samuel comes from the redactor of Jgs, who felt the need of making the last of the judges the agent of transition to the monarchy.

The story of the vocation of Samuel (1 S 1–3) affirms his prophetic character and his divine commission. It is a midrash*.

The anointing of David (1 S 16:1–13) is also a midrash. Samuel is already conceived as a prophet when this was written; the elected king who replaced Saul was also designated by the prophetic word and the ritual which symbolized the giving of the spirit*.

In 1 Ch 6:13, 18 Samuel is given an artificial Levite genealogy in the clan of Gershom*; the sacred functions which he fulfills in 1 S could not, in the mind of the Chronicler, have been assumed unless he were a member of a priestly family. With David he is represented as appointing Levites to their offices (1 Ch 9:22). In Je 15:1 he is mentioned with Moses as one who intercedes for Israel; this allusion seems to echo 1 S 7:9.

Later biblical references reflect the final compilation of 1–2 S and not its sources.

Ps 99:6 probably refers to his priestly genealogy; he is mentioned with Moses and Aaron and calls on the name of Yahweh. In BS 46:13–20 he is primarily a prophet, but also a judge. In AA 3:24; 13:20 he is a prophet, in Heb 11:32 a judge.

It is apparent that the literary traditions concerning Samuel are complex; but those historians who accept only the earliest as authentic and treat the others as unhistorical entirely seem to oversimplify. The figure of Samuel also appears to be complex. Admitting that the prophetic reflections are not pure narrative, there must be some reason why Samuel was thought important enough to be made the spokesman of the antimonarchic "school." He was probably not a "judge" in the sense of the other judges. Neither was he a prophet in the sense of the later prophets. But he is the earliest religious figure after Moses who resembles a prophet, and the prophetic school was not wrong in seeing in him the earliest representative of prophecy. Very probably his true character was leader of the sons of the prophets (cf PROPHET); this position would explain both his importance in the foundation of the monarchy and the ambiguity of his attitude. Where the promonarchic tradition has simplified Samuel in one direction by making him the organ of election, the antimonarchic tradition has preserved traditions of a conflict both in the soul of Israel and in the soul of Samuel, who spoke for that group in Israel which feared kingship as a secularization of Israelite faith. Although the account shows later origin, there is nothing to compel one to think that the tradition of a deadly conflict between prophecy, represented by Samuel, and the monarchy is unhistorical. Prophecy was as yet not as well defined, and the priesthood suffered a shattering blow in the extermination of the house of Eli* and the destruction of Shiloh*. The point of the story of the ark (1 S 4–6 + 2 S 6) is that the ark needs the monarchy. Someone had to speak for the faith of Israel in the covenant of the 12-tribe amphictyony and in the simple life of the Israelite peasant who rejected Canaanite civilization, wealth, and conquest. This tradition found its spokesman in the memories of Samuel. Samuel elected the king as the representative of Yahweh, and he felt empowered to repudiate him with the same authority. Whether his own theory, if we so call a practice which was never presented in theory, was viable or not is another question; the theory seems to have been that the prophet should actually rule the king, and thus Samuel claimed for prophecy a power which it did not possess. This kind of theocracy was impractical; the traditions show that Samuel's repudiation of Saul was politically ineffective. It was necessary for prophecy to find another and a higher level on which to present the will of Yahweh to the king. In the duel of the two it was Samuel who was rejected by Israel; the Israelites would not accept a political spokesman of Yahweh.

Samuel, Books of. 1–2 S were originally a single book. It was divided into two in the LXX and in the Vg; the division into two was introduced into the Hb text in 1448. The LXX entitled the books 1–2 "Kingdoms," and the Lt Bibles entitled them 1–2 "Kings," making 1–2 K into 3–4 "Kings." This title is employed in the Douay OT and some other Eng OT versions; it causes an unfortunate confusion in references to the books. Rabbinical tradition attributed the books to Samuel; to support this attribution reference is made to 1 Ch 29:29 f, but this verse scarcely means 1–2 S by "the chronicles of Samuel, Nathan, and Gad." Samuel is inactive after 1 S 15 and his death is recorded in 1 S 25:1.

1. *Contents.* 1 S 1–7, Samuel: 1–3 birth and vocation of Samuel; 4–6, story of the ark; 7, victory of the Philistines, Samuel as judge.

1 S 8–15, Samuel and Saul: 8–11, election of Saul; 12, Samuel's farewell; 13–14, Saul's victories; 15, Saul's rejection.

1 S 16–31, Saul and David: 16, anointing of David and his introduction at court; 17, David and Goliath; 18–20, David at court; 21–27, David the outlaw; 28, Saul at Endor; 29–30, David with the Philistines; 31, defeat and death of Saul.

1 S 1–8, David king of Israel and Judah: 1, death of Saul; 2–4, David king in Hebron; 5, David king of Israel, victories over Philistines, taking of Jerusalem; 6, the ark introduced to Jerusalem; 7, the oracle of Nathan; 8, lists.

2 S 9–20, the family history of David: 9, the house of Saul; 10–12, victory over the Ammonites and David's adultery; 13–18, rebellion of Absalom; 19, David's return; 20, rebellion of Sheba.

2 S 21–24, appendices: 21:1–15, revenge executed upon the house of Saul; 21:16–22, feats of David's heroes; 22, psalm; 23:1–7, last words of David; 23:8–39, David's heroes; 24, the census and the plague.

The book exhibits signs of obvious compilation such as doublets, divergences, and interruptions. Samuel appears as a prophet in 1 S 1–3, as a judge in 1 S 7 + 12, as a seer in 1 S 9. Israel assembles at Mizpah in 1 S 10:17, at Gilgal in 1 S 11:15. There are two accounts of the beginning of the monarchy, one promonarchic (1 S 9:1–10:

16 + 11), one antimonarchic (1 S 8 + 10: 17–25 + 12). In 1 S 13:16–14:46 Saul appears as a devout king; there are two accounts of his rejection (13:7–15 and 15). The story of Saul and David exhibits a series of doublets as follows:

David's introduction at court: 16:14–23 and 17:1–18:5 (17:1–18:5 is itself composite). The LXX removes the inconcinnity of David meeting Saul for the first time twice by omitting 17:12–31.

18:10–11 and 19:9–10, attempts on David's life.

18:12–16 and 28–30, David's success and popularity.

18:17–19 and 20–27, promise of Saul's daughter.

19:1–7 and 20:1–10 + 18–39, Jonathan's intervention on behalf of David.

19:10–17 and 20:1–21:1, David's flight.

23:1–13 and 19–28, betrayal of David by those whom he protects; 24 and 26, David spares Saul's life.

28:3–25 + 31 and 1 S 29–30 + 2 S 1:1–16, death of Saul.

2. *Theories of composition and sources.* These evidences of compilation have furnished modern scholars a base upon which they erect theoretical constructions of the original materials and of the processes by which they were compiled in their present form. Most of the older theories attempted to find in 1–2 S continuations of the Pnt* sources J and E. It is paradoxical that while the analysis of the text is commonly accepted, the well identified documents called J and E cannot be surely recognized in 1–2 S; there are sources discernible, but they must be attributed to other origins. O. Eissfeldt among contemporary scholars has most seriously defended the division of the material between E and J; for Eissfeldt, however, J includes the documents L (the "lay" source) which he himself has analyzed in the Pnt. To E is attributed most of the account of Samuel's vocation, the antimonarchic account of the election of Saul, the anointing of David, the rejection of Saul, and one series of the doublets of David's life; the character of E, he believes, is to be found in such stories as 1 S 21:11–16, which is a "spiritualization" of David's service with the Philistines. To J + L are attributed the story of the ark, the promonarchic account of Saul's election, the family history of David (J), the account of David's accession and the taking of Jerusalem (L). This analysis does not, however, show the characteristics which identify these documents in the Pnt; in the following exposition the work of A. Weiser, which takes a broader and, it seems, more probable view, is used as a base.

Weiser points out that the compilers of

1–2 S and of the documents from which the work arose put the material together in a more mechanical manner and did not produce such a literary and ideological document as J. The origin of the book must be conceived in a different manner; Weiser calls it a process of expansion and interpretation of traditions over a long period of time. This process is a theological interpretation of history. The monarchy in fact was a critical factor in the development of the belief and history of Israel; its effects were mixed and it elicited different responses according to the background of those who considered it and according to the change in its historical situation (cf KING). The difficulties attendant upon the monarchy were present from its very beginning; 1–2 S reflect these early difficulties as they were related in tradition, and also the reflections upon them in different circles and in different periods. Weiser begins with what most critics agree can be easily defined as originally independent literary unities.

a) 1 S 4–6 + 2 S 6, a history of the ark. This story, which follows the story of the vocation of Samuel in the present text, knows nothing of Samuel. The stories are extremely popular, with an exaggerated element of wonder; they attest faith in the ark as the symbol of Yahweh's saving presence, but they unquestionably attest also a doubt; unless Israel is faithful to Yahweh, the symbol loses its power. The ark, in the. minds of the authors of the story, does not belong in a tent nor in the battle lines of Israel; it is a sacred cult object which kills those who touch it and brings catastrophe when it is not properly venerated. Its proper home is the sanctuary attached to the royal palace, and the story ends with its introduction by David to Jerusalem, where Yahweh's king and Yahweh's ark are the heart of Israel. The most probable source for this story is the Jerusalem priesthood, and Weiser believes it should be dated in the reign of David or of Solomon.

b) 1 S 9:1–10:16 + 13–14, the rise of Saul. Weiser believes this "unity" consists of several detached stories strung together loosely. It ends with a citation from a document in 1 S 14:47–52. The promonarchic account of the origin of the kingship is composed from popular tradition; romantic traits are evident throughout. Samuel is here the seer whose function is to dedicate the king, but the king is the' savior of Israel. 1 S 13 is compiled from other popular traditions, "soldiers' memories." Saul appears in this document as a figure worthy of honor and respect; Weiser believes therefore that its source is the tribe of Benjamin and its date not too long after the event. 13:1–15,

the story of the rejection, has been worked in by a later hand; it was necessary to explain why Saul was defeated and replaced by David. This addition may have come originally from a Judahite source; but in its present form it gives Samuel a priestly character.

c) 1 S 16:14–2 S 5, the rise of David. The original story ends with 2 S 5:10, 12. The theme of the story is obvious: how David, the shepherd boy, became king of all Israel in spite of difficulties and dangers which seemed insurmountable. He succeeded because Yahweh was with him and not with Saul. This story, however, probably knew nothing of David's anointing as related in 1 S 16:1–13 nor of Saul's rejection. Yahweh wanted David as king and brought him successfully through all obstacles. There is no element of wonder in the story; Yahweh accomplishes His design through the course of human events. David is endowed with the kind of wisdom* which wins success. This section contains the doublets mentioned above. Weiser attributes these not to documentary sources but to the luxuriance of oral tradition, which tells favorite stories in various ways. The author collected and arranged the variants.

The original story was expanded by the addition of 2 S 5:17–25. 8:1 ff was further added by the editor who put 2 S 6–7 in their present position from other sources. The author of the original story was probably a scribe of David's court. It is in this sense that the appellation of "Jahwist" (J) is justified; it is most probable that the J of the Pnt was also a scribe of David's court. The history of early Israel and the history of the early monarchy were produced by the same school of writers. One may probably attribute the institution and intention of this school to David himself. In uniting Israel and Judah in his monarchy he wished the traditions of the tribes to be fused into a single tradition which would identify as one the nation which he had created and merge its dangerous diversities. The attempt was not entirely successful on the political level.

d) 2 S 9–20, the family history of David. This section, of unquestioned literary unity, is universally admired as the greatest single monument of Israelite prose narrative; indeed, no narrative of comparable merit is known before it in any literature of the world, and few Gk historians were able to write as well. The author is detached and objective; he lets the words and actions of his characters tell what the characters were. The story moves rapidly and consistently, it is vivid; there is no marvelous element, but the story is profoundly religious. It is the story of a sin which displeased Yahweh (2 S 11:27) and of the tragedy which followed it, the wreck of a family, of lives, and nearly of a kingdom. No prophet spoke more forcefully of the malice of sin, but this writer does it quietly without rhetoric; history is the witness of Yahweh's righteousness.

It is probable that the writer went far beyond what his commission required; for the entire story is ended in 1 K 1–2 with the accession of Solomon, and its author was probably a court scribe of Solomon who was commissioned to write the history of the succession in order to show that Solomon, the younger son, was the legitimate successor of David. Some scholars have suggested persons engaged in the action such as Abiathar* or Ahimaaz* as the author; these can be no more than educated guesses, but it is sure that the author gathered his information from such primary sources. One is here in the presence of the David of history more than in any other part of the book.

Weiser believes that these four complexes arose as a result of the burst of national-historical consciousness which must have followed the erection of David's kingdom of all Israel and his victories. This was the period of national birth, and its heroic stories (like the stories of the American war of independence) were sure to be recounted with a new flash of pride and with a new faith; for they were the stories of Yahweh's saving acts for Israel. Weiser suggests that they were also the subject of formal recitals at court, after the manner of ballad singers; these rather than the popular stories would form the basis of the accounts.

These early national traditions were subjected to an important transformation by later theological reflection, mostly from prophetic circles. The later kingship was not the messianic institution of David's reign; it split into two kingdoms and in the opinion of many was an instrument of religious and moral corruption. From these reflections the following materials were added:

1 S 15, the rejection of Saul for disobedience to a prophetic command.

1 S 28, prophetic pronouncement of doom upon Saul for the same reason. The author here probably drew upon a genuine piece of tradition; the realism of the story is remarkable. Saul's fall into superstition made him the victim of the necromancer's wiles, but the story exhibits a strange pity for Saul, the tragic failure.

1 S 8 + 10:17–27, the antimonarchic account of Saul's election. The election of a king is a defection from Yahweh and from the prophetic word; Yahweh permitted this defection and punished it with royal tyranny.

1 S 7: Samuel's victory over the Philistines.

This unhistorical account is a midrash*; Samuel could not have defeated the Philistines, whose power appears undiminished in later chapters. The story affirms through narrative that victory lies in the prophetic word.

1 S 1–3, the vocation of Samuel. Samuel is conceived as a prophet in this story (as he is not in the earlier complexes), and the genuinity of his prophetic mission is affirmed in the story of his divine election and mandate.

1 S 13:7–15 (cf above).

1 S 16:1–13, the anointing of David. This is also a midrash; it authenticates David through the prophetic word and emphasizes further the rejection of Saul.

These pieces do not form a literary unity. It is evident from their content that the theme is the conflict of prophet and king, of religious and secular power, of two charismatic figures. This conflict was never perfectly resolved in Israel. These materials affirm the rights and mission of the prophet with the king as a charismatic leader, and the power of the prophet to rebuke and even to depose a king. The ideological connection between these materials and the events related of Elijah* and Elisha* is evident, and the prophetic circles of N Israel appear to be the principal sources. These are the circles associated with the Pnt source E, and hence there is some justification for this attribution, as there is for J (cf above); but the justification rests upon a community of thought, not upon literary identity.

The book was submitted to the redaction which produced the Deuteronomic history*; but the Deuteronomic writing is limited to passages in 1 S 2 and 7. It is most probable that the liturgical pieces and poems were introduced after the Deuteronomic redaction.

Weiser sums up the composition of the book thus:

I. The existence of detached popular and court traditions (1 S 11; 13; 2 S 10 ff; 1 S 9 f; 1 S 4–6; 2 S 6–7), lists and annals (2 S 8:21–23; 2 S 1:17–27; 3:33 f).

II. Historical writing using detached traditions (1 S 9:1–11:13; 1 S 16:14–2 S 5; 2 S 9–20).

III. The compilation and unification of the materials of II into a chronological scheme with the addition of other traditions, some parallel and some new.

IV. The prophetic transformation of the tradition into a theological interpretation of a conspectus of history (1 S 1–3 + 7 + 8 + 10:17 ff + 12 + 15 + 16:1–13 + 28).

V. Deuteronomic redaction.

VI. Insertion of poems (1 S 2:1–10; 2 S 22; 23:1–7) and expansions in 1 S 17 and 18.

3. *Literary form and historical character.* It is evident from the above summary that

1-2 S contain almost all varieties of historical narrative. Since the books are the only source for the period which they cover, the material must be examined with the greatest critical care. The weakness of Egypt and Mesopotamia during this period was the political factor which permitted David to create the kingdom of Israel; but it also means that there are no documentary sources from these regions for the period of the early monarchy. In general 1-2 S contain valuable material for the reconstruction of the history of the rise of the monarchy; cf DAVID; KING; SAMUEL; SAUL.

4. *Theology*. The above summary also shows that we should speak of theologies rather than a theology of the book of Samuel. A proper title of the book would be the origin of the Davidic monarchy; this is what the book relates, and it was probably what the scribes whose work lies at the basis of the book were commissioned to write. These men viewed the monarchy as a divine institution by which Yahweh saved Israel in a crisis. The passing charismatic leadership of the judges became permanent in the king. But as soon as there was a king the problem arose of the relation of the king, a secular ruler, to the sacral character of Israel as the people of Yahweh. The king could not be above Yahweh, and so in some sense he must be subject to the prophet, the spokesman of Yahweh. The historical kingship did not fulfill its early promise; the reflective narratives ask why this happened. Is it the failure of kings to accept the will of Yahweh, or did Israel as a whole rebel against Yahweh in seeking the political form of monarchy? Israel, as we have said, never resolved the problem, and its two aspects are asserted in subsequent books of the OT: the ideal of the monarchy lives in the idea of the king* Messiah*, and the antimonarchical school lives in the prophets who see no king in the future of Israel. Cf KING.

Sanballat (Hb *sanballaṭ*, Akkadian *sin-muballiṭ*, "[the god] Sin gives life"), a personal name; governor of the district of Samaria* under the Persians in the time of Nehemiah. Despite his Akkadian name he seems to have been a worshiper of Yahweh; in 408 BC the Jews of Elephantine* in Egypt sent a letter to Shelemiah and Delaiah, the sons of Sanballat, at Samaria, reporting the destruction of their temple (ANET 492). These are names compounded with Yahweh. Nehemiah represents Sanballat as hostile to the community of Jerusalem (Ne 2:10, 19), in particular to Nehemiah's project of rebuilding the walls of Jerusalem, against which armed attack was threatened (Ne 3:33 ff). When the threat failed, Sanballat attempted to persuade Nehemiah to meet him in a conference outside Jerusalem; Nehemiah, fearing that he would be seized, refused the meeting (Ne 6:1-14). One of the priests of Jerusalem was a son-in-law of Sanballat; Nehemiah expelled him from Jerusalem (Ne 13:28). In fairness to Sanballat it should be recalled that the Jews of Jerusalem refused the overtures of the Samaritans* to take part in the rebuilding of the temple; when Nehemiah came the hostility was already firmly established.

Sandals (Hb *na'alayim* [dual], Gk *hypodēma*

Assyrian sculptures showing military boots.

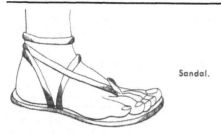

Sandal.

[sing]). The ordinary footwear in OT and NT times was a leather sole fastened to the foot by thongs drawn between the first and second toe and tied about the ankle. The sandal thong is a cheap article (Gn 14:23), and the rich are said to sell the needy for the pair of sandals which he gives in pledge, again an example of a cheap article (Am 2:6; 8:6). The sandals were to be worn during the Passover* meal, at which the diners were dressed for travel, and were normally removed when one entered the house (Ex 12:11). They were also removed when one was in mourning (Ezk 24:17, 23). To have no sandals was a sign of the destitution of captives in war (Is 20:2). The sandal had certain symbolic meanings which exhibit no consistent pattern. The removal of the sandal in the ceremony of the renunciation of the levirate* marriage signified the renunciation of a power or a right (Dt 25:9 f; Rt 4:7 f). To cast one's sandal upon another was a sign of dominion (Pss 60:10; 108:10). The sandals were removed when one entered holy ground (Ex 3:5; Jos 5:15); modern Moslems demand that all who enter a mosque remove or cover their shoes. To tie or loose the thongs of the sandals was the work of a body servant (Mk 1:7; Lk 3:16; Jn 1:27; AA 13:25; Mt 3:11 has "carry his sandals"). The disciples are to take no sandals with them on their mission as a sign of their poverty (Mt 10:10; Lk 10:4).

Sanhedrin. Cf COUNCIL.

Sapphira (Gk *sapphira*, Aramaic *šappīrā'*, "good" or " beautiful"), a personal name; wife of Ananias*, who with her husband sold a piece of property and gave the proceeds to the Church, withholding part of the price. Both of them fell dead when Peter charged them with lying (AA 5:1–11). The story is a midrash* of the type found in the Pnt; the obligation of a law is illustrated by an anecdote in which a violation of the law is severely punished, even by death.

Sarah (Hb *sārāh*, "princess"), wife of Abraham*. Until Gn 17:15 she is called Sarai (Hb *sārāi*), which appears to be a dialectal variant of Sarah; the presence of two names in the traditions was explained by a divine change of the name signifying election (cf ABRAHAM). The patronymic of Sarah is not given, which is striking; it was not even invented. She is said to be the sister (half sister) of Abraham in the E story of Sarah and Abimelech (Gn 20:12); this detail is not found in the J story of Sarah and the Pharaoh (Gn 12:10–18), and probably was created by the storytellers to justify the use of this device by the patriarchs. Sarah was barren (Gn 11:31). The promise of a son to Abraham and Sarah appears in the J cycle (Gn 18:6–17); here Sarah laughs at the promise, thus furnishing an occasion to explain the name of her son Isaac*. It appears also in P (Gn 17:15–19). Because of her barrenness Sarah gave her slave Hagar* to Abraham as a substitute, but expelled her because of pride; the substitution is paralleled in the Nuzu* tablets (cf MARRIAGE), but such expulsion was prohibited. In one tradition the expulsion occurred before the birth of Ishmael (Gn 16:1–8 [J]), in another after the birth of Isaac (Gn 21:1–12 [E]). The beauty of Sarah, the ancestress of Israel, was traditional, and there are two stories of how she was taken into the harem of a foreign ruler: the Pharaoh (Gn 12:10–18 [J]) and Abimelech (Gn 20:2–18 [E]). She is represented in the J narratives with a vivacious and well defined character, proud, quick to anger, hardly the submissive and demure wife, a bustling and generous hostess and easily amused, ready for the give and take of conversation with her man and his guests. These are not necessarily traits of the historical Sarah; she is described as the kind of wife whom the Bedu chieftain finds attractive, except for the curse of sterility. This curse is removed by the blessing* which is conferred upon her husband.

Sarah died at Hebron and was buried in the cave of Machpelah* (Gn 23; 25:10; 49:31). In Is 51:2 she and Abraham are the rock and quarry from which Israel was hewn; the prophet recalls that her fertility was the result of a divine promise.

In the NT Sarah is mentioned in the epistles. Paul refers to her barrenness as an occasion of Abraham's faith (Rm 4:19). Christians are the descendants of Abraham because they, like Isaac, are children of promise (Rm 9:9). Sarah is the free woman whose son is a son of promise; by allegory she is the heavenly Jerusalem (Gal 4:21–30). She conceived by faith (Heb 11:11). She is a model of wifely obedience who called her husband lord (1 Pt 3:6).

Sardis (Gk *sardeis*, meaning uncertain), modern Sart, a city of Asia Minor 50 mi E of

Smyrna. The ancient city lay on the right bank of the Pactolus on the slopes of Mt Tmolus. It was the capital of the kingdom of Lydia*. It was taken by Cyrus* in 546 BC and became the administrative capital of the satrapy of Asia Minor. It lay at the W terminus of the royal road from Susa*. It passed from Persian dominion to the Seleucid kingdom, then to the kingdom of Pergamum*, then to Rome. Its importance under these powers was less than it had been in the Persian period, but it was still large and prosperous, famous for its handicrafts. It was badly damaged by an earthquake in AD 17. It was excavated by an American expedition 1910–1914, and another expedition was begun by Harvard and Cornell in 1958. Ruins from Roman times include an odeum, a stadium, a theater, a senate house, possibly a gymnasium, a bath, and a temple of Artemis, here identified with the Asian mother goddess Cybele. Its Christian church was established in the apostolic period; it is one of the seven churches of Apc (1:11; 3:1, 4).

Sarepta. Cf ZAREPHATH.

Sargon (Hb *sargōn*, Akkadian *šarru-kin*, "legitimate king" [perhaps a title]), king of Assyria 722–705 BC. The reign of Sargon was a period of wide and successful conquest for the Assyrian empire. Sargon was victorious in the three most important frontier areas: Armenia, which he reduced to impotence; Babylon*, where he suppressed a rebellion (cf MERODACH-BALADAN) and proclaimed himself king; and Syria and Palestine. Sargon succeeded Shalmaneser V while Samaria* was under siege and received the capitulation. He deported 27,290 Israelites and settled the country with peoples from Mesopotamia. He established an Assyrian province in Syria-Palestine, excepting Judah, the kingdoms of E Palestine, Philistia, and the city states of Phoenicia, which were vassal kingdoms. Is 20:1 alludes to his suppression of the rebellion of Ashdod* in 711 BC; the strange prophetic action of Isaiah was intended to dissuade Hezekiah* from taking part in the rebellion. Sargon built a palace at Dur-Sharrukin, modern Khorsabad, which is one of the great monuments of Assyrian architecture. He was killed in battle at a time and place not exactly recorded. Cf records of Sargon in ANET 284–287.

Satan (Hb *satan*), in the OT the word always appears with the article, "the *satan*," except in 1 Ch 21:1, where it is a proper name; this is a development of later thought (cf below). The LXX often renders the word by *diabolos* (whence Eng "devil"), "accuser" or "slanderer"; in the NT the Gk words

satanas, satan, and diabolos are used indifferently. The basic meaning of *satan* is an accuser in a court of law; most occurrences of the word in the OT, however, show its use in the metaphorical sense of adversary.

1. *OT.* The word means an accuser in Ps 109:6, and a military or political adversary in 1 S 29:4; 2 S 19:23; 1 K 5:18. The adversaries raised up against Solomon (1 K 11:14, 23, 25), however, suggest the use of the word which appears later; for these adversaries are raised up by Yahweh in punishment for the sins of Solomon. In BS 21:27 the word is simply adversary. In other uses the adversary is a celestial being. The angel stands in the way of Balaam's* journey to Balak* (Nm 22:22, 32).

The concept of the *satan* which appears to be the basis for later Jewish speculations appears in Jb 1:6 ff; 2:1 ff. Here the sons of Elohim are gathered in what seems to be a heavenly assembly or assizes. Among them is the *satan*. He is not an evil spirit of the kind which appears in Mesopotamian and in later Jewish literature (cf DEMON); he is an accuser, a heavenly officer or prosecutor, whose function it is to question and to test the genuinity of human virtue. To accomplish his work he has the power to inflict evil on men — sickness, natural catastrophes, human agents. The concept is partly theological and partly mythological; the evils which in ancient superstition were attributed to demons are here attributed to an agency of Yahweh. The purpose of these misfortunes is to test the reactions of men; virtue is not genuine unless it sustains adversity. This conception of an accuser is echoed in Zc 3:1–2. In 1 Ch 21:1 the plague which in the older conception was the work of Yahweh, is in the most recent conception of the Chronicler attributed to this agent of catastrophe and punishment; he now has a proper name, Satan.

2. *Jewish literature.* In the apocryphal literature Satan (or the devil, *diabolos*) acquires a more definite form. The work of temptation which in Jb is a testing has become a work of malice, and the evils which Satan has the power to inflict are wrought because of his hatred of men. Satan is the prince of evil spirits, and the devil's treasure house is full of the poison of evil spirits. The spirit of hate works with Satan to accomplish the death of man. Man must be able to distinguish the angel of the Lord from the angel of Satan; the devil flees those who live in righteousness. In the life of Adam and Eve Satan (also called the devil here) is the tempter of Eve in Eden; he is not identified with the serpent but speaks through the serpent, disguising him-

self as an angel of God. When Adam asks him the reason for his malicious hatred of men, Satan explains that he was expelled from heaven by Michael* because he refused to adore man, the image of God. In the book of Enoch the word is used in the plural, "the satans"; they tempt the angels, slander pious men before God, and punish the damned. Satan disappears in the millennium* and in the messianic age; it is not clear whether he disappears through annihilation or through restraint. WS 2:24, which attributes the entrance of death into the world to the envy of the devil, shows the influence of the apocryphal books. Most of these conceptions are echoed in the NT.

3. *NT*. There is no appreciable difference in meaning between the NT titles *satanas* and *diabolos*. Satan is also called the strong one (Mt 12:29; Mk 3:27; Lk 11:21), the evil one (Mt 13:19 +), the prince of this world (Jn 12:31). Satan is a tempter who even tempts Jesus (Mt 4:1; Mk 1:13; Lk 4:2). When Peter attempts to dissuade Jesus from His passion, Jesus calls him Satan; his thoughts are human, not divine (Mt 16:23; Mk 8:33). Satan takes the seed of the word from the mouth of those who receive it (Mt 13:19; Mk 4:15; Lk 8:12). Satan put the betrayal of Jesus into the heart of Judas* (Jn 13:2), and then entered Judas for the consummation of the deed (Lk 22:3; Jn 13:27). Satan tries to sift the disciples like wheat (Lk 22:31). He filled the heart of Ananias* with deceit (AA 5:3). He tempts with designs (1 Co 7:5; 2 Co 2:11) and with wiles (Eph 6:11) and with snares (1 Tm 3:7; 2 Tm 2:26). He disguises himself as an angel of light (2 Co 11:14). He seduces some of the faithful (1 Tm 5:15). He is the enemy who sows cockle in the field of the Lord's wheat (Mt 13:39; Lk 8:12). He is like a roaring lion seeking prey (1 Pt 5:8). Christians should give him no room to work (Eph 4:27).

Satan also has power to do bodily harm. He has a house and a kingdom (Mt 12:26; Mk 3:23, 26; Lk 11:18). He claims that all the kingdoms of the world are in his power (Lk 4:6). Luke so constructs the temptation narrative as to show that the power of Satan, which is frustrated in the temptation "until an opportunity" (Lk 4:13), finds its opportunity in the passion of Jesus, the hour of the power of darkness (Lk 22:53). The power of Satan is the power of darkness opposed to the power of light also in AA 26:18. Satan bound a paralyzed woman for 18 years (Lk 13:16), and his angel is the "thorn in the flesh" from which Paul suffered (2 Co 12:7). It is to Satan as the agent of bodily harm that sinners and adversaries of the apostles are delivered (1 Co 5:5; 1 Tm 1:20). Satan hindered Paul from making a journey to Thessalonica (1 Th 2:18). The Antichrist* comes with the active power of Satan (2 Th 2:9). In the millennium Satan is bound in the pit (Apc 20:2); he is then released and permitted to work destruction in the final world period (Apc 20:7). But the time granted to the devil is short (Apc 12:12). He has the power to kill (Heb 2:14).

But Satan is subject to the power of God and is ultimately to be subdued. Jesus saw Satan fall from heaven (Lk 10:18); this obscure saying is not to be taken as a reference to the preexistence of Jesus nor as an affirmation of the Jewish story of the fall of the angels, but as an allusion to the pride which goes before a fall. An explicit allusion to the story of the fall is found in Apc 12:9–10; here Satan is identified with the great dragon of ancient mythology (cf CREATION) and the serpent of the story of Paradise: he is cast down from heaven by Michael. Eternal fire is prepared for the devil and his angels (Mt 25:41). If Christians resist the devil he will flee from them (Js 4:7); God will crush Satan under their feet (Rm 16:20).

The sons of the devil, as opposed to the sons of God, are those who do not do righteousness and do not love their brothers (1 Jn 3:10). He who sins is from the devil, and the devil was a sinner from the beginning (1 Jn 3:8). Jesus calls the Jews sons of the devil, who is a murderer from the beginning; the truth is not in him (Jn 8:44). Judas himself is called a devil (Jn 6:70). Heretical doctrine is the "deep things of Satan" (Apc 2:24), and a heretical sect identified only as pseudo-Jews is called the synagogue of Satan (Apc 2:9; 3:9). The throne of Satan and the place where Satan dwells was found in Pergamum; this cryptic allusion probably signifies one or more of Pergamum's famous sanctuaries, perhaps the altar of Zeus or the temple of Caesar.

On the meaning and value of this use of material from Jewish apocryphal literature cf DEMON.

Satrap. Cf PERSIA.

Saul (Hb *šā'ûl*, "asked [of Yahweh]"?), the explanation of the name of Samuel* as "asked" (1 S 1:20) leads some scholars to the suspicion that the story of the birth of Samuel was first told of the birth of Saul. The name is borne by three men in the OT and one in the NT; the best known OT figure is the first king of Israel.

1. Saul ben Kish was a man of Benjamin, handsome (1 S 9:2), who stood head and shoulders above other men. The account of

his election as king and of his reign is compiled from several sources: a promonarchic source using materials sympathetic to Saul, an antimonarchic source hostile to Saul, and the history of David, also hostile to Saul (cf SAMUEL, BOOKS OF). The historical Saul is somewhat difficult to recover with precision. The occasion of his election as king was the aggression of the Philistines*, who had defeated Israel severely at Aphek* and established themselves as overlords with garrison troops in the hill country of Israel (1 S 13:3). The promonarchic source tells of Saul's election by divine revelation to Samuel when Saul went in search of his father's asses (1 S 9:2–10:16). This source relates his anointing, the symbol of the spirit*, and the descent of the spirit upon Saul (1 S 10:6, 10–13); Saul is thus authenticated as a charismatic leader like the judges*. The antimonarchic source makes his election the result of the lot*, a much less manifest sign of divine choice (1 S 10:17–25). The story of Saul's rescue of Jabesh-gilead* from the attack of Nahash* of Ammon* (1 S 11:1–11) is possibly a third account of Saul's election in which he was acclaimed as king because of his charismatic leadership (1 S 11:6) in this instance; in the compilation which preceded the present text this episode was arranged to follow 10:16. Saul then took up the major danger facing Israel, drew the Philistine occupation troops into battle and drove them from the hill country (1 S 13:2–14:46). This was not an incursion into Philistine territory and left the Philistines free for later attacks, which they made; but it cleared the heartland of Israel and made it more difficult for the Philistines to invade. In this account Saul does not look good as a leader; he is somewhat indecisive, especially compared to Jonathan*, the real hero of the story, slow to take advantage of Jonathan's assault on the Philistines, and then drives the troops beyond the point of fatigue. The archival material cited in 1 S 14:47–52 mentions victories of Saul over Moab, Ammon, Edom, Zobah, and Amalek in addition.

Saul was rejected as king by Samuel. One account (1 S 13:8–15) makes the occasion Saul's arrogation of the priestly office; this is probably a later interpretation of the break, since it is doubtful that the priestly monopoly of sacrifice existed at this early period, and Samuel was no more a priest than Saul. The second account (1 S 15) makes the occasion Saul's failure to execute the ban* against Amalek. This is more likely to preserve genuine historical memories, but the occasion was really deeper; it was the failure to reach an understanding on the religious character of the king and his relation to the spokesman of Yahweh (cf KING; SAMUEL). Samuel's de-

position of Saul seems to have had no effect; Saul continued to reign and Samuel retired. People were scarcely in a mood to reject the only successful leader they had known against the Philistines. But in the narrative the removal of the prophet's blessings has disastrous effects later on.

There are two accounts of the introduction of David into Saul's service (16:14–23; 17). The first of these contains the important notice that Saul was troubled by an evil spirit from Yahweh which David soothed by his music. In both David appears as a warrior whose success and popularity aroused the jealousy of Saul (1 S 18:1–9), who in a rage threw his weapon at David; there are parallel accounts of this incident (1 S 18:10 f; 19:9 f). Saul promised his daughter Merab* to David but actually gave him a younger daughter, Michal*, after exacting the bridal price of 100 Philistine foreskins — a price which, it was hoped, David would lose his life trying to earn. Jonathan and Michal, the son and daughter of Saul, were both sympathetic to David; Jonathan interceded for David, incurring Saul's anger, and both of them aided David to escape; these are related in parallel accounts (1 S 19:1–8, 11–24; 20:24–33; 21). In his pursuit of David, Saul committed the ghastly crime of slaughtering the entire priesthood of Nob* (1 S 22:11 ff). He continued his pursuit of David through the desert* of Judah; there are two parallel accounts of how his life was spared by David (1 S 24 + 26), and the pursuit was finally abandoned, but without a reconciliation. One wonders what Saul was doing about the Philistines while he went after David. The Philistines mounted a major offensive into Israel. Saul, who had not faced such a force before, went in panic to consult a witch at Endor* (1 S 28). This dramatic scene no doubt preserves a genuine historical memory, although the details are largely the construction of the storyteller; Saul did consult a witch and received, as might be expected, an unfavorable response. His army was defeated and he and his three sons were killed at the battle of Mt Gilboa*, both in 1 S 31 and in 2 S 1; the two accounts of his death agree that it was suicidal, one account making it self-inflicted and the other making it the request of Saul to a passerby. The rescue of his body from Beth-shan* by the men of Jabesh-gilead attests their gratitude and shows the kind of loyalty which Saul could inspire.

The dates of Saul can be reached only generally by reckoning back from Rehoboam*, the first fixed date of the early monarchy. The data of 1 S 13:1 have been corrupted; W. F. Albright estimates that Saul reigned 1020–1000 BC. The extent of his kingdom is also uncertain; it seems unlikely that it included the entire 12-tribe confederacy. In particular it seems that it did not include Judah; there are other reasons for maintaining the distinction between Israel* and Judah*, and the service of David with the Philistines is more easily understood on the assumption that he was a professional soldier who hired his services and was not a subject who owed fealty to Saul. Saul's gesture on behalf of Jabesh-gilead recognized the community of Israel in E Palestine with Israel in W Palestine, and this must have been shown in other ways; it is to be noticed that Ishbaal* transferred the seat of the monarchy E of the Jordan after the Philistine conquest of W Palestine. As a king Saul was a military leader rather than a genuine ruler; there is no evidence of any organization of the kingdom nor of any lawmaking or judicial activity. His citadel at Gibeah* has been excavated; it was a modest fortress.

The character of Saul is complex and tragic. Historians generally agree that he suffered from mental derangement. This was the "evil spirit" from Yahweh which troubled him, and it makes more intelligible his pathological jealousy and hatred of David, his murderous assaults on David and the priests of Nob and his neglect of his duty while he engaged in a vain pursuit of his adversary, the alienation of even his children from him. These traits are not merely the result of a deliberate effort of the court historians of David to blacken his reputation; there is no evidence that they made this attempt, and the story was sufficient in itself. David himself in the opinion of almost all modern critics composed the tribute to Saul found in 2 S 1:19–26, one of the great pieces of early Israelite poetry. He was solicitous for the family of Saul (cf ISHBAAL; MERIBAAL), although the family maintained a cordial hatred of David in some of its members (2 S 16:5, 8). This may have been stimulated by David's yielding to the Gibeonites* in their claim for blood revenge on the house of Saul (2 S 21); the episode which was responsible for this claim is not elsewhere recorded. The actions of Saul as they are reported in his later years appear to be the deeds of an abnormal mind. How much this inner weakness was aided by external events is difficult to say. The traditions contain allusions to the fact that Saul felt he was abandoned by Yahweh (1 S 28:6, 15), as he felt that he was abandoned by his family and retainers in favor of David (1 S 18:8; 20:30–32; 22:7–8, 13). One may suspect that Samuel's repudiation preyed upon his mind; in addition he had the Philistine threat. When he saw or thought he saw his own reign endangered by the rise of David his mind gave.

The achievements of Saul were substantial. He gave Israel a focus around which its consciousness of union could take form. By clearing the hill country of Philistines he made it difficult for them to invade in force and created an Israel solid enough to survive in E Palestine even after a shattering defeat. He built up an armed force with some pride and experience of success. It was due to Saul more than to any one else that there was an Israel whose elders could invite David to be their king (2 S 5:1); the monarchy of David arose from the monarchy of Saul.

Gibeah retained his name in the days of Isaiah (10:29). His pursuit of David is reflected in some Ps titles (52:2; 54:2; 57:1; 59:1). The Chronicler sums up formally the unfavorable judgment on him implicit in the antimonarchic source (1 Ch 10:13 f). His genealogy appears in 1 Ch 8:33; 9:39.

2. Saul was the Jewish name of Paul*. He is called Saul in AA from his first appearance (7:58) until the two names are noticed in 13:9.

Savior. Cf SALVATION.

Saw. Flint saws with serrated edges were in use in Palestine even in the Iron Age; they were of necessity small. Excavation also discloses saws of bronze and of iron. The saw is illustrated in Egyptian art (ANEP 122, 123). Here it appears as a broad curved blade, angled at one end to form a handle; there is no trace of a wooden handle. The workman applies one hand to the handle and the other to the back of the blade; the wood to be sawn is held stationary by binding it with cord to another piece of wood inserted into the ground. The OT mentions saws for stone masonry as well as for wood (1 K 7:9). David put the prisoners of Rabbah to work with saws and other tools (2 S 12:31); by one of the more sensational misreadings of the OT 1 Ch 20:3 reads that he sawed them with saws. Assyria is compared to a saw wielded by the hand of Yahweh (Is 10:15).

Scapegoat. Cf ATONEMENT, DAY OF; AZAZEL.

Scarlet. Cf DYE.

Scepter (Hb šēbeṭ, "rod" or "staff," which can be used as a weapon [Ex 21:20; Mi 4:14 +], especially the shepherd's staff [Ps 23:4; Mi 7:14, both of the staff of Yahweh the shepherd of Israel]). The scepter as the symbol of royalty or other official position is mentioned frequently in the OT. It was carried by kings and other rulers (Gn 49:10; Nm 24:17; Pss 2:9; 45:7; Is 14:5; Ezk

19:11, 14; Am 1:5, 8) and may by metonymy signify the king. The word *šēbeṭ* also signifies a tribe; the sheikhs carried scepters which distinguished the tribe which they headed. The scepter is often represented in ancient Near Eastern art as carried both by gods and men; in Egypt many of the gods carried a scepter which identified them. Cf ANEP 383 (Egyptian, shepherd's crook), 414 (Egyptian, mace), 442 (Assyrian, mace), 461 (Hittite, mace), 463 (Persian, long staff), 470 (Canaanite, long staff slightly curved), 549 (Egyptian, the staff with the *ankh,* the sign of life, of Ptah), 556 (Egyptian, the scourge and the crook of Osiris).

Sceva (Gk *skeuas,* etymology uncertain), head of a Jewish priestly family whose sons, attempting to exorcise a demoniac in the name of Jesus and Paul, were attacked by the demoniac (AA 19:14). The name occurs in other historians of the Hellenistic-Roman period.

Scorpion (Hb *'aḳrab,* Gk *skorpios,* one of the *Arachnidae*). The animal is shaped like a lobster, 4 in to 6 in long. The scorpion has a long tail with a venomous sting. It is carnivorous, eating insects and worms. It lurks under stones and in walls. It is common in Palestine and Syria, especially in the desert regions. Its sting is painful to human beings and causes some illness, but it is not fatal unless the swelling of the wound obstructs breathing. About a dozen species are known in Palestine; they are black, yellow, brown, white, red, and striped. Dt 8:15 alludes to their infestation of the desert; metaphorically one's enemies (Ezk 2:6) or a wicked woman (BS 26:7) are compared to a scorpion. Rehoboam threatened to scourge the Israelites with scorpions, scourges equipped with barbs (1 K 12:11, 14; 2 Ch 10:11, 14). The scorpion is compared to an egg in size and color (Lk 11:12).

The pass of Akrabbim, "Scorpion Pass," probably derives its name from the presence of the animals. It lay of the S frontier of Judah (Jos 15:3), which was also the frontier of Israel (Nm 34:4) and the frontier of the Amorites* (Jgs 1:36). It was the scene of a raid of Judas* upon the Idumaeans (1 Mc 5:3; Gk *akrabattēnē*). It is identified with the modern Nakb es safa, a defile which connects the Arabah* with the Negeb*.

Scourge. Flogging or scourging as a legal punishment was common in the ancient world, but OT references to it are rare. Dt 25:1–3 limits the number of blows in legal punishment to 40; it may be assumed that this humanitarian law of Dt is a reform of earlier practice which, as usual, left the number of blows to the discretion of the judge or of the agent of execution. The type of scourge employed is not indicated; Hb *šôṭ* is used to designate a horsewhip (Na 3:2; Pr 26:3), and possibly no specific type of scourge was employed for punishment. Forced labor was done under the scourge of the overseer, who appears in Egyptian art with this symbol of office; the scourging with which Rehoboam* threatened the Israelites (1 K 12:11, 14; 2 Ch 10:11, 14) was the scourge of the master of forced labor. Assyria is the scourge of Yahweh (Is 28:15, 18); but Yahweh Himself smites the Assyrian with scourge and staff as He has smitten other enemies (Is 10:24–26). Metaphorically the scourge is a misfortune (Jb 9:23).

In NT times under Roman law scourging was a penalty which was inflicted on slaves and provincials; the law severely prohibited the scourging of Roman citizens. Scourging was done as a prelude to execution or as a punishment for lesser offenses or as a part of the questioning of witnesses. It was either the *flagellatio* or the *verberatio,* the first inflicted with the *flagellum* and the second with the *fasces.* The *flagellum* was made of thongs of leather equipped with fragments of bone or even of metal. This was the punishment inflicted on Jesus (Mt 27:26; Mk 15:15; Jn 19:1; Lk mentions the proposal of scourging [23:16] but not the execution). There is a difference in the place of the scourging in the passion in Mt-Mk as contrasted with Jn. In Mt-Mk the scourging is a prelude to the execution of the death sentence; in Jn (possibly hinted also in Lk) the scourging appears to be done as a substitute for the death penalty demanded by the Jews. The scourge as a punishment of slaves is often mentioned in Roman literature, where it is called *horribile;* the punishment was often fatal. The *verberatio* was done at the order and in the presence of a magistrate who was entitled to an escort of *lictores,* who carried axes bound in a bundle of rods; the rods were employed for the flogging, Paul received this punishment at Philippi (AA 16:22) and in 2 Co 11:25 says that he received it three times, in spite of the Roman citizenship to which he appealed at Philippi. He was threatened with the lash by a tribune at Jerusalem as part of his interrogation, but escaped this by an appeal to his citizenship (AA 22:24 ff). Paul mentions stripes as a hazard of the apostolate (2 Co 6:5). The apostles were flogged by the Jewish authorities in Jerusalem for preaching the Gospel (AA 5:40). This was done according to the Jewish practice which limited the blows to 39, one less than the number prescribed in Dt 25:1–3. Paul mentions that he received 39 lashes from the Jews five times (2 Co 11:24).

Scribe. The professional scribe appears in both Egypt and Mesopotamia in the earliest periods in which writing was used. In very few cultures have reading and writing

Egyptian scribe.

been skills which were widely diffused through the general population; the complicated systems of writing both in Egypt and Mesopotamia made it even more difficult for more than a few to master these skills. Reading and writing were basic in the advance of material civilization and of public administration in Egypt and Mesopotamia; the mercantile and industrial activities of these communities and the bureaucracy of government were rendered possible by the keeping of vast written records. It is doubtful that the kings, officers, nobles, and merchants who directed these enterprises were themselves literate; they depended on their scribes for all the vital information they needed for their decisions. Since the scribe was thus the only man who really was in control of the information, it was only natural that his advice should come to be important. In both Egypt and Mesopotamia we see that the scribe could advance to the highest levels of commercial and political management.

The only schools in the proper sense of the word in the ancient Near East were the scribal schools; these were the centers where wisdom* and wisdom literature were devel-

oped. In fact the scribes were the possessors and the transmitters of all the learning of the ancient world. The literary remains show us that they produced the administrative records of government and business and personal correspondence of individuals; they also produced and copied the literature, religious and secular, which has been preserved, the historical records, the mathematical, astronomical, and medical literature. The scribes were the professional learned men — one might almost say the intellectuals of the ancient Near East. The wisdom literature in its origins is a professional handbook in which the scribe learns the practical wisdom which will teach him good conduct and further his advancement. The literature betrays some class snobbery; the scribe knew his opportunities and spoke with contempt of those who lacked these opportunities, particularly of men doomed to manual labor.

Scribes appear frequently in the art of Egypt and Mesopotamia, and their ubiquity attests their importance. ANEP 460 shows an Aramaean scribe in an audience with the king. Assyrian battle and victory scenes rarely fail to represent the scribes recording the booty and prisoners taken (ANEP 235, 236, 364, 367, 370). As an officer close to the king an Egyptian scribe introduces a party of nomads to a royal audience (ANEP 3). Egyptian scribes appear in a goldsmith's shop (ANEP 133) and on the staff of the tax collector (ANEP 231). The Egyptian scribe frequently if not always did his work seated in a squatting posture with his tablet spread upon his knees (ANEP 230) or resting on one knee with the tablet placed upon the other (ANEP 231, 232). The Assyrian scribe, on the other hand, is usually represented standing. The tools of the Egyptian scribe were his pen, a palette with the dry components of his ink*, and a water jar for mixing the ink (ANEP 233–234). The scribe carried his tools with him and is recognized in art by their presence.

The scribe possibly is a military officer in Jgs 5:14, where the text is suspected by most critics, and in 1 Mc 5:42. As a royal officer the scribe appears in the list of David's cabinet officers (2 S 8:17; 20:25; 1 Ch 18:16). Scholars suggest that David organized his administration on the model of the Egyptian court, where the scribe was an essential officer; and it is altogether likely that the strength of his administration compared with the simple chieftainship of Saul was derived from this organization. The royal scribe appears as a high officer of state also in the reigns of Solomon (1 K 4:3; two scribes are mentioned), Jehoash* (2 K 12:11), Hezekiah* (2 K 18:18, 37; 19:2; Is 36:3, 22; 37:2 +), Uzziah* (2 Ch 16:11),

Josiah* (2 K 22:3 ff), Jehoiakim* (Je 36:10 ff), and Zedekiah* (2 K 25:19; Je 37:15, 20; 52:25). Nehemiah was assisted by scribes in his government (Ne 13:13). These passages show that the scribe was one of the principal officers of the royal administration, if not indeed the highest officer, but they reveal little of his duties and responsibilities. 1 Ch 27:32 mentions Jonathan as a scribe and a counselor; the book is late, but the identification of the two offices in a single person is not unlikely. It is very probable that the scribe mentioned by name in the royal cabinet is the chief of the scribal office where subordinates did most of the actual writing. Many modern scholars think that one of the chief tasks set upon the scribal office by David and Solomon was not only the keeping of annals and archives, but the compilation of the traditions and beliefs of Israel from existing written sources and from popular oral tradition; these offices were thus the places where the actual writing of the Old Testament was begun. Hezekiah's scribe Shebna* was one of the commission which went to negotiate with the commander of the army of Sennacherib*. The scribe of Jehoash with the chief priest supervises the administration of the funds for the repair of the temple (2 K 12:11). The scribe was a channel to the king; when Hilkiah* discovered the book of the law*, he brought it to Shaphan the scribe (2 K 22:3 ff), and when Baruch read the discourses of Jeremiah in the temple, the report was brought to the scribe (Je 36:10 ff); it is to be noticed that all the royal officers meet in the office of the scribe. Jeremiah was later put in the house of Zedekiah's scribe (Je 37:15, 20). 1 Ch 24:6 commits the keeping of the priestly rolls to the royal scribe, and 2 Ch 26:11 the keeping of the army rolls. 1 Ch 2:55 mentions Jabez as a whole town of scribes; many modern scholars are inclined to accept this and such guild towns as a genuine historical memory. In such towns were the scribal schools where the craft was taught by tradition from father to son. Ezekiel has a scribe accompany the celestial destroyers of Jerusalem, as the scribe accompanied the armies of Mesopotamia (Ezk 9:2 f). A last pathetic tribute to the importance of the royal scribe of Judah was his selection by Nebuchadnezzar* to be a member of the group of officers executed at Riblah (2 K 25:19; Je 52:25). The Psalmist compares his tongue to the pen of a rapid scribe (Ps 45:2).

The scribe first appears in a sense leading toward his meaning in Judaism and the NT in Je 8:8; the prophet says that the false pen of the scribes has turned the law of Yahweh into a lie. The scribal office

among its other works copied the monuments of Israel's legal traditions, which were also religious traditions; Jeremiah here must refer to some work of compilation and redaction which he asserts distorts the law of Yahweh. Ezra*, "the rapid scribe in the law of Yahweh" (Ezr 7:6), "learned in the words of the commandments of Yahweh" (Ezr 7:11) is the scribe of Judaism: a man learned in the law. Ezra read the law to the community of Jerusalem (Ne 8:1 ff), and modern criticism sees in him and in the scribes of Babylon the men who were responsible for compiling the law into a form identical or substantially identical with the present Pnt*. The scribes who acted as representatives of the Jews to Alcimus* (1 Mc 5:42) and the heroic scribe Eleazar* (2 Mc 6:18) were also members of this scribal class.

NT. The Jewish scribe in NT times is the scholar and the intellectual of Judaism, who receives the title rabbi*. His scholarship was the knowledge of the law, which he regarded as the sum of wisdom and the only true learning. His position in the Jewish community was a respected position of leadership; it is somewhat surprising but revealing that Mt 7:29 says that Jesus taught with authority, not like the scribes. This may refer to the fact that the teaching of Jesus was His own, not a compilation of quotations from the law and the traditions of the elders. The scribe as such was not a member of any Jewish sect or party (cf PHARISEES; SADDUCEES), but in fact most of the scribes were Pharisees, adhering to the strict interpretation of the law. Jesus was a threat to their influence, and most of the NT references show their hostility to Him. There are a few references to their teaching. Herod asks the scribes where the Messiah is to be born; this is a problem of biblical interpretation which was exactly their field of interest (Mt 2:4). They teach that the Messiah is the son of David (Mk 12:35, not mentioned in the parallels in Mt-Lk). They teach that Elijah* is the precursor of the Messiah (Mk 9:11; Mt 17:10). Jesus gives them the authority of Moses; they sit on his chair, but they impose heavy burdens by their rigorous interpretation and they close the kingdom of heaven to those who desire to enter (Mt 23:2, 13–15). They are zealous in making proselytes* (Mt 23:15). Jesus scores their vanity and their love of signs of respect (Mt 23:38; Lk 20:46). Their doctrine produces a righteousness* which Jesus tells His disciples they must exceed if they wish to enter the kingdom of heaven (Mt 5:20).

The hostility of the scribes to Jesus begins early in His public life and endures toward the community which He founded. His claim to forgive sins they call blasphemy (Mt 9:3; Mk 2:6; Lk 5:21). They ask Jesus for a sign from heaven to prove His authority (Mt 12:38). They object to the neglect of ritual washing (Mt 15:1; Mk 7:1). Jesus enumerates them among His enemies in His predictions of the passion (Mt 16:21; 20:18; Mk 8:31; 10:33; Lk 9:22). They are among the objectors to the acclamations which Jesus received on His final entry into Jerusalem (Mt 21:15). They find fault with the friendliness of Jesus toward publicans and sinners (Mk 2:16; Lk 5:30; 15:2). They charge that Jesus is in league with Beelzebul* in His exorcisms (Mk 3:22). With the chief priests they plot the death of Jesus (Mk 11:18; 14:1; Lk 19:47). They challenge the authority of Jesus (Mk 11:27). They watch Him closely for violations of the Sabbath (Lk 6:7). They slander Jesus to the public (Lk 11:53). They attempt to seize Him (Lk 20:19). They introduce a woman taken in adultery in order to pose an insoluble problem (Jn 8:3). With others they are active in the passion. They are present at the hearing before Caiaphas* (Mt 26:57; Mk 14:53). They are members of the arresting party (Mk 14:43). They take part in the meeting of the council (Lk 23:10) and accuse Jesus before Herod (Lk 23:10). They mock Jesus as He dies on the cross (Mt 27:41; Mk 15:31). They take part in the examinations of the apostles (AA 4:5) and of Stephen* (AA 6:12). The pattern of hostility which emerges is composed of their belief that Jesus was a threat to the integrity of the law, which to them was the very heart of Judaism; and only if their devotion to the law is recognized can the profundity of their hostility to Jesus and their refusal to admit any possible validity of His claims be understood.

But these men cherished the traditions of Judaism, and it would be wrong to think that this prejudiced hostility possessed the entire body of scribes. The offer of a scribe to join the company of Jesus was met by a statement of the demands which the offer implied, but the offer could not have been a hostile gesture (Mt 8:19). The scribe who is learned in the kingdom of God brings out old and new treasures (Mt 13:52); here the scribe learned in the kingdom is probably contrasted with the scribe learned in the law, but the same term is used to describe the wise man of the Gospel. The scribe who asked Jesus what was the first and greatest commandment accepted His answer and was told that he was not far from the kingdom of God (Mk 12:28–34). The scribes praised Jesus for His confutation of the Sadducees (Lk 20:39); this

praise, of course, was probably mixed with partisan motives, but it shows that their minds were not entirely closed. In the same doctrinal issue of the resurrection some of the scribes defended Paul (AA 23:9). It is altogether probable that the first Christian communities included some scribes among their members, and indeed the NT itself shows the influence of rabbinical interpretation*.

The scribe as a political officer is mentioned only in AA 19:35 (Ephesus).

Scripture. Cf BIBLE.

Scroll. Cf BOOK.

Scrolls, Dead Sea. Cf QUMRAN.

Scythians. A nomadic barbarian people whose original home was in central Asia E of the Caspian Sea and N of the Caucasus range. They appear in Assyrian records as invading the empire from 670 to 612 BC and the Assyrians, unable to halt them, accepted them as allies. Their migration was due to pressure of other nomadic peoples from the N and E, and they settled in Asia and in Europe N of the Black Sea and the Danube. Their territory N of the Danube was invaded by Darius I of Persia in 512 BC. Herodotus reports a major incursion of the Scythians which passed through Syria and Palestine and reached the border of Egypt. Many interpreters have identified this incursion with the invasion from the N mentioned in Je 1:13–15; 4:5–6:26. Recent scholars believe that Herodotus or his sources exaggerated the extent and seriousness of the Scythian incursion and deny any reference to it in the OT. During the Gk period the city of Beth-shan* acquired the name of Scythopolis.

2 Mc 4:47 alludes to the proverbial barbarism of the Scythians; in Gk "to act like a Scythian" means to show the extreme of boorishness. Col 3:11 enumerates them among the disparate peoples who become one in Christ.

Scythopolis. Cf BETH-SHAN.

Sea. "The sea" without qualification in the Bible almost always means the Mediterranean, but the word *yām* is applied to other bodies of water also (cf DEAD SEA; GALILEE, SEA OF; RED SEA). "Seawards" is the usual designation of the westward point of direction. The Israelites were never a seagoing people, and the two most famous Israelite sea travelers mentioned in the Bible, Jonah* and Paul*, were both cast into the sea. Many mentions of the sea exhibit an uncertainty and even a fear of the sea. This is partly due to the geographical character of the Palestinian coast, which has no natural harbors (in contrast with Phoenicia) and does not encourage sea travel; furthermore, the prevailing W winds drive the sea against the shore in a manner which makes it usually rough and often furious. Paul mentions three shipwrecks which he experienced and includes perils of the sea among the dangers of his mission (2 Co 11:25 f). Ps 107:23–30 is a famous passage which describes the terrors of those who go down to the sea in ships and experience a storm from which Yahweh delivers them. It is Yahweh who stirs up the storms of the sea (Je 31:35). In contrast with these passages Ps 104:25 views the sea with some appreciation: the sea is great and wide, teeming with life, and ships travel on its surface; it is a work of Yahweh's wisdom. The other component of the Israelite fear of the sea is derived from cosmological-theological motives. The sea is the monster of chaos in ancient myths of creation* which the creative deity overcomes; and several OT allusions (cf below) describe the sea as a monster under restraint. One of the names of the adversary of the creative deity in the mythological poems of Ugarit* is Yamm, "Sea."

The account of creation in Gn 1:9 f (P) represents the sea as created by the division of the primeval waters from the land. The Bible often alludes to the creation of the sea by Yahweh; it is a witness of His supreme power (Ne 9:6; Ps 24:2; Jon 1:9; AA 4:24; Apc 10:6 +). Yahweh calls the waters of the sea and pours them out (Am 5:8); He tramples the waves of the sea (Jb 9:8). The conception of the sea as a monster restrained is clear in Jb 38:8–11; Yahweh sets its boundaries beyond which it may not pass (cf also Pr 8:29). It is implied also in the rebuke of Yahweh which dries up the sea (Is 50:2; Na 1:4); these passages possibly allude also to the exodus*, where Yahweh exhibits His power over the sea by dividing it for the passage of Israel (Ex 14:15 +). In Ps 114:3 the division is caused when the sea flees in terror at the sight of Yahweh. The exodus is reenacted in the deliverance of Israel from exile (Is 11:15). Yahweh is present even at the uttermost boundaries of the sea (Ps 139:9). The sea and all its monsters are invited to praise Yahweh (Ps 148:7). The power of Jesus is manifest in His rebuke of the wind and the waves (Mt 8:23–27; Mk 4:35–41; Lk 8:22–25), which recalls these OT passages. It is no doubt the cosmological-mythological background which makes the author of Apc exclude the sea from the new heavens and the new earth (21:1). To this writer it

is a hostile element which has no place in a world where the peace of Yahweh reigns.

In ancient cosmogony the visible sea was a portion of the vast abyss upon which the earth rested (Ps 24:2). It is the source of springs and rivers (Jb 38:16). In the collapse of the earth into chaos which is the deluge* in P the fountains of the great infernal abyss are broken and the abyss rises to submerge the earth (Gn 7:11). This conception is found also in the cosmology of Mesopotamia.

The bronze "sea" which stood in the court of the temple of Solomon's court is described under TEMPLE.

Seal. In the ancient world, where the skills of reading and writing were not generally diffused, the seal served as a signature. Only the seal was valid in law. Three types were in use: the scarab, an Egyptian type shaped like a beetle (Gk *skarabos*) with the figure of the beetle on the upper side and the impression on the base: the cylinder seal, a Mesopotamian type always containing a pictorial strip; and the stamp seal, most common in Palestine but found also in Syria. The scarabs found in Palestine are amulets* rather than seals, and the devices found on the base are meaningless decorations. The seal was usually made of semiprecious stone; it was vital that the seal (almost universally intaglio) preserve its sharpness of outline. Some of the finest art of the ancient Near East appears in glyptic art, which is little larger than microscopic in scale. The Mesopotamian seals are a rich source of information on mythology, from which the scenes on the seals are taken (ANEP 672–706); without some literary information from other sources they are extremely obscure, but when the myth can be identified from literary sources details are found in glyptic art which are not mentioned in the literature. The seal was hung on a cord about the neck (Gn 38:18) or on the arm (SS 8:6) or on the wrist (Je 22:24). Gn 38:18 shows its use as a personal identification and a pledge; SS 8:6 and Je 22:24 that it was regarded as something to be kept on the person at all times.

Palestinian seals, mostly Israelite, come from 800–500 BC and more than 150 are now known. Where pictorial designs appear foreign influence is evident — Egyptian, Canaanite, Mesopotamian. The pictorial designs are merely decorative; unlike Mesopotamian seals and scarabs, which were identified merely by their design, Palestinian seals usually have the name of the owner. The pictorial designs favor wild animals or winged figures drawn from mythology. A common Israelite type gives the name (+

Mesopotamian cylinder seal impressions.

patronymic in some) and the office of the owner. These are valuable sources of information for early Hb writing and furnish a supplement to biblical nomenclature. Some of the names are biblical (not necessarily the same person), but where they are known only from the seals they show the same type of name formation. It is a question whether the absence of pictorial decoration on most Israelite seals is due to religious motives (cf IMAGE). Some offices mentioned in the Bible are found also in seals; some of the seals have the title "slave of . . ." (the king or of a private person), slave* here being the title of an office of high responsibility. An interesting seal contains the name of Gedaliah* who was "over the house" (master of the palace).

Three of the best known Hb seals are illustrated in ANEP 276–278. 276 is the seal of Shema slave of Jeroboam* (II), with a lion (a popular motif). 277 is the seal of Jaazaniah* slave of the king, with a fighting cock. 278 has no decoration and shows the name and title in two panels, Eliakim* steward (?) of YKWN, the contemporary writing of the OT YHWYKYN, Jehoiachin*.

Secundus (Gk *sekundos*, Lt *secundus*, "second"), a personal name; one of the party of Thessalonians who accompanied Paul on his journey from Greece to Syria (AA 20:4).

Seer. Cf PROPHET.

Segub (Hb *segûb*, "exalted"?), youngest son of Hiel* of Bethel, who rebuilt Jericho and set up its gates "in his youngest son"; the phrase is thought to signify the offering of the sons of Hiel as foundation sacrifices (1 K 16:34).

Seir (Hb *sē'îr*), a geographical name; Seir is associated with Esau* and Edom* and the association is expressed in a play on the words *sē'ār*, "goat," and *sā'îr*, "hairy," in Gn 25:25; 27:11, 23. The name appears as the designation of a land, of a mountain, and as a gentilic. There is no doubt that the mountain is the chain which extends SW of the Dead Sea along the W side of the Arabah*, rising to an average height of 5000 ft. The name was later extended to the corresponding mountain chain on the E side of the Arabah. As a territorial designation the term is used more loosely of the region adjacent to the mountain chain, substantially identical with the territory of Edom. In tradition the Horites* were the pre-Edomite inhabitants of the region (Gn 14:6; 36:30). The eponymous ancestor Seir the Horite (Gn 36:20 f; 1 Ch 1:38) is a good example of the personification of a geographical name into the ancestor of the clans who dwell there. Israelite tradition itself recognized that the claim of Edom to Seir and its settlement there were older than its own claim to Canaan. It was the region of Esau the brother of Jacob (Gn 32:4; 33:14, 16; 36:8 f; Nm 24:18; Dt 2:4 ff; Jos 24:4). Dt 1:44 places the land of Seir S of the hill country of the Amorites beginning in the neighborhood of Hormah*, which is not itself precisely located. It lay between Horeb* and Kadesh-barnea* (Dt 1:2); this tradition is some help in locating these two points. The Israelites passed around Mt Seir to the S to avoid encroaching on Edomite territory (Dt 2:1–5). An isolated tradition in 1 Ch 4:42 relates that clans of Simeon* settled in Mt Seir. The mountain becomes a loose designation of its inhabitants as "the men of Seir or Mt Seir" (2 Ch 20:10, 22 f; 25:11, 14); these must be the Edomites. Ezk 35 contains an oracle against Mt Seir (contrasted with the mountains of Israel, which are blessed in 36), alluding to the plundering of Judahite territory by Edom after the fall of Jerusalem in 587 BC. Yahweh twice comes from Seir in a theophany* (Dt 33:2; Jgs 5:4); this probably means merely the S, the region of the theophanies of Sinai* and Kadesh-barnea*.

It is probable that the name first belonged to the mountain and was then extended to the region. The frequent use of the name indicates that it was a much older designation of the region than the settlement of Edom.

Sela (Hb sela', "rock"), the name of a town. Sela was taken from the Edomites* by Amaziah* of Judah and renamed Joktheel (2 K 14:7). Tribute was sent from Sela to Jerusalem (Is 16:1; the passage causes some confusion, since the context concerns Moab, not Edom). The border of the Amorites extended from Sela along the pass of Akrabbim* (Jgs 1:36); some geographers believe that this indicates a different Sela. Sela was an Edomite royal city or citadel. Many scholars locate it at Petra, which later became the Nabataean capital and is one of the most celebrated sites of the Near East. This great mass of red sandstone, approachable only through a narrow gorge, over a mile long, is itself an extremely strong site. But scholars believe that Sela should be located precisely on the summit of Umm el Biyarah in the Petra complex; this rock mass rises almost sheer to a height of 3700 ft above sea level and several hundred ft above the adjacent terrain. It is suggested that this is the rock meant in 2 Ch 25:12, where the victory of Amaziah is further embroidered by the story that the Judahites threw 10,000 Edomite prisoners from "the rock." It is also seen in "the clefts of the rock" in which Edom is said to build its nest (Je 49:16; Ob 3).

Selah. Cf PSALMS.

Seleucia (Gk seleukia), the city of Seleucia Pieria, named after Seleucus*; the seaport of Antioch* in Syria, located 28 mi from Antioch and 5 mi N of the mouth of the River Orontes. It was one of the coastal cities conquered by Ptolemy VI Philometor in his attempt to recover Palestine and Syria (1 Mc 11:8), and was the port from which Paul and Barnabas embarked to Cyprus on their first missionary journey (AA 13:4). The excavation of the site has not recovered remains earlier than the Christian period.

Seleucid, Seleucus. The Seleucid dynasty ruled the Gk kingdom of Syria from a few years after the death of Alexander the Great to the collapse of the dynasty in the early 1st century BC. The dynasty is named after its founder Seleucus I Nicator, one of the generals of Alexander called the Diadochi ("successors"). In a conference of the Diadochi held in 320 BC at Triparadisus (Riblah*) in Syria Seleucus was allotted Babylonia as his portion of Alexander's conquests. In the war which followed the conference Seleucus was attacked by Antigonus of Asia Minor and fled to Ptolemy I of Egypt. The defeat of Antigonus by the other Diadochi in 312 marks the beginning of the Seleucid era, after which the dates in Mc are computed. Seleucus took the title of king in 305 BC. After the battle of Ipsus in Asia Minor in 301 Seleucus' kingdom was expanded to include Armenia, Cappadocia, and N Syria. In 281, after his victory over Lysimachus at Corupedion, Seleucus added Asia Minor. This vast territory, stretching from the Indus to the Aegean, lacked inner unity and was subject to constant disturbance. Seleucus I and his successor Antiochus I Soter attempted to unify the kingdom by the foundation of Gk and Macedonian military colonies throughout the realm. These became the great Hellenistic cities of the Near East, and were the centers through which Hellenism* was diffused in Near Eastern countries. The center and strength of the kingdom lay in Cilicia, N Syria, and Mesopotamia.

During the reign of Seleucus Ptolemy II occupied all of Syria S of the Lebanon and Damascus in 301. Seleucus was not inclined to dispute the Ptolemies' possession of Palestine. In 278, however, Ptolemy II invaded N Syria and was defeated by Antiochus I in 276. The wars and quarrels which ensued were patched up by the marriage of Antiochus I to Berenice, daughter of Ptolemy II, in 253 (Dn 11:6). This measure proved disastrous. Antiochus repudiated his first wife Laodice and her son to marry Berenice. Antiochus died in 257, Ptolemy in 246, and Laodice gathered a party to fight for the succession of her son. She succeeded in assassinating Berenice and her son, and the son of Laodice succeeded as Seleucus II in 246. The war dragged on between Seleucus II and Ptolemy III until 241.

Antiochus III the Great received his appellative even in ancient times; he was the most ambitious and able of the Seleucid rulers, although his ambition led to a nearly fatal blow to the kingdom. His attempt to annex Palestine to the Seleucid kingdom began with invasion which carried him as far as Jerusalem in 218. The following year, however, he was defeated at Raphia on the frontier by Sosibius, the general of Ptolemy IV. This defeat halted his attempts on Palestine; but he spent the following years consolidating and expanding his territories in Asia Minor, Armenia, and in the E as far as the Indus. When he returned to the invasion of Palestine in 202 he was successful, and his defeat of Ptolemy V at Panion (Dan*) in 198 took Palestine from the Ptolemies permanently. In Asia Minor, however, he was in trouble. Cities and kingdoms there which did not wish the Seleucids to rule them invoked the aid of Rome, now free of its war with Hannibal. The war began in 192 and was a series of defeats for Antiochus which ended at the battle of Magnesia in 190. Antiochus in the treaty renounced all claims in Asia Minor W of the Taurus range and left his successor a badly depleted treasury.

On the successors of Antiochus III, who were concerned with Jewish history during the Maccabean period, cf the relevant articles. The dynasty dissolved after the death of Antiochus VII Sidetes in 128 into a number of factions supporting rival Seleucid claimants to the throne. The territory of the kingdom was taken in large portions by neighboring kingdoms to the N and E, and order was restored only by Roman intervention under Sulla in Asia Minor and under Pompey in Palestine.

Seleucus I Nicator 305–280
Antiochus I Soter 280–261
Antiochus II Theos 261–246
Seleucus II Callinicus 246–226
Seleucus III Ceraunus 226–223
Antiochus III the Great 223–187
Seleucus IV Philopator 187–175
*Antiochus IV Epiphanes 175–163
*Antiochus V Eupator 163–161
*Demetrius I Soter 161–150
*Alexander Balas 150–145
*Demetrius II Nicator 145–138
*Antiochus VI Dionysius 145–142
*Antiochus VII Sidetes 138–128
*Demetrius II Nicator 128–125

The unnamed king of 2 Mc 3:7, who sent Heliodorus* to raid the temple treasury of Jerusalem, is Seleucus IV Philopator (187–175). His death is mentioned in 2 Mc 4:7; the author probably did not know of his assassination by his minister Heliodorus.

Semitic. On the basis of Gn 10:21–31 the name Semitic has been since 1781 (Schlozer

and Eichhorn) applied to a group of languages and of peoples of the Near East. Gn 10 (cf TABLE OF NATIONS) is partly artificial and includes under "Hamitic" (cf HAM) peoples who were ethnically and linguistically Semitic. The Semitic language group is arranged artificially as follows:

Northeast Semitic (Babylonia and Assyria): Akkadian*, with Babylonian* and Assyrian* dialects.

Northwest Semitic (upper Mesopotamia, Syria, Palestine): Aramaic*, Canaanite*, Phoenician*, Hebrew*.

Southern Semitic (Arabia, Ethiopia): Arabic*, Ethiopic.

Certain characteristics of the Semitic languages are noted under HEBREW.

As an ethnographic term Semitic designates a group with certain distinctive physical characteristics, in particular olive complexion, large straight nose and heavy dark beard and hair. The hooked nose popularly associated with Semitic types is actually Hittite*. This type was identified in ancient Egyptian art and can easily be distinguished from non-Semitic peoples: Egyptians, Sumerians, Hittites, Philistines. It is probable that the Arabian peninsula is the motherland of all the Semitic peoples; the deserts of Arabia produce more people than they can support, and migrations into the surrounding fertile territory occur from the beginning of the recorded history of the Near East. The culture of the Semitic peoples in the desert area is nomadic*; peasant and urban cultures were adopted after their migrations.

Gn 10:21–31 includes among Semitic peoples Elamites*, Assyrians*, Hebrews*, Aramaeans*, and Arabian* tribes. Ethnically the Elamites should be excluded from this group: the Canaanites*, some Arabian tribes, and the Babylonians (classified as Hamitic in Gn 10:6–20) should also be counted as Semitic; on the principle of arrangement cf TABLE OF NATIONS. In historical times (after 3000 BC) the Semitic peoples appear in the geographical area designated "the Fertile Crescent" by J. H. Breasted. This is a stretch of arable land which, beginning at the SE extremity at the mouth of the Tigris* and Euphrates*, extends NW through the valleys of these rivers to N Syria, where it turns S along the coast of Syria and Palestine and then, interrupted by the desert between Palestine and Egypt, continues S up the valley of the Nile*. This geographical area was a single cultural complex in the ancient world and is the ancient Near East; Egypt, however, was Semitic neither in language nor in race, and its culture had peculiarities which distinguish it from the Semitic peoples elsewhere through the Crescent. Within the Crescent non-Semitic peoples appear as occasional isolated pieces (cf HITTITES; HURRIANS; HYKSOS; PHILISTINES; SUMERIANS). This Crescent, it will be observed, bounds the Syrian and Arabian deserts. A. B. Cook defined the area as the "Semitic quadrilateral." This is an uneven rectangle bounded on its NE side by the Zagros Mts E of the Tigris and the Persian Gulf, on its NW side by the highlands of Armenia and Anatolia and the Mediterranean, on its SW side by the Red Sea, and on its SE side by the Indian Ocean. This area is somewhat deceptive in that Egypt is excluded from its cultural complex; but it designates the Semitic countries more accurately, which are the Arabian peninsula and the regions contiguous to it as far as the mountain and sea barriers mentioned above. On the place of this region in the history of early civilizations cf ASSYRIA; BABYLONIA; SUMERIANS.

Senir. Cf HERMON.

Sennacherib (Hb *sanḥērîb,* Assyrian *sin-aheriba,* "[the god] Sin has increased the brothers"), king of Assyria 705–681 BC. Sennacherib was the son of Sargon. At his accession he was greeted by a general rebellion through much of the Assyrian empire, with its two principal centers at Babylon under the leadership of Merodach-baladan and in Syria and Palestine under the leadership of Hezekiah* of Judah with the assistance of Egypt. Sennacherib's rapid campaigns in Babylonia suppressed the rebellion in Mesopotamia and in 701 he moved against Syria and Palestine. Outside of Judah and the cities of Philistia no effective resistance was offered; the Egyptian forces were defeated at Eltekeh, and Jerusalem was forced to capitulate. The rebellion in Babylon, however, was not completely suppressed; and Sennacherib determined to remove this center of discontent. In 689 he razed the city of Babylon to the ground and transferred the shrine of Marduk to Nineveh*. This act was regarded as barbarous; Babylon was an old and venerable city and a focus of Mesopotamian religion and civilization. There are no records of Sennacherib after 689; the records of his successor make it clear that he was assassinated by his sons, who then contested the succession of the younger son Esarhaddon*, designated as successor by Sennacherib. The OT (2 K 19:37) adds their names, Adrammelech* and Sharezer* (called his sons in 2 Ch 21:31), and the place of the murder, the temple of Nisroch* (either at Kalah or at Nineveh). On the question of whether 2 K 18–19; Is 36–37 relate one campaign or two distinct campaigns against Judah cf HEZEKIAH. Herodotus relates a campaign of Sennacherib

against Egypt which in the chronology of the rulers of Egypt (cf TIRHAKAH) cannot be identified with the campaign of 701. This campaign was arrested by field mice, which gnawed the leather straps and thongs of the army. This bit of popular tradition is thought by scholars to reflect a more serious nonmilitary factor: an attack of the bubonic plague.

Sennacherib was a patron of the ancient Assyrian royal city Nineveh, to which he restored the royal residence and where he built extensively. For the records of Sennacherib cf ANET 287–288.

Sepharad (Hb *sᵉpārad,* meaning uncertain), a place to which the Jews of Jerusalem were exiled (Ob 20). The name is otherwise unknown, and modern scholars suggest Sardis* in Asia Minor or a region of Media. The name Sephardic to designate a Jewish synagogue rite is derived from this name.

Sepharvaim (Hb *sᵉparwayim;* meaning uncertain), a city conquered by the Assyrians. People of Sepharvaim were settled in Samaria and worshiped the gods Adrammelech* and Anammelech* (2 K 17:24, 31). The Assyrian general boasts of the conquest of Sepharvaim in enumerating his victories to the legation of Hezekiah (2 K 18:34; 19:13; Is 36:19; 37:13). The situation of Sepharvaim is unknown; in the passages cited above it is enumerated with cities of Mesopotamia and of Syria. In the enumerations it stands next to cities of Syria and is probably to be located in this region.

Septuagint (Lt *septuaginta,* "seventy"), the name commonly given to the Jewish Gk version of the OT made in the pre-Christian period. The name is derived from the spurious letter of Aristeas which pretends to give an account of the origin of the version. Aristeas, a Jewish scholar of the 2nd century BC, is made to say that Ptolemy II Philadelphus (283–246 BC) wished to have a translation of the Jewish sacred books in the great library which he founded at Alexandria*. At his request 72 men, 6 from each of the 12 tribes, were sent from Jerusalem to make the translation. The story was later embroidered: the 72 were put into separate cells on the island of Pharos, each completed his translation in 72 days, and they were found to be identical. Of these stories historians preserve only the place and in general the date of the version. There is no doubt that it was made in Alexandria for the large Jewish community of that city; and it can scarcely be earlier than 250 BC. The language accords with an Alexandrian origin. Scholars believe that it is a private version, but this is by no means certain; liturgical needs may have been at least in part a motive for the work. The prologue of BS, written about 130 BC, mentions the existence of Gk translations of "the law, the prophets, and the other books." This corresponds to the threefold division of the Jewish canon* and establishes very probably the date by which the LXX was completed.

Some recent scholars have insisted that *the* LXX conceived as a single work or a single project is a fiction; they believe that it is a collection of various versions of various books, done by many hands independently, and that there were other independent versions which have not been preserved. Whether one goes to this extreme or not, it is manifest that the LXX is not the work of a single translator; at times different translators can be discerned within a single book. Certainly there is no compelling reason to assert that the version was made under a single direction. It is altogether probable that the Pnt, as that part of the OT which the Jews venerated most highly, was translated first, and this may have been done for liturgical use. At least some of the other books appear to be private versions. The LXX included books which are not preserved in Hb or had no Hb original; cf CANON.

The quality of the LXX as a translation is uneven and has been thus analyzed by A. Vaccari: in adherence to the original, SS and Ec are servile, Pss, Prophets (except Dn) are literal, Pnt and historical books are faithful, Jb, Pr, Dn, Est are free or paraphrastic; In Gk idiom Jb, Pr are best, Pnt, Jos, Is are mediocre, others are inferior; in understanding of the Hb text Pnt is best, Is, minor prophets, Jb, Pr are worst, others are mediocre. In this analysis the LXX as a whole does not come off well as a version, and indeed it is not adequate from any point of view; it was done without the modern aids to the translator such as dictionaries, grammars, concordances, and commentaries, by men apparently who knew little Hb and were not skilled in Gk composition.

The LXX is not only a translation, it is also the first interpretation of the OT. The translators lived in a world of Jewish thought which is the world of the P source of the Pnt* and of the Chronicler*, and to some degree they were influenced by Gk ideas. Hence many of the raw anthropomorphisms and anthropopathisms of early Israelite literature were removed ("hand" becomes "power," "rock" becomes "help" etc). The divine name Yahweh (cf GOD), which was no longer pronounced at this time, was replaced by the word *kyrios* (lord*), which renders the Hb word Adonai substituted for Yahweh in the reading of the Bible, but is also a divine and royal title in Hellenistic culture. The Hb word *ḥesed* (cf LOVE) was rendered by *eleos,* "mercy" or "pity," and the Hb word *ṣedeḳ* (cf RIGHTEOUS) by *dikaiosynē,* "justice," and two fundamental ideas of Israelite belief experienced a substantial alteration. Similar examples of interpretation are numerous.

The text which the translators used was not the MT which we have, and not all of the variant readings in the LXX are due by any means to faulty translation or scribal error. The existence and character of this text is now better known from the MSS of Qumran*, which contain some fragments of the Hb text of the OT which belong with the LXX and not with the MT.

The LXX enjoyed great authority among the Jews of the Diaspora into the 1st century AD. It was the Gk Bible, and for this reason it was adopted by Christians when they began to evangelize the Hellenistic world. Christians adopted it with even greater enthusiasm than the Jews; it became the Bible of the Church in the first generation of Christians, and 300 of the 350 citations from the OT in the NT are quoted according to the LXX. This, however, is scarcely an indication of the influence of the LXX in forming the religious terminology of the NT. The great theological words of the NT come from the Hb through the LXX, although the NT does not always follow the interpretation of the LXX.

The authority of the LXX was likewise accepted by the Gk and Lt fathers of the Church, and many of them express the belief, based on the story of Pseudo-Aristeas, that the LXX also was inspired (cf INSPIRATION). As the Fathers understood it this opinion cannot be sustained; but a more modern restatement of the inspiration of the LXX has been proposed, especially by P. Benoit, which has met with some acceptance; but most scholars are hesitant to receive it. The opinion of Benoit is deduced from a revision of the concept of inspiration and views the LXX, as noted above, as an interpretation of the OT. The NT has often incorporated this interpretation in itself, and Benoit sees no difference in the attitude of the NT writers toward the interpretation from their attitude toward the original. Other scholars believe that this question is better answered by an explanation drawn from the principles of interpretation implicit in the practice of the writers of the NT (cf INTERPRETATION).

Other Gk versions. There is little doubt that the acceptance of the LXX and its use by Christians led the Jews to reject it. Some rabbis said that darkness covered the earth for three days when the LXX was written; others said that that day was as sad for Israel as the day of the golden calf. But there were still Jews in the Hellenistic cities who needed Gk versions, and others were prepared under Jewish auspices.

Aquila: he is reported to be a pagan official who was converted to Christianity and then to Judaism. His translation was made about AD 130. It survives only in fragments. It was an extraordinary achievement of servility; each Hb word is represented by one Gk word, which means that it is often unintelligible without the Hb text. It was for this reason much admired by the Jews.

Symmachus: a proselyte to Judaism from the Ebionites or the Samaritans. The date is uncertain; the version is probably assigned to the reign of Marcus Aurelius (161–180) or Septimus Severus (193–211). Jerome praised the version for its effort to render the sense rather than the words and for some attention to elegance of style, qualities which Jerome claimed for his own Lt version of the OT (cf VULGATE). The version survives only in fragments.

Theodotion: he is reported to have passed from paganism to Marcionism to Judaism. Epiphanius placed the version in the reign of Commodus (180–192). Jerome described the version as a revision of the LXX, and this description is borne out by the Dn of Theodotion; the LXX Dn has been replaced in most MSS by Theodotion. Otherwise his version survives only in fragments.

Recensions of the LXX. The universal employment of the LXX in the first three Christian centuries meant the multiplication of copies and a consequent deterioration of the text. Ancient sources attribute recensions of the text to Hesychius of Alexandria and Lucian of Antioch, both about AD 300; how successful their work was is not known, and modern scholars believe they have found traces of these recensions in the MS tradition. The principal recension of the LXX was made by Origen (+ AD 254) at Caesarea in Palestine, and this recension was extremely important in the subsequent history of the text. The recension of Origen was motivated by a desire to furnish Christians with a LXX text which could be used in controversies with Jews and would preserve Christians from the embarrassment of quoting texts which were absent from the Hb text or read differently there. The work which Origen prepared would show this at a glance. It was called the Hexapla (Gk *hex,* "six," from its six columns), and showed the Hb text and the various Gk versions in parallel columns, arranged as follows:

1	2	3
Hb text	Hb in Gk characters	Aquila

4	5	6
Symmachus	LXX	Theodotion

Since only one Hb word was given in each line, it is evident that the work was of enormous dimensions; it has been calculated that it would fill about 50 volumes (cf BOOK). It is doubtful that any copy of the entire original was ever made. The preparation occupied Origen from 228 to 240; it was preserved with the rest of his great library at Caesarea by his school. Jerome consulted it and its existence is attested for the end of the 6th century. It probably perished during the Moslem conquest of Palestine. It is known that copies were made of the last four columns, omitting the Hb text and its transcription into Gk characters. That which was copied most frequently was the 5th column, the LXX, and Origen's editorial treatment of this column confused the MS tradition. The text was edited according to his purpose as indicated above. Where the LXX had no correspondence in the Hb, Origen marked such passages at the beginning and the end. Where the Hb text had no correspondence in the LXX Origen supplied the missing material from Theodotion or some other version and marked the beginning and the end. Where the LXX has a different order of the text from the Hb, Origen altered it to fit the Hb and marked such passages in both texts. This text is called the Hexaplaric text. It is easy to imagine what happens when the Hexaplaric text is copied slavishly with no attention even to Origen's diacritical marks, and scarcely any MS of the LXX has been preserved which has not been to some degree affected by these editorial revisions.

The earliest MSS of the LXX are the fragments from Qumran*, probably from the latter half of the 1st century AD. The John Rylands Gk papyrus 458 (Manchester) contains 15 verses of Dt from the 2nd century AD. 2nd century fragments are found in the Chester Beatty papyri. The oldest codices are the Vaticanus and Sinaiticus, both of the 4th century AD; Vaticanus lacks Gn 1–45 and about 30 Pss. The LXX was first printed in the Alcala Polyglot 1514–1517, followed shortly by the Aldine edition (Venice, 1518–1519). No complete critical edition exists; two such editions have been many years in preparation, one at Cambridge and one at Göttingen, and both have been partially published.

Sepulcher. Cf BURIAL.

Seraiah (Hb *s^erāyāh*, "Yahweh is strong"?), personal name borne by several men in the OT. **1.** David's scribe* (2 S 8:17); this is possibly the adopted Hb name of the scribe Sheva* (2 S 20:25). **2.** Chief priest of Jerusalem, one of the royal officers executed by Nebuchadnezzar* at Riblah* (2 S 25:18; Je 52:24). **3.** One of the marauding captains who joined the company of Gedaliah* at Mizpah (Je 40:8), possibly the same man who went on an embassy to Babylon with Zedekiah (Je 51:59-61), called "officer of the rest," i.e., quartermaster. **4.** Father of Ezra (Ezr 7:1). **5.** One of the officers of Jehoiakim* sent to arrest Jeremiah (Je 36:26). The name is borne by six others in the OT.

Seraph (Hb *sārāp*, pl *s^erāpîm*, whence Eng seraphim; a superhuman being of uncertain character and function). The etymology (*SRP*) suggests "fiery one," "burning one." This is somewhat supported by the appearance of the seraphim in the vision of Is 6:2, 6 not so much by the fact that a seraph uses tongs to bring a live coal from the altar flame, but because fire* is the element of deity; the seraphim may be conceived as personifications of the tongues of flame of the theophany, as the cherub* is sometimes identified with the storm cloud. The form of the seraphim is only vaguely indicated in Is 6; they have six wings, two covering their face and two their feet (a euphemism for the sexual organs), and two for flight. They could be therefore either anthropomorphic or theriomorphic. They form part of the heavenly retinue of Yahweh (cf ANGEL) and sing the triple "Holy," the hymn of adoration. If they are to be identified with the seraphs mentioned in Nm 21:6, 8 and Is 14:29, they appear also as emissaries of Yahweh to execute His judgments; and this identification should probably be made. In Nm 21:6 they are called "seraph serpents"; in Nm 21:8 both terms are used, but not together. The material identification of these agents of vengeance with venomous serpents is somewhat crass; it seems better to understand them as emissaries of judgment with no indication of their material character. The personification of a tongue of flame as a winged serpentine being does not strain the imagination, and this is probably the material form in which they were imagined. The brazen serpent* was an image of such a heavenly being, and it is not impossible that the story of the seraphs in the desert was formed from a tradition associated with the brazen serpent as a cult object. This story is probably alluded to in Dt 8:15; Is 30:6, where the desert is called a land of winged seraphs. The winged seraph appears as an emissary of vengeance on Philistia in Is 14:29; here it is parallel with a word found only once in the OT, which almost certainly signifies viper, suggesting again the serpentine form of the seraph.

Sergius Paulus (Lt *sergius paulus*), a personal name; Roman proconsul of Cyprus*, who invited Paul and Barnabas to speak before him. They were controverted by a magician named Bar Jesus* or Elymas*. Sergius Paulus, impressed by the blinding of the magician at Paul's words, accepted the faith (AA 13:7-12). This is not improbable; at this period the Roman government had no quarrel with Christianity, and a high official could accept it as easily as he could be initiated into the mysteries. The Sergius Paulus mentioned by Pliny the Elder and in some inscriptions of Cyprus, Asia Minor, and Rome, is possibly the man mentioned in AA 13.

Serpent. There are at least 33 species of serpent in Palestine, several of them venomous, and allusions to the serpent are common in the Bible. As a symbolic figure the serpent is important in the religions of the ancient Near East and in OT and NT. The serpent is a demonic figure in many regions of the world, and it is such in the mythology of Mesopotamia, Persia, Egypt, Greece, and Rome. As a demonic figure it may be beneficent or maleficent. The serpent is a divine or demonic symbol on Mesopotamian boundary stones (ANEP 519, 520) and is included among the gods who are invoked to bring imprecations on the trespasser of the boundary. A serpent-headed dragon appears on the Ishtar Gate of Babylon* as a guardian spirit of the gate (ANEP 761). More commonly it is a maleficent demon; there can be no doubt of its character where it is grasped in the hand of the Lamashtu (cf DEMON) of Mesopotamia (ANEP 657, 660). The repulsive demon partly represented in ANEP 658 has tail and penis terminating in serpents' heads.

The serpent is not only a demonic figure; it is also a divine figure or a divine emblem, but its symbolism here becomes obscure. Its association with the deities of fertility, however, is assured. The nude Canaanite goddess of fertility is represented in Egyptian scenes grasping a serpent in the hand (ANEP 470-474). It is possibly represented as draped around a goddess (ANEP 480); this representation is regarded as certain by W. F. Albright for a plaque of a goddess which he discovered in Tell Beit Mirsim. Entwined serpents are identified by H. Frankfort as accompanying the god of fertility or as his symbol (ANEP 511, 675). It may therefore

a) Mesopotamian vase showing demon and serpent.
b) Divine image with entwined serpent, from a
Syrian shrine in Rome. c) The goddess Kadesh holding the lotus and serpents. d) A serpentine dragon
in a Mesopotamian seal impression.

be asked whether this is not the symbolism intended where the serpent figures are not explicitly identified, such as the serpents draped about cult objects from Beth-shan (ANEP 585, 590) and Assyria, or the god represented as a serpent figure (ANEP 692). As a symbol of fertility the serpent becomes a figure of life and health as in the modern caduceus, the emblem of medicine, which is derived from the emblem of the Gk healing god Asklepios (cf SALVATION).

The serpent is also a cosmic figure, identified with the monster of chaos which is conquered by the creative deity (cf CREATION). As such it is the very emblem of the powers of evil and darkness. This serpentine character of the monster of chaos is explicit in the mythological texts of Ugarit*. The symbolism of the serpent is not therefore uniform and must be identified by the con

text in which the symbol appears. The symbolism of the ancient Near East must be recalled in explaining the symbolic value of the serpent in the Bible.

As a celestial demonic figure, the emissary of Yahweh, the serpent is noticed under SERAPH. The serpent as a cosmic figure appears in some OT allusions: Yahweh smites the fleeing serpent, the twisted serpent, and the dragon in the sea (Jb 26:13; Is 27:1). This adversary of the creative deity appears in the mythological texts of Ugarit described in the identical words which are used in Is 27:1. Am 9:3 alludes to the serpent on the floor of the sea*, the cosmic serpent.

More obscure and much more discussed is the symbolism of the serpent in Gn 3. The identification of the serpent with Satan* occurs only in late Jewish literature, from which it passed to the NT (WS 2:24; 2 Co

11:3; and cf below). No concept of a demonic figure such as Satan can be traced in Israelite belief of the period when Gn 3 must be dated (cf PENTATEUCH). Since the symbolic value of the serpent was so common in the ancient Near East, it seems altogether probable that both writer and readers would see symbolic value in the serpent of Eden; and here as elsewhere the symbolism must be identified from the literary context as it is from artistic contexts. Even in early Jewish interpretation the symbolism of the serpent was referred to the fertility motif (cf above); and identification of the primeval sin as the use or abuse of sex, which was so common in rabbinical and patristic interpretation, has a long history. The literary context of a nude couple suggests the symbolism of the fertility cult (unknown to the rabbinical and patristic interpreters), and the curse of both the man and the woman in Gn 3:15 ff deals with the area of fertility: childbearing for the woman, the cultivation of the soil for the man. Some modern interpreters have suggested that the seduction of man and woman by the serpent is a mythological representation of the seduction of Israel by the deities of fertility, which to the writer of the story is the fundamental sin of Israel. It is not impossible that this motif is combined implicitly with the motif of the cosmic serpent. The serpent of Gn 3 is represented as a serpent (outside of his loquacity), but the curse of the serpent (Gn 3:14 f) reduces him to his natural serpentine character, and it is conceivable that this is intended to be another version of the victory of Yahweh over the cosmic serpent.

In the messianic age the serpent becomes harmless (Is 11:8). The promise of protection in Ps 91:13 includes the power to tread upon serpents. These passages may be allusions to Gn 3:14 f; they are at the base of Mk 16:18; Lk 10:19, where it is one of the signs of the mission of the disciples of Jesus that they have power over serpents. It is perhaps not fanciful to see here allusions to the victory of Jesus over the serpent, a reenactment of the cosmic drama of creation. This appears to be clearly the meaning of the serpent dragon in Apc 12:3–17; 20:2. The serpent here is expressly identified with Satan and the devil, and the "ancient serpent" can scarcely be any other than the serpent of Gn 3. It is evident that this is the cosmic serpent, the symbol of the powers of evil and darkness. The flood of water which the serpent pours from its mouth (Apc 12:15) is probably borrowed remotely from Mesopotamian mythology. The cosmic serpent takes on the character of Satan in apocalyptic literature; he is cast out of heaven by Michael* (Apc

12:7 f) and bound for the period of the millennium* (Apc 20:2). The woman and the serpent appear here in the reenactment of the drama of Eden and of creation; the mythological images which were employed in early times to signify the beginnings are employed to signify the end. God restores things to their beginning by reversing the course of events by which man fell.

Servant of the Lord. The servant of Yahweh is a figure who appears in Is 40–55. The origin of the passages in which the servant appears and the identity of the servant are two of the most celebrated questions of the OT, discussed at great length through almost the entire history of exegesis and particularly in recent years. As yet no solution to these questions can be proposed which is universally accepted; in this article the views most commonly held are summarized.

The Servant poems were first isolated as a distinct literary unity by B. Duhm in 1892. He defined them as the following passages: Is 42:1–4; 49:1–6; 50:4–9; 52:13–53:12. Duhm attributed these poems to a different and later author from the author of Is 40–55, believing them to be a separate unity. Some later critics expand the poems to include 42:5–7 and 50:10–11 (cf below). The identification of the poems as a distinct literary unity is almost universally accepted; some critics, however, believe they are the work of the author of Is 40–55, and others believe they come from several authors. These critical views arise less from accepted critical grounds than from the difficulty of identifying the Servant.

The content of the poems:

42:1–4: Yahweh is the speaker; He describes the call and mission of one who is to bring forth judgment and righteousness in the whole earth.

49:1–6: the Servant is the speaker; he describes his election (cf Je 1:5), his equipment as a speaker, the difficulty of his labor, his mission to gather Israel and to be a light and a mediator of salvation to the earth.

50:4–9: the Servant is the speaker; he describes his mission as a teacher, opposition to his mission, and his assurance of success in the assistance of Yahweh.

52:13–53:12: the speakers are Yahweh (52:13–15) and unidentified persons (53:1–12). The Servant suffers and dies, possibly by execution but certainly with an evil reputation. His death is mysterious because of his innocence; the mystery is revealed as the vicarious atoning merit of his death, vindicated by his resurrection.

The critical question does not admit an obvious solution, as noted above. Recent critics have pointed out numerous affinities in language and conception between the Servant poems and the rest of Is 40–55; other critics observe that these affinities may come from a school rather than from the same author. The insertion of the poems in their present context is a puzzle viewed from any angle, whether the insertion comes from the author of Is 40–55 or from an editor. It should be noticed that the first three poems are fitted into the context by expansions or commentaries (42:7–9; 49:7–12 or 7–13; 50:10–11, a response to 50:4–9 which some critics include in the 3rd poem). These expansions take up words and ideas of the poems and treat them in the style of Second Isaiah; one could suspect that the poems were earlier, not later than Second Isaiah, and that Second Isaiah himself inserted them in his work and added the commentaries.

The title "Servant" (lit *'ebed,* "slave") has a wide background in the OT which is without doubt present in the mind of the writer, but does not determine whom he meant by the servant. The remote background lies in the title "slave of the king"; this is an honorific title of an official who ranks high in responsibility and in proximity to the monarch. When one who addresses the king uses the polite circumlocution "your slave" he expresses his humility in the royal presence. The same humility appears when the polite phrase is used by one who addresses Yahweh (e.g., Moses, Ex 4:10; Nm 11:11; Dt 3:24). As an honorific title it is applied to Moses often (Ex 14:31; Nm 12:7 f +), David (2 S 3:18; 1 K 11:34, 36; Ps 89:4, 21 +; David is called "my servant whom I have chosen," cf Is 42:1), Zerubbabel (Hg 2:23; Zc 3:8), Elijah (1 K 18:36; 2 K 9:36; 10:10), Ahijah and other prophets (1 K 14:18); "my servants the prophets" is a common phrase in the Deuteronomic history (2 K 9:7; 17:13, 23; 2:10 +). J. Jeremias has noticed that the servant designates both the king and the prophet, and that interpreters have generally elected either one line or the other in identifying the Servant. It seems possible that the poet chose the title precisely because it is neutral and does not put the Servant in one class or the other of traditional charismatic leader. The title "servant" permits him to recall all those who were instruments of Yahweh's saving deeds, whether Moses, the king, or the prophet; the title may be conceived as suggesting either a collective ideal figure who combines all these leaders or an ideal individual figure who possesses all the gifts of charismatic leadership. Cf below.

The history of Jewish interpretation shows vacillation in the understanding of the Servant. Ultimately it reached the view which has become traditional in Jewish interpretation and is accepted by many modern scholars (cf below), that the Servant is Israel personified as an individual. But this does not appear to have been the earliest Jewish interpretation, and it seems that it arose as a response to the use of Is 53 by Christian apologetes. In the apocryphal work, the Testament of Benjamin, there is an obscure reference to a Messiah of the house of Joseph who suffers. The messianic titles "the Elect One" and "the Righteous One" in the books of Enoch are thought by many to echo the Servant poems. In the scheme of Jewish eschatology the messianic time of troubles which preceded the judgment included the suffering or even the death of the Messiah. But in general Jewish interpretation rejected the idea of a suffering and dying Messiah. The Targum of Is 53 completely perverts the meaning of the text; the sufferings mentioned are transferred to the Gentile nations and the poem becomes a declaration of the establishment of the messianic reign in Israel.

Modern theories of the identity of the Servant may be classified as individual or collective, and a third group which attempts to combine the individual and the collective. The problem is extremely difficult and very few of the theories can be dismissed as fanciful; the studied obscurity of the poet (for that is what it is) leaves room for the proponents of the theories to base their opinion on the text.

A very common view, which seems to be losing ground among modern interpreters, is that the Servant is the people Israel. This view is not without justification; Israel is called the Servant of Yahweh several times in Second Isaiah (41:8 f; 44:1 f; 44:21; 42:19; 45:4; 48:20), and once in the poems themselves (49:3). Against this view is the mission of the Servant to Israel (49:5–6) and the probability that the unnamed speakers in 53:1–12 are themselves Israelites. Hence some have refined this view; the Servant is not the historic Israel, but the ideal Israel whose mission is described in the poems, or more concretely the pious nucleus of Israel, the remnant* of the prophets or the ancestors of the later Pharisees*. In the words of J. Lindblom, "the Servant embodies an idea, and that idea is the mission of Israel to the world." C. C. Torrey defined the Servant as the personified Israel or Israel's representative. It seems that the identity of the Servant with Israel must be preserved in some way unless one takes the desperate measure of assigning the passages which seem to assert this identity to other authors or to glossators, as many have suggested for Is 49:3.

The individual theories which identify the Servant with a historic figure have proposed a great number of individuals: Zerubbabel, Jehoiachin (as representatives of the Davidic dynasty); Moses; the prophet author himself; some anonymous figure known to the prophet; Jeremiah. Some have proposed Israel in some poems, the prophet or the Messiah in others. A number of recent writers of the Scandinavian school have connected the Servant with the king* as a saving cultic figure. The Mesopotamian and Canaanite liturgy of the New Year* festival included the ritual suffering of the king as the cultic representative of the dying and rising god of fertility. I. Engnell has seen in the poems a remodeling of liturgical poems which incorporate this ritual suffering. A. Bentzen identifies the Servant as the prophet himself, conceived as a second Moses whose mission is to lead Israel from exile to the messianic kingdom as Moses led Israel from Egypt to the promised land. Others see in the Servant the institution of prophecy — a refinement of the collective theory.

The question arises here of the royal and prophetic lines of interpretation mentioned above. In spite of the skillful argument of Scandinavian scholars, the Servant appears to be more of a prophet than a king. He is charismatic, endowed with the spirit* (42:1, which may be found in both prophet and king), he speaks but does not proclaim (42:2), his weapon is his speech (49:2), he is a teacher (50:4). On the other hand, he brings forth judgment* (42:3 f, parallel to *tôrāh,* instruction [cf LAW]), he is a light and a medium of salvation (49:6); these do suggest the king. The question seems best answered if we suppose, as suggested above, that the title Servant designates precisely more than a prophet or a king, more even than a second Moses. The work of the Servant has its climax in a manner which is related of no other charismatic leader, that he makes himself a sin offering, heals others through his innocent suffering, and brings judgment and righteousness (victory, vindication) through his death and not through his conquests. This is a unique conception which demands a new title.

That interpretation seems preferable which succeeds best in incorporating most of the elements found in other views. Such an interpretation, based on the "corporate personality" of Israelite thought, has been proposed by C. R. North and H. H. Rowley and others. The corporate personality, which is easily verified in the OT, is seen in those individuals who head and represent a group, and in their character and experiences exhibit the character and experiences of the group which they represent. Such were the patriarchs and such was David. Jacob-Israel was in a way Israel. The Servant also is

Israel because in his person he recapitulates the gifts and the mission of Israel. The revelation of the Servant is that salvation comes through suffering. Such a conception must have been future in the mind of the writer. It does not appear that to him the Servant was identified with the Messiah. It is another view of the salvation of Israel which he did not attempt to synthesize with the messianic king. The profundity of this insight is matched in the OT perhaps only in Jb*. It is a revelation of the mind of God which is proposed after reflection on the historic experience of Israel; more than any other prophetic passage it leads to the Gospels. But it is not a mere prediction; its obscurity, while it is studied, comes from no desire to conceal an identity which the writer knew. This, he says, must be the real destiny of Israel and her leadership.

NT. In the NT the title Servant is applied to Jesus in AA 3:13; 3:26; 4:27, 30. The Servant poems are quoted in Mt 8:17 (loose use of 53:4 with reference to healing); 12: 18–21; Lk 22:37, referring to the passion; Lk 2:32; Rm 15:21; 4:25. It is remarkable that the words of the baptism of Jesus (Mt 3:17; Mk 1:11; Lk 3:22) are an almost exact quotation of Is 42:1; and it is probable, as many interpreters suggest, that the original form of this saying was a quotation of Is 42:1 with the change of servant to son. J. Jeremias suggests that the title of Servant belonged to the early Palestinian preaching of the Church but was little used in the Gentile churches, where the title of slave seemed degrading; Gk has no phrase to correspond to the Hb "slave of the king." The same scholar thinks that "servant" has been replaced by "lamb" in Jn 1:29, 36; cf LAMB. The Servant songs are very probably implicit in a number of other passages which use their words or their conceptions: 1 Co 15: 3–5, the passion in the Scriptures; Mt 26:28; Mk 14:24; Lk 22:20; 1 Co 11:23–25 ("for you" and "for many" in the formula of the Eucharist); Rm 8:34; Phl 2:6–11 (Jesus took the form of a slave); Mt 20:28; Mk 10:45; 1 Tm 2:6; (Jesus gave Himself as a ransom); Mk 9:12 (it is written that the Son of Man must suffer); 1 Pt 2:21–25, a chain of phrases from Is 53:5–6, 9, 12; 3:18 (He died for our sins, the righteous for the unrighteous); 1 Jn 2:2; 4:10 (expiation for our sins); 3:5; Jn 10:11, 15, 17 (Jesus lays down His life). It is obvious that most of these quotations and allusions turn upon the passion. It is not too much to say that the conception of the atoning and redeeming death in the NT is a development of the idea of the Servant.

This development is not to be regarded as the work of the apostles themselves.

The witness of the Gospels is that this essential feature of the life and mission of Jesus is one which they, with the mass of Judaism, found most difficult to understand and accept. The identification of Jesus with the Servant is best attributed to Jesus Himself. The title and the conception, as observed, permitted Him to assume a role which fell into none of the existing categories of charismatic leader and savior. This brought out the novelty of His character and at the same time presented Him as the fulfillment of all the elements of Israel's gifts and missions. It furnished a biblical basis for His teaching on the atoning passion and death, and on the meaning of suffering and death in human experience.

The identity of the Servant and Israel is paralleled by the identity of Jesus and the Church. Jesus is the Servant who brings Israel to fullness; He is the true and the perfect "corporate personality," one with the Church which is His body. This great conception has many roots in the OT, and one of them is the conception of the Servant who suffers in his own person and who sanctifies the sufferings of the group which he represents.

Seth (Hb *šēt*, "he placed"?), son of Adam and Eve, with whom Yahweh "replaced" Abel, whence the fanciful explanation of his name, father of Enosh* (Gn 4:25 f, J). In the genealogy of P, which ignores Cain and Abel, Seth is the eldest son of Adam. The story of Cain and Abel probably was not a part of the original genealogical traditions, and the name of Seth presented a convenient point of conjunction. Possibly Seth is a parallel figure to Enoch*, "dedication," in the building of the first city; the name could be rendered "he founded."

Seven. The number seven is significant in almost every culture; but the reason for this significance is too obscure to be explained. Some have suggested that it comes from the 7 planets; but the number is significant among peoples who are ignorant of the 7 planets. Others suggest that it comes from the 4 phases of the moon, which come in periods of 7 days; the week therefore is the original number from which the significance is derived. Seven as a meaningful number appears in Mesopotamia, Egypt and Canaan and frequently in both OT and NT. A seven-headed dragon is slain by Baal in the mythology of Ugarit*. The significance of 7 in the Bible is fairly obvious; it means totality, fullness, completeness. At times it is multiplied by itself (7×7 or 7×70); this does not signify excess, but rather the removal of limit implied in totality. Thus

Cain* is avenged 7 times, Lamech 7×70 (Gn 4:24). There are 7 fat years and 7 lean years in Egypt (Gn 41:2 ff). Samson's hair is bound in 7 locks (Jgs 16:13). In the fall of Judah 7 women attempt to marry one man (Is 4:1). Balak erects 7 altars for 7 victims (Nm 23:1). Ruth is better than 7 sons (Rt 4:15). The boy who is raised by Elisha sneezes 7 times and revives (2 K 4:35). The Israelites march 7 days around Jericho (Jos 6:1 ff). There are 7 pre-Israelite peoples of Canaan (Dt 7:1). The 6 days of creation followed by a 7th day of rest are the complete and perfect work (Gn 2:1-3). There are 70 peoples in the world (Gn 10) and 70 in the family of Jacob (Gn 46:27; Ex 1:5). The 70 elders of Nm 11 are actually 72, 6 for each tribe, and so too the 70 disciples of Lk 10:1. The number seven is important in ritual actions; this is observed in particular in the magical rites of Mesopotamia. There are 7 days of Mazzoth* (Ex 12:15, 19). The number recurs often in the rites of ritual purification (Lv 12–15). Naaman must wash 7 times in the Jordan (2 K 5:10). The Hb word for 7, *šeba'*, is identical with the root of the word *šāba'* "to swear"; and some think that the Hb word for swear is derived from an original rite of the oath in which the number 7 was used.

The same idea of fullness and totality is seen in the NT use of the number. The Sadducees propose a case of 7 brothers who married the same woman (Mt 22:25; Mk 12:20; Lk 20:29). The 7 loaves which are multiplied leave 7 baskets of fragments (Mt 15:34, 37; Mk 8:5, 8). The evil spirit who returns after exorcism brings 7 other spirits worse than himself (Mt 12:45; Lk 11:26). Seven demons were expelled from Mary Magdalen (Lk 8:2). The symbolism of 7 is extremely prominent in Apc: there are 7 churches (1:4), lamps (1:13), stars (1:16), spirits (1:4; 4:5), seals (5:1), trumpets (8:2), serpent heads (12:3), plagues (15:1), and other examples. Seven men were appointed to assist the Twelve in Jerusalem (AA 6:2 ff).

A refinement of the symbolism of the number is seen in Mt 18:21 f as contrasted with Lk 17:4. In Lk seven times, the number of totality and perfection, is stated as the number of times when forgiveness should be granted; Mt, however, multiplies 7×70 and signifies what is not so clear in the formula of Lk, that the perfection of forgiveness signified by 7 consists in the removal of any limit to the number of times when one should forgive.

Shaalbim (Hb *ša'albîm* and *sa'ǎlabbîn*, meaning uncertain), a town in the original territory of Dan* adjacent to Judah (Jos 19:42), occupied by the Amorites* even after the settlement of Dan (Jgs 1:35), in Solomon's 2nd district (1 K 4:9). It is probably to be identified with the modern Selbit, about 2 mi NNW of Amwas.

Shaddai. Cf GOD.

Shadrach (Hb šadrak), the Babylonian name given to Daniel's* companion Hananiah (Dn 1:7). The etymology is uncertain; older scholars suggested suduraku, "command of [the god] Aku." The name is possibly a deliberate corruption of a name formed from the divine name Marduk*.

Shalim or **Shaalim** (Hb ša'ᵃlîm, meaning uncertain), a region where Saul sought his father's asses (1 S 9:4), not otherwise identified, probably to be located on the W slope of the hill country of Ephraim*.

Shalisha (Hb šālišāh, meaning uncertain), a region mentioned with Shalim* (1 S 9:4), no doubt near the town of Baal-shalisha, which is probably to be located SW of Samaria*.

Shallum (Hb šallûm, personal name; meaning uncertain, probably shortened from the root SLM [cf PEACE]). **1.** King of Israel 745 BC, who gained the throne by the assassination of Zechariah* and was himself assassinated by Menahem* after a reign of one month (2 K 15:10–15).
2. Son of Josiah* and king of Judah who was taken away to captivity. The name Shallum is given this king only in Je 22:11; 1 Ch 3:15; he is called Jehoahaz* in 2 K 23:31 ff; 2 Ch 36:1 ff. Jehoahaz was probably his throne name.
The name was very popular, especially in the later monarchy and postexilic period, and is borne by at least 12 others in the OT.

Shalman (Hb šalman). He destroyed Beth-Arbel* in battle (Ho 10:14). The episode is otherwise unknown. Some scholars see in Shalman a shortened form of Shalmaneser* V of Assyria* (727–722), who conquered the territory of Israel after it rebelled; others suggest a Moabite prince Salamanu, mentioned in the annals of Tiglath-pileser* III of Assyria (745–727).

Shalmaneser (Hb šalman'eṣer, Akkadian sulman-asaridu, "[the god] Shulman is prince"). Shalmaneser V, king of Assyria 727–722. When Hoshea* of Israel rebelled, Shalmaneser imprisoned him; the resistance of Samaria continued without the king and Shalmaneser besieged the city for three years

(2 K 17:3–5; 18:9 f). He died shortly before the capitulation (not mentioned in the OT) and was succeeded by Sargon*, who received the surrender and ended the kingdom of Israel. Almost the entire reign of Shalmaneser was consumed with the suppression of the rebellion in Syria and Phoenicia and Palestine, of which the Israelite rebellion was only a part. Historians suspect that he may have been assassinated; his successor Sargon was not his son, but the Assyrian records on this point are obscure.

Shamgar (Hb šamgar, etymology uncertain; it cannot be a Hb name, and it has been suggested that it is Hurrian*). Shamgar son of Anath slew 600 Philistines with an ox goad (Jgs 3:31), an exploit which recalls the feat of Samson with the jawbone of an ass (Jgs 15:15), and thus "he also" delivered Israel. The song of Deborah refers to "the days of Shamgar ben Anath," and there seems to be no good reason to distinguish the two. Shamgar is not called a judge; he appears to be a Canaanite prince who helped to save Israel by fighting against the common enemy, the Philistines. Jgs 5:6 hints that he may have been otherwise an enemy of Israel.

Shamir (Hb šāmîr, "place of thistles"?). **1.** A town in the hill country of Judah (Jos 15:48). The ancient name survives in Khirbet Sumara, about 12 mi SW of Hebron; Khirbet el Bireh nearby is also suggested.
2. A town in the hill country of Ephraim, the home of the judge Tola (Jgs 10:1 f). This is perhaps the site of the later Samaria*.

Shaphan (Hb šāpān, "rock badger"), a personal name which appears frequently in the period of Jeremiah. Shaphan was the scribe of Josiah* who received the book of the law* from Hilkiah* the priest and brought it to Josiah (2 K 22; 2 Ch 34). A son of Shaphan, Ahikam*, appears as an officer of the king at the same time (2 K 22:12 +); some scholars question the identity of this Shaphan with the scribe. Elasah son of Shaphan is one of the men sent in a diplomatic mission to Nebuchadnezzar by Zedekiah* who took with them the letter of Jeremiah to the exiles (Je 29:3). Gemariah son of Shaphan was the scribe of Jehoiakim* (Je 36:10 ff). Jaazaniah son of Shaphan sits with the 70 elders adoring foreign gods (Ezk 8:11). The relative dates of these men are all near enough to permit the hypothesis that they are sons of one and the same Shaphan, a scribe whose large family entered the royal service. It is to be noted that the members of this family appear as well disposed toward Jeremiah; their assistance to him in his troubles with the kings and other officers is mentioned several times (cf AHIKAM; GEDALIAH). The family appear to have been loyal worshipers of Yahweh.

Shaphat (Hb *šapaṭ*, "he judges"), possibly shortened from Jehoshaphat*, a personal name borne by several men in the OT, including the father of Elisha* (1 K 19:16 +).

Sharezer (Hb *sar'eṣer*, "may he protect the king"), personal name; one of the murderers of Sennacherib* (2 K 19:37); the murderers are called his sons but not named in 2 Ch 21:31. That Sennacherib was murdered by his sons is attested in the Assyrian records. Sharezer is very probably to be identified with the eponymous *limmu* officer listed for the year of the murder, Nabu-sar-usur.

Sharon (Hb *šārôn*, always with the article, "the Sharon"; possibly derived from the root *YSR*, "to be level," hence "the plain"). The plain of Sharon is the central section of the coastal plain of Palestine extending roughly from Mt Carmel* in the N to Joppa* in the S, a distance of about 45 mi. Its maximum width is about 12 mi. It is rarely mentioned in the Bible; Is 33:9; 35:2 suggest luxuriant vegetation. 1 Ch 27:29 mentions pastures of David in Sharon, and Is 65:10 also speaks of pasture there. Aphek* is the only OT town which can be located in Sharon (Jos 12:18). The "rose of Sharon" (SS 2:1) is a crocus. In the NT Sharon is mentioned only AA 9:35 with Lydda*.

It is evident that the plain of Sharon was nearly totally uninhabited in OT times, despite the fact that its soil is fertile and it is well watered by several perennial streams which rise in the mountains. The reason for its emptiness lies probably in the fact that it is extremely marshy. Near the coast it is spotted with shifting sand dunes. In ancient times it was probably thickly forested. These factors taken together discouraged agriculture. The main road between Egypt and Syria passed through the plain of Sharon, but it hugged the foothills to avoid the marshes. The plain was never a part of Israel and of Israelite life.

Sharuhen (Hb *šārûhen*, meaning uncertain), a town in Simeon* (Jos 19:6). A parallel list in 1 Ch 4, which contains several variations in the names of towns, reads Shaaraim in 4:31 where Sharuhen appears in Jos 19:6. Shilhim is probably another variant of Sharuhen in a list of the towns of Judah (Jos 15:32) which is substantially identical with the Simeon list of Jos 19. The site is identified with the modern Tell el Farah about 15 mi SSE of Gaza*. The name Sharuhen is con-

firmed by the Egyptian records of Ahmose I (1570–1545), founder of the 18th dynasty, who expelled the Hyksos* from Egypt (ANET 233, 235). These records relate that Sharuhen was a Hyksos fortress which was taken by the Egyptians after a siege of three years. Sharuhen appears again later in the 18th and 19th dynasties as an important Egyptian base in Palestine. A brief excavation of Tell el Farah was conducted by the British School of Archaeology directed by Sir Flinders Petrie. The excavation showed that the city was destroyed in the 9th century BC and was left unoccupied for four centuries; this indicates that the list of Simeon must be earlier than 900 BC. A large brick wall 23 ft thick was dated in the 10th century; it is suggested that this was a construction of the Pharaoh Shishak* during his campaign in Palestine.

Shaveh (Hb *šāweh*, "plain"?), a valley where Abraham* met Melchizedek* after his victory over the kings of the E (Gn 14:17). A gloss in this verse identifies the valley of Shaveh with the valley of the king, where Absalom* erected his memorial (2 S 18:18). Josephus locates it near Jerusalem, and no more precise location can be given.

Shaving. Cf BEARD; RAZOR.

Shavsha. Cf SHIVA.

Shealtiel (Hb *šᵉ'altî'ēl*, "I have asked El"), father of Zerubbabel* (Hg 1:1, 12, 14; 2:2, 23; Ezr 3:2, 8; 5:2; Ne 12:1), but uncle of Zerubbabel in 1 Ch 3:17; son of Jechoniah* in 1 Ch 3:17; Mt 1:12, but son of Neri in Lk 3:27. These variations must be reduced to variations in the genealogical records from which these passages were taken.

Shear-jashub (Hb *šᵉ'ar-yāšûb*, "a remnant will return"), son of Isaiah* (Is 7:3). On the prophetic significance of the name cf REMNANT.

Sheba (Hb *šᵉbā'*, meaning uncertain), a geographic and gentilic name. Sheba is frequently mentioned with Arabian tribes and there is no doubt that it is Arabian and is definitely to be located in the SW corner of the Arabian peninsula, the modern Yemen. In the Table* of Nations Sheba appears both as a descendant of Ham* (Gn 10:7; 1 Ch 1:9, with Dedan, a son of Raamah) and as a descendant of Shem* (Gn 10:28; 1 Ch 1:22, a son of Joktan* with several Arabian tribes). In Gn 25:3 and 1 Ch 1:32 it is reckoned with Dedan as a descendant of Abraham and Keturah* through Jokshan. It is mentioned with Dedan in Ezk 38:13, with Seba in Ps 72:10. Sheba appears also in Assyrian records. There are several allusions to Sheba as a trading center. It traded gold, spices, and precious stones with Solomon* (1 K 10:1 ff; 2 Ch 9:1 ff) and with Tyre* (Ezk 27:22). Is 60:6 mentions its gold and incense*, and Je 6:20 its incense. The travelers of Sheba (Jb 6:19) are traders.

The exploration of S Arabia, in particular the American expedition to Yemen of 1950 which was rudely interrupted by the incredible barbarism of the Yemenites, have cast much light on the trading position of Sheba in the ancient world and on the mission of the queen of Sheba to the court of Solomon (1 K 10; 2 Ch 9). Assyrian records of the 8th-7th centuries mention five Arabian queens by name, which furnishes a curious and revealing parallel to this feminine domination. The Sabaeans, originally nomadic, had by the 10th century BC established a kingdom which controlled the trade routes connecting Arabia and regions farther E with Palestine and Syria. The description of the Sabaeans as nomad raiders in Jb 1:15 is an archaism. The expansion of Sabaean trade was made possible by the collapse of Egyptian trade relations with Arabia after the New Kingdom. The mission of the queen of Sheba, described in the romantic language of popular tradition, can scarcely have been anything else but a trade mission. The expansion of Sabaean trade was simultaneous with the expansion of Israelite trade through Solomon's port of Ezion-geber* and his Red Sea fleet.

Shebat (Hb *šᵉbaṭ*, derived from Akkadian *sabaṭu* [cf CALENDAR]), the 11th month of the year (February-March).

Shebna (Hb *šebnā'*, shortened from Shebaniah?), a personal name. Shebna, majordomo ("over the house") of Hezekiah*, is the object of an invective in Is 22:15-19. For building himself a magnificent tomb the prophet threatens him with exile and with deposition from his office, to be replaced by Eliakim*. In 2 K 18:18, 26, 37; 19:2; Is 36:3, 11, 22; 37:2 Eliakim appears as majordomo and Shebna as scribe among the officers of Hezekiah who negotiated with the Assyrian commander representing Sennacherib*. This is less than a complete fulfillment of the prophet's threat; the office of scribe* was scarcely less important than the office of majordomo.

Shechem (Hb *šᵉkem*, "shoulder? [of mountain]"), a town of central Palestine. Since the beginning of the 20th century there is no doubt that the site is located at Tell Balatah. It lies about 40 mi N of Jerusalem and about 1 mi E of Nablus. The

mound sits at the entrance of the pass which is traversed by the road from Jerusalem to N Palestine. To N, E, and S it looks out upon a broad fertile plain. The site has been excavated by a German expedition led by E. Sellin and R. Welter 1925-1934 and by an American expedition led by G. E. Wright since 1956. The results of the early expedition were poorly observed and recorded, but the later expedition has learned much about the history of the site.

A city existed on the site at the beginning of the 3rd millennium BC and perhaps earlier. Shechem is mentioned in the Egyptian execration texts of the 19th-18th centuries BC (ANET 329) and it was taken by the Pharaoh Sesostris III (1878-1841 BC; ANET 230). An Egyptian geographical text of the 13th century BC mentions the mountain of Shechem (ANET 477). During the period of the Amarna* Letters Shechem was evidently an important political center (ANET 485-487, 489). It was a focus of rebellion against Egyptian rule under its king Labayu and his sons, who are accused of "giving Shechem to the Apiru" (cf HEBREW). This cannot be related to the settlement of the Israelites in Canaan according to the evidence as it is known at present.

The Israelite traditions concerning Shechem are complex. Abraham stopped there, experienced a theophany at the oak of Moreh, and built an altar. This story connects Abraham with the sanctuary and the sacred oak of Shechem; but the city is more closely connected with Jacob. Jacob settled at Shechem on his return from Mesopotamia, and to him also is attributed the construction of an altar (Gn 33:18 f). Jacob became a landholder in Shechem by purchase. Gn 34 relates the rape of Dinah*, the establishment of a *connubium* between the sons of Israel and the Bene Hamor*, "sons of the ass," who held Shechem, and the sack of Shechem by Simeon* and Levi*. With this episode is possibly connected Gn 48:22, which attributed to Jacob the claim that he took Shechem from the Amorite with his sword and his bow. Even on the hypothesis that these are variant traditions of an Israelite attack on Shechem, it is difficult to relate this to the history of the city. There is no conquest of Shechem in Jos and Jgs, and the city appears as Canaanite but friendly to Israel. Furthermore, it was the center of Israelite cult in the early period of the settlement, the city of the covenant (cf below). Unless this tradition is to be regarded as entirely unhistorical, it is tempting to relate it to the troubled period of the Amarna Letters and the passage of Shechem from Egyptian control to the Apiru (cf above); the people who lived in Shechem when the

Israelites entered the country and who joined the covenant of Israel could have incorporated their own traditions of the acquisition of Shechem into the traditions of Jacob and Israel; cf ISRAEL.

Shechem appears as an Israelite center in the time of Joshua; it was the scene of the assembly when Joshua imposed the covenant* upon Israel (Jos 24), which here probably includes those elements of Israel which were residing in the country at the time when the "Israelite" group entered from Egypt. An echo of this tradition in another form (P) is possibly preserved in the story of the burial of foreign gods by Jacob at Shechem (Gn 35:4). Shechem is also the scene of the festival of the renewal of the covenant described in Dt 27; Jos 8:30–35. The question then arises whether the Baal-berith, "lord of the covenant," worshiped in the temple of Shechem (Jgs 8:33; 9:4, 46) and treated by the Deuteronomic redactor of Jgs 8:33 as a Canaanite god, was not Yahweh Himself.

The story of Abimelech* adds to the complexity of the traditions. Shechem was ruled by an aristocracy, the 70 sons of Jerubbaal, identified in the traditions with Gideon* of Manasseh. This identification is not altogether certain; but the ruling clan seems to have been Israelite. Abimelech incited the Shechemites to rebellion and had himself proclaimed king; but strangely he did not establish his royal residence at Shechem. The Shechemites rebelled against Abimelech who destroyed the city and its citadel, the tower (migdal) of Shechem. The story does not make this quarrel more than a dispute between the Shechemites and an Israelite freebooter and his followers; and the attack on Shechem, which can scarcely have been a total destruction, did not seriously interrupt the life and the importance of Shechem.

Shechem is associated with Manasseh in the Gideon-Abimelech stories and is included in Manasseh in the boundary list (Jos 17:7); but it is identified with Mt Ephraim in Jos 20:7; 21:21, with Ephraim in 1 Ch 7:28. These divergences probably come from an administrative division of the monarchy which altered old tribal lines. Shechem was the scene of the assembly of all Israel where Rehoboam went to be acclaimed as king; it is to be noted that Shechem and not Jerusalem was the center where this assembly met (1 K 12). After the schism Jeroboam "built" (i.e., fortified) Shechem and made it the royal city (1 K 12:25). For reasons which are unknown he moved the royal residence to Tirzah*, and with this move the importance of Shechem comes to an end. The change was possibly motivated by the search for a more defensible site; Shechem lies in a plain and could be fortified well enough to resist the siege warfare of the Bronze Age; but it was more vulnerable to the improved techniques of warfare of the Iron Age.

Other scattered allusions contribute little to the history of the site. It was a city of refuge* and a levitical city (cf LEVI; Jos 20:7; 21:21; 1 Ch 6:52). Pss 60:8; 108:8, a Judahite war song, alludes to "the division of Shechem." Ho 6:9 alludes to murder committed by priests on the way to Shechem. Je 41:5 mentions 80 pilgrims from Samaria* and Shechem who came to mourn the destruction of the temple of Jerusalem. The site was occupied during the Gk period. The city was captured by John Hyrcanus (cf HASMONEAN) in 107 BC. It was destroyed in AD 67, probably by Vespasian, and abandoned.

The excavations have identified a large E gate with double entry (outer and inner) of a type as yet not paralleled in Palestinian sites. The gate was evidently the most strongly fortified point of the defenses, as the point most open to attack; but the ruins showed that it had been forced several times. The gate was flanked by basalt orthostats. It was built in the 17th century BC and its final destruction is with probability attributed to John Hyrcanus. A cyclopean wall and the remains of a citadel on the NW corners and heavy earthwork plastered walls are attributed to the Hyksos* of the 17th century BC. A large temple, 65 ft by 80 ft, with walls 16 ft thick, is with probability identified with the temple of Baalberith. A granary was built over this temple in the Israelite period. The temple was a migdal or a fortress temple of a type paralleled elsewhere in Palestinian sites and mentioned in Jgs 9:46. Standing stones were found before the temple; these are the cult symbol (maṣṣēbāh) mentioned so frequently in the OT. The date of the destruction of the temple cannot be established precisely; it could fall within the period of Abimelech. The temple was built in the 17th century and remodeled later. No evidence of occupation between the 8th and 4th centuries BC has been found; but this could be accidental. The evidence for a thriving city of the Gk period, about 300–100 BC, is abundant. BS 50:26 refers to "the foolish people who dwell in Shechem," the Samaritans*. The Hellenistic city was surrounded by a casemate wall. There is evidence of the violent destruction of the Hyksos city, probably by the Egyptians, and of the Israelite city; this destruction is with probability attributed to the Aramaeans about 800 BC, a period of Israelite weakness.

Sheep. Sheep and goats are the chief support of pastoral peoples. The sheep furnishes clothing (cf WOOL), milk, butter, cheese, and meat. The flocks of the pasture lands of Palestine were and are large, but the tribute of Mesha* of Moab to the king of Israel of 100,000 lambs and the wool of 100,000 rams (2 K 3:4) is possibly exaggerated by popular tradition, and the number of victims sacrificed at the dedication of the temple of Solomon, 120,000 (1 K 8:63) is certainly exaggerated. But the number of 100 sheep for the daily provision of the household of Solomon (1 K 4:23) does not appear to be so notably exaggerated; this, however, is the height of luxurious living, since the ordinary Israelite ate mutton only at a festival. The plateaus of E Palestine and the mountains of Palestine and Syria offer abundant good pasture country for sheep. The animal can live off a light grass cover and therefore can be pastured in the desert itself when the winter rains bring growth and all year in semiarid reaches. The sheep need be watered only once a day. Sheep yean in the spring, and the season is one of activity and festive celebrations. The male is normally the sacrificial animal. The ram's horn* was a musical instrument. The fat-tailed sheep now bred in Palestine were probably found there in ancient times also. The remarkably large and heavy tail of this breed sometimes yields 10 lbs of pure fat, which is esteemed as a delicacy. Both white (Ps 147:16; Is 1:18; Dn 7:9) and brown sheep (Gn 30:32–42) were bred.

Allusions to sheep and to sheep raising are very numerous in the Bible. The annual shearing of sheep is mentioned in Gn 31:19; 38:12; 1 S 25:4 ff, and the festivities which accompanied this activity are mentioned in 2 S 13:25–27. The care of sheep is also mentioned and is a rich source of theological imagery (cf SHEPHERD). The sheep must be protected from wild beasts, theft, and inclement weather (Gn 31:39–40). The shepherd defended the sheep against lions and bears with his naked hands (1 S 17:34), and sometimes died in the defense of the flock (Jn 10:15). The shepherd leads the sheep to water and protects them (Ps 23:1–4). Vivid pictures of the daily watering of the sheep at a well and of the meetings and quarrels which occurred there are seen in Gn 29:2–11; Ex 2:16–21. In inclement weather sheep were sheltered in folds in caves (1 S 24:3). Lambs and sheep which were ill or injured were carried by the shepherd (Is 40:11). The shepherd used dogs to help him (Jb 30:1). Sheep need to be led, and the shepherd goes to great trouble to find the sheep which has strayed; this becomes a figure of the care of God for the sinner (Mt 18:12–14; Lk 15:3–7). Even

on the Sabbath a man would rescue a sheep which had fallen into a pit (Mt 12:11). A people is often called a flock whose shepherd is God or the king (2 S 24:17; Pss 77:21; 78:52; 80:1; Is 63:11; Je 13:20; 27:6; Ezk 34:2 ff), and a people without leadership is sheep without a shepherd (Nm 27:17; 1 K 22:17; Mt 9:36; Mk 6:34). The sinner is a sheep which has strayed (Ps 119:176; Is 53:6; 1 Pt 2:25). Jesus applies to His passion the words of Zc 13:7: when the shepherd is struck the sheep are scattered (Mt 26:31; Mk 14:27). For the world judgment Mt 25:32 ff uses a figure drawn from daily life; the sheep and the goats, which pasture together, are separated from each other for shearing and marketing. Sheep recognize the voice of their own shepherd and learn to obey voice commands (Jn 10:3–4); they fear strangers and will not be led by them.

Sheep gate. This gate of Jerusalem is mentioned in Ne 3:1, 32 (rebuilding of the gate); 12:39, and the pool of Bethzatha is located near the sheep gate (Jn 5:2). The allusions in Ne suit a point in the N wall of the city near the NE corner, therefore near the temple area. The identification of the pool with the pool beneath a Byzantine church in the property of the Church of St Anne, in charge of the White Fathers, has long been accepted and suits the spot; cf BETHESDA.

Shekel. Cf MONEY; WEIGHTS AND MEASURES.

Shelah (Hb šēlāh, etymology uncertain), personal and clan name. The third son of Judah* and the only surviving son in Gn 38 after the deaths of Er* and Onan*; he was refused in marriage to Tamar*. The clan of Shelah is enumerated among the clans of Judah in Gn 46:12; Nm 26:20; 1 Ch 2:3. The families of the clan are enumerated in 1 Ch 4:21–23; they included linen workers and potters, and one family which "ruled in Moab."

Shem (Hb šēm, etymology uncertain), eldest son of Noah* (Gn 5:32; 6:10; 7:13; 10:1; 11:10–11; 1 Ch 1:4, 17, 24). With Japheth* he showed respect for his father when Noah became intoxicated and so received a blessing (Gn 9:18–27). The blessing is attributed in Israelite folklore to the figure whom they represented as their own ancestor (Gn 10:21–31; 11:10–26). On the grouping of peoples in Gn 10:21 ff cf TABLE OF NATIONS.

Shemaiah (Hb šᵉmaʻyāh, šᵉmaʻyāhû, "Yahweh has heard"), personal name.

1. A prophet who warned Rehoboam*

against war with the seceding kingdom of Israel (1 K 12:22–24). Since prophets appear as encouraging and approving the establishment of the kingdom of Israel, it is natural that Shemaiah should disapprove any measures which might be calculated to restore the union. The Chronicler attributes to Shemaiah a theological explanation of the raid of the Pharaoh Shishak* on Judah (2 Ch 12:5–8) and quotes him as a chronicler of the reign of Rehoboam (2 Ch 12:15; cf CHRONICLES).

2. A prophet of the time of Jeremiah, one of the prophets who predicted that Judah would survive the power of Babylon and wrote from Babylon to have Jeremiah silenced. Jeremiah threatened that he would have no children (Je 29:24–32). The name is common in the postexilic period, especially as a Levitical name.

Shemeber (Hb *šem'ēber*, etymology uncertain), king of Zeboim*, one of the five Canaanite kings attacked and defeated by the raiding Mesopotamian kings and rescued by Abraham (Gn 14:2).

Shemer (Hb *šemer*, etymology uncertain), the person or possibly clan from which Omri* purchased the hill on which Samaria* was built (1 K 16:24). The name of the city is derived from the name of the owner. The name also appears as an Israelite name and as a place name of unknown location.

Sheol (Hb *šᵉ'ôl*, etymology uncertain; represented in Gk by *hadēs*, the name of the underworld in Gk mythology). Sheol is the underworld as the abode of the dead. Ancient Near Eastern thought conceived the world as structured in three levels: the heavens, the earth, and the underworld. The underworld consists of the subterranean ocean (CREATION; SEA), beneath which is Sheol, the abode of the dead. The picture is not entirely consistent, for Sheol is often mentioned parallel with the "pit," the grave; when the earth is opened for burial of the dead, the grave is an entrance to Sheol. Here we deal only with the conception of Sheol as a place; the OT conception of death is treated under DEATH; LIFE; MAN; SOUL.

In a number of passages Sheol means no more than death or the grave, and to go to Sheol = to die. One who dies a tranquil natural death is said to go down to Sheol in peace* (1 K 2:6, 9; Jb 21:13) and one whose last years are embittered by grief goes down to Sheol in sorrow (Gn 37:35; 42:38; 44:29, 31). Sheol is mentioned with death and the grave as the last end of man (Ps 55:16). No one can deliver himself from

the power of Sheol (Ps 89:49); one who descends to Sheol does not come up (Jb 7:9). Sheol is a pit, a place of darkness, worms, and dust; these seem to represent the tomb (Jb 17:13–16). When Dathan and the rebels against Moses were swallowed up in an earthquake, they are said to go down to Sheol alive, a peculiarly horrible death (Nm 16:30, 33), for it comes suddenly without any preliminary weakening, which is itself an approach of death and Sheol (cf below). So the wicked lie in wait for their victim; like Sheol, they swallow him alive (Pr 1:12).

The conception of Sheol as a place of darkness and dust is a commonplace in the ancient Near East and is paralleled in the Akkadian version of the myth of the descent of Ishtar into the underworld (ANET 107–109). The underworld is described as "the dark house, the abode of Irkalla, the land of no return, from which there is no way back, where the entrants are bereft of light, where dust is their fare and clay their food, where they see no light, where over bolt and door is spread dust." This, like the biblical passages, expresses the fear and horror of death as the inevitable and final term of life, where man is left in the dust and darkness of the tomb. J. Pedersen has called Sheol "the non-world."

The state of the deceased in Sheol is one of utter inactivity; it is less a positive conception of survival than a picturesque denial of all that is meant by life and activity. Sheol does not thank Yahweh, nor death praise Him (Is 38:18). There is no remembrance or praise of Yahweh in Sheol (Ps 6:6). There is no work, no thought, no knowledge, no wisdom in Sheol (Ez 9:10). Yahweh does not remember the dead; they lie in regions dark and deep; He works no wonders for the dead; the Rephaim* do not praise Him; His love and His faithfulness are not declared in Sheol and Abaddon*; His wonders are not known in the darkness, nor His saving deeds in the land of forgetfulness (Ps 88:5–13). The most picturesque description of the inactivity of the dead appears in Is 14:9–11; Sheol is aroused to greet the great king; and the shades of earlier kings, who sit motionless on their thrones in Sheol, acclaim his coming because he is now as powerless as they; maggots are his bed, and worms his covering. Ezk 32:17–32 enumerates the kings and warriors who have fallen by the sword; all of them lie helpless in the pit, in Sheol. The emptiness of Sheol is the final negation of the pomp and power of the conqueror. Jb 14:13, however, exhibits a conception of Sheol which approaches the conception of later Judaism (cf below); he expresses the impossible desire that God would hide him or preserve him in Sheol until the time of his vindication.

Sheol is conceived as a power which one may by occult means convert to one's end. The men of Judah make a covenant with death and a pact with Sheol (Is 28:15, 18). The passage is obscure and may mean either that death and Sheol are occult powers or that the political alliances of Judah are a covenant by which the destroying powers of death and Sheol agree to spare Judah. Sheol is a power from which Yahweh can ransom; but He does not choose to do so, and invokes the plagues and destruction of death and Sheol against His people Israel (Ho 13:14). Sheol is personified as a monster which opens its mouth to devour (Is 5:14; Ps 141:7). Sheol and Abaddon are never sated (Pr 27:20; 30:16). Its greed is great (Hab 2:5). Love is as strong as death, and jealousy is as cruel as Sheol (SS 8:6). Sheol is sometimes conceived in the Mesopotamian manner as a palace fortress with gates and bars (Is 38:10), the chambers of death (Pr 7:27).

Sheol is death, and one whose life is in danger thinks himself on the road to Sheol or already there. Yahweh brings men down to Sheol and raises them up (1 S 2:6) One in danger is entangled in the cords of Sheol (2 S 22:6; Ps 18:6), or is even in the belly of Sheol, submerged in the abyss, at the roots of the mountains, forever enclosed behind bars (Jon 2:3–6). He is threatened by the snares of death and the pangs of Sheol (Ps 116:3). He is reckoned among those who go down to the pit (Ps 88:5–13), consigned to the gates of Sheol (Is 38:10). Sheol is particularly a danger for sinners: death is their shepherd and Sheol their home (Ps 49:15). Sheol snatches them (Jb 24:19); they go dumbfounded to Sheol (Ps 31:18), they depart to Sheol (Ps 9:18). The adulterous woman travels to death and Sheol (Pr 5:5), and her house is the way to Sheol (Pr 7:27); her guests are already in the depths of Sheol (Pr 9:18). There is not yet in such passages a conception of a punishment of the wicked after death; the threat is the threat of a sudden and untimely death, which in wisdom literature is regarded as the sure portion of the wicked. Illness and danger are encroachments upon life; they diminish it and hence are a form of death and Sheol, which are present and active when illness and danger come. From Sheol Yahweh and Yahweh alone can deliver (1 S 2:6; Pss 16:10; 30:4; 49:16; 86:13; 116:3 ff; Jon 2:3 ff). Wisdom also leads to life and avoids Sheol (Pr 15:24); and the wise man saves the life of his son from Sheol by chastising him (Pr 23:14).

Sheol is one of the limits of the universe, and it is a mark of Yahweh's power and knowledge that they reach even to Sheol. His anger burns to Sheol (Dt 32:22), and one who flees to Sheol cannot escape His presence (Ps 139:8) or His vengeance (Am 9:2). Sheol and Abaddon are open and naked to Yahweh (Pr 15:11; Jb 26:6). Isaiah asks Ahaz to request a sign either in heaven above or in Sheol beneath i.e., within the limits of the entire universe (Is 7:11); for Yahweh's power reaches everywhere.

In the thought of intertestamental Judaism Sheol becomes a place for the wicked only, but the conception is not consistent in the literature; where Sheol is the place of the wicked after death, the righteous are taken to Paradise*. The place of the punishment of the wicked is Gehenna*, a development of Sheol which is distinguished from it.

In the NT Sheol (Gk *hadēs*) appears in several forms, although the word is not common. Ps 16:10 is quoted and applied to Jesus in AA 2:27 in connection with the resurrection, deliverance from death. 1 Co 15:55 quotes Ho 13:14, but it is to be noted that Sheol/Hades is replaced by death. Capernaum will be brought down to Hades (Mt 11:23; Lk 10:15), which here means destruction. The power of the risen Christ is shown by His possession of the keys of death and Hades (Apc 1:18). Hades as a destructive power follows death, the fourth horseman of the Apc (6:8). Apc 20:13 f exhibits a conception of Sheol which is found in Judaism also: in the final catastrophe death and Sheol, which are temporary places of storage for the deceased, give up the dead for final judgment, and then are themselves destroyed. Hades becomes a place of torment, scarcely to be distinguished from Gehenna, in Lk 16:23. Hades is also a destructive power in Mt 16:18, where Jesus promises that the gates of Hades shall not overcome His Church. The gates are here the power of the palace fortress; Hades is the agent of destruction, not expressly identified with cosmic or human agents, and the passage means that the Church is indestructible.

Shephatiah (Hb *šᵉpaṭyāh, šᵉpaṭyāhu,* "Yahweh has judged"), a personal name; son of Mattan, one of the officers of Zedekiah* who heard Jeremiah's counsel to the people of Jerusalem to surrender to the Babylonians, reported to the king that the prophet was seditious, and demanded that he be executed; they cast Jeremiah into a cistern (Je 38:1 ff). The name was also borne by a son of David (2 S 3:4; 1 Ch 3:3) and by several others, especially in the postexilic period.

Shephelah (Hb *šᵉpēlāh,* "the low," and hence in many Eng Bibles "the lowland"; more recent translations prefer to transliterate the Hb word, since "lowland" is misleading here). The name designates a range of limestone foothills of the central mountain range of Judah, which begins N of a line drawn W from Jerusalem and continues S of the ancient Debir* (Tell Beit Mirsim), where it merges into the plateau of the Negeb*. These foothills are a unique feature of Palestinian geography; nothing like them appears between the central range of Samaria* and Galilee* and the sea. They are gently sloping, rounded or conical, rising to an altitude of 330–1500 ft, cut by a number of wadis E and W; but the distinctive feature of the Shephelah is the series of longitudinal N–S valleys which divide the foothills sharply from the central range. In ancient times this valley was lined with fortified towns. This valley and the Shephelah are compared by geographers to an outer bulwark and a moat of the fortress of the uplands of Judah. Historically the Shephelah has been the battleground of Judah on the W, and indeed still is; for Israel holds the Shephelah, while Jordan retains possession of the central mountain range. The proximity of the Shephelah to the mountains and its defensive importance can be easily appreciated from the summits of the central range near Hebron, where one can see the foothills, the coastal plain, and the Mediterranean.

The wadis which cut the Shephelah E and W are the lines of communication between the mountains of Judah and the coastal plain, and the names of the towns located in them show their historic importance. They are, N to S: (1) the valley of Aijalon, where the two Beth-horons are located, leading to Jerusalem and Bethel via Gibeon, the scene of Joshua's defeat of the Canaanite league (Jos 10). (2) the valley of Sorek, followed by the modern railway from Jaffa to Jerusalem; here are located Beth-shemesh, Zorah, and Timnah, where the exploits of Samson occurred, and Gezer and Ekron lie in the plain on this route. (3) the valley of Elah, where Libnah and Azekah are located, the scene of the duel of David and Goliath. (4) the valley of Zephathah, the site of Mareshah and Eleutheropolis. There follow to the S the valleys of Gath, of Lachish, of Eglon, and of Debir, which are not named in the Bible.

The region is fertile; it produces grain, vineyards, and olive groves, and was well wooded in ancient times. It was perhaps the most thickly settled part of Israel; the town names and the remains of ancient towns are more numerous in the Shephelah than in any other part of the country. It was the scene of most of the battles between Philistines and Israelites until it was finally secured by David, who subdued the Philistines.

The name occurs 20 times in the Bible, usually distinguished from other geographical areas: the Negeb, the Arabah*, the mountains, the desert, the coastal plain (Dt 1:7; Jos 9:1; 10:40; 12:8; Jgs 1:9; Je 17:26; 32:44; 33:13; Ob 19; Zc 7:7; 2 Ch 26:10). Allusions are made to the large number of sycamore and olive trees in the Shephelah (1 K 10:27; 1 Ch 27:28; 2 Ch 1:15; 9:27). The towns of the Shephelah are listed in Jos 15:33–36; most of these are towns of Dan*, whose original territory lay in the Shephelah before its migration to Dan in the N. 2 Ch 28:18 alludes to raids on the Shephelah made in the reign of Ahaz by the Philistines.

Shepherd. 1. *OT.* The nomadic herdsman is one of the earliest figures of the Near East; Hb tradition recognizes this and places Abel* the herdsman at the beginning of its story of primitive man, although culturally the herdsman is now known to be a much more recent figure. The story of Cain* and Abel (Gn 4:2 ff) reflects the perpetual feud between the peasant and the herdsman; each of these classes regards the other as hostile to his interests. Cultivation of the land restricts the right of free pasture, and the pasture of flocks damages the lands and crops of the peasant. The peasant thinks that the shepherd is a starveling bandit; the shepherd thinks that the peasant is a mean-spirited digger.

The type of pasture available in biblical regions (cf SHEEP) imposes upon the shepherd the necessity of the nomadic life; he must travel with his flock from one pasture to another as the seasons change (cf NOMAD). Sheep find grass even where there appears to be little and need to be watered only once daily; but they must be led to both pasture and water. The shepherd also leads them to shelter in inclement weather and defends them against beasts of prey and bandits. The life of the shepherd is described by Jacob in his plea to Laban (Gn 31:38–41). David boasted that he killed lions and bears with his naked hands when they attacked his father's flocks (1 S 17:34–37). The shepherd establishes a remarkable rapport with his flock; they recognize his voice and distinguish it from others and learn to obey commands given by voice. They seem to have perfect confidence in their shepherd and follow him wherever he leads. The shepherd keeps the flock together, going to great trouble to search out strayed sheep, knowing

a) Hermes as the good shepherd. b) An early Christian statue of Christ as the good shepherd.

that the flock will docilely remain together until he returns. The care of the flocks under the supervision of the men of the tribe or clan is often entrusted to girls (Gn 29:6–10; Ex 2:16–19). The Israelites identified themselves in Egypt as shepherds; the nomadic shepherd was well known on the frontiers of Egypt (Gn 46:32, 34; 47:3). That the shepherd was an abomination to the Egyptians is not otherwise attested (Gn 43:32); this verse probably alludes to the Egyptians' detestation for the Hyksos* overlords who invaded Egypt from Canaan, the country of the nomadic shepherds.

In the ancient Near East the title of shepherd was applied both to kings and to gods. Lipit-Ishtar of Isin is the wise shepherd, the humble shepherd (ANET 159), and Hammurabi is the shepherd of the people (ANET 164, 165). The god Shamash is addressed as shepherd (ANET 387). The OT theological use of the title, however, shows some variation from the Mesopotamian use. The king of Israel is never called the shepherd directly; and the title as applied to Yahweh is not conventional, but is elaborated with a wealth of imagery drawn from the life of the shepherd. The title of shepherd is given to the rulers of the people, who include the king, the royal officers, the elders, all who have authority. It includes also the judges*, the heroes of Jgs (2 S 7:7). Almost all of the uses of the title find fault with the shepherds for failure to meet their responsibilities (Je 2:8); they are stupid

(Je 10:21), they scatter the flock (Je 23:1–2), they lead the people astray (Je 50:6), they are unfaithful (Ezk 34:2–10), they have no understanding (Is 56:11 f). Therefore the prophetic threats of disaster fall with special force upon the shepherds of Israel (Je 22:22; 25:34–36). In the messianic restoration Yahweh will give His people shepherds after His own heart (Je 3:15; 23:4); the prince from Bethlehem will feed his flock in the strength of Yahweh (Mi 5:3). Cyrus* is the shepherd of Yahweh who leads the people of Yahweh back to their own land (Is 44:28). The schism of Israel will be healed in the messianic future, and Israel will be one nation under one shepherd (Ezk 34:23; 37:22, 24; this passage is echoed in Jn 10:16).

Yahweh is the true shepherd of Israel (Gn 49:24), who leads Joseph like a flock (Ps 80:2), carries His sheep (Ps 28:9), leads them (Pss 77:21; 78:52), gathers the remnants (Je 23:3), guards Israel (Je 31:10), restores Israel to its pasture (Je 23:3; 50:19). Yahweh as the shepherd of the Israelite is described in the classic Ps 23:1–4. He is the shepherd of the messianic restoration, who gathers the strays, leads them to their own pasture, binds up their wounds, and keeps them in peaceful order (Ezk 34:11–22). The image of Yahweh as shepherd is a prominent messianic motif.

2. *NT.* Shepherds appear outside of the figurative sense in the NT only in the nativity account of Lk 2:8–20. Critics now generally

believe that they belong to the oldest phase of the nativity tradition, along with the manger. The son of David, the king who had been a shepherd, was born in Bethlehem, the city of David, in a cave sheepfold, and the news of His birth was first manifested to shepherds. There is no doubt a contrast intended between shepherds, the poor and ignorant, and the leaders of Judaism.

The figure of the shepherd is applied to Jesus both by Himself and by others. Both His own mission and the first mission of His disciples is exclusively to the lost sheep of the house of Israel (Mt 10:6; 15:24). He is the shepherd who leaves the 99 sheep alone in the desert to search out one stray, and His joy at the recovery of a single sinner is like the joy of the shepherd who finds the stray (Mt 18:12–14; Lk 15:3–7). His arrest and His passion leave His disciples scattered like sheep when the shepherd is struck (Mt 26:31 f; Mk 14:27 f, quoting Zc 13:7). In the final judgment He acts as a shepherd who separates the sheep and the goats after they have shared a common pasture (Mt 25:32). He is the great shepherd (Heb 13:20), the chief shepherd (1 Pt 5:4).

The figure of the good shepherd (Jn 10:1–6, 10–16) is interrupted by the figure of Jesus as the door of the sheepfold (10:7–9), and many critics have suspected some disarrangement either in the text or in the oral traditions. The passage is certainly arranged somewhat loosely, but no satisfactory rearrangement imposes itself. The figure is an echo of Ezk 34:11–22, but it is treated with originality. The emphasis of the parable falls upon the mutual knowledge of Jesus and His followers and His devotion to the flock, culminating in His saving death. The unity of one flock under one shepherd in particular is an echo of Ezk 34:23; 37:22, 24; not only the unity of the flock, but the apostolic mission of the Church is expressed in Jn. The figure of Jesus as the good shepherd was a favorite in the early Christian centuries, and perhaps the earliest artistic representations of Jesus show Him as the good shepherd.

The title of shepherd is applied also to officers of the Church. Shepherds are included among the officers enumerated in Eph 4:11; but whether they can be understood as officers distinct from the others listed is difficult to decide. The elders are addressed as shepherds of the flock in AA 20:28; 1 Pt 5:2–4; in the later passage Jesus the chief shepherd is proposed as their model. Peter* is given in a distinctive way the office of shepherd in Jn 21:15–17; the solemn threefold repetition of the mission, which is not shared by the other apostles in

this context, is clear evidence of the eminence of Peter among the apostles in the primitive Christian community. The figure of the shepherd has passed into common use in the title of pastor (Lt *pastor,* shepherd) given to the chief ecclesiastical officers in the entire Church, the diocese, and the parish.

Sheshach (Hb *šēšak,* which appears in "the king of Sheshach" [Je 25:26; 51:41]), the word is a cipher for Babel (Babylon), formed by the rabbinical device called *Athbash,* in which a word is concealed by substituting the last letter of the alphabet for the first (Th = A), the second last for the second (Sh = B) etc. The word may be original in Je 51:41, which is a later portion of the book. Why it should appear in these two passages is not known. Many modern translations replace the word by Babylon.

Sheshbazzar (Hb *šešbaṣṣar,* a personal name; the name is obviously a corruption of a Babylonian name, but the original form is uncertain; probably *šamaš-apal-uṣur* or *sin-apal-uṣur,* "[the god] Shamash or [the god] Sin protect the son"). Sheshbazzar was a prince of Judah who received from Cyrus the vessels taken from the temple of Jerusalem for transport back to the city (Ezr 1:8, 11). According to the Aramaic source of Ezr (cf EZRA-NEHEMIAH) Sheshbazzar received the vessels, was appointed governor (*pᵉḥāh*) by Cyrus, and laid the foundations of the new temple in Jerusalem (Ezr 5:14–16). Sheshbazzar and Zerubbabel* have a number of features in common: both lead the caravan back to Jerusalem (this is not expressly stated of Sheshbazzar but must be assumed, since he appears with authority at both ends of the journey); both lay the foundations of the temple; Sheshbazzar is called a prince of Judah, and Zerubbabel is a grandson of Jehoiachin*; both have the title of governor. These data have led many historians to identify the two. Most recent writers, however, believe they were two distinct individuals. That a Mesopotamian Jew should have a Babylonian name is no difficulty, but it seems highly improbable that the same man should have two Babylonian names (Zerubbabel is also a Babylonian name). The activities of the two are not so closely identified that Sheshbazzar cannot have begun projects which Zerubbabel completed. John Bright has further suggested that the Chronicler has telescoped the careers of the two men. Some scholars identify Sheshbazzar with Shenazzar of 1 Ch 3:18; in this hypothesis Zerubbabel was the nephew of Sheshbazzar as well as his successor. The office which Sheshbazzar held is not definitely known; he may have been the governor of a new province of Judah (if it was established at this early date), or deputy governor of the district of Judah in the province of Samaria, or a special agent appointed for the mission of resettling Jerusalem and rebuilding the temple. The title "prince of Judah" makes it altogether unlikely that he was a Babylonian in the Persian civil service.

Sheth (Hb *šē't,* only in Nm 24:17), the sons of Sheth who with Moab and Edom will be crushed by Israel. The *Sutu* in the Amarna* Letters designate nomadic tribesmen who were in Egyptian service (W. F. Albright, ANET 490), and the name is possibly to be connected with this group. J. A. Wilson suggests *Shutu* in .the Egyptian execration texts of the 12th–13th dynasties (ANET 329).

Shethar-Bozenai (Aramaic *š*e*tar bôz*e*nai*), a Persian officer of the province of Abarnahara (W of the Euphrates) who questioned the permission to the Jews to rebuild the temple of Jerusalem (Ezr 5:3, 6). The name is probably Persian; the second component, *bauzana,* means deliverer, and the first component is probably a divine name (Mithra?).

Sheva (Hb *š*e*wā'*), the name of David's scribe* in 2 S 20:25; the name of the officer in 1 Ch 18:16 is Shavsha (Hb *šawšā'*), in 2 S 8:17 Seraiah*, and in the list of Solomon's officers Elihoreph and Ahijah sons of Shisha (Hb *šīšā'*) are scribes. Sheva-Shavsha-Shisha-Seraiah are in all probability the same individual, and Shavsha is more probably the original form. The name appears to be foreign; Hurrian has been suggested, but it seems quite certain that David formed his cabinet after Egyptian models, and Shavsha may have been an Egyptian. The name Seraiah may have been adopted as an Israelite name.

Shewbread. This traditional Eng word comes from the King James Version of the Bible. It designates what is usually called in Hb the bread of the presence (lit "bread of the face": Ex 25:30; 35:13; 39:36; 40:23; Nm 4:7; 1 S 21:5–7; 1 K 7:48; 2 Ch 4:19). It is called "the bread of the row" (set forth in rows) in 1 Ch 9:32; 23:29; Ne 10:34, and "the row of bread" in 2 Ch 13:11. From the Gk *artoi tēs protheseōs,* bread to be set forth, came the literal Vg translation *panes propositionis,* again literally and unintelligibly rendered in the Douay OT as loaves of proposition.

The directions in Lv 24:5–9 state that 12 loaves are to be baked of fine flour and set in two rows of 6 each with frankincense in each row before Yahweh. Fresh bread is to be set forth on each Sabbath and the priests eat the loaves of the preceding week. In 1 S 21:5–7 the loaves could be eaten by laymen provided they were sexually continent for an undetermined length of time; the bread was holy*. The bread was placed in the holy place on a table constructed for the purpose; in Ex 25:23–30 the table is made of acacia wood, but in the temple of Solomon the table was of gold (1 K 7:48; 2 Ch 4:19).

The passages which allude to the bread of the presence are all late except 1 S 21:5–7; this passage shows that the bread was an early Israelite practice. The appearance of the bread in the tent sanctuary of Nob suggests that it was a nomadic rite; bread is the staple food of the nomad, and it is likely that the bread of the presence was originally set forth each day rather than each week. The bread of the presence can scarcely be called a sacrifice in the proper sense of the term; its original symbolism was no doubt that of a food offering to the deity, but this is not explicit in the OT. It may be regarded as a ritual survival from the earlier period retained because it was customary with no more than a vague idea of its symbolism.

Shibboleth (Hb *šibbolet,* "ear of grain"), the word was used as a test after Jephthath's* defeat of the Ephraimites to catch the fugitives of Ephraim at the fords of the Jordan. The passage shows a dialectal difference between the speech of Gilead* and the speech of Ephraim; the men of Ephraim could not sound the consonant Shin (š). In a few rare instances in biblical Hb there is a variation between Shin (š) and Samech or Sin (s).

Shield. In the equipment of the armored soldier two types of shield appear in practically every culture: the large shield, the shield proper, usually oblong with perhaps the top curved and often made in a concavo-convex form so as partly to enclose the body; and the small shield or buckler, usually round, carried on the left arm. The shield is used where maintaining a defensive line is important, or moving a line of attack without breaking ranks; the buckler gives the individual soldier more mobility. The ancient shield or buckler was usually made of leather with a wooden or wicker frame (it was combustible, Ezk 39:9), and was anointed with oil to keep it smooth (2 S 1:21; Is 22:6) and covered when not in use (Is 22:6). Types of shield and buckler and their use in warfare are illustrated in

a) Assyrian relief sculpture showing various types of shields. b) Assyrian shield. c) Assyrian sculpture showing a team of two archers with a shield bearer.

ANEP: 36, a dumbbell shaped Hittite buckler; the round buckler, 37, 59, 184, 332, 369, 372, 494, 496. The round buckler was carried by horsemen, 164. The Egyptian shield and buckler both appear oblong with the top side curving to a point (180, 344). The use of the large shield carried by a line

of infantry in close formation is seen in 300. The Assyrians employed the large shield, as tall as a man and curved at the top and sides, to protect the archers during assault (368, 373).

In Hb the large shield is called the *ṣinnāh*, the buckler the *māgēn*. The large shield, when used by the aristocratic knight of the Philistines, was carried by a bearer (1 S 17:7, 41). Solomon made 200 large ornamental shields of gold to be hung in the house of the forest of Lebanon (1 K 10:16; 2 Ch 9:15). Ezk 26:8 alludes to the "roof of shields" in siege warfare; this, like the *testudo* of Roman warfare, was made by the shields of the assaulting force carried in such a way as to protect both the sides and the head from missiles thrown from the walls. The buckler sometimes, if not usually, had a boss in the center (Jb 15:26). Solomon made 300 gold bucklers also to be hung in the house of the forest of Lebanon (1 K 10:17).

Yahweh's favor covers the Psalmist like a shield (Ps 5:13), and His fidelity is shield and buckler (Ps 91:4). Yahweh is frequently called a buckler (this type of armor more readily suggested itself to the poet than the large shield; Pss 3:4; 18:3, 31; 28:7; 33:20; 59:12; 84:12; 115:9–11; 119:114; 144:2; Pr 2:7 30:5), or is said to furnish a buckler (Ps 18:36). Yahweh is the buckler of Abraham (Gn 15:1). Kings are the bucklers of their people (Pss 47:10; 84:10; 89:19).

In the spiritual armor of the Christian faith is the shield (Eph 6:16); the shield here is the *thyreos,* the long oblong shield.

Shihor (Hb *šiḥôr,* "waters of Horus?"), a stream, located E of Egypt in Jos 13:3 and in 1 Ch 13:5, where it is the boundary of Israel, possibly identified with the Wadi el Arish, the "torrent of Egypt" mentioned elsewhere as the boundary of Egypt and Canaan. In Je 2:18 it appears to designate the Nile, and in Is 23:3 the grain of Shihor certainly designates an Egyptian stream; it is parallel to the Nile in the 2nd half of the verse. Geographers believe that it designates an E arm of the Nile in the Delta.

Shiloh (Hb *šilô, šilōh,* meaning uncertain), a town identified with the modern Seilun, 9 mi NNE of Bethel*, in the central mountain range. Shiloh appears in Jos 18:1, 8–10; 19:51; 21:2; 22:9, 12; Jgs 18:31 as the place of the tabernacle* and the place of the general assembly of Israel (displacing Shechem*). Jgs 21:19–21 describes it in the same terms, adding the information that an annual vineyard feast of Yahweh (probably identical with the feast of Tabernacles*) was celebrated there. Shiloh is here the scene of the rape of the girls of Shiloh by the Benjaminite survivors of the intertribal war. These passages are all of later literary origin, but the tradition of Shiloh as a central shrine and a place of assembly is confirmed by earlier passages. Shiloh is the scene of 1 S

1:3. The shrine is maintained by a hereditary priesthood headed by Eli*; Israelites come to Shiloh to celebrate an annual pilgrim feast; it is the place of sacrifice and the place where the ark is kept. From Shiloh the ark was taken into battle and lost to the Philistines* (1 S 4). Shiloh is therefore the central shrine of the Israelite amphictyonic confederacy (cf ISRAEL): the reason for the selection of Shiloh is not clear. There are several literary allusions to a destruction of Shiloh (Je 7:12, 14; 26:6, 9, and in particular the veiled allusion in Ps 78:60), but no explicit account of this disaster is preserved in the OT. Indeed there is room for suspicion that it was deliberately not preserved; Je 7:12, 14; 26:6, 9 employs Shiloh as an example to show that Yahweh has no respect even for places which are dedicated to His worship, and that He can destroy Jerusalem as He destroyed Shiloh. The shock which this declaration caused shows the horror which the Israelites must have felt when Yahweh did not even protect His own holy place. Excavations conducted by a Danish expedition 1930–1932 showed that Shiloh was destroyed about 1050 BC and abandoned for several centuries; the destruction is therefore most probably to be attributed to the Philistines after their victory at Aphek*. The priesthood of Shiloh continued as custodians of the shrine of Yahweh first at Nob* and then at Jerusalem until Abiathar* was deposed by Solomon (1 K 2:27). The origin of the prophet Ahijah* from Shiloh (1 K 14:2, 4) suggests at least a village settlement on or near the site; and Je 41:5 indicates settlement there in the 6th century.

Shimei (Hb *šim'eî,* shortened from *š^ema'yāh,* "Yahweh has heard?"), a personal name; the son of Gera, of the tribe of Benjamin, a kinsman of Saul. The attitude of the household and kinsmen of Saul toward David was probably expressed by Shimei when he cursed David as a murderer when David was forced to flee Jerusalem before Absalom (2 S 16:5–13); and it is probable also that not a few of Saul's tribe of Benjamin shared these sentiments. When David recovered his power Shimei was less than heroic in his abject apology (2 S 19:17–24). If 1 K 2:8 f be accepted as a genuine historical note, then it is obvious, as J. Bright remarks, that David did not really forgive Shimei; but in the disturbed conditions of the time David could not arouse further hostility by an unnecessary act of vengeance. Several historians have suggested that the testament of David and his commission to Solomon to execute vengeance upon Shimei and others in 1 K 2 is rather an expression of what the authors thought the mind of David was than of an actual commission given to Solomon. There is no compelling reason to think that such a commission was out of character with David; in his view justice demanded the vengeance which policy had prevented him from executing. Nor did Solomon act directly, but "in wisdom" (1 K 2:9); he laid an impossibly severe restriction upon Shimei and had him executed at the first violation (1 K 2:36–45).

Shimron (Hb *šimron*, meaning uncertain), a Canaanite city ruled by a king, one of the N confederacy of cities defeated by Joshua (Jos 11:1, Shimron-meron in Jos 12:20), enumerated among the cities on the frontier of Zebulun (Jos 19:15). It may be probably identified with the modern Semuniyeh, about 5 mi W of Nazareth.

Shin. The 21st letter of the Hb alphabet, which has two values, š and s.

Shinab (Hb *šin'āb*, etymology uncertain), king of Admah*, one of the five Canaanite kings raided by the Mesopotamian kings and rescued by Abraham* (Gn 14:2).

Shinar (Hb *šin'ār;* some scholars have suggested that this is the Hb form of the word Sumer [cf SUMERIANS]). In any case the area designated by the name is Babylonia,

the S portion of the valley of the Tigris and Euphrates. It is the land of the kingdom of Nimrod* (Gn 10:10) and of the tower of Babel* (Gn 11:2) and of the kingdom of Amraphel* (Gn 14:2, 9). Achan* stole a mantle from Shinar (Jos 7:21). It is one of the places where the Jews of the Diaspora* are found (Is 11:11) and the land of Nebuchadnezzar* (Dn 1:2). It is the place where a house (temple) is to be built for the woman Wickedness (Zc 5:11).

Ship. The ship of the ancient world exhibited no really new development in technique from earliest times down to the Roman period. It was made of wood, constructed with keel, ribs, and planking caulked with tar. Both ends of the keel projected well above the level of the deck and were ornamented with figureheads. Until the Roman period the ship had a single mast with square sail; later a foremast and foresail were added. The steering assembly usually consisted of two oars, one projecting from each side of the stern; but sometimes a single broad-bladed paddle was employed. By 400 BC the merchant ship was usually completely decked; before that time the ship was decked at least fore and aft, with an awning on the stern deck (Ezk 27:7). The ship scarcely exceeded 100 ft in length. The warship (called "longship" in both Gk and Lt) was

Assyrian representation of a Phoenician warship.

built with a proportion of about 7:1 for greater speed and maneuverability; the merchant ship had a proportion of about 4:1, was built higher and was more seaworthy. The capacity of the ship is difficult to estimate; in Roman times a few vessels which had a capacity of over 1000 tons were famous; the average merchant vessel probably had a capacity of 50–100 tons. The ship was shallow draught, about 3–4 ft. The average speed for a merchant vessel may have been 3–4 knots. The merchant ship depended chiefly upon the sail, which was supplemented by long sweeps (Is 33:21; Ezk 27:8, 29); the warship, whose maneuverability was of vital importance, carried a mast and sail but in combat depended upon its banks of oars. The sea traveler voyaged under primitive and crowded conditions; the ship in which Paul was wrecked carried 276 persons (AA 23:37). It is not surprising that Horace said that a man who embarked on the high seas in such a crate must have oak and three-ply bronze about his heart; yet sea travel was generally preferred as the safest, cheapest, and most comfortable journey.

Some ancient ships are illustrated in ANEP. 41–42 show a ship of very shallow draught with at least a half-deck, a double demountable mast of a type which did not come into general use, and a steering assembly of three oars. 111 shows a single-masted vessel with a crow's nest at the mast head and a sounding pole employed at the bow. 341 shows a warship with an exaggerated crescent shaped keel, a single mast and sail, a crow's nest, a bank of rowers, and a single paddle used as a rudder.

Sea commerce was well established in the 2nd millennium BC between Crete and the Aegean islands on the one hand and Asia on the other. From 1000 to 750 BC the Mediterranean commerce was completely dominated by the Phoenicians*; after 750 the Phoenician commerce was seriously impeded by the Assyrian wars, and at the same time the Greeks began the expansion which gave them the control of maritime commerce until the Roman conquests. The Phoenicians sailed to the W extremity of the Mediterranean. Israelite commerce in the Red Sea (cf EZION-GEBER; SOLOMON) was handled by Phoenician mariners. The "ship of Tarshish" was a Phoenician vessel of unusual size and sturdiness; cf TARSHISH.

Ancient navigation was severely restricted by the absence of the compass. The Phoenicians knew celestial navigation, which enabled them to pursue the voyage at night; but even so ancient mariners often harbored or beached their vessels for the night. The ancient ship sailed hugging the coastline or hopping from one to another of the many islands which dot the Mediterranean. Hence the crow's nest shown in ancient representations was a very important feature of the vessel. To sail close to the shore added to the hazards of the voyage, which were numerous enough already. The ship could not be maneuvered in a gale; shipwrecks were a common event, and the mariner had no protection against shipwreck except to find harbor before the storm overtook him. Hence the prognostication of stormy weather was a highly prized nautical skill. A ship which was in danger of a storm or which could not reach its port before winter put into the nearest harbor until sailing weather reappeared, even if this meant spending the entire winter in the strange port. Sailing was not attempted between the fall and the spring equinox; AA 27:9 notes that Paul's voyage was prolonged beyond the fast at the beginning of the Jewish year in September, and Paul advised wintering at Fair Havens. The captain, like many other mariners, preferred to risk the profit from finishing the voyage without the expensive delay in winter quarters. In addition to storms piracy was a genuine danger until Julius Caesar wiped out the pirates' nests in Asia Minor.

Shiphrah (Hb *šiprāh*, etymology uncertain), one of the two midwives who disobeyed the command of the Pharaoh to kill the male children of the Hebrews (Ex 1:15).

Shishak (Hb *šîšak*, but probably the original writing was *šûšak*, meaning uncertain), the Pharaoh Shoshenk or Sheshonk I (935–914 BC), 1st king of the 22nd dynasty. Shoshenk was a Libyan military chieftain in Egyptian service who seized the throne from the weak 21st dynasty with the project of reestablishing Egypt as an imperial power. This meant control of Palestine, and it was no doubt with this in mind that Shoshenk gave asylum to Jeroboam*, the adversary of Solomon (1 K 11:40). Shoshenk's campaign against Palestine occurred in the 5th year of Rehoboam* (918 BC); the OT relates only that he sacked Jerusalem (1 K 14:25 f). 2 Ch 12:2–9 introduces a theological commentary; a prophetic discourse explains the invasion as a punishment of sin, but when Judah repents the disaster is mitigated. Shoshenk's inscription on the wall of one of the temples of Karnak enlarges the story. The list of Palestinian cities which he claims he conquered (partially given in ANET 242–243; Jerusalem is strangely not included) numbers 156 and extends from Edom to N Palestine. While the list may exaggerate his achievements, fragments of a stele of Shoshenk found at Megiddo* show that the

The inscription of Shishak at Karnak. The figures represent defeated enemy peoples, identified by name.

campaign was extensive. Some historians suggest that Shoshenk was invited to attack Judah by his former client, Jeroboam, and that Shoshenk, with much more ambitious plans in mind, raided the territory of Israel as well. The campaign had no enduring results; the internal weakness of Egypt did not permit her to maintain a foreign empire.

Shittim (Hb *šiṭṭîm*, always with the definite article; "the acacias"?), The site of the Israelite camp E of the Jordan and NE of the Dead Sea before the crossing of the Jordan (Jos 2:1; 3:1); here occurred the episode of the cult of Baal Peor* (Nm 25:1). The place is called Abel Shittim in Nm 33:49 ("field of the acacias"). In Mi 6:5 the events from Shittim to Gilgal designate the crossing of the Jordan. The valley of Shittim (Jl 4:18) can be located only near Jerusalem.

Shoa (Hb *šô'a* [Ezk 23:23]), apparently a Mesopotamian tribe, probably to be located on the Diyala, an E tributary of the Tigris.

Shobach (Hb *šôbak* [2 S 10:16, 18], written *šôpak* in 1 Ch 19:16, 18, meaning and etymology uncertain), military commander of the Aramaean king Hadadezer*, who was killed in the battle of Helam* while fighting as an ally of the Ammonites against David.

Shobi (Hb *šōbî*, meaning and etymology uncertain), son of Nahash of Rabbah, one of the group which met David with supplies and assistance when he fled from Absalom (2 S 17:27); the Ammonites remained loyal to David during the uprising.

Shoe. Cf SANDAL.

Shua (Hb *šû'a*), father of the Canaanite wife of Judah (unnamed, Gn 38:2); from the patronymic a proper name Bath-shua is constructed in 1 Ch 2:3. Bathsheba*, mother of Solomon, is called Bath-shua in 1 Ch 3:5, probably by scribal error. The name appears to be connected with the word "salvation," and is possibly an abbreviation from which the divine component has been omitted.

Shulammite (Hb *šûlammît*), a title given to the bride in SS 7:1 during the "dance of the camp" (cf SONG OF SOLOMON). The meaning and etymology of the title are obscure and several explanations have been proposed: (1) "Shulammite" should be read Shunemite, with an allusion to Abishag of Shunem*, the companion of David* and the most beautiful girl of all Israel (1 K 1:2–4); it is supposed that "Shunemite" came to mean "a beauty." (2) Shulammite is a feminized form of Solomon and is equivalent to "queen." (3) The word is an otherwise unknown appelative of the Canaanite fertility goddess, the patroness of beauty and sexual appeal.

Shunem (Hb *šûnēm*, meaning uncertain), a town; listed among the cities of Issachar* (Jos 19:18); the site of the Philistine camp before the battle of Mt Gilboa* (1 S 28:4); the home of Abishag*, the companion of David (1 K 1:3, 15; 2:17, 21); the home of a woman who gave Elisha* food and lodging, and whose son he raised to life (2 K 4:8–37). Shunem is identified with the modern Solem at the foot of Jebel Dahi (the hill of Moreh*) in the plain of Esdraelon*, about 4 mi N of Jezreel*. Shunem is mentioned in the lists of Palestinian towns conquered by Thutmose III and Shoshenk I (ANET 243).

Shur (Hb *šûr*), a geographical name which designates the steppes SW of Palestine and E of Egypt and N of the deserts of the Sinai peninsula. The Hb word suggests *šûr*, "wall," and some geographers have thought that the name alludes to the line of fortresses constructed by the Egyptians to protect the

E frontier of Egypt. The region is the scene of the flight of Hagar* in the account of J (Gn 16:7). Abraham dwelt for a time in the Negeb* between Kadesh* and Shur (Gn 20:1). The Israelites traversed the desert of Shur after crossing of the Sea of Reeds (Ex 15:22). The area from Havilah* to Shur was the home of the Amalekites* and other nomad tribes (Gn 25:18; 1 S 15:7; 27:8).

Shushan. Cf SUSA.

Sibbecai (Hb *sibbekāi*, meaning and etymology uncertain, possibly an abbreviation or a foreign name), one of David's heroes who slew a Philistine giant (2 S 21:18; 1 Ch 11:29; 27:11). On the basis of the parallel in 1 Ch 27:11 Sibbecai is probably to be read for Mebunnai in 2 S 23:27.

Sibboleth. Cf SHIBBOLETH.

Siddim (Hb *siddîm*, always with the definite article, meaning and etymology uncertain), the valley of Siddim, the scene of the battle between the Canaanite and the Mesopotamian kings (Gn 14:3, 8, 10), identified with the Dead Sea in the gloss of Gn 14:3; the presence of bitumen pits is noticed in Gn 14:10. Since the Dead Sea existed in prehistoric times, the simple view that the valley of Siddim is the present basin of the Dead Sea cannot be sustained. Several modern scholars, however, believe that the valley can be identified with the S portion of the Dead Sea, the shallowest portion of the Sea and nearly cut off from the main body by the peninsula of El Lisan ("the tongue"). There are indications that this bay was created in historic times by an earthquake which permitted the sea to cover land previously occupied and cultivated.

Sidon (Hb *ṣîdôn*, meaning uncertain), a city of Phoenicia*, located at the modern Saida, 28 mi S of Beirut and 25 mi N of Tyre*. In ancient times the city had a double harbor protected by an island and was divided into two cities, the island port city and the mainland fortress. The modern city covers the remains of ancient Sidon; a Phoenician necropolis and the ruins of a temple of Eshmun are situated near the city.

The antiquity of Sidon cannot be ascertained; it was in existence in the first part of the 2nd millennium BC. Before the rise of Cretan sea power in this period Sidon had a commercial empire with a chain of markets and colonies on the mainland of Asia. During the 2nd millennium it was the leader of the Phoenician cities; in ancient documents "Sidonian" often designates the inhabitants of the Phoenician coast, as we use Phoenicians (e.g., to live in quiet and security after the manner of the Sidonians, Jgs 18:7). After the 11th century Sidon yielded its hegemony to Tyre*, possibly because of the capture of Sidon by the Philistines. In the Amarna* Letters Zimreda of Sidon is mentioned as dealing with Aziru, the enemy of Egypt. Tiglath-pileser I of Assyria (1112–1074) includes Sidon among the cities from which he received tribute. It appears also among the tributaries mentioned by Ashur-nasir-pal II (883–859), Shalmaneser III (858–824), and Adad-nirari III (810–783). Sidon was a leader in the rebellion at the accession of Sennacherib (705–681), who relates that he conquered Sidon, forced its king Luli to

The harbor of Sidon.

flee overseas, and installed Ethbaal as king. Abdi-milkutta of Sidon rebelled against Esarhaddon (680–669), who conquered and destroyed the city. It is listed among the satellite kingdoms of Nebuchadnezzar. It passed under Persian dominion with no resistance and was the headquarters of a district of the Persian satrapy of "across the river." The city still retained its satellite king; Tabnit of Sidon rebelled against Artaxerxes III Ochus (358–338), who inflicted upon the city the greatest disaster in its history; it was sacked and burned and 40,000 inhabitants (perhaps exaggerated) were slaughtered. The city recovered in time to surrender to Alexander without resistance in 332 and add its ships to his fleet. After the division of Alexander's empire Sidon with the rest of Phoenicia was held by the Ptolemies* through the 3rd century; the siege of the city by Antiochus III was interrupted by a message from Rome, but the city ultimately passed to the Seleucids*. It was a free city in the Roman province of Syria and was one of the Hellenistic cities which received donations from Herod the Great. The maritime traditions of Sidon are attested in the Aramaic proverb, "Do not show an Arab the sea or a Sidonian the desert, for their work is different" (ANET 430).

In the Table* of Nations Sidon is the eldest son of Canaan (Gn 10:15; 1 Ch 1:13); this attests the leadership of Sidon in the 2nd millennium BC. Sidon is often mentioned as a boundary point: the flank of Zebulun* (Gn 49:13), the limit of Canaanite territory (Gn 10:19), the boundary of Asher* at "Sidon the Great" (Jos 19:28), the limit of David's kingdom (2 S 24:6), the limit of Joshua's pursuit of the Canaanite kings of the N (Jos 11:8). Laish* and Zarephath* were satellite cities of Sidon (Jgs 18:28; 1 K 17:9). Sidon remained Canaanite after the Israelite settlement (Jgs 1:31). Sidon is often mentioned with Tyre in the OT; this with other extrabiblical indications shows the close relationships between the two cities during the period of the hegemony of Tyre, 1000–750 BC. Sidon is mentioned alone or more frequently with Tyre in prophetic threatening oracles (Is 23:2, 4, 12; Je 47:4; Ezk 28:20–23; Zc 9:2; Jl 4:4). It is one of the cities and kingdoms which must drink the cup of Yahweh's wrath (Je 25:22). Sidon was one of the states which sent ambassadors to Zedekiah* to urge him to join the rebellion against Nebuchadnezzar (Je 27:3). The metaphorical ship of Tyre has Sidonian oarsmen (Ezk 27:8). In the wars of the Maccabean period Sidon and other cities launched attacks upon the Jews of Galilee (1 Mc 5:15).

Jesus reached the neighborhood of Tyre and Sidon (Mt 15:21; Mk 7:24, 31). This does not signify a departure from Jewish territory, but an approach to the frontier of Jewish and Phoenician territory. People from Tyre and Sidon, which means Jews from these cities, came to hear Jesus (Mk 3:8; Lk 6:17). Jesus uses Tyre and Sidon as examples of deep-seated paganism which would have been converted if they had received the ministry which He performed in the cities of Galilee, and therefore they will be more favorably treated in the judgment (Mt 11:21 f; Lk 10:13 f). AA 12:20 alludes to a quarrel between the citizens of Sidon and Herod Agrippa*; the Phoenician cities were included in his kingdom. It was the first port at which Paul's ship harbored on his journey to Rome (AA 27:3).

Siege. The techniques of siege warfare advanced in antiquity at a more rapid pace than the techniques of defensive engineering, and there are many more records of successful sieges than of failures. The simplest technique was the complete enclosure of the fortress so as to cut off food and water. This required a heavy advantage in manpower, some siege engineering (cf below), inexhaustible patience, and in Palestine was particularly ineffective; cities were built where water was available, and the besieging force could easily find that its food and water were exhausted first. Hence the siege was planned so as to culminate in a successful assault upon the walls. This demanded circumvallation, a complete enclosure of the fortress by earthworks and wooden palisades, engines for sapping and breaching the walls, and offensive and defensive engines for the assault.

Circumvallation was employed early; Thutmose II besieged Megiddo* with earthworks and palisades (ANET 237) and it was employed by Joab against Abel-beth-maacah (2 S 20:15). Dt 20:19 ff prohibits the cutting down of fruit trees during a siege; these would be employed in the construction of palisades. A word which is translated "siegeworks" is used in Is 29:3, 7, lit "pressures." Ezk 4:2; 21:27; 26:8 f; Na 2:6 mention circumvallation, mounds, battering rams, and axes. The axes were used against gates; the mounds or ramps were earthworks constructed up to the level of the top of the wall to permit a frontal assault; they were opposed by piling up the top of the wall. Both Egyptian and Assyrian art represent sieges in some detail. Egyptian siege technique is illustrated in ANEP 311 (mining of the walls, scaling ladders, and the picturesque detail of a defender listening at the wall in order to detect the sound of the sappers), 330 (assault with scaling ladders), 334, 344 (scaling ladders and axes employed against the gate), 346 (the defense of the wall, which is manned by pikemen). The besieger employed all the means available: enclosure, mining or breaching the walls, assault. Any one could succeed, or the pressure of all at once forced the defense to give at some point. The Assyrians refined the technique of siege beyond anything previously known, and their record against fortresses was impressive. More important than the technique perhaps was the Assyrian readiness to take the time and the pains necessary to conclude the siege. Sennacherib mentions the use of ramps, the ram, assault, and mines in his siege warfare (ANET 288). These are illustrated in ANEP: 362, 365 show sappers and the use of scaling ladders, and a feature which the Assyrians greatly refined, although they probably did not invent it; this is the cover of the assault columns and the sappers by a heavy archery fire, which is shown regularly in Assyrian representations of siege and was obviously of great importance. 368 shows another Assyrian invention, the ram which moved on a wheeled vehicle and was entirely covered against missiles from above and from the sides; it was moved to the wall on a ramp. 372–373 show the same device moving on a track of logs, with the interesting feature of one man detailed with a bucket of water to put out fires on the cover which might be started by firebrands dropped from the walls.

In the Gk and Hellenistic periods the technique was further improved by better methods of ramming and mining and by the introduction of two new devices, the catapult and the siege tower. The catapult appears after 400 BC, although some scholars suspect that it was used by the Assyrians. The movable siege tower on wheels was a formidable device of several stories with a drop bridge to the wall which brought the assault column right to the defenders. The. towers used by Alexander, who was the first in history to take Tyre by any means, had 20 stories and stood about 160 ft high. The upper stories of these towers were manned by archers who covered the assault column on the bridge. These siege engines were used in Palestine* in the Maccabean period (1 Mc 11:20) and were also used by the Jews (1 Mc 13:44, Simon's assault on Gezer).

The Bible mentions a number of notable sieges: the siege of Jabesh-gilead by Nahash of Ammon, relieved by Saul (1 S 11:1 ff); the siege of Samaria by Ben-hadad of Damascus, which reduced the inhabitants to starvation until the Aramaeans were forced to lift the siege (2 K 7:24 ff), and by Shalmaneser V of Assyria, which was ended by capitulation after three years (2 K 17:5); the siege of Tyre by Nebuchadnezzar, which was lifted after 13 years (Ezk 29:18); the siege of Jerusalem by Nebuchadnezzar, which lasted 18 months and was ended by assault after the wall was breached (2 K 25:1 ff). The greatest siege of Palestinian history and the best known is the siege of Jerusalem by Titus from March to July in AD 70, which is described in detail by Josephus, the city was taken by assault in several stages. As each defense line was breached the defenders formed another rampart within, and the victory was achieved at a heavy cost of life of attackers and defenders.

Sign. The basic meaning of the sign in biblical thought is the symbol which indicates the existence or the presence of that which it signifies; it directs the attention to the reality signified. Rarely it is used in the sense of omen or portent as understood in divination*, the sign of the coming event (Is 44:25; Je 10:2). The biblical conception of the sign of the coming event is quite different from the omen of divination· (cf below). The sign is the standard, the symbolic identification of the tribe (Nm 2:2) or the military standard (Ps 74:4); the symbolic standard identifies the reality which it symbolizes and distinguishes it from other realities. The sign is an assurance that a promise will be kept (Jos 2:12 f); in the context this sign can be only the solemn asseveration confirmed by an oath. When the psalmist asks Yahweh to produce a sign for good (Ps 86:17), the sign is an assurance of the favor of Yahweh; the quality of the sign is no doubt to be understood in the common use of sign as a manifest work of Yahweh (cf below). The sign is a symbolic reminder of a past event: the memorial stones of the crossing of the Jordan (Jos 4:6), the censers of Korah and his company (Nm 17:3), the rod of Aaron as a memorial of the exclusive priesthood conferred upon him (Nm 17:25). The recitation of the saving deeds of Yahweh are a sign and a memorial on the hand and the brow (Ex 13:9, 16; Dt 6:8; 11:18), literally fulfilled in Judaism by the wearing of phylacteries*. The altar and pillar to be erected in Egypt are signs and witnesses of Yahweh (Is 19:20). The sign is a witness: the Jews of the diaspora* are a sign made by Yahweh, for their restoration will exhibit His saving power and will (Is 66:19). The punishments which Yahweh sends upon Israel are a sign attesting His righteousness (Dt 28:46; Ezk 14:8). The symbolic actions of Isaiah are a sign which both affirms and signifies the defeat of Israel (Is 20:3). The rainbow is a symbol and witness of the covenant (Gn 9:12, 13, 17); so likewise circumcision (Gn 17:11) and the Sabbath (Ex 31:13, 17; Ezk 20:12, 20) are external observances which attest the covenant which Yahweh has made with Abraham or with Israel. Redeemed Israel is a sign of the saving power and will of Yahweh, an eternal sign (Is 55:13).

The sign then comes to mean a piece of proof or evidence (Jb 21:29), but of a particular type: the evidence of truth which cannot be ascertained by experience and observation, the proof that Yahweh is speaking or acting. The sign of this type must be a wonderful event: it is the prediction of an event which is shortly to occur (Ex 3:12; 1 S 2:34; 10:1, 7, 9; 2 K 19:29; Is 37:30; Je 44:29 f), a wonder of any character whatever (Jgs 6:17), "from heaven above to Sheol beneath" (Is 7:11, 14), a celestial phenomenon (2 K 20:8 f; Is 38:7, 22), or it may be arbitrarily elected by the inquirer from among the various possibilities, as Jonathan took a sign of Yahweh's will from one of the two answers which the Philistines could give to his challenge (1 S 14:10). This episode shows the Israelite conception of sign more clearly; Yahweh was always present and active, and a sign need not be wonderful; Yahweh could manifest Himself in any way in which He chose.

From the combination of the ideas of proof and of wonder arises the most common theological use of sign in the OT, by which the word signifies a wonderful deed of Yahweh without explicit reference to the evidential character of the deed; in the enumeration "signs, portents, and wonders" the three words become nearly synonymous. The "signs" most frequently mentioned in this sense are the saving deeds of the exodus* (Ex 4:8, 9, 17, 28, 30; 7:3; 8:19; 10:1, 2; Nm 14:11, 22; Dt 11:3; 4:34; 7:19; 26:8; 29:2; 6:22; 34:11; Ne 9:10; Jos 24: 17; Pss 78:43; 105:27; 135:9; Je 32:20 f). The Israelite could expect like signs to terrify the enemies of Israel in later times (Ps 65:9) and was disappointed when they did not occur (Ps 74:9). The Gk writer of WS uses the word both in the sense of an indication of the future (WS 8:8) and of a wonder (10:16), adding his own reflection that the discernment and the performance of signs are works of wisdom. Too rigid a view of the Hb idea of the sign is prevented by the Hb belief that a false prophet could perform a sign (Dt 13:2–3); if this happened, the Israelite must take his traditional belief as his controlling evidence and reject any sign which was presented in opposition to it.

In the NT the most common use of the word is to indicate the demonstrative wonder, in the same sense explained above in the OT (Mk 16:17, 20; Lk 23:8; AA 4:16, 22; 2:43; 4:30; 5:12; 6:8; 7:36; 14:3; 15:12; 8:13; 2:22; Rm 15:19; Heb 2:4). The sign is also the piece of evidence (Paul's signature at the end of his letters, 2 Th 3:17). It is the evidence of the messianic event (Lk 2:12), and the disciples expect to learn what signs will indicate the coming of the eschatological event (Mt 24:3; Mk 13:4; Lk 21:7). Mt 24:30 mentions the appearance of the sign of the Son of Man in the sky, but does not tell what it is. The attitude of the Jews toward the sign is shown by their questions of Jesus (Mt 12:38–40; 16:1–4; Mk 8:11 f; Lk 11:29 f); if anyone made such claims as Jesus, he should validate the claims by the production of some demonstrative wonder. Paul also attests the demand of the Jews for signs (1 Co 1:22). The response of Jesus seems to indicate a certain impatience with this desire for "signs"; faith* should be given Him because of what He is. Jn exhibits a greater preoccupation with the sign than do the other Gospels; not only is the demand for a sign mentioned more frequently, but Jesus Himself is represented as appealing to the sign in a way which is not found in the other Gospels (Jn 2:11, 18; 3:2; 4:48, 54; 6:2, 14, 26, 30; 7:31; 9:16; 23). This emphasis of Jn is perhaps due to his desire to show that what the Jews demand was really exhibited by Jesus.

The gift of tongues is a sign not to believers, but to unbelievers (1 Co 14:22); it is the kind of wonder which astonishes, and the believer does not need this. Jesus is "a sign which is contradicted" (Lk 2:34); the phrase is obscure, but emphasizes the basic truth that the person of Jesus Himself is the great sign which needs no other confirmation, and the sign which arouses most opposition. Circumcision is a sign and seal i.e., a proof of the righteousness of the law (Rm 4:11). The genuine apostle is recognized by certain signs, which here are not wonderful deeds (2 Co 12:12) but credentials. The Parousia* is preceded by signs in the heavens; these are disturbances of the natural order, the wonderful. The signs in the sky of Apc 12:1, 3 (the woman clothed with the sun, the dragon) and 15:1 (the seven angels with seven plagues) are symbolic figures. Finally, the same caution concerning the validity of signs is found both in NT and OT; for false Messiahs and false prophets (Mt 24:24; Mk 13:22), the Antichrist* (2 Th 2:9), the beast (Apc 13:13 f), the spirits of demons (Apc 16:14), and the false prophet (Apc 19:20) will produce signs. The wonderful event is therefore not of itself demonstrative, but must be taken in conjunction with the entire character of its agent and his message.

Sihon (Hb *sîḥôn*, meaning and etymology uncertain), an Amorite* king, whose kingdom lay E of the Dead Sea and N of the Arnon. According to Nm 21:21–27 the Israelites asked permission to traverse his land; when he offered armed opposition, Israel destroyed his army and occupied his kingdom. Nm 21:27–30 adds a fragment of a song and an explanation that Sihon's Amorite kingdom had been formed of territory wrested from Moab*. The territory was given to Reuben* and Gad* (Jos 13:21, 27), to Reuben, Gad and Manasseh* (Nm 32:33). There are several allusions to this victory as a saving deed of Yahweh (Dt 1:4 +; Jos 2:10; Ne 9:22; Pss 135:11; 136:19; Je 48:45 quotes Nm 21:27–30). Israel's conquest of Sihon is urged as a basis of the Israelite claim to the territory against Moab (Jgs 11:19–21). While the picture of the conquest of Canaan is not simple, it should be noticed that this claim, like other Israelite claims in E Palestine, is placed by the traditions before Joshua, and thus very probably represents claims earlier than the entrance of the Joseph tribes from Egypt. The allusions are frequent and suggest a notable victory. The conquest is more probably attributed to Gad than to the Israelites who came out of Egypt.

Silas (Gk *silas*, from Aramaic *šeʾîlāʾ*, "Saul"), a personal name; a leading member of the Church of Jerusalem and a prophet, who was sent with Judas as a delegate of the Church of Jerusalem to accompany Paul and Barnabas to Antioch to communicate the liberties granted the Gentile Christians by the council of Jerusalem (AA 15:22–35). On the occasion of the quarrel of Paul and Barnabas because of John Mark*, Paul chose Silas to accompany him on his 2nd journey (AA 15:36–41). The journey took them to the cities of Lycaonia*, Galatia*, and Phrygia*, and Silas was one of the first Christian missionaries to reach the continent of Europe (AA 16:1–10). Silas shared Paul's imprisonment and release at Philippi* and with him was involved in the riot at Thessalonica* (AA 16:11–17:9). When Paul left Berea* because of disturbances there, Silas remained in the city (AA 17:10–15) and rejoined Paul at Corinth (AA 18:5). The Silvanus (Gk *siluanos*) who with Timothy is mentioned by Paul in 1 Th 1:1; 2 Th 1:1, and who helped Paul preach the Gospel at Corinth (2 Co 1:19) is regarded as the same person; 1–2 Th were written from Corinth, and Silvanus is easily understood as a variant Gk form of the Semitic name

or as a Gk second name used in addition to the Semitic name. Silvanus also appears in 1 Pt 5:12 as the man through whom the letter is sent; some scholars believe that this means not only that he was the messenger, but that he was also the author of the epistle.

Siloam (Gk *siloam*, from Hb *šilôaḥ*), which occurs only in Is 8:6 as the name of a canal or tunnel probably connected with the spring of Gihon*, but whose location is uncertain. It was earlier than the tunnel of Hezekiah. The Hb word probably means "sender." The pool into which the water of the tunnel of Hezekiah was deposited lay on the western slope of the hill of Zion. The modern pool, which bears the name of Siloam, is a much later construction, but it is still fed through the tunnel of Hezekiah. The pool at this site in NT times is identified with the pool of Siloam of Jn 9:7, 11, and the tower which fell during its construction was in the neighborhood (Lk 13:4).

Silvanus. Cf SILAS.

Silver. The first use of silver occurred in prehistoric times; but it appears to have been discovered later than gold*. Egypt had gold-bearing ores but no silver, and it did not become common in Egypt until the 18th dynasty, when it was imported from the Hittites*. The Phoenicians* imported silver into Asia from Spain; besides Spain, silver was mined in Asia Minor, Armenia, and in the Gk period in Attica. At least in the 2nd millennium BC unminted silver became the general medium of exchange; both the Akkadian *kaspu* and the Hb *kesep* are frequently used in contexts where they signify "money" or "price." Silver-bearing ores were mined in shafts (Jb 28:1). The refining process was a later discovery, scarcely earlier than 1000 BC. The ore was smelted into stannum, a mixture of silver and lead, which was then refined in the furnace. Early methods could not produce a temperature sufficiently high for the manufacture of pure silver. Silver was less used in jewelry than gold; it was more difficult to handle. Most frequently it was hammered and was often used as plating. Casting was a later development. The OT mentions the brightness of silver metaphorically (Ps 68:14). It frequently signifies wealth (Gn 13:2; Ex 21:21). It was less valuable than gold; on the ratio of silver to gold cf GOLD. It was booty in war (Jgs 5:19; 2 S 8:11 +). It is frequently mentioned as a measure of weight and value (cf WEIGHTS AND MEASURES) and as money or price. Since it was not minted in the early period, silver was always weighed out in payment. Among silver vessels mentioned are the cup of Joseph (Gn 44:2), the trumpets of the tabernacle (Nm 10:2), unidentified vessels (Gn 24:53), and idols frequently. The silversmiths of Ephesus manufactured miniature silver temples of Artemis and incited a riot against the Christians when they feared that conversions to Christianity would cut into their trade (AA 19:24 ff).

Simeon (Hb šimʿôn, etymology and meaning uncertain; the etymology given in Gn 29:33 from "Yahweh has heard" is popular), a personal and tribal name; the 2nd son of Jacob* and Leah* and one of the 12 tribes of Israel (Gn 29:33; 35:23). The census of the tribe of Simeon is given in Nm 1:22 f; 2:12. Simeon is associated with Levi* in the sack of Shechem* in revenge for the rape of Dinah* (Gn 34:25–30); it is doubtless in allusion to this story that Simeon and Levi are cursed for their ferocity and said to be dispersed and scattered in Israel (Gn 49:5–7). Simeon accompanies Judah in the conquest of the territory of Judah (Jgs 1:3, 17). The territory of Simeon (Jos 19:1–9, the list of cities of Simeon) is located in the Negeb* around Beersheba*. These are cities of Judah in Jos 15:21–32; it may be supposed that the list of Judah comes from a later period when Simeon no longer existed as a distinct tribal group. Such a disappearance of the tribe is suggested by the absence of Simeon from the blessing of Moses (Dt 33). The cities of Simeon form an enclave in the territory of Judah; the redactor of Jos explains this from the fact that the territory of Judah was too extensive for Judah. The explanation is probably more complex; cf below. 1 Ch 4:24–43 lists the clans of Simeon and mentions migrations of the tribe, described as nomadic, to Gedor and Mt Seir*.

Similar questions arise concerning Simeon*, Reuben*, and Levi*. The three tribes are ranked as the eldest, which implies antiquity; all three likewise appear as diminished and as losing their land or completely dispossessed of it. It may be supposed that they were the oldest of the Israelite groups which belonged to Canaan and did not enter the country in the 13th century. The story of Shechem puts Simeon in the central highlands and not in the Negeb; from the dimly remembered story one may deduce an attempt at the conquest of Shechem, perhaps successful, but which issued in the expulsion of Simeon and Levi and the settlement of Simeon under the patronage of Judah in the Negeb. It was still strong enough to form a member of the 12-tribe confederacy, but

must have been absorbed by Judah at an early date, probably before the monarchy.

Simon (Gk simōn), a personal name; the Gk name was often adopted by men who had the Hb name Simeon. **1.** 2nd son of Mattathias* (1 Mc 2:3), surnamed Thassi, called "a man of discretion" in the testament of Mattathias (2 Mc 2:65) and respected as counselor in the Maccabean movement of independence. He was sent to Galilee by his brother Judas* to assist the Jews there; he defeated the Seleucid forces in several skirmishes but finally evacuated the Jewish population of Galilee. After the death of Judas he joined Jonathan* in flight to Tekoa* and assisted in Jonathan's reprisal against the Nabateans (1 Mc 9:33–42). He was left by Jonathan in command at Bethbasi and repelled the siege of the town by Bacchides* (1 Mc 9:62–68). He was an officer in Jonathan's defeat of Apollonius* (1 Mc 10:82). After Jonathan was confirmed in the high priesthood by Antiochus VI he was appointed governor; Simon led the campaign in which Beth-zur* was finally taken from the Seleucid forces (1 Mc 11:59, 65 f). He took Joppa* and fortified Adida (1 Mc 12:33 f, 38). He succeeded to the supreme military and political office after the capture of Jonathan by Tryphon* (1 Mc 13–16). He fortified Jerusalem and discouraged Tryphon from attacking. He was forced to send ransom for Jonathan and the sons of Jonathan as hostages, although he knew the demand was insincere. He recovered the body of Jonathan and erected a family mausoleum at Modin* in grand style, no doubt similar to the large mausoleums which can be seen near Jerusalem today; the narrator says that it was visible from the Mediterranean. Simon supported Demetrius II in his campaign to seize the throne from Tryphon, and in return for his support achieved the goal of the Maccabean wars: remission of tribute and practical independence (1 Mc 13:36 ff). The Jews began to date a new era from this year, the 170th Seleucid year 142–141 BC. Simon took Gezer* and expelled the foreign garrison from the citadel of Jerusalem. Simon's administration afforded the first period of peace which the country had known for a generation (1 Mc 14:4 ff). He renewed diplomatic relations with Rome and secured a document sent to the nations and kingdoms of the E Mediterranean assuring the friendship of the Romans for the Jews. The deeds of Simon were engraved on tablets of bronze. Antiochus VII, who claimed the throne of Syria after his brother Demetrius* II had been captured by the Parthians, was not satisfied with the liberties granted the Jews; and in spite of Simon's support of his claim, demanded the surrender of Joppa and Gezer and other towns and the payment of a heavy tribute. Simon refused; an expeditionary force commanded by Cendebaeus* was defeated by the Jews under the command of Simon's sons. Simon and his sons were treacherously assassinated by his son-in-law Ptolemy Abubus, governor of Jericho. 2 Mc adds little about Simon, mentioning that he was an officer in Judas' defeat of Nicanor* (8:22), that he commanded a force which was left to contain the Idumeans (10:19 f), and that he was checked in his encounters with Nicanor (14:17); on the attitude of the author of 2 Mc toward the Hasmoneans cf MACCABEES, BOOKS OF. Simon did not take the title of king, probably because he was not of the line of David and felt that the people would not support it; his title was "prince of the people of El" (1 Mc 14:28). He was likewise not eligible for the office of high priest, a difficulty which haunted the Hasmonean line during its entire history, and it was understood that he held the office "until a true prophet should appear" to decide the question (1 Mc 14:41).

2. A man of Benjamin, governor of the temple under the high priest Onias*. Because of a quarrel with the high priest he gave an exaggerated report of the treasures to the governor Apollonius* which was the cause of the raid of Heliodorus* on the temple (2 Mc 3). Simon continued his hostility by accusations of Onias at court (2 Mc 4:1 ff). Simon was the brother of Menelaus*, who later obtained the high priesthood.

3. Simon II, son of Onias* II, high priest about the time of Ben Sira (BS 50:1 ff). Josephus relates that this Simon was deeply involved in the factional strife which followed the battle of Panium (198 BC) in which Antiochus III conquered Palestine from the Ptolemies, and that he was won from the Seleucid faction to the Ptolemy faction. Cf TOBIAS.

4. The original name of the apostle Peter*.

5. One of the Twelve, called "the Canaanite" (Mt 10:4; Mk 3:18), "the Zealot*" (Lk 6:15; AA 1:13). Lk has translated the word which has been confused with Canaanite, Aramaic ḳan'an, "zealot"; the title probably indicates that Simon had formerly been a member of this party. Nothing is known of him otherwise.

6. A kinsman of Jesus (Mt 13:55; Mk 6:3), possibly identical with Simon the Zealot.

7. Simon of Cyrene*, was was pressed into assisting Jesus to carry the cross from the judgment seat to Calvary (Mt 27:32; Mk 15:21; Lk 23:26). Mk notes that he was the father of two well known Christians, Alexander and Rufus.

8. The father of Judas* Iscariot (Jn 6:71; 12:4; 13:2, 26).

9. Simon the leper, the host of Jesus on the occasion when a woman anointed his head and washed his feet (Mt 26:6–13; Mk 14:3–9). Cf LEPER.

10. A Pharisee, the host of Jesus in Lk's version of the anointing (Lk 7:36–50; cf # 9 above), which appears to combine the anointing of Bethany with another event.

11. Simon the tanner, a Christian of Joppa*, the host of Peter when Peter received the centurion Cornelius* (AA 9:43; 10:6, 17, 32).

12. A magician of Samaria, esteemed by his followers as "the Great Power of God," a title which suggests that he headed a Gnostic cult (AA 8:9–24). He was converted by the preaching of the apostles, but was apparently most impressed by the charismata which accompanied the giving of the spirit* and desired to purchase the gift for money. From him the vice of simony, commercial traffic in sacred things, takes its name.

Sin. 1. *OT*. There is no word in Hb which means precisely theological sin; Hb uses a large variety of words, each of which has a profane use, to designate sin, and a comparison of these shows the OT conception of sin. It is impossible to cite even a small portion of the passages in which these words occur. The word which is commonly translated sin is *ḥeṭ'*, *ḥaṭṭa't*; lit like the Gk *hamartia* the verb means "to miss the mark." This signifies not merely an intellectual error in judgment but a failure to attain a goal. The literal sense is not foremost in a common use of the Akkadian cognate noun, which is technically a word for rebellion; and the word "sin" is used in this sense by Hezekiah* of his rebellion against his Assyrian overlord (2 K 18:14). It is also used of a breach of an agreement between nations and peoples; Jephthah denies that Israel has sinned by aggression (Jgs 11:27). In the personal relation of lord and vassal which existed between Saul and David sin is disloyalty by either party to the agreement (1 S 19:4; 24:12; 26:21). Sin is the failure of an inferior to fulfill his obligations (Gn 31:36; 42:22) or of the host to fulfill his duty of hospitality (Gn 20:9). On the basis of these and other passages J. Pedersen remarks that the kernel of sin is a breach of covenant*. But the same writer also observes, considering the basic meaning of "miss the mark," failure to achieve an objective, that sin is a nonaction; this consideration of sin as a failure is seen in other words also.

The word 'āwôn, usually translated "iniquity," means a deviation; here also the element of failure and of distortion is seen. Iniquity means that reality has become what ought not to exist. In common use iniquity signifies concretely "guilt," the distortion which remains as a result of the iniquitous act. Guilt is conceived as burden too heavy for the sinner to carry (Gn 4:13; Ps 38:5; Is 1:4). The sin of Judah is engraved on its heart like an inscription in stone (Je 17:1); it is like the rust which eats into a metal vessel (Ezk 24:6). These metaphors attempt to express the damage of sin to the sinner; his guilt is not only a liability before Yahweh, but also a corruption of the person. This idea is frequently expressed in other metaphors; cf below. Guilt as liability before Yahweh is expressed by the word 'āšām; this is a responsibility which remains until it is removed. Most frequently the word is used of the guilt of ritual infractions, which are not conceived as genuinely malicious; there is no ritual atonement for sins committed with "a high hand" (Nm 15:30), with deliberate malice. Related to the idea of 'āwôn is the word šegāgāh, "a straying"; the sinner leaves the path which leads to his destination and is lost. His life is aimless, and he will surely perish.

Several words signify that sin is rebellion (pāša', mārad, mārāh). Mārāh signifies primarily the rebellion of a child against its parents; pāša' signifies more properly rebellion against a political superior (1 K 12:19; 2 K 8:20) and is applied to rebellion against Yahweh (Is 1:2; Je 2:29; Am 4:4; Ho 7:13). In these words, as in ḥaṭṭa't sin signifies the act by which a community is dissolved (Pedersen). It is important to observe that the political conception of overlord and vassal in the ancient world is conceived as a personal rather than a political relation in our sense; when sin is called a breach of the covenant and a sin against the law of Yahweh (Ho 8:1), the prophet is not thinking of a legal offense. His words arise from the background of the covenant* understood as an act of beneficence by the sovereign toward the vassal, and rebellion is not an impersonal severing of relations but a personal offense, an insult which arouses anger*. Ultimately the sinner hates Yahweh (Ex 20:5; Dt 5:9). The personal element is clearer in the rebellion of the child against its parents, and in the word mārad, which signifies rather the disposition to rebellion: obstinacy, contentiousness, a refractory disposition. The legal element is more prominent in the word reša', which signifies formally legal guilt, the guilt of one who has been declared guilty by a legal process, therefore a criminal; in this sense the usual Eng translation of "wicked" is accurate.

"Disorder" seems too feeble a word to use as a summary of the words ra', "evil"; tô 'ēbāh, "abomination"; 'awel, "twisted." The evil is that which lacks its proper form; ra' also means ugly. The abomination is that which Yahweh finds intolerable, which He rejects and loathes. That which is twisted is also that which lacks proper form and shape, which is crippled and distorted. Related to these words is the designation of sin as šeḳer, "a lie"; this word can be applied not only to mendacity, but to any sin. The sinner acts deceitfully — not that he can successfully deceive Yahweh, but that he pretends to be something which he is not. The lie is a denial of reality by speech; sin is a denial of reality by action. The usage is not unlike Plato's phrase, "the lie in the soul," which is far more pernicious than the lie in the mouth, for the sinner believes his own lie.

Sin is often called folly, and the sinner is a fool* (Dt 32:6; Je 4: 22; 5:21). This can be used as an extenuating word, but in the OT a self-made fool is not treated with sympathy. One who deliberately releases a harmful influence is a fool (cf below). For sin is also trouble ('awen); that this one word should signify sin, affliction, and sorrow is perhaps as revealing as anything which can be said about the OT conception of sin. The sinner is a troublemaker, not only for himself but for his neighbor as well. The extent to which he makes trouble is explicit in Gn 3–11 and in the prophetic and Deuteronomic theologies of sin; cf below.

The origin of sin raises two questions: its psychological origin and its historical origin. Ultimately these resolve into a single answer. The psychological origin of sin is altogether clear in the OT and it is impossible to cite all the relevant passages. Sin arises from the lack of knowledge* of God (Ho 2:8; 4:1, 6); here the Hb conception of knowledge must be recalled. Lack of knowledge is a refusal to know i.e., to accept God, to recognize His reality. Sin arises from the evil heart (Je 7:24). There is never any question in the OT whether sin is a deliberate and willful act for which man must bear full responsibility. There is no suspicion of any compulsion or neurosis, nor of any failure of society which excuses the individual. Sin is indeed a breakdown of society, and the prophets often speak of this; but society breaks down because of the failure of its members.

The historical origin of sin is really the question of original sin, and this in turn resolves itself ultimately into the question of how sin can enter a universe governed by the saving power and will of God. To this mystery the OT offers no solution; indeed it is more accurate to say that it does not consider the mystery. The narrative of Gn 3 (cf ADAM; EVE; PARADISE; and related articles) attributes sin to the free choice of man in his primitive condition. when he was not subject to the burden of sin and of evil desires which the OT recognizes in historic man. Man is indeed tempted by agents outside himself; the narrative affirms that he has the power to resist temptation, and the fine psychological insight of the story shows how and why he yields. Man yields because he wants something which is not his. By this first sin the good relations between Yahweh and the sons of man are destroyed and in some ways irreparably destroyed; man can repent, he can receive forgiveness and a covenant with Yahweh, but there is no thought of a return to Paradise unless Yahweh himself restores man to his original bliss. In its present context Gn 3 should not be considered apart from Gn 4–11, to which it is an introduction. This collection of originally detached anecdotes is intended to show how sin, once admitted into the world, spreads until "all flesh corrupts its way" (Gn 6:12). Malicious man does not halt his wickedness, which can have no issue except the catastrophe of the deluge*; for Yahweh must destroy sinful man. After the deluge Yahweh seems almost to accept the fact that "the bent of man's heart is evil from his youth" (Gn 8:21) and resolves not to punish man by another deluge. But it is no part of the author's intention to imply that Yahweh ceases to punish sin; it is his intention to show that Yahweh's punishments of sin are tempered by mercy and are less than one could expect.

The result of the sin of Gn 3 is the curse*, and this is the result of every sin. In Gn 3 the curse falls upon man in an unspoiled universe; the author reduces the discord between man and the universe to the sin which ruptured his community with God. The OT response to the mystery of evil is to absolve God from all blame. The first and dominant effect of sin is death (cf also Ezk 18:4); sin is the denial of life, and one can paraphrase the OT by saying that in its view the sinner dies a little each time he sins. The conception that sin brings curse and disaster is again so dominant in the OT that quotations are impossible. The wisdom* literature has many graphic descriptions of the disaster which overtakes the sinner; cf e.g., Jb 18:5–21. The "penitential psalms" (e.g., Ps 38; 51) exhibit the belief that the sinner experiences disaster until he repents and asks for deliverance. The historical books contain a number of passages which approach the tragic in their story of men who sin and by their sinful action release forces which ultimately destroy them: Abimelech* (Jgs 9), David* (2 S 12–20), Ahab* (1 K 21–22; 2 K 9–10). These narratives affirm clearly the freedom and responsibility of the individuals, while at the same time they show the inevitable consequences of actions which break down the morality of society. The theology of sin reaches its culmination in the prophets, who interpret the fall of Israel as the necessary consequence of national guilt. Amos asks whether there is evil in the city which Yahweh has not done (Am 3:6). For sin releases the most destructive force of all, the anger* of Yahweh. The OT explanation of the mystery of evil, if one can call it an explanation, is that there is no disaster or affliction in the personal or social life of man or in nature which is not to be attributed to the sin of man; no matter to what degree man suffers, it is no more than the just result of his deeds.

2. *Judaism.* In Judaism the consciousness of sin and guilt appears even heightened; the literature of Judaism was written after the terrifying judgment of the fall of the kingdoms of Israel and Judah. But between the literature of Judaism and the later books of the OT on the one hand and the early books of the OT on the other there is a difference. Judaism sought security in the law* and hence considers sin primarily an offense against the law, and the early view of sin as a personal offense against Yahweh is less prominent. In many circles of Pharisaic Judaism the malice of sin was perceived only obscurely. Since one was perfect by the observance of the law as interpreted by the Pharisees, all who did not maintain Pharisaic observance were sinners. The Gentiles were sinners by definition simply because they were not Jews. Actually this involved a frivolous view of sin which is the object of polemic in the NT.

On the devil as a cause of sin cf DEMON; SATAN. The connection of the devil with sin is late in the OT and appears in Judaism more prominently than it does in the NT. The appearance of the devil as a tempter does not affect the basic biblical belief that man is himself the responsible agent of his sin.

3. *NT.* The NT designates sin by the Gk words *hamartia* and *hamartēma*. In the NT these become theological terms; the Christian concept of sin does not appear in the classical Gk use of these words. The background of the NT idea of sin is the OT idea sketched above; this background is taken for granted and is not explicit. The NT adds new elements to the concept. These elements

can be summed up with Stählin under three heads: (1) sin as a single act; (2) sin as a state or condition, especially prominent in Paul and John; (3) sin as a power, also prominent in Paul and John. The novel element of the NT conception of sin is the presentation of Jesus as the conqueror of sin, which appears in almost every NT book and is most explicit in those writings where sin is discussed at greater length. The NT does not by this presentation diminish the biblical idea of the malice of sin; it rather emphasizes the magnitude and the truly divine character of the saving deed of Jesus. In the OT only God can deliver man from sin; in the NT God does deliver man.

I. *The Synoptic Gospels.* Some writers have said that there is no theology of sin in the Synoptic Gospels i.e., in the words of Jesus Himself; and it is remarkable that most occurrences of the word in the Synoptics deal with the forgiveness of sin. Jesus is the conqueror of sin, and it is this which makes Him the associate and friend of sinners whom He calls to repentance (Mt 9:10, 13; 11:19; Lk 7:34; 15:1–2; 19:7). The charge of the Pharisees that He consorted with sinners reflects the narrowness of Pharisaism. Jesus by these associations did not condone sin; He called to repentance and by His kindness made real to man the divine mercy and disposition to forgive. He could state the malice of sin; sins come from the heart and they alone defile a man (Mt 15:18–19; Mk 7:20–22). Sin was the wandering of the son from the house of his father (Lk 15:18, 21), and it can scarcely be denied that the attitude toward sin expressed in the parable of the prodigal son is one of the revolutionary ideas of the NT. The sinner need only ask forgiveness (Lk 18:13 ff). There is joy in heaven at the return of the sinner (Lk 15:7, 10).

II. *John.* The malice of sin is more explicit in the Johannine writings. Sin is lawlessness (1 Jn 3:4), it is unrighteousness (1 Jn 5:17). He who sins is from the devil (1 Jn 3:8) and is the slave of sin (Jn 8:34). Sin is the lust of the flesh, the lust of the eyes, and the pride of life (1 Jn 2:16). The sinner loves darkness* rather than the light* (Jn 3:19 f). The word is more common in Jn than in the Synoptics; and it more commonly signifies not the single act but a state or condition induced by the evil act. Like the guilt of the OT, the sin endures in the sinner. It is a peculiar feature of the Johannine conception that sin is often opposed to truth; as in the OT, the sin is a lie. The result of sin is death (1 Jn 5:16 f). This passage is the only one in the NT in which a distinction between deadly or mortal sins and sins which are not deadly is explicit.

This is not, it seems, the distinction between mortal and venial which has become traditional in Catholic theology. The deadly sin is a sin for which one need not pray; the author does not specify, but it is very probable that he means the sin of unbelief in one who has received the faith.

In Jn also Jesus is the conqueror of sin. Himself sinless (Jn 8:46; 1 Jn 3:5), He is the lamb* who takes away the sins of the world (Jn 1:29). He is the atoning sacrifice for the sins of the whole world (1 Jn 2:2; 4:10), He takes away our sins (1 Jn 3:5).

II. *Paul.* The fullest theology of sin in the NT appears in the writings of Paul, and practically this entire theology appears in the first part of Rm. The entire Gentile world is corrupted by sin; Paul does not excuse this corruption, since it comes from their refusal to recognize God, who in turn has abandoned them to their own unworthy desires (Rm 1:18–32). But Paul does not accept the Jewish division of the world into Jews and sinners. Possession of the law does not mean victory over sin, and observance of the law cannot establish righteousness*. The law can only make man aware of his sin. Both Jew and Greek are "under sin"; all men have sinned, and do not attain to the glory of God (Rm 2:1–3:31). In this first part of the discourse a number of new points appear. Paul treats sin not only as a state or condition, but as the human condition. Again without excusing any one — for sin is a deliberate act — he presents a world in which sin reigns without any hope being offered of escape; sin is a power. These elements are elaborated in Rm 5–8.

How sin became the human condition is the point of Rm 5:12–21. Paul traces the condition back to the sin narrated in Gn 3. When the first man sinned he sundered harmonious relations with God for the entire race. Paul argues this from the universality of death; it is OT belief that sin brings death, and Paul concludes from the fact that all men die that all men are sinners, even though they have not sinned personally. This is the Pauline doctrine of original sin, which, it must be noticed, goes beyond the beliefs implicit in Gn 3. This doctrine is intelligible only if one understands sin here in the Pauline conception of a state or condition or a power which is released. He does not mean and explicitly rejects the idea that men share in some way in the personal act of the ancestor; they do share in the condition which this act produced, a condition in which they are "enemies of God" (Rm 5:10). The belief likewise cannot be understood without reference to the biblical belief of solidarity and the representative personality (cf SERVANT OF THE LORD). This is a mysterious reality which Paul accepts rather than explains, but it is vital to his teaching; were it not for solidarity of the representative person with the society which he represents, it would be impossible for the deliverance to be as total as the curse. It is his point in this passage that the deliverance from sin effected by Jesus Christ reaches as far as the damage done by sin.

Since death is the effect of sin, Paul goes on to point out that sin is overcome by death: the death of Jesus Christ and the share of the Christian in the death of Christ. It is by dying with Christ to sin that the Christian escapes sin. Sin reigns, the sinner is a slave to sin; it is overcome by the reign of Christ and complete submission to Him (Rm 6:1–23). Through this death comes life. It is not only by death with Christ but by rising with Him that the Christian attains new life (1 Co 15:3, 17; Gal 1:4).

The seat of sin as a power is in the flesh*. Sin is a kind of pseudo-law, in opposition to the law of Moses. It enslaves man so that he is unable to do what is right even when he wishes. Man lacks the resources to deliver himself from this slavery; only Jesus Christ can liberate him (Rm 7:1–25). This teaching of Paul is the source of the theological teaching concerning concupiscence, a teaching which is among the most sharply discussed points of theology. Paul does not teach the inevitability of sin in a way which excuses man from responsibility; even if one were to concede that here, as elsewhere, he emphasizes a point of doctrine which can be qualified only by other parts of his writings, the qualifications can be found. Paul is aware of the powerful impulses in nature which move men to wrongdoing. Sin is not indeed inevitable if man can resist it; Paul does not affirm failure so much as he affirms perpetual conflict between the law of reason and the law of the flesh. In this conflict man need not be defeated, but neither can he achieve victory except through Jesus Christ. Christ has freed us from this pseudo-law by His death, by dwelling in our hearts, by His spirit taking possession of us (Rm 8:1–17). Hence in Paul more than in any NT book does Jesus appear as the conqueror of sin.

The NT writings also speak of the nature and malice of sin in other contexts. For Paul what is not from faith* as a principle of action is sin (Rm 14:23). Js 1:14 f contains a picturesque description of temptation in which the author affirms the responsibility of the sinner; one is tempted by one's own desire, and it is one's own desire that brings forth sin; sin in turn brings forth death. The same epistle (4:17) observes that to know what is right and not to do it is sin.

Sin offering. Cf SACRIFICE.

Sin (Hb *sîn,* meaning uncertain), a geographical name. 1. A frontier city of Egypt, most probably the ancient Pelusium on the E frontier (Ezk 30:15 f). In Ezk 30:16 many critics read Syene* instead of Sin.

2. The desert of Sin, between Elim and Sinai* (Ex 16:1; 17:1; Nm 33:11 f). These passages all come from the late P source. Modern geographers locate the desert of Sin in the region of Debbet er Ramleh, in the Sinai peninsula S of Jebel et Tih. Cf SINAI.

Sinai (Hb *sînaî,* meaning and etymology uncertain), the name given to a mountain and a desert, in the present Pnt* the scene of the theophany to Israel and the revelations of Moses, the giving of the covenant, and of the events in the exodus* from Ex 19:1 to Nm 10:11. The name Sinai occurs rarely in the J source (cf PENTATEUCH; Ex 19:20, 23; 34:2, 4); most occurrences of the name appear in the P source, and in the E and D sources the name of the mountain of revelation and covenant is Horeb*. This has led several modern critics to suspect that the J account of the theophany had no local name attached to it, and that Sinai has been inserted in Ex 19 and 34 by a redactor; this hypothesis is rejected by many scholars, and no definitive judgment can be given. The occurrences of the name outside the Pnt are rare. In Jgs 5:5, an early poem, Yahweh is called "He of Sinai" (now regarded as a more probable translation than the usual "this is Sinai"), and this indicates an early connection of Yahweh with Sinai. The poem is not equally informative on the location of Sinai; Yahweh comes from Seir* and Edom* in Jgs 5:4, and if no other information were available it would be concluded that Sinai is located in the territory of Edom. Dt 33:2, a less ancient poem, probably from the period of the monarchy, mentions Sinai as the point from which Yahweh appears, and associates it with Seir, Paran*, and Meribath-Kadesh*. Other allusions are based on the traditions of the Pnt (Ne 9:13; Ps 68:9; BS 48:7; AA 7:30); and the location of Sinai in Arabia*, a vague geographical term (Gal 4:24 f), strengthens the suspicion that even in the earliest period of the settlement in Palestine the exact geographical location of Sinai (also called Horeb) was not known by the Israelites; it lay to the S, and nothing further could be asserted.

The traditional location of Sinai places it in the peninsula of Sinai, which is a triangular piece of land about 260 mi N-S and about 150 mi wide at the N, lying between the Gulf of Suez and the Gulf of

The mountains of the Sinai peninsula.

Aqaba. A belt of sand about 15 mi wide stretches across the N; a rocky plateau then rises through a distance of 150 mi through the N and central part of the peninsula to the granite mountain chain of the S. The entire peninsula is extremely arid desert; outside of a few oases there is practically no vegetation, and communications are difficult. The mountain chain rises to 8000 ft at its highest; Jebel Musa ("mountain of Moses"), the traditional scene of the events of Ex-Nm, is about 7500 ft high. The desert of Sinai is usually identified with the plain er-Raha, which lies at the foot of Ras es-Safsafeh near Jebel Musa. The steep and bare red granite peaks in the vast desert form indeed an awesome scene of stark grandeur, and the identification is attractive to the imagination; but it cannot be regarded as certainly established. There is no evidence that the identification is earlier than the 4th century AD, and it is noticed above that it is doubtful that the exact location was known during the period of the Hb monarchy. There are reasons for questioning the identification, although these are not peremptory. The Egyptians exploited copper and turquoise mines in the mountains of the S from predynastic times to the 20th dynasty, and archaeological exploration suggests that the peninsula, which now supports about 10,000 scattered nomads in dire poverty, had settlements in the 2nd millennium BC. It seems unlikely that the Israelites would have headed for an area which was under Egyptian military control. Furthermore, many scholars think a volcano is indicated by the phenomena of Ex 19:16–19, and there are no volcanoes active or extinct in the mountains of Sinai. For these reasons some scholars locate Sinai in NW Arabia, E of the Gulf of Aqaba, where there are extinct volcanoes. Others, believing the volcanic phenomena can be understood as the description of a mountain storm or as additions of popular tradition, identify Sinai with Kadesh* or place it in the N part of the Sinai peninsula. Still others believe that the traditional location is as good as any other suggested; they point out that the Egyptian activity in the peninsula varied in location and in intensity. Because of the rarity of the name in the J traditions, some suggest that it is not possible to identify the group which had the Sinai experience, and that it is possible that the presence of Moses and the covenant at Sinai comes from a fusion of several traditions.

The alphabetic inscriptions of Sinai are among the earliest examples of alphabetic writing; cf ALPHABET. An Egyptian inscription of 1840–1790 BC speaks with feeling of the heat of the mining region.

Sinites. A geographical or tribal name. **1.** Hb *sînî*, one of the sons of Canaan* (Gn 10:17; 1 Ch 1:15); they are to be located in the traditional Canaanite territory, probably in the N, but more definite location is impossible. **2.** Hb *sînîm*, "the land of the Sinites" (Is 49:12); most modern cities read s^ewēnîm here; cf SYENE.

Sirach. Cf BEN SIRA.

Sirion. Another name of Mt Hermon*.

Sisera (Hb sîs^erā', probably a Hittite name; etymology uncertain), in Jgs 4 the commander of the armies of Jabin* king of Hazor*, but in Jgs 5 Jabin is not mentioned and Sisera appears to be a Canaanite king, which is probably more faithful to historical reality. Sisera was defeated by the Israelites led by Barak* and Deborah* and assassinated by Jael* when he sought refuge in her tent.

Sitnah (Hb sitnāh, "hostility"?), the name of a well dug by Isaac* (Gn 26:21).

Siwan (Hb siwan, an Akkadian loan word), the 3rd month of the Hb calendar (May-June).

Slave, slavery. The Sumerian word for slave means lit "foreigner"; this etymology does not appear in the other languages of the ancient Near East, but the Sumerian word suggests that the chief source of slaves in earliest times and through most of ancient history was prisoners of war. The Assyrian records often contain exact enumerations of the prisoners taken; they were the most valuable form of booty. A number of allusions show that brigandage and piracy were also sources of supply for slaves. A few prophetic passages allude to slave dealing by Phoenicians, Philistines, and Greeks (Ezk 27:13; Jl 3:6; Am 1:6, 9). Kidnapping was punished by death in the code of Hammurabi (# 14, ANET 166) and in Hb law (Ex 21:16; Dt 24:7). Slaves were most frequently acquired by the individual owner by purchase; a number of sale contracts are preserved from Mesopotamia (ANET 221). Hammurabi provides that the sale is void if the slave contracts epilepsy within 30 days of the sale (# 278, ANET 177), and that the purchaser is liable to any claim which lies against the slave (# 279, ibid). If a native Babylonian slave purchased abroad should be proved to belong to a Babylonian owner, the slave must be restored at the buyer's loss (# 280, ibid); but if the slave is a foreigner, the claimant must reimburse the buyer the price which he paid for the slave (# 281, ibid). These are instances of the principle of distinction between native and foreign slaves which was common in most ancient peoples. Lv 25:35 ff forbids the enslavement of Hebrews by Hebrews, but permits the enslavement of foreigners. Ex-

posure of unwanted infants, usually girls, was also a source of slaves. The sale could be a voluntary self-sale; contracts of Nuzu exhibit these transactions (ANET 220), which possibly have a background unknown to us. A father could sell his children into slavery; the sale was often masked under a formula of adoption. The self-sale, voluntary or involuntary, was a means of meeting insolvency; this is probably the type of slavery mentioned in Ex 21:1-6; Dt 15:12 ff, and it is explicitly called slavery for debt in Lv 25:35 ff. Hb law of Ex 21:1 ff; Dt 15:12 ff prescribes a six-year limit of slavery for debt, after which the slave has the option of his liberty or the voluntary acceptance of perpetual slavery. In Lv 25:35 ff the limit is the next year of jubilee*. Hammurabi, on the contrary (# 117, ANET 170-171), has a three-year limit of slavery for debt. Natural increase was another source of slavery; male and female slaves were mated.

The slave was legally a chattel with no human rights. Male and female slaves were mated, not married, and their children were the property of the owner. Even in Hb law the wife and children of the slave remained with the owner after the slave was freed if the wife had been given him by the owner; they shared his freedom only if he had them before enslavement (Ex 21:3 f). Ancient documents speak of the mark of the slave without describing it; Hammurabi (# 227, ANET 176) prescribes death for the removal of the mark from the slave of another, so the mark does not seem to have been a brand or other permanent disfigurement. Scholars suggest a tag or a tattoo; permanent marks may have been made on runaways, especially if they repeated the attempt. The laws always distinguish between violence done to slaves and to freemen; death or injury to a slave is penalized by damages to be paid to his owner: (Hammurabi [# 199, 213, 214, ANET 175], the Hittite laws [ANET 189-190], Ex 21:32). Hb law, however, punishes the man who kills his slave if the slave dies instantly, but not if the slave survives the blow for a day or two (Ex 21:20 f), and frees the slave who is seriously injured by his owner (Ex 21:26 f). In Greece and possibly among other peoples also the evidence of a slave was not valid in law unless it was taken under torture; the slave was not capable of the oath of a freeman. Slavery was the punishment of a thief who could not restore stolen goods (Ex 22:3).

The position of the female slave was always different from that of the male slave; any female slave could be employed for the pleasure of her master, and if she were acquired precisely for this purpose certain laws governed the relationship. The concubine did not enjoy the privilege of release after 6 years; but she could not be sold, and retained her rights to food, clothing, and sexual commerce if her owner married another woman; if he deprived her of these rights she was freed. If a man acquired a concubine for his son she was to be treated as a daughter (Ex 21:7–11). If a man acquired a concubine from the prisoners of war, he must either marry her or free her, and she was not to be sold or mistreated (Dt 21:10–14). We have several instances of a concubine furnished to the husband by the wife, who owned the slave, a practice which is regulated by law at Nuzu* (Gn 16:1 ff; 30:3, 9); a slave so given could not be sold. If a man recognized the children of the slave as his own, they shared equally in the inheritance with the children of the free wife; if he did not recognize them, the mother and the children were freed (Hammurabi [# 173, ANET 170–171]).

A slave could marry a free woman (1 Ch 2:35, Nuzu). The children of such a union did not belong to the owner of the slave (Hammurabi [# 175, ANET 174]). If the slave died, the owner and the widow divided his goods equally (Hammurabi [# 176, ibid]). In Mesopotamia and probably elsewhere a slave could acquire a peculium; he could invest this or purchase his freedom with it, and contracts of investment by slaves are preserved. Ziba* seems to be a slave who owns slaves (2 S 9:10). Hammurabi # 176 (cf above) supposes that a slave can have an estate; this is seen also in the Hittite laws, which assess a slave for damages (ANET 193–194).

Fugitive slaves were punished severely, but less severely than those who assisted them; the death penalty is rare in law for slaves, whose death was a loss to their owner. For denying ownership the slave loses an ear (Hammurabi [# 282, ANET 177]). Even for striking a freeman the Mesopotamian slave was punished by the loss of an ear (Hammurabi [# 205, ANET 175]). Hammurabi prescribes death for helping or harboring a runaway slave, and prescribes a reward of 2 shekels of silver for the return of a fugitive (# 15–20, ANET 166–167); the Hittite laws also grant a reward for the return of a fugitive (ANET 190). The early code of Lipit-ishtar is milder, demanding only the return of the slave or the payment of 15 shekels of silver. Dt 23:16 is unique in the ancient Near East in forbidding the return of a fugitive slave, and it represents later Hb law. The OT alludes to several runaways (Gn 16:6; 1 S 25:10; 1 K 2:39). Besides slaves held by private owners there were state slaves, i.e., slaves of the king (cf

below) and temple slaves, acquired by donations and private dedications. These were found also in Israel; they were called nᵉtînîm ("given," "dedicated"). While they are mentioned only in 1 Ch, Ezr, and Ne in the postexilic community, the institution is ascribed to David and almost certainly goes back to the monarchy. The institution is also attributed to Joshua in the story of the Gibeonites (Jos 9:23, 27). This can scarcely be entirely historical, since the Gibeonites do not appear elsewhere as temple slaves, but it attests the antiquity of temple slavery in Israel. The excavations of Nelson Glueck at Ezion-geber* disclosed mining and smelting operations of Solomon which scholars believe were done under such intolerable conditions that slave labor must have been employed. 1 K 9:21 relates that Solomon raised a slave labor force from the Canaanites within his kingdom.

The number of slaves in the general population of the ancient world is difficult to estimate; scholars think that there were never many in Mesopotamia or in Israel. In the postexilic community of Jerusalem, which perhaps was not typical, slaves were ⅙ of the total population (Ne 7:67). In Greece, on the other hand, where 400,000 slaves were counted in Attica in 309 BC, slaves accounted for more than half the total population; it is thought that a similar proportion was found in Rome under the empire. The price of slaves is also difficult to estimate in terms of real value; the 30 shekels of silver which are damages for a slave gored by an ox (Ex 21:32) seems high. I. Mendelssohn calculates that the price of a slave was equivalent to 3–5 years pay of hired labor; since the slave had to be supported, hired labor was actually cheaper. Slave labor does not seem to have been an economically sound investment; both in Mesopotamia and in Rome slave labor in agriculture was more expensive to the owner than, tenant farming, and there seem also to have been few slaves at any period engaged in the skilled crafts. In general slaves were employed in domestic service, which meant that most of them were a luxury of the rich; the ordinary owner may have had a slave or a family of slaves to help him in his work.

While the slave was legally a chattel, human solidarity broke through the law. There is no protest against the institution as such in all ancient literature of the Near East except Jb 31:15, which appeals to common humanity. BS 33:24–31, written in the 3rd century BC, is a paradoxical combination of recommendations of severe punishment and hard work for slaves joined to counsel to treat the slave like oneself and a brother; the passage no doubt reflects the tension in the soul of many a devout and kindly slave owner. The houseborn slave was in a different position socially if not legally from the purchased slave. He was a member of the family; he was given charge of large houses and estates (Gn 24:2; Mt 24:45 f), was entrusted with responsible missions even on intimate family affairs (Gn 24), enjoyed easy and familiar relations and gave advice which was respected (Jgs 19:11; 1 S 9:5–10; 25: 14–17; 2 K 5:2–3), ate with his owner as a guest of another (1 S 9:22), and could inherit the entire estate of an owner who died without a male heir (Gn 15:2; Pr 17:2). Dt often recommends that the Israelites remember that they were themselves slaves in Egypt and that they should deal with their slaves humanely (Dt 5:15; 15:15; 16:12; 24:18, 22). The slaves of Israelites, at least if they were houseborn, were members of the Israelite religious community, enjoying the Sabbath rest (Ex 20:10; 23:12), receiving circumcision* (Gn 17:12 f, 23, 27), and partaking in the major festivals (Ex 12:44; Dt 12:12, 18; 16:11, 14).

The term "slave" is used metaphorically. In polite address the inferior speaks of himself to the superior as a slave (Gn 32:18; 43:28; Nm 32:25; Rt 3:9; 1 S 25:41 +). The vassal king uses the same language to his overlord (2 K 16:7). The "slaves of the king" usually do not designate the state slaves mentioned above, but rather his household and his retinue; it is difficult to say whether these were really slaves or not (Gn 40:20; 41:10; 1 S 16:17; 18:22; 19:1; 21:8; 28:27; 2 S 11:13; 1 K 1:47; Pr 14:35 +). "The slave of the king" (2 K 22:12; 2 Ch 24:20) is very probably a high ranking cabinet officer; this title has been found on a Hb seal* from the time of Jeroboam II. Possibly "the slave of the high priest" (Mt 26:51; Mk 14:47; Lk 22:50) is also a high ranking officer of the temple. It is this usage, it seems, and not the literal sense, which lies behind the religious use of the term in the OT. The worshipers of Yahweh are His slaves (often), and the prophets are the slaves of Yahweh in a special sense (Je 25:4; Am 3:7; cf SERVANT OF THE LORD).

Allusions to slavery in the Gospels are casual and describe the inferior position of slaves (Mt 10:24 f; Lk 17:7–10; Jn 8:35) and their services (Lk 12:35–40). Jesus demands that one who would be first among His disciples should be the slave of all; from this passage (Mt 20:27; Mk 10:44) comes the designation of the Roman Pontiff as "slave of the slaves of God." The religious use of the term is not common in the NT. The apostles are called slaves of the Lord, echoing the use of slave to signify a royal officer (AA 4:29; 16:17; Gal 1:10); the title,

"slave of God" (Js 1:1; Tt 1:1) or "slave of Jesus Christ" (Rm 1:1; Phl 1:1; Jd 1) is used in the titles of some of the epistles. Man can be a slave to sin (Jn 8:34; Rm 6:17, 20) or to righteousness (Rm 6:18) or to God (Rm 6:22). But the conception of man's relation to God as slavery does not fit well the NT revelation of adoption* and is not characteristic. Paul contrasts the sonship of the Christian with the condition of the slave (Gal 4:1 ff), and Jesus says the disciples are no longer slaves but friends (Jn 15:15). Jesus is said to assume the form of a slave in the incarnation (Phl 2:7), which is synonymous with "the likeness of a man" in the same verse; man is an adopted son by grace, but a slave of God by nature.

It has often been a source of wonder and even of scandal that the NT seems to take a neutral attitude toward slavery, accepting it as a social fact. The epistles contain recommendations to slaves to be obedient and to masters to be kindly (Eph 6:5–9; Col 3:22–4:1; 1 Tm 6:1 f; 1 Pt 2:18). Phm is a warm recommendation to an owner to receive a runaway with kindness not as a slave but as a brother — a strong hint, it appears, that Paul thinks he should be manumitted. Those who are dissatisfied with this neutrality fail to observe the true character of Christian social reform, which is very well illustrated in slavery. The NT does not attack the institution directly, but attacks the principle of inequality on which chattel slavery was based. The slave need not seek liberty, for he is a freedman of the Lord as the owner is a slave of the Lord (1 Co 7:21–23). There is no distinction between slave and free in Christ Jesus; all are baptized in one spirit to form one body (1 Co 12:13; Gal 3:28; Col 3:11). The principles of Christian love* and unity made it impossible for the Christian to regard another man as a chattel, and thus made slavery impracticable. Historically Christianity has been the only effective destroyer of slavery.

Sling. The use of the sling as a weapon is extremely ancient, and there was no change in its technique from the earliest period to Roman times. It consisted of a hollow pocket of leather or other fabric to which were attached two cords about 12–18 in long. The missile was whirled about with the hand and projected by the release of one of the cords from the grasp. Many ancient sources attest the accuracy of the skilled slinger, and stories such as those of the slingers of Benjamin (Jgs 20:16) and of David's killing of Goliath* (1 S 17:40, 49) are not exaggerated. Slingers were part of the regular military complement (Jgs 20:16; 1 K 3:25; 1 Ch 12:2; 2 Ch 26:14). The ambidextrous

Assyrian slingers.

slinger was particularly esteemed (Jgs 20:16; 1 Ch 12:2). The slinger did not depend as did David on finding his missiles by chance; the rounded stones, 2–3 in. in diameter, found in abundance in Palestinian sites, are evidently shaped and polished. In Greek and Roman times the slingstone in war was replaced by a smaller lead pellet which was more deadly. A slinger is represented among the defenders of Lachish (ANEP 373).

Smith. In Hb folklore the smith's craft was invented by Tubal-cain* (Gn 4:22), and it is probable that this hero was the eponymous ancestor of the Kenites*, who in the opinion of many scholars were nomad tinkers of the type who still pursue the trade in the desert. Early Israel certainly lacked the skill to work iron* and the Philistines held the monopoly for a time (1 S 13:19–22). Solomon employed a smith from Tyre for the bronze work of the temple* (1 K 7:14). The Israelites acquired the skill under the monarchy and there are several allusions to the craft (1 K 6:7; 2 Ch 24:12; Is 41:7; 44:12; Je 6:29; 23:29). Smiths were included among the skilled artisans deported from Jerusalem by Nebuchadnezzar (2 K 24:14). BS 38:28 describes the work of the smith and notes that it makes him unfit for wisdom.

Smyrna (Gk *smyrna*, meaning uncertain), a city of Asia Minor, the seat of one of the seven churches of Apc (1:11; 2:8). The site is occupied by the modern Izmir, the largest city of Asia Minor. It lies at the head of the gulf into which the river Hermus empties. "Old Smyrna" lay at the NE corner of the gulf; the date of its foundation is unknown. The city was captured by Alyattes of Lydia in 627 BC and for the next 300 years a

village occupied the site. A new foundation was established after Alexander's conquest of Sardis at the present site of the city around the base of Mt Pagus. In Roman times the city was renowned for its wealth, its buildings, and as a center of science and medicine. In commercial and political importance it yielded to Ephesus*. The date and the founder of its Christian community are unknown.

Snow. Snow is rare in Palestine. In the central mountains flurries of snow, which melt almost immediately, may occur every winter; a heavy fall may occur every 5 to 10 years, and the roads are blocked perhaps every 30 years. In the plateau of E Palestine with its lower temperatures snow is much more common. In the higher mountains of the Lebanon* and the Anti-Lebanon* snow falls and remains during the entire winter; Mt Hermon* retains some snow all year, and these snows are the source of the Jordan. The snows of Lebanon feed the rivers of the country.

Snow is mentioned most frequently in the Bible in poetic books and in metaphorical language. "White as snow" is a commonplace: forgiveness of sins (Ps 51:9; Is 1:18), garments (Mt 28:3; Apc 1:14), complexion (Lam 4:7), leprosy* (Ex 4:6; Nm 12:10; 2 K 5:27). The perennial snows of Hermon are compared to deeply ingrained habits (Je 18:14). Honor to a fool is like snow in the summer (Pr 26:1). The water of a snow-fed mountain stream is a refreshing drink (Pr 25:13). Job knows snow-fed streams (6:16; 24:19). Snow is sent at the command of Yahweh to water the earth (Pss 147:16; 148:8; Jb 37:6; Is 55:10); it is kept in storehouses until its use (Jb 38:22). One who has warm garments does not fear snow (Pr 31:21). Actual snowfall is mentioned rarely (2 S 23:20; 1 Ch 11:22). An unusually heavy snow prevented Tryphon* from moving his army (1 Mc 13:22).

So. (Hb *sô*), a king of Egypt with whom Hoshea* of Israel conspired to rebel against Assyria (2 K 17:4). Most scholars believe the name should be vocalized *sewe'* and identify him with Sib'e, the commander (Akkadian *turtan*) of Egypt mentioned by Sargon* as an ally of Hanno of Gaza*, defeated by the Assyrians shortly after the fall of Samaria. The inexact "king" of 2 K 17:4 reflects the unsettled condition of Egypt at the time; the country was divided among several small Delta states, one of which no doubt was the kingdom to which Sib'e owed allegiance.

Soap. Soap or some cleansing agent is mentioned for clothing in Mal 3:2, possibly in

Jn 9:30, and for the person in Jn 2:22, perhaps in exaggeration. That such agents were used may be assumed; they were probably composed by the mixture of ashes or some similar gritty particles with a fatty substance. Natron, a natural carbonate of soda found in the Near East, was used as a cleansing agent.

Socoh (Hb *sôkōh,* meaning unknown), the name of three towns. **1.** The modern Khirbet Shuweikeh in the Wadi es Sant (cf SHEPHELAH) E of Azekah*; a city of Judah (Jos 15:35): the site of the Philistine camp when David fought Goliath (1 S 17:1); fortified by Rehoboam (2 Ch 11:7); raided by the Philistines in the time of Ahaz (2 Ch 28:18). **2.** The modern Khirbet Shuweikeh SSW of Hebron; a city of Judah in the hill country (Jos 15:48); associated with the clan of Heber, called its "father" (1 Ch 4:18). **3.** The modern Tell er Ras, WNW of Samaria, or Shuweikeh N of Tulkarm; in Solomon's 3rd district (1 K 4:10).

Sodom (Hb *sᵉdōm,* meaning and etymology uncertain), a city in the neighborhood of the Dead Sea*. It is usually mentioned with Gomorrah and was one of five cities of the region (Sodom, Gomorrah, Admah, Zeboim, Zoar). The area was chosen by Lot as his home when he separated from Abraham and was as fair as the garden of Yahweh (Gn 13:10–13). The king of Sodom was one of the kings rescued by Abraham (Gn 14:2 ff). After Abraham entertained Yahweh and His two companions, the investigation of the wickedness of Sodom is announced; Abraham pleads with Yahweh to spare the city for the sake of even a few righteous men who might be found there, and Yahweh promises to do this (Gn 18: 20–33). When the two messengers of Yahweh are received as guests by Lot, the men of Sodom attempt to assault them; from this episode the unnatural vice. of sodomy is named. Lot and his family are then warned to leave the city, and the towns are destroyed by a rain of fire and sulphur from the heavens (Gn 19:24), and the next day smoke rose from the land like smoke from a kiln (Gn 19:28). The story of Sodom and Gomorrah was deeply imbedded in Israelite tradition; it becomes a proverbial example of the anger and judgment of Yahweh (Dt 29:22 f; WS 10:6; Is 1:9; Je 20:16; 49:18; 50:40; Lam 4:6; Am 4:11; Zp 2:9; Lk 17:29; 2 Pt 2:6; Jd 7). The wickedness of Sodom is also proverbial as the extreme of depravity (Dt 32:32; Is 1:10; Je 23:14; Ezk 16:46–56; Mt 10:15; 11:23 f; Lk 10:12; Apc 11:8).

The story presents some problems in liter-

ary and historical criticism. It is often supposed that the site of the cities is now covered by the S bay of the Dead Sea S of the peninsula el Lisan (cf SIDDIM); but the narrative never suggests that the cities were covered by the sea. The description of the area as "fair like the garden of Yahweh" is entirely unfit for the Dead Sea region in its present state; and while exploration has indicated that the Jordan valley was more thickly settled in prehistoric times than it has been since, it seems doubtful that this was ever true of the shores of the Dead Sea. The possibility must be accepted that there is no indication where the cities were located.

The story appears to be somewhat violently joined to the story of Abraham. It is difficult to establish with certainty that Abraham was a contemporary of the disaster. The story is filled with obvious folklore traits which indicate that it is constructed from fragmentary memories. It is now a theological narrative; the disaster is explained as a judgment of God on the sins of the cities. Yahweh does indeed spare sinful men in order not to destroy the righteous mingled with the wicked; but there are no righteous in Sodom save Lot and his family, and they are taken out of the city before the disaster. The reasoning concerning such strokes of God's anger is similar to the reasoning in the story of the deluge*.

On the assumption that the cities lay in the traditional location, some modern scholars have sought an explanation of the story in the geology of the area. The region lies on the fault of the Jordan valley, which is subject to earthquakes*. Bituminous and petroleum deposits have been found in the region of the Dead Sea, and some ancient writers attest the presence of gases. It is supposed that an earthquake released combustible materials and gases, which when ignited could cause a terrible destruction of the kind related in Gn 19.

Solomon (Hb *šᵉlōmōh;* meaning not entirely clear, but derived from *šālôm,* "peace," "prosperity"), son and successor of David* as king of Israel. Solomon was probably a throne name taken at accession; at birth the name Jedidiah* was given him (2 S 12: 25). The dates of Solomon's reign are about 961–922 BC; these are not established by contemporary records but are estimated by calculating back from fixed dates in later periods.

The story of Solomon's accession is the final portion of the court history of David (1 K 1–2). Solomon, born of Bathsheba* at Jerusalem (2 S 5:14; 12:24 f; 1 Ch 3:5; 14:4), was younger than several of his brothers, but was the son of David's favorite wife. Evidently no principle of succession by primogeniture or by anything else had yet been established, and the eldest surviving son, Adonijah*, assisted by Joab* and Abiathar*, assumed that he would succeed. The candidacy of Solomon was supported by his mother, Nathan*, and Benaiah*, now a more powerful military commander than Joab. Whether anything deeper than personal differences divided these factions is hard to say. It is also hard to say that the promise to which Bathsheba alluded (1 K 1:13, 17) had ever been delivered. It is clear that Nathan and Bathsheba feared the same fate which overtook the partisans of Adonijah. David had Solomon proclaimed coregent and thus abruptly arrested the claims of Adonijah. Solomon appears inactive in these affairs; but he showed himself active enough after his accession by exterminating Joab and Adonijah, not without pretext, and by exiling Abiathar and deposing him from the priesthood. Included in the killings was Shimei* of Benjamin, who as far as is known had no part in the question of the succession. Some historians have been skeptical about the testament of David (1 K 2:2–9) in which the killing of Joab and Shimei is recommended, believing it to be a propaganda document justifying Solomon's acts. The statement, however, is altogether in accord with Hb thought patterns and the events of David's life, and it is not out of character with David.

Solomon's long reign was a period of peace, with a few possible interruptions which were not of great proportions and may have been passed over lightly in the text (cf below), of growth in wealth and prosperity, foreign trade, and building. On his greatest building projects cf PALACE; TEMPLE. On his mining and smelting operations, not mentioned in the Bible, cf EZION-GEBER. On his foreign trade with Red Sea countries cf OPHIR; SHEBA. Solomon's chariot cities and store cities (1 K 9:19; 2 Ch 8:6) were intended for administrative purposes and for control of his own subjects. To him is credited the introduction of the chariot as a military weapon (1 K 4:26; 10:26); when David captured chariots, the lack of skilled operators and the rough terrain of the country made them useless, and he destroyed the chariots and hamstrung the horses (2 S 8:4). Megiddo* is the best preserved example of a chariot and store city, and the stalls for 450 horses show that the figures of 1400 chariots and 12,000 horsemen (1 K 10:26) are scarcely exaggerated. Solomon neither bred horses nor manufactured chariots; he had a controlling position as middleman in the trade of horses from Kue

(Cilicia*) and chariots from Egypt (1 K 10:28 f).

Solomon's great building program was impossible without heavy taxes, and in the ancient world the most common tax upon the general population was forced labor. There is no doubt that foreign trade, of which the king held a monopoly, brought in extensive revenue, but not enough to support either the building program or the lavish style of living of the court (1 K 4:22 f). Forced labor was an institution accepted in Egypt and Mesopotamia but foreign to Hb customs and traditions, and it was deeply resented by the Israelites (cf JEROBOAM; REHOBOAM). It had already been introduced by David (2 S 20:24). The traditions are somewhat at variance on this question; 1 K 5:27 says that Solomon imposed forced labor on all Israel; 1 K 9:20–22 limits the forced labor to the Canaanites (2 Ch 8:7–9). The petition of the Israelites at the accession of Rehoboam (1 K 12:4) indicates that 1 K 5:27 is accurate, and that the other passages are an interpretation intended to remove this odious trait from Solomon. One should very probably distinguish between the forced labor of the Israelites and the Canaanites; it appears that Solomon enslaved many of the Canaanite population as royal slaves*.

In order to administer the collection of revenues and the draft of forced labor Solomon reorganized the kingdom into 12 districts. The list of the districts (1 K 4:7–19) covers the territory outside of Judah, and hence it is not clear that the number 12 is intended to correspond to the 12 tribes; according to 4:7 they correspond to the 12 months of the year, each district being responsible for the provision of the royal household for one month. What may have been included in the expenses of "the king's house" is not stated. The document from which the list is compiled had suffered a tear on the right hand side at the beginning, and the names of the first four officers are lost; only their patronymics are preserved. The list should be read "X son of Hur" etc. The 12 districts do not follow the old tribal lines, and most historians assume that this was deliberate; Solomon intended to weaken the old tribal ties and loyalties and attach the subjects to the king. The project was probably successful as far as dissolving the tribes was concerned, but it did not attach the people to the throne. The absence of Judah from the list is interpreted by many to mean that Judah, as the king's own tribe, was exempt from this taxation. G. E. Wright and F. M. Cross have proposed with more probability that Judah had already been organized into administrative districts by David. This, they believe, was the purpose of the census of David (2 S 24), and they believe that this organization may explain why the men of Judah followed the revolt of Absalom with such enthusiasm. Solomon's districts were apparently retained by the kings of Israel after the schism. The districts can be located as follows: (1) the highlands of Ephraim, including Ephraim and part of Manasseh. (2) The former territory of Dan in the Shephelah. (3) Difficult to define, but included most of the territory of Manasseh. (4) The N coastal plain and Mt Carmel. (5) The territory of Manasseh S of the plain of Esdraelon, including Megiddo and Beth-shan. (6) In E Palestine, the territory of Machir, Bashan, and Argob. (7) The N portion of Gilead. (8) Naphtali and the N territory of Dan. (9) Asher and Zebulun. (10) Issachar, the plain of Esdraelon and S Galilee. (11) Benjamin. (12) The S portion of Gilead. From our knowledge it seems that these districts were quite unequal in population and resources, and an equal distribution of responsibility would have worked a great hardship on some districts.

Solomon retained close diplomatic relations with Egypt* and Tyre* (cf HIRAM). His marriage to an Egyptian princess shows both the height to which Israel had risen and the weakness to which Egypt had fallen; in the period of the Egyptian empire of the 18th dynasty the request of the greatest power for marriage to an Egyptian princess was an impertinence. The princess was treated with greater dignity than any other member of the harem, and the city of Gezer* was captured by the Pharaoh and presented to Solomon as her dowry* (1 K 3:1; 7:8; 9:16, 24). Tyre was the principal agent in Solomon's sea trade and in his building.

The wealth of Solomon was proverbial (Mt 6:29; Lk 12:27), and tradition preserved glowing pictures of the kingdom during his reign (1 K 4:20 f, 25; 9:10–14; 10:14–1, 27). The historian finds it necessary to add some reservations. The wealth attributed to Solomon and his court did not permit much to slip down into the general population. This must be considered as a factor in the rebellion of Jeroboam. The existence of a small class of extremely wealthy people and the grinding poverty of the majority, mentioned so often by the prophets, should be attributed to the reign of Solomon for its origin. The delivery of 20 towns of Galilee to Hiram of Tyre (1 K 9:10–14) indicates that Solomon had badly overextended himself.

The Deuteronomic compiler has grouped the sins of Solomon and the reverses which he suffered at the end of his story (1 K 11). Actually his marriages to foreign wives and his patronage of their cult must have occurred throughout his reign. As late as the reign of Josiah* the high places attributed to Solomon were still in existence (2 K 23:13). The somewhat astonishing harem of Solomon, 700 wives and 300 concubines (1 K 11:4), is no doubt exaggerated by popular tradition, but it is a clue to the life of the grand monarch. His reputation as a lover is alluded to in SS*. The reverses of Solomon likewise belong to some extent in the early part of his reign. Hadad*, a prince of Edom, was subsidized by the Pharaoh to make trouble for Solomon; we must see here a change of dynasty in Egypt after Solomon's marriage to the Pharaoh's daughter. To what extent Hadad succeeded is doubtful, since there was no interference with Solomon's mining and commercial operations at Ezion-geber (1 K 11:14–22). More serious was the independent kingdom which the brigand Rezon* established at Damascus* (1 K 11:23–25); this kingdom was later a threat to the kingdom of Israel. There was also an abortive rebellion in Israel itself led by Jeroboam* with the support of some of the prophets (1 K 11:26–40); no details are given and the seriousness of the episode cannot be determined. The treatment of the Deuteronomic historian can be compared with the treatment of the Chronicler (1 Ch 28–2 Ch 9), who omits the story of the succession and replaces it with an orderly commission of David, omits the districts, and has no allusion to Solomon's sins and reverses.

Solomon was in tradition the father of Israelite wisdom* and wisdom literature (1 K 3:1–28; 4:29–34; 10:23 f; Pr 1:10; 10:1; 25:1). At the base of these allusions modern historians see a great literary movement in the reign of Solomon, probably begun under David (cf SCRIBE). In this movement should be placed the Yahwist history of early Israel (cf PENTATEUCH) and other collections of material from the period of the settlement and the judges*, most of which was preserved orally and was first written under the monarchy. Literature here as in other periods of history came as an expression of a new national consciousness and an awareness that the people is a historical factor. The keeping of annals and chronicles is a part of the same movement. The unification of the tribes under the monarchy made it highly desirable, if the consciousness of a single Israel under one king was to arise, to collate and to fuse the various tribal traditions. In this literary movement one should also include the collection in writing of Israelite wisdom.

Modern historians are generally adverse rather than favorable in their judgment of Solomon. He inherited a strong kingdom from David and maintained it; but its collapse after his death leads to suspicions that it was not well maintained. The increase in Israel's wealth was matched by an increase in extravagance, and the benefits of David's conquests and Solomon's trade were not diffused. His attempt to unify Judah and Israel obviously failed, and it is suspected that his treatment of the northern tribes exhibited favoritism to Judah.

Solomon's porch. Cf TEMPLE.

Son. Cf FAMILY.

Son of God. 1. *OT*. The title son of God is applied in the OT to heavenly beings (cf ANGEL; Gn 6:2; Pss 29:1; 89:7; Jb 1:6; 2:1; 38:7). In this usage the title probably has its roots in primitive conceptions of heavenly beings as members of the divine and superhuman order of being. In common Hb idiom the "son" of any collective noun is a member of the species which the noun designates. The title is applied to the people Israel as a whole (Ex 4:22; Dt 14:1; 32:19; Is 1:2; 43:6; Je 31:9, 20; Ho 2:1; 11:1 +). In this use the title is another way of expressing the covenant* relationship of Yahweh and Israel and signifies the adoption* of Israel by Yahweh. The title in later usage signifies the devout Israelite, even as an individual person (Ps 73:15; WS 2:13, 18; 5:5 +). Divine adoption in a unique sense, based also upon a covenant and promises, was attributed to the Davidic king* (2 S 7:14; 1 Ch 22:10; Pss 2:7; 89:28). Adoption signifies acceptance by Yahweh, His peculiar love and care, and responsibilities and obedience imposed upon Israel, the devout Israelite, or the king. The title does not in the OT reflect the Egyptian conception of the king as Horus the son of Re.

2. *NT*. The title is applied frequently to Jesus in the NT (31 times in the Synoptic Gospels, 42 times in the epistles, 23 times in Jn, where the title is most frequent, 3 times in AA, once in Apc).

Modern writers point out that the term is more congenial to a Hellenistic than to a Jewish background; in Gk the title is frequently given to demigods, heroes, kings, and priests. This may be granted; but the NT use of the title does not reflect this Hellenistic background. Neither does it reflect the OT background; Son of God is not a messianic title in Judaism. The title becomes a means by which the early Church expressed its faith in the absolutely unique character of Jesus. The use of the term reflects the developed faith of Easter and Pentecost. It is not obvious, however, that the title always meant precisely the same thing in all the NT writings, and it seems possible to trace a development.

I. *The Synoptic Gospels.* The phrase "son of God" in Mk 1:1 is missing in the best MSS. The title appears in the annunciation* tive (Lk 1:32, 35). The title is used by demoniacs (Mt 8:29; Mk 3:11; 5:7; Lk 4:41; 8:28), where the supernatural power of Jesus is exhibited. The object of the temptation of Jesus was to ascertain whether He was the son of God (Mt 4:3, 6; Lk 4:3, 9). The confession of the centurion is probably to be conceived in Hellenistic terms (Mt 27:54; Mk 15:39); but the Gospels place this confession at the summit of the life of Jesus, the moment when His redeeming work is accomplished. The taunt of the Jews (Mt 27:43) is strangely reminiscent of WS 2:13, 18; it seems to allude to the claims of Jesus Himself (cf below) and perhaps echoes the conception of the devout Jew as a son of God. The title is used in the confessions of the disciples (Mt 14:33) and Peter (Mt 16:16), both occurring in exceptionally dramatic situations.

The most solemn use of the title is in the scenes of the baptism Mt 3:17; Mk 1:11; Lk 3:22; cf Jn 1:34) and in the transfiguration (Mt 17:5; Mk 9:7; Lk 9:35; cf 2 Pt 1:17). Here the title comes from the Father and authenticates the Son as His emissary. The sentence echoes the Servant* passage of Is 42:1; the servant of God turns out to be His Son. In the baptism the Spirit comes upon the Son (Is 11:2; 61:1). Such a declaration from the Father obviously raises the sonship of Jesus above the common OT use of the phrase. It is altogether improbable that the phrase is derived from the application of Ps 2:7 to Jesus, as it is in AA 13:33; Heb 1:5; 5:5; rather the application comes from the existing use of the title. The same is to be said of the application of Ho 11:1 in Mt 2:15.

Jesus applies the title to Himself. In the attestation demanded by the high priest Jesus accepts the title, and adds a prediction of His second coming in order to remove all doubt of its meaning (Mt 26:63 f; Mk 14:61 f). This obviously signifies a unique and supernatural sonship. In Mt 21:37 f; Mk 12:6 Jesus describes Himself as the son of the owner of the vineyard slain by the vintners. Mt 11:27 ff; Lk 10:22 ff connect the title with a mutual knowledge of Father and Son which is shared by no one; only the Son in virtue of this intimate knowledge can reveal the Father. Why, then, is knowledge attributed to the Father which is denied to the Son (Mt 24:36; Mk 13:32)? This celebrated problem has not been solved to universal satisfaction. One can say only that the conception of His sonship as described by Jesus admits a piece of knowledge which the Incarnate Son does not share.

One may with P. Bonnard summarize the title in the Synoptics as indicating that Jesus is sent by the Father, possesses the Spirit, is the Son who realizes in His own person the sonship of Israel, the unique Son and heir who represents the Father to men, and who enjoys an exclusive and intimate union with the Father.

II. *The Epistles.* To a remarkable degree the divine sonship of Jesus is associated with His redeeming death; to perceive fully the meaning and the efficacy of the redemption it is necessary to understand who He is that dies (Rm 5:10; 8:32; Gal 4:4; Col 1:13; Heb 6:6). These texts in almost every instance also emphasize that the Father has sent or delivered the Son to the redeeming death. So also in Heb 4:14; 7:28 the priesthood of Jesus is the one final and perfect priesthood because He is anointed with sonship. As the Son Jesus is the revealer of the Father surpassing the prophets (Heb 1:2); here are added the attributes of the supremacy of the Son and His function in creation. For Paul Jesus is declared i.e., revealed as the Son of God in His resurrection; before this event men might question the title, but not after it. He is the term to which creation tends and is the one through whom all creation becomes subject to the Father (1 Co 15:28). The sonship of Jesus is the operative principle of the adoption of Christians; through fellowship with the Son men reach the Father (1 Co 1:9); this idea is expressed more frequently in Jn (cf below). Faith in the Son of God (Gal 2:20) and knowledge of the Son of God (Eph 4:13) are things by which the Christian lives. Salvation is the transfer into His realm (Col 1:13). In the epistles the preexistence of the Son becomes evident, an idea not explicit in the Synoptics. The divine nature, divine origin, and divine power of the Son are such that we cannot suppose that these are the fruits of adoption. The only Son cannot be distinguished from other men unless His personal relation to the Father antecedes His appearance in the flesh. In the epistles the title affirms the divinity of Jesus and differentiates Him from the Father, who is signified by the title "God" (Gk *ho theos;* cf GOD).

III. Jn. The use of the title in Jn presupposes the reflection evident in the epistles. In the confessions of Nathanael (Jn 1:49) and of Martha (Jn 11:27) it is possible that the title has acquired a messianic significance. More commonly it expresses the intimate union of the Son with the Father; this is a perfect union of their operations, in

virtue of which the Son receives from the Father the power to judge and to confer life (Jn 5:19–26). Because of the close union of the Father and the Son Jn emphasizes that the Son is entitled to the glorification proper to His sonship, and that the Father will glorify Him (Jn 11:4; 17:1). The Son is the redeemer whom the Father has given; the love which the Father has for the Son makes Him the medium through which the world is saved and men receive eternal life (Jn 3:16–18; 1 Jn 4:9, 13). To this purpose the Father has committed all things to Him (Jn 3:35 f). Hence it is faith in the Son which brings eternal life (Jn 6:40; 20:31; 1 Jn 5:13). The sonship of Jesus is the principle of the adoption of Christians (Jn 1:12); fellowship with the Son is fellowship with the Father (1 Jn 1:3). Confession of the Son brings men to union with the Father, and without union with the Son no one reaches the Father (1 Jn 2:22–24). Throughout the Johannine writings the preexistence of the Son is a divine condition is evidently supposed.

In the NT "Son of God" is a soteriological rather than a metaphysical title. The unique relation of Jesus the Son of God with the Father enables Him to mediate between the Father and mankind and gives His saving acts and His intercession a unique efficacy. Were He not the Son, it is inconceivable that men should receive the adoption which He confers, which is a far more intimate union with God than the OT adoption of Israel. Were He not the Son, the Father could not have for Him the love which makes His offering of Himself so acceptable. There are, of course, metaphysical implications in the title, and these implications are the source of the great theological discussions of the 3rd–5th centuries AD; but the NT itself is not explicitly conscious of these metaphysical implications and therefore does not answer explicitly the metaphysical questions which can be asked.

Son of Man (Aramaic *bar nāšā'*), in this phrase "son" (or daughter) prefixed to a collective noun indicates an individual member of the species; the Gk and Eng translations are excessively literal, since the phrase means "the man" or "a man." The translation has the merit, however, of bringing out the distinctive character of the title in the Gospels. It is a messianic title, occurring 70 times in the Synoptics, 12 times in Jn, and outside of the Gospels only in AA 7:56, where Stephen alludes to Dn 7:13. Mt 26:64; Mk 14:62; Lk 22:69; and Apc 1:13; 14:14, also allude to Dn 7:13.

The title is used in Dn 7:13 f to designate "one like a man" who appears on the clouds before the Ancient of Days and receives a kingdom. This figure symbolizes Israel (7:18, 22, 27). It is suggested by some scholars that "the man" is connected with a figure of Iranian mythology called Primordial Man, the first man who is deified and who will return in the final period of the world to inaugurate the kingdom of God. The figure is obscure in Iranian mythology and this suggestion is rejected by many scholars; but it appears that the son of man in Enoch and 4 Esdras (cf APOCRYPHAL ROOKS) does depend on non-Jewish mythology, as well as on Dn 7:13. The Son of Man appears before the Ancient of Days; he is the righteous one who reveals all hidden treasures; he is chosen by the Lord of spirits as judge; he overcomes kings and powerful ones and sinners (Enoch 46). His name is pronounced in the presence of the Lord of spirits before creation; he is a staff for the righteous and holy; he is the light and hope of peoples, adored and praised by all; he is chosen and hidden before creation and remains with the Lord throughout eternity; men are saved in his name (Enoch 48). The saved will eat and drink with him (Enoch 62). He sits on a throne and judgment is given him (Enoch 69). He appears as a man flying on the clouds whose glance and voice make all things tremble. He defeats a great host with the flame which issues from his mouth. He is kept for a long time to the last day; through him creation is saved and a new order established; he is the son of the Most High (4 Esdras 13). The question arises whether the NT notion of the Son of Man shows any influence of these conceptions. It is difficult to deny any influence whatever. It is also difficult to suppose that Jesus would deliberately invoke such a figure as the Son of Man of Enoch, nor does this seem to have been the effect of the phrase on those who heard it.

It is remarkable not only that the phrase does not occur in the epistles, but also that in the Gospels it is used only by Jesus. To most scholars this is evidence that the title was original with Jesus Himself, and that its abandonment outside the Gospels is due not only to its Semitic character, which would make it foreign to a Hellenistic audience, but also is a tribute to the originality. But to what extent was it a messianic title in current usage? This question admits no certain answer; it cannot be determined how widely known the conceptions of Enoch were. The title rather suggests than affirms and invites those who hear it to inquire further about its meaning. As a reflection of Dn 7:13 it suggests that Jesus is the new Israel. Some modern scholars have solved the difficulty by denying that the title was used by Jesus; they believe that it is a messianic title, deliberately echoing Dn and Enoch, which was given to Jesus by the primitive Church. Against this is the quite distinctive use of the title by Jesus alone. Others have suggested that the Son of Man, when used in the 3rd person by Jesus of an apocalyptic-eschatological figure, does not designate Himself but the Son of Man of Dn and Enoch; the identification again was made by the primitive Church. Of these hypotheses one must say that they raise as many difficulties as they solve.

The uses of the phrase in the Synoptics can be classified under 5 heads:

(1) in a context in which Jesus speaks of His human condition: He has no place to lay His head (Mt 8:20; Lk 9:58), He comes eating and drinking (Mt 11:19; Lk 7:34).

(2) in contexts where superhuman powers are attributed to Jesus: power to forgive sins (Mt 9:6; Mk 2:10; Lk 5:24) and lordship over the Sabbath (Mt 12:8; Mk 2:28; Lk 6:5). These are really connected with the following group.

(3) in contexts which describe the messianic mission of Jesus: sower of the word of God (Mt 13:37), He for whom the disciples must suffer (Lk 6:22; Mt 5:11 has "me"), He who seeks and saves the lost (Lk 19:10), He whom men must identify (Mt 16:13); the sin of speaking against the Son of Man (Mt 12:32; Lk 12:10).

(4) a much more numerous group of texts in which the passion and death are attributed to the Son of Man (Mt 12:40; 17:12, 22; 20:18; Mk 9:31; 10:33; Lk 9:44; 11:30; 18:31). He serves and gives His life for many (Mt 20:28; 26:2, 24, 45; Mk 8:31; 9:12; 10:45; 14:21, 41; Lk 9:22; 22:22, 48; 24:7). These are so numerous that one may conclude that it is precisely as Son of Man that Jesus suffers and dies; how this affects the meaning of the title is discussed below.

(5) another large group of passages which speak of the apocalyptic-eschatological coming of the Son of Man in the end of time; this is a coming in glory on the clouds accompanied by angels and is obviously derived from Dn 7:13 (Mt 10:23; 13:41; 16:28; Lk 9:26; the resurrection, Mt 17:9; 24:27, 30, 37, 39, 44; 25:31; Mk 9:9; 13:26; Lk 17:24, 26; 21:27); of particular interest is the solemn profession of the Second Coming in the process of Jesus before Caiaphas, Mt 26:64; Mk 14:62; Lk 12:8; 22:69; where Mt 10:32 has "I"; Lk 17:22; 18:8. In this coming the Son of Man is enthroned at the right hand of God and receives the judicial power over all men (Mt 13:41; 16:27; 19:28; 25:31 ff; 26:64; Mk 14:62; Lk 22:69).

It is evident that the merging of these themes in a single title is not derived from any earlier source; and the attribution of the themes to the primitive community or to different circles of the community rather evades the problem than solves it. It is evident from the title itself that it emphasizes the humanity of Jesus and His community with other men. It is His humanity that makes Him capable of suffering, and thus it is under this title that He experiences His passion. But it must be noticed that the Son of Man of Dn and the apocryphal books is not a suffering figure; this trait we must attribute to the fusion of the Son of Man with the Suffering Servant* of the Lord. To attribute a step so fundamental in the concept of redemption and salvation to any other than Jesus Himself seems captious; the NT affirms constantly that the redeeming passion and death was a mystery unintelligible to the disciples which Jesus explained with difficulty. It must be granted, of course, that they did not perceive that the passion and death were a victory until the fullness of the faith of Easter and Pentecost; but they attribute this faith to the teaching of Jesus Himself. The title, which suggested nothing of the national traits of the Davidic king-messiah, was apt as a vehicle for the suffering Servant. In this sense it seems Jesus must have chosen and used the title.

The attribution of the apocalyptic-eschatological traits to the Son of man raises another question; and interpreters believe that it may here legitimately be asked how much of #5 above is due to the words of Jesus Himself and how much to the teaching of the primitive Church interpreting His person and mission. Much of the eschatology of the Synoptic Gospels is simply a development of the scene of Dn 7:13 f; and it seems possible and likely that the Church interpreted the title Son of Man in the light of this passage, although Jesus had not done so Himself. By this interpretation the paradox of the suffering and glorified Son of Man reflected the paradox, or rather the mystery, of Jesus Himself, who is glorified through His passion and death.

In Jn the title takes on some new features. As in the Synoptics, the Son of Man is judge (Jn 5:27). The references to the suffering of the Son of Man all mention His "elevation" on the cross (Jn 3:14; 8:28; 12:34); the elevation stands in contrast to His descent (Jn 3:13). In Jn the Son of Man is clearly preexistent; as He came down from heaven, so He ascends to the place from which He came (Jn 6:62). He is a heavenly being, a medium between heaven and earth upon which angels rise and descend (Jn 1:51). The humanity of the Son of

Man appears eminently in His sacramental work; if one does not eat His flesh and drink His blood, one cannot have eternal life (Jn 6:27, 53). Through the Eucharist the faithful have intimate communion with the Son of Man in His humanity. Faith in the Son of Man is demanded (Jn 9:35). The Son of Man must be glorified; He is already glorified by the Father whom He glorifies (Jn 13:31) by the demonstration of His sonship; and He awaits a further hour of glorification (Jn 12:23), which must be His passion and His vindication by resurrection. In Jn the Son of Man has lost the apocalyptic traits of the Synoptics and has become the preexistent being. This is not, however, a reformation of the concept according, to the salvation-myth of Primordial Man; for the Son of Man in Jn redeems by His death. Only in Jn does the title elicit a question about the identity of the Son of Man (Jn 9:35; 12:34). One wonders whether only Jn has preserved a question which, it seems, must have been asked. In the context of Jn the question is a response to the presentation of the Son of Man as a mysterious heavenly being, and the question shows how difficult it was for the Jews to grasp the revelation of the preexistent heavenly Son of Man.

Song. Cf PSALMS.

Song of Songs. The Hb title of this book is "song of songs [best of songs] which is for [by?] Solomon." In Eng it is also called the Song of Songs, in the Douay OT "canticle of canticles" after Vg *canticum canticorum*. In the Hb Bible the book appears in the 3rd portion of the canon*, the Writings or Hagiographa; in the Gk and Vg it is strangely classified with the wisdom* books, with which it has nothing in common except an attribution to Solomon. SS is unique in its literary form in the OT; cf below.

1. *Contents.* It is impossible to set forth even a summary of the contents without committing oneself to a theory about the interpretation of the book; the following outline simply enumerates the distinct songs or song fragments which can be found in the book; their arrangement and interrelation is discussed below.

1:1–4, praise of the beloved; 1:5–6, an outdoor girl; 1:7–8, dialogue; 1:9–17, lovers' antiphons; 2:1–7, the rose of Sharon; 2:8–14, love in the springtime; 2:15, the little foxes; 2:16–17, surrender; 3:1–5, desire; 3:6–11, the wedding parade; 4:1–7, beauty; 4:8–9, love call; 4:9–5:1, dialogue; 5:2–7, the test of love; 5:8–6:3, praise of the lover; 6:4–7, beauty; 6:8–9, one is my dove; 6:10–12, bright as the sun; 7:1–6, the sword dance; 7:7–10, dialogue; 7:11–14, love in the vineyard; 8:1-4, brother and sister; 8:5-7, strong as death; 8:8-10, the fortress; 8:11-12, Solomon's vineyard; 8:13-14, in the garden.

2. *Authorship and Date.* The attribution to Solomon* in the title is pseudonymous; Solomon had a reputation as a great lover. Modern critics place the book in the postexilic period, arguing principally from the presence of Aramaic and Gk words. The book may contain much older materials. It is doubtful whether one can speak of a unity of authorship; cf below.

3. *Canonicity.* The candid erotic character of much of the book has caused difficulties even from early times; and it should be added that there is even more erotic symbolism than appears on the surface. A Talmudic tradition relates that the place of the book in the canon was disputed by some rabbis in a synod held at Jamnia in Palestine about AD 100. The book was saved by the arguments of a number of influential rabbis. The great Rabbi Akiba excluded from the resurrection those who sang selections from SS at banquets. The argument against its canonicity has been urged by medieval and modern interpreters.

4. *Interpretation.* From the rabbinical discussions mentioned above down to modern times it has been assumed antecedently by many interpreters that erotic poetry cannot be found in a sacred and inspired book. Therefore the book must have another than its superficial meaning, and on this assumption it has been declared by most ancient, medieval, and modern interpreters to be a parable or an allegory. If it is a parable, then it must have some unity other than the unity of a random collection of love lyrics. This unity has been interpreted dramatically by a number of scholars. The characters are thought to be two, the Shulammite and her shepherd lover, or three with the addition of Solomon; and a chorus of voices is usually added. With two characters the drama moves from the beginning of love to its fulfillment. With three characters a dramatic struggle is introduced; the maiden is in love with her shepherd lover, but Solomon appears and wishes to take her into his harem. Impressed by the purity of the love of the rustic pair, he abandons the effort and permits the two lovers to marry. A further refinement of the dramatic theory presents Solomon making his advances to the maiden in the disguise of a shepherd. In modern interpretation the dramatic theory has very few defenders, not only because of the absence of any form of the drama in ancient Israel, but also because one must rewrite the book in order to convert it into a drama. A recent example of the unity conceived

in the book as the expression of the growth of love is seen in an arrangement accepted by A. Gelin, A. Robert, H. Lusseau and a number of others. The poems are reduced to five: Introduction: 1:1-4. I. 1:5-2:7. II. 2:8-3:5. III. 3:6-5:1. IV. 5:2-6:3. V. 6:4-8:3. These poems are said each to exhibit a rhythm of tension and repose; the tension consists in the mutual love and the mutual search of the two lovers for each other, ending in the repose of mutual possession. The repose is not final until the conclusion, 8:4-7a. 8:7b-13 are regarded as additions.

The reality symbolized by the parable is proposed as the love between Yahweh and Israel. The image of matrimonial love is often used in the OT to express the love of Yahweh for His people (cf LOVE; MARRIAGE). This interpretation was proposed by Jewish interpreters and in the Talmudic story mentioned above is the decisive reason why the book was preserved as canonical. Christian interpreters have adapted the same principle to the Church, the New Israel, and propose SS as a parabolic description of the union of Christ and the Church (cf MARRIAGE). Several ancient and modern interpreters go farther and expand the parable into an allegory, finding meaning in each of the details of the book. Such interpretations admit no control in the principles of exegesis and are often fanciful; modern exegesis rejects them. Christian interpreters from the Middle Ages have often identified the bride of SS with the Virgin Mary, and a number of such applications of SS occur in the liturgy. These uses must be judged accommodated; while they no doubt serve as expressions of piety and devotion, it is quite impossible to suppose that they touch the genuine meaning of the book. The same judgment is valid of the interpretation of SS of the love of Christ and the individual Christian soul, frequently used by mystical writers.

There are certain difficulties against the parabolic interpretation, perhaps none of which are convincing. There is no trace of this interpretation in SS itself. When SS is compared with the prophetic passages in which the image of matrimonial love is employed, the contrast is evident; in the prophets the identity of Yahweh and Israel is clear and explicit. The parable must be introduced into SS from outside. Furthermore, if SS is regarded as indecent and unworthy of inspiration unless it receive a spiritual interpretation, one must ask whether the symbol itself also should not meet the standards of decency implicit in this principle. If the material of SS is indecent in itself, is it not also unworthy of employment as a symbol of divine love?

These considerations lead many to seek an interpretation in the literature and culture of the ancient Near East. It is now known that love lyrics were included in this literature; cf Egyptian love lyrics (ANET 467–469), which have interesting contacts with SS in three points: the allusions to nature; the addresses "brother" and "sister" used by lovers; the "sickness" of love. Observations of Syrian wedding customs made by Wetzstein, the German consul in Syria in 1873, exhibited some interesting parallels. The bride and groom are "king" and "queen." for a week; they are drawn on a threshing sledge which serves as a palanquin (cf SS 3:6–11); the bride performs a dance with a naked sword (cf the "dance of the camp" SS 6:13–7:6). The Arabic song called the *wasf* is a description of the charms of the lover and the beloved, sung by each to the other; the charms are enumerated from head to foot, or from foot to head (cf SS 4:1–5; 5:10–16; 6:13–7:6). The uninhibited character of wedding festivities is known to all travelers in the modern Near East, and wedding festivities are alluded to in the OT (Gn 29:27 f; Jgs 14:10–18; Je 16:9; 25:10; Ps 45 is a wedding song). The value of some of these observations is questioned by many scholars; they believe that a projection from modern customs to ancient Israelite customs is unjustified, and they find some of the parallels exaggerated. It appears that the sword dance and the *wasf* are valid points of comparison; but the view of Wetzstein, accepted by many scholars, that SS is a collection of songs for wedding festivities, seems to go beyond the evidence.

Some scholars believe that SS is a collection of songs from the liturgy of the sacred marriage, which was a part of the fertility ritual (cf BAAL and related articles). This view deals simply with the origin of the songs and not with their use and interpretation by Israelites; it is possible that the songs were collected with no knowledge of their origin, or that they were adapted to the parabolic interpretation. The majority of scholars finds this opinion difficult; the revulsion of Israelite religion against the cults of fertility was so extreme that it is hard to imagine how this liturgy could have been adapted in any way. Here also, as in the parabolic interpretation, evidence in the text itself fails.

The view that SS is a collection of love songs need not fall on the ground that erotic poetry is of itself too indecent for inclusion in the Bible. One must first observe that the candor of ancient Israel concerning love and sexual processes — a candor which can be seen in every less sophisticated people — is considered bad taste in modern society. Good taste and basic morality must not be confused; this is Puritanism. In any hypothesis the language of SS will be offensive to modern ears; but this does not argue that it is morally offensive. A similar candor is seen throughout the OT. A sympathetic understanding of SS is impossible unless one is willing to admit that looser standards of discourse than our own are permissible.

A second point is that the subject of erotic poetry need not be illicit love, although the history of this literary form shows little interest in anything else. The love which is at the base of marriage, however, is in any sound morality not only good but even holy; the matrimonial consent, which signifies the surrender of the body, is identified by the Church with the sacrament of marriage. There is no reason why anything so free from moral reproach should not be the object of praise in a sacred book as well as in a profane book, and why the praise should not include praise of the joy which love communicates to the partners. Unless this love and joy are morally wrong, the praise of them can scarcely be morally wrong. Modern interpreters therefore are more inclined to see in SS a collection of love lyrics, not necessarily arranged in a pattern, which affirm the goodness and the joy of sexual love, an affirmation which stands in no opposition whatever to the highest ideals of Christian morality.

It is sometimes urged that the secular interpretation of SS has been condemned by the Fifth Ecumenical Council (AD 553), which rejected the opinion of Theodore of Mopsuestia as offensive to pious ears. Theodore is quoted as saying that SS celebrates the wedding of Solomon with the Egyptian princess. This statement needs several reservations: we have not the work of Theodore himself, who was frequently and badly misquoted in the Acts of the Council; we have no exact record of what the Council actually said in its condemnation; and it is quite false to say that anything but the parabolic interpretation is a secular interpretation. SS, understood as the praise of legitimate matrimonial love, is precisely directed against a "secular" view of love and marriage. Praise of what is morally good is not purely secular, even if the morally good happens, as in this instance, to be also satisfying to human desires.

Sons of the Prophets. Cf PROPHETS.

Soothsayer. Cf DIVINATION.

Sopater (Gk *sōpater*, hypocoristicon of Sosipater*), a personal name; the son of Pyrrhus, a Christian of Berea* who was one of Paul's company on his journey from Greece to Jerusalem (AA 20:4). Many scholars identify him with Sosipater*.

Sorcery. Cf MAGIC.

Sorek (Hb sōrēk, meaning and etymology uncertain), the wadi in which dwelt Delilah*, the mistress of Samson* (Jgs 16:4). Geographers identify it with the Wadi es Surar, the second of the five wadis which cross the Shephelah* W to E. The wadi was also the scene of some other famous episodes of Israelite history. In the valley are located Zorah*, Eshtaol* and Timnah*, which occur in the story of Samson, Beth-shemesh*, and possibly Kirjah-jearim*. The valley is the road taken by the cattle when the ark* was returned to the Israelites by the Philistines (1 S 4:12). The wadi is formed by the junction of three watercourses from the central highlands. It is the route followed by the modern railway from Jaffa to Jerusalem.

Sosipater (Gk sōsipatros, "savior of the father"?), a personal name. **1.** One of the officers of Judas* who led the force which defeated the Seleucid commander Timotheus* and who released Timotheus after his capture (2 Mc 12:19–25). **2.** A fellow countryman (fellow Jew) whom Paul associates with his greetings to the Romans from Corinth (Rm 16:21); probably identical with Sopater*.

Sosthenes (Gk sōsthenēs, "saving strength?") a personal name. **1.** Leader of the synagogue of Corinth after Crispus*, who became a Christian. The Jews attempted to charge Paul with irreligion before the governor Gallio*, who refused to hear the case; the Jews then beat Sosthenes in the presence of the governor who ignored the riot (AA 18:12–17). The beating was probably the outcome of resentment at the failure of Sosthenes to give what they considered a proper presentation of the case. **2.** A colleague of Paul, associated with him in the greetings to the Corinthians from Ephesus (1 Co 1:1). Even in patristic times the identification of #1 with #2 has been proposed; the quarrel of his fellow Jews with Sosthenes may have been the needed incitement to embrace the new faith.

Soul. **1.** OT. The word "soul" is used in Eng Bibles to translate the Hb nepeš. The translation is unfortunate; soul in common speech reflects a complex of ideas which go back to Gk philosophy as refined by medieval scholasticism. In the philosophy of Plato the soul is a pure spiritual principle, the subject of thought, really distinct from the body, and immortal; in Platonism the soul is really man. In Aristotelian philosophy the soul is united with the body as a form united to matter; it is the subject of thought, but its spirituality and immortality are less evident. In scholasticism the spirituality and immortality of Platonism are explicitly united with the Aristotelian conception of form, and the soul becomes a subsistent spiritual form. Hb nepeš reflects none of these ideas; since the word is important in the Hb concept of man, its uses are summarized here.

The nepeš is distinguished from the flesh* (Dt 12:23; Is 10:18), but not precisely as noncarnal in the sense in which spirit* is opposed to flesh. Elsewhere the nepeš shares the experiences of the flesh; it is mentioned in parallelism with the flesh (Jb 14:22); both experience grief and pain (Pss 42:5, 7; 131:2; Jb 30:16) and share other experiences (cf below). The nepeš departs at death (Gn 35:18; 1 K 17:21 f; Jb 11:20; 31:39; Je 15:9), but it does not survive as a living being. The nepeš mēt ("dead nepeš," a contradiction in terms in Gk philosophy) is simply a deceased person (Lv 21:11; Nm 6:6 +; usually without mēt, Lv 19:28; 21:1; Nm 9:6 f +). The deliverance of the nepeš from Sheol* is often the object of prayer or thanksgiving (Pss 16:10; 30:4; 49:16; 86:13; 89:49; Pr 23:14 +); but it must be noticed that these passages deal with the preservation of one's life from death, not with the evocation of a separate spiritual being from the dead.

The constitution of man as a nepeš is explicitly described only in Gn 2:7; by the reception of the breath of God into the nostrils man becomes a "living nepeš." The nepeš is not here identical with "the breath of life" which man receives from God; the living nepeš is man as he is once he begins to live. He is no longer a "dead nepeš." It is remarkable and not entirely intelligible that the phrase nepeš hayyāh is used here only of man; elsewhere it is used of animals (Gn 2:19, where many critics suspect the phrase is glossed; Gn 1:20, 24; 9:12, 15 f +). Animals are said either to be nepeš hayyāh or the nepeš hayyāh is said to be within them (Gn 1:30 +); since the two phrases occur in the same literary context, it is scarcely a sign of divergent concepts of the nepeš, but rather an evidence of its flexibility.

The association of the nepeš with life* is so close that the word is often best translated by life; but to think that the nepeš means life is as deceptive as it is to think that it means soul. When one's life is in danger, it is the nepeš that survives or is spared (Gn 12:13; 19:20; 1 K 20:32; Je 38:17, 20 +). A common formula of the oath* is "as your nepeš lives" (1 S 1:26; 17:55; 20:3; 25:6;

2 S 11:11; 14:19; 2 K 2:2, 4, 6; 4:30 +). Thus the *nepeš* itself lives rather than serves as the principle of life, just as the *nepeš* also dies (Nm 23:10; Jgs 16:30; Ezk 18:4, 20 +; *nepeš mēt* above). An attack on one's *nepeš* is an attack on one's life (Ps 69:2; Je 4:10). To risk one's *nepeš* is to risk one's life (Nm 17:3; Jgs 5:18; 2 S 23:17; 1 K 2:23; Pr 7:23 +); a more picturesque phrase is to put one's *nepeš* in one's hand (Jgs 12:3; 1 S 19:5; 28:21; Jb 13:14). To seek one's *nepeš* is to seek one's life (Ex 4:19; 1 S 20:1; 22:23; 23:15 +, very common). To strike the *nepeš* is to deliver a fatal blow (Gn 37:21; Dt 19:6, 11; Je 40:14 f), and to take the *nepeš* is to take the life (1 K 19:4; Ps 31:14; Pr 1:19). The law of retaliation demands a *nepeš* for a *nepeš* (Ex 21:23; Dt 19:21; 2 S 14:7). These phrases can be translated "life for life," but the same translation is slightly misleading when one pledges one's own *nepeš* for the security of another's *nepeš* (Jos 2:14) or demands a *nepeš* for the *nepeš* of an escaped prisoner (1 K 20:39, 42; 2 K 10:24). To escape from death is to deliver one's *nepeš* (Jos 2:13; 1 S 19:11; 2 S 19:6; 1 K 11:12 +, common). To take a millstone as a pledge is to take the *nepeš* (Dt 24:6); obviously the exacting creditor does not take life, but takes an essential tool of food production and thus lays an aggressive hand on the *nepeš*.

In a large number of phrases *nepeš* can be best translated by "self" or by the personal pronoun (Gn 49:6; Nm 23:10; 30:3 ff; Jgs 16:30; Jb 9:21; Pss 25:13; 124:7; Is 3:9; 43:4; 46:2; 51:23 +). The *nepeš* can be guarded (Dt 4:9 +); one loves another as one loves one's own *nepeš* (1 S 18:1, 3); one proves one's *nepeš* righteous* (Je 3:11); one should not deceive one's *nepeš* (Je 37:9); one brings evil against one's *nepeš* (Je 26:19). Related to this use is another large group of passages where *nepeš* is best translated *person* (Lv 24:17 f; Pr 11:25; 19:15; Jb 16:4). *Nepeš* is used for a general relative pronoun, "any one who . . ." (Dt 24:7; 27:25; Ezk 18:4 ff +, very common). In enumerations of persons the sum is rendered as a number of *nᵉpašôt* (plural: Dt 10:22; Jos 10:28 ff +, very common).

The *nepeš* is the seat of appetites, including quite carnal appetites: hunger (Ps 107:9; Pr 27:7) and thirst (Ps 42:3; 63:2; Je 31:25 +), and when the appetite is satisfied the *nepeš* is filled (Is 56:11; 58:10; Ezk 7:19 +). Pleasant words are sweet to the *nepeš* (Pr 16:24). The *nepeš* is greedy (Ps 17:9), and Sheol enlarges its *nepeš* to swallow up its prey (Is 5:14). The *nepeš* is also the seat of emotions: desire (Dt 12:20; 14:26; 1 S 2:16; 2 S 3:21 +, very common). According to one's *nepeš* means according to one's desire (Dt 21:14; 23:25; Ps 105:22; Je 34:16 +). To lift up the *nepeš* to something is to desire it (Dt 24:15; 2 S 14:14; Pr 19:8; Je 22:27; Ho 4:8 +). The *nepeš* loathes (Lv 26:11; Je 14:19 +). It experiences sorrow, distress, discontent, bitterness (Gn 42:21; 1 S 22:2; 2 S 17:8; Jb 3:20; 30:35; Is 15:4; 19:10; Je 13:17;), joy (Pss 35:9; 86:4; 94:19; Is 61:10 +), love (Gn 34:3, 8; Ps 63:9; SS 1:7; 3:1–4; Je 12:7), hatred (2 S 5:8; Is 1:14; Je 6:8; Ezk 23:17 f), impatience (Nm 21:4; Jgs 10:16; 16:16 +). The soul can be revived, which usually means to refresh or to cheer (1 K 17:21 f; Rt 4:15; Ps 19:8; Pr 25:13). The verb *nāpaš*, lit "to ensoul," means to refresh (Ex 23:12; 31:17; 2 S 16:14). "To know the *nepeš* of the stranger" is to know how it feels to be a stranger (Ex 23:9).

The *nepeš* is occasionally the subject of mental and volitional processes which are usually attributed to the heart*: knowing (Ps 139:14; Pr 19:4), thinking (Est 4:13; Pr 23:7), choosing (Jb 7:15), refusing (Ps 77:3; Jb 6:7); the *nepeš* sins (Lv 4:2, 27; Nm 15:27; Ezk 18:4, 20).

This survey shows that the concept signified by *nepeš* can be signified by no single word in modern languages; we must seek the basic meaning and describe it. J. Pedersen has said that man in his total essence is a *nepeš;* E. Jacob calls the *nepeš* a psychophysical totality. Pedersen adds that the *nepeš* is a totality with a peculiar stamp; it is not conceived abstractly and essentially but concretely and existentially as *this nepeš* in this concrete manner and condition of being. Whether he does not add something foreign when he says that the will is the whole of the tendency of the *nepeš* is not clear. He notes that the singular is used of the *nepeš* of a group (Gn 23:8; Nm 11:6; 21:5; Pss 33:20; 44:26) and sees the *nepeš* of a group, like the *nepeš* of the individual, conceived as a psychic unity and totality. The key word in these analyses is totality, but one must go beyond this. The basic meaning can be best understood, it seems, in those uses where *nepeš* is translated by self or person, but it is the concrete existing self. It is the self precisely as personal, as the conscious subject of action and passion, as distinct from other selves (or group selves, as Pedersen has noticed). Consciousness is life, the manifestation of the *nepeš*. It is not insignificant that the *nepeš* is not the subject of sensations; these are attributed to the external corporal organs of sense, for the self thinks of itself as distinct from its eyes, ears, hands, etc. Perhaps the Ego of modern psychology comes closer to a parallel with *nepeš* than any other word, and *nepeš* is the Hb word which comes nearest to person in the psychological sense, i.e., a conscious subject.

In the OT the Gk concept of soul (*psychē*) appears only in WS (cf 3:1; as preexisting in 8:19–20). The immortality of WS is the enduring life of the *psychē*. But the author of the book has been touched by Gk philosophy very lightly and is not acquainted with the complexities of the Gk concept; cf WISDOM OF SOLOMON.

2. *NT.* The NT employs the Gk *psychē*, translated in Eng by soul; in many passages where it means the self or the person recent translations paraphrase it. The NT use of the term is heavily dependent on the OT use and shows little or no effect of Gk philosophical concepts. The *psychē* is associated with life. It leaves the body at death (Lk 12:20). To seek the *psychē* is to seek the life (Mt 2:20; Rm 11:3). One may give, put or surrender one's *psychē* (Mt 20:28; Mk 10:45; Jn 10:11; 13:37 f; 15:13, 17; AA 15:26; 1 Th 2:8) and one may risk one's *psychē* (Rm 16:4; Phl 2:30). The *psychē* is sustained by food (Mt 6:25; Lk 12:22 f). Love of one's *psychē* is love of life (Apc 12:11). Paul counts his *psychē* as nothing as long as he fulfills his mission (AA 20:24). Loss of *psychē* means simply loss of life (AA 27:10, 22). Only Apc exhibits an idea of the survival of the *psychē* in an undefined state of burial (6:9); the *psychē* of the righteous is restored to life in the millennium (Apc 20:4). These conceptions appear in rabbinical and apocalyptic Judaism. The NT employs the phrase "living *psychē*" (Apc 16:3; 1 Co 15:45) and uses *psychē* to signify person (Mk 3:4; Lk 6:9; AA 2:41, 43; 3:23; Rm 2:9; 13:1). In these uses, as in the use of *psychē* to signify life, the NT adds nothing to the OT conception of *nepeš*.

The *psychē* is the seat of desire and satisfaction (Lk 12:19), sorrow, (Mt 26:38; Mk 14:34); it is troubled (Jn 12:27; AA 15:24), exalted (Lk 1:46). It is pierced by grief as by a sword (Lk 2:35). It doubts (Jn 10:24). Slander "makes the *psychē* evil" i.e., hostile (AA 14:2). It experiences encouragement (AA 14:22), pain (Rm 2:9; 2 Pt 2:8), weariness (Heb 12:3), love; genuine love is love from the whole *psychē* (Mt 22:37; Mk 12:30; Lk 10:27, from Dt 6:5; 10:12; 11:13). One should do the will of God from the *psychē* (Eph 6:6; Col 3:23). Unity is described as being of one *psychē* (Phl 1:27; one heart and one *psychē*, AA 4:32). This summary likewise shows no difference in the language of the NT from the language of the OT, and no difference in conception.

A difference is seen in the conception of the *psychē* as the seat of supernatural life*

and the object of supernatural salvation*; both of these words are charged with theological as well as with profane meaning (Heb 10:39; Js 1:21; 1 Pt 1:9). Men can kill the body but not the *psychē;* God can destroy both into Gehenna* (Mt 10:39). The life lost here is evidently not natural life; for the *psychē* dies; it is the new life of the Christian. The loss of the *psychē* is a total loss for which the entire world is no compensation (Mt 16:26; Mk 8:36 f), since this involves the loss of supernatural life. The rest which Jesus gives to the *psychē* is not mere refreshment, but the security of salvation (Mt 11:29). In the supernatural life the *psychē* becomes holy (1 Pt 1:22). It is entrusted to God in a new way (1 Pt 4:19). Hope*, the assurance of salvation, is the anchor of the *psychē* (Heb 6:19). One gains i.e., assures possession of one's *psychē* by patience (Lk 21:19); secure possession of the *psychē* is possible by the promise of eternal life. As the seat of supernatural life, the *psychē* is subject to temptation (1 Pt 2:11; 2 Pt 2:14). Under the same aspect the *psychē* is the object of pastoral care, first of Christ, the shepherd and overseer of *psychai* (1 Pt 2:25), then of apostles and other officers of the Church (2 Co 12:15); Heb 13:17).

It is against this background that the paradoxical hatred of his own *psychē* is demanded of the disciple of Jesus (Lk 14:26); still more paradoxically Jesus says that one who wishes to save his *psychē* loses it, and that one who loses his *psychē* for the sake of Jesus finds it or saves it (Mt 16:25; Mk 8:35; Lk 9:24). The paradox is removed by the explanation of Jn 12:25; he who hates his *psychē* in this world saves it for eternal life. The paradox lies not in the double meaning of *psychē* as life and as soul, but in the double meaning of love and hatred, saving and losing. What the world thinks is love and care of the *psychē* is actually and effectively hatred, for it destroys the self; the self lives only by refusing what the world offers and accepting Jesus instead. By this one saves one's *psychē* for eternal life; but the world regards such treatment of the self as hatred.

The use of the adjective *psychikos* is rare and slightly different. This word signifies the natural as opposed to the spiritual (1 Co 15:46), the man endowed with natural life but lacking the spirit* (1 Co 2:14; Jd 19), the body with natural life as opposed to the spiritual body of the resurrection (1 Co 15:44). Many scholars suggest that this use of the term comes from Gnosticism.

The *psychē* as the seat of supernatural life and the object of salvation furnishes a basis for the common idioms such as "saving one's soul," "care of souls" etc. In common speech, however, the Gk concept of *psychē* as a distinct spiritual principle is usually read into the term, and thus the concept of salvation and eternal life may become Platonic rather than biblical. The *psychē* in the NT is still the totality of the self as a living and conscious subject, and it is the totality of the self which is saved for eternal life. The novelty of the NT belief does not arise from a new idea of the *nepeš-psychē*, but from a radically new revelation of the meaning of life and salvation.

Spain. Mentioned in the Bible in 1 Mc 8:3 among the conquests of Rome. The Spanish wars of 197–179 BC had subdued the Iberian peninsula and given Rome access to the silver and gold mines of Spain (mentioned in 1 Mc 8:3); but the complete subjugation of the country was not completed until the wars of 154–133 BC, which occurred after the date of Judas*. Rm 15:23, 28 suggests that Paul made a definite decision to go to Spain, but there is no evidence that this plan was ever realized.

Sparta. The famous city of the Peloponnesus in Greece is mentioned in 1 Mc 12:2 as the object of an alliance sought by Jonathan*. The letter of Jonathan is given in 12:5–18, the letter of Arius, king of Sparta, in 12:19–23. Simon* wrote to renew the alliance and received a friendly answer (1 Mc 14:16–23). Sparta was one of the states to which the Roman letter affirming alliance with the Jews was addressed (1 Mc 15:23). The fanciful kinship asserted by the Jews with the Spartans (1 Mc 12:7) was often found in ancient treaties of alliance. The Sparta whose alliance the Jews sought was an enfeebled shadow of the state which dominated Greece through the 4th century BC, and at the time maintained its leadership in Greece only by its relations with Rome, which had conquered the Macedonians in 197 BC. Kinship with the Spartans is also asserted of Jason*, who fled there and died (2 Mc 5:9).

Spear. Spear is a generic term for a weapon consisting of a long wooden shaft terminating in a metal point; it includes the javelin, which is cast, and the pike or lance, with a longer handle, which is a thrusting weapon. In Hb the *kîdōn* is clearly a javelin (Jos 8:18); this weapon was probably about 4 ft long in the handle, and the warrior carried it or a supply of them slung over his back (1 S 17:6). In the hand of the skilled warrior the javelin could be a deadly weapon; this can be observed in the modern athletic competition of the javelin, in which distance rather than accuracy is prized. It seems that the modern athlete throws a much longer and heavier weapon (about 8½ ft) than the ancient warriors who instituted the game. The Hb *hᵃnît*, like Eng spear, seems to cover both pike and javelin. It also was cast (1 S 18:10 f; 19:9 f; 20:33); it was long enough for a man to lean upon (2 S 1:6). The word "strike," which describes Abner's* killing of Asahel*, can mean either close combat or use of a missile. Close combat is indicated in 2 S 23:21. The spears represented in ancient art are not of such a size that a strong practiced warrior could not cast them. The *rōmah,* mentioned less frequently (Jgs 5:8; Je 46:4; used as a weapon for slashing 1 K 18:28), seems to have been the pike, at least 6 ft long. The *hᵃnît* was carried by a warrior in the field (1 S 22:6), and was stuck in the ground to indicate the quarters of the king (1 S 26:7 ff); this custom has survived into modern times among the Bedu; a spear stuck in the ground indicates the tent of the sheikh. The butt, not the point, was placed in the ground, and was often equipped with a shoe of some fabric for this purpose. No shafts, of course, have been preserved, but bronze and iron heads are found in Palestinian sites in quantity. The most common shape is a blade broad at the base and narrowing to a point. The simplest way of attaching the head to the shaft was by forcing a small sharp metal point into the wood; more refined techniques employed a hollow metal shaft, sometimes pierced to receive nails.

Ancient art shows that the pike was the basic offensive weapon of the foot soldier. It was used by all peoples with no perceptible difference in style, and is illustrated abundantly in ANEP: Hittite (36, 37), Assyrian (174, 372–373, 173), Egyptian

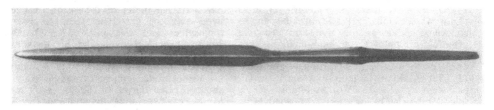

Spear point.

(180), Canaanite (346), Persian (30), the Sea Peoples (59), Sumerian (163), Babylonian (308). ANEP 39 shows a Hittite soldier armed with bow and spear, and 172 a Hittite archer in a chariot armed with a spear also. An Egyptian painting (ANEP 12) shows its use in hunting. ANEP 300 shows Sumerian massed infantry armed with pikes. ANEP 308 shows its use by a Babylonian soldier dispatching an enemy. Assyrian horsemen were armed with lances (ANEP 375). In the NT the spear is mentioned only in the passion narrative of Jn 19:34.

Spikenard. Cf NARD.

Spinning. Spinning is the operation by which fibers are drawn and twisted into thread. The skill was known in prehistoric times, but scarcely any substantial improvement in technique was made before the 18th century AD. In ancient Palestine the fibers in use were wool* (Jb 31:20), goat's* hair (Ex 35:26), camel's* hair (2 K 1:3; Mt 3:4), and flax* (Jos 2:6). The only tool employed in antiquity was the spindle. A perforated whorl of stone or ceramic was used to weight the spindle and hold it steady during rotation. The twisted fiber was placed upon the spindle, which was then rotated upon the thigh or between thumb and forefinger; the thread was drawn by letting the spindle hang by the thread, the thread was wound upon the spindle, and the operation was repeated. Spindle whorls are always numerous in Palestinian excavations. The practice of the craft is illustrated in ANEP 142–144. The laboriousness of the process is suggested in Mt 6:28; Lk 12:27. Spinning was one of the tasks of the industrious housewife (Pr 31:19).

Spirit. 1. *OT.* The Hb word *rûaḥ* does not admit translation by any single Eng word; nor is it entirely correct to say that it sometimes means breath, sometimes wind, sometimes spirit, etc. It is a single word with a single basic meaning; to grasp its meaning we must examine what is said of it. In the article below we use the word *spirit* throughout the first part simply to render the Hb word.

Spirit sometimes signifies the breath (Jb 15:30; 19:17); there is no spirit in idols (Lam 4:20; Hab 2:19 +). Breath can be conceived either as the sign and principle of life (cf below) or as something unsubstantial; a man utters windy words (Jb 16:3; cf Jb 6:26). False prophets are spirit (Je 5:13). Man is merely a spirit which passes away (Ps 78:39). An empty life is spirit (Jb 7:7); spurious knowledge is windy or "spiritual" (Jb 15:2). The vain

pursuit of human desires is a striving for spirit (Ec 1:14; 2:11, 17, 26; 4:4, 6; 6:9).

Breath is the movement of air, and the movement of air is the wind, by which spirit can very frequently be translated. The element of breath is sometimes obscured in a personification of the wind as a winged being (2 S 22:11; Ps 18:11; Ho 4:19) or as the messenger of Yahweh (Ps 104:4). The wind is the breath of Yahweh, and thus spirit becomes an agent of power; it is the creative command of Yahweh (Ps 33:6) or an agent which destroys the wicked (the spirit of the messianic king, Is 11:4). The acceleration of the breath in anger makes spirit synonymous with anger; it is the spirit of the nostrils (cf God, Ex 15:8; 2 S 22:6; Jb 4:9 +; of man, Is 25:4).

Spirit is the principle of life and of vital activity. The spirit of life is the breath (Gn 6:17; 7:15, 22; BS 38:23; WS 15:11, 16; 16:14). The breath is the breath of God, the wind, communicated to man by divine inspiration (Gn 2:7, where the word spirit is not used). Yahweh forms spirit (Zc 12:1), gives it (Is 42:5; 2 Mc 7:22 f), and it goes back to Him at death (Ec 12:7). This conception of spirit underlies Ec 3:19–21, where the spirit of man and the spirit of the beasts are identified; spirit leaves man just as it leaves the beast, and there is no difference in where it goes. This is not a conception of spirit as soul*, and indeed such a conception occurs nowhere in the OT. Spirit as a principle of life is almost always considered as a foreign element to man, given by God and taken back by Him; it is never conceived as a personal being. It is the spirit of Eloah in one's nostrils (Jb 27:3). God preserves it (Jb 10:12) and takes it (Tb 3:6; Bar 2:17). Yahweh decrees that His spirit shall not remain in man because man is flesh* (Gn 6:3); man is here seen not only as carnal but as sinful, unable to be sustained even by the spirit of Yahweh, the life-giving breath, more than a short span of years. While man lives he can speak of the life of his spirit (Is 38:16), but the spirit is not man's after death. When Yahweh takes away His spirit living beings die; when He sends it forth they are created, and thus He renews the face of the earth (Ps 104:29–30; cf Jb 34:14; Is 57:16; Jdt 16:14). The dry scattered bones of the vision of Ezekiel need only the life-giving spirit to assemble themselves and rise (Ezk 37:5 ff). When Job's* spirit is broken and his days extinguished, his vitality is diminished (Jb 17:1).

Spirit in man is also vitality as activity, as disposition, temper, courage. Loss of spirit in the queen of Sheba is surrender to the overwhelming magnificence of Soloman (1 K 10:5 +). The spirit is vexed (1

K 20:5), it revives (Gn 45:27) or returns (Jgs 15:19; 1 S 30:12) after sorrow or fatigue. Spirit fails warriors when they face superior forces (Jos 5:1; Jdt 7:19). Yahweh cuts off the spirit of princes by inspiring fear in them (Ps 76:13). The spirit faints or does not remain erect (Jos 2:11; Ps 77:4 +). One who rules one's spirit controls his temper (Pr 16:22; 25:28), and the spirit of the angry man subsides when his anger ends (Jgs 8:3). The quick-tempered man is short of spirit (Ex 6:9; Mi 2:7; Pr 14:29 +). The spirit is troubled (Gn 41:8), bitter (Gn 26:35), crushed (Ezk 21:14). When a man makes an important decision, Yahweh is said to arouse his spirit (Ezr 1:5; Je 51:11; Hg 1:14). The spirit exhibits traits of character or behavior: there is a spirit of fornication (Ho 4:12; 5:4), of jealousy (Nm 5:14), of dizziness (Is 19:14), of judgment (Is 28:6), of discernment (Pr 17:27). In texts which are mostly late the spirit also exhibits intellectual operations: it is wise (Ex 28:3; Dt 34:9; WS 7:7), it forms devices (Ezk 11:5), thoughts enter the spirit (Ezk 20:32), it has understanding (BS 39:6). It appears as a principle of conversion; the penitent asks Yahweh to renew a firm spirit in him (Ps 51:12) and affirms that a broken spirit, a spirit which has been humiliated, is a true sacrifice (Ps 51:19). The messianic regeneration of Israel is the creation of a new heart* and a new spirit (Ezk 11:19; 18:31; 36:26).

The spirit of Yahweh or the spirit of God (Elohim) is a force which has unique effects upon man. The two are not the same; the spirit of Elohim is a neutral or indifferent force, and the spirit of Yahweh is a force which operates the works of Yahweh the savior and the judge. The spirit of Yahweh is often the force which inspires prophecy (Nm 11:17 ff; 24:2; 2 S 23:2; 1 Ch 12:18; Is 61:1; Mi 3:8; Ezk 2:2; 3:12, 14, 24; 8:3; 11:1, 5, 24; 37:1; 43:5; Ne 9:30; Zc 7:12). The prophet is a man of the spirit (Ho 9:7). In the messianic age a general outpouring of the spirit will give all of Israel prophetic insight (Jl 3:1–2). It is to be noticed that except for Ho 9:7 these passages are very probably postexilic; and the spirit as an inspiring agent does not appear in the early prophetic literature, where the inspiration consists in hearing the word* of Yahweh. A point of transition is seen in Ezk, where the spirit has a prominence unparalleled in other prophetic books. The prophetic spirit in the early period was the force which inspired the ecstatic worship of the sons of the prophets (1 S 10:6, 10; 19:20, 23). The spirit of Yahweh which carries off Elijah is not an inspiring agent but an unknown and unidentified agent (1 K

18:12; 2 K 2:16). The spirit can also be an evil spirit sent as a punishing agent; Saul was afflicted by such an evil spirit (1 S 16:14–16, 23; 18:10; 19:9). The distinction between the spirit of Yahweh and the spirit of Elohim is carefully observed in these and similar passages; the evil spirit is called the evil spirit of Elohim or the evil spirit from Yahweh, but not the evil spirit of Yahweh; hence most critics correct the reading of 1 K 19:9. Yahweh sends a lying spirit to false prophets (1 K 22:21 ff). He sends an evil spirit between Abimelech* and the men of Shechem* (Jgs 9:23). In these passages the spirit emerges as the cause of phenomena to which no perceptible cause can be assigned: insanity in Saul, self-deception in the prophets, hostility between partners in crime.

The spirit of Yahweh is a charismatic spirit when it is imparted to those who have an office in Israel: judges (Jgs 3:10; 11:29; 6:34; 13:25; 14:6, 19; 15:14), kings (1 S 11:6; 16:13 f), in particular the messianic king (Is 11:2), the servant* of the Lord (Is 42:1), Cyrus* (Is 48:16), craftsmen (Ex 31:3; 35:31). In later literature it is diffused upon the whole people in the messianic regeneration (Is 32:15; Ezk 39:29; Zc 12:10) and upon wise men (Jb 32:8; Pr 1:23). The spirit not only confers upon those who receive it the qualities necessary to fulfill their mission, but also inspires them to deeds above and beyond the expected and their normal habits and powers; and this is the true sign of the spirit, that a man rises above his habits and attainments. It is also to be noticed that the spirit is a passing charisma in the judges and in Saul, but reposes permanently upon David and upon the messianic king.

There is apparent a development in the direction of a hypostatization of the spirit, not in the sense that it is conceived as a person but as a substantial source of force and activity. It is the creative force of Yahweh (Gn 1:2). It impels the chariot of Ezekiel (Ezk 1:12, 20 f; 10:17), for it is the divine element of power. It is the saving power of Yahweh; Israel is delivered not by power or strength but by His spirit in Zc 4:6. It is the pervading divine presence either in the world or in Yahweh's guidance of Israel (Ps 139:7; WS 1:7; Is 63:10 f; Hg 2:5). It is Yahweh's holy spirit (Ps 51:9; Is 63:10 f, a rare phrase) or His good spirit (Ne 9:20; Ps 143:10).

In summary, the spirit in the OT, originally the wind and the breath, is conceived as a divine dynamic entity by which Yahweh accomplishes His ends: it saves, it is a creative and charismatic power, and as an agent of His anger it is a demonic power. It remains impersonal. Like the wind, neither its origin nor its course can be discovered, and hence to it are attributed the effects which men find mysterious. It is contrasted to flesh; spirit is opposed to flesh as man is to El, divinity (Is 31:3). This does not mean spiritual in the sense of immaterial; there is no evidence that a concept of the immaterial was developed in the OT. Spirit is opposed not to the material (for which there is no Hb word) but to flesh: the mortal, corruptible, weak and sinful element in man. Spirit is not flesh; and the OT could say no more about it.

The writings of extrabiblical Judaism use the term spirit in senses which go beyond the OT and which affected the NT use of the term. Both angels and demons are called spirits. The spirit of man is a principle of animal and psychic functions, and its use becomes nearly synonymous with *nepeš* (cf SOUL). Judaism, perhaps influenced by Gk thought, introduces a dualism of spirit and body in man which does not appear in the OT; the spirit is a preexisting element of heavenly origin which survives death and is preserved in a kind of storage chamber until the resurrection. The spirit of God is predominantly the spirit of prophecy and revelation, and it becomes the inspiring agent of the writing of the law*. It is a principle of righteousness in man. It is by no means clear that the spirit acquires personal character in the writings of Judaism; the personification of the spirit goes beyond the OT but not clearly beyond metaphor. The dualism of the good and the evil spirit is basic in the theology of Qumran*; the life of man is a conflict between the influence of these two spirits. The Qumran documents speak of the spirit of man in senses similar to those of other Jewish literature as the self, the understanding, or the character of man.

2. *NT*. The Gk word which is translated spirit is *pneuma*. The original meaning and use of this word is much like the meaning and use of the Hb *rûᵃh;* it is the movement of the air, primarily either breath or wind. The NT, however, brings to the Gk word the OT background sketched above; and the primary meaning of the word is rare in the NT. In the following paragraphs *spirit* represents the Gk *pneuma;* as above, its meaning is sought in its usage. The NT writers vary in emphasis and meaning and the word is treated according to the separate writers.

I. *Mt and Mk*. There are some instances of the use of the word to signify evil spirits; this is the usual expression in Mk, while Mt prefers to use the word demon. "In the spirit" (Mk 2:8; 8:12 +) means simply inwardly. The spirit is the principle of life which departs at death (Mt 27:50). The

spirit which is willing in contrast to the flesh which is weak (Mt 26:41; Mk 14:38) is the principle of good actions as opposed to the sinful inclinations of the flesh. These uses do not differ from OT uses.

The conception of the spirit as the power of God exhibits some of the novelty of the NT which is more fully developed in Paul and John (cf below). It is the power which drives Jesus into the desert (Mk 1:12, an expression avoided in Mt 4:1), and the power by which Jesus expels demons (Mt 12:28; Lk 11:20 has the "finger" of God). The spirit inspires the sacred writers of the OT (David, Mt 22:43; Mk 12:36). The sin of speaking against the holy spirit is not forgiven (Mt 12:32; Mk 3:29; Lk 12:10). This difficult conception is best explained from the context as a denial of the principle by which sin is forgiven; this principle is the saving will of God, which is manifest and operative in the exorcism of demons by Jesus.

The spirit is given, first of all to Jesus Himself in the baptism (Mt 3:13–17; Mk 1:9–11). The repose of the spirit upon Jesus together with the word of the Father authenticates Him as the Messiah (cf Is 11: 1 ff). In the infancy narrative of Mt (1:18, 20) the conception of Jesus is attributed to the holy spirit; this is not only a denial of human paternity but also an affirmation that His coming is a work of the mysterious saving power of God so often mentioned in the OT (cf above). The spirit is also given to the disciples of Jesus, and the spirit will speak in them when they are called upon to bear witness to Jesus (Mt 24:20; Mk 13:11). John the Baptist contrasts his own baptism with the baptism of Jesus, which confers the holy spirit (Mt 3:11); the holy spirit and fire of the baptism of Mk 1:8 is no doubt an allusion to the event of Pentecost*. On the poor in spirit of Mt 5:3 cf POOR.

The baptismal formula of Mt 28:19 is obviously a striking departure from these uses mentioned; and it is possible that this verse, like others in Mt, represents a much more developed form of belief. The listing of the three under "the name" is perhaps the most explicit declaration of the personal character of the spirit in the entire NT; but it must be noticed that the very designation of spirit shows that the personality of the spirit is not to be conceived in the most obvious fashion; cf below.

The spirit is rare in Mt-Mk compared to the writings of Luke, Paul, and John. E Schweizer thinks this reflects their fidelity they do not read back into the words of Jesus Himself beliefs which became articulate only after Pentecost and the experiences of the primitive Church. The spirit in Mt-Mk is generally the OT spirit applied to the person and mission of Jesus. Outside of Mt 28:19 it cannot be called a personal being nor a being distinct from the Father.

II. *Lk and AA.* The spirit becomes much more prominent in these writings. This appears first of all in Jesus Himself, who is influenced in His movements (Lk 4:1, 14) and inspired to speak (Lk 10:21) by the spirit. Lk's account of the baptism of Jesus (3:12 f) and of the conception of Jesus by the spirit (1:35) does not differ from the accounts of Mt-Mk. Lk adds a new element in His presentation of Jesus as the dispenser of the spirit to the Church (Lk 24:49; AA 2:33). This is a prelude to the presentation of the growth of the Church in AA as the work of the spirit.

To modern readers the use of the term in AA and Paul and to a degree in the synoptic Gospels is ambiguous. The spirit is called either a spirit (without the definite article) or the spirit (with the definite article). It is qualified by the adjective holy or the genitives "of God," "of the Lord," "of Jesus." The term, however, is rarely ambiguous to the degree that it is uncertain whether the spirit of God, the holy spirit, which emerges as a distinct entity, is meant. Whether we should remove the ambiguity by the use of capital letters (the Holy Spirit) is not always certain; in the following paragraphs the capital letters are not used without, however, implying anything concerning the personal identity of the spirit.

The spirit dominates AA. When it comes upon the disciples, they are given power and become witnesses of Jesus throughout the world (AA 1:8). The transformation of the disciples by the reception of the spirit (AA 2:3 ff) marks the birth of the Church. As the spirit was in Jesus, so now the spirit is in the Church. The apostles are filled with the holy spirit, and the Church herself possesses the spirit and is empowered to confer it upon her members (AA 2:38; 4:8, 31; 6:8; 9:17; 11:24; 7:55; 13:52; 19:2). The presence of the spirit manifests itself externally in such phenomena as the gift of tongues and prophecy; these manifestations witness the present activity of God in the Church (AA 2:3 ff; 10:47; 11:17; 15:8). The spirit teaches the disciples what to say (Lk 12:12); it is power from above (Lk 24:49). It reveals the mysteries of God (Lk 1:41, 67; AA 11:28; 13:9) and inspires prophecy, fulfilling the words of Jl (AA 2:18). It is a spirit of wisdom (AA 6:3), of faith (AA 6:5), of encouragement (AA 9:31), of joy (AA 13:52). The spirit directs the officers of the Church in important decisions (AA 13:2; 15:28; 20:

28). The Father gives the spirit in answer to prayer (Lk 11:13), and the spirit is conferred upon each believer at baptism (AA 19:2, 6; 2:38 f; 15:8 f; 8:16–18; 9:17; 10:44; 11:16 f). The coming of the spirit presupposes faith in the believer. The spirit was conferred by the rite of the imposition of hands (AA 8:14–17; 19:6; cf CONFIRMATION). In AA the spirit is a divine dynamic force, the charismatic spirit of the OT, which moves the apostles to preach and witness Jesus and empowers them to feats of courage and eloquence which are entirely beyond the personal capacities of these men as they appear in the Gospels. The spirit is not restricted to the charismatic leaders, but is given with the messianic fullness to the entire body of believers.

The Lucan writings also contain a few uses of spirit in the meaning of the vital principle or the inner disposition of man (Lk 1:47, 80; 8:55; 23:46; AA 7:59). In Lk 24:37, 39 it is used in the popular sense of ghost.

III. *Paul.* The theology of the spirit becomes still more elaborate in Paul; but it is still unreflecting and consequently is not always entirely consistent. The spirit is basically the divine and heavenly dynamic force; it is conceived as peculiarly existing in Jesus (and specifically in the risen Jesus), as pervading the body of Jesus which is the Church, and as apportioned to the members of the Church. Jesus is the son of David in the flesh but the son of God in power according to the spirit (Rm 1:3); the unique possession of the spirit by Jesus and the unique power which flows from this possession reveal His true reality, which is the reality of the spiritual sphere, i.e., the divine and heavenly sphere. Similarly Jesus is manifest in the flesh but proved righteous in the spirit (1 Tm 3:16).

Paul once identifies Jesus with the spirit as a basis for the remark that where the spirit of the Lord is, there is liberty (2 Co 3:17). Such an identification obviously cannot be made of two distinct personalities. The spirit here must mean the divine and heavenly level of being, which is proper to the risen Jesus; His existence is now "spiritual," not carnal. Because His existence is now that of spirit, He exists in a larger sense and in a more intimate union with His Church than can be conceived for one who exists in the flesh. In the same sense the new covenant is spirit which gives life in contrast to the old covenant which is letter and kills (2 Co 3:6), and it is called a covenant of spirit (2 Co 3:8). The freedom of the spirit is freedom from the power of sin and death. The body of Jesus which is the Church is a "spiritual" body which admits the believers as its members. Thus he who adheres to the Lord is one spirit (1 Co 6:17); the believers are baptized into one body, saturated with one spirit (1 Co 12:13). By his union with the spirit, the divine reality of the risen Jesus, the believer rises in a spiritual body (1 Co 15: 35–50), of which Jesus is the quickening spirit (1 Co 15:45). In this conception the spirit of the OT as a creative and life-giving force is transferred to the risen Jesus in the Church.

As a result of this union with Christ the spirit dwells in the individual believer, and thus the believer is in the spirit (Rm 8:9), in the divine manner of existence communicated through Christ. The believer as an individual and the Church as a whole are the temple of the indwelling spirit (1 Co 3:16; 6:19; 8:11). With the gift of the spirit comes the adoption* of the Christian as the son of God (Rm 8:16; Gal 4:6). The present possession of the spirit is a foretaste (Rm 8:23) and a pledge (2 Co 1:22; 5:5) of the eschatological salvation of the Christian.

The spirit in the Christian is a principle of the life and activity proper to the Christian. The spirit enables the Christian to pray (Rm 8:15, 26 f; 1 Co 12:3; Gal 4:6). The distinctive effect of the spirit is the "gifts" such as prophecy and tongues (1 Co 12 and 14); these and similar manifestations are a witness to the risen Christ and the security of the Christian hope (Rm 15:19; 1 Co 14:14–16; 2:4 f; Gal 3:5). The spirit is a power of faith; it reveals and searches out the "deep things" of God, His saving deeds, which are known and understood by the Christian only through the spirit which he possesses (1 Co 2:10–16); so it is called a spirit of faith (2 Co 4:13). From faith the Christian has hope by the spirit (Gal 5:5). The spirit is the principle by which the Christian lives a life worthy of the Christian. He serves God in a new spirit, not in the old letter (Rm 7:6; 8:9). Those who live in the spirit must walk in the spirit (Gal 5:25), and by sowing for the spirit they shall reap eternal life from the spirit (Gal 6:8). The spirit is the principle of love*, the most characteristic of Christian virtues; the love of God is poured into the heart by the spirit which is given (Rm 5:5), and the spirit awakens love in the Christian (Col 1:8); it is likewise the principle of the mutual love of Christians (Gal 5:13–36; Rm 15:30).

The spirit stands in antithesis to the flesh. The flesh is understood both as the law and as the inner inclination to sin. The spirit is not gained by the works of the law (Gal 3:2; 5). The Christian serves the spirit, not the law and the flesh (Phl 3:3). Righteousness is achieved by circumcision* in the spirit, not circumcision of the flesh (Rm 2:29), and true sonship of Abraham* is sonship in the spirit, not in the flesh (Gal 4:29). There is a conflict in man between the spirit and the flesh considered as sin (Gal 5:17). The flesh is a principle of corruption, the spirit a principle of eternal life (Gal 6:8). The Christian walks not by the flesh but by the spirit (Rm 8:4) and lives if he kills the deeds of the flesh by the spirit (Rm 8:13). Flesh as law and flesh as sin are taken together in this, that neither is a principle of salvation, and in this they are opposed to the spirit.

The spirit also appears in Paul as the seat of consciousness and psychic functions (1 Co 7:34; 2 Co 7:1), equivalent to the soul* (Phl 1:27; cf 2 Co 2:13; 7:5; 1 Co 16:18). It sometimes designates the person (1 Co 2:11; Gal 6:18; Phl 4:23; 1 Th 5:28). In 1 Co 5:3–5 the spirit of Paul, present when he is absent, must be his power as an apostle and his personal influence. At times Paul seems nearly to identify the spirit as the conscious self and the spirit as the heavenly level of being into which the Christian is transformed; and indeed he does regard the transformation of the Christian as total, or at least it ought to be total, so that the Christian thinks and says and does nothing except in virtue of the indwelling spirit.

The spirit is not obviously and explicitly conceived as a distinct divine personal being in Paul. The occasional personifications which he employs do not go beyond the personifications found in the OT and in Judaism. The prevailing conception is that of the pervading new divine life communicated to the Church by Jesus. Here (as in Mt 28:19) we meet an enumeration of Jesus, God (= the Father), and the spirit (2 Co 13:13) which goes beyond the general idea of the spirit in Paul and opens the possibility of seeing that the new life is ultimately the work of a personal reality, like the creative and saving deeds of the Father and of Jesus Christ. As is noted above, the name of spirit and the character of the reality and the works of the spirit demand that we enlarge our idea of the divine personality.

IV. *John.* In Jn, as P. Menoud has observed, the spirit works in and through Jesus; the association is perhaps even more intimate than the association in Paul. Jn does not emphasize the giving of the spirit in the baptism of Jesus (Jn 1:33). While he states that the spirit is not given in measure (Jn 3:34), the prevailing conception in Jn is the conception of a reality rather external to the Christian than internal. Baptism is a birth of water and spirit (Jn

3:5–8); the antithesis of flesh and spirit in this passage is characteristic of Jn. The play on *pneuma* as wind and as a vital and creative force in Jn 3:8 cannot be translated; the dynamism of the spirit is given the free and unpredictable power of the wind. Because God is spirit He is to be worshiped in spirit and truth (Jn 4:24). E. Schweizer notes that this is not a denial of external cult; to worship God in spirit is to worship Him in His manifest divine reality, which is incarnate in Jesus Christ. So Schweizer finds that Jn's "worship in spirit and truth" is equivalent to Paul's "in Christ." The verse so understood shows the same idea of the pervading divine reality which is seen in Paul.

The spirit as opposed to flesh is a principle of the Christian life; and the words of Jesus, which are the revelation of God, are spirit and life (Jn 6:63). Christ gives the spirit (1 Jn 3:24; 4:13), which is streams of life for the believer (Jn 7:38 f). The Pentecostal experience moves Jn to add here that the spirit was not given before Jesus was glorified. Only Jn (20:22) presents the spirit as a power conferred upon the apostles enabling them to remove sin by a forgiving* act. The spirit is conferred by the symbolic act of breathing; as God inspired life into the body of man (Gn 2:7), so Jesus communicates His spirit here.

The spirit is most prominent in Jn as the Paraclete*, the spirit of truth (Jn 14:17; 15:26; 16:13) which dwells in the apostles (Jn 14:17), which the world does not know (Jn 14:17), which is sent by the Father and by Jesus (Jn 14:24, 26; 15:26), proceeds from the Father (Jn 15:27), teaches (Jn 14:26), witnesses (Jn 15:26; 1 Jn 5:6), convicts the world of sin (Jn 16:8–11), does not speak of itself (Jn 16:13), comes after Jesus (Jn 16:7), remains forever (Jn 14:16), reveals the true reality of Jesus (Jn 14:26; 16:13). Here perhaps a distinct personal reality is more explicitly asserted than elsewhere in the NT. The Paraclete shares His functions with Jesus, but the distinction between the two seems evident; the Paraclete is in the continuing life of the Church what Jesus is in its foundation. The caution concerning the nature of the personality of the spirit already made is to be entered again; the obscurity of its character makes it difficult to enunciate it more clearly.

V. *Other NT Writings.* The other books of the NT do not go beyond the categories already mentioned. Of the writings connected with the Pauline epistles, Eph is the most important. Here the spirit is the power of growth of the Church (3:16), the principle of prayer (5:18), and of revelation (1:17; 3:5; 6:17). The spirit is the vital principle of the body of the Church

(4:4). It is a seal given at baptism marking the Christian as belonging to Christ (1:13; 4:30). In 2 Tm 1:7 the spirit is a principle of power and love and temperance; it is the indwelling spirit (2 Tm 1:14). In Tt 3:5 baptism is the renewal of the holy spirit. Heb 2:4 conceives the spirit as imparted to the faithful.

Js 4:5 presents the indwelling spirit. In 1 Pt 1:2 the spirit is an agent of holiness; it rests upon those who suffer for Christ (4:14). It is the principle of the life of the risen Christ (3:18) and of the life of the risen Christian (4:6). Elsewhere in the epistles the spirit is most frequently the spirit which inspires the sacred books; cf also Apc 1:10; 17:3; 21:10, the spirit of prophecy and revelation. Apc also uses the term of the seven angels (1:4; 4:5; 5:6) and of evil spirits (16:13 f; 18:2).

Staff (Hb *maṭṭeh, šēbeṭ, makkēl,* translated in Eng rod or staff, signify the long wooden staff which was an indispensable tool for the Israelite male). It was carried by the traveler (Ex 12:11) and the warrior (1 S 14:27). The ass is driven by it (Nm 22: 27). It is a reaping tool (Is 28:27) and in emergencies can be used to uncover a spring or a well (Nm 21:18). It is carried by the shepherd and is a symbol of Yahweh's protection of His people (Ps 23:4; Mi 7:14). It is a defensive weapon against human or animal aggressors. One leans on it when fatigued, and it is a metaphor for support (Ezk 4:16; 14:13 +). It is the symbol of the military officer (Jgs 5:14) and of the ruler, the scepter*. The rod of the overseer beats the laborers (Is 9:3; 14:5) and is a symbol of oppression (Is 10:24–26; 14:29). The rod means punishment (Pr 22:8, 15; 29:15; 10:13; 26:3; 1 Co 4:21 +), and is the symbol of the punishing anger of Yahweh (2 S 7:14; Ps 89:33; Is 10:5, 15; 30: 31; Ezk 20:37; Lam 3:1). The rod is an instrument by which Yahweh works wonders (Ex 4:2 ff, 17; 7:15 ff; 8:1, 12; 9:23; 10:13; Nm 20:8 f; 2 K 4:29 ff). The poor traveler has nothing but a staff (Gn 32:10). The variation between the commission to the apostles to take only one staff (Mk 6:8) and to take none (Mt 10:10; Lk 9:3) is not significant; both mean to take nothing, to travel as poor men. The staff of the sheikh was decorated to identify him and the tribe which he headed, and the words for staff are used to signify a tribe*. The owner of the staff, if he were the head of a house, could be identified by his staff, which must have had some device (Gn 38:18, 25).

Star. The OT is emphatic in asserting that Yahweh created the stars, and that He created them for light and for the reckoning of time (Gn 1:16; Ps 8:4; 136:9; Je 31:35). He numbers them and calls them by name (Ps 147:4). Personified, they are invited to praise Him (Ps 148:3), and in Jb 38:7 they are imagined as joining in song on the day of creation. The emphasis on their creation is to some extent polemic; Israel was influenced by the astral cults of Mesopotamia (cf HOST OF HEAVEN: Am 5:26; Dt 4:19). Allusions to astrology are few in the OT (Is 47:13). The stars are the absolute in height under the throne of Yahweh (Jb 22:12), and the height of human ambition, infringing upon the prerogatives of deity, is to strive to reach the stars (Is 14:13; Ob 4). In the apocalyptic judgment the stars are darkened or disturbed in their course or fall from the heavens (Is 13:10; Ezk 32:7; Jl 2:10; 4:15; Dn 8:10; Mt 24:29; Mk 13:25; Lk 21:25; Apc 6:13; 8:10–12; 9:1; 12:4). The darkening of the stars is a metaphor for old age (Ec 12:2) and the object of a mighty curse. As weapons of Yahweh they fight against Sisera* (Jgs 5:20); the rainfall during the battle impeded his chariots. The stars are dim before God (Jb 25:5). The righteous will shine like stars (Dn 12:3); Paul, perhaps developing this passage, compares the differences in the glory of the elect to the degrees of brightness of the stars (1 Co 15:41). The wicked, on the other hand, are stars which have wandered from their courses (Jd 19). The seven churches of Apc are seven stars (Apc 1:16, 20; 2:1; 3:1). The morning star is awarded to the righteous (Apc 2:28); there is probably no intended connection between this line and the title of morning star given to Jesus (Apc 22:16). The 12 stars with which the woman of Apc 12:1 is crowned are probably the 12 tribes of Israel. AA 27:20 alludes not only to the darkness of the storm but to the impossibility of celestial navigation; cf SHIP.

The usual translation of Nm 24:17, "a star will rise from Jacob," is questioned by W. F. Albright; cf BALAAM. The star of Bethlehem (Mt 2:2, 7, 9–10) is a unique case. Throughout the Bible the conception of the stars is the conception of the universe in the ancient Semitic world; cf CREATION. In this conception the star of Bethlehem moves easily. Modern interpreters are forced to look for a conjunction of stars which suits the event in its date and its course, or failing this — and it has failed — to suppose the creation for the purpose of a celestial luminous source. More recent interpreters suggest that the character of the episode indicates that the story of the star of Bethlehem is a midrash* formed upon Nm 24:17; when the Messiah appears the star of Jacob

rises and is discerned by those to whom God reveals it.

Stater. Cf MONEY.

Stephanas (Gk *stephanas,* perhaps nickname for *stephanephoros,* "crown bearer"), a Christian of Corinth, whose household was the first to be baptized (by Paul himself) in Achaea and who served the Church (1 Co 1:16; 16:15). He was one of the mission which reported to Paul at Ephesus and presumably carried 1 Co back to Corinth.

Stephen (Gk *stephanos,* "crown"). Stephen was a Jew of the Diaspora* living in Jerusalem (one of the group called Hellenists, AA 6:1; cf GREEK) who accepted Christianity. Because of a dissension between the Palestinian Jewish Christians and those of the Diaspora Stephen and six others were appointed to provide for the care of the needy of the community while the Twelve confined themselves to preaching (AA 6:1–6). The Seven, however, also preached; but it appears that they spoke only to the Jews of the Diaspora; only these are mentioned as disputing with Stephen (AA 6:9 f), and it was these who charged him before the council*. The burden of the charge was a prediction of the destruction of the temple and of the change of the law (AA 6:13 f); these charges can scarcely have been false. Jesus Himself predicted the one, and Stephen anticipated Paul in his attitude toward the law. The discourse of Stephen before the council is more artfully composed than appears on the surface; it enumerates the revelations and saving deeds of Yahweh, all outside Palestine, quotes Amos' criticism of sacrifice*, mentions the tabernacle* as the dwelling of Yahweh, and closes with the temple of Solomon, which is evidently described as a lapse from primitive and genuine religion. The peroration charges the Jews with killing the prophets and finally Jesus. The discourse very probably represents the earliest preaching of Christian converts from the Diaspora, which denied any peculiar holiness to the law, the temple, sacrificial ritual, and the Promised Land. This was judged blasphemy and Stephen was stoned* according to the law. Lk notes the presence of Saul (AA 8:1); the death of Stephen was the occasion of an event of momentous importance in the early Church.

It is probable that the differences between Palestinian and Hellenistic Jewish Christians went deeper than the distribution of goods. No doubt the question was already raised about the attitude of the Church toward Judaism and its obligations, not only for Gentiles but also for Hellenistic Jews. The question which it took a generation to solve and which was a pivotal point in the theology of Paul and the conception of salvation and the Church (cf GENTILE; LAW and related articles) is proposed in the discourse of Stephen, and a solution hardly less radical than that of Paul is suggested.

Steward. The usual translation of the Gk *oekonomos,* the manager of a large household or estate, who might be a slave. The name also designated a municipal officer (Rm 16:23, treasurer?). The steward had the management of the children of the owner (Gal 4:2). Jesus proposes the faithful steward as the example of the responsible Christian (Lk 12:42). The apostles are managers of the mysteries of God (1 Co 4:1–2; Tt 1:7), and the Christian is a steward of the grace of God (1 Pt 4:10). Jesus commends the dishonest steward of the parable (Lk 16:1 ff) not for his dishonesty but for his foresight; the Christian, who knows of the coming judgment, should exhibit greater foresight than the worldling.

Stones, precious. The use of precious and semiprecious stones in the ancient world, including Palestine, is shown by archaeology, which often discovers articles in which they are used. Palestine produces none of its own and had to import them. The names used to designate precious stones in the Bible are often of uncertain meaning; the three principal enumerations appear in the description of the breastplate of the high priest (Ex 28: 17–20; 39:10–13), the jewels of the king of Tyre (Ezk 28:13), and the walls of the heavenly Jerusalem (Apc 21:18–20). With no attempt to relate the Eng names to the Hb words, the precious stones mentioned in the Bible most probably include the following: agate, amethyst, beryl, carbuncle, chalcedony, chrysoprase, cornelian, diamond(?), emerald, jacinth, jasper, onyx, opal, quartz, ruby, sapphire, sardonyx, topaz.

Stoning. Stoning is a form of execution often mentioned in the Bible. Often it appears as a form of lynch law, and indeed this may have been the earliest form in which it occurred; it is mentioned as threatened (Ex 17:4; Nm 14:10; 1 S 30:6; Lk 20:6; AA 5:26; 14:5) and as done (1 K 12:18, Adoram; AA 14:19; 2 Co 11:25, Paul, who did not die from the stoning). When Shimei stoned David, he was probably trying to initiate a lynching (2 S 16:6). Jesus was threatened with stoning (Jn 8:59; 10:31, 33; 11:8). He charged the Jews with stoning the prophets (Mt 21:35; 23:37; Lk 13:34); the only OT allusion to the stoning of a prophet occurs in 2 Ch 24:21

(Zechariah*). The laws of the Pnt prescribe stoning for the following crimes: idolatry (Dt 13:10; 17:5); blasphemy (Lv 24:14; cf 1 K 21:10; Jn 10:33); child sacrifice (Lv 20:2); divination (Lv 20:27); Sabbath violation (Nm 15:32 ff); adultery (Dt 22:22 f; cf Ezk 16:40; 23:47; Jn 8:4 f); fornication by an unmarried woman (Dt 22:21); rebellion of children (Dt 21:20 f); and the ox that gores (Ex 21:28). It may be assumed that stoning is the penalty for other crimes in which the manner of execution is not specified.

Since Palestine is perhaps the stoniest of all areas in the world, one may suspect that the penalty came into use because of its convenience; in the laws of Hammurabi the most common penalty is drowning in the river, likewise convenient. The condemned is to be taken outside the town (where there are more stones; Lv 24:14, 23; Nm 15:36; 1 K 21:10, 13; AA 7:58); the witnesses to the charge cast the first stones (Lv 24:14; Dt 13:9; 17:7). But the penalty involves more than convenience. It is a community action in which each member takes part, thus sharing the judgment and the punishment, and in which no single person strikes the fatal blow. Originally the penalty reflected the conception of blood guilt; stoning is not the shedding of blood as the Israelites understood it, and thus no one incurred blood guilt.

Stranger. Stranger in the Bible designates one who is not a member of the social group. In early Israelite society, which was patriarchal, the stranger was a person who was not a member of the tribe. With the settlement and the rise of the monarchy, the stranger came to mean non-Israelite, roughly equivalent to our "alien." In all societies, even in modern civilization, the foreigner, while not an enemy by definition, as he is said to be in more primitive societies, is nonetheless strange and somewhat an object of suspicions. In early Israel the stranger was theoretically an enemy. This attitude extended to the stranger as a group and as remote. When the stranger entered the Israelite community as a guest, he was entitled to hospitality*. The OT exhibits a paradoxical combination of theoretical hostility to the stranger and practical friendliness and readiness to receive him. Contacts between Israelites and foreigners were constant. The theoretical hostility appears in such passages as Dt 7:1–7; 9:1–5; 12:1–3, in which the Israelites are commanded to exterminate the Canaanites. The history of the settlement shows that this was never done, and that the passage of Dt is a theoretical emphasis upon the religious difference between Israel and its neighbors. The great danger from foreigners in the time of Dt was that Israelites might adopt foreign religious beliefs and practices. Hence no communication with them beyond the necessary minimum was permitted. In Judaism the term foreigner becomes equivalent to heathen, a worshiper of false gods (2 Mc 10:2, 5). Some of the prophetic books contain oracles against foreign nations, "burdens" (Is 13–23; Je 46–51; Ezk 29–32; Na). These passages, which express hostility and predict the downfall of foreign nations, are often difficult for modern readers. They have, however, a basis in Israelite belief. The foreign nations, not recognizing the supremacy of Yahweh, must be brought to recognize His supremacy, and this can only mean their submission to Him. As claiming a power which belongs only to Yahweh they must fall, and they must be punished for their refusal to submit to even elementary morality. The school of Dt also expresses its opposition to foreigners by certain prohibitions of marriage*. These prohibitions also appear to be of later origin; the OT contains many instances of marriage between Israelites and foreigners.

The stranger could dwell in Israel either as a temporary guest or as a permanent resident alien (gēr or tôšāb). No distinction in meaning between gēr and tôšāb can be traced, and it is probable that the two words come from different sources or traditions. Some critics think that tôšāb, "dweller," is a later term. Gēr is often rendered in older Eng versions by "sojourner." The position of the gēr can be observed in the narratives. Abraham was a gēr in Egypt and in Canaan (Gn 12:10; 17:8; 20:1; 21:34; 23:4). Lot was a gēr in Sodom (Gn 19:9), and Isaac was a gēr in Canaan (Gn 26:3). Jacob and his clan were gērîm in Egypt (Gn 47:4), and Israelite tradition recalled that the fathers were gērîm in Egypt (Ex 22:20; 23:9; Dt 23:8). A Levite was a gēr in Bethlehem, from which he moved to Ephraim (Jgs 17:7 f), and another Levite appears as a gēr in Ephraim (Jgs 19:1). The Levites as a landless tribe no doubt had the status of gērîm. Moses was a gēr in Midian (Ex 2:22), and Elimelech became a gēr in Moab because of a famine (Rt 1:1). The men of Beeroth were gērîm in Israel (2 S 4:3), and fugitives from Moab were admitted into Israel as gērîm (Is 16:4). The status of the gēr was often uncertain, without any explicit guarantee of his rights and assurance of protection. Thus in Gn 12:12 ff; 20:2 ff; 26:6 ff Abraham and Isaac fear that their wives will be taken into the harem of the ruler of the land, which is narrated as happening in each instance. The codes of Israelite law give no explicit cata-

logue of the rights and duties of the gēr. They commend him as the object of charity (Dt 10:18; 14:29) and prohibit the oppression of the gēr (Ex 22:20; 23:9). These, together with such allusions as Ps 94:6 suggest that the gēr was often mistreated. The gēr was granted equal rights with the Israelites before the law (Dt 1:16) and was entitled to asylum for homicide (Nm 35:15; Jos 20:9). It is said explicitly of David's family that they were under the patronage of the king of Moab when David sent them to escape the anger of Saul (1 S 22:3). David himself later became a gēr in the military service of Achish of Gath (1 S 27:1 ff; 29:1 ff). Because he was a gēr the Philistine leaders did not trust him to take part in the war against Israel (1 S 29). Ittai* of Gath, a gēr, appears in the personal military service of David (2 S 15:19). There is no indication outside these passages that the gēr was a client of any person, clan, or tribe, although it is extremely probable that the gēr had to attach himself to some such patron. It seems that the gēr was not bound to military service, although he could hire himself, like David and Ittai, as a mercenary warrior. Some passages suggest that in early Israel and the early monarchy the gēr could be a landowner. When Abraham, a gēr at Hebron, wished to purchase a piece of ground for the burial of his family, the right to purchase was not granted until it had been submitted to the council of the city (Gn 23:4 ff). Other passages contrast the gēr with the "inhabitant" in such a way as to suggest the same thing (Lv 25:35; Pss 78:55; 105:11 ff). R. de Vaux believes that in the early period the gēr could not be a landowner, but supported himself by his hired labor (Dt 24:14). Ezk 47:22 ff prescribes that the gēr shall draw his lot for property equally with the Israelite; but this is a much later passage. Despite the danger of oppression to which the gēr was subject and his limited rights of land ownership, it was possible for them to become wealthy (Dt 28:43 f). The gēr could take no part in the deliberations of the assembly of the clan, tribe, or city. The gēr was not a cultic person; he could, however, at least in later Israel, become a cultic person by circumcision. The gēr was forbidden to eat meat with the blood (Lv 17:10 ff) and was obliged to follow the Israelite laws of sexual morality (Lv 18:26). These laws did not bind the gēr as strictly as they bound the Israelite (Dt 14:21). The gēr was entitled to the Sabbath rest (Ex 20:10; Dt 5:14). It is implied in Lv 17:8 that the gēr could offer sacrifice, cf also Lv 22:18; Nm 15:15, a later passage, imposes one law for the native Israelite and for the alien. The gērîm in preexilic Israel were quite probably the Canaanite population which had not been assimilated into Israel by marriage or adoption. The men of Beeroth were one such group which had retained its identity (2 S 4:3); there were probably others. The *gēr,* however, appears more frequently as an isolated individual or family and not as a distinct group.

Theologically Israel was a *gēr* who dwelt in the land of Yahweh, not its own (1 Ch 29:15; Lv 25:23). The individual Israelite also thought of himself as a *gēr* of Yahweh (Ps 38:13; 118:19).

The attitude of the primitive Church toward the foreigner was revolutionary, and the large number of foreigners who joined the community soon outnumbered the Jewish members. The OT conception of the *gēr* appears in the NT. The Christian is not a *gēr* but a citizen of the kingdom of God (Eph 2:19). With reference to this present world, however, the Christian who is a citizen of the kingdom of heaven is a *gēr* (1 Pt 1:1, 17; 2:11).

Succoth (Hb *sukkôt,* "tents"). **1.** A town probably located at the modern Tell Deirallah on the right bank of the Jabbok* in the Jordan valley E of Shechem*. A popular tradition connected the name with a camp of Jacob (Gn 33:17). It lay in the territory of Gad* (Jos 13:27). The elders of Succoth refused aid to Gideon in his pursuit of the Midianites, and he took revenge upon them (Jgs 8:5–7, 14–16). It is mentioned as a point of reference near Solomon's bronze foundry (1 K 7:46; 2 Ch 4:17). The valley of Succoth is alluded to in Pss 60:8; 108:8. **2.** A point on the exodus* of the Israelites from Egypt between Raamses* and Etham, Egyptian Tkw (Ex 12:37; 13:20; Nm 33:5 f). It is identified with the modern Tell el Mashuta in the Wadi Tumilat in the E Delta, about 8 mi E of the site of ancient Pithom*.

Sumerians. The name of the earliest inhabitants of Mesopotamia of whom there are historical records. The Sumerians are not mentioned in the Bible; but their cultural contributions to later Mesopotamian civilization, which had great influence on Israelite culture, were so great and so original that they must be included in a study of the biblical background. Sumerian cities explored by archaeology include Uruk (biblical Erech*), Lagash (modern Tello), Nippur (modern Niffer), Shuruppak (modern Fara), Ur* (modern Muqayyar), Eridu (modern Tell Abu Shahrein), Kish (modern el Oheimir), Jemdet Nasr (ancient name unknown), Eshnunna (modern Tell Asmar), and some others of less importance. These explorations have recovered tens of thousands of Sumerian tablets and revealed extensive remains of Sumerian cities and temples. The Sumerian language can now be read by scholars and the history of Sumer from the beginning of written records reconstructed and dated with some assurance. This is a remarkable achievement; as recently as 1915 leading scholars denied that the Sumerians ever existed.

The language of the Sumerians belongs to the agglutinative type (Turkish, Finnish, Hungarian). As yet it has been connected with no known language group. The racial type of the Sumerians is well described in their own art, but their racial connections are likewise unknown; they were not a Semitic people. They probably entered Mesopotamia via the Persian Gulf about 3000 BC. They were not the aboriginal inhabitants of the country. The geographical name Sumer in ancient times designated lower Mesopotamia from the mouth of the Diyala to the Persian Gulf. The shoreline at the mouth of the Tigris and Euphrates has advanced at least 65–70 mi in historic times by deposits of silt; Eridu, the southernmost of the Sumerian cities, once lay on the seacoast.

1. History. Uruk VI–IV period (named after the archaeological levels of Uruk): before 2800 BC. During this period the Sumerians appear organized in cities which are temple* communities. The god is the king of the city and the temple is the owner of the land; the people are the servants and tenants of the temple. Writing and art are known and monumental temples are erected. Commerce and the crafts and the division of labor permit fuller realization of natural resources.

Jemdet Nasr period, 2800–2600 BC. Very little is known of the history. The period seems to have ended in a catastrophe.

Mesilim period, before and after 2600 BC; named after a king of Kish. There appears a tendency for independent city-states to league themselves under one king as an overlord.

Ur I period, 2500–2350 BC. Ur was the dominant power among the Sumerian cities. Its wealth and artistic progress are evident from the royal tombs excavated by C. L. Woolley. Its kings have left numerous inscriptions and records. Much information also comes from the city of Lagash through documents, inscriptions, and statues. The vulture stele of Eannatum celebrates a victory of Lagash over the city of Umma. Urukagina of Lagash instituted social reforms in which he limited the power of the temples and great landlords in favor of the lower classes. With him the dynasty of Lagash ended; the city was destroyed by the invasion of Umma.

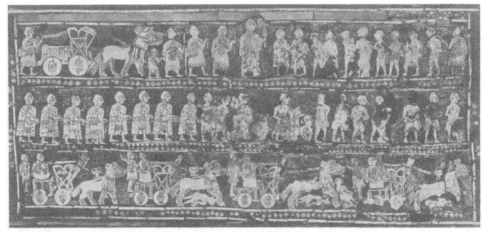

a) and b) Sumerian triumph scenes showing procession, prisoners of war and booty, and banquet scene. c) Gudea of Lagash in posture of adoration. d) Monument of Ur-Nina.

Lugalzaggisi, king of Umma, then claimed the title of "king of the lands" over all Sumer; but his empire was destroyed by an Akkadian* invasion from the N.

Akkadian dynasty, 2350–2150. Under a series of able kings, of whom Sargon and Naram-Sin were outstanding, the Akkadian empire extended throughout Mesopotamia. The empire incited an outburst of artistic and literary effort as the Akkadians inherited the cultural legacy of Sumer. The victory stele of Naram-Sin is perhaps the greatest artistic monument of the period. The contacts of Mesopotamian peoples with western peoples were closer than ever before. Under the successor of Naram-Sin, Shar-kali-sharri, the Akkadian dynasty lost its vigor and Mesopotamia was invaded by barbarous tribes from the E, the Guti, who wrecked and destroyed the cities of Sumer. Their unstable domination was short-lived and was followed by a period of Sumerian restoration.

Ur III period, 2067–1955. The victory over the Guti was achieved by Utu-hengal of Uruk; but the hegemony of Sumer was taken from him by Ur-nammu of Ur. The peace of the period is described in the inscriptions of Gudea of Lagash, a satellite city of Ur; Gudea engaged in no military campaigns, but was devoted to the welfare of his people and to his building enterprises, in particular the building of temples, for Gudea was the most devout of all Sumerian rulers. The peace did not endure. Sumer was threatened both by the growing Semitic power to the N and by Elam* from the E. The last three kings of Ur had Semitic names. Sumerian civilization survived for a short time in the dynasties of Isin (1970–1735) and Larsa (1960–1698), but the Sumerians as a people disappear at the beginning of the 2nd millennium.

Some recent scholars, in particular Americans, prefer other designations for the periods of Sumerian history:

Warka (Uruk) 3250–3000
Jemdet Nasr 3000–2800

These two are sometimes called the Proto-literate period.

Early Dynastic (Protodynastic)	
I	2900–2700
II	2700–2600
IIIa	2600–2500
IIIb	2500–2350
Akkadian dynasty	2350–2180
Guti invasion	2180–2060
Ur III	2060–1950

2. Culture. The contributions of Sumer to Mesopotamian civilization include, as mentioned above, the very conception of city life and civic organization. This also includes the concept and practice of law. In 1947 fragments of a code of Lipit-Ishtar, king of Isin in the first half of the 19th century BC, written in Sumerian, were discovered. In 1948 a fragment of the code of Bilalama of Eshnunna, also in Sumerian and about 70 years earlier than Lipit-Ishtar, was discovered. These are both antedated by a tablet of a code of Ur-nammu of Ur, about 2050 BC, and it is altogether possible that the codification of Sumerian law may be much older than Ur III. The Sumerians developed the monumental architecture and fortifications which are necessary for city life; these were the models which the later Semitic peoples developed. The art of Sumer appears to best advantage in its cylinder seals; but the Sumerians also employed sculpture in the round and relief sculpture. The style is distinctive and original, although the technique is primitive, and the Semitic peoples developed a technique of their own. For subjects and style and motif and symbols of the divine, however, they retained Sumerian features.

The most important Sumerian invention was the cuneiform* script. This was first used for records and accounts. Sumerian literature is a later development. That it is preserved at all is largely due to the temple scribes of the Semitic peoples. Sumerian survived as a sacred language after it had ceased to live, and the Semitic scribes copied and translated much Sumerian material. The temple scribes of Nippur, however, seem to have made a deliberate effort to collect the entire Sumerian literary tradition. The types of literature include wisdom* collections, historical texts and chronicles, omen literature, and religious and mythological texts. The religion and mythology of Sumer had a predominant influence in the religion and mythology of the Semitic peoples of Mesopotamia. Originally Sumerian deities of the same type and sometimes of the same name worshiped by the Semitic peoples included the fertility goddess Inanna (Akkadian Ishtar), her consort Dumuzi (Tammuz) and the cycle of death and resurrection; the "nameless" gods, the Anunnaki and the Igigi; the cosmic triad of Anu (the heavens) Enlil (the upper air), and Enki (the lower waters, Akkadian Ea); the sun god Utu (Akkadian Shamash) and the moon god Nanna (Akkadian Sin). The Akkadians followed the Sumerian practice of building the ziggurat, the step-tower beside the temple (cf BABEL, TOWER OF). The Mesopotamian belief in demons* is Sumerian in origin. The hymns, divination* texts and incantations of Mesopotamia are derived from Sumerian originals. Among Sumerian myths the most important for biblical studies is the myth of the deluge*, found in the Akkadian epic of Gilgamesh*, which has a Sumerian original. There is also a Sumerian myth of the descent of Inanna into the nether world which is imitated in the Akkadian myth of Ishtar and is related to the cult of fertility. The Sumerian belief in the afterlife is vague and the epic of Gilgamesh expresses despair, but one startling and so far unparalleled burial practice must be mentioned; in the royal tombs of Ur I there often appeared a large number of bodies, which in the greatest tomb discovered numbered 80. This tomb was extremely rich in artistic objects and ornaments of gold and silver. The bodies were undisturbed and the presence of small flasks suggested that all 80 entered the tomb when the king was buried and drank poison. The literature discloses no motive for this practice; it does not, however, as some scholars think, imply a belief in an afterlife.

Sun. In both Egypt* and Mesopotamia* the sun was an extremely important religious symbol; a large number of gods in both countries are solar deities. The Hb word *šemeš* is cognate to the Akkadian Shamash, a solar deity who was a god of justice. Allusions to the cult of the sun in Israel are few; it was venerated in the astral cults of the 7th century (cf HOST OF HEAVEN: 2 K 23:5; Je 8:2). Horses and chariots dedicated to the sun stood in the temple of Yahweh during this period (2 K 23:11). In the time of Ezekiel* a cult of the sun with incense was conducted in the temple (Ezk 8:16). As a natural body the sun was a creature of Yahweh; it was created after light*, which was conceived as a distinct being, indeed the primary being associated with deity. The sun is merely a bearer of light (Gn 1:16). It moves in obedience to the command of Yahweh (Jb 9:7; Mt 5:45). Its place in poetry is small; a notable exception is the description of the sun emerging like a strong young man to run its course (Ps 19:5–7). Some scholars suggest the Pss here employ a Canaanite original. The darkening of the sun is one of the phenomena of the apocalyptic judgment (Is 13:10; 30:26; Mt 24:29; Mk 13:24; Apc 6:12; 8:12; 9:2). The heavenly Jerusalem will need no sun, for the glory of the Lamb will be brighter than the sun (Apc 21:23; 22:5). God is called the sun of the Psalmist (Ps 84:12). The brightness of the sun is a metaphor for glory (Apc 12:1 +), and the power of sunstroke to harm both man and vegetation is known (2 K 4:19 ff; Jon 4:6–8; Ps 121:6; Is 49:10).

The sun is said to stand still during Joshua's battle at Gibeon (Jos 10:12–14) and to recede 10 steps (on the sun dial?; Is 38:7 f). These can scarcely be rationalized into natural phenomena. The first is a quotation from a war song glossed by the compiler; the second is a symbol of the prolongation of the life of Hezekiah*, which is conceived as the regress of time.

Susa (Hb *šûšān*, meaning uncertain), a city of the Persians; a royal residence (Ne 1:1 and Est *passim,* where it is the scene of the narrative; the scene of the vision of Dn in 8:2 ff). The remains of ancient Susa lie in Iran about 160 mi N of Abadan at the mouth of the Shatt el Arab, the confluence of the Tigris* and the Euphrates*. The site has been excavated extensively by a French archaeological mission which began its work in 1897; the results have been extremely illuminating for the history of ancient Elam and Persia. The most famous discovery at the site was a stele on which the laws of Hammurabi* were inscribed; the stele had been taken to Susa from Babylon as a trophy of war.

The origins of the city lie in prehistoric times. The levels of occupation showed a correlation with other cultures of early Mesopotamia; Susa I (4000–3500 BC) corresponded to the culture of Tell Obeid, a transitional period (3400–3100 BC) to Uruk, and Susa II (3100–2900 BC) to Jemdet Nasr. Susa II is the period of Akkadian immigration in S Mesopotamia. The city became the center of the Elamite* political organization about 2500 BC and remained the Elamite royal residence until the destruction of the kingdom and the city of Susa by Ashur-banipal of Assyria in 640 BC. The city was occupied by the Persians and rebuilt magnificently by Darius I; it became the winter residence of the Persian kings and the chief administrative center of the Persian empire. It was the base from which Alexander marched into India. It passed into the hands of the Seleucid* kingdom, who lost it to the Parthians.

Susa of the Persian period was a large city, marked by four distinct tells or mounds. The Tell of the Apadana was the site of the palace and audience hall built by Darius; this is "Susa the fortress" (castle, citadel in some Eng versions) of the OT. The tell of the acropolis was the site of the Elamite royal city. The tell of the royal city was the quarters of the officers and personnel of the palace and the court. The tell of the city of the artisans was a smaller and later extension of the site in the Persian period.

Susanna (Hb *šûšan*, "lily"), a personal name; the heroine of the story of Dn 13. Susanna the wife of Joakim was the object of the lustful desire of two elders of the Babylonian

Jewish community. They trapped her in the garden of her home while she was bathing and threatened to accuse her of adultery unless she yielded to their desires. She refused and was tried and condemned on their accusation. On the way to execution Daniel refused to accept the verdict, and on his examination of the elders the falsehood was detected and the elders were executed.

Susanna is called the world's first detective story, and it is one of the passages of the Bible which most recommends itself simply as a story in its own right. It is, of course, an entirely fictitious narrative with drama and suspense. It does exhibit the common wisdom* theme of innocence defended and malice punished. Some scholars suggest that its purpose is more precise and that it is a midrash* intended to point out abuses in judicial procedure.

The chapter does not exist in Hb and is not in the Jewish and Protestant canon*. It is not unlikely that Daniel was not the original hero of the story and became the hero only when Susanna was appended to Dn. A Hb original is suggested by several scholars; against this opinion are the puns in 13:54 f; 58 f, which are possible only in Gk: *schinos* (mastic) = *schizein* (split); *prinos* (liveoak) = *priein*, (saw). The interrogation of the elders is the denouement of the story and a rewriting of the passage in another language seems unlikely. No date can be assigned except a date later than Dn itself.

Swear. Cf OATH.

Swine. The swine is enumerated among the unclean animals (Lv 11:7; Dt 14:8; cf CLEAN). No particular prejudice appears in the list; the swine is unclean because, while it cleaves the hoof, it does not chew the cud. It is mentioned rarely elsewhere. To offer swine is a profane sacrifice (Is 66:3). The eating of pork mentioned in Is 55:4; 66:17 seems to be part of certain superstitious rites. In the Maccabean period abstention from pork became one of the key symbols of Jewish observance; and it has remained such a symbol into modern times. Sacrifice of swine was prescribed by Antiochus* IV as a part of his program to assimilate the Jews to the Greeks (1 Mc 1:47). There are stories, not certainly historical, of Eleazar* (2 Mc 6:18 ff) and the seven brothers (2 Mc 7:1 ff) who submitted to torture and death rather than eat pork. The golden ring in the swine's snout (Pr 11:22) is the extreme of the incongruous.

The saying of Jesus, "Do not cast your pearls before swine" (Mt 7:6) is paralleled in classical Greek and reflects the repugnance which Jews felt for the animal. When the prodigal son of the parable had to herd swine (Lk 15:15 f) he fell as low as a Jew could fall. 2 Pt 2:22 quotes the proverb about the sow returning to the mire to illustrate the obdurate sinner. The episode of the demoniac and the swine (Mt 8:30–32; Mk 5:11–13, 16; Lk 8:32 f), in which the demons, expelled by Jesus, are permitted by Him to take possession of a herd of swine, which they then drive to death in the sea, is one of the more spectacular exorcisms of the Gospel. Possibly the story of the exorcism has here been enlarged by symbolism; the demon of the story is "unclean," and its proper dwelling is the unclean animal, the swine. But the sacred soil of the land of promise cannot bear the unclean animal or the unclean demon in the presence of the Messiah, and it rejects both of them.

Sword. The sword is made in two types, each of which is attested from early times: the rapier or thrust sword, made with a pointed double-edged blade narrow in proportion to its length, and the saber or slashing sword, curved with a single-edged blade. An Oriental modification of the saber is the scimitar, which has an exaggerated curve, almost semicircular, which resembles the blade of a sickle. Hb has no words to distinguish the various types of sword; *hereb* designates them all. Neither does Hb have a word for dagger, which is a thrusting weapon with a blade no longer than 16 in. The weapon used by Ehud* (Jgs 3:12 f) and Joab* on two occasions (2 S 3:27; 20:8) was a dagger, since it was concealed beneath the garments. Representations in ancient art and archaeological remains show little change in technique over the entire ancient period except for improvements in the attachment of the blade to the handle. The material of the sword was changed from bronze to iron in the late 2nd millennium BC. During the period when the Philistines maintained a monopoly or iron* in Palestine the Israelites had no swords (1 S 13:19, 22). The sword was kept in a leather sheath and was worn at the girdle, usually simply stuck under the girdle (ANEP 28, 36, 40 +); a Hittite prince is depicted wearing a baldric (ANEP 461). The Hittite sword is a straight rapier represented as longer than the blade used by other peoples (ANEP 36, 40); the Assyrians (ANEP 174 +) and the Sea Peoples (ANEP 59) have a shorter weapon which, like the Roman infantry weapon, was scarcely longer than a dagger. This was intended for close combat and could be employed for thrusting or for slashing. It is a matter of interest that the short infantry sword in the ancient world always overcame the broad saber in the long run; it was more easily handled and permitted mass attack. The scimitar (Canaanite, ANEP 48, 468; Egyptian, 338; Palestinian, 176, 496; Babylonian, 699; Assyrian, 706) is thought by some scholars to have been a ceremonial weapon rather than a practical weapon of war.

In the OT "one who draws a sword" is a man of military age. To kill "at the mouth [edge] of the sword" is to kill after the manner of the sword i.e., without quarter. The sword was part of the normal equipment of the warrior. A war cry of Israel on one occasion was "the sword of Yahweh and of Gideon" (Jgs 7:20). Metaphorically the slanderous tongue is a sword (Pss 55:21; 57:5; 59:8; Pr 12:18; 30:14). The sword is often represented as a monster which devours (Dt 32:42; 2 S 2:26; Is 1:20; Je 2:30; 12:12; 46:10 +). "The sword" metaphorically means war, and it is often sent or drawn by Yahweh (Lv 26:6, 25; 2 S 11:25; Je 5:12; 46:16; Ezk 7:15). It also means violence (2 S 12:10). The sword is an instrument by which Yahweh punishes (1 Ch 21:12; Ps 7:12; Is 34:5 f; 66:16; Apc 19:15). This is the theme of Ezekiel's Song of the Sword (Ezk 21:13–22). "Sword, famine and pestilence" is a triple threat against Judah often found in Jeremiah. In the messianic peace swords will be beaten into ploughshares (Is 2:4; Mi 4:3); this phrase is inverted for the apocalyptic judgment, when ploughshares will be beaten into swords (Jl 4:10).

In Gk the short sword (*machaira*), the broad sword or saber (*rhomphaia*) and the rapier (*xiphos*) are distinguished; but the NT uses only the first two of these somewhat loosely. The sword symbolizes authority (Rm 13:4); this probably reflects the Roman legal term *ius gladii*, the right of capital punishment. The sword was an instrument of execution (AA 12:2; Heb 11:37). The rider on the red horse who bears a sword (Apc 6:4) is war. Metaphorically the sword means sorrow (Lk 2:35). The sword of persecution cannot separate the Christian from the love of Christ (Rm 8:35). The sword which proceeds from the mouth of the Servant* of the Lord (Is 49:2) and from the mouth of the Lamb (Apc 1:16; 2:12, 16) is the word* of God. This sword of the spirit, the word of God is part of the armor of the Christian (Eph 6:17). The word of God, sharper than a two-edged sword, penetrates the innermost part of man (Heb 4:12); the word of God in these passages is not the written word of the sacred books, but the revealed word of the prophet and the apostle, and in particular the word of Jesus. It confutes His enemies, furnishes the Christian with a defense, and forces every man to a decision by stripping him of pretense and excuse.

The use of the sword in the defense of Jesus at His arrest (Mt 26:51; Mk 14:47; Lk 22:49 f; Jn 18:10 f) is the occasion of a saying reported only in Mt 26:52: they who take the sword shall perish by the sword. Jesus said that He came to bring not peace but a sword (Mt 10:34), where the context clearly indicates that the sword means hostility aroused by faith in Him. Mt 26:52 makes explicit what is implicit in the other Gospels concerning His attitude to the use of violence in His defense; He sharply rejects it. But the generalization goes beyond a particular occasion and can be interpreted as nothing but a total repudiation of the use of arms and violence. This is altogether in harmony with other sayings of the Gospel (Mt 5:38–48; Lk 6:27–30, 32–36); an appeal to violence ultimately produces nothing except the destruction of him who appeals to it. This need not be understood as a moral repudiation but simply as a declaration of the futility of violence; and Christians who believe that there is a legitimate violence must themselves consider how they suit their belief with the judgment of Jesus on violence. It seems that the minimum of respect for the words of the Gospel would prevent anyone from advocating the use of violence to advance the work of Jesus Christ.

It is possible that Lk 22:35–38 preserves the same saying in a different form. The warning of Jesus to obtain swords is evidently metaphorical, a warning to prepare for combat; and the shallow literal understanding of the words by the disciples is left by Lk to collapse of its own weight. In the context immediately before the passion of Jesus no explanation that this is not the time for swordplay was necessary.

Sychar (Gk *sychar,* meaning uncertain), a town in Samaria near the well of Jacob* where Jesus met and conversed with the Samaritan woman (Jn 4:6). Several have identified Sychar with the village of Askar, about 3 mi N of the well of Jacob. The name of Askar, however, is recent, and it is much more probable that Sychar is a Gk corruption of Shechem*.

Syene (Hb *sᵉwēnēh,* meaning uncertain), a place mentioned in Ezk 29:10; 30:6 as the S frontier of Egypt. The place is to be identified with the modern Assuan, 560 mi S of the Mediterranean and a few miles N of the 1st cataract of the Nile* and the traditional boundary point in ancient times between Egypt and Cush* (Nubia). The quarries of Aswan were the source of the rose granite used extensively in the building and sculpture of ancient Egypt. The city lies opposite the island of Elephantine*, the site of a Jewish military colony in the 5th century BC.

Synagogue (Gk *synagōgē*, "assembly" or "collection"), the Gk name of Jewish places of assembly for prayer and instruction (Hb *ḳahāl*, Aramaic *bēt kᵉnîstā'*). The synagogue arose as a result of the destruction of the temple of Jerusalem in 587 BC and of the dispersion of the Jews outside Palestine (cf DIASPORA). A cult centered upon the temple ritual was impossible, and the synagogue was organized as a substitute to maintain Jewish unity in faith and worship. The earliest synagogues were doubtless purely private gatherings in private dwellings. The origin of the synagogue cannot be certainly dated; it is generally agreed that it goes back at least to the time of Ezra, and possibly to the period of the Exile in Babylonia. The synagogues may be meant by "the assemblies of El" in Ps 74:8, a postexilic psalm. By NT times the synagogue was an established and essential part of Jewish life and cult. The synagogue had become a distinct building erected for the purpose; and it was found in every Palestinian town of any size and in cities outside Palestine where there was a community of Jews. In Capernaum* the synagogue was built by the gift of a Gentile (Lk 7:5). In large cities there were several synagogues; the "synagogue of the freedmen" (Hellenistic Jews) is mentioned in Jerusalem (AA 6:9).

The synagogue was not, like the temple, a house where the deity dwelt, but a meeting house for prayer and the study of the law. It was a lay organization; sacrifice had no place in the synagogue cult, and if a priest happened to be present he was, except for certain courtesies, not distinguished from other members of the congregation. The government of the synagogue was committed to the elders* of the synagogue, who were probably the elders of the community. The management and maintenance of the synagogue and the order of the services were in charge of an *archisynagogus* or "ruler of the synagogue" (Lk 8:41; AA 18:8, 17 +). The synagogue had certain judicial and punitive powers (Mt 10:7; 23:34; Mk 13:9; Lk 21:12; 12:11; AA 9:2; 22:19; 26:11). There were no officers appointed to conduct the services; these were conducted by members of the congregation or by guests, both by invitation. The courtesy shown guests was of no small importance in the missionary journeys of Christian apostles (cf below). How often the synagogue had an elementary school for the instruction of children during the NT period cannot be determined.

Services were held in the synagogue on the Sabbath* and on feast days. Men and women were segregated in the seating. The services began with the recitation of the *Shema* (Dt 6:4 ff), the Jewish profession of faith. This was followed by a long prayer recited by one of the congregation; originally improvised, the prayers acquired a set form which was copied in manuals. A section of the law was read in Hb, followed by a translation or paraphrase into the vernacular (cf TARGUM) and then by a homily upon the passage read, again improvised by a member of the congregation (AA 15:21). The reading of the prophets was added early to the reading of the Law. If a priest were present, the services were concluded by the recitation of the sacerdotal blessing (Nm 6:24–26). The services were gradually expanded by the addition of other prayers and the singing of psalms. The Pnt* was arranged in a cycle of reading which covered the entire Pnt in three years.

The oldest remains of a synagogue are found near Alexandria from 250–200 BC. The Jewish-Roman war of AD 66–70 seems to have caused the demolition of most of the Palestinian synagogues, as there are no remains which are certainly earlier than the 3rd century AD. It is unlikely that there was any notable modification in the style of the building, which was basically very simple; it consisted of a rectangular hall, usually in the basilica style with a nave and two side aisles. The entrance had one or three doors with a vestibule and possibly a portico. In these later synagogues the segregation of the sexes was accomplished by a gallery on two sides and the rear, in which the women sat. The synagogue was furnished with an ark or chest in which the scroll of the law was kept, the tribune on which speakers and readers stood, a table, lamps, and horns and trumpets for ceremonial purposes. The ark of the law occupied the central position against the front wall and was heavily decorated with hangings; the construction of an apse in which the ark was placed was possibly introduced under the influence of Christian churches. Adjoining the main room were smaller rooms for work and storage and often one or more open courts. One of the storage rooms was the *genizah*. Here MSS of the law which were worn, damaged, or incorrectly written were stored; to destroy them was not permitted. The *genizah* of the synagogue of Old Cairo has disclosed a large number of old and important MSS. The synagogue of Capernaum* is the best preserved Palestinian synagogue; like the others, it comes from the 3rd century AD. Talmudic tradition relates that a rabbinical opinion of the 3rd or 4th century permitted the decoration of synagogues; several of the remains exhibit mosaic floors with decorative patterns, and the remarkable synagogue of Dura Europos on the Euphrates had its walls decorated with paintings of biblical scenes. These paintings came from the same atelier and perhaps from the same artist who decorated the pagan temple of Dura Europos. In NT times and earlier it is likely that most Jews would have regarded such decorations as a violation of the second commandment. The synagogue of Capernaum was spacious, about 83 ft by 61 ft.

More than any other single factor the synagogue was responsible for the survival of Judaism as a religion and of the Jews as a distinct people against the powerful assimilative forces of Hellenism*. It was not only a place where the law and the traditions were preserved and explained; it was also a meeting place of the Jewish community. The great discovery that Judaism could exist as an active religion without a temple and temple cult was the decisive factor in creating the idea of a religion which was first of all a faith and a way of life.

The synagogue was also of vital importance in the origins and growth of Christianity. Jesus attended the synagogue regularly and made it one of the places in which He taught (Mt 4:23; 9:35; 12:9; Mk 1:39; 3:1; Lk 4:15; 6:6; 13:10; Jn 18:20). His procedure often began from the synagogue functions of the reading of the Bible and the homily, which gave Him an occasion to announce the gospel; this procedure in the synagogue of Nazareth* is described in Lk 4:16–21. Other episodes are noted in the synagogue of Capernaum (Mk 1:21 ff; Jn 6:59).

Even closer is the connection between the synagogue and the preaching of the gospel by the apostles. Paul began his preaching in the synagogue of Damascus (AA 9:20); and in his journeys it was his practice to go first to the synagogue of the city where, as a guest, he would be invited to give a homily. This procedure is mentioned explicitly as followed at Salamis in Cyprus (AA 13:5), Antioch of Pisidia (AA 13:14), Iconium (AA 14:1), Thessalonica (AA 17:1), Berea (AA 17:10), Corinth (AA 18:4), and Ephesus (AA 19:8). In most of these places Paul's visit to the synagogue ended in quarrels and sometimes in violence. It should not be thought that Paul's visits to the synagogue were a kind of infiltration of the Jewish community; Paul and his associates thought of themselves as Jews announcing the messianic salvation of Israel, and they abandoned the synagogues only when the Jews repudiated them. It is obvious how important the network of synagogues visited by Paul was for the diffusion of the gospel in Asia and the mainland of Europe.

The synagogue was also of importance in the development of the Christian cult. In Jewish Christian communities their own assembly was called a synagogue (Js 2:2). The worship of the Christian community, changed from the Sabbath to the day following, was organized around the synagogue service of prayer and the reading of the Bible, to which Christians added the celebration of the *agape* and the Eucharist*. There in essence and substance is the ritual of the Mass. The early communities had elders* to govern them like the synagogue, ministers (deacons*) to assist in the services and management of the assembly; and the Christian overseer (*episkopos,* bishop) in his earliest form was probably closely related in office and functions to the *archisynagogus.*

Synoptic Question. In modern biblical criticism the term Synoptic Question or Synoptic Problem designates the question which arises from the relations of Mt-Mk-Lk and leads to the question of their origins. The problem is raised only in modern criticism i.e., not before the late 18th century. In earlier biblical study the problem was conceived as a problem of harmonization, solved most frequently by simply conflating the variant details of the Gospels.

The problem arises from the substantial agreement of Mt-Mk-Lk in content and in form, and the numerous and striking divergences in details. No similar problem is found in either ancient or modern literature. No satisfactory and universally accepted solution of the problem has been proposed, and many critics feel that it is unlikely that such a solution will emerge. The hypotheses suggested, summarized below, all contain elements of a solution, and each in its own way has contributed to the ultimate purpose of literary criticism, which is a better understanding of the Gospels; but no single solution can be proposed as anything more than a hypothesis.

It is important that the problem be grasped, the problem of "the synoptic fact." Certain terms are employed to simplify the discussion: by "the triple tradition" is meant material which is found in Mt-Mk-Lk; by "the double tradition" is meant material which is found in Mt-Lk (for reasons which will appear below, the term is not employed to designate Mt-Mk or Lk-Mk material, which is designated simply as Mk or "Marcan"); a "simple tradition" is material which is proper to any one of the three. Taking Mk as the standard, the triple tradition is found in 330 verses out of 661 in Mk (excluding Mk 16:9–20), 330 out of 1068 in Mt, 330 out of 1150 in Lk. The double tradition is found in 230 verses of Mt and of Lk. The simple traditions are found in 50 verses of Mk; 315–330 verses of Mt; 500–600 verses of Lk. The use of Mk is different in Mt and in Lk. Mt contains all of Mk except 40–50 verses. Lk includes about 350 verses of Mk; of the rest, some is simply omitted, and reasons for the omission can be suggested: Lk did not relate two episodes which seemed to make the same point; he omitted passages which appeared difficult or unimportant for Gentile readers. But elsewhere he relates the same episodes which Mk relates from other sources: Mk 1:16–20 = Lk 5:1–11; Mk 3:22–30 = Lk 11:14–23; 12:10; Mk 4:30–32 = Lk 13:18 f; Mk 6:1–6 = Lk 4:16–30; Mk 9:42–48 = Lk 17:1 f; Mk 9:49 f = Lk 14:34 f; Mk 10:11 f = Lk 16:18; Mk 10:31 = Lk 13:30; Mk 10:35–45 = Lk 22:24–27; Mk 12:28–34 = Lk 10:25–28; Mk 13:15 f = Lk 17:31; Mk 13:21–23 = Lk 17:23; Mk 13:33–37 = Lk 12:35–40; Mk 14:27–31 = Lk 22:31–34.

Structure. The arrangement and structure of the three shows both agreement and divergence. All show the same basic arrangement of the events of the public life of Jesus: preparation (John the Baptist, baptism and temptation of Jesus), ministry in Galilee, journey to Jerusalem, Passion and Resurrection. Furthermore, even in smaller groupings the arrangement of the events is often remarkably similar. The same groupings appear in Mk 1:21–45 = Mt 7:28–8:16; Mk 2:1–22 = Mt 9:1–17; Mk 2:23–3:6 = Mt 12:1–14; Mk 3:22–4:34 = Mt 12:22–13:34; Mk 4:35–5:20 = Mt 8:18–34; Mk 5:21–43 = Mt 9:18–26. Lk follows Mk more faithfully than Mt does, inserting his own material as a rule without disturbing the order of Mk. But these agreements in arrangement are found amid surprising disagreements; the list of Mt-Mk groupings just cited shows that the groupings in Mt diverge from the general order of Mk, and there are other divergences as well. Lk places the call of the disciples after the first preaching of Jesus at Capernaum (5:1–11), and Mk places it before (1:16–20). Mk places the rejection of Jesus at Nazareth at the conclusion of the Galilean ministry (6:1–6), Lk places it at the beginning (4:16–30). The order found in both Mk 1:21–6:13 and Lk 4:31–9:6 is at variance with the order found in Mt 4:23–13:58. Even in single episodes inversion appears (the temptation of Jesus, Mt 4:1–11; Lk 4:1–13).

Details. Complete agreement in details is not to be expected; what is not expected is the number of curious and quite close agreements in detail, although no strict pattern

of agreement emerges; if it did, the Synoptic problem would be solved. As examples may be cited: Mt 4:18 = Mk 1:16; Mt 9:6 = Mk 2:10 = Lk 5:24; Mt 3:7b–10 = Lk 3:7b–9. In addition there are agreements in the use of rare or vulgar Gk words in two or even in three. The agreement appears in citations of the OT which follow neither the Hb text nor the LXX e.g. Mt 3:3 = Mk 1:3 = Lk 3:4; Mt 11:10 = Mk 1:2 = Lk 7:27. The use of the OT seems to postulate a *florilegium* of texts collected by Christians; cf GOSPEL.

Here likewise agreement is found in the midst of variations. Many of the variations may be reduced to literary polish by Mt or Lk, others to variant translations of a single Aramaic original. In others this explanation does not explain. Léon-Dufour cites passages where the Gospels exhibit the same fixed structure with a variation of words (Mt 23:13 = Lk 11:52; Mt 12:27 = Mk 3:29 vs Lk 11:21 f), and other passages where words are fixed but the structure is varied; i.e., identical words are found in different places, with different meanings, situations, or functions (Mt 15:27 vs Mk 7:28; Mk 4:19 vs Lk 8:14; Mt 22:25 vs Mk 12:20; Mt 9:19 vs Mk 5:24; Mt 10:27 vs Lk 12:3; Mt 27:50 vs Mk 15:37; Mt 13:55 vs Mk 6:5).

The problem can be stated thus: the numerous agreements seem to demand literary interdependence of the Gospels; the numerous divergences, additions, and omissions seem to exclude literary interdependence. Since the late 18th century the hypotheses proposed to explain the Synoptic fact fall into three classes: oral tradition as a common source; literary interdependence; one or more common documentary sources.

I. Oral Tradition. In modern criticism the primacy and the importance of oral tradition in the formation of the Gospels is almost universally admitted (cf GOSPEL). It is rejected with almost the same universality as a single adequate answer to the Synoptic Question, which precisely is concerned with the triple tradition. Oral tradition may more easily be invoked for simple traditions; the elements of oral style can be discerned in the Gospels, although these do not prove that the material could not have been written before it was incorporated into the canonical Gospels. Oral tradition helps to explain the divergences of the Gospels; it can scarcely account for their agreements.

II. Literary Interdependence. In its simplest form this theory proposes that one Gospel is the source of the others, or that two are the source of the third. In this simple form it is almost universally abandoned by scholars. The question of interdependence, however, is vital to any explanation of the Synoptic Problem; and the following conclusions are now generally accepted by scholars.

Mk is independent of Mt-Lk. This critical affirmation of the priority of Mk (called a "dogma" by some who doubt it) is almost universally received. Mt here means the canonical Gk Gospel; cf below for possible earlier forms of Mt. The conclusion, critics think, is imposed by Mk's brevity, which is not the work of an abbreviator, and by the vivid and primitive features of his style (cf MARK).

Lk depends on Mk. The dependence is generally accepted; the nature and extent of the dependence is disputed. For the "Marcan sections" (Lk 4:31–6:19; 8:4–9:50; 18:15–21:38) there seems to be little room for argument. But one must note some doublets in Lk, in which the same episode appears both in the Marcan sections and in Lucan sections: 8:16 = 11:33; 8:17 = 12:2; 11:43 = 12:38; 9:5 = 10:10; 9:23 = 14:27; 9:24 = 17:33. Such phenomena postulate another source somewhat parallel to Mk. L. Vaganay has noted agreements of Mt-Lk against Mk, emphasizing "negative agreements" i.e., both Mt and Lk omit details which appear in Mk. For these reasons a simple dependence of Lk on Mk is an insufficient explanation. Some scholars have supposed that Lk did not have the canonical Mk but a more primitive form, Proto-Mark or *Urmarkus*. This theory is generally abandoned. L. Vaganay has proposed that Lk had both Mk and a Gk translation of the Aramaic Mt, which is not the same as the canonical Mt, and that he did not simply "follow" Mk but used him. In fact no satisfactory statement of the dependence has yet been proposed; but the dependence must be maintained.

Mt depends on Mk. This is widely affirmed, but it is disputed vigorously; the hypothesis of the priority of Mt has never been entirely excluded from criticism. A dependence is apparent in the triple tradition; but in Mt also there are doublets which occur in the Marcan sections and in the Matthaean sections (5:29 f = 18:8 f; 5:31 f = 19:9; 10:38 f = 16:24 f; 17:20 = 21:21). Here also the Mt-Lk agreements (cf above) are significant. Some scholars suggest that a common source of Mt-Mk will explain the agreements better than the hypothesis of dependence. A satisfactory statement of the dependence of Mt on Mk has not been proposed; but it seems that it too must be maintained, although with more reserve than the dependence of Lk on Mk.

III. Documentary Hypotheses. The older view that a single Aramaic gospel lay behind the three canonical Gospels is generally rejected as insufficient to explain the variations. In criticism for nearly 100 years the most popular hypothesis has been the "Two-Document Hypothesis." In spite of numerous variations proposed by scholars, the theory has retained a basic scheme which can be summarized thus: Mk, the first Gospel, arose from the oral gospel; in addition to Mk a documentary source nearly as early as Mk but unknown to Mk was compiled which contained a collection of sayings (*Logia*) of Jesus, and this is the document mentioned by Papias (cf MATTHEW; MARK). This document (first suggested by Schleiermacher in 1832) is usually called Q (German *Quelle*, source). Mt and Lk both employed Mk and Q as their principal sources, adapting the material to the different circles which they intended to reach. In addition Mt and Mk had special sources for the material proper to each. The Infancy* and the Passion* narratives set a special problem by themselves.

In this simple and elementary form the hypothesis is insufficient, and most who have proposed it have modified it in some respects. But it has the merit of simplicity and economy; it is easy for refinements to become so numerous and complex that they quickly become unreal. The difficulties are real. Perhaps the major unsolved problem for the Two-Document Hypothesis is that the phenomena which postulate the existence of Q appear in the narratives also i.e., the existence of material which is common to Mt-Lk but not found in Mk. Another difficulty is the form and character of Q, on which critics have never reached a consensus. It was by hypothesis not a gospel but a collection of sayings; but no one is sure whether it was random or structured, topical or chronological or topographical, or whether it must not have included incidents as well as sayings. These problems led many critics to suggest various strata in Q, but it was seen that fragmentation destroyed one of the Two Documents and made it a hypothesis of Mk + numerous fragmentary documents. B. H. Streeter believed that the relations of Lk to Q demanded an additional document which he called Proto-Lk; this consisted of Q + the Lucan material. Many say that Q is simply the necessary second documentary source and do not attempt to reconstruct its contents; this seems to be a confession of defeat.

A fault of the classical Two-Document Hypothesis was that it was conceived almost entirely in literary terms and took no account of oral tradition. The study of oral tradition and literary forms (cf GOSPEL) has rendered it impossible to conceive the origins of the Gospels simply as a writing process.

Some recent theories have attempted to incorporate the element of oral tradition into a theory of literary origins; none of these has yet won wide acceptance.

L. Vaganay has proposed a complex hypothesis (which, he says, is required by the complexity of the problem). At the base lies oral tradition, both in Aramaic and in Gk. This body of tradition was first fixed in writing in what Vaganay calls "Essays," small collections of words or incidents or both. The first writing of these in "gospel" form was the Aramaic Mt, which was not identical with the canonical Mt. Another early collection he calls simply "The Source," consisting of sayings and discourses; this also was written in Aramaic. Both of these were translated into Gk. Mk, the earliest canonical Gospel, used as sources the Gk translation of Aramaic Mt and that body of oral tradition which represented the catechesis of Peter. The canonical Mt used as sources Mk and the Gk translations both of Aramaic Mt and the Source, and elements of the oral tradition of the catechesis of Peter. Lk used as sources Mk, both Gk translations, and in addition elements of the oral tradition. Vaganay believes that Mt is the best representative of the original Aramaic gospel. The system has been criticized for what seems unnecessary complexity; for reconstructing the Two-Document Hypothesis, which Vaganay wishes to reject, with Q under another name; and for presenting no good reason why Mk should have been written.

P. Parker has suggested a Proto-Mt used by Mt and Mk, but known to Lk only through Mk, and Q (which is not the classical Q), used by Mt and Lk. Mt is independent of Mk. This theory also is criticized because it escapes the priority of Mk; it is difficult to understand why Mk should be written as anything but the first gospel.

L. Cerfaux and X. Léon-Dufour, with differences in detail, have incorporated some of these elements into a hypothesis which is more flexible but less definite; it may be called a hypothesis of oral tradition and multiple documentation. In the beginning is the body of oral tradition, which, however, soon begins to crystallize in variant forms in different localities — Palestine, Antioch, Rome, perhaps other places. From the tradition arises small collections, principally of sayings but not exclusively, prepared as handbooks to aid the memory of preachers. From these come an Aramaic systematization, which corresponds to the Aramaic Mt or Proto-Mt, which was translated into Gk. From this in turn rise other particular traditions; for oral tradition does not cease with these early fixations in writing, but continues

to expand and modify the gospel. These particular traditions, three in number, issue in the canonical Gospels. No other documentary source is postulated. Léon-Dufour places oral tradition both at the beginning of the process and at the end, just before our Gospels were written. There need be in this hypothesis no literary contacts between our Gospels at all; literary contacts there were, but they occurred in the presynoptic phases of development. Only by this multiple documentation, say its proponents, can the unique pattern of harmony and divergence be explained.

The theory renounces two documents and interdependence and combines two elements, oral tradition and a single written gospel, each of which is insufficient to explain the Synoptic problem. Critics ask whether the two together have the strength which neither has alone. Multiple documentation approaches the fragmentation of documentary sources, which critics regard as evasion; men do not write fragments. The theory, if it is to stand, must be supported by extensive studies of particular passages; and it is not certain that even this would give it the necessary evidence. It also raises the question which other recent hypotheses raise; if there were a single gospel document, why were others written? Furthermore, the agreements of the three are such that a literary process and not an oral process seems required; but the agreements cannot be reduced to a single document.

It is impossible to render a firm judgment on contemporary theories of the origins of the Gospels. Each has evidence in its favor, each has what appears to be decisive difficulties against it. No doubt the solution, if one is to be found, lies in the direction of oral tradition rather than in the direction of documents.

Syntyche (Gk *syntychē,* "happy event"), a personal name; a woman of Philippi* (Phl 4:2), urged by Paul to reconcile her quarrel with Evodia*.

Syracuse (Gk *syrakūsae,* meaning uncertain), a large and important city on the E coast of Sicily; the ship on which Paul traveled to Rome put in at Syracuse for three days on the voyage between Malta and Rhegium (AA 28:12).

Syria (Gk *syria,* possibly a corruption of *assyria**), a geographical name. As a general regional name Syria designates the part of W Asia bounded by the Taurus Mts on the N, the Euphrates on the E, Palestine on the S, and the Mediterranean on the W. As a modern political name Syria designates the above area with the exception of a strip S of the Taurus, which belongs to Turkey, and the S part of the coastal plain with the Lebanon and the Beqa, which belongs to Lebanon. In the NT the name designates the Roman province of Syria, erected in 64 BC and governed by an imperial legate who resided in Antioch (Mt 4:24; Lk 2:2; AA 15:23, 41; 18:18; 20:3; 21:3; Gal 1:21). The province of Syria included Palestine in addition to the area mentioned above.

Geographically Syria exhibits the same contours as Palestine; a coastal plain of varying width (cf PHOENICIA), the Lebanon range, the valley of the Beqa, the Anti-Lebanon, a plateau which fades off into the steppes and the Syrian desert. It is distinguished from Palestine by a number of rivers (the Orontes, the Euphrates, the Litany [ancient Leontes]), a more abundant rainfall, and particularly by the plateau which lies E of the Anti-Lebanon range. This high flat plain has deep arable soil and more rainfall than the plateau of E Palestine.

On the political history of the region cf ARAMAEANS; PHOENICIA; SELEUCID; and related articles. In addition it may be remarked that the region of Syria is one of the most interesting examples of the fusion of Oriental and Hellenistic cultures, which exhibits itself in a striking mixture in religious cults, architecture and art, and literature. Similarly the region in the 3rd–1st millennia BC produced a strongly mixed culture which exhibited native, Egyptian, and Mesopotamian traits.

Syriac Versions. Syriac designates several dialects of Aramaic* which arose in the early centuries of the Christian era in the old Aramaic speaking regions, which roughly include the modern Israel and Jordan, Syria, Lebanon, the portion of Turkey adjacent to Syria, and Iraq. The dialects of Syriac fall into two principal groups, eastern and western. As a living language Syriac fell into disuse with the Mohammedan conquests and yielded to Arabic; it now survives as a liturgical language in some dissident eastern churches and in a few isolated pockets.

After the Gk version (cf SEPTUAGINT) the Syriac versions of the OT are the oldest to be made into a vernacular, and the NT versions are perhaps older than any other; they are very near the Old Latin versions in age. They are grouped here according to OT and NT.

OT. The Peshitto OT: Syriac Peshitto means "the simple," although the more precise meaning of the term is uncertain; "simple" here may mean the text in common use (= "vulgate") or the text which

was considered the most easily understood. The Peshitto OT was the work of several translators who were possibly Jewish Christians. It was translated from Hb in the 1st or 2nd century AD, but includes the deuterocanonical books (cf CANON). To a surprising degree the Peshitto often agrees with the LXX against MT; this seems more probably due to later revisions of the Peshitto and not to the Hb text which the translators employed.

The Philoxenian version is named after Philoxenus, the Monophysite bishop of Mabbug, who had the version made in the early 6th century. It was made from the Gk, not the Hb, and practically nothing of the version remains.

The Syro-palestinian OT was also made from the Gk sometime between the 4th and 6th centuries for the Christians who spoke western Syriac. It is preserved in lectionaries.

The Syro-hexapla was a translation from the LXX* as it was edited in the Hexapla of Origen. It is the work of Paul of Tella in 616–617. It is preserved in fragments, and is one of the most important witnesses for the work of Origen.

NT. The Old Syriac versions are the versions older than the Peshitto NT (cf below). These were replaced in common use by the Peshitto and have survived only in fragments.

The Syro-curetonian version is named after W. Cureton, who published the version in 1858. It contains 80 pages of a Gospel lectionary and was probably produced in the 3rd or 4th century.

The Syro-sinaiticus version was discovered in 1892 in the monastery of St. Catherine on Mt Sinai by two English ladies, Mrs. Lewis and Mrs. Gibson. It contains ¾ of the Gospels and was probably produced about AD 200.

The *Diatessaron* (Gk "through four") of the heretic Tatian of the 2nd century, Syrian by birth but Gk speaking, is the earliest harmony of the Gospels and if it was produced in Syriac is the oldest Syriac version. It has long been uncertain whether it was produced in Syriac or was a later Syriac version of a Gk harmony. The discovery of a 2nd century fragment of the harmony in Gk seems to indicate that it was produced in Gk.

The Peshitto NT was in existence in the 5th century; how much earlier than this it was produced cannot be determined. It has been suggested by several scholars that it is the work of the famous Rabbula, bishop of Edessa 411–435.

The Philoxenian NT (cf above) was a revision of the Peshitto NT.

The Syro-palestinian NT was produced with the Syro-palestinian OT (cf above).

The Syro-harclean NT is named after its producer, Thomas of Harkel [Heraclea]; it was made in the 7th century.

Syrophoenician. The name given to the woman of Mk 7:26 (called a Canaanite* in Mt 15:22). Mk also calls her a "Greek," which here means much the same as Gentile*. The name indicates that she lived in the region of Phoenicia* in the province of Syria*. While Phoenicia was not a distinct administrative unit in Roman government, the awareness of its distinct cultural identity exhibited in this word is paralleled in other ancient writers.

Syrtis. The Syrtis mentioned in AA 27:17 is the gulf called Syrtis Major by the ancients; it lies off the coast of Libya W of the promontory of Cyrenaica. The shallow depths and shifting sand banks of this body of water made it dangerous and it was much feared by ancient navigators. The smaller Syrtis Minor lies W of Syrtis Major off the peninsula of Tunisia.

T

Taanach (Hb *ta'anak,* "barrier"?), a city in the territory of Manasseh* (Jos 17:11) and a Levitical* city (Jos 21:25). The site is identified with the modern Tell Taannek, about 5 mi S of the site of Megiddo*. Like Megiddo, Taanach lay near the pass which gives access between the coastal plain and the plain of Esdraelon*, and possession of Taanach gave control of the road. Taanach appears in the list of Canaanite cities conquered by Joshua (Jos 12:21); this schematic list, however, contains the names of cities which remained Canaanite long after Joshua. Jgs 1:27 includes it among the Canaanite cities not conquered by Israel, and it probably did not become Israelite until the monarchy. It was the scene of Barak's* defeat of the Canaanites (Jgs 5:19). It was included in Solomon's 5th district (1 K 4:12). Although the city lay in the territory of Manasseh, 1 Ch 7:29 preserves a tradition that it was settled by clans of Ephraim*. Taanach is mentioned in the account of the capture of Megiddo by Thutmose III (ANET 235–236) and appears in the list of Palestinian cities conquered by Shishak*. The site was excavated by a German expedition directed by E. Sellin 1901–1904. A number of cuneiform* letters were discovered which come from about 100 years before the Amarna* Letters, but are similar in character. The letters show that Taanach was the residence of an Egyptian governor. Comparative archaeology of Taanach and Megiddo indicates that the occupation of the two sites was complementary rather than simultaneous; when one site flourished, the other was occupied by a village or not occupied at all. Jgs 5:19 suggests that Taanach was occupied at the time of Barak's battle and that Megiddo lay in ruins. Both, however, were occupied in Solomon's reign. The earliest occupation of Taanach revealed by excavation was in the 26th century BC.

Tabeel (Hb *ṭāb'ēl,* "El is good," cf Akkadian *tab-ilum*), a personal name. **1.** Patronymic of the unnamed "son of Tabeel" whom Pekah* of Israel and Rezin* of Damascus intended to install as king of Judah in place of Ahaz* (Is 7:6). Ben Tabeel was probably an Aramaean prince of Damascus, but some think it may be Rezin himself.
2. An Aramaean, an official of the Persian government, one of the authors of the letter quoted in Ezr 4:7 ff; on the problems connected with this letter cf EZRA-NEHEMIAH.

Taberah (Hb *tab'ērāh,* "burning"?, "pasture"?), the place where some of the Israelites were struck by "the fire of Yahweh" (lightning; Nm 11:3; Dt 9:22). If the etymology of "pasture" is correct, the name offers a good example of a popular tradition which creates an event out of a paronomastic etymology of a name. The site cannot be identified.

Tabernacle (Lt *tabernaculum,* "tent"), the name often used in Eng versions to designate the sacred cultic tent of ancient Israel. The plan of the tabernacle and its furniture is set forth in Ex 25–31; the execution of the plan is narrated in Ex 35–40 in almost the identical words with changes from jussive to narrative.

It is obvious that the tabernacle is a fusion of desert motifs and temple motifs. The materials of the tabernacle, the tent curtains and the acacia wood of the frames, are desert products; but the dimensions and the structure of the tabernacle are those of the temple of Solomon. The frame of the tent is made of 48 wooden frames, 15 ft high by 27 in wide, composed of three vertical arms joined by three cross pieces. These are set in wooden supports and over them are hung two large curtains (decorated like the paneling of the temple of Solomon), one of which forms the larger room, the Holy Place, and the other the smaller room, the Holy of Holies or Most Holy Place. Over these are spread three covers. The Holy Place and the Most Holy Place are separated by a veil. The tabernacle stands in the center of the Israelite camp (Nm 2); it is the place of the visible manifestation of Yahweh in the cloud and the glory* (Ex 40:34–38 +).

The tabernacle has two names in Hb: *miškān,* "dwelling," signifies that the tabernacle is the place where Yahweh dwells among His people. This is the common temple motif of the ancient Near East. The other name, *'ōhel mō'ēd,* "tent of meeting," is more peculiarly Israelite. The "meeting" of the name is not the meeting of men in assembly to worship, but the meeting of Yahweh and Israel through Moses. The tabernacle is the place of revelation.

Many older critics regarded the tabernacle as a projection of the temple into Israel's nomadic past, a creation of the late priestly source without any historical foundation. More recent investigations have shown that this judgment is too sweeping. It is not as certain (without testing), as many critics judge, that the tabernacle as described would not stand up and could not be carried. Here it is necessary to distinguish between the details of the tabernacle and the idea of the tabernacle. It is easily conceded that the priestly source, lacking any details about the tabernacle, turned the temple of Solomon (or rather the second temple built along the same lines) to a tent; many of the materials of the furnishings of the tabernacle seem to be beyond the resources of a nomadic tribe. F. M. Cross, however, would modify even this judgment; he suggests that the tabernacle as described is the tent shrine erected by David (cf below), and that the priestly source employed genuine traditions about its structure.

Both biblical data and extrabiblical information make the existence of an early portable tent shrine not only possible but extremely probable. Historians now are in general agreement with the thesis of M. Noth that premonarchic Israel was an amphictyony organized about a central shrine (cf ISRAEL); the traditions of Israel indicate that the earliest form of this central shrine was a tent and not a building, and these traditions are found in documents earlier than the late priestly source. From the J source there is the account of a tent of meeting which stood outside the camp, was guarded by Joshua, and where Moses received divine revelation (Ex 33:7–11). The tent as a place of revelation appears again in Nm 11:24 f; 12:4–10; 14:10. The P tradition that it was set up at Shiloh* (Jos 18:1; 19:51) is supported by 1 S 2:22. When David brought the ark to Jerusalem he pitched a tent for it (2 S 6:17). That this was merely temporary is contradicted by the entire story of the oracle of Nathan which presupposes that a tent was the normal and traditional dwelling of the ark (2 S 7:6) and that David's temple project was a novelty for the ark. The tent still existed at the beginning of the reign of Solomon, and Joab fled there for sanctuary (1 K 2:28 f). When the temple of Solomon was finished the ark was transferred from the tabernacle to the temple (1 K 8:4).

This biblical evidence is supported by the existence of portable tent shrines among nomads of the Syrian desert which were still in use until recent times. These shrines are certainly of great antiquity; they are not Islamic in origin, and similar shrines are attested by ancient writers of the classical period; one such shrine is represented on a relief of the temple of Bel at Palmyra. These shrines are smaller than the tabernacle of Israel as it is described; but we have no certain information of the size of the original tabernacle, and the similarities in conception and use here seem more decisive than the size. These tent shrines head the movements of the tribes and their attacks in war; and by a remarkable coincidence many of them have a leather covering like the tabernacle of Ex 26:14; 36:19; the leather of the Bedu tent shrines is dyed red.

According to Ex 25:9 + the tabernacle is constructed according to heavenly pattern or model shown to Moses on the mountain. This expresses the common ancient Near Eastern conception that the earthly temple is the imitation and counterpart of the heavenly temple, the dwelling of the deity. This feature of the tabernacle is echoed in the NT allusions to the tabernacle. Jesus is the priest of the heavenly tabernacle, which is the true tabernacle (Heb 8:2, 5). The tabernacle of the Christians is the heavenly tabernacle, a greater and more perfect tabernacle not made with hands (Heb 9:11 f). The heavenly tent of meeting appears in Apc 15:5; and the new heavenly Jerusalem is the tabernacle of God with men (Apc 21:3). In the messianism of these passages the original divine and heavenly tabernacle, imitated in the cult of the law, descends to earth.

Tabernacles, Feast of. The early name of this feast in the code of the covenant (Ex 23:16) and the Yahwist decalogue (Ex 34:22; cf LAW; PENTATEUCH) is the Feast of Ingathering (Hb *'āsîp*). These early laws prescribe that it is to be kept at the "end" or the "beginning" of the year; the phrase is obscure enough to admit either translation, and the feast falls in the 7th month or Tishri (cf CALENDAR) at just the point where the spring calendar and the autumn calendar overlap. In the autumn calendar Tabernacles combines a harvest festival with the beginning of the year (cf NEW YEAR); it is this combination which causes some obscurity in the meaning of the feast. Elsewhere in the OT Tabernacles is called the feast of Booths (Hb *sukkôt*, Lt *tabernacula*, Eng *tabernacles*). Dt 16:13–15 prescribes its celebration for seven days; it is a harvest festival for the fruits of the threshing floor and the wine press, and is a feast of rejoicing. With Passover* and Pentecost* it is a feast which is to be celebrated at the sanctuary. The connection established in Dt 16 with the threshing floor is obscure; the autumn is not the season of the grain harvest. Dt 26:1–11 adds an interesting prescription; the principal offering of the individual is a basket of harvest fruits with the recital of the saving acts by which Yahweh delivered His people from Egypt and gave them possession of the promised land, what G. von Rad has called the Credo of early Israel. This Credo makes the feast a commemoration of the acquisition of the Promised Land. Dt 31:10–13 in addition prescribes the reading of the law of Dt at the feast every 7th year. Lv 23:34–36, 39–43 (the 2nd section appears to be a later supplement) prescribes a 7-day festival with the carrying of palms and branches and introduces the dwelling in booths made of leafy branches as a commemoration of the desert sojourn of Israel. The commemoration is related to the Credo of Dt 26; but scholars are doubtful that the booths originally symbolized the desert sojourn, which was a dwelling in tents, not in booths. They direct attention to the common practice of living in booths in the fields during the harvest, and suggest that this is a feature of the harvest festival which has been "historicized" into a commemoration of the desert sojourn. Ne 8:14–18 describes the postexilic celebration of the feast; it includes living in booths and the reading of the law. Nm 29:12–28 lists the sacrifices prescribed for the 7 days of the feast. The temple of Solomon was dedicated at the feast of Tabernacles (1 K 8:2, 65, here and elsewhere called "the feast," which indicated its importance). The feast is coincidental with the Canaanite grape festival of Shechem (Jgs 9:27), which included a sacred meal in the temple, and is certainly connected with it. The feast of Jgs 21:21 f, at which maidens danced in the vineyards, must be the feast of tabernacles; some scholars have suggested that the feast included a ritual rape of the maidens, a feature of the Canaanite harvest feast.

Like Passover*, Tabernacles combines an agricultural motif and a historical motif; but the historical motif is less clear than the motif of Passover, and recent scholars have proposed a number of divergent theories. Several scholars have suggested that the feast under the monarchy was also a feast of the dedication of the temple, basing this opinion on 1 K 8, which they understand as a ritual directive rather than a historical narrative. This feast included an annual procession in which the ark was introduced into the temple, commemorating both the dedication of the temple and the introduction of the ark into Jerusalem by David (2 S 6). Ps 24 is suggested as a hymn for this festival. H. J. Kraus has expanded this interpretation and sees in Tabernacles a royal Zion festival commemorating the election of the dynasty of David and of Jerusalem as the site of the temple; here the agricultural motif is almost completely obscured. G. von Rad, basing his opinion principally on Dt 26, believes that Tabernacles was a renewal of the covenant; the regular reading of the law (Dt 31:10 ff) falls in with this interpretation. A. R. Johnson and others call attention to Zc 14:16–19, which describes the feast of tabernacles as a worship of Yahweh the king and connect the feast with the New Year*, which it follows very closely, as a part of the feast of the kingship and enthronement of Yahweh. The same passage of Zc threatens those who fail to observe the feast with the punishment of drought; and Johnson thinks that the feast was also a petition for the beginning of the rainy season, which normally begins a month or so after the feast of Tabernacles.

These opinions all have some degree of probability and employ material from the OT which does not easily suit any simple and general theory. The failure of any theory to win general acceptance shows at least that the history of the feast and the development of its meaning is much more complex than one might think, and no definitive solution can be given.

According to the Talmud* people lived in booths for the seven days of the feast. On the first night of the feast the temple area was brightly illuminated by lamps and torches; ceremonial dancing was done by this illumination. Daily there was a procession around the altar; the worshipers carried a branch in one hand (*lûlāb*) and a fruit (*'etrôg*) in the other, and Ps 118 was sung. The priests marched around the altar 7 times. On the last day a vessel of water was brought to the temple from the pool of Siloam and poured out before the altar of burnt offerings. Horns and trumpets were blown at all the great moments of the feast.

In the NT the feast is certainly mentioned only once; it is the feast which Jesus attended secretly after refusing to go publicly (Jn 7). The rivers of water (Jn 7:37 f) may be an allusion to the libation rite of the feast (cf above). The title of "light of the world" which Jesus gave Himself (Jn 8:12) may have been spoken during the illuminations of the feast of Tabernacles.

Tabitha (Aramaic *ṭabycṭā'*, "gazelle"), the Aramaic name of Dorcas*, a woman of Joppa raised from the dead by Peter (AA 9:36–40).

Table of Nations. The name frequently given to the genealogy of Noah* and his sons (Gn 10; substantially reproduced in 1 Ch 1:4–24). The list is constructed on the Hb principle of genealogy*, which uses the genealogy to represent connections other than those of carnal descent. The Table describes the world and its peoples as known to the writer; this world is the lands adjacent to the E Mediterranean. Beginning with the N coast of Africa W of Egypt and moving counterclockwise, this area includes N Africa (modern Libya), Egypt and Nubia, the Arabian peninsula, Palestine and Syria, Mesopotamia and the Iranian plateau, Asia Minor and possibly the N coast of the Black Sea, the Aegean archipelago and continental Greece, very probably S Italy and Sardinia, possibly Spain and Phoenician colonies in N Africa, in Tunisia. The principles of the grouping of peoples under the sons of Noah are geographical; peoples who live in adjoining lands and who speak cognate languages are grouped together. Thus the sons of Japheth are Indo-European, the sons of Shem are Semite (the name is retained by modern ethnology), and the sons of Ham are Hamitic i.e., African. The motives for exceptions in these groupings are historical and geographical. Thus the Elamites are included with the Semites, although they were not linguistically and ethnically related; but Elam was adjacent to Mesopotamia and shared its history and culture. Canaan and the Arabian tribes are included with the Hamites, possibly as a reflection of the long Egyptian dominion over these territories. The data on Assyria under the Hamite genealogy are misplaced, possibly because of a confusion in the understanding of Cush*. Further details can be found under the separate articles.

The peoples and their relations fall best into a period about the 10th century BC. The Table is principally from the source P of Pnt*, with a few notes interspersed which seem to be from J. But the material is older than the P source. As a historical conception of "one world" the Table is unique in ancient Near Eastern literature; and the historical conception arises from a theological conception. Israel is located in a world which is governed by the one God, Yahweh. In this world Yahweh has elected the people Israel as His own people of covenant. The unity of humanity described in genealogical terms is religious rather than biological.

Tabor (Hb *tābôr*, meaning uncertain), Mt Tabor of the OT is the modern Jebel et Tor, which rises in the NE corner of the plain of Esdraelon to a height of 1850 ft. The mountain stands isolated in the plain and rises steeply; it is more impressive in appearance than its relatively low height would suggest, and this is mentioned parallel with Mt Hermon* (Ps 89:13) and Carmel* (Je 46:18) as a large and prominent mountain. It lay on the boundary of Issachar* (Jos 19:22), and gave its name to Chisloth-tabor in the plain of Esdraelon (Jos 19:12) and Aznoth-tabor, also in the plain, on the boundary of Naphtali. Mt Tabor was the site of the camp of Barak* (Jgs 4:6, 12, 14) and

the scene of the killing of Gideon's brothers by the Midianites* (Jgs 8:18). The allusion to the priests "who were a snare at Tabor" (Ho 5:1) is obscure and may refer to a cult site on the mountain. The oak of Tabor (1 S 10:3) lay near Bethel; modern critics suspect the integrity of the text. The name also belongs to a town of Zebulun (1 Ch 6:62) whose location is unknown. Mt Tabor is one of the sites suggested in tradition for the Transfiguration; the scene of this event is not named in the Gospels. The probable presence of a village on the summit in NT times makes this identification improbable.

Tab-rimmon (Hb *ṭab-rimmōn*, "[the god] Ramman is good"), a personal name; the Hb represents the Aramaic name of the father of Ben-hadad*, king of Damascus (1 K 15:18).

Tadmor (Hb *tadmōr*, meaning uncertain), one of the fortress cities built by Solomon* (1 K 9:18; 2 Ch 8:4). The name represents the ancient Aramaic name of the famous caravan city called in Hellenistic and Roman times Palmyra, which lies in the Syrian desert about 100 mi E of Homs. The ancient name is preserved in Arabic Tudmur, the name of the modern village. It is altogether improbable that Solomon's building projects involved a site so far from Israel; and the consonantal text of 1 K 9:18 reads Tamar*, which is correct.

Tahpanhes (Hb *tahpanḥēs*, probably representing Egyptian *T-h-p-nhsj*, meaning uncertain), fortress of the Nubian, or with W. F. Albright, fortress of Pinehas, an Egyptian general of the 11th century BC; identified by Albright with Tell Defneh in the E Delta region of Egypt (Gk *daphnae*), by A. Alt not with a town but with a region E of Tanis* in the same area. Ezk 30:18 reads the name *teḥapneḥēs;* the consonantal text of Je 2:16 reads *taḥpenēs,* but the vocalized text reads Tahpanhes. It is mentioned as a N border point of Egypt (Ezk 30:18), as a prominent Egyptian city (Je 2:16), and as a place where Judahites fleeing from Palestine settled (Je 43:7–9; 44:1). Jeremiah buried stones in the ground at Tahpanhes as a symbolic threat against Egypt; the stones were the foundation of the throne of Nebuchadnezzar in Egypt (Je 43:9–13).

Tahpenes (Hb *taḥpenēs,* an Egyptian personal name of uncertain meaning), it is nearly identical with Tahpanhes*, a place name; the queen of the unnamed Pharaoh who furnished asylum to Hadad* of Edom

(1 K 11:19 f). Je 2:16 reads Tahpenes in the consonantal text for Tahpanhes.

Talent. Cf MONEY.

Talitha cumi. The critical Gk text reads *talitha kūm* in Mk 5:41; the received text *talitha kūmī* is grammatically accurate but represents an editorial correction. The Gk is a transliteration of the Aramaic *talyᵉtā kûmî*, "maiden, stand up."

Talmai (Hb *talmai*, meaning and etymology uncertain), similar personal names are found in Nabatean* inscriptions. **1.** The Aramaean* king of Geshur*, whose daughter Maacah* was one of the wives of David and mother of Absalom* (2 S 3:3; 1 Ch 3:2). Absalom fled to his court after the murder of Amnon* (2 S 13:37). **2.** One of the sons of Anak*, a chieftain of Hebron*, conquered and expelled by Caleb* (Nm 13:22; Jos 15:14; Jgs 1:10).

Talmud (Aramaic *talmûd,* "teaching"), the name of a collection of Jewish rabbinical literature. The name Talmud properly belongs to only a part of the collection, but it is popularly used to designate the entire collection. The origins and divisions of the Talmud are somewhat complex.

The core of the Talmudic literature is a collection of rabbinical opinions called the *Mishna;* this collection was made by Rabbi Judah ha-Nasi in AD 200. The rabbis whose opinions are collected in the Mishna are called *Tannaim,* "teachers." The language of the Mishna is Hebrew, but a later development of the language called Neo-Hebrew or Mishnic Hebrew. The Mishna is divided into 6 parts or "orders" (*seder*): (1) Seeds. (2) Feasts. (3) Women. (4) Damages. (5) Holiness. (6) [Levitical] Cleanliness. Each *seder* is divided into a number of treatises (*masseket*), and each treatise into chapters or sections (*perek*). The total number of treatises in the Mishna is 63.

The Mishna itself became after its publication the subject of rabbinical study, and two commentaries upon the Mishna, composed by compiling the opinions of rabbis who lived after the Mishna, were prepared. Each of these is called the *Gemara* or the *Talmud* indifferently; they are distinguished by their place of origin as the Palestinian Talmud, prepared in the rabbinical schools of Palestine, and the Babylonian Talmud, prepared in the schools of Babylonia. The language of the two Talmuds is Aramaic, Palestinian Aramaic in the Palestinian Talmud and Eastern Aramaic in the Babylonian Talmud. The rabbis whose opinions are collected in the Talmud are called *Amoraim,* "speakers," "interpreters." The date and the first editor of the Jerusalem Talmud are obscure; it was possibly completed before AD 450. It contains comments on the first 4 seders of the Mishna and part of the 6th, a total of 39 of the 63 treatises. The Babylonian Talmud was substantially completed by AD 500, and received some additions during the 6th and 7th centuries; the rabbis of these two centuries are called *Saboraim,* "thinkers."

There are other bodies of rabbinical literature similar in form and content. The *Tosefta* (additions) is a collection of opinions of the Tannaim found outside the Mishna. The source and origin of this collection is obscure. The *Baraita* is a collection of opinions of the Tannaim found in the Talmud but not in the Mishna. There are collections of halakhic midrash (cf below) from the pre-Mishna period arranged according to the books of the Pnt: *Mekhilta* on Ex; *Sifra* on Lv; *Sifre* on Nm-Dt. Gn, which contains few laws, was of less interest in rabbinical discussions.

The Mishna-Talmud can be described generally as an interpretation of the law*, i.e., of the Pnt as a divinely revealed guide of morals and conduct. Almost any description, however, fails to describe the form and contents of the collections. The object of the interpretation is chiefly to settle problems of casuistry: to determine the obligations of the law as precisely as possible. The Mishna follows the titles of its treatises with some fidelity; but titles and subtitles are no guide to the Talmud, since the discussion often wanders remotely from the subject with which the discussion is begun. The traditions of the elders are treated as of equal value with the law and are submitted to the same discussion and interpretation; cf LAW; SCRIBE.

The roots of rabbinical interpretation lie in the late pre-Christian centuries; since the interpretations were transmitted orally until AD 200, one cannot always be certain that the Talmud illustrates rabbinical interpretation of the NT period. Talmudic interpretation may be distinguished into literal and practical. The literal seeks to discover the meaning of the text; this is not the investigation of the literal sense as it is understood in modern interpretation*, but it is distinguished from the practical, of which it forms a basis. The practical interpretation (Hb *midrash**) is of two kinds: the *halakha* (lit "walking"), which deduces rules of conduct; and the *haggadah* (lit "narrative"), which deduces homiletic conclusions and applications from the text. The *haggadah* often draws its conclusions from a biblical narrative by retelling the narrative with generous embellishments; cf MIDRASH.

Talmudic interpretation often seems arbitrary to modern students; but the number of rules of interpretation contained in rabbinical traditions shows that it was the intention of the rabbis not to be arbitrary. Seven fundamental rules are attributed to the great Rabbi Hillel, 13 to Rabbi Ishmael, 32 to Rabbi ben Jose, others to Aqiba. What Talmudic interpretation lacks, painstaking as it is, is principles of modern criticism and of literary forms. The principle that every detail of the text has meaning is valid, but when it is applied to such questions as variations in spelling, why this order of words is used rather than that, why a word is repeated three times rather than twice, and when the meaning of a word or of a precept is explained by appealing to another passage which has nothing in common except a catchword, the principle is pressed beyond endurance. Were the rabbis pretending to deal with the modern "literal sense," their exegesis would often be meaningless. But they actually did not distinguish a literal sense from the conclusions and applications which they deduced; they constructed an edifice of doctrine and discipline upon the law as a basis, and they were satisfied if the law gave them the suitable word or idea which they needed. It is rather important to grasp and understand rabbinical interpretation with sympathy, since most NT interpretation of the OT reflects rabbinical principles.

As a guide to the history of the NT period the Talmud must be used with extremely critical care. The rabbis and their compilers were nearly unconscious historically; and the opinions and customs which they cite are not distinguished according to periods of history. The Jewish life and thought of the Talmud is not the Jewish life and thought of the NT period simply, and while this mine of information often does illustrate the NT, it has also misled scholars who projected elements of the Talmudic period into the NT period, where they had not yet appeared.

Tamar (Hb *tāmār*, "palm"), a personal and a local name. **1.** A Canaanite woman (Gn 38), taken by Judah as wife for his son Er*, and after Er's death for Onan*. When Judah withheld his third son Shelah out of superstition, Tamar disguised herself with the veil of a temple prostitute and seduced Judah himself. When Judah threatened her with the punishment of burning for fornication — as a widow promised to Shelah she was under Judah's paternal power — she produced evidence that Judah was her accomplice. She bore twin sons who have the names of the Judahite clans Perez* and Zerah* (1

Ch 2:4). On the legal questions involved cf LEVIRATE MARRIAGE. The morality of the characters of the story is Canaanite rather than Israelite, and the story is one of the points which illustrates the Canaanite background of the tribe of Judah. The action of Tamar was taken to secure her rights as a widow, and for this reason Judah admitted that she was more in the right than he was (Gn 38:26). In the ancient world Tamar was admired as a woman of determination and adroitness. She is mentioned in the blessing of Ruth (Rt 4:12) and in the genealogy of Jesus (Mt 1:3).

2. The daughter of David and Maacah* and full sister of Absalom*, the victim of the incestuous rape of Amnon* (2 S 13). For this crime Absalom later murdered Amnon and had to flee the country.

3. Daughter of Absalom (2 S 14:27), doubtless named after her unfortunate aunt, and like her aunt (2 S 13:1) admired for her beauty.

4. A town in the S of Palestine (Ezk 47:19; 48:28); Tamar is read instead of Tadmor* in the consonantal text of 1 K 9:18 for a fortress city of Solomon*. The site is identified by some with Hazazontamar*, by others with the modern Kurnub, 22 mi SE of Beersheba*.

Tammuz (Hb *tammûz*, a divine name). Ezk 8:14 describes women weeping for Tammuz at the N gate of the temple. Ritual lamentations for this god have been preserved from Mesopotamia which illustrate the cult mentioned here. Tammuz (Sumerian *Du-mu-zi*) is an ancient Mesopotamian god, perhaps a deified human being. He is one of the many forms of the god whose death and resurrection represents the cycle of vegetation and fertility. He is the legendary king of Badtibira who ruled for 36,000 years before the deluge (ANET 265); a variant legend makes him king of Uruk for 100 years. He is closely connected with the female goddess of fertility, the Sumerian Inanna and the Akkadian Ishtar. He is a shepherd or a fisherman, the lover of Ishtar. A Sumerian poem describes his suit of Inanna (ANET 41–42). He is represented in seals as the protector of the flocks against wild beasts. The later version of the poem of the descent of Ishtar into the underworld connects this adventure with the recall of Tammuz from the dead (ANET 109). He also appears as one of the gatekeepers of the gate of Anu (ANET 101); perfect consistency in Mesopotamian mythology is rarely attained. The allusion to the Tammuz-Ishtar myth in the epic of Gilgamesh* (ANET 84) is bitterly sarcastic; Ishtar is here a nymphomaniac who destroys the lovers whom she seduces. In the opinion of some scholars the deified king Tammuz is represented in the fertility cult by the reigning king, through whom as Tammuz men partake of the divine nature of Inanna-Ishtar, the principle of life and fertility.

Tanning. Cf LEATHER.

Tappuah (Hb *tappuᵃh*, "apple"), a place name. **1.** A town of Judah* in the Shephelah* (Jos 15:34), Gk Tephon, fortified by Jonathan* (1 Mc 9:50); identified with the modern Beit Nettif, about 13 mi W of Bethlehem.
2. A town of Ephraim*, also called En Tappuah (Jos 17:7 f), on the boundary of Ephraim (Jos 16:8), included in the list of Canaanite towns taken by Joshua (Jos 12: 17). It is identified with the modern Sheikh Abu Zared, 33 mi N of Jerusalem. Tappuah should be read for Tiphsah in 2 K 15:16; the town was sacked by Menahem* because it did not recognize him as king.

Tares (Gk *zizanion,* pl *zizania*), the "tares" of the Authorized Version and the "cockle" of the Rheims NT, replaced in more modern versions by "weeds," probably darnel or cheat.

Targum. (Aramaic *targûm*, "translation"). After the exile Hb as the language of the Jews was replaced by Aramaic*, and at an early date the Hb of the OT was no longer intelligible to many Jews when it was read in the synagogue. Hence the reading of the OT was supplemented by a translation into the vernacular, rendered after the reading of each verse or sometimes of two or three verses. At first it was the duty of the translator to improvise; not only was he allowed no written translation, he was not even allowed to refer to the Hb text. At an early date, however, the improvisation was replaced by written versions; a Targum is an Aramaic version, the language spoken in Palestine, Syria, and Mesopotamia.
The earliest written Targum mentioned in Jewish literature was a Targum of Job of the 1st century AD; it is doubtless this document of which fragments have been found at Qumran*. Qumran has yielded several other fragments of Targums. The scattered pieces of Targums in many large libraries show the number and diversity of these versions. The Targum is a somewhat unique type of translation. Babylonian Targums appear to have been so literal as to be at times servile; Palestinian Targums are free, paraphrastic, expansive, and sometimes are commentaries rather than translations. The Targum of Is 53, for instance, completely in-

verts the meaning of the original by removing all idea of suffering and turning the passage into a description of the glorious and triumphant Messiah.
The two best known Palestinian Targums are the Targum of Onkelos on the Pnt and the Targum of Jonathan on the Prophets (the historical books Jos, 2 K and Is, Je, Ezk, the 12 prophets). In their present form these can scarcely be older than the 5th century AD. The attributions to Onkelos (Aquila) and Jonathan (Theodotion) are literary fictions; for the Gk versions attributed to these men cf SEPTUAGINT. A complete copy of a Palestinian Targum on the Pnt was discovered in the Vatican Library in 1956.
The Targums have a real value in the criticism of the text, but their use demands great critical caution. They often confirm a reading or a form of text found elsewhere, but their witness alone is of little value.

Tarshish (Hb *taršîš*), a local name. Many scholars follow the suggestion of W. F. Albright that *taršîš* is a Phoenician loan word meaning "refinery," a place where metal is melted and refined. This etymology has implications for the location of Tarshish; cf below. In the Table* of Nations Tarshish is a descendant of Japheth* and a son of Javan* (Gn 10:4; 1 Ch 1:7). The daughter of Tarshish, a poetic apostrophe for a city, is addressed in the lamentation of Tyre in Is 23:10, and the inhabitants of Tyre are invited to flee to Tarshish (Is 23:6). It is mentioned together with Put* and Lud* in Is 66:19. Ezk 38:13 mentions its merchants, and Ezk 27:12 lists its articles of trade with Tyre as metals: silver, iron, tin, and lead. Je 10:9 mentions its silver. Ps 72:10 invites Tarshish and the islands to worship the messianic king. The ships that travel to Tarshish on the Red Sea (2 Ch 20:36 f) come from a misunderstanding of the term "Tarshish ship." The same misunderstanding lurks in Jonah's journey to Tarshish (Jon 1:3; 4:2). The name occurs elsewhere in the phrase "ships of Tarshish" (1 K 10:22; 22:49; 2 Ch 9:21; Ps 48:8; Is 2:16; 23:1, 4; 60:9; Ezk 27:25; Jon 1:3). Tarshish was long identified with the classical Tartessos on the Atlantic coast of Spain at the mouth of the Guadalquivir N of Cadiz. The name also occurs in a text of Esarhaddon* of Assyria and in a Phoenician inscription of the 9th century BC from Sardinia. W. F. Albright, however, has cast serious doubt upon this identification, and he is followed by many. There could scarcely have been Phoenician colonies in Spain as early as this inscription; therefore he suggests that it is a common noun, "refinery," and was given to Phoenician colonies in Sardinia where metal was mined and worked. Thus the local name Tarshish may have belonged to several places. A *"Tarshish* ship" has long been understood as a large strongly built vessel capable of the long voyage to Spain. In Albright's explanation it is still a large ship, as the biblical allusions suggest, but it is a "refinery ship" constructed for the transportation of the heavy cargo of smelted metal. The biblical use of the name indicates that one of the refineries was given the name by a kind of preeminence, but it is not possible to determine which is meant.

Tarsus (Gk *tarsos,* meaning uncertain), a city of Asia Minor, the native city of Paul (AA 22:3). He returned to Tarsus after he was forced to leave Jerusalem (AA 9:30) and remained there until he was approached by Barnabas concerning participation in preaching to the Greeks (AA 11:25). Paul with local pride calls Tarsus "no mean city" (AA 21:39), and his boast was not without justification. The age of the foundation is uncertain; it is first mentioned in the Black Obelisk of Shalmaneser III of Assyria (858–824 BC). Its history during the Assyrian, Babylonian, and Persian periods is obscure. 2 Mc 4:30 mentions an insurrection of Tarsus against Antiochus* IV Epiphanes. In NT times Tarsus was a large and prosperous port and commercial center. It lies on the Cydnus river about 20 mi from the sea at the foothills of the Taurus Mts on the SE coast of Turkey. Its harbor lay at the mouth of the Cydnus; in ancient times the river was navigable from the sea to the city, but it has long been silted up. Roads from Tarsus reached the interior of Asia Minor through the Cilician Gates of the Taurus and to N Syria through the Amanus Gates. Tarsus was made a free city by Mark Antony; its privileges were confirmed and enlarged by Augustus. It was a celebrated center of learning which produced a number of famous scholars, and its schools of Stoic philosophy enjoyed special respect. Culturally and religiously Tarsus was a splendid example of the amalgamation of Hellenistic, Anatolian, and Syrian elements. Speculation on the influence of this busy and cosmopolitan center on the mind of Paul is fascinating but scarcely conclusive; it is unlikely, however, that Paul would have possessed his remarkable gift of assimilation with a less cosmopolitan background.

Tartan (Hb *tartān*), an Assyrian officer mentioned in 2 K 18:17; Is 20:1; in some Eng versions rendered Tartan, in others by commander, officer. The word represents Akkadian *turtanu* and designates the commander-in-chief of the army, the officer second to the king.

Tattenai (Aramaic *tattᶜnai*), an Aramaic name? satrap of the Persian satrapy of *Ebernahara,* "across the river" [Euphrates]. In Ezr 5:3–6:13 Tattenai inquired of the Jews what authority they had to rebuild the temple of Jerusalem and referred the question to Darius for confirmation from the royal archives. Darius confirmed the authorization granted by Cyrus and ordered Tattenai to support the project from the royal treasury.

Tau. The 22nd and last letter of the Hb alphabet, with the value of *t.*

Teach, teaching. 1. *OT.* There is no allusion to academic instruction in the OT; that schools existed is known (cf SCRIBE), but the nearest approach to academic instruction is illustrated by the allusions to teaching in the wisdom* literature. These allusions, however, tell us nothing about the conception of teaching nor its techniques. We can deduce that ancient wisdom teaching was the same type which was used in the rabbinical schools and which is still the usual method in the schools of the Near East: it is the communication of an assigned text to rote memory. The work of the teacher before the days of the printed page was to communicate the text and to hear the recitation.

Two Hb words, slightly different in meaning, designate teaching. *Limmēd* seems to mean primarily "to drill," "to exercise," "to train"; it is used of the training of an ox (Je 31:18). The object of teaching is knowledge* (Ec 12:9 +), "ways" i.e., rules of conduct (Ps 51:15; Je 2:33 +), statutes (Dt 4:5 +), how to speak (Je 9:4 +), to swear (Je 12:16), the cult of the Baal (Je 9:13), the words of Yahweh (Dt 11:19), the skills of war (2 S 22:35; Ps 18:35; Jgs 3:2), songs (2 S 1:18, emended text; Dt 31:19; Je 9:19), the book of the law (2 Ch 17:7–9). *Hôrāh* signifies primarily "to show," "to point out," "to inform." The object of teaching when signified by this word scarcely differs from the object of *limmēd:* right conduct (2 K 12:3), judgments* (Ps 119:102 +), what to do (Ex 4:15 +), what to say (Ex 4:12 +), the good and right way (1 S 12:23), the cult of Yahweh (2 K 17:28), the difference between clean and unclean (Lv 14:57), statutes (Lv 10:11 +), laws and commandments (Ex 24:12 +), knowledge (Is 28:9), righteousness (Ho 10:12). *Limmēd* sometimes designates priestly instruction (2 Ch 17:7–9), but *hôrāh* is a technical term for priestly instruction (Lv 14:57; 10:11; 2 K 12:3 +), and the word *tôrāh,* law*, means literally "instruction." It is remarkable how the religious content of teaching is mentioned more frequently than secular instruction; this is of importance in the understanding of the NT use of the word, and also as an original development of Israelite religion: the appearance of doctrine, teaching, as an element of religion. Yahweh is the first teacher, who teaches Moses His *torah,* His statutes and judgments, His ways; and the tradition of teaching thus established is transmitted and applied by the priests, one of whose offices is teaching the revealed truth. The teacher in the OT, whether sacred or secular, is conceived primarily as a revealer. The disciple is a listener. Obviously teaching of this kind is neither theoretical nor specialized; it is addressed to the whole man, not to the intellect, and the acceptance of the teaching is the acceptance of Yahweh revealing Himself as the lord and savior of Israel. This acceptance demands a total surrender; the teaching is a teaching of life.

2. *Gk.* The antithesis between teaching in the OT and the Platonic concept of teaching must be noticed; it is the Platonic concept which influences educational thinking and practice, and which can easily be read into the Bible, where it does not belong. The Gks, the real discoverers of the human intellect and its operations, are also the true discoverers of teaching as an intellectual or otherwise specialized instruction. The essential Gk contribution to the idea of teaching is exhibited in all Gk teaching, whether it be instruction in arts and crafts, athletics, or intellectual theory; this is the conception of teaching as a dialogue, the Socratic form rendered classical by Plato but scarcely original as a process with Socrates and Plato. The teacher is more than a revealer; it is his function to arouse the student's aptitudes by the presentation of problems and to cultivate the student's use of his powers by demanding that he exercise them.

In pointing out this difference between Hb and Gk teaching no value judgment is implied; the idea of teaching needs both conceptions. The effect of the Gk idea of teaching on human intellectual development is too vast to be calculated, and even religious teaching cannot now dispense with it. But neither can the Hb idea of teaching be dismissed; it is based upon the conviction that a body of truth exists which the student needs to learn by the "revelation" of the teacher.

3. *NT.* Jesus was a teacher; this title is given Him more frequently than any other. The use of the word, its contexts, and the description of His teaching show that He acted and was regarded by others as a teacher in the Jewish sense of the word (cf RABBI; SCRIBE): a teacher of the Law*, of the Scriptures (Mt 10:24 f; Lk 2:46; Jn 3:10), as the title is also applied to John the Baptist (Lk 3:12). He gathered a group of disciples*, as the rabbi gathering disciples, and His relations with them were those of the rabbi. They rendered services to the master (Mt 8:18 ff; 21:1 ff; 26:17 ff; Mk 4:35 ff; 11:1 ff; 14:12 ff; Lk 8:22 ff; 19:28 ff; 22:7 ff). He is explicitly described as a teacher of the law, one who teaches the way of God truthfully (Mt 22:16; Mk 12:14; Lk 20:21), and He is asked the type of question which the teacher is asked (Mt 22:36; Lk 10:25). The place of His teaching was often the synagogue* (Mt 4:23; 9:35; 13:54; Mk 6:2; Lk 4:15, 31; 6:6 +).

The content and method of His teaching were largely those of the teacher of the law. When the content of His teaching is mentioned, it is often an exposition of the Scripture, or it takes its point of departure from such an explanation. The teachings (Mt 5:2) which are collected in the "Sermon on the Mount" (Mt 5–7) begin in most cases with a discussion of some biblical text. As such a teacher He was a familiar and acceptable figure in the Jewish community; it was the originality of the form and content of His teaching and His departures from the rigid pattern of rabbinical teaching which aroused hostility. For He was not a mere expounder of traditional teaching; He taught His own positive doctrine and based it upon His personal authority. In the exposition of the Scriptures His teaching was ultimately a biblical demonstration that the kingdom of God had arrived and was fulfilled in Him. Even His teaching on the passion, we may be sure, was a biblical explanation of redemptive suffering (Mk 8:31). He taught the disciples how to pray (Lk 11:1). His teaching took on the character of prophecy, indeed of a new Moses, the first of Israel's teachers. Hence His teaching caused admiration and astonishment because it was "teaching with power" (Mt 7:29; Mk 1:22; 11:18). In His teaching are included the parables*; these were chosen as vehicles of the most original parts of His teaching, the doctrines in which He went beyond the traditional exposition of the Scriptures. In the parables also there is a touch of the Socratic-Platonic dialogue; He leaves the listener with questions to which He has given the answer, but the listener must form the answer for Himself.

In Jn the authority of the teaching of Jesus is more explicitly based on His divine commission. The teaching of Jesus is not His own but the teaching of Him who sent Jesus (Jn 7:16); Jesus says what the Father has taught Him (Jn 8:28). The Paraclete* will teach the disciples what Jesus has said to them (Jn 14:26), and all Christians will be taught by the "anointing" of Jesus, which must mean the spirit* (1 Jn 2:27). These passages introduce the idea of an interior divine teaching, and return to the OT idea of God as the teacher. Jesus therefore is the teacher as revealer; He does not explain the *torah* but proposes a new *torah;* and His teaching in turn is incorporated with the Scriptures in the teaching of the primitive Church.

The early Church distinguished between teaching and preaching*; and it appears that teaching retains the basic meaning of instruction in the Scriptures, now enlarged to signify an apologetic demonstration from the Scriptures that Jesus is the Messiah, and instruction based on the teaching of Jesus Himself. Thus the content of the apostolic preaching of Mt 28:19 is "all that I have commanded you." This was the general content of the teaching of the apostles in Jerusalem (AA 4:2; 5:25, 42), further specified as the word of the Lord (AA 15:35), the word of God (AA 18:11), the "things concerning Jesus" (AA 18:25). The word is not common in Paul; R. Rengstorff has suggested that "teaching" in the Jewish sense was not possible in Gentile churches. Paul denies that he received his Gospel from any one's teaching (Gal 1:12). His own teaching is "his ways in Christ" (1 Co 4:17). But as the churches developed, a body of teaching based on the Scriptures and the teaching of Jesus was developed; this could be called wisdom (Col 1:28), the faith (Col 2:7), traditions (2 Th 2:15); ultimately the object of Christian teaching was Christ (Eph 4:21). Teaching included pastoral-ethical instruction (Rm 12:7). As Christianity developed, the need of teachers and instruction grew with it: for Christianity, like the faith of Israel (cf above) was based upon a body of revealed truth, "taught" by God, which had to be assimilated. Teachers therefore appear among the officers of the Church (1 Co 12: 28 f; Eph 4:11). In the pastoral epistles teaching is a part of the office of apostle (1 Tm 2:7; 2 Tm 3:11) and of the office of bishop (2 Tm 4:3 +). With the cessation of the apostolic office the preservation and explanation of apostolic traditions became of primary importance; this was "sound doctrine" (1 Tm 1:10; 2 Tm 4:3; Tt 1:9; 2:1). Preaching was addressed to nonbelievers; for those who had accepted the faith an explanation of their belief was necessary.

Tekel. Cf MENE; TEKEL; UPHARSIN.

Tekoa (Hb *tᵉḳôꜥᵃ*, meaning uncertain), a place name; a town of Judah, the home city of the prophet Amos* (Am 1:1), of David's hero Ira (2 S 23:26; 1 Ch 11:28; 27:9), and of the wise woman introduced by Joab* to trick David into forgiving Absalom* (2 S 14:2 ff). It was settled by the Judahite clan of Ashur (1 Ch 2:24; 4:5). It was one of Rehoboam's* fortified cities (2 Ch 11:6). Tekoa was one of the towns resettled by the Jewish community after the exile* (Ne 3:5, 27).

The site is identified with Khirbet Teqoa, about 10 mi S of Jerusalem. There are no remains from anything before the Byzantine period; it is a bare windswept height with a magnificent view of the Dead Sea and the cliffs of Moab, from which the wilderness of Judah slopes down abruptly to the Dead Sea. This part of the desert is the "desert of Tekoa" (2 Ch 20:20), into which Jonathan and Simon fled from the attack of Bacchides* (1 Mc 9:33). Tekoa is not mentioned in the lists of Jos, which may suggest that it was a Judahite foundation.

Tel-abib (Hb *tel-'ābîb,* "hill of the ear [of grain]"), the settlement of the exiled Jews in Babylonia where Ezekiel lived. Some scholars suggest that the name of the town is a Hebraization of Akkadian *til abubi,* "hill of the deluge." The site is unknown. "Hill" here means a mound created by continuous occupation; cf TELL.

Telassar (Hb *tᵉla'ssar,* meaning uncertain), a town of Eden conquered by the Assyrians (2 K 19:12; Is 37:12), otherwise unknown.

Tell. The Arabic *tell* appears in biblical Hb as *tēl* and designates a mound created by long occupation of a site. In the Near East (Turkey, Syria, Palestine, Mesopotamia, Iraq) the mound, often an isolated eminence in the otherwise flat land of a plain or plateau, takes a very characteristic appearance which is easily recognized. The origins of the mound lie usually in village culture; the site was erected principally because of the availability of water, but it was even more desirable if a natural eminence which offered some defense was adjacent to the water source. The tell is the creation not only of buildings and other debris of occupation — in the ancient Near East there seems to have been little effort to clear debris from towns and cities — but also of interruption of occupation due to war, famine, disease, or similar disasters. When this happened the site was abandoned as it stood, and the erosion of rain and wind rounded off the top and sides. The artificial elevation thus created made the site even more desirable for the next occupation. It is these successive layers of occupation, like the layers of a cake, which make it possible for the archaeologist to sort out the various periods of occupation and reconstruct the history of the site. The usual tell of the Near East resembles a truncated cone or more frequently a hogback ridge. In old settlements the depth of the debris reaches an astonishing height; Tell es-Sultan (Jericho*) contained 80 ft of debris which was deposited during occupation from Neolithic times (6800 BC) to Iron Age II (the Israelite monarchy).

Tell el Amarna. Cf AMARNA.

Tema (Hb *têma'*, meaning uncertain), a place name and tribal name of Arabia; a son of Ishmael* with other Arabian peoples (Gn 25:15; 1 Ch 1:30), inhabitants of the desert (Is 21:14) and caravan traders (Jb 6:19), the object of a threatening oracle with other Arabian peoples (Je 25:23). The name survives in Teima, an oasis of the part of the Arabian desert called the Nefud in N central Arabia.

Teman (Hb *têmān*, "the south"?), a place name; a region of Edom (Je 49:7; Ezk 25:13; Am 1:12; Ob 9) mentioned with Dedan* (Ezk 25:13), famous for its wise men (Je 49:7), the place from which Yahweh appears (Hab 3:3; mentioned with Mt Paran*); genealogically reckoned a descendant of Esau and a son of Eliphaz (Gn 36:11, 15, 42; 1 Ch 1:36, 53). The situation is unknown except that it must be in the territory of Edom. Very frequently in the OT *têmān* is used to signify simply "south" as a point of direction.

Temple. In both Egypt and Mesopotamia the temple was the house of the god where he was served by the priests and not a house of assembly for the worshipers. When the worshipers came to the temple they were admitted only to the temple courts; the temple building was too small to admit any more than a few at one time. The rites of prayer and sacrifice conducted before the public were conducted in the court outside the temple. The Egyptians conceived the temple as a symbol of the world itself; in Mesopotamia the earthly temple was a counterpart of the heavenly temple.

In both Egypt and Mesopotamia the temple had more immediate effect upon the civic and economic life of the people. The earliest cities of Sumerian times were actually temple communities; the god was the king of the city and the temple was the landowner. The entire people were servants and tenants of the temple. Even after this conception of society had changed the temple remained a focus of communal life. The temples appear as great landowners in Egypt and in Mesopotamia. They employed a large staff of priests and priestesses, and in addition craftsmen, peasants, shepherds, fishermen, cooks, bakers, and other workers. The temple taxes lay upon all; and the vast storehouses of the temple made it a bank and a treasury. Its economic activities made it a marketing center and an industrial area. The temples were the first place where writing appears; the temple staff included a large number of scribes, and its archives and records were extensive. These temple libraries also contained historical, mythological, and religious literature such as hymns, prayers, and cultic ritual directions, and the literature of magic* and divination. We may infer by analogy that the Jerusalem temple was also a civic, cultural, and economic center.

1. *The Temple of Solomon.* The Hb word for temple *hêkāl,* is borrowed from Akkadian *ekallu,* Sumerian *e-gal,* "great house," applied in Akkadian more frequently to palace than to temple. The temple is also called simply "the house" or "the house of Yahweh." The idea of building a temple came to David* when he established his palace in Jerusalem, which he took from the Jebusites and made the royal residence (2 S 7:1 ff). The oracle of Nathan, which is principally directed to the promise of an eternal dynasty of David, begins (2 S 7:5–7; 1 Ch 17:3–7) with an apparent rejection and an appeal to Israelite tradition that Yahweh dwelt, like His originally nomadic people, only in a tent, a movable shrine (cf TABERNACLE). The oracle goes on to authenticate the temple, which is to be built by David's son. In 1 Ch 28:3 the failure of David to build the temple is rationalized; he is "a man of blood," a warrior. The site of the temple was traditionally the threshing floor of Araunah* (2 S 24:16 ff), where David built an altar to commemorate the arresting of the plague.

There is no doubt that the site of Solomon's temple was the site of the present Haram-esh-Sharif in Jerusalem; but there are no archaeological remains. The description of the temple in 1 K 6:1 ff leaves much to be desired. The architecture and style must have been Phoenician, since the temple was planned and built by the architects and workmen of Hiram* of Tyre* (1 K 5:1 ff); there would be no satisfactory parallel except a 10th century Phoenician temple, which we do not have.

The temple was a part of the palace* enclosure; this appears also in Assyrian palaces, although it is probably oversimplifying to call the temple "a royal chapel." Most archaeologists believe that there was a public gate

a) Restoration of the temple of Anu-Adad

b) Pylon of the temple of Edfu.

c) Detail of the arch of Titus, showing the spoils of the temple of Jerusalem.

to the temple court so that the worshipers would not have to pass through the palace courts; the king, however, had his own gate from the palace to the temple court. The temple probably lay to the N of the palace. The building of the temple took seven years (1 K 6:37 f); it is not surprising that the palace, which was a much more extensive project, took 13 years (1 K 7:1). The stone was hewn to shape in the quarry and the woodwork was prefabricated, so that "sound of hammer and axe and any tool was not heard in the temple while it was being built" (1 K 6:7).

No data are given of the temple court or courts, which must have existed. The temple building itself was 90 ft long × 30 ft wide × 45 ft high. It is not clear whether these are inside or outside measurements. The porch was 30 ft wide, the width of the building, and 15 ft deep; it is not clear whether it was salient or recessed. Its height is given in 2 Ch 3:4 as 180 ft: this figure seems impossible.

No precise parallel to the porch is known from which we can deduce its structure. The tripartite structure of the temple is seen in a Canaanite temple of Tell Tainat in Syria of the 9th century BC. The side chambers offer another difficulty in reconstruction; they may have been built actually within the wall, but the structural difficulties which this would involve lead most modern scholars to think of them as wings projecting parallel to the wall. It is commonly assumed, since there is no mention of light or ventilation, that they were storage chambers. Before the temple were two free standing columns of bronze surmounted with decorated capitals. Their purpose is not given, but scholars believe they were more than merely decorative. W. F. Albright has suggested that they were fire-pillars of cosmic significance, recalling the pillar of smoke and the pillar of fire of the exodus*. The names, *Yakin*, "he will establish," and *Boaz*, "in strength," may be the first words of their inscriptions. From the porch double doors of olive wood led into the "holy place" (to which the word *hêkāl*, cf above, is often applied); this was 60 ft long × 30 ft wide × 45 ft high. The entire interior was paneled with cedar carved with floral decorations, palms, and cherubim. The room was illuminated by windows, probably clerestory latticed windows. The holy place contained cultic apparatus: the golden altar of incense, the table of the shewbread*, ten lampstands, and other utensils. Two double doors led into the "holy of holies" or most holy place, where reposed the ark* of the covenant. This was a cube 30 ft on a side. The difference between the height of the holy place and the most holy place is evident; it is more probable that the floor of the most holy place stood higher than the floor of the holy place than it is that the ceiling was lower. This room also was paneled with cedar with gold inlay. Two large cherubim of cedar stood over the ark, each 15 ft high and with a 15 foot wingspread, so that they filled the room. The roof was probably made of beaten earth (cf HOUSE); it was probably surrounded by a crenelated parapet attested in other ancient Near Eastern buildings. No illumination of the most holy place is mentioned at all and it was probably totally dark, never entered by the worshipers and rarely by the priests (cf 1 K 8:12 f)

The court in front of the temple contained the bronze altar of whole burnt offerings. This is described in 2 Ch 4:1 as 30 ft long, 30 ft wide, and 15 ft high, so that it must have been ascended by a flight of steps; similar altar steps are found elsewhere in the Near East. Some scholars have suggested that it was a step tower of three stages in the form of the Mesopotamian *ziggurat*. A bronze platform 7½ ft long × 7½ ft wide × 4½ ft high upon which Solomon knelt during his prayer is paralleled by a representation from Ugarit* which shows a worshiper kneeling upon a similar platform; the platform is not mentioned elsewhere in the OT. Its purpose, as suggested by A Parrot, may have been to aid in projecting the voice of the officiant. The bronze "sea" was an immense reservoir 7½ ft high with a diameter of 15 ft. It was supported by twelve figures of oxen, three oriented toward each of the four cardinal points of the compass. This recalls the sacred lake found adjacent to Egyptian temples; its size and shape seem to make it impractical for simple water storage. It may therefore symbolize the primeval sea which Yahweh conquered (cf CREATION) and upon which He sits enthroned (Ps 29: 10). Ten mobile bronze lavers for carrying water stood in the court. These were highly decorated with carvings. They rested upon square supports 6 ft on a side and 4½ ft wide and were themselves 6 ft in diameter These also seem a little too large for easy use and it has been suggested that they also were symbolic; but no definite symbolism has been found. Similar lavers but smaller have been found in temples of Crete.

The temple was the scene of more than one critical event in the history of Judah Its treasures were emptied several times to pay tribute or to buy alliances (1 K 14:26 15:18; 2 K 12:18; 16:8; 18:15). The infant king Jehoash was hidden in the priests apartments for six years (2 K 11:3) from the murderous intentions of Athaliah*; he was then proclaimed king in the temple and

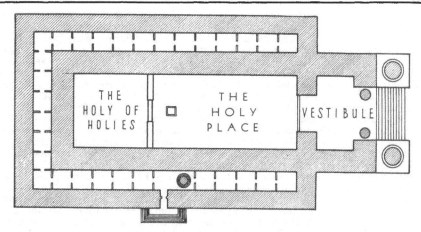

Plan of the sanctuary of Herod's temple.

Athaliah herself was killed just outside the temple enclosure (2 K 11:9 ff). Hezekiah spread the letter from the Assyrian ambassadors in the temple and there prayed for deliverance (2 K 19:14 ff). Hilkiah* discovered the "book of the torah of Yahweh" (cf DEUTERONOMY) which was the basis of the reforms of Josiah* in the temple library (2 K 22:8). Josiah and the people then made a covenant with Yahweh in the temple (2 K 23:3 f). The temple of Solomon was destroyed by the Babylonians in 587 BC.

2. *The Temple of Zerubbabel.* No data whatever are given concerning the structure of this temple, which was begun in 537 BC, interrupted by objections from neighboring peoples, resumed in 520 BC, and dedicated in 515 BC. It stood until the beginning of Herod's new temple in 19 BC. It was no doubt of the same dimensions and structure as the temple of Solomon but much inferior in the richness of its decorations (Ezr 3:12; Hg 2:3).

3. *The Temple of Herod*.* Among the many building projects of Herod was included a new temple at Jerusalem. His motives were probably less devotional than political; this gift to the Jews would remove some of the hostility which they felt toward him as an Idumean and a man whose religion was more heathen than Jewish. He spared no expense in producing a grand temple complex. He put 10,000 men to work and trained 1000 priests as masons so that they could work on the most sacred parts of the temple. The building was begun in 19 BC and finished in 10 years, but the work of decoration was carried on for some years afterwards. The Pharisees observed that "this temple has been under construction for 46 years" (Jn 2:20). It was completely fin-

ished in AD 64, six years before it was burned down in the Roman attack on Jerusalem. The descriptions of the temple come from Josephus and Talmudic traditions.

The entire enclosure according to Josephus was twice as large as the earlier enclosure. It was a trapezoid measuring 2350 ft in its perimeter. There were eight gates: two on the S, four on the W, one on the N, and one on the E. One "ascended" to the temple (Lk 18:10) through the S gates by covered vaulted passages. The gates in the W were connected with the city by viaducts over the valley of the Tyropoeon. The E gate, near the site of the present "Golden Gate," was probably the gate used by Jesus on Palm Sunday (Mt 21:12; Mk 11:11; Lk 19:45). The entire enclosure was divided into several courts. The largest, the court of the Gentiles, was accessible on all four sides, unless the temple itself lay against the W wall. The court of the Gentiles was bordered by colonnades on all four sides. The royal porch lay on the S and the porch of Solomon (Jn 10:22; AA 3:11; 5:12) on the E. The "pinnacle of the temple" (Mt 4:5; Lk 4:9) is not certainly located; many scholars believe it designates the wall of the SE corner, where the ground plunges steeply toward the Kidron. The court of the Gentiles was accessible to anyone. It was separated from the temple and the other courts by a balustrade with inscriptions prohibiting Gentiles from entering the interior courts under pain of death; two copies of this inscription have been discovered. The sacred enclosure formed a rectangle in the W center of the court of the Gentiles. It was raised upon a terrace, walled, and entered by 9 gates: 4 on the N, 4 on the S, and one on the E. The E gate was the most ornate, the Corinthian gate of Josephus and the beautiful gate of AA 3:2. The first court reached from the E was the court of the women, five steps above the court of the Gentiles, beyond which women might not pass. Here there were alms boxes for contributions for the cult (Mk 12:41 ff; Lk 21:1) and the treasury of Jn 8:20. The next court to the W was the court of Israel or the court of the men, raised five steps above the court of the women. It was 280 ft × 202 ft. It was entered by 3 gates on the N, 3 on the S, and one on the E, which was probably the Nicanor gate, named after a generous Jewish donor from Alexandria. The court of Israel was the place of the worshipers during the incense offering (Lk 1:10). It is probably the scene of the prayer of the Pharisee (Lk 18:11) and of the disciples (Lk 24:53) and of Paul's fulfillment of his vow (AA 21:26). From the court of Israel one passed into the court of the priests, which surrounded the temple building. The altar of whole burnt offerings in the court of the priests stood between the gate of Nicanor and the temple and was ascended by a ramp from the S. It probably stood where one may now see the mass of native rock within the Dome of the Rock. The temple building maintained the tripartite division of Solomon's temple. The porch was reached by an ascent of 12 steps above the court of the priests; it was much larger than Solomon's porch, 150 ft wide and 150 ft high. The porch was entered through a great doorway 60 ft wide and 30 ft high. Another doorway 30 ft wide and 15 ft high led from the porch into the holy place, 60 ft long × 30 ft wide × 60 ft high. No details are given concerning the decoration of the holy place; it contained the altar of incense, the table of the shewbread, and the seven-branched lampstand (represented on the arch of Titus). The most holy place was a cube 30 ft on a side; the floor was possibly raised as in the temple of Solomon. It was entirely empty and totally dark; it was entered only by the high priest once a year on the Day of Atonement*. The most holy place was separated from the holy place by a veil; the rending of the veil at the death of Jesus (Mk 15:38; Mt 27:51) is a symbolic narrative signifying the access of all peoples to God through the death of Jesus.

The entire temple building was surrounded by small chambers as was the temple of Solomon. The external proportions of the building were rendered regular according to the dimensions of the porch by the erection of a large room, whose purpose is unknown, above the entire sanctuary. The temple building was composed of white limestone ornamented with gold plating and gilded pinnacles, so that it must have been a truly impressive sight.

4. *Theological Significance of the temple.* I. The Temple in the OT. The OT exhibits an ambivalent attitude toward the temple. As the seat and symbol of the presence of Yahweh among His people it is the scene of Isaiah's vision of Yahweh the king, his perception of Yahweh's holiness, and his prophetic commission (Is 6:1 ff). In the messianic era "the mountain of the house of Yahweh" becomes the highest of all mountains to which all peoples resort for instruction and the word of Yahweh (Is 2:1 ff; Mi 4:1 ff). The temple will be a house of prayer for all peoples (Is 56:7), who will bring their wealth for the service of the temple (Is 60:1 ff), and the glory of the temple of Zerubbabel will exceed the glory of the temple of Solomon (Hg 2:6–9). To this temple will come Yahweh and the angel of the covenant (Mal 3:1). Here the temple is one of the Hebrew institutions, like kingdom and priesthood, in terms of which the messianic fulfillment is conceived. Another stream of thought, however, conceives the temple as disappearing in the messianic fulfillment. Je 7:1 ff denies the false security in the presence of Yahweh which the Israelites found in the temple and predicts its destruction (cf 26:1 ff). Mi 3:12 also predicts the destruction of the temple. Is 66:1 denies the necessity of a temple. Ezk 40–42 describes the new temple of the messianic Jerusalem in detail. The description is ideal but is based on the temple of Solomon. Ezekiel enhances the sacredness of the temple area by setting it off in a series of zones and courts. He also provides chambers and offices for the priests and for cultic utensils. The temple becomes the source of a stream of living water which fertilizes the desert of Judah and sweetens the water of the Dead Sea (47:1 ff), a symbolism which recurs in Zc 14:8. The temple of Ezekiel is constructed after a heavenly model, as was the tabernacle* (Ex 26:30); the idea of the heavenly model also appears in Mesopotamia.

II. The temple in the NT. Jesus was often in the temple and appears to have fulfilled His duty as a Jew of taking part in its public cult. The episode in which he was lost for three days and was found in the temple was the occasion of a cryptic saying, "Did you not know that I must be in the things of my father?" The Gk phrase, "the things of my father," is translated by some "my father's business," by others, "my father's house." The translation "my father's house" seems more intelligible. It answers the question asked by Mary: "Why did you look for me? Did you not know that I would be in the temple?" The encounter with the scribes and teachers probably took place either in the temple porticoes or in the temple schoolroom; these were also the scenes of the teaching of Jesus in the temple and of discussions with questioners, which are mentioned several times (Mt 21:23; 26:55; Mk 11:27; 12:35; 14:49; Lk 20:1; 22:53). This public teaching is emphasized in Jn 18:20. Jesus taught no secret or esoteric doctrine; He had nothing to conceal and there was no lack of witnesses to what He had taught. In harmony with his interest in the Jerusalem ministry of Jesus John refers more frequently to teaching in the temple than do the other Gospels (7:14, 28; 8:20, 59; 10:23; 11:56). The respect of Jesus for the temple was all that could be desired. He called it the house of God (Mt 12:4; Lk 6:4), a house of prayer (Mt 21:13; Mk 11:17; Lk 19:46) and the house of His Father (Jn 2:16). The temple is holy because of Him who dwells in it, and it sanctifies the objects it contains (Mt 23:16–21). Jesus paid the temple tax, although He asserted His freedom from it (Mt 17:24–27).

The episode of the cleansing of the temple is related in all four Gospels (Mt 21:12 f; Mk 11:15–17; Lk 19:45 f; Jn 2:14–17). Jn places it at the beginning of the public career and the Synoptics place it at the end. Exegetes are divided on which position represents the chronological order. K. L. Schmidt, followed by V. Taylor, suggests that the episode in the pre-Gospel tradition was related without any chronological setting and was arranged according to the plan of each tradition: Jn places it at the beginning as a keynote declaration, and the synoptic tradition at the end to relate it to the charge laid at the trial of Jesus based on his saying in this episode: destroy this temple and in three days I will rebuild it. The saying is connected with the episode only in Jn. Mt 26:61 and Mk 14:58 report it at the trial. There are modal differences (Mt, "I can destroy"; Mk, "I will destroy"; Jn. "destroy." Mk adds "made with hands," "not made with hands"). Jn alone explains that the temple is His body. Few would doubt that this saying belongs to the original traditions; its meaning, however, is obscure, unless it is considered as the saying which lies at the root of the theological consideration of the temple in the apostolic writings (cf below). Jesus here affirms that He Himself becomes the cultic center, the place where God is present in His dwelling; as such He is greater than the temple (Mt 12:6). It is in harmony with this saying that He should have predicted the destruction of the temple, as all the synoptics relate (Mt 24:2; Mk 13:2; Lk 21:6). This echoes the words of Jeremiah and Micah (cf above) and taken with the saying about the raising of a new temple gives full meaning to the messianic view of the temple of Isaiah and Ezekiel.

Like Jesus, the members of the primitive Christian community of Jerusalem took part in the temple worship (AA 2:46; 3:1; 22:17); like Him, the apostles taught in the temple (AA 5:12, 20, 25, 42). In the first years of the community the break between Christianity and Judaism had not yet become apparent. Even Paul, when he was in Jerusalem, took part in the temple cult (AA 21:26; 24:6, 12, 18; 26:21). But an antitemple motif appears in the charge laid against Stephen*, in which he is said to have quoted the saying of Jesus, "Destroy this temple" (AA 6:14). In his discourse before the council Stephen did nothing to refute the charge; rather by quoting Is 66:1 he implies that there is no need of temple worship. A similar thought is expressed in Paul's discourse at Athens (AA 17:24); this discourse, however, is addressed to Greeks and refers primarily to their temples. It is possible, following the suggestion of some scholars, to discern in the Hellenistic Jewish community represented by Stephen the beginnings of the rejection of the temple cult. Paul denied its necessity for Gentile Christians.

Ultimately the theological significance of the temple in the NT is based on the saying of Jesus which identifies His body with the new temple. His body in turn is identified with the Church, and the Church herself is the new temple (1 Co 3:9, 16 f; 2 Co 6:16; Eph 2:19–22). The Church is now the place of God's presence, not merely symbolic, but real through the indwelling of the Spirit. Thus the Church is holy like the temple, and it can never live in friendship with idolatry. The apostles and prophets are the foundations of the temple and Christ Jesus is its cornerstone and principle of unity. The Christians are the living stones of this temple and its consecrated priesthood. Paul also makes the individual Christian the temple in which the Spirit dwells; for the body which is profaned by fornication is the body of the individual Christian (1 Co 6:19).

The heavenly temple of which the earthly temple is the counterpart appears in Apc 3:12; 7:15; 11:19; 14:15, 17; 15:5, 8; 16:1. But the vision of the heavenly temple vanishes in the descent of new Jerusalem in 21:2 ff. When the earth is renewed by the descent of the heavenly city, there is no temple in the city, because the Lord God and the Lamb are its temple. This is not an inconsistency in the visions; rather here on the last page of the Bible the symbolism of the temple arrives at its fullness. For the symbolic presence of God among His people is at last replaced by His dwelling among them.

Temptation. 1. *OT*. Hb *nāsāh* means "to try" or "to test." When it is used of a person, it means to elicit some personal response to show either what the person can do or what the person will do. "Temptation" in the common meaning of the word is a test of a person's disposition and will rather than his abilities. In this sense God is said to tempt man. God tempted Abraham by commanding him to sacrifice Isaac, despite the promise of a numerous progeny (Gn 22:1-19; BS 44:20; 1 Mc 2:52). The theophany of Sinai is a coming of God in order to tempt Israel (Ex 20:20). God tempts the Israelites to see in what way they will walk (Jgs 2:22; WS 11:9). Service of God demands readiness to be tempted (BS 2:1), and wisdom tempts the wise man with her judgments (BS 4:17). One who has not been tempted knows little (BS 34:10). God delivers the righteous in temptations (BS 33:1); and the righteous is proved by temptation, like gold in the furnace (WS 3:5 f). The temptation of Job by the Satan*, who acts with God's permission, is very circumstantially described (Jb 1-2). This passage together with the temptation of Abraham (Gn 22) shows what is meant in the OT by God's temptation of man; it is primarily the visitation of unmerited suffering upon man, the kind of suffering which shakes man's faith in the accepted doctrine of retribution according to one's deeds. It is therefore principally a temptation, a testing of man's faith. Underneath the idea of temptation is the anthropomorphic conception of God searching out information after the manner of a man; this early view is more apparent in the story of Abraham and in Ex 20:20. Temptation reveals a man's true disposition and will toward God and the sincerity of his righteousness, and thus it is a discovery.

The narrative of Gn 3:1-19 recounts a temptation in which God is not the tempter; the agent who tempts is the serpent*. The temptation attributed to God consists in the prohibition of the tree of life. The story is a masterful description of the psychology of temptation; the resistance, the hesitation and weakening, and the final surrender of the woman, are thoroughly true to life.

Man also tempts God. This appears in its classic form in the story of Massah* (temptation; Ex 17:1-7, alluded to in Pss 78:17 f, 40 f; 95:8 f; 106:14). Dt 6:16 warns the Israelites not to tempt God as did their fathers, a warning repeated in BS 18:23. To tempt God is "not to recognize His power and not to take His saving will seriously" (Seesemann); it is to exhibit unbelief as the Israelites did in the episode of the scouts (Nm 14:22). To tempt God is, in a very anthropomorphic conception, to bait Him, to see how far His patience can be tried before His anger breaks out. This is the temptation of God which Ahaz* refused (Is 7:12); his plea was hypocritical, for he had already determined to seek salvation from Assyria and not from Yahweh.

2. *NT*. In the NT Satan or the devil appears more frequently as the agent of temptation (1 Co 7:5; 1 Th 3:5; 1 Pt 5:8 f). Temptation of faith (1 Th 3:5) and of continence (1 Co 7:5) are mentioned in particular. Temptation itself is to be avoided through vigilance (Gal 6:1), and God promises that He will keep the Christian from temptation (Apc 3:10). He keeps the righteous from temptation (2 Pt 2:9). In these passages temptation is conceived as an evil in itself; it is seduction to which man is likely to yield. In the same sense Jesus warns His disciples to pray that they may not come into temptation, for the reason that however willing the spirit may be, the flesh is weak (Mt 26:41; Mk 14:38; Lk 22:46). It is in this sense that the petition of the Lord's prayer that the Father may not lead us into temptation is to be understood (Mt 6:13; Lk 11:4). In the biblical thought of the OT, which is implicit here, God may very well lead one into temptation, as He did Job and Abraham. The prayer asks that the Christian may be delivered from the seduction of sin, in the sense in which this deliverance is assured in Apc 3:10; 2 Pt 2:9. Paul refines the idea of temptation in 1 Co 10:13 by defining it as the temptation which is "human," common to man in his earthly condition. God's fidelity to His promise assures the Christian that God permits no temptation beyond one's strength but provides an issue from the temptation. This defines more closely the deliverance from temptation which is asked in the Lord's Prayer.

In Js 1:2, 12-15 temptation is conceived not as an evil to be avoided but as a blessing for which to be grateful. Temptation here is the test or trial rather than the seduction; it is a return to the OT sense of the word. It is temptation that produces steadfastness in the faith and wins the crown of life. Js denies that God tempts anyone, not the flat contradiction of biblical doctrine which it seems to be; with Paul he agrees that God, far from wishing anyone to commit evil, alone makes it possible for one not to commit evil. The source of temptation is not to be found in God but in one's own disorderly desires, which produce sin. Js would seem to agree that no one is tempted unless he wishes. The temptation in 1:13–15 is not precisely the trial of 1:2, 12, in which one should rejoice; and the wavering of Js shows the mystery of the fact of temptation, in which opportunities and incitements to do evil are the thing which ultimately prove the Christian. Paul speaks of suffering in Rm 5:3 f in much the same terms which Js uses; suffering produces endurance, proof, and firm hope; as in the OT (cf above), the test which God put man to is the test of unmerited suffering.

The temptation of God by man is rare in the NT; it occurs only in the lie of Sapphira* to Peter (AA 5:9) and in Peter's use of the phrase to refer to the imposition of the law upon the Gentiles (AA 15:10). This is a genuine OT use of the word; the imposition of the law is a doubt of the power and will of God to save through Christ.

The temptation of Jesus Himself is mentioned in Heb 2:18; 4:15 and in the Gospels (Mt 4:1–11; Mk 1:12–13; Lk 4:1–13). It is evident that Heb and the Gospels are not talking about the same thing, and indeed it is difficult to specify what Heb refers to. Heb 5:7–9 suggests that by the temptations of Jesus the Gethsemani experience is meant, although the word is not used in the Gospels. The temptations of Jesus enable Him to assist those who are tempted (Heb 2:18); for He can sympathize with us, having been tempted as we are in every respect apart from sin (Heb 4:15). "Like us" does not indicate that Jesus experienced either concupiscence or the danger of consent but that in Gethsemani, like us, He felt the full weight of unmerited suffering.

The episode of the temptation is reported in only summary form in Mk 1:12 f, and it is quite possible that Mk was unacquainted with the fuller form of Mt 4:1–11; Lk 4:1–13. These differ in the order of the temptations: Mt, bread, the temple pinnacle, the mountain top; Lk, bread, the mountain top, the temple pinnacle. The order of Mt is more studiously climactic. Recent interpreters believe the explanation of this episode is to be sought in doctrinal symbolism rather than in the real course of events. The episode describes the kind of Messiah Jesus was, and by implication what kind of society the Church, the new Israel is: it lives by the word of God, it does not challenge God's promises, and it adores and serves God alone and not the world. Jesus rejects in anticipation the temptations to which His Church will be submitted.

Ten Commandments. Cf DECALOGUE.

Tent. It is dwelling in the tent rather than a house which distinguishes the nomad* from the peasant. In Arabic there is no specific word for tent; the tent is "a house of hair."

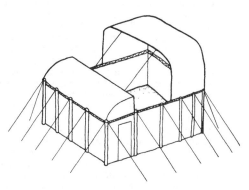

The tent used by the king during military campaigns, from an Assyrian relief sculpture.

Hb distinguishes the tent (*'ōhel*) from the house (*bayit*). In the primitive history of Gn the invention of tent-dwelling and the nomadic shepherd life is attributed to Jabal* (Gn 4:20). Through the Pnt the patriarchs and the early Israelites are tent-dwelling nomadic shepherds; they did not begin to live in houses and till the soil until after the settlement in Canaan. The nomadic past of Israel survived in memory and in a number of archaic features in speech and language; cf NOMAD. Even under the monarchy the cry with which secession from David* and from Rehoboam was declared was "To your tents, Israel" (2 S 20:1; 1 K 12:16). The figurative use of the tent is fairly common for the home, the person, the life (cf Je 10:20; Lk 16:9; 2 Co 5:1, 4 +). In the time of Jeremiah the Rechabites* clung to the nomadic life as a religious practice (Je 35:6–10). The proper home of Yahweh the God of Israel was a tent (cf TABERNACLE).

K. Galling has observed that the use of tents for military encampment was exceptional; it is attested for Israelites (2 S 11:11), Aramaeans (2 K 7:7), and Babylonians (Je 37:10). Each of these instances refers to a besieging army (cf SIEGE). Assyrian military tents are represented in art (ANEP 170, 171, 374).

The form of the ancient tent is not described in the literature, but it probably did not differ substantially from the tent of modern Bedu. The tent covering was woven from camel hair or goat hair; the goat is usually black, and so are the tents (SS 1:5). The wool of Cilician goats (*cilicium*, "hair cloth") was much prized; Paul, a native of Cilicia, was a tentmaker by trade (AA 18:3) i.e., a weaver of goat hair fabric. The ordinary family tent of the Bedu is rectangular in shape; the coverings are supported by at least 9 tent poles; more are used by richer and more important heads of families. The rectangle is arranged in 3 rows of poles. The door of the tent is covered by a hanging which is left open during the day to anyone. The family tent is divided by a curtain into at least two rooms, one of which is the harem reserved for women and children (Gn 18:9). Access to this room is reserved to the head of the family; ancient custom punished invasion of the harem by death. The pitching and striking of the tent is the work of the women, who do it very rapidly; the mallet for the tent pegs is a domestic tool (Jgs 4:21; 5:26). Each tent pole is attached by ropes to tent pegs driven in the ground outside the tent. The Assyrian tents pictured in ANEP 170, 171, 374 are circular tents; these are supported on a center post and four outer poles.

Terah (Hb *terah*, meaning uncertain), a personal name; son of Nahor* and father of Abraham (Gn 11:24–32; 1 Ch 1:26). Terah migrated with his family from Ur* to go to Canaan, but settled in Haran* instead, where he died. The name Terah appears in cuneiform sources in the place name Til-Turakhi, "mound of Turakh" (cf TELL). Like Haran and Nahor* it appears as both a personal name and a place name. With them it strengthens the connection between Abraham and NW Mesopotamia. More probably Terah is a clan name which was given to the city, or vice versa, and which is hypostatized in the genealogy of the patriarchs.

Teraphim. Cf IMAGE.

Tertius (Lt *tertius,* "third [son?]"), the scribe* who wrote Rm (Rm 16:22).

Tertullus (Lt *tertullus*), a *rhetor* or professional advocate, presumably of Jerusalem, hired by Ananias* and the elders who accompanied him to present their charges against Paul before Felix* at Caesarea (AA 24:1–8).

Testament. The Old Testament and the New Testament are the principal divisions of the Christian Bible. The word testament is derived from Lt *testamentum,* employed to translate Gk *diathēkē. Diathēkē* means either a last will or an agreement, and *testamentum,* which means a last will, was unfortunately chosen. *Diathēkē* in the Bible signifies covenant*; cf also BIBLE.

Teth. The 9th letter of the Hb alphabet, with the value of *t.*

Tetrarch (Gk *tetrarchēs,* lit "ruler of the 4th part of a region"; but in general use signified a satellite prince who ranked below a king in dignity). In the NT the title is given to Herod Antipas* (Mt 14:1; Lk 3:19; 9:7; AA 13:1), the tetrarch of Galilee, and to another son of Herod, Philip*, tetrarch of Ituraea and Trachonitis, and to Lysanias*, tetrarch of Abilene (Lk 3:1). Their territories came from the kingdom of Herod* the Great, divided by Augustus after the death of Herod.

Text. 1. *OT.* The Hb text tradition of the OT reposes principally upon some hundreds of MSS, none earlier than the medieval period, and all exhibiting a remarkable uniformity. The text is not entirely satisfactory, exhibiting numerous obvious corruptions and alterations which cannot render the original. It is only within recent years that critics have been able to go behind this received text and ascertain to some extent the history by which the text arrived at its present form.

The uniformity of the received text is due to a rigid Jewish textual tradition which at some point took great care to preserve the text which then existed; variations were excluded by editorial work and the text thus obtained was preserved from further variation by severe regulations governing the copying of the text. It is not possible to trace the preparation of the text; but the transmission since the 6th century AD is known to be the work of rabbis called Massoretes (Hb *massōrāh,* "tradition"); the text which comes from their work, the modern received text, is called the Massoretic text [MT]. Up to the 6th or 7th century AD the Hb text was copied as it had always been written, with consonantal signs alone; the Hb alphabet contains no vowel signs. The pronunciation of the text therefore was preserved only by living oral tradition, which was subject to dialectical variations. The Syriac alphabet likewise contains no vowel signs, and as early as the 4th century AD Syriac MSS were written with small points or tiny Gk letters to indicate the vocalization of the text. It is not unlikely that the vowel signs added to the Hb text by the Massoretes were contrived in imitation of the Syriac signs. There were two principal schools of Massoretes, the Eastern (Babylonian) and the Western (Palestinian), with smaller groups within each of these schools. Several systems of adding points to the consonantal text were devised; that which finally survived and appears in almost all MSS is called the Tiberian system (after Tiberias* in Galilee). In addition to points indicating the vowels the Massoretes added other points to indicate the pronunciation of certain consonants, the doubling of consonants, accents which indicated both stress and the phrasing to be followed in synagogue reading. The small or marginal Massorah called attention to any peculiarities in the text, such as rare words, ambiguous spelling, or unusual writing. Some of these peculiarities show the mechanical and rigorous fidelity of the Massoretes to their text; a few letters written accidentally larger than others were written large in all copies; a letter raised and inserted between two other letters, the usual way of correcting omissions in MSS ancient and modern, was retained in its raised position. The great or final Massorah at the end of each book collected statistics which helped the copyist to check the accuracy of his copy; it gave the number of letters, words, and verses in the book, the middle letter, word, and verse, and mnemotechnical combinations to aid in the exact memorizing of the statistics. The success of the Massoretic canons is shown by the total disappearance of significant variations in MT. A recent achievement of textual research has been the recovery of MSS which stand closer to the tradition with which the Massoretes began. The more important of the two schools is the Western school, and in particular the texts associated with two great families, the family of ben Asher, of which the names are known for five successive generations, and the family of ben Naphtali. MT is the text of ben Asher. Few MSS of the ben Naphtali tradition are known; the most famous is preserved at Karlsruhe and was written in 1105. Of the ben Asher tradition there exist the Pnt of the British Museum, dated 820–850 by Ginsburg, more recently dated 950 by Kahle; the Prophets of Moses ben Asher IV, written 895, long preserved in the Sephardic synagogue of Aleppo, now in Cairo. The oldest complete Hb text was a text of Aaron ben Asher of 950, preserved in the same Aleppo synagogue and now in Israel. Paul Kahle earlier found a copy of this MS in Leningrad, dated 1008, and it was the Leningrad MS that was employed as the basic text in the present critical edition of the Hb text, Kahle's 3rd edition of Kittel's *Biblica Hebraica* (1929–1937). Until this edition appeared, all printed Hb Bibles had followed the text of the first complete printed Hb Bible, prepared by Jacob ben Chayyim and published by Bomberg in Venice 1524–1525.

Earlier text traditions were disclosed by the MSS of Qumran*, which contained a complete scroll of Is and another fragmentary scroll of Is, extensive fragments of Pss, Lv, 1–2 S, Nm, Je, Ex, Dn, 12 prophets, and fragments of every book of the Hb Bible except Est. Prior to these discoveries critics of the Hb text depended principally on the LXX without any assurance that the variations of the LXX do not represent the aberrations of translators and copyists rather than a different and older text tradition. The Qumran scrolls, which come from the 1st century BC and some of the 2nd, show that the LXX text tradition is the base of the Qumran MSS of 1–2 S, Jos, 1–2 K, and the LXX tradition appears with the MT tradition in Je. The existence of the LXX text type in Hb is in the opinion of most scholars thus verified for the 1st century BC, if not earlier. F. M. Cross suggests that there were three pre-Christian recensions, reflected in MT, LXX, and the Samaritan* Pnt, and that all of these were found in Palestine; the LXX tradition is not, as most have thought, an exclusively Egyptian recension.

Criticism can do no more than recover substantial portions of these older traditions; but the Hb text of the OT is still substantially MT. It must be added that the fidelity of MT as a witness of the original is not in question; the number and importance of the places where it has failed to preserve the original are small.

2. *NT*. The textual tradition of the NT depends principally upon MSS of the Gk NT. The ancient versions of the NT are less important as direct witnesses, but of no small value in fixing the date and provenance and interrelation of the principal witnesses. No more than a few of the major MSS can be listed here. All the MSS come from the codex type of MS (cf BOOK).

I. The papyrus MSS which come from the 2nd–3rd centuries AD are the oldest witnesses. Almost all of them come from Egypt.

A. John Rylands Papyrus, containing Jn 18:31–33, 37–38; AD 150. Small as it is, this fragment attests the existence and diffusion of Jn within 50 years of the traditional date of Jn.

B. Bodmer Papyrii: P^{66}, Jn 1–14 (except 6:12–35), c AD 200; P^{72}, Jd and 1–2 Pt, 3rd century; P^{74}, portions of AA, Js, 1–2 Pt, 1–3 Jn, 7th century; P^{75}, Lk and Jn, AD 175–225.

C. A papyrus from Dura Europos containing a fragment of Tatian's *Diatessaron* (cf SYRIAC); 220.

D. Oxyrhynchus Papyri, fragments of Jn and Heb; 220 +.

E. Chester Beatty Papyri: P^{45}, 2 pages of Mt, 6 pages of Mk, 7 pages of Lk, 2 pages of Jn, 13 pages of AA. P^{46}, 86 pages of Pauline epistles (56 pages in Chester Beatty collection, 30 pages at University of Michigan). P^{47}, Apc 9–17. The Chester Beatty Papyri also come from the 3rd century.

II. Parchment Mss.

Papyrus* was a cheaper material than the more durable and expensive parchment*; with the 4th century parchment codices of the Bible begin to appear. Many of these are copies of the entire Bible in Gk; here only the NT portions are mentioned.

A. Codex Vaticanus (B): NT except for Pastoral Epistles, Heb, Apc. 4th century.

B. Codex Sinaiticus (S): entire NT; 4th century.

C. Codex Alexandrinus (A): NT, missing Mt, 2 chapters of Jn, 8 chapters of 2 Co; early 5th century.

D. Codex Ephrem (C): a palimpsest from which the NT was erased and which was reused for the homilies of Ephrem. Infrared photography makes it possible to recover the material without the earlier chemical processes used, which were very likely to damage the MS. Contains 145 pages of the original 238 pages of the NT; 5th century.

E. Codex Washingtonianus (W): Gospels; 5th century.

F. Codex Bezae (D): Gospels and AA in Gk and Lt; 6th century.

G. Codex Claromontanus (D_2): Pauline epistles; 6th century.

These and other MSS down to the 9th century, written in Gk capital letters, are called uncials or majuscules. No uncials later than the 10th century are preserved. In minuscule or cursive MSS the letters are connected and the form of the letter is modified as in modern cursive script. The earliest cursive MS is dated 835.

The total number of MSS of the NT is difficult to tabulate, since new discoveries have appeared very frequently; this has been especially true of the papyri. A general estimate of the total gives about 4500 +: about 240 uncials, 2500 cursives, 75 papyri, about 1800 lectionaries; a lectionary is a book of passages of the Epistles and Gospels for liturgical use. Of these 53 contain the entire NT.

The NT is the best established ancient literature by so great a margin that no comparison with Gk and Lt literature is possible. The number of MSS earlier than the medieval period is scarcely ever more than two or three for any writer, and some ancient writers are known from only one MS. The problems of NT textual criticism arise from an embarrassment of riches, not from poverty of material.

3. *Criticism of the NT Text*. The first printed Gk NT was edited by Erasmus and published at Basel in 1516. This edition was prepared hastily from a few MSS possessed by the Dominican convent of Basel. The edition of Erasmus was followed by the Gk text of the Alcala Polyglot Bible in 1522, whose text did not differ substantially from the text of Erasmus. These printings were used by the Paris printer Étienne and by Theodore Beza of Geneva in the late 16th century and the text thus diffused appeared in all subsequent printings. The Elzevir brothers of Leyden described this text in their 1633 printing as "textus ab omnibus receptus," the text universally accepted; and it remained the standard text in all printings until the late 19th century. Dissatisfaction with the text arose among isolated scholars in the 18th and early 19th centuries; the examination of MSS showed that the received text was not attested by all witnesses. No printed edition, however, abandoned the received text; Tischendorff, who discovered the Codex Sinaiticus (cf above) was the first to print the NT from another text; he employed his own discovery (1869–1872).

The number of MSS of the NT known by 1850 was far greater than before. In the 18th century scholars had introduced the genealogical principle in order to bring the number of MSS into some classification. The genealogical principle groups MSS according to their characteristics, particularly the variations which they share as a group against other MSS, and concludes from this comparison to the character of the group in general. The genealogical principle supposes that such groups come from a common ancestor; if this ancestor exists, copies of it can be ignored. By comparison of the groups, or rather of the MSS which represent the ancestor of the group, it is possible to conclude to the relative antiquity of the MSS and to the degree of their fidelity to the original. The classic application of this principle was the edition of Westcott and Hort in 1881, which abandoned the received text in favor of the text found in the Vaticanus and Sinaiticus MSS (cf above). Their classification of the families has been modified by later studies, and contemporary critics group the MSS in these families:

Western (a misnomer given to this family because it was first noticed in Old Latin versions): its principal witnesses are D and some papyri. The MSS of this family remove some striking or graphic expressions which were thought offensive, harmonize the accounts of the same events in the Synoptic Gospels, and expand or omit from obviously theological motives. The text type is as old as the 3rd century, perhaps the 2nd.

Alexandrian: Westcott and Hort called this the "Neutral" family on the assumption that it was free of editorial treatment and thus represented the original text with fewest modifications. The principal witnesses are the Codex Vaticanus and the Codex Sinaiticus, and the Westcott and Hort text was prepared from these MSS. The text has been employed in almost all subsequent printed editions of the NT, and editors who have attempted to displace it have not convinced scholars that they were successful. It is no longer regarded as "Neutral" and is thought to exhibit editorial alterations like the other families; but they are fewer in number.

Antioch-Constantinople (called Syrian by Westcott and Hort): this family is represented by almost all the cursive MSS and some uncials and therefore by most of the extant MSS. It was therefore by sheer probability the text most likely to be found by Erasmus and the Alcala editors and became the received text used in all printed editions before Tischendorff. It was also judged by Westcott and Hort and all later critics to be the least faithful witness of the text; it is a revised text, altered in the interest of elegance and clarity, with harmonization in the Synoptic Gospels.

Caesarean (Palestinian): this is the most recently identified family, thought to be the text prepared by Origen at Caesarea in Palestine. It is not as well represented in the MSS as the other families and not as well identified. It is a compromise between the Western and the Alexandrian families, polished but to a lesser degree than the Antioch-Constantinople text.

These families are attributed on the genealogical principle to recensions, by which are meant texts prepared from already variant copies in an effort to remove the variations. They are recognized by common traits, in particular by "common faults." No family therefore represents the original MS (archetype); but the judgment of Westcott and Hort that the Alexandrian family is most free of alterations is still the judgment of critics. The number of variations in the MS tradition is vast simply because of the large number of MSS; it has been calculated that there are 200,000 variations in the 150,000 words of the NT. None of these are serious and few of them are more than trivial. Modern critics, however, are less confident than Westcott and Hort that they can find a family which exactly reproduces the original. The wealth of material permits critics to compare the evidence relying chiefly on two principles: (1) That reading is superior which best explains the variant readings; (2) That reading is superior which best agrees with the known habits and tendencies of the author. There is general agreement that $\frac{7}{8}$ to $\frac{9}{10}$ of the text of the NT is critically above suspicion; this is a far higher degree of fidelity than can be affirmed for any other piece of ancient literature.

Thaddaeus (Gk *thaddaios,* Aramaic *thaddai*), one of the Twelve (cf APOSTLE); the name occurs only in the lists of Mt 10:3; Mk 3:18; Lk has Jude* (6:16; AA 1:13).

Thank offering. Cf SACRIFICE.

Theater. The theater is mentioned in the

The theater of Dionysius at Athens.

Bible only in AA 19:29, 31 as the place at which the mob of Ephesus converged in the riot against Christians. The word is used in the sense of spectacle, what is seen in the theater, in 1 Co 4:9. A theater for dramatic presentations was built in every Hellenistic city; they were often quite large, with an auditorium seating several thousand people, and could therefore be used also for public assemblies.

Thebes. From the Gk name (*thēbai*) of the Egyptian city *uese*, Hb *nō'* (Na 3:8 *nō' 'āmôn*); the great city of ancient Egypt on the site of the modern Luxor and Karnak in upper Egypt. Thebes first appeared in history at the end of Old Kingdom (cf EGYPT) and became the royal city in the 11th and 12th dynasties. It became the royal city again during the 18th dynasty; it was a Theban prince under whose leadership the Egyptians expelled the Hyksos*. These dynasties were the greatest periods of ancient Egypt. Thebes became the royal city for the last time in the 25th (Ethiopian) dynasty; it was taken and destroyed by Ashur-bani-pal of Assyria in 633 BC. This is alluded to in Na 3:8; the prophet asks if Nineveh is greater than Thebes and mentions the water ramparts of Thebes. These may be simply the Nile on whose banks the city sat; it is quite possible that the city had moats in addition. The city is the object of prophetic threats in Je 46:25; Ezk 30:14–16. The ruins of Thebes are the most extensive of Egypt. They include the temples of Karnak and Luxor on the E bank of the river, the site of the ancient city, and on the W bank the vast necropolis of the Valley of the Kings, the Valley of the Queens, the mortuary temples of Deir el Bahari and Medinet Habu and Ramses II, and a number of smaller temples besides. The "Colossi of Memnon," two badly worn figures about 65 ft high, are really figures of the Pharaoh Amenhotep III; the building before which they stood has been entirely removed.

Thebez (Hb *tebeṣ*, meaning uncertain), a town near Shechem; Abimelech* was killed during the siege of Thebez by a millstone which a woman threw from the wall (Jgs 9:50–55). The ignominious death of a warrior at the hands of a woman became proverbial in Israel (2 S 11:21). Thebez is identified with the modern Tubas, about 10 mi ENE of Nablus in the Wadi Farah.

Theophany (Gk *theophania*, "appearance of God"), the name given to the well defined and characteristic concept and imagery exhibited in a number of passages of the OT. The theophany is an appearance or manifestation of Yahweh in character and attributes which reveal His divinity and power, and is thereby distinguished from other appearances in which He is known as the revealer. The place from which Yahweh appears in the theophany, if it is mentioned, is almost always the S: Seir (Jgs 4:4) or Teman and Paran (Dt 33:2; Hab 3:3), and it may be assumed that it is in the S in other passages where the direction is not mentioned. The S is not the direction from which storms come in Palestine, and this shows that the theophany is not merely a personification of the storm; the S is the region of the original manifestation of Yahweh to Israel in the exodus* and covenant* traditions. The theophany therefore supposes that this region is the proper home of Yahweh. In Ezk 1:4 the theophany appears from the N; Yahweh, like other travelers, makes the trip from Canaan to Babylonia through N Syria and Mesopotamia and arrives from the N. Similarly in the later Ps 50:2 the theophany appears from Zion, the place where Yahweh dwells. The theophany is a manifestation of Yahweh in natural convulsions: earthquake (Jgs 4:4 f; Pss 18:8; 68:8; 77:19; 97:4; Is 6:4; Mi 1:4; Na 1:5; Hab 3:6), rain (Jgs 4:4; Pss 68:8; 77:18; Hab 3:9), clouds (Pss 18:11; 50:3; 77:19; 104:3; Ezk 1:4; Na 1:3; Hab 3:7), which are also signified by smoke (Ps 18:9; Is 6:4) or darkness (Pss 18:10, 12; 97:2) and possibly by the cherubim* (Ps 18:11), wind (Pss 18:11; 50:3; 77:19; 104:3 f; Ezk 1:4; Na 1:3; Hab 3:7), hail (Ps 18:13), lightning (Dt 33:2; Pss 18:14 f; 50:3; 77:18; 97:3 f; 104:4; Ezk 1:4; Hab 3:4), thunder (Pss 18:14; 77:18), pestilence and plague (Hab 3:5), drying up of sea and rivers (Ps 77:20; Na 1:4). When the passages in which these allusions appear are compared, a common and almost conventional pattern of imagery emerges, despite the variations between the brief allusions of one or two lines and the elaborate expansions such as Ps 18:8–16 (2 S 22:8–16); Hab 3:3–15. The pattern is the violent desert thunderstorm combined with the earthquake; while the earthquake* is unfortunately common in Palestine and adjacent lands, it is not an ordinary accompaniment of the thunderstorm. Possibly allusions refer to the trembling of the ground which occurs during a violent thunderstorm, but the allusions describe a trembling which is much stronger. The theophany is more than an identification of Yahweh with the storm, an identification which is seen in the conception of the god Hadad*, although several traits of the theophany can be paralleled in ancient Near Eastern literature and art. The most frequent occasion of the theophany is the appearance of Yahweh as the savior* of His people from their enemies. Salvation is also judgment* upon the enemies, and this attribute of Yahweh is apparent in the theophany. The theophany therefore combines the concept of Yahweh as lord of nature with the concept of Yahweh as lord of history. It is through His control of nature that Yahweh acts to execute His will in the events of history, and the course of nature is integrated into His plan of salvation and judgment.

The theophany is so distinctively Israelite that it seems impossible to reduce it to the mythological images of the storm and the storm god. It is most probably rooted in the traditions of Sinai and the exodus. In the Sinai traditions (Ex 19:16–19) Yahweh is revealed in the convulsions of nature which are characteristic of the theophany — clouds and smoke, thunder, earthquake; in these convulsions He is manifested as the covenant God who imposes His moral will upon Israel and displays His power to vindicate His will. Some modern scholars have suggested that the theophany was liturgically reenacted in a covenant festival through a procession with the ark*; the cherubim* of the ark are one of the motifs of the theophany.

The remarkable theophany of Elijah (1 K 19:11–13) is a deliberate reversal of the conventional theophany and thereby the introduction of a new conception of the saving and judging works of Yahweh. Elijah learns that Yahweh is not in the conventional signs of the theophany — earthquake, wind, and thunder. Yahweh is present in a barely perceptible breeze. His saving works are accomplished not only through the power and violence which is symbolized by the imagery of the theophany, but also through His unseen government of events, no less effective because it exhibits no perceptible display.

Theophilus (Gk *theophilos,* "beloved of god"), a personal name; the Christian otherwise unknown to whom Lk dedicated the gospel (Lk 1:3) and AA (1:1).

Thessalonians, Epistles to the. On the church to which these letters were addressed cf THESSALONICA.

1. *Contents:*

1 Th.

1:1, salutation.

1:1–2:13, refutation of Jewish calumnies: 1:2–10, the work of the spirit in Thessalonica; 2:1–13, Paul's purity of intention in preaching.

2:13–20, the persecution by the Jews.

3:1–13, the mission of Timothy.

4:1–5:22, exhortations.

4:3–8, love and chastity; 4:9–10, fraternal love; 4:10–12, industry; 4:13–18, assurance of the resurrection; 5:1–11, the judgment is to be awaited in faith, hope, and love; 5:12–22, counsels on community life.

2 Th.

1:1–2, salutations; 1:3–10, thanksgiving for the patience of the Thessalonians in persecution; 1:11–12, prayer for their perseverance.

2:1–12, instruction on the Parousia.

2:13–3:5, exhortation to perseverance, request for prayers.

3:6–15, exhortations to industry and obedience.

3:17–18, salutation.

2. *Authorship.* 1–2 Th were probably used by Ignatius of Antioch; they appear in Marcion's canon of the NT and in the Canon of Muratori (cf CANON) and tradition is unanimous in attributing them to Paul. Modern criticism does not question the attribution of 1 Th, but a number of scholars have raised questions about 2 Th. Their doubts are based on some admitted differences of style between the two; and the uniformity of vocabulary of 1–2 Th with each other and with other Pauline letters is explained by some as due to the fact that an imitator has compiled 2 Th as a cento from 1 Th. More serious is the argument from the apparent inconsistency of 2 Th 2:1–12 with 1 Th 4:13–5:11; the change, it is urged, was made by the imitator in order to remove the misconception of an imminent Parousia; Paul, who has given the basis for the misconception, can hardly be imagined to reverse himself within such a short time. Those who maintain the Pauline origin of 2 Th cannot allow more than a few months between the two; some limit the interval to a few weeks or even a few days. If the two were so near each other in time, the question arises why 2 Th does not refer to 1 Th, or at least mention it. The differences in style are not serious, and they do not affect the fact that the personality of Paul seems to emerge in both letters. But it must be granted that this sense of unity is not a rigorous demonstration; and it is better to leave the possibility open that 2 Th does not come from Paul but from his school, an explanation which must be accepted for some other letters of the Pauline corpus.

3. *Date and Occasion.* 1 Th is the first of all Paul's letters and is to be dated early in his sojourn at Corinth in AD 50 during his second journey, not long after his departure from Thessalonica. 2 Th, if it is the work of Paul, is most probably to be dated a few months after 1 Th. The occasion of the letter is seen from the contents;

it is a response to a question of the Thessalonians concerning the fate of those who might be living when the Parousia occurred. The implication that they might be deprived of the glorious resurrection is not clear to us, but it seems to have been their worry; cf RESURRECTION. To this doubt Paul answers that all shall be translated to glory whether they pass through death and resurrection or not. 2 Th clearly corrects an impression that the Day of the Lord is near and warns of signs which will indicate its coming. These signs, obscure to us, formed part of the apostolic teaching (cf ANTICHRIST; DAY OF THE LORD; JUDGMENT). It must be admitted that Paul's use of the first personal pronoun in 1 Th readily lends itself to the impression that the Parousia is to be an event of the present generation. 2 Th does not deny the possibility, but states clearly that it may not occur in this generation, and leaves the impression that the writer does not expect it in his generation. If both letters are from Paul, one can say only that his thinking on this question had not crystallized; and it is not impossible that the corrective comes from him directly. For it is clear from the exhortations of both letters that the belief in an imminent Parousia is not of itself a wholesome moral influence; the exhortations to industry show that some thought it unnecessary to work for their living any longer, and other exhortations imply that the imminence of the Parousia led some to take a last fling. The proper attitude of the Christian before the event is set forth in both letters with no difference: patience, faith, confident hope, mutual love, and Christian living.

The question which occasions the letters permits Paul to set forth general exhortations on conduct which become a set feature of his later letters.

Thessalonica (Gk *thessalonikē*, meaning uncertain), a city of Macedonia at the head of the Thermaic Gulf, about 75 mi W of Philippi, the modern Saloniki. The city was founded in 315 BC and was named after a sister of Alexander the Great. It had and has a good harbor, a fertile hinterland, and connections into the mainland; the modern Saloniki is the second largest city of Greece. It lay on the Via Egnatia, the Roman road which connected Italy with Byzantium. In NT times it was a free city. Thessalonica was reached by Paul on his second missionary journey (AA 17:1–15); his affection for the church which he founded there is apparent in 1–2 Th. He was very well received by the Gentiles, but the Jews of Thessalonica were unusually hostile; they incited a riot against Jason, one of Paul's

converts, and Paul and Silas fled secretly to Berea. The Jews of Thessalonica sent emissaries after them to lay charges before the magistrates. The city is also mentioned in passing in Phl 4:16; 2 Tm 4:10. Some remains of late Roman arches can be seen in Saloniki, but the large modern city makes excavation impossible.

Theudas (Gk *theudas*, a contraction of some name beginning with *theos*, "god"). In AA 5:36 Gamaliel alludes to a rebellion of four hundred men led by Theudas which was suppressed and concludes from this example that the apostles should not be molested, since their work will come to nothing if it is not of God. Josephus relates a messianic movement led by Theudas who promised his followers that he would divide the Jordan like Joshua and lead them across; the movement was attacked by the cavalry of the procurator Cuspius Fadus, the followers were killed or imprisoned, and Theudas was beheaded. This event occurred in AD 44, some years after the encounter of the apostles with the council of Jerusalem must have occurred. To presuppose a similar earlier insurrection led by another Theudas seems contrived; it is evident that the composer of the discourse put in the mouth of Gamaliel did not have access to accurate chronological records, and that Theudas appears in the discourse by an anachronism.

Thomas (Gk *thōmas*, Aramaic *teômā'*, "twin"), one of the Twelve, mentioned in the lists (Mt 10:3; Mk 3:18; Lk 6:15 AA 1:13). In Jn the Gk *didymus*, "twin," is added to the name; inscriptions suggest that this was never used as a surname, and indeed it is possible that the personal name of Thomas has not been preserved. Thomas is given unusual prominence in Jn; in 11:16 he urges the Twelve to accompany Jesus into Judea and die with Him, in 14:5 he asks where Jesus is going and how they may know the way, and in 21:2 he is one of the group which goes fishing and meets the risen Jesus. Jn 11:16 suggests a generous and impetuous temperament, which is not what is suggested by the most famous incident in which Thomas appears, the episode which has created the phrase "doubting Thomas" (Jn 20:24–29). Here, as in Jn 14:5, Thomas is the occasion for the recording of a saying of Jesus; the difficulty which Thomas experienced was even greater for those who lived after the first generation of Christians, and their faith is even more laudable than the faith of the witnesses. The prominence of Thomas in Jn is no doubt partly responsible for the numerous legends of Thomas and the apocryphal* literature which gathered about his name; none of this material has any historical value.

Thorn. The thorn (with which we may include the bramble and the briar) is abundant in Palestine, there are probably nearly twenty species mentioned in the Bible which cannot be distinguished. Thorns are a feature of wild uncultivated land (Jb 30:7; Is 5:6; 7:23; 32:13; 34:13; 55:13; Ho 9:6; 10:8; Zp 2:9 +), and prophetic oracles which threaten desolation of the land announce that it will be overgrown with thorns. Thorns are an obstacle to agriculture which must be cleared from the land (Gn 3:18; Pr 24:30; Mt 13:7, 22; Mk 4:7, 18; Lk 8:7, 14; +). In a country where wood was not abundant thorns were a common fuel, as they are in modern times (Ps 58:9; Ec 7:6); but they were also a fire hazard, whether growing wild near the fields or stacked for fuel (Ex 22:6; Is 9:18; 10:17 +). Gideon punished the inhospitable men of Succoth with thorns (Jgs 8:7, 16) in a way which is not described, probably by dragging them through a thorn patch — grisly enough but probably not fatal. Thorns are frequent in biblical imagery. The wicked are like thorns, useless and painful and dangerous (2 S 23:6; Mi 7:4 +), and likewise one's enemies are like thorns (Jos 23:13; Ezk 28:24 +). "A way hedged in with thorns" is a path through thorn patches, a life of difficulty and misfortune (Pr 15:19; 22:5; Ho 2:6). In the parable of Jotham (Jgs 9:8–15) the trees refuse the election as king, and it is accepted by the unproductive thorn bush, which threatens the other trees with destruction by fire if they do not obey. Jeremiah warns not to sow among thorns (Je 4:3), and Jesus illustrates the impossibility of good works from a bad intention by asking if one gathers grapes from thorns (Mt 7:16; Lk 6:44). The crown of thorns placed on the head of Jesus by the Roman soldiers appears in three of the four Gospels (Mt 27:29; Mk 15:17; Jn 19:2, 5). Christian art and the common popular explanation represents this crown as a chaplet woven from shoots of the rose vine and laid upon the head. While thorns are plentiful in Palestine, rose vines are not, and the common species of thorn are too long to permit such a weaving. The crown of thorns is far more probably an imitation of the radiate crown* worn by kings and divine figures in the Hellenistic figures symbolizing the rays of the sun; this crown is familiar to all Americans, since it is a crown of this type which appears on the Statue of Liberty. The spikes of the thorns were set so as to rise from the crown of the head.

Thousand. The number 1000 does not appear in the Bible with any obvious symbolic value (cf NUMBER); it sometimes signifies the immense, a number too large to be counted. The use of the number 1000 in early Hb traditions, which often gives impossibly high totals of population, has long been a difficulty, often solved by assuming that 1000 here meant simply a number too great to be counted. G. E. Mendenhall, following a suggestion made many years ago by Flinders Petrie, has proposed that 1000 (Hb 'elep) is a technical sociological term whose meaning was unknown by the final compilers of the Pnt. It appears to have signified a subsection of a tribe*, more precisely that subsection which was obliged to furnish a quota of men under their own leader for military service in the militia of the tribal confederacy. This term is illustrated in Jgs 6:10 (Gideon's 'elep is the smallest 'elep in Manasseh*), Mi 5:1 (Bethlehem is too small to be an 'elep of Judah), and in 1 S 23:23 (Saul hunted David in all the 'ᵃlāpîm of Judah). In particular Mendenhall illustrates the disappearance of the original meaning of the term from Jgs 7:3 ff: the 32,000 men of Jgs 7:3 are actually identical with the 300 men of Jgs 7:6 ff, since the 300 are the warriors levied from the 32 'ᵃlāpîm of Manasseh. The story of the dismissal of the fearful and of the test of drinking water is a later midrash* designed to reconcile the two numbers given in tradition, 32 'ᵃlāpîm (understood as 32,000) and 300. The basis of the misunderstanding, according to Mendenhall, lay in the change of the meaning of the term under the monarchy. Saul probably and David certainly organized part at least of the army under the direct command of the king through officers of the units appointed by the king and responsible to him. These officers were not tribal leaders but professional soldiers. In this organization the 'elep, for purposes of efficiency, usually had a number of men close to the meaning of the word, 1000. Later compilers took the word in this sense, which was the only sense they knew. Applying this principle to such passages as the census of Nm 1:26 Mendenhall reaches a total of warriors which is in agreement with the numbers of armies as related in ancient extrabiblical records.

Threshing. The threshing floor in ancient Palestinian villages, as in modern times, was usually set upon a convenient high point near the village where the prevailing west wind could be utilized for winnowing*. It was a rock floor, either natural or artificially terraced, and was usually communally owned; some large owners had their own threshing floors (2 S 24:16, Araunah*). During the harvest the workers and owners slept on the threshing floor to protect the grain (Rt 3:7); freshly harvested grain could be stolen by thieves or marauders (1 S 23:1). In many parts of the ancient world and doubtless also in Israel the grain was threshed by driving oxen over the piles of grain who trampled it with their hooves; a humanitarian law (Dt 25:4) prohibited the muzzling of the animals employed in threshing. There are, however, several references to the threshing sledge, a wooden frame holding sharp stones or metal points on its underside and weighted down with stones (2 S 24:22; Is 28:27; 41:15; Am 1:3). The threshing wagon (Is 28:28) was no doubt similar except that it was equipped with wheels. The same passage (Is 28:27 f) alludes to different methods of threshing — sledge, flail, wagon — used for different kinds of grain. Threshing is often mentioned in figures of speech; it is a metaphor for the harsh treatment of a defeated enemy in war (2 K 13:7; Is 41:15; Je 51:33; Ho 13:3; Am 1:3; Mi 4:13) or for the judgments of Yahweh (Is 25:10; Hab 3:12). The underbelly of the crocodile is compared to the teeth of the threshing sledge (Jb 41:22).

Throne. The throne need not be a large and decorated seat; but in the art and literature of the ancient Near East the chair in which the king alone sits and which symbolizes royalty is a universal motif. In the OT the throne is the chair of the king in Egypt (Gn 41:40) and in Israel (2 S 14:9; 1 K 16:11; 22:10; Ps 45:7 +). The queen mother also has a throne (1 K 2:19), and after the monarchy ended the throne was the seat of the governor (Ne 3:7). The firstborn son of the king shared his throne (Ex 11:5; 12:29). The throne is the symbol of kingship as it is in Eng (2 S 3:10; Is 14:13), and to the throne are given the attributes of judgment, fidelity, and righteousness which belong to the king (Is 16:5). In Judah the throne of David* acquires a peculiar dignity because of the covenant of Yahweh promising David an eternal dynasty, and the royal throne of Judah retained the title of throne of David under his successors down to the fall of the monarchy (1 K 1:13, 35, 46; 2:12, 24, 33, 45; 2:12, 24, 33, 45; Ps 89:5, 30; Is 9:6; Je 13:13; 17:25; 22:30). Like human kings, Yahweh the king is imagined as enthroned (1 K 22:19; Ps 47:9; WS 18:15; Is 6:1; Je 14:21; Ezk 1:26); heaven is the throne of Yahweh (Is 66:1) or Jerusalem (Je 3:17).

Jesus also uses the designation of heaven as the throne of God (Mt 5:34; 23:22). The throne of David is mentioned in Lk 1:32; AA 2:30; Heb 1:8; it is the throne of the Messiah. The throne of the Son of Man is a heavenly throne on which he is manifested in the Parousia*; it is a throne of judgment (Mt 25:31). The throne and the judgment are also granted to the Twelve (Mt 19:28). In the great final judgment

An Assyrian king seated on the throne, receiving homage of defeated enemies.

thrones are set forth for those who are granted the power to judge (Apc 20:4). The throne of God is the center of the vision of Apc 4; it is surrounded by the 24 thrones of the 24 elders. The throne of God is the great white throne (Apc 20:11). It is the throne of grace (Heb 4:16). The throne of Satan* in Pergamum* is probably a temple (Apc 2:13). The beast who exercises power over the earth sits upon a throne (Apc 13:2; 16:10). In Col 1:16 thrones are an order of angels*; the title appears in Enoch and the Testament of Levi (cf APOCRYPHAL BOOKS) and probably is derived from popular Jewish belief.

The thrones of ancient kings are frequently represented in art; the throne of Solomon was gold-plated with ivory inlay, decorated with a calf's head on the back and lions supporting the arm rests, and was placed on a dais raised by six steps with two lions on each step (1 K 10:18–20). The description resembles a Canaanite throne with sphinx arm rests pictured on a Megiddo* ivory* (ANEP 332; cf also ANEP 456, 458). The throne is sometimes represented as a plain seat with neither arms nor back, or only with back (Persian, ANEP 460). The throne is often represented with a footstool (Assyrian, ANEP 371; Aramaean, ANEP 460), and the arm rests are usually decorated with animal figures such as bulls' heads (ANEP 460) or lion's heads (cf above); an Assyrian throne has three panels of human figures carved upon the sides and arm rests (ANEP 371). A Sumerian throne is supported by geese and rests on water (ANEP 507). The throne is sometimes an armless and backless cushioned stool, certainly portable, which is the model of the bishop's faldstool (Egyptian, ANEP 405). The splendid throne of Tut-ankh-amon, recovered from his tomb and preserved in the museum of Cairo is richly decorated; its arm rests are winged serpent figures, the legs and feet are feline, the arm rests end in lions' heads, and the panel of the back is decorated with a domestic scene showing the king and his queen in their garden. The throne is of wood with gold and ivory inlays.

Thummim. Cf URIM and THUMMIM.

Thunder. Hb has no specific word for thunder; it designates thunder by *kôl*, which means sound, such as a voice. The thunder is the voice of Yahweh (Ex 9:23 ff; Ps 46:7; 104:7; Jb 37:4; BS 43:17; Is 30:30 f; Je 10:13; 51:16; Am 1:2; Jl 2:11; 4:16). As the voice of Yahweh it is one of the motifs of the theophany* (Ex 19:16; 20:18; 2 S 22:14; Ps 18:14; 77:18 f). The voice of Yahweh is heard when He comes to defend

His people in battle (1 S 7:10); but the most frequent context of the voice of Yahweh is judgment*. It may be the sign of Yahweh's approval (1 S 12:17 f). The voice of Yahweh is the refrain of the magnificent poem of Ps 29, which follows the course of the thunderstorm across the land. In the NT the conception of thunder as the voice of God appears in Jn 12:29 and Apc, and there rather frequently. It is one of the theophany motifs (Apc 4:5; 8:5; 11:19; 16:18) which initiate each change in the eschatological drama of Apc. It is also the voice of an angel (Apc 6:1) and the music of the heavenly harps (Apc 14:2) and of the heavenly hymn of triumph (Apc 19:6). The "seven thunders" of Apc 10:3 f are obscure; the number seven* indicates fullness, and this is possibly what is meant here. In Apc the "voice of Yahweh" has become the sound or noise of heaven, faintly audible on earth, signifying judgment or triumph.

Thyatira (Gk *thyatira*, meaning uncertain), a city of Asia Minor; it lay between Sardis* and Pergamum* on the river Lycus, on the frontier of Mysia and Lydia. Lydia of Thyatira was the first of Paul's converts at Philippi*; the purple dye industry of which she was a commercial representative was the great industry of Thyatira, and the guild of dyers appears in a number of inscriptions. Archaeological exploration has recovered some of the fine monumental buildings erected at Thyatira by the Attalid dynasty of Pergamum. Thyatira was one of the seven churches addressed in Apc (1:11; 2:18–29). The history of its foundation is not known. The city was the seat of a cult headed by a certain Jezebel, possibly a pseudonym, which investigated "the deep things of Satan."

Tiamat. Cf CREATION.

Tiberias (Gk *tiberias*), modern et-Tabariyeh, a city on the SW shore of the Sea of Galilee, where the hills come quite close to the lake. It was founded by Herod Antipas as the capital of his tetrarchy (AD 18–20), and named after Tiberius Caesar*. The site had previously been used for a burying ground and was therefore unclean (cf CLEAN); the city seems to have been entirely Gentile in NT times. It is mentioned only in Jn 6:23 (boats came from Tiberias), Jn 6:1; 21:1 (Sea of Tiberias). Jesus is not said to have entered the city, and the common opinion of interpreters is that He never did. It was the largest and most important city of the region of the lake.

Tiberius. Tiberius Claudius Nero, born 42

BC, adopted son and successor of Augustus*, emperor of Rome AD 14–37; his mother Livia divorced the father of Tiberius and married Augustus. The beginning of the ministry of John the Baptist is dated in the 15th year of Tiberius (Lk 3:1), between August, AD 28, and August, AD 29. This is the only chronological datum for the life of Jesus. It is known, however, that at Antioch* a variant calculation of imperial years in the first century was used; if Lk was written in Antioch and was affected by this calculation, the date may have to be revised to the year between Oct 1, AD 27, and Sept 30, AD 28. Tiberius is not recorded to have acted directly on Palestine. He recalled Pilate* after the procurator had suppressed a popular movement with much bloodshed.

Tibni (Hb *tibnî*, similar to the Phoenician name *tabnit;* meaning uncertain), son of Ginath, a claimant to the throne of Israel after Omri's* killing of Zimri* (1 K 16:21 f). The claim was serious; a large part of Israel, perhaps more than half, accepted Tibni as king, and according to the data of 1 K 16:15, 23 it took four years for Omri to suppress the rival king.

Tidal. (Hb *tid'al*, meaning uncertain), king of Goyim, one of the four Mesopotamian kings who invaded Canaan and were routed by Abraham* (Gn 14:1 ff). No name of the period known from extrabiblical records fits except Tudhalias, the name of several Hittite* kings, one of whom reigned in the 17th century BC. King of Goyim is lit "king of nations" (Hb *goyim*), perhaps a corruption of a gentilic name.

Tiglath-pileser (Hb *tiglat pil'eṣer*, Akkadian *tukulti-apil-esarra*, "my help is the son of Esharra [Ninurta]"), Tiglath-pileser III, king of Assyria 745–727 BC. Before the accession of Tiglath-pileser Assyrian power had fallen to a low estate under a series of weak kings. Tiglath-pileser attained the throne by a coup d'état of which the details are not known; he was not a member of the reigning royal family. From his accession he exhibited extraordinary ability and industry; he is the true founder of the Assyrian empire, which endured for 100 years after his death. He conquered the Aramaean* tribes of Babylonia and made himself king of Babylon; this attempt to settle the Babylonian question by personal union of the two monarchies of Babylon and Assyria was imitated by some of his successors. He transported many of the peoples of Babylonia to other regions of the empire; he was the first to practice transportation on a large scale with the deliberate purpose of breaking national and tribal consciousness and uniting all subjects under the one monarchy of Assyria. His attempt to conquer the dangerous kingdom of Urartu in Armenia was unsuccessful. He enjoyed much greater success in Syria and Palestine. He conquered Galilee and Gilead in 734 BC and incorporated them into an Assyrian province. Damascus* was defeated and razed in 732; this kingdom also was incorporated into an Assyrian province. Other kings of Syria and Palestine submitted and paid tribute.

The OT mentions Tiglath-pileser's conquest of Galilee and Gilead (2 K 15:29; 1 Ch 5:6, 26). It adds to his records the information that Ahaz* paid tribute and asked for an alliance and defense against Israel and Damascus (2 K 16:7–9; 2 Ch 28:20); this step was rebuked by Isaiah (7:10–14). After the conquest of Damascus Ahaz went to Damascus to make his submission to Tiglath-pileser (2 K 16:10). Tiglath-pileser is called Pul* in 2 K 15:19, which mentions the tribute paid him by Menahem* of Israel, and in 1 Ch 5:26.

Tigris (Hb *ḥiddeḳel*, Akkadian *idiklat*, from Sumerian *idigna*, "fast flowing"?), a river of Mesopotamia. The Tigris is formed by two branches, both of which rise in the mountains of Armenia near Lake Van and Lake Geuljik. Its length to its mouth at the Persian Gulf is 600 mi. Its principal tributaries, all flowing in from the E, are the Greater Zab, the Little Zab, the Adhem, and the Diyala. The Tigris joins the Euphrates above the mouth of the rivers to form the Shatt el Arab, which flows through a marshy area. Although the sources of the Tigris and the Euphrates lie near each other, the Tigris flows more directly than the Euphrates and is only half as long; it also carries a larger volume of water at a more rapid current than the Euphrates, and its floods are more violent. The average width of the river for most of its length is about ¼ mi, and its average depth at high water about 25 ft. Near Baghdad the Tigris and the Euphrates are only 3–5 mi apart; in ancient times the two streams were connected by canals which served both for irrigation and for navigation. The great cities of ancient Assyria *lay on or near the Tigris. It is mentioned in the Bible only as one of the four rivers of Paradise* (Gn 2:14); as the scene of a vision of Daniel (Dn 10:4); as the stream in which Tobias caught the fish from which he obtained the means of exorcising the demon of Sarah and of curing his father's blindness (Tb 6:1).

The Tigris at Bagdad.

Tile. Tiles were not used for the roofs of Palestinian houses*. Where Mk 2:4 narrates that the friends of the paralytic dug a hole in the earth roof of the house, Lk 5:19, which arose in an Antiochene milieu, was unaware of the type of roof used in Palestinian houses; the story therefore is told in terms of the only roof which the writer knew, and describes how the friends of the paralytic removed the tiles in order to let the sick man down to the room below.

Timaeus. Cf BARTIMAEUS.

Time. The Bible contains no abstract philosophy of time as the universal measure of movement such as we find in Gk philosophy. The Hb and Gk words which are translated "time" indicate a point of time; and the point is identified by the event which is associated with it. The biblical conception of time is governed by the thought that time is ordered by the succession of events which are expected in due time. This is erected into a rigid scheme in Ec 4:1–8, which affirms a time for everything; but this is not the important point of his statement. The things which he enumerates are set forth in pairs of opposites, each of which neutralizes the other; this supports his thesis that all things return to the beginning and that there is nothing new under the sun. The appointed times of events permit no breakthrough of a new force. This is a pessimistic meditation of the sage (cf ECCLESIASTES); here as elsewhere Ec exposes considerations which make one doubt about the reality of salvation. Were the scheme of time so rigid, no divine intervention could be conceived.

The rigidity of the scheme of Ec, however, is a faithful if exaggerated part of biblical thinking even about salvation; for salvation comes in its time (Gk *kairos*). This set time is not understood as postulated by preceding events, as the time of death follows the time of birth and the time of harvest follows the time of sowing. The time of salvation is retained by the Father in His own power, and it is revealed to no man; it cannot be predicted as can the succession of events in nature and human affairs (AA 1:7). Instruction of the time is not a part of Christian doctrine (1 Th 5:1 f). The explicit statement that the Father keeps the times in His own power is the element of biblical belief which answers the doubt to which Ec gives expression; "the times" are the course of events, all of which lead up to the time, the *Kairos* of salvation and judgment. The process by which the *Kairos* is reached is not the result of casual coincidence.

In speaking of the *Kairos* as the climax of time, the Bible does not call it the *Kairos* exclusively. Each step in the process of time is a *Kairos* in the sense that it is a critical time, a decisive moment which hastens or retards the *Kairos* of salvation* and judgment*. Here biblical time seems in a way to coalesce into a single *Kairos;* for the salvation and the judgment of God are exhibited in each instant, and the responsibility of man to rise to the *Kairos* never ceases. Hence it can be said that the present moment in biblical thought recapitulates the entire past, at the same time as it contains the entire future. This conception explains many NT passages in which a distinction between the present *kairos* and the eschatological *Kairos* is not made. This thought pattern is not explained by the mere assumption that the first generation of Christians thought the Parousia* was near; it is understood only if one realizes that in biblical thought the Parousia is in a sense present in the initial stages of the process which initiates its coming.

In the NT the *Kairos* in the primary sense is the time of the coming of Jesus; this is the salvation event in which the *Kairos* is fulfilled, the event which is demanded by the process of history. The coming of Jesus here does not mean only His birth and His life in Palestine, but His arrival and permanence in the Church in which He lives. With His coming the time has come and the reign of God is near (Mk 1:15); His redeeming death happens in the *Kairos* (Rm 5:6). It is the *Kairos* in which God has revealed His word (Tt 1:3); it is the great event which is the object of divine witness (1 Tm 2:6). The *Kairos* initiated by the coming of Jesus is the time to do good (Gal 6:10); the Christian must make the most of the *Kairos*, lit must make a profit of it (Eph 5:16; Col 4:5). More particularly, the *kairos* of Jesus is the time of His death; Mt 26:18 uses *kairos* in the same sense in which Jn and the other Gospels use the word hour*. His coming is the *kairos* when God visits Jerusalem (Lk 19:44), which the Jews should be able to interpret (Lk 12:56). It is the *kairos* when the Christian should rise from sleep, for salvation comes nearer (Rm 13:11).

The coming of Jesus is the great *Kairos*, the initial point which reaches its fulfillment in the accomplishment of salvation and judgment; hence it is the eschatological moment which is most frequently called the *Kairos* in the NT. This is the *Kairos* when the mysterious "restrainer" (cf ANTICHRIST) will be revealed (2 Th 2:6), the *Kairos* of judgment (Mk 13:33; 1 Pt 4:17; Apc 11:18), of the epiphany of Jesus (1 Tm 6:15), of the coming of the Lord (1 Co 4:5). The *Kairos* is conceived as eschatological when the demons ask Jesus whether He has come to torture them before the *Kairos* (Mt 8:29). In this time God will elevate the believers (1 Pt 5:6). It is the last *Kairos* (1 Pt 1:5). With this last *Kairos* time, which began with creation, comes to an end; there is no further development of history, no event, and no set time. There begins another age which is not reckoned by movement toward a term.

Timnah (Hb *timnāh*, meaning uncertain), a local name: **1.** A town in the hill country of Judah (Jos 15:57), the place where Judah held his sheepshearing (Gn 38:12–14), raided by the Philistines in the reign of Ahaz* (2 Ch 28:18). It is identified with

the modern Khirbet Tibneh about 10 mi W of Bethlehem.

2. A town of Dan (Jos 19:43) on the frontier of Judah (Jos 15:10), the home of Samson's Philistine wife (Jgs 14:1–5; 15:6). It is identified with the modern Khirbet Tibneh in the Shephelah* in the Wadi es Sarar, a short distance W of Bethshemesh*.

Timnath-serah (Hb *timnat-heres*, meaning uncertain), the town where Joshua was given landed property by Israel and the place where he was buried (Jos 19:50; 24:30; Jgs 2:9). It lay in the hill country of Ephraim and is identified with the modern Khirbet Tibneh SSW of Shechem* and about 10 mi NE of Bethel. It is called *Timnat-serah* in Jos 19:50; 24:30 and *Timnath-heres* in Jgs 2:9; critics regard this latter form as the correct name.

Timotheus. A local Seleucid commander in Palestine, defeated by Judas* in the Maccabean wars. In 1 Mc 5 Timotheus is the commander in E Palestine, defeated in several skirmishes and in two battles which are described as major engagements. Judas, however, was unable to hold E Palestine and removed the entire Jewish population W of the Jordan. A parallel account appears in 2 Mc 12; here, however, the geography is more uncertain, and the author has merged two campaigns reported in 1 Mc 5, one in the coastal plain and the other in E Palestine. 2 Mc adds the interesting detail that Timotheus was captured by the Jews and obtained his release by threats against Jewish hostages, members of the families of Dositheus and Sosipater, the officers who captured him. On the variations in the two accounts cf MACCABEES, BOOKS OF.

Timothy (Gk *timotheos*, "honoring the god"), a disciple and companion of Paul. Timothy was a native of Lystra* in Lycaonia, the son of a Gk father and a Jewish Christian mother; because of his Jewish mother Paul permitted him to receive circumcision (AA 16:1–3). According to 2 Tm 1:5 his mother's name was Eunice and his grandmother's name Lois; and it was Lois who first became a Christian. Paul took Timothy as an associate when he passed Lystra on his second missionary journey. Timothy remained at Berea with Silas when Paul was forced to leave suddenly (AA 17:14 f) and rejoined Paul at Corinth, where it appears that he remained during the period of Paul's preaching in Corinth. He was sent to Macedonia with Erastus before Paul's 3rd journey (AA 19:22) and was among the company with which Paul returned from his 3rd journey (AA 20:4).

Timothy is associated with Paul in the initial salutations of 2 Co 1:1; Phl 1:1; Col 1:1; 1 Th 1:1; 2 Th 1:1; Phm 1, and in the final salutation of Rm 16:21. He was sent to Corinth by Paul in the troubles which preceded the writing of 1 Co (1 Co 4:17), and another mission was planned after the writing of the letter (1 Co 16:10). Paul alludes to Timothy's association with him in the evangelization of Corinth (2 Co 1:19). A mission of Timothy to Philippi was planned when Phl was written (Phl 2:19). Timothy went to Thessalonica to investigate and report before the writing of 1 Th (1 Th 3:2, 6). Heb 13:23 alludes to the imprisonment and release of Timothy. These allusions show that Timothy was one of Paul's most intimate and trusted associates. No other genuine information about him is found in ancient sources.

On the epistles addressed to Timothy cf PASTORIAL EPISTLES.

Tin. Tin is an essential component in the manufacture of bronze* and was known to the Israelites, although it is rarely mentioned in the Bible. It is included in a list of metals in Nm 31:22. Ezk 22:18, 20 alludes to the smelting of metals, including tin. Tin was imported by Tyre* from Tarshish* i.e., refineries. The metal is not found in or near Palestine. The Phoenicians could have found deposits in countries bordering on the Adriatic, and it probably reached them from Spain and from Great Britain through the hands of other merchants. Before the Phoenician exploitation of Mediterranean sources tin could have been imported into W Asia from Persia and Armenia.

Tiphsah (Hb *tipsaḥ*, meaning uncertain), the N limit of the kingdom of Solomon (1 K 5:4). Tiphsah is identical with the Thapsacus of the Gks, the modern Dibseh at the confluence of the Belikh and the Euphrates, about 75 mi E of Aleppo. In ancient times there was an important ford of the Euphrates at this point. Tiphsah in 2 K 15:16 should probably be read Tappuah*.

Tiras (Hb *tîrās*), a gentilic name; in the Table* of Nations a son of Japheth* (Gn 10:2; 1 Ch 1:5). The name is very probably to be connected with the *tw-rj-š-,'* of Ramses III, one of the Sea Peoples (cf EGYPT) and the *tyrsenoi* of Herodotus; several scholars suggest the Etruscans.

Tirhakah (Hb *tirhāḳāh*, Egytian *t-h-rw-a*), Taharko king of Ethiopia who came to at-

tack Sennacherib* during his campaign in Judah (2 K 19:9; Is 37:9). Taharko was the 4th king of the 25th (Nubian) dynasty of Egypt (690–664 BC). During his reign the Assyrians under Esarhaddon* invaded and conquered Egypt and destroyed Thebes*, and Taharko withdrew to Napata in Nubia. The Assyrian overlordship endured 7 years, and Taharko recovered his kingdom. The allusion to Taharko in 2 K 19:9; Is 37:9 cannot be reconciled with the campaign of Sennacherib in 701 BC. W. F. Albright and others argue from this allusion and from other indications that the OT has conflated accounts of two different campaigns; cf HEZEKIAH; SENNACHERIB.

Tirshatha (Hb *tiršātā'*, always with the definite article), a title given to the Persian governor of Judah (Ezr 2:63; Ne 7:65, 70; 8:9; 10:2). Many recent Eng versions translate "governor." The word possibly represents Persian *taršta*, an official title.

Tirzah (Hb *tirṣāh*, meaning uncertain), a Canaanite town included in the list of towns conquered by Joshua (Jos 12:24); the royal residence of the kings of Israel under Jeroboam* (1 K 14:17), Baasha* (1 K 15:21, 33; 16:6), Elah* (1 K 16:8 f), Zimri* (1 K 16:15). Zimri was besieged in Tirzah by Omri* (1 K 16:17). It was the royal residence of Omri for 6 years; the capital was then transferred to Samaria* (1 K 16:23). Menahem* came from Tirzah (2 K 15:14); it is mentioned as part of the territory of Tappuah* (2 K 15:16). The beloved is called "beautiful as Tirzah" (SS 6:4).

Tirzah is probably identified with Tell el Farah, about 7 mi NE of Nablus. Excavations conducted by the École Biblique de Jérusalem since 1946 have disclosed a large and presumably important city situated on the heights about the Wadi Farah. The site was occupied from the Chalcolithic period, abandoned from EB II to MB II, and reoccupied in the early Israelite period, and abandoned in the 9th century. This suits Omri's change of the capital; but the inclusion of Tirzah in the list of Jos 12 must be an anachronism if Tell el Farah is Tirzah. A building called tentatively the "Palace" was uncovered; it was built in two phases, one possibly the building of Jeroboam I, the other the remodeling of Omri. Nothing was found to identify the site positively with Tirzah, but the identification is regarded as quite probable by most scholars.

Tishbite. Cf ELIJAH.

Tishri. The 7th month of the Hb calendar* (Sept–Oct).

Tithe. The tithe is a tenth part taken as a tax. In the OT the tithe appears as a religious tax; the practice is old and not limited to Israel, and the tithes paid to Melchizedek by Abraham (Gn 14:20) and promised to Yahweh by Jacob (Gn 28:22) may well represent old cultic practices. The oldest certain allusion to tithes is Am 4:4, which mentions tithes paid at Bethel. The law of Dt 14:22–29 (cf Dt 26:12–15) prescribes annual tithes of grain, wine, oil, and firstlings. Two years out of three these are to furnish the food for the sacred banquet; in the 3rd year the tithes go to the poor. A later law reflects a change in cultic practices and no doubt an increase in the number of cultic personnel and their exclusive occupation in the temple; the law of Nm 18:21–32 grants the tithes of all Israel to the Levites, and the Levites are in turn to pay a tithe of what they receive to the priests. The law of Lv 27:30–33 is intermediate between these two, saying only that the tithes are holy to Yahweh but not specifying their use further. Ne 10:37 relates that the postexilic community pledged itself to pay tithes according to the law of Nm 18:21 ff. Mal 3:8–12 complains that the postexilic community is lax and unfaithful in the payment of tithes. The practice is alluded to in 1 Mc 3:49. Demetrius confirmed tithes and freed them from royal taxation (1 Mc 10:31). 1 Mc 11:35 refers to a royal tithe collected for the crown.

In the NT the payment of all tithes was a proof of the piety of the Pharisee (Lk 18:12). The tithes of the OT were levied only on the produce of the grains, vines, and flocks; the Pharisees extended the obligation to even the smallest herbs (Mt 23:23; Lk 11:42). Heb 7:1–10 argues elaborately from Abraham's tithes to Melchizedek that the priesthood of Christ according to Melchizedek is greater than the priesthood of Aaron; for Aaron paid tithes to Melchizedek through his ancestor Abraham, in whose loins he was, and tithes are paid by the lesser to the greater.

Tittle. In many Eng versions the translation of Gk *keraia*, "little horn," in Mt 5:18; Lk 16:17, indicating that not even the smallest portion of the law will pass away. The *keraia* was a small ornamental hook or projection on the ends of many Hb letters in the script used in NT times, substantially the same script which is still in use.

Titus (Lt *titus*), a disciple and associate of Paul. Titus does not appear in AA and nothing is known of his antecedents. He was a companion of Paul on his journey to Jerusalem (Gal 2:1); because he was a Gentile Paul would not permit him to be circumcised (Gal 2:3). He was Paul's emissary to Corinth between the writing of 1 Co and 2 Co; Paul relates his own anxiety at Titus's failure to meet him in Troas, where he was expected (2 Co 2:13), his joy when Titus met him in Macedonia with news from Corinth (2 Co 7:6), and Titus's own joy at the attitude of the Corinthians (2 Co 7:13 f); it seems clear that Titus was unknown to the Corinthians when he was sent on this delicate mission, and that the mission was successful. Paul states his intention to send Titus back to Corinth as his representative for the collection to be taken up for the Jerusalem community (2 Co 8:6, 16 f). Paul calls him "my partner and fellow worker in your service" (2 Co 8:23) and praises him for taking no advantage of the Corinthians (2 Co 12:18). 2 Tm 4:10 alludes to a mission of Titus to Dalmatia. According to Tt 1:4 Paul left him in Crete* to correct abuses and appoint elders. Ancient sources contain no other genuine information.

On the letter addressed to Titus cf PASTORAL EPISTLES.

Tob (Hb *ṭôb*, meaning uncertain), the region where Jephthah* lived as a bandit (Jgs 11:3, 5) and from which the Ammonites hired mercenary Aramaean troops to resist David (2 S 10:6, 8). It was inhabited by Jews in Maccabean times (1 Mc 5:13; 2 Mc 12:17). The region certainly must lie in E Palestine and very probably in the N in the region of Bashan*. The name may survive in the modern et-Taiyibeh, about 10 mi ESE of Deraa.

Tobiah (Hb *ṭôbiyyāh*, "Yahweh is good"), a personal name. Tobiah was one of the Jews who returned from Babylon; his association with Zerubbabel* suggests that he was an important and respected man (Zc 6:10, 14). It is somewhat surprising to find the sons of Tobiah listed among those Jews who could not prove their Jewish descent from the genealogical tables (Ezr 2:60; Ne 7:62); but there is no reason to suppose that we are dealing with two different families. It is possible that the clan of Tobiah, excluded from the Jerusalem community, moved to E Palestine and there established itself as local nobility. Tobiah the Ammonite was one of the adversaries of Nehemiah*, who calls him the slave, the Ammonite (Ne 2:10, 19; 3:35; 4:1; 6:1, 12–14). Yet Tobiah was not an Ammonite; he was related to Jewish nobles (Ne 6:17–19) and to a priestly family (Ne 13:4), and received from the priests a chamber in the temple for his own use, from which Nehemiah expelled him (Ne 13:7 f). The appellative "the slave" is most probably based on a double meaning; Tobiah was "slave of the king" (cf SLAVE) i.e., a royal officer; his association with Sanballat* and his obvious power as an adversary of Nehemiah show that he was governor of E Palestine, as Nehemiah was governor of Judah. The family of the Tobiads continue prominent in Palestinian history into the Maccabean period; they appear frequently in Josephus and are now known from Egyptian papyri. These papyri indicate that the Tobiads of the 3rd century continued to hold under the Ptolemies the office of governor of E Palestine. Hyrcanus, son of Tobiah, had a deposit in the temple in the time of Seleucus IV (2 Mc 3:11); the quarrel with the Jerusalem authorities had been healed. The ruins of Araq el Amir, in the hills of E Palestine about halfway between the Jordan and Amman, are the ruins of the castle and fortress of the Tobiads. The ruins show a large complex of buildings on a spacious artificial terrace; behind them in the limestone hills were cut extensive galleries and chambers, furnishing an inner citadel of defense. The name Tobiah is inscribed on the limestone in Hb characters.

Tobit (Tobias), Book of. Tobit is a Gk form of Hb *Tobiah*, which is also Grecized as Tobias. In Tb the name of Tobit is given to the father, the name of Tobias to the son.

1. *Contents:* 1:1–22, the deportation of Tobit from Israel in the reign of Shalmaneser* of Assyria and his good works; 2:1–3:6, the blindness of Tobit and his patient acceptance of his trial; 3:7–17, the affliction of Sarah*, daughter of Raguel*, by the demon Asmodaeus*; 4:1–21, Tobit commissions Tobias to collect a debt from their kinsman Gabael* and instructs him on good conduct; 5:1–22, Tobias meets the angel Raphael* who agrees to accompany him on the journey to Rages*; 6:1–18, the journey and the catching of the fish by which Tobit and Sarah are to be cured; 7:1–8:21, the marriage of Tobias and Sarah and the expulsion of Asmodaeus; 9:1–11:19, the return and the cure of Tobit's blindness; 12:1–22, the revelation of the identity of Raphael; 13:1–18, the song of Tobit; 14:1–15, the prophecy of Tobit and his death.

2. *Text and Language.* Tb is preserved in Gk; the Gk MSS exhibit considerable variations in the text, which was very freely transmitted. Jerome made his version from an Aramaic MS, but it was done hastily and it is impossible to establish any critical conclusions from the Vg version. The Qumran* MSS include 3 fragmentary copies of the Aramaic text of Tb and one fragment of a Hb text. J. T. Milik believes that Aramaic is the original language of the book and

that both Gk and Hb are versions of the Aramaic.

3. *Authorship and Date.* The authorship can be identified only in general; the contents of the book and its teaching (cf below) suggest very strongly that the book is of Palestinian origin. The date is estimated by most critics about 200 BC. Tb contains no allusion to the belief in the resurrection, and it does not clearly reflect the troubles of the Maccabean period, although it does describe the devout Jew who suffers for his observance of Judaism.

4. *Teaching and Literary Form.* While Tb is couched in the form of a narrative, it is scarcely possible that anything in it can be historical except perhaps the names of some of the characters. The historical situation of Tb corresponds to nothing that is known of the period in which the episodes are placed. Tb is wisdom literature rather than historical literature. Its thesis is that the righteous man should sustain himself patiently in troubles in the assurance that God will deliver him; it represents the simple and naive wisdom which is discussed in Jb*. In addition to the main thesis of the narrative the wisdom of Tb is supplemented by the discourses of the characters. Tb and his son are images of genuine Jewish piety of the later postexilic period. Piety consists in the observance of the law. Some good works are given special praise: almsgiving (1:3–8, 16 f; 2:2; 4:5–19; 12:8), observance of the laws of cleanliness* (1:10–12; 2:6), the burying of the dead (1:18 f; 2:4–8; 12:13), the honoring of God (12:7 f, 17 f, 22), thanksgiving (8:5–9, 16 f; 11:14–17 +). The book contains many prayers which illustrate Jewish piety (3:1–6, 11–15; 9:15–17; 13:1–18 +). The life lived quietly in the practice of such virtues and sustained in the face of adversity is the life recommended to the man who wishes to live in the true path of virtue.

In some details Tb exhibits foreign influence. The story of Tb himself bears some resemblances to a widely diffused story of "the grateful dead," which relates how a man is helped by a companion and protector who is ultimately revealed as the spirit of one whose corpse he buried. In Tb the motif of the burial of the dead is present, but the grateful dead is replaced by the angel Raphael. This adaptation is made in accordance with Jewish belief. Asmodaeus is the name of a Persian demon. The author knows the story of Ahikar*, to whose hero he alludes; and the story of Ahikar, a righteous man who suffers injustice, has some superficial resemblance to the story of Tb in its thesis; but Tb is an independent composition.

The angelology of Tb is considerably advanced beyond the angelology of older books of the OT; cf ANGEL; RAPHAEL. The elements of this angelology can be traced in the literature of extrabiblical Judaism, and it is not necessary to seek them in non-Jewish literature.

Tb is accepted in the canon* of the Catholic Church, but it does not appear in Protestant and Jewish canons.

Togarmah (Hb *tōgarmāh,* meaning uncertain), a geographical name; descendant of Japheth* and son of Gomer* (Gn 10:3; 1 Ch 1:6). Togarmah exported horses to Tyre (Ezk 27:14) and appears in the army of Gog* (Ezk 38:6). A connection is suggested between Togarmah and Takarama of the Hittite texts, Tilgarimmu of the Assyrian texts. This region is located between the Antitaurus and the Euphrates by Forrer, a little to the E to the banks of the Euphrates between Samosata and Melita by Goetze.

Toi. Cf TOU.

Tola (Hb *tôlā',* meaning and etymology uncertain). **1.** A clan of Issachar* (Gn 46:13; Nm 26:23; 1 Ch 7:1 f). **2.** A minor judge, a man of Issachar, son of Puah, who lived at Shamir in the hill country of Ephraim (Jgs 10:1 f). Possibly the judge is to be identified with the clan.

Tomb. Cf BURIAL.

Tongue. Like other bodily organs, the tongue in the Bible is often hypostatized and given moral attributes which belong to the person. While the tongue is the organ of taste, it is much more frequently mentioned as the organ of speech, and by metonymy means speech itself. The tongue is boastful (Ps 12:4), deceitful (Ps 120:3 +, very often), smooth and seductive (Pr 6:24), lying (Ps 109:2 +, very often). The tongue is a scourge (Jb 5:21), it is whetted like a sword (Ps 64:4), it is like a serpent's tongue (Ps 140:4), like a sharp sword (Ps 57:5), like a bow and arrow (Je 9:27). "The man of tongue" is a slanderer (Ps 140:12). Death and life are in the power of the tongue (Pr 18:21). The enemies of Je plan to kill him with the tongue (Je 18:18). Not all words of the tongue are sinful; the healing tongue is a tree of life (Pr 15:4), and the tongue of the righteous is choice silver (Pr 10:20). But the faults of the tongue are more numerous and obvious than its virtues, and the sages warn against them. BS 19:16 asks who has not sinned with his tongue, and assures us that a man's tongue is his downfall (BS

5:13). The tongue may destroy one (BS 22:27), and the man who does not slip with his tongue is blessed (BS 25:8). Like the Pss, BS is much aware of the harm which can be done by the slanderous tongue (BS 28:13–23). In the NT also are admonitions to restrain the tongue; he who fails to bridle his tongue has no true religion (Js 1:26). To commit no sin with the tongue is to be perfect; the tongue is the little rudder which directs the whole ship, it is a fire, it is the only animal which cannot be tamed (Js 3:2–12).

A special question is raised by the meaning of "tongue" in the passages which mention "speaking in tongues" (Mk 16:17; AA 2:4–11; 10:46; 19:6; 1 Co 14). Here tongue is speech or language. It is a speech which is unintelligible to the listeners (except in AA 2:4–11, cf below); it is a fruit of the outpouring of the spirit, particularly at baptism (AA 10:46; 19:6), and in some churches becomes a routine part of the cult which needs regulation (1 Co 14). It is addressed not to men but to God (1 Co 14:2), it edifies the speaker rather than those who hear him (1 Co 14:4), it must be interpreted (1 Co 14:5–19, 27), it is a sign for unbelievers, not for believers (1 Co 14:22).

Scholars have pointed out certain seeming parallels in Gk religions and in Oriental cults; other scholars have rejected these parallels entirely. A moderate position between a simple affirmation of identity and a simple denial of any relationship at all seems more defensible. It is established that one of the effects of religious exaltation in certain Hellenistic and Oriental circles was the utterance of unintelligible speech. This phenomenon may be taken as a cultural background which makes the appearance of the unintelligible "tongues" of the early Christian churches an appropriate sign of exaltation in the Hellenistic-Oriental world, and which offers some explanation of the gradual disappearance of tongues.

In AA 2:4–11, however, the phenomenon of tongues is described not as unintelligible but intelligible speech; each of the foreign groups present understood his own language. The historical reality of the event is affirmed by many interpreters; but it also exhibits certain traces of symbolism. The speech of the apostles, intelligible to foreign peoples, is the message of the Church addressed to all nations. It is the spirit* which enables the Church to make her message intelligible to all nations. The Church breaks out of the geographical and linguistic barriers of Judaism. T. Zahn suggested that the narrative signified a reversal of the story of the tower of Babel* and the beginning of the restoration of the unity of mankind. These considerations suggest that the event has been enlarged by some midrashic* considerations.

Tophet (Hb *tōpet*, "fire place"?), the name of the high place in the valley of Ge-hinnom* near Jerusalem*, the shrine of Molech* (2 K 23:10; Je 7:31 f), where human sacrifices were offered. It was profaned by Josiah (2 K 23:10), but Jeremiah still speaks of Tophet and its cult, threatening that it will be filled with dead bodies and will become a burying ground (Je 7:31 f; 19:6, 11 f) and that Jerusalem itself will become a Tophet, a place of burning (Je 19:13 f). Is 30:33 uses the term simply to mean fireplace, the place where corpses are burned.

Torah. Cf LAW.

Tou (Hb *tōʿû* in 1 Ch 18:9 f, Toi, *tōʿî* in 2 S 8:9 f), king of Hamath*, a contemporary and an ally of David.

Tower. The towers mentioned in the OT are not all the same kind of structure. The tower may be a flimsy isolated structure in a vineyard (Is 5:2) or in the open country (2 Ch 26:10) which served as observation posts against wild beasts or thieves. Watchtowers for military observation stood on high points outside the cities; the approach of a hostile army could be signalled by smoke (2 K 17:9; 18:8; 1 Ch 27:25; 2 Ch 26:9; Is 2:15). The wall of a city was strengthened by the erection of towers at gates and other points of weakness (cf FORTIFICATIONS). The tower of a city sometimes means its central citadel, which was defended after the city walls were breached; the tower of Shechem* was probably a temple fortress (Jgs 9:46–49). Such citadels are probably meant by other towers which are named after a city (Jgs 8:17), or which appear as part of the name of a city (names compounded with *migdal*). The beloved in SS 7:5 is called a tower of ivory.

Trachonitis. Cf BASHAN.

Tradition. In the NT the concept of tradition (Gk noun, *paradosis;* verb, *paradidonai*), is used of the teaching of the rabbis, handed down from one generation to another by oral tradition (cf TALMUD; Mt 15:2–6; Mk 7:3–13; AA 6:14; Gal 1:14). A human tradition not identified, possibly Jewish traditions, is an obstacle to the faith (Col 2:8).

Christian belief becomes the object of tradition. This is explicitly said of the narrative of the Eucharistic institution (1 Co 11:23) and of the gospel* summary in 1 Co 15:3 ff; the word suggests that here Paul is using fixed formulae for these recitals.

The word also is applied to what is apparently the more general teaching of Paul (1 Co 11:2), his teaching concerning the Day of the Lord (2 Th 2:15) and rules of conduct (2 Th 3:6), to which the believers should hold fast. Tradition includes the faith (Jd 3) and "the holy commandment" (2 Pt 2:21).

The importance of tradition in the formation of the Gospels and the teaching of the primitive Church is touched in GOSPEL; TEACHING and related articles. The first generations of the Church were no doubt accustomed to communicate their beliefs by the means which were familiar to them from the rabbinical schools: the oral transmission of the material to disciples. The text quoted above and others which do not contain the word "tradition" attest the existence of a common body of material which is summed up as gospel and teaching and which was traced to the apostles* and witnesses* of the life of Jesus Himself. It was of importance that this tradition should be preserved without deformation; and fidelity to the received tradition was the ultimate assurance that the doctrine proposed was genuine. Revelation* was the word* of Jesus: the word incarnate, i.e., His life and person, and the word which He spoke, i.e., His sayings. This revelation was the object of tradition; the spirit* indeed taught the Church, but communicated no new word beyond that which Jesus had incarnated and uttered. The content of the revelation, once Jesus no longer dwelt on earth, was secured only by the faithful preservation and transmission of the word among His followers. Tradition must therefore be included among the constitutive elements of the primitive Christian community.

Transfiguration (Gk *metamorphōsis*), in Gk mythology the word designates the change of form and appearance of which the gods were believed capable. The use of the word to designate the episode related in Mt 17:1–8; Mk 2:8; Lk 9:28–36 has no connection with the mythological use of the term. The revelation made to Peter, James, and John in this passage has no parallel in OT or NT, and it is impossible to reconstruct it completely. But the themes and the symbolism used to convey the experience are clear and derived from other biblical passages, and the theological significance of the revelation is not obscure. It is not irrelevant that Lk 9:32 signifies a sleep of the disciples which must be understood as ecstatic in character. Mt depends on Mk for his account of the episode; Lk has derived some features from an independent source, thought by some critics to be Johannine. The situation of the episode in all three Gospels is after the first prediction of the passion, and this position in meaningful; the transfiguration gives the predictions of the passion a necessary clarification. It should be noted that it is a constant theme of the Synoptic Gospels that this clarification was not understood by the disciples before the resurrection. The change described in the appearance of Jesus suggests the change which is implied in the resurrection narratives and which made it difficult for the disciples to recognize Him; cf RESURRECTION. The transformation of the body into glory in the resurrection is also mentioned by Paul (1 Co 15:40–44); it is a change into the likeness of the glory of Jesus produced by the contemplation of His glory (2 Co 3:18). Light* and glory in the OT are elements of the theophany*, the sensible presence of God. The whiteness mentioned in the passage is the luminous quality of glory; it belongs also to the Risen Christ in Apc 1:14 +. The cloud* also is an element of the theophany of the OT. The cloud and the formula of the utterance of the Father are derived from the baptism* of Jesus. The unnamed mountain (cf TABOR) on which the episode takes place suggests the mountain of the revelation of Moses, Sinai-Horeb. Moses and Elijah represent the law* and the prophets*, the sacred literature and tradition of Israel which foretell the passion and the glorification of the Messiah. Lk 9:31 makes explicit the relation of the two with the passion of Jesus. The tabernacles desired by Peter echo the tabernacle* of the OT as the place where Yahweh dwells among His people. The postponement of the revelation of the vision until after the resurrection (Mt 17:9; Mk 9:9) suggests the failure of the disciples to understand the relation of the passion and glorification of Jesus until after His resurrection.

The transfiguration is much more than a doublet of the baptism of Jesus or a misplaced resurrection apparition. It is a statement that the Son of Man even in His earthly existence is the glorious Son of Man who is recognized in His glory after His passion and resurrection. Following upon the prediction of the passion, it is a revelation of the truth that glory follows the passion. The fullness of the meaning of the attestation that Jesus is the Son of God sent by His Father is perceived in the climactic episodes of His earthly life. The tremendous and mysterious content of this revelation is so overpowering that it can be described only in the symbolism of ecstasy and vision. The theology of the transfiguration is entirely one with the theology of Phl 2:6–11, where Paul probes the significance of Jesus' emptying of Himself, the meaning of God's taking to Himself the human condition.

The transfiguration is mentioned in 2 Pt 1:16–18. The vision of glory in Jn 1:14 is not a reference to the transfiguration; on the Johannine conception of glory cf GLORY.

Trespass Offering. Cf SACRIFICE.

Tribe (Hb šebeṭ or maṭṭeh, both meaning "staff" or "rod," referring to the tribal standard). Tribal organization is the social form of the modern Bedu and is the universal social form of nomadic peoples known to history. The tribe is an autonomous group which acknowledges no higher authority than its own. This is the essence of the tribe, and numbers are irrelevant to the constitution of a tribe, although the numbers of the tribe are important in determining its ability to assert its sovereignty effectively. The basis of tribal union is blood kinship, real or achieved by legal fiction; all members of the tribe are "brothers." The tribe considers itself as descended from one common ancestor, who is often eponymous; the tribe is often called "the sons of X." The concept of ancestry is not altered by another common designation, "the house of X"; thus in the OT both terms appear, and some groups, such as Joseph, are normally called "the house" and not "the sons" or even "the tribe." In modern Bedu tribes the eponymous ancestor is often invented; the name of the ancestor may be a geographical name or an appellative. Similar inventions are quite probable for at least some of the tribes of Israel*. But the eponymous ancestor should not be on principle regarded as a fictitious character; the origins of the tribe, however, are much more complex than the simple genealogical scheme suggests. It is not altogether correct to think of the tribe as the fusion of family or clans, neither of which units is able to survive independently in the nomadic culture; as remarked above, the tribe is the autonomous unit, and this is the primary unit. The modern tribe is divided into clans, which in turn are subdivided into individual familes, and the same organzation is reflected in the OT: family [bēt'ab], clan [mišpāḥāh], tribe [šēbet, maṭṭeh]. This organization appears most frequently in the writing of the P source of the Pnt* and the Chronicler*, both of which are much later than the tribal society of Israel; but they are so similar to the modern tribal organization that they can scarcely be late literary fictions and must represent old traditions of tribal organization. The clan is the effective social unit within the tribe; it is the clan of which the tribesman is a member, and it is the clan which imposes tribal obligations such as blood vengeance. Many tribes no doubt have arisen from the fusion of clans, but this is only one way in which tribes arise; they may also arise from fusion of smaller tribes. Ultimately the tribe is the self-sufficient autonomous group. Once a tribe exists, it can expand by the adoption of clans or individual families. A tribe can arise by fission of large clans from the parent tribe. In such fissions the genealogical relations are remembered. Likewise when smaller groups are adopted by a tribe an artificial genealogical relationship is created; for membership is blood kinship, without which the tribal obligations would not be valid. Such tribal relationships appear in the OT. Abraham and Lot illustrate tribal fission (Gn 13). The adoption of clans appears in the relations of Judah* and Caleb*. The absorption of a weak tribe by a stronger appears in Judah and Simeon*. A tribe which either split, retaining the same name, or merged separate groups in separated territories, is Manasseh*. Simeon and Levi* both disappeared as tribes.

The tribe is headed by a sheikh (lit "old man"; cf Hb zākēn, "elder"). In modern tribes the office is generally hereditary with reservations; the son of the sheikh may be displaced by another if he shows incompetence. The position is, however, generally retained in the same family and clan. The authority of the sheikh is paternal, but in practice it is not often such. Each clan also is headed by a sheikh, and decisions must be reached by common agreement. The sheikh imposes his will rather by force of character and diplomatic tact than by authority. In theory he is the bravest and strongest warrior of the tribe, and in practice he should not be notably inferior in these qualities. "Intelligence and the sword" were the two qualities of the sheikh mentioned by an Arab to a European traveler, A. Jaussen. The sheikh determines the movements of the tribe to seek pasture, leads them in war and raids, and is the judge of disputes.

The tribe claims a territory, usually not very precisely defined, in which it pastures its flocks; the size of the territory depends upon the size of the tribe, the amount of pasture available — for the tribe does not like to cover large areas simply for the pleasure of moving — and the ability of the tribe to enforce its claims. The territory must include water sources which are claimed exclusively by the tribe or shared with other tribes; water rights are more clearly defined than land rights, and are often a cause of quarrels.

The family solidarity of the tribe imposes certain obligations which admit no excuse. The tribesman must serve the tribe in wars and raids. A certain community of goods is practiced; he who has more must contribute to the survival of the tribe by assisting those who have less. The obligation of blood revenge (cf AVENGER) is sacred. The tribesmen must exhibit hospitality*. Beyond these duties the tribe gives its members a surprising amount of freedom. But the effective exercise of freedom is somewhat limited. It is the solidarity of the tribe which makes it the most effective social form for survival in the desert. The individual can survive only as a member of the tribe, and the close social solidarity which tribal life demands is reflected in much of both OT and NT.

The tribal structure of ancient Israel was a 12-tribe confederation. The origins and the operation of this confederacy are obscure in many details. The tribal structure of Israel, well adapted to the nomadic life, was less adapted to town and village life, where geographical rather than tribal connections became important. The organization of the monarchy left little room for the functions of tribal society, which was not much more than a memory during the monarchy. It is indeed remarkable that it continued so strong as a memory; this is due to the importance of Israel as a theological conception more than to its importance as a social structure.

Trinity. The trinity of God is defined by the Church as the belief that in God are three persons who subsist in one nature. The belief as so defined was reached only in the 4th and 5th centuries AD and hence is not explicitly and formally a biblical belief. The trinity of persons within the unity of nature is defined in terms of "person" and "nature" which are Gk philosophical terms; actually the terms do not appear in the Bible. The trinitarian definitions arose as the result of long controversies in which these terms and others such as "essence" and "substance" were erroneously applied to God by some theologians. The ultimate affirmation of trinity of persons and unity of nature was declared by the Church to be the only correct way in which these terms could be used.

The elements of the trinity of persons within the unity of nature in the Bible appear in the use of the terms Father*, Son*, and Spirit*. The personal reality of the Spirit emerged more slowly than the personal reality of Father and Son, which are personal terms. On the application of the name of Spirit to the Son in the Pauline writings cf SPIRIT. The unity of nature does not appear as a problem in the Bible, and indeed could only arise when a philosophical investigation of the term nature as applied to God was begun. In the NT the Father is "the God" (Gk ho theos), and Jesus is "the Son of the God" (ho hyios tou theou). The

Spirit is "the spirit of the God" or "the holy spirit," in this context a synonymous term. Deity is conceived not in the Gk term of nature but rather as a level of being, "the holy"; between this level and the level of "flesh*" there is an impassable gulf. Impassable, that is, by man; it is bridged by Jesus, the Son, who renders it possible for men to be adopted sons. Without an explicit formula the NT leaves no room to think that Jesus is Himself an object of the adoption which He communicates to others. He knows the Father and reveals Him. He therefore belongs to the divine level of being; and there is no question at all about the Spirit belonging to the divine level of being. What is less clear about the Spirit is His personal reality; often He is mentioned in language in which His personal reality is not explicit. This distinction between God and flesh is the NT basis for the affirmation of the unity of nature; the very identification of the Father with "the God" shows that the NT writers intend to distinguish the Son and the Spirit from the Father. The NT does not approach the metaphysical problem of subordination, as it approaches no metaphysical problem. It offers no room for a statement of the relations of Father, Son, and Spirit which would imply that one of them is more or less properly on the divine level of being than another. In Jewish thought of the time the son and the spirit are angels; it does not even take the trouble explicitly to deny it. At the same time, it is necessary to recall that in Catholic belief the trinity of persons within the unity of nature is a mystery which ultimately escapes understanding; and in no respect is it more mysterious than in the relations of the persons to each other. "Son" and "Spirit" do not express perfect identity and are not intended to express it; the distinction of persons is not merely numerical but reposes upon a mysterious personality or character in each one which is unknown in its ultimate reality. The Church has declared that any statement of this distinction which reduces the divinity of any of the persons is a false statement; equally false would be a statement which would deny their personal distinction. The notions of Father, Son, and Spirit are revealed that we may know God better; and the theologian should explore these ideas.

The OT does not contain suggestions or foreshadowing of the trinity of persons. What it does contain are the words which the NT employs to express the trinity of persons such as Father, Son, Word, Spirit, etc. A study of these words shows us how the revelation of God in the NT advances beyond the revelation of God in the OT. The same study of these words and their background is the best way to arrive at an understanding of the distinction of persons as it is stated in the NT.

Troas (Gk *trōas*), the extreme NW region of the province of Asia* and the peninsula of Asia Minor, a few mi S of the Hellespont. The name preserves the name of the ancient city of Troy, which lay in the plain of Troas. In NT times the name of the city of the region was Alexandrian Troas, but the city is called simply Troas in the NT. The city was made a Roman colony by Augustus and enjoyed favored treatment because of the legendary connection between fugitives from Troy and early Latium. Paul* sailed from Troas on his 2nd missionary journey (AA 16:8, 11); this was the first contact of Christian missionaries with Europe. It was also the point where he was joined by a party of Macedonians who accompanied him on his trip to Jerusalem (AA 20:5 ff). There was by this time a church established in Troas; Paul preached there and cured a young man named Eutychus who fell from a window while dozing during Paul's sermon. The founding of this church is not mentioned directly; Paul's allusion in 2 Co 2:12 indicates that it was his own foundation, but this can have occurred on neither of the visits mentioned above. 2 Tm 4:13 alludes to still another visit.

Trophimus (Gk *trophimos,* "nourishing"), a Christian of Ephesus* who accompanied Paul on his journey to Jerusalem (AA 20:4) and was the innocent occasion of the riot against Paul in the temple (AA 21:29). 2 Tm 4:20 mentions that he fell ill at Miletus and was left there.

Trumpet. The trumpet as distinguished from the horn* is made of metal, has a long straight stem and a bell mouth; the OT mentions trumpets of silver, but they were no doubt more commonly of bronze. Jewish trumpets are represented among the trophies on the arch of Titus. The OT mentions their use both for secular and cultic purposes, much more commonly cultic. They sounded the entrance of the monarch (2 K 11:14; 2 Ch 23:13) and the alarm in war (Ho 5:8). In the cult they sounded the religious assembly and announced the beginning of a feast day (Nm 10:1 ff). They were included in the musical instruments of the temple (2 K 12:13; 1 Ch 16:42; 2 Ch 5:12). They were sounded before the ark in procession (1 Ch 15:24, 28; 16:6), during the temple sacrifice (2 Ch 29:28), and are mentioned as used on such solemn occasions as the dedication of the temple (2 Ch 7:6) and the foundation of the second temple (Ezr 3:10). Most references to the trumpet occur in late books, and this suggests that they were more used in the post-exilic period. The sounding of the trumpet by the priests before battle, while reported in a late source (2 Ch 13:14), may very well reflect an early custom.

In the NT the trumpet becomes eschatological and apocalyptic. Seven angels each sound a trumpet, and each blast of the trumpet is followed by a natural catastrophe (Apc 8:2–9, 11). The sound of the trumpet calls the elect for the final gathering (Mt 24:31), and the dead are awakened to the resurrection by the angel's trumpet (1 Co 15:52; 1 Th 4:16).

Truth. 1. *OT.* The difference between the patterns of Hb and Gk speech is clearly exhibited in the idea of truth; Hb has no distinct word for true and truth. These ideas are expressed by *'emet* and cognate words, which are treated under FAITH. The true in Hb is that to which one can give belief, whether it is a person or a thing. The basis upon which belief rests is the solidity of the object, or perhaps better its reality; it is steadfast and unchanging; it does not collapse upon testing or examination or stress. Hence one can rely upon it; it will not betray one's confidence. The failure to distinguish "truth" as a concept and to express it by a word distinct from the words for belief and fidelity is in harmony with the generally nonintellectual character of Hb expressions which we think of primarily as intellectual. The true is not merely an object of intellectual assent, but something which demands a personal commitment. In a sense one can be said to choose or accept the truth rather than assent to it. The lie, on the contrary is not solidly real, and therefore not dependable. It is spurious, not the reality which it pretends to be or which it is alleged to be. The lie, like the truth, is understood in terms of the personal commitment of the person to whom it is presented; they are both challenges which elicit a personal response.

2. *NT.* The NT use of *alēthēs, alētheia,* reflects both the Hb words *'emet* and its cognates and the classical Gk use of the word. To some extent the Gk words also signify the real and the genuine, and in this they are not totally dissimilar from the Hb words. But the difference is apparent in this, that truth to the Gk is reality as intellectually apprehended; truth is known rather than believed and trusted, which is the characteristic Hb manner of speech.

In such phrases as "speak the truth," "witness the truth" etc the NT use of the word carries no peculiar force (Mk 5:33; Lk 4:25; Jn 5:31; 4:37; 16:7; 19:35; AA 26:25; Rm 9:1; 2 Co 12:6; Tt 1:13). Similarly truth in the meaning of truthfulness or sincerity is the same as in ordinary usage (Mt 22:16; Mk 12:14; Jn 3:33; 7:18; 8:26; 1 Co 5:8; 2 Co 6:8; 7:14; Phl 1:18). When the apostle is called a teacher of the nations in all fidelity and sincerity, however, the word acquires some of the overtones noted below (1 Tm 2:7). The truth of judgment is its justice (Jn 8:16). The OT meaning of the truth as the solid and steadfast appears in a reference to the steadfast grace of God (1 Pt 5:12). Not infrequently, especially where truth stands in opposition to unrighteousness (Rm 2:8; 1 Co 13:6) or is mentioned parallel with righteousness (Eph 4:24; 5:9; 6:14; perhaps Js 5:19; Phl 4:8) truth seems to be synonymous with righteousness as an attribute of character and conduct, and this is probably the meaning of "to be truthful in love" (Eph 4:16). The true is the real or the genuine as opposed to the unreal or the spurious: the true God (1 Th 1:9; Apc 6:10; cf also AA 12:9; Jn 10:41; 4:18). Truth is predicated in Jn in some passages in a rather peculiar sense, always of Jesus: the true light (Jn 1:9), the true vine (Jn 15:1). His body is true food and His blood is true drink (Jn 6:55). In the same sense the heavenly tabernacle is the true tabernacle (Heb 8:2). True here means more than real or genuine; it is real in the sense of permanent and lasting, and its permanence is rooted in its heavenly and incorruptible character. One might almost take "true" here as signifying the primordial, the archetype of which earthly food and drink, earthly light, earthly vines are an imitation and a participation, deriving their reality from the heavenly archetype.

R. Bultmann pointed out that truth in Jn has a peculiar and distinctively Christian force. The word is common in Jn, and is frequently combined with other key Johannine words such as light* and life*. The Johannine force is evident in the dialogue of Jn 8. The truth which Jesus presents is something which can be known (in the Hb sense of knowledge*) and it liberates (Jn 8:32). It is clear from Jn 8:34 that the truth liberates from sin, not from ignorance. This truth Jesus hears from God and tells to men (Jn 8:40); and from Jn 8:45 truth is seen to be synonymous with the words of God. In this truth the devil did not stand, and the truth is not in him (Jn 8:44). Jesus has come to witness this truth, and every one who belongs to the truth hears His voice (Jn 18:37). This is the statement which moved Pilate to end the examination with the question, "What is truth?" In Pilate Jn represents the world as asking this question, and his Gospel affirms that Jesus alone can answer it. Jesus prays that His disciples may be sanctified in truth, which is the word of the Father (Jn 17:17, 19). Jesus Himself is the way, the truth, and the life (Jn 14:6); He is the only-begotten Son, full of grace and truth (Jn 1:14). The genuine worshipers of the Father will worship Him in spirit* and in truth (Jn 4:23). The spirit which Jesus sends is the spirit of truth who will teach the disciples all truth (Jn 14:17; 15:26; 16:13). This is the truth which Jesus speaks or witnesses (Jn 5:33 +). It is very probably this truth, and not genuinity and sincerity, which is implied when Christians are told to love not in word or speech but in deed and in truth (1 Jn 3:18).

The Johannine idea of truth as described by Bultmann emerges from these passages; truth is the divinely revealed reality of God, manifested in the words and the person of Jesus Christ. This is the ultimate and the supreme truth; in contrast to the truth of God and the truth which is God and Jesus Christ human speech and thought and ambitions and achievements are falsehoods. Without this truth man is ignorant and deceived. Although the sentence does not appear formally as such, the Johannine writings equivalently affirm that God and God alone is truth.

This conception of truth is not exclusively Johannine in the NT; and it is not at all evident that the Johannine phrases represent the last phase in the development. Here as elsewhere, whatever may be said about the probable date of the Johannine writings, there are serious reasons for asking whether the Johannine thought is not a primitive rather than a later stage of NT thought. In the epistles the truth is often the gospel or the word of God. The law contained the embodiment or formulation (Gk *morphōsis*) of knowledge and truth; it is possible that *morphōsis* is here the form as contrasted with the fullness of knowledge and truth in the gospel. Jesus Christ is the truth, and the truth is in Him (Eph 4:21). We can do nothing against the truth, but only for it (2 Co 13:8). The activity of the apostle is the manifestation of the truth (2 Co 4:2). The truth which is believed by the Christian (Gal 5:7) and to which the Christian owes submission (1 Pt 1:22) is the truth revealed and preached. The word of truth in 2 Co 6:7; Col 1:5; Eph 1:13 is evidently the preaching of the gospel. The truth is to be recognized (1 Tm 2:4; 2 Tm 3:7; Heb 10:26). The love of the truth saves (2 Th 2:10–12). The Church* is the pillar and ground of the truth (1 Tm 3:15). Those who teach and believe false doctrines are bereft of the truth (1 Tm 6:5), have swerved from the truth (2 Tm 2:18), oppose the truth (2 Tm 3:8), turn away from the truth (2 Tm 4:4), reject the truth (Tt 1:14). This is probably the sense of the word in Js 3:14; 5:19, which speak of being false to the truth and wandering from the truth.

Against the explicit background of the Johannine writings it seems clear that the same idea of the truth as the revealed divine reality is implicit in these phrases of the epistles. The absence of the word in this sense from the Synoptic Gospels stands in contrast to Jn.

Truth seems to be used in a somewhat singular sense in the NT and more akin to the Gk usage in Rm 1:18, 25. The truth of God here is what is known of God (Rm 1:19). The context indicates that this truth is not the divine reality revealed in the gospel and in Jesus Christ, but the divine reality as perceived by human reason. For Paul the manifestation of God's power and divinity in His works is a kind of revelation*, and men are guilty for not recognizing and accepting it. But this meaning of truth is not characteristic of the Pauline writings; as in Jn, the truth is usually the revelation of God through and in Jesus Christ, and there is no other truth than this. Truth here is not the intellectual perception of reality, but the solid and firm reality of God which is reached through faith and which saves.

Tryphaena (Gk *tryphaena*, "delicately raised"), a Christian woman of Rome, greeted by Paul among the workers for the Lord (Rm 16:12). The name is found in Gk inscriptions.

Tryphon (Gk *tryphōn*, "reveler"), Diodotus, surnamed Tryphon; held the office of "King's Friend" under Alexander* Balas. After Demetrius II had defeated Alexander and become king of Syria, Tryphon brought the son of Alexander, Antiochus VI Dionysius, only a boy, from Arabia where he had been reared, and proclaimed him king, declaring himself regent (145 BC; 1 Mc 11:39 f). Because of quarrels with Demetrius, the Jews led by Jonathan* accepted him, as did many others, and Tryphon expelled Demetrius from Antioch (1 Mc 11:54–56). Demetrius, however, retained possession of enough of the kingdom to mount a war of resistance later. Tryphon had the boy king confirm Jonathan as high priest (1 Mc 11:57 ff). Tryphon proved a bad choice; he was a rapacious and murderous plunderer, and the dissatisfaction of the Jews soon became obvious. Tryphon invaded Palestine, but was not strong enough to carry on a campaign; he invited Jonathan to a conference at Ptolemais* and by treachery murdered his escort and held Jonathan prisoner (1 Mc 12:39–53). Believing that the Jews would be lost without their leader, he again invaded their country; but meeting resistance, he offered to release Jonathan for ransom. The offer was manifestly insincere, but the ransom had to be paid. Tryphon did not break off the invasion; it was halted by a snowstorm, and since Jonathan was of no further use Tryphon had him killed (143 BC; 1 Mc 13:12–24). Tryphon returned to Antioch, assassinated Antiochus VI, and proclaimed himself *autocratōr* of Syria (142 BC; 1 Mc 13:31 f). His tyranny made it possible for the brother of Demetrius II, Antiochus VII, to invade the country and take the title of king. Tryphon, expelled from Antioch (139–138 BC), was besieged in Dor* (1 Mc 15:10–14, 25), escaped to Orthosia and then to Apamea, where he died.

Tryphosa (Gk *tryphōsa,* meaning uncertain), a Christian woman of Rome, greeted by Paul as one of the workers in the Lord (Rm 16:12). The name appears in Gk inscriptions.

Tubal (Hb *tŭbal,* meaning uncertain), a geographical and gentilic name; son of Japheth* (Gn 10:2; 1 Ch 1:5); traded slaves and bronze objects with Tyre (Ezk 27:13); the land of Gog* (Ezk 38:2 f; 39:1); often mentioned with Meshech* (Gn 10:2; 1 Ch 1:5; Ezk 27:13; 32:26; 83:2 f; 39:1); exiled Jews resided there (Is 66:19). Tubal is very probably identical with the *tibarēnoi* of Herodotus, located SE of the Black Sea.

Tubal-cain (Hb *tubal-ḳayin*), one of the three culture heroes, sons of Lamech* (Gn 4:22), the inventor of metallurgy. The assonance of the three names (Jabal, Jubal, Tubal) suggests that Cain* is an addition to the original name; Cain means smith in Hb and some cognate languages. It is possible also, however, that Cain appeared as a smith in other stories and has been conflated with Tubal here; cf KENITES.

Tychicus (Gk *tychikos,* a personal name, possibly "under the patronage of [the goddess] Tyche [fortune]"), an associate of Paul mentioned rather frequently in the NT. He was an Asian, probably of Ephesus, one of the group who met Paul at Troas and accompanied him on his journey to Jerusalem (AA 20:4). He appears as the bearer of Eph (Eph 6:21) and of Col 4:7. 2 Tm 4:12 places him at Ephesus, sent there by Paul (an allusion possibly based on Eph

6:21), and Tt 3:12 refers to an intended mission of Tychicus from Paul to Titus in Crete.

Type, typology. (Gk *typos* means lit "an impression"; then "a copy," "image," "pattern" or "model," "example"). The type and typological interpretation of the Bible is an exposition which presents the persons, institutions or events of the OT as "types" of persons, events or institutions in the NT; the variations in typological interpretation turn precisely on what the interpreter understands by type. The principles of typology were formally set forth by Origen of Alexandria (+ AD 254), although he does not use the word type. In his writings and in many of the writings of the Fathers there is no clear distinction between type and allegory*. The interpretation arose from the problem of meeting the arguments of the Jews, who refused to admit that Christ is the fulfillment of the OT, and from the heresy of Marcion, who denied that the OT was a part of the Christian revelation. These arguments forced Christian interpreters to find some way of "Christianizing" the OT; and Origen distinguished between the letter, the surface and obvious meaning of the text, and the spirit, the Christian meaning which is perceived only by the reader who is guided by the Holy Spirit. When the OT does not obviously speak of Christ, it speaks of Him in type, figure, or allegory which prefigure the Christian event. The principle was especially useful in interpreting those passages of the OT which were nearly unintelligible or which dealt with Israelite laws and institutions which were abandoned in Christianity and at times appeared to be in contradiction with Christian belief and institutions. The search for prefiguration led the Fathers frequently to find typical significance in merely material details; e.g. the red cord hung from the window of the house of Rahab* in Jericho, the sign which saved the house from the slaughter of the people of the city, was a type in its color of the saving blood of Christ. Such interpretations appear now as fanciful, and were regarded as unsound by the exegetes of the school of Antioch (Chrysostom, Theodore of Mopsuestia); but the Alexandrian interpreters accepted a principle drawn from Jewish interpreters that the Bible had all the meaning which one could extract from it. This principle is sound only if it is joined with sound methods of ascertaining the meaning.

The biblical base of typology rests on the two occurrences of the word *typos* in the Pauline writings in the sense of pattern or example. Adam is called a type of Christ (Rm 5:14); and the Israelites are called "types" for the Christian in their adventures in the desert sojourn (Ex-Nm; 1 Co 10:6). Paul finds that the common element in Adam and Christ is the effect of the action of one on many. He finds a type of baptism in the passage of Israel through the sea and a type of the Eucharist in the food and drink which the Israelites were given in the desert. On this basis and on the use of typology in the Church in the patristic period and since, modern interpreters do not question the legitimacy of typological interpretation; they do believe that the definition of typology implicit in the writings of the Fathers is antiquated. Historical and critical interpretation makes it impossible to take many of the typological interpretations of the Fathers seriously.

P. Grelot has pointed out that typology is not exegesis in the proper sense but a theological interpretation of the contents of the Bible. This type of interpretation is older than the NT. In Is 40–55 the restoration of Israel after the exile* is described in terms of the exodus, of which the restoration is in a sense a reenactment. Besides the two passages in which *typos* occurs there are a large number of NT passages in which the events of the NT are described in OT terms. Modern studies have revealed that this is much deeper in the NT than the Fathers realized. The definition of the principles of typology in modern studies is not yet clearly stated; but that typology which rests on merely material and verbal coincidences is rejected. Typology in the genuine sense arises from an inner and organic connection between the OT and the NT; the task of modern biblical theology is to define this connection.

The definition must affirm the unity of OT and NT; the unity is the unity of one God and one mystery of salvation. The resemblances between the persons and the events and institutions of OT and NT exhibit not merely external features in common; they exhibit the personal attributes of God and the nature of God's plan and will to save. Because of this unity typology can be found in each of the great ideas and events of the history of salvation. References to theological topics in this dictionary show how the same idea is developed in OT and NT and how it grows in fullness of meaning. Through these characteristic themes the revelation of God advances from a comparatively primitive stage in Israel to the knowledge of God in Christ. Thus Jesus is presented as a new Moses and a new Israel as well as the Messiah; but the idea of Messiah itself as expressed in His life and person goes beyond the OT conception, which is therefore not a real "prediction" of the

NT reality; cf JESUS CHRIST. The Church also is the new Israel and the new Jerusalem, the people of God and the city of God.

This understanding of typology is developmental rather than prefigurative and predictive; and if anyone wishes to say that in this respect it is not the typology of the Fathers, he is free to raise this objection. But he should remember that the developmental understanding of the connection of OT and NT is as deeply rooted in patristic interpretation as are typology and allegory; and it suits historical and critical interpretation, which must ultimately be rejected if one returns to the principles of Alexandrian interpretation. Typology in modern interpretation accepts the fact that the revelation of the NT is made in the patterns of thought and language of the OT, which it transforms because its contents exceed these patterns. The NT cannot be understood, nor the degree to which it is a transformation, unless the OT is as well understood as is possible. Thus one returns to what seems to be a better statement of the fundamental principle of typology: that God created a people, a culture and a history precisely that this people, culture, and history might become the vehicle of the revelation of Himself which reached its fullness in Jesus Christ.

Tyrannus (Gk *tyrannos*, "absolute sovereign"), a personal name found in inscriptions; the owner of the hall or large room (Gk *scholē*) where Paul taught at Ephesus for two years after he was compelled to withdraw from the synagogue* (AA 19:9). The *scholē* was a large room for academic instruction and discussion (whence Eng *school*); such rooms were attached to the gymnasium* in every Hellenistic city, where possibly this *scholē* was located. It is not clear whether Tyrannus was the teacher (probably of rhetoric) or simply the landlord.

Tyre (Hb *ṣōr*, related to *ṣur*, "the rock"), a city of Phoenicia*, the modern Sur about 50 mi S of Beirut. The modern town is situated on a peninsula connected with the mainland by a narrow neck; the peninsula is the ancient island of Tyre, about a mile long N-S. The neck was created by the causeway built by Alexander (cf below) and the junction with the mainland remained permanent. The ancient island had two bays which served as harbors and ports: the N bay, called the Sidonian harbor, which is still in use, and the S bay called the Egyptian harbor. In ancient times the two harbors were protected by breakwaters, remnants of which can still be seen. The ancient Tyre consisted of two cities, the island city and the mainland city; the mainland city had a distinct name, which appears as Ushu in Akkadian texts and Uzu in Egyptian texts. Capture of the mainland city permitted conquerors to claim the capture of Tyre; the island city resisted sieges by Shalmaneser V, Sennacherib, Esarhaddon, Ashur-bani-pal, and Nebuchadnezzar, and was first taken by Alexander. Alexander's success was due not only to the construction of the causeway, but even more to the control of the sea, which in earlier sieges was controlled by Tyre.

It seems practically certain that Tyre was in existence by 2100 BC. Several convergent traditions represent Tyre as a foundation from Sidon*; but these traditions may refer to the rebuilding of Tyre in the 12th century BC (cf below). Tyre is mentioned in the execration texts of the 12th-13th dynasties of Egypt (19th–18th centuries BC; ANET 477), and in the lists of Palestinian and Syrian towns claimed by Amenhotep III, Seti I, and Ramses III (ANET 243). The Amarna* Letters include letters from Abdi-milki of Tyre. With other coastal cities Tyre was destroyed in the invasion of the Sea Peoples (cf EGYPT; PHILISTINES) in the 12th century; it was rebuilt in the same century by Sidonians. With the 11th century begins the preeminence of Tyre among the Phoenician cities, its control of Mediterranean commerce, and its position as the great port and market of exchange between the Near Eastern mainland and the coasts of the Mediterranean basin. Tyre established colonies in Cyprus, Sicily, Sardinia, N Africa, and Spain; its most famous colony was Carthage, which after the 8th century became more powerful than the mother city. During these centuries Tyre enjoyed close relations with Israel (cf below). The Assyrian advance to the W gradually but surely undermined Tyre's position. The island city, as noted above, was too strong for capture, but Assyrian control of the mainland made Tyre dependent upon Assyria for continued trade. The policy of Tyre was usually to pay tribute to Assyria, which the city could well afford, and continue its trading activities unhampered. Tribute from Tyre is claimed by Ashur-nasir-pal II (883–859), Shalmaneser III (858–824), Adadnirari III (810–783), and Tiglath-pileser III (745–727), who mentions the name of the king as Hiram. Shalmaneser III represents the payment of tribute from Tyre on a sculptured bronze gate (ANEP 356). Shalmaneser V (727–722) and Sargon (721–705) conducted an unsuccessful campaign against Tyre 725–715. Tyre joined the rebellion against Sennacherib (705–681); Sennacherib reduced the mainland city but not the island, and tribute was resumed. Esarhaddon (680–669) also took

the mainland city when tribute was withheld; he relates that Tyre was one of the Phoenician cities which contributed cedar* to his building projects. Ashur-bani-pal (668–630) likewise claims tribute; he also besieged the mainland city and records a negotiated peace. The drain of the Assyrian wars combined with the growth of Tyrian colonies and the rise of Gk sea power to reduce the commercial importance of Tyre after the 8th century; its western colonies were by this time Carthaginian rather than Tyrian. Tyre was besieged unsuccessfully by Nebuchadnezzar* for 14 years (587–574, Ezk 29:18–20); here also Tyre finally paid tribute. The king of Tyre is listed among the courtiers of Nebuchadnezzar (ANET 308). Tyre was a part of the Persian empire. It resisted Alexander, who took it after the siege of 7 months in 332 and destroyed about half of the city. It was rebuilt in 313 and remained in the Seleucid* kingdom until 64 BC, when Pompey erected the Roman province of Syria. But after the conquest of Alexander, Tyre was a minor port. Tyre was included in the kingdom of Herod the Great and received donations from him.

The absence of Tyre from the Table* of Nations (Gn 10) is striking, and suggests that this list must have been composed before Tyre had attained its eminence. It is mentioned as the limit of David's kingdom (2 S 24:7). Close relations with Israel existed during the reigns of David* and Solomon* (cf HIRAM). The influence of Tyre culturally and religiously was incalculable; the civilization of the monarchy borrowed more from Tyre than from all other sources combined. The temple* of Solomon was built by Tyrian craftsmen after Tyrian models. The religious influence of Tyre was most considerable in the reign of Ahab*, whose queen Jezebel* introduced the cult of Melkart, the Baal of Tyre, and promoted it by violence (cf ELIJAH; ELISHA). The female consort of the Baal, Asherah, is mentioned in the Ugaritic* texts. The revolution of Jehu* seems to have broken off these close relations permanently; whether it is connected with this event or not, the prophetic allusions to Tyre are entirely hostile. Am 1:9 threatens Tyre with destruction because of the slave trade; the slave trade and plunder are also charged against Tyre in Jl 4:4. Tyre is one of the kingdoms which must drink the cup of wrath (Je 25:22), and to which Jeremiah issued his warning to submit to Nebuchadnezzar (Je 27:3); the city is threatened in Je 47:4. For reasons which are not entirely clear Tyre is very prominent in Ezk; possibly not all these oracles are original with Ezekiel himself. The city is threatened in Ezk 26 (there is a clear allusion to the two cities of island and mainland in 26:6, 8), the king of Tyre in Ezk 28:1–19. The mythological allusions in Ezk 28 are remarkable, and to some extent reflect Canaanite mythology. Ezk 27 contains the description of Tyre as a ship, and in 27:12–25 is an enumeration of the nations who traded with Tyre and the articles of trade; this is a valuable source for ancient commerce. Is 23 also predicts the downfall of Tyre; the passage calls Tyre a city "whose merchants are princes" (23:8). A gloss in 23:13 identifies the Babylonians and not the Assyrians as the destroyers of Tyre; this can refer only to the mainland city (cf above). The date of Is 23 is uncertain, but it must be earlier than the siege of Tyre by Nebuchadnezzar The threats against Tyre are continued in Zc 9:2 ff, a late work which may allude to the conquest of Alexander. Tyre appears as a city of merchants in the postexilic period; its merchants violated the Sabbath in Jerusalem (Ne 13:16). Cedar for the second temple was obtained from Tyre, as it had been for the first (Ezr 3:7). Ps 45:13 seems to allude to a period of friendly relations with Tyre, while Ps 87:4 includes Tyre among the enemies of Israel. Ps 87:4, like Is 23:17 f, alludes to a future recognition by Tyre of the supremacy of Yahweh. Quinquennial games at Tyre in honor of Heracles are mentioned in 2 Mc 4:18.

Tyre is usually mentioned with Sidon* in the Gospels (Mt 11:21 f; 15:21; Mk 3:8; 7:24 (Tyre alone), 31; Lk 6:17; 10:13 f). It was the mainland port at which Paul arrived on his voyage to Jerusalem; there was already a Christian community in Tyre at this time (AA 21:3–7).

U

Ucal (Hb *'ŭkāl*), a wise man mentioned in Pr 30:1; the explanation of the name is obscure and the name is not otherwise known.

Ugarit. An ancient city of the coast of Syria at the site of the modern Ras Shamra, 8 mi N of Latakia. The city lay near the coast; its harbor and port were situated at the bay of Minet el Beida. The ruins, at that time completely buried, were discovered by chance in 1928; the site was very thoroughly excavated by a French mission in a series of campaigns 1929–1933 and excavations have been continued since 1946. The site was extraordinarily rich and was unique in the number of literary remains which were found. The name of the city appears in the documents of Mari*, Amarna*, and the Hittite* documents of Boghazkoy. The site was occupied in the Neolithic period (4th millennium BC). It was destroyed by fire between the 24th and 22nd centuries BC (a period of widespread destruction which has left traces in most Near Eastern sites). It was allied with Egypt during the 19th century and remained under Egyptian influence or control for several hundred years. Ugarit was ruled by a conquering Hurrian (cf HORITE) aristocracy from the 18th to the 16th centuries. The period of Egyptian domination during the 18th and 19th dynasties was ancient Ugarit's most prosperous period, and the period from which most of its remains and documents come. The city suffered from a disastrous earthquake in 1365 BC, but was rebuilt. It was destroyed in the invasion of the Sea Peoples (cf EGYPT; PHILISTINES) about 1200 BC and was totally and permanently abandoned. The most impressive of its ruins was the great palace-fortress complex of the 15th century (cf PALACE). It was here that the royal archives were found. The temple quarter contained several temples, of which the largest was the temple of Dagon*; here were found the religious and mythological texts. In addition a large number of ordinary dwellings afforded a much clearer knowledge of the living conditions of Canaanites of the Middle and Late Bronze Age.

The literary remains comprised several hundred texts. These were written in cuneiform Akkadian, Egyptian, Canaanite in cuneiform script, and in Canaanite in the Ugaritic alphabetic* script, unknown before the discovery. The royal archives of the palace contained administrative and economic documents; these added to our knowledge of the political and diplomatic history of the period and of trade, commerce, manufacture, and daily life. The large number of lists of personal names show the ethnic composition of the people of Ugarit and their neighbors. More significant for biblical studies were the religious and mythological texts. These were the first literary records of Canaanite religion, alluded to so frequently in the OT. Canaanite gods known only by name in the OT were identified in their persons and functions and in the mythology of Canaan. A number of cultic practices likewise known only by allusion were recognized in the Canaanite cultic pattern, which had considerable influence on Israelite cultic practices. The character of Canaanite myth was perceived to be not merely recitative; the myth was the story of the cosmic event which was reenacted in the accompanying ritual. Superficially the number of parallels between Canaanite and Hb literature was large, and it is now apparent that Hb literary forms, original as they are in many respects, were not created by the Hebrews; they were adopted from the larger culture of which Israel was a sharer. The poetry of Ugarit exhibits a parallelism identical with that of the Bible. A number of literary phrases or mythological allusions are found verbally identical in Ugarit and in the OT: the epithet of "Rider of the Clouds" applied to Baal and to Yahweh (Ps 68:5); the mythological monster Lotan, the OT Leviathan* (Is 27:1 +); the mountain or the recesses of the N the seat of the gods (Ps 48:3; Is 14:13); the blessing with the dew of heaven and the fat of the earth (Gn 27:28, 39); the blood of the grape (Gn 49:11); the curse of no dew and no rain (2 S 1:21); the rite of boiling a kid in milk (Ex 23:19; 34:26).

The religion of Ugarit is regarded as the basic religion of Canaan with local variations which cannot always be sorted out. It is a nature religion whose gods and goddesses are identified with natural forces, in particular the forces of fertility. The mythology represents the cycle of nature — the annual renewal and death of vegetation and the course of the seasons — as a cosmic struggle between divine personal beings. The ritual integrates the worshipers with the cycle and with the divine forces which maintain the cycle. Since the principle of fertility is the principle of reproduction by sexual process, both the myth and the ritual contain candidly obscene elements in which sexual processes are dramatically enacted and recited.

The residence of the gods, as noted above, is the mythological mountain of the N, Sapan (biblical Sapon). The head of the pantheon is El, the progenitor of the gods, often called "El the Bull." He is a venerable figure of not very effective supremacy, and he is not active in the myths, which revolve about his sons and daughters. Of these the greatest is no doubt Aleyan Baal, in whom the Baal* of the OT is recognized. His most frequent titles are "Rider of the Clouds," and "Mighty." He is the male principle of fertility whose annual death and resurrection is the central event of the mythical cycle. As Hadd or Hadad* he is the god of the storm. He is opposed by various adversaries, not very clearly distinguished and probably the result of the fusion of various mythologies; here as throughout the religion of Ugarit the warning of W. F. Albright that the Canaanite gods have a remarkably fluid character which permits one to pass into another should be remembered. One of these adversaries is called Yamm, "Sea," and Nahar, "River"; it is not clear that this adversary is identified with the dragon monster Lotan. This being reflects the ancient widely diffused myth of creation*, which is a victory of the creative deity over the monster of chaos. Another adversary of Baal is Mot, "Death," who represents the forces of death: the underworld, aridity and barrenness; he is possibly identical with Resheph*. Dagan (biblical Dagon*) is a grain god, the father of Baal, doubtless important but not active in the myths. A number of lesser deities or semidivine beings appear: Shahar and Shalem, "the beautiful and gracious gods," Dawn and Sunset, whom El begets by seducing two women; Koshar-wa-Hasis, "Adroit-and Deft," the craftsman; the goddess Nikkal. The principal goddesses are possibly different forms of the same conception, the deified female principle of sex. The consort of El is Asherah*, "the Lady Asherah of the Sea," who is less active than two younger goddesses. Ashtar (Astarte*) is the goddess of sexual passion and vigor and of fecundity and is also the goddess of warfare; the lust of sex and the lust of blood are two violent passions more closely related than one might think. "The Virgin Anath" is the sister and the consort of Baal; as a goddess of sex and war she is hard to distinguish from Astarte. Both these goddesses are represented in Egyptian art of the 19th dynasty; they appear nude standing upon the back of an animal and usually holding a lotus and a serpent.

The mythological poems were found in fragments, and reconstruction of the proper sequence has not been an easy task; furthermore, there are a number of important gaps. The summary below follows the translation of H. L. Ginsberg (ANET 129–155). The largest cycle of poems deals with Baal and Anath. El grants permission for the erection of a palace for Yamm and Nahar. Baal, who has no palace, is delivered into subjection to Yamm and Nahar. In anger Baal attacks first their messengers and then Yamm and Nahar and overcomes them. Several gods petition El to permit the erection of a palace for Baal. Its erection is peculiar; it is constructed of precious materials, a fire is then kindled in the palace which burns for six days, and on the 7th day the fire goes out and the palace stands finished. After a gap Anath appears slaughtering people by the thousands until she wades in blood to her neck, and finally she threatens El himself; the occasion of the conflict is not mentioned nor its issue, but it appears to happen on behalf of Baal. There is a fragmentary allusion to the combat of El with Lotan, and after another gap Baal is now dead, the victim of the attack of Mot. Anath buries him with a great funeral and slays Mot; she treats him like grain, winnowing him and grinding him and sowing him. By rites which are missing Baal is restored to life, as is Mot, and the two engage in combat; the issue of the combat is missing, and in the last part of the poem preserved Baal has intercourse with Anath and is enthroned in his palace. The fluidity mentioned by Albright is apparent; but the nature motif of the god of vegetation slain and rising to defeat his enemies is clear. It is clear also that the survival of the male principle is secured by the aid of the female principle; in the union of these two is the recurrent but never final victory of life over death.

The Legend of Keret. Keret, a favorite of El, loses all his sons. At the behest of El he attacks with his army Pabel, king of Udum, and threatens destruction unless he receives princess Hurriya, daughter of Pabel, as his wife. Hurriya bears him sons. Thereafter Keret falls seriously ill and is cured by a messenger of El. The poem breaks off here; it is very probably a variation of the naturistic myth.

Aqhat and Danel. Danel (cf DANIEL), a devout and pious man, is childless. Through prayer and the intercession of Baal before El he obtains a son, Aqhat. Danel then receives a bow from the gods which he gives to Aqhat. Anath covets the bow and asks Aqhat for it; when he refuses it, she plots its theft, but through the mistake of her helper Aqhat is killed. Danel curses the killer, and his daughter Peghat discovers the killer and avenges the murder. The rest of the story is lost; it is thought that this also is a variation of the vegetation myth in which Aqhat is restored to life for part of the year. The myth is related to the myth of Adonis, who is killed by Ishtar.

Ulai (Hb *'ûlāi,* Akkadian Ulaa), the modern Disful Karun, a stream flowing in a southerly direction E of Susa; the scene of one of the visions of Daniel (Dn 8:2, 16).

Unclean. Cf CLEAN.

Unleavened Bread. Cf MAZZOTH.

Uphaz (Hb *'ûpāz,* "gold"?), a gold bearing land mentioned in Je 10:9; Dn 10:5. The name is otherwise unattested; most critics believe that Ophir* should be read in Je 10:9 and *'ûpāz,* (= "gold") in Dn 10:5.

Ur (Hb *'ûr,* Akkadian *uri,* meaning uncertian), a city of Mesopotamia; the site is the modern Tell Mugheir about 200 mi SSE of Baghdad and a few miles from the mouth of the Euphrates. Ur is the city from which Terah*, the father of Abraham, migrated to Haran* (Gn 11:28, 31; 15:7; Ne 9:7). The city is always given the anachronistic epithet "Ur of the Chaldees" (cf CHALDEANS). The tradition of Ur, however, appears only in the latest of the sources of the Pnt*, and the city is not mentioned in the LXX; a number of modern critics believe that the tradition is a later intrusion. The migration, if the tradition is genuine, was very probably connected with the disturbances at the end of the 3rd Dynasty of Ur (cf below).

The site was identified by Taylor in 1853 and was systematically excavated on a large scale by a joint expedition of the British Museum and the University of Pennsylvania 1922–1934, directed by Sir Leonard Woolley. The site proved extremely rich, and the number and quality of the objects discovered and the size of the building complexes contributed immensely to our knowledge of the history and culture of Mesopotamia. Ur was inhabited at the end of the Neolithic Age (4000–3400 BC). It was a satellite city of Uruk (biblical Erech*) until the 1st Dynasty of Ur, which freed itself from Uruk about 2700 BC. The 1st Dynasty of Ur, beginning about 2700 BC, comprised 5 kings who reigned 177 years; they made Ur the metropolis of Mesopotamia. The city was conquered by Eannatum of Lagash about 2530 BC. After Sargon of Agade Ur remained under Akkadian domination until the Guti invasion largely wrecked Mesopotamian civilization. The rise of Mesopotamia after the Guti invasion was a Sumerian renascence of which Ur was the center.

The 3rd Dynasty of Ur began with Urnammu about 2120 BC, who made the city independent and took the title "king of Sumer and Akkad." The dynasty included 4 other kings; they carried on a series of campaigns against Elam*. The city could not sustain its power and fell about 2015 BC. Ur was destroyed by the Elamites and the 3rd Dynasty was ended. With the rest of the country Ur passed under the Amorite domination of the 1st Dynasty of Babylon*. The city steadily declined in importance thereafter.

The excavations revealed the remains of the ziggurat or step tower (cf BABEL, TOWER OF), substantially built of brick under the 3rd Dynasty and remodeled in the neo-Babylonian period. Woolley concluded that the original tower had three stages, and that the neo-Babylonian reconstruction had 5 or 7 stages. A small temple stood on the summit. There were traces of stairways by which the stages were reached. The ziggurat stood in one corner of the great temple complex built around the court of Nanna, the moon god. Remains of brick temples of the 1st Dynasty were found, but most of the structures were of later construction. The principal temples were built in honor of Nanna and the goddess Nin-gal. Adjacent to the temple enclosure were a large number of tombs of the shaft type; Woolley's identification of these as royal tombs has been seriously questioned by many scholars. The amount of gold and jewelry and the quality of weapons, vessels, and jewels were astonishing. More remarkable was the discovery of mass burials; one double tomb (one chamber above the other) contained 74 skeletons (of which 68 were female). These were so arranged that archaeologists were forced to conclude that the persons died willingly, either by suicide or execution; the method by which death was inflicted has not been identified. No explanation of these mass burials has been generally accepted.

Urbanus (Lt *urbanus,* "city dweller"), a Christian of Rome and a fellow worker of Paul, to whom Paul sends greetings in Rm 16:9. The name appears in several Lt inscriptions.

Uriah (Hb *'ûrîyyāh,* "my light is Yah[weh]"), a personal name. **1.** Uriah the Hittite, one of David's* 30 heroes (2 S 23:39; 1 Ch 11:41), the husband of Bath-sheba*, whom David seduced. Since Uriah was a foreigner, some scholars have suggested that his name is a Hebraization of the Hurrian *ariya.* When Bath-sheba became pregnant, her life and David's reputation were seriously endangered, and David brought Uriah from the campaign against Rabbath Ammon and attempted both by suggestion and by intoxication to get him to sleep with his wife. Uriah's refusal may have been motivated by suspicion; his excuse was his unwillingness to enjoy love while his comrades were still in the field of war, but there are several reasons for thinking that continence was imposed to some extent upon Israelite soldiers during a campaign. David then arranged secretly with Joab that Uriah should be exposed in battle and then abandoned to the enemy (2 S 11). The crime is called by the Deuteronomic historian the one exception to an otherwise blameless life (1 K 15:5). It is alluded to in the genealogy of Jesus (Mt 1:6).

2. Priest in the reign of Ahaz* who constructed the altar* in the temple* according to the Assyrian model which Ahaz saw at Damascus (2 K 16:10–16) and invoked as a witness to a prophecy by Isaiah (Is 8:2). One of his descendants appears as priest in the time of Ezra (Ezr 8:33).

The name is borne by two others in the OT.

Urim and Thummim (Hb '*ûrîm* and *tŭmmîm*, lit "lights" and "integrity;" but these meanings are very doubtful). The P source of the Pnt* describes them as worn in the breastplate of the high priest (Ex 28:30; Lv 8:8). Dt 33:8, an earlier source, assigns them to Levi*. In 1 S 28:6 the Urim are mentioned as one of the means by which Yahweh can be consulted. The Urim (or Urim and Thummim) are an oracular device also in the later books; in Ezr 2:63 (= Ne 7:65) a cultic problem is postponed until there shall be a priest to consult Urim and Thummim. In Nm 27:21 the priest is to inquire by the judgment of Urim.

These passages give no description of Urim and Thummim. The late sources, however, probably preserve early traditions in their implications that Urim and Thummim could be carried in the priestly breastplate. It is probable they were two objects carried in a pocket; the drawing of the object at random was a form of the lot by which questions could be answered in the affirmative or negative. No more information than this could be obtained.

There are a number of references to consultations of Yahweh in the early books of the Bible which were probably conducted through Urim and Thummim, although the names do not appear. The choice by elimination, especially where the elimination proceeds by groups and individuals, was surely conducted by a lot which responded only Yes or No (Jos 7:14; Jgs 1:2; 20:18; 1 S 10:22; 14:37, 41). When David fled from Saul and was joined by the priest Abiathar*, one of the things which Abiathar brought was the ephod*, which seems to have contained the oracular device. David consulted it once in a question of Yes and No (1 S 23:9) and once in a choice by elimination (2 S 2:1).

There are no later references to the device except those mentioned above, and it appears that the priestly oracle fell into disuse after the beginning of the monarchy; the priest wore it only as a decorative part of his vestments. Urim and Thummim were an extremely primitive device for ascertaining the will of the deity; indeed, their use can scarcely be distinguished from divination*. With the growth of religious enlightenment in Israel it seems that it was perceived that such a device had no place in the cult of Yahweh.

Usury. Cf LOAN.

Uz (Hb '*ûṣ*, meaning uncertain), a geographical and gentilic name. In the Table* of Nations Uz appears as the son of Aram (cf ARAMAEANS; Gn 10:23; 1 Ch 1:17) and in Gn 22:21 as the son of Nahor* and the uncle of Aram. Both of these associations connect Uz with NW Mesopotamia. The same clan or place can scarcely be meant in other passages where the association is clearly or implicitly with Edom*. Uz is an Edomite clan (Gn 36:28; 1 Ch 1:42), and it is associated with Edom in Lam 4:21. It is the home of Job not otherwise identified (Jb 1:1), but the homes of the friends of Job are found in or near Edom. Je 25:20 mentions its kings among contemporary rulers but gives no geographical clue. The name is not elsewhere attested.

Uzal (Hb '*ûzāl*, meaning uncertain), in the Table* of Nations an Arabian clan, a son of Joktan* (Gn 10:27; 1 Ch 1:21); by an emendation accepted by modern critics based on the LXX text Uzal is mentioned in Ezk 27:19 as a producer of wine. The name is possibly connected with the pre-Islamic name of the city of Sana in Yemen.

Uzza, Uzzah (Hb '*ŭzzā'*, '*ŭzzāh*, perhaps both variant nicknames from Uzziah*). **1.** Son of Abinadab, who died suddenly when he touched the ark to keep it from falling, called Uzza and Uzzah (2 S 6:3–8; 1 Ch 13:7–11). The story of Uzza may have a historical basis which can scarcely be defined; it has become a story which illustrates the power of the holiness of the ark.

2. Uzza, a clan of Benjamin (1 Ch 8:7).

3. The garden of Uzza in or near Jerusalem, the site of the tombs of Manasseh* and Amon* (2 K 21:18, 26). The site is unknown.

4. Uzza, a clan of temple slaves in the company of Ezra* (Ezr 2:49; Ne 7:51), probably identical with # 5.

5. A Levite clan, a son of Merari* (1 Ch 6:14).

Uzziah (Hb *'uzzīyyāh,* "my strength is Yah[weh]), king of Judah 783–742 BC, son and successor of Amaziah*. He is also called Azariah* (2 K 14:21; 15:1, 6–8). He was installed by the people of Judah (as opposed to the royal family and the court) after the deposition of Amaziah. The name Uzziah is no doubt a throne name given at this unusual accession. His long reign is briefly reported in 2 K 14:21 f; 15:1–7; 2 Ch 26; but the reign coincided with a period of Assyrian weakness and inactivity, and archaeology together with this opportunity suggests that his reign was peaceful and prosperous. He restored the port of Elath*, which indicates that he also resumed the sea trade; and the control of Elath implies control of Edom and the country S of Judah. Before his death he contracted leprosy* and his son Jotham* ruled as regent.

2 Ch 26 adds a number of details: his victories over the Philistines and some desert tribes; the fortification of Jerusalem; his organization and equipment of the army. The explanation of his leprosy in 2 Ch 26 illustrates the Chronicler's theological rewriting of history; the disease is explained as a punishment of sin, which consisted in his arrogation to himself of the priestly prerogative of offering incense.

Tiglath-pileser III of Assyria mentions a victory over Azriau of Lauda (ANET 282–283). In spite of the similarity of the names, the identity of this king with Azariah-Uzziah is contested by many historians. There are chronological difficulties; Tiglath-pileser acceded to the throne in 742, after the date at which Uzziah must have retired from government. It is possible that the kingdom was still conducted in his name. It is difficult to explain the silence of the OT concerning a defeat as massive as that recorded by Tiglath-pileser; but it is not impossible that the Assyrian exaggerated his conquest, and that nothing more serious occurred than a coalition of Uzziah with other kings of the Syrian coast which failed to check the Assyrian advance.

V

Vashti (Hb *waštî*, a personal name, probably Persian, etymology and meaning uncertain), queen of Ahasuerus*. She refused to present herself before his guests at a banquet to display her beauty, and was deposed as queen. She was replaced by Esther* (Est 1–2). The episode and the person can scarcely be historical. The story shows little acquaintance with Persian manners. Herodotus gives the name of Xerxes' queen as Amestris, and shows no knowledge of any episode such as that related in Est 1–2 and no suggestion that she was deposed.

Vau. The 6th letter of the Hb alphabet, with the value *w*.

Veil. The wearing of the veil by women is an ancient and widespread custom with diversified symbolism. It is very frequently a sign of mourning; but this use of the veil appears unrelated to the symbolism of the veil which is found in the Bible and in the ancient Near East. It is apparent from many scenes such as Gn 12:14 f; 24:15 f; 26:7 + that Israelite women did not usually wear the veil. Hence the veiling of Rebekah when she meets Isaac, her prospective husband, for the first time must have a special significance. The substitution of Leah* for Rachel* in the marriage of Jacob (Gn 29: 23–25) is more easily understood if Leah were veiled. The inference is justified that the veil was worn by women at the time of marriage and at the consummation of the marriage; possibly the veil was worn regularly during marital intercourse. The wearing of the veil by Tamar* at her meeting with Judah (Gn 38:14 f) identified her as a prostitute; this likewise suggests that the veil was the costume of sexual intercourse. If this is the correct conclusion concerning Israelite practice, it was at variance with the Middle Assyrian law (ANET 183); this law prescribes that wives, widows, and daughters of gentlemen, and concubines who are accepted as members of the harem must wear the veil. A temple prostitute must wear the veil if she is married; she may not wear the veil if she is unmarried. A professional prostitute may not wear the veil. Since the temple prostitute represented the goddess in cultic fornication, it is difficult to suppose that the veil among the Assyrians identified the woman with Ishtar. The variation in Israelite practice, however, permits one to suppose that this identification was made in

Canaanite practice. The representation of female figures nude except for the veil (ANEP 222, 224) also suggests that the veil was the costume of intercourse; the veil is not so easily perceived on some Palestinian figurines (ANEP 469). The precise manner in which the veil was used in rites of divination cannot be described; but some sexual significance is altogether likely.

Another symbolism of the veil appears in the veil of Moses (Ex 34:29–35). Here the veil is worn when Moses speaks in the name of Yahweh. The explanation given in the text is the preternatural brightness of Moses's countenance after communication with Yahweh. This is probably a later popular explanation of a rite whose meaning was no longer known. It is suggested that the veil masked the face of the prophet so that his own person was concealed when he spoke the word of Yahweh in the person of Yahweh. Paul deduces still another symbolism from the veil of Moses in 2 Co 3:7–18; the veil signifies the obscurity of the knowledge of God given through the law* in contrast with the fullness of the knowledge revealed by Christ.

Paul's precept that women should wear a veil during worship (1 Co 11:5 ff) is obscure; no background in Hellenistic customs similar to the OT and Mesopotamian background mentioned above is known which would explain the precept. Without such information scholars generally believe that Paul here tried to introduce customs of Oriental decorum (as practiced, for example, in his own city of Tarsus*) into Corinth. The custom has been retained in all Christian groups.

Vengeance. Cf AVENGER.

Versions. Cf ENGLISH VERSIONS; SEPTUAGINT; SYRIAC; TARGUM; VULGATE.

Village (Hb *kāpār*, cognate to Arabic *kefr*, is a rare word in the OT). Villages are usually called the "daughters" of a larger "city*," which is by definition a walled community. In ancient as in modern Palestine* the peasants live in small village communities which are surrounded by the ground which they work. These villages could be as large as a city, but lacked the fortified enclosure. They were simply organized in families and clans headed by their elders*. The clustering of families in villages was necessary to secure protection; furthermore, the village was unlikely to have more than one water source, around which the houses were built. In time of war the villagers moved into the nearest fortified city. It seems likely that the majority of the population of ancient Israel dwelt in villages.

Vine. Allusions to viniculture in the Bible indicate that it was as common in ancient times as it is in modern times. The vine was usually planted on the slopes of hills, which were less suitable for the planting

Ancient Egyptian representation of the plucking of grapes.

of cereals. The ground must be cleared of stones and terraced. The vineyard is secured against predatory animals by an enclosing wall or hedge; the ground must be cultivated with a hoe or mattock. A watchtower is built for additional protection. These steps are described in Is 5:2–7. In addition the passage mentions a vat hewn in the rock in the vineyard itself, a feature which has been disclosed by archaeology (cf WINE). The vine was allowed to grow in the manner best suited to the location: either creeping freely on the ground or climbing trees (Ezk 19:11; Lk 13:6). Props were possibly used also but are not mentioned; the practice of cradling vines between trees does not seem to have been in use before Roman times. A vine arbor, however, is shown on an Egyptian painting (ANEP 156). The care of the vine demanded maintenance of the wall or hedge (Pr 24:30 f), weeding (*ibid*), watering (Is 27:3), pruning (Jn 15:2). The vintage harvest was a festive occasion; cf TABERNACLES. Such a festival is mentioned in Shiloh* in Jgs 21:19 ff; it included dancing in the fields by the maidens of the town. The festival was a time of joy and gladness, with songs and shouts of triumph in the vineyards (Is 16:10). The grapes were picked with a cutting hook (Apc 14:18 f); in the Egyptian painting (ANET 156) no cutting tool is depicted.

Metaphorically the vine is Israel (Ps 80: 9 ff; Je 2:21; Ezk 15:1 ff; Ho 10:1); wisdom (BS 24:17); the wife (Ps 128:3); the royal house of Judah (Ezk 19:10 ff). Israel is the vine as the peculiar object of the care of Yahweh, as the vine is the object of the care of its grower, and the plant from which he expects most fruit. The *be'ušîm* of Is 5:2, 4, mentioned only here, usually translated in Eng "wild grapes," is obscure. The word means lit "stinking," and suggests grapes which rot before they are ripe. The vine is also a figure of luxuriant growth (BS 24:17; Ezk 19:11 ff; Ho 10:1), and of fertility (Ps 128:3).

Jesus calls Himself the vine and His disciples the branches (Jn 15:1 ff). The figure is not used in this sense elsewhere; it signifies the close union between Jesus and the disciples, and corresponds in Jn to the figure of the body* in Paul*. The disciples derive their power to bear fruit (which means probably not only the work of the apostolate but also the achievement of Christian life) only by a vital union with Jesus, a sharing of the same life which is the source of power and activity.

Vinegar (Hb *ḥōmeṣ* and Gk *oxos*, designate sour wine or wine vinegar). It was cheaper than ordinary wine and for that reason was preferred by the poor. It was spiced or diluted with water. Taken alone it was not extremely palatable; it set the teeth on edge (Pr 10:26) and was not offered to a friend (Ps 69:22). Like other alcoholic beverages it was forbidden to the Nazirite* (Nm 6:3). It was used as bread dip (Rt 2:14). It was effective for quenching the thirst; many readers of the Gospel, understanding by vinegar in Mt 27:48; Mk 15:36; Lk 23:36; Jn 19:28 f the modern condiment, have thought that the action of the soldier was gratuitous petty cruelty to a dying man; actually the soldier shared with Jesus the drink which the soldiers themselves were drinking.

Virgin. In ancient Semitic religions virginity was one of the two contradictory attributes of the goddess, who united in herself virginity and fecundity. In popular belief the virgin was endowed with great desirability and greater fertility than the woman who had known man. Thus "the virgin" is one of the titles of the goddess Anath of Ugarit. Socially the virgin was the unmarried daughter who was still under the power of her father* (cf FAMILY). In common usage the Hb word *betûlāh* and the Gk word *parthenos* do not always emphasize the physical integrity of the woman, but designate her as unmarried; indeed it appears that she would not in ordinary speech lose this technical designation before marriage, even if she lost her physical integrity. Normally the virgin was married shortly after she reached puberty (cf MARRIAGE). In actual usage the word is often the equivalent of the Eng "girl." Virginity was not a thing to be maintained; when the daughter of Jephthah* and her virgin companions wished some time to bewail her virginity, what they mourned was her death before attaining the fulfillment of her womanhood in marriage (Jgs 11:37 f). In Israel the law discloses the esteem which Israelites placed upon virginity in the bride. The man who seduces a virgin must either marry her or pay the father her bridal price (Ex 22:15); he has damaged her value in the matrimonial market. The high priest must take a virgin bride (Lv 21:14 f). The Israelite may incur the uncleanness of mourning for a virgin sister, because she has no man to mourn her (Lv 21:3). Dt 22:13–21 legislates for a charge laid by a man that his wife was not found a virgin. The parents of the bride (presumably responsible for her virginity) are to prove her virginity by "evidence"; this visible evidence can scarcely be anything but the bloodstained garments of the nuptial couch, retained by the parents as proof of the rupture of the hymen. If the charge is false, the slanderous husband is flogged and fined and forbidden to divorce the wife whom he has slandered; but if there is no evidence of virginity, the guilty woman is stoned.

In poetry "virgin" is often employed as a pathetic address: "virgin daughter of Zion" +. The city or county thus addressed is personified as a young woman; the figure represents her helplessness. It is usually employed in contexts of threat, which liken the city or country to a girl who was defenseless against the lust of conquering soldiers.

Virginity as an ascetic ideal appears in the NT. The explicit recommendations of the ideal are not numerous; Christian tradition has leaned as much upon the life of Jesus Himself and the virgin birth (cf MARY) as it has upon the words of the NT. Jesus Himself recommends virginity only in Mt 19:12; cf EUNUCH. The ideal is proposed explicitly by Paul (1 Co 7:1, 8, 25–38). The recommendation is made in his own name; he has no command of the Lord (1 Co 7:25). The recommendation is based upon "the instant necessity" (1 Co 7:26) which Paul does not define and upon the difficulties of divided loyalty (7:32–34). It is most unlikely that the phrase "instant necessity" refers to the impending eschatological judgment; it is not elsewhere used to describe this judgment. Because of the

"instant necessity" virginity is recommended as part of a more general recommendation that no one should change his state of life. Yet a certain eschatological urgency is implied in 1 Co 7:29–31; and the eschatological urgency of the judgment* dominates Paul's thinking in general, as it does here. The "form of the world" is transitory, and the demands which marriage makes upon one add to the difficulties of serving God (1 Co 7:32–34). This recommendation, Paul is well aware, is meant only for a few; for the vast majority of Christians, marriage is not only lawful but necessary (1 Co 7:2, 9, 38 f).

The meaning of 1 Co 7:36–38 is ambiguous. The man and the virgin of the passage are understood by some to be the virgin and her father, by others to be the virgin and her betrothed, and by others to be the virgin residing in the household of a man who has engaged himself to protect her virginity. In the first hypothesis it is supposed that the virgin has not her own decision concerning marriage, but is given in marriage by her father. The second hypothesis implies a recommendation of virginal espousals or even of virginal marriage. The third hypothesis postulates an early Christian practice which made it possible for young women to leave their father's house (and thus escape being given in marriage) and reside where they could preserve their virginity.

Virginity in men is praised in Apc 14:4 as creating a special bond of union with Jesus.

Vision. Vision as an ecstatic experience and as a medium of revelation occupies a surprisingly small place in the Bible. In the stories of the patriarchs there appears a type of vision which is commonplace: "Yahweh appeared and said . . ." (Gn 12:7; 17:1; 26:2, 24; 35:9; 1 K 3:5; 9:2 +). In these passages the emphasis falls upon the speech and not the vision (cf REVELATION; WORD), and it is evident that the vision is anthropomorphic realism added to the message. With Moses the visionary experience occupies a larger place; the vision of the burning bush (Ex 3) is a prelude to a dialogue, but the vision itself is a revelation of the divine reality (cf FIRE); for fire is the element of deity. The traditions of the visions of Moses are not uniform; on one side there is the consistent tradition that Moses was granted a personal experience of Yahweh which is unique, and which is most easily described as vision, and on the other side is a rationalization of the traditions of Moses according to the basic belief that no man can see Yahweh and live. The first of these is expressed in Nm 12:6–8, which distinguishes the personal familiarity of Yahweh with Moses as with no other man; the second is expressed in Ex 33:18 ff, where Moses is permitted to see the back of Yahweh, but not His face. Behind this somewhat crude realism is an effort to reconcile the traditions of Moses with the invisibility of Yahweh. The tradition of the elders of Israel (Ex 24:10 f) even grants to them a vision of Yahweh; this appears to be parallel to a communication to them of the spirit* (Nm 12:24 ff).

In the prophetic literature the vision is remarkably rare, except in the later prophets. The visions of Amos (Am 7:1, 4, 7 f; 8:1 f) are exceptional in the book; but their originality cannot be questioned, and they show that the vision is not foreign to early prophecy. It should be observed, however, that the object of the vision is not an invisible reality (cf Je 1:11–13); in both Jeremiah and Amos the object of vision is an ordinary object of daily experience which becomes an object of prophetic significance. In the vision of the basket of fruit (Am 8:1 f) and the vision of the almond twig (Je 1:11) the significance comes from a play on words; it is here the word and not the vision which is important. In Is 6 and Ezk 1 are contained inaugural visions; there can be little doubt that the prophetic career of each of the prophets began with some transforming mystical experience, but only in these two books is the experience described as a vision. Both Je 23:16 and Ezk 12:24; 13:6 ff speak of vision as characteristic of false rather than of genuine prophecy. Whether Ezekiel's visions of Jerusalem (Ezk 8–9) should be called visions is questionable; the prophet or his editors have gone to some trouble to describe the experience as a translation of the prophet to Jerusalem. While this creates problems (cf EZEKIEL), it does not suggest clairvoyance of distant events.

It seems altogether probable that a distinction should be drawn between the few visions of the earlier prophetic books and the visions which appear so frequently in the later books, such as Zc 1–6 and Dn 7–8. In the later books the vision has become a purely literary form which permits the prophet to employ rich imagery and symbolism. The distinction is not intended to suggest that there is no literary quality to the visions of the earlier prophets, for there certainly is; they too employ symbolism. But it is employed with a comparatively greater restraint which hints at a genuine and profound experience which is described in veiled language. The prevailing conception of revelation as the word in the earlier prophets suggests very strongly that the visionary element in the prophetic experience remained at a minimum.

The NT exhibits the same type of conventional revelation by appearance and speech mentioned above (AA 9:10; 16:9; 18:9; 23:11; 27:23); the appearance is sometimes the appearance of an angel (Lk 1:11, 22; 2:13). This prominence of the angel as contrasted with the OT is probably an effect of the tendency of contemporary Judaism to introduce angels as mediators of divine revelation and divine activity. In these conventional phrases, as in the OT, it is the message and not the vision which is significant. Otherwise visions are rare in the NT, as they are in the OT. The few which are related at some length, such as the vision of the baptism of Jesus (Mt 3:16; Mk 1:10; Lk 3:21; Jn 1:32) and the vision by which Peter perceives that the law of unclean foods does not oblige Christians (AA 10:10–16) have an obvious symbolic meaning; cf also TRANSFIGURATION. Paul speaks of celestial visions and revelations (2 Co 12:1 ff), but he also places the emphasis upon the word and not upon the vision. The NT here is in sharp contrast to the apocalyptic literature of Judaism, where the vision is the prevailing manner in which the seer describes his revelation. In such visions as the baptism, the transfiguration, and the vision of Peter, it is likely that the visionary form is employed to set forth a revealed truth in concrete symbolic form. The visions of Apc echo the visions of the later prophetic books in form and conception.

Vision in Jn has a peculiar element; it seems that Jn feels compelled to describe the novelty and clarity of the Christian revelation in terms of vision. The OT belief that God is invisible is expressed in the NT also (1 Jn 3:6; 4:12, 20; Jn 1:18; 1 Tm 1:17; 6:16 +); but Jn describes the seeing of Jesus in the flesh as a vision of the Father (Jn 12:44; 14:9). Furthermore, this vision of Jesus, if it is accompanied by faith, confers everlasting life* (Jn 6:40). The seeing of Jesus is an encounter with the Father which commands a decision from him who sees Jesus; the Jews also see Him, but they have seen and hated both Him and the Father (Jn 14:24). The vision of Jesus in the flesh, then, is a "vision" in the sense of a saving vision only if it is a vision of faith; for His fullness is not revealed in the incarnation. Those who believe can expect to see Him ascend where He was before (Jn 6:62). The seeing of the Father in Jesus is parallel to the Johannine emphasis upon hearing the word of the Father spoken by Jesus (Jn 5:24 +).

Against this background the story of

Thomas* can be regarded, it seems, only as an explanation of an implicit problem posed in the early Church; what of those who have not experienced this saving vision? The words addressed to Thomas (Jn 20:29) make it clear that it is the faith of those who saw Jesus and not the sensible vision itself which is the saving experience. Once again the Bible recurs to the word, which lives on in the preaching of the Church; to hear the word generates faith as effectively as the encounter with the incarnate word, which did not save the Jews.

The eschatological vision of God, which has become for many centuries of Christian theology the technical term for realized salvation ("beatific vision") is rare in the NT. The belief in the invisibility of God to man perseveres in the NT, as noticed above. The promise of the vision of God is found in the words of Jesus Himself (Mt 5:8); and against the background of Jewish thought it is remarkable that the promise is uttered without any further refinement or expansion. The explanation is found in the other beatitudes, which contain other parallel phrases to designate realized salvation. It may be more than coincidental that the vision of God which is promised to the peacemakers in Mt 5:8 is the fruit of love in 1 Co 13:12. Paul contrasts the eschatological vision with the dim view seen in a mirror*, and chooses a phrase "face to face" which has echoes in the traditions of Moses (cf above); the paradoxical impact of the phrase must have been evident to Paul. Similarly Paul alludes to the veil* of Moses (2 Co 3:12-18). The veil concealed the glory of the Lord reflected in the countenance of Moses; by a turn of phrase Paul puts the veil on the Jews instead of on Moses, and contrasts them with the Christian who beholds the glory of the Lord with unveiled countenance. In 1 Jn 3:2 the writer says simply that we shall see Him as He is, and that the vision transforms the seer into the likeness of God.

Vow. In modern theology a vow is defined as a deliberate promise to God of a good which is better than its opposite and is possible. A vow is an act of worship affirming the divinity of the being to whom the promise is made. Vows are mentioned frequently in the OT and belong to the oldest Israelite cultic practices: Jacob's vow to worship at Bethel (Gn 28:20), Israel's vow in order to obtain a victory in battle (Nm 21:2), Hannah's* vow in order to obtain a son (1 S 1:11), Absalom's vow of sacrifice (2 S 15:8 f), David's vow to provide a dwelling for the ark* (Ps 132:2). The vow of Jephthah is a special case (Jgs 11:30 ff); it was thoughtlessly made and

executed with intolerable rigidity, but it illustrates the seriousness of the vow in early Israel. The Nazirite* vow is also a special case (Nm 6). Vows could be made to a false god as to the true God (Je 44:25). There are frequent allusions to the duty of fulfilling vows (Dt 23:22 ff; Pss 22:26; 50:14; 56:13; 61:9; 65:2; 66:13; 76:12; Jb 22:27; Ec 5:4 f; Is 19:21; Jon 2:9), and the evasion of a vow is cursed (Mal 1:14). The obligation is so serious that one should not make a rash and inconsiderate vow, nor should one postpone its fulfillment (Pr 20:25; BS 18:22-24). The usual motive of a vow was to strengthen one's petition in prayer; the Gk word *euchē* designates both vow and prayer. The object of the vow could be any object or action within one's power; thus Hannah offered her unborn son. Usually, however, the object of the vow was a sacrifice, and such vows are regulated in the laws of the Pnt concerning sacrifice. The flesh of the votive offering had a lower degree of holiness than the flesh of the thank offering (Lv 7:16 f). In the law of Dt vows, like other sacrifices, are to be fulfilled only at the central sanctuary (Dt 12:6, 11, 17, 26). The victim is to be without blemish (Lv 22:18 ff). Two sets of peculiar regulations suggest that the fulfillment of vows was often more difficult than the votant had suspected. Lv 27:1-8 provides for the commutation of vows for money; and Nm 30 prescribes that the vows of women who are dependent upon a man may be annulled by the father or the husband.

In the NT the vow is mentioned only twice: a vow of Paul (AA 18:18) and the vow of four Christians of Jerusalem (AA 21:23 f). The reference to the shaving of the head suggests that both of these were Nazirite* vows.

Vulgate (Lt *vulgata*, "common" or "usual"), the name given since the 13th century to the Lt version of the Bible made by St Jerome (Eusebius Sophronius Hieronymus). The Vg was the last of a series of Lt versions made in the early Church, now called the Old Lt versions.

Old Lt versions. Gk was the common language of the early Church, as it was the common language of the Roman Empire. Lt versions were not made until there was a sufficient number of Christians in the Lt speaking parts of the empire who knew no Gk to create a demand for Lt versions. The origin of the Old Lt versions is unknown; it is probably that they first arose in the Lt speaking provinces of N Africa, Gaul, or N Italy. A document of 180 indicates the existence of a Lt version in Africa. The Old Lt survives only in extensive fragments, and no

MS is earlier than the 5th century. The variations in the MS tradition are so great that scholars disagree whether there was one Lt version or several. The evidence does not permit a definitive answer to the question; the probability seems to lie in favor of several. If there was only one, it very early divided into two text types, the African and the European. It is probably the European which Augustine mentions under the name of *Itala* (Italian).

No great merit can be attributed to the Old Lt. It was made from the LXX and the translators had little Lt and less Gk. It was slavishly literal and often unintelligible. The translators were not educated men and produced without intending it one of the greatest monuments of vulgar unlettered Lt of the period. The uncritical and careless multiplication of copies soon produced a state of corruption which demanded attention. The mandate of Pope Damasus initiated Jerome on his great work.

In 382 Damasus entrusted Jerome with a revision of the Gospels. This work was done 383–384 and appears in the modern Vg. Jerome by good fortune employed better Gk texts than those which later became common and are the base of the Received Text (cf TEXT). Himself a well educated rhetorician, Jerome's language here as in the rest of his translation combines the popular speech with correct but relaxed Lt prose. Jerome left Rome in 384 after the death of his patron Damasus; possibly this is responsible for his failure to revise the other NT books. The existing Vg NT is indeed a revision, and it has gone under Jerome's name since 450; but indirect allusions in his writings and the Lt text he himself employs make it most unlikely that he revised the epistles. The text of the present Vg of the rest of the NT existed in 406; but its authors and provenance are unknown. At the same time Jerome revised the Pss; his interest, like that of Damasus, was at this time primarily liturgical. This revision was made according to the LXX and had no particular merit.

Jerome went to Palestine from Rome, finally settling in Bethlehem, and there he resumed the study of Hb, which he had begun when he lived as a monk near Antioch for a few years prior to 379. At Caesarea he discovered the famous library of Origen and text of the Hexapla (cf SEPTUAGINT); he was so stirred by the superiority of this text that he revised Jb, 1–2 Ch, Pr, Pss, SS according to the Hexapla. All of this except one book was lost or stolen; and perhaps it was this disaster which led Jerome to the decision to abandon revision of the Old Lt and translate the OT entirely from the Hb.

He had already adopted the view that the books which are not found in Hb are not canonical (cf CANON). The work was done between 390 and 405; at the insistence of friends, he produced a new and somewhat careless version of Jdt and Tb, but left the other deuterocanonical books in the Old Lt, the form in which they still appear in the Vg. The translation was a private enterprise and received no official sanction before the Council of Trent (cf below). It was received with considerable opposition, and won its way only on its evident superiority; after the time of Charlemagne, whose scholar, Alcuin, was a great promoter of the version, it was in undisputed possession in the Lt Church.

It is this acceptance which makes the Vg so important in the history of the Bible and of theology; and it is to be observed that no man before Jerome or among his contemporaries and very few men for many centuries afterwards were so well qualified to do the work. He had learned Hb well, and did not hesitate to ask Jewish opinions on interpretation. Without critical training he had an excellent sense of MSS. He was a skilled Latinist and wrote in a popular and supple but elegant style. His faults were beyond his own possibilities of correction. In accepting the Hb text he uncritically rejected the LXX as a witness. Where the Hb is difficult and he is uncertain, he either becomes so slavishly literal as to be unintelligible or he paraphrases with bold conjectures. Rabbinical exegesis affected his judgment. He annoys frequently by translating proper names instead of transliterating them. He often misunderstood poetry, and his translation fails to render the mood and style of poetry. He is best in the historical books, followed by Jb; in the prophetic books he more frequently falls into literalism; Ec, SS, are less polished; and Tb and Jdt are so free as to be undisciplined.

The problems of the Vg can be said only to have begun with its production. It was multiplied by careless copying, and the recensions of Cassiodorus (570), Alcuin (800), Theodulf (821), Lanfranc (1089), and Stephen Harding (+ 1134) failed to establish a reliable text. The rise of Paris as the center of theological studies was responsible for the Paris text, as it was called; this text was established in general use, but it was far from faithful to the original. The Paris text was printed by Gutenberg at Mainz 1450–1452, and it was copied in subsequent printings, of which there were over 100 before 1500. Dissatisfaction with the text led Sanctes Pagnini and Cajetan to undertake new Lt versions in the early 16th century.

The Council of Trent prescribed a new

and corrected edition of the Vg in 1546. This was begun at Louvain under private auspices; a commission appointed at Rome dragged in its work, and nothing was done until Sixtus V (1585–1590) forced its completion by his personal intervention. His own work, however, was judged unfit for publication; it was revised immediately after his death, and the Clementine Vg (Clement VIII), published 1592–1593, has remained in common use. A commission was appointed by St Pius X in 1907 to prepare a critical edition; the work is carried on by the monks of the Benedictine monastery of St Jerome in Rome.

In the same decree the Council of Trent declared that the Vg is the "authentic" text to be used in the Lt Church. This decree, often misunderstood, was finally interpreted by Pius XII in 1943. The authenticity which the Council intended was juridical, not critical. This means that the Vg is authenticated by its long use in the Church as free of error in faith and morals and is therefore a safe source of Catholic doctrine. Its critical authenticity is not affirmed in detail nor even as a whole except to that degree which makes it a substantially faithful witness of the original text. Its use is prescribed in public ecclesiastical acts; but the original texts have that superior critical authenticity which is theirs by nature, and translations into the vernacular for common use are not only permitted but encouraged in *Divino Afflante Spiritu* (Pius XII, 1943).

W

War. Details of the tactics and techniques of war are given under separate articles on armor* and the various weapons; cf also ARMY; FORTIFICATIONS; HOST; SIEGE. War was a normal state in the ancient world of the Near East; there are few years of record without campaigning. The ancient war was a candid war of conquest or looting. Both of these ends were sanctified by the religious character of war, which was fought on behalf of the gods of the people and under the leadership and protection of the gods. The cruelty and barbarism of ancient war were equally candid; ancient war is shocking only because it involved the primitive means of personal effort, and could not achieve the vast mechanical horrors of modern warfare. Prisoners of war had no rights whatever; the entire population could be enslaved, unless the defeated enemy were regarded as a menace to the victor; if it were, the male population could be exterminated or mutilated. Destruction of conquered towns was a normal act of the victor.

The time for beginning a campaign was the spring (2 S 11:1), which afforded at least six months of movement before the rainy season. War could not be carried on actively in the winter. The trumpet summoned the men to war (Jgs 3:27; 2 S 20:1). The ancient battle was often no more than a melee of confused fighting; indeed, it could be no more than a rush of two shouting groups toward each other until one group yielded to panic; after that the battle was flight and slaughter. The war cry was intended to stimulate courage and to inspire terror (Nm 10:9; 1 S 17:52). The more successful warring nations of the ancient world, however, knew the importance of discipline and mass movement; cf SPEAR. The armies used projectiles (cf BOW; SLING) before they came to close quarters, and preferred to keep close ranks and force their way with pikes rather than permit the attack to degenerate into private quarrels. Ancient sources refer several times to a complete loss of discipline when victory was achieved and the camp or city of the enemy was open to plunder. The infantry column was the backbone of offensive war; the chariot* was useful only on open ground, and mounted men, a relatively late military innovation, annoyed infantry rather than harmed it. The ancient commanders knew the importance of fortified positions which made the attacker come up to them (1 S 14:4). Strategy included such deceptions as the ambush (Jos 8:3 ff), and the division of forces for an attack in the rear (2 S 5:22–25) or a pincer movement (2 S 10:9–14). The defenders preferred strong entrenchments (cf FORTIFICATIONS), but techniques to force them were successful if handled with determination (cf SIEGE). Espionage or scouting of the enemy's strength before attack was used (Nm 13:1 ff; Jos 2:1 ff; 2 S 10:3). It is not clear that ancient Near Eastern warfare included the single combat of champions such as the combats described in Homer, and which were the main events of medieval warfare until the battle of Crécy. Such combats are reported of David* and Goliath* (1 S 17) and at the battle of Joab and Abner at Gibeon (2 S 2:14–16); but here possibly Mycenean practices had been introduced through the Philistines*.

In Israel, at least until the monarchy, war was the holy war. The wars of Israel were the wars of Yahweh (Ex 17:16; Nm 21:14; 1 S 25:28). The war of Israel against Amalek* was the execution of the anger* of Yahweh (1 S 28:18). The technical phrase for initiating war was to "sanctify" war and warriors i.e., to place them in a state of holiness for a holy activity (Je 6:4; Jl 4:9; Mi 3:5). It seems probable that this consecration included abstinence from sexual activity (1 S 21:6; 2 S 11:4). Yahweh was present in the camp (Dt 23:15) through the symbolic presence of the ark* (1 S 4:7; 2 S 11:11); it does not appear that the ark was still carried into war after Solomon*. A motto of Israel was "Yahweh is my standard [of war]" (Ex 17:15). Yahweh Himself is called a warrior (Ex 15:3; Ps 24:8); He fights on behalf of Israel (Ex 14:14; Dt 1:30; 32:41; Jos 10:14, 42; 23:10; 24:12; Jgs 5:23), He sends panic among His enemies (Ex 23:27 f) or hailstones (Jos 10:10 f). The theophany* is often connected with war. Yahweh delivers the enemy into the hand of Israel (Jos 2:24; 6:2, 16; Jgs 3:28; 1 S 23:4; 1 K 20:28). Victory is not achieved by the strength or the numbers or the weapons of Israel, but by the help of Yahweh (Jgs 7:2 ff; 1 S 14:6; 17:45, 47). It is Yahweh who leads the armies of Israel (Jgs 4:14; Dt 20:4; 2 S 5:24) and who gives the victory (Ex 15:14–16; 23:27 f). The enemies of Israel are the enemies of Yahweh (Jgs 5:23, 31). War and battle were preceded by the consultation of Yahweh and sacrifice (1 S 13:9; 14:19). The priestly

Assyrian soldier crossing a river by boat.

Assyrian relief sculpture showing attack by siege ramp and mobile battering ram, and removal of prisoners of war and booty.

ideal of a sacred war is set forth in the midrash* of Nm 31: the fulfillment of all the prescribed ritual and the ban* upon the prisoners and the booty. The law of war of Dt 20 is another and earlier rationalization of war; it is an effort to make it more humane both in its demands upon the combatants and in the treatment of conquered enemies, but it retains the ideal of the ban for Canaanites. The law possibly reflects the change in the character of war from the holy war of the tribal confederacy to the organized political wars of the monarchy. The change in the concept of war was merely a reflection of the change in the state and the change in the composition of the army. The state was now the king*; the army* was still the levy of Israel, the host*, but its nucleus was a corps of professional soldiers who were the personal guard of the king. The frequency of war has filled the Bible with metaphors drawn from war which are too numerous to cite; cf articles on the separate weapons and related subjects.

Modern readers find the Israelite concept of the holy war a primitive type of morality; this it is, but it is doubtfully more primitive than the modern concept of war. Where the Bible relates the thought patterns of early Israel, it does not seem to rise above the thought of its time; and its conception of Yahweh as a warrior was an imperfect apprehension of His reality and activity. The Bible itself presents the elements which permit man to emancipate himself from the idea of war, which is primitive in ancient or modern times. Several passages of the prophets expressly renounce war as a means of the salvation of Israel. War is a judgment of Yahweh on Israel (Is 5:25–30; Je 5:15; Am 5:27; 6:14 +; cf SWORD). The prophets assert that the military means by which Israel thinks to escape judgment are sure to fail; not their security, but their mere survival is assured only by faith* (Is 2:15; 30:15–17; 31:1–3; 22:8–11; Je 21:3–10; 27; 34:1–5; 38:2–4; Ho 8:14; 10:13 f; 14:4; Am 2:15). These passages should not be rationalized out of existence; they declare the futility of war as a means of assuring the only good which war promises, the security of the warring nation. Presumably they would approve war as a national policy only if a nation were not under the judgment of Yahweh.

The NT takes no different position, although it is not explicit; since the early Christian community was not a political society and had no part in determining policy, the question did not arise as it did for the prophets. Soldiers pass through the NT (cf CENTURION) and their calling is not noticed except that John* the Baptist warned them not to abuse their power (Lk 3:14). The saying of Jesus concerning the sword* is relevant (Mt 26:52); Jesus seems to have no expectation of abolishing war, but He affirms that it destroys those who engage in it. Warfare appears frequently in metaphors which describe the Christian life or illustrate the preaching of the gospel; Jesus uses it in parables (Mt 22:7; Lk 11:17; 14:31 f), Paul alludes to military service to illustrate the apostolate (1 Co 9:7) and to the trumpet which summons to war (1 Co 14:8). The apostle should fight the good fight (1 Tm 1:18) as a good soldier of Jesus Christ (2 Tm 2:3 f). The warfare of the Christian is waged against the powers of evil (Eph 6:12).

The eschatological judgment is described as a war both in OT and NT. The messianic king is a victorious warrior (Pss 2; 110:5–7) Ezk 38–39 describes the attack and defeat of Gog*. The theme of the eschatological war is much more prominent in the apocryphal* literature, which is now supplemented by the Qumran* scroll of the war of the sons of light against the sons of darkness. A striking difference between the Qumran conception and the biblical conception is that in the biblical conception the hostile forces are scattered by the power of God or by angelic forces; in Qumran it is a combat between two groups of men. The sons of light, of course, win a miraculously certain and easy victory by the power of God, but they are the active combatants. In the NT the imagery of the apocalyptic war appears only in Apc 12:7, the war between the angels led by Michael and the dragon, and Apc 20:9, where the forces of the dragon are annihilated in their final attack by the power of God.

Water. The average rainfall* of Palestine is sufficient to support agriculture; but the country lacks rivers, perennial streams, and lakes and is more arid than Europe or most of North America. Furthermore, the steppes and the desert* lie close to Palestine proper. Hence the Bible exhibits an awareness of the meaning of water for life and of the dire consequences which follow when it falls. The imagery of the Bible is rich in symbols drawn from water.

Water was secured from springs and wells* or by preserving rain water in cisterns*. The Bible mentions a number of pools connected with towns: Gibeon* (2 S 2:13), Hebron* (2 S 4:12), Samaria* (1 K 22:38), Jerusalem (Is 7:3; 22:9, 11; 36:2; Ne 2:14; Jn 5:2, 4; 9:7, 11; cf GIHON). Archaeology has uncovered a number of complex hydraulic installations for channeling and storing water both from springs or wells and from rainfall. Water was sold on the streets of ancient Jerusalem (Is 55:1), as it is in modern Near Eastern cities. Water rights were often the occasion of bickering (cf WELL), but they could be obtained by payment (Nm 20:19). Rare as water might be, courtesy demanded that a drink be offered to the thirsty traveler, even if it had to be drawn from a deep well (Gn 24:17; Jb 22:7; Is 32:6; Mt 10:42; 25:42; Mk 9:41; Lk 7:44; Jn 4:7). The refreshing quality of water is not unworthy of the Israelite poet (Pss 23:2; 42:2; Pr 25:25). "Living water," which is water from a well or spring or stream, is preferred to the water of pools and cisterns. The drawing of water is the work of women (Gn 24:11; 1 S 9:11; Jn 4:7), and this can still be seen in the towns and villages of the Near East; it is this which gives point to Jesus' direction that His disciples should look for a man carrying a vessel of water (Mt 14:13; Lk 22:10).

Water is used in religious ablutions (cf CLEAN); it is the element of the basic Christian initiation of baptism*, in which almost its entire symbolism appears (cf below). Water has a cosmic significance; H. G. May has shown that "many waters" or "mighty waters" (mayim rabbim), which is a threat of destruction, signifies not merely a flood or torrent but the waters of the primeval chaos (cf CREATION). Water is the primordial element (Gn 1:2); it is not enumerated among the works of creation, but is presupposed. In the Paradise story the growth of vegetation begins with the flow of the four rivers of Paradise (Gn 2:10 ff). It may be asked whether the story of the drawing of Moses from the water (Ex 2:3–10) may not be composed to present in him the symbolic saving which he later brings to Israel. The might of Yahweh in saving Israel appears in His power over water; He corrupts water, the life of Egypt (Ex 7:20), and divides the water through which Israel survives and in which the Egyptians perish (Ex 14:21–30). In the passage through the desert He produces water for Israel (Ex 15:23–25; 17:6; Nm 20:8–11).

In biblical imagery water is life and salvation. The saving acts of Yahweh for Israel are compared to the production of water, especially to the production of water in the desert (Is 35:7; 41:18; 43:19; 44:3). The Israelite who feels separated from Yahweh is like an arid desert (Pss 63:2; 143:6). Yahweh is a source of living water (Je 2:13; 17:13); Jesus applies the same figure to Himself, promising to give living water which is eternal life (Jn 4:10, 13 f; 7:37–39). The care and providence of Yahweh are expressed as His leading one beside still waters (Ps 23:2). The righteous is like a tree planted beside living water, which does not fail (Ps 1:3; Je 17:8). The mouth of the righteous (Pr 10:11) or the teaching of the wise (Pr 13:14) or wisdom is a spring of life (Pr 16:22). The righteous king is a blessing to his people like streams of water in an arid land (Is 32:2). The pleasures of love are compared to refreshing water in the admonition to the husband to drink water from his own cistern (Pr 5:15).

The eschatological Jerusalem cannot be conceived without its stream of living water. Ezk 47:1–12 sees a spring which issues from the temple and becomes a mighty river on its passage to the Jordan valley, regenerating the land with vitality. This image is resumed in Apc 22:1 in the river of the water of life flowing from beneath the throne in the new Jerusalem. In Apc 7:17; 21:6 the salvation of the righteous is the reception of water from the fountain of life.

The imagery of water appears in other aspects; it is the symbol of the perishable. Job will forget his misery like waters that have passed (Jb 11:6). Human beings are mortal, they are like water spilt on the ground (2 S 14:14). The Psalmist prays that the wicked will vanish like water that runs off (Ps 58:8). What H. G. May has explained as cosmic symbolism appears in water as a destructive threat. This symbolism is certainly present in the conception of the sea* and the story of the deluge*. The thunder of many peoples (Is 17:12), the storm of waters which overwhelm Israel (Is 28:2, 17) are the invasion of enemies. Assyria overflows Israel like the mighty river (Is 8:7 ff). Waters rise from the N like a flood (Je 47:2). The prophets here recur to the symbolism of the chaotic sea to describe the coming disaster; the "mighty waters" destroy the existing order. The same image is applied even to personal distress in the Pss (32:6; 69:3, 16), and deliverance is granted when Yahweh draws the petitioner from "mighty waters." These two principal themes are merged in baptism; immersion in water is the death of the neophyte to sin and self, but the water is at the same time the water of eternal life.

Wave Offering. Cf SACRIFICE.

Way (Hb *derek*, Gk *hodos*) is used in the Bible not only in its literal sense but frequently in several metaphorical and theological senses.

1. *OT.* Way means simply the life of man or a part of it: human experience, fortune, or misfortune. This is the way which Yahweh sees (Jb 31:4) and knows (Ps 139:3; Jb 23:10); in such contexts to know

one's way is to regard it with favor, to take care of one (cf KNOWLEDGE). Man does not understand his way (Pr 20:24), the meaning of his life and the term to which the way leads. Afflicted Israel says that its way is hidden from Yahweh, He does not observe its misfortunes (Is 40:27). The righteous commits his way to Yahweh (Ps 37:5), who preserves the way of His saints (Pr 2:8) and sends His angels to guard the righteous in his ways (Ps 91:11). The way of all the earth is death (1 K 2:2). Man's ignorance of his way may lead to a way which he thinks right but which ends in death (Pr 14:12). The house of the harlot is the way to Sheol (Pr 7:27).

Very frequently the way of a man is ethical; it designates his manner of life and conduct. Thus one must eat the fruit of one's way (Pr 1:31) or have one's way returned upon one's head (1 K 8:32). Moses instructs the Israelites in the way in which they should walk (Ex 18:20). Punishment comes because of one's ways and deeds (Je 4:18). No one declares the way of the wicked to his face (Jb 21:31). The moral corruption of mankind is described as "all flesh had corrupted its way" (Gn 6:12). "The way of Jeroboam" (1 K 15:34 +) is the cultic deviation of sanctuaries outside of Jerusalem. "One heart and one way" (Je 32:39; the textual evidence also suggests "a new heart and a new way") signifies the unity of disposition and conduct which will be found in the restored Judah. The instructions of the wise are a way of life (Pr 6:23). The way of peace* is conduct which assures peace (Is 59:8). One's way may be good, upright, righteous, perfect, or evil, obstinate, lying, crooked (very common, especially in wisdom literature).

The way of man in particular is the way shown him by the will of Yahweh; this sense also is frequent, and way sometimes does not appear to differ from commandment. This is the way(s) which Yahweh has commanded (Dt 5:23; Ex 32:8; Je 7:23). The righteous man keeps the ways of Yahweh (2 S 22:22). These are the ways which please Yahweh (Pr 16:7). The will of Yahweh is the good and right way in which Samuel instructs the Israelites (1 S 12:23). The will of Yahweh is the true way from which the wicked wander (WS 5:6). It is the way of Yahweh (Je 5:4 f), the way of life (Ps 16:11). The way of wisdom (Jb 28:13, 23) appears to be a pregnant use of the word; the way of wisdom is the way where wisdom can be found; but it is found only with God, whom one must attain to be wise.

The way of the wicked is both their wicked manner of life and the direction toward perdition in which the way tends. Jeremiah wonders why the way of the wicked prospers (Je 12:1). But the wicked are judged according to their ways (Ezk 7:8); God visits their ways upon them (Ho 4:9) and repays men according to their ways (Je 17:10). The wicked will be forced to remember their ways (Ezk 16:61). Yahweh desires that the wicked should turn from his way and live (Ezk 18:23; 33:11).

The ways of God are not merely the ways of good conduct but likewise they are the ways which lead to salvation. Yahweh leads Israel in the way in which it should go (Ps 25:9; Is 2:3; 48:17) the good way (1 K 8:36). This is the way of wisdom which the wise man teaches (Pr 4:11), the ways which Israel pretends to desire to know (Is 58:2).

In another sense the ways of God are His manners of conduct, His plans and His deeds. The ways of Yahweh are love* and fidelity (Ps 25:10). They are right and the righteous walk in them (Ho 14:10); this line, probably from a glossator, does not mean by ways the will of God concerning conduct, but His actions in history, in which the righteous walk by understanding and accepting them. The deeds of Yahweh in history are the ways which the Israelites call crooked (Ezk 33:17); it is not the ways of Yahweh that are crooked, but the actions of the Israelites. The plans and deeds of Yahweh are His thoughts and ways which are not the thoughts and ways of men; they are as far above the ways of men as the heavens are above the earth (Is 55:8 f).

It is doubtful that the explicit teaching of "the two ways" which appears in Christian literature after the apostolic age appears in the OT; at best it is not prominent. Yahweh knows the way of the righteous, but the way of the wicked perishes (Ps 1:6). The way of the righteous is light, and the way of the wicked is darkness (Pr 4:18 f). The way here is both the manner of life and the term to which it leads. In the Manual of Discipline of Qumran* the doctrine of the two ways which belong to the two spirits of light and darkness appears in a form which is quite similar to its form in the postapostolic literature. The way of life and the way of death (Je 21:8) do not refer to way in the general sense, but to the decision to be made in a particular situation, the choice of surrender to the Babylonians or resistance.

2. *NT*. Jesus alludes to the narrow gate and the confined way which lead to life and the broad gate and wide way which lead to perdition (Mt 7:13 f); the parallel in Lk 13:23 f mentions only two doors and is given in response to a question concerning

the number of the saved. Some commentators believe that the context of Mt, or rather its lack of context, represents the original sense of the saying more fully. The narrow gate and way are not the general path to salvation, but represent the invitation to discipleship, an invitation which is accepted by few.

Jesus Himself appears as the way in two passages. In Heb 9:8; 10:19 f He represents a way into the sanctuary which was not available through the Levitical priesthood. Jesus is here the way as the priest who offers the effective redeeming sacrifice. In Jn 14:4–6, in answer to a question about where He is going and the way in which He is going, Jesus says He is the Way, the Truth, and the Life. In spite of the immediately preceding context, the saying is not purely eschatological. Jesus is the Way by being the Truth and the Life, a source of revelation and regeneration. It is His sonship which establishes Him as mediator. He is the Way soteriologically by His saving death and ecclesially by His constitution of the Church which becomes concretely identified with Him as the Way. Possibly John intends an antithesis to the Law*, regarded by the Jews as exclusively the Way of God (cf above).

Way means a way of life and conduct, but specifically the Christian way of life or some aspect of it. Love is the excellent way which Paul shows the Corinthians (1 Co 12:31). The way of truth which is reviled (2 Pt 2:2) and the way of righteousness which it would be better for apostates not to have known (2 Pt 2:21) may be the Christian ideal of conduct, but it more probably designates the gospel, Christian faith as a whole. The way is also the unstable or wandering way of the sinner (Js 1:8; 5:20). The way of God is the way commanded by God (Mt 22:16; Mk 12:14; Lk 20:21); the phrase is put in the mouth of the Jews and has the OT sense. Paul speaks of his ways in Christ Jesus which he teaches in every church (1 Co 4:17); this must signify his gospel, with particular reference to instructions in Christian conduct. The way of the Lord (AA 18:25) or the way of God (AA 18:26) is the belief in which converts are instructed; the way of salvation is proclaimed by the apostles (AA 16:17).

Christianity is designated simply as "the Way" (AA 9:2; 19:9, 23; 22:4; 24:14, 22). This usage does not appear elsewhere and has no known antecedents. It must reflect a particular and probably local designation. It appears to be an abbreviation of "the Way of God" or "the Way of the Lord." It exhibits the early Christian conception of their belief as more than a set of propositions which could be taught or a code of moral principles; it was the revealed will of God operating in history through Jesus Christ, giving direction to human life. Christianity is more than a faith; it is a way of life.

Wealth. 1. *OT*. In the older books of the OT no definite attitude toward wealth appears; it is simply a gift of Yahweh (Gn 31:5–9; Dt 28:3–7). In early Israel wealth was not a social or moral problem; no one acquired great wealth and a minority group of the wealthy in opposition to the mass of the poor had not yet arisen. Even after the social division of rich and poor* which developed under the monarchy the criticism of the prophets dealt more with the protection of the poor than with the rich as a distinct class. There is, however, a steady refrain of charges against the rich that they oppress the poor, exact debts without mercy, and drive the poor into enslavement (Is 10:1 f; 2:25–31; Ezk 22:25–29; Am 2:6 f; 3:10; 5:11 f; Mi 2:1 ff), which carries the implication that no one could acquire and retain great wealth except by dishonest means. Both Isaiah (3:16; 4:1) and Amos (5:8–10) speak of the wives of the wealthy who by their demands for luxury impel their husbands to acquire wealth by dishonest actions. These texts indicate the existence of a small class of wealthy who were greedy and rapacious and who were utterly unscrupulous in their business. The existence of this class was a weakness of the social fabric of Israel and a solvent of the ancient unity of clan and tribe derived from the nomadic* past of early Israel. The class arose under the monarchy and under its patronage, and very probably had its origin in the officers of the court, whose position gave them opportunities to amass wealth.

The wisdom* literature exhibits an ambivalent attitude toward wealth. At times wealth is praised and admired. It is the fruit of wisdom (Pr 24:3 f; 3:16) or of diligence (Pr 10:4; 11:16); it is the reward of humility and the fear of Yahweh (Pr 10:22). The drunkard will never become rich (BS 19:1). The blessing of Yahweh brings wealth (Pr 10:22). The difference between wealth and poverty can be viewed in a detached manner; the poor man is hated, while the rich has many friends (Pr 14:20). The rich man's wealth is his fortress, the poor man's poverty is his ruin (Pr 10:15; 18:11). More frequently wealth is viewed unfavorably. BS draws a number of antitheses between the rich and the poor which are not laudatory of the rich. The rich man does wrong and adds a threat while the poor must apologize when he is wronged (BS 13:3). When the rich man falls, there are many to help him; when he speaks, all are silent (BS 13:22 f). When the rich man rests from his toil to amass wealth he enjoys luxury; if the poor man rests, he becomes destitute (BS 31:3). Wealth and poverty are not adequate criteria of a man's worth; the rich man is honored for his wealth, the poor for his knowledge (BS 10:30). The rich is wise in his own eyes, and an intelligent poor man tests him (Pr 28:11). Who trusts in his riches will fail (Pr 11:28). The honest poor man is better than the dishonest rich man (Pr 28:6). Wealth is good without sin, and poverty is called evil by the impious (BS 13:24). The covetousness of gold is a spiritual danger which leads to many sins (BS 31:5–10). The man who makes wealth his stronghold and trusts not in God will fail (Ps 52:9). Wealth is not the supreme good; health (BS 30:14 ff) or a good name (Pr 22:1) or wisdom (WS 7:8) is better than riches. A man is careful to amass wealth and then dies and leaves it to others (BS 11:18 f). Wealth does not satisfy; it breeds anxiety, can damage its possessor, and may ultimately be lost leaving the man with nothing for his toil (Ec 5:10–20). Wealth deprives its owner of sleep (BS 31:1 f).

These passages of the wisdom literature are instances of "the piety of the poor" (cf POOR). To some extent they reflect the effort of the sages to find contentment in poverty by reflections on the disadvantages of wealth, its temptations, and the moral obliquity which in the ancient world seemed a prerequisite for the acquisition of wealth. The sayings of the wise are echoed in some passages of the NT.

2. *NT.* The words of Jesus Himself are more frequently directed to a positive approach toward poverty than to a negative criticism of wealth (cf POOR). The classic text for wealth and poverty is the parable of the rich man who rejected the invitation of Jesus to follow Him (Mt 19:16–30); Mk 10:17–31; Lk 18:18–30). The episode elicits the sayings about the difficulty which the rich have in entering the kingdom of heaven, compared to the passage of a camel through the eye of a needle. While this saying contains hyperbole, it can scarcely mean anything but moral impossibility; Jesus makes wealth an insuperable obstacle to salvation, and offers no solution of the difficulty except that one should give away one's riches. Attempts to rationalize this saying into something else have no success. Jesus also draws a comparison between the contributions of the rich to the temple and the contribution of an impoverished widow (Mk 12:41–44; Lk 21:1–4). The gift which does not actually deprive the giver of something

but comes from his superfluity is of no account. A striking contrast between the extremes of wealth and poverty is presented in the parable of Dives and Lazarus (Lk 16:19–31); the sin of Dives consists in no more than living in luxury while dire poverty is near. The passages in which Jesus speaks of wealth are few, but they do not lack strength of language.

Wealth is mentioned even less frequently in the epistles. Avarice leads men into all temptations and sins; it is the root of all evil (1 Tm 6:9 f). James, in this as in other things the heir of OT wisdom, has the most vigorous polemic against wealth. The rich man ought to rejoice when he is impoverished because of the fate of the rich (Js 1:10 f). The rich who humiliate the poor forget that the poor are God's chosen (Js 2:1–9). A dreadful vengeance will overtake the rich who have deprived the poor of their wages and who live in luxury (Js 5:1–6).

Weaving. The materials used in ancient weaving were linen, wool, or goat's hair. In Israel weaving was women's work (1 S 2:19; Pr 31:17, 24) and was a part of the domestic chores; with economic growth in

Women weaving, an Egyptian tomb painting.

Israel, as in other ancient peoples, guilds of professional weavers appeared (1 Ch 4:21). The loom most commonly used was a horizontal loom similar to the type which is still used in domestic weaving in the Near East and is represented in Egyptian art (ANEP 142, 143). The loom was formed by two beams, one of which was placed behind two pegs driven into the ground which held it when pulled taut; the other beam was attached by a cord at each of its ends to a single peg which permitted the warp to be drawn taut. The warp was stretched between these two beams; its threads were separated by movable rods so that the shuttle passed above and below alternate threads. The twisting of several threads together and the more complex alternation of threads in the warp allowed greater strength and variety of fabric. The superior work of professional weavers was imported from abroad: Babylonia (Jos 7:21), Egypt (Ezk 27:7), Phoenicia (Ezk 27:16). The vertical frame loom was also in use; loom weights are found frequently in excavation of Palestinian sites.

The industry is not often mentioned in the Bible. The shaft of Goliath's spear was like a weaver's beam (1 S 17:7); the comparison refers to thickness. Jb 7:6 compares the movement of the days of Job's life to the movements of the shuttle; the comparison refers less to the swiftness of the passage of time than to the monotony of the shuttle movement, which makes no progress. Since the ancient loom could produce a bolt of cloth no more than a few feet wide and a few yards long, the mantle of Jesus woven without seam in one piece (Jn 19:23 f) must have been a remarkable piece of work.

Wedding. Cf MARRIAGE.

Week. Cf SABBATH; SEVEN.

Weeks, Feast of. Cf PENTECOST.

Weights and Measures. The weights and measures mentioned in the Bible are not entirely certain either in their relation to each other or in their conversion into modern standards. There was no official standard such as we know in modern times, although references to "the royal weight" (2 S 14:26) in Israel* and in other countries indicate that the palace weights and measures were the standard by which revenue was measured; no doubt this was the standard generally followed.

Weight: The Hb weights appear to have followed the Babylonian system.

50 shekels = 1 mina; 60 minas = 1 talent.

The Babylonian talent is estimated at 133⅓ lbs (60.6 kg). This cannot certainly be extended to Hb weights. A number of Mesopotamian weights have been found (ANEP 117–121); weights found in Palestinian excavations average 11.4–11.5 gm per shekel.

Measures of surface: the measures of surface are calculated upon the arm and hand: 4 fingers (Hb 'esba') = 1 palm (Hb ṭōpaḥ); 3 palms = 1 span (Hb zeret); 2 spans = 1 cubit (Hb 'ammāh). The cubit is the length of the arm from the fingertips to the elbow, about 18 in (45.8–52.5 cm). For larger distances the unit of measures was the reed, about 10½ ft. Only in the Gk

period did Gk measures come into use. The stadion = 607 ft (192 m). The Roman mile (Mt 5:41) = 1620 yards. Area was measured by the yoke, the area which a team of oxen could plow in one day. In Mesopotamia this was ⅔ acre, in Rome ⅝ acre.

Measures of volume: these combine a duodecimal system (Babylonian in origin) with a decimal system. 1 ḥōmer = 180 kab or 720 log; 1 lōg = 0.89 pt (0.54 lt), 1 kab = 1:78 qts (2.3 lt). 1 ḥōmer (10 bushels) = 2 letek; 1 letek = 5 'êpāh or bat; 1 'êpāh = 1 bushel = 39:3 lt = 3 seʾāh; 1 seʾāh = 2.67 gals = 6.6 lt = 2 hin; 1 ḥōmer = 100 'ōmer ('issārôn). The ḥōmer is lit an ass, the load which an ass can carry.

A number of biblical references to dishonest weights and measures as an abomination to Yahweh (Pr 11:1; 20:10, 23; Mi 6:11) and to Yahweh's concern for honest weights and measures (Pr 16:11) show that the variation in Palestinian weights is not due merely to carelessness; they also suggest that some standard, no doubt the royal weight, was regarded as legal. The Israelite laws prescribe honest weights and measures with a serious tone (Dt 25:13–16; Lv 19:36). Allusions show that the merchant carried his own weights with him in his bag of merchandise.

Well. The water table of Palestine permits the digging of wells in most parts of the country. Exploration of ancient sites shows that their wells were carefully built and solidly walled. In some instances, as the famous well of Jacob near Shechem*, the depth exceeds 100 ft. When the well served a walled city, the mouth was sometimes closed and concealed with stones and the well was entered by a subterranean passage cut in the rock. Where the terrain permitted the water was diverted through subterranean tunnels so that it flowed into the city. Pools also were constructed where possible for the more convenient watering of animals; where there was no pool, animals were watered by the cumbersome and slow use of the water jar (Gn 24:11, 20). Water was usually drawn from the well by the most primitive device, the vessel attached to a rope. The well was covered by a large slab; the slab of Gn 29:3, which could be moved only when a number of men were present, may have been installed in order to insure that no shepherd could water his flocks ahead of the others. The successful digging of a well was an occasion of rejoicing (Gn 26:33) which at least once was celebrated in song (Nm 21:17 f); the song suggests that the digging of the well was a ceremonial process in which each of the heads of the various clans took a ceremonial part, perhaps as a token of his part ownership of the well. The ownership of wells was an object of dispute (Gn 26:19). To stop up a well was an act of personal hostility (Gn 26:15) or of war (2 K 3:19). The well was the scene of disputes (Ex 2:16); but as the place where the community gathered, it was also a place where music was heard (Jgs 5:11) and was normally the scene of lively social intercourse.

Whale. The whale which appears in many older Eng versions is an incorrect translation; the *tannin* is a large fish of uncertain species, perhaps signifying in some passages the mythological sea* monster.

Wheat. Wheat was cultivated in Palestine in the Bronze Age and has always been the principal cereal product of the country. It can be grown in almost every part of the country, with particular success in the coastal plain, the plain of Esdraelon*, the plateau of E Palestine*, and the valleys of the central mountain range. The wheat is planted after the autumn rains have softened the ground sufficiently for plowing and is harvested in the spring. Cf BREAD; MILL; THRESHING. The grain was also eaten raw, prepared by rubbing it in the hands (Dt 23:26; Mt 12:1 f; Mk 2:23; Lk 6:1). It could be made more palatable by parching (Lv 23:14) or roasting (Rt 2:14); parched grain was easily provided in an emergency (1 S 17:17; 25:18; 2 S 17:28). "The fat of the wheat" (Dt 32:14; Ps 81:17) is the best and finest of the grain. The grain of wheat is used by Jesus as a figure of His own death from which life* comes (Jn 12:24) and by Paul of the body (1 Co 15:36–44), which cannot be transformed into the new life of the resurrection* unless, like the grain, it first dies. Both these figures use popular speech, for the grain which is sown does not die; but it is buried, and this permits the figure.

Whole-burnt Offering. Cf SACRIFICE.

Widow. In ancient society the independent woman did not exist; she was a member of a family and dependent either upon her father or upon her husband. The position of a widow could therefore be difficult. She wore clothing to designate her condition (Gn 38:14, 19). She could not inherit from her husband, and in the early period she was a part of the inheritance of the eldest son. If she was childless she returned to her father's house (Gn 38:11; Lv 22:13; Rt 1:8). She could marry again (1 Co 7:8), although priests were not allowed to marry widows unless they were widows of priests

(Lv 21:14). The woman who had no man to defend her rights was an obvious victim for the exactions of a creditor (2 K 4:1 ff; Jb 24:3) and for any type of oppression (Jb 22:9; 24:21; Ezk 22:7); the "murder" of widows in Ps 94:6 may be a hyperbole, except that exactions and dishonest oppression could reduce the widow to starvation. The widow had no defender at law and was therefore at the mercy of dishonest judges (Is 1:23; 10:2; 2 S 14:4 ff; Lk 18:3). Israelite law extended protection to them by prohibiting injustice in the cases of widows (Ex 22:22; Dt 24:17), including a curse upon injustice (Dt 27:19); but the allusions elsewhere in the OT show that such a general law with no practical implementation was a lifeless ideal. The prophets include the oppression of widows in the crimes with which they charge the Israelites (Is 1:17; Je 7:6; Zc 7:10). Je 22:3 warns the king himself against this crime, and Mal 3:5 makes Yahweh the protector of widows. Jesus spoke of those who prayed at great length while they devoured the houses of widows (Mk 12:40; Lk 20:47). Among Job's boasts is his charity to the widow (Jb 29:13; 31:16). Widows were granted a share of the sacrificial festivals (Dt 16:11, 14) and the tithes* (Dt 14:28 f; 26:12) and were permitted to glean in the fields after the harvest (Dt 24:19–21), and the owner was not to reap so thoroughly that he left nothing for them. The story of Naomi* illustrates the plight of a widow who lost all her male kin.

The primitive Church made the practical care of its widows a concern. It provided food for them (AA 6:1) and Dorcas* is praised because she made clothing for widows (AA 9:39). Care of widows and orphans is one of the two elements of genuine religion mentioned in Js 1:27. It is indicated in 1 Tm 5:3–16 that the care of widows had become well organized. There was an approved list of widows who might receive care from the Church. They had to be 60 years of age and childless; if they had relatives, their care fell upon the relatives and the Church would not substitute. The accepted widow must have established a reputation of good life and was expected to devote herself entirely to prayer and good works. The animus of the writer against younger widows is severe and it is hard to see how he expected them to be supported, if they were in straits, except by a second marriage.

Wife. Cf FAMILY; MARRIAGE.

Wilderness. Cf DESERT.

Wind. Cf PALESTINE (Climate); SPIRIT.

Window. The ordinary house in ancient times probably had no more than one window; this helped to keep the house cool in summer and warm in winter. No remains which show ancient windows have been preserved, but artistic representations suggest that they were usually small. Since there was no glass, they were covered by mats, curtains, or wooden shutters. The window was covered in addition by a grill or bars. The modern Palestinian peasant stuffs his windows with stones during the winter, and the practice may be ancient. The window, i.e., the shutter or mat, could be opened. The grill or lattice allowed people to look out (Gn 26:8; Jgs 5:28; 2 S 6:16; Pr 7:6) or in (SS 2:9). Dome windows were large enough to let a person through (Jos 2:15; 1 S 19:12; Je 9:20; 2 Co 11:32), and thieves could enter through the windows (Jl 2:9). The windows mentioned in the temple of Solomon (1 K 6:4) and in the house of the forest of Lebanon (1 K 7:4 f) are not described; many modern scholars think they were clerestory windows. Je 22:14 rebukes Jehoiakim* for building windows in his palace. It is quite probable that the palace window mentioned here and in 2 K 9:30 ff (from which Jezebel* was thrown) is a "window of appearance" of the type represented in Egyptian palaces. These were large windows opening upon a balcony in which the Pharaoh and his family appeared to receive the acclamations and the homage of the people who stood below.

The artistic motif of "the woman in the window" (ANEP 131) is not fully explained. This representation of a woman looking through a window may possibly represent the goddess Ishtar as a harlot.

Wine. The production of wine is prehistoric in the Near East. The invention of wine is attributed to Noah* (Gn 9:20 ff), who is here a culture hero; the account takes a somewhat mixed view, since Noah first experiences intoxication. Wine was the usual drink with meals and is very frequently mentioned in the Bible. Palestine itself was a wine producing country; some wines of other regions are mentioned as especially good (Lebanon, Ho 14:8; Helbon, Ezk 27:18). Gk levels of occupation in Palestine contain many stamped Rhodian jar handles; the wine of Rhodes was prized in the ancient world. Wine is a gift and a blessing of Yahweh (Dt 7:13; Pr 3:10 f; Ho 2:10; Jl 2:24), which He withdraws in punishment (Dt 28:30, 39; Ho 2:11; 9:2; Am 5:11; Zp 1:13). The wine press usually stood in the vineyard; the excavations at Gibeon*, which show that this town was an important center of wine manufacture, have uncovered several such installations, which appear at other sites also. The press consisted of two troughs cut in a rock at different levels with a drain leading from the upper level to the lower level. The first press was done by treading with the feet (Ne 13:15); this was a festive occupation carried on with shouts (Je 25:30; 48:33) and to the accompaniment of music (illustrated in ANEP 90, 156). The grapes were then pressed by means of a beam weighted with a stone or as illustrated in ANEP 155 by the use of poles which served as levers for weights. The treading of the

Egyptian tomb painting showing harvesting and treading of grapes.

grapes is a figure for the punishing wrath of Yahweh (Is 63:2 ff; Je 25:30; 48:33; Lam 1:15). The juice was stored in vats or in skin vessels for fermentation; new skins were necessary for this process (Mt 9:17; Mk 2:22; Lk 5:37 f). No method of storing unfermented juice was known. The excavations of Gibeon disclosed over 40 large vats cut in the rock with a capacity of several thousand gallons each. Some of these were plastered and could store wine in such large quantities; most were unplastered and must have held the wine in jars. The temperature of the vats when covered was a constant 65° F at all seasons. Wine was not only taken with meals but was also carried as part of the provision of the traveler (Jgs 19:19) and is noted as part of the provisions of garrison troops (2 Ch 11:11). Wine was cut with water (2 Mc 15:39) in the Gk period, and Is 1:22 indicates that it was done also in the earlier periods, although it is not praised in this passage. The Israelites also very probably flavored their wine with spices as other peoples did. The term "blood of the grape" (Gn 49:11; Dt 32:14; BS 50:15) indicates that most Palestinian wine was red. More and better wine was expected at festivities (1 S 25:36; 2 S 13:28; WS 2:7; Is 5:12; Jn 2:1–11). Lk 10:34 suggests that wine was used as a soothing external medication, and 1 Tm 5:23 recommends it as good for the stomach. Mourners were served a "cup of consolation" (Je 16:7). Intemperance was common enough, and the Bible contains a number of unfavorable references to excessive drinking; cf DRUNKENNESS. Wine is praised; it rejoices gods and men (Jgs 9:13); it gladdens the heart of man (Ps 104:15), it gladdens life (Ex 10:19), it makes the heart exult (Zc 10:7), it cheers the spirits of the depressed (Pr 31:6). It is used in figures of speech. Wine cut by water is a character weakened by sin (Is 1:22). It is a figure of the delights of love (SS 5:1; 8:2). It is also used unfavorably; it is the seductions of the great harlot (Apc 14:8; 17:4), and it is the intoxicating cup of God's anger* (cf DRUNKENNESS).

The attitude of Jesus toward wine, like that of the entire Bible, is neutral, praising its use and finding fault in its intemperate use. Certainly the production of wine at Cana* (Jn 2:1–11) scarcely supports any belief that Jesus or the primitive Church regarded the use of wine as sinful in itself.

The religious use of wine in the OT is not important. It accompanies sacrifices* as a libation. The abstinence from wine practiced by the Nazirites* and the Rechabites* was due to the peculiar vow and the peculiar

traditions respectively. On the sacramental character of wine in the NT cf EUCHARIST.

Winnow. Winnowing follows threshing* in the processing of grain*. The threshed grain lying on the threshing floor is tossed into the air when a strong wind is blowing; the chaff is carried off and the heavier grain falls to the ground. A pitchfork shaped like a shovel is used to toss the grain. The actual process is mentioned in the Bible only in Rt 3:2; other references to winnowing speak of the process as a metaphor for the judgment of Yahweh. The wind separates the grain from the chaff (Is 41:16; Je 4:11; Ezk 5:2, 10); these metaphors compare the scattering of Israel during the exile* to winnowing. He employs the winnowing fork (Is 30:24; Je 15:7; Mt 3:12; Lk 3:17).

Wisdom, Wisdom literature. 1. *OT.* Wisdom and wisdom literature in the OT are connected with wisdom and wisdom literature in the larger ancient Near East; comparative studies of the now abundant literature of this type make it clear that wisdom was international in character, that the conception of wisdom was substantially the same everywhere, with important modifications introduced in the OT (cf below), and that there was a wide exchange of wise sayings. Israel was aware that its wisdom had antecedents in the E, in Egypt and in Edom, which had a great reputation for its sages (1 K 5:10 f; Je 49:7). A number of the most important of these texts are collected in ANET: from Egypt come the instruction of Ptah-hotep (2450 BC, ANET 412–414), the instruction of Meri-ka-re (2100 BC, ANET 414–418), the instruction of Amen-em-het (1960 BC, ANET 418–419), the instruction of Hor-dedef (1250–1150 BC, but from earlier material, ANET 419–420), the instruction of Ani (19th dynasty, ANET 420–421), the instruction of Amen-em-opet (10th-6th centuries BC, ANET 421–424; cf PROVERBS). Akkadian maxims of uncertain date are given in ANET 425–427. This literature is very much of a type. It consists of maxims on how to conduct oneself in speech and deportment in such a way as to dispose others favorably, to foster one's own success and advancement, and to live free of anxiety which arises from hostility, opposition, and failure. The origin of these maxims is found in the class of professional scribes* who kept the records and administered the business of palaces and temples. Many of these collections are found in schoolboy copies; the young men were trained in the manners of a good scribe while they learned their letters. This class was the first to cultivate wisdom; it was a wisdom which consisted in a knowledge of how to act. Its maxims seem largely political and motivated by enlightened self-interest; nevertheless, a code which has as its ideal to avoid giving offense will not fall beneath a certain level. Whatever the motivation, the counsels of the sages are moral in character; truthfulness, moderation, chastity, kindliness, honesty, and other basic virtues of society are a part of the trained and disciplined officer of the court. Furthermore, it was thought that wisdom could be learned only by instruction; it was the collective sum of experience, and the young man learned it by docile attention to his elders or not at all.

The writings of the sages in some instances went beyond maxims of conduct and contain reflections on problems of life, of good and evil. Such are the Egyptian dialogue of the man with his soul (ANET 405–407), the Babylonian poem "Lord of Wisdom" (ANET 434–437; cf JOB), the dialogue of master and servant (ANET 437–438), the dialogue of human misery (ANET 438–440). The affinities of these works lie with Jb and Ec; they question the justice of human life and experience, the problem of the success of wickedness and the failure of righteousness, the proper attitude which a man should take before unhappiness. Their tone is pessimistic; they come from periods of defeat and depression, and they exhibit the failure of religious faith in Egypt and Mesopotamia to furnish principles by which one might meet these problems.

Israelite wisdom is also practical, a skill in action. Wisdom is the word which designates the skill of the craftsman (Ex 31:6; 35:10; 1 K 7:14; 1 Ch 22:15; 2 Ch 2:6, 11 f; Is 40:20 +). It is displayed in the skill with which a man fulfills an office or a responsibility: it is the wisdom of the administrator (Gn 41:39), the prudence of the chieftain and the leader (Dt 1:13, 15; 34:9). It can be morally neutral, to say the least; the devious plan which Jonadab* suggested by which Amnon* might rape Tamar* is called wise (2 S 13:3), and so is the craft by which Solomon is expected to create a trap for Joab* (1 K 2:9). David is credited with shrewdness, "wisdom," in seeing through the fictitious case of the woman of Tekoa (2 S 14:20). Wisdom to render judgment is required in the judge (1 K 3:28).

The content of much Israelite wisdom was maxims of conduct (cf BEN SIRA; PROVERBS). Solomon's wisdom was displayed in his discourses on trees, plants, animals, and reptiles (1 K 5:13); this knowledge was not a primitive science, but the empirical observation by which the behavior and characteristics of

plants and animals could be used to form similes which illustrate human life and experience; many such similes appear in the wisdom literature, often taking the form of the riddle*. Israelite wisdom more frequently concerns itself with the problems of life and experience (cf ECCLESIASTES; JOB; WISDOM OF SOLOMON). These books obviously do not contain a philosophical wisdom; they are without dialectic and do not think in abstract terms. Their purpose is rather to teach the wise man how to live with these problems than to reach intellectual satisfaction in their solution.

Israelite wisdom, like the wisdom of other peoples, was the product of the scribal schools and the scribal class; this class first appeared under the monarchy and followed Egyptian models in administration and procedure (cf SCRIBE). Wisdom is gained by counsel and instruction (Pr 1:5; 12:15; 13:14; 19:20 +), and the young man is frequently admonished to accept instruction. Wisdom comes from association with the wise (Pr 13:20). The tradition of wisdom begins with primordial man (Ezk 28:12). The wise man accepts correction and instruction (Pr 9:8 f; 21:11); he is always learning, where the fool* refuses to learn.

The existence of professional sages is suggested by the description of Ahithophel* (2 S 16:23) and by the sages whose charisma is counsel (Je 18:18). The scribes boasted that they had wisdom (Je 8:8). Women also were respected for their wisdom and counsel (2 S 14:2; 20:16; Jgs 5:29); these women were probably professional advisers. The professional wise man no doubt developed from the scribal class as a rule, although his distinction must have rested upon some degree of proved experience.

Israelite wisdom was modified by its relation to faith in Yahweh, which gives it a character of its own. Both Egypt and Mesopotamia had gods who were venerated for their wisdom, but these gods were, like the counselers, specialists. Yahweh alone is truly wise; His wisdom is exhibited in creation* (Pr 3:19; Jb 38–39; BS 42:15–43:33 f). The wisdom of Yahweh is also knowledge of how to do things; and the knowledge which lies behind the greatest of all works, creation, is the highest of all wisdom. Wisdom appears as personified, accompanying Yahweh in His creation (Pr 8:22–36), as a heavenly being (BS 24:1–22), reflecting the majesty and attributes of divinity (WS 7:24–8:1). This hypostatic wisdom can be compared to the divine word* in the OT; it remains a personification, since it is clearly not identified with Yahweh nor is it a distinct created being. It is created from eternity (BS 1:4). Wisdom is also personified as a woman who gives instruction (Pr 8:1–21), and as the heavenly being who descends to dwell in Israel (BS 24:8 ff; cf below). Wisdom is not personified in Jb 28; it is a treasure which men cannot discover, for it is found only with God, who grants it to men. The wisdom of God is seen not only in His creation but in His management of human history in a mysterious way (Jb 12:13 ff). It even appears in His skill in bringing "evil" i.e., disaster (Is 31:2).

Wisdom, while learned from tradition (cf above), is ultimately a gift of Yahweh (Pr 2:6; BS 1:1). The wisdom of Joseph in government and the wisdom of Solomon in judging are from God (Gn 41:38; 1 K 3:28), as is the wisdom of the craftsman (Ex 31:6 +). The beginning or the essence of wisdom is the fear of Yahweh, without which there is no true wisdom (Pr 1:7; 9:10; 15:23; Jb 28:28; BS 1:14, 16, 18, 20). Man therefore must not be wise in his own opinion (Pr 3:10; 26:12 +), nor is wisdom an object of boasting (Je 9:22). That wisdom is a gift of Yahweh is the point of the somewhat midrashic account of Solomon's prayer and its answer (1 K 3:5–14); and this gift includes all other desirable things, which only wisdom can secure. The peak of wisdom therefore is understanding of the deeds of Yahweh, especially His judgments (Je 9:11; Ho 14:10).

In Dt 4:6 appears a theme which is prominent in BS and WS and dominates the later concept of wisdom, the theme that wisdom is the observation of the law. In BS 24:23–34 the celestial wisdom which descends to dwell in Israel is the law; and knowledge of the law is the true wisdom which belongs to the scribe alone and is not possessed by men whose work gives them no time to study the law (BS 38:24–39:11). The same conception of the heavenly wisdom which descends as the law is seen in Bar 3:9–4:3; it is not so clear in WS, whose conception of wisdom is not free of Gk influence (cf WISDOM OF SOLOMON). This is the wisdom which is the guide of life, the key to success and happiness (BS 4:11–20; 6:18–33; 14:20–15:8). Here the later wisdom books are true to the earlier Israelite traditions, which identified wisdom with the fear of Yahweh; wisdom is therefore a moral as well as a practical way of life, and the sages end with the conclusion that morality is a practical way of life. One may notice a slight deviation in Ec (2:16, 19; 6:8; 1:18). Wisdom as a successful way of life has its disillusionments, and Ec gives expression to them. Craftsmanship in good living is not enough to satisfy, and conventional wisdom does not answer all questions and solve all problems. Jb* is extremely critical of traditional conventional wisdom for its failure to meet the paradoxes of life.

Wisdom divides mankind into two classes, the wise and the foolish, and does not conceive a passage from one to the other; this is a schematic, not a realistic view, and the two classes as such, of course, remain irreconcilably divided. The young man is foolish by definition, but he can learn wisdom; if he has not acquired wisdom with maturity, he is hopelessly a fool. Folly* (which is more than mental defects) is the root of failure and unhappiness; in deference to the traditional sages, their simplification of the relation between wisdom and success and happiness must be qualified by their assurance that success and happiness could never be assured by folly. The doctrine stood in need of some nuances and was open to criticism when its simplism was pressed too closely and too literally.

The wisdom literature alone in the OT directs attention explicitly to the problems of the individual person; it is free of peculiarly national traits and of messianism. Its merit is that it does draw attention to the importance of the business of daily life of the man who is not very important, and its emphasis on the fact that life is unity and integrity which must be preserved from the disintegration of folly is not misplaced.

The style and content of wisdom and wisdom literature run through most of the books of the OT; many of these allusions are noticed under articles on the separate books.

2. *NT*. The NT use of "wise" and "wisdom" is affected not only by the OT background of the words but also by the meaning of *sophos, sophia* in Gk to designate philosophical knowledge. This is especially apparent in Paul.

I. Gospels. Jesus grew in wisdom as an adult should (Lk 2:52); the understanding which He displayed as a boy (Lk 2:47) was not precocious, but proper to an intelligent and alert child. When He appeared as a teacher, i.e., as a professional wise man, His acquaintances wondered where He had acquired wisdom, which could not be obtained without schooling (Mt 13:54; Mk 6:2); this is the wisdom of the scribes, not of the practical man. The scribes are also the wise from whom God has concealed the revelation of Jesus (Mt 11:25; Lk 10:21). Wise men with prophets and scribes were the messengers of God in the OT (Mt 23:34). The wisdom of God which speaks in Lk 11:49 is a paraphrase for God Himself. Jesus promises His disciples "mouth and wisdom" i.e., skill in speech (Lk 21:15). The wisdom which is proved right by her deeds (Mt 11:19; Lk 7:35) is the wisdom of God which is demonstrated to be true wisdom by its results.

II. Epistles. God alone has true wisdom, which is too deep for man to search out (Rm 11:33; 16:27) and manifold (Eph 3:10). Christian wisdom, like OT wisdom, is a gift of God (Eph 1:8; Col 1:9). The ability to speak the word of wisdom is a charismatic gift (1 Co 12:8). The spirit of wisdom is given by God (Eph 1:17). Wisdom is taught by the apostle who proposes the Christian revelation (Col 1:28); Paul rejects carnal wisdom as a means of presenting his message (2 Co 1:12). Christians should admonish each other with wisdom (Col 3:16) and make it a principle of prudent dealing with those outside the Church (Col 4:5). They should distinguish true wisdom from spurious wisdom (Col 2:23). The wisdom which comes from above is proved to be genuine by right conduct (Js 3:13–15); it is a wisdom for good (Rm 16:19).

The wisdom of this world makes its possessors think themselves wise when they are foolish (Rm 1:22). Wisdom here seems to have the technical meaning of philosophical knowledge; these are the wise to whom God's power and divinity are known by reason through His creation, and who stifle the truth of God (Rm 1:18–21); they appear to be professional learned men.

Whether the same type of wisdom is intended by Paul in his polemic against worldly wisdom (1 Co 1:17–2:7) is not clear; but the allusions to wisdom in speech (1 Co 1:17, 20; 2:1, 4, 6) suggest that this is the wisdom intended, the learning in rhetoric and philosophy which some apparently found missing in Paul's discourses. Here Paul defines true Christian wisdom; it is Christ, and Christ nailed to the cross (1 Co 1:18, 22; 2:2). This is the wisdom of God which is folly to the world, but which confounds the wisdom of the world. Christ is the wisdom of God (1 Co 1:24); the wisdom of God is therefore revelation, unattainable by human searching. It does not need presentation by the wisdom of the rhetorical speaker (1 Co 2:4). It is the revelation of God's hidden wisdom and secret purpose, His plan of salvation for mankind through Christ crucified (1 Co 2:7–10). Hence the wise of this world must become fools to acquire the wisdom of God, for the wisdom of the world is folly to God (1 Co 3:18 f). All the treasures of the wisdom of God are in Christ (Col 2:3).

The conception of Christ as the wisdom of God may echo the conception of wisdom as personified (cf above); in particular it seems to respond to the conception of wisdom as the law. The law* was for the Jew the means of revelation and salvation. Christ

has come to fulfill the law, i.e., to fulfill its purpose of revelation and salvation. He is the true knowledge communicated by God, the key to union with God and to a successful and happy life. Wisdom also finds in Him its fulfillment.

Wisdom of Solomon. WS is preserved in Gk and is not included in the Protestant and Jewish canon*.

1. *Contents:*

1–5, wisdom and human destiny; fate of righteous and wicked.

1:1–16, warning against wickedness; 2:1–20, thoughts of the impious; 2:21–24, blindness of impious; 3:1–9, salvation of the righteous; 3:10–4:6, punishment of the impious; 4:7–14, explanation of the premature death of the righteous; 4:14–20, sure retribution for the impious; 5:1–14, remorse of impious; 5:15–23, eternal life of righteous and annihilation of impious.

6–9, origin and nature of wisdom and means of acquiring it.

6:1–11, exhortation to rulers; 6:12–20, wisdom confers power; 6:21–25, enduring power of wise rulers; 7:1–14, wisdom granted to prayer; 7:15–22, God gives wisdom; 7:22–8:1, nature of wisdom; 8:2–21, search and acquisition of wisdom; 9:1–11, thanksgiving for wisdom; 9:12–18, excellence of wisdom.

10–19, wisdom of God in history of Israel* (13–15, digression on idolatry).

10:1–21, wisdom protects patriarchs; 10:21–12:2, hymn of praise; 12:3–11, God's mercy to Israel and to Canaan; 12:12–18, praise of God's righteousness; 12:19–22, God's righteousness an example to men; 12:23–27, judgment on the unrighteous (Egyptians); 13:1–3, denunciation of idolatry; 13:4–9, God known through His works; 13:10–19, folly of idolatry; 14:1–31, evil effects of idolatry; 15:1–6, Israel's fidelity to God; 15:7–17, folly of idolatry, 15:18–16:14, punishments of Egypt and of Israel; 16:15–29, punishments of Egypt through nature; 17:1–18:4, plagues of Egypt; 18:5–19, death of firstborn; 18:20–25, deliverance of Israel; 19:1–12, crossing of sea; 19:13–17, punishment of Egyptians, 19:18–22, transmutation of elements.

2. *Author and Date.* The book is written in the person of Solomon (1:1; 6:1–11, 21; 7:5; 8:9–15); this pseudonym is a literary artifice. The original language of the book is Gk. The background of Gk ideas and the interest of the author suggest a Jew of Alexandria*; and the development of the thought, which is late but earlier than Philo, falls best about 50 BC. The book is addressed to Jews who are so impressed by Hellenistic

learning and civilization that their faith is in danger. The enemies of 1–5 are not Gentiles but renegade Jews; the author combats their materialism, hedonism, and idolatry.

3. *Doctrine*. WS attacks the great problem of life, the problem of sin and evil, which is the problem of Jb and Ec and of some of the wisdom* literature of the ancient Near East. His solution of the problem in general is that one can meet the problem only by fidelity to the beliefs and traditions of Israel. These are summed up in wisdom and the law. Wisdom is a gift of God. Genuine wisdom means belief in the one God of Israel and fidelity to His law. Wisdom delivers the believer from all evil; this is illustrated by a review of the saving deeds of God for the patriarchs and for the Israelites in Egypt, the very country where Jews are now beginning to abandon their faith. The review of the history is an example of midrash*; it is composed with great freedom of imagination and the element of wonder is heightened.

The exposition of the author is considerably modified by his introduction of an idea which is Gk and not Hb: the immortality of the soul. The soul is conceived as a *pneuma* (spirit*), which bears resemblances to the Stoic conception; the idea of the body as a tent (9:15) is found in Pythagoreanism and Platonism. Other Platonic conceptions appear in 2:23; 6:18 f. Gk style also is evident in his composition; it is not a collection of maxims but follows consecutive discourse in the manner of Gk philosophical writings. The extent of Gk influence should not be exaggerated; the author's knowledge of Gk philosophy was superficial and could be gained by conversation. But the conception of immortality of the righteous and the annihilation of the wicked, which is basic to his argument, has a form which can be recognized as Gk. In a manner not Gk the origin of evil is attributed to the devil (2:24).

The concept of wisdom is traditional, but it has at the same time some refinement and subtlety which possibly reflect Gk patterns. The knowledge which wisdom communicates is the knowledge of Gk natural science (7:17–21; 8:8). Wisdom is creative, the artificer of all things (7:22). The description of personified wisdom (7:22–8:1) is obviously intended to represent wisdom in a more spiritual form which belongs to God and emanates from Him into holy souls. Residing there, this emanating wisdom is the principle of all virtues and of security. Evidently the identification of wisdom with the law is somewhat relaxed in this conception; rather than the document, the revelation as an internal principle is the guide of life.

The wisdom of God in creation is emphasized less than in other wisdom books. Instead it becomes prominent in history. The power of nature which creation implies is exhibited even more wonderfully in the deliverance of Israel, and the author emphasized the elements as instruments of God's wisdom. Possibly this emphasis is a response to Gk philosophical thinking about the elements, which are themselves primary principles in much of Gk thought; Jewish belief makes them the willing servants of the creator, and sees their movements as directed entirely by His purposes of salvation and judgment.

Witch. Cf DIVINATION; MAGIC.

Witness. 1. *OT*. In Israelite law the evidence of witnesses was required for the conviction of a crime. The evidence of one witness was not enough; two or three were required (Nm 35:30; Dt 19:15). In a charge of murder (and presumably on any capital charge) it was the duty of the witnesses to cast the first stone (Dt 17:6 f). Nm 5:13 provides an ordeal* for a woman charged with adultery without witnesses; this is the only charge which had any legal standing without witnesses. The Israelite law, like Mesopotamian law, exhibits no rules of evidence; the examination of witnesses was left to the discretion of the judges. The story of Susanna* illustrates the necessity for care in the examination of witnesses and is perhaps partly a polemic against hasty verdicts. Ex 23:1 prohibits false witness; the numerous allusions to false witness (1 K 21:10–13; Pr 6:19; 12:17, 19; 19:5, 9; 21:28; 14:25; Pss 27:12; 35:11 +) show that the law was not entirely strong on this point in practice. Dt 19:18 f imposes upon the false witness the penalty of the charge which he lays falsely. Witnesses were also required for contracts, as in Mesopotamian law; Israelite law in this matter is not as full and precise as Mesopotamian law, but legal practice went beyond the laws of the Pnt. The contract of sale described in Je 32 was witnessed by men whose seals were placed upon the two copies of the contract (Je 32:10, 25, 44). In simpler practice the witness was a mere verbal attestation of those present (Rt 4:9); but such transactions were to be performed at the gate* where most of the adult male population would be found at certain times. A "witness" could also be a symbol, such as a heap of stones (Gn 31:44–54) or lambs offered in sacrifice (Gn 21:30). Yahweh was invoked as a witness in the oath (1 S 20:23, 42; 12:5f; 1 Mc 2:37) of a solemn affirmation or agreement. Witness acquires a theological significance in a number of passages. Yahweh is invoked as a witness against the crimes of Israel (Je 29:23; Mi 3:8; Mal 3:5). Job invokes the witness in heaven in favor of his innocence (Jb 16:19). Yahweh is a witness of what is in man's heart (WS 1:6). David is a witness of Yahweh's fidelity to His covenant; the attestation here is not by testimony but by mere existence; the promised restoration of the dynasty is itself the assurance (Ps 89:38). The memorial stones which Joshua erects are witnesses of the covenant which he imposed upon Israel (Jos 24:27). The book of the law which Israel fails to observe is the witness of their rebellion; it attests the will of Yahweh which Israel has refused to obey (Dt 31:26). The song of Moses is a witness against Israel; it is a recitation of charges (Dt 31:19).

Second Isaiah conceives the declaration of Yahweh's divinity before the nations as a legal process. Israel by its survival of the disasters of the exile is a witness that Yahweh alone is a saving God (Is 43:9–13). It is also a witness of the fulfillment of prophecy; for Yahweh's saving acts have been foretold (Is 44:7–11). Yahweh is a witness against the nations also (Zp 3:8) who have in their pride refused to acknowledge Him.

2. *NT.* Strathmann has pointed out that in both biblical and profane Gk the word *martys* and its cognates (*martyria, martyrion*) are used both in the legal sense of the attestation of a fact and the transferred sense of the attestation of a truth; the distinction lies between the fact which falls under observation and the truth which is not observed but is reached by reasoning or by faith. The legal use of witness in the NT needs no comment. In the trial of Jesus the profession of Jesus Himself is taken by Caiaphas* to dispense with the need of witnesses (Mt 26:65; Mk 14:63). The NT also has instances of false witnesses besides the trial of Jesus (AA 6:13; 7:58). The law of Dt 17:6 f; 19:15 concerning the need of more than one witness is several times applied properly or in a transferred sense to a situation within the Christian community (2 Co 13:1; 1 Tm 5:19). A Christian who cannot settle a dispute with his brother by private conversations should state his complaint before two or three witnesses before he takes it to the entire Church (Mt 18:16). By a play on words Jesus makes the Jews witnesses of the murder of the prophets by their ancestors through the erection of the tombs of the prophets (Mt 23:31; Lk 11:48). God is invoked as witness in solemn asseverations (Rm 1:9; 2 Co 1:23; Phl 1:8; 1 Th 2:5). Apparently the confession of faith was recited in the presence of witnesses (1 Tm 6:12). Those who have heard the teaching of Paul are called its witnesses (2 Tm 2:2). The "cloud of witness" (Heb 12:1) is the assembly of the heroes of faith who are recited in Heb 11; their passage through trial attests that faith is powerful enough to carry the Christian through his trials. In a transferred sense Epimenides is quoted as a witness to the moral character of the Cretans (Tt 1:113).

Strathmann has also pointed out that Lk and AA exhibit a concept of witness which is peculiar to those books: the apostles are witnesses of Jesus (Lk 24:47; AA 1:8, 22; 5:32; 2:32; 3:15; 10:39–43; 13:31). They attest His death and resurrection* and indeed all the events of His public life, since the successor of Judas as witness must be selected from those who were members of the company from the baptism of John to the ascension (AA 1:22). They are not merely witnesses of fact, however; they are more properly witnesses to the meaning of the facts, that these are saving events. This meaning of events which they witness is not an object of observation but a truth known by faith in the revelation of Jesus Christ. Similarly Peter is a witness of the sufferings of Christ (1 Pt 5:1). It is therefore somewhat surprising to find that Paul (AA 22:15; 26:16) and Stephen (AA 22:20) are also called witnesses, since neither of them was present at the events. It seems, as Strathmann has pointed out, that here the witness of fact and the witness of the truth*, the meaning of the saving event, have begun to merge; and importance is attached primarily to the witness of the truth. God is a witness of the preaching of the Church (AA 15:8) and of the piety of Abel (Heb 11:4 f). The preaching of the Church is witnessed by the Scripture (AA 10:43; Rm 3:21; Heb 7:8, 17) and by the Holy Spirit speaking in the Scriptures (Heb 10:15). The Lord bears witness to the preaching by signs and wonders (AA 14:3).

In the Johannine writings the idea of witness acquires greater importance. Apc 2:13; 17:6 are perhaps the earliest uses of the word in what later becomes the technical sense of *martyr;* this is not apparent in the witness of the two prophets (Apc 11:3). As in Lk (cf above), the apostles are witnesses to the life and death of Jesus (Jn 15:27; 21:24; 1 Jn 1:2; 4:14); but the use of the word elsewhere in the Johannine writings shows that the witness is here given to the truth of the saving events rather than to fact. John the Baptist bears witness to the light (Jn 1:7 f) and that Jesus is the Messiah (Jn 1:15). The witness concerning Jesus attests that He is the Son of God (Jn 1:34), that the Father sent Him (Jn

5:36), that God gave us eternal life and that this life is in His son (1 Jn 5:10 f). Jesus is witnessed by the Father, by John the Baptist, and by the Scriptures (Jn 5:31–39). He is witnessed by His works (Jn 10:25) and by the spirit (Jn 15:26). Jesus Himself witnesses what He has seen and heard (Jn 3:11, 32) and came into the world to witness the truth (Jn 18:38). He is the object of the three witnesses: the spirit which works in the Church, the water of baptism, and the blood of His sacrifice (1 Jn 5:7 f).

Witness is used several times in the Gospels to signify an express or symbolic attestation of unbelief (Mt 10:18; 24:14; Mk 1:44; 6:11; 13:9; Lk 9:5), as the law is such a witness in the OT (cf above).

The NT idea of witness, whether in the proper sense of attestation by a person to a fact or the transferred sense of attestation of a truth or symbolic attestation by a thing, is not the conception of "evidence" of modern law nor the "evidence" of scientific demonstration. "Witness" in OT and NT is primarily the affirmation of a person; it is subject to examination, but the examination consists in seeing whether more than one person makes the attestation. If this is verified, it was the part of the reasonable man to accept the witness. Witness is never an impersonal marshaling of facts, but always remains a personal attestation, even when the attestation by personification is attached to a thing rather than a person. In a sense therefore the distinction between witness of fact and witness of truth is a modern distinction which has no meaning in the Bible. Whether to fact or to truth in our sense, the witness consists in the commitment of a person to the truth which he attests.

The supreme commitment of a person to truth is the commitment of his life. This is implied in Apc 2:13; 17:6 (cf above). The use of the Gk word *martys* (Eng martyr) to designate one who suffers death for the Christian faith appears in the 2nd century AD and has passed into common usage.

Wizard. Cf MAGIC.

Woman. 1. *In the Near East, Greece, and Rome.* In the ancient Near East woman generally had no rights as a free person; she was always subject to a man, either her father or her husband. The inferior position of woman in ancient law is treated under ADULTERY; DIVORCE; DOWRY; FAMILY; INHERITANCE; MARRIAGE; PROSTITUTION; WIDOW and related articles. By chance a section of the Middle Assyrian laws which have survived deals almost entirely with women (ANET 180–185). These laws may not be altogether representative of Mesopotamia; in many respects their casual treatment of woman, such as retaliation of damages on the innocent wife or daughter of the offender, is savage. But even these laws admit a kind of common law marriage (# 34, p 183) and suppose that a widow may have property of her own; if a widow marries and moves into her husband's house, he acquires all her property; but if the husband moves into her house, she acquires all his property (# 35, *ibid*). Legal practice in Mesopotamia, at least in some periods and in some places, permitted woman to act as a legal agent; women appear as owners, buyers, sellers, defendants, and plaintiffs in contracts.

The legal inferiority of woman is paradoxically opposed to the conception of the fertility goddess who is wife and mother. The goddess represents woman as the source of life; but she also represents woman as the instrument of sexual pleasure, and in the grosser conceptions of the cult this is her highest function. It seems that the overemphasis upon the sexual function of woman involved a loss of dignity as a member of society and as a full partner in matrimony. It is apparent from the laws of Mesopotamia that a high degree of freedom and possibly a position of greater esteem and dignity belonged to women of the temple personnel, whether priestesses or cultic prostitutes.

While it is difficult to generalize about the position of women in Greece, it is clear that at Athens the wife had a social position almost as low as the woman of the E; her life was strictly confined to the home and her one responsibility was the bearing and rearing of legitimate children. It was accepted that the womanly graces and the cultivation of wit and intelligence were permitted only to the professional companions (*hetaera*), who were more than mere prostitutes; they furnished entertaining conversation and diversions. As in the Near East, marital fidelity was not imposed upon the husband. Gk marriage, however, was monogamous. Both in Greece and in the Near East there are numerous allusions to the popular belief that woman is by instinct a nymphomaniac; it is assumed that no woman can be trusted to remain faithful unless she is closely watched.

Roman law and custom imposed a severe power of the father over both sons and daughters (*patria potestas*); but the position of the wife and mother of a family was higher both in legal rights and in dignity than in Greece or the E. Indeed, in the period of the later Republic and the early empire (the period of the New Testament) many contemporary writers regarded the freedom of women to associate freely with men and to share their social activities and public entertainments, such as the theater and the games, as a social deterioration. The freedom of women in Rome imposed no restraint upon sexual license either for men or for women. The excavations of Pompeii have disclosed that this ancient resort town was a vast brothel.

2. *In the OT.* The legal position of woman in the OT is treated in the articles cited at the beginning of this article. We may notice some additional instances of the subordination of the woman to the man; she is his property, which he may use in his own defense (Gn 12:12–20; 20:2; 19:8; Jgs 19:24–27). In one version of the decalogue* the wife is enumerated with the property (Ex 20:17). Women apparently did not usually eat with men (Gn 18:9; Rt 2:14).

While the legal position of Hb women was perhaps inferior to the position of women in Mesopotamia, their social position and dignity seem to have been superior. The mother is expressly included in the precepts of honor and obedience which sons must pay to parents (Ex 20:12; Lv 19:3; Dt 5:16; 21:18). Women took part in festive celebrations; indeed, their song and dancing was one of the principal elements of the celebration (Ex 15:20; Jgs 11:34; 1 S 18:6; Ps 68:25). They also took part in cultic festivals (Dt 12:12; Jgs 13:20, 23; 1 S 1:1–4; 2 S 6:19). The women of the Bible whose stories are related because of their intelligence or devotion form an interesting group: Rahab (Jos 2), Michal (1 S 19:11 ff), Abigail (1 S 25:14 ff), Rizpah (2 S 21:7 ff), the woman of Shunem (2 K 4:8 ff); the pictures of the wives of patriarchs — Sarah, Hagar, Rebekah, Rachel, Leah — and of Jezebel, Delilah, and Athaliah are more mixed, but one can hardly say that women of this type represent a depressed class. Deborah* is a Hb heroine, and the women of Rt are depicted with all the qualities of womanhood. In later literature Judith* and Esther* are heroines.

Hb law also contains provisions which afford woman special protection: the law of the captive in war (Dt 21:10 ff), of the wife who is falsely charged with premarital intercourse (Dt 22:13 ff), of the girl who is raped (Dt 22:28 ff). It must be granted that such laws are exceptional; one may deduce that the position of women was guaranteed by custom rather than by law.

The most significant OT passage which deals with the position of woman is Gn 2–3. In Gn 2 woman is represented as a helper "like man," of his species, "bone of

his bone and flesh of his flesh," for whom man leaves his parents and lives with his wife. Equality seems to be implied in the narrative; and the implication is made clear in Gn 3:16, where the existing inferiority of woman, her subjection to the man and her dependence upon him for sexual fulfillment which is the root of her subjection, is attributed to a curse. The inferiority of woman is thus presented as a deterioration from the primitive and unspoiled condition of man.

The work of women was long and hard; theirs were the milling, the baking, the procuring of fuel and water, spinning, weaving, sewing, the care of the house (in nomadic life the care and pitching and striking of the tent as well as its manufacture), the care of children. It is altogether probable that, like women in the modern Near East, they also shared in the tilling of the soil: plowing and sowing, reaping, threshing, although these are properly the responsibilities of men. The responsibilities of the Hb woman, however, were partly compensated by the freedom of movement which she enjoyed within the community, whether she were a wife or an unmarried daughter (Gn 24:13 ff; Ex 2:16; Dt 12:12; Jgs 21:21; 2 S 6).

The wisdom literature of the OT exhibits a strain which can only be called misogyny. Men, especially young men, are warned against the seductions of the prostitute and the adulteress (Pr 6:24–26; 7:5–27). A golden ring in a swine's snout is a woman fair and foolish (Pr 11:22). The sages are aware of the monotony of the nagging wife (Pr 19:13; 21:9; 25:24; 27:15). Ben Sira warns of the danger of wine and women (BS 19:2) and the ease with which man is seduced by feminine beauty (BS 9:3–9). He finds women quarrelsome, talkative, malicious, deceiving men by their beauty (BS 25:16 ff), envious, drunkards, promiscuous (BS 26:6–12), and concludes with the statement that sin began with a woman and because of her we all die (BS 25:24). Amos (4:1ff) and Isaiah (3:16 ff) find fault with the frivolity and extravagance of the women of Samaria and Jerusalem. Such passages illustrate the fact that the wisdom literature is a speculum of wise sayings of all sorts; the sages' opinion of women is mixed, which is hardly surprising. Against these passages must be set others in which a good wife is called good fortune and a gift of Yahweh and a crown to her husband (Pr 18:22; 19:14; 12:4; BS 26:1–4) and in which all the virtues of a good wife are enumerated (Pr 31:10 ff). BS 36:21–26 notices that a man needs a wife, and lists her qualities (26:13–18): beauty, intelligence, silence, discipline, modesty, diligence as a housekeeper. The misogyny of the sages is an indirect testimonial that woman was not the depressed and helpless thing which one might deduce from studying the law alone. Misogyny reaches an even higher pitch in the rabbinical literature; the wise man thanks God that he has not made him a Gentile or a slave or a woman.

3. *In the NT.* The NT attitude toward women is hardly revolutionary in the proper sense; yet it proposes principles which are in opposition both to the social and legal depression of women of the E and the excessive emancipation of women in Rome.

The dealings of Jesus with women are revealing. He has an awareness of the daily life and tasks of women and an interest in them which is shown in the parables: baking (Mt 13:33), the lost coin (Lk 15:8 ff), the widow with a lawsuit (Lk 18:1 ff), the girls who form the bridal party (Mt 25:1 ff). He performs miracles at the request of women just as He performs them for men: Peter's mother-in-law (Mt 8:14 f; Mk 1:29–31; Lk 4:38 f), the daughter of Jairus and the woman with a hemorrhage (Mt 9:18–26; Mk 5:21–43; Lk 8:40–56), the woman of Syria (Mt 15:21–28; Mk 7:24–30), the woman with a deformed back (Lk 13:10–17), the widow of Naim (Lk 7:11–17). He accepted the anointing offered Him by a woman and defended her against criticism (Mt 26:10; Mk 14:6). His needs were served by a group of devoted women (Lk 8:2 f), many of whom witnessed His death and resurrection. His relations with Martha and Mary were those of close and familiar friendship (Lk 10:38–42; Jn 11). He spoke without embarrassment to a strange woman at the well of Jacob, which the disciples apparently thought a departure from good form (Jn 4:7 ff, 27). These episodes reveal in Jesus a total absence of the misogyny (cf above) and the assumption of the inferiority of woman which prevailed in the Jewish world of His time. His teaching in this respect is not revolutionary, but His conduct is.

From the beginning of the primitive Church women appear as full members (AA 1:14; 12:12), and a number of women converts are singled out for mention (AA 16:13 f; 17:4, 12, 34). Women took an active part in the life of the Church, doing good works as well as receiving them (AA 6:1; 9:36 ff; 16:15). These good works included assistance to the apostles in their ministry, not indeed in the preaching and teaching, but in rendering practical assistance, which is several times acknowledged (Rm 16:1, 3, 6, 12 f; 1 Co 16:19). Priscilla* shared with Aquila* the office of instruction (AA 18:26). There is an apparent discord between 1 Co 11:4, which permits women to pray and to speak in the church, and 1 Co 14:34 f, which imposes silence upon them; the discord is best explained by supposing that only charismatically inspired speech is permitted to women. The imposition of silence and submission in church in 1 Tm 2:11 probably comes from a slightly later period and is intended to be total.

The theoretical position of woman is not often mentioned outside of the discussion of marriage*, but the few texts are important. 1 Tm 2:15, which affirms that women will be saved through motherhood, does not go beyond the OT conception of woman's fulfillment. 1 Pt 3:7 affirms that woman is a full partner with man of the Christian life, but urges that she be cherished because she is the weaker sex; the weakness meant here is probably not merely physical. In Paul a certain tension appears. Woman is and ought to be subject to man, and Paul adduces theological arguments to show that the subjection should be maintained (1 Co 11:3, 7, 10; 14:35; Col 3:18; Eph 5:21 f). On the other hand, he affirms the mutual interdependence of the two sexes (1 Co 11:11–12) and affirms that in Christ there is no difference between male and female, the clearest statement of the dignity of woman in the NT. The apparent antinomy probably arises because Paul, conditioned by the customs of the society in which he lived, saw in the emancipation of woman in the Roman world a breakdown of genuine morality. Rather than surrender to the general relaxed morals Christians should maintain what to Paul was the traditional and solid basis of Jewish family life, even though he knew that the subjection of women was the result of a curse. With the removal of the curse of sin the subjection also should be removed, but not by a sudden upheaval of society. The principle is established, and as men and women grow in the life of regeneration woman also will recover the position which is rightly hers by nature and lost by sin.

Wood. It is probable that Palestine had more forest in ancient times than it has now, although it can never have been heavily wooded; allusions to the necessity of clearing the highlands of Ephraim* (Jos 17:15–18) and to the forest or thicket of the Negeb* (Ezk 21:2) could not be made today. Of the woods available the sycamore was the usual construction material (Is 9:6). The pine (or olive? 1 K 6:23) and the cypress (Is 37:24; Ezk 27:5) and the oak (Ezk 27:5; Is 6:13; 44:14; Zc 11:2) were superior and consequently rarer. The best of all woods was the cedar* obtained from Lebanon. The rarity of wood made stone a cheaper material, but allusions show its use in beams and pillars of houses, floor boards and paneling (these were luxuries, cf Je 22:14), ships, doors, and gates, doorposts and frames, tables and chairs, carts and sledges, weapons; and there was enough wood available to be used for gibbets (Dt 21:22; Jos 10:26). It is, of course, extremely rare that archaeologists find articles of wood preserved. The tools used in carpentry can be identified from the Bible and from archaeology; it is surprising how often tools of flint appear even long after the introduction of metal. The tools include axe, saw, chisel, hammer, and nails. The use of wood for fuel was probably limited to cultic purposes and perhaps the palaces of the wealthy; the common fuel was thorns* or dried dung (Ezk 4:12–16). David and Solomon imported carpenters from Tyre for work on their palaces; this does not imply that the Israelites had no carpenters, but that their craftsmanship was inferior (2 S 5:11; 1 K 5:6). Israelite carpenters appear later in the monarchy (2 K 12:12; 24:14).

In the NT "the wood" is used to designate simply the cross on which Jesus died (AA 5:30; 10:39; 13:29; 1 Pt 2:24), a usage which becomes common in later Christian literature.

Wool. The economy of Palestine was pastoral as well as agricultural, and wool was one of its most important products (Ho 2:5, 9 +). It was the most common material of clothing; linen* was much more expensive. Wool was offered among the first fruits (Dt 18:4). Both white and brown sheep* were cultivated; the white wool was more highly esteemed (Is 1:18). Wool was dyed* (Pr 31:22). The preparation of wool was the task of the housewife (Pr 31:13). Wool was traded from Damascus to Tyre (Ezk 27:13). Mesha* of Moab paid his annual tribute to Israel in sheep and wool (2 K 3:4). The moth was known (Is 51:8; Mt 6:19–20). The weaving of wool and linen threads in a single fabric was prohibited in Hb law (Lv 19:19; Dt 22:11), together with the yoking of animals of different species and the sowing of different seeds in one field. This law against "mixtures" probably had a religious background, but its meaning is unknown.

Word. 1. *OT*. The Hebrews shared with most of the ancient Semitic world and many peoples of widely scattered cultures a belief in the distinct reality of the spoken word as a dynamic entity. Often this belief degenerates into magic; but magic is rather a perversion of a genuine belief in the power of the word. The spoken word is more important in a culture which writes little or not at all; the permanence which writing gives the word is supplied by the belief in the continuing reality of the spoken word. This is most clearly seen in words which are uttered with solemnity, such as the words of covenant*, marriage, contracts, promises, and similar commitments; and it is seen also in words which reach from the present into the future, such as blessings* and curses*. The reality and power of the word are rooted in the personality who utters the word; it is a release of psychic energy and when it is uttered with power it posits the reality which it signifies. Isaac could not recall the blessing which he conferred upon Jacob (Gn 27); in modern law a contract with such an error concerning the identity of the person would easily be invalidated. But the psychic energy could not be recalled, nor could it be summoned again; Isaac could give Esau only another and an inferior blessing, since the first blessing had exhausted his power. Jacob himself was a victim of a similar deception when he was given Leah* instead of Rachel in marriage (Gn 29:20–27); the solemnly spoken word of the marriage covenant could not be recalled. The mother of Micah cursed the thief who stole her silver; when her son in fear restored the silver, she could not withdraw the curse, but sent a blessing after it to neutralize it (Jgs 17:1–2). The woman accused of adultery had to drink water into which had been washed the written imprecation which she uttered herself; if she were guilty, the power of the word would destroy her capacity to bear (Nm 5:12–31).

The dynamic reality of the word is accompanied by its dianoetic reality (O. Procksch). Hb uses "word" where we use "thing" or "deed." The word as name* gives the thing intelligibility; but the thing does not acquire full reality until it gets a name and becomes intelligible. In conferring the name the person exercises the dynamism by which he makes the thing real; in knowing the name the person exercises his dynamism in the reverse direction and "apprehends" the word-thing.

The word of God in the OT refers most frequently to the word of the prophet*. The word was the charisma of the prophet, as instruction (cf LAW) was of the priest* and counsel of the wise* man (Je 18:18). The word of Yahweh comes to the prophet as a dynamic entity with its distinct reality, a word-thing which the prophet receives. It is an expansion of the living personality of Yahweh and it has the power derived from

Him. Yahweh puts His word in the mouth of Jeremiah (1:9), and the conscious possession of the word distinguishes the true from the false prophet (Je 23:16–28). The word makes the vision intelligible (1 K 22:17–23; Is 6:1 ff; Ezk 1:1–28). Amos' vision of a basket of late summer fruit, *ḳayiṣ*, suggests "end," *ḳeṣ* (Am 8:1–3), and Jeremiah's vision of an almond twig, *šāḳēd,* suggests "watching," *šōḳēd*. These are not mere plays on words; the power-laden word posits the reality which it signifies. The word-thing seen is shown by Yahweh; the prophet transforms the word-thing which signifies into the word-thing which is signified.

As Jeremiah (1:9) received the word of Yahweh in his mouth, so Ezekiel (2:9–3:3) devoured a scroll on which the word of Yahweh was written. To Jeremiah the word was a burning fire shut up in his bones which he could not contain (Je 20:7–9). These suggest that the prophetic experience of the word is more than a simple hearing; it is the experience of a distinct and compelling reality. The personality of the prophet is invaded through the word by the personality of Yahweh.

The word is often said "to be fulfilled," or "to come," or "to be established." When this happens, the reality of the word-thing reaches its fullness. The word of Yahweh may be called sacramental in the sense that it effects what it signifies. Events occur according to the prophetic word of Yahweh, such as the annihilation of the house of Jeroboam proclaimed by Ahijah (1 K 15:29), of the house of Baasha proclaimed by Jehu (1 K 16:12), the death of Ahaziah according to the word of Elijah (2 K 1:17), the deaths of Ahab and Jezebel (2 K 9:26, 36), the extermination of the house of Ahab (2 K 10:17). Jeremiah's power to uproot and to tear down, to destroy and to ruin, to build and to plant consists in his power to utter the prophetic word which proclaims these events (Je 1:9–10). The word of Yahweh is like fire, like a hammer that shatters rock (Je 23:29). Yahweh hews with the prophets and kills with the words of His mouth (Ho 6:5). These passages show that the conception of the prophetic word is more than prediction-fulfillment; the word accomplishes the reality which it posits. Like the rain and snow, it does not return without accomplishing that for which it was sent (Is 55:10 f). It is eternal with the eternity of the will which it embodies (Is 40:8). When it falls upon Israel, it has an explosive force like a delayed-action bomb (Is 9:8 ff). It is, as Grether and Procksch have described it, the nerve or hinge of biblical history which initiates each crisis in Israel's historic march.

The divine utterance is the first recorded event in the OT (Gn 1:3). It comes at the deluge (Gn 6:7), the call of Abraham (Gn 12:1), the call of Moses (Ex 3), the call of Samuel (1 S 3), the election (1 S 9:17; 10:17–24) and rejection (1 S 15:10) of Saul, the election of David (1 S 16:12), the establishment of the eternal dynasty of David (2 S 7), the punishment of David's sin (2 S 12), the schism of the monarchy (1 K 11:31 ff). History is a process which is governed by the word of Yahweh; rather history is the word of Yahweh, the reality which fulfills His utterance. The word of history is dynamic in that it accomplishes what it signifies, dianoetic in that it renders history intelligible. As a release of psychic energy history is also a revelation of Him who utters the word.

The word of Yahweh is a creative agent (Gn 1; Pss 33:6, 9; 147:4; 15–18; Is 40:26; 48:13). Creation is a word-thing which is heard even though it does not speak, because it is the word uttered by the creator (Ps 19:2–5). Nature, like history, is also a word which reveals Yahweh who speaks it.

With Dt there appears the conception of the written law* as the word of Yahweh. This term was, it seems, applied in older collections to the "apodictic" imperatives like the ten words (cf DECALOGUE; Ex 34:28; Dt 4:13; 10:4). This word of Yahweh is the life of Israel (Dt 32:47; 8:3). Ultimately this conception developed into the conception of the sacred books as the word of God.

2. *NT.* Some scholars formerly thought that the NT conception of the word was influenced by the *mēmrā',* "word," which appears in the rabbinical writings as a personified attribute of God. This opinion is no longer sustained; the *mēmrā'* is a part of a pattern of thought which, to protect the divine transcendence, multiplied intermediate agents, personal and impersonal, between God and creation. The destroying word which leaped from heaven to slay the firstborn of the Egyptians (WS 18:14–16) is more characteristic of this rabbinical speculation than of OT usage.

I. *Mt and Mk.* The word is comparatively rare in Mt and Mk. It signifies the gospel*, the *euangelion* proclaimed by Jesus (Mk 2:2; 4:33; 8:32). In the parable of the sower (Mt 13:18–23; Mk 4:13–20; Lk 8:11–15) it appears in a somewhat hypostatized form. The usage, while not common, already illustrates the conception of the word which prevails in the rest of the NT; the gospel is the successor of the prophetic word (cf above) and must be received with the same submission. Only once the word appears as a dynamic utterance which expels demons (Mt 8:16).

II. *Lk and AA*. Luke also uses word of the gospel proclaimed by Jesus (5:1; 4:32). He differs from Mt and Mk in using frequently the term "word of God" to designate the gospel (5:1; 8:11, 21; 11:28). In AA the word is the gospel proclaimed by the apostles, and it appears frequently (AA 4:4, 29–31; 6:4; 8:4; 10:44; 11:1, 29; 10:36; 13:44, 48; 13:26; 16:6, 32; 17:11; 18:5; 19:20; 20:32). It is more frequently called the word of God (AA 4:29–31; 6:7; 10:36; 11:1; 13:44; 16:32) or the word of the Lord (AA 12:24; 13:48); this latter term applies to the gospel the technical term for the prophetic utterance in the OT. It is once called "the word of the gospel" (AA 15:7). It is personified; it grows and becomes strong (AA 19:20), it grows and is enlarged (AA 12:24; 6:7). It is sent as well as spoken (AA 10:36), it is received (AA 17:11 +) as well as heard. The work of the apostles is "the service of the word" (AA 6:4). It has the saving attributes of the gospel; it is the word of salvation (AA 13:26), the word of grace (AA 20:32), the words of this life (AA 5:20).

III. *The Pauline writings*. Here also the word is most frequently the gospel (1 Co 14:36; 2 Co 2:17; 6:7; Gal 6:6; Eph 1:13; Phl 1:14; Col 1:5; 4:2; 1 Th 1:6, 8; 2:13; 2 Th 3:1; 2 Tm 2:9, 15; 4:2; Tt 1:3). It is called the word of God (1 Co 14:36; 2 Co 2:17; 4:2; Eph 6:17; Phl 1:14; Col 1:25; 1 Th 2:13), the word of the Lord (1 Th 1:8; 2 Th 3:1), once the word of Christ (Rm 10:17). The word also signifies a single saying (1 Tm 1:15; 3:1), the source of which is not given; but it does not appear to be a saying of Jesus. The word is revealed through the preaching* (Tt 1:3); here a distinction is made between the content and the preaching which indicates that the word is regarded as distinct entity. The word is also the object of catechesis (Gal 6:6). Faith comes only from hearing, and hearing comes from the preaching of the word (Rm 10:17).

The personification of the word and its conception as a distinct dynamic reality is more sharply nuanced in the Pauline corpus. The word preached to the Thessalonians resounded from them (1 Th 2:8). The word is active in those who believe (1 Th 2:13). The word runs and is glorified (2 Th 3:1); here the word is more closely identified with God, for glory* is due to God alone. It goes out from one and comes to another (1 Co 14:36). It is not bound, even though its preachers are imprisoned (2 Tm 2:9). It is not to be sold cheaply (2 Co 2:17) nor to be tampered with (2 Co 4:2). The word has saving attributes: it is the word of reconciliation between God and man (2 Co 5:19),

the word of truth (2 Co 6:7; Eph 1:13; Col 1:5; 2 Tm 2:15). The word of the cross (1 Co 1:18) is probably the preaching of the redeeming death (1 Co 1:23). In Col 1:25; 4:2 the word is identified with the mystery which is the content of Paul's preaching; this mystery in turn is identified with Christ Himself, or rather with the "Christ-fact" (Kittel), the saving event, an idea which approaches Jn 1:1 ff (cf below).

IV. *In other epistles*. Here also the word is the gospel (Heb 13:7; Js 1:18, 21; 1 Pt 2:8; 3:1) and the word of God (Heb 13:7; 1 Pt 1:23). It is planted in the believer and has the power to save (Js 1:21). The living and abiding word of God is an immortal seed through which the believer is born anew (1 Pt 1:23). The two-edged sword of Heb 4:12 f and the sword of the spirit which is the word of God (Eph 6:17), however, appear to suggest more than the gospel and its preaching. The sword of Heb appears as the revealed will of God, more precisely His revealed judgment, which forces a decision from all those who hear the word. This theme is not apparent in the sword of the spirit of Eph; but the image of the sword, paralleled only here and in Apc 19:11 ff (cf below) suggests that the word is conceived in OT terms as a dynamic entity. It is the divine utterance which effects deliverance from the attacks of evil.

V. *The Johannine writings*. In the Johannine writings a different conception and emphasis appear. In Jn the word is not the gospel but the utterances of Jesus Himself. These, however, are emphatically the words of the Father which Jesus speaks. Thus, while Jesus speaks of "my word" (Jn 5:24; 8:43, 51; 12:47–50; 14:23; 15:20 +), the word is not His but the Father's (Jn 8:55; 14:24; 17:6, 14, 17), the word which the Father has given Him (Jn 17:8). The Father commands Him what He should speak (Jn 13:47–50). He does not speak of Himself (Jn 14:10). Thus when the word is called the word of God (Jn 3:34; 8:47) the phrase receives a nuance which it does not have in the other NT writings. The new emphasis in Jn is a part of the teaching of the 4th Gospel that Jesus and the Father are one (Jn 10:30). The unity in word and in work between the Father and Jesus in Jn is not the unity of the OT prophet with God in the word of God which the prophet speaks, but a unity more profound and personal. It reflects the conception of Jesus as the word in the prologue of Jn (cf below). The word of the Father is truth (Jn 17:17) and he who listens to the word of Jesus has eternal life (Jn 5:24). Peculiar to Jn is the conception of the word as something which "abides" in the one who hears it (Jn 5:38; 15:7; 1 Jn 2:14) and as something in which the believer abides (Jn 8:31); here the word is hypostatized as a permanent reality.

The rider on the white horse of Apc 19:11–16 is called the word of God. The sword which proceeds from his mouth is also the dynamic prophetic word which accomplishes the destruction which it pronounces, although this is not explicit. The name king of kings and lord of lords makes it difficult to see in this apparition any other than Jesus Himself appearing in His eschatological function (Dupont). The title does not refer to the revealed saving utterance, but to the word of judgment. Elsewhere in Apc the word is identified not with the gospel but with witness to Jesus rendered by the Church and its members (1:9; 6:9; 12:11; 20:4). This change of emphasis no doubt reflects the troubles of the Christian community at the time of the writing of Apc.

The prologue of 1 Jn (1:1–3) speaks of what the apostles have heard, seen, contemplated, and handled about the "word of life." The repeated expressions of direct experience go beyond the "hearing" of the spoken word and at least suggest that Jn enlarges the conception of word to signify the entire experience of Jesus by the apostles. It is not as clear here as it is in the prologue of Jn that Jesus Himself is the word, but the writer moves in the same circle of ideas, in particular the life-giving virtue of the word.

The prologue of Jn (1:1–14) synthesizes in the identification of Jesus with the word all the leading themes of the 4th Gospel: the identity of Jesus with the Father (1:1) and the personal distinction of Jesus and the Father, Jesus as the life of mankind (1:4, 13) and as the light which brings life (1:4 f, 9). Here also appears the word as the creative agent, a motif not common elsewhere in the NT (1:3, 10). The hypostatization of the word as a distinct dynamic reality here reaches its "fulfillment"; Jesus Himself achieved all that the word of God is said to achieve in the OT, and the word becomes flesh* and pitches His tent among men (1:14). He is also the word which reveals the glory of the Father which He shares (1:14). This word is the summit and the fullness of the self-revelation of God through His word (1:18), and the agent through which God accomplishes the salvation which this word signifies. Both Kittel and Starcky point out an implicit antithesis in the prologue between the law*, the word spoken through Moses, and Christ, who is Himself the saving word uttered by the Father; the antithesis becomes explicit in 1:17 and lies

chiefly in grace* and truth* of which the incarnate word is full (1:14).

While the hypostatic word is original with Jn, the elements which are synthesized are common NT teaching. The preexistence of Jesus is stated or implied in Rm 1:4; 8:3; 1 Co 10:3 f; 2 Co 8:9; Gal 4:4; Phl 2:6 ff; Col 1:16. Christ as the creative agent appears in Col 1:15 ff; Heb 1:2 ff.

It seems unnecessary to seek antecedents and connections of the Johannine conception of the incarnate word either in the speculations of Philo Judaeus, who conceives a hypostatized word as an intermediate being, or in the philosophical atmosphere of Stoicism, which represented the world as animated by *logos* as an intelligent principle. The background of OT and NT sketched here present all the elements in which the conception is easily traced, and it is best understood as an insight which is developed from biblical ideas.

Work. Work in the Bible is the work of God or the work of man. The work of God is creation (Gn 2:2 f; Pss 103:22; 104:13, 24; BS 16:26 f; 39:14 +). The heavens are the work of His hands (Pss 8:4; 102:26). The works of God reveal the workman (WS 13:1 ff). In particular man is the work of God's hands (Jb 10:3; 14:15; Is 64:8); this designation of man is pathetic, expressing the peculiar interest which God takes in man. The conception of creation as a work is a counterweight to the conception of creation as a victory through combat; it expresses better than the image of the combat the complete domination of God over creation and the ease with which He creates.

The work of God is also accomplished in history. Salvation is the work of God (Is 29:23; 45:11); restored Israel is His work (Is 60:21). The course of Israel's history is a recitation of His works of salvation (Dt 3:24; Jos 24:31; Jgs 2:7, 10; Pss 66:3, 5; 77:13). But judgment is also His work (Is 5:12, 19; 28:21; Apc 15:3). The image of work represents God as really and immanently active in the course of history, which He effects with the same power by which He creates the world.

Jn speaks of the works of the Father (Jn 9:3) and of the works which Jesus and the Father perform in union (Jn 5:20; 9:4; 14:10–12) and of the works of Jesus (Jn 5:36; 7:3, 21). The work of Jesus is the work which His Father has given Him to do (Jn 17:4); His works demonstrate that He has been sent by the Father (Jn 10:25, 32, 37 f). The work which God gives men to do is faith (Jn 6:29 f). Neither the works of the Father nor the works of Jesus should be considered simply as miracles; Jn echoes the OT conception of the saving and judging work of God (cf above) which He does in history. Jesus is the work of God incarnate, as He is the word* incarnate. The work is the revelation of the Father, the redemption of man, the victory over sin; work is the issue of power, and the power of God dwells in Jesus.

The other NT writings do not use the word *work* of God in a consistent pattern. The work of God is the spiritual edification of the community (Rm 14:20), the apostolate (AA 5:38; 13:2; 1 Co 16:10; Phl 2:30). The Christian life in the individual Christian is God's work (1 Co 15:58); the regeneration and the perfection of the Christian is the good work which God has begun and which He will finish (Phl 1:6). The charismata are the work of God in man (1 Co 12:6).

The work of man is viewed under two aspects in Gn 2:15, where it is the destiny for which man is placed in the garden, and in Gn 3:17–19, where it is a curse. The change comes through the sin of man; his proper destiny, by which he should have been integrated into nature, is now a toil and a frustration because nature is no longer submissive to him. In the Pauline writings work is accepted as a necessary part of human responsibility (Eph 4:28; 1 Th 4:11; 2 Th 3:10–12), and by work here is meant the work of the hands. In Judaism of NT times the work of the hands was by no means contemned; even the rabbis made it a point of pride to know a trade by which they could support themselves, and Paul himself was a tentmaker, a trade to which he resorted in his apostolic travels.

The works of man in the sense of deeds are sometimes viewed with deep pessimism; they are works of darkness (Rm 13:12; Eph 5:11), works of the flesh (Gal 5:19), wicked works (Jn 3:19). Even the works of the law are regarded by Paul as of no saving value (Rm 3:20, 28; Gal 2:16; 3:2, 10). On the antithesis of faith and works cf FAITH; it is a principle of NT theology that the works of man are totally ineffective to achieve the righteousness* which saves. Once one has received faith, however, the works of faith are demanded (Gal 5:6; 1 Th 1:3; 2 Th 1:11; Js 1:25; 2:17); these are deeds which are done in accordance with the Christian standards of righteousness and from the motive of faith and love. The works of faith are considered less as works which effect man's salvation than as necessary consequences of the principle of salvation which he has received in the new life in Christ.

World. There is no single Hb word which can be translated *world*. When the visible universe is mentioned in a single phrase it is "heaven* and earth*"; but this phrase does not mean "world." The world (Gk *kosmos*) is conceived in Gk and modern thought as a systematic whole constituted by some unifying principle; in ancient Semitic thought the "world" was a sum of conflicting forces; cf CREATION. The Gk word *kosmos* for world appears in the OT only in late Gk books, and its use shows the influence of Gk usage. God made the world (WS 9:9), He is its creator (2 Mc 7:23; 13:14), its ruler (2 Mc 12:15), its king (2 Mc 7:5). It has a "constitution," a unifying principle (WS 7:17). The gods of the nations are its alleged rulers (WS 13:2). The world fights for God and for the righteous (WS 5:20; 16:17). *Kosmos* is also used to signify not the universe but the earth: man is created to manage the world (WS 9:3); the temple is honored over the whole world (2 Mc 3:12). Death and idolatry have entered the world (WS 2:24; 14:14). The world also means humanity: Adam is the first formed father of the world (WS 10:1), Noah was the hope of the world (WS 14:6), the wise are the salvation of the world (WS 6:24).

In the NT *kosmos* is both a cosmological and a theological term; it is far more common in the theological sense, but the two uses sometimes merge. God is the creator of the *kosmos* (AA 17:24); it was made through the Word* (Jn 1:10). The *kosmos* belongs to Christians (1 Co 3:22). The addition of "all in it" (AA 17:24) echoes Hb "heaven and earth and all in them" and is Hb in thought rather than Gk; the *kosmos* is conceived as a spatial container, as it is in Jn 21:25. The *kosmos* is of limited duration: it has its age (Eph 2:2), its end (Mt 13:40) and its beginning (Mt 24:21), which is its creation (Rm 1:20) or its foundation (Mt 25:34; Lk 11:50; Jn 17:24; Eph 1:4; Heb 4:3; 9:26; 1 Pt 1:20; Apc 13:8). The "foundation" of the world is an echo of OT language concerning creation. The world (1 Jn 2:17) and its form (1 Co 7:31) passes away. The elements of the world which are served and which are in some sense hostile to God (cf below; Gal 4:3; Col 2:8, 20) are obscure; some understand them as the Law*, others as the elemental spirits which appear in Hellenistic syncretism.

The world is also the dwelling place of man: it is the scene of kingdoms (Mt 4:8) and nations (Lk 12:30). This is the world which it is no profit to gain at the cost of one's soul* (Mt 16:26; Mk 8:36; Lk 9:25). It is the world into which the apostles are sent (Mt 26:13; Mk 16:15; cf Rm 1:8). The world is mankind, the world of which the disciples are the light (Mt 5:14), of which Paul is the refuse (1 Co 4:9), before which he is a spectacle (1 Co 4:9). The world as the dwelling place of man or as mankind, however, is more frequently conceived in connection with the world in a theological sense.

The world in a theological sense is the world as the scene of the process of salvation; it is not merely the scene but one of the protagonists of the drama, for the world is mankind as fallen, as alienated from God and hostile to God and to Jesus Christ. This conception is most frequent in the Pauline writings and in Jn, less frequent in the epistles and scarcely found at all in the Synoptic Gospels. The world stands in opposition to God; there is the spirit* of the world and the spirit of God (1 Co 2:12). The wisdom, strength, and nobility of the world are the folly, weakness, and ignobility of God (1 Co 1:20-28; 3:19). The base of the opposition is found in the sinfulness of the world, the sin which entered the world through one man (Rm 5:12). Because of sin the world lies under God's judgment (Rm 3:6, 19; 1 Co 6:2; 11:32). It was the rulers of the world who crucified Christ (1 Co 2:8), not "rulers of the world" in the sense of imperial rulers but rulers whose power is in the world and comes from the world.

The world is hostile to God, but God is not hostile to the world. In Christ God reconciles the world to Himself (2 Co 5:19; Rm 11:15). Christ came into the world to save sinners (1 Tm 1:15). But as long as the world remains unredeemed, Christians cannot identify themselves with it. Anxiety about the affairs of this world turns one from God (1 Co 7:33). The Christian must deal with the world as if he were not dealing with it (1 Co 7:31); he must not live as if he still belonged to the world (Col 2:20). Paul is crucified to the world, and the world to him (Gal 6:14). Religion means to keep oneself unspotted from the world (Js 1:27), and friendship with the world is enmity with God (Js 4:4). The Christian must not be conformed to this world (Rm 12:2). On the other hand, the Christian cannot simply go out of this world in order to avoid contact with sinners (1 Co 5:10).

In Jn the world becomes more prominent, and the opposition between God and Christ and the world is more sharply polarized. The purpose of God's salvation is the world and the mission of the Son is to it. He is the light of the world (Jn 1:9; 3:19; 8:12; 9:5; 12:46). Jn speaks frequently of the coming of Christ (the Son, the Word) into the world (3:17; 9:39; 10:36; 11:27; 12:46 f; 16:28; 17:18; 18:37; 1 Jn 4:9); this is never a simple coming, but has overtones of coming with a mission. Although Jesus comes into the world, He is not of the world (Jn 8:23). The world is loved by God so much that He sent His only son, and the mission of the Son is not to condemn but to save (Jn 3:16 f). He is the lamb* who takes away the sin of the world (Jn 1:29), and the propitiation for the sins of the whole world (1 Jn 2:2). He gives life to the world (Jn 6:33).

But sinful humanity, to whom this mission of salvation comes, does not receive the mission nor the emissary; and it is in this aspect that the "world" in Jn becomes polarized into a kind of anti-God, a constant reality which is neither saved nor capable of salvation. The world recognizes and acknowledges neither Jesus nor the Father (Jn 1:10; 17:25); indeed, the world hates Jesus (Jn 7:7; 15:18). The world is under judgment (Jn 12:31), as is the ruler of the world (Jn 16:11), who has no power over Jesus (Jn 14:30). "The ruler of this world" is an obscure phrase which many interpreters understand to mean Satan*, and this interpretation is possible. Other interpreters suggest that the ruler of this world is a collective personification of mankind unredeemed and hostile to God which sets itself up as an opposing power. The identification of Satan with the world as combined powers of evil is suggested in such verses as Jn 17:15; Jesus does not pray that the disciples be kept out of the world, but that the Father will protect them from the evil one. For the world Jesus does not pray (Jn 17:9); here certainly unredeemed humanity is conceived as a constant. The world can be redeemed and reconciled to God only by ceasing to be the world. The disciples, although they are men and live in the world as the universe and the scene of human life, do not belong to the world, as Jesus does not (Jn 15:19). The world cannot receive the spirit nor recognize Him (Jn 14:17). When the world must be brought to believe that the Father has sent Jesus and that He loves the disciples (Jn 17:21, 23), it is not clearly a salutary recognition which is implied. The disciples are not to love the world (1 Jn 2:15); mankind in general is not meant, but mankind as the personified hostile power, for one is to love one's fellowmen. Jesus has overcome the world (Jn 16:33), He has broken its power; but His victory consists in His redeeming act, His surrender to love fulfilled in death. The disciples also overcome the world by their faith (1 Jn 5:4 f), the faith which refuses to acknowledge the power of the world and thus reduces it to impotence.

Such passages are the root of the "otherworldliness" or "unworldliness" which is a feature of historic Christianity. It is important to grasp the true meaning of "the world" in the NT in order that "unworldliness" may not be mere narrowness and intolerance, or mere external distinction from other men in manners and customs. Christians, like Jesus, are in the world and have a mission to the world and overcome it eventually by love and only by love. To obtain the victory they must not identify themselves with the world as a power hostile to God, but neither can they lose their identity with the world as the creature of God, as the stage of the processes of salvation, and as unredeemed mankind.

Worm. The worm is an agent of destruction which often appears in metaphors describing the corruptibility and the mortality of the flesh*. One who expects death thinks of himself as consumed by worms (Jb 17:14; 21:26). Job in his mortal illness thinks of himself as already consumed by worms (Jb 7:5); this is a more probable interpretation than that some disease which issues in consumption by worms is imagined. The worms alluded to in the traditions of the death of Antiochus Epiphanes (2 Mc 9:9) and Herod Agrippa (AA 12:23) are also very probably a popular story which gave these two persecutors the horror of the phenomena of the grave while they were still living. The worm which does not die (Is 66:24; Mk 9:48) is a metaphor of "eternal death*" rather than of some eternal punishment.

Wormwood (Hb *la'ᵃnāh,* Gk *apsinthos*), the plant *Artemisia.* Because of its bitter taste it is employed as a metaphor for sin (Dt 29:17; Am 5:7; 6:12), divine punishment (Je 9:14; 23:15; Lam 3:15, 19), disaster (Pr 5:4). The star of Apc 8:11 named Wormwood falls from the sky and renders water poisonous.

Writing. Cf ALPHABET; BOOK; CUNEIFORM; INK; OSTRACA; PAPYRUS; PARCHMENT; PEN; SCRIBE.

X

Xerxes. Cf AHASUERUS.

Y

Yahweh. Cf GOD.

Year. Cf CALENDAR; NEW YEAR.

Yod. The 10th letter of the Hb alphabet, with the value of *y*.

Yoke. The yoke employed in ancient Palestine was similar to the yoke which is still in use. It consisted of a heavy wooden bar laid upon the shoulders of the draught animals (oxen or asses) and attached to the animals by pins and thongs which passed around and under their throats. A longer pin attached the yoke to the shaft. The iron yoke of Dt 28:48 and Jeremiah's symbolic action (Je 27–28) was not in practical use; the iron symbolized the heavy oppression of a foreign conqueror. The yoke is a symbol of submission, not always with the implication of oppression (Gn 27:40; Lv 26:13; 1 K 12; 2 Ch 10; Is 9:3; 14:25; Je 30:8; 10:27; Ho 11:4). It is a symbol of submission to Yahweh (Je 2:20) and of the obligation of the law (AA 15:10; Gal 5:1). Slavery is a yoke (1 Tm 6:1). The yoke of Jesus imposes obligations which are easy to bear (Mt 11:29 f). To put the yoke upon an ox was to use it for the first time, hence to profane it (cf HOLY); oxen which were employed for sacred purposes (drawing the ark, 1 S 6:7; atonement for murder, Dt 21:3 ff) should never have been yoked.

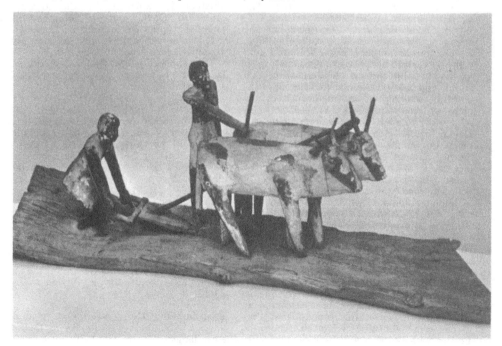

Ancient Egyptian model showing plowing and yoked oxen.

Z

Zacchaeus (Gk *zacchaios*, Hb *zakkai*, probably an abbreviated name [Ne 3:20; Ezr 2:9]), the name appears in inscriptions. The Gk name is borne by one of the officers of Judas* (2 Mc 10:19). Zacchaeus was the chief tax collector of Jericho, a Jew, who went to see Jesus from curiosity; he had the reputation of being unobservant. Jesus invited Himself to the home of Zacchaeus for dinner, and Zacchaeus was moved to make restitution of ill-gotten gains and to give to the poor (Lk 19:1–10). The story of the dignitary, small of stature, who climbed a tree to see the distinguished visitor and was called down like a small boy is told with humor.

Zacharias. Cf ZECHARIAH.

Zachary. Cf ZECHARIAH.

Zadok (Hb *ṣādôḳ*, "righteous"? possibly an abbreviated name, possibly also a Canaanite divine name; a connection has been noticed with Melchizedek* of Jerusalem), son of Ahitub, appointed priest with Ahimelech* by David (2 S 8:17; 1 Ch 18:16). The name is borne by six others in the OT. When David fled from Jerusalem at the beginning of the rebellion of Absalom*, Zadok and the other priests followed him with the ark*; but David instructed them to remain with the ark in Jerusalem, and Zadok and his son Ahimaaz* were of assistance in sending David intelligence of the plans of Absalom (2 S 15:24–35; 17:15; 18:19–27). Zadok was the spokesman for David to the elders of Judah concerning the return of the king (2 S 19:12). During the last days of David, Zadok did not adopt the cause of Adonijah* with his brother priest Abiathar*, but joined the party of Solomon, and was commissioned by David to anoint Solomon king (1 K 1:8, 26, 32–45). For this loyalty he was rewarded by Solomon with the office of chief priest to replace the deposed Abiathar (1 K 2:35). He was succeeded by his son Azariah as priest (1 K 4:2; the text is obscure, cf ELIHOREPH); 1 K 4:4 is misplaced in its present position from the list of David's officers. In the restored temple of Ezekiel only the sons of Zadok are permitted to serve as priests, on the ground that they alone were faithful to Yahweh when the Levites with the rest of Israel were unfaithful (Ezk 40:46; 43:19; 44:15; 48:11). A number of details are added in 1 Ch. Zadok appears in the Levite genealogy in the clan of Kohath* as a descendant of Eleazar* (1 Ch 5:34; 24:3–6), and as the representative of the family of Aaron among Israelite officers (1 Ch 27:17). He was appointed priest of the high place of Gibeon* by David (1 Ch 16:39) and is listed among the priests who bring the ark to Jerusalem (1 Ch 15:11).

Many scholars believe that these data of 1 Ch do not represent genuine traditions. They suggest that the inclusion of Zadok in the Levite and Aaronite genealogies, in view of Ezekiel's distinction between the Zadokites and Levites, must be an artificial connection established in a later period when the priesthood was identified exclusively with the family of Aaron, although it was in fact held by the Zadokites in the postexilic temple. These scholars suggest that Zadok was himself neither an Israelite nor a Levite but priest of the Jebusite shrine of Jerusalem who adopted the cult of Yahweh when David took Jerusalem. The advance of Zadok over the line of Eli* represented by Abiathar is explained by the loyalty of Zadok to David and to Solomon, while Abiathar supported Adonijah. These views have some probability but do not admit rigorous demonstration; cf PRIEST.

The connection of Zadok-Zadokite with Sadducee* is favored by some scholars, but is doubtful.

Zalmon (Hb *ṣalmōn*, "sparkling"). **1.** a mountain, which the context of Jgs 9:48 suggests is near Shechem*; modern geographers think it is the name of a slope or promontory of Ebal* or Gerizim*. The name occurs again in Ps 68:15 with no indication of its location. **2.** a personal name; one of David's heroes (2 S 23:28).

Zalmunna (Hb *ṣalmunnāʿ*, etymology uncertain), a Moabite chieftain who with Zebah* was pursued by Gideon* into E Palestine, captured, and executed in blood revenge for their killing of Gideon's brothers (Jgs 8:4–21). On the literary criticism of the story cf GIDEON. The victory is alluded to in Ps 83:12.

Zamzummmim (Hb *zamzummîm*, etymology uncertain but probably alludes to their foreign language), in Dt 2:20 mentioned as the Ammonite name of the pre-Israelite inhabitants of Canaan* elsewhere called Rephaim*.

Zaphenath-paneah (Hb *ṣāpᶜnat pa'nēⁿḥ*, Egyptian *Da-p',-nt(r)-'wf-'nh*, "the god speaks and he lives"), the Egyptian name given Joseph when he entered the service of the Pharaoh (Gn 41:45).

Zaphon (Hb *ṣāpôn*, "north"), a town of Gad in the Jordan valley on the E bank, where the Ephraimites crossed to meet Jephthah* (Jos 13:27; Jgs 12:1). It is probably identified with the modern Tell el Qos a few miles NNE of Succoth*.

Zarephath (Hb *ṣārᶜpat*, Gk *sarepta*, meaning uncertain), a city of ancient Phoenicia, modern Sarafand, about 10 mi S of Sidon*; the modern village has moved a short distance away from the coast. The ancient city had a fine harbor of three small bays. The city was a center of the manufacture of glass*. Very few ruins from ancient times have survived. It lay on the border of Phoenicia (Ob 20). Elijah sojourned at Zarephath during the famine in Israel with a widow, for whom he provided oil and whose son he raised from illness (1 K 17:8–24). Jesus alludes to this episode to illustrate the unbelief of the Jews as contrasted with Gentiles (Lk 4:26).

Zarethan (Hb *ṣārᶜtan*, meaning uncertain), a town in or near the Jordan valley on the W bank of the river, near the fords at Adam (Damiyyeh; Jos 3:16); near Bethshan in Solomon's 5th district (1 K 4:12, but the text is obscure); the site of Solomon's bronze foundry (1 K 7:46). It is usually identified with Qarn es Sartabeh, W of Damiyyeh and 19 mi N of Jericho, the site of Herod's fortress of Alexandreion; Tell es Saidiyeh 11 mi N of Damiyyeh is also suggested.

Zayin. The 7th letter of the Hb alphabet, with the value of *z*.

Zealots (Gk *zēlōtēs*, "one who shows zeal and enthusiasm"). In NT times the Zealots were a Jewish sect which represented the extreme of fanatic nationalism. Their belief in the messianism of the OT was entirely limited to the recovery of Jewish independence; they believed in the worship of Yahweh alone and were convinced that acceptance of foreign domination and payment of taxes to a foreign ruler was a blasphemy against Yahweh. The party seems to have originated in the revolt against the census taken under Quirinius (on the question of the date cf CENSUS; QUIRINIUS).

The sect was a minority and was regarded by other Jews with distaste at least. Their tactics were those of the modern political terrorists; they raided and killed frequently, attacking both foreigners and Jews whom they suspected of what is more recently called "collaboration." They carried the art of assassination to such a point of skill that the Romans called them *sicarii* ("stabbers") from their practice of concealing a dagger beneath the garments for stealthy use in crowded areas. Their largest concerted effort before the outbreak of the Jewish war was a raid of reprisal on Samaria for an assault on Jewish pilgrims under the procurator Ventidius Cumanus (48–52). Their fanaticism and their tactics are illustrated in the life of Paul, who was threatened with assassination by a group of men (AA 23:12–15). One of the disciples of Jesus, Simon*, was called the Zealot; he was probably a former member of the sect. They were chiefly responsible for the outbreak of the rebellion against Rome in 66, and forced the moderates to accept the rebellion even against their will; and during the next few years they obtained control of Jerusalem by the suppression or murder of those who opposed their extreme policies. They maintained pockets of resistance in the country after the fall of Jerusalem, and the movement survived long enough to break out again in the rebellion of 132–135 under Hadrian.

A connection between the Zealots and the Qumran* sect has been sought by some scholars but is not established. Recently F. W. Farmer has examined the material concerning the Zealots anew. Our principal source for the Zealots is Josephus, who is extremely hostile to them, calling them assassins and brigands. F. W. Farmer suggests that Josephus has blackened their reputation unduly and proposes that the Zealots were the spiritual heirs of the Maccabees*, preserving the same ideals of independence and religion and employing tactics which, on the hypothesis that Josephus gives a prejudiced report, did not differ substantially from the tactics of the Maccabees. They differ from the Maccabees, Farmer thinks, only in their failure.

Zebah (Hb *zebaḥ*, "born on the day of the sacrifice [*zebah*]"?), a Midianite chieftain executed with Zalmunna* in revenge for Gideon's brothers (Jgs 8:4–21; Ps 83:12).

Zebedee (Gk *zebedaios*, Hb *zabdî*, abbreviated from *zabdî'ēl* or *zabdîyāh*, "gift of El or gift of Yahweh"), a personal name; father of the apostles James* and John*, with whom they were mending their nets when Jesus called them (Mt 4:21; Mk 1:19 f); mentioned briefly otherwise only as father of the two.

Zeboim. The one Eng name represents the two Hb words. **1.** ṣᵉbōʾîm, always mentioned with Admah, one of the five cities of the plain destroyed with Sodom (Gn 10:19; 14:2, 8) and thus an example of Yahweh's anger (Dt 29:22; Ho 11:8). The site is unknown; cf SODOM. **2.** ṣᵉbōʾîm ("hyenas"?), a town in the territory of Benjamin (Ne 11:34), "toward the desert" presumably to the E (1 S 13:18). The site is unknown.

Zebul (Hb zᵉbŭl, "prince"?), a personal name; governor of Shechem* under Abimelech* during the insurrection of Gaal* (Jgs 9:28–41).

Zebulun (Hb zᵉbûlûn, "prince"?), son of Jacob* and Leah* and one of the 12 tribes of Israel*. The story of his birth (Gn 30:20) connects the name with Hb zbl, "to bear" or "to tolerate"; but the word is found only here in biblical Hb and the etymology given above is preferable. Gn 30:20 seems to suggest a play also on the word zbd, "reward." Zebulun occurs in the lists of the sons of Israel (Gn 35:28; Ex 1:3; 1 Ch 2:1); the clans of Zebulun are listed in Gn 46:14. In the census of Nm 1:30 f Zebulun is given 57,400, in the census of Nm 26:26 60,500; cf CENSUS; THOUSAND. The territory is defined in Jos 19:10–16; it lies in lower Galilee N of Mt Carmel and the plain of Esdraelon and borders on the coastal plain. Both Gn 49:13 and Dt 33:18 allude to the dwelling of Zebulun by the seashore and to its access to ships; but the territory described does not give access to the sea directly, and Zebulun would be the only Israelite tribe which reached the sea. It is therefore more probable that it had access to the sea through relations with the Canaanite cities of the coast. Jgs 1:30 mentions Canaanite cities which remained in Canaanite hands, but no details are given anywhere of Zebulun's entrance into its territory. On its place in the Israelite tribal confederacy cf ISRAEL; LEAH. Zebulun with Naphtali* fought against Sisera* under the leadership of Barak* and Deborah* (Jgs 4:6, 10; 5:18) and is mentioned among the tribes summoned by Gideon* (Jgs 6:35). It appears in the processional march of Ps 68:28. It was the tribe of the minor judge Elon* (Jgs 12:11 f). The Levitical* cities of Zebulun are listed in 1 Ch 6:48, 62; Jos 21:34 f. Is 8:23 alludes to the conquest of Galilee by Tiglath-pileser* III of Assyria in 734. The name Zebulun occurs in the Egyptian Execration Texts of the 19th–18th

centuries BC (ANET 329) as the name of a prince of Shutu (possibly Moab).

Zechariah (Hb zᵉkaryāh, "Yahweh has remembered"), a very common personal name in the Bible; only a few who bear it are mentioned here.
1. Son and successor of Jeroboam* II as king of Israel; he acceded to the throne in 746 BC and was assassinated by Shallum* after six months (2 K 14:29; 15:8–11). The political background of the assassination is unknown, but it initiated a period of internecine strife and anarchy which endured until the fall of the kingdom of Israel.
2. Son of Jehoiada, a prophet in the reign of Jehoash* of Judah who was stoned in the court of the temple (2 Ch 24:20–23).
3. A prophet of the time of Uzziah* of Judah (2 Ch 26:5).
4. A prophet of the postexilic period; cf ZECHARIAH, BOOK OF. The patronymic, son of Berechiah, would identify this prophet with the prophet killed between the temple and the altar (Mt 23:35; Lk 11:51). The allusion of Mt-Lk, however, must be to #2 above, particularly since his is the last murder mentioned in the Hb Bible (which ends with 2 Ch) while Abel* is the first (Mt-Lk [ibid]). The use of the patronymic of the literary prophet can be attributed only to some carelessness in the oral tradition of the discourse.
5. Gk zacharias, father of John the Baptist. He was a priest; the birth of a son to himself and his wife, who had no children, was announced by the angel Gabriel* while he offered incense in the temple. When he doubted, the sign of the promise was his dumbness until the birth of the child (Lk 1:5–25). After the birth of the child Zachary recovered his speech when the child was given his name; to him is attributed the song Benedictus (Lk 1:59–79). The story of Zachary contains elements of midrash* (cf INFANCY GOSPELS). With the initiation of the messianic era the beginnings of Israelite traditions, which included the promise of a son to an aging childless couple, Abraham* and Sarah*, are recalled; in the composition of the story elements are employed which recall the stories of the births of Samson* and Samuel*. Gabriel is the angel who announces to Daniel* the coming restoration of Israel.

Zechariah, Book of. The 11th of the minor prophets. The book falls into two parts, 1–8 and 9–14, of which only the first can be attributed to Zc. The dates found in 1–8 (1:1, 7; 7:1) fall between 520 and 518 BC, after the return of Jews to Jerusalem from

Babylon and shortly before the dedication of the rebuilt temple in 515. Zechariah is called the son of Berechiah in Zc 1:1, 7, the son of Iddo in Ezr 5:1; 6:14, and he is identified by most scholars with the Zechariah of the priestly family of Iddo mentioned in Ne 12:16. This uncertainty concerning his father's name is not easily resolved; his membership in the priestly family of Iddo may account for the appearance of Iddo as the name of his father.

1. *Contents* (1–8) consisting principally of eight nocturnal visions.

1:1, title; 1:2–6, admonition to repentance; 1:8–17, vision of the horsemen, promises of restoration; 1:18–21, vision of the four horns and the four smiths; 2:1–5, vision of the man with the measuring line; 2:6–9, summons to the exiles; 2:10–13, promises of restoration; 3:1–7, vision of the purification of Joshua; 3:8–10, the servant Branch; 4:1–6a + 10b–14, the vision of the lamp and the two olive trees; 4:6b–10a, promises of deliverance and the rebuilding of the temple; 5:1–11, visions of the flying scroll and the woman Wickedness in the measure; 6:1–8, vision of the four chariots; 6:9–15, coronation of Zerubbabel; 7:1–3 + 8:18–19, fasting turned into joy; 7:4–14, righteousness rather than fasting; 8:1–17, promises of restoration; 8:18–23, the glory of Jerusalem.

2. *Composition*. Few critics question the attribution of the discourses to Zechariah, but most of them believe that the original collection has been interrupted by insertions. The outline above shows the place of these insertions into the series of the visions. There is also a change in the person; the prophet speaks in the first person in 1:7–6:8. The additions made by the editors, however, are taken from the words of Zechariah; nothing in the material suggests a different origin. The question concerning the· fast (7:1–3) is not answered until 8:18 f; 7:4 ff, which draws a contrast between fasting and interior morality, comes here because of the catchword. The song of 2:10–13 is inserted on the same principle, and 3:8–10 after 3:1–7.

A particular problem is created by the present text of 6:9–15, which relates the coronation of the high priest Joshua under the title "Branch." The messianic title "Branch" is given to the descendant of David in Je 23:5; 33:15 (cf Ps 132:17), and critics are right in affirming unanimously that the name which stood originally in this passage was Zerubbabel. On the possible historical reasons which lie behind the altered text cf ZERUBBABEL.

3. *Theology* (1–8). The dominant note of Zc 1–8 is messianism. The prophet proposes a revelation of a new national-religious messianic community to be established in Palestine with its center in Jerusalem. The time of the messianic salvation is near, and the rebuilding of the temple is the sign and initiation of its coming. In the messianic period the nations will be defeated (2:1–4, 10–13), the temple (1:16) and Jerusalem will be rebuilt (8:3), Yahweh will come to dwell with His people (2:14; 8:3), the exiles will be gathered (6:15; 7:7 f), the nations will worship Yahweh (2:15; 8:20–23), there will be peace and joy (3:10; 8:12), and sin will be removed (3:9; 5:1–11). The messianism of Zechariah does not rise to the highest level of OT conceptions; on the other hand, it is not merely national but includes a purification of the community which is presupposed for its union with Yahweh.

A number of modern scholars (Eissfeldt, Johnson +) have proposed that Zechariah is an example of the cultic prophet* whose function it was to speak the word of Yahweh during cultic functions. The priesthood of Zechariah supports this view concerning him, as well as his activity in 3:6–6:9–15. His own conception of prophecy and prophetic inspiration differs from the conception of earlier prophets. While he still hears and speaks the word* of Yahweh, the vision has become a normal vehicle of communicating his message; and the vision in Zechariah is an evident literary device and not a psychological experience. With the vision comes his preference for stating things in symbols and images; the explanation of the symbol is the message.

4. *Contents* (9–14).

9:1–8, threats against neighboring peoples; 9:9–17, coming of the messianic king, victory over enemies; 10:1–2, against divination; 10:3–11:3, the ingathering and the restoration of all Israel; 11:4–17; 13:7–9, punishment of the foolish shepherds; 12:1–14, the power of Jerusalem and the defeat of the nations; 13:1–6, the end of prophecy; 14:1–21, the restoration of Jerusalem and Palestine and the destruction of enemies.

5. *Authorship and Date*. The difference between Zc 1–8 and 9–14 was noticed as early as the 18th century. Older views were that 9–11 were written shortly before the fall of Israel in 721 BC, and 12–14 shortly before the fall of Judah in the period 609–587 BC. The ascription of Zc 11:12 f to Jeremiah in Mt 27:9 f, a celebrated problem, may possibly be explained by an uncertainty in the division of the text of the prophetic books. Modern scholars are convinced that 9–14 cannot be older materials added to the work of a more recent prophet; they are agreed that 9–14 come from the Gk period after the conquests of Alexander.

Allusions to such peoples as Egypt and Assyria are deliberate archaisms to conceal the true identity of the peoples whom the prophet means; the Bible reader would recognize that Egypt means the Egypt of the Ptolemies* and Assyria the kingdom of the Seleucids*. 11:4–17 + 13:7–9 as well as 12:1–13:6, in particular 12:10–14, must refer to definite events. Unfortunately they cannot be certainly attached to any known events of the Gk period, and the date must remain open all the way from the late 4th century to the Maccabean period.

Modern critics are likewise agreed that 9–11 and 12–14 do not come from a single author; differences of style and conception and possibly of background, although it is more difficult to affirm this without qualification, are explained more easily on the hypothesis of different authors. There is no reason to suppose more than two authors, except for 14, which appears to be constructed of a series of utterances added successively.

6. *Theology (9–14)*. Messianism is also the dominant note of 9–14, but messianism has become strongly apocalyptic*. The accomplishment of the messianic salvation coincides with the end time. Israel is established as a cultic theocracy which the powers of the world attack in vain. The messianism centers upon the house of David, which is not, however, treated with unreserved veneration; like Israel as a whole, the house of David also needs purification. The most striking feature of the messianism cf Zc 9–14 is the appearance of the Messiah of the poor* (9:9); with the disappearance of the monarchy for several centuries the external features of the messianic ruler are not the trappings of royalty. He has become identified with the devout class of postexilic Judaism called the poor. This is the only feature of royal messianism which was explicitly accepted by Jesus (Mt 21:1–9; Mk 11:1–10; Lk 19:28–38), and He deliberately reenacted the saying of Zc.

Zc 13:3–7 marks the end of prophecy in a remarkable way. The background of the passage cannot be traced; but it is evident that it comes from a period when it was no longer possible for anyone to claim the title of prophet, and suggests that the Jewish community knew only false prophets, and apparently many of them. It was the belief of Judaism of the NT period and earlier that the next prophet to appear would be the precursor of the Messiah.

Zedekiah (Hb *ṣidḳîyyāh*, "Yahweh is my righteousness"), personal name.
1. A prophet of the reign of Ahab*, who predicted victory for Ahab at Ramoth-

gilead* and was disputed by Micaiah* (1 K 22:11, 24; 2 Ch 18:10, 23).
2. A prophet who lived in Babylon in the time of Jeremiah threatened by Jeremiah with punishment for crimes and false prophecy (Je 29:21 f); he was probably involved in an abortive rebellion.
3. Son of Josiah*, brother of Jehoiakim* and uncle and successor of Jehoiachin*; the last king of Judah (597–587). His name was Mattaniah; he was installed as king by Nebuchadnezzar*, who gave him the throne name of Zedekiah, doubtless as a sign of his vassalage to Babylon. Zedekiah is prominent in Je; he appears as well intentioned but weak and vacillating and unable to resist the pressure put upon him by his courtiers. Zedekiah and the court were the object of a threatening oracle of Jeremiah shortly after the defeat of 598–597 (Je 24:8–10). Zedekiah plotted revolt with other subject peoples, who sent ambassadors to Jerusalem to plan action; the move was denounced by Jeremiah as sure to fail (Je 27). During the siege of Jerusalem by the Babylonians Jeremiah consistently urged surrender upon the king and his nobles, and rebuked Zedekiah for the dishonesty shown by the people of Jerusalem in releasing their slaves and then repossessing them (Je 34). Zedekiah nevertheless respected Jeremiah as a genuine prophet and asked him for an oracle; Jeremiah promised defeat if resistance were continued (Je 21). Zedekiah asked Jeremiah to pray for the people (Je 37:3–4). When the prophet left the city during the interruption of the siege, the officers of Zedekiah demanded that he be imprisoned for desertion; the king asked Jeremiah for another oracle, and received only the same threat of defeat; but he granted Jeremiah's petition for better quarters (Je 37:11–21). Jeremiah continued his preaching in favor of surrender, and the officers demanded that he be executed. In order to avoid the shedding of blood, he was put into a cistern; but Zedekiah at the urging of one of his slaves permitted his release. The question of surrender was discussed once more; the king appears to have believed Jeremiah, but could not follow his advice for fear of shame (Je 38). When the city was finally breached, Zedekiah and a small band fled toward the Jordan. They were overtaken and captured and taken to Nebuchadnezzar at Riblah*, where the unfortunate Zedekiah received the full penalty of rebellion. His sons were executed in his presence, he himself was blinded and taken in chains to Babylon, where apparently he died; no more is reported of him. Not all his subjects regarded him as a legitimate king, since he had been installed by a foreign power, and perhaps Jeremiah was among

them; for he seems to treat Jehoiachin as the last of the dynasty of David. Jehoiachin retained the title of king after the death of Zedekiah. The dealings of Zedekiah with Jeremiah show that he was not an unbeliever; but he was totally unable to control the fanatics of the patriotic party.

Zeeb (Hb $z^{e'}\bar{e}b$, "jackal"), one of the princes of Midian defeated and killed by Gideon* (Jgs 7:25; 8:3). The victory is alluded to in Ps 83:12.

Zelophehad (Hb $ṣ^clophād$, meaning uncertain), a clan of Machir* (Nm 26:33; Jos 17:3; 1 Ch 7:15). The clan of Zelophehad is the object of a midrash* (Nm 27:1-11; 36:1-12) which explains the law permitting daughters to inherit where there are no sons, provided they marry within the clan of their father.

Zenas (Gk $z\bar{e}n\hat{a}s$, possibly shortened form of $z\bar{e}nod\bar{o}pas$, "gift of Zeus"), a Christian and a "lawyer" (Tt 3:13); the title does not indicate whether Zenas was skilled in the Jewish law* or in Roman law.

Zephaniah. The 9th of the minor prophets. 1. *Contents.* 1:1, title; 1:2-6, 8-13, the day of the doom of the world (2-3) and of Jerusalem (4-6; 8:13); 1:7, 14-18, the day of Yahweh; 2:1-3, invitation to repentance; 2:4-15, oracles against foreign nations (4-7, Philistines; 8-11, Moab and Ammon; 12, Ethiopia; 13-15, Assyria): 3:1-7, threat against Jerusalem; 3:8-13, judgment of the wicked and deliverance of the remnant; 3:14-20, the deliverance and the glory of Israel. 2. *Criticism.* The book is substantially attributed to Zephaniah by almost all modern critics, who date it in the first part of the reign of Josiah* (640-609 BC). For reasons stated below it should be dated earlier than 621. Nothing is known of the life and person of Zephaniah. His genealogy carried back to four generations (1:1) is extremely unusual and led many older writers to conclude that the Hezekiah* mentioned must be the king of Judah; but the bare mention of the name does not support this opinion. The historical crisis of Zephaniah is with difficulty identified with the invasion of the Scythians, as several older writers supposed. Historians now question the accuracy of the sources of Herodotus, who reports this invasion, and some even question the fact itself. The "invasion" of the Scythians left little if any traces in the literature and archaelogical remains of Syria and Palestine as they are known to us.

The present form of the book is a later compilation. The three elements in its structure (threats, oracles against foreign nations, promises) appear also in the compilations of Is 1-35; the LXX of Je; Ezk. Some portions are identified by their content and style as additions. 1:2-3 generalizes the threat against Jerusalem. 1:7 is displaced from its original position before 1:14. The conception and language of 1:17 f are stilted and commonplace in comparison to the preceding lines. The oracles against Moab and Ammon (2:8-11), like Je 49:1-6; Ezk 25:1-11, refer to the predatory attacks of Moab and Ammon against Judah after the Babylonian conquest of 587 BC and are probably later than this event. 3:9-20 appears to be an addition entirely or in part; in particular, the dispersion in foreign lands (3:10, 20) must be later than the Babylonian conquest.

3. *Theology.* Zephaniah does not allude to the Deuteronomic reform of Josiah in 621 BC. The sins which he attacks are the superstitions of the reigns of Manasseh* and Amon* and the early years of Josiah: the cults of Baal* and Milcom* and astral cults (1:4 f). He mentions the Philistine cultic practice of leaping over the temple threshold (1:9; 1 S 5:5). He anticipates Jeremiah's condemnation of priests and prophets (3:4; Je 2:8). Like Jeremiah, he speaks more of superstitution than of antisocial vices, although these are among the sins of Judah (3:3). For practical purposes he identifies Jerusalem with all of Judah. He is aware of an approaching crisis of history, the collapse of the Assyrian empire after the death of Ashur-bani-pal in 626 BC. The conflict of empires which began with the revolt of Babylon in 625 BC endured for 20 years and had among its effects the fall of the kingdom of Judah. This crisis is the day of Yahweh (1:7, 14-18), an intervention of Yahweh in history in a theophany* of power and judgment.

Zephaniah is faithful to the prophetic tradition in his conception of sin and judgment; but he is one of the less original of the prophets. The day of Yahweh comes from Am 5:18-20 and Is 2:10-21. His denunciation of pride and his praise of humility seem to depend on Is 2:10-17. The remnant (3:12 f) echoes the theme of Isaiah*. The remnant is purified in judgment (3:13), as in Is 1:25-27. The language and conceptions in which the deliverance and glory of Israel are presented show similarities to Is 49:14-50:3; 51:1-52:12; 60-61.

Zephaniah does not appear in the NT. His description of the day of Yahweh has influenced the popular image of "Judgment Day" through the medieval hymn *Dies irae,* which drew its inspiration not directly from

Zephaniah but from the use of Zp 1:14–15 in the responses of the Office of the Dead.

Zephath. Cf HORMAH.

Zerah (Hb *zerah*, "flash"?). **1.** A clan of Edom (Gn 36:13, 17; 1 Ch 1:37). **2.** Another Edomite clan (Gn 36:33; 1 Ch 1:44). **3.** A clan of Judah, which drew its origin from the story of Judah and Tamar* (Gn 38:30; 46:12; Nm 26:20; Jos 7:1, 17 f, 24; 22:20; 1 Ch 2:4, 6; 9:6; 27:8, 11, 13; Ne 11:24). From this clan came the wise men and musicians Ethan* and Heman* (1 K 5:11; Pss 88:1; 89:1). **4.** A clan of Simeon (Nm 26:13, 1 Ch 4:24). **5.** A Levite clan (1 Ch 6:6, 26). **6.** A Cushite chieftain who invaded Judah in the reign of Asa* and was defeated (2 Ch 14:8 ff).

It is doubtful that all these clans of the same name are distinct. The territory of all of them lies in the S. The wise men Ethan and Heman suggest the Edomite* tradition of wisdom. It is possible that the Edomite clan of Zerah merged with Judah and acquired a fictitious Judahite genealogy in the story of Tamar. Elements of the clan may have merged with Simeon also; but the relations of Simeon with Judah are themselves problematic.

Zered (Hb *zered*, meaning uncertain), a wadi crossed by the Israelites on their journey from the desert to Jericho. It lay S of the Arnon* and the Israelites encamped "in" the wadi (Nm 21:12; Dt 2:13 f). The Zered is generally identified with the Wadi el Hesa, about 60 mi S of the Arnon (and therefore too far for a single day's journey, as suggested by Nm 21:12); it is a perennial stream in its lower reaches and flows into the SE corner of the Dead Sea. It is possibly the stream meant in Is 15:7; 2 K 3:16–20. The Wadi el Hesa is a broad deep canyon several mi wide, easily large enough for a nomad encampment.

Zeresh (Hb *zereš*, probably a Persian name; meaning uncertain), the wife of Haman*, to whom is credited the suggestion for the erection of the lofty gibbet on which her husband and her sons were hung (Est 5:10, 14; 6:13).

Zerubbabel (Hb *zᵉrŭbbābel*, Akkadian *zer-babili*, "offspring of [born in] Babylon"), son of Shealtiel, a descendant of David, governor of Judah* during the postexilic period at the time of the rebuilding of the temple (1 Ch 3:19; Ne 12:47; Hg 1:1, 12). He is credited with beginning the rebuilding of the temple; it is not clear that he was

in Jerusalem when the task was completed (Ezr 3:2, 8; 5:2; Hg 1:14; 2:4). It is not certain that he should also be credited with leading one of the first parties of Jews to return to Jerusalem from Babylon (Ezr 2:2; Ne 7:7; 12:1); possibly his career has here been telescoped with the career of Sheshbazzar*. He refused to let the residents of the land cooperate with the rebuilding of the temple and thus helped to stimulate the ill feeling that issued in the Samaritan* schism (Ezr 4:2 f). He was a contemporary of the high priest Joshua*.

The major problem concerning Zerubbabel is the messianic titles with which he is greeted by Haggai (2:21–23) and Zechariah (4:6–10). Both of these passages appear to greet him as the representative of the restored dynasty of David, which he was only in so far as a descendant of David again ruled in Jerusalem, although he was installed as governor by a foreign imperial power. The signet ring of Hg 2:23 recalls the threat of Je 22:24. To the prophets, however, this was an attestation of the fidelity of Yahweh to His promises and an assurance of the survival of an Israel, however reduced, ruled by the house of David. Critics are unanimous in seeing in Zc 6:9–14 an account of the crowning of Zerubbabel by Zechariah; but the name of Zerubbabel has been removed from the text and the name of Joshua substituted. This at least reflects the fact that in the years following Nehemiah and Ezra the high priest was the civil as well as the religious head of the Jewish community and its representative with the imperial government. The question is whether the messianic oracles and the account of the crowning reflect anything more. Some modern historians have proposed the theory that this formal installation of the dynasty of David was treated by the Persian government as an act of rebellion and that Zerubbabel (who is not mentioned again) was deposed from his office; some say he was executed. The evidence does not support such an elaborate theory; it must be conceded, however, that a coronation of a king would require some explanation to the Persian government. It is not impossible that such an explanation could be given. The absence of Zerubbabel from the scene subsequently need not be explained by his deposition and still less by his execution; other causes may have intervened. The alteration in the text of Zc 6:9–14, however, remains an unsolved problem. It is possible that the Persian government took no violent positive action, but preferred not to have a governor of the house of David, and ultimately found it most satisfactory to have the priest as its representative. The alteration of the text would then reflect this increase in the importance of the priesthood.

Zeruiah (Hb ṣˢrûyāh, "perfumed with mastic"?), sister of David* and mother of Joab*, Abishai*, and Asahel* (1 Ch 2:16); elsewhere the name appears only with the names of her sons. It is curious that the name of her husband and the father of her sons is never mentioned; it is quite unusual for men to be distinguished by the name of their mother and not their father.

Zeus (Gk zeus), the supreme god of the classical Gk pantheon. Antiochus* Epiphanes dedicated a temple to Zeus Xenios (Zeus the patron of hospitality) on Mt Gerizim* and wished to dedicate the temple of Jerusalem to Zeus of Olympus, the mountain of the gods in Gk mythology (2 Mc 6:2). At Lystra*, where there was a temple of Zeus, the citizens greeted Barnabas* as Zeus and Paul as Hermes* (AA 14:12).

Ziba (Hb ṣîbā', etymology uncertain), a personal name; a slave of the house of Saul who informed David of the survival of Jonathan's son Mephibosheth* and was committed by David with the care of Mephibosheth and the estate which David gave him (2 S 9:2–12). Ziba met David with provisions when David fled from Absalom and charged his master with disloyalty to David; David promised him the estates of Mephibosheth (2 S 16:1–4). Ziba met David when he returned victorious (2 S 19:18). Mephibosheth, however, charged that Ziba had slandered him; David apparently believed neither entirely and divided the estates between them (2 S 19:24–30).

Ziklag (Hb ṣiḳlag, etymology uncertain), a town of Judah in the list of Jos 15:31, but a town of Simeon in the lists of Jos 19:5; 1 Ch 4:30; on the relations of these tribes cf JUDAH; SIMEON. The town was given to David as a fief by Achish*, king of Gath (1 S 27:6), and it was David's residence until he moved to Hebron* (2 S 1:1; 4:10; 1 Ch 12:1, 20). It was raided and burned by the Amalekites during the absence of David and his band (1 S 30:1–26). Ziklag was resettled after the exile (Ne 11:28). The site is not certain; it is usually identified with Tell el Khuweilifeh in the Negeb*, about 12 mi NNW of Beersheba*.

Zillah (Hb ṣillāh, "shadow"?), wife of Lamech* (Gn 4:19, 22 f), the first polygamist, and the mother of Tubal-cain* and Naamah.

Zilpah (Hb zilpāh, "short-nosed"?), a per-

sonal name; the slave of Jacob's wife Leah*, to whom she was given by Laban* (Gn 29:24). As a substitute for the wife she bore Gad* and Asher* (Gn 30:9–12; 35:26; 46:18).

Zimri (Hb zimrî, shortened from zˢmaryāh?), a personal name; an officer of Elah*, king of Israel, who assassinated Elah and his entire family at Tirzah. Zimri reigned only a week; when the city was besieged by Omri*, general of the army, Zimri burned the palace and died in the fire (876 BC; 1 K 16:9–20). His name was hurled at Jehu* by Jezebel* as an epithet meaning assassin (2 K 9:31) The name is borne by three others in the OT. It also appears as a gentilic name designating an Arabian tribe (Je 25:25); it is probably identical with Zimran (Gn 25:2; 1 Ch 1:32).

Zin (Hb ṣin, meaning uncertain), a desert region which lay at the S boundary of Canaan (Nm 13:21; 34:3 f) and of Judah (Jos 15:1, 3), in which Kadesh* and Meribah* were located (Nm 20:1; 27:14; 33:36; Dt 32:51). These data place it S of the Negeb* and E of the Arabah*.

Zion. Cf JERUSALEM.

Ziph (Hb zîp, meaning uncertain). **1.** A town of Judah* (Jos 15:24); probably identified with Khirbet ez Zeifeh in the Negeb*, SE of Hebron*. **2.** A town of Judah (Jos 15:55) which gives its name to a portion of the desert on the E slope of the mountains over the Dead Sea*; the men of this town betrayed David* to Saul* when David was in flight (1 S 23:14 f, 19, 24; 26:1 f; Ps 54:2). It is called a "son" of Mareshah* (1 Ch 2:42), which suggests a foundation from this town. It is one of the cities fortified by Rehoboam* (2 Ch 11:8). It is probably identified with Khirbet ez Zif, about 3 mi SE of Hebron.

Zipporah (Hb ṣippōrāh, "sparrow"?), a personal name; daughter of Jethro*, priest of Midian, and wife of Moses (Ex 2:21). On the circumcision* of the son of Moses by Zipporah (Ex 4:24–26) cf CIRCUMCISION; MOSES. Zipporah and her two sons were not, however, in Egypt when the Israelites left it, and were brought to Moses by Jethro, with whom they had stayed (Ex 18:2–5).

Zoan (Hb ṣō'an, meaning uncertain), a city of Egypt, founded 7 years after Hebron* (Nm 13:22). "The fields of Zoan" were the scene of the saving acts of Yahweh (Ps 78:12, 43). The princes of Zoan are threatened in Is 19:11, 13; Zoan is the residence of the royal officers (Is 30:4). Ezekiel threatened Zoan with burning (Ezk 30:14). Zoan is identical with an important Egyptian city which has several names in history. As Avaris it was the royal residence of the Hyksos* kings and lay in or near Goshen*, where the Israelites lived. Avaris was taken and destroyed by Ahmose I, the founder of the 18th dynasty, and seems to have remained unoccupied until the 19th dynasty (ANET 231–233). A stele of the 19th dynasty found at the site celebrates the 400th anniversary of the foundation of the city (ANET 253); the stele is to be dated 1320–1310, the foundation of Avaris 1720–1710. The city was rebuilt in the 19th dynasty; most of the work was done by Ramses II (1290–1224) in the magnificent style for which it is celebrated; it was given the name of Pi-Ramses, city of Ramses (Ex 1:11). A document of the 19th dynasty praises the beauty of Pi-Ramses (ANET 470–471). The city was called Tanis after 1100 bc. It was the royal residence at times during the 21–23 dynasties (1085–720 bc) and under Tirhakah* of the 25th (Nubian) dynasty. The city was sacked by Ashur-banipal of Assyria (668 bc).

Most scholars place Tanis at San-el-Hagar in NE Egypt S of Lake Menzaleh; others place it at Qantir in the same region. This site, nearest the border of Palestine, was strongest for the Hyksos, who dominated both countries; and the same geographical advantage moved Ramses II to make it his royal residence rather than Thebes*. The site was excavated by Mariette and Petrie; the excavations conducted by Pierre Montet 1929–1932 were much more important and restored the history of the site. The Hyksos fortifications, the remains of the great structures of Ramses II, and the 400-year stele were discovered in these campaigns. Ramses II built a great temple to Seth, the god of the Hyksos, to whom his family traced their lineage.

Zoar (Hb ṣôʿar), called by the alternate name of Bela in Gn 14:2, 8; one of the five cities of the plain (Gn 13:10; 14:2, 8), and the only one which escaped destruction (Gn 19: 22 f, 30). A pun on the name Zoar and misʿar, "small," appears in Gn 19:21 f. Indications of its location place it in the Jordan valley (Dt 34:3) near Moab (Is 15:5; Je 48:34). The location cannot be defined more precisely.

Zobah (Hb šôbāh, šôbāʾ; meaning uncertain), an Aramaean* kingdom. There was war between Saul* and Zobah (1 S 14:47). Zobah sent mercenary forces to assist Hanun* of Ammon when he was attacked by David*; they were defeated (2 S 10:6–8; 1 Ch 19:6). It was probably after their campaign that David attacked Zobah in reprisal and defeated its king Hadadezer completely, making Zobah a subject kingdom (2 S 8:3–12; 1 Ch 18:3–10). A former officer of Hadadezer of Zobah named Rezon became a bandit chief and established himself king of Damascus in Solomon's reign (1 K 11:23). The kingdom of Zobah was located in the N portion of the valley between the Lebanon and the Anti-Lebanon. Assyrian records indicate that it was large, reaching as far as the Euphrates* to the N, and was even a threat to Assyria, which was weak in the 10th century.

Zorah (Hb ṣŭrʿāh, meaning uncertain), a town of Dan (Jos 19:41); after the migration of the Danites (Jgs 18:2, 8, 11) the town became Judahite (Jos 15:33; 1 Ch 4:2). 1 Ch 2:53 suggests that Zorah was settled from Kirjath-jearim*. Zorah was the home of Samson* (Jgs 13:2, 25; 16:31). It was one of the cities fortified by Rehoboam (2 Ch 11:10) and one of the cities resettled after the exile (Ne 11:29). Zorah is the modern Sarah in the valley of Sorek* in the Shephelah*, about 15 mi W of Jerusalem.

Zur. Cf BETH ZUR.